I0816518

the Peoples' BIBLE

the Peoples' BIBLE

New Revised Standard Version with the Apocrypha

Editors

Curtiss Paul DeYoung

Wilda C. Gafney

Leticia A. Guardiola-Sáenz

George "Tink" Tinker

Frank M. Yamada

Fortress Press

Minneapolis

THE PEOPLES' BIBLE
New Revised Standard Version with the Apocrypha

Fortress Press Publishing Team for *The Peoples' Bible*: Scott Tunseth and Neil Elliott, project directors; J. Michael West, Editor-in-Chief; Josh Messner, Development Editor; Jessica Hillstrom, Project Editor; John Goodman, Designer

Cougrr Graphics, Thomas Ristow, Kathleen Ristow, typesetters; Donn McLellan, copyeditor; Peachtree Editorial, proofreader; Sally Messner, proofreader

ISBN: 978-1-5064-8249-1

Printed in China

Contents

The Bible at the Crossroad of Cultures

The Old Testament

The Apocryphal/Deuterocanonical Books

The New Testament

Additional Resources

Introduction
to *The Peoples' Bible*

Why *The Peoples' Bible*?

The United States is rapidly becoming a nation of widely different cultures with a multiplicity of worldviews. Similar diversification is evident around the globe, particularly in the major cities of the world. By the mid-point of the twenty-first century, whites of European descent are expected to constitute less than 50 percent of the total U.S. population, in a nation with a plurality of races, ethnicities, and cultures.

It is easy for the members of any dominant majority group to imagine themselves at the center of things, and others as peripheral. Given a long history in which European conquest and colonialism were intertwined with Christian missionary efforts among other lands and peoples, including North America; and given the particular history of slavery, conquest, and wave after wave of immigration that has produced the present diversity in the United States, it has long been possible for white Christians of European descent to imagine that the Bible was "theirs" more than it belonged to others. They could read themselves into the biblical story, spontaneously identifying themselves with the people of God. But the rich diversity of communities of faith has now made impossible the assumption that any one people "owns" the Bible. We are pleased to present *The Peoples' Bible,* a study Bible that speaks to this new reality.

Multicultural perspectives and culture-critical methods are squarely at home in contemporary biblical scholarship, but until now, teachers and religious leaders who have wanted to explore these issues with their students and congregations have necessarily relied on "extra" resources—texts or commentaries alongside a study Bible, for example. The inevitable impression is that the questions raised in multicultural and culture-critical scholarship are somehow extraneous questions, brought by marginalized "others" to a Bible that remains transcendent, universally authoritative, and ethnically "neutral."

The Peoples' Bible shatters the misperception that the Bible is somehow "color-" and "culture-blind." Through informative and stimulating articles and introductions by renowned biblical scholars from richly diverse backgrounds, thought-provoking study notes, and a beautiful four-color gallery that highlights the myriad ways in which our cultural backgrounds determine our perceptions, *The Peoples' Bible* opens our eyes to the complex interactions of peoples, at cultural crossroads through centuries of history, that gave rise to our Bible. This resource draws us into a new encounter with Scripture as the product of many cultures, at home in many cultures, and shows that the Bible really is a peoples' Bible.

The Peoples' Bible seeks to reach a mass audience of people who have often felt left out and voiceless in their encounter with other study Bibles. These include people at the grassroots as well as people in the academy. In order to give voice to those who have been silenced by dominant narratives in Western culture, *The Peoples' Bible* offers some of the best insights of scholars from a wide array of different cultures and ethnicities, writing in accessible language. The editorial team and writers are comprised of scholars from communities traditionally underrepresented in mainstream biblical scholarship in the United States, whose perspectives have consequently been underrepresented in study Bibles as well: African Americans, Asian Americans, Latinas/os, and Native Americans. Some white interpreters who have a track record offering perspectives rarely heard have also contributed to this study Bible, and the editors have sought a balance of men and women writers as well.

The New Revised Standard Version (NRSV) of the Bible has been selected by the editors and the publisher as the translation for *The Peoples' Bible*. This choice was made because of the NRSV's wide acceptance for accuracy in translation from the original languages of the Bible and for its effort to use gender-inclusive language in order to communicate in a modern idiom.

The Perspective of *The Peoples' Bible*

The Peoples' Bible envisions the Bible as a crossroads: both a place of collision and of convergence. On the journey of biblical interpretation, there are collisions between one or another culture and Scripture, between cultures themselves, between dominant and marginal perspectives, and across imbalances of power in society. These realities are reflected here as scholars often present multiple perspectives on a biblical text. Yet the Bible is also a place of convergence, where people meet at the crossroads, finding points of common ground and shared interest.

The Peoples' Bible gives the Bible back to the reader and invites a peoples' interpretation of Scripture through each reader's own unique social lens. Readers will resonate with voices speaking from life settings similar to their own. Biblical narratives will engage readers in ways that prompt reflection on their own life journeys. How we read the Bible, like our understanding of life itself, is affected by many dimensions, including our age, gender, race, culture, socioeconomic class, religion, ability, sexual orientation, and nation of origin. *The Peoples' Bible* taps into this reservoir of feeling and insight to inform the reader's understanding of these ancient texts. Studying the Bible with only one's own set of lived experiences or educational viewpoints limits the possibilities for gaining meaning from biblical texts. This study Bible brings together the interpretive lenses of scholars from many peoples, whose many perspectives produce a mosaic of wisdom and affirmation. The reader's own view is enriched by the vast cultural diversity of scholarly knowledge offered in *The Peoples' Bible*.

Not only does *The Peoples' Bible* offer the reader the space to explore Scripture from multiple social locations, it also invites a fresh discussion of the critical issues facing citizens of the twenty-first century. Many people have rejected biblical faith, believing that it has no power to address contemporary racism and injustice. The writers in this study Bible engage with passion the Bible's potential for social justice and liberation, originally meant for times long ago yet still proclaiming a timely word today. They also describe how the biblical authors struggled with the limitations of their own settings as they tried to interpret God's will and work. The essays and introductions in *The Peoples' Bible* speak with a refreshing candor about how, throughout history, the Bible has been manipulated and misused to support colonization, slavery, genocide, ethnic cleansing, sexism, and a host of other forms of oppression. The residue of oppression still marks much current biblical interpretation and theological musing. The publication of *The Peoples' Bible* marks a new era of inclusion and freedom in which all peoples and all voices are welcome to the table of biblical interpretation—a process that we hope will serve as a catalyst for a more just society and a reconciled human family.

How *The Peoples' Bible* is different

In order to appreciate the wealth of meaning in Scripture, it is often necessary to recognize and set aside, at least momentarily, our own culture-bound assumptions so that we can understand the perspectives of other people. This study Bible embraces multiple cultural approaches that reflect the current cultural mosaic in the United States. It relies on established historical-critical, literary-critical, and social-scientific methods, but also on the perspectives of postcolonial, feminist, and Afrocentric criticism, to name a few. *The Peoples' Bible* highlights interpretations that emerge from diverse and particular contexts.

We are committed to the possibility that all may learn to read the Bible as we have never read it before, from social locations where we have never stood before. For example, men may learn to read Scripture through the eyes of women; those accustomed to reading the Bible from the perspective of the dominant culture may read through the eyes of those at the margins; and so on. Precisely because biblical interpretation differs from one cultural perspective to the next, and from one social location to the next, any of us who wish to gain a deeper understanding of the Bible must involve ourselves in what may well feel like a risky endeavor: to listen to the Bible by listening to one another. It is toward that end that we are pleased to offer *The Peoples' Bible.*

The Editors

George "Tink" Tinker — I am an enrolled member of the Osage (*Wazhazhe*) Nation and Professor of American Indian Cultures and Religious Traditions at Iliff School of Theology. I have taught at Iliff for nearly twenty years, bringing an Indian perspective to a predominantly Euro-American school. As an American Indian academic originally trained in biblical studies (Ph.D., Graduate Theological Union), I am committed to a scholarly endeavor that takes seriously both the liberation of Indian peoples from their historic oppression as colonized communities and the liberation of white Americans, the historic colonizers and oppressors of Indian peoples.

Wilda C. Gafney — I teach the "scriptures of Israel"—by which I mean a wealth of literature including the Hebrew Bible (the scriptures of contemporary Judaism); the ancient Jewish writings treasured by many Christians as the Apocrypha or Deutero-canonical biblical writings; the Septuagint, the Greek translation of Jewish scriptures made in North Africa; the Samaritan Pentateuch; and the writings represented in the Dead Sea Scrolls. As a black feminist with postcolonial commitments to and beyond the African Diaspora, my interest in these overlapping bodies of literature and their languages leads me to explore how translations, theories, and practices either open up or cover up biblical texts. I am an Episcopal priest who is a member of two congregations, the African Episcopal Church of St. Thomas and the Dorshei Derekh Reconstructionist (Jewish) Minyan, both in Philadelphia.

Frank M. Yamada — I am Sansei, third-generation Japanese American, who grew up on the West Coast of California, which locates me one generation after the internment of over 200,000 Japanese and Japanese Americans during World War II. I grew up in a nominally Buddhist home, before converting to Christianity when I was in college. I received my training as a scholar at a Protestant seminary, where historical criticism was the dominant form of investigation. Ironically, this is also where I began to develop interest in the destabilizing practice of postmodern biblical interpretation. All of these forces of cultural conflict and fusion are reflected in my identity—a hybrid construction that seeks to refuse oversimplified characterizations of Asia or America in my Asian American body. Because of my identity, I am often drawn to conflicts and contradictions in the biblical text, seeing them not as a problem to be fixed, but as difficult and sometimes painful openings into another people's understanding of the world and God.

Leticia A. Guardiola-Sáenz — Just as the Bible has shaped the way I read and understand my life, my life has shaped the way I read and understand the Bible. Through my experiences as a Latina woman of Mexican heritage, born and bred in the bicultural borderlands between Mexico and the United States, I have come to appreciate and read the Bible as a hybrid text where many borders, voices, and meanings converge. So, as a reader, believer, and lecturer of the Christian Scripture, I find myself constantly negotiating and contesting the meanings and stories of the Bible as I seek to responsibly interpret and appropriate its message in a culture and time that is thousands of years and miles away from its original context. Ultimately, my goals as an informed reader of the Bible are to empower minority readers as

 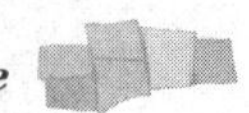

agents of historical change in the ongoing process of decolonization and liberation, to dismantle oppressive interpretations, and to offer inclusive and transformative readings that can bring about justice and liberation for all of God's creation.

Curtiss Paul DeYoung — I am a white male of Dutch and English ancestry who is a citizen of the United States, ordained in the Church of God (Anderson, Ind.), and Professor of Reconciliation Studies at Bethel University. My biblical interpretation has been transformed from a de facto Eurocentric bias to a more multicultural perspective through theological training at Howard University School of Divinity and years of reading biblical scholars and theologians from Native American, Asian, Latin American, African, Arab, and African American perspectives. My racial self-understanding was interrupted at age fifty with the genealogical discovery of a black ancestor. My cultural self-understanding has been affected by socialization in African American communities and by the consciousness raised by multiple visits to South Africa and Palestine/Israel. As a person with race, class, and male privileges in the United States, I have committed my life to social justice and reconciliation. This collision of birthright privilege and experiential transformation informs my interpretation of the Bible.

How to Use
The Peoples' Bible

This Bible was developed to help students and readers understand how people from different cultures, from different parts of the world, read and understand the Bible. No single, exclusive way to approach the Bible is proposed here because there are so many possible ways to interpret its writings. Rather, *The Peoples' Bible* gathers the voices of different interpreters from different social locations as a way of encouraging students and readers to recognize that *all* Bible interpreters are people whose cultures of origin and social locations influence their scholarship. Similarly, *The Peoples' Bible* encourages students and readers to reflect on how *their* cultures and social locations continue to shape them as Bible readers and interpreters.

In general, *The Peoples' Bible* is intended to help each reader find his or her own voice in and through the text, and also to hear the voices of others. This is done best when the Bible is read and studied in the midst of socially diverse groups and communities, where a multiplicity of voices can come alive. Many resources in this study Bible encourage this process.

The editors have invited a wide range of scholars to contribute overviews of the major sections of the Hebrew Scriptures, the Apocrypha, and the Second (traditionally, New) Testament, and to introduce each book of the Bible. The reader is encouraged to read the relevant section overview and book introduction prior to studying a certain text or an entire book. This helps to set the stage for informed and inclusive interpretation. Study notes have been placed throughout the books of the Bible to draw the reader's attention to particular scriptural passages that offer examples of how culture and interpretation intersect. These can be occasions for individual reflection—*How does this voice resemble my own? How is it different?*—and for group discussion as well: *How have the historical experiences of different peoples shaped the ways we hear the Bible? How do they challenge assumptions we have taken for granted? Does our encounter with the Bible help us recognize the ways we establish our own identities at cultural crossroads today, whether through connection with others or through contrast and conflict?*

A number of articles raise issues or suggest strategies for interpretation that readers may apply to the larger narrative of the Bible, not just to particular texts, books, or sections. Several essays delve deeply into the role of culture in the biblical narratives and how culture affects our present-day view of the Bible. These essays place the reader at a crossroads where the perspectives of Native American, Latina/o, Asian American, and African American cultures meet. They alert us to the nuances of particularity and to the possibilities for conflict and collision, as well as for convergence and community, in the process of interpretation. The impact of culture is also noted in the diversity of views of the biblical God and in the ways a culturally rooted Jesus of Nazareth was transformed over history to serve processes of cultural domination. Other essays explore the ways traditional forms of interpretation have sanctified exclusivist worldviews; the role played by one or another empire in shaping biblical history and subsequent interpretation; and the tensions present when Christians set about to interpret the Hebrew Scriptures. An article discussing the Bible as an instrument of reconciliation moves from the realm of theory to that of action and activism.

Visual resources have been selected to enhance the reader's experience. Readers will find the maps helpful for relating the biblical stories to actual landscapes. A color art gallery provides angles of vision into the biblical narratives that are sometimes inaccessible through words alone.

Using *The Peoples' Bible* in the Classroom

Professors of biblical studies or religion who wish to bring multicultural perspectives and the diversity of interpretive options into the classroom will find *The Peoples' Bible* a welcome resource. Some possibilities include the following:

Instructors who have shaped their courses around the histories that produced the biblical writings will want to rely on the section and book introductions, which emphasize the social and historical dynamics behind the text, and on articles discussing the Bible as a text of culture, the role of empires, and the biblical representations of God.

Instructors wishing to emphasize the literary character of the biblical writings will also want to use the section and book introductions and the study notes to direct their students' attention to particular aspects of the text that have caught the ear, and eye, of one or another community.

Those wishing to teach methods of biblical interpretation may note that *The Peoples' Bible* is a study Bible with a difference. By design, the text of the Bible printed here does not include the headings, marginal notes, or running commentary that in other study Bibles can give the impression that a particular passage has a single, authoritative meaning. Here the section and book introductions are designed to invite students into diverse encounters with the biblical text. Students should think of the writer of each introduction, not as making authoritative pronouncements on the meaning of a text, but as offering to accompany the reader with an informed but nevertheless personally inflected perspective.

Teachers who intend to use a survey or introductory textbook in their course will see that the articles at the beginning of *The Peoples' Bible* recognize the importance of historical- and literary-critical methods. Teachers who intend to assign only a classroom Bible will appreciate the succinct attention these articles give to the importance of history, identity, and culture in the formation of the biblical writings and in their subsequent interpretation.

Instructors may wish to use specific classroom techniques with *The Peoples' Bible.* For example:

An instructor may wish to draw attention to the distinctiveness of one or another writer's perspective, asking students: How does the writer's cultural background, the experience of his or her people, shape his or her reading of the Bible? How does your reading reflect your own sense of social and cultural identity?

The study notes may be used as occasions for classroom conversation: How does the perspective of the writer draw us into the biblical text? How does the writer open up a new insight into the text? How might the experience of other peoples provide different insights?

The images in the art gallery might be used to focus attention in a more intuitive, nonverbal way. Which images are more familiar? Which less? Which images draw you into a connection with another culture? Which draw you into the Bible so that you experience it in a new way?

The introductory articles might be relied upon to focus students' reading and discussion of the biblical materials. For one or another biblical book, students might be asked: How are different understandings of God evident in the text? How have the dynamics of the rise and fall of empires shaped the text? Or: Have Christians read this text differently from Jews or others? How might any of us come to read the text differently today?

Instructors who wish to incorporate the Bible as a resource in courses on social justice, peace or reconciliation studies, or similar courses in a humanities curriculum might well do something similar. They might rely on the articles on the Bible in cultures and the Bible as an instrument of reconciliation and ask: How has this text been taken up and wielded as an instrument of harm in conflicts between ethnic groups, between nations, or between social classes? How has the text served as a resource for healing and reconciliation? How might it serve as such today?

Using *The Peoples' Bible* in Congregational Settings

Congregational leaders and teachers will find *The Peoples' Bible* a valuable resource for worship, education, and mission. Preachers may find that regular use of *The Peoples' Bible* alerts them to the different ways the Bible—and things said about it from the pulpit—may strike the ears of persons from different backgrounds and social locations. Congregations may wish to adopt *The Peoples' Bible* as their pew Bible as a sign of welcome and an occasion for opening their shared life to others at the margins.

Bible teachers in the congregation, working with youth and adults alike, may appreciate the way *The Peoples' Bible* highlights the perspective of the reader and stimulates exploration and question, rather than providing set answers.

Finally, those who seek to call their congregations outward into greater engagement with a divided and troubled world may find in *The Peoples' Bible* a useful spur to mission. Here is a Bible that acknowledges the diversity of ways, hurtful and healing alike, in which different groups and peoples have experienced sacred Scripture. Here is a Bible that challenges the assumption that any one group may possess Scripture as its own or control its interpretation. Here is a Bible that may invite readers more deeply into an encounter with a God who desires to be recognized as the creator of *all* the peoples of the earth and to be known as the reconciler of *all* peoples who learn to live together in community with one another in ever greater harmony.

Additional resources for this volume can be found online at www.fortresspress.com/peoplesbible.

Contributors

John J. Ahn
Austin Seminary
Obadiah, Zephaniah

Randall C. Bailey
Interdenominational Theological Center
The Bible as a Text of Cultures
Genesis

Angela Bauer-Levesque
Episcopal Divinity School
Jeremiah
Study notes

Frederick Houk Borsch
The Lutheran Theological Seminary at Philadelphia
Baruch, The Letter of Jeremiah, Psalm 151

Alejandro F. Botta
Boston University School of Theology
Ezra, Nehemiah

Valerie Bridgeman
Memphis Theological Seminary
Amos, Habakkuk
Study notes

David G. Burke
NIDA Institute for Biblical Scholarship of the American Bible Society, dean emeritus
Study notes

Greg Carey
Lancaster Theological Seminary
Revelation

Choi Hee An
Boston University School of Theology
Women, Culture, and The Bible

Stephanie Buckhanon Crowder
Belmont University
Luke

David Cortés-Fuentes
San Francisco Theological Seminary of Southern California
1 Peter, 2 Peter, Jude

Gregory Lee Cuéllar
Texas A & M University
1 Chronicles, 2 Chronicles

Steed Vernyl Davidson
Pacific Lutheran Theological Seminary
Haggai, Zechariah
Study notes

Stacy Davis
Saint Mary's College
1 Esdras, 2 Esdras, 3 Maccabees, 4 Maccabees, The Prayer of Manasseh

Miguel A. De La Torre
Iliff School of Theology
Study notes

Curtiss Paul DeYoung
Bethel University
Editorial Team (Originating editor; responsibility for Articles; Art; Maps)
The Bible as an Instrument of Reconciliation; Jesus and Cultures (with Leticia A. Guardiola-Saénz)
Study notes

Rubén R. Dupertuis
Trinity University
Introduction to Acts

Nicole Wilkinson Duran
Trinity Presbyterian Church, Bryn Mawr, Penn.
The Bible as a Text in Cultures: Euro-Americans
Esther (Greek)

Neil Elliott
Fortress Press
The Bible and Empire
Study notes

Cain Hope Felder
Howard University School of Divinity
Introduction to the Gospels
Philemon

Wilda C. Gafney
Lutheran Theological Seminary at Philadelphia
Editorial Team (responsibility for Hebrew Bible; Apocrypha)
Introduction to the Apocryphal/ Deuterocanonical Books
Numbers, Judges, Ruth, Judith, Azariah and the Three Jews, Susanna, Bel and the Dragon
Study notes

Francisco García-Treto
Trinity University
Introduction to Wisdom and Poetry
1 Kings, 2 Kings

Leticia A. Guardiola-Sáenz
Seattle University
Editorial Team (responsibility for New Testament)
Culture and Identity (with Frank M. Yamada); Jesus and Cultures (with Curtiss Paul DeYoung)
Matthew

Alice Hunt
Chicago Theological Seminary
Song of Solomon

Willa E. M. Johnson
University of Mississippi
Esther

Craig S. Keener
Palmer Theological Seminary
1 John, 2 John, 3 John

Hyun Chul Paul Kim
Methodist Theological School in Ohio
Isaiah

Uriah Y. Kim
Hartford Seminary
Introduction to the Historical Books
1 Samuel, 2 Samuel

Cheryl A. Kirk-Duggan
Shaw University Divinity School
Job, Lamentations
Study notes

Kosuke Koyama
Union Theological Seminary, emeritus
God of the Bible and the Peoples of the Earth

Barbara M. Leung Lai
Tyndale Seminary
Daniel

Ediberto López-Rodríguez
Seminario Evangélico de Puerto Rico
Galatians

Francisco Lozada, Jr.
Brite Divinity School, Texas Christian University
The Bible as a Text in Cultures: Latinas/os

Claude F. Mariottini
Northern Baptist Theological Seminary
Jonah, Joel

Aquiles Ernesto Martínez
Reinhardt College
Philippians

James Earl Massey
Anderson University, School of Theology, emeritus
Hebrews

Dora R. Mbuwayesango
Hood Theological Seminary
Joshua

Madeline McClenney-Sadler
ExodusFoundation.org
Leviticus, Ecclesiastes

Raj Nadella
Seabury-Western Theological Seminary
Ephesians

Lai Ling Elizabeth Ngan
Truett Theological Seminary, Baylor University
Introduction to the Prophets
Hosea

Margaret Aymer Oget
Interdenominational Theological Center
James
Study notes

Jorge Pixley
Seminario Teológico Bautista, Managua, emeritus
Exodus

Anathea E. Portier-Young
Duke Divinity School
Tobit, 1 Maccabees, 2 Maccabees
Study notes

Emerson Byron Powery
Lee University
Mark

Stephen Breck Reid
Bethany Theological Seminary
Psalms

Henry W. Morisada Rietz
Grinnell College
Introduction to the General Letters and Revelation

Joseph F. Scrivner
Samford University
Proverbs

Fernando F. Segovia
Divinity School, Vanderbilt University
The Bible as a Text in Cultures: An Introduction
John

Abraham Smith
Southern Methodist University
1 Thessalonians, 2 Thessalonians

Daniel L. Smith-Christopher
Loyola Marymount University
Micah, Nahum

Aída Besançon Spencer
Gordon-Conwell Theological Seminary
1 Timothy, 2 Timothy, Titus

Elsa Tamez
United Bible Societies & Universidad Bíblica Latinoamericana
Introduction to the Pauline Letters
Romans

George "Tink" Tinker
Iliff School of Theology
Editorial Team (responsibility for Articles; Art)
The Bible as a Text in Cultures: Native Americans

Scott Tunseth
Fortress Press
Wisdom of Solomon, Sirach
Study notes

Osvaldo D. Vena
Garrett Evangelical Theological Seminary
Malachi

Demetrius K. Williams
Marquette University
1 Corinthians, 2 Corinthians

Johanna W. H. van Wijk-Bos
Louisville Presbyterian Theological Seminary
Responsible Christian Exegesis of Hebrew Scripture

Vincent L. Wimbush
Claremont Graduate University
The Bible as a Text in Cultures: African Americans

Frank M. Yamada
McCormick Theological Seminary
Editorial Team (responsibility for Hebrew Bible)
The Bible as a Text in Cultures: Asian Americans
Culture and Identity (with Leticia Guardiola-Sáenz)
Introduction to the Pentateuch
Deuteronomy
Study notes

Gale A. Yee
Episcopal Divinity School
Ezekiel

Gordon Zerbe
Canadian Mennonite University
Colossians

Study Notes Key

ABL – Angela Baurer-Levesque
APY – Anathea E. Portier-Young
CKD – Cheryl A. Kirk-Duggan
CPD – Curtiss Paul DeYoung
DB – David G. Burke
FY – Frank M. Yamada
MAO – Margaret Aymer Oget
MDLT – Miguel A. De La Torre
NE – Neil Elliott
ST – Scott Tunseth
SVD – Steed Vernyl Davidson
VB – Valerie Bridgeman
WG – Wilda C. Gafney

Preface
to the New Revised Standard Version

This preface is addressed to you by the Committee of translators, who wish to explain, as briefly as possible, the origin and character of our work. The publication of our revision is yet another step in the long, continual process of making the Bible available in the form of the English language that is most widely current in our day. To summarize in a single sentence: the New Revised Standard Version of the Bible is an authorized revision of the Revised Standard Version, published in 1952, which was a revision of the American Standard Version, published in 1901, which, in turn, embodied earlier revisions of the King James Version, published in 1611.

In the course of time, the King James Version came to be regarded as "the Authorized Version." With good reason it has been termed "the noblest monument of English prose," and it has entered, as no other book has, into the making of the personal character and the public institutions of the English-speaking peoples. We owe to it an incalculable debt.

Yet the King James Version has serious defects. By the middle of the nineteenth century, the development of biblical studies and the discovery of many biblical manuscripts more ancient than those on which the King James Version was based made it apparent that these defects were so many as to call for revision. The task was begun, by authority of the Church of England, in 1870. The (British) Revised Version of the Bible was published in 1881-1885; and the American Standard Version, its variant embodying the preferences of the American scholars associated with the work, was published, as was mentioned above, in 1901. In 1928 the copyright of the latter was acquired by the International Council of Religious Education and thus passed into the ownership of the Churches of the United States and Canada that were associated in this Council through their boards of education and publication.

The Council appointed a committee of scholars to have charge of the text of the American Standard Version and to undertake inquiry concerning the need for further revision. After studying the questions whether or not revision should be undertaken, and if so, what its nature and extent should be, in 1937 the Council authorized a revision. The scholars who served as members of the Committee worked in two sections, one dealing with the Old Testament and one with the New Testament. In 1946 the Revised Standard Version of the New Testament was published. The publication of the Revised Standard Version of the Bible, containing the Old and New Testaments, took place on September 30, 1952. A translation of the *Apocryphal/Deuterocanonical* Books of the Old Testament followed in 1957. In 1977 this collection was issued in an expanded edition, containing three additional texts received by Eastern

Orthodox communions (3 and 4 Maccabees and Psalm 151). Thereafter the Revised Standard Version gained the distinction of being officially authorized for use by all major Christian churches: Protestant, Anglican, Roman Catholic, and Eastern Orthodox.

The Revised Standard Version Bible Committee is a continuing body, comprising about thirty members, both men and women. Ecumenical in representation, it includes scholars affiliated with various Protestant denominations, as well as several Roman Catholic members, an Eastern Orthodox member, and a Jewish member who serves in the Old Testament section. For a period of time, the Committee included several members from Canada and from England.

Because no translation of the Bible is perfect or is acceptable to all groups of readers, and because discoveries of older manuscripts and further investigation of linguistic features of the text continue to become available, renderings of the Bible have proliferated. During the years following the publication of the Revised Standard Version, twenty-six other English translations and revisions of the Bible were produced by committees and by individual scholars—not to mention twenty-five other translations and revisions of the New Testament alone. One of the latter was the second edition of the RSV New Testament, issued in 1971, twenty-five years after its initial publication.

Following the publication of the RSV Old Testament in 1952, significant advances were made in the discovery and interpretation of documents in Semitic languages related to Hebrew. In addition to the information that had become available in the late 1940s from the Dead Sea texts of Isaiah and Habakkuk, subsequent acquisitions from the same area brought to light many other early copies of all the books of the Hebrew Scriptures (except Esther), though most of these copies are fragmentary. During the same period early Greek manuscript copies of books of the New Testament also became available.

In order to take these discoveries into account, along with recent studies of documents in Semitic languages related to Hebrew, in 1974 the Policies Committee of the Revised Standard Version, which is a standing committee of the National Council of the Churches of Christ in the U.S.A., authorized the preparation of a revision of the entire RSV Bible.

For the Old Testament the Committee has made use of the *Biblia Hebraica Stuttgartensia* (1977; ed. sec. emendata, 1983). This is an edition of the Hebrew and Aramaic text as current early in the Christian era and fixed by Jewish scholars (the "Masoretes") of the sixth to the ninth centuries. The vowel signs, which were added by the Masoretes, are accepted in the main, but where a more probable and convincing reading can be obtained by assuming different vowels, this has been done. No notes are given in such cases, because the vowel points are less ancient and reliable than the consonants. When an alternative reading given by the Masoretes is translated in a footnote, this is identified by the words "Another reading is."

Departures from the consonantal text of the best manuscripts have been made only where it seems clear that errors in copying had been made before the text was standardized. Most of the corrections adopted are based on the ancient versions (translations into Greek, Aramaic, Syriac, and Latin), which were made prior to the time of the work of the Masoretes and which therefore may reflect earlier forms of the Hebrew text. In such instances a footnote specifies the version or versions from which the correction has been derived and also gives a translation of the Masoretic Text. Where it was deemed appropriate to do so, information is supplied in footnotes from subsidiary Jewish traditions concerning other textual readings (the *Tiqqune Sopherim,* "emendations of the scribes"). These are identified in the footnotes as "Ancient Heb tradition."

Occasionally it is evident that the text has suffered in transmission and that none of the versions provides a satisfactory restoration. Here we can only follow the best judgment of competent scholars as to the most probable reconstruction of the original text. Such reconstructions are indicated in footnotes by the abbreviation Cn ("Correction"), and a translation of the Masoretic Text is added.

For the Apocryphal/Deuterocanonical Books of the Old Testament, the Committee has made use of a number of texts. For most of these books, the basic Greek text from which the present translation was made is the edition of the Septuagint prepared by Alfred Rahlfs and published by the Württemberg Bible Society (Stuttgart, 1935). For several of the books, the more recently published individual volumes of the Göttingen Septuagint project were utilized. For the book of Tobit, it was decided to follow the form of the Greek text found in codex Sinaiticus (supported as it is by evidence from Qumran); where this text is defective, it was supplemented and corrected by other Greek manuscripts. For the three Additions to Daniel (namely, Susanna, the Prayer of Azariah and the Song of the Three Jews, and Bel and the Dragon) the Committee continued to use the Greek version attributed to Theodotion (the so-called "Theodotion-Daniel"). In translating Ecclesiasticus (Sirach), while constant reference was made to the Hebrew fragments of a large portion of this book (those discovered at Qumran and Masada as well as those recovered from the Cairo Geniza), the Committee generally followed the Greek text (including verse numbers) published by Joseph Ziegler in the Göttingen Septuagint (1965). But in many places the Committee has translated the Hebrew text when this provides a reading that is clearly superior to the Greek; the Syriac and Latin versions were also consulted throughout and occasionally adopted. The basic text adopted in rendering 2 Esdras is the Latin version given in *Biblia Sacra,* edited by Robert Weber (Stuttgart, 1971). This was supplemented by consulting the Latin text as edited by R. L. Bensly (1895) and by Bruno Violet (1910), as well as by taking into account the several Oriental versions of 2 Esdras, namely, the Syriac, Ethiopic, Arabic (two forms, referred to as Arabic 1 and Arabic 2), Armenian, and Georgian versions. Finally, since the Additions to the Book of Esther are disjointed and quite unintelligible as they stand in most editions of the Apocrypha, we have provided them with their original context by translating the whole of the Greek version of Esther from Robert Hanhart's Göttingen edition (1983).

For the New Testament the Committee has based its work on the most recent edition of *The Greek New Testament,* prepared by an interconfessional and international committee and published by the United Bible Societies (1966; 3rd ed. corrected, 1983; information concerning changes to be introduced into the critical apparatus of the forthcoming 4th edition was available to the Committee). As in that edition, double brackets are used to enclose a few passages that are generally regarded to be later additions to the text, but which we have retained because of their evident antiquity and their importance in the textual tradition. Only in very rare instances have we replaced the text or the punctuation of the Bible Societies' edition by an alternative that seemed to us to be superior. Here and there in the footnotes, the phrase "Other ancient authorities read," identifies alternative readings preserved by Greek manuscripts and early versions. In both Testaments alternative renderings of the text are indicated by the word "Or."

As for the style of English adopted for the present revision, among the mandates given to the Committee in 1980 by the Division of Education and Ministry of the National Council of Churches of Christ (which now holds the copyright of the RSV Bible) was the directive to continue in the tradition of the King James Bible, but to introduce such changes as are warranted on the basis of accuracy, clarity, euphony, and current English usage. Within the constraints set by the original texts and by the mandates of the Division, the Committee has followed the maxim, "As literal as possible, as free as necessary." As a consequence, the New Revised Standard Version (NRSV) remains essentially a literal translation. Paraphrastic renderings have been adopted only sparingly, and then chiefly to compensate for a deficiency in the English language—the lack of a common gender third person singular pronoun.

During the almost half a century since the publication of the RSV, many in the churches have become sensitive to the danger of linguistic sexism arising from the inherent bias of the English language towards the masculine gender, a bias that in the case of the Bible has often restricted or obscured the meaning of the original text. The mandates from the Division specified that, in references to men and women, masculine-oriented language should be eliminated as far as this can be done without altering passages that reflect the historical situation of ancient patriarchal culture. As can be appreciated, more than once the Committee found that the several mandates stood in tension and even in conflict. The various concerns had to be balanced case by case in order to provide a faithful and acceptable rendering without using contrived English. Only very occasionally has the pronoun "he" or "him" been retained in passages where the reference may have been to a woman as well as to a man; for example, in several legal texts in

Leviticus and Deuteronomy. In such instances of formal, legal language, the options of either putting the passage in the plural or of introducing additional nouns to avoid masculine pronouns in English seemed to the Committee to obscure the historic structure and literary character of the original. In the vast majority of cases, however, inclusiveness has been attained by simple rephrasing or by introducing plural forms when this does not distort the meaning of the passage. Of course, in narrative and in parable no attempt was made to generalize the sex of individual persons.

Another aspect of style will be detected by readers who compare the more stately English rendering of the Old Testament with the less formal rendering adopted for the New Testament. For example, the traditional distinction between *shall* and *will* in English has been retained in the Old Testament as appropriate in rendering a document that embodies what may be termed the classic form of Hebrew, while in the New Testament the abandonment of such distinctions in the usage of the future tense in English reflects the more colloquial nature of the koine Greek used by most New Testament authors except when they are quoting the Old Testament.

Careful readers will notice that here and there in the Old Testament the word LORD (or in certain cases GOD) is printed in capital letters. This represents the traditional manner in English versions of rendering the Divine Name, the "Tetragrammaton" (see the notes on Exodus 3:14, 15), following the precedent of the ancient Greek and Latin translators and the long established practice in the reading of the Hebrew Scriptures in the synagogue. While it is almost if not quite certain that the Name was originally pronounced "Yahweh," this pronunciation was not indicated when the Masoretes added vowel sounds to the consonantal Hebrew text. To the four consonants YHWH of the Name, which had come to be regarded as too sacred to be pronounced, they attached vowel signs indicating that in its place should be read the Hebrew word *Adonai* meaning "Lord" (or *Elohim* meaning "God"). Ancient Greek translators employed the word *Kyrios* ("Lord") for the Name. The Vulgate likewise used the Latin word *Dominus* ("Lord"). The form "Jehovah" is of late medieval origin; it is a combination of the consonants of the Divine Name and the vowels attached to it by the Masoretes but belonging to an entirely different word. Although the American Standard Version (1901) had used "Jehovah" to render the Tetragrammaton (the sound of Y being represented by J and the sound of W by V, as in Latin), for two reasons the Committees that produced the RSV and the NRSV returned to the more familiar usage of the King James Version. (1) The word "Jehovah" does not accurately represent any form of the Name ever used in Hebrew. (2) The use of any proper name for the one and only God, as though there were other gods from whom the true God had to be distinguished, began to be discontinued in Judaism before the Christian era and is inappropriate for the universal faith of the Christian Church.

It will be seen that in the Psalms and in other prayers addressed to God, the archaic second person singular pronouns *(thee, thou, thine)* and verb forms *(art, hast, hadst)* are no longer used. Although some readers may regret this change, it should be pointed out that in the original languages neither the Old Testament nor the New makes any linguistic distinction between addressing a human being and addressing the Deity. Furthermore, in the tradition of the King James Version one will not expect to find the use of capital letters for pronouns that refer to the Deity—such capitalization is an unnecessary innovation that has only recently been introduced into a few English translations of the Bible. Finally, we have left to the discretion of the licensed publishers such matters as section headings, cross-references, and clues to the pronunciation of proper names.

This new version seeks to preserve all that is best in the English Bible as it has been known and used through the years. It is intended for use in public reading and congregational worship, as well as in private study, instruction, and meditation. We have resisted the temptation to introduce terms and phrases that merely reflect current moods, and have tried to put the message of the Scriptures in simple, enduring words and expressions that are worthy to stand in the great tradition of the King James Bible and its predecessors.

In traditional Judaism and Christianity, the Bible has been more than a historical document to be preserved or a classic of literature to be cherished and admired; it is recognized as the unique record of God's dealings with people over the ages. The Old Testament sets forth the call of a special people to enter into covenant relation with the God of justice and steadfast love and to bring God's law to the nations. The New Testament records the life and work of Jesus Christ, the one in whom "the Word became flesh," as well as describes the rise and spread of the early Christian Church. The Bible carries its full message, not to those who regard it simply as a noble literary heritage of the past or who wish to use it to enhance political purposes and advance otherwise desirable goals, but to all persons and communities who read it so that they may discern and understand what God is saying to them. That message must not be disguised in phrases that are no longer clear, or hidden under words that have changed or lost their meaning; it must be presented in language that is direct and plain and meaningful to people today. It is the hope and prayer of the translators that this version of the Bible may continue to hold a large place in congregational life and to speak to all readers, young and old alike, helping them to understand and believe and respond to its message.

For the Committee,
BRUCE M. METZGER

Books of the Bible in Alphabetical Order
with Abbreviations

Apocryphal/Deuterocanonical books are in italics.

Abbreviations

In the notes to the books of the Old Testament the following abbreviations are used:

Ant.	Josephus, *Antiquities of the Jews*
Aram	Aramaic
BCE	Before Common Era
CE	Common Era
Ch., chs.	Chapter, chapters
Cn	Correction; made where the text has suffered in transmission and the versions provide no satisfactory restoration but where the Revised Standard Bible Committee agrees with the judgment of competent scholars as to the most probable reconstruction of the original text.
Gk	Septuagint, Greek version of the Old Testament
Heb	Hebrew of the consonantal Masoretic Text of the Old Testament
Josephus	Flavius Josephus (Jewish historian, about CE 37 to about 95)
Macc.	The book(s) of the Maccabees
Ms(s)	Manuscript(s)
MT	The Hebrew of the pointed Masoretic Text of the Old Testament
OL	Old Latin
Q Ms(s)	Manuscript(s) found at Qumran by the Dead Sea
Sam	Samaritan Hebrew text of the Old Testament
Syr	Syriac Version of the Old Testament
Syr H	Syriac Version of Origen's Hexapla
Tg	Targum
v., vv.	Verse, verses
Vg	Vulgate, Latin Version of the Old Testament

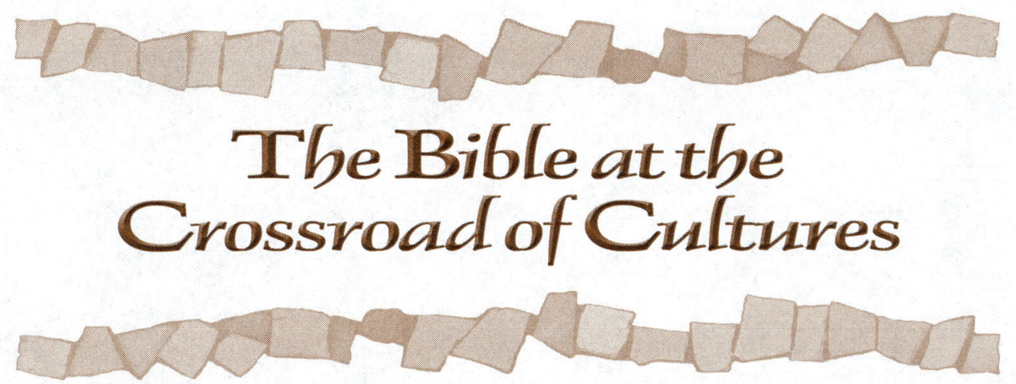
The Bible at the
Crossroad of Cultures

Culture and Identity

Frank M. Yamada and Leticia A. Guardiola-Sáenz

If there is one clear commonality between twenty-first-century readers of the Bible and the peoples of the biblical world, it is that each of us, like each of them, belongs to a culture and has an identity. Of course, our contemporary cultures and identities also set us apart, in various ways, from the peoples of the Bible. How, then, can understanding culture and identity help us understand the biblical text, considering our sameness but without losing sight of our differences?

Our initial encounter with culture and the process of identity formation is subtle and imperceptible; it begins with our first breath. Our first interactions with those who care for us and with the environment we share with them give us our first appreciation of sameness and difference; we learn to reject or to accept certain differences in other people. Later, as we grow and pass through the stages of life, participating in new cultural spaces such as school, church, workplace, and community, we encounter other ways to value diversity, which can either affirm or challenge our earlier perceptions. Sadly, more often than not, we are socially trained to assimilate that which is similar to us and reject that which is different from us. What is similar and familiar appeals to our trust, but what is different and strange tends to trigger fear and suspicion in us.

But as nations are becoming more and more culturally diverse because of immigration and political, social, and economic factors, the face of the world is changing and new identities and cultural spaces are emerging. With these changes we are offered an opportunity to gain a new appreciation for the richness of diversity.

Within this new social reality, understanding culture and the process of identity formation not only can give us new light to appreciate the social complexities of the biblical text; it can also help us realize how our own cultural diversity as readers affects the ways we read the Bible and live in a multicultural world.

Defining Culture

Culture is a word we commonly use but rarely define. Culture can be explained as the sum total of our everyday practices and "texts"—the ways we live everyday life, our behavior, beliefs, social interactions, and all human production, such as food, clothing, art, ideology, institutions, and, most importantly, language. Culture is the collective space where the meanings we produce are assimilated or resisted; it is the battleground where the ideologies of those in power are established or dissolved; it is the public and private terrain where we create our personal and social identities. Culture—with its values, points of view, and traditions—shapes the way we see life, understand the world, define ourselves, think, act, create community, relate to others, and express our sense of belonging to family, groups, and nations.

All the creation, expression, and transmission of culture and identity is only possible through the fundamental vehicle of language. Through language we create meaning to express ourselves, and because meaning can only be understood in context, language is intrinsically connected to culture. Through the acquisition of language we enter into a cultural dialogue already in progress as we go through a process of socialization.

Language is fundamental for cultural identity: it shapes our perception of reality, past and present. Our native languages express our identity and culture in ways that no foreign language can. Language is a maker of identity; when languages disappear, cultures die. Losing a native language means losing aspects of a culture and an identity. On the other hand, speaking other languages creates the opportunity for different or multiple identities as we immerse ourselves into other cultures. As a strategy of colonization, native languages were suppressed in order to undermine a native people's

sense of nation, community, culture, and therefore identity. In some other instances, immigrants who arrive in a new country, or later generations of their offspring, have refused to speak their native language to avoid being identified with a certain group. This is a way of erasing an identity that is not equally valued in a new context.

With the help of technology, we have managed to increase our mobility in the world more than ever before. Now we find ourselves negotiating our identities in a new world where multiple cultures converge in neighboring spaces in most big cities. With an abundance of new cultural traits around us, we find ourselves constantly modifying our identities, looking for new ways to communicate with others in a changing world.

Identity Formation

Identity, or how we speak about ourselves, can be defined in different ways. The spectrum of definitions ranges from those that assign autonomy and power to the self—as a being not only in control of the process of self-definition but also capable of changing social structures—to those that barely recognize the existence of the individual. The latter definitions assert that the multiple external forces at play in the formation of our identities hardly give us any control over the ways we define ourselves, let alone any power to create change apart from what current social structures allow.

Identity formation is complex and not easily defined, but three main ideas are crucial in this process. First, identities are shaped by power relations; they are created in relation to outsiders (thus Western representations of the non-Western "other" in terms of ethnic identities are often seen as subordinated to the West). Second, identities are not unified; they are fragmented, ruptured, discontinuous, and contradictory. We are split among political allegiances; we have multiple identities that sometimes struggle within us. Third, identities are constantly in flux; they are always changing, not fixed products; they are productions in process.

By and large, although we could say that there are some genetic predispositions involved, the formation of identity is mostly a social process. Even identity markers such as ethnicity, skin color, gender, sexual orientation, or physical disabilities cannot really be said to affect our identity because of biological predispositions; rather, they are identity markers because of the cultural value we have assigned to such characteristics.

Identity is formed within culture and in relation to those around us. We learn to become ourselves by observing others, mirroring behaviors, trying out new patterns of action, following in the steps of those we admire, or by those we feel pressured to imitate. Our identity is formed in community, and therefore understanding others helps us understand ourselves.

Even before we can speak, the formation of our identity has already started. We come into a world that has a culture and a language with ready-made labels, names, and expectations that begin to shape our identity even without our knowledge. At first, our existence is automatically explained through those labels. Later on, once we have acquired language and a sense of the culture that surrounds us, we can escape some of those labels and choose others on our own. Our power to define who we are is limited, however, by language, a system already established by society before we participate in it.

Despite the sense of being trapped by language, identity is fluid and dynamic. It changes as we move in life and adopt new cultures, new ideologies, new beliefs, new languages. Identity is in constant motion, just as culture and language are, which in turn helps us create new and complex identities shaped by our cultural heritage, family, geography, religion, and social identity. Identity is a *process*. At any moment, identity is only a snapshot of a person who continues to grow, develop, and identify herself or himself in diverse ways. We are not born with an essence of identity within ourselves that we need to discover; identity is rather a social and public process linked to the personal and emotional ways we define ourselves at different conscious and unconscious levels.

The construction of our identity is not an abstract process in a vacuum; it is historically grounded in culture and involves a lot of emotions and feelings. For many it can be traumatic as we move from childhood to adulthood, if we do not find the support to be ourselves in the face of stressful or even harmful social and cultural expectations.

Our identities are also grounded in larger histories. Just as our nations are characterized geographically by specific terrains shaped by natural forces over time—mountains, rivers, deserts, and plains—so our identities are affected by government, religious, educational, and other cultural institutions that have been shaped by the sweep of history.

Culture, Identity, and the Bible

As complex as it may sound, we all experience culture and identity in our daily lives, and it is through these social realities that we learn to understand the world that surrounds us. As we read the Bible, we should keep in mind that although we may find some stories very familiar because of our experiences in life, it is still important to ponder the stories in their own cultural context before translating their message into our own. Just because we find a point of correlation between a biblical story and our own lives does not mean that we can ignore the temporal and cultural gap between us and the Bible. Some of the most oppressive readings of the Bible arise, for example, when we lose track of the liberating message of a text and seek instead to reproduce the cultural settings of the text—trying, say, to reproduce the social mores of the first-century church in a twenty-first-century context.

As we explore aspects of culture and identity in the Bible, we should also keep in mind that just as we are constantly negotiating our identity in complex cultural settings, the people of the Bible were also negotiating their own identities in the midst of different cultures. In the First Testament we see the Hebrews forming a new identity as the people of God in the midst of a hostile environment, surrounded by cities and nations with different and often opposing cultures and customs. Later we see a similar struggle in the Second Testament when those who believed in Jesus were called to adopt a new identity in the midst of political, cultural, and religious opposition. In both cases, the process of identity formation as people of God became a constant struggle as men and women seemed at times to adopt the identity of those around them as a strategy of survival, and at other times to strive to establish a clearly different identity that distinguished them from their neighbors—even when that might have implied oppression, violence, and death.

Culture and Identity in the Bible

Most discussions among biblical scholars about cultural identity focus on the issue of ethnicity. For example, scholars tend to understand Israelite identity in relationship to Israel's emergence and history as a nation—from a confederation of tribes to a monarchy, from a divided monarchy to Assyrian and Babylonian deportations, from exile to repatriating peoples in the province of Yehud (Judah). In contemporary North America, especially in the United States, while ethnicity also plays an important role for cultural groups, the issue of race is one of the key identifying marks of cultural identity, especially for people of color. "Race" usually refers to particular physical traits (for example, skin color) around which groups understand a common culture. However, the division of peoples into racial categories is arbitrary, varying from one Western society to another and having no basis in human genetics. The practice developed among the pioneers of the social sciences in the West and had racist underpinnings and assumptions. In spite of this history, African Americans, Latina/o Americans, and Asian Americans have continued to use these racial designations strategically to build community and to obtain a collective political and social voice.

Contemporary understandings of racial identity are not used as prominently in the Bible to mark identity as are ethnicity or religion. Historically, "ethnicity" tends to refer to issues of identity that are related to the identity of a people or a nation. In biblical terminology, the Greek word *ethnos*, from which we derive the word *ethnicity*, refers to a people or a nation (although in the New Testament the NRSV consistently translates the plural *ethnē* as "Gentiles"). In early Judaism, and in the New Testament (where early Christians of whatever ancestry often considered themselves to be in continuity with Judaism), other "peoples" or "nations" fell under the generic collective term *ethnē*.

The writers of the Hebrew Bible assumed that their place in and perspective of the world was normative for all humankind. The contemporary reader of the biblical text must recognize, however, that the Hebrew Bible is told from the perspective of a small, colonized group of peoples who lived in successive generations in the land first called Canaan. Most of these writings were compiled in the sixth and fifth centuries BCE, though some books, sources, and texts were written earlier in Israel's history. Moreover, most of the biblical authors wrote from the perspective of the southern kingdom of Judah (928–586 BCE), which had its capital in Jerusalem. Northern traditions are still present in a significant way, but the point of view is heavily skewed toward that of the Southern Kingdom. All these factors influence the way that a people understood its identity as Israel and how Israel came to be represented in relation to other peoples in the biblical text.

National identity, or ethnicity, certainly plays a large role in Israel's self-understanding. Israelite traditions show an awareness of different national identities within Canaan

 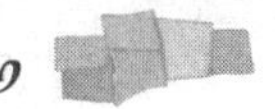

and beyond, represented in the various nation lists that appear in biblical narrative and law (Gen 10; Deut 7:1) and in oracles against the nations within prophetic materials (Amos 1–2; Jer 46–51). As far as the biblical text indicates, Israelite cultural identity tends to understand itself as fundamentally different from these foreign "others." Hence, in Deuteronomy 7, part of what makes Israel a chosen nation before its God is its religious and cultural distinctiveness from the surrounding peoples. Israelites are not to worship as those other peoples do, nor are they to make covenants with them or intermarry with them (see Deut 7:1–6). Thus, the people are called to be holy, that is, separate or set apart to their God. This language of religious and cultural distinctiveness must be understood in light of Israel's status as a small nation in the shadow of great empires. Archaeologists and biblical scholars now recognize that the cultural artifacts and religious traditions of earliest Israel were actually very consistent with the traditions from surrounding Canaanite society. In fact, on the basis of its similarity in material culture, many scholars now hold that early Israel was ethnically indistinguishable from the Canaanites. They further contend that the sharp differentiation that later biblical writers, living under the aegis of the Persian Empire, sought to maintain between Israelite and "Canaanite" is not as much related to an actual ethnic difference between their ancestors and the people of Canaan as it is a cultural, social, or religious construction serving particular purposes in the sixth and fifth centuries BCE. We can certainly understand the perceived need for constructing such a difference. When small groups or peoples feel the impact of larger empires (such as the Egyptian, Assyrian, Babylonian, or Persian empires), the need for cultural identity and particularity increases. Thus, in the Hebrew Bible we see ancient Israel constructing its self-understanding as religiously and culturally unique: they are a chosen people who are in a special relationship to their God.

Within the New Testament, the language of cultural specificity and religious uniqueness takes on a similar tone. Even though some early Christians saw their missionary activity as being inclusive of the whole world (Matt 28:19; Acts 1:8), cultural identity in early Christian groups was often maintained by dividing the world into two parts—God's chosen people (the elect, understood as the church) and outsiders, who are often described as the "other" nations (the "Gentiles"). While the early apostolic communities sought to join Jews and non-Jews together in the circle of those who were considered chosen (a process that plays out in different ways through the letters of Paul and the book of Acts), that very distinction shows that the cultural assumptions of Roman-era Judaism remained strong among these communities. We see in Paul's letters the concern to establish a new identity for non-Jewish believers that is neither Jewish nor "Gentile" (see, for example, 1 Cor 5:1, where the NRSV translates *ethnesin* as "pagans"). When later New Testament writings begin to speak of Jews (or "Judeans"; in Greek, *Ioudaioi*) as the "other," scholars see evidence that the composition of the early Christian movement shifted decisively from a Jewish to a non-Jewish majority, probably soon after the fall of Jerusalem in 70 CE. The reader of biblical material must remember that, similar to what we find in the Hebrew Bible, the New Testament writings represent the perspectives of small groups of people living under an imperial authority (so the traditions of Jesus' birth are set within an environment of Roman occupation: Matt 2; Luke 2:1-2). Even though the Christian church was later accepted by the Roman Emperor Constantine, the New Testament writings show a more conflicted relationship between early Christian identity and empire. But the drive to establish group identity by distinguishing insiders from outsiders, whether those outsiders are "Gentiles" or Jews, may be understood as different responses to the pressures of an imperial culture.

Culture and Identity of Readers

It is well beyond the scope of this essay to address the multiplicity of contemporary readers and the cultural contexts in which they seek to find meaning in the Bible. However, one of the important features of *The Peoples' Bible* is that it represents a shift in the way scholars approach the biblical writings. Indeed, in recent decades, scholars of both the Hebrew Bible and New Testament have increasingly recognized the importance of identifying the cultural and social location of readers in a more disciplined and concrete way. For most of the nineteenth and twentieth centuries, a method of investigation known as historical criticism had been the dominant mode of scholarly exploration of the biblical text. In its basic form, historical criticism, which emerged in Europe among other intellectual developments in the Enlightenment, believed that contemporary readers must set aside their own self-understanding in order to examine the historical contexts of the biblical authors and readers. In this way, historical critics understood that contemporary readers' biases could substantially influence the ways they read the text. Hence, historical critics recognized the importance—and in their minds the potential danger—of people reading their own self-interest into the Bible.

What historical critics often failed to recognize, however, was that their own ways of reading were not universal principles through which the biblical text became evidently clear to all peoples of the world. Historical criticism itself is a culturally contextualized approach to the biblical text—one that is heavily shaped within the context of post-Enlightenment Europe, especially Germany. It served the purpose of helping biblical scholars to be objective in their approach to the biblical text. This objectivity had at least two functions. First, similar to broader trends within theology, biblical criticism was seeking to define itself as a legitimate form of "scientific" inquiry (in German, *Wissenschaft*). Within this methodology, objectivity became an important value in presenting biblical criticism as a legitimate form of knowledge within European intellectual life. Second, biblical scholarship during this time sought to distance itself from the traditional and confessional interpretations that emerged from faith traditions. Hence, objective, disinterested inquiry was championed as a way to create a safeguard against interpretations of the Bible that sought to reinforce the positions of the church in an age of increased secularization.

During the last third of the twentieth century, which saw the emergence of racial and cultural identities following the Civil Rights era, biblical scholars and theologians began to understand the vitality and importance of new perspectives from African Americans, Latinas/os, Asian Americans, Native Americans, and many other historically marginalized groups. In his important essay "Toward a Hermeneutics of the Diaspora: A Hermeneutics of Otherness and Engagement" (1995), Fernando Segovia argued that biblical scholarship must take seriously the "real reader" of the Bible. Segovia's argument represents a larger trend in biblical scholarship that moves beyond historical criticism's objective reader and fully engages the social and cultural location of real readers with the same disciplined rigor that has been a hallmark of biblical scholarship from its inception. This shift highlights the important role that a reader's cultural context plays in generating meaning in relation to the biblical material. Hence, within culturally contextual biblical interpretation, scholars and readers find importance not only in the cultures of ancient Israel, Judaism, and early Christianity, but they also highlight the significant contributions of people of color to the interpretation of the biblical text. All interpreters, regardless of their social location, benefit from the powerful interpretative insights of African Americans and Latin American liberation theologians in their expositions of the exodus and liberation narratives of the Hebrew Bible. Native American and Palestinian perspectives on the conquest narratives, in which readers often find themselves sympathizing with invaded Canaanites, help all of us to understand the problematic side of the language of chosenness that is so prevalent in both the First and Second Testaments. Asian American interpretations of the Ruth and Esther stories help all of us to see the various cultural nuances and conflicting responses that happen when a group seeks to establish their identity in a dominant culture that sees them only as foreign others.

Culture and Identity in our Reading of the Bible

Culture, whether it is understood through identity markers such as race, ethnicity, class, gender, or sexual orientation, affects the way we understand the biblical text. But this does not lead us toward a negative understanding of Babel—the confusion of too many tongues all speaking different languages. Rather, this great polyphony of different cultural voices challenges the assumption that one can learn only through the limited experience of voices similar to one's own. Within all of the great religions of the world that assume some form of god or gods, we find a common theme: human beings do not learn from what is similar to them but from what is different. Within the Bible, people of faith also maintain that humans have a great capacity to be transformed when they come in contact with the holy Other, whose desire it is to dwell among human beings. What goes for human interactions with the divine holds true as well for human-to-human interactions. We learn from difference. We can be mutually transformed as we listen attentively to our very different understandings of the God that we may encounter in and through the biblical text.

As we read the Bible, let us keep in mind that culture shapes our faith and how we read. Since meaning is bound to context, there is no single general understanding of the Bible that will be valid for everyone; understanding is always particularized, modified by our context.

Cultural diversity is an integral part of who we are. Learning to appreciate its richness can help us overcome our biases, our racism and our discrimination, so that we can see our interdependency with others. We are formed in light of others who have preceded us. Devaluing or seeking to destroy cultural diversity hinders and limits our understanding of the world and of the Word. Valuing diversity and the richness that it brings makes us stronger as a people and allows us to discover and respect the otherness in ourselves as well.

The Bible as a Text of Cultures

Randall C. Bailey

One of the difficulties in approaching the Bible is that we have been conditioned to look at it as "the Word of God," which gives it a sense of universalism and timelessness, and elevates it as a reality above culture. This way of viewing the Bible has helped in transporting it from one culture to another; it has also made it easier for people to read the Bible as though their own cultural biases were embodied in the text itself. The sense that there is but one way to view the text and only one way to interpret it has been reinforced by a view that "our way of doing it is the right way." Too often we have failed to look at the biblical text as a cultural production within its own time and geographical location, and we have not recognized that our interpretations of the biblical text have been prodded and shaped by our own cultural understandings and time. This has robbed us, as readers, of the rich textures of the text and, ironically, has inflated the importance of our own readings to equal the high status we have attributed to the Bible itself.

One exception to this way of reading comes when we see something in the text that is embarrassing or upsetting. For example, in Genesis 16, Sarai tells Abram to have sex with her Egyptian slave, Hagar, so that Sarai can take Hagar's baby as a way of fulfilling God's promise to Abram—that he will be the father of a great nation (Gen 16:1-6). We readily recognize that this is about raping a slave, as we would see it in our own time. Yet we seek to explain it away, saying, for example, "That is just how it was in those times. This wasn't sexual abuse—it was just the custom of people back then." At a wedding in Cana, in John's gospel, Jesus responds to his mother, "Woman, what concern is that to you and to me?" (John 2:4). Most of us know that were we to address our own mothers that way, we probably wouldn't be able to finish the sentence! But since Jesus is the speaker, we imagine, "That must have been a term of endearment in those days." In other words, we have been trained to read the Bible as though there isn't much difference between the culture of our time and place and that of the text—*except* when it becomes so obviously problematic that we assert, rightly or wrongly, that the culture behind the biblical text must have been dramatically different from our own!

Scripture and Culture

In approaching the biblical text, we should understand that the books that finally won places in the canon were not originally written by people who thought they were contributing to such a limited and authoritative collection. There was no collection, no Bible, and no plan for a Bible when people first composed the books that ended up in the Hebrew Bible, or First Testament. There was no doctrine of inspiration of the writings in either the First or Second Testament at the time those writings were being composed. (True, 2 Tim 3:16 states, "All scripture is inspired by God and is useful for teaching, for reproof, for correction, and for training in righteousness." But at the time that verse was written, only the Hebrew Bible and the Septuagint, that is, the Greek translation of the Hebrew Bible, had been compiled as Scripture. Even those two collections did not agree as to which books should be included or excluded, nor regarding order or wording of those books. The statement in 2 Timothy cannot refer to the New Testament, which wasn't assembled into its current order until some two hundred years later.) The doctrine of the Bible's inspiration as an article of faith is a modern concept, developed in response to the critical study of the Bible in the eighteenth and nineteenth centuries.

The authors of the books we find in our Bibles today were writing to people of their time, exploring ideas of what life was about and how God wanted them to live. They were talking to people of their era, in languages, and using metaphors and symbols

that made sense to their contemporaries. It isn't surprising that the biblical authors primarily used symbols and ideas that would make sense to *men* from the upper classes—their readers—because in the ancient world only upper-class men were taught to read and write. Some examples help make the point clear.

In the world of ancient Judah and Israel, polygamy—the marriage of a man to several women at the same time—was the norm. Thus, we see that Jacob was married to Leah and Rachel (Gen 29:21-30); David was married to Michal (1 Sam 18:27), Abigail (1 Sam 25:42), Bathsheba (2 Sam 11:27), and other women as well (2 Sam 15:16). Solomon is reported to have married 700 princesses and 300 concubines (1 Kgs 11:3)! In the New Testament, we read that a bishop can only have been married once (1 Tim 3:2)—but we are not told that this was a requirement for other "Followers of the Way," much later called Christians. Today, however, we practice monogamy as though it were a clear biblical mandate.

An interesting aspect of this reading of the biblical text is that when African and other men who practice polygamy convert to Christianity, they often are required to divorce all but one of their wives. Given the clear acceptance of this marriage style in much of the Bible, it is a matter of curiosity—and of concern—to see that the church has often disrupted families because of false claims about "what the Bible says." While Paul in 1 Corinthians 7 speaks positively regarding marriage, he describes it as a distant second choice to asceticism and celibacy, and as an alternative appropriate only for those who cannot live his own lifestyle.

The ancient world also knew the practice of levirate marriage. In essence, when a man died without a male heir, his brother was to impregnate the widow, so that the first son born to her would carry the name of the deceased man. This practice is the basis of the story of Tamar in Genesis 38, of Ruth and Boaz in Ruth 3–4, and of the question the Sadducees pose to Jesus about a woman who had multiple husbands (Matt 22:23-30). It may surprise us to note that Jesus says nothing to question the practice of levirate marriage. Here again, understanding a culture different from our own helps us better understand what is going on in the Bible.

Scholars have noted that the royal administrations of David and Solomon's courts use the Egyptian form of government in the incorporation of the offices of recorder and secretary (2 Sam 8:15-18; 20:23-26; 1 Kgs 4:1-6). Even in this example we see a wider pattern in the Bible: the political life of ancient Israel and Judah was influenced by the ways of the peoples and nations with whom they lived and interacted. Similarly, Jesus likely spoke Aramaic and, as many scholars have observed, would probably have been perceived by many of his contemporaries in Galilee and Judah as a prophet with a politically incendiary message. That his speeches come to us in Greek means that early on they were subjected to a certain Greco-Roman spin—as incongruous, I imagine, as presenting Billy Graham's sermons in hip-hop.

There is evidence that biblical writers borrowed directly from other cultures. For instance, Ps 110:1-3a says:

> The LORD says to my lord,
> "Sit at my right hand
> until I make your enemies your footstool."
> 2 The LORD sends out from Zion
> your mighty scepter.
> Rule in the midst of your foes.
> 3 Your people will offer themselves willingly
> on the day you lead your forces
> on the holy mountains.

Here "the LORD" is a reference to God. On the other hand, "my lord" is a reference to the king—note the "scepter" in verse 2 and "your people" being led in verse 3. In verse 1, the statement that the king's enemies will be his footstool appears to be a direct reference to Egyptian court custom: the Pharaoh was seated on a throne, with his feet on a stool that bore the carved names of his enemies.

In the New Testament we have lists that scholars call the Household Codes (Eph 5:22—6:9; Col 3:18—4:1; 1 Pet 2:18—3:7). These passages talk about relationships of wives and husbands, children and parents, and slaves and masters. To varying degrees they talk not only about the responsibility of the subordinate members of each pair to the dominant ones; they also to some extent instruct the dominant ones to be nice to their subordinates. Although we know of no Greco-Roman document that bears such instructions, the ordering of God, husband, wife, child, and slave is a

New Testament adaptation of the social organization of families in the Greco-Roman world. In other words, these instructions tell the members of the early Followers of the Way groups that they should be organized in line with Roman customs.

Different Cultural Views within Scripture

Within the biblical writings as well we find examples of writers debating with other writers over issues of culture and cultural theologies. For example, 2 Sam 24:1 states, "Again the anger of the LORD was kindled against Israel, and he incited David against them, saying, 'Go, count the people of Israel and Judah.'" As the story has it, once David does what God incited him to do, he is punished and given three choices: three years of famine, being pursued by his enemies for three months, or three days of pestilence. He chooses pestilence (vv. 13-15). We may be surprised to hear of a biblical character being punished for doing what God urged him to do, until we recognize that there are other places in the books of Samuel—for example 1 Sam 16:14 which tells us that God sent an evil spirit on Saul—where God is described as doing good and bad things to people. The writers of Chronicles—probably written in the fifth century BCE—didn't like this theology. So when the same story is retold, 1 Chron 21:1 states that "Satan"—not God!—"stood up against Israel, and incited David to count the people of Israel." Chronicles was written during the Persian period, when Yehud (Judah) was a colony of Persia. The writers of Chronicles were influenced by Persian thought and theology, including a dualism that posed one power, responsible for good, against another power responsible for evil. The writers of Chronicles could blame Satan for inciting David to do something that would get him and the nation into trouble—a conception that wasn't available to the earlier writers of Samuel, because they lived in a different time and a different culture. The contrast allows us to recognize that those who today chant "God is good—all the time!" agree more closely with the theology of 1 Chronicles than that of 2 Samuel.

Similarly, in the New Testament, when Paul is asked whether it is all right to eat meat purchased in the marketplace (that is, meat that had been sacrificed to other gods), he responds that, yes, it is: since our God is God of all the earth, sacrificing to other gods was nothing more than wasted activity on the part of the Corinthian butchers and those making the sacrifice (1 Cor 10:25-29). His only disclaimer is that eating such meat is not allowed if someone else is offended by the practice. Paul takes the stand that when there is a conflict between the practices of the broader culture and tenets of the faith, unless the issue is one of crucial import, believers should "go along with the flow" culturally.

But the writer of Revelation totally disagrees on this and other issues. Addressing meat sacrificed to idols, he compares it to fornication and presents the risen Christ as threatening harm to those who do it (Rev 2:14-16). So this writer says one should not accommodate to culture but, rather, stand fast.

Here again we have two different biblical writers addressing the same episode or situation and taking different positions. Paul may have regarded the prospect of making it to Rome as a high point in his career; Luke certainly presents his preaching in Agrippa's court as a climax of Paul's story in Acts. The writer of Revelation, on the other hand, was living through a time of great persecution by the Romans, so he viewed any accommodation to them or their culture as evil. Two different biblical writers, at different times and under different social circumstances, disagree—and both of their contrary positions end up in the biblical text. Perhaps we should take this as a signal that those who put the Bible together recognized that culture and times influence theology, and that there is more than one way to look at things.

Readers from different cultures and different times have looked at the same text and come up with radically different ways of interpreting the text. The Pilgrims who migrated to North America in the seventeenth century read Exod 3:7-8:

> Then the LORD said, "I have observed the misery of my people who are in Egypt; I have heard their cry on account of their taskmasters. Indeed, I know their sufferings, [8]and I have come down to deliver them from the Egyptians, and to bring them up out of that land to a good and broad land, a land flowing with milk and honey, to the country of the Canaanites, the Hittites, the Amorites, the Perizzites, the Hivites, and the Jebusites."

The Pilgrims saw this passage as inspiration to leave their homes in England, where they were being persecuted for their religious beliefs, move to Holland, and then to travel to the "New World," which they called the "Promised Land." They saw both their leaving their place of oppression and their taking the lands of the native peoples

in the Americas as following divine warrant. The Afrikaner Dutch Reformed Church in South Africa read that text in much the same way.

Enslaved Africans in the Americas heard those same verses as saying that God would free them from enslavement. They sang "Go Down, Moses," and interpreted their experience as paralleling Israel's. They even called Harriett Tubman the "Black Moses." Their hopes for manumission were inspired by such biblical passages. As a biblical scholar I find it interesting that enslavers and enslaved alike looked on the same passage as a way of justifying their actions, and as a Black man in the United States, I consider it of utmost importance that we all reflect deeply on that fact.

Latin American liberation theologians also looked to the Exodus story as a way of arguing that God had a special "preferential option" for the poor. They saw this narrative as encouragement to struggle against oppressors in their context. South African theologians opposed to apartheid appropriated this text in similar ways, and for similar reasons.

But some Native American theologians challenged black and liberation theologians on their use of the Exodus paradigm. They noted that the liberation of the people of Israel, spoken of in verse 7, is followed by a foreshadowing of the conquest of the Canaanites in verse 8. The God of liberation, they declared, was also a God of dispossession. Given their experience with the conquest of their lands in the Americas, these Native American theologians found themselves identifying more with the Canaanites than with the Israelites. They asked black and liberation theologians why they didn't also identify with the Canaanites, given their oppression at the hands of those who had come from Europe and had brought many of them to the Americas as slaves.

Reading Out, Reading In

We read what Scripture says differently—and sometimes we may be reading what we believe as much as what Scripture itself says! Some have read Genesis 19, the story of the destruction of Sodom and Gomorrah, as a condemnation of homosexuals. That argument is based on one way of reading verse 5, which says the men of these cities "called to Lot, 'Where are the men who came to you tonight? Bring them out to us, so that we may know them.' " If we assume that the word *know* here means—as we often put it—"to know *in the biblical sense,*" that is, sexually, then we might further assume that the men of Sodom are making a sexually threatening request. This view finds some reinforcement in Lot's response in verses 7-8:

> I beg you, my brothers, do not act so wickedly. Look, I have two daughters who have not known a man; let me bring them out to you, and do to them as you please; only do nothing to these men, for they have come under the shelter of my roof.

Lot responds as if he thinks this is a sexual request and feels that letting his neighbors rape his daughters is better than letting them rape his male guests. Part of our problem is that many contemporary readers would agree with Lot on both counts!

However, several observations call that interpretation into question. When the Lord tells Abraham that these cities are to be destroyed (18:20-21), there is no description of the behaviors to which the Lord objects. Further, we regularly recognize the difference between gang rape (which may be carried out against vulnerable persons—prisoners, for example, in prison or military settings—by men who understand themselves as heterosexual) and same-gender sexuality. The men of Sodom and Gomorrah might well have expected to assault Lot's guests and then go home to their wives. Finally, Ezek 16:48-49 clearly suggests that the sin of Sodom was its lack of hospitality; nothing indicates it had to do with homosexuality.

Others have argued that this story is really about the sexual abuse of daughters. The verb *know* appears twice later, in Gen 19:33 and 35, when Lot's daughters committed incest with their drunken father. We read that Lot "did not know" when his daughter "lay down or when she rose." Clearly, in these verses the verb refers to awareness, not to knowing in the sense of sexual activity. Could it be that the men of Sodom just wanted knowledge of who was in the city? Note that it is *Lot* who thinks their request has sexual intention, and responds by offering his daughters for abuse. Lot is not the most morally reliable of characters. Later he seeks to exonerate himself with regard to incest with his daughters by saying that he was so drunk, he didn't know what was happening. Those who regard the "sin of Sodom" as simply a lack of hospitality might bear in mind that Lot's understanding of hospitality is to sacrifice his daughters. My point is that often our readings are shaped by what in a passage seems either to help or to hurt us; often we ignore what else is going on, either in the passage or in our own interpretations.

Another example is presented in the Magnificat, Mary's song in Luke 1:46-55, which reads in part:

My soul magnifies the Lord,
    and my spirit rejoices in God my Savior,
for he has looked with favor on the lowliness of his servant.
    Surely, from now on all generations will call me blessed;
for the Mighty One has done great things for me,
    and holy is his name.

This song often is held up as an example of how the women in the Gospel according to Luke hold a special role. So, for example, the birth story in Matthew 1 concentrates on Joseph and his feelings, but Luke's account of the birth concentrates on Mary and even allows her to speak. The song ends with verses 52-55:

He has brought down the powerful from their thrones,
    and lifted up the lowly;
he has filled the hungry with good things,
    and sent the rich away empty.
He has helped his servant Israel,
    in remembrance of his mercy,
according to the promise he made to our ancestors,
    to Abraham and to his descendants forever.

Churches that celebrate and lift up Mary for veneration and prayer look to this song as validating their claims of her special role in the life of Jesus. After all, there is no Song of Joseph. This song has also had great appeal to some liberation theologians, because it speaks of a God of reversal who helps the oppressed. These verses strengthen the claim of a special option for the poor in the Gospels.

Yet there are feminists and womanists who ask, How long will women have to put themselves in harm's way to save others and to be part of the struggle? How long will women, even when involved in shared community struggles, be expected to do "women's work" rather than taking true leadership roles? These critics see Mary's song as a way of encouraging women to go along, even in times of struggle, and to put themselves in jeopardy. Again we see that wherever one enters the story—whether in line with one's own experience, that of one's people, or of one's race, gender, social class, or sexual orientation—may dictate how one reads and interprets a text.

Sometimes we feel compelled to take other people's readings and make them our own. At other times we may feel compelled to struggle with these texts, to discern how they fit—or whether they fit—with our lives. For these texts not only grow out of certain historical and cultural contexts, they are also read and interpreted by people who live in very different contexts. Perhaps our goal could be to hear one another's readings and to see what is guiding them. Perhaps in this we can learn to see the richness in the texts, in the interpretations—and in the interpreters.

The Bible as a Text in Cultures: An Introduction

Fernando F. Segovia

Biblical interpretation involves widely differing ways of reading the text. For instance, a dogmatic-theological reading is used as official church doctrines are formulated. An ecclesial-liturgical reading is concerned with the conduct and worship of the church. A popular-devotional reading is at work in the daily practices and common piety of church members. Cultural readings of the text show up in literature, music, art, film, and the like. Social readings pertain to politics or the economy. And the academic-scholarly tradition puts the text into the world of higher education and knowledge production. Each of these reading traditions can be varied and complex, using any number of approaches or perspectives.

Ideally, biblical criticism—a term reserved for the academic-scholarly strand—should have within its angle of vision and study *all* of these reading traditions. Historically, however, that has not been the case. The discipline has mostly confined itself to analysis of its own trajectories and discourses. As a result, biblical criticism has pursued the study of the Bible as a text "in culture" but not "in cultures." *Culture* should be understood broadly, as meaning not only cultural production of symbols but also the material matrix of a culture. Consequently, it would be better to say that biblical criticism has pursued the study of the Bible as a text "in society and culture," but not "in societies and cultures." Thus, until recently, biblical criticism has pursued such study as focused solely on ancient society and culture.

Within this narrow academic way of seeing, any mention of contemporary Euro-American readings or of African American, Asian American, Latina/o American, or Native American readings of the Bible was unthinkable. For me to specify that my own reading had something to do with my particular social location—as someone born and raised in Cuba, who had lived first in the world of the colonized as a citizen of a dependent country, and then in the world of the colonizer, as a member of what was in the United States a minority ethnic group—would have been regarded as intrusive and ruled out of order. The appearance of *The Peoples' Bible* is one indication that this situation no longer pertains. To understand this transformation it is necessary to retrace the history of the discipline.

The Rise of Biblical Criticism

Biblical criticism emerged as a tradition of reading in the early part of the nineteenth century, following upon the ferment of the French Revolution and paralleling the rise of several other areas of studies now formally pursued as disciplines in higher education. Its aim was to understand the texts of the Bible within their respective contexts, cultural as well as material, and, in so doing, to liberate the Bible from the doctrinal constraints placed upon it by the church. For this task of contextualization, biblical criticism was inspired by another new academic discipline of the time, historical studies. Biblical criticism latched onto the new historical methodology in its own investigation of texts from the past, yielding what could be described as an "umbrella" model or paradigm—a model of models—of interpretation that became known as historical criticism. The historical-critical method, which over time came to encompass a succession of varying but related models or angles of inquiry, proved dominant for about 150 years, right up to the final quarter of the twentieth century.

For historical criticism, the core challenge of contextualization was to bridge the historical gap that was perceived to exist between ancient writings and modern readers. This was done in a way that would avoid both reading the present back into the past (anachronism) *and* reading the critic's individual concerns and interests (or those of the critic's group) into the texts. This required, first, amassing as much historical knowledge as possible about the material and cultural realities of the particular

time and place of the text being read, particularly focusing on religious knowledge and practices. Second, because scholars wanted to avoid reading the critic's personal concerns and interests into the text, they technically called the task of interpretation *exegesis,* meaning "reading out of" the text, or letting the texts speak for themselves. Its opposite, *eisegesis,* "reading into" the text, or imposing on it the personal agenda of the modern reader, was considered to be a fundamental misreading of the text.

Historical criticism, then, represented itself as a scientific method, objective and impartial in character, trying to understand the original meaning of the ancient texts in their own contexts, within the limits of the evidence available to us. For proper learning and deployment of the method, it was necessary for critics to put aside all markers and preoccupations of identity, removing themselves from their own material and cultural contexts and become instead universal and informed readers. In the eyes of historical criticism, therefore, all other reading traditions were deemed to be fundamentally defective, yielding inaccurate and compromised perceptions of the past. Biblical criticism had set itself up as the one proper key to unlock the biblical past—the Bible in (ancient) society and culture—and hence the norm for any and all interpretation of the Bible.

New Approaches

The ascendency of this mode of biblical criticism was unchallenged until the mid-1970s. The challenge to establish biblical criticism followed the social ferment of the 1960s and ran parallel to the way similar questions were being asked across the humanities and social sciences. Following the earlier example of historical criticism itself, new models posed themselves as a liberation from the constraints imposed upon biblical interpretation by the old historical criticism. The challenge came from two different sides.

On the one hand, the first stirrings of what would eventually become two new umbrella models signaled a parting of the ways with traditional historical criticism. Literary criticism, interested in texts as texts rather than as windows to the world, turned to literary studies (narratology, reader response, rhetoric, psychology) for direction. Sociocultural criticism, focused on social contexts as contexts rather than as mere backdrops for texts, looked to the social sciences (sociology, anthropology) for its grounding. From each direction, and in very different ways, the reigning view of a

faithful retrieval of the past by neutral critics began to undergo destabilization. The literary turn showed that texts were multidimensional, that readers were actively involved in producing the meaning of texts, and that this process produced multiple readings. The sociocultural turn accentuated the placement of texts and readers in society and culture, and hence emphasized the gap between antiquity and modernity. This first deviation from the standing paradigm arose from within the discipline itself: it was pursued by its traditional practitioners, dissatisfied as they were with the state of affairs in criticism.

On the other hand, the new undertaking of what would in time become another umbrella model, ideological criticism, was more intent on identifying and analyzing relations of power in society and culture. Ideological criticism marked another dramatic departure from traditional historical criticism. For instance, feminist criticism pressed the question of gender constructions and gender relations, while liberation criticism questioned the effects of political economy and social class on biblical texts. These developments seriously shattered what had been an entrenched view of the objective and impartial recovery of the text's meaning and its history. The established critical tradition was instead portrayed as thoroughly situated and interested—highly patriarchal as well as highly middle-class in nature—despite its claim to and its mask of objectivity.

New Interpreters, New Locations

This second deviation from the ruling paradigm originated outside the traditional ranks of the discipline and involved a variety of newcomers, such as women scholars from the dominant culture in the West and male scholars from the non-Western world—especially Latin America at first—who had pursued graduate studies in the West. Ideological criticism continued to develop through the 1980s and 1990s as literary and sociocultural criticism as well as feminist and liberation criticism solidified and increased their hold. Minority criticism pursued racial-ethnic constructions and relations; queer criticism attended to sexual constructions and relations; and postcolonial criticism raised the issue of imperial-colonial relations. As a result, any claim to a single correct reading by informed and universal critics stood demolished. The older established critical tradition was again depicted as profoundly biased and not nearly as objective as it had claimed. It was now seen to be highly Euro-American, heterosexual, and empire-based. New models challenged the old model as having masked its

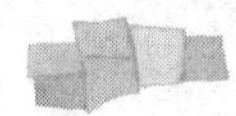

social location and political agenda under the guise of objectivity. More importantly, this further shift from the standing paradigm was generated by people whose social location was even farther outside the traditional discipline: men and women scholars from non-Western minority groups in the West, especially African Americans at first; gay and lesbian scholars from within the West; and men and women scholars from the former colonies of the West.

By the end of the century, biblical criticism had come full circle since its inception, paralleling similar developments in other fields of study. The changes in question were momentous. Instead of a single defining model, several competing models were now in operation and in dialogue with one another. Instead of a privileged and normative model standing guard over interpretation, the presence of a variety of models alongside one another yielded acknowledgment of multiple points of entry and multiple results in interpretation. Instead of readings producing a faithful recovery of meaning and history from the past, readings were now regarded as contextualized and "perspectival," offering constructions or representations of meaning and history that were themselves subject to critical analysis. Instead of critics who sought to transcend material and cultural contexts through scientific methodology, critics now emerged as embodying cultural contexts and engaged in those contexts, worthy of critical analysis in their own right.

Biblical criticism could now be envisioned in a different way altogether. Its objects of study were no longer only the texts and contexts of antiquity, as envisioned by traditional historical criticism, but also the modern and postmodern interpretations of ancient texts and contexts and the interpreters behind such interpretations. With the scientific ideals of objectivity and impartiality in retreat, biblical criticism now pursued more fully the study of the Bible as a text "in cultures and societies," meaning simultaneously in antiquity, modernity, and postmodernity. Texts, interpretations, and interpreters were now seen as not independent of one another but rather thoroughly enmeshed in and constitutive of one another.

The new lens provided by ideological criticism focused on the biblical text in terms of placement and ideology in society and culture, and hence on unequal relations of power. Suddenly, it was not only acceptable but imperative to critique the dominant tradition of interpretation, identified with Euro-American readings and the world of the North Atlantic, most evident in tradional historical criticism but present as well in the umbrella models of literary and sociocultural criticism. Now it was acceptable and imperative to speak of feminist, liberationist, minority, queer, and postcolonial readings. Now it was possible and necessary to speak of African American, Asian American, Latina/o, and Native American readings, where the central axis of discussion was the problem of race and ethnicity, in association with such related concepts as migration, the "nation," borders, racialization, and ethnicization. In each case, and in minority criticism as a whole, the discussion became at once ever more subtle and ever more complex. This is the state of affairs at present in biblical criticism.

Moving beyond the Circle of Experts

But a further and crucial development in the discipline needs to be mentioned. As a result of this transformation, there has been a fundamental change in attitude toward the other major traditions of reading the Bible. Biblical critics no longer work alone, apart from a world of others who read the Bible. Given all this emphasis on location and agenda regarding texts, readings, and readers coming from sociocultural and especially ideological criticism, plus the intense focus on the multiple voices of texts, the agency of readers, and the diversity of readings coming from literary and ideological criticism, another principle of established criticism had to give way. Biblical analysis could no longer be restricted to the experts, to the world of learned readings and readers. The line of argument was clear and to the point. If the academic-scholarly tradition of reading was no longer viewed as guaranteeing proper and impartial interpretation, but constituted at all times a situated and positioned exercise in reading, why should criticism not extend its field of vision to the other reading traditions? If the goal of contextualization was no longer considered applicable only to the texts of antiquity (via a faithful recapturing of past meaning and history) but was now construed as applicable to *all* constructions of the past and their agents (given their character as localized and engaged), why should criticism not include similar representations and their agents from the other reading traditions? In sum, why should the use of the Bible in the theological-dogmatic, the ecclesial-liturgical, the popular-devotional, and the cultural-social reading traditions not be subject to the same degree of attention and analysis?

Countless possibilities for research opened up as a result. Why not examine the use of the Bible in works of popular theology or in official church pronouncements? Why not explore appeals to the Bible in missionary endeavors or in preaching traditions?

Why not inquire into applications of the Bible in small church communities or in daily religious practices? Why not examine invocations of the Bible in works of poetry or in political discourse? Such a move signaled a much more expansive view of criticism, involving a broad conception of the Bible as text and of interpretation as task. The biblical writings no longer constituted just texts from the past bearing stable meanings. Now they represented living texts, drawn upon and reconfigured in ever so many ways, to ever so many ends, and with ever so many consequences. And biblical interpretation no longer represented simply an exercise in writing the history of ancient times, as if to retrieve one stable meaning from the past; now interpreters were fully aware of the problem of claiming to represent what history was "about" or what it "meant." Interpretation now became an exercise in cultural studies as well, attentive to all applications, their objectives, and their consequences.

Putting Our Interpretations in Context

With this extension of criticism into other reading traditions, a further principle of established criticism was revisited as well: the limitation of comparative analysis to the historical times and cultural areas of the ancient texts. For the goal of contextualized interpretation, comparative analysis of both symbolic and material aspects of culture was essential so that the biblical texts could be set as fully as possible—and thus explained as fully as possible—within their historical and cultural frameworks. As criticism moved to include analysis of modern and postmodern interpretations and interpreters, comparative analysis underwent an initial and corresponding expansion. It became imperative to situate such interpretations and interpreters, as constructive renditions of the biblical text, within their respective social-cultural contexts in modernity and postmodernity. Now, as criticism proceeded to include other major reading traditions as constructive renditions of the biblical texts, comparative analysis followed suit. It became similarly imperative, first, to situate such interpretations and interpreters within their respective social-cultural contexts; second, to place such interpretations and interpreters alongside one another, either within the same context or across a variety of contexts; and third, to place such interpretations and interpreters alongside the academic-scholarly tradition, either within the same context or across a variety of contexts.

By the end of the twentieth century biblical criticism had indeed come full circle. These changes proved as momentous as those at its beginning. Instead of setting

firm boundaries around the academic-scholarly tradition, other reading traditions were brought under its critical gaze. Instead of reserving comparative analysis to the academic-scholarly tradition, other reading traditions were now brought into critical juxtaposition with the academic-scholarly tradition and with one another. This was truly biblical criticism in a different key. Its object of study now comprehended all other major traditions of reading and their discourses. As a result, biblical criticism now pursued in full the study of the Bible "in societies and cultures"—in the world of learning as well as in all cultural appeals to it and renditions of it.

Within this comprehensive perspective, the issue of location and ideology in society and culture—that is, of power relations—was in the foreground in all areas of inquiry. Now it was not only imperative to speak of a dominant Euro-American tradition of interpretation in biblical criticism; it was proper to keep such a dimension in mind in *all* reading traditions. Now it was not only imperative to speak of feminist, liberationist, minority, queer, and postcolonial traditions of interpretation in criticism; it was proper to keep *all* such dimensions in mind across the other reading traditions. Now it was not only imperative to speak of African American, Asian American, Latina/o American, and Native American traditions of interpretation in criticism; it was proper to keep such dimensions in mind throughout the other reading traditions. In such minority approaches, the problematic of race and ethnicity and their related concepts functioned as the axis of discussion. The result in each case, as in minority criticism as a whole, was an even more subtle and more complex discussion. This is the present state of affairs in biblical criticism.

The result of this recent transformation has been, for many, a far more demanding, far more engaging, and far more fulfilling conception and practice of the discipline. Today's biblical criticism continues to look back to the past, but it also looks around in the present and forward to the future. It is a biblical criticism in full dialogue with others, within the discipline, across disciplines, across societies and cultures, and across all realms of societies and cultures. In sum, it is a criticism for which the Bible has become truly a text *in societies and cultures*.

The Bible as a Text in Cultures: African Americans

Vincent L. Wimbush

African American engagements with the Bible suggest much not only about who the people of the Bible are, how they sound and think, and what they mean and communicate but also about how Scripture functions in society and culture. African American use of the Bible as Scripture is varied and wide-ranging and has a storied history. These engagements should be understood as reflections of a people's long and continuing efforts to define and empower themselves. They are at once "readings" of the people and of the worlds with which they were forced to negotiate. These engagements reflect the people's consistent aspiration for power to signify upon, speak back to, and reshape the worlds and situations forced upon them.

One useful way to capture the complexity of African Americans' engagement with the Bible is through use of a framework of historical "readings." Such a schema will account for some of the recurring sentiments, practices, and orientations of a large segment of a people who have been called by many names, all reflecting marginal status, but in recent times most often "African Americans." The sketch presented here is organized historically, but the characteristics of each "reading" extend across the different types of readings, allowing us to observe different stages in orientation to the world.

First Reading: Awe and Fear—Initial Negotiation of the Bible and the New World

From the beginning of their captivity in different parts of the west coast of Africa and their traumatic translation to the Americas, where they experienced slavery and subjugation, peoples of African descent were confronted with the "civilizing" and missionizing agenda of the white-controlled system of black enslavement. One of the most important ideological tools used to advance this agenda was the Bible, held in common as an iconic text by all the European slave-trading nations.

Testimonies from European sailors, teachers, and missionaries, on the one hand, and from African, African American, and Afro-British autobiographies of the eighteenth and nineteenth centuries on the other, register the Africans' initial lack of understanding of European socio-religious orientations and their uneasy socialization into them. In arrogant presumption, European cultures violently imposed particular types of psycho-social scripts (ways of being), forms, and practices of literacy that at first frustrated the "conversion" of the Africans made to be slaves. Scripting and literacy per se were not the issue. But not only were the Africans on the whole incapable of meeting the culture-specific literacy requirements for conversion; they were not emotionally disposed toward the book religion of the slavers. The notion of the divine communicating via a book was odd and scary, as should have been expected upon first contact. But at the same time, Africans perceived behind such a notion something awesome, mysterious, fascinating, and full of potential for future negotiation and empowerment. This was the period of the foundation and cultivation of the folk traditions among the Africans made slaves in the Americas. The complex engagement with the Bible was an important part of the cultivation of such traditions.

Second Reading: Critique and Accommodation

Not until the late eighteenth century, with the phenomenal growth of dissenting, evangelical movements in England and in its colonies that were about to become the United States, did large numbers of the mostly enslaved Africans in the latter began to engage the Bible explicitly and in ways that were more and more self-interested. Finding themselves directly appealed to by the new evangelicals and revivalists in vivid, emotional biblical language, and seeing that nearly the entire white world explained its power and authority by appeal to the Bible, the Africans could hardly fail to be drawn closer to it. With great ingenuity, reflecting their awareness of their situation

and the times, they began to change the Bible from the sacred book of the white, aristocratic slavers and the mostly lower-class dissenting evangelical exhorters into a close-at-hand source of psychic-spiritual power and of hope. It offered inspiration for learning and language that was ready-made for a stinging, if veiled, critique of their situation. The Bible became for them a freighted site of social memory.

This reading extends well into the late twentieth century and may be considered the most popular, significant, and certainly the most enduring of the readings. It antedates but came to define and shape the independent African American churches and denominations that began in the late eighteenth century, as well as schools, colleges, and other organizations throughout the nineteenth century. It supplied the rhetoric and fueled many of the ideological-political positions of the civil rights movements and related campaigns of the mid-twentieth century. This reading of the Bible played an important role in the cultivation, in the late nineteenth to mid-twentieth century, of worldviews, initiatives, and political orientations that offered "racial uplift" to African Americans.

This reading—of both the Bible and of U.S. culture—expressed considerable ambivalence. It was at once critical and accommodationist. On the one hand, its respect for the primarily Protestant canon reflected its desire to be included within the nation's mainstream. On the other hand, its interpretations, including some burgeoning black "nationalist" sentiments, were on the whole from a social and ideological location "from below" and outside the mainstream—and these interpretations projected a blistering critique of Bible-believing, slave-holding, racist America.

Third Reading: Critique from the Margins among the Marginal

Another reading was cultivated in the early decades of the twentieth century, primarily in urban centers of the United States. It reflected the sentiments of rural and small-town residents who migrated to the big cities in search of better job opportunities, greater social freedom, and a sense of power. These displaced individuals formed new religious communities that gave them a sense of solidarity.

The reading of the Bible and of the world among such communities also reflected a particular attitude about society and culture. It was a more critical, even radical, attitude about America. It held out little hope of full integration into the mainstream. The

United States was seen as racist and arrogant, and was to be rejected as such. The use of the Bible and the creation and uses of other religious texts clearly reflect this attitude. Among the movements associated with such an attitude were the Garvey Movement, Father Divine and the Peace Mission Movement, the Black Jews, the Nation of Islam, the Spiritual churches, and the Pentecostal movement. These fairly marginal groups involving marginal peoples exerted considerable pressure upon mainstream groups to take note of the sentiments and practices to be found at the margins. But as a nonconfederated mix of communities, these folks remained marginal in numbers and power only for a few generations. They and the reading they fostered have in many respects come in the last few decades to define the center of African American religious life, including engagement with the Bible.

Fourth Reading: Fundamentalism—Leaving Race Behind

Another African American reading of the Bible and American culture emerged as a significant phenomenon in the late twentieth century. Sometimes called Fundamentalism, it was and continues to be in many respects a reaction to both the accommodationist and the separatist readings discussed above. This particular reading of the Bible is a sharp departure from the traditional African American use of the Bible. To be sure, African Americans have historically been evangelical in their religious sensibilities. For example, many African Americans continue to attach primary importance to the Bible as guide in all domains of life, including religious doctrine, morality, and ethics. Yet for a variety of reasons—including the politics of literacy and class divisions within and beyond religious denominations and also the richness of oral traditions and sensibilities among African peoples—most African Americans have historically been much more inclined toward playfulness and ingenuity than toward doctrinalism and moralism in their engagement with the Bible. In much the same way that the rise of Fundamentalism among whites in the early decades of the twentieth century represented a rejection of modernism, so within the world of African Americans a turn toward the universalism and color blindness offered in Fundamentalism can be seen as rejecting the significance of the particularities of African Americans' historical experiences.

The growth of such a reading, seen in the change in orientation of more traditional African American churches and in the founding of new churches and alliances with white Fundamentalist denominations and organizations, has resulted in the height-

ening of some tensions and the deepening of some fault lines within African America. These tensions are especially evident with regard to political initiatives and alliances.

Drawing the Circle More Widely: Women's Reading

In evidence throughout the history of African American readings of the Bible are the special readings of African American women. From Phyllis Wheatley to modern womanist interpreters, women have not only participated in each of the readings distinguished above; they have also constructed and transmitted those readings. Across all of these readings, differences in historical periods, locations, classes, and other factors notwithstanding, women collectively have for the most part added special emphases and intensities. Especially important has been their radical challenge to their male contemporaries, in every historical period and situation, to be consistent in striving for the prophetic ideals of justice and fairness.

Seen as a thread running through the story of a historically enslaved and subjugated people, we may see the Bible as a freighted cultural and political phenomenon, and a site for poignant social memories. Seen through this people's history, the Bible should not be viewed merely as holding different meanings for African Americans. The Bible must no longer be solely the object of historical criticism. We should see it as a focal point in critical histories of peoples and their journeys, orientations, practices, and politics.

The Bible as a Text in Cultures: Latinas/os

Francisco Lozada, Jr.

What distinguishes a Latina/o reading of the Bible from a European-Anglo reading or an African American, Asian American, or Native American reading of the Bible, to name only a few perspectives? One way to address this question is to examine the various ways Latinas/os have read the Bible through the lens of our experiences of *diaspora*—that is, of being unsettled, traveling, and resettling. These experiences are understood broadly; they involve not only an external diaspora, traveling from home country to host country, but also an internal diaspora, movement within a home or host country.

People and communities leave their home countries (into an external diaspora) for many reasons: political (for example, civil unrest or colonialism), economic (for example, globalization, scarcity of jobs), cultural (for example, social migration to reunite with family or escape religious intolerance), and those related to acts of nature (like earthquakes and hurricanes). Internal diasporas also have many causes: socioeconomic (searching for jobs), political (to escape anti-immigration laws), cultural (for example, in the United states, English-only laws), and, again, acts of nature (such as famines). Diaspora has traditionally been viewed in a temporally linear way, assuming that after the experience of resettlement, the diaspora experience ceases, both physically and mentally. But a more inclusive view sees diaspora as a temporally circular event that entails an ongoing experience. In other words, with every new wave of migration from Latin America, the process of diaspora starts over again for people from that particular country of origin, and for the Latina/o community in general. In addition, this circular understanding includes the view that diaspora involves social psychology and, in particular, the memory of many Latinas/os. This sense of diaspora is reflected in the titles of some biblical and theological books, including *Galilean Journey, Strangers in our Own Land,* and *A Dream Unfinished.*

Finally, the idea of diaspora is not fixed and stable but is fluid, extending beyond the first generations. Still, we should not assume that all Latinas/os have given a lot of reflection to either the concept or experience of diaspora.

A word about what I mean when I use the term *Latina/o*. It is Spanish nomenclature that is often mistranslated in English as "Latin." But Latina/o usually refers to communities whose cultural roots are traced to Latin America rather than to Spain. It is also a term that suggests permanency in the United States and that one has agency in claiming this identity for oneself. Finally, it is a term that is used loosely in the collective community, so as not to overshadow the unique cultural and historical particularities of the various Latina/o communities in the United States—Mexicans, Cubans, Puerto Ricans, Dominicans, Guatemalans, Salvadorans, Costa Ricans, Colombians, Venezuelans, Argentineans, and so on.

Being Unsettled or Uprooted

Due to the violent encounter of indigenous American peoples with the Spanish empire in the sixteenth to the eighteenth centuries and to the colonial and imperial involvement of the United States throughout much of Latin America and the Caribbean from the nineteenth century to the present, the history of Latinas/os in the United States involves a great deal of dislocation and migration to and within the United States. Many Mexican Latinas/os in the U.S. Southwest found their political identity changed overnight, against their will, when the United States acquired the Southwest territory (known by Chicanos/as as *Aztlán*) after the Mexican-U.S. War and the Treaty of Guadalupe Hidalgo in 1848. Similarly, Puerto Ricans became subjects of the United States overnight with the colonization of their island in 1898. Such

experiences of colonialism led many Latin Americans to unsettle themselves, within their home countries, as well as from their homelands to various host countries, including the United States. This experience of being uprooted is reflected in the way many Latinas/os read the Bible and is part of what we mean by a Latina/o perspective. It is especially visible in the reading strategies, principles, and assumptions of many Latina/o Christians.

Prior to the 1980s, the traditional way to read the Christian Scriptures was to borrow from the long-reigning and normative model of historical criticism. This model, focused primarily on identifying the written sources used by biblical authors, the oral traditions, histories, and settings behind the biblical texts, and the authors' special emphases and theologies, became a dominant way to read the Christian Scriptures. It was the way many Latinas/os learned to read the Bible, particularly if they were trained to read in the United States or Europe or by institutions in Latin America informed by historical criticism. As U.S. power and influence increased throughout the nineteenth and twentieth centuries, so did the dominance of the historical-critical approach. However, certain forces began to create a kind of uprootedness among Latin American scholars in the field of biblical studies. Leaving behind the traditional methods (but not altogether), many (including Latinas/os in the United States) began to depart from the historical-critical approach. These scholars began to challenge its principles of positivism and universality and to abandon its notions that meaning is apolitical and that the reader is invisible. This departure led many Latinas/os to borrow from the theology of liberation the interpretive push to decolonize and contextualize the experience of the interpreter. One of the earliest examples of this is Virgilio Elizondo's *Galilean Journey: A Mexican American Promise.* He draws from the historical, social, and theological experiences of Mexican Americans to read the Gospels through the experience of *mestizaje,* the cultural and racial intermixing of the Mexican people following the often violent cultural encounter between the Spanish (Roman Catholic) and indigenous communities of the Southwest. Elizondo argued that both Jesus and Mexican Americans were *mestizos;* that is, they were marginalized and outcasts within their societies. Another example is Justo González's strategy of reading "in Spanish," reflected in his book *Mañana: Christian Theology from a Hispanic Perspective,* in which he reads the Christian Scriptures from the experiences of exile (as a stranger in a new land) and oppression. Both readings are representative of this uprootedness. Dissatisfied with historical criticism's promises of prosperity, Latinos and Latinas stood up and began to travel to a new interpretive location. Drawing upon their experience of being unsettled, they began to explore where to go next. At the same time, filled as they were with a new consciousness and dismayed by dead-end historical-critical readings, they embarked on the risk of a new journey, back and forth sometimes, to "el norte," across the sea, and crossing the Southwest, always toward a new terrain, always in the hope of something new for them and their community.

Travel: Crossing Borders and Waters

The experience of travel is not the same for all Latinas/os. These journeys are as diverse and unique as are the identities within the community. For many, it is extremely dangerous, while for others it is relatively safe. Some travel because of civil war (for example, Central Americans, Argentineans), political repression (Cubans, Dominicans), or economic disparity (Puerto Ricans, Mexicans). Others engage in social migration to rejoin family, as many women and children are doing today to join husbands and fathers who cannot travel back to their home country because of stricter immigration policies. Some travel because people of their sexual orientation are persecuted. Diasporic communities are just as diverse. Some are considered migrants (legal or "illegal"); others are viewed as political exiles and refugees. Some travel across state lines (for example, from Texas to Oklahoma) as internally displaced migrants, while others travel across national boundaries—which may involve crossing treacherous deserts or rivers. The diasporic experience of travel is distinctive for each of the Latina/o communities in the United States and diverse within each particular national or ethnic group as well. This experience of travel is usually a matter of crossing borders and waters. That is reflected in the biblical reading strategies of many Latina/os, and it is another part of what is meant by a Latina/o perspective.

The experience of travel is the moment of searching—of trying to find space to stake one's own claim, to speak one's own voice, within the academic world of biblical studies as well as throughout various ecclesial communities and the larger society. Travel is also a moment of combating the closing of the borders of the mind, of opting for perforated borders and "crossing over" into different discourses. Much of this sense of combativeness was due to the experience of cultural clash when Latinas/os arrived physically in the United States, or perhaps only later when they felt that their consciousness had arrived in the United States. Many Latinas/os began to experience systematic mistreatment in their host country, and as a result they inevitably turned their experience, language, and culture into tools of resistance. They sought to achieve full equality within their host country and within the Christian tradition. Many who were trained in the rich tradition of historical criticism "migrated" to other discoures—ranging from literary criticism to cultural studies, as well as to initial collaborations with other modes of interpretation, particularly that of liberation—that were reshaping the field of biblical studies. Traveling back and forth across borders was a common enough experience, allowing Latinos and Latinas to draw nourishment from their various homelands and, at the same time, to come under the influence of other discourses and ways of reading. Many of their readings now are infused with the cultural and ethnic pride that was awakened by the cultural clash of travel—but that also owes much to being *in* the United States but not really part of it.

This cultural clash also exists within both academy and church. As a result, Latina/o culture and language were employed in strategies of resistance and as tools to demand full equality within the host society. This spirit of resistance is part of what makes up the Latina/o perspective.

This experience of the diaspora is perhaps best represented by Harold J. Recinos's reading approach, which some have called *barrio* reading. Reading the Christian Bible through the lens of the experience of the inner city (the barrio), with its socioeconomic third-world conditions that make the people poor, Recinos correlates the marginalized experiences of the people in the world behind the biblical text with the marginalized people (Latinas/os) in front *of* the text. In effect, his strategy is crossing over, back and forth, between two different worlds. In the biblical scholarship from the early 1990s we find that many readings of the Bible begin with the social location of the reader and involve a similar crossing-over. This approach is sometimes called social-location hermeneutics, and it typically begins readings with the expression "I read from the perspective of…" or "My social location is…" Another scholar who represents this diasporic travel experience is Ada María Isasi-Díaz. Drawing upon her experience as a *mujerista* (womanist) theologian, she reads the Bible with a hermeneutic of suspicion and recovery. That is, she seeks to reclaim the voice of women that has been suppressed or obscured in the biblical text, in order to reclaim the Latina voice within the contemporary community.

A Latina/o perspective is conscious of the reader's social location and of the purpose of interpretation, which is to challenge any negative representation of Latinas/os in the United States, in the academy, and in ecclesial communities. Latina/o interpretation works with the principle that all readings of the Bible are socially- and culturally-located constructions. Thus all meaning is particular. And drawing from their experience of diaspora, Latinas/os seek to negotiate where interpretation itself is to be located. Latina/o interpreters continue to look back to their homelands at the same time they look forward to their new home.

Resettlement: Transforming Space and Voice

The experience of resettlement varies among Latina/o communities. Latinas/os have resettled in all regions of the United States. Many of these resettlements have led to the formation of new transnational identities, that is, the creation of new social identities that span borders, thus creating dual or multiple identifications. Sometimes this is reflected in new modes of cultural production, such as new hybrid cultures (for example, the Nuevo Latina/o cuisine, or *Reguettón,* a blending of many Latin American musical styles). Recently, transnational identities have allowed Latinas/os—Mexicans or Cubans in the United States, for example—to influence the economics and politics of their homeland countries as well as their host countries through monetary remittances. Finally, transnational identities allow Latinos and Latinas to change or transform their particular locales to reflect their home cultures (think, for example, of Little Havana, Club San Lorenzo, Puerto Rico, or La Michoacán). I characterize this moment as one of "transforming space and voice." Respect shown to the culture of the host country is reciprocated by the host country respecting its various Latina/o communities. This transformation is also part of what is meant by a Latina/o perspective.

During this experience of resettlement, many Latinas/os are beginning to establish their homes in the host country. This is particularly reflected among those Latinas/os who have been in the United States since the 1960s or even earlier in the twentieth century, as well as by their children (second- and third-generation Latinas/os). These younger people are beginning not only to draw from their grandparents' cultures and homelands, but also to fuse them with other Latina/o and marginalized cultures found throughout the United States. What results is a cultural amalgamation, among Latinas/os themselves and others, through intermarriage, through shared knowledge

regarding food, traditions, music, language, and religion, through uniting to combat anti-Latina/o ethnic racism, and through people of different cultural and ethnic identities being shunted into the same segregated neighborhoods, areas, and churches throughout the United States. During this period of resettlement, Latinas/os aim to preserve their language and their traditions, and gradually fuse them with other cultures in the United States. The result is a postcolonial hybridity or ambiguity as a way to survive within their new home. This "transforming space and voice" is also part of what makes up a Latina/o perspective.

This transformation is best represented in Fernando F. Segovia's reading strategy of intercultural hermeneutics and his push to make the discipline of biblical studies more interdisciplinary. Segovia seeks to bring biblical studies into dialogue with other discourses, whether it is with other theoretical discourses (around feminism, racism, sexuality) or with the cultural production of any contemporary period (such as globalization). A Cuban American, Segovia reads the Bible out of his own Latino context, using postcolonial studies as the optic or lens in which to read the Bible and providing interpretive strategies that other colonized people may use if they prove liberating, or refuse if they prove oppressive. Another representative example is the reading strategy of Efraín Agosto. Using postcolonial studies, Agosto reads Philippians, for example, through the lens of the colonization of Puerto Rico by the United States. This reading provides readers a way to reinsert the voices of the colonized (Puerto Ricans) back into history with the colonized voices in the text. In effect, Agosto entertains a dialogue between the colonization evident in the text and the colonization of Puerto Rico.

It should be evident that reading the Bible through the perspective of the Latina/o experience includes diverse possibilities, as reflected in the diverse makeup of the community. Any attempt to flatten this collective diversity fails to capture the unique characteristics of the community. The framework of diasporic experience is one small way to understand not only the diversity of experiences and cultures among Latinos and Latinas, but also how they read the Bible through their cultures. All diasporas are different, and every diaspora is poignant—but every diaspora also holds the possibility of leading new, hybrid lives filled with much hope.

The Bible as a Text in Cultures: Native Americans

George "Tink" Tinker

American Indians will read a biblical text differently than Amer-European readers because they live a distinctly different cultural reality. Sometimes American Indian cultures and our historical experiences of conquest mean that the biblical text collides with our idea of good in the world.

Take, for example, the Exodus story. American Indians will always see themselves as the aboriginal Canaanite owners of land that has been invaded. The Pilgrims and Puritans arriving in America saw the situation in exactly those terms, calling themselves the "new Israel" as they justified their invasion and theft of Indian property. In the nineteenth century, in the age of imperialism, German scholars read the exodus as a pure act of colonial conquest. By the late twentieth century, on the other hand, some scholars were arguing for understanding the emergence of Israel in Canaan on the model of a peasant revolt. Those last two interpretations present a significant problem for Native American readers. The Indian reading of Exodus will always raise hackles, because Indians will always identify with the Canaanites as indigenous, colonized peoples.

This is problematic enough on the face of it, but there is another, more serious, dilemma inherent in the Euro-Christian/Indian intersection. While we will not deal here with the place of Scriptures in the faith of Indian Christians, we have to notice that Christian Scriptures cannot have the same place among Indian Christians as they do in Amer-European church communities. The missionary imposition of the Hebrew Bible on Native American Christians as an "Old Testament," a practice that denominations continue today, has two primary effects that prove destructive for Native American communities. First, it challenges the validity of Native American traditions, which were castigated as "demonic" by the missionaries. Second, it inherently prescribes replacing one's own history with someone else's as a prerequisite for conversion. Christian conversion typically mandates the learning and embracing of a completely foreign history—the history of Israel and Judaic Palestine—as one's own. Today many Indian Christians are increasingly insisting that their own historic covenants with the Creator, once labeled demonic by the missionaries, should receive continued respect and attention. Many Indians participate both in church liturgies and in their own tribe's ancient traditional ceremonies.

Time, Space, and the Kingdom of God

We will mention here two significant cultural differences between American Indian and Euro-Western peoples that deeply affect interpretation of biblical text. First, American Indian peoples are characteristically spatial in their thinking, while Euro-Western folk tend strongly toward being temporal thinkers, emphasizing time as a priority. Second, the radical individualism of Euro-Western people continues to be distinctly foreign to American Indians because it is opposed to an Indian worldview.

If we take a single text, Mark 1:14-15, as an example, the foundational Indian cultural perception of spatiality changes the reading of the text from one focused on time and eschatology—the theology of the last days of the world—to one much more interested in a theology of creation. At stake here is the interpretation of the "kingdom" of God (*basileia tou theou* in Greek). As it stands in the Greek or in a literal English translation, this metaphor presents a particular challenge for any American Indian reader or listener. Beyond the inherent sexism of the usual "kingdom" translation, the concept is problematic simply because Indian peoples in North America never functioned with political systems that included ruling monarchs. For American Indian peoples, who come out of communities that are historically more egalitarian and genuinely democratic and participatory, the kingdom metaphor is culturally foreign

and must be completely recast. The only possible point of comparison for the notion of *basileia* (bah-si-LAY-ah) in Indian experience might be the Bureau of Indian Affairs or the U.S. War Department!

Comparing an American Indian interpretation of *basileia* (kingdom) with those generally proposed by Western biblical scholars will show how the principles of creation and spatiality might function. Euro-Western scholarly discussion for the last century has assumed a universal validity across cultures, when otherness and difference may have been much closer to reality. Until recently, these scholars interpreted the meaning of *basileia* as related to time, based on contemporary notions of eschatology. That is, the only appropriate question to ask about the *basileia* has been, *When* will the kingdom come? It is not that scholars did not consider other possibilities. The question of where has been consistently dismissed! A wide variety of temporal answers have been argued, each generating a new technical term. We have been given notions of "realized eschatology," "actualized eschatology," "immanent eschatology," and "future eschatology." But each merely addresses a different perspective on the time-related "when-will-the-kingdom-come" question.

It seems obvious enough that spatial categories do not necessarily exclude the temporal, or vice versa; but the orientation assumed by the interpreter becomes crucial. In the Gospel of Mark especially—the verses cited above notwithstanding—there seems to be a distinct sense of the priority of the spatial in its language. Any Indian reader of Mark, or of the other two Synoptic Gospels, Matthew and Luke, is bound to think first of all about the question Where? with regard to *basileia*. An American Indian reading, then, must begin with a spatial understanding of the *basileia* as a place where God rules. That place, in the Indian mind, must be the place God created, namely, the world in which we exist. Thus, *basileia* is read spatially, as a creation metaphor.

My argument is that those two different ways of thinking have to do with time and space, the when and the where of the *basileia* in Mark. Space and time are not necessarily two dimensions of equal value in human thinking. For any given culture, one is usually primary, the other secondary. American Indian people tend to think out of a spatial cosmology. Their most fundamental and powerful images, metaphors, and myths have to do primarily with space and places. An American Indian spatial interpretation raises the likelihood that all of Western biblical scholarship has worked for a century with a transcultural blind spot. Why, after all, would the kingdom of God not be a realm or a place where God rules, or a community that God rules?

For the Western intellectual tradition, time is primary, and space is a subordinate category. From notions of progress to the casual revelation that "time is money," from the sacred hour on Sunday morning and the seven-day cycle of work, play, and spiritual obligation, to the assumption of progress in philosophical and scientific inquiry in the West, time always reigns supreme. In much of Western thought, all of space is rendered a mere function of time. It is no wonder that the *basileia tou theou* (kingdom of God) is also discussed consistently as a function of time.

An American Indian spatial reading of the Gospels combines spatiality and creation, resulting in a reading that naturally understands *basileia* as a creation metaphor that images ideal harmony and balance. It represents a symbolic value whose parameters might be outlined as follows. First, the Gospels seem to view divine rule as something that is in process. It is drawing near. It is emerging (Mark 1:15). Yet it is also "among" us, in our midst (Luke 17:21). It is something that can be experienced by the faithful here and now, even if only anticipated, while its full emergence is still in the future. Second, the symbolic value captured by this imagery in no small part includes a view of an ideal world. Finally, the structural definition of that ideal world is, above all else, relational and spatial.

The imagery of divine rule in the Hebrew Scriptures is essentially creation imagery. That is, the ideal world symbolically represented in the Hebrew Bible builds on the divine origin of the cosmos as an ideal past and points to an ideal future. American Indian readers would assume that the ideal world is the real world of creation in an ideal relationship of harmony and balance with the creator. It is relational, first because it implies a relationship between the created order of things and its creator and, second, because it implies a relationship between all created things. As the creator, *theos* (God, in the Christian Scriptures) is the rightful ruler of all. Hence, the ideal world to which Jesus points in the Gospels is precisely the realization of that proper relationship between creator and created in the real, spatial world of creation.

For an American Indian reader of the Bible's creation stories, whether human beings were created first of all the mammals or last of all the "createds" is not nearly as im-

portant as affirming the harmony and balance of the created order. While the balance of that order is repeatedly shaken by the human creatures, it is still the ideal state of being that we attempt to restore. While the ideal state of balance and harmony can never be achieved for all time, all—meaning all of creation—are part of the ongoing process of restoring balance. In his letter to the Romans, Paul says that all of creation groans in travail, that is, in childbirth (Rom 8:22). A Christian Indian perspective would naturally assume that Paul sees the Christ-event as having the same purpose as Indian ceremonies: to restore a world in travail.

In this American Indian interpretation, the *basileia* must be understood as all-inclusive. That is, if it symbolizes the harmony and balance of all creation, then it must include all things created. In an American Indian anthropology, the *basileia* must include two-legged, four-legged, winged, and all the living moving ones, since all are created by the creator and leader of all existence. The *basileia* is inclusive of all human beings, whether or not all recognize the divine creator. Those who are considered to be standing outside the kingdom are there because they have somehow excluded themselves by failing to recognize the balance and harmony intended in creation. This state of unawareness is often the result of an individual's attempts to establish her or his own sense of control within or over the creation.

While Native Americans know little about either rulers or kingdoms, only a spatial response to the question Where? begins to make any sense of the metaphor. Whatever the *basileia* is, it must be a place. The verb *ēngizein* ("the kingdom has drawn near," Mark 1:15) allows for and even predicates a primary meaning of spatial nearness. In Luke 17:21, Jesus instructs the Pharisees that the *basileia* is "in your midst" (*entos hymas*), that is, already spatially present. Removing the Amer-European emphasis of temporality of course lessens the emphasis on the future establishment of God's kingdom. In an American Indian reading, the *basileia* has little, if anything, to do with what happens in the future. Rather, it is concerned with how one images oneself in the present in relationship to the Creator and to the rest of creation.

The Kingdom, Repentance, and Restoration

In Mark 1:15 the *basileia* is linked with the imperative, *metanoiete* (repent). We need not discuss at length the nature of the word for time in this verse. It is enough to acknowledge the cyclical and seasonal nature of *kairos* (meaning the "right or opportune moment"), used here, over against the more linear concept of *chronos* (meaning "continuing time"). The mention of a time element should not distract us from a spatial, and now creational, understanding. More important for a Native American reading is a spatial understanding of *metanoiete.* Here the underlying meaning of the Aramaic-Hebrew *shuv* (return) is spatial, rather than the having the Greek notion of "change of mind." Repentance is key to the establishment of divine oversight, because it involves a return to God and a proper understanding of God's rule over all of creation.

Feeling sorry for one's sins is not part of repentance at all, although that may be the initial act of confession. In the Acts of the Apostles, repentance does not yet carry a penitential, emotive connotation but instead carries the Hebrew sense of *return.* In Acts 2:37-39, people feel penitential emotion (they are "cut to the heart") as a result of Peter's sermon and come to him and the others to ask what they must do. His response: "Repent, and be baptized." Since they already feel sorry for their sins, "repent" here cannot imply the Latin *penitentio,* penitence. The Hebrew notion of repentance really is calling on God's people to recognize the divine rule of God, to return to God, to return to the ideal relationship between Creator and created, to live in the spatiality of creation fully aware of God's rule, of human createdness, and of the interrelatedness of all the createds.

In the Native American world, we recognize that interrelatedness as a peer relationship between the two-leggeds and all the others—four-legged, winged, and other living, moving things. This is the real world within which we hope to actualize the ideal world of creational balance and harmony.

These examples only begin to articulate an American Indian reading of the Christian Bible. That this reading of the *basileia* may be quite unlike standard Amer-European interpretations should signal that in a multicultural, pluralistic world of diversity there will necessarily be many readings of the Bible. A single normative interpretation seems to be further from reality today than ever.

The Bible as a Text in Cultures: Asian Americans

Frank M. Yamada

Asian American biblical interpretation reflects the diverse perspectives and experiences of peoples from many different ethnic backgrounds, whose ancestry can be traced back to the various nations and rich cultures that make up Asia. The question "How does one read the Bible from an Asian American perspective?" is complicated. For many Asians in the United States, their experience of the Bible has been heavily shaped by missionaries from the West who sought to convert peoples of Asian descent to Christianity and to Western cultural ideals. The Bible, however, is just one influence among many religious texts and traditions for Asian groups within the United States. The very term "Asian American" complicates biblical interpretation from this U.S. cultural location. Asian Americans include peoples from China, Japan, Korea, Vietnam, the Philippines, India, Thailand, Laos, and many other nations. Because of this, it is difficult to identify a single or unified Asian American way of being. Though each of these groups would maintain the importance of their ethnic heritage for understanding community identity, no one group can speak for the others. Moreover, the history of U.S. racism, both in law and in culture, has affected the ways these groups and individuals have experienced life in the United States. To understand Asian American biblical interpretation, one must first begin to understand the complex experiences, cultures, and histories that emerge from Asian peoples who live in the United States.

It is necessary to make an important qualification. The term *Asian American* has been a useful and politically strategic classification. During the civil rights movement, this identification helped unite peoples of different Asian ethnicities to gain a more unified and powerful political voice. Since that time, several Asian American organizations, activist groups, and student agencies have benefited from the collective energies that come from such diverse gatherings. In the latter part of the twentieth century, Asian American studies programs began to emerge at universities and colleges around the country, especially in or near big cities and on either coast. Asian Americans are now also more prominently visible throughout popular culture, even as many pernicious stereotypes persist.

The civil rights energy and the social activism surrounding the racial classification "Asian American" suggest that it has been a helpful designation for many Asian peoples within the United States. But it is also inherently limiting. The category does not take into account the many and varied ethnicities and cultures that are an important part of the lives of Asians living in America. Even within a single ethnic designation, such as Japanese American, for example, it is difficult for one to take into account generational, geographical, cultural, and social differences. A Japanese American who grew up during World War II on the West Coast will have a different perspective than one who grew up in Hawaii during those same years. Similarly, a Nisei (second generation) female will think very differently about gender roles than a Sansei (third generation) male like myself. One begins to see the difficulty in defining what it means to be Asian American when one expands these few examples to include all of the ethnic and cultural groups that make up the rich diversity of Asians in the United States.

Additionally, Christianity has had a long and complicated relationship to Asia, which affects the ways Asians receive the Bible. The Bible was introduced to many Asian countries within the context of Western European colonialism. Different forms of U.S. Christianity, including Evangelical, mainline, and Roman Catholic traditions, have all had a major impact on the practice of Asian American Christians. Because this racial designation is both useful and problematic, Asians in the United States are empowered through the building of Asian and Asian American communities, while they simultaneously seek to resist oversimplified stereotypes of Asians within Western culture.

 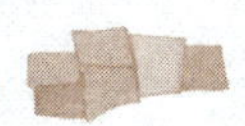

It is difficult, therefore, to suggest that there can be a single, unified way to understand how Asian Americans read the Bible. Asian American biblical interpretation is as diverse as the many different ethnic groups that make up the peoples of Asian descent in the United States. One helpful way to understand Asian Americans and their relationship to the Bible is to examine the historical experiences of these peoples and the history of the development of Asian American theological thought.

The Experience of Asian Americans

Themes of exclusion and the persistence of community characterize the history of Asians in the United States. Asians began immigrating to the United States as early as the eighteenth century, with large groups from East Asia, especially the Chinese and Japanese, relocating to the United States in the 1800s. Many worked on the railroads during their westward expansion in the latter third of the nineteenth century. With this new wave of immigrants came fear from the existing populations. Legislation soon followed that sought to limit the population of Asians in the United States. Congress passed a series of laws that prohibited Asians from gaining citizenship or owning property, including the Chinese Exclusion Act of 1882. The Immigration Exclusion Act, also passed in 1882, halted further migration of the Chinese to the United States.

During World War II, after the Japanese bombed Pearl Harbor, President Franklin D. Roosevelt signed Executive Order 9066, which allowed for the imprisonment of more than 120,000 Japanese and Japanese Americans into internment camps, located mostly in remote areas of the western continental United States. Many families were only given forty-eight hours to pack up their belongings and relocate to the camps. The government enforced this legislation without due process of law, even though many in the camps were U.S. citizens by birth. Forty years later, the Commission on Wartime Relocation and Internment of Civilians determined that the government's actions were unjustified, based as they were primarily in racism and war hysteria. The government issued an official apology and provided a financial settlement to survivors of the camps, but the effects of the camps have been devastating and long-lasting in the Japanese American community.

More recently, groups primarily from South Asia have experienced violence and hostility in the aftermath of the terrorist attacks that occurred on September 11, 2001.

In this case, racism has been manifested in religious and ethnic stereotypes. Asians in America, whether or not they were religiously observant Muslims, faced discrimination at the hands of a nation gripped with fear, suspicion, and prejudice. Islam, similar to other monotheistic religions, is multifaceted and complex. It is neither more nor less inherently violent than the other Abrahamic monotheistic religions, Christianity and Judaism. In a culture of fear, however, people's irrational actions and thought processes took hold. Thus, even other Asian American religious groups, which differ from Islam in their religious practices and beliefs, were often identified erroneously as "Middle-Eastern terrorists" by an uninformed American public after the attacks. For example, many Sikhs, who wear traditional head coverings as part of their religious observance, were publicly harassed or violently assaulted shortly after 9/11. This happened in spite of the clear religious differences between Sikhs and Muslims. Similar incidents were reported among Hindus of Asian descent. In these cases, stereotypes of Middle-Eastern Islamic terrorists were projected upon peoples who were neither Middle Eastern nor Muslims and whose religious practice discourages violence against others.

Even though Asian Americans have contributed greatly to U.S. history and society, stereotypes of Asians exist within contemporary U.S. culture. Two such stereotypes are prominent: the "model minority" and the perpetual foreigner. Because certain Asian Americans have been relatively successful in American society, they are often viewed as a model minority. On the surface, this stereotype could be viewed as a positive description. However, the idea of the model minority is problematic for Asian Americans, both internally and externally. Internally, it limits identity. For many, the designation means that Asian Americans are good citizens who do not cause problems. Thus, this stereotype doesn't envision Asian Americans engaging in the sorts of civil disobedience or dissent that were typical in the 1960s and 1970s. Moreover, the model-minority label makes invisible those Asian Americans who do, in fact, suffer from poverty or social dislocation. Externally, this stereotype also creates tension between Asian Americans and other people of color, since it functions within the dominant society to pit one racial group against another.

The second dominant stereotype of Asians in American culture is the perpetual foreigner. Even though some Asian American groups have been in the United States for centuries, spanning many generations, the Asian population continues to be por-

trayed in American culture as foreign or alien. Asian American men and women are commonly depicted in the media as exotic, often speaking with a heavy accent. In some cases, Asian foreignness is characterized as disloyalty or untrustworthiness. Even as late as 1999, the U.S. government falsely accused Wen Ho Lee, a Taiwanese American scientist, of being a spy for the Chinese government in a highly publicized case that ultimately proved embarrassing for U.S. officials. The perpetual-foreigner stereotype is tied to the history of Asian immigration to the United States—a history in which legislation such as the Chinese Exclusion Act sought to keep Asians foreign to protect the status quo. The perpetual-foreigner label is another way the dominant U.S. culture tells people of Asian descent that they are not wanted or that their acceptance in this country has limits.

In spite of this history and culture of exclusion, Asian American communities have persisted and flourished. Peoples from Asia continue to immigrate to the United States, building communities that grow and thrive. During the 1960s, Asian American activist groups worked toward social change during the civil rights movement, resulting in empowerment and political voice. Religious centers, including Christian churches from a variety of traditions, are locations in which Asian American identity and culture is fostered. For example, immigrant churches continue to serve as both worship centers and places where future generations can practice the language and culture of their ancestry. Asian Americans as a group tend to be upwardly mobile socially and economically, integrating well into mainstream American society. Asian American studies programs are now well established at universities and colleges across the nation. Moreover, in the twenty-first century many Asians in the United States, including mixed-race Asian Americans, have become prominent public figures and celebrities in politics, sports, literature, the media, and other areas. The communities of Asian America continue to grow and expand in vital and diverse ways.

Issues in Asian American Biblical Interpretation

The experience and culture of Asian Americans informs how these communities read the Bible. However, there are specific factors within the academic study of the Bible that have also contributed to what we know as Asian American biblical interpretation. For most of the nineteenth and twentieth centuries, biblical scholars employed a method of study called historical criticism. This useful methodology, developed primarily in Germany, had a lasting impact on modern biblical scholarship. Historical

criticism emphasizes that the meaning of a text must be situated in its original context in history. But in the 1970s and 1980s, biblical scholars began to emphasize the importance of recognizing the role the *reader's culture* plays in developing the meaning of a text. For example, someone reading from an African American perspective would not necessarily see the same things in a text as someone coming from a white, Western-European understanding. It is from within this change of perspective in scholarship that Asian American biblical interpretation emerges.

Asian American academic study of the Bible has its roots in Asian American theology, which began to blossom in the last three decades of the previous century. These scholars, primarily from Protestant Christian traditions, began to write theologies that emphasized the experiences of Asians in the United States. Therefore, ideas such as marginality and *liminality* (the experience of being in an ambiguous in-between or "threshold" state) became prominent. As in all liberation theologies, when one understands God from the perspective of the margins, important themes begin to emerge. For example, Jesus' status as mediating between humanity and deity within the Christian Scriptures allows us to understand him as someone who responds to those who are marginalized in society. Much of Asian American experience, especially in early generations, is described as being located *between* two worlds—their land of origin and the United States. Because of this, Asian American theology identifies with a God who is on the margins or who works in those in-between places. Thus, Asian American theology is based in the experiences of Asians in the United States, stressing the rich cultural and religious heritages that come from the continent of Asia.

Asian American biblical scholarship has followed a similar trajectory. Biblical scholars have sought to read the Bible through characters and themes that emphasize margins or spaces in-between. In the Abraham-Sarah stories, for example, an Asian American reading might understand the marginalized status of a childless couple in the ancient world, who are wandering in a place between their land of origin and an unknown destination promised to them by God. One would also be attentive to characters such as Hagar and Ishmael, whom God blesses even when they are excluded from the center because of their ethnic (Egyptian) difference.

Asian American scholars also have used cultural and religious themes from Asia to help in their understanding of the Bible. Some have sought to see tensions within the

biblical texts through the lens of yin-yang. Rather than thinking of diverse opinions as opposites, this East-Asian philosophical idea understands differences as mutually intertwined—not either/or but both/and. Thus, the differentiations God/human, grace/law, or insider/outsider are held together in tension. Still other scholars have stressed the similarities between biblical understandings of human existence with religious ideas within Taoism, Buddhism, or Confucian thought.

The trajectories described above have greatly enhanced biblical interpretation from the context of Asian America. These themes, however, have tended to stress the Asianness of Asian American biblical interpretation. Ideas such as marginality or liminality make most sense among early generations, where the context of immigration is central. But later generations do not have the same longing for homeland that their parents or grandparents experienced. For Asian Americans who have been in the United States for three to five or more generations, their relationship to the U.S. context is complicated and conflicted in a different way. Themes such as hybridity or the fluidity of identity become more important. Interpretations in this vein might stress the ways that biblical identity is conflicted rather than stable. Within this interpretative mode one might ponder, for example, how the identity "Israelite" is developed largely to deflect another identity, "Canaanite." Israel's religious practice is fully dependent on Canaanite religion, even as it tries to be different from it. Later-generation Asian American biblical interpretation would complicate clear distinctions between Asian and American, between Israelite and Canaanite, or between Jew and Gentile, preferring instead to see the complexity that is inherent in any cultural identity.

Asian American biblical interpretation is as complex and diverse as the many different ethnicities, cultures, and experiences that make up the populations of Asians in the United States. While the inherent diversity within Asian America threatens the usefulness of this racial designation, Asian Americans continue to form alliances across these social boundaries to form meaningful communities. This movement in Asian American theology and biblical scholarship mirrors what is happening in churches across the nation as later generations form congregations through their shared experience of growing up as Asians in America. This meaningful connection suggests that generations of Asians in the United States will continue to generate biblical interpretations that will empower their understanding of God at work in their midst and give voice to their own rich cultural heritages.

The Bible as a Text in Cultures: Euro-Americans

Nicole Wilkinson Duran

The Bible, which in the Christian use of the term includes Hebrew and Greek writings, has nowhere else exerted the kind of deep influence on culture that it has had in the West. Europe certainly had religious and cultural traditions before the Bible was introduced. But as long as it has been called "the West," the Bible has been profoundly involved in its history. Robert Alter has maintained that the linear quality of Hebrew narrative constituted a revolution in literary culture and that the Bible consequently stands as the most influential source for Western literature and historiography. Certainly one cannot read European literature without becoming familiar with biblical themes and stories. The Bible has exerted a major influence on most elements of Western culture, from art to astronomy.

Like most peoples of the world, the peoples of the West have always read the Bible in translation. The native speakers of biblical Hebrew and *koine*, or common, Greek were not Westerners, and Westerners, once there was a West, on the whole did not read or speak those languages. When Christianity became the official religion of the Roman Empire, it made sense to translate the Hebrew, Aramaic, and Greek of the original texts into Latin, at the time the most common spoken language in the Empire. This translation was quickly seen as sacred in itself. The holy words of Scripture, and of the Christian Mass in which it played an integral role, were Latin words, even among peoples who did not understand Latin. The Bible could exert its strong cultural influence only because of the mediation of the clergy, who, unlike the populace, were literate in Latin and interpreted the text to common Christians, both by translating it and by making it relevant.

In far too many cases, the ecclesiastical hierarchy interpreted and taught its clergy to interpret the Bible to serve its own interests. The poor were poor as part of God's plan, merely lower links on what came to be known as the Great Chain of Being. Earthly authorities, said these interpreters of the church's Bible, were ordained by God, as were slavery, war, chauvinism of all kinds, and even torture.

The Legacies of the Reformation and Enlightenment

For centuries after the West became predominantly Christian, the Bible's worldview mingled with that of Western culture almost imperceptibly. Sometimes the Bible adapted and reshaped native European traditions, with the result that we (I speak as a person of white European descent) learned to portray biblical saints with the sun god's radiant halo, and to read three wise men into Matthew's story because three was for us a magical number. During the Reformation some of this interplay of older culture with biblical interpretation was noted and, in a word, protested. Various strains of the Protestant movement rejected certain elements of interaction between the Bible and native cultures: the array of local gods alongside Christian saints and the adoption of the winter solstice as the birth of Christ, for example. The Protestant ideal was to cleanse the Bible of cultural influences and to cleanse the church—and the culture—of every authority but the Bible. Of course this ideal was never achieved. Cultural influences can be reshaped, but they cannot be undone. The Bible, like any text, cannot be received except through human hands, mediated and interpreted by culture.

But if Protestant leaders wanted to free the Bible of certain "foreign" cultural entanglements, most concluded that it was neither possible nor desirable to have a Bible free of all cultures except those of biblical times. Not surprisingly, these European Protestants looked with some favor on their own culture. Eventually, they understood the Bible to give authority to the rise of European power and to European imperialism. The biblical mandate to conquer the promised land and destroy idolaters, as well as

Christ's command in Matthew (the "great commission") to go out into all the world, lent support and offered satisfying rationalizations for those who sought adventure, trade, power, and wealth in the European imperial project, from the Crusades to the conquest of the Americas and beyond.

On the other hand, some of those same biblically supported ventures brought back news that seemed to threaten the Bible's authority. Europe's science for the first time came into conflict with what was understood to be the worldview of the Bible. If the Bible said that God created humanity as the pinnacle of creation, then surely the earth, humanity's home, was the point around which the heavens turned. To threaten that inference, as new astronomical discoveries did, was to diminish the Bible and, perhaps more importantly, detract from the authority of the Bible's appointed interpreters. For the first time, what were understood as advances in European culture were shunned by the church. The unity of religion and elite culture had been broken.

The rift between at least one stream of European culture and the biblical text became a central issue during the Enlightenment. The concept of natural law seemed to fly in the face of the Bible's miracle stories, and it was difficult to enlist the Bible on the side of equality and democracy when it had historically been one of the greatest defenders of hierarchy. Secularism became almost a belief system in itself, and the cultural space for those who had no use for any religion widened considerably. In response, those who stayed with some form of the church regrouped into two separate camps—camps that continue in the West, with little development, to this day and are particularly evident in U.S. Christianity.

On one side are those who see the rift between the Bible and the Enlightenment as a series of errors in the insights, premises, and conclusions of the Enlightenment. From this perspective, the Enlightenment's very establishment of a secular space from which to begin contemplating the world and humanity emerges as its central error. The concept of natural law must be flawed, since it fails to take into account God's complete freedom and excludes miracles from the start. Likewise, the Enlightenment value on equality, particularly when applied to gender, is seen as based on human vanity; it flies in the face of biblical teaching that long had been understood to be confirmed in biological realities. At the same time, writers and preachers from this perspective often insist that the Bible is supported by scientific facts (appealing, paradoxically, to an Enlightenment category), if the scientific facts are properly interpreted. But like the Bible's influence, the influence of the Enlightenment is difficult to escape, even among those who would like to.

On the other hand, some portions of the church attempt to make peace with the Enlightenment, while still holding onto the Bible. This school of thought reads the biblical story of creation, for example, as symbolic and theological, a narrative about God's relationship to all things, rather than as a historical or scientific account. The resurrection, rather than requiring a hole in the fabric of natural law, likewise becomes symbolic and a statement about God and Jesus, rather than a miracle verifiable by science. In this view, the Bible's value lies not in its usefulness as a compendium of all knowledge worthy of the name but as a story that centers and frames human history. The weakness of this position has been its relatively weak hold on the biblical text or on Christianity in general. Its aversion to dogma and its sympathy for secular thought has meant, at least until recently, that its supporters are reluctant to claim much of anything for the Bible—least of all to speak out loudly in defense of the Bible as Scripture or as definitive in some way for human life.

With the problematic exception of the United States, the West has effectively given the Bible away in its travels to other parts of the globe, often forcing Christian Scripture upon peoples who did not want it, while back home in Europe the Bible—or at least active public participation in the church—dwindled into a pale relic. In the United States, however, the Bible remains culturally prominent. Our courts hear lawsuits about monumental governmental displays of the Ten Commandments. Our politicians cite Scripture when they can. Our news magazines run cover stories on new interpretations of the biblical Jesus. Historically, arguments both for and against such major issues as slavery, abortion rights, and stem-cell research have been couched in biblical language.

Conservative politicians and citizens often reinvent the American Revolution as a biblically based event organized by faithful Christians, although it in fact emerged directly from Enlightenment secularism and included prominent atheists and deists as well as the occasional churchgoer. The religious revivals washing over the country almost since its founding have raised the Bible to new heights in American public life. It remains on those heights—though often unread—offering a sacred space for some

and simply a distinguishing feature of the landscape for others. Perhaps it is because of our lack of a common cultural history—for the United States is a country made up of people descended from immigrants, slaves, and the battered remains of once prosperous indigenous peoples—that Euro-Americans have looked so often to the Bible as a foundation on which to build some kind of commonality, by force if necessary.

The Legacy of Apocalypse

Much political rhetoric and cultural production across the U.S. spectrum continues to draw on the biblical imagery and drama of apocalypse. It is no accident that when Joseph Conrad's novel *Heart of Darkness* was Americanized in film, the subject became war and the title became *Apocalypse Now.* Visions of the end time fueled the nonviolent force of the civil rights movement but also produced the Branch Davidians and their arsenals in Waco, Texas. From the Civil War to the post-9/11 "War on Terror," every U.S. conflict has been effectively sold to the public, in song, slogan, and speech, as a biblical confrontation between good and evil. Likewise, the U.S. branch of the environmental movement almost relishes its prophecies of impending doom, rhetoric shaped and informed by biblical prophecy. We seem to be in love with the apocalypse—ready to read each cultural or historic change as a sign that it is coming, and prepared to break down history's doors and drag it in if it delays too long.

Many citizens of the United States love the Bible best at its end—the end of the book and the end of the world. The urgency of ultimate justice intoxicates us so that, as a historian of the Ku Klux Klan once wrote, "being an American is a heady experience." At the end of the world, after all—facing the ultimate enemy, whether that means God's own enemy or that of the planet—all bets are off; all forgiveness is at an end; and all violence and torment, as well as all sacrifice and effort, are justified. Then the biblical message of God's overarching justice is at its most powerful and most volatile, like the terrifying power of the atom, or that of the nation itself. Like a child with a gun, we are consumed equally by visions of justice, vengeance, and chaos, visions we aspire to make reality, even as we fear that they may mean our own destruction.

The challenge for us who read the Bible as inheritors of these distinctive European and Euro-American legacies is to read with discernment. How can we negotiate these mixed and often conflicting visions in order to contribute with others to a just and peaceable world?

Jesus and Cultures

Leticia A. Guardiola-Sáenz and Curtiss Paul DeYoung

Throughout the centuries and around the world, almost every culture has represented Jesus in characteristic ways that are relevant and appropriate to the faith, ideologies, and social contexts of a people. The resulting titles, names, images, and symbols used to speak of and to characterize Jesus are as diverse as the readers of the biblical text. Jesus can also be appreciated in a wide range of imagery that goes from the classic works of art found in museums around the globe to the contemporary renditions of pop art images and movies.

The representations of Jesus are so many that it would be impossible to cover all of them in this short article. What we offer here is a small sample, highlighting the cultural context from where they have emerged. First, we look at some of the images of Jesus as described in the New Testament, within his own culture and the culture of the early church. Then we briefly describe the quest for Jesus within the academic culture; and finally we present some of the ways Jesus has been depicted in contemporary cultures.

Jesus in His Culture

Right from the start, the New Testament validates the plurality of images of Jesus by giving voice to the unique perspectives of four evangelists (the Gospel writers, from the Greek word *euangelion,* "gospel"). The Gospels, our main sources for a life of Jesus, give him many different names and titles that convey particular roles and symbolize distinct aspects of his identity. Despite their similarities, each Gospel renders a particular representation of Jesus. In Matthew, for example, Jesus is predominantly presented as the teacher, the rabbi; for Mark, Jesus is the suffering son of God; the Gospel of Luke highlights Jesus as the savior of the world; and in John, Jesus is the incarnate Word (from the Greek *logos*). Together with these titles, some of the most familiar names and images of Jesus in the New Testament are Messiah or Christ, Son of David, Son of Man, King of Kings, Lord of Lords, Almighty, Lamb of God, High Priest, Light of the World, and Good Shepherd. All of these are linked to particular aspects of Israel's experience.

The influence behind the formation of these images of Jesus comes mainly from three cultural arenas: the political, the religious and philosophical, and the economic.

The first influence involves political reality not only in ancient Judea but also in the neighboring nations. After the Babylonian destruction of Jerusalem, the Jews who returned from Babylon included in their sacred writings the expectation of a future king, anointed (in Hebrew, *moshiach*) as the great David had been, who would free them from foreign domination and oppression. It is important not to exaggerate the scope of this expectation, as if all Jews were "waiting for a messiah." Early Jewish literature, in the Hebrew Bible and outside it, shows a wide range of expectations for priestly, royal, military, or even heavenly figures who would bring salvation, alongside movements to reform worship in the temple or law observance among the common people. In the era of Roman rule in Judea, the language of kingship or messiahship was apparently most used in a number of brief popular movements that rallied around militant figures (termed "bandits" by the Romans) whose careers were inevitably short-lived. Typically, such movements did not devote their energy to leaving literary remains for posterity.

The idealized expectation of a messiah nevertheless was crucial to the circles that first acclaimed Jesus as Messiah (in Greek, *christos*) or Son of David. It was in these circles that the concept of a suffering Messiah, who would die to cleanse the people of their sins, first appeared, based on innovative readings of Psalms 22 and 69 and Isaiah 53 (notice, for example, how phrases from Psalm 22 are woven into the accounts of Jesus'

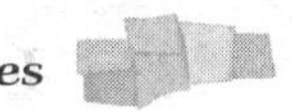

crucifixion in the Gospels). This concept was never part of earlier Jewish expectations, however, and these passages of Scripture were never read as referring to a messiah before the Jesus movement.

The conception of a suffering and dying messiah helped the first believers in Jesus to understand his death, and in subsequent centuries Christian theologians developed it into the predominant understanding of salvation through the atoning death of Jesus. More recently, however, theologians have noted that an overemphasis on the divine necessity of the Messiah's suffering has the potential to make suffering as such seem a spiritual necessity. Historically, just such interpretations have brought much pain when they have been used—in contexts of slavery, conquest, imperialism, and the subjugation of classes of people—to tell the mistreated that their suffering is somehow justified.

New Testament images of Jesus were also influenced by the political context of Roman imperial rule. In the midst of an oppressive empire, ruled by emperors who were hailed as sons of God, saviors of the world, kings, and lords, it was a bold move—but a crucially important one—for emergent Christianity to acknowledge Jesus as the true Savior of the world, the only begotten Son of God, the King of kings, the Lord of lords, and the Almighty who would redeem his people from oppression. Early Christianity did not dismiss Jewish expectations of a powerful warrior-messiah, one capable of neutralizing the power of foreign adversaries like Rome. Instead, in the distinctive doctrine of the second coming of the messiah, believers assigned the traditional roles of Jewish messianic expectation—ruling over the earth in peace, subduing enemies, securing justice, restoring the oppressed—to Jesus at his future advent (see for example 1 Cor 15:24-28 or the prophecy of Rome's defeat in Rev 18).

The second cultural arena that influenced images of Jesus is the world of religious and philosophical experience and practice. The images of Jesus as the *great high priest* and Lamb of God derive from Israel's worship. The first, predominant in Hebrews, announces Jesus as the supreme mediator who surpasses all human priests who had served in the temple; the second speaks of Jesus as embodying and surpassing the sacrificial rituals in which the blood of an unblemished lamb was offered in expiation for sins (Lev 4:32). The New Testament writings, and especially the Gospel of John, refer to Jesus as the sacrificial lamb, unblemished and innocent, offered to expiate the sins of the people. It is interesting that the lamb for the sin offering had to be a female. A similar application of feminine imagery to Jesus appears when he is represented as the personification of divine Wisdom (1 Cor 1:24, 30). Wisdom personified (the Hebrew, *Hokmah,* and Greek, *Sophia,* are both feminine nouns) appears and speaks in Proverbs 8 and became the subject of greater speculation among more philosophically minded Hellenistic Jews (Philo and the author of the Wisdom of Solomon). Such speculation apparently stands behind the masculine metaphor of the *Logos* in the Gospel of John. *Logos* and the imagery of Jesus as Light of the world both emerge from the cosmopolitan, hellenized society in which the church grew in the late first and early second centuries; they are related to the Greek philosophical view of the creating force that originates and sustains the order of the cosmos.

The third cultural arena of influence is Israel's agrarian society. In a land of shepherds, whose livelihoods depend on taking good care of their flocks, the image of a good shepherd is greatly valued. The New Testament—and many of the earliest visual representations of Jesus in Christian art—represent him as the *Good Shepherd* who takes great care and protects the flock (see John 10:1-5), just as YHWH did (Psalm 23).

The plurality of images of Jesus in the New Testament opened the door for new interpretations, some coming from theologians and teachers in the church, past and present, but many others coming from ordinary readers who have felt invited to appropriate Jesus in personal ways.

Jesus in Academic Culture

In an effort to explain Jesus of Nazareth as a historical figure—apart from the interpretations of the church and the faithful appropriations of individual believers—scholars have used modern historical methods to analyze the Gospels in their cultural context. This historically oriented scholarship, begun at the end of the eighteenth century, is known as "The Quest for the Historical Jesus." As controversial as some of the reconstructions of the "historical Jesus" have been, it is important to learn about them, because they help us understand the cultural conceptions and expectations that Jesus' followers may have had of him, and they help present-day readers understand better what the New Testament says about him. The contemporary quest for the historical Jesus has its roots in the Enlightenment, when the Bible became an object of historical science and of the historical-critical method. The quest for the historical Jesus thus far can be explained succinctly as a three-phase endeavor: the first or original quest (late eighteenth to early twentieth century); the second or new quest (early 1950s to early 1970s); and a third quest (late 1970s to the present).

First Quest

Attempting to depart from what they considered the unreal and "inhuman" Christ of faith created by the institutionalized church of the fourth and fifth centuries, the first "questers" for the historical Jesus stripped away the cloths of dogma and faith, hoping to find the human Jesus they assumed was hidden in the Gospels. Some of these interpreters proposed that Jesus should be seen in political terms, having had messianic intentions, thinking of himself as future king of a new kingdom, and at last entering Jerusalem and trying to seize power as a worldly messiah. Others sought to re-create Jesus' mental and social outlook, depicting him as a supporter of a pure worship, a religion with no priests or external rites, based on feelings and emotions—an idealist who highlighted the infinite value of the human soul and had as his core message love and the fatherhood of God. The goal of this first quest was to recover the Jesus of history hidden behind the Christ of faith, and its main result was the realization that the Gospels were products of faith, not historical records. By the end of the nineteenth century a consensus had emerged that the Jesus of history had been lost behind the Christ of faith.

The original quest ended when, at the beginning of the twentieth century, William Wrede and Albert Schweitzer challenged these interpreters, revealing their biases and subjectivity in creating modern, liberal images of Jesus with whom they felt more comfortable. Schweitzer proposed a counter-image of Jesus, in light of his religious-historical context, as an eschatological enthusiast who, claiming to be the Messiah, sought to bring God's longed-for kingdom but instead died tragically on the cross.

Second Quest

Following Schweitzer's work, many academic interpreters became convinced that the Gospels offered no reliable accounts as sources for the historical figure of Jesus. In the 1950s, however, in the wake of the Second World War and influenced by the existentialist philosophy of Søren Kierkegaard and Martin Heidegger, a "new quest" for Jesus began. Its proponents believed that the New Testament evangelists had said little about the person and life of Jesus because they were not interested in those details. What had mattered to them, rather, was the question of how to interpret our existence when confronted with Christ's teaching.

With such an existentialist message, these scholars took it as their task in this new quest to seek out the history embedded in the early church's *kerygma* (proclamation), understanding that the Gospels had no historical interest apart from faith. Their goal was to reconstruct the historical context where the message about Jesus, the *kerygma,* was preached, rather than to reconstruct the historical Jesus per se.

Third Quest

By the late 1970s, after the decline of existentialism and a period in which the quest for the historical Jesus became dormant, something of a renaissance in Jesus scholarship started a third quest, which has been characterized by its widely contrasting representations of Jesus and by a lack of a common methodology. There are, however, three points of consensus: the image of Jesus as an eschatological prophet has faded; a new image of Jesus as teacher has emerged; and the social world of Jesus has become central to the quest.

The goal of the third quest has been to free Jesus from the prison of Scriptures, where we have incarcerated him. Some of the portraits of Jesus that emerge from this third quest see him as a Jewish-Cynic peasant; a prophet of restoration eschatology; a Hellenistic-type Cynic sage; an egalitarian prophet of Wisdom; a social prophet; and a spirit person.

In the end, it may seem to some that the logic behind the battle between the Christ of Christian faith and the Jesus of history has destroyed both figures, leaving no winner. The result of the quest for the historical Jesus has been in some cases an ahistorical Jesus, dispossessed both from his Jewishness and from the community of faith that portrayed him in the Gospels. On the other hand, the Christ of faith has become "unbelievable" because he had been so extremely divinized and removed from the sociocultural context of what Christians affirm as the incarnation. In the same way that too much light or too little light prevents us from seeing clearly, polarizing the question of Jesus' identity in the stark terms of history versus Christian faith may prevent us from understanding him in new ways, including ways that accept the tension inherent in the Christian claim of his full humanity *and* his full divinity. Some of this new light has come through the images of Jesus current in contexts outside the West.

Jesus in Multicultural Contexts

In the same way that the cultural context of ancient Israel and the context of the Roman Empire influenced the titles and representations of Jesus, every cultural context in Christian history has contributed its own particular images of Jesus. For the Christianized Platonic philosophy of the third century, Jesus was essentially the Cosmic Christ, the *Logos* who ruled the universe and in whom all things had their being. In a sixth-century mosaic, dressed in Roman armor and driving the chariot of the sun (in the figure of Apollo), Jesus was transformed into the Christ Militant. For the medieval Benedictines, Jesus became a monastic figure who simultaneously ruled the world. In the Renaissance he was turned into the Universal Man (though distinctly European!). As themes of judgment came to the fore in popular European imagination, the Reformers found in Christ the Mirror of God's parental love that justified the sinner. For the philosophers of the Enlightenment, he became the Teacher of Common Sense. The multicultural quest for Jesus today emerges as a response to contemporary racism, the colonial captivity of much of the world, and the thwarting of indigenous images of Jesus.

Dominant White Eurocentric Images

When Jesus of Nazareth walked in Galilee, he looked visibly like his first-century Galilean Jewish contemporaries and shared their common culture. He came culturally from the region today called the Middle East, and he was ethnically like others descending from Afro-Asiatic Hebrews. Yet the image of Jesus that has been pervasive throughout much of the world is that of a white Northern European male with fair hair and blue eyes. How did that white Jesus become the prevailing image?

The earliest representations of Jesus were symbols such as a fish or a lamb. Early likenesses of Jesus show him as a beardless young man with a brown complexion. Only under the Byzantine Empire of the fifth and sixth centuries—which often depicted Jesus, with a beard and his hair parted down the middle, after the fashion of the Byzantine court, as a monarch, seated on a throne, his hand raised in command—did artists begin to create what has come to be the standard representation of Jesus. Like other regions, Europe developed culturally relevant representations of Christ for communicating the biblical story of Jesus.

But why did Europe's culturally appropriate Christ become the dominant image of the historical Jesus beyond Europe? The "European" Christ image was used to support European colonial expansion into Africa, Asia, and the Americas, as well as the genocide of indigenous peoples and the capture and enslavement of black Africans. In effect, a white likeness of Jesus served the purpose of being God's stamp of approval on the actions of white conquerors and demonstrated that the white "race" was superior to peoples of color by virtue of the whiteness of Jesus.

Missionaries from Europe could have discarded the Western images of Jesus upon arrival in Africa, the Americas, Asia, and the islands of the great oceans. With the help of indigenous people, new images of Jesus could have been shaped that spoke powerfully to the people encountered. But this did not happen. The propagation of white images of Jesus continues even to our own time through media portrayals in movies and television, as well as in the pictures of nearly every Bible produced for use around the world.

The effects of a Western image of a white Jesus have been far-reaching. In contexts outside of Europe, the whiteness of the image makes Jesus seem like a foreigner, a stranger, or even an enemy. If your oppressor is white and the oppressor's image of Jesus is white, it appears that Jesus has endorsed your domination—an impression the oppressors were often only too happy to promote. In this way, the Jesus who taught the love of enemies (Matt 5:44, Luke 6:27) has repeatedly been transformed into the enemy, a monarch who presides over brutal oppression carried out by those who look like he does.

When white Western images of Jesus appear in contexts outside of Europe, Jesus seems like a captive of the West. This makes it difficult for non-European people to understand Jesus as separate from those who brought him from Europe. When the Bible is interpreted from a Western bias, Christian faith and Western culture come to appear synonymous. White images of Jesus subtly give the impression that European and Euro-American ways of thinking and acting are normative. The effects of regarding Western Christianity as the normative and superior form of the Christian faith demeans any other form of Christianity, including ancient rites like the Eastern Orthodox Church and the Egyptian Coptic Church.

White images of Jesus have been used to deny the biblical message of liberation. The Jesus who preached good news to the poor and freedom for the oppressed (Luke

4:16–19) was altered to sustain systems of exploitation. For example, the religion of the slaveholder in the United States required only a belief in the incarnation (God made flesh in Jesus Christ): there was limited concern for the historical Jesus. Christianity was a religion of right belief. As long as one subscribed to the right belief or doctrine, one could enslave people in good conscience. Slave masters forced enslaved Africans to bow down in worship to this white image who looked racially like the brutal overseer. But the effects on white people in the United States have been no less troubling. In order to bless slavery and condone the white man's divine right to own Africans, the Bible was stripped of its liberating power. The Jesus that preached, practiced, and prayed for freedom and liberation was replaced with a Christ who was a symbol of right belief. Christian faith was domesticated, stultified into a pale reflection of white power and privilege.

Restoring Culturally Appropriate Images of Jesus

Today we know that the colonizer, the slaveholder, and the white supremacist lied about Jesus. Yet the image of a white Jesus remains deeply imbedded in our psyches. In order to change perceptions, people need to see that Jesus was not white. Jesus must be returned to his rightful place in a faith with roots in Africa and Asia. Even white people may need an Afro-Asiatic Jesus to be set free from racism. Whites who assent to an Afro-Asiatic Jesus will find it more difficult to accept society's racial hierarchy.

There is also a need for culturally relevant depictions. Some Native Americans describe Jesus as a respected spiritual leader. Latina/o scholars living in the United States have connected with a Galilean Jesus who knows the experience of feeling cut off from one's culture of origin and unaccepted by the dominant culture in a new land. African Americans have claimed a black Jesus who is friend, fellow sufferer, confidant, and liberator. Of course, the historical Jesus with African blood flowing through his veins (at least one drop!) could easily blend in among the wide range of skin colors and hues found in the AfricanAmerican community today.

Jesus must also be internationalized. Asian scholars remind us that the Jesus of history lived and breathed on the Asian continent. We need to reclaim this cultural connection. Latin American images of Jesus are diverse and include traditional portrayals of the infant Jesus and the suffering Jesus, as well as modern images such as the Indian Jesus, the black Jesus, the revolutionary Jesus, and Jesus as friend and liberator of women. Africans are contributing images of Jesus like Greatest Ancestor, First Ancestor, Elder Brother, Healer, Liberator, and Mother (or Nurturer of Life).

It is interesting to note that there are also some representations of Jesus coming from Asian non-Christian contexts. Within Islam, Jesus has been known as *Isa Masih* (Jesus the Messiah). Isa is known as one of God's most prominent and beloved prophets, who was called to guide the people of Israel. A Hindu view of Jesus recognizes him as one of the *Avataras,* the incarnations of the divine. Within Buddhism he has been called *Bodhisattva* ("one whose existence is enlightenment"), a being whose wisdom lies in the commitment to redeem all of life.

In our contemporary multicultural context, Jesus is emerging with new faces that are relevant to those who live in a culture different from the West. Following are a few examples.

Jesus the Liberator

In the midst of the economic oppression of poverty, the social oppression of dehumanization, and the spiritual oppression of sin, Jesus has emerged in Latin America as liberator from all oppressions. Jesus' miracles in the Gospels are seen not so much as demonstrations of Jesus' divinity but as actions of liberation that freed the oppressed as a consequence of their participating in the creation of God's kingdom. Jesus' followers must do what Jesus did: generate partial liberations in anticipation of the future liberation of all that God will bring about. As liberator, Jesus is also seen as a prophet who questioned the religious-political authorities and demanded justice, challenging the oppressive systems of his time. This image gives hope and liberation to the powerless to demand justice. Jesus the liberator does not arise exclusively from Latin America: a similar Jesus has emerged from the realities of oppression and poverty in Asian and African nations and of racism in the United States.

Jesus the Galilean–Mestizo

This Jesus emerges from the Latina/o reality of marginality in the United States. Jesus' identity as a Galilean, on the boundaries of Judean culture, is a symbol of marginality, a mirror where the marginalized community today can find a clear cultural identity. This Galilean Jesus was a human being with no particular privilege (Phil 2:6-7); he even assumed the form of a slave, in the eyes of the slaveholder less than human. He came into the world of the voiceless, the sick, the hungry, and the oppressed, not to do things for them, but to become one of them. The challenge of this Jesus today is to understand what Galilee was and what it means to be a Galilean today, and to seek out those who live on the cultural margins in today's world. It is there, in the most unsuspected places, that God continues to work.

Jesus the Ancestor

In some African cultures the concept of communion with the dead is an important part of their worldview. Those relatives who have died acquire a sacred status that implies supernatural powers and closeness to God. In that position they can act as mediators between God and humanity. For many, the deceased ancestors are liturgical companions of the living. Being an ancestor is more than simply having died; it means one lived an exemplary life, was married and transmitted life to another generation, then died a natural death. With the intention of translating the Christian faith into categories that are familiar to African people, the image of Jesus as Ancestor conveys the important role of Jesus as mediator between God and humans. A complementary understanding of Jesus as Elder Brother emphasizes his companionship in daily life.

Jesus as Chief

The concept of chief among some African communities is that of the guardian. The chief is the leader over political and religious matters in the community and is seen as a hero who can conquer enemies in both the earthly and the spiritual realms. Located at the intersection of both realms, the chief receives strength and authority from the ancestors and is considered an ancestor himself. In such position the chief is mediator between members of the tribe, the ancestors, and even those who have not been born. The identity of the community is derived from the chief. Just as the chief mediates between the tribe and the ancestors and gives identity to the community, Jesus mediates blessings to the church from God and gives identity to the church.

The Peoples' Jesus

As history shows, each of us has a particular vision of Jesus that may be influenced by our faith, ideologies, traditions, experiences, and all the other cultural elements that play a role in shaping our vision of reality and our own identity. No matter how diverse all these individual images of Jesus are, it is always important to acknowledge his historical context in first-century Judea and the fact that Jesus was a Jew. When our images of Jesus are divested of his cultural and ethnic background, they risk becoming anti-Semitic.

With so many images of Jesus available already, it is impossible not to ask, is there a limit to the images and representations of Jesus that we can create? Our answer: Not really. As long as diverse people come to Jesus, approaching him with particular images in mind, personalizing their own distinct encounters with him and perhaps coming to call upon him with distinct names, there will be no such limit. However, we could say that a limit is set by the spirit of love and liberation that the gospels convey. Images that depict a Jesus contrary to the spirit of the Gospels go beyond that limit. It should be inconceivable, for example, to represent Jesus as someone who meant to inflict oppression and pain. Imperialist images of Jesus, or the Aryan, Nazi Jesus who sponsored racism, or a violent, armed, revolutionary Jesus—all are distortions of the gospel depiction of a Jesus who preached the love of God.

The first-century Jesus of Nazareth had a particular culture and a distinct ethnic look. Jesus as the Christ has come to reside in all cultures, embraces all cultures, and speaks forth from all cultures. The Jesus of history and the Jesus who emerges from the pages of the Bible has come to be and remains the peoples' Jesus.

The Bible as an Instrument of Reconciliation

Curtiss Paul DeYoung

The biblical story commences in an idyllic garden setting in Genesis, with God creating the world and breathing life into the first human couple. The Bible concludes in Revelation in an envisioned future utopian paradise where all of humanity is gathered around the throne of God in perfect unity. Between creation and eternity the biblical story juxtaposes human alienation and God's desire for reconciliation. For us who live in a post-biblical, pre-paradise world, the Bible still remains a powerful source for understanding separation and God's hope for reconciliation.

The Hebrew Scriptures illustrate the story of God's relationship with the entire human family by highlighting a particular relationship between God and the Hebrew people. The narrative emerging from the pages of the Hebrew Scriptures describes the cycle of separation and reunion in the Hebrew peoples' relationship with God. Yet God never gives up on humanity and constantly pursues a relationship with the peoples of the earth.

One of the most powerful stories illustrating God's love for the Hebrew people is found in the writings of the prophet Hosea. Hosea's relentless pursuit of his unfaithful wife serves as a prophetic parable of God's constant pursuit of a relationship with humanity. This theme of relational reconciliation with God, or atonement (at-one-ment), is found throughout the Hebrew Scriptures. There are also many examples of alienation and reconciliation within the human family itself, including Adam and Eve, Jacob and Esau, Joseph and his brothers, Queen Esther (representing the Jews) and King Ahasuerus (the Persians). The Hebrew Scriptures offer insights into the dynamics that produce just relationships among people.

In the New Testament Gospels, Jesus of Nazareth is the model of reconciliation with God and others. The Gospel writers went to great lengths to present Jesus as a radically inclusive person and an exemplar of reconciliation. Their accounts of his birth and upbringing describe a relevant preparation for his reconciling task. Mary gave birth to Jesus in a livestock barn (Luke 2:7). Poor and despised shepherds in Palestine witnessed the event (2:8-20). Rich magi from Asia went to Bethlehem to see the infant Jesus, and the family escaped to the continent of Africa as refugees (Matt 2:1-15). Jesus the Jew was raised in Galilee of the nations (NRSV: "Gentiles," Matt 4:15). While Jesus maintained his own Jewish cultural and religious identity, he was enriched by various cultural elements from many nations.

The ministry of Jesus was also radically inclusive, beginning with his choice of disciples. He selected both a tax collector who collaborated with the Roman Empire and a zealot who called for the violent revolutionary overthrow of Rome (Matt 10:2-4; Luke 6:14-16). Jesus took the unheard of step of including a number of women in the circle of his followers (Matt 27: 55-56; Mark 15:40-41; Luke 8:2-3). His broad table fellowship reached to individuals outside of his socioeconomic class and ethnic/cultural world. Even at the death of Jesus, an African named Simon of Cyrene carried his cross (Matt 27:32; Mark 15:21; Luke 23:26) and a Roman centurion uttered words of faith (Matt 27:54; Mark 15:39).

In Acts and the apostolic writings Jesus the Christ, by virtue of his death and resurrection, is presented as the mediator between God and humanity, person and person, group and group. The apostle Paul and his circle of disciples were the theologians of reconciliation for the first-century church. The Greek words for "reconciliation" or "reconcile," *katallassō, katallagē, apokatallassō,* are used only a few times (Rom 5:10, 11; 11:15; 2 Cor 5:18, 19; Eph 2:16; and Col 1:20, 22), but are a powerful way of

expressing the meaning of the life, death, resurrection, and abiding presence of Jesus Christ. Biblical reconciliation implies friendship with God and each other, radical change and the transformation of a relationship or of a society, and the restoration of harmony.

The biblical discussions are not limited to embracing a loving God in relationship or affirming a good theology of reconciliation. Those of us who read the Bible as Scripture understand biblical reconciliation as a message we must announce and a ministry we must pursue. We are called to become God's "ambassadors" of reconciliation (2 Corinthians 5), working as catalysts for inclusive community, peace among nations, social transformation in society, and unity amidst religious diversity. The following biblical resources can empower us in that ambassadorial work.

Reconciliation and Inclusive Community

Congregations in the first century, as described in the Acts of the Apostles and in the Pauline letters, present an inviting possibility for developing a community that is inclusive. The mother church in Jerusalem (Acts 2–6) was a multilingual congregation of Jews from Jerusalem, Galilee, and the broader Roman Empire. The community was also diverse socioeconomically. The faith community in Antioch of Syria (Acts 11, 13; Galatians 2) was founded by Greek-speaking Jewish leaders originating from North Africa and Cyprus. From its beginning the Antioch congregation was multiethnic, including not only Jews raised in different cultural settings but Greeks and others. They had a multicultural and multiracial leadership team and survived a possible schism along ethnic lines through a courageous confrontation by the apostle Paul (Galatians 2). In Acts 13 and subsequent chapters, the author narrates the founding of many other congregations launched on the model of multiethnic inclusiveness found in Antioch. In many first-century congregations, women also emerged as leaders. (See Rom 16:1-15, where Paul mentions thirty-four church leaders, sixteen of whom are women.)

The congregations in the first-century church offer insights for reconciliation and creating inclusive communities through their empowering ministry with the poor, spiritual disciplines, courageous social action, and bilingual, multicultural, and gender-inclusive leadership teams. The New Testament details both the successes and failures of these faith communities in their efforts to be ministers of reconciliation.

Reconciliation and Peace among Nations

The Bible not only portrays the possibility of unity in faith communities; it also offers a vision for peace among nations. The prophet Isaiah proclaimed, "They shall beat their swords into plowshares, and their spears into pruning hooks; nation shall not lift up a sword against a nation, neither shall they learn war any more" (Isa 2:4). The author of Revelation saw a time when "a great multitude that no one could count, from every nation, from all tribes and peoples and languages" would be gathered together (Rev 7:9).

One of the most dramatic biblical episodes of two nations reconciling is the reunion of Jacob and Esau (Genesis 32–33). At the surface this seems to be only the reconciliation of two estranged brothers. And it is that. But by the time they met, after years of separation, they were no longer just individuals but growing communities—soon to be nations. The meeting of these leaders of two large tribal groups provides clues to the possibilities of peacemaking among nations in our own day.

Before the meeting, Jacob, the offender, sent gifts ahead to symbolically replace what he had taken from his brother Esau. He surmised, "I may appease him with the present that goes ahead of me, and afterwards I shall see his face; perhaps he will accept me" (Gen 32:20). Then Jacob spent the night prior to the meeting wrestling with God, purifying his motives, and preparing for the worst. The encounter with God left him wounded and ready to meet his brother with humility and repentance—"I have seen God face to face, and yet my life is preserved" (32:30). On the appointed day Jacob went ahead of the others and led his nation to meet Esau "bowing himself to the ground seven times, until he came near his brother" (33:3).

It seems that Esau, the offended, had also met with God. When he saw his brother Jacob he "ran to meet him, and fell on his neck and kissed him, and they wept" (33:4). Jacob came to the meeting with humility and a demonstrated willingness to make reparation. Esau came to the meeting ready to forgive and seek a new future for the relationship. Esau at first refused Jacob's gifts, saying he already had enough. But Jacob insisted, "If I find favor with you, then accept my present from my hand; for truly to see your face is like seeing the face of God (for) God has dealt graciously with me" (33:10-11).

Peace in the world becomes a greater possibility when the leaders of nations embrace the spirit of Jacob and Esau. Too often kings, queens, prime ministers, presidents, and other leaders approach the table of international dialogue with an agenda that is informed by a sense of ethnic or racial superiority, a punitive desire for revenge, self-centered arrogance, and an apparent lack of interest in an inclusive view of humanity or of social justice. These two biblical leaders of emerging nations had such a strong desire for reconciliation they set aside real and rightful feelings of hurt, anger, shame, fear, vengeance, and the like. A biblical framework for peace among nations requires leaders and citizens who emulate the attitudes and actions of Esau and Jacob.

Reconciliation and Social Transformation

Another key component of reconciliation is a focus on social transformation for justice. As noted above, 2 Cor 5:1—6:2 calls us to be ambassadors of reconciliation. "As we work together with [God], we urge you also not to accept the grace of God in vain. For he says, 'At an acceptable time I have listened to you, and on a day of salvation I have helped you.' See, now is the acceptable time; see, now is the day of salvation!" (6:1-2). Paul's quote from Isaiah 49 echoes Jesus' quotation of Isaiah 61 in Luke 4:18-19. The language of the "day of salvation" and "the year of the Lord's favor" speaks of the year of Jubilee (Leviticus 25)—that great ideal placed in the legal code of the Hebrew people to ensure that social justice defined their community and nationhood. (Unfortunately, there is no record of it ever having been practiced.) In Luke 4, Jesus appeals to this divine intention in his opening sermon. In 2 Corinthians, Paul links the ministry of reconciliation with the prophetic call to social justice. Our reconciliation with God leads to reconciliation with each other. This means on the macro level the creation of a society that practices social justice.

Paul makes the link between social justice and reconciliation even clearer in Galatians 3:28. "There is no longer Jew or Greek, there is no longer slave or free, there is no longer male and female; for all of you are one in Christ Jesus." These words were part of a baptismal formula from the earliest days of the first-century church. This creedal statement was used to initiate new members into a reconciling faith that removed socially constructed boundaries and hierarchies and replaced them with relationships and societal interactions based on social justice.

Too often people of faith choose to focus on reconciliation with God but not with others. Others reconcile relationally across human boundaries but do not address the societal issues that created the boundaries. A biblical perspective calls for an integrated approach to reconciliation that includes our relationship with God, our relationship with other people, the dismantling of oppressive social structures that cause division, and the creation of just societies and nations.

Reconciliation and Religious Diversity

The biblical writers focus primarily on the story of the Hebrew people and then of Jesus and the first-century Christians. Therefore, there is little in the Bible that speaks directly to interfaith reconciliation. Given the extreme conflicts in the twentieth century and beyond that involve the three major Abrahamic religions—Judaism, Christianity, and Islam—there is one biblical story that might symbolize the needed reconciliation. Jews and Christians claim Abraham as their father through Isaac, and Muslims claim Abraham through Ishmael. The story in Genesis 25 of Ishmael and Isaac coming together to bury their father could serve as a catalyst for reconciliation among these monotheistic religions. The story is simple. Upon Abraham's death at 175 years, "His sons Isaac and Ishmael buried him in the cave of Machpelah, in the field of Ephron son of Zohar the Hittite, east of Mamre, the field that Abraham purchased from the Hittites. There Abraham was buried, with his wife Sarah" (vv. 9-10). Ishmael, the older son and spiritual ancestor of Islam, joined together with his brother, Isaac, spiritual ancestor of Judaism and Christianity, and they buried their father Abraham in Hebron.

The biblical stories of Ishmael and Isaac reveal a history of favoritism, prejudice, manipulation, rejection, victimization, and mixed blessing. Yet the death of Abraham provided a reason for setting aside problematic histories and convoluted relationships to focus on a shared love and responsibility. Judaism, Christianity, and Islam share much in their understanding of faith, the importance of peace and social justice, and God's love for humanity. They also share a problematic history and convoluted relationships. The story of Ishmael and Isaac together burying their father, Abraham, offers a message to Judaism, Christianity, and Islam in our day: Set aside histories and present animosities in order to focus on a world that desperately needs the values of compassion, reconciliation, social justice, and peace at the core of your respective faiths.

Reconciliation and Community

Usually the work of reconciliation is complex and multifaceted. Reconciliation issues are often intertwined and not easily separated. The Bible also offers scriptural resources for this reality. Paul's admonition in Gal 3:28 implies that race, gender, and socioeconomic class are all intertwined justice issues and that reconciliation cannot succeed without a strategy to address each that is simultaneous and interlinked.

A good biblical example of the complicated and multifaceted nature of reconciliation is the story of Jesus in conversation with a woman from Samaria by Jacob's well (John 4:4-42). This interchange represented differences in culture, gender, socioeconomic class, status, religion, and more. As the story is read, it becomes evident that Jesus arrived at the encounter unashamed of the differences and well prepared for the nuances of such a conversation. This allowed reconciliation to occur rather than for alienation to fester further. Jesus engages with this Samaritan woman in public. As a Jewish male and itinerant rabbi, Jesus rejected social norms when he spoke publicly to a woman, requested a drink from a Samaritan, and was seen with a person of questionable moral standards. This single act of welcoming the woman from Samaria to a relational encounter meant Jesus had to cross at least three social boundaries. He could not decide to focus only on ethnic reconciliation, or gender inclusion, or moral questions. Jesus had to embrace all of who this woman was and he did it publicly, without any embarrassment or hesitation.

Not only was Jesus bold in a public display of his reconciliation intentions, he was also well prepared for the encounter. Most likely Jesus did not know that he was going to meet a Samaritan woman on this day. What Jesus did know was that his call to be a reconciler would lead him to all kinds of encounters, so he had to prepare himself even before the event. Given the proximity of Samaria, it seems that Jesus was likely familiar with their culture and religion. This is apparent in how he presents himself and his messianic mission to the woman. The Samaritans were seeking a messiah who would reveal truth and restore belief. When Jesus told the woman things about her life that he would have no way of knowing, he was not saying something about her. Rather, Jesus was revealing something about himself. He was informing her that he was the Revealer (*Taheb*), the Messiah. The woman told her neighbors, "Come and see a man who told me everything I have ever done! He cannot be the Messiah, can he?" (John 4:29). Jesus' knowledge of Samaritan culture and religious beliefs hurried the process of reconciliation at Jacob's well that day.

The theme of reconciliation runs throughout the Bible. Reconciliation calls us to inclusive communities, peace among nations, social transformation, and relationships across religions. Jesus said to the woman in Samaria, "Woman, believe me, the hour is coming when you worship the Father neither on this mountain nor in Jerusalem" (John 4:21). Reconciliation calls us to such a time: a future era when neither race, culture, gender, socioeconomic class, religion, nor any other designator will serve as our primary identity or the identity we ascribe to others. Biblical reconciliation propels us to embrace our ultimate identity as humans created in the image of God, that is, as children of God.

The Bible and Empire

Neil Elliott

Introductions to the Bible ordinarily discuss the rise and fall of empires as the background of biblical history, and for good reason. For most of recorded history, the peoples living in the land once called Canaan, later Israel, and still later Palestine, have lived under the sway of outside powers. From Egypt and its Canaanite vassal kings to the Hittite empire, the Mesopotamian empires of Asshur and Babylon, later Persia, then the Greeks and the Hellenistic Seleucids, and still later the Roman Empire—throughout this long history, empires exerted control over the land and the labor of the people who lived on it.

That history continued, of course, after the biblical period, with the Byzantine Empire; the rise of Islam and the Arab Caliphates; European Crusader kingdoms; and the Mamluk and Ottoman Empires. Following World War I, the land was controlled under the British Mandate. After World War II, the United Nations partitioned the land and created the State of Israel. Following the war of 1967, Israel occupied the Palestinian territories, continuing to hold them today under the plea of self-defense and with the indispensable protection from international sanction provided by the United States. The oil resources of the Middle East are only one reason—but an undeniably important one—that powerful foreign nations continue to influence the fortunes of people living in the land.

But there are other, more pressing reasons to consider the Bible's relationship to empire. In the 1960s and 1970s, many formerly colonized peoples in Africa, Asia, and South America began to throw off the rule of European and North American powers, following the example of India in the 1940s (and Haiti in 1791). These same peoples throughout the world are nevertheless keenly aware of the powerful continuing legacy of colonialism. Deprived of much of the natural wealth of their lands, often stripped of their cultural heritage, their kinship and community structures ravaged, and their new governments too often independent only in name, people of the "global South," and the surviving native peoples of North America as well, know that their futures are inevitably shaped by the political, economic, and military power of the same industrialized nations that formerly ruled them directly.

Because the Bible was so often wielded as an instrument of European and North American imperialism, justifying policies of genocide, enslavement, and cultural extinction, formerly colonized peoples now look upon the Bible with tremendous ambivalence. The profoundly varied ways that different communities have experienced the Bible—and come to read it for themselves—are well represented throughout the essays in this volume. This essay will focus on the role of imperialism in constraining the imaginations of the people who wrote the Bible itself. The communities who produced the Bible thought of themselves, their world, their God, and the future in ways that bear the unmistakable imprint of empire. These themes are at the center of biblical scholarship today.

The Emergence of "Israel" in Canaan

How did a people called "Israel" emerge in the land of Canaan in the thirteenth through eleventh centuries BCE? The Bible itself offers a conflicted picture. The book of Joshua tells of a swift and decisive military conquest of Canaan, carried out by a single people, Israel, who had been led miraculously out of slavery in Egypt and across the Sinai wilderness (according to the epic related earlier in Exodus–Deuteronomy). These people, also called "Hebrews," shared the lineage of Abraham, who had left his home in Ur (in modern Iraq) in answer to the call of a god he had not known before (Genesis 11–12). But the Bible also declares that "a mixed crowd" left Egypt with the

Israelites (Exod 12:37-38); and after Joshua's time, the book of Judges describes Israel's failure to drive out "the Canaanites" and their continued struggle against Canaanite influences. The traditional picture of a decisive Israelite "conquest" that dispossessed and destroyed the Canaanites is called into question within the Bible itself.

Critical assessment of all the biblical, archaeological, and extrabiblical literary evidence suggests a much more complicated history. The Hebrews (*'ibrim*) may have begun not as a distinct ethnic group but as a social class in Canaan. Canaanite documents (like the Amarna letters) refer to *hapiru* either as outsiders or persons of low status, or as political opponents who set themselves against the kings of Canaan's city-states and their Egyptian overlords. At least some of the *hapiru* settled in the highlands, beyond Egypt's reach; others controlled cities in defiance of Egypt. If the origins of the Hebrews are to be found here, it would appear that Israel first emerged in the hills of Canaan as the result of a social and cultural phenomenon, achieved in part through the displacement of peoples as Egypt's power over the land subsided, and in part through the overthrow of Canaanite cities from within as well as without. The term *Israel* first described a network of cities, villages, and clans, made up (on this theory) not of one but of different ethnicities, joined in cooperative agriculture, the sharing of resources, and responsibilities for mutual defense.

According to the Bible, this new people gathered around ceremonies and symbols that represented the centrality of the God of liberation in their shared life. Joshua 24 may reflect typical occasions on which the dispossessed were drawn to this new people and incorporated into it. They recited a common history that looked back to an unnamed migrant ancestor, "a wandering Aramean" (Deut 26:5). Note that it is Abraham's departure from Ur, not his "Aramaean" ethnicity, that makes him paradigmatic: see Deut 26:5-9. They spoke of miraculous deliverance from slavery in Egypt at the hands of a God who listened to the cries of the oppressed. That story was likely brought into Canaan originally by escaped slaves, but the story would have spoken just as powerfully to the people of the land who had borne the brunt of oppression by Egypt's vassal kings. (If one of Israel's most ancient poems is Miriam's celebration of the defeat of Pharaoh's army at the Red Sea, or Sea of Reeds, Exod 15:20-21, another celebrates the deliverance, at Deborah's hand, of "the peasantry" of Canaan from "the mighty," Judg 5:1-31.) They called upon God under the name YHWH, an enigmatic name, later read (but not spoken) in Hebrew, and translated into Greek and English as "Lord" (and so printed in the NRSV; see note at Exodus 3). The name probably originally meant "creator," and it was linked from the beginning with the downfall of earthly lords.

A decided antagonism to empire marks the earliest symbols that united this people. The identification of YHWH as the God of liberation is the first commandment given to the new people (according to Exod 20:2; compare Deut 6:12; 26:7-9). They were to worship this God alone and never to carve any image of God (Exod 20:4-6; compare Deut 4:15-20). In the context of ancient Near-Eastern empires, in which the gods were regularly carved in the likeness of a human monarch, that prohibition conveyed a clear message: the glory of YHWH the deliverer was incompatible with the grasping claims of pharaohs and kings. To similar and startling effect, early Israel gathered for prayer, or went into battle, around the most disconcerting of symbols: the ark of the covenant, which resembled the portable thrones of other ancient Near-Eastern deities—except that it was conspicuously empty! (See 1 Samuel 4–6.)

The Rise of the Kingdom Israel

In the eleventh century BCE, the waning of Egyptian power allowed a new people to invade the coastland of Canaan. The Philistines brought superior iron-age weapons to their conflict with bronze-age Israel. In a scenario often repeated in history, the militarily weaker people were able eventually to thwart more powerful opponents through collective effort and stealth. They gathered around a fearless bandit leader whose courage, loyalty, and cunning gained him tremendous popular support. This was David; and just as Saul, his predecessor, was raised up as "king" after leading an Israelite victory in the field, so the tales of David's daring exploits—single-handedly defeating a more powerful Philistine warrior, tricking Philistine raiders who mistook him for an ally, and at last capturing the fortified city of Jerusalem with a small band of warriors, and without bloodshed—amply explain his rise to power as Israel's most renowned king (see 1 Samuel).

David moved swiftly to unite the people behind his monarchy, establishing Jerusalem as his capital and bringing the ark of the covenant into his city (2 Sam 6:12-19). David's reign and that of his son, Solomon, was the first period of Israelite independence. It is not surprising that Israel's first national epic, fragments of which scholars find in Genesis, Exodus, and Numbers, was written in this period or that it expressed buoyant defiance of imperial values (see the introduction to the Pentateuch).

While Mesopotamian creation accounts began with a city and its king being lowered from heaven, this Israelite epic spoke of a man and a woman bearing the image of God (Gen 1:26-27) as they walked, naked and unashamed, in a paradisal garden. Kings, cities, and the makings of sacrifice and warfare were not yet in sight (Gen 2:4-25). The epic moved from promises made to the ancestor Abraham toward their fulfillment in the reign of Solomon (compare Genesis 15 with the map of David and Solomon's reign). The centerpiece of this narrative was the exodus from Egypt, now elaborated as a great contest in which YHWH manifested his power at Pharaoh's expense. Everything that imperial Egypt held sacred—from the cleansing waters of the Nile and the fertile fields along its banks, to the Pharaoh's firstborn son, whose succession would guarantee dynastic stability, to the power to control the bodies of slaves through the threat of violence, represented in Pharaoh's mighty chariots—all this was polluted, struck down, or emptied of force (Exodus 3–15). Strikingly, Egyptian records give not a hint that the empire of the pharaohs ever faced a catastrophe like that described in Exodus; to the contrary, Egypt continued to influence Israel's history for centuries. The power of the exodus story lay not in its objective reporting of ancient history but in its potency to shape a new people around the imagination of a world where imperial power was no longer decisive.

Contested Memory

The preceding account necessarily reads beneath and behind the biblical narratives, which reflect later efforts to manage the memory of Israel's origins. Like an archaeological tell or a geologist's trench, the Bible provides a wealth of information but often in complex layers that require critical interpretation. The Bible presents not a single voice but a chorus of sometimes conflicting voices struggling to articulate what YHWH had done, was doing, and would do in the future.

We find tensions between different views of Israel's monarchy, for example. In some of the psalms a distinct theological narrative appears, resembling the kingship ideology of other ancient Near-Eastern empires. Probably developed in the court of David and Solomon, this "Zion theology" represents YHWH's chief work in the world as the establishment of the royal city, Zion (the sacred name for David's Jerusalem), and of the king himself, through whose benevolent rule alone YHWH would bring justice to the earth (see Psalms 48 and 72). On the other hand, the books of Samuel and Kings present episodes in which one or another individual or group protests the actions of a king as excessive. Solomon's son Rehoboam's harsh rule was (according to 1 Kings 12) the occasion for the kingdom's division into a northern ("Israel") and a southern kingdom ("Judah"), a fault line that neighboring nations were eager to exploit. When in the eighth century the Assyrian Empire threatened the Northern Kingdom, the prophets Amos and Hosea read the geopolitical power shift as a warning from YHWH against the nation's infidelity and injustice. Similarly, Isaiah of Jerusalem warned the Southern Kingdom that what seemed pragmatic alliances with neighboring kingdoms was a failure to trust YHWH.

While we cannot identify a single institutional location for the rise of prophecy in Israel, the prophetic writings testify to sites and practices of advice and criticism, addressed to the monarch or the ruling class, in the name of YHWH and on behalf of the poor and needy. The book of Amos gives glimpses of the tensions when both an opposition prophet and the officials of a royal sanctuary claimed to speak for the same God. A similar tension appears elsewhere as the contrast between "true" and "false" prophets (see for example 1 Kings 22). While it is impossible to speak of a single "prophetic perspective," the tendency of the prophets to speak of YHWH as the sovereign God who governed earthly affairs would prove fatefully decisive when hostile empires loomed on Israel's horizon.

YHWH *and the* Imagination *of* Empires

Unable to imagine the YHWH who had formed Israel through the defeat of mighty Egypt as in any way inferior to the gods of other empires, the prophets made the daring move of imagining the empire of Assyria and, later, of Babylon as themselves the instruments through which YHWH threatened judgment on a disobedient Israel. Although the book of Jeremiah shows that this viewpoint was unpopular in a nation that understood YHWH as their protector, after Babylon's capture of Jerusalem and deportation of many of its people to exile (587–86 BCE), what had been unpopular became self-evident. That Israel's defeat at the hands of Babylon was the expression of YHWH's anger seemed, paradoxically, to prove that YHWH alone was truly God. The necessary corollary of belief in YHWH's supremacy was the acceptance of humil-

iation at the hands of imperial powers as the will of heaven—a belief that subsequent empires would find little enough reason to challenge.

The Documents of Colonial Judah

It was in Babylonian exile that the priestly and scribal elite of defeated Judah assembled the great compositional units of the Hebrew Bible: the Torah; the scrolls of the Prophets; and the epic history that reaches from Joshua to 2 Kings, called the Former Prophets in Jewish tradition and the Deuteronomistic History in contemporary scholarship. When Babylon in turn fell to the Persian empire—an event that the Second Isaiah (Isaiah 40–55) hailed as a new exodus, YHWH's unprecedented deliverance of his people—members of the exile community were allowed to return to their homeland (see Ezra and Nehemiah). They "restored" Judah, not as a vassal kingdom but as a tributary temple-state ruled by priests on behalf of their Persian overlords. The documents the exiles had created became the constitution of reorganized Judah. We may read the Torah and Prophets, then, as the artifacts of a colonial situation.

The returning elite had to negotiate the competing claims of the Persian Empire and of the indigenous population who worked the land. In their final form, the writings they placed at the center of the people framed earlier traditions around themes that implicitly showed the people their place in the colonial order. The account of creation and the earth's primeval history revealed a priestly focus on order and on the necessity of sacrifice to recover from catastrophe (Genesis 1–9). The grumblings and apostasies of an unworthy and recalcitrant people punctuated the account of the exodus and the wandering in the wilderness (Exodus–Numbers). Only repeated priestly interventions saved the people from much-deserved wrath; indeed, the presence of YHWH among the people was possible only because of a system of sacrifice. When Israel entered the land of Canaan, worship and the ingathering of tithes and offerings were to be centralized under priestly supervision in Jerusalem.

The postexile Torah warned that kings—the hallmark of sovereign nations—would prove disastrous unless they submitted to priestly supervision (Deut 17:14-20). Prophecy, originally an urgent challenge to the present, was redefined as the authoritative voice of the past (Deut 18:15-22). These two themes would govern the whole of the Deuteronomistic History as well. The Torah now concluded with warnings to the people, issued on the far side of the Jordan river, that their own willful disobedience to their covenant with God would make them unworthy of the land they were about to inhabit—a lesson illustrated at length in the history. Israel's early life as a federation of tribes was now recast in Judges as life under the shadow of self-destructive lawlessness and anarchy; the epic of the great king David was retold as a warning against the dangers of monarchic power. The succession of kings in Israel and Judah was evaluated according to a simple criterion: those kings who had obeyed "true" prophets and supported centralized worship in Jerusalem were good kings; those who had tolerated alternative modes of popular religion were evil. The artificiality of this scheme is apparent when one compares the evaluation of the "evil" Manasseh, who reigned for fifty-five years, to the reformer Josiah, who was struck down in battle—in punishment, the history insists, for the sins of Manasseh! (2 Kgs 21:1—23:30).

For the Deuteronomistic historians, Manasseh's sin was not the tolerance of Israelite popular religion but promotion of the "abominable practices of the nations" that YHWH had driven out "before the people" (2 Kgs 21:2). A single theological agenda informs the book of Deuteronomy and the Deuteronomistic History alike, according to which the greatest danger to Israel's future is the contagion of a "Canaanite" past. The book of Joshua represents Israel's violent conquest of Canaan as obedience to YHWH's command to invade the land and to exterminate and replace its unworthy inhabitants (explicit, for example, in Deut 20:16-18).

Long read as an actual description of divinely ordained conquest, this narrative has borne terrible fruit in recent centuries as the empires of Christianized Europe expanded into new lands. Their reading of Joshua emboldened more recent conquerors to view the indigenous peoples of the lands they invaded as inferior and expendable. In North America, the equation of European settlers with a "new Israel" and the native peoples with the unworthy inhabitants of a "new Canaan" was explicit (see "The Bible as a text in Cultures: Native American"). Later secularized as the "manifest destiny" of the Anglo-Saxon race, this theme fueled violent American imperialist expansion throughout the late nineteenth and early twentieth centuries. But read as the product of the colonial elite in Persian-controlled Judah, the biblical command to "drive out" the Canaanites appears rather as a spasm of spectacularly violent wishful thinking. The reformers' zeal to suppress what they regarded as corrupting influences among their own people led them to rewrite Israelite origins as a sacred campaign to exterminate the contagion of the Canaanite population.

The messages of the prophets were assembled into scrolls and edited to convey a dominant rhythm of disobedience, judgment, repentance, and restoration—the same rhythm rehearsed in the Deuteronomistic History. YHWH's covenantal faithfulness was constant and undeserved. The fulfillment of ancient hopes was projected into a distant future and made dependent on the precarious prospect of the people's renewed obedience.

There were dissenting voices. The books of Job and Ecclesiastes (in Hebrew, *Qoheleth*, "the Preacher") protested, in their own ways, the crude equation of misfortune and defeat with divine judgment. The intimate narrative of Ruth has been read as an oblique rebuttal to Ezra's "reforms"; and the strident tone in some postexilic prophecy (for example, Isaiah 56–66) reveals controversies regarding the welfare of groups excluded from temple worship.

The Disciplining of Hope

Torah and temple alike were sites of contention between the national and religious aspirations of the Judean population—who by the second century BCE seem to have accepted both as ordained by God—and the successive Hellenistic and Roman empires that tried, ultimately without success, to cultivate a compliant ruling class in the land. Nothing so stirred up hopes for a future free of foreign domination as the successful uprising of the Maccabees against a brutally repressive Hellenistic rule (167–64 BCE; see 1 and 2 Maccabees). Judean independence was short-lived, however. The Hasmonean dynasty that followed the Maccabean revolt secured its position through pragmatic compromises with Hellenistic rulers that alienated many of the priestly class. We can see a range of responses in the splintering of the Judean priestly and lay ruling class into factions or schools: the Pharisees and Sadducees who appear later in the gospels, for example, and the dissenters who withdrew from what they considered a corrupt temple to wait near the Dead Sea for YHWH's purging of Jerusalem (according to the generally accepted reading of the Dead Sea Scrolls). We can also recognize the knife-edge of negotiating the colonial situation in the flourishing of short stories that depict devout Judeans living faithfully in a foreign court (Esther, Daniel 1–6, and the story of Joseph in Genesis 37–48). When the colonizing power became intolerably harsh, the genre of apocalyptic vision offered heavenly reassurance that God remained in control and would vindicate the righteous in a spectacular redemption, if they only endured (Daniel 7–12, soon followed by an explosion of other apocalyptic writings).

In 63 BCE the intervention of the Roman general Pompey effectively made the Hasmonean dynasty a client kingdom of Rome (lamented in the Psalms of Solomon). Priestly and scribal elites facilitated the payment of tribute to Rome from the temple treasuries; in so doing, they may also have protected the people from bearing more directly the brunt of Roman demands. Some of the leaders of resistance to Rome also came from priestly circles, as did, at last, some of the instigators of revolt in 66 CE.

These aspects of the colonial situation characterized the world in which Jesus of Nazareth lived and died. The fact that Jesus was crucified beneath the derisive Roman title "King of the Jews" (see Mark 15:25 and parallels) requires that we understand him against the context of Roman imperialism. The Romans crucified rebels and fugitive slaves, including thousands of Judeans in the course of the first century CE, to punish the insubordinate and to display their bodies as a warning to others.

Scholars debate which aspects of the gospels point us reliably to Jesus' own practice. There are nevertheless ample reasons to explain why Jesus was among Rome's victims. For example, though they appear now as allegories of God's dealings with the world, Jesus' parables may originally have functioned to shine the harsh light of the prophetic tradition on the fundamental injustice of the Roman economy in Palestine—juxtaposing sharecroppers and day laborers with cruel landowners and indifferent landlords. He apparently preached a coming reversal of fortunes (compare Matt 5:1-12 and Luke 6:20-26); he urged a mutual reliance among the poor that would have cut against the grain of Roman patronage, land appropriation, and taxation. He and his disciples are depicted performing exorcisms, as did other itinerant Judean wonder-workers in his day; but Jesus presented these as an assault on the present reign of Satan (see Mark 3), at a time when Roman propaganda boasted of having inaugurated a golden age of peace and justice. At length, Jesus made a dramatic entrance into Jerusalem, during Passover—a time when nationalist feeling was most intense—at the head of an excited crowd who hailed him as the Messiah. He entered the outer court of the temple and staged a disturbance there. While the gospels disagree on his motives, comparison with similar actions by other Jews suggests that he intended a protest against a temple regime that some saw as collaborating with Rome (see Mark 11:7-18 and parallels).

Scholars also debate the precise responsibility for Jesus' arrest and execution. But there is near universal recognition that the ultimate responsibility for crucifixion lay with the Roman governor, Pilate, whom we know from other sources to have been spectacularly brutal (in marked contrast to his portrayal in the gospels). Any of the actions just described might have provoked a reaction from agents of the temple regime, eager to maintain a precarious balance and avoid the sort of spectacular collective punishment of which Rome had repeatedly shown itself all too capable. (The high priest expresses this logic in a statement that may, ironically, hold a kernel of historical truth: see John 11:49-50.) The gospels give troubling hints of broader unrest: Mark makes oblique reference to an "insurrection" (15:7), and reports that Jesus was crucified between two "bandits" (Mark 15:27). We must go outside the gospels for evidence that a number of first-century Judeans similarly gathered crowds, staged provocative actions against the Roman client regime in Jerusalem, and were cut down, their followers scattered.

The Sublimation of Hope

During the forty years between the death of Jesus and the earliest of the New Testament gospels, an international movement sprang up, centered in Jerusalem and including Judeans and non-Judeans alike in small assemblies that honored Jesus as Israel's true Messiah, miraculously raised from the dead. Our primary source for this period, and consequently for what account we should give of the spread of this movement beyond Palestine, remains controversial. On one account, the apostle Paul sought to move beyond the chafing boundaries of Jewish practice to establish a universal religion that transcended ethnic limitations. On another account, any "universalism" purchased at the price of Jewish identity is a false universalism; the interpretation of Paul thus becomes a conflict in cultural values. The controversy is compounded by writings in the New Testament that many scholars contend were falsely attributed to Paul (see the Introduction to the Pauline Letters).

All the New Testament gospels were penned years after Paul's death—and more importantly, in the aftermath of the Roman war that put down a rebellious Judea and destroyed the temple (66–70 CE). Though all of the gospels affirm that Jesus had been raised from death and would return to usher in a messianic future, the gospel writers thus faced circumstances that seemed to disconfirm those hopes. Each responded, in his own way, by providing Jesus a messianic past. Matthew and Luke specified his Davidic lineage and recounted the sort of birth prodigies and miracles that Hellenistic readers would have expected of heaven's favorite. They and Mark reframed Jesus' parables as allegorical teachings about God's sublime nature; and with John they set Jesus in opposition primarily to corrupt, venal, and hypocritical Jewish religious leaders who mercilessly imposed the Torah's purity codes to defraud and oppress the poor. The gospels all ascribed Jesus' failure to bring in the messianic age to his devout refusal to seize power inappropriately (see the "temptation" scene in Matthew 3 and Luke 4) and to his obedience to a divine "necessity" that he die on behalf of others. Most fatefully, they attributed primary responsibility for his death not to Roman colonial policy but to the malice and dishonesty of the Jewish leadership in Jerusalem, the weak and ineffectual character of the Roman governor, and the fickleness of the Jewish mob. The crowd's paradigmatic choice of Barabbas, a murderous rebel, over Jesus, whom even Pilate identifies as an innocent man, seals not only Jesus' fate but that of the city itself; for as Jesus' own words make clear, the city's rejection of him will bring down the judgment of God (see especially Matthew 21–24).

In the decades after the horrors of Nazism, churches around the world repudiated the notion, prevalent in some Christian communities, that the Jewish people were culpable for the death of Jesus. In general, however, churches have not as readily embraced the insights of critical scholarship into the pivotal—but historically improbable—role that notion plays in the plot of the various gospels. By portraying Jesus' fate as a miscarriage of justice for which hostile Jews were responsible, rather than as the predictable consequence of his own actions and words, the gospels implicitly disavowed the cause of defeated Judea and presented belief in Jesus as politically innocuous. In this way the gospels, too, reveal themselves as no less the products of a colonial situation than the Torah and Prophets of the Hebrew Bible.

To the Present

In the decades following the apostolic age, Christian theology focused increasingly on Jesus' divine nature and on the necessity of his atoning death. The ancient priestly logic of sacrifice, which Judaism reinterpreted metaphorically after the temple was destroyed, became central to Christian atonement theology (as seen already in the Letter to the Hebrews). The political significance of the actions that led to Jesus' death was minimized, however. The thoroughly Judean character of his hope had become a liability, and the dejudaization of Jesus, evident already in early Christianity, continues even to the present.

 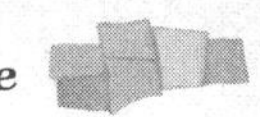

In the fourth century, with the advent of a Christian emperor of the Roman Empire, the heavenly Jesus himself came to be represented in the likeness of a monarch: bearded, clothed in purple, and seated on a throne, his hand raised in command. That imperial depiction of Jesus as all-ruler ("Pantocrator") is one of the most widely recognized images in our world.

Closer to our own time, imperial powers have wielded the Bible as an instrument of colonization. Yet from time to time, the colonized have also found in the Bible sparks to ignite resistance and the struggle for liberation. In our own day, leaders of the world's most powerful nation have candidly spoken of the possibility, even the necessity, of a benevolent imperialism and have appealed to the imperative of "national security" in laying claim to the resources of peoples from Venezuela to Iraq and beyond. In the two-thirds world, however, theologians describe devastating war, the proliferation of national security states, the forced displacement of millions of human beings, and the hijacking of national economies for the benefit of transnational corporations as the true nature of a new global imperialism, the savage face of capitalism.

Those who turn to the Bible as a compass as they try faithfully to navigate a course through these realities face great challenges, for the Bible presents a complex and bewildering legacy. Contemporary scholarship shows us that the sweep of biblical story was marked by the rise and fall of empires. We should hardly be surprised that the Bible's contents have been shaped by their sway.

The challenges facing contemporary readers of the Bible are, first, to recognize how powerfully the Bible itself was shaped by political realities. Second, and just as important, we may recognize the ways in which religious perceptions and practices in our own day—including the very definition of what counts as religion—have been shaped by the complex and subtle pressures of imperial culture. In the United States in particular, the rise of a powerful civil religion, the popularity of escapist fiction about the "rapture," and, paradoxically, the simultaneous marginalization of alternative religious voices from the public sphere are but a few important consequences of those pressures.

My own awareness of these pressures is admittedly limited: I live fairly comfortably as a well-educated, middle class, white professional male. My efforts at raising the issues just named from an Episcopal pulpit are generally tolerated by my congregation, either because of their liberal inclinations or their forgiving spirit! But perhaps these are symptoms of the problem I have been describing: many of us are quite comfortable with the religion in which we find ourselves, and many of those who have been most moved by the gospel's demands have either moved on or have been made to feel unwelcome in the church. For all of us, the responsibilities to reassess the biblical heritage critically and to reevaluate the ways the Bible has shaped our perceptions of our global neighbors and what we owe them remain nothing less than moral imperatives.

The God of the Bible and the Peoples of the Earth

Kosuke Koyama

Speaking of "God"

The English word "god" is used in different ways. In general, when we speak of a "god" we mean a being who is beyond us, larger, wiser, and more powerful than we are. Routinely we speak of "God" (with a capital "G") as the one such being who actually exists, and we think of God in personal terms. On further reflection, we may realize we do not mean to refer to one more being alongside others but to a mysterious, invisible, and transcendent reality that is beyond all other beings—in traditional Christian terms, a Creator who is unlike all that is created—and that eludes being captured by human thought: in the words God speaks in Isaiah, "For my thoughts are not your thoughts, nor are your ways my ways.... For as the heavens are higher than the earth, so are my ways higher than your ways and my thoughts than your thoughts" (55:8-9).

Some people have insisted that the reality we call God transcends even our understanding of what it means to be a person. The prominent scholar of religions Rudolf Otto described the human experience of a mystery that is at once fearsome and fascinating as the source of all religious expression. Though the character and intensity of this experience surely varies, this phrase describes what we can find in many diverse cultures. Some scholars who study cultures say that every language and dialect of the several thousand spoken in the world has a word that can be translated "deity(ies)" or "god(s)": *kami* in Japanese, *nkulunkulu* in Zulu, *mwari* in Shona, *khuda* in Tamil, *siong-te* in Chinese, *allah* in Javanese, *theos* in Greek, and so on. This is a remarkable fact, suggesting that every culture has some conception of a transcendent being or beings. Whether or not they speak of God in personal terms, in many cultures people perceive that they not only can speak about this transcendent reality but can be personally connected with it.

To be religious means being aware of such a connection. Dag Hammarskjöld, general secretary of the United Nations, wrote,

> I don't know Who—or what—put the question, I don't know when it was put. I don't even remember answering. But at some moment I did answer Yes to Someone—or Something—and from that hour I was certain that existence is meaningful and that, therefore, my life, in self-surrender, had a goal.[1]

A similar experience, from another culture, comes to us from the great Indian writer, Rabindranath Tagore:

> Almost every morning in the early hour of the dusk, I would run out from my bed in a great hurry to greet the first pink flush of the dawn through the shivering branches of the palm trees.... The sky seemed to bring to me the call of a personal companionship, and all my heart—my whole body in fact—used to drink in at a draught the overflowing light and peace of those silent hours.... I am certain that I felt a larger meaning of my own self when the barrier vanished between me and what was beyond myself.[2]

The Bible, too, offers scenes of encounters with God that are filled with awe and wonder: Moses's encounter with the LORD in a bush that "was blazing, yet it was not consumed" (Exod 3:1-6), for example, or Isaiah's vision of the LORD in the Jerusalem temple (6:1-13).

Israel's "One God"

In the great story of human awareness of the transcendent that reaches back to the dawn of civilization, the ancient people of Israel in the Near East made a remarkable contribution. The Hebrew Bible (what Christians call the Old Testament) gives evidence that from its beginnings as a people, Israel was keenly aware of the wealth of religious ideas and practices around and among them. Though other gods were worshiped in Israel, the Bible always presents that phenomenon as faithlessness and false worship, and depicts Israel's very life as founded on a relationship with one unique God. That God—whose name, spelled in Hebrew YHWH, is represented in the New Revised Standard Version by the form "the LORD"—was originally perceived as supreme among a host of gods: "For the LORD your God is God of gods and Lord of lords" (Deut 10:17; see Deut 13:2, Pss 77:13, 86:8, and Isa 44:6). Sometimes another god is specifically distinguished as a "strange god" or a "foreign god" (Ps 81:9).

Israel understood the LORD as the Creator of all things, who rules the world with sovereign freedom, justice, and love. Eventually, Israel came to hold a genuinely monotheistic faith, believing that the LORD was the only truly existing God:

> Thus says the LORD, the King of Israel, and his Redeemer, the LORD of hosts: I am the first and I am the last; besides me there is no god. (Isa 44:6)

This belief did not come immediately, or easily. The story of Israel's faith involves tortuous spiritual struggles both within Israel and against the polytheistic god-talk of the surrounding nations. The Hebrew Bible is fearlessly honest about the intensity of that struggle, though looking back on Israel's history the biblical authors also sought to portray their own monotheistic faith as a clear and obvious truth from the beginning. This required portraying alternative beliefs within Israel as the "stiff-necked" duplicity and faithlessness of some—at times, of the majority—in Israel (Exod 32:9, Jer 7:24). Through the prophet Hosea, the LORD complains against the worship of Baal within Israel: "She did not know that it was I who gave her the grain, the wine, and the oil, and who lavished upon her silver and gold that they used for Baal" (Hos 2:8). Again, we read of the spectacular contest between the prophet Elijah and 450 prophets of Baal in 1 Kgs 18:1-40.

The LORD insists that "You must not worship any other god, because the LORD, whose name is Impassioned, is an impassioned God" (Exod 34:14, the JPS *Tanakh* translation). This is not just a matter of "jealousy," as the NRSV translates the verse; in the Bible's perspective, "any other god" also refers to any god who allows injustice, cruelty, and the use of power to control people. Such gods must not be worshiped. Though the biblical God is sometimes depicted as responding in anger and wrath against an unfaithful nation, this is only one aspect of a larger and more comprehensive portrayal of the LORD yearning passionately for a relationship of mutual faithfulness with Israel and, indeed, the whole human race.

God Shows No Partiality

Israel's ancient faith in one God has decisively influenced the fundamental character of Judaism, Christianity, and Islam alike. Because Israel recognized one God over all people, the love, freedom, and justice of this one God apply to all people equally. This meant in particular that God showed no partiality or favoritism for the rich and powerful against the needy. So God speaks in Jeremiah:

> For if you truly amend your ways and your doings, if you truly act justly one with another, if you do not oppress the alien, the orphan, and the widow, or shed innocent blood in this place and if you do not go after other gods to your own hurt, then I will dwell with you in this place, in the land that I gave of old to your ancestors forever and ever. (Jer 7:5-7)

The message is clear: the worship of God must be expressed by doing justice, loving kindness, and walking humbly with God " (Mic 6:8). It will be seen in acts of loving the neighbor as one loves oneself (Lev 19:18). The same theme is voiced in the New Testament, as "the king" (here meaning the Messiah, the risen Jesus) says at the last judgment:

> I was hungry and you gave me food, I was thirsty and you gave me something to drink, I was a stranger and you welcomed me. I was naked and you gave me clothing, I was sick and you took care of me, I was in prison and you visited me. (Matt 25:35-36)

God's impartiality also means that the biblical God's purposes extended to all nations, not just to Israel (Isa 42:6-7; 49:6)—a theme picked up by Jews speaking in the New

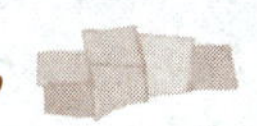

Testament as well (Luke 1:29-32; Rom 3:29-30). Israel's God was never a tribal god but the universal God, the God of all nations and all peoples who "judges the world with righteousness... [and] the peoples with equity" (Ps 9:8). The ancient promise given to Abraham was repeatedly reaffirmed: "in you all the families of the earth shall be blessed" (Gen 12:3). This is, so to speak, an "ecumenical God," from the Greek word for the peoples of the inhabited world (*oikoumenē*).

The ecumenical God is "the Creator of the ends of the earth" (Isa 40:28). The apostle Paul reaffirms the ecumenicity of the God of Israel: "Is God the God of Jews only? Is he not the God of Gentiles also? Yes, of Gentiles also, since God is one"(Rom 3:29). The words first spoken in Israel are now spoken to all the peoples of the earth: The whole cosmos is within the concern of this God. In the story of Pentecost (Acts 2), we read that the gospel is not limited to one specific language or culture but is spoken in many languages. Thus the horizon of the message of healing is widened: it becomes multicultural, inter-religious, inter-ethnic, international, and even cosmic. "All things came into being" through the Word, declares the Gospel of John, "and without him not one thing came into being. What has come into being in him was life, and the life was the light of all people" (John 1:3-4).

The ancient psalmist sings that God "who keeps Israel will neither slumber nor sleep" (Ps 121:4). The profound ecumenicity of the biblical God suggests that the same promise extends to all people, of any nation and any faith. "The one who keeps Nigerians will neither slumber nor sleep"; "the one who keeps Buddhists will neither slumber nor sleep."

The Word of the Biblical God and the Religions of the World

The inhabited world is the world of many religions. One scholar of religions, Mircea Eliade, has listed forty-four different religions. These religions, like human languages, are constantly encountering and influencing one another. The meeting of religions affects human spirituality with its languages and cultures, bringing about change and growth. Some religious symbols may cease to be meaningful, and new symbols may take their places. Some religions have transcended initial ethnic boundaries to become universal religions (for example, Islam and Buddhism). Judaism, Christianity, and Islam all revere the biblical patriarch Abraham, and are called the Abrahamic religions: the growth and diversity of each religion expresses the biblical promise to Abraham, that he should be "the ancestor of a multitude of nations" (Gen 17:4-5).

The Bible insists that truth is one. That implies that truth found in Judaism and Christianity does not diminish the authenticity of truth found in other religions. Mahatma Gandhi expressed his understanding of a "public religion" when he said, "instead of saying God is Truth, I have been saying Truth is God." Similarly, the Jewish thinker Martin Buber wrote, "If one dares to turn towards the unknown God, to go to meet Him, to call to Him, Reality is present."[3]

The Buddha declares that our principal problem is greed; in the Hindu tradition, what you do to others will visit you without fail. We can read the Bible in order to separate ourselves from others; but as the American writer James Baldwin puts it, "one cannot demonize others without demonizing oneself." The very diversity of forms in which the Bible expresses the word of God—prose, poems, songs, visions, dreams, narratives, law, history, prophecy, accusation, vindication, maxims—and the wealth of picture-language for God's word, which can be like "drippings of the honeycomb" (Ps 19:10) or like "a hammer that breaks a rock in pieces" (Jer 23:29)—suggests that the breadth and depth of God's word cannot be contained by human religious knowledge.

Abraham Heschel wrote that the prophets tell "God's experiences of history." The Psalmist declares, "If I ascend to heaven, you are there; if I make my bed in Sheol, you are there" (Ps 139:8). Do not such texts in the Bible itself affirm that truths found in diverse human communities, such as the various expressions of what the so-called Golden Rule (Matt 7:12), point to a single truth of history? Empathy is a universal value, as the African proverb suggests: "One who would take a pointed stick to poke a baby bird should first try it on oneself to feel how it hurts." If we wish to learn the depth of "God's experiences of history," we are wise to listen to the experiences of those who are strangers to us.

The Holy God Who Cares

God is always "God in relationship." To say, "God is" is to say, "God cares." "Can a woman forget her nursing child, or show no compassion for the child of her womb? Even these may forget, yet I will not forget you" (Isa 49:15; see Luke 13:34). Israel's God is a holy God (Isa 6:3), and holiness means separation: there is an unbridgeable

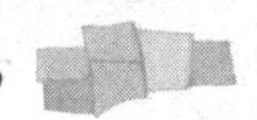

distance between the holy God and humanity in what the Bible can call our uncleanness (Isa 6:5). Yet the Bible also likens this holy God to a woman with her nursing child! Here God is described as reaching out to overcome this distance. The prophet Hosea expresses the deeply felt desire of God for connection: "How can I give you up, Ephraim?" (11:8). The Gospel of John depicts the Word of God reaching across the separation between God and humanity: "And the Word became flesh and lived among us" (1:14). The Gospel of Mark portrays Jesus reaching across social boundaries for connection with others, prompting questions from observers: "Why does he eat with tax collectors and sinners?" (Mark 2:16). Jesus responds: "I have come to call not the righteous but sinners" (Mark 2:17).

The holy God cannot be boxed in. "Even heaven and the highest heaven cannot contain you," King Solomon prays at the dedication of the Jerusalem temple (1 Kgs 8:27). Christians affirm this transcendence, declaring (for example, in the words of the Westminster Shorter Catechism) that "God is a Spirit, infinite, eternal, and unchangeable in his being, wisdom, power, holiness, justice, goodness, and truth." Even this impressive chain of words "cannot contain" God, any more than statements like the Apostles' Creed could "contain" God. "Death no longer has dominion over him [Jesus]," wrote the apostle Paul to the Romans (6:9). If even death cannot contain the power of God, why should we imagine we could "box in" God with our cultural, religious, ethical, moral, and theological words? As New Testament scholar Eduard Schweizer writes, our teaching and our theology cannot ultimately convey the reality of "the living God":

> It may even hinder his coming, though it may be totally correct. It is exactly the most correct and orthodox teaching that would suggest that we had got hold of God. Then he can no longer come in his surprising ways.[4]

A "boxed in" God is a convenient God, a portable God—but not the God of the Bible. "Their idols are like scarecrows in a cucumber field, and they cannot speak; they have to be carried for they cannot walk," declares Jeremiah (10:5). But God is not like a scarecrow in a cucumber field!

The holy God described in the Bible is invisible, which is one way to describe God's holiness. Yet the Bible also includes Job's hope for vindication: "in my flesh I shall see

God" (19:26), and Jesus' saying, "Blessed are the pure in heart, for they will see God" (Matt 5:8). The pure in heart practice what Jeremiah said: "...do not oppress the alien, the orphan, and the widow" (7:6). And 1 John suggests that when we love other people, who are visible, we are showing love for the invisible (1 John 4:20). Love particularly strangers, orphans, and widows! Pay special attention to the welfare of children throughout the world. "Whoever welcomes this child in my name welcomes me, and whoever welcomes me welcomes the one who sent me," Jesus says (Luke 9:48). In welcoming children, we are welcoming God. In others, we "see" God.

It is our relationship with what we can see that determines our relationship with the invisible God. If we may "see" God in our neighbors (Matt 25:40, John 13:35), then it is possible to "see" God anywhere, at any time! The reality that Jesus called the kingdom of God comes when we learn to see the "image of God" (Gen 1:27) in our neighbors and in ourselves. The apostle Paul spoke of the kingdom of God as "righteousness and peace and joy in the Holy Spirit" (Rom 14:17-19). Similarly, in loving the planet earth, our ecological concern (our care for our own home, from the Greek *oikos,* "house"), we "see" the Creator and Sustainer of the universe (see Ps 104:19). On the other hand, when we abuse our neighbors, we are also giving offense to God. Oppressing our neighbors is making "wrongful use of the name of the LORD your God" (Exod 20:7).

The God of the Bible and the God of Jesus

For Christians, God is best understood by looking to Jesus as Lord. The New Testament proclaims one God as "the Father, from whom are all things and for whom we exist, and one Lord, Jesus Christ" (1 Cor 8:6). While belief in Jesus' unique relationship to God is the most distinguishing hallmark of Christianity, the New Testament presents that relationship less as a doctrine to be believed than as an invitation. Jesus called God "Father," *abba* (using an Aramaic word indicating a close intimacy: Mark 14:36; compare Rom 8:15), and taught his disciples to address God as "Our Father in heaven" (Matt 6:9).

As feminist theologians have correctly insisted, New Testament language about God as "father" does not mean that God is a male person. Though biblical representations of God often use masculine pronouns and metaphors, the Bible also affirms that God transcends gender definition. Human beings, male and female, are alike created in

God's image (Gen 1:27); and virtually alone in the religious cultures of the ancient world, the God of Israel—and the God of the early church—did not have a "consort." Though we must take account of the patriarchal cultures in which the biblical writings were produced, we may also understand biblical language of God as "father" as a way of speaking metaphorically of "One who devotedly loves and cares."

Of course, the New Testament references to God as "father" often mean to affirm more: that God is to be understood as the "father" of Jesus Christ. "Whoever has seen me has seen the Father," Jesus declares in the Fourth Gospel (John 14:9; compare 10:38). Even in that Gospel, however, the relationship between Jesus and the Father is not a mere object of belief: it is a matter of participating in the "works" of God (see John 14:12, 15, 21). Elsewhere in the New Testament we find expressed the idea that following Jesus is a way to respond to God, or in the words of the prophet Micah, "to do justice, and to love kindness, and to walk humbly with your God" (Mic 6:8). The apostle Paul affirms that even people "who do not possess the law" may "do instinctively what the law requires" and that these may be justified before God (Rom 2:13-16). In Matthew's Gospel, Jesus declares that God's standard of judgment is simply whether we have met the most basic needs of others: providing food to the hungry, drink to the thirsty, welcoming the stranger, clothing the naked, caring for the sick, and visiting those in prison (Matt 25:31-46).

Though differences in religious belief often divide people, we find in many religions—and in important passages in the Bible as well—a vision that transcends difference: the affirmation that the God of the Bible, and the God of Jesus, is best honored when we live in peace, honoring one another in justice and mercy. As the apostle Paul exhorts the Philippians, "Finally beloved, whatever is true, whatever is honorable, whatever is just, whatever is pure, whatever is pleasing, whatever is commendable, if there is any excellence and if there is anything worthy of praise, think about these things" (Phil 4:8).

Women, Culture, and the Bible

Choi Hee An

How we see ourselves shapes how we see the peoples of the Bible. But because of the importance of the Bible in Western culture, and especially in the history of the imposition of Western culture on other cultures through colonialism and imperialism, the reverse is also true: how the peoples of the Bible are represented to us influences the way we see ourselves and others.

Because of its predominance as a symbol in Western colonial cultures, the Bible and its values have been identified with the dominant values of those cultures. When this has meant that privileged classes in colonial cultures—whites, males, the powerful, and so on—have been identified with the peoples at the center of biblical narrative, the result has been the subordination, marginalization, and exclusion of nonprivileged others as the "others" of the Bible.

It has been easier in Western culture for privileged classes to identify themselves with the "we" of the Bible. At the same time, others—immigrants and foreign women, for example—have found just that identification difficult. The Bible has been regularly employed to define a "we" that marginalizes and excludes others in various ways—

for example, through racism, classism, sexism and heterosexism, prejudices regarding different ages and different body abilities, and the prejudices of colonial powers toward the colonized.

The prominent forms of biblical interpretation in colonial cultures have regularly made these hierarchical ideologies appear natural. Consciously or unconsciously, Western interpreters have identified white Western males as the normative "we" of the Bible; but they have also identified, and thus devalued and negated, any other possible "we"—we women, we the marginalized, we the oppressed, we ethnic minorities, we immigrants—as the biblical "other." This dominant way of reading the Bible in colonial situations has consecrated white domination at the same time it has denied sacredness to other religious practices and cultures as "uncivilized," without moral or historical value. The way conventional biblical scholarship has discussed historical "backgrounds" to the Bible mirrors the way colonial culture has taught the colonized to habitually think of themselves, with their many religions and cultures, as "objects of investigation," in the phrase of postcolonial theorist Gayatri Chakravorty Spivak. Further, using the Bible to legitimate the supremacy of Western white males has led to the fusion of the biblical value of fearing the one God with obedience to Western colonial power.

Reading the Bible as a "Foreign Woman"

Especially in the case of women who are immigrants, foreigners, or members of ethnic minorities in Western societies, approaching the Bible intentionally requires renegotiating what "we" means and who "we" are. Immigrant women like myself (I come from Korea), who find themselves an ethnic minority in a new land, have experienced the Bible as a symbol of Western colonial control—but also as a resource that offers them their own voice and legitimacy, an instrument through which their own voices can come to be heard.

In the transition from their own countries to life in a new land, immigrant women become "foreign." They are impelled to adapt from thinking of themselves as "we," as they could do in their own countries, to seeing themselves as "the other." They acquire a marginalized identity, exacerbated in the European and North American contexts by severe racism and unbounded individualism. When such women have read the Bible and tried to find a place for themselves in its story, they have often been compelled to erase their own unique ethnic memories, to forget their own histories,

traditions, and cultures, in order to try to adopt the perspective of white culture and its religion, Christianity. Too often the place that Western culture assigns them in the biblical story is that of "the other."

But such forgetting of themselves remains incomplete. These women struggle to sustain their existence by remembering who they once were, reintroducing memories that become dangerous to the assumptions of white Western domination. Only by struggling to retrieve their own histories can these women discern what it means to be faithful and to live out their own lives authentically before the divine. Interpreting the Bible can be an important resource in this process.

The Place of the Foreign Woman in the Bible

The Bible is not a single book but has always been the object of multiple and diverse readings. However, the predominant biblical interpretation in the West has presumed that the Bible speaks with a single voice and this singular voice is best understood and interpreted from within Western culture in general and the Western Christian tradition in particular. But this presumed unity is false. It could only be maintained through a sort of interpretive violence that privileged Western culture and denied any significance to the wide variety of other communities, not least the diversity of ethnic immigrant women. Ironically, this presumption of Western superiority has often been considered the "universal" perspective. Claims to read the Bible from any of the many alternative perspectives found in the majority of the world's peoples has too often been considered tendentious.

Within the presuppositions of this colonial pattern of interpretation, the only space relegated in the Bible to immigrant, foreign, and ethnic-minority women are a handful of images of non-Israelite women in the biblical narratives. But Euro-American scholarship has repeatedly read these images—for example, Rahab, Canaanite women in general, Tamar, Ruth, the wife of Uriah, or the unnamed Samaritan woman in John 4—through the lens of the contemporary valuation of immigrant or foreign women. Thus these biblical women are valued only as they could be assimilated as members of ethnic minorities within the normative people, "Israel" or "the church." These "outsider" women are often further characterized as unclean, impure, manipulative, illicitly sexual, and/or disloyal to their own countries and to the colonizers' countries as well.

Nowhere is this interpretive strategy more evident than in discussions of Matthew's genealogy of Jesus, which famously includes non-Israelite women. It is not unusual to find Matthew's inclusion of these women interpreted as affirming the necessity that outsiders, especially non-Israelites, be transformed in Christ. On this view, these foreign women obtained salvation and inclusion in the genealogy of the Messiah because they joined Israel, relinquishing their previous histories and identities. Without such transforming inclusion, the immigrant or foreign women of the Bible signify only dangerous seductiveness, or weakness—as when they are represented as the victims of the patriarchal oppression of their own native ethnic cultures, from which they must be rescued (by Christ or the Christians). In such interpretation, the saving incorporation into the normative people mirrors the solicitude of sympathetic white feminist or liberal theologians for immigrant and foreign women in their own contemporary culture.

When elite Western interpreters characterize non-Israelite women in the Bible in culturally marginalized terms, they implicitly disparage contemporary immigrant and foreign women as well. This tendency can perhaps best be read in interpretations of the story of Rahab. Some white feminists have described Rahab as a heroine, a faithful woman, and as Phyllis Bird put it, as the "pagan confessor," one who could discern what her neighbors failed to see and thus "committed her life to the people of Yahweh." However positively this characterization is meant, to immigrant and ethnic-minority women it evokes the culturally loaded image of the converted prostitute, the native woman who placed her sympathies with the conquerors (or fell in love with them or had sex with them), saving them and offering them assistance against her own people by embracing the colonizing religion and culture wholeheartedly. As Kwok Pui-Lan points out, Rahab becomes in effect a Canaanite Pocahontas, the "good native" who acquiesces voluntarily to the conquerors, offering them her body as well as her protection and assistance and, in so doing, enabling the subjugation of her own people. In biblical accounts Rahab's previous religion was condemned and her culture was portrayed as sexually lascivious and impure (see Lev 17–18; Deut 7:1-5). Thus, to welcome the Israelites, she was forced to despise her own people's religion and culture, erasing the knowledge of all that she had known in her past life. In subsequent readings of the text, she was held up (in Timothy Tseng's phrase) as "a model minority" who successfully adopted the colonizer's culture, being changed from a sexually illicit and heretic non-Israelite

to a faithfully civilized woman. She could be cited in colonial efforts to proselytize colonized peoples. She nevertheless remained, so far as the book of Joshua was concerned, a foreigner, an alien, and an outsider.

In a constant effort to distinguish the biblical "we" from the biblical "other," this colonial-preferred interpretation discriminates not only against Rahab the Canaanite, but also against the ethnic identities, cultures, traditions, languages, and spiritual practices of all immigrant and foreign women. It both presumes and implicitly represents the legitimacy of colonial domination, thus putting in suspense the legitimacy of these women's memories and traditions and precluding any notion that they might participate in divine creativity as do the normative "people of God."

Finding One's Own Place in the Bible

Paradoxically, immigrant and ethnic-minority women have also read the Bible in ways that offer them an alternative to the place assigned them by colonial cultures and a way to understand who they are before God in their situation as immigrants, "foreigners," and "others." These alternative reading strategies start from remembering the historical injuries of colonialism. By remembering the experiences of colonial intervention and immigration, women start to integrate their previous selves with their current situation in new and imaginative ways.

They are compelled to adapt to a new situation—not just to survive but to try to live in hope. Their memories, ethnic identities, and consciousness of their own history and culture may appear as dangerously different in a new and often oppressive world. When immigrants were in their own land, their orientation was to the community, to "us." When they move into a new land, the land of the (former or present) colonial power, they are forced to think more individually—not just as "I" but "I as the other," an identity shaped by the racism and individualism of the new culture. When they experience a clash between their former "we" identity and the new "I as other" identity, they may try to engage both identities in a transformative way and to create a new self: "I and We among others." I call this the struggle to establish a postcolonial self. This self is characterized by connection rather than separation, and it can become the core of a new identity. In this evolution, colonial struggles are not experienced as historic baggage to leave behind but as part of a history that immigrant women deliberately carry with them as they move, not just *into* a new culture but *beyond* it, to participate in global-majority communities.

In this process, the Bible can provide a space for women that is not just the marginalized space assigned by the legacy of colonial interpretation. By reinterpreting non-Israelite women's lives in light of their own, immigrant and "foreign" women revalue those biblical figures and themselves, no longer as the colonial "other" but as participants in a greater "we" in which we are aware of our own power for transformation.

For example, immigrant and "foreign" women can find in the story of Naomi and Ruth a biblical image in which solidarity is nurtured not only among one's own ethnic group but also among the many immigrant, ethnic minority, and "foreign" communities that surround us. Ruth chose to stay in the society to which she had immigrated not only out of necessity for her own survival as a widow but also out of solidarity with Naomi—that is, out of the solidarity of "I and we among others." This was not an easy choice. It involved inevitable danger. She risked enduring bitter experiences of marginalization in her new culture, but she accepted the risk in order to cherish her relationship with her mother-in-law. This was an expression not of patriarchal virtue but of an embraced connectedness with Naomi, also an "other," as "we."

Reading the story of Ruth in this way challenges the individualistic orientation of Western culture, which emphasizes the difference between "we" and "other." It opens a space for a new "we" to be realized, a "we" that welcomes our different ethnicities and honors our histories without accepting the marginalized status of "other." The solidarity Ruth shows in choosing to live with Naomi is an instance of resistance against the social forces that would marginalize them both. Reading the story this way allows the Bible to become a space for immigrant women—and other "others"—to exercise, communally and individually, a different way of being "we" together.

Such a reading does not come easily, especially in a society where the Bible enjoys tremendous importance but, as we have seen, is usually read as a unitary voice that legitimizes the distinction between a normative "we" and marginalized "others."

But such a reading frees the Bible from the role of legitimizing the privileged and powerful in Western society. The presence of the “foreign” woman belies and resists the normative representation of “the other” in the biblical text and in contemporary global society alike, and opens up the possibility that the Bible will be a space of solidarity and welcome.

Responsible Christian Exegesis of Hebrew Scripture

Johanna W. H. van Wijk-Bos

How we read Holy Scripture has been important as long as there has been a text to read.

One of the earliest examples of what might be called "Christian exegesis" is found in the Gospel of Luke, written at least two generations after Jesus' death. The scene depicts a conversation between Jesus and an expert in the Torah (Luke 10.25-29; compare Mt 22.34-40, Mk 12.28-34). Here is my translation:

> And, look, a certain expert in the Torah stood up to test him and said: "Teacher, what must I do to obtain eternal life?" And he said to him: "What is written in the Torah? How do you read?" He answered: "You shall love the Holy One your God with your entire heart and with all your soul and all your strength and your whole mind, and your neighbor as yourself." He said to him: "You answered correctly. Do this and live." He wanting to justify himself, said to Jesus: "And who is my neighbor?"

Luke presents Jesus as confronted by a member of his community who knows the most important part of Scripture for his day, the Torah. He is an expert in reading and interpreting what he reads in the Torah. Luke paints the incident as a confrontation. This person stood up to test Jesus, as if laying a trap. Contrary to what we might expect, he asks Jesus a question not about interpretation, but rather about action. He asks: "What must I *do*?"

Jesus excelled at clever interaction with members of his own faith community and turns the question right back into his questioner's field of expertise. He asks, "What is written in the Torah? How do you read?" In other words, if you want to know what to do, pay attention not only to *what* you read, but to *how* you read.

Exegesis and Responsibility

Exegesis, a Greek word meaning "interpretation" or "explanation," is the study of the biblical text. Exegetes intend to provide a solid foundation for reading the Bible. Exegesis is a technical word, and many exegetes are specialists who concentrate on this technical work. Yet all of us who are interested in the Bible—who read it, who study it, who listen to it being taught and preached—are in an informal way exegetes of the text. Exegesis, reading the text, is of crucial importance because it is directly connected to our actions. When we ask how to read we are also and always asking what to do.

Those of us who are Christians do Christian exegesis, meaning that we read the Bible from the perspective that in Jesus the God of Israel became incarnate so that Gentiles might become a beloved community, taken into covenant by the God who is revealed in Israel's Scripture. That part of the Bible, which in Christianity has traditionally been called the Old Testament, we also call *Hebrew Scripture* out of respect for the faith that recognizes this book as its Bible. (Jews also call it *Miqra'*.) Christian exegetes are aware that in reading this part of the Bible we are in sacred literature that was not in the first place created for our benefit and that is still the entire Bible for Judaism, a faith with adherents around the world. Although the term *Hebrew Scripture* has its own shortcomings, it does not imply that these writings are in any way surpassed or superseded, as the term *Old Testament* might.

Christian exegetes must read Hebrew Scripture responsibly. We may begin by assuming that, like the Torah expert in Luke 10, Christian exegetes are responsible to both

God and our neighbor. We are responsible to God as we read, insofar as we consider the Bible to be the sacred literature that speaks to us of God's dealings with us and with all creation. We are responsible to God insofar as we believe that God addresses contemporary believers somehow through the words of these texts. Before reading from the Bible on Sunday morning, many Christian preachers may invite their congregations to listen to these words as *a* or *the* word of God.

Exegetes are also responsible to our neighbors in our work. First, we are responsible to the neighbors of the past, those who in faith spoke and eventually wrote these texts, the community that went before, the "great . . . cloud of witnesses" of Heb 12:1. Exegetes are responsible to all who have devoted themselves to reading these texts so that it might benefit them, strengthen their faith, and guide their actions. Next, exegetes are responsible to our neighbors today. They include those who are potentially hurt and alienated by a certain way of reading the Bible; neighbors who belong to another community of faith; and neighbors within our own community who read, study, and listen so they may hear as fully as possible from these texts about God and God's will for their lives.

Responsibility after the Holocaust

What, then, constitutes responsible Christian exegesis of Hebrew Scripture? First and foremost, responsibility to the neighbor requires that Christian exegesis of the Hebrew Scripture proceeds from an awareness that we read the Bible today in a post-Holocaust world. We are aware that previous Christian ways of reading at the very least contributed to a political climate that made the Holocaust (or Shoah) possible. The Holocaust has forever changed the way in which the Hebrew Bible is read theologically by Jews and Christians alike.

Second, responsible Christian exegesis acknowledges that Judaism has its own legitimate claim on these sacred texts, comprising a community of direct descendants of the people who produced the Hebrew Scriptures, who have their own centuries-long tradition of interpretation. Third, responsible Christian exegesis recognizes that there is a connection between the idea that the Hebrew Bible is somehow incomplete or unfulfilled without the "New" Testament and active Christian persecution of the Jews and defamation of Judaism throughout the centuries. Christian exegesis must repent of past actions of discrimination and persecution against Jews, and insist on reading both Testaments from a perspective of honor and respect for Jewish sisters and brothers and their faith convictions. Finally, responsible Christian exegesis understands the Christian faith community to be in great need of direction for its way of life—for its relation to God and neighbor. It looks to directives in the Hebrew Scriptures to complete and deepen the instructions given to the early followers of Jesus, and at times even to correct these later directives, especially as found in the epistles of the New Testament. This responsibility means attempting at every turn to dissolve the tension between gospel and Torah found in much traditional Christian exegesis, insofar as gospel is identified with Christianity and Torah with Judaism. In all these ways, Christian interpreters exercise responsibility to the neighbor.

What about responsibility to God? Responsible Christian exegesis of the Hebrew Bible takes seriously the conviction that Christians believe in one God who is revealed in two parts of the Bible, in Christian terminology the Old and the New Testament. It affirms that the good news, the gospel, of God's presence with the world permeates the entire Bible, and did not begin with the arrival of Jesus Christ. Moreover, responsible Christian exegesis of the Hebrew Scriptures recognizes that the witness of the Hebrew Bible to the God of Israel does not need the witness of the New Testament to speak fully of God and God's presence in the world. Conversely, however, this kind of exegesis understands that the witness of the New Testament is incomplete and can be easily misunderstood without the foundational testimony of the Hebrew Scripture.

Responsible Christian exegesis takes note of the entire Hebrew Bible, not just the parts that fit with certain New Testament texts, and engages in a continuous reading of the biblical text. This is a particular challenge when a church lectionary takes fragments of a book of the Hebrew Bible out of context and juxtaposes them with fragments from a New Testament writing. In light of the responsibilities discussed here, it is desirable to provide for the continuous reading of a book—or of a complete unit within a book—of the Hebrew Bible and to do the same with Second Testament writings (though not in isolation from the Hebrew text). Such procedures allow us to engage First and Second Testament texts in conversation with each other and thus to arrive at a Christian interpretation that takes a full account of the diverse voices of Scripture.

In many ways, irresponsible Christian exegesis represents the opposite of what has just been described. Irresponsible Christian exegesis of the Hebrew Scriptures ignores

 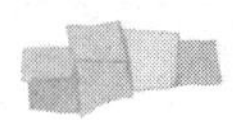

the events of the Holocaust/Shoah and how Christian anti-Judaism contributed to make those events possible. It ignores, as far as possible, the existence of contemporary Judaism and the contributions that Jewish tradition has made to interpretation of the biblical text. Irresponsible Christian exegesis continues to view Christianity as superior to Judaism and as the sole true inheritor of the promises made to ancient Israel. It judges the Hebrew Scriptures to be unfulfilled and incomplete without the witness of the "New" Testament and considers the community that produced these sacred texts ultimately to be a failure.

This type of exegesis understands the New Testament to be the final arbiter of the value of biblical texts in revealing God and speaking of the Christian life to the believer. It understands texts of Hebrew Scripture to have revelatory value only insofar as they speak to the revelation of God in Christ. Thus, an irresponsible Christian exegesis never reads texts from the Hebrew Scriptures unless they are followed by, and in practice subordinated to, New Testament texts in Sunday morning preaching. New Testament texts, on the other hand, may be read and preached on their own during large parts of the so-called Christian year. Such practices imply that New Testament texts are self-sufficient to describe what is worthwhile and to speak of God to the community.

Finally and more subtly, irresponsible Christian exegesis ignores the historical context of the Hebrew Scriptures and the significance and meaning of the election of ancient Israel as God's covenant community. It ignores the distance in time and space between the Christian reader or listener and texts from the Hebrew Scriptures and reads them only as they have application to the church and the contemporary Christian reader.

The problems with this type of Christian exegesis are multiple. It sustains barriers between two faiths and their adherents who by common sense ought to consider each other sister faiths. It blocks avenues to the richness of the biblical text as God's self-revelation. It has created the impression among many Christians that the Bible speaks of *two* deities, one threatening and violent, of which the Hebrew Scripture speaks, and one loving and kind, to which the New Testament testifies. Such exegesis in effect not only ignores the existence and contributions of contemporary Judaism, but erases the historical roots of the Jews. In this way, it belongs on a continuum of indifference and hostility toward Jews, a continuum with a long history of persecution of Jews that culminated in Christian complicity in the Holocaust/Shoah.

Irresponsible Christian exegesis of Hebrew Scripture not only belies the self-understanding and identity of believing Jews but also prevents Christians from a full sense of their own identity as believers in the God of the Bible. In the end, this kind of exegesis is irresponsible to God, to neighbors both past and present, and to the self as well.

Examples of Reading

The roots of the sort of irresponsible Christian interpretation of Hebrew Scripture discussed here are very deep. The fifth-century bishop Augustine of Hippo, for example, was one of the first theologians to put anti-Jewish interpretation of the Bible on the Christian map with his reference to Jews as a "cursed people" (*Faust.,* 12.11). But it is not difficult to find examples of irresponsible Christian exegesis of Hebrew Scriptures today, not only in many Christian churches in the United States, but also in scholarship. Introductory textbooks on the Old Testament rarely make a consideration of the Holocaust/Shoah a primary point of departure, or even consider it at all. Recognition of the Holocaust's importance is thus often confined to "specialized" literature. While today one rarely encounters such crass hostility toward the Jewish neighbor as found in Augustine, it is not so unusual to hear a sermon on an Old or New Testament text in which the existence of the Jews and their faith is completely ignored, making the Jews as invisible as if Hitler had been successful with his program of extermination. In Christian scholarship, too, one not infrequently meets generalizations about Israel and Jews in the past tense, as if they no longer existed, and to their covenant with God as obsolete and superseded. This is often especially egregious in Christian theological and historical discussions of Jesus that set him in opposition to the benighted attitudes and practices of his contemporaries, as in some modern liberationist theologies. Christian theologians may then read the "Old Testament" as pointing to the *church* as the "New Israel," or to the Exodus as a paradigm for the liberation of the oppressed, without acknowledging the particularity of the original covenant people. They may ignore the continuing covenant relationship that another community has with God or imply that the other community's relationship has ended in failure so that Christians may lay claim to all the promises made to that original covenant people.

Who Is Our Neighbor?

Taking our cue from the Gospel story with which we began, with the Torah expert we may well ask: "Who is our neighbor?" When Jesus responds with the story of the Samaritan who rescued the victim of a robbery, he points to both neighborly action and the recipient of this action. The one to whom we should show the love of neighbor may not be like us, may not be of our "family." In this regard, Luke places Jesus in a direct line with Torah's teaching concerning love for God and neighbor, which ultimately means love for the *stranger* (see Lev. 19:34). The stranger need not be distant or an outsider; the stranger may be one close by—but different. Responsible Christian exegesis will read the Hebrew Scriptures especially with an eye toward the Jewish neighbor. If Christians do not read in ways that directly connect them in compassionate action to this particular neighbor, how can they aspire to read in ways that lead to the love of any neighbor?

The Old Testament

Commonly Known as the Hebrew Bible

The Pentateuch

INTRODUCTION

Frank M. Yamada

THE FIRST FIVE BOOKS of the Hebrew Bible or Old Testament (Genesis–Deuteronomy) are generally called the Pentateuch among Christians and some biblical scholars. In Jewish tradition the Five Books of Moses are known as the Torah. The Hebrew word *torah* literally means "teaching" or "instruction" and refers to what is the heart of the Hebrew Scriptures in both content and importance. The story lines within this collection stretch from the creation of the world and humanity to Moses's last speech on the plains of Moab as the Israelites prepare to enter into the land of promise. The Pentateuch, however, contains various forms of literature from many time periods. These five books have played a formative role in the religious beliefs and imagination of many Christian, Jewish, and Muslim traditions. The Pentateuch has also been one of the primary points of emphasis in modern biblical scholarship. In fact, one can trace the developments in the scholarly study of the Bible by surveying the history of Pentateuchal research. With such well-known stories as Adam and Eve in the Garden of Eden, Noah and the flood, the *Akedah* (or "Binding" of Isaac), the exodus, the Ten Commandments, and God's provision of manna in the wilderness, it is no wonder that these texts have inspired generations of people for millennia.

One must distinguish between the narrative arc found within the Pentateuch, beginning with creation and ending on the plains of Moab, and the historical contexts out of which the traditions in these books emerge. Historically, scholars agree that the Pentateuch is a compilation of sources, traditions, folktales, and legal material from different historical periods. Four primary sources have been identified within Genesis–Deuteronomy. The J and E sources, Yahwist and Elohist respectively, also known as the Epic Tradition, make up the main story line of the Pentateuch narrative. Both sources were written during the Israelite monarchy. Whereas the Yahwist source contains the perspective of the Southern Kingdom of Judah, the Elohist reflects ideas and themes associated with Israel, the Northern Kingdom. The J story line begins in the Garden of Eden (Gen 2:4b) and extends into Israel's journey through the Sinai wilderness. The D, for Deuteronomic, source is comprised of significant portions of the book of Deuteronomy and was written largely during the time of Josiah's reign (late-seventh century BCE). Finally, the P, for Priestly, document contains mostly cultic, genealogical, and narrative material written by a priestly school or group after the Babylonian exile (587 BCE). Genesis begins with the Priestly account of creation and its well-known phrase, "In the beginning..." (Gen 1:1). Hebrew scholars differ on exactly how that phrase should be translated.

Because of this complex textual process, the resulting five books are a richly diverse collection that includes many different and even conflicting perspectives contained within it. For example, the Priestly account of creation depicts a well-ordered creation, with a sovereign God (*Elohim* in Hebrew) who structures the natural order through divine command. In this first creation story, plants and animals are created before humans, with humans made last as the climax of God's work. Immediately following the P version, the Yahwist's account of creation begins (Gen 2:4b) in a garden. The deity, represented by the divine name ("LORD" in most translations), forms humanity out of the ground. Animals are created *after* the human in response to Adam's need for companionship (Gen 2:18). Both accounts are self-contained creation stories. They provide different points of emphasis and depart from each other in significant ways—different names and images of the deity, different order of creation, and so on. Both accounts, however, are included in the biblical witness without significant editing to blur the variations. Thus the diverse and complex nature of the Pentateuch suggests that the final form of this collection was intended to reflect and keep in tension the various traditions that made up Israel's historical self-understanding. It is important to note, however, that textual versions such as the Samaritan Pentateuch, the Septuagint (a Greek translation), and fragments from the Dead Sea Scrolls represent different lines of tradition and thus point to other communities with textual traditions of their own.

The basic structure of the Pentateuch follows a narrative progression from creation to the journey of a particular ancestral family that becomes a nation. Here is an outline:

- Genesis: Creation to the ancestors
  - Genesis 1–11: Stories about creation and early humanity
  - Genesis 12–50: Stories about the ancestors

Exodus: Liberation from Egypt to revelation at Sinai
   Exodus 1:1—15:21: Exodus from Egypt
   Exodus 15:22—40:38: Journeys in the wilderness and revelation at Sinai

Leviticus: Revelation at Sinai continued
   Leviticus 1:1—27:34: Laws concerning worship and holiness

Numbers: Wanderings in the wilderness
   Numbers 1:1—25:18: The first generation in the wilderness
   Numbers 26:1—36:13: The second generation in the wilderness

Deuteronomy: Re-proclamation of the covenant
   Deuteronomy 1:1—30:20: Moses re-proclaims the covenant
   Deuteronomy 31:1—34:12: Moses's farewell and death

The plot line of the Pentateuch starts universally, beginning with the creation of the world and humanity. Genesis 1–11 contains universal stories about the beginning of human civilization and addresses common themes such as mortality and death (Gen 3, Garden of Eden), violence between human beings (Gen 4, Cain and Abel), God's comprehensive judgment through flood (6–9), and the creation of different languages and cultures (Gen 11, Tower of Babel). In 12–50, the narrative focuses on the particular family line of Abraham and Sarah, from whom God promises to make a great nation (Gen 12:2). This couple's progeny eventually become the tribes of Israel. A persistent theme throughout the ancestral stories is how the divine promise reaches fulfillment in spite of the circumstances and human decisions that threaten it. The theme of barrenness is frequent and appears in the stories of Sarah, Rebekah, and Rachel. In each case, God eventually opens the woman's womb. The most significant story that involves an endangerment of the promise is in Genesis 22, where God tests Abraham by asking him to sacrifice his only son, Isaac, as a burnt offering.

At the end of Genesis, Jacob and his family migrate south to Egypt, where Joseph had found favor in the household of Pharaoh. The book of Exodus begins with how the Israelites fell out of favor with a later pharaoh and were subjugated to slavery. Exodus 1–15 describes how the LORD delivers Israel from their bondage in Egypt. After a series of plagues, the Israelites are released. The climax of Israel's liberation occurs with the event at the sea, where the LORD delivers them miraculously. In the wilderness of Sinai, Moses receives the revelation of God, which will become the basis of Israelite community (Exod 19:1—34:35). The book of Leviticus, an extensive collection of laws with a primary focus on worship, is placed in the middle of the Torah and is set in the context of God's revelation at Sinai. The largest section of the book, 17:1—26:46, known as the Holiness Code, stresses this theme repeatedly. God's people are to be holy just as the LORD their God is holy (Lev 19:2).

The book of Numbers moves the narrative plot forward from the Mount Sinai event and tells of the people's wanderings in the wilderness. Themes of sin and rebellion recur in these stories, resulting in judgment and death. An entire generation of Israelites perishes in the wilderness journeys. Standing in tension with the theme of human rebellion is the equally persistent idea of God's provision in the wilderness. The LORD provides both water and manna to sustain the people on their journey. Numbers ends with a new generation poised to enter into God's promises and ready to go into the land.

In Deuteronomy, the Pentateuch concludes with Moses's final speech to Israel prior to their entrance into Canaan. The book contains a re-proclamation of the covenant that the LORD made with Israel on Mount Horeb, Deuteronomy's term for Sinai. The themes of Deuteronomy, however, are more than a simple rearticulation of earlier ideas. The book emphasizes the distinct character of Israel and its God. One of the primary motifs in the book is found in Deut 6:4-5, known as the Shema (*shema* in Hebrew is the first word in this passage and means "hear" or "listen"). The passage reads: "Hear, O Israel: The LORD is our God, the LORD alone. You shall love the LORD your God with all your heart, and with all your soul, and with all your might." The LORD is one, and therefore the people of Israel should be one and should worship the LORD exclusively. In practice this means that the people of Israel are to distinguish themselves from other nations in their community and worship. Similarly, they should worship in a central place of the LORD's choosing. As the last of the five books of Moses, Deuteronomy serves as a transition. It ends with the death of Moses, the pivotal figure who led the young nation out of Egypt. Moses is the central character in the Pentateuch, the Israelite prophet par excellence (cf. Deut 34:10-12). His death marks the end of an era and hence is an appropriate conclusion to the Pentateuch. But the trajectories in Deuteronomy are central in the Former Prophets that follow. Many of Deuteronomy's themes can be found in Joshua, Judges, 1 and 2 Samuel, and 1 and 2 Kings. It is useful to think of Deuteronomy as a fulcrum point between the Pentateuch and the Former Prophets: it concludes the Torah and anticipates the continuing story of Israel.

The Pentateuch includes many possible points of entry for Asian American readers and communities of color in general. I am a *Sansei,* a third-generation Japanese American. The individual stories within these first five books have been a rich resource for the Asian American communities of which I have been a part. The theme of *ancestors* reminds us that our beliefs, religious practice, and culture are not accidents but were preserved and maintained through the actions of those who came before us. As an Asian American reader, I am struck by the fact that the Torah chooses to tell its history not only through the lens of national events but through the particular struggles and triumphs of ancestors. Early missionaries to Asia discouraged the practice of ancestor worship, a community and family ritual that is common in many cultures of the world, including Asia. The biblical witness, however, while stopping short of the worship of ancestors, emphasizes the important role of ancestral faith and belief. In fact, the Torah tells its story primarily through the vehicle of ancestral lineage. When the LORD remembers Israel, who is suffering from the bondage of slavery in Egypt, the reason for God's remembrance is located in the promises made to the ancestors. In fact, the LORD is identified as "the God of Abraham, the God of Isaac, and the God of Jacob" (Exod 3:6).

Another important theme for this Asian American reader is found in the exodus. Following in the footsteps of African American interpreters and Latin American liberation theologians, many Asian Americans have continued to find meaning in the story of God's liberation of Israel from Egypt. The image of a God who liberates oppressed peoples continues to inspire communities that have experienced hostility within American society. The Asian American experience is one of exclusion. Legislation such as the Chinese Exclusion Act of 1882, which sought to restrict immigration to the United States, and government-sanctioned racism, as seen in the internment of Japanese Americans during World War II, points to a history of prejudice and fear toward people of Asian descent. In the first decade of the twenty-first century, South Asians who live in the United States have become targets of violence and hate crimes. The biblical idea of a God who liberates and sides with the oppressed provides a strong theological image from which the Asian American community can continue to build its self-understanding. Just as God loves justice and sides with those who are oppressed, so too Asian American community can be built on themes of liberation, siding with those in any community who suffer from injustice or prejudice at the hands of others.

Genesis

As the first book in the Hebrew Bible, Genesis speaks to beginnings. It opens with two differing stories on the creation of the universe (1:1—2:4a) and of the earth (2:4b-25). It contains narratives of the first family (chs. 3–4), first city (11:1-9), and the beginnings of the Hebrew people (chs. 12–50). Scholars have long noted how the creation story in Genesis 1 and the flood stories in chapters 6–9 are patterned on similar stories found in ancient Mesopotamia and how the creation story in Genesis 2 is patterned on creation stories in ancient Egypt. This borrowing from other cultures was common. As 2:10-14 claims, the Garden of Eden extended from Africa (ancient Cush/Ethiopia) to Mesopotamia (Euphrates River). All ancient cultures presented creation as controlled by their god(s) and set in their own backyards. Similarly, the idea of the seas being gathered into "one place" (1:9) is explained by people's knowledge of the Mediterranean. While the story line of Genesis goes from a *universal* story of the beginning (chs. 1–5) and rebeginning (chs. 6–11) of humanity to a story of a *particular* people, the descendants of Abram/Abraham (12–50), many different nations, cultures, and ethnicities are mentioned and engaged. The Table of Nations (Genesis 10) is an attempt to describe the interrelatedness of nations in the "known world" by depicting them as the descendants of Noah's three sons, Japheth, Ham, and Shem. Within the stories of Abraham's descendants are stories of the beginnings of Israel's neighbors, the Moabites and Ammonites (19:37-8), Ishmaelites (21:17-18), and the Edomites (36:1). In this way there is a claim that these nations were tribally related to Israel just as Lot, Ishmael, and Esau were related to Abraham and Jacob, though they were not from Israel, the line that God favored.

These stories were composed in a society that valued men more than women. The lists of generations in Genesis 4–5 and 29:31—30:24 are lists primarily of men. The promises made by God for a great nation stemming from Abraham are given to men (12:1-3; 15:7-21; 28:13-15). Divine promises to women are about giving birth to sons (16:11-12; 25:23). The women who are important characters in the story, for example Sarah in 21:9-11 and Rebekah in 27:6-9, 46, are all depicted as trying to ensure a social place for their sons. Polygamy was the basic form of family assumed in the stories about the ancestors. God is depicted as male and is referred to as the God of Abraham (24:42), the God of Abraham and Isaac (28:13), or the God of your father (43:23; 46:3) and never the God of your mother(s). Finally, the sign of the covenant for Israel, circumcision, is only given to the men (17:10-12a).

In the society in which these stories were written, it was normal for people to own slaves. Sarai/Sarah has an Egyptian slave, Hagar (16:1). Abraham has a slave, Eliezer (15:2). Laban gives his daughters female slaves as marriage presents (29:24, 29). Potiphar buys Joseph as a slave (39:1). All these slaves are exploited sexually. The women are forced to have sex with the slave master to

produce children (16:2, 4; 30:3-12), and the male slaves have to be circumcised and service their slave masters (17:12; 24:2). As an African American, whose people were enslaved in the United States, I am always concerned about such passages in the Bible that present slave society as acceptable to the people and God of the Book. Bible translators often soften this abuse of slaves by calling these characters "servants" or maids. But such distinctions reflect the translators' embarrassment about the text, not the true social and cultural distinctions of those ancient societies.

Finally, some of the stories found in Genesis have played a major role in supporting political positions. Environmentalists adopt the biblical idea of God calling the creation "good" in Genesis 1. The divine curses on Adam and Eve (3:16-19) have been used to support concepts of men controlling women and their bodies. The so-called "Curse of Ham" (9:26-27)—really a set of curses on Canaan—was used to sanction the enslavement of Africans in Europe and the Americas. The destruction of Sodom and Gomorrah has been interpreted as a story of homosexuality rather than one of the sexual exploitation of daughters (19:8, 26, 33, 36) and has been used to sanction the oppression of gays and lesbians. The Lord's killing of Onan because he ended sex with Tamar before climax (38:9-10) is used as an argument against masturbation and contraceptives.

The good news about Genesis is that as we read the book, we have much to discuss, especially as it relates to our own lives, views of God, humanity, and the world in which we live. As we continue to interpret this richly diverse collection of texts, we engage interpreters past and present and participate in an ongoing dialogue with ancients and contemporaries who seek to locate their place in the world from "the beginning."

— ***Randall C. Bailey***

1 In the beginning when God created[a] the heavens and the earth, 2 the earth was a formless
void and darkness covered the face of the deep,
while a wind from God[b] swept over the face of the
waters. 3 Then God said, "Let there be light"; and
there was light. 4 And God saw that the light was
good; and God separated the light from the darkness. 5 God called the light Day, and the darkness
he called Night. And there was evening and there
was morning, the first day.
6 And God said, "Let there be a dome in the
midst of the waters, and let it separate the waters
from the waters." 7 So God made the dome and
separated the waters that were under the dome
from the waters that were above the dome. And it
was so. 8 God called the dome Sky. And there was
evening and there was morning, the second day.
9 And God said, "Let the waters under the
sky be gathered together into one place, and let
the dry land appear." And it was so. 10 God called
the dry land Earth, and the waters that were gathered together he called Seas. And God saw that

[a] Or *when God began to create* or *In the beginning God created*

[b] Or *while the spirit of God* or *while a mighty wind*

Genesis 1:1-2

The first two depictions of God are masculine—literally, "When beginning, he, God created"—(v. 1) *and* feminine—"The Spirit of God, she was brooding"—(v. 2), foreshadowing human creation in the divine image as male and female in 1:27. Most translations of the Bible obscure the gender of God's Spirit, leaving readers with the erroneous impression that the Scriptures use only masculine language when describing God. Throughout the Hebrew Bible, God's Spirit is feminine; in the Christian Scriptures, the Spirit is neuter.

— ***WG***

it was good. 11 Then God said, "Let the earth put
forth vegetation: plants yielding seed, and fruit
trees of every kind on earth that bear fruit with
the seed in it." And it was so. 12 The earth brought
forth vegetation: plants yielding seed of every
kind, and trees of every kind bearing fruit with
the seed in it. And God saw that it was good.
13 And there was evening and there was morning,
the third day.

14 And God said, "Let there be lights in the
dome of the sky to separate the day from the
night; and let them be for signs and for seasons
and for days and years, 15 and let them be lights in
the dome of the sky to give light upon the earth."
And it was so. 16 God made the two great lights—
the greater light to rule the day and the lesser
light to rule the night—and the stars. 17 God set
them in the dome of the sky to give light upon the
earth, 18 to rule over the day and over the night,
and to separate the light from the darkness. And
God saw that it was good. 19 And there was evening and there was morning, the fourth day.

20 And God said, "Let the waters bring forth
swarms of living creatures, and let birds fly above
the earth across the dome of the sky." 21 So God
created the great sea monsters and every living
creature that moves, of every kind, with which
the waters swarm, and every winged bird of
every kind. And God saw that it was good. 22 God
blessed them, saying, "Be fruitful and multiply
and fill the waters in the seas, and let birds multiply on the earth." 23 And there was evening and
there was morning, the fifth day.

24 And God said, "Let the earth bring forth
living creatures of every kind: cattle and creeping things and wild animals of the earth of every
kind." And it was so. 25 God made the wild animals of the earth of every kind, and the cattle of
every kind, and everything that creeps upon the
ground of every kind. And God saw that it was
good.

26 Then God said, "Let us make humankind[a]
in our image, according to our likeness; and let
them have dominion over the fish of the sea, and
over the birds of the air, and over the cattle, and
over all the wild animals of the earth,[b] and over
every creeping thing that creeps upon the earth."

27 So God created humankind[a] in his image,
in the image of God he created them;[c]
male and female he created them.

28 God blessed them, and God said to them, "Be
fruitful and multiply, and fill the earth and subdue it; and have dominion over the fish of the sea
and over the birds of the air and over every living thing that moves upon the earth." 29 God said,
"See, I have given you every plant yielding seed
that is upon the face of all the earth, and every
tree with seed in its fruit; you shall have them for
food. 30 And to every beast of the earth, and to
every bird of the air, and to everything that creeps
on the earth, everything that has the breath of
life, I have given every green plant for food." And
it was so. 31 God saw everything that he had made,
and indeed, it was very good. And there was evening and there was morning, the sixth day.

2 Thus the heavens and the earth were finished,
and all their multitude. 2 And on the seventh
day God finished the work that he had done, and
he rested on the seventh day from all the work
that he had done. 3 So God blessed the seventh
day and hallowed it, because on it God rested
from all the work that he had done in creation.

[a] Heb *adam* [b] Syr: Heb *and over all the earth* [c] Heb *him*

Genesis 2

The biblical story of creation tells us that God created one couple who became the parents of all people on earth. In striking contrast to other creation stories in the ancient Near East, no kings, no thrones, no walled cities appear "in the beginning." Not only do the first people bear no mark of ethnicity—the Bible affirms that all peoples come from a single origin—but they are without nationality. In the Acts of the Apostles, Paul will later declare that God has limited the times and boundaries of all nations (Acts 17:26); all rise and fall in history, and none is eternal. While the royal imagery of other ancient Near Eastern cultures depicted the gods in kingly regalia, seated enthroned and giving commands like monarchs, in Genesis the image of God is borne by two people who stand naked and defenseless in a garden. How fitting that a prominent Israeli human rights organization has chosen the name *B'tselem*—"in the image."

— *DB, NE*

4 These are the generations of the heavens
and the earth when they were created.
In the day that the LORD[a] God made the
earth and the heavens, 5when no plant of the
field was yet in the earth and no herb of the field
had yet sprung up—for the LORD God had not
caused it to rain upon the earth, and there was
no one to till the ground; 6but a stream would
rise from the earth, and water the whole face
of the ground— 7then the LORD God formed
man from the dust of the ground,[b] and breathed
into his nostrils the breath of life; and the man became a living being. 8And the LORD God planted
a garden in Eden, in the east; and there he put the
man whom he had formed. 9Out of the ground
the LORD God made to grow every tree that is
pleasant to the sight and good for food, the tree
of life also in the midst of the garden, and the tree
of the knowledge of good and evil.

10 A river flows out of Eden to water the
garden, and from there it divides and becomes
four branches. 11The name of the first is Pishon;
it is the one that flows around the whole land of
Havilah, where there is gold; 12and the gold of
that land is good; bdellium and onyx stone are
there. 13The name of the second river is Gihon;
it is the one that flows around the whole land
of Cush. 14The name of the third river is Tigris,
which flows east of Assyria. And the fourth river
is the Euphrates.
15 The LORD God took the man and put him
in the garden of Eden to till it and keep it. 16And
the LORD God commanded the man, "You may
freely eat of every tree of the garden; 17but of
the tree of the knowledge of good and evil you

Genesis 2:8-10

The Hebrew geographic term *Eden* is a loanword from the ancient Mesopotamian culture of Sumer, signifying that the tradition of the "garden of God" owes much to that culture. That Eden was located in what was later called Mesopotamia is implied by the names of two rivers, the Tigris and Euphrates, that flow the length of that once-fertile land (now Iraq). But another river, the Gihon, "flows around the whole land of Cush" (now Ethiopia), and contemporary archaeological discoveries and linguistic evidence point to eastern Africa as the point where our species began. Eden suddenly appears much larger than a "garden"! The man and woman placed in Eden bear generic names: *Adam* (the common Hebrew word for "human" and closely related to *adamah*, "earth," from which he was molded) and *Chawwah* or Eve (a word meaning "living" or "mother of life"). Even though Western culture has long imaged them as white, European-looking people, the narrative in Genesis 2 clearly identifies them as the ancestors of all human beings.

— *DB, NE*

[a] Heb YHWH, as in other places where "LORD" is spelled with capital letters (see also Exod 3.14–15 with notes).

[b] Or *formed a man* (Heb *adam*) *of dust from the ground* (Heb *adamah*)

shall not eat, for in the day that you eat of it you
shall die."
18 Then the LORD God said, "It is not good
that the man should be alone; I will make him
a helper as his partner." 19 So out of the ground
the LORD God formed every animal of the field
and every bird of the air, and brought them to the
man to see what he would call them; and whatever the man called every living creature, that
was its name. 20 The man gave names to all cattle,
and to the birds of the air, and to every animal of
the field; but for the man[a] there was not found a
helper as his partner. 21 So the LORD God caused
a deep sleep to fall upon the man, and he slept;
then he took one of his ribs and closed up its place
with flesh. 22 And the rib that the LORD God had
taken from the man he made into a woman and
brought her to the man. 23 Then the man said,

"This at last is bone of my bones
  and flesh of my flesh;
this one shall be called Woman,[b]
  for out of Man[c] this one was taken."

24 Therefore a man leaves his father and his mother
and clings to his wife, and they become one flesh.
25 And the man and his wife were both naked, and
were not ashamed.

3 Now the serpent was more crafty than any
other wild animal that the LORD God had
made. He said to the woman, "Did God say, 'You
shall not eat from any tree in the garden'?" 2 The
woman said to the serpent, "We may eat of the
fruit of the trees in the garden; 3 but God said,
'You shall not eat of the fruit of the tree that is
in the middle of the garden, nor shall you touch
it, or you shall die.'" 4 But the serpent said to the
woman, "You will not die; 5 for God knows that
when you eat of it your eyes will be opened, and
you will be like God,[d] knowing good and evil."
6 So when the woman saw that the tree was good
for food, and that it was a delight to the eyes,
and that the tree was to be desired to make one
wise, she took of its fruit and ate; and she also
gave some to her husband, who was with her,
and he ate. 7 Then the eyes of both were opened,
and they knew that they were naked; and they
sewed fig leaves together and made loincloths for
themselves.
8 They heard the sound of the LORD God
walking in the garden at the time of the evening
breeze, and the man and his wife hid themselves
from the presence of the LORD God among the
trees of the garden. 9 But the LORD God called to
the man, and said to him, "Where are you?" 10 He
said, "I heard the sound of you in the garden,
and I was afraid, because I was naked; and I hid
myself." 11 He said, "Who told you that you were
naked? Have you eaten from the tree of which
I commanded you not to eat?" 12 The man said,
"The woman whom you gave to be with me, she
gave me fruit from the tree, and I ate." 13 Then the
LORD God said to the woman, "What is this that
you have done?" The woman said, "The serpent
tricked me, and I ate." 14 The LORD God said to
the serpent,

"Because you have done this,
  cursed are you among all animals
  and among all wild creatures;
upon your belly you shall go,
  and dust you shall eat
  all the days of your life.
15 I will put enmity between you and the
    woman,
  and between your offspring and hers;
he will strike your head,
  and you will strike his heel."

16 To the woman he said,

"I will greatly increase your pangs in
    childbearing;
  in pain you shall bring forth children,
yet your desire shall be for your husband,
  and he shall rule over you."

17 And to the man[e] he said,

"Because you have listened to the voice of
    your wife,
  and have eaten of the tree
about which I commanded you,
  'You shall not eat of it,'
cursed is the ground because of you;
  in toil you shall eat of it all the days of your
    life;

[a] Or *for Adam* [b] Heb *ishshah* [c] Heb *ish* [d] Or *gods* [e] Or *to Adam*

18 thorns and thistles it shall bring forth for you;
and you shall eat the plants of the field.
19 By the sweat of your face
you shall eat bread
until you return to the ground,
for out of it you were taken;
you are dust,
and to dust you shall return."

20 The man named his wife Eve,[a] because she
was the mother of all living. 21And the LORD God
made garments of skins for the man[b] and for his
wife, and clothed them.

22 Then the LORD God said, "See, the man
has become like one of us, knowing good and
evil; and now, he might reach out his hand and
take also from the tree of life, and eat, and live forever"— 23therefore the LORD God sent him forth
from the garden of Eden, to till the ground from
which he was taken. 24He drove out the man; and
at the east of the garden of Eden he placed the
cherubim, and a sword flaming and turning to
guard the way to the tree of life.

4 Now the man knew his wife Eve, and she
conceived and bore Cain, saying, "I have produced[c] a man with the help of the LORD." 2Next
she bore his brother Abel. Now Abel was a keeper
of sheep, and Cain a tiller of the ground. 3In the
course of time Cain brought to the LORD an offering of the fruit of the ground,4and Abel for his
part brought of the firstlings of his flock, their fat
portions. And the LORD had regard for Abel and
his offering, 5but for Cain and his offering he had
no regard. So Cain was very angry, and his countenance fell. 6The LORD said to Cain, "Why are
you angry, and why has your countenance fallen?
7If you do well, will you not be accepted? And if
you do not do well, sin is lurking at the door; its
desire is for you, but you must master it."

8 Cain said to his brother Abel, "Let us go
out to the field."[d] And when they were in the
field, Cain rose up against his brother Abel, and
killed him. 9Then the LORD said to Cain, "Where
is your brother Abel?" He said, "I do not know;
am I my brother's keeper?" 10And the LORD said,
"What have you done? Listen; your brother's
blood is crying out to me from the ground! 11And
now you are cursed from the ground, which has
opened its mouth to receive your brother's blood
from your hand. 12When you till the ground, it
will no longer yield to you its strength; you will
be a fugitive and a wanderer on the earth." 13Cain
said to the LORD, "My punishment is greater than
I can bear! 14Today you have driven me away
from the soil, and I shall be hidden from your
face; I shall be a fugitive and a wanderer on the
earth, and anyone who meets me may kill me."
15Then the LORD said to him, "Not so![e] Whoever
kills Cain will suffer a sevenfold vengeance." And
the LORD put a mark on Cain, so that no one who
came upon him would kill him. 16Then Cain went
away from the presence of the LORD, and settled
in the land of Nod,[f] east of Eden.

17 Cain knew his wife, and she conceived
and bore Enoch; and he built a city, and named it
Enoch after his son Enoch. 18To Enoch was born
Irad; and Irad was the father of Mehujael, and
Mehujael the father of Methushael, and Methushael the father of Lamech. 19Lamech took two
wives; the name of the one was Adah, and the
name of the other Zillah. 20Adah bore Jabal; he
was the ancestor of those who live in tents and
have livestock. 21His brother's name was Jubal;
he was the ancestor of all those who play the lyre
and pipe. 22Zillah bore Tubal-cain, who made all
kinds of bronze and iron tools. The sister of
Tubal-cain was Naamah.

23 Lamech said to his wives:
"Adah and Zillah, hear my voice;
you wives of Lamech, listen to what I say:
I have killed a man for wounding me,
a young man for striking me.
24 If Cain is avenged sevenfold,
truly Lamech seventy-sevenfold."

25 Adam knew his wife again, and she bore a
son and named him Seth, for she said, "God has
appointed[g] for me another child instead of Abel,

[a] In Heb *Eve* resembles the word for *living* [b] Or *for Adam*
[d] Sam Gk Syr Compare Vg: MT lacks *Let us go out to the field*
[g] The verb in Heb resembles the word for *Seth*

[c] The verb in Heb resembles the word for *Cain*
[e] Gk Syr Vg: Heb *Therefore* [f] That is *Wandering*

because Cain killed him." 26To Seth also a son
was born, and he named him Enosh. At that time
people began to invoke the name of the LORD.

5 This is the list of the descendants of Adam.
When God created humankind,[a] he made
them[b] in the likeness of God. 2Male and female
he created them, and he blessed them and named
them "Humankind"[c] when they were created.

3 When Adam had lived one hundred thirty
years, he became the father of a son in his likeness,
according to his image, and named him Seth. 4The
days of Adam after he became the father of Seth
were eight hundred years; and he had other sons
and daughters. 5Thus all the days that Adam lived
were nine hundred thirty years; and he died.

6 When Seth had lived one hundred five
years, he became the father of Enosh. 7Seth lived
after the birth of Enosh eight hundred seven
years, and had other sons and daughters. 8Thus
all the days of Seth were nine hundred twelve
years; and he died.

9 When Enosh had lived ninety years, he
became the father of Kenan. 10Enosh lived after
the birth of Kenan eight hundred fifteen years,
and had other sons and daughters. 11Thus all the
days of Enosh were nine hundred five years; and
he died.

12 When Kenan had lived seventy years, he
became the father of Mahalalel. 13Kenan lived after the birth of Mahalalel eight hundred and forty
years, and had other sons and daughters. 14Thus
all the days of Kenan were nine hundred and ten
years; and he died.

15 When Mahalalel had lived sixty-five years,
he became the father of Jared. 16Mahalalel lived
after the birth of Jared eight hundred thirty years,
and had other sons and daughters. 17Thus all the
days of Mahalalel were eight hundred ninety-five
years; and he died.

18 When Jared had lived one hundred sixty-
two years he became the father of Enoch. 19Jared
lived after the birth of Enoch eight hundred years,
and had other sons and daughters. 20Thus all the
days of Jared were nine hundred sixty-two years;
and he died.

21 When Enoch had lived sixty-five years, he
became the father of Methuselah. 22Enoch walked
with God after the birth of Methuselah three
hundred years, and had other sons and daughters.
23Thus all the days of Enoch were three hundred
sixty-five years. 24Enoch walked with God; then
he was no more, because God took him.

25 When Methuselah had lived one hundred
eighty-seven years, he became the father of Lamech. 26Methuselah lived after the birth of Lamech seven hundred eighty-two years, and had
other sons and daughters. 27Thus all the days of
Methuselah were nine hundred sixty-nine years;
and he died.

28 When Lamech had lived one hundred
eighty-two years, he became the father of a
son; 29he named him Noah, saying, "Out of the
ground that the LORD has cursed this one shall
bring us relief from our work and from the toil
of our hands." 30Lamech lived after the birth of
Noah five hundred ninety-five years, and had
other sons and daughters. 31Thus all the days of
Lamech were seven hundred seventy-seven years;
and he died.

32 After Noah was five hundred years old,
Noah became the father of Shem, Ham, and
Japheth.

6 When people began to multiply on the face
of the ground, and daughters were born to
them, 2the sons of God saw that they were fair;
and they took wives for themselves of all that they
chose. 3Then the LORD said, "My spirit shall not
abide[c] in mortals forever, for they are flesh; their
days shall be one hundred twenty years." 4The
Nephilim were on the earth in those days—and
also afterward—when the sons of God went in
to the daughters of humans, who bore children
to them. These were the heroes that were of old,
warriors of renown.

5 The LORD saw that the wickedness of humankind was great in the earth, and that every
inclination of the thoughts of their hearts was
only evil continually. 6And the LORD was sorry
that he had made humankind on the earth, and
it grieved him to his heart. 7So the LORD said, "I

[a] Heb *adam* [b] Heb *him* [c] Meaning of Heb uncertain

will blot out from the earth the human beings I have created—people together with animals and creeping things and birds of the air, for I am sorry that I have made them." 8 But Noah found favor in the sight of the LORD.

9 These are the descendants of Noah. Noah was a righteous man, blameless in his generation; Noah walked with God. 10 And Noah had three sons, Shem, Ham, and Japheth.

11 Now the earth was corrupt in God's sight, and the earth was filled with violence. 12 And God saw that the earth was corrupt; for all flesh had corrupted its ways upon the earth. 13 And God said to Noah, "I have determined to make an end of all flesh, for the earth is filled with violence because of them; now I am going to destroy them along with the earth. 14 Make yourself an ark of cypress[a] wood; make rooms in the ark, and cover it inside and out with pitch. 15 This is how you are to make it: the length of the ark three hundred cubits, its width fifty cubits, and its height thirty cubits. 16 Make a roof[b] for the ark, and finish it to a cubit above; and put the door of the ark in its side; make it with lower, second, and third decks. 17 For my part, I am going to bring a flood of waters on the earth, to destroy from under heaven all flesh in which is the breath of life; everything that is on the earth shall die. 18 But I will establish my covenant with you; and you shall come into the ark, you, your sons, your wife, and your sons' wives with you. 19 And of every living thing, of all flesh, you shall bring two of every kind into the ark, to keep them alive with you; they shall be male and female. 20 Of the birds according to their kinds, and of the animals according to their kinds, of every creeping thing of the ground according to its kind, two of every kind shall come in to you, to keep them alive. 21 Also take with you every kind of food that is eaten, and store it up; and it shall serve as food for you and for them." 22 Noah did this; he did all that God commanded him.

7 Then the LORD said to Noah, "Go into the ark, you and all your household, for I have seen that you alone are righteous before me in this generation. 2 Take with you seven pairs of all clean animals, the male and its mate; and a pair of the animals that are not clean, the male and its mate; 3 and seven pairs of the birds of the air also, male and female, to keep their kind alive on the face of all the earth. 4 For in seven days I will send rain on the earth for forty days and forty nights; and every living thing that I have made I will blot out from the face of the ground." 5 And Noah did all that the LORD had commanded him.

6 Noah was six hundred years old when the flood of waters came on the earth. 7 And Noah with his sons and his wife and his sons' wives went into the ark to escape the waters of the flood. 8 Of clean animals, and of animals that are not clean, and of birds, and of everything that creeps on the ground, 9 two and two, male and female, went into the ark with Noah, as God had commanded Noah. 10 And after seven days the waters of the flood came on the earth.

11 In the six hundredth year of Noah's life, in the second month, on the seventeenth day of the month, on that day all the fountains of the great deep burst forth, and the windows of the heavens were opened. 12 The rain fell on the earth forty days and forty nights. 13 On the very same day Noah with his sons, Shem and Ham and Japheth, and Noah's wife and the three wives of his sons entered the ark, 14 they and every wild animal of every kind, and all domestic animals of every kind, and every creeping thing that creeps on the earth, and every bird of every kind—every bird, every winged creature. 15 They went into the ark with Noah, two and two of all flesh in which there was the breath of life. 16 And those that entered, male and female of all flesh, went in as God had commanded him; and the LORD shut him in.

17 The flood continued forty days on the earth; and the waters increased, and bore up the ark, and it rose high above the earth. 18 The waters swelled and increased greatly on the earth; and the ark floated on the face of the waters. 19 The waters swelled so mightily on the earth that all the high mountains under the whole heaven were covered; 20 the waters swelled above the mountains, covering them fifteen cubits deep. 21 And all flesh died

[a] Meaning of Heb uncertain [b] Or *window*

that moved on the earth, birds, domestic animals, wild animals, all swarming creatures that swarm on the earth, and all human beings; [22] everything on dry land in whose nostrils was the breath of life died. [23] He blotted out every living thing that was on the face of the ground, human beings and animals and creeping things and birds of the air; they were blotted out from the earth. Only Noah was left, and those that were with him in the ark. [24] And the waters swelled on the earth for one hundred fifty days.

8 But God remembered Noah and all the wild animals and all the domestic animals that were with him in the ark. And God made a wind blow over the earth, and the waters subsided; [2] the fountains of the deep and the windows of the heavens were closed, the rain from the heavens was restrained, [3] and the waters gradually receded from the earth. At the end of one hundred fifty days the waters had abated; [4] and in the seventh month, on the seventeenth day of the month, the ark came to rest on the mountains of Ararat. [5] The waters continued to abate until the tenth month; in the tenth month, on the first day of the month, the tops of the mountains appeared.

6 At the end of forty days Noah opened the window of the ark that he had made [7] and sent out the raven; and it went to and fro until the waters were dried up from the earth. [8] Then he sent out the dove from him, to see if the waters had subsided from the face of the ground; [9] but the dove found no place to set its foot, and it returned to him to the ark, for the waters were still on the face of the whole earth. So he put out his hand and took it and brought it into the ark with him. [10] He waited another seven days, and again he sent out the dove from the ark; [11] and the dove came back to him in the evening, and there in its beak was a freshly plucked olive leaf; so Noah knew that the waters had subsided from the earth. [12] Then he waited another seven days, and sent out the dove; and it did not return to him any more.

13 In the six hundred first year, in the first month, on the first day of the month, the waters were dried up from the earth; and Noah removed the covering of the ark, and looked, and saw that the face of the ground was drying. [14] In the second month, on the twenty-seventh day of the month, the earth was dry. [15] Then God said to Noah, [16] "Go out of the ark, you and your wife, and your sons and your sons' wives with you. [17] Bring out with you every living thing that is with you of all flesh—birds and animals and every creeping thing that creeps on the earth—so that they may abound on the earth, and be fruitful and multiply on the earth." [18] So Noah went out with his sons and his wife and his sons' wives. [19] And every animal, every creeping thing, and every bird, everything that moves on the earth, went out of the ark by families.

20 Then Noah built an altar to the LORD, and took of every clean animal and of every clean bird, and offered burnt offerings on the altar. [21] And when the LORD smelled the pleasing odor, the LORD said in his heart, "I will never again curse the ground because of humankind, for the inclination of the human heart is evil from youth; nor will I ever again destroy every living creature as I have done.

22 As long as the earth endures,
seedtime and harvest, cold and heat,
summer and winter, day and night,
shall not cease."

9 God blessed Noah and his sons, and said to them, "Be fruitful and multiply, and fill the earth. [2] The fear and dread of you shall rest on every animal of the earth, and on every bird of the air, on everything that creeps on the ground, and on all the fish of the sea; into your hand they are delivered. [3] Every moving thing that lives shall be food for you; and just as I gave you the green plants, I give you everything. [4] Only, you shall not eat flesh with its life, that is, its blood. [5] For your own lifeblood I will surely require a reckoning: from every animal I will require it and from human beings, each one for the blood of another, I will require a reckoning for human life.

6 Whoever sheds the blood of a human,
by a human shall that person's blood be shed;
for in his own image
God made humankind.

[7] And you, be fruitful and multiply, abound on the earth and multiply in it."

8 Then God said to Noah and to his sons with
him, 9"As for me, I am establishing my covenant
with you and your descendants after you, 10and
with every living creature that is with you, the
birds, the domestic animals, and every animal of
the earth with you, as many as came out of the
ark.[a] 11I establish my covenant with you, that
never again shall all flesh be cut off by the waters
of a flood, and never again shall there be a flood
to destroy the earth." 12God said, "This is the sign
of the covenant that I make between me and you
and every living creature that is with you, for all
future generations: 13I have set my bow in the
clouds, and it shall be a sign of the covenant between me and the earth. 14When I bring clouds
over the earth and the bow is seen in the clouds,
15I will remember my covenant that is between
me and you and every living creature of all flesh;
and the waters shall never again become a flood
to destroy all flesh. 16When the bow is in the
clouds, I will see it and remember the everlasting covenant between God and every living creature of all flesh that is on the earth." 17God said
to Noah, "This is the sign of the covenant that I
have established between me and all flesh that is
on the earth."

18 The sons of Noah who went out of the
ark were Shem, Ham, and Japheth. Ham was the
father of Canaan. 19These three were the sons
of Noah; and from these the whole earth was
peopled.

20 Noah, a man of the soil, was the first to
plant a vineyard. 21He drank some of the wine
and became drunk, and he lay uncovered in his
tent. 22And Ham, the father of Canaan, saw the
nakedness of his father, and told his two brothers outside. 23Then Shem and Japheth took a garment, laid it on both their shoulders, and walked
backward and covered the nakedness of their father; their faces were turned away, and they did
not see their father's nakedness. 24When Noah
awoke from his wine and knew what his youngest
son had done to him, 25he said,

"Cursed be Canaan;
lowest of slaves shall he be to his brothers."

26He also said,
"Blessed by the LORD my God be Shem;
and let Canaan be his slave.
27 May God make space for[b] Japheth,
and let him live in the tents of Shem;
and let Canaan be his slave."

28 After the flood Noah lived three hundred
fifty years. 29All the days of Noah were nine hundred fifty years; and he died.

10 These are the descendants of Noah's sons,
Shem, Ham, and Japheth; children were
born to them after the flood.

2 The descendants of Japheth: Gomer, Magog, Madai, Javan, Tubal, Meshech, and Tiras.

Genesis 10

Rather than any objective historical account of genealogies, the Table of Nations in Gen 10 presents us with a theologically motivated catalogue of people. The Table not only ends with the descendants of Shem but does so in a way consciously stylised to accentuate the importance of the descendants of Shem among the peoples of the earth. About this, the author of the genealogy in 1 Chron 1:17-34 is most explicit inasmuch as of all the descendants of the sons of Noah those descended from Shem receive the most elaborate attention.... In this long progression, the theological presuppositions of a particular ethnic group displace any concern for objective historiography and ethnography. The descendants of Noah apart from those of Shem are increasingly insignificant and gain access to the text only as they serve as foils to demonstrate the priority of the Israelites.

The subtle process being described may consequently be called "sacralisation" because it represents an attempt on the part of succeeding generations of one ethnic group to construe salvation history in terms distinctly favourable to it as opposed to others. Here, ethnic particularity evolves with a certain divine vindication and inevitably the dangers of rank racism lie just beneath the surface.[5]

— Cain Hope Felder

[a] Gk: Heb adds *every animal of the earth* [b] Heb *yapht*, a play on *Japheth*

3The descendants of Gomer: Ashkenaz, Riphath, and Togarmah. 4The descendants of Javan: Elishah, Tarshish, Kittim, and Rodanim.[a] 5From these the coastland peoples spread. These are the descendants of Japheth[b] in their lands, with their own language, by their families, in their nations.

6 The descendants of Ham: Cush, Egypt, Put, and Canaan. 7The descendants of Cush: Seba, Havilah, Sabtah, Raamah, and Sabteca. The descendants of Raamah: Sheba and Dedan. 8Cush became the father of Nimrod; he was the first on earth to become a mighty warrior. 9He was a mighty hunter before the LORD; therefore it is said, "Like Nimrod a mighty hunter before the LORD." 10The beginning of his kingdom was Babel, Erech, and Accad, all of them in the land of Shinar. 11From that land he went into Assyria, and built Nineveh, Rehoboth-ir, Calah, and 12Resen between Nineveh and Calah; that is the great city. 13Egypt became the father of Ludim, Anamim, Lehabim, Naphtuhim, 14Pathrusim, Casluhim, and Caphtorim, from which the Philistines come.[c]

15 Canaan became the father of Sidon his firstborn, and Heth, 16and the Jebusites, the Amorites, the Girgashites, 17the Hivites, the Arkites, the Sinites, 18the Arvadites, the Zemarites, and the Hamathites. Afterward the families of the Canaanites spread abroad. 19And the territory of the Canaanites extended from Sidon, in the direction of Gerar, as far as Gaza, and in the direction of Sodom, Gomorrah, Admah, and Zeboiim, as far as Lasha. 20These are the descendants of Ham, by their families, their languages, their lands, and their nations.

21 To Shem also, the father of all the children of Eber, the elder brother of Japheth, children were born. 22The descendants of Shem: Elam, Asshur, Arpachshad, Lud, and Aram. 23The descendants of Aram: Uz, Hul, Gether, and Mash. 24Arpachshad became the father of Shelah; and Shelah became the father of Eber. 25To Eber were born two sons: the name of the one was Peleg,[d] for in his days the earth was divided, and his brother's name was Joktan. 26Joktan became the father of Almodad, Sheleph, Hazarmaveth, Jerah, 27Hadoram, Uzal, Diklah, 28Obal, Abimael, Sheba, 29Ophir, Havilah, and Jobab; all these were the descendants of Joktan. 30The territory in which they lived extended from Mesha in the direction of Sephar, the hill country of the east. 31These are the descendants of Shem, by their families, their languages, their lands, and their nations.

32 These are the families of Noah's sons, according to their genealogies, in their nations; and from these the nations spread abroad on the earth after the flood.

11 Now the whole earth had one language and the same words. 2And as they migrated from the east,[e] they came upon a plain in the land of Shinar and settled there. 3And they said to one another, "Come, let us make bricks, and burn them thoroughly." And they had brick for stone, and bitumen for mortar. 4Then they said, "Come, let us build ourselves a city, and a tower with its top in the heavens, and let us make

Genesis 11:1-9

The Tower of Babel story is often read as one of sin and punishment. This reading can be problematic for interpreters who value diversity, for whom the many cultures of the world are a gift and not a curse. Another way to read this story, however, is to see the larger pattern within Genesis 1–11, a pattern that moves from sin to judgment to grace. At the end of each episode, human rebellion is met with divine judgment, after which the LORD shows some act of kindness—clothing Adam and Eve, marking Cain to protect him from further retribution, making a covenant with Noah and humanity, and so on. Similarly, in Genesis 11, the LORD divides the people from each other in order to thwart their effort—but then in an act of divine graciousness gives to the peoples of the earth the gift of diverse languages and cultures.

—FY

[a] Heb Mss Sam Gk See 1 Chr 1.7: MT *Dodanim* [b] Compare verses 20, 31. Heb lacks *These are the descendants of Japheth*

[c] Cn: Heb *Casluhim, from which the Philistines come, and Caphtorim* [d] That is *Division* [e] Or *migrated eastward*

a name for ourselves; otherwise we shall be scattered abroad upon the face of the whole earth."
5 The LORD came down to see the city and the
tower, which mortals had built. 6 And the LORD
said, "Look, they are one people, and they have all
one language; and this is only the beginning of
what they will do; nothing that they propose to do
will now be impossible for them. 7 Come, let us go
down, and confuse their language there, so that
they will not understand one another's speech."
8 So the LORD scattered them abroad from there
over the face of all the earth, and they left off
building the city. 9 Therefore it was called Babel,
because there the LORD confused[a] the language of
all the earth; and from there the LORD scattered
them abroad over the face of all the earth.

10 These are the descendants of Shem. When
Shem was one hundred years old, he became the
father of Arpachshad two years after the flood;
11 and Shem lived after the birth of Arpachshad
five hundred years, and had other sons and
daughters.

12 When Arpachshad had lived thirty-five
years, he became the father of Shelah; 13 and
Arpachshad lived after the birth of Shelah four
hundred three years, and had other sons and
daughters.

14 When Shelah had lived thirty years, he
became the father of Eber; 15 and Shelah lived
after the birth of Eber four hundred three years,
and had other sons and daughters.

16 When Eber had lived thirty-four years, he
became the father of Peleg; 17 and Eber lived after
the birth of Peleg four hundred thirty years, and
had other sons and daughters.

18 When Peleg had lived thirty years, he became the father of Reu; 19 and Peleg lived after
the birth of Reu two hundred nine years, and had
other sons and daughters.

20 When Reu had lived thirty-two years, he
became the father of Serug; 21 and Reu lived after
the birth of Serug two hundred seven years, and
had other sons and daughters.

22 When Serug had lived thirty years, he became the father of Nahor; 23 and Serug lived after
the birth of Nahor two hundred years, and had
other sons and daughters.

24 When Nahor had lived twenty-nine years,
he became the father of Terah; 25 and Nahor lived
after the birth of Terah one hundred nineteen
years, and had other sons and daughters.

26 When Terah had lived seventy years, he
became the father of Abram, Nahor, and Haran.

27 Now these are the descendants of Terah.
Terah was the father of Abram, Nahor, and Haran; and Haran was the father of Lot. 28 Haran
died before his father Terah in the land of his
birth, in Ur of the Chaldeans. 29 Abram and Nahor took wives; the name of Abram's wife was
Sarai, and the name of Nahor's wife was Milcah.
She was the daughter of Haran the father of
Milcah and Iscah. 30 Now Sarai was barren; she
had no child.

31 Terah took his son Abram and his grandson Lot son of Haran, and his daughter-in-law
Sarai, his son Abram's wife, and they went out
together from Ur of the Chaldeans to go into the
land of Canaan; but when they came to Haran,
they settled there. 32 The days of Terah were two
hundred five years; and Terah died in Haran.

12 Now the LORD said to Abram, "Go from
your country and your kindred and your
father's house to the land that I will show you.
2 I will make of you a great nation, and I will
bless you, and make your name great, so that you
will be a blessing. 3 I will bless those who bless
you, and the one who curses you I will curse;
and in you all the families of the earth shall be
blessed."[b]

4 So Abram went, as the LORD had told him;
and Lot went with him. Abram was seventy-five
years old when he departed from Haran. 5 Abram
took his wife Sarai and his brother's son Lot, and
all the possessions that they had gathered, and the
persons whom they had acquired in Haran; and
they set forth to go to the land of Canaan. When
they had come to the land of Canaan, 6 Abram
passed through the land to the place at Shechem,
to the oak[c] of Moreh. At that time the Canaanites
were in the land. 7 Then the LORD appeared to

[a] Heb *balal*, meaning *to confuse* [b] Or *by you all the families of the earth shall bless themselves* [c] Or *terebinth*

Genesis 12:1-7

Abraham has been claimed as the ancestor of three monotheistic religions: Judaism, Christianity, and Islam. Because of this, the character of Abraham represents both the shared heritage and the inherent diversity among these religious traditions. One cannot minimize the importance of this common connection to one ancestor; however, one also cannot ignore the centuries-long conflict between these three religions. In this sense, the promise given to Abraham—that in him "all the families of the earth shall be blessed"—still awaits fulfillment.

—*FY*

Abram, and said, "To your offspring[a] I will give this land." So he built there an altar to the LORD, who had appeared to him. [8] From there he moved on to the hill country on the east of Bethel, and pitched his tent, with Bethel on the west and Ai on the east; and there he built an altar to the LORD and invoked the name of the LORD. [9] And Abram journeyed on by stages toward the Negeb.

10 Now there was a famine in the land. So Abram went down to Egypt to reside there as an alien, for the famine was severe in the land. [11] When he was about to enter Egypt, he said to his wife Sarai, "I know well that you are a woman beautiful in appearance; [12] and when the Egyptians see you, they will say, 'This is his wife'; then they will kill me, but they will let you live. [13] Say you are my sister, so that it may go well with me because of you, and that my life may be spared on your account." [14] When Abram entered Egypt the Egyptians saw that the woman was very beautiful. [15] When the officials of Pharaoh saw her, they praised her to Pharaoh. And the woman was taken into Pharaoh's house. [16] And for her sake he dealt well with Abram; and he had sheep, oxen, male donkeys, male and female slaves, female donkeys, and camels.

17 But the LORD afflicted Pharaoh and his house with great plagues because of Sarai, Abram's wife. [18] So Pharaoh called Abram, and said, "What is this you have done to me? Why did you not tell me that she was your wife? [19] Why did you say, 'She is my sister,' so that I took her for my wife? Now then, here is your wife, take her, and be gone." [20] And Pharaoh gave his men orders concerning him; and they set him on the way, with his wife and all that he had.

13 So Abram went up from Egypt, he and his wife, and all that he had, and Lot with him, into the Negeb.

2 Now Abram was very rich in livestock, in silver, and in gold. [3] He journeyed on by stages from the Negeb as far as Bethel, to the place where his tent had been at the beginning, between Bethel and Ai, [4] to the place where he had made an altar at the first; and there Abram called on the name of the LORD. [5] Now Lot, who went with Abram, also had flocks and herds and tents, [6] so that the land could not support both of them living together; for their possessions were so great that they could not live together, [7] and there was strife between the herders of Abram's livestock and the herders of Lot's livestock. At that time the Canaanites and the Perizzites lived in the land.

8 Then Abram said to Lot, "Let there be no strife between you and me, and between your herders and my herders; for we are kindred. [9] Is not the whole land before you? Separate yourself from me. If you take the left hand, then I will go to the right; or if you take the right hand, then I will go to the left." [10] Lot looked about him, and saw that the plain of the Jordan was well watered everywhere like the garden of the LORD, like the land of Egypt, in the direction of Zoar; this was before the LORD had destroyed Sodom and Gomorrah. [11] So Lot chose for himself all the plain of the Jordan, and Lot journeyed eastward; thus they separated from each other. [12] Abram settled in the land of Canaan, while Lot settled among the cities of the Plain and moved his tent as far as Sodom. [13] Now the people of Sodom were wicked, great sinners against the LORD.

14 The LORD said to Abram, after Lot had separated from him, "Raise your eyes now, and

[a] Heb *seed*

look from the place where you are, northward and
southward and eastward and westward; 15for all
the land that you see I will give to you and to your
offspring[a] forever. 16I will make your offspring
like the dust of the earth; so that if one can count
the dust of the earth, your offspring also can be
counted. 17Rise up, walk through the length and
the breadth of the land, for I will give it to you."
18So Abram moved his tent, and came and settled
by the oaks[b] of Mamre, which are at Hebron; and
there he built an altar to the LORD.

14 In the days of King Amraphel of Shinar,
King Arioch of Ellasar, King Chedorlaomer of Elam, and King Tidal of Goiim, 2these
kings made war with King Bera of Sodom, King
Birsha of Gomorrah, King Shinab of Admah,
King Shemeber of Zeboiim, and the king of Bela
(that is, Zoar). 3All these joined forces in the Valley of Siddim (that is, the Dead Sea).[c] 4Twelve
years they had served Chedorlaomer, but in the
thirteenth year they rebelled. 5In the fourteenth
year Chedorlaomer and the kings who were
with him came and subdued the Rephaim in
Ashteroth-karnaim, the Zuzim in Ham, the Emim
in Shaveh-kiriathaim, 6and the Horites in the hill
country of Seir as far as El-paran on the edge of
the wilderness; 7then they turned back and came
to En-mishpat (that is, Kadesh), and subdued
all the country of the Amalekites, and also the
Amorites who lived in Hazazon-tamar. 8Then the
king of Sodom, the king of Gomorrah, the king of
Admah, the king of Zeboiim, and the king of Bela
(that is, Zoar) went out, and they joined battle
in the Valley of Siddim 9with King Chedorlaomer
of Elam, King Tidal of Goiim, King Amraphel of
Shinar, and King Arioch of Ellasar, four kings
against five. 10Now the Valley of Siddim was full
of bitumen pits; and as the kings of Sodom and
Gomorrah fled, some fell into them, and the rest
fled to the hill country. 11So the enemy took all
the goods of Sodom and Gomorrah, and all their
provisions, and went their way; 12they also took
Lot, the son of Abram's brother, who lived in Sodom, and his goods, and departed.

13 Then one who had escaped came and told
Abram the Hebrew, who was living by the oaks[b]
of Mamre the Amorite, brother of Eshcol and of
Aner; these were allies of Abram. 14When Abram
heard that his nephew had been taken captive, he
led forth his trained men, born in his house, three
hundred eighteen of them, and went in pursuit as
far as Dan. 15He divided his forces against them
by night, he and his servants, and routed them
and pursued them to Hobah, north of Damascus.
16Then he brought back all the goods, and also
brought back his nephew Lot with his goods, and
the women and the people.

17 After his return from the defeat of Chedorlaomer and the kings who were with him, the
king of Sodom went out to meet him at the Valley of Shaveh (that is, the King's Valley). 18And
King Melchizedek of Salem brought out bread
and wine; he was priest of God Most High.[d] 19He
blessed him and said,

"Blessed be Abram by God Most High,[d]
maker of heaven and earth;
20 and blessed be God Most High,[d]
who has delivered your enemies into
your hand!"

And Abram gave him one-tenth of everything.
21Then the king of Sodom said to Abram, "Give
me the persons, but take the goods for yourself."
22But Abram said to the king of Sodom, "I have
sworn to the LORD, God Most High,[d] maker of
heaven and earth, 23that I would not take a thread
or a sandal-thong or anything that is yours, so
that you might not say, 'I have made Abram rich.'
24I will take nothing but what the young men
have eaten, and the share of the men who went
with me—Aner, Eshcol, and Mamre. Let them
take their share."

15 After these things the word of the LORD
came to Abram in a vision, "Do not be
afraid, Abram, I am your shield; your reward shall
be very great." 2But Abram said, "O Lord GOD,
what will you give me, for I continue childless,
and the heir of my house is Eliezer of Damascus?"[e] 3And Abram said, "You have given me no
offspring, and so a slave born in my house is to be
my heir." 4But the word of the LORD came to him,

[a] Heb *seed* [b] Or *terebinths* [c] Heb *Salt Sea* [d] Heb *El Elyon* [e] Meaning of Heb uncertain

"This man shall not be your heir; no one but your
very own issue shall be your heir." 5He brought
him outside and said, "Look toward heaven and
count the stars, if you are able to count them."
Then he said to him, "So shall your descendants
be." 6And he believed the LORD; and the LORD[a]
reckoned it to him as righteousness.

7 Then he said to him, "I am the LORD who
brought you from Ur of the Chaldeans, to give you
this land to possess." 8But he said, "O Lord GOD,
how am I to know that I shall possess it?" 9He said
to him, "Bring me a heifer three years old, a female goat three years old, a ram three years old,
a turtledove, and a young pigeon." 10He brought
him all these and cut them in two, laying each half
over against the other; but he did not cut the birds
in two. 11And when birds of prey came down on
the carcasses, Abram drove them away.

12 As the sun was going down, a deep sleep
fell upon Abram, and a deep and terrifying darkness descended upon him. 13Then the LORD[a] said
to Abram, "Know this for certain, that your offspring shall be aliens in a land that is not theirs,
and shall be slaves there, and they shall be oppressed for four hundred years; 14but I will bring
judgment on the nation that they serve, and afterward they shall come out with great possessions.
15As for yourself, you shall go to your ancestors
in peace; you shall be buried in a good old age.
16And they shall come back here in the fourth
generation; for the iniquity of the Amorites is not
yet complete."

17 When the sun had gone down and it was
dark, a smoking fire pot and a flaming torch
passed between these pieces. 18On that day the
LORD made a covenant with Abram, saying, "To
your descendants I give this land, from the river of
Egypt to the great river, the river Euphrates, 19the
land of the Kenites, the Kenizzites, the Kadmon-
ites, 20the Hittites, the Perizzites, the Rephaim,
21the Amorites, the Canaanites, the Girgashites,
and the Jebusites."

16 Now Sarai, Abram's wife, bore him no
children. She had an Egyptian slave-
girl whose name was Hagar, 2and Sarai said to
Abram, "You see that the LORD has prevented me
from bearing children; go in to my slave-girl; it
may be that I shall obtain children by her." And
Abram listened to the voice of Sarai. 3So, after
Abram had lived ten years in the land of Canaan,
Sarai, Abram's wife, took Hagar the Egyptian, her
slave-girl, and gave her to her husband Abram as
a wife. 4He went in to Hagar, and she conceived;
and when she saw that she had conceived, she
looked with contempt on her mistress. 5Then
Sarai said to Abram, "May the wrong done to
me be on you! I gave my slave-girl to your embrace, and when she saw that she had conceived,
she looked on me with contempt. May the LORD
judge between you and me!" 6But Abram said to
Sarai, "Your slave-girl is in your power; do to her
as you please." Then Sarai dealt harshly with her,
and she ran away from her.

7 The angel of the LORD found her by a spring
of water in the wilderness, the spring on the way
to Shur. 8And he said, "Hagar, slave-girl of Sarai,
where have you come from and where are you
going?" She said, "I am running away from my
mistress Sarai." 9The angel of the LORD said to
her, "Return to your mistress, and submit to her."

Genesis 16

The story of Hagar is particularly significant to readers of African descent. The enslavement of this African woman has resonances with the American experience of slavery, including forcible impregnation of the enslaved by their owners. Ironically, in verse 3 Hagar is given to Abram as a "wife" in the same category as Sarai. In verse 6 Sarai violently abuses Hagar. The same verb will be used in Exodus to describe the oppression of the Israelites at the hands of the Egyptians. Verse 10 details the canon's first angelic annunciation and promise of a dynasty to a woman. And verse 13 records Hagar's naming of God. She is the only human person in the Scriptures to name God.

— *WG*

[a] Heb *he*

10The angel of the LORD also said to her, "I will so
greatly multiply your offspring that they cannot
be counted for multitude." 11And the angel of the
LORD said to her,

"Now you have conceived and shall bear a
son;
you shall call him Ishmael,[a]
for the LORD has given heed to your
affliction.
12 He shall be a wild ass of a man,
with his hand against everyone,
and everyone's hand against him;
and he shall live at odds with all his kin."

13So she named the LORD who spoke to her, "You
are El-roi";[b] for she said, "Have I really seen God
and remained alive after seeing him?"[c] 14There-
fore the well was called Beer-lahai-roi;[d] it lies between Kadesh and Bered.

15 Hagar bore Abram a son; and Abram
named his son, whom Hagar bore, Ishmael.
16Abram was eighty-six years old when Hagar
bore him[e] Ishmael.

17 When Abram was ninety-nine years old,
the LORD appeared to Abram, and said
to him, "I am God Almighty;[f] walk before me,
and be blameless. 2And I will make my covenant
between me and you, and will make you exceedingly numerous." 3Then Abram fell on his face;
and God said to him, 4"As for me, this is my covenant with you: You shall be the ancestor of a multitude of nations. 5No longer shall your name be
Abram,[g] but your name shall be Abraham;[h] for I
have made you the ancestor of a multitude of nations. 6I will make you exceedingly fruitful; and
I will make nations of you, and kings shall come
from you. 7I will establish my covenant between
me and you, and your offspring after you throughout their generations, for an everlasting covenant,
to be God to you and to your offspring[i] after you.
8And I will give to you, and to your offspring after you, the land where you are now an alien, all
the land of Canaan, for a perpetual holding; and I
will be their God."

9 God said to Abraham, "As for you, you
shall keep my covenant, you and your offspring
after you throughout their generations. 10This
is my covenant, which you shall keep, between
me and you and your offspring after you: Every
male among you shall be circumcised. 11You
shall circumcise the flesh of your foreskins, and
it shall be a sign of the covenant between me and
you. 12Throughout your generations every male
among you shall be circumcised when he is eight
days old, including the slave born in your house
and the one bought with your money from any
foreigner who is not of your offspring. 13Both the
slave born in your house and the one bought with
your money must be circumcised. So shall my
covenant be in your flesh an everlasting covenant.
14Any uncircumcised male who is not circumcised in the flesh of his foreskin shall be cut off
from his people; he has broken my covenant."

15 God said to Abraham, "As for Sarai your
wife, you shall not call her Sarai, but Sarah shall
be her name. 16I will bless her, and moreover I
will give you a son by her. I will bless her, and she
shall give rise to nations; kings of peoples shall
come from her." 17Then Abraham fell on his face
and laughed, and said to himself, "Can a child be
born to a man who is a hundred years old? Can
Sarah, who is ninety years old, bear a child?"
18And Abraham said to God, "O that Ishmael
might live in your sight!" 19God said, "No, but
your wife Sarah shall bear you a son, and you shall
name him Isaac.[j] I will establish my covenant with
him as an everlasting covenant for his offspring
after him. 20As for Ishmael, I have heard you; I
will bless him and make him fruitful and exceedingly numerous; he shall be the father of twelve
princes, and I will make him a great nation. 21But
my covenant I will establish with Isaac, whom
Sarah shall bear to you at this season next year."
22And when he had finished talking with him,
God went up from Abraham.

23 Then Abraham took his son Ishmael and
all the slaves born in his house or bought with

[a] That is *God hears* [b] Perhaps *God of seeing* or *God who sees* [c] Meaning of Heb uncertain [d] That is *the Well of the Living One who sees me* [e] Heb *Abram* [f] Traditional rendering of Heb *El Shaddai* [g] That is *exalted ancestor* [h] Here taken to mean *ancestor of a multitude* [i] Heb *seed* [j] That is *he laughs*

his money, every male among the men of Abraham's house, and he circumcised the flesh of their foreskins that very day, as God had said to him. 24 Abraham was ninety-nine years old when he was circumcised in the flesh of his foreskin. 25 And his son Ishmael was thirteen years old when he was circumcised in the flesh of his foreskin. 26 That very day Abraham and his son Ishmael were circumcised; 27 and all the men of his house, slaves born in the house and those bought with money from a foreigner, were circumcised with him.

18 The LORD appeared to Abraham[a] by the oaks[b] of Mamre, as he sat at the entrance of his tent in the heat of the day. 2 He looked up and saw three men standing near him. When he saw them, he ran from the tent entrance to meet them, and bowed down to the ground. 3 He said, "My lord, if I find favor with you, do not pass by your servant. 4 Let a little water be brought, and wash your feet, and rest yourselves under the tree. 5 Let me bring a little bread, that you may refresh yourselves, and after that you may pass on—since you have come to your servant." So they said, "Do as you have said." 6 And Abraham hastened into the tent to Sarah, and said, "Make ready quickly three measures[c] of choice flour, knead it, and make cakes." 7 Abraham ran to the herd, and took a calf, tender and good, and gave it to the servant, who hastened to prepare it. 8 Then he took curds and milk and the calf that he had prepared, and set it before them; and he stood by them under the tree while they ate.

9 They said to him, "Where is your wife Sarah?" And he said, "There, in the tent." 10 Then one said, "I will surely return to you in due season, and your wife Sarah shall have a son." And Sarah was listening at the tent entrance behind him. 11 Now Abraham and Sarah were old, advanced in age; it had ceased to be with Sarah after the manner of women. 12 So Sarah laughed to herself, saying, "After I have grown old, and my husband is old, shall I have pleasure?" 13 The LORD said to Abraham, "Why did Sarah laugh, and say, 'Shall I indeed bear a child, now that I am old?' 14 Is anything too wonderful for the LORD? At the set time I will return to you, in due season, and Sarah shall have a son." 15 But Sarah denied, saying, "I did not laugh"; for she was afraid. He said, "Oh yes, you did laugh."

16 Then the men set out from there, and they looked toward Sodom; and Abraham went with them to set them on their way. 17 The LORD said, "Shall I hide from Abraham what I am about to do, 18 seeing that Abraham shall become a great and mighty nation, and all the nations of the

[a] Heb *him* [b] Or *terebinths* [c] Heb *seahs*

Genesis 18:1-10

In the "heat of the day," Sarah is in the tent and Abraham is sitting at its entrance when he sees three strangers standing nearby. Are they robbers? Are they hot, tired, and hungry? Abraham offers them water and the shade of a nearby tree. Sarah, Abraham, and a servant prepare a meal for them. Before leaving, the grateful guests—who in fact are the LORD—promise that the couple, although "advanced in age," soon will have a son. Robert E. Meagher argues that much of what today passes for hospitality is but a watered-down version of the ancient and real thing:

> Hospitality has become a harmless urbane quality in the order of... civility, politeness, and table manners. It is on the verge of being regarded as a matter of personality,... not far removed from the peculiar oblivion spread ever wider by our obsession with the particular and the private. If we manage, across some period of time, not to be rude to our friends within our own house... we are deemed hospitable.... We forget that properly hospitality has to do with unrecognizable strangers.... [A]ncient hospitality is first and primarily a bond between utter strangers.[6]

—DB

earth shall be blessed in him?[a] 19No, for I have
chosen[b] him, that he may charge his children and
his household after him to keep the way of the
LORD by doing righteousness and justice; so that
the LORD may bring about for Abraham what he
has promised him." 20Then the LORD said, "How
great is the outcry against Sodom and Gomorrah
and how very grave their sin! 21I must go down
and see whether they have done altogether according to the outcry that has come to me; and if
not, I will know."

22 So the men turned from there, and went
toward Sodom, while Abraham remained standing before the LORD.[c] 23Then Abraham came near
and said, "Will you indeed sweep away the righteous with the wicked? 24Suppose there are fifty
righteous within the city; will you then sweep
away the place and not forgive it for the fifty righteous who are in it? 25Far be it from you to do such
a thing, to slay the righteous with the wicked, so
that the righteous fare as the wicked! Far be that
from you! Shall not the Judge of all the earth do
what is just?" 26And the LORD said, "If I find at
Sodom fifty righteous in the city, I will forgive the
whole place for their sake." 27Abraham answered,
"Let me take it upon myself to speak to the Lord, I
who am but dust and ashes. 28Suppose five of the
fifty righteous are lacking? Will you destroy the
whole city for lack of five?" And he said, "I will
not destroy it if I find forty-five there." 29Again he
spoke to him, "Suppose forty are found there." He
answered, "For the sake of forty I will not do it."
30Then he said, "Oh do not let the Lord be angry if I speak. Suppose thirty are found there." He
answered, "I will not do it, if I find thirty there."
31He said, "Let me take it upon myself to speak
to the Lord. Suppose twenty are found there." He
answered, "For the sake of twenty I will not destroy it." 32Then he said, "Oh do not let the Lord
be angry if I speak just once more. Suppose ten
are found there." He answered, "For the sake of
ten I will not destroy it." 33And the LORD went
his way, when he had finished speaking to Abraham; and Abraham returned to his place.

19 The two angels came to Sodom in the evening, and Lot was sitting in the gateway of
Sodom. When Lot saw them, he rose to meet them,
and bowed down with his face to the ground. 2He
said, "Please, my lords, turn aside to your servant's
house and spend the night, and wash your feet;
then you can rise early and go on your way." They
said, "No; we will spend the night in the square."
3But he urged them strongly; so they turned aside
to him and entered his house; and he made them
a feast, and baked unleavened bread, and they ate.
4But before they lay down, the men of the city, the
men of Sodom, both young and old, all the people
to the last man, surrounded the house; 5and they
called to Lot, "Where are the men who came to
you tonight? Bring them out to us, so that we may
know them." 6Lot went out of the door to the men,
shut the door after him, 7and said, "I beg you, my
brothers, do not act so wickedly. 8Look, I have two
daughters who have not known a man; let me bring
them out to you, and do to them as you please;
only do nothing to these men, for they have come
under the shelter of my roof." 9But they replied,
"Stand back!" And they said, "This fellow came
here as an alien, and he would play the judge! Now
we will deal worse with you than with them." Then
they pressed hard against the man Lot, and came
near the door to break it down. 10But the men inside reached out their hands and brought Lot into
the house with them, and shut the door. 11And
they struck with blindness the men who were at
the door of the house, both small and great, so that
they were unable to find the door.

12 Then the men said to Lot, "Have you anyone else here? Sons-in-law, sons, daughters, or
anyone you have in the city—bring them out of
the place. 13For we are about to destroy this place,
because the outcry against its people has become
great before the LORD, and the LORD has sent us
to destroy it." 14So Lot went out and said to his
sons-in-law, who were to marry his daughters,
"Up, get out of this place; for the LORD is about
to destroy the city." But he seemed to his sons-in-
law to be jesting.

[a] Or *and all the nations of the earth shall bless themselves by him* [b] Heb *known*
[c] Another ancient tradition reads *while the LORD remained standing before Abraham*

15 When morning dawned, the angels urged
Lot, saying, “Get up, take your wife and your two
daughters who are here, or else you will be consumed in the punishment of the city.” 16 But he lingered; so the men seized him and his wife and his
two daughters by the hand, the LORD being merciful to him, and they brought him out and left him
outside the city. 17 When they had brought them
outside, they[a] said, “Flee for your life; do not look
back or stop anywhere in the Plain; flee to the
hills, or else you will be consumed.” 18 And Lot
said to them, “Oh, no, my lords; 19 your servant
has found favor with you, and you have shown me
great kindness in saving my life; but I cannot flee
to the hills, for fear the disaster will overtake me
and I die. 20 Look, that city is near enough to flee
to, and it is a little one. Let me escape there—is
it not a little one?—and my life will be saved!”
21 He said to him, “Very well, I grant you this favor
too, and will not overthrow the city of which you
have spoken. 22 Hurry, escape there, for I can do
nothing until you arrive there.” Therefore the city
was called Zoar.[b] 23 The sun had risen on the earth
when Lot came to Zoar.

24 Then the LORD rained on Sodom and
Gomorrah sulfur and fire from the LORD out of
heaven; 25 and he overthrew those cities, and all
the Plain, and all the inhabitants of the cities,
and what grew on the ground. 26 But Lot’s wife,
behind him, looked back, and she became a pillar
of salt.

27 Abraham went early in the morning to the
place where he had stood before the LORD; 28 and
he looked down toward Sodom and Gomorrah
and toward all the land of the Plain and saw the
smoke of the land going up like the smoke of a
furnace.

29 So it was that, when God destroyed the
cities of the Plain, God remembered Abraham,
and sent Lot out of the midst of the overthrow,
when he overthrew the cities in which Lot had
settled.

30 Now Lot went up out of Zoar and settled
in the hills with his two daughters, for he was
afraid to stay in Zoar; so he lived in a cave with
his two daughters. 31 And the firstborn said to
the younger, “Our father is old, and there is not
a man on earth to come in to us after the manner
of all the world. 32 Come, let us make our father
drink wine, and we will lie with him, so that we
may preserve offspring through our father.” 33 So
they made their father drink wine that night; and
the firstborn went in, and lay with her father; he
did not know when she lay down or when she
rose. 34 On the next day, the firstborn said to the
younger, “Look, I lay last night with my father; let
us make him drink wine tonight also; then you go
in and lie with him, so that we may preserve offspring through our father.” 35 So they made their
father drink wine that night also; and the younger
rose, and lay with him; and he did not know when
she lay down or when she rose. 36 Thus both the
daughters of Lot became pregnant by their father. 37 The firstborn bore a son, and named him
Moab; he is the ancestor of the Moabites to this
day. 38 The younger also bore a son and named
him Ben-ammi; he is the ancestor of the Ammonites to this day.

20 From there Abraham journeyed toward
the region of the Negeb, and settled between Kadesh and Shur. While residing in Gerar
as an alien, 2 Abraham said of his wife Sarah, “She
is my sister.” And King Abimelech of Gerar sent
and took Sarah. 3 But God came to Abimelech
in a dream by night, and said to him, “You are
about to die because of the woman whom you
have taken; for she is a married woman.” 4 Now
Abimelech had not approached her; so he said,
“Lord, will you destroy an innocent people? 5 Did
he not himself say to me, ‘She is my sister’? And
she herself said, ‘He is my brother.’ I did this in
the integrity of my heart and the innocence of my
hands.” 6 Then God said to him in the dream, “Yes,
I know that you did this in the integrity of your
heart; furthermore it was I who kept you from
sinning against me. Therefore I did not let you
touch her. 7 Now then, return the man’s wife; for
he is a prophet, and he will pray for you and you
shall live. But if you do not restore her, know that
you shall surely die, you and all that are yours.”

[a] Gk Syr Vg: Heb *he* [b] That is *Little*

8 So Abimelech rose early in the morning, and called all his servants and told them all
these things; and the men were very much afraid.
9 Then Abimelech called Abraham, and said to
him, "What have you done to us? How have I
sinned against you, that you have brought such
great guilt on me and my kingdom? You have
done things to me that ought not to be done."
10 And Abimelech said to Abraham, "What were
you thinking of, that you did this thing?" 11 Abraham said, "I did it because I thought, There is no
fear of God at all in this place, and they will kill
me because of my wife. 12 Besides, she is indeed
my sister, the daughter of my father but not the
daughter of my mother; and she became my wife.
13 And when God caused me to wander from my
father's house, I said to her, 'This is the kindness
you must do me: at every place to which we come,
say of me, He is my brother.'" 14 Then Abimelech
took sheep and oxen, and male and female slaves,
and gave them to Abraham, and restored his wife
Sarah to him. 15 Abimelech said, "My land is before you; settle where it pleases you." 16 To Sarah
he said, "Look, I have given your brother a thousand pieces of silver; it is your exoneration before
all who are with you; you are completely vindicated." 17 Then Abraham prayed to God; and God
healed Abimelech, and also healed his wife and
female slaves so that they bore children. 18 For the
LORD had closed fast all the wombs of the house
of Abimelech because of Sarah, Abraham's wife.

21 The LORD dealt with Sarah as he had said,
and the LORD did for Sarah as he had
promised. 2 Sarah conceived and bore Abraham a
son in his old age, at the time of which God had
spoken to him. 3 Abraham gave the name Isaac to
his son whom Sarah bore him. 4 And Abraham
circumcised his son Isaac when he was eight days
old, as God had commanded him. 5 Abraham was
a hundred years old when his son Isaac was born
to him. 6 Now Sarah said, "God has brought laughter for me; everyone who hears will laugh with
me." 7 And she said, "Who would ever have said
to Abraham that Sarah would nurse children? Yet
I have borne him a son in his old age."

8 The child grew, and was weaned; and Abraham made a great feast on the day that Isaac was
weaned. 9 But Sarah saw the son of Hagar the
Egyptian, whom she had borne to Abraham,
playing with her son Isaac.[a] 10 So she said to Abraham, "Cast out this slave woman with her son;
for the son of this slave woman shall not inherit
along with my son Isaac." 11 The matter was very
distressing to Abraham on account of his son.
12 But God said to Abraham, "Do not be distressed because of the boy and because of your
slave woman; whatever Sarah says to you, do as
she tells you, for it is through Isaac that offspring
shall be named for you. 13 As for the son of the
slave woman, I will make a nation of him also,
because he is your offspring." 14 So Abraham rose
early in the morning, and took bread and a skin
of water, and gave it to Hagar, putting it on her
shoulder, along with the child, and sent her away.
And she departed, and wandered about in the
wilderness of Beer-sheba.

15 When the water in the skin was gone, she
cast the child under one of the bushes. 16 Then she
went and sat down opposite him a good way off,
about the distance of a bowshot; for she said, "Do
not let me look on the death of the child." And as
she sat opposite him, she lifted up her voice and
wept. 17 And God heard the voice of the boy; and
the angel of God called to Hagar from heaven,
and said to her, "What troubles you, Hagar? Do
not be afraid; for God has heard the voice of the
boy where he is. 18 Come, lift up the boy and hold
him fast with your hand, for I will make a great
nation of him." 19 Then God opened her eyes and
she saw a well of water. She went, and filled the
skin with water, and gave the boy a drink.

20 God was with the boy, and he grew up;
he lived in the wilderness, and became an expert
with the bow. 21 He lived in the wilderness of
Paran; and his mother got a wife for him from the
land of Egypt.

22 At that time Abimelech, with Phicol the
commander of his army, said to Abraham, "God
is with you in all that you do; 23 now therefore
swear to me here by God that you will not deal

[a] Gk Vg: Heb lacks *with her son Isaac*

falsely with me or with my offspring or with my
posterity, but as I have dealt loyally with you, you
will deal with me and with the land where you
have resided as an alien." 24 And Abraham said, "I
swear it."

25 When Abraham complained to Abimelech
about a well of water that Abimelech's servants
had seized, 26 Abimelech said, "I do not know who
has done this; you did not tell me, and I have not
heard of it until today." 27 So Abraham took sheep
and oxen and gave them to Abimelech, and the
two men made a covenant. 28 Abraham set apart
seven ewe lambs of the flock. 29 And Abimelech
said to Abraham, "What is the meaning of these
seven ewe lambs that you have set apart?" 30 He
said, "These seven ewe lambs you shall accept
from my hand, in order that you may be a witness for me that I dug this well." 31 Therefore that
place was called Beer-sheba;[a] because there both
of them swore an oath. 32 When they had made a
covenant at Beer-sheba, Abimelech, with Phicol
the commander of his army, left and returned to
the land of the Philistines. 33 Abraham[b] planted
a tamarisk tree in Beer-sheba, and called there
on the name of the LORD, the Everlasting God.[c]
34 And Abraham resided as an alien many days in
the land of the Philistines.

22 After these things God tested Abraham.
He said to him, "Abraham!" And he said,
"Here I am." 2 He said, "Take your son, your only
son Isaac, whom you love, and go to the land of
Moriah, and offer him there as a burnt offering
on one of the mountains that I shall show you."
3 So Abraham rose early in the morning, saddled
his donkey, and took two of his young men with
him, and his son Isaac; he cut the wood for the
burnt offering, and set out and went to the place
in the distance that God had shown him. 4 On the
third day Abraham looked up and saw the place
far away. 5 Then Abraham said to his young men,
"Stay here with the donkey; the boy and I will
go over there; we will worship, and then we will
come back to you." 6 Abraham took the wood of
the burnt offering and laid it on his son Isaac, and
he himself carried the fire and the knife. So the
two of them walked on together. 7 Isaac said to his
father Abraham, "Father!" And he said, "Here I
am, my son." He said, "The fire and the wood are
here, but where is the lamb for a burnt offering?"
8 Abraham said, "God himself will provide the
lamb for a burnt offering, my son." So the two of
them walked on together.

Genesis 22:1-19

The Binding of Isaac, in Hebrew, the *Akedah*, serves as a textual monument for both Jewish and Christian communities, attesting to the obedience and faithfulness of Israel's ancestors. There is a great deal of pathos in this story, centered in God's troubling command for Abraham to sacrifice his son and in the father's apparent willingness to carry out the act. Reading the story in a positive light requires regarding God's providence of an alternative sacrifice (22:8, 13-14) as an acceptable resolution to the story. In the Qur'an, the chosen child is not Isaac but Ishmael, and in Islamic traditions, Ishmael's obedience to the divine command parallels Abraham's. In the Hebrew Bible, the Isaac/Ishmael traditions conclude with the two brothers reuniting to bury their common father together (25:9).

— FY

9 When they came to the place that God had
shown him, Abraham built an altar there and laid
the wood in order. He bound his son Isaac, and
laid him on the altar, on top of the wood. 10 Then
Abraham reached out his hand and took the
knife to kill[d] his son. 11 But the angel of the LORD
called to him from heaven, and said, "Abraham,
Abraham!" And he said, "Here I am." 12 He said,
"Do not lay your hand on the boy or do anything to him; for now I know that you fear God,
since you have not withheld your son, your only
son, from me." 13 And Abraham looked up and
saw a ram, caught in a thicket by its horns.
Abraham went and took the ram and offered it
up as a burnt offering instead of his son. 14 So
Abraham called that place "The LORD will

[a] That is *Well of seven* or *Well of the oath* [b] Heb *He* [c] Or *the LORD, El Olam* [d] Or *to slaughter*

provide";[a] as it is said to this day, "On the mount
of the LORD it shall be provided."[b]
15 The angel of the LORD called to Abraham
a second time from heaven, 16and said, "By myself I have sworn, says the LORD: Because you
have done this, and have not withheld your son,
your only son, 17I will indeed bless you, and I will
make your offspring as numerous as the stars of
heaven and as the sand that is on the seashore.
And your offspring shall possess the gate of their
enemies, 18and by your offspring shall all the nations of the earth gain blessing for themselves, because you have obeyed my voice." 19So Abraham
returned to his young men, and they arose and
went together to Beer-sheba; and Abraham lived
at Beer-sheba.
20 Now after these things it was told Abraham, "Milcah also has borne children, to your
brother Nahor: 21Uz the firstborn, Buz his brother,
Kemuel the father of Aram, 22Chesed, Hazo, Pil-
dash, Jidlaph, and Bethuel." 23Bethuel became
the father of Rebekah. These eight Milcah bore to
Nahor, Abraham's brother. 24Moreover, his concubine, whose name was Reumah, bore Tebah,
Gaham, Tahash, and Maacah.
23 Sarah lived one hundred twenty-seven
years; this was the length of Sarah's
life. 2And Sarah died at Kiriath-arba (that is,
Hebron) in the land of Canaan; and Abraham
went in to mourn for Sarah and to weep for
her. 3Abraham rose up from beside his dead,
and said to the Hittites, 4"I am a stranger and
an alien residing among you; give me property
among you for a burying place, so that I may
bury my dead out of my sight." 5The Hittites answered Abraham, 6"Hear us, my lord; you are a
mighty prince among us. Bury your dead in the
choicest of our burial places; none of us will
withhold from you any burial ground for burying your dead." 7Abraham rose and bowed to
the Hittites, the people of the land. 8He said to
them, "If you are willing that I should bury my
dead out of my sight, hear me, and entreat for
me Ephron son of Zohar, 9so that he may give
me the cave of Machpelah, which he owns; it is
at the end of his field. For the full price let him
give it to me in your presence as a possession
for a burying place." 10Now Ephron was sitting
among the Hittites; and Ephron the Hittite answered Abraham in the hearing of the Hittites,
of all who went in at the gate of his city, 11"No,
my lord, hear me; I give you the field, and I give
you the cave that is in it; in the presence of my
people I give it to you; bury your dead." 12Then
Abraham bowed down before the people of the
land. 13He said to Ephron in the hearing of the
people of the land, "If you only will listen to me!
I will give the price of the field; accept it from
me, so that I may bury my dead there." 14Ephron
answered Abraham, 15"My lord, listen to me;
a piece of land worth four hundred shekels of
silver—what is that between you and me? Bury
your dead." 16Abraham agreed with Ephron;
and Abraham weighed out for Ephron the silver
that he had named in the hearing of the Hittites,
four hundred shekels of silver, according to the
weights current among the merchants.
17 So the field of Ephron in Machpelah,
which was to the east of Mamre, the field with the
cave that was in it and all the trees that were in
the field, throughout its whole area, passed 18to
Abraham as a possession in the presence of the
Hittites, in the presence of all who went in at the
gate of his city. 19After this, Abraham buried Sarah
his wife in the cave of the field of Machpelah facing Mamre (that is, Hebron) in the land of Canaan. 20The field and the cave that is in it passed
from the Hittites into Abraham's possession as a
burying place.
24 Now Abraham was old, well advanced in
years; and the LORD had blessed Abraham in all things. 2Abraham said to his servant,
the oldest of his house, who had charge of all that
he had, "Put your hand under my thigh 3and I will
make you swear by the LORD, the God of heaven
and earth, that you will not get a wife for my son
from the daughters of the Canaanites, among
whom I live, 4but will go to my country and to my
kindred and get a wife for my son Isaac." 5The servant said to him, "Perhaps the woman may not be

[a] Or *will see;* Heb traditionally transliterated *Jehovah Jireh* [b] Or *he shall be seen*

Genesis 24

Rebekah's family of origin is matriarchal, countering the notion that patriarchy was universal in biblical Israel. Some of the characteristics of her family are that her father, Bethuel, is identified as the son of his mother, Milcah, in verse 24, and the family home is described as belonging to Rebekah's mother in verse 28. It is also noteworthy that when Rebekah agrees to marry in verse 58, the choice is hers. Later, in 29:12, Rebekah's son also identifies himself as the son of his mother, not his father.

— *WG*

willing to follow me to this land; must I then take your son back to the land from which you came?" 6Abraham said to him, "See to it that you do not take my son back there. 7The Lord, the God of heaven, who took me from my father's house and from the land of my birth, and who spoke to me and swore to me, 'To your offspring I will give this land,' he will send his angel before you, and you shall take a wife for my son from there. 8But if the woman is not willing to follow you, then you will be free from this oath of mine; only you must not take my son back there." 9So the servant put his hand under the thigh of Abraham his master and swore to him concerning this matter.

10 Then the servant took ten of his master's camels and departed, taking all kinds of choice gifts from his master; and he set out and went to Aram-naharaim, to the city of Nahor. 11He made the camels kneel down outside the city by the well of water; it was toward evening, the time when women go out to draw water. 12And he said, "O Lord, God of my master Abraham, please grant me success today and show steadfast love to my master Abraham. 13I am standing here by the spring of water, and the daughters of the townspeople are coming out to draw water. 14Let the girl to whom I shall say, 'Please offer your jar that I may drink,' and who shall say, 'Drink, and I will water your camels'—let her be the one whom you have appointed for your servant Isaac. By this I shall know that you have shown steadfast love to my master."

15 Before he had finished speaking, there was Rebekah, who was born to Bethuel son of Milcah, the wife of Nahor, Abraham's brother, coming out with her water jar on her shoulder. 16The girl was very fair to look upon, a virgin, whom no man had known. She went down to the spring, filled her jar, and came up. 17Then the servant ran to meet her and said, "Please let me sip a little water from your jar." 18"Drink, my lord," she said, and quickly lowered her jar upon her hand and gave him a drink. 19When she had finished giving him a drink, she said, "I will draw for your camels also, until they have finished drinking." 20So she quickly emptied her jar into the trough and ran again to the well to draw, and she drew for all his camels. 21The man gazed at her in silence to learn whether or not the Lord had made his journey successful.

22 When the camels had finished drinking, the man took a gold nose-ring weighing a half shekel, and two bracelets for her arms weighing ten gold shekels, 23and said, "Tell me whose daughter you are. Is there room in your father's house for us to spend the night?" 24She said to him, "I am the daughter of Bethuel son of Milcah, whom she bore to Nahor." 25She added, "We have plenty of straw and fodder and a place to spend the night." 26The man bowed his head and worshiped the Lord 27and said, "Blessed be the Lord, the God of my master Abraham, who has not forsaken his steadfast love and his faithfulness toward my master. As for me, the Lord has led me on the way to the house of my master's kin."

28 Then the girl ran and told her mother's household about these things. 29Rebekah had a brother whose name was Laban; and Laban ran out to the man, to the spring. 30As soon as he had seen the nose-ring, and the bracelets on his sister's arms, and when he heard the words of his sister Rebekah, "Thus the man spoke to me," he went to the man; and there he was, standing by the camels at the spring. 31He said, "Come in, O blessed of the Lord. Why do you stand outside when I have prepared the house and a place for the camels?" 32So the man came into the

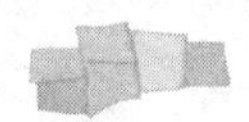

house; and Laban unloaded the camels, and gave
him straw and fodder for the camels, and water to
wash his feet and the feet of the men who were
with him. 33 Then food was set before him to eat;
but he said, "I will not eat until I have told my er-
rand." He said, "Speak on."

34 So he said, "I am Abraham's servant. 35 The
LORD has greatly blessed my master, and he has
become wealthy; he has given him flocks and
herds, silver and gold, male and female slaves,
camels and donkeys. 36 And Sarah my master's
wife bore a son to my master when she was old;
and he has given him all that he has. 37 My master
made me swear, saying, 'You shall not take a wife
for my son from the daughters of the Canaanites,
in whose land I live; 38 but you shall go to my father's house, to my kindred, and get a wife for my
son.' 39 I said to my master, 'Perhaps the woman
will not follow me.' 40 But he said to me, 'The
LORD, before whom I walk, will send his angel
with you and make your way successful. You
shall get a wife for my son from my kindred, from
my father's house. 41 Then you will be free from
my oath, when you come to my kindred; even if
they will not give her to you, you will be free from
my oath.'

42 "I came today to the spring, and said,
'O LORD, the God of my master Abraham, if now
you will only make successful the way I am going! 43 I am standing here by the spring of water;
let the young woman who comes out to draw, to
whom I shall say, "Please give me a little water
from your jar to drink," 44 and who will say to me,
"Drink, and I will draw for your camels also"—let
her be the woman whom the LORD has appointed
for my master's son.'

45 "Before I had finished speaking in my
heart, there was Rebekah coming out with her
water jar on her shoulder; and she went down to
the spring, and drew. I said to her, 'Please let me
drink.' 46 She quickly let down her jar from her
shoulder, and said, 'Drink, and I will also water
your camels.' So I drank, and she also watered the
camels. 47 Then I asked her, 'Whose daughter are
you?' She said, 'The daughter of Bethuel, Nahor's
son, whom Milcah bore to him.' So I put the ring
on her nose, and the bracelets on her arms. 48 Then
I bowed my head and worshiped the LORD, and
blessed the LORD, the God of my master Abraham, who had led me by the right way to obtain
the daughter of my master's kinsman for his son.
49 Now then, if you will deal loyally and truly with
my master, tell me; and if not, tell me, so that I
may turn either to the right hand or to the left."

50 Then Laban and Bethuel answered, "The
thing comes from the LORD; we cannot speak to
you anything bad or good. 51 Look, Rebekah is before you, take her and go, and let her be the wife
of your master's son, as the LORD has spoken."

52 When Abraham's servant heard their
words, he bowed himself to the ground before
the LORD. 53 And the servant brought out jewelry
of silver and of gold, and garments, and gave them
to Rebekah; he also gave to her brother and to her
mother costly ornaments. 54 Then he and the men
who were with him ate and drank, and they spent
the night there. When they rose in the morning,
he said, "Send me back to my master." 55 Her
brother and her mother said, "Let the girl remain
with us a while, at least ten days; after that she
may go." 56 But he said to them, "Do not delay me,
since the LORD has made my journey successful;
let me go that I may go to my master." 57 They said,
"We will call the girl, and ask her." 58 And they
called Rebekah, and said to her, "Will you go with
this man?" She said, "I will." 59 So they sent away
their sister Rebekah and her nurse along with
Abraham's servant and his men. 60 And they
blessed Rebekah and said to her,

"May you, our sister, become
thousands of myriads;
may your offspring gain possession
of the gates of their foes."

61 Then Rebekah and her maids rose up, mounted
the camels, and followed the man; thus the servant took Rebekah, and went his way.

62 Now Isaac had come from[a] Beer-lahai-roi,
and was settled in the Negeb. 63 Isaac went out in
the evening to walk[b] in the field; and looking up,
he saw camels coming. 64 And Rebekah looked

[a] Syr Tg: Heb *from coming to* [b] Meaning of Heb word is uncertain

up, and when she saw Isaac, she slipped quickly from the camel, [65]and said to the servant, "Who is the man over there, walking in the field to meet us?" The servant said, "It is my master." So she took her veil and covered herself. [66]And the servant told Isaac all the things that he had done. [67]Then Isaac brought her into his mother Sarah's tent. He took Rebekah, and she became his wife; and he loved her. So Isaac was comforted after his mother's death.

25 Abraham took another wife, whose name was Keturah. [2]She bore him Zimran, Jokshan, Medan, Midian, Ishbak, and Shuah. [3]Jokshan was the father of Sheba and Dedan. The sons of Dedan were Asshurim, Letushim, and Leummim. [4]The sons of Midian were Ephah, Epher, Hanoch, Abida, and Eldaah. All these were the children of Keturah. [5]Abraham gave all he had to Isaac. [6]But to the sons of his concubines Abraham gave gifts, while he was still living, and he sent them away from his son Isaac, eastward to the east country.

7 This is the length of Abraham's life, one hundred seventy-five years. [8]Abraham breathed his last and died in a good old age, an old man and full of years, and was gathered to his people. [9]His sons Isaac and Ishmael buried him in the cave of Machpelah, in the field of Ephron son of Zohar the Hittite, east of Mamre, [10]the field that Abraham purchased from the Hittites. There Abraham was buried, with his wife Sarah. [11]After the death of Abraham God blessed his son Isaac. And Isaac settled at Beer-lahai-roi.

12 These are the descendants of Ishmael, Abraham's son, whom Hagar the Egyptian, Sarah's slave-girl, bore to Abraham. [13]These are the names of the sons of Ishmael, named in the order of their birth: Nebaioth, the firstborn of Ishmael; and Kedar, Adbeel, Mibsam, [14]Mishma, Dumah, Massa, [15]Hadad, Tema, Jetur, Naphish, and Kedemah. [16]These are the sons of Ishmael and these are their names, by their villages and by their encampments, twelve princes according to their tribes. [17](This is the length of the life of Ishmael, one hundred thirty-seven years; he breathed his last and died, and was gathered to his people.) [18]They settled from Havilah to Shur, which is opposite Egypt in the direction of Assyria; he settled down[a] alongside of[b] all his people.

19 These are the descendants of Isaac, Abraham's son: Abraham was the father of Isaac, [20]and Isaac was forty years old when he married Rebekah, daughter of Bethuel the Aramean of Paddan-aram, sister of Laban the Aramean. [21]Isaac prayed to the LORD for his wife, because she was barren; and the LORD granted his prayer, and his wife Rebekah conceived. [22]The children struggled together within her; and she said, "If it is to be this way, why do I live?"[c] So she went to inquire of the LORD. [23]And the LORD said to her,

"Two nations are in your womb,
  and two peoples born of you shall be divided;
the one shall be stronger than the other,
  the elder shall serve the younger."

[24]When her time to give birth was at hand, there were twins in her womb. [25]The first came out red, all his body like a hairy mantle; so they named him Esau. [26]Afterward his brother came out, with his hand gripping Esau's heel; so he was named Jacob.[d] Isaac was sixty years old when she bore them.

Genesis 25:1-6

Ancient Israelites had a two-tier marriage practice, consisting of primary and secondary wives. Abraham had three primary wives, Sarah, Hagar, and Keturah, and an unknown number of secondary wives, called concubines in verse 6. Concubinage—sexual access without relational responsibilities—does not adequately describe the latter form of marriage. The language in Judges 19, "husband" and "father-in-law," makes clear that this is a true marriage. Yet the story of Abraham and his wives demonstrates that children born in a secondary marriage are not entitled to an inheritance.

— WG

[a] Heb *he fell* [b] Or *down in opposition to* [c] Syr: Meaning of Heb uncertain [d] That is *He takes by the heel* or *He supplants*

27 When the boys grew up, Esau was a skillful
hunter, a man of the field, while Jacob was a quiet
man, living in tents. 28 Isaac loved Esau, because
he was fond of game; but Rebekah loved Jacob.
29 Once when Jacob was cooking a stew,
Esau came in from the field, and he was famished.
30 Esau said to Jacob, "Let me eat some of that red
stuff, for I am famished!" (Therefore he was called
Edom.[a]) 31 Jacob said, "First sell me your birthright." 32 Esau said, "I am about to die; of what use
is a birthright to me?" 33 Jacob said, "Swear to me
first."[b] So he swore to him, and sold his birthright
to Jacob. 34 Then Jacob gave Esau bread and lentil
stew, and he ate and drank, and rose and went his
way. Thus Esau despised his birthright.

26 Now there was a famine in the land, besides the former famine that had occurred
in the days of Abraham. And Isaac went to Gerar,
to King Abimelech of the Philistines. 2 The LORD
appeared to Isaac[c] and said, "Do not go down to
Egypt; settle in the land that I shall show you.
3 Reside in this land as an alien, and I will be with
you, and will bless you; for to you and to your descendants I will give all these lands, and I will fulfill the oath that I swore to your father Abraham.
4 I will make your offspring as numerous as the
stars of heaven, and will give to your offspring all
these lands; and all the nations of the earth shall
gain blessing for themselves through your offspring, 5 because Abraham obeyed my voice and
kept my charge, my commandments, my statutes,
and my laws."
6 So Isaac settled in Gerar. 7 When the men of
the place asked him about his wife, he said, "She
is my sister"; for he was afraid to say, "My wife,"
thinking, "or else the men of the place might kill
me for the sake of Rebekah, because she is attractive in appearance." 8 When Isaac had been there
a long time, King Abimelech of the Philistines
looked out of a window and saw him fondling his
wife Rebekah. 9 So Abimelech called for Isaac, and
said, "So she is your wife! Why then did you say,
'She is my sister'?" Isaac said to him, "Because I
thought I might die because of her." 10 Abimelech
said, "What is this you have done to us? One of
the people might easily have lain with your wife,
and you would have brought guilt upon us." 11 So
Abimelech warned all the people, saying, "Whoever touches this man or his wife shall be put to
death."
12 Isaac sowed seed in that land, and in the
same year reaped a hundredfold. The LORD
blessed him, 13 and the man became rich; he
prospered more and more until he became very
wealthy. 14 He had possessions of flocks and herds,
and a great household, so that the Philistines envied him. 15 (Now the Philistines had stopped up
and filled with earth all the wells that his father's
servants had dug in the days of his father Abraham.) 16 And Abimelech said to Isaac, "Go away
from us; you have become too powerful for us."
17 So Isaac departed from there and camped
in the valley of Gerar and settled there. 18 Isaac
dug again the wells of water that had been dug in
the days of his father Abraham; for the Philistines
had stopped them up after the death of Abraham;
and he gave them the names that his father had
given them. 19 But when Isaac's servants dug in
the valley and found there a well of spring water, 20 the herders of Gerar quarreled with Isaac's
herders, saying, "The water is ours." So he called
the well Esek,[d] because they contended with him.
21 Then they dug another well, and they quarreled
over that one also; so he called it Sitnah.[e] 22 He
moved from there and dug another well, and they
did not quarrel over it; so he called it Rehoboth,[f]
saying, "Now the LORD has made room for us,
and we shall be fruitful in the land."
23 From there he went up to Beer-sheba.
24 And that very night the LORD appeared to
him and said, "I am the God of your father Abraham; do not be afraid, for I am with you and will
bless you and make your offspring numerous for
my servant Abraham's sake." 25 So he built an altar there, called on the name of the LORD, and
pitched his tent there. And there Isaac's servants
dug a well.
26 Then Abimelech went to him from Gerar,

[a] That is *Red* [b] Heb *today* [c] Heb *him* [d] That is *Contention* [e] That is *Enmity* [f] That is *Broad places* or *Room*

with Ahuzzath his adviser and Phicol the commander of his army. 27 Isaac said to them, "Why have you come to me, seeing that you hate me and have sent me away from you?" 28 They said, "We see plainly that the LORD has been with you; so we say, let there be an oath between you and us, and let us make a covenant with you 29 so that you will do us no harm, just as we have not touched you and have done to you nothing but good and have sent you away in peace. You are now the blessed of the LORD." 30 So he made them a feast, and they ate and drank. 31 In the morning they rose early and exchanged oaths; and Isaac set them on their way, and they departed from him in peace. 32 That same day Isaac's servants came and told him about the well that they had dug, and said to him, "We have found water!" 33 He called it Shibah;[a] therefore the name of the city is Beer-sheba[b] to this day.

34 When Esau was forty years old, he married Judith daughter of Beeri the Hittite, and Basemath daughter of Elon the Hittite; 35 and they made life bitter for Isaac and Rebekah.

27 When Isaac was old and his eyes were dim so that he could not see, he called his elder son Esau and said to him, "My son"; and he answered, "Here I am." 2 He said, "See, I am old; I do not know the day of my death. 3 Now then, take your weapons, your quiver and your bow, and go out to the field, and hunt game for me. 4 Then prepare for me savory food, such as I like, and bring it to me to eat, so that I may bless you before I die."

5 Now Rebekah was listening when Isaac spoke to his son Esau. So when Esau went to the field to hunt for game and bring it, 6 Rebekah said to her son Jacob, "I heard your father say to your brother Esau, 7 'Bring me game, and prepare for me savory food to eat, that I may bless you before the LORD before I die.' 8 Now therefore, my son, obey my word as I command you. 9 Go to the flock, and get me two choice kids, so that I may prepare from them savory food for your father, such as he likes; 10 and you shall take it to your father to eat, so that he may bless you before he dies." 11 But Jacob said to his mother Rebekah, "Look, my brother Esau is a hairy man, and I am a man of smooth skin. 12 Perhaps my father will feel me, and I shall seem to be mocking him, and bring a curse on myself and not a blessing." 13 His mother said to him, "Let your curse be on me, my son; only obey my word, and go, get them for me." 14 So he went and got them and brought them to his mother; and his mother prepared savory food, such as his father loved. 15 Then Rebekah took the best garments of her elder son Esau, which were with her in the house, and put them on her younger son Jacob; 16 and she put the skins of the kids on his hands and on the smooth part of his neck. 17 Then she handed the savory food, and the bread that she had prepared, to her son Jacob.

18 So he went in to his father, and said, "My father"; and he said, "Here I am; who are you, my son?" 19 Jacob said to his father, "I am Esau your firstborn. I have done as you told me; now sit up and eat of my game, so that you may bless me." 20 But Isaac said to his son, "How is it that you have found it so quickly, my son?" He answered, "Because the LORD your God granted me success." 21 Then Isaac said to Jacob, "Come near, that I may feel you, my son, to know whether you are really my son Esau or not." 22 So Jacob went up to his father Isaac, who felt him and said, "The voice is Jacob's voice, but the hands are the hands of Esau." 23 He did not recognize him, because his hands were hairy like his brother Esau's hands; so he blessed him. 24 He said, "Are you really my son Esau?" He answered, "I am." 25 Then he said, "Bring it to me, that I may eat of my son's game and bless you." So he brought it to him, and he ate; and he brought him wine, and he drank. 26 Then his father Isaac said to him, "Come near and kiss me, my son." 27 So he came near and kissed him; and he smelled the smell of his garments, and blessed him, and said,

"Ah, the smell of my son
is like the smell of a field that the LORD
has blessed.
28 May God give you of the dew of heaven,
and of the fatness of the earth,

[a] A word resembling the word for *oath* [b] That is *Well of the oath* or *Well of seven*

and plenty of grain and wine.
29 Let peoples serve you,
and nations bow down to you.
Be lord over your brothers,
and may your mother's sons bow down to
you.
Cursed be everyone who curses you,
and blessed be everyone who blesses you!"

30 As soon as Isaac had finished blessing
Jacob, when Jacob had scarcely gone out from
the presence of his father Isaac, his brother Esau
came in from his hunting. 31 He also prepared
savory food, and brought it to his father. And he
said to his father, "Let my father sit up and eat of
his son's game, so that you may bless me." 32 His
father Isaac said to him, "Who are you?" He answered, "I am your firstborn son, Esau." 33 Then
Isaac trembled violently, and said, "Who was it
then that hunted game and brought it to me, and
I ate it all[a] before you came, and I have blessed
him?—yes, and blessed he shall be!" 34 When
Esau heard his father's words, he cried out with
an exceedingly great and bitter cry, and said to his
father, "Bless me, me also, father!" 35 But he said,
"Your brother came deceitfully, and he has taken
away your blessing." 36 Esau said, "Is he not rightly
named Jacob?[b] For he has supplanted me these
two times. He took away my birthright; and look,
now he has taken away my blessing." Then he
said, "Have you not reserved a blessing for me?"
37 Isaac answered Esau, "I have already made him
your lord, and I have given him all his brothers as
servants, and with grain and wine I have sustained
him. What then can I do for you, my son?" 38 Esau
said to his father, "Have you only one blessing,
father? Bless me, me also, father!" And Esau lifted
up his voice and wept.

39 Then his father Isaac answered him:
"See, away from[c] the fatness of the earth shall
your home be,
and away from[d] the dew of heaven on
high.
40 By your sword you shall live,
and you shall serve your brother;
but when you break loose,[e]
you shall break his yoke from your neck."

41 Now Esau hated Jacob because of the
blessing with which his father had blessed him,
and Esau said to himself, "The days of mourning
for my father are approaching; then I will kill my
brother Jacob." 42 But the words of her elder son
Esau were told to Rebekah; so she sent and called
her younger son Jacob and said to him, "Your
brother Esau is consoling himself by planning to
kill you. 43 Now therefore, my son, obey my voice;
flee at once to my brother Laban in Haran, 44 and
stay with him a while, until your brother's fury
turns away— 45 until your brother's anger against
you turns away, and he forgets what you have
done to him; then I will send, and bring you back
from there. Why should I lose both of you in
one day?"

46 Then Rebekah said to Isaac, "I am weary
of my life because of the Hittite women. If Jacob
marries one of the Hittite women such as these,
one of the women of the land, what good will my
life be to me?"

28 Then Isaac called Jacob and blessed him,
and charged him, "You shall not marry
one of the Canaanite women. 2 Go at once to
Paddan-aram to the house of Bethuel, your mother's father; and take as wife from there one of the
daughters of Laban, your mother's brother. 3 May
God Almighty[f] bless you and make you fruitful
and numerous, that you may become a company
of peoples. 4 May he give to you the blessing of
Abraham, to you and to your offspring with you,
so that you may take possession of the land where
you now live as an alien—land that God gave to
Abraham." 5 Thus Isaac sent Jacob away; and he
went to Paddan-aram, to Laban son of Bethuel
the Aramean, the brother of Rebekah, Jacob's and
Esau's mother.

6 Now Esau saw that Isaac had blessed Jacob
and sent him away to Paddan-aram to take a wife
from there, and that as he blessed him he charged
him, "You shall not marry one of the Canaanite
women," 7 and that Jacob had obeyed his father

[a] Cn: Heb *of all* [b] That is *He supplants* or *He takes by the heel* [c] Or *See, of* [d] Or *and of*
[e] Meaning of Heb uncertain [f] Traditional rendering of Heb *El Shaddai*

and his mother and gone to Paddan-aram. 8 So
when Esau saw that the Canaanite women did
not please his father Isaac, 9 Esau went to Ishmael
and took Mahalath daughter of Abraham's son
Ishmael, and sister of Nebaioth, to be his wife in
addition to the wives he had.

10 Jacob left Beer-sheba and went toward
Haran. 11 He came to a certain place and stayed
there for the night, because the sun had set. Taking one of the stones of the place, he put it under
his head and lay down in that place. 12 And he
dreamed that there was a ladder[a] set up on the
earth, the top of it reaching to heaven; and the
angels of God were ascending and descending
on it. 13 And the LORD stood beside him[b] and
said, "I am the LORD, the God of Abraham your
father and the God of Isaac; the land on which
you lie I will give to you and to your offspring;
14 and your offspring shall be like the dust of
the earth, and you shall spread abroad to the
west and to the east and to the north and to the
south; and all the families of the earth shall be
blessed[c] in you and in your offspring. 15 Know
that I am with you and will keep you wherever
you go, and will bring you back to this land;
for I will not leave you until I have done what
I have promised you." 16 Then Jacob woke from
his sleep and said, "Surely the LORD is in this
place—and I did not know it!" 17 And he was
afraid, and said, "How awesome is this place!
This is none other than the house of God, and
this is the gate of heaven."

18 So Jacob rose early in the morning, and
he took the stone that he had put under his head
and set it up for a pillar and poured oil on the
top of it. 19 He called that place Bethel;[d] but the
name of the city was Luz at the first. 20 Then Jacob made a vow, saying, "If God will be with me,
and will keep me in this way that I go, and will
give me bread to eat and clothing to wear, 21 so
that I come again to my father's house in peace,
then the LORD shall be my God, 22 and this stone,
which I have set up for a pillar, shall be God's
house; and of all that you give me I will surely
give one-tenth to you."

29 Then Jacob went on his journey, and came
to the land of the people of the east. 2 As
he looked, he saw a well in the field and three
flocks of sheep lying there beside it; for out of
that well the flocks were watered. The stone on
the well's mouth was large, 3 and when all the
flocks were gathered there, the shepherds would
roll the stone from the mouth of the well, and water the sheep, and put the stone back in its place
on the mouth of the well.

4 Jacob said to them, "My brothers, where
do you come from?" They said, "We are from
Haran." 5 He said to them, "Do you know Laban
son of Nahor?" They said, "We do." 6 He said to
them, "Is it well with him?" "Yes," they replied,
"and here is his daughter Rachel, coming with
the sheep." 7 He said, "Look, it is still broad daylight; it is not time for the animals to be gathered together. Water the sheep, and go, pasture
them." 8 But they said, "We cannot until all the
flocks are gathered together, and the stone is
rolled from the mouth of the well; then we water the sheep."

9 While he was still speaking with them, Rachel came with her father's sheep; for she kept
them. 10 Now when Jacob saw Rachel, the daughter of his mother's brother Laban, and the sheep
of his mother's brother Laban, Jacob went up
and rolled the stone from the well's mouth, and
watered the flock of his mother's brother Laban.
11 Then Jacob kissed Rachel, and wept aloud.
12 And Jacob told Rachel that he was her father's
kinsman, and that he was Rebekah's son; and she
ran and told her father.

13 When Laban heard the news about his sister's son Jacob, he ran to meet him; he embraced
him and kissed him, and brought him to his
house. Jacob[e] told Laban all these things, 14 and
Laban said to him, "Surely you are my bone and
my flesh!" And he stayed with him a month.

15 Then Laban said to Jacob, "Because you
are my kinsman, should you therefore serve me
for nothing? Tell me, what shall your wages be?"
16 Now Laban had two daughters; the name of the
elder was Leah, and the name of the younger was

[a] Or *stairway* or *ramp* [b] Or *stood above it* [c] Or *shall bless themselves* [d] That is *House of God* [e] Heb *He*

Rachel. 17 Leah's eyes were lovely,[a] and Rachel was graceful and beautiful. 18 Jacob loved Rachel; so he said, "I will serve you seven years for your younger daughter Rachel." 19 Laban said, "It is better that I give her to you than that I should give her to any other man; stay with me." 20 So Jacob served seven years for Rachel, and they seemed to him but a few days because of the love he had for her.

21 Then Jacob said to Laban, "Give me my wife that I may go in to her, for my time is completed." 22 So Laban gathered together all the people of the place, and made a feast. 23 But in the evening he took his daughter Leah and brought her to Jacob; and he went in to her. 24 (Laban gave his maid Zilpah to his daughter Leah to be her maid.) 25 When morning came, it was Leah! And Jacob said to Laban, "What is this you have done to me? Did I not serve with you for Rachel? Why then have you deceived me?" 26 Laban said, "This is not done in our country—giving the younger before the firstborn. 27 Complete the week of this one, and we will give you the other also in return for serving me another seven years." 28 Jacob did so, and completed her week; then Laban gave him his daughter Rachel as a wife. 29 (Laban gave his maid Bilhah to his daughter Rachel to be her maid.) 30 So Jacob went in to Rachel also, and he loved Rachel more than Leah. He served Laban[b] for another seven years.

31 When the LORD saw that Leah was unloved, he opened her womb; but Rachel was barren. 32 Leah conceived and bore a son, and she named him Reuben;[c] for she said, "Because the LORD has looked on my affliction; surely now my husband will love me." 33 She conceived again and bore a son, and said, "Because the LORD has heard[d] that I am hated, he has given me this son also"; and she named him Simeon. 34 Again she conceived and bore a son, and said, "Now this time my husband will be joined[e] to me, because I have borne him three sons"; therefore he was named Levi. 35 She conceived again and bore a son, and said, "This time I will praise[f] the LORD"; therefore she named him Judah; then she ceased bearing.

30 When Rachel saw that she bore Jacob no children, she envied her sister; and she said to Jacob, "Give me children, or I shall die!" 2 Jacob became very angry with Rachel and said, "Am I in the place of God, who has withheld from you the fruit of the womb?" 3 Then she said, "Here is my maid Bilhah; go in to her, that she may bear upon my knees and that I too may have children through her." 4 So she gave him her maid Bilhah as a wife; and Jacob went in to her. 5 And Bilhah conceived and bore Jacob a son. 6 Then Rachel said, "God has judged me, and has also heard my voice and given me a son"; therefore she named him Dan.[g] 7 Rachel's maid Bilhah conceived again and bore Jacob a second son. 8 Then Rachel said, "With mighty wrestlings I have wrestled[h] with my sister, and have prevailed"; so she named him Naphtali.

9 When Leah saw that she had ceased bearing children, she took her maid Zilpah and gave her to Jacob as a wife. 10 Then Leah's maid Zilpah bore Jacob a son. 11 And Leah said, "Good fortune!" so she named him Gad.[i] 12 Leah's maid Zilpah bore Jacob a second son. 13 And Leah said, "Happy am I! For the women will call me happy"; so she named him Asher.[j]

14 In the days of wheat harvest Reuben went and found mandrakes in the field, and brought them to his mother Leah. Then Rachel said to Leah, "Please give me some of your son's mandrakes." 15 But she said to her, "Is it a small matter that you have taken away my husband? Would you take away my son's mandrakes also?" Rachel said, "Then he may lie with you tonight for your son's mandrakes." 16 When Jacob came from the field in the evening, Leah went out to meet him, and said, "You must come in to me; for I have hired you with my son's mandrakes." So he lay with her that night. 17 And God heeded Leah, and she conceived and bore Jacob a fifth son. 18 Leah said, "God has given me my hire[k] because I gave my maid to my husband"; so she named him Issachar.

[a] Meaning of Heb uncertain [b] Heb *him* [c] That is *See, a son* [d] Heb *shama* [e] Heb *lawah* [f] Heb *hodah*
[g] That is *He judged* [h] Heb *niphtal* [i] That is *Fortune* [j] That is *Happy* [k] Heb *sakar*

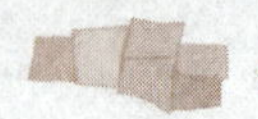

19And Leah conceived again, and she bore Jacob a sixth son. 20Then Leah said, "God has endowed me with a good dowry; now my husband will honor[a] me, because I have borne him six sons"; so she named him Zebulun. 21Afterwards she bore a daughter, and named her Dinah.

22 Then God remembered Rachel, and God heeded her and opened her womb. 23She conceived and bore a son, and said, "God has taken away my reproach"; 24and she named him Joseph,[b] saying, "May the LORD add to me another son!"

25 When Rachel had borne Joseph, Jacob said to Laban, "Send me away, that I may go to my own home and country. 26Give me my wives and my children for whom I have served you, and let me go; for you know very well the service I have given you." 27But Laban said to him, "If you will allow me to say so, I have learned by divination that the LORD has blessed me because of you; 28name your wages, and I will give it." 29Jacob said to him, "You yourself know how I have served you, and how your cattle have fared with me. 30For you had little before I came, and it has increased abundantly; and the LORD has blessed you wherever I turned. But now when shall I provide for my own household also?" 31He said, "What shall I give you?" Jacob said, "You shall not give me anything; if you will do this for me, I will again feed your flock and keep it: 32let me pass through all your flock today, removing from it every speckled and spotted sheep and every black lamb, and the spotted and speckled among the goats; and such shall be my wages. 33So my honesty will answer for me later, when you come to look into my wages with you. Every one that is not speckled and spotted among the goats and black among the lambs, if found with me, shall be counted stolen." 34Laban said, "Good! Let it be as you have said." 35But that day Laban removed the male goats that were striped and spotted, and all the female goats that were speckled and spotted, every one that had white on it, and every lamb that was black, and put them in charge of his sons; 36and he set a distance of three days' journey between himself and Jacob, while Jacob was pasturing the rest of Laban's flock.

37 Then Jacob took fresh rods of poplar and almond and plane, and peeled white streaks in them, exposing the white of the rods. 38He set the rods that he had peeled in front of the flocks in the troughs, that is, the watering places, where the flocks came to drink. And since they bred when they came to drink, 39the flocks bred in front of the rods, and so the flocks produced young that were striped, speckled, and spotted. 40Jacob separated the lambs, and set the faces of the flocks toward the striped and the completely black animals in the flock of Laban; and he put his own droves apart, and did not put them with Laban's flock. 41Whenever the stronger of the flock were breeding, Jacob laid the rods in the troughs before the eyes of the flock, that they might breed among the rods, 42but for the feebler of the flock he did not lay them there; so the feebler were Laban's, and the stronger Jacob's. 43Thus the man grew exceedingly rich, and had large flocks, and male and female slaves, and camels and donkeys.

31 Now Jacob heard that the sons of Laban were saying, "Jacob has taken all that was our father's; he has gained all this wealth from what belonged to our father." 2And Jacob saw that Laban did not regard him as favorably as he did before. 3Then the LORD said to Jacob, "Return to the land of your ancestors and to your kindred, and I will be with you." 4So Jacob sent and called Rachel and Leah into the field where his flock was, 5and said to them, "I see that your father does not regard me as favorably as he did before. But the God of my father has been with me. 6You know that I have served your father with all my strength; 7yet your father has cheated me and changed my wages ten times, but God did not permit him to harm me. 8If he said, 'The speckled shall be your wages,' then all the flock bore speckled; and if he said, 'The striped shall be your wages,' then all the flock bore striped. 9Thus God has taken away the livestock of your father, and given them to me.

10 "During the mating of the flock I once

[a] Heb *zabal* [b] That is *He adds*

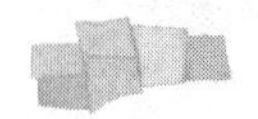

had a dream in which I looked up and saw that
the male goats that leaped upon the flock were
striped, speckled, and mottled. 11Then the angel
of God said to me in the dream, 'Jacob,' and I said,
'Here I am!' 12And he said, 'Look up and see that
all the goats that leap on the flock are striped,
speckled, and mottled; for I have seen all that
Laban is doing to you. 13I am the God of Bethel,[a]
where you anointed a pillar and made a vow to
me. Now leave this land at once and return to the
land of your birth.'" 14Then Rachel and Leah answered him, "Is there any portion or inheritance
left to us in our father's house? 15Are we not regarded by him as foreigners? For he has sold us,
and he has been using up the money given for us.
16All the property that God has taken away from
our father belongs to us and to our children; now
then, do whatever God has said to you."

17 So Jacob arose, and set his children and
his wives on camels; 18and he drove away all his
livestock, all the property that he had gained, the
livestock in his possession that he had acquired in
Paddan-aram, to go to his father Isaac in the land
of Canaan.

19 Now Laban had gone to shear his sheep,
and Rachel stole her father's household gods.
20And Jacob deceived Laban the Aramean, in
that he did not tell him that he intended to flee.
21So he fled with all that he had; starting out he
crossed the Euphrates,[b] and set his face toward
the hill country of Gilead.

22 On the third day Laban was told that Jacob had fled. 23So he took his kinsfolk with him
and pursued him for seven days until he caught
up with him in the hill country of Gilead. 24But
God came to Laban the Aramean in a dream by
night, and said to him, "Take heed that you say
not a word to Jacob, either good or bad."

25 Laban overtook Jacob. Now Jacob had
pitched his tent in the hill country, and Laban
with his kinsfolk camped in the hill country of
Gilead. 26Laban said to Jacob, "What have you
done? You have deceived me, and carried away
my daughters like captives of the sword. 27Why
did you flee secretly and deceive me and not tell
me? I would have sent you away with mirth and
songs, with tambourine and lyre. 28And why did
you not permit me to kiss my sons and my daughters farewell? What you have done is foolish. 29It
is in my power to do you harm; but the God of
your father spoke to me last night, saying, 'Take
heed that you speak to Jacob neither good nor
bad.' 30Even though you had to go because you
longed greatly for your father's house, why did
you steal my gods?" 31Jacob answered Laban, "Because I was afraid, for I thought that you would
take your daughters from me by force. 32But anyone with whom you find your gods shall not live.
In the presence of our kinsfolk, point out what I
have that is yours, and take it." Now Jacob did not
know that Rachel had stolen the gods.[c]

33 So Laban went into Jacob's tent, and into
Leah's tent, and into the tent of the two maids,
but he did not find them. And he went out of
Leah's tent, and entered Rachel's. 34Now Rachel
had taken the household gods and put them in
the camel's saddle, and sat on them. Laban felt all
about in the tent, but did not find them. 35And
she said to her father, "Let not my lord be angry that I cannot rise before you, for the way of
women is upon me." So he searched, but did not
find the household gods.

36 Then Jacob became angry, and upbraided
Laban. Jacob said to Laban, "What is my offense?
What is my sin, that you have hotly pursued me?
37Although you have felt about through all my
goods, what have you found of all your household goods? Set it here before my kinsfolk and
your kinsfolk, so that they may decide between
us two. 38These twenty years I have been with
you; your ewes and your female goats have not
miscarried, and I have not eaten the rams of your
flocks. 39That which was torn by wild beasts I did
not bring to you; I bore the loss of it myself; of
my hand you required it, whether stolen by day
or stolen by night. 40It was like this with me:
by day the heat consumed me, and the cold by
night, and my sleep fled from my eyes. 41These
twenty years I have been in your house; I served
you fourteen years for your two daughters, and

[a] Cn: Meaning of Heb uncertain [b] Heb *the river* [c] Heb *them*

six years for your flock, and you have changed
my wages ten times. 42 If the God of my father,
the God of Abraham and the Fear[a] of Isaac, had
not been on my side, surely now you would have
sent me away empty-handed. God saw my affliction and the labor of my hands, and rebuked you
last night."

43 Then Laban answered and said to Jacob,
"The daughters are my daughters, the children
are my children, the flocks are my flocks, and
all that you see is mine. But what can I do today
about these daughters of mine, or about their
children whom they have borne? 44 Come now,
let us make a covenant, you and I; and let it be
a witness between you and me." 45 So Jacob took
a stone, and set it up as a pillar. 46 And Jacob said
to his kinsfolk, "Gather stones," and they took
stones, and made a heap; and they ate there by
the heap. 47 Laban called it Jegar-sahadutha:[b] but
Jacob called it Galeed.[c] 48 Laban said, "This heap
is a witness between you and me today." Therefore he called it Galeed, 49 and the pillar[d] Mizpah,[e]
for he said, "The LORD watch between you and
me, when we are absent one from the other. 50 If
you ill-treat my daughters, or if you take wives in
addition to my daughters, though no one else is
with us, remember that God is witness between
you and me."

51 Then Laban said to Jacob, "See this heap
and see the pillar, which I have set between you
and me. 52 This heap is a witness, and the pillar
is a witness, that I will not pass beyond this heap
to you, and you will not pass beyond this heap
and this pillar to me, for harm. 53 May the God
of Abraham and the God of Nahor"—the God of
their father—"judge between us." So Jacob swore
by the Fear[a] of his father Isaac, 54 and Jacob offered a sacrifice on the height and called his kinsfolk to eat bread; and they ate bread and tarried
all night in the hill country.

55[f] Early in the morning Laban rose up, and
kissed his grandchildren and his daughters and
blessed them; then he departed and returned
home.

32 Jacob went on his way and the angels of
God met him; 2 and when Jacob saw them
he said, "This is God's camp!" So he called that
place Mahanaim.[g]

3 Jacob sent messengers before him to his
brother Esau in the land of Seir, the country of
Edom, 4 instructing them, "Thus you shall say to
my lord Esau: Thus says your servant Jacob, 'I
have lived with Laban as an alien, and stayed until
now; 5 and I have oxen, donkeys, flocks, male and
female slaves; and I have sent to tell my lord, in
order that I may find favor in your sight.'"

6 The messengers returned to Jacob, saying,
"We came to your brother Esau, and he is coming to meet you, and four hundred men are with
him." 7 Then Jacob was greatly afraid and distressed; and he divided the people that were with
him, and the flocks and herds and camels, into
two companies, 8 thinking, "If Esau comes to the
one company and destroys it, then the company
that is left will escape."

9 And Jacob said, "O God of my father Abraham and God of my father Isaac, O LORD who
said to me, 'Return to your country and to your
kindred, and I will do you good,' 10 I am not worthy of the least of all the steadfast love and all the
faithfulness that you have shown to your servant,
for with only my staff I crossed this Jordan; and
now I have become two companies. 11 Deliver
me, please, from the hand of my brother, from
the hand of Esau, for I am afraid of him; he may
come and kill us all, the mothers with the children. 12 Yet you have said, 'I will surely do you
good, and make your offspring as the sand of the
sea, which cannot be counted because of their
number.'"

13 So he spent that night there, and from
what he had with him he took a present for his
brother Esau, 14 two hundred female goats and
twenty male goats, two hundred ewes and twenty
rams, 15 thirty milch camels and their colts, forty
cows and ten bulls, twenty female donkeys and
ten male donkeys. 16 These he delivered into the
hand of his servants, every drove by itself, and

[a] Meaning of Heb uncertain [b] In Aramaic *The heap of witness* [c] In Hebrew *The heap of witness*
[d] Compare Sam: MT lacks *the pillar* [e] That is *Watchpost* [f] Ch 32.1 in Heb [g] Here taken to mean *Two camps*

said to his servants, "Pass on ahead of me, and
put a space between drove and drove." 17He instructed the foremost, "When Esau my brother
meets you, and asks you, 'To whom do you
belong? Where are you going? And whose are
these ahead of you?' 18then you shall say, 'They
belong to your servant Jacob; they are a present
sent to my lord Esau; and moreover he is behind
us.'" 19He likewise instructed the second and
the third and all who followed the droves, "You
shall say the same thing to Esau when you meet
him, 20and you shall say, 'Moreover your servant
Jacob is behind us.'" For he thought, "I may appease him with the present that goes ahead of
me, and afterwards I shall see his face; perhaps
he will accept me." 21So the present passed on
ahead of him; and he himself spent that night in
the camp.

22 The same night he got up and took his two
wives, his two maids, and his eleven children, and
crossed the ford of the Jabbok. 23He took them
and sent them across the stream, and likewise
everything that he had. 24Jacob was left alone;
and a man wrestled with him until daybreak.
25When the man saw that he did not prevail
against Jacob, he struck him on the hip socket;
and Jacob's hip was put out of joint as he wrestled
with him. 26Then he said, "Let me go, for the day
is breaking." But Jacob said, "I will not let you go,
unless you bless me." 27So he said to him, "What
is your name?" And he said, "Jacob." 28Then the
man[a] said, "You shall no longer be called Jacob,
but Israel,[b] for you have striven with God and
with humans,[c] and have prevailed." 29Then Jacob asked him, "Please tell me your name." But
he said, "Why is it that you ask my name?" And
there he blessed him. 30So Jacob called the place
Peniel,[d] saying, "For I have seen God face to face,
and yet my life is preserved." 31The sun rose upon
him as he passed Penuel, limping because of his
hip. 32Therefore to this day the Israelites do not
eat the thigh muscle that is on the hip socket,
because he struck Jacob on the hip socket at the
thigh muscle.

33 Now Jacob looked up and saw Esau coming, and four hundred men with him. So
he divided the children among Leah and Rachel
and the two maids. 2He put the maids with their
children in front, then Leah with her children, and
Rachel and Joseph last of all. 3He himself went
on ahead of them, bowing himself to the ground
seven times, until he came near his brother.

4 But Esau ran to meet him, and embraced
him, and fell on his neck and kissed him, and they
wept. 5When Esau looked up and saw the women
and children, he said, "Who are these with you?"
Jacob said, "The children whom God has graciously given your servant." 6Then the maids drew
near, they and their children, and bowed down;
7Leah likewise and her children drew near and
bowed down; and finally Joseph and Rachel drew
near, and they bowed down. 8Esau said, "What do
you mean by all this company that I met?" Jacob
answered, "To find favor with my lord." 9But Esau
said, "I have enough, my brother; keep what you
have for yourself." 10Jacob said, "No, please; if I
find favor with you, then accept my present from
my hand; for truly to see your face is like seeing
the face of God—since you have received me
with such favor. 11Please accept my gift that is
brought to you, because God has dealt graciously
with me, and because I have everything I want."
So he urged him, and he took it.

12 Then Esau said, "Let us journey on our
way, and I will go alongside you." 13But Jacob said
to him, "My lord knows that the children are frail
and that the flocks and herds, which are nursing,
are a care to me; and if they are overdriven for
one day, all the flocks will die. 14Let my lord pass
on ahead of his servant, and I will lead on slowly,
according to the pace of the cattle that are before
me and according to the pace of the children, until I come to my lord in Seir."

15 So Esau said, "Let me leave with you some
of the people who are with me." But he said,
"Why should my lord be so kind to me?" 16So
Esau returned that day on his way to Seir. 17But
Jacob journeyed to Succoth,[e] and built himself a

[a] Heb *he* [b] That is *The one who strives with God* or *God strives* [c] Or *with divine and human beings*
[d] That is *The face of God* [e] That is *Booths*

house, and made booths for his cattle; therefore
the place is called Succoth.
18 Jacob came safely to the city of Shechem,
which is in the land of Canaan, on his way from
Paddan-aram; and he camped before the city.
19 And from the sons of Hamor, Shechem's father,
he bought for one hundred pieces of money[a] the
plot of land on which he had pitched his tent.
20 There he erected an altar and called it El-Elohe-
Israel.[b]

34 Now Dinah the daughter of Leah, whom
she had borne to Jacob, went out to visit
the women of the region. 2 When Shechem son
of Hamor the Hivite, prince of the region, saw
her, he seized her and lay with her by force. 3 And
his soul was drawn to Dinah daughter of Jacob;
he loved the girl, and spoke tenderly to her. 4 So
Shechem spoke to his father Hamor, saying, "Get
me this girl to be my wife."

5 Now Jacob heard that Shechem[c] had defiled his daughter Dinah; but his sons were with
his cattle in the field, so Jacob held his peace until
they came. 6 And Hamor the father of Shechem
went out to Jacob to speak with him, 7 just as the
sons of Jacob came in from the field. When they
heard of it, the men were indignant and very
angry, because he had committed an outrage in
Israel by lying with Jacob's daughter, for such a
thing ought not to be done.

8 But Hamor spoke with them, saying, "The
heart of my son Shechem longs for your daughter; please give her to him in marriage. 9 Make
marriages with us; give your daughters to us, and
take our daughters for yourselves. 10 You shall live
with us; and the land shall be open to you; live
and trade in it, and get property in it." 11 Shechem
also said to her father and to her brothers, "Let
me find favor with you, and whatever you say to
me I will give. 12 Put the marriage present and gift
as high as you like, and I will give whatever you
ask me; only give me the girl to be my wife."

13 The sons of Jacob answered Shechem and
his father Hamor deceitfully, because he had defiled their sister Dinah. 14 They said to them, "We
cannot do this thing, to give our sister to one who
is uncircumcised, for that would be a disgrace to
us. 15 Only on this condition will we consent to
you: that you will become as we are and every
male among you be circumcised. 16 Then we will
give our daughters to you, and we will take your
daughters for ourselves, and we will live among
you and become one people. 17 But if you will not
listen to us and be circumcised, then we will take
our daughter and be gone."

18 Their words pleased Hamor and Hamor's
son Shechem. 19 And the young man did not delay to do the thing, because he was delighted with
Jacob's daughter. Now he was the most honored
of all his family. 20 So Hamor and his son Shechem
came to the gate of their city and spoke to the men

Genesis 34:12

Kwok Pui-lan, a theologian from Hong Kong, has observed that "the genderized and sexualized nature of dowry brings into sharp relief the collateral that the majority of the world's women must pay" and asks "what role religions and cultural ideologies have played to justify the unequal burden on the vast number of women."[7] In many contemporary cultures the dowry is money or goods given to the bride by her father to elevate her status in the eyes of the bridegroom's family. The pressure to produce a worthy dowry has led to economic hardship or chaos for many families.

In ancient Israel, however, the dowry worked the other way: the bridegroom's father paid a "brideprice" (*mohar*, in Hebrew) to the bride's father. It was not technically a purchase of property (though in the Ten Commandments the wife is mentioned as if she were property, along with house, servants, and animals. Rather the *mohar* was seen as compensation to the bride's household for its loss of an economic contributor. Thus it is translated as "marriage present" in Gen 34:12.

— *DB*

[a] Heb *one hundred qesitah* [b] That is *God, the God of Israel* [c] Heb *he*

of their city, saying, 21“These people are friendly
with us; let them live in the land and trade in it,
for the land is large enough for them; let us take
their daughters in marriage, and let us give them
our daughters. 22Only on this condition will they
agree to live among us, to become one people:
that every male among us be circumcised as they
are circumcised. 23Will not their livestock, their
property, and all their animals be ours? Only let
us agree with them, and they will live among us.”
24And all who went out of the city gate heeded
Hamor and his son Shechem; and every male was
circumcised, all who went out of the gate of his
city.

25 On the third day, when they were still in
pain, two of the sons of Jacob, Simeon and Levi,
Dinah’s brothers, took their swords and came
against the city unawares, and killed all the males.
26They killed Hamor and his son Shechem with
the sword, and took Dinah out of Shechem’s
house, and went away. 27And the other sons of
Jacob came upon the slain, and plundered the
city, because their sister had been defiled. 28They
took their flocks and their herds, their donkeys,
and whatever was in the city and in the field. 29All
their wealth, all their little ones and their wives,
all that was in the houses, they captured and made
their prey. 30Then Jacob said to Simeon and Levi,
“You have brought trouble on me by making me
odious to the inhabitants of the land, the Canaanites and the Perizzites; my numbers are few, and if
they gather themselves against me and attack me,
I shall be destroyed, both I and my household.”
31But they said, “Should our sister be treated like
a whore?”

35 God said to Jacob, “Arise, go up to Bethel,
and settle there. Make an altar there to the
God who appeared to you when you fled from
your brother Esau.” 2So Jacob said to his household and to all who were with him, “Put away
the foreign gods that are among you, and purify
yourselves, and change your clothes; 3then come,
let us go up to Bethel, that I may make an altar
there to the God who answered me in the day of
my distress and has been with me wherever I have
gone.” 4So they gave to Jacob all the foreign gods
that they had, and the rings that were in their
ears; and Jacob hid them under the oak that was
near Shechem.

5 As they journeyed, a terror from God fell
upon the cities all around them, so that no one pursued them. 6Jacob came to Luz (that is, Bethel),
which is in the land of Canaan, he and all the
people who were with him, 7and there he built
an altar and called the place El-bethel,[a] because
it was there that God had revealed himself to him
when he fled from his brother. 8And Deborah,
Rebekah’s nurse, died, and she was buried under an oak below Bethel. So it was called Allon-
bacuth.[b]

9 God appeared to Jacob again when he
came from Paddan-aram, and he blessed him.
10God said to him, “Your name is Jacob; no longer shall you be called Jacob, but Israel shall be
your name.” So he was called Israel. 11God said
to him, “I am God Almighty:[c] be fruitful and
multiply; a nation and a company of nations
shall come from you, and kings shall spring from
you. 12The land that I gave to Abraham and Isaac
I will give to you, and I will give the land to your
offspring after you.” 13Then God went up from
him at the place where he had spoken with him.
14Jacob set up a pillar in the place where he had
spoken with him, a pillar of stone; and he poured
out a drink offering on it, and poured oil on it.
15So Jacob called the place where God had spoken with him Bethel.

16 Then they journeyed from Bethel; and
when they were still some distance from Ephrath,
Rachel was in childbirth, and she had hard labor.
17When she was in her hard labor, the midwife
said to her, “Do not be afraid; for now you will
have another son.” 18As her soul was departing
(for she died), she named him Ben-oni;[d] but his
father called him Benjamin.[e] 19So Rachel died,
and she was buried on the way to Ephrath (that
is, Bethlehem), 20and Jacob set up a pillar at her
grave; it is the pillar of Rachel’s tomb, which is

[a] That is *God of Bethel* [b] That is *Oak of weeping* [c] Traditional rendering of Heb *El Shaddai*
[d] That is *Son of my sorrow* [e] That is *Son of the right hand* or *Son of the South*

there to this day. 21 Israel journeyed on, and
pitched his tent beyond the tower of Eder.

22 While Israel lived in that land, Reuben
went and lay with Bilhah his father's concubine;
and Israel heard of it.

Now the sons of Jacob were twelve. 23 The sons
of Leah: Reuben (Jacob's firstborn), Simeon,
Levi, Judah, Issachar, and Zebulun. 24 The sons
of Rachel: Joseph and Benjamin. 25 The sons of
Bilhah, Rachel's maid: Dan and Naphtali. 26 The
sons of Zilpah, Leah's maid: Gad and Asher.
These were the sons of Jacob who were born to
him in Paddan-aram.

27 Jacob came to his father Isaac at Mamre,
or Kiriath-arba (that is, Hebron), where Abraham
and Isaac had resided as aliens. 28 Now the days of
Isaac were one hundred eighty years. 29 And Isaac
breathed his last; he died and was gathered to his
people, old and full of days; and his sons Esau and
Jacob buried him.

36 These are the descendants of Esau (that
is, Edom). 2 Esau took his wives from the
Canaanites: Adah daughter of Elon the Hittite,
Oholibamah daughter of Anah son[a] of Zibeon the
Hivite, 3 and Basemath, Ishmael's daughter, sister
of Nebaioth. 4 Adah bore Eliphaz to Esau; Basemath bore Reuel; 5 and Oholibamah bore Jeush,
Jalam, and Korah. These are the sons of Esau who
were born to him in the land of Canaan.

6 Then Esau took his wives, his sons, his
daughters, and all the members of his household,
his cattle, all his livestock, and all the property
he had acquired in the land of Canaan; and he
moved to a land some distance from his brother
Jacob. 7 For their possessions were too great for
them to live together; the land where they were
staying could not support them because of their
livestock. 8 So Esau settled in the hill country of
Seir; Esau is Edom.

9 These are the descendants of Esau, ancestor of the Edomites, in the hill country of Seir.
10 These are the names of Esau's sons: Eliphaz son
of Adah the wife of Esau; Reuel, the son of Esau's
wife Basemath. 11 The sons of Eliphaz were Teman, Omar, Zepho, Gatam, and Kenaz. 12 (Timna
was a concubine of Eliphaz, Esau's son; she bore
Amalek to Eliphaz.) These were the sons of Adah,
Esau's wife. 13 These were the sons of Reuel: Nahath, Zerah, Shammah, and Mizzah. These were
the sons of Esau's wife, Basemath. 14 These were
the sons of Esau's wife Oholibamah, daughter
of Anah son[b] of Zibeon: she bore to Esau Jeush,
Jalam, and Korah.

15 These are the clans[c] of the sons of Esau.
The sons of Eliphaz the firstborn of Esau: the
clans[c] Teman, Omar, Zepho, Kenaz, 16 Korah, Gatam, and Amalek; these are the clans[c] of Eliphaz
in the land of Edom; they are the sons of Adah.
17 These are the sons of Esau's son Reuel: the clans[c]
Nahath, Zerah, Shammah, and Mizzah; these are
the clans[c] of Reuel in the land of Edom; they are
the sons of Esau's wife Basemath. 18 These are the
sons of Esau's wife Oholibamah: the clans[c] Jeush,
Jalam, and Korah; these are the clans[c] born of
Esau's wife Oholibamah, the daughter of Anah.
19 These are the sons of Esau (that is, Edom), and
these are their clans.[c]

20 These are the sons of Seir the Horite, the
inhabitants of the land: Lotan, Shobal, Zibeon,
Anah, 21 Dishon, Ezer, and Dishan; these are the
clans[c] of the Horites, the sons of Seir in the land
of Edom. 22 The sons of Lotan were Hori and
Heman; and Lotan's sister was Timna. 23 These
are the sons of Shobal: Alvan, Manahath, Ebal,
Shepho, and Onam. 24 These are the sons of Zibeon: Aiah and Anah; he is the Anah who found
the springs[d] in the wilderness, as he pastured the
donkeys of his father Zibeon. 25 These are the children of Anah: Dishon and Oholibamah daughter
of Anah. 26 These are the sons of Dishon: Hem-
dan, Eshban, Ithran, and Cheran. 27 These are the
sons of Ezer: Bilhan, Zaavan, and Akan. 28 These
are the sons of Dishan: Uz and Aran. 29 These are
the clans[c] of the Horites: the clans[c] Lotan, Shobal, Zibeon, Anah, 30 Dishon, Ezer, and Dishan;
these are the clans[c] of the Horites, clan by clan[e] in
the land of Seir.

31 These are the kings who reigned in the

[a] Sam Gk Syr: Heb *daughter* [b] Gk Syr: Heb *daughter* [c] Or *chiefs* [d] Meaning of Heb uncertain
[e] Or *chief by chief*

land of Edom, before any king reigned over the
Israelites. 32Bela son of Beor reigned in Edom,
the name of his city being Dinhabah. 33Bela died,
and Jobab son of Zerah of Bozrah succeeded him
as king. 34Jobab died, and Husham of the land of
the Temanites succeeded him as king. 35Husham
died, and Hadad son of Bedad, who defeated
Midian in the country of Moab, succeeded him
as king, the name of his city being Avith. 36Hadad
died, and Samlah of Masrekah succeeded him as
king. 37Samlah died, and Shaul of Rehoboth on
the Euphrates succeeded him as king. 38Shaul
died, and Baal-hanan son of Achbor succeeded
him as king. 39Baal-hanan son of Achbor died,
and Hadar succeeded him as king, the name of
his city being Pau; his wife's name was Mehetabel,
the daughter of Matred, daughter of Me-zahab.

40 These are the names of the clans[a] of Esau,
according to their families and their localities by
their names: the clans[a] Timna, Alvah, Jetheth,
41Oholibamah, Elah, Pinon, 42Kenaz, Teman,
Mibzar, 43Magdiel, and Iram; these are the clans[a]
of Edom (that is, Esau, the father of Edom), according to their settlements in the land that they
held.

37 Jacob settled in the land where his father
had lived as an alien, the land of Canaan.
2This is the story of the family of Jacob.

Joseph, being seventeen years old, was shepherding the flock with his brothers; he was a
helper to the sons of Bilhah and Zilpah, his father's wives; and Joseph brought a bad report of
them to their father. 3Now Israel loved Joseph
more than any other of his children, because he
was the son of his old age; and he had made him
a long robe with sleeves.[b] 4But when his brothers saw that their father loved him more than all
his brothers, they hated him, and could not speak
peaceably to him.

5 Once Joseph had a dream, and when he
told it to his brothers, they hated him even more.
6He said to them, "Listen to this dream that I
dreamed. 7There we were, binding sheaves in the
field. Suddenly my sheaf rose and stood upright;
then your sheaves gathered around it, and bowed
down to my sheaf." 8His brothers said to him,
"Are you indeed to reign over us? Are you indeed
to have dominion over us?" So they hated him
even more because of his dreams and his words.

9 He had another dream, and told it to his
brothers, saying, "Look, I have had another
dream: the sun, the moon, and eleven stars were
bowing down to me." 10But when he told it to his
father and to his brothers, his father rebuked him,
and said to him, "What kind of dream is this that
you have had? Shall we indeed come, I and your
mother and your brothers, and bow to the ground
before you?" 11So his brothers were jealous of
him, but his father kept the matter in mind.

12 Now his brothers went to pasture their
father's flock near Shechem. 13And Israel said to
Joseph, "Are not your brothers pasturing the flock
at Shechem? Come, I will send you to them." He
answered, "Here I am." 14So he said to him, "Go
now, see if it is well with your brothers and with
the flock; and bring word back to me." So he sent
him from the valley of Hebron.

He came to Shechem, 15and a man found
him wandering in the fields; the man asked him,
"What are you seeking?" 16"I am seeking my
brothers," he said; "tell me, please, where they
are pasturing the flock." 17The man said, "They
have gone away, for I heard them say, 'Let us go
to Dothan.'" So Joseph went after his brothers,
and found them at Dothan. 18They saw him from
a distance, and before he came near to them, they
conspired to kill him. 19They said to one another,
"Here comes this dreamer. 20Come now, let us
kill him and throw him into one of the pits; then
we shall say that a wild animal has devoured him,
and we shall see what will become of his dreams."
21But when Reuben heard it, he delivered him out
of their hands, saying, "Let us not take his life."
22Reuben said to them, "Shed no blood; throw
him into this pit here in the wilderness, but lay
no hand on him"—that he might rescue him out
of their hand and restore him to his father. 23So
when Joseph came to his brothers, they stripped
him of his robe, the long robe with sleeves[c] that
he wore; 24and they took him and threw him

[a] Or *chiefs* [b] Traditional rendering (compare Gk): *a coat of many colors*; meaning of Heb uncertain [c] See note on 37.3

into a pit. The pit was empty; there was no water
in it.
25 Then they sat down to eat; and looking up
they saw a caravan of Ishmaelites coming from
Gilead, with their camels carrying gum, balm,
and resin, on their way to carry it down to Egypt.
26 Then Judah said to his brothers, "What profit
is it if we kill our brother and conceal his blood?
27 Come, let us sell him to the Ishmaelites, and
not lay our hands on him, for he is our brother,
our own flesh." And his brothers agreed. 28 When
some Midianite traders passed by, they drew Joseph up, lifting him out of the pit, and sold him
to the Ishmaelites for twenty pieces of silver. And
they took Joseph to Egypt.
29 When Reuben returned to the pit and saw
that Joseph was not in the pit, he tore his clothes.
30 He returned to his brothers, and said, "The
boy is gone; and I, where can I turn?" 31 Then
they took Joseph's robe, slaughtered a goat, and
dipped the robe in the blood. 32 They had the
long robe with sleeves[a] taken to their father, and
they said, "This we have found; see now whether
it is your son's robe or not." 33 He recognized it,
and said, "It is my son's robe! A wild animal has
devoured him; Joseph is without doubt torn to
pieces." 34 Then Jacob tore his garments, and put
sackcloth on his loins, and mourned for his son
many days. 35 All his sons and all his daughters
sought to comfort him; but he refused to be comforted, and said, "No, I shall go down to Sheol
to my son, mourning." Thus his father bewailed
him. 36 Meanwhile the Midianites had sold him in
Egypt to Potiphar, one of Pharaoh's officials, the
captain of the guard.

38 It happened at that time that Judah went
down from his brothers and settled near
a certain Adullamite whose name was Hirah.
2 There Judah saw the daughter of a certain Canaanite whose name was Shua; he married her
and went in to her. 3 She conceived and bore a
son; and he named him Er. 4 Again she conceived
and bore a son whom she named Onan. 5 Yet again
she bore a son, and she named him Shelah. She[b]
was in Chezib when she bore him. 6 Judah took
a wife for Er his firstborn; her name was Tamar.
7 But Er, Judah's firstborn, was wicked in the sight
of the LORD, and the LORD put him to death.
8 Then Judah said to Onan, "Go in to your brother's wife and perform the duty of a brother-in-law
to her; raise up offspring for your brother." 9 But
since Onan knew that the offspring would not be
his, he spilled his semen on the ground whenever
he went in to his brother's wife, so that he would
not give offspring to his brother. 10 What he did
was displeasing in the sight of the LORD, and he
put him to death also. 11 Then Judah said to his
daughter-in-law Tamar, "Remain a widow in your
father's house until my son Shelah grows up"—
for he feared that he too would die, like his brothers. So Tamar went to live in her father's house.
12 In course of time the wife of Judah, Shua's
daughter, died; when Judah's time of mourning
was over,[c] he went up to Timnah to his sheepshearers, he and his friend Hirah the Adullamite.
13 When Tamar was told, "Your father-in-law is
going up to Timnah to shear his sheep," 14 she put
off her widow's garments, put on a veil, wrapped
herself up, and sat down at the entrance to Enaim,
which is on the road to Timnah. She saw that
Shelah was grown up, yet she had not been given
to him in marriage. 15 When Judah saw her, he
thought her to be a prostitute, for she had covered her face. 16 He went over to her at the roadside, and said, "Come, let me come in to you," for
he did not know that she was his daughter-in-law.
She said, "What will you give me, that you may
come in to me?" 17 He answered, "I will send
you a kid from the flock." And she said, "Only
if you give me a pledge, until you send it." 18 He
said, "What pledge shall I give you?" She replied,
"Your signet and your cord, and the staff that is in
your hand." So he gave them to her, and went in
to her, and she conceived by him. 19 Then she got
up and went away, and taking off her veil she put
on the garments of her widowhood.
20 When Judah sent the kid by his friend
the Adullamite, to recover the pledge from the
woman, he could not find her. 21 He asked the
townspeople, "Where is the temple prostitute

[a] See note on 37.3 [b] Gk: Heb *He* [c] Heb *when Judah was comforted*

Genesis 38:21

The Hebrew word that is inappropriately translated "temple prostitute" throughout the canon literally means "holy woman" and indicates a woman in religious service outside the sanctioned religion of biblical Israel. The biblical authors demonized people who practiced other religions and in the case of such "holy women" identified them as prostitues—an identification that biblical scholars have only recently called seriously into doubt. What will it take for people truly to respect religious differences among the earth's peoples?

— *WG*

who was at Enaim by the wayside?" But they said,
"No prostitute has been here." 22So he returned to
Judah, and said, "I have not found her; moreover
the townspeople said, 'No prostitute has been
here.'" 23Judah replied, "Let her keep the things
as her own, otherwise we will be laughed at; you
see, I sent this kid, and you could not find her."

24 About three months later Judah was told,
"Your daughter-in-law Tamar has played the
whore; moreover she is pregnant as a result of
whoredom." And Judah said, "Bring her out, and
let her be burned." 25As she was being brought
out, she sent word to her father-in-law, "It was
the owner of these who made me pregnant." And
she said, "Take note, please, whose these are, the
signet and the cord and the staff." 26Then Judah
acknowledged them and said, "She is more in the
right than I, since I did not give her to my son
Shelah." And he did not lie with her again.

27 When the time of her delivery came, there
were twins in her womb. 28While she was in
labor, one put out a hand; and the midwife took
and bound on his hand a crimson thread, saying,
"This one came out first." 29But just then he drew
back his hand, and out came his brother; and she
said, "What a breach you have made for yourself!"
Therefore he was named Perez.[a] 30Afterward his
brother came out with the crimson thread on his
hand; and he was named Zerah.[b]

39 Now Joseph was taken down to Egypt,
and Potiphar, an officer of Pharaoh, the
captain of the guard, an Egyptian, bought him
from the Ishmaelites who had brought him down
there. 2The LORD was with Joseph, and he became a successful man; he was in the house of his
Egyptian master. 3His master saw that the LORD
was with him, and that the LORD caused all that
he did to prosper in his hands. 4So Joseph found
favor in his sight and attended him; he made him
overseer of his house and put him in charge of all
that he had. 5From the time that he made him
overseer in his house and over all that he had, the
LORD blessed the Egyptian's house for Joseph's
sake; the blessing of the LORD was on all that he
had, in house and field. 6So he left all that he had
in Joseph's charge; and, with him there, he had no
concern for anything but the food that he ate.

Now Joseph was handsome and good-looking.
7And after a time his master's wife cast her eyes
on Joseph and said, "Lie with me." 8But he refused and said to his master's wife, "Look, with
me here, my master has no concern about anything in the house, and he has put everything
that he has in my hand. 9He is not greater in this
house than I am, nor has he kept back anything
from me except yourself, because you are his
wife. How then could I do this great wickedness,
and sin against God?" 10And although she spoke
to Joseph day after day, he would not consent
to lie beside her or to be with her. 11One day,
however, when he went into the house to do his
work, and while no one else was in the house,
12she caught hold of his garment, saying, "Lie
with me!" But he left his garment in her hand,
and fled and ran outside. 13When she saw that
he had left his garment in her hand and had fled
outside, 14she called out to the members of her
household and said to them, "See, my husband[c]
has brought among us a Hebrew to insult us! He
came in to me to lie with me, and I cried out with
a loud voice; 15and when he heard me raise my
voice and cry out, he left his garment beside me,

[a] That is *A breach* [b] That is *Brightness*; perhaps alluding to the crimson thread [c] Heb *he*

and fled outside." 16 Then she kept his garment by
her until his master came home, 17 and she told
him the same story, saying, "The Hebrew servant, whom you have brought among us, came in
to me to insult me; 18 but as soon as I raised my
voice and cried out, he left his garment beside
me, and fled outside."

19 When his master heard the words that his
wife spoke to him, saying, "This is the way your
servant treated me," he became enraged. 20 And
Joseph's master took him and put him into the
prison, the place where the king's prisoners were
confined; he remained there in prison. 21 But the
LORD was with Joseph and showed him steadfast
love; he gave him favor in the sight of the chief
jailer. 22 The chief jailer committed to Joseph's care
all the prisoners who were in the prison, and whatever was done there, he was the one who did it.
23 The chief jailer paid no heed to anything that was
in Joseph's care, because the LORD was with him;
and whatever he did, the LORD made it prosper.

40 Some time after this, the cupbearer of
the king of Egypt and his baker offended
their lord the king of Egypt. 2 Pharaoh was angry
with his two officers, the chief cupbearer and the
chief baker, 3 and he put them in custody in the
house of the captain of the guard, in the prison
where Joseph was confined. 4 The captain of the
guard charged Joseph with them, and he waited
on them; and they continued for some time in
custody. 5 One night they both dreamed—the
cupbearer and the baker of the king of Egypt,
who were confined in the prison—each his own
dream, and each dream with its own meaning.
6 When Joseph came to them in the morning, he
saw that they were troubled. 7 So he asked Pharaoh's officers, who were with him in custody in
his master's house, "Why are your faces downcast today?" 8 They said to him, "We have had
dreams, and there is no one to interpret them."
And Joseph said to them, "Do not interpretations
belong to God? Please tell them to me."

9 So the chief cupbearer told his dream to
Joseph, and said to him, "In my dream there was a
vine before me, 10 and on the vine there were three
branches. As soon as it budded, its blossoms came
out and the clusters ripened into grapes. 11 Pharaoh's cup was in my hand; and I took the grapes
and pressed them into Pharaoh's cup, and placed
the cup in Pharaoh's hand." 12 Then Joseph said to
him, "This is its interpretation: the three branches
are three days; 13 within three days Pharaoh will
lift up your head and restore you to your office;
and you shall place Pharaoh's cup in his hand, just
as you used to do when you were his cupbearer.
14 But remember me when it is well with you;
please do me the kindness to make mention of me
to Pharaoh, and so get me out of this place. 15 For
in fact I was stolen out of the land of the Hebrews;
and here also I have done nothing that they should
have put me into the dungeon."

16 When the chief baker saw that the interpretation was favorable, he said to Joseph, "I also
had a dream: there were three cake baskets on
my head, 17 and in the uppermost basket there
were all sorts of baked food for Pharaoh, but the
birds were eating it out of the basket on my head."
18 And Joseph answered, "This is its interpretation: the three baskets are three days; 19 within
three days Pharaoh will lift up your head—from
you!—and hang you on a pole; and the birds will
eat the flesh from you."

20 On the third day, which was Pharaoh's
birthday, he made a feast for all his servants, and
lifted up the head of the chief cupbearer and the
head of the chief baker among his servants. 21 He
restored the chief cupbearer to his cupbearing,
and he placed the cup in Pharaoh's hand; 22 but
the chief baker he hanged, just as Joseph had interpreted to them. 23 Yet the chief cupbearer did
not remember Joseph, but forgot him.

41 After two whole years, Pharaoh dreamed
that he was standing by the Nile, 2 and
there came up out of the Nile seven sleek and fat
cows, and they grazed in the reed grass. 3 Then
seven other cows, ugly and thin, came up out of
the Nile after them, and stood by the other cows
on the bank of the Nile. 4 The ugly and thin cows
ate up the seven sleek and fat cows. And Pharaoh
awoke. 5 Then he fell asleep and dreamed a second
time; seven ears of grain, plump and good, were
growing on one stalk. 6 Then seven ears, thin and
blighted by the east wind, sprouted after them.
7 The thin ears swallowed up the seven plump and

full ears. Pharaoh awoke, and it was a dream. [8]In the morning his spirit was troubled; so he sent and called for all the magicians of Egypt and all its wise men. Pharaoh told them his dreams, but there was no one who could interpret them to Pharaoh.

9 Then the chief cupbearer said to Pharaoh, "I remember my faults today. [10]Once Pharaoh was angry with his servants, and put me and the chief baker in custody in the house of the captain of the guard. [11]We dreamed on the same night, he and I, each having a dream with its own meaning. [12]A young Hebrew was there with us, a servant of the captain of the guard. When we told him, he interpreted our dreams to us, giving an interpretation to each according to his dream. [13]As he interpreted to us, so it turned out; I was restored to my office, and the baker was hanged."

14 Then Pharaoh sent for Joseph, and he was hurriedly brought out of the dungeon. When he had shaved himself and changed his clothes, he came in before Pharaoh. [15]And Pharaoh said to Joseph, "I have had a dream, and there is no one who can interpret it. I have heard it said of you that when you hear a dream you can interpret it." [16]Joseph answered Pharaoh, "It is not I; God will give Pharaoh a favorable answer." [17]Then Pharaoh said to Joseph, "In my dream I was standing on the banks of the Nile; [18]and seven cows, fat and sleek, came up out of the Nile and fed in the reed grass. [19]Then seven other cows came up after them, poor, very ugly, and thin. Never had I seen such ugly ones in all the land of Egypt. [20]The thin and ugly cows ate up the first seven fat cows, [21]but when they had eaten them no one would have known that they had done so, for they were still as ugly as before. Then I awoke. [22]I fell asleep a second time[a] and I saw in my dream seven ears of grain, full and good, growing on one stalk, [23]and seven ears, withered, thin, and blighted by the east wind, sprouting after them; [24]and the thin ears swallowed up the seven good ears. But when I told it to the magicians, there was no one who could explain it to me."

25 Then Joseph said to Pharaoh, "Pharaoh's dreams are one and the same; God has revealed to Pharaoh what he is about to do. [26]The seven good cows are seven years, and the seven good ears are seven years; the dreams are one. [27]The seven lean and ugly cows that came up after them are seven years, as are the seven empty ears blighted by the east wind. They are seven years of famine. [28]It is as I told Pharaoh; God has shown to Pharaoh what he is about to do. [29]There will come seven years of great plenty throughout all the land of Egypt. [30]After them there will arise seven years of famine, and all the plenty will be forgotten in the land of Egypt; the famine will consume the land. [31]The plenty will no longer be known in the land because of the famine that will follow, for it will be very grievous. [32]And the doubling of Pharaoh's dream means that the thing is fixed by God, and God will shortly bring it about. [33]Now therefore let Pharaoh select a man who is discerning and wise, and set him over the land of Egypt. [34]Let Pharaoh proceed to appoint overseers over the land, and take one-fifth of the produce of the land of Egypt during the seven plenteous years. [35]Let them gather all the food of these good years that are coming, and lay up grain under the authority of Pharaoh for food in the cities, and let them keep it. [36]That food shall be a reserve for the land against the seven years of famine that are to befall the land of Egypt, so that the land may not perish through the famine."

37 The proposal pleased Pharaoh and all his servants. [38]Pharaoh said to his servants, "Can we find anyone else like this—one in whom is the spirit of God?" [39]So Pharaoh said to Joseph, "Since God has shown you all this, there is no one so discerning and wise as you. [40]You shall be over my house, and all my people shall order themselves as you command; only with regard to the throne will I be greater than you." [41]And Pharaoh said to Joseph, "See, I have set you over all the land of Egypt." [42]Removing his signet ring from his hand, Pharaoh put it on Joseph's hand; he arrayed him in garments of fine linen, and put a gold chain around his neck. [43]He had him ride in the chariot of his second-in-command; and they

[a] Gk Syr Vg: Heb lacks *I fell asleep a second time*

cried out in front of him, "Bow the knee!"[a] Thus
he set him over all the land of Egypt. 44Moreover
Pharaoh said to Joseph, "I am Pharaoh, and without your consent no one shall lift up hand or foot
in all the land of Egypt." 45Pharaoh gave Joseph
the name Zaphenath-paneah; and he gave him
Asenath daughter of Potiphera, priest of On, as
his wife. Thus Joseph gained authority over the
land of Egypt.

Genesis 41:45

Joseph's marriage to Asenath means that two of the twelve tribes, Ephraim and Manasseh, will be half-Egyptian. Combined with Abram's origin from Chaldean Ur (once in Babylon, now in Iraq) in 11:27-28, the implication is that Israelite identity is a social, not biological or racial, identity. As important as are differences across human communities, there is only one human race.

— *WG*

46 Joseph was thirty years old when he entered the service of Pharaoh king of Egypt. And
Joseph went out from the presence of Pharaoh,
and went through all the land of Egypt. 47Dur-
ing the seven plenteous years the earth produced
abundantly. 48He gathered up all the food of the
seven years when there was plenty[b] in the land of
Egypt, and stored up food in the cities; he stored
up in every city the food from the fields around it.
49So Joseph stored up grain in such abundance—
like the sand of the sea—that he stopped measuring it; it was beyond measure.
50 Before the years of famine came, Joseph had
two sons, whom Asenath daughter of Potiphera,
priest of On, bore to him. 51Joseph named the firstborn Manasseh,[c] "For," he said, "God has made me
forget all my hardship and all my father's house."
52The second he named Ephraim,[d] "For God has
made me fruitful in the land of my misfortunes."
53 The seven years of plenty that prevailed in
the land of Egypt came to an end; 54and the seven
years of famine began to come, just as Joseph
had said. There was famine in every country, but
throughout the land of Egypt there was bread.
55When all the land of Egypt was famished, the
people cried to Pharaoh for bread. Pharaoh said to
all the Egyptians, "Go to Joseph; what he says to
you, do." 56And since the famine had spread over
all the land, Joseph opened all the storehouses,[e]
and sold to the Egyptians, for the famine was
severe in the land of Egypt. 57Moreover, all the
world came to Joseph in Egypt to buy grain,
because the famine became severe throughout
the world.

42 When Jacob learned that there was grain
in Egypt, he said to his sons, "Why do
you keep looking at one another? 2I have heard,"
he said, "that there is grain in Egypt; go down
and buy grain for us there, that we may live and
not die." 3So ten of Joseph's brothers went down
to buy grain in Egypt. 4But Jacob did not send
Joseph's brother Benjamin with his brothers, for
he feared that harm might come to him. 5Thus the
sons of Israel were among the other people who
came to buy grain, for the famine had reached the
land of Canaan.
6 Now Joseph was governor over the land;
it was he who sold to all the people of the land.
And Joseph's brothers came and bowed themselves before him with their faces to the ground.
7When Joseph saw his brothers, he recognized
them, but he treated them like strangers and
spoke harshly to them. "Where do you come
from?" he said. They said, "From the land of
Canaan, to buy food." 8Although Joseph had
recognized his brothers, they did not recognize
him. 9Joseph also remembered the dreams that
he had dreamed about them. He said to them,
"You are spies; you have come to see the nakedness of the land!" 10They said to him, "No, my
lord; your servants have come to buy food. 11We
are all sons of one man; we are honest men; your

[a] *Abrek,* apparently an Egyptian word similar in sound to the Hebrew word meaning *to kneel* [b] Sam Gk: MT *the seven years that were* [c] That is *Making to forget* [d] From a Hebrew word meaning *to be fruitful*
[e] Gk Vg Compare Syr: Heb *opened all that was in* (or, *among*) *them*

servants have never been spies." 12But he said to
them, "No, you have come to see the nakedness
of the land!" 13They said, "We, your servants,
are twelve brothers, the sons of a certain man
in the land of Canaan; the youngest, however, is
now with our father, and one is no more." 14But
Joseph said to them, "It is just as I have said to
you; you are spies! 15Here is how you shall be
tested: as Pharaoh lives, you shall not leave this
place unless your youngest brother comes here!
16Let one of you go and bring your brother,
while the rest of you remain in prison, in order
that your words may be tested, whether there
is truth in you; or else, as Pharaoh lives, surely
you are spies." 17And he put them all together in
prison for three days.

18 On the third day Joseph said to them,
"Do this and you will live, for I fear God: 19if
you are honest men, let one of your brothers
stay here where you are imprisoned. The rest
of you shall go and carry grain for the famine
of your households, 20and bring your youngest
brother to me. Thus your words will be verified,
and you shall not die." And they agreed to do so.
21They said to one another, "Alas, we are paying
the penalty for what we did to our brother; we
saw his anguish when he pleaded with us, but
we would not listen. That is why this anguish
has come upon us." 22Then Reuben answered
them, "Did I not tell you not to wrong the boy?
But you would not listen. So now there comes a
reckoning for his blood." 23They did not know
that Joseph understood them, since he spoke
with them through an interpreter. 24He turned
away from them and wept; then he returned and
spoke to them. And he picked out Simeon and
had him bound before their eyes. 25Joseph then
gave orders to fill their bags with grain, to return
every man's money to his sack, and to give them
provisions for their journey. This was done for
them.

26 They loaded their donkeys with their
grain, and departed. 27When one of them opened
his sack to give his donkey fodder at the lodging place, he saw his money at the top of the
sack. 28He said to his brothers, "My money has
been put back; here it is in my sack!" At this they
lost heart and turned trembling to one another,
saying, "What is this that God has done to us?"

29 When they came to their father Jacob in
the land of Canaan, they told him all that had
happened to them, saying, 30"The man, the lord
of the land, spoke harshly to us, and charged us
with spying on the land. 31But we said to him,
'We are honest men, we are not spies. 32We are
twelve brothers, sons of our father; one is no
more, and the youngest is now with our father in
the land of Canaan.' 33Then the man, the lord of
the land, said to us, 'By this I shall know that you
are honest men: leave one of your brothers with
me, take grain for the famine of your households,
and go your way. 34Bring your youngest brother
to me, and I shall know that you are not spies but

Genesis 42

At the time Joseph had become vizier of Egypt, all the lands at the eastern end of the Mediterranean began to suffer from severe drought and famine. Joseph had supervised the stockpiling of grains in Egypt during the earlier plentiful years. Rather than starve, the sons of Jacob, Jacob himself, and their entire clan finally left their home in Canaan and became refugees in Egypt. In our own day, refugee and displaced populations and migration movements have become global phenomena, the sheer magnitude of which indicates that they are symptoms of a sick or unjust world order. The Central Committee of the World Council of Churches observes that it is usually "the countries which can least afford the presence of refugees that have the largest number of them. These . . . countries pay a high price in terms of domestic instability and deferred development, and yet, though they are often reluctant hosts to their refugees, remarkable instances of generosity to the homeless and uprooted can be cited."[8]

— DB

honest men. Then I will release your brother to
you, and you may trade in the land.'"
35 As they were emptying their sacks, there in
each one's sack was his bag of money. When they
and their father saw their bundles of money, they
were dismayed. 36And their father Jacob said to
them, "I am the one you have bereaved of children:
Joseph is no more, and Simeon is no more, and
now you would take Benjamin. All this has happened to me!" 37Then Reuben said to his father,
"You may kill my two sons if I do not bring him
back to you. Put him in my hands, and I will bring
him back to you." 38But he said, "My son shall not
go down with you, for his brother is dead, and he
alone is left. If harm should come to him on the
journey that you are to make, you would bring
down my gray hairs with sorrow to Sheol."

43 Now the famine was severe in the land.
2And when they had eaten up the grain
that they had brought from Egypt, their father
said to them, "Go again, buy us a little more
food." 3But Judah said to him, "The man solemnly
warned us, saying, 'You shall not see my face unless your brother is with you.' 4If you will send
our brother with us, we will go down and buy you
food; 5but if you will not send him, we will not go
down, for the man said to us, 'You shall not see
my face, unless your brother is with you.'" 6Israel
said, "Why did you treat me so badly as to tell
the man that you had another brother?" 7They
replied, "The man questioned us carefully about
ourselves and our kindred, saying, 'Is your father
still alive? Have you another brother?' What we
told him was in answer to these questions. Could
we in any way know that he would say, 'Bring
your brother down'?" 8Then Judah said to his father Israel, "Send the boy with me, and let us be
on our way, so that we may live and not die—you
and we and also our little ones. 9I myself will be
surety for him; you can hold me accountable for
him. If I do not bring him back to you and set him
before you, then let me bear the blame forever.
10If we had not delayed, we would now have returned twice."
11 Then their father Israel said to them,
"If it must be so, then do this: take some of the
choice fruits of the land in your bags, and carry
them down as a present to the man—a little balm
and a little honey, gum, resin, pistachio nuts,
and almonds. 12Take double the money with
you. Carry back with you the money that was
returned in the top of your sacks; perhaps it was
an oversight. 13Take your brother also, and be on
your way again to the man; 14may God Almighty[a]
grant you mercy before the man, so that he may
send back your other brother and Benjamin. As
for me, if I am bereaved of my children, I am bereaved." 15So the men took the present, and they
took double the money with them, as well as
Benjamin. Then they went on their way down to
Egypt, and stood before Joseph.
16 When Joseph saw Benjamin with them,
he said to the steward of his house, "Bring the
men into the house, and slaughter an animal and
make ready, for the men are to dine with me at
noon." 17The man did as Joseph said, and brought
the men to Joseph's house. 18Now the men were
afraid because they were brought to Joseph's
house, and they said, "It is because of the money,
replaced in our sacks the first time, that we have
been brought in, so that he may have an opportunity to fall upon us, to make slaves of us and take
our donkeys." 19So they went up to the steward
of Joseph's house and spoke with him at the entrance to the house. 20They said, "Oh, my lord,
we came down the first time to buy food; 21and
when we came to the lodging place we opened
our sacks, and there was each one's money in
the top of his sack, our money in full weight. So
we have brought it back with us. 22Moreover we
have brought down with us additional money to
buy food. We do not know who put our money
in our sacks." 23He replied, "Rest assured, do not
be afraid; your God and the God of your father
must have put treasure in your sacks for you; I received your money." Then he brought Simeon out
to them. 24When the steward[b] had brought the
men into Joseph's house, and given them water,
and they had washed their feet, and when he had
given their donkeys fodder, 25they made the pres-

[a] Traditional rendering of Heb *El Shaddai* [b] Heb *the man*

ent ready for Joseph's coming at noon, for they
had heard that they would dine there.
26 When Joseph came home, they brought
him the present that they had carried into the
house, and bowed to the ground before him. 27 He
inquired about their welfare, and said, "Is your
father well, the old man of whom you spoke? Is
he still alive?" 28 They said, "Your servant our father is well; he is still alive." And they bowed their
heads and did obeisance. 29 Then he looked up
and saw his brother Benjamin, his mother's son,
and said, "Is this your youngest brother, of whom
you spoke to me? God be gracious to you, my
son!" 30 With that, Joseph hurried out, because he
was overcome with affection for his brother, and
he was about to weep. So he went into a private
room and wept there. 31 Then he washed his face
and came out; and controlling himself he said,
"Serve the meal." 32 They served him by himself,
and them by themselves, and the Egyptians who
ate with him by themselves, because the Egyptians could not eat with the Hebrews, for that is
an abomination to the Egyptians. 33 When they
were seated before him, the firstborn according to his birthright and the youngest according
to his youth, the men looked at one another in
amazement. 34 Portions were taken to them from
Joseph's table, but Benjamin's portion was five
times as much as any of theirs. So they drank and
were merry with him.

44 Then he commanded the steward of his
house, "Fill the men's sacks with food, as
much as they can carry, and put each man's money
in the top of his sack. 2 Put my cup, the silver cup,
in the top of the sack of the youngest, with his
money for the grain." And he did as Joseph told
him. 3 As soon as the morning was light, the men
were sent away with their donkeys. 4 When they
had gone only a short distance from the city,
Joseph said to his steward, "Go, follow after the
men; and when you overtake them, say to them,
'Why have you returned evil for good? Why have
you stolen my silver cup?[a] 5 Is it not from this that
my lord drinks? Does he not indeed use it for divination? You have done wrong in doing this.'"
6 When he overtook them, he repeated these
words to them. 7 They said to him, "Why does my
lord speak such words as these? Far be it from
your servants that they should do such a thing!
8 Look, the money that we found at the top of our
sacks, we brought back to you from the land of
Canaan; why then would we steal silver or gold
from your lord's house? 9 Should it be found with
any one of your servants, let him die; moreover
the rest of us will become my lord's slaves." 10 He
said, "Even so; in accordance with your words,
let it be: he with whom it is found shall become
my slave, but the rest of you shall go free." 11 Then
each one quickly lowered his sack to the ground,
and each opened his sack. 12 He searched, beginning with the eldest and ending with the youngest; and the cup was found in Benjamin's sack.
13 At this they tore their clothes. Then each one
loaded his donkey, and they returned to the city.
14 Judah and his brothers came to Joseph's
house while he was still there; and they fell to the
ground before him. 15 Joseph said to them, "What
deed is this that you have done? Do you not know
that one such as I can practice divination?" 16 And
Judah said, "What can we say to my lord? What
can we speak? How can we clear ourselves? God
has found out the guilt of your servants; here we
are then, my lord's slaves, both we and also the
one in whose possession the cup has been found."
17 But he said, "Far be it from me that I should do
so! Only the one in whose possession the cup was
found shall be my slave; but as for you, go up in
peace to your father."
18 Then Judah stepped up to him and said,
"O my lord, let your servant please speak a word
in my lord's ears, and do not be angry with your
servant; for you are like Pharaoh himself. 19 My
lord asked his servants, saying, 'Have you a father
or a brother?' 20 And we said to my lord, 'We have
a father, an old man, and a young brother, the
child of his old age. His brother is dead; he alone
is left of his mother's children, and his father loves
him.' 21 Then you said to your servants, 'Bring him
down to me, so that I may set my eyes on him.'
22 We said to my lord, 'The boy cannot leave his

[a] Gk Compare Vg: Heb lacks *Why have you stolen my silver cup?*

father, for if he should leave his father, his father
would die.’ 23Then you said to your servants, ‘Unless your youngest brother comes down with you,
you shall see my face no more.’ 24When we went
back to your servant my father we told him the
words of my lord. 25And when our father said,
‘Go again, buy us a little food,’ 26we said, ‘We cannot go down. Only if our youngest brother goes
with us, will we go down; for we cannot see the
man’s face unless our youngest brother is with us.’
27Then your servant my father said to us, ‘You
know that my wife bore me two sons; 28one left
me, and I said, Surely he has been torn to pieces;
and I have never seen him since. 29If you take
this one also from me, and harm comes to him,
you will bring down my gray hairs in sorrow to
Sheol.’ 30Now therefore, when I come to your servant my father and the boy is not with us, then,
as his life is bound up in the boy’s life, 31when
he sees that the boy is not with us, he will die;
and your servants will bring down the gray hairs
of your servant our father with sorrow to Sheol.
32For your servant became surety for the boy to
my father, saying, ‘If I do not bring him back to
you, then I will bear the blame in the sight of my
father all my life.’ 33Now therefore, please let your
servant remain as a slave to my lord in place of the
boy; and let the boy go back with his brothers.
34For how can I go back to my father if the boy is
not with me? I fear to see the suffering that would
come upon my father.”

45 Then Joseph could no longer control
himself before all those who stood by
him, and he cried out, “Send everyone away from
me.” So no one stayed with him when Joseph
made himself known to his brothers. 2And he
wept so loudly that the Egyptians heard it, and
the household of Pharaoh heard it. 3Joseph said
to his brothers, “I am Joseph. Is my father still
alive?” But his brothers could not answer him, so
dismayed were they at his presence.

4 Then Joseph said to his brothers, “Come
closer to me.” And they came closer. He said, “I
am your brother, Joseph, whom you sold into
Egypt. 5And now do not be distressed, or angry
with yourselves, because you sold me here; for
God sent me before you to preserve life. 6For the
famine has been in the land these two years; and
there are five more years in which there will be
neither plowing nor harvest. 7God sent me before you to preserve for you a remnant on earth,
and to keep alive for you many survivors. 8So
it was not you who sent me here, but God; he
has made me a father to Pharaoh, and lord of all
his house and ruler over all the land of Egypt.
9Hurry and go up to my father and say to him,
‘Thus says your son Joseph, God has made me
lord of all Egypt; come down to me, do not delay. 10You shall settle in the land of Goshen, and
you shall be near me, you and your children and
your children’s children, as well as your flocks,
your herds, and all that you have. 11I will provide
for you there—since there are five more years of
famine to come—so that you and your household, and all that you have, will not come to poverty.’ 12And now your eyes and the eyes of my
brother Benjamin see that it is my own mouth
that speaks to you. 13You must tell my father
how greatly I am honored in Egypt, and all that
you have seen. Hurry and bring my father down
here.” 14Then he fell upon his brother Benjamin’s
neck and wept, while Benjamin wept upon his
neck. 15And he kissed all his brothers and wept
upon them; and after that his brothers talked
with him.

16 When the report was heard in Pharaoh’s
house, “Joseph’s brothers have come,” Pharaoh
and his servants were pleased. 17Pharaoh said to
Joseph, “Say to your brothers, ‘Do this: load your
animals and go back to the land of Canaan. 18Take
your father and your households and come to me,
so that I may give you the best of the land of Egypt,
and you may enjoy the fat of the land.’ 19You are
further charged to say, ‘Do this: take wagons from
the land of Egypt for your little ones and for your
wives, and bring your father, and come. 20Give no
thought to your possessions, for the best of all the
land of Egypt is yours.’”

21 The sons of Israel did so. Joseph gave them
wagons according to the instruction of Pharaoh,
and he gave them provisions for the journey. 22To
each one of them he gave a set of garments; but to
Benjamin he gave three hundred pieces of silver
and five sets of garments. 23To his father he sent

the following: ten donkeys loaded with the good things of Egypt, and ten female donkeys loaded with grain, bread, and provision for his father on the journey. 24 Then he sent his brothers on their way, and as they were leaving he said to them, "Do not quarrel[a] along the way."

25 So they went up out of Egypt and came to their father Jacob in the land of Canaan. 26 And they told him, "Joseph is still alive! He is even ruler over all the land of Egypt." He was stunned; he could not believe them. 27 But when they told him all the words of Joseph that he had said to them, and when he saw the wagons that Joseph had sent to carry him, the spirit of their father Jacob revived. 28 Israel said, "Enough! My son Joseph is still alive. I must go and see him before I die."

46 When Israel set out on his journey with all that he had and came to Beer-sheba, he offered sacrifices to the God of his father Isaac. 2 God spoke to Israel in visions of the night, and said, "Jacob, Jacob." And he said, "Here I am." 3 Then he said, "I am God,[b] the God of your father; do not be afraid to go down to Egypt, for I will make of you a great nation there. 4 I myself will go down with you to Egypt, and I will also bring you up again; and Joseph's own hand shall close your eyes."

5 Then Jacob set out from Beer-sheba; and the sons of Israel carried their father Jacob, their little ones, and their wives, in the wagons that Pharaoh had sent to carry him. 6 They also took their livestock and the goods that they had acquired in the land of Canaan, and they came into Egypt, Jacob and all his offspring with him, 7 his sons, and his sons' sons with him, his daughters, and his sons' daughters; all his offspring he brought with him into Egypt.

8 Now these are the names of the Israelites, Jacob and his offspring, who came to Egypt. Reuben, Jacob's firstborn, 9 and the children of Reuben: Hanoch, Pallu, Hezron, and Carmi. 10 The children of Simeon: Jemuel, Jamin, Ohad, Jachin, Zohar, and Shaul,[c] the son of a Canaanite woman. 11 The children of Levi: Gershon, Kohath, and Merari. 12 The children of Judah: Er, Onan, Shelah, Perez, and Zerah (but Er and Onan died in the land of Canaan); and the children of Perez were Hezron and Hamul. 13 The children of Issachar: Tola, Puvah, Jashub,[d] and Shimron. 14 The children of Zebulun: Sered, Elon, and Jahleel 15 (these are the sons of Leah, whom she bore to Jacob in Paddan-aram, together with his daughter Dinah; in all his sons and his daughters numbered thirty-three). 16 The children of Gad: Ziphion, Haggi, Shuni, Ezbon, Eri, Arodi, and Areli. 17 The children of Asher: Imnah, Ishvah, Ishvi, Beriah, and their sister Serah. The children of Beriah: Heber and Malchiel 18 (these are the children of Zilpah, whom Laban gave to his daughter Leah; and these she bore to Jacob—sixteen persons). 19 The children of Jacob's wife Rachel: Joseph and Benjamin. 20 To Joseph in the land of Egypt were born Manasseh and Ephraim, whom Asenath daughter of Potiphera, priest of On, bore to him. 21 The children of Benjamin: Bela, Becher, Ashbel, Gera, Naaman, Ehi, Rosh, Muppim, Huppim, and Ard 22 (these are the children of Rachel, who were born to Jacob—fourteen persons in all). 23 The children of Dan: Hashum.[e] 24 The children of Naphtali: Jahzeel, Guni, Jezer, and Shillem 25 (these are the children of Bilhah, whom Laban gave to his daughter Rachel, and these she bore to Jacob—seven persons in all). 26 All the persons belonging to Jacob who came into Egypt, who were his own offspring, not including the wives of his sons, were sixty-six persons in all.

Genesis 46:15

The total number of Jacob's sons and daughters is thirty-three. If he has only the twelve sons, then he has twenty-one daughters. Only the name of Dinah, whose story is told in chapter 34, is preserved in the text.

— WG

[a] Or *be agitated* [b] Heb *the God* [c] Or *Saul* [d] Compare Sam Gk Num 26.24; 1 Chr 7.1: MT *Iob*
[e] Gk: Heb *Hushim*

27 The children of Joseph, who were born to him
in Egypt, were two; all the persons of the house
of Jacob who came into Egypt were seventy.
28 Israel[a] sent Judah ahead to Joseph to lead
the way before him into Goshen. When they
came to the land of Goshen, 29 Joseph made
ready his chariot and went up to meet his father
Israel in Goshen. He presented himself to him,
fell on his neck, and wept on his neck a good
while. 30 Israel said to Joseph, "I can die now,
having seen for myself that you are still alive."
31 Joseph said to his brothers and to his father's
household, "I will go up and tell Pharaoh, and
will say to him, 'My brothers and my father's
household, who were in the land of Canaan,
have come to me. 32 The men are shepherds, for
they have been keepers of livestock; and they
have brought their flocks, and their herds, and
all that they have.' 33 When Pharaoh calls you,
and says, 'What is your occupation?' 34 you shall
say, 'Your servants have been keepers of livestock from our youth even until now, both we
and our ancestors'—in order that you may settle
in the land of Goshen, because all shepherds are
abhorrent to the Egyptians."

47 So Joseph went and told Pharaoh, "My
father and my brothers, with their flocks
and herds and all that they possess, have come
from the land of Canaan; they are now in the land
of Goshen." 2 From among his brothers he took
five men and presented them to Pharaoh. 3 Pharaoh said to his brothers, "What is your occupation?" And they said to Pharaoh, "Your servants
are shepherds, as our ancestors were." 4 They said
to Pharaoh, "We have come to reside as aliens in
the land; for there is no pasture for your servants'
flocks because the famine is severe in the land of
Canaan. Now, we ask you, let your servants settle
in the land of Goshen." 5 Then Pharaoh said to
Joseph, "Your father and your brothers have come
to you. 6 The land of Egypt is before you; settle
your father and your brothers in the best part of
the land; let them live in the land of Goshen; and
if you know that there are capable men among
them, put them in charge of my livestock."
7 Then Joseph brought in his father Jacob, and
presented him before Pharaoh, and Jacob blessed
Pharaoh. 8 Pharaoh said to Jacob, "How many are
the years of your life?" 9 Jacob said to Pharaoh,
"The years of my earthly sojourn are one hundred
thirty; few and hard have been the years of my life.
They do not compare with the years of the life of
my ancestors during their long sojourn." 10 Then
Jacob blessed Pharaoh, and went out from the
presence of Pharaoh. 11 Joseph settled his father
and his brothers, and granted them a holding in
the land of Egypt, in the best part of the land, in
the land of Rameses, as Pharaoh had instructed.
12 And Joseph provided his father, his brothers,
and all his father's household with food, according to the number of their dependents.
13 Now there was no food in all the land, for
the famine was very severe. The land of Egypt
and the land of Canaan languished because of
the famine. 14 Joseph collected all the money to
be found in the land of Egypt and in the land
of Canaan, in exchange for the grain that they
bought; and Joseph brought the money into Pharaoh's house. 15 When the money from the land
of Egypt and from the land of Canaan was spent,
all the Egyptians came to Joseph, and said, "Give
us food! Why should we die before your eyes?
For our money is gone." 16 And Joseph answered,
"Give me your livestock, and I will give you food
in exchange for your livestock, if your money
is gone." 17 So they brought their livestock to
Joseph; and Joseph gave them food in exchange
for the horses, the flocks, the herds, and the donkeys. That year he supplied them with food in
exchange for all their livestock. 18 When that year
was ended, they came to him the following year,
and said to him, "We can not hide from my lord
that our money is all spent; and the herds of cattle
are my lord's. There is nothing left in the sight of
my lord but our bodies and our lands. 19 Shall we
die before your eyes, both we and our land? Buy
us and our land in exchange for food. We with our
land will become slaves to Pharaoh; just give us
seed, so that we may live and not die, and that the
land may not become desolate."

[a] Heb *He*

Genesis 47:19-21

Ironically, Joseph is credited with enslaving Egyptians well before the Egyptians enslave his descendants in Exodus.

— *WG*

20 So Joseph bought all the land of Egypt
for Pharaoh. All the Egyptians sold their fields,
because the famine was severe upon them; and
the land became Pharaoh's. 21 As for the people,
he made slaves of them[a] from one end of Egypt
to the other. 22 Only the land of the priests he did
not buy; for the priests had a fixed allowance from
Pharaoh, and lived on the allowance that Pharaoh
gave them; therefore they did not sell their land.
23 Then Joseph said to the people, "Now that I
have this day bought you and your land for Pharaoh, here is seed for you; sow the land. 24 And at
the harvests you shall give one-fifth to Pharaoh,
and four-fifths shall be your own, as seed for the
field and as food for yourselves and your households, and as food for your little ones." 25 They
said, "You have saved our lives; may it please my
lord, we will be slaves to Pharaoh." 26 So Joseph
made it a statute concerning the land of Egypt,
and it stands to this day, that Pharaoh should have
the fifth. The land of the priests alone did not become Pharaoh's.

27 Thus Israel settled in the land of Egypt,
in the region of Goshen; and they gained possessions in it, and were fruitful and multiplied
exceedingly. 28 Jacob lived in the land of Egypt
seventeen years; so the days of Jacob, the years of
his life, were one hundred forty-seven years.

29 When the time of Israel's death drew near,
he called his son Joseph and said to him, "If I
have found favor with you, put your hand under
my thigh and promise to deal loyally and truly
with me. Do not bury me in Egypt. 30 When I lie
down with my ancestors, carry me out of Egypt
and bury me in their burial place." He answered,
"I will do as you have said." 31 And he said, "Swear
to me"; and he swore to him. Then Israel bowed
himself on the head of his bed.

48 After this Joseph was told, "Your father
is ill." So he took with him his two sons,
Manasseh and Ephraim. 2 When Jacob was told,
"Your son Joseph has come to you," he[b] summoned his strength and sat up in bed. 3 And Jacob
said to Joseph, "God Almighty[c] appeared to me
at Luz in the land of Canaan, and he blessed me,
4 and said to me, 'I am going to make you fruitful and increase your numbers; I will make of
you a company of peoples, and will give this land
to your offspring after you for a perpetual holding.' 5 Therefore your two sons, who were born
to you in the land of Egypt before I came to you
in Egypt, are now mine; Ephraim and Manasseh
shall be mine, just as Reuben and Simeon are. 6 As
for the offspring born to you after them, they shall
be yours. They shall be recorded under the names
of their brothers with regard to their inheritance.
7 For when I came from Paddan, Rachel, alas, died
in the land of Canaan on the way, while there was
still some distance to go to Ephrath; and I buried
her there on the way to Ephrath" (that is, Bethlehem).

8 When Israel saw Joseph's sons, he said,
"Who are these?" 9 Joseph said to his father, "They
are my sons, whom God has given me here." And
he said, "Bring them to me, please, that I may
bless them." 10 Now the eyes of Israel were dim
with age, and he could not see well. So Joseph
brought them near him; and he kissed them and
embraced them. 11 Israel said to Joseph, "I did not
expect to see your face; and here God has let me
see your children also." 12 Then Joseph removed
them from his father's knees,[d] and he bowed
himself with his face to the earth. 13 Joseph took
them both, Ephraim in his right hand toward Israel's left, and Manasseh in his left hand toward
Israel's right, and brought them near him. 14 But
Israel stretched out his right hand and laid it on
the head of Ephraim, who was the younger, and
his left hand on the head of Manasseh, crossing

[a] Sam Gk Compare Vg: MT *He removed them to the cities* [b] Heb *Israel* [c] Traditional rendering of Heb *El Shaddai*
[d] Heb *from his knees*

his hands, for Manasseh was the firstborn. 15He
blessed Joseph, and said,

"The God before whom my ancestors
Abraham and Isaac walked,
the God who has been my shepherd all my
life to this day,
16 the angel who has redeemed me from all
harm, bless the boys;
and in them let my name be perpetuated, and
the name of my ancestors Abraham
and Isaac;
and let them grow into a multitude on the
earth."

17 When Joseph saw that his father laid his
right hand on the head of Ephraim, it displeased
him; so he took his father's hand, to remove it
from Ephraim's head to Manasseh's head. 18Jo-
seph said to his father, "Not so, my father! Since
this one is the firstborn, put your right hand on
his head." 19But his father refused, and said, "I
know, my son, I know; he also shall become a
people, and he also shall be great. Nevertheless
his younger brother shall be greater than he, and
his offspring shall become a multitude of nations."
20So he blessed them that day, saying,

"By you[a] Israel will invoke blessings, saying,
'God make you[a] like Ephraim and like
Manasseh.'"

So he put Ephraim ahead of Manasseh. 21Then
Israel said to Joseph, "I am about to die, but God
will be with you and will bring you again to the
land of your ancestors. 22I now give to you one
portion[b] more than to your brothers, the portion[b]
that I took from the hand of the Amorites with
my sword and with my bow."

49 Then Jacob called his sons, and said:
"Gather around, that I may tell you what
will happen to you in days to come.

2 Assemble and hear, O sons of Jacob;
listen to Israel your father.

3 Reuben, you are my firstborn,
my might and the first fruits of my vigor,
excelling in rank and excelling in power.
4 Unstable as water, you shall no longer excel
because you went up onto your father's
bed;
then you defiled it—you[c] went up onto my
couch!

5 Simeon and Levi are brothers;
weapons of violence are their swords.
6 May I never come into their council;
may I not be joined to their company—
for in their anger they killed men,
and at their whim they hamstrung oxen.
7 Cursed be their anger, for it is fierce,
and their wrath, for it is cruel!
I will divide them in Jacob,
and scatter them in Israel.

8 Judah, your brothers shall praise you;
your hand shall be on the neck of your
enemies;
your father's sons shall bow down before
you.
9 Judah is a lion's whelp;
from the prey, my son, you have gone up.
He crouches down, he stretches out like a
lion,
like a lioness—who dares rouse him up?
10 The scepter shall not depart from Judah,
nor the ruler's staff from between his feet,
until tribute comes to him;[d]
and the obedience of the peoples is his.
11 Binding his foal to the vine
and his donkey's colt to the choice vine,
he washes his garments in wine
and his robe in the blood of grapes;
12 his eyes are darker than wine,
and his teeth whiter than milk.

13 Zebulun shall settle at the shore of the sea;
he shall be a haven for ships,
and his border shall be at Sidon.

14 Issachar is a strong donkey,
lying down between the sheepfolds;

[a] *you* here is singular in Heb [b] Or *mountain slope* (Heb *shekem*, a play on the name of the town and district of Shechem)
[c] Gk Syr Tg: Heb *he* [d] Or *until Shiloh comes* or *until he comes to Shiloh* or (with Syr) *until he comes to whom it belongs*

15 he saw that a resting place was good,
and that the land was pleasant;
so he bowed his shoulder to the burden,
and became a slave at forced labor.

16 Dan shall judge his people
as one of the tribes of Israel.
17 Dan shall be a snake by the roadside,
a viper along the path,
that bites the horse's heels
so that its rider falls backward.

18 I wait for your salvation, O LORD.

19 Gad shall be raided by raiders,
but he shall raid at their heels.

20 Asher's[a] food shall be rich,
and he shall provide royal delicacies.

21 Naphtali is a doe let loose
that bears lovely fawns.[b]

22 Joseph is a fruitful bough,
a fruitful bough by a spring;
his branches run over the wall.[c]
23 The archers fiercely attacked him;
they shot at him and pressed him hard.
24 Yet his bow remained taut,
and his arms[d] were made agile
by the hands of the Mighty One of Jacob,
by the name of the Shepherd, the Rock of
Israel,
25 by the God of your father, who will help
you,
by the Almighty[e] who will bless you
with blessings of heaven above,
blessings of the deep that lies beneath,
blessings of the breasts and of the womb.
26 The blessings of your father
are stronger than the blessings of the
eternal mountains,
the bounties[f] of the everlasting hills;
may they be on the head of Joseph,
on the brow of him who was set apart from
his brothers.

27 Benjamin is a ravenous wolf,
in the morning devouring the prey,
and at evening dividing the spoil."

28 All these are the twelve tribes of Israel,
and this is what their father said to them when
he blessed them, blessing each one of them with
a suitable blessing.
29 Then he charged them, saying to them,
"I am about to be gathered to my people. Bury
me with my ancestors—in the cave in the field
of Ephron the Hittite, 30 in the cave in the field at
Machpelah, near Mamre, in the land of Canaan,
in the field that Abraham bought from Ephron
the Hittite as a burial site. 31 There Abraham
and his wife Sarah were buried; there Isaac and
his wife Rebekah were buried; and there I buried Leah— 32 the field and the cave that is in it
were purchased from the Hittites." 33 When Jacob
ended his charge to his sons, he drew up his feet
into the bed, breathed his last, and was gathered
to his people.

50 Then Joseph threw himself on his father's
face and wept over him and kissed him.
2 Joseph commanded the physicians in his service
to embalm his father. So the physicians embalmed
Israel; 3 they spent forty days in doing this, for
that is the time required for embalming. And the
Egyptians wept for him seventy days.
4 When the days of weeping for him were
past, Joseph addressed the household of Pharaoh,
"If now I have found favor with you, please speak
to Pharaoh as follows: 5 My father made me swear
an oath; he said, 'I am about to die. In the tomb
that I hewed out for myself in the land of Canaan,
there you shall bury me.' Now therefore let me go
up, so that I may bury my father; then I will return." 6 Pharaoh answered, "Go up, and bury your
father, as he made you swear to do."

[a] Gk Vg Syr: Heb *From Asher* [b] Or *that gives beautiful words* [c] Meaning of Heb uncertain
[d] Heb *the arms of his hands* [e] Traditional rendering of Heb *Shaddai*
[f] Cn Compare Gk: Heb *of my progenitors to the boundaries*

7 So Joseph went up to bury his father. With him went up all the servants of Pharaoh, the elders of his household, and all the elders of the land of Egypt, 8 as well as all the household of Joseph, his brothers, and his father's household. Only their children, their flocks, and their herds were left in the land of Goshen. 9 Both chariots and charioteers went up with him. It was a very great company. 10 When they came to the threshing floor of Atad, which is beyond the Jordan, they held there a very great and sorrowful lamentation; and he observed a time of mourning for his father seven days. 11 When the Canaanite inhabitants of the land saw the mourning on the threshing floor of Atad, they said, "This is a grievous mourning on the part of the Egyptians." Therefore the place was named Abel-mizraim;[a] it is beyond the Jordan. 12 Thus his sons did for him as he had instructed them. 13 They carried him to the land of Canaan and buried him in the cave of the field at Machpelah, the field near Mamre, which Abraham bought as a burial site from Ephron the Hittite. 14 After he had buried his father, Joseph returned to Egypt with his brothers and all who had gone up with him to bury his father.

15 Realizing that their father was dead, Joseph's brothers said, "What if Joseph still bears a grudge against us and pays us back in full for all the wrong that we did to him?" 16 So they approached[b] Joseph, saying, "Your father gave this instruction before he died, 17 'Say to Joseph: I beg you, forgive the crime of your brothers and the wrong they did in harming you.' Now therefore please forgive the crime of the servants of the God of your father." Joseph wept when they spoke to him. 18 Then his brothers also wept,[c] fell down before him, and said, "We are here as your slaves." 19 But Joseph said to them, "Do not be afraid! Am I in the place of God? 20 Even though you intended to do harm to me, God intended it for good, in order to preserve a numerous people, as he is doing today. 21 So have no fear; I myself will provide for you and your little ones." In this way he reassured them, speaking kindly to them.

22 So Joseph remained in Egypt, he and his father's household; and Joseph lived one hundred ten years. 23 Joseph saw Ephraim's children of the third generation; the children of Machir son of Manasseh were also born on Joseph's knees.

24 Then Joseph said to his brothers, "I am about to die; but God will surely come to you, and bring you up out of this land to the land that he swore to Abraham, to Isaac, and to Jacob." 25 So Joseph made the Israelites swear, saying, "When God comes to you, you shall carry up my bones from here." 26 And Joseph died, being one hundred ten years old; he was embalmed and placed in a coffin in Egypt.

[a] That is *mourning* (or *meadow*) *of Egypt* [b] Gk Syr: Heb *they commanded* [c] Cn: Heb *also came*

Other Old Testaments

Episcopal bishop and theologian Steven Charleston, a citizen of the Choctaw Nation, writes that the indigenous peoples of the Americas have their own "Old Testament," that is, "their own original covenant relationship with the Creator and their own original understanding of God prior to the birth of Christ. It is a tradition that has evolved over centuries. It tells of the active, living, revealing presence of God in relation to Native People through generations of Native life and experience. It asserts that God was not an absentee landlord for North America. God was here, on this continent among this people, in covenant, in relation, in life. Like Israel itself, Native America proclaims that God is a God of all times and of all places and of all peoples."[9]

— *CDY*

Exodus

THE BOOK OF EXODUS is the centerpiece of the Torah (or Pentateuch)—the five books of Moses that begin the Hebrew scriptures, for Christians the Old Testament. Exodus tells the story of how YHWH, the God of Israel, freed a group of slaves in Egypt and brought them to YHWH's chosen mountain in the desert to give them laws by which they should live. It is the foundational story of the people of Israel, celebrated to this day by the Jews on Passover. These liberated people will become, says YHWH, a special property (*segullah*) among all the peoples of the earth (19:5). Much of the Torah is devoted to the laws revealed at Sinai so that this special people might share the holiness of YHWH. That Exodus is so foundational for Jewish identity makes this a difficult book for many Christians to identify with—unless they are poor or oppressed Christians in Latin America and other places around the world.

The content of Exodus can be characterized in three great sections. In chapters 1–15, YHWH hears the cries of the oppressed slaves in Egypt and calls a prophet, Moses, to lead them to freedom. God had promised Moses that he would give the people land in Canaan (3:8), but when they escape from Egypt they find themselves in a desert. Chapters 15–18 tell of the people's wanderings in the desert that lead them to the "wilderness of Sinai" (19:1). Now, in chapters 19–40, comes the third and longest section, the revelation of laws to guide the life of the people in their new social situation—to assure that they act justly toward one another *and* maintain the holiness of YHWH.

Reading Exodus in Latin America

I am the son of a medical doctor and a nurse who worked in a Baptist Hospital in Managua, Nicaragua. Though I am a U.S. citizen, my schooling through high school was done in Managua in Spanish. Later, my work with peasant native communities in Mexico, at the Seminario Bautista de México and the Instituto Teológico de Estudios Superiores, opened my eyes to the reality of most rural peoples of the world. I became convinced that if the Christian gospel had nothing for them, it had nothing at all. In his *Notebooks of 1858* and in *Capital*, Karl Marx gave a theoretical framework, and liberation theology gave the theological basis for a word to these poor.

Many Christian readers of the Bible in Latin America—and almost all of the Native (Indian) communities here—are peasants. Peasants are people who feel wedded to the land, of which they feel they are a part. They produce much of their own food and clothing, selling some surplus production in grains and animals to meet needs they cannot supply for themselves, such as salt and shoes. But with the penetration of capitalist agriculture in the last one hundred years, they have seen their way of life threatened—and in many cases destroyed—by imported grains, which sell for less than their costs of production, and by the sale and use of fertilizers and pesticides that were unnecessary in their traditional way of producing food. Many believe that Monsanto, Cargill, Dole, and other multinational corporations have driven them off land that God gave them and forced them into urban slums.

These peasants, whether living on the land or displaced into slums, are a majority of the Bible readers in Latin America and among them liberation theology emerged. With little economic sophistication, they nevertheless readily identify their oppressor as Neoliberalism or globalization. Those are *today's* names for Pharaoh as the peasants read Exodus in the context of their cultural situation. As the enslaved peasants of Egypt cried for liberation from Pharaoh, Latin America's peasants cry for liberation from Neoliberalism and the effects of economic globalization.

Others, including many of Latin America's more urbanized Christians, believe the root cause of their problems is control of their economies and political life by the world's leading imperial power, the United States. That empire, by determining what they should produce, destroys their *internal* national markets. It often determines what their democracy should look like, thus uprooting their political life from national realities. When things do not satisfy the U.S. empire, its troops or proxies intervene by destroying their coca fields or making certain that Latin American debts are directed to the "right" creditors. So, at the beginning of the twenty-first century, Pharaoh for them is the United States, and liberation means freedom from bondage to the United States; figures like Fidel Castro and Hugo Chávez become to them like Moses and Aaron.

The Composition of Exodus

The original story of the exodus from Egypt—as opposed to the story narrated in the book—must have arisen, and been told and retold, among the peasant people who rose up against the kings of the Canaanite plains and emigrated to the underpopulated hills of Canaan. That is the influential interpretation that Norman Gottwald proposed in his book *The Tribes of Yahweh*. The laws of the so-called Covenant Code (20:22—23:19), though probably put together later in the monarchical period, still reflect aspects of peasant life, the life of the original tellers of the exodus story.

The book of Exodus owes its present form to the scribes of Yehud (Judah), a Persian province (538–322 BCE). Under priestly dominance, laws that make up the bulk of Exodus 24:15—40:38, what scholars call the Priestly Code—became prominent as the people strove to maintain their holiness under foreign hegemony.

— Jorge Pixley

1 These are the names of the sons of Israel
who came to Egypt with Jacob, each with his
household: 2 Reuben, Simeon, Levi, and Judah,
3 Issachar, Zebulun, and Benjamin, 4 Dan and
Naphtali, Gad and Asher. 5 The total number of
people born to Jacob was seventy. Joseph was
already in Egypt. 6 Then Joseph died, and all his
brothers, and that whole generation. 7 But the

Israelites were fruitful and prolific; they multiplied and grew exceedingly strong, so that the
land was filled with them.

8 Now a new king arose over Egypt, who did
not know Joseph. 9He said to his people, "Look,
the Israelite people are more numerous and more
powerful than we. 10Come, let us deal shrewdly
with them, or they will increase and, in the
event of war, join our enemies and fight against
us and escape from the land." 11Therefore they
set taskmasters over them to oppress them with
forced labor. They built supply cities, Pithom and
Rameses, for Pharaoh. 12But the more they were
oppressed, the more they multiplied and spread,
so that the Egyptians came to dread the Israelites.
13The Egyptians became ruthless in imposing
tasks on the Israelites, 14and made their lives bitter with hard service in mortar and brick and in
every kind of field labor. They were ruthless in all
the tasks that they imposed on them.

15 The king of Egypt said to the Hebrew midwives, one of whom was named Shiphrah and the
other Puah, 16"When you act as midwives to the
Hebrew women, and see them on the birthstool,
if it is a boy, kill him; but if it is a girl, she shall
live." 17But the midwives feared God; they did
not do as the king of Egypt commanded them,
but they let the boys live. 18So the king of Egypt
summoned the midwives and said to them, "Why
have you done this, and allowed the boys to live?"
19The midwives said to Pharaoh, "Because the
Hebrew women are not like the Egyptian wom-
en; for they are vigorous and give birth before
the midwife comes to them." 20So God dealt well
with the midwives; and the people multiplied
and became very strong. 21And because the midwives feared God, he gave them families. 22Then
Pharaoh commanded all his people, "Every boy
that is born to the Hebrews[a] you shall throw into
the Nile, but you shall let every girl live."

2 Now a man from the house of Levi went and
married a Levite woman. 2The woman conceived and bore a son; and when she saw that he
was a fine baby, she hid him three months. 3When
she could hide him no longer she got a papyrus
basket for him, and plastered it with bitumen and
pitch; she put the child in it and placed it among
the reeds on the bank of the river. 4His sister stood
at a distance, to see what would happen to him.

5 The daughter of Pharaoh came down to
bathe at the river, while her attendants walked beside the river. She saw the basket among the reeds
and sent her maid to bring it. 6When she opened
it, she saw the child. He was crying, and she took
pity on him. "This must be one of the Hebrews'
children," she said. 7Then his sister said to Pharaoh's daughter, "Shall I go and get you a nurse
from the Hebrew women to nurse the child for
you?" 8Pharaoh's daughter said to her, "Yes." So
the girl went and called the child's mother. 9Pha-
raoh's daughter said to her, "Take this child and
nurse it for me, and I will give you your wages." So
the woman took the child and nursed it. 10When
the child grew up, she brought him to Pharaoh's
daughter, and she took him as her son. She named
him Moses,[b] "because," she said, "I drew him out[c]
of the water."

11 One day, after Moses had grown up, he
went out to his people and saw their forced labor.
He saw an Egyptian beating a Hebrew, one of his
kinsfolk. 12He looked this way and that, and seeing no one he killed the Egyptian and hid him in
the sand. 13When he went out the next day, he
saw two Hebrews fighting; and he said to the one
who was in the wrong, "Why do you strike your

Exodus 1:15-22

Confronted by Pharaoh, the Hebrew midwives deceive him by playing on his own racism. Their preposterous excuse—that "the Hebrew women are not like the Egyptian women" but are too "vigorous," almost like wild animals—seems quite plausible to him. Their sly answer reflects the cunning on which subject peoples must often rely as they navigate the treacherous ways of an oppressive culture.

— *NE*

[a] Sam Gk Tg: Heb lacks *to the Hebrews* [b] Heb *Mosheh* [c] Heb *mashah*

fellow Hebrew?" 14He answered, "Who made
you a ruler and judge over us? Do you mean to
kill me as you killed the Egyptian?" Then Moses was afraid and thought, "Surely the thing is
known." 15When Pharaoh heard of it, he sought
to kill Moses.

But Moses fled from Pharaoh. He settled in
the land of Midian, and sat down by a well. 16The
priest of Midian had seven daughters. They came
to draw water, and filled the troughs to water their
father's flock. 17But some shepherds came and
drove them away. Moses got up and came to their
defense and watered their flock. 18When they returned to their father Reuel, he said, "How is it
that you have come back so soon today?" 19They
said, "An Egyptian helped us against the shepherds; he even drew water for us and watered the
flock." 20He said to his daughters, "Where is he?
Why did you leave the man? Invite him to break
bread." 21Moses agreed to stay with the man, and
he gave Moses his daughter Zipporah in marriage. 22She bore a son, and he named him Gershom; for he said, "I have been an alien[a] residing
in a foreign land."

23 After a long time the king of Egypt died.
The Israelites groaned under their slavery, and
cried out. Out of the slavery their cry for help rose
up to God. 24God heard their groaning, and God
remembered his covenant with Abraham, Isaac,
and Jacob. 25God looked upon the Israelites, and
God took notice of them.

3 Moses was keeping the flock of his father-in-
law Jethro, the priest of Midian; he led his
flock beyond the wilderness, and came to Horeb,
the mountain of God. 2There the angel of the
LORD appeared to him in a flame of fire out of
a bush; he looked, and the bush was blazing, yet
it was not consumed. 3Then Moses said, "I must
turn aside and look at this great sight, and see why
the bush is not burned up." 4When the LORD saw
that he had turned aside to see, God called to him
out of the bush, "Moses, Moses!" And he said,
"Here I am." 5Then he said, "Come no closer! Remove the sandals from your feet, for the place on
which you are standing is holy ground." 6He said
further, "I am the God of your father, the God of
Abraham, the God of Isaac, and the God of Jacob." And Moses hid his face, for he was afraid to
look at God.

7 Then the LORD said, "I have observed the
misery of my people who are in Egypt; I have
heard their cry on account of their taskmasters.
Indeed, I know their sufferings, 8and I have come
down to deliver them from the Egyptians, and
to bring them up out of that land to a good and
broad land, a land flowing with milk and honey,
to the country of the Canaanites, the Hittites,
the Amorites, the Perizzites, the Hivites, and
the Jebusites. 9The cry of the Israelites has now
come to me; I have also seen how the Egyptians
oppress them. 10So come, I will send you to
Pharaoh to bring my people, the Israelites, out
of Egypt." 11But Moses said to God, "Who am
I that I should go to Pharaoh, and bring the Israelites out of Egypt?" 12He said, "I will be with
you; and this shall be the sign for you that it
is I who sent you: when you have brought the

Exodus 3:7

Although Genesis has already introduced the name YHWH ("the LORD"), Moses' encounter is an awesome epiphany in which the hitherto unknown identity of the one true God is revealed. God's self-disclosure offers a sort of etymology of the divine name; the Hebrew *'ehyeh 'asher 'ehyeh* ("I AM WHO I AM," v. 14) plays on the verb *hayah,* "to be," perhaps suggesting (improbably) that the name YHWH comes from the same verb. More important are the terms in which this God chooses to be introduced: as "the LORD, the God of your ancestors," implying that the deliverance to come is motivated by divine faithfulness to the promises given to Abraham in Genesis but also as the one who hears the cry of the oppressed. What a breathtaking revelation in a world where the gods were often represented as listening only to kings!

— ***NE***

[a] Heb *ger*

people out of Egypt, you shall worship God on
this mountain."
13 But Moses said to God, "If I come to the
Israelites and say to them, 'The God of your ancestors has sent me to you,' and they ask me, 'What is
his name?' what shall I say to them?" 14God said to
Moses, "I AM WHO I AM."[a] He said further, "Thus
you shall say to the Israelites, 'I AM has sent me to
you.'" 15God also said to Moses, "Thus you shall
say to the Israelites, 'The LORD,[b] the God of your
ancestors, the God of Abraham, the God of Isaac,
and the God of Jacob, has sent me to you':

This is my name forever,
and this my title for all generations.

16Go and assemble the elders of Israel, and say
to them, 'The LORD, the God of your ancestors,
the God of Abraham, of Isaac, and of Jacob, has
appeared to me, saying: I have given heed to you
and to what has been done to you in Egypt. 17I
declare that I will bring you up out of the misery
of Egypt, to the land of the Canaanites, the Hittites, the Amorites, the Perizzites, the Hivites, and
the Jebusites, a land flowing with milk and honey.'
18They will listen to your voice; and you and the
elders of Israel shall go to the king of Egypt and
say to him, 'The LORD, the God of the Hebrews,
has met with us; let us now go a three days' journey into the wilderness, so that we may sacrifice
to the LORD our God.' 19I know, however, that
the king of Egypt will not let you go unless compelled by a mighty hand.[c] 20So I will stretch out
my hand and strike Egypt with all my wonders
that I will perform in it; after that he will let you
go. 21I will bring this people into such favor with
the Egyptians that, when you go, you will not
go empty-handed; 22each woman shall ask her
neighbor and any woman living in the neighbor's
house for jewelry of silver and of gold, and clothing, and you shall put them on your sons and
on your daughters; and so you shall plunder the
Egyptians."

4 Then Moses answered, "But suppose they do
not believe me or listen to me, but say, 'The
LORD did not appear to you.'" 2The LORD said
to him, "What is that in your hand?" He said, "A
staff." 3And he said, "Throw it on the ground." So
he threw the staff on the ground, and it became
a snake; and Moses drew back from it. 4Then the
LORD said to Moses, "Reach out your hand, and
seize it by the tail"—so he reached out his hand
and grasped it, and it became a staff in his hand—
5"so that they may believe that the LORD, the
God of their ancestors, the God of Abraham, the
God of Isaac, and the God of Jacob, has appeared
to you."
6 Again, the LORD said to him, "Put your
hand inside your cloak." He put his hand into
his cloak; and when he took it out, his hand was
leprous,[d] as white as snow. 7Then God said, "Put
your hand back into your cloak"—so he put his
hand back into his cloak, and when he took it
out, it was restored like the rest of his body— 8"If
they will not believe you or heed the first sign,
they may believe the second sign. 9If they will
not believe even these two signs or heed you, you
shall take some water from the Nile and pour it
on the dry ground; and the water that you shall
take from the Nile will become blood on the dry
ground."
10 But Moses said to the LORD, "O my Lord,
I have never been eloquent, neither in the past
nor even now that you have spoken to your servant; but I am slow of speech and slow of tongue."
11Then the LORD said to him, "Who gives speech
to mortals? Who makes them mute or deaf, seeing or blind? Is it not I, the LORD? 12Now go, and
I will be with your mouth and teach you what you
are to speak." 13But he said, "O my Lord, please
send someone else." 14Then the anger of the LORD
was kindled against Moses and he said, "What of
your brother Aaron the Levite? I know that he
can speak fluently; even now he is coming out to
meet you, and when he sees you his heart will be
glad. 15You shall speak to him and put the words
in his mouth; and I will be with your mouth and
with his mouth, and will teach you what you shall

[a] Or *I AM WHAT I AM* or *I WILL BE WHAT I WILL BE* [b] The word "LORD" when spelled with capital letters stands for the divine name, *YHWH*, which is here connected with the verb *hayah*, "to be" [c] Gk Vg: Heb *no, not by a mighty hand*
[d] A term for several skin diseases; precise meaning uncertain

do. 16He indeed shall speak for you to the people; he shall serve as a mouth for you, and you shall serve as God for him. 17Take in your hand this staff, with which you shall perform the signs."

18 Moses went back to his father-in-law Jethro and said to him, "Please let me go back to my kindred in Egypt and see whether they are still living." And Jethro said to Moses, "Go in peace." 19The LORD said to Moses in Midian, "Go back to Egypt; for all those who were seeking your life are dead." 20So Moses took his wife and his sons, put them on a donkey, and went back to the land of Egypt; and Moses carried the staff of God in his hand.

21 And the LORD said to Moses, "When you go back to Egypt, see that you perform before Pharaoh all the wonders that I have put in your power; but I will harden his heart, so that he will not let the people go. 22Then you shall say to Pharaoh, 'Thus says the LORD: Israel is my firstborn son. 23I said to you, "Let my son go that he may worship me." But you refused to let him go; now I will kill your firstborn son.'"

24 On the way, at a place where they spent the night, the LORD met him and tried to kill him. 25But Zipporah took a flint and cut off her son's foreskin, and touched Moses'[a] feet with it, and said, "Truly you are a bridegroom of blood to me!" 26So he let him alone. It was then she said, "A bridegroom of blood by circumcision."

27 The LORD said to Aaron, "Go into the wilderness to meet Moses." So he went; and he met him at the mountain of God and kissed him. 28Moses told Aaron all the words of the LORD with which he had sent him, and all the signs with which he had charged him. 29Then Moses and Aaron went and assembled all the elders of the Israelites. 30Aaron spoke all the words that the LORD had spoken to Moses, and performed the signs in the sight of the people. 31The people believed; and when they heard that the LORD had given heed to the Israelites and that he had seen their misery, they bowed down and worshiped.

5 Afterward Moses and Aaron went to Pharaoh and said, "Thus says the LORD, the God of Israel, 'Let my people go, so that they may celebrate a festival to me in the wilderness.'" 2But Pharaoh said, "Who is the LORD, that I should heed him and let Israel go? I do not know the LORD, and I will not let Israel go." 3Then they said, "The God of the Hebrews has revealed himself to us; let us go a three days' journey into the wilderness to sacrifice to the LORD our God, or he will fall upon us with pestilence or sword." 4But the king of Egypt said to them, "Moses and Aaron, why are you taking the people away from their work? Get to your labors!" 5Pharaoh continued, "Now they are more numerous than the people of the land[b] and yet you want them to stop working!" 6That same day Pharaoh commanded the taskmasters of the people, as well as their supervisors, 7"You shall no longer give the people straw to make bricks, as before; let them go and gather straw for themselves. 8But you shall require of them the same quantity of bricks as they have made previously; do not diminish it, for they are lazy; that is why they cry, 'Let us go and offer sacrifice to our God.' 9Let heavier work be laid on them; then they will labor at it and pay no attention to deceptive words."

10 So the taskmasters and the supervisors of the people went out and said to the people, "Thus says Pharaoh, 'I will not give you straw. 11Go and get straw yourselves, wherever you can find it; but your work will not be lessened in the least.'" 12So the people scattered throughout the land of Egypt, to gather stubble for straw. 13The taskmasters were urgent, saying, "Complete your work, the same daily assignment as when you were given straw." 14And the supervisors of the Israelites, whom Pharaoh's taskmasters had set over them, were beaten, and were asked, "Why did you not finish the required quantity of bricks yesterday and today, as you did before?"

15 Then the Israelite supervisors came to Pharaoh and cried, "Why do you treat your servants like this? 16No straw is given to your servants, yet they say to us, 'Make bricks!' Look how your servants are beaten! You are unjust to your own people."[c] 17He said, "You are lazy, lazy; that is

[a] Heb *his* [b] Sam: Heb *The people of the land are now many* [c] Gk Compare Syr Vg: Heb *beaten, and the sin of your people*

why you say, 'Let us go and sacrifice to the LORD.' 18 Go now, and work; for no straw shall be given you, but you shall still deliver the same number of bricks." 19 The Israelite supervisors saw that they were in trouble when they were told, "You shall not lessen your daily number of bricks." 20 As they left Pharaoh, they came upon Moses and Aaron who were waiting to meet them. 21 They said to them, "The LORD look upon you and judge! You have brought us into bad odor with Pharaoh and his officials, and have put a sword in their hand to kill us."

22 Then Moses turned again to the LORD and said, "O LORD, why have you mistreated this people? Why did you ever send me? 23 Since I first came to Pharaoh to speak in your name, he has mistreated this people, and you have done nothing at all to deliver your people."

6 Then the LORD said to Moses, "Now you shall see what I will do to Pharaoh: Indeed, by a mighty hand he will let them go; by a mighty hand he will drive them out of his land."

2 God also spoke to Moses and said to him: "I am the LORD. 3 I appeared to Abraham, Isaac, and Jacob as God Almighty,[a] but by my name 'The LORD'[b] I did not make myself known to them. 4 I also established my covenant with them, to give them the land of Canaan, the land in which they resided as aliens. 5 I have also heard the groaning of the Israelites whom the Egyptians are holding as slaves, and I have remembered my covenant. 6 Say therefore to the Israelites, 'I am the LORD, and I will free you from the burdens of the Egyptians and deliver you from slavery to them. I will redeem you with an outstretched arm and with mighty acts of judgment. 7 I will take you as my people, and I will be your God. You shall know that I am the LORD your God, who has freed you from the burdens of the Egyptians. 8 I will bring you into the land that I swore to give to Abraham, Isaac, and Jacob; I will give it to you for a possession. I am the LORD.'" 9 Moses told this to the Israelites; but they would not listen to Moses, because of their broken spirit and their cruel slavery.

10 Then the LORD spoke to Moses, 11 "Go and tell Pharaoh king of Egypt to let the Israelites go out of his land." 12 But Moses spoke to the LORD, "The Israelites have not listened to me; how then shall Pharaoh listen to me, poor speaker that I am?"[c] 13 Thus the LORD spoke to Moses and Aaron, and gave them orders regarding the Israelites and Pharaoh king of Egypt, charging them to free the Israelites from the land of Egypt.

14 The following are the heads of their ancestral houses: the sons of Reuben, the firstborn of Israel: Hanoch, Pallu, Hezron, and Carmi; these are the families of Reuben. 15 The sons of Simeon: Jemuel, Jamin, Ohad, Jachin, Zohar, and Shaul,[d] the son of a Canaanite woman; these are the families of Simeon. 16 The following are the names of the sons of Levi according to their genealogies: Gershon,[e] Kohath, and Merari, and the length of Levi's life was one hundred thirty-seven years. 17 The sons of Gershon:[e] Libni and Shimei, by their families. 18 The sons of Kohath: Amram, Izhar, Hebron, and Uzziel, and the length of Kohath's life was one hundred thirty-three years. 19 The sons of Merari: Mahli and Mushi. These are the families of the Levites according to their genealogies. 20 Amram married Jochebed his father's sister and she bore him Aaron and Moses, and the length of Amram's life was one hundred thirty-seven years. 21 The sons of Izhar: Korah, Nepheg, and Zichri. 22 The sons of Uzziel: Mishael, Elzaphan, and Sithri. 23 Aaron married Elisheba, daughter of Amminadab and sister of Nahshon, and she bore him Nadab, Abihu, Eleazar, and Ithamar. 24 The sons of Korah: Assir, Elkanah, and Abiasaph; these are the families of the Korahites. 25 Aaron's son Eleazar married one of the daughters of Putiel, and she bore him Phinehas. These are the heads of the ancestral houses of the Levites by their families.

26 It was this same Aaron and Moses to whom the LORD said, "Bring the Israelites out of the land of Egypt, company by company." 27 It was they who spoke to Pharaoh king of Egypt to bring the Israelites out of Egypt, the same Moses and Aaron.

[a] Traditional rendering of Heb *El Shaddai* [b] Heb *YHWH*; see note at 3.15 [c] Heb *me? I am uncircumcised of lips*

[d] Or *Saul* [e] Also spelled *Gershom*; see 2.22

28 On the day when the LORD spoke to Moses in the land of Egypt, 29he said to him, "I am
the LORD; tell Pharaoh king of Egypt all that I am
speaking to you." 30But Moses said in the LORD's
presence, "Since I am a poor speaker,[a] why would
Pharaoh listen to me?"

7 The LORD said to Moses, "See, I have made
you like God to Pharaoh, and your brother
Aaron shall be your prophet. 2You shall speak all
that I command you, and your brother Aaron shall
tell Pharaoh to let the Israelites go out of his land.
3But I will harden Pharaoh's heart, and I will multiply my signs and wonders in the land of Egypt.
4When Pharaoh does not listen to you, I will lay
my hand upon Egypt and bring my people the Israelites, company by company, out of the land of
Egypt by great acts of judgment. 5The Egyptians
shall know that I am the LORD, when I stretch out
my hand against Egypt and bring the Israelites
out from among them." 6Moses and Aaron did
so; they did just as the LORD commanded them.
7Moses was eighty years old and Aaron eighty-
three when they spoke to Pharaoh.

8 The LORD said to Moses and Aaron, 9"When
Pharaoh says to you, 'Perform a wonder,' then you
shall say to Aaron, 'Take your staff and throw it
down before Pharaoh, and it will become a snake.'"
10So Moses and Aaron went to Pharaoh and did as
the LORD had commanded; Aaron threw down
his staff before Pharaoh and his officials, and it
became a snake. 11Then Pharaoh summoned the
wise men and the sorcerers; and they also, the
magicians of Egypt, did the same by their secret
arts. 12Each one threw down his staff, and they became snakes; but Aaron's staff swallowed up theirs.
13Still Pharaoh's heart was hardened, and he would
not listen to them, as the LORD had said.

14 Then the LORD said to Moses, "Pharaoh's
heart is hardened; he refuses to let the people go.
15Go to Pharaoh in the morning, as he is going
out to the water; stand by at the river bank to
meet him, and take in your hand the staff that was
turned into a snake. 16Say to him, 'The LORD, the
God of the Hebrews, sent me to you to say, "Let
my people go, so that they may worship me in the
wilderness." But until now you have not listened.
17Thus says the LORD, "By this you shall know
that I am the LORD." See, with the staff that is in
my hand I will strike the water that is in the Nile,
and it shall be turned to blood. 18The fish in the
river shall die, the river itself shall stink, and the
Egyptians shall be unable to drink water from
the Nile.'" 19The LORD said to Moses, "Say to
Aaron, 'Take your staff and stretch out your hand
over the waters of Egypt—over its rivers, its canals, and its ponds, and all its pools of water—so
that they may become blood; and there shall be
blood throughout the whole land of Egypt, even
in vessels of wood and in vessels of stone.'"

20 Moses and Aaron did just as the LORD
commanded. In the sight of Pharaoh and of his
officials he lifted up the staff and struck the water in the river, and all the water in the river was
turned into blood, 21and the fish in the river died.
The river stank so that the Egyptians could not
drink its water, and there was blood throughout
the whole land of Egypt. 22But the magicians of
Egypt did the same by their secret arts; so Pharaoh's heart remained hardened, and he would
not listen to them, as the LORD had said. 23Pha-
raoh turned and went into his house, and he did
not take even this to heart. 24And all the Egyptians had to dig along the Nile for water to drink,
for they could not drink the water of the river.

25 Seven days passed after the LORD had
struck the Nile.

Exodus 7:7

If Moses is eighty and Aaron is eighty-three when they demand Israel's freedom, how old is Miriam? Her age is not given in the text, but in Exodus 2, Moses's sister is older than he, so much so that she is able to negotiate with Pharaoh's daughter. The story of Miriam, Aaron, and Moses is, among other things, the story of empowered elders; they are all well beyond "retirement age."

— *WG*

[a] Heb *am uncircumcised of lips*; see 6.12

Exodus 7:14-16

Black ministers, from slavery to last Sunday morning, standing in pulpits in the sprawling urban metropolis and in rural, dusty Southern counties, have been preaching deliverance from the early days of the Republic, the slave Republic, to the automated, mechanized society of urban America. Said the preacher . . . "Go down Moses, way down to Egypt land and tell old Pharaoh to let my people go." When the preacher didn't say it, the choirs . . . would sing it to the beat of their own pulse and rhythm . . . . Within minutes the entire church would be singing. No pianos, no organs—just shining, smiling faces lifting their voices to a universal tune of freedom, singing again and again, "Go down Moses, way down to Egypt land, tell old Pharaoh let my people go." Nobody stopped to take the time to write a dissertation on freedom. Freedom was in the air. The preacher, moved by his people, stood and yelled, "Set the captives free." While in the midst of all the shouts of jubilation and joy, the church kept singing, "Let my people go."[10]

— Willie K. Smith

8 [a]Then the LORD said to Moses, "Go to Pharaoh and say to him, 'Thus says the LORD:
Let my people go, so that they may worship me.
2 If you refuse to let them go, I will plague your
whole country with frogs. 3 The river shall swarm
with frogs; they shall come up into your palace,
into your bedchamber and your bed, and into
the houses of your officials and of your people,[b]
and into your ovens and your kneading bowls.
4 The frogs shall come up on you and on your
people and on all your officials.'" 5 [c]And the LORD
said to Moses, "Say to Aaron, 'Stretch out your
hand with your staff over the rivers, the canals,
and the pools, and make frogs come up on the
land of Egypt.'" 6 So Aaron stretched out his hand
over the waters of Egypt; and the frogs came up
and covered the land of Egypt. 7 But the magicians
did the same by their secret arts, and brought
frogs up on the land of Egypt.

8 Then Pharaoh called Moses and Aaron, and
said, "Pray to the LORD to take away the frogs from
me and my people, and I will let the people go to
sacrifice to the LORD." 9 Moses said to Pharaoh,
"Kindly tell me when I am to pray for you and for
your officials and for your people, that the frogs
may be removed from you and your houses and
be left only in the Nile." 10 And he said, "Tomorrow." Moses said, "As you say! So that you may
know that there is no one like the LORD our God,
11 the frogs shall leave you and your houses and
your officials and your people; they shall be left
only in the Nile." 12 Then Moses and Aaron went
out from Pharaoh; and Moses cried out to the
LORD concerning the frogs that he had brought
upon Pharaoh.[d] 13 And the LORD did as Moses requested: the frogs died in the houses, the court-
yards, and the fields. 14 And they gathered them
together in heaps, and the land stank. 15 But when
Pharaoh saw that there was a respite, he hardened
his heart, and would not listen to them, just as the
LORD had said.

16 Then the LORD said to Moses, "Say to Aaron, 'Stretch out your staff and strike the dust of the
earth, so that it may become gnats throughout the
whole land of Egypt.'" 17 And they did so; Aaron
stretched out his hand with his staff and struck
the dust of the earth, and gnats came on humans
and animals alike; all the dust of the earth turned
into gnats throughout the whole land of Egypt.
18 The magicians tried to produce gnats by their
secret arts, but they could not. There were gnats
on both humans and animals. 19 And the magicians said to Pharaoh, "This is the finger of God!"
But Pharaoh's heart was hardened, and he would
not listen to them, just as the LORD had said.

20 Then the LORD said to Moses, "Rise early
in the morning and present yourself before Pharaoh, as he goes out to the water, and say to him,
'Thus says the LORD: Let my people go, so that
they may worship me. 21 For if you will not let my
people go, I will send swarms of flies on you, your
officials, and your people, and into your houses;
and the houses of the Egyptians shall be filled
with swarms of flies; so also the land where they

[a] Ch 7.26 in Heb [b] Gk: Heb *upon your people* [c] Ch 8.1 in Heb [d] Or *frogs, as he had agreed with Pharaoh*

live. 22 But on that day I will set apart the land of
Goshen, where my people live, so that no swarms
of flies shall be there, that you may know that I the
LORD am in this land. 23 Thus I will make a distinction[a] between my people and your people. This
sign shall appear tomorrow.'" 24 The LORD did
so, and great swarms of flies came into the house
of Pharaoh and into his officials' houses; in all of
Egypt the land was ruined because of the flies.
25 Then Pharaoh summoned Moses and
Aaron, and said, "Go, sacrifice to your God within the land." 26 But Moses said, "It would not be
right to do so; for the sacrifices that we offer to
the LORD our God are offensive to the Egyptians.
If we offer in the sight of the Egyptians sacrifices
that are offensive to them, will they not stone
us? 27 We must go a three days' journey into the
wilderness and sacrifice to the LORD our God as
he commands us." 28 So Pharaoh said, "I will let
you go to sacrifice to the LORD your God in the
wilderness, provided you do not go very far away.
Pray for me." 29 Then Moses said, "As soon as I
leave you, I will pray to the LORD that the swarms
of flies may depart tomorrow from Pharaoh, from
his officials, and from his people; only do not let
Pharaoh again deal falsely by not letting the people go to sacrifice to the LORD."
30 So Moses went out from Pharaoh and
prayed to the LORD. 31 And the LORD did as
Moses asked: he removed the swarms of flies
from Pharaoh, from his officials, and from his
people; not one remained. 32 But Pharaoh hardened his heart this time also, and would not let
the people go.

9 Then the LORD said to Moses, "Go to Pharaoh, and say to him, 'Thus says the LORD,
the God of the Hebrews: Let my people go, so
that they may worship me. 2 For if you refuse to let
them go and still hold them, 3 the hand of the
LORD will strike with a deadly pestilence your
livestock in the field: the horses, the donkeys, the
camels, the herds, and the flocks. 4 But the LORD
will make a distinction between the livestock of
Israel and the livestock of Egypt, so that nothing
shall die of all that belongs to the Israelites.'" 5 The
LORD set a time, saying, "Tomorrow the LORD
will do this thing in the land." 6 And on the next
day the LORD did so; all the livestock of the Egyptians died, but of the livestock of the Israelites not
one died. 7 Pharaoh inquired and found that not
one of the livestock of the Israelites was dead. But
the heart of Pharaoh was hardened, and he would
not let the people go.
8 Then the LORD said to Moses and Aaron,
"Take handfuls of soot from the kiln, and let Moses throw it in the air in the sight of Pharaoh. 9 It
shall become fine dust all over the land of Egypt,
and shall cause festering boils on humans and
animals throughout the whole land of Egypt."
10 So they took soot from the kiln, and stood before Pharaoh, and Moses threw it in the air, and
it caused festering boils on humans and animals.
11 The magicians could not stand before Moses
because of the boils, for the boils afflicted the
magicians as well as all the Egyptians. 12 But the
LORD hardened the heart of Pharaoh, and he
would not listen to them, just as the LORD had
spoken to Moses.
13 Then the LORD said to Moses, "Rise up
early in the morning and present yourself before
Pharaoh, and say to him, 'Thus says the LORD,
the God of the Hebrews: Let my people go, so
that they may worship me. 14 For this time I will
send all my plagues upon you yourself, and upon
your officials, and upon your people, so that you
may know that there is no one like me in all the
earth. 15 For by now I could have stretched out my
hand and struck you and your people with pestilence, and you would have been cut off from the
earth. 16 But this is why I have let you live: to show
you my power, and to make my name resound
through all the earth. 17 You are still exalting yourself against my people, and will not let them go.
18 Tomorrow at this time I will cause the heaviest
hail to fall that has ever fallen in Egypt from the
day it was founded until now. 19 Send, therefore,
and have your livestock and everything that you
have in the open field brought to a secure place;
every human or animal that is in the open field
and is not brought under shelter will die when

[a] Gk Vg: Heb *will set redemption*

the hail comes down upon them.'" 20 Those officials of Pharaoh who feared the word of the LORD hurried their slaves and livestock off to a secure place. 21 Those who did not regard the word of the LORD left their slaves and livestock in the open field.

22 The LORD said to Moses, "Stretch out your hand toward heaven so that hail may fall on the whole land of Egypt, on humans and animals and all the plants of the field in the land of Egypt." 23 Then Moses stretched out his staff toward heaven, and the LORD sent thunder and hail, and fire came down on the earth. And the LORD rained hail on the land of Egypt; 24 there was hail with fire flashing continually in the midst of it, such heavy hail as had never fallen in all the land of Egypt since it became a nation. 25 The hail struck down everything that was in the open field throughout all the land of Egypt, both human and animal; the hail also struck down all the plants of the field, and shattered every tree in the field. 26 Only in the land of Goshen, where the Israelites were, there was no hail.

27 Then Pharaoh summoned Moses and Aaron, and said to them, "This time I have sinned; the LORD is in the right, and I and my people are in the wrong. 28 Pray to the LORD! Enough of God's thunder and hail! I will let you go; you need stay no longer." 29 Moses said to him, "As soon as I have gone out of the city, I will stretch out my hands to the LORD; the thunder will cease, and there will be no more hail, so that you may know that the earth is the LORD's. 30 But as for you and your officials, I know that you do not yet fear the LORD God." 31 (Now the flax and the barley were ruined, for the barley was in the ear and the flax was in bud. 32 But the wheat and the spelt were not ruined, for they are late in coming up.) 33 So Moses left Pharaoh, went out of the city, and stretched out his hands to the LORD; then the thunder and the hail ceased, and the rain no longer poured down on the earth. 34 But when Pharaoh saw that the rain and the hail and the thunder had ceased, he sinned once more and hardened his heart, he and his officials. 35 So the heart of Pharaoh was hardened, and he would not let the Israelites go, just as the LORD had spoken through Moses.

10 Then the LORD said to Moses, "Go to Pharaoh; for I have hardened his heart and the heart of his officials, in order that I may show these signs of mine among them, 2 and that you may tell your children and grandchildren how I have made fools of the Egyptians and what signs I have done among them—so that you may know that I am the LORD."

Exodus 10:1

The dramatic power of the LORD's contest with Pharaoh owes much to the skillful narrative: Pharaoh's repeated concessions, then the reversals as he hardens his heart, increase the dramatic tension of the story. But at length it is the LORD who hardens Pharaoh's heart, "in order that I may show these signs of mine among them, and that you may tell your children and grandchildren how I have made fools of the Egyptians . . . so that you may know that I am the LORD" (10:1-2). While some interpreters have sought scientific explanations for the plagues, the power of the story is quite intentionally mythical: all that is sacred in Egyptian culture and religion—the water of the Nile, the fertility of the fields, even the perpetuity of the Pharaoh's lineage—all are defiled, polluted, or destroyed. At last the war machines of a great world empire are destroyed, not by an opposing army but by the miraculous power of a God who hears the cries of the oppressed and acts to deliver them.

—*NE*

3 So Moses and Aaron went to Pharaoh, and said to him, "Thus says the LORD, the God of the Hebrews, 'How long will you refuse to humble yourself before me? Let my people go, so that they may worship me. 4 For if you refuse to let my people go, tomorrow I will bring locusts into your country. 5 They shall cover the surface of the land, so that no one will be able to see the land. They shall devour the last remnant left you after the hail, and they shall devour every tree of yours that grows in the field. 6 They shall fill your houses, and the houses of all your officials and of all the Egyptians—something that neither your

parents nor your grandparents have seen, from the day they came on earth to this day.’ ” Then he turned and went out from Pharaoh.

7 Pharaoh’s officials said to him, “How long shall this fellow be a snare to us? Let the people go, so that they may worship the LORD their God; do you not yet understand that Egypt is ruined?” 8 So Moses and Aaron were brought back to Pharaoh, and he said to them, “Go, worship the LORD your God! But which ones are to go?” 9 Moses said, “We will go with our young and our old; we will go with our sons and daughters and with our flocks and herds, because we have the LORD’s festival to celebrate.” 10 He said to them, “The LORD indeed will be with you, if ever I let your little ones go with you! Plainly, you have some evil purpose in mind. 11 No, never! Your men may go and worship the LORD, for that is what you are asking.” And they were driven out from Pharaoh’s presence.

12 Then the LORD said to Moses, “Stretch out your hand over the land of Egypt, so that the locusts may come upon it and eat every plant in the land, all that the hail has left.” 13 So Moses stretched out his staff over the land of Egypt, and the LORD brought an east wind upon the land all that day and all that night; when morning came, the east wind had brought the locusts. 14 The locusts came upon all the land of Egypt and settled on the whole country of Egypt, such a dense swarm of locusts as had never been before, nor ever shall be again. 15 They covered the surface of the whole land, so that the land was black; and they ate all the plants in the land and all the fruit of the trees that the hail had left; nothing green was left, no tree, no plant in the field, in all the land of Egypt. 16 Pharaoh hurriedly summoned Moses and Aaron and said, “I have sinned against the LORD your God, and against you. 17 Do forgive my sin just this once, and pray to the LORD your God that at the least he remove this deadly thing from me.” 18 So he went out from Pharaoh and prayed to the LORD. 19 The LORD changed the wind into a very strong west wind, which lifted the locusts and drove them into the Red Sea;[a] not a single locust was left in all the country of Egypt. 20 But the LORD hardened Pharaoh’s heart, and he would not let the Israelites go.

21 Then the LORD said to Moses, “Stretch out your hand toward heaven so that there may be darkness over the land of Egypt, a darkness that can be felt.” 22 So Moses stretched out his hand toward heaven, and there was dense darkness in all the land of Egypt for three days. 23 People could not see one another, and for three days they could not move from where they were; but all the Israelites had light where they lived. 24 Then Pharaoh summoned Moses, and said, “Go, worship the LORD. Only your flocks and your herds shall remain behind. Even your children may go with you.” 25 But Moses said, “You must also let us have sacrifices and burnt offerings to sacrifice to the LORD our God. 26 Our livestock also must go with us; not a hoof shall be left behind, for we must choose some of them for the worship of the LORD our God, and we will not know what to use to worship the LORD until we arrive there.” 27 But the LORD hardened Pharaoh’s heart, and he was unwilling to let them go. 28 Then Pharaoh said to him, “Get away from me! Take care that you do not see my face again, for on the day you see my face you shall die.” 29 Moses said, “Just as you say! I will never see your face again.”

11 The LORD said to Moses, “I will bring one more plague upon Pharaoh and upon Egypt; afterwards he will let you go from here; indeed, when he lets you go, he will drive you away. 2 Tell the people that every man is to ask his neighbor and every woman is to ask her neighbor for objects of silver and gold.” 3 The LORD gave the people favor in the sight of the Egyptians. Moreover, Moses himself was a man of great importance in the land of Egypt, in the sight of Pharaoh’s officials and in the sight of the people.

4 Moses said, “Thus says the LORD: About midnight I will go out through Egypt. 5 Every firstborn in the land of Egypt shall die, from the firstborn of Pharaoh who sits on his throne to the firstborn of the female slave who is behind the handmill, and all the firstborn of the live-

[a] Or *Sea of Reeds*

stock. 6Then there will be a loud cry throughout the whole land of Egypt, such as has never been or will ever be again. 7But not a dog shall growl at any of the Israelites—not at people, not at animals—so that you may know that the LORD makes a distinction between Egypt and Israel. 8Then all these officials of yours shall come down to me, and bow low to me, saying, 'Leave us, you and all the people who follow you.' After that I will leave." And in hot anger he left Pharaoh.

9 The LORD said to Moses, "Pharaoh will not listen to you, in order that my wonders may be multiplied in the land of Egypt." 10Moses and Aaron performed all these wonders before Pharaoh; but the LORD hardened Pharaoh's heart, and he did not let the people of Israel go out of his land.

12 The LORD said to Moses and Aaron in the land of Egypt: 2This month shall mark for you the beginning of months; it shall be the first month of the year for you. 3Tell the whole congregation of Israel that on the tenth of this month they are to take a lamb for each family, a lamb for each household. 4If a household is too small for a whole lamb, it shall join its closest neighbor in obtaining one; the lamb shall be divided in proportion to the number of people who eat of it. 5Your lamb shall be without blemish, a year-old male; you may take it from the sheep or from the goats. 6You shall keep it until the fourteenth day of this month; then the whole assembled congregation of Israel shall slaughter it at twilight. 7They shall take some of the blood and put it on the two doorposts and the lintel of the houses in which they eat it. 8They shall eat the lamb that same night; they shall eat it roasted over the fire with unleavened bread and bitter herbs. 9Do not eat any of it raw or boiled in water, but roasted over the fire, with its head, legs, and inner organs. 10You shall let none of it remain until the morning; anything that remains until the morning you shall burn. 11This is how you shall eat it: your loins girded, your sandals on your feet, and your staff in your hand; and you shall eat it hurriedly. It is the passover of the LORD. 12For I will pass through the land of Egypt that night, and I will strike down every firstborn in the land of Egypt, both human beings and animals; on all the gods of Egypt I will execute judgments: I am the LORD. 13The blood shall be a sign for you on the houses where you live: when I see the blood, I will pass over you, and no plague shall destroy you when I strike the land of Egypt.

14 This day shall be a day of remembrance for you. You shall celebrate it as a festival to the LORD; throughout your generations you shall observe it as a perpetual ordinance. 15Seven days you shall eat unleavened bread; on the first day you shall remove leaven from your houses, for whoever eats leavened bread from the first day until the seventh day shall be cut off from Israel. 16On the first day you shall hold a solemn assembly, and on the seventh day a solemn assembly; no work shall be done on those days; only what everyone must eat, that alone may be prepared by you. 17You shall observe the festival of unleavened bread, for on this very day I brought your companies out of the land of Egypt: you shall observe this day throughout your generations as a perpetual ordinance. 18In the first month, from the evening of the fourteenth day until the evening of the twenty-first day, you shall eat unleavened bread. 19For seven days no leaven shall be found in your houses; for whoever eats what is leavened shall be cut off from the congregation of Israel, whether an alien or a native of the land. 20You shall eat nothing leavened; in all your settlements you shall eat unleavened bread.

21 Then Moses called all the elders of Israel and said to them, "Go, select lambs for your families, and slaughter the passover lamb. 22Take a bunch of hyssop, dip it in the blood that is in the basin, and touch the lintel and the two doorposts with the blood in the basin. None of you shall go outside the door of your house until morning. 23For the LORD will pass through to strike down the Egyptians; when he sees the blood on the lintel and on the two doorposts, the LORD will pass over that door and will not allow the destroyer to enter your houses to strike you down. 24You shall observe this rite as a perpetual ordinance for you and your children. 25When you come to the land that the LORD will give you, as he has promised, you shall keep this observance. 26And when your

children ask you, 'What do you mean by this observance?' 27 you shall say, 'It is the passover sacrifice to the LORD, for he passed over the houses
of the Israelites in Egypt, when he struck down
the Egyptians but spared our houses.'" And the
people bowed down and worshiped.
28 The Israelites went and did just as the
LORD had commanded Moses and Aaron.
29 At midnight the LORD struck down all the
firstborn in the land of Egypt, from the firstborn
of Pharaoh who sat on his throne to the firstborn
of the prisoner who was in the dungeon, and all
the firstborn of the livestock. 30 Pharaoh arose
in the night, he and all his officials and all the
Egyptians; and there was a loud cry in Egypt, for
there was not a house without someone dead.
31 Then he summoned Moses and Aaron in the
night, and said, "Rise up, go away from my people, both you and the Israelites! Go, worship the
LORD, as you said. 32 Take your flocks and your
herds, as you said, and be gone. And bring a blessing on me too!"
33 The Egyptians urged the people to hasten their departure from the land, for they said,
"We shall all be dead." 34 So the people took their
dough before it was leavened, with their kneading
bowls wrapped up in their cloaks on their shoulders. 35 The Israelites had done as Moses told
them; they had asked the Egyptians for jewelry of
silver and gold, and for clothing, 36 and the LORD
had given the people favor in the sight of the
Egyptians, so that they let them have what they
asked. And so they plundered the Egyptians.
37 The Israelites journeyed from Rameses
to Succoth, about six hundred thousand men on
foot, besides children. 38 A mixed crowd also went
up with them, and livestock in great numbers,
both flocks and herds. 39 They baked unleavened
cakes of the dough that they had brought out of
Egypt; it was not leavened, because they were
driven out of Egypt and could not wait, nor had
they prepared any provisions for themselves.
40 The time that the Israelites had lived in
Egypt was four hundred thirty years. 41 At the end
of four hundred thirty years, on that very day, all
the companies of the LORD went out from the
land of Egypt. 42 That was for the LORD a night of
vigil, to bring them out of the land of Egypt. That
same night is a vigil to be kept for the LORD by all
the Israelites throughout their generations.
43 The LORD said to Moses and Aaron: This
is the ordinance for the passover: no foreigner
shall eat of it, 44 but any slave who has been purchased may eat of it after he has been circumcised; 45 no bound or hired servant may eat of it.
46 It shall be eaten in one house; you shall not take
any of the animal outside the house, and you shall
not break any of its bones. 47 The whole congregation of Israel shall celebrate it. 48 If an alien who
resides with you wants to celebrate the passover
to the LORD, all his males shall be circumcised;
then he may draw near to celebrate it; he shall be
regarded as a native of the land. But no uncircumcised person shall eat of it; 49 there shall be one
law for the native and for the alien who resides
among you.
50 All the Israelites did just as the LORD had
commanded Moses and Aaron. 51 That very day
the LORD brought the Israelites out of the land of
Egypt, company by company.

13 The LORD said to Moses: 2 Consecrate to
me all the firstborn; whatever is the first
to open the womb among the Israelites, of human
beings and animals, is mine.
3 Moses said to the people, "Remember this
day on which you came out of Egypt, out of the
house of slavery, because the LORD brought you
out from there by strength of hand; no leavened
bread shall be eaten. 4 Today, in the month of
Abib, you are going out. 5 When the LORD brings
you into the land of the Canaanites, the Hittites,
the Amorites, the Hivites, and the Jebusites,
which he swore to your ancestors to give you, a
land flowing with milk and honey, you shall keep
this observance in this month. 6 Seven days you
shall eat unleavened bread, and on the seventh
day there shall be a festival to the LORD. 7 Unleavened bread shall be eaten for seven days;
no leavened bread shall be seen in your possession, and no leaven shall be seen among you in
all your territory. 8 You shall tell your child on that
day, 'It is because of what the LORD did for me
when I came out of Egypt.' 9 It shall serve for you
as a sign on your hand and as a reminder on your

forehead, so that the teaching of the LORD may
be on your lips; for with a strong hand the LORD
brought you out of Egypt. 10You shall keep this
ordinance at its proper time from year to year.

11 "When the LORD has brought you into
the land of the Canaanites, as he swore to you
and your ancestors, and has given it to you, 12you
shall set apart to the LORD all that first opens the
womb. All the firstborn of your livestock that are
males shall be the LORD's. 13But every firstborn
donkey you shall redeem with a sheep; if you do
not redeem it, you must break its neck. Every firstborn male among your children you shall redeem.
14When in the future your child asks you, 'What
does this mean?' you shall answer, 'By strength
of hand the LORD brought us out of Egypt, from
the house of slavery. 15When Pharaoh stubbornly
refused to let us go, the LORD killed all the firstborn in the land of Egypt, from human firstborn
to the firstborn of animals. Therefore I sacrifice to
the LORD every male that first opens the womb,
but every firstborn of my sons I redeem.' 16It shall
serve as a sign on your hand and as an emblem[a]
on your forehead that by strength of hand the
LORD brought us out of Egypt."

17 When Pharaoh let the people go, God did
not lead them by way of the land of the Philistines, although that was nearer; for God thought,
"If the people face war, they may change their
minds and return to Egypt." 18So God led the
people by the roundabout way of the wilderness
toward the Red Sea.[b] The Israelites went up out of
the land of Egypt prepared for battle. 19And Moses took with him the bones of Joseph who had
required a solemn oath of the Israelites, saying,
"God will surely take notice of you, and then you
must carry my bones with you from here." 20They
set out from Succoth, and camped at Etham, on
the edge of the wilderness. 21The LORD went in
front of them in a pillar of cloud by day, to lead
them along the way, and in a pillar of fire by night,
to give them light, so that they might travel by day
and by night. 22Neither the pillar of cloud by day
nor the pillar of fire by night left its place in front
of the people.

14 Then the LORD said to Moses: 2Tell the
Israelites to turn back and camp in front
of Pi-hahiroth, between Migdol and the sea, in
front of Baal-zephon; you shall camp opposite
it, by the sea. 3Pharaoh will say of the Israelites,
"They are wandering aimlessly in the land; the
wilderness has closed in on them." 4I will harden
Pharaoh's heart, and he will pursue them, so that I
will gain glory for myself over Pharaoh and all his
army; and the Egyptians shall know that I am the
LORD. And they did so.

5 When the king of Egypt was told that the
people had fled, the minds of Pharaoh and his officials were changed toward the people, and they
said, "What have we done, letting Israel leave
our service?" 6So he had his chariot made ready,
and took his army with him; 7he took six hundred picked chariots and all the other chariots of
Egypt with officers over all of them. 8The LORD
hardened the heart of Pharaoh king of Egypt and
he pursued the Israelites, who were going out
boldly. 9The Egyptians pursued them, all Pharaoh's horses and chariots, his chariot drivers and
his army; they overtook them camped by the sea,
by Pi-hahiroth, in front of Baal-zephon.

10 As Pharaoh drew near, the Israelites looked
back, and there were the Egyptians advancing
on them. In great fear the Israelites cried out to
the LORD. 11They said to Moses, "Was it because
there were no graves in Egypt that you have taken
us away to die in the wilderness? What have you
done to us, bringing us out of Egypt? 12Is this not
the very thing we told you in Egypt, 'Let us alone
and let us serve the Egyptians'? For it would have
been better for us to serve the Egyptians than to
die in the wilderness." 13But Moses said to the
people, "Do not be afraid, stand firm, and see the
deliverance that the LORD will accomplish for
you today; for the Egyptians whom you see today
you shall never see again. 14The LORD will fight
for you, and you have only to keep still."

15 Then the LORD said to Moses, "Why do
you cry out to me? Tell the Israelites to go forward. 16But you lift up your staff, and stretch out
your hand over the sea and divide it, that the

[a] Or *as a frontlet*; meaning of Heb uncertain [b] Or *Sea of Reeds*

Israelites may go into the sea on dry ground.
17 Then I will harden the hearts of the Egyptians
so that they will go in after them; and so I will gain
glory for myself over Pharaoh and all his army, his
chariots, and his chariot drivers. 18 And the Egyptians shall know that I am the LORD, when I have
gained glory for myself over Pharaoh, his chariots, and his chariot drivers."

19 The angel of God who was going before
the Israelite army moved and went behind them;
and the pillar of cloud moved from in front of
them and took its place behind them. 20 It came
between the army of Egypt and the army of Israel. And so the cloud was there with the darkness,
and it lit up the night; one did not come near the
other all night.

21 Then Moses stretched out his hand over
the sea. The LORD drove the sea back by a strong
east wind all night, and turned the sea into dry
land; and the waters were divided. 22 The Israelites
went into the sea on dry ground, the waters forming a wall for them on their right and on their left.
23 The Egyptians pursued, and went into the sea
after them, all of Pharaoh's horses, chariots, and
chariot drivers. 24 At the morning watch the LORD
in the pillar of fire and cloud looked down upon
the Egyptian army, and threw the Egyptian army
into panic. 25 He clogged[a] their chariot wheels so
that they turned with difficulty. The Egyptians
said, "Let us flee from the Israelites, for the LORD
is fighting for them against Egypt."

26 Then the LORD said to Moses, "Stretch
out your hand over the sea, so that the water may
come back upon the Egyptians, upon their chariots and chariot drivers." 27 So Moses stretched
out his hand over the sea, and at dawn the sea
returned to its normal depth. As the Egyptians
fled before it, the LORD tossed the Egyptians into
the sea. 28 The waters returned and covered the
chariots and the chariot drivers, the entire army
of Pharaoh that had followed them into the sea;
not one of them remained. 29 But the Israelites
walked on dry ground through the sea, the waters forming a wall for them on their right and on
their left.

30 Thus the LORD saved Israel that day from
the Egyptians; and Israel saw the Egyptians dead
on the seashore. 31 Israel saw the great work that
the LORD did against the Egyptians. So the people feared the LORD and believed in the LORD
and in his servant Moses.

15 Then Moses and the Israelites sang this
song to the LORD:

"I will sing to the LORD, for he has triumphed
gloriously;
horse and rider he has thrown into the sea.
2 The LORD is my strength and my might,[b]
and he has become my salvation;
this is my God, and I will praise him,
my father's God, and I will exalt him.
3 The LORD is a warrior;
the LORD is his name.

4 "Pharaoh's chariots and his army he cast into
the sea;
his picked officers were sunk in the Red
Sea.[c]
5 The floods covered them;
they went down into the depths like a
stone.
6 Your right hand, O LORD, glorious in
power—
your right hand, O LORD, shattered the
enemy.
7 In the greatness of your majesty you
overthrew your adversaries;
you sent out your fury, it consumed them
like stubble.
8 At the blast of your nostrils the waters
piled up,
the floods stood up in a heap;
the deeps congealed in the heart of the sea.
9 The enemy said, 'I will pursue, I will overtake,
I will divide the spoil, my desire shall have
its fill of them.
I will draw my sword, my hand shall
destroy them.'
10 You blew with your wind, the sea covered
them;
they sank like lead in the mighty waters.

[a] Sam Gk Syr: MT *removed* [b] Or *song* [c] Or *Sea of Reeds*

11 "Who is like you, O LORD, among the gods?
Who is like you, majestic in holiness,
awesome in splendor, doing wonders?
12 You stretched out your right hand,
the earth swallowed them.

13 "In your steadfast love you led the people
whom you redeemed;
you guided them by your strength to your
holy abode.
14 The peoples heard, they trembled;
pangs seized the inhabitants of Philistia.
15 Then the chiefs of Edom were dismayed;
trembling seized the leaders of Moab;
all the inhabitants of Canaan melted away.
16 Terror and dread fell upon them;
by the might of your arm, they became still
as a stone
until your people, O LORD, passed by,
until the people whom you acquired
passed by.
17 You brought them in and planted them
on the mountain of your own
possession,
the place, O LORD, that you made your
abode,
the sanctuary, O LORD, that your hands
have established.
18 The LORD will reign forever and ever."

19 When the horses of Pharaoh with his
chariots and his chariot drivers went into the sea,
the LORD brought back the waters of the sea upon
them; but the Israelites walked through the sea
on dry ground.
20 Then the prophet Miriam, Aaron's sister, took a tambourine in her hand; and all the
women went out after her with tambourines and
with dancing. 21 And Miriam sang to them:
"Sing to the LORD, for he has triumphed
gloriously;
horse and rider he has thrown into the sea."
22 Then Moses ordered Israel to set out from
the Red Sea,[a] and they went into the wilderness
of Shur. They went three days in the wilderness
and found no water. 23 When they came to Marah,
they could not drink the water of Marah because
it was bitter. That is why it was called Marah.[b]
24 And the people complained against Moses,
saying, "What shall we drink?" 25 He cried out to
the LORD; and the LORD showed him a piece of
wood;[c] he threw it into the water, and the water
became sweet.

There the LORD[d] made for them a statute and
an ordinance and there he put them to the test.
26 He said, "If you will listen carefully to the voice
of the LORD your God, and do what is right in his
sight, and give heed to his commandments and
keep all his statutes, I will not bring upon you
any of the diseases that I brought upon the Egyptians; for I am the LORD who heals you."
27 Then they came to Elim, where there were
twelve springs of water and seventy palm trees;
and they camped there by the water.

16 The whole congregation of the Israelites
set out from Elim; and Israel came to the
wilderness of Sin, which is between Elim and Sinai, on the fifteenth day of the second month after
they had departed from the land of Egypt. 2 The
whole congregation of the Israelites complained
against Moses and Aaron in the wilderness. 3 The
Israelites said to them, "If only we had died by the
hand of the LORD in the land of Egypt, when we
sat by the fleshpots and ate our fill of bread; for
you have brought us out into this wilderness to
kill this whole assembly with hunger."
4 Then the LORD said to Moses, "I am going
to rain bread from heaven for you, and each day
the people shall go out and gather enough for that
day. In that way I will test them, whether they will
follow my instruction or not. 5 On the sixth day,
when they prepare what they bring in, it will be
twice as much as they gather on other days." 6 So
Moses and Aaron said to all the Israelites, "In the
evening you shall know that it was the LORD who
brought you out of the land of Egypt, 7 and in the
morning you shall see the glory of the LORD, because he has heard your complaining against the
LORD. For what are we, that you complain against
us?" 8 And Moses said, "When the LORD gives you
meat to eat in the evening and your fill of bread

[a] Or *Sea of Reeds* [b] That is *Bitterness* [c] Or *a tree* [d] Heb *he*

in the morning, because the LORD has heard the
complaining that you utter against him—what
are we? Your complaining is not against us but
against the LORD."
9 Then Moses said to Aaron, "Say to the
whole congregation of the Israelites, 'Draw near
to the LORD, for he has heard your complaining.' "
10And as Aaron spoke to the whole congregation
of the Israelites, they looked toward the wilderness, and the glory of the LORD appeared in the
cloud. 11The LORD spoke to Moses and said, 12"I
have heard the complaining of the Israelites; say
to them, 'At twilight you shall eat meat, and in the
morning you shall have your fill of bread; then
you shall know that I am the LORD your God.' "
13 In the evening quails came up and covered
the camp; and in the morning there was a layer of
dew around the camp. 14When the layer of dew
lifted, there on the surface of the wilderness was a
fine flaky substance, as fine as frost on the ground.
15When the Israelites saw it, they said to one another, "What is it?"[a] For they did not know what
it was. Moses said to them, "It is the bread that
the LORD has given you to eat. 16This is what the
LORD has commanded: 'Gather as much of it as
each of you needs, an omer to a person according
to the number of persons, all providing for those
in their own tents.' " 17The Israelites did so, some
gathering more, some less. 18But when they measured it with an omer, those who gathered much
had nothing over, and those who gathered little
had no shortage; they gathered as much as each
of them needed. 19And Moses said to them, "Let
no one leave any of it over until morning." 20But
they did not listen to Moses; some left part of it
until morning, and it bred worms and became
foul. And Moses was angry with them. 21Morn-
ing by morning they gathered it, as much as each
needed; but when the sun grew hot, it melted.
22 On the sixth day they gathered twice as
much food, two omers apiece. When all the leaders of the congregation came and told Moses,
23he said to them, "This is what the LORD has
commanded: 'Tomorrow is a day of solemn rest,
a holy sabbath to the LORD; bake what you want
to bake and boil what you want to boil, and all
that is left over put aside to be kept until morning.' " 24So they put it aside until morning, as
Moses commanded them; and it did not become
foul, and there were no worms in it. 25Moses said,
"Eat it today, for today is a sabbath to the LORD;
today you will not find it in the field. 26Six days
you shall gather it; but on the seventh day, which
is a sabbath, there will be none."
27 On the seventh day some of the people
went out to gather, and they found none. 28The
LORD said to Moses, "How long will you refuse
to keep my commandments and instructions?
29See! The LORD has given you the sabbath,
therefore on the sixth day he gives you food for
two days; each of you stay where you are; do not
leave your place on the seventh day." 30So the
people rested on the seventh day.
31 The house of Israel called it manna; it was
like coriander seed, white, and the taste of it was
like wafers made with honey. 32Moses said, "This
is what the LORD has commanded: 'Let an omer
of it be kept throughout your generations, in order that they may see the food with which I fed
you in the wilderness, when I brought you out of
the land of Egypt.' " 33And Moses said to Aaron,
"Take a jar, and put an omer of manna in it, and
place it before the LORD, to be kept throughout
your generations." 34As the LORD commanded
Moses, so Aaron placed it before the covenant,[b]
for safekeeping. 35The Israelites ate manna forty
years, until they came to a habitable land; they ate
manna, until they came to the border of the land
of Canaan. 36An omer is a tenth of an ephah.

17 From the wilderness of Sin the whole congregation of the Israelites journeyed by
stages, as the LORD commanded. They camped at
Rephidim, but there was no water for the people
to drink. 2The people quarreled with Moses, and
said, "Give us water to drink." Moses said to them,
"Why do you quarrel with me? Why do you test
the LORD?" 3But the people thirsted there for
water; and the people complained against Moses
and said, "Why did you bring us out of Egypt, to
kill us and our children and livestock with thirst?"

[a] Or *"It is manna"* (Heb *man hu*, see verse 31) [b] Or *treaty* or *testimony*; Heb *eduth*

4 So Moses cried out to the LORD, "What shall I do
with this people? They are almost ready to stone
me." 5 The LORD said to Moses, "Go on ahead of
the people, and take some of the elders of Israel
with you; take in your hand the staff with which
you struck the Nile, and go. 6 I will be standing
there in front of you on the rock at Horeb. Strike
the rock, and water will come out of it, so that the
people may drink." Moses did so, in the sight of
the elders of Israel. 7 He called the place Massah[a]
and Meribah,[b] because the Israelites quarreled
and tested the LORD, saying, "Is the LORD among
us or not?"

8 Then Amalek came and fought with Israel
at Rephidim. 9 Moses said to Joshua, "Choose
some men for us and go out, fight with Amalek.
Tomorrow I will stand on the top of the hill with
the staff of God in my hand." 10 So Joshua did as
Moses told him, and fought with Amalek, while
Moses, Aaron, and Hur went up to the top of
the hill. 11 Whenever Moses held up his hand,
Israel prevailed; and whenever he lowered his
hand, Amalek prevailed. 12 But Moses' hands
grew weary; so they took a stone and put it under him, and he sat on it. Aaron and Hur held
up his hands, one on one side, and the other on
the other side; so his hands were steady until the
sun set. 13 And Joshua defeated Amalek and his
people with the sword.

14 Then the LORD said to Moses, "Write this
as a reminder in a book and recite it in the hearing
of Joshua: I will utterly blot out the remembrance
of Amalek from under heaven." 15 And Moses
built an altar and called it, The LORD is my banner. 16 He said, "A hand upon the banner of the
LORD![c] The LORD will have war with Amalek
from generation to generation."

18 Jethro, the priest of Midian, Moses' father-
in-law, heard of all that God had done for
Moses and for his people Israel, how the LORD
had brought Israel out of Egypt. 2 After Moses
had sent away his wife Zipporah, his father-in-law
Jethro took her back, 3 along with her two sons.
The name of the one was Gershom (for he said, "I
have been an alien[d] in a foreign land"), 4 and the
name of the other, Eliezer[e] (for he said, "The God
of my father was my help, and delivered me from
the sword of Pharaoh"). 5 Jethro, Moses' father-
in-law, came into the wilderness where Moses
was encamped at the mountain of God, bringing
Moses' sons and wife to him. 6 He sent word to
Moses, "I, your father-in-law Jethro, am coming
to you, with your wife and her two sons." 7 Moses went out to meet his father-in-law; he bowed
down and kissed him; each asked after the other's
welfare, and they went into the tent. 8 Then Moses
told his father-in-law all that the LORD had done
to Pharaoh and to the Egyptians for Israel's sake,
all the hardship that had beset them on the way,
and how the LORD had delivered them. 9 Jethro
rejoiced for all the good that the LORD had done
to Israel, in delivering them from the Egyptians.

10 Jethro said, "Blessed be the LORD, who
has delivered you from the Egyptians and from
Pharaoh. 11 Now I know that the LORD is greater
than all gods, because he delivered the people
from the Egyptians,[f] when they dealt arrogantly
with them." 12 And Jethro, Moses' father-in-law,
brought a burnt offering and sacrifices to God;
and Aaron came with all the elders of Israel to eat
bread with Moses' father-in-law in the presence
of God.

13 The next day Moses sat as judge for the
people, while the people stood around him from
morning until evening. 14 When Moses' father-in-
law saw all that he was doing for the people, he
said, "What is this that you are doing for the people? Why do you sit alone, while all the people
stand around you from morning until evening?"
15 Moses said to his father-in-law, "Because the
people come to me to inquire of God. 16 When
they have a dispute, they come to me and I decide between one person and another, and I make
known to them the statutes and instructions of
God." 17 Moses' father-in-law said to him, "What
you are doing is not good. 18 You will surely wear
yourself out, both you and these people with you.
For the task is too heavy for you; you cannot do

[a] That is *Test* [b] That is *Quarrel* [c] Cn: Meaning of Heb uncertain [d] Heb *ger* [e] Heb *Eli,* my God; *ezer,* help

[f] The clause *because . . . Egyptians* has been transposed from verse 10

it alone. [19]Now listen to me. I will give you counsel, and God be with you! You should represent
the people before God, and you should bring
their cases before God; [20]teach them the statutes
and instructions and make known to them the
way they are to go and the things they are to do.
[21]You should also look for able men among all
the people, men who fear God, are trustworthy,
and hate dishonest gain; set such men over them
as officers over thousands, hundreds, fifties, and
tens. [22]Let them sit as judges for the people at all
times; let them bring every important case to you,
but decide every minor case themselves. So it will
be easier for you, and they will bear the burden
with you. [23]If you do this, and God so commands
you, then you will be able to endure, and all these
people will go to their home in peace."
24 So Moses listened to his father-in-law and
did all that he had said. [25]Moses chose able men
from all Israel and appointed them as heads over
the people, as officers over thousands, hundreds,
fifties, and tens. [26]And they judged the people at
all times; hard cases they brought to Moses, but
any minor case they decided themselves. [27]Then
Moses let his father-in-law depart, and he went
off to his own country.

19 On the third new moon after the Israelites had gone out of the land of Egypt,
on that very day, they came into the wilderness
of Sinai. [2]They had journeyed from Rephidim,
entered the wilderness of Sinai, and camped in
the wilderness; Israel camped there in front of
the mountain. [3]Then Moses went up to God; the
LORD called to him from the mountain, saying,
"Thus you shall say to the house of Jacob, and tell
the Israelites: [4]You have seen what I did to the
Egyptians, and how I bore you on eagles' wings
and brought you to myself. [5]Now therefore, if you
obey my voice and keep my covenant, you shall
be my treasured possession out of all the peoples.
Indeed, the whole earth is mine, [6]but you shall
be for me a priestly kingdom and a holy nation.
These are the words that you shall speak to the
Israelites."
7 So Moses came, summoned the elders of
the people, and set before them all these words
that the LORD had commanded him. [8]The people
all answered as one: "Everything that the LORD
has spoken we will do." Moses reported the words
of the people to the LORD. [9]Then the LORD said
to Moses, "I am going to come to you in a dense
cloud, in order that the people may hear when I
speak with you and so trust you ever after."

When Moses had told the words of the people
to the LORD, [10]the LORD said to Moses: "Go to
the people and consecrate them today and tomorrow. Have them wash their clothes [11]and
prepare for the third day, because on the third
day the LORD will come down upon Mount Sinai
in the sight of all the people. [12]You shall set limits for the people all around, saying, 'Be careful
not to go up the mountain or to touch the edge
of it. Any who touch the mountain shall be put
to death. [13]No hand shall touch them, but they
shall be stoned or shot with arrows;[a] whether
animal or human being, they shall not live.' When
the trumpet sounds a long blast, they may go up
on the mountain." [14]So Moses went down from
the mountain to the people. He consecrated the
people, and they washed their clothes. [15]And he
said to the people, "Prepare for the third day; do
not go near a woman."

Exodus 19:10-15

Compare God's instructions in verses 10-13 with Moses' instructions in verse 15. Moses adds the prohibition against intimacy. What else does he add? How are we to distinguish the "word of Moses" from the "word of God"? Since Moses is not held accountable for these additions, how flexible is the divine word to be perceived?

— *WG*

16 On the morning of the third day there
was thunder and lightning, as well as a thick
cloud on the mountain, and a blast of a trumpet
so loud that all the people who were in the camp

[a] Heb lacks *with arrows*

trembled. 17Moses brought the people out of the
camp to meet God. They took their stand at the
foot of the mountain. 18Now Mount Sinai was
wrapped in smoke, because the LORD had descended upon it in fire; the smoke went up like
the smoke of a kiln, while the whole mountain
shook violently. 19As the blast of the trumpet
grew louder and louder, Moses would speak and
God would answer him in thunder. 20When the
LORD descended upon Mount Sinai, to the top of
the mountain, the LORD summoned Moses to the
top of the mountain, and Moses went up. 21Then
the LORD said to Moses, "Go down and warn the
people not to break through to the LORD to look;
otherwise many of them will perish. 22Even the
priests who approach the LORD must consecrate
themselves or the LORD will break out against
them." 23Moses said to the LORD, "The people
are not permitted to come up to Mount Sinai; for
you yourself warned us, saying, 'Set limits around
the mountain and keep it holy.'" 24The LORD said
to him, "Go down, and come up bringing Aaron
with you; but do not let either the priests or the
people break through to come up to the LORD;
otherwise he will break out against them." 25So
Moses went down to the people and told them.

20 Then God spoke all these words:
2 I am the LORD your God, who brought
you out of the land of Egypt, out of the house
of slavery; 3you shall have no other gods before[a] me.

Exodus 20:1

In Jewish tradition, the first commandment is simply the LORD's self-disclosure as the God "who brought you out of the land of Egypt, out of the house of slavery." As in the encounter with Moses from the burning bush in Exodus 3, the LORD wishes to be known as the God who hears the cries of the oppressed and acts to deliver them.

— *NE*

4 You shall not make for yourself an idol,
whether in the form of anything that is in heaven
above, or that is on the earth beneath, or that is
in the water under the earth. 5You shall not bow
down to them or worship them; for I the LORD
your God am a jealous God, punishing children
for the iniquity of parents, to the third and the
fourth generation of those who reject me, 6but
showing steadfast love to the thousandth generation[b] of those who love me and keep my commandments.

7 You shall not make wrongful use of the
name of the LORD your God, for the LORD will
not acquit anyone who misuses his name.

8 Remember the sabbath day, and keep it
holy. 9Six days you shall labor and do all your
work. 10But the seventh day is a sabbath to the
LORD your God; you shall not do any work—
you, your son or your daughter, your male or
female slave, your livestock, or the alien resident
in your towns. 11For in six days the LORD made
heaven and earth, the sea, and all that is in them,
but rested the seventh day; therefore the LORD
blessed the sabbath day and consecrated it.

12 Honor your father and your mother, so
that your days may be long in the land that the
LORD your God is giving you.

13 You shall not murder.[c]

14 You shall not commit adultery.

15 You shall not steal.

16 You shall not bear false witness against
your neighbor.

17 You shall not covet your neighbor's house;
you shall not covet your neighbor's wife, or male
or female slave, or ox, or donkey, or anything that
belongs to your neighbor.

18 When all the people witnessed the thunder and lightning, the sound of the trumpet,
and the mountain smoking, they were afraid[d]
and trembled and stood at a distance, 19and said
to Moses, "You speak to us, and we will listen;
but do not let God speak to us, or we will die."
20Moses said to the people, "Do not be afraid; for
God has come only to test you and to put the fear
of him upon you so that you do not sin." 21Then

[a] Or *besides* [b] Or *to thousands* [c] Or *kill* [d] Sam Gk Syr Vg: MT *they saw*

the people stood at a distance, while Moses drew near to the thick darkness where God was.

22 The LORD said to Moses: Thus you shall say to the Israelites: "You have seen for yourselves that I spoke with you from heaven. 23You shall not make gods of silver alongside me, nor shall you make for yourselves gods of gold. 24You need make for me only an altar of earth and sacrifice on it your burnt offerings and your offerings of well-being, your sheep and your oxen; in every place where I cause my name to be remembered I will come to you and bless you. 25But if you make for me an altar of stone, do not build it of hewn stones; for if you use a chisel upon it you profane it. 26You shall not go up by steps to my altar, so that your nakedness may not be exposed on it."

21 These are the ordinances that you shall set before them:

2 When you buy a male Hebrew slave, he shall serve six years, but in the seventh he shall go out a free person, without debt. 3If he comes in single, he shall go out single; if he comes in married, then his wife shall go out with him. 4If his master gives him a wife and she bears him sons or daughters, the wife and her children shall be her master's and he shall go out alone. 5But if the slave declares, "I love my master, my wife, and my children; I will not go out a free person," 6then his master shall bring him before God.[a] He shall be brought to the door or the doorpost; and his master shall pierce his ear with an awl; and he shall serve him for life.

7 When a man sells his daughter as a slave, she shall not go out as the male slaves do. 8If she does not please her master, who designated her for himself, then he shall let her be redeemed; he shall have no right to sell her to a foreign people, since he has dealt unfairly with her. 9If he designates her for his son, he shall deal with her as with a daughter. 10If he takes another wife to himself, he shall not diminish the food, clothing, or marital rights of the first wife.[b] 11And if he does not do these three things for her, she shall go out without debt, without payment of money.

12 Whoever strikes a person mortally shall be put to death. 13If it was not premeditated, but came about by an act of God, then I will appoint for you a place to which the killer may flee. 14But if someone willfully attacks and kills another by treachery, you shall take the killer from my altar for execution.

15 Whoever strikes father or mother shall be put to death.

16 Whoever kidnaps a person, whether that person has been sold or is still held in possession, shall be put to death.

17 Whoever curses father or mother shall be put to death.

18 When individuals quarrel and one strikes the other with a stone or fist so that the injured party, though not dead, is confined to bed, 19but recovers and walks around outside with the help of a staff, then the assailant shall be free of liability, except to pay for the loss of time, and to arrange for full recovery.

20 When a slaveowner strikes a male or female slave with a rod and the slave dies immediately, the owner shall be punished. 21But if the slave survives a day or two, there is no punishment; for the slave is the owner's property.

22 When people who are fighting injure a pregnant woman so that there is a miscarriage, and yet no further harm follows, the one responsible shall be fined what the woman's husband demands, paying as much as the judges determine. 23If any harm follows, then you shall give life for life, 24eye for eye, tooth for tooth, hand for hand, foot for foot, 25burn for burn, wound for wound, stripe for stripe.

26 When a slaveowner strikes the eye of a male or female slave, destroying it, the owner shall let the slave go, a free person, to compensate for the eye. 27If the owner knocks out a tooth of a male or female slave, the slave shall be let go, a free person, to compensate for the tooth.

28 When an ox gores a man or a woman to death, the ox shall be stoned, and its flesh shall not be eaten; but the owner of the ox shall not be liable. 29If the ox has been accustomed to gore in the past, and its owner has been warned but has

[a] Or *to the judges* [b] Heb *of her*

not restrained it, and it kills a man or a woman,
the ox shall be stoned, and its owner also shall
be put to death. 30If a ransom is imposed on the
owner, then the owner shall pay whatever is imposed for the redemption of the victim's life. 31If
it gores a boy or a girl, the owner shall be dealt
with according to this same rule. 32If the ox gores
a male or female slave, the owner shall pay to the
slaveowner thirty shekels of silver, and the ox
shall be stoned.

33 If someone leaves a pit open, or digs a pit
and does not cover it, and an ox or a donkey falls
into it, 34the owner of the pit shall make restitution, giving money to its owner, but keeping the
dead animal.

35 If someone's ox hurts the ox of another,
so that it dies, then they shall sell the live ox and
divide the price of it; and the dead animal they
shall also divide. 36But if it was known that the ox
was accustomed to gore in the past, and its owner
has not restrained it, the owner shall restore ox
for ox, but keep the dead animal.

22 [a]When someone steals an ox or a sheep,
and slaughters it or sells it, the thief
shall pay five oxen for an ox, and four sheep for
a sheep.[b] The thief shall make restitution, but if
unable to do so, shall be sold for the theft. 4When
the animal, whether ox or donkey or sheep, is
found alive in the thief's possession, the thief
shall pay double.

2[c] If a thief is found breaking in, and is beaten
to death, no bloodguilt is incurred; 3but if it happens after sunrise, bloodguilt is incurred.

5 When someone causes a field or vineyard
to be grazed over, or lets livestock loose to graze
in someone else's field, restitution shall be made
from the best in the owner's field or vineyard.

6 When fire breaks out and catches in thorns
so that the stacked grain or the standing grain or
the field is consumed, the one who started the fire
shall make full restitution.

7 When someone delivers to a neighbor
money or goods for safekeeping, and they are
stolen from the neighbor's house, then the thief,
if caught, shall pay double. 8If the thief is not
caught, the owner of the house shall be brought
before God,[d] to determine whether or not the
owner had laid hands on the neighbor's goods.

9 In any case of disputed ownership involving ox, donkey, sheep, clothing, or any other loss,
of which one party says, "This is mine," the case
of both parties shall come before God;[d] the one
whom God condemns[e] shall pay double to the
other.

10 When someone delivers to another a donkey, ox, sheep, or any other animal for safekeeping,
and it dies or is injured or is carried off, without
anyone seeing it, 11an oath before the LORD shall
decide between the two of them that the one has
not laid hands on the property of the other; the
owner shall accept the oath, and no restitution
shall be made. 12But if it was stolen, restitution
shall be made to its owner. 13If it was mangled by
beasts, let it be brought as evidence; restitution
shall not be made for the mangled remains.

14 When someone borrows an animal from
another and it is injured or dies, the owner not
being present, full restitution shall be made. 15If
the owner was present, there shall be no restitution; if it was hired, only the hiring fee is due.

16 When a man seduces a virgin who is not
engaged to be married, and lies with her, he shall
give the bride-price for her and make her his wife.
17But if her father refuses to give her to him, he
shall pay an amount equal to the bride-price for
virgins.

18 You shall not permit a female sorcerer to
live.

19 Whoever lies with an animal shall be put
to death.

20 Whoever sacrifices to any god, other than
the LORD alone, shall be devoted to destruction.

21 You shall not wrong or oppress a resident
alien, for you were aliens in the land of Egypt.
22You shall not abuse any widow or orphan. 23If
you do abuse them, when they cry out to me, I
will surely heed their cry; 24my wrath will burn,
and I will kill you with the sword, and your

[a] Ch 21.37 in Heb [b] Verses 2, 3, and 4 rearranged thus: 3b, 4, 2, 3a [c] Ch 22.1 in Heb [d] Or *before the judges*
[e] Or *the judges condemn*

Exodus 22:25-27

From the beginning Israel knew about the divine demand for mercy. In the language of the divine rights in the Old Testament this is expressed very concretely in law formulas: "If you lend money to the poor with you, then you shall not be to him as a usurer. You shall not impose interest upon him. If you take your fellow man's coat as a pledge, you shall give it back to him before sunset. Because this is his only blanket.... But if he will cry to me, I will hear him, because I am merciful."

By this example... it becomes clear how divine rights constitute human rights. They are the concrete order by which we "invent" human rights and apply them in concrete cases. Human rights are the social execution of the divine rights. That is why we should never set human rights as absolute, because we would be raising them to the level of divine rights and be putting human justice and mercy on a divine level. This means also that we must at all times reexamine and redevelop (reconsider) the meaning of human rights.... [H]uman rights must be fought for, in order that they will be carried through and applied in realizing the divine rights.[11]

— Helmut Frenz

wives shall become widows and your children
orphans.
25 If you lend money to my people, to the
poor among you, you shall not deal with them as
a creditor; you shall not exact interest from them.
26 If you take your neighbor's cloak in pawn, you
shall restore it before the sun goes down; 27 for it
may be your neighbor's only clothing to use as
cover; in what else shall that person sleep? And
if your neighbor cries out to me, I will listen, for I
am compassionate.
28 You shall not revile God, or curse a leader
of your people.
29 You shall not delay to make offerings from
the fullness of your harvest and from the outflow
of your presses.[a]
The firstborn of your sons you shall give to
me. 30 You shall do the same with your oxen and
with your sheep: seven days it shall remain with
its mother; on the eighth day you shall give it
to me.
31 You shall be people consecrated to me;
therefore you shall not eat any meat that is mangled by beasts in the field; you shall throw it to
the dogs.
23 You shall not spread a false report. You
shall not join hands with the wicked to
act as a malicious witness. 2 You shall not follow a
majority in wrongdoing; when you bear witness
in a lawsuit, you shall not side with the majority
so as to pervert justice; 3 nor shall you be partial
to the poor in a lawsuit.
4 When you come upon your enemy's ox or
donkey going astray, you shall bring it back.
5 When you see the donkey of one who hates
you lying under its burden and you would hold
back from setting it free, you must help to set it
free.[a]
6 You shall not pervert the justice due to
your poor in their lawsuits. 7 Keep far from a false
charge, and do not kill the innocent and those in
the right, for I will not acquit the guilty. 8 You shall
take no bribe, for a bribe blinds the officials, and
subverts the cause of those who are in the right.
9 You shall not oppress a resident alien; you

Exodus 23:9

"You must not oppress the strangers; you know how a stranger feels, for you lived as strangers in the land of Egypt." These protective commandments for the strangers are not formulated as timeless humanitarian or philanthropic principles; they are motivated by the historical experience of Israel, because the people of Israel themselves have experienced alienation and slavery in their history, and therefore they are able and obliged to put themselves in the position of the strangers and to identify with them. Any condescending or patronizing attitude over against strangers is excluded.[12]

— Gerhard Hoffmann

[a] Meaning of Heb uncertain

know the heart of an alien, for you were aliens in
the land of Egypt.
10 For six years you shall sow your land and
gather in its yield; 11but the seventh year you
shall let it rest and lie fallow, so that the poor of
your people may eat; and what they leave the wild
animals may eat. You shall do the same with your
vineyard, and with your olive orchard.
12 Six days you shall do your work, but on
the seventh day you shall rest, so that your ox and
your donkey may have relief, and your homeborn
slave and the resident alien may be refreshed.
13Be attentive to all that I have said to you. Do
not invoke the names of other gods; do not let
them be heard on your lips.
14 Three times in the year you shall hold a
festival for me. 15You shall observe the festival
of unleavened bread; as I commanded you, you
shall eat unleavened bread for seven days at the
appointed time in the month of Abib, for in it you
came out of Egypt.
No one shall appear before me empty-handed.
16 You shall observe the festival of harvest,
of the first fruits of your labor, of what you sow
in the field. You shall observe the festival of ingathering at the end of the year, when you gather
in from the field the fruit of your labor. 17Three
times in the year all your males shall appear before the Lord GOD.
18 You shall not offer the blood of my sacrifice with anything leavened, or let the fat of my
festival remain until the morning.
19 The choicest of the first fruits of your
ground you shall bring into the house of the
LORD your God.
You shall not boil a kid in its mother's milk.
20 I am going to send an angel in front of you,
to guard you on the way and to bring you to the
place that I have prepared. 21Be attentive to him
and listen to his voice; do not rebel against him,
for he will not pardon your transgression; for my
name is in him.
22 But if you listen attentively to his voice
and do all that I say, then I will be an enemy to
your enemies and a foe to your foes.
23 When my angel goes in front of you, and
brings you to the Amorites, the Hittites, the
Perizzites, the Canaanites, the Hivites, and the
Jebusites, and I blot them out, 24you shall not
bow down to their gods, or worship them, or follow their practices, but you shall utterly demolish them and break their pillars in pieces. 25You
shall worship the LORD your God, and I[a] will
bless your bread and your water; and I will take
sickness away from among you. 26No one shall
miscarry or be barren in your land; I will fulfill
the number of your days. 27I will send my terror
in front of you, and will throw into confusion all
the people against whom you shall come, and I
will make all your enemies turn their backs to
you. 28And I will send the pestilence[b] in front of
you, which shall drive out the Hivites, the Canaanites, and the Hittites from before you. 29I
will not drive them out from before you in one
year, or the land would become desolate and the
wild animals would multiply against you. 30Little
by little I will drive them out from before you,
until you have increased and possess the land. 31I
will set your borders from the Red Sea[c] to the sea
of the Philistines, and from the wilderness to the
Euphrates; for I will hand over to you the inhabitants of the land, and you shall drive them out
before you. 32You shall make no covenant with
them and their gods. 33They shall not live in your
land, or they will make you sin against me; for if
you worship their gods, it will surely be a snare
to you.

24 Then he said to Moses, "Come up to the
LORD, you and Aaron, Nadab, and Abihu,
and seventy of the elders of Israel, and worship
at a distance. 2Moses alone shall come near the
LORD; but the others shall not come near, and
the people shall not come up with him."
3 Moses came and told the people all the
words of the LORD and all the ordinances; and
all the people answered with one voice, and said,
"All the words that the LORD has spoken we will
do." 4And Moses wrote down all the words of the
LORD. He rose early in the morning, and built
an altar at the foot of the mountain, and set up

[a] Gk Vg: Heb *he* [b] Or *hornets*: Meaning of Heb uncertain [c] Or *Sea of Reeds*

twelve pillars, corresponding to the twelve tribes of Israel. 5 He sent young men of the people of Israel, who offered burnt offerings and sacrificed oxen as offerings of well-being to the LORD. 6 Moses took half of the blood and put it in basins, and half of the blood he dashed against the altar. 7 Then he took the book of the covenant, and read it in the hearing of the people; and they said, "All that the LORD has spoken we will do, and we will be obedient." 8 Moses took the blood and dashed it on the people, and said, "See the blood of the covenant that the LORD has made with you in accordance with all these words."

9 Then Moses and Aaron, Nadab, and Abihu, and seventy of the elders of Israel went up, 10 and they saw the God of Israel. Under his feet there was something like a pavement of sapphire stone, like the very heaven for clearness. 11 God[a] did not lay his hand on the chief men of the people of Israel; also they beheld God, and they ate and drank.

12 The LORD said to Moses, "Come up to me on the mountain, and wait there; and I will give you the tablets of stone, with the law and the commandment, which I have written for their instruction." 13 So Moses set out with his assistant Joshua, and Moses went up into the mountain of God. 14 To the elders he had said, "Wait here for us, until we come to you again; for Aaron and Hur are with you; whoever has a dispute may go to them."

15 Then Moses went up on the mountain, and the cloud covered the mountain. 16 The glory of the LORD settled on Mount Sinai, and the cloud covered it for six days; on the seventh day he called to Moses out of the cloud. 17 Now the appearance of the glory of the LORD was like a devouring fire on the top of the mountain in the sight of the people of Israel. 18 Moses entered the cloud, and went up on the mountain. Moses was on the mountain for forty days and forty nights.

25 The LORD said to Moses: 2 Tell the Israelites to take for me an offering; from all whose hearts prompt them to give you shall receive the offering for me. 3 This is the offering that you shall receive from them: gold, silver, and bronze, 4 blue, purple, and crimson yarns and fine linen, goats' hair, 5 tanned rams' skins, fine leather,[b] acacia wood, 6 oil for the lamps, spices for the anointing oil and for the fragrant incense, 7 onyx stones and gems to be set in the ephod and for the breastpiece. 8 And have them make me a sanctuary, so that I may dwell among them. 9 In accordance with all that I show you concerning the pattern of the tabernacle and of all its furniture, so you shall make it.

10 They shall make an ark of acacia wood; it shall be two and a half cubits long, a cubit and a half wide, and a cubit and a half high. 11 You shall overlay it with pure gold, inside and outside you shall overlay it, and you shall make a molding of gold upon it all around. 12 You shall cast four rings of gold for it and put them on its four feet, two rings on the one side of it, and two rings on the other side. 13 You shall make poles of acacia wood, and overlay them with gold. 14 And you shall put the poles into the rings on the sides of the ark, by which to carry the ark. 15 The poles shall remain in the rings of the ark; they shall not be taken from it. 16 You shall put into the ark the covenant[c] that I shall give you.

17 Then you shall make a mercy seat[d] of pure gold; two cubits and a half shall be its length, and a cubit and a half its width. 18 You shall make two cherubim of gold; you shall make them of hammered work, at the two ends of the mercy seat.[e] 19 Make one cherub at the one end, and one cherub at the other; of one piece with the mercy seat[e] you shall make the cherubim at its two ends. 20 The cherubim shall spread out their wings above, overshadowing the mercy seat[e] with their wings. They shall face one to another; the faces of the cherubim shall be turned toward the mercy seat.[e] 21 You shall put the mercy seat[e] on the top of the ark; and in the ark you shall put the covenant[c] that I shall give you. 22 There I will meet with you, and from above the mercy seat,[e] from between the two cherubim that are on the ark of the covenant,[c] I will deliver to you all my commands for the Israelites.

[a] Heb *He* [b] Meaning of Heb uncertain [c] Or *treaty,* or *testimony;* Heb *eduth* [d] Or *a cover* [e] Or *the cover*

23 You shall make a table of acacia wood,
two cubits long, one cubit wide, and a cubit and
a half high. 24 You shall overlay it with pure gold,
and make a molding of gold around it. 25 You shall
make around it a rim a handbreadth wide, and a
molding of gold around the rim. 26 You shall make
for it four rings of gold, and fasten the rings to the
four corners at its four legs. 27 The rings that hold
the poles used for carrying the table shall be close
to the rim. 28 You shall make the poles of acacia
wood, and overlay them with gold, and the table
shall be carried with these. 29 You shall make its
plates and dishes for incense, and its flagons and
bowls with which to pour drink offerings; you
shall make them of pure gold. 30 And you shall set
the bread of the Presence on the table before me
always.

31 You shall make a lampstand of pure gold.
The base and the shaft of the lampstand shall be
made of hammered work; its cups, its calyxes,
and its petals shall be of one piece with it; 32 and
there shall be six branches going out of its sides,
three branches of the lampstand out of one side
of it and three branches of the lampstand out of
the other side of it; 33 three cups shaped like almond blossoms, each with calyx and petals, on
one branch, and three cups shaped like almond
blossoms, each with calyx and petals, on the
other branch—so for the six branches going out
of the lampstand. 34 On the lampstand itself there
shall be four cups shaped like almond blossoms,
each with its calyxes and petals. 35 There shall be
a calyx of one piece with it under the first pair of
branches, a calyx of one piece with it under the
next pair of branches, and a calyx of one piece
with it under the last pair of branches—so for
the six branches that go out of the lampstand.
36 Their calyxes and their branches shall be of
one piece with it, the whole of it one hammered
piece of pure gold. 37 You shall make the seven
lamps for it; and the lamps shall be set up so as to
give light on the space in front of it. 38 Its snuffers
and trays shall be of pure gold. 39 It, and all these
utensils, shall be made from a talent of pure gold.
40 And see that you make them according to the
pattern for them, which is being shown you on
the mountain.

26 Moreover you shall make the tabernacle
with ten curtains of fine twisted linen,
and blue, purple, and crimson yarns; you shall
make them with cherubim skillfully worked into
them. 2 The length of each curtain shall be twenty-
eight cubits, and the width of each curtain four
cubits; all the curtains shall be of the same size.
3 Five curtains shall be joined to one another;
and the other five curtains shall be joined to one
another. 4 You shall make loops of blue on the
edge of the outermost curtain in the first set; and
likewise you shall make loops on the edge of the
outermost curtain in the second set. 5 You shall
make fifty loops on the one curtain, and you shall
make fifty loops on the edge of the curtain that is
in the second set; the loops shall be opposite one
another. 6 You shall make fifty clasps of gold, and
join the curtains to one another with the clasps,
so that the tabernacle may be one whole.

7 You shall also make curtains of goats' hair
for a tent over the tabernacle; you shall make
eleven curtains. 8 The length of each curtain shall
be thirty cubits, and the width of each curtain
four cubits; the eleven curtains shall be of the
same size. 9 You shall join five curtains by themselves, and six curtains by themselves, and the
sixth curtain you shall double over at the front of
the tent. 10 You shall make fifty loops on the edge
of the curtain that is outermost in one set, and
fifty loops on the edge of the curtain that is outermost in the second set.

11 You shall make fifty clasps of bronze, and
put the clasps into the loops, and join the tent
together, so that it may be one whole. 12 The part
that remains of the curtains of the tent, the half
curtain that remains, shall hang over the back of
the tabernacle. 13 The cubit on the one side, and
the cubit on the other side, of what remains in the
length of the curtains of the tent, shall hang over
the sides of the tabernacle, on this side and that
side, to cover it. 14 You shall make for the tent a
covering of tanned rams' skins and an outer covering of fine leather.[a]

[a] Meaning of Heb uncertain

15 You shall make upright frames of acacia wood for the tabernacle. 16 Ten cubits shall be the length of a frame, and a cubit and a half the width of each frame. 17 There shall be two pegs in each frame to fit the frames together; you shall make these for all the frames of the tabernacle. 18 You shall make the frames for the tabernacle: twenty frames for the south side; 19 and you shall make forty bases of silver under the twenty frames, two bases under the first frame for its two pegs, and two bases under the next frame for its two pegs; 20 and for the second side of the tabernacle, on the north side twenty frames, 21 and their forty bases of silver, two bases under the first frame, and two bases under the next frame; 22 and for the rear of the tabernacle westward you shall make six frames. 23 You shall make two frames for corners of the tabernacle in the rear; 24 they shall be separate beneath, but joined at the top, at the first ring; it shall be the same with both of them; they shall form the two corners. 25 And so there shall be eight frames, with their bases of silver, sixteen bases; two bases under the first frame, and two bases under the next frame.

26 You shall make bars of acacia wood, five for the frames of the one side of the tabernacle, 27 and five bars for the frames of the other side of the tabernacle, and five bars for the frames of the side of the tabernacle at the rear westward. 28 The middle bar, halfway up the frames, shall pass through from end to end. 29 You shall overlay the frames with gold, and shall make their rings of gold to hold the bars; and you shall overlay the bars with gold. 30 Then you shall erect the tabernacle according to the plan for it that you were shown on the mountain.

31 You shall make a curtain of blue, purple, and crimson yarns, and of fine twisted linen; it shall be made with cherubim skillfully worked into it. 32 You shall hang it on four pillars of acacia overlaid with gold, which have hooks of gold and rest on four bases of silver. 33 You shall hang the curtain under the clasps, and bring the ark of the covenant[a] in there, within the curtain; and the curtain shall separate for you the holy place from the most holy. 34 You shall put the mercy seat[b] on the ark of the covenant[a] in the most holy place. 35 You shall set the table outside the curtain, and the lampstand on the south side of the tabernacle opposite the table; and you shall put the table on the north side.

36 You shall make a screen for the entrance of the tent, of blue, purple, and crimson yarns, and of fine twisted linen, embroidered with needlework. 37 You shall make for the screen five pillars of acacia, and overlay them with gold; their hooks shall be of gold, and you shall cast five bases of bronze for them.

27 You shall make the altar of acacia wood, five cubits long and five cubits wide; the altar shall be square, and it shall be three cubits high. 2 You shall make horns for it on its four corners; its horns shall be of one piece with it, and you shall overlay it with bronze. 3 You shall make pots for it to receive its ashes, and shovels and basins and forks and firepans; you shall make all its utensils of bronze. 4 You shall also make for it a grating, a network of bronze; and on the net you shall make four bronze rings at its four corners. 5 You shall set it under the ledge of the altar so that the net shall extend halfway down the altar. 6 You shall make poles for the altar, poles of acacia wood, and overlay them with bronze; 7 the poles shall be put through the rings, so that the poles shall be on the two sides of the altar when it is carried. 8 You shall make it hollow, with boards. They shall be made just as you were shown on the mountain.

9 You shall make the court of the tabernacle. On the south side the court shall have hangings of fine twisted linen one hundred cubits long for that side; 10 its twenty pillars and their twenty bases shall be of bronze, but the hooks of the pillars and their bands shall be of silver. 11 Likewise for its length on the north side there shall be hangings one hundred cubits long, their pillars twenty and their bases twenty, of bronze, but the hooks of the pillars and their bands shall be of silver. 12 For the width of the court on the west side there shall be fifty cubits of hangings, with ten

[a] Or *treaty*, or *testimony*; Heb *eduth* [b] Or *the cover*

pillars and ten bases. 13The width of the court on
the front to the east shall be fifty cubits. 14There
shall be fifteen cubits of hangings on the one side,
with three pillars and three bases. 15There shall be
fifteen cubits of hangings on the other side, with
three pillars and three bases. 16For the gate of the
court there shall be a screen twenty cubits long,
of blue, purple, and crimson yarns, and of fine
twisted linen, embroidered with needlework; it
shall have four pillars and with them four bases.
17All the pillars around the court shall be banded
with silver; their hooks shall be of silver, and their
bases of bronze. 18The length of the court shall
be one hundred cubits, the width fifty, and the
height five cubits, with hangings of fine twisted
linen and bases of bronze. 19All the utensils of the
tabernacle for every use, and all its pegs and all
the pegs of the court, shall be of bronze.

20 You shall further command the Israelites
to bring you pure oil of beaten olives for the light,
so that a lamp may be set up to burn regularly.
21In the tent of meeting, outside the curtain that
is before the covenant,[a] Aaron and his sons shall
tend it from evening to morning before the LORD.
It shall be a perpetual ordinance to be observed
throughout their generations by the Israelites.

28 Then bring near to you your brother
Aaron, and his sons with him, from among
the Israelites, to serve me as priests—Aaron and
Aaron's sons, Nadab and Abihu, Eleazar and
Ithamar. 2You shall make sacred vestments for the
glorious adornment of your brother Aaron. 3And
you shall speak to all who have ability, whom I
have endowed with skill, that they make Aaron's
vestments to consecrate him for my priesthood.
4These are the vestments that they shall make: a
breastpiece, an ephod, a robe, a checkered tunic,
a turban, and a sash. When they make these sacred vestments for your brother Aaron and his
sons to serve me as priests, 5they shall use gold,
blue, purple, and crimson yarns, and fine linen.

6 They shall make the ephod of gold, of blue,
purple, and crimson yarns, and of fine twisted lin-
en, skillfully worked. 7It shall have two shoulder-
pieces attached to its two edges, so that it may
be joined together. 8The decorated band on it
shall be of the same workmanship and materials, of gold, of blue, purple, and crimson yarns,
and of fine twisted linen. 9You shall take two
onyx stones, and engrave on them the names of
the sons of Israel, 10six of their names on the one
stone, and the names of the remaining six on the
other stone, in the order of their birth. 11As a gem-
cutter engraves signets, so you shall engrave the
two stones with the names of the sons of Israel;
you shall mount them in settings of gold filigree.
12You shall set the two stones on the shoulder-
pieces of the ephod, as stones of remembrance
for the sons of Israel; and Aaron shall bear their
names before the LORD on his two shoulders for
remembrance. 13You shall make settings of gold
filigree, 14and two chains of pure gold, twisted
like cords; and you shall attach the corded chains
to the settings.

15 You shall make a breastpiece of judgment,
in skilled work; you shall make it in the style of
the ephod; of gold, of blue and purple and crimson yarns, and of fine twisted linen you shall
make it. 16It shall be square and doubled, a span
in length and a span in width. 17You shall set in it
four rows of stones. A row of carnelian,[b] chrysolite, and emerald shall be the first row; 18and the
second row a turquoise, a sapphire,[c] and a moonstone; 19and the third row a jacinth, an agate, and
an amethyst; 20and the fourth row a beryl, an
onyx, and a jasper; they shall be set in gold filigree. 21There shall be twelve stones with names
corresponding to the names of the sons of Israel;
they shall be like signets, each engraved with its
name, for the twelve tribes. 22You shall make for
the breastpiece chains of pure gold, twisted like
cords; 23and you shall make for the breastpiece
two rings of gold, and put the two rings on the two
edges of the breastpiece. 24You shall put the two
cords of gold in the two rings at the edges of the
breastpiece; 25the two ends of the two cords you
shall attach to the two settings, and so attach it in
front to the shoulder-pieces of the ephod. 26You
shall make two rings of gold, and put them at the
two ends of the breastpiece, on its inside edge

[a] Or *treaty*, or *testimony*; Heb *eduth*
[b] The identity of several of these stones is uncertain
[c] Or *lapis lazuli*

next to the ephod. 27 You shall make two rings of
gold, and attach them in front to the lower part of
the two shoulder-pieces of the ephod, at its joining above the decorated band of the ephod. 28 The
breastpiece shall be bound by its rings to the rings
of the ephod with a blue cord, so that it may lie on
the decorated band of the ephod, and so that the
breastpiece shall not come loose from the ephod.
29 So Aaron shall bear the names of the sons of Israel in the breastpiece of judgment on his heart
when he goes into the holy place, for a continual
remembrance before the LORD. 30 In the breastpiece of judgment you shall put the Urim and the
Thummim, and they shall be on Aaron's heart
when he goes in before the LORD; thus Aaron
shall bear the judgment of the Israelites on his
heart before the LORD continually.

31 You shall make the robe of the ephod all
of blue. 32 It shall have an opening for the head in
the middle of it, with a woven binding around the
opening, like the opening in a coat of mail,[a] so that
it may not be torn. 33 On its lower hem you shall
make pomegranates of blue, purple, and crimson
yarns, all around the lower hem, with bells of gold
between them all around— 34 a golden bell and
a pomegranate alternating all around the lower
hem of the robe. 35 Aaron shall wear it when he
ministers, and its sound shall be heard when he
goes into the holy place before the LORD, and
when he comes out, so that he may not die.

36 You shall make a rosette of pure gold, and
engrave on it, like the engraving of a signet, "Holy
to the LORD." 37 You shall fasten it on the turban
with a blue cord; it shall be on the front of the
turban. 38 It shall be on Aaron's forehead, and
Aaron shall take on himself any guilt incurred in
the holy offering that the Israelites consecrate as
their sacred donations; it shall always be on his
forehead, in order that they may find favor before
the LORD.

39 You shall make the checkered tunic of fine
linen, and you shall make a turban of fine linen,
and you shall make a sash embroidered with
needlework.

40 For Aaron's sons you shall make tunics and
sashes and headdresses; you shall make them for
their glorious adornment. 41 You shall put them
on your brother Aaron, and on his sons with him,
and shall anoint them and ordain them and consecrate them, so that they may serve me as priests.
42 You shall make for them linen undergarments
to cover their naked flesh; they shall reach from
the hips to the thighs; 43 Aaron and his sons shall
wear them when they go into the tent of meeting,
or when they come near the altar to minister in
the holy place; or they will bring guilt on themselves and die. This shall be a perpetual ordinance
for him and for his descendants after him.

29 Now this is what you shall do to them to
consecrate them, so that they may serve
me as priests. Take one young bull and two rams
without blemish, 2 and unleavened bread, unleavened cakes mixed with oil, and unleavened
wafers spread with oil. You shall make them of
choice wheat flour. 3 You shall put them in one
basket and bring them in the basket, and bring
the bull and the two rams. 4 You shall bring Aaron
and his sons to the entrance of the tent of meeting, and wash them with water. 5 Then you shall
take the vestments, and put on Aaron the tunic
and the robe of the ephod, and the ephod, and
the breastpiece, and gird him with the decorated
band of the ephod; 6 and you shall set the turban
on his head, and put the holy diadem on the turban. 7 You shall take the anointing oil, and pour
it on his head and anoint him. 8 Then you shall
bring his sons, and put tunics on them, 9 and you
shall gird them with sashes[b] and tie headdresses
on them; and the priesthood shall be theirs by a
perpetual ordinance. You shall then ordain Aaron
and his sons.

10 You shall bring the bull in front of the
tent of meeting. Aaron and his sons shall lay
their hands on the head of the bull, 11 and you
shall slaughter the bull before the LORD, at the
entrance of the tent of meeting, 12 and shall take
some of the blood of the bull and put it on the
horns of the altar with your finger, and all the rest
of the blood you shall pour out at the base of the
altar. 13 You shall take all the fat that covers the

[a] Meaning of Heb uncertain [b] Gk: Heb *sashes, Aaron and his sons*

entrails, and the appendage of the liver, and the
two kidneys with the fat that is on them, and turn
them into smoke on the altar. 14But the flesh of
the bull, and its skin, and its dung, you shall burn
with fire outside the camp; it is a sin offering.

15 Then you shall take one of the rams, and
Aaron and his sons shall lay their hands on the
head of the ram, 16and you shall slaughter the
ram, and shall take its blood and dash it against
all sides of the altar. 17Then you shall cut the ram
into its parts, and wash its entrails and its legs,
and put them with its parts and its head, 18and
turn the whole ram into smoke on the altar; it is a
burnt offering to the LORD; it is a pleasing odor,
an offering by fire to the LORD.

19 You shall take the other ram; and Aaron
and his sons shall lay their hands on the head of
the ram, 20and you shall slaughter the ram, and
take some of its blood and put it on the lobe of
Aaron's right ear and on the lobes of the right
ears of his sons, and on the thumbs of their right
hands, and on the big toes of their right feet, and
dash the rest of the blood against all sides of the
altar. 21Then you shall take some of the blood that
is on the altar, and some of the anointing oil, and
sprinkle it on Aaron and his vestments and on his
sons and his sons' vestments with him; then he
and his vestments shall be holy, as well as his sons
and his sons' vestments.

22 You shall also take the fat of the ram, the fat
tail, the fat that covers the entrails, the appendage
of the liver, the two kidneys with the fat that is on
them, and the right thigh (for it is a ram of ordination), 23and one loaf of bread, one cake of bread
made with oil, and one wafer, out of the basket of
unleavened bread that is before the LORD; 24and
you shall place all these on the palms of Aaron
and on the palms of his sons, and raise them as an
elevation offering before the LORD. 25Then you
shall take them from their hands, and turn them
into smoke on the altar on top of the burnt offering of pleasing odor before the LORD; it is an
offering by fire to the LORD.

26 You shall take the breast of the ram of
Aaron's ordination and raise it as an elevation
offering before the LORD; and it shall be your
portion. 27You shall consecrate the breast that
was raised as an elevation offering and the thigh
that was raised as an elevation offering from the
ram of ordination, from that which belonged to
Aaron and his sons. 28These things shall be a perpetual ordinance for Aaron and his sons from the
Israelites, for this is an offering; and it shall be an
offering by the Israelites from their sacrifice of offerings of well-being, their offering to the LORD.

29 The sacred vestments of Aaron shall be
passed on to his sons after him; they shall be
anointed in them and ordained in them. 30The
son who is priest in his place shall wear them sev-
en days, when he comes into the tent of meeting
to minister in the holy place.

31 You shall take the ram of ordination, and
boil its flesh in a holy place; 32and Aaron and his
sons shall eat the flesh of the ram and the bread
that is in the basket, at the entrance of the tent
of meeting. 33They themselves shall eat the food
by which atonement is made, to ordain and consecrate them, but no one else shall eat of them,
because they are holy. 34If any of the flesh for
the ordination, or of the bread, remains until the
morning, then you shall burn the remainder with
fire; it shall not be eaten, because it is holy.

35 Thus you shall do to Aaron and to his sons,
just as I have commanded you; through seven
days you shall ordain them. 36Also every day you
shall offer a bull as a sin offering for atonement.
Also you shall offer a sin offering for the altar,
when you make atonement for it, and shall anoint
it, to consecrate it. 37Seven days you shall make
atonement for the altar, and consecrate it, and
the altar shall be most holy; whatever touches the
altar shall become holy.

38 Now this is what you shall offer on the altar: two lambs a year old regularly each day. 39One
lamb you shall offer in the morning, and the other
lamb you shall offer in the evening; 40and with
the first lamb one-tenth of a measure of choice
flour mixed with one-fourth of a hin of beaten
oil, and one-fourth of a hin of wine for a drink
offering. 41And the other lamb you shall offer in
the evening, and shall offer with it a grain offering and its drink offering, as in the morning, for a
pleasing odor, an offering by fire to the LORD. 42It
shall be a regular burnt offering throughout your

generations at the entrance of the tent of meeting
before the LORD, where I will meet with you, to
speak to you there. 43 I will meet with the Israelites there, and it shall be sanctified by my glory;
44 I will consecrate the tent of meeting and the
altar; Aaron also and his sons I will consecrate,
to serve me as priests. 45 I will dwell among the Israelites, and I will be their God. 46 And they shall
know that I am the LORD their God, who brought
them out of the land of Egypt that I might dwell
among them; I am the LORD their God.

30 You shall make an altar on which to offer
incense; you shall make it of acacia wood.
2 It shall be one cubit long, and one cubit wide;
it shall be square, and shall be two cubits high;
its horns shall be of one piece with it. 3 You shall
overlay it with pure gold, its top, and its sides all
around and its horns; and you shall make for it a
molding of gold all around. 4 And you shall make
two golden rings for it; under its molding on two
opposite sides of it you shall make them, and they
shall hold the poles with which to carry it. 5 You
shall make the poles of acacia wood, and overlay
them with gold. 6 You shall place it in front of the
curtain that is above the ark of the covenant,[a]
in front of the mercy seat[b] that is over the covenant,[a] where I will meet with you. 7 Aaron shall
offer fragrant incense on it; every morning when
he dresses the lamps he shall offer it, 8 and when
Aaron sets up the lamps in the evening, he shall
offer it, a regular incense offering before the
LORD throughout your generations. 9 You shall
not offer unholy incense on it, or a burnt offering,
or a grain offering; and you shall not pour a drink
offering on it. 10 Once a year Aaron shall perform
the rite of atonement on its horns. Throughout
your generations he shall perform the atonement
for it once a year with the blood of the atoning sin
offering. It is most holy to the LORD.

11 The LORD spoke to Moses: 12 When you
take a census of the Israelites to register them,
at registration all of them shall give a ransom for
their lives to the LORD, so that no plague may
come upon them for being registered. 13 This is
what each one who is registered shall give: half
a shekel according to the shekel of the sanctuary
(the shekel is twenty gerahs), half a shekel as an
offering to the LORD. 14 Each one who is registered, from twenty years old and upward, shall
give the LORD's offering. 15 The rich shall not give
more, and the poor shall not give less, than the
half shekel, when you bring this offering to the
LORD to make atonement for your lives. 16 You
shall take the atonement money from the Israelites and shall designate it for the service of the
tent of meeting; before the LORD it will be a reminder to the Israelites of the ransom given for
your lives.

17 The LORD spoke to Moses: 18 You shall
make a bronze basin with a bronze stand for
washing. You shall put it between the tent of
meeting and the altar, and you shall put water
in it; 19 with the water[c] Aaron and his sons shall
wash their hands and their feet. 20 When they go
into the tent of meeting, or when they come near
the altar to minister, to make an offering by fire to
the LORD, they shall wash with water, so that they
may not die. 21 They shall wash their hands and
their feet, so that they may not die: it shall be a
perpetual ordinance for them, for him and for his
descendants throughout their generations.

22 The LORD spoke to Moses: 23 Take the finest spices: of liquid myrrh five hundred shekels,
and of sweet-smelling cinnamon half as much,
that is, two hundred fifty, and two hundred fifty
of aromatic cane, 24 and five hundred of cassia—
measured by the sanctuary shekel—and a hin of
olive oil; 25 and you shall make of these a sacred
anointing oil blended as by the perfumer; it shall
be a holy anointing oil. 26 With it you shall anoint
the tent of meeting and the ark of the covenant,[a]
27 and the table and all its utensils, and the lampstand and its utensils, and the altar of incense,
28 and the altar of burnt offering with all its utensils, and the basin with its stand; 29 you shall
consecrate them, so that they may be most holy;
whatever touches them will become holy. 30 You
shall anoint Aaron and his sons, and consecrate
them, in order that they may serve me as priests.
31 You shall say to the Israelites, "This shall be my

[a] Or *treaty*, or *testimony*; Heb *eduth* [b] Or *the cover* [c] Heb *it*

holy anointing oil throughout your generations.
32It shall not be used in any ordinary anointing
of the body, and you shall make no other like it
in composition; it is holy, and it shall be holy to
you. 33Whoever compounds any like it or whoever puts any of it on an unqualified person shall
be cut off from the people."

34 The LORD said to Moses: Take sweet
spices, stacte, and onycha, and galbanum, sweet
spices with pure frankincense (an equal part of
each), 35and make an incense blended as by the
perfumer, seasoned with salt, pure and holy;
36and you shall beat some of it into powder, and
put part of it before the covenant[a] in the tent of
meeting where I shall meet with you; it shall be
for you most holy. 37When you make incense according to this composition, you shall not make it
for yourselves; it shall be regarded by you as holy
to the LORD. 38Whoever makes any like it to use
as perfume shall be cut off from the people.

31 The LORD spoke to Moses: 2See, I have
called by name Bezalel son of Uri son of
Hur, of the tribe of Judah: 3and I have filled him
with divine spirit,[b] with ability, intelligence, and
knowledge in every kind of craft, 4to devise artistic designs, to work in gold, silver, and bronze, 5in
cutting stones for setting, and in carving wood, in
every kind of craft. 6Moreover, I have appointed
with him Oholiab son of Ahisamach, of the tribe
of Dan; and I have given skill to all the skillful, so
that they may make all that I have commanded
you: 7the tent of meeting, and the ark of the covenant,[a] and the mercy seat[c] that is on it, and all
the furnishings of the tent, 8the table and its utensils, and the pure lampstand with all its utensils,
and the altar of incense, 9and the altar of burnt
offering with all its utensils, and the basin with
its stand, 10and the finely worked vestments,
the holy vestments for the priest Aaron and the
vestments of his sons, for their service as priests,
11and the anointing oil and the fragrant incense
for the holy place. They shall do just as I have
commanded you.

12 The LORD said to Moses: 13You yourself
are to speak to the Israelites: "You shall keep my
sabbaths, for this is a sign between me and you
throughout your generations, given in order that
you may know that I, the LORD, sanctify you.
14You shall keep the sabbath, because it is holy
for you; everyone who profanes it shall be put
to death; whoever does any work on it shall be
cut off from among the people. 15Six days shall
work be done, but the seventh day is a sabbath
of solemn rest, holy to the LORD; whoever does
any work on the sabbath day shall be put to death.
16Therefore the Israelites shall keep the sabbath,
observing the sabbath throughout their generations, as a perpetual covenant. 17It is a sign forever between me and the people of Israel that in
six days the LORD made heaven and earth, and on
the seventh day he rested, and was refreshed."

18 When God[d] finished speaking with Moses
on Mount Sinai, he gave him the two tablets of
the covenant,[a] tablets of stone, written with the
finger of God.

32 When the people saw that Moses delayed
to come down from the mountain, the
people gathered around Aaron, and said to him,
"Come, make gods for us, who shall go before us;
as for this Moses, the man who brought us up out
of the land of Egypt, we do not know what has
become of him." 2Aaron said to them, "Take off
the gold rings that are on the ears of your wives,
your sons, and your daughters, and bring them
to me." 3So all the people took off the gold rings
from their ears, and brought them to Aaron. 4He
took the gold from them, formed it in a mold,[e]
and cast an image of a calf; and they said, "These
are your gods, O Israel, who brought you up out
of the land of Egypt!" 5When Aaron saw this, he
built an altar before it; and Aaron made proclamation and said, "Tomorrow shall be a festival
to the LORD." 6They rose early the next day, and
offered burnt offerings and brought sacrifices of
well-being; and the people sat down to eat and
drink, and rose up to revel.

7 The LORD said to Moses, "Go down at
once! Your people, whom you brought up out of

[a] Or *treaty*, or *testimony*; Heb *eduth* [b] Or *with the spirit of God* [c] Or *the cover* [d] Heb *he*
[e] Or *fashioned it with a graving tool*; Meaning of Heb uncertain

the land of Egypt, have acted perversely; 8they have been quick to turn aside from the way that I commanded them; they have cast for themselves an image of a calf, and have worshiped it and sacrificed to it, and said, 'These are your gods, O Israel, who brought you up out of the land of Egypt!' " 9The LORD said to Moses, "I have seen this people, how stiff-necked they are. 10Now let me alone, so that my wrath may burn hot against them and I may consume them; and of you I will make a great nation."

11 But Moses implored the LORD his God, and said, "O LORD, why does your wrath burn hot against your people, whom you brought out of the land of Egypt with great power and with a mighty hand? 12Why should the Egyptians say, 'It was with evil intent that he brought them out to kill them in the mountains, and to consume them from the face of the earth'? Turn from your fierce wrath; change your mind and do not bring disaster on your people. 13Remember Abraham, Isaac, and Israel, your servants, how you swore to them by your own self, saying to them, 'I will multiply your descendants like the stars of heaven, and all this land that I have promised I will give to your descendants, and they shall inherit it forever.' " 14And the LORD changed his mind about the disaster that he planned to bring on his people.

15 Then Moses turned and went down from the mountain, carrying the two tablets of the covenant[a] in his hands, tablets that were written on both sides, written on the front and on the back. 16The tablets were the work of God, and the writing was the writing of God, engraved upon the tablets. 17When Joshua heard the noise of the people as they shouted, he said to Moses, "There is a noise of war in the camp." 18But he said,

"It is not the sound made by victors,
or the sound made by losers;
it is the sound of revelers that I hear."

19As soon as he came near the camp and saw the calf and the dancing, Moses' anger burned hot, and he threw the tablets from his hands and broke them at the foot of the mountain. 20He took the calf that they had made, burned it with fire, ground it to powder, scattered it on the water, and made the Israelites drink it.

21 Moses said to Aaron, "What did this people do to you that you have brought so great a sin upon them?" 22And Aaron said, "Do not let the anger of my lord burn hot; you know the people, that they are bent on evil. 23They said to me, 'Make us gods, who shall go before us; as for this Moses, the man who brought us up out of the land of Egypt, we do not know what has become of him.' 24So I said to them, 'Whoever has gold, take it off'; so they gave it to me, and I threw it into the fire, and out came this calf!"

25 When Moses saw that the people were running wild (for Aaron had let them run wild, to the derision of their enemies), 26then Moses stood in the gate of the camp, and said, "Who is on the LORD's side? Come to me!" And all the sons of Levi gathered around him. 27He said to them, "Thus says the LORD, the God of Israel, 'Put your sword on your side, each of you! Go back and forth from gate to gate throughout the camp, and each of you kill your brother, your friend, and your neighbor.' " 28The sons of Levi did as Moses commanded, and about three thousand of the people fell on that day. 29Moses said, "Today you have ordained yourselves[b] for the service of the LORD, each one at the cost of a son or a brother, and so have brought a blessing on yourselves this day."

30 On the next day Moses said to the people, "You have sinned a great sin. But now I will go up to the LORD; perhaps I can make atonement for your sin." 31So Moses returned to the LORD and said, "Alas, this people has sinned a great sin; they have made for themselves gods of gold. 32But now, if you will only forgive their sin—but if not, blot me out of the book that you have written." 33But the LORD said to Moses, "Whoever has sinned against me I will blot out of my book. 34But now go, lead the people to the place about which I have spoken to you; see, my angel shall go in front of you. Nevertheless, when the day comes for punishment, I will punish them for their sin."

35 Then the LORD sent a plague on the peo-

[a] Or *treaty*, or *testimony*; Heb *eduth* [b] Gk Vg Compare Tg: Heb *Today ordain yourselves*

ple, because they made the calf—the one that
Aaron made.
33 The LORD said to Moses, “Go, leave this
place, you and the people whom you have
brought up out of the land of Egypt, and go to the
land of which I swore to Abraham, Isaac, and Jacob, saying, ‘To your descendants I will give it.’ 2 I
will send an angel before you, and I will drive out
the Canaanites, the Amorites, the Hittites, the
Perizzites, the Hivites, and the Jebusites. 3 Go up
to a land flowing with milk and honey; but I will
not go up among you, or I would consume you on
the way, for you are a stiff-necked people.”
4 When the people heard these harsh words,
they mourned, and no one put on ornaments.
5 For the LORD had said to Moses, “Say to the Israelites, ‘You are a stiff-necked people; if for a single moment I should go up among you, I would
consume you. So now take off your ornaments,
and I will decide what to do to you.’ ” 6 Therefore
the Israelites stripped themselves of their ornaments, from Mount Horeb onward.
7 Now Moses used to take the tent and pitch it
outside the camp, far off from the camp; he called
it the tent of meeting. And everyone who sought
the LORD would go out to the tent of meeting,
which was outside the camp. 8 Whenever Moses
went out to the tent, all the people would rise
and stand, each of them, at the entrance of their
tents and watch Moses until he had gone into the
tent. 9 When Moses entered the tent, the pillar of
cloud would descend and stand at the entrance
of the tent, and the LORD would speak with
Moses. 10 When all the people saw the pillar of
cloud standing at the entrance of the tent, all the
people would rise and bow down, all of them, at
the entrance of their tent. 11 Thus the LORD used
to speak to Moses face to face, as one speaks to
a friend. Then he would return to the camp; but
his young assistant, Joshua son of Nun, would not
leave the tent.
12 Moses said to the LORD, “See, you have
said to me, ‘Bring up this people’; but you have not
let me know whom you will send with me. Yet you
have said, ‘I know you by name, and you have also
found favor in my sight.’ 13 Now if I have found favor in your sight, show me your ways, so that I may
know you and find favor in your sight. Consider
too that this nation is your people.” 14 He said, “My
presence will go with you, and I will give you rest.”
15 And he said to him, “If your presence will not
go, do not carry us up from here. 16 For how shall
it be known that I have found favor in your sight,
I and your people, unless you go with us? In this
way, we shall be distinct, I and your people, from
every people on the face of the earth.”
17 The LORD said to Moses, “I will do the
very thing that you have asked; for you have
found favor in my sight, and I know you by name.”
18 Moses said, “Show me your glory, I pray.” 19 And
he said, “I will make all my goodness pass before
you, and will proclaim before you the name, ‘The
LORD’;[a] and I will be gracious to whom I will be
gracious, and will show mercy on whom I will
show mercy. 20 But,” he said, “you cannot see my
face; for no one shall see me and live.” 21 And the
LORD continued, “See, there is a place by me
where you shall stand on the rock; 22 and while
my glory passes by I will put you in a cleft of the
rock, and I will cover you with my hand until I
have passed by; 23 then I will take away my hand,
and you shall see my back; but my face shall not
be seen.”
34 The LORD said to Moses, “Cut two tablets
of stone like the former ones, and I will
write on the tablets the words that were on the
former tablets, which you broke. 2 Be ready in the
morning, and come up in the morning to Mount
Sinai and present yourself there to me, on the top
of the mountain. 3 No one shall come up with
you, and do not let anyone be seen throughout all
the mountain; and do not let flocks or herds graze
in front of that mountain.” 4 So Moses cut two
tablets of stone like the former ones; and he rose
early in the morning and went up on Mount Sinai, as the LORD had commanded him, and took
in his hand the two tablets of stone. 5 The LORD
descended in the cloud and stood with him there,
and proclaimed the name, “The LORD.”[a] 6 The
LORD passed before him, and proclaimed,

[a] Heb *YHWH*; see note at 3.15

"The LORD, the LORD,
a God merciful and gracious,
slow to anger,
and abounding in steadfast love and
faithfulness,
7 keeping steadfast love for the thousandth
generation,[a]
forgiving iniquity and transgression and sin,
yet by no means clearing the guilty,
but visiting the iniquity of the parents
upon the children
and the children's children,
to the third and the fourth generation."

8 And Moses quickly bowed his head toward the
earth, and worshiped. 9 He said, "If now I have
found favor in your sight, O Lord, I pray, let the
Lord go with us. Although this is a stiff-necked
people, pardon our iniquity and our sin, and take
us for your inheritance."

10 He said: I hereby make a covenant. Before
all your people I will perform marvels, such as
have not been performed in all the earth or in any
nation; and all the people among whom you live
shall see the work of the LORD; for it is an awesome thing that I will do with you.

11 Observe what I command you today. See,
I will drive out before you the Amorites, the Canaanites, the Hittites, the Perizzites, the Hivites,
and the Jebusites. 12 Take care not to make a covenant with the inhabitants of the land to which
you are going, or it will become a snare among
you. 13 You shall tear down their altars, break
their pillars, and cut down their sacred poles[b]
14 (for you shall worship no other god, because
the LORD, whose name is Jealous, is a jealous
God). 15 You shall not make a covenant with the
inhabitants of the land, for when they prostitute
themselves to their gods and sacrifice to their
gods, someone among them will invite you, and
you will eat of the sacrifice. 16 And you will take
wives from among their daughters for your sons,
and their daughters who prostitute themselves
to their gods will make your sons also prostitute
themselves to their gods.

17 You shall not make cast idols.

18 You shall keep the festival of unleavened
bread. Seven days you shall eat unleavened bread,
as I commanded you, at the time appointed in
the month of Abib; for in the month of Abib you
came out from Egypt.

19 All that first opens the womb is mine, all
your male[c] livestock, the firstborn of cow and
sheep. 20 The firstborn of a donkey you shall redeem with a lamb, or if you will not redeem it you
shall break its neck. All the firstborn of your sons
you shall redeem.

No one shall appear before me empty-
handed.

21 Six days you shall work, but on the seventh day you shall rest; even in plowing time and
in harvest time you shall rest. 22 You shall observe
the festival of weeks, the first fruits of wheat harvest, and the festival of ingathering at the turn of
the year. 23 Three times in the year all your males
shall appear before the LORD God, the God of
Israel. 24 For I will cast out nations before you,
and enlarge your borders; no one shall covet your
land when you go up to appear before the LORD
your God three times in the year.

25 You shall not offer the blood of my sacrifice with leaven, and the sacrifice of the festival of
the passover shall not be left until the morning.

26 The best of the first fruits of your ground
you shall bring to the house of the LORD your
God.

You shall not boil a kid in its mother's milk.

27 The LORD said to Moses: Write these
words; in accordance with these words I have
made a covenant with you and with Israel. 28 He
was there with the LORD forty days and forty
nights; he neither ate bread nor drank water. And
he wrote on the tablets the words of the covenant,
the ten commandments.[d]

29 Moses came down from Mount Sinai. As
he came down from the mountain with the two
tablets of the covenant[e] in his hand, Moses did
not know that the skin of his face shone because
he had been talking with God. 30 When Aaron

[a] Or *for thousands* [b] Heb *Asherim* [c] Gk Theodotion Vg Tg: Meaning of Heb uncertain [d] Heb *words*
[e] Or *treaty*, or *testimony*; Heb *eduth*

and all the Israelites saw Moses, the skin of his
face was shining, and they were afraid to come
near him. 31 But Moses called to them; and Aaron
and all the leaders of the congregation returned
to him, and Moses spoke with them. 32 Afterward
all the Israelites came near, and he gave them in
commandment all that the LORD had spoken
with him on Mount Sinai. 33 When Moses had
finished speaking with them, he put a veil on his
face; 34 but whenever Moses went in before the
LORD to speak with him, he would take the veil
off, until he came out; and when he came out, and
told the Israelites what he had been commanded,
35 the Israelites would see the face of Moses, that
the skin of his face was shining; and Moses would
put the veil on his face again, until he went in to
speak with him.

35 Moses assembled all the congregation of
the Israelites and said to them: These are
the things that the LORD has commanded you
to do:

2 Six days shall work be done, but on the seventh day you shall have a holy sabbath of solemn
rest to the LORD; whoever does any work on it
shall be put to death. 3 You shall kindle no fire in
all your dwellings on the sabbath day.

4 Moses said to all the congregation of the
Israelites: This is the thing that the LORD has
commanded: 5 Take from among you an offering
to the LORD; let whoever is of a generous heart
bring the LORD's offering: gold, silver, and
bronze; 6 blue, purple, and crimson yarns, and
fine linen; goats' hair, 7 tanned rams' skins,
and fine leather;[a] acacia wood, 8 oil for the light,
spices for the anointing oil and for the fragrant
incense, 9 and onyx stones and gems to be set in
the ephod and the breastpiece.

10 All who are skillful among you shall come
and make all that the LORD has commanded: the
tabernacle, 11 its tent and its covering, its clasps
and its frames, its bars, its pillars, and its bases;
12 the ark with its poles, the mercy seat,[b] and the
curtain for the screen; 13 the table with its poles
and all its utensils, and the bread of the Presence;
14 the lampstand also for the light, with its utensils and its lamps, and the oil for the light; 15 and
the altar of incense, with its poles, and the anointing oil and the fragrant incense, and the screen for
the entrance, the entrance of the tabernacle; 16 the
altar of burnt offering, with its grating of bronze,
its poles, and all its utensils, the basin with its
stand; 17 the hangings of the court, its pillars and
its bases, and the screen for the gate of the court;
18 the pegs of the tabernacle and the pegs of the
court, and their cords; 19 the finely worked vestments for ministering in the holy place, the holy
vestments for the priest Aaron, and the vestments
of his sons, for their service as priests.

20 Then all the congregation of the Israelites
withdrew from the presence of Moses. 21 And
they came, everyone whose heart was stirred, and
everyone whose spirit was willing, and brought
the LORD's offering to be used for the tent of meeting, and for all its service, and for the sacred vestments. 22 So they came, both men and women; all
who were of a willing heart brought brooches and
earrings and signet rings and pendants, all sorts of
gold objects, everyone bringing an offering of gold
to the LORD. 23 And everyone who possessed blue
or purple or crimson yarn or fine linen or goats'
hair or tanned rams' skins or fine leather,[a] brought
them. 24 Everyone who could make an offering of
silver or bronze brought it as the LORD's offering; and everyone who possessed acacia wood of
any use in the work, brought it. 25 All the skillful
women spun with their hands, and brought what
they had spun in blue and purple and crimson
yarns and fine linen; 26 all the women whose hearts
moved them to use their skill spun the goats' hair.
27 And the leaders brought onyx stones and gems
to be set in the ephod and the breastpiece, 28 and
spices and oil for the light, and for the anointing
oil, and for the fragrant incense. 29 All the Israelite
men and women whose hearts made them willing
to bring anything for the work that the LORD had
commanded by Moses to be done, brought it as a
freewill offering to the LORD.

30 Then Moses said to the Israelites: See, the
LORD has called by name Bezalel son of Uri son of
Hur, of the tribe of Judah; 31 he has filled him with

[a] Meaning of Heb uncertain [b] Or *the cover*

divine spirit,[a] with skill, intelligence, and knowledge in every kind of craft, 32to devise artistic designs, to work in gold, silver, and bronze, 33in cutting stones for setting, and in carving wood, in every kind of craft. 34And he has inspired him to teach, both him and Oholiab son of Ahisamach, of the tribe of Dan. 35He has filled them with skill to do every kind of work done by an artisan or by a designer or by an embroiderer in blue, purple, and crimson yarns, and in fine linen, or by a weaver—by any sort of artisan or skilled designer.

36 Bezalel and Oholiab and every skillful one to whom the LORD has given skill and understanding to know how to do any work in the construction of the sanctuary shall work in accordance with all that the LORD has commanded.

2 Moses then called Bezalel and Oholiab and every skillful one to whom the LORD had given skill, everyone whose heart was stirred to come to do the work; 3and they received from Moses all the freewill offerings that the Israelites had brought for doing the work on the sanctuary. They still kept bringing him freewill offerings every morning, 4so that all the artisans who were doing every sort of task on the sanctuary came, each from the task being performed, 5and said to Moses, "The people are bringing much more than enough for doing the work that the LORD has commanded us to do." 6So Moses gave command, and word was proclaimed throughout the camp: "No man or woman is to make anything else as an offering for the sanctuary." So the people were restrained from bringing; 7for what they had already brought was more than enough to do all the work.

8 All those with skill among the workers made the tabernacle with ten curtains; they were made of fine twisted linen, and blue, purple, and crimson yarns, with cherubim skillfully worked into them. 9The length of each curtain was twenty-eight cubits, and the width of each curtain four cubits; all the curtains were of the same size.

10 He joined five curtains to one another, and the other five curtains he joined to one another. 11He made loops of blue on the edge of the outermost curtain of the first set; likewise he made them on the edge of the outermost curtain of the second set; 12he made fifty loops on the one curtain, and he made fifty loops on the edge of the curtain that was in the second set; the loops were opposite one another. 13And he made fifty clasps of gold, and joined the curtains one to the other with clasps; so the tabernacle was one whole.

14 He also made curtains of goats' hair for a tent over the tabernacle; he made eleven curtains. 15The length of each curtain was thirty cubits, and the width of each curtain four cubits; the eleven curtains were of the same size. 16He joined five curtains by themselves, and six curtains by themselves. 17He made fifty loops on the edge of the outermost curtain of the one set, and fifty loops on the edge of the other connecting curtain. 18He made fifty clasps of bronze to join the tent together so that it might be one whole. 19And he made for the tent a covering of tanned rams' skins and an outer covering of fine leather.[b]

20 Then he made the upright frames for the tabernacle of acacia wood. 21Ten cubits was the length of a frame, and a cubit and a half the width of each frame. 22Each frame had two pegs for fitting together; he did this for all the frames of the tabernacle. 23The frames for the tabernacle he made in this way: twenty frames for the south side; 24and he made forty bases of silver under the twenty frames, two bases under the first frame for its two pegs, and two bases under the next frame for its two pegs. 25For the second side of the tabernacle, on the north side, he made twenty frames 26and their forty bases of silver, two bases under the first frame and two bases under the next frame. 27For the rear of the tabernacle westward he made six frames. 28He made two frames for corners of the tabernacle in the rear. 29They were separate beneath, but joined at the top, at the first ring; he made two of them in this way, for the two corners. 30There were eight frames with their bases of silver: sixteen bases, under every frame two bases.

31 He made bars of acacia wood, five for the

[a] Or *the spirit of God* [b] Meaning of Heb uncertain

frames of the one side of the tabernacle, 32 and
five bars for the frames of the other side of the
tabernacle, and five bars for the frames of the tabernacle at the rear westward. 33 He made the middle bar to pass through from end to end halfway
up the frames. 34 And he overlaid the frames with
gold, and made rings of gold for them to hold the
bars, and overlaid the bars with gold.

35 He made the curtain of blue, purple, and
crimson yarns, and fine twisted linen, with cherubim skillfully worked into it. 36 For it he made four
pillars of acacia, and overlaid them with gold;
their hooks were of gold, and he cast for them
four bases of silver. 37 He also made a screen for
the entrance to the tent, of blue, purple, and crimson yarns, and fine twisted linen, embroidered
with needlework; 38 and its five pillars with their
hooks. He overlaid their capitals and their bases
with gold, but their five bases were of bronze.

37 Bezalel made the ark of acacia wood; it
was two and a half cubits long, a cubit
and a half wide, and a cubit and a half high. 2 He
overlaid it with pure gold inside and outside, and
made a molding of gold around it. 3 He cast for it
four rings of gold for its four feet, two rings on
its one side and two rings on its other side. 4 He
made poles of acacia wood, and overlaid them
with gold, 5 and put the poles into the rings on
the sides of the ark, to carry the ark. 6 He made
a mercy seat[a] of pure gold; two cubits and a half
was its length, and a cubit and a half its width.
7 He made two cherubim of hammered gold; at
the two ends of the mercy seat[a] he made them,
8 one cherub at the one end, and one cherub at the
other end; of one piece with the mercy seat[a] he
made the cherubim at its two ends. 9 The cherubim spread out their wings above, overshadowing
the mercy seat[a] with their wings. They faced one
another; the faces of the cherubim were turned
toward the mercy seat.[a]

10 He also made the table of acacia wood, two
cubits long, one cubit wide, and a cubit and a half
high. 11 He overlaid it with pure gold, and made a
molding of gold around it. 12 He made around it a
rim a handbreadth wide, and made a molding of
gold around the rim. 13 He cast for it four rings of
gold, and fastened the rings to the four corners at
its four legs. 14 The rings that held the poles used
for carrying the table were close to the rim. 15 He
made the poles of acacia wood to carry the table,
and overlaid them with gold. 16 And he made the
vessels of pure gold that were to be on the table,
its plates and dishes for incense, and its bowls and
flagons with which to pour drink offerings.

17 He also made the lampstand of pure gold.
The base and the shaft of the lampstand were
made of hammered work; its cups, its calyxes, and
its petals were of one piece with it. 18 There were
six branches going out of its sides, three branches
of the lampstand out of one side of it and three
branches of the lampstand out of the other side
of it; 19 three cups shaped like almond blossoms,
each with calyx and petals, on one branch, and
three cups shaped like almond blossoms, each
with calyx and petals, on the other branch—so for
the six branches going out of the lampstand. 20 On
the lampstand itself there were four cups shaped
like almond blossoms, each with its calyxes and
petals. 21 There was a calyx of one piece with it
under the first pair of branches, a calyx of one
piece with it under the next pair of branches, and
a calyx of one piece with it under the last pair of
branches. 22 Their calyxes and their branches were
of one piece with it, the whole of it one hammered
piece of pure gold. 23 He made its seven lamps and
its snuffers and its trays of pure gold. 24 He made it
and all its utensils of a talent of pure gold.

25 He made the altar of incense of acacia
wood, one cubit long, and one cubit wide; it was
square, and was two cubits high; its horns were of
one piece with it. 26 He overlaid it with pure gold,
its top, and its sides all around, and its horns; and
he made for it a molding of gold all around, 27 and
made two golden rings for it under its molding,
on two opposite sides of it, to hold the poles with
which to carry it. 28 And he made the poles of acacia wood, and overlaid them with gold.

29 He made the holy anointing oil also, and
the pure fragrant incense, blended as by the perfumer.

[a] Or *a cover*

38 He made the altar of burnt offering also of acacia wood; it was five cubits long, and five cubits wide; it was square, and three cubits high. 2 He made horns for it on its four corners; its horns were of one piece with it, and he overlaid it with bronze. 3 He made all the utensils of the altar, the pots, the shovels, the basins, the forks, and the firepans: all its utensils he made of bronze. 4 He made for the altar a grating, a network of bronze, under its ledge, extending halfway down. 5 He cast four rings on the four corners of the bronze grating to hold the poles; 6 he made the poles of acacia wood, and overlaid them with bronze. 7 And he put the poles through the rings on the sides of the altar, to carry it with them; he made it hollow, with boards.

8 He made the basin of bronze with its stand of bronze, from the mirrors of the women who served at the entrance to the tent of meeting.

9 He made the court; for the south side the hangings of the court were of fine twisted linen, one hundred cubits long; 10 its twenty pillars and their twenty bases were of bronze, but the hooks of the pillars and their bands were of silver. 11 For the north side there were hangings one hundred cubits long; its twenty pillars and their twenty bases were of bronze, but the hooks of the pillars and their bands were of silver. 12 For the west side there were hangings fifty cubits long, with ten pillars and ten bases; the hooks of the pillars and their bands were of silver. 13 And for the front to the east, fifty cubits. 14 The hangings for one side of the gate were fifteen cubits, with three pillars and three bases. 15 And so for the other side; on each side of the gate of the court were hangings of fifteen cubits, with three pillars and three bases. 16 All the hangings around the court were of fine twisted linen. 17 The bases for the pillars were of bronze, but the hooks of the pillars and their bands were of silver; the overlaying of their capitals was also of silver, and all the pillars of the court were banded with silver. 18 The screen for the entrance to the court was embroidered with needlework in blue, purple, and crimson yarns and fine twisted linen. It was twenty cubits long and, along the width of it, five cubits high, corresponding to the hangings of the court. 19 There were four pillars; their four bases were of bronze, their hooks of silver, and the overlaying of their capitals and their bands of silver. 20 All the pegs for the tabernacle and for the court all around were of bronze.

21 These are the records of the tabernacle, the tabernacle of the covenant,[a] which were drawn up at the commandment of Moses, the work of the Levites being under the direction of Ithamar son of the priest Aaron. 22 Bezalel son of Uri son of Hur, of the tribe of Judah, made all that the LORD commanded Moses; 23 and with him was Oholiab son of Ahisamach, of the tribe of Dan, engraver, designer, and embroiderer in blue, purple, and crimson yarns, and in fine linen.

24 All the gold that was used for the work, in all the construction of the sanctuary, the gold from the offering, was twenty-nine talents and seven hundred thirty shekels, measured by the sanctuary shekel. 25 The silver from those of the congregation who were counted was one hundred talents and one thousand seven hundred seventy-five shekels, measured by the sanctuary shekel; 26 a beka a head (that is, half a shekel, measured by the sanctuary shekel), for everyone who was counted in the census, from twenty years old and upward, for six hundred three thousand, five hundred fifty men. 27 The hundred talents of silver were for casting the bases of the sanctuary, and the bases of the curtain; one hundred bases for the hundred talents, a talent for a base. 28 Of the thousand seven hundred seventy-five shekels he made hooks for the pillars, and overlaid their capitals and made bands for them. 29 The bronze that was contributed was seventy talents, and two thousand four hundred shekels; 30 with it he made the bases for the entrance of the tent of meeting, the bronze altar and the bronze grating for it and all the utensils of the altar, 31 the bases all around the court, and the bases of the gate of the court, all the pegs of the tabernacle, and all the pegs around the court.

39 Of the blue, purple, and crimson yarns they made finely worked vestments, for

[a] Or *treaty*, or *testimony*; Heb *eduth*

ministering in the holy place; they made the sacred vestments for Aaron; as the LORD had commanded Moses.
2 He made the ephod of gold, of blue, purple, and crimson yarns, and of fine twisted linen.
3 Gold leaf was hammered out and cut into threads
to work into the blue, purple, and crimson yarns
and into the fine twisted linen, in skilled design.
4 They made for the ephod shoulder-pieces,
joined to it at its two edges. 5 The decorated band
on it was of the same materials and workmanship,
of gold, of blue, purple, and crimson yarns, and of
fine twisted linen; as the LORD had commanded
Moses.
6 The onyx stones were prepared, enclosed
in settings of gold filigree and engraved like the
engravings of a signet, according to the names of
the sons of Israel. 7 He set them on the shoulder-
pieces of the ephod, to be stones of remembrance
for the sons of Israel; as the LORD had commanded Moses.
8 He made the breastpiece, in skilled work,
like the work of the ephod, of gold, of blue, purple, and crimson yarns, and of fine twisted linen.
9 It was square; the breastpiece was made double, a span in length and a span in width when
doubled. 10 They set in it four rows of stones. A
row of carnelian,[a] chrysolite, and emerald was
the first row; 11 and the second row, a turquoise, a
sapphire,[b] and a moonstone; 12 and the third row,
a jacinth, an agate, and an amethyst; 13 and the
fourth row, a beryl, an onyx, and a jasper; they
were enclosed in settings of gold filigree. 14 There
were twelve stones with names corresponding to
the names of the sons of Israel; they were like signets, each engraved with its name, for the twelve
tribes. 15 They made on the breastpiece chains of
pure gold, twisted like cords; 16 and they made
two settings of gold filigree and two gold rings,
and put the two rings on the two edges of the
breastpiece; 17 and they put the two cords of gold
in the two rings at the edges of the breastpiece.
18 Two ends of the two cords they had attached
to the two settings of filigree; in this way they
attached it in front to the shoulder-pieces of the
ephod. 19 Then they made two rings of gold, and
put them at the two ends of the breastpiece, on
its inside edge next to the ephod. 20 They made
two rings of gold, and attached them in front to
the lower part of the two shoulder-pieces of the
ephod, at its joining above the decorated band of
the ephod. 21 They bound the breastpiece by its
rings to the rings of the ephod with a blue cord,
so that it should lie on the decorated band of the
ephod, and that the breastpiece should not come
loose from the ephod; as the LORD had commanded Moses.
22 He also made the robe of the ephod woven all of blue yarn; 23 and the opening of the robe
in the middle of it was like the opening in a coat
of mail,[c] with a binding around the opening, so
that it might not be torn. 24 On the lower hem of
the robe they made pomegranates of blue, purple, and crimson yarns, and of fine twisted linen.
25 They also made bells of pure gold, and put the
bells between the pomegranates on the lower
hem of the robe all around, between the pomegranates; 26 a bell and a pomegranate, a bell and
a pomegranate all around on the lower hem of
the robe for ministering; as the LORD had commanded Moses.
27 They also made the tunics, woven of fine
linen, for Aaron and his sons, 28 and the turban
of fine linen, and the headdresses of fine linen,
and the linen undergarments of fine twisted
linen, 29 and the sash of fine twisted linen, and
of blue, purple, and crimson yarns, embroidered
with needlework; as the LORD had commanded
Moses.
30 They made the rosette of the holy diadem
of pure gold, and wrote on it an inscription, like
the engraving of a signet, "Holy to the LORD."
31 They tied to it a blue cord, to fasten it on the
turban above; as the LORD had commanded
Moses.
32 In this way all the work of the tabernacle
of the tent of meeting was finished; the Israelites had done everything just as the LORD had
commanded Moses. 33 Then they brought the
tabernacle to Moses, the tent and all its utensils,

[a] The identification of several of these stones is uncertain [b] Or *lapis lazuli* [c] Meaning of Heb uncertain

its hooks, its frames, its bars, its pillars, and its bases; 34 the covering of tanned rams' skins and the covering of fine leather,[a] and the curtain for the screen; 35 the ark of the covenant[b] with its poles and the mercy seat;[c] 36 the table with all its utensils, and the bread of the Presence; 37 the pure lampstand with its lamps set on it and all its utensils, and the oil for the light; 38 the golden altar, the anointing oil and the fragrant incense, and the screen for the entrance of the tent; 39 the bronze altar, and its grating of bronze, its poles, and all its utensils; the basin with its stand; 40 the hangings of the court, its pillars, and its bases, and the screen for the gate of the court, its cords, and its pegs; and all the utensils for the service of the tabernacle, for the tent of meeting; 41 the finely worked vestments for ministering in the holy place, the sacred vestments for the priest Aaron, and the vestments of his sons to serve as priests. 42 The Israelites had done all of the work just as the LORD had commanded Moses. 43 When Moses saw that they had done all the work just as the LORD had commanded, he blessed them.

40 The LORD spoke to Moses: 2 On the first day of the first month you shall set up the tabernacle of the tent of meeting. 3 You shall put in it the ark of the covenant,[b] and you shall screen the ark with the curtain. 4 You shall bring in the table, and arrange its setting; and you shall bring in the lampstand, and set up its lamps. 5 You shall put the golden altar for incense before the ark of the covenant,[b] and set up the screen for the entrance of the tabernacle. 6 You shall set the altar of burnt offering before the entrance of the tabernacle of the tent of meeting, 7 and place the basin between the tent of meeting and the altar, and put water in it. 8 You shall set up the court all around, and hang up the screen for the gate of the court. 9 Then you shall take the anointing oil, and anoint the tabernacle and all that is in it, and consecrate it and all its furniture, so that it shall become holy. 10 You shall also anoint the altar of burnt offering and all its utensils, and consecrate the altar, so that the altar shall be most holy. 11 You shall also anoint the basin with its stand, and consecrate it. 12 Then you shall bring Aaron and his sons to the entrance of the tent of meeting, and shall wash them with water, 13 and put on Aaron the sacred vestments, and you shall anoint him and consecrate him, so that he may serve me as priest. 14 You shall bring his sons also and put tunics on them, 15 and anoint them, as you anointed their father, that they may serve me as priests: and their anointing shall admit them to a perpetual priesthood throughout all generations to come.

16 Moses did everything just as the LORD had commanded him. 17 In the first month in the second year, on the first day of the month, the tabernacle was set up. 18 Moses set up the tabernacle; he laid its bases, and set up its frames, and put in its poles, and raised up its pillars; 19 and he spread the tent over the tabernacle, and put the covering of the tent over it; as the LORD had commanded Moses. 20 He took the covenant[b] and put it into the ark, and put the poles on the ark, and set the mercy seat[c] above the ark; 21 and he brought the ark into the tabernacle, and set up the curtain for screening, and screened the ark of the covenant;[b] as the LORD had commanded Moses. 22 He put the table in the tent of meeting, on the north side of the tabernacle, outside the curtain, 23 and set the bread in order on it before the LORD; as the LORD had commanded Moses. 24 He put the lampstand in the tent of meeting, opposite the table on the south side of the tabernacle, 25 and set up the lamps before the LORD; as the LORD had commanded Moses. 26 He put the golden altar in the tent of meeting before the curtain, 27 and offered fragrant incense on it; as the LORD had commanded Moses. 28 He also put in place the screen for the entrance of the tabernacle. 29 He set the altar of burnt offering at the entrance of the tabernacle of the tent of meeting, and offered on it the burnt offering and the grain offering as the LORD had commanded Moses. 30 He set the basin between the tent of meeting and the altar, and put water in it for washing, 31 with which Moses and Aaron and his sons washed their hands and their feet. 32 When they went into the tent of meet-

[a] Meaning of Heb uncertain [b] Or *treaty*, or *testimony*; Heb *eduth* [c] Or *the cover*

ing, and when they approached the altar, they washed; as the LORD had commanded Moses. 33He set up the court around the tabernacle and the altar, and put up the screen at the gate of the court. So Moses finished the work.

34 Then the cloud covered the tent of meeting, and the glory of the LORD filled the tabernacle. 35Moses was not able to enter the tent of meeting because the cloud settled upon it, and the glory of the LORD filled the tabernacle. 36Whenever the cloud was taken up from the tabernacle, the Israelites would set out on each stage of their journey; 37but if the cloud was not taken up, then they did not set out until the day that it was taken up. 38For the cloud of the LORD was on the tabernacle by day, and fire was in the cloud[a] by night, before the eyes of all the house of Israel at each stage of their journey.

[a] Heb *it*

The Legacy of Exodus

The Exodus story has been an important story of freedom for many different peoples, especially among African Americans and Latin American and Asian liberation theologians. The theme of a God who sides with the marginalized and oppressed has resonated with those who live under the burden or threat of colonialism. But this great biblical theme comes with the difficult idea that God chooses a particular people. Below is a small sampling of commentators on the Exodus from a collection of essays in *Voices from the Margin* (ed. R. S. Sugirtharajah):

> "So the exodus account clearly shows that justice means taking sides with the oppressed. From this our text draws the theological principle that God's impartiality makes God love the orphan and the widow with preference" (George Pixley).[13]
>
> "The God of the Bible, hitherto the God who saves and liberates, has come to be viewed by Palestinians as partial and discriminating" (Naim Ateek).[14]
>
> "The land, Yahweh decided, belonged to these former slaves from Egypt and Yahweh planned on giving it to them—using the same power used against the enslaving Egyptians to defeat the indigenous inhabitants of Canaan. Yahweh the deliverer became Yahweh the conqueror. The obvious characters in the story for Native Americans to identify with are the Canaanites, the people who already lived in the promised land" (Robert Allen Warrior).[15]

—FY

Leviticus

Leviticus, the third book of the Pentateuch, positioned between Exodus and Numbers, is one of the least studied books in contemporary churches. However, it is one of the most important books if we desire to understand the ethical system and religious practices of the Hebrew people, delivered by God from Egyptian bondage. In Hebrew, its title is the first word of the book, *wayyiqrā'*—"and he called." In the Greek translation of this book, its title is *Levitikon*, which probably refers generally to priestly ideals and issues. Leviticus, the English title, is the Latin rendering of the Greek.

We know that Leviticus was carefully copied over the centuries, because fragments found at Qumran do not reveal any meaningful variations from the much later manuscripts of the Masoretic tradition. The book's contents reveal stratification; that is, there are multiple layers reflecting multiple life settings. Thus, we do not need to assign the entire book of Leviticus to any one period or provide a single date for its composition, though much of the terminology of Leviticus points toward a pre-exilic date, during the First Temple period. Scholars divide the book's chapters in different ways to study its content:

1–7	Sacrificial System
8–10	Ordination of Priests
11–16	System of Purity and Impurity
17–26	Holiness Code
27	Appendix

Or it may be divided into two sections:

1–16	Manual for Priests
17–27	Teachings Addressed to the Israelite People

The key to understanding Leviticus is to remember that the first half of the book provides instructions for priests, and the second half provides instructions about how the Israelites should live and treat one another. Its emphasis on holiness and holy behavior is a timeless admonition for believers all over the world. For the priests who recorded Leviticus 17–26, holiness must govern sexual relationships, relationships with strangers, relationships with enemies, and relationships with foreigners. Chapter 19 is where we first find a word from heaven that is timeless: "love your neighbor as yourself" (19:18). That is repeated in the New Testament, and Jesus introduced it as one of the two greatest commandments (Mark 12:31).

Holiness is an important touchstone in many churches and especially in many African American churches. To be holy is to love one's neighbor, even if the neighbor happens to be an enemy.

The rationale for the pursuit of holiness is simple: we must be holy because God is holy (19:2). In this way, we may read Leviticus as constructing cultural identity through its religious and ethical ideals. Religious values are often a significant factor in the shaping of ethnic and racial identity. The book of Leviticus provides us with such an example, as holiness becomes a marker that defines the community of God's people and governs their interactions with one another.

My own reading of the Hebrew Scriptures has been shaped by many people and perspectives: a southern Baptist mother and an Episcopalian father, a conservative college campus ministry, liberation and womanist theology, feminism, and doctoral training in the Hebrew Scriptures. If I had to select the single most important theological influence on my understanding of scripture, however, it would be the theological reflections of men and women I met at the homeless shelter on 2nd and D Street between 1986 and 1993. With particular regard to the themes of holiness in the book of Leviticus, I contend that all of us should grapple with what it might mean to be holy as we pass by a person in need on the street. Many of our homeless brothers and sisters are trying to return home from prison. The biblical precepts are clear: they require that we love homeless and formerly incarcerated persons—I might add: by any means necessary. I dedicate this introduction to homeless and formerly incarcerated friends everywhere.

— ***Madeline McClenney-Sadler***

1 The Lord summoned Moses and spoke to
him from the tent of meeting, saying: 2 Speak
to the people of Israel and say to them: When any
of you bring an offering of livestock to the Lord,
you shall bring your offering from the herd or
from the flock.
3 If the offering is a burnt offering from the
herd, you shall offer a male without blemish; you
shall bring it to the entrance of the tent of meeting, for acceptance in your behalf before the
Lord. 4 You shall lay your hand on the head of
the burnt offering, and it shall be acceptable in
your behalf as atonement for you. 5 The bull shall
be slaughtered before the Lord; and Aaron's
sons the priests shall offer the blood, dashing
the blood against all sides of the altar that is at
the entrance of the tent of meeting. 6 The burnt
offering shall be flayed and cut up into its parts.
7 The sons of the priest Aaron shall put fire on
the altar and arrange wood on the fire. 8 Aaron's
sons the priests shall arrange the parts, with the
head and the suet, on the wood that is on the fire
on the altar; 9 but its entrails and its legs shall be
washed with water. Then the priest shall turn the
whole into smoke on the altar as a burnt offering, an offering by fire of pleasing odor to the
Lord.
10 If your gift for a burnt offering is from the
flock, from the sheep or goats, your offering shall
be a male without blemish. 11 It shall be slaughtered on the north side of the altar before the
Lord, and Aaron's sons the priests shall dash its
blood against all sides of the altar. 12 It shall be cut
up into its parts, with its head and its suet, and
the priest shall arrange them on the wood that is
on the fire on the altar; 13 but the entrails and the
legs shall be washed with water. Then the priest
shall offer the whole and turn it into smoke on

the altar; it is a burnt offering, an offering by fire
of pleasing odor to the LORD.
14 If your offering to the LORD is a burnt offering of birds, you shall choose your offering from
turtledoves or pigeons. 15 The priest shall bring it
to the altar and wring off its head, and turn it into
smoke on the altar; and its blood shall be drained
out against the side of the altar. 16 He shall remove
its crop with its contents[a] and throw it at the east
side of the altar, in the place for ashes. 17 He shall
tear it open by its wings without severing it. Then
the priest shall turn it into smoke on the altar, on
the wood that is on the fire; it is a burnt offering, an
offering by fire of pleasing odor to the LORD.

2 When anyone presents a grain offering to
the LORD, the offering shall be of choice
flour; the worshiper shall pour oil on it, and put
frankincense on it, 2 and bring it to Aaron's sons
the priests. After taking from it a handful of the
choice flour and oil, with all its frankincense, the
priest shall turn this token portion into smoke on
the altar, an offering by fire of pleasing odor to the
LORD. 3 And what is left of the grain offering shall
be for Aaron and his sons, a most holy part of the
offerings by fire to the LORD.
4 When you present a grain offering baked
in the oven, it shall be of choice flour: unleavened cakes mixed with oil, or unleavened wafers
spread with oil. 5 If your offering is grain prepared
on a griddle, it shall be of choice flour mixed with
oil, unleavened; 6 break it in pieces, and pour oil
on it; it is a grain offering. 7 If your offering is
grain prepared in a pan, it shall be made of choice
flour in oil. 8 You shall bring to the LORD the grain
offering that is prepared in any of these ways; and
when it is presented to the priest, he shall take
it to the altar. 9 The priest shall remove from the
grain offering its token portion and turn this into
smoke on the altar, an offering by fire of pleasing odor to the LORD. 10 And what is left of the
grain offering shall be for Aaron and his sons; it
is a most holy part of the offerings by fire to the
LORD.
11 No grain offering that you bring to the
LORD shall be made with leaven, for you must not
turn any leaven or honey into smoke as an offering by fire to the LORD. 12 You may bring them to
the LORD as an offering of choice products, but
they shall not be offered on the altar for a pleasing
odor. 13 You shall not omit from your grain offerings the salt of the covenant with your God; with
all your offerings you shall offer salt.
14 If you bring a grain offering of first fruits
to the LORD, you shall bring as the grain offering of your first fruits coarse new grain from fresh
ears, parched with fire. 15 You shall add oil to it
and lay frankincense on it; it is a grain offering.
16 And the priest shall turn a token portion of it
into smoke—some of the coarse grain and oil
with all its frankincense; it is an offering by fire
to the LORD.

3 If the offering is a sacrifice of well-being, if
you offer an animal of the herd, whether male
or female, you shall offer one without blemish before the LORD. 2 You shall lay your hand on the
head of the offering and slaughter it at the entrance of the tent of meeting; and Aaron's sons
the priests shall dash the blood against all sides
of the altar. 3 You shall offer from the sacrifice of
well-being, as an offering by fire to the LORD, the
fat that covers the entrails and all the fat that is
around the entrails; 4 the two kidneys with the fat
that is on them at the loins, and the appendage of
the liver, which he shall remove with the kidneys.
5 Then Aaron's sons shall turn these into smoke
on the altar, with the burnt offering that is on the
wood on the fire, as an offering by fire of pleasing
odor to the LORD.
6 If your offering for a sacrifice of well-being
to the LORD is from the flock, male or female, you
shall offer one without blemish. 7 If you present a
sheep as your offering, you shall bring it before
the LORD 8 and lay your hand on the head of the
offering. It shall be slaughtered before the tent of
meeting, and Aaron's sons shall dash its blood
against all sides of the altar. 9 You shall present its
fat from the sacrifice of well-being, as an offering
by fire to the LORD: the whole broad tail, which
shall be removed close to the backbone, the fat
that covers the entrails, and all the fat that is

[a] Meaning of Heb uncertain

around the entrails; 10the two kidneys with the
fat that is on them at the loins, and the appendage of the liver, which you shall remove with the
kidneys. 11Then the priest shall turn these into
smoke on the altar as a food offering by fire to the
LORD.

12 If your offering is a goat, you shall bring it
before the LORD 13and lay your hand on its head;
it shall be slaughtered before the tent of meeting;
and the sons of Aaron shall dash its blood against
all sides of the altar. 14You shall present as your
offering from it, as an offering by fire to the LORD,
the fat that covers the entrails, and all the fat that
is around the entrails; 15the two kidneys with the
fat that is on them at the loins, and the appendage of the liver, which you shall remove with the
kidneys. 16Then the priest shall turn these into
smoke on the altar as a food offering by fire for a
pleasing odor.

All fat is the LORD's. 17It shall be a perpetual
statute throughout your generations, in all your
settlements: you must not eat any fat or any
blood.

4 The LORD spoke to Moses, saying, 2Speak
to the people of Israel, saying: When anyone
sins unintentionally in any of the LORD's commandments about things not to be done, and
does any one of them:

3 If it is the anointed priest who sins, thus
bringing guilt on the people, he shall offer for the
sin that he has committed a bull of the herd without blemish as a sin offering to the LORD. 4He
shall bring the bull to the entrance of the tent
of meeting before the LORD and lay his hand on
the head of the bull; the bull shall be slaughtered
before the LORD. 5The anointed priest shall take
some of the blood of the bull and bring it into the
tent of meeting. 6The priest shall dip his finger in
the blood and sprinkle some of the blood seven
times before the LORD in front of the curtain of
the sanctuary. 7The priest shall put some of the
blood on the horns of the altar of fragrant incense
that is in the tent of meeting before the LORD;
and the rest of the blood of the bull he shall pour
out at the base of the altar of burnt offering, which
is at the entrance of the tent of meeting. 8He shall
remove all the fat from the bull of sin offering:
the fat that covers the entrails and all the fat that
is around the entrails; 9the two kidneys with the
fat that is on them at the loins; and the appendage of the liver, which he shall remove with the
kidneys, 10just as these are removed from the ox
of the sacrifice of well-being. The priest shall turn
them into smoke upon the altar of burnt offering.
11But the skin of the bull and all its flesh, as well
as its head, its legs, its entrails, and its dung—
12all the rest of the bull—he shall carry out to a
clean place outside the camp, to the ash heap, and
shall burn it on a wood fire; at the ash heap it shall
be burned.

13 If the whole congregation of Israel errs unintentionally and the matter escapes the notice of
the assembly, and they do any one of the things
that by the LORD's commandments ought not to
be done and incur guilt; 14when the sin that they
have committed becomes known, the assembly
shall offer a bull of the herd for a sin offering and
bring it before the tent of meeting. 15The elders of
the congregation shall lay their hands on the head
of the bull before the LORD, and the bull shall
be slaughtered before the LORD. 16The anointed
priest shall bring some of the blood of the bull
into the tent of meeting, 17and the priest shall dip
his finger in the blood and sprinkle it seven times
before the LORD, in front of the curtain. 18He
shall put some of the blood on the horns of the altar that is before the LORD in the tent of meeting;
and the rest of the blood he shall pour out at the
base of the altar of burnt offering that is at the entrance of the tent of meeting. 19He shall remove
all its fat and turn it into smoke on the altar. 20He
shall do with the bull just as is done with the bull
of sin offering; he shall do the same with this. The
priest shall make atonement for them, and they
shall be forgiven. 21He shall carry the bull outside
the camp, and burn it as he burned the first bull;
it is the sin offering for the assembly.

22 When a ruler sins, doing unintentionally
any one of all the things that by commandments
of the LORD his God ought not to be done and
incurs guilt, 23once the sin that he has committed is made known to him, he shall bring as his
offering a male goat without blemish. 24He shall
lay his hand on the head of the goat; it shall be

slaughtered at the spot where the burnt offering
is slaughtered before the LORD; it is a sin offering.
25The priest shall take some of the blood of the
sin offering with his finger and put it on the horns
of the altar of burnt offering, and pour out the
rest of its blood at the base of the altar of burnt
offering. 26All its fat he shall turn into smoke on
the altar, like the fat of the sacrifice of well-being.
Thus the priest shall make atonement on his behalf for his sin, and he shall be forgiven.

27 If anyone of the ordinary people among
you sins unintentionally in doing any one of the
things that by the LORD's commandments ought
not to be done and incurs guilt, 28when the sin
that you have committed is made known to you,
you shall bring a female goat without blemish as
your offering, for the sin that you have committed. 29You shall lay your hand on the head of the
sin offering; and the sin offering shall be slaughtered at the place of the burnt offering. 30The
priest shall take some of its blood with his finger
and put it on the horns of the altar of burnt offering, and he shall pour out the rest of its blood at
the base of the altar. 31He shall remove all its fat,
as the fat is removed from the offering of well-
being, and the priest shall turn it into smoke on
the altar for a pleasing odor to the LORD. Thus the
priest shall make atonement on your behalf, and
you shall be forgiven.

32 If the offering you bring as a sin offering
is a sheep, you shall bring a female without blemish. 33You shall lay your hand on the head of the
sin offering; and it shall be slaughtered as a sin
offering at the spot where the burnt offering is
slaughtered. 34The priest shall take some of the
blood of the sin offering with his finger and put
it on the horns of the altar of burnt offering, and
pour out the rest of its blood at the base of the
altar. 35You shall remove all its fat, as the fat of the
sheep is removed from the sacrifice of well-being,
and the priest shall turn it into smoke on the altar, with the offerings by fire to the LORD. Thus
the priest shall make atonement on your behalf
for the sin that you have committed, and you shall
be forgiven.

5 When any of you sin in that you have heard a
public adjuration to testify and—though able
to testify as one who has seen or learned of the
matter—do not speak up, you are subject to punishment. 2Or when any of you touch any unclean
thing—whether the carcass of an unclean beast
or the carcass of unclean livestock or the carcass
of an unclean swarming thing—and are unaware
of it, you have become unclean, and are guilty.
3Or when you touch human uncleanness—any
uncleanness by which one can become unclean—
and are unaware of it, when you come to know
it, you shall be guilty. 4Or when any of you utter aloud a rash oath for a bad or a good purpose,
whatever people utter in an oath, and are unaware
of it, when you come to know it, you shall in any
of these be guilty. 5When you realize your guilt
in any of these, you shall confess the sin that you
have committed. 6And you shall bring to the
LORD, as your penalty for the sin that you have
committed, a female from the flock, a sheep or a
goat, as a sin offering; and the priest shall make
atonement on your behalf for your sin.

7 But if you cannot afford a sheep, you shall
bring to the LORD, as your penalty for the sin that
you have committed, two turtledoves or two pigeons, one for a sin offering and the other for a
burnt offering. 8You shall bring them to the priest,
who shall offer first the one for the sin offering,
wringing its head at the nape without severing it.
9He shall sprinkle some of the blood of the sin
offering on the side of the altar, while the rest of
the blood shall be drained out at the base of the
altar; it is a sin offering. 10And the second he shall
offer for a burnt offering according to the regulation. Thus the priest shall make atonement on
your behalf for the sin that you have committed,
and you shall be forgiven.

11 But if you cannot afford two turtledoves or
two pigeons, you shall bring as your offering for
the sin that you have committed one-tenth of an
ephah of choice flour for a sin offering; you shall
not put oil on it or lay frankincense on it, for it is a
sin offering. 12You shall bring it to the priest, and
the priest shall scoop up a handful of it as its memorial portion, and turn this into smoke on the
altar, with the offerings by fire to the LORD; it is
a sin offering. 13Thus the priest shall make atonement on your behalf for whichever of these sins

you have committed, and you shall be forgiven.
Like the grain offering, the rest shall be for the
priest.

14 The LORD spoke to Moses, saying:
15 When any of you commit a trespass and sin
unintentionally in any of the holy things of the
LORD, you shall bring, as your guilt offering to
the LORD, a ram without blemish from the flock,
convertible into silver by the sanctuary shekel; it
is a guilt offering. 16 And you shall make restitution for the holy thing in which you were remiss,
and shall add one-fifth to it and give it to the
priest. The priest shall make atonement on your
behalf with the ram of the guilt offering, and you
shall be forgiven.

17 If any of you sin without knowing it, doing
any of the things that by the LORD's commandments ought not to be done, you have incurred
guilt, and are subject to punishment. 18 You shall
bring to the priest a ram without blemish from
the flock, or the equivalent, as a guilt offering; and
the priest shall make atonement on your behalf
for the error that you committed unintentionally,
and you shall be forgiven. 19 It is a guilt offering;
you have incurred guilt before the LORD.

6 [a] The LORD spoke to Moses, saying: 2 When
any of you sin and commit a trespass
against the LORD by deceiving a neighbor in a
matter of a deposit or a pledge, or by robbery, or
if you have defrauded a neighbor, 3 or have found
something lost and lied about it—if you swear
falsely regarding any of the various things that
one may do and sin thereby— 4 when you have
sinned and realize your guilt, and would restore
what you took by robbery or by fraud or the
deposit that was committed to you, or the lost
thing that you found, 5 or anything else about
which you have sworn falsely, you shall repay
the principal amount and shall add one-fifth to
it. You shall pay it to its owner when you realize
your guilt. 6 And you shall bring to the priest, as
your guilt offering to the LORD, a ram without
blemish from the flock, or its equivalent, for a
guilt offering. 7 The priest shall make atonement
on your behalf before the LORD, and you shall
be forgiven for any of the things that one may do
and incur guilt thereby.

8 [b] The LORD spoke to Moses, saying: 9 Command Aaron and his sons, saying: This is the ritual of the burnt offering. The burnt offering itself
shall remain on the hearth upon the altar all night
until the morning, while the fire on the altar shall
be kept burning. 10 The priest shall put on his
linen vestments after putting on his linen undergarments next to his body; and he shall take up
the ashes to which the fire has reduced the burnt
offering on the altar, and place them beside the
altar. 11 Then he shall take off his vestments and
put on other garments, and carry the ashes out
to a clean place outside the camp. 12 The fire on
the altar shall be kept burning; it shall not go out.
Every morning the priest shall add wood to it, lay
out the burnt offering on it, and turn into smoke
the fat pieces of the offerings of well-being. 13 A
perpetual fire shall be kept burning on the altar;
it shall not go out.

14 This is the ritual of the grain offering: The
sons of Aaron shall offer it before the LORD, in
front of the altar. 15 They shall take from it a handful of the choice flour and oil of the grain offering,
with all the frankincense that is on the offering,
and they shall turn its memorial portion into
smoke on the altar as a pleasing odor to the LORD.
16 Aaron and his sons shall eat what is left of it; it
shall be eaten as unleavened cakes in a holy place;
in the court of the tent of meeting they shall eat it.
17 It shall not be baked with leaven. I have given it
as their portion of my offerings by fire; it is most
holy, like the sin offering and the guilt offering.
18 Every male among the descendants of Aaron
shall eat of it, as their perpetual due throughout
your generations, from the LORD's offerings by
fire; anything that touches them shall become
holy.

19 The LORD spoke to Moses, saying: 20 This
is the offering that Aaron and his sons shall offer to the LORD on the day when he is anointed:
one-tenth of an ephah of choice flour as a regular
offering, half of it in the morning and half in the
evening. 21 It shall be made with oil on a griddle;

[a] Ch 5.20 in Heb [b] Ch 6.1 in Heb

you shall bring it well soaked, as a grain offering
of baked[a] pieces, and you shall present it as a
pleasing odor to the LORD. 22 And so the priest,
anointed from among Aaron's descendants as
a successor, shall prepare it; it is the LORD's—a
perpetual due—to be turned entirely into smoke.
23 Every grain offering of a priest shall be wholly
burned; it shall not be eaten.

24 The LORD spoke to Moses, saying:
25 Speak to Aaron and his sons, saying: This is the
ritual of the sin offering. The sin offering shall be
slaughtered before the LORD at the spot where
the burnt offering is slaughtered; it is most holy.
26 The priest who offers it as a sin offering shall
eat of it; it shall be eaten in a holy place, in the
court of the tent of meeting. 27 Whatever touches
its flesh shall become holy; and when any of its
blood is spattered on a garment, you shall wash
the bespattered part in a holy place. 28 An earthen
vessel in which it was boiled shall be broken;
but if it is boiled in a bronze vessel, that shall be
scoured and rinsed in water. 29 Every male among
the priests shall eat of it; it is most holy. 30 But no
sin offering shall be eaten from which any blood
is brought into the tent of meeting for atonement
in the holy place; it shall be burned with fire.

7 This is the ritual of the guilt offering. It is
most holy; 2 at the spot where the burnt offering is slaughtered, they shall slaughter the guilt
offering, and its blood shall be dashed against all
sides of the altar. 3 All its fat shall be offered: the
broad tail, the fat that covers the entrails, 4 the two
kidneys with the fat that is on them at the loins,
and the appendage of the liver, which shall be
removed with the kidneys. 5 The priest shall turn
them into smoke on the altar as an offering by fire
to the LORD; it is a guilt offering. 6 Every male
among the priests shall eat of it; it shall be eaten
in a holy place; it is most holy.

7 The guilt offering is like the sin offering,
there is the same ritual for them; the priest who
makes atonement with it shall have it. 8 So, too,
the priest who offers anyone's burnt offering shall
keep the skin of the burnt offering that he has
offered. 9 And every grain offering baked in the
oven, and all that is prepared in a pan or on a griddle, shall belong to the priest who offers it. 10 But
every other grain offering, mixed with oil or dry,
shall belong to all the sons of Aaron equally.

11 This is the ritual of the sacrifice of the offering of well-being that one may offer to the LORD.
12 If you offer it for thanksgiving, you shall offer
with the thank offering unleavened cakes mixed
with oil, unleavened wafers spread with oil, and
cakes of choice flour well soaked in oil. 13 With
your thanksgiving sacrifice of well-being you
shall bring your offering with cakes of leavened
bread. 14 From this you shall offer one cake from
each offering, as a gift to the LORD; it shall belong
to the priest who dashes the blood of the offering of well-being. 15 And the flesh of your thanksgiving sacrifice of well-being shall be eaten on the
day it is offered; you shall not leave any of it until
morning. 16 But if the sacrifice you offer is a votive
offering or a freewill offering, it shall be eaten on
the day that you offer your sacrifice, and what is
left of it shall be eaten the next day; 17 but what
is left of the flesh of the sacrifice shall be burned
up on the third day. 18 If any of the flesh of your
sacrifice of well-being is eaten on the third day, it
shall not be acceptable, nor shall it be credited to
the one who offers it; it shall be an abomination,
and the one who eats of it shall incur guilt.

19 Flesh that touches any unclean thing shall
not be eaten; it shall be burned up. As for other
flesh, all who are clean may eat such flesh. 20 But
those who eat flesh from the LORD's sacrifice of
well-being while in a state of uncleanness shall
be cut off from their kin. 21 When any one of you
touches any unclean thing—human uncleanness
or an unclean animal or any unclean creature—
and then eats flesh from the LORD's sacrifice of
well-being, you shall be cut off from your kin.

22 The LORD spoke to Moses, saying: 23 Speak
to the people of Israel, saying: You shall eat no
fat of ox or sheep or goat. 24 The fat of an animal
that died or was torn by wild animals may be put
to any other use, but you must not eat it. 25 If any
one of you eats the fat from an animal of which
an offering by fire may be made to the LORD, you

[a] Meaning of Heb uncertain

who eat it shall be cut off from your kin. 26You
must not eat any blood whatever, either of bird or
of animal, in any of your settlements. 27Any one
of you who eats any blood shall be cut off from
your kin.
28 The LORD spoke to Moses, saying:
29Speak to the people of Israel, saying: Any one of
you who would offer to the Lord your sacrifice of
well-being must yourself bring to the LORD your
offering from your sacrifice of well-being. 30Your
own hands shall bring the LORD's offering by fire;
you shall bring the fat with the breast, so that the
breast may be raised as an elevation offering before the LORD. 31The priest shall turn the fat into
smoke on the altar, but the breast shall belong to
Aaron and his sons. 32And the right thigh from
your sacrifices of well-being you shall give to the
priest as an offering; 33the one among the sons of
Aaron who offers the blood and fat of the offering
of well-being shall have the right thigh for a portion. 34For I have taken the breast of the elevation offering, and the thigh that is offered, from
the people of Israel, from their sacrifices of well-
being, and have given them to Aaron the priest
and to his sons, as a perpetual due from the people
of Israel. 35This is the portion allotted to Aaron
and to his sons from the offerings made by fire to
the LORD, once they have been brought forward
to serve the LORD as priests; 36these the LORD
commanded to be given them, when he anointed
them, as a perpetual due from the people of Israel
throughout their generations.
37 This is the ritual of the burnt offering, the
grain offering, the sin offering, the guilt offering, the offering of ordination, and the sacrifice
of well-being, 38which the LORD commanded
Moses on Mount Sinai, when he commanded
the people of Israel to bring their offerings to the
LORD, in the wilderness of Sinai.
8 The LORD spoke to Moses, saying: 2Take
Aaron and his sons with him, the vestments,
the anointing oil, the bull of sin offering, the two
rams, and the basket of unleavened bread; 3and
assemble the whole congregation at the entrance
of the tent of meeting. 4And Moses did as the
LORD commanded him. When the congregation was assembled at the entrance of the tent of
meeting, 5Moses said to the congregation, "This
is what the LORD has commanded to be done."
6 Then Moses brought Aaron and his sons
forward, and washed them with water. 7He put
the tunic on him, fastened the sash around him,
clothed him with the robe, and put the ephod
on him. He then put the decorated band of the
ephod around him, tying the ephod to him with
it. 8He placed the breastpiece on him, and in the
breastpiece he put the Urim and the Thummim.
9And he set the turban on his head, and on the
turban, in front, he set the golden ornament, the
holy crown, as the LORD commanded Moses.
10 Then Moses took the anointing oil and
anointed the tabernacle and all that was in it, and
consecrated them. 11He sprinkled some of it on
the altar seven times, and anointed the altar and
all its utensils, and the basin and its base, to consecrate them. 12He poured some of the anointing
oil on Aaron's head and anointed him, to consecrate him. 13And Moses brought forward Aaron's
sons, and clothed them with tunics, and fastened
sashes around them, and tied headdresses on
them, as the LORD commanded Moses.
14 He led forward the bull of sin offering;
and Aaron and his sons laid their hands upon
the head of the bull of sin offering, 15and it was
slaughtered. Moses took the blood and with his
finger put some on each of the horns of the altar,
purifying the altar; then he poured out the blood
at the base of the altar. Thus he consecrated it, to
make atonement for it. 16Moses took all the fat
that was around the entrails, and the appendage
of the liver, and the two kidneys with their fat,
and turned them into smoke on the altar. 17But
the bull itself, its skin and flesh and its dung, he
burned with fire outside the camp, as the LORD
commanded Moses.
18 Then he brought forward the ram of burnt
offering. Aaron and his sons laid their hands on
the head of the ram, 19and it was slaughtered.
Moses dashed the blood against all sides of the
altar. 20The ram was cut into its parts, and Moses
turned into smoke the head and the parts and the
suet. 21And after the entrails and the legs were
washed with water, Moses turned into smoke the
whole ram on the altar; it was a burnt offering for

a pleasing odor, an offering by fire to the Lord, as
the Lord commanded Moses.
22 Then he brought forward the second ram,
the ram of ordination. Aaron and his sons laid
their hands on the head of the ram, 23and it was
slaughtered. Moses took some of its blood and
put it on the lobe of Aaron's right ear and on the
thumb of his right hand and on the big toe of his
right foot. 24After Aaron's sons were brought forward, Moses put some of the blood on the lobes
of their right ears and on the thumbs of their right
hands and on the big toes of their right feet; and
Moses dashed the rest of the blood against all
sides of the altar. 25He took the fat—the broad
tail, all the fat that was around the entrails, the
appendage of the liver, and the two kidneys with
their fat—and the right thigh. 26From the basket
of unleavened bread that was before the Lord, he
took one cake of unleavened bread, one cake of
bread with oil, and one wafer, and placed them
on the fat and on the right thigh. 27He placed all
these on the palms of Aaron and on the palms of
his sons, and raised them as an elevation offering
before the Lord. 28Then Moses took them from
their hands and turned them into smoke on the
altar with the burnt offering. This was an ordination offering for a pleasing odor, an offering by
fire to the Lord. 29Moses took the breast and
raised it as an elevation offering before the Lord;
it was Moses' portion of the ram of ordination, as
the Lord commanded Moses.
30 Then Moses took some of the anointing
oil and some of the blood that was on the altar
and sprinkled them on Aaron and his vestments,
and also on his sons and their vestments. Thus he
consecrated Aaron and his vestments, and also
his sons and their vestments.
31 And Moses said to Aaron and his sons,
"Boil the flesh at the entrance of the tent of
meeting, and eat it there with the bread that is in
the basket of ordination offerings, as I was commanded, 'Aaron and his sons shall eat it'; 32and
what remains of the flesh and the bread you shall
burn with fire. 33You shall not go outside the
entrance of the tent of meeting for seven days,
until the day when your period of ordination is
completed. For it will take seven days to ordain
you; 34as has been done today, the Lord has
commanded to be done to make atonement for
you. 35You shall remain at the entrance of the tent
of meeting day and night for seven days, keeping
the Lord's charge so that you do not die; for so I
am commanded." 36Aaron and his sons did all the
things that the Lord commanded through Moses.

9 On the eighth day Moses summoned Aaron
and his sons and the elders of Israel. 2He said
to Aaron, "Take a bull calf for a sin offering and a
ram for a burnt offering, without blemish, and offer them before the Lord. 3And say to the people
of Israel, 'Take a male goat for a sin offering; a calf
and a lamb, yearlings without blemish, for a burnt
offering; 4and an ox and a ram for an offering of
well-being to sacrifice before the Lord; and a
grain offering mixed with oil. For today the Lord
will appear to you.' " 5They brought what Moses
commanded to the front of the tent of meeting; and the whole congregation drew near and
stood before the Lord. 6And Moses said, "This
is the thing that the Lord commanded you to
do, so that the glory of the Lord may appear
to you." 7Then Moses said to Aaron, "Draw near
to the altar and sacrifice your sin offering and your
burnt offering, and make atonement for yourself
and for the people; and sacrifice the offering of
the people, and make atonement for them; as the
Lord has commanded."
8 Aaron drew near to the altar, and slaughtered the calf of the sin offering, which was for
himself. 9The sons of Aaron presented the blood
to him, and he dipped his finger in the blood and
put it on the horns of the altar; and the rest of the
blood he poured out at the base of the altar. 10But
the fat, the kidneys, and the appendage of the
liver from the sin offering he turned into smoke
on the altar, as the Lord commanded Moses;
11and the flesh and the skin he burned with fire
outside the camp.
12 Then he slaughtered the burnt offering.
Aaron's sons brought him the blood, and he dashed
it against all sides of the altar. 13And they brought
him the burnt offering piece by piece, and the head,
which he turned into smoke on the altar. 14He
washed the entrails and the legs and, with the burnt
offering, turned them into smoke on the altar.

15 Next he presented the people's offering.
He took the goat of the sin offering that was for
the people, and slaughtered it, and presented it as
a sin offering like the first one. [16]He presented the
burnt offering, and sacrificed it according to regulation. [17]He presented the grain offering, and,
taking a handful of it, he turned it into smoke on
the altar, in addition to the burnt offering of the
morning.

18 He slaughtered the ox and the ram as a
sacrifice of well-being for the people. Aaron's sons
brought him the blood, which he dashed against
all sides of the altar, [19]and the fat of the ox and of
the ram—the broad tail, the fat that covers the entrails, the two kidneys and the fat on them,[a] and
the appendage of the liver. [20]They first laid the fat
on the breasts, and the fat was turned into smoke
on the altar; [21]and the breasts and the right thigh
Aaron raised as an elevation offering before the
Lord, as Moses had commanded.

22 Aaron lifted his hands toward the people
and blessed them; and he came down after sacrificing the sin offering, the burnt offering, and the
offering of well-being. [23]Moses and Aaron entered the tent of meeting, and then came out and
blessed the people; and the glory of the Lord appeared to all the people. [24]Fire came out from the
Lord and consumed the burnt offering and the
fat on the altar; and when all the people saw it,
they shouted and fell on their faces.

10 Now Aaron's sons, Nadab and Abihu,
each took his censer, put fire in it, and laid
incense on it; and they offered unholy fire before
the Lord, such as he had not commanded them.
[2]And fire came out from the presence of the
Lord and consumed them, and they died before
the Lord. [3]Then Moses said to Aaron, "This is
what the Lord meant when he said,

'Through those who are near me
I will show myself holy,
and before all the people
I will be glorified.'"

And Aaron was silent.

4 Moses summoned Mishael and Elzaphan,
sons of Uzziel the uncle of Aaron, and said to
them, "Come forward, and carry your kinsmen
away from the front of the sanctuary to a place
outside the camp." [5]They came forward and carried them by their tunics out of the camp, as Moses had ordered. [6]And Moses said to Aaron and
to his sons Eleazar and Ithamar, "Do not dishevel
your hair, and do not tear your vestments, or you
will die and wrath will strike all the congregation;
but your kindred, the whole house of Israel, may
mourn the burning that the Lord has sent. [7]You
shall not go outside the entrance of the tent of
meeting, or you will die; for the anointing oil of
the Lord is on you." And they did as Moses had
ordered.

8 And the Lord spoke to Aaron: [9]Drink no
wine or strong drink, neither you nor your sons,
when you enter the tent of meeting, that you may
not die; it is a statute forever throughout your
generations. [10]You are to distinguish between the
holy and the common, and between the unclean
and the clean; [11]and you are to teach the people
of Israel all the statutes that the Lord has spoken
to them through Moses.

12 Moses spoke to Aaron and to his remaining sons, Eleazar and Ithamar: Take the grain
offering that is left from the Lord's offerings by
fire, and eat it unleavened beside the altar, for it
is most holy; [13]you shall eat it in a holy place, because it is your due and your sons' due, from the
offerings by fire to the Lord; for so I am commanded. [14]But the breast that is elevated and the
thigh that is raised, you and your sons and daughters as well may eat in any clean place; for they
have been assigned to you and your children from
the sacrifices of the offerings of well-being of the
people of Israel. [15]The thigh that is raised and the
breast that is elevated they shall bring, together
with the offerings by fire of the fat, to raise for an
elevation offering before the Lord; they are to be
your due and that of your children forever, as the
Lord has commanded.

16 Then Moses made inquiry about the goat
of the sin offering, and—it had already been
burned! He was angry with Eleazar and Ithamar,
Aaron's remaining sons, and said, [17]"Why did

[a] Gk: Heb *the broad tail, and that which covers, and the kidneys*

you not eat the sin offering in the sacred area? For
it is most holy, and God[a] has given it to you that
you may remove the guilt of the congregation, to
make atonement on their behalf before the LORD.
18Its blood was not brought into the inner part of
the sanctuary. You should certainly have eaten it
in the sanctuary, as I commanded." 19And Aaron
spoke to Moses, "See, today they offered their
sin offering and their burnt offering before the
LORD; and yet such things as these have befallen
me! If I had eaten the sin offering today, would it
have been agreeable to the LORD?" 20And when
Moses heard that, he agreed.

11 The LORD spoke to Moses and Aaron,
saying to them: 2Speak to the people of
Israel, saying:

From among all the land animals, these are the
creatures that you may eat. 3Any animal that has
divided hoofs and is cleft-footed and chews the
cud—such you may eat. 4But among those that
chew the cud or have divided hoofs, you shall not
eat the following: the camel, for even though it
chews the cud, it does not have divided hoofs;
it is unclean for you. 5The rock badger, for even
though it chews the cud, it does not have divided
hoofs; it is unclean for you. 6The hare, for even
though it chews the cud, it does not have divided
hoofs; it is unclean for you. 7The pig, for even
though it has divided hoofs and is cleft-footed, it
does not chew the cud; it is unclean for you. 8Of
their flesh you shall not eat, and their carcasses
you shall not touch; they are unclean for you.

9 These you may eat, of all that are in the waters. Everything in the waters that has fins and
scales, whether in the seas or in the streams—
such you may eat. 10But anything in the seas or
the streams that does not have fins and scales, of
the swarming creatures in the waters and among
all the other living creatures that are in the waters—they are detestable to you 11and detestable
they shall remain. Of their flesh you shall not eat,
and their carcasses you shall regard as detestable.
12Everything in the waters that does not have fins
and scales is detestable to you.

13 These you shall regard as detestable
among the birds. They shall not be eaten; they
are an abomination: the eagle, the vulture, the osprey, 14the buzzard, the kite of any kind; 15every
raven of any kind; 16the ostrich, the nighthawk,
the sea gull, the hawk of any kind; 17the little owl,
the cormorant, the great owl, 18the water hen, the
desert owl,[b] the carrion vulture, 19the stork, the
heron of any kind, the hoopoe, and the bat.[c]

20 All winged insects that walk upon all fours
are detestable to you. 21But among the winged
insects that walk on all fours you may eat those
that have jointed legs above their feet, with which
to leap on the ground. 22Of them you may eat:
the locust according to its kind, the bald locust
according to its kind, the cricket according to its
kind, and the grasshopper according to its kind.
23But all other winged insects that have four feet
are detestable to you.

24 By these you shall become unclean; whoever touches the carcass of any of them shall be
unclean until the evening, 25and whoever carries
any part of the carcass of any of them shall wash
his clothes and be unclean until the evening.
26Every animal that has divided hoofs but is not
cleft-footed or does not chew the cud is unclean
for you; everyone who touches one of them shall
be unclean. 27All that walk on their paws, among
the animals that walk on all fours, are unclean for
you; whoever touches the carcass of any of them
shall be unclean until the evening, 28and the one
who carries the carcass shall wash his clothes
and be unclean until the evening; they are unclean for you.

29 These are unclean for you among the
creatures that swarm upon the earth: the wea-
sel, the mouse, the great lizard according to its
kind, 30the gecko, the land crocodile, the lizard,
the sand lizard, and the chameleon. 31These are
unclean for you among all that swarm; whoever
touches one of them when they are dead shall be
unclean until the evening. 32And anything upon
which any of them falls when they are dead shall
be unclean, whether an article of wood or cloth
or skin or sacking, any article that is used for any
purpose; it shall be dipped into water, and it shall

[a] Heb *he* [b] Or *pelican* [c] Identification of several of the birds in verses 13–19 is uncertain

be unclean until the evening, and then it shall be
clean. 33 And if any of them falls into any earthen
vessel, all that is in it shall be unclean, and you
shall break the vessel. 34 Any food that could be
eaten shall be unclean if water from any such vessel comes upon it; and any liquid that could be
drunk shall be unclean if it was in any such vessel. 35 Everything on which any part of the carcass
falls shall be unclean; whether an oven or stove,
it shall be broken in pieces; they are unclean, and
shall remain unclean for you. 36 But a spring or a
cistern holding water shall be clean, while whatever touches the carcass in it shall be unclean. 37 If
any part of their carcass falls upon any seed set
aside for sowing, it is clean; 38 but if water is put
on the seed and any part of their carcass falls on
it, it is unclean for you.

39 If an animal of which you may eat dies, anyone who touches its carcass shall be unclean until
the evening. 40 Those who eat of its carcass shall
wash their clothes and be unclean until the evening; and those who carry the carcass shall wash
their clothes and be unclean until the evening.

41 All creatures that swarm upon the earth
are detestable; they shall not be eaten. 42 Whatever moves on its belly, and whatever moves on all
fours, or whatever has many feet, all the creatures
that swarm upon the earth, you shall not eat; for
they are detestable. 43 You shall not make yourselves detestable with any creature that swarms;
you shall not defile yourselves with them, and so
become unclean. 44 For I am the LORD your God;
sanctify yourselves therefore, and be holy, for I
am holy. You shall not defile yourselves with any
swarming creature that moves on the earth. 45 For
I am the LORD who brought you up from the land
of Egypt, to be your God; you shall be holy, for I
am holy.

46 This is the law pertaining to land animal
and bird and every living creature that moves
through the waters and every creature that
swarms upon the earth, 47 to make a distinction
between the unclean and the clean, and between
the living creature that may be eaten and the living creature that may not be eaten.

12 The LORD spoke to Moses, saying: 2 Speak
to the people of Israel, saying:

If a woman conceives and bears a male child,
she shall be ceremonially unclean seven days; as
at the time of her menstruation, she shall be unclean. 3 On the eighth day the flesh of his foreskin
shall be circumcised. 4 Her time of blood purification shall be thirty-three days; she shall not touch
any holy thing, or come into the sanctuary, until
the days of her purification are completed. 5 If
she bears a female child, she shall be unclean two
weeks, as in her menstruation; her time of blood
purification shall be sixty-six days.

6 When the days of her purification are completed, whether for a son or for a daughter, she
shall bring to the priest at the entrance of the tent
of meeting a lamb in its first year for a burnt offering, and a pigeon or a turtledove for a sin offering. 7 He shall offer it before the LORD, and make
atonement on her behalf; then she shall be clean
from her flow of blood. This is the law for her who
bears a child, male or female. 8 If she cannot afford
a sheep, she shall take two turtledoves or two pigeons, one for a burnt offering and the other for a
sin offering; and the priest shall make atonement
on her behalf, and she shall be clean.

13 The LORD spoke to Moses and Aaron,
saying:

2 When a person has on the skin of his body
a swelling or an eruption or a spot, and it turns
into a leprous[a] disease on the skin of his body, he
shall be brought to Aaron the priest or to one of
his sons the priests. 3 The priest shall examine the
disease on the skin of his body, and if the hair in
the diseased area has turned white and the disease appears to be deeper than the skin of his
body, it is a leprous[a] disease; after the priest has
examined him he shall pronounce him ceremonially unclean. 4 But if the spot is white in the skin
of his body, and appears no deeper than the skin,
and the hair in it has not turned white, the priest
shall confine the diseased person for seven days.
5 The priest shall examine him on the seventh day,
and if he sees that the disease is checked and the
disease has not spread in the skin, then the priest

[a] A term for several skin diseases; precise meaning uncertain

shall confine him seven days more. 6 The priest
shall examine him again on the seventh day, and
if the disease has abated and the disease has not
spread in the skin, the priest shall pronounce him
clean; it is only an eruption; and he shall wash
his clothes, and be clean. 7 But if the eruption
spreads in the skin after he has shown himself to
the priest for his cleansing, he shall appear again
before the priest. 8 The priest shall make an examination, and if the eruption has spread in the
skin, the priest shall pronounce him unclean; it is
a leprous[a] disease.

9 When a person contracts a leprous[a] disease, he shall be brought to the priest. 10 The
priest shall make an examination, and if there is a
white swelling in the skin that has turned the hair
white, and there is quick raw flesh in the swelling,
11 it is a chronic leprous[a] disease in the skin of his
body. The priest shall pronounce him unclean; he
shall not confine him, for he is unclean. 12 But if
the disease breaks out in the skin, so that it covers
all the skin of the diseased person from head to
foot, so far as the priest can see, 13 then the priest
shall make an examination, and if the disease
has covered all his body, he shall pronounce him
clean of the disease; since it has all turned white,
he is clean. 14 But if raw flesh ever appears on him,
he shall be unclean; 15 the priest shall examine
the raw flesh and pronounce him unclean. Raw
flesh is unclean, for it is a leprous[a] disease. 16 But
if the raw flesh again turns white, he shall come to
the priest; 17 the priest shall examine him, and if
the disease has turned white, the priest shall pronounce the diseased person clean. He is clean.

18 When there is on the skin of one's body a
boil that has healed, 19 and in the place of the boil
there appears a white swelling or a reddish-white
spot, it shall be shown to the priest. 20 The priest
shall make an examination, and if it appears
deeper than the skin and its hair has turned white,
the priest shall pronounce him unclean; this is a
leprous[a] disease, broken out in the boil. 21 But if
the priest examines it and the hair on it is not
white, nor is it deeper than the skin but has abated,
the priest shall confine him seven days. 22 If it
spreads in the skin, the priest shall pronounce him
unclean; it is diseased. 23 But if the spot remains in
one place and does not spread, it is the scar of the
boil; the priest shall pronounce him clean.

24 Or, when the body has a burn on the skin
and the raw flesh of the burn becomes a spot,
reddish-white or white, 25 the priest shall examine
it. If the hair in the spot has turned white and it appears deeper than the skin, it is a leprous[a] disease;
it has broken out in the burn, and the priest shall
pronounce him unclean. This is a leprous[a] disease.
26 But if the priest examines it and the hair in the
spot is not white, and it is no deeper than the skin
but has abated, the priest shall confine him seven
days. 27 The priest shall examine him the seventh
day; if it is spreading in the skin, the priest shall
pronounce him unclean. This is a leprous[a] disease.
28 But if the spot remains in one place and does
not spread in the skin but has abated, it is a swelling from the burn, and the priest shall pronounce
him clean; for it is the scar of the burn.

29 When a man or woman has a disease on
the head or in the beard, 30 the priest shall examine the disease. If it appears deeper than the skin
and the hair in it is yellow and thin, the priest
shall pronounce him unclean; it is an itch, a leprous[a] disease of the head or the beard. 31 If the
priest examines the itching disease, and it appears
no deeper than the skin and there is no black hair
in it, the priest shall confine the person with the
itching disease for seven days. 32 On the seventh
day the priest shall examine the itch; if the itch
has not spread, and there is no yellow hair in it,
and the itch appears to be no deeper than the
skin, 33 he shall shave, but the itch he shall not
shave. The priest shall confine the person with
the itch for seven days more. 34 On the seventh
day the priest shall examine the itch; if the itch
has not spread in the skin and it appears to be no
deeper than the skin, the priest shall pronounce
him clean. He shall wash his clothes and be clean.
35 But if the itch spreads in the skin after he was
pronounced clean, 36 the priest shall examine
him. If the itch has spread in the skin, the priest
need not seek for the yellow hair; he is unclean.

[a] A term for several skin diseases; precise meaning uncertain

37 But if in his eyes the itch is checked, and black hair has grown in it, the itch is healed, he is clean; and the priest shall pronounce him clean.

38 When a man or a woman has spots on the skin of the body, white spots, 39 the priest shall make an examination, and if the spots on the skin of the body are of a dull white, it is a rash that has broken out on the skin; he is clean.

40 If anyone loses the hair from his head, he is bald but he is clean. 41 If he loses the hair from his forehead and temples, he has baldness of the forehead but he is clean. 42 But if there is on the bald head or the bald forehead a reddish-white diseased spot, it is a leprous[a] disease breaking out on his bald head or his bald forehead. 43 The priest shall examine him; if the diseased swelling is reddish-white on his bald head or on his bald forehead, which resembles a leprous[a] disease in the skin of the body, 44 he is leprous,[a] he is unclean. The priest shall pronounce him unclean; the disease is on his head.

45 The person who has the leprous[a] disease shall wear torn clothes and let the hair of his head be disheveled; and he shall cover his upper lip and cry out, "Unclean, unclean." 46 He shall remain unclean as long as he has the disease; he is unclean. He shall live alone; his dwelling shall be outside the camp.

47 Concerning clothing: when a leprous[a] disease appears in it, in woolen or linen cloth, 48 in warp or woof of linen or wool, or in a skin or in anything made of skin, 49 if the disease shows greenish or reddish in the garment, whether in warp or woof or in skin or in anything made of skin, it is a leprous[a] disease and shall be shown to the priest. 50 The priest shall examine the disease, and put the diseased article aside for seven days. 51 He shall examine the disease on the seventh day. If the disease has spread in the cloth, in warp or woof, or in the skin, whatever be the use of the skin, this is a spreading leprous[a] disease; it is unclean. 52 He shall burn the clothing, whether diseased in warp or woof, woolen or linen, or anything of skin, for it is a spreading leprous[a] disease; it shall be burned in fire.

53 If the priest makes an examination, and the disease has not spread in the clothing, in warp or woof or in anything of skin, 54 the priest shall command them to wash the article in which the disease appears, and he shall put it aside seven days more. 55 The priest shall examine the diseased article after it has been washed. If the diseased spot has not changed color, though the disease has not spread, it is unclean; you shall burn it in fire, whether the leprous[a] spot is on the inside or on the outside.

56 If the priest makes an examination, and the disease has abated after it is washed, he shall tear the spot out of the cloth, in warp or woof, or out of skin. 57 If it appears again in the garment, in warp or woof, or in anything of skin, it is spreading; you shall burn with fire that in which the disease appears. 58 But the cloth, warp or woof, or anything of skin from which the disease disappears when you have washed it, shall then be washed a second time, and it shall be clean.

59 This is the ritual for a leprous[a] disease in a cloth of wool or linen, either in warp or woof, or in anything of skin, to decide whether it is clean or unclean.

14 The Lord spoke to Moses, saying: 2 This shall be the ritual for the leprous[a] person at the time of his cleansing:

He shall be brought to the priest; 3 the priest shall go out of the camp, and the priest shall make an examination. If the disease is healed in the leprous[a] person, 4 the priest shall command that two living clean birds and cedarwood and crimson yarn and hyssop be brought for the one who is to be cleansed. 5 The priest shall command that one of the birds be slaughtered over fresh water in an earthen vessel. 6 He shall take the living bird with the cedarwood and the crimson yarn and the hyssop, and dip them and the living bird in the blood of the bird that was slaughtered over the fresh water. 7 He shall sprinkle it seven times upon the one who is to be cleansed of the leprous[a] disease; then he shall pronounce him clean, and he shall let the living bird go into the open field. 8 The one who is to be cleansed shall wash his clothes, and

[a] A term for several skin diseases; precise meaning uncertain

shave off all his hair, and bathe himself in water,
and he shall be clean. After that he shall come
into the camp, but shall live outside his tent seven
days. 9 On the seventh day he shall shave all his
hair: of head, beard, eyebrows; he shall shave all
his hair. Then he shall wash his clothes, and bathe
his body in water, and he shall be clean.

10 On the eighth day he shall take two male
lambs without blemish, and one ewe lamb in
its first year without blemish, and a grain offering of three-tenths of an ephah of choice flour
mixed with oil, and one log[a] of oil. 11 The priest
who cleanses shall set the person to be cleansed,
along with these things, before the LORD, at the
entrance of the tent of meeting. 12 The priest shall
take one of the lambs, and offer it as a guilt offering, along with the log[a] of oil, and raise them as
an elevation offering before the LORD. 13 He shall
slaughter the lamb in the place where the sin
offering and the burnt offering are slaughtered
in the holy place; for the guilt offering, like the
sin offering, belongs to the priest: it is most holy.
14 The priest shall take some of the blood of the
guilt offering and put it on the lobe of the right
ear of the one to be cleansed, and on the thumb
of the right hand, and on the big toe of the right
foot. 15 The priest shall take some of the log[a] of
oil and pour it into the palm of his own left hand,
16 and dip his right finger in the oil that is in his left
hand and sprinkle some oil with his finger seven
times before the LORD. 17 Some of the oil that remains in his hand the priest shall put on the lobe
of the right ear of the one to be cleansed, and on
the thumb of the right hand, and on the big toe of
the right foot, on top of the blood of the guilt
offering. 18 The rest of the oil that is in the priest's
hand he shall put on the head of the one to be
cleansed. Then the priest shall make atonement
on his behalf before the LORD: 19 the priest shall
offer the sin offering, to make atonement for the
one to be cleansed from his uncleanness. Afterward he shall slaughter the burnt offering; 20 and
the priest shall offer the burnt offering and the
grain offering on the altar. Thus the priest shall
make atonement on his behalf and he shall be
clean.

21 But if he is poor and cannot afford so
much, he shall take one male lamb for a guilt
offering to be elevated, to make atonement on his
behalf, and one-tenth of an ephah of choice flour
mixed with oil for a grain offering and a log[a] of
oil; 22 also two turtledoves or two pigeons, such
as he can afford, one for a sin offering and the
other for a burnt offering. 23 On the eighth day
he shall bring them for his cleansing to the priest,
to the entrance of the tent of meeting, before the
LORD; 24 and the priest shall take the lamb of the
guilt offering and the log[a] of oil, and the priest
shall raise them as an elevation offering before
the LORD. 25 The priest shall slaughter the lamb
of the guilt offering and shall take some of the
blood of the guilt offering, and put it on the lobe
of the right ear of the one to be cleansed, and on
the thumb of the right hand, and on the big toe of
the right foot. 26 The priest shall pour some of the
oil into the palm of his own left hand, 27 and shall
sprinkle with his right finger some of the oil that
is in his left hand seven times before the LORD.
28 The priest shall put some of the oil that is in his
hand on the lobe of the right ear of the one to be
cleansed, and on the thumb of the right hand, and
the big toe of the right foot, where the blood of
the guilt offering was placed. 29 The rest of the oil
that is in the priest's hand he shall put on the head
of the one to be cleansed, to make atonement on
his behalf before the LORD. 30 And he shall offer,
of the turtledoves or pigeons such as he can afford, 31 one[b] for a sin offering and the other for
a burnt offering, along with a grain offering; and
the priest shall make atonement before the LORD
on behalf of the one being cleansed. 32 This is the
ritual for the one who has a leprous[c] disease, who
cannot afford the offerings for his cleansing.

33 The LORD spoke to Moses and Aaron,
saying:

34 When you come into the land of Canaan,
which I give you for a possession, and I put a leprous[c] disease in a house in the land of your pos-

[a] A liquid measure [b] Gk Syr: Heb *afford, 31 such as he can afford, one*

[c] A term for several skin diseases; precise meaning uncertain

session, 35 the owner of the house shall come and tell the priest, saying, "There seems to me to be some sort of disease in my house." 36 The priest shall command that they empty the house before the priest goes to examine the disease, or all that is in the house will become unclean; and afterward the priest shall go in to inspect the house. 37 He shall examine the disease; if the disease is in the walls of the house with greenish or reddish spots, and if it appears to be deeper than the surface, 38 the priest shall go outside to the door of the house and shut up the house seven days. 39 The priest shall come again on the seventh day and make an inspection; if the disease has spread in the walls of the house, 40 the priest shall command that the stones in which the disease appears be taken out and thrown into an unclean place outside the city. 41 He shall have the inside of the house scraped thoroughly, and the plaster that is scraped off shall be dumped in an unclean place outside the city. 42 They shall take other stones and put them in the place of those stones, and take other plaster and plaster the house.

43 If the disease breaks out again in the house, after he has taken out the stones and scraped the house and plastered it, 44 the priest shall go and make inspection; if the disease has spread in the house, it is a spreading leprous[a] disease in the house; it is unclean. 45 He shall have the house torn down, its stones and timber and all the plaster of the house, and taken outside the city to an unclean place. 46 All who enter the house while it is shut up shall be unclean until the evening; 47 and all who sleep in the house shall wash their clothes; and all who eat in the house shall wash their clothes.

48 If the priest comes and makes an inspection, and the disease has not spread in the house after the house was plastered, the priest shall pronounce the house clean; the disease is healed. 49 For the cleansing of the house he shall take two birds, with cedarwood and crimson yarn and hyssop, 50 and shall slaughter one of the birds over fresh water in an earthen vessel, 51 and shall take the cedarwood and the hyssop and the crimson yarn, along with the living bird, and dip them in the blood of the slaughtered bird and the fresh water, and sprinkle the house seven times. 52 Thus he shall cleanse the house with the blood of the bird, and with the fresh water, and with the living bird, and with the cedarwood and hyssop and crimson yarn; 53 and he shall let the living bird go out of the city into the open field; so he shall make atonement for the house, and it shall be clean.

54 This is the ritual for any leprous[a] disease: for an itch, 55 for leprous[a] diseases in clothing and houses, 56 and for a swelling or an eruption or a spot, 57 to determine when it is unclean and when it is clean. This is the ritual for leprous[a] diseases.

15 The LORD spoke to Moses and Aaron, saying: 2 Speak to the people of Israel and say to them:

When any man has a discharge from his member,[b] his discharge makes him ceremonially unclean. 3 The uncleanness of his discharge is this: whether his member[b] flows with his discharge, or his member[b] is stopped from discharging, it is uncleanness for him. 4 Every bed on which the one with the discharge lies shall be unclean; and everything on which he sits shall be unclean. 5 Anyone who touches his bed shall wash his clothes, and bathe in water, and be unclean until the evening. 6 All who sit on anything on which the one with the discharge has sat shall wash their clothes, and bathe in water, and be unclean until the evening. 7 All who touch the body of the one with the discharge shall wash their clothes, and bathe in water, and be unclean until the evening. 8 If the one with the discharge spits on persons who are clean, then they shall wash their clothes, and bathe in water, and be unclean until the evening. 9 Any saddle on which the one with the discharge rides shall be unclean. 10 All who touch anything that was under him shall be unclean until the evening, and all who carry such a thing shall wash their clothes, and bathe in water, and be unclean until the evening. 11 All those whom the one with the discharge touches without his having rinsed his hands in water shall wash their clothes, and bathe in water, and be unclean until

[a] A term for several skin diseases; precise meaning uncertain

[b] Heb *flesh*

the evening. 12 Any earthen vessel that the one with the discharge touches shall be broken; and every vessel of wood shall be rinsed in water.

13 When the one with a discharge is cleansed of his discharge, he shall count seven days for his cleansing; he shall wash his clothes and bathe his body in fresh water, and he shall be clean. 14 On the eighth day he shall take two turtledoves or two pigeons and come before the Lord to the entrance of the tent of meeting and give them to the priest. 15 The priest shall offer them, one for a sin offering and the other for a burnt offering; and the priest shall make atonement on his behalf before the Lord for his discharge.

16 If a man has an emission of semen, he shall bathe his whole body in water, and be unclean until the evening. 17 Everything made of cloth or of skin on which the semen falls shall be washed with water, and be unclean until the evening. 18 If a man lies with a woman and has an emission of semen, both of them shall bathe in water, and be unclean until the evening.

19 When a woman has a discharge of blood that is her regular discharge from her body, she shall be in her impurity for seven days, and whoever touches her shall be unclean until the evening. 20 Everything upon which she lies during her impurity shall be unclean; everything also upon which she sits shall be unclean. 21 Whoever touches her bed shall wash his clothes, and bathe in water, and be unclean until the evening. 22 Whoever touches anything upon which she sits shall wash his clothes, and bathe in water, and be unclean until the evening; 23 whether it is the bed or anything upon which she sits, when he touches it he shall be unclean until the evening. 24 If any man lies with her, and her impurity falls on him, he shall be unclean seven days; and every bed on which he lies shall be unclean.

25 If a woman has a discharge of blood for many days, not at the time of her impurity, or if she has a discharge beyond the time of her impurity, all the days of the discharge she shall continue in uncleanness; as in the days of her impurity, she shall be unclean. 26 Every bed on which she lies during all the days of her discharge shall be treated as the bed of her impurity; and everything on which she sits shall be unclean, as in the uncleanness of her impurity. 27 Whoever touches these things shall be unclean, and shall wash his clothes, and bathe in water, and be unclean until the evening. 28 If she is cleansed of her discharge, she shall count seven days, and after that she shall be clean. 29 On the eighth day she shall take two turtledoves or two pigeons and bring them to the priest at the entrance of the tent of meeting. 30 The priest shall offer one for a sin offering and the other for a burnt offering; and the priest shall make atonement on her behalf before the Lord for her unclean discharge.

31 Thus you shall keep the people of Israel separate from their uncleanness, so that they do not die in their uncleanness by defiling my tabernacle that is in their midst.

32 This is the ritual for those who have a discharge: for him who has an emission of semen, becoming unclean thereby, 33 for her who is in the infirmity of her period, for anyone, male or female, who has a discharge, and for the man who lies with a woman who is unclean.

16 The Lord spoke to Moses after the death of the two sons of Aaron, when they drew near before the Lord and died. 2 The Lord said to Moses:

Tell your brother Aaron not to come just at any time into the sanctuary inside the curtain before the mercy seat[a] that is upon the ark, or he will die; for I appear in the cloud upon the mercy seat.[a] 3 Thus shall Aaron come into the holy place: with a young bull for a sin offering and a ram for a burnt offering. 4 He shall put on the holy linen tunic, and shall have the linen undergarments next to his body, fasten the linen sash, and wear the linen turban; these are the holy vestments. He shall bathe his body in water, and then put them on. 5 He shall take from the congregation of the people of Israel two male goats for a sin offering, and one ram for a burnt offering.

6 Aaron shall offer the bull as a sin offering for himself, and shall make atonement for himself

[a] Or *the cover*

and for his house. 7 He shall take the two goats and set them before the LORD at the entrance of the tent of meeting; 8 and Aaron shall cast lots on the two goats, one lot for the LORD and the other lot for Azazel.[a] 9 Aaron shall present the goat on which the lot fell for the LORD, and offer it as a sin offering; 10 but the goat on which the lot fell for Azazel[a] shall be presented alive before the LORD to make atonement over it, that it may be sent away into the wilderness to Azazel.[a]

11 Aaron shall present the bull as a sin offering for himself, and shall make atonement for himself and for his house; he shall slaughter the bull as a sin offering for himself. 12 He shall take a censer full of coals of fire from the altar before the LORD, and two handfuls of crushed sweet incense, and he shall bring it inside the curtain 13 and put the incense on the fire before the LORD, that the cloud of the incense may cover the mercy seat[b] that is upon the covenant,[c] or he will die. 14 He shall take some of the blood of the bull, and sprinkle it with his finger on the front of the mercy seat,[b] and before the mercy seat[b] he shall sprinkle the blood with his finger seven times.

15 He shall slaughter the goat of the sin offering that is for the people and bring its blood inside the curtain, and do with its blood as he did with the blood of the bull, sprinkling it upon the mercy seat[b] and before the mercy seat.[b] 16 Thus he shall make atonement for the sanctuary, because of the uncleannesses of the people of Israel, and because of their transgressions, all their sins; and so he shall do for the tent of meeting, which remains with them in the midst of their uncleannesses. 17 No one shall be in the tent of meeting from the time he enters to make atonement in the sanctuary until he comes out and has made atonement for himself and for his house and for all the assembly of Israel. 18 Then he shall go out to the altar that is before the LORD and make atonement on its behalf, and shall take some of the blood of the bull and of the blood of the goat, and put it on each of the horns of the altar. 19 He shall sprinkle some of the blood on it with his finger seven times, and cleanse it and hallow it from the uncleannesses of the people of Israel.

20 When he has finished atoning for the holy place and the tent of meeting and the altar, he shall present the live goat. 21 Then Aaron shall lay both his hands on the head of the live goat, and confess over it all the iniquities of the people of Israel, and all their transgressions, all their sins, putting them on the head of the goat, and sending it away into the wilderness by means of someone designated for the task.[d] 22 The goat shall bear on itself all their iniquities to a barren region; and the goat shall be set free in the wilderness.

23 Then Aaron shall enter the tent of meeting, and shall take off the linen vestments that he put on when he went into the holy place, and shall leave them there. 24 He shall bathe his body in water in a holy place, and put on his vestments; then he shall come out and offer his burnt offering and the burnt offering of the people, making atonement for himself and for the people. 25 The fat of the sin offering he shall turn into smoke on the altar. 26 The one who sets the goat free for Azazel[a] shall wash his clothes and bathe his body in water, and afterward may come into the camp. 27 The bull of the sin offering and the goat of the sin offering, whose blood was brought in to make atonement in the holy place, shall be taken outside the camp; their skin and their flesh and their dung shall be consumed in fire. 28 The one who burns them shall wash his clothes and bathe his body in water, and afterward may come into the camp.

29 This shall be a statute to you forever: In the seventh month, on the tenth day of the month, you shall deny yourselves,[e] and shall do no work, neither the citizen nor the alien who resides among you. 30 For on this day atonement shall be made for you, to cleanse you; from all your sins you shall be clean before the LORD. 31 It is a sabbath of complete rest to you, and you shall deny yourselves;[e] it is a statute forever. 32 The priest who is anointed and consecrated as priest in his father's place shall make atonement, wearing the

[a] Traditionally rendered *a scapegoat* [b] Or *the cover* [c] Or *treaty*, or *testament*; Heb *eduth*
[d] Meaning of Heb uncertain [e] Or *shall fast*

linen vestments, the holy vestments. 33 He shall
make atonement for the sanctuary, and he shall
make atonement for the tent of meeting and for
the altar, and he shall make atonement for the
priests and for all the people of the assembly.
34 This shall be an everlasting statute for you, to
make atonement for the people of Israel once in
the year for all their sins. And Moses did as the
LORD had commanded him.

17 The LORD spoke to Moses:
2 Speak to Aaron and his sons and to all
the people of Israel and say to them: This is what
the LORD has commanded. 3 If anyone of the
house of Israel slaughters an ox or a lamb or a goat
in the camp, or slaughters it outside the camp,
4 and does not bring it to the entrance of the tent
of meeting, to present it as an offering to the
LORD before the tabernacle of the LORD, he shall
be held guilty of bloodshed; he has shed blood,
and he shall be cut off from the people. 5 This is in
order that the people of Israel may bring their
sacrifices that they offer in the open field, that
they may bring them to the LORD, to the priest at
the entrance of the tent of meeting, and offer
them as sacrifices of well-being to the LORD. 6 The
priest shall dash the blood against the altar of the
LORD at the entrance of the tent of meeting, and
turn the fat into smoke as a pleasing odor to the
LORD, 7 so that they may no longer offer their sacrifices for goat-demons, to whom they prostitute
themselves. This shall be a statute forever to them
throughout their generations.

8 And say to them further: Anyone of the
house of Israel or of the aliens who reside among
them who offers a burnt offering or sacrifice, 9 and
does not bring it to the entrance of the tent of
meeting, to sacrifice it to the LORD, shall be cut
off from the people.

10 If anyone of the house of Israel or of the
aliens who reside among them eats any blood,
I will set my face against that person who eats
blood, and will cut that person off from the people. 11 For the life of the flesh is in the blood; and
I have given it to you for making atonement for
your lives on the altar; for, as life, it is the blood
that makes atonement. 12 Therefore I have said to
the people of Israel: No person among you shall
eat blood, nor shall any alien who resides among
you eat blood. 13 And anyone of the people of
Israel, or of the aliens who reside among them,
who hunts down an animal or bird that may be
eaten shall pour out its blood and cover it with
earth.

14 For the life of every creature—its blood
is its life; therefore I have said to the people of
Israel: You shall not eat the blood of any creature,
for the life of every creature is its blood; whoever
eats it shall be cut off. 15 All persons, citizens or
aliens, who eat what dies of itself or what has been
torn by wild animals, shall wash their clothes, and
bathe themselves in water, and be unclean until
the evening; then they shall be clean. 16 But if they
do not wash themselves or bathe their body, they
shall bear their guilt.

18 The LORD spoke to Moses, saying:
2 Speak to the people of Israel and say to
them: I am the LORD your God. 3 You shall not do
as they do in the land of Egypt, where you lived,
and you shall not do as they do in the land of Canaan, to which I am bringing you. You shall not
follow their statutes. 4 My ordinances you shall
observe and my statutes you shall keep, following
them: I am the LORD your God. 5 You shall keep
my statutes and my ordinances; by doing so one
shall live: I am the LORD.

6 None of you shall approach anyone near of
kin to uncover nakedness: I am the LORD. 7 You
shall not uncover the nakedness of your father,
which is the nakedness of your mother; she is
your mother, you shall not uncover her nakedness. 8 You shall not uncover the nakedness of
your father's wife; it is the nakedness of your
father. 9 You shall not uncover the nakedness of
your sister, your father's daughter or your mother's daughter, whether born at home or born
abroad. 10 You shall not uncover the nakedness of
your son's daughter or of your daughter's daughter, for their nakedness is your own nakedness.
11 You shall not uncover the nakedness of your
father's wife's daughter, begotten by your father,
since she is your sister. 12 You shall not uncover
the nakedness of your father's sister; she is your
father's flesh. 13 You shall not uncover the nakedness of your mother's sister, for she is your moth-

er's flesh. 14 You shall not uncover the nakedness
of your father's brother, that is, you shall not approach his wife; she is your aunt. 15 You shall not
uncover the nakedness of your daughter-in-law:
she is your son's wife; you shall not uncover her
nakedness. 16 You shall not uncover the nakedness
of your brother's wife; it is your brother's nakedness. 17 You shall not uncover the nakedness of a
woman and her daughter, and you shall not take[a]
her son's daughter or her daughter's daughter to
uncover her nakedness; they are your[b] flesh; it
is depravity. 18 And you shall not take[a] a woman
as a rival to her sister, uncovering her nakedness
while her sister is still alive.

19 You shall not approach a woman to uncover her nakedness while she is in her menstrual
uncleanness. 20 You shall not have sexual relations
with your kinsman's wife, and defile yourself with
her. 21 You shall not give any of your offspring to
sacrifice them[c] to Molech, and so profane the
name of your God: I am the LORD. 22 You shall
not lie with a male as with a woman; it is an
abomination. 23 You shall not have sexual relations with any animal and defile yourself with it,
nor shall any woman give herself to an animal to
have sexual relations with it: it is perversion.

24 Do not defile yourselves in any of these
ways, for by all these practices the nations I am
casting out before you have defiled themselves.
25 Thus the land became defiled; and I punished
it for its iniquity, and the land vomited out its inhabitants. 26 But you shall keep my statutes and
my ordinances and commit none of these abominations, either the citizen or the alien who resides
among you 27 (for the inhabitants of the land, who
were before you, committed all of these abominations, and the land became defiled); 28 otherwise the land will vomit you out for defiling it,
as it vomited out the nation that was before you.
29 For whoever commits any of these abominations shall be cut off from their people. 30 So keep
my charge not to commit any of these abominations that were done before you, and not to defile
yourselves by them: I am the LORD your God.

19 The LORD spoke to Moses, saying:
2 Speak to all the congregation of the people of Israel and say to them: You shall be holy,
for I the LORD your God am holy. 3 You shall each
revere your mother and father, and you shall keep
my sabbaths: I am the LORD your God. 4 Do not
turn to idols or make cast images for yourselves: I
am the LORD your God.

5 When you offer a sacrifice of well-being to
the LORD, offer it in such a way that it is acceptable in your behalf. 6 It shall be eaten on the same
day you offer it, or on the next day; and anything
left over until the third day shall be consumed in
fire. 7 If it is eaten at all on the third day, it is an
abomination; it will not be acceptable. 8 All who
eat it shall be subject to punishment, because they
have profaned what is holy to the LORD; and any
such person shall be cut off from the people.

9 When you reap the harvest of your land,
you shall not reap to the very edges of your field,
or gather the gleanings of your harvest. 10 You
shall not strip your vineyard bare, or gather the
fallen grapes of your vineyard; you shall leave
them for the poor and the alien: I am the LORD
your God.

11 You shall not steal; you shall not deal
falsely; and you shall not lie to one another.
12 And you shall not swear falsely by my name,
profaning the name of your God: I am the LORD.

13 You shall not defraud your neighbor; you
shall not steal; and you shall not keep for yourself the wages of a laborer until morning. 14 You
shall not revile the deaf or put a stumbling block
before the blind; you shall fear your God: I am
the LORD.

15 You shall not render an unjust judgment;
you shall not be partial to the poor or defer to the
great: with justice you shall judge your neighbor.
16 You shall not go around as a slanderer[d] among
your people, and you shall not profit by the blood[e]
of your neighbor: I am the LORD.

17 You shall not hate in your heart anyone
of your kin; you shall reprove your neighbor, or
you will incur guilt yourself. 18 You shall not take

[a] Or *marry* [b] Gk: Heb lacks *your* [c] Heb *to pass them over* [d] Meaning of Heb uncertain
[e] Heb *stand against the blood*

vengeance or bear a grudge against any of your
people, but you shall love your neighbor as yourself: I am the LORD.
19 You shall keep my statutes. You shall not
let your animals breed with a different kind; you
shall not sow your field with two kinds of seed;
nor shall you put on a garment made of two different materials.
20 If a man has sexual relations with a woman
who is a slave, designated for another man but
not ransomed or given her freedom, an inquiry
shall be held. They shall not be put to death, since
she has not been freed; 21 but he shall bring a guilt
offering for himself to the LORD, at the entrance
of the tent of meeting, a ram as guilt offering.
22 And the priest shall make atonement for him
with the ram of guilt offering before the LORD for
his sin that he committed; and the sin he committed shall be forgiven him.
23 When you come into the land and plant all
kinds of trees for food, then you shall regard their
fruit as forbidden;[a] three years it shall be forbidden[b] to you, it must not be eaten. 24 In the fourth
year all their fruit shall be set apart for rejoicing
in the LORD. 25 But in the fifth year you may eat
of their fruit, that their yield may be increased for
you: I am the LORD your God.
26 You shall not eat anything with its blood.
You shall not practice augury or witchcraft. 27 You
shall not round off the hair on your temples or
mar the edges of your beard. 28 You shall not make
any gashes in your flesh for the dead or tattoo any
marks upon you: I am the LORD.
29 Do not profane your daughter by making
her a prostitute, that the land not become prostituted and full of depravity. 30 You shall keep my
sabbaths and reverence my sanctuary: I am the
LORD.
31 Do not turn to mediums or wizards; do
not seek them out, to be defiled by them: I am
the LORD your God.
32 You shall rise before the aged, and defer
to the old; and you shall fear your God: I am the
LORD.
33 When an alien resides with you in your
land, you shall not oppress the alien. 34 The alien
who resides with you shall be to you as the citizen
among you; you shall love the alien as yourself,
for you were aliens in the land of Egypt: I am the
LORD your God.
35 You shall not cheat in measuring length,
weight, or quantity. 36 You shall have honest balances, honest weights, an honest ephah, and
an honest hin: I am the LORD your God, who
brought you out of the land of Egypt. 37 You shall
keep all my statutes and all my ordinances, and
observe them: I am the LORD.

20 The LORD spoke to Moses, saying: 2 Say
further to the people of Israel:
Any of the people of Israel, or of the aliens
who reside in Israel, who give any of their offspring to Molech shall be put to death; the people

[a] Heb *as their uncircumcision* [b] Heb *uncircumcision*

Leviticus 19:32

From an interview with Swiss physician Paul Tournier:

Q: On the basis of conversations you have had with your patients, both men and women, do you have the feeling that old people are rather despised, or that they feel despised?

That is because of the prejudice of society which values a person in terms of productivity. There is a kind of prejudice which disparages old age, against which we must fight tooth and nail, because human beings are not validated by work; it is work which has its value because it comes from human beings. . . . Some, who were afraid of retirement, have suddenly seen that it presents the possibility of new human horizons . . . the capabilty of offering much fuller life than the working life that precedes it, which is often a form of slavery.[16]

of the land shall stone them to death. 3I myself
will set my face against them, and will cut them
off from the people, because they have given of
their offspring to Molech, defiling my sanctuary
and profaning my holy name. 4And if the people
of the land should ever close their eyes to them,
when they give of their offspring to Molech, and
do not put them to death, 5I myself will set my
face against them and against their family, and
will cut them off from among their people, them
and all who follow them in prostituting themselves to Molech.

6 If any turn to mediums and wizards, prostituting themselves to them, I will set my face
against them, and will cut them off from the
people. 7Consecrate yourselves therefore, and be
holy; for I am the LORD your God. 8Keep my statutes, and observe them; I am the LORD; I sanctify
you. 9All who curse father or mother shall be put
to death; having cursed father or mother, their
blood is upon them.

10 If a man commits adultery with the wife
of[a] his neighbor, both the adulterer and the adulteress shall be put to death. 11The man who lies
with his father's wife has uncovered his father's
nakedness; both of them shall be put to death;
their blood is upon them. 12If a man lies with
his daughter-in-law, both of them shall be put
to death; they have committed perversion, their
blood is upon them. 13If a man lies with a male
as with a woman, both of them have committed an abomination; they shall be put to death;
their blood is upon them. 14If a man takes a wife
and her mother also, it is depravity; they shall be
burned to death, both he and they, that there may
be no depravity among you. 15If a man has sexual
relations with an animal, he shall be put to death;
and you shall kill the animal. 16If a woman approaches any animal and has sexual relations with
it, you shall kill the woman and the animal; they
shall be put to death, their blood is upon them.

17 If a man takes his sister, a daughter of his
father or a daughter of his mother, and sees her
nakedness, and she sees his nakedness, it is a disgrace, and they shall be cut off in the sight of their
people; he has uncovered his sister's nakedness,
he shall be subject to punishment. 18If a man lies
with a woman having her sickness and uncovers her nakedness, he has laid bare her flow and
she has laid bare her flow of blood; both of them
shall be cut off from their people. 19You shall not
uncover the nakedness of your mother's sister or
of your father's sister, for that is to lay bare one's
own flesh; they shall be subject to punishment.
20If a man lies with his uncle's wife, he has uncovered his uncle's nakedness; they shall be subject to punishment; they shall die childless. 21If
a man takes his brother's wife, it is impurity; he
has uncovered his brother's nakedness; they shall
be childless.

22 You shall keep all my statutes and all my
ordinances, and observe them, so that the land to
which I bring you to settle in may not vomit you
out. 23You shall not follow the practices of the
nation that I am driving out before you. Because
they did all these things, I abhorred them. 24But
I have said to you: You shall inherit their land,
and I will give it to you to possess, a land flowing
with milk and honey. I am the LORD your God; I
have separated you from the peoples. 25You shall
therefore make a distinction between the clean
animal and the unclean, and between the unclean
bird and the clean; you shall not bring abomination on yourselves by animal or by bird or by anything with which the ground teems, which I have
set apart for you to hold unclean. 26You shall be
holy to me; for I the LORD am holy, and I have
separated you from the other peoples to be mine.

27 A man or a woman who is a medium or a
wizard shall be put to death; they shall be stoned
to death, their blood is upon them.

21 The LORD said to Moses: Speak to the
priests, the sons of Aaron, and say to
them:

No one shall defile himself for a dead person
among his relatives, 2except for his nearest kin:
his mother, his father, his son, his daughter, his
brother; 3likewise, for a virgin sister, close to him
because she has had no husband, he may defile
himself for her. 4But he shall not defile himself as

[a] Heb repeats *if a man commits adultery with the wife of*

a husband among his people and so profane himself. 5They shall not make bald spots upon their heads, or shave off the edges of their beards, or make any gashes in their flesh. 6They shall be holy to their God, and not profane the name of their God; for they offer the LORD's offerings by fire, the food of their God; therefore they shall be holy. 7They shall not marry a prostitute or a woman who has been defiled; neither shall they marry a woman divorced from her husband. For they are holy to their God, 8and you shall treat them as holy, since they offer the food of your God; they shall be holy to you, for I the LORD, I who sanctify you, am holy. 9When the daughter of a priest profanes herself through prostitution, she profanes her father; she shall be burned to death.

10 The priest who is exalted above his fellows, on whose head the anointing oil has been poured and who has been consecrated to wear the vestments, shall not dishevel his hair, nor tear his vestments. 11He shall not go where there is a dead body; he shall not defile himself even for his father or mother. 12He shall not go outside the sanctuary and thus profane the sanctuary of his God; for the consecration of the anointing oil of his God is upon him: I am the LORD. 13He shall marry only a woman who is a virgin. 14A widow, or a divorced woman, or a woman who has been defiled, a prostitute, these he shall not marry. He shall marry a virgin of his own kin, 15that he may not profane his offspring among his kin; for I am the LORD; I sanctify him.

16 The LORD spoke to Moses, saying: 17Speak to Aaron and say: No one of your offspring throughout their generations who has a blemish may approach to offer the food of his God. 18For no one who has a blemish shall draw near, one who is blind or lame, or one who has a mutilated face or a limb too long, 19or one who has a broken foot or a broken hand, 20or a hunchback, or a dwarf, or a man with a blemish in his eyes or an itching disease or scabs or crushed testicles. 21No descendant of Aaron the priest who has a blemish shall come near to offer the LORD's offerings by fire; since he has a blemish, he shall not come near to offer the food of his God. 22He may eat the food of his God, of the most holy as well as of the holy. 23But he shall not come near the curtain or approach the altar, because he has a blemish, that he may not profane my sanctuaries; for I am the LORD; I sanctify them. 24Thus Moses spoke to Aaron and to his sons and to all the people of Israel.

22 The LORD spoke to Moses, saying: 2Direct Aaron and his sons to deal carefully with the sacred donations of the people of Israel, which they dedicate to me, so that they may not profane my holy name; I am the LORD. 3Say to them: If anyone among all your offspring throughout your generations comes near the sacred donations, which the people of Israel dedicate to the LORD, while he is in a state of uncleanness, that person shall be cut off from my presence: I am the LORD. 4No one of Aaron's offspring who has a leprous[a] disease or suffers a discharge may eat of the sacred donations until he is clean. Whoever touches anything made unclean by a corpse or a man who has had an emission of semen, 5and whoever touches any swarming thing by which he may be made unclean or any human being by whom he may be made unclean—whatever his uncleanness may be— 6the person who touches any such shall be unclean until evening and shall not eat of the sacred donations unless he has washed his body in water. 7When the sun sets he shall be clean; and afterward he may eat of the sacred donations, for they are his food. 8That which died or was torn by wild animals he shall not eat, becoming unclean by it: I am the LORD. 9They shall keep my charge, so that they may not incur guilt and die in the sanctuary[b] for having profaned it: I am the LORD; I sanctify them.

10 No lay person shall eat of the sacred donations. No bound or hired servant of the priest shall eat of the sacred donations; 11but if a priest acquires anyone by purchase, the person may eat of them; and those that are born in his house may eat of his food. 12If a priest's daughter marries a layman, she shall not eat of the offering of the sacred donations; 13but if a priest's daughter

[a] A term for several skin diseases; precise meaning uncertain

[b] Vg: Heb *incur guilt for it and die in it*

is widowed or divorced, without offspring, and
returns to her father's house, as in her youth, she
may eat of her father's food. No lay person shall
eat of it. 14If a man eats of the sacred donation
unintentionally, he shall add one-fifth of its value
to it, and give the sacred donation to the priest.
15No one shall profane the sacred donations of
the people of Israel, which they offer to the LORD,
16causing them to bear guilt requiring a guilt offering, by eating their sacred donations: for I am the
LORD; I sanctify them.

17 The LORD spoke to Moses, saying: 18Speak
to Aaron and his sons and all the people of Israel
and say to them: When anyone of the house of
Israel or of the aliens residing in Israel presents
an offering, whether in payment of a vow or as a
freewill offering that is offered to the LORD as a
burnt offering, 19to be acceptable in your behalf
it shall be a male without blemish, of the cattle or
the sheep or the goats. 20You shall not offer anything that has a blemish, for it will not be acceptable in your behalf.

21 When anyone offers a sacrifice of well-
being to the LORD, in fulfillment of a vow or as
a freewill offering, from the herd or from the
flock, to be acceptable it must be perfect; there
shall be no blemish in it. 22Anything blind, or
injured, or maimed, or having a discharge or an
itch or scabs—these you shall not offer to the
LORD or put any of them on the altar as offerings
by fire to the LORD. 23An ox or a lamb that has a
limb too long or too short you may present for a
freewill offering; but it will not be accepted for
a vow. 24Any animal that has its testicles bruised
or crushed or torn or cut, you shall not offer to
the LORD; such you shall not do within your land,
25nor shall you accept any such animals from a
foreigner to offer as food to your God; since they
are mutilated, with a blemish in them, they shall
not be accepted in your behalf.

26 The LORD spoke to Moses, saying: 27When
an ox or a sheep or a goat is born, it shall remain
seven days with its mother, and from the eighth
day on it shall be acceptable as the LORD's offering by fire. 28But you shall not slaughter, from the
herd or the flock, an animal with its young on the
same day. 29When you sacrifice a thanksgiving
offering to the LORD, you shall sacrifice it so that
it may be acceptable in your behalf. 30It shall be
eaten on the same day; you shall not leave any of
it until morning: I am the LORD.

31 Thus you shall keep my commandments
and observe them: I am the LORD. 32You shall
not profane my holy name, that I may be sanctified among the people of Israel: I am the LORD; I
sanctify you, 33I who brought you out of the land
of Egypt to be your God: I am the LORD.

23 The LORD spoke to Moses, saying: 2Speak
to the people of Israel and say to them:
These are the appointed festivals of the LORD
that you shall proclaim as holy convocations, my
appointed festivals.

3 Six days shall work be done; but the seventh
day is a sabbath of complete rest, a holy convocation; you shall do no work: it is a sabbath to the
LORD throughout your settlements.

4 These are the appointed festivals of the
LORD, the holy convocations, which you shall
celebrate at the time appointed for them. 5In the
first month, on the fourteenth day of the month,
at twilight,[a] there shall be a passover offering to
the LORD, 6and on the fifteenth day of the same
month is the festival of unleavened bread to the
LORD; seven days you shall eat unleavened bread.
7On the first day you shall have a holy convocation; you shall not work at your occupations. 8For
seven days you shall present the LORD's offerings
by fire; on the seventh day there shall be a holy
convocation: you shall not work at your occupations.

9 The LORD spoke to Moses: 10Speak to the
people of Israel and say to them: When you enter the land that I am giving you and you reap its
harvest, you shall bring the sheaf of the first fruits
of your harvest to the priest. 11He shall raise the
sheaf before the LORD, that you may find acceptance; on the day after the sabbath the priest
shall raise it. 12On the day when you raise the
sheaf, you shall offer a lamb a year old, without
blemish, as a burnt offering to the LORD. 13And

[a] Heb *between the two evenings*

the grain offering with it shall be two-tenths of
an ephah of choice flour mixed with oil, an offering by fire of pleasing odor to the LORD; and the
drink offering with it shall be of wine, one-fourth
of a hin. 14 You shall eat no bread or parched grain
or fresh ears until that very day, until you have
brought the offering of your God: it is a statute
forever throughout your generations in all your
settlements.

15 And from the day after the sabbath, from
the day on which you bring the sheaf of the elevation offering, you shall count off seven weeks;
they shall be complete. 16 You shall count until
the day after the seventh sabbath, fifty days; then
you shall present an offering of new grain to the
LORD. 17 You shall bring from your settlements
two loaves of bread as an elevation offering, each
made of two-tenths of an ephah; they shall be of
choice flour, baked with leaven, as first fruits to the
LORD. 18 You shall present with the bread seven
lambs a year old without blemish, one young
bull, and two rams; they shall be a burnt offering
to the LORD, along with their grain offering and
their drink offerings, an offering by fire of pleasing
odor to the LORD. 19 You shall also offer one male
goat for a sin offering, and two male lambs a year
old as a sacrifice of well-being. 20 The priest shall
raise them with the bread of the first fruits as an
elevation offering before the LORD, together with
the two lambs; they shall be holy to the LORD
for the priest. 21 On that same day you shall make
proclamation; you shall hold a holy convocation;
you shall not work at your occupations. This is a
statute forever in all your settlements throughout
your generations.

22 When you reap the harvest of your land,
you shall not reap to the very edges of your field,
or gather the gleanings of your harvest; you shall
leave them for the poor and for the alien: I am the
LORD your God.

23 The LORD spoke to Moses, saying: 24 Speak
to the people of Israel, saying: In the seventh
month, on the first day of the month, you shall
observe a day of complete rest, a holy convocation commemorated with trumpet blasts. 25 You
shall not work at your occupations; and you shall
present the LORD's offering by fire.

26 The LORD spoke to Moses, saying: 27 Now,
the tenth day of this seventh month is the day of
atonement; it shall be a holy convocation for you:
you shall deny yourselves[a] and present the LORD's
offering by fire; 28 and you shall do no work during
that entire day; for it is a day of atonement, to make
atonement on your behalf before the LORD your
God. 29 For anyone who does not practice self-
denial[b] during that entire day shall be cut off from
the people. 30 And anyone who does any work during that entire day, such a one I will destroy from
the midst of the people. 31 You shall do no work: it
is a statute forever throughout your generations in
all your settlements. 32 It shall be to you a sabbath
of complete rest, and you shall deny yourselves;[a]
on the ninth day of the month at evening, from
evening to evening you shall keep your sabbath.

33 The LORD spoke to Moses, saying: 34 Speak
to the people of Israel, saying: On the fifteenth
day of this seventh month, and lasting seven days,
there shall be the festival of booths[c] to the LORD.
35 The first day shall be a holy convocation; you
shall not work at your occupations. 36 Seven days
you shall present the LORD's offerings by fire; on
the eighth day you shall observe a holy convocation and present the LORD's offerings by fire; it
is a solemn assembly; you shall not work at your
occupations.

37 These are the appointed festivals of the
LORD, which you shall celebrate as times of holy
convocation, for presenting to the LORD offerings by fire—burnt offerings and grain offerings,
sacrifices and drink offerings, each on its proper
day— 38 apart from the sabbaths of the LORD,
and apart from your gifts, and apart from all your
votive offerings, and apart from all your freewill
offerings, which you give to the LORD.

39 Now, the fifteenth day of the seventh
month, when you have gathered in the produce of
the land, you shall keep the festival of the LORD,
lasting seven days; a complete rest on the first
day, and a complete rest on the eighth day. 40 On
the first day you shall take the fruit of majestic[d]

[a] Or *shall fast* [b] Or *does not fast* [c] Or *tabernacles*: Heb *succoth* [d] Meaning of Heb uncertain

trees, branches of palm trees, boughs of leafy
trees, and willows of the brook; and you shall rejoice before the LORD your God for seven days.
41You shall keep it as a festival to the LORD seven
days in the year; you shall keep it in the seventh
month as a statute forever throughout your generations. 42You shall live in booths for seven days;
all that are citizens in Israel shall live in booths,
43so that your generations may know that I made
the people of Israel live in booths when I brought
them out of the land of Egypt: I am the LORD
your God.

44 Thus Moses declared to the people of Israel the appointed festivals of the LORD.

24 The LORD spoke to Moses, saying: 2Com-
mand the people of Israel to bring you
pure oil of beaten olives for the lamp, that a light
may be kept burning regularly. 3Aaron shall set it
up in the tent of meeting, outside the curtain of
the covenant,[a] to burn from evening to morning
before the LORD regularly; it shall be a statute
forever throughout your generations. 4He shall
set up the lamps on the lampstand of pure gold[b]
before the LORD regularly.

5 You shall take choice flour, and bake twelve
loaves of it; two-tenths of an ephah shall be in
each loaf. 6You shall place them in two rows, six
in a row, on the table of pure gold.[c] 7You shall put
pure frankincense with each row, to be a token
offering for the bread, as an offering by fire to the
LORD. 8Every sabbath day Aaron shall set them
in order before the LORD regularly as a commitment of the people of Israel, as a covenant forever.
9They shall be for Aaron and his descendants,
who shall eat them in a holy place, for they are
most holy portions for him from the offerings by
fire to the LORD, a perpetual due.

10 A man whose mother was an Israelite and
whose father was an Egyptian came out among
the people of Israel; and the Israelite woman's
son and a certain Israelite began fighting in the
camp. 11The Israelite woman's son blasphemed
the Name in a curse. And they brought him to
Moses—now his mother's name was Shelomith,
daughter of Dibri, of the tribe of Dan— 12and
they put him in custody, until the decision of the
LORD should be made clear to them.

13 The LORD said to Moses, saying: 14Take
the blasphemer outside the camp; and let all
who were within hearing lay their hands on his
head, and let the whole congregation stone him.
15And speak to the people of Israel, saying: Anyone who curses God shall bear the sin. 16One
who blasphemes the name of the LORD shall be
put to death; the whole congregation shall stone
the blasphemer. Aliens as well as citizens, when
they blaspheme the Name, shall be put to death.
17Anyone who kills a human being shall be put
to death. 18Anyone who kills an animal shall
make restitution for it, life for life. 19Anyone who
maims another shall suffer the same injury in return: 20fracture for fracture, eye for eye, tooth for
tooth; the injury inflicted is the injury to be suffered. 21One who kills an animal shall make restitution for it; but one who kills a human being
shall be put to death. 22You shall have one law for
the alien and for the citizen: for I am the LORD
your God. 23Moses spoke thus to the people of
Israel; and they took the blasphemer outside the
camp, and stoned him to death. The people of Israel did as the LORD had commanded Moses.

25 The LORD spoke to Moses on Mount Sinai, saying: 2Speak to the people of Israel
and say to them: When you enter the land that I
am giving you, the land shall observe a sabbath
for the LORD. 3Six years you shall sow your field,
and six years you shall prune your vineyard, and
gather in their yield; 4but in the seventh year
there shall be a sabbath of complete rest for the
land, a sabbath for the LORD: you shall not sow
your field or prune your vineyard. 5You shall not
reap the aftergrowth of your harvest or gather the
grapes of your unpruned vine: it shall be a year of
complete rest for the land. 6You may eat what the
land yields during its sabbath—you, your male
and female slaves, your hired and your bound
laborers who live with you; 7for your livestock
also, and for the wild animals in your land all its
yield shall be for food.

8 You shall count off seven weeks[d] of years,

[a] Or *treaty*, or *testament*; Heb *eduth* [b] Heb *pure lampstand* [c] Heb *pure table* [d] Or *sabbaths*

seven times seven years, so that the period of
seven weeks of years gives forty-nine years. 9Then
you shall have the trumpet sounded loud; on the
tenth day of the seventh month—on the day of
atonement—you shall have the trumpet sounded
throughout all your land. 10And you shall hallow
the fiftieth year and you shall proclaim liberty
throughout the land to all its inhabitants. It shall
be a jubilee for you: you shall return, every one
of you, to your property and every one of you to
your family. 11That fiftieth year shall be a jubilee for you: you shall not sow, or reap the aftergrowth, or harvest the unpruned vines. 12For it is
a jubilee; it shall be holy to you: you shall eat only
what the field itself produces.

13 In this year of jubilee you shall return,
every one of you, to your property. 14When
you make a sale to your neighbor or buy from
your neighbor, you shall not cheat one another.
15When you buy from your neighbor, you shall
pay only for the number of years since the jubilee;
the seller shall charge you only for the remaining
crop years. 16If the years are more, you shall increase the price, and if the years are fewer, you
shall diminish the price; for it is a certain number
of harvests that are being sold to you. 17You shall
not cheat one another, but you shall fear your
God; for I am the Lord your God.

18 You shall observe my statutes and faithfully keep my ordinances, so that you may live on
the land securely. 19The land will yield its fruit,
and you will eat your fill and live on it securely.
20Should you ask, "What shall we eat in the seventh year, if we may not sow or gather in our
crop?" 21I will order my blessing for you in the
sixth year, so that it will yield a crop for three
years. 22When you sow in the eighth year, you
will be eating from the old crop; until the ninth
year, when its produce comes in, you shall eat the
old. 23The land shall not be sold in perpetuity, for
the land is mine; with me you are but aliens and
tenants. 24Throughout the land that you hold,
you shall provide for the redemption of the land.

25 If anyone of your kin falls into difficulty
and sells a piece of property, then the next of kin
shall come and redeem what the relative has sold.
26If the person has no one to redeem it, but then
prospers and finds sufficient means to do so, 27the
years since its sale shall be computed and the difference shall be refunded to the person to whom
it was sold, and the property shall be returned.
28But if there are not sufficient means to recover
it, what was sold shall remain with the purchaser
until the year of jubilee; in the jubilee it shall be
released, and the property shall be returned.

29 If anyone sells a dwelling house in a walled
city, it may be redeemed until a year has elapsed
since its sale; the right of redemption shall be one
year. 30If it is not redeemed before a full year has
elapsed, a house that is in a walled city shall pass

Leviticus 25:23

In the Bible land is a gift, that is, it remains God's property.... Though it is the farmers who sow the seed on the land, it is not they who produce its fruits, but in their sowing there is a promise of what the earth will bring forth—the fruit. Thus bread, like life, is a gift.... In contrast to this, colonialists do not await the gift; they conquer, subdue and exploit the land and the people. Colonialists want quick profits, not life; and in their quest they destroy land (by soil erosion), people (by slavery and eviction) and even themselves, for they take up credits which they then have to repay ten-fold (foreign debt). Gift or conquest: which of these bestows salvation and life upon us? We conclude with a text of the Qu'chua Indians:

> *Everything that injures the earth also injures the children of earth. The Indian is a child of earth. The earth is our life and our freedom. The great lords of the earth do not understand the indigenous people because they enslave the earth itself. They are strangers who come by night and steal everything they want from the earth. To them one piece of earth is like another.... The landless Indian is like a rootless tree by the wayside. Everyone who injures the earth injures also the children of the earth.*[17]

— ***Michael Knoch***

in perpetuity to the purchaser, throughout the
generations; it shall not be released in the jubilee.
31 But houses in villages that have no walls around
them shall be classed as open country; they may
be redeemed, and they shall be released in the jubilee. 32 As for the cities of the Levites, the Levites
shall forever have the right of redemption of the
houses in the cities belonging to them. 33 Such
property as may be redeemed from the Levites—
houses sold in a city belonging to them—shall be
released in the jubilee; because the houses in the
cities of the Levites are their possession among
the people of Israel. 34 But the open land around
their cities may not be sold; for that is their possession for all time.

35 If any of your kin fall into difficulty and
become dependent on you,[a] you shall support
them; they shall live with you as though resident
aliens. 36 Do not take interest in advance or otherwise make a profit from them, but fear your God;
let them live with you. 37 You shall not lend them
your money at interest taken in advance, or provide them food at a profit. 38 I am the LORD your
God, who brought you out of the land of Egypt,
to give you the land of Canaan, to be your God.

39 If any who are dependent on you become
so impoverished that they sell themselves to you,
you shall not make them serve as slaves. 40 They
shall remain with you as hired or bound laborers.
They shall serve with you until the year of the jubilee. 41 Then they and their children with them
shall be free from your authority; they shall go
back to their own family and return to their ancestral property. 42 For they are my servants, whom I
brought out of the land of Egypt; they shall not
be sold as slaves are sold. 43 You shall not rule over
them with harshness, but shall fear your God.
44 As for the male and female slaves whom you
may have, it is from the nations around you that
you may acquire male and female slaves. 45 You
may also acquire them from among the aliens residing with you, and from their families that are
with you, who have been born in your land; and
they may be your property. 46 You may keep them
as a possession for your children after you, for
them to inherit as property. These you may treat
as slaves, but as for your fellow Israelites, no one
shall rule over the other with harshness.

47 If resident aliens among you prosper, and
if any of your kin fall into difficulty with one
of them and sell themselves to an alien, or to a
branch of the alien's family, 48 after they have sold
themselves they shall have the right of redemption; one of their brothers may redeem them,
49 or their uncle or their uncle's son may redeem
them, or anyone of their family who is of their
own flesh may redeem them; or if they prosper
they may redeem themselves. 50 They shall compute with the purchaser the total from the year
when they sold themselves to the alien until the
jubilee year; the price of the sale shall be applied
to the number of years: the time they were with
the owner shall be rated as the time of a hired laborer. 51 If many years remain, they shall pay for
their redemption in proportion to the purchase
price; 52 and if few years remain until the jubilee
year, they shall compute thus: according to the
years involved they shall make payment for their
redemption. 53 As a laborer hired by the year they
shall be under the alien's authority, who shall not,
however, rule with harshness over them in your
sight. 54 And if they have not been redeemed in
any of these ways, they and their children with
them shall go free in the jubilee year. 55 For to
me the people of Israel are servants; they are my
servants whom I brought out from the land of
Egypt: I am the LORD your God.

26 You shall make for yourselves no idols
and erect no carved images or pillars, and
you shall not place figured stones in your land, to
worship at them; for I am the LORD your God.
2 You shall keep my sabbaths and reverence my
sanctuary: I am the LORD.

3 If you follow my statutes and keep my
commandments and observe them faithfully, 4 I
will give you your rains in their season, and the
land shall yield its produce, and the trees of the
field shall yield their fruit. 5 Your threshing shall
overtake the vintage, and the vintage shall overtake the sowing; you shall eat your bread to the

[a] Meaning of Heb uncertain

full, and live securely in your land. 6And I will
grant peace in the land, and you shall lie down,
and no one shall make you afraid; I will remove
dangerous animals from the land, and no sword
shall go through your land. 7You shall give chase
to your enemies, and they shall fall before you
by the sword. 8Five of you shall give chase to a
hundred, and a hundred of you shall give chase
to ten thousand; your enemies shall fall before
you by the sword. 9I will look with favor upon
you and make you fruitful and multiply you; and
I will maintain my covenant with you. 10You shall
eat old grain long stored, and you shall have to
clear out the old to make way for the new. 11I will
place my dwelling in your midst, and I shall not
abhor you. 12And I will walk among you, and will
be your God, and you shall be my people. 13I am
the LORD your God who brought you out of the
land of Egypt, to be their slaves no more; I have
broken the bars of your yoke and made you walk
erect.

14 But if you will not obey me, and do not
observe all these commandments, 15if you spurn
my statutes, and abhor my ordinances, so that
you will not observe all my commandments, and
you break my covenant, 16I in turn will do this
to you: I will bring terror on you; consumption
and fever that waste the eyes and cause life to pine
away. You shall sow your seed in vain, for your enemies shall eat it. 17I will set my face against you,
and you shall be struck down by your enemies;
your foes shall rule over you, and you shall flee
though no one pursues you. 18And if in spite of
this you will not obey me, I will continue to punish you sevenfold for your sins. 19I will break your
proud glory, and I will make your sky like iron and
your earth like copper. 20Your strength shall be
spent to no purpose: your land shall not yield its
produce, and the trees of the land shall not yield
their fruit.

21 If you continue hostile to me, and will not
obey me, I will continue to plague you sevenfold
for your sins. 22I will let loose wild animals against
you, and they shall bereave you of your children
and destroy your livestock; they shall make you
few in number, and your roads shall be deserted.

23 If in spite of these punishments you have
not turned back to me, but continue hostile to
me, 24then I too will continue hostile to you: I
myself will strike you sevenfold for your sins. 25I
will bring the sword against you, executing vengeance for the covenant; and if you withdraw
within your cities, I will send pestilence among
you, and you shall be delivered into enemy hands.
26When I break your staff of bread, ten women
shall bake your bread in a single oven, and they
shall dole out your bread by weight; and though
you eat, you shall not be satisfied.

27 But if, despite this, you disobey me, and
continue hostile to me, 28I will continue hostile
to you in fury; I in turn will punish you myself
sevenfold for your sins. 29You shall eat the flesh
of your sons, and you shall eat the flesh of your
daughters. 30I will destroy your high places and
cut down your incense altars; I will heap your carcasses on the carcasses of your idols. I will abhor
you. 31I will lay your cities waste, will make your
sanctuaries desolate, and I will not smell your
pleasing odors. 32I will devastate the land, so that
your enemies who come to settle in it shall be appalled at it. 33And you I will scatter among the nations, and I will unsheathe the sword against you;
your land shall be a desolation, and your cities a
waste.

34 Then the land shall enjoy[a] its sabbath
years as long as it lies desolate, while you are in
the land of your enemies; then the land shall rest,
and enjoy[a] its sabbath years. 35As long as it lies
desolate, it shall have the rest it did not have on
your sabbaths when you were living on it. 36And
as for those of you who survive, I will send faint-
ness into their hearts in the lands of their enemies; the sound of a driven leaf shall put them
to flight, and they shall flee as one flees from the
sword, and they shall fall though no one pursues. 37They shall stumble over one another, as if
to escape a sword, though no one pursues; and
you shall have no power to stand against your enemies. 38You shall perish among the nations, and
the land of your enemies shall devour you. 39And

[a] Or *make up for*

those of you who survive shall languish in the
land of your enemies because of their iniquities;
also they shall languish because of the iniquities
of their ancestors.
40 But if they confess their iniquity and the
iniquity of their ancestors, in that they committed treachery against me and, moreover, that
they continued hostile to me— 41so that I, in
turn, continued hostile to them and brought
them into the land of their enemies; if then their
uncircumcised heart is humbled and they make
amends for their iniquity, 42then will I remember
my covenant with Jacob; I will remember also my
covenant with Isaac and also my covenant with
Abraham, and I will remember the land. 43For
the land shall be deserted by them, and enjoy[a]
its sabbath years by lying desolate without them,
while they shall make amends for their iniquity,
because they dared to spurn my ordinances, and
they abhorred my statutes. 44Yet for all that, when
they are in the land of their enemies, I will not
spurn them, or abhor them so as to destroy them
utterly and break my covenant with them; for I
am the LORD their God; 45but I will remember
in their favor the covenant with their ancestors
whom I brought out of the land of Egypt in the
sight of the nations, to be their God: I am the
LORD.
46 These are the statutes and ordinances and
laws that the LORD established between himself
and the people of Israel on Mount Sinai through
Moses.

27 The LORD spoke to Moses, saying:
2Speak to the people of Israel and say to
them: When a person makes an explicit vow to
the LORD concerning the equivalent for a human
being, 3the equivalent for a male shall be: from
twenty to sixty years of age the equivalent shall
be fifty shekels of silver by the sanctuary shekel.
4If the person is a female, the equivalent is thirty
shekels. 5If the age is from five to twenty years of
age, the equivalent is twenty shekels for a male
and ten shekels for a female. 6If the age is from
one month to five years, the equivalent for a male
is five shekels of silver, and for a female the equivalent is three shekels of silver. 7And if the person
is sixty years old or over, then the equivalent for a
male is fifteen shekels, and for a female ten shekels. 8If any cannot afford the equivalent, they shall
be brought before the priest and the priest shall
assess them; the priest shall assess them according to what each one making a vow can afford.
9 If it concerns an animal that may be brought
as an offering to the LORD, any such that may be
given to the LORD shall be holy. 10Another shall
not be exchanged or substituted for it, either
good for bad or bad for good; and if one animal is
substituted for another, both that one and its substitute shall be holy. 11If it concerns any unclean
animal that may not be brought as an offering to
the LORD, the animal shall be presented before
the priest. 12The priest shall assess it: whether
good or bad, according to the assessment of the
priest, so it shall be. 13But if it is to be redeemed,
one-fifth must be added to the assessment.
14 If a person consecrates a house to the
LORD, the priest shall assess it: whether good
or bad, as the priest assesses it, so it shall stand.
15And if the one who consecrates the house
wishes to redeem it, one-fifth shall be added to its
assessed value, and it shall revert to the original
owner.
16 If a person consecrates to the LORD any inherited landholding, its assessment shall be in accordance with its seed requirements: fifty shekels
of silver to a homer of barley seed. 17If the person
consecrates the field as of the year of jubilee, that
assessment shall stand; 18but if the field is consecrated after the jubilee, the priest shall compute
the price for it according to the years that remain
until the year of jubilee, and the assessment shall
be reduced. 19And if the one who consecrates
the field wishes to redeem it, then one-fifth shall
be added to its assessed value, and it shall revert
to the original owner; 20but if the field is not redeemed, or if it has been sold to someone else,
it shall no longer be redeemable. 21But when the
field is released in the jubilee, it shall be holy to the
LORD as a devoted field; it becomes the priest's
holding. 22If someone consecrates to the LORD a

[a] Or *make up for*

field that has been purchased, which is not a part
of the inherited landholding, 23the priest shall
compute for it the proportionate assessment up
to the year of jubilee, and the assessment shall be
paid as of that day, a sacred donation to the LORD.
24In the year of jubilee the field shall return to the
one from whom it was bought, whose holding the
land is. 25All assessments shall be by the sanctuary shekel: twenty gerahs shall make a shekel.

26 A firstling of animals, however, which as
a firstling belongs to the LORD, cannot be consecrated by anyone; whether ox or sheep, it is the
LORD's. 27If it is an unclean animal, it shall be ransomed at its assessment, with one-fifth added; if it
is not redeemed, it shall be sold at its assessment.

28 Nothing that a person owns that has been
devoted to destruction for the LORD, be it human
or animal, or inherited landholding, may be sold
or redeemed; every devoted thing is most holy to
the LORD. 29No human beings who have been devoted to destruction can be ransomed; they shall
be put to death.

30 All tithes from the land, whether the seed
from the ground or the fruit from the tree, are the
LORD's; they are holy to the LORD. 31If persons
wish to redeem any of their tithes, they must add
one-fifth to them. 32All tithes of herd and flock,
every tenth one that passes under the shepherd's
staff, shall be holy to the LORD. 33Let no one inquire whether it is good or bad, or make substitution for it; if one makes substitution for it, then
both it and the substitute shall be holy and cannot be redeemed.

34 These are the commandments that the
LORD gave to Moses for the people of Israel on
Mount Sinai.

Numbers

The stories in Numbers are a continuation of the exodus saga. Many of the most familiar stories from the wilderness sojourn of the Israelites occur in Numbers. Examples include the presence of the pillar of cloud and fire; provision of quails, the appearance of poisonous serpents, and a healing sculpted serpent; the sending of spies into Canaan; and murmuring and wandering on the part of the people. As the conclusion of the narrative that began in Exodus—and following a lengthy sermonic interlude formed by Leviticus—Numbers is significant for anyone interested in the theme of liberation in the Hebrew Scriptures.

I approach the biblical narrative as an African American woman with feminist commitments. My identity, like all identities, is complex and constructed. As an African American Christian, I have been socialized to read the text from the dominant perspective and to identify with the Israelites—but that is an ironic posture for anyone in the African diaspora. While the Israelites are Afro-Asiatic, the Egyptians are continental Africans. The traditional and dominant interpretation of the exodus saga among U.S. and European Christians characterizes the Africans as enemies of God's people. The exodus story that is continued in Numbers is read as liberative for Jewish, African American, Feminist, Queer, and many other readers. But it is not liberative for indigenous readers. Native peoples in the Americas as well as colonized peoples in Asia and Africa encounter a text in which God dispossesses the inhabitants of the land. In the history of American expansion and European colonization, the broader Exodus narrative was used to justify invasion, slavery, colonization, segregation, and other violent intercultural practices.

Numbers gets its English title from its Greek version, *Arithmoi*. The book's Hebrew title, *BeMidbar*—"In the Wilderness"—comes from the fifth word (in Hebrew) in the first verse. The name Numbers in Greek, Latin, English, and other translations comes from the census that begins the book (1:1-4). This census, really a military muster (as are those in chapters 4 and 26), is a reminder that in spite of claims of a divine promise, entry into an inhabited land will not be seamless, or bloodless.

Among the more significant—but less familiar—narratives in Numbers are: a ritual for establishing the guilt of a suspected adulteress in 5:11-31; the establishment (and revision) of a community rule for female and male Nazirites in 6:1-8 and 30:1-5; Moses' questioning of God's parenting skills in chapter 11; conflict between Miriam, Moses, and Aaron in chapter 12; the fire-serpent and fire-serpent sculpture in 21:4-9 (described by Rabbi Arthur Waskow as a "copper copperhead"); the story of Balaam the gentile prophet in chapters 22–24; the stories of Mahlah, Noah, Hoglah, Milcah, and Tirzah—the women for whom traditional inheritance law was changed—in 27:1-11 and 36:1-12; and the initiation of rape-marriage, in which young girls are abducted and forced into marriage in 31:1-20.

Numbers marks the end of the exodus journey and the beginning of Israelite self-determination. It also marks the passage into death—and not yet into the Promised Land—of the first generation to experience liberation. Numbers ends with the emergence of a new generation who will experience the fulfillment of the promise of liberation, eventually. However, the books of Joshua and Judges have very different portraits of how this liberation was experienced.

— ***Wilda C. Gafney***

1 The LORD spoke to Moses in the wilderness
of Sinai, in the tent of meeting, on the first day
of the second month, in the second year after they
had come out of the land of Egypt, saying: 2 Take
a census of the whole congregation of Israelites,
in their clans, by ancestral houses, according to
the number of names, every male individually;
3 from twenty years old and upward, everyone in
Israel able to go to war. You and Aaron shall enroll
them, company by company. 4 A man from each
tribe shall be with you, each man the head of his
ancestral house. 5 These are the names of the men
who shall assist you:

From Reuben, Elizur son of Shedeur.
6 From Simeon, Shelumiel son of Zurishaddai.
7 From Judah, Nahshon son of Amminadab.
8 From Issachar, Nethanel son of Zuar.
9 From Zebulun, Eliab son of Helon.
10 From the sons of Joseph:
from Ephraim, Elishama son of Ammihud;
from Manasseh, Gamaliel son of Pedahzur.
11 From Benjamin, Abidan son of Gideoni.
12 From Dan, Ahiezer son of Ammishaddai.
13 From Asher, Pagiel son of Ochran.
14 From Gad, Eliasaph son of Deuel.
15 From Naphtali, Ahira son of Enan.

16 These were the ones chosen from the congregation, the leaders of their ancestral tribes, the
heads of the divisions of Israel.

17 Moses and Aaron took these men who had
been designated by name, 18 and on the first day
of the second month they assembled the whole
congregation together. They registered themselves
in their clans, by their ancestral houses, according
to the number of names from twenty years old and
upward, individually, 19 as the LORD commanded
Moses. So he enrolled them in the wilderness
of Sinai.

20 The descendants of Reuben, Israel's firstborn, their lineage, in their clans, by their ancestral houses, according to the number of names,
individually, every male from twenty years old
and upward, everyone able to go to war: 21 those
enrolled of the tribe of Reuben were forty-six
thousand five hundred.

22 The descendants of Simeon, their lineage,
in their clans, by their ancestral houses, those
of them that were numbered, according to the
number of names, individually, every male from
twenty years old and upward, everyone able to
go to war: 23 those enrolled of the tribe of Simeon
were fifty-nine thousand three hundred.

24 The descendants of Gad, their lineage, in
their clans, by their ancestral houses, according to
the number of the names, from twenty years old
and upward, everyone able to go to war: 25 those
enrolled of the tribe of Gad were forty-five thousand six hundred fifty.

26 The descendants of Judah, their lineage, in
their clans, by their ancestral houses, according
to the number of names, from twenty years old
and upward, everyone able to go to war: 27 those
enrolled of the tribe of Judah were seventy-four
thousand six hundred.

28 The descendants of Issachar, their lineage,
in their clans, by their ancestral houses, according
to the number of names, from twenty years old
and upward, everyone able to go to war: 29 those
enrolled of the tribe of Issachar were fifty-four
thousand four hundred.

30 The descendants of Zebulun, their lineage,
in their clans, by their ancestral houses, according
to the number of names, from twenty years old
and upward, everyone able to go to war: 31 those
enrolled of the tribe of Zebulun were fifty-seven
thousand four hundred.

32 The descendants of Joseph, namely, the
descendants of Ephraim, their lineage, in their
clans, by their ancestral houses, according to the
number of names, from twenty years old and upward, everyone able to go to war: 33 those enrolled
of the tribe of Ephraim were forty thousand five
hundred.

34 The descendants of Manasseh, their lineage, in their clans, by their ancestral houses,
according to the number of names, from twenty
years old and upward, everyone able to go to war:
35 those enrolled of the tribe of Manasseh were
thirty-two thousand two hundred.

36 The descendants of Benjamin, their lineage, in their clans, by their ancestral houses,
according to the number of names, from twenty
years old and upward, everyone able to go to war:
37 those enrolled of the tribe of Benjamin were
thirty-five thousand four hundred.

38 The descendants of Dan, their lineage, in
their clans, by their ancestral houses, according
to the number of names, from twenty years old
and upward, everyone able to go to war: 39 those
enrolled of the tribe of Dan were sixty-two thousand seven hundred.

40 The descendants of Asher, their lineage, in
their clans, by their ancestral houses, according to
the number of names, from twenty years old and
upward, everyone able to go to war: 41 those enrolled of the tribe of Asher were forty-one thousand five hundred.

42 The descendants of Naphtali, their lineage,
in their clans, by their ancestral houses, according
to the number of names, from twenty years old
and upward, everyone able to go to war: 43 those
enrolled of the tribe of Naphtali were fifty-three
thousand four hundred.

44 These are those who were enrolled, whom
Moses and Aaron enrolled with the help of the
leaders of Israel, twelve men, each representing
his ancestral house. 45 So the whole number of the
Israelites, by their ancestral houses, from twenty
years old and upward, everyone able to go to war
in Israel— 46 their whole number was six hundred
three thousand five hundred fifty. 47 The Levites,
however, were not numbered by their ancestral
tribe along with them.

48 The LORD had said to Moses: 49 Only the
tribe of Levi you shall not enroll, and you shall
not take a census of them with the other Israelites. 50 Rather you shall appoint the Levites over
the tabernacle of the covenant,[a] and over all its
equipment, and over all that belongs to it; they
are to carry the tabernacle and all its equipment,
and they shall tend it, and shall camp around the
tabernacle. 51 When the tabernacle is to set out,
the Levites shall take it down; and when the
tabernacle is to be pitched, the Levites shall set
it up. And any outsider who comes near shall be
put to death. 52 The other Israelites shall camp in
their respective regimental camps, by companies;
53 but the Levites shall camp around the tabernacle of the covenant,[a] that there may be no wrath
on the congregation of the Israelites; and the
Levites shall perform the guard duty of the tabernacle of the covenant.[a] 54 The Israelites did so;
they did just as the LORD commanded Moses.

2 The LORD spoke to Moses and Aaron, saying: 2 The Israelites shall camp each in their
respective regiments, under ensigns by their ancestral houses; they shall camp facing the tent of
meeting on every side. 3 Those to camp on the

[a] Or *treaty*, or *testimony*; Heb *eduth*

east side toward the sunrise shall be of the regimental encampment of Judah by companies. The
leader of the people of Judah shall be Nahshon
son of Amminadab, 4with a company as enrolled
of seventy-four thousand six hundred. 5Those to
camp next to him shall be the tribe of Issachar.
The leader of the Issacharites shall be Nethanel
son of Zuar, 6with a company as enrolled of fifty-
four thousand four hundred. 7Then the tribe of
Zebulun: The leader of the Zebulunites shall be
Eliab son of Helon, 8with a company as enrolled
of fifty-seven thousand four hundred. 9The total
enrollment of the camp of Judah, by companies,
is one hundred eighty-six thousand four hundred.
They shall set out first on the march.

10 On the south side shall be the regimental encampment of Reuben by companies. The
leader of the Reubenites shall be Elizur son of
Shedeur, 11with a company as enrolled of forty-
six thousand five hundred. 12And those to camp
next to him shall be the tribe of Simeon. The
leader of the Simeonites shall be Shelumiel son
of Zurishaddai, 13with a company as enrolled of
fifty-nine thousand three hundred. 14Then the
tribe of Gad: The leader of the Gadites shall be
Eliasaph son of Reuel, 15with a company as enrolled of forty-five thousand six hundred fifty.
16The total enrollment of the camp of Reuben,
by companies, is one hundred fifty-one thousand
four hundred fifty. They shall set out second.

17 The tent of meeting, with the camp of the
Levites, shall set out in the center of the camps;
they shall set out just as they camp, each in position, by their regiments.

18 On the west side shall be the regimental encampment of Ephraim by companies. The
leader of the people of Ephraim shall be Elishama
son of Ammihud, 19with a company as enrolled
of forty thousand five hundred. 20Next to him
shall be the tribe of Manasseh. The leader of the
people of Manasseh shall be Gamaliel son of Pedahzur, 21with a company as enrolled of thirty-
two thousand two hundred. 22Then the tribe of
Benjamin: The leader of the Benjaminites shall
be Abidan son of Gideoni, 23with a company as
enrolled of thirty-five thousand four hundred.
24The total enrollment of the camp of Ephraim,
by companies, is one hundred eight thousand one
hundred. They shall set out third on the march.

25 On the north side shall be the regimental
encampment of Dan by companies. The leader
of the Danites shall be Ahiezer son of Ammishaddai, 26with a company as enrolled of sixty-
two thousand seven hundred. 27Those to camp
next to him shall be the tribe of Asher. The leader
of the Asherites shall be Pagiel son of Ochran,
28with a company as enrolled of forty-one thousand five hundred. 29Then the tribe of Naphtali:
The leader of the Naphtalites shall be Ahira son of
Enan, 30with a company as enrolled of fifty-three
thousand four hundred. 31The total enrollment
of the camp of Dan is one hundred fifty-seven
thousand six hundred. They shall set out last, by
companies.[a]

32 This was the enrollment of the Israelites
by their ancestral houses; the total enrollment in
the camps by their companies was six hundred
three thousand five hundred fifty. 33Just as the
LORD had commanded Moses, the Levites were
not enrolled among the other Israelites.

34 The Israelites did just as the LORD had
commanded Moses: They camped by regiments,
and they set out the same way, everyone by clans,
according to ancestral houses.

3 This is the lineage of Aaron and Moses at the
time when the LORD spoke with Moses on
Mount Sinai. 2These are the names of the sons of
Aaron: Nadab the firstborn, and Abihu, Eleazar,
and Ithamar; 3these are the names of the sons of
Aaron, the anointed priests, whom he ordained
to minister as priests. 4Nadab and Abihu died
before the LORD when they offered unholy fire
before the LORD in the wilderness of Sinai, and
they had no children. Eleazar and Ithamar served
as priests in the lifetime of their father Aaron.

5 Then the LORD spoke to Moses, saying:
6Bring the tribe of Levi near, and set them before Aaron the priest, so that they may assist him.
7They shall perform duties for him and for the
whole congregation in front of the tent of meet-

[a] Compare verses 9, 16, 24: Heb *by their regiments*

ing, doing service at the tabernacle; 8they shall be
in charge of all the furnishings of the tent of meeting, and attend to the duties for the Israelites as
they do service at the tabernacle. 9You shall give
the Levites to Aaron and his descendants; they
are unreservedly given to him from among the Israelites. 10But you shall make a register of Aaron
and his descendants; it is they who shall attend to
the priesthood, and any outsider who comes near
shall be put to death.

11 Then the LORD spoke to Moses, saying: 12I hereby accept the Levites from among
the Israelites as substitutes for all the firstborn
that open the womb among the Israelites. The
Levites shall be mine, 13for all the firstborn are
mine; when I killed all the firstborn in the land of
Egypt, I consecrated for my own all the firstborn
in Israel, both human and animal; they shall be
mine. I am the LORD.

14 Then the LORD spoke to Moses in the
wilderness of Sinai, saying: 15Enroll the Levites
by ancestral houses and by clans. You shall enroll
every male from a month old and upward. 16So
Moses enrolled them according to the word of the
LORD, as he was commanded. 17The following
were the sons of Levi, by their names: Gershon,
Kohath, and Merari. 18These are the names of the
sons of Gershon by their clans: Libni and Shimei.
19The sons of Kohath by their clans: Amram,
Izhar, Hebron, and Uzziel. 20The sons of Merari
by their clans: Mahli and Mushi. These are the
clans of the Levites, by their ancestral houses.

21 To Gershon belonged the clan of the Libnites and the clan of the Shimeites; these were
the clans of the Gershonites. 22Their enrollment,
counting all the males from a month old and upward, was seven thousand five hundred. 23The clans
of the Gershonites were to camp behind the tabernacle on the west, 24with Eliasaph son of Lael
as head of the ancestral house of the Gershonites.
25The responsibility of the sons of Gershon in the
tent of meeting was to be the tabernacle, the tent
with its covering, the screen for the entrance of
the tent of meeting, 26the hangings of the court,
the screen for the entrance of the court that
is around the tabernacle and the altar, and its
cords—all the service pertaining to these.

27 To Kohath belonged the clan of the Amramites, the clan of the Izharites, the clan of the
Hebronites, and the clan of the Uzzielites; these
are the clans of the Kohathites. 28Counting all the
males, from a month old and upward, there were
eight thousand six hundred, attending to the duties of the sanctuary. 29The clans of the Kohathites
were to camp on the south side of the tabernacle,
30with Elizaphan son of Uzziel as head of the
ancestral house of the clans of the Kohathites.
31Their responsibility was to be the ark, the table,
the lampstand, the altars, the vessels of the sanctuary with which the priests minister, and the
screen—all the service pertaining to these. 32El-
eazar son of Aaron the priest was to be chief over
the leaders of the Levites, and to have oversight
of those who had charge of the sanctuary.

33 To Merari belonged the clan of the Mahlites and the clan of the Mushites: these are the
clans of Merari. 34Their enrollment, counting all
the males from a month old and upward, was six
thousand two hundred. 35The head of the ancestral house of the clans of Merari was Zuriel son
of Abihail; they were to camp on the north side
of the tabernacle. 36The responsibility assigned
to the sons of Merari was to be the frames of the
tabernacle, the bars, the pillars, the bases, and all
their accessories—all the service pertaining to
these; 37also the pillars of the court all around,
with their bases and pegs and cords.

38 Those who were to camp in front of the
tabernacle on the east—in front of the tent of
meeting toward the east—were Moses and Aaron
and Aaron's sons, having charge of the rites
within the sanctuary, whatever had to be done for
the Israelites; and any outsider who came near
was to be put to death. 39The total enrollment of
the Levites whom Moses and Aaron enrolled at
the commandment of the LORD, by their clans,
all the males from a month old and upward, was
twenty-two thousand.

40 Then the LORD said to Moses: Enroll all
the firstborn males of the Israelites, from a month
old and upward, and count their names. 41But
you shall accept the Levites for me—I am the
LORD—as substitutes for all the firstborn among
the Israelites, and the livestock of the Levites as

substitutes for all the firstborn among the livestock of the Israelites. 42 So Moses enrolled all
the firstborn among the Israelites, as the LORD
commanded him. 43 The total enrollment, all the
firstborn males from a month old and upward,
counting the number of names, was twenty-two
thousand two hundred seventy-three.

44 Then the LORD spoke to Moses, saying:
45 Accept the Levites as substitutes for all the firstborn among the Israelites, and the livestock of
the Levites as substitutes for their livestock; and
the Levites shall be mine. I am the LORD. 46 As the
price of redemption of the two hundred seventy-
three of the firstborn of the Israelites, over and
above the number of the Levites, 47 you shall accept five shekels apiece, reckoning by the shekel
of the sanctuary, a shekel of twenty gerahs. 48 Give
to Aaron and his sons the money by which the
excess number of them is redeemed. 49 So Moses
took the redemption money from those who
were over and above those redeemed by the Levites; 50 from the firstborn of the Israelites he took
the money, one thousand three hundred sixty-
five shekels, reckoned by the shekel of the sanctuary; 51 and Moses gave the redemption money to
Aaron and his sons, according to the word of the
LORD, as the LORD had commanded Moses.

4 The LORD spoke to Moses and Aaron, saying: 2 Take a census of the Kohathites separate from the other Levites, by their clans and
their ancestral houses, 3 from thirty years old up
to fifty years old, all who qualify to do work relating to the tent of meeting. 4 The service of the Kohathites relating to the tent of meeting concerns
the most holy things.

5 When the camp is to set out, Aaron and
his sons shall go in and take down the screening
curtain, and cover the ark of the covenant[a] with
it; 6 then they shall put on it a covering of fine
leather,[b] and spread over that a cloth all of blue,
and shall put its poles in place. 7 Over the table
of the bread of the Presence they shall spread a
blue cloth, and put on it the plates, the dishes
for incense, the bowls, and the flagons for the
drink offering; the regular bread also shall be on
it; 8 then they shall spread over them a crimson
cloth, and cover it with a covering of fine leather,[b]
and shall put its poles in place. 9 They shall take a
blue cloth, and cover the lampstand for the light,
with its lamps, its snuffers, its trays, and all the
vessels for oil with which it is supplied; 10 and
they shall put it with all its utensils in a covering
of fine leather,[b] and put it on the carrying frame.
11 Over the golden altar they shall spread a blue
cloth, and cover it with a covering of fine leather,[b]
and shall put its poles in place; 12 and they shall
take all the utensils of the service that are used in
the sanctuary, and put them in a blue cloth, and
cover them with a covering of fine leather,[b] and
put them on the carrying frame. 13 They shall take
away the ashes from the altar, and spread a purple
cloth over it; 14 and they shall put on it all the
utensils of the altar, which are used for the service there, the firepans, the forks, the shovels, and
the basins, all the utensils of the altar; and they
shall spread on it a covering of fine leather,[b] and
shall put its poles in place. 15 When Aaron and his
sons have finished covering the sanctuary and all
the furnishings of the sanctuary, as the camp sets
out, after that the Kohathites shall come to carry
these, but they must not touch the holy things, or
they will die. These are the things of the tent of
meeting that the Kohathites are to carry.

16 Eleazar son of Aaron the priest shall have
charge of the oil for the light, the fragrant incense,
the regular grain offering, and the anointing oil,
the oversight of all the tabernacle and all that is in
it, in the sanctuary and in its utensils.

17 Then the LORD spoke to Moses and Aaron,
saying: 18 You must not let the tribe of the clans
of the Kohathites be destroyed from among the
Levites. 19 This is how you must deal with them
in order that they may live and not die when they
come near to the most holy things: Aaron and
his sons shall go in and assign each to a particular
task or burden. 20 But the Kohathites[c] must not go
in to look on the holy things even for a moment;
otherwise they will die.

21 Then the LORD spoke to Moses, saying:
22 Take a census of the Gershonites also, by their

[a] Or *treaty*, or *testimony*; Heb *eduth* [b] Meaning of Heb uncertain [c] Heb *they*

ancestral houses and by their clans; 23from thirty
years old up to fifty years old you shall enroll them,
all who qualify to do work in the tent of meeting. 24This is the service of the clans of the Gershonites, in serving and bearing burdens: 25They
shall carry the curtains of the tabernacle, and the
tent of meeting with its covering, and the outer
covering of fine leather[a] that is on top of it, and
the screen for the entrance of the tent of meeting,
26and the hangings of the court, and the screen for
the entrance of the gate of the court that is around
the tabernacle and the altar, and their cords, and
all the equipment for their service; and they shall
do all that needs to be done with regard to them.
27All the service of the Gershonites shall be at the
command of Aaron and his sons, in all that they
are to carry, and in all that they have to do; and
you shall assign to their charge all that they are
to carry. 28This is the service of the clans of the
Gershonites relating to the tent of meeting, and
their responsibilities are to be under the oversight
of Ithamar son of Aaron the priest.

29 As for the Merarites, you shall enroll them
by their clans and their ancestral houses; 30from
thirty years old up to fifty years old you shall enroll them, everyone who qualifies to do the work
of the tent of meeting. 31This is what they are
charged to carry, as the whole of their service in
the tent of meeting: the frames of the tabernacle,
with its bars, pillars, and bases, 32and the pillars
of the court all around with their bases, pegs, and
cords, with all their equipment and all their related service; and you shall assign by name the objects that they are required to carry. 33This is the
service of the clans of the Merarites, the whole of
their service relating to the tent of meeting, under
the hand of Ithamar son of Aaron the priest.

34 So Moses and Aaron and the leaders of
the congregation enrolled the Kohathites, by
their clans and their ancestral houses, 35from
thirty years old up to fifty years old, everyone
who qualified for work relating to the tent of
meeting; 36and their enrollment by clans was two
thousand seven hundred fifty. 37This was the enrollment of the clans of the Kohathites, all who
served at the tent of meeting, whom Moses and
Aaron enrolled according to the commandment
of the LORD by Moses.

38 The enrollment of the Gershonites, by
their clans and their ancestral houses, 39from
thirty years old up to fifty years old, everyone
who qualified for work relating to the tent of
meeting— 40their enrollment by their clans and
their ancestral houses was two thousand six hundred thirty. 41This was the enrollment of the clans
of the Gershonites, all who served at the tent of
meeting, whom Moses and Aaron enrolled according to the commandment of the LORD.

42 The enrollment of the clans of the Merarites, by their clans and their ancestral houses,
43from thirty years old up to fifty years old, everyone who qualified for work relating to the tent of
meeting— 44their enrollment by their clans was
three thousand two hundred. 45This is the enrollment of the clans of the Merarites, whom Moses
and Aaron enrolled according to the commandment of the LORD by Moses.

46 All those who were enrolled of the Levites, whom Moses and Aaron and the leaders of
Israel enrolled, by their clans and their ancestral
houses, 47from thirty years old up to fifty years
old, everyone who qualified to do the work of service and the work of bearing burdens relating to
the tent of meeting, 48their enrollment was eight
thousand five hundred eighty. 49According to the
commandment of the LORD through Moses they
were appointed to their several tasks of serving or
carrying; thus they were enrolled by him, as the
LORD commanded Moses.

5 The LORD spoke to Moses, saying: 2Com-
mand the Israelites to put out of the camp
everyone who is leprous,[b] or has a discharge, and
everyone who is unclean through contact with a
corpse; 3you shall put out both male and female,
putting them outside the camp; they must not
defile their camp, where I dwell among them.
4The Israelites did so, putting them outside the
camp; as the LORD had spoken to Moses, so the
Israelites did.

5 The LORD spoke to Moses, saying: 6Speak

[a] Meaning of Heb uncertain [b] A term for several skin diseases; precise meaning uncertain

to the Israelites: When a man or a woman wrongs another, breaking faith with the LORD, that person incurs guilt 7and shall confess the sin that has been committed. The person shall make full restitution for the wrong, adding one-fifth to it, and giving it to the one who was wronged. 8If the injured party has no next of kin to whom restitution may be made for the wrong, the restitution for wrong shall go to the LORD for the priest, in addition to the ram of atonement with which atonement is made for the guilty party. 9Among all the sacred donations of the Israelites, every gift that they bring to the priest shall be his. 10The sacred donations of all are their own; whatever anyone gives to the priest shall be his.

11 The LORD spoke to Moses, saying: 12Speak to the Israelites and say to them: If any man's wife goes astray and is unfaithful to him, 13if a man has had intercourse with her but it is hidden from her husband, so that she is undetected though she has defiled herself, and there is no witness against her since she was not caught in the act; 14if a spirit of jealousy comes on him, and he is jealous of his wife who has defiled herself; or if a spirit of jealousy comes on him, and he is jealous of his wife, though she has not defiled herself; 15then the man shall bring his wife to the priest. And he shall bring the offering required for her, one-tenth of an ephah of barley flour. He shall pour no oil on it and put no frankincense on it, for it is a grain offering of jealousy, a grain offering of remembrance, bringing iniquity to remembrance.

16 Then the priest shall bring her near, and set her before the LORD; 17the priest shall take holy water in an earthen vessel, and take some of the dust that is on the floor of the tabernacle and put it into the water. 18The priest shall set the woman before the LORD, dishevel the woman's hair, and place in her hands the grain offering of remembrance, which is the grain offering of jealousy. In his own hand the priest shall have the water of bitterness that brings the curse. 19Then the priest shall make her take an oath, saying, "If no man has lain with you, if you have not turned aside to uncleanness while under your husband's authority, be immune to this water of bitterness that brings the curse. 20But if you have gone astray while under your husband's authority, if you have defiled yourself and some man other than your husband has had intercourse with you," 21—let the priest make the woman take the oath of the curse and say to the woman—"the LORD make you an execration and an oath among your people, when the LORD makes your uterus drop, your womb discharge; 22now may this water that brings the curse enter your bowels and make your womb discharge, your uterus drop!" And the woman shall say, "Amen. Amen."

23 Then the priest shall put these curses in writing, and wash them off into the water of bitterness. 24He shall make the woman drink the water of bitterness that brings the curse, and the water that brings the curse shall enter her and cause bitter pain. 25The priest shall take the grain offering of jealousy out of the woman's hand, and shall elevate the grain offering before the LORD and bring it to the altar; 26and the priest shall take a handful of the grain offering, as its memorial portion, and turn it into smoke on the altar, and afterward shall make the woman drink the water. 27When he has made her drink the water, then, if she has defiled herself and has been unfaithful to her husband, the water that brings the curse shall enter into her and cause bitter pain, and her womb shall discharge, her uterus drop, and the woman shall become an execration among her people. 28But if the woman has not defiled herself and is clean, then she shall be immune and be able to conceive children.

29 This is the law in cases of jealousy, when a wife, while under her husband's authority, goes astray and defiles herself, 30or when a spirit of jealousy comes on a man and he is jealous of his wife; then he shall set the woman before the LORD, and the priest shall apply this entire law to her. 31The man shall be free from iniquity, but the woman shall bear her iniquity.

6 The LORD spoke to Moses, saying: 2Speak to the Israelites and say to them: When either men or women make a special vow, the vow of a nazirite,[a] to separate themselves to the LORD,

[a] That is *one separated* or *one consecrated*

3they shall separate themselves from wine and
strong drink; they shall drink no wine vinegar or
other vinegar, and shall not drink any grape juice
or eat grapes, fresh or dried. 4All their days as nazirites[a] they shall eat nothing that is produced by
the grapevine, not even the seeds or the skins.

5 All the days of their nazirite vow no razor
shall come upon the head; until the time is completed for which they separate themselves to the
LORD, they shall be holy; they shall let the locks
of the head grow long.

6 All the days that they separate themselves to
the LORD they shall not go near a corpse. 7Even
if their father or mother, brother or sister, should
die, they may not defile themselves; because their
consecration to God is upon the head. 8All their
days as nazirites[a] they are holy to the LORD.

9 If someone dies very suddenly nearby, defiling the consecrated head, then they shall shave
the head on the day of their cleansing; on the
seventh day they shall shave it. 10On the eighth
day they shall bring two turtledoves or two young
pigeons to the priest at the entrance of the tent
of meeting, 11and the priest shall offer one as a
sin offering and the other as a burnt offering, and
make atonement for them, because they incurred
guilt by reason of the corpse. They shall sanctify
the head that same day, 12and separate themselves
to the LORD for their days as nazirites,[a] and bring
a male lamb a year old as a guilt offering. The former time shall be void, because the consecrated
head was defiled.

13 This is the law for the nazirites[a] when the
time of their consecration has been completed:
they shall be brought to the entrance of the tent
of meeting, 14and they shall offer their gift to the
LORD, one male lamb a year old without blemish as a burnt offering, one ewe lamb a year old
without blemish as a sin offering, one ram without blemish as an offering of well-being, 15and a
basket of unleavened bread, cakes of choice flour
mixed with oil and unleavened wafers spread
with oil, with their grain offering and their drink
offerings. 16The priest shall present them before
the LORD and offer their sin offering and burnt
offering, 17and shall offer the ram as a sacrifice
of well-being to the LORD, with the basket of
unleavened bread; the priest also shall make the
accompanying grain offering and drink offering.
18Then the nazirites[a] shall shave the consecrated
head at the entrance of the tent of meeting, and
shall take the hair from the consecrated head and
put it on the fire under the sacrifice of well-being.
19The priest shall take the shoulder of the ram,
when it is boiled, and one unleavened cake out of
the basket, and one unleavened wafer, and shall
put them in the palms of the nazirites,[a] after they
have shaved the consecrated head. 20Then the
priest shall elevate them as an elevation offering
before the LORD; they are a holy portion for the
priest, together with the breast that is elevated
and the thigh that is offered. After that the nazirites[a] may drink wine.

21 This is the law for the nazirites[a] who take
a vow. Their offering to the LORD must be in accordance with the nazirite[a] vow, apart from what
else they can afford. In accordance with whatever
vow they take, so they shall do, following the law
for their consecration.

22 The LORD spoke to Moses, saying: 23Speak
to Aaron and his sons, saying, Thus you shall
bless the Israelites: You shall say to them,

24 The LORD bless you and keep you;
25 the LORD make his face to shine upon you,
and be gracious to you;
26 the LORD lift up his countenance upon you,
and give you peace.

27 So they shall put my name on the Israelites, and I will bless them.

7 On the day when Moses had finished setting up the tabernacle, and had anointed and
consecrated it with all its furnishings, and had
anointed and consecrated the altar with all its
utensils, 2the leaders of Israel, heads of their ancestral houses, the leaders of the tribes, who were
over those who were enrolled, made offerings.
3They brought their offerings before the LORD,
six covered wagons and twelve oxen, a wagon for
every two of the leaders, and for each one an ox;
they presented them before the tabernacle. 4Then

[a] That is *those separated* or *those consecrated*

the LORD said to Moses: 5Accept these from
them, that they may be used in doing the service
of the tent of meeting, and give them to the Levites, to each according to his service. 6So Moses
took the wagons and the oxen, and gave them to
the Levites. 7Two wagons and four oxen he gave
to the Gershonites, according to their service;
8and four wagons and eight oxen he gave to the
Merarites, according to their service, under the
direction of Ithamar son of Aaron the priest. 9But
to the Kohathites he gave none, because they
were charged with the care of the holy things that
had to be carried on the shoulders.

10 The leaders also presented offerings for
the dedication of the altar at the time when it was
anointed; the leaders presented their offering before the altar. 11The LORD said to Moses: They
shall present their offerings, one leader each day,
for the dedication of the altar.

12 The one who presented his offering the
first day was Nahshon son of Amminadab, of the
tribe of Judah; 13his offering was one silver plate
weighing one hundred thirty shekels, one silver
basin weighing seventy shekels, according to
the shekel of the sanctuary, both of them full of
choice flour mixed with oil for a grain offering;
14one golden dish weighing ten shekels, full of incense; 15one young bull, one ram, one male lamb
a year old, for a burnt offering; 16one male goat
for a sin offering; 17and for the sacrifice of well-
being, two oxen, five rams, five male goats, and
five male lambs a year old. This was the offering
of Nahshon son of Amminadab.

18 On the second day Nethanel son of Zuar,
the leader of Issachar, presented an offering; 19he
presented for his offering one silver plate weighing one hundred thirty shekels, one silver basin
weighing seventy shekels, according to the shekel
of the sanctuary, both of them full of choice flour
mixed with oil for a grain offering; 20one golden
dish weighing ten shekels, full of incense; 21one
young bull, one ram, one male lamb a year old, as
a burnt offering; 22one male goat as a sin offering;
23and for the sacrifice of well-being, two oxen,
five rams, five male goats, and five male lambs a
year old. This was the offering of Nethanel son
of Zuar.

24 On the third day Eliab son of Helon, the
leader of the Zebulunites: 25his offering was one
silver plate weighing one hundred thirty shekels,
one silver basin weighing seventy shekels, according to the shekel of the sanctuary, both of
them full of choice flour mixed with oil for a grain
offering; 26one golden dish weighing ten shekels,
full of incense; 27one young bull, one ram, one
male lamb a year old, for a burnt offering; 28one
male goat for a sin offering; 29and for the sacrifice
of well-being, two oxen, five rams, five male goats,
and five male lambs a year old. This was the offering of Eliab son of Helon.

30 On the fourth day Elizur son of Shedeur,
the leader of the Reubenites: 31his offering was
one silver plate weighing one hundred thirty
shekels, one silver basin weighing seventy shekels,
according to the shekel of the sanctuary, both of
them full of choice flour mixed with oil for a grain
offering; 32one golden dish weighing ten shekels,
full of incense; 33one young bull, one ram, one
male lamb a year old, for a burnt offering; 34one
male goat for a sin offering; 35and for the sacrifice
of well-being, two oxen, five rams, five male goats,
and five male lambs a year old. This was the offering of Elizur son of Shedeur.

36 On the fifth day Shelumiel son of Zurishaddai, the leader of the Simeonites: 37his offering was one silver plate weighing one hundred
thirty shekels, one silver basin weighing seventy
shekels, according to the shekel of the sanctuary,
both of them full of choice flour mixed with oil
for a grain offering; 38one golden dish weighing
ten shekels, full of incense; 39one young bull, one
ram, one male lamb a year old, for a burnt offering; 40one male goat for a sin offering; 41and for
the sacrifice of well-being, two oxen, five rams,
five male goats, and five male lambs a year old.
This was the offering of Shelumiel son of Zurishaddai.

42 On the sixth day Eliasaph son of Deuel,
the leader of the Gadites: 43his offering was one
silver plate weighing one hundred thirty shekels,
one silver basin weighing seventy shekels, according to the shekel of the sanctuary, both of
them full of choice flour mixed with oil for a grain
offering; 44one golden dish weighing ten shekels,

full of incense; 45 one young bull, one ram, one
male lamb a year old, for a burnt offering; 46 one
male goat for a sin offering; 47 and for the sacrifice
of well-being, two oxen, five rams, five male goats,
and five male lambs a year old. This was the offering of Eliasaph son of Deuel.

48 On the seventh day Elishama son of Ammihud, the leader of the Ephraimites: 49 his offering was one silver plate weighing one hundred
thirty shekels, one silver basin weighing seventy
shekels, according to the shekel of the sanctuary,
both of them full of choice flour mixed with oil
for a grain offering; 50 one golden dish weighing
ten shekels, full of incense; 51 one young bull, one
ram, one male lamb a year old, for a burnt offering; 52 one male goat for a sin offering; 53 and for
the sacrifice of well-being, two oxen, five rams,
five male goats, and five male lambs a year old.
This was the offering of Elishama son of Ammihud.

54 On the eighth day Gamaliel son of Pedahzur, the leader of the Manassites: 55 his offering
was one silver plate weighing one hundred thirty
shekels, one silver basin weighing seventy shekels,
according to the shekel of the sanctuary, both of
them full of choice flour mixed with oil for a grain
offering; 56 one golden dish weighing ten shekels,
full of incense; 57 one young bull, one ram, one
male lamb a year old, for a burnt offering; 58 one
male goat for a sin offering; 59 and for the sacrifice
of well-being, two oxen, five rams, five male goats,
and five male lambs a year old. This was the offering of Gamaliel son of Pedahzur.

60 On the ninth day Abidan son of Gideoni,
the leader of the Benjaminites: 61 his offering was
one silver plate weighing one hundred thirty
shekels, one silver basin weighing seventy shekels,
according to the shekel of the sanctuary, both of
them full of choice flour mixed with oil for a grain
offering; 62 one golden dish weighing ten shekels,
full of incense; 63 one young bull, one ram, one
male lamb a year old, for a burnt offering; 64 one
male goat for a sin offering; 65 and for the sacrifice
of well-being, two oxen, five rams, five male goats,
and five male lambs a year old. This was the offering of Abidan son of Gideoni.

66 On the tenth day Ahiezer son of Ammishaddai, the leader of the Danites: 67 his offering
was one silver plate weighing one hundred thirty
shekels, one silver basin weighing seventy shekels,
according to the shekel of the sanctuary, both of
them full of choice flour mixed with oil for a grain
offering; 68 one golden dish weighing ten shekels,
full of incense; 69 one young bull, one ram, one
male lamb a year old, for a burnt offering; 70 one
male goat for a sin offering; 71 and for the sacrifice
of well-being, two oxen, five rams, five male goats,
and five male lambs a year old. This was the offering of Ahiezer son of Ammishaddai.

72 On the eleventh day Pagiel son of Ochran,
the leader of the Asherites: 73 his offering was one
silver plate weighing one hundred thirty shekels,
one silver basin weighing seventy shekels, according to the shekel of the sanctuary, both of
them full of choice flour mixed with oil for a grain
offering; 74 one golden dish weighing ten shekels,
full of incense; 75 one young bull, one ram, one
male lamb a year old, for a burnt offering; 76 one
male goat for a sin offering; 77 and for the sacrifice
of well-being, two oxen, five rams, five male goats,
and five male lambs a year old. This was the offering of Pagiel son of Ochran.

78 On the twelfth day Ahira son of Enan, the
leader of the Naphtalites: 79 his offering was one
silver plate weighing one hundred thirty shekels,
one silver basin weighing seventy shekels, according to the shekel of the sanctuary, both of
them full of choice flour mixed with oil for a grain
offering; 80 one golden dish weighing ten shekels,
full of incense; 81 one young bull, one ram, one
male lamb a year old, for a burnt offering; 82 one
male goat for a sin offering; 83 and for the sacrifice
of well-being, two oxen, five rams, five male goats,
and five male lambs a year old. This was the offering of Ahira son of Enan.

84 This was the dedication offering for the
altar, at the time when it was anointed, from
the leaders of Israel: twelve silver plates, twelve
silver basins, twelve golden dishes, 85 each silver
plate weighing one hundred thirty shekels and
each basin seventy, all the silver of the vessels
two thousand four hundred shekels according to
the shekel of the sanctuary, 86 the twelve golden
dishes, full of incense, weighing ten shekels apiece

according to the shekel of the sanctuary, all the
gold of the dishes being one hundred twenty
shekels; 87 all the livestock for the burnt offering
twelve bulls, twelve rams, twelve male lambs a
year old, with their grain offering; and twelve male
goats for a sin offering; 88 and all the livestock for
the sacrifice of well-being twenty-four bulls, the
rams sixty, the male goats sixty, the male lambs a
year old sixty. This was the dedication offering for
the altar, after it was anointed.

89 When Moses went into the tent of meeting to speak with the LORD,[a] he would hear the
voice speaking to him from above the mercy seat[b]
that was on the ark of the covenant[c] from between
the two cherubim; thus it spoke to him.

8 The LORD spoke to Moses, saying: 2 Speak
to Aaron and say to him: When you set up
the lamps, the seven lamps shall give light in
front of the lampstand. 3 Aaron did so; he set up
its lamps to give light in front of the lampstand,
as the LORD had commanded Moses. 4 Now this
was how the lampstand was made, out of hammered work of gold. From its base to its flowers,
it was hammered work; according to the pattern
that the LORD had shown Moses, so he made the
lampstand.

5 The LORD spoke to Moses, saying: 6 Take
the Levites from among the Israelites and cleanse
them. 7 Thus you shall do to them, to cleanse
them: sprinkle the water of purification on them,
have them shave their whole body with a razor
and wash their clothes, and so cleanse themselves. 8 Then let them take a young bull and its
grain offering of choice flour mixed with oil, and
you shall take another young bull for a sin offering. 9 You shall bring the Levites before the tent of
meeting, and assemble the whole congregation of
the Israelites. 10 When you bring the Levites before the LORD, the Israelites shall lay their hands
on the Levites, 11 and Aaron shall present the
Levites before the LORD as an elevation offering
from the Israelites, that they may do the service
of the LORD. 12 The Levites shall lay their hands
on the heads of the bulls, and he shall offer the
one for a sin offering and the other for a burnt
offering to the LORD, to make atonement for the
Levites. 13 Then you shall have the Levites stand
before Aaron and his sons, and you shall present
them as an elevation offering to the LORD.

14 Thus you shall separate the Levites from
among the other Israelites, and the Levites shall
be mine. 15 Thereafter the Levites may go in to
do service at the tent of meeting, once you have
cleansed them and presented them as an elevation offering. 16 For they are unreservedly given to
me from among the Israelites; I have taken them
for myself, in place of all that open the womb, the
firstborn of all the Israelites. 17 For all the firstborn among the Israelites are mine, both human
and animal. On the day that I struck down all the
firstborn in the land of Egypt I consecrated them
for myself, 18 but I have taken the Levites in place
of all the firstborn among the Israelites. 19 Moreover, I have given the Levites as a gift to Aaron
and his sons from among the Israelites, to do the
service for the Israelites at the tent of meeting,
and to make atonement for the Israelites, in order
that there may be no plague among the Israelites
for coming too close to the sanctuary.

20 Moses and Aaron and the whole congregation of the Israelites did with the Levites accordingly; the Israelites did with the Levites just
as the LORD had commanded Moses concerning
them. 21 The Levites purified themselves from sin
and washed their clothes; then Aaron presented
them as an elevation offering before the LORD,
and Aaron made atonement for them to cleanse
them. 22 Thereafter the Levites went in to do
their service in the tent of meeting in attendance
on Aaron and his sons. As the LORD had commanded Moses concerning the Levites, so they
did with them.

23 The LORD spoke to Moses, saying: 24 This
applies to the Levites: from twenty-five years old
and upward they shall begin to do duty in the service of the tent of meeting; 25 and from the age
of fifty years they shall retire from the duty of
the service and serve no more. 26 They may assist
their brothers in the tent of meeting in carrying
out their duties, but they shall perform no ser-

[a] Heb *him* [b] Or *the cover* [c] Or *treaty*, or *testimony*; Heb *eduth*

vice. Thus you shall do with the Levites in assign-
ing their duties.

9 The LORD spoke to Moses in the wilderness
of Sinai, in the first month of the second year
after they had come out of the land of Egypt, saying: 2 Let the Israelites keep the passover at its
appointed time. 3 On the fourteenth day of this
month, at twilight,[a] you shall keep it at its appointed time; according to all its statutes and all
its regulations you shall keep it. 4 So Moses told
the Israelites that they should keep the passover.
5 They kept the passover in the first month, on the
fourteenth day of the month, at twilight,[a] in the
wilderness of Sinai. Just as the LORD had commanded Moses, so the Israelites did. 6 Now there
were certain people who were unclean through
touching a corpse, so that they could not keep the
passover on that day. They came before Moses and
Aaron on that day, 7 and said to him, "Although we
are unclean through touching a corpse, why must
we be kept from presenting the LORD's offering at
its appointed time among the Israelites?" 8 Moses
spoke to them, "Wait, so that I may hear what the
LORD will command concerning you."

9 The LORD spoke to Moses, saying: 10 Speak
to the Israelites, saying: Anyone of you or your
descendants who is unclean through touching a
corpse, or is away on a journey, shall still keep the
passover to the LORD. 11 In the second month on
the fourteenth day, at twilight,[a] they shall keep it;
they shall eat it with unleavened bread and bitter
herbs. 12 They shall leave none of it until morning, nor break a bone of it; according to all the
statute for the passover they shall keep it. 13 But
anyone who is clean and is not on a journey, and
yet refrains from keeping the passover, shall be
cut off from the people for not presenting the
LORD's offering at its appointed time; such a one
shall bear the consequences for the sin. 14 Any
alien residing among you who wishes to keep
the passover to the LORD shall do so according
to the statute of the passover and according to its
regulation; you shall have one statute for both the
resident alien and the native.

15 On the day the tabernacle was set up,
the cloud covered the tabernacle, the tent of the
covenant;[b] and from evening until morning it
was over the tabernacle, having the appearance
of fire. 16 It was always so: the cloud covered it
by day[c] and the appearance of fire by night.
17 Whenever the cloud lifted from over the tent,
then the Israelites would set out; and in the place
where the cloud settled down, there the Israelites
would camp. 18 At the command of the LORD the
Israelites would set out, and at the command of
the LORD they would camp. As long as the cloud
rested over the tabernacle, they would remain
in camp. 19 Even when the cloud continued over
the tabernacle many days, the Israelites would
keep the charge of the LORD, and would not
set out. 20 Sometimes the cloud would remain a
few days over the tabernacle, and according to
the command of the LORD they would remain
in camp; then according to the command of
the LORD they would set out. 21 Sometimes the
cloud would remain from evening until morning; and when the cloud lifted in the morning,
they would set out, or if it continued for a day
and a night, when the cloud lifted they would set
out. 22 Whether it was two days, or a month, or
a longer time, that the cloud continued over the
tabernacle, resting upon it, the Israelites would
remain in camp and would not set out; but when
it lifted they would set out. 23 At the command
of the LORD they would camp, and at the command of the LORD they would set out. They kept
the charge of the LORD, at the command of the
LORD by Moses.

10 The LORD spoke to Moses, saying: 2 Make
two silver trumpets; you shall make them
of hammered work; and you shall use them for
summoning the congregation, and for breaking
camp. 3 When both are blown, the whole congregation shall assemble before you at the entrance
of the tent of meeting. 4 But if only one is blown,
then the leaders, the heads of the tribes of Israel,
shall assemble before you. 5 When you blow an
alarm, the camps on the east side shall set out;
6 when you blow a second alarm, the camps on
the south side shall set out. An alarm is to be

[a] Heb *between the two evenings* [b] Or *treaty*, or *testimony*; Heb *eduth* [c] Gk Syr Vg: Heb lacks *by day*

blown whenever they are to set out. [7]But when the assembly is to be gathered, you shall blow, but you shall not sound an alarm. [8]The sons of Aaron, the priests, shall blow the trumpets; this shall be a perpetual institution for you throughout your generations. [9]When you go to war in your land against the adversary who oppresses you, you shall sound an alarm with the trumpets, so that you may be remembered before the LORD your God and be saved from your enemies. [10]Also on your days of rejoicing, at your appointed festivals, and at the beginnings of your months, you shall blow the trumpets over your burnt offerings and over your sacrifices of well-being; they shall serve as a reminder on your behalf before the LORD your God: I am the LORD your God.

11 In the second year, in the second month, on the twentieth day of the month, the cloud lifted from over the tabernacle of the covenant.[a] [12]Then the Israelites set out by stages from the wilderness of Sinai, and the cloud settled down in the wilderness of Paran. [13]They set out for the first time at the command of the LORD by Moses. [14]The standard of the camp of Judah set out first, company by company, and over the whole company was Nahshon son of Amminadab. [15]Over the company of the tribe of Issachar was Nethanel son of Zuar; [16]and over the company of the tribe of Zebulun was Eliab son of Helon.

17 Then the tabernacle was taken down, and the Gershonites and the Merarites, who carried the tabernacle, set out. [18]Next the standard of the camp of Reuben set out, company by company; and over the whole company was Elizur son of Shedeur. [19]Over the company of the tribe of Simeon was Shelumiel son of Zurishaddai, [20]and over the company of the tribe of Gad was Eliasaph son of Deuel.

21 Then the Kohathites, who carried the holy things, set out; and the tabernacle was set up before their arrival. [22]Next the standard of the Ephraimite camp set out, company by company, and over the whole company was Elishama son of Ammihud. [23]Over the company of the tribe of Manasseh was Gamaliel son of Pedahzur, [24]and over the company of the tribe of Benjamin was Abidan son of Gideoni.

25 Then the standard of the camp of Dan, acting as the rear guard of all the camps, set out, company by company, and over the whole company was Ahiezer son of Ammishaddai. [26]Over the company of the tribe of Asher was Pagiel son of Ochran, [27]and over the company of the tribe of Naphtali was Ahira son of Enan. [28]This was the order of march of the Israelites, company by company, when they set out.

29 Moses said to Hobab son of Reuel the Midianite, Moses' father-in-law, "We are setting out for the place of which the LORD said, 'I will give it to you'; come with us, and we will treat you well; for the LORD has promised good to Israel." [30]But he said to him, "I will not go, but I will go back to my own land and to my kindred." [31]He said, "Do not leave us, for you know where we should camp in the wilderness, and you will serve as eyes for us. [32]Moreover, if you go with us, whatever good the LORD does for us, the same we will do for you."

33 So they set out from the mount of the LORD three days' journey with the ark of the covenant of the LORD going before them three days' journey, to seek out a resting place for them, [34]the cloud of the LORD being over them by day when they set out from the camp.

35 Whenever the ark set out, Moses would say,

"Arise, O LORD, let your enemies be
scattered,
and your foes flee before you."

[36]And whenever it came to rest, he would say,

"Return, O LORD of the ten thousand
thousands of Israel."[b]

11 Now when the people complained in the hearing of the LORD about their misfortunes, the LORD heard it and his anger was kindled. Then the fire of the LORD burned against them, and consumed some outlying parts of the camp. [2]But the people cried out to Moses; and Moses prayed to the LORD, and the fire abated. [3]So that place was called Taberah,[c] because the fire of the LORD burned against them.

[a] Or *treaty*, or *testimony*; Heb *eduth* [b] Meaning of Heb uncertain [c] That is *Burning*

Numbers 11:1-6

Michael Walzer has observed that "wherever people know the Bible, and experience oppression, the Exodus has sustained their spirits and (sometimes) inspired their resistance."[2] Numbers is different. Here the wilderness generation is depicted as fickle, sometimes cowardly, even base in their preference for the delicacies of Egypt over the austere subsistence diet of manna. The Gospel of John plays upon similar themes as Jesus rebukes the crowds for seeking "food that perishes" (John 6:26-27). Neither text justifies those with full stomachs showing disdain for the poor simply because they are preoccupied with securing their daily bread. The challenge posed in Numbers is that of perseverance in the hard work of forging a new, free people. That work requires sacrifice, but the sacrifice must be freely chosen.[18]

— *NE*

4 The rabble among them had a strong craving; and the Israelites also wept again, and said,
"If only we had meat to eat! 5We remember the
fish we used to eat in Egypt for nothing, the
cucumbers, the melons, the leeks, the onions,
and the garlic; 6but now our strength is dried
up, and there is nothing at all but this manna to
look at."

7 Now the manna was like coriander seed,
and its color was like the color of gum resin. 8The
people went around and gathered it, ground it in
mills or beat it in mortars, then boiled it in pots
and made cakes of it; and the taste of it was like
the taste of cakes baked with oil. 9When the dew
fell on the camp in the night, the manna would
fall with it.

10 Moses heard the people weeping throughout their families, all at the entrances of their
tents. Then the LORD became very angry, and
Moses was displeased. 11So Moses said to the
LORD, "Why have you treated your servant so
badly? Why have I not found favor in your sight,
that you lay the burden of all this people on me?
12Did I conceive all this people? Did I give birth
to them, that you should say to me, 'Carry them
in your bosom, as a nurse carries a sucking child,
to the land that you promised on oath to their
ancestors'? 13Where am I to get meat to give to
all this people? For they come weeping to me
and say, 'Give us meat to eat!' 14I am not able
to carry all this people alone, for they are too
heavy for me. 15If this is the way you are going
to treat me, put me to death at once—if I have
found favor in your sight—and do not let me see
my misery."

16 So the LORD said to Moses, "Gather for
me seventy of the elders of Israel, whom you
know to be the elders of the people and officers
over them; bring them to the tent of meeting, and
have them take their place there with you. 17I will
come down and talk with you there; and I will
take some of the spirit that is on you and put it on
them; and they shall bear the burden of the people along with you so that you will not bear it all
by yourself. 18And say to the people: Consecrate
yourselves for tomorrow, and you shall eat meat;

Numbers 11:11-15

Moses asks a series of rhetorical questions in verses 12-13, railing against God and demanding to know why God is treating him so badly. In his protest, Moses describes himself as a man trying to do a woman's job and God as the woman whose job Moses is forced to perform because she has abdicated her responsibilities. Moses did not give birth to them, God did. Moses is not equipped to nurse God's children; God must feed them. Using a feminine pronoun for God, Moses gives his notice as God's nanny in verse 15. In doing so Moses becomes the only person in the Bible to use a feminine pronoun for God.

— *WG*

for you have wailed in the hearing of the LORD,
saying, 'If only we had meat to eat! Surely it was
better for us in Egypt.' Therefore the LORD will
give you meat, and you shall eat. 19You shall eat
not only one day, or two days, or five days, or ten
days, or twenty days, 20but for a whole month—
until it comes out of your nostrils and becomes
loathsome to you—because you have rejected
the LORD who is among you, and have wailed before him, saying, 'Why did we ever leave Egypt?'"
21But Moses said, "The people I am with number six hundred thousand on foot; and you say, 'I
will give them meat, that they may eat for a whole
month'! 22Are there enough flocks and herds
to slaughter for them? Are there enough fish in
the sea to catch for them?" 23The LORD said to
Moses, "Is the LORD's power limited?[a] Now you
shall see whether my word will come true for you
or not."

24 So Moses went out and told the people
the words of the LORD; and he gathered seventy
elders of the people, and placed them all around
the tent. 25Then the LORD came down in the
cloud and spoke to him, and took some of the
spirit that was on him and put it on the seventy elders; and when the spirit rested upon them, they
prophesied. But they did not do so again.

26 Two men remained in the camp, one
named Eldad, and the other named Medad, and
the spirit rested on them; they were among those
registered, but they had not gone out to the tent,
and so they prophesied in the camp. 27And a
young man ran and told Moses, "Eldad and Medad are prophesying in the camp." 28And Joshua
son of Nun, the assistant of Moses, one of his
chosen men,[b] said, "My lord Moses, stop them!"
29But Moses said to him, "Are you jealous for
my sake? Would that all the LORD's people were
prophets, and that the LORD would put his spirit
on them!" 30And Moses and the elders of Israel
returned to the camp.

31 Then a wind went out from the LORD, and
it brought quails from the sea and let them fall
beside the camp, about a day's journey on this
side and a day's journey on the other side, all
around the camp, about two cubits deep on the
ground. 32So the people worked all that day and
night and all the next day, gathering the quails;
the least anyone gathered was ten homers; and
they spread them out for themselves all around
the camp. 33But while the meat was still between
their teeth, before it was consumed, the anger of
the LORD was kindled against the people, and the
LORD struck the people with a very great plague.
34So that place was called Kibroth-hattaavah,[c] because there they buried the people who had the
craving. 35From Kibroth-hattaavah the people
journeyed to Hazeroth.

12 While they were at Hazeroth, Miriam
and Aaron spoke against Moses because
of the Cushite woman whom he had married (for
he had indeed married a Cushite woman); 2and
they said, "Has the LORD spoken only through
Moses? Has he not spoken through us also?" And
the LORD heard it. 3Now the man Moses was very
humble,[d] more so than anyone else on the face of
the earth. 4Suddenly the LORD said to Moses,
Aaron, and Miriam, "Come out, you three, to the
tent of meeting." So the three of them came out.
5Then the LORD came down in a pillar of cloud,
and stood at the entrance of the tent, and called
Aaron and Miriam; and they both came forward.
6And he said, "Hear my words:

When there are prophets among you,
  I the LORD make myself known to them in visions;
  I speak to them in dreams.
7 Not so with my servant Moses;
  he is entrusted with all my house.
8 With him I speak face to face— clearly, not in riddles;
  and he beholds the form of the LORD.

Why then were you not afraid to speak against my
servant Moses?" 9And the anger of the LORD was
kindled against them, and he departed.

10 When the cloud went away from over
the tent, Miriam had become leprous,[e] as white
as snow. And Aaron turned towards Miriam and

[a] Heb *LORD's hand too short?* [b] Or *of Moses from his youth* [c] That is *Graves of craving* [d] Or *devout*
[e] A term for several skin diseases; precise meaning uncertain

saw that she was leprous. 11Then Aaron said to Moses, "Oh, my lord, do not punish us[a] for a sin that we have so foolishly committed. 12Do not let her be like one stillborn, whose flesh is half consumed when it comes out of its mother's womb." 13And Moses cried to the LORD, "O God, please heal her." 14But the LORD said to Moses, "If her father had but spit in her face, would she not bear her shame for seven days? Let her be shut out of the camp for seven days, and after that she may be brought in again." 15So Miriam was shut out of the camp for seven days; and the people did not set out on the march until Miriam had been brought in again. 16After that the people set out from Hazeroth, and camped in the wilderness of Paran.

13 The LORD said to Moses, 2"Send men to spy out the land of Canaan, which I am giving to the Israelites; from each of their ancestral tribes you shall send a man, every one a leader among them." 3So Moses sent them from the wilderness of Paran, according to the command of the LORD, all of them leading men among the Israelites. 4These were their names: From the tribe of Reuben, Shammua son of Zaccur; 5from the tribe of Simeon, Shaphat son of Hori; 6from the tribe of Judah, Caleb son of Jephunneh; 7from the tribe of Issachar, Igal son of Joseph; 8from the tribe of Ephraim, Hoshea son of Nun; 9from the tribe of Benjamin, Palti son of Raphu; 10from the tribe of Zebulun, Gaddiel son of Sodi; 11from the tribe of Joseph (that is, from the tribe of Manasseh), Gaddi son of Susi; 12from the tribe of Dan, Ammiel son of Gemalli; 13from the tribe of Asher, Sethur son of Michael; 14from the tribe of Naphtali, Nahbi son of Vophsi; 15from the tribe of Gad, Geuel son of Machi. 16These were the names of the men whom Moses sent to spy out the land. And Moses changed the name of Hoshea son of Nun to Joshua.

17 Moses sent them to spy out the land of Canaan, and said to them, "Go up there into the Negeb, and go up into the hill country, 18and see what the land is like, and whether the people who live in it are strong or weak, whether they are few or many, 19and whether the land they live in is good or bad, and whether the towns that they live in are unwalled or fortified, 20and whether the land is rich or poor, and whether there are trees in it or not. Be bold, and bring some of the fruit of the land." Now it was the season of the first ripe grapes.

21 So they went up and spied out the land from the wilderness of Zin to Rehob, near Lebo-hamath. 22They went up into the Negeb, and came to Hebron; and Ahiman, Sheshai, and Talmai, the Anakites, were there. (Hebron was built seven years before Zoan in Egypt.) 23And they came to the Wadi Eshcol, and cut down from there a branch with a single cluster of grapes, and they carried it on a pole between two of them. They also brought some pomegranates and figs. 24That place was called the Wadi Eshcol,[b] because of the cluster that the Israelites cut down from there.

25 At the end of forty days they returned from spying out the land. 26And they came to Moses and Aaron and to all the congregation of the Israelites in the wilderness of Paran, at Kadesh; they brought back word to them and to all the congregation, and showed them the fruit of the land. 27And they told him, "We came to the land to which you sent us; it flows with milk and honey, and this is its fruit. 28Yet the people who live in the land are strong, and the towns are fortified and very large; and besides, we saw the descendants of Anak there. 29The Amalekites live in the land of the Negeb; the Hittites, the Jebusites, and the Amorites live in the hill country; and the Canaanites live by the sea, and along the Jordan."

30 But Caleb quieted the people before Moses, and said, "Let us go up at once and occupy it, for we are well able to overcome it." 31Then the men who had gone up with him said, "We are not able to go up against this people, for they are stronger than we." 32So they brought to the Israelites an unfavorable report of the land that they had spied out, saying, "The land that we have gone through as spies is a land that devours its inhabitants; and all the people that we saw in it are of great size. 33There we saw the Nephilim

[a] Heb *do not lay sin upon us* [b] That is *Cluster*

(the Anakites come from the Nephilim); and to
ourselves we seemed like grasshoppers, and so we
seemed to them."

14 Then all the congregation raised a loud
cry, and the people wept that night. 2 And
all the Israelites complained against Moses and
Aaron; the whole congregation said to them,
"Would that we had died in the land of Egypt! Or
would that we had died in this wilderness! 3 Why
is the LORD bringing us into this land to fall by
the sword? Our wives and our little ones will become booty; would it not be better for us to go
back to Egypt?" 4 So they said to one another,
"Let us choose a captain, and go back to Egypt."

5 Then Moses and Aaron fell on their faces
before all the assembly of the congregation of the
Israelites. 6 And Joshua son of Nun and Caleb son
of Jephunneh, who were among those who had
spied out the land, tore their clothes 7 and said to
all the congregation of the Israelites, "The land
that we went through as spies is an exceedingly
good land. 8 If the LORD is pleased with us, he will
bring us into this land and give it to us, a land that
flows with milk and honey. 9 Only, do not rebel
against the LORD; and do not fear the people
of the land, for they are no more than bread for
us; their protection is removed from them, and
the LORD is with us; do not fear them." 10 But the
whole congregation threatened to stone them.

Then the glory of the LORD appeared at the
tent of meeting to all the Israelites. 11 And the
LORD said to Moses, "How long will this people
despise me? And how long will they refuse to
believe in me, in spite of all the signs that I have
done among them? 12 I will strike them with pestilence and disinherit them, and I will make of
you a nation greater and mightier than they."

13 But Moses said to the LORD, "Then the
Egyptians will hear of it, for in your might you
brought up this people from among them, 14 and
they will tell the inhabitants of this land. They
have heard that you, O LORD, are in the midst
of this people; for you, O LORD, are seen face to
face, and your cloud stands over them and you go
in front of them, in a pillar of cloud by day and
in a pillar of fire by night. 15 Now if you kill this
people all at one time, then the nations who have
heard about you will say, 16 'It is because the LORD
was not able to bring this people into the land he
swore to give them that he has slaughtered them
in the wilderness.' 17 And now, therefore, let the
power of the LORD be great in the way that you
promised when you spoke, saying,

18 'The LORD is slow to anger,
and abounding in steadfast love,
forgiving iniquity and transgression,
but by no means clearing the guilty,
visiting the iniquity of the parents
upon the children
to the third and the fourth generation.'

19 Forgive the iniquity of this people according
to the greatness of your steadfast love, just as you
have pardoned this people, from Egypt even until
now."

20 Then the LORD said, "I do forgive, just as
you have asked; 21 nevertheless—as I live, and as
all the earth shall be filled with the glory of the
LORD— 22 none of the people who have seen
my glory and the signs that I did in Egypt and
in the wilderness, and yet have tested me these
ten times and have not obeyed my voice, 23 shall
see the land that I swore to give to their ancestors; none of those who despised me shall see it.
24 But my servant Caleb, because he has a different spirit and has followed me wholeheartedly, I
will bring into the land into which he went, and
his descendants shall possess it. 25 Now, since the
Amalekites and the Canaanites live in the valleys,
turn tomorrow and set out for the wilderness by
the way to the Red Sea."[a]

26 And the LORD spoke to Moses and to
Aaron, saying: 27 How long shall this wicked congregation complain against me? I have heard the
complaints of the Israelites, which they complain
against me. 28 Say to them, "As I live," says the
LORD, "I will do to you the very things I heard
you say: 29 your dead bodies shall fall in this very
wilderness; and of all your number, included in
the census, from twenty years old and upward,
who have complained against me, 30 not one of

[a] Or *Sea of Reeds*

you shall come into the land in which I swore to
settle you, except Caleb son of Jephunneh and
Joshua son of Nun. 31But your little ones, who
you said would become booty, I will bring in, and
they shall know the land that you have despised.
32But as for you, your dead bodies shall fall in this
wilderness. 33And your children shall be shepherds in the wilderness for forty years, and shall
suffer for your faithlessness, until the last of your
dead bodies lies in the wilderness. 34According
to the number of the days in which you spied
out the land, forty days, for every day a year, you
shall bear your iniquity, forty years, and you shall
know my displeasure." 35I the LORD have spoken;
surely I will do thus to all this wicked congregation gathered together against me: in this wilderness they shall come to a full end, and there they
shall die.

36 And the men whom Moses sent to spy
out the land, who returned and made all the
congregation complain against him by bringing
a bad report about the land— 37the men who
brought an unfavorable report about the land
died by a plague before the LORD. 38But Joshua
son of Nun and Caleb son of Jephunneh alone
remained alive, of those men who went to spy
out the land.

39 When Moses told these words to all the Israelites, the people mourned greatly. 40They rose
early in the morning and went up to the heights
of the hill country, saying, "Here we are. We will
go up to the place that the LORD has promised,
for we have sinned." 41But Moses said, "Why do
you continue to transgress the command of the
LORD? That will not succeed. 42Do not go up, for
the LORD is not with you; do not let yourselves
be struck down before your enemies. 43For the
Amalekites and the Canaanites will confront you
there, and you shall fall by the sword; because you
have turned back from following the LORD, the
LORD will not be with you." 44But they presumed
to go up to the heights of the hill country, even
though the ark of the covenant of the LORD, and
Moses, had not left the camp. 45Then the Amalekites and the Canaanites who lived in that hill
country came down and defeated them, pursuing
them as far as Hormah.

15 The LORD spoke to Moses, saying: 2Speak
to the Israelites and say to them: When
you come into the land you are to inhabit, which
I am giving you, 3and you make an offering
by fire to the LORD from the herd or from the
flock—whether a burnt offering or a sacrifice,
to fulfill a vow or as a freewill offering or at your
appointed festivals—to make a pleasing odor for
the LORD, 4then whoever presents such an offering to the LORD shall present also a grain offering, one-tenth of an ephah of choice flour, mixed
with one-fourth of a hin of oil. 5Moreover, you
shall offer one-fourth of a hin of wine as a drink
offering with the burnt offering or the sacrifice,
for each lamb. 6For a ram, you shall offer a grain
offering, two-tenths of an ephah of choice flour
mixed with one-third of a hin of oil; 7and as a
drink offering you shall offer one-third of a hin
of wine, a pleasing odor to the LORD. 8When
you offer a bull as a burnt offering or a sacrifice,
to fulfill a vow or as an offering of well-being to
the LORD, 9then you shall present with the bull a
grain offering, three-tenths of an ephah of choice
flour, mixed with half a hin of oil, 10and you shall
present as a drink offering half a hin of wine, as an
offering by fire, a pleasing odor to the LORD.

11 Thus it shall be done for each ox or ram, or
for each of the male lambs or the kids. 12Accord-
ing to the number that you offer, so you shall do
with each and every one. 13Every native Israelite
shall do these things in this way, in presenting an
offering by fire, a pleasing odor to the LORD. 14An
alien who lives with you, or who takes up permanent residence among you, and wishes to offer an
offering by fire, a pleasing odor to the LORD, shall
do as you do. 15As for the assembly, there shall be
for both you and the resident alien a single statute, a perpetual statute throughout your generations; you and the alien shall be alike before the
LORD. 16You and the alien who resides with you
shall have the same law and the same ordinance.

17 The LORD spoke to Moses, saying: 18Speak
to the Israelites and say to them: After you come
into the land to which I am bringing you, 19when-
ever you eat of the bread of the land, you shall
present a donation to the LORD. 20From your
first batch of dough you shall present a loaf as a

donation; you shall present it just as you present a
donation from the threshing floor. 21 Throughout
your generations you shall give to the LORD a donation from the first of your batch of dough.

22 But if you unintentionally fail to observe
all these commandments that the LORD has
spoken to Moses— 23 everything that the LORD
has commanded you by Moses, from the day
the LORD gave commandment and thereafter,
throughout your generations— 24 then if it was
done unintentionally without the knowledge of
the congregation, the whole congregation shall
offer one young bull for a burnt offering, a pleasing
odor to the LORD, together with its grain offering
and its drink offering, according to the ordinance,
and one male goat for a sin offering. 25 The priest
shall make atonement for all the congregation of
the Israelites, and they shall be forgiven; it was
unintentional, and they have brought their offering, an offering by fire to the LORD, and their sin
offering before the LORD, for their error. 26 All the
congregation of the Israelites shall be forgiven, as
well as the aliens residing among them, because
the whole people was involved in the error.

27 An individual who sins unintentionally
shall present a female goat a year old for a sin
offering. 28 And the priest shall make atonement
before the LORD for the one who commits an error, when it is unintentional, to make atonement
for the person, who then shall be forgiven. 29 For
both the native among the Israelites and the alien
residing among them—you shall have the same
law for anyone who acts in error. 30 But whoever
acts high-handedly, whether a native or an alien,
affronts the LORD, and shall be cut off from among
the people. 31 Because of having despised the word
of the LORD and broken his commandment, such
a person shall be utterly cut off and bear the guilt.

32 When the Israelites were in the wilderness, they found a man gathering sticks on the
sabbath day. 33 Those who found him gathering
sticks brought him to Moses, Aaron, and to the
whole congregation. 34 They put him in custody,
because it was not clear what should be done to
him. 35 Then the LORD said to Moses, "The man
shall be put to death; all the congregation shall
stone him outside the camp." 36 The whole congregation brought him outside the camp and
stoned him to death, just as the LORD had commanded Moses.

37 The LORD said to Moses: 38 Speak to the
Israelites, and tell them to make fringes on the
corners of their garments throughout their generations and to put a blue cord on the fringe at
each corner. 39 You have the fringe so that, when
you see it, you will remember all the commandments of the LORD and do them, and not follow
the lust of your own heart and your own eyes.
40 So you shall remember and do all my commandments, and you shall be holy to your God.
41 I am the LORD your God, who brought you out
of the land of Egypt, to be your God: I am the
LORD your God.

16 Now Korah son of Izhar son of Kohath
son of Levi, along with Dathan and Abiram sons of Eliab, and On son of Peleth—
descendants of Reuben—took 2 two hundred fifty
Israelite men, leaders of the congregation, chosen
from the assembly, well-known men,[a] and they
confronted Moses. 3 They assembled against Moses and against Aaron, and said to them, "You
have gone too far! All the congregation are holy,
every one of them, and the LORD is among them.
So why then do you exalt yourselves above the assembly of the LORD?" 4 When Moses heard it, he
fell on his face. 5 Then he said to Korah and all his
company, "In the morning the LORD will make
known who is his, and who is holy, and who will
be allowed to approach him; the one whom he
will choose he will allow to approach him. 6 Do
this: take censers, Korah and all your[b] company,
7 and tomorrow put fire in them, and lay incense
on them before the LORD; and the man whom
the LORD chooses shall be the holy one. You Levites have gone too far!" 8 Then Moses said to Korah, "Hear now, you Levites! 9 Is it too little for
you that the God of Israel has separated you from
the congregation of Israel, to allow you to approach him in order to perform the duties of the
LORD's tabernacle, and to stand before the con-

[a] Cn: Heb *and they confronted Moses, and two hundred fifty men . . . well-known men* [b] Heb *his*

gregation and serve them? [10]He has allowed you
to approach him, and all your brother Levites
with you; yet you seek the priesthood as well!
[11]Therefore you and all your company have gathered together against the LORD. What is Aaron
that you rail against him?"

12 Moses sent for Dathan and Abiram sons
of Eliab; but they said, "We will not come! [13]Is it
too little that you have brought us up out of a land
flowing with milk and honey to kill us in the wilderness, that you must also lord it over us? [14]It is
clear you have not brought us into a land flowing
with milk and honey, or given us an inheritance
of fields and vineyards. Would you put out the
eyes of these men? We will not come!"

15 Moses was very angry and said to the
LORD, "Pay no attention to their offering. I have
not taken one donkey from them, and I have not
harmed any one of them." [16]And Moses said to
Korah, "As for you and all your company, be present tomorrow before the LORD, you and they and
Aaron; [17]and let each one of you take his censer,
and put incense on it, and each one of you present his censer before the LORD, two hundred
fifty censers; you also, and Aaron, each his censer." [18]So each man took his censer, and they put
fire in the censers and laid incense on them, and
they stood at the entrance of the tent of meeting
with Moses and Aaron. [19]Then Korah assembled
the whole congregation against them at the entrance of the tent of meeting. And the glory of the
LORD appeared to the whole congregation.

20 Then the LORD spoke to Moses and to
Aaron, saying: [21]Separate yourselves from this
congregation, so that I may consume them in
a moment. [22]They fell on their faces, and said,
"O God, the God of the spirits of all flesh, shall
one person sin and you become angry with the
whole congregation?"

23 And the LORD spoke to Moses, saying:
[24]Say to the congregation: Get away from the
dwellings of Korah, Dathan, and Abiram. [25]So
Moses got up and went to Dathan and Abiram;
the elders of Israel followed him. [26]He said to the
congregation, "Turn away from the tents of these
wicked men, and touch nothing of theirs, or you
will be swept away for all their sins." [27]So they got
away from the dwellings of Korah, Dathan, and
Abiram; and Dathan and Abiram came out and
stood at the entrance of their tents, together with
their wives, their children, and their little ones.
[28]And Moses said, "This is how you shall know
that the LORD has sent me to do all these works;
it has not been of my own accord: [29]If these people die a natural death, or if a natural fate comes
on them, then the LORD has not sent me. [30]But if
the LORD creates something new, and the ground
opens its mouth and swallows them up, with all
that belongs to them, and they go down alive into
Sheol, then you shall know that these men have
despised the LORD."

31 As soon as he finished speaking all these
words, the ground under them was split apart.
[32]The earth opened its mouth and swallowed
them up, along with their households—everyone
who belonged to Korah and all their goods. [33]So
they with all that belonged to them went down
alive into Sheol; the earth closed over them, and
they perished from the midst of the assembly.
[34]All Israel around them fled at their outcry, for
they said, "The earth will swallow us too!" [35]And
fire came out from the LORD and consumed the
two hundred fifty men offering the incense.

36[a] Then the LORD spoke to Moses, saying:
[37]Tell Eleazar son of Aaron the priest to take the
censers out of the blaze; then scatter the fire far
and wide. [38]For the censers of these sinners have
become holy at the cost of their lives. Make them
into hammered plates as a covering for the altar,
for they presented them before the LORD and
they became holy. Thus they shall be a sign to the
Israelites. [39]So Eleazar the priest took the bronze
censers that had been presented by those who
were burned; and they were hammered out as a
covering for the altar— [40]a reminder to the Israelites that no outsider, who is not of the descendants of Aaron, shall approach to offer incense
before the LORD, so as not to become like Korah
and his company—just as the LORD had said to
him through Moses.

[a] Ch 17.1 in Heb

41 On the next day, however, the whole congregation of the Israelites rebelled against Moses
and against Aaron, saying, "You have killed the
people of the LORD." 42 And when the congregation had assembled against them, Moses and
Aaron turned toward the tent of meeting; the
cloud had covered it and the glory of the LORD
appeared. 43 Then Moses and Aaron came to the
front of the tent of meeting, 44 and the LORD
spoke to Moses, saying, 45 "Get away from this
congregation, so that I may consume them in a
moment." And they fell on their faces. 46 Moses
said to Aaron, "Take your censer, put fire on it
from the altar and lay incense on it, and carry
it quickly to the congregation and make atonement for them. For wrath has gone out from the
LORD; the plague has begun." 47 So Aaron took it
as Moses had ordered, and ran into the middle
of the assembly, where the plague had already
begun among the people. He put on the incense,
and made atonement for the people. 48 He stood
between the dead and the living; and the plague
was stopped. 49 Those who died by the plague
were fourteen thousand seven hundred, besides
those who died in the affair of Korah. 50 When the
plague was stopped, Aaron returned to Moses at
the entrance of the tent of meeting.

17 [a] The LORD spoke to Moses, saying:
2 Speak to the Israelites, and get twelve
staffs from them, one for each ancestral house,
from all the leaders of their ancestral houses.
Write each man's name on his staff, 3 and write
Aaron's name on the staff of Levi. For there shall
be one staff for the head of each ancestral house.
4 Place them in the tent of meeting before the covenant,[b] where I meet with you. 5 And the staff of
the man whom I choose shall sprout; thus I will
put a stop to the complaints of the Israelites that
they continually make against you. 6 Moses spoke
to the Israelites; and all their leaders gave him
staffs, one for each leader, according to their ancestral houses, twelve staffs; and the staff of Aaron
was among theirs. 7 So Moses placed the staffs before the LORD in the tent of the covenant.[b]

8 When Moses went into the tent of the covenant[b] on the next day, the staff of Aaron for the
house of Levi had sprouted. It put forth buds, produced blossoms, and bore ripe almonds. 9 Then
Moses brought out all the staffs from before the
LORD to all the Israelites; and they looked, and
each man took his staff. 10 And the LORD said to
Moses, "Put back the staff of Aaron before the
covenant,[b] to be kept as a warning to rebels, so
that you may make an end of their complaints
against me, or else they will die." 11 Moses did so;
just as the LORD commanded him, so he did.

12 The Israelites said to Moses, "We are perishing; we are lost, all of us are lost! 13 Everyone
who approaches the tabernacle of the LORD will
die. Are we all to perish?"

18 The LORD said to Aaron: You and your
sons and your ancestral house with you
shall bear responsibility for offenses connected
with the sanctuary, while you and your sons alone
shall bear responsibility for offenses connected
with the priesthood. 2 So bring with you also your
brothers of the tribe of Levi, your ancestral tribe,
in order that they may be joined to you, and serve
you while you and your sons with you are in front
of the tent of the covenant.[b] 3 They shall perform
duties for you and for the whole tent. But they
must not approach either the utensils of the sanctuary or the altar, otherwise both they and you
will die. 4 They are attached to you in order to
perform the duties of the tent of meeting, for all
the service of the tent; no outsider shall approach
you. 5 You yourselves shall perform the duties of
the sanctuary and the duties of the altar, so that
wrath may never again come upon the Israelites.
6 It is I who now take your brother Levites from
among the Israelites; they are now yours as a gift,
dedicated to the LORD, to perform the service of
the tent of meeting. 7 But you and your sons with
you shall diligently perform your priestly duties
in all that concerns the altar and the area behind
the curtain. I give your priesthood as a gift;[c] any
outsider who approaches shall be put to death.

8 The LORD spoke to Aaron: I have given
you charge of the offerings made to me, all the
holy gifts of the Israelites; I have given them to

[a] Ch 17.16 in Heb [b] Or *treaty*, or *testimony*; Heb *eduth* [c] Heb *as a service of gift*

you and your sons as a priestly portion due you
in perpetuity. 9This shall be yours from the most
holy things, reserved from the fire: every offering
of theirs that they render to me as a most holy
thing, whether grain offering, sin offering, or
guilt offering, shall belong to you and your sons.
10As a most holy thing you shall eat it; every male
may eat it; it shall be holy to you. 11This also is
yours: I have given to you, together with your
sons and daughters, as a perpetual due, whatever
is set aside from the gifts of all the elevation offerings of the Israelites; everyone who is clean in
your house may eat them. 12All the best of the
oil and all the best of the wine and of the grain,
the choice produce that they give to the LORD, I
have given to you. 13The first fruits of all that is in
their land, which they bring to the LORD, shall be
yours; everyone who is clean in your house may
eat of it. 14Every devoted thing in Israel shall be
yours. 15The first issue of the womb of all creatures, human and animal, which is offered to the
LORD, shall be yours; but the firstborn of human
beings you shall redeem, and the firstborn of unclean animals you shall redeem. 16Their redemption price, reckoned from one month of age, you
shall fix at five shekels of silver, according to the
shekel of the sanctuary (that is, twenty gerahs).
17But the firstborn of a cow, or the firstborn of
a sheep, or the firstborn of a goat, you shall not
redeem; they are holy. You shall dash their blood
on the altar, and shall turn their fat into smoke
as an offering by fire for a pleasing odor to the
LORD; 18but their flesh shall be yours, just as the
breast that is elevated and as the right thigh are
yours. 19All the holy offerings that the Israelites
present to the LORD I have given to you, together
with your sons and daughters, as a perpetual due;
it is a covenant of salt forever before the LORD
for you and your descendants as well. 20Then the
LORD said to Aaron: You shall have no allotment
in their land, nor shall you have any share among
them; I am your share and your possession among
the Israelites.

21 To the Levites I have given every tithe in
Israel for a possession in return for the service
that they perform, the service in the tent of meeting. 22From now on the Israelites shall no longer
approach the tent of meeting, or else they will incur guilt and die. 23But the Levites shall perform
the service of the tent of meeting, and they shall
bear responsibility for their own offenses; it shall
be a perpetual statute throughout your generations. But among the Israelites they shall have no
allotment, 24because I have given to the Levites
as their portion the tithe of the Israelites, which
they set apart as an offering to the LORD. Therefore I have said of them that they shall have no
allotment among the Israelites.

25 Then the LORD spoke to Moses, saying:
26You shall speak to the Levites, saying: When
you receive from the Israelites the tithe that I
have given you from them for your portion, you
shall set apart an offering from it to the LORD, a
tithe of the tithe. 27It shall be reckoned to you as
your gift, the same as the grain of the threshing
floor and the fullness of the wine press. 28Thus
you also shall set apart an offering to the LORD
from all the tithes that you receive from the Israelites; and from them you shall give the LORD's
offering to the priest Aaron. 29Out of all the gifts
to you, you shall set apart every offering due to
the LORD; the best of all of them is the part to
be consecrated. 30Say also to them: When you
have set apart the best of it, then the rest shall be
reckoned to the Levites as produce of the threshing floor, and as produce of the wine press. 31You
may eat it in any place, you and your households;
for it is your payment for your service in the tent
of meeting. 32You shall incur no guilt by reason of
it, when you have offered the best of it. But you
shall not profane the holy gifts of the Israelites,
on pain of death.

19 The LORD spoke to Moses and Aaron,
saying: 2This is a statute of the law that the
LORD has commanded: Tell the Israelites to bring
you a red heifer without defect, in which there is
no blemish and on which no yoke has been laid.
3You shall give it to the priest Eleazar, and it shall
be taken outside the camp and slaughtered in
his presence. 4The priest Eleazar shall take some
of its blood with his finger and sprinkle it seven
times towards the front of the tent of meeting.
5Then the heifer shall be burned in his sight; its
skin, its flesh, and its blood, with its dung, shall

be burned. 6The priest shall take cedarwood, hyssop, and crimson material, and throw them into
the fire in which the heifer is burning. 7Then the
priest shall wash his clothes and bathe his body
in water, and afterwards he may come into the
camp; but the priest shall remain unclean until
evening. 8The one who burns the heifer[a] shall
wash his clothes in water and bathe his body in
water; he shall remain unclean until evening.
9Then someone who is clean shall gather up the
ashes of the heifer, and deposit them outside the
camp in a clean place; and they shall be kept for
the congregation of the Israelites for the water for
cleansing. It is a purification offering. 10The one
who gathers the ashes of the heifer shall wash his
clothes and be unclean until evening.

This shall be a perpetual statute for the Israelites and for the alien residing among them.
11Those who touch the dead body of any human
being shall be unclean seven days. 12They shall
purify themselves with the water on the third day
and on the seventh day, and so be clean; but if they
do not purify themselves on the third day and on
the seventh day, they will not become clean. 13All
who touch a corpse, the body of a human being
who has died, and do not purify themselves, defile
the tabernacle of the LORD; such persons shall be
cut off from Israel. Since water for cleansing was
not dashed on them, they remain unclean; their
uncleanness is still on them.

14 This is the law when someone dies in a
tent: everyone who comes into the tent, and everyone who is in the tent, shall be unclean seven
days. 15And every open vessel with no cover fastened on it is unclean. 16Whoever in the open
field touches one who has been killed by a sword,
or who has died naturally,[b] or a human bone, or
a grave, shall be unclean seven days. 17For the
unclean they shall take some ashes of the burnt
purification offering, and running water shall be
added in a vessel; 18then a clean person shall take
hyssop, dip it in the water, and sprinkle it on the
tent, on all the furnishings, on the persons who
were there, and on whoever touched the bone,
the slain, the corpse, or the grave. 19The clean
person shall sprinkle the unclean ones on the
third day and on the seventh day, thus purifying
them on the seventh day. Then they shall wash
their clothes and bathe themselves in water, and
at evening they shall be clean. 20Any who are unclean but do not purify themselves, those persons
shall be cut off from the assembly, for they have
defiled the sanctuary of the LORD. Since the water for cleansing has not been dashed on them,
they are unclean.

21 It shall be a perpetual statute for them.
The one who sprinkles the water for cleansing
shall wash his clothes, and whoever touches the
water for cleansing shall be unclean until evening.
22Whatever the unclean person touches shall be
unclean, and anyone who touches it shall be unclean until evening.

20 The Israelites, the whole congregation,
came into the wilderness of Zin in the
first month, and the people stayed in Kadesh.
Miriam died there, and was buried there.

2 Now there was no water for the congregation; so they gathered together against Moses and
against Aaron. 3The people quarreled with Moses
and said, "Would that we had died when our
kindred died before the LORD! 4Why have you
brought the assembly of the LORD into this wilderness for us and our livestock to die here? 5Why
have you brought us up out of Egypt, to bring us
to this wretched place? It is no place for grain, or
figs, or vines, or pomegranates; and there is no
water to drink." 6Then Moses and Aaron went
away from the assembly to the entrance of the
tent of meeting; they fell on their faces, and the
glory of the LORD appeared to them. 7The LORD
spoke to Moses, saying: 8Take the staff, and assemble the congregation, you and your brother
Aaron, and command the rock before their eyes
to yield its water. Thus you shall bring water out
of the rock for them; thus you shall provide drink
for the congregation and their livestock.

9 So Moses took the staff from before the
LORD, as he had commanded him. 10Moses and
Aaron gathered the assembly together before the
rock, and he said to them, "Listen, you rebels,

[a] Heb *it* [b] Heb lacks *naturally*

shall we bring water for you out of this rock?" 11 Then Moses lifted up his hand and struck the rock twice with his staff; water came out abundantly, and the congregation and their livestock drank. 12 But the LORD said to Moses and Aaron, "Because you did not trust in me, to show my holiness before the eyes of the Israelites, therefore you shall not bring this assembly into the land that I have given them." 13 These are the waters of Meribah,[a] where the people of Israel quarreled with the LORD, and by which he showed his holiness.

14 Moses sent messengers from Kadesh to the king of Edom, "Thus says your brother Israel: You know all the adversity that has befallen us: 15 how our ancestors went down to Egypt, and we lived in Egypt a long time; and the Egyptians oppressed us and our ancestors; 16 and when we cried to the LORD, he heard our voice, and sent an angel and brought us out of Egypt; and here we are in Kadesh, a town on the edge of your territory. 17 Now let us pass through your land. We will not pass through field or vineyard, or drink water from any well; we will go along the King's Highway, not turning aside to the right hand or to the left until we have passed through your territory."

18 But Edom said to him, "You shall not pass through, or we will come out with the sword against you." 19 The Israelites said to him, "We will stay on the highway; and if we drink of your water, we and our livestock, then we will pay for it. It is only a small matter; just let us pass through on foot." 20 But he said, "You shall not pass through." And Edom came out against them with a large force, heavily armed. 21 Thus Edom refused to give Israel passage through their territory; so Israel turned away from them.

22 They set out from Kadesh, and the Israelites, the whole congregation, came to Mount Hor. 23 Then the LORD said to Moses and Aaron at Mount Hor, on the border of the land of Edom, 24 "Let Aaron be gathered to his people. For he shall not enter the land that I have given to the Israelites, because you rebelled against my command at the waters of Meribah. 25 Take Aaron and his son Eleazar, and bring them up Mount Hor; 26 strip Aaron of his vestments, and put them on his son Eleazar. But Aaron shall be gathered to his people,[b] and shall die there." 27 Moses did as the LORD had commanded; they went up Mount Hor in the sight of the whole congregation. 28 Moses stripped Aaron of his vestments, and put them on his son Eleazar; and Aaron died there on the top of the mountain. Moses and Eleazar came down from the mountain. 29 When all the congregation saw that Aaron had died, all the house of Israel mourned for Aaron thirty days.

21 When the Canaanite, the king of Arad, who lived in the Negeb, heard that Israel was coming by the way of Atharim, he fought against Israel and took some of them captive. 2 Then Israel made a vow to the LORD and said, "If you will indeed give this people into our hands, then we will utterly destroy their towns." 3 The LORD listened to the voice of Israel, and handed over the Canaanites; and they utterly destroyed them and their towns; so the place was called Hormah.[c]

4 From Mount Hor they set out by the way to the Red Sea,[d] to go around the land of Edom; but the people became impatient on the way. 5 The people spoke against God and against Moses, "Why have you brought us up out of Egypt to die in the wilderness? For there is no food and no water, and we detest this miserable food." 6 Then the LORD sent poisonous[e] serpents among the people, and they bit the people, so that many Israelites died. 7 The people came to Moses and said, "We have sinned by speaking against the LORD and against you; pray to the LORD to take away the serpents from us." So Moses prayed for the people. 8 And the LORD said to Moses, "Make a poisonous[f] serpent, and set it on a pole; and everyone who is bitten shall look at it and live." 9 So Moses made a serpent of bronze, and put it upon a pole; and whenever a serpent bit someone, that person would look at the serpent of bronze and live.

[a] That is *Quarrel* [b] Heb lacks *to his people* [c] Heb *Destruction* [d] Or *Sea of Reeds* [e] Or *fiery*; Heb *seraphim*
[f] Or *fiery*; Heb *seraph*

10 The Israelites set out, and camped in
Oboth. 11 They set out from Oboth, and camped
at Iye-abarim, in the wilderness bordering Moab
toward the sunrise. 12 From there they set out, and
camped in the Wadi Zered. 13 From there they set
out, and camped on the other side of the Arnon,
in[a] the wilderness that extends from the boundary of the Amorites; for the Arnon is the boundary of Moab, between Moab and the Amorites.
14 Wherefore it is said in the Book of the Wars of
the LORD,

"Waheb in Suphah and the wadis.
The Arnon 15 and the slopes of the wadis
that extend to the seat of Ar,
and lie along the border of Moab."[b]

16 From there they continued to Beer;[c] that
is the well of which the LORD said to Moses,
"Gather the people together, and I will give them
water." 17 Then Israel sang this song:

"Spring up, O well!—Sing to it!—
18 the well that the leaders sank,
that the nobles of the people dug,
with the scepter, with the staff."

From the wilderness to Mattanah, 19 from Mattanah to Nahaliel, from Nahaliel to Bamoth, 20 and
from Bamoth to the valley lying in the region of
Moab by the top of Pisgah that overlooks the
wasteland.[d]

21 Then Israel sent messengers to King Sihon of the Amorites, saying, 22 "Let me pass
through your land; we will not turn aside into
field or vineyard; we will not drink the water of
any well; we will go by the King's Highway until we have passed through your territory." 23 But
Sihon would not allow Israel to pass through his
territory. Sihon gathered all his people together,
and went out against Israel to the wilderness; he
came to Jahaz, and fought against Israel. 24 Israel
put him to the sword, and took possession of his
land from the Arnon to the Jabbok, as far as to the
Ammonites; for the boundary of the Ammonites
was strong. 25 Israel took all these towns, and Israel settled in all the towns of the Amorites, in
Heshbon, and in all its villages. 26 For Heshbon
was the city of King Sihon of the Amorites, who
had fought against the former king of Moab and
captured all his land as far as the Arnon. 27 Therefore the ballad singers say,

"Come to Heshbon, let it be built;
let the city of Sihon be established.
28 For fire came out from Heshbon,
flame from the city of Sihon.
It devoured Ar of Moab,
and swallowed up[e] the heights of the
Arnon.
29 Woe to you, O Moab!
You are undone, O people of Chemosh!
He has made his sons fugitives,
and his daughters captives,
to an Amorite king, Sihon.
30 So their posterity perished
from Heshbon[f] to Dibon,
and we laid waste until fire spread to
Medeba."[g]

31 Thus Israel settled in the land of the Amorites. 32 Moses sent to spy out Jazer; and they captured its villages, and dispossessed the Amorites
who were there.

33 Then they turned and went up the road to
Bashan; and King Og of Bashan came out against
them, he and all his people, to battle at Edrei.
34 But the LORD said to Moses, "Do not be afraid
of him; for I have given him into your hand, with
all his people, and all his land. You shall do to him
as you did to King Sihon of the Amorites, who
ruled in Heshbon." 35 So they killed him, his sons,
and all his people, until there was no survivor left;
and they took possession of his land.

22 The Israelites set out, and camped in the
plains of Moab across the Jordan from
Jericho. 2 Now Balak son of Zippor saw all that
Israel had done to the Amorites. 3 Moab was in
great dread of the people, because they were so
numerous; Moab was overcome with fear of the
people of Israel. 4 And Moab said to the elders of
Midian, "This horde will now lick up all that is
around us, as an ox licks up the grass of the field."
Now Balak son of Zippor was king of Moab at

[a] Gk: Heb *which is in* [b] Meaning of Heb uncertain [c] That is *Well* [d] Or *Jeshimon* [e] Gk: Heb *and the lords of*
[f] Gk: Heb *we have shot at them; Heshbon has perished* [g] Compare Sam Gk: Meaning of MT uncertain

that time. 5He sent messengers to Balaam son of
Beor at Pethor, which is on the Euphrates, in the
land of Amaw,[a] to summon him, saying, "A people has come out of Egypt; they have spread over
the face of the earth, and they have settled next to
me. 6Come now, curse this people for me, since
they are stronger than I; perhaps I shall be able
to defeat them and drive them from the land; for
I know that whomever you bless is blessed, and
whomever you curse is cursed."

7 So the elders of Moab and the elders of
Midian departed with the fees for divination in
their hand; and they came to Balaam, and gave
him Balak's message. 8He said to them, "Stay here
tonight, and I will bring back word to you, just as
the LORD speaks to me"; so the officials of Moab
stayed with Balaam. 9God came to Balaam and
said, "Who are these men with you?" 10Balaam
said to God, "King Balak son of Zippor of Moab,
has sent me this message: 11'A people has come
out of Egypt and has spread over the face of the
earth; now come, curse them for me; perhaps I
shall be able to fight against them and drive them
out.'" 12God said to Balaam, "You shall not go
with them; you shall not curse the people, for
they are blessed." 13So Balaam rose in the morning, and said to the officials of Balak, "Go to your
own land, for the LORD has refused to let me go
with you." 14So the officials of Moab rose and
went to Balak, and said, "Balaam refuses to come
with us."

15 Once again Balak sent officials, more
numerous and more distinguished than these.
16They came to Balaam and said to him, "Thus
says Balak son of Zippor: 'Do not let anything
hinder you from coming to me; 17for I will surely
do you great honor, and whatever you say to me
I will do; come, curse this people for me.'" 18But
Balaam replied to the servants of Balak, "Although
Balak were to give me his house full of silver and
gold, I could not go beyond the command of the
LORD my God, to do less or more. 19You remain
here, as the others did, so that I may learn what
more the LORD may say to me." 20That night God
came to Balaam and said to him, "If the men have
come to summon you, get up and go with them;
but do only what I tell you to do." 21So Balaam
got up in the morning, saddled his donkey, and
went with the officials of Moab.

22 God's anger was kindled because he was
going, and the angel of the LORD took his stand
in the road as his adversary. Now he was riding on
the donkey, and his two servants were with him.
23The donkey saw the angel of the LORD standing in the road, with a drawn sword in his hand;
so the donkey turned off the road, and went into
the field; and Balaam struck the donkey, to turn it
back onto the road. 24Then the angel of the LORD
stood in a narrow path between the vineyards,
with a wall on either side. 25When the donkey
saw the angel of the LORD, it scraped against the
wall, and scraped Balaam's foot against the wall;
so he struck it again. 26Then the angel of the LORD
went ahead, and stood in a narrow place, where
there was no way to turn either to the right or to
the left. 27When the donkey saw the angel of the
LORD, it lay down under Balaam; and Balaam's
anger was kindled, and he struck the donkey with
his staff. 28Then the LORD opened the mouth of
the donkey, and it said to Balaam, "What have I
done to you, that you have struck me these three
times?" 29Balaam said to the donkey, "Because
you have made a fool of me! I wish I had a sword
in my hand! I would kill you right now!" 30But
the donkey said to Balaam, "Am I not your donkey, which you have ridden all your life to this
day? Have I been in the habit of treating you this
way?" And he said, "No."

31 Then the LORD opened the eyes of Balaam, and he saw the angel of the LORD standing
in the road, with his drawn sword in his hand; and
he bowed down, falling on his face. 32The angel of
the LORD said to him, "Why have you struck your
donkey these three times? I have come out as an
adversary, because your way is perverse[b] before
me. 33The donkey saw me, and turned away from
me these three times. If it had not turned away
from me, surely just now I would have killed you
and let it live." 34Then Balaam said to the angel of
the LORD, "I have sinned, for I did not know that

[a] Or *land of his kinsfolk* [b] Meaning of Heb uncertain

you were standing in the road to oppose me. Now
therefore, if it is displeasing to you, I will return
home.” 35The angel of the LORD said to Balaam,
“Go with the men; but speak only what I tell you
to speak.” So Balaam went on with the officials
of Balak.
36 When Balak heard that Balaam had come,
he went out to meet him at Ir-moab, on the
boundary formed by the Arnon, at the farthest
point of the boundary. 37Balak said to Balaam,
“Did I not send to summon you? Why did you
not come to me? Am I not able to honor you?”
38Balaam said to Balak, “I have come to you now,
but do I have power to say just anything? The
word God puts in my mouth, that is what I must
say.” 39Then Balaam went with Balak, and they
came to Kiriath-huzoth. 40Balak sacrificed oxen
and sheep, and sent them to Balaam and to the
officials who were with him.
41 On the next day Balak took Balaam and
brought him up to Bamoth-baal; and from there
he could see part of the people of Israel.[a]

23 1Then Balaam said to Balak, “Build me
seven altars here, and prepare seven bulls and
seven rams for me.” 2Balak did as Balaam had
said; and Balak and Balaam offered a bull and a
ram on each altar. 3Then Balaam said to Balak,
“Stay here beside your burnt offerings while I go
aside. Perhaps the LORD will come to meet me.
Whatever he shows me I will tell you.” And he
went to a bare height.
4 Then God met Balaam; and Balaam said to
him, “I have arranged the seven altars, and have
offered a bull and a ram on each altar.” 5The LORD
put a word in Balaam’s mouth, and said, “Return
to Balak, and this is what you must say.” 6So he
returned to Balak,[b] who was standing beside his
burnt offerings with all the officials of Moab.
7Then Balaam[c] uttered his oracle, saying:

“Balak has brought me from Aram,
the king of Moab from the eastern
mountains:
‘Come, curse Jacob for me;
Come, denounce Israel!’
8 How can I curse whom God has not cursed?
How can I denounce those whom the
LORD has not denounced?
9 For from the top of the crags I see him,
from the hills I behold him.
Here is a people living alone,
and not reckoning itself among the
nations!
10 Who can count the dust of Jacob,
or number the dust-cloud[d] of Israel?
Let me die the death of the upright,
and let my end be like his!”

11 Then Balak said to Balaam, “What have
you done to me? I brought you to curse my enemies, but now you have done nothing but bless
them.” 12He answered, “Must I not take care to
say what the LORD puts into my mouth?”
13 So Balak said to him, “Come with me to
another place from which you may see them; you
shall see only part of them, and shall not see them
all; then curse them for me from there.” 14So he
took him to the field of Zophim, to the top of Pisgah. He built seven altars, and offered a bull and a
ram on each altar. 15Balaam said to Balak, “Stand
here beside your burnt offerings, while I meet
the LORD over there.” 16The LORD met Balaam,
put a word into his mouth, and said, “Return to
Balak, and this is what you shall say.” 17When he
came to him, he was standing beside his burnt
offerings with the officials of Moab. Balak said to
him, “What has the LORD said?” 18Then Balaam
uttered his oracle, saying:

“Rise, Balak, and hear;
listen to me, O son of Zippor:
19 God is not a human being, that he should lie,
or a mortal, that he should change his
mind.
Has he promised, and will he not do it?
Has he spoken, and will he not fulfill it?
20 See, I received a command to bless;
he has blessed, and I cannot revoke it.
21 He has not beheld misfortune in Jacob;
nor has he seen trouble in Israel.
The LORD their God is with them,
acclaimed as a king among them.
22 God, who brings them out of Egypt,

[a] Heb lacks *of Israel* [b] Heb *him* [c] Heb *he* [d] Or *fourth part*

is like the horns of a wild ox for them.
23 Surely there is no enchantment against Jacob,
no divination against Israel;
now it shall be said of Jacob and Israel,
'See what God has done!'
24 Look, a people rising up like a lioness,
and rousing itself like a lion!
It does not lie down until it has eaten the
prey
and drunk the blood of the slain."

25 Then Balak said to Balaam, "Do not curse
them at all, and do not bless them at all." 26 But Balaam answered Balak, "Did I not tell you, 'Whatever the LORD says, that is what I must do'?"

27 So Balak said to Balaam, "Come now,
I will take you to another place; perhaps it will
please God that you may curse them for me from
there." 28 So Balak took Balaam to the top of Peor,
which overlooks the wasteland.[a] 29 Balaam said to
Balak, "Build me seven altars here, and prepare
seven bulls and seven rams for me." 30 So Balak
did as Balaam had said, and offered a bull and a
ram on each altar.

24 Now Balaam saw that it pleased the LORD
to bless Israel, so he did not go, as at other
times, to look for omens, but set his face toward
the wilderness. 2 Balaam looked up and saw Israel camping tribe by tribe. Then the spirit of
God came upon him, 3 and he uttered his oracle,
saying:
"The oracle of Balaam son of Beor,
the oracle of the man whose eye is clear,[b]
4 the oracle of one who hears the words of
God,
who sees the vision of the Almighty,[c]
who falls down, but with eyes uncovered:
5 how fair are your tents, O Jacob,
your encampments, O Israel!
6 Like palm groves that stretch far away,
like gardens beside a river,
like aloes that the LORD has planted,
like cedar trees beside the waters.
7 Water shall flow from his buckets,
and his seed shall have abundant water,
his king shall be higher than Agag,
and his kingdom shall be exalted.
8 God who brings him out of Egypt,
is like the horns of a wild ox for him;
he shall devour the nations that are his foes
and break their bones.
He shall strike with his arrows.[d]
9 He crouched, he lay down like a lion,
and like a lioness; who will rouse him up?
Blessed is everyone who blesses you,
and cursed is everyone who curses you."

10 Then Balak's anger was kindled against
Balaam, and he struck his hands together. Balak
said to Balaam, "I summoned you to curse my enemies, but instead you have blessed them these
three times. 11 Now be off with you! Go home! I
said, 'I will reward you richly,' but the LORD has
denied you any reward." 12 And Balaam said to
Balak, "Did I not tell your messengers whom you
sent to me, 13 'If Balak should give me his house
full of silver and gold, I would not be able to go
beyond the word of the LORD, to do either good
or bad of my own will; what the LORD says, that
is what I will say'? 14 So now, I am going to my
people; let me advise you what this people will do
to your people in days to come."

15 So he uttered his oracle, saying:
"The oracle of Balaam son of Beor,
the oracle of the man whose eye is clear,[b]
16 the oracle of one who hears the words of
God,
and knows the knowledge of the Most
High,[e]
who sees the vision of the Almighty,[c]
who falls down, but with his eyes
uncovered:
17 I see him, but not now;
I behold him, but not near—
a star shall come out of Jacob,
and a scepter shall rise out of Israel;
it shall crush the borderlands[f] of Moab,
and the territory[g] of all the Shethites.
18 Edom will become a possession,
Seir a possession of its enemies,[h]

[a] Or *overlooks Jeshimon* [b] Or *closed* or *open* [c] Traditional rendering of Heb *Shaddai* [d] Meaning of Heb uncertain
[e] Or *of Elyon* [f] Or *forehead* [g] Some Mss read *skull* [h] Heb *Seir, its enemies, a possession*

while Israel does valiantly.
19 One out of Jacob shall rule,
and destroy the survivors of Ir."
20 Then he looked on Amalek, and uttered
his oracle, saying:
"First among the nations was Amalek,
but its end is to perish forever."
21 Then he looked on the Kenite, and uttered
his oracle, saying:
"Enduring is your dwelling place,
and your nest is set in the rock;
22 yet Kain is destined for burning.
How long shall Asshur take you away
captive?"
23 Again he uttered his oracle, saying:
"Alas, who shall live when God does this?
24 But ships shall come from Kittim
and shall afflict Asshur and Eber;
and he also shall perish forever."
25 Then Balaam got up and went back to his
place, and Balak also went his way.

25 While Israel was staying at Shittim, the
people began to have sexual relations
with the women of Moab. 2 These invited the people to the sacrifices of their gods, and the people
ate and bowed down to their gods. 3 Thus Israel
yoked itself to the Baal of Peor, and the LORD's
anger was kindled against Israel. 4 The LORD said
to Moses, "Take all the chiefs of the people, and
impale them in the sun before the LORD, in order
that the fierce anger of the LORD may turn away
from Israel." 5 And Moses said to the judges of
Israel, "Each of you shall kill any of your people
who have yoked themselves to the Baal of Peor."
6 Just then one of the Israelites came and
brought a Midianite woman into his family, in the
sight of Moses and in the sight of the whole congregation of the Israelites, while they were weeping at the entrance of the tent of meeting. 7 When
Phinehas son of Eleazar, son of Aaron the priest,
saw it, he got up and left the congregation. Taking a spear in his hand, 8 he went after the Israelite
man into the tent, and pierced the two of them,
the Israelite and the woman, through the belly. So
the plague was stopped among the people of Israel. 9 Nevertheless those that died by the plague
were twenty-four thousand.
10 The LORD spoke to Moses, saying:
11 "Phinehas son of Eleazar, son of Aaron the
priest, has turned back my wrath from the Israelites by manifesting such zeal among them on my
behalf that in my jealousy I did not consume the
Israelites. 12 Therefore say, 'I hereby grant him my
covenant of peace. 13 It shall be for him and for
his descendants after him a covenant of perpetual
priesthood, because he was zealous for his God,
and made atonement for the Israelites.'"
14 The name of the slain Israelite man, who
was killed with the Midianite woman, was Zimri
son of Salu, head of an ancestral house belonging to the Simeonites. 15 The name of the Midianite woman who was killed was Cozbi daughter
of Zur, who was the head of a clan, an ancestral
house in Midian.
16 The LORD said to Moses, 17 "Harass the
Midianites, and defeat them; 18 for they have harassed you by the trickery with which they deceived you in the affair of Peor, and in the affair
of Cozbi, the daughter of a leader of Midian, their
sister; she was killed on the day of the plague that
resulted from Peor."

26 After the plague the LORD said to Moses
and to Eleazar son of Aaron the priest,
2 "Take a census of the whole congregation of the
Israelites, from twenty years old and upward, by
their ancestral houses, everyone in Israel able to
go to war." 3 Moses and Eleazar the priest spoke
with them in the plains of Moab by the Jordan
opposite Jericho, saying, 4 "Take a census of the
people,[a] from twenty years old and upward," as
the LORD commanded Moses.

The Israelites, who came out of the land of
Egypt, were:
5 Reuben, the firstborn of Israel. The descendants of Reuben: of Hanoch, the clan of the
Hanochites; of Pallu, the clan of the Palluites; 6 of
Hezron, the clan of the Hezronites; of Carmi, the
clan of the Carmites. 7 These are the clans of the
Reubenites; the number of those enrolled was
forty-three thousand seven hundred thirty. 8 And

[a] Heb lacks *take a census of the people*: Compare verse 2

the descendants of Pallu: Eliab. 9 The descendants
of Eliab: Nemuel, Dathan, and Abiram. These are
the same Dathan and Abiram, chosen from the
congregation, who rebelled against Moses and
Aaron in the company of Korah, when they rebelled against the LORD, 10 and the earth opened
its mouth and swallowed them up along with
Korah, when that company died, when the fire
devoured two hundred fifty men; and they became a warning. 11 Notwithstanding, the sons of
Korah did not die.

12 The descendants of Simeon by their clans:
of Nemuel, the clan of the Nemuelites; of Jamin,
the clan of the Jaminites; of Jachin, the clan of the
Jachinites; 13 of Zerah, the clan of the Zerahites;
of Shaul, the clan of the Shaulites.[a] 14 These are
the clans of the Simeonites, twenty-two thousand
two hundred.

15 The children of Gad by their clans: of
Zephon, the clan of the Zephonites; of Haggi,
the clan of the Haggites; of Shuni, the clan of
the Shunites; 16 of Ozni, the clan of the Oznites;
of Eri, the clan of the Erites; 17 of Arod, the clan
of the Arodites; of Areli, the clan of the Arelites.
18 These are the clans of the Gadites: the number
of those enrolled was forty thousand five hundred.

19 The sons of Judah: Er and Onan; Er and
Onan died in the land of Canaan. 20 The descendants of Judah by their clans were: of Shelah, the
clan of the Shelanites; of Perez, the clan of the
Perezites; of Zerah, the clan of the Zerahites.
21 The descendants of Perez were: of Hezron, the
clan of the Hezronites; of Hamul, the clan of
the Hamulites. 22 These are the clans of Judah: the
number of those enrolled was seventy-six thousand five hundred.

23 The descendants of Issachar by their
clans: of Tola, the clan of the Tolaites; of Puvah,
the clan of the Punites; 24 of Jashub, the clan of
the Jashubites; of Shimron, the clan of the Shim-
ronites. 25 These are the clans of Issachar: sixty-
four thousand three hundred enrolled.

26 The descendants of Zebulun by their
clans: of Sered, the clan of the Seredites; of Elon,
the clan of the Elonites; of Jahleel, the clan of the
Jahleelites. 27 These are the clans of the Zebulunites; the number of those enrolled was sixty
thousand five hundred.

28 The sons of Joseph by their clans: Manasseh and Ephraim. 29 The descendants of Manasseh: of Machir, the clan of the Machirites; and
Machir was the father of Gilead; of Gilead, the
clan of the Gileadites. 30 These are the descendants of Gilead: of Iezer, the clan of the Iezerites;
of Helek, the clan of the Helekites; 31 and of Asriel, the clan of the Asrielites; and of Shechem, the
clan of the Shechemites; 32 and of Shemida, the
clan of the Shemidaites; and of Hepher, the clan
of the Hepherites. 33 Now Zelophehad son of Hepher had no sons, but daughters: and the names of
the daughters of Zelophehad were Mahlah, Noah,
Hoglah, Milcah, and Tirzah. 34 These are the clans
of Manasseh; the number of those enrolled was
fifty-two thousand seven hundred.

35 These are the descendants of Ephraim according to their clans: of Shuthelah, the clan of the
Shuthelahites; of Becher, the clan of the Becher-
ites; of Tahan, the clan of the Tahanites. 36 And
these are the descendants of Shuthelah: of Eran,
the clan of the Eranites. 37 These are the clans of
the Ephraimites: the number of those enrolled
was thirty-two thousand five hundred. These are
the descendants of Joseph by their clans.

38 The descendants of Benjamin by their
clans: of Bela, the clan of the Belaites; of Ashbel,
the clan of the Ashbelites; of Ahiram, the clan
of the Ahiramites; 39 of Shephupham, the clan
of the Shuphamites; of Hupham, the clan of the
Huphamites. 40 And the sons of Bela were Ard
and Naaman: of Ard, the clan of the Ardites; of
Naaman, the clan of the Naamites. 41 These are
the descendants of Benjamin by their clans; the
number of those enrolled was forty-five thousand
six hundred.

42 These are the descendants of Dan by their
clans: of Shuham, the clan of the Shuhamites.
These are the clans of Dan by their clans. 43 All the
clans of the Shuhamites: sixty-four thousand four
hundred enrolled.

[a] Or *Saul . . . Saulites*

44 The descendants of Asher by their families: of Imnah, the clan of the Imnites; of Ishvi,
the clan of the Ishvites; of Beriah, the clan of
the Beriites. 45 Of the descendants of Beriah: of
Heber, the clan of the Heberites; of Malchiel,
the clan of the Malchielites. 46 And the name of
the daughter of Asher was Serah. 47 These are the
clans of the Asherites: the number of those enrolled was fifty-three thousand four hundred.

48 The descendants of Naphtali by their
clans: of Jahzeel, the clan of the Jahzeelites; of
Guni, the clan of the Gunites; 49 of Jezer, the clan
of the Jezerites; of Shillem, the clan of the Shil-
lemites. 50 These are the Naphtalites[a] by their
clans: the number of those enrolled was forty-five
thousand four hundred.

51 This was the number of the Israelites enrolled: six hundred and one thousand seven hundred thirty.

52 The LORD spoke to Moses, saying: 53 To
these the land shall be apportioned for inheritance according to the number of names. 54 To a
large tribe you shall give a large inheritance, and
to a small tribe you shall give a small inheritance;
every tribe shall be given its inheritance according to its enrollment. 55 But the land shall be apportioned by lot; according to the names of their
ancestral tribes they shall inherit. 56 Their inheritance shall be apportioned according to lot between the larger and the smaller.

57 This is the enrollment of the Levites
by their clans: of Gershon, the clan of the Gershonites; of Kohath, the clan of the Kohathites; of
Merari, the clan of the Merarites. 58 These are the
clans of Levi: the clan of the Libnites, the clan of
the Hebronites, the clan of the Mahlites, the clan
of the Mushites, the clan of the Korahites. Now
Kohath was the father of Amram. 59 The name
of Amram's wife was Jochebed daughter of Levi,
who was born to Levi in Egypt; and she bore to
Amram: Aaron, Moses, and their sister Miriam.
60 To Aaron were born Nadab, Abihu, Eleazar, and
Ithamar. 61 But Nadab and Abihu died when they
offered unholy fire before the LORD. 62 The number of those enrolled was twenty-three thousand,
every male one month old and upward; for they
were not enrolled among the Israelites because
there was no allotment given to them among the
Israelites.

63 These were those enrolled by Moses and
Eleazar the priest, who enrolled the Israelites in
the plains of Moab by the Jordan opposite Jericho. 64 Among these there was not one of those
enrolled by Moses and Aaron the priest, who had
enrolled the Israelites in the wilderness of Sinai.
65 For the LORD had said of them, "They shall
die in the wilderness." Not one of them was left,
except Caleb son of Jephunneh and Joshua son
of Nun.

27 Then the daughters of Zelophehad came
forward. Zelophehad was son of Hepher
son of Gilead son of Machir son of Manasseh
son of Joseph, a member of the Manassite clans.
The names of his daughters were: Mahlah, Noah,
Hoglah, Milcah, and Tirzah. 2 They stood before
Moses, Eleazar the priest, the leaders, and all
the congregation, at the entrance of the tent of
meeting, and they said, 3 "Our father died in the
wilderness; he was not among the company of
those who gathered themselves together against
the LORD in the company of Korah, but died for
his own sin; and he had no sons. 4 Why should the
name of our father be taken away from his clan
because he had no son? Give to us a possession
among our father's brothers."

5 Moses brought their case before the LORD.
6 And the LORD spoke to Moses, saying: 7 The
daughters of Zelophehad are right in what they
are saying; you shall indeed let them possess an
inheritance among their father's brothers and
pass the inheritance of their father on to them.
8 You shall also say to the Israelites, "If a man dies,
and has no son, then you shall pass his inheritance on to his daughter. 9 If he has no daughter,
then you shall give his inheritance to his brothers. 10 If he has no brothers, then you shall give his
inheritance to his father's brothers. 11 And if his
father has no brothers, then you shall give his inheritance to the nearest kinsman of his clan, and
he shall possess it. It shall be for the Israelites a

[a] Heb *clans of Naphtali*

statute and ordinance, as the LORD commanded
Moses."
12 The LORD said to Moses, "Go up this
mountain of the Abarim range, and see the land
that I have given to the Israelites. 13When you
have seen it, you also shall be gathered to your
people, as your brother Aaron was, 14because
you rebelled against my word in the wilderness of
Zin when the congregation quarreled with me.[a]
You did not show my holiness before their eyes
at the waters." (These are the waters of Meribath-
kadesh in the wilderness of Zin.) 15Moses spoke
to the LORD, saying, 16"Let the LORD, the God of
the spirits of all flesh, appoint someone over the
congregation 17who shall go out before them and
come in before them, who shall lead them out
and bring them in, so that the congregation of the
LORD may not be like sheep without a shepherd."
18So the LORD said to Moses, "Take Joshua son
of Nun, a man in whom is the spirit, and lay your
hand upon him; 19have him stand before Eleazar
the priest and all the congregation, and commission him in their sight. 20You shall give him some
of your authority, so that all the congregation of
the Israelites may obey. 21But he shall stand before Eleazar the priest, who shall inquire for him
by the decision of the Urim before the LORD; at
his word they shall go out, and at his word they
shall come in, both he and all the Israelites with
him, the whole congregation." 22So Moses did as
the LORD commanded him. He took Joshua and
had him stand before Eleazar the priest and the
whole congregation; 23he laid his hands on him
and commissioned him—as the LORD had directed through Moses.

28 The LORD spoke to Moses, saying: 2Com-
mand the Israelites, and say to them: My
offering, the food for my offerings by fire, my
pleasing odor, you shall take care to offer to me
at its appointed time. 3And you shall say to them,
This is the offering by fire that you shall offer to
the LORD: two male lambs a year old without
blemish, daily, as a regular offering. 4One lamb
you shall offer in the morning, and the other lamb
you shall offer at twilight;[b] 5also one-tenth of an
ephah of choice flour for a grain offering, mixed
with one-fourth of a hin of beaten oil. 6It is a regular burnt offering, ordained at Mount Sinai for
a pleasing odor, an offering by fire to the LORD.
7Its drink offering shall be one-fourth of a hin for
each lamb; in the sanctuary you shall pour out a
drink offering of strong drink to the LORD. 8The
other lamb you shall offer at twilight[b] with a grain
offering and a drink offering like the one in the
morning; you shall offer it as an offering by fire, a
pleasing odor to the LORD.
9 On the sabbath day: two male lambs a year
old without blemish, and two-tenths of an ephah
of choice flour for a grain offering, mixed with oil,
and its drink offering— 10this is the burnt offering for every sabbath, in addition to the regular
burnt offering and its drink offering.
11 At the beginnings of your months you
shall offer a burnt offering to the LORD: two
young bulls, one ram, seven male lambs a year old
without blemish; 12also three-tenths of an ephah
of choice flour for a grain offering, mixed with oil,
for each bull; and two-tenths of choice flour for
a grain offering, mixed with oil, for the one ram;
13and one-tenth of choice flour mixed with oil as
a grain offering for every lamb—a burnt offering
of pleasing odor, an offering by fire to the LORD.
14Their drink offerings shall be half a hin of wine
for a bull, one-third of a hin for a ram, and one-
fourth of a hin for a lamb. This is the burnt offering of every month throughout the months of the
year. 15And there shall be one male goat for a sin
offering to the LORD; it shall be offered in addition to the regular burnt offering and its drink
offering.
16 On the fourteenth day of the first month
there shall be a passover offering to the LORD.
17And on the fifteenth day of this month is a festival; seven days shall unleavened bread be eaten.
18On the first day there shall be a holy convocation. You shall not work at your occupations. 19You
shall offer an offering by fire, a burnt offering to
the LORD: two young bulls, one ram, and seven
male lambs a year old; see that they are without
blemish. 20Their grain offering shall be of choice

[a] Heb lacks *with me* [b] Heb *between the two evenings*

flour mixed with oil: three-tenths of an ephah shall you offer for a bull, and two-tenths for a ram; 21 one-tenth shall you offer for each of the seven lambs; 22 also one male goat for a sin offering, to make atonement for you. 23 You shall offer these in addition to the burnt offering of the morning, which belongs to the regular burnt offering. 24 In the same way you shall offer daily, for seven days, the food of an offering by fire, a pleasing odor to the LORD; it shall be offered in addition to the regular burnt offering and its drink offering. 25 And on the seventh day you shall have a holy convocation; you shall not work at your occupations.

26 On the day of the first fruits, when you offer a grain offering of new grain to the LORD at your festival of weeks, you shall have a holy convocation; you shall not work at your occupations. 27 You shall offer a burnt offering, a pleasing odor to the LORD: two young bulls, one ram, seven male lambs a year old. 28 Their grain offering shall be of choice flour mixed with oil, three-tenths of an ephah for each bull, two-tenths for one ram, 29 one-tenth for each of the seven lambs; 30 with one male goat, to make atonement for you. 31 In addition to the regular burnt offering with its grain offering, you shall offer them and their drink offering. They shall be without blemish.

29 On the first day of the seventh month you shall have a holy convocation; you shall not work at your occupations. It is a day for you to blow the trumpets, 2 and you shall offer a burnt offering, a pleasing odor to the LORD: one young bull, one ram, seven male lambs a year old without blemish. 3 Their grain offering shall be of choice flour mixed with oil, three-tenths of one ephah for the bull, two-tenths for the ram, 4 and one-tenth for each of the seven lambs; 5 with one male goat for a sin offering, to make atonement for you. 6 These are in addition to the burnt offering of the new moon and its grain offering, and the regular burnt offering and its grain offering, and their drink offerings, according to the ordinance for them, a pleasing odor, an offering by fire to the LORD.

7 On the tenth day of this seventh month you shall have a holy convocation, and deny yourselves;[a] you shall do no work. 8 You shall offer a burnt offering to the LORD, a pleasing odor: one young bull, one ram, seven male lambs a year old. They shall be without blemish. 9 Their grain offering shall be of choice flour mixed with oil, three-tenths of an ephah for the bull, two-tenths for the one ram, 10 one-tenth for each of the seven lambs; 11 with one male goat for a sin offering, in addition to the sin offering of atonement, and the regular burnt offering and its grain offering, and their drink offerings.

12 On the fifteenth day of the seventh month you shall have a holy convocation; you shall not work at your occupations. You shall celebrate a festival to the LORD seven days. 13 You shall offer a burnt offering, an offering by fire, a pleasing odor to the LORD: thirteen young bulls, two rams, fourteen male lambs a year old. They shall be without blemish. 14 Their grain offering shall be of choice flour mixed with oil, three-tenths of an ephah for each of the thirteen bulls, two-tenths for each of the two rams, 15 and one-tenth for each of the fourteen lambs; 16 also one male goat for a sin offering, in addition to the regular burnt offering, its grain offering and its drink offering.

17 On the second day: twelve young bulls, two rams, fourteen male lambs a year old without blemish, 18 with the grain offering and the drink offerings for the bulls, for the rams, and for the lambs, as prescribed in accordance with their number; 19 also one male goat for a sin offering, in addition to the regular burnt offering and its grain offering, and their drink offerings.

20 On the third day: eleven bulls, two rams, fourteen male lambs a year old without blemish, 21 with the grain offering and the drink offerings for the bulls, for the rams, and for the lambs, as prescribed in accordance with their number; 22 also one male goat for a sin offering, in addition to the regular burnt offering and its grain offering and its drink offering.

23 On the fourth day: ten bulls, two rams, fourteen male lambs a year old without blemish, 24 with the grain offering and the drink offerings

[a] Or *and fast*

for the bulls, for the rams, and for the lambs, as
prescribed in accordance with their number;
25 also one male goat for a sin offering, in addition
to the regular burnt offering, its grain offering
and its drink offering.

26 On the fifth day: nine bulls, two rams,
fourteen male lambs a year old without blemish,
27 with the grain offering and the drink offerings
for the bulls, for the rams, and for the lambs, as
prescribed in accordance with their number;
28 also one male goat for a sin offering, in addition
to the regular burnt offering and its grain offering
and its drink offering.

29 On the sixth day: eight bulls, two rams,
fourteen male lambs a year old without blemish,
30 with the grain offering and the drink offerings
for the bulls, for the rams, and for the lambs, as
prescribed in accordance with their number;
31 also one male goat for a sin offering, in addition
to the regular burnt offering, its grain offering,
and its drink offerings.

32 On the seventh day: seven bulls, two rams,
fourteen male lambs a year old without blemish,
33 with the grain offering and the drink offerings
for the bulls, for the rams, and for the lambs, as
prescribed in accordance with their number;
34 also one male goat for a sin offering, besides the
regular burnt offering, its grain offering, and its
drink offering.

35 On the eighth day you shall have a solemn
assembly; you shall not work at your occupations.
36 You shall offer a burnt offering, an offering by
fire, a pleasing odor to the LORD: one bull, one
ram, seven male lambs a year old without blemish, 37 and the grain offering and the drink offerings for the bull, for the ram, and for the lambs,
as prescribed in accordance with their number;
38 also one male goat for a sin offering, in addition
to the regular burnt offering and its grain offering
and its drink offering.

39 These you shall offer to the LORD at your
appointed festivals, in addition to your votive
offerings and your freewill offerings, as your
burnt offerings, your grain offerings, your drink
offerings, and your offerings of well-being.

40[a] So Moses told the Israelites everything
just as the LORD had commanded Moses.

30 Then Moses said to the heads of the tribes
of the Israelites: This is what the LORD
has commanded. 2 When a man makes a vow to
the LORD, or swears an oath to bind himself by
a pledge, he shall not break his word; he shall do
according to all that proceeds out of his mouth.

3 When a woman makes a vow to the LORD,
or binds herself by a pledge, while within her
father's house, in her youth, 4 and her father
hears of her vow or her pledge by which she has
bound herself, and says nothing to her; then all
her vows shall stand, and any pledge by which
she has bound herself shall stand. 5 But if her father expresses disapproval to her at the time that
he hears of it, no vow of hers, and no pledge by
which she has bound herself, shall stand; and the
LORD will forgive her, because her father had expressed to her his disapproval.

6 If she marries, while obligated by her vows
or any thoughtless utterance of her lips by which
she has bound herself, 7 and her husband hears
of it and says nothing to her at the time that he
hears, then her vows shall stand, and her pledges
by which she has bound herself shall stand. 8 But
if, at the time that her husband hears of it, he expresses disapproval to her, then he shall nullify the
vow by which she was obligated, or the thoughtless utterance of her lips, by which she bound herself; and the LORD will forgive her. 9 (But every
vow of a widow or of a divorced woman, by which
she has bound herself, shall be binding upon her.)
10 And if she made a vow in her husband's house,
or bound herself by a pledge with an oath, 11 and
her husband heard it and said nothing to her, and
did not express disapproval to her, then all her
vows shall stand, and any pledge by which she
bound herself shall stand. 12 But if her husband
nullifies them at the time that he hears them, then
whatever proceeds out of her lips concerning her
vows, or concerning her pledge of herself, shall
not stand. Her husband has nullified them, and
the LORD will forgive her. 13 Any vow or any binding oath to deny herself,[b] her husband may allow

[a] Ch 30.1 in Heb [b] Or *to fast*

to stand, or her husband may nullify. 14 But if her
husband says nothing to her from day to day,[a]
then he validates all her vows, or all her pledges,
by which she is obligated; he has validated them,
because he said nothing to her at the time that
he heard of them. 15 But if he nullifies them some
time after he has heard of them, then he shall bear
her guilt.

16 These are the statutes that the LORD commanded Moses concerning a husband and his
wife, and a father and his daughter while she is
still young and in her father's house.

31 The LORD spoke to Moses, saying,
2 "Avenge the Israelites on the Midianites;
afterward you shall be gathered to your people."
3 So Moses said to the people, "Arm some of your
number for the war, so that they may go against
Midian, to execute the LORD's vengeance on
Midian. 4 You shall send a thousand from each
of the tribes of Israel to the war." 5 So out of the
thousands of Israel, a thousand from each tribe
were conscripted, twelve thousand armed for battle. 6 Moses sent them to the war, a thousand from
each tribe, along with Phinehas son of Eleazar
the priest,[b] with the vessels of the sanctuary and
the trumpets for sounding the alarm in his hand.
7 They did battle against Midian, as the LORD had
commanded Moses, and killed every male. 8 They
killed the kings of Midian: Evi, Rekem, Zur, Hur,
and Reba, the five kings of Midian, in addition
to others who were slain by them; and they also
killed Balaam son of Beor with the sword. 9 The Israelites took the women of Midian and their little
ones captive; and they took all their cattle, their
flocks, and all their goods as booty. 10 All their
towns where they had settled, and all their encampments, they burned, 11 but they took all the
spoil and all the booty, both people and animals.
12 Then they brought the captives and the booty
and the spoil to Moses, to Eleazar the priest, and
to the congregation of the Israelites, at the camp
on the plains of Moab by the Jordan at Jericho.

13 Moses, Eleazar the priest, and all the leaders of the congregation went to meet them outside the camp. 14 Moses became angry with the
officers of the army, the commanders of thousands and the commanders of hundreds, who
had come from service in the war. 15 Moses said
to them, "Have you allowed all the women to
live? 16 These women here, on Balaam's advice,
made the Israelites act treacherously against the
LORD in the affair of Peor, so that the plague
came among the congregation of the LORD.
17 Now therefore, kill every male among the little ones, and kill every woman who has known
a man by sleeping with him. 18 But all the young
girls who have not known a man by sleeping with
him, keep alive for yourselves. 19 Camp outside
the camp seven days; whoever of you has killed
any person or touched a corpse, purify yourselves
and your captives on the third and on the seventh
day. 20 You shall purify every garment, every article of skin, everything made of goats' hair, and
every article of wood."

21 Eleazar the priest said to the troops who
had gone to battle: "This is the statute of the law
that the LORD has commanded Moses: 22 gold,
silver, bronze, iron, tin, and lead— 23 everything
that can withstand fire, shall be passed through
fire, and it shall be clean. Nevertheless it shall also
be purified with the water for purification; and
whatever cannot withstand fire, shall be passed
through the water. 24 You must wash your clothes
on the seventh day, and you shall be clean; afterward you may come into the camp."

25 The LORD spoke to Moses, saying, 26 "You
and Eleazar the priest and the heads of the ancestral houses of the congregation make an inventory of the booty captured, both human and
animal. 27 Divide the booty into two parts, between the warriors who went out to battle and
all the congregation. 28 From the share of the warriors who went out to battle, set aside as tribute
for the LORD, one item out of every five hundred,
whether persons, oxen, donkeys, sheep, or goats.
29 Take it from their half and give it to Eleazar
the priest as an offering to the LORD. 30 But from
the Israelites' half you shall take one out of every
fifty, whether persons, oxen, donkeys, sheep, or
goats—all the animals—and give them to the

[a] Or *from that day to the next* [b] Gk: Heb adds *to the war*

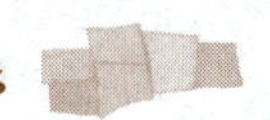

Levites who have charge of the tabernacle of the
Lord."
31 Then Moses and Eleazar the priest did as
the Lord had commanded Moses:
32 The booty remaining from the spoil that
the troops had taken totaled six hundred seventy-
five thousand sheep, 33seventy-two thousand oxen,
34sixty-one thousand donkeys, 35and thirty-two
thousand persons in all, women who had not
known a man by sleeping with him.
36 The half-share, the portion of those who
had gone out to war, was in number three hundred thirty-seven thousand five hundred sheep
and goats, 37and the Lord's tribute of sheep
and goats was six hundred seventy-five. 38The
oxen were thirty-six thousand, of which the
Lord's tribute was seventy-two. 39The donkeys
were thirty thousand five hundred, of which the
Lord's tribute was sixty-one. 40The persons were
sixteen thousand, of which the Lord's tribute
was thirty-two persons. 41Moses gave the tribute,
the offering for the Lord, to Eleazar the priest, as
the Lord had commanded Moses.
42 As for the Israelites' half, which Moses
separated from that of the troops, 43the congregation's half was three hundred thirty-seven
thousand five hundred sheep and goats, 44thirty-
six thousand oxen, 45thirty thousand five hundred donkeys, 46and sixteen thousand persons.
47From the Israelites' half Moses took one of
every fifty, both of persons and of animals, and
gave them to the Levites who had charge of the
tabernacle of the Lord; as the Lord had commanded Moses.
48 Then the officers who were over the thousands of the army, the commanders of thousands
and the commanders of hundreds, approached
Moses, 49and said to Moses, "Your servants have
counted the warriors who are under our command, and not one of us is missing. 50And we
have brought the Lord's offering, what each of
us found, articles of gold, armlets and bracelets,
signet rings, earrings, and pendants, to make
atonement for ourselves before the Lord." 51Mo-
ses and Eleazar the priest received the gold from
them, all in the form of crafted articles. 52And all
the gold of the offering that they offered to the
Lord, from the commanders of thousands and
the commanders of hundreds, was sixteen thousand seven hundred fifty shekels. 53(The troops
had all taken plunder for themselves.) 54So Moses
and Eleazar the priest received the gold from the
commanders of thousands and of hundreds, and
brought it into the tent of meeting as a memorial
for the Israelites before the Lord.

32 Now the Reubenites and the Gadites
owned a very great number of cattle.
When they saw that the land of Jazer and the
land of Gilead was a good place for cattle, 2the
Gadites and the Reubenites came and spoke to
Moses, to Eleazar the priest, and to the leaders of
the congregation, saying, 3"Ataroth, Dibon, Jazer,
Nimrah, Heshbon, Elealeh, Sebam, Nebo, and
Beon— 4the land that the Lord subdued before
the congregation of Israel—is a land for cattle;
and your servants have cattle." 5They continued,
"If we have found favor in your sight, let this land
be given to your servants for a possession; do not
make us cross the Jordan."
6 But Moses said to the Gadites and to the
Reubenites, "Shall your brothers go to war while
you sit here? 7Why will you discourage the hearts
of the Israelites from going over into the land that
the Lord has given them? 8Your fathers did this,
when I sent them from Kadesh-barnea to see the
land. 9When they went up to the Wadi Eshcol and
saw the land, they discouraged the hearts of the
Israelites from going into the land that the Lord
had given them. 10The Lord's anger was kindled
on that day and he swore, saying, 11'Surely none
of the people who came up out of Egypt, from
twenty years old and upward, shall see the land
that I swore to give to Abraham, to Isaac, and to
Jacob, because they have not unreservedly followed me— 12none except Caleb son of Jephunneh the Kenizzite and Joshua son of Nun, for they
have unreservedly followed the Lord.' 13And the
Lord's anger was kindled against Israel, and he
made them wander in the wilderness for forty
years, until all the generation that had done evil
in the sight of the Lord had disappeared. 14And
now you, a brood of sinners, have risen in place of
your fathers, to increase the Lord's fierce anger
against Israel! 15If you turn away from following

him, he will again abandon them in the wilderness; and you will destroy all this people."
16 Then they came up to him and said, "We
will build sheepfolds here for our flocks, and
towns for our little ones, 17but we will take up
arms as a vanguard[a] before the Israelites, until
we have brought them to their place. Meanwhile
our little ones will stay in the fortified towns because of the inhabitants of the land. 18We will not
return to our homes until all the Israelites have
obtained their inheritance. 19We will not inherit
with them on the other side of the Jordan and beyond, because our inheritance has come to us on
this side of the Jordan to the east."
20 So Moses said to them, "If you do this—if
you take up arms to go before the LORD for the
war, 21and all those of you who bear arms cross
the Jordan before the LORD, until he has driven
out his enemies from before him 22and the land
is subdued before the LORD—then after that you
may return and be free of obligation to the LORD
and to Israel, and this land shall be your possession before the LORD. 23But if you do not do this,
you have sinned against the LORD; and be sure
your sin will find you out. 24Build towns for your
little ones, and folds for your flocks; but do what
you have promised."
25 Then the Gadites and the Reubenites said
to Moses, "Your servants will do as my lord commands. 26Our little ones, our wives, our flocks,
and all our livestock shall remain there in the
towns of Gilead; 27but your servants will cross
over, everyone armed for war, to do battle for the
LORD, just as my lord orders."
28 So Moses gave command concerning
them to Eleazar the priest, to Joshua son of Nun,
and to the heads of the ancestral houses of the Israelite tribes. 29And Moses said to them, "If the
Gadites and the Reubenites, everyone armed for
battle before the LORD, will cross over the Jordan
with you and the land shall be subdued before
you, then you shall give them the land of Gilead
for a possession; 30but if they will not cross over
with you armed, they shall have possessions
among you in the land of Canaan." 31The Gadites
and the Reubenites answered, "As the LORD has
spoken to your servants, so we will do. 32We will
cross over armed before the LORD into the land
of Canaan, but the possession of our inheritance
shall remain with us on this side of[b] the Jordan."
33 Moses gave to them—to the Gadites and
to the Reubenites and to the half-tribe of Manasseh son of Joseph—the kingdom of King
Sihon of the Amorites and the kingdom of King
Og of Bashan, the land and its towns, with the
territories of the surrounding towns. 34And the
Gadites rebuilt Dibon, Ataroth, Aroer, 35Atroth-
shophan, Jazer, Jogbehah, 36Beth-nimrah, and
Beth-haran, fortified cities, and folds for sheep.
37And the Reubenites rebuilt Heshbon, Elealeh,
Kiriathaim, 38Nebo, and Baal-meon (some names
being changed), and Sibmah; and they gave
names to the towns that they rebuilt. 39The descendants of Machir son of Manasseh went to
Gilead, captured it, and dispossessed the Amorites who were there; 40so Moses gave Gilead to
Machir son of Manasseh, and he settled there.
41Jair son of Manasseh went and captured their
villages, and renamed them Havvoth-jair.[c] 42And
Nobah went and captured Kenath and its villages,
and renamed it Nobah after himself.

33 These are the stages by which the Israelites went out of the land of Egypt in
military formation under the leadership of Moses
and Aaron. 2Moses wrote down their starting
points, stage by stage, by command of the LORD;
and these are their stages according to their starting places. 3They set out from Rameses in the first
month, on the fifteenth day of the first month; on
the day after the passover the Israelites went out
boldly in the sight of all the Egyptians, 4while
the Egyptians were burying all their firstborn,
whom the LORD had struck down among them.
The LORD executed judgments even against their
gods.
5 So the Israelites set out from Rameses, and
camped at Succoth. 6They set out from Succoth,
and camped at Etham, which is on the edge of
the wilderness. 7They set out from Etham, and
turned back to Pi-hahiroth, which faces Baal-

[a] Cn: Heb *hurrying* [b] Heb *beyond* [c] That is *the villages of Jair*

zephon; and they camped before Migdol. 8 They set out from Pi-hahiroth, passed through the sea into the wilderness, went a three days' journey in the wilderness of Etham, and camped at Marah. 9 They set out from Marah and came to Elim; at Elim there were twelve springs of water and seventy palm trees, and they camped there. 10 They set out from Elim and camped by the Red Sea.[a] 11 They set out from the Red Sea[a] and camped in the wilderness of Sin. 12 They set out from the wilderness of Sin and camped at Dophkah. 13 They set out from Dophkah and camped at Alush. 14 They set out from Alush and camped at Rephidim, where there was no water for the people to drink. 15 They set out from Rephidim and camped in the wilderness of Sinai. 16 They set out from the wilderness of Sinai and camped at Kibroth-hattaavah. 17 They set out from Kibroth-hattaavah and camped at Hazeroth. 18 They set out from Hazeroth and camped at Rithmah. 19 They set out from Rithmah and camped at Rimmon-perez. 20 They set out from Rimmon-perez and camped at Libnah. 21 They set out from Libnah and camped at Rissah. 22 They set out from Rissah and camped at Kehelathah. 23 They set out from Kehelathah and camped at Mount Shepher. 24 They set out from Mount Shepher and camped at Haradah. 25 They set out from Haradah and camped at Makheloth. 26 They set out from Makheloth and camped at Tahath. 27 They set out from Tahath and camped at Terah. 28 They set out from Terah and camped at Mithkah. 29 They set out from Mithkah and camped at Hashmonah. 30 They set out from Hashmonah and camped at Moseroth. 31 They set out from Moseroth and camped at Bene-jaakan. 32 They set out from Bene-jaakan and camped at Hor-haggidgad. 33 They set out from Hor-haggidgad and camped at Jotbathah. 34 They set out from Jotbathah and camped at Abronah. 35 They set out from Abronah and camped at Ezion-geber. 36 They set out from Ezion-geber and camped in the wilderness of Zin (that is, Kadesh). 37 They set out from Kadesh and camped at Mount Hor, on the edge of the land of Edom.

38 Aaron the priest went up Mount Hor at the command of the LORD and died there in the fortieth year after the Israelites had come out of the land of Egypt, on the first day of the fifth month. 39 Aaron was one hundred twenty-three years old when he died on Mount Hor.

40 The Canaanite, the king of Arad, who lived in the Negeb in the land of Canaan, heard of the coming of the Israelites.

41 They set out from Mount Hor and camped at Zalmonah. 42 They set out from Zalmonah and camped at Punon. 43 They set out from Punon and camped at Oboth. 44 They set out from Oboth and camped at Iye-abarim, in the territory of Moab. 45 They set out from Iyim and camped at Dibon-gad. 46 They set out from Dibon-gad and camped at Almon-diblathaim. 47 They set out from Almon-diblathaim and camped in the mountains of Abarim, before Nebo. 48 They set out from the mountains of Abarim and camped in the plains of Moab by the Jordan at Jericho; 49 they camped by the Jordan from Beth-jeshimoth as far as Abel-shittim in the plains of Moab.

50 In the plains of Moab by the Jordan at Jericho, the LORD spoke to Moses, saying: 51 Speak to the Israelites, and say to them: When you cross over the Jordan into the land of Canaan, 52 you shall drive out all the inhabitants of the land from before you, destroy all their figured stones, destroy all their cast images, and demolish all their high places. 53 You shall take possession of the land and settle in it, for I have given you the land to possess. 54 You shall apportion the land by lot according to your clans; to a large one you shall give a large inheritance, and to a small one you shall give a small inheritance; the inheritance shall belong to the person on whom the lot falls; according to your ancestral tribes you shall inherit. 55 But if you do not drive out the inhabitants of the land from before you, then those whom you let remain shall be as barbs in your eyes and thorns in your sides; they shall trouble you in the land where you are settling. 56 And I will do to you as I thought to do to them.

[a] Or *Sea of Reeds*

34 The LORD spoke to Moses, saying: 2 Command the Israelites, and say to them: When you enter the land of Canaan (this is the land that shall fall to you for an inheritance, the land of Canaan, defined by its boundaries), 3 your south sector shall extend from the wilderness of Zin along the side of Edom. Your southern boundary shall begin from the end of the Dead Sea[a] on the east; 4 your boundary shall turn south of the ascent of Akrabbim, and cross to Zin, and its outer limit shall be south of Kadesh-barnea; then it shall go on to Hazar-addar, and cross to Azmon; 5 the boundary shall turn from Azmon to the Wadi of Egypt, and its termination shall be at the Sea.

6 For the western boundary, you shall have the Great Sea and its[b] coast; this shall be your western boundary.

7 This shall be your northern boundary: from the Great Sea you shall mark out your line to Mount Hor; 8 from Mount Hor you shall mark it out to Lebo-hamath, and the outer limit of the boundary shall be at Zedad; 9 then the boundary shall extend to Ziphron, and its end shall be at Hazar-enan; this shall be your northern boundary.

10 You shall mark out your eastern boundary from Hazar-enan to Shepham; 11 and the boundary shall continue down from Shepham to Riblah on the east side of Ain; and the boundary shall go down, and reach the eastern slope of the sea of Chinnereth; 12 and the boundary shall go down to the Jordan, and its end shall be at the Dead Sea.[a] This shall be your land with its boundaries all around.

13 Moses commanded the Israelites, saying: This is the land that you shall inherit by lot, which the LORD has commanded to give to the nine tribes and to the half-tribe; 14 for the tribe of the Reubenites by their ancestral houses and the tribe of the Gadites by their ancestral houses have taken their inheritance, and also the half-tribe of Manasseh; 15 the two tribes and the half-tribe have taken their inheritance beyond the Jordan at Jericho eastward, toward the sunrise.

16 The LORD spoke to Moses, saying: 17 These are the names of the men who shall apportion the land to you for inheritance: the priest Eleazar and Joshua son of Nun. 18 You shall take one leader of every tribe to apportion the land for inheritance. 19 These are the names of the men: Of the tribe of Judah, Caleb son of Jephunneh. 20 Of the tribe of the Simeonites, Shemuel son of Ammihud. 21 Of the tribe of Benjamin, Elidad son of Chislon. 22 Of the tribe of the Danites a leader, Bukki son of Jogli. 23 Of the Josephites: of the tribe of the Manassites a leader, Hanniel son of Ephod, 24 and of the tribe of the Ephraimites a leader, Kemuel son of Shiphtan. 25 Of the tribe of the Zebulunites a leader, Eli-zaphan son of Parnach. 26 Of the tribe of the Issacharites a leader, Paltiel son of Azzan. 27 And of the tribe of the Asherites a leader, Ahihud son of Shelomi. 28 Of the tribe of the Naphtalites a leader, Pedahel son of Ammihud. 29 These were the ones whom the LORD commanded to apportion the inheritance for the Israelites in the land of Canaan.

35 In the plains of Moab by the Jordan at Jericho, the LORD spoke to Moses, saying: 2 Command the Israelites to give, from the inheritance that they possess, towns for the Levites to live in; you shall also give to the Levites pasture lands surrounding the towns. 3 The towns shall be theirs to live in, and their pasture lands shall be for their cattle, for their livestock, and for all their animals. 4 The pasture lands of the towns, which you shall give to the Levites, shall reach from the wall of the town outward a thousand cubits all around. 5 You shall measure, outside the town, for the east side two thousand cubits, for the south side two thousand cubits, for the west side two thousand cubits, and for the north side two thousand cubits, with the town in the middle; this shall belong to them as pasture land for their towns.

6 The towns that you give to the Levites shall include the six cities of refuge, where you shall permit a slayer to flee, and in addition to them you shall give forty-two towns. 7 The towns that you give to the Levites shall total forty-eight,

[a] Heb *Salt Sea* [b] Syr: Heb lacks *its*

with their pasture lands. 8And as for the towns
that you shall give from the possession of the
Israelites, from the larger tribes you shall take
many, and from the smaller tribes you shall take
few; each, in proportion to the inheritance that it
obtains, shall give of its towns to the Levites.
9 The LORD spoke to Moses, saying: 10Speak
to the Israelites, and say to them: When you cross
the Jordan into the land of Canaan, 11then you
shall select cities to be cities of refuge for you,
so that a slayer who kills a person without intent
may flee there. 12The cities shall be for you a refuge from the avenger, so that the slayer may not
die until there is a trial before the congregation.
13 The cities that you designate shall be six
cities of refuge for you: 14you shall designate
three cities beyond the Jordan, and three cities in
the land of Canaan, to be cities of refuge. 15These
six cities shall serve as refuge for the Israelites,
for the resident or transient alien among them,
so that anyone who kills a person without intent
may flee there.
16 But anyone who strikes another with
an iron object, and death ensues, is a murderer;
the murderer shall be put to death. 17Or anyone
who strikes another with a stone in hand that
could cause death, and death ensues, is a murderer; the murderer shall be put to death. 18Or
anyone who strikes another with a weapon of
wood in hand that could cause death, and death
ensues, is a murderer; the murderer shall be put
to death. 19The avenger of blood is the one who
shall put the murderer to death; when they meet,
the avenger of blood shall execute the sentence.
20Likewise, if someone pushes another from hatred, or hurls something at another, lying in wait,
and death ensues, 21or in enmity strikes another
with the hand, and death ensues, then the one
who struck the blow shall be put to death; that
person is a murderer; the avenger of blood shall
put the murderer to death, when they meet.
22 But if someone pushes another suddenly
without enmity, or hurls any object without lying
in wait, 23or, while handling any stone that could
cause death, unintentionally[a] drops it on another
and death ensues, though they were not enemies,
and no harm was intended, 24then the congregation shall judge between the slayer and the avenger
of blood, in accordance with these ordinances;
25and the congregation shall rescue the slayer
from the avenger of blood. Then the congregation shall send the slayer back to the original city
of refuge. The slayer shall live in it until the death
of the high priest who was anointed with the holy
oil. 26But if the slayer shall at any time go outside
the bounds of the original city of refuge, 27and is
found by the avenger of blood outside the bounds
of the city of refuge, and is killed by the avenger,
no bloodguilt shall be incurred. 28For the slayer
must remain in the city of refuge until the death
of the high priest; but after the death of the high
priest the slayer may return home.
29 These things shall be a statute and ordinance for you throughout your generations wherever you live.
30 If anyone kills another, the murderer shall
be put to death on the evidence of witnesses; but
no one shall be put to death on the testimony of
a single witness. 31Moreover you shall accept no
ransom for the life of a murderer who is subject
to the death penalty; a murderer must be put to
death. 32Nor shall you accept ransom for one
who has fled to a city of refuge, enabling the fugitive to return to live in the land before the death
of the high priest. 33You shall not pollute the land
in which you live; for blood pollutes the land, and
no expiation can be made for the land, for the
blood that is shed in it, except by the blood of the
one who shed it. 34You shall not defile the land
in which you live, in which I also dwell; for I the
LORD dwell among the Israelites.
36 The heads of the ancestral houses of the
clans of the descendants of Gilead son of
Machir son of Manasseh, of the Josephite clans,
came forward and spoke in the presence of Moses
and the leaders, the heads of the ancestral houses
of the Israelites; 2they said, "The LORD commanded my lord to give the land for inheritance
by lot to the Israelites; and my lord was commanded by the LORD to give the inheritance of

[a] Heb *without seeing*

our brother Zelophehad to his daughters. 3 But if
they are married into another Israelite tribe, then
their inheritance will be taken from the inheritance of our ancestors and added to the inheritance of the tribe into which they marry; so it will
be taken away from the allotted portion of our inheritance. 4 And when the jubilee of the Israelites
comes, then their inheritance will be added to the
inheritance of the tribe into which they have married; and their inheritance will be taken from the
inheritance of our ancestral tribe."

5 Then Moses commanded the Israelites according to the word of the LORD, saying, "The
descendants of the tribe of Joseph are right in
what they are saying. 6 This is what the LORD commands concerning the daughters of Zelophehad,
'Let them marry whom they think best; only it
must be into a clan of their father's tribe that they
are married, 7 so that no inheritance of the Israelites shall be transferred from one tribe to another;
for all Israelites shall retain the inheritance of their
ancestral tribes. 8 Every daughter who possesses an
inheritance in any tribe of the Israelites shall marry
one from the clan of her father's tribe, so that all
Israelites may continue to possess their ancestral
inheritance. 9 No inheritance shall be transferred
from one tribe to another; for each of the tribes of
the Israelites shall retain its own inheritance.' "

10 The daughters of Zelophehad did as
the LORD had commanded Moses. 11 Mahlah,
Tirzah, Hoglah, Milcah, and Noah, the daughters of Zelophehad, married sons of their father's
brothers. 12 They were married into the clans of
the descendants of Manasseh son of Joseph, and
their inheritance remained in the tribe of their
father's clan.

13 These are the commandments and the
ordinances that the LORD commanded through
Moses to the Israelites in the plains of Moab by
the Jordan at Jericho.

Deuteronomy

DEUTERONOMY IS THE FIFTH BOOK in the Pentateuch. The name of the book comes from Greek and means "second law." The Hebrew name is *'elleh haddebarim*, "these are the words." Both of these names point to two different aspects of the book. In Jewish tradition, there is only one Torah. However, this last book of the Five Books of Moses represents a preached law, or a re-situating of Israel's covenant with its God for a new setting and a later generation. The Hebrew title comes from the first two words of the book and is descriptive of the contents. Deuteronomy is written as the final speech—or series of speeches—from Moses. Hence, it represents a last will and testament of this legendary leader of Israel.

The book is set on the plains of Moab prior to the children of Israel's entrance into the land of Canaan. In this way, Deuteronomy is a boundary document. It attempts to set forth Israel's identity, grounded firmly in God's revelation on the mountain, as the people seek to enter into God's promises made to the ancestors. As Israel is about to cross borders into a new land, Moses reminds the people of their distinctiveness, constructing boundaries for Israel's identity as a chosen community.

In 2 Kings 22–23, a "book of the law" is found in the temple during the reign of Josiah. The young king proceeds to reform the religious life of Israel according to the stipulation of this document, presumably with the assistance of his advisers, since he was only eight years old. Among the many named counselors are Jedidah, his queen mother (2 Kgs 22:1), and Huldah, the court prophet (2 Kgs 22:16-20), the latter providing the definitive word of the LORD in response to the royal inquiry about the "words of this book" (2 Kgs 22:13). Many scholars have associated this "book of the law" with large portions of Deuteronomy. Themes such as the LORD's intolerance of foreign shrines and altars, the oneness of God and of Israel, and the centralization of worship at a place of the LORD's choosing parallel the political and religious reforms of Josiah. Hence, scholars have dated significant portions of Deuteronomy to the last third of the seventh century BCE, during the reign of Josiah. After the fall of the Northern Kingdom in 722, the language of Israel's oneness and the LORD's oneness (cf. Deut 6:4-5) represented an attempt to reestablish an ideal version of the former United Kingdom, one Israel. Scholars also have recognized that other portions of the book are written from a perspective after the Babylonian exile (587 BCE), long after the monarchy had collapsed. In this way, the specter of exile came to provide another re-contextualization of earlier ideas and themes. The idea of constructing an identity for the people of God in a promised land creates quite a different image when seen through the eyes of exile rather than through the lens of monarchy.

Deuteronomy is comprised of four sections, each beginning with an editorial comment that describes Moses' role as he re-situates the covenant for this new stage of Israel's journey and prepares the people for life beyond the Jordan (see 1:1-5; 4:44-49; 29:1; and 31:1-2). The first section (1:1—4:43) provides an introduction to the book as Moses summarizes Israel's wandering in the wilderness. The second and central section, 4:44—28:68, is a re-proclamation of the law that was revealed at Horeb (Sinai in other biblical traditions). In 29:1—30:20, the covenant is renewed on the plains of Moab. Moses exhorts the Israelites to choose life by being faithful to the "commandments, decrees, and ordinances" of the LORD their God (30:16). The book ends with the events surrounding Moses' death. This last section (31:1—34:12) includes Moses' commissioning of Joshua, a song of Moses, a final blessing, and the death and burial of this "prophet" (34:10) of Israel.

Deuteronomy 6:4-6 represents one of the central themes in the book. This passage, also known as the *Shema* (verse 4 begins with this Hebrew command, meaning "hear" or "listen"), calls Israel to locate their identity in a God who is one and who alone should be worshipped. The notion of exclusive worship of the LORD should be reflected in the Israelite community, which should be similarly unified as one people under the covenant of its God. This distinctiveness is reflected in Deuteronomy's laws through its emphasis on Israelite worship and social order over against Canaanite culture and practices. The theme of oneness can also be found in Deuteronomy's insistence that worship should be at one site, a place of the LORD's choosing. These themes in Deuteronomy can be understood as an exercise in constructing identity. To *be* Israel, the people must, on the one hand, be wholly dedicated to the LORD, and on the other they must distinguish themselves from the practices of other peoples. Group identity is created through the erection of cultural and religious boundaries. Both in its historical context and in its canonical/literary context, the authors and editors of this book sought to make clear what was distinctly Israelite for their day and age.

Establishing and maintaining cultural identity is a necessary and sometimes problematic business. There is a fine line between creating group boundaries to preserve a cultural heritage and erecting walls or fences to keep others out. I am a *Sansei*—a third-generation Japanese American. This double-edged sword of cultural identity bears itself out in my family's histories and in my own experience. Traditions, religion, and community have helped to preserve some aspects of Japanese culture for generations of Japanese Americans. Thus, culture can act as a force that binds together people of similar ethnic background, making them one. However, the Japanese in America have also been labeled as the cultural "other," or foreigner. During World War II, in a time of war hysteria, people of Japanese descent were perceived as threats by those who could not recognize the Japanese as belonging in America. This was made most clear when the U.S. Government unjustly imprisoned some 120,000 Japanese and Japanese Americans in camps throughout the West Coast without due process of law. In that case, cultural identity was the rationale that was used to exclude—setting "American" culture over against those of Japanese descent. Because of this double-edged nature of culture—the ability to both include and exclude—it is important to read the themes in Deuteronomy in context rather than assume them to be universal. The special nature of a place and people in relationship to their God can quickly turn into a rationale for the expulsion or extermination of a foreign "other."

— ***Frank M. Yamada***

1 These are the words that Moses spoke to all
Israel beyond the Jordan—in the wilderness,
on the plain opposite Suph, between Paran and
Tophel, Laban, Hazeroth, and Di-zahab. 2 (By
the way of Mount Seir it takes eleven days to
reach Kadesh-barnea from Horeb.) 3 In the fortieth year, on the first day of the eleventh month,
Moses spoke to the Israelites just as the LORD
had commanded him to speak to them. 4 This was
after he had defeated King Sihon of the Amorites,
who reigned in Heshbon, and King Og of Bashan,
who reigned in Ashtaroth and[a] in Edrei. 5 Beyond
the Jordan in the land of Moab, Moses undertook
to expound this law as follows:

6 The LORD our God spoke to us at Horeb,
saying, "You have stayed long enough at this
mountain. 7 Resume your journey, and go into
the hill country of the Amorites as well as into the
neighboring regions—the Arabah, the hill country, the Shephelah, the Negeb, and the seacoast—
the land of the Canaanites and the Lebanon, as
far as the great river, the river Euphrates. 8 See, I
have set the land before you; go in and take possession of the land that I[b] swore to your ancestors, to Abraham, to Isaac, and to Jacob, to give to
them and to their descendants after them."

9 At that time I said to you, "I am unable by
myself to bear you. 10 The LORD your God has
multiplied you, so that today you are as numerous
as the stars of heaven. 11 May the LORD, the God
of your ancestors, increase you a thousand times
more and bless you, as he has promised you!
12 But how can I bear the heavy burden of your
disputes all by myself? 13 Choose for each of your
tribes individuals who are wise, discerning, and
reputable to be your leaders." 14 You answered me,
"The plan you have proposed is a good one." 15 So
I took the leaders of your tribes, wise and reputable individuals, and installed them as leaders over
you, commanders of thousands, commanders of
hundreds, commanders of fifties, commanders
of tens, and officials, throughout your tribes. 16 I
charged your judges at that time: "Give the members of your community a fair hearing, and judge
rightly between one person and another, whether
citizen or resident alien. 17 You must not be partial in judging: hear out the small and the great
alike; you shall not be intimidated by anyone, for
the judgment is God's. Any case that is too hard
for you, bring to me, and I will hear it." 18 So I
charged you at that time with all the things that
you should do.

19 Then, just as the LORD our God had
ordered us, we set out from Horeb and went
through all that great and terrible wilderness that
you saw, on the way to the hill country of the
Amorites, until we reached Kadesh-barnea. 20 I
said to you, "You have reached the hill country of
the Amorites, which the LORD our God is giving
us. 21 See, the LORD your God has given the land
to you; go up, take possession, as the LORD, the
God of your ancestors, has promised you; do not
fear or be dismayed."

22 All of you came to me and said, "Let us
send men ahead of us to explore the land for us
and bring back a report to us regarding the route
by which we should go up and the cities we will
come to." 23 The plan seemed good to me, and
I selected twelve of you, one from each tribe.
24 They set out and went up into the hill country,
and when they reached the Valley of Eshcol they
spied it out 25 and gathered some of the land's
produce, which they brought down to us. They
brought back a report to us, and said, "It is a good
land that the LORD our God is giving us."

26 But you were unwilling to go up. You rebelled against the command of the LORD your
God; 27 you grumbled in your tents and said, "It
is because the LORD hates us that he has brought
us out of the land of Egypt, to hand us over to the
Amorites to destroy us. 28 Where are we headed?
Our kindred have made our hearts melt by reporting, 'The people are stronger and taller than we;
the cities are large and fortified up to heaven! We
actually saw there the offspring of the Anakim!' "
29 I said to you, "Have no dread or fear of them.
30 The LORD your God, who goes before you, is
the one who will fight for you, just as he did for
you in Egypt before your very eyes, 31 and in the
wilderness, where you saw how the LORD your

[a] Gk Syr Vg Compare Josh 12.4: Heb lacks *and* [b] Sam Gk: MT *the LORD*

God carried you, just as one carries a child, all
the way that you traveled until you reached this
place. 32But in spite of this, you have no trust in
the LORD your God, 33who goes before you on
the way to seek out a place for you to camp, in fire
by night, and in the cloud by day, to show you the
route you should take."
34 When the LORD heard your words, he was
wrathful and swore: 35"Not one of these—not
one of this evil generation—shall see the good
land that I swore to give to your ancestors, 36ex-
cept Caleb son of Jephunneh. He shall see it, and
to him and to his descendants I will give the land
on which he set foot, because of his complete fidelity to the LORD." 37Even with me the LORD
was angry on your account, saying, "You also shall
not enter there. 38Joshua son of Nun, your assistant, shall enter there; encourage him, for he is the
one who will secure Israel's possession of it. 39And
as for your little ones, who you thought would become booty, your children, who today do not yet
know right from wrong, they shall enter there; to
them I will give it, and they shall take possession
of it. 40But as for you, journey back into the wilderness, in the direction of the Red Sea."[a]
41 You answered me, "We have sinned against
the LORD! We are ready to go up and fight, just
as the LORD our God commanded us." So all of
you strapped on your battle gear, and thought it
easy to go up into the hill country. 42The LORD
said to me, "Say to them, 'Do not go up and do
not fight, for I am not in the midst of you; otherwise you will be defeated by your enemies.'"
43Although I told you, you would not listen. You
rebelled against the command of the LORD and
presumptuously went up into the hill country.
44The Amorites who lived in that hill country
then came out against you and chased you as bees
do. They beat you down in Seir as far as Hormah.
45When you returned and wept before the LORD,
the LORD would neither heed your voice nor pay
you any attention.
46 After you had stayed at Kadesh as many
days as you did,

2 1we journeyed back into the
wilderness, in the direction of the Red Sea,[a]
as the LORD had told me and skirted Mount Seir
for many days. 2Then the LORD said to me: 3"You
have been skirting this hill country long enough.
Head north, 4and charge the people as follows:
You are about to pass through the territory of
your kindred, the descendants of Esau, who live
in Seir. They will be afraid of you, so, be very careful 5not to engage in battle with them, for I will
not give you even so much as a foot's length of
their land, since I have given Mount Seir to Esau
as a possession. 6You shall purchase food from
them for money, so that you may eat; and you
shall also buy water from them for money, so that
you may drink. 7Surely the LORD your God has
blessed you in all your undertakings; he knows
your going through this great wilderness. These
forty years the LORD your God has been with
you; you have lacked nothing." 8So we passed by
our kin, the descendants of Esau who live in Seir,
leaving behind the route of the Arabah, and leaving behind Elath and Ezion-geber.
When we had headed out along the route of
the wilderness of Moab, 9the LORD said to me:
"Do not harass Moab or engage them in battle, for
I will not give you any of its land as a possession,
since I have given Ar as a possession to the descendants of Lot." 10(The Emim—a large and numerous people, as tall as the Anakim—had formerly
inhabited it. 11Like the Anakim, they are usually
reckoned as Rephaim, though the Moabites call
them Emim. 12Moreover, the Horim had formerly inhabited Seir, but the descendants of Esau
dispossessed them, destroying them and settling
in their place, as Israel has done in the land that
the LORD gave them as a possession.) 13"Now
then, proceed to cross over the Wadi Zered."
So we crossed over the Wadi Zered. 14And
the length of time we had traveled from Kadesh-
barnea until we crossed the Wadi Zered was
thirty-eight years, until the entire generation
of warriors had perished from the camp, as the
LORD had sworn concerning them. 15Indeed, the
LORD's own hand was against them, to root them
out from the camp, until all had perished.
16 Just as soon as all the warriors had died

[a] Or *Sea of Reeds*

off from among the people, 17 the LORD spoke to me, saying, 18 "Today you are going to cross the boundary of Moab at Ar. 19 When you approach the frontier of the Ammonites, do not harass them or engage them in battle, for I will not give the land of the Ammonites to you as a possession, because I have given it to the descendants of Lot." 20 (It also is usually reckoned as a land of Rephaim. Rephaim formerly inhabited it, though the Ammonites call them Zamzummim, 21 a strong and numerous people, as tall as the Anakim. But the LORD destroyed them from before the Ammonites so that they could dispossess them and settle in their place. 22 He did the same for the descendants of Esau, who live in Seir, by destroying the Horim before them so that they could dispossess them and settle in their place even to this day. 23 As for the Avvim, who had lived in settlements in the vicinity of Gaza, the Caphtorim, who came from Caphtor, destroyed them and settled in their place.) 24 "Proceed on your journey and cross the Wadi Arnon. See, I have handed over to you King Sihon the Amorite of Heshbon, and his land. Begin to take possession by engaging him in battle. 25 This day I will begin to put the dread and fear of you upon the peoples everywhere under heaven; when they hear report of you, they will tremble and be in anguish because of you."

26 So I sent messengers from the wilderness of Kedemoth to King Sihon of Heshbon with the following terms of peace: 27 "If you let me pass through your land, I will travel only along the road; I will turn aside neither to the right nor to the left. 28 You shall sell me food for money, so that I may eat, and supply me water for money, so that I may drink. Only allow me to pass through on foot— 29 just as the descendants of Esau who live in Seir have done for me and likewise the Moabites who live in Ar—until I cross the Jordan into the land that the LORD our God is giving us." 30 But King Sihon of Heshbon was not willing to let us pass through, for the LORD your God had hardened his spirit and made his heart defiant in order to hand him over to you, as he has now done.

31 The LORD said to me, "See, I have begun to give Sihon and his land over to you. Begin now to take possession of his land." 32 So when Sihon came out against us, he and all his people for battle at Jahaz, 33 the LORD our God gave him over to us; and we struck him down, along with his offspring and all his people. 34 At that time we captured all his towns, and in each town we utterly destroyed men, women, and children. We left not a single survivor. 35 Only the livestock we kept as spoil for ourselves, as well as the plunder of the towns that we had captured. 36 From Aroer on the edge of the Wadi Arnon (including the town that is in the wadi itself) as far as Gilead, there was no citadel too high for us. The LORD our God gave everything to us. 37 You did not encroach, however, on the land of the Ammonites, avoiding the whole upper region of the Wadi Jabbok as well as the towns of the hill country, just as[a] the LORD our God had charged.

3 When we headed up the road to Bashan, King Og of Bashan came out against us, he and all his people, for battle at Edrei. 2 The LORD said to me, "Do not fear him, for I have handed him over to you, along with his people and his land. Do to him as you did to King Sihon of the Amorites, who reigned in Heshbon." 3 So the LORD our God also handed over to us King Og of Bashan and all his people. We struck him down until not a single survivor was left. 4 At that time we captured all his towns; there was no citadel that we did not take from them—sixty towns, the whole region of Argob, the kingdom of Og in Bashan. 5 All these were fortress towns with high walls, double gates, and bars, besides a great many villages. 6 And we utterly destroyed them, as we had done to King Sihon of Heshbon, in each city utterly destroying men, women, and children. 7 But all the livestock and the plunder of the towns we kept as spoil for ourselves.

8 So at that time we took from the two kings of the Amorites the land beyond the Jordan, from the Wadi Arnon to Mount Hermon 9 (the Sidonians call Hermon Sirion, while the Amorites call it Senir), 10 all the towns of the tableland, the whole of Gilead, and all of Bashan, as

[a] Gk Tg: Heb *and all*

far as Salecah and Edrei, towns of Og's kingdom
in Bashan. 11(Now only King Og of Bashan was
left of the remnant of the Rephaim. In fact his
bed, an iron bed, can still be seen in Rabbah of
the Ammonites. By the common cubit it is nine
cubits long and four cubits wide.) 12As for the
land that we took possession of at that time, I
gave to the Reubenites and Gadites the territory
north of Aroer,[a] that is on the edge of the Wadi
Arnon, as well as half the hill country of Gilead
with its towns, 13and I gave to the half-tribe of
Manasseh the rest of Gilead and all of Bashan,
Og's kingdom. (The whole region of Argob: all
that portion of Bashan used to be called a land
of Rephaim; 14Jair the Manassite acquired the
whole region of Argob as far as the border of the
Geshurites and the Maacathites, and he named
them—that is, Bashan—after himself, Havvoth-
jair,[b] as it is to this day.) 15To Machir I gave Gilead.
16And to the Reubenites and the Gadites I gave
the territory from Gilead as far as the Wadi Arnon,
with the middle of the wadi as a boundary, and
up to the Jabbok, the wadi being boundary of the
Ammonites; 17the Arabah also, with the Jordan
and its banks, from Chinnereth down to the sea of
the Arabah, the Dead Sea,[c] with the lower slopes
of Pisgah on the east.

18 At that time, I charged you as follows: "Although the LORD your God has given you this land
to occupy, all your troops shall cross over armed
as the vanguard of your Israelite kin. 19Only your
wives, your children, and your livestock—I know
that you have much livestock—shall stay behind
in the towns that I have given to you. 20When the
LORD gives rest to your kindred, as to you, and
they too have occupied the land that the LORD
your God is giving them beyond the Jordan, then
each of you may return to the property that I have
given to you." 21And I charged Joshua as well
at that time, saying: "Your own eyes have seen
everything that the LORD your God has done to
these two kings; so the LORD will do to all the
kingdoms into which you are about to cross.
22Do not fear them, for it is the LORD your God
who fights for you."

23 At that time, too, I entreated the LORD,
saying: 24"O Lord GOD, you have only begun
to show your servant your greatness and your
might; what god in heaven or on earth can perform deeds and mighty acts like yours! 25Let
me cross over to see the good land beyond the
Jordan, that good hill country and the Lebanon."
26But the LORD was angry with me on your account and would not heed me. The LORD said
to me, "Enough from you! Never speak to me of
this matter again! 27Go up to the top of Pisgah
and look around you to the west, to the north, to
the south, and to the east. Look well, for you shall
not cross over this Jordan. 28But charge Joshua,
and encourage and strengthen him, because it is
he who shall cross over at the head of this people
and who shall secure their possession of the land
that you will see." 29So we remained in the valley
opposite Beth-peor.

4 So now, Israel, give heed to the statutes and
ordinances that I am teaching you to observe,
so that you may live to enter and occupy the land
that the LORD, the God of your ancestors, is giving you. 2You must neither add anything to what I
command you nor take away anything from it, but
keep the commandments of the LORD your God
with which I am charging you. 3You have seen for
yourselves what the LORD did with regard to the
Baal of Peor—how the LORD your God destroyed
from among you everyone who followed the Baal
of Peor, 4while those of you who held fast to the
LORD your God are all alive today.

5 See, just as the LORD my God has charged
me, I now teach you statutes and ordinances for
you to observe in the land that you are about to
enter and occupy. 6You must observe them diligently, for this will show your wisdom and discernment to the peoples, who, when they hear all
these statutes, will say, "Surely this great nation is
a wise and discerning people!" 7For what other
great nation has a god so near to it as the LORD
our God is whenever we call to him? 8And what
other great nation has statutes and ordinances as
just as this entire law that I am setting before you
today?

[a] Heb *territory from Aroer* [b] That is *Settlement of Jair* [c] Heb *Salt Sea*

9 But take care and watch yourselves closely, so as neither to forget the things that your eyes have seen nor to let them slip from your mind all the days of your life; make them known to your children and your children's children— 10how you once stood before the LORD your God at Horeb, when the LORD said to me, "Assemble the people for me, and I will let them hear my words, so that they may learn to fear me as long as they live on the earth, and may teach their children so"; 11you approached and stood at the foot of the mountain while the mountain was blazing up to the very heavens, shrouded in dark clouds. 12Then the LORD spoke to you out of the fire. You heard the sound of words but saw no form; there was only a voice. 13He declared to you his covenant, which he charged you to observe, that is, the ten commandments;[a] and he wrote them on two stone tablets. 14And the LORD charged me at that time to teach you statutes and ordinances for you to observe in the land that you are about to cross into and occupy.

15 Since you saw no form when the LORD spoke to you at Horeb out of the fire, take care and watch yourselves closely, 16so that you do not act corruptly by making an idol for yourselves, in the form of any figure—the likeness of male or female, 17the likeness of any animal that is on the earth, the likeness of any winged bird that flies in the air, 18the likeness of anything that creeps on the ground, the likeness of any fish that is in the water under the earth. 19And when you look up to the heavens and see the sun, the moon, and the stars, all the host of heaven, do not be led astray and bow down to them and serve them, things that the LORD your God has allotted to all the peoples everywhere under heaven. 20But the LORD has taken you and brought you out of the iron-smelter, out of Egypt, to become a people of his very own possession, as you are now.

21 The LORD was angry with me because of you, and he vowed that I should not cross the Jordan and that I should not enter the good land that the LORD your God is giving for your possession. 22For I am going to die in this land without crossing over the Jordan, but you are going to cross over to take possession of that good land. 23So be careful not to forget the covenant that the LORD your God made with you, and not to make for yourselves an idol in the form of anything that the LORD your God has forbidden you. 24For the LORD your God is a devouring fire, a jealous God.

25 When you have had children and children's children, and become complacent in the land, if you act corruptly by making an idol in the form of anything, thus doing what is evil in the sight of the LORD your God, and provoking him to anger, 26I call heaven and earth to witness against you today that you will soon utterly perish from the land that you are crossing the Jordan to occupy; you will not live long on it, but will be utterly destroyed. 27The LORD will scatter you among the peoples; only a few of you will be left among the nations where the LORD will lead you. 28There you will serve other gods made by human hands, objects of wood and stone that neither see, nor hear, nor eat, nor smell. 29From there you will seek the LORD your God, and you will find him if you search after him with all your heart and soul. 30In your distress, when all these things have happened to you in time to come, you will return to the LORD your God and heed him. 31Because the LORD your God is a merciful God, he will neither abandon you nor destroy you; he will not forget the covenant with your ancestors that he swore to them.

32 For ask now about former ages, long before your own, ever since the day that God created human beings on the earth; ask from one end of heaven to the other: has anything so great as this ever happened or has its like ever been heard of? 33Has any people ever heard the voice of a god speaking out of a fire, as you have heard, and lived? 34Or has any god ever attempted to go and take a nation for himself from the midst of another nation, by trials, by signs and wonders, by war, by a mighty hand and an outstretched arm, and by terrifying displays of power, as the LORD your God did for you in Egypt before your

[a] Heb *the ten words*

very eyes? 35To you it was shown so that you
would acknowledge that the LORD is God; there
is no other besides him. 36From heaven he made
you hear his voice to discipline you. On earth he
showed you his great fire, while you heard his
words coming out of the fire. 37And because he
loved your ancestors, he chose their descendants
after them. He brought you out of Egypt with
his own presence, by his great power, 38driving
out before you nations greater and mightier than
yourselves, to bring you in, giving you their land
for a possession, as it is still today. 39So acknowledge today and take to heart that the LORD is
God in heaven above and on the earth beneath;
there is no other. 40Keep his statutes and his commandments, which I am commanding you today
for your own well-being and that of your descendants after you, so that you may long remain in
the land that the LORD your God is giving you
for all time.

41 Then Moses set apart on the east side of
the Jordan three cities 42to which a homicide
could flee, someone who unintentionally kills another person, the two not having been at enmity
before; the homicide could flee to one of these
cities and live: 43Bezer in the wilderness on the
tableland belonging to the Reubenites, Ramoth
in Gilead belonging to the Gadites, and Golan in
Bashan belonging to the Manassites.

44 This is the law that Moses set before the
Israelites. 45These are the decrees and the statutes
and ordinances that Moses spoke to the Israelites
when they had come out of Egypt, 46beyond the
Jordan in the valley opposite Beth-peor, in the
land of King Sihon of the Amorites, who reigned
at Heshbon, whom Moses and the Israelites defeated when they came out of Egypt. 47They occupied his land and the land of King Og of Bashan,
the two kings of the Amorites on the eastern side
of the Jordan: 48from Aroer, which is on the edge
of the Wadi Arnon, as far as Mount Sirion[a] (that
is, Hermon), 49together with all the Arabah on
the east side of the Jordan as far as the Sea of the
Arabah, under the slopes of Pisgah.

5 Moses convened all Israel, and said to them:
Hear, O Israel, the statutes and ordinances
that I am addressing to you today; you shall learn
them and observe them diligently. 2The LORD
our God made a covenant with us at Horeb. 3Not
with our ancestors did the LORD make this covenant, but with us, who are all of us here alive
today. 4The LORD spoke with you face to face at
the mountain, out of the fire. 5(At that time I was
standing between the LORD and you to declare to
you the words[b] of the LORD; for you were afraid
because of the fire and did not go up the mountain.) And he said:

6 I am the LORD your God, who brought you
out of the land of Egypt, out of the house of slavery; 7you shall have no other gods before[c] me.

8 You shall not make for yourself an idol,
whether in the form of anything that is in heaven
above, or that is on the earth beneath, or that is
in the water under the earth. 9You shall not bow
down to them or worship them; for I the LORD
your God am a jealous God, punishing children
for the iniquity of parents, to the third and fourth
generation of those who reject me, 10but showing
steadfast love to the thousandth generation[d] of
those who love me and keep my commandments.

11 You shall not make wrongful use of the
name of the LORD your God, for the LORD will
not acquit anyone who misuses his name.

Deuteronomy 5:8

The Ten Commandments here differ only slightly from their form in Exodus 20. The prohibition from making or worshiping images would have had a particular edge in the ancient near east, where the gods were routinely depicted in carvings as crowned monarchs, seated on thrones and wielding scepters, giving their laws to earthly kings. The command not to make an idol means, in part: never imagine the God of the exodus in the likeness of a king!

— NE

[a] Syr: Heb *Sion* [b] Q Mss Sam Gk Syr Vg Tg: MT *word* [c] Or *besides* [d] Or *to thousands*

12 Observe the sabbath day and keep it holy,
as the LORD your God commanded you. 13 Six
days you shall labor and do all your work. 14 But
the seventh day is a sabbath to the LORD your
God; you shall not do any work—you, or your
son or your daughter, or your male or female
slave, or your ox or your donkey, or any of your
livestock, or the resident alien in your towns, so
that your male and female slave may rest as well
as you. 15 Remember that you were a slave in the
land of Egypt, and the LORD your God brought
you out from there with a mighty hand and an
outstretched arm; therefore the LORD your God
commanded you to keep the sabbath day.

16 Honor your father and your mother, as
the LORD your God commanded you, so that
your days may be long and that it may go well
with you in the land that the LORD your God is
giving you.

17 You shall not murder.[a]

18 Neither shall you commit adultery.

19 Neither shall you steal.

20 Neither shall you bear false witness against
your neighbor.

21 Neither shall you covet your neighbor's
wife.

Neither shall you desire your neighbor's house,
or field, or male or female slave, or ox, or donkey,
or anything that belongs to your neighbor.

22 These words the LORD spoke with a loud
voice to your whole assembly at the mountain, out
of the fire, the cloud, and the thick darkness, and
he added no more. He wrote them on two stone
tablets, and gave them to me. 23 When you heard
the voice out of the darkness, while the mountain
was burning with fire, you approached me, all the
heads of your tribes and your elders; 24 and you
said, "Look, the LORD our God has shown us his
glory and greatness, and we have heard his voice
out of the fire. Today we have seen that God may
speak to someone and the person may still live.
25 So now why should we die? For this great fire
will consume us; if we hear the voice of the LORD
our God any longer, we shall die. 26 For who is
there of all flesh that has heard the voice of the
living God speaking out of fire, as we have, and
remained alive? 27 Go near, you yourself, and hear
all that the LORD our God will say. Then tell us
everything that the LORD our God tells you, and
we will listen and do it."

28 The LORD heard your words when you
spoke to me, and the LORD said to me: "I have
heard the words of this people, which they have
spoken to you; they are right in all that they
have spoken. 29 If only they had such a mind as
this, to fear me and to keep all my commandments always, so that it might go well with them
and with their children forever! 30 Go say to them,
'Return to your tents.' 31 But you, stand here by
me, and I will tell you all the commandments, the
statutes and the ordinances, that you shall teach
them, so that they may do them in the land that I
am giving them to possess." 32 You must therefore
be careful to do as the LORD your God has commanded you; you shall not turn to the right or to
the left. 33 You must follow exactly the path that
the LORD your God has commanded you, so that
you may live, and that it may go well with you,
and that you may live long in the land that you
are to possess.

6 Now this is the commandment—the statutes
and the ordinances—that the LORD your
God charged me to teach you to observe in the
land that you are about to cross into and occupy,
2 so that you and your children and your children's
children may fear the LORD your God all the days
of your life, and keep all his decrees and his commandments that I am commanding you, so that
your days may be long. 3 Hear therefore, O Israel,
and observe them diligently, so that it may go well
with you, and so that you may multiply greatly in
a land flowing with milk and honey, as the LORD,
the God of your ancestors, has promised you.

4 Hear, O Israel: The LORD is our God, the
LORD alone.[b] 5 You shall love the LORD your God
with all your heart, and with all your soul, and
with all your might. 6 Keep these words that I am
commanding you today in your heart. 7 Recite
them to your children and talk about them when
you are at home and when you are away, when

[a] Or *kill* [b] Or *The LORD our God is one LORD,* or *The LORD our God, the LORD is one,* or *The LORD is our God, the LORD is one*

you lie down and when you rise. 8 Bind them as
a sign on your hand, fix them as an emblem[a] on
your forehead, 9 and write them on the doorposts
of your house and on your gates.

10 When the LORD your God has brought
you into the land that he swore to your ancestors, to Abraham, to Isaac, and to Jacob, to give
you—a land with fine, large cities that you did
not build, 11 houses filled with all sorts of goods
that you did not fill, hewn cisterns that you did
not hew, vineyards and olive groves that you did
not plant—and when you have eaten your fill,
12 take care that you do not forget the LORD, who
brought you out of the land of Egypt, out of the
house of slavery. 13 The LORD your God you shall
fear; him you shall serve, and by his name alone
you shall swear. 14 Do not follow other gods, any
of the gods of the peoples who are all around you,
15 because the LORD your God, who is present
with you, is a jealous God. The anger of the LORD
your God would be kindled against you and he
would destroy you from the face of the earth.

16 Do not put the LORD your God to the
test, as you tested him at Massah. 17 You must diligently keep the commandments of the LORD your
God, and his decrees, and his statutes that he has
commanded you. 18 Do what is right and good in
the sight of the LORD, so that it may go well with
you, and so that you may go in and occupy the
good land that the LORD swore to your ancestors
to give you, 19 thrusting out all your enemies from
before you, as the LORD has promised.

20 When your children ask you in time to
come, "What is the meaning of the decrees and
the statutes and the ordinances that the LORD
our God has commanded you?" 21 then you shall
say to your children, "We were Pharaoh's slaves
in Egypt, but the LORD brought us out of Egypt
with a mighty hand. 22 The LORD displayed before
our eyes great and awesome signs and wonders
against Egypt, against Pharaoh and all his household. 23 He brought us out from there in order to
bring us in, to give us the land that he promised
on oath to our ancestors. 24 Then the LORD commanded us to observe all these statutes, to fear
the LORD our God, for our lasting good, so as to
keep us alive, as is now the case. 25 If we diligently observe this entire commandment before the
LORD our God, as he has commanded us, we will
be in the right."

7 When the LORD your God brings you into
the land that you are about to enter and occupy, and he clears away many nations before
you—the Hittites, the Girgashites, the Amorites,
the Canaanites, the Perizzites, the Hivites, and
the Jebusites, seven nations mightier and more
numerous than you— 2 and when the LORD your
God gives them over to you and you defeat them,

[a] Or *as a frontlet*

Deuteronomy 7:1-2

Although it is not unusual today to hear characterizations of Islam as a violent religion, those who treasure the Bible as sacred scripture might well consider that in several places the Qur'an places strict limits on the resort to violence and force. On the other hand, in Deuteronomy God is represented as commanding wholesale slaughter of a people ("you must utterly destroy them . . . show them no mercy," Deut. 7:2). No one is to be spared, and the indigenous culture of Canaan is to be obliterated as well. The book of Judges, and archaeological evidence as well, show that in fact the Hebrews did not carry out such complete and wholesale destruction. Some scholars suggest that these commands represent the "wishful thinking" of later scribes who lament the residual practices of ancient Canaanite religion; but wistful or not, the commands to slaughter others in the name of God have had disastrous consequences in history—most notably in the destruction of native American peoples and the eradication of their cultures in a continent that many of the Europeans regarded as a "New Canaan."

— *NE*

then you must utterly destroy them. Make no covenant with them and show them no mercy. 3Do
not intermarry with them, giving your daughters
to their sons or taking their daughters for your
sons, 4for that would turn away your children
from following me, to serve other gods. Then the
anger of the LORD would be kindled against you,
and he would destroy you quickly. 5But this is
how you must deal with them: break down their
altars, smash their pillars, hew down their sacred
poles,[a] and burn their idols with fire. 6For you are
a people holy to the LORD your God; the LORD
your God has chosen you out of all the peoples on
earth to be his people, his treasured possession.

7 It was not because you were more numerous than any other people that the LORD set his
heart on you and chose you—for you were the
fewest of all peoples. 8It was because the LORD
loved you and kept the oath that he swore to your
ancestors, that the LORD has brought you out
with a mighty hand, and redeemed you from the
house of slavery, from the hand of Pharaoh king
of Egypt. 9Know therefore that the LORD your
God is God, the faithful God who maintains covenant loyalty with those who love him and keep
his commandments, to a thousand generations,
10and who repays in their own person those who
reject him. He does not delay but repays in their
own person those who reject him. 11Therefore,
observe diligently the commandment—the statutes and the ordinances—that I am commanding
you today.

12 If you heed these ordinances, by diligently
observing them, the LORD your God will maintain with you the covenant loyalty that he swore
to your ancestors; 13he will love you, bless you,
and multiply you; he will bless the fruit of your
womb and the fruit of your ground, your grain
and your wine and your oil, the increase of your
cattle and the issue of your flock, in the land that
he swore to your ancestors to give you. 14You
shall be the most blessed of peoples, with neither
sterility nor barrenness among you or your livestock. 15The LORD will turn away from you every
illness; all the dread diseases of Egypt that you
experienced, he will not inflict on you, but he will
lay them on all who hate you. 16You shall devour
all the peoples that the LORD your God is giving
over to you, showing them no pity; you shall not
serve their gods, for that would be a snare to you.

17 If you say to yourself, "These nations are
more numerous than I; how can I dispossess
them?" 18do not be afraid of them. Just remember what the LORD your God did to Pharaoh and
to all Egypt, 19the great trials that your eyes saw,
the signs and wonders, the mighty hand and the
outstretched arm by which the LORD your God
brought you out. The LORD your God will do the
same to all the peoples of whom you are afraid.
20Moreover, the LORD your God will send the
pestilence[b] against them, until even the survivors
and the fugitives are destroyed. 21Have no dread
of them, for the LORD your God, who is present with you, is a great and awesome God. 22The
LORD your God will clear away these nations
before you little by little; you will not be able to
make a quick end of them, otherwise the wild
animals would become too numerous for you.
23But the LORD your God will give them over to
you, and throw them into great panic, until they
are destroyed. 24He will hand their kings over to
you and you shall blot out their name from under
heaven; no one will be able to stand against you,
until you have destroyed them. 25The images of
their gods you shall burn with fire. Do not covet
the silver or the gold that is on them and take it
for yourself, because you could be ensnared by it;
for it is abhorrent to the LORD your God. 26Do
not bring an abhorrent thing into your house, or
you will be set apart for destruction like it. You
must utterly detest and abhor it, for it is set apart
for destruction.

8 This entire commandment that I command
you today you must diligently observe, so
that you may live and increase, and go in and occupy the land that the LORD promised on oath
to your ancestors. 2Remember the long way that
the LORD your God has led you these forty years
in the wilderness, in order to humble you, testing you to know what was in your heart, whether

[a] Heb *Asherim* [b] Or *hornets*: Meaning of Heb uncertain

or not you would keep his commandments. 3He
humbled you by letting you hunger, then by feeding you with manna, with which neither you nor
your ancestors were acquainted, in order to make
you understand that one does not live by bread
alone, but by every word that comes from the
mouth of the LORD.[a] 4The clothes on your back
did not wear out and your feet did not swell these
forty years. 5Know then in your heart that as a
parent disciplines a child so the LORD your God
disciplines you. 6Therefore keep the commandments of the LORD your God, by walking in his
ways and by fearing him. 7For the LORD your
God is bringing you into a good land, a land with
flowing streams, with springs and underground
waters welling up in valleys and hills, 8a land of
wheat and barley, of vines and fig trees and pomegranates, a land of olive trees and honey, 9a land
where you may eat bread without scarcity, where
you will lack nothing, a land whose stones are
iron and from whose hills you may mine copper.
10You shall eat your fill and bless the LORD your
God for the good land that he has given you.

11 Take care that you do not forget the LORD
your God, by failing to keep his commandments,
his ordinances, and his statutes, which I am commanding you today. 12When you have eaten your
fill and have built fine houses and live in them,
13and when your herds and flocks have multiplied, and your silver and gold is multiplied, and
all that you have is multiplied, 14then do not exalt yourself, forgetting the LORD your God, who
brought you out of the land of Egypt, out of the
house of slavery, 15who led you through the great
and terrible wilderness, an arid wasteland with
poisonous[b] snakes and scorpions. He made water flow for you from flint rock, 16and fed you in
the wilderness with manna that your ancestors
did not know, to humble you and to test you, and
in the end to do you good. 17Do not say to yourself, "My power and the might of my own hand
have gotten me this wealth." 18But remember
the LORD your God, for it is he who gives you
power to get wealth, so that he may confirm his
covenant that he swore to your ancestors, as he
is doing today. 19If you do forget the LORD your
God and follow other gods to serve and worship
them, I solemnly warn you today that you shall
surely perish. 20Like the nations that the LORD
is destroying before you, so shall you perish, because you would not obey the voice of the LORD
your God.

9 Hear, O Israel! You are about to cross the
Jordan today, to go in and dispossess nations
larger and mightier than you, great cities, fortified to the heavens, 2a strong and tall people, the
offspring of the Anakim, whom you know. You
have heard it said of them, "Who can stand up to
the Anakim?" 3Know then today that the LORD
your God is the one who crosses over before you
as a devouring fire; he will defeat them and subdue them before you, so that you may dispossess
and destroy them quickly, as the LORD has promised you.

4 When the LORD your God thrusts them out
before you, do not say to yourself, "It is because
of my righteousness that the LORD has brought
me in to occupy this land"; it is rather because of
the wickedness of these nations that the LORD is
dispossessing them before you. 5It is not because
of your righteousness or the uprightness of your
heart that you are going in to occupy their land;
but because of the wickedness of these nations
the LORD your God is dispossessing them before
you, in order to fulfill the promise that the LORD
made on oath to your ancestors, to Abraham, to
Isaac, and to Jacob.

6 Know, then, that the LORD your God is not
giving you this good land to occupy because of
your righteousness; for you are a stubborn people.
7Remember and do not forget how you provoked
the LORD your God to wrath in the wilderness;
you have been rebellious against the LORD from
the day you came out of the land of Egypt until
you came to this place.

8 Even at Horeb you provoked the LORD
to wrath, and the LORD was so angry with you
that he was ready to destroy you. 9When I went
up the mountain to receive the stone tablets, the
tablets of the covenant that the LORD made with

[a] Or *by anything that the LORD decrees* [b] Or *fiery*; Heb *seraph*

you, I remained on the mountain forty days and
forty nights; I neither ate bread nor drank water.
10 And the LORD gave me the two stone tablets
written with the finger of God; on them were all
the words that the LORD had spoken to you at the
mountain out of the fire on the day of the assembly. 11 At the end of forty days and forty nights the
LORD gave me the two stone tablets, the tablets of
the covenant. 12 Then the LORD said to me, "Get
up, go down quickly from here, for your people
whom you have brought from Egypt have acted
corruptly. They have been quick to turn from the
way that I commanded them; they have cast an
image for themselves." 13 Furthermore the LORD
said to me, "I have seen that this people is indeed
a stubborn people. 14 Let me alone that I may destroy them and blot out their name from under
heaven; and I will make of you a nation mightier
and more numerous than they."

15 So I turned and went down from the
mountain, while the mountain was ablaze; the
two tablets of the covenant were in my two hands.
16 Then I saw that you had indeed sinned against
the LORD your God, by casting for yourselves an
image of a calf; you had been quick to turn from
the way that the LORD had commanded you. 17 So
I took hold of the two tablets and flung them
from my two hands, smashing them before your
eyes. 18 Then I lay prostrate before the LORD as
before, forty days and forty nights; I neither ate
bread nor drank water, because of all the sin you
had committed, provoking the LORD by doing
what was evil in his sight. 19 For I was afraid that
the anger that the LORD bore against you was so
fierce that he would destroy you. But the LORD
listened to me that time also. 20 The LORD was so
angry with Aaron that he was ready to destroy
him, but I interceded also on behalf of Aaron at
that same time. 21 Then I took the sinful thing you
had made, the calf, and burned it with fire and
crushed it, grinding it thoroughly, until it was reduced to dust; and I threw the dust of it into the
stream that runs down the mountain.

22 At Taberah also, and at Massah, and at
Kibroth-hattaavah, you provoked the LORD
to wrath. 23 And when the LORD sent you from
Kadesh-barnea, saying, "Go up and occupy the
land that I have given you," you rebelled against
the command of the LORD your God, neither
trusting him nor obeying him. 24 You have been
rebellious against the LORD as long as he has[a]
known you.

25 Throughout the forty days and forty nights
that I lay prostrate before the LORD when the
LORD intended to destroy you, 26 I prayed to
the LORD and said, "Lord GOD, do not destroy
the people who are your very own possession,
whom you redeemed in your greatness, whom
you brought out of Egypt with a mighty hand.
27 Remember your servants, Abraham, Isaac,
and Jacob; pay no attention to the stubbornness of this people, their wickedness and their
sin, 28 otherwise the land from which you have
brought us might say, 'Because the LORD was not
able to bring them into the land that he promised
them, and because he hated them, he has brought
them out to let them die in the wilderness.' 29 For
they are the people of your very own possession,
whom you brought out by your great power and
by your outstretched arm."

10 At that time the LORD said to me, "Carve
out two tablets of stone like the former
ones, and come up to me on the mountain, and
make an ark of wood. 2 I will write on the tablets
the words that were on the former tablets, which
you smashed, and you shall put them in the ark."
3 So I made an ark of acacia wood, cut two tablets of stone like the former ones, and went up
the mountain with the two tablets in my hand.
4 Then he wrote on the tablets the same words as
before, the ten commandments[b] that the LORD
had spoken to you on the mountain out of the fire
on the day of the assembly; and the LORD gave
them to me. 5 So I turned and came down from
the mountain, and put the tablets in the ark that I
had made; and there they are, as the LORD commanded me.

6 (The Israelites journeyed from Beeroth-
bene-jaakan[c] to Moserah. There Aaron died, and
there he was buried; his son Eleazar succeeded

[a] Sam Gk: MT *I have* [b] Heb *the ten words* [c] Or *the wells of the Bene-jaakan*

him as priest. 7From there they journeyed to Gudgodah, and from Gudgodah to Jotbathah, a land with flowing streams. 8At that time the LORD set apart the tribe of Levi to carry the ark of the covenant of the LORD, to stand before the LORD to minister to him, and to bless in his name, to this day. 9Therefore Levi has no allotment or inheritance with his kindred; the LORD is his inheritance, as the LORD your God promised him.)

10 I stayed on the mountain forty days and forty nights, as I had done the first time. And once again the LORD listened to me. The LORD was unwilling to destroy you. 11The LORD said to me, "Get up, go on your journey at the head of the people, that they may go in and occupy the land that I swore to their ancestors to give them."

12 So now, O Israel, what does the LORD your God require of you? Only to fear the LORD your God, to walk in all his ways, to love him, to serve the LORD your God with all your heart and with all your soul, 13and to keep the commandments of the LORD your God[a] and his decrees that I am commanding you today, for your own well-being. 14Although heaven and the heaven of heavens belong to the LORD your God, the earth with all that is in it, 15yet the LORD set his heart in love on your ancestors alone and chose you, their descendants after them, out of all the peoples, as it is today. 16Circumcise, then, the foreskin of your heart, and do not be stubborn any longer. 17For the LORD your God is God of gods and Lord of lords, the great God, mighty and awesome, who is not partial and takes no bribe, 18who executes justice for the orphan and the widow, and who loves the strangers, providing them food and clothing. 19You shall also love the stranger, for you were strangers in the land of Egypt. 20You shall fear the LORD your God; him alone you shall worship; to him you shall hold fast, and by his name you shall swear. 21He is your praise; he is your God, who has done for you these great and awesome things that your own eyes have seen. 22Your ancestors went down to Egypt seventy persons; and now the LORD your God has made you as numerous as the stars in heaven.

11 You shall love the LORD your God, therefore, and keep his charge, his decrees, his ordinances, and his commandments always. 2Remember today that it was not your children (who have not known or seen the discipline of the LORD your God), but it is you who must acknowledge his greatness, his mighty hand and his outstretched arm, 3his signs and his deeds that he did in Egypt to Pharaoh, the king of Egypt, and to all his land; 4what he did to the Egyptian army, to

[a] Q Ms Gk Syr: MT lacks *your God*

Deuteronomy 10:17-19

[Henri Nouwen wrote that] "the paradox of hospitality is that it wants to create an emptiness, not a fearful emptiness, but a friendly emptiness where strangers can enter and discover themselves as created free; free to sing their own songs, speak their own languages, dance their own dances; free also to leave and follow their own vocations. Hospitality is not a subtle invitation to adopt the lifestyle of the host, but the gift of a chance for the guest to find his own."

This paradox has special application to our relations in the public life. Hospitality means letting the stranger remain a stranger while offering acceptance nonetheless. It means honoring the fact that strangers already have a relationship—rooted in our common humanity—without having to build one on intimate interpersonal knowledge, without having to become friends. It means valuing the strangeness of the stranger—even letting the stranger speak a language you cannot speak or sing a song you cannot join with—resisting the temptation to reduce the relation to some lowest common denominator, since all language and all music is already human. It means meeting the stranger's needs while allowing him or her simply to be, without attempting to make the stranger over into a modified version of ourselves.[19]

— Parker J. Palmer

their horses and chariots, how he made the water
of the Red Sea[a] flow over them as they pursued
you, so that the LORD has destroyed them to this
day; 5 what he did to you in the wilderness, until
you came to this place; 6 and what he did to Dathan and Abiram, sons of Eliab son of Reuben,
how in the midst of all Israel the earth opened its
mouth and swallowed them up, along with their
households, their tents, and every living being in
their company; 7 for it is your own eyes that have
seen every great deed that the LORD did.

8 Keep, then, this entire commandment that
I am commanding you today, so that you may
have strength to go in and occupy the land that
you are crossing over to occupy, 9 and so that you
may live long in the land that the LORD swore to
your ancestors to give them and to their descendants, a land flowing with milk and honey. 10 For
the land that you are about to enter to occupy is
not like the land of Egypt, from which you have
come, where you sow your seed and irrigate by
foot like a vegetable garden. 11 But the land that
you are crossing over to occupy is a land of hills
and valleys, watered by rain from the sky, 12 a land
that the LORD your God looks after. The eyes of
the LORD your God are always on it, from the beginning of the year to the end of the year.

13 If you will only heed his every commandment[b] that I am commanding you today—loving
the LORD your God, and serving him with all
your heart and with all your soul— 14 then he[c]
will give the rain for your land in its season, the
early rain and the later rain, and you will gather
in your grain, your wine, and your oil; 15 and he[c]
will give grass in your fields for your livestock,
and you will eat your fill. 16 Take care, or you will
be seduced into turning away, serving other gods
and worshiping them, 17 for then the anger of the
LORD will be kindled against you and he will shut
up the heavens, so that there will be no rain and
the land will yield no fruit; then you will perish
quickly off the good land that the LORD is giving
you.

18 You shall put these words of mine in your
heart and soul, and you shall bind them as a sign
on your hand, and fix them as an emblem[d] on your
forehead. 19 Teach them to your children, talking
about them when you are at home and when you
are away, when you lie down and when you rise.
20 Write them on the doorposts of your house and
on your gates, 21 so that your days and the days of
your children may be multiplied in the land that
the LORD swore to your ancestors to give them,
as long as the heavens are above the earth.

22 If you will diligently observe this entire
commandment that I am commanding you, loving the LORD your God, walking in all his ways,
and holding fast to him, 23 then the LORD will
drive out all these nations before you, and you
will dispossess nations larger and mightier than
yourselves. 24 Every place on which you set foot
shall be yours; your territory shall extend from
the wilderness to the Lebanon and from the
River, the river Euphrates, to the Western Sea.
25 No one will be able to stand against you; the
LORD your God will put the fear and dread of you
on all the land on which you set foot, as he promised you.

26 See, I am setting before you today a blessing and a curse: 27 the blessing, if you obey the
commandments of the LORD your God that I am
commanding you today; 28 and the curse, if you
do not obey the commandments of the LORD
your God, but turn from the way that I am commanding you today, to follow other gods that you
have not known.

29 When the LORD your God has brought
you into the land that you are entering to occupy,
you shall set the blessing on Mount Gerizim and
the curse on Mount Ebal. 30 As you know, they are
beyond the Jordan, some distance to the west, in
the land of the Canaanites who live in the Arabah,
opposite Gilgal, beside the oak[e] of Moreh.

31 When you cross the Jordan to go in to occupy the land that the LORD your God is giving
you, and when you occupy it and live in it, 32 you
must diligently observe all the statutes and ordinances that I am setting before you today.

[a] Or *Sea of Reeds* [b] Compare Gk: Heb *my commandments* [c] Sam Gk Vg: MT *I* [d] Or *as a frontlet*
[e] Gk Syr: Compare Gen 12.6; Heb *oaks* or *terebinths*

12 These are the statutes and ordinances that
you must diligently observe in the land
that the LORD, the God of your ancestors, has
given you to occupy all the days that you live on
the earth.

2 You must demolish completely all the
places where the nations whom you are about
to dispossess served their gods, on the mountain
heights, on the hills, and under every leafy tree.
3 Break down their altars, smash their pillars, burn
their sacred poles[a] with fire, and hew down the
idols of their gods, and thus blot out their name
from their places. 4 You shall not worship the
LORD your God in such ways. 5 But you shall seek
the place that the LORD your God will choose out
of all your tribes as his habitation to put his name
there. You shall go there, 6 bringing there your
burnt offerings and your sacrifices, your tithes
and your donations, your votive gifts, your freewill offerings, and the firstlings of your herds and
flocks. 7 And you shall eat there in the presence of
the LORD your God, you and your households together, rejoicing in all the undertakings in which
the LORD your God has blessed you.

8 You shall not act as we are acting here today, all of us according to our own desires, 9 for
you have not yet come into the rest and the possession that the LORD your God is giving you.
10 When you cross over the Jordan and live in the
land that the LORD your God is allotting to you,
and when he gives you rest from your enemies all
around so that you live in safety, 11 then you shall
bring everything that I command you to the place
that the LORD your God will choose as a dwelling for his name: your burnt offerings and your
sacrifices, your tithes and your donations, and
all your choice votive gifts that you vow to the
LORD. 12 And you shall rejoice before the LORD
your God, you together with your sons and your
daughters, your male and female slaves, and the
Levites who reside in your towns (since they have
no allotment or inheritance with you).

13 Take care that you do not offer your burnt
offerings at any place you happen to see. 14 But
only at the place that the LORD will choose in
one of your tribes—there you shall offer your
burnt offerings and there you shall do everything
I command you.

15 Yet whenever you desire you may slaughter
and eat meat within any of your towns, according
to the blessing that the LORD your God has given
you; the unclean and the clean may eat of it, as
they would of gazelle or deer. 16 The blood, however, you must not eat; you shall pour it out on
the ground like water. 17 Nor may you eat within
your towns the tithe of your grain, your wine,
and your oil, the firstlings of your herds and your
flocks, any of your votive gifts that you vow, your
freewill offerings, or your donations; 18 these you
shall eat in the presence of the LORD your God
at the place that the LORD your God will choose,
you together with your son and your daughter,
your male and female slaves, and the Levites
resident in your towns, rejoicing in the presence
of the LORD your God in all your undertakings.
19 Take care that you do not neglect the Levite as
long as you live in your land.

20 When the LORD your God enlarges your
territory, as he has promised you, and you say, "I
am going to eat some meat," because you wish to
eat meat, you may eat meat whenever you have
the desire. 21 If the place where the LORD your
God will choose to put his name is too far from
you, and you slaughter as I have commanded you
any of your herd or flock that the LORD has given
you, then you may eat within your towns whenever you desire. 22 Indeed, just as gazelle or deer is
eaten, so you may eat it; the unclean and the clean
alike may eat it. 23 Only be sure that you do not
eat the blood; for the blood is the life, and you
shall not eat the life with the meat. 24 Do not eat
it; you shall pour it out on the ground like water.
25 Do not eat it, so that all may go well with you
and your children after you, because you do what
is right in the sight of the LORD. 26 But the sacred
donations that are due from you, and your votive
gifts, you shall bring to the place that the LORD
will choose. 27 You shall present your burnt offerings, both the meat and the blood, on the altar of
the LORD your God; the blood of your other sac-

[a] Heb *Asherim*

rifices shall be poured out beside[a] the altar of the
LORD your God, but the meat you may eat.
28 Be careful to obey all these words that I
command you today,[b] so that it may go well with
you and with your children after you forever, because you will be doing what is good and right in
the sight of the LORD your God.

29 When the LORD your God has cut off before you the nations whom you are about to enter
to dispossess them, when you have dispossessed
them and live in their land, 30take care that you
are not snared into imitating them, after they
have been destroyed before you: do not inquire
concerning their gods, saying, "How did these
nations worship their gods? I also want to do the
same." 31You must not do the same for the LORD
your God, because every abhorrent thing that the
LORD hates they have done for their gods. They
would even burn their sons and their daughters
in the fire to their gods. 32[c]You must diligently observe everything that I command you; do not add
to it or take anything from it.

13 [d] If prophets or those who divine by
dreams appear among you and promise
you omens or portents, 2and the omens or the
portents declared by them take place, and they
say, "Let us follow other gods" (whom you have
not known) "and let us serve them," 3you must
not heed the words of those prophets or those
who divine by dreams; for the LORD your God
is testing you, to know whether you indeed love
the LORD your God with all your heart and soul.
4The LORD your God you shall follow, him alone
you shall fear, his commandments you shall keep,
his voice you shall obey, him you shall serve, and
to him you shall hold fast. 5But those prophets or
those who divine by dreams shall be put to death
for having spoken treason against the LORD your
God—who brought you out of the land of Egypt
and redeemed you from the house of slavery—to
turn you from the way in which the LORD your
God commanded you to walk. So you shall purge
the evil from your midst.

6 If anyone secretly entices you—even if it is
your brother, your father's son or[e] your mother's
son, or your own son or daughter, or the wife you
embrace, or your most intimate friend—saying,
"Let us go worship other gods," whom neither you
nor your ancestors have known, 7any of the gods of
the peoples that are around you, whether near you
or far away from you, from one end of the earth
to the other, 8you must not yield to or heed any
such persons. Show them no pity or compassion
and do not shield them. 9But you shall surely kill
them; your own hand shall be first against them to
execute them, and afterwards the hand of all the
people. 10Stone them to death for trying to turn
you away from the LORD your God, who brought
you out of the land of Egypt, out of the house of
slavery. 11Then all Israel shall hear and be afraid,
and never again do any such wickedness.
12 If you hear it said about one of the towns
that the LORD your God is giving you to live in,
13that scoundrels from among you have gone out
and led the inhabitants of the town astray, saying, "Let us go and worship other gods," whom
you have not known, 14then you shall inquire and
make a thorough investigation. If the charge is established that such an abhorrent thing has been
done among you, 15you shall put the inhabitants
of that town to the sword, utterly destroying it
and everything in it—even putting its livestock
to the sword. 16All of its spoil you shall gather
into its public square; then burn the town and all
its spoil with fire, as a whole burnt offering to the
LORD your God. It shall remain a perpetual ruin,
never to be rebuilt. 17Do not let anything devoted
to destruction stick to your hand, so that the
LORD may turn from his fierce anger and show
you compassion, and in his compassion multiply
you, as he swore to your ancestors, 18if you obey
the voice of the LORD your God by keeping all
his commandments that I am commanding you
today, doing what is right in the sight of the LORD
your God.

14 You are children of the LORD your God.
You must not lacerate yourselves or shave

[a] Or *on* [b] Gk Sam Syr: MT lacks *today* [c] Ch 13.1 in Heb [d] Ch 13.2 in Heb
[e] Sam Gk Compare Tg: MT lacks *your father's son or*

your forelocks for the dead. 2For you are a people
holy to the LORD your God; it is you the LORD
has chosen out of all the peoples on earth to be
his people, his treasured possession.
3 You shall not eat any abhorrent thing.
4These are the animals you may eat: the ox, the
sheep, the goat, 5the deer, the gazelle, the roebuck,
the wild goat, the ibex, the antelope, and the
mountain-sheep. 6Any animal that divides the
hoof and has the hoof cleft in two, and chews
the cud, among the animals, you may eat. 7Yet of
those that chew the cud or have the hoof cleft you
shall not eat these: the camel, the hare, and the
rock badger, because they chew the cud but do
not divide the hoof; they are unclean for you.
8And the pig, because it divides the hoof but does
not chew the cud, is unclean for you. You shall
not eat their meat, and you shall not touch their
carcasses.
9 Of all that live in water you may eat these:
whatever has fins and scales you may eat. 10And
whatever does not have fins and scales you shall
not eat; it is unclean for you.
11 You may eat any clean birds. 12But these
are the ones that you shall not eat: the eagle, the
vulture, the osprey, 13the buzzard, the kite of any
kind; 14every raven of any kind; 15the ostrich, the
nighthawk, the sea gull, the hawk of any kind;
16the little owl and the great owl, the water hen
17and the desert owl,[a] the carrion vulture and the
cormorant, 18the stork, the heron of any kind; the
hoopoe and the bat.[b] 19And all winged insects are
unclean for you; they shall not be eaten. 20You
may eat any clean winged creature.
21 You shall not eat anything that dies of
itself; you may give it to aliens residing in your
towns for them to eat, or you may sell it to a foreigner. For you are a people holy to the LORD
your God.
You shall not boil a kid in its mother's milk.
22 Set apart a tithe of all the yield of your
seed that is brought in yearly from the field. 23In
the presence of the LORD your God, in the place
that he will choose as a dwelling for his name, you
shall eat the tithe of your grain, your wine, and
your oil, as well as the firstlings of your herd and
flock, so that you may learn to fear the LORD your
God always. 24But if, when the LORD your God
has blessed you, the distance is so great that you
are unable to transport it, because the place where
the LORD your God will choose to set his name
is too far away from you, 25then you may turn it
into money. With the money secure in hand, go
to the place that the LORD your God will choose;
26spend the money for whatever you wish—
oxen, sheep, wine, strong drink, or whatever you
desire. And you shall eat there in the presence of
the LORD your God, you and your household rejoicing together. 27As for the Levites resident in
your towns, do not neglect them, because they
have no allotment or inheritance with you.
28 Every third year you shall bring out the
full tithe of your produce for that year, and store
it within your towns; 29the Levites, because they
have no allotment or inheritance with you, as
well as the resident aliens, the orphans, and the
widows in your towns, may come and eat their fill
so that the LORD your God may bless you in all
the work that you undertake.

15 Every seventh year you shall grant a remission of debts. 2And this is the manner of
the remission: every creditor shall remit the claim
that is held against a neighbor, not exacting it of a
neighbor who is a member of the community, because the LORD's remission has been proclaimed.
3Of a foreigner you may exact it, but you must remit your claim on whatever any member of your
community owes you. 4There will, however, be
no one in need among you, because the LORD is
sure to bless you in the land that the LORD your
God is giving you as a possession to occupy, 5if
only you will obey the LORD your God by diligently observing this entire commandment that I
command you today. 6When the LORD your God
has blessed you, as he promised you, you will
lend to many nations, but you will not borrow;
you will rule over many nations, but they will not
rule over you.
7 If there is among you anyone in need, a
member of your community in any of your towns

[a] Or *pelican* [b] Identification of several of the birds in verses 12–18 is uncertain

Deuteronomy 15:1-18

This chapter presents the Torah command for the Sabbatical Year, a practice that sought to assure that in every seventh year debts would be cancelled for any Israelite citizen, so that no one would get trapped in unending poverty or, worse, have to sell themselves into bond-slavery. The Sabbatical Year aims to assure that "There will... be no one in need among you... if only you will obey the LORD your God by diligently observing this entire commandment" (15:4). But reality intrudes in verses 7-8: "If there is among you anyone in need,... do not be hard-hearted or tight-fisted toward your needy neighbor. You should rather open your hand, willingly lending enough to meet the need." Verse 11 admits that "there will never cease to be some in need on the earth" and says God's command is: "Open your hand to the poor and needy neighbor in your land."

Verses 12-18 are about persons so poor they are forced to sell themselves into slavery to escape their debts. The Israelite ideal was that no one be impoverished, but there was a realistic recognition that poverty would never disappear. The aim was to hold it in check and help—as a community—to alleviate it.

— *DB*

within the land that the LORD your God is giving
you, do not be hard-hearted or tight-fisted toward
your needy neighbor. 8 You should rather open
your hand, willingly lending enough to meet the
need, whatever it may be. 9 Be careful that you
do not entertain a mean thought, thinking, "The
seventh year, the year of remission, is near," and
therefore view your needy neighbor with hostility and give nothing; your neighbor might cry to
the LORD against you, and you would incur guilt.
10 Give liberally and be ungrudging when you do
so, for on this account the LORD your God will
bless you in all your work and in all that you undertake. 11 Since there will never cease to be some
in need on the earth, I therefore command you,
"Open your hand to the poor and needy neighbor
in your land."

12 If a member of your community, whether
a Hebrew man or a Hebrew woman, is sold[a] to
you and works for you six years, in the seventh
year you shall set that person free. 13 And when
you send a male slave[b] out from you a free person, you shall not send him out empty-handed.
14 Provide liberally out of your flock, your threshing floor, and your wine press, thus giving to him
some of the bounty with which the LORD your
God has blessed you. 15 Remember that you were
a slave in the land of Egypt, and the LORD your
God redeemed you; for this reason I lay this command upon you today. 16 But if he says to you, "I
will not go out from you," because he loves you
and your household, since he is well off with you,
17 then you shall take an awl and thrust it through
his earlobe into the door, and he shall be your
slave[c] forever.

You shall do the same with regard to your female slave.[d]

18 Do not consider it a hardship when you
send them out from you free persons, because for
six years they have given you services worth the
wages of hired laborers; and the LORD your God
will bless you in all that you do.

19 Every firstling male born of your herd and
flock you shall consecrate to the LORD your God;
you shall not do work with your firstling ox nor
shear the firstling of your flock. 20 You shall eat it,
you together with your household, in the presence of the LORD your God year by year at the
place that the LORD will choose. 21 But if it has
any defect—any serious defect, such as lameness
or blindness—you shall not sacrifice it to the
LORD your God; 22 within your towns you may
eat it, the unclean and the clean alike, as you
would a gazelle or deer. 23 Its blood, however, you
must not eat; you shall pour it out on the ground
like water.

16 Observe the month[e] of Abib by keeping
the passover to the LORD your God, for in
the month of Abib the LORD your God brought

[a] Or *sells himself or herself* [b] Heb *him* [c] Or *bondman* [d] Or *bondwoman* [e] Or *new moon*

you out of Egypt by night. 2You shall offer the passover sacrifice to the LORD your God, from the flock and the herd, at the place that the LORD will choose as a dwelling for his name. 3You must not eat with it anything leavened. For seven days you shall eat unleavened bread with it—the bread of affliction—because you came out of the land of Egypt in great haste, so that all the days of your life you may remember the day of your departure from the land of Egypt. 4No leaven shall be seen with you in all your territory for seven days; and none of the meat of what you slaughter on the evening of the first day shall remain until morning. 5You are not permitted to offer the passover sacrifice within any of your towns that the LORD your God is giving you. 6But at the place that the LORD your God will choose as a dwelling for his name, only there shall you offer the passover sacrifice, in the evening at sunset, the time of day when you departed from Egypt. 7You shall cook it and eat it at the place that the LORD your God will choose; the next morning you may go back to your tents. 8For six days you shall continue to eat unleavened bread, and on the seventh day there shall be a solemn assembly for the LORD your God, when you shall do no work.

9 You shall count seven weeks; begin to count the seven weeks from the time the sickle is first put to the standing grain. 10Then you shall keep the festival of weeks to the LORD your God, contributing a freewill offering in proportion to the blessing that you have received from the LORD your God. 11Rejoice before the LORD your God—you and your sons and your daughters, your male and female slaves, the Levites resident in your towns, as well as the strangers, the orphans, and the widows who are among you—at the place that the LORD your God will choose as a dwelling for his name. 12Remember that you were a slave in Egypt, and diligently observe these statutes.

13 You shall keep the festival of booths[a] for seven days, when you have gathered in the produce from your threshing floor and your wine press. 14Rejoice during your festival, you and your sons and your daughters, your male and female slaves, as well as the Levites, the strangers, the orphans, and the widows resident in your towns. 15Seven days you shall keep the festival to the LORD your God at the place that the LORD will choose; for the LORD your God will bless you in all your produce and in all your undertakings, and you shall surely celebrate.

16 Three times a year all your males shall appear before the LORD your God at the place that he will choose: at the festival of unleavened bread, at the festival of weeks, and at the festival of booths.[a] They shall not appear before the LORD empty-handed; 17all shall give as they are able, according to the blessing of the LORD your God that he has given you.

18 You shall appoint judges and officials throughout your tribes, in all your towns that the LORD your God is giving you, and they shall render just decisions for the people. 19You must not distort justice; you must not show partiality; and you must not accept bribes, for a bribe blinds the eyes of the wise and subverts the cause of those who are in the right. 20Justice, and only justice, you shall pursue, so that you may live and occupy the land that the LORD your God is giving you.

21 You shall not plant any tree as a sacred pole[b] beside the altar that you make for the LORD your God; 22nor shall you set up a stone pillar—things that the LORD your God hates.

17 You must not sacrifice to the LORD your God an ox or a sheep that has a defect, anything seriously wrong; for that is abhorrent to the LORD your God.

2 If there is found among you, in one of your towns that the LORD your God is giving you, a man or woman who does what is evil in the sight of the LORD your God, and transgresses his covenant 3by going to serve other gods and worshiping them—whether the sun or the moon or any of the host of heaven, which I have forbidden—4and if it is reported to you or you hear of it, and you make a thorough inquiry, and the charge is proved true that such an abhorrent thing has occurred in Israel, 5then you shall bring out to your

[a] Or *tabernacles*; Heb *succoth* [b] Heb *Asherah*

gates that man or that woman who has committed
this crime and you shall stone the man or woman
to death. 6On the evidence of two or three witnesses the death sentence shall be executed; a
person must not be put to death on the evidence
of only one witness. 7The hands of the witnesses
shall be the first raised against the person to execute the death penalty, and afterward the hands
of all the people. So you shall purge the evil from
your midst.

8 If a judicial decision is too difficult for you
to make between one kind of bloodshed and another, one kind of legal right and another, or one
kind of assault and another—any such matters of
dispute in your towns—then you shall immediately go up to the place that the LORD your God
will choose, 9where you shall consult with the
levitical priests and the judge who is in office in
those days; they shall announce to you the decision in the case. 10Carry out exactly the decision
that they announce to you from the place that the
LORD will choose, diligently observing everything
they instruct you. 11You must carry out fully the
law that they interpret for you or the ruling that
they announce to you; do not turn aside from the
decision that they announce to you, either to the
right or to the left. 12As for anyone who presumes
to disobey the priest appointed to minister there
to the LORD your God, or the judge, that person
shall die. So you shall purge the evil from Israel.
13All the people will hear and be afraid, and will
not act presumptuously again.

14 When you have come into the land that
the LORD your God is giving you, and have taken
possession of it and settled in it, and you say, "I
will set a king over me, like all the nations that
are around me," 15you may indeed set over you a
king whom the LORD your God will choose. One
of your own community you may set as king over
you; you are not permitted to put a foreigner over
you, who is not of your own community. 16Even
so, he must not acquire many horses for himself,
or return the people to Egypt in order to acquire
more horses, since the LORD has said to you, "You
must never return that way again." 17And he must
not acquire many wives for himself, or else his
heart will turn away; also silver and gold he must
not acquire in great quantity for himself. 18When
he has taken the throne of his kingdom, he shall
have a copy of this law written for him in the presence of the levitical priests. 19It shall remain with
him and he shall read in it all the days of his life,
so that he may learn to fear the LORD his God,
diligently observing all the words of this law and
these statutes, 20neither exalting himself above
other members of the community nor turning
aside from the commandment, either to the right
or to the left, so that he and his descendants may
reign long over his kingdom in Israel.

18 The levitical priests, the whole tribe of
Levi, shall have no allotment or inheritance within Israel. They may eat the sacrifices
that are the LORD's portion[a] 2but they shall have
no inheritance among the other members of the
community; the LORD is their inheritance, as he
promised them.

3 This shall be the priests' due from the
people, from those offering a sacrifice, whether
an ox or a sheep: they shall give to the priest the
shoulder, the two jowls, and the stomach. 4The
first fruits of your grain, your wine, and your oil,
as well as the first of the fleece of your sheep, you
shall give him. 5For the LORD your God has chosen Levi[b] out of all your tribes, to stand and minister in the name of the LORD, him and his sons
for all time.

6 If a Levite leaves any of your towns, from
wherever he has been residing in Israel, and comes
to the place that the LORD will choose (and he
may come whenever he wishes), 7then he may
minister in the name of the LORD his God, like
all his fellow-Levites who stand to minister there
before the LORD. 8They shall have equal portions
to eat, even though they have income from the
sale of family possessions.[a]

9 When you come into the land that the
LORD your God is giving you, you must not learn
to imitate the abhorrent practices of those nations. 10No one shall be found among you who
makes a son or daughter pass through fire, or

[a] Meaning of Heb uncertain [b] Heb *him*

who practices divination, or is a soothsayer, or
an augur, or a sorcerer, 11 or one who casts spells,
or who consults ghosts or spirits, or who seeks
oracles from the dead. 12 For whoever does these
things is abhorrent to the LORD; it is because
of such abhorrent practices that the LORD your
God is driving them out before you. 13 You must
remain completely loyal to the LORD your God.
14 Although these nations that you are about to
dispossess do give heed to soothsayers and diviners, as for you, the LORD your God does not permit you to do so.
15 The LORD your God will raise up for you
a prophet[a] like me from among your own people;
you shall heed such a prophet.[b] 16 This is what
you requested of the LORD your God at Horeb
on the day of the assembly when you said: "If I
hear the voice of the LORD my God any more, or
ever again see this great fire, I will die." 17 Then the
LORD replied to me: "They are right in what they
have said. 18 I will raise up for them a prophet[a]
like you from among their own people; I will
put my words in the mouth of the prophet,[c] who
shall speak to them everything that I command.
19 Anyone who does not heed the words that the
prophet[d] shall speak in my name, I myself will
hold accountable. 20 But any prophet who speaks
in the name of other gods, or who presumes to
speak in my name a word that I have not commanded the prophet to speak—that prophet shall
die." 21 You may say to yourself, "How can we recognize a word that the LORD has not spoken?"
22 If a prophet speaks in the name of the LORD
but the thing does not take place or prove true,
it is a word that the LORD has not spoken. The
prophet has spoken it presumptuously; do not be
frightened by it.

19 When the LORD your God has cut off the
nations whose land the LORD your God
is giving you, and you have dispossessed them
and settled in their towns and in their houses,
2 you shall set apart three cities in the land that
the LORD your God is giving you to possess. 3 You
shall calculate the distances[e] and divide into three
regions the land that the LORD your God gives
you as a possession, so that any homicide can flee
to one of them.
4 Now this is the case of a homicide who
might flee there and live, that is, someone who
has killed another person unintentionally when
the two had not been at enmity before: 5 Suppose
someone goes into the forest with another to cut
wood, and when one of them swings the ax to
cut down a tree, the head slips from the handle
and strikes the other person who then dies; the
killer may flee to one of these cities and live. 6 But
if the distance is too great, the avenger of blood in
hot anger might pursue and overtake and put the
killer to death, although a death sentence was not
deserved, since the two had not been at enmity
before. 7 Therefore I command you: You shall set
apart three cities.
8 If the LORD your God enlarges your territory, as he swore to your ancestors—and he will
give you all the land that he promised your ancestors to give you, 9 provided you diligently observe
this entire commandment that I command you
today, by loving the LORD your God and walking always in his ways—then you shall add three
more cities to these three, 10 so that the blood of
an innocent person may not be shed in the land
that the LORD your God is giving you as an inheritance, thereby bringing bloodguilt upon you.
11 But if someone at enmity with another
lies in wait and attacks and takes the life of that
person, and flees into one of these cities, 12 then
the elders of the killer's city shall send to have the
culprit taken from there and handed over to the
avenger of blood to be put to death. 13 Show no
pity; you shall purge the guilt of innocent blood
from Israel, so that it may go well with you.
14 You must not move your neighbor's
boundary marker, set up by former generations,
on the property that will be allotted to you in
the land that the LORD your God is giving you
to possess.
15 A single witness shall not suffice to convict a person of any crime or wrongdoing in connection with any offense that may be committed.
Only on the evidence of two or three witnesses

[a] Or *prophets* [b] Or *such prophets* [c] Or *mouths of the prophets* [d] Heb *he* [e] Or *prepare roads to them*

shall a charge be sustained. 16If a malicious witness comes forward to accuse someone of wrongdoing, 17then both parties to the dispute shall
appear before the LORD, before the priests and
the judges who are in office in those days, 18and
the judges shall make a thorough inquiry. If the
witness is a false witness, having testified falsely
against another, 19then you shall do to the false
witness just as the false witness had meant to
do to the other. So you shall purge the evil from
your midst. 20The rest shall hear and be afraid,
and a crime such as this shall never again be committed among you. 21Show no pity: life for life,
eye for eye, tooth for tooth, hand for hand, foot
for foot.

20 When you go out to war against your
enemies, and see horses and chariots, an
army larger than your own, you shall not be afraid
of them; for the LORD your God is with you, who
brought you up from the land of Egypt. 2Before
you engage in battle, the priest shall come forward and speak to the troops, 3and shall say to
them: "Hear, O Israel! Today you are drawing
near to do battle against your enemies. Do not
lose heart, or be afraid, or panic, or be in dread
of them; 4for it is the LORD your God who goes
with you, to fight for you against your enemies,
to give you victory." 5Then the officials shall address the troops, saying, "Has anyone built a new
house but not dedicated it? He should go back to
his house, or he might die in the battle and another dedicate it. 6Has anyone planted a vineyard
but not yet enjoyed its fruit? He should go back
to his house, or he might die in the battle and another be first to enjoy its fruit. 7Has anyone become engaged to a woman but not yet married
her? He should go back to his house, or he might
die in the battle and another marry her." 8The officials shall continue to address the troops, saying, "Is anyone afraid or disheartened? He should
go back to his house, or he might cause the heart
of his comrades to melt like his own." 9When the
officials have finished addressing the troops, then
the commanders shall take charge of them.

10 When you draw near to a town to fight
against it, offer it terms of peace. 11If it accepts
your terms of peace and surrenders to you, then all
the people in it shall serve you at forced labor. 12If
it does not submit to you peacefully, but makes
war against you, then you shall besiege it; 13and
when the LORD your God gives it into your hand,
you shall put all its males to the sword. 14You may,
however, take as your booty the women, the children, livestock, and everything else in the town,
all its spoil. You may enjoy the spoil of your enemies, which the LORD your God has given you.
15Thus you shall treat all the towns that are very
far from you, which are not towns of the nations
here. 16But as for the towns of these peoples that
the LORD your God is giving you as an inheritance, you must not let anything that breathes
remain alive. 17You shall annihilate them—the
Hittites and the Amorites, the Canaanites and
the Perizzites, the Hivites and the Jebusites—just
as the LORD your God has commanded, 18so that
they may not teach you to do all the abhorrent
things that they do for their gods, and you thus
sin against the LORD your God.

19 If you besiege a town for a long time, making war against it in order to take it, you must not
destroy its trees by wielding an ax against them.
Although you may take food from them, you must
not cut them down. Are trees in the field human
beings that they should come under siege from
you? 20You may destroy only the trees that you
know do not produce food; you may cut them
down for use in building siegeworks against the
town that makes war with you, until it falls.

21 If, in the land that the LORD your God
is giving you to possess, a body is found
lying in open country, and it is not known who
struck the person down, 2then your elders and
your judges shall come out to measure the distances to the towns that are near the body. 3The
elders of the town nearest the body shall take a
heifer that has never been worked, one that has
not pulled in the yoke; 4the elders of that town
shall bring the heifer down to a wadi with running water, which is neither plowed nor sown,
and shall break the heifer's neck there in the wadi.
5Then the priests, the sons of Levi, shall come forward, for the LORD your God has chosen them to
minister to him and to pronounce blessings in the
name of the LORD, and by their decision all cases

of dispute and assault shall be settled. 6 All the
elders of that town nearest the body shall wash
their hands over the heifer whose neck was broken
in the wadi, 7 and they shall declare: "Our hands
did not shed this blood, nor were we witnesses to
it. 8 Absolve, O LORD, your people Israel, whom
you redeemed; do not let the guilt of innocent
blood remain in the midst of your people Israel."
Then they will be absolved of bloodguilt. 9 So you
shall purge the guilt of innocent blood from your
midst, because you must do what is right in the
sight of the LORD.
10 When you go out to war against your enemies, and the LORD your God hands them over
to you and you take them captive, 11 suppose you
see among the captives a beautiful woman whom
you desire and want to marry, 12 and so you bring
her home to your house: she shall shave her head,
pare her nails, 13 discard her captive's garb, and
shall remain in your house a full month, mourning for her father and mother; after that you may
go in to her and be her husband, and she shall
be your wife. 14 But if you are not satisfied with
her, you shall let her go free and not sell her for
money. You must not treat her as a slave, since
you have dishonored her.
15 If a man has two wives, one of them loved
and the other disliked, and if both the loved and
the disliked have borne him sons, the firstborn
being the son of the one who is disliked, 16 then
on the day when he wills his possessions to his
sons, he is not permitted to treat the son of the
loved as the firstborn in preference to the son of
the disliked, who is the firstborn. 17 He must acknowledge as firstborn the son of the one who is
disliked, giving him a double portion[a] of all that
he has; since he is the first issue of his virility, the
right of the firstborn is his.
18 If someone has a stubborn and rebellious
son who will not obey his father and mother, who
does not heed them when they discipline him,
19 then his father and his mother shall take hold
of him and bring him out to the elders of his town
at the gate of that place. 20 They shall say to the
elders of his town, "This son of ours is stubborn
and rebellious. He will not obey us. He is a glutton and a drunkard." 21 Then all the men of the
town shall stone him to death. So you shall purge
the evil from your midst; and all Israel will hear,
and be afraid.
22 When someone is convicted of a crime
punishable by death and is executed, and you
hang him on a tree, 23 his corpse must not remain
all night upon the tree; you shall bury him that
same day, for anyone hung on a tree is under
God's curse. You must not defile the land that the
LORD your God is giving you for possession.

22 You shall not watch your neighbor's ox or
sheep straying away and ignore them; you
shall take them back to their owner. 2 If the owner
does not reside near you or you do not know who
the owner is, you shall bring it to your own house,
and it shall remain with you until the owner claims
it; then you shall return it. 3 You shall do the same
with a neighbor's donkey; you shall do the same
with a neighbor's garment; and you shall do the
same with anything else that your neighbor loses
and you find. You may not withhold your help.
4 You shall not see your neighbor's donkey or
ox fallen on the road and ignore it; you shall help
to lift it up.
5 A woman shall not wear a man's apparel,
nor shall a man put on a woman's garment; for
whoever does such things is abhorrent to the
LORD your God.
6 If you come on a bird's nest, in any tree or
on the ground, with fledglings or eggs, with the
mother sitting on the fledglings or on the eggs,
you shall not take the mother with the young.
7 Let the mother go, taking only the young for
yourself, in order that it may go well with you and
you may live long.
8 When you build a new house, you shall
make a parapet for your roof; otherwise you
might have bloodguilt on your house, if anyone
should fall from it.
9 You shall not sow your vineyard with a second kind of seed, or the whole yield will have to
be forfeited, both the crop that you have sown
and the yield of the vineyard itself.

[a] Heb *two-thirds*

10 You shall not plow with an ox and a donkey yoked together.

11 You shall not wear clothes made of wool
and linen woven together.

12 You shall make tassels on the four corners
of the cloak with which you cover yourself.

13 Suppose a man marries a woman, but after
going in to her, he dislikes her 14 and makes up
charges against her, slandering her by saying, "I
married this woman; but when I lay with her, I
did not find evidence of her virginity." 15 The father of the young woman and her mother shall
then submit the evidence of the young woman's
virginity to the elders of the city at the gate. 16 The
father of the young woman shall say to the elders:
"I gave my daughter in marriage to this man but
he dislikes her; 17 now he has made up charges
against her, saying, 'I did not find evidence of
your daughter's virginity.' But here is the evidence
of my daughter's virginity." Then they shall spread
out the cloth before the elders of the town. 18 The
elders of that town shall take the man and punish
him; 19 they shall fine him one hundred shekels of
silver (which they shall give to the young woman's father) because he has slandered a virgin of
Israel. She shall remain his wife; he shall not be
permitted to divorce her as long as he lives.

20 If, however, this charge is true, that evidence of the young woman's virginity was not
found, 21 then they shall bring the young woman
out to the entrance of her father's house and the
men of her town shall stone her to death, because
she committed a disgraceful act in Israel by prostituting herself in her father's house. So you shall
purge the evil from your midst.

22 If a man is caught lying with the wife of
another man, both of them shall die, the man
who lay with the woman as well as the woman. So
you shall purge the evil from Israel.

23 If there is a young woman, a virgin already
engaged to be married, and a man meets her in
the town and lies with her, 24 you shall bring both
of them to the gate of that town and stone them
to death, the young woman because she did not
cry for help in the town and the man because he
violated his neighbor's wife. So you shall purge
the evil from your midst.

25 But if the man meets the engaged woman
in the open country, and the man seizes her and
lies with her, then only the man who lay with her
shall die. 26 You shall do nothing to the young
woman; the young woman has not committed an
offense punishable by death, because this case is
like that of someone who attacks and murders a
neighbor. 27 Since he found her in the open country, the engaged woman may have cried for help,
but there was no one to rescue her.

28 If a man meets a virgin who is not engaged, and seizes her and lies with her, and they
are caught in the act, 29 the man who lay with
her shall give fifty shekels of silver to the young
woman's father, and she shall become his wife.
Because he violated her he shall not be permitted
to divorce her as long as he lives.

30[a] A man shall not marry his father's wife,
thereby violating his father's rights.[b]

23 No one whose testicles are crushed or
whose penis is cut off shall be admitted to
the assembly of the LORD.

2 Those born of an illicit union shall not be
admitted to the assembly of the LORD. Even to
the tenth generation, none of their descendants
shall be admitted to the assembly of the LORD.

3 No Ammonite or Moabite shall be admitted to the assembly of the LORD. Even to the
tenth generation, none of their descendants
shall be admitted to the assembly of the LORD,
4 because they did not meet you with food and
water on your journey out of Egypt, and because
they hired against you Balaam son of Beor, from
Pethor of Mesopotamia, to curse you. 5 (Yet the
LORD your God refused to heed Balaam; the
LORD your God turned the curse into a blessing
for you, because the LORD your God loved you.)
6 You shall never promote their welfare or their
prosperity as long as you live.

7 You shall not abhor any of the Edomites, for
they are your kin. You shall not abhor any of the
Egyptians, because you were an alien residing in
their land. 8 The children of the third generation

[a] Ch 23.1 in Heb [b] Heb *uncovering his father's skirt*

that are born to them may be admitted to the assembly of the LORD.
9 When you are encamped against your enemies you shall guard against any impropriety.
10 If one of you becomes unclean because
of a nocturnal emission, then he shall go outside
the camp; he must not come within the camp.
11When evening comes, he shall wash himself
with water, and when the sun has set, he may
come back into the camp.
12 You shall have a designated area outside
the camp to which you shall go. 13With your
utensils you shall have a trowel; when you relieve
yourself outside, you shall dig a hole with it and
then cover up your excrement. 14Because the
LORD your God travels along with your camp, to
save you and to hand over your enemies to you,
therefore your camp must be holy, so that he may
not see anything indecent among you and turn
away from you.
15 Slaves who have escaped to you from their
owners shall not be given back to them. 16They
shall reside with you, in your midst, in any place
they choose in any one of your towns, wherever
they please; you shall not oppress them.
17 None of the daughters of Israel shall be a
temple prostitute; none of the sons of Israel shall
be a temple prostitute. 18You shall not bring the
fee of a prostitute or the wages of a male prostitute[a] into the house of the LORD your God in
payment for any vow, for both of these are abhorrent to the LORD your God.
19 You shall not charge interest on loans to
another Israelite, interest on money, interest on
provisions, interest on anything that is lent. 20On
loans to a foreigner you may charge interest, but
on loans to another Israelite you may not charge
interest, so that the LORD your God may bless
you in all your undertakings in the land that you
are about to enter and possess.
21 If you make a vow to the LORD your God,
do not postpone fulfilling it; for the LORD your
God will surely require it of you, and you would
incur guilt. 22But if you refrain from vowing, you
will not incur guilt. 23Whatever your lips utter
you must diligently perform, just as you have
freely vowed to the LORD your God with your
own mouth.
24 If you go into your neighbor's vineyard,
you may eat your fill of grapes, as many as you
wish, but you shall not put any in a container.
25 If you go into your neighbor's standing
grain, you may pluck the ears with your hand,
but you shall not put a sickle to your neighbor's
standing grain.

24 Suppose a man enters into marriage with
a woman, but she does not please him because he finds something objectionable about her,
and so he writes her a certificate of divorce, puts
it in her hand, and sends her out of his house; she
then leaves his house 2and goes off to become another man's wife. 3Then suppose the second man
dislikes her, writes her a bill of divorce, puts it in
her hand, and sends her out of his house (or the
second man who married her dies); 4her first husband, who sent her away, is not permitted to take
her again to be his wife after she has been defiled;
for that would be abhorrent to the LORD, and you
shall not bring guilt on the land that the LORD
your God is giving you as a possession.
5 When a man is newly married, he shall not
go out with the army or be charged with any related duty. He shall be free at home one year, to
be happy with the wife whom he has married.
6 No one shall take a mill or an upper millstone in pledge, for that would be taking a life in
pledge.
7 If someone is caught kidnaping another
Israelite, enslaving or selling the Israelite, then
that kidnaper shall die. So you shall purge the evil
from your midst.
8 Guard against an outbreak of a leprous[b] skin
disease by being very careful; you shall carefully
observe whatever the levitical priests instruct
you, just as I have commanded them. 9Remem-
ber what the LORD your God did to Miriam on
your journey out of Egypt.
10 When you make your neighbor a loan of
any kind, you shall not go into the house to take
the pledge. 11You shall wait outside, while the

[a] Heb *a dog* [b] A term for several skin diseases; precise meaning uncertain

person to whom you are making the loan brings
the pledge out to you. 12If the person is poor, you
shall not sleep in the garment given you as[a] the
pledge. 13You shall give the pledge back by sunset, so that your neighbor may sleep in the cloak
and bless you; and it will be to your credit before
the LORD your God.

14 You shall not withhold the wages of poor
and needy laborers, whether other Israelites or
aliens who reside in your land in one of your
towns. 15You shall pay them their wages daily before sunset, because they are poor and their livelihood depends on them; otherwise they might
cry to the LORD against you, and you would incur
guilt.

16 Parents shall not be put to death for their
children, nor shall children be put to death for
their parents; only for their own crimes may persons be put to death.

17 You shall not deprive a resident alien or
an orphan of justice; you shall not take a widow's
garment in pledge. 18Remember that you were a
slave in Egypt and the LORD your God redeemed
you from there; therefore I command you to do
this.

19 When you reap your harvest in your field
and forget a sheaf in the field, you shall not go
back to get it; it shall be left for the alien, the orphan, and the widow, so that the LORD your God
may bless you in all your undertakings. 20When
you beat your olive trees, do not strip what is
left; it shall be for the alien, the orphan, and the
widow.

21 When you gather the grapes of your vineyard, do not glean what is left; it shall be for the
alien, the orphan, and the widow. 22Remember
that you were a slave in the land of Egypt; therefore I am commanding you to do this.

25 Suppose two persons have a dispute and
enter into litigation, and the judges decide between them, declaring one to be in the
right and the other to be in the wrong. 2If the one
in the wrong deserves to be flogged, the judge
shall make that person lie down and be beaten in
his presence with the number of lashes proportionate to the offense. 3Forty lashes may be given
but not more; if more lashes than these are given,
your neighbor will be degraded in your sight.

4 You shall not muzzle an ox while it is treading out the grain.

5 When brothers reside together, and one
of them dies and has no son, the wife of the deceased shall not be married outside the family to a
stranger. Her husband's brother shall go in to her,
taking her in marriage, and performing the duty
of a husband's brother to her, 6and the firstborn
whom she bears shall succeed to the name of the
deceased brother, so that his name may not be
blotted out of Israel. 7But if the man has no desire
to marry his brother's widow, then his brother's
widow shall go up to the elders at the gate and
say, "My husband's brother refuses to perpetuate
his brother's name in Israel; he will not perform
the duty of a husband's brother to me." 8Then the
elders of his town shall summon him and speak
to him. If he persists, saying, "I have no desire to
marry her," 9then his brother's wife shall go up to
him in the presence of the elders, pull his sandal
off his foot, spit in his face, and declare, "This is
what is done to the man who does not build up
his brother's house." 10Throughout Israel his family shall be known as "the house of him whose
sandal was pulled off."

11 If men get into a fight with one another,
and the wife of one intervenes to rescue her husband from the grip of his opponent by reaching
out and seizing his genitals, 12you shall cut off her
hand; show no pity.

13 You shall not have in your bag two kinds
of weights, large and small. 14You shall not have
in your house two kinds of measures, large and
small. 15You shall have only a full and honest
weight; you shall have only a full and honest measure, so that your days may be long in the land
that the LORD your God is giving you. 16For all
who do such things, all who act dishonestly, are
abhorrent to the LORD your God.

17 Remember what Amalek did to you on
your journey out of Egypt, 18how he attacked you
on the way, when you were faint and weary, and

[a] Heb lacks *the garment given you as*

struck down all who lagged behind you; he did
not fear God. 19 Therefore when the LORD your
God has given you rest from all your enemies on
every hand, in the land that the LORD your God is
giving you as an inheritance to possess, you shall
blot out the remembrance of Amalek from under
heaven; do not forget.

26 When you have come into the land that
the LORD your God is giving you as an inheritance to possess, and you possess it, and settle
in it, 2 you shall take some of the first of all the
fruit of the ground, which you harvest from the
land that the LORD your God is giving you, and
you shall put it in a basket and go to the place that
the LORD your God will choose as a dwelling for
his name. 3 You shall go to the priest who is in office at that time, and say to him, "Today I declare
to the LORD your God that I have come into the
land that the LORD swore to our ancestors to give
us." 4 When the priest takes the basket from your
hand and sets it down before the altar of the LORD
your God, 5 you shall make this response before
the LORD your God: "A wandering Aramean
was my ancestor; he went down into Egypt and
lived there as an alien, few in number, and there
he became a great nation, mighty and populous.
6 When the Egyptians treated us harshly and afflicted us, by imposing hard labor on us, 7 we cried
to the LORD, the God of our ancestors; the LORD
heard our voice and saw our affliction, our toil,
and our oppression. 8 The LORD brought us out
of Egypt with a mighty hand and an outstretched
arm, with a terrifying display of power, and with
signs and wonders; 9 and he brought us into this
place and gave us this land, a land flowing with
milk and honey. 10 So now I bring the first of the
fruit of the ground that you, O LORD, have given
me." You shall set it down before the LORD your
God and bow down before the LORD your God.
11 Then you, together with the Levites and the
aliens who reside among you, shall celebrate with
all the bounty that the LORD your God has given
to you and to your house.

12 When you have finished paying all the
tithe of your produce in the third year (which
is the year of the tithe), giving it to the Levites,
the aliens, the orphans, and the widows, so that

Deuteronomy 26:1-11

For Israel, identification with the strangers does not belong in the realm of ethics, but rather in the realm of the creed. In Deut 26:1-11 we find this creed in a very interesting context, namely in connection with a liturgy of thanksgiving. . . . In the deuteronomic liturgy of thanksgiving, however, Israel confessed not the gods of fertility and of the soil, but the God of the unsettled, of the homeless and of the slaves: "My father was a wandering Aramaean. He went down into Egypt to find refuge there . . . and Yahweh brought us out of Egypt with a mighty hand and outstretched arm, . . . brought us here and gave us this land."

And after having remembered the fathers and mothers of Israel who were strangers themselves, Israel is called by God to celebrate together with the strangers in their midst: . . . "Then you are to feast on all the good things Yahweh has given you, you and your household and with you the Levite and the stranger who lives among you." Texts and contexts like this make clear that biblical Israel does not find its identity in "blood and soil," nor in the loyalty to the gods of the soil. Its progenitor was not a god or demigod who belonged to the land and the land to him; it was rather a "wandering Aramaean," that is, a homeless migrant and nomad and refugee.[20]

— Gerhard Hoffmann

they may eat their fill within your towns, 13 then
you shall say before the LORD your God: "I have
removed the sacred portion from the house, and
I have given it to the Levites, the resident aliens,
the orphans, and the widows, in accordance with
your entire commandment that you commanded
me; I have neither transgressed nor forgotten any
of your commandments: 14 I have not eaten of it
while in mourning; I have not removed any of it
while I was unclean; and I have not offered any of
it to the dead. I have obeyed the LORD my God,
doing just as you commanded me. 15 Look down
from your holy habitation, from heaven, and bless
your people Israel and the ground that you have
given us, as you swore to our ancestors—a land
flowing with milk and honey."

16 This very day the LORD your God is commanding you to observe these statutes and ordinances; so observe them diligently with all your
heart and with all your soul. 17 Today you have
obtained the LORD's agreement: to be your God;
and for you to walk in his ways, to keep his statutes, his commandments, and his ordinances,
and to obey him. 18 Today the LORD has obtained
your agreement: to be his treasured people, as he
promised you, and to keep his commandments;
19 for him to set you high above all nations that
he has made, in praise and in fame and in honor;
and for you to be a people holy to the LORD your
God, as he promised.

27 Then Moses and the elders of Israel
charged all the people as follows: Keep
the entire commandment that I am commanding
you today. 2 On the day that you cross over the
Jordan into the land that the LORD your God is
giving you, you shall set up large stones and cover
them with plaster. 3 You shall write on them all
the words of this law when you have crossed over,
to enter the land that the LORD your God is giving you, a land flowing with milk and honey, as
the LORD, the God of your ancestors, promised
you. 4 So when you have crossed over the Jordan, you shall set up these stones, about which
I am commanding you today, on Mount Ebal,
and you shall cover them with plaster. 5 And you
shall build an altar there to the LORD your God,
an altar of stones on which you have not used an
iron tool. 6 You must build the altar of the LORD
your God of unhewn[a] stones. Then offer up burnt
offerings on it to the LORD your God, 7 make sacrifices of well-being, and eat them there, rejoicing
before the LORD your God. 8 You shall write on
the stones all the words of this law very clearly.

9 Then Moses and the levitical priests spoke
to all Israel, saying: Keep silence and hear, O Israel! This very day you have become the people of
the LORD your God. 10 Therefore obey the LORD
your God, observing his commandments and his
statutes that I am commanding you today.

11 The same day Moses charged the people
as follows: 12 When you have crossed over the
Jordan, these shall stand on Mount Gerizim for
the blessing of the people: Simeon, Levi, Judah,
Issachar, Joseph, and Benjamin. 13 And these shall
stand on Mount Ebal for the curse: Reuben, Gad,
Asher, Zebulun, Dan, and Naphtali. 14 Then the
Levites shall declare in a loud voice to all the Israelites:

15 "Cursed be anyone who makes an idol or
casts an image, anything abhorrent to the LORD,
the work of an artisan, and sets it up in secret." All
the people shall respond, saying, "Amen!"

16 "Cursed be anyone who dishonors father
or mother." All the people shall say, "Amen!"

17 "Cursed be anyone who moves a neighbor's boundary marker." All the people shall say,
"Amen!"

18 "Cursed be anyone who misleads a blind
person on the road." All the people shall say,
"Amen!"

19 "Cursed be anyone who deprives the
alien, the orphan, and the widow of justice." All
the people shall say, "Amen!"

20 "Cursed be anyone who lies with his father's wife, because he has violated his father's
rights."[b] All the people shall say, "Amen!"

21 "Cursed be anyone who lies with any animal." All the people shall say, "Amen!"

22 "Cursed be anyone who lies with his sister,
whether the daughter of his father or the daughter
of his mother." All the people shall say, "Amen!"

23 "Cursed be anyone who lies with his
mother-in-law." All the people shall say, "Amen!"

24 "Cursed be anyone who strikes down
a neighbor in secret." All the people shall say,
"Amen!"

25 "Cursed be anyone who takes a bribe to
shed innocent blood." All the people shall say,
"Amen!"

26 "Cursed be anyone who does not uphold
the words of this law by observing them." All the
people shall say, "Amen!"

28 If you will only obey the LORD your
God, by diligently observing all his commandments that I am commanding you today,
the LORD your God will set you high above all

[a] Heb *whole* [b] Heb *uncovered his father's skirt*

the nations of the earth; [2]all these blessings shall
come upon you and overtake you, if you obey the
LORD your God:
3 Blessed shall you be in the city, and blessed
shall you be in the field.
4 Blessed shall be the fruit of your womb, the
fruit of your ground, and the fruit of your livestock, both the increase of your cattle and the issue of your flock.
5 Blessed shall be your basket and your
kneading bowl.
6 Blessed shall you be when you come in, and
blessed shall you be when you go out.
7 The LORD will cause your enemies who rise
against you to be defeated before you; they shall
come out against you one way, and flee before
you seven ways. [8]The LORD will command the
blessing upon you in your barns, and in all that
you undertake; he will bless you in the land that
the LORD your God is giving you. [9]The LORD will
establish you as his holy people, as he has sworn
to you, if you keep the commandments of the
LORD your God and walk in his ways. [10]All the
peoples of the earth shall see that you are called
by the name of the LORD, and they shall be afraid
of you. [11]The LORD will make you abound in
prosperity, in the fruit of your womb, in the fruit
of your livestock, and in the fruit of your ground
in the land that the LORD swore to your ancestors to give you. [12]The LORD will open for you
his rich storehouse, the heavens, to give the rain
of your land in its season and to bless all your
undertakings. You will lend to many nations, but
you will not borrow. [13]The LORD will make you
the head, and not the tail; you shall be only at
the top, and not at the bottom—if you obey the
commandments of the LORD your God, which I
am commanding you today, by diligently observing them, [14]and if you do not turn aside from any
of the words that I am commanding you today,
either to the right or to the left, following other
gods to serve them.

15 But if you will not obey the LORD your
God by diligently observing all his commandments and decrees, which I am commanding you
today, then all these curses shall come upon you
and overtake you:

16 Cursed shall you be in the city, and cursed
shall you be in the field.
17 Cursed shall be your basket and your
kneading bowl.
18 Cursed shall be the fruit of your womb,
the fruit of your ground, the increase of your cattle and the issue of your flock.
19 Cursed shall you be when you come in,
and cursed shall you be when you go out.
20 The LORD will send upon you disaster,
panic, and frustration in everything you attempt
to do, until you are destroyed and perish quickly,
on account of the evil of your deeds, because you
have forsaken me. [21]The LORD will make the pestilence cling to you until it has consumed you off
the land that you are entering to possess. [22]The
LORD will afflict you with consumption, fever,
inflammation, with fiery heat and drought, and
with blight and mildew; they shall pursue you
until you perish. [23]The sky over your head shall
be bronze, and the earth under you iron. [24]The
LORD will change the rain of your land into powder, and only dust shall come down upon you
from the sky until you are destroyed.
25 The LORD will cause you to be defeated
before your enemies; you shall go out against
them one way and flee before them seven ways.
You shall become an object of horror to all the
kingdoms of the earth. [26]Your corpses shall be
food for every bird of the air and animal of the
earth, and there shall be no one to frighten them
away. [27]The LORD will afflict you with the boils
of Egypt, with ulcers, scurvy, and itch, of which
you cannot be healed. [28]The LORD will afflict you
with madness, blindness, and confusion of mind;
[29]you shall grope about at noon as blind people
grope in darkness, but you shall be unable to find
your way; and you shall be continually abused
and robbed, without anyone to help. [30]You shall
become engaged to a woman, but another man
shall lie with her. You shall build a house, but not
live in it. You shall plant a vineyard, but not enjoy
its fruit. [31]Your ox shall be butchered before your
eyes, but you shall not eat of it. Your donkey shall
be stolen in front of you, and shall not be restored
to you. Your sheep shall be given to your enemies,
without anyone to help you. [32]Your sons and

daughters shall be given to another people, while
you look on; you will strain your eyes looking for
them all day but be powerless to do anything. 33A
people whom you do not know shall eat up the
fruit of your ground and of all your labors; you
shall be continually abused and crushed, 34and
driven mad by the sight that your eyes shall see.
35The LORD will strike you on the knees and on
the legs with grievous boils of which you cannot
be healed, from the sole of your foot to the crown
of your head. 36The LORD will bring you, and the
king whom you set over you, to a nation that neither you nor your ancestors have known, where
you shall serve other gods, of wood and stone.
37You shall become an object of horror, a proverb, and a byword among all the peoples where
the LORD will lead you.

38 You shall carry much seed into the field but
shall gather little in, for the locust shall consume
it. 39You shall plant vineyards and dress them, but
you shall neither drink the wine nor gather the
grapes, for the worm shall eat them. 40You shall
have olive trees throughout all your territory, but
you shall not anoint yourself with the oil, for your
olives shall drop off. 41You shall have sons and
daughters, but they shall not remain yours, for
they shall go into captivity. 42All your trees and
the fruit of your ground the cicada shall take over.
43Aliens residing among you shall ascend above
you higher and higher, while you shall descend
lower and lower. 44They shall lend to you but you
shall not lend to them; they shall be the head and
you shall be the tail.

45 All these curses shall come upon you, pursuing and overtaking you until you are destroyed,
because you did not obey the LORD your God, by
observing the commandments and the decrees
that he commanded you. 46They shall be among
you and your descendants as a sign and a portent
forever.

47 Because you did not serve the LORD your
God joyfully and with gladness of heart for the
abundance of everything, 48therefore you shall
serve your enemies whom the LORD will send
against you, in hunger and thirst, in nakedness
and lack of everything. He will put an iron yoke
on your neck until he has destroyed you. 49The
LORD will bring a nation from far away, from the
end of the earth, to swoop down on you like an
eagle, a nation whose language you do not understand, 50a grim-faced nation showing no respect
to the old or favor to the young. 51It shall consume the fruit of your livestock and the fruit of
your ground until you are destroyed, leaving you
neither grain, wine, and oil, nor the increase of
your cattle and the issue of your flock, until it has
made you perish. 52It shall besiege you in all your
towns until your high and fortified walls, in which
you trusted, come down throughout your land;
it shall besiege you in all your towns throughout
the land that the LORD your God has given you.
53In the desperate straits to which the enemy
siege reduces you, you will eat the fruit of your
womb, the flesh of your own sons and daughters
whom the LORD your God has given you. 54Even
the most refined and gentle of men among you
will begrudge food to his own brother, to the wife
whom he embraces, and to the last of his remaining children, 55giving to none of them any of the
flesh of his children whom he is eating, because
nothing else remains to him, in the desperate
straits to which the enemy siege will reduce you
in all your towns. 56She who is the most refined
and gentle among you, so gentle and refined that
she does not venture to set the sole of her foot
on the ground, will begrudge food to the husband
whom she embraces, to her own son, and to her
own daughter, 57begrudging even the afterbirth
that comes out from between her thighs, and the
children that she bears, because she is eating them
in secret for lack of anything else, in the desperate
straits to which the enemy siege will reduce you
in your towns.

58 If you do not diligently observe all the
words of this law that are written in this book,
fearing this glorious and awesome name, the
LORD your God, 59then the LORD will overwhelm both you and your offspring with severe
and lasting afflictions and grievous and lasting
maladies. 60He will bring back upon you all the
diseases of Egypt, of which you were in dread,
and they shall cling to you. 61Every other malady
and affliction, even though not recorded in the
book of this law, the LORD will inflict on you

until you are destroyed. 62 Although once you were as numerous as the stars in heaven, you shall be left few in number, because you did not obey the LORD your God. 63 And just as the LORD took delight in making you prosperous and numerous, so the LORD will take delight in bringing you to ruin and destruction; you shall be plucked off the land that you are entering to possess. 64 The LORD will scatter you among all peoples, from one end of the earth to the other; and there you shall serve other gods, of wood and stone, which neither you nor your ancestors have known. 65 Among those nations you shall find no ease, no resting place for the sole of your foot. There the LORD will give you a trembling heart, failing eyes, and a languishing spirit. 66 Your life shall hang in doubt before you; night and day you shall be in dread, with no assurance of your life. 67 In the morning you shall say, "If only it were evening!" and at evening you shall say, "If only it were morning!"—because of the dread that your heart shall feel and the sights that your eyes shall see. 68 The LORD will bring you back in ships to Egypt, by a route that I promised you would never see again; and there you shall offer yourselves for sale to your enemies as male and female slaves, but there will be no buyer.

29 [a] These are the words of the covenant that the LORD commanded Moses to make with the Israelites in the land of Moab, in addition to the covenant that he had made with them at Horeb.

2 [b] Moses summoned all Israel and said to them: You have seen all that the LORD did before your eyes in the land of Egypt, to Pharaoh and to all his servants and to all his land, 3 the great trials that your eyes saw, the signs, and those great wonders. 4 But to this day the LORD has not given you a mind to understand, or eyes to see, or ears to hear. 5 I have led you forty years in the wilderness. The clothes on your back have not worn out, and the sandals on your feet have not worn out; 6 you have not eaten bread, and you have not drunk wine or strong drink—so that you may know that I am the LORD your God. 7 When you came to this place, King Sihon of Heshbon and King Og of Bashan came out against us for battle, but we defeated them. 8 We took their land and gave it as an inheritance to the Reubenites, the Gadites, and the half-tribe of Manasseh. 9 Therefore diligently observe the words of this covenant, in order that you may succeed[c] in everything that you do.

10 You stand assembled today, all of you, before the LORD your God—the leaders of your tribes,[d] your elders, and your officials, all the men of Israel, 11 your children, your women, and the aliens who are in your camp, both those who cut your wood and those who draw your water— 12 to enter into the covenant of the LORD your God, sworn by an oath, which the LORD your God is making with you today; 13 in order that he may establish you today as his people, and that he may be your God, as he promised you and as he swore to your ancestors, to Abraham, to Isaac, and to Jacob. 14 I am making this covenant, sworn by an oath, not only with you who stand here with us today before the LORD our God, 15 but also with those who are not here with us today. 16 You know how we lived in the land of Egypt, and how we came through the midst of the nations through which you passed. 17 You have seen their detestable things, the filthy idols of wood and stone, of silver and gold, that were among them. 18 It may be that there is among you a man or woman, or a family or tribe, whose heart is already turning away from the LORD our God to serve the gods of those nations. It may be that there is among you a root sprouting poisonous and bitter growth. 19 All who hear the words of this oath and bless themselves, thinking in their hearts, "We are safe even though we go our own stubborn ways" (thus bringing disaster on moist and dry alike)[e]— 20 the LORD will be unwilling to pardon them, for the LORD's anger and passion will smoke against them. All the curses written in this book will descend on them, and the LORD will blot out their names from under heaven. 21 The LORD will single them out from all the

[a] Ch 28.69 in Heb [b] Ch 29.1 in Heb [c] Or *deal wisely*
[e] Meaning of Heb uncertain

[d] Gk Syr: Heb *your leaders, your tribes*

tribes of Israel for calamity, in accordance with
all the curses of the covenant written in this book
of the law. 22The next generation, your children
who rise up after you, as well as the foreigner who
comes from a distant country, will see the devastation of that land and the afflictions with which
the LORD has afflicted it— 23all its soil burned
out by sulfur and salt, nothing planted, nothing
sprouting, unable to support any vegetation, like
the destruction of Sodom and Gomorrah, Admah and Zeboiim, which the LORD destroyed in
his fierce anger— 24they and indeed all the nations will wonder, "Why has the LORD done thus
to this land? What caused this great display of
anger?" 25They will conclude, "It is because they
abandoned the covenant of the LORD, the God of
their ancestors, which he made with them when
he brought them out of the land of Egypt. 26They
turned and served other gods, worshiping them,
gods whom they had not known and whom he
had not allotted to them; 27so the anger of the
LORD was kindled against that land, bringing on
it every curse written in this book. 28The LORD
uprooted them from their land in anger, fury, and
great wrath, and cast them into another land, as is
now the case." 29The secret things belong to the
LORD our God, but the revealed things belong to
us and to our children forever, to observe all the
words of this law.

30 When all these things have happened
to you, the blessings and the curses that
I have set before you, if you call them to mind
among all the nations where the LORD your God
has driven you, 2and return to the LORD your
God, and you and your children obey him with
all your heart and with all your soul, just as I am
commanding you today, 3then the LORD your
God will restore your fortunes and have compassion on you, gathering you again from all the
peoples among whom the LORD your God has
scattered you. 4Even if you are exiled to the ends
of the world,[a] from there the LORD your God
will gather you, and from there he will bring you
back. 5The LORD your God will bring you into
the land that your ancestors possessed, and you
will possess it; he will make you more prosperous
and numerous than your ancestors.

6 Moreover, the LORD your God will circumcise your heart and the heart of your descendants,
so that you will love the LORD your God with all
your heart and with all your soul, in order that you
may live. 7The LORD your God will put all these
curses on your enemies and on the adversaries
who took advantage of you. 8Then you shall again
obey the LORD, observing all his commandments
that I am commanding you today, 9and the LORD
your God will make you abundantly prosperous
in all your undertakings, in the fruit of your body,
in the fruit of your livestock, and in the fruit of
your soil. For the LORD will again take delight in
prospering you, just as he delighted in prospering your ancestors, 10when you obey the LORD
your God by observing his commandments and
decrees that are written in this book of the law,
because you turn to the LORD your God with all
your heart and with all your soul.

11 Surely, this commandment that I am commanding you today is not too hard for you, nor
is it too far away. 12It is not in heaven, that you
should say, "Who will go up to heaven for us, and
get it for us so that we may hear it and observe it?"
13Neither is it beyond the sea, that you should
say, "Who will cross to the other side of the sea
for us, and get it for us so that we may hear it and
observe it?" 14No, the word is very near to you;
it is in your mouth and in your heart for you to
observe.

15 See, I have set before you today life and
prosperity, death and adversity. 16If you obey the
commandments of the LORD your God[b] that I am
commanding you today, by loving the LORD your
God, walking in his ways, and observing his commandments, decrees, and ordinances, then you
shall live and become numerous, and the LORD
your God will bless you in the land that you are
entering to possess. 17But if your heart turns away
and you do not hear, but are led astray to bow
down to other gods and serve them, 18I declare to
you today that you shall perish; you shall not live
long in the land that you are crossing the Jordan

[a] Heb *of heaven* [b] Gk: Heb lacks *If you obey the commandments of the LORD your God*

to enter and possess. 19 I call heaven and earth to witness against you today that I have set before you life and death, blessings and curses. Choose life so that you and your descendants may live, 20 loving the LORD your God, obeying him, and holding fast to him; for that means life to you and length of days, so that you may live in the land that the LORD swore to give to your ancestors, to Abraham, to Isaac, and to Jacob.

31 When Moses had finished speaking all[a] these words to all Israel, 2 he said to them: "I am now one hundred twenty years old. I am no longer able to get about, and the LORD has told me, 'You shall not cross over this Jordan.' 3 The LORD your God himself will cross over before you. He will destroy these nations before you, and you shall dispossess them. Joshua also will cross over before you, as the LORD promised. 4 The LORD will do to them as he did to Sihon and Og, the kings of the Amorites, and to their land, when he destroyed them. 5 The LORD will give them over to you and you shall deal with them in full accord with the command that I have given to you. 6 Be strong and bold; have no fear or dread of them, because it is the LORD your God who goes with you; he will not fail you or forsake you."

7 Then Moses summoned Joshua and said to him in the sight of all Israel: "Be strong and bold, for you are the one who will go with this people into the land that the LORD has sworn to their ancestors to give them; and you will put them in possession of it. 8 It is the LORD who goes before you. He will be with you; he will not fail you or forsake you. Do not fear or be dismayed."

9 Then Moses wrote down this law, and gave it to the priests, the sons of Levi, who carried the ark of the covenant of the LORD, and to all the elders of Israel. 10 Moses commanded them: "Every seventh year, in the scheduled year of remission, during the festival of booths,[b] 11 when all Israel comes to appear before the LORD your God at the place that he will choose, you shall read this law before all Israel in their hearing. 12 Assemble the people—men, women, and children, as well as the aliens residing in your towns—so that they may hear and learn to fear the LORD your God and to observe diligently all the words of this law, 13 and so that their children, who have not known it, may hear and learn to fear the LORD your God, as long as you live in the land that you are crossing over the Jordan to possess."

14 The LORD said to Moses, "Your time to die is near; call Joshua and present yourselves in the tent of meeting, so that I may commission him." So Moses and Joshua went and presented themselves in the tent of meeting, 15 and the LORD appeared at the tent in a pillar of cloud; the pillar of cloud stood at the entrance to the tent.

16 The LORD said to Moses, "Soon you will lie down with your ancestors. Then this people will begin to prostitute themselves to the foreign gods in their midst, the gods of the land into which they are going; they will forsake me, breaking my covenant that I have made with them. 17 My anger will be kindled against them in that day. I will forsake them and hide my face from them; they will become easy prey, and many terrible troubles will come upon them. In that day they will say, 'Have not these troubles come upon us because our God is not in our midst?' 18 On that day I will surely hide my face on account of all the evil they have done by turning to other gods. 19 Now therefore write this song, and teach it to the Israelites; put it in their mouths, in order that this song may be a witness for me against the Israelites. 20 For when I have brought them into the land flowing with milk and honey, which I promised on oath to their ancestors, and they have eaten their fill and grown fat, they will turn to other gods and serve them, despising me and breaking my covenant. 21 And when many terrible troubles come upon them, this song will confront them as a witness, because it will not be lost from the mouths of their descendants. For I know what they are inclined to do even now, before I have brought them into the land that I promised them on oath." 22 That very day Moses wrote this song and taught it to the Israelites.

23 Then the LORD commissioned Joshua son of Nun and said, "Be strong and bold, for you

[a] Q Ms Gk: MT *Moses went and spoke* [b] Or *tabernacles*; Heb *succoth*

shall bring the Israelites into the land that I promised them; I will be with you."
24 When Moses had finished writing down
in a book the words of this law to the very end,
25 Moses commanded the Levites who carried the
ark of the covenant of the LORD, saying, 26 "Take
this book of the law and put it beside the ark of
the covenant of the LORD your God; let it remain
there as a witness against you. 27 For I know well
how rebellious and stubborn you are. If you already have been so rebellious toward the LORD
while I am still alive among you, how much more
after my death! 28 Assemble to me all the elders of
your tribes and your officials, so that I may recite
these words in their hearing and call heaven and
earth to witness against them. 29 For I know that
after my death you will surely act corruptly, turning aside from the way that I have commanded
you. In time to come trouble will befall you, because you will do what is evil in the sight of the
LORD, provoking him to anger through the work
of your hands."

30 Then Moses recited the words of this
song, to the very end, in the hearing of the whole
assembly of Israel:

32 Give ear, O heavens, and I will speak;
let the earth hear the words of my
mouth.
2 May my teaching drop like the rain,
my speech condense like the dew;
like gentle rain on grass,
like showers on new growth.
3 For I will proclaim the name of the LORD;
ascribe greatness to our God!

4 The Rock, his work is perfect,
and all his ways are just.
A faithful God, without deceit,
just and upright is he;
5 yet his degenerate children have dealt falsely
with him,[a]
a perverse and crooked generation.
6 Do you thus repay the LORD,
O foolish and senseless people?
Is not he your father, who created you,
who made you and established you?
7 Remember the days of old,
consider the years long past;
ask your father, and he will inform you;
your elders, and they will tell you.
8 When the Most High[b] apportioned the
nations,
when he divided humankind,
he fixed the boundaries of the peoples
according to the number of the gods;[c]
9 the LORD's own portion was his people,
Jacob his allotted share.

10 He sustained[d] him in a desert land,
in a howling wilderness waste;
he shielded him, cared for him,
guarded him as the apple of his eye.
11 As an eagle stirs up its nest,
and hovers over its young;
as it spreads its wings, takes them up,
and bears them aloft on its pinions,
12 the LORD alone guided him;
no foreign god was with him.
13 He set him atop the heights of the land,
and fed him with[e] produce of the field;
he nursed him with honey from the crags,
with oil from flinty rock;
14 curds from the herd, and milk from the flock,
with fat of lambs and rams;
Bashan bulls and goats,
together with the choicest wheat—
you drank fine wine from the blood of
grapes.
15 Jacob ate his fill;[f]
Jeshurun grew fat, and kicked.
You grew fat, bloated, and gorged!
He abandoned God who made him,
and scoffed at the Rock of his salvation.
16 They made him jealous with strange gods,
with abhorrent things they provoked him.
17 They sacrificed to demons, not God,
to deities they had never known,
to new ones recently arrived,

[a] Meaning of Heb uncertain [b] Traditional rendering of Heb *Elyon* [c] Q Ms Compare Gk Tg: MT *the Israelites*
[d] Sam Gk Compare Tg: MT *found* [e] Sam Gk Syr Tg: MT *he ate* [f] Q Mss Sam Gk: MT lacks *Jacob ate his fill*

Deuteronomy 32:13-18

God our Mother: The last phrase of verse 18 can also be translated "You forgot the God who writhed in labor with you." God nurses Israel in verses 13-14. These are examples of divine maternity. God also writhes in labor to give birth to the mountains in Ps 90:2 and the hills in Job 15:7. The biblical authors were comfortable describing God in maternal terms. Contemporary readers frequently choose one gender for God by appealing to some scriptures while censoring others. The inclusion of masculine and feminine divine language reminds us that God transcends our categories.

— *WG*

whom your ancestors had not feared.
18 You were unmindful of the Rock that bore
you;[a]
you forgot the God who gave you birth.

19 The LORD saw it, and was jealous;[b]
he spurned[c] his sons and daughters.
20 He said: I will hide my face from them,
I will see what their end will be;
for they are a perverse generation,
children in whom there is no faithfulness.
21 They made me jealous with what is no god,
provoked me with their idols.
So I will make them jealous with what is no
people,
provoke them with a foolish nation.
22 For a fire is kindled by my anger,
and burns to the depths of Sheol;
it devours the earth and its increase,
and sets on fire the foundations of the
mountains.
23 I will heap disasters upon them,
spend my arrows against them:
24 wasting hunger,
burning consumption,
bitter pestilence.
The teeth of beasts I will send against them,
with venom of things crawling in the dust.
25 In the street the sword shall bereave,
and in the chambers terror,
for young man and woman alike,
nursing child and old gray head.
26 I thought to scatter them[d]
and blot out the memory of them from
humankind;
27 but I feared provocation by the enemy,
for their adversaries might misunderstand
and say, "Our hand is triumphant;
it was not the LORD who did all this."

28 They are a nation void of sense;
there is no understanding in them.
29 If they were wise, they would understand
this;
they would discern what the end
would be.
30 How could one have routed a thousand,
and two put a myriad to flight,
unless their Rock had sold them,
the LORD had given them up?
31 Indeed their rock is not like our Rock;
our enemies are fools.[d]
32 Their vine comes from the vinestock of
Sodom,
from the vineyards of Gomorrah;
their grapes are grapes of poison,
their clusters are bitter;
33 their wine is the poison of serpents,
the cruel venom of asps.

34 Is not this laid up in store with me,
sealed up in my treasuries?
35 Vengeance is mine, and recompense,
for the time when their foot shall slip;
because the day of their calamity is at hand,
their doom comes swiftly.

36 Indeed the LORD will vindicate his people,
have compassion on his servants,
when he sees that their power is gone,

[a] Or *that begot you* [b] Q Mss Gk: MT lacks *was jealous* [c] Cn: Heb *he spurned because of provocation*
[d] Gk: Meaning of Heb uncertain

neither bond nor free remaining.
37 Then he will say: Where are their gods,
the rock in which they took refuge,
38 who ate the fat of their sacrifices,
and drank the wine of their libations?
Let them rise up and help you,
let them be your protection!

39 See now that I, even I, am he;
there is no god besides me.
I kill and I make alive;
I wound and I heal;
and no one can deliver from my hand.
40 For I lift up my hand to heaven,
and swear: As I live forever,
41 when I whet my flashing sword,
and my hand takes hold on judgment;
I will take vengeance on my adversaries,
and will repay those who hate me.
42 I will make my arrows drunk with blood,
and my sword shall devour flesh—
with the blood of the slain and the
captives,
from the long-haired enemy.

43 Praise, O heavens,[a] his people,
worship him, all you gods![b]
For he will avenge the blood of his children,[c]
and take vengeance on his adversaries;
he will repay those who hate him,[b]
and cleanse the land for his people.[d]

44 Moses came and recited all the words of
this song in the hearing of the people, he and
Joshua[e] son of Nun. 45When Moses had finished
reciting all these words to all Israel, 46he said to
them: "Take to heart all the words that I am giving in witness against you today; give them as a
command to your children, so that they may diligently observe all the words of this law. 47This is
no trifling matter for you, but rather your very
life; through it you may live long in the land that
you are crossing over the Jordan to possess."

48 On that very day the LORD addressed
Moses as follows: 49"Ascend this mountain of
the Abarim, Mount Nebo, which is in the land
of Moab, across from Jericho, and view the land
of Canaan, which I am giving to the Israelites for
a possession; 50you shall die there on the mountain that you ascend and shall be gathered to your
kin, as your brother Aaron died on Mount Hor
and was gathered to his kin; 51because both of
you broke faith with me among the Israelites at
the waters of Meribath-kadesh in the wilderness
of Zin, by failing to maintain my holiness among
the Israelites. 52Although you may view the land
from a distance, you shall not enter it—the land
that I am giving to the Israelites."

33 This is the blessing with which Moses, the
man of God, blessed the Israelites before
his death. 2He said:

The LORD came from Sinai,
and dawned from Seir upon us;[f]
he shone forth from Mount Paran.
With him were myriads of holy ones;[g]
at his right, a host of his own.[h]
3 Indeed, O favorite among[i] peoples,
all his holy ones were in your charge;
they marched at your heels,
accepted direction from you.
4 Moses charged us with the law,
as a possession for the assembly of Jacob.
5 There arose a king in Jeshurun,
when the leaders of the people
assembled—
the united tribes of Israel.

6 May Reuben live, and not die out,
even though his numbers are few.

7And this he said of Judah:
O LORD, give heed to Judah,
and bring him to his people;
strengthen his hands for him,[j]
and be a help against his adversaries.

[a] Q Ms Gk: MT *nations* [b] Q Ms Gk: MT lacks this line [c] Q Ms Gk: MT *his servants* [d] Q Ms Sam Gk Vg: MT *his land his people* [e] Sam Gk Syr Vg: MT *Hoshea* [f] Gk Syr Vg Compare Tg: Heb *upon them* [g] Cn Compare Gk Sam Syr Vg: MT *He came from Ribeboth-kodesh,* [h] Cn Compare Gk: meaning of Heb uncertain [i] Or *O lover of the* [j] Cn: Heb *with his hands he contended*

8 And of Levi he said:
Give to Levi[a] your Thummim,
and your Urim to your loyal one,
whom you tested at Massah,
with whom you contended at the waters of Meribah;
9 who said of his father and mother,
"I regard them not";
he ignored his kin,
and did not acknowledge his children.
For they observed your word,
and kept your covenant.
10 They teach Jacob your ordinances,
and Israel your law;
they place incense before you,
and whole burnt offerings on your altar.
11 Bless, O LORD, his substance,
and accept the work of his hands;
crush the loins of his adversaries,
of those that hate him, so that they do not rise again.

12 Of Benjamin he said:
The beloved of the LORD rests in safety—
the High God[b] surrounds him all day long—
the beloved[c] rests between his shoulders.

13 And of Joseph he said:
Blessed by the LORD be his land,
with the choice gifts of heaven above,
and of the deep that lies beneath;
14 with the choice fruits of the sun,
and the rich yield of the months;
15 with the finest produce of the ancient mountains,
and the abundance of the everlasting hills;
16 with the choice gifts of the earth and its fullness,
and the favor of the one who dwells on Sinai.[d]
Let these come on the head of Joseph,
on the brow of the prince among his brothers.
17 A firstborn[e] bull—majesty is his!
His horns are the horns of a wild ox;
with them he gores the peoples,
driving them to[f] the ends of the earth;
such are the myriads of Ephraim,
such the thousands of Manasseh.

18 And of Zebulun he said:
Rejoice, Zebulun, in your going out;
and Issachar, in your tents.
19 They call peoples to the mountain;
there they offer the right sacrifices;
for they suck the affluence of the seas
and the hidden treasures of the sand.

20 And of Gad he said:
Blessed be the enlargement of Gad!
Gad lives like a lion;
he tears at arm and scalp.
21 He chose the best for himself,
for there a commander's allotment was reserved;
he came at the head of the people,
he executed the justice of the LORD,
and his ordinances for Israel.

22 And of Dan he said:
Dan is a lion's whelp
that leaps forth from Bashan.

23 And of Naphtali he said:
O Naphtali, sated with favor,
full of the blessing of the LORD,
possess the west and the south.

24 And of Asher he said:
Most blessed of sons be Asher;
may he be the favorite of his brothers,
and may he dip his foot in oil.
25 Your bars are iron and bronze;
and as your days, so is your strength.

26 There is none like God, O Jeshurun,
who rides through the heavens to your help,

[a] Q Ms Gk: MT lacks *Give to Levi* [b] Heb *above him* [c] Heb *he* [d] Cn: Heb *in the bush* [e] Q Ms Gk Syr Vg: MT *His firstborn* [f] Cn: Heb *the peoples, together*

majestic through the skies.
27 He subdues the ancient gods,[a]
shatters[b] the forces of old;[c]
he drove out the enemy before you,
and said, "Destroy!"
28 So Israel lives in safety,
untroubled is Jacob's abode[d]
in a land of grain and wine,
where the heavens drop down dew.
29 Happy are you, O Israel! Who is like you,
a people saved by the LORD,
the shield of your help,
and the sword of your triumph!
Your enemies shall come fawning to you,
and you shall tread on their backs.

34 Then Moses went up from the plains of
Moab to Mount Nebo, to the top of Pisgah, which is opposite Jericho, and the LORD
showed him the whole land: Gilead as far as Dan,
2 all Naphtali, the land of Ephraim and Manasseh,
all the land of Judah as far as the Western Sea, 3 the
Negeb, and the Plain—that is, the valley of Jericho,
the city of palm trees—as far as Zoar. 4 The LORD
said to him, "This is the land of which I swore to
Abraham, to Isaac, and to Jacob, saying, 'I will
give it to your descendants'; I have let you see it
with your eyes, but you shall not cross over there."
5 Then Moses, the servant of the LORD, died there
in the land of Moab, at the LORD's command. 6 He
was buried in a valley in the land of Moab, opposite Beth-peor, but no one knows his burial place
to this day. 7 Moses was one hundred twenty years
old when he died; his sight was unimpaired and
his vigor had not abated. 8 The Israelites wept for
Moses in the plains of Moab thirty days; then the
period of mourning for Moses was ended.

9 Joshua son of Nun was full of the spirit of
wisdom, because Moses had laid his hands on
him; and the Israelites obeyed him, doing as the
LORD had commanded Moses.

10 Never since has there arisen a prophet in
Israel like Moses, whom the LORD knew face to
face. 11 He was unequaled for all the signs and
wonders that the LORD sent him to perform in
the land of Egypt, against Pharaoh and all his servants and his entire land, 12 and for all the mighty
deeds and all the terrifying displays of power that
Moses performed in the sight of all Israel.

[a] Or *The eternal God is a dwelling place* [b] Cn: Heb *from underneath* [c] Or *the everlasting arms* [d] Or *fountain*

The Historical Books

INTRODUCTION

Uriah Y. Kim

The Historical Books, a part of the Christian Bible (and *The Peoples' Bible*), includes several books—Joshua, Judges, 1 and 2 Samuel, and 1 and 2 Kings—that appear in the Jewish tradition as the Former Prophets, part of the *Nevi'im* ("Prophets"), the second division of scripture. Jewish tradition recognized that the material in Joshua–Kings was somehow similar to, yet different from the prophetic writings—Isaiah, Jeremiah, Ezekiel, and the Book of the Twelve, Hosea through Malachi—that in that tradition are called the Latter Prophets (see the Introduction to the Prophets, beginning on p. 810). The emphasis in these writings on the role of prophets and the recurring theme of "prophecy and fulfillment," in which the word of God is given to a prophet and then fulfilled in events that happen "according to the word of God," give them a prophetic flavor.

The Deuteronomistic History

In contemporary biblical scholarship these books are viewed as theologically and editorially connected in a self-contained work called the Deuteronomistic History. This work recounts a history of ancient Israel from its entrance into and settlement in Canaan (Joshua and Judges), to the establishment of the dynasty of David (1–2 Samuel), then to the division of the kingdom (1 Kings), and finally to the fall of Samaria and Jerusalem (2 Kings). This work is influenced by the ideals expounded in Deuteronomy, believed to be "the book of the law" mentioned in it (see 2 Kgs 22:8).

There are several overarching themes or messages in the Deuteronomistic History. From the perspective of the Babylonian exile, one theme shows that the Babylonian captivity was a result of centuries of Israel's unfaithfulness to its God, and therefore that God was justified in punishing the people. Some see a message of hope in the way the Deuteronomistic History

ends with the report of the release of an exiled Davidic king from prison (2 Kgs 25:27-30), affirming a theme of God's special relation with the house of David that runs through the books of Samuel and Kings. Another theme is a call for repentance, prominent in the book of Judges, exhorting the people to turn back to God from their infidelity and to trust God to forgive and deliver them. Many scholars believe that a pre-exilic edition of the Deuteronomistic History was composed during King Josiah's reign (640–609 BCE). Two themes would have been especially powerful in the time of Josiah: the sinfulness of Jeroboam, founding king of the Northern Kingdom, who established illegitimate sanctuaries in Dan and Bethel and thus brought about the fall of that kingdom; and the faithfulness of David and God's promise of loyalty to David and his house.

In genre, the Deuteronomistic History is one of the first examples of historical narrative of a people, and it invites its readers to read it as history. Therefore, it is critical to have some knowledge of the historical background of events depicted in this work. Until the eighth century BCE, Judah, the Southern Kingdom, and Israel, the Northern Kingdom, were involved in regional conflicts with neighboring political entities but free from interference from the major powers outside the region, namely Egypt and the Mesopotamian powers, Assyria and Babylon. In the middle of the eighth century, however, the Neo-Assyrians invaded Syria-Palestine and eventually conquered the Northern Kingdom of Israel, sacking Samaria in 722 (2 Kings 17). Judah was spared the same fate when the Assyrian campaign against Jerusalem in 701 was thwarted miraculously, according to 2 Kings 18–19. However, even Josiah's faithful implementation of the "book of the law" (2 Kings 22–23) could not prevent what seemed like Judah's irrevocable march toward judgment. In 598, Jerusalem surrendered to Nebuchadnezzar, the king of the Neo-Babylonian Empire (2 Kings 24), which had replaced the Neo-Assyrian Empire toward the end of the seventh century. When Jerusalem rebelled against Nebuchadnezzar, he conquered Jerusalem, destroyed its temple, and took many of its residents back to Babylon in 586 (2 Kings 25). The books of the Deuteronomistic History are written against that background.

Joshua. The book of Joshua opens with God instructing Joshua to take possession of the land of Canaan, promising him sweeping successes if he obeys the book of the law (1:1-9). Obedience to God's instructions is a key theme in Joshua. The supposed quick campaign to conquer Canaan starts at a very slow pace. The procession across the Jordan (ch. 3), the setting of twelve stones as a memorial (ch. 4), the circumcision of the new generation, and the observance of the Passover (5:1-12) read more like priestly narratives than martial reports. Most of the subsequent conquest narrative centers around two cities in central Canaan, Jericho and Ai (chs. 6–9). The pace of the conquest narrative picks up with the description of the defeat of kings in the south (ch. 10) and the defeat of kings in the north (ch. 11), ending with the statement that Joshua "took the whole land" and "the land had rest from war" (11:23). It is critical to note that God's command to "utterly destroy" the indigenous people (8:26; 10:28-43;11:1-23) is understood as a matter of faith, as a demonstration of obedience that propels the narrative forward; it should not be read as a moral precedent. Joshua then distributes the land according to the tribal allotments (chs. 12–22) and draws territorial boundaries. One has to wonder whether these artificial territorial boundaries followed or cut across cultural and ethnic boundaries that probably existed among the people of Canaan. Joshua ends with Joshua's farewell speech to the people, exhorting them to be faithful to God (ch. 23), and with a renewal of the covenant with God at Shechem (24:1-28).

Judges. Despite claims in Joshua that Israel was able to conquer the entire land, the book of Judges describes the Israelites' ongoing conflict with local Canaanite tribes, emerging kingdoms, and the Philistines, who arrived about the same time as the Israelites. The Israelites were forewarned not to follow the gods of their neighbors and that they would be turned over to their enemies if they did not show loyalty to their God (2:11-15). This threat is carried out in chapters 2–16, where each crisis begins with the formulaic saying that the Israelites had done "evil in the sight of the Lord," followed by the Israelites being handed over to their foes (3:7-8; 3:12; 4:1-2; 6:1; 10:6-7; 13:1). But each time the people repent of their infidelity, God is moved by their cry and raises a judge to deliver them from their suffering. This pattern of apostasy, persecution at the hand of their enemies, repentance, and God's deliverance through the judges is repeated until the narrative reaches the last part of the book (chs. 17–21). This section describes a complete disintegration of moral and religious integrity and a tragic civil war between Benjamin and the rest of Israel. Judges ends on an ominous note—"In those days there was no king in Israel; all the people did what was right in their own eyes" (17:6; 18:1; 19:1; 21:25)—driving home the point that these atrocities happened because there was no king.

First and Second Samuel. In the two books of Samuel—originally one book—there are voices for and against the establishment of a kingship. The story opens with Hannah's petition to the Lord for a son by Elkanah (ch. 1). After her son is born, she praises God in a prayer that predicts God's anointing of a king (1 Sam 2:1-10). Her son, Samuel, faithful as he is, is not the anointed one, however; neither are *his* sons (1 Samuel 8). Saul is anointed by God but is quickly rejected for another (1 Samuel 13, 15). God chooses a ruddy shepherd boy (1 Samuel 16). Once David appears, the narrative focuses on why he, and not Saul, is God's choice. The narrative ends with the ignominious death of Saul (1 Samuel 31). The story of David's rise to kingship continues until it culminates in 2 Samuel 5 when David becomes king of Judah and Israel. In 2 Samuel, David secures his kingdom through the founding of Jerusalem as his capital (2 Samuel 5) and military successes against the Philistines and other neighboring peoples (2 Samuel 8). Then the story takes an abrupt turn for the worse and begins what scholars call the Succession Narrative (2 Samuel 9–20), which recounts internal problems that threaten David's reign. Second Samuel ends with a collection of stories and poems associated with David (2 Samuel 21–24), which includes a song of David (2 Samuel 22) that parallels Hannah's song and expresses a full-blown theology of a divinely established monarchy.

First and Second Kings. First Kings continues the narrative that began with a young, daring,

and charismatic David and now describes him as an old, impotent, and fragile man waiting for his death (1 Kings 1). David, however, is not finished yet. He has enough strength and sense to utter his last wishes and to put his son Solomon on the throne (1 Kgs 2:1-12). Solomon is famous for his wisdom, but his most important achievement is the building of the temple in Jerusalem (1 Kings 5–8). Upon his death, the kingdom is divided into the Northern Kingdom of Israel, led by Jeroboam, and the Southern Kingdom of Judah, ruled by Solomon's son Rehoboam (1 Kgs 12:1-32). Israel is condemned from the start, because Jeroboam commits the ultimate sin when he sets up royal shrines outside Jerusalem (1 Kgs 12:25-32). From this point on, each king is judged according to his loyalty to God as specified in "the book of the law," especially the law commanding all worship to be concentrated at one chosen site (compare Deuteronomy 12), which we should understand to mean the Jerusalem temple.

The narrative pays a great deal of attention to the house of Omri and is especially critical of Ahab (1 Kgs 17:1—2 Kgs 10:31). Then Samaria, the capital of Israel, falls to the Assyrians (2 Kings 17). Judah lasted another century and a half after the fall of Israel. It was miraculously delivered from the Assyrian aggression (2 Kings 18–20), perhaps due to Hezekiah's faithfulness. Only Hezekiah and Josiah receive unconditional praise from the narrator for their uncompromising loyalty to God and for abolishing the "high places," that is, local shrines for the common people outside Jerusalem (2 Kgs 18:1-8; 22:1-2; 23:24-25). However, even Josiah's unprecedented obedience to the instructions in the "book of the law" is unable to prevent God's long-delayed judgment on Judah. Nebuchadnezzar conquers Jerusalem, destroys the temple, and takes many of its inhabitants to Babylon (2 Kgs 24:8—25:21). Second Kings ends with an intriguing note that Jehoiachin, the Davidic king who was taken captive to Babylon, is released from prison in Babylon (25:27-30).

The centralization of worship and sacrifice implemented by Hezekiah and Josiah was an attempt to shut down the worship at the "high places." This policy forced the people to come to the Jerusalem temple, the royal shrine of the house of David, for sacrifice and worship. That made the people's access to God more difficult and costly. There also were other popular religious practices in which the common people participated but which were deemed illegitimate by the official religion of the kingdom.

It would have been easy for the people of Israel to resign themselves to the fact that political powers greater than they, namely the Mesopotamian empires, controlled their history. However, the Deuteronomistic History (and all of the Historical Books) clearly show that the Israelites believed that their history, aspirations, and destiny were guided by their God. They wrote a history of their own, without appropriating the ideologies and assumptions of the empires. The Historical Books are a testimony to Israel's faith that they were the subjects of their own history and that their God was its divine agent.

Other Historical Books

The Christian Bible interrupts the Deuteronomistic History by inserting Ruth between Judges and 1 Samuel and adds 1 and 2 Chronicles, Ezra and Nehemiah (all of which come from the restored Judah of the fifth century BCE) and the book of Esther. The latter books are included in Jewish scripture among the *Kethuvim,* or writings (see the introductions to these books).

Ruth. This winsome story is not as forcefully didactic as the Deuteronomistic History, but delivers a message nonetheless. It moves from lack (famine and the deaths of husbands, which leave Naomi and Ruth vulnerable) to fulfillment (as the two women make a new home for themselves in Bethlehem). If, as many scholars hold, it was written in the period of return from exile (586-500 BCE), it may bear a more pointed message: that the concern expressed in Ezra and Nehemiah to separate Israelite men from foreign women (like the Moabite Ruth) is misguided. In Jewish scripture Ruth is one of the five *megilloth,* scrolls read on special occasions (the Song of Solomon, during Passover; Ruth, at Shavuot or the Feast of Weeks; Lamentations, on the Ninth of Av; Ecclesiastes, at Sukkoth; and Esther, at Purim). The Christian Bible places Ruth between Joshua and Judges because it narrates a time before the rise of the monarchy.

1 and 2 Chronicles. These books, written in the period of Judah's restoration, "chronicle" some of the same history narrated in the books of Samuel and Kings (and indeed refer to them), but from a distinct theological perspective (see the introductions to those books). Their name in the Greek Septuagint, *paraleipomena* (literally "things left out"), suggests they are "supplemental" to the Deuteronomistic History, but they convey a vision all their own.

Ezra and Nehemiah. These two books in the Christian Bible are a single book in the Hebrew Bible; they pick up the narrative where 2 Chronicles leaves off. Because they describe the organization of a people in a restored Judah gathered around the Torah—which had been given its final form in exile—historians find these books of inestimable value for the history of early Judaism.

Esther. Also one of the *megilloth,* Esther is read at Purim, the feast that celebrates the deliverance that the book narrates. As the introduction to that book suggests, Esther may be more valuable as an inspiring story of courage and resourcefulness on the part of faithful Jews in a foreign environment than as a historical account. Though the plot revolves around the working of retributive justice, the God of Israel is never named (a perceived lack that was made up by additions to the Greek version of Daniel, which stand in the Apocrypha: see the introduction there).

I can appreciate Israel's determination to write its own history, despite the fact that it was not one of the region's great powers. In many ways I am no different from others in the United States in having multiple identities, for everyone is a mixture of cultures and ethnicities. I am ethnically Korean, culturally American, and "racially" Asian. However, due to identity politics in the United States, some people are more likely to be considered "foreign" than others. As a member of a minority community whose history is relegated to the margin of the historical narrative of the United States, I believe it is important to understand a history of Asian Americans or other groups without always referencing the national history of the United States. Creating or adopting a history of a people independent of a national history is an important step for a minority community.

Joshua

The book of Joshua presents the fulfillment of the promise of land to the Israelites' ancestors. This fulfillment began with Moses leading the people from Egypt, through Sinai, to the verge of the Promised Land in the plains of Moab (Exodus–Deuteronomy). Joshua presents the movement of the Israelites from the plains of Moab into Canaan. Two major types of activities are reported in the book. The first half of the book (chs. 1–12) is concerned with the Israelites' dispossession of the Canaanites from the land. The second half (chs. 13–24) recounts the division of the land among the Israelites. Both the dispossession of the Canaanites and the settlement of the Israelites are presented as sanctioned, indeed as achieved, by Israel's God, YHWH.

The land-distribution narratives show how the land was divided among the Israelites according to YHWH's command. The focus of these narratives is on the people's internal unity. Despite tribal and geographical boundaries, Israel is united in the covenant with YHWH who had given them the land. However, this positive message is undermined significantly by the message of exclusivity in the first half of the book; God is portrayed as favoring one people, Israel, to the exclusion of all others. Chapters 1–12 are problematic because they are full of violence and destruction, which God sanctions. To me, an African person whose ancestors experienced dispossession and exploitation at the hands of Europeans invaders, these narratives (6:1—12:24) are very disturbing, as they seem to be a blueprint for the barbaric acts that were carried out much later in southern Africa. The disturbing nature of these narratives is compounded by the historical alliance between the European missionaries and plunderers who brought the Bible and its God to that region.

In these narratives the conquest of the land is presented in an epic style, focused on the capture of a few key cities and the practice of *herem*. The Hebrew word *herem* has connotations ranging from "thing devoted to YHWH," to "ban," to "utter destruction." In Joshua, *herem* entails the utter destruction of the enemy. Thus Israel's occupation of the land involved systematic pillaging and the killing of the current inhabitants. The practice of the ban is demonstrated in the first battle at Jericho (6:1-24). The Israelites are guaranteed victory before they even set foot in the city. All they have to do is follow YHWH's instructions. When Jericho falls, they proceed to apply the *herem* requirement: All breathing things, "men and women, young and old, oxen, sheep, and donkeys," are killed (6:16-21). Only one Jericho family is spared, the family of Rahab, the Canaanite prostitute who had assisted the foreign spies earlier and kept their secret. While humans and other living things are killed, silver, gold, and vessels of bronze and iron are considered holy, that is, taken and set apart for YHWH. The city is burned down, along with everything in it except for Rahab's family, the silver, gold, and bronze and iron vessels (6:24).

The seriousness of the *herem* ban is demonstrated by Israel's initial failure to defeat Ai because the Israelite Achan secretly saved some of the treasures at Jericho for himself (7:1-5). Only after Achan and his family are destroyed (7:18-26) does the second attack on Ai result in victory (8:1-29). Ironically, in this episode the *herem* law is relaxed a little to allow the Israelites to keep spoil and livestock as "booty"; however, all humans are killed. Except for Rahab's family, the escape of other indigenous peoples from utter destruction is viewed as against YHWH's will. The fate of the Gibeonites, who tricked the Israelites into making a covenant with them, is to be "hewers of wood and drawers of water for the congregation and for the altar of the LORD" (9:27). Future divine dispossession is promised for other lands still undefeated when Joshua distributes the land (13:1-7).

The portrayal of God's exclusive favor in these narratives is troubling and difficult to reconcile with other biblical portrayals of God. The divine sanction of the extermination and dispossession of the indigenous peoples of Canaan is disturbing. Material goods such as gold, silver, bronze, and iron are deemed more precious than human life. The picture of God as a partisan deity, favoring one nation at the expense of others, is also disturbing.

These accounts of the conquest and settlement by the Israelites were written during the exilic or early postexilic period with the purpose of forging an identity among those who longed to return to Judah. These accounts define those who legitimately deserve to be in the land of Canaan. They seek to inspire the returnees to fulfill what they believe was God's original purpose for them. The exclusive ideology of Joshua is dangerous because history shows that it can be put into practice. A belief in exclusive divine favor for one people can lead to genocide and extermination of other entire peoples.

— ***Dora R. Mbuwayesango***

1 After the death of Moses the servant of the
LORD, the LORD spoke to Joshua son of Nun,
Moses' assistant, saying, 2"My servant Moses is
dead. Now proceed to cross the Jordan, you and
all this people, into the land that I am giving to
them, to the Israelites. 3Every place that the sole
of your foot will tread upon I have given to you, as
I promised to Moses. 4From the wilderness and
the Lebanon as far as the great river, the river Euphrates, all the land of the Hittites, to the Great
Sea in the west shall be your territory. 5No one
shall be able to stand against you all the days of
your life. As I was with Moses, so I will be with
you; I will not fail you or forsake you. 6Be strong
and courageous; for you shall put this people in
possession of the land that I swore to their ancestors to give them. 7Only be strong and very courageous, being careful to act in accordance with
all the law that my servant Moses commanded
you; do not turn from it to the right hand or to
the left, so that you may be successful wherever
you go. 8This book of the law shall not depart out
of your mouth; you shall meditate on it day and
night, so that you may be careful to act in accordance with all that is written in it. For then you
shall make your way prosperous, and then you
shall be successful. 9I hereby command you: Be
strong and courageous; do not be frightened or
dismayed, for the LORD your God is with you
wherever you go."

10 Then Joshua commanded the officers of
the people, 11 "Pass through the camp, and command the people: 'Prepare your provisions; for in
three days you are to cross over the Jordan, to go
in to take possession of the land that the LORD
your God gives you to possess.'"

12 To the Reubenites, the Gadites, and the
half-tribe of Manasseh Joshua said, 13 "Remember the word that Moses the servant of the LORD
commanded you, saying, 'The LORD your God is
providing you a place of rest, and will give you
this land.' 14 Your wives, your little ones, and your
livestock shall remain in the land that Moses gave
you beyond the Jordan. But all the warriors among
you shall cross over armed before your kindred
and shall help them, 15 until the LORD gives rest
to your kindred as well as to you, and they too
take possession of the land that the LORD your
God is giving them. Then you shall return to your
own land and take possession of it, the land that
Moses the servant of the LORD gave you beyond
the Jordan to the east."

16 They answered Joshua: "All that you have
commanded us we will do, and wherever you
send us we will go. 17 Just as we obeyed Moses
in all things, so we will obey you. Only may the
LORD your God be with you, as he was with
Moses! 18 Whoever rebels against your orders
and disobeys your words, whatever you command, shall be put to death. Only be strong and
courageous."

2 Then Joshua son of Nun sent two men secretly from Shittim as spies, saying, "Go, view
the land, especially Jericho." So they went, and
entered the house of a prostitute whose name was
Rahab, and spent the night there. 2 The king of
Jericho was told, "Some Israelites have come here
tonight to search out the land." 3 Then the king of
Jericho sent orders to Rahab, "Bring out the men
who have come to you, who entered your house,
for they have come only to search out the whole
land." 4 But the woman took the two men and
hid them. Then she said, "True, the men came to
me, but I did not know where they came from.
5 And when it was time to close the gate at dark,
the men went out. Where the men went I do not
know. Pursue them quickly, for you can overtake
them." 6 She had, however, brought them up to
the roof and hidden them with the stalks of flax
that she had laid out on the roof. 7 So the men
pursued them on the way to the Jordan as far as
the fords. As soon as the pursuers had gone out,
the gate was shut.

8 Before they went to sleep, she came up to
them on the roof 9 and said to the men: "I know
that the LORD has given you the land, and that
dread of you has fallen on us, and that all the
inhabitants of the land melt in fear before you.
10 For we have heard how the LORD dried up the
water of the Red Sea[a] before you when you came
out of Egypt, and what you did to the two kings
of the Amorites that were beyond the Jordan, to
Sihon and Og, whom you utterly destroyed. 11 As
soon as we heard it, our hearts melted, and there
was no courage left in any of us because of you.
The LORD your God is indeed God in heaven
above and on earth below. 12 Now then, since I
have dealt kindly with you, swear to me by the
LORD that you in turn will deal kindly with my
family. Give me a sign of good faith 13 that you
will spare my father and mother, my brothers and
sisters, and all who belong to them, and deliver
our lives from death." 14 The men said to her, "Our

Joshua 2:1-21

While earlier feminist interpreters saw in Rahab a resourceful woman taking her future into her own hands, more recently women reading her story from postcolonial situations have insisted that we attend to more than Rahab's gender alone. She is a woman turned against her own people in a narrative dominated by the theme of righteous conquest, and of the impurity and unworthiness of the Canaanites. Is she a heroine? A sellout? A victim of colonization? If I join the text in applauding her initiative, have I assumed the perspective of the invader?

—NE

[a] Or *Sea of Reeds*

life for yours! If you do not tell this business of ours, then we will deal kindly and faithfully with you when the LORD gives us the land."

15 Then she let them down by a rope through the window, for her house was on the outer side of the city wall and she resided within the wall itself. 16 She said to them, "Go toward the hill country, so that the pursuers may not come upon you. Hide yourselves there three days, until the pursuers have returned; then afterward you may go your way." 17 The men said to her, "We will be released from this oath that you have made us swear to you 18 if we invade the land and you do not tie this crimson cord in the window through which you let us down, and you do not gather into your house your father and mother, your brothers, and all your family. 19 If any of you go out of the doors of your house into the street, they shall be responsible for their own death, and we shall be innocent; but if a hand is laid upon any who are with you in the house, we shall bear the responsibility for their death. 20 But if you tell this business of ours, then we shall be released from this oath that you made us swear to you." 21 She said, "According to your words, so be it." She sent them away and they departed. Then she tied the crimson cord in the window.

22 They departed and went into the hill country and stayed there three days, until the pursuers returned. The pursuers had searched all along the way and found nothing. 23 Then the two men came down again from the hill country. They crossed over, came to Joshua son of Nun, and told him all that had happened to them. 24 They said to Joshua, "Truly the LORD has given all the land into our hands; moreover all the inhabitants of the land melt in fear before us."

3 Early in the morning Joshua rose and set out from Shittim with all the Israelites, and they came to the Jordan. They camped there before crossing over. 2 At the end of three days the officers went through the camp 3 and commanded the people, "When you see the ark of the covenant of the LORD your God being carried by the levitical priests, then you shall set out from your place. Follow it, 4 so that you may know the way you should go, for you have not passed this way before. Yet there shall be a space between you and it, a distance of about two thousand cubits; do not come any nearer to it." 5 Then Joshua said to the people, "Sanctify yourselves; for tomorrow the LORD will do wonders among you." 6 To the priests Joshua said, "Take up the ark of the covenant, and pass on in front of the people." So they took up the ark of the covenant and went in front of the people.

7 The LORD said to Joshua, "This day I will begin to exalt you in the sight of all Israel, so that they may know that I will be with you as I was with Moses. 8 You are the one who shall command the priests who bear the ark of the covenant, 'When you come to the edge of the waters of the Jordan, you shall stand still in the Jordan.'" 9 Joshua then said to the Israelites, "Draw near and hear the words of the LORD your God." 10 Joshua said, "By this you shall know that among you is the living God who without fail will drive out from before you the Canaanites, Hittites, Hivites, Perizzites, Girgashites, Amorites, and Jebusites: 11 the ark of the covenant of the Lord of all the earth is going to pass before you into the Jordan. 12 So now select twelve men from the tribes of Israel, one from each tribe. 13 When the soles of the feet of the priests who bear the ark of the LORD, the Lord of all the earth, rest in the waters of the Jordan, the waters of the Jordan flowing from above shall be cut off; they shall stand in a single heap."

14 When the people set out from their tents to cross over the Jordan, the priests bearing the ark of the covenant were in front of the people. 15 Now the Jordan overflows all its banks throughout the time of harvest. So when those who bore the ark had come to the Jordan, and the feet of the priests bearing the ark were dipped in the edge of the water, 16 the waters flowing from above stood still, rising up in a single heap far off at Adam, the city that is beside Zarethan, while those flowing toward the sea of the Arabah, the Dead Sea,[a] were wholly cut off. Then the people crossed over opposite Jericho. 17 While all Israel were crossing

[a] Heb *Salt Sea*

over on dry ground, the priests who bore the ark
of the covenant of the LORD stood on dry ground
in the middle of the Jordan, until the entire nation finished crossing over the Jordan.

4 When the entire nation had finished crossing over the Jordan, the LORD said to Joshua:
2“Select twelve men from the people, one from
each tribe, 3and command them, ‘Take twelve
stones from here out of the middle of the Jordan,
from the place where the priests’ feet stood, carry
them over with you, and lay them down in the
place where you camp tonight.’ ” 4Then Joshua
summoned the twelve men from the Israelites,
whom he had appointed, one from each tribe.
5Joshua said to them, “Pass on before the ark of
the LORD your God into the middle of the Jordan,
and each of you take up a stone on his shoulder,
one for each of the tribes of the Israelites, 6so that
this may be a sign among you. When your children ask in time to come, ‘What do those stones
mean to you?’ 7then you shall tell them that the
waters of the Jordan were cut off in front of the
ark of the covenant of the LORD. When it crossed
over the Jordan, the waters of the Jordan were cut
off. So these stones shall be to the Israelites a memorial forever.”

8 The Israelites did as Joshua commanded.
They took up twelve stones out of the middle of
the Jordan, according to the number of the tribes
of the Israelites, as the LORD told Joshua, carried
them over with them to the place where they
camped, and laid them down there. 9(Joshua set
up twelve stones in the middle of the Jordan, in
the place where the feet of the priests bearing the
ark of the covenant had stood; and they are there
to this day.)

10 The priests who bore the ark remained
standing in the middle of the Jordan, until everything was finished that the LORD commanded
Joshua to tell the people, according to all that Moses had commanded Joshua. The people crossed
over in haste. 11As soon as all the people had finished crossing over, the ark of the LORD, and the
priests, crossed over in front of the people. 12The
Reubenites, the Gadites, and the half-tribe of Manasseh crossed over armed before the Israelites,
as Moses had ordered them. 13About forty thousand armed for war crossed over before the LORD
to the plains of Jericho for battle.

14 On that day the LORD exalted Joshua in
the sight of all Israel; and they stood in awe of
him, as they had stood in awe of Moses, all the
days of his life.

15 The LORD said to Joshua, 16“Command
the priests who bear the ark of the covenant,[a] to
come up out of the Jordan.” 17Joshua therefore
commanded the priests, “Come up out of the Jordan.” 18When the priests bearing the ark of the
covenant of the LORD came up from the middle
of the Jordan, and the soles of the priests’ feet
touched dry ground, the waters of the Jordan returned to their place and overflowed all its banks,
as before.

19 The people came up out of the Jordan on
the tenth day of the first month, and they camped
in Gilgal on the east border of Jericho. 20Those
twelve stones, which they had taken out of the
Jordan, Joshua set up in Gilgal, 21saying to the
Israelites, “When your children ask their parents
in time to come, ‘What do these stones mean?’
22then you shall let your children know, ‘Israel
crossed over the Jordan here on dry ground.’
23For the LORD your God dried up the waters of
the Jordan for you until you crossed over, as the
LORD your God did to the Red Sea,[b] which he
dried up for us until we crossed over, 24so that all
the peoples of the earth may know that the hand
of the LORD is mighty, and so that you may fear
the LORD your God forever.”

5 When all the kings of the Amorites beyond
the Jordan to the west, and all the kings of the
Canaanites by the sea, heard that the LORD had
dried up the waters of the Jordan for the Israelites
until they had crossed over, their hearts melted,
and there was no longer any spirit in them, because of the Israelites.

2 At that time the LORD said to Joshua, “Make
flint knives and circumcise the Israelites a second
time.” 3So Joshua made flint knives, and circumcised the Israelites at Gibeath-haaraloth.[c] 4This is

[a] Or *treaty*, or *testimony*; Heb *eduth*

[b] Or *Sea of Reeds*

[a] That is *the Hill of the Foreskins*

the reason why Joshua circumcised them: all the
males of the people who came out of Egypt, all
the warriors, had died during the journey through
the wilderness after they had come out of Egypt.
[5]Although all the people who came out had been
circumcised, yet all the people born on the journey through the wilderness after they had come
out of Egypt had not been circumcised. [6]For the
Israelites traveled forty years in the wilderness,
until all the nation, the warriors who came out of
Egypt, perished, not having listened to the voice
of the LORD. To them the LORD swore that he
would not let them see the land that he had sworn
to their ancestors to give us, a land flowing with
milk and honey. [7]So it was their children, whom
he raised up in their place, that Joshua circumcised; for they were uncircumcised, because they
had not been circumcised on the way.

8 When the circumcising of all the nation
was done, they remained in their places in the
camp until they were healed. [9]The LORD said to
Joshua, "Today I have rolled away from you the
disgrace of Egypt." And so that place is called Gilgal[a] to this day.

10 While the Israelites were camped in Gilgal they kept the passover in the evening on the
fourteenth day of the month in the plains of Jericho. [11]On the day after the passover, on that very
day, they ate the produce of the land, unleavened
cakes and parched grain. [12]The manna ceased on
the day they ate the produce of the land, and the
Israelites no longer had manna; they ate the crops
of the land of Canaan that year.

13 Once when Joshua was by Jericho, he
looked up and saw a man standing before him
with a drawn sword in his hand. Joshua went to
him and said to him, "Are you one of us, or one of
our adversaries?" [14]He replied, "Neither; but as
commander of the army of the LORD I have now
come." And Joshua fell on his face to the earth
and worshiped, and he said to him, "What do you
command your servant, my lord?" [15]The commander of the army of the LORD said to Joshua,
"Remove the sandals from your feet, for the place
where you stand is holy." And Joshua did so.

[a] Related to Heb *galal* to roll

6 Now Jericho was shut up inside and out because of the Israelites; no one came out and
no one went in. [2]The LORD said to Joshua, "See,
I have handed Jericho over to you, along with its
king and soldiers. [3]You shall march around the
city, all the warriors circling the city once. Thus
you shall do for six days, [4]with seven priests bearing seven trumpets of rams' horns before the ark.
On the seventh day you shall march around the
city seven times, the priests blowing the trumpets. [5]When they make a long blast with the ram's
horn, as soon as you hear the sound of the trumpet, then all the people shall shout with a great
shout; and the wall of the city will fall down flat,
and all the people shall charge straight ahead."
[6]So Joshua son of Nun summoned the priests
and said to them, "Take up the ark of the covenant, and have seven priests carry seven trumpets
of rams' horns in front of the ark of the LORD."
[7]To the people he said, "Go forward and march
around the city; have the armed men pass on before the ark of the LORD."

8 As Joshua had commanded the people, the
seven priests carrying the seven trumpets of rams'
horns before the LORD went forward, blowing
the trumpets, with the ark of the covenant of the
LORD following them. [9]And the armed men went
before the priests who blew the trumpets; the
rear guard came after the ark, while the trumpets
blew continually. [10]To the people Joshua gave
this command: "You shall not shout or let your

Joshua 6:1-27

Though the siege and destruction of Jericho is one of the most memorable scenes in the Bible, archaeological excavations to date indicate that at the time Israel is represented as entering Canaan, the site of Jericho had been long abandoned; the absence of any fortifications (the "walls of Jericho") is difficult to reconcile with the biblical account.

— *NE*

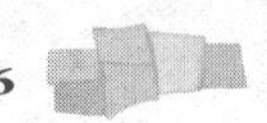

voice be heard, nor shall you utter a word, until the day I tell you to shout. Then you shall shout." 11So the ark of the LORD went around the city, circling it once; and they came into the camp, and spent the night in the camp.

12 Then Joshua rose early in the morning, and the priests took up the ark of the LORD. 13The seven priests carrying the seven trumpets of rams' horns before the ark of the LORD passed on, blowing the trumpets continually. The armed men went before them, and the rear guard came after the ark of the LORD, while the trumpets blew continually. 14On the second day they marched around the city once and then returned to the camp. They did this for six days.

15 On the seventh day they rose early, at dawn, and marched around the city in the same manner seven times. It was only on that day that they marched around the city seven times. 16And at the seventh time, when the priests had blown the trumpets, Joshua said to the people, "Shout! For the LORD has given you the city. 17The city and all that is in it shall be devoted to the LORD for destruction. Only Rahab the prostitute and all who are with her in her house shall live because she hid the messengers we sent. 18As for you, keep away from the things devoted to destruction, so as not to covet[a] and take any of the devoted things and make the camp of Israel an object for destruction, bringing trouble upon it. 19But all silver and gold, and vessels of bronze and iron, are sacred to the LORD; they shall go into the treasury of the LORD." 20So the people shouted, and the trumpets were blown. As soon as the people heard the sound of the trumpets, they raised a great shout, and the wall fell down flat; so the people charged straight ahead into the city and captured it. 21Then they devoted to destruction by the edge of the sword all in the city, both men and women, young and old, oxen, sheep, and donkeys.

22 Joshua said to the two men who had spied out the land, "Go into the prostitute's house, and bring the woman out of it and all who belong to her, as you swore to her." 23So the young men who had been spies went in and brought Rahab out, along with her father, her mother, her brothers, and all who belonged to her—they brought all her kindred out—and set them outside the camp of Israel. 24They burned down the city, and everything in it; only the silver and gold, and the vessels of bronze and iron, they put into the treasury of the house of the LORD. 25But Rahab the prostitute, with her family and all who belonged to her, Joshua spared. Her family[b] has lived in Israel ever since. For she hid the messengers whom Joshua sent to spy out Jericho.

26 Joshua then pronounced this oath, saying,

"Cursed before the LORD be anyone who tries
to build this city—this Jericho!
At the cost of his firstborn he shall lay its foundation,
and at the cost of his youngest he shall set up its gates!"

27 So the LORD was with Joshua; and his fame was in all the land.

7 But the Israelites broke faith in regard to the devoted things: Achan son of Carmi son of Zabdi son of Zerah, of the tribe of Judah, took some of the devoted things; and the anger of the LORD burned against the Israelites.

2 Joshua sent men from Jericho to Ai, which is near Beth-aven, east of Bethel, and said to them, "Go up and spy out the land." And the men went up and spied out Ai. 3Then they returned to Joshua and said to him, "Not all the people need go up; about two or three thousand men should go up and attack Ai. Since they are so few, do not make the whole people toil up there." 4So about three thousand of the people went up there; and they fled before the men of Ai. 5The men of Ai killed about thirty-six of them, chasing them from outside the gate as far as Shebarim and killing them on the slope. The hearts of the people melted and turned to water.

6 Then Joshua tore his clothes, and fell to the ground on his face before the ark of the LORD until the evening, he and the elders of Israel; and they

[a] Gk: Heb *devote to destruction* Compare 7.21 [b] Heb *She*

put dust on their heads. 7Joshua said, "Ah, Lord GOD! Why have you brought this people across the Jordan at all, to hand us over to the Amorites so as to destroy us? Would that we had been content to settle beyond the Jordan! 8O Lord, what can I say, now that Israel has turned their backs to their enemies! 9The Canaanites and all the inhabitants of the land will hear of it, and surround us, and cut off our name from the earth. Then what will you do for your great name?"

10 The LORD said to Joshua, "Stand up! Why have you fallen upon your face? 11Israel has sinned; they have transgressed my covenant that I imposed on them. They have taken some of the devoted things; they have stolen, they have acted deceitfully, and they have put them among their own belongings. 12Therefore the Israelites are unable to stand before their enemies; they turn their backs to their enemies, because they have become a thing devoted for destruction themselves. I will be with you no more, unless you destroy the devoted things from among you. 13Proceed to sanctify the people, and say, "Sanctify yourselves for tomorrow; for thus says the LORD, the God of Israel, "There are devoted things among you, O Israel; you will be unable to stand before your enemies until you take away the devoted things from among you." 14In the morning therefore you shall come forward tribe by tribe. The tribe that the LORD takes shall come near by clans, the clan that the LORD takes shall come near by households, and the household that the LORD takes shall come near one by one. 15And the one who is taken as having the devoted things shall be burned with fire, together with all that he has, for having transgressed the covenant of the LORD, and for having done an outrageous thing in Israel.'"

16 So Joshua rose early in the morning, and brought Israel near tribe by tribe, and the tribe of Judah was taken. 17He brought near the clans of Judah, and the clan of the Zerahites was taken; and he brought near the clan of the Zerahites, family by family,[a] and Zabdi was taken. 18And he brought near his household one by one, and Achan son of Carmi son of Zabdi son of Zerah, of the tribe of Judah, was taken. 19Then Joshua said to Achan, "My son, give glory to the LORD God of Israel and make confession to him. Tell me now what you have done; do not hide it from me." 20And Achan answered Joshua, "It is true; I am the one who sinned against the LORD God of Israel. This is what I did: 21when I saw among the spoil a beautiful mantle from Shinar, and two hundred shekels of silver, and a bar of gold weighing fifty shekels, then I coveted them and took them. They now lie hidden in the ground inside my tent, with the silver underneath."

22 So Joshua sent messengers, and they ran to the tent; and there it was, hidden in his tent with the silver underneath. 23They took them out of the tent and brought them to Joshua and all the Israelites; and they spread them out before the LORD. 24Then Joshua and all Israel with him took Achan son of Zerah, with the silver, the mantle, and the bar of gold, with his sons and daughters, with his oxen, donkeys, and sheep, and his tent and all that he had; and they brought them up to the Valley of Achor. 25Joshua said, "Why did you bring trouble on us? The LORD is bringing trouble on you today." And all Israel stoned him to death; they burned them with fire, cast stones on them, 26and raised over him a great heap of stones that remains to this day. Then the LORD turned from his burning anger. Therefore that place to this day is called the Valley of Achor.[b]

8 Then the LORD said to Joshua, "Do not fear or be dismayed; take all the fighting men with you, and go up now to Ai. See, I have handed over to you the king of Ai with his people, his city, and his land. 2You shall do to Ai and its king as you did to Jericho and its king; only its spoil and its livestock you may take as booty for yourselves. Set an ambush against the city, behind it."

3 So Joshua and all the fighting men set out to go up against Ai. Joshua chose thirty thousand warriors and sent them out by night 4with the command, "You shall lie in ambush against the city, behind it; do not go very far from the city, but all of you stay alert. 5I and all the people who are with me will approach the city. When they

[a] Mss Syr: MT *man by man* [b] That is *Trouble*

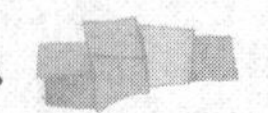

come out against us, as before, we shall flee from
them. 6They will come out after us until we have
drawn them away from the city; for they will say,
"They are fleeing from us, as before.' While we
flee from them, 7you shall rise up from the ambush and seize the city; for the LORD your God
will give it into your hand. 8And when you have
taken the city, you shall set the city on fire, doing
as the LORD has ordered; see, I have commanded
you." 9So Joshua sent them out; and they went to
the place of ambush, and lay between Bethel and
Ai, to the west of Ai; but Joshua spent that night
in the camp.[a]

10 In the morning Joshua rose early and mustered the people, and went up, with the elders of
Israel, before the people to Ai. 11All the fighting
men who were with him went up, and drew near
before the city, and camped on the north side of
Ai, with a ravine between them and Ai. 12Taking
about five thousand men, he set them in ambush
between Bethel and Ai, to the west of the city.
13So they stationed the forces, the main encampment that was north of the city and its rear guard
west of the city. But Joshua spent that night in the
valley. 14When the king of Ai saw this, he and all
his people, the inhabitants of the city, hurried out
early in the morning to the meeting place facing
the Arabah to meet Israel in battle; but he did
not know that there was an ambush against him
behind the city. 15And Joshua and all Israel made
a pretense of being beaten before them, and fled
in the direction of the wilderness. 16So all the
people who were in the city were called together
to pursue them, and as they pursued Joshua they
were drawn away from the city. 17There was not a
man left in Ai or Bethel who did not go out after
Israel; they left the city open, and pursued Israel.

18 Then the LORD said to Joshua, "Stretch
out the sword that is in your hand toward Ai; for I
will give it into your hand." And Joshua stretched
out the sword that was in his hand toward the
city. 19As soon as he stretched out his hand, the
troops in ambush rose quickly out of their place
and rushed forward. They entered the city, took
it, and at once set the city on fire. 20So when the
men of Ai looked back, the smoke of the city was
rising to the sky. They had no power to flee this
way or that, for the people who fled to the wilderness turned back against the pursuers. 21When
Joshua and all Israel saw that the ambush had
taken the city and that the smoke of the city was
rising, then they turned back and struck down
the men of Ai. 22And the others came out from
the city against them; so they were surrounded
by Israelites, some on one side, and some on the
other; and Israel struck them down until no one
was left who survived or escaped. 23But the king
of Ai was taken alive and brought to Joshua.

24 When Israel had finished slaughtering
all the inhabitants of Ai in the open wilderness
where they pursued them, and when all of them
to the very last had fallen by the edge of the
sword, all Israel returned to Ai, and attacked it
with the edge of the sword. 25The total of those
who fell that day, both men and women, was
twelve thousand—all the people of Ai. 26For
Joshua did not draw back his hand, with which
he stretched out the sword, until he had utterly
destroyed all the inhabitants of Ai. 27Only the
livestock and the spoil of that city Israel took as
their booty, according to the word of the LORD
that he had issued to Joshua. 28So Joshua burned
Ai, and made it forever a heap of ruins, as it is to
this day. 29And he hanged the king of Ai on a tree
until evening; and at sunset Joshua commanded,
and they took his body down from the tree, threw
it down at the entrance of the gate of the city, and
raised over it a great heap of stones, which stands
there to this day.

30 Then Joshua built on Mount Ebal an altar
to the LORD, the God of Israel, 31just as Moses
the servant of the LORD had commanded the Israelites, as it is written in the book of the law of
Moses, "an altar of unhewn[b] stones, on which no
iron tool has been used"; and they offered on it
burnt offerings to the LORD, and sacrificed offerings of well-being. 32And there, in the presence of
the Israelites, Joshua[c] wrote on the stones a copy
of the law of Moses, which he had written. 33All
Israel, alien as well as citizen, with their elders

[a] Heb *among the people* [b] Heb *whole* [c] Heb *he*

and officers and their judges, stood on opposite sides of the ark in front of the levitical priests who carried the ark of the covenant of the LORD, half of them in front of Mount Gerizim and half of them in front of Mount Ebal, as Moses the servant of the LORD had commanded at the first, that they should bless the people of Israel. 34 And afterward he read all the words of the law, blessings and curses, according to all that is written in the book of the law. 35 There was not a word of all that Moses commanded that Joshua did not read before all the assembly of Israel, and the women, and the little ones, and the aliens who resided among them.

9 Now when all the kings who were beyond the Jordan in the hill country and in the lowland all along the coast of the Great Sea toward Lebanon—the Hittites, the Amorites, the Canaanites, the Perizzites, the Hivites, and the Jebusites—heard of this, 2 they gathered together with one accord to fight Joshua and Israel.

3 But when the inhabitants of Gibeon heard what Joshua had done to Jericho and to Ai, 4 they on their part acted with cunning: they went and prepared provisions,[a] and took worn-out sacks for their donkeys, and wineskins, worn-out and torn and mended, 5 with worn-out, patched sandals on their feet, and worn-out clothes; and all their provisions were dry and moldy. 6 They went to Joshua in the camp at Gilgal, and said to him and to the Israelites, "We have come from a far country; so now make a treaty with us." 7 But the Israelites said to the Hivites, "Perhaps you live among us; then how can we make a treaty with you?" 8 They said to Joshua, "We are your servants." And Joshua said to them, "Who are you? And where do you come from?" 9 They said to him, "Your servants have come from a very far country, because of the name of the LORD your God; for we have heard a report of him, of all that he did in Egypt, 10 and of all that he did to the two kings of the Amorites who were beyond the Jordan, King Sihon of Heshbon, and King Og of Bashan who lived in Ashtaroth. 11 So our elders and all the inhabitants of our country said to us, 'Take provisions in your hand for the journey; go to meet them, and say to them, "We are your servants; come now, make a treaty with us." ' 12 Here is our bread; it was still warm when we took it from our houses as our food for the journey, on the day we set out to come to you, but now, see, it is dry and moldy; 13 these wineskins were new when we filled them, and see, they are burst; and these garments and sandals of ours are worn out from the very long journey." 14 So the leaders[b] partook of their provisions, and did not ask direction from the LORD. 15 And Joshua made peace with them, guaranteeing their lives by a treaty; and the leaders of the congregation swore an oath to them.

16 But when three days had passed after they had made a treaty with them, they heard that they were their neighbors and were living among them. 17 So the Israelites set out and reached their cities on the third day. Now their cities were Gibeon, Chephirah, Beeroth, and Kiriath-jearim. 18 But the Israelites did not attack them, because the leaders of the congregation had sworn to them by the LORD, the God of Israel. Then all the congregation murmured against the leaders. 19 But all the leaders said to all the congregation, "We have sworn to them by the LORD, the God of Israel, and now we must not touch them. 20 This is what we will do to them: We will let them live, so that wrath may not come upon us, because of the oath that we swore to them." 21 The leaders said to them, "Let them live." So they became hewers of wood and drawers of water for all the congregation, as the leaders had decided concerning them.

22 Joshua summoned them, and said to them, "Why did you deceive us, saying, 'We are very far from you,' while in fact you are living among us? 23 Now therefore you are cursed, and some of you shall always be slaves, hewers of wood and drawers of water for the house of my God." 24 They answered Joshua, "Because it was told to your servants for a certainty that the LORD your God had commanded his servant Moses to give you all the land, and to destroy all the inhabitants

[a] Cn: Meaning of Heb uncertain [b] Gk: Heb *men*

of the land before you; so we were in great fear
for our lives because of you, and did this thing.
25And now we are in your hand: do as it seems
good and right in your sight to do to us." 26This is
what he did for them: he saved them from the Israelites; and they did not kill them. 27But on that
day Joshua made them hewers of wood and drawers of water for the congregation and for the altar
of the LORD, to continue to this day, in the place
that he should choose.

10 When King Adoni-zedek of Jerusalem
heard how Joshua had taken Ai, and had
utterly destroyed it, doing to Ai and its king as
he had done to Jericho and its king, and how the
inhabitants of Gibeon had made peace with Israel and were among them, 2he[a] became greatly
frightened, because Gibeon was a large city, like
one of the royal cities, and was larger than Ai, and
all its men were warriors. 3So King Adoni-zedek
of Jerusalem sent a message to King Hoham
of Hebron, to King Piram of Jarmuth, to King
Japhia of Lachish, and to King Debir of Eglon,
saying, 4"Come up and help me, and let us attack Gibeon; for it has made peace with Joshua
and with the Israelites." 5Then the five kings of
the Amorites—the king of Jerusalem, the king of
Hebron, the king of Jarmuth, the king of Lachish,
and the king of Eglon—gathered their forces, and
went up with all their armies and camped against
Gibeon, and made war against it.

6 And the Gibeonites sent to Joshua at the
camp in Gilgal, saying, "Do not abandon your
servants; come up to us quickly, and save us, and
help us; for all the kings of the Amorites who live
in the hill country are gathered against us." 7So
Joshua went up from Gilgal, he and all the fighting force with him, all the mighty warriors. 8The
LORD said to Joshua, "Do not fear them, for I
have handed them over to you; not one of them
shall stand before you." 9So Joshua came upon
them suddenly, having marched up all night from
Gilgal. 10And the LORD threw them into a panic
before Israel, who inflicted a great slaughter on
them at Gibeon, chased them by the way of the
ascent of Beth-horon, and struck them down
as far as Azekah and Makkedah. 11As they fled
before Israel, while they were going down the
slope of Beth-horon, the LORD threw down huge
stones from heaven on them as far as Azekah, and
they died; there were more who died because of
the hailstones than the Israelites killed with the
sword.

12 On the day when the LORD gave the
Amorites over to the Israelites, Joshua spoke to
the LORD; and he said in the sight of Israel,

"Sun, stand still at Gibeon,
and Moon, in the valley of Aijalon."
13 And the sun stood still, and the moon
stopped,
until the nation took vengeance on their
enemies.

Is this not written in the Book of Jashar? The sun
stopped in midheaven, and did not hurry to set
for about a whole day. 14There has been no day
like it before or since, when the LORD heeded a
human voice; for the LORD fought for Israel.

15 Then Joshua returned, and all Israel with
him, to the camp at Gilgal.

16 Meanwhile, these five kings fled and hid
themselves in the cave at Makkedah. 17And it was
told Joshua, "The five kings have been found, hidden in the cave at Makkedah." 18Joshua said, "Roll
large stones against the mouth of the cave, and set
men by it to guard them; 19but do not stay there
yourselves; pursue your enemies, and attack them
from the rear. Do not let them enter their towns,
for the LORD your God has given them into your
hand." 20When Joshua and the Israelites had finished inflicting a very great slaughter on them,
until they were wiped out, and when the survivors had entered into the fortified towns, 21all
the people returned safe to Joshua in the camp at
Makkedah; no one dared to speak[b] against any of
the Israelites.

22 Then Joshua said, "Open the mouth of the
cave, and bring those five kings out to me from
the cave." 23They did so, and brought the five
kings out to him from the cave, the king of Jerusalem, the king of Hebron, the king of Jarmuth, the
king of Lachish, and the king of Eglon. 24When

[a] Heb *they* [b] Heb *moved his tongue*

they brought the kings out to Joshua, Joshua
summoned all the Israelites, and said to the chiefs
of the warriors who had gone with him, "Come
near, put your feet on the necks of these kings."
Then they came near and put their feet on their
necks. 25 And Joshua said to them, "Do not be
afraid or dismayed; be strong and courageous; for
thus the LORD will do to all the enemies against
whom you fight." 26 Afterward Joshua struck them
down and put them to death, and he hung them
on five trees. And they hung on the trees until
evening. 27 At sunset Joshua commanded, and
they took them down from the trees and threw
them into the cave where they had hidden themselves; they set large stones against the mouth of
the cave, which remain to this very day.

28 Joshua took Makkedah on that day, and
struck it and its king with the edge of the sword;
he utterly destroyed every person in it; he left no
one remaining. And he did to the king of Makkedah as he had done to the king of Jericho.

29 Then Joshua passed on from Makkedah,
and all Israel with him, to Libnah, and fought
against Libnah. 30 The LORD gave it also and its
king into the hand of Israel; and he struck it with
the edge of the sword, and every person in it; he
left no one remaining in it; and he did to its king
as he had done to the king of Jericho.

31 Next Joshua passed on from Libnah, and
all Israel with him, to Lachish, and laid siege to
it, and assaulted it. 32 The LORD gave Lachish into
the hand of Israel, and he took it on the second
day, and struck it with the edge of the sword, and
every person in it, as he had done to Libnah.

33 Then King Horam of Gezer came up to
help Lachish; and Joshua struck him and his people, leaving him no survivors.

34 From Lachish Joshua passed on with all
Israel to Eglon; and they laid siege to it, and assaulted it; 35 and they took it that day, and struck
it with the edge of the sword; and every person
in it he utterly destroyed that day, as he had done
to Lachish.

36 Then Joshua went up with all Israel from
Eglon to Hebron; they assaulted it, 37 and took it,
and struck it with the edge of the sword, and its
king and its towns, and every person in it; he left
no one remaining, just as he had done to Eglon,
and utterly destroyed it with every person in it.

38 Then Joshua, with all Israel, turned back
to Debir and assaulted it, 39 and he took it with its
king and all its towns; they struck them with the
edge of the sword, and utterly destroyed every
person in it; he left no one remaining; just as he
had done to Hebron, and, as he had done to Libnah and its king, so he did to Debir and its king.

40 So Joshua defeated the whole land, the hill
country and the Negeb and the lowland and the
slopes, and all their kings; he left no one remaining, but utterly destroyed all that breathed, as the
LORD God of Israel commanded. 41 And Joshua
defeated them from Kadesh-barnea to Gaza,
and all the country of Goshen, as far as Gibeon.
42 Joshua took all these kings and their land at one
time, because the LORD God of Israel fought for
Israel. 43 Then Joshua returned, and all Israel with
him, to the camp at Gilgal.

11 When King Jabin of Hazor heard of this,
he sent to King Jobab of Madon, to the
king of Shimron, to the king of Achshaph, 2 and
to the kings who were in the northern hill country, and in the Arabah south of Chinneroth, and
in the lowland, and in Naphoth-dor on the west,
3 to the Canaanites in the east and the west, the
Amorites, the Hittites, the Perizzites, and the Jebusites in the hill country, and the Hivites under
Hermon in the land of Mizpah. 4 They came out,
with all their troops, a great army, in number like
the sand on the seashore, with very many horses
and chariots. 5 All these kings joined their forces,
and came and camped together at the waters of
Merom, to fight with Israel.

6 And the LORD said to Joshua, "Do not be
afraid of them, for tomorrow at this time I will
hand over all of them, slain, to Israel; you shall
hamstring their horses, and burn their chariots
with fire." 7 So Joshua came suddenly upon them
with all his fighting force, by the waters of Merom,
and fell upon them. 8 And the LORD handed them
over to Israel, who attacked them and chased
them as far as Great Sidon and Misrephoth-maim,
and eastward as far as the valley of Mizpeh. They
struck them down, until they had left no one remaining. 9 And Joshua did to them as the LORD

commanded him; he hamstrung their horses, and burned their chariots with fire.

10 Joshua turned back at that time, and took Hazor, and struck its king down with the sword. Before that time Hazor was the head of all those kingdoms. 11 And they put to the sword all who were in it, utterly destroying them; there was no one left who breathed, and he burned Hazor with fire. 12 And all the towns of those kings, and all their kings, Joshua took, and struck them with the edge of the sword, utterly destroying them, as Moses the servant of the LORD had commanded. 13 But Israel burned none of the towns that stood on mounds except Hazor, which Joshua did burn. 14 All the spoil of these towns, and the livestock, the Israelites took for their booty; but all the people they struck down with the edge of the sword, until they had destroyed them, and they did not leave any who breathed. 15 As the LORD had commanded his servant Moses, so Moses commanded Joshua, and so Joshua did; he left nothing undone of all that the LORD had commanded Moses.

16 So Joshua took all that land: the hill country and all the Negeb and all the land of Goshen and the lowland and the Arabah and the hill country of Israel and its lowland, 17 from Mount Halak, which rises toward Seir, as far as Baal-gad in the valley of Lebanon below Mount Hermon. He took all their kings, struck them down, and put them to death. 18 Joshua made war a long time with all those kings. 19 There was not a town that made peace with the Israelites, except the Hivites, the inhabitants of Gibeon; all were taken in battle. 20 For it was the LORD's doing to harden their hearts so that they would come against Israel in battle, in order that they might be utterly destroyed, and might receive no mercy, but be exterminated, just as the LORD had commanded Moses.

21 At that time Joshua came and wiped out the Anakim from the hill country, from Hebron, from Debir, from Anab, and from all the hill country of Judah, and from all the hill country of Israel; Joshua utterly destroyed them with their towns. 22 None of the Anakim was left in the land of the Israelites; some remained only in Gaza, in Gath, and in Ashdod. 23 So Joshua took the whole land, according to all that the LORD had spoken to Moses; and Joshua gave it for an inheritance to Israel according to their tribal allotments. And the land had rest from war.

12 Now these are the kings of the land, whom the Israelites defeated, whose land they occupied beyond the Jordan toward the east, from the Wadi Arnon to Mount Hermon, with all the Arabah eastward: 2 King Sihon of the Amorites who lived at Heshbon, and ruled from Aroer, which is on the edge of the Wadi Arnon, and from the middle of the valley as far as the river Jabbok, the boundary of the Ammonites, that is, half of Gilead, 3 and the Arabah to the Sea of Chinneroth eastward, and in the direction of Beth-jeshimoth, to the sea of the Arabah, the Dead Sea,[a] southward to the foot of the slopes of Pisgah; 4 and King Og[b] of Bashan, one of the last of the Rephaim, who lived at Ashtaroth and at Edrei 5 and ruled over Mount Hermon and Salecah and all Bashan to the boundary of the Geshurites and the

[a] Heb *Salt Sea* [b] Gk: Heb *the boundary of King Og*

Joshua 11:23

The statement that "Joshua took the whole land" (11:23) is difficult to reconcile with the indications in the later book of Judges that Israel continued to live side-by-side with Canaanites, and at times to struggle against them, for generations to come (see Judg 1:1, 2:3, 3:5). Some scholars regard this statement as an attempt to give Joshua primary credit for the "conquest"; others wonder whether the term *conquest* is the best way to describe the emergence of Israel in Canaan.

—*NE*

Maacathites, and over half of Gilead to the
boundary of King Sihon of Heshbon. 6 Moses, the
servant of the LORD, and the Israelites defeated
them; and Moses the servant of the LORD gave
their land for a possession to the Reubenites and
the Gadites and the half-tribe of Manasseh.

7 The following are the kings of the land
whom Joshua and the Israelites defeated on the
west side of the Jordan, from Baal-gad in the valley of Lebanon to Mount Halak, that rises toward
Seir (and Joshua gave their land to the tribes of
Israel as a possession according to their allotments, 8 in the hill country, in the lowland, in the
Arabah, in the slopes, in the wilderness, and in
the Negeb, the land of the Hittites, Amorites, Canaanites, Perizzites, Hivites, and Jebusites):

9 the king of Jericho one
the king of Ai, which is next to Bethel one
10 the king of Jerusalem one
the king of Hebron one
11 the king of Jarmuth one
the king of Lachish one
12 the king of Eglon one
the king of Gezer one
13 the king of Debir one
the king of Geder one
14 the king of Hormah one
the king of Arad one
15 the king of Libnah one
the king of Adullam one
16 the king of Makkedah one
the king of Bethel one
17 the king of Tappuah one
the king of Hepher one
18 the king of Aphek one
the king of Lasharon one
19 the king of Madon one
the king of Hazor one
20 the king of Shimron-meron one
the king of Achshaph one
21 the king of Taanach one
the king of Megiddo one
22 the king of Kedesh one
the king of Jokneam in Carmel one
23 the king of Dor in Naphath-dor one
the king of Goiim in Galilee,[a] one
24 the king of Tirzah one
thirty-one kings in all.

13 Now Joshua was old and advanced in
years; and the LORD said to him, "You
are old and advanced in years, and very much
of the land still remains to be possessed. 2 This is
the land that still remains: all the regions of the
Philistines, and all those of the Geshurites 3 (from
the Shihor, which is east of Egypt, northward to
the boundary of Ekron, it is reckoned as Canaanite; there are five rulers of the Philistines, those
of Gaza, Ashdod, Ashkelon, Gath, and Ekron),
and those of the Avvim 4 in the south; all the
land of the Canaanites, and Mearah that belongs
to the Sidonians, to Aphek, to the boundary of
the Amorites, 5 and the land of the Gebalites,
and all Lebanon, toward the east, from Baal-gad
below Mount Hermon to Lebo-hamath, 6 all the
inhabitants of the hill country from Lebanon to
Misrephoth-maim, even all the Sidonians. I will
myself drive them out from before the Israelites;
only allot the land to Israel for an inheritance, as
I have commanded you. 7 Now therefore divide
this land for an inheritance to the nine tribes and
the half-tribe of Manasseh."

8 With the other half-tribe of Manasseh[b] the
Reubenites and the Gadites received their inheritance, which Moses gave them, beyond the Jordan
eastward, as Moses the servant of the LORD gave
them: 9 from Aroer, which is on the edge of the
Wadi Arnon, and the town that is in the middle
of the valley, and all the tableland from[c] Medeba
as far as Dibon; 10 and all the cities of King Sihon
of the Amorites, who reigned in Heshbon, as far
as the boundary of the Ammonites; 11 and Gilead,
and the region of the Geshurites and Maacathites,
and all Mount Hermon, and all Bashan to Salecah;
12 all the kingdom of Og in Bashan, who reigned
in Ashtaroth and in Edrei (he alone was left of
the survivors of the Rephaim); these Moses had
defeated and driven out. 13 Yet the Israelites did
not drive out the Geshurites or the Maacathites;
but Geshur and Maacath live within Israel to
this day.

[a] Gk: Heb *Gilgal* [b] Cn: Heb *With it* [c] Compare Gk: Heb lacks *from*

14 To the tribe of Levi alone Moses gave no
inheritance; the offerings by fire to the LORD God
of Israel are their inheritance, as he said to them.
15 Moses gave an inheritance to the tribe of
the Reubenites according to their clans. 16Their
territory was from Aroer, which is on the edge
of the Wadi Arnon, and the town that is in the
middle of the valley, and all the tableland by
Medeba; 17with Heshbon, and all its towns that
are in the tableland; Dibon, and Bamoth-baal,
and Beth-baal-meon, 18and Jahaz, and Kedemoth, and Mephaath, 19and Kiriathaim, and Sibmah, and Zereth-shahar on the hill of the valley,
20and Beth-peor, and the slopes of Pisgah, and
Beth-jeshimoth, 21that is, all the towns of the
tableland, and all the kingdom of King Sihon of
the Amorites, who reigned in Heshbon, whom
Moses defeated with the leaders of Midian, Evi
and Rekem and Zur and Hur and Reba, as princes
of Sihon, who lived in the land. 22Along with the
rest of those they put to death, the Israelites also
put to the sword Balaam son of Beor, who practiced divination. 23And the border of the Reubenites was the Jordan and its banks. This was the
inheritance of the Reubenites according to their
families with their towns and villages.
24 Moses gave an inheritance also to the tribe
of the Gadites, according to their families. 25Their
territory was Jazer, and all the towns of Gilead,
and half the land of the Ammonites, to Aroer,
which is east of Rabbah, 26and from Heshbon to
Ramath-mizpeh and Betonim, and from Mahanaim to the territory of Debir,[a] 27and in the valley
Beth-haram, Beth-nimrah, Succoth, and Zaphon,
the rest of the kingdom of King Sihon of Heshbon, the Jordan and its banks, as far as the lower
end of the Sea of Chinnereth, eastward beyond
the Jordan. 28This is the inheritance of the Gadites according to their clans, with their towns and
villages.
29 Moses gave an inheritance to the half-tribe
of Manasseh; it was allotted to the half-tribe of
the Manassites according to their families. 30Their
territory extended from Mahanaim, through
all Bashan, the whole kingdom of King Og of
Bashan, and all the settlements of Jair, which are
in Bashan, sixty towns, 31and half of Gilead, and
Ashtaroth, and Edrei, the towns of the kingdom
of Og in Bashan; these were allotted to the people of Machir son of Manasseh according to their
clans—for half the Machirites.
32 These are the inheritances that Moses distributed in the plains of Moab, beyond the Jordan
east of Jericho. 33But to the tribe of Levi Moses
gave no inheritance; the LORD God of Israel is
their inheritance, as he said to them.

14 These are the inheritances that the Israelites received in the land of Canaan, which
the priest Eleazar, and Joshua son of Nun, and the
heads of the families of the tribes of the Israelites
distributed to them. 2Their inheritance was by
lot, as the LORD had commanded Moses for the
nine and one-half tribes. 3For Moses had given
an inheritance to the two and one-half tribes beyond the Jordan; but to the Levites he gave no inheritance among them. 4For the people of Joseph
were two tribes, Manasseh and Ephraim; and no
portion was given to the Levites in the land, but
only towns to live in, with their pasture lands
for their flocks and herds. 5The Israelites did as
the LORD commanded Moses; they allotted the
land.
6 Then the people of Judah came to Joshua
at Gilgal; and Caleb son of Jephunneh the Kenizzite said to him, "You know what the LORD
said to Moses the man of God in Kadesh-barnea
concerning you and me. 7I was forty years old
when Moses the servant of the LORD sent me
from Kadesh-barnea to spy out the land; and I
brought him an honest report. 8But my companions who went up with me made the heart of the
people melt; yet I wholeheartedly followed the
LORD my God. 9And Moses swore on that day,
saying, "Surely the land on which your foot has
trodden shall be an inheritance for you and your
children forever, because you have wholeheartedly followed the LORD my God.' 10And now, as
you see, the LORD has kept me alive, as he said,
these forty-five years since the time that the
LORD spoke this word to Moses, while Israel was

[a] Gk Syr Vg: Heb *Lidebir*

journeying through the wilderness; and here I am today, eighty-five years old. 11I am still as strong today as I was on the day that Moses sent me; my strength now is as my strength was then, for war, and for going and coming. 12So now give me this hill country of which the LORD spoke on that day; for you heard on that day how the Anakim were there, with great fortified cities; it may be that the LORD will be with me, and I shall drive them out, as the LORD said."

13 Then Joshua blessed him, and gave Hebron to Caleb son of Jephunneh for an inheritance. 14So Hebron became the inheritance of Caleb son of Jephunneh the Kenizzite to this day, because he wholeheartedly followed the LORD, the God of Israel. 15Now the name of Hebron formerly was Kiriath-arba;[a] this Arba was[b] the greatest man among the Anakim. And the land had rest from war.

15 The lot for the tribe of the people of Judah according to their families reached southward to the boundary of Edom, to the wilderness of Zin at the farthest south. 2And their south boundary ran from the end of the Dead Sea,[c] from the bay that faces southward; 3it goes out southward of the ascent of Akrabbim, passes along to Zin, and goes up south of Kadesh-barnea, along by Hezron, up to Addar, makes a turn to Karka, 4passes along to Azmon, goes out by the Wadi of Egypt, and comes to its end at the sea. This shall be your south boundary. 5And the east boundary is the Dead Sea,[c] to the mouth of the Jordan. And the boundary on the north side runs from the bay of the sea at the mouth of the Jordan; 6and the boundary goes up to Beth-hoglah, and passes along north of Beth-arabah; and the boundary goes up to the Stone of Bohan, Reuben's son; 7and the boundary goes up to Debir from the Valley of Achor, and so northward, turning toward Gilgal, which is opposite the ascent of Adummim, which is on the south side of the valley; and the boundary passes along to the waters of En-shemesh, and ends at En-rogel; 8then the boundary goes up by the valley of the son of Hinnom at the southern slope of the Jebusites (that is, Jerusalem); and the boundary goes up to the top of the mountain that lies over against the valley of Hinnom, on the west, at the northern end of the valley of Rephaim; 9then the boundary extends from the top of the mountain to the spring of the Waters of Nephtoah, and from there to the towns of Mount Ephron; then the boundary bends around to Baalah (that is, Kiriath-jearim); 10and the boundary circles west of Baalah to Mount Seir, passes along to the northern slope of Mount Jearim (that is, Chesalon), and goes down to Beth-shemesh, and passes along by Timnah; 11the boundary goes out to the slope of the hill north of Ekron, then the boundary bends around to Shikkeron, and passes along to Mount Baalah, and goes out to Jabneel; then the boundary comes to an end at the sea. 12And the west boundary was the Mediterranean with its coast. This is the boundary surrounding the people of Judah according to their families.

13 According to the commandment of the LORD to Joshua, he gave to Caleb son of Jephunneh a portion among the people of Judah, Kiriath-arba,[a] that is, Hebron (Arba was the father of Anak). 14And Caleb drove out from there the three sons of Anak: Sheshai, Ahiman, and Talmai, the descendants of Anak. 15From there he went up against the inhabitants of Debir; now the name of Debir formerly was Kiriath-sepher. 16And Caleb said, "Whoever attacks Kiriath-sepher and takes it, to him I will give my daughter Achsah as wife." 17Othniel son of Kenaz, the brother of Caleb, took it; and he gave him his daughter Achsah as wife. 18When she came to him, she urged him to ask her father for a field. As she dismounted from her donkey, Caleb said to her, "What do you wish?" 19She said to him, "Give me a present; since you have set me in the land of the Negeb, give me springs of water as well." So Caleb gave her the upper springs and the lower springs.

20 This is the inheritance of the tribe of the people of Judah according to their families. 21The towns belonging to the tribe of the people of Judah in the extreme south, toward the bound-

[a] That is *the city of Arba* [b] Heb lacks *this Arba was* [c] Heb *Salt Sea*

ary of Edom, were Kabzeel, Eder, Jagur, [22]Kinah,
Dimonah, Adadah, [23]Kedesh, Hazor, Ithnan,
[24]Ziph, Telem, Bealoth, [25]Hazor-hadattah,
Kerioth-hezron (that is, Hazor), [26]Amam, Shema,
Moladah, [27]Hazar-gaddah, Heshmon, Beth-pelet,
[28]Hazar-shual, Beer-sheba, Biziothiah, [29]Baalah,
Iim, Ezem, [30]Eltolad, Chesil, Hormah, [31]Ziklag,
Madmannah, Sansannah, [32]Lebaoth, Shilhim,
Ain, and Rimmon: in all, twenty-nine towns,
with their villages.

33 And in the lowland, Eshtaol, Zorah, Ashnah, [34]Zanoah, En-gannim, Tappuah, Enam,
[35]Jarmuth, Adullam, Socoh, Azekah, [36]Shaaraim,
Adithaim, Gederah, Gederothaim: fourteen
towns with their villages.

37 Zenan, Hadashah, Migdal-gad, [38]Dilan,
Mizpeh, Jokthe-el, [39]Lachish, Bozkath, Eglon,
[40]Cabbon, Lahmam, Chitlish, [41]Gederoth, Beth-
dagon, Naamah, and Makkedah: sixteen towns
with their villages.

42 Libnah, Ether, Ashan, [43]Iphtah, Ashnah,
Nezib, [44]Keilah, Achzib, and Mareshah: nine
towns with their villages.

45 Ekron, with its dependencies and its villages; [46]from Ekron to the sea, all that were near
Ashdod, with their villages.

47 Ashdod, its towns and its villages; Gaza,
its towns and its villages; to the Wadi of Egypt,
and the Great Sea with its coast.

48 And in the hill country, Shamir, Jattir,
Socoh, [49]Dannah, Kiriath-sannah (that is, Debir),
[50]Anab, Eshtemoh, Anim, [51]Goshen, Holon, and
Giloh: eleven towns with their villages.

52 Arab, Dumah, Eshan, [53]Janim, Beth-
tappuah, Aphekah, [54]Humtah, Kiriath-arba (that
is, Hebron), and Zior: nine towns with their villages.

55 Maon, Carmel, Ziph, Juttah, [56]Jezreel,
Jokdeam, Zanoah, [57]Kain, Gibeah, and Timnah:
ten towns with their villages.

58 Halhul, Beth-zur, Gedor, [59]Maarath, Beth-
anoth, and Eltekon: six towns with their villages.

60 Kiriath-baal (that is, Kiriath-jearim) and
Rabbah: two towns with their villages.

61 In the wilderness, Beth-arabah, Middin,
Secacah, [62]Nibshan, the City of Salt, and En-
gedi: six towns with their villages.

63 But the people of Judah could not drive
out the Jebusites, the inhabitants of Jerusalem;
so the Jebusites live with the people of Judah in
Jerusalem to this day.

16 The allotment of the Josephites went from
the Jordan by Jericho, east of the waters
of Jericho, into the wilderness, going up from Jericho into the hill country to Bethel; [2]then going
from Bethel to Luz, it passes along to Ataroth, the
territory of the Archites; [3]then it goes down westward to the territory of the Japhletites, as far as
the territory of Lower Beth-horon, then to Gezer,
and it ends at the sea.

4 The Josephites—Manasseh and Ephraim—
received their inheritance.

5 The territory of the Ephraimites by their
families was as follows: the boundary of their inheritance on the east was Ataroth-addar as far as
Upper Beth-horon, [6]and the boundary goes from
there to the sea; on the north is Michmethath;
then on the east the boundary makes a turn toward Taanath-shiloh, and passes along beyond it
on the east to Janoah, [7]then it goes down from
Janoah to Ataroth and to Naarah, and touches
Jericho, ending at the Jordan. [8]From Tappuah
the boundary goes westward to the Wadi Kanah,
and ends at the sea. Such is the inheritance of
the tribe of the Ephraimites by their families, [9]to-
gether with the towns that were set apart for the
Ephraimites within the inheritance of the Manassites, all those towns with their villages. [10]They
did not, however, drive out the Canaanites who
lived in Gezer: so the Canaanites have lived within
Ephraim to this day but have been made to do
forced labor.

17 Then allotment was made to the tribe of
Manasseh, for he was the firstborn of Joseph. To Machir the firstborn of Manasseh, the
father of Gilead, were allotted Gilead and Bashan,
because he was a warrior. [2]And allotments were
made to the rest of the tribe of Manasseh, by
their families, Abiezer, Helek, Asriel, Shechem,
Hepher, and Shemida; these were the male descendants of Manasseh son of Joseph, by their
families.

3 Now Zelophehad son of Hepher son of
Gilead son of Machir son of Manasseh had no

sons, but only daughters; and these are the names
of his daughters: Mahlah, Noah, Hoglah, Milcah,
and Tirzah. 4They came before the priest Eleazar
and Joshua son of Nun and the leaders, and said,
"The LORD commanded Moses to give us an inheritance along with our male kin." So according
to the commandment of the LORD he gave them
an inheritance among the kinsmen of their father.
5Thus there fell to Manasseh ten portions, besides
the land of Gilead and Bashan, which is on the
other side of the Jordan, 6because the daughters
of Manasseh received an inheritance along with
his sons. The land of Gilead was allotted to the
rest of the Manassites.

7 The territory of Manasseh reached from
Asher to Michmethath, which is east of Shechem;
then the boundary goes along southward to the
inhabitants of En-tappuah. 8The land of Tappuah
belonged to Manasseh, but the town of Tappuah
on the boundary of Manasseh belonged to the
Ephraimites. 9Then the boundary went down to
the Wadi Kanah. The towns here, to the south of
the wadi, among the towns of Manasseh, belong
to Ephraim. Then the boundary of Manasseh
goes along the north side of the wadi and ends at
the sea. 10The land to the south is Ephraim's and
that to the north is Manasseh's, with the sea forming its boundary; on the north Asher is reached,
and on the east Issachar. 11Within Issachar and
Asher, Manasseh had Beth-shean and its villages,
Ibleam and its villages, the inhabitants of Dor and
its villages, the inhabitants of En-dor and its villages, the inhabitants of Taanach and its villages,
and the inhabitants of Megiddo and its villages
(the third is Naphath).[a] 12Yet the Manassites
could not take possession of those towns; but the
Canaanites continued to live in that land. 13But
when the Israelites grew strong, they put the Canaanites to forced labor, but did not utterly drive
them out.

14 The tribe of Joseph spoke to Joshua, saying, "Why have you given me but one lot and
one portion as an inheritance, since we are a
numerous people, whom all along the LORD has
blessed?" 15And Joshua said to them, "If you are
a numerous people, go up to the forest, and clear
ground there for yourselves in the land of the Perizzites and the Rephaim, since the hill country of
Ephraim is too narrow for you." 16The tribe of Joseph said, "The hill country is not enough for us;
yet all the Canaanites who live in the plain have
chariots of iron, both those in Beth-shean and its
villages and those in the Valley of Jezreel." 17Then
Joshua said to the house of Joseph, to Ephraim
and Manasseh, "You are indeed a numerous
people, and have great power; you shall not have
one lot only, 18but the hill country shall be yours,
for though it is a forest, you shall clear it and possess it to its farthest borders; for you shall drive
out the Canaanites, though they have chariots of
iron, and though they are strong."

18 Then the whole congregation of the Israelites assembled at Shiloh, and set up
the tent of meeting there. The land lay subdued
before them.

2 There remained among the Israelites seven
tribes whose inheritance had not yet been apportioned. 3So Joshua said to the Israelites, "How
long will you be slack about going in and taking
possession of the land that the LORD, the God
of your ancestors, has given you? 4Provide three
men from each tribe, and I will send them out
that they may begin to go throughout the land,
writing a description of it with a view to their
inheritances. Then come back to me. 5They shall
divide it into seven portions, Judah continuing in
its territory on the south, and the house of Joseph
in their territory on the north. 6You shall describe
the land in seven divisions and bring the description here to me; and I will cast lots for you here
before the LORD our God. 7The Levites have no
portion among you, for the priesthood of the
LORD is their heritage; and Gad and Reuben and
the half-tribe of Manasseh have received their
inheritance beyond the Jordan eastward, which
Moses the servant of the LORD gave them."

8 So the men started on their way; and Joshua
charged those who went to write the description
of the land, saying, "Go throughout the land and
write a description of it, and come back to me;

[a] Meaning of Heb uncertain

and I will cast lots for you here before the LORD
in Shiloh." 9So the men went and traversed the
land and set down in a book a description of it by
towns in seven divisions; then they came back to
Joshua in the camp at Shiloh, 10and Joshua cast
lots for them in Shiloh before the LORD; and
there Joshua apportioned the land to the Israelites, to each a portion.

11 The lot of the tribe of Benjamin according
to its families came up, and the territory allotted
to it fell between the tribe of Judah and the tribe
of Joseph. 12On the north side their boundary began at the Jordan; then the boundary goes up to
the slope of Jericho on the north, then up through
the hill country westward; and it ends at the wilderness of Beth-aven. 13From there the boundary
passes along southward in the direction of Luz, to
the slope of Luz (that is, Bethel), then the boundary goes down to Ataroth-addar, on the mountain
that lies south of Lower Beth-horon. 14Then the
boundary goes in another direction, turning on
the western side southward from the mountain
that lies to the south, opposite Beth-horon, and
it ends at Kiriath-baal (that is, Kiriath-jearim), a
town belonging to the tribe of Judah. This forms
the western side. 15The southern side begins at
the outskirts of Kiriath-jearim; and the boundary
goes from there to Ephron,[a] to the spring of the
Waters of Nephtoah; 16then the boundary goes
down to the border of the mountain that overlooks the valley of the son of Hinnom, which is
at the north end of the valley of Rephaim; and it
then goes down the valley of Hinnom, south of
the slope of the Jebusites, and downward to En-
rogel; 17then it bends in a northerly direction
going on to En-shemesh, and from there goes to
Geliloth, which is opposite the ascent of Adummim; then it goes down to the Stone of Bohan,
Reuben's son; 18and passing on to the north of
the slope of Beth-arabah[b] it goes down to the Arabah; 19then the boundary passes on to the north
of the slope of Beth-hoglah; and the boundary
ends at the northern bay of the Dead Sea,[c] at
the south end of the Jordan: this is the southern
border. 20The Jordan forms its boundary on the
eastern side. This is the inheritance of the tribe of
Benjamin, according to its families, boundary by
boundary all around.

21 Now the towns of the tribe of Benjamin
according to their families were Jericho, Beth-
hoglah, Emek-keziz, 22Beth-arabah, Zemaraim,
Bethel, 23Avvim, Parah, Ophrah, 24Chephar-
ammoni, Ophni, and Geba—twelve towns with
their villages: 25Gibeon, Ramah, Beeroth, 26Miz-
peh, Chephirah, Mozah, 27Rekem, Irpeel, Tar-
alah, 28Zela, Haeleph, Jebus[d] (that is, Jerusalem),
Gibeah[e] and Kiriath-jearim[f]—fourteen towns
with their villages. This is the inheritance of the
tribe of Benjamin according to its families.

19 The second lot came out for Simeon, for
the tribe of Simeon, according to its families; its inheritance lay within the inheritance of
the tribe of Judah. 2It had for its inheritance Beer-
sheba, Sheba, Moladah, 3Hazar-shual, Balah,
Ezem, 4Eltolad, Bethul, Hormah, 5Ziklag, Beth-
marcaboth, Hazar-susah, 6Beth-lebaoth, and
Sharuhen—thirteen towns with their villages;
7Ain, Rimmon, Ether, and Ashan—four towns
with their villages; 8together with all the villages
all around these towns as far as Baalath-beer, Ramah of the Negeb. This was the inheritance of the
tribe of Simeon according to its families. 9The inheritance of the tribe of Simeon formed part of
the territory of Judah; because the portion of the
tribe of Judah was too large for them, the tribe
of Simeon obtained an inheritance within their
inheritance.

10 The third lot came up for the tribe of Zebulun, according to its families. The boundary of
its inheritance reached as far as Sarid; 11then its
boundary goes up westward, and on to Maralah,
and touches Dabbesheth, then the wadi that is
east of Jokneam; 12from Sarid it goes in the other
direction eastward toward the sunrise to the
boundary of Chisloth-tabor; from there it goes to
Daberath, then up to Japhia; 13from there it passes
along on the east toward the sunrise to Gath-
hepher, to Eth-kazin, and going on to Rimmon

[a] Cn See 15.9. Heb *westward* [b] Gk: Heb *to the slope over against the Arabah* [c] Heb *Salt Sea* [d] Gk Syr Vg: Heb *the Jebusite* [e] Heb *Gibeath* [f] Gk: Heb *Kiriath*

it bends toward Neah; 14then on the north the boundary makes a turn to Hannathon, and it ends at the valley of Iphtah-el; 15and Kattath, Nahalal, Shimron, Idalah, and Bethlehem—twelve towns with their villages. 16This is the inheritance of the tribe of Zebulun, according to its families—these towns with their villages.

17 The fourth lot came out for Issachar, for the tribe of Issachar, according to its families. 18Its territory included Jezreel, Chesulloth, Shunem, 19Hapharaim, Shion, Anaharath, 20Rabbith, Kishion, Ebez, 21Remeth, En-gannim, En-haddah, Beth-pazzez; 22the boundary also touches Tabor, Shahazumah, and Beth-shemesh, and its boundary ends at the Jordan—sixteen towns with their villages. 23This is the inheritance of the tribe of Issachar, according to its families—the towns with their villages.

24 The fifth lot came out for the tribe of Asher according to its families. 25Its boundary included Helkath, Hali, Beten, Achshaph, 26Allammelech, Amad, and Mishal; on the west it touches Carmel and Shihor-libnath, 27then it turns eastward, goes to Beth-dagon, and touches Zebulun and the valley of Iphtah-el northward to Beth-emek and Neiel; then it continues in the north to Cabul, 28Ebron, Rehob, Hammon, Kanah, as far as Great Sidon; 29then the boundary turns to Ramah, reaching to the fortified city of Tyre; then the boundary turns to Hosah, and it ends at the sea; Mahalab,[a] Achzib, 30Ummah, Aphek, and Rehob—twenty-two towns with their villages. 31This is the inheritance of the tribe of Asher according to its families—these towns with their villages.

32 The sixth lot came out for the tribe of Naphtali, for the tribe of Naphtali, according to its families. 33And its boundary ran from Heleph, from the oak in Zaanannim, and Adami-nekeb, and Jabneel, as far as Lakkum; and it ended at the Jordan; 34then the boundary turns westward to Aznoth-tabor, and goes from there to Hukkok, touching Zebulun at the south, and Asher on the west, and Judah on the east at the Jordan. 35The fortified towns are Ziddim, Zer, Hammath, Rakkath, Chinnereth, 36Adamah, Ramah, Hazor, 37Kedesh, Edrei, En-hazor, 38Iron, Migdal-el, Horem, Beth-anath, and Beth-shemesh—nineteen towns with their villages. 39This is the inheritance of the tribe of Naphtali according to its families—the towns with their villages.

40 The seventh lot came out for the tribe of Dan, according to its families. 41The territory of its inheritance included Zorah, Eshtaol, Ir-shemesh, 42Shaalabbin, Aijalon, Ithlah, 43Elon, Timnah, Ekron, 44Eltekeh, Gibbethon, Baalath, 45Jehud, Bene-berak, Gath-rimmon, 46Me-jarkon, and Rakkon at the border opposite Joppa. 47When the territory of the Danites was lost to them, the Danites went up and fought against Leshem, and after capturing it and putting it to the sword, they took possession of it and settled in it, calling Leshem, Dan, after their ancestor Dan. 48This is the inheritance of the tribe of Dan, according to their families—these towns with their villages.

49 When they had finished distributing the several territories of the land as inheritances, the Israelites gave an inheritance among them to Joshua son of Nun. 50By command of the LORD they gave him the town that he asked for, Timnath-serah in the hill country of Ephraim; he rebuilt the town, and settled in it.

51 These are the inheritances that the priest Eleazar and Joshua son of Nun and the heads of the families of the tribes of the Israelites distributed by lot at Shiloh before the LORD, at the entrance of the tent of meeting. So they finished dividing the land.

20 Then the LORD spoke to Joshua, saying, 2"Say to the Israelites, "Appoint the cities of refuge, of which I spoke to you through Moses, 3so that anyone who kills a person without intent or by mistake may flee there; they shall be for you a refuge from the avenger of blood. 4The slayer shall flee to one of these cities and shall stand at the entrance of the gate of the city, and explain the case to the elders of that city; then the fugitive shall be taken into the city, and given a place, and shall remain with them. 5And if the avenger of blood is in pursuit, they shall not give up the

[a] Cn Compare Gk: Heb *Mehebel*

slayer, because the neighbor was killed by mistake, there having been no enmity between them
before. 6 The slayer shall remain in that city until
there is a trial before the congregation, until the
death of the one who is high priest at the time:
then the slayer may return home, to the town in
which the deed was done.'"
7 So they set apart Kedesh in Galilee in the
hill country of Naphtali, and Shechem in the hill
country of Ephraim, and Kiriath-arba (that is,
Hebron) in the hill country of Judah. 8 And beyond the Jordan east of Jericho, they appointed
Bezer in the wilderness on the tableland, from
the tribe of Reuben, and Ramoth in Gilead, from
the tribe of Gad, and Golan in Bashan, from the
tribe of Manasseh. 9 These were the cities designated for all the Israelites, and for the aliens residing among them, that anyone who killed a person
without intent could flee there, so as not to die by
the hand of the avenger of blood, until there was
a trial before the congregation.

Joshua 20:1-9

The "cities of refuge" are sometimes hailed as biblical antecedents to the modern principles of asylum and the presumption of innocence. It stands in definite tension with the practice, described elsewhere in Joshua, of utter destruction of Canaanite cities and peoples that have been "devoted" to YHWH (the biblical idea of *herem*).

—*NE*

21 Then the heads of the families of the
Levites came to the priest Eleazar and to
Joshua son of Nun and to the heads of the families
of the tribes of the Israelites; 2 they said to them
at Shiloh in the land of Canaan, "The LORD commanded through Moses that we be given towns
to live in, along with their pasture lands for our
livestock." 3 So by command of the LORD the Israelites gave to the Levites the following towns and
pasture lands out of their inheritance.
4 The lot came out for the families of the Kohathites. So those Levites who were descendants
of Aaron the priest received by lot thirteen towns
from the tribes of Judah, Simeon, and Benjamin.
5 The rest of the Kohathites received by
lot ten towns from the families of the tribe of
Ephraim, from the tribe of Dan, and the half-tribe
of Manasseh.
6 The Gershonites received by lot thirteen
towns from the families of the tribe of Issachar,
from the tribe of Asher, from the tribe of Naphtali,
and from the half-tribe of Manasseh in Bashan.
7 The Merarites according to their families
received twelve towns from the tribe of Reuben,
the tribe of Gad, and the tribe of Zebulun.
8 These towns and their pasture lands the
Israelites gave by lot to the Levites, as the LORD
had commanded through Moses.
9 Out of the tribe of Judah and the tribe of
Simeon they gave the following towns mentioned
by name, 10 which went to the descendants of
Aaron, one of the families of the Kohathites who
belonged to the Levites, since the lot fell to them
first. 11 They gave them Kiriath-arba (Arba being
the father of Anak), that is Hebron, in the hill
country of Judah, along with the pasture lands
around it. 12 But the fields of the town and its villages had been given to Caleb son of Jephunneh
as his holding.
13 To the descendants of Aaron the priest
they gave Hebron, the city of refuge for the slayer,
with its pasture lands, Libnah with its pasture
lands, 14 Jattir with its pasture lands, Eshtemoa
with its pasture lands, 15 Holon with its pasture
lands, Debir with its pasture lands, 16 Ain with
its pasture lands, Juttah with its pasture lands,
and Beth-shemesh with its pasture lands—nine
towns out of these two tribes. 17 Out of the tribe
of Benjamin: Gibeon with its pasture lands, Geba
with its pasture lands, 18 Anathoth with its pasture lands, and Almon with its pasture lands—
four towns. 19 The towns of the descendants of
Aaron—the priests—were thirteen in all, with
their pasture lands.
20 As to the rest of the Kohathites belonging to the Kohathite families of the Levites, the
towns allotted to them were out of the tribe of
Ephraim. 21 To them were given Shechem, the
city of refuge for the slayer, with its pasture lands

in the hill country of Ephraim, Gezer with its
pasture lands, 22 Kibzaim with its pasture lands,
and Beth-horon with its pasture lands—four
towns. 23 Out of the tribe of Dan: Elteke with its
pasture lands, Gibbethon with its pasture lands,
24 Aijalon with its pasture lands, Gath-rimmon
with its pasture lands—four towns. 25 Out of the
half-tribe of Manasseh: Taanach with its pasture
lands, and Gath-rimmon with its pasture lands—
two towns. 26 The towns of the families of the rest
of the Kohathites were ten in all, with their pasture lands.

27 To the Gershonites, one of the families
of the Levites, were given out of the half-tribe of
Manasseh, Golan in Bashan with its pasture lands,
the city of refuge for the slayer, and Beeshterah
with its pasture lands—two towns. 28 Out of the
tribe of Issachar: Kishion with its pasture lands,
Daberath with its pasture lands, 29 Jarmuth with
its pasture lands, En-gannim with its pasture
lands—four towns. 30 Out of the tribe of Asher:
Mishal with its pasture lands, Abdon with its pasture lands, 31 Helkath with its pasture lands, and
Rehob with its pasture lands—four towns. 32 Out
of the tribe of Naphtali: Kedesh in Galilee with
its pasture lands, the city of refuge for the slayer,
Hammoth-dor with its pasture lands, and Kartan
with its pasture lands—three towns. 33 The towns
of the several families of the Gershonites were in
all thirteen, with their pasture lands.

34 To the rest of the Levites—the Merarite
families—were given out of the tribe of Zebulun:
Jokneam with its pasture lands, Kartah with its
pasture lands, 35 Dimnah with its pasture lands,
Nahalal with its pasture lands—four towns.
36 Out of the tribe of Reuben: Bezer with its pasture lands, Jahzah with its pasture lands, 37 Kedemoth with its pasture lands, and Mephaath with
its pasture lands—four towns. 38 Out of the tribe
of Gad: Ramoth in Gilead with its pasture lands,
the city of refuge for the slayer, Mahanaim with
its pasture lands, 39 Heshbon with its pasture
lands, Jazer with its pasture lands—four towns
in all. 40 As for the towns of the several Merarite families, that is, the remainder of the families
of the Levites, those allotted to them were twelve
in all.

41 The towns of the Levites within the holdings of the Israelites were in all forty-eight towns
with their pasture lands. 42 Each of these towns
had its pasture lands around it; so it was with all
these towns.

43 Thus the LORD gave to Israel all the land
that he swore to their ancestors that he would
give them; and having taken possession of it, they
settled there. 44 And the LORD gave them rest on
every side just as he had sworn to their ancestors;
not one of all their enemies had withstood them,
for the LORD had given all their enemies into
their hands. 45 Not one of all the good promises
that the LORD had made to the house of Israel
had failed; all came to pass.

22 Then Joshua summoned the Reubenites,
the Gadites, and the half-tribe of Manasseh, 2 and said to them, "You have observed all
that Moses the servant of the LORD commanded
you, and have obeyed me in all that I have commanded you; 3 you have not forsaken your kindred these many days, down to this day, but have
been careful to keep the charge of the LORD your
God. 4 And now the LORD your God has given
rest to your kindred, as he promised them; therefore turn and go to your tents in the land where
your possession lies, which Moses the servant of
the LORD gave you on the other side of the Jordan. 5 Take good care to observe the commandment and instruction that Moses the servant of
the LORD commanded you, to love the LORD
your God, to walk in all his ways, to keep his commandments, and to hold fast to him, and to serve
him with all your heart and with all your soul."
6 So Joshua blessed them and sent them away, and
they went to their tents.

7 Now to the one half of the tribe of Manasseh
Moses had given a possession in Bashan; but to
the other half Joshua had given a possession beside their fellow Israelites in the land west of the
Jordan. And when Joshua sent them away to their
tents and blessed them, 8 he said to them, "Go
back to your tents with much wealth, and with
very much livestock, with silver, gold, bronze,
and iron, and with a great quantity of clothing;
divide the spoil of your enemies with your kindred." 9 So the Reubenites and the Gadites and

 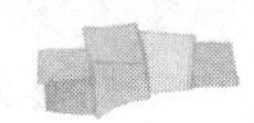

the half-tribe of Manasseh returned home, parting from the Israelites at Shiloh, which is in the land of Canaan, to go to the land of Gilead, their own land of which they had taken possession by command of the LORD through Moses.

10 When they came to the region[a] near the Jordan that lies in the land of Canaan, the Reubenites and the Gadites and the half-tribe of Manasseh built there an altar by the Jordan, an altar of great size. 11The Israelites heard that the Reubenites and the Gadites and the half-tribe of Manasseh had built an altar at the frontier of the land of Canaan, in the region[b] near the Jordan, on the side that belongs to the Israelites. 12And when the people of Israel heard of it, the whole assembly of the Israelites gathered at Shiloh, to make war against them.

13 Then the Israelites sent the priest Phinehas son of Eleazar to the Reubenites and the Gadites and the half-tribe of Manasseh, in the land of Gilead, 14and with him ten chiefs, one from each of the tribal families of Israel, every one of them the head of a family among the clans of Israel. 15They came to the Reubenites, the Gadites, and the half-tribe of Manasseh, in the land of Gilead, and they said to them, 16"Thus says the whole congregation of the LORD, 'What is this treachery that you have committed against the God of Israel in turning away today from following the LORD, by building yourselves an altar today in rebellion against the LORD? 17Have we not had enough of the sin at Peor from which even yet we have not cleansed ourselves, and for which a plague came upon the congregation of the LORD, 18that you must turn away today from following the LORD! If you rebel against the LORD today, he will be angry with the whole congregation of Israel tomorrow. 19But now, if your land is unclean, cross over into the LORD's land where the LORD's tabernacle now stands, and take for yourselves a possession among us; only do not rebel against the LORD, or rebel against us[c] by building yourselves an altar other than the altar of the LORD our God. 20Did not Achan son of Zerah break faith in the matter of the devoted things, and wrath fell upon all the congregation of Israel? And he did not perish alone for his iniquity!' "

21 Then the Reubenites, the Gadites, and the half-tribe of Manasseh said in answer to the heads of the families of Israel, 22"The LORD, God of gods! The LORD, God of gods! He knows; and let Israel itself know! If it was in rebellion or in breach of faith toward the LORD, do not spare us today 23for building an altar to turn away from following the LORD; or if we did so to offer burnt offerings or grain offerings or offerings of well-being on it, may the LORD himself take vengeance. 24No! We did it from fear that in time to come your children might say to our children, 'What have you to do with the LORD, the God of Israel? 25For the LORD has made the Jordan a boundary between us and you, you Reubenites and Gadites; you have no portion in the LORD.' So your children might make our children cease to worship the LORD. 26Therefore we said, 'Let us now build an altar, not for burnt offering, nor for sacrifice, 27but to be a witness between us and you, and between the generations after us, that we do perform the service of the LORD in his presence with our burnt offerings and sacrifices and offerings of well-being; so that your children may never say to our children in time to come, "You have no portion in the LORD." ' 28And we thought, If this should be said to us or to our descendants in time to come, we could say, 'Look at this copy of the altar of the LORD, which our ancestors made, not for burnt offerings, nor for sacrifice, but to be a witness between us and you.' 29Far be it from us that we should rebel against the LORD, and turn away this day from following the LORD by building an altar for burnt offering, grain offering, or sacrifice, other than the altar of the LORD our God that stands before his tabernacle!"

30 When the priest Phinehas and the chiefs of the congregation, the heads of the families of Israel who were with him, heard the words that the Reubenites and the Gadites and the Manassites spoke, they were satisfied. 31The priest Phinehas son of Eleazar said to the Reubenites and the Gadites and the Manassites, "Today we

[a] Or *to Geliloth* [a] Or *at Geliloth* [c] Or *make rebels of us*

know that the LORD is among us, because you
have not committed this treachery against the
LORD; now you have saved the Israelites from the
hand of the LORD."

32 Then the priest Phinehas son of Eleazar
and the chiefs returned from the Reubenites and
the Gadites in the land of Gilead to the land of
Canaan, to the Israelites, and brought back word
to them. 33 The report pleased the Israelites; and
the Israelites blessed God and spoke no more
of making war against them, to destroy the land
where the Reubenites and the Gadites were settled. 34 The Reubenites and the Gadites called the
altar Witness;[a] "For," said they, "it is a witness between us that the LORD is God."

23 A long time afterward, when the LORD
had given rest to Israel from all their enemies all around, and Joshua was old and well
advanced in years, 2 Joshua summoned all Israel,
their elders and heads, their judges and officers,
and said to them, "I am now old and well advanced in years; 3 and you have seen all that the
LORD your God has done to all these nations for
your sake, for it is the LORD your God who has
fought for you. 4 I have allotted to you as an inheritance for your tribes those nations that remain,
along with all the nations that I have already cut
off, from the Jordan to the Great Sea in the west.
5 The LORD your God will push them back before
you, and drive them out of your sight; and you
shall possess their land, as the LORD your God
promised you. 6 Therefore be very steadfast to
observe and do all that is written in the book of
the law of Moses, turning aside from it neither to
the right nor to the left, 7 so that you may not be
mixed with these nations left here among you,
or make mention of the names of their gods, or
swear by them, or serve them, or bow yourselves
down to them, 8 but hold fast to the LORD your
God, as you have done to this day. 9 For the LORD
has driven out before you great and strong nations; and as for you, no one has been able to
withstand you to this day. 10 One of you puts to
flight a thousand, since it is the LORD your God
who fights for you, as he promised you. 11 Be very
careful, therefore, to love the LORD your God.
12 For if you turn back, and join the survivors
of these nations left here among you, and intermarry with them, so that you marry their women
and they yours, 13 know assuredly that the LORD
your God will not continue to drive out these nations before you; but they shall be a snare and a
trap for you, a scourge on your sides, and thorns
in your eyes, until you perish from this good land
that the LORD your God has given you.

14 "And now I am about to go the way of all
the earth, and you know in your hearts and souls,
all of you, that not one thing has failed of all the
good things that the LORD your God promised
concerning you; all have come to pass for you,
not one of them has failed. 15 But just as all the
good things that the LORD your God promised
concerning you have been fulfilled for you, so
the LORD will bring upon you all the bad things,
until he has destroyed you from this good land
that the LORD your God has given you. 16 If you
transgress the covenant of the LORD your God,
which he enjoined on you, and go and serve other
gods and bow down to them, then the anger of
the LORD will be kindled against you, and you
shall perish quickly from the good land that he
has given to you."

24 Then Joshua gathered all the tribes of
Israel to Shechem, and summoned the elders, the heads, the judges, and the officers of Israel; and they presented themselves before God.
2 And Joshua said to all the people, "Thus says the
LORD, the God of Israel: Long ago your ancestors—Terah and his sons Abraham and Nahor—
lived beyond the Euphrates and served other
gods. 3 Then I took your father Abraham from beyond the River and led him through all the land of
Canaan and made his offspring many. I gave him
Isaac; 4 and to Isaac I gave Jacob and Esau. I gave
Esau the hill country of Seir to possess, but Jacob
and his children went down to Egypt. 5 Then I sent
Moses and Aaron, and I plagued Egypt with what
I did in its midst; and afterwards I brought you
out. 6 When I brought your ancestors out of Egypt,
you came to the sea; and the Egyptians pursued

[a] Cn Compare Syr: Heb lacks *Witness*

your ancestors with chariots and horsemen to the Red Sea.[a] 7When they cried out to the LORD, he put darkness between you and the Egyptians, and made the sea come upon them and cover them; and your eyes saw what I did to Egypt. Afterwards you lived in the wilderness a long time. 8Then I brought you to the land of the Amorites, who lived on the other side of the Jordan; they fought with you, and I handed them over to you, and you took possession of their land, and I destroyed them before you. 9Then King Balak son of Zippor of Moab, set out to fight against Israel. He sent and invited Balaam son of Beor to curse you, 10but I would not listen to Balaam; therefore he blessed you; so I rescued you out of his hand. 11When you went over the Jordan and came to Jericho, the citizens of Jericho fought against you, and also the Amorites, the Perizzites, the Canaanites, the Hittites, the Girgashites, the Hivites, and the Jebusites; and I handed them over to you. 12I sent the hornet[b] ahead of you, which drove out before you the two kings of the Amorites; it was not by your sword or by your bow. 13I gave you a land on which you had not labored, and towns that you had not built, and you live in them; you eat the fruit of vineyards and oliveyards that you did not plant.

14 "Now therefore revere the LORD, and serve him in sincerity and in faithfulness; put away the gods that your ancestors served beyond the River and in Egypt, and serve the LORD. 15Now if you are unwilling to serve the LORD, choose this day whom you will serve, whether the gods your ancestors served in the region beyond the River or the gods of the Amorites in whose land you are living; but as for me and my household, we will serve the LORD."

16 Then the people answered, "Far be it from us that we should forsake the LORD to serve other gods; 17for it is the LORD our God who brought us and our ancestors up from the land of Egypt, out of the house of slavery, and who did those great signs in our sight. He protected us along all the way that we went, and among all the peoples through whom we passed; 18and the LORD drove out before us all the peoples, the Amorites who lived in the land. Therefore we also will serve the LORD, for he is our God."

19 But Joshua said to the people, "You cannot serve the LORD, for he is a holy God. He is a jealous God; he will not forgive your transgressions or your sins. 20If you forsake the LORD and serve foreign gods, then he will turn and do you harm, and consume you, after having done you good." 21And the people said to Joshua, "No, we will serve the LORD!" 22Then Joshua said to the people, "You are witnesses against yourselves that you have chosen the LORD, to serve him." And they said, "We are witnesses." 23He said, "Then put away the foreign gods that are among you, and incline your hearts to the LORD, the God of Israel." 24The people said to Joshua, "The LORD our God we will serve, and him we will obey." 25So Joshua made a covenant with the people that day, and made statutes and ordinances for them at Shechem. 26Joshua wrote these words in the book of the law of God; and he took a large stone, and set it up there under the oak in the sanctuary of the LORD. 27Joshua said to all the people, "See, this stone shall be a witness against us; for it has heard all the words of the LORD that he spoke to us; therefore it shall be a witness against you, if you deal falsely with your God." 28So Joshua sent the people away to their inheritances.

29 After these things Joshua son of Nun, the servant of the LORD, died, being one hundred ten

Joshua 24:1-28

In this ceremony, often regarded as a "renewal" of the covenant at Sinai, Joshua calls on his audience to "put away the foreign gods that are among you" (24:23). Some interpreters read this as an indication that membership in Israel was a matter not of lineage but of loyalty. According to the biblical narrative, the allure of "foreign gods" remained a danger within Israel for generations to come.

— NE

[a] Or *Sea of Reeds* [b] Meaning of Heb uncertain

years old. 30 They buried him in his own inheritance at Timnath-serah, which is in the hill country of Ephraim, north of Mount Gaash.
31 Israel served the LORD all the days of
Joshua, and all the days of the elders who outlived
Joshua and had known all the work that the LORD
did for Israel.
32 The bones of Joseph, which the Israelites had brought up from Egypt, were buried at
Shechem, in the portion of ground that Jacob had
bought from the children of Hamor, the father
of Shechem, for one hundred pieces of money;[a]
it became an inheritance of the descendants of
Joseph.
33 Eleazar son of Aaron died; and they buried him at Gibeah, the town of his son Phinehas,
which had been given him in the hill country of
Ephraim.

[a] Heb *one hundred qesitah*

Judges

JUDGES 1:27-36 PAINTS a portrait of the settlement of Canaan that is markedly different than the one sketched in Joshua. Judges indicates that the tribes did not drive out the inhabitants of the land, whereas Joshua recounts numerous unequivocal military victories. Judges 1:34-36 show that Joseph's descendants continued in his ways; they forced the indigenous people into service—just as Joseph's adopted Egyptian people had earlier forced their own kindred into bondage (see Gen 47:19-26)—in spite of their own recent liberation from slavery.

There are several narratives of note in Judges: the story of Deborah, Barak, and Jael in chapters 4–5; Gideon in 6–8; Abimelech in 9; Jephthah and his daughter in 11; Samson and his women in 13–16; Micah, his mother, and their religion in 17; the Levite, his wife, and her murderers in 19; and the rape of the Shilonite women in 20–21. Each of these stories involves folk who are in some way marginal: outsiders, members of undistinguished tribes, illegitimate children, thieves, makers and worshipers of images, abused and murdered women. Some of them describe horrible violence. As a woman from a marginalized, African American community and as a feminist biblical scholar, the book of Judges fascinates me.

Judges presents several narratives that turn on women's participation in warfare. The Deborah saga is introduced by a description of her predecessor, Shamgar ben Anat (whose name indicates either that he is the son of a woman named Anat, meaning his mother was named for the Canaanite warrior goddess, or that he is such a great warrior that he is perceived as semi-divine, as was Achilles). Deborah's saga includes the story of Jael, the woman who executes Sisera. Subsequent revisions of the biblical narrative erase Deborah and Jael: First Samuel 12:11 says that YHWH sent Barak to deliver Israel, without mentioning Deborah; and Hebrews 11:32 also lists Barak as the sole deliverer.

Jael is the first woman in the Scriptures to be called "most blessed of women" (5:24; Judith is the second, and Miryam, Mary of Nazareth, is the third). According to the Song of Deborah (ch. 5), Jael was so important that time was measured by her life; verse 6 speaks of events "in the days of Jael. . . ." Jael can also be understood as an avenger of raped women, for Sisera's mother is represented (5:30) as boasting that her son is delayed because he is dividing up girls as spoil—literally, "dividing the woman-flesh" (she uses a Hebrew word for a woman's reproductive system).

Judges includes two particularly vicious stories of violence against women, the "sacrifice" of Jephthah's daughter (Judges 11) and the rape, murder, and dismemberment of an anonymous Levite's secondary wife in Judges 19. In Judges 20, the Benjaminites refuse to hand over the men of Gibeah who raped and murdered the Levite's *pilegesh* (the Hebrew word refers to a wife of secondary status). Israel goes to war against Benjamin, killing twenty-five thousand male warriors. The remaining Israelite tribes swear not to give their daughters in marriage to the six hundred survivors of Benjamin. Since the Gadite warriors of Jabesh-gilead did not join in the battle, these tribes also decide to annihilate their warriors, men and boys, and sexually active women, and to seize four hundred sexually uninitiated girls as wives for the Benjaminite warriors. But because these girls were insufficient in number, the tribes decide to abduct the innocent daughters of faithful Israelites from the house of God at Shiloh. The Benjaminites abduct young women performing a cultic service at the Shiloh shrine, in this case liturgical dance, as wives.

The abduction and rape of the Shilonite girls marks the end of Judges and is summed up with the refrain: "In those days there was no king in Israel; all the people did what was right in their own eyes" (21:25). Episodes of violence against women throughout the book thus serve an ideological purpose: to show that Israel's life without a king is wild, chaotic, and destructive.

To be sure, Judges also presents the intriguing story of the first king in Israel—a king before Saul ben Kish of the tribe of Benjamin, Gideon's son Abimelech ben Jerubbaal (see Judges 9). We read in 9:22 that Abimelech ruled three years, much longer than many later kings in the divided monarchy. He consolidated his reign by killing all of his brothers that he could find—sixty-nine; the youngest hid successfully. Abimelech also killed all of the people of Shechem in the fields outside of the city (9:42-45), then burned the nobles of Shechem in the temple of El-berith. Abimelech was dealt a deathblow by an unnamed woman; but he asked a young man to kill him before he died of his wounds, so that no one would say a woman killed him.

Unlike many other biblical texts, where such violence is narrated but not condemned, Judges provides an editorial conclusion: Every sin, transgression, and atrocity recorded in its pages results from the lack of a king. The refrain "there was no king in Israel" is repeated four times: at 17:6, 18:1, 19:1, and 21:25. Judges thus prepares for the account of the rise of Israel's monarchy in 1–2 Samuel. In this respect it should be read as a document of pro-monarchical propaganda.

— ***Wilda C. Gafney***

1 After the death of Joshua, the Israelites inquired of the Lord, "Who shall go up first for us against the Canaanites, to fight against them?"
2 The Lord said, "Judah shall go up. I hereby give
the land into his hand." 3 Judah said to his brother
Simeon, "Come up with me into the territory allotted to me, that we may fight against the Canaanites; then I too will go with you into the territory allotted to you." So Simeon went with him. 4 Then
Judah went up and the Lord gave the Canaanites and the Perizzites into their hand; and they
defeated ten thousand of them at Bezek. 5 They
came upon Adoni-bezek at Bezek, and fought against him, and defeated the Canaanites and the
Perizzites. 6 Adoni-bezek fled; but they pursued
him, and caught him, and cut off his thumbs and

Judges 1:1

The people's cry, "Who shall go up first for us against the Canaanites?" indicates that Israel's conquest of the land under Joshua was not as complete as the book of Joshua suggests. Some scholars see evidence here that the biblical picture of wholesale conquest was the wishful thinking of later biblical writers, who still contended against "Canaanite" impulses in their own time.

— *NE*

big toes. 7Adoni-bezek said, "Seventy kings with
their thumbs and big toes cut off used to pick up
scraps under my table; as I have done, so God has
paid me back." They brought him to Jerusalem,
and he died there.
8 Then the people of Judah fought against
Jerusalem and took it. They put it to the sword
and set the city on fire. 9Afterward the people of
Judah went down to fight against the Canaanites
who lived in the hill country, in the Negeb, and
in the lowland. 10Judah went against the Canaanites who lived in Hebron (the name of Hebron
was formerly Kiriath-arba); and they defeated
Sheshai and Ahiman and Talmai.
11 From there they went against the inhabitants of Debir (the name of Debir was formerly
Kiriath-sepher). 12Then Caleb said, "Whoever
attacks Kiriath-sepher and takes it, I will give him
my daughter Achsah as wife." 13And Othniel son
of Kenaz, Caleb's younger brother, took it; and he
gave him his daughter Achsah as wife. 14When
she came to him, she urged him to ask her father
for a field. As she dismounted from her donkey,
Caleb said to her, "What do you wish?" 15She said
to him, "Give me a present; since you have set me
in the land of the Negeb, give me also Gulloth-
mayim."[a] So Caleb gave her Upper Gulloth and
Lower Gulloth.
16 The descendants of Hobab[b] the Kenite,
Moses' father-in-law, went up with the people
of Judah from the city of palms into the wilderness of Judah, which lies in the Negeb near Arad.
Then they went and settled with the Amalekites.[c]
17Judah went with his brother Simeon, and they
defeated the Canaanites who inhabited Zephath,
and devoted it to destruction. So the city was
called Hormah. 18Judah took Gaza with its territory, Ashkelon with its territory, and Ekron with
its territory. 19The LORD was with Judah, and he
took possession of the hill country, but could not
drive out the inhabitants of the plain, because
they had chariots of iron. 20Hebron was given to
Caleb, as Moses had said; and he drove out from
it the three sons of Anak. 21But the Benjaminites
did not drive out the Jebusites who lived in Jerusalem; so the Jebusites have lived in Jerusalem
among the Benjaminites to this day.
22 The house of Joseph also went up against
Bethel; and the LORD was with them. 23The
house of Joseph sent out spies to Bethel (the
name of the city was formerly Luz). 24When
the spies saw a man coming out of the city, they
said to him, "Show us the way into the city, and
we will deal kindly with you." 25So he showed
them the way into the city; and they put the city
to the sword, but they let the man and all his family go. 26So the man went to the land of the Hittites and built a city, and named it Luz; that is its
name to this day.
27 Manasseh did not drive out the inhabitants of Beth-shean and its villages, or Taanach
and its villages, or the inhabitants of Dor and its
villages, or the inhabitants of Ibleam and its villages, or the inhabitants of Megiddo and its villages; but the Canaanites continued to live in that
land. 28When Israel grew strong, they put the Canaanites to forced labor, but did not in fact drive
them out.
29 And Ephraim did not drive out the Canaanites who lived in Gezer; but the Canaanites
lived among them in Gezer.
30 Zebulun did not drive out the inhabitants
of Kitron, or the inhabitants of Nahalol; but the
Canaanites lived among them, and became subject to forced labor.
31 Asher did not drive out the inhabitants of

[a] That is *Basins of Water* [b] Gk: Heb lacks *Hobab* [c] See 1 Sam 15.6: Heb *people*

Acco, or the inhabitants of Sidon, or of Ahlab, or
of Achzib, or of Helbah, or of Aphik, or of Rehob;
32 but the Asherites lived among the Canaanites,
the inhabitants of the land; for they did not drive
them out.

33 Naphtali did not drive out the inhabitants of Beth-shemesh, or the inhabitants of
Beth-anath, but lived among the Canaanites, the
inhabitants of the land; nevertheless the inhabitants of Beth-shemesh and of Beth-anath became
subject to forced labor for them.

34 The Amorites pressed the Danites back
into the hill country; they did not allow them
to come down to the plain. 35 The Amorites continued to live in Har-heres, in Aijalon, and in
Shaalbim, but the hand of the house of Joseph
rested heavily on them, and they became subject
to forced labor. 36 The border of the Amorites ran
from the ascent of Akrabbim, from Sela and upward.

2 Now the angel of the LORD went up from
Gilgal to Bochim, and said, "I brought you up
from Egypt, and brought you into the land that I
had promised to your ancestors. I said, 'I will never
break my covenant with you. 2 For your part, do
not make a covenant with the inhabitants of this
land; tear down their altars.' But you have not
obeyed my command. See what you have done!
3 So now I say, I will not drive them out before
you; but they shall become adversaries[a] to you,
and their gods shall be a snare to you." 4 When
the angel of the LORD spoke these words to all
the Israelites, the people lifted up their voices and
wept. 5 So they named that place Bochim,[b] and
there they sacrificed to the LORD.

6 When Joshua dismissed the people, the Israelites all went to their own inheritances to take
possession of the land. 7 The people worshiped
the LORD all the days of Joshua, and all the days
of the elders who outlived Joshua, who had seen
all the great work that the LORD had done for Israel. 8 Joshua son of Nun, the servant of the LORD,
died at the age of one hundred ten years. 9 So they
buried him within the bounds of his inheritance
in Timnath-heres, in the hill country of Ephraim,
north of Mount Gaash. 10 Moreover, that whole
generation was gathered to their ancestors, and
another generation grew up after them, who did
not know the LORD or the work that he had done
for Israel.

11 Then the Israelites did what was evil in the
sight of the LORD and worshiped the Baals; 12 and
they abandoned the LORD, the God of their ancestors, who had brought them out of the land of
Egypt; they followed other gods, from among the
gods of the peoples who were all around them,
and bowed down to them; and they provoked the
LORD to anger. 13 They abandoned the LORD, and
worshiped Baal and the Astartes. 14 So the anger of
the LORD was kindled against Israel, and he gave
them over to plunderers who plundered them,
and he sold them into the power of their enemies
all around, so that they could no longer withstand
their enemies. 15 Whenever they marched out,
the hand of the LORD was against them to bring
misfortune, as the LORD had warned them and
sworn to them; and they were in great distress.

16 Then the LORD raised up judges, who delivered them out of the power of those who plundered them. 17 Yet they did not listen even to their
judges; for they lusted after other gods and bowed
down to them. They soon turned aside from the
way in which their ancestors had walked, who
had obeyed the commandments of the LORD;

Judges 2:1-5

In contrast to the usual biblical picture of a wholesale conquest of Canaan by Israel, here the LORD indicates that he will *not* drive out the inhabitants of the land. The passage surely gives us a glimpse into the historical reality in later centuries and suggests to some scholars that the struggle was not between *peoples*—Israel against the various peoples inhabiting Canaan—but between *allegiances*—to the LORD alone, or to the LORD alongside other gods: see 3:5-7.

— *NE*

[a] OL Vg Compare Gk: Heb *sides* [b] That is *Weepers*

they did not follow their example. 18Whenever
the LORD raised up judges for them, the LORD
was with the judge, and he delivered them from
the hand of their enemies all the days of the
judge; for the LORD would be moved to pity by
their groaning because of those who persecuted
and oppressed them. 19But whenever the judge
died, they would relapse and behave worse than
their ancestors, following other gods, worshiping them and bowing down to them. They would
not drop any of their practices or their stubborn
ways. 20So the anger of the LORD was kindled
against Israel; and he said, "Because this people
have transgressed my covenant that I commanded
their ancestors, and have not obeyed my voice,
21I will no longer drive out before them any of the
nations that Joshua left when he died." 22In order
to test Israel, whether or not they would take care
to walk in the way of the LORD as their ancestors
did, 23the LORD had left those nations, not driving them out at once, and had not handed them
over to Joshua.

3 Now these are the nations that the LORD
left to test all those in Israel who had no experience of any war in Canaan 2(it was only that
successive generations of Israelites might know
war, to teach those who had no experience of it
before): 3the five lords of the Philistines, and all
the Canaanites, and the Sidonians, and the Hivites who lived on Mount Lebanon, from Mount
Baal-hermon as far as Lebo-hamath. 4They were
for the testing of Israel, to know whether Israel
would obey the commandments of the LORD,
which he commanded their ancestors by Moses.
5So the Israelites lived among the Canaanites, the
Hittites, the Amorites, the Perizzites, the Hivites,
and the Jebusites; 6and they took their daughters
as wives for themselves, and their own daughters
they gave to their sons; and they worshiped their
gods.

7 The Israelites did what was evil in the sight
of the LORD, forgetting the LORD their God, and
worshiping the Baals and the Asherahs. 8Therefore
the anger of the LORD was kindled against Israel,
and he sold them into the hand of King Cushan-
rishathaim of Aram-naharaim; and the Israelites
served Cushan-rishathaim eight years. 9But when
the Israelites cried out to the LORD, the LORD
raised up a deliverer for the Israelites, who delivered them, Othniel son of Kenaz, Caleb's younger
brother. 10The spirit of the LORD came upon him,
and he judged Israel; he went out to war, and the
LORD gave King Cushan-rishathaim of Aram into
his hand; and his hand prevailed over Cushan-
rishathaim. 11So the land had rest forty years.
Then Othniel son of Kenaz died.

12 The Israelites again did what was evil in
the sight of the LORD; and the LORD strengthened King Eglon of Moab against Israel, because
they had done what was evil in the sight of the
LORD. 13In alliance with the Ammonites and the
Amalekites, he went and defeated Israel; and they
took possession of the city of palms. 14So the Israelites served King Eglon of Moab eighteen years.

15 But when the Israelites cried out to the
LORD, the LORD raised up for them a deliverer,
Ehud son of Gera, the Benjaminite, a left-handed
man. The Israelites sent tribute by him to King
Eglon of Moab. 16Ehud made for himself a
sword with two edges, a cubit in length; and he
fastened it on his right thigh under his clothes.
17Then he presented the tribute to King Eglon
of Moab. Now Eglon was a very fat man. 18When
Ehud had finished presenting the tribute, he sent
the people who carried the tribute on their way.
19But he himself turned back at the sculptured
stones near Gilgal, and said, "I have a secret message for you, O king." So the king said,[a] "Silence!"
and all his attendants went out from his presence.
20Ehud came to him, while he was sitting alone
in his cool roof chamber, and said, "I have a message from God for you." So he rose from his seat.
21Then Ehud reached with his left hand, took the
sword from his right thigh, and thrust it into Eglon's[b] belly; 22the hilt also went in after the blade,
and the fat closed over the blade, for he did not
draw the sword out of his belly; and the dirt came
out.[c] 23Then Ehud went out into the vestibule,[d]
and closed the doors of the roof chamber on him,
and locked them.

[a] Heb *he said* [b] Heb *his* [c] With Tg Vg: Meaning of Heb uncertain [d] Meaning of Heb uncertain

24 After he had gone, the servants came.
When they saw that the doors of the roof chamber were locked, they thought, "He must be re-
lieving himself[a] in the cool chamber." 25So they
waited until they were embarrassed. When he
still did not open the doors of the roof chamber,
they took the key and opened them. There was
their lord lying dead on the floor.

26 Ehud escaped while they delayed, and
passed beyond the sculptured stones, and escaped to Seirah. 27When he arrived, he sounded
the trumpet in the hill country of Ephraim; and
the Israelites went down with him from the hill
country, having him at their head. 28He said to
them, "Follow after me; for the LORD has given
your enemies the Moabites into your hand." So
they went down after him, and seized the fords
of the Jordan against the Moabites, and allowed
no one to cross over. 29At that time they killed
about ten thousand of the Moabites, all strong,
able-bodied men; no one escaped. 30So Moab
was subdued that day under the hand of Israel.
And the land had rest eighty years.

31 After him came Shamgar son of Anath,
who killed six hundred of the Philistines with an
oxgoad. He too delivered Israel.

4 The Israelites again did what was evil in the
sight of the LORD, after Ehud died. 2So the
LORD sold them into the hand of King Jabin of
Canaan, who reigned in Hazor; the commander
of his army was Sisera, who lived in Harosheth-
ha-goiim. 3Then the Israelites cried out to the
LORD for help; for he had nine hundred chariots
of iron, and had oppressed the Israelites cruelly
twenty years.

4 At that time Deborah, a prophetess, wife
of Lappidoth, was judging Israel. 5She used to
sit under the palm of Deborah between Ramah
and Bethel in the hill country of Ephraim; and
the Israelites came up to her for judgment. 6She
sent and summoned Barak son of Abinoam from
Kedesh in Naphtali, and said to him, "The LORD,
the God of Israel, commands you, 'Go, take position at Mount Tabor, bringing ten thousand from
the tribe of Naphtali and the tribe of Zebulun. 7I
will draw out Sisera, the general of Jabin's army,
to meet you by the Wadi Kishon with his chariots and his troops; and I will give him into your
hand.' " 8Barak said to her, "If you will go with me,
I will go; but if you will not go with me, I will
not go." 9And she said, "I will surely go with you;
nevertheless, the road on which you are going
will not lead to your glory, for the LORD will sell
Sisera into the hand of a woman." Then Deborah
got up and went with Barak to Kedesh. 10Barak
summoned Zebulun and Naphtali to Kedesh;
and ten thousand warriors went up behind him;
and Deborah went up with him.

11 Now Heber the Kenite had separated
from the other Kenites,[b] that is, the descendants
of Hobab the father-in-law of Moses, and had encamped as far away as Elon-bezaanannim, which
is near Kedesh.

12 When Sisera was told that Barak son of
Abinoam had gone up to Mount Tabor, 13Sisera
called out all his chariots, nine hundred chariots
of iron, and all the troops who were with him,
from Harosheth-ha-goiim to the Wadi Kishon.
14Then Deborah said to Barak, "Up! For this is
the day on which the LORD has given Sisera into
your hand. The LORD is indeed going out before
you." So Barak went down from Mount Tabor
with ten thousand warriors following him. 15And
the LORD threw Sisera and all his chariots and
all his army into a panic[c] before Barak; Sisera
got down from his chariot and fled away on foot,
16while Barak pursued the chariots and the army
to Harosheth-ha-goiim. All the army of Sisera fell
by the sword; no one was left.

17 Now Sisera had fled away on foot to the
tent of Jael wife of Heber the Kenite; for there
was peace between King Jabin of Hazor and the
clan of Heber the Kenite. 18Jael came out to meet
Sisera, and said to him, "Turn aside, my lord, turn
aside to me; have no fear." So he turned aside to
her into the tent, and she covered him with a rug.
19Then he said to her, "Please give me a little water
to drink; for I am thirsty." So she opened a skin of
milk and gave him a drink and covered him. 20He
said to her, "Stand at the entrance of the tent, and

[a] Heb *covering his feet* [b] Heb *from the Kain* [c] Heb adds *to the sword*; compare verse 16

if anybody comes and asks you, 'Is anyone here?'
say, 'No.'" 21 But Jael wife of Heber took a tent
peg, and took a hammer in her hand, and went
softly to him and drove the peg into his temple,
until it went down into the ground—he was lying
fast asleep from weariness—and he died. 22 Then,
as Barak came in pursuit of Sisera, Jael went out
to meet him, and said to him, "Come, and I will
show you the man whom you are seeking." So
he went into her tent; and there was Sisera lying
dead, with the tent peg in his temple.

23 So on that day God subdued King Jabin
of Canaan before the Israelites. 24 Then the hand
of the Israelites bore harder and harder on King
Jabin of Canaan, until they destroyed King Jabin
of Canaan.

5 Then Deborah and Barak son of Abinoam
sang on that day, saying:

2 "When locks are long in Israel,
when the people offer themselves
willingly—
bless[a] the LORD!

3 "Hear, O kings; give ear, O princes;
to the LORD I will sing,
I will make melody to the LORD, the God
of Israel.

4 "LORD, when you went out from Seir,
when you marched from the region of
Edom,
the earth trembled,
and the heavens poured,
the clouds indeed poured water.
5 The mountains quaked before the LORD, the
One of Sinai,
before the LORD, the God of Israel.

6 "In the days of Shamgar son of Anath,
in the days of Jael, caravans ceased
and travelers kept to the byways.
7 The peasantry prospered in Israel,
they grew fat on plunder,
because you arose, Deborah,
arose as a mother in Israel.

8 When new gods were chosen,
then war was in the gates.
Was shield or spear to be seen
among forty thousand in Israel?
9 My heart goes out to the commanders of
Israel
who offered themselves willingly among
the people.
Bless the LORD.

10 "Tell of it, you who ride on white donkeys,
you who sit on rich carpets[b]
and you who walk by the way.
11 To the sound of musicians[b] at the watering
places,
there they repeat the triumphs of the
LORD,
the triumphs of his peasantry in Israel.

"Then down to the gates marched the
people of the LORD.

12 "Awake, awake, Deborah!
Awake, awake, utter a song!
Arise, Barak, lead away your captives,
O son of Abinoam.
13 Then down marched the remnant of the
noble;
the people of the LORD marched down for
him[c] against the mighty.

Judges 5:2-31

The Song of Deborah is widely regarded as one of the oldest pieces of Hebrew poetry in Scripture (alongside the Song of Miriam in Exod 15:20-21). Here, however, the Lord is praised not for delivering slaves from Egyptian slave masters but "the peasantry" of the land from the rich and powerful. The passage suggests to some scholars that the origins of Israel are to be found, at least in part, in social conflict within Canaanite society.

—*NE*

[a] Or *You who offer yourselves willingly among the people, bless* [b] Meaning of Heb uncertain [c] Gk: Heb *me*

14 From Ephraim they set out[a] into the valley,[b]
following you, Benjamin, with your kin;
from Machir marched down the
commanders,
and from Zebulun those who bear the
marshal's staff;
15 the chiefs of Issachar came with Deborah,
and Issachar faithful to Barak;
into the valley they rushed out at his heels.
Among the clans of Reuben
there were great searchings of heart.
16 Why did you tarry among the sheepfolds,
to hear the piping for the flocks?
Among the clans of Reuben
there were great searchings of heart.
17 Gilead stayed beyond the Jordan;
and Dan, why did he abide with the ships?
Asher sat still at the coast of the sea,
settling down by his landings.
18 Zebulun is a people that scorned death;
Naphtali too, on the heights of the field.

19 "The kings came, they fought;
then fought the kings of Canaan,
at Taanach, by the waters of Megiddo;
they got no spoils of silver.
20 The stars fought from heaven,
from their courses they fought against
Sisera.
21 The torrent Kishon swept them away,
the onrushing torrent, the torrent Kishon.
March on, my soul, with might!

22 "Then loud beat the horses' hoofs
with the galloping, galloping of his steeds.

23 "Curse Meroz, says the angel of the LORD,
curse bitterly its inhabitants,
because they did not come to the help of the
LORD,
to the help of the LORD against the mighty.

24 "Most blessed of women be Jael,
the wife of Heber the Kenite,
of tent-dwelling women most blessed.

25 He asked water and she gave him milk,
she brought him curds in a lordly bowl.
26 She put her hand to the tent peg
and her right hand to the workmen's
mallet;
she struck Sisera a blow,
she crushed his head,
she shattered and pierced his temple.
27 He sank, he fell,
he lay still at her feet;
at her feet he sank, he fell;
where he sank, there he fell dead.

28 "Out of the window she peered,
the mother of Sisera gazed[c] through the
lattice:
'Why is his chariot so long in coming?
Why tarry the hoofbeats of his chariots?'
29 Her wisest ladies make answer,
indeed, she answers the question herself:
30 'Are they not finding and dividing the
spoil?—
A girl or two for every man;
spoil of dyed stuffs for Sisera,
spoil of dyed stuffs embroidered,
two pieces of dyed work embroidered for
my neck as spoil?'

31 "So perish all your enemies, O LORD!
But may your friends be like the sun as it
rises in its might."

And the land had rest forty years.

6 The Israelites did what was evil in the sight of
the LORD, and the LORD gave them into the
hand of Midian seven years. 2 The hand of Midian
prevailed over Israel; and because of Midian the
Israelites provided for themselves hiding places
in the mountains, caves and strongholds. 3 For
whenever the Israelites put in seed, the Midianites and the Amalekites and the people of the
east would come up against them. 4 They would
encamp against them and destroy the produce of
the land, as far as the neighborhood of Gaza, and
leave no sustenance in Israel, and no sheep or ox

[a] Cn: Heb *From Ephraim their root* [b] Gk: Heb *in Amalek* [c] Gk Compare Tg: Heb *exclaimed*

or donkey. 5 For they and their livestock would come up, and they would even bring their tents, as thick as locusts; neither they nor their camels could be counted; so they wasted the land as they came in. 6 Thus Israel was greatly impoverished because of Midian; and the Israelites cried out to the LORD for help.

7 When the Israelites cried to the LORD on account of the Midianites, 8 the LORD sent a prophet to the Israelites; and he said to them, "Thus says the LORD, the God of Israel: I led you up from Egypt, and brought you out of the house of slavery; 9 and I delivered you from the hand of the Egyptians, and from the hand of all who oppressed you, and drove them out before you, and gave you their land; 10 and I said to you, 'I am the LORD your God; you shall not pay reverence to the gods of the Amorites, in whose land you live.' But you have not given heed to my voice."

11 Now the angel of the LORD came and sat under the oak at Ophrah, which belonged to Joash the Abiezrite, as his son Gideon was beating out wheat in the wine press, to hide it from the Midianites. 12 The angel of the LORD appeared to him and said to him, "The LORD is with you, you mighty warrior." 13 Gideon answered him, "But sir, if the LORD is with us, why then has all this happened to us? And where are all his wonderful deeds that our ancestors recounted to us, saying, 'Did not the LORD bring us up from Egypt?' But now the LORD has cast us off, and given us into the hand of Midian." 14 Then the LORD turned to him and said, "Go in this might of yours and deliver Israel from the hand of Midian; I hereby commission you." 15 He responded, "But sir, how can I deliver Israel? My clan is the weakest in Manasseh, and I am the least in my family." 16 The LORD said to him, "But I will be with you, and you shall strike down the Midianites, every one of them." 17 Then he said to him, "If now I have found favor with you, then show me a sign that it is you who speak with me. 18 Do not depart from here until I come to you, and bring out my present, and set it before you." And he said, "I will stay until you return."

19 So Gideon went into his house and prepared a kid, and unleavened cakes from an ephah of flour; the meat he put in a basket, and the broth he put in a pot, and brought them to him under the oak and presented them. 20 The angel of God said to him, "Take the meat and the unleavened cakes, and put them on this rock, and pour out the broth." And he did so. 21 Then the angel of the LORD reached out the tip of the staff that was in his hand, and touched the meat and the unleavened cakes; and fire sprang up from the rock and consumed the meat and the unleavened cakes; and the angel of the LORD vanished from his sight. 22 Then Gideon perceived that it was the angel of the LORD; and Gideon said, "Help me, Lord GOD! For I have seen the angel of the LORD face to face." 23 But the LORD said to him, "Peace be to you; do not fear, you shall not die." 24 Then Gideon built an altar there to the LORD, and called it, The LORD is peace. To this day it still stands at Ophrah, which belongs to the Abiezrites.

25 That night the LORD said to him, "Take your father's bull, the second bull seven years old, and pull down the altar of Baal that belongs to your father, and cut down the sacred pole[a] that is beside it; 26 and build an altar to the LORD your God on the top of the stronghold here, in proper order; then take the second bull, and offer it as a burnt offering with the wood of the sacred pole[a] that you shall cut down." 27 So Gideon took ten of his servants, and did as the LORD had told him; but because he was too afraid of his family and the townspeople to do it by day, he did it by night.

28 When the townspeople rose early in the morning, the altar of Baal was broken down, and the sacred pole[a] beside it was cut down, and the second bull was offered on the altar that had been built. 29 So they said to one another, "Who has done this?" After searching and inquiring, they were told, "Gideon son of Joash did it." 30 Then the townspeople said to Joash, "Bring out your son, so that he may die, for he has pulled down the altar of Baal and cut down the sacred pole[a] beside it." 31 But Joash said to all who were arrayed against him, "Will you contend for Baal?

[a] Heb *Asherah*

Or will you defend his cause? Whoever contends
for him shall be put to death by morning. If he is a
god, let him contend for himself, because his altar
has been pulled down." 32 Therefore on that day
Gideon[a] was called Jerubbaal, that is to say, "Let
Baal contend against him," because he pulled
down his altar.

33 Then all the Midianites and the Amalekites and the people of the east came together, and
crossing the Jordan they encamped in the Valley
of Jezreel. 34 But the spirit of the LORD took possession of Gideon; and he sounded the trumpet,
and the Abiezrites were called out to follow him.
35 He sent messengers throughout all Manasseh,
and they too were called out to follow him. He
also sent messengers to Asher, Zebulun, and
Naphtali, and they went up to meet them.

36 Then Gideon said to God, "In order to
see whether you will deliver Israel by my hand,
as you have said, 37 I am going to lay a fleece of
wool on the threshing floor; if there is dew on
the fleece alone, and it is dry on all the ground,
then I shall know that you will deliver Israel
by my hand, as you have said." 38 And it was so.
When he rose early next morning and squeezed
the fleece, he wrung enough dew from the fleece
to fill a bowl with water. 39 Then Gideon said to
God, "Do not let your anger burn against me, let
me speak one more time; let me, please, make
trial with the fleece just once more; let it be dry
only on the fleece, and on all the ground let there
be dew." 40 And God did so that night. It was dry
on the fleece only, and on all the ground there
was dew.

7 Then Jerubbaal (that is, Gideon) and all the
troops that were with him rose early and
encamped beside the spring of Harod; and the
camp of Midian was north of them, below[b] the
hill of Moreh, in the valley.

2 The LORD said to Gideon, "The troops with
you are too many for me to give the Midianites
into their hand. Israel would only take the credit
away from me, saying, 'My own hand has delivered me.' 3 Now therefore proclaim this in the
hearing of the troops, 'Whoever is fearful and
trembling, let him return home.'" Thus Gideon
sifted them out;[c] twenty-two thousand returned,
and ten thousand remained.

4 Then the LORD said to Gideon, "The troops
are still too many; take them down to the water
and I will sift them out for you there. When I say,
'This one shall go with you,' he shall go with you;
and when I say, 'This one shall not go with you,'
he shall not go." 5 So he brought the troops down
to the water; and the LORD said to Gideon, "All
those who lap the water with their tongues, as a
dog laps, you shall put to one side; all those who
kneel down to drink, putting their hands to their
mouths,[d] you shall put to the other side." 6 The
number of those that lapped was three hundred;
but all the rest of the troops knelt down to drink
water. 7 Then the LORD said to Gideon, "With the
three hundred that lapped I will deliver you, and
give the Midianites into your hand. Let all the
others go to their homes." 8 So he took the jars of
the troops from their hands,[e] and their trumpets;
and he sent all the rest of Israel back to their own
tents, but retained the three hundred. The camp
of Midian was below him in the valley.

9 That same night the LORD said to him, "Get
up, attack the camp; for I have given it into your
hand. 10 But if you fear to attack, go down to the
camp with your servant Purah; 11 and you shall
hear what they say, and afterward your hands
shall be strengthened to attack the camp." Then
he went down with his servant Purah to the outposts of the armed men that were in the camp.
12 The Midianites and the Amalekites and all the
people of the east lay along the valley as thick as
locusts; and their camels were without number,
countless as the sand on the seashore. 13 When
Gideon arrived, there was a man telling a dream
to his comrade; and he said, "I had a dream, and
in it a cake of barley bread tumbled into the camp
of Midian, and came to the tent, and struck it so
that it fell; it turned upside down, and the tent
collapsed." 14 And his comrade answered, "This is
no other than the sword of Gideon son of Joash,

[a] Heb *he* [b] Heb *from* [c] Cn: Heb *home, and depart from Mount Gilead'"* [d] Heb places the words *putting their hands to their mouths* after the word *lapped* in verse 6 [e] Cn: Heb *So the people took provisions in their hands*

a man of Israel; into his hand God has given Midian and all the army."
15 When Gideon heard the telling of the
dream and its interpretation, he worshiped; and
he returned to the camp of Israel, and said, "Get
up; for the LORD has given the army of Midian
into your hand." 16After he divided the three hundred men into three companies, and put trumpets
into the hands of all of them, and empty jars, with
torches inside the jars, 17he said to them, "Look
at me, and do the same; when I come to the outskirts of the camp, do as I do. 18When I blow the
trumpet, I and all who are with me, then you also
blow the trumpets around the whole camp, and
shout, 'For the LORD and for Gideon!'"
19 So Gideon and the hundred who were
with him came to the outskirts of the camp at the
beginning of the middle watch, when they had
just set the watch; and they blew the trumpets
and smashed the jars that were in their hands.
20So the three companies blew the trumpets and
broke the jars, holding in their left hands the
torches, and in their right hands the trumpets to
blow; and they cried, "A sword for the LORD and
for Gideon!" 21Every man stood in his place all
around the camp, and all the men in camp ran;
they cried out and fled. 22When they blew the
three hundred trumpets, the LORD set every
man's sword against his fellow and against all the
army; and the army fled as far as Beth-shittah
toward Zererah,[a] as far as the border of Abel-
meholah, by Tabbath. 23And the men of Israel
were called out from Naphtali and from Asher
and from all Manasseh, and they pursued after
the Midianites.
24 Then Gideon sent messengers throughout
all the hill country of Ephraim, saying, "Come
down against the Midianites and seize the waters
against them, as far as Beth-barah, and also the
Jordan." So all the men of Ephraim were called
out, and they seized the waters as far as Beth-
barah, and also the Jordan. 25They captured the
two captains of Midian, Oreb and Zeeb; they
killed Oreb at the rock of Oreb, and Zeeb they
killed at the wine press of Zeeb, as they pursued
the Midianites. They brought the heads of Oreb
and Zeeb to Gideon beyond the Jordan.

8 Then the Ephraimites said to him, "What
have you done to us, not to call us when you
went to fight against the Midianites?" And they
upbraided him violently. 2So he said to them,
"What have I done now in comparison with you?
Is not the gleaning of the grapes of Ephraim better than the vintage of Abiezer? 3God has given
into your hands the captains of Midian, Oreb and
Zeeb; what have I been able to do in comparison
with you?" When he said this, their anger against
him subsided.
4 Then Gideon came to the Jordan and
crossed over, he and the three hundred who were
with him, exhausted and famished.[b] 5So he said to
the people of Succoth, "Please give some loaves of
bread to my followers, for they are exhausted, and
I am pursuing Zebah and Zalmunna, the kings of
Midian." 6But the officials of Succoth said, "Do
you already have in your possession the hands of
Zebah and Zalmunna, that we should give bread
to your army?" 7Gideon replied, "Well then, when
the LORD has given Zebah and Zalmunna into
my hand, I will trample your flesh on the thorns
of the wilderness and on briers." 8From there he
went up to Penuel, and made the same request of
them; and the people of Penuel answered him as
the people of Succoth had answered. 9So he said
to the people of Penuel, "When I come back victorious, I will break down this tower."
10 Now Zebah and Zalmunna were in Kar-
kor with their army, about fifteen thousand men,
all who were left of all the army of the people of
the east; for one hundred twenty thousand men
bearing arms had fallen. 11So Gideon went up by
the caravan route east of Nobah and Jogbehah,
and attacked the army; for the army was off its
guard. 12Zebah and Zalmunna fled; and he pursued them and took the two kings of Midian, Zebah and Zalmunna, and threw all the army into
a panic.
13 When Gideon son of Joash returned from
the battle by the ascent of Heres, 14he caught a
young man, one of the people of Succoth, and

[a] Another reading is *Zeredah* [b] Gk: Heb *pursuing*

questioned him; and he listed for him the officials and elders of Succoth, seventy-seven people. 15Then he came to the people of Succoth,
and said, "Here are Zebah and Zalmunna, about
whom you taunted me, saying, 'Do you already
have in your possession the hands of Zebah and
Zalmunna, that we should give bread to your
troops who are exhausted?'" 16So he took the
elders of the city and he took thorns of the wilderness and briers and with them he trampled[a]
the people of Succoth. 17He also broke down the
tower of Penuel, and killed the men of the city.

18 Then he said to Zebah and Zalmunna,
"What about the men whom you killed at Tabor?" They answered, "As you are, so were they,
every one of them; they resembled the sons of a
king." 19And he replied, "They were my brothers,
the sons of my mother; as the LORD lives, if you
had saved them alive, I would not kill you." 20So
he said to Jether his firstborn, "Go kill them!" But
the boy did not draw his sword, for he was afraid,
because he was still a boy. 21Then Zebah and Zalmunna said, "You come and kill us; for as the man
is, so is his strength." So Gideon proceeded to kill
Zebah and Zalmunna; and he took the crescents
that were on the necks of their camels.

22 Then the Israelites said to Gideon, "Rule
over us, you and your son and your grandson
also; for you have delivered us out of the hand of
Midian." 23Gideon said to them, "I will not rule
over you, and my son will not rule over you; the
LORD will rule over you." 24Then Gideon said
to them, "Let me make a request of you; each of
you give me an earring he has taken as booty."
(For the enemy[b] had golden earrings, because
they were Ishmaelites.) 25"We will willingly give
them," they answered. So they spread a garment,
and each threw into it an earring he had taken as
booty. 26The weight of the golden earrings that he
requested was one thousand seven hundred shekels of gold (apart from the crescents and the pendants and the purple garments worn by the kings
of Midian, and the collars that were on the necks
of their camels). 27Gideon made an ephod of it
and put it in his town, in Ophrah; and all Israel
prostituted themselves to it there, and it became
a snare to Gideon and to his family. 28So Midian
was subdued before the Israelites, and they lifted
up their heads no more. So the land had rest forty
years in the days of Gideon.

29 Jerubbaal son of Joash went to live in his
own house. 30Now Gideon had seventy sons, his
own offspring, for he had many wives. 31His concubine who was in Shechem also bore him a son,
and he named him Abimelech. 32Then Gideon
son of Joash died at a good old age, and was buried in the tomb of his father Joash at Ophrah of
the Abiezrites.

33 As soon as Gideon died, the Israelites re-
lapsed and prostituted themselves with the Baals,
making Baal-berith their god. 34The Israelites did
not remember the LORD their God, who had rescued them from the hand of all their enemies on
every side; 35and they did not exhibit loyalty to
the house of Jerubbaal (that is, Gideon) in return
for all the good that he had done to Israel.

9 Now Abimelech son of Jerubbaal went to
Shechem to his mother's kinsfolk and said to
them and to the whole clan of his mother's family,
2"Say in the hearing of all the lords of Shechem,
'Which is better for you, that all seventy of the
sons of Jerubbaal rule over you, or that one rule
over you?' Remember also that I am your bone
and your flesh." 3So his mother's kinsfolk spoke
all these words on his behalf in the hearing of all
the lords of Shechem; and their hearts inclined
to follow Abimelech, for they said, "He is our
brother." 4They gave him seventy pieces of silver
out of the temple of Baal-berith with which Abimelech hired worthless and reckless fellows, who
followed him. 5He went to his father's house at
Ophrah, and killed his brothers the sons of Jerubbaal, seventy men, on one stone; but Jotham,
the youngest son of Jerubbaal, survived, for he
hid himself. 6Then all the lords of Shechem and
all Beth-millo came together, and they went and
made Abimelech king, by the oak of the pillar[c] at
Shechem.

7 When it was told to Jotham, he went and
stood on the top of Mount Gerizim, and cried

[a] With verse 7, Compare Gk: Heb *he taught* [b] Heb *they* [c] Cn: Meaning of Heb uncertain

aloud and said to them, "Listen to me, you lords of Shechem, so that God may listen to you.

8 The trees once went out
to anoint a king over themselves.
So they said to the olive tree,
'Reign over us.'
9 The olive tree answered them,
'Shall I stop producing my rich oil
by which gods and mortals are honored,
and go to sway over the trees?'
10 Then the trees said to the fig tree,
'You come and reign over us.'
11 But the fig tree answered them,
'Shall I stop producing my sweetness
and my delicious fruit,
and go to sway over the trees?'
12 Then the trees said to the vine,
'You come and reign over us.'
13 But the vine said to them,
'Shall I stop producing my wine
that cheers gods and mortals,
and go to sway over the trees?'
14 So all the trees said to the bramble,
'You come and reign over us.'
15 And the bramble said to the trees,
'If in good faith you are anointing me king
over you,
then come and take refuge in my shade;
but if not, let fire come out of the bramble
and devour the cedars of Lebanon.'

16 "Now therefore, if you acted in good faith
and honor when you made Abimelech king, and if
you have dealt well with Jerubbaal and his house,
and have done to him as his actions deserved—
17 for my father fought for you, and risked his life,
and rescued you from the hand of Midian; 18 but
you have risen up against my father's house this
day, and have killed his sons, seventy men on one
stone, and have made Abimelech, the son of his
slave woman, king over the lords of Shechem,
because he is your kinsman— 19 if, I say, you
have acted in good faith and honor with Jerubbaal and with his house this day, then rejoice in
Abimelech, and let him also rejoice in you; 20 but
if not, let fire come out from Abimelech, and devour the lords of Shechem, and Beth-millo; and
let fire come out from the lords of Shechem, and
from Beth-millo, and devour Abimelech." 21 Then
Jotham ran away and fled, going to Beer, where he
remained for fear of his brother Abimelech.

22 Abimelech ruled over Israel three years.
23 But God sent an evil spirit between Abimelech
and the lords of Shechem; and the lords of
Shechem dealt treacherously with Abimelech.
24 This happened so that the violence done to the
seventy sons of Jerubbaal might be avenged[a] and
their blood be laid on their brother Abimelech,
who killed them, and on the lords of Shechem,
who strengthened his hands to kill his brothers.
25 So, out of hostility to him, the lords of Shechem
set ambushes on the mountain tops. They robbed
all who passed by them along that way; and it was
reported to Abimelech.

26 When Gaal son of Ebed moved into
Shechem with his kinsfolk, the lords of Shechem
put confidence in him. 27 They went out into the
field and gathered the grapes from their vineyards, trod them, and celebrated. Then they went
into the temple of their god, ate and drank, and
ridiculed Abimelech. 28 Gaal son of Ebed said,
"Who is Abimelech, and who are we of Shechem,
that we should serve him? Did not the son of
Jerubbaal and Zebul his officer serve the men of
Hamor father of Shechem? Why then should we
serve him? 29 If only this people were under my
command! Then I would remove Abimelech; I
would say[b] to him, 'Increase your army, and come
out.' "

30 When Zebul the ruler of the city heard the
words of Gaal son of Ebed, his anger was kindled.
31 He sent messengers to Abimelech at Arumah,[c]
saying, "Look, Gaal son of Ebed and his kinsfolk
have come to Shechem, and they are stirring up[d]
the city against you. 32 Now therefore, go by night,
you and the troops that are with you, and lie in
wait in the fields. 33 Then early in the morning, as
soon as the sun rises, get up and rush on the city;
and when he and the troops that are with him
come out against you, you may deal with them as
best you can."

[a] Heb *might come* [b] Gk: Heb *and he said* [c] Cn See 9.41. Heb *Tormah* [d] Cn: Heb *are besieging*

34 So Abimelech and all the troops with him
got up by night and lay in wait against Shechem in
four companies. 35 When Gaal son of Ebed went
out and stood in the entrance of the gate of the
city, Abimelech and the troops with him rose
from the ambush. 36 And when Gaal saw them,
he said to Zebul, "Look, people are coming down
from the mountain tops!" And Zebul said to him,
"The shadows on the mountains look like people
to you." 37 Gaal spoke again and said, "Look, people are coming down from Tabbur-erez, and one
company is coming from the direction of Elon-
meonenim."[a] 38 Then Zebul said to him, "Where
is your boast[b] now, you who said, 'Who is Abimelech, that we should serve him?' Are not these
the troops you made light of? Go out now and
fight with them." 39 So Gaal went out at the head
of the lords of Shechem, and fought with Abimelech. 40 Abimelech chased him, and he fled before him. Many fell wounded, up to the entrance
of the gate. 41 So Abimelech resided at Arumah;
and Zebul drove out Gaal and his kinsfolk, so that
they could not live on at Shechem.

42 On the following day the people went
out into the fields. When Abimelech was told,
43 he took his troops and divided them into three
companies, and lay in wait in the fields. When he
looked and saw the people coming out of the city,
he rose against them and killed them. 44 Abimelech and the company that was[c] with him rushed
forward and stood at the entrance of the gate of
the city, while the two companies rushed on all
who were in the fields and killed them. 45 Abimelech fought against the city all that day; he took
the city, and killed the people that were in it; and
he razed the city and sowed it with salt.

46 When all the lords of the Tower of
Shechem heard of it, they entered the stronghold
of the temple of El-berith. 47 Abimelech was told
that all the lords of the Tower of Shechem were
gathered together. 48 So Abimelech went up to
Mount Zalmon, he and all the troops that were
with him. Abimelech took an ax in his hand, cut
down a bundle of brushwood, and took it up and
laid it on his shoulder. Then he said to the troops
with him, "What you have seen me do, do quickly,
as I have done." 49 So every one of the troops cut
down a bundle and following Abimelech put it
against the stronghold, and they set the stronghold on fire over them, so that all the people of
the Tower of Shechem also died, about a thousand men and women.

50 Then Abimelech went to Thebez, and encamped against Thebez, and took it. 51 But there
was a strong tower within the city, and all the men
and women and all the lords of the city fled to it
and shut themselves in; and they went to the roof
of the tower. 52 Abimelech came to the tower, and
fought against it, and came near to the entrance
of the tower to burn it with fire. 53 But a certain
woman threw an upper millstone on Abimelech's
head, and crushed his skull. 54 Immediately he
called to the young man who carried his armor
and said to him, "Draw your sword and kill me,
so people will not say about me, 'A woman killed
him.'" So the young man thrust him through, and
he died. 55 When the Israelites saw that Abimelech
was dead, they all went home. 56 Thus God repaid
Abimelech for the crime he committed against
his father in killing his seventy brothers; 57 and
God also made all the wickedness of the people
of Shechem fall back on their heads, and on them
came the curse of Jotham son of Jerubbaal.

10 After Abimelech, Tola son of Puah son
of Dodo, a man of Issachar, who lived at
Shamir in the hill country of Ephraim, rose to deliver Israel. 2 He judged Israel twenty-three years.
Then he died, and was buried at Shamir.

3 After him came Jair the Gileadite, who
judged Israel twenty-two years. 4 He had thirty
sons who rode on thirty donkeys; and they had
thirty towns, which are in the land of Gilead, and
are called Havvoth-jair to this day. 5 Jair died, and
was buried in Kamon.

6 The Israelites again did what was evil in the
sight of the LORD, worshiping the Baals and the
Astartes, the gods of Aram, the gods of Sidon,
the gods of Moab, the gods of the Ammonites,
and the gods of the Philistines. Thus they abandoned the LORD, and did not worship him. 7 So

[a] That is *Diviners' Oak* [b] Heb *mouth* [c] Vg and some Gk Mss: Heb *companies that were*

the anger of the LORD was kindled against Israel,
and he sold them into the hand of the Philistines
and into the hand of the Ammonites, 8and they
crushed and oppressed the Israelites that year.
For eighteen years they oppressed all the Israelites that were beyond the Jordan in the land of the
Amorites, which is in Gilead. 9The Ammonites
also crossed the Jordan to fight against Judah and
against Benjamin and against the house of
Ephraim; so that Israel was greatly distressed.

10 So the Israelites cried to the LORD, saying, "We have sinned against you, because we
have abandoned our God and have worshiped the
Baals." 11And the LORD said to the Israelites, "Did
I not deliver you[a] from the Egyptians and from
the Amorites, from the Ammonites and from the
Philistines? 12The Sidonians also, and the Amalekites, and the Maonites, oppressed you; and you
cried to me, and I delivered you out of their hand.
13Yet you have abandoned me and worshiped
other gods; therefore I will deliver you no more.
14Go and cry to the gods whom you have chosen;
let them deliver you in the time of your distress."
15And the Israelites said to the LORD, "We have
sinned; do to us whatever seems good to you; but
deliver us this day!" 16So they put away the foreign
gods from among them and worshiped the LORD;
and he could no longer bear to see Israel suffer.

17 Then the Ammonites were called to arms,
and they encamped in Gilead; and the Israelites
came together, and they encamped at Mizpah.
18The commanders of the people of Gilead said
to one another, "Who will begin the fight against
the Ammonites? He shall be head over all the inhabitants of Gilead."

11 Now Jephthah the Gileadite, the son of a
prostitute, was a mighty warrior. Gilead
was the father of Jephthah. 2Gilead's wife also
bore him sons; and when his wife's sons grew up,
they drove Jephthah away, saying to him, "You
shall not inherit anything in our father's house;
for you are the son of another woman." 3Then
Jephthah fled from his brothers and lived in the
land of Tob. Outlaws collected around Jephthah
and went raiding with him.

4 After a time the Ammonites made war
against Israel. 5And when the Ammonites made
war against Israel, the elders of Gilead went to
bring Jephthah from the land of Tob. 6They said
to Jephthah, "Come and be our commander, so
that we may fight with the Ammonites." 7But
Jephthah said to the elders of Gilead, "Are you
not the very ones who rejected me and drove me
out of my father's house? So why do you come to
me now when you are in trouble?" 8The elders of
Gilead said to Jephthah, "Nevertheless, we have
now turned back to you, so that you may go with
us and fight with the Ammonites, and become
head over us, over all the inhabitants of Gilead."
9Jephthah said to the elders of Gilead, "If you
bring me home again to fight with the Ammonites, and the LORD gives them over to me, I will
be your head." 10And the elders of Gilead said to
Jephthah, "The LORD will be witness between
us; we will surely do as you say." 11So Jephthah
went with the elders of Gilead, and the people
made him head and commander over them; and
Jephthah spoke all his words before the LORD at
Mizpah.

12 Then Jephthah sent messengers to the
king of the Ammonites and said, "What is there
between you and me, that you have come to me
to fight against my land?" 13The king of the Ammonites answered the messengers of Jephthah,
"Because Israel, on coming from Egypt, took
away my land from the Arnon to the Jabbok and
to the Jordan; now therefore restore it peaceably."
14Once again Jephthah sent messengers to the
king of the Ammonites 15and said to him: "Thus
says Jephthah: Israel did not take away the land of
Moab or the land of the Ammonites, 16but when
they came up from Egypt, Israel went through
the wilderness to the Red Sea[b] and came to
Kadesh. 17Israel then sent messengers to the king
of Edom, saying, 'Let us pass through your land';
but the king of Edom would not listen. They also
sent to the king of Moab, but he would not consent. So Israel remained at Kadesh. 18Then they
journeyed through the wilderness, went around
the land of Edom and the land of Moab, arrived

[a] Heb lacks *Did I not deliver you* [b] Or *Sea of Reeds*

on the east side of the land of Moab, and camped
on the other side of the Arnon. They did not
enter the territory of Moab, for the Arnon was
the boundary of Moab. [19]Israel then sent messengers to King Sihon of the Amorites, king of
Heshbon; and Israel said to him, 'Let us pass
through your land to our country.' [20]But Sihon
did not trust Israel to pass through his territory;
so Sihon gathered all his people together, and encamped at Jahaz, and fought with Israel. [21]Then
the LORD, the God of Israel, gave Sihon and all
his people into the hand of Israel, and they defeated them; so Israel occupied all the land of the
Amorites, who inhabited that country. [22]They occupied all the territory of the Amorites from the
Arnon to the Jabbok and from the wilderness to
the Jordan. [23]So now the LORD, the God of Israel, has conquered the Amorites for the benefit
of his people Israel. Do you intend to take their
place? [24]Should you not possess what your god
Chemosh gives you to possess? And should we
not be the ones to possess everything that the
LORD our God has conquered for our benefit?
[25]Now are you any better than King Balak son of
Zippor of Moab? Did he ever enter into conflict
with Israel, or did he ever go to war with them?
[26]While Israel lived in Heshbon and its villages,
and in Aroer and its villages, and in all the towns
that are along the Arnon, three hundred years,
why did you not recover them within that time?
[27]It is not I who have sinned against you, but you
are the one who does me wrong by making war
on me. Let the LORD, who is judge, decide today
for the Israelites or for the Ammonites." [28]But the
king of the Ammonites did not heed the message
that Jephthah sent him.

29 Then the spirit of the LORD came upon
Jephthah, and he passed through Gilead and
Manasseh. He passed on to Mizpah of Gilead,
and from Mizpah of Gilead he passed on to the
Ammonites. [30]And Jephthah made a vow to the
LORD, and said, "If you will give the Ammonites
into my hand, [31]then whoever comes out of the
doors of my house to meet me, when I return victorious from the Ammonites, shall be the LORD's,
to be offered up by me as a burnt offering." [32]So
Jephthah crossed over to the Ammonites to fight
against them; and the LORD gave them into his
hand. [33]He inflicted a massive defeat on them
from Aroer to the neighborhood of Minnith,
twenty towns, and as far as Abel-keramim. So the
Ammonites were subdued before the people of
Israel.

34 Then Jephthah came to his home at Mizpah; and there was his daughter coming out to
meet him with timbrels and with dancing. She
was his only child; he had no son or daughter except her. [35]When he saw her, he tore his clothes,

Judges 11:29-40

The horrible tragedy of Jephthah's daughter is told here. Jephthah, one of the judges, was the son of an Israelite father and a Canaanite mother, and was therefore driven from his home and disinherited (11:1-2). Turned to banditry, his reputation grew until the people of Gilead sought his help against Ammonite invaders. Jephthah agrees and makes a rash vow: if God grants victory, he will sacrifice as a thank offering the first person he encounters upon return home. Tragically it is his own *daughter,* unnamed here, that he meets first, and slays. Peggy L. Day comments:

> Israelite women told the story of Jephthah's daughter in the context of a rite of passage from immaturity to adolescence. In her landmark work *In a Different Voice,* Carol Gilligan has traced women's moral development through an adolescent stage of total self-sacrifice to mature recognition that they must take their own well-being as well as others' well-being into account when making moral decisions.... [W]omen today...would do well to hear Gilligan's voice as it resonates with the words of Jepththah's daughter who, as archetype of female adolescence, resolved a moral dilemma by completely ignoring her own well-being.[21]

— ***DB***

and said, "Alas, my daughter! You have brought
me very low; you have become the cause of great
trouble to me. For I have opened my mouth to
the LORD, and I cannot take back my vow." 36 She
said to him, "My father, if you have opened your
mouth to the LORD, do to me according to what
has gone out of your mouth, now that the LORD
has given you vengeance against your enemies,
the Ammonites." 37 And she said to her father,
"Let this thing be done for me: Grant me two
months, so that I may go and wander[a] on the
mountains, and bewail my virginity, my companions and I." 38 "Go," he said and sent her away for
two months. So she departed, she and her companions, and bewailed her virginity on the mountains. 39 At the end of two months, she returned to
her father, who did with her according to the vow
he had made. She had never slept with a man. So
there arose an Israelite custom that 40 for four days
every year the daughters of Israel would go out to
lament the daughter of Jephthah the Gileadite.

12 The men of Ephraim were called to arms,
and they crossed to Zaphon and said
to Jephthah, "Why did you cross over to fight
against the Ammonites, and did not call us to go
with you? We will burn your house down over
you!" 2 Jephthah said to them, "My people and
I were engaged in conflict with the Ammonites
who oppressed us[b] severely. But when I called
you, you did not deliver me from their hand.
3 When I saw that you would not deliver me, I
took my life in my hand, and crossed over against
the Ammonites, and the LORD gave them into my
hand. Why then have you come up to me this day,
to fight against me?" 4 Then Jephthah gathered all
the men of Gilead and fought with Ephraim; and
the men of Gilead defeated Ephraim, because
they said, "You are fugitives from Ephraim, you
Gileadites—in the heart of Ephraim and Manasseh."[c] 5 Then the Gileadites took the fords of
the Jordan against the Ephraimites. Whenever
one of the fugitives of Ephraim said, "Let me
go over," the men of Gilead would say to him,
"Are you an Ephraimite?" When he said, "No,"
6 they said to him, "Then say Shibboleth," and he
said, "Sibboleth," for he could not pronounce it
right. Then they seized him and killed him at the
fords of the Jordan. Forty-two thousand of the
Ephraimites fell at that time.

7 Jephthah judged Israel six years. Then
Jephthah the Gileadite died, and was buried in
his town in Gilead.[d]

8 After him Ibzan of Bethlehem judged Israel. 9 He had thirty sons. He gave his thirty daughters in marriage outside his clan and brought in
thirty young women from outside for his sons.
He judged Israel seven years. 10 Then Ibzan died,
and was buried at Bethlehem.

11 After him Elon the Zebulunite judged Israel; and he judged Israel ten years. 12 Then Elon
the Zebulunite died, and was buried at Aijalon in
the land of Zebulun.

13 After him Abdon son of Hillel the Pirathonite judged Israel. 14 He had forty sons and
thirty grandsons, who rode on seventy donkeys;
he judged Israel eight years. 15 Then Abdon son of
Hillel the Pirathonite died, and was buried at Pirathon in the land of Ephraim, in the hill country
of the Amalekites.

13 The Israelites again did what was evil in
the sight of the LORD, and the LORD gave
them into the hand of the Philistines forty years.

2 There was a certain man of Zorah, of the
tribe of the Danites, whose name was Manoah.
His wife was barren, having borne no children.
3 And the angel of the LORD appeared to the
woman and said to her, "Although you are barren,
having borne no children, you shall conceive and
bear a son. 4 Now be careful not to drink wine or
strong drink, or to eat anything unclean, 5 for you
shall conceive and bear a son. No razor is to come
on his head, for the boy shall be a nazirite[e] to God
from birth. It is he who shall begin to deliver Israel from the hand of the Philistines." 6 Then the
woman came and told her husband, "A man of
God came to me, and his appearance was like that
of an angel[f] of God, most awe-inspiring; I did not
ask him where he came from, and he did not tell

[a] Cn: Heb *go down* [b] Gk OL, Syr H: Heb lacks *who oppressed us* [c] Meaning of Heb uncertain: Gk omits *because . . . Manasseh* [d] Gk: Heb *in the towns of Gilead* [e] That is *one separated* or *one consecrated* [f] Or *the angel*

me his name; 7 but he said to me, 'You shall conceive and bear a son. So then drink no wine or
strong drink, and eat nothing unclean, for the boy
shall be a nazirite[a] to God from birth to the day
of his death.'"
8 Then Manoah entreated the LORD, and
said, "O LORD, I pray, let the man of God whom
you sent come to us again and teach us what we
are to do concerning the boy who will be born."
9 God listened to Manoah, and the angel of God
came again to the woman as she sat in the field;
but her husband Manoah was not with her. 10 So
the woman ran quickly and told her husband,
"The man who came to me the other day has appeared to me." 11 Manoah got up and followed his
wife, and came to the man and said to him, "Are
you the man who spoke to this woman?" And he
said, "I am." 12 Then Manoah said, "Now when
your words come true, what is to be the boy's rule
of life; what is he to do?" 13 The angel of the LORD
said to Manoah, "Let the woman give heed to all
that I said to her. 14 She may not eat of anything
that comes from the vine. She is not to drink wine
or strong drink, or eat any unclean thing. She is to
observe everything that I commanded her."
15 Manoah said to the angel of the LORD,
"Allow us to detain you, and prepare a kid for
you." 16 The angel of the LORD said to Manoah,
"If you detain me, I will not eat your food; but if
you want to prepare a burnt offering, then offer it
to the LORD." (For Manoah did not know that he
was the angel of the LORD.) 17 Then Manoah said
to the angel of the LORD, "What is your name, so
that we may honor you when your words come
true?" 18 But the angel of the LORD said to him,
"Why do you ask my name? It is too wonderful."
19 So Manoah took the kid with the grain
offering, and offered it on the rock to the LORD,
to him who works[b] wonders.[c] 20 When the flame
went up toward heaven from the altar, the angel
of the LORD ascended in the flame of the altar
while Manoah and his wife looked on; and they
fell on their faces to the ground. 21 The angel of
the LORD did not appear again to Manoah and
his wife. Then Manoah realized that it was the angel of the LORD. 22 And Manoah said to his wife,
"We shall surely die, for we have seen God." 23 But
his wife said to him, "If the LORD had meant to
kill us, he would not have accepted a burnt offering and a grain offering at our hands, or shown
us all these things, or now announced to us such
things as these."
24 The woman bore a son, and named him
Samson. The boy grew, and the LORD blessed
him. 25 The spirit of the LORD began to stir him in
Mahaneh-dan, between Zorah and Eshtaol.

14 Once Samson went down to Timnah, and
at Timnah he saw a Philistine woman.
2 Then he came up, and told his father and mother,
"I saw a Philistine woman at Timnah; now get her
for me as my wife." 3 But his father and mother
said to him, "Is there not a woman among your
kin, or among all our[d] people, that you must go to
take a wife from the uncircumcised Philistines?"
But Samson said to his father, "Get her for me,
because she pleases me." 4 His father and mother
did not know that this was from the LORD; for
he was seeking a pretext to act against the Philistines. At that time the Philistines had dominion
over Israel.
5 Then Samson went down with his father
and mother to Timnah. When he came to the
vineyards of Timnah, suddenly a young lion
roared at him. 6 The spirit of the LORD rushed on
him, and he tore the lion apart barehanded as one
might tear apart a kid. But he did not tell his father
or his mother what he had done. 7 Then he went
down and talked with the woman, and she pleased
Samson. 8 After a while he returned to marry her,
and he turned aside to see the carcass of the lion,
and there was a swarm of bees in the body of the
lion, and honey. 9 He scraped it out into his hands,
and went on, eating as he went. When he came to
his father and mother, he gave some to them, and
they ate it. But he did not tell them that he had
taken the honey from the carcass of the lion.
10 His father went down to the woman, and
Samson made a feast there as the young men

[a] That is *one separated* or *one consecrated* [b] Gk Vg: Heb *and working* [c] Heb *wonders, while Manoah and his wife looked on*
[d] Cn: Heb *my*

were accustomed to do. 11When the people saw
him, they brought thirty companions to be with
him. 12Samson said to them, "Let me now put a
riddle to you. If you can explain it to me within
the seven days of the feast, and find it out, then I
will give you thirty linen garments and thirty festal garments. 13But if you cannot explain it to me,
then you shall give me thirty linen garments and
thirty festal garments." So they said to him, "Ask
your riddle; let us hear it." 14He said to them,

"Out of the eater came something to eat.
Out of the strong came something sweet."

But for three days they could not explain the
riddle.

15 On the fourth[a] day they said to Samson's
wife, "Coax your husband to explain the riddle to
us, or we will burn you and your father's house
with fire. Have you invited us here to impoverish
us?" 16So Samson's wife wept before him, saying,
"You hate me; you do not really love me. You have
asked a riddle of my people, but you have not explained it to me." He said to her, "Look, I have not
told my father or my mother. Why should I tell
you?" 17She wept before him the seven days that
their feast lasted; and because she nagged him, on
the seventh day he told her. Then she explained
the riddle to her people. 18The men of the town
said to him on the seventh day before the sun
went down,

"What is sweeter than honey?
What is stronger than a lion?"

And he said to them,

"If you had not plowed with my heifer,
you would not have found out my riddle."

19Then the spirit of the LORD rushed on him, and
he went down to Ashkelon. He killed thirty men
of the town, took their spoil, and gave the festal
garments to those who had explained the riddle.
In hot anger he went back to his father's house.
20And Samson's wife was given to his companion,
who had been his best man.

15 After a while, at the time of the wheat harvest, Samson went to visit his wife, bringing along a kid. He said, "I want to go into my
wife's room." But her father would not allow him
to go in. 2Her father said, "I was sure that you had
rejected her; so I gave her to your companion. Is
not her younger sister prettier than she? Why not
take her instead?" 3Samson said to them, "This
time, when I do mischief to the Philistines, I will
be without blame." 4So Samson went and caught
three hundred foxes, and took some torches; and
he turned the foxes[b] tail to tail, and put a torch between each pair of tails. 5When he had set fire to
the torches, he let the foxes go into the standing
grain of the Philistines, and burned up the shocks
and the standing grain, as well as the vineyards
and[c] olive groves. 6Then the Philistines asked,
"Who has done this?" And they said, "Samson,
the son-in-law of the Timnite, because he has
taken Samson's wife and given her to his companion." So the Philistines came up, and burned her
and her father. 7Samson said to them, "If this is
what you do, I swear I will not stop until I have
taken revenge on you." 8He struck them down
hip and thigh with great slaughter; and he went
down and stayed in the cleft of the rock of Etam.

9 Then the Philistines came up and encamped
in Judah, and made a raid on Lehi. 10The men of
Judah said, "Why have you come up against us?"
They said, "We have come up to bind Samson,
to do to him as he did to us." 11Then three thousand men of Judah went down to the cleft of the
rock of Etam, and they said to Samson, "Do you
not know that the Philistines are rulers over us?
What then have you done to us?" He replied, "As
they did to me, so I have done to them." 12They
said to him, "We have come down to bind you, so
that we may give you into the hands of the Philistines." Samson answered them, "Swear to me that
you yourselves will not attack me." 13They said to
him, "No, we will only bind you and give you into
their hands; we will not kill you." So they bound
him with two new ropes, and brought him up
from the rock.

14 When he came to Lehi, the Philistines
came shouting to meet him; and the spirit of the
LORD rushed on him, and the ropes that were on
his arms became like flax that has caught fire, and
his bonds melted off his hands. 15Then he found

[a] Gk Syr: Heb *seventh* [b] Heb *them* [c] Gk Tg Vg: Heb lacks *and*

a fresh jawbone of a donkey, reached down and
took it, and with it he killed a thousand men.
16 And Samson said,

"With the jawbone of a donkey,
heaps upon heaps,
with the jawbone of a donkey
I have slain a thousand men."

17 When he had finished speaking, he threw away
the jawbone; and that place was called Ramath-
lehi.[a]

18 By then he was very thirsty, and he called
on the LORD, saying, "You have granted this great
victory by the hand of your servant. Am I now to
die of thirst, and fall into the hands of the uncircumcised?" 19 So God split open the hollow place
that is at Lehi, and water came from it. When he
drank, his spirit returned, and he revived. Therefore it was named En-hakkore,[b] which is at Lehi
to this day. 20 And he judged Israel in the days of
the Philistines twenty years.

16 Once Samson went to Gaza, where he
saw a prostitute and went in to her. 2 The
Gazites were told,[c] "Samson has come here." So
they circled around and lay in wait for him all
night at the city gate. They kept quiet all night,
thinking, "Let us wait until the light of the morning; then we will kill him." 3 But Samson lay only
until midnight. Then at midnight he rose up, took
hold of the doors of the city gate and the two
posts, pulled them up, bar and all, put them on
his shoulders, and carried them to the top of the
hill that is in front of Hebron.

4 After this he fell in love with a woman in
the valley of Sorek, whose name was Delilah.
5 The lords of the Philistines came to her and said
to her, "Coax him, and find out what makes his
strength so great, and how we may overpower
him, so that we may bind him in order to subdue
him; and we will each give you eleven hundred
pieces of silver." 6 So Delilah said to Samson,
"Please tell me what makes your strength so great,
and how you could be bound, so that one could
subdue you." 7 Samson said to her, "If they bind
me with seven fresh bowstrings that are not dried
out, then I shall become weak, and be like anyone
else." 8 Then the lords of the Philistines brought
her seven fresh bowstrings that had not dried
out, and she bound him with them. 9 While men
were lying in wait in an inner chamber, she said
to him, "The Philistines are upon you, Samson!"
But he snapped the bowstrings, as a strand of fi-
ber snaps when it touches the fire. So the secret of
his strength was not known.

10 Then Delilah said to Samson, "You have
mocked me and told me lies; please tell me how
you could be bound." 11 He said to her, "If they
bind me with new ropes that have not been used,
then I shall become weak, and be like anyone
else." 12 So Delilah took new ropes and bound him
with them, and said to him, "The Philistines are
upon you, Samson!" (The men lying in wait were
in an inner chamber.) But he snapped the ropes
off his arms like a thread.

13 Then Delilah said to Samson, "Until now
you have mocked me and told me lies; tell me how
you could be bound." He said to her, "If you weave
the seven locks of my head with the web and make
it tight with the pin, then I shall become weak, and
be like anyone else." 14 So while he slept, Delilah
took the seven locks of his head and wove them
into the web,[d] and made them tight with the pin.
Then she said to him, "The Philistines are upon
you, Samson!" But he awoke from his sleep, and
pulled away the pin, the loom, and the web.

15 Then she said to him, "How can you say,
'I love you,' when your heart is not with me? You
have mocked me three times now and have not
told me what makes your strength so great." 16 Finally, after she had nagged him with her words
day after day, and pestered him, he was tired to
death. 17 So he told her his whole secret, and said
to her, "A razor has never come upon my head; for
I have been a nazirite[e] to God from my mother's
womb. If my head were shaved, then my strength
would leave me; I would become weak, and be
like anyone else."

18 When Delilah realized that he had told her
his whole secret, she sent and called the lords of

[a] That is *The Hill of the Jawbone* [b] That is *The Spring of the One who Called* [c] Gk: Heb lacks *were told*
[d] Compare Gk: in verses 13–14, Heb lacks *and make it tight . . . into the web* [e] That is *one separated* or *one consecrated*

the Philistines, saying, "This time come up, for he
has told his whole secret to me." Then the lords of
the Philistines came up to her, and brought the
money in their hands. 19She let him fall asleep
on her lap; and she called a man, and had him
shave off the seven locks of his head. He began
to weaken,[a] and his strength left him. 20Then she
said, "The Philistines are upon you, Samson!"
When he awoke from his sleep, he thought, "I
will go out as at other times, and shake myself
free." But he did not know that the LORD had left
him. 21So the Philistines seized him and gouged
out his eyes. They brought him down to Gaza and
bound him with bronze shackles; and he ground
at the mill in the prison. 22But the hair of his head
began to grow again after it had been shaved.

23 Now the lords of the Philistines gathered
to offer a great sacrifice to their god Dagon, and
to rejoice; for they said, "Our god has given Samson our enemy into our hand." 24When the people saw him, they praised their god; for they said,
"Our god has given our enemy into our hand,
the ravager of our country, who has killed many
of us." 25And when their hearts were merry, they
said, "Call Samson, and let him entertain us." So
they called Samson out of the prison, and he performed for them. They made him stand between
the pillars; 26and Samson said to the attendant
who held him by the hand, "Let me feel the pillars on which the house rests, so that I may lean
against them." 27Now the house was full of men
and women; all the lords of the Philistines were
there, and on the roof there were about three
thousand men and women, who looked on while
Samson performed.

28 Then Samson called to the LORD and
said, "Lord GOD, remember me and strengthen
me only this once, O God, so that with this one
act of revenge I may pay back the Philistines for
my two eyes."[b] 29And Samson grasped the two
middle pillars on which the house rested, and
he leaned his weight against them, his right hand
on the one and his left hand on the other. 30Then
Samson said, "Let me die with the Philistines."
He strained with all his might; and the house fell
on the lords and all the people who were in it. So
those he killed at his death were more than those
he had killed during his life. 31Then his brothers
and all his family came down and took him and
brought him up and buried him between Zorah
and Eshtaol in the tomb of his father Manoah. He
had judged Israel twenty years.

17 There was a man in the hill country of
Ephraim whose name was Micah. 2He
said to his mother, "The eleven hundred pieces
of silver that were taken from you, about which
you uttered a curse, and even spoke it in my
hearing,—that silver is in my possession; I took it;
but now I will return it to you."[c] And his mother
said, "May my son be blessed by the LORD!"
3Then he returned the eleven hundred pieces of
silver to his mother; and his mother said, "I consecrate the silver to the LORD from my hand for
my son, to make an idol of cast metal." 4So when
he returned the money to his mother, his mother
took two hundred pieces of silver, and gave it to
the silversmith, who made it into an idol of cast
metal; and it was in the house of Micah. 5This
man Micah had a shrine, and he made an ephod
and teraphim, and installed one of his sons, who
became his priest. 6In those days there was no
king in Israel; all the people did what was right in
their own eyes.

7 Now there was a young man of Bethlehem
in Judah, of the clan of Judah. He was a Levite
residing there. 8This man left the town of Bethlehem in Judah, to live wherever he could find
a place. He came to the house of Micah in the
hill country of Ephraim to carry on his work.[d]
9Micah said to him, "From where do you come?"
He replied, "I am a Levite of Bethlehem in Judah, and I am going to live wherever I can find a
place." 10Then Micah said to him, "Stay with me,
and be to me a father and a priest, and I will give
you ten pieces of silver a year, a set of clothes, and
your living."[e] 11The Levite agreed to stay with the

[a] Gk: Heb *She began to torment him* [b] Or *so that I may be avenged upon the Philistines for one of my two eyes* [c] The words *but now I will return it to you* are transposed from the end of verse 3 in Heb [d] Or *Ephraim, continuing his journey* [e] Heb *living, and the Levite went*

man; and the young man became to him like one
of his sons. 12 So Micah installed the Levite, and
the young man became his priest, and was in the
house of Micah. 13 Then Micah said, "Now I know
that the LORD will prosper me, because the Levite has become my priest."

18 In those days there was no king in Israel.
And in those days the tribe of the Dan-
ites was seeking for itself a territory to live in; for
until then no territory among the tribes of Israel
had been allotted to them. 2 So the Danites sent
five valiant men from the whole number of their
clan, from Zorah and from Eshtaol, to spy out the
land and to explore it; and they said to them, "Go,
explore the land." When they came to the hill
country of Ephraim, to the house of Micah, they
stayed there. 3 While they were at Micah's house,
they recognized the voice of the young Levite;
so they went over and asked him, "Who brought
you here? What are you doing in this place? What
is your business here?" 4 He said to them, "Micah
did such and such for me, and he hired me, and I
have become his priest." 5 Then they said to him,
"Inquire of God that we may know whether the
mission we are undertaking will succeed." 6 The
priest replied, "Go in peace. The mission you are
on is under the eye of the LORD."

7 The five men went on, and when they came
to Laish, they observed the people who were there
living securely, after the manner of the Sidonians,
quiet and unsuspecting, lacking[a] nothing on
earth, and possessing wealth.[b] Furthermore, they
were far from the Sidonians and had no dealings
with Aram.[c] 8 When they came to their kinsfolk
at Zorah and Eshtaol, they said to them, "What
do you report?" 9 They said, "Come, let us go up
against them; for we have seen the land, and it is
very good. Will you do nothing? Do not be slow
to go, but enter in and possess the land. 10 When
you go, you will come to an unsuspecting people.
The land is broad—God has indeed given it into
your hands—a place where there is no lack of
anything on earth."

11 Six hundred men of the Danite clan,
armed with weapons of war, set out from Zorah and Eshtaol, 12 and went up and encamped
at Kiriath-jearim in Judah. On this account that
place is called Mahaneh-dan[d] to this day; it is
west of Kiriath-jearim. 13 From there they passed
on to the hill country of Ephraim, and came to
the house of Micah.

14 Then the five men who had gone to spy
out the land (that is, Laish) said to their comrades, "Do you know that in these buildings there
are an ephod, teraphim, and an idol of cast metal?
Now therefore consider what you will do." 15 So
they turned in that direction and came to the
house of the young Levite, at the home of Micah,
and greeted him. 16 While the six hundred men
of the Danites, armed with their weapons of war,
stood by the entrance of the gate, 17 the five men
who had gone to spy out the land proceeded to
enter and take the idol of cast metal, the ephod,
and the teraphim.[e] The priest was standing by the
entrance of the gate with the six hundred men
armed with weapons of war. 18 When the men
went into Micah's house and took the idol of cast
metal, the ephod, and the teraphim, the priest
said to them, "What are you doing?" 19 They said
to him, "Keep quiet! Put your hand over your
mouth, and come with us, and be to us a father
and a priest. Is it better for you to be priest to the
house of one person, or to be priest to a tribe and
clan in Israel?" 20 Then the priest accepted the
offer. He took the ephod, the teraphim, and the
idol, and went along with the people.

21 So they resumed their journey, putting the
little ones, the livestock, and the goods in front
of them. 22 When they were some distance from
the home of Micah, the men who were in the
houses near Micah's house were called out, and
they overtook the Danites. 23 They shouted to the
Danites, who turned around and said to Micah,
"What is the matter that you come with such a
company?" 24 He replied, "You take my gods that
I made, and the priest, and go away, and what
have I left? How then can you ask me, 'What is
the matter?'" 25 And the Danites said to him, "You

[a] Cn Compare 18.10: Meaning of Heb uncertain [b] Meaning of Heb uncertain [c] Symmachus: Heb *with anyone*
[d] That is *Camp of Dan* [e] Compare 17.4, 5; 18.14: Heb *teraphim and the cast metal*

had better not let your voice be heard among us
or else hot-tempered fellows will attack you, and
you will lose your life and the lives of your household." 26Then the Danites went their way. When
Micah saw that they were too strong for him, he
turned and went back to his home.

27 The Danites, having taken what Micah
had made, and the priest who belonged to him,
came to Laish, to a people quiet and unsuspecting, put them to the sword, and burned down
the city. 28There was no deliverer, because it
was far from Sidon and they had no dealings
with Aram.[a] It was in the valley that belongs to
Beth-rehob. They rebuilt the city, and lived in it.
29They named the city Dan, after their ancestor
Dan, who was born to Israel; but the name of the
city was formerly Laish. 30Then the Danites set
up the idol for themselves. Jonathan son of Gershom, son of Moses,[b] and his sons were priests
to the tribe of the Danites until the time the land
went into captivity. 31So they maintained as their
own Micah's idol that he had made, as long as the
house of God was at Shiloh.

19 In those days, when there was no king in
Israel, a certain Levite, residing in the remote parts of the hill country of Ephraim, took
to himself a concubine from Bethlehem in Judah.
2But his concubine became angry with[c] him, and
she went away from him to her father's house at
Bethlehem in Judah, and was there some four
months. 3Then her husband set out after her, to
speak tenderly to her and bring her back. He had
with him his servant and a couple of donkeys.
When he reached[d] her father's house, the girl's
father saw him and came with joy to meet him.
4His father-in-law, the girl's father, made him
stay, and he remained with him three days; so
they ate and drank, and he[e] stayed there. 5On the
fourth day they got up early in the morning, and
he prepared to go; but the girl's father said to his
son-in-law, "Fortify yourself with a bit of food,
and after that you may go." 6So the two men sat
and ate and drank together; and the girl's father
said to the man, "Why not spend the night and
enjoy yourself?" 7When the man got up to go,
his father-in-law kept urging him until he spent
the night there again. 8On the fifth day he got up
early in the morning to leave; and the girl's father
said, "Fortify yourself." So they lingered[f] until the
day declined, and the two of them ate and drank.[g]
9When the man with his concubine and his servant got up to leave, his father-in-law, the girl's father, said to him, "Look, the day has worn on until
it is almost evening. Spend the night. See, the day
has drawn to a close. Spend the night here and
enjoy yourself. Tomorrow you can get up early in
the morning for your journey, and go home."

10 But the man would not spend the night;
he got up and departed, and arrived opposite
Jebus (that is, Jerusalem). He had with him a
couple of saddled donkeys, and his concubine
was with him. 11When they were near Jebus, the
day was far spent, and the servant said to his master, "Come now, let us turn aside to this city of
the Jebusites, and spend the night in it." 12But his
master said to him, "We will not turn aside into a
city of foreigners, who do not belong to the people of Israel; but we will continue on to Gibeah."
13Then he said to his servant, "Come, let us try
to reach one of these places, and spend the night
at Gibeah or at Ramah." 14So they passed on and
went their way; and the sun went down on them
near Gibeah, which belongs to Benjamin. 15They
turned aside there, to go in and spend the night
at Gibeah. He went in and sat down in the open
square of the city, but no one took them in to
spend the night.

16 Then at evening there was an old man
coming from his work in the field. The man was
from the hill country of Ephraim, and he was residing in Gibeah. (The people of the place were
Benjaminites.) 17When the old man looked up
and saw the wayfarer in the open square of the
city, he said, "Where are you going and where do
you come from?" 18He answered him, "We are
passing from Bethlehem in Judah to the remote
parts of the hill country of Ephraim, from which
I come. I went to Bethlehem in Judah; and I am

[a] Cn Compare verse 7: Heb *with anyone* [b] Another reading is *son of Manasseh* [c] Gk OL: Heb *prostituted herself against* [d] Gk: Heb *she brought him to* [e] Compare verse 7 and Gk: Heb *they* [f] Cn: Heb *Linger* [g] Gk: Heb lacks *and drank*

going to my home.[a] Nobody has offered to take
me in. 19We your servants have straw and fodder for our donkeys, with bread and wine for me
and the woman and the young man along with
us. We need nothing more." 20The old man said,
"Peace be to you. I will care for all your wants;
only do not spend the night in the square." 21So
he brought him into his house, and fed the donkeys; they washed their feet, and ate and drank.

22 While they were enjoying themselves, the
men of the city, a perverse lot, surrounded the
house, and started pounding on the door. They
said to the old man, the master of the house,
"Bring out the man who came into your house,
so that we may have intercourse with him." 23And
the man, the master of the house, went out to
them and said to them, "No, my brothers, do
not act so wickedly. Since this man is my guest,
do not do this vile thing. 24Here are my virgin
daughter and his concubine; let me bring them
out now. Ravish them and do whatever you want
to them; but against this man do not do such a
vile thing." 25But the men would not listen to
him. So the man seized his concubine, and put
her out to them. They wantonly raped her, and
abused her all through the night until the morning. And as the dawn began to break, they let her
go. 26As morning appeared, the woman came and
fell down at the door of the man's house where
her master was, until it was light.

27 In the morning her master got up, opened
the doors of the house, and when he went out
to go on his way, there was his concubine lying
at the door of the house, with her hands on the
threshold. 28"Get up," he said to her, "we are going." But there was no answer. Then he put her
on the donkey; and the man set out for his home.
29When he had entered his house, he took a knife,
and grasping his concubine he cut her into twelve
pieces, limb by limb, and sent her throughout all
the territory of Israel. 30Then he commanded the
men whom he sent, saying, "Thus shall you say
to all the Israelites, 'Has such a thing ever happened[b] since the day that the Israelites came up
from the land of Egypt until this day? Consider
it, take counsel, and speak out.' "

20 Then all the Israelites came out, from
Dan to Beer-sheba, including the land of
Gilead, and the congregation assembled in one
body before the LORD at Mizpah. 2The chiefs of
all the people, of all the tribes of Israel, presented
themselves in the assembly of the people of God,
four hundred thousand foot-soldiers bearing
arms. 3(Now the Benjaminites heard that the
people of Israel had gone up to Mizpah.) And the
Israelites said, "Tell us, how did this criminal act
come about?" 4The Levite, the husband of the
woman who was murdered, answered, "I came to
Gibeah that belongs to Benjamin, I and my concubine, to spend the night. 5The lords of Gibeah
rose up against me, and surrounded the house at
night. They intended to kill me, and they raped
my concubine until she died. 6Then I took my
concubine and cut her into pieces, and sent her
throughout the whole extent of Israel's territory;
for they have committed a vile outrage in Israel.
7So now, you Israelites, all of you, give your advice and counsel here."

8 All the people got up as one, saying, "We
will not any of us go to our tents, nor will any of
us return to our houses. 9But now this is what we
will do to Gibeah: we will go up[c] against it by lot.
10We will take ten men of a hundred throughout
all the tribes of Israel, and a hundred of a thousand, and a thousand of ten thousand, to bring
provisions for the troops, who are going to repay[d]
Gibeah of Benjamin for all the disgrace that they
have done in Israel." 11So all the men of Israel
gathered against the city, united as one.

12 The tribes of Israel sent men through all
the tribe of Benjamin, saying, "What crime is
this that has been committed among you? 13Now
then, hand over those scoundrels in Gibeah, so
that we may put them to death, and purge the
evil from Israel." But the Benjaminites would
not listen to their kinsfolk, the Israelites. 14The
Benjaminites came together out of the towns to
Gibeah, to go out to battle against the Israelites.

[a] Gk Compare 19.29. Heb *to the house of the LORD* [b] Compare Gk: Heb 30*And all who saw it said, "Such a thing has not happened or been seen* [c] Gk: Heb lacks *we will go up* [d] Compare Gk: Meaning of Heb uncertain

15 On that day the Benjaminites mustered twenty-six thousand armed men from their towns, besides the inhabitants of Gibeah. 16 Of all this force, there were seven hundred picked men who were left-handed; every one could sling a stone at a hair, and not miss. 17 And the Israelites, apart from Benjamin, mustered four hundred thousand armed men, all of them warriors.

18 The Israelites proceeded to go up to Bethel, where they inquired of God, "Which of us shall go up first to battle against the Benjaminites?" And the LORD answered, "Judah shall go up first."

19 Then the Israelites got up in the morning, and encamped against Gibeah. 20 The Israelites went out to battle against Benjamin; and the Israelites drew up the battle line against them at Gibeah. 21 The Benjaminites came out of Gibeah, and struck down on that day twenty-two thousand of the Israelites. 23[a] The Israelites went up and wept before the LORD until the evening; and they inquired of the LORD, "Shall we again draw near to battle against our kinsfolk the Benjaminites?" And the LORD said, "Go up against them." 22 The Israelites took courage, and again formed the battle line in the same place where they had formed it on the first day.

24 So the Israelites advanced against the Benjaminites the second day. 25 Benjamin moved out against them from Gibeah the second day, and struck down eighteen thousand of the Israelites, all of them armed men. 26 Then all the Israelites, the whole army, went back to Bethel and wept, sitting there before the LORD; they fasted that day until evening. Then they offered burnt offerings and sacrifices of well-being before the LORD. 27 And the Israelites inquired of the LORD (for the ark of the covenant of God was there in those days, 28 and Phinehas son of Eleazar, son of Aaron, ministered before it in those days), saying, "Shall we go out once more to battle against our kinsfolk the Benjaminites, or shall we desist?" The LORD answered, "Go up, for tomorrow I will give them into your hand."

29 So Israel stationed men in ambush around Gibeah. 30 Then the Israelites went up against the Benjaminites on the third day, and set themselves in array against Gibeah, as before. 31 When the Benjaminites went out against the army, they were drawn away from the city. As before they began to inflict casualties on the troops, along the main roads, one of which goes up to Bethel and the other to Gibeah, as well as in the open country, killing about thirty men of Israel. 32 The Benjaminites thought, "They are being routed before us, as previously." But the Israelites said, "Let us retreat and draw them away from the city toward the roads." 33 The main body of the Israelites drew back its battle line to Baal-tamar, while those Israelites who were in ambush rushed out of their place west[b] of Geba. 34 There came against Gibeah ten thousand picked men out of all Israel, and the battle was fierce. But the Benjaminites did not realize that disaster was close upon them.

35 The LORD defeated Benjamin before Israel; and the Israelites destroyed twenty-five thousand one hundred men of Benjamin that day, all of them armed.

36 Then the Benjaminites saw that they were defeated.[c]

The Israelites gave ground to Benjamin, because they trusted to the troops in ambush that they had stationed against Gibeah. 37 The troops in ambush rushed quickly upon Gibeah. Then they put the whole city to the sword. 38 Now the agreement between the main body of Israel and the men in ambush was that when they sent up a cloud of smoke out of the city 39 the main body of Israel should turn in battle. But Benjamin had begun to inflict casualties on the Israelites, killing about thirty of them; so they thought, "Surely they are defeated before us, as in the first battle." 40 But when the cloud, a column of smoke, began to rise out of the city, the Benjaminites looked behind them—and there was the whole city going up in smoke toward the sky! 41 Then the main body of Israel turned, and the Benjaminites were dismayed, for they saw that disaster was close upon them. 42 Therefore they turned away from the Israelites in the direction of the wilderness; but the

[a] Verses 22 and 23 are transposed [b] Gk Vg: Heb *in the plain* [c] This sentence is continued by verse 45.

battle overtook them, and those who came out
of the city[a] were slaughtering them in between.[b]
43 Cutting down[c] the Benjaminites, they pursued
them from Nohah[d] and trod them down as far
as a place east of Gibeah. 44 Eighteen thousand
Benjaminites fell, all of them courageous fighters.
45 When they turned and fled toward the wilderness to the rock of Rimmon, five thousand of them
were cut down on the main roads, and they were
pursued as far as Gidom, and two thousand of
them were slain. 46 So all who fell that day of Benjamin were twenty-five thousand arms-bearing
men, all of them courageous fighters. 47 But six
hundred turned and fled toward the wilderness
to the rock of Rimmon, and remained at the rock
of Rimmon for four months. 48 Meanwhile, the Israelites turned back against the Benjaminites, and
put them to the sword—the city, the people, the
animals, and all that remained. Also the remaining towns they set on fire.

21 Now the Israelites had sworn at Mizpah,
"No one of us shall give his daughter in
marriage to Benjamin." 2 And the people came to
Bethel, and sat there until evening before God,
and they lifted up their voices and wept bitterly.
3 They said, "O LORD, the God of Israel, why has
it come to pass that today there should be one
tribe lacking in Israel?" 4 On the next day, the people got up early, and built an altar there, and offered burnt offerings and sacrifices of well-being.
5 Then the Israelites said, "Which of all the tribes
of Israel did not come up in the assembly to the
LORD?" For a solemn oath had been taken concerning whoever did not come up to the LORD to
Mizpah, saying, "That one shall be put to death."
6 But the Israelites had compassion for Benjamin
their kin, and said, "One tribe is cut off from Israel this day. 7 What shall we do for wives for those
who are left, since we have sworn by the LORD
that we will not give them any of our daughters
as wives?"

8 Then they said, "Is there anyone from
the tribes of Israel who did not come up to the
LORD to Mizpah?" It turned out that no one
from Jabesh-gilead had come to the camp, to the
assembly. 9 For when the roll was called among
the people, not one of the inhabitants of Jabesh-
gilead was there. 10 So the congregation sent
twelve thousand soldiers there and commanded
them, "Go, put the inhabitants of Jabesh-gilead
to the sword, including the women and the little
ones. 11 This is what you shall do; every male and
every woman that has lain with a male you shall
devote to destruction." 12 And they found among
the inhabitants of Jabesh-gilead four hundred
young virgins who had never slept with a man
and brought them to the camp at Shiloh, which is
in the land of Canaan.

13 Then the whole congregation sent word to
the Benjaminites who were at the rock of Rimmon, and proclaimed peace to them. 14 Benjamin returned at that time; and they gave them
the women whom they had saved alive of the
women of Jabesh-gilead; but they did not suffice
for them.

15 The people had compassion on Benjamin because the LORD had made a breach in
the tribes of Israel. 16 So the elders of the congregation said, "What shall we do for wives for
those who are left, since there are no women left
in Benjamin?" 17 And they said, "There must be
heirs for the survivors of Benjamin, in order that
a tribe may not be blotted out from Israel. 18 Yet
we cannot give any of our daughters to them as
wives." For the Israelites had sworn, "Cursed be
anyone who gives a wife to Benjamin." 19 So they
said, "Look, the yearly festival of the LORD is taking place at Shiloh, which is north of Bethel, on
the east of the highway that goes up from Bethel
to Shechem, and south of Lebonah." 20 And they
instructed the Benjaminites, saying, "Go and lie
in wait in the vineyards, 21 and watch; when the
young women of Shiloh come out to dance in
the dances, then come out of the vineyards and
each of you carry off a wife for himself from the
young women of Shiloh, and go to the land of
Benjamin. 22 Then if their fathers or their brothers come to complain to us, we will say to them,

[a] Compare Vg and some Gk Mss: Heb *cities* [b] Compare Syr: Meaning of Heb uncertain [c] Gk: Heb *Surrounding*
[d] Gk: Heb *pursued them at their resting place*

'Be generous and allow us to have them; because
we did not capture in battle a wife for each man.
But neither did you incur guilt by giving your
daughters to them.'" 23The Benjaminites did
so; they took wives for each of them from the
dancers whom they abducted. Then they went
and returned to their territory, and rebuilt the
towns, and lived in them. 24So the Israelites
departed from there at that time by tribes and
families, and they went out from there to their
own territories.

25 In those days there was no king in Israel;
all the people did what was right in their own
eyes.

Ruth

The book of Ruth is the story of the mother of the Messiah. In the Hebrew Bible, David is the most significant character identified as God's *meshiach* or anointed (*christos* in Greek). Jesus of Nazareth is the only character identified as God's anointed in the New Testament. Ruth is named in the genealogies of both David (Ruth 4:17-22) and Jesus (Matt 1:5-16).

As a member of both Jewish and Christian congregations, I am interested in Ruth's nearly identical role in both traditions. As a woman and a feminist biblical scholar, I am also interested in the women's relationships with one another and the sexual undertones in the story of Ruth. As an African American, I am interested in the cultural intersections in the text.

The story of Ruth begins with trauma—she and Orpah are abducted from their home in Moab and forced into marriage in an Israelite family struggling to survive a famine. The "taking" of the women in 1:4 is done with the same verb that describes the abduction and rape of the young girls in Shiloh in Judg 21:23, where it is translated as "abducted." The grooms die before producing children. The three women, Naomi and her daughters-in-law, Ruth and Orpah, are left to fend for themselves. Since the younger women are clearly not pregnant, they are of no use to Naomi, who tries to get rid of them. Ruth, however, decides to cast her lot with Naomi and Naomi's God, while Orpah goes to reclaim her lost life in her homeland.

The Moabite identity of Ruth and Orpah is interesting. Israel and Moab were perpetually embittered. In Israel's accounting, the people of Moab had come into being through an incestuous relationship between Lot and his daughters in Gen 19:37. Throughout the narrative, Ruth is identified as a Moabite woman; she seems never to lose her outsider status in spite of her beautiful poetic vow to Naomi in 1:16-17:

Do not beg me to leave you anymore, woman,
or to turn back from following you, woman.
For where you go, woman, I will go;
where you rest, woman, I will rest;
your people, woman, will be my people;
and your God, woman, will be my God.
Where you die, woman, I will die
and there I will be buried.
May YHWH do this to me and more
if anything but death separates me from you, woman.
(author's translation)

While Naomi laments her circumstances, Ruth goes to work to support them. Naomi's land-owning kinsman notices Ruth following the reapers and gleaning grain in his fields and instructs his laborers to leave her extra grain. He also instructs them not to touch or injure Ruth—a verb now translated as "bother" in 2:9. Boaz's protection of Ruth underscores the vulnerability of poor, hungry women to physical and sexual abuse. It also prompts the question: Did Boaz protect *all* of the vulnerable women on his property?

The dramatic climax of the story is the after-hours tryst between Boaz and Ruth. Naomi advises Ruth to wait until it is dark and Boaz is well fed and intoxicated before lying down with him (3:3). She also tells Ruth to do whatever Boaz tells her, which, combined with the Hebrew expression "uncover his feet" (3:4), has a sexual connotation. (The word for feet in biblical Hebrew is regularly a euphemism for the genitalia.) Boaz accepts Ruth's offer of herself in marriage, and they discuss terms. After this, Boaz tells Ruth to lie back down with him until morning. Their activities are not elaborated upon.

The story of Ruth ends with the withdrawal of another potential suitor, Ruth's marriage to Boaz, and the birth of their son, Obed. At their union, all the people in the community bless Ruth and Boaz. Their prayer is that Ruth will be fertile. When Ruth gives birth, all the women bless Naomi, naming her as the baby's beneficiary; and the women name him Obed, from the verb that means both to serve and to worship.

The story of Ruth ends with the name of David, Ruth's most famous descendant at the point the text was composed, written, and received. The conclusion decenters Ruth in order to make a point about the messiah's lineage: even Israel's greatest king was descended from a poor, vulnerable woman from a despised foreign nation.

— ***Wilda C. Gafney***

1 In the days when the judges ruled, there was
a famine in the land, and a certain man of
Bethlehem in Judah went to live in the country of
Moab, he and his wife and two sons. 2 The name
of the man was Elimelech and the name of his
wife Naomi, and the names of his two sons were
Mahlon and Chilion; they were Ephrathites from
Bethlehem in Judah. They went into the country
of Moab and remained there. 3 But Elimelech, the
husband of Naomi, died, and she was left with her
two sons. 4 These took Moabite wives; the name
of the one was Orpah and the name of the other
Ruth. When they had lived there about ten years,
5 both Mahlon and Chilion also died, so that the
woman was left without her two sons and her
husband.

6 Then she started to return with her
daughters-in-law from the country of Moab, for
she had heard in the country of Moab that the
Lord had considered his people and given them
food. 7 So she set out from the place where she
had been living, she and her two daughters-in-
law, and they went on their way to go back to
the land of Judah. 8 But Naomi said to her two
daughters-in-law, "Go back each of you to your
mother's house. May the Lord deal kindly with

you, as you have dealt with the dead and with me.
9 The LORD grant that you may find security, each
of you in the house of your husband." Then she
kissed them, and they wept aloud. 10 They said to
her, "No, we will return with you to your people."
11 But Naomi said, "Turn back, my daughters,
why will you go with me? Do I still have sons in
my womb that they may become your husbands?
12 Turn back, my daughters, go your way, for I am
too old to have a husband. Even if I thought there
was hope for me, even if I should have a husband
tonight and bear sons, 13 would you then wait until they were grown? Would you then refrain from
marrying? No, my daughters, it has been far more
bitter for me than for you, because the hand of
the LORD has turned against me." 14 Then they
wept aloud again. Orpah kissed her mother-in-
law, but Ruth clung to her.

15 So she said, "See, your sister-in-law has
gone back to her people and to her gods; return
after your sister-in-law." 16 But Ruth said,

"Do not press me to leave you
  or to turn back from following you!
Where you go, I will go;
  where you lodge, I will lodge;
your people shall be my people,
  and your God my God.
17 Where you die, I will die—
  there will I be buried.
May the LORD do thus and so to me,
  and more as well,
if even death parts me from you!"

18 When Naomi saw that she was determined to
go with her, she said no more to her.

19 So the two of them went on until they
came to Bethlehem. When they came to Bethlehem, the whole town was stirred because of them;
and the women said, "Is this Naomi?" 20 She said
to them,

"Call me no longer Naomi,[a]
  call me Mara,[b]
  for the Almighty[c] has dealt bitterly with me.
21 I went away full,
  but the LORD has brought me back empty;
why call me Naomi
  when the LORD has dealt harshly with[d] me,
  and the Almighty[c] has brought calamity
    upon me?"

22 So Naomi returned together with Ruth
the Moabite, her daughter-in-law, who came back
with her from the country of Moab. They came
to Bethlehem at the beginning of the barley harvest.

2 Now Naomi had a kinsman on her husband's
side, a prominent rich man, of the family of
Elimelech, whose name was Boaz. 2 And Ruth the
Moabite said to Naomi, "Let me go to the field and
glean among the ears of grain, behind someone

[a] That is *Pleasant* [b] That is *Bitter* [c] Traditional rendering of Heb *Shaddai* [d] Or *has testified against*

Ruth 1:15-22

Readers of the Old Testament have long contrasted the negative view of marriage with foreigners represented by Ezra and the apparently more positive attitude represented in Ruth. The latter is nonetheless a profoundly ambiguous book. On the one hand, the story can be read as written against Ezra: as a testament to ethnic universalism, where even the enemy Moab is welcomed. Kinship is so open, that a (former?) Moabite can become the ancestor of David—and by extension of Jesus. On the other hand, even after she joins Naomi and the Israelites, Ruth continues to be referred to as the Moabite. In this reading, rather than fostering ethnic universalism, the book of Ruth testifies to failed assimilation. No matter how far Ruth goes, she can never leave her ugly past behind. One way to more positively construe the Moabite references…would be to see them not as reminding Ruth of her ugly past but as welcoming her to keep her original identity. But this reading is difficult to sustain in the light of the anti-Moabite, anti-mixed-marriage rhetoric found elsewhere in the Hebrew Bible. Is Ruth a heroine—or a betrayer of her own people, like the indigenous woman Malinche who accompanied Cortés on his conquest of South America?[22]

— Francisco García-Treto

in whose sight I may find favor." She said to her,
"Go, my daughter." 3So she went. She came and
gleaned in the field behind the reapers. As it happened, she came to the part of the field belonging
to Boaz, who was of the family of Elimelech. 4Just
then Boaz came from Bethlehem. He said to the
reapers, "The LORD be with you." They answered,
"The LORD bless you." 5Then Boaz said to his servant who was in charge of the reapers, "To whom
does this young woman belong?" 6The servant
who was in charge of the reapers answered, "She
is the Moabite who came back with Naomi from
the country of Moab. 7She said, 'Please, let me
glean and gather among the sheaves behind the
reapers.' So she came, and she has been on her
feet from early this morning until now, without
resting even for a moment."[a]

8 Then Boaz said to Ruth, "Now listen, my
daughter, do not go to glean in another field
or leave this one, but keep close to my young
women. 9Keep your eyes on the field that is being reaped, and follow behind them. I have ordered the young men not to bother you. If you
get thirsty, go to the vessels and drink from what
the young men have drawn." 10Then she fell prostrate, with her face to the ground, and said to him,
"Why have I found favor in your sight, that you
should take notice of me, when I am a foreigner?"
11But Boaz answered her, "All that you have done
for your mother-in-law since the death of your
husband has been fully told me, and how you left
your father and mother and your native land and
came to a people that you did not know before.
12May the LORD reward you for your deeds, and
may you have a full reward from the LORD, the
God of Israel, under whose wings you have come
for refuge!" 13Then she said, "May I continue to
find favor in your sight, my lord, for you have
comforted me and spoken kindly to your servant,
even though I am not one of your servants."

14 At mealtime Boaz said to her, "Come here,
and eat some of this bread, and dip your morsel in
the sour wine." So she sat beside the reapers, and
he heaped up for her some parched grain. She ate
until she was satisfied, and she had some left over.
15When she got up to glean, Boaz instructed his
young men, "Let her glean even among the standing sheaves, and do not reproach her. 16You must
also pull out some handfuls for her from the bundles, and leave them for her to glean, and do not
rebuke her."

17 So she gleaned in the field until evening.
Then she beat out what she had gleaned, and it
was about an ephah of barley. 18She picked it up
and came into the town, and her mother-in-law
saw how much she had gleaned. Then she took
out and gave her what was left over after she herself had been satisfied. 19Her mother-in-law said
to her, "Where did you glean today? And where
have you worked? Blessed be the man who took
notice of you." So she told her mother-in-law with
whom she had worked, and said, "The name of the
man with whom I worked today is Boaz." 20Then
Naomi said to her daughter-in-law, "Blessed be he
by the LORD, whose kindness has not forsaken the
living or the dead!" Naomi also said to her, "The
man is a relative of ours, one of our nearest kin."[b]
21Then Ruth the Moabite said, "He even said to
me, 'Stay close by my servants, until they have
finished all my harvest.'" 22Naomi said to Ruth,
her daughter-in-law, "It is better, my daughter,
that you go out with his young women, otherwise
you might be bothered in another field." 23So she
stayed close to the young women of Boaz, gleaning until the end of the barley and wheat harvests;
and she lived with her mother-in-law.

3 Naomi her mother-in-law said to her, "My
daughter, I need to seek some security for
you, so that it may be well with you. 2Now here
is our kinsman Boaz, with whose young women
you have been working. See, he is winnowing
barley tonight at the threshing floor. 3Now wash
and anoint yourself, and put on your best clothes
and go down to the threshing floor; but do not
make yourself known to the man until he has finished eating and drinking. 4When he lies down,
observe the place where he lies; then, go and uncover his feet and lie down; and he will tell you
what to do." 5She said to her, "All that you tell me
I will do."

[a] Compare Gk Vg: Meaning of Heb uncertain [b] Or *one with the right to redeem*

6 So she went down to the threshing floor and
did just as her mother-in-law had instructed her.
7When Boaz had eaten and drunk, and he was
in a contented mood, he went to lie down at the
end of the heap of grain. Then she came stealthily
and uncovered his feet, and lay down. 8At midnight the man was startled, and turned over, and
there, lying at his feet, was a woman! 9He said,
"Who are you?" And she answered, "I am Ruth,
your servant; spread your cloak over your servant,
for you are next-of-kin."[a] 10He said, "May you be
blessed by the LORD, my daughter; this last instance of your loyalty is better than the first; you
have not gone after young men, whether poor or
rich. 11And now, my daughter, do not be afraid, I
will do for you all that you ask, for all the assembly
of my people know that you are a worthy woman.
12But now, though it is true that I am a near kinsman, there is another kinsman more closely related
than I. 13Remain this night, and in the morning, if
he will act as next-of-kin[a] for you, good; let him
do it. If he is not willing to act as next-of-kin[a] for
you, then, as the LORD lives, I will act as next-of-
kin[a] for you. Lie down until the morning."

14 So she lay at his feet until morning, but
got up before one person could recognize another; for he said, "It must not be known that the
woman came to the threshing floor." 15Then he
said, "Bring the cloak you are wearing and hold
it out." So she held it, and he measured out six
measures of barley, and put it on her back; then
he went into the city. 16She came to her mother-
in-law, who said, "How did things go with you,[b]
my daughter?" Then she told her all that the man
had done for her, 17saying, "He gave me these six
measures of barley, for he said, 'Do not go back
to your mother-in-law empty-handed.'" 18She
replied, "Wait, my daughter, until you learn how
the matter turns out, for the man will not rest, but
will settle the matter today."

4 No sooner had Boaz gone up to the gate and
sat down there than the next-of-kin,[a] of whom
Boaz had spoken, came passing by. So Boaz said,
"Come over, friend; sit down here." And he went
over and sat down. 2Then Boaz took ten men of
the elders of the city, and said, "Sit down here"; so
they sat down. 3He then said to the next-of-kin,[a]
"Naomi, who has come back from the country of
Moab, is selling the parcel of land that belonged
to our kinsman Elimelech. 4So I thought I would
tell you of it, and say: Buy it in the presence of
those sitting here, and in the presence of the elders of my people. If you will redeem it, redeem
it; but if you will not, tell me, so that I may know;
for there is no one prior to you to redeem it, and
I come after you." So he said, "I will redeem it."
5Then Boaz said, "The day you acquire the field
from the hand of Naomi, you are also acquiring
Ruth[c] the Moabite, the widow of the dead man,
to maintain the dead man's name on his inheritance." 6At this, the next-of-kin[a] said, "I cannot
redeem it for myself without damaging my own
inheritance. Take my right of redemption yourself, for I cannot redeem it."

7 Now this was the custom in former times in
Israel concerning redeeming and exchanging: to
confirm a transaction, the one took off a sandal
and gave it to the other; this was the manner of

Ruth 4:5, 10

Whether the book of Ruth is dated early or late, and quite aside from any question of the historicity of the narrative, the reader is summoned to explain how it ever got into the canon, given the fact that the events and relationships described deviate so sharply from the Deuteronomic code (23:1-5).... Eight times in the text Ruth's foreignness is stressed.... Is the writer saying that despite past history, despite the obvious risk, despite the Law, people are not to be excluded from God's community for reasons they cannot alter? Communities will of course go on building walls because they are thought to be needed to assure the group's identity. Walls also provide a sense, often a false sense, of stability and security. But in God's family walls are self-defeating if they are used for the purpose of keeping out people—any people—who are seeking to be members of the family.[23]

— Alan Neely

[a] Or *one with the right to redeem* [b] Or *"Who are you,* [c] OL Vg: Heb *from the hand of Naomi and from Ruth*

attesting in Israel. 8 So when the next-of-kin[a] said
to Boaz, "Acquire it for yourself," he took off his
sandal. 9 Then Boaz said to the elders and all the
people, "Today you are witnesses that I have acquired from the hand of Naomi all that belonged
to Elimelech and all that belonged to Chilion and
Mahlon. 10 I have also acquired Ruth the Moabite,
the wife of Mahlon, to be my wife, to maintain
the dead man's name on his inheritance, in order
that the name of the dead may not be cut off from
his kindred and from the gate of his native place;
today you are witnesses." 11 Then all the people
who were at the gate, along with the elders, said,
"We are witnesses. May the LORD make the
woman who is coming into your house like Rachel and Leah, who together built up the house
of Israel. May you produce children in Ephrathah
and bestow a name in Bethlehem; 12 and, through
the children that the LORD will give you by this
young woman, may your house be like the house
of Perez, whom Tamar bore to Judah."

13 So Boaz took Ruth and she became his
wife. When they came together, the LORD made
her conceive, and she bore a son. 14 Then the
women said to Naomi, "Blessed be the LORD, who
has not left you this day without next-of-kin;[a] and
may his name be renowned in Israel! 15 He shall
be to you a restorer of life and a nourisher of your
old age; for your daughter-in-law who loves you,
who is more to you than seven sons, has borne
him." 16 Then Naomi took the child and laid him in
her bosom, and became his nurse. 17 The women
of the neighborhood gave him a name, saying, "A
son has been born to Naomi." They named him
Obed; he became the father of Jesse, the father
of David.

18 Now these are the descendants of Perez:
Perez became the father of Hezron, 19 Hezron
of Ram, Ram of Amminadab, 20 Amminadab
of Nahshon, Nahshon of Salmon, 21 Salmon of
Boaz, Boaz of Obed, 22 Obed of Jesse, and Jesse
of David.

[a] Or *one with the right to redeem*

1 Samuel

First and Second Samuel, originally one book, are included in the Prophets, the second section of the three-part Jewish scriptures (Torah, Prophets, and Writings) that Christians call the Old Testament. It made sense to view these books as prophetic because in them prophets such as Samuel, Nathan, and Gad play critical roles in advancing God's history, and the theme of prophecy and fulfillment is prominent throughout. In contemporary biblical scholarship the two books are viewed as part of the Deuteronomistic History (Joshua, Judges, 1–2 Samuel, and 1–2 Kings), which recounts a history of ancient Israel from its entrance into and settlement in Canaan (Joshua and Judges), to the establishment of the house of David (1–2 Samuel), to the division of the kingdom (1 Kings), and finally to the fall of Samaria and Jerusalem (2 Kings).

First Samuel responds to the problem noted at the end of Judges: "In those days there was no king in Israel; all the people did what was right in their own eyes" (Judg 21:25). There are voices for and against the establishment of kingship in 1 Samuel. The people of Israel were in transition, moving from one form of governance—tribal confederacy practiced during the period of Judges—to another—monarchy as practiced by their neighbors.

The story opens with a petition for a son by a barren woman named Hannah (1 Samuel 1). When God grants her appeal she praises God with a song, which predicts God's anointing of a king (1 Sam 2:1-11). The importance of having a male child in the biblical culture finds parallel in certain modern cultures, where male children are still preferred over a female child. This may not be the case in much of the West but is still the case in many parts of the world, perhaps more for cultural reasons than for economic reasons, as it was in the past. Hannah's son Samuel, faithful as he is, is not the one for whom the people are waiting; neither are his sons (1 Samuel 8). Saul, who appears physically superior to all others, is anointed by God but is quickly rejected (1 Samuel 13 and 15). Later in the story, God chooses a ruddy shepherd boy to be anointed (1 Samuel 16). Once David appears in the narrative, 1 Samuel focuses on why David is God's choice instead of Saul. The book ends with the ignominious death of Saul (1 Samuel 31). The story of David's rise to kingship continues in 2 Samuel.

First Samuel takes place during the time when Canaan was free from political powers outside the region; but there were conflicts within. Israel was one among several groups of people that wanted to establish or maintain their territories in Canaan. It was a time when there were more crossroads where these peoples interacted, often in conflict, than exact boundaries. The drawing of various kinds of boundaries—territorial, cultural, ethnic—was an ongoing process at the time. The Israelites saw themselves as different from their neighbors, especially from their archenemy the Philistines, whom they called the uncircumcised. They were, however, not very different ethnically

or culturally from other peoples in Canaan, some who also practiced circumcision. Moreover, the relationship between David and the Philistines was ambivalent. David defeated Goliath of Gath to win the support of the people (1 Samuel 17) but served King Achish of Gath, a Philistine city, as the king's bodyguard (1 Sam 27:1—28:2). Later David's bodyguard was made up of the Cherethites and the Pelethites (2 Sam 8:18), who were closely associated with the Philistines. When David had to flee Jerusalem due to Absalom, Ittai the Gittite, who was in charge of six hundred Gittites (soldiers from Gath), escorted David (2 Sam 15:18-23).

My reading of 1 Samuel is colored by my experience as a member of a minority community in the United States. Together and separately, various groups construct the nation's cultural landscape. However, culture is often shaped through *collisions* between a dominant group and minority groups. When reading 1 Samuel, I pay attention to the interaction between various competing ethnic and religious groups.

— ***Uriah Y. Kim***

1 There was a certain man of Ramathaim, a
Zuphite[a] from the hill country of Ephraim,
whose name was Elkanah son of Jeroham son of
Elihu son of Tohu son of Zuph, an Ephraimite.
2He had two wives; the name of the one was Hannah, and the name of the other Peninnah. Peninnah had children, but Hannah had no children.

3 Now this man used to go up year by year
from his town to worship and to sacrifice to the
LORD of hosts at Shiloh, where the two sons of Eli,
Hophni and Phinehas, were priests of the LORD.
4On the day when Elkanah sacrificed, he would
give portions to his wife Peninnah and to all her
sons and daughters; 5but to Hannah he gave a
double portion,[b] because he loved her, though
the LORD had closed her womb. 6Her rival used
to provoke her severely, to irritate her, because
the LORD had closed her womb. 7So it went on
year by year; as often as she went up to the house
of the LORD, she used to provoke her. Therefore
Hannah wept and would not eat. 8Her husband
Elkanah said to her, "Hannah, why do you weep?
Why do you not eat? Why is your heart sad? Am
I not more to you than ten sons?"

9 After they had eaten and drunk at Shiloh,
Hannah rose and presented herself before the
LORD.[c] Now Eli the priest was sitting on the seat
beside the doorpost of the temple of the LORD.
10She was deeply distressed and prayed to the
LORD, and wept bitterly. 11She made this vow:
"O LORD of hosts, if only you will look on the
misery of your servant, and remember me, and
not forget your servant, but will give to your servant a male child, then I will set him before you
as a nazirite[d] until the day of his death. He shall
drink neither wine nor intoxicants,[e] and no razor
shall touch his head."

12 As she continued praying before the
LORD, Eli observed her mouth. 13Hannah was
praying silently; only her lips moved, but her

[a] Compare Gk and 1 Chr 6.35–36: Heb *Ramathaim-zophim* [b] Syr: Meaning of Heb uncertain [c] Gk: Heb lacks *and presented herself before the LORD* [d] That is *one separated* or *one consecrated*
[e] Cn Compare Gk Q Ms 1.22: MT *then I will give him to the LORD all the days of his life*

voice was not heard; therefore Eli thought she
was drunk. 14So Eli said to her, "How long will
you make a drunken spectacle of yourself? Put
away your wine." 15But Hannah answered, "No,
my lord, I am a woman deeply troubled; I have
drunk neither wine nor strong drink, but I have
been pouring out my soul before the LORD. 16Do
not regard your servant as a worthless woman,
for I have been speaking out of my great anxiety
and vexation all this time." 17Then Eli answered,
"Go in peace; the God of Israel grant the petition
you have made to him." 18And she said, "Let your
servant find favor in your sight." Then the woman
went to her quarters,[a] ate and drank with her husband,[b] and her countenance was sad no longer.[c]

19 They rose early in the morning and worshiped before the LORD; then they went back
to their house at Ramah. Elkanah knew his wife
Hannah, and the LORD remembered her. 20In
due time Hannah conceived and bore a son. She
named him Samuel, for she said, "I have asked
him of the LORD."

21 The man Elkanah and all his household
went up to offer to the LORD the yearly sacrifice,
and to pay his vow. 22But Hannah did not go up,
for she said to her husband, "As soon as the child
is weaned, I will bring him, that he may appear in
the presence of the LORD, and remain there forever; I will offer him as a nazirite[d] for all time."[e]
23Her husband Elkanah said to her, "Do what
seems best to you, wait until you have weaned
him; only—may the LORD establish his word."[f]
So the woman remained and nursed her son, until she weaned him. 24When she had weaned him,
she took him up with her, along with a three-year-
old bull,[g] an ephah of flour, and a skin of wine.
She brought him to the house of the LORD at
Shiloh; and the child was young. 25Then they
slaughtered the bull, and they brought the child
to Eli. 26And she said, "Oh, my lord! As you live,
my lord, I am the woman who was standing here
in your presence, praying to the LORD. 27For this
child I prayed; and the LORD has granted me the
petition that I made to him. 28Therefore I have
lent him to the LORD; as long as he lives, he is
given to the LORD."

She left him there for[h] the LORD.

2 Hannah prayed and said,
"My heart exults in the LORD;
my strength is exalted in my God.[i]
My mouth derides my enemies,
because I rejoice in my[j] victory.

2 "There is no Holy One like the LORD,
no one besides you;
there is no Rock like our God.
3 Talk no more so very proudly,
let not arrogance come from your mouth;
for the LORD is a God of knowledge,
and by him actions are weighed.
4 The bows of the mighty are broken,
but the feeble gird on strength.
5 Those who were full have hired themselves
out for bread,
but those who were hungry are fat with
spoil.
The barren has borne seven,
but she who has many children is forlorn.
6 The LORD kills and brings to life;
he brings down to Sheol and raises up.
7 The LORD makes poor and makes rich;
he brings low, he also exalts.
8 He raises up the poor from the dust;
he lifts the needy from the ash heap,
to make them sit with princes
and inherit a seat of honor.[k]
For the pillars of the earth are the LORD's,
and on them he has set the world.

9 "He will guard the feet of his faithful ones,
but the wicked shall be cut off in darkness;
for not by might does one prevail.

[a] Gk: Heb *went her way* [b] Gk: Heb lacks *and drank with her husband* [c] Gk: Meaning of Heb uncertain [d] That is *one separated* or *one consecrated* [e] Cn Compare Q Ms: MT lacks *I will offer him as a nazirite for all time* [f] MT: Q Ms Gk Compare Syr *that which goes out of your mouth* [g] Q Ms Gk Syr: MT *three bulls* [h] Gk (Compare Q Ms) and Gk at 2.11: MT *And he* (that is, Elkanah) *worshiped there before* [i] Gk: Heb *the LORD* [j] Q Ms: MT *your* [k] Gk (Compare Q Ms) adds *He grants the vow of the one who vows, and blesses the years of the just*

10 The LORD! His adversaries shall be shattered;
the Most High[a] will thunder in heaven.
The LORD will judge the ends of the earth;
he will give strength to his king,
and exalt the power of his anointed."

11 Then Elkanah went home to Ramah, while
the boy remained to minister to the LORD, in the
presence of the priest Eli.

12 Now the sons of Eli were scoundrels; they
had no regard for the LORD 13or for the duties of
the priests to the people. When anyone offered
sacrifice, the priest's servant would come, while
the meat was boiling, with a three-pronged fork
in his hand, 14and he would thrust it into the
pan, or kettle, or caldron, or pot; all that the fork
brought up the priest would take for himself.[b]
This is what they did at Shiloh to all the Israelites
who came there. 15Moreover, before the fat was
burned, the priest's servant would come and say
to the one who was sacrificing, "Give meat for the
priest to roast; for he will not accept boiled meat
from you, but only raw." 16And if the man said to
him, "Let them burn the fat first, and then take
whatever you wish," he would say, "No, you must
give it now; if not, I will take it by force." 17Thus
the sin of the young men was very great in the
sight of the LORD; for they treated the offerings
of the LORD with contempt.

18 Samuel was ministering before the LORD,
a boy wearing a linen ephod. 19His mother used
to make for him a little robe and take it to him
each year, when she went up with her husband to
offer the yearly sacrifice. 20Then Eli would bless
Elkanah and his wife, and say, "May the LORD
repay[c] you with children by this woman for the
gift that she made to[d] the LORD"; and then they
would return to their home.

21 And[e] the LORD took note of Hannah; she
conceived and bore three sons and two daughters.
And the boy Samuel grew up in the presence
of the LORD.

22 Now Eli was very old. He heard all that
his sons were doing to all Israel, and how they lay
with the women who served at the entrance to
the tent of meeting. 23He said to them, "Why do
you do such things? For I hear of your evil dealings
from all these people. 24No, my sons; it is not
a good report that I hear the people of the LORD
spreading abroad. 25If one person sins against another,
someone can intercede for the sinner with
the LORD;[f] but if someone sins against the LORD,
who can make intercession?" But they would not
listen to the voice of their father; for it was the
will of the LORD to kill them.

26 Now the boy Samuel continued to grow
both in stature and in favor with the LORD and
with the people.

27 A man of God came to Eli and said to him,
"Thus the LORD has said, 'I revealed[g] myself to
the family of your ancestor in Egypt when they
were slaves[h] to the house of Pharaoh. 28I chose
him out of all the tribes of Israel to be my priest,
to go up to my altar, to offer incense, to wear an
ephod before me; and I gave to the family of your
ancestor all my offerings by fire from the people
of Israel. 29Why then look with greedy eye[i] at my
sacrifices and my offerings that I commanded,
and honor your sons more than me by fattening
yourselves on the choicest parts of every offering
of my people Israel?' 30Therefore the LORD the
God of Israel declares: 'I promised that your family
and the family of your ancestor should go in
and out before me forever'; but now the LORD
declares: 'Far be it from me; for those who honor
me I will honor, and those who despise me shall
be treated with contempt. 31See, a time is coming
when I will cut off your strength and the strength
of your ancestor's family, so that no one in your
family will live to old age. 32Then in distress you
will look with greedy eye[j] on all the prosperity
that shall be bestowed upon Israel; and no one in
your family shall ever live to old age. 33The only
one of you whom I shall not cut off from my altar
shall be spared to weep out his[k] eyes and grieve

[a] Cn Heb *against him he* [b] Gk Syr Vg: Heb *with it* [c] Q Ms Gk: MT *give* [d] Q Ms Gk: MT *for the petition that she asked of* [e] Q Ms Gk: MT *When* [f] Gk Compare Q Ms: MT *another, God will mediate for him* [g] Gk Tg Syr: Heb *Did I reveal* [h] Q Ms Gk: MT lacks *slaves* [i] Q Ms Gk: MT *then kick* [j] Q Ms Gk: MT *will kick* [k] Q Ms Gk: MT *your*

his[a] heart; all the members of your household
shall die by the sword.[b] 34 The fate of your two
sons, Hophni and Phinehas, shall be the sign to
you—both of them shall die on the same day.
35 I will raise up for myself a faithful priest, who
shall do according to what is in my heart and in
my mind. I will build him a sure house, and he
shall go in and out before my anointed one forever. 36 Everyone who is left in your family shall
come to implore him for a piece of silver or a loaf
of bread, and shall say, Please put me in one of the
priest's places, that I may eat a morsel of bread.' "

3 Now the boy Samuel was ministering to the
LORD under Eli. The word of the LORD was
rare in those days; visions were not widespread.

2 At that time Eli, whose eyesight had begun
to grow dim so that he could not see, was lying
down in his room; 3 the lamp of God had not yet
gone out, and Samuel was lying down in the temple of the LORD, where the ark of God was. 4 Then
the LORD called, "Samuel! Samuel!"[c] and he said,
"Here I am!" 5 and ran to Eli, and said, "Here
I am, for you called me." But he said, "I did not
call; lie down again." So he went and lay down.
6 The LORD called again, "Samuel!" Samuel got
up and went to Eli, and said, "Here I am, for you
called me." But he said, "I did not call, my son;
lie down again." 7 Now Samuel did not yet know
the LORD, and the word of the LORD had not yet
been revealed to him. 8 The LORD called Samuel
again, a third time. And he got up and went to
Eli, and said, "Here I am, for you called me." Then
Eli perceived that the LORD was calling the boy.
9 Therefore Eli said to Samuel, "Go, lie down; and
if he calls you, you shall say, 'Speak, LORD, for
your servant is listening.' " So Samuel went and
lay down in his place.

10 Now the LORD came and stood there,
calling as before, "Samuel! Samuel!" And Samuel
said, "Speak, for your servant is listening." 11 Then
the LORD said to Samuel, "See, I am about to
do something in Israel that will make both ears
of anyone who hears of it tingle. 12 On that day I
will fulfill against Eli all that I have spoken concerning his house, from beginning to end. 13 For I
have told him that I am about to punish his house
forever, for the iniquity that he knew, because
his sons were blaspheming God,[d] and he did not
restrain them. 14 Therefore I swear to the house
of Eli that the iniquity of Eli's house shall not be
expiated by sacrifice or offering forever."

15 Samuel lay there until morning; then
he opened the doors of the house of the LORD.
Samuel was afraid to tell the vision to Eli. 16 But
Eli called Samuel and said, "Samuel, my son." He
said, "Here I am." 17 Eli said, "What was it that he
told you? Do not hide it from me. May God do so
to you and more also, if you hide anything from
me of all that he told you." 18 So Samuel told him
everything and hid nothing from him. Then he
said, "It is the LORD; let him do what seems good
to him."

19 As Samuel grew up, the LORD was with
him and let none of his words fall to the ground.
20 And all Israel from Dan to Beer-sheba knew that
Samuel was a trustworthy prophet of the LORD.
21 The LORD continued to appear at Shiloh, for
the LORD revealed himself to Samuel at Shiloh

4 by the word of the LORD. 1 And the word of
Samuel came to all Israel.

In those days the Philistines mustered for
war against Israel,[e] and Israel went out to battle
against them;[f] they encamped at Ebenezer, and
the Philistines encamped at Aphek. 2 The Philistines drew up in line against Israel, and when
the battle was joined,[g] Israel was defeated by the
Philistines, who killed about four thousand men
on the field of battle. 3 When the troops came to
the camp, the elders of Israel said, "Why has the
LORD put us to rout today before the Philistines?
Let us bring the ark of the covenant of the LORD
here from Shiloh, so that he may come among us
and save us from the power of our enemies." 4 So
the people sent to Shiloh, and brought from there
the ark of the covenant of the LORD of hosts, who
is enthroned on the cherubim. The two sons of

[a] Q Ms Gk: Heb *your* [b] Q Ms See Gk: MT *die like mortals* [c] Q Ms Gk See 3.10: MT *the LORD called Samuel*
[d] Another reading is *for themselves* [e] Gk: Heb lacks *In those days the Philistines mustered for war against Israel*
[f] Gk: Heb *against the Philistines* [g] Meaning of Heb uncertain

Eli, Hophni and Phinehas, were there with the
ark of the covenant of God.
5 When the ark of the covenant of the LORD
came into the camp, all Israel gave a mighty
shout, so that the earth resounded. 6When the
Philistines heard the noise of the shouting, they
said, "What does this great shouting in the camp
of the Hebrews mean?" When they learned that
the ark of the LORD had come to the camp, 7the
Philistines were afraid; for they said, "Gods have[a]
come into the camp." They also said, "Woe to us!
For nothing like this has happened before. 8Woe
to us! Who can deliver us from the power of these
mighty gods? These are the gods who struck the
Egyptians with every sort of plague in the wilderness. 9Take courage, and be men, O Philistines,
in order not to become slaves to the Hebrews as
they have been to you; be men and fight."
10 So the Philistines fought; Israel was defeated, and they fled, everyone to his home. There
was a very great slaughter, for there fell of Israel
thirty thousand foot soldiers. 11The ark of God
was captured; and the two sons of Eli, Hophni
and Phinehas, died.
12 A man of Benjamin ran from the battle
line, and came to Shiloh the same day, with
his clothes torn and with earth upon his head.
13When he arrived, Eli was sitting upon his seat
by the road watching, for his heart trembled for
the ark of God. When the man came into the city
and told the news, all the city cried out. 14When
Eli heard the sound of the outcry, he said, "What
is this uproar?" Then the man came quickly and
told Eli. 15Now Eli was ninety-eight years old and
his eyes were set, so that he could not see. 16The
man said to Eli, "I have just come from the battle;
I fled from the battle today." He said, "How did
it go, my son?" 17The messenger replied, "Israel
has fled before the Philistines, and there has also
been a great slaughter among the troops; your
two sons also, Hophni and Phinehas, are dead,
and the ark of God has been captured." 18When
he mentioned the ark of God, Eli[b] fell over backward from his seat by the side of the gate; and his
neck was broken and he died, for he was an old
man, and heavy. He had judged Israel forty years.
19 Now his daughter-in-law, the wife of Phinehas, was pregnant, about to give birth. When she
heard the news that the ark of God was captured,
and that her father-in-law and her husband were
dead, she bowed and gave birth; for her labor
pains overwhelmed her. 20As she was about to
die, the women attending her said to her, "Do not
be afraid, for you have borne a son." But she did
not answer or give heed. 21She named the child
Ichabod, meaning, "The glory has departed from
Israel," because the ark of God had been captured
and because of her father-in-law and her husband.
22She said, "The glory has departed from Israel,
for the ark of God has been captured."

5 When the Philistines captured the ark of
God, they brought it from Ebenezer to Ashdod; 2then the Philistines took the ark of God and
brought it into the house of Dagon and placed it
beside Dagon. 3When the people of Ashdod rose
early the next day, there was Dagon, fallen on his
face to the ground before the ark of the LORD. So
they took Dagon and put him back in his place.
4But when they rose early on the next morning,
Dagon had fallen on his face to the ground before the ark of the LORD, and the head of Dagon
and both his hands were lying cut off upon the
threshold; only the trunk of[c] Dagon was left to
him. 5This is why the priests of Dagon and all
who enter the house of Dagon do not step on the
threshold of Dagon in Ashdod to this day.
6 The hand of the LORD was heavy upon the
people of Ashdod, and he terrified and struck
them with tumors, both in Ashdod and in its
territory. 7And when the inhabitants of Ashdod
saw how things were, they said, "The ark of the
God of Israel must not remain with us; for his
hand is heavy on us and on our god Dagon." 8So
they sent and gathered together all the lords of
the Philistines, and said, "What shall we do with
the ark of the God of Israel?" The inhabitants
of Gath replied, "Let the ark of God be moved
on to us."[d] So they moved the ark of the God of

[a] Or *A god has* [b] Heb *he* [c] Heb lacks *the trunk of*
[d] Gk Compare Q Ms: MT *They answered, "Let the ark of the God of Israel be brought around to Gath."*

Israel to Gath.[a] 9But after they had brought it to Gath,[b] the hand of the LORD was against the city, causing a very great panic; he struck the inhabitants of the city, both young and old, so that tumors broke out on them. 10So they sent the ark of the God of Israel[c] to Ekron. But when the ark of God came to Ekron, the people of Ekron cried out, "Why[d] have they brought around to us[e] the ark of the God of Israel to kill us[e] and our[f] people?" 11They sent therefore and gathered together all the lords of the Philistines, and said, "Send away the ark of the God of Israel, and let it return to its own place, that it may not kill us and our people." For there was a deathly panic[g] throughout the whole city. The hand of God was very heavy there; 12those who did not die were stricken with tumors, and the cry of the city went up to heaven.

6 The ark of the LORD was in the country of the Philistines seven months. 2Then the Philistines called for the priests and the diviners and said, "What shall we do with the ark of the LORD? Tell us what we should send with it to its place." 3They said, "If you send away the ark of the God of Israel, do not send it empty, but by all means return him a guilt offering. Then you will be healed and will be ransomed;[h] will not his hand then turn from you?" 4And they said, "What is the guilt offering that we shall return to him?" They answered, "Five gold tumors and five gold mice, according to the number of the lords of the Philistines; for the same plague was upon all of you and upon your lords. 5So you must make images of your tumors and images of your mice that ravage the land, and give glory to the God of Israel; perhaps he will lighten his hand on you and your gods and your land. 6Why should you harden your hearts as the Egyptians and Pharaoh hardened their hearts? After he had made fools of them, did they not let the people go, and they departed? 7Now then, get ready a new cart and two milch cows that have never borne a yoke, and yoke the cows to the cart, but take their calves home, away from them. 8Take the ark of the LORD and place it on the cart, and put in a box at its side the figures of gold, which you are returning to him as a guilt offering. Then send it off, and let it go its way. 9And watch; if it goes up on the way to its own land, to Beth-shemesh, then it is he who has done us this great harm; but if not, then we shall know that it is not his hand that struck us; it happened to us by chance."

10 The men did so; they took two milch cows and yoked them to the cart, and shut up their calves at home. 11They put the ark of the LORD on the cart, and the box with the gold mice and the images of their tumors. 12The cows went straight in the direction of Beth-shemesh along one highway, lowing as they went; they turned neither to the right nor to the left, and the lords of the Philistines went after them as far as the border of Beth-shemesh.

13 Now the people of Beth-shemesh were reaping their wheat harvest in the valley. When they looked up and saw the ark, they went with rejoicing to meet it.[i] 14The cart came into the field of Joshua of Beth-shemesh, and stopped there. A large stone was there; so they split up the wood of the cart and offered the cows as a burnt offering to the LORD. 15The Levites took down the ark of the LORD and the box that was beside it, in which were the gold objects, and set them upon the large stone. Then the people of Beth-shemesh offered burnt offerings and presented sacrifices on that day to the LORD. 16When the five lords of the Philistines saw it, they returned that day to Ekron.

17 These are the gold tumors, which the Philistines returned as a guilt offering to the LORD: one for Ashdod, one for Gaza, one for Ashkelon, one for Gath, one for Ekron; 18also the gold mice, according to the number of all the cities of the Philistines belonging to the five lords, both fortified cities and unwalled villages. The great stone, beside which they set down the ark of the LORD, is a witness to this day in the field of Joshua of Beth-shemesh.

[a] Gk: Heb lacks *to Gath* [b] Q Ms: MT lacks *to Gath* [c] Q Ms Gk: MT lacks *of Israel* [d] Q Ms Gk: MT lacks *Why* [e] Heb *me* [f] Heb *my* [g] Q Ms reads *a panic from the LORD* [h] Q Ms Gk: MT *and it will be known to you* [i] Gk: Heb *rejoiced to see it*

19 The descendants of Jeconiah did not rejoice with the people of Beth-shemesh when they
greeted[a] the ark of the LORD; and he killed seventy men of them.[b] The people mourned because
the LORD had made a great slaughter among
the people. 20 Then the people of Beth-shemesh
said, "Who is able to stand before the LORD,
this holy God? To whom shall he go so that we
may be rid of him?" 21 So they sent messengers
to the inhabitants of Kiriath-jearim, saying, "The
Philistines have returned the ark of the LORD.
7 Come down and take it up to you." 1 And the
people of Kiriath-jearim came and took up
the ark of the LORD, and brought it to the house
of Abinadab on the hill. They consecrated his son,
Eleazar, to have charge of the ark of the LORD.

2 From the day that the ark was lodged at
Kiriath-jearim, a long time passed, some twenty
years, and all the house of Israel lamented[c] after
the LORD.

3 Then Samuel said to all the house of Israel,
"If you are returning to the LORD with all your
heart, then put away the foreign gods and the
Astartes from among you. Direct your heart to
the LORD, and serve him only, and he will deliver
you out of the hand of the Philistines." 4 So Israel
put away the Baals and the Astartes, and they
served the LORD only.

5 Then Samuel said, "Gather all Israel at Mizpah, and I will pray to the LORD for you." 6 So they
gathered at Mizpah, and drew water and poured
it out before the LORD. They fasted that day, and
said, "We have sinned against the LORD." And
Samuel judged the people of Israel at Mizpah.

7 When the Philistines heard that the people
of Israel had gathered at Mizpah, the lords of the
Philistines went up against Israel. And when the
people of Israel heard of it they were afraid of
the Philistines. 8 The people of Israel said to Samuel, "Do not cease to cry out to the LORD our
God for us, and pray that he may save us from the
hand of the Philistines." 9 So Samuel took a sucking lamb and offered it as a whole burnt offering
to the LORD; Samuel cried out to the LORD for
Israel, and the LORD answered him. 10 As Samuel
was offering up the burnt offering, the Philistines
drew near to attack Israel; but the LORD thundered with a mighty voice that day against the Philistines and threw them into confusion; and they
were routed before Israel. 11 And the men of Israel
went out of Mizpah and pursued the Philistines,
and struck them down as far as beyond Beth-car.

12 Then Samuel took a stone and set it up
between Mizpah and Jeshanah,[d] and named it
Ebenezer;[e] for he said, "Thus far the LORD has
helped us." 13 So the Philistines were subdued
and did not again enter the territory of Israel; the
hand of the LORD was against the Philistines all
the days of Samuel. 14 The towns that the Philistines had taken from Israel were restored to Israel,
from Ekron to Gath; and Israel recovered their
territory from the hand of the Philistines. There
was peace also between Israel and the Amorites.

15 Samuel judged Israel all the days of his life.
16 He went on a circuit year by year to Bethel, Gilgal, and Mizpah; and he judged Israel in all these
places. 17 Then he would come back to Ramah, for
his home was there; he administered justice there
to Israel, and built there an altar to the LORD.

8 When Samuel became old, he made his sons
judges over Israel. 2 The name of his firstborn
son was Joel, and the name of his second, Abijah;
they were judges in Beer-sheba. 3 Yet his sons did
not follow in his ways, but turned aside after gain;
they took bribes and perverted justice.

4 Then all the elders of Israel gathered together and came to Samuel at Ramah, 5 and said to
him, "You are old and your sons do not follow in
your ways; appoint for us, then, a king to govern
us, like other nations." 6 But the thing displeased
Samuel when they said, "Give us a king to govern
us." Samuel prayed to the LORD, 7 and the LORD
said to Samuel, "Listen to the voice of the people
in all that they say to you; for they have not rejected you, but they have rejected me from being
king over them. 8 Just as they have done to me,[f]

[a] Gk: Heb *And he killed some of the people of Beth-shemesh, because they looked into* [b] Heb *killed seventy men, fifty thousand men* [c] Meaning of Heb uncertain [d] Gk Syr: Heb *Shen* [e] That is *Stone of Help*
[f] Gk: Heb lacks *to me*

from the day I brought them up out of Egypt to
this day, forsaking me and serving other gods, so
also they are doing to you. 9Now then, listen to
their voice; only—you shall solemnly warn them,
and show them the ways of the king who shall
reign over them."

10 So Samuel reported all the words of the
LORD to the people who were asking him for a
king. 11He said, "These will be the ways of the
king who will reign over you: he will take your
sons and appoint them to his chariots and to be
his horsemen, and to run before his chariots;
12and he will appoint for himself commanders of
thousands and commanders of fifties, and some
to plow his ground and to reap his harvest, and to
make his implements of war and the equipment
of his chariots. 13He will take your daughters to
be perfumers and cooks and bakers. 14He will
take the best of your fields and vineyards and olive orchards and give them to his courtiers. 15He
will take one-tenth of your grain and of your
vineyards and give it to his officers and his courtiers. 16He will take your male and female slaves,
and the best of your cattle[a] and donkeys, and
put them to his work. 17He will take one-tenth
of your flocks, and you shall be his slaves. 18And
in that day you will cry out because of your king,
whom you have chosen for yourselves; but the
LORD will not answer you in that day."

19 But the people refused to listen to the voice
of Samuel; they said, "No! but we are determined
to have a king over us, 20so that we also may be
like other nations, and that our king may govern
us and go out before us and fight our battles."
21When Samuel had heard all the words of the
people, he repeated them in the ears of the LORD.
22The LORD said to Samuel, "Listen to their voice
and set a king over them." Samuel then said to the
people of Israel, "Each of you return home."

9 There was a man of Benjamin whose name
was Kish son of Abiel son of Zeror son of
Becorath son of Aphiah, a Benjaminite, a man
of wealth. 2He had a son whose name was Saul,
a handsome young man. There was not a man
among the people of Israel more handsome than
he; he stood head and shoulders above everyone else.

3 Now the donkeys of Kish, Saul's father, had
strayed. So Kish said to his son Saul, "Take one of
the boys with you; go and look for the donkeys."
4He passed through the hill country of Ephraim
and passed through the land of Shalishah, but
they did not find them. And they passed through
the land of Shaalim, but they were not there. Then
he passed through the land of Benjamin, but they
did not find them.

5 When they came to the land of Zuph, Saul
said to the boy who was with him, "Let us turn
back, or my father will stop worrying about the
donkeys and worry about us." 6But he said to him,
"There is a man of God in this town; he is a man
held in honor. Whatever he says always comes
true. Let us go there now; perhaps he will tell
us about the journey on which we have set out."
7Then Saul replied to the boy, "But if we go, what
can we bring the man? For the bread in our sacks
is gone, and there is no present to bring to the
man of God. What have we?" 8The boy answered
Saul again, "Here, I have with me a quarter shekel
of silver; I will give it to the man of God, to tell us
our way." 9(Formerly in Israel, anyone who went
to inquire of God would say, "Come, let us go to
the seer"; for the one who is now called a prophet
was formerly called a seer.) 10Saul said to the boy,
"Good; come, let us go." So they went to the town
where the man of God was.

11 As they went up the hill to the town, they
met some girls coming out to draw water, and
said to them, "Is the seer here?" 12They answered,
"Yes, there he is just ahead of you. Hurry; he has
come just now to the town, because the people
have a sacrifice today at the shrine. 13As soon as
you enter the town, you will find him, before he
goes up to the shrine to eat. For the people will
not eat until he comes, since he must bless the
sacrifice; afterward those eat who are invited.
Now go up, for you will meet him immediately."
14So they went up to the town. As they were
entering the town, they saw Samuel coming out
toward them on his way up to the shrine.

[a] Gk: Heb *young men*

15 Now the day before Saul came, the LORD
had revealed to Samuel: 16 “Tomorrow about this
time I will send to you a man from the land of
Benjamin, and you shall anoint him to be ruler
over my people Israel. He shall save my people
from the hand of the Philistines; for I have seen
the suffering of[a] my people, because their outcry
has come to me.” 17 When Samuel saw Saul, the
LORD told him, “Here is the man of whom I spoke
to you. He it is who shall rule over my people.”
18 Then Saul approached Samuel inside the gate,
and said, “Tell me, please, where is the house of
the seer?” 19 Samuel answered Saul, “I am the seer;
go up before me to the shrine, for today you shall
eat with me, and in the morning I will let you go
and will tell you all that is on your mind. 20 As for
your donkeys that were lost three days ago, give no
further thought to them, for they have been found.
And on whom is all Israel’s desire fixed, if not on
you and on all your ancestral house?” 21 Saul answered, “I am only a Benjaminite, from the least of
the tribes of Israel, and my family is the humblest
of all the families of the tribe of Benjamin. Why
then have you spoken to me in this way?”

22 Then Samuel took Saul and his servant-
boy and brought them into the hall, and gave
them a place at the head of those who had been
invited, of whom there were about thirty. 23 And
Samuel said to the cook, “Bring the portion I gave
you, the one I asked you to put aside.” 24 The cook
took up the thigh and what went with it[b] and set
them before Saul. Samuel said, “See, what was
kept is set before you. Eat; for it is set[c] before you
at the appointed time, so that you might eat with
the guests.”[d]

So Saul ate with Samuel that day. 25 When they
came down from the shrine into the town, a bed
was spread for Saul[e] on the roof, and he lay down
to sleep.[f] 26 Then at the break of dawn[g] Samuel
called to Saul upon the roof, “Get up, so that I
may send you on your way.” Saul got up, and both
he and Samuel went out into the street.

27 As they were going down to the outskirts
of the town, Samuel said to Saul, “Tell the boy to
go on before us, and when he has passed on, stop
here yourself for a while, that I may make known

10 to you the word of God.” 1 Samuel took a
vial of oil and poured it on his head, and
kissed him; he said, “The LORD has anointed you
ruler over his people Israel. You shall reign over
the people of the LORD and you will save them
from the hand of their enemies all around. Now
this shall be the sign to you that the LORD has
anointed you ruler[h] over his heritage: 2 When you
depart from me today you will meet two men
by Rachel’s tomb in the territory of Benjamin at
Zelzah; they will say to you, ‘The donkeys that
you went to seek are found, and now your father
has stopped worrying about them and is worrying about you, saying: What shall I do about my
son?’ 3 Then you shall go on from there further
and come to the oak of Tabor; three men going
up to God at Bethel will meet you there, one carrying three kids, another carrying three loaves of
bread, and another carrying a skin of wine. 4 They
will greet you and give you two loaves of bread,
which you shall accept from them. 5 After that you
shall come to Gibeath-elohim,[i] at the place where
the Philistine garrison is; there, as you come to
the town, you will meet a band of prophets coming down from the shrine with harp, tambourine,
flute, and lyre playing in front of them; they will
be in a prophetic frenzy. 6 Then the spirit of the
LORD will possess you, and you will be in a prophetic frenzy along with them and be turned into
a different person. 7 Now when these signs meet
you, do whatever you see fit to do, for God is
with you. 8 And you shall go down to Gilgal ahead
of me; then I will come down to you to present
burnt offerings and offer sacrifices of well-being.
Seven days you shall wait, until I come to you and
show you what you shall do.”

9 As he turned away to leave Samuel, God
gave him another heart; and all these signs were

[a] Gk: Heb lacks *the suffering of* [b] Meaning of Heb uncertain [c] Q Ms Gk: MT *it was kept* [d] Cn: Heb *it was kept for you, saying, I have invited the people* [e] Gk: Heb *and he spoke with Saul* [f] Gk: Heb lacks *and he lay down to sleep* [g] Gk: Heb *and they arose early and at break of dawn* [h] Gk: Heb lacks *over his people Israel. You shall . . . anointed you ruler* [i] Or *the Hill of God*

fulfilled that day. 10When they were going from there[a] to Gibeah,[b] a band of prophets met him; and the spirit of God possessed him, and he fell into a prophetic frenzy along with them. 11When all who knew him before saw how he prophesied with the prophets, the people said to one another, "What has come over the son of Kish? Is Saul also among the prophets?" 12A man of the place answered, "And who is their father?" Therefore it became a proverb, "Is Saul also among the prophets?" 13When his prophetic frenzy had ended, he went home.[c]

14 Saul's uncle said to him and to the boy, "Where did you go?" And he replied, "To seek the donkeys; and when we saw they were not to be found, we went to Samuel." 15Saul's uncle said, "Tell me what Samuel said to you." 16Saul said to his uncle, "He told us that the donkeys had been found." But about the matter of the kingship, of which Samuel had spoken, he did not tell him anything.

17 Samuel summoned the people to the LORD at Mizpah 18and said to them,[d] "Thus says the LORD, the God of Israel, 'I brought up Israel out of Egypt, and I rescued you from the hand of the Egyptians and from the hand of all the kingdoms that were oppressing you.' 19But today you have rejected your God, who saves you from all your calamities and your distresses; and you have said, 'No! but set a king over us.' Now therefore present yourselves before the LORD by your tribes and by your clans."

20 Then Samuel brought all the tribes of Israel near, and the tribe of Benjamin was taken by lot. 21He brought the tribe of Benjamin near by its families, and the family of the Matrites was taken by lot. Finally he brought the family of the Matrites near man by man,[e] and Saul the son of Kish was taken by lot. But when they sought him, he could not be found. 22So they inquired again of the LORD, "Did the man come here?"[f] and the LORD said, "See, he has hidden himself among the baggage." 23Then they ran and brought him from there. When he took his stand among the people, he was head and shoulders taller than any of them. 24Samuel said to all the people, "Do you see the one whom the LORD has chosen? There is no one like him among all the people." And all the people shouted, "Long live the king!"

25 Samuel told the people the rights and duties of the kingship; and he wrote them in a book and laid it up before the LORD. Then Samuel sent all the people back to their homes. 26Saul also went to his home at Gibeah, and with him went warriors whose hearts God had touched. 27But some worthless fellows said, "How can this man save us?" They despised him and brought him no present. But he held his peace.

Now Nahash, king of the Ammonites, had been grievously oppressing the Gadites and the Reubenites. He would gouge out the right eye of each of them and would not grant Israel a deliverer. No one was left of the Israelites across the Jordan whose right eye Nahash, king of the Ammonites, had not gouged out. But there were seven thousand men who had escaped from the Ammonites and had entered Jabesh-gilead.[g]

11 About a month later,[h] Nahash the Ammonite went up and besieged Jabesh-gilead; and all the men of Jabesh said to Nahash, "Make a treaty with us, and we will serve you." 2But Nahash the Ammonite said to them, "On this condition I will make a treaty with you, namely that I gouge out everyone's right eye, and thus put disgrace upon all Israel." 3The elders of Jabesh said to him, "Give us seven days' respite that we may send messengers through all the territory of Israel. Then, if there is no one to save us, we will give ourselves up to you." 4When the messengers came to Gibeah of Saul, they reported the matter in the hearing of the people; and all the people wept aloud.

5 Now Saul was coming from the field behind the oxen; and Saul said, "What is the matter with the people, that they are weeping?" So they told him the message from the inhabitants of Jabesh.

[a] Gk: Heb *they came there* [b] Or *the hill* [c] Cn: Heb *he came to the shrine* [d] Heb *to the people of Israel* [e] Gk: Heb lacks *Finally . . . man by man* [f] Gk: Heb *Is there yet a man to come here?* [g] Q Ms Compare Josephus, *Antiquities* VI.v.1 (68–71): MT lacks *Now Nahash . . . entered Jabesh-gilead.* [h] Q Ms Gk: MT lacks *About a month later*

6And the spirit of God came upon Saul in power
when he heard these words, and his anger was
greatly kindled. 7He took a yoke of oxen, and cut
them in pieces and sent them throughout all the
territory of Israel by messengers, saying, "Whoever does not come out after Saul and Samuel,
so shall it be done to his oxen!" Then the dread
of the LORD fell upon the people, and they came
out as one. 8When he mustered them at Bezek,
those from Israel were three hundred thousand,
and those from Judah seventy[a] thousand. 9They
said to the messengers who had come, "Thus shall
you say to the inhabitants of Jabesh-gilead: 'Tomorrow, by the time the sun is hot, you shall have
deliverance.'" When the messengers came and
told the inhabitants of Jabesh, they rejoiced. 10So
the inhabitants of Jabesh said, "Tomorrow we
will give ourselves up to you, and you may do to
us whatever seems good to you." 11The next day
Saul put the people in three companies. At the
morning watch they came into the camp and cut
down the Ammonites until the heat of the day;
and those who survived were scattered, so that no
two of them were left together.

12 The people said to Samuel, "Who is it that
said, 'Shall Saul reign over us?' Give them to us so
that we may put them to death." 13But Saul said,
"No one shall be put to death this day, for today
the LORD has brought deliverance to Israel."

14 Samuel said to the people, "Come, let us
go to Gilgal and there renew the kingship." 15So
all the people went to Gilgal, and there they
made Saul king before the LORD in Gilgal. There
they sacrificed offerings of well-being before the
LORD, and there Saul and all the Israelites rejoiced greatly.

12 Samuel said to all Israel, "I have listened
to you in all that you have said to me, and
have set a king over you. 2See, it is the king who
leads you now; I am old and gray, but my sons
are with you. I have led you from my youth until
this day. 3Here I am; testify against me before the
LORD and before his anointed. Whose ox have I
taken? Or whose donkey have I taken? Or whom
have I defrauded? Whom have I oppressed? Or
from whose hand have I taken a bribe to blind my
eyes with it? Testify against me[b] and I will restore
it to you." 4They said, "You have not defrauded
us or oppressed us or taken anything from the
hand of anyone." 5He said to them, "The LORD is
witness against you, and his anointed is witness
this day, that you have not found anything in my
hand." And they said, "He is witness."

6 Samuel said to the people, "The LORD is
witness, who[c] appointed Moses and Aaron and
brought your ancestors up out of the land of
Egypt. 7Now therefore take your stand, so that
I may enter into judgment with you before the
LORD, and I will declare to you[d] all the saving
deeds of the LORD that he performed for you
and for your ancestors. 8When Jacob went into
Egypt and the Egyptians oppressed them,[e] then
your ancestors cried to the LORD and the LORD
sent Moses and Aaron, who brought forth your
ancestors out of Egypt, and settled them in this
place. 9But they forgot the LORD their God; and
he sold them into the hand of Sisera, commander
of the army of King Jabin of[f] Hazor, and into
the hand of the Philistines, and into the hand of
the king of Moab; and they fought against them.
10Then they cried to the LORD, and said, 'We
have sinned, because we have forsaken the LORD,
and have served the Baals and the Astartes; but
now rescue us out of the hand of our enemies,
and we will serve you.' 11And the LORD sent Jerubbaal and Barak,[g] and Jephthah, and Samson,[h]
and rescued you out of the hand of your enemies
on every side; and you lived in safety. 12But when
you saw that King Nahash of the Ammonites
came against you, you said to me, 'No, but a king
shall reign over us,' though the LORD your God
was your king. 13See, here is the king whom you
have chosen, for whom you have asked; see, the
LORD has set a king over you. 14If you will fear
the LORD and serve him and heed his voice and
not rebel against the commandment of the LORD,

[a] Q Ms Gk: MT *thirty* [b] Gk: Heb lacks *Testify against me* [c] Gk: Heb lacks *is witness, who* [d] Gk: Heb lacks *and I will declare to you* [e] Gk: Heb lacks *and the Egyptians oppressed them* [f] Gk: Heb lacks *King Jabin of* [g] Gk Syr: Heb *Bedan* [h] Gk: Heb *Samuel*

and if both you and the king who reigns over you will follow the LORD your God, it will be well; 15but if you will not heed the voice of the LORD, but rebel against the commandment of the LORD, then the hand of the LORD will be against you and your king.[a] 16Now therefore take your stand and see this great thing that the LORD will do before your eyes. 17Is it not the wheat harvest today? I will call upon the LORD, that he may send thunder and rain; and you shall know and see that the wickedness that you have done in the sight of the LORD is great in demanding a king for yourselves." 18So Samuel called upon the LORD, and the LORD sent thunder and rain that day; and all the people greatly feared the LORD and Samuel.

19 All the people said to Samuel, "Pray to the LORD your God for your servants, so that we may not die; for we have added to all our sins the evil of demanding a king for ourselves." 20And Samuel said to the people, "Do not be afraid; you have done all this evil, yet do not turn aside from following the LORD, but serve the LORD with all your heart; 21and do not turn aside after useless things that cannot profit or save, for they are useless. 22For the LORD will not cast away his people, for his great name's sake, because it has pleased the LORD to make you a people for himself. 23Moreover as for me, far be it from me that I should sin against the LORD by ceasing to pray for you; and I will instruct you in the good and the right way. 24Only fear the LORD, and serve him faithfully with all your heart; for consider what great things he has done for you. 25But if you still do wickedly, you shall be swept away, both you and your king."

13 Saul was . . .[b] years old when he began to reign; and he reigned . . . and two[c] years over Israel.

2 Saul chose three thousand out of Israel; two thousand were with Saul in Michmash and the hill country of Bethel, and a thousand were with Jonathan in Gibeah of Benjamin; the rest of the people he sent home to their tents. 3Jonathan defeated the garrison of the Philistines that was at Geba; and the Philistines heard of it. And Saul blew the trumpet throughout all the land, saying, "Let the Hebrews hear!" 4When all Israel heard that Saul had defeated the garrison of the Philistines, and also that Israel had become odious to the Philistines, the people were called out to join Saul at Gilgal.

5 The Philistines mustered to fight with Israel, thirty thousand chariots, and six thousand horsemen, and troops like the sand on the seashore in multitude; they came up and encamped at Michmash, to the east of Beth-aven. 6When the Israelites saw that they were in distress (for the troops were hard pressed), the people hid themselves in caves and in holes and in rocks and in tombs and in cisterns. 7Some Hebrews crossed the Jordan to the land of Gad and Gilead. Saul was still at Gilgal, and all the people followed him trembling.

8 He waited seven days, the time appointed by Samuel; but Samuel did not come to Gilgal, and the people began to slip away from Saul.[d] 9So Saul said, "Bring the burnt offering here to me, and the offerings of well-being." And he offered the burnt offering. 10As soon as he had finished offering the burnt offering, Samuel arrived; and Saul went out to meet him and salute him. 11Samuel said, "What have you done?" Saul replied, "When I saw that the people were slipping away from me, and that you did not come within the days appointed, and that the Philistines were mustering at Michmash, 12I said, 'Now the Philistines will come down upon me at Gilgal, and I have not entreated the favor of the LORD'; so I forced myself, and offered the burnt offering." 13Samuel said to Saul, "You have done foolishly; you have not kept the commandment of the LORD your God, which he commanded you. The LORD would have established your kingdom over Israel forever, 14but now your kingdom will not continue; the LORD has sought out a man after his own heart; and the LORD has appointed him to be ruler over his people, because you have not kept what the LORD commanded you." 15And Samuel left and went on his way from Gilgal.[e] The

[a] Gk: Heb *and your ancestors* [b] The number is lacking in the Heb text (the verse is lacking in the Septuagint). [c] *Two* is not the entire number; something has dropped out. [d] Heb *him* [e] Gk: Heb *went up from Gilgal to Gibeah of Benjamin*

rest of the people followed Saul to join the army;
they went up from Gilgal toward Gibeah of Benjamin.[a]

Saul counted the people who were present
with him, about six hundred men. 16 Saul, his son
Jonathan, and the people who were present with
them stayed in Geba of Benjamin; but the Philistines encamped at Michmash. 17 And raiders
came out of the camp of the Philistines in three
companies; one company turned toward Ophrah,
to the land of Shual, 18 another company turned
toward Beth-horon, and another company turned
toward the mountain[b] that looks down upon the
valley of Zeboim toward the wilderness.

19 Now there was no smith to be found
throughout all the land of Israel; for the Philistines said, "The Hebrews must not make swords
or spears for themselves"; 20 so all the Israelites
went down to the Philistines to sharpen their
plowshares, mattocks, axes, or sickles;[c] 21 The
charge was two-thirds of a shekel[d] for the plowshares and for the mattocks, and one-third of
a shekel for sharpening the axes and for setting
the goads.[e] 22 So on the day of the battle neither
sword nor spear was to be found in the possession of any of the people with Saul and Jonathan;
but Saul and his son Jonathan had them.

23 Now a garrison of the Philistines had gone
out to the pass of Michmash.

14 1 One day
Jonathan son of Saul said to the young
man who carried his armor, "Come, let us go over
to the Philistine garrison on the other side." But
he did not tell his father. 2 Saul was staying in the
outskirts of Gibeah under the pomegranate tree
that is at Migron; the troops that were with him
were about six hundred men, 3 along with Ahijah
son of Ahitub, Ichabod's brother, son of Phinehas
son of Eli, the priest of the LORD in Shiloh, carrying an ephod. Now the people did not know that
Jonathan had gone. 4 In the pass,[f] by which Jonathan tried to go over to the Philistine garrison,
there was a rocky crag on one side and a rocky
crag on the other; the name of the one was Bozez,
and the name of the other Seneh. 5 One crag rose
on the north in front of Michmash, and the other
on the south in front of Geba.

6 Jonathan said to the young man who carried
his armor, "Come, let us go over to the garrison of
these uncircumcised; it may be that the LORD will
act for us; for nothing can hinder the LORD from
saving by many or by few." 7 His armor-bearer
said to him, "Do all that your mind inclines to.[g] I
am with you; as your mind is, so is mine."[h] 8 Then
Jonathan said, "Now we will cross over to those
men and will show ourselves to them. 9 If they
say to us, 'Wait until we come to you,' then we
will stand still in our place, and we will not go up
to them. 10 But if they say, 'Come up to us,' then
we will go up; for the LORD has given them into
our hand. That will be the sign for us." 11 So both
of them showed themselves to the garrison of
the Philistines; and the Philistines said, "Look,
Hebrews are coming out of the holes where
they have hidden themselves." 12 The men of the

[a] Gk: Heb lacks *The rest . . . of Benjamin* [b] Cn Compare Gk: Heb *toward the border* [c] Gk: Heb *plowshare* [d] Heb *was a pim* [e] Cn: Meaning of Heb uncertain [f] Heb *Between the passes* [g] Gk: Heb *Do all that is in your mind. Turn* [h] Gk: Heb lacks *so is mine*

1 Samuel 13:19-22

Israel—a people of the Late Bronze Age—confronted the Philistines, who had mastered the smelting of iron and controlled the distribution of iron implements (and weapons). Not for the first time in history, military technology seemed to determine the fates of peoples—until Jonathan and his armor-bearer defeat a vastly superior force through courage and cunning, an event that causes the earth to quake (14:15); similar courage brought victory to the young David against the armored giant Goliath (ch. 17).

—*NE*

garrison hailed Jonathan and his armor-bearer,
saying, "Come up to us, and we will show you
something." Jonathan said to his armor-bearer,
"Come up after me; for the LORD has given them
into the hand of Israel." 13Then Jonathan climbed
up on his hands and feet, with his armor-bearer
following after him. The Philistines[a] fell before
Jonathan, and his armor-bearer, coming after
him, killed them. 14In that first slaughter Jonathan and his armor-bearer killed about twenty
men within an area about half a furrow long in an
acre[b] of land. 15There was a panic in the camp, in
the field, and among all the people; the garrison
and even the raiders trembled; the earth quaked;
and it became a very great panic.

16 Saul's lookouts in Gibeah of Benjamin
were watching as the multitude was surging back
and forth.[c] 17Then Saul said to the troops that
were with him, "Call the roll and see who has gone
from us." When they had called the roll, Jonathan
and his armor-bearer were not there. 18Saul said
to Ahijah, "Bring the ark[d] of God here." For at
that time the ark[d] of God went with the Israelites.
19While Saul was talking to the priest, the tumult
in the camp of the Philistines increased more and
more; and Saul said to the priest, "Withdraw your
hand." 20Then Saul and all the people who were
with him rallied and went into the battle; and
every sword was against the other, so that there
was very great confusion. 21Now the Hebrews
who previously had been with the Philistines and
had gone up with them into the camp turned and
joined the Israelites who were with Saul and Jonathan. 22Likewise, when all the Israelites who had
gone into hiding in the hill country of Ephraim
heard that the Philistines were fleeing, they too
followed closely after them in the battle. 23So the
LORD gave Israel the victory that day.

The battle passed beyond Beth-aven, and the troops with Saul numbered altogether about ten thousand men. The battle spread out over the hill country of Ephraim.

24 Now Saul committed a very rash act on
that day.[e] He had laid an oath on the troops, saying, "Cursed be anyone who eats food before it
is evening and I have been avenged on my enemies." So none of the troops tasted food. 25All
the troops[f] came upon a honeycomb; and there
was honey on the ground. 26When the troops
came upon the honeycomb, the honey was dripping out; but they did not put their hands to their
mouths, for they feared the oath. 27But Jonathan had not heard his father charge the troops
with the oath; so he extended the staff that was
in his hand, and dipped the tip of it in the honeycomb, and put his hand to his mouth; and his
eyes brightened. 28Then one of the soldiers said,
"Your father strictly charged the troops with an
oath, saying, 'Cursed be anyone who eats food
this day.' And so the troops are faint." 29Then
Jonathan said, "My father has troubled the land;
see how my eyes have brightened because I tasted
a little of this honey. 30How much better if today
the troops had eaten freely of the spoil taken from
their enemies; for now the slaughter among the
Philistines has not been great."

31 After they had struck down the Philistines
that day from Michmash to Aijalon, the troops
were very faint; 32so the troops flew upon the
spoil, and took sheep and oxen and calves, and
slaughtered them on the ground; and the troops
ate them with the blood. 33Then it was reported
to Saul, "Look, the troops are sinning against the
LORD by eating with the blood." And he said,
"You have dealt treacherously; roll a large stone
before me here."[g] 34Saul said, "Disperse yourselves among the troops, and say to them, 'Let
all bring their oxen or their sheep, and slaughter
them here, and eat; and do not sin against the
LORD by eating with the blood.'" So all of the
troops brought their oxen with them that night,
and slaughtered them there. 35And Saul built an
altar to the LORD; it was the first altar that he
built to the LORD.

36 Then Saul said, "Let us go down after the
Philistines by night and despoil them until the
morning light; let us not leave one of them." They
said, "Do whatever seems good to you." But the

[a] Heb *They* [b] Heb *yoke* [c] Gk: Heb *they went and there* [d] Gk *the ephod* [e] Gk: Heb *The Israelites were distressed that day* [f] Heb *land* [g] Gk: Heb *me this day*

priest said, "Let us draw near to God here." 37So
Saul inquired of God, "Shall I go down after the
Philistines? Will you give them into the hand of
Israel?" But he did not answer him that day. 38Saul
said, "Come here, all you leaders of the people;
and let us find out how this sin has arisen today.
39For as the LORD lives who saves Israel, even if
it is in my son Jonathan, he shall surely die!" But
there was no one among all the people who answered him. 40He said to all Israel, "You shall be
on one side, and I and my son Jonathan will be on
the other side." The people said to Saul, "Do what
seems good to you." 41Then Saul said, "O LORD
God of Israel, why have you not answered your
servant today? If this guilt is in me or in my son
Jonathan, O LORD God of Israel, give Urim; but
if this guilt is in your people Israel,[a] give Thummim." And Jonathan and Saul were indicated by
the lot, but the people were cleared. 42Then Saul
said, "Cast the lot between me and my son Jonathan." And Jonathan was taken.

43 Then Saul said to Jonathan, "Tell me what
you have done." Jonathan told him, "I tasted a
little honey with the tip of the staff that was in
my hand; here I am, I will die." 44Saul said, "God
do so to me and more also; you shall surely die,
Jonathan!" 45Then the people said to Saul, "Shall
Jonathan die, who has accomplished this great
victory in Israel? Far from it! As the LORD lives,
not one hair of his head shall fall to the ground;
for he has worked with God today." So the people
ransomed Jonathan, and he did not die. 46Then
Saul withdrew from pursuing the Philistines; and
the Philistines went to their own place.

47 When Saul had taken the kingship over
Israel, he fought against all his enemies on every
side—against Moab, against the Ammonites,
against Edom, against the kings of Zobah, and
against the Philistines; wherever he turned he
routed them. 48He did valiantly, and struck down
the Amalekites, and rescued Israel out of the
hands of those who plundered them.

49 Now the sons of Saul were Jonathan,
Ishvi, and Malchishua; and the names of his two
daughters were these: the name of the firstborn
was Merab, and the name of the younger, Michal.
50The name of Saul's wife was Ahinoam daughter of Ahimaaz. And the name of the commander
of his army was Abner son of Ner, Saul's uncle;
51Kish was the father of Saul, and Ner the father
of Abner was the son of Abiel.

52 There was hard fighting against the Philistines all the days of Saul; and when Saul saw
any strong or valiant warrior, he took him into his
service.

15 Samuel said to Saul, "The LORD sent me
to anoint you king over his people Israel;
now therefore listen to the words of the LORD.
2Thus says the LORD of hosts, 'I will punish the
Amalekites for what they did in opposing the Israelites when they came up out of Egypt. 3Now
go and attack Amalek, and utterly destroy all that
they have; do not spare them, but kill both man
and woman, child and infant, ox and sheep, camel
and donkey.'"

4 So Saul summoned the people, and numbered them in Telaim, two hundred thousand
foot soldiers, and ten thousand soldiers of Judah.
5Saul came to the city of the Amalekites and lay
in wait in the valley. 6Saul said to the Kenites,
"Go! Leave! Withdraw from among the Amalekites, or I will destroy you with them; for you
showed kindness to all the people of Israel when
they came up out of Egypt." So the Kenites withdrew from the Amalekites. 7Saul defeated the
Amalekites, from Havilah as far as Shur, which is
east of Egypt. 8He took King Agag of the Amalekites alive, but utterly destroyed all the people
with the edge of the sword. 9Saul and the people
spared Agag, and the best of the sheep and of the
cattle and of the fatlings, and the lambs, and all
that was valuable, and would not utterly destroy
them; all that was despised and worthless they utterly destroyed.

10 The word of the LORD came to Samuel:
11"I regret that I made Saul king, for he has turned
back from following me, and has not carried out
my commands." Samuel was angry; and he cried
out to the LORD all night. 12Samuel rose early in
the morning to meet Saul, and Samuel was told,

[a] Vg Compare Gk: Heb [41] *Saul said to the LORD, the God of Israel*

"Saul went to Carmel, where he set up a monument for himself, and on returning he passed on
down to Gilgal." 13 When Samuel came to Saul,
Saul said to him, "May you be blessed by the
LORD; I have carried out the command of the
LORD." 14 But Samuel said, "What then is this
bleating of sheep in my ears, and the lowing of
cattle that I hear?" 15 Saul said, "They have brought
them from the Amalekites; for the people spared
the best of the sheep and the cattle, to sacrifice to
the LORD your God; but the rest we have utterly
destroyed." 16 Then Samuel said to Saul, "Stop! I
will tell you what the LORD said to me last night."
He replied, "Speak."

17 Samuel said, "Though you are little in your
own eyes, are you not the head of the tribes of
Israel? The LORD anointed you king over Israel.
18 And the LORD sent you on a mission, and said,
'Go, utterly destroy the sinners, the Amalekites,
and fight against them until they are consumed.'
19 Why then did you not obey the voice of the
LORD? Why did you swoop down on the spoil,
and do what was evil in the sight of the LORD?"
20 Saul said to Samuel, "I have obeyed the voice of
the LORD, I have gone on the mission on which
the LORD sent me, I have brought Agag the king
of Amalek, and I have utterly destroyed the Amalekites. 21 But from the spoil the people took
sheep and cattle, the best of the things devoted to
destruction, to sacrifice to the LORD your God in
Gilgal." 22 And Samuel said,

"Has the LORD as great delight in burnt
offerings and sacrifices,
as in obedience to the voice of the LORD?
Surely, to obey is better than sacrifice,
and to heed than the fat of rams.
23 For rebellion is no less a sin than divination,
and stubbornness is like iniquity and
idolatry.
Because you have rejected the word of the
LORD,
he has also rejected you from being king."

24 Saul said to Samuel, "I have sinned; for
I have transgressed the commandment of the
LORD and your words, because I feared the people and obeyed their voice. 25 Now therefore, I
pray, pardon my sin, and return with me, so that
I may worship the LORD." 26 Samuel said to Saul, "I
will not return with you; for you have rejected the
word of the LORD, and the LORD has rejected you
from being king over Israel." 27 As Samuel turned
to go away, Saul caught hold of the hem of his
robe, and it tore. 28 And Samuel said to him, "The
LORD has torn the kingdom of Israel from you this
very day, and has given it to a neighbor of yours,
who is better than you. 29 Moreover the Glory of
Israel will not recant[a] or change his mind; for he
is not a mortal, that he should change his mind."
30 Then Saul[b] said, "I have sinned; yet honor me
now before the elders of my people and before
Israel, and return with me, so that I may worship
the LORD your God." 31 So Samuel turned back
after Saul; and Saul worshiped the LORD.

32 Then Samuel said, "Bring Agag king of the
Amalekites here to me." And Agag came to him
haltingly.[c] Agag said, "Surely this is the bitterness
of death."[d] 33 But Samuel said,

"As your sword has made women childless,
so your mother shall be childless among
women."

And Samuel hewed Agag in pieces before the
LORD in Gilgal.

34 Then Samuel went to Ramah; and Saul
went up to his house in Gibeah of Saul. 35 Samuel
did not see Saul again until the day of his death,
but Samuel grieved over Saul. And the LORD was
sorry that he had made Saul king over Israel.

16 The LORD said to Samuel, "How long will
you grieve over Saul? I have rejected him
from being king over Israel. Fill your horn with
oil and set out; I will send you to Jesse the Bethlehemite, for I have provided for myself a king
among his sons." 2 Samuel said, "How can I go?
If Saul hears of it, he will kill me." And the LORD
said, "Take a heifer with you, and say, 'I have
come to sacrifice to the LORD.' 3 Invite Jesse to
the sacrifice, and I will show you what you shall
do; and you shall anoint for me the one whom I

[a] Q Ms Gk: MT *deceive* [b] Heb *he* [c] Cn Compare Gk: Meaning of Heb uncertain
[d] Q Ms Gk: MT *Surely the bitterness of death is past*

name to you." 4 Samuel did what the LORD commanded, and came to Bethlehem. The elders of the city came to meet him trembling, and said, "Do you come peaceably?" 5 He said, "Peaceably; I have come to sacrifice to the LORD; sanctify yourselves and come with me to the sacrifice." And he sanctified Jesse and his sons and invited them to the sacrifice.

6 When they came, he looked on Eliab and thought, "Surely the LORD's anointed is now before the LORD."[a] 7 But the LORD said to Samuel, "Do not look on his appearance or on the height of his stature, because I have rejected him; for the LORD does not see as mortals see; they look on the outward appearance, but the LORD looks on the heart." 8 Then Jesse called Abinadab, and made him pass before Samuel. He said, "Neither has the LORD chosen this one." 9 Then Jesse made Shammah pass by. And he said, "Neither has the LORD chosen this one." 10 Jesse made seven of his sons pass before Samuel, and Samuel said to Jesse, "The LORD has not chosen any of these." 11 Samuel said to Jesse, "Are all your sons here?" And he said, "There remains yet the youngest, but he is keeping the sheep." And Samuel said to Jesse, "Send and bring him; for we will not sit down until he comes here." 12 He sent and brought him in. Now he was ruddy, and had beautiful eyes, and was handsome. The LORD said, "Rise and anoint him; for this is the one." 13 Then Samuel took the horn of oil, and anointed him in the presence of his brothers; and the spirit of the LORD came mightily upon David from that day forward. Samuel then set out and went to Ramah.

14 Now the spirit of the LORD departed from Saul, and an evil spirit from the LORD tormented him. 15 And Saul's servants said to him, "See now, an evil spirit from God is tormenting you. 16 Let our lord now command the servants who attend you to look for someone who is skillful in playing the lyre; and when the evil spirit from God is upon you, he will play it, and you will feel better." 17 So Saul said to his servants, "Provide for me someone who can play well, and bring him to me." 18 One of the young men answered, "I have seen a son of Jesse the Bethlehemite who is skillful in playing, a man of valor, a warrior, prudent in speech, and a man of good presence; and the LORD is with him." 19 So Saul sent messengers to Jesse, and said, "Send me your son David who is with the sheep." 20 Jesse took a donkey loaded with bread, a skin of wine, and a kid, and sent them by his son David to Saul. 21 And David came to Saul, and entered his service. Saul loved him greatly, and he became his armor-bearer. 22 Saul sent to Jesse, saying, "Let David remain in my service, for he has found favor in my sight." 23 And whenever the evil spirit from God came upon Saul, David took the lyre and played it with his hand, and Saul would be relieved and feel better, and the evil spirit would depart from him.

17 Now the Philistines gathered their armies for battle; they were gathered at Socoh, which belongs to Judah, and encamped between Socoh and Azekah, in Ephes-dammim. 2 Saul and the Israelites gathered and encamped in the valley of Elah, and formed ranks against the Philistines. 3 The Philistines stood on the mountain on the one side, and Israel stood on the mountain on the other side, with a valley between them. 4 And there came out from the camp of the Philistines a champion named Goliath, of Gath, whose height was six[b] cubits and a span. 5 He had a helmet of bronze on his head, and he was armed with a coat of mail; the weight of the coat was five thousand shekels of bronze. 6 He had greaves of bronze on his legs and a javelin of bronze slung between his shoulders. 7 The shaft of his spear was like a weaver's beam, and his spear's head weighed six hundred shekels of iron; and his shield-bearer went before him. 8 He stood and shouted to the ranks of Israel, "Why have you come out to draw up for battle? Am I not a Philistine, and are you not servants of Saul? Choose a man for yourselves, and let him come down to me. 9 If he is able to fight with me and kill me, then we will be your servants; but if I prevail against him and kill him, then you shall be our servants and serve us." 10 And the Philistine said, "Today I defy the ranks of Israel! Give me a man, that we may fight

[a] Heb *him* [b] MT: Q Ms Gk *four*

together." [11]When Saul and all Israel heard these
words of the Philistine, they were dismayed and
greatly afraid.

12 Now David was the son of an Ephrathite of
Bethlehem in Judah, named Jesse, who had eight
sons. In the days of Saul the man was already old
and advanced in years.[a] [13]The three eldest sons of
Jesse had followed Saul to the battle; the names of
his three sons who went to the battle were Eliab
the firstborn, and next to him Abinadab, and the
third Shammah. [14]David was the youngest; the
three eldest followed Saul, [15]but David went back
and forth from Saul to feed his father's sheep at
Bethlehem. [16]For forty days the Philistine came
forward and took his stand, morning and evening.

17 Jesse said to his son David, "Take for your
brothers an ephah of this parched grain and these
ten loaves, and carry them quickly to the camp
to your brothers; [18]also take these ten cheeses to
the commander of their thousand. See how your
brothers fare, and bring some token from them."

19 Now Saul, and they, and all the men of
Israel, were in the valley of Elah, fighting with
the Philistines. [20]David rose early in the morning,
left the sheep with a keeper, took the provisions,
and went as Jesse had commanded him. He
came to the encampment as the army was going
forth to the battle line, shouting the war cry. [21]Israel
and the Philistines drew up for battle, army
against army. [22]David left the things in charge of
the keeper of the baggage, ran to the ranks, and
went and greeted his brothers. [23]As he talked
with them, the champion, the Philistine of Gath,
Goliath by name, came up out of the ranks of the
Philistines, and spoke the same words as before.
And David heard him.

24 All the Israelites, when they saw the man,
fled from him and were very much afraid. [25]The
Israelites said, "Have you seen this man who has
come up? Surely he has come up to defy Israel.
The king will greatly enrich the man who kills
him, and will give him his daughter and make
his family free in Israel." [26]David said to the men
who stood by him, "What shall be done for the
man who kills this Philistine, and takes away the
reproach from Israel? For who is this uncircumcised
Philistine that he should defy the armies
of the living God?" [27]The people answered him
in the same way, "So shall it be done for the man
who kills him."

28 His eldest brother Eliab heard him talking
to the men; and Eliab's anger was kindled
against David. He said, "Why have you come
down? With whom have you left those few sheep
in the wilderness? I know your presumption and
the evil of your heart; for you have come down
just to see the battle." [29]David said, "What have
I done now? It was only a question." [30]He turned
away from him toward another and spoke in the
same way; and the people answered him again as
before.

31 When the words that David spoke were
heard, they repeated them before Saul; and he

1 Samuel 17:12

Although David is named as the youngest of at least eight sons of Jesse of Bethlehem (17:12-14) and had at least two sisters whose names we know, Abigail and Zeruiah (1 Chr 2:16), his mother's name is not preserved in the Bible. In the Talmud the rabbis record her name, Nizbeth bat Adael, and explain that it was not written in Scripture in order to hide it from the *minim*, the heretics—meaning primarily Christians.

While the Gospel of Matthew traces Jesus' ancestry back to Solomon, the son of David and Bathsheba, eight of David's wives are named in Scripture (1 Chr 3:1-9), including Michal, Saul's daughter (2 Sam 6:23), with whom he had no children, and Bathsheba (2 Samuel 11–12) and Abigail (1 Samuel 25). He also had many unnamed primary and secondary wives, who also gave birth to his children (1 Chr 3:9; 14:3). Nineteen of his sons and one daughter are named—but he also had numerous other unnamed sons and daughters.

— WG

[a] Gk Syr: Heb *among men*

sent for him. 32David said to Saul, "Let no one's
heart fail because of him; your servant will go and
fight with this Philistine." 33Saul said to David,
"You are not able to go against this Philistine to
fight with him; for you are just a boy, and he has
been a warrior from his youth." 34But David said
to Saul, "Your servant used to keep sheep for his
father; and whenever a lion or a bear came, and
took a lamb from the flock, 35I went after it and
struck it down, rescuing the lamb from its mouth;
and if it turned against me, I would catch it by the
jaw, strike it down, and kill it. 36Your servant has
killed both lions and bears; and this uncircumcised Philistine shall be like one of them, since he
has defied the armies of the living God." 37David
said, "The LORD, who saved me from the paw of
the lion and from the paw of the bear, will save
me from the hand of this Philistine." So Saul said
to David, "Go, and may the LORD be with you!"

38 Saul clothed David with his armor; he put
a bronze helmet on his head and clothed him with
a coat of mail. 39David strapped Saul's sword over
the armor, and he tried in vain to walk, for he was
not used to them. Then David said to Saul, "I cannot walk with these; for I am not used to them."
So David removed them. 40Then he took his staff
in his hand, and chose five smooth stones from
the wadi, and put them in his shepherd's bag, in
the pouch; his sling was in his hand, and he drew
near to the Philistine.

41 The Philistine came on and drew near
to David, with his shield-bearer in front of him.
42When the Philistine looked and saw David, he
disdained him, for he was only a youth, ruddy
and handsome in appearance. 43The Philistine
said to David, "Am I a dog, that you come to me
with sticks?" And the Philistine cursed David by
his gods. 44The Philistine said to David, "Come
to me, and I will give your flesh to the birds of the
air and to the wild animals of the field." 45But David said to the Philistine, "You come to me with
sword and spear and javelin; but I come to you
in the name of the LORD of hosts, the God of the
armies of Israel, whom you have defied. 46This
very day the LORD will deliver you into my hand,
and I will strike you down and cut off your head;
and I will give the dead bodies of the Philistine
army this very day to the birds of the air and to
the wild animals of the earth, so that all the earth
may know that there is a God in Israel, 47and that
all this assembly may know that the LORD does
not save by sword and spear; for the battle is the
LORD's and he will give you into our hand."

48 When the Philistine drew nearer to meet
David, David ran quickly toward the battle line
to meet the Philistine. 49David put his hand in
his bag, took out a stone, slung it, and struck the
Philistine on his forehead; the stone sank into his
forehead, and he fell face down on the ground.

50 So David prevailed over the Philistine
with a sling and a stone, striking down the Philistine and killing him; there was no sword in David's hand. 51Then David ran and stood over the
Philistine; he grasped his sword, drew it out of its
sheath, and killed him; then he cut off his head
with it.

When the Philistines saw that their champion was dead, they fled. 52The troops of Israel
and Judah rose up with a shout and pursued the
Philistines as far as Gath[a] and the gates of Ekron,
so that the wounded Philistines fell on the way
from Shaaraim as far as Gath and Ekron. 53The
Israelites came back from chasing the Philistines,
and they plundered their camp. 54David took the
head of the Philistine and brought it to Jerusalem; but he put his armor in his tent.

55 When Saul saw David go out against the
Philistine, he said to Abner, the commander of
the army, "Abner, whose son is this young man?"
Abner said, "As your soul lives, O king, I do not
know." 56The king said, "Inquire whose son the
stripling is." 57On David's return from killing the
Philistine, Abner took him and brought him before Saul, with the head of the Philistine in his
hand. 58Saul said to him, "Whose son are you,
young man?" And David answered, "I am the son
of your servant Jesse the Bethlehemite."

18 When David[b] had finished speaking to
Saul, the soul of Jonathan was bound to
the soul of David, and Jonathan loved him as his

[a] Gk Syr: Heb *Gai* [b] Heb *he*

own soul. 2 Saul took him that day and would not
let him return to his father's house. 3 Then Jonathan made a covenant with David, because he
loved him as his own soul. 4 Jonathan stripped
himself of the robe that he was wearing, and gave
it to David, and his armor, and even his sword
and his bow and his belt. 5 David went out and
was successful wherever Saul sent him; as a result,
Saul set him over the army. And all the people,
even the servants of Saul, approved.

6 As they were coming home, when David
returned from killing the Philistine, the women
came out of all the towns of Israel, singing and
dancing, to meet King Saul, with tambourines,
with songs of joy, and with musical instruments.[a]
7 And the women sang to one another as they
made merry,

"Saul has killed his thousands,
and David his ten thousands."

8 Saul was very angry, for this saying displeased
him. He said, "They have ascribed to David ten
thousands, and to me they have ascribed thousands; what more can he have but the kingdom?"
9 So Saul eyed David from that day on.

10 The next day an evil spirit from God
rushed upon Saul, and he raved within his house,
while David was playing the lyre, as he did day
by day. Saul had his spear in his hand; 11 and Saul
threw the spear, for he thought, "I will pin David
to the wall." But David eluded him twice.

12 Saul was afraid of David, because the
LORD was with him but had departed from Saul.
13 So Saul removed him from his presence, and
made him a commander of a thousand; and David marched out and came in, leading the army.
14 David had success in all his undertakings; for
the LORD was with him. 15 When Saul saw that he
had great success, he stood in awe of him. 16 But
all Israel and Judah loved David; for it was he who
marched out and came in leading them.

17 Then Saul said to David, "Here is my elder daughter Merab; I will give her to you as a
wife; only be valiant for me and fight the LORD's
battles." For Saul thought, "I will not raise a hand
against him; let the Philistines deal with him."
18 David said to Saul, "Who am I and who are my
kinsfolk, my father's family in Israel, that I should
be son-in-law to the king?" 19 But at the time when
Saul's daughter Merab should have been given to
David, she was given to Adriel the Meholathite
as a wife.

20 Now Saul's daughter Michal loved David.
Saul was told, and the thing pleased him. 21 Saul
thought, "Let me give her to him that she may be
a snare for him and that the hand of the Philistines may be against him." Therefore Saul said to
David a second time,[b] "You shall now be my son-
in-law." 22 Saul commanded his servants, "Speak
to David in private and say, 'See, the king is delighted with you, and all his servants love you;
now then, become the king's son-in-law.'" 23 So
Saul's servants reported these words to David in
private. And David said, "Does it seem to you a
little thing to become the king's son-in-law, seeing
that I am a poor man and of no repute?" 24 The
servants of Saul told him, "This is what David
said." 25 Then Saul said, "Thus shall you say to David, 'The king desires no marriage present except
a hundred foreskins of the Philistines, that he may
be avenged on the king's enemies.'" Now Saul
planned to make David fall by the hand of the
Philistines. 26 When his servants told David these
words, David was well pleased to be the king's son-
in-law. Before the time had expired, 27 David rose
and went, along with his men, and killed one hundred[c] of the Philistines; and David brought their
foreskins, which were given in full number to the
king, that he might become the king's son-in-law.
Saul gave him his daughter Michal as a wife. 28 But
when Saul realized that the LORD was with David,
and that Saul's daughter Michal loved him, 29 Saul
was still more afraid of David. So Saul was David's
enemy from that time forward.

30 Then the commanders of the Philistines
came out to battle; and as often as they came out,
David had more success than all the servants of
Saul, so that his fame became very great.

19 Saul spoke with his son Jonathan and with
all his servants about killing David. But
Saul's son Jonathan took great delight in David.

[a] Or *triangles*, or *three-stringed instruments* [b] Heb *by two* [c] Gk Compare 2 Sam 3.14: Heb *two hundred*

2 Jonathan told David, "My father Saul is trying to
kill you; therefore be on guard tomorrow morning; stay in a secret place and hide yourself. 3 I
will go out and stand beside my father in the field
where you are, and I will speak to my father about
you; if I learn anything I will tell you." 4 Jonathan
spoke well of David to his father Saul, saying to
him, "The king should not sin against his servant
David, because he has not sinned against you,
and because his deeds have been of good service
to you; 5 for he took his life in his hand when he
attacked the Philistine, and the LORD brought
about a great victory for all Israel. You saw it,
and rejoiced; why then will you sin against an innocent person by killing David without cause?"
6 Saul heeded the voice of Jonathan; Saul swore,
"As the LORD lives, he shall not be put to death."
7 So Jonathan called David and related all these
things to him. Jonathan then brought David to
Saul, and he was in his presence as before.

8 Again there was war, and David went out to
fight the Philistines. He launched a heavy attack
on them, so that they fled before him. 9 Then an
evil spirit from the LORD came upon Saul, as he
sat in his house with his spear in his hand, while
David was playing music. 10 Saul sought to pin
David to the wall with the spear; but he eluded
Saul, so that he struck the spear into the wall. David fled and escaped that night.

11 Saul sent messengers to David's house to
keep watch over him, planning to kill him in the
morning. David's wife Michal told him, "If you
do not save your life tonight, tomorrow you will
be killed." 12 So Michal let David down through
the window; he fled away and escaped. 13 Michal
took an idol[a] and laid it on the bed; she put a net[b]
of goats' hair on its head, and covered it with the
clothes. 14 When Saul sent messengers to take David, she said, "He is sick." 15 Then Saul sent the
messengers to see David for themselves. He said,
"Bring him up to me in the bed, that I may kill
him." 16 When the messengers came in, the idol[c]
was in the bed, with the covering[b] of goats' hair
on its head. 17 Saul said to Michal, "Why have you
deceived me like this, and let my enemy go, so
that he has escaped?" Michal answered Saul, "He
said to me, 'Let me go; why should I kill you?'"

18 Now David fled and escaped; he came to
Samuel at Ramah, and told him all that Saul had
done to him. He and Samuel went and settled at
Naioth. 19 Saul was told, "David is at Naioth in Ramah." 20 Then Saul sent messengers to take David.
When they saw the company of the prophets in a
frenzy, with Samuel standing in charge of[b] them,
the spirit of God came upon the messengers of
Saul, and they also fell into a prophetic frenzy.
21 When Saul was told, he sent other messengers,
and they also fell into a frenzy. Saul sent messengers again the third time, and they also fell into
a frenzy. 22 Then he himself went to Ramah. He
came to the great well that is in Secu;[d] he asked,
"Where are Samuel and David?" And someone
said, "They are at Naioth in Ramah." 23 He went
there, toward Naioth in Ramah; and the spirit of
God came upon him. As he was going, he fell into
a prophetic frenzy, until he came to Naioth in Ramah. 24 He too stripped off his clothes, and he too
fell into a frenzy before Samuel. He lay naked all
that day and all that night. Therefore it is said, "Is
Saul also among the prophets?"

20 David fled from Naioth in Ramah. He
came before Jonathan and said, "What
have I done? What is my guilt? And what is my
sin against your father that he is trying to take
my life?" 2 He said to him, "Far from it! You shall
not die. My father does nothing either great
or small without disclosing it to me; and why
should my father hide this from me? Never!"
3 But David also swore, "Your father knows well
that you like me; and he thinks, 'Do not let Jonathan know this, or he will be grieved.' But truly,
as the LORD lives and as you yourself live, there
is but a step between me and death." 4 Then Jonathan said to David, "Whatever you say, I will do
for you." 5 David said to Jonathan, "Tomorrow is
the new moon, and I should not fail to sit with
the king at the meal; but let me go, so that I may
hide in the field until the third evening. 6 If your

[a] Heb *took the teraphim* [b] Meaning of Heb uncertain [c] Heb *the teraphim*
[d] Gk reads *to the well of the threshing floor on the bare height*

father misses me at all, then say, 'David earnestly asked leave of me to run to Bethlehem his city; for there is a yearly sacrifice there for all the family.' 7 If he says, 'Good!' it will be well with your servant; but if he is angry, then know that evil has been determined by him. 8 Therefore deal kindly with your servant, for you have brought your servant into a sacred covenant[a] with you. But if there is guilt in me, kill me yourself; why should you bring me to your father?" 9 Jonathan said, "Far be it from you! If I knew that it was decided by my father that evil should come upon you, would I not tell you?" 10 Then David said to Jonathan, "Who will tell me if your father answers you harshly?" 11 Jonathan replied to David, "Come, let us go out into the field." So they both went out into the field.

12 Jonathan said to David, "By the LORD, the God of Israel! When I have sounded out my father, about this time tomorrow, or on the third day, if he is well disposed toward David, shall I not then send and disclose it to you? 13 But if my father intends to do you harm, the LORD do so to Jonathan, and more also, if I do not disclose it to you, and send you away, so that you may go in safety. May the LORD be with you, as he has been with my father. 14 If I am still alive, show me the faithful love of the LORD; but if I die,[b] 15 never cut off your faithful love from my house, even if the LORD were to cut off every one of the enemies of David from the face of the earth." 16 Thus Jonathan made a covenant with the house of David, saying, "May the LORD seek out the enemies of David." 17 Jonathan made David swear again by his love for him; for he loved him as he loved his own life.

18 Jonathan said to him, "Tomorrow is the new moon; you will be missed, because your place will be empty. 19 On the day after tomorrow, you shall go a long way down; go to the place where you hid yourself earlier, and remain beside the stone there.[b] 20 I will shoot three arrows to the side of it, as though I shot at a mark. 21 Then I will send the boy, saying, 'Go, find the arrows.' If I say to the boy, 'Look, the arrows are on this side of you, collect them,' then you are to come, for, as the LORD lives, it is safe for you and there is no danger. 22 But if I say to the young man, 'Look, the arrows are beyond you,' then go; for the LORD has sent you away. 23 As for the matter about which you and I have spoken, the LORD is witness[c] between you and me forever."

24 So David hid himself in the field. When the new moon came, the king sat at the feast to eat. 25 The king sat upon his seat, as at other times, upon the seat by the wall. Jonathan stood, while Abner sat by Saul's side; but David's place was empty.

26 Saul did not say anything that day; for he thought, "Something has befallen him; he is not clean, surely he is not clean." 27 But on the second day, the day after the new moon, David's place was empty. And Saul said to his son Jonathan, "Why has the son of Jesse not come to the feast, either yesterday or today?" 28 Jonathan answered Saul, "David earnestly asked leave of me to go to Bethlehem; 29 he said, 'Let me go; for our family is holding a sacrifice in the city, and my brother has commanded me to be there. So now, if I have found favor in your sight, let me get away, and see my brothers.' For this reason he has not come to the king's table."

30 Then Saul's anger was kindled against Jonathan. He said to him, "You son of a perverse, rebellious woman! Do I not know that you have chosen the son of Jesse to your own shame, and to the shame of your mother's nakedness? 31 For as long as the son of Jesse lives upon the earth, neither you nor your kingdom shall be established. Now send and bring him to me, for he shall surely die." 32 Then Jonathan answered his father Saul, "Why should he be put to death? What has he done?" 33 But Saul threw his spear at him to strike him; so Jonathan knew that it was the decision of his father to put David to death. 34 Jonathan rose from the table in fierce anger and ate no food on the second day of the month, for he was grieved for David, and because his father had disgraced him.

35 In the morning Jonathan went out into

[a] Heb *a covenant of the LORD* [b] Meaning of Heb uncertain [c] Gk: Heb lacks *witness*

the field to the appointment with David, and
with him was a little boy. 36 He said to the boy,
"Run and find the arrows that I shoot." As the
boy ran, he shot an arrow beyond him. 37 When
the boy came to the place where Jonathan's arrow
had fallen, Jonathan called after the boy and said,
"Is the arrow not beyond you?" 38 Jonathan called
after the boy, "Hurry, be quick, do not linger."
So Jonathan's boy gathered up the arrows and
came to his master. 39 But the boy knew nothing;
only Jonathan and David knew the arrangement.
40 Jonathan gave his weapons to the boy and said
to him, "Go and carry them to the city." 41 As soon
as the boy had gone, David rose from beside the
stone heap[a] and prostrated himself with his face
to the ground. He bowed three times, and they
kissed each other, and wept with each other;
David wept the more.[b] 42 Then Jonathan said to
David, "Go in peace, since both of us have sworn
in the name of the LORD, saying, 'The LORD shall
be between me and you, and between my descendants and your descendants, forever.' " He got up
and left; and Jonathan went into the city.[c]

21 [d] David came to Nob to the priest Ahimelech. Ahimelech came trembling to meet
David, and said to him, "Why are you alone,
and no one with you?" 2 David said to the priest
Ahimelech, "The king has charged me with a
matter, and said to me, 'No one must know anything of the matter about which I send you, and
with which I have charged you.' I have made an
appointment[e] with the young men for such and
such a place. 3 Now then, what have you at hand?
Give me five loaves of bread, or whatever is here."
4 The priest answered David, "I have no ordinary bread at hand, only holy bread—provided
that the young men have kept themselves from
women." 5 David answered the priest, "Indeed
women have been kept from us as always when
I go on an expedition; the vessels of the young
men are holy even when it is a common journey; how much more today will their vessels be
holy?" 6 So the priest gave him the holy bread;
for there was no bread there except the bread of
the Presence, which is removed from before the
LORD, to be replaced by hot bread on the day it
is taken away.

7 Now a certain man of the servants of Saul
was there that day, detained before the LORD; his
name was Doeg the Edomite, the chief of Saul's
shepherds.

8 David said to Ahimelech, "Is there no spear
or sword here with you? I did not bring my sword
or my weapons with me, because the king's business required haste." 9 The priest said, "The sword
of Goliath the Philistine, whom you killed in the
valley of Elah, is here wrapped in a cloth behind
the ephod; if you will take that, take it, for there is
none here except that one." David said, "There is
none like it; give it to me."

10 David rose and fled that day from Saul; he
went to King Achish of Gath. 11 The servants of
Achish said to him, "Is this not David the king of
the land? Did they not sing to one another of him
in dances,

'Saul has killed his thousands,
and David his ten thousands'?"

12 David took these words to heart and was very
much afraid of King Achish of Gath. 13 So he
changed his behavior before them; he pretended
to be mad when in their presence.[f] He scratched
marks on the doors of the gate, and let his spittle
run down his beard. 14 Achish said to his servants,
"Look, you see the man is mad; why then have
you brought him to me? 15 Do I lack madmen,
that you have brought this fellow to play the madman in my presence? Shall this fellow come into
my house?"

22 David left there and escaped to the cave
of Adullam; when his brothers and all his
father's house heard of it, they went down there
to him. 2 Everyone who was in distress, and everyone who was in debt, and everyone who was
discontented gathered to him; and he became
captain over them. Those who were with him
numbered about four hundred.

3 David went from there to Mizpeh of Moab.
He said to the king of Moab, "Please let my father

[a] Gk: Heb *from beside the south* [b] Vg: Meaning of Heb uncertain [c] This sentence is 21.1 in Heb [d] Ch 21.2 in Heb
[e] Q Ms Vg Compare Gk: Meaning of MT uncertain [f] Heb *in their hands*

and mother come[a] to you, until I know what God
will do for me." 4He left them with the king of
Moab, and they stayed with him all the time that
David was in the stronghold. 5Then the prophet
Gad said to David, "Do not remain in the stronghold; leave, and go into the land of Judah." So David left, and went into the forest of Hereth.

6 Saul heard that David and those who were
with him had been located. Saul was sitting at
Gibeah, under the tamarisk tree on the height,
with his spear in his hand, and all his servants
were standing around him. 7Saul said to his servants who stood around him, "Hear now, you
Benjaminites; will the son of Jesse give every one
of you fields and vineyards, will he make you all
commanders of thousands and commanders of
hundreds? 8Is that why all of you have conspired
against me? No one discloses to me when my son
makes a league with the son of Jesse, none of you
is sorry for me or discloses to me that my son has
stirred up my servant against me, to lie in wait, as
he is doing today." 9Doeg the Edomite, who was
in charge of Saul's servants, answered, "I saw the
son of Jesse coming to Nob, to Ahimelech son of
Ahitub; 10he inquired of the LORD for him, gave
him provisions, and gave him the sword of Goliath the Philistine."

11 The king sent for the priest Ahimelech son
of Ahitub and for all his father's house, the priests
who were at Nob; and all of them came to the
king. 12Saul said, "Listen now, son of Ahitub." He
answered, "Here I am, my lord." 13Saul said to him,
"Why have you conspired against me, you and the
son of Jesse, by giving him bread and a sword, and
by inquiring of God for him, so that he has risen
against me, to lie in wait, as he is doing today?"

14 Then Ahimelech answered the king,
"Who among all your servants is so faithful as
David? He is the king's son-in-law, and is quick[b]
to do your bidding, and is honored in your house.
15Is today the first time that I have inquired of
God for him? By no means! Do not let the king
impute anything to his servant or to any member
of my father's house; for your servant has known
nothing of all this, much or little." 16The king said,

1 Samuel 22:11-23

Though Saul is ruthless in pursuing David, even ordering the slaughter of priests who had assisted him, David swears that he will protect those who fight with him. The courage, cunning, and loyalty David shows even to the king who seeks to kill him make David one of the most attractive heroes in literature—but make the tragedy of his fall (in 2 Samuel) even more poignant.

— *NE*

"You shall surely die, Ahimelech, you and all your
father's house." 17The king said to the guard who
stood around him, "Turn and kill the priests of
the LORD, because their hand also is with David; they knew that he fled, and did not disclose
it to me." But the servants of the king would not
raise their hand to attack the priests of the LORD.
18Then the king said to Doeg, "You, Doeg, turn
and attack the priests." Doeg the Edomite turned
and attacked the priests; on that day he killed
eighty-five who wore the linen ephod. 19Nob, the
city of the priests, he put to the sword; men and
women, children and infants, oxen, donkeys, and
sheep, he put to the sword.

20 But one of the sons of Ahimelech son of
Ahitub, named Abiathar, escaped and fled after
David. 21Abiathar told David that Saul had killed
the priests of the LORD. 22David said to Abiathar,
"I knew on that day, when Doeg the Edomite
was there, that he would surely tell Saul. I am responsible[c] for the lives of all your father's house.
23Stay with me, and do not be afraid; for the one
who seeks my life seeks your life; you will be safe
with me."

23 Now they told David, "The Philistines
are fighting against Keilah, and are robbing the threshing floors." 2David inquired of the
LORD, "Shall I go and attack these Philistines?"
The LORD said to David, "Go and attack the Philistines and save Keilah." 3But David's men said
to him, "Look, we are afraid here in Judah; how

[a] Syr Vg: Heb *come out* [b] Heb *and turns aside* [c] Gk Vg: Meaning of Heb uncertain

much more then if we go to Keilah against the
armies of the Philistines?" 4Then David inquired
of the LORD again. The LORD answered him, "Yes,
go down to Keilah; for I will give the Philistines
into your hand." 5So David and his men went to
Keilah, fought with the Philistines, brought away
their livestock, and dealt them a heavy defeat.
Thus David rescued the inhabitants of Keilah.

6 When Abiathar son of Ahimelech fled to
David at Keilah, he came down with an ephod in
his hand. 7Now it was told Saul that David had
come to Keilah. And Saul said, "God has given[a]
him into my hand; for he has shut himself in by
entering a town that has gates and bars." 8Saul
summoned all the people to war, to go down to
Keilah, to besiege David and his men. 9When David learned that Saul was plotting evil against him,
he said to the priest Abiathar, "Bring the ephod
here." 10David said, "O LORD, the God of Israel,
your servant has heard that Saul seeks to come
to Keilah, to destroy the city on my account.
11And now, will[b] Saul come down as your servant
has heard? O LORD, the God of Israel, I beseech
you, tell your servant." The LORD said, "He will
come down." 12Then David said, "Will the men of
Keilah surrender me and my men into the hand of
Saul?" The LORD said, "They will surrender you."
13Then David and his men, who were about six
hundred, set out and left Keilah; they wandered
wherever they could go. When Saul was told that
David had escaped from Keilah, he gave up the
expedition. 14David remained in the strongholds
in the wilderness, in the hill country of the Wilderness of Ziph. Saul sought him every day, but
the LORD[c] did not give him into his hand.

15 David was in the Wilderness of Ziph at
Horesh when he learned that[d] Saul had come out
to seek his life. 16Saul's son Jonathan set out and
came to David at Horesh; there he strengthened
his hand through the LORD.[e] 17He said to him,
"Do not be afraid; for the hand of my father Saul
shall not find you; you shall be king over Israel,
and I shall be second to you; my father Saul also
knows that this is so." 18Then the two of them
made a covenant before the LORD; David remained at Horesh, and Jonathan went home.

19 Then some Ziphites went up to Saul at
Gibeah and said, "David is hiding among us in
the strongholds of Horesh, on the hill of Hachilah, which is south of Jeshimon. 20Now, O king,
whenever you wish to come down, do so; and
our part will be to surrender him into the king's
hand." 21Saul said, "May you be blessed by the
LORD for showing me compassion! 22Go and
make sure once more; find out exactly where he
is, and who has seen him there; for I am told that
he is very cunning. 23Look around and learn all
the hiding places where he lurks, and come back
to me with sure information. Then I will go with
you; and if he is in the land, I will search him out
among all the thousands of Judah." 24So they set
out and went to Ziph ahead of Saul.

David and his men were in the wilderness of
Maon, in the Arabah to the south of Jeshimon.
25Saul and his men went to search for him. When
David was told, he went down to the rock and
stayed in the wilderness of Maon. When Saul
heard that, he pursued David into the wilderness
of Maon. 26Saul went on one side of the mountain, and David and his men on the other side of
the mountain. David was hurrying to get away
from Saul, while Saul and his men were closing
in on David and his men to capture them. 27Then
a messenger came to Saul, saying, "Hurry and
come; for the Philistines have made a raid on
the land." 28So Saul stopped pursuing David, and
went against the Philistines; therefore that place
was called the Rock of Escape.[f] 29[g]David then
went up from there, and lived in the strongholds
of En-gedi.

24 When Saul returned from following the
Philistines, he was told, "David is in the
wilderness of En-gedi." 2Then Saul took three
thousand chosen men out of all Israel, and went
to look for David and his men in the direction of
the Rocks of the Wild Goats. 3He came to the

[a] Gk Tg: Heb *made a stranger of* [b] Q Ms Compare Gk: MT *Will the men of Keilah surrender me into his hand? Will* [c] Q Ms Gk: MT *God* [d] Or *saw that* [e] Compare Q Ms Gk: MT *God* [f] Or *Rock of Division*; meaning of Heb uncertain [g] Ch 24.1 in Heb

sheepfolds beside the road, where there was a cave; and Saul went in to relieve himself.[a] Now David and his men were sitting in the innermost parts of the cave. 4 The men of David said to him, "Here is the day of which the LORD said to you, 'I will give your enemy into your hand, and you shall do to him as it seems good to you.'" Then David went and stealthily cut off a corner of Saul's cloak. 5 Afterward David was stricken to the heart because he had cut off a corner of Saul's cloak. 6 He said to his men, "The LORD forbid that I should do this thing to my lord, the LORD's anointed, to raise my hand against him; for he is the LORD's anointed." 7 So David scolded his men severely and did not permit them to attack Saul. Then Saul got up and left the cave, and went on his way.

8 Afterwards David also rose up and went out of the cave and called after Saul, "My lord the king!" When Saul looked behind him, David bowed with his face to the ground, and did obeisance. 9 David said to Saul, "Why do you listen to the words of those who say, 'David seeks to do you harm'? 10 This very day your eyes have seen how the LORD gave you into my hand in the cave; and some urged me to kill you, but I spared[b] you. I said, 'I will not raise my hand against my lord; for he is the LORD's anointed.' 11 See, my father, see the corner of your cloak in my hand; for by the fact that I cut off the corner of your cloak, and did not kill you, you may know for certain that there is no wrong or treason in my hands. I have not sinned against you, though you are hunting me to take my life. 12 May the LORD judge between me and you! May the LORD avenge me on you; but my hand shall not be against you. 13 As the ancient proverb says, 'Out of the wicked comes forth wickedness'; but my hand shall not be against you. 14 Against whom has the king of Israel come out? Whom do you pursue? A dead dog? A single flea? 15 May the LORD therefore be judge, and give sentence between me and you. May he see to it, and plead my cause, and vindicate me against you."

16 When David had finished speaking these words to Saul, Saul said, "Is this your voice, my son David?" Saul lifted up his voice and wept. 17 He said to David, "You are more righteous than I; for you have repaid me good, whereas I have repaid you evil. 18 Today you have explained how you have dealt well with me, in that you did not kill me when the LORD put me into your hands. 19 For who has ever found an enemy, and sent the enemy safely away? So may the LORD reward you with good for what you have done to me this day. 20 Now I know that you shall surely be king, and that the kingdom of Israel shall be established in your hand. 21 Swear to me therefore by the LORD that you will not cut off my descendants after me, and that you will not wipe out my name from my father's house." 22 So David swore this to Saul. Then Saul went home; but David and his men went up to the stronghold.

25 Now Samuel died; and all Israel assembled and mourned for him. They buried him at his home in Ramah.

Then David got up and went down to the wilderness of Paran.

2 There was a man in Maon, whose property was in Carmel. The man was very rich; he had three thousand sheep and a thousand goats. He was shearing his sheep in Carmel. 3 Now the name of the man was Nabal, and the name of his wife Abigail. The woman was clever and beautiful, but the man was surly and mean; he was a Calebite. 4 David heard in the wilderness that Nabal was shearing his sheep. 5 So David sent ten young men; and David said to the young men, "Go up to Carmel, and go to Nabal, and greet him in my name. 6 Thus you shall salute him: 'Peace be to you, and peace be to your house, and peace be to all that you have. 7 I hear that you have shearers; now your shepherds have been with us, and we did them no harm, and they missed nothing, all the time they were in Carmel. 8 Ask your young men, and they will tell you. Therefore let my young men find favor in your sight; for we have come on a feast day. Please give whatever you have at hand to your servants and to your son David.'"

9 When David's young men came, they said

[a] Heb *to cover his feet* [b] Gk Syr Tg Vg: Heb *it* (my eye) *spared*

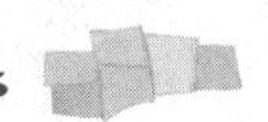

all this to Nabal in the name of David; and then
they waited. 10But Nabal answered David's servants, "Who is David? Who is the son of Jesse?
There are many servants today who are breaking
away from their masters. 11Shall I take my bread
and my water and the meat that I have butchered
for my shearers, and give it to men who come
from I do not know where?" 12So David's young
men turned away, and came back and told him all
this. 13David said to his men, "Every man strap
on his sword!" And every one of them strapped
on his sword; David also strapped on his sword;
and about four hundred men went up after David,
while two hundred remained with the baggage.

14 But one of the young men told Abigail,
Nabal's wife, "David sent messengers out of the
wilderness to salute our master; and he shouted
insults at them. 15Yet the men were very good to
us, and we suffered no harm, and we never missed
anything when we were in the fields, as long as
we were with them; 16they were a wall to us both
by night and by day, all the while we were with
them keeping the sheep. 17Now therefore know
this and consider what you should do; for evil
has been decided against our master and against
all his house; he is so ill-natured that no one can
speak to him."

18 Then Abigail hurried and took two hundred loaves, two skins of wine, five sheep ready
dressed, five measures of parched grain, one hundred clusters of raisins, and two hundred cakes of
figs. She loaded them on donkeys 19and said to
her young men, "Go on ahead of me; I am coming after you." But she did not tell her husband
Nabal. 20As she rode on the donkey and came
down under cover of the mountain, David and
his men came down toward her; and she met
them. 21Now David had said, "Surely it was in
vain that I protected all that this fellow has in the
wilderness, so that nothing was missed of all that
belonged to him; but he has returned me evil for
good. 22God do so to David[a] and more also, if by
morning I leave so much as one male of all who
belong to him."

23 When Abigail saw David, she hurried and
alighted from the donkey, and fell before David
on her face, bowing to the ground. 24She fell at
his feet and said, "Upon me alone, my lord, be the
guilt; please let your servant speak in your ears,
and hear the words of your servant. 25My lord, do
not take seriously this ill-natured fellow, Nabal;
for as his name is, so is he; Nabal[b] is his name, and
folly is with him; but I, your servant, did not see
the young men of my lord, whom you sent.

26 "Now then, my lord, as the LORD lives,
and as you yourself live, since the LORD has restrained you from bloodguilt and from taking
vengeance with your own hand, now let your enemies and those who seek to do evil to my lord be
like Nabal. 27And now let this present that your
servant has brought to my lord be given to the
young men who follow my lord. 28Please forgive
the trespass of your servant; for the LORD will
certainly make my lord a sure house, because my
lord is fighting the battles of the LORD; and evil
shall not be found in you so long as you live. 29If
anyone should rise up to pursue you and to seek
your life, the life of my lord shall be bound in the
bundle of the living under the care of the LORD
your God; but the lives of your enemies he shall
sling out as from the hollow of a sling. 30When
the LORD has done to my lord according to all the
good that he has spoken concerning you, and has
appointed you prince over Israel, 31my lord shall
have no cause of grief, or pangs of conscience, for
having shed blood without cause or for having
saved himself. And when the LORD has dealt well
with my lord, then remember your servant."

32 David said to Abigail, "Blessed be the
LORD, the God of Israel, who sent you to meet me
today! 33Blessed be your good sense, and blessed
be you, who have kept me today from bloodguilt
and from avenging myself by my own hand! 34For
as surely as the LORD the God of Israel lives, who
has restrained me from hurting you, unless you
had hurried and come to meet me, truly by morning there would not have been left to Nabal so
much as one male." 35Then David received from
her hand what she had brought him; he said to
her, "Go up to your house in peace; see, I have

[a] Gk Compare Syr: Heb *the enemies of David* [b] That is *Fool*

heeded your voice, and I have granted your petition."
36 Abigail came to Nabal; he was holding
a feast in his house, like the feast of a king. Nabal's heart was merry within him, for he was very
drunk; so she told him nothing at all until the
morning light. 37 In the morning, when the wine
had gone out of Nabal, his wife told him these
things, and his heart died within him; he became
like a stone. 38 About ten days later the LORD
struck Nabal, and he died.
39 When David heard that Nabal was dead,
he said, "Blessed be the LORD who has judged
the case of Nabal's insult to me, and has kept back
his servant from evil; the LORD has returned the
evildoing of Nabal upon his own head." Then
David sent and wooed Abigail, to make her his
wife. 40 When David's servants came to Abigail
at Carmel, they said to her, "David has sent us
to you to take you to him as his wife." 41 She rose
and bowed down, with her face to the ground,
and said, "Your servant is a slave to wash the feet
of the servants of my lord." 42 Abigail got up hurriedly and rode away on a donkey; her five maids
attended her. She went after the messengers of
David and became his wife.
43 David also married Ahinoam of Jezreel;
both of them became his wives. 44 Saul had given
his daughter Michal, David's wife, to Palti son of
Laish, who was from Gallim.

26 Then the Ziphites came to Saul at Gibeah,
saying, "David is in hiding on the hill of
Hachilah, which is opposite Jeshimon."[a] 2 So Saul
rose and went down to the Wilderness of Ziph,
with three thousand chosen men of Israel, to seek
David in the Wilderness of Ziph. 3 Saul encamped
on the hill of Hachilah, which is opposite Jeshimon[a] beside the road. But David remained in
the wilderness. When he learned that Saul had
come after him into the wilderness, 4 David sent
out spies, and learned that Saul had indeed arrived. 5 Then David set out and came to the place
where Saul had encamped; and David saw the
place where Saul lay, with Abner son of Ner, the
commander of his army. Saul was lying within
the encampment, while the army was encamped
around him.
6 Then David said to Ahimelech the Hittite,
and to Joab's brother Abishai son of Zeruiah,
"Who will go down with me into the camp to
Saul?" Abishai said, "I will go down with you."
7 So David and Abishai went to the army by night;
there Saul lay sleeping within the encampment,
with his spear stuck in the ground at his head;
and Abner and the army lay around him. 8 Abishai
said to David, "God has given your enemy into
your hand today; now therefore let me pin him
to the ground with one stroke of the spear; I will
not strike him twice." 9 But David said to Abishai,
"Do not destroy him; for who can raise his hand
against the LORD's anointed, and be guiltless?"
10 David said, "As the LORD lives, the LORD will
strike him down; or his day will come to die;
or he will go down into battle and perish. 11 The
LORD forbid that I should raise my hand against
the LORD's anointed; but now take the spear that
is at his head, and the water jar, and let us go." 12 So
David took the spear that was at Saul's head and
the water jar, and they went away. No one saw it,
or knew it, nor did anyone awake; for they were
all asleep, because a deep sleep from the LORD
had fallen upon them.
13 Then David went over to the other side,
and stood on top of a hill far away, with a great
distance between them. 14 David called to the
army and to Abner son of Ner, saying, "Abner!
Will you not answer?" Then Abner replied, "Who
are you that calls to the king?" 15 David said to
Abner, "Are you not a man? Who is like you in
Israel? Why then have you not kept watch over
your lord the king? For one of the people came
in to destroy your lord the king. 16 This thing that
you have done is not good. As the LORD lives,
you deserve to die, because you have not kept
watch over your lord, the LORD's anointed. See
now, where is the king's spear, or the water jar
that was at his head?"
17 Saul recognized David's voice, and said,
"Is this your voice, my son David?" David said,
"It is my voice, my lord, O king." 18 And he added,

[a] Or *opposite the wasteland*

"Why does my lord pursue his servant? For what have I done? What guilt is on my hands? 19 Now therefore let my lord the king hear the words of his servant. If it is the LORD who has stirred you up against me, may he accept an offering; but if it is mortals, may they be cursed before the LORD, for they have driven me out today from my share in the heritage of the LORD, saying, 'Go, serve other gods.' 20 Now therefore, do not let my blood fall to the ground, away from the presence of the LORD; for the king of Israel has come out to seek a single flea, like one who hunts a partridge in the mountains."

21 Then Saul said, "I have done wrong; come back, my son David, for I will never harm you again, because my life was precious in your sight today; I have been a fool, and have made a great mistake." 22 David replied, "Here is the spear, O king! Let one of the young men come over and get it. 23 The LORD rewards everyone for his righteousness and his faithfulness; for the LORD gave you into my hand today, but I would not raise my hand against the LORD's anointed. 24 As your life was precious today in my sight, so may my life be precious in the sight of the LORD, and may he rescue me from all tribulation." 25 Then Saul said to David, "Blessed be you, my son David! You will do many things and will succeed in them." So David went his way, and Saul returned to his place.

27 David said in his heart, "I shall now perish one day by the hand of Saul; there is nothing better for me than to escape to the land of the Philistines; then Saul will despair of seeking me any longer within the borders of Israel, and I shall escape out of his hand." 2 So David set out and went over, he and the six hundred men who were with him, to King Achish son of Maoch of Gath. 3 David stayed with Achish at Gath, he and his troops, every man with his household, and David with his two wives, Ahinoam of Jezreel, and Abigail of Carmel, Nabal's widow. 4 When Saul was told that David had fled to Gath, he no longer sought for him.

5 Then David said to Achish, "If I have found favor in your sight, let a place be given me in one of the country towns, so that I may live there; for why should your servant live in the royal city with you?" 6 So that day Achish gave him Ziklag; therefore Ziklag has belonged to the kings of Judah to this day. 7 The length of time that David lived in the country of the Philistines was one year and four months.

8 Now David and his men went up and made raids on the Geshurites, the Girzites, and the Amalekites; for these were the landed settlements from Telam[a] on the way to Shur and on to the land of Egypt. 9 David struck the land, leaving neither man nor woman alive, but took away the sheep, the oxen, the donkeys, the camels, and the clothing, and came back to Achish. 10 When Achish asked, "Against whom[b] have you made a raid today?" David would say, "Against the Negeb of Judah," or "Against the Negeb of the Jerahmeelites," or, "Against the Negeb of the Kenites." 11 David left neither man nor woman alive to be brought back to Gath, thinking, "They might tell about us, and say, 'David has done so and so.'" Such was his practice all the time he lived in the country of the Philistines. 12 Achish trusted David, thinking, "He has made himself utterly abhorrent to his people Israel; therefore he shall always be my servant."

28 In those days the Philistines gathered their forces for war, to fight against Israel. Achish said to David, "You know, of course, that you and your men are to go out with me in the army." 2 David said to Achish, "Very well, then you shall know what your servant can do." Achish said to David, "Very well, I will make you my bodyguard for life."

3 Now Samuel had died, and all Israel had mourned for him and buried him in Ramah, his own city. Saul had expelled the mediums and the wizards from the land. 4 The Philistines assembled, and came and encamped at Shunem. Saul gathered all Israel, and they encamped at Gilboa. 5 When Saul saw the army of the Philistines, he was afraid, and his heart trembled greatly. 6 When Saul inquired of the LORD, the LORD did not

[a] Compare Gk 15.4: Heb *from of old* [b] Q Ms Gk Vg: MT lacks *whom*

answer him, not by dreams, or by Urim, or by
prophets. 7 Then Saul said to his servants, "Seek
out for me a woman who is a medium, so that I
may go to her and inquire of her." His servants
said to him, "There is a medium at Endor."

8 So Saul disguised himself and put on other
clothes and went there, he and two men with
him. They came to the woman by night. And he
said, "Consult a spirit for me, and bring up for me
the one whom I name to you." 9 The woman said
to him, "Surely you know what Saul has done,
how he has cut off the mediums and the wizards
from the land. Why then are you laying a snare
for my life to bring about my death?" 10 But Saul
swore to her by the LORD, "As the LORD lives, no
punishment shall come upon you for this thing."
11 Then the woman said, "Whom shall I bring
up for you?" He answered, "Bring up Samuel for
me." 12 When the woman saw Samuel, she cried
out with a loud voice; and the woman said to
Saul, "Why have you deceived me? You are Saul!"
13 The king said to her, "Have no fear; what do
you see?" The woman said to Saul, "I see a divine
being[a] coming up out of the ground." 14 He said to
her, "What is his appearance?" She said, "An old
man is coming up; he is wrapped in a robe." So
Saul knew that it was Samuel, and he bowed with
his face to the ground, and did obeisance.

15 Then Samuel said to Saul, "Why have you
disturbed me by bringing me up?" Saul answered,
"I am in great distress, for the Philistines are warring against me, and God has turned away from
me and answers me no more, either by prophets
or by dreams; so I have summoned you to tell me
what I should do." 16 Samuel said, "Why then do
you ask me, since the LORD has turned from you
and become your enemy? 17 The LORD has done
to you just as he spoke by me; for the LORD has
torn the kingdom out of your hand, and given it
to your neighbor, David. 18 Because you did not
obey the voice of the LORD, and did not carry
out his fierce wrath against Amalek, therefore the
LORD has done this thing to you today. 19 Moreover the LORD will give Israel along with you into
the hands of the Philistines; and tomorrow you
and your sons shall be with me; the LORD will
also give the army of Israel into the hands of the
Philistines."

20 Immediately Saul fell full length on the
ground, filled with fear because of the words of
Samuel; and there was no strength in him, for
he had eaten nothing all day and all night. 21 The
woman came to Saul, and when she saw that he
was terrified, she said to him, "Your servant has
listened to you; I have taken my life in my hand,
and have listened to what you have said to me.
22 Now therefore, you also listen to your servant;
let me set a morsel of bread before you. Eat, that
you may have strength when you go on your way."
23 He refused, and said, "I will not eat." But his
servants, together with the woman, urged him;
and he listened to their words. So he got up from
the ground and sat on the bed. 24 Now the woman
had a fatted calf in the house. She quickly slaughtered it, and she took flour, kneaded it, and baked
unleavened cakes. 25 She put them before Saul
and his servants, and they ate. Then they rose and
went away that night.

29 Now the Philistines gathered all their
forces at Aphek, while the Israelites were
encamped by the fountain that is in Jezreel. 2 As
the lords of the Philistines were passing on by
hundreds and by thousands, and David and his
men were passing on in the rear with Achish,
3 the commanders of the Philistines said, "What
are these Hebrews doing here?" Achish said to
the commanders of the Philistines, "Is this not
David, the servant of King Saul of Israel, who has
been with me now for days and years? Since he
deserted to me I have found no fault in him to this
day." 4 But the commanders of the Philistines were
angry with him; and the commanders of the Philistines said to him, "Send the man back, so that
he may return to the place that you have assigned
to him; he shall not go down with us to battle, or
else he may become an adversary to us in the battle. For how could this fellow reconcile himself to
his lord? Would it not be with the heads of the
men here? 5 Is this not David, of whom they sing
to one another in dances,

[a] Or *a god*; or *gods*

'Saul has killed his thousands,
and David his ten thousands'?"
6 Then Achish called David and said to him,
"As the LORD lives, you have been honest, and
to me it seems right that you should march out
and in with me in the campaign; for I have found
nothing wrong in you from the day of your coming to me until today. Nevertheless the lords
do not approve of you. 7So go back now; and
go peaceably; do nothing to displease the lords
of the Philistines." 8David said to Achish, "But
what have I done? What have you found in your
servant from the day I entered your service until
now, that I should not go and fight against the
enemies of my lord the king?" 9Achish replied
to David, "I know that you are as blameless in
my sight as an angel of God; nevertheless, the
commanders of the Philistines have said, 'He
shall not go up with us to the battle.' 10Now then
rise early in the morning, you and the servants
of your lord who came with you, and go to the
place that I appointed for you. As for the evil report, do not take it to heart, for you have done
well before me.[a] Start early in the morning, and
leave as soon as you have light." 11So David set
out with his men early in the morning, to return
to the land of the Philistines. But the Philistines
went up to Jezreel.

30 Now when David and his men came to
Ziklag on the third day, the Amalekites
had made a raid on the Negeb and on Ziklag.
They had attacked Ziklag, burned it down, 2and
taken captive the women and all[b] who were in it,
both small and great; they killed none of them,
but carried them off, and went their way. 3When
David and his men came to the city, they found
it burned down, and their wives and sons and
daughters taken captive. 4Then David and the
people who were with him raised their voices and
wept, until they had no more strength to weep.
5David's two wives also had been taken captive,
Ahinoam of Jezreel, and Abigail the widow of
Nabal of Carmel. 6David was in great danger;
for the people spoke of stoning him, because all
the people were bitter in spirit for their sons and
daughters. But David strengthened himself in the
LORD his God.
7 David said to the priest Abiathar son of
Ahimelech, "Bring me the ephod." So Abiathar
brought the ephod to David. 8David inquired of
the LORD, "Shall I pursue this band? Shall I overtake them?" He answered him, "Pursue; for you
shall surely overtake and shall surely rescue." 9So
David set out, he and the six hundred men who
were with him. They came to the Wadi Besor,
where those stayed who were left behind. 10But
David went on with the pursuit, he and four hundred men; two hundred stayed behind, too exhausted to cross the Wadi Besor.
11 In the open country they found an Egyptian, and brought him to David. They gave him
bread and he ate; they gave him water to drink;
12they also gave him a piece of fig cake and two
clusters of raisins. When he had eaten, his spirit
revived; for he had not eaten bread or drunk water for three days and three nights. 13Then David
said to him, "To whom do you belong? Where are
you from?" He said, "I am a young man of Egypt,
servant to an Amalekite. My master left me behind because I fell sick three days ago. 14We had
made a raid on the Negeb of the Cherethites and
on that which belongs to Judah and on the Negeb
of Caleb; and we burned Ziklag down." 15David
said to him, "Will you take me down to this raiding party?" He said, "Swear to me by God that
you will not kill me, or hand me over to my master, and I will take you down to them."

1 Samuel 30:1-25

David is portrayed not only as a courageous and cunning warrior but as a loyal commander: after a raid to rescue the kidnapped families of his own warriors, David refuses to divide spoil only among those who participated in the raid, insisting that all his troops would "share alike" (vv. 23-25).

—*NE*

[a] Gk: Heb lacks *and go to the place . . . done well before me*

[b] Gk: Heb lacks *and all*

16 When he had taken him down, they were
spread out all over the ground, eating and drinking
and dancing, because of the great amount of spoil
they had taken from the land of the Philistines and
from the land of Judah. 17David attacked them
from twilight until the evening of the next day. Not
one of them escaped, except four hundred young
men, who mounted camels and fled. 18David recovered all that the Amalekites had taken; and David rescued his two wives. 19Nothing was missing,
whether small or great, sons or daughters, spoil or
anything that had been taken; David brought back
everything. 20David also captured all the flocks
and herds, which were driven ahead of the other
cattle; people said, "This is David's spoil."
21 Then David came to the two hundred men
who had been too exhausted to follow David, and
who had been left at the Wadi Besor. They went
out to meet David and to meet the people who
were with him. When David drew near to the
people he saluted them. 22Then all the corrupt
and worthless fellows among the men who had
gone with David said, "Because they did not go
with us, we will not give them any of the spoil
that we have recovered, except that each man may
take his wife and children, and leave." 23But David said, "You shall not do so, my brothers, with
what the LORD has given us; he has preserved
us and handed over to us the raiding party that
attacked us. 24Who would listen to you in this
matter? For the share of the one who goes down
into the battle shall be the same as the share of
the one who stays by the baggage; they shall share
alike." 25From that day forward he made it a statute and an ordinance for Israel; it continues to
the present day.
26 When David came to Ziklag, he sent part
of the spoil to his friends, the elders of Judah,
saying, "Here is a present for you from the spoil
of the enemies of the LORD"; 27it was for those
in Bethel, in Ramoth of the Negeb, in Jattir, 28in
Aroer, in Siphmoth, in Eshtemoa, 29in Racal, in
the towns of the Jerahmeelites, in the towns of the
Kenites, 30in Hormah, in Bor-ashan, in Athach,
31in Hebron, all the places where David and his
men had roamed.

31 Now the Philistines fought against Israel;
and the men of Israel fled before the Philistines, and many fell[a] on Mount Gilboa. 2The
Philistines overtook Saul and his sons; and the
Philistines killed Jonathan and Abinadab and
Malchishua, the sons of Saul. 3The battle pressed
hard upon Saul; the archers found him, and he
was badly wounded by them. 4Then Saul said to
his armor-bearer, "Draw your sword and thrust
me through with it, so that these uncircumcised
may not come and thrust me through, and make
sport of me." But his armor-bearer was unwilling;
for he was terrified. So Saul took his own sword
and fell upon it. 5When his armor-bearer saw that
Saul was dead, he also fell upon his sword and
died with him. 6So Saul and his three sons and his
armor-bearer and all his men died together on the
same day. 7When the men of Israel who were on
the other side of the valley and those beyond the
Jordan saw that the men of Israel had fled and that
Saul and his sons were dead, they forsook their
towns and fled; and the Philistines came and occupied them.
8 The next day, when the Philistines came
to strip the dead, they found Saul and his three
sons fallen on Mount Gilboa. 9They cut off his
head, stripped off his armor, and sent messengers
throughout the land of the Philistines to carry
the good news to the houses of their idols and to
the people. 10They put his armor in the temple of
Astarte;[b] and they fastened his body to the wall of
Beth-shan. 11But when the inhabitants of Jabesh-
gilead heard what the Philistines had done to Saul,
12all the valiant men set out, traveled all night
long, and took the body of Saul and the bodies of
his sons from the wall of Beth-shan. They came to
Jabesh and burned them there. 13Then they took
their bones and buried them under the tamarisk
tree in Jabesh, and fasted seven days.

[a] Heb *and they fell slain* [b] Heb plural

2 Samuel

Second Samuel opens with David learning of Saul's death, thus picking up the story where 1 Samuel left off. The people of Judah immediately anoint David their king upon the news of Saul's death (2 Sam 2:1-4). Several years of war ensue between David's men and those who remain loyal to the house of Saul. When Ish-bosheth (or Ishbaal, in NRSV), son of Saul, is assassinated by his own servants (2 Samuel 4), the people of the northern tribes also embrace David as their king, making David king of Judah and Israel (2 Sam 5:1-5). It is important to note that the southern tribes and the northern tribes are distinguished throughout the narrative. In some ways, we might say the people of Judah under David's leadership *conquered* the people of Israel. It was to David's credit that the two distinct peoples came together as one nation. However, their union was tenuous; they always were only a crisis away from going their separate ways.

David secures his kingdom by establishing his capital in Jerusalem (2 Sam 5:6-16) and through military successes against the Philistines and other neighboring peoples (2 Samuel 8). However, the story takes an abrupt turn for the worse in 2 Samuel 11 when David has an affair with Bathsheba and has Uriah the Hittite killed. The subsequent chapters (2 Samuel 13–20) are filled with internal problems that threaten David's reign and put succession in jeopardy. Second Samuel ends with a collection of stories and poems associated with David (2 Samuel 21–24). These include a song of David (2 Samuel 22–23) that expresses a full-blown theology of a firmly established monarchy—a far cry from the earlier theology of a people gathered around the God of the exodus.

Jerusalem is a crossroads where different cultural and ethnic groups converge in peace but sometimes collide in violence. David conquers Jerusalem, a city belonging to the Jebusites, and builds his house there (2 Sam 5:6-12). The Jebusites were probably assimilated into Israel; at least, they were not exterminated. This is indicated by the fact that David buys land from a Jebusite that would become the site of the temple (2 Sam 24:18-25). Moreover, David, who is from the tribe of Judah, secures the loyalty of the northern tribes by bringing the ark of the covenant, which is associated with the northern religious tradition, into Jerusalem (2 Samuel 6). The Cherethites, the Pelethites, and the Gittites were David's inner circle of soldiers. Uriah the Hittite, an officer with a perfectly good Yahwistic name—indicating perhaps that Uriah was culturally and religiously an Israelite—has a house in Jerusalem and is married to Bathsheba (2 Samuel 11). She is an Israelite woman whose father, Eliam, shows up in the list of mighty warriors with her husband (2 Sam 23:34) and whose grandfather Ahithophel is a prominent member of David's court (2 Sam 15:12). But David has Uriah killed to cover up his affair with Bathsheba, triggering a series of violent acts that take place in the "city of peace."

I am ethnically Korean and culturally Northern American. There are predicaments and privileges that come with being a cultural hybrid in a society where the normative cultural identity is that of one particular racial group—white Americans of mostly European descent. If I let the normative identity politics define who I am, I will forever be marked a foreigner, just as Uriah the Hittite was labeled a foreigner in the text. I ask: What makes one an Israelite? What makes one an American?

— ***Uriah Y. Kim***

1 After the death of Saul, when David had returned from defeating the Amalekites, David remained two days in Ziklag. 2On the third
day, a man came from Saul's camp, with his
clothes torn and dirt on his head. When he came
to David, he fell to the ground and did obeisance. 3David said to him, "Where have you
come from?" He said to him, "I have escaped
from the camp of Israel." 4David said to him,
"How did things go? Tell me!" He answered,
"The army fled from the battle, but also many of
the army fell and died; and Saul and his son Jonathan also died." 5Then David asked the young
man who was reporting to him, "How do you
know that Saul and his son Jonathan died?" 6The
young man reporting to him said, "I happened
to be on Mount Gilboa; and there was Saul leaning on his spear, while the chariots and the
horsemen drew close to him. 7When he looked
behind him, he saw me, and called to me. I answered, 'Here sir.' 8And he said to me, 'Who are
you?' I answered him, 'I am an Amalekite.' 9He
said to me, 'Come, stand over me and kill me;
for convulsions have seized me, and yet my life
still lingers.' 10So I stood over him, and killed
him, for I knew that he could not live after he
had fallen. I took the crown that was on his head
and the armlet that was on his arm, and I have
brought them here to my lord."
11 Then David took hold of his clothes and
tore them; and all the men who were with him
did the same. 12They mourned and wept, and
fasted until evening for Saul and for his son Jonathan, and for the army of the LORD and for the
house of Israel, because they had fallen by the
sword. 13David said to the young man who had
reported to him, "Where do you come from?"
He answered, "I am the son of a resident alien,
an Amalekite." 14David said to him, "Were you
not afraid to lift your hand to destroy the LORD's
anointed?" 15Then David called one of the young
men and said, "Come here and strike him down."
So he struck him down and he died. 16David said
to him, "Your blood be on your head; for your
own mouth has testified against you, saying, 'I
have killed the LORD's anointed.'"
17 David intoned this lamentation over
Saul and his son Jonathan. 18(He ordered that
The Song of the Bow[a] be taught to the people
of Judah; it is written in the Book of Jashar.) He
said:

19 Your glory, O Israel, lies slain upon your high
 places!
 How the mighty have fallen!
20 Tell it not in Gath,
 proclaim it not in the streets of Ashkelon;
 or the daughters of the Philistines will
 rejoice,
 the daughters of the uncircumcised will
 exult.

[a] Heb *that The Bow*

21 You mountains of Gilboa,
let there be no dew or rain upon you,
nor bounteous fields![a]
For there the shield of the mighty was
defiled,
the shield of Saul, anointed with oil no
more.

22 From the blood of the slain,
from the fat of the mighty,
the bow of Jonathan did not turn back,
nor the sword of Saul return empty.

23 Saul and Jonathan, beloved and lovely!
In life and in death they were not divided;
they were swifter than eagles,
they were stronger than lions.

24 O daughters of Israel, weep over Saul,
who clothed you with crimson, in luxury,
who put ornaments of gold on your
apparel.

25 How the mighty have fallen
in the midst of the battle!

Jonathan lies slain upon your high places.
26 I am distressed for you, my brother
Jonathan;
greatly beloved were you to me;
your love to me was wonderful,
passing the love of women.

27 How the mighty have fallen,
and the weapons of war perished!

2 After this David inquired of the LORD, "Shall
I go up into any of the cities of Judah?" The
LORD said to him, "Go up." David said, "To which
shall I go up?" He said, "To Hebron." 2So David
went up there, along with his two wives, Ahinoam of Jezreel, and Abigail the widow of Nabal
of Carmel. 3David brought up the men who were
with him, every one with his household; and they
settled in the towns of Hebron. 4Then the people
of Judah came, and there they anointed David
king over the house of Judah.

When they told David, "It was the people of
Jabesh-gilead who buried Saul," 5David sent messengers to the people of Jabesh-gilead, and said to
them, "May you be blessed by the LORD, because
you showed this loyalty to Saul your lord, and
buried him! 6Now may the LORD show steadfast love and faithfulness to you! And I too will
reward you because you have done this thing.
7Therefore let your hands be strong, and be valiant; for Saul your lord is dead, and the house of
Judah has anointed me king over them."

8 But Abner son of Ner, commander of Saul's
army, had taken Ishbaal[b] son of Saul, and brought
him over to Mahanaim. 9He made him king over
Gilead, the Ashurites, Jezreel, Ephraim, Benjamin, and over all Israel. 10Ishbaal,[b] Saul's son,
was forty years old when he began to reign over
Israel, and he reigned two years. But the house
of Judah followed David. 11The time that David
was king in Hebron over the house of Judah was
seven years and six months.

12 Abner son of Ner, and the servants of Ishbaal[b] son of Saul, went out from Mahanaim to
Gibeon. 13Joab son of Zeruiah, and the servants
of David, went out and met them at the pool
of Gibeon. One group sat on one side of
the pool, while the other sat on the other side of
the pool. 14Abner said to Joab, "Let the young
men come forward and have a contest before us."
Joab said, "Let them come forward." 15So they
came forward and were counted as they passed
by, twelve for Benjamin and Ishbaal[b] son of Saul,
and twelve of the servants of David. 16Each
grasped his opponent by the head, and thrust his
sword in his opponent's side; so they fell down
together. Therefore that place was called Helkath-
hazzurim,[c] which is at Gibeon. 17The battle was
very fierce that day; and Abner and the men of
Israel were beaten by the servants of David.

18 The three sons of Zeruiah were there,
Joab, Abishai, and Asahel. Now Asahel was as
swift of foot as a wild gazelle. 19Asahel pursued

[a] Meaning of Heb uncertain
[b] Gk Compare 1 Chr 8.33; 9.39: Heb *Ish-bosheth*, "man of shame"
[c] That is *Field of Sword-edges*

2 Samuel 2:18

The three sons of Zeruiah are David's nephews and chief warriors (Zeruiah is identified as David's sister in 1 Chr 2:13-16). Unusually, Zeruiah's sons are known by her name, not their father's. Here we find that David has another sister, Abigail; we learn about David's father and brothers in the story of his anointing in 1 Samuel 16. But what about David's mother? We learn later—in 1 Sam 22:3—that David sends her into hiding with his father. We know that family trees and relationships are more complicated than those presented in the Scriptures. It falls to the reader to read between the lines in search of the characters who make the story possible.

— *WG*

Abner, turning neither to the right nor to the left
as he followed him. 20Then Abner looked back
and said, "Is it you, Asahel?" He answered, "Yes,
it is." 21Abner said to him, "Turn to your right or
to your left, and seize one of the young men, and
take his spoil." But Asahel would not turn away
from following him. 22Abner said again to Asahel, "Turn away from following me; why should I
strike you to the ground? How then could I show
my face to your brother Joab?" 23But he refused
to turn away. So Abner struck him in the stomach
with the butt of his spear, so that the spear came
out at his back. He fell there, and died where he
lay. And all those who came to the place where
Asahel had fallen and died, stood still.

24 But Joab and Abishai pursued Abner. As
the sun was going down they came to the hill of
Ammah, which lies before Giah on the way to
the wilderness of Gibeon. 25The Benjaminites
rallied around Abner and formed a single band;
they took their stand on the top of a hill. 26Then
Abner called to Joab, "Is the sword to keep devouring forever? Do you not know that the end
will be bitter? How long will it be before you order your people to turn from the pursuit of their
kinsmen?" 27Joab said, "As God lives, if you had
not spoken, the people would have continued to
pursue their kinsmen, not stopping until morning." 28Joab sounded the trumpet and all the
people stopped; they no longer pursued Israel or
engaged in battle any further.

29 Abner and his men traveled all that night
through the Arabah; they crossed the Jordan,
and, marching the whole forenoon,[a] they came to
Mahanaim. 30Joab returned from the pursuit of
Abner; and when he had gathered all the people
together, there were missing of David's servants
nineteen men besides Asahel. 31But the servants
of David had killed of Benjamin three hundred
sixty of Abner's men. 32They took up Asahel and
buried him in the tomb of his father, which was at
Bethlehem. Joab and his men marched all night,
and the day broke upon them at Hebron.

3 There was a long war between the house of
Saul and the house of David; David grew
stronger and stronger, while the house of Saul became weaker and weaker.

2 Sons were born to David at Hebron: his
firstborn was Amnon, of Ahinoam of Jezreel; 3his
second, Chileab, of Abigail the widow of Nabal
of Carmel; the third, Absalom son of Maacah,
daughter of King Talmai of Geshur; 4the fourth,
Adonijah son of Haggith; the fifth, Shephatiah
son of Abital; 5and the sixth, Ithream, of David's
wife Eglah. These were born to David in Hebron.

6 While there was war between the house of
Saul and the house of David, Abner was making
himself strong in the house of Saul. 7Now Saul had
a concubine whose name was Rizpah daughter of
Aiah. And Ishbaal[b] said to Abner, "Why have you
gone in to my father's concubine?" 8The words of
Ishbaal[c] made Abner very angry; he said, "Am I a
dog's head for Judah? Today I keep showing loyalty to the house of your father Saul, to his brothers, and to his friends, and have not given you into
the hand of David; and yet you charge me now
with a crime concerning this woman. 9So may
God do to Abner and so may he add to it! For just
what the LORD has sworn to David, that will I accomplish for him, 10to transfer the kingdom from
the house of Saul, and set up the throne of David

[a] Meaning of Heb uncertain [b] Heb *And he* [c] Gk Compare 1 Chr 8.33; 9.39: Heb *Ish-bosheth*, "man of shame"

over Israel and over Judah, from Dan to Beer-
sheba." 11And Ishbaal[a] could not answer Abner
another word, because he feared him.

12 Abner sent messengers to David at Hebron,[b] saying, "To whom does the land belong?
Make your covenant with me, and I will give you
my support to bring all Israel over to you." 13He
said, "Good; I will make a covenant with you. But
one thing I require of you: you shall never appear
in my presence unless you bring Saul's daughter
Michal when you come to see me." 14Then David
sent messengers to Saul's son Ishbaal,[c] saying,
"Give me my wife Michal, to whom I became engaged at the price of one hundred foreskins of the
Philistines." 15Ishbaal[c] sent and took her from her
husband Paltiel the son of Laish. 16But her husband went with her, weeping as he walked behind
her all the way to Bahurim. Then Abner said to
him, "Go back home!" So he went back.

17 Abner sent word to the elders of Israel,
saying, "For some time past you have been seeking David as king over you. 18Now then bring
it about; for the LORD has promised David:
Through my servant David I will save my people
Israel from the hand of the Philistines, and from
all their enemies." 19Abner also spoke directly to
the Benjaminites; then Abner went to tell David
at Hebron all that Israel and the whole house of
Benjamin were ready to do.

20 When Abner came with twenty men to
David at Hebron, David made a feast for Abner
and the men who were with him. 21Abner said to
David, "Let me go and rally all Israel to my lord
the king, in order that they may make a covenant
with you, and that you may reign over all that
your heart desires." So David dismissed Abner,
and he went away in peace.

22 Just then the servants of David arrived
with Joab from a raid, bringing much spoil with
them. But Abner was not with David at Hebron,
for David[d] had dismissed him, and he had gone
away in peace. 23When Joab and all the army that
was with him came, it was told Joab, "Abner son
of Ner came to the king, and he has dismissed
him, and he has gone away in peace." 24Then
Joab went to the king and said, "What have you
done? Abner came to you; why did you dismiss
him, so that he got away? 25You know that Abner
son of Ner came to deceive you, and to learn your
comings and goings and to learn all that you
are doing."

26 When Joab came out from David's presence, he sent messengers after Abner, and they
brought him back from the cistern of Sirah; but
David did not know about it. 27When Abner
returned to Hebron, Joab took him aside in the
gateway to speak with him privately, and there
he stabbed him in the stomach. So he died for
shedding[e] the blood of Asahel, Joab's[f] brother.
28Afterward, when David heard of it, he said, "I
and my kingdom are forever guiltless before the
LORD for the blood of Abner son of Ner. 29May
the guilt[g] fall on the head of Joab, and on all his
father's house; and may the house of Joab never
be without one who has a discharge, or who is
leprous,[h] or who holds a spindle, or who falls
by the sword, or who lacks food!" 30So Joab and
his brother Abishai murdered Abner because he
had killed their brother Asahel in the battle at
Gibeon.

31 Then David said to Joab and to all the
people who were with him, "Tear your clothes,
and put on sackcloth, and mourn over Abner."
And King David followed the bier. 32They buried Abner at Hebron. The king lifted up his voice
and wept at the grave of Abner, and all the people
wept. 33The king lamented for Abner, saying,

"Should Abner die as a fool dies?
34 Your hands were not bound,
your feet were not fettered;
as one falls before the wicked
you have fallen."

And all the people wept over him again. 35Then
all the people came to persuade David to eat
something while it was still day; but David swore,
saying, "So may God do to me, and more, if I taste
bread or anything else before the sun goes down!"
36All the people took notice of it, and it pleased

[a] Heb *And he* [b] Gk: Heb *where he was* [c] Heb *Ish-bosheth* [d] Heb *he* [e] Heb lacks *shedding* [f] Heb *his*
[g] Heb *May it* [h] A term for several skin diseases; precise meaning uncertain

them; just as everything the king did pleased all
the people. 37 So all the people and all Israel understood that day that the king had no part in the
killing of Abner son of Ner. 38 And the king said to
his servants, "Do you not know that a prince and
a great man has fallen this day in Israel? 39 Today I
am powerless, even though anointed king; these
men, the sons of Zeruiah, are too violent for me.
The LORD pay back the one who does wickedly in
accordance with his wickedness!"

4 When Saul's son Ishbaal[a] heard that Abner had died at Hebron, his courage failed,
and all Israel was dismayed. 2 Saul's son had two
captains of raiding bands; the name of the one
was Baanah, and the name of the other Rechab.
They were sons of Rimmon a Benjaminite from
Beeroth—for Beeroth is considered to belong
to Benjamin. 3 (Now the people of Beeroth had
fled to Gittaim and are there as resident aliens
to this day).

4 Saul's son Jonathan had a son who was
crippled in his feet. He was five years old when
the news about Saul and Jonathan came from Jezreel. His nurse picked him up and fled; and, in her
haste to flee, it happened that he fell and became
lame. His name was Mephibosheth.[b]

5 Now the sons of Rimmon the Beerothite,
Rechab and Baanah, set out, and about the heat
of the day they came to the house of Ishbaal,[c]
while he was taking his noonday rest. 6 They
came inside the house as though to take wheat,
and they struck him in the stomach; then Rechab
and his brother Baanah escaped.[d] 7 Now they
had come into the house while he was lying on
his couch in his bedchamber; they attacked him,
killed him, and beheaded him. Then they took his
head and traveled by way of the Arabah all night
long. 8 They brought the head of Ishbaal[c] to David
at Hebron and said to the king, "Here is the head
of Ishbaal,[c] son of Saul, your enemy, who sought
your life; the LORD has avenged my lord the king
this day on Saul and on his offspring."

9 David answered Rechab and his brother
Baanah, the sons of Rimmon the Beerothite, "As
the LORD lives, who has redeemed my life out
of every adversity, 10 when the one who told me,
'See, Saul is dead,' thought he was bringing good
news, I seized him and killed him at Ziklag—this
was the reward I gave him for his news. 11 How
much more then, when wicked men have killed
a righteous man on his bed in his own house!
And now shall I not require his blood at your
hand, and destroy you from the earth?" 12 So David commanded the young men, and they killed
them; they cut off their hands and feet, and hung
their bodies beside the pool at Hebron. But the
head of Ishbaal[c] they took and buried in the tomb
of Abner at Hebron.

5 Then all the tribes of Israel came to David at
Hebron, and said, "Look, we are your bone and
flesh. 2 For some time, while Saul was king over us,
it was you who led out Israel and brought it in. The
LORD said to you: It is you who shall be shepherd of
my people Israel, you who shall be ruler over Israel."
3 So all the elders of Israel came to the king at Hebron; and King David made a covenant with them
at Hebron before the LORD, and they anointed
David king over Israel. 4 David was thirty years old
when he began to reign, and he reigned forty years.
5 At Hebron he reigned over Judah seven years and
six months; and at Jerusalem he reigned over all
Israel and Judah thirty-three years.

6 The king and his men marched to Jerusalem
against the Jebusites, the inhabitants of the land,
who said to David, "You will not come in here,
even the blind and the lame will turn you back"—
thinking, "David cannot come in here." 7 Nevertheless David took the stronghold of Zion, which
is now the city of David. 8 David had said on
that day, "Whoever would strike down the Jebusites, let him get up the water shaft to attack the
lame and the blind, those whom David hates."[e]
Therefore it is said, "The blind and the lame shall
not come into the house." 9 David occupied the
stronghold, and named it the city of David. David
built the city all around from the Millo inward.
10 And David became greater and greater, for the
LORD, the God of hosts, was with him.

[a] Heb lacks *Ishbaal* [b] In 1 Chr 8.34 and 9.40, *Merib-baal* [c] Heb *Ish-bosheth* [d] Meaning of Heb of verse 6 uncertain
[e] Another reading is *those who hate David*

11 King Hiram of Tyre sent messengers to
David, along with cedar trees, and carpenters and
masons who built David a house. 12David then
perceived that the LORD had established him
king over Israel, and that he had exalted his kingdom for the sake of his people Israel.
13 In Jerusalem, after he came from Hebron,
David took more concubines and wives; and
more sons and daughters were born to David.
14These are the names of those who were born
to him in Jerusalem: Shammua, Shobab, Nathan,
Solomon, 15Ibhar, Elishua, Nepheg, Japhia, 16El-
ishama, Eliada, and Eliphelet.
17 When the Philistines heard that David
had been anointed king over Israel, all the Philistines went up in search of David; but David
heard about it and went down to the stronghold.
18Now the Philistines had come and spread out
in the valley of Rephaim. 19David inquired of the
LORD, "Shall I go up against the Philistines? Will
you give them into my hand?" The LORD said to
David, "Go up; for I will certainly give the Philistines into your hand." 20So David came to Baal-
perazim, and David defeated them there. He said,
"The LORD has burst forth against[a] my enemies
before me, like a bursting flood." Therefore that
place is called Baal-perazim.[b] 21The Philistines
abandoned their idols there, and David and his
men carried them away.
22 Once again the Philistines came up, and
were spread out in the valley of Rephaim. 23When
David inquired of the LORD, he said, "You shall
not go up; go around to their rear, and come upon
them opposite the balsam trees. 24When you hear
the sound of marching in the tops of the balsam
trees, then be on the alert; for then the LORD has
gone out before you to strike down the army of
the Philistines." 25David did just as the LORD had
commanded him; and he struck down the Philistines from Geba all the way to Gezer.

6 David again gathered all the chosen men of
Israel, thirty thousand. 2David and all the
people with him set out and went from Baale-
judah, to bring up from there the ark of God,
which is called by the name of the LORD of hosts
who is enthroned on the cherubim. 3They carried
the ark of God on a new cart, and brought it out
of the house of Abinadab, which was on the hill.
Uzzah and Ahio,[c] the sons of Abinadab, were driving the new cart 4with the ark of God;[d] and Ahio[c]
went in front of the ark. 5David and all the house
of Israel were dancing before the LORD with all
their might, with songs[e] and lyres and harps and
tambourines and castanets and cymbals.
6 When they came to the threshing floor of
Nacon, Uzzah reached out his hand to the ark
of God and took hold of it, for the oxen shook
it. 7The anger of the LORD was kindled against
Uzzah; and God struck him there because he
reached out his hand to the ark;[f] and he died
there beside the ark of God. 8David was angry
because the LORD had burst forth with an out-
burst upon Uzzah; so that place is called Perez-
uzzah,[g] to this day. 9David was afraid of the LORD
that day; he said, "How can the ark of the LORD
come into my care?" 10So David was unwilling to
take the ark of the LORD into his care in the city
of David; instead David took it to the house of
Obed-edom the Gittite. 11The ark of the LORD
remained in the house of Obed-edom the Gittite
three months; and the LORD blessed Obed-edom
and all his household.
12 It was told King David, "The LORD has
blessed the household of Obed-edom and all that
belongs to him, because of the ark of God." So
David went and brought up the ark of God from
the house of Obed-edom to the city of David
with rejoicing; 13and when those who bore the
ark of the LORD had gone six paces, he sacrificed
an ox and a fatling. 14David danced before the
LORD with all his might; David was girded with
a linen ephod. 15So David and all the house of Israel brought up the ark of the LORD with shouting, and with the sound of the trumpet.
16 As the ark of the LORD came into the city
of David, Michal daughter of Saul looked out of

[a] Heb *paraz* [b] That is *Lord of Bursting Forth* [c] Or *and his brother* [d] Compare Gk: Heb *and brought it out of the house of Abinadab, which was on the hill with the ark of God* [e] Q Ms Gk 1 Chr 13.8: Heb *fir trees* [f] 1 Chr 13.10 Compare Q Ms: Meaning of Heb uncertain [g] That is *Bursting Out Against Uzzah*

the window, and saw King David leaping and
dancing before the LORD; and she despised him
in her heart.
17 They brought in the ark of the LORD,
and set it in its place, inside the tent that David had pitched for it; and David offered burnt
offerings and offerings of well-being before the
LORD. 18When David had finished offering the
burnt offerings and the offerings of well-being,
he blessed the people in the name of the LORD
of hosts, 19and distributed food among all the
people, the whole multitude of Israel, both men
and women, to each a cake of bread, a portion of
meat,[a] and a cake of raisins. Then all the people
went back to their homes.
20 David returned to bless his household.
But Michal the daughter of Saul came out to
meet David, and said, "How the king of Israel
honored himself today, uncovering himself today before the eyes of his servants' maids, as any
vulgar fellow might shamelessly uncover himself!" 21David said to Michal, "It was before the
LORD, who chose me in place of your father and
all his household, to appoint me as prince over
Israel, the people of the LORD, that I have danced
before the LORD. 22I will make myself yet more
contemptible than this, and I will be abased in my
own eyes; but by the maids of whom you have
spoken, by them I shall be held in honor." 23And
Michal the daughter of Saul had no child to the
day of her death.
7 Now when the king was settled in his house,
and the LORD had given him rest from all
his enemies around him, 2the king said to the
prophet Nathan, "See now, I am living in a house
of cedar, but the ark of God stays in a tent." 3Na-
than said to the king, "Go, do all that you have in
mind; for the LORD is with you."
4 But that same night the word of the LORD
came to Nathan: 5Go and tell my servant David:
Thus says the LORD: Are you the one to build me
a house to live in? 6I have not lived in a house
since the day I brought up the people of Israel
from Egypt to this day, but I have been moving
about in a tent and a tabernacle. 7Wherever I have
moved about among all the people of Israel, did
I ever speak a word with any of the tribal leaders[b]
of Israel, whom I commanded to shepherd my
people Israel, saying, "Why have you not built me
a house of cedar?" 8Now therefore thus you shall
say to my servant David: Thus says the LORD of
hosts: I took you from the pasture, from following the sheep to be prince over my people Israel;
9and I have been with you wherever you went,
and have cut off all your enemies from before
you; and I will make for you a great name, like the
name of the great ones of the earth. 10And I will
appoint a place for my people Israel and will plant
them, so that they may live in their own place, and
be disturbed no more; and evildoers shall afflict
them no more, as formerly, 11from the time that
I appointed judges over my people Israel; and I
will give you rest from all your enemies. Moreover the LORD declares to you that the LORD will
make you a house. 12When your days are fulfilled
and you lie down with your ancestors, I will raise
up your offspring after you, who shall come forth
from your body, and I will establish his kingdom.
13He shall build a house for my name, and I will
establish the throne of his kingdom forever. 14I
will be a father to him, and he shall be a son to
me. When he commits iniquity, I will punish
him with a rod such as mortals use, with blows
inflicted by human beings. 15But I will not take[c]
my steadfast love from him, as I took it from Saul,
whom I put away from before you. 16Your house
and your kingdom shall be made sure forever before me;[d] your throne shall be established forever.
17In accordance with all these words and with all
this vision, Nathan spoke to David.
18 Then King David went in and sat before
the LORD, and said, "Who am I, O Lord GOD,
and what is my house, that you have brought me
thus far? 19And yet this was a small thing in your
eyes, O Lord GOD; you have spoken also of your
servant's house for a great while to come. May
this be instruction for the people,[e] O Lord GOD!
20And what more can David say to you? For you

[a] Vg: Meaning of Heb uncertain [b] Or *any of the tribes* [c] Gk Syr Vg 1 Chr 17.13: Heb *shall not depart* [d] Gk Heb Mss: MT *before you*; Compare 2 Sam 7.26, 29 [e] Meaning of Heb uncertain

know your servant, O Lord GOD! 21 Because of
your promise, and according to your own heart,
you have wrought all this greatness, so that your
servant may know it. 22 Therefore you are great,
O LORD God; for there is no one like you, and
there is no God besides you, according to all that
we have heard with our ears. 23 Who is like your
people, like Israel? Is there another[a] nation on
earth whose God went to redeem it as a people,
and to make a name for himself, doing great and
awesome things for them,[b] by driving out[c] before
his people nations and their gods?[d] 24 And you
established your people Israel for yourself to be
your people forever; and you, O LORD, became
their God. 25 And now, O LORD God, as for the
word that you have spoken concerning your servant and concerning his house, confirm it forever; do as you have promised. 26 Thus your name
will be magnified forever in the saying, 'The
LORD of hosts is God over Israel'; and the house
of your servant David will be established before
you. 27 For you, O LORD of hosts, the God of Israel, have made this revelation to your servant,
saying, 'I will build you a house'; therefore your
servant has found courage to pray this prayer to
you. 28 And now, O Lord GOD, you are God, and
your words are true, and you have promised this
good thing to your servant; 29 now therefore may
it please you to bless the house of your servant, so
that it may continue forever before you; for you,
O Lord GOD, have spoken, and with your blessing shall the house of your servant be blessed
forever."

8 Some time afterward, David attacked the Philistines and subdued them; David took Metheg-
ammah out of the hand of the Philistines.

2 He also defeated the Moabites and, making
them lie down on the ground, measured them
off with a cord; he measured two lengths of cord
for those who were to be put to death, and one
length[e] for those who were to be spared. And the
Moabites became servants to David and brought
tribute.

3 David also struck down King Hadadezer
son of Rehob of Zobah, as he went to restore his
monument[f] at the river Euphrates. 4 David took
from him one thousand seven hundred horsemen, and twenty thousand foot soldiers. David
hamstrung all the chariot horses, but left enough
for a hundred chariots. 5 When the Arameans
of Damascus came to help King Hadadezer of
Zobah, David killed twenty-two thousand men of
the Arameans. 6 Then David put garrisons among
the Arameans of Damascus; and the Arameans
became servants to David and brought tribute.
The LORD gave victory to David wherever he
went. 7 David took the gold shields that were carried by the servants of Hadadezer, and brought
them to Jerusalem. 8 From Betah and from
Berothai, towns of Hadadezer, King David took
a great amount of bronze.

9 When King Toi of Hamath heard that David had defeated the whole army of Hadadezer,
10 Toi sent his son Joram to King David, to greet
him and to congratulate him because he had
fought against Hadadezer and defeated him.
Now Hadadezer had often been at war with Toi.
Joram brought with him articles of silver, gold,
and bronze; 11 these also King David dedicated to
the LORD, together with the silver and gold that
he dedicated from all the nations he subdued,
12 from Edom, Moab, the Ammonites, the Philistines, Amalek, and from the spoil of King Hadadezer son of Rehob of Zobah.

13 David won a name for himself. When he
returned, he killed eighteen thousand Edomites[g]
in the Valley of Salt. 14 He put garrisons in Edom;
throughout all Edom he put garrisons, and all
the Edomites became David's servants. And the
LORD gave victory to David wherever he went.

15 So David reigned over all Israel; and David administered justice and equity to all his
people. 16 Joab son of Zeruiah was over the army;
Jehoshaphat son of Ahilud was recorder; 17 Zadok
son of Ahitub and Ahimelech son of Abiathar
were priests; Seraiah was secretary; 18 Benaiah

[a] Gk: Heb *one* [b] Heb *you* [c] Gk 1 Chr 17.21: Heb *for your land* [d] Cn: Heb *before your people, whom you redeemed for yourself from Egypt, nations and its gods* [e] Heb *one full length* [f] Compare 1 Sam 15.12 and 2 Sam 18.18
[g] Gk: Heb *returned from striking down eighteen thousand Arameans*

son of Jehoiada was over[a] the Cherethites and the
Pelethites; and David's sons were priests.

9 David asked, "Is there still anyone left of the
house of Saul to whom I may show kindness
for Jonathan's sake?" 2Now there was a servant of
the house of Saul whose name was Ziba, and he
was summoned to David. The king said to him,
"Are you Ziba?" And he said, "At your service!"
3The king said, "Is there anyone remaining of the
house of Saul to whom I may show the kindness
of God?" Ziba said to the king, "There remains
a son of Jonathan; he is crippled in his feet." 4The
king said to him, "Where is he?" Ziba said to
the king, "He is in the house of Machir son of
Ammiel, at Lo-debar." 5Then King David sent
and brought him from the house of Machir son
of Ammiel, at Lo-debar. 6Mephibosheth[b] son of
Jonathan son of Saul came to David, and fell on
his face and did obeisance. David said, "Mephibosheth!"[b] He answered, "I am your servant."
7David said to him, "Do not be afraid, for I will
show you kindness for the sake of your father
Jonathan; I will restore to you all the land of your
grandfather Saul, and you yourself shall eat at my
table always." 8He did obeisance and said, "What
is your servant, that you should look upon a dead
dog such as I?"

9 Then the king summoned Saul's servant
Ziba, and said to him, "All that belonged to Saul
and to all his house I have given to your master's
grandson. 10You and your sons and your servants
shall till the land for him, and shall bring in the
produce, so that your master's grandson may have
food to eat; but your master's grandson Mephibosheth[b] shall always eat at my table." Now Ziba had
fifteen sons and twenty servants. 11Then Ziba said
to the king, "According to all that my lord the king
commands his servant, so your servant will do."
Mephibosheth[b] ate at David's[c] table, like one of
the king's sons. 12Mephibosheth[b] had a young son
whose name was Mica. And all who lived in Ziba's
house became Mephibosheth's[d] servants. 13Me-
phibosheth[b] lived in Jerusalem, for he always ate at
the king's table. Now he was lame in both his feet.

10 Some time afterward, the king of the Ammonites died, and his son Hanun succeeded him. 2David said, "I will deal loyally with
Hanun son of Nahash, just as his father dealt loyally with me." So David sent envoys to console
him concerning his father. When David's envoys
came into the land of the Ammonites, 3the princes
of the Ammonites said to their lord Hanun, "Do
you really think that David is honoring your father just because he has sent messengers with
condolences to you? Has not David sent his envoys to you to search the city, to spy it out, and to
overthrow it?" 4So Hanun seized David's envoys,
shaved off half the beard of each, cut off their garments in the middle at their hips, and sent them
away. 5When David was told, he sent to meet
them, for the men were greatly ashamed. The
king said, "Remain at Jericho until your beards
have grown, and then return."

6 When the Ammonites saw that they had
become odious to David, the Ammonites sent
and hired the Arameans of Beth-rehob and the
Arameans of Zobah, twenty thousand foot soldiers, as well as the king of Maacah, one thousand
men, and the men of Tob, twelve thousand men.
7When David heard of it, he sent Joab and all the
army with the warriors. 8The Ammonites came
out and drew up in battle array at the entrance of
the gate; but the Arameans of Zobah and of Rehob, and the men of Tob and Maacah, were by
themselves in the open country.

9 When Joab saw that the battle was set
against him both in front and in the rear, he chose
some of the picked men of Israel, and arrayed
them against the Arameans; 10the rest of his men
he put in the charge of his brother Abishai, and
he arrayed them against the Ammonites. 11He
said, "If the Arameans are too strong for me, then
you shall help me; but if the Ammonites are too
strong for you, then I will come and help you.
12Be strong, and let us be courageous for the sake
of our people, and for the cities of our God; and
may the LORD do what seems good to him." 13So
Joab and the people who were with him moved

[a] Syr Tg Vg 20.23; 1 Chr 18.17: Heb lacks *was over* [b] Or *Merib-baal*: See 4.4 note [c] Gk: Heb *my* [d] Or *Merib-baal's*: See 4.4 note

forward into battle against the Arameans; and
they fled before him. 14When the Ammonites saw
that the Arameans fled, they likewise fled before
Abishai, and entered the city. Then Joab returned
from fighting against the Ammonites, and came
to Jerusalem.
15 But when the Arameans saw that they had
been defeated by Israel, they gathered themselves
together. 16Hadadezer sent and brought out the
Arameans who were beyond the Euphrates; and
they came to Helam, with Shobach the commander of the army of Hadadezer at their head.
17When it was told David, he gathered all Israel
together, and crossed the Jordan, and came to
Helam. The Arameans arrayed themselves against
David and fought with him. 18The Arameans fled
before Israel; and David killed of the Arameans
seven hundred chariot teams, and forty thousand horsemen,[a] and wounded Shobach the
commander of their army, so that he died there.
19When all the kings who were servants of Hadadezer saw that they had been defeated by Israel,
they made peace with Israel, and became subject
to them. So the Arameans were afraid to help the
Ammonites any more.

11 In the spring of the year, the time when
kings go out to battle, David sent Joab
with his officers and all Israel with him; they ravaged the Ammonites, and besieged Rabbah. But
David remained at Jerusalem.
2 It happened, late one afternoon, when David rose from his couch and was walking about
on the roof of the king's house, that he saw from
the roof a woman bathing; the woman was very
beautiful. 3David sent someone to inquire about
the woman. It was reported, "This is Bathsheba
daughter of Eliam, the wife of Uriah the Hittite."
4So David sent messengers to get her, and she
came to him, and he lay with her. (Now she was
purifying herself after her period.) Then she returned to her house. 5The woman conceived; and
she sent and told David, "I am pregnant."
6 So David sent word to Joab, "Send me Uriah
the Hittite." And Joab sent Uriah to David. 7When
Uriah came to him, David asked how Joab and the
people fared, and how the war was going. 8Then
David said to Uriah, "Go down to your house,
and wash your feet." Uriah went out of the king's
house, and there followed him a present from the
king. 9But Uriah slept at the entrance of the king's
house with all the servants of his lord, and did
not go down to his house. 10When they told David, "Uriah did not go down to his house," David
said to Uriah, "You have just come from a journey. Why did you not go down to your house?"
11Uriah said to David, "The ark and Israel and Judah remain in booths;[b] and my lord Joab and the
servants of my lord are camping in the open field;
shall I then go to my house, to eat and to drink,
and to lie with my wife? As you live, and as your
soul lives, I will not do such a thing." 12Then David said to Uriah, "Remain here today also, and tomorrow I will send you back." So Uriah remained
in Jerusalem that day. On the next day, 13David
invited him to eat and drink in his presence and
made him drunk; and in the evening he went out
to lie on his couch with the servants of his lord,
but he did not go down to his house.
14 In the morning David wrote a letter to
Joab, and sent it by the hand of Uriah. 15In the
letter he wrote, "Set Uriah in the forefront of the
hardest fighting, and then draw back from him, so
that he may be struck down and die." 16As Joab

2 Samuel 11:1-27

The moral preoccupations of Western Christianity have often led to a focus on David's adultery with Bathsheba. In the perspective of the biblical authors, however, the magnitude of his moral corruption is seen only in what follows. David orders the murder of Bathsheba's husband, a loyal warrior, in the front line; when he hears that his forces have suffered heavy casualties, he responds with the cynical equivalent of "war is hell" (v. 25). Long gone is the loyal chieftain of 1 Samuel; David has become a caricature of the war-monger who blithely sends brave soldiers to their deaths.

—*NE*

[a] 1 Chr 19.18 and some Gk Mss read *foot soldiers* [b] Or *at Succoth*

was besieging the city, he assigned Uriah to the
place where he knew there were valiant warriors.
17 The men of the city came out and fought with
Joab; and some of the servants of David among
the people fell. Uriah the Hittite was killed as
well. 18 Then Joab sent and told David all the news
about the fighting; 19 and he instructed the messenger, “When you have finished telling the king
all the news about the fighting, 20 then, if the
king’s anger rises, and if he says to you, ‘Why did
you go so near the city to fight? Did you not know
that they would shoot from the wall? 21 Who
killed Abimelech son of Jerubbaal?[a] Did not a
woman throw an upper millstone on him from
the wall, so that he died at Thebez? Why did you
go so near the wall?’ then you shall say, ‘Your servant Uriah the Hittite is dead too.’ ”

22 So the messenger went, and came and
told David all that Joab had sent him to tell. 23 The
messenger said to David, “The men gained an advantage over us, and came out against us in the
field; but we drove them back to the entrance of
the gate. 24 Then the archers shot at your servants
from the wall; some of the king’s servants are
dead; and your servant Uriah the Hittite is dead
also.” 25 David said to the messenger, “Thus you
shall say to Joab, ‘Do not let this matter trouble
you, for the sword devours now one and now
another; press your attack on the city, and overthrow it.’ And encourage him.”

26 When the wife of Uriah heard that her
husband was dead, she made lamentation for
him. 27 When the mourning was over, David sent
and brought her to his house, and she became his
wife, and bore him a son.

But the thing that David had done displeased
12 the LORD, 1 and the LORD sent Nathan to
David. He came to him, and said to him,
“There were two men in a certain city, the one rich
and the other poor. 2 The rich man had very many
flocks and herds; 3 but the poor man had nothing
but one little ewe lamb, which he had bought. He
brought it up, and it grew up with him and with
his children; it used to eat of his meager fare, and
drink from his cup, and lie in his bosom, and it
was like a daughter to him. 4 Now there came a
traveler to the rich man, and he was loath to take
one of his own flock or herd to prepare for the
wayfarer who had come to him, but he took the
poor man’s lamb, and prepared that for the guest
who had come to him.” 5 Then David’s anger was
greatly kindled against the man. He said to Nathan, “As the LORD lives, the man who has done
this deserves to die; 6 he shall restore the lamb
fourfold, because he did this thing, and because
he had no pity.”

7 Nathan said to David, “You are the man!
Thus says the LORD, the God of Israel: I anointed
you king over Israel, and I rescued you from the
hand of Saul; 8 I gave you your master’s house,
and your master’s wives into your bosom, and
gave you the house of Israel and of Judah; and
if that had been too little, I would have added as
much more. 9 Why have you despised the word of
the LORD, to do what is evil in his sight? You have
struck down Uriah the Hittite with the sword,
and have taken his wife to be your wife, and have
killed him with the sword of the Ammonites.
10 Now therefore the sword shall never depart
from your house, for you have despised me, and
have taken the wife of Uriah the Hittite to be
your wife. 11 Thus says the LORD: I will raise up
trouble against you from within your own house;
and I will take your wives before your eyes, and
give them to your neighbor, and he shall lie with
your wives in the sight of this very sun. 12 For you
did it secretly; but I will do this thing before all
Israel, and before the sun.” 13 David said to Nathan, “I have sinned against the LORD.” Nathan
said to David, “Now the LORD has put away your
sin; you shall not die. 14 Nevertheless, because by
this deed you have utterly scorned the LORD,[b] the
child that is born to you shall die.” 15 Then Nathan
went to his house.

The LORD struck the child that Uriah’s wife
bore to David, and it became very ill. 16 David
therefore pleaded with God for the child; David fasted, and went in and lay all night on the

[a] Gk Syr Judg 7.1: Heb *Jerubbesheth*

[b] Ancient scribal tradition: Compare 1 Sam 25.22 note: Heb *scorned the enemies of the LORD*

ground. 17The elders of his house stood beside him, urging him to rise from the ground; but he would not, nor did he eat food with them. 18On the seventh day the child died. And the servants of David were afraid to tell him that the child was dead; for they said, "While the child was still alive, we spoke to him, and he did not listen to us; how then can we tell him the child is dead? He may do himself some harm." 19But when David saw that his servants were whispering together, he perceived that the child was dead; and David said to his servants, "Is the child dead?" They said, "He is dead."

20 Then David rose from the ground, washed, anointed himself, and changed his clothes. He went into the house of the LORD, and worshiped; he then went to his own house; and when he asked, they set food before him and he ate. 21Then his servants said to him, "What is this thing that you have done? You fasted and wept for the child while it was alive; but when the child died, you rose and ate food." 22He said, "While the child was still alive, I fasted and wept; for I said, 'Who knows? The LORD may be gracious to me, and the child may live.' 23But now he is dead; why should I fast? Can I bring him back again? I shall go to him, but he will not return to me."

24 Then David consoled his wife Bathsheba, and went to her, and lay with her; and she bore a son, and he named him Solomon. The LORD loved him, 25and sent a message by the prophet Nathan; so he named him Jedidiah,[a] because of the LORD.

26 Now Joab fought against Rabbah of the Ammonites, and took the royal city. 27Joab sent messengers to David, and said, "I have fought against Rabbah; moreover, I have taken the water city. 28Now, then, gather the rest of the people together, and encamp against the city, and take it; or I myself will take the city, and it will be called by my name." 29So David gathered all the people together and went to Rabbah, and fought against it and took it. 30He took the crown of Milcom[b] from his head; the weight of it was a talent of gold, and in it was a precious stone; and it was placed on David's head. He also brought forth the spoil of the city, a very great amount. 31He brought out the people who were in it, and set them to work with saws and iron picks and iron axes, or sent them to the brickworks. Thus he did to all the cities of the Ammonites. Then David and all the people returned to Jerusalem.

13 Some time passed. David's son Absalom had a beautiful sister whose name was Tamar; and David's son Amnon fell in love with her. 2Amnon was so tormented that he made himself ill because of his sister Tamar, for she was a virgin and it seemed impossible to Amnon to do anything to her. 3But Amnon had a friend whose name was Jonadab, the son of David's brother Shimeah; and Jonadab was a very crafty man. 4He said to him, "O son of the king, why are you so haggard morning after morning? Will you not tell me?" Amnon said to him, "I love Tamar, my brother Absalom's sister." 5Jonadab said to him, "Lie down on your bed, and pretend to be ill; and when your father comes to see you, say to him, 'Let my sister Tamar come and give me something to eat, and prepare the food in my sight, so that I may see it and eat it from her hand.'" 6So Amnon lay down, and pretended to be ill; and when the king came to see him, Amnon said to the king, "Please let my sister Tamar come and make a couple of cakes in my sight, so that I may eat from her hand."

7 Then David sent home to Tamar, saying, "Go to your brother Amnon's house, and prepare food for him." 8So Tamar went to her brother Amnon's house, where he was lying down. She took dough, kneaded it, made cakes in his sight, and baked the cakes. 9Then she took the pan and set them[c] out before him, but he refused to eat. Amnon said, "Send out everyone from me." So everyone went out from him. 10Then Amnon said to Tamar, "Bring the food into the chamber, so that I may eat from your hand." So Tamar took the cakes she had made, and brought them into the chamber to Amnon her brother. 11But when she brought them near him to eat, he took hold of her, and said to her, "Come, lie with me, my

[a] That is *Beloved of the* LORD [b] Gk See 1 Kings 11.5, 33: Heb *their kings* [c] Heb *and poured*

sister." [12]She answered him, "No, my brother, do not force me; for such a thing is not done in Israel; do not do anything so vile! [13]As for me, where could I carry my shame? And as for you, you would be as one of the scoundrels in Israel. Now therefore, I beg you, speak to the king; for he will not withhold me from you." [14]But he would not listen to her; and being stronger than she, he forced her and lay with her.

15 Then Amnon was seized with a very great loathing for her; indeed, his loathing was even greater than the lust he had felt for her. Amnon said to her, "Get out!" [16]But she said to him, "No, my brother;[a] for this wrong in sending me away is greater than the other that you did to me." But he would not listen to her. [17]He called the young man who served him and said, "Put this woman out of my presence, and bolt the door after her." [18](Now she was wearing a long robe with sleeves; for this is how the virgin daughters of the king were clothed in earlier times.[b]) So his servant put her out, and bolted the door after her. [19]But Tamar put ashes on her head, and tore the long robe that she was wearing; she put her hand on her head, and went away, crying aloud as she went.

20 Her brother Absalom said to her, "Has Amnon your brother been with you? Be quiet for now, my sister; he is your brother; do not take this to heart." So Tamar remained, a desolate woman, in her brother Absalom's house. [21]When King David heard of all these things, he became very angry, but he would not punish his son Amnon, because he loved him, for he was his firstborn.[c] [22]But Absalom spoke to Amnon neither good nor bad; for Absalom hated Amnon, because he had raped his sister Tamar.

23 After two full years Absalom had sheepshearers at Baal-hazor, which is near Ephraim, and Absalom invited all the king's sons. [24]Absalom came to the king, and said, "Your servant has sheepshearers; will the king and his servants please go with your servant?" [25]But the king said to Absalom, "No, my son, let us not all go, or else we will be burdensome to you." He pressed him, but he would not go but gave him his blessing. [26]Then Absalom said, "If not, please let my brother Amnon go with us." The king said to him, "Why should he go with you?" [27]But Absalom pressed him until he let Amnon and all the king's sons go with him. Absalom made a feast like a king's feast.[d] [28]Then Absalom commanded his servants, "Watch when Amnon's heart is merry with wine, and when I say to you, 'Strike Amnon,' then kill him. Do not be afraid; have I not myself commanded you? Be courageous and valiant." [29]So the servants of Absalom did to Amnon as Absalom had commanded. Then all the king's sons rose, and each mounted his mule and fled.

30 While they were on the way, the report came to David that Absalom had killed all the king's sons, and not one of them was left. [31]The king rose, tore his garments, and lay on the ground; and all his servants who were standing by tore their garments. [32]But Jonadab, the son of David's brother Shimeah, said, "Let not my lord suppose that they have killed all the young men the king's sons; Amnon alone is dead. This has been determined by Absalom from the day Amnon[e] raped his sister Tamar. [33]Now therefore, do not let my lord the king take it to heart, as if all the king's sons were dead; for Amnon alone is dead."

34 But Absalom fled. When the young man who kept watch looked up, he saw many people coming from the Horonaim road[f] by the side of the mountain. [35]Jonadab said to the king, "See, the king's sons have come; as your servant said, so it has come about." [36]As soon as he had finished speaking, the king's sons arrived, and raised their voices and wept; and the king and all his servants also wept very bitterly.

37 But Absalom fled, and went to Talmai son of Ammihud, king of Geshur. David mourned for his son day after day. [38]Absalom, having fled to Geshur, stayed there three years. [39]And the heart of[g] the king went out, yearning for Absalom; for he was now consoled over the death of Amnon.

[a] Cn Compare Gk Vg: Meaning of Heb uncertain [b] Cn: Heb *were clothed in robes* [c] Q Ms Gk: MT lacks *but he would not punish . . . firstborn* [d] Gk Compare Q Ms: MT lacks *Absalom made a feast like a king's feast* [e] Heb *he* [f] Cn Compare Gk: Heb *the road behind him* [g] Q Ms Gk: MT *And David*

14 Now Joab son of Zeruiah perceived that
the king's mind was on Absalom. 2Joab
sent to Tekoa and brought from there a wise
woman. He said to her, "Pretend to be a mourner;
put on mourning garments, do not anoint yourself with oil, but behave like a woman who has
been mourning many days for the dead. 3Go to
the king and speak to him as follows." And Joab
put the words into her mouth.

4 When the woman of Tekoa came to the
king, she fell on her face to the ground and did
obeisance, and said, "Help, O king!" 5The king
asked her, "What is your trouble?" She answered,
"Alas, I am a widow; my husband is dead. 6Your
servant had two sons, and they fought with one
another in the field; there was no one to part
them, and one struck the other and killed him.
7Now the whole family has risen against your servant. They say, 'Give up the man who struck his
brother, so that we may kill him for the life of his
brother whom he murdered, even if we destroy
the heir as well.' Thus they would quench my one
remaining ember, and leave to my husband neither name nor remnant on the face of the earth."

8 Then the king said to the woman, "Go to
your house, and I will give orders concerning
you." 9The woman of Tekoa said to the king, "On
me be the guilt, my lord the king, and on my father's house; let the king and his throne be guiltless." 10The king said, "If anyone says anything to
you, bring him to me, and he shall never touch
you again." 11Then she said, "Please, may the king
keep the LORD your God in mind, so that the
avenger of blood may kill no more, and my son
not be destroyed." He said, "As the LORD lives,
not one hair of your son shall fall to the ground."

12 Then the woman said, "Please let your servant speak a word to my lord the king." He said,
"Speak." 13The woman said, "Why then have you
planned such a thing against the people of God?
For in giving this decision the king convicts himself, inasmuch as the king does not bring his banished one home again. 14We must all die; we are
like water spilled on the ground, which cannot
be gathered up. But God will not take away a life;
he will devise plans so as not to keep an outcast
banished forever from his presence.[a] 15Now I
have come to say this to my lord the king because
the people have made me afraid; your servant
thought, 'I will speak to the king; it may be that
the king will perform the request of his servant.
16For the king will hear, and deliver his servant
from the hand of the man who would cut both me
and my son off from the heritage of God.' 17Your
servant thought, 'The word of my lord the king
will set me at rest'; for my lord the king is like
the angel of God, discerning good and evil. The
LORD your God be with you!"

18 Then the king answered the woman, "Do
not withhold from me anything I ask you." The
woman said, "Let my lord the king speak." 19The
king said, "Is the hand of Joab with you in all this?"
The woman answered and said, "As surely as you
live, my lord the king, one cannot turn right or left
from anything that my lord the king has said. For
it was your servant Joab who commanded me; it
was he who put all these words into the mouth of
your servant. 20In order to change the course of
affairs your servant Joab did this. But my lord has
wisdom like the wisdom of the angel of God to
know all things that are on the earth."

21 Then the king said to Joab, "Very well, I
grant this; go, bring back the young man Absalom." 22Joab prostrated himself with his face to
the ground and did obeisance, and blessed the
king; and Joab said, "Today your servant knows
that I have found favor in your sight, my lord the
king, in that the king has granted the request of
his servant." 23So Joab set off, went to Geshur,
and brought Absalom to Jerusalem. 24The king
said, "Let him go to his own house; he is not to
come into my presence." So Absalom went to his
own house, and did not come into the king's presence.

25 Now in all Israel there was no one to be
praised so much for his beauty as Absalom; from
the sole of his foot to the crown of his head there
was no blemish in him. 26When he cut the hair
of his head (for at the end of every year he used
to cut it; when it was heavy on him, he cut it), he

[a] Meaning of Heb uncertain

weighed the hair of his head, two hundred shekels by the king's weight. 27 There were born to Absalom three sons, and one daughter whose name
was Tamar; she was a beautiful woman.
28 So Absalom lived two full years in Jerusalem, without coming into the king's presence.
29 Then Absalom sent for Joab to send him to the
king; but Joab would not come to him. He sent
a second time, but Joab would not come. 30 Then
he said to his servants, "Look, Joab's field is next
to mine, and he has barley there; go and set it
on fire." So Absalom's servants set the field on
fire. 31 Then Joab rose and went to Absalom at
his house, and said to him, "Why have your servants set my field on fire?" 32 Absalom answered
Joab, "Look, I sent word to you: Come here, that
I may send you to the king with the question,
'Why have I come from Geshur? It would be better for me to be there still.' Now let me go into
the king's presence; if there is guilt in me, let him
kill me!" 33 Then Joab went to the king and told
him; and he summoned Absalom. So he came to
the king and prostrated himself with his face to
the ground before the king; and the king kissed
Absalom.

15 After this Absalom got himself a chariot
and horses, and fifty men to run ahead
of him. 2 Absalom used to rise early and stand
beside the road into the gate; and when anyone
brought a suit before the king for judgment, Absalom would call out and say, "From what city
are you?" When the person said, "Your servant
is of such and such a tribe in Israel," 3 Absalom
would say, "See, your claims are good and right;
but there is no one deputed by the king to hear
you." 4 Absalom said moreover, "If only I were
judge in the land! Then all who had a suit or
cause might come to me, and I would give them
justice." 5 Whenever people came near to do
obeisance to him, he would put out his hand and
take hold of them, and kiss them. 6 Thus Absalom did to every Israelite who came to the king
for judgment; so Absalom stole the hearts of the
people of Israel.
7 At the end of four[a] years Absalom said to
the king, "Please let me go to Hebron and pay
the vow that I have made to the LORD. 8 For your
servant made a vow while I lived at Geshur in
Aram: If the LORD will indeed bring me back to
Jerusalem, then I will worship the LORD in Hebron."[b] 9 The king said to him, "Go in peace." So
he got up, and went to Hebron. 10 But Absalom
sent secret messengers throughout all the tribes
of Israel, saying, "As soon as you hear the sound
of the trumpet, then shout: Absalom has become
king at Hebron!" 11 Two hundred men from Jerusalem went with Absalom; they were invited
guests, and they went in their innocence, knowing nothing of the matter. 12 While Absalom was
offering the sacrifices, he sent for[c] Ahithophel the
Gilonite, David's counselor, from his city Giloh.
The conspiracy grew in strength, and the people
with Absalom kept increasing.
13 A messenger came to David, saying, "The
hearts of the Israelites have gone after Absalom."
14 Then David said to all his officials who were with
him at Jerusalem, "Get up! Let us flee, or there
will be no escape for us from Absalom. Hurry, or
he will soon overtake us, and bring disaster down
upon us, and attack the city with the edge of the
sword." 15 The king's officials said to the king,
"Your servants are ready to do whatever our lord
the king decides." 16 So the king left, followed by
all his household, except ten concubines whom
he left behind to look after the house. 17 The king
left, followed by all the people; and they stopped
at the last house. 18 All his officials passed by him;
and all the Cherethites, and all the Pelethites, and
all the six hundred Gittites who had followed him
from Gath, passed on before the king.
19 Then the king said to Ittai the Gittite, "Why
are you also coming with us? Go back, and stay
with the king; for you are a foreigner, and also an
exile from your home. 20 You came only yesterday,
and shall I today make you wander about with
us, while I go wherever I can? Go back, and take
your kinsfolk with you; and may the LORD show[d]
steadfast love and faithfulness to you." 21 But Ittai answered the king, "As the LORD lives, and as
my lord the king lives, wherever my lord the king

[a] Gk Syr: Heb *forty* [b] Gk Mss: Heb lacks *in Hebron* [c] Or *he sent* [d] Gk Compare 2.6: Heb lacks *may the LORD show*

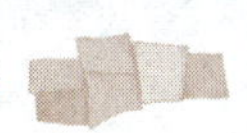

may be, whether for death or for life, there also
your servant will be." 22David said to Ittai, "Go
then, march on." So Ittai the Gittite marched on,
with all his men and all the little ones who were
with him. 23The whole country wept aloud as all
the people passed by; the king crossed the Wadi
Kidron, and all the people moved on toward the
wilderness.

24 Abiathar came up, and Zadok also, with all
the Levites, carrying the ark of the covenant of
God. They set down the ark of God, until the people had all passed out of the city. 25Then the king
said to Zadok, "Carry the ark of God back into
the city. If I find favor in the eyes of the LORD,
he will bring me back and let me see both it and
the place where it stays. 26But if he says, 'I take no
pleasure in you,' here I am, let him do to me what
seems good to him." 27The king also said to the
priest Zadok, "Look,[a] go back to the city in peace,
you and Abiathar,[b] with your two sons, Ahimaaz
your son, and Jonathan son of Abiathar. 28See, I
will wait at the fords of the wilderness until word
comes from you to inform me." 29So Zadok and
Abiathar carried the ark of God back to Jerusalem, and they remained there.

30 But David went up the ascent of the
Mount of Olives, weeping as he went, with his
head covered and walking barefoot; and all the
people who were with him covered their heads
and went up, weeping as they went. 31David was
told that Ahithophel was among the conspirators
with Absalom. And David said, "O LORD, I pray
you, turn the counsel of Ahithophel into foolishness."

32 When David came to the summit, where
God was worshiped, Hushai the Archite came
to meet him with his coat torn and earth on his
head. 33David said to him, "If you go on with me,
you will be a burden to me. 34But if you return to
the city and say to Absalom, 'I will be your servant, O king; as I have been your father's servant
in time past, so now I will be your servant,' then
you will defeat for me the counsel of Ahithophel.
35The priests Zadok and Abiathar will be with
you there. So whatever you hear from the king's
house, tell it to the priests Zadok and Abiathar.
36Their two sons are with them there, Zadok's
son Ahimaaz and Abiathar's son Jonathan; and by
them you shall report to me everything you hear."
37So Hushai, David's friend, came into the city,
just as Absalom was entering Jerusalem.

16 When David had passed a little beyond
the summit, Ziba the servant of Mephibosheth[c] met him, with a couple of donkeys
saddled, carrying two hundred loaves of bread,
one hundred bunches of raisins, one hundred of
summer fruits, and one skin of wine. 2The king
said to Ziba, "Why have you brought these?"
Ziba answered, "The donkeys are for the king's
household to ride, the bread and summer fruit for
the young men to eat, and the wine is for those
to drink who faint in the wilderness." 3The king
said, "And where is your master's son?" Ziba said
to the king, "He remains in Jerusalem; for he said,
'Today the house of Israel will give me back my
grandfather's kingdom.' " 4Then the king said to
Ziba, "All that belonged to Mephibosheth[c] is now
yours." Ziba said, "I do obeisance; let me find favor in your sight, my lord the king."

5 When King David came to Bahurim, a
man of the family of the house of Saul came out
whose name was Shimei son of Gera; he came
out cursing. 6He threw stones at David and at all
the servants of King David; now all the people
and all the warriors were on his right and on his

2 Samuel 16:5-14

Reduced to fleeing the army of his rebellious son like any war refugee, David is cursed and accused of murder—his crimes against Uriah, and others, are public knowledge. But in the perspective of the biblical authors, his moral reclamation begins when he refuses to destroy his accuser: he acknowledges, with a humility all too rare among governments, that the dissenting voice may be the voice of God.

—NE

[a] Gk: Heb *Are you a seer* or *Do you see?* [b] Cn: Heb lacks *and Abiathar* [c] Or *Merib-baal*: See 4.4 note

left. 7Shimei shouted while he cursed, "Out! Out!
Murderer! Scoundrel! 8The LORD has avenged on
all of you the blood of the house of Saul, in whose
place you have reigned; and the LORD has given
the kingdom into the hand of your son Absalom.
See, disaster has overtaken you; for you are a man
of blood."

9 Then Abishai son of Zeruiah said to the
king, "Why should this dead dog curse my lord
the king? Let me go over and take off his head."
10But the king said, "What have I to do with you,
you sons of Zeruiah? If he is cursing because the
LORD has said to him, 'Curse David,' who then
shall say, 'Why have you done so?'" 11David said
to Abishai and to all his servants, "My own son
seeks my life; how much more now may this Benjaminite! Let him alone, and let him curse; for the
LORD has bidden him. 12It may be that the LORD
will look on my distress,[a] and the LORD will repay me with good for this cursing of me today."
13So David and his men went on the road, while
Shimei went along on the hillside opposite him
and cursed as he went, throwing stones and fling-
ing dust at him. 14The king and all the people who
were with him arrived weary at the Jordan;[b] and
there he refreshed himself.

15 Now Absalom and all the Israelites[c] came
to Jerusalem; Ahithophel was with him. 16When
Hushai the Archite, David's friend, came to Absalom, Hushai said to Absalom, "Long live the king!
Long live the king!" 17Absalom said to Hushai, "Is
this your loyalty to your friend? Why did you not
go with your friend?" 18Hushai said to Absalom,
"No; but the one whom the LORD and this people and all the Israelites have chosen, his I will be,
and with him I will remain. 19Moreover, whom
should I serve? Should it not be his son? Just as I
have served your father, so I will serve you."

20 Then Absalom said to Ahithophel, "Give
us your counsel; what shall we do?" 21Ahithophel
said to Absalom, "Go in to your father's concubines, the ones he has left to look after the house;
and all Israel will hear that you have made yourself odious to your father, and the hands of all
who are with you will be strengthened." 22So they
pitched a tent for Absalom upon the roof; and
Absalom went in to his father's concubines in the
sight of all Israel. 23Now in those days the counsel
that Ahithophel gave was as if one consulted the
oracle[d] of God; so all the counsel of Ahithophel
was esteemed, both by David and by Absalom.

17 Moreover Ahithophel said to Absalom,
"Let me choose twelve thousand men,
and I will set out and pursue David tonight. 2I
will come upon him while he is weary and discouraged, and throw him into a panic; and all the
people who are with him will flee. I will strike
down only the king, 3and I will bring all the people back to you as a bride comes home to her husband. You seek the life of only one man,[e] and all
the people will be at peace." 4The advice pleased
Absalom and all the elders of Israel.

5 Then Absalom said, "Call Hushai the Archite also, and let us hear too what he has to say."
6When Hushai came to Absalom, Absalom said
to him, "This is what Ahithophel has said; shall
we do as he advises? If not, you tell us." 7Then
Hushai said to Absalom, "This time the counsel
that Ahithophel has given is not good." 8Hushai
continued, "You know that your father and his
men are warriors, and that they are enraged, like
a bear robbed of her cubs in the field. Besides,
your father is expert in war; he will not spend the
night with the troops. 9Even now he has hidden
himself in one of the pits, or in some other place.
And when some of our troops[f] fall at the first attack, whoever hears it will say, 'There has been
a slaughter among the troops who follow Absalom.' 10Then even the valiant warrior, whose
heart is like the heart of a lion, will utterly melt
with fear; for all Israel knows that your father is a
warrior, and that those who are with him are valiant warriors. 11But my counsel is that all Israel
be gathered to you, from Dan to Beer-sheba, like
the sand by the sea for multitude, and that you
go to battle in person. 12So we shall come upon
him in whatever place he may be found, and we
shall light on him as the dew falls on the ground;

[a] Gk Vg: Heb *iniquity* [b] Gk: Heb lacks *at the Jordan* [c] Gk: Heb *all the people, the men of Israel* [d] Heb *word*
[e] Gk: Heb *like the return of the whole (is) the man whom you seek* [f] Gk Mss: Heb *some of them*

and he will not survive, nor will any of those
with him. 13If he withdraws into a city, then all
Israel will bring ropes to that city, and we shall
drag it into the valley, until not even a pebble is
to be found there." 14Absalom and all the men of
Israel said, "The counsel of Hushai the Archite is
better than the counsel of Ahithophel." For the
LORD had ordained to defeat the good counsel of
Ahithophel, so that the LORD might bring ruin
on Absalom.

15 Then Hushai said to the priests Zadok and
Abiathar, "Thus and so did Ahithophel counsel
Absalom and the elders of Israel; and thus and so
I have counseled. 16Therefore send quickly and
tell David, 'Do not lodge tonight at the fords of
the wilderness, but by all means cross over; otherwise the king and all the people who are with him
will be swallowed up.'" 17Jonathan and Ahimaaz
were waiting at En-rogel; a servant-girl used to go
and tell them, and they would go and tell King
David; for they could not risk being seen entering
the city. 18But a boy saw them, and told Absalom;
so both of them went away quickly, and came to
the house of a man at Bahurim, who had a well in
his courtyard; and they went down into it. 19The
man's wife took a covering, stretched it over the
well's mouth, and spread out grain on it; and
nothing was known of it. 20When Absalom's servants came to the woman at the house, they said,
"Where are Ahimaaz and Jonathan?" The woman
said to them, "They have crossed over the brook[a]
of water." And when they had searched and could
not find them, they returned to Jerusalem.

21 After they had gone, the men came up out
of the well, and went and told King David. They
said to David, "Go and cross the water quickly;
for thus and so has Ahithophel counseled against
you." 22So David and all the people who were
with him set out and crossed the Jordan; by daybreak not one was left who had not crossed the
Jordan.

23 When Ahithophel saw that his counsel
was not followed, he saddled his donkey and
went off home to his own city. He set his house in
order, and hanged himself; he died and was buried in the tomb of his father.

24 Then David came to Mahanaim, while
Absalom crossed the Jordan with all the men of
Israel. 25Now Absalom had set Amasa over the
army in the place of Joab. Amasa was the son of a
man named Ithra the Ishmaelite,[b] who had married Abigal daughter of Nahash, sister of Zeruiah,
Joab's mother. 26The Israelites and Absalom encamped in the land of Gilead.

27 When David came to Mahanaim, Shobi
son of Nahash from Rabbah of the Ammonites,
and Machir son of Ammiel from Lo-debar, and
Barzillai the Gileadite from Rogelim, 28brought
beds, basins, and earthen vessels, wheat, barley,
meal, parched grain, beans and lentils,[c] 29honey
and curds, sheep, and cheese from the herd, for
David and the people with him to eat; for they
said, "The troops are hungry and weary and
thirsty in the wilderness."

18 Then David mustered the men who were
with him, and set over them commanders of thousands and commanders of hundreds.
2And David divided the army into three groups:[d]
one third under the command of Joab, one third
under the command of Abishai son of Zeruiah,
Joab's brother, and one third under the command
of Ittai the Gittite. The king said to the men, "I
myself will also go out with you." 3But the men
said, "You shall not go out. For if we flee, they will
not care about us. If half of us die, they will not
care about us. But you are worth ten thousand
of us;[e] therefore it is better that you send us help
from the city." 4The king said to them, "Whatever
seems best to you I will do." So the king stood at
the side of the gate, while all the army marched
out by hundreds and by thousands. 5The king
ordered Joab and Abishai and Ittai, saying, "Deal
gently for my sake with the young man Absalom."
And all the people heard when the king gave orders to all the commanders concerning Absalom.

6 So the army went out into the field against
Israel; and the battle was fought in the forest of
Ephraim. 7The men of Israel were defeated there

[a] Meaning of Heb uncertain [b] 1 Chr 2.17: Heb *Israelite* [c] Heb *and lentils and parched grain* [d] Gk: Heb *sent forth the army* [e] Gk Vg Symmachus: Heb *for now there are ten thousand such as we*

by the servants of David, and the slaughter there
was great on that day, twenty thousand men. 8 The
battle spread over the face of all the country; and
the forest claimed more victims that day than the
sword.

9 Absalom happened to meet the servants
of David. Absalom was riding on his mule, and
the mule went under the thick branches of a great
oak. His head caught fast in the oak, and he was
left hanging[a] between heaven and earth, while the
mule that was under him went on. 10 A man saw it,
and told Joab, "I saw Absalom hanging in an oak."
11 Joab said to the man who told him, "What, you
saw him! Why then did you not strike him there
to the ground? I would have been glad to give you
ten pieces of silver and a belt." 12 But the man said
to Joab, "Even if I felt in my hand the weight of
a thousand pieces of silver, I would not raise my
hand against the king's son; for in our hearing the
king commanded you and Abishai and Ittai, saying: For my sake protect the young man Absalom!
13 On the other hand, if I had dealt treacherously
against his life[b] (and there is nothing hidden from
the king), then you yourself would have stood
aloof." 14 Joab said, "I will not waste time like this
with you." He took three spears in his hand, and
thrust them into the heart of Absalom, while he
was still alive in the oak. 15 And ten young men,
Joab's armor-bearers, surrounded Absalom and
struck him, and killed him.

16 Then Joab sounded the trumpet, and the
troops came back from pursuing Israel, for Joab
restrained the troops. 17 They took Absalom,
threw him into a great pit in the forest, and raised
over him a very great heap of stones. Meanwhile
all the Israelites fled to their homes. 18 Now Absalom in his lifetime had taken and set up for
himself a pillar that is in the King's Valley, for he
said, "I have no son to keep my name in remembrance"; he called the pillar by his own name. It is
called Absalom's Monument to this day.

19 Then Ahimaaz son of Zadok said, "Let me
run, and carry tidings to the king that the LORD
has delivered him from the power of his enemies."
20 Joab said to him, "You are not to carry tidings today; you may carry tidings another day, but today
you shall not do so, because the king's son is dead."
21 Then Joab said to a Cushite, "Go, tell the king
what you have seen." The Cushite bowed before
Joab, and ran. 22 Then Ahimaaz son of Zadok said
again to Joab, "Come what may, let me also run
after the Cushite." And Joab said, "Why will you
run, my son, seeing that you have no reward[c] for
the tidings?" 23 "Come what may," he said, "I will
run." So he said to him, "Run." Then Ahimaaz ran
by the way of the Plain, and outran the Cushite.

24 Now David was sitting between the two
gates. The sentinel went up to the roof of the gate
by the wall, and when he looked up, he saw a man
running alone. 25 The sentinel shouted and told
the king. The king said, "If he is alone, there are
tidings in his mouth." He kept coming, and drew
near. 26 Then the sentinel saw another man running; and the sentinel called to the gatekeeper
and said, "See, another man running alone!" The
king said, "He also is bringing tidings." 27 The sentinel said, "I think the running of the first one is
like the running of Ahimaaz son of Zadok." The
king said, "He is a good man, and comes with
good tidings."

28 Then Ahimaaz cried out to the king, "All is
well!" He prostrated himself before the king with
his face to the ground, and said, "Blessed be the
LORD your God, who has delivered up the men
who raised their hand against my lord the king."
29 The king said, "Is it well with the young man
Absalom?" Ahimaaz answered, "When Joab sent
your servant,[d] I saw a great tumult, but I do not
know what it was." 30 The king said, "Turn aside,
and stand here." So he turned aside, and stood
still.

31 Then the Cushite came; and the Cushite
said, "Good tidings for my lord the king! For the
LORD has vindicated you this day, delivering you
from the power of all who rose up against you."
32 The king said to the Cushite, "Is it well with the
young man Absalom?" The Cushite answered,
"May the enemies of my lord the king, and all

[a] Gk Syr Tg: Heb *was put* [b] Another reading is *at the risk of my life* [c] Meaning of Heb uncertain
[d] Heb *the king's servant, your servant*

who rise up to do you harm, be like that young
man."

33[a] The king was deeply moved, and went up
to the chamber over the gate, and wept; and as he
went, he said, "O my son Absalom, my son, my
son Absalom! Would I had died instead of you,
O Absalom, my son, my son!"

19 It was told Joab, "The king is weeping and
mourning for Absalom." 2 So the victory
that day was turned into mourning for all the
troops; for the troops heard that day, "The king is
grieving for his son." 3 The troops stole into the
city that day as soldiers steal in who are ashamed
when they flee in battle. 4 The king covered his
face, and the king cried with a loud voice, "O my
son Absalom, O Absalom, my son, my son!"
5 Then Joab came into the house to the king, and
said, "Today you have covered with shame the
faces of all your officers who have saved your life
today, and the lives of your sons and your daughters, and the lives of your wives and your concubines, 6 for love of those who hate you and for
hatred of those who love you. You have made it
clear today that commanders and officers are
nothing to you; for I perceive that if Absalom
were alive and all of us were dead today, then you
would be pleased. 7 So go out at once and speak
kindly to your servants; for I swear by the LORD,
if you do not go, not a man will stay with you this
night; and this will be worse for you than any disaster that has come upon you from your youth
until now." 8 Then the king got up and took his
seat in the gate. The troops were all told, "See, the
king is sitting in the gate"; and all the troops came
before the king.

Meanwhile, all the Israelites had fled to their
homes. 9 All the people were disputing throughout all the tribes of Israel, saying, "The king delivered us from the hand of our enemies, and
saved us from the hand of the Philistines; and
now he has fled out of the land because of Absalom. 10 But Absalom, whom we anointed over us,
is dead in battle. Now therefore why do you say
nothing about bringing the king back?"

11 King David sent this message to the priests
Zadok and Abiathar, "Say to the elders of Judah,
'Why should you be the last to bring the king back
to his house? The talk of all Israel has come to the
king.[b] 12 You are my kin, you are my bone and my
flesh; why then should you be the last to bring
back the king?' 13 And say to Amasa, 'Are you not
my bone and my flesh? So may God do to me, and
more, if you are not the commander of my army
from now on, in place of Joab.'" 14 Amasa[c] swayed
the hearts of all the people of Judah as one, and
they sent word to the king, "Return, both you
and all your servants." 15 So the king came back to
the Jordan; and Judah came to Gilgal to meet the
king and to bring him over the Jordan.

16 Shimei son of Gera, the Benjaminite, from
Bahurim, hurried to come down with the people
of Judah to meet King David; 17 with him were a
thousand people from Benjamin. And Ziba, the
servant of the house of Saul, with his fifteen sons
and his twenty servants, rushed down to the Jordan ahead of the king, 18 while the crossing was
taking place,[d] to bring over the king's household,
and to do his pleasure.

Shimei son of Gera fell down before the king,
as he was about to cross the Jordan, 19 and said to
the king, "May my lord not hold me guilty or remember how your servant did wrong on the day
my lord the king left Jerusalem; may the king not
bear it in mind. 20 For your servant knows that I
have sinned; therefore, see, I have come this day,
the first of all the house of Joseph to come down
to meet my lord the king." 21 Abishai son of Zeruiah answered, "Shall not Shimei be put to death
for this, because he cursed the LORD's anointed?"
22 But David said, "What have I to do with you,
you sons of Zeruiah, that you should today become an adversary to me? Shall anyone be put to
death in Israel this day? For do I not know that
I am this day king over Israel?" 23 The king said
to Shimei, "You shall not die." And the king gave
him his oath.

24 Mephibosheth[e] grandson of Saul came
down to meet the king; he had not taken care

[a] Ch 19.1 in Heb [b] Gk: Heb *to the king, to his house* [c] Heb *He* [d] Cn: Heb *the ford crossed*
[e] Or *Merib-baal*: See 4.4 note

of his feet, or trimmed his beard, or washed his
clothes, from the day the king left until the day
he came back in safety. 25When he came from Jerusalem to meet the king, the king said to him,
"Why did you not go with me, Mephibosheth?"[a]
26He answered, "My lord, O king, my servant deceived me; for your servant said to him, 'Saddle
a donkey for me,[b] so that I may ride on it and
go with the king.' For your servant is lame. 27He
has slandered your servant to my lord the king.
But my lord the king is like the angel of God; do
therefore what seems good to you. 28For all my
father's house were doomed to death before my
lord the king; but you set your servant among
those who eat at your table. What further right
have I, then, to appeal to the king?" 29The king
said to him, "Why speak any more of your affairs? I have decided: you and Ziba shall divide
the land." 30Mephibosheth[a] said to the king, "Let
him take it all, since my lord the king has arrived
home safely."

31 Now Barzillai the Gileadite had come
down from Rogelim; he went on with the king to
the Jordan, to escort him over the Jordan. 32Bar-
zillai was a very aged man, eighty years old. He
had provided the king with food while he stayed
at Mahanaim, for he was a very wealthy man.
33The king said to Barzillai, "Come over with
me, and I will provide for you in Jerusalem at my
side." 34But Barzillai said to the king, "How many
years have I still to live, that I should go up with
the king to Jerusalem? 35Today I am eighty years
old; can I discern what is pleasant and what is
not? Can your servant taste what he eats or what
he drinks? Can I still listen to the voice of singing
men and singing women? Why then should your
servant be an added burden to my lord the king?
36Your servant will go a little way over the Jordan
with the king. Why should the king recompense
me with such a reward? 37Please let your servant
return, so that I may die in my own town, near
the graves of my father and my mother. But here
is your servant Chimham; let him go over with
my lord the king; and do for him whatever seems
good to you." 38The king answered, "Chimham
shall go over with me, and I will do for him whatever seems good to you; and all that you desire of
me I will do for you." 39Then all the people crossed
over the Jordan, and the king crossed over; the
king kissed Barzillai and blessed him, and he returned to his own home. 40The king went on to
Gilgal, and Chimham went on with him; all the
people of Judah, and also half the people of Israel,
brought the king on his way.

41 Then all the people of Israel came to the
king, and said to him, "Why have our kindred the
people of Judah stolen you away, and brought
the king and his household over the Jordan, and
all David's men with him?" 42All the people of Judah answered the people of Israel, "Because the
king is near of kin to us. Why then are you angry
over this matter? Have we eaten at all at the king's
expense? Or has he given us any gift?" 43But the
people of Israel answered the people of Judah,
"We have ten shares in the king, and in David also
we have more than you. Why then did you despise us? Were we not the first to speak of bringing back our king?" But the words of the people
of Judah were fiercer than the words of the people
of Israel.

20 Now a scoundrel named Sheba son of
Bichri, a Benjaminite, happened to be
there. He sounded the trumpet and cried out,

"We have no portion in David,
no share in the son of Jesse!
Everyone to your tents, O Israel!"

2So all the people of Israel withdrew from David
and followed Sheba son of Bichri; but the people
of Judah followed their king steadfastly from the
Jordan to Jerusalem.

3 David came to his house at Jerusalem; and
the king took the ten concubines whom he had
left to look after the house, and put them in a
house under guard, and provided for them, but
did not go in to them. So they were shut up until
the day of their death, living as if in widowhood.

4 Then the king said to Amasa, "Call the men
of Judah together to me within three days, and
be here yourself." 5So Amasa went to summon
Judah; but he delayed beyond the set time that

[a] Or *Merib-baal*: See 4.4 note [b] Gk Syr Vg: Heb *said, 'I will saddle a donkey for myself*

had been appointed him. 6 David said to Abishai,
"Now Sheba son of Bichri will do us more harm
than Absalom; take your lord's servants and pursue him, or he will find fortified cities for himself,
and escape from us." 7 Joab's men went out after
him, along with the Cherethites, the Pelethites,
and all the warriors; they went out from Jerusalem to pursue Sheba son of Bichri. 8 When they
were at the large stone that is in Gibeon, Amasa
came to meet them. Now Joab was wearing a soldier's garment and over it was a belt with a sword
in its sheath fastened at his waist; as he went forward it fell out. 9 Joab said to Amasa, "Is it well
with you, my brother?" And Joab took Amasa by
the beard with his right hand to kiss him. 10 But
Amasa did not notice the sword in Joab's hand;
Joab struck him in the belly so that his entrails
poured out on the ground, and he died. He did
not strike a second blow.

Then Joab and his brother Abishai pursued
Sheba son of Bichri. 11 And one of Joab's men
took his stand by Amasa, and said, "Whoever favors Joab, and whoever is for David, let him follow Joab." 12 Amasa lay wallowing in his blood on
the highway, and the man saw that all the people
were stopping. Since he saw that all who came by
him were stopping, he carried Amasa from the
highway into a field, and threw a garment over
him. 13 Once he was removed from the highway,
all the people went on after Joab to pursue Sheba
son of Bichri.

14 Sheba[a] passed through all the tribes of Israel to Abel of Beth-maacah;[b] and all the Bich-
rites[c] assembled, and followed him inside. 15 Joab's
forces[d] came and besieged him in Abel of Beth-
maacah; they threw up a siege ramp against the
city, and it stood against the rampart. Joab's forces
were battering the wall to break it down. 16 Then a
wise woman called from the city, "Listen! Listen!
Tell Joab, 'Come here, I want to speak to you.' "
17 He came near her; and the woman said, "Are
you Joab?" He answered, "I am." Then she said to
him, "Listen to the words of your servant." He answered, "I am listening." 18 Then she said, "They
used to say in the old days, 'Let them inquire at
Abel'; and so they would settle a matter. 19 I am
one of those who are peaceable and faithful in Israel; you seek to destroy a city that is a mother in
Israel; why will you swallow up the heritage of
the LORD?" 20 Joab answered, "Far be it from me,
far be it, that I should swallow up or destroy!
21 That is not the case! But a man of the hill country of Ephraim, called Sheba son of Bichri, has
lifted up his hand against King David; give him
up alone, and I will withdraw from the city." The
woman said to Joab, "His head shall be thrown
over the wall to you." 22 Then the woman went to
all the people with her wise plan. And they cut off
the head of Sheba son of Bichri, and threw it out
to Joab. So he blew the trumpet, and they dispersed from the city, and all went to their homes,
while Joab returned to Jerusalem to the king.

23 Now Joab was in command of all the army
of Israel;[e] Benaiah son of Jehoiada was in command of the Cherethites and the Pelethites; 24 Adoram was in charge of the forced labor; Jehoshaphat son of Ahilud was the recorder; 25 Sheva
was secretary; Zadok and Abiathar were priests;
26 and Ira the Jairite was also David's priest.

21 Now there was a famine in the days of David for three years, year after year; and David inquired of the LORD. The LORD said, "There
is bloodguilt on Saul and on his house, because
he put the Gibeonites to death." 2 So the king
called the Gibeonites and spoke to them. (Now
the Gibeonites were not of the people of Israel,
but of the remnant of the Amorites; although the
people of Israel had sworn to spare them, Saul had
tried to wipe them out in his zeal for the people of
Israel and Judah.) 3 David said to the Gibeonites,
"What shall I do for you? How shall I make expiation, that you may bless the heritage of the
LORD?" 4 The Gibeonites said to him, "It is not a
matter of silver or gold between us and Saul or his
house; neither is it for us to put anyone to death
in Israel." He said, "What do you say that I should
do for you?" 5 They said to the king, "The man
who consumed us and planned to destroy us, so

[a] Heb *He* [b] Compare 20.15: Heb *and Beth-maacah* [c] Compare Gk Vg: Heb *Berites* [d] Heb *They*
[e] Cn: Heb *Joab to all the army, Israel*

that we should have no place in all the territory of Israel— 6let seven of his sons be handed over to us, and we will impale them before the LORD at Gibeon on the mountain of the LORD."[a] The king said, "I will hand them over."

7 But the king spared Mephibosheth,[b] the son of Saul's son Jonathan, because of the oath of the LORD that was between them, between David and Jonathan son of Saul. 8The king took the two sons of Rizpah daughter of Aiah, whom she bore to Saul, Armoni and Mephibosheth;[b] and the five sons of Merab[c] daughter of Saul, whom she bore to Adriel son of Barzillai the Meholathite; 9he gave them into the hands of the Gibeonites, and they impaled them on the mountain before the LORD. The seven of them perished together. They were put to death in the first days of harvest, at the beginning of barley harvest.

10 Then Rizpah the daughter of Aiah took sackcloth, and spread it on a rock for herself, from the beginning of harvest until rain fell on them from the heavens; she did not allow the birds of the air to come on the bodies[d] by day, or the wild animals by night. 11When David was told what Rizpah daughter of Aiah, the concubine of Saul, had done, 12David went and took the bones of Saul and the bones of his son Jonathan from the people of Jabesh-gilead, who had stolen them from the public square of Beth-shan, where the Philistines had hung them up, on the day the Philistines killed Saul on Gilboa. 13He brought up from there the bones of Saul and the bones of his son Jonathan; and they gathered the bones of those who had been impaled. 14They buried the bones of Saul and of his son Jonathan in the land of Benjamin in Zela, in the tomb of his father Kish; they did all that the king commanded. After that, God heeded supplications for the land.

15 The Philistines went to war again with Israel, and David went down together with his servants. They fought against the Philistines, and David grew weary. 16Ishbi-benob, one of the descendants of the giants, whose spear weighed three hundred shekels of bronze, and who was fitted out with new weapons,[e] said he would kill David. 17But Abishai son of Zeruiah came to his aid, and attacked the Philistine and killed him. Then David's men swore to him, "You shall not go out with us to battle any longer, so that you do not quench the lamp of Israel."

18 After this a battle took place with the Philistines, at Gob; then Sibbecai the Hushathite killed Saph, who was one of the descendants of the giants. 19Then there was another battle with the Philistines at Gob; and Elhanan son of Jaare-oregim, the Bethlehemite, killed Goliath the Gittite, the shaft of whose spear was like a weaver's beam. 20There was again war at Gath, where there was a man of great size, who had six fingers on each hand, and six toes on each foot, twenty-four in number; he too was descended from the giants. 21When he taunted Israel, Jonathan son of David's brother Shimei, killed him. 22These four were descended from the giants in Gath; they fell by the hands of David and his servants.

22 David spoke to the LORD the words of this song on the day when the LORD delivered him from the hand of all his enemies, and from the hand of Saul. 2He said:

The LORD is my rock, my fortress, and my
    deliverer,
3 my God, my rock, in whom I take refuge,
my shield and the horn of my salvation,
    my stronghold and my refuge,
    my savior; you save me from violence.
4 I call upon the LORD, who is worthy to be
    praised,
    and I am saved from my enemies.

5 For the waves of death encompassed me,
    the torrents of perdition assailed me;
6 the cords of Sheol entangled me,
    the snares of death confronted me.

7 In my distress I called upon the LORD;
    to my God I called.
From his temple he heard my voice,
    and my cry came to his ears.

[a] Cn Compare Gk and 21.9: Heb *at Gibeah of Saul, the chosen of the LORD* [b] Or *Merib-baal*: See 4.4 note
[c] Two Heb Mss Syr Compare Gk: MT *Michal* [d] Heb *them* [e] Heb *was belted anew*

8 Then the earth reeled and rocked;
the foundations of the heavens trembled
and quaked, because he was angry.
9 Smoke went up from his nostrils,
and devouring fire from his mouth;
glowing coals flamed forth from him.
10 He bowed the heavens, and came down;
thick darkness was under his feet.
11 He rode on a cherub, and flew;
he was seen upon the wings of the wind.
12 He made darkness around him a canopy,
thick clouds, a gathering of water.
13 Out of the brightness before him
coals of fire flamed forth.
14 The LORD thundered from heaven;
the Most High uttered his voice.
15 He sent out arrows, and scattered them
—lightning, and routed them.
16 Then the channels of the sea were seen,
the foundations of the world were laid
bare
at the rebuke of the LORD,
at the blast of the breath of his nostrils.

17 He reached from on high, he took me,
he drew me out of mighty waters.
18 He delivered me from my strong enemy,
from those who hated me;
for they were too mighty for me.
19 They came upon me in the day of my
calamity,
but the LORD was my stay.
20 He brought me out into a broad place;
he delivered me, because he delighted
in me.

21 The LORD rewarded me according to my
righteousness;
according to the cleanness of my hands he
recompensed me.
22 For I have kept the ways of the LORD,
and have not wickedly departed from my
God.
23 For all his ordinances were before me,
and from his statutes I did not turn aside.
24 I was blameless before him,
and I kept myself from guilt.
25 Therefore the LORD has recompensed me
according to my righteousness,
according to my cleanness in his sight.

26 With the loyal you show yourself loyal;
with the blameless you show yourself
blameless;
27 with the pure you show yourself pure,
and with the crooked you show yourself
perverse.
28 You deliver a humble people,
but your eyes are upon the haughty to
bring them down.
29 Indeed, you are my lamp, O LORD,
the LORD lightens my darkness.
30 By you I can crush a troop,
and by my God I can leap over a wall.
31 This God—his way is perfect;
the promise of the LORD proves true;
he is a shield for all who take refuge in
him.

32 For who is God, but the LORD?
And who is a rock, except our God?
33 The God who has girded me with strength[a]
has opened wide my path.[b]
34 He made my[c] feet like the feet of deer,
and set me secure on the heights.
35 He trains my hands for war,
so that my arms can bend a bow of bronze.
36 You have given me the shield of your
salvation,
and your help[d] has made me great.
37 You have made me stride freely,
and my feet do not slip;
38 I pursued my enemies and destroyed them,
and did not turn back until they were
consumed.
39 I consumed them; I struck them down, so
that they did not rise;
they fell under my feet.

[a] Q Ms Gk Syr Vg Compare Ps 18.32: MT *God is my strong refuge* [b] Meaning of Heb uncertain [c] Another reading is *his*
[d] Q Ms: MT *your answering*

40 For you girded me with strength for the battle;
you made my assailants sink under me.
41 You made my enemies turn their backs to me,
those who hated me, and I destroyed them.
42 They looked, but there was no one to save them;
they cried to the LORD, but he did not answer them.
43 I beat them fine like the dust of the earth,
I crushed them and stamped them down like the mire of the streets.

44 You delivered me from strife with the peoples;[a]
you kept me as the head of the nations;
people whom I had not known served me.
45 Foreigners came cringing to me;
as soon as they heard of me, they obeyed me.
46 Foreigners lost heart,
and came trembling out of their strongholds.

47 The LORD lives! Blessed be my rock,
and exalted be my God, the rock of my salvation,
48 the God who gave me vengeance
and brought down peoples under me,
49 who brought me out from my enemies;
you exalted me above my adversaries,
you delivered me from the violent.

50 For this I will extol you, O LORD, among the nations,
and sing praises to your name.
51 He is a tower of salvation for his king,
and shows steadfast love to his anointed,
to David and his descendants forever.

23 Now these are the last words of David:
The oracle of David, son of Jesse,
the oracle of the man whom God exalted,[b]
the anointed of the God of Jacob,
the favorite of the Strong One of Israel:

2 The spirit of the LORD speaks through me,
his word is upon my tongue.
3 The God of Israel has spoken,
the Rock of Israel has said to me:
One who rules over people justly,
ruling in the fear of God,
4 is like the light of morning,
like the sun rising on a cloudless morning,
gleaming from the rain on the grassy land.

5 Is not my house like this with God?
For he has made with me an everlasting covenant,
ordered in all things and secure.
Will he not cause to prosper
all my help and my desire?
6 But the godless are[c] all like thorns that are thrown away;
for they cannot be picked up with the hand;
7 to touch them one uses an iron bar
or the shaft of a spear.
And they are entirely consumed in fire on the spot.[d]

8 These are the names of the warriors whom
David had: Josheb-basshebeth a Tachemonite;
he was chief of the Three;[e] he wielded his spear[f]
against eight hundred whom he killed at one
time.
9 Next to him among the three warriors was
Eleazar son of Dodo son of Ahohi. He was with
David when they defied the Philistines who were
gathered there for battle. The Israelites withdrew,
10 but he stood his ground. He struck down the
Philistines until his arm grew weary, though his
hand clung to the sword. The LORD brought
about a great victory that day. Then the people
came back to him—but only to strip the dead.
11 Next to him was Shammah son of Agee,
the Hararite. The Philistines gathered together
at Lehi, where there was a plot of ground full of

[a] Gk: Heb *from strife with my people* [b] Q Ms: MT *who was raised on high* [c] Heb *But worthlessness* [d] Heb *in sitting*
[e] Gk Vg Compare 1 Chr 11.11: Meaning of Heb uncertain [f] 1 Chr 11.11: Meaning of Heb uncertain

lentils; and the army fled from the Philistines.
12But he took his stand in the middle of the plot,
defended it, and killed the Philistines; and the
LORD brought about a great victory.
13 Towards the beginning of harvest three
of the thirty[a] chiefs went down to join David at
the cave of Adullam, while a band of Philistines
was encamped in the valley of Rephaim. 14David
was then in the stronghold; and the garrison of
the Philistines was then at Bethlehem. 15David
said longingly, "O that someone would give me
water to drink from the well of Bethlehem that
is by the gate!" 16Then the three warriors broke
through the camp of the Philistines, drew water
from the well of Bethlehem that was by the gate,
and brought it to David. But he would not drink
of it; he poured it out to the LORD, 17for he said,
"The LORD forbid that I should do this. Can I
drink the blood of the men who went at the risk
of their lives?" Therefore he would not drink it.
The three warriors did these things.
18 Now Abishai son of Zeruiah, the brother
of Joab, was chief of the Thirty.[b] With his spear
he fought against three hundred men and killed
them, and won a name beside the Three. 19He
was the most renowned of the Thirty,[c] and became their commander; but he did not attain to
the Three.
20 Benaiah son of Jehoiada was a valiant
warrior[d] from Kabzeel, a doer of great deeds;
he struck down two sons of Ariel[e] of Moab. He
also went down and killed a lion in a pit on a day
when snow had fallen. 21And he killed an Egyptian, a handsome man. The Egyptian had a spear
in his hand; but Benaiah went against him with
a staff, snatched the spear out of the Egyptian's
hand, and killed him with his own spear. 22Such
were the things Benaiah son of Jehoiada did, and
won a name beside the three warriors. 23He was
renowned among the Thirty, but he did not attain
to the Three. And David put him in charge of his
bodyguard.
24 Among the Thirty were Asahel brother
of Joab; Elhanan son of Dodo of Bethlehem;
25Shammah of Harod; Elika of Harod; 26Helez
the Paltite; Ira son of Ikkesh of Tekoa; 27Abiezer
of Anathoth; Mebunnai the Hushathite; 28Zal-
mon the Ahohite; Maharai of Netophah; 29He-
leb son of Baanah of Netophah; Ittai son of Ribai
of Gibeah of the Benjaminites; 30Benaiah of Pirathon; Hiddai of the torrents of Gaash; 31Abi-
albon the Arbathite; Azmaveth of Bahurim;
32Eliahba of Shaalbon; the sons of Jashen: Jonathan 33son of[f] Shammah the Hararite; Ahiam
son of Sharar the Hararite; 34Eliphelet son of
Ahasbai of Maacah; Eliam son of Ahithophel the
Gilonite; 35Hezro[g] of Carmel; Paarai the Arbite;
36Igal son of Nathan of Zobah; Bani the Gadite;
37Zelek the Ammonite; Naharai of Beeroth, the
armor-bearer of Joab son of Zeruiah; 38Ira the
Ithrite; Gareb the Ithrite; 39Uriah the Hittite—
thirty-seven in all.

24 Again the anger of the LORD was kindled against Israel, and he incited David
against them, saying, "Go, count the people of Israel and Judah." 2So the king said to Joab and the
commanders of the army,[h] who were with him,
"Go through all the tribes of Israel, from Dan to
Beer-sheba, and take a census of the people, so
that I may know how many there are." 3But Joab
said to the king, "May the LORD your God increase the number of the people a hundredfold,
while the eyes of my lord the king can still see it!
But why does my lord the king want to do this?"
4But the king's word prevailed against Joab and
the commanders of the army. So Joab and the
commanders of the army went out from the presence of the king to take a census of the people of
Israel. 5They crossed the Jordan, and began from[i]
Aroer and from the city that is in the middle of
the valley, toward Gad and on to Jazer. 6Then they
came to Gilead, and to Kadesh in the land of the
Hittites;[j] and they came to Dan, and from Dan[k]

[a] Heb adds *head* [b] Two Heb Mss Syr: MT *Three* [c] Syr Compare 1 Chr 11.25: Heb *Was he the most renowned of the Three?* [d] Another reading is *the son of Ish-hai* [e] Gk: Heb lacks *sons of* [f] Gk: Heb lacks *son of* [g] Another reading is *Hezrai* [h] 1 Chr 21.2 Gk: Heb *to Joab the commander of the army* [i] Gk Mss: Heb *encamped in Aroer south of* [j] Gk: Heb *to the land of Tahtim-hodshi* [k] Cn Compare Gk: Heb *they came to Dan-jaan and*

they went around to Sidon, 7 and came to the fortress of Tyre and to all the cities of the Hivites
and Canaanites; and they went out to the Negeb
of Judah at Beer-sheba. 8 So when they had gone
through all the land, they came back to Jerusalem
at the end of nine months and twenty days. 9 Joab
reported to the king the number of those who had
been recorded: in Israel there were eight hundred
thousand soldiers able to draw the sword, and
those of Judah were five hundred thousand.

10 But afterward, David was stricken to the
heart because he had numbered the people. David said to the LORD, "I have sinned greatly in
what I have done. But now, O LORD, I pray you,
take away the guilt of your servant; for I have
done very foolishly." 11 When David rose in the
morning, the word of the LORD came to the
prophet Gad, David's seer, saying, 12 "Go and say
to David: Thus says the LORD: Three things I offer[a] you; choose one of them, and I will do it to
you." 13 So Gad came to David and told him; he
asked him, "Shall three[b] years of famine come to
you on your land? Or will you flee three months
before your foes while they pursue you? Or shall
there be three days' pestilence in your land? Now
consider, and decide what answer I shall return to
the one who sent me." 14 Then David said to Gad,
"I am in great distress; let us fall into the hand of
the LORD, for his mercy is great; but let me not
fall into human hands."

15 So the LORD sent a pestilence on Israel
from that morning until the appointed time; and
seventy thousand of the people died, from Dan
to Beer-sheba. 16 But when the angel stretched
out his hand toward Jerusalem to destroy it, the
LORD relented concerning the evil, and said to
the angel who was bringing destruction among
the people, "It is enough; now stay your hand."
The angel of the LORD was then by the threshing
floor of Araunah the Jebusite. 17 When David saw
the angel who was destroying the people, he said
to the LORD, "I alone have sinned, and I alone
have done wickedly; but these sheep, what have
they done? Let your hand, I pray, be against me
and against my father's house."

18 That day Gad came to David and said to
him, "Go up and erect an altar to the LORD on
the threshing floor of Araunah the Jebusite."
19 Following Gad's instructions, David went up,
as the LORD had commanded. 20 When Araunah
looked down, he saw the king and his servants
coming toward him; and Araunah went out and
prostrated himself before the king with his face
to the ground. 21 Araunah said, "Why has my lord
the king come to his servant?" David said, "To
buy the threshing floor from you in order to build
an altar to the LORD, so that the plague may be
averted from the people." 22 Then Araunah said
to David, "Let my lord the king take and offer up
what seems good to him; here are the oxen for the
burnt offering, and the threshing sledges and the
yokes of the oxen for the wood. 23 All this, O king,
Araunah gives to the king." And Araunah said to
the king, "May the LORD your God respond favorably to you."

24 But the king said to Araunah, "No, but
I will buy them from you for a price; I will not
offer burnt offerings to the LORD my God that
cost me nothing." So David bought the threshing
floor and the oxen for fifty shekels of silver. 25 David built there an altar to the LORD, and offered
burnt offerings and offerings of well-being. So the
LORD answered his supplication for the land, and
the plague was averted from Israel.

[a] Or *hold over* [b] 1 Chr 21.12 Gk: Heb *seven*

1 Kings

The Book of Kings—the division into "first" and "second" parts did not originally refer to two separate books—is a theological meditation on the religious and historical paths taken by the states of Judah and Israel. The theological point of view of 1 and 2 Kings is consistent with that of the other books of the Former Prophets (as distinguished from the Latter Prophets) of the Jewish canon—Joshua, Judges, Samuel, and Kings. Contemporary scholars call these books the Deuteronomistic History because, in their interpretation of the history of Israel from the conquest of the land of Canaan to the Babylonian overthrow of nation and temple, they build on Deuteronomy's distinctive views of the relationship the Lord established with a certain people. That relationship is marked by concepts such as covenant and election, recast by the framers of Deuteronomy in the ideological fires of religious reformation and nationalistic recovery that were kindled in the times of Kings Hezekiah and Josiah of Judah. Faithfulness to the Lord—which for the Deuteronomistic writers meant exclusive monotheistic worship and strict observance of Torah, especially on the part of the kings of David's line, who were for the authors the only rightful rulers of the Lord's people—is the key to enjoyment of the blessings of election, in particular possession of the land of Canaan. The opposite leads to calamity, national ruin, and the ultimate catastrophe of exile.

The story begins in 1 Kgs 1:1—11:43 with the death of David and the beginning of Solomon's reign in Jerusalem, under whom the growth and glory of the city culminates in the building of the temple. However, even Solomon, the builder of the temple, in the end succumbs to following other gods, a sin the writers of Kings identify as the cause for the split of the kingdoms (1 Kgs 11:1-13.)

The rest of 1 Kings (12:1—22:53) takes the story from the split of the northern tribes of Israel from Judah, resulting from the rebellion of Jeroboam son of Nebat against Rehoboam son of Solomon to the accession of Ahaziah son of Ahab to the throne in Samaria. The story alternates between the kings of Israel and Judah, driven by a categorical rejection of the possibility that anything good could ever be said about a northern king. So Omri, arguably one of the most successful and powerful of the kings of Israel, is given much less prominence in the story (1 Kgs 16:23-28) than his weak son Ahab, who is presented as the feckless husband of evil Queen Jezebel, and roundly condemned by Elijah (1 Kgs 16:29—22:40). The role of pointing out the failures of the rulers of Israel and Judah falls to prophetic figures, such as Elijah, who in 1 Kings appears on the scene not only to confront the cult of Baal (1 Kings 18) but to rebuke Ahab for his injustice and to speak prophecies of doom that, in a promise-then-fulfillment scheme, are basic elements of the plot of the work (1 Kings 21).

— *Francisco García-Treto*

1 King David was old and advanced in years;
and although they covered him with clothes,
he could not get warm. 2So his servants said to
him, "Let a young virgin be sought for my lord
the king, and let her wait on the king, and be his
attendant; let her lie in your bosom, so that my
lord the king may be warm." 3So they searched
for a beautiful girl throughout all the territory of
Israel, and found Abishag the Shunammite, and
brought her to the king. 4The girl was very beautiful. She became the king's attendant and served
him, but the king did not know her sexually.

5 Now Adonijah son of Haggith exalted
himself, saying, "I will be king"; he prepared for
himself chariots and horsemen, and fifty men
to run before him. 6His father had never at any
time displeased him by asking, "Why have you
done thus and so?" He was also a very handsome
man, and he was born next after Absalom. 7He
conferred with Joab son of Zeruiah and with the
priest Abiathar, and they supported Adonijah.
8But the priest Zadok, and Benaiah son of Jehoiada, and the prophet Nathan, and Shimei, and
Rei, and David's own warriors did not side with
Adonijah.

9 Adonijah sacrificed sheep, oxen, and fatted
cattle by the stone Zoheleth, which is beside En-
rogel, and he invited all his brothers, the king's
sons, and all the royal officials of Judah, 10but he
did not invite the prophet Nathan or Benaiah or
the warriors or his brother Solomon.

11 Then Nathan said to Bathsheba, Solomon's
mother, "Have you not heard that Adonijah son
of Haggith has become king and our lord David
does not know it? 12Now therefore come, let me
give you advice, so that you may save your own
life and the life of your son Solomon. 13Go in at
once to King David, and say to him, 'Did you not,
my lord the king, swear to your servant, saying:
Your son Solomon shall succeed me as king, and
he shall sit on my throne? Why then is Adonijah
king?' 14Then while you are still there speaking
with the king, I will come in after you and confirm your words."

15 So Bathsheba went to the king in his room.
The king was very old; Abishag the Shunammite
was attending the king. 16Bathsheba bowed and
did obeisance to the king, and the king said,
"What do you wish?" 17She said to him, "My
lord, you swore to your servant by the LORD your
God, saying: Your son Solomon shall succeed me
as king, and he shall sit on my throne. 18But now
suddenly Adonijah has become king, though you,
my lord the king, do not know it. 19He has sacrificed oxen, fatted cattle, and sheep in abundance,
and has invited all the children of the king, the
priest Abiathar, and Joab the commander of the
army; but your servant Solomon he has not invited. 20But you, my lord the king—the eyes of all
Israel are on you to tell them who shall sit on the
throne of my lord the king after him. 21Otherwise
it will come to pass, when my lord the king sleeps
with his ancestors, that my son Solomon and I
will be counted offenders."

22 While she was still speaking with the king,
the prophet Nathan came in. 23The king was told,
"Here is the prophet Nathan." When he came in
before the king, he did obeisance to the king,
with his face to the ground. 24Nathan said, "My
lord the king, have you said, 'Adonijah shall succeed me as king, and he shall sit on my throne'?
25For today he has gone down and has sacrificed
oxen, fatted cattle, and sheep in abundance, and
has invited all the king's children, Joab the commander[a] of the army, and the priest Abiathar,
who are now eating and drinking before him, and
saying, 'Long live King Adonijah!' 26But he did
not invite me, your servant, and the priest Zadok,
and Benaiah son of Jehoiada, and your servant
Solomon. 27Has this thing been brought about
by my lord the king and you have not let your servants know who should sit on the throne of my
lord the king after him?"

28 King David answered, "Summon Bathsheba to me." So she came into the king's presence, and stood before the king. 29The king swore,
saying, "As the LORD lives, who has saved my life
from every adversity, 30as I swore to you by the
LORD, the God of Israel, 'Your son Solomon shall
succeed me as king, and he shall sit on my throne

[a] Gk: Heb *the commanders*

in my place,' so will I do this day." 31 Then Bathsheba bowed with her face to the ground, and did
obeisance to the king, and said, "May my lord
King David live forever!"

32 King David said, "Summon to me the
priest Zadok, the prophet Nathan, and Benaiah
son of Jehoiada." When they came before the
king, 33 the king said to them, "Take with you
the servants of your lord, and have my son Solomon ride on my own mule, and bring him down
to Gihon. 34 There let the priest Zadok and the
prophet Nathan anoint him king over Israel; then
blow the trumpet, and say, 'Long live King Solomon!' 35 You shall go up following him. Let him
enter and sit on my throne; he shall be king in my
place; for I have appointed him to be ruler over
Israel and over Judah." 36 Benaiah son of Jehoiada
answered the king, "Amen! May the LORD, the
God of my lord the king, so ordain. 37 As the
LORD has been with my lord the king, so may he
be with Solomon, and make his throne greater
than the throne of my lord King David."

38 So the priest Zadok, the prophet Nathan,
and Benaiah son of Jehoiada, and the Cherethites
and the Pelethites, went down and had Solomon
ride on King David's mule, and led him to Gihon.
39 There the priest Zadok took the horn of oil
from the tent and anointed Solomon. Then they
blew the trumpet, and all the people said, "Long
live King Solomon!" 40 And all the people went
up following him, playing on pipes and rejoicing
with great joy, so that the earth quaked at their
noise.

41 Adonijah and all the guests who were with
him heard it as they finished feasting. When Joab
heard the sound of the trumpet, he said, "Why is
the city in an uproar?" 42 While he was still speaking, Jonathan son of the priest Abiathar arrived.
Adonijah said, "Come in, for you are a worthy
man and surely you bring good news." 43 Jonathan
answered Adonijah, "No, for our lord King David
has made Solomon king; 44 the king has sent with
him the priest Zadok, the prophet Nathan, and
Benaiah son of Jehoiada, and the Cherethites and
the Pelethites; and they had him ride on the king's
mule; 45 the priest Zadok and the prophet Nathan
have anointed him king at Gihon; and they have
gone up from there rejoicing, so that the city is in
an uproar. This is the noise that you heard. 46 Solomon now sits on the royal throne. 47 Moreover
the king's servants came to congratulate our lord
King David, saying, 'May God make the name of
Solomon more famous than yours, and make his
throne greater than your throne.' The king bowed
in worship on the bed 48 and went on to pray thus,
'Blessed be the LORD, the God of Israel, who today has granted one of my offspring[a] to sit on my
throne and permitted me to witness it.'"

49 Then all the guests of Adonijah got up
trembling and went their own ways. 50 Adonijah, fearing Solomon, got up and went to grasp
the horns of the altar. 51 Solomon was informed,
"Adonijah is afraid of King Solomon; see, he has
laid hold of the horns of the altar, saying, 'Let
King Solomon swear to me first that he will not
kill his servant with the sword.'" 52 So Solomon
responded, "If he proves to be a worthy man,
not one of his hairs shall fall to the ground; but if
wickedness is found in him, he shall die." 53 Then
King Solomon sent to have him brought down
from the altar. He came to do obeisance to King
Solomon; and Solomon said to him, "Go home."

2 When David's time to die drew near, he
charged his son Solomon, saying: 2 "I am
about to go the way of all the earth. Be strong,
be courageous, 3 and keep the charge of the LORD
your God, walking in his ways and keeping his
statutes, his commandments, his ordinances, and
his testimonies, as it is written in the law of Moses, so that you may prosper in all that you do and
wherever you turn. 4 Then the LORD will establish
his word that he spoke concerning me: 'If your
heirs take heed to their way, to walk before me in
faithfulness with all their heart and with all their
soul, there shall not fail you a successor on the
throne of Israel.'

5 "Moreover you know also what Joab son
of Zeruiah did to me, how he dealt with the
two commanders of the armies of Israel, Abner
son of Ner, and Amasa son of Jether, whom he

[a] Gk: Heb *one*

murdered, retaliating in time of peace for blood
that had been shed in war, and putting the blood
of war on the belt around his waist, and on the
sandals on his feet. 6 Act therefore according to
your wisdom, but do not let his gray head go
down to Sheol in peace. 7 Deal loyally, however,
with the sons of Barzillai the Gileadite, and let
them be among those who eat at your table; for
with such loyalty they met me when I fled from
your brother Absalom. 8 There is also with you
Shimei son of Gera, the Benjaminite from Bahurim, who cursed me with a terrible curse on
the day when I went to Mahanaim; but when he
came down to meet me at the Jordan, I swore to
him by the LORD, 'I will not put you to death with
the sword.' 9 Therefore do not hold him guiltless,
for you are a wise man; you will know what you
ought to do to him, and you must bring his gray
head down with blood to Sheol."

10 Then David slept with his ancestors, and
was buried in the city of David. 11 The time that
David reigned over Israel was forty years; he
reigned seven years in Hebron, and thirty-three
years in Jerusalem. 12 So Solomon sat on the
throne of his father David; and his kingdom was
firmly established.

13 Then Adonijah son of Haggith came to
Bathsheba, Solomon's mother. She asked, "Do
you come peaceably?" He said, "Peaceably."
14 Then he said, "May I have a word with you?"
She said, "Go on." 15 He said, "You know that the
kingdom was mine, and that all Israel expected
me to reign; however, the kingdom has turned
about and become my brother's, for it was his
from the LORD. 16 And now I have one request to
make of you; do not refuse me." She said to him,
"Go on." 17 He said, "Please ask King Solomon—
he will not refuse you—to give me Abishag the
Shunammite as my wife." 18 Bathsheba said, "Very
well; I will speak to the king on your behalf."

19 So Bathsheba went to King Solomon, to
speak to him on behalf of Adonijah. The king rose
to meet her, and bowed down to her; then he sat
on his throne, and had a throne brought for the
king's mother, and she sat on his right. 20 Then she
said, "I have one small request to make of you; do
not refuse me." And the king said to her, "Make
your request, my mother; for I will not refuse
you." 21 She said, "Let Abishag the Shunammite
be given to your brother Adonijah as his wife."
22 King Solomon answered his mother, "And why
do you ask Abishag the Shunammite for Adonijah? Ask for him the kingdom as well! For he is
my elder brother; ask not only for him but also
for the priest Abiathar and for Joab son of Zeruiah!" 23 Then King Solomon swore by the LORD,
"So may God do to me, and more also, for Adonijah has devised this scheme at the risk of his life!
24 Now therefore as the LORD lives, who has established me and placed me on the throne of my
father David, and who has made me a house as he
promised, today Adonijah shall be put to death."
25 So King Solomon sent Benaiah son of Jehoiada;
he struck him down, and he died.

26 The king said to the priest Abiathar, "Go to
Anathoth, to your estate; for you deserve death.
But I will not at this time put you to death, because you carried the ark of the Lord GOD before
my father David, and because you shared in all
the hardships my father endured." 27 So Solomon
banished Abiathar from being priest to the LORD,
thus fulfilling the word of the LORD that he had
spoken concerning the house of Eli in Shiloh.

28 When the news came to Joab—for Joab
had supported Adonijah though he had not supported Absalom—Joab fled to the tent of the
LORD and grasped the horns of the altar. 29 When
it was told King Solomon, "Joab has fled to the
tent of the LORD and now is beside the altar,"
Solomon sent Benaiah son of Jehoiada, saying,
"Go, strike him down." 30 So Benaiah came to the
tent of the LORD and said to him, "The king commands, 'Come out.'" But he said, "No, I will die
here." Then Benaiah brought the king word again,
saying, "Thus said Joab, and thus he answered
me." 31 The king replied to him, "Do as he has said,
strike him down and bury him; and thus take
away from me and from my father's house the
guilt for the blood that Joab shed without cause.
32 The LORD will bring back his bloody deeds on
his own head, because, without the knowledge
of my father David, he attacked and killed with
the sword two men more righteous and better
than himself, Abner son of Ner, commander of

the army of Israel, and Amasa son of Jether, commander of the army of Judah. 33So shall their
blood come back on the head of Joab and on the
head of his descendants forever; but to David,
and to his descendants, and to his house, and to
his throne, there shall be peace from the LORD
forevermore." 34Then Benaiah son of Jehoiada
went up and struck him down and killed him; and
he was buried at his own house near the wilderness. 35The king put Benaiah son of Jehoiada over
the army in his place, and the king put the priest
Zadok in the place of Abiathar.
36 Then the king sent and summoned Shimei,
and said to him, "Build yourself a house in Jerusalem, and live there, and do not go out from there
to any place whatever. 37For on the day you go
out, and cross the Wadi Kidron, know for certain
that you shall die; your blood shall be on your
own head." 38And Shimei said to the king, "The
sentence is fair; as my lord the king has said, so
will your servant do." So Shimei lived in Jerusalem many days.
39 But it happened at the end of three years
that two of Shimei's slaves ran away to King
Achish son of Maacah of Gath. When it was told
Shimei, "Your slaves are in Gath," 40Shimei arose
and saddled a donkey, and went to Achish in
Gath, to search for his slaves; Shimei went and
brought his slaves from Gath. 41When Solomon
was told that Shimei had gone from Jerusalem
to Gath and returned, 42the king sent and summoned Shimei, and said to him, "Did I not make
you swear by the LORD, and solemnly adjure you,
saying, 'Know for certain that on the day you go
out and go to any place whatever, you shall die'?
And you said to me, 'The sentence is fair; I accept.' 43Why then have you not kept your oath
to the LORD and the commandment with which
I charged you?" 44The king also said to Shimei,
"You know in your own heart all the evil that you
did to my father David; so the LORD will bring
back your evil on your own head. 45But King
Solomon shall be blessed, and the throne of David shall be established before the LORD forever."
46Then the king commanded Benaiah son of Jehoiada; and he went out and struck him down,
and he died.

So the kingdom was established in the hand
of Solomon.

3 Solomon made a marriage alliance with
Pharaoh king of Egypt; he took Pharaoh's
daughter and brought her into the city of David,
until he had finished building his own house and
the house of the LORD and the wall around Jerusalem. 2The people were sacrificing at the high
places, however, because no house had yet been
built for the name of the LORD.
3 Solomon loved the LORD, walking in the
statutes of his father David; only, he sacrificed
and offered incense at the high places. 4The
king went to Gibeon to sacrifice there, for that
was the principal high place; Solomon used to
offer a thousand burnt offerings on that altar.
5At Gibeon the LORD appeared to Solomon
in a dream by night; and God said, "Ask what I
should give you." 6And Solomon said, "You have
shown great and steadfast love to your servant
my father David, because he walked before you
in faithfulness, in righteousness, and in uprightness of heart toward you; and you have kept for
him this great and steadfast love, and have given
him a son to sit on his throne today. 7And now,
O LORD my God, you have made your servant
king in place of my father David, although I am
only a little child; I do not know how to go out or
come in. 8And your servant is in the midst of the
people whom you have chosen, a great people, so
numerous they cannot be numbered or counted.
9Give your servant therefore an understanding mind to govern your people, able to discern
between good and evil; for who can govern this
your great people?"
10 It pleased the Lord that Solomon had
asked this. 11God said to him, "Because you have
asked this, and have not asked for yourself long
life or riches, or for the life of your enemies, but
have asked for yourself understanding to discern
what is right, 12I now do according to your word.
Indeed I give you a wise and discerning mind; no
one like you has been before you and no one like
you shall arise after you. 13I give you also what
you have not asked, both riches and honor all
your life; no other king shall compare with you.
14If you will walk in my ways, keeping my statutes

and my commandments, as your father David
walked, then I will lengthen your life."
15 Then Solomon awoke; it had been a dream.
He came to Jerusalem where he stood before the
ark of the covenant of the LORD. He offered up
burnt offerings and offerings of well-being, and
provided a feast for all his servants.
16 Later, two women who were prostitutes
came to the king and stood before him. 17The
one woman said, "Please, my lord, this woman
and I live in the same house; and I gave birth
while she was in the house. 18Then on the third
day after I gave birth, this woman also gave birth.
We were together; there was no one else with us
in the house, only the two of us were in the house.
19Then this woman's son died in the night, because
she lay on him. 20She got up in the middle of the
night and took my son from beside me while your
servant slept. She laid him at her breast, and laid
her dead son at my breast. 21When I rose in the
morning to nurse my son, I saw that he was dead;
but when I looked at him closely in the morning,
clearly it was not the son I had borne." 22But the
other woman said, "No, the living son is mine,
and the dead son is yours." The first said, "No, the
dead son is yours, and the living son is mine." So
they argued before the king.
23 Then the king said, "The one says, 'This is
my son that is alive, and your son is dead'; while
the other says, 'Not so! Your son is dead, and my
son is the living one.'" 24So the king said, "Bring
me a sword," and they brought a sword before
the king. 25The king said, "Divide the living boy
in two; then give half to the one, and half to the
other." 26But the woman whose son was alive said
to the king—because compassion for her son
burned within her—"Please, my lord, give her the
living boy; certainly do not kill him!" The other
said, "It shall be neither mine nor yours; divide
it." 27Then the king responded: "Give the first
woman the living boy; do not kill him. She is his
mother." 28All Israel heard of the judgment that
the king had rendered; and they stood in awe of
the king, because they perceived that the wisdom
of God was in him, to execute justice.

4 King Solomon was king over all Israel, 2and
these were his high officials: Azariah son of
Zadok was the priest; 3Elihoreph and Ahijah
sons of Shisha were secretaries; Jehoshaphat son
of Ahilud was recorder; 4Benaiah son of Jehoiada
was in command of the army; Zadok and Abiathar were priests; 5Azariah son of Nathan was
over the officials; Zabud son of Nathan was priest
and king's friend; 6Ahishar was in charge of the
palace; and Adoniram son of Abda was in charge
of the forced labor.
7 Solomon had twelve officials over all Israel,
who provided food for the king and his household; each one had to make provision for one
month in the year. 8These were their names: Ben-
hur, in the hill country of Ephraim; 9Ben-deker,
in Makaz, Shaalbim, Beth-shemesh, and Elon-
beth-hanan; 10Ben-hesed, in Arubboth (to him
belonged Socoh and all the land of Hepher);
11Ben-abinadab, in all Naphath-dor (he had
Taphath, Solomon's daughter, as his wife); 12Ba-
ana son of Ahilud, in Taanach, Megiddo, and all
Beth-shean, which is beside Zarethan below Jezreel, and from Beth-shean to Abel-meholah, as far
as the other side of Jokmeam; 13Ben-geber, in
Ramoth-gilead (he had the villages of Jair son of
Manasseh, which are in Gilead, and he had the
region of Argob, which is in Bashan, sixty great
cities with walls and bronze bars); 14Ahinadab
son of Iddo, in Mahanaim; 15Ahimaaz, in Naphtali (he had taken Basemath, Solomon's daughter,
as his wife); 16Baana son of Hushai, in Asher and
Bealoth; 17Jehoshaphat son of Paruah, in Issachar; 18Shimei son of Ela, in Benjamin; 19Geber
son of Uri, in the land of Gilead, the country of
King Sihon of the Amorites and of King Og of
Bashan. And there was one official in the land
of Judah.
20 Judah and Israel were as numerous as the
sand by the sea; they ate and drank and were
happy. 21[a]Solomon was sovereign over all the
kingdoms from the Euphrates to the land of the
Philistines, even to the border of Egypt; they
brought tribute and served Solomon all the days
of his life.

[a] Ch 5.1 in Heb

22 Solomon's provision for one day was
thirty cors of choice flour, and sixty cors of meal,
23ten fat oxen, and twenty pasture-fed cattle, one
hundred sheep, besides deer, gazelles, roebucks,
and fatted fowl. 24For he had dominion over all
the region west of the Euphrates from Tiphsah
to Gaza, over all the kings west of the Euphrates;
and he had peace on all sides. 25During Solomon's
lifetime Judah and Israel lived in safety, from Dan
even to Beer-sheba, all of them under their vines
and fig trees. 26Solomon also had forty thousand
stalls of horses for his chariots, and twelve thousand horsemen. 27Those officials supplied provisions for King Solomon and for all who came to
King Solomon's table, each one in his month; they
let nothing be lacking. 28They also brought to the
required place barley and straw for the horses and
swift steeds, each according to his charge.

29 God gave Solomon very great wisdom, discernment, and breadth of understanding as vast
as the sand on the seashore, 30so that Solomon's
wisdom surpassed the wisdom of all the people
of the east, and all the wisdom of Egypt. 31He was
wiser than anyone else, wiser than Ethan the Ezrahite, and Heman, Calcol, and Darda, children
of Mahol; his fame spread throughout all the
surrounding nations. 32He composed three thousand proverbs, and his songs numbered a thousand and five. 33He would speak of trees, from the
cedar that is in the Lebanon to the hyssop that
grows in the wall; he would speak of animals, and
birds, and reptiles, and fish. 34People came from
all the nations to hear the wisdom of Solomon;
they came from all the kings of the earth who had
heard of his wisdom.

5 [a] Now King Hiram of Tyre sent his servants
to Solomon, when he heard that they had
anointed him king in place of his father; for Hiram had always been a friend to David. 2Solomon
sent word to Hiram, saying, 3"You know that
my father David could not build a house for the
name of the LORD his God because of the warfare
with which his enemies surrounded him, until
the LORD put them under the soles of his feet.[b]
4But now the LORD my God has given me rest on
every side; there is neither adversary nor misfortune. 5So I intend to build a house for the name
of the LORD my God, as the LORD said to my father David, 'Your son, whom I will set on your
throne in your place, shall build the house for my
name.' 6Therefore command that cedars from the
Lebanon be cut for me. My servants will join your
servants, and I will give you whatever wages you
set for your servants; for you know that there is
no one among us who knows how to cut timber
like the Sidonians."

7 When Hiram heard the words of Solomon,
he rejoiced greatly, and said, "Blessed be the
LORD today, who has given to David a wise son
to be over this great people." 8Hiram sent word
to Solomon, "I have heard the message that you
have sent to me; I will fulfill all your needs in the
matter of cedar and cypress timber. 9My servants
shall bring it down to the sea from the Lebanon;
I will make it into rafts to go by sea to the place
you indicate. I will have them broken up there for
you to take away. And you shall meet my needs
by providing food for my household." 10So Hiram
supplied Solomon's every need for timber of cedar and cypress. 11Solomon in turn gave Hiram
twenty thousand cors of wheat as food for his
household, and twenty cors of fine oil. Solomon
gave this to Hiram year by year. 12So the LORD
gave Solomon wisdom, as he promised him.
There was peace between Hiram and Solomon;
and the two of them made a treaty.

13 King Solomon conscripted forced labor
out of all Israel; the levy numbered thirty thousand men. 14He sent them to the Lebanon, ten
thousand a month in shifts; they would be a
month in the Lebanon and two months at home;
Adoniram was in charge of the forced labor. 15Sol-
omon also had seventy thousand laborers and
eighty thousand stonecutters in the hill country,
16besides Solomon's three thousand three hundred supervisors who were over the work, having
charge of the people who did the work. 17At the
king's command, they quarried out great, costly
stones in order to lay the foundation of the house
with dressed stones. 18So Solomon's builders and

[a] Ch 5.15 in Heb [b] Gk Tg Vg: Heb *my feet* or *his feet*

Hiram's builders and the Gebalites did the stone-
cutting and prepared the timber and the stone to
build the house.

6 In the four hundred eightieth year after the
Israelites came out of the land of Egypt, in
the fourth year of Solomon's reign over Israel, in
the month of Ziv, which is the second month, he
began to build the house of the LORD. 2 The house
that King Solomon built for the LORD was sixty
cubits long, twenty cubits wide, and thirty cubits
high. 3 The vestibule in front of the nave of the
house was twenty cubits wide, across the width of
the house. Its depth was ten cubits in front of the
house. 4 For the house he made windows with recessed frames.[a] 5 He also built a structure against
the wall of the house, running around the walls
of the house, both the nave and the inner sanctuary; and he made side chambers all around. 6 The
lowest story[b] was five cubits wide, the middle
one was six cubits wide, and the third was seven
cubits wide; for around the outside of the house
he made offsets on the wall in order that the supporting beams should not be inserted into the
walls of the house.

7 The house was built with stone finished at
the quarry, so that neither hammer nor ax nor any
tool of iron was heard in the temple while it was
being built.

8 The entrance for the middle story was on
the south side of the house: one went up by wind-
ing stairs to the middle story, and from the middle story to the third. 9 So he built the house, and
finished it; he roofed the house with beams and
planks of cedar. 10 He built the structure against
the whole house, each story[c] five cubits high, and
it was joined to the house with timbers of cedar.

11 Now the word of the LORD came to Solomon, 12 "Concerning this house that you are
building, if you will walk in my statutes, obey my
ordinances, and keep all my commandments by
walking in them, then I will establish my promise
with you, which I made to your father David. 13 I
will dwell among the children of Israel, and will
not forsake my people Israel."

14 So Solomon built the house, and finished
it. 15 He lined the walls of the house on the inside
with boards of cedar; from the floor of the house
to the rafters of the ceiling, he covered them on
the inside with wood; and he covered the floor
of the house with boards of cypress. 16 He built
twenty cubits of the rear of the house with boards
of cedar from the floor to the rafters, and he built
this within as an inner sanctuary, as the most holy
place. 17 The house, that is, the nave in front of the
inner sanctuary, was forty cubits long. 18 The cedar within the house had carvings of gourds and
open flowers; all was cedar, no stone was seen.
19 The inner sanctuary he prepared in the innermost part of the house, to set there the ark of the
covenant of the LORD. 20 The interior of the inner
sanctuary was twenty cubits long, twenty cubits
wide, and twenty cubits high; he overlaid it with
pure gold. He also overlaid the altar with cedar.[d]
21 Solomon overlaid the inside of the house with
pure gold, then he drew chains of gold across, in
front of the inner sanctuary, and overlaid it with
gold. 22 Next he overlaid the whole house with
gold, in order that the whole house might be perfect; even the whole altar that belonged to the inner sanctuary he overlaid with gold.

23 In the inner sanctuary he made two
cherubim of olivewood, each ten cubits high.
24 Five cubits was the length of one wing of the
cherub, and five cubits the length of the other
wing of the cherub; it was ten cubits from the tip
of one wing to the tip of the other. 25 The other
cherub also measured ten cubits; both cherubim
had the same measure and the same form. 26 The
height of one cherub was ten cubits, and so was
that of the other cherub. 27 He put the cherubim
in the innermost part of the house; the wings of
the cherubim were spread out so that a wing of
one was touching the one wall, and a wing of the
other cherub was touching the other wall; their
other wings toward the center of the house were
touching wing to wing. 28 He also overlaid the
cherubim with gold.

29 He carved the walls of the house all around
about with carved engravings of cherubim, palm
trees, and open flowers, in the inner and outer

[a] Gk: Meaning of Heb uncertain [b] Gk: Heb *structure* [c] Heb lacks *each story* [d] Meaning of Heb uncertain

rooms. 30The floor of the house he overlaid with
gold, in the inner and outer rooms.
31 For the entrance to the inner sanctuary
he made doors of olivewood; the lintel and the
doorposts were five-sided.[a] 32He covered the two
doors of olivewood with carvings of cherubim,
palm trees, and open flowers; he overlaid them
with gold, and spread gold on the cherubim and
on the palm trees.
33 So also he made for the entrance to the
nave doorposts of olivewood, four-sided each,
34and two doors of cypress wood; the two leaves
of the one door were folding, and the two leaves
of the other door were folding. 35He carved cherubim, palm trees, and open flowers, overlaying
them with gold evenly applied upon the carved
work. 36He built the inner court with three
courses of dressed stone to one course of cedar
beams.
37 In the fourth year the foundation of the
house of the LORD was laid, in the month of Ziv.
38In the eleventh year, in the month of Bul, which
is the eighth month, the house was finished in all
its parts, and according to all its specifications.
He was seven years in building it.

7 Solomon was building his own house thirteen years, and he finished his entire house.
2 He built the House of the Forest of the Lebanon one hundred cubits long, fifty cubits wide,
and thirty cubits high, built on four rows of cedar
pillars, with cedar beams on the pillars. 3It was
roofed with cedar on the forty-five rafters, fifteen
in each row, which were on the pillars. 4There
were window frames in the three rows, facing
each other in the three rows. 5All the doorways
and doorposts had four-sided frames, opposite,
facing each other in the three rows.
6 He made the Hall of Pillars fifty cubits long
and thirty cubits wide. There was a porch in front
with pillars, and a canopy in front of them.
7 He made the Hall of the Throne where he
was to pronounce judgment, the Hall of Justice,
covered with cedar from floor to floor.
8 His own house where he would reside, in
the other court back of the hall, was of the same
construction. Solomon also made a house like
this hall for Pharaoh's daughter, whom he had
taken in marriage.
9 All these were made of costly stones, cut
according to measure, sawed with saws, back and
front, from the foundation to the coping, and
from outside to the great court. 10The foundation
was of costly stones, huge stones, stones of eight
and ten cubits. 11There were costly stones above,
cut to measure, and cedarwood. 12The great court
had three courses of dressed stone to one layer of
cedar beams all around; so had the inner court of
the house of the LORD, and the vestibule of the
house.
13 Now King Solomon invited and received
Hiram from Tyre. 14He was the son of a widow of
the tribe of Naphtali, whose father, a man of Tyre,
had been an artisan in bronze; he was full of skill,
intelligence, and knowledge in working bronze.
He came to King Solomon, and did all his work.
15 He cast two pillars of bronze. Eighteen cubits was the height of the one, and a cord of twelve
cubits would encircle it; the second pillar was the
same.[b] 16He also made two capitals of molten
bronze, to set on the tops of the pillars; the height
of the one capital was five cubits, and the height
of the other capital was five cubits. 17There were
nets of checker work with wreaths of chain work
for the capitals on the tops of the pillars; seven[c]
for the one capital, and seven[c] for the other capital. 18He made the columns with two rows around
each latticework to cover the capitals that were
above the pomegranates; he did the same with
the other capital. 19Now the capitals that were on
the tops of the pillars in the vestibule were of lily-
work, four cubits high. 20The capitals were on the
two pillars and also above the rounded projection
that was beside the latticework; there were two
hundred pomegranates in rows all around; and so
with the other capital. 21He set up the pillars at
the vestibule of the temple; he set up the pillar on
the south and called it Jachin; and he set up the
pillar on the north and called it Boaz. 22On the

[a] Meaning of Heb uncertain
[b] Cn: Heb *and a cord of twelve cubits encircled the second pillar*; Compare Jer 52.21
[c] Heb: Gk *a net*

tops of the pillars was lily-work. Thus the work of
the pillars was finished.
23 Then he made the molten sea; it was
round, ten cubits from brim to brim, and five cubits high. A line of thirty cubits would encircle
it completely. 24Under its brim were panels all
around it, each of ten cubits, surrounding the
sea; there were two rows of panels, cast when it
was cast. 25It stood on twelve oxen, three facing
north, three facing west, three facing south, and
three facing east; the sea was set on them. The
hindquarters of each were toward the inside. 26Its
thickness was a handbreadth; its brim was made
like the brim of a cup, like the flower of a lily; it
held two thousand baths.[a]
27 He also made the ten stands of bronze;
each stand was four cubits long, four cubits wide,
and three cubits high. 28This was the construction
of the stands: they had borders; the borders were
within the frames; 29on the borders that were set
in the frames were lions, oxen, and cherubim.
On the frames, both above and below the lions
and oxen, there were wreaths of beveled work.
30Each stand had four bronze wheels and axles
of bronze; at the four corners were supports for a
basin. The supports were cast with wreaths at the
side of each. 31Its opening was within the crown
whose height was one cubit; its opening was
round, as a pedestal is made; it was a cubit and a
half wide. At its opening there were carvings; its
borders were four-sided, not round. 32The four
wheels were underneath the borders; the axles
of the wheels were in the stands; and the height
of a wheel was a cubit and a half. 33The wheels
were made like a chariot wheel; their axles, their
rims, their spokes, and their hubs were all cast.
34There were four supports at the four corners
of each stand; the supports were of one piece
with the stands. 35On the top of the stand there
was a round band half a cubit high; on the top of
the stand, its stays and its borders were of one
piece with it. 36On the surfaces of its stays and
on its borders he carved cherubim, lions, and
palm trees, where each had space, with wreaths
all around. 37In this way he made the ten stands;
all of them were cast alike, with the same size and
the same form.
38 He made ten basins of bronze; each basin
held forty baths,[a] each basin measured four cubits; there was a basin for each of the ten stands.
39He set five of the stands on the south side
of the house, and five on the north side of the
house; he set the sea on the southeast corner of
the house.
40 Hiram also made the pots, the shovels,
and the basins. So Hiram finished all the work
that he did for King Solomon on the house of the
LORD: 41the two pillars, the two bowls of the capitals that were on the tops of the pillars, the two
latticeworks to cover the two bowls of the capitals that were on the tops of the pillars; 42the four
hundred pomegranates for the two latticeworks,
two rows of pomegranates for each latticework,
to cover the two bowls of the capitals that were
on the pillars; 43the ten stands, the ten basins on
the stands; 44the one sea, and the twelve oxen underneath the sea.
45 The pots, the shovels, and the basins, all
these vessels that Hiram made for King Solomon
for the house of the LORD were of burnished
bronze. 46In the plain of the Jordan the king
cast them, in the clay ground between Succoth
and Zarethan. 47Solomon left all the vessels un-
weighed, because there were so many of them;
the weight of the bronze was not determined.
48 So Solomon made all the vessels that were
in the house of the LORD: the golden altar, the
golden table for the bread of the Presence, 49the
lampstands of pure gold, five on the south side
and five on the north, in front of the inner sanctuary; the flowers, the lamps, and the tongs, of
gold; 50the cups, snuffers, basins, dishes for incense, and firepans, of pure gold; the sockets for
the doors of the innermost part of the house, the
most holy place, and for the doors of the nave of
the temple, of gold.
51 Thus all the work that King Solomon did
on the house of the LORD was finished. Solomon
brought in the things that his father David had
dedicated, the silver, the gold, and the vessels,

[a] A Heb measure of volume

and stored them in the treasuries of the house of
the LORD.

8 Then Solomon assembled the elders of Israel
and all the heads of the tribes, the leaders of
the ancestral houses of the Israelites, before King
Solomon in Jerusalem, to bring up the ark of the
covenant of the LORD out of the city of David,
which is Zion. 2All the people of Israel assembled
to King Solomon at the festival in the month
Ethanim, which is the seventh month. 3And all
the elders of Israel came, and the priests carried the ark. 4So they brought up the ark of the
LORD, the tent of meeting, and all the holy vessels that were in the tent; the priests and the Levites brought them up. 5King Solomon and all the
congregation of Israel, who had assembled before
him, were with him before the ark, sacrificing
so many sheep and oxen that they could not be
counted or numbered. 6Then the priests brought
the ark of the covenant of the LORD to its place, in
the inner sanctuary of the house, in the most holy
place, underneath the wings of the cherubim.
7For the cherubim spread out their wings over
the place of the ark, so that the cherubim made
a covering above the ark and its poles. 8The poles
were so long that the ends of the poles were seen
from the holy place in front of the inner sanctuary; but they could not be seen from outside;
they are there to this day. 9There was nothing in
the ark except the two tablets of stone that Moses had placed there at Horeb, where the LORD
made a covenant with the Israelites, when they
came out of the land of Egypt. 10And when the
priests came out of the holy place, a cloud filled
the house of the LORD, 11so that the priests could
not stand to minister because of the cloud; for the
glory of the LORD filled the house of the LORD.

12 Then Solomon said,

"The LORD has said that he would dwell in
thick darkness.

13 I have built you an exalted house,
a place for you to dwell in forever."

14 Then the king turned around and blessed
all the assembly of Israel, while all the assembly
of Israel stood. 15He said, "Blessed be the LORD,
the God of Israel, who with his hand has fulfilled
what he promised with his mouth to my father
David, saying, 16'Since the day that I brought my
people Israel out of Egypt, I have not chosen a
city from any of the tribes of Israel in which to
build a house, that my name might be there; but
I chose David to be over my people Israel.' 17My
father David had it in mind to build a house for
the name of the LORD, the God of Israel. 18But
the LORD said to my father David, 'You did
well to consider building a house for my name;
19nevertheless you shall not build the house, but
your son who shall be born to you shall build the
house for my name.' 20Now the LORD has upheld
the promise that he made; for I have risen in the
place of my father David; I sit on the throne of
Israel, as the LORD promised, and have built the
house for the name of the LORD, the God of Israel. 21There I have provided a place for the ark,
in which is the covenant of the LORD that he
made with our ancestors when he brought them
out of the land of Egypt."

22 Then Solomon stood before the altar of
the LORD in the presence of all the assembly of
Israel, and spread out his hands to heaven. 23He
said, "O LORD, God of Israel, there is no God like
you in heaven above or on earth beneath, keeping covenant and steadfast love for your servants
who walk before you with all their heart, 24the
covenant that you kept for your servant my father David as you declared to him; you promised
with your mouth and have this day fulfilled with
your hand. 25Therefore, O LORD, God of Israel,
keep for your servant my father David that which
you promised him, saying, 'There shall never fail
you a successor before me to sit on the throne of
Israel, if only your children look to their way, to
walk before me as you have walked before me.'
26Therefore, O God of Israel, let your word be
confirmed, which you promised to your servant
my father David.

27 "But will God indeed dwell on the earth?
Even heaven and the highest heaven cannot contain you, much less this house that I have built!
28Regard your servant's prayer and his plea,
O LORD my God, heeding the cry and the prayer
that your servant prays to you today; 29that your
eyes may be open night and day toward this
house, the place of which you said, My name shall

be there,' that you may heed the prayer that your
servant prays toward this place. 30 Hear the plea of
your servant and of your people Israel when they
pray toward this place; O hear in heaven your
dwelling place; heed and forgive.

31 "If someone sins against a neighbor and is
given an oath to swear, and comes and swears before your altar in this house, 32 then hear in heaven,
and act, and judge your servants, condemning
the guilty by bringing their conduct on their own
head, and vindicating the righteous by rewarding
them according to their righteousness.

33 "When your people Israel, having sinned
against you, are defeated before an enemy but turn
again to you, confess your name, pray and plead
with you in this house, 34 then hear in heaven,
forgive the sin of your people Israel, and bring
them again to the land that you gave to their ancestors.

35 "When heaven is shut up and there is no
rain because they have sinned against you, and
then they pray toward this place, confess your
name, and turn from their sin, because you punish[a] them, 36 then hear in heaven, and forgive the
sin of your servants, your people Israel, when you
teach them the good way in which they should
walk; and grant rain on your land, which you have
given to your people as an inheritance.

37 "If there is famine in the land, if there is
plague, blight, mildew, locust, or caterpillar; if
their enemy besieges them in any[b] of their cities; whatever plague, whatever sickness there is;
38 whatever prayer, whatever plea there is from
any individual or from all your people Israel,
all knowing the afflictions of their own hearts
so that they stretch out their hands toward this
house; 39 then hear in heaven your dwelling place,
forgive, act, and render to all whose hearts you
know—according to all their ways, for only you
know what is in every human heart— 40 so that
they may fear you all the days that they live in the
land that you gave to our ancestors.

41 "Likewise when a foreigner, who is not
of your people Israel, comes from a distant land
because of your name 42—for they shall hear of
your great name, your mighty hand, and your
outstretched arm—when a foreigner comes and
prays toward this house, 43 then hear in heaven
your dwelling place, and do according to all that
the foreigner calls to you, so that all the peoples
of the earth may know your name and fear you, as
do your people Israel, and so that they may know
that your name has been invoked on this house
that I have built.

44 "If your people go out to battle against
their enemy, by whatever way you shall send
them, and they pray to the LORD toward the city
that you have chosen and the house that I have
built for your name, 45 then hear in heaven their
prayer and their plea, and maintain their cause.

46 "If they sin against you—for there is no
one who does not sin—and you are angry with
them and give them to an enemy, so that they are
carried away captive to the land of the enemy, far
off or near; 47 yet if they come to their senses in
the land to which they have been taken captive,
and repent, and plead with you in the land of
their captors, saying, 'We have sinned, and have
done wrong; we have acted wickedly'; 48 if they
repent with all their heart and soul in the land of
their enemies, who took them captive, and pray
to you toward their land, which you gave to their
ancestors, the city that you have chosen, and the
house that I have built for your name; 49 then hear
in heaven your dwelling place their prayer and
their plea, maintain their cause 50 and forgive your
people who have sinned against you, and all their
transgressions that they have committed against
you; and grant them compassion in the sight of
their captors, so that they may have compassion
on them 51 (for they are your people and heritage,
which you brought out of Egypt, from the midst
of the iron-smelter). 52 Let your eyes be open to
the plea of your servant, and to the plea of your
people Israel, listening to them whenever they
call to you. 53 For you have separated them from
among all the peoples of the earth, to be your heritage, just as you promised through Moses, your
servant, when you brought our ancestors out of
Egypt, O Lord GOD."

[a] Or *when you answer* [b] Gk Syr: Heb *in the land*

54 Now when Solomon finished offering all
this prayer and this plea to the LORD, he arose
from facing the altar of the LORD, where he had
knelt with hands outstretched toward heaven;
55 he stood and blessed all the assembly of Israel
with a loud voice:

56 "Blessed be the LORD, who has given
rest to his people Israel according to all that he
promised; not one word has failed of all his good
promise, which he spoke through his servant
Moses. 57 The LORD our God be with us, as he
was with our ancestors; may he not leave us or
abandon us, 58 but incline our hearts to him, to
walk in all his ways, and to keep his commandments, his statutes, and his ordinances, which he
commanded our ancestors. 59 Let these words of
mine, with which I pleaded before the LORD, be
near to the LORD our God day and night, and
may he maintain the cause of his servant and the
cause of his people Israel, as each day requires;
60 so that all the peoples of the earth may know
that the LORD is God; there is no other. 61 Therefore devote yourselves completely to the LORD
our God, walking in his statutes and keeping his
commandments, as at this day."

62 Then the king, and all Israel with him,
offered sacrifice before the LORD. 63 Solomon
offered as sacrifices of well-being to the LORD
twenty-two thousand oxen and one hundred
twenty thousand sheep. So the king and all the
people of Israel dedicated the house of the LORD.
64 The same day the king consecrated the middle
of the court that was in front of the house of the
LORD; for there he offered the burnt offerings
and the grain offerings and the fat pieces of the
sacrifices of well-being, because the bronze altar
that was before the LORD was too small to receive
the burnt offerings and the grain offerings and
the fat pieces of the sacrifices of well-being.

65 So Solomon held the festival at that time,
and all Israel with him—a great assembly, people
from Lebo-hamath to the Wadi of Egypt—before
the LORD our God, seven days.[a] 66 On the eighth
day he sent the people away; and they blessed the
king, and went to their tents, joyful and in good
spirits because of all the goodness that the LORD
had shown to his servant David and to his people
Israel.

9 When Solomon had finished building the
house of the LORD and the king's house and
all that Solomon desired to build, 2 the LORD
appeared to Solomon a second time, as he had
appeared to him at Gibeon. 3 The LORD said to
him, "I have heard your prayer and your plea,
which you made before me; I have consecrated
this house that you have built, and put my name
there forever; my eyes and my heart will be there
for all time. 4 As for you, if you will walk before
me, as David your father walked, with integrity of
heart and uprightness, doing according to all that
I have commanded you, and keeping my statutes
and my ordinances, 5 then I will establish your
royal throne over Israel forever, as I promised
your father David, saying, 'There shall not fail you
a successor on the throne of Israel.'

6 "If you turn aside from following me, you
or your children, and do not keep my commandments and my statutes that I have set before you,
but go and serve other gods and worship them,
7 then I will cut Israel off from the land that I have
given them; and the house that I have consecrated for my name I will cast out of my sight; and
Israel will become a proverb and a taunt among
all peoples. 8 This house will become a heap of
ruins;[b] everyone passing by it will be astonished,
and will hiss; and they will say, 'Why has the
LORD done such a thing to this land and to this
house?' 9 Then they will say, 'Because they have
forsaken the LORD their God, who brought their
ancestors out of the land of Egypt, and embraced
other gods, worshiping them and serving them;
therefore the LORD has brought this disaster
upon them.'"

10 At the end of twenty years, in which Solomon had built the two houses, the house of the
LORD and the king's house, 11 King Hiram of Tyre
having supplied Solomon with cedar and cypress
timber and gold, as much as he desired, King
Solomon gave to Hiram twenty cities in the land
of Galilee. 12 But when Hiram came from Tyre to

[a] Compare Gk: Heb *seven days and seven days, fourteen days*

[b] Syr Old Latin: Heb *will become high*

see the cities that Solomon had given him, they
did not please him. 13 Therefore he said, "What
kind of cities are these that you have given me, my
brother?" So they are called the land of Cabul[a] to
this day. 14 But Hiram had sent to the king one
hundred twenty talents of gold.

15 This is the account of the forced labor that
King Solomon conscripted to build the house
of the LORD and his own house, the Millo and
the wall of Jerusalem, Hazor, Megiddo, Gezer
16 (Pharaoh king of Egypt had gone up and captured Gezer and burned it down, had killed the
Canaanites who lived in the city, and had given
it as dowry to his daughter, Solomon's wife; 17 so
Solomon rebuilt Gezer), Lower Beth-horon,
18 Baalath, Tamar in the wilderness, within the
land, 19 as well as all of Solomon's storage cities,
the cities for his chariots, the cities for his cavalry, and whatever Solomon desired to build, in
Jerusalem, in Lebanon, and in all the land of his
dominion. 20 All the people who were left of the
Amorites, the Hittites, the Perizzites, the Hivites,
and the Jebusites, who were not of the people of
Israel— 21 their descendants who were still left
in the land, whom the Israelites were unable to
destroy completely—these Solomon conscripted
for slave labor, and so they are to this day. 22 But
of the Israelites Solomon made no slaves; they
were the soldiers, they were his officials, his commanders, his captains, and the commanders of
his chariotry and cavalry.

23 These were the chief officers who were
over Solomon's work: five hundred fifty, who had
charge of the people who carried on the work.

24 But Pharaoh's daughter went up from the
city of David to her own house that Solomon had
built for her; then he built the Millo.

25 Three times a year Solomon used to offer
up burnt offerings and sacrifices of well-being
on the altar that he built for the LORD, offering
incense[b] before the LORD. So he completed the
house.

26 King Solomon built a fleet of ships at
Ezion-geber, which is near Eloth on the shore of
the Red Sea,[c] in the land of Edom. 27 Hiram sent
his servants with the fleet, sailors who were familiar with the sea, together with the servants of
Solomon. 28 They went to Ophir, and imported
from there four hundred twenty talents of gold,
which they delivered to King Solomon.

10 When the queen of Sheba heard of the
fame of Solomon (fame due to[d] the name
of the LORD), she came to test him with hard
questions. 2 She came to Jerusalem with a very
great retinue, with camels bearing spices, and
very much gold, and precious stones; and when
she came to Solomon, she told him all that was on
her mind. 3 Solomon answered all her questions;
there was nothing hidden from the king that he
could not explain to her. 4 When the queen of
Sheba had observed all the wisdom of Solomon,
the house that he had built, 5 the food of his table,
the seating of his officials, and the attendance of
his servants, their clothing, his valets, and his
burnt offerings that he offered at the house of the
LORD, there was no more spirit in her.

6 So she said to the king, "The report was true
that I heard in my own land of your accomplishments and of your wisdom, 7 but I did not believe
the reports until I came and my own eyes had seen
it. Not even half had been told me; your wisdom
and prosperity far surpass the report that I had
heard. 8 Happy are your wives![e] Happy are these
your servants, who continually attend you and
hear your wisdom! 9 Blessed be the LORD your
God, who has delighted in you and set you on the
throne of Israel! Because the LORD loved Israel
forever, he has made you king to execute justice
and righteousness." 10 Then she gave the king one
hundred twenty talents of gold, a great quantity
of spices, and precious stones; never again did
spices come in such quantity as that which the
queen of Sheba gave to King Solomon.

11 Moreover, the fleet of Hiram, which
carried gold from Ophir, brought from Ophir
a great quantity of almug wood and precious
stones. 12 From the almug wood the king made
supports for the house of the LORD, and for the

[a] Perhaps meaning *a land good for nothing* [b] Gk: Heb *offering incense with it that was* [c] Or *Sea of Reeds* [d] Meaning of Heb uncertain [e] Gk Syr: Heb *men*

king's house, lyres also and harps for the singers; no such almug wood has come or been seen to this day.

13 Meanwhile King Solomon gave to the queen of Sheba every desire that she expressed, as well as what he gave her out of Solomon's royal bounty. Then she returned to her own land, with her servants.

14 The weight of gold that came to Solomon in one year was six hundred sixty-six talents of
gold, 15besides that which came from the trad-
ers and from the business of the merchants, and from all the kings of Arabia and the governors
of the land. 16King Solomon made two hundred
large shields of beaten gold; six hundred shekels
of gold went into each large shield. 17He made
three hundred shields of beaten gold; three minas of gold went into each shield; and the king put them in the House of the Forest of Lebanon.
18The king also made a great ivory throne, and
overlaid it with the finest gold. 19The throne had
six steps. The top of the throne was rounded in the back, and on each side of the seat were arm rests and two lions standing beside the arm rests,
20while twelve lions were standing, one on each
end of a step on the six steps. Nothing like it was
ever made in any kingdom. 21All King Solomon's
drinking vessels were of gold, and all the vessels of the House of the Forest of Lebanon were of pure gold; none were of silver—it was not considered as anything in the days of Solomon. 22For
the king had a fleet of ships of Tarshish at sea with the fleet of Hiram. Once every three years the fleet of ships of Tarshish used to come bringing gold, silver, ivory, apes, and peacocks.[a]

23 Thus King Solomon excelled all the kings
of the earth in riches and in wisdom. 24The whole
earth sought the presence of Solomon to hear his
wisdom, which God had put into his mind. 25Ev-
ery one of them brought a present, objects of silver and gold, garments, weaponry, spices, horses, and mules, so much year by year.

26 Solomon gathered together chariots and horses; he had fourteen hundred chariots and twelve thousand horses, which he stationed in the chariot cities and with the king in Jerusalem.
27The king made silver as common in Jerusalem
as stones, and he made cedars as numerous as
the sycamores of the Shephelah. 28Solomon's im-
port of horses was from Egypt and Kue, and the king's traders received them from Kue at a price.
29A chariot could be imported from Egypt for
six hundred shekels of silver, and a horse for one hundred fifty; so through the king's traders they were exported to all the kings of the Hittites and the kings of Aram.

1 Kings 10:26—11:8

Although King Solomon is popularly known for his surpassing wisdom (10:23-25), the Deuteronomistic editors are critical of Solomon because he took many foreign wives and accumulated prize horses (10:26-29); he thus appears to be the target of Moses' warning in Deuteronomy 17:14-20. His condemnation for promoting the worship of other gods outside Jerusalem (11:4-8) echoes Deuteronomy's insistence on one God, one nation, one chosen king, and one city where the LORD's name dwells. But the Deuteronomists blame his behavior on his foreign wives, who "turned away his heart" (11:3). The ethnocentric and androcentric bias of the text resembles the stereotypes that women of Asian descent face in U.S. culture, where they are often characterized as exotic, foreign, and as the sexualized other.

—*FY*

11 King Solomon loved many foreign women along with the daughter of Pharaoh: Moabite, Ammonite, Edomite, Sidonian, and Hittite women, 2from the nations concerning which
the LORD had said to the Israelites, "You shall not enter into marriage with them, neither shall they with you; for they will surely incline your heart to follow their gods"; Solomon clung to
these in love. 3Among his wives were seven hun-
dred princesses and three hundred concubines;
and his wives turned away his heart. 4For when

[a] Or *baboons*

Solomon was old, his wives turned away his heart after other gods; and his heart was not true to the LORD his God, as was the heart of his father David. 5For Solomon followed Astarte the goddess of the Sidonians, and Milcom the abomination of the Ammonites. 6So Solomon did what was evil in the sight of the LORD, and did not completely follow the LORD, as his father David had done. 7Then Solomon built a high place for Chemosh the abomination of Moab, and for Molech the abomination of the Ammonites, on the mountain east of Jerusalem. 8He did the same for all his foreign wives, who offered incense and sacrificed to their gods.

9 Then the LORD was angry with Solomon, because his heart had turned away from the LORD, the God of Israel, who had appeared to him twice, 10and had commanded him concerning this matter, that he should not follow other gods; but he did not observe what the LORD commanded. 11Therefore the LORD said to Solomon, "Since this has been your mind and you have not kept my covenant and my statutes that I have commanded you, I will surely tear the kingdom from you and give it to your servant. 12Yet for the sake of your father David I will not do it in your lifetime; I will tear it out of the hand of your son. 13I will not, however, tear away the entire kingdom; I will give one tribe to your son, for the sake of my servant David and for the sake of Jerusalem, which I have chosen."

14 Then the LORD raised up an adversary against Solomon, Hadad the Edomite; he was of the royal house in Edom. 15For when David was in Edom, and Joab the commander of the army went up to bury the dead, he killed every male in Edom 16(for Joab and all Israel remained there six months, until he had eliminated every male in Edom); 17but Hadad fled to Egypt with some Edomites who were servants of his father. He was a young boy at that time. 18They set out from Midian and came to Paran; they took people with them from Paran and came to Egypt, to Pharaoh king of Egypt, who gave him a house, assigned him an allowance of food, and gave him land. 19Hadad found great favor in the sight of Pharaoh, so that he gave him his sister-in-law for a wife, the sister of Queen Tahpenes. 20The sister of Tahpenes gave birth by him to his son Genubath, whom Tahpenes weaned in Pharaoh's house; Genubath was in Pharaoh's house among the children of Pharaoh. 21When Hadad heard in Egypt that David slept with his ancestors and that Joab the commander of the army was dead, Hadad said to Pharaoh, "Let me depart, that I may go to my own country." 22But Pharaoh said to him, "What do you lack with me that you now seek to go to your own country?" And he said, "No, do let me go."

23 God raised up another adversary against Solomon,[a] Rezon son of Eliada, who had fled from his master, King Hadadezer of Zobah. 24He gathered followers around him and became leader of a marauding band, after the slaughter by David; they went to Damascus, settled there, and made him king in Damascus. 25He was an adversary of Israel all the days of Solomon, making trouble as Hadad did; he despised Israel and reigned over Aram.

26 Jeroboam son of Nebat, an Ephraimite of Zeredah, a servant of Solomon, whose mother's name was Zeruah, a widow, rebelled against the king. 27The following was the reason he rebelled against the king. Solomon built the Millo, and closed up the gap in the wall[b] of the city of his father David. 28The man Jeroboam was very able, and when Solomon saw that the young man was industrious he gave him charge over all the forced labor of the house of Joseph. 29About that time, when Jeroboam was leaving Jerusalem, the prophet Ahijah the Shilonite found him on the road. Ahijah had clothed himself with a new garment. The two of them were alone in the open country 30when Ahijah laid hold of the new garment he was wearing and tore it into twelve pieces. 31He then said to Jeroboam: Take for yourself ten pieces; for thus says the LORD, the God of Israel, "See, I am about to tear the kingdom from the hand of Solomon, and will give you ten tribes. 32One tribe will remain his, for the sake of my servant

[a] Heb *him* [b] Heb lacks *in the wall*

David and for the sake of Jerusalem, the city that I
have chosen out of all the tribes of Israel. 33This is
because he has[a] forsaken me, worshiped Astarte
the goddess of the Sidonians, Chemosh the god
of Moab, and Milcom the god of the Ammonites,
and has[a] not walked in my ways, doing what is
right in my sight and keeping my statutes and my
ordinances, as his father David did. 34Neverthe-
less I will not take the whole kingdom away from
him but will make him ruler all the days of his life,
for the sake of my servant David whom I chose
and who did keep my commandments and my
statutes; 35but I will take the kingdom away from
his son and give it to you—that is, the ten tribes.
36Yet to his son I will give one tribe, so that my
servant David may always have a lamp before me
in Jerusalem, the city where I have chosen to put
my name. 37I will take you, and you shall reign
over all that your soul desires; you shall be king
over Israel. 38If you will listen to all that I command you, walk in my ways, and do what is right
in my sight by keeping my statutes and my commandments, as David my servant did, I will be
with you, and will build you an enduring house,
as I built for David, and I will give Israel to you.
39For this reason I will punish the descendants of
David, but not forever." 40Solomon sought therefore to kill Jeroboam; but Jeroboam promptly fled
to Egypt, to King Shishak of Egypt, and remained
in Egypt until the death of Solomon.

41 Now the rest of the acts of Solomon, all
that he did as well as his wisdom, are they not
written in the Book of the Acts of Solomon? 42The
time that Solomon reigned in Jerusalem over all
Israel was forty years. 43Solomon slept with his
ancestors and was buried in the city of his father
David; and his son Rehoboam succeeded him.

12 Rehoboam went to Shechem, for all Israel
had come to Shechem to make him king.
2When Jeroboam son of Nebat heard of it (for he
was still in Egypt, where he had fled from King
Solomon), then Jeroboam returned from[b] Egypt.
3And they sent and called him; and Jeroboam and
all the assembly of Israel came and said to Rehoboam, 4"Your father made our yoke heavy. Now
therefore lighten the hard service of your father
and his heavy yoke that he placed on us, and we
will serve you." 5He said to them, "Go away for
three days, then come again to me." So the people
went away.

6 Then King Rehoboam took counsel with
the older men who had attended his father Solomon while he was still alive, saying, "How do you
advise me to answer this people?" 7They answered
him, "If you will be a servant to this people today
and serve them, and speak good words to them
when you answer them, then they will be your
servants forever." 8But he disregarded the advice
that the older men gave him, and consulted with
the young men who had grown up with him and
now attended him. 9He said to them, "What do
you advise that we answer this people who have
said to me, 'Lighten the yoke that your father put
on us'?" 10The young men who had grown up
with him said to him, "Thus you should say to this
people who spoke to you, 'Your father made our
yoke heavy, but you must lighten it for us'; thus
you should say to them, 'My little finger is thicker
than my father's loins. 11Now, whereas my father
laid on you a heavy yoke, I will add to your yoke.
My father disciplined you with whips, but I will
discipline you with scorpions.'"

12 So Jeroboam and all the people came to
Rehoboam the third day, as the king had said,
"Come to me again the third day." 13The king
answered the people harshly. He disregarded the
advice that the older men had given him 14and
spoke to them according to the advice of the
young men, "My father made your yoke heavy,
but I will add to your yoke; my father disciplined
you with whips, but I will discipline you with
scorpions." 15So the king did not listen to the
people, because it was a turn of affairs brought
about by the LORD that he might fulfill his word,
which the LORD had spoken by Ahijah the Shilonite to Jeroboam son of Nebat.

16 When all Israel saw that the king would
not listen to them, the people answered the king,

"What share do we have in David?
We have no inheritance in the son of Jesse.

[a] Gk Syr Vg: Heb *they have* [b] Gk Vg Compare 2 Chr 10.2: Heb *lived in*

To your tents, O Israel!
Look now to your own house, O David."
So Israel went away to their tents. 17But Rehoboam reigned over the Israelites who were living
in the towns of Judah. 18When King Rehoboam
sent Adoram, who was taskmaster over the forced
labor, all Israel stoned him to death. King Rehoboam then hurriedly mounted his chariot to flee
to Jerusalem. 19So Israel has been in rebellion
against the house of David to this day.

20 When all Israel heard that Jeroboam had
returned, they sent and called him to the assembly and made him king over all Israel. There was
no one who followed the house of David, except
the tribe of Judah alone.

21 When Rehoboam came to Jerusalem, he
assembled all the house of Judah and the tribe of
Benjamin, one hundred eighty thousand chosen
troops to fight against the house of Israel, to restore the kingdom to Rehoboam son of Solomon.
22But the word of God came to Shemaiah the
man of God: 23Say to King Rehoboam of Judah,
son of Solomon, and to all the house of Judah and
Benjamin, and to the rest of the people, 24"Thus
says the LORD, You shall not go up or fight against
your kindred the people of Israel. Let everyone go
home, for this thing is from me." So they heeded
the word of the LORD and went home again, according to the word of the LORD.

25 Then Jeroboam built Shechem in the hill
country of Ephraim, and resided there; he went
out from there and built Penuel. 26Then Jeroboam said to himself, "Now the kingdom may
well revert to the house of David. 27If this people
continues to go up to offer sacrifices in the house
of the LORD at Jerusalem, the heart of this people
will turn again to their master, King Rehoboam of
Judah; they will kill me and return to King Rehoboam of Judah." 28So the king took counsel, and
made two calves of gold. He said to the people,[a]
"You have gone up to Jerusalem long enough.
Here are your gods, O Israel, who brought you up
out of the land of Egypt." 29He set one in Bethel,
and the other he put in Dan. 30And this thing became a sin, for the people went to worship before
the one at Bethel and before the other as far as
Dan.[b] 31He also made houses[c] on high places, and
appointed priests from among all the people, who
were not Levites. 32Jeroboam appointed a festival
on the fifteenth day of the eighth month like the
festival that was in Judah, and he offered sacrifices
on the altar; so he did in Bethel, sacrificing to the
calves that he had made. And he placed in Bethel
the priests of the high places that he had made.
33He went up to the altar that he had made in
Bethel on the fifteenth day in the eighth month,
in the month that he alone had devised; he appointed a festival for the people of Israel, and he
went up to the altar to offer incense.

13 While Jeroboam was standing by the altar
to offer incense, a man of God came out
of Judah by the word of the LORD to Bethel 2and
proclaimed against the altar by the word of the
LORD, and said, "O altar, altar, thus says the LORD:
'A son shall be born to the house of David, Josiah
by name; and he shall sacrifice on you the priests
of the high places who offer incense on you, and
human bones shall be burned on you.' " 3He gave a
sign the same day, saying, "This is the sign that the
LORD has spoken: 'The altar shall be torn down,
and the ashes that are on it shall be poured out.' "
4When the king heard what the man of God cried
out against the altar at Bethel, Jeroboam stretched
out his hand from the altar, saying, "Seize him!"
But the hand that he stretched out against him
withered so that he could not draw it back to himself. 5The altar also was torn down, and the ashes
poured out from the altar, according to the sign
that the man of God had given by the word of the
LORD. 6The king said to the man of God, "Entreat
now the favor of the LORD your God, and pray
for me, so that my hand may be restored to me."
So the man of God entreated the LORD; and the
king's hand was restored to him, and became as
it was before. 7Then the king said to the man of
God, "Come home with me and dine, and I will
give you a gift." 8But the man of God said to the
king, "If you give me half your kingdom, I will not
go in with you; nor will I eat food or drink water
in this place. 9For thus I was commanded by the

[a] Gk: Heb *to them* [b] Compare Gk: Heb *went to the one as far as Dan* [c] Gk Vg Compare 13.32: Heb *a house*

word of the LORD: You shall not eat food, or drink
water, or return by the way that you came." 10So he
went another way, and did not return by the way
that he had come to Bethel.

11 Now there lived an old prophet in Bethel.
One of his sons came and told him all that the man
of God had done that day in Bethel; the words
also that he had spoken to the king, they told to
their father. 12Their father said to them, "Which
way did he go?" And his sons showed him the way
that the man of God who came from Judah had
gone. 13Then he said to his sons, "Saddle a donkey for me." So they saddled a donkey for him,
and he mounted it. 14He went after the man of
God, and found him sitting under an oak tree. He
said to him, "Are you the man of God who came
from Judah?" He answered, "I am." 15Then he
said to him, "Come home with me and eat some
food." 16But he said, "I cannot return with you, or
go in with you; nor will I eat food or drink water
with you in this place; 17for it was said to me by
the word of the LORD: You shall not eat food or
drink water there, or return by the way that you
came." 18Then the other[a] said to him, "I also am a
prophet as you are, and an angel spoke to me by
the word of the LORD: Bring him back with you
into your house so that he may eat food and drink
water." But he was deceiving him. 19Then the man
of God[a] went back with him, and ate food and
drank water in his house.

20 As they were sitting at the table, the
word of the LORD came to the prophet who
had brought him back; 21and he proclaimed to
the man of God who came from Judah, "Thus
says the LORD: Because you have disobeyed the
word of the LORD, and have not kept the commandment that the LORD your God commanded
you, 22but have come back and have eaten food
and drunk water in the place of which he said to
you, 'Eat no food, and drink no water,' your body
shall not come to your ancestral tomb." 23After
the man of God[a] had eaten food and had drunk,
they saddled for him a donkey belonging to the
prophet who had brought him back. 24Then as he
went away, a lion met him on the road and killed
him. His body was thrown in the road, and the
donkey stood beside it; the lion also stood beside
the body. 25People passed by and saw the body
thrown in the road, with the lion standing by
the body. And they came and told it in the town
where the old prophet lived.

26 When the prophet who had brought him
back from the way heard of it, he said, "It is the
man of God who disobeyed the word of the LORD;
therefore the LORD has given him to the lion,
which has torn him and killed him according to
the word that the LORD spoke to him." 27Then he
said to his sons, "Saddle a donkey for me." So they
saddled one, 28and he went and found the body
thrown in the road, with the donkey and the lion
standing beside the body. The lion had not eaten
the body or attacked the donkey. 29The prophet
took up the body of the man of God, laid it on the
donkey, and brought it back to the city,[b] to mourn
and to bury him. 30He laid the body in his own
grave; and they mourned over him, saying, "Alas,
my brother!" 31After he had buried him, he said to
his sons, "When I die, bury me in the grave in
which the man of God is buried; lay my bones beside his bones. 32For the saying that he proclaimed
by the word of the LORD against the altar in
Bethel, and against all the houses of the high
places that are in the cities of Samaria, shall surely
come to pass."

33 Even after this event Jeroboam did not
turn from his evil way, but made priests for the
high places again from among all the people;
any who wanted to be priests he consecrated for
the high places. 34This matter became sin to the
house of Jeroboam, so as to cut it off and to destroy it from the face of the earth.

14 At that time Abijah son of Jeroboam fell
sick. 2Jeroboam said to his wife, "Go, disguise yourself, so that it will not be known that
you are the wife of Jeroboam, and go to Shiloh;
for the prophet Ahijah is there, who said of me
that I should be king over this people. 3Take with
you ten loaves, some cakes, and a jar of honey,
and go to him; he will tell you what shall happen
to the child."

[a] Heb *he* [b] Gk: Heb *he came to the town of the old prophet*

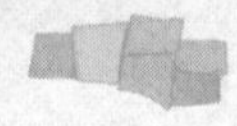

4 Jeroboam's wife did so; she set out and
went to Shiloh, and came to the house of Ahijah.
Now Ahijah could not see, for his eyes were dim
because of his age. 5 But the LORD said to Ahijah,
"The wife of Jeroboam is coming to inquire of
you concerning her son; for he is sick. Thus and
thus you shall say to her."

When she came, she pretended to be another
woman. 6 But when Ahijah heard the sound
of her feet, as she came in at the door, he said,
"Come in, wife of Jeroboam; why do you pretend
to be another? For I am charged with heavy tidings for you. 7 Go, tell Jeroboam, 'Thus says the
LORD, the God of Israel: Because I exalted you
from among the people, made you leader over
my people Israel, 8 and tore the kingdom away
from the house of David to give it to you; yet
you have not been like my servant David, who
kept my commandments and followed me with
all his heart, doing only that which was right in
my sight, 9 but you have done evil above all those
who were before you and have gone and made for
yourself other gods, and cast images, provoking
me to anger, and have thrust me behind your
back; 10 therefore, I will bring evil upon the house
of Jeroboam. I will cut off from Jeroboam every
male, both bond and free in Israel, and will consume the house of Jeroboam, just as one burns up
dung until it is all gone. 11 Anyone belonging to
Jeroboam who dies in the city, the dogs shall eat;
and anyone who dies in the open country, the
birds of the air shall eat; for the LORD has spoken.'
12 Therefore set out, go to your house. When your
feet enter the city, the child shall die. 13 All Israel
shall mourn for him and bury him; for he alone
of Jeroboam's family shall come to the grave, because in him there is found something pleasing
to the LORD, the God of Israel, in the house of
Jeroboam. 14 Moreover the LORD will raise up for
himself a king over Israel, who shall cut off the
house of Jeroboam today, even right now![a]

15 "The LORD will strike Israel, as a reed is
shaken in the water; he will root up Israel out
of this good land that he gave to their ancestors,
and scatter them beyond the Euphrates, because
they have made their sacred poles,[b] provoking the
LORD to anger. 16 He will give Israel up because of
the sins of Jeroboam, which he sinned and which
he caused Israel to commit."

17 Then Jeroboam's wife got up and went
away, and she came to Tirzah. As she came to the
threshold of the house, the child died. 18 All Israel
buried him and mourned for him, according to
the word of the LORD, which he spoke by his servant the prophet Ahijah.

19 Now the rest of the acts of Jeroboam, how
he warred and how he reigned, are written in the
Book of the Annals of the Kings of Israel. 20 The
time that Jeroboam reigned was twenty-two
years; then he slept with his ancestors, and his
son Nadab succeeded him.

21 Now Rehoboam son of Solomon reigned
in Judah. Rehoboam was forty-one years old when
he began to reign, and he reigned seventeen years
in Jerusalem, the city that the LORD had chosen
out of all the tribes of Israel, to put his name there.
His mother's name was Naamah the Ammonite.
22 Judah did what was evil in the sight of the LORD;
they provoked him to jealousy with their sins that
they committed, more than all that their ancestors
had done. 23 For they also built for themselves high
places, pillars, and sacred poles[b] on every high hill
and under every green tree; 24 there were also male
temple prostitutes in the land. They committed all
the abominations of the nations that the LORD
drove out before the people of Israel.

25 In the fifth year of King Rehoboam, King
Shishak of Egypt came up against Jerusalem; 26 he
took away the treasures of the house of the LORD
and the treasures of the king's house; he took everything. He also took away all the shields of gold
that Solomon had made; 27 so King Rehoboam
made shields of bronze instead, and committed
them to the hands of the officers of the guard,
who kept the door of the king's house. 28 As often
as the king went into the house of the LORD, the
guard carried them and brought them back to the
guardroom.

29 Now the rest of the acts of Rehoboam, and
all that he did, are they not written in the Book

[a] Meaning of Heb uncertain [b] Heb *Asherim*

of the Annals of the Kings of Judah? 30There was war between Rehoboam and Jeroboam continually. 31Rehoboam slept with his ancestors and was buried with his ancestors in the city of David. His mother's name was Naamah the Ammonite. His son Abijam succeeded him.

15 Now in the eighteenth year of King Jeroboam son of Nebat, Abijam began to reign over Judah. 2He reigned for three years in Jerusalem. His mother's name was Maacah daughter of Abishalom. 3He committed all the sins that his father did before him; his heart was not true to the LORD his God, like the heart of his father David. 4Nevertheless for David's sake the LORD his God gave him a lamp in Jerusalem, setting up his son after him, and establishing Jerusalem; 5because David did what was right in the sight of the LORD, and did not turn aside from anything that he commanded him all the days of his life, except in the matter of Uriah the Hittite. 6The war begun between Rehoboam and Jeroboam continued all the days of his life. 7The rest of the acts of Abijam, and all that he did, are they not written in the Book of the Annals of the Kings of Judah? There was war between Abijam and Jeroboam. 8Abijam slept with his ancestors, and they buried him in the city of David. Then his son Asa succeeded him.

9 In the twentieth year of King Jeroboam of Israel, Asa began to reign over Judah; 10he reigned forty-one years in Jerusalem. His mother's name was Maacah daughter of Abishalom. 11Asa did what was right in the sight of the LORD, as his father David had done. 12He put away the male temple prostitutes out of the land, and removed all the idols that his ancestors had made. 13He also removed his mother Maacah from being queen mother, because she had made an abominable image for Asherah; Asa cut down her image and burned it at the Wadi Kidron. 14But the high places were not taken away. Nevertheless the heart of Asa was true to the LORD all his days. 15He brought into the house of the LORD the votive gifts of his father and his own votive gifts—silver, gold, and utensils.

16 There was war between Asa and King Baasha of Israel all their days. 17King Baasha of Israel went up against Judah, and built Ramah, to prevent anyone from going out or coming in to King Asa of Judah. 18Then Asa took all the silver and the gold that were left in the treasures of the house of the LORD and the treasures of the king's house, and gave them into the hands of his servants. King Asa sent them to King Ben-hadad son of Tabrimmon son of Hezion of Aram, who resided in Damascus, saying, 19"Let there be an alliance between me and you, like that between my father and your father: I am sending you a present of silver and gold; go, break your alliance with King Baasha of Israel, so that he may withdraw from me." 20Ben-hadad listened to King Asa, and sent the commanders of his armies against the cities of Israel. He conquered Ijon, Dan, Abel-beth-maacah, and all Chinneroth, with all the land of Naphtali. 21When Baasha heard of it, he stopped building Ramah and lived in Tirzah. 22Then King Asa made a proclamation to all Judah, none was exempt: they carried away the stones of Ramah and its timber, with which Baasha had been building; with them King Asa built Geba of Benjamin and Mizpah. 23Now the rest of all the acts of Asa, all his power, all that he did, and the cities that he built, are they not written in the Book of the Annals of the Kings of Judah? But in his old age he was diseased in his feet. 24Then Asa slept with his ancestors, and was buried with his ancestors in the city of his father David; his son Jehoshaphat succeeded him.

25 Nadab son of Jeroboam began to reign over Israel in the second year of King Asa of Judah; he reigned over Israel two years. 26He did what was evil in the sight of the LORD, walking in the way of his ancestor and in the sin that he caused Israel to commit.

27 Baasha son of Ahijah, of the house of Issachar, conspired against him; and Baasha struck him down at Gibbethon, which belonged to the Philistines; for Nadab and all Israel were laying siege to Gibbethon. 28So Baasha killed Nadab[a] in the third year of King Asa of Judah, and

[a] Heb *him*

succeeded him. 29 As soon as he was king, he
killed all the house of Jeroboam; he left to the
house of Jeroboam not one that breathed, until
he had destroyed it, according to the word of the
LORD that he spoke by his servant Ahijah the Shilonite— 30 because of the sins of Jeroboam that
he committed and that he caused Israel to commit, and because of the anger to which he provoked the LORD, the God of Israel.

31 Now the rest of the acts of Nadab, and all
that he did, are they not written in the Book of the
Annals of the Kings of Israel? 32 There was war between Asa and King Baasha of Israel all their days.

33 In the third year of King Asa of Judah,
Baasha son of Ahijah began to reign over all Israel
at Tirzah; he reigned twenty-four years. 34 He did
what was evil in the sight of the LORD, walking in
the way of Jeroboam and in the sin that he caused
Israel to commit.

16 The word of the LORD came to Jehu son
of Hanani against Baasha, saying, 2 "Since
I exalted you out of the dust and made you leader
over my people Israel, and you have walked in
the way of Jeroboam, and have caused my people
Israel to sin, provoking me to anger with their
sins, 3 therefore, I will consume Baasha and his
house, and I will make your house like the house
of Jeroboam son of Nebat. 4 Anyone belonging to
Baasha who dies in the city the dogs shall eat; and
anyone of his who dies in the field the birds of the
air shall eat."

5 Now the rest of the acts of Baasha, what
he did, and his power, are they not written in the
Book of the Annals of the Kings of Israel? 6 Baasha
slept with his ancestors, and was buried at Tirzah;
and his son Elah succeeded him. 7 Moreover the
word of the LORD came by the prophet Jehu son
of Hanani against Baasha and his house, both because of all the evil that he did in the sight of the
LORD, provoking him to anger with the work of
his hands, in being like the house of Jeroboam,
and also because he destroyed it.

8 In the twenty-sixth year of King Asa of Judah, Elah son of Baasha began to reign over Israel
in Tirzah; he reigned two years. 9 But his servant
Zimri, commander of half his chariots, conspired
against him. When he was at Tirzah, drinking
himself drunk in the house of Arza, who was
in charge of the palace at Tirzah, 10 Zimri came
in and struck him down and killed him, in the
twenty-seventh year of King Asa of Judah, and
succeeded him.

11 When he began to reign, as soon as he
had seated himself on his throne, he killed all the
house of Baasha; he did not leave him a single
male of his kindred or his friends. 12 Thus Zimri
destroyed all the house of Baasha, according to
the word of the LORD, which he spoke against
Baasha by the prophet Jehu— 13 because of all
the sins of Baasha and the sins of his son Elah
that they committed, and that they caused Israel
to commit, provoking the LORD God of Israel to
anger with their idols. 14 Now the rest of the acts
of Elah, and all that he did, are they not written in
the Book of the Annals of the Kings of Israel?

15 In the twenty-seventh year of King Asa
of Judah, Zimri reigned seven days in Tirzah.
Now the troops were encamped against Gibbethon, which belonged to the Philistines, 16 and
the troops who were encamped heard it said,
"Zimri has conspired, and he has killed the king";
therefore all Israel made Omri, the commander
of the army, king over Israel that day in the camp.
17 So Omri went up from Gibbethon, and all Israel with him, and they besieged Tirzah. 18 When
Zimri saw that the city was taken, he went into
the citadel of the king's house; he burned down
the king's house over himself with fire, and
died— 19 because of the sins that he committed,
doing evil in the sight of the LORD, walking in the
way of Jeroboam, and for the sin that he committed, causing Israel to sin. 20 Now the rest of the
acts of Zimri, and the conspiracy that he made,
are they not written in the Book of the Annals of
the Kings of Israel?

21 Then the people of Israel were divided
into two parts; half of the people followed Tibni
son of Ginath, to make him king, and half followed Omri. 22 But the people who followed
Omri overcame the people who followed Tibni
son of Ginath; so Tibni died, and Omri became
king. 23 In the thirty-first year of King Asa of Judah, Omri began to reign over Israel; he reigned
for twelve years, six of them in Tirzah.

24 He bought the hill of Samaria from Shemer for two talents of silver; he fortified the hill,
and called the city that he built, Samaria, after the
name of Shemer, the owner of the hill.
25 Omri did what was evil in the sight of the
LORD; he did more evil than all who were before
him. 26For he walked in all the way of Jeroboam
son of Nebat, and in the sins that he caused Israel
to commit, provoking the LORD, the God of Israel, to anger by their idols. 27Now the rest of the
acts of Omri that he did, and the power that he
showed, are they not written in the Book of the
Annals of the Kings of Israel? 28Omri slept with
his ancestors, and was buried in Samaria; his son
Ahab succeeded him.
29 In the thirty-eighth year of King Asa of Judah, Ahab son of Omri began to reign over Israel;
Ahab son of Omri reigned over Israel in Samaria
twenty-two years. 30Ahab son of Omri did evil
in the sight of the LORD more than all who were
before him.
31 And as if it had been a light thing for him
to walk in the sins of Jeroboam son of Nebat, he
took as his wife Jezebel daughter of King Ethbaal
of the Sidonians, and went and served Baal, and
worshiped him. 32He erected an altar for Baal
in the house of Baal, which he built in Samaria.
33Ahab also made a sacred pole.[a] Ahab did more
to provoke the anger of the LORD, the God of
Israel, than had all the kings of Israel who were
before him. 34In his days Hiel of Bethel built Jericho; he laid its foundation at the cost of Abiram
his firstborn, and set up its gates at the cost of his
youngest son Segub, according to the word of the
LORD, which he spoke by Joshua son of Nun.

17 Now Elijah the Tishbite, of Tishbe[b] in
Gilead, said to Ahab, "As the LORD the
God of Israel lives, before whom I stand, there
shall be neither dew nor rain these years, except
by my word." 2The word of the LORD came to
him, saying, 3"Go from here and turn eastward,
and hide yourself by the Wadi Cherith, which
is east of the Jordan. 4You shall drink from the
wadi, and I have commanded the ravens to feed
you there." 5So he went and did according to the
word of the LORD; he went and lived by the Wadi
Cherith, which is east of the Jordan. 6The ravens
brought him bread and meat in the morning,
and bread and meat in the evening; and he drank
from the wadi. 7But after a while the wadi dried
up, because there was no rain in the land.
8 Then the word of the LORD came to him,
saying, 9"Go now to Zarephath, which belongs
to Sidon, and live there; for I have commanded
a widow there to feed you." 10So he set out and
went to Zarephath. When he came to the gate of
the town, a widow was there gathering sticks; he
called to her and said, "Bring me a little water in
a vessel, so that I may drink." 11As she was going
to bring it, he called to her and said, "Bring me a
morsel of bread in your hand." 12But she said, "As
the LORD your God lives, I have nothing baked,
only a handful of meal in a jar, and a little oil in a
jug; I am now gathering a couple of sticks, so that
I may go home and prepare it for myself and my
son, that we may eat it, and die." 13Elijah said to
her, "Do not be afraid; go and do as you have said;
but first make me a little cake of it and bring it to
me, and afterwards make something for yourself
and your son. 14For thus says the LORD the God
of Israel: The jar of meal will not be emptied and
the jug of oil will not fail until the day that the
LORD sends rain on the earth." 15She went and
did as Elijah said, so that she as well as he and her
household ate for many days. 16The jar of meal
was not emptied, neither did the jug of oil fail,
according to the word of the LORD that he spoke
by Elijah.
17 After this the son of the woman, the mistress of the house, became ill; his illness was so
severe that there was no breath left in him. 18She
then said to Elijah, "What have you against me,
O man of God? You have come to me to bring
my sin to remembrance, and to cause the death
of my son!" 19But he said to her, "Give me your
son." He took him from her bosom, carried him
up into the upper chamber where he was lodging,
and laid him on his own bed. 20He cried out to
the LORD, "O LORD my God, have you brought
calamity even upon the widow with whom I am

[a] Heb *Asherah* [b] Gk: Heb *of the settlers*

staying, by killing her son?" 21Then he stretched
himself upon the child three times, and cried out
to the LORD, "O LORD my God, let this child's
life come into him again." 22The LORD listened to
the voice of Elijah; the life of the child came into
him again, and he revived. 23Elijah took the child,
brought him down from the upper chamber into
the house, and gave him to his mother; then Elijah said, "See, your son is alive." 24So the woman
said to Elijah, "Now I know that you are a man
of God, and that the word of the LORD in your
mouth is truth."

18 After many days the word of the LORD
came to Elijah, in the third year of the
drought,[a] saying, "Go, present yourself to Ahab;
I will send rain on the earth." 2So Elijah went to
present himself to Ahab. The famine was severe in
Samaria. 3Ahab summoned Obadiah, who was in
charge of the palace. (Now Obadiah revered the
LORD greatly; 4when Jezebel was killing off the
prophets of the LORD, Obadiah took a hundred
prophets, hid them fifty to a cave, and provided
them with bread and water.) 5Then Ahab said to
Obadiah, "Go through the land to all the springs
of water and to all the wadis; perhaps we may find
grass to keep the horses and mules alive, and not
lose some of the animals." 6So they divided the
land between them to pass through it; Ahab went
in one direction by himself, and Obadiah went in
another direction by himself.

7 As Obadiah was on the way, Elijah met him;
Obadiah recognized him, fell on his face, and
said, "Is it you, my lord Elijah?" 8He answered
him, "It is I. Go, tell your lord that Elijah is here."
9And he said, "How have I sinned, that you would
hand your servant over to Ahab, to kill me? 10As
the LORD your God lives, there is no nation or
kingdom to which my lord has not sent to seek
you; and when they would say, 'He is not here,' he
would require an oath of the kingdom or nation,
that they had not found you. 11But now you say,
'Go, tell your lord that Elijah is here.' 12As soon as
I have gone from you, the spirit of the LORD will
carry you I know not where; so, when I come and
tell Ahab and he cannot find you, he will kill me,
although I your servant have revered the LORD
from my youth. 13Has it not been told my lord
what I did when Jezebel killed the prophets of the
LORD, how I hid a hundred of the LORD's prophets fifty to a cave, and provided them with bread
and water? 14Yet now you say, 'Go, tell your lord
that Elijah is here'; he will surely kill me." 15Elijah
said, "As the LORD of hosts lives, before whom
I stand, I will surely show myself to him today."
16So Obadiah went to meet Ahab, and told him;
and Ahab went to meet Elijah.

17 When Ahab saw Elijah, Ahab said to him,
"Is it you, you troubler of Israel?" 18He answered,
"I have not troubled Israel; but you have, and
your father's house, because you have forsaken
the commandments of the LORD and followed
the Baals. 19Now therefore have all Israel assemble for me at Mount Carmel, with the four hundred fifty prophets of Baal and the four hundred
prophets of Asherah, who eat at Jezebel's table."

20 So Ahab sent to all the Israelites, and assembled the prophets at Mount Carmel. 21Elijah
then came near to all the people, and said, "How
long will you go limping with two different opinions? If the LORD is God, follow him; but if Baal,
then follow him." The people did not answer him
a word. 22Then Elijah said to the people, "I, even
I only, am left a prophet of the LORD; but Baal's
prophets number four hundred fifty. 23Let two
bulls be given to us; let them choose one bull
for themselves, cut it in pieces, and lay it on the
wood, but put no fire to it; I will prepare the other
bull and lay it on the wood, but put no fire to it.
24Then you call on the name of your god and I
will call on the name of the LORD; the god who
answers by fire is indeed God." All the people answered, "Well spoken!" 25Then Elijah said to the
prophets of Baal, "Choose for yourselves one bull
and prepare it first, for you are many; then call on
the name of your god, but put no fire to it." 26So
they took the bull that was given them, prepared
it, and called on the name of Baal from morning
until noon, crying, "O Baal, answer us!" But there
was no voice, and no answer. They limped about
the altar that they had made. 27At noon Elijah

[a] Heb lacks *of the drought*

mocked them, saying, “Cry aloud! Surely he is a
god; either he is meditating, or he has wandered
away, or he is on a journey, or perhaps he is asleep
and must be awakened.” 28 Then they cried aloud
and, as was their custom, they cut themselves
with swords and lances until the blood gushed
out over them. 29 As midday passed, they raved on
until the time of the offering of the oblation, but
there was no voice, no answer, and no response.

30 Then Elijah said to all the people, “Come
closer to me”; and all the people came closer to
him. First he repaired the altar of the Lord that
had been thrown down; 31 Elijah took twelve
stones, according to the number of the tribes of
the sons of Jacob, to whom the word of the Lord
came, saying, “Israel shall be your name”; 32 with
the stones he built an altar in the name of the
Lord. Then he made a trench around the altar,
large enough to contain two measures of seed.
33 Next he put the wood in order, cut the bull in
pieces, and laid it on the wood. He said, “Fill four
jars with water and pour it on the burnt offering
and on the wood.” 34 Then he said, “Do it a second
time”; and they did it a second time. Again he
said, “Do it a third time”; and they did it a third
time, 35 so that the water ran all around the altar,
and filled the trench also with water.

36 At the time of the offering of the oblation,
the prophet Elijah came near and said, “O Lord,
God of Abraham, Isaac, and Israel, let it be known
this day that you are God in Israel, that I am your
servant, and that I have done all these things at
your bidding. 37 Answer me, O Lord, answer me,
so that this people may know that you, O Lord,
are God, and that you have turned their hearts
back.” 38 Then the fire of the Lord fell and consumed the burnt offering, the wood, the stones,
and the dust, and even licked up the water that
was in the trench. 39 When all the people saw it,
they fell on their faces and said, “The Lord indeed is God; the Lord indeed is God.” 40 Elijah
said to them, “Seize the prophets of Baal; do not
let one of them escape.” Then they seized them;
and Elijah brought them down to the Wadi Kishon, and killed them there.

41 Elijah said to Ahab, “Go up, eat and
drink; for there is a sound of rushing rain.” 42 So
Ahab went up to eat and to drink. Elijah went
up to the top of Carmel; there he bowed himself
down upon the earth and put his face between
his knees. 43 He said to his servant, “Go up now,
look toward the sea.” He went up and looked,
and said, “There is nothing.” Then he said, “Go
again seven times.” 44 At the seventh time he said,
“Look, a little cloud no bigger than a person’s
hand is rising out of the sea.” Then he said, “Go
say to Ahab, ‘Harness your chariot and go down
before the rain stops you.’ ” 45 In a little while the
heavens grew black with clouds and wind; there
was a heavy rain. Ahab rode off and went to Jezreel. 46 But the hand of the Lord was on Elijah;
he girded up his loins and ran in front of Ahab to
the entrance of Jezreel.

19 Ahab told Jezebel all that Elijah had done,
and how he had killed all the prophets
with the sword. 2 Then Jezebel sent a messenger
to Elijah, saying, “So may the gods do to me, and
more also, if I do not make your life like the life
of one of them by this time tomorrow.” 3 Then
he was afraid; he got up and fled for his life, and
came to Beer-sheba, which belongs to Judah; he
left his servant there.

4 But he himself went a day’s journey into the
wilderness, and came and sat down under a solitary broom tree. He asked that he might die: “It
is enough; now, O Lord, take away my life, for
I am no better than my ancestors.” 5 Then he lay
down under the broom tree and fell asleep. Suddenly an angel touched him and said to him, “Get
up and eat.” 6 He looked, and there at his head was
a cake baked on hot stones, and a jar of water. He
ate and drank, and lay down again. 7 The angel of
the Lord came a second time, touched him, and
said, “Get up and eat, otherwise the journey will
be too much for you.” 8 He got up, and ate and
drank; then he went in the strength of that food
forty days and forty nights to Horeb the mount of
God. 9 At that place he came to a cave, and spent
the night there.

Then the word of the Lord came to him, saying, “What are you doing here, Elijah?” 10 He answered, “I have been very zealous for the Lord,
the God of hosts; for the Israelites have forsaken
your covenant, thrown down your altars, and

killed your prophets with the sword. I alone am
left, and they are seeking my life, to take it away."
11 He said, "Go out and stand on the mountain before the LORD, for the LORD is about to
pass by." Now there was a great wind, so strong
that it was splitting mountains and breaking
rocks in pieces before the LORD, but the LORD
was not in the wind; and after the wind an earthquake, but the LORD was not in the earthquake;
12 and after the earthquake a fire, but the LORD
was not in the fire; and after the fire a sound of
sheer silence. 13 When Elijah heard it, he wrapped
his face in his mantle and went out and stood at
the entrance of the cave. Then there came a voice
to him that said, "What are you doing here, Elijah?" 14 He answered, "I have been very zealous
for the LORD, the God of hosts; for the Israelites
have forsaken your covenant, thrown down your
altars, and killed your prophets with the sword.
I alone am left, and they are seeking my life, to
take it away." 15 Then the LORD said to him, "Go,
return on your way to the wilderness of Damascus; when you arrive, you shall anoint Hazael
as king over Aram. 16 Also you shall anoint Jehu
son of Nimshi as king over Israel; and you shall
anoint Elisha son of Shaphat of Abel-meholah as
prophet in your place. 17 Whoever escapes from
the sword of Hazael, Jehu shall kill; and whoever
escapes from the sword of Jehu, Elisha shall kill.
18 Yet I will leave seven thousand in Israel, all the
knees that have not bowed to Baal, and every
mouth that has not kissed him."
19 So he set out from there, and found Elisha
son of Shaphat, who was plowing. There were
twelve yoke of oxen ahead of him, and he was
with the twelfth. Elijah passed by him and threw
his mantle over him. 20 He left the oxen, ran after
Elijah, and said, "Let me kiss my father and my
mother, and then I will follow you." Then Elijah[a]
said to him, "Go back again; for what have I done
to you?" 21 He returned from following him, took
the yoke of oxen, and slaughtered them; using the
equipment from the oxen, he boiled their flesh,
and gave it to the people, and they ate. Then he set
out and followed Elijah, and became his servant.

20 King Ben-hadad of Aram gathered all his
army together; thirty-two kings were with
him, along with horses and chariots. He marched
against Samaria, laid siege to it, and attacked it.
2 Then he sent messengers into the city to King
Ahab of Israel, and said to him: "Thus says Ben-
hadad: 3 Your silver and gold are mine; your fairest wives and children also are mine." 4 The king
of Israel answered, "As you say, my lord, O king,
I am yours, and all that I have." 5 The messengers
came again and said: "Thus says Ben-hadad: I
sent to you, saying, 'Deliver to me your silver
and gold, your wives and children'; 6 nevertheless
I will send my servants to you tomorrow about
this time, and they shall search your house and
the houses of your servants, and lay hands on
whatever pleases them,[b] and take it away."
7 Then the king of Israel called all the elders
of the land, and said, "Look now! See how this
man is seeking trouble; for he sent to me for my
wives, my children, my silver, and my gold; and I
did not refuse him." 8 Then all the elders and all
the people said to him, "Do not listen or consent."
9 So he said to the messengers of Ben-hadad, "Tell
my lord the king: All that you first demanded of
your servant I will do; but this thing I cannot do."
The messengers left and brought him word again.
10 Ben-hadad sent to him and said, "The gods do
so to me, and more also, if the dust of Samaria will
provide a handful for each of the people who follow me." 11 The king of Israel answered, "Tell him:
One who puts on armor should not brag like one
who takes it off." 12 When Ben-hadad heard this
message—now he had been drinking with the
kings in the booths—he said to his men, "Take
your positions!" And they took their positions
against the city.
13 Then a certain prophet came up to King
Ahab of Israel and said, "Thus says the LORD,
Have you seen all this great multitude? Look, I
will give it into your hand today; and you shall
know that I am the LORD." 14 Ahab said, "By
whom?" He said, "Thus says the LORD, By the
young men who serve the district governors."
Then he said, "Who shall begin the battle?" He

[a] Heb *he* [b] Gk Syr Vg: Heb *you*

answered, "You." 15 Then he mustered the young
men who served the district governors, two hundred thirty-two; after them he mustered all the
people of Israel, seven thousand.

16 They went out at noon, while Ben-hadad
was drinking himself drunk in the booths, he and
the thirty-two kings allied with him. 17 The young
men who served the district governors went out
first. Ben-hadad had sent out scouts,[a] and they
reported to him, "Men have come out from Samaria." 18 He said, "If they have come out for
peace, take them alive; if they have come out for
war, take them alive."

19 But these had already come out of the
city: the young men who served the district governors, and the army that followed them. 20 Each
killed his man; the Arameans fled and Israel pursued them, but King Ben-hadad of Aram escaped
on a horse with the cavalry. 21 The king of Israel
went out, attacked the horses and chariots, and
defeated the Arameans with a great slaughter.

22 Then the prophet approached the king of
Israel and said to him, "Come, strengthen yourself, and consider well what you have to do; for in
the spring the king of Aram will come up against
you."

23 The servants of the king of Aram said to
him, "Their gods are gods of the hills, and so they
were stronger than we; but let us fight against
them in the plain, and surely we shall be stronger
than they. 24 Also do this: remove the kings, each
from his post, and put commanders in place of
them; 25 and muster an army like the army that
you have lost, horse for horse, and chariot for
chariot; then we will fight against them in the
plain, and surely we shall be stronger than they."
He heeded their voice, and did so.

26 In the spring Ben-hadad mustered the
Arameans and went up to Aphek to fight against
Israel. 27 After the Israelites had been mustered
and provisioned, they went out to engage them;
the people of Israel encamped opposite them like
two little flocks of goats, while the Arameans filled
the country. 28 A man of God approached and
said to the king of Israel, "Thus says the LORD:
Because the Arameans have said, 'The LORD is
a god of the hills but he is not a god of the valleys,' therefore I will give all this great multitude
into your hand, and you shall know that I am the
LORD." 29 They encamped opposite one another
seven days. Then on the seventh day the battle
began; the Israelites killed one hundred thousand Aramean foot soldiers in one day. 30 The rest
fled into the city of Aphek; and the wall fell on
twenty-seven thousand men that were left.

Ben-hadad also fled, and entered the city to
hide. 31 His servants said to him, "Look, we have
heard that the kings of the house of Israel are
merciful kings; let us put sackcloth around our
waists and ropes on our heads, and go out to the
king of Israel; perhaps he will spare your life."
32 So they tied sackcloth around their waists, put
ropes on their heads, went to the king of Israel,
and said, "Your servant Ben-hadad says, 'Please
let me live.'" And he said, "Is he still alive? He is
my brother." 33 Now the men were watching for
an omen; they quickly took it up from him and
said, "Yes, Ben-hadad is your brother." Then he
said, "Go and bring him." So Ben-hadad came out
to him; and he had him come up into the chariot. 34 Ben-hadad[b] said to him, "I will restore the
towns that my father took from your father; and
you may establish bazaars for yourself in Damascus, as my father did in Samaria." The king of Israel responded,[c] "I will let you go on those terms."
So he made a treaty with him and let him go.

35 At the command of the LORD a certain
member of a company of prophets[d] said to another, "Strike me!" But the man refused to strike
him. 36 Then he said to him, "Because you have
not obeyed the voice of the LORD, as soon as
you have left me, a lion will kill you." And when
he had left him, a lion met him and killed him.
37 Then he found another man and said, "Strike
me!" So the man hit him, striking and wounding
him. 38 Then the prophet departed, and waited
for the king along the road, disguising himself
with a bandage over his eyes. 39 As the king
passed by, he cried to the king and said, "Your
servant went out into the thick of the battle;

[a] Heb lacks *scouts* [b] Heb *He* [c] Heb lacks *The king of Israel responded* [d] Heb *of the sons of the prophets*

then a soldier turned and brought a man to me,
and said, 'Guard this man; if he is missing, your
life shall be given for his life, or else you shall
pay a talent of silver.' 40While your servant was
busy here and there, he was gone." The king of
Israel said to him, "So shall your judgment be;
you yourself have decided it." 41Then he quickly
took the bandage away from his eyes. The king
of Israel recognized him as one of the prophets.
42Then he said to him, "Thus says the LORD,
'Because you have let the man go whom I had
devoted to destruction, therefore your life shall
be for his life, and your people for his people.'"
43The king of Israel set out toward home, resentful and sullen, and came to Samaria.

21 Later the following events took place:
Naboth the Jezreelite had a vineyard in
Jezreel, beside the palace of King Ahab of Samaria. 2And Ahab said to Naboth, "Give me your
vineyard, so that I may have it for a vegetable garden, because it is near my house; I will give you a
better vineyard for it; or, if it seems good to you,
I will give you its value in money." 3But Naboth
said to Ahab, "The LORD forbid that I should give
you my ancestral inheritance." 4Ahab went home
resentful and sullen because of what Naboth the
Jezreelite had said to him; for he had said, "I will
not give you my ancestral inheritance." He lay
down on his bed, turned away his face, and would
not eat.

5 His wife Jezebel came to him and said,
"Why are you so depressed that you will not eat?"
6He said to her, "Because I spoke to Naboth the
Jezreelite and said to him, 'Give me your vineyard
for money; or else, if you prefer, I will give you
another vineyard for it'; but he answered, 'I will
not give you my vineyard.'" 7His wife Jezebel said
to him, "Do you now govern Israel? Get up, eat
some food, and be cheerful; I will give you the
vineyard of Naboth the Jezreelite."

8 So she wrote letters in Ahab's name and
sealed them with his seal; she sent the letters to
the elders and the nobles who lived with Naboth
in his city. 9She wrote in the letters, "Proclaim a
fast, and seat Naboth at the head of the assembly; 10seat two scoundrels opposite him, and
have them bring a charge against him, saying,
'You have cursed God and the king.' Then take
him out, and stone him to death." 11The men of
his city, the elders and the nobles who lived in his
city, did as Jezebel had sent word to them. Just as
it was written in the letters that she had sent to
them, 12they proclaimed a fast and seated Naboth
at the head of the assembly. 13The two scoundrels
came in and sat opposite him; and the scoundrels
brought a charge against Naboth, in the presence

1 Kings 21

King Ahab's marriage to Jezebel, daughter of the Phoenician king, had brought new trade and prosperity to Israel by the mid-800s BCE. While the normative biblical view is that land is a gift from God and something all persons could own, the story of Naboth's vineyard shows us the opposite understanding at work in Israel (whether because of "Canaanite" influence or the corruption of power): all land belonged to the king, who could dispense it or take it back at his will. When Naboth refuses to surrender his vineyard to the king, Ahab is constrained by Israelite tradition; but Jezebel feels no such constraints. She has Naboth eliminated and seizes the vineyard by a kind of royal right of eminent domain. The experience is common enough throughout the world today; Michael Knoch writes about his work with another land-rights activist among the Kaigang Indians of Brazil, whose reservation land is coveted by others:

> Since the Portuguese colonial era land has been regarded as an object of conquest and exploitation... and at the disposal of those with influence and power,... not the soil inherited from one's ancestors.... We drove back to Porto Allegre, tired but sharing in the struggle of many people for their land. Maggie Nkwe frequently quoted Isaiah 32:18, "My people will live in peaceful dwelling places, in secure homes in undisturbed places of rest."[24]

— DB

of the people, saying, "Naboth cursed God and
the king." So they took him outside the city, and
stoned him to death. 14 Then they sent to Jezebel,
saying, "Naboth has been stoned; he is dead."
15 As soon as Jezebel heard that Naboth had
been stoned and was dead, Jezebel said to Ahab,
"Go, take possession of the vineyard of Naboth
the Jezreelite, which he refused to give you for
money; for Naboth is not alive, but dead." 16 As
soon as Ahab heard that Naboth was dead, Ahab
set out to go down to the vineyard of Naboth the
Jezreelite, to take possession of it.
17 Then the word of the LORD came to Elijah the Tishbite, saying: 18 Go down to meet King
Ahab of Israel, who rules[a] in Samaria; he is now in
the vineyard of Naboth, where he has gone to take
possession. 19 You shall say to him, "Thus says the
LORD: Have you killed, and also taken possession?" You shall say to him, "Thus says the LORD:
In the place where dogs licked up the blood of
Naboth, dogs will also lick up your blood."
20 Ahab said to Elijah, "Have you found me,
O my enemy?" He answered, "I have found you.
Because you have sold yourself to do what is evil
in the sight of the LORD, 21 I will bring disaster
on you; I will consume you, and will cut off from
Ahab every male, bond or free, in Israel; 22 and I
will make your house like the house of Jeroboam
son of Nebat, and like the house of Baasha son of
Ahijah, because you have provoked me to anger
and have caused Israel to sin. 23 Also concerning
Jezebel the LORD said, 'The dogs shall eat Jezebel
within the bounds of Jezreel.' 24 Anyone belonging to Ahab who dies in the city the dogs shall
eat; and anyone of his who dies in the open country the birds of the air shall eat."
25 (Indeed, there was no one like Ahab, who
sold himself to do what was evil in the sight of
the LORD, urged on by his wife Jezebel. 26 He
acted most abominably in going after idols, as the
Amorites had done, whom the LORD drove out
before the Israelites.)
27 When Ahab heard those words, he tore
his clothes and put sackcloth over his bare flesh;
he fasted, lay in the sackcloth, and went about de-
jectedly. 28 Then the word of the LORD came to
Elijah the Tishbite: 29 "Have you seen how Ahab
has humbled himself before me? Because he has
humbled himself before me, I will not bring the
disaster in his days; but in his son's days I will
bring the disaster on his house."

22 For three years Aram and Israel continued
without war. 2 But in the third year King
Jehoshaphat of Judah came down to the king of
Israel. 3 The king of Israel said to his servants, "Do
you know that Ramoth-gilead belongs to us, yet
we are doing nothing to take it out of the hand of
the king of Aram?" 4 He said to Jehoshaphat, "Will
you go with me to battle at Ramoth-gilead?" Jehoshaphat replied to the king of Israel, "I am as
you are; my people are your people, my horses
are your horses."
5 But Jehoshaphat also said to the king of
Israel, "Inquire first for the word of the LORD."
6 Then the king of Israel gathered the prophets
together, about four hundred of them, and said to
them, "Shall I go to battle against Ramoth-gilead,
or shall I refrain?" They said, "Go up; for the
LORD will give it into the hand of the king." 7 But
Jehoshaphat said, "Is there no other prophet of
the LORD here of whom we may inquire?" 8 The
king of Israel said to Jehoshaphat, "There is still
one other by whom we may inquire of the LORD,
Micaiah son of Imlah; but I hate him, for he never
prophesies anything favorable about me, but only
disaster." Jehoshaphat said, "Let the king not say
such a thing." 9 Then the king of Israel summoned
an officer and said, "Bring quickly Micaiah son
of Imlah." 10 Now the king of Israel and King Jehoshaphat of Judah were sitting on their thrones,
arrayed in their robes, at the threshing floor at the
entrance of the gate of Samaria; and all the prophets were prophesying before them. 11 Zedekiah
son of Chenaanah made for himself horns of
iron, and he said, "Thus says the LORD: With
these you shall gore the Arameans until they are
destroyed." 12 All the prophets were prophesying
the same and saying, "Go up to Ramoth-gilead
and triumph; the LORD will give it into the hand
of the king."

[a] Heb *who is*

13 The messenger who had gone to summon Micaiah said to him, "Look, the words of the prophets with one accord are favorable to the king; let your word be like the word of one of them, and speak favorably." 14But Micaiah said, "As the LORD lives, whatever the LORD says to me, that I will speak."

15 When he had come to the king, the king said to him, "Micaiah, shall we go to Ramoth-gilead to battle, or shall we refrain?" He answered him, "Go up and triumph; the LORD will give it into the hand of the king." 16But the king said to him, "How many times must I make you swear to tell me nothing but the truth in the name of the LORD?" 17Then Micaiah[a] said, "I saw all Israel scattered on the mountains, like sheep that have no shepherd; and the LORD said, 'These have no master; let each one go home in peace.' " 18The king of Israel said to Jehoshaphat, "Did I not tell you that he would not prophesy anything favorable about me, but only disaster?"

1 *Kings* 22:1-38

This prophetic showdown, pitting a single prophet who speaks the LORD's word against hundreds of opposing prophets, gives an intriguing glimpse into Israelite prophecy. The kings of Judah and Israel are able to call upon hundreds of "professional" prophets who stand ready to affirm God's support of a war on which the kings have set their hearts. The story is heavy with irony, of course. The kings see through Micaiah's flattering lie, as if they already know that the LORD opposes them. Micaiah then describes another, heavenly court where the LORD receives counsel, and that true counsel—which only Micaiah discerns—is to confound the kings by inspiring false counsel from their prophets. Despite the transparent irony of this story and the "post-mortem" evaluation of prophecy recommended in Deut 18:21-22, the confrontation recounted here shows that discerning true prophecy was never a straightforward matter in Israel.

—*NE*

19 Then Micaiah[a] said, "Therefore hear the word of the LORD: I saw the LORD sitting on his throne, with all the host of heaven standing beside him to the right and to the left of him. 20And the LORD said, 'Who will entice Ahab, so that he may go up and fall at Ramoth-gilead?' Then one said one thing, and another said another, 21until a spirit came forward and stood before the LORD, saying, 'I will entice him.' 22'How?' the LORD asked him. He replied, 'I will go out and be a lying spirit in the mouth of all his prophets.' Then the LORD[a] said, 'You are to entice him, and you shall succeed; go out and do it.' 23So you see, the LORD has put a lying spirit in the mouth of all these your prophets; the LORD has decreed disaster for you."

24 Then Zedekiah son of Chenaanah came up to Micaiah, slapped him on the cheek, and said, "Which way did the spirit of the LORD pass from me to speak to you?" 25Micaiah replied, "You will find out on that day when you go in to hide in an inner chamber." 26The king of Israel then ordered, "Take Micaiah, and return him to Amon the governor of the city and to Joash the king's son, 27and say, 'Thus says the king: Put this fellow in prison, and feed him on reduced rations of bread and water until I come in peace.' " 28Micaiah said, "If you return in peace, the LORD has not spoken by me." And he said, "Hear, you peoples, all of you!"

29 So the king of Israel and King Jehoshaphat of Judah went up to Ramoth-gilead. 30The king of Israel said to Jehoshaphat, "I will disguise myself and go into battle, but you wear your robes." So the king of Israel disguised himself and went into battle. 31Now the king of Aram had commanded the thirty-two captains of his chariots, "Fight with no one small or great, but only with the king of Israel." 32When the captains of the chariots saw Jehoshaphat, they said, "It is surely the king of Israel." So they turned to fight against him; and Jehoshaphat cried out. 33When the captains of the chariots saw that it was not the king of Israel, they turned back from pursuing him. 34But a certain man drew his bow and unknowingly struck the king of Israel between the scale

[a] Heb *he*

armor and the breastplate; so he said to the driver
of his chariot, "Turn around, and carry me out of
the battle, for I am wounded." 35 The battle grew
hot that day, and the king was propped up in his
chariot facing the Arameans, until at evening he
died; the blood from the wound had flowed into
the bottom of the chariot. 36 Then about sunset a
shout went through the army, "Every man to his
city, and every man to his country!"

37 So the king died, and was brought to Samaria; they buried the king in Samaria. 38 They
washed the chariot by the pool of Samaria; the
dogs licked up his blood, and the prostitutes
washed themselves in it,[a] according to the word
of the LORD that he had spoken. 39 Now the rest
of the acts of Ahab, and all that he did, and the
ivory house that he built, and all the cities that he
built, are they not written in the Book of the Annals of the Kings of Israel? 40 So Ahab slept with
his ancestors; and his son Ahaziah succeeded
him.

41 Jehoshaphat son of Asa began to reign
over Judah in the fourth year of King Ahab of
Israel. 42 Jehoshaphat was thirty-five years old
when he began to reign, and he reigned twenty-
five years in Jerusalem. His mother's name was
Azubah daughter of Shilhi. 43 He walked in all the
way of his father Asa; he did not turn aside from
it, doing what was right in the sight of the LORD;
yet the high places were not taken away, and the
people still sacrificed and offered incense on the
high places. 44 Jehoshaphat also made peace with
the king of Israel.

45 Now the rest of the acts of Jehoshaphat,
and his power that he showed, and how he waged
war, are they not written in the Book of the Annals of the Kings of Judah? 46 The remnant of the
male temple prostitutes who were still in the land
in the days of his father Asa, he exterminated.

47 There was no king in Edom; a deputy was
king. 48 Jehoshaphat made ships of the Tarshish
type to go to Ophir for gold; but they did not go,
for the ships were wrecked at Ezion-geber. 49 Then
Ahaziah son of Ahab said to Jehoshaphat, "Let
my servants go with your servants in the ships,"
but Jehoshaphat was not willing. 50 Jehoshaphat
slept with his ancestors and was buried with his
ancestors in the city of his father David; his son
Jehoram succeeded him.

51 Ahaziah son of Ahab began to reign over
Israel in Samaria in the seventeenth year of King
Jehoshaphat of Judah; he reigned two years over
Israel. 52 He did what was evil in the sight of the
LORD, and walked in the way of his father and
mother, and in the way of Jeroboam son of Nebat,
who caused Israel to sin. 53 He served Baal and
worshiped him; he provoked the LORD, the God
of Israel, to anger, just as his father had done.

[a] Heb lacks *in it*

2 Kings

Second Kings 1:1—17:41 continues the story of the divided kingdoms of Judah and Israel begun in 1 Kings (see the Introduction to 1 Kings). This is a story increasingly marked by foreign intervention on the part of Aram and Assyria, a story in which the prophet Elijah plays a major part. It is at his instigation that Jehu carries out a military coup in which the House of Omri is overthrown. Chapter 17 briefly recounts the fall of Samaria to the Assyrians (vv. 1-6), then follows with a Deuteronomistic justification of the doom of the kingdom (7-23) and a negative appraisal of the population settled by the Assyrians in the north, based on their mixed ethnicity (24-41).

Second Kings 18:1—25:30 moves quickly to the fall of Judah and Jerusalem to Babylonia. This is not a simple event, but a historical process in which the growing darkness is twice lit by the reigns of two reforming kings, Hezekiah (2 Kgs 18:1-8) and his grandson Josiah (2 Kgs 22:1—23:25). The other side of the Deuteronomistic claim—that a return to faithfulness to the Lord would reverse the results of breaking the covenant, voiced in Solomon's prayer at the dedication of the temple (1 Kgs 8:46-53)—echoes in the final notice (2 Kgs 25:27-30) that an heir of the house of David remained in Babylonia, leaving open the possibility of return and restoration.

My personal history as a Cuban exile has made me wary of the dangers of too-simple explanations of national catastrophes, particularly when they fan the fires of zealotry and flatten those who are blamed into the position of irredeemable *other*. I read Kings with care, understanding that its trust in God's covenant faithfulness and its offer of return and redemption are in truth for *all* God's people.

— ***Francisco García-Treto***

1 After the death of Ahab, Moab rebelled against Israel.

2 Ahaziah had fallen through the lattice in his upper chamber in Samaria, and lay injured; so he sent messengers, telling them, "Go, inquire of Baal-zebub, the god of Ekron, whether I shall recover from this injury." 3But the angel of the Lord said to Elijah the Tishbite, "Get up, go to meet the messengers of the king of Samaria, and say to them, 'Is it because there is no God in Israel that you are going to inquire of Baal-zebub, the god of Ekron?' 4Now therefore thus says

the LORD, 'You shall not leave the bed to which
you have gone, but you shall surely die.'" So Elijah went.
5 The messengers returned to the king, who
said to them, "Why have you returned?" [6]They
answered him, "There came a man to meet us,
who said to us, 'Go back to the king who sent you,
and say to him: Thus says the LORD: Is it because
there is no God in Israel that you are sending to
inquire of Baal-zebub, the god of Ekron? Therefore you shall not leave the bed to which you have
gone, but shall surely die.'" [7]He said to them,
"What sort of man was he who came to meet
you and told you these things?" [8]They answered
him, "A hairy man, with a leather belt around his
waist." He said, "It is Elijah the Tishbite."
9 Then the king sent to him a captain of fifty
with his fifty men. He went up to Elijah, who
was sitting on the top of a hill, and said to him,
"O man of God, the king says, 'Come down.'"
[10]But Elijah answered the captain of fifty, "If I
am a man of God, let fire come down from
heaven and consume you and your fifty." Then fire
came down from heaven, and consumed him and
his fifty.
11 Again the king sent to him another captain
of fifty with his fifty. He went up[a] and said to him,
"O man of God, this is the king's order: Come
down quickly!" [12]But Elijah answered them, "If I
am a man of God, let fire come down from heaven
and consume you and your fifty." Then the fire of
God came down from heaven and consumed him
and his fifty.
13 Again the king sent the captain of a third
fifty with his fifty. So the third captain of fifty
went up, and came and fell on his knees before
Elijah, and entreated him, "O man of God, please
let my life, and the life of these fifty servants of
yours, be precious in your sight. [14]Look, fire
came down from heaven and consumed the two
former captains of fifty men with their fifties; but
now let my life be precious in your sight." [15]Then
the angel of the LORD said to Elijah, "Go down
with him; do not be afraid of him." So he set out
and went down with him to the king, [16]and said
to him, "Thus says the LORD: Because you have
sent messengers to inquire of Baal-zebub, the god
of Ekron,—is it because there is no God in Israel
to inquire of his word?—therefore you shall not
leave the bed to which you have gone, but you
shall surely die."
17 So he died according to the word of the
LORD that Elijah had spoken. His brother,[b] Jehoram succeeded him as king in the second year
of King Jehoram son of Jehoshaphat of Judah, because Ahaziah had no son. [18]Now the rest of the
acts of Ahaziah that he did, are they not written in
the Book of the Annals of the Kings of Israel?

2 Now when the LORD was about to take Elijah
up to heaven by a whirlwind, Elijah and Elisha were on their way from Gilgal. [2]Elijah said to
Elisha, "Stay here; for the LORD has sent me as far
as Bethel." But Elisha said, "As the LORD lives, and
as you yourself live, I will not leave you." So they
went down to Bethel. [3]The company of prophets[c]
who were in Bethel came out to Elisha, and said
to him, "Do you know that today the LORD will
take your master away from you?" And he said,
"Yes, I know; keep silent."
4 Elijah said to him, "Elisha, stay here; for the
LORD has sent me to Jericho." But he said, "As
the LORD lives, and as you yourself live, I will not
leave you." So they came to Jericho. [5]The company of prophets[c] who were at Jericho drew near
to Elisha, and said to him, "Do you know that
today the LORD will take your master away from
you?" And he answered, "Yes, I know; be silent."
6 Then Elijah said to him, "Stay here; for the
LORD has sent me to the Jordan." But he said, "As
the LORD lives, and as you yourself live, I will not
leave you." So the two of them went on. [7]Fifty
men of the company of prophets[c] also went, and
stood at some distance from them, as they both
were standing by the Jordan. [8]Then Elijah took
his mantle and rolled it up, and struck the water; the water was parted to the one side and to
the other, until the two of them crossed on dry
ground.
9 When they had crossed, Elijah said to Elisha, "Tell me what I may do for you, before I am

[a] Gk Compare verses 9, 13: Heb *He answered* [b] Gk Syr: Heb lacks *His brother* [c] Heb *sons of the prophets*

taken from you." Elisha said, "Please let me inherit
a double share of your spirit." 10He responded,
"You have asked a hard thing; yet, if you see me
as I am being taken from you, it will be granted
you; if not, it will not." 11As they continued walking and talking, a chariot of fire and horses of fire
separated the two of them, and Elijah ascended in
a whirlwind into heaven. 12Elisha kept watching
and crying out, "Father, father! The chariots of
Israel and its horsemen!" But when he could no
longer see him, he grasped his own clothes and
tore them in two pieces.

13 He picked up the mantle of Elijah that
had fallen from him, and went back and stood on
the bank of the Jordan. 14He took the mantle of
Elijah that had fallen from him, and struck the
water, saying, "Where is the LORD, the God of
Elijah?" When he had struck the water, the water
was parted to the one side and to the other, and
Elisha went over.

15 When the company of prophets[a] who were
at Jericho saw him at a distance, they declared,
"The spirit of Elijah rests on Elisha." They came
to meet him and bowed to the ground before
him. 16They said to him, "See now, we have fifty
strong men among your servants; please let them
go and seek your master; it may be that the spirit
of the LORD has caught him up and thrown him
down on some mountain or into some valley." He
responded, "No, do not send them." 17But when
they urged him until he was ashamed, he said,
"Send them." So they sent fifty men who searched
for three days but did not find him. 18When
they came back to him (he had remained at Jericho), he said to them, "Did I not say to you, Do
not go?"

19 Now the people of the city said to Elisha,
"The location of this city is good, as my lord sees;
but the water is bad, and the land is unfruitful."
20He said, "Bring me a new bowl, and put salt in
it." So they brought it to him. 21Then he went to
the spring of water and threw the salt into it, and
said, "Thus says the LORD, I have made this water wholesome; from now on neither death nor
miscarriage shall come from it." 22So the water
has been wholesome to this day, according to the
word that Elisha spoke.

23 He went up from there to Bethel; and
while he was going up on the way, some small
boys came out of the city and jeered at him, saying, "Go away, baldhead! Go away, baldhead!"
24When he turned around and saw them, he
cursed them in the name of the LORD. Then two
she-bears came out of the woods and mauled
forty-two of the boys. 25From there he went on to
Mount Carmel, and then returned to Samaria.

3 In the eighteenth year of King Jehoshaphat
of Judah, Jehoram son of Ahab became king
over Israel in Samaria; he reigned twelve years.
2He did what was evil in the sight of the LORD,
though not like his father and mother, for he removed the pillar of Baal that his father had made.
3Nevertheless he clung to the sin of Jeroboam
son of Nebat, which he caused Israel to commit;
he did not depart from it.

4 Now King Mesha of Moab was a sheep
breeder, who used to deliver to the king of Israel
one hundred thousand lambs, and the wool of
one hundred thousand rams. 5But when Ahab
died, the king of Moab rebelled against the king of
Israel. 6So King Jehoram marched out of Samaria
at that time and mustered all Israel. 7As he went
he sent word to King Jehoshaphat of Judah, "The
king of Moab has rebelled against me; will you go
with me to battle against Moab?" He answered, "I
will; I am with you, my people are your people,
my horses are your horses." 8Then he asked, "By
which way shall we march?" Jehoram answered,
"By the way of the wilderness of Edom."

9 So the king of Israel, the king of Judah, and
the king of Edom set out; and when they had made
a roundabout march of seven days, there was no
water for the army or for the animals that were
with them. 10Then the king of Israel said, "Alas!
The LORD has summoned us, three kings, only to
be handed over to Moab." 11But Jehoshaphat said,
"Is there no prophet of the LORD here, through
whom we may inquire of the LORD?" Then one of
the servants of the king of Israel answered, "Elisha son of Shaphat, who used to pour water on

[a] Heb *sons of the prophets*

the hands of Elijah, is here." 12Jehoshaphat said,
"The word of the LORD is with him." So the king
of Israel and Jehoshaphat and the king of Edom
went down to him.

13 Elisha said to the king of Israel, "What
have I to do with you? Go to your father's prophets or to your mother's." But the king of Israel
said to him, "No; it is the LORD who has summoned us, three kings, only to be handed over
to Moab." 14Elisha said, "As the LORD of hosts
lives, whom I serve, were it not that I have regard
for King Jehoshaphat of Judah, I would give you
neither a look nor a glance. 15But get me a musician." And then, while the musician was playing,
the power of the LORD came on him. 16And he
said, "Thus says the LORD, 'I will make this wadi
full of pools.' 17For thus says the LORD, 'You shall
see neither wind nor rain, but the wadi shall be
filled with water, so that you shall drink, you,
your cattle, and your animals.' 18This is only a trifle in the sight of the LORD, for he will also hand
Moab over to you. 19You shall conquer every fortified city and every choice city; every good tree
you shall fell, all springs of water you shall stop
up, and every good piece of land you shall ruin
with stones." 20The next day, about the time of
the morning offering, suddenly water began to
flow from the direction of Edom, until the country was filled with water.

21 When all the Moabites heard that the kings
had come up to fight against them, all who were
able to put on armor, from the youngest to the
oldest, were called out and were drawn up at the
frontier. 22When they rose early in the morning,
and the sun shone upon the water, the Moabites
saw the water opposite them as red as blood.
23They said, "This is blood; the kings must have
fought together, and killed one another. Now then,
Moab, to the spoil!" 24But when they came to the
camp of Israel, the Israelites rose up and attacked
the Moabites, who fled before them; as they entered Moab they continued the attack.[a] 25The
cities they overturned, and on every good piece
of land everyone threw a stone, until it was covered; every spring of water they stopped up, and
every good tree they felled. Only at Kir-hareseth
did the stone walls remain, until the slingers
surrounded and attacked it. 26When the king of
Moab saw that the battle was going against him,
he took with him seven hundred swordsmen to
break through, opposite the king of Edom; but
they could not. 27Then he took his firstborn son
who was to succeed him, and offered him as a
burnt offering on the wall. And great wrath came
upon Israel, so they withdrew from him and returned to their own land.

4 Now the wife of a member of the company
of prophets[b] cried to Elisha, "Your servant
my husband is dead; and you know that your
servant feared the LORD, but a creditor has come
to take my two children as slaves." 2Elisha said
to her, "What shall I do for you? Tell me, what
do you have in the house?" She answered, "Your
servant has nothing in the house, except a jar of
oil." 3He said, "Go outside, borrow vessels from
all your neighbors, empty vessels and not just a
few. 4Then go in, and shut the door behind you
and your children, and start pouring into all these
vessels; when each is full, set it aside." 5So she left
him and shut the door behind her and her children; they kept bringing vessels to her, and she
kept pouring. 6When the vessels were full, she
said to her son, "Bring me another vessel." But
he said to her, "There are no more." Then the oil
stopped flowing. 7She came and told the man of
God, and he said, "Go sell the oil and pay your
debts, and you and your children can live on the
rest."

8 One day Elisha was passing through Shunem, where a wealthy woman lived, who urged him
to have a meal. So whenever he passed that way,
he would stop there for a meal. 9She said to her
husband, "Look, I am sure that this man who regularly passes our way is a holy man of God. 10Let
us make a small roof chamber with walls, and put
there for him a bed, a table, a chair, and a lamp, so
that he can stay there whenever he comes to us."

11 One day when he came there, he went up to

[a] Compare Gk Syr: Meaning of Heb uncertain [b] Heb *the sons of the prophets*

the chamber and lay down there. 12 He said to his
servant Gehazi, "Call the Shunammite woman."
When he had called her, she stood before him.
13 He said to him, "Say to her, Since you have
taken all this trouble for us, what may be done
for you? Would you have a word spoken on your
behalf to the king or to the commander of the
army?" She answered, "I live among my own people." 14 He said, "What then may be done for her?"
Gehazi answered, "Well, she has no son, and her
husband is old." 15 He said, "Call her." When he
had called her, she stood at the door. 16 He said,
"At this season, in due time, you shall embrace a
son." She replied, "No, my lord, O man of God;
do not deceive your servant."

17 The woman conceived and bore a son at
that season, in due time, as Elisha had declared
to her.

18 When the child was older, he went out one
day to his father among the reapers. 19 He complained to his father, "Oh, my head, my head!"
The father said to his servant, "Carry him to his
mother." 20 He carried him and brought him to his
mother; the child sat on her lap until noon, and
he died. 21 She went up and laid him on the bed
of the man of God, closed the door on him, and
left. 22 Then she called to her husband, and said,
"Send me one of the servants and one of the donkeys, so that I may quickly go to the man of God
and come back again." 23 He said, "Why go to him
today? It is neither new moon nor sabbath." She
said, "It will be all right." 24 Then she saddled the
donkey and said to her servant, "Urge the animal
on; do not hold back for me unless I tell you."
25 So she set out, and came to the man of God at
Mount Carmel.

When the man of God saw her coming, he
said to Gehazi his servant, "Look, there is the
Shunammite woman; 26 run at once to meet her,
and say to her, Are you all right? Is your husband
all right? Is the child all right?" She answered, "It
is all right." 27 When she came to the man of God
at the mountain, she caught hold of his feet. Gehazi approached to push her away. But the man
of God said, "Let her alone, for she is in bitter
distress; the LORD has hidden it from me and
has not told me." 28 Then she said, "Did I ask my
lord for a son? Did I not say, Do not mislead me?"
29 He said to Gehazi, "Gird up your loins, and take
my staff in your hand, and go. If you meet anyone, give no greeting, and if anyone greets you,
do not answer; and lay my staff on the face of the
child." 30 Then the mother of the child said, "As
the LORD lives, and as you yourself live, I will not
leave without you." So he rose up and followed
her. 31 Gehazi went on ahead and laid the staff on
the face of the child, but there was no sound or
sign of life. He came back to meet him and told
him, "The child has not awakened."

32 When Elisha came into the house, he saw
the child lying dead on his bed. 33 So he went
in and closed the door on the two of them, and
prayed to the LORD. 34 Then he got up on the
bed[a] and lay upon the child, putting his mouth
upon his mouth, his eyes upon his eyes, and his
hands upon his hands; and while he lay bent over
him, the flesh of the child became warm. 35 He
got down, walked once to and fro in the room,
then got up again and bent over him; the child
sneezed seven times, and the child opened his
eyes. 36 Elisha[b] summoned Gehazi and said, "Call
the Shunammite woman." So he called her. When
she came to him, he said, "Take your son." 37 She
came and fell at his feet, bowing to the ground;
then she took her son and left.

38 When Elisha returned to Gilgal, there was
a famine in the land. As the company of prophets was[c] sitting before him, he said to his servant,
"Put the large pot on, and make some stew for
the company of prophets."[d] 39 One of them went
out into the field to gather herbs; he found a wild
vine and gathered from it a lapful of wild gourds,
and came and cut them up into the pot of stew,
not knowing what they were. 40 They served some
for the men to eat. But while they were eating
the stew, they cried out, "O man of God, there
is death in the pot!" They could not eat it. 41 He
said, "Then bring some flour." He threw it into the
pot, and said, "Serve the people and let them eat."
And there was nothing harmful in the pot.

[a] Heb lacks *on the bed* [b] Heb *he* [c] Heb *sons of the prophets were* [d] Heb *sons of the prophet*

42 A man came from Baal-shalishah, bringing food from the first fruits to the man of God:
twenty loaves of barley and fresh ears of grain in
his sack. Elisha said, "Give it to the people and let
them eat." 43 But his servant said, "How can I set
this before a hundred people?" So he repeated,
"Give it to the people and let them eat, for thus
says the LORD, 'They shall eat and have some
left.'" 44 He set it before them, they ate, and had
some left, according to the word of the LORD.

5 Naaman, commander of the army of the
king of Aram, was a great man and in high
favor with his master, because by him the LORD
had given victory to Aram. The man, though a
mighty warrior, suffered from leprosy.[a] 2 Now the
Arameans on one of their raids had taken a young
girl captive from the land of Israel, and she served
Naaman's wife. 3 She said to her mistress, "If only
my lord were with the prophet who is in Samaria!
He would cure him of his leprosy."[a] 4 So Naaman[b]
went in and told his lord just what the girl from
the land of Israel had said. 5 And the king of Aram
said, "Go then, and I will send along a letter to the
king of Israel."

He went, taking with him ten talents of silver,
six thousand shekels of gold, and ten sets of garments. 6 He brought the letter to the king of Israel,
which read, "When this letter reaches you, know
that I have sent to you my servant Naaman, that
you may cure him of his leprosy."[a] 7 When the
king of Israel read the letter, he tore his clothes
and said, "Am I God, to give death or life, that this
man sends word to me to cure a man of his leprosy?[a] Just look and see how he is trying to pick a
quarrel with me."

8 But when Elisha the man of God heard that
the king of Israel had torn his clothes, he sent a
message to the king, "Why have you torn your
clothes? Let him come to me, that he may learn
that there is a prophet in Israel." 9 So Naaman
came with his horses and chariots, and halted
at the entrance of Elisha's house. 10 Elisha sent a
messenger to him, saying, "Go, wash in the Jordan
seven times, and your flesh shall be restored and
you shall be clean." 11 But Naaman became angry
and went away, saying, "I thought that for me he
would surely come out, and stand and call on the
name of the LORD his God, and would wave his
hand over the spot, and cure the leprosy![a] 12 Are
not Abana[c] and Pharpar, the rivers of Damascus,
better than all the waters of Israel? Could I not
wash in them, and be clean?" He turned and went
away in a rage. 13 But his servants approached
and said to him, "Father, if the prophet had commanded you to do something difficult, would you
not have done it? How much more, when all he
said to you was, 'Wash, and be clean'?" 14 So he
went down and immersed himself seven times
in the Jordan, according to the word of the man
of God; his flesh was restored like the flesh of a
young boy, and he was clean.

15 Then he returned to the man of God, he
and all his company; he came and stood before
him and said, "Now I know that there is no God
in all the earth except in Israel; please accept a
present from your servant." 16 But he said, "As the
LORD lives, whom I serve, I will accept nothing!"
He urged him to accept, but he refused. 17 Then
Naaman said, "If not, please let two mule-loads
of earth be given to your servant; for your servant
will no longer offer burnt offering or sacrifice to
any god except the LORD. 18 But may the LORD
pardon your servant on one count: when my
master goes into the house of Rimmon to worship there, leaning on my arm, and I bow down
in the house of Rimmon, when I do bow down
in the house of Rimmon, may the LORD pardon
your servant on this one count." 19 He said to him,
"Go in peace."

But when Naaman had gone from him a short
distance, 20 Gehazi, the servant of Elisha the
man of God, thought, "My master has let that
Aramean Naaman off too lightly by not accepting
from him what he offered. As the LORD lives, I
will run after him and get something out of him."
21 So Gehazi went after Naaman. When Naaman
saw someone running after him, he jumped down
from the chariot to meet him and said, "Is everything all right?" 22 He replied, "Yes, but my master
has sent me to say, 'Two members of a company

[a] A term for several skin diseases; precise meaning uncertain [b] Heb *he* [c] Another reading is *Amana*

of prophets[a] have just come to me from the hill
country of Ephraim; please give them a talent
of silver and two changes of clothing.' " 23 Naaman said, "Please accept two talents." He urged
him, and tied up two talents of silver in two bags,
with two changes of clothing, and gave them to
two of his servants, who carried them in front of
Gehazi.[b] 24 When he came to the citadel, he took
the bags[c] from them, and stored them inside; he
dismissed the men, and they left.

25 He went in and stood before his master;
and Elisha said to him, "Where have you been,
Gehazi?" He answered, "Your servant has not
gone anywhere at all." 26 But he said to him, "Did
I not go with you in spirit when someone left
his chariot to meet you? Is this a time to accept
money and to accept clothing, olive orchards and
vineyards, sheep and oxen, and male and female
slaves? 27 Therefore the leprosy[d] of Naaman shall
cling to you, and to your descendants forever." So
he left his presence leprous,[d] as white as snow.

6 Now the company of prophets[a] said to Elisha, "As you see, the place where we live under your charge is too small for us. 2 Let us go to
the Jordan, and let us collect logs there, one for
each of us, and build a place there for us to live."
He answered, "Do so." 3 Then one of them said,
"Please come with your servants." And he answered, "I will." 4 So he went with them. When
they came to the Jordan, they cut down trees.
5 But as one was felling a log, his ax head fell into
the water; he cried out, "Alas, master! It was borrowed." 6 Then the man of God said, "Where did
it fall?" When he showed him the place, he cut off
a stick, and threw it in there, and made the iron
float. 7 He said, "Pick it up." So he reached out his
hand and took it.

8 Once when the king of Aram was at war
with Israel, he took counsel with his officers. He
said, "At such and such a place shall be my camp."
9 But the man of God sent word to the king of Israel, "Take care not to pass this place, because the
Arameans are going down there." 10 The king of
Israel sent word to the place of which the man of
God spoke. More than once or twice he warned
such a place[e] so that it was on the alert.

11 The mind of the king of Aram was greatly
perturbed because of this; he called his officers
and said to them, "Now tell me who among us
sides with the king of Israel?" 12 Then one of his
officers said, "No one, my lord king. It is Elisha,
the prophet in Israel, who tells the king of Israel
the words that you speak in your bedchamber."
13 He said, "Go and find where he is; I will send
and seize him." He was told, "He is in Dothan."
14 So he sent horses and chariots there and a great
army; they came by night, and surrounded the
city.

15 When an attendant of the man of God
rose early in the morning and went out, an army
with horses and chariots was all around the city.
His servant said, "Alas, master! What shall we
do?" 16 He replied, "Do not be afraid, for there are
more with us than there are with them." 17 Then
Elisha prayed: "O LORD, please open his eyes
that he may see." So the LORD opened the eyes
of the servant, and he saw; the mountain was
full of horses and chariots of fire all around Elisha. 18 When the Arameans[f] came down against
him, Elisha prayed to the LORD, and said, "Strike
this people, please, with blindness." So he struck
them with blindness as Elisha had asked. 19 Elisha said to them, "This is not the way, and this
is not the city; follow me, and I will bring you
to the man whom you seek." And he led them
to Samaria.

20 As soon as they entered Samaria, Elisha
said, "O LORD, open the eyes of these men so that
they may see." The LORD opened their eyes, and
they saw that they were inside Samaria. 21 When
the king of Israel saw them he said to Elisha, "Father, shall I kill them? Shall I kill them?" 22 He answered, "No! Did you capture with your sword
and your bow those whom you want to kill? Set
food and water before them so that they may eat
and drink; and let them go to their master." 23 So
he prepared for them a great feast; after they ate
and drank, he sent them on their way, and they

[a] Heb *sons of the prophets* [b] Heb *him* [c] Heb lacks *the bags* [d] A term for several skin diseases; precise meaning uncertain [e] Heb *warned it* [f] Heb *they*

went to their master. And the Arameans no longer came raiding into the land of Israel.
24 Some time later King Ben-hadad of Aram
mustered his entire army; he marched against
Samaria and laid siege to it. 25As the siege continued, famine in Samaria became so great that
a donkey's head was sold for eighty shekels of
silver, and one-fourth of a kab of dove's dung for
five shekels of silver. 26Now as the king of Israel
was walking on the city wall, a woman cried out
to him, "Help, my lord king!" 27He said, "No! Let
the LORD help you. How can I help you? From
the threshing floor or from the wine press?"
28But then the king asked her, "What is your
complaint?" She answered, "This woman said to
me, 'Give up your son; we will eat him today, and
we will eat my son tomorrow.' 29So we cooked my
son and ate him. The next day I said to her, 'Give
up your son and we will eat him.' But she has hidden her son." 30When the king heard the words
of the woman he tore his clothes—now since he
was walking on the city wall, the people could see
that he had sackcloth on his body underneath—
31and he said, "So may God do to me, and more,
if the head of Elisha son of Shaphat stays on his
shoulders today." 32So he dispatched a man from
his presence.

Now Elisha was sitting in his house, and the
elders were sitting with him. Before the messenger arrived, Elisha said to the elders, "Are
you aware that this murderer has sent someone to take off my head? When the messenger comes, see that you shut the door and hold
it closed against him. Is not the sound of his
master's feet behind him?" 33While he was still
speaking with them, the king[a] came down to
him and said, "This trouble is from the LORD!
Why should I hope in the LORD any longer?"

7 1But Elisha said, "Hear the word of the
LORD: thus says the LORD, Tomorrow about
this time a measure of choice meal shall be sold
for a shekel, and two measures of barley for a
shekel, at the gate of Samaria." 2Then the captain
on whose hand the king leaned said to the man
of God, "Even if the LORD were to make windows
in the sky, could such a thing happen?" But he
said, "You shall see it with your own eyes, but you
shall not eat from it."

3 Now there were four leprous[b] men outside
the city gate, who said to one another, "Why
should we sit here until we die? 4If we say, 'Let
us enter the city,' the famine is in the city, and we
shall die there; but if we sit here, we shall also die.
Therefore, let us desert to the Aramean camp; if
they spare our lives, we shall live; and if they kill
us, we shall but die." 5So they arose at twilight to
go to the Aramean camp; but when they came to
the edge of the Aramean camp, there was no one
there at all. 6For the Lord had caused the Aramean
army to hear the sound of chariots, and of horses,
the sound of a great army, so that they said to one
another, "The king of Israel has hired the kings of
the Hittites and the kings of Egypt to fight against
us." 7So they fled away in the twilight and abandoned their tents, their horses, and their donkeys
leaving the camp just as it was, and fled for their
lives. 8When these leprous[b] men had come to the
edge of the camp, they went into a tent, ate and
drank, carried off silver, gold, and clothing, and
went and hid them. Then they came back, entered another tent, carried off things from it, and
went and hid them.

9 Then they said to one another, "What we
are doing is wrong. This is a day of good news;
if we are silent and wait until the morning light,
we will be found guilty; therefore let us go and
tell the king's household." 10So they came and
called to the gatekeepers of the city, and told
them, "We went to the Aramean camp, but there
was no one to be seen or heard there, nothing but
the horses tied, the donkeys tied, and the tents
as they were." 11Then the gatekeepers called out
and proclaimed it to the king's household. 12The
king got up in the night, and said to his servants,
"I will tell you what the Arameans have prepared
against us. They know that we are starving; so
they have left the camp to hide themselves in the
open country, thinking, 'When they come out of
the city, we shall take them alive and get into the
city.'" 13One of his servants said, "Let some men

[a] See 7.2: Heb *messenger* [b] A term for several skin diseases; precise meaning uncertain

take five of the remaining horses, since those left
here will suffer the fate of the whole multitude of
Israel that have perished already;[a] let us send and
find out." 14 So they took two mounted men, and
the king sent them after the Aramean army, saying, "Go and find out." 15 So they went after them
as far as the Jordan; the whole way was littered
with garments and equipment that the Arameans
had thrown away in their haste. So the messengers returned, and told the king.

16 Then the people went out, and plundered
the camp of the Arameans. So a measure of
choice meal was sold for a shekel, and two measures of barley for a shekel, according to the word
of the LORD. 17 Now the king had appointed the
captain on whose hand he leaned to have charge
of the gate; the people trampled him to death in
the gate, just as the man of God had said when
the king came down to him. 18 For when the man
of God had said to the king, "Two measures of
barley shall be sold for a shekel, and a measure of
choice meal for a shekel, about this time tomorrow in the gate of Samaria," 19 the captain had answered the man of God, "Even if the LORD were
to make windows in the sky, could such a thing
happen?" And he had answered, "You shall see it
with your own eyes, but you shall not eat from it."
20 It did indeed happen to him; the people trampled him to death in the gate.

8 Now Elisha had said to the woman whose
son he had restored to life, "Get up and go
with your household, and settle wherever you
can; for the LORD has called for a famine, and it
will come on the land for seven years." 2 So the
woman got up and did according to the word of
the man of God; she went with her household
and settled in the land of the Philistines seven
years. 3 At the end of the seven years, when the
woman returned from the land of the Philistines,
she set out to appeal to the king for her house and
her land. 4 Now the king was talking with Gehazi
the servant of the man of God, saying, "Tell me
all the great things that Elisha has done." 5 While
he was telling the king how Elisha had restored a
dead person to life, the woman whose son he had
restored to life appealed to the king for her house
and her land. Gehazi said, "My lord king, here
is the woman, and here is her son whom Elisha
restored to life." 6 When the king questioned the
woman, she told him. So the king appointed an
official for her, saying, "Restore all that was hers,
together with all the revenue of the fields from
the day that she left the land until now."

7 Elisha went to Damascus while King Ben-
hadad of Aram was ill. When it was told him,
"The man of God has come here," 8 the king
said to Hazael, "Take a present with you and go
to meet the man of God. Inquire of the LORD
through him, whether I shall recover from this
illness." 9 So Hazael went to meet him, taking a
present with him, all kinds of goods of Damascus,
forty camel loads. When he entered and stood
before him, he said, "Your son King Ben-hadad of
Aram has sent me to you, saying, 'Shall I recover
from this illness?'" 10 Elisha said to him, "Go,
say to him, 'You shall certainly recover'; but the
LORD has shown me that he shall certainly die."
11 He fixed his gaze and stared at him, until he was
ashamed. Then the man of God wept. 12 Hazael
asked, "Why does my lord weep?" He answered,
"Because I know the evil that you will do to the
people of Israel; you will set their fortresses on
fire, you will kill their young men with the sword,
dash in pieces their little ones, and rip up their
pregnant women." 13 Hazael said, "What is your
servant, who is a mere dog, that he should do
this great thing?" Elisha answered, "The LORD
has shown me that you are to be king over Aram."
14 Then he left Elisha, and went to his master
Ben-hadad,[b] who said to him, "What did Elisha
say to you?" And he answered, "He told me that
you would certainly recover." 15 But the next day
he took the bed-cover and dipped it in water and
spread it over the king's face, until he died. And
Hazael succeeded him.

16 In the fifth year of King Joram son of Ahab
of Israel,[c] Jehoram son of King Jehoshaphat of
Judah began to reign. 17 He was thirty-two years

[a] Compare Gk Syr Vg: Meaning of Heb uncertain [b] Heb lacks *Ben-hadad*
[c] Gk Syr: Heb adds *Jehoshaphat being king of Judah,*

old when he became king, and he reigned eight
years in Jerusalem. 18 He walked in the way of the
kings of Israel, as the house of Ahab had done, for
the daughter of Ahab was his wife. He did what
was evil in the sight of the LORD. 19 Yet the LORD
would not destroy Judah, for the sake of his servant David, since he had promised to give a lamp
to him and to his descendants forever.

20 In his days Edom revolted against the rule
of Judah, and set up a king of their own. 21 Then
Joram crossed over to Zair with all his chariots.
He set out by night and attacked the Edomites
and their chariot commanders who had surrounded him;[a] but his army fled home. 22 So
Edom has been in revolt against the rule of Judah
to this day. Libnah also revolted at the same time.
23 Now the rest of the acts of Joram, and all that he
did, are they not written in the Book of the Annals of the Kings of Judah? 24 So Joram slept with
his ancestors, and was buried with them in the
city of David; his son Ahaziah succeeded him.

25 In the twelfth year of King Joram son of
Ahab of Israel, Ahaziah son of King Jehoram of
Judah began to reign. 26 Ahaziah was twenty-two
years old when he began to reign; he reigned one
year in Jerusalem. His mother's name was Athaliah, a granddaughter of King Omri of Israel.
27 He also walked in the way of the house of Ahab,
doing what was evil in the sight of the LORD, as
the house of Ahab had done, for he was son-in-
law to the house of Ahab.

28 He went with Joram son of Ahab to wage
war against King Hazael of Aram at Ramoth-
gilead, where the Arameans wounded Joram.
29 King Joram returned to be healed in Jezreel
of the wounds that the Arameans had inflicted
on him at Ramah, when he fought against King
Hazael of Aram. King Ahaziah son of Jehoram of
Judah went down to see Joram son of Ahab in Jezreel, because he was wounded.

9 Then the prophet Elisha called a member of
the company of prophets[b] and said to him,
"Gird up your loins; take this flask of oil in your
hand, and go to Ramoth-gilead. 2 When you arrive, look there for Jehu son of Jehoshaphat, son
of Nimshi; go in and get him to leave his companions, and take him into an inner chamber. 3 Then
take the flask of oil, pour it on his head, and say,
'Thus says the LORD: I anoint you king over Israel.' Then open the door and flee; do not linger."

4 So the young man, the young prophet, went
to Ramoth-gilead. 5 He arrived while the commanders of the army were in council, and he announced, "I have a message for you, commander."
"For which one of us?" asked Jehu. "For you,
commander." 6 So Jehu[c] got up and went inside;
the young man poured the oil on his head, saying
to him, "Thus says the LORD the God of Israel:
I anoint you king over the people of the LORD,
over Israel. 7 You shall strike down the house of
your master Ahab, so that I may avenge on Jezebel
the blood of my servants the prophets, and the
blood of all the servants of the LORD. 8 For the
whole house of Ahab shall perish; I will cut off
from Ahab every male, bond or free, in Israel.
9 I will make the house of Ahab like the house
of Jeroboam son of Nebat, and like the house of
Baasha son of Ahijah. 10 The dogs shall eat Jezebel
in the territory of Jezreel, and no one shall bury
her." Then he opened the door and fled.

11 When Jehu came back to his master's officers, they said to him, "Is everything all right?
Why did that madman come to you?" He answered them, "You know the sort and how they
babble." 12 They said, "Liar! Come on, tell us!" So
he said, "This is just what he said to me: 'Thus says
the LORD, I anoint you king over Israel.'" 13 Then
hurriedly they all took their cloaks and spread
them for him on the bare[a] steps; and they blew
the trumpet, and proclaimed, "Jehu is king."

14 Thus Jehu son of Jehoshaphat son of Nimshi conspired against Joram. Joram with all Israel
had been on guard at Ramoth-gilead against King
Hazael of Aram; 15 but King Joram had returned
to be healed in Jezreel of the wounds that the
Arameans had inflicted on him, when he fought
against King Hazael of Aram. So Jehu said, "If this
is your wish, then let no one slip out of the city
to go and tell the news in Jezreel." 16 Then Jehu
mounted his chariot and went to Jezreel, where

[a] Meaning of Heb uncertain [b] Heb *sons of the prophets* [c] Heb *he*

Joram was lying ill. King Ahaziah of Judah had
come down to visit Joram.
17 In Jezreel, the sentinel standing on the
tower spied the company of Jehu arriving, and
said, "I see a company." Joram said, "Take a horseman; send him to meet them, and let him say, 'Is
it peace?' " 18 So the horseman went to meet him;
he said, "Thus says the king, 'Is it peace?' " Jehu
responded, "What have you to do with peace?
Fall in behind me." The sentinel reported, saying,
"The messenger reached them, but he is not coming back." 19 Then he sent out a second horseman,
who came to them and said, "Thus says the king,
'Is it peace?' " Jehu answered, "What have you to
do with peace? Fall in behind me." 20 Again the
sentinel reported, "He reached them, but he is
not coming back. It looks like the driving of Jehu
son of Nimshi; for he drives like a maniac."
21 Joram said, "Get ready." And they got his
chariot ready. Then King Joram of Israel and King
Ahaziah of Judah set out, each in his chariot, and
went to meet Jehu; they met him at the property of Naboth the Jezreelite. 22 When Joram saw
Jehu, he said, "Is it peace, Jehu?" He answered,
"What peace can there be, so long as the many
whoredoms and sorceries of your mother Jezebel
continue?" 23 Then Joram reined about and fled,
saying to Ahaziah, "Treason, Ahaziah!" 24 Jehu
drew his bow with all his strength, and shot Joram
between the shoulders, so that the arrow pierced
his heart; and he sank in his chariot. 25 Jehu said to
his aide Bidkar, "Lift him out, and throw him on
the plot of ground belonging to Naboth the Jezreelite; for remember, when you and I rode side
by side behind his father Ahab how the LORD uttered this oracle against him: 26 'For the blood of
Naboth and for the blood of his children that I
saw yesterday, says the LORD, I swear I will repay
you on this very plot of ground.' Now therefore
lift him out and throw him on the plot of ground,
in accordance with the word of the LORD."
27 When King Ahaziah of Judah saw this, he
fled in the direction of Beth-haggan. Jehu pursued him, saying, "Shoot him also!" And they
shot him[a] in the chariot at the ascent to Gur,
which is by Ibleam. Then he fled to Megiddo, and
died there. 28 His officers carried him in a chariot
to Jerusalem, and buried him in his tomb with his
ancestors in the city of David.
29 In the eleventh year of Joram son of Ahab,
Ahaziah began to reign over Judah.
30 When Jehu came to Jezreel, Jezebel heard
of it; she painted her eyes, and adorned her head,
and looked out of the window. 31 As Jehu entered
the gate, she said, "Is it peace, Zimri, murderer of
your master?" 32 He looked up to the window and
said, "Who is on my side? Who?" Two or three
eunuchs looked out at him. 33 He said, "Throw
her down." So they threw her down; some of her
blood spattered on the wall and on the horses,
which trampled on her. 34 Then he went in and
ate and drank; he said, "See to that cursed woman
and bury her; for she is a king's daughter." 35 But
when they went to bury her, they found no more
of her than the skull and the feet and the palms of
her hands. 36 When they came back and told him,
he said, "This is the word of the LORD, which he
spoke by his servant Elijah the Tishbite, 'In the
territory of Jezreel the dogs shall eat the flesh of
Jezebel; 37 the corpse of Jezebel shall be like dung
on the field in the territory of Jezreel, so that no
one can say, This is Jezebel.' "

10 Now Ahab had seventy sons in Samaria.
So Jehu wrote letters and sent them to Samaria, to the rulers of Jezreel,[b] to the elders, and to
the guardians of the sons of[c] Ahab, saying, 2 "Since
your master's sons are with you and you have at
your disposal chariots and horses, a fortified city,
and weapons, 3 select the son of your master who
is the best qualified, set him on his father's throne,
and fight for your master's house." 4 But they were
utterly terrified and said, "Look, two kings could
not withstand him; how then can we stand?"
5 So the steward of the palace, and the governor
of the city, along with the elders and the guardians, sent word to Jehu: "We are your servants; we
will do anything you say. We will not make anyone king; do whatever you think right." 6 Then he
wrote them a second letter, saying, "If you are on
my side, and if you are ready to obey me, take the

[a] Syr Vg Compare Gk: Heb lacks *and they shot him* [b] Or *of the city*; Vg Compare Gk [c] Gk: Heb lacks *of the sons of*

heads of your master's sons and come to me at Jezreel tomorrow at this time." Now the king's sons,
seventy persons, were with the leaders of the city,
who were charged with their upbringing. 7When
the letter reached them, they took the king's sons
and killed them, seventy persons; they put their
heads in baskets and sent them to him at Jezreel.
8When the messenger came and told him, "They
have brought the heads of the king's sons," he said,
"Lay them in two heaps at the entrance of the gate
until the morning." 9Then in the morning when
he went out, he stood and said to all the people,
"You are innocent. It was I who conspired against
my master and killed him; but who struck down
all these? 10Know then that there shall fall to the
earth nothing of the word of the LORD, which the
LORD spoke concerning the house of Ahab; for
the LORD has done what he said through his servant Elijah." 11So Jehu killed all who were left of
the house of Ahab in Jezreel, all his leaders, close
friends, and priests, until he left him no survivor.

12 Then he set out and went to Samaria. On
the way, when he was at Beth-eked of the Shepherds, 13Jehu met relatives of King Ahaziah of
Judah and said, "Who are you?" They answered,
"We are kin of Ahaziah; we have come down to
visit the royal princes and the sons of the queen
mother." 14He said, "Take them alive." They took
them alive, and slaughtered them at the pit of Beth-
eked, forty-two in all; he spared none of them.

15 When he left there, he met Jehonadab son
of Rechab coming to meet him; he greeted him,
and said to him, "Is your heart as true to mine as
mine is to yours?"[a] Jehonadab answered, "It is."
Jehu said,[b] "If it is, give me your hand." So he gave
him his hand. Jehu took him up with him into
the chariot. 16He said, "Come with me, and see
my zeal for the LORD." So he[c] had him ride in his
chariot. 17When he came to Samaria, he killed all
who were left to Ahab in Samaria, until he had
wiped them out, according to the word of the
LORD that he spoke to Elijah.

18 Then Jehu assembled all the people and
said to them, "Ahab offered Baal small service;
but Jehu will offer much more. 19Now therefore
summon to me all the prophets of Baal, all his
worshipers, and all his priests; let none be missing, for I have a great sacrifice to offer to Baal;
whoever is missing shall not live." But Jehu was
acting with cunning in order to destroy the
worshipers of Baal. 20Jehu decreed, "Sanctify a
solemn assembly for Baal." So they proclaimed
it. 21Jehu sent word throughout all Israel; all
the worshipers of Baal came, so that there was
no one left who did not come. They entered
the temple of Baal, until the temple of Baal was
filled from wall to wall. 22He said to the keeper of
the wardrobe, "Bring out the vestments for all
the worshipers of Baal." So he brought out the
vestments for them. 23Then Jehu entered the
temple of Baal with Jehonadab son of Rechab;
he said to the worshipers of Baal, "Search and
see that there is no worshiper of the LORD here
among you, but only worshipers of Baal." 24Then
they proceeded to offer sacrifices and burnt offerings.

Now Jehu had stationed eighty men outside,
saying, "Whoever allows any of those to escape
whom I deliver into your hands shall forfeit his
life." 25As soon as he had finished presenting the
burnt offering, Jehu said to the guards and to the
officers, "Come in and kill them; let no one escape." So they put them to the sword. The guards
and the officers threw them out, and then went
into the citadel of the temple of Baal. 26They
brought out the pillar[d] that was in the temple of
Baal, and burned it. 27Then they demolished the
pillar of Baal, and destroyed the temple of Baal,
and made it a latrine to this day.

28 Thus Jehu wiped out Baal from Israel.
29But Jehu did not turn aside from the sins of Jeroboam son of Nebat, which he caused Israel to
commit—the golden calves that were in Bethel
and in Dan. 30The LORD said to Jehu, "Because
you have done well in carrying out what I consider right, and in accordance with all that was
in my heart have dealt with the house of Ahab,
your sons of the fourth generation shall sit on the

[a] Gk: Heb *Is it right with your heart, as my heart is with your heart?* [b] Gk: Heb lacks *Jehu said* [c] Gk Syr Tg: Heb *they*
[d] Gk Vg Syr Tg: Heb *pillars*

throne of Israel." 31But Jehu was not careful to follow the law of the LORD the God of Israel with all
his heart; he did not turn from the sins of Jeroboam, which he caused Israel to commit.
32 In those days the LORD began to trim off
parts of Israel. Hazael defeated them throughout
the territory of Israel: 33from the Jordan eastward, all the land of Gilead, the Gadites, the Reubenites, and the Manassites, from Aroer, which is
by the Wadi Arnon, that is, Gilead and Bashan.
34Now the rest of the acts of Jehu, all that he did,
and all his power, are they not written in the Book
of the Annals of the Kings of Israel? 35So Jehu
slept with his ancestors, and they buried him in
Samaria. His son Jehoahaz succeeded him. 36The
time that Jehu reigned over Israel in Samaria was
twenty-eight years.

11 Now when Athaliah, Ahaziah's mother,
saw that her son was dead, she set about to
destroy all the royal family. 2But Jehosheba, King
Joram's daughter, Ahaziah's sister, took Joash son
of Ahaziah, and stole him away from among the
king's children who were about to be killed; she
put[a] him and his nurse in a bedroom. Thus she[b]
hid him from Athaliah, so that he was not killed;
3he remained with her six years, hidden in the
house of the LORD, while Athaliah reigned over
the land.
4 But in the seventh year Jehoiada summoned the captains of the Carites and of the
guards and had them come to him in the house
of the LORD. He made a covenant with them and
put them under oath in the house of the LORD;
then he showed them the king's son. 5He commanded them, "This is what you are to do: one-
third of you, those who go off duty on the sabbath
and guard the king's house 6(another third being
at the gate Sur and a third at the gate behind the
guards), shall guard the palace; 7and your two
divisions that come on duty in force on the sabbath and guard the house of the LORD[c] 8shall surround the king, each with weapons in hand; and
whoever approaches the ranks is to be killed. Be
with the king in his comings and goings."
9 The captains did according to all that the
priest Jehoiada commanded; each brought his
men who were to go off duty on the sabbath, with
those who were to come on duty on the sabbath,
and came to the priest Jehoiada. 10The priest delivered to the captains the spears and shields that
had been King David's, which were in the house
of the LORD; 11the guards stood, every man with
his weapons in his hand, from the south side of
the house to the north side of the house, around
the altar and the house, to guard the king on
every side. 12Then he brought out the king's son,
put the crown on him, and gave him the covenant;[d] they proclaimed him king, and anointed
him; they clapped their hands and shouted,
"Long live the king!"
13 When Athaliah heard the noise of the
guard and of the people, she went into the house
of the LORD to the people; 14when she looked,
there was the king standing by the pillar, according to custom, with the captains and the trumpeters beside the king, and all the people of the land
rejoicing and blowing trumpets. Athaliah tore her
clothes and cried, "Treason! Treason!" 15Then
the priest Jehoiada commanded the captains who
were set over the army, "Bring her out between
the ranks, and kill with the sword anyone who
follows her." For the priest said, "Let her not be
killed in the house of the LORD." 16So they laid
hands on her; she went through the horses' entrance to the king's house, and there she was put
to death.
17 Jehoiada made a covenant between the
LORD and the king and people, that they should
be the LORD's people; also between the king and
the people. 18Then all the people of the land went
to the house of Baal, and tore it down; his altars
and his images they broke in pieces, and they
killed Mattan, the priest of Baal, before the altars.
The priest posted guards over the house of the
LORD. 19He took the captains, the Carites, the
guards, and all the people of the land; then they
brought the king down from the house of the
LORD, marching through the gate of the guards to

[a] With 2 Chr 22.11: Heb lacks *she put* [b] Gk Syr Vg Compare 2 Chr 22.11: Heb *they* [c] Heb *the LORD to the king*
[d] Or *treaty* or *testimony*; Heb *eduth*

the king's house. He took his seat on the throne of
the kings. 20So all the people of the land rejoiced;
and the city was quiet after Athaliah had been
killed with the sword at the king's house.

21[a] Jehoash[b] was seven years old when he began to reign.

12 In the seventh year of Jehu, Jehoash began
to reign; he reigned forty years in Jerusalem. His mother's name was Zibiah of Beer-sheba.
2Jehoash did what was right in the sight of the
LORD all his days, because the priest Jehoiada instructed him. 3Nevertheless the high places were
not taken away; the people continued to sacrifice
and make offerings on the high places.

4 Jehoash said to the priests, "All the money
offered as sacred donations that is brought into
the house of the LORD, the money for which each
person is assessed—the money from the assessment of persons—and the money from the voluntary offerings brought into the house of the
LORD, 5let the priests receive from each of the donors; and let them repair the house wherever any
need of repairs is discovered." 6But by the twenty-
third year of King Jehoash the priests had made
no repairs on the house. 7Therefore King Jehoash
summoned the priest Jehoiada with the other
priests and said to them, "Why are you not repairing the house? Now therefore do not accept any
more money from your donors but hand it over
for the repair of the house." 8So the priests agreed
that they would neither accept more money
from the people nor repair the house.

9 Then the priest Jehoiada took a chest, made
a hole in its lid, and set it beside the altar on the
right side as one entered the house of the LORD;
the priests who guarded the threshold put in it all
the money that was brought into the house of the
LORD. 10Whenever they saw that there was a great
deal of money in the chest, the king's secretary
and the high priest went up, counted the money
that was found in the house of the LORD, and tied
it up in bags. 11They would give the money that
was weighed out into the hands of the workers
who had the oversight of the house of the LORD;
then they paid it out to the carpenters and the
builders who worked on the house of the LORD,
12to the masons and the stonecutters, as well as to
buy timber and quarried stone for making repairs
on the house of the LORD, as well as for any outlay
for repairs of the house. 13But for the house of the
LORD no basins of silver, snuffers, bowls, trumpets, or any vessels of gold, or of silver, were made
from the money that was brought into the house
of the LORD, 14for that was given to the workers
who were repairing the house of the LORD with
it. 15They did not ask an accounting from those
into whose hand they delivered the money to pay
out to the workers, for they dealt honestly. 16The
money from the guilt offerings and the money
from the sin offerings was not brought into the
house of the LORD; it belonged to the priests.

17 At that time King Hazael of Aram went
up, fought against Gath, and took it. But when
Hazael set his face to go up against Jerusalem,
18King Jehoash of Judah took all the votive gifts
that Jehoshaphat, Jehoram, and Ahaziah, his ancestors, the kings of Judah, had dedicated, as well
as his own votive gifts, all the gold that was found
in the treasuries of the house of the LORD and of
the king's house, and sent these to King Hazael of
Aram. Then Hazael withdrew from Jerusalem.

19 Now the rest of the acts of Joash, and all
that he did, are they not written in the Book of
the Annals of the Kings of Judah? 20His servants
arose, devised a conspiracy, and killed Joash in
the house of Millo, on the way that goes down
to Silla. 21It was Jozacar son of Shimeath and Jehozabad son of Shomer, his servants, who struck
him down, so that he died. He was buried with
his ancestors in the city of David; then his son
Amaziah succeeded him.

13 In the twenty-third year of King Joash son
of Ahaziah of Judah, Jehoahaz son of Jehu
began to reign over Israel in Samaria; he reigned
seventeen years. 2He did what was evil in the sight
of the LORD, and followed the sins of Jeroboam
son of Nebat, which he caused Israel to sin; he did
not depart from them. 3The anger of the LORD
was kindled against Israel, so that he gave them
repeatedly into the hand of King Hazael of Aram,

[a] Ch 12.1 in Heb [b] Another spelling is *Joash*; see verse 19

then into the hand of Ben-hadad son of Hazael.
4But Jehoahaz entreated the LORD, and the LORD
heeded him; for he saw the oppression of Israel,
how the king of Aram oppressed them. 5There-
fore the LORD gave Israel a savior, so that they
escaped from the hand of the Arameans; and the
people of Israel lived in their homes as formerly.
6Nevertheless they did not depart from the sins
of the house of Jeroboam, which he caused Israel
to sin, but walked[a] in them; the sacred pole[b] also
remained in Samaria. 7So Jehoahaz was left with
an army of not more than fifty horsemen, ten
chariots and ten thousand footmen; for the king
of Aram had destroyed them and made them like
the dust at threshing. 8Now the rest of the acts of
Jehoahaz and all that he did, including his might,
are they not written in the Book of the Annals of
the Kings of Israel? 9So Jehoahaz slept with his
ancestors, and they buried him in Samaria; then
his son Joash succeeded him.

10 In the thirty-seventh year of King Joash
of Judah, Jehoash son of Jehoahaz began to reign
over Israel in Samaria; he reigned sixteen years.
11He also did what was evil in the sight of the
LORD; he did not depart from all the sins of Jeroboam son of Nebat, which he caused Israel to
sin, but he walked in them. 12Now the rest of the
acts of Joash, and all that he did, as well as the
might with which he fought against King Amaziah of Judah, are they not written in the Book
of the Annals of the Kings of Israel? 13So Joash
slept with his ancestors, and Jeroboam sat upon
his throne; Joash was buried in Samaria with the
kings of Israel.

14 Now when Elisha had fallen sick with the
illness of which he was to die, King Joash of Israel went down to him, and wept before him, crying, "My father, my father! The chariots of Israel
and its horsemen!" 15Elisha said to him, "Take a
bow and arrows"; so he took a bow and arrows.
16Then he said to the king of Israel, "Draw the
bow"; and he drew it. Elisha laid his hands on the
king's hands. 17Then he said, "Open the window
eastward"; and he opened it. Elisha said, "Shoot";
and he shot. Then he said, "The LORD's arrow of
victory, the arrow of victory over Aram! For you
shall fight the Arameans in Aphek until you have
made an end of them." 18He continued, "Take the
arrows"; and he took them. He said to the king of
Israel, "Strike the ground with them"; he struck
three times, and stopped. 19Then the man of God
was angry with him, and said, "You should have
struck five or six times; then you would have
struck down Aram until you had made an end of
it, but now you will strike down Aram only three
times."

20 So Elisha died, and they buried him. Now
bands of Moabites used to invade the land in the
spring of the year. 21As a man was being buried,
a marauding band was seen and the man was
thrown into the grave of Elisha; as soon as the
man touched the bones of Elisha, he came to life
and stood on his feet.

22 Now King Hazael of Aram oppressed Israel all the days of Jehoahaz. 23But the LORD was
gracious to them and had compassion on them;
he turned toward them, because of his covenant
with Abraham, Isaac, and Jacob, and would not
destroy them; nor has he banished them from his
presence until now.

24 When King Hazael of Aram died, his son
Ben-hadad succeeded him. 25Then Jehoash son of
Jehoahaz took again from Ben-hadad son of Haz-
ael the towns that he had taken from his father
Jehoahaz in war. Three times Joash defeated him
and recovered the towns of Israel.

14 In the second year of King Joash son of
Joahaz of Israel, King Amaziah son of
Joash of Judah, began to reign. 2He was twenty-
five years old when he began to reign, and he
reigned twenty-nine years in Jerusalem. His
mother's name was Jehoaddin of Jerusalem. 3He
did what was right in the sight of the LORD, yet
not like his ancestor David; in all things he did
as his father Joash had done. 4But the high places
were not removed; the people still sacrificed and
made offerings on the high places. 5As soon as
the royal power was firmly in his hand he killed
his servants who had murdered his father the
king. 6But he did not put to death the children of

[a] Gk Syr Tg Vg: Heb *he walked* [b] Heb *Asherah*

the murderers; according to what is written in the
book of the law of Moses, where the LORD commanded, "The parents shall not be put to death
for the children, or the children be put to death
for the parents; but all shall be put to death for
their own sins."

7 He killed ten thousand Edomites in the
Valley of Salt and took Sela by storm; he called it
Jokthe-el, which is its name to this day.

8 Then Amaziah sent messengers to King Jehoash son of Jehoahaz, son of Jehu, of Israel, saying, "Come, let us look one another in the face."
9 King Jehoash of Israel sent word to King Amaziah of Judah, "A thornbush on Lebanon sent to a
cedar on Lebanon, saying, 'Give your daughter to
my son for a wife'; but a wild animal of Lebanon
passed by and trampled down the thornbush.
10 You have indeed defeated Edom, and your heart
has lifted you up. Be content with your glory, and
stay at home; for why should you provoke trouble
so that you fall, you and Judah with you?"

11 But Amaziah would not listen. So King
Jehoash of Israel went up; he and King Amaziah
of Judah faced one another in battle at Beth-
shemesh, which belongs to Judah. 12 Judah was
defeated by Israel; everyone fled home. 13 King
Jehoash of Israel captured King Amaziah of Judah
son of Jehoash, son of Ahaziah, at Beth-shemesh;
he came to Jerusalem, and broke down the wall
of Jerusalem from the Ephraim Gate to the Corner Gate, a distance of four hundred cubits. 14 He
seized all the gold and silver, and all the vessels
that were found in the house of the LORD and in
the treasuries of the king's house, as well as hostages; then he returned to Samaria.

15 Now the rest of the acts that Jehoash did,
his might, and how he fought with King Amaziah
of Judah, are they not written in the Book of the
Annals of the Kings of Israel? 16 Jehoash slept with
his ancestors, and was buried in Samaria with the
kings of Israel; then his son Jeroboam succeeded
him.

17 King Amaziah son of Joash of Judah lived
fifteen years after the death of King Jehoash son of
Jehoahaz of Israel. 18 Now the rest of the deeds of
Amaziah, are they not written in the Book of the
Annals of the Kings of Judah? 19 They made a conspiracy against him in Jerusalem, and he fled to
Lachish. But they sent after him to Lachish, and
killed him there. 20 They brought him on horses;
he was buried in Jerusalem with his ancestors in
the city of David. 21 All the people of Judah took
Azariah, who was sixteen years old, and made
him king to succeed his father Amaziah. 22 He
rebuilt Elath and restored it to Judah, after King
Amaziah[a] slept with his ancestors.

23 In the fifteenth year of King Amaziah son
of Joash of Judah, King Jeroboam son of Joash of
Israel began to reign in Samaria; he reigned forty-
one years. 24 He did what was evil in the sight of
the LORD; he did not depart from all the sins of
Jeroboam son of Nebat, which he caused Israel to
sin. 25 He restored the border of Israel from Lebo-
hamath as far as the Sea of the Arabah, according
to the word of the LORD, the God of Israel, which
he spoke by his servant Jonah son of Amittai, the
prophet, who was from Gath-hepher. 26 For the
LORD saw that the distress of Israel was very bitter; there was no one left, bond or free, and no
one to help Israel. 27 But the LORD had not said
that he would blot out the name of Israel from
under heaven, so he saved them by the hand of
Jeroboam son of Joash.

28 Now the rest of the acts of Jeroboam, and
all that he did, and his might, how he fought,
and how he recovered for Israel Damascus and
Hamath, which had belonged to Judah, are they
not written in the Book of the Annals of the Kings
of Israel? 29 Jeroboam slept with his ancestors, the
kings of Israel; his son Zechariah succeeded him.

15 In the twenty-seventh year of King Jeroboam of Israel King Azariah son of Amaziah of Judah began to reign. 2 He was sixteen
years old when he began to reign, and he reigned
fifty-two years in Jerusalem. His mother's name
was Jecoliah of Jerusalem. 3 He did what was right
in the sight of the LORD, just as his father Amaziah had done. 4 Nevertheless the high places were
not taken away; the people still sacrificed and
made offerings on the high places. 5 The LORD

[a] Heb *the king*

struck the king, so that he was leprous[a] to the day
of his death, and lived in a separate house. Jotham
the king's son was in charge of the palace, governing the people of the land. 6 Now the rest of the
acts of Azariah, and all that he did, are they not
written in the Book of the Annals of the Kings
of Judah? 7 Azariah slept with his ancestors; they
buried him with his ancestors in the city of David; his son Jotham succeeded him.

8 In the thirty-eighth year of King Azariah of
Judah, Zechariah son of Jeroboam reigned over
Israel in Samaria six months. 9 He did what was
evil in the sight of the LORD, as his ancestors had
done. He did not depart from the sins of Jeroboam son of Nebat, which he caused Israel to sin.
10 Shallum son of Jabesh conspired against him,
and struck him down in public and killed him,
and reigned in place of him. 11 Now the rest of
the deeds of Zechariah are written in the Book of
the Annals of the Kings of Israel. 12 This was the
promise of the LORD that he gave to Jehu, "Your
sons shall sit on the throne of Israel to the fourth
generation." And so it happened.

13 Shallum son of Jabesh began to reign in
the thirty-ninth year of King Uzziah of Judah; he
reigned one month in Samaria. 14 Then Menahem
son of Gadi came up from Tirzah and came to
Samaria; he struck down Shallum son of Jabesh
in Samaria and killed him; he reigned in place of
him. 15 Now the rest of the deeds of Shallum, including the conspiracy that he made, are written
in the Book of the Annals of the Kings of Israel.
16 At that time Menahem sacked Tiphsah, all who
were in it and its territory from Tirzah on; because they did not open it to him, he sacked it.
He ripped open all the pregnant women in it.

17 In the thirty-ninth year of King Azariah
of Judah, Menahem son of Gadi began to reign
over Israel; he reigned ten years in Samaria. 18 He
did what was evil in the sight of the LORD; he did
not depart all his days from any of the sins of Jeroboam son of Nebat, which he caused Israel to
sin. 19 King Pul of Assyria came against the land;
Menahem gave Pul a thousand talents of silver,
so that he might help him confirm his hold on
the royal power. 20 Menahem exacted the money
from Israel, that is, from all the wealthy, fifty shekels of silver from each one, to give to the king of
Assyria. So the king of Assyria turned back, and
did not stay there in the land. 21 Now the rest of
the deeds of Menahem, and all that he did, are
they not written in the Book of the Annals of the
Kings of Israel? 22 Menahem slept with his ancestors, and his son Pekahiah succeeded him.

23 In the fiftieth year of King Azariah of Judah, Pekahiah son of Menahem began to reign
over Israel in Samaria; he reigned two years. 24 He
did what was evil in the sight of the LORD; he did
not turn away from the sins of Jeroboam son of
Nebat, which he caused Israel to sin. 25 Pekah son
of Remaliah, his captain, conspired against him
with fifty of the Gileadites, and attacked him in
Samaria, in the citadel of the palace along with
Argob and Arieh; he killed him, and reigned in
place of him. 26 Now the rest of the deeds of Pekahiah, and all that he did, are written in the Book
of the Annals of the Kings of Israel.

27 In the fifty-second year of King Azariah of
Judah, Pekah son of Remaliah began to reign over
Israel in Samaria; he reigned twenty years. 28 He
did what was evil in the sight of the LORD; he did
not depart from the sins of Jeroboam son of Nebat, which he caused Israel to sin.

29 In the days of King Pekah of Israel, King
Tiglath-pileser of Assyria came and captured
Ijon, Abel-beth-maacah, Janoah, Kedesh, Hazor,
Gilead, and Galilee, all the land of Naphtali; and
he carried the people captive to Assyria. 30 Then
Hoshea son of Elah made a conspiracy against
Pekah son of Remaliah, attacked him, and killed
him; he reigned in place of him, in the twentieth
year of Jotham son of Uzziah. 31 Now the rest of
the acts of Pekah, and all that he did, are written
in the Book of the Annals of the Kings of Israel.

32 In the second year of King Pekah son of
Remaliah of Israel, King Jotham son of Uzziah of
Judah began to reign. 33 He was twenty-five years
old when he began to reign and reigned sixteen
years in Jerusalem. His mother's name was Je-
rusha daughter of Zadok. 34 He did what was right

[a] A term for several skin diseases; precise meaning uncertain

in the sight of the LORD, just as his father Uzziah had done. 35 Nevertheless the high places were not removed; the people still sacrificed and made offerings on the high places. He built the upper gate of the house of the LORD. 36 Now the rest of the acts of Jotham, and all that he did, are they not written in the Book of the Annals of the Kings of Judah? 37 In those days the LORD began to send King Rezin of Aram and Pekah son of Remaliah against Judah. 38 Jotham slept with his ancestors, and was buried with his ancestors in the city of David, his ancestor; his son Ahaz succeeded him.

16 In the seventeenth year of Pekah son of Remaliah, King Ahaz son of Jotham of Judah began to reign. 2 Ahaz was twenty years old when he began to reign; he reigned sixteen years in Jerusalem. He did not do what was right in the sight of the LORD his God, as his ancestor David had done, 3 but he walked in the way of the kings of Israel. He even made his son pass through fire, according to the abominable practices of the nations whom the LORD drove out before the people of Israel. 4 He sacrificed and made offerings on the high places, on the hills, and under every green tree.

5 Then King Rezin of Aram and King Pekah son of Remaliah of Israel came up to wage war on Jerusalem; they besieged Ahaz but could not conquer him. 6 At that time the king of Edom[a] recovered Elath for Edom,[b] and drove the Judeans from Elath; and the Edomites came to Elath, where they live to this day. 7 Ahaz sent messengers to King Tiglath-pileser of Assyria, saying, "I am your servant and your son. Come up, and rescue me from the hand of the king of Aram and from the hand of the king of Israel, who are attacking me." 8 Ahaz also took the silver and gold found in the house of the LORD and in the treasures of the king's house, and sent a present to the king of Assyria. 9 The king of Assyria listened to him; the king of Assyria marched up against Damascus, and took it, carrying its people captive to Kir; then he killed Rezin.

10 When King Ahaz went to Damascus to meet King Tiglath-pileser of Assyria, he saw the altar that was at Damascus. King Ahaz sent to the priest Uriah a model of the altar, and its pattern, exact in all its details. 11 The priest Uriah built the altar; in accordance with all that King Ahaz had sent from Damascus, just so did the priest Uriah build it, before King Ahaz arrived from Damascus. 12 When the king came from Damascus, the king viewed the altar. Then the king drew near to the altar, went up on it, 13 and offered his burnt offering and his grain offering, poured his drink offering, and dashed the blood of his offerings of well-being against the altar. 14 The bronze altar that was before the LORD he removed from the front of the house, from the place between his altar and the house of the LORD, and put it on the north side of his altar. 15 King Ahaz commanded the priest Uriah, saying, "Upon the great altar offer the morning burnt offering, and the evening grain offering, and the king's burnt offering, and his grain offering, with the burnt offering of all the people of the land, their grain offering, and their drink offering; then dash against it all the blood of the burnt offering, and all the blood of the sacrifice; but the bronze altar shall be for me to inquire by." 16 The priest Uriah did everything that King Ahaz commanded.

17 Then King Ahaz cut off the frames of the stands, and removed the laver from them; he removed the sea from the bronze oxen that were under it, and put it on a pediment of stone. 18 The covered portal for use on the sabbath that had been built inside the palace, and the outer entrance for the king he removed from[c] the house of the LORD. He did this because of the king of Assyria. 19 Now the rest of the acts of Ahaz that he did, are they not written in the Book of the Annals of the Kings of Judah? 20 Ahaz slept with his ancestors, and was buried with his ancestors in the city of David; his son Hezekiah succeeded him.

17 In the twelfth year of King Ahaz of Judah, Hoshea son of Elah began to reign in Samaria over Israel; he reigned nine years. 2 He did what was evil in the sight of the LORD, yet not like the kings of Israel who were before him. 3 King

[a] Cn: Heb *King Rezin of Aram* [b] Cn: Heb *Aram* [c] Cn: Heb lacks *from*

Shalmaneser of Assyria came up against him; Hoshea became his vassal, and paid him tribute. 4 But the king of Assyria found treachery in Hoshea; for he had sent messengers to King So of Egypt, and offered no tribute to the king of Assyria, as he had done year by year; therefore the king of Assyria confined him and imprisoned him.

5 Then the king of Assyria invaded all the land and came to Samaria; for three years he besieged it. 6 In the ninth year of Hoshea the king of Assyria captured Samaria; he carried the Israelites away to Assyria. He placed them in Halah, on the Habor, the river of Gozan, and in the cities of the Medes.

7 This occurred because the people of Israel had sinned against the LORD their God, who had brought them up out of the land of Egypt from under the hand of Pharaoh king of Egypt. They had worshiped other gods 8 and walked in the customs of the nations whom the LORD drove out before the people of Israel, and in the customs that the kings of Israel had introduced.[a] 9 The people of Israel secretly did things that were not right against the LORD their God. They built for themselves high places at all their towns, from watchtower to fortified city; 10 they set up for themselves pillars and sacred poles[b] on every high hill and under every green tree; 11 there they made offerings on all the high places, as the nations did whom the LORD carried away before them. They did wicked things, provoking the LORD to anger; 12 they served idols, of which the LORD had said to them, "You shall not do this." 13 Yet the LORD warned Israel and Judah by every prophet and every seer, saying, "Turn from your evil ways and keep my commandments and my statutes, in accordance with all the law that I commanded your ancestors and that I sent to you by my servants the prophets." 14 They would not listen but were stubborn, as their ancestors had been, who did not believe in the LORD their God. 15 They despised his statutes, and his covenant that he made with their ancestors, and the warnings that he gave them. They went after false idols and became false; they followed the nations that were around them, concerning whom the LORD had commanded them that they should not do as they did. 16 They rejected all the commandments of the LORD their God and made for themselves cast images of two calves; they made a sacred pole,[c] worshiped all the host of heaven, and served Baal. 17 They made their sons and their daughters pass through fire; they used divination and augury; and they sold themselves to do evil in the sight of the LORD, provoking him to anger. 18 Therefore the LORD was very angry with Israel and removed them out of his sight; none was left but the tribe of Judah alone.

19 Judah also did not keep the commandments of the LORD their God but walked in the customs that Israel had introduced. 20 The LORD rejected all the descendants of Israel; he punished them and gave them into the hand of plunderers, until he had banished them from his presence.

21 When he had torn Israel from the house of David, they made Jeroboam son of Nebat king. Jeroboam drove Israel from following the LORD and made them commit great sin. 22 The people of Israel continued in all the sins that Jeroboam committed; they did not depart from them 23 until the LORD removed Israel out of his sight, as he had foretold through all his servants the prophets. So Israel was exiled from their own land to Assyria until this day.

24 The king of Assyria brought people from Babylon, Cuthah, Avva, Hamath, and Sepharvaim, and placed them in the cities of Samaria in place of the people of Israel; they took possession of Samaria, and settled in its cities. 25 When they first settled there, they did not worship the LORD; therefore the LORD sent lions among them, which killed some of them. 26 So the king of Assyria was told, "The nations that you have carried away and placed in the cities of Samaria do not know the law of the god of the land; therefore he has sent lions among them; they are killing them, because they do not know the law of the god of the land." 27 Then the king of Assyria commanded, "Send there one of the priests whom you carried away from there; let him[d] go and live there, and teach

[a] Meaning of Heb uncertain [b] Heb *Asherim* [c] Heb *Asherah* [d] Syr Vg: Heb *them*

2 Kings 17:24-28

What is the relationship between the citizens of Samaria, the capital city of the Northern Kingdom, and the hated Samaritans of the New Testament? Many of the original Samarians were exiled by the Assyrians when Samaria fell in 720 BCE. The poor and unskilled were left behind and joined by forced migrants from other subjugated peoples. Along with diverse ethnic origins, the groups have diverse religious practices. Because a Levite priest must be brought in to teach them to worship the God of Israel to stave off lion attacks, they are regarded as having insincere, inadequate faith. The groups intermarried and became the people known as Samaritans.

— *WG*

them the law of the god of the land." 28So one of
the priests whom they had carried away from Samaria came and lived in Bethel; he taught them
how they should worship the LORD.
29 But every nation still made gods of its own
and put them in the shrines of the high places
that the people of Samaria had made, every nation in the cities in which they lived; 30the people
of Babylon made Succoth-benoth, the people of
Cuth made Nergal, the people of Hamath made
Ashima; 31the Avvites made Nibhaz and Tartak;
the Sepharvites burned their children in the fire
to Adrammelech and Anammelech, the gods of
Sepharvaim. 32They also worshiped the LORD
and appointed from among themselves all sorts
of people as priests of the high places, who sacrificed for them in the shrines of the high places.
33So they worshiped the LORD but also served
their own gods, after the manner of the nations
from among whom they had been carried away.
34To this day they continue to practice their former customs.
They do not worship the LORD and they do not
follow the statutes or the ordinances or the law or
the commandment that the LORD commanded
the children of Jacob, whom he named Israel.
35The LORD had made a covenant with them and
commanded them, "You shall not worship other
gods or bow yourselves to them or serve them
or sacrifice to them, 36but you shall worship the
LORD, who brought you out of the land of Egypt
with great power and with an outstretched arm;
you shall bow yourselves to him, and to him you
shall sacrifice. 37The statutes and the ordinances
and the law and the commandment that he wrote
for you, you shall always be careful to observe.
You shall not worship other gods; 38you shall
not forget the covenant that I have made with
you. You shall not worship other gods, 39but you
shall worship the LORD your God; he will deliver
you out of the hand of all your enemies." 40They
would not listen, however, but they continued to
practice their former custom.
41 So these nations worshiped the LORD, but
also served their carved images; to this day their
children and their children's children continue to
do as their ancestors did.

18 In the third year of King Hoshea son of
Elah of Israel, Hezekiah son of King Ahaz
of Judah began to reign. 2He was twenty-five years
old when he began to reign; he reigned twenty-
nine years in Jerusalem. His mother's name was
Abi daughter of Zechariah. 3He did what was
right in the sight of the LORD just as his ancestor
David had done. 4He removed the high places,
broke down the pillars, and cut down the sacred
pole.[a] He broke in pieces the bronze serpent that
Moses had made, for until those days the people
of Israel had made offerings to it; it was called
Nehushtan. 5He trusted in the LORD the God of
Israel; so that there was no one like him among all
the kings of Judah after him, or among those who
were before him. 6For he held fast to the LORD;
he did not depart from following him but kept
the commandments that the LORD commanded
Moses. 7The LORD was with him; wherever he
went, he prospered. He rebelled against the king
of Assyria and would not serve him. 8He attacked
the Philistines as far as Gaza and its territory,
from watchtower to fortified city.
9 In the fourth year of King Hezekiah, which

[a] Heb *Asherah*

was the seventh year of King Hoshea son of Elah of Israel, King Shalmaneser of Assyria came up against Samaria, besieged it, [10]and at the end of three years, took it. In the sixth year of Hezekiah, which was the ninth year of King Hoshea of Israel, Samaria was taken. [11]The king of Assyria carried the Israelites away to Assyria, settled them in Halah, on the Habor, the river of Gozan, and in the cities of the Medes, [12]because they did not obey the voice of the LORD their God but transgressed his covenant—all that Moses the servant of the LORD had commanded; they neither listened nor obeyed.

13 In the fourteenth year of King Hezekiah, King Sennacherib of Assyria came up against all the fortified cities of Judah and captured them. [14]King Hezekiah of Judah sent to the king of Assyria at Lachish, saying, "I have done wrong; withdraw from me; whatever you impose on me I will bear." The king of Assyria demanded of King Hezekiah of Judah three hundred talents of silver and thirty talents of gold. [15]Hezekiah gave him all the silver that was found in the house of the LORD and in the treasuries of the king's house. [16]At that time Hezekiah stripped the gold from the doors of the temple of the LORD, and from the doorposts that King Hezekiah of Judah had overlaid and gave it to the king of Assyria. [17]The king of Assyria sent the Tartan, the Rabsaris, and the Rabshakeh with a great army from Lachish to King Hezekiah at Jerusalem. They went up and came to Jerusalem. When they arrived, they came and stood by the conduit of the upper pool, which is on the highway to the Fuller's Field. [18]When they called for the king, there came out to them Eliakim son of Hilkiah, who was in charge of the palace, and Shebnah the secretary, and Joah son of Asaph, the recorder.

19 The Rabshakeh said to them, "Say to Hezekiah: Thus says the great king, the king of Assyria: On what do you base this confidence of yours? [20]Do you think that mere words are strategy and power for war? On whom do you now rely, that you have rebelled against me? [21]See, you are relying now on Egypt, that broken reed of a staff, which will pierce the hand of anyone who leans on it. Such is Pharaoh king of Egypt to all who rely on him. [22]But if you say to me, 'We rely on the LORD our God,' is it not he whose high places and altars Hezekiah has removed, saying to Judah and to Jerusalem, 'You shall worship before this altar in Jerusalem'? [23]Come now, make a wager with my master the king of Assyria: I will give you two thousand horses, if you are able on your part to set riders on them. [24]How then can you repulse a single captain among the least of my master's servants, when you rely on Egypt for chariots and for horsemen? [25]Moreover, is it without the LORD that I have come up against this place to destroy it? The LORD said to me, Go up against this land, and destroy it."

26 Then Eliakim son of Hilkiah, and Shebnah, and Joah said to the Rabshakeh, "Please speak to your servants in the Aramaic language, for we understand it; do not speak to us in the language of Judah within the hearing of the people who are on the wall." [27]But the Rabshakeh said to them, "Has my master sent me to speak these words to your master and to you, and not to the people sitting on the wall, who are doomed with you to eat their own dung and to drink their own urine?"

28 Then the Rabshakeh stood and called out in a loud voice in the language of Judah, "Hear the word of the great king, the king of Assyria! [29]Thus says the king: 'Do not let Hezekiah deceive you, for he will not be able to deliver you out of my hand. [30]Do not let Hezekiah make you rely on the LORD by saying, The LORD will surely deliver us, and this city will not be given into the hand of the king of Assyria.' [31]Do not listen to Hezekiah; for thus says the king of Assyria: 'Make your peace with me and come out to me; then every one of you will eat from your own vine and your own fig tree, and drink water from your own cistern, [32]until I come and take you away to a land like your own land, a land of grain and wine, a land of bread and vineyards, a land of olive oil and honey, that you may live and not die. Do not listen to Hezekiah when he misleads you by saying, The LORD will deliver us. [33]Has any of the gods of the nations ever delivered its land out of the hand of the king of Assyria? [34]Where are the gods of Hamath and Arpad? Where are the gods of Sepharvaim, Hena, and Ivvah? Have they de-

livered Samaria out of my hand? 35 Who among
all the gods of the countries have delivered their
countries out of my hand, that the LORD should
deliver Jerusalem out of my hand?' "

36 But the people were silent and answered
him not a word, for the king's command was, "Do
not answer him." 37 Then Eliakim son of Hilkiah,
who was in charge of the palace, and Shebna the
secretary, and Joah son of Asaph, the recorder,
came to Hezekiah with their clothes torn and told
him the words of the Rabshakeh.

19 When King Hezekiah heard it, he tore his
clothes, covered himself with sackcloth,
and went into the house of the LORD. 2 And he
sent Eliakim, who was in charge of the palace, and
Shebna the secretary, and the senior priests, covered with sackcloth, to the prophet Isaiah son of
Amoz. 3 They said to him, "Thus says Hezekiah,
This day is a day of distress, of rebuke, and of disgrace; children have come to the birth, and there
is no strength to bring them forth. 4 It may be that
the LORD your God heard all the words of the
Rabshakeh, whom his master the king of Assyria
has sent to mock the living God, and will rebuke
the words that the LORD your God has heard;
therefore lift up your prayer for the remnant that
is left." 5 When the servants of King Hezekiah
came to Isaiah, 6 Isaiah said to them, "Say to your
master, 'Thus says the LORD: Do not be afraid
because of the words that you have heard, with
which the servants of the king of Assyria have
reviled me. 7 I myself will put a spirit in him, so
that he shall hear a rumor and return to his own
land; I will cause him to fall by the sword in his
own land.' "

8 The Rabshakeh returned, and found the
king of Assyria fighting against Libnah; for he
had heard that the king had left Lachish. 9 When
the king[a] heard concerning King Tirhakah of
Ethiopia,[b] "See, he has set out to fight against
you," he sent messengers again to Hezekiah, saying, 10 "Thus shall you speak to King Hezekiah of
Judah: Do not let your God on whom you rely deceive you by promising that Jerusalem will not be
given into the hand of the king of Assyria. 11 See,
you have heard what the kings of Assyria have
done to all lands, destroying them utterly. Shall
you be delivered? 12 Have the gods of the nations
delivered them, the nations that my predecessors destroyed, Gozan, Haran, Rezeph, and the
people of Eden who were in Telassar? 13 Where is
the king of Hamath, the king of Arpad, the king of
the city of Sepharvaim, the king of Hena, or the
king of Ivvah?"

14 Hezekiah received the letter from the hand
of the messengers and read it; then Hezekiah
went up to the house of the LORD and spread it
before the LORD. 15 And Hezekiah prayed before
the LORD, and said: "O LORD the God of Israel,
who are enthroned above the cherubim, you are
God, you alone, of all the kingdoms of the earth;
you have made heaven and earth. 16 Incline your
ear, O LORD, and hear; open your eyes, O LORD,
and see; hear the words of Sennacherib, which he
has sent to mock the living God. 17 Truly, O LORD,
the kings of Assyria have laid waste the nations
and their lands, 18 and have hurled their gods into
the fire, though they were no gods but the work
of human hands—wood and stone—and so they
were destroyed. 19 So now, O LORD our God, save
us, I pray you, from his hand, so that all the kingdoms of the earth may know that you, O LORD,
are God alone."

20 Then Isaiah son of Amoz sent to Hezekiah,
saying, "Thus says the LORD, the God of Israel:
I have heard your prayer to me about King Sennacherib of Assyria. 21 This is the word that the
LORD has spoken concerning him:

She despises you, she scorns you—
  virgin daughter Zion;
she tosses her head—behind your back,
  daughter Jerusalem.

22 "Whom have you mocked and reviled?
  Against whom have you raised your voice
and haughtily lifted your eyes?
  Against the Holy One of Israel!
23 By your messengers you have mocked the
    Lord,
  and you have said, 'With my many chariots

[a] Heb *he* [b] Or *Nubia*; Heb *Cush*

I have gone up the heights of the mountains,
to the far recesses of Lebanon;
I felled its tallest cedars,
its choicest cypresses;
I entered its farthest retreat,
its densest forest.
24 I dug wells
and drank foreign waters,
I dried up with the sole of my foot
all the streams of Egypt.'

25 "Have you not heard
that I determined it long ago?
I planned from days of old
what now I bring to pass,
that you should make fortified cities
crash into heaps of ruins,
26 while their inhabitants, shorn of strength,
are dismayed and confounded;
they have become like plants of the field
and like tender grass,
like grass on the housetops,
blighted before it is grown.

27 "But I know your rising[a] and your sitting,
your going out and coming in,
and your raging against me.
28 Because you have raged against me
and your arrogance has come to my ears,
I will put my hook in your nose
and my bit in your mouth;
I will turn you back on the way
by which you came.

29 "And this shall be the sign for you: This
year you shall eat what grows of itself, and in the
second year what springs from that; then in the
third year sow, reap, plant vineyards, and eat their
fruit. 30 The surviving remnant of the house of Judah shall again take root downward, and bear fruit
upward; 31 for from Jerusalem a remnant shall go
out, and from Mount Zion a band of survivors.
The zeal of the LORD of hosts will do this.
32 "Therefore thus says the LORD concerning
the king of Assyria: He shall not come into this
city, shoot an arrow there, come before it with a
shield, or cast up a siege ramp against it. 33 By the
way that he came, by the same he shall return; he
shall not come into this city, says the LORD. 34 For
I will defend this city to save it, for my own sake
and for the sake of my servant David."
35 That very night the angel of the LORD set
out and struck down one hundred eighty-five
thousand in the camp of the Assyrians; when
morning dawned, they were all dead bodies.
36 Then King Sennacherib of Assyria left, went
home, and lived at Nineveh. 37 As he was worshiping in the house of his god Nisroch, his sons
Adrammelech and Sharezer killed him with the
sword, and they escaped into the land of Ararat.
His son Esar-haddon succeeded him.

20 In those days Hezekiah became sick and
was at the point of death. The prophet
Isaiah son of Amoz came to him, and said to him,
"Thus says the LORD: Set your house in order, for
you shall die; you shall not recover." 2 Then Hezekiah turned his face to the wall and prayed to the
LORD: 3 "Remember now, O LORD, I implore
you, how I have walked before you in faithfulness
with a whole heart, and have done what is good in
your sight." Hezekiah wept bitterly. 4 Before Isaiah had gone out of the middle court, the word
of the LORD came to him: 5 "Turn back, and say
to Hezekiah prince of my people, Thus says the
LORD, the God of your ancestor David: I have
heard your prayer, I have seen your tears; indeed,
I will heal you; on the third day you shall go up
to the house of the LORD. 6 I will add fifteen years
to your life. I will deliver you and this city out of
the hand of the king of Assyria; I will defend this
city for my own sake and for my servant David's
sake." 7 Then Isaiah said, "Bring a lump of figs. Let
them take it and apply it to the boil, so that he
may recover."
8 Hezekiah said to Isaiah, "What shall be
the sign that the LORD will heal me, and that I
shall go up to the house of the LORD on the third
day?" 9 Isaiah said, "This is the sign to you from
the LORD, that the LORD will do the thing that he
has promised: the shadow has now advanced ten

[a] Gk Compare Isa 37.27 Q Ms: MT lacks *rising*

intervals; shall it retreat ten intervals?" 10Heze-
kiah answered, "It is normal for the shadow to
lengthen ten intervals; rather let the shadow retreat ten intervals." 11The prophet Isaiah cried to
the LORD; and he brought the shadow back the
ten intervals, by which the sun[a] had declined on
the dial of Ahaz.

12 At that time King Merodach-baladan son
of Baladan of Babylon sent envoys with letters
and a present to Hezekiah, for he had heard that
Hezekiah had been sick. 13Hezekiah welcomed
them;[b] he showed them all his treasure house, the
silver, the gold, the spices, the precious oil, his armory, all that was found in his storehouses; there
was nothing in his house or in all his realm that
Hezekiah did not show them. 14Then the prophet
Isaiah came to King Hezekiah, and said to him,
"What did these men say? From where did they
come to you?" Hezekiah answered, "They have
come from a far country, from Babylon." 15He
said, "What have they seen in your house?" Hezekiah answered, "They have seen all that is in my
house; there is nothing in my storehouses that I
did not show them."

16 Then Isaiah said to Hezekiah, "Hear the
word of the LORD: 17Days are coming when all
that is in your house, and that which your ancestors have stored up until this day, shall be carried
to Babylon; nothing shall be left, says the LORD.
18Some of your own sons who are born to you
shall be taken away; they shall be eunuchs in the
palace of the king of Babylon." 19Then Hezekiah
said to Isaiah, "The word of the LORD that you
have spoken is good." For he thought, "Why not,
if there will be peace and security in my days?"

20 The rest of the deeds of Hezekiah, all his
power, how he made the pool and the conduit
and brought water into the city, are they not written in the Book of the Annals of the Kings of Judah? 21Hezekiah slept with his ancestors; and his
son Manasseh succeeded him.

21 Manasseh was twelve years old when he
began to reign; he reigned fifty-five years
in Jerusalem. His mother's name was Hephzibah.
2He did what was evil in the sight of the LORD,
following the abominable practices of the nations that the LORD drove out before the people
of Israel. 3For he rebuilt the high places that his
father Hezekiah had destroyed; he erected altars
for Baal, made a sacred pole,[c] as King Ahab of Israel had done, worshiped all the host of heaven,
and served them. 4He built altars in the house of
the LORD, of which the LORD had said, "In Jerusalem I will put my name." 5He built altars for all
the host of heaven in the two courts of the house
of the LORD. 6He made his son pass through fire;
he practiced soothsaying and augury, and dealt
with mediums and with wizards. He did much
evil in the sight of the LORD, provoking him to
anger. 7The carved image of Asherah that he had
made he set in the house of which the LORD said
to David and to his son Solomon, "In this house,
and in Jerusalem, which I have chosen out of all
the tribes of Israel, I will put my name forever;
8I will not cause the feet of Israel to wander any
more out of the land that I gave to their ancestors, if only they will be careful to do according to
all that I have commanded them, and according
to all the law that my servant Moses commanded
them." 9But they did not listen; Manasseh misled
them to do more evil than the nations had done
that the LORD destroyed before the people of
Israel.

10 The LORD said by his servants the prophets, 11"Because King Manasseh of Judah has committed these abominations, has done things more
wicked than all that the Amorites did, who were
before him, and has caused Judah also to sin with
his idols; 12therefore thus says the LORD, the God
of Israel, I am bringing upon Jerusalem and Judah
such evil that the ears of everyone who hears of
it will tingle. 13I will stretch over Jerusalem the
measuring line for Samaria, and the plummet
for the house of Ahab; I will wipe Jerusalem as
one wipes a dish, wiping it and turning it upside
down. 14I will cast off the remnant of my heritage,
and give them into the hand of their enemies;
they shall become a prey and a spoil to all their
enemies, 15because they have done what is evil
in my sight and have provoked me to anger, since

[a] Syr See Isa 38.8 and Tg: Heb *it* [b] Gk Vg Syr: Heb *When Hezekiah heard about them* [c] Heb *Asherah*

the day their ancestors came out of Egypt, even
to this day."
16 Moreover Manasseh shed very much innocent blood, until he had filled Jerusalem from
one end to another, besides the sin that he caused
Judah to sin so that they did what was evil in the
sight of the LORD.
17 Now the rest of the acts of Manasseh, all
that he did, and the sin that he committed, are
they not written in the Book of the Annals of
the Kings of Judah? 18Manasseh slept with his
ancestors, and was buried in the garden of his
house, in the garden of Uzza. His son Amon succeeded him.
19 Amon was twenty-two years old when he
began to reign; he reigned two years in Jerusalem.
His mother's name was Meshullemeth daughter
of Haruz of Jotbah. 20He did what was evil in
the sight of the LORD, as his father Manasseh
had done. 21He walked in all the way in which
his father walked, served the idols that his father
served, and worshiped them; 22he abandoned
the LORD, the God of his ancestors, and did not
walk in the way of the LORD. 23The servants of
Amon conspired against him, and killed the king
in his house. 24But the people of the land killed
all those who had conspired against King Amon,
and the people of the land made his son Josiah
king in place of him. 25Now the rest of the acts
of Amon that he did, are they not written in the
Book of the Annals of the Kings of Judah? 26He
was buried in his tomb in the garden of Uzza;
then his son Josiah succeeded him.

22 Josiah was eight years old when he began
to reign; he reigned thirty-one years in Jerusalem. His mother's name was Jedidah daughter of Adaiah of Bozkath. 2He did what was right
in the sight of the LORD, and walked in all the way
of his father David; he did not turn aside to the
right or to the left.
3 In the eighteenth year of King Josiah, the
king sent Shaphan son of Azaliah, son of Meshullam, the secretary, to the house of the LORD, saying, 4"Go up to the high priest Hilkiah, and have
him count the entire sum of the money that has
been brought into the house of the LORD, which
the keepers of the threshold have collected from
the people; 5let it be given into the hand of the
workers who have the oversight of the house of the
LORD; let them give it to the workers who are at
the house of the LORD, repairing the house, 6that
is, to the carpenters, to the builders, to the masons;
and let them use it to buy timber and quarried
stone to repair the house. 7But no accounting shall
be asked from them for the money that is delivered
into their hand, for they deal honestly."
8 The high priest Hilkiah said to Shaphan the
secretary, "I have found the book of the law in the
house of the LORD." When Hilkiah gave the book
to Shaphan, he read it. 9Then Shaphan the secretary came to the king, and reported to the king,
"Your servants have emptied out the money that
was found in the house, and have delivered it into
the hand of the workers who have oversight of the
house of the LORD." 10Shaphan the secretary informed the king, "The priest Hilkiah has given me
a book." Shaphan then read it aloud to the king.
11 When the king heard the words of the
book of the law, he tore his clothes. 12Then the
king commanded the priest Hilkiah, Ahikam son
of Shaphan, Achbor son of Micaiah, Shaphan the
secretary, and the king's servant Asaiah, saying,
13"Go, inquire of the LORD for me, for the people,
and for all Judah, concerning the words of this
book that has been found; for great is the wrath of
the LORD that is kindled against us, because our
ancestors did not obey the words of this book, to
do according to all that is written concerning us."
14 So the priest Hilkiah, Ahikam, Achbor,
Shaphan, and Asaiah went to the prophetess
Huldah the wife of Shallum son of Tikvah, son
of Harhas, keeper of the wardrobe; she resided in
Jerusalem in the Second Quarter, where they consulted her. 15She declared to them, "Thus says the
LORD, the God of Israel: Tell the man who sent
you to me, 16Thus says the LORD, I will indeed
bring disaster on this place and on its inhabitants—all the words of the book that the king of
Judah has read. 17Because they have abandoned
me and have made offerings to other gods, so that
they have provoked me to anger with all the work
of their hands, therefore my wrath will be kindled
against this place, and it will not be quenched.
18But as to the king of Judah, who sent you to in-

quire of the LORD, thus shall you say to him, Thus
says the LORD, the God of Israel: Regarding the
words that you have heard, 19because your heart
was penitent, and you humbled yourself before
the LORD, when you heard how I spoke against
this place, and against its inhabitants, that they
should become a desolation and a curse, and because you have torn your clothes and wept before
me, I also have heard you, says the LORD. 20There-
fore, I will gather you to your ancestors, and you
shall be gathered to your grave in peace; your eyes
shall not see all the disaster that I will bring on this
place." They took the message back to the king.

23 Then the king directed that all the elders
of Judah and Jerusalem should be gathered to him. 2The king went up to the house of
the LORD, and with him went all the people of Judah, all the inhabitants of Jerusalem, the priests,
the prophets, and all the people, both small and
great; he read in their hearing all the words of the
book of the covenant that had been found in the
house of the LORD. 3The king stood by the pillar
and made a covenant before the LORD, to follow
the LORD, keeping his commandments, his decrees, and his statutes, with all his heart and all
his soul, to perform the words of this covenant
that were written in this book. All the people
joined in the covenant.

4 The king commanded the high priest
Hilkiah, the priests of the second order, and
the guardians of the threshold, to bring out of
the temple of the LORD all the vessels made for
Baal, for Asherah, and for all the host of heaven;
he burned them outside Jerusalem in the fields
of the Kidron, and carried their ashes to Bethel.
5He deposed the idolatrous priests whom the
kings of Judah had ordained to make offerings in
the high places at the cities of Judah and around
Jerusalem; those also who made offerings to Baal,
to the sun, the moon, the constellations, and all
the host of the heavens. 6He brought out the
image of[a] Asherah from the house of the LORD,
outside Jerusalem, to the Wadi Kidron, burned it
at the Wadi Kidron, beat it to dust and threw the
dust of it upon the graves of the common people.
7He broke down the houses of the male temple
prostitutes that were in the house of the LORD,
where the women did weaving for Asherah. 8He
brought all the priests out of the towns of Judah,
and defiled the high places where the priests had
made offerings, from Geba to Beer-sheba; he
broke down the high places of the gates that were
at the entrance of the gate of Joshua the governor of the city, which were on the left at the gate
of the city. 9The priests of the high places, however, did not come up to the altar of the LORD
in Jerusalem, but ate unleavened bread among
their kindred. 10He defiled Topheth, which is in

[a] Heb lacks *image of*

2 Kings 23:10

African-Americans are acutely aware of the high costs of the poor stewardship of human resources in our national life. Dr. C. Eric Lincoln . . . reminds us that our racial madness has exacted an enormous toll of the American potential in the form of poverty, ignorance, race hatred, self-hatred, high mortality, low morality, insecurity, ethical compromise, and selective exclusion of the ordinary common values we all helped to create. Lincoln's description of the loss is jarring: "We shall never know what potential genius, black and white, has been sacrificed to the racial Moloch which designated some of us keepers and others to be kept. . . . What great music was never written; what miracles of medicine remain undiscovered; what strategies for peace and understanding among the nations of the world have never been developed because we have been preoccupied with building fences and closing the doors which eliminate the kept and enervate the keepers . . . to the impairment of our common capacity to get on with the Dream we once dared to believe in?"[25]

— Clarice J. Martin, quoting C. Eric Lincoln

the valley of Ben-hinnom, so that no one would make a son or a daughter pass through fire as an offering to Molech. 11He removed the horses that the kings of Judah had dedicated to the sun, at the entrance to the house of the LORD, by the chamber of the eunuch Nathan-melech, which was in the precincts;[a] then he burned the chariots of the sun with fire. 12The altars on the roof of the upper chamber of Ahaz, which the kings of Judah had made, and the altars that Manasseh had made in the two courts of the house of the LORD, he pulled down from there and broke in pieces, and threw the rubble into the Wadi Kidron. 13The king defiled the high places that were east of Jerusalem, to the south of the Mount of Destruction, which King Solomon of Israel had built for Astarte the abomination of the Sidonians, for Chemosh the abomination of Moab, and for Milcom the abomination of the Ammonites. 14He broke the pillars in pieces, cut down the sacred poles,[b] and covered the sites with human bones.

15 Moreover, the altar at Bethel, the high place erected by Jeroboam son of Nebat, who caused Israel to sin—he pulled down that altar along with the high place. He burned the high place, crushing it to dust; he also burned the sacred pole.[c] 16As Josiah turned, he saw the tombs there on the mount; and he sent and took the bones out of the tombs, and burned them on the altar, and defiled it, according to the word of the LORD that the man of God proclaimed,[d] when Jeroboam stood by the altar at the festival; he turned and looked up at the tomb of the man of God who had predicted these things. 17Then he said, "What is that monument that I see?" The people of the city told him, "It is the tomb of the man of God who came from Judah and predicted these things that you have done against the altar at Bethel." 18He said, "Let him rest; let no one move his bones." So they let his bones alone, with the bones of the prophet who came out of Samaria. 19Moreover, Josiah removed all the shrines of the high places that were in the towns of Samaria, which kings of Israel had made, provoking the LORD to anger; he did to them just as he had done at Bethel. 20He slaughtered on the altars all the priests of the high places who were there, and burned human bones on them. Then he returned to Jerusalem.

21 The king commanded all the people, "Keep the passover to the LORD your God as prescribed in this book of the covenant." 22No such passover had been kept since the days of the judges who judged Israel, even during all the days of the kings of Israel and of the kings of Judah; 23but in the eighteenth year of King Josiah this passover was kept to the LORD in Jerusalem.

24 Moreover Josiah put away the mediums, wizards, teraphim,[e] idols, and all the abominations that were seen in the land of Judah and in Jerusalem, so that he established the words of the law that were written in the book that the priest Hilkiah had found in the house of the LORD. 25Before him there was no king like him, who turned to the LORD with all his heart, with all his soul, and with all his might, according to all the law of Moses; nor did any like him arise after him.

26 Still the LORD did not turn from the fierceness of his great wrath, by which his anger was kindled against Judah, because of all the provocations with which Manasseh had provoked him. 27The LORD said, "I will remove Judah also out of my sight, as I have removed Israel; and I will reject this city that I have chosen, Jerusalem, and the house of which I said, My name shall be there."

28 Now the rest of the acts of Josiah, and all that he did, are they not written in the Book of the Annals of the Kings of Judah? 29In his days Pharaoh Neco king of Egypt went up to the king of Assyria to the river Euphrates. King Josiah went to meet him; but when Pharaoh Neco met him at Megiddo, he killed him. 30His servants carried him dead in a chariot from Megiddo, brought him to Jerusalem, and buried him in his own tomb. The people of the land took Jehoahaz son of Josiah, anointed him, and made him king in place of his father.

[a] Meaning of Heb uncertain [b] Heb *Asherim* [c] Heb *Asherah* [d] Gk: Heb *proclaimed, who had predicted these things*
[e] Or *household gods*

31 Jehoahaz was twenty-three years old when
he began to reign; he reigned three months in Jerusalem. His mother's name was Hamutal daughter of Jeremiah of Libnah. 32He did what was evil
in the sight of the LORD, just as his ancestors had
done. 33Pharaoh Neco confined him at Riblah in
the land of Hamath, so that he might not reign
in Jerusalem, and imposed tribute on the land of
one hundred talents of silver and a talent of gold.
34Pharaoh Neco made Eliakim son of Josiah king
in place of his father Josiah, and changed his name
to Jehoiakim. But he took Jehoahaz away; he
came to Egypt, and died there. 35Jehoiakim gave
the silver and the gold to Pharaoh, but he taxed
the land in order to meet Pharaoh's demand for
money. He exacted the silver and the gold from
the people of the land, from all according to their
assessment, to give it to Pharaoh Neco.

36 Jehoiakim was twenty-five years old when
he began to reign; he reigned eleven years in Jerusalem. His mother's name was Zebidah daughter
of Pedaiah of Rumah. 37He did what was evil in
the sight of the LORD, just as all his ancestors had
done.

24 In his days King Nebuchadnezzar of Babylon came up; Jehoiakim became his servant for three years; then he turned and rebelled
against him. 2The LORD sent against him bands
of the Chaldeans, bands of the Arameans, bands
of the Moabites, and bands of the Ammonites; he
sent them against Judah to destroy it, according
to the word of the LORD that he spoke by his servants the prophets. 3Surely this came upon Judah
at the command of the LORD, to remove them
out of his sight, for the sins of Manasseh, for all
that he had committed, 4and also for the innocent blood that he had shed; for he filled Jerusalem with innocent blood, and the LORD was not
willing to pardon. 5Now the rest of the deeds of
Jehoiakim, and all that he did, are they not written in the Book of the Annals of the Kings of Judah? 6So Jehoiakim slept with his ancestors; then
his son Jehoiachin succeeded him. 7The king of
Egypt did not come again out of his land, for the
king of Babylon had taken over all that belonged
to the king of Egypt from the Wadi of Egypt to
the River Euphrates.

8 Jehoiachin was eighteen years old when he
began to reign; he reigned three months in Jerusalem. His mother's name was Nehushta daughter of Elnathan of Jerusalem. 9He did what was
evil in the sight of the LORD, just as his father had
done.

10 At that time the servants of King Nebuchadnezzar of Babylon came up to Jerusalem, and
the city was besieged. 11King Nebuchadnezzar of
Babylon came to the city, while his servants were
besieging it; 12King Jehoiachin of Judah gave
himself up to the king of Babylon, himself, his
mother, his servants, his officers, and his palace
officials. The king of Babylon took him prisoner
in the eighth year of his reign.

13 He carried off all the treasures of the
house of the LORD, and the treasures of the king's
house; he cut in pieces all the vessels of gold in
the temple of the LORD, which King Solomon of
Israel had made, all this as the LORD had foretold.
14He carried away all Jerusalem, all the officials,
all the warriors, ten thousand captives, all the artisans and the smiths; no one remained, except
the poorest people of the land. 15He carried away
Jehoiachin to Babylon; the king's mother, the
king's wives, his officials, and the elite of the land,
he took into captivity from Jerusalem to Babylon.
16The king of Babylon brought captive to Babylon
all the men of valor, seven thousand, the artisans
and the smiths, one thousand, all of them strong
and fit for war. 17The king of Babylon made Mattaniah, Jehoiachin's uncle, king in his place, and
changed his name to Zedekiah.

18 Zedekiah was twenty-one years old when
he began to reign; he reigned eleven years in Jerusalem. His mother's name was Hamutal daughter
of Jeremiah of Libnah. 19He did what was evil in
the sight of the LORD, just as Jehoiakim had done.
20Indeed, Jerusalem and Judah so angered the
LORD that he expelled them from his presence.

Zedekiah rebelled against the king of Bab-
25 ylon. 1And in the ninth year of his reign,
in the tenth month, on the tenth day of
the month, King Nebuchadnezzar of Babylon
came with all his army against Jerusalem, and
laid siege to it; they built siegeworks against it
all around. 2So the city was besieged until the

eleventh year of King Zedekiah. 3On the ninth
day of the fourth month the famine became so
severe in the city that there was no food for the
people of the land. 4Then a breach was made
in the city wall;[a] the king with all the soldiers
fled[b] by night by the way of the gate between
the two walls, by the king's garden, though the
Chaldeans were all around the city. They went in
the direction of the Arabah. 5But the army of the
Chaldeans pursued the king, and overtook him in
the plains of Jericho; all his army was scattered,
deserting him. 6Then they captured the king and
brought him up to the king of Babylon at Riblah,
who passed sentence on him. 7They slaughtered
the sons of Zedekiah before his eyes, then put out
the eyes of Zedekiah; they bound him in fetters
and took him to Babylon.

8 In the fifth month, on the seventh day of
the month—which was the nineteenth year of
King Nebuchadnezzar, king of Babylon—Nebuzaradan, the captain of the bodyguard, a servant
of the king of Babylon, came to Jerusalem. 9He
burned the house of the LORD, the king's house,
and all the houses of Jerusalem; every great house
he burned down. 10All the army of the Chaldeans
who were with the captain of the guard broke
down the walls around Jerusalem. 11Nebuzara-
dan the captain of the guard carried into exile
the rest of the people who were left in the city
and the deserters who had defected to the king
of Babylon—all the rest of the population. 12But
the captain of the guard left some of the poorest
people of the land to be vinedressers and tillers
of the soil.

13 The bronze pillars that were in the house
of the LORD, as well as the stands and the
bronze sea that were in the house of the LORD,
the Chaldeans broke in pieces, and carried the
bronze to Babylon. 14They took away the pots,
the shovels, the snuffers, the dishes for incense,
and all the bronze vessels used in the temple service, 15as well as the firepans and the basins. What
was made of gold the captain of the guard took
away for the gold, and what was made of silver,
for the silver. 16As for the two pillars, the one sea,
and the stands, which Solomon had made for the
house of the LORD, the bronze of all these vessels
was beyond weighing. 17The height of the one
pillar was eighteen cubits, and on it was a bronze
capital; the height of the capital was three cubits;
latticework and pomegranates, all of bronze, were
on the capital all around. The second pillar had
the same, with the latticework.

18 The captain of the guard took the chief
priest Seraiah, the second priest Zephaniah, and
the three guardians of the threshold; 19from the
city he took an officer who had been in command
of the soldiers, and five men of the king's council
who were found in the city; the secretary who was
the commander of the army who mustered the
people of the land; and sixty men of the people
of the land who were found in the city. 20Nebu-
zaradan the captain of the guard took them, and
brought them to the king of Babylon at Riblah.
21The king of Babylon struck them down and put
them to death at Riblah in the land of Hamath. So
Judah went into exile out of its land.

22 He appointed Gedaliah son of Ahikam
son of Shaphan as governor over the people who
remained in the land of Judah, whom King Nebuchadnezzar of Babylon had left. 23Now when all
the captains of the forces and their men heard
that the king of Babylon had appointed Gedaliah
as governor, they came with their men to Gedaliah at Mizpah, namely, Ishmael son of Nethaniah,
Johanan son of Kareah, Seraiah son of Tanhumeth the Netophathite, and Jaazaniah son of the
Maacathite. 24Gedaliah swore to them and their
men, saying, "Do not be afraid because of the
Chaldean officials; live in the land, serve the king
of Babylon, and it shall be well with you." 25But
in the seventh month, Ishmael son of Nethaniah
son of Elishama, of the royal family, came with
ten men; they struck down Gedaliah so that he
died, along with the Judeans and Chaldeans who
were with him at Mizpah. 26Then all the people,
high and low,[c] and the captains of the forces set
out and went to Egypt; for they were afraid of the
Chaldeans.

27 In the thirty-seventh year of the exile of

[a] Heb lacks *wall* [b] Gk Compare Jer 39.4; 52.7: Heb lacks *the king* and lacks *fled* [c] Or *young and old*

King Jehoiachin of Judah, in the twelfth month, on the twenty-seventh day of the month, King Evil-merodach of Babylon, in the year that he began to reign, released King Jehoiachin of Judah from prison; 28he spoke kindly to him, and gave him a seat above the other seats of the kings who were with him in Babylon. 29So Jehoiachin put aside his prison clothes. Every day of his life he dined regularly in the king's presence. 30For his allowance, a regular allowance was given him by the king, a portion every day, as long as he lived.

1 Chronicles

The books of Chronicles are inspired by the events of Israel's exile in Babylon and the return from exile. In recounting these events, Chronicles reconstructs a distinct cultural memory of the people of Israel. For the Chronicler (as the anonymous author of these books is known), the exile and return represent far more than theological metaphors. From beginning to end, these traumatic events ordered all of Israel's past into a tension between two fundamental experiences: sojourning and settlement. Hence the readers of Chronicles are led to remember a people who were once "strangers in the land, wandering from nation to nation" (1 Chr 16:19-20), whom YHWH then "brought… out of the land of Egypt" (2 Chr 7:22; see 1Chr 17:5, 21; 2 Chr 5:10; 20:10) to live in "the land that you [YHWH] gave to them and to their ancestors" (2 Chr 6:25; see 1 Chr 16:18; 22:18; 28:8; 2 Chr 33:8). The tension between sojourn and settlement, exile and return not only brings structure to the Chronicler's memory of ancient Israel; it also defines Israel's experience in terms of its relationship to the Neo-Babylonian and Persian empires that shaped—and ultimately shattered—Israel's monarchical past.

It is apparent that in Judah's exile (587 BCE), key aspects of Israel's past were subsumed to the ideological requirements of the Neo-Babylonian Empire. As with any event in which peoples are displaced from their territories, the exile had the consequence of effacing some of the crucial particularities of Israelite identity and silencing the subjects who constituted it, such as the tribes of Judah, Levi, and Benjamin, the Davidic dynasty, the Levites, the Jerusalem temple, the priesthood, and the Judean cult. These subjects of ancient Israel's past re-emerge in the books of Chronicles in such a way as to allow the Jews returning from exile to recover a collective Israelite identity. As with any recovery of cultural identity, the Chronicler turns to the resources of the past: archives, including genealogical records, the writings of prophets, and royal court records, many of which are cited explicitly, and (in the view of many scholars) the books of Samuel and Kings as well. The Chronicler combines these resources to forge a text that will transmit a collective Israelite identity and mobilize support for Israel's cultic and political institutions. Throughout the text the Chronicler reveals that the archives on which he draws are a record of Israel's past at the same time that it points to the people's future.

The books of Chronicles can be divided into three major sections. First comes the genealogical section (1 Chr 1–9). This section merits readers' close attention and critical consideration, for in it, the Chronicler legitimates Israel's divine claim to land ownership and governance in the region of Palestine. The genealogies do not merely summarize the prehistory of Israel and Judah before the monarchical period and the temple system; the lists are a strategically crafted composition that attempts to delineate the true Israel. Although imbued with theological meaning, the genealogical

lists address the question of identity and inheritance in a very immediate way. The next sections are the accounts of David and Solomon (1 Chr 10—2 Chr 9); and the accounts of the kings of Judah (2 Chr 10–36). The whole comes to a conclusion on a note of hope (2 Chr 36:22-23) that in Jewish tradition is the final word in Scripture.

As a self-identified Mexican American from the Southwest, my reading of the exilic context of 1 Chronicles is informed profoundly by the Hispanic American reality and experience of exile in the United States. As an academic in biblical studies, I find that the Jewish experience of Diaspora in 587 BCE becomes an unavoidable frame of reference because of its pertinence to the development of the Hebrew Bible.

— ***Gregory Lee Cuéllar***

1 Adam, Seth, Enosh; 2 Kenan, Mahalalel, Jared; 3 Enoch, Methuselah, Lamech; 4 Noah,
Shem, Ham, and Japheth.
5 The descendants of Japheth: Gomer, Magog, Madai, Javan, Tubal, Meshech, and Tiras.
6 The descendants of Gomer: Ashkenaz, Diphath,[a]
and Togarmah. 7 The descendants of Javan: Elishah, Tarshish, Kittim, and Rodanim.[b]
8 The descendants of Ham: Cush, Egypt, Put,
and Canaan. 9 The descendants of Cush: Seba,
Havilah, Sabta, Raama, and Sabteca. The descendants of Raamah: Sheba and Dedan. 10 Cush became the father of Nimrod; he was the first to be
a mighty one on the earth.
11 Egypt became the father of Ludim,
Anamim, Lehabim, Naphtuhim, 12 Pathrusim,
Casluhim, and Caphtorim, from whom the Philistines come.[c]
13 Canaan became the father of Sidon his
firstborn, and Heth, 14 and the Jebusites, the
Amorites, the Girgashites, 15 the Hivites, the
Arkites, the Sinites, 16 the Arvadites, the Zemarites, and the Hamathites.
17 The descendants of Shem: Elam, Asshur,
Arpachshad, Lud, Aram, Uz, Hul, Gether, and
Meshech.[d] 18 Arpachshad became the father of
Shelah; and Shelah became the father of Eber.
19 To Eber were born two sons: the name of the
one was Peleg (for in his days the earth was divided), and the name of his brother Joktan.
20 Joktan became the father of Almodad, Sheleph,
Hazarmaveth, Jerah, 21 Hadoram, Uzal, Diklah,
22 Ebal, Abimael, Sheba, 23 Ophir, Havilah, and
Jobab; all these were the descendants of Joktan.
24 Shem, Arpachshad, Shelah; 25 Eber, Peleg,
Reu; 26 Serug, Nahor, Terah; 27 Abram, that is,
Abraham.
28 The sons of Abraham: Isaac and Ishmael.
29 These are their genealogies: the firstborn of
Ishmael, Nebaioth; and Kedar, Adbeel, Mibsam,
30 Mishma, Dumah, Massa, Hadad, Tema, 31 Jetur,
Naphish, and Kedemah. These are the sons of Ishmael. 32 The sons of Keturah, Abraham's concubine: she bore Zimran, Jokshan, Medan, Midian,
Ishbak, and Shuah. The sons of Jokshan: Sheba
and Dedan. 33 The sons of Midian: Ephah, Epher,
Hanoch, Abida, and Eldaah. All these were the
descendants of Keturah.

[a] Gen 10.3 *Ripath*; See Gk Vg [b] Gen 10.4 *Dodanim*; See Syr Vg [c] Heb *Casluhim, from which the Philistines come, Caphtorim*; See Am 9.7, Jer 47.4 [d] *Mash* in Gen 10.23

34 Abraham became the father of Isaac. The
sons of Isaac: Esau and Israel. 35 The sons of Esau:
Eliphaz, Reuel, Jeush, Jalam, and Korah. 36 The
sons of Eliphaz: Teman, Omar, Zephi, Gatam,
Kenaz, Timna, and Amalek. 37 The sons of Reuel:
Nahath, Zerah, Shammah, and Mizzah.

38 The sons of Seir: Lotan, Shobal, Zibeon,
Anah, Dishon, Ezer, and Dishan. 39 The sons of
Lotan: Hori and Homam; and Lotan's sister was
Timna. 40 The sons of Shobal: Alian, Manahath,
Ebal, Shephi, and Onam. The sons of Zibeon:
Aiah and Anah. 41 The sons of Anah: Dishon. The
sons of Dishon: Hamran, Eshban, Ithran, and
Cheran. 42 The sons of Ezer: Bilhan, Zaavan, and
Jaakan.[a] The sons of Dishan:[b] Uz and Aran.

43 These are the kings who reigned in the
land of Edom before any king reigned over the
Israelites: Bela son of Beor, whose city was
called Dinhabah. 44 When Bela died, Jobab son of
Zerah of Bozrah succeeded him. 45 When Jobab
died, Husham of the land of the Temanites succeeded him. 46 When Husham died, Hadad son
of Bedad, who defeated Midian in the country
of Moab, succeeded him; and the name of his
city was Avith. 47 When Hadad died, Samlah of
Masrekah succeeded him. 48 When Samlah died,
Shaul[c] of Rehoboth on the Euphrates succeeded
him. 49 When Shaul[c] died, Baal-hanan son of
Achbor succeeded him. 50 When Baal-hanan
died, Hadad succeeded him; the name of his city
was Pai, and his wife's name Mehetabel daughter
of Matred, daughter of Me-zahab. 51 And Hadad
died.

The clans[d] of Edom were: clans[d] Timna, Aliah,[e]
Jetheth, 52 Oholibamah, Elah, Pinon, 53 Kenaz,
Teman, Mibzar, 54 Magdiel, and Iram; these are
the clans[d] of Edom.

2 These are the sons of Israel: Reuben, Simeon,
Levi, Judah, Issachar, Zebulun, 2 Dan, Joseph,
Benjamin, Naphtali, Gad, and Asher. 3 The sons of
Judah: Er, Onan, and Shelah; these three the Ca-
naanite woman Bath-shua bore to him. Now Er,
Judah's firstborn, was wicked in the sight of the
LORD, and he put him to death. 4 His daughter-in-
law Tamar also bore him Perez and Zerah. Judah
had five sons in all.

5 The sons of Perez: Hezron and Hamul.
6 The sons of Zerah: Zimri, Ethan, Heman, Calcol, and Dara,[f] five in all. 7 The sons of Carmi:
Achar, the troubler of Israel, who transgressed in
the matter of the devoted thing; 8 and Ethan's son
was Azariah.

9 The sons of Hezron, who were born to
him: Jerahmeel, Ram, and Chelubai. 10 Ram became the father of Amminadab, and Amminadab became the father of Nahshon, prince of the
sons of Judah. 11 Nahshon became the father of
Salma, Salma of Boaz, 12 Boaz of Obed, Obed of
Jesse. 13 Jesse became the father of Eliab his firstborn, Abinadab the second, Shimea the third,
14 Nethanel the fourth, Raddai the fifth, 15 Ozem
the sixth, David the seventh; 16 and their sisters
were Zeruiah and Abigail. The sons of Zeruiah:
Abishai, Joab, and Asahel, three. 17 Abigail bore
Amasa, and the father of Amasa was Jether the
Ishmaelite.

18 Caleb son of Hezron had children by his
wife Azubah, and by Jerioth; these were her sons:
Jesher, Shobab, and Ardon. 19 When Azubah
died, Caleb married Ephrath, who bore him Hur.
20 Hur became the father of Uri, and Uri became
the father of Bezalel.

21 Afterward Hezron went in to the daughter of Machir father of Gilead, whom he married when he was sixty years old; and she bore
him Segub; 22 and Segub became the father of
Jair, who had twenty-three towns in the land of
Gilead. 23 But Geshur and Aram took from them
Havvoth-jair, Kenath and its villages, sixty towns.
All these were descendants of Machir, father of
Gilead. 24 After the death of Hezron, in Caleb-
ephrathah, Abijah wife of Hezron bore him Ashhur, father of Tekoa.

25 The sons of Jerahmeel, the firstborn of
Hezron: Ram his firstborn, Bunah, Oren, Ozem,
and Ahijah. 26 Jerahmeel also had another wife,
whose name was Atarah; she was the mother of
Onam. 27 The sons of Ram, the firstborn of Je-

[a] Or *and Akan*; See Gen 36.27 [b] See 1.38: Heb *Dishon* [c] Or *Saul* [d] Or *chiefs* [e] Or *Alvah*; See Gen 36.40
[f] Or *Darda*; Compare Syr Tg some Gk Mss; See 1 Kings 4.31

rahmeel: Maaz, Jamin, and Eker. 28The sons of
Onam: Shammai and Jada. The sons of Shammai:
Nadab and Abishur. 29The name of Abishur's
wife was Abihail, and she bore him Ahban and
Molid. 30The sons of Nadab: Seled and Appaim;
and Seled died childless. 31The son[a] of Appaim:
Ishi. The son[a] of Ishi: Sheshan. The son[a] of
Sheshan: Ahlai. 32The sons of Jada, Shammai's
brother: Jether and Jonathan; and Jether died
childless. 33The sons of Jonathan: Peleth and
Zaza. These were the descendants of Jerahmeel.
34Now Sheshan had no sons, only daughters; but
Sheshan had an Egyptian slave, whose name was
Jarha. 35So Sheshan gave his daughter in marriage to his slave Jarha; and she bore him Attai.
36Attai became the father of Nathan, and Nathan
of Zabad. 37Zabad became the father of Ephlal,
and Ephlal of Obed. 38Obed became the father of
Jehu, and Jehu of Azariah. 39Azariah became the
father of Helez, and Helez of Eleasah. 40Eleasah
became the father of Sismai, and Sismai of Shallum. 41Shallum became the father of Jekamiah,
and Jekamiah of Elishama.

42 The sons of Caleb brother of Jerahmeel:
Mesha[b] his firstborn, who was father of Ziph.
The sons of Mareshah father of Hebron. 43The
sons of Hebron: Korah, Tappuah, Rekem, and
Shema. 44Shema became father of Raham, father of Jorkeam; and Rekem became the father
of Shammai. 45The son of Shammai: Maon;
and Maon was the father of Beth-zur. 46Ephah
also, Caleb's concubine, bore Haran, Moza, and
Gazez; and Haran became the father of Gazez.
47The sons of Jahdai: Regem, Jotham, Geshan,
Pelet, Ephah, and Shaaph. 48Maacah, Caleb's
concubine, bore Sheber and Tirhanah. 49She
also bore Shaaph father of Madmannah, Sheva
father of Machbenah and father of Gibea; and
the daughter of Caleb was Achsah. 50These were
the descendants of Caleb.

The sons[c] of Hur the firstborn of Ephrathah:
Shobal father of Kiriath-jearim, 51Salma father
of Bethlehem, and Hareph father of Beth-gader.
52Shobal father of Kiriath-jearim had other sons:
Haroeh, half of the Menuhoth. 53And the families of Kiriath-jearim: the Ithrites, the Puthites,
the Shumathites, and the Mishraites; from these
came the Zorathites and the Eshtaolites. 54The
sons of Salma: Bethlehem, the Netophathites,
Atroth-beth-joab, and half of the Manahathites,
the Zorites. 55The families also of the scribes that
lived at Jabez: the Tirathites, the Shimeathites,
and the Sucathites. These are the Kenites who
came from Hammath, father of the house of
Rechab.

3 These are the sons of David who were born
to him in Hebron: the firstborn Amnon, by
Ahinoam the Jezreelite; the second Daniel, by
Abigail the Carmelite; 2the third Absalom, son of
Maacah, daughter of King Talmai of Geshur; the
fourth Adonijah, son of Haggith; 3the fifth Shephatiah, by Abital; the sixth Ithream, by his wife
Eglah; 4six were born to him in Hebron, where
he reigned for seven years and six months. And
he reigned thirty-three years in Jerusalem. 5These
were born to him in Jerusalem: Shimea, Shobab,
Nathan, and Solomon, four by Bath-shua, daughter of Ammiel; 6then Ibhar, Elishama, Eliphelet,
7Nogah, Nepheg, Japhia, 8Elishama, Eliada, and
Eliphelet, nine. 9All these were David's sons, besides the sons of the concubines; and Tamar was
their sister.

10 The descendants of Solomon: Rehoboam,
Abijah his son, Asa his son, Jehoshaphat his son,
11Joram his son, Ahaziah his son, Joash his son,
12Amaziah his son, Azariah his son, Jotham his
son, 13Ahaz his son, Hezekiah his son, Manasseh
his son, 14Amon his son, Josiah his son. 15The
sons of Josiah: Johanan the firstborn, the second
Jehoiakim, the third Zedekiah, the fourth Shallum. 16The descendants of Jehoiakim: Jeconiah
his son, Zedekiah his son; 17and the sons of Jeconiah, the captive: Shealtiel his son, 18Malchiram,
Pedaiah, Shenazzar, Jekamiah, Hoshama, and
Nedabiah; 19The sons of Pedaiah: Zerubbabel
and Shimei; and the sons of Zerubbabel: Meshullam and Hananiah, and Shelomith was their
sister; 20and Hashubah, Ohel, Berechiah, Hasadiah, and Jushab-hesed, five. 21The sons of Hananiah: Pelatiah and Jeshaiah, his son[d] Rephaiah,

[a] Heb *sons* [b] Gk reads *Mareshah* [c] Gk Vg: Heb *son* [d] Gk Compare Syr Vg: Heb *sons of*

his son[a] Arnan, his son[a] Obadiah, his son[a] Shecaniah. 22 The son[b] of Shecaniah: Shemaiah. And
the sons of Shemaiah: Hattush, Igal, Bariah, Neariah, and Shaphat, six. 23 The sons of Neariah: Elioenai, Hizkiah, and Azrikam, three. 24 The sons
of Elioenai: Hodaviah, Eliashib, Pelaiah, Akkub,
Johanan, Delaiah, and Anani, seven.

4 The sons of Judah: Perez, Hezron, Carmi,
Hur, and Shobal. 2 Reaiah son of Shobal became the father of Jahath, and Jahath became the
father of Ahumai and Lahad. These were the families of the Zorathites. 3 These were the sons[c] of
Etam: Jezreel, Ishma, and Idbash; and the name
of their sister was Hazzelelponi, 4 and Penuel was
the father of Gedor, and Ezer the father of Hu-
shah. These were the sons of Hur, the firstborn of
Ephrathah, the father of Bethlehem. 5 Ashhur father of Tekoa had two wives, Helah and Naarah;
6 Naarah bore him Ahuzzam, Hepher, Temeni,
and Haahashtari.[d] These were the sons of Naarah.
7 The sons of Helah: Zereth, Izhar,[e] and Ethnan.
8 Koz became the father of Anub, Zobebah, and
the families of Aharhel son of Harum. 9 Jabez was
honored more than his brothers; and his mother
named him Jabez, saying, "Because I bore him
in pain." 10 Jabez called on the God of Israel, saying, "Oh that you would bless me and enlarge
my border, and that your hand might be with
me, and that you would keep me from hurt and
harm!" And God granted what he asked. 11 Chelub the brother of Shuhah became the father of
Mehir, who was the father of Eshton. 12 Eshton
became the father of Beth-rapha, Paseah, and
Tehinnah the father of Ir-nahash. These are the
men of Recah. 13 The sons of Kenaz: Othniel and
Seraiah; and the sons of Othniel: Hathath and
Meonothai.[f] 14 Meonothai became the father of
Ophrah; and Seraiah became the father of Joab
father of Ge-harashim,[g] so-called because they
were artisans. 15 The sons of Caleb son of Jephun-
neh: Iru, Elah, and Naam; and the son[b] of Elah:
Kenaz. 16 The sons of Jehallelel: Ziph, Ziphah,
Tiria, and Asarel. 17 The sons of Ezrah: Jether,
Mered, Epher, and Jalon. These are the sons of
Bithiah, daughter of Pharaoh, whom Mered
married;[h] and she conceived and bore[i] Miriam,
Shammai, and Ishbah father of Eshtemoa. 18 And
his Judean wife bore Jered father of Gedor, Heber
father of Soco, and Jekuthiel father of Zanoah.
19 The sons of the wife of Hodiah, the sister of
Naham, were the fathers of Keilah the Garmite
and Eshtemoa the Maacathite. 20 The sons of Shi-
mon: Amnon, Rinnah, Ben-hanan, and Tilon.
The sons of Ishi: Zoheth and Ben-zoheth. 21 The
sons of Shelah son of Judah: Er father of Lecah,
Laadah father of Mareshah, and the families of
the guild of linen workers at Beth-ashbea; 22 and
Jokim, and the men of Cozeba, and Joash, and
Saraph, who married into Moab but returned to
Lehem[j] (now the records[k] are ancient). 23 These
were the potters and inhabitants of Netaim and
Gederah; they lived there with the king in his
service.

24 The sons of Simeon: Nemuel, Jamin, Jarib,
Zerah, Shaul;[l] 25 Shallum was his son, Mibsam
his son, Mishma his son. 26 The sons of Mishma:
Hammuel his son, Zaccur his son, Shimei his son.
27 Shimei had sixteen sons and six daughters; but
his brothers did not have many children, nor did
all their family multiply like the Judeans. 28 They
lived in Beer-sheba, Moladah, Hazar-shual, 29 Bilhah, Ezem, Tolad, 30 Bethuel, Hormah, Ziklag,
31 Beth-marcaboth, Hazar-susim, Beth-biri, and
Shaaraim. These were their towns until David became king. 32 And their villages were Etam, Ain,
Rimmon, Tochen, and Ashan, five towns, 33 along
with all their villages that were around these
towns as far as Baal. These were their settlements.
And they kept a genealogical record.

34 Meshobab, Jamlech, Joshah son of Amaziah, 35 Joel, Jehu son of Joshibiah son of Seraiah
son of Asiel, 36 Elioenai, Jaakobah, Jeshohaiah,
Asaiah, Adiel, Jesimiel, Benaiah, 37 Ziza son of
Shiphi son of Allon son of Jedaiah son of Shimri

[a] Gk Compare Syr Vg: Heb *sons of* [b] Heb *sons* [c] Gk Compare Vg: Heb *the father* [d] Or *Ahashtari* [e] Another reading is *Zohar* [f] Gk Vg: Heb lacks *and Meonothai* [g] That is *Valley of artisans* [h] The clause: *These are . . . married* is transposed from verse 18 [i] Heb lacks *and bore* [j] Vg Compare Gk: Heb *and Jashubi-lahem* [k] Or *matters* [l] Or *Saul*

son of Shemaiah— 38these mentioned by name
were leaders in their families, and their clans increased greatly. 39They journeyed to the entrance
of Gedor, to the east side of the valley, to seek
pasture for their flocks, 40where they found rich,
good pasture, and the land was very broad, quiet,
and peaceful; for the former inhabitants there
belonged to Ham. 41These, registered by name,
came in the days of King Hezekiah of Judah, and
attacked their tents and the Meunim who were
found there, and exterminated them to this day,
and settled in their place, because there was pasture there for their flocks. 42And some of them,
five hundred men of the Simeonites, went to
Mount Seir, having as their leaders Pelatiah, Neariah, Rephaiah, and Uzziel, sons of Ishi; 43they
destroyed the remnant of the Amalekites that had
escaped, and they have lived there to this day.

5 The sons of Reuben the firstborn of Israel.
(He was the firstborn, but because he defiled his father's bed his birthright was given to
the sons of Joseph son of Israel, so that he is not
enrolled in the genealogy according to the birthright; 2though Judah became prominent among
his brothers and a ruler came from him, yet the
birthright belonged to Joseph.) 3The sons of
Reuben, the firstborn of Israel: Hanoch, Pallu,
Hezron, and Carmi. 4The sons of Joel: Shemaiah
his son, Gog his son, Shimei his son, 5Micah his
son, Reaiah his son, Baal his son, 6Beerah his son,
whom King Tilgath-pilneser of Assyria carried
away into exile; he was a chieftain of the Reubenites. 7And his kindred by their families, when the
genealogy of their generations was reckoned: the
chief, Jeiel, and Zechariah, 8and Bela son of Azaz,
son of Shema, son of Joel, who lived in Aroer, as
far as Nebo and Baal-meon. 9He also lived to the
east as far as the beginning of the desert this side
of the Euphrates, because their cattle had multiplied in the land of Gilead. 10And in the days of
Saul they made war on the Hagrites, who fell by
their hand; and they lived in their tents throughout all the region east of Gilead.

11 The sons of Gad lived beside them in the
land of Bashan as far as Salecah: 12Joel the chief,
Shapham the second, Janai, and Shaphat in
Bashan. 13And their kindred according to their
clans: Michael, Meshullam, Sheba, Jorai, Jacan,
Zia, and Eber, seven. 14These were the sons of
Abihail son of Huri, son of Jaroah, son of Gilead,
son of Michael, son of Jeshishai, son of Jahdo, son
of Buz; 15Ahi son of Abdiel, son of Guni, was
chief in their clan; 16and they lived in Gilead, in
Bashan and in its towns, and in all the pasture
lands of Sharon to their limits. 17All of these were
enrolled by genealogies in the days of King
Jotham of Judah, and in the days of King Jeroboam of Israel.

18 The Reubenites, the Gadites, and the half-
tribe of Manasseh had valiant warriors, who carried shield and sword, and drew the bow, expert
in war, forty-four thousand seven hundred sixty,
ready for service. 19They made war on the Hagrites, Jetur, Naphish, and Nodab; 20and when
they received help against them, the Hagrites
and all who were with them were given into their
hands, for they cried to God in the battle, and he
granted their entreaty because they trusted in
him. 21They captured their livestock: fifty thousand of their camels, two hundred fifty thousand
sheep, two thousand donkeys, and one hundred
thousand captives. 22Many fell slain, because the
war was of God. And they lived in their territory
until the exile.

23 The members of the half-tribe of Manasseh lived in the land; they were very numerous from Bashan to Baal-hermon, Senir, and
Mount Hermon. 24These were the heads of their
clans: Epher,[a] Ishi, Eliel, Azriel, Jeremiah, Hodaviah, and Jahdiel, mighty warriors, famous men,
heads of their clans. 25But they transgressed
against the God of their ancestors, and prostituted themselves to the gods of the peoples of
the land, whom God had destroyed before them.
26So the God of Israel stirred up the spirit of King
Pul of Assyria, the spirit of King Tilgath-pilneser
of Assyria, and he carried them away, namely,
the Reubenites, the Gadites, and the half-tribe of
Manasseh, and brought them to Halah, Habor,
Hara, and the river Gozan, to this day.

[a] Gk Vg: Heb *and Epher*

6[a] The sons of Levi: Gershom,[b] Kohath, and Merari. 2 The sons of Kohath: Amram, Izhar, Hebron, and Uzziel. 3 The children of Amram: Aaron, Moses, and Miriam. The sons of Aaron: Nadab, Abihu, Eleazar, and Ithamar. 4 Eleazar became the father of Phinehas, Phinehas of Abishua, 5 Abishua of Bukki, Bukki of Uzzi, 6 Uzzi of Zerahiah, Zerahiah of Meraioth, 7 Meraioth of Amariah, Amariah of Ahitub, 8 Ahitub of Zadok, Zadok of Ahimaaz, 9 Ahimaaz of Azariah, Azariah of Johanan, 10 and Johanan of Azariah (it was he who served as priest in the house that Solomon built in Jerusalem). 11 Azariah became the father of Amariah, Amariah of Ahitub, 12 Ahitub of Zadok, Zadok of Shallum, 13 Shallum of Hilkiah, Hilkiah of Azariah, 14 Azariah of Seraiah, Seraiah of Jehozadak; 15 and Jehozadak went into exile when the LORD sent Judah and Jerusalem into exile by the hand of Nebuchadnezzar.

16[c] The sons of Levi: Gershom, Kohath, and Merari. 17 These are the names of the sons of Gershom: Libni and Shimei. 18 The sons of Kohath: Amram, Izhar, Hebron, and Uzziel. 19 The sons of Merari: Mahli and Mushi. These are the clans of the Levites according to their ancestry. 20 Of Gershom: Libni his son, Jahath his son, Zimmah his son, 21 Joah his son, Iddo his son, Zerah his son, Jeatherai his son. 22 The sons of Kohath: Amminadab his son, Korah his son, Assir his son, 23 Elkanah his son, Ebiasaph his son, Assir his son, 24 Tahath his son, Uriel his son, Uzziah his son, and Shaul his son. 25 The sons of Elkanah: Amasai and Ahimoth, 26 Elkanah his son, Zophai his son, Nahath his son, 27 Eliab his son, Jeroham his son, Elkanah his son. 28 The sons of Samuel: Joel[d] his firstborn, the second Abijah.[e] 29 The sons of Merari: Mahli, Libni his son, Shimei his son, Uzzah his son, 30 Shimea his son, Haggiah his son, and Asaiah his son.

31 These are the men whom David put in charge of the service of song in the house of the LORD, after the ark came to rest there. 32 They ministered with song before the tabernacle of the tent of meeting, until Solomon had built the house of the LORD in Jerusalem; and they performed their service in due order. 33 These are the men who served; and their sons were: Of the Kohathites: Heman, the singer, son of Joel, son of Samuel, 34 son of Elkanah, son of Jeroham, son of Eliel, son of Toah, 35 son of Zuph, son of Elkanah, son of Mahath, son of Amasai, 36 son of Elkanah, son of Joel, son of Azariah, son of Zephaniah, 37 son of Tahath, son of Assir, son of Ebiasaph, son of Korah, 38 son of Izhar, son of Kohath, son of Levi, son of Israel; 39 and his brother Asaph, who stood on his right, namely, Asaph son of Berechiah, son of Shimea, 40 son of Michael, son of Baaseiah, son of Malchijah, 41 son of Ethni, son of Zerah, son of Adaiah, 42 son of Ethan, son of Zimmah, son of Shimei, 43 son of Jahath, son of Gershom, son of Levi. 44 On the left were their kindred the sons of Merari: Ethan son of Kishi, son of Abdi, son of Malluch, 45 son of Hashabiah, son of Amaziah, son of Hilkiah, 46 son of Amzi, son of Bani, son of Shemer, 47 son of Mahli, son of Mushi, son of Merari, son of Levi; 48 and their kindred the Levites were appointed for all the service of the tabernacle of the house of God.

49 But Aaron and his sons made offerings on the altar of burnt offering and on the altar of incense, doing all the work of the most holy place, to make atonement for Israel, according to all that Moses the servant of God had commanded. 50 These are the sons of Aaron: Eleazar his son, Phinehas his son, Abishua his son, 51 Bukki his son, Uzzi his son, Zerahiah his son, 52 Meraioth his son, Amariah his son, Ahitub his son, 53 Zadok his son, Ahimaaz his son.

54 These are their dwelling places according to their settlements within their borders: to the sons of Aaron of the families of Kohathites—for the lot fell to them first— 55 to them they gave Hebron in the land of Judah and its surrounding pasture lands, 56 but the fields of the city and its villages they gave to Caleb son of Jephunneh. 57 To the sons of Aaron they gave the cities of refuge: Hebron, Libnah with its pasture lands, Jattir,

[a] Ch 5.27 in Heb [b] Heb *Gershon*, variant of *Gershom*; See 6.16 [c] Ch 6.1 in Heb [d] Gk Syr Compare verse 33 and 1 Sam 8.2: Heb lacks *Joel* [e] Heb reads *Vashni, and Abijah* for *the second Abijah*, taking *the second* as a proper name

Eshtemoa with its pasture lands, 58 Hilen[a] with its pasture lands, Debir with its pasture lands, 59 Ashan with its pasture lands, and Beth-shemesh with its pasture lands. 60 From the tribe of Benjamin, Geba with its pasture lands, Alemeth with its pasture lands, and Anathoth with its pasture lands. All their towns throughout their families were thirteen.

61 To the rest of the Kohathites were given by lot out of the family of the tribe, out of the half-tribe, the half of Manasseh, ten towns. 62 To the Gershomites according to their families were allotted thirteen towns out of the tribes of Issachar, Asher, Naphtali, and Manasseh in Bashan. 63 To the Merarites according to their families were allotted twelve towns out of the tribes of Reuben, Gad, and Zebulun. 64 So the people of Israel gave the Levites the towns with their pasture lands. 65 They also gave them by lot out of the tribes of Judah, Simeon, and Benjamin these towns that are mentioned by name.

66 And some of the families of the sons of Kohath had towns of their territory out of the tribe of Ephraim. 67 They were given the cities of refuge: Shechem with its pasture lands in the hill country of Ephraim, Gezer with its pasture lands, 68 Jokmeam with its pasture lands, Beth-horon with its pasture lands, 69 Aijalon with its pasture lands, Gath-rimmon with its pasture lands; 70 and out of the half-tribe of Manasseh, Aner with its pasture lands, and Bileam with its pasture lands, for the rest of the families of the Kohathites.

71 To the Gershomites: out of the half-tribe of Manasseh: Golan in Bashan with its pasture lands and Ashtaroth with its pasture lands; 72 and out of the tribe of Issachar: Kedesh with its pasture lands, Daberath[b] with its pasture lands, 73 Ramoth with its pasture lands, and Anem with its pasture lands; 74 out of the tribe of Asher: Mashal with its pasture lands, Abdon with its pasture lands, 75 Hukok with its pasture lands, and Rehob with its pasture lands; 76 and out of the tribe of Naphtali: Kedesh in Galilee with its pasture lands, Hammon with its pasture lands, and Kiriathaim with its pasture lands. 77 To the rest of the Merarites out of the tribe of Zebulun: Rimmono with its pasture lands, Tabor with its pasture lands, 78 and across the Jordan from Jericho, on the east side of the Jordan, out of the tribe of Reuben: Bezer in the steppe with its pasture lands, Jahzah with its pasture lands, 79 Kedemoth with its pasture lands, and Mephaath with its pasture lands; 80 and out of the tribe of Gad: Ramoth in Gilead with its pasture lands, Mahanaim with its pasture lands, 81 Heshbon with its pasture lands, and Jazer with its pasture lands.

7 The sons[c] of Issachar: Tola, Puah, Jashub, and Shimron, four. 2 The sons of Tola: Uzzi, Rephaiah, Jeriel, Jahmai, Ibsam, and Shemuel, heads of their ancestral houses, namely of Tola, mighty warriors of their generations, their number in the days of David being twenty-two thousand six hundred. 3 The son[d] of Uzzi: Izrahiah. And the sons of Izrahiah: Michael, Obadiah, Joel, and Isshiah, five, all of them chiefs; 4 and along with them, by their generations, according to their ancestral houses, were units of the fighting force, thirty-six thousand, for they had many wives and sons. 5 Their kindred belonging to all the families of Issachar were in all eighty-seven thousand mighty warriors, enrolled by genealogy.

6 The sons of Benjamin: Bela, Becher, and Jediael, three. 7 The sons of Bela: Ezbon, Uzzi, Uzziel, Jerimoth, and Iri, five, heads of ancestral houses, mighty warriors; and their enrollment by genealogies was twenty-two thousand thirty-four. 8 The sons of Becher: Zemirah, Joash, Eliezer, Elioenai, Omri, Jeremoth, Abijah, Anathoth, and Alemeth. All these were the sons of Becher; 9 and their enrollment by genealogies, according to their generations, as heads of their ancestral houses, mighty warriors, was twenty thousand two hundred. 10 The sons of Jediael: Bilhan. And the sons of Bilhan: Jeush, Benjamin, Ehud, Chenaanah, Zethan, Tarshish, and Ahishahar. 11 All these were the sons of Jediael according to the heads of their ancestral houses, mighty warriors, seventeen thousand two hundred, ready for service in war. 12 And Shuppim and Huppim were the sons of Ir, Hushim the son[d] of Aher.

[a] Other readings *Hilez, Holon*; See Josh 21.15 [b] Or *Dobrath* [c] Syr Compare Vg: Heb *And to the sons* [d] Heb *sons*

13 The descendants of Naphtali: Jahziel,
Guni, Jezer, and Shallum, the descendants of
Bilhah.
14 The sons of Manasseh: Asriel, whom his
Aramean concubine bore; she bore Machir the
father of Gilead. 15 And Machir took a wife for
Huppim and for Shuppim. The name of his sister was Maacah. And the name of the second was
Zelophehad; and Zelophehad had daughters.
16 Maacah the wife of Machir bore a son, and she
named him Peresh; the name of his brother was
Sheresh; and his sons were Ulam and Rekem.
17 The son[a] of Ulam: Bedan. These were the sons
of Gilead son of Machir, son of Manasseh. 18 And
his sister Hammolecheth bore Ishhod, Abiezer,
and Mahlah. 19 The sons of Shemida were Ahian,
Shechem, Likhi, and Aniam.
20 The sons of Ephraim: Shuthelah, and
Bered his son, Tahath his son, Eleadah his son,
Tahath his son, 21 Zabad his son, Shuthelah his
son, and Ezer and Elead. Now the people of Gath,
who were born in the land, killed them, because
they came down to raid their cattle. 22 And their
father Ephraim mourned many days, and his
brothers came to comfort him. 23 Ephraim[b] went
in to his wife, and she conceived and bore a son;
and he named him Beriah, because disaster[c] had
befallen his house. 24 His daughter was Sheerah,
who built both Lower and Upper Beth-horon, and
Uzzen-sheerah. 25 Rephah was his son, Resheph
his son, Telah his son, Tahan his son, 26 Ladan his
son, Ammihud his son, Elishama his son, 27 Nun[d]
his son, Joshua his son. 28 Their possessions and
settlements were Bethel and its towns, and eastward Naaran, and westward Gezer and its towns,
Shechem and its towns, as far as Ayyah and its
towns; 29 also along the borders of the Manassites, Beth-shean and its towns, Taanach and its
towns, Megiddo and its towns, Dor and its towns.
In these lived the sons of Joseph son of Israel.
30 The sons of Asher: Imnah, Ishvah, Ishvi,
Beriah, and their sister Serah. 31 The sons of Beriah: Heber and Malchiel, who was the father of
Birzaith. 32 Heber became the father of Japhlet,
Shomer, Hotham, and their sister Shua. 33 The
sons of Japhlet: Pasach, Bimhal, and Ashvath.
These are the sons of Japhlet. 34 The sons of Shemer: Ahi, Rohgah, Hubbah, and Aram. 35 The
sons of Helem[e] his brother: Zophah, Imna, She-
lesh, and Amal. 36 The sons of Zophah: Suah,
Harnepher, Shual, Beri, Imrah, 37 Bezer, Hod,
Shamma, Shilshah, Ithran, and Beera. 38 The sons
of Jether: Jephunneh, Pispa, and Ara. 39 The sons
of Ulla: Arah, Hanniel, and Rizia. 40 All of these
were men of Asher, heads of ancestral houses, select mighty warriors, chief of the princes. Their
number enrolled by genealogies, for service in
war, was twenty-six thousand men.

8 Benjamin became the father of Bela his firstborn, Ashbel the second, Aharah the third,
2 Nohah the fourth, and Rapha the fifth. 3 And
Bela had sons: Addar, Gera, Abihud,[f] 4 Abishua,
Naaman, Ahoah, 5 Gera, Shephuphan, and Huram. 6 These are the sons of Ehud (they were
heads of ancestral houses of the inhabitants of
Geba, and they were carried into exile to Manahath): 7 Naaman,[g] Ahijah, and Gera, that is,
Heglam,[h] who became the father of Uzza and
Ahihud. 8 And Shaharaim had sons in the country
of Moab after he had sent away his wives Hushim
and Baara. 9 He had sons by his wife Hodesh:
Jobab, Zibia, Mesha, Malcam, 10 Jeuz, Sachia, and
Mirmah. These were his sons, heads of ancestral

1 Chronicles 7:23-24

Sheerah, the daughter or granddaughter of Ephraim—the text is not clear—is the only woman in the Scriptures identified as a city builder. Among her cities are the twin cities of Upper and Lower Beth Horon that endured from the settlement of Canaan until the time of Solomon, who fortified them. The city she named after herself—Uzzen Sheerah, "Give ear to..." or "Listen to Sheerah"—is lost, but not her legacy.

— *WG*

[a] Heb *sons* [b] Heb *He* [c] Heb *beraah* [d] Here spelled *Non*; see Ex 33.11 [e] Or *Hotham*; see 7.32 [f] Or *father of Ehud*; see 8.6 [g] Heb *and Naaman* [h] Or *he carried them into exile*

houses. 11He also had sons by Hushim: Abitub and Elpaal. 12The sons of Elpaal: Eber, Misham, and Shemed, who built Ono and Lod with its towns, 13and Beriah and Shema (they were heads of ancestral houses of the inhabitants of Aijalon, who put to flight the inhabitants of Gath); 14and Ahio, Shashak, and Jeremoth. 15Zebadiah, Arad, Eder, 16Michael, Ishpah, and Joha were sons of Beriah. 17Zebadiah, Meshullam, Hizki, Heber, 18Ishmerai, Izliah, and Jobab were the sons of Elpaal. 19Jakim, Zichri, Zabdi, 20Elienai, Zillethai, Eliel, 21Adaiah, Beraiah, and Shimrath were the sons of Shimei. 22Ishpan, Eber, Eliel, 23Abdon, Zichri, Hanan, 24Hananiah, Elam, Anthothijah, 25Iphdeiah, and Penuel were the sons of Shashak. 26Shamsherai, Shehariah, Athaliah, 27Jaareshiah, Elijah, and Zichri were the sons of Jeroham. 28These were the heads of ancestral houses, according to their generations, chiefs. These lived in Jerusalem.

29 Jeiel[a] the father of Gibeon lived in Gibeon, and the name of his wife was Maacah. 30His firstborn son: Abdon, then Zur, Kish, Baal,[b] Nadab, 31Gedor, Ahio, Zecher, 32and Mikloth, who became the father of Shimeah. Now these also lived opposite their kindred in Jerusalem, with their kindred. 33Ner became the father of Kish, Kish of Saul,[c] Saul[c] of Jonathan, Malchishua, Abinadab, and Esh-baal; 34and the son of Jonathan was Merib-baal; and Merib-baal became the father of Micah. 35The sons of Micah: Pithon, Melech, Tarea, and Ahaz. 36Ahaz became the father of Jehoaddah; and Jehoaddah became the father of Alemeth, Azmaveth, and Zimri; Zimri became the father of Moza. 37Moza became the father of Binea; Raphah was his son, Eleasah his son, Azel his son. 38Azel had six sons, and these are their names: Azrikam, Bocheru, Ishmael, Sheariah, Obadiah, and Hanan; all these were the sons of Azel. 39The sons of his brother Eshek: Ulam his firstborn, Jeush the second, and Eliphelet the third. 40The sons of Ulam were mighty warriors, archers, having many children and grandchildren, one hundred fifty. All these were Benjaminites.

9 So all Israel was enrolled by genealogies; and these are written in the Book of the Kings of Israel. And Judah was taken into exile in Babylon because of their unfaithfulness. 2Now the first to live again in their possessions in their towns were Israelites, priests, Levites, and temple servants.

3 And some of the people of Judah, Benjamin, Ephraim, and Manasseh lived in Jerusalem: 4Uthai son of Ammihud, son of Omri, son of Imri, son of Bani, from the sons of Perez son of Judah. 5And of the Shilonites: Asaiah the firstborn, and his sons. 6Of the sons of Zerah: Jeuel and their kin, six hundred ninety. 7Of the Benjaminites: Sallu son of Meshullam, son of Hodaviah, son of Hassenuah, 8Ibneiah son of Jeroham, Elah son of Uzzi, son of Michri, and Meshullam son of Shephatiah, son of Reuel, son of Ibnijah; 9and their kindred according to their generations, nine hundred fifty-six. All these were heads of families according to their ancestral houses.

10 Of the priests: Jedaiah, Jehoiarib, Jachin, 11and Azariah son of Hilkiah, son of Meshullam, son of Zadok, son of Meraioth, son of Ahitub, the chief officer of the house of God; 12and Adaiah son of Jeroham, son of Pashhur, son of Malchijah, and Maasai son of Adiel, son of Jahzerah, son of Meshullam, son of Meshillemith, son of Immer; 13besides their kindred, heads of their ancestral houses, one thousand seven hundred sixty, qualified for the work of the service of the house of God.

14 Of the Levites: Shemaiah son of Hasshub, son of Azrikam, son of Hashabiah, of the sons of Merari; 15and Bakbakkar, Heresh, Galal, and Mattaniah son of Mica, son of Zichri, son of Asaph; 16and Obadiah son of Shemaiah, son of Galal, son of Jeduthun, and Berechiah son of Asa, son of Elkanah, who lived in the villages of the Netophathites.

17 The gatekeepers were: Shallum, Akkub, Talmon, Ahiman; and their kindred Shallum was the chief, 18stationed previously in the king's gate on the east side. These were the gatekeepers of the camp of the Levites. 19Shallum son of Kore, son of Ebiasaph, son of Korah, and his kindred

[a] Compare 9.35: Heb lacks *Jeiel* [b] Gk Ms adds *Ner*; Compare 8.33 and 9.36 [c] Or *Shaul*

of his ancestral house, the Korahites, were in charge of the work of the service, guardians of the thresholds of the tent, as their ancestors had been in charge of the camp of the LORD, guardians of the entrance. 20 And Phinehas son of Eleazar was chief over them in former times; the LORD was with him. 21 Zechariah son of Meshelemiah was gatekeeper at the entrance of the tent of meeting. 22 All these, who were chosen as gatekeepers at the thresholds, were two hundred twelve. They were enrolled by genealogies in their villages. David and the seer Samuel established them in their office of trust. 23 So they and their descendants were in charge of the gates of the house of the LORD, that is, the house of the tent, as guards. 24 The gatekeepers were on the four sides, east, west, north, and south; 25 and their kindred who were in their villages were obliged to come in every seven days, in turn, to be with them; 26 for the four chief gatekeepers, who were Levites, were in charge of the chambers and the treasures of the house of God. 27 And they would spend the night near the house of God; for on them lay the duty of watching, and they had charge of opening it every morning.

28 Some of them had charge of the utensils of service, for they were required to count them when they were brought in and taken out. 29 Others of them were appointed over the furniture, and over all the holy utensils, also over the choice flour, the wine, the oil, the incense, and the spices. 30 Others, of the sons of the priests, prepared the mixing of the spices, 31 and Mattithiah, one of the Levites, the firstborn of Shallum the Korahite, was in charge of making the flat cakes. 32 Also some of their kindred of the Kohathites had charge of the rows of bread, to prepare them for each sabbath.

33 Now these are the singers, the heads of ancestral houses of the Levites, living in the chambers of the temple free from other service, for they were on duty day and night. 34 These were heads of ancestral houses of the Levites, according to their generations; these leaders lived in Jerusalem.

35 In Gibeon lived the father of Gibeon, Jeiel, and the name of his wife was Maacah. 36 His firstborn son was Abdon, then Zur, Kish, Baal, Ner, Nadab, 37 Gedor, Ahio, Zechariah, and Mikloth; 38 and Mikloth became the father of Shimeam; and these also lived opposite their kindred in Jerusalem, with their kindred. 39 Ner became the father of Kish, Kish of Saul, Saul of Jonathan, Malchishua, Abinadab, and Esh-baal; 40 and the son of Jonathan was Merib-baal; and Merib-baal became the father of Micah. 41 The sons of Micah: Pithon, Melech, Tahrea, and Ahaz;[a] 42 and Ahaz became the father of Jarah, and Jarah of Alemeth, Azmaveth, and Zimri; and Zimri became the father of Moza. 43 Moza became the father of Binea; and Rephaiah was his son, Eleasah his son, Azel his son. 44 Azel had six sons, and these are their names: Azrikam, Bocheru, Ishmael, Sheariah, Obadiah, and Hanan; these were the sons of Azel.

10 Now the Philistines fought against Israel; and the men of Israel fled before the Philistines, and fell slain on Mount Gilboa. 2 The Philistines overtook Saul and his sons; and the Philistines killed Jonathan and Abinadab and Malchishua, sons of Saul. 3 The battle pressed hard on Saul; and the archers found him, and he was wounded by the archers. 4 Then Saul said to his armor-bearer, "Draw your sword, and thrust me through with it, so that these uncircumcised may not come and make sport of me." But his armor-bearer was unwilling, for he was terrified. So Saul took his own sword and fell on it. 5 When his armor-bearer saw that Saul was dead, he also fell on his sword and died. 6 Thus Saul died; he and his three sons and all his house died together. 7 When all the men of Israel who were in the valley saw that the army[b] had fled and that Saul and his sons were dead, they abandoned their towns and fled; and the Philistines came and occupied them.

8 The next day when the Philistines came to strip the dead, they found Saul and his sons fallen on Mount Gilboa. 9 They stripped him and took his head and his armor, and sent messengers

[a] Compare 8.35: Heb lacks *and Ahaz* [b] Heb *they*

throughout the land of the Philistines to carry
the good news to their idols and to the people.
10They put his armor in the temple of their gods,
and fastened his head in the temple of Dagon.
11But when all Jabesh-gilead heard everything
that the Philistines had done to Saul, 12all the valiant warriors got up and took away the body of
Saul and the bodies of his sons, and brought them
to Jabesh. Then they buried their bones under the
oak in Jabesh, and fasted seven days.

13 So Saul died for his unfaithfulness; he was
unfaithful to the LORD in that he did not keep
the command of the LORD; moreover, he had
consulted a medium, seeking guidance, 14and did
not seek guidance from the LORD. Therefore the
LORD[a] put him to death and turned the kingdom
over to David son of Jesse.

11 Then all Israel gathered together to David at Hebron and said, "See, we are your
bone and flesh. 2For some time now, even while
Saul was king, it was you who commanded the
army of Israel. The LORD your God said to you: It
is you who shall be shepherd of my people Israel,
you who shall be ruler over my people Israel." 3So
all the elders of Israel came to the king at Hebron,
and David made a covenant with them at Hebron
before the LORD. And they anointed David king
over Israel, according to the word of the LORD by
Samuel.

4 David and all Israel marched to Jerusalem,
that is Jebus, where the Jebusites were, the inhabitants of the land. 5The inhabitants of Jebus said
to David, "You will not come in here." Nevertheless David took the stronghold of Zion, now the
city of David. 6David had said, "Whoever attacks
the Jebusites first shall be chief and commander."
And Joab son of Zeruiah went up first, so he became chief. 7David resided in the stronghold;
therefore it was called the city of David. 8He built
the city all around, from the Millo in complete
circuit; and Joab repaired the rest of the city.
9And David became greater and greater, for the
LORD of hosts was with him.

10 Now these are the chiefs of David's warriors, who gave him strong support in his kingdom, together with all Israel, to make him king,
according to the word of the LORD concerning
Israel. 11This is an account of David's mighty warriors: Jashobeam, son of Hachmoni,[b] was chief
of the Three;[c] he wielded his spear against three
hundred whom he killed at one time.

12 And next to him among the three warriors
was Eleazar son of Dodo, the Ahohite. 13He was
with David at Pas-dammim when the Philistines
were gathered there for battle. There was a plot
of ground full of barley. Now the people had fled
from the Philistines, 14but he and David took
their stand in the middle of the plot, defended
it, and killed the Philistines; and the LORD saved
them by a great victory.

15 Three of the thirty chiefs went down to
the rock to David at the cave of Adullam, while
the army of Philistines was encamped in the valley of Rephaim. 16David was then in the stronghold; and the garrison of the Philistines was then
at Bethlehem. 17David said longingly, "O that
someone would give me water to drink from the
well of Bethlehem that is by the gate!" 18Then the
Three broke through the camp of the Philistines,
and drew water from the well of Bethlehem that
was by the gate, and they brought it to David.
But David would not drink of it; he poured it out
to the LORD, 19and said, "My God forbid that I
should do this. Can I drink the blood of these
men? For at the risk of their lives they brought it."
Therefore he would not drink it. The three warriors did these things.

20 Now Abishai,[d] the brother of Joab, was
chief of the Thirty.[e] With his spear he fought
against three hundred and killed them, and won
a name beside the Three. 21He was the most renowned[f] of the Thirty,[e] and became their commander; but he did not attain to the Three.

22 Benaiah son of Jehoiada was a valiant man[g]
of Kabzeel, a doer of great deeds; he struck down
two sons of[h] Ariel of Moab. He also went down

[a] Heb *he* [b] Or *a Hachmonite* [c] Compare 2 Sam 23.8: Heb *Thirty* or *captains* [d] Gk Vg Tg Compare 2 Sam 23.18: Heb *Abshai* [e] Syr: Heb *Three* [f] Compare 2 Sam 23.19: Heb *more renowned among the two* [g] Syr: Heb *the son of a valiant man* [h] See 2 Sam 23.20: Heb lacks *sons of*

and killed a lion in a pit on a day when snow had
fallen. 23And he killed an Egyptian, a man of great
stature, five cubits tall. The Egyptian had in his
hand a spear like a weaver's beam; but Benaiah
went against him with a staff, snatched the spear
out of the Egyptian's hand, and killed him with
his own spear. 24Such were the things Benaiah
son of Jehoiada did, and he won a name beside
the three warriors. 25He was renowned among
the Thirty, but he did not attain to the Three. And
David put him in charge of his bodyguard.

26 The warriors of the armies were Asahel
brother of Joab, Elhanan son of Dodo of Bethlehem, 27Shammoth of Harod,[a] Helez the Pelonite,
28Ira son of Ikkesh of Tekoa, Abiezer of Anathoth,
29Sibbecai the Hushathite, Ilai the Ahohite,
30Maharai of Netophah, Heled son of Baanah of
Netophah, 31Ithai son of Ribai of Gibeah of the
Benjaminites, Benaiah of Pirathon, 32Hurai of the
wadis of Gaash, Abiel the Arbathite, 33Azmaveth
of Baharum, Eliahba of Shaalbon, 34Hashem[b] the
Gizonite, Jonathan son of Shagee the Hararite,
35Ahiam son of Sachar the Hararite, Eliphal son
of Ur, 36Hepher the Mecherathite, Ahijah the
Pelonite, 37Hezro of Carmel, Naarai son of Ez-
bai, 38Joel the brother of Nathan, Mibhar son of
Hagri, 39Zelek the Ammonite, Naharai of Beeroth, the armor-bearer of Joab son of Zeruiah, 40Ira
the Ithrite, Gareb the Ithrite, 41Uriah the Hittite,
Zabad son of Ahlai, 42Adina son of Shiza the
Reubenite, a leader of the Reubenites, and thirty
with him, 43Hanan son of Maacah, and Joshaphat
the Mithnite, 44Uzzia the Ashterathite, Shama
and Jeiel sons of Hotham the Aroerite, 45Jediael
son of Shimri, and his brother Joha the Tizite,
46Eliel the Mahavite, and Jeribai and Joshaviah
sons of Elnaam, and Ithmah the Moabite, 47Eliel,
and Obed, and Jaasiel the Mezobaite.

12 The following are those who came to David at Ziklag, while he could not move
about freely because of Saul son of Kish; they
were among the mighty warriors who helped him
in war. 2They were archers, and could shoot arrows and sling stones with either the right hand
or the left; they were Benjaminites, Saul's kindred. 3The chief was Ahiezer, then Joash, both
sons of Shemaah of Gibeah; also Jeziel and Pelet
sons of Azmaveth; Beracah, Jehu of Anathoth,
4Ishmaiah of Gibeon, a warrior among the Thirty
and a leader over the Thirty; Jeremiah,[c] Jahaziel,
Johanan, Jozabad of Gederah, 5Eluzai,[d] Jerimoth,
Bealiah, Shemariah, Shephatiah the Haruphite;
6Elkanah, Isshiah, Azarel, Joezer, and Jashobeam,
the Korahites; 7and Joelah and Zebadiah, sons of
Jeroham of Gedor.

8 From the Gadites there went over to David
at the stronghold in the wilderness mighty and experienced warriors, expert with shield and spear,
whose faces were like the faces of lions, and who
were swift as gazelles on the mountains: 9Ezer
the chief, Obadiah second, Eliab third, 10Mish-
mannah fourth, Jeremiah fifth, 11Attai sixth, Eliel
seventh, 12Johanan eighth, Elzabad ninth, 13Jer-
emiah tenth, Machbannai eleventh. 14These Gadites were officers of the army, the least equal to a
hundred and the greatest to a thousand. 15These
are the men who crossed the Jordan in the first
month, when it was overflowing all its banks, and
put to flight all those in the valleys, to the east and
to the west.

16 Some Benjaminites and Judahites came
to the stronghold to David. 17David went out to
meet them and said to them, "If you have come to
me in friendship, to help me, then my heart will
be knit to you; but if you have come to betray me
to my adversaries, though my hands have done
no wrong, then may the God of our ancestors see
and give judgment." 18Then the spirit came upon
Amasai, chief of the Thirty, and he said,

"We are yours, O David;
 and with you, O son of Jesse!
Peace, peace to you,
 and peace to the one who helps you!
 For your God is the one who helps you."

Then David received them, and made them officers of his troops.

[a] Compare 2 Sam 23.25: Heb *the Harorite* [b] Compare Gk and 2 Sam 23.32: Heb *the sons of Hashem* [c] Heb verse 5
[d] Heb verse 6

19 Some of the Manassites deserted to David when he came with the Philistines for the battle against Saul. (Yet he did not help them, for the rulers of the Philistines took counsel and sent him away, saying, "He will desert to his master Saul at the cost of our heads.") 20 As he went to Ziklag these Manassites deserted to him: Adnah, Jozabad, Jediael, Michael, Jozabad, Elihu, and Zillethai, chiefs of the thousands in Manasseh. 21 They helped David against the band of raiders,[a] for they were all warriors and commanders in the army. 22 Indeed from day to day people kept coming to David to help him, until there was a great army, like an army of God.

23 These are the numbers of the divisions of the armed troops who came to David in Hebron to turn the kingdom of Saul over to him, according to the word of the LORD. 24 The people of Judah bearing shield and spear numbered six thousand eight hundred armed troops. 25 Of the Simeonites, mighty warriors, seven thousand one hundred. 26 Of the Levites four thousand six hundred. 27 Jehoiada, leader of the house of Aaron, and with him three thousand seven hundred. 28 Zadok, a young warrior, and twenty-two commanders from his own ancestral house. 29 Of the Benjaminites, the kindred of Saul, three thousand, of whom the majority had continued to keep their allegiance to the house of Saul. 30 Of the Ephraimites, twenty thousand eight hundred, mighty warriors, notables in their ancestral houses. 31 Of the half-tribe of Manasseh, eighteen thousand, who were expressly named to come and make David king. 32 Of Issachar, those who had understanding of the times, to know what Israel ought to do, two hundred chiefs, and all their kindred under their command. 33 Of Zebulun, fifty thousand seasoned troops, equipped for battle with all the weapons of war, to help David[b] with singleness of purpose. 34 Of Naphtali, a thousand commanders, with whom there were thirty-seven thousand armed with shield and spear. 35 Of the Danites, twenty-eight thousand six hundred equipped for battle. 36 Of Asher, forty thousand seasoned troops ready for battle. 37 Of the Reubenites and Gadites and the half-tribe of Manasseh from beyond the Jordan, one hundred twenty thousand armed with all the weapons of war.

38 All these, warriors arrayed in battle order, came to Hebron with full intent to make David king over all Israel; likewise all the rest of Israel were of a single mind to make David king. 39 They were there with David for three days, eating and drinking, for their kindred had provided for them. 40 And also their neighbors, from as far away as Issachar and Zebulun and Naphtali, came bringing food on donkeys, camels, mules, and oxen—abundant provisions of meal, cakes of figs, clusters of raisins, wine, oil, oxen, and sheep, for there was joy in Israel.

13 David consulted with the commanders of the thousands and of the hundreds, with every leader. 2 David said to the whole assembly of Israel, "If it seems good to you, and if it is the will of the LORD our God, let us send abroad to our kindred who remain in all the land of Israel, including the priests and Levites in the cities that have pasture lands, that they may come together to us. 3 Then let us bring again the ark of our God to us; for we did not turn to it in the days of Saul." 4 The whole assembly agreed to do so, for the thing pleased all the people.

5 So David assembled all Israel from the Shihor of Egypt to Lebo-hamath, to bring the ark of God from Kiriath-jearim. 6 And David and all Israel went up to Baalah, that is, to Kiriath-jearim, which belongs to Judah, to bring up from there the ark of God, the LORD, who is enthroned on the cherubim, which is called by his[c] name. 7 They carried the ark of God on a new cart, from the house of Abinadab, and Uzzah and Ahio[d] were driving the cart. 8 David and all Israel were dancing before God with all their might, with song and lyres and harps and tambourines and cymbals and trumpets.

9 When they came to the threshing floor of Chidon, Uzzah put out his hand to hold the ark, for the oxen shook it. 10 The anger of the LORD was kindled against Uzzah; he struck him down because he put out his hand to the ark; and he

[a] Or *as officers of his troops* [b] Gk: Heb lacks *David* [c] Heb lacks *his* [d] Or *and his brother*

died there before God. 11 David was angry because the LORD had burst out against Uzzah;
so that place is called Perez-uzzah[a] to this day.
12 David was afraid of God that day; he said,
"How can I bring the ark of God into my care?"
13 So David did not take the ark into his care into
the city of David; he took it instead to the house
of Obed-edom the Gittite. 14 The ark of God remained with the household of Obed-edom in his
house three months, and the LORD blessed the
household of Obed-edom and all that he had.

14 King Hiram of Tyre sent messengers to
David, along with cedar logs, and masons
and carpenters to build a house for him. 2 David
then perceived that the LORD had established
him as king over Israel, and that his kingdom was
highly exalted for the sake of his people Israel.

3 David took more wives in Jerusalem, and
David became the father of more sons and daughters. 4 These are the names of the children whom
he had in Jerusalem: Shammua, Shobab, and
Nathan; Solomon, 5 Ibhar, Elishua, and Elpelet;
6 Nogah, Nepheg, and Japhia; 7 Elishama, Bee-
liada, and Eliphelet.

8 When the Philistines heard that David had
been anointed king over all Israel, all the Philistines went up in search of David; and David heard
of it and went out against them. 9 Now the Philistines had come and made a raid in the valley of
Rephaim. 10 David inquired of God, "Shall I go up
against the Philistines? Will you give them into
my hand?" The LORD said to him, "Go up, and I
will give them into your hand." 11 So he went up
to Baal-perazim, and David defeated them there.
David said, "God has burst out[b] against my enemies by my hand, like a bursting flood." Therefore
that place is called Baal-perazim.[c] 12 They abandoned their gods there, and at David's command
they were burned.

13 Once again the Philistines made a raid in
the valley. 14 When David again inquired of God,
God said to him, "You shall not go up after them;
go around and come on them opposite the balsam trees. 15 When you hear the sound of marching in the tops of the balsam trees, then go out to
battle; for God has gone out before you to strike
down the army of the Philistines." 16 David did as
God had commanded him, and they struck down
the Philistine army from Gibeon to Gezer. 17 The
fame of David went out into all lands, and the
LORD brought the fear of him on all nations.

15 David[d] built houses for himself in the city
of David, and he prepared a place for the
ark of God and pitched a tent for it. 2 Then David
commanded that no one but the Levites were to
carry the ark of God, for the LORD had chosen
them to carry the ark of the LORD and to minister to him forever. 3 David assembled all Israel
in Jerusalem to bring up the ark of the LORD to
its place, which he had prepared for it. 4 Then David gathered together the descendants of Aaron
and the Levites: 5 of the sons of Kohath, Uriel the
chief, with one hundred twenty of his kindred;
6 of the sons of Merari, Asaiah the chief, with
two hundred twenty of his kindred; 7 of the sons
of Gershom, Joel the chief, with one hundred
thirty of his kindred; 8 of the sons of Elizaphan,
Shemaiah the chief, with two hundred of his kindred; 9 of the sons of Hebron, Eliel the chief, with
eighty of his kindred; 10 of the sons of Uzziel, Amminadab the chief, with one hundred twelve of
his kindred.

11 David summoned the priests Zadok and
Abiathar, and the Levites Uriel, Asaiah, Joel,
Shemaiah, Eliel, and Amminadab. 12 He said to
them, "You are the heads of families of the Levites; sanctify yourselves, you and your kindred,
so that you may bring up the ark of the LORD, the
God of Israel, to the place that I have prepared for
it. 13 Because you did not carry it the first time,[e]
the LORD our God burst out against us, because
we did not give it proper care." 14 So the priests
and the Levites sanctified themselves to bring up
the ark of the LORD, the God of Israel. 15 And the
Levites carried the ark of God on their shoulders
with the poles, as Moses had commanded according to the word of the LORD.

16 David also commanded the chiefs of the

[a] That is *Bursting Out Against Uzzah* [b] Heb *paraz* [c] That is *Lord of Bursting Out* [d] Heb *He*
[e] Meaning of Heb uncertain

Levites to appoint their kindred as the singers to
play on musical instruments, on harps and lyres
and cymbals, to raise loud sounds of joy. 17So
the Levites appointed Heman son of Joel; and
of his kindred Asaph son of Berechiah; and of
the sons of Merari, their kindred, Ethan son of
Kushaiah; 18and with them their kindred of the
second order, Zechariah, Jaaziel, Shemiramoth,
Jehiel, Unni, Eliab, Benaiah, Maaseiah, Mattithiah, Eliphelehu, and Mikneiah, and the gatekeepers Obed-edom and Jeiel. 19The singers
Heman, Asaph, and Ethan were to sound bronze
cymbals; 20Zechariah, Aziel, Shemiramoth, Jehiel, Unni, Eliab, Maaseiah, and Benaiah were to
play harps according to Alamoth; 21but Mattithiah, Eliphelehu, Mikneiah, Obed-edom, Jeiel,
and Azaziah were to lead with lyres according to
the Sheminith. 22Chenaniah, leader of the Levites in music, was to direct the music, for he understood it. 23Berechiah and Elkanah were to be
gatekeepers for the ark. 24Shebaniah, Joshaphat,
Nethanel, Amasai, Zechariah, Benaiah, and Eliezer, the priests, were to blow the trumpets before
the ark of God. Obed-edom and Jehiah also were
to be gatekeepers for the ark.

25 So David and the elders of Israel, and the
commanders of the thousands, went to bring up
the ark of the covenant of the LORD from the
house of Obed-edom with rejoicing. 26And because God helped the Levites who were carrying
the ark of the covenant of the LORD, they sacrificed seven bulls and seven rams. 27David was
clothed with a robe of fine linen, as also were all
the Levites who were carrying the ark, and the
singers, and Chenaniah the leader of the music of
the singers; and David wore a linen ephod. 28So
all Israel brought up the ark of the covenant of the
LORD with shouting, to the sound of the horn,
trumpets, and cymbals, and made loud music on
harps and lyres.

29 As the ark of the covenant of the LORD
came to the city of David, Michal daughter of
Saul looked out of the window, and saw King David leaping and dancing; and she despised him in
her heart.

16 They brought in the ark of God, and set
it inside the tent that David had pitched
for it; and they offered burnt offerings and offerings of well-being before God. 2When David
had finished offering the burnt offerings and the
offerings of well-being, he blessed the people in
the name of the LORD; 3and he distributed to
every person in Israel—man and woman alike—
to each a loaf of bread, a portion of meat,[a] and a
cake of raisins.

4 He appointed certain of the Levites as ministers before the ark of the LORD, to invoke, to
thank, and to praise the LORD, the God of Israel.
5Asaph was the chief, and second to him Zechariah, Jeiel, Shemiramoth, Jehiel, Mattithiah,
Eliab, Benaiah, Obed-edom, and Jeiel, with harps
and lyres; Asaph was to sound the cymbals, 6and
the priests Benaiah and Jahaziel were to blow
trumpets regularly, before the ark of the covenant
of God.

7 Then on that day David first appointed the
singing of praises to the LORD by Asaph and his
kindred.

8 O give thanks to the LORD, call on his name,
make known his deeds among the peoples.
9 Sing to him, sing praises to him,
tell of all his wonderful works.
10 Glory in his holy name;
let the hearts of those who seek the LORD
rejoice.
11 Seek the LORD and his strength,
seek his presence continually.
12 Remember the wonderful works he has done,
his miracles, and the judgments he uttered,
13 O offspring of his servant Israel,[b]
children of Jacob, his chosen ones.

14 He is the LORD our God;
his judgments are in all the earth.
15 Remember his covenant forever,
the word that he commanded, for a
thousand generations,
16 the covenant that he made with Abraham,
his sworn promise to Isaac,

[a] Compare Gk Syr Vg: Meaning of Heb uncertain [b] Another reading is *Abraham* (compare Ps 105.6)

17 which he confirmed to Jacob as a statute,
to Israel as an everlasting covenant,
18 saying, "To you I will give the land of Canaan
as your portion for an inheritance."

19 When they were few in number,
of little account, and strangers in the land,[a]
20 wandering from nation to nation,
from one kingdom to another people,
21 he allowed no one to oppress them;
he rebuked kings on their account,
22 saying, "Do not touch my anointed ones;
do my prophets no harm."

23 Sing to the LORD, all the earth.
Tell of his salvation from day to day.
24 Declare his glory among the nations,
his marvelous works among all the
peoples.
25 For great is the LORD, and greatly to be
praised;
he is to be revered above all gods.
26 For all the gods of the peoples are idols,
but the LORD made the heavens.
27 Honor and majesty are before him;
strength and joy are in his place.

28 Ascribe to the LORD, O families of the
peoples,
ascribe to the LORD glory and strength.
29 Ascribe to the LORD the glory due his name;
bring an offering, and come before him.
Worship the LORD in holy splendor;
30 tremble before him, all the earth.
The world is firmly established; it shall
never be moved.
31 Let the heavens be glad, and let the earth
rejoice,
and let them say among the nations, "The
LORD is king!"
32 Let the sea roar, and all that fills it;
let the field exult, and everything in it.
33 Then shall the trees of the forest sing for joy
before the LORD, for he comes to judge
the earth.
34 O give thanks to the LORD, for he is good;
for his steadfast love endures forever.

35 Say also:
"Save us, O God of our salvation,
and gather and rescue us from among the
nations,
that we may give thanks to your holy name,
and glory in your praise.
36 Blessed be the LORD, the God of Israel,
from everlasting to everlasting."
Then all the people said "Amen!" and praised the
LORD.

37 David left Asaph and his kinsfolk there before the ark of the covenant of the LORD to minister regularly before the ark as each day required,
38 and also Obed-edom and his[b] sixty-eight kinsfolk; while Obed-edom son of Jeduthun and Hosah were to be gatekeepers. 39 And he left the priest
Zadok and his kindred the priests before the tabernacle of the LORD in the high place that was at
Gibeon, 40 to offer burnt offerings to the LORD on
the altar of burnt offering regularly, morning and
evening, according to all that is written in the law
of the LORD that he commanded Israel. 41 With
them were Heman and Jeduthun, and the rest
of those chosen and expressly named to render
thanks to the LORD, for his steadfast love endures
forever. 42 Heman and Jeduthun had with them
trumpets and cymbals for the music, and instruments for sacred song. The sons of Jeduthun were
appointed to the gate.

43 Then all the people departed to their
homes, and David went home to bless his household.

17 Now when David settled in his house,
David said to the prophet Nathan, "I am
living in a house of cedar, but the ark of the covenant of the LORD is under a tent." 2 Nathan said
to David, "Do all that you have in mind, for God
is with you."

3 But that same night the word of the LORD
came to Nathan, saying: 4 Go and tell my servant
David: Thus says the LORD: You shall not build
me a house to live in. 5 For I have not lived in a

[a] Heb *in it* [b] Gk Syr Vg: Heb *their*

house since the day I brought out Israel to this
very day, but I have lived in a tent and a tabernacle.[a] 6Wherever I have moved about among
all Israel, did I ever speak a word with any of the
judges of Israel, whom I commanded to shepherd
my people, saying, Why have you not built me a
house of cedar? 7Now therefore thus you shall
say to my servant David: Thus says the LORD of
hosts: I took you from the pasture, from following the sheep, to be ruler over my people Israel;
8and I have been with you wherever you went,
and have cut off all your enemies before you; and
I will make for you a name, like the name of the
great ones of the earth. 9I will appoint a place for
my people Israel, and will plant them, so that they
may live in their own place, and be disturbed no
more; and evildoers shall wear them down no
more, as they did formerly, 10from the time that
I appointed judges over my people Israel; and I
will subdue all your enemies.

Moreover I declare to you that the LORD will
build you a house. 11When your days are fulfilled
to go to be with your ancestors, I will raise up
your offspring after you, one of your own sons,
and I will establish his kingdom. 12He shall build
a house for me, and I will establish his throne
forever. 13I will be a father to him, and he shall
be a son to me. I will not take my steadfast love
from him, as I took it from him who was before
you, 14but I will confirm him in my house and in
my kingdom forever, and his throne shall be established forever. 15In accordance with all these
words and all this vision, Nathan spoke to David.

16 Then King David went in and sat before
the LORD, and said, "Who am I, O LORD God,
and what is my house, that you have brought me
thus far? 17And even this was a small thing in
your sight, O God; you have also spoken of your
servant's house for a great while to come. You
regard me as someone of high rank,[b] O LORD
God! 18And what more can David say to you for
honoring your servant? You know your servant.
19For your servant's sake, O LORD, and according to your own heart, you have done all these
great deeds, making known all these great things.
20There is no one like you, O LORD, and there is
no God besides you, according to all that we have
heard with our ears. 21Who is like your people
Israel, one nation on the earth whom God went
to redeem to be his people, making for yourself a
name for great and terrible things, in driving out
nations before your people whom you redeemed
from Egypt? 22And you made your people Israel
to be your people forever; and you, O LORD, became their God.

23 "And now, O LORD, as for the word that
you have spoken concerning your servant and
concerning his house, let it be established forever, and do as you have promised. 24Thus your
name will be established and magnified forever
in the saying, 'The LORD of hosts, the God of Israel, is Israel's God'; and the house of your servant David will be established in your presence.
25For you, my God, have revealed to your servant
that you will build a house for him; therefore
your servant has found it possible to pray before
you. 26And now, O LORD, you are God, and you
have promised this good thing to your servant;
27therefore may it please you to bless the house
of your servant, that it may continue forever before you. For you, O LORD, have blessed and are
blessed[c] forever."

18 Some time afterward, David attacked the
Philistines and subdued them; he took
Gath and its villages from the Philistines.

2 He defeated Moab, and the Moabites became subject to David and brought tribute.

3 David also struck down King Hadadezer of
Zobah, toward Hamath,[b] as he went to set up a
monument at the river Euphrates. 4David took
from him one thousand chariots, seven thousand
cavalry, and twenty thousand foot soldiers. David
hamstrung all the chariot horses, but left one hundred of them. 5When the Arameans of Damascus
came to help King Hadadezer of Zobah, David
killed twenty-two thousand Arameans. 6Then
David put garrisons[d] in Aram of Damascus; and
the Arameans became subject to David, and

[a] Gk 2 Sam 7.6: Heb *but I have been from tent to tent and from tabernacle* [b] Meaning of Heb uncertain [c] Or *and it is blessed* [d] Gk Vg 2 Sam 8.6 Compare Syr: Heb lacks *garrisons*

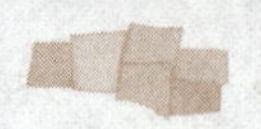

brought tribute. The LORD gave victory to David wherever he went. 7David took the gold shields that were carried by the servants of Hadadezer, and brought them to Jerusalem. 8From Tibhath and from Cun, cities of Hadadezer, David took a vast quantity of bronze; with it Solomon made the bronze sea and the pillars and the vessels of bronze.

9 When King Tou of Hamath heard that David had defeated the whole army of King Hadadezer of Zobah, 10he sent his son Hadoram to King David, to greet him and to congratulate him, because he had fought against Hadadezer and defeated him. Now Hadadezer had often been at war with Tou. He sent all sorts of articles of gold, of silver, and of bronze; 11these also King David dedicated to the LORD, together with the silver and gold that he had carried off from all the nations, from Edom, Moab, the Ammonites, the Philistines, and Amalek.

12 Abishai son of Zeruiah killed eighteen thousand Edomites in the Valley of Salt. 13He put garrisons in Edom; and all the Edomites became subject to David. And the LORD gave victory to David wherever he went.

14 So David reigned over all Israel; and he administered justice and equity to all his people. 15Joab son of Zeruiah was over the army; Jehoshaphat son of Ahilud was recorder; 16Zadok son of Ahitub and Ahimelech son of Abiathar were priests; Shavsha was secretary; 17Benaiah son of Jehoiada was over the Cherethites and the Pelethites; and David's sons were the chief officials in the service of the king.

19 Some time afterward, King Nahash of the Ammonites died, and his son succeeded him. 2David said, "I will deal loyally with Hanun son of Nahash, for his father dealt loyally with me." So David sent messengers to console him concerning his father. When David's servants came to Hanun in the land of the Ammonites, to console him, 3the officials of the Ammonites said to Hanun, "Do you think, because David has sent consolers to you, that he is honoring your father? Have not his servants come to you to search and to overthrow and to spy out the land?" 4So Hanun seized David's servants, shaved them, cut off their garments in the middle at their hips, and sent them away; 5and they departed. When David was told about the men, he sent messengers to them, for they felt greatly humiliated. The king said, "Remain at Jericho until your beards have grown, and then return."

6 When the Ammonites saw that they had made themselves odious to David, Hanun and the Ammonites sent a thousand talents of silver to hire chariots and cavalry from Mesopotamia, from Aram-maacah and from Zobah. 7They hired thirty-two thousand chariots and the king of Maacah with his army, who came and camped before Medeba. And the Ammonites were mustered from their cities and came to battle. 8When David heard of it, he sent Joab and all the army of the warriors. 9The Ammonites came out and drew up in battle array at the entrance of the city, and the kings who had come were by themselves in the open country.

10 When Joab saw that the line of battle was set against him both in front and in the rear, he chose some of the picked men of Israel and arrayed them against the Arameans; 11the rest of his troops he put in the charge of his brother Abishai, and they were arrayed against the Ammonites. 12He said, "If the Arameans are too strong for me, then you shall help me; but if the Ammonites are too strong for you, then I will help you. 13Be strong, and let us be courageous for our people and for the cities of our God; and may the LORD do what seems good to him." 14So Joab and the troops who were with him advanced toward the Arameans for battle; and they fled before him. 15When the Ammonites saw that the Arameans fled, they likewise fled before Abishai, Joab's brother, and entered the city. Then Joab came to Jerusalem.

16 But when the Arameans saw that they had been defeated by Israel, they sent messengers and brought out the Arameans who were beyond the Euphrates, with Shophach the commander of the army of Hadadezer at their head. 17When David was informed, he gathered all Israel together, crossed the Jordan, came to them, and drew up his forces against them. When David set the battle in array against the Arameans, they fought

with him. 18 The Arameans fled before Israel; and
David killed seven thousand Aramean charioteers
and forty thousand foot soldiers, and also killed
Shophach the commander of their army. 19 When
the servants of Hadadezer saw that they had been
defeated by Israel, they made peace with David,
and became subject to him. So the Arameans were
not willing to help the Ammonites any more.

20 In the spring of the year, the time when
kings go out to battle, Joab led out the
army, ravaged the country of the Ammonites, and
came and besieged Rabbah. But David remained
at Jerusalem. Joab attacked Rabbah, and overthrew it. 2 David took the crown of Milcom[a] from
his head; he found that it weighed a talent of gold,
and in it was a precious stone; and it was placed
on David's head. He also brought out the booty of
the city, a very great amount. 3 He brought out the
people who were in it, and set them to work[b] with
saws and iron picks and axes.[c] Thus David did to
all the cities of the Ammonites. Then David and
all the people returned to Jerusalem.

4 After this, war broke out with the Philistines
at Gezer; then Sibbecai the Hushathite killed
Sippai, who was one of the descendants of the
giants; and the Philistines were subdued. 5 Again
there was war with the Philistines; and Elhanan
son of Jair killed Lahmi the brother of Goliath the
Gittite, the shaft of whose spear was like a weaver's beam. 6 Again there was war at Gath, where
there was a man of great size, who had six fingers
on each hand, and six toes on each foot, twenty-
four in number; he also was descended from the
giants. 7 When he taunted Israel, Jonathan son of
Shimea, David's brother, killed him. 8 These were
descended from the giants in Gath; they fell by
the hand of David and his servants.

21 Satan stood up against Israel, and incited
David to count the people of Israel. 2 So
David said to Joab and the commanders of the
army, "Go, number Israel, from Beer-sheba to
Dan, and bring me a report, so that I may know
their number." 3 But Joab said, "May the LORD increase the number of his people a hundredfold!
Are they not, my lord the king, all of them my
lord's servants? Why then should my lord require
this? Why should he bring guilt on Israel?" 4 But
the king's word prevailed against Joab. So Joab departed and went throughout all Israel, and came
back to Jerusalem. 5 Joab gave the total count of
the people to David. In all Israel there were one
million one hundred thousand men who drew
the sword, and in Judah four hundred seventy
thousand who drew the sword. 6 But he did not
include Levi and Benjamin in the numbering, for
the king's command was abhorrent to Joab.

7 But God was displeased with this thing,
and he struck Israel. 8 David said to God, "I have
sinned greatly in that I have done this thing. But
now, I pray you, take away the guilt of your servant; for I have done very foolishly." 9 The LORD
spoke to Gad, David's seer, saying, 10 "Go and say
to David, 'Thus says the LORD: Three things I offer you; choose one of them, so that I may do it to
you.'" 11 So Gad came to David and said to him,
"Thus says the LORD, 'Take your choice: 12 either
three years of famine; or three months of devastation by your foes, while the sword of your enemies overtakes you; or three days of the sword
of the LORD, pestilence on the land, and the angel
of the LORD destroying throughout all the territory of Israel.' Now decide what answer I shall return to the one who sent me." 13 Then David said
to Gad, "I am in great distress; let me fall into the
hand of the LORD, for his mercy is very great; but
let me not fall into human hands."

14 So the LORD sent a pestilence on Israel;
and seventy thousand persons fell in Israel. 15 And
God sent an angel to Jerusalem to destroy it; but
when he was about to destroy it, the LORD took
note and relented concerning the calamity; he
said to the destroying angel, "Enough! Stay your
hand." The angel of the LORD was then standing by
the threshing floor of Ornan the Jebusite. 16 David
looked up and saw the angel of the LORD standing between earth and heaven, and in his hand a
drawn sword stretched out over Jerusalem. Then
David and the elders, clothed in sackcloth, fell on

[a] Gk Vg See 1 Kings 11.5, 33: MT *of their king* [b] Compare 2 Sam 12.31: Heb *and he sawed*
[c] Compare 2 Sam 12.31: Heb *saws*

their faces. 17And David said to God, "Was it not
I who gave the command to count the people?
It is I who have sinned and done very wickedly.
But these sheep, what have they done? Let your
hand, I pray, O LORD my God, be against me and
against my father's house; but do not let your
people be plagued!"

18 Then the angel of the LORD commanded
Gad to tell David that he should go up and erect
an altar to the LORD on the threshing floor of
Ornan the Jebusite. 19So David went up following Gad's instructions, which he had spoken in
the name of the LORD. 20Ornan turned and saw
the angel; and while his four sons who were with
him hid themselves, Ornan continued to thresh
wheat. 21As David came to Ornan, Ornan looked
and saw David; he went out from the threshing
floor, and did obeisance to David with his face
to the ground. 22David said to Ornan, "Give me
the site of the threshing floor that I may build on
it an altar to the LORD—give it to me at its full
price—so that the plague may be averted from
the people." 23Then Ornan said to David, "Take
it; and let my lord the king do what seems good
to him; see, I present the oxen for burnt offerings,
and the threshing sledges for the wood, and the
wheat for a grain offering. I give it all." 24But King
David said to Ornan, "No; I will buy them for
the full price. I will not take for the LORD what is
yours, nor offer burnt offerings that cost me nothing." 25So David paid Ornan six hundred shekels
of gold by weight for the site. 26David built there
an altar to the LORD and presented burnt offerings and offerings of well-being. He called upon
the LORD, and he answered him with fire from
heaven on the altar of burnt offering. 27Then
the LORD commanded the angel, and he put his
sword back into its sheath.

28 At that time, when David saw that the
LORD had answered him at the threshing floor of
Ornan the Jebusite, he made his sacrifices there.
29For the tabernacle of the LORD, which Moses had made in the wilderness, and the altar of
burnt offering were at that time in the high place
at Gibeon; 30but David could not go before it to
inquire of God, for he was afraid of the sword of
the angel of the LORD.

22 1Then David said,
"Here shall be the house of the LORD God
and here the altar of burnt offering for Israel."

2 David gave orders to gather together the
aliens who were residing in the land of Israel, and
he set stonecutters to prepare dressed stones for
building the house of God. 3David also provided
great stores of iron for nails for the doors of the
gates and for clamps, as well as bronze in quantities beyond weighing, 4and cedar logs without
number—for the Sidonians and Tyrians brought
great quantities of cedar to David. 5For David
said, "My son Solomon is young and inexperienced, and the house that is to be built for the
LORD must be exceedingly magnificent, famous
and glorified throughout all lands; I will therefore
make preparation for it." So David provided materials in great quantity before his death.

6 Then he called for his son Solomon and
charged him to build a house for the LORD, the
God of Israel. 7David said to Solomon, "My son,
I had planned to build a house to the name of
the LORD my God. 8But the word of the LORD
came to me, saying, 'You have shed much blood
and have waged great wars; you shall not build
a house to my name, because you have shed so
much blood in my sight on the earth. 9See, a son
shall be born to you; he shall be a man of peace. I
will give him peace from all his enemies on every
side; for his name shall be Solomon,[a] and I will
give peace[b] and quiet to Israel in his days. 10He
shall build a house for my name. He shall be a son
to me, and I will be a father to him, and I will establish his royal throne in Israel forever.' 11Now,
my son, the LORD be with you, so that you may
succeed in building the house of the LORD your
God, as he has spoken concerning you. 12Only,
may the LORD grant you discretion and understanding, so that when he gives you charge over
Israel you may keep the law of the LORD your
God. 13Then you will prosper if you are careful to
observe the statutes and the ordinances that the
LORD commanded Moses for Israel. Be strong
and of good courage. Do not be afraid or dis-

[a] Heb *Shelomoh* [b] Heb *shalom*

mayed. 14With great pains I have provided for the
house of the LORD one hundred thousand talents
of gold, one million talents of silver, and bronze
and iron beyond weighing, for there is so much of
it; timber and stone too I have provided. To these
you must add more. 15You have an abundance of
workers: stonecutters, masons, carpenters, and
all kinds of artisans without number, skilled in
working 16gold, silver, bronze, and iron. Now begin the work, and the LORD be with you."
17 David also commanded all the leaders of
Israel to help his son Solomon, saying, 18"Is not
the LORD your God with you? Has he not given
you peace on every side? For he has delivered the
inhabitants of the land into my hand; and the
land is subdued before the LORD and his people.
19Now set your mind and heart to seek the LORD
your God. Go and build the sanctuary of the
LORD God so that the ark of the covenant of the
LORD and the holy vessels of God may be brought
into a house built for the name of the LORD."

23

When David was old and full of days, he
made his son Solomon king over Israel.
2 David assembled all the leaders of Israel
and the priests and the Levites. 3The Levites,
thirty years old and upward, were counted, and
the total was thirty-eight thousand. 4"Twenty-
four thousand of these," David said, "shall have
charge of the work in the house of the LORD, six
thousand shall be officers and judges, 5four thousand gatekeepers, and four thousand shall offer
praises to the LORD with the instruments that
I have made for praise." 6And David organized
them in divisions corresponding to the sons of
Levi: Gershon,[a] Kohath, and Merari.
7 The sons of Gershon[b] were Ladan and
Shimei. 8The sons of Ladan: Jehiel the chief,
Zetham, and Joel, three. 9The sons of Shimei:
Shelomoth, Haziel, and Haran, three. These were
the heads of families of Ladan. 10And the sons of
Shimei: Jahath, Zina, Jeush, and Beriah. These
four were the sons of Shimei. 11Jahath was the
chief, and Zizah the second; but Jeush and Beriah
did not have many sons, so they were enrolled as
a single family.

12 The sons of Kohath: Amram, Izhar, Hebron, and Uzziel, four. 13The sons of Amram:
Aaron and Moses. Aaron was set apart to consecrate the most holy things, so that he and his
sons forever should make offerings before the
LORD, and minister to him and pronounce blessings in his name forever; 14but as for Moses the
man of God, his sons were to be reckoned among
the tribe of Levi. 15The sons of Moses: Gershom
and Eliezer. 16The sons of Gershom: Shebuel the
chief. 17The sons of Eliezer: Rehabiah the chief;
Eliezer had no other sons, but the sons of Rehabiah were very numerous. 18The sons of Izhar:
Shelomith the chief. 19The sons of Hebron: Jeriah
the chief, Amariah the second, Jahaziel the third,
and Jekameam the fourth. 20The sons of Uzziel:
Micah the chief and Isshiah the second.
21 The sons of Merari: Mahli and Mushi. The
sons of Mahli: Eleazar and Kish. 22Eleazar died
having no sons, but only daughters; their kindred, the sons of Kish, married them. 23The sons
of Mushi: Mahli, Eder, and Jeremoth, three.
24 These were the sons of Levi by their ancestral houses, the heads of families as they were
enrolled according to the number of the names of
the individuals from twenty years old and upward
who were to do the work for the service of the
house of the LORD. 25For David said, "The LORD,
the God of Israel, has given rest to his people; and
he resides in Jerusalem forever. 26And so the Levites no longer need to carry the tabernacle or any
of the things for its service"— 27for according to
the last words of David these were the number of
the Levites from twenty years old and upward—
28"but their duty shall be to assist the descendants
of Aaron for the service of the house of the LORD,
having the care of the courts and the chambers,
the cleansing of all that is holy, and any work for
the service of the house of God; 29to assist also
with the rows of bread, the choice flour for the
grain offering, the wafers of unleavened bread, the
baked offering, the offering mixed with oil, and
all measures of quantity or size. 30And they shall
stand every morning, thanking and praising the
LORD, and likewise at evening, 31and whenever

[a] Or *Gershom*; See 1 Chr 6.1, note, and 23.15 [b] Vg Compare Gk Syr: Heb *to the Gershonite*

burnt offerings are offered to the LORD on sabbaths, new moons, and appointed festivals, according to the number required of them, regularly
before the LORD. 32Thus they shall keep charge of
the tent of meeting and the sanctuary, and shall
attend the descendants of Aaron, their kindred,
for the service of the house of the LORD."

24 The divisions of the descendants of Aaron
were these. The sons of Aaron: Nadab,
Abihu, Eleazar, and Ithamar. 2But Nadab and
Abihu died before their father, and had no sons;
so Eleazar and Ithamar became the priests. 3Along
with Zadok of the sons of Eleazar, and Ahimelech
of the sons of Ithamar, David organized them according to the appointed duties in their service.
4Since more chief men were found among the
sons of Eleazar than among the sons of Ithamar,
they organized them under sixteen heads of ancestral houses of the sons of Eleazar, and eight of
the sons of Ithamar. 5They organized them by lot,
all alike, for there were officers of the sanctuary
and officers of God among both the sons of Eleazar and the sons of Ithamar. 6The scribe Shemaiah son of Nethanel, a Levite, recorded them
in the presence of the king, and the officers, and
Zadok the priest, and Ahimelech son of Abiathar,
and the heads of ancestral houses of the priests
and of the Levites; one ancestral house being
chosen for Eleazar and one chosen for Ithamar.

7 The first lot fell to Jehoiarib, the second to
Jedaiah, 8the third to Harim, the fourth to Seo-
rim, 9the fifth to Malchijah, the sixth to Mijamin, 10the seventh to Hakkoz, the eighth to
Abijah, 11the ninth to Jeshua, the tenth to Shecaniah, 12the eleventh to Eliashib, the twelfth to Ja-
kim, 13the thirteenth to Huppah, the fourteenth
to Jeshebeab, 14the fifteenth to Bilgah, the sixteenth to Immer, 15the seventeenth to Hezir, the
eighteenth to Happizzez, 16the nineteenth to Pethahiah, the twentieth to Jehezkel, 17the twenty-
first to Jachin, the twenty-second to Gamul, 18the
twenty-third to Delaiah, the twenty-fourth to
Maaziah. 19These had as their appointed duty in
their service to enter the house of the LORD according to the procedure established for them by
their ancestor Aaron, as the LORD God of Israel
had commanded him.

20 And of the rest of the sons of Levi: of the
sons of Amram, Shubael; of the sons of Shubael,
Jehdeiah. 21Of Rehabiah: of the sons of Rehabiah, Isshiah the chief. 22Of the Izharites, Shelomoth; of the sons of Shelomoth, Jahath. 23The
sons of Hebron:[a] Jeriah the chief,[b] Amariah the
second, Jahaziel the third, Jekameam the fourth.
24The sons of Uzziel, Micah; of the sons of Micah,
Shamir. 25The brother of Micah, Isshiah; of the
sons of Isshiah, Zechariah. 26The sons of Merari:
Mahli and Mushi. The sons of Jaaziah: Beno.[c]
27The sons of Merari: of Jaaziah, Beno,[c] Shoham,
Zaccur, and Ibri. 28Of Mahli: Eleazar, who had
no sons. 29Of Kish, the sons of Kish: Jerahmeel.
30The sons of Mushi: Mahli, Eder, and Jerimoth.
These were the sons of the Levites according to
their ancestral houses. 31These also cast lots corresponding to their kindred, the descendants of
Aaron, in the presence of King David, Zadok,
Ahimelech, and the heads of ancestral houses of
the priests and of the Levites, the chief as well as
the youngest brother.

25 David and the officers of the army also set
apart for the service the sons of Asaph,
and of Heman, and of Jeduthun, who should
prophesy with lyres, harps, and cymbals. The
list of those who did the work and of their duties was: 2Of the sons of Asaph: Zaccur, Joseph,
Nethaniah, and Asarelah, sons of Asaph, under
the direction of Asaph, who prophesied under
the direction of the king. 3Of Jeduthun, the sons
of Jeduthun: Gedaliah, Zeri, Jeshaiah, Shimei,[d]
Hashabiah, and Mattithiah, six, under the direction of their father Jeduthun, who prophesied with
the lyre in thanksgiving and praise to the LORD.
4Of Heman, the sons of Heman: Bukkiah, Mattaniah, Uzziel, Shebuel, and Jerimoth, Hananiah,
Hanani, Eliathah, Giddalti, and Romamti-ezer,
Joshbekashah, Mallothi, Hothir, Mahazioth. 5All
these were the sons of Heman the king's seer, according to the promise of God to exalt him; for

[a] See 23.19: Heb lacks *Hebron* [b] See 23.19: Heb lacks *the chief* [c] Or *his son*: Meaning of Heb uncertain
[d] One Ms: Gk: MT lacks *Shimei*

God had given Heman fourteen sons and three
daughters. 6They were all under the direction
of their father for the music in the house of the
LORD with cymbals, harps, and lyres for the service of the house of God. Asaph, Jeduthun, and
Heman were under the order of the king. 7They
and their kindred, who were trained in singing to
the LORD, all of whom were skillful, numbered
two hundred eighty-eight. 8And they cast lots for
their duties, small and great, teacher and pupil
alike.
9 The first lot fell for Asaph to Joseph; the
second to Gedaliah, to him and his brothers and
his sons, twelve; 10the third to Zaccur, his sons
and his brothers, twelve; 11the fourth to Izri,
his sons and his brothers, twelve; 12the fifth to
Nethaniah, his sons and his brothers, twelve;
13the sixth to Bukkiah, his sons and his brothers,
twelve; 14the seventh to Jesarelah,[a] his sons and
his brothers, twelve; 15the eighth to Jeshaiah, his
sons and his brothers, twelve; 16the ninth to Mattaniah, his sons and his brothers, twelve; 17the
tenth to Shimei, his sons and his brothers, twelve;
18the eleventh to Azarel, his sons and his brothers, twelve; 19the twelfth to Hashabiah, his sons
and his brothers, twelve; 20to the thirteenth, Shubael, his sons and his brothers, twelve; 21to the
fourteenth, Mattithiah, his sons and his brothers,
twelve; 22to the fifteenth, to Jeremoth, his sons
and his brothers, twelve; 23to the sixteenth, to
Hananiah, his sons and his brothers, twelve; 24to
the seventeenth, to Joshbekashah, his sons and
his brothers, twelve; 25to the eighteenth, to Hanani, his sons and his brothers, twelve; 26to the
nineteenth, to Mallothi, his sons and his brothers, twelve; 27to the twentieth, to Eliathah, his
sons and his brothers, twelve; 28to the twenty-
first, to Hothir, his sons and his brothers, twelve;
29to the twenty-second, to Giddalti, his sons and
his brothers, twelve; 30to the twenty-third, to
Mahazioth, his sons and his brothers, twelve; 31to
the twenty-fourth, to Romamti-ezer, his sons and
his brothers, twelve.

26 As for the divisions of the gatekeepers:
of the Korahites, Meshelemiah son of
Kore, of the sons of Asaph. 2Meshelemiah had
sons: Zechariah the firstborn, Jediael the second,
Zebadiah the third, Jathniel the fourth, 3Elam
the fifth, Jehohanan the sixth, Eliehoenai the
seventh. 4Obed-edom had sons: Shemaiah the
firstborn, Jehozabad the second, Joah the third,
Sachar the fourth, Nethanel the fifth, 5Ammiel
the sixth, Issachar the seventh, Peullethai the
eighth; for God blessed him. 6Also to his son Shemaiah sons were born who exercised authority
in their ancestral houses, for they were men of
great ability. 7The sons of Shemaiah: Othni, Re-
phael, Obed, and Elzabad, whose brothers were
able men, Elihu and Semachiah. 8All these, sons
of Obed-edom with their sons and brothers, were
able men qualified for the service; sixty-two of
Obed-edom. 9Meshelemiah had sons and brothers, able men, eighteen. 10Hosah, of the sons of
Merari, had sons: Shimri the chief (for though he
was not the firstborn, his father made him chief),
11Hilkiah the second, Tebaliah the third, Zechariah the fourth: all the sons and brothers of Hosah totaled thirteen.
12 These divisions of the gatekeepers, corresponding to their leaders, had duties, just as
their kindred did, ministering in the house of the
LORD; 13and they cast lots by ancestral houses,
small and great alike, for their gates. 14The lot
for the east fell to Shelemiah. They cast lots also
for his son Zechariah, a prudent counselor, and
his lot came out for the north. 15Obed-edom's
came out for the south, and to his sons was allotted the storehouse. 16For Shuppim and Hosah it
came out for the west, at the gate of Shallecheth
on the ascending road. Guard corresponded to
guard. 17On the east there were six Levites each
day,[b] on the north four each day, on the south
four each day, as well as two and two at the storehouse; 18and for the colonnade[c] on the west there
were four at the road and two at the colonnade.[c]
19These were the divisions of the gatekeepers
among the Korahites and the sons of Merari.
20 And of the Levites, Ahijah had charge of
the treasuries of the house of God and the treasuries of the dedicated gifts. 21The sons of Ladan,

[a] Or *Asarelah*; see 25.2 [b] Gk: Heb lacks *each day* [c] Heb *parbar*: meaning uncertain

the sons of the Gershonites belonging to Ladan,
the heads of families belonging to Ladan the Gershonite: Jehieli.[a]
22 The sons of Jehieli, Zetham and his brother
Joel, were in charge of the treasuries of the house
of the LORD. 23 Of the Amramites, the Izharites,
the Hebronites, and the Uzzielites: 24 Shebuel
son of Gershom, son of Moses, was chief officer
in charge of the treasuries. 25 His brothers: from
Eliezer were his son Rehabiah, his son Jeshaiah,
his son Joram, his son Zichri, and his son Shelomoth. 26 This Shelomoth and his brothers were in
charge of all the treasuries of the dedicated gifts
that King David, and the heads of families, and
the officers of the thousands and the hundreds,
and the commanders of the army, had dedicated.
27 From booty won in battles they dedicated gifts
for the maintenance of the house of the LORD.
28 Also all that Samuel the seer, and Saul son
of Kish, and Abner son of Ner, and Joab son of
Zeruiah had dedicated—all dedicated gifts were
in the care of Shelomoth[b] and his brothers.

29 Of the Izharites, Chenaniah and his sons
were appointed to outside duties for Israel, as
officers and judges. 30 Of the Hebronites, Hashabiah and his brothers, one thousand seven
hundred men of ability, had the oversight of
Israel west of the Jordan for all the work of the
LORD and for the service of the king. 31 Of the
Hebronites, Jerijah was chief of the Hebronites.
(In the fortieth year of David's reign search was
made, of whatever genealogy or family, and men
of great ability among them were found at Jazer
in Gilead.) 32 King David appointed him and his
brothers, two thousand seven hundred men of
ability, heads of families, to have the oversight of
the Reubenites, the Gadites, and the half-tribe
of the Manassites for everything pertaining to
God and for the affairs of the king.

27 This is the list of the people of Israel, the
heads of families, the commanders of the
thousands and the hundreds, and their officers
who served the king in all matters concerning the
divisions that came and went, month after month
throughout the year, each division numbering
twenty-four thousand:

2 Jashobeam son of Zabdiel was in charge of
the first division in the first month; in his division
were twenty-four thousand. 3 He was a descendant
of Perez, and was chief of all the commanders of
the army for the first month. 4 Dodai the Ahohite was in charge of the division of the second
month; Mikloth was the chief officer of his division. In his division were twenty-four thousand.
5 The third commander, for the third month, was
Benaiah son of the priest Jehoiada, as chief; in his
division were twenty-four thousand. 6 This is the
Benaiah who was a mighty man of the Thirty and
in command of the Thirty; his son Ammizabad
was in charge of his division.[c] 7 Asahel brother of
Joab was fourth, for the fourth month, and his son
Zebadiah after him; in his division were twenty-
four thousand. 8 The fifth commander, for the fifth
month, was Shamhuth, the Izrahite; in his division
were twenty-four thousand. 9 Sixth, for the sixth
month, was Ira son of Ikkesh the Tekoite; in his
division were twenty-four thousand. 10 Seventh,
for the seventh month, was Helez the Pelonite,
of the Ephraimites; in his division were twenty-
four thousand. 11 Eighth, for the eighth month,
was Sibbecai the Hushathite, of the Zerahites; in
his division were twenty-four thousand. 12 Ninth,
for the ninth month, was Abiezer of Anathoth,
a Benjaminite; in his division were twenty-four
thousand. 13 Tenth, for the tenth month, was Maharai of Netophah, of the Zerahites; in his division were twenty-four thousand. 14 Eleventh, for
the eleventh month, was Benaiah of Pirathon, of
the Ephraimites; in his division were twenty-four
thousand. 15 Twelfth, for the twelfth month, was
Heldai the Netophathite, of Othniel; in his division were twenty-four thousand.

16 Over the tribes of Israel, for the Reubenites, Eliezer son of Zichri was chief officer; for
the Simeonites, Shephatiah son of Maacah; 17 for
Levi, Hashabiah son of Kemuel; for Aaron, Zadok; 18 for Judah, Elihu, one of David's brothers;
for Issachar, Omri son of Michael; 19 for Zebulun,

[a] The Hebrew text of verse 21 is confused [b] Gk Compare 26.28: Heb *Shelomith*
[c] Gk Vg: Heb *Ammizabad was his division*

Ishmaiah son of Obadiah; for Naphtali, Jerimoth son of Azriel; 20 for the Ephraimites, Hoshea son of Azaziah; for the half-tribe of Manasseh, Joel son of Pedaiah; 21 for the half-tribe of Manasseh in Gilead, Iddo son of Zechariah; for Benjamin, Jaasiel son of Abner; 22 for Dan, Azarel son of Jeroham. These were the leaders of the tribes of Israel. 23 David did not count those below twenty years of age, for the LORD had promised to make Israel as numerous as the stars of heaven. 24 Joab son of Zeruiah began to count them, but did not finish; yet wrath came upon Israel for this, and the number was not entered into the account of the Annals of King David.

25 Over the king's treasuries was Azmaveth son of Adiel. Over the treasuries in the country, in the cities, in the villages and in the towers, was Jonathan son of Uzziah. 26 Over those who did the work of the field, tilling the soil, was Ezri son of Chelub. 27 Over the vineyards was Shimei the Ramathite. Over the produce of the vineyards for the wine cellars was Zabdi the Shiphmite. 28 Over the olive and sycamore trees in the Shephelah was Baal-hanan the Gederite. Over the stores of oil was Joash. 29 Over the herds that pastured in Sharon was Shitrai the Sharonite. Over the herds in the valleys was Shaphat son of Adlai. 30 Over the camels was Obil the Ishmaelite. Over the donkeys was Jehdeiah the Meronothite. Over the flocks was Jaziz the Hagrite. 31 All these were stewards of King David's property.

32 Jonathan, David's uncle, was a counselor, being a man of understanding and a scribe; Jehiel son of Hachmoni attended the king's sons. 33 Ahithophel was the king's counselor, and Hushai the Archite was the king's friend. 34 After Ahithophel came Jehoiada son of Benaiah, and Abiathar. Joab was commander of the king's army.

28 David assembled at Jerusalem all the officials of Israel, the officials of the tribes, the officers of the divisions that served the king, the commanders of the thousands, the commanders of the hundreds, the stewards of all the property and cattle of the king and his sons, together with the palace officials, the mighty warriors, and all the warriors. 2 Then King David rose to his feet and said: "Hear me, my brothers and my people. I had planned to build a house of rest for the ark of the covenant of the LORD, for the footstool of our God; and I made preparations for building. 3 But God said to me, 'You shall not build a house for my name, for you are a warrior and have shed blood.' 4 Yet the LORD God of Israel chose me from all my ancestral house to be king over Israel forever; for he chose Judah as leader, and in the house of Judah my father's house, and among my father's sons he took delight in making me king over all Israel. 5 And of all my sons, for the LORD has given me many, he has chosen my son Solomon to sit upon the throne of the kingdom of the LORD over Israel. 6 He said to me, 'It is your son Solomon who shall build my house and my courts, for I have chosen him to be a son to me, and I will be a father to him. 7 I will establish his kingdom forever if he continues resolute in keeping my commandments and my ordinances, as he is today.' 8 Now therefore in the sight of all Israel, the assembly of the LORD, and in the hearing of our God, observe and search out all the commandments of the LORD your God; that you may possess this good land, and leave it for an inheritance to your children after you forever.

9 "And you, my son Solomon, know the God of your father, and serve him with single mind and willing heart; for the LORD searches every mind, and understands every plan and thought. If you seek him, he will be found by you; but if you forsake him, he will abandon you forever. 10 Take heed now, for the LORD has chosen you to build a house as the sanctuary; be strong, and act."

11 Then David gave his son Solomon the plan of the vestibule of the temple, and of its houses, its treasuries, its upper rooms, and its inner chambers, and of the room for the mercy seat;[a] 12 and the plan of all that he had in mind: for the courts of the house of the LORD, all the surrounding chambers, the treasuries of the house of God, and the treasuries for dedicated gifts; 13 for the divisions of the priests and of the Levites, and all

[a] Or *the cover*

the work of the service in the house of the LORD;
for all the vessels for the service in the house of
the LORD, 14 the weight of gold for all golden
vessels for each service, the weight of silver vessels for each service, 15 the weight of the golden
lampstands and their lamps, the weight of gold
for each lampstand and its lamps, the weight of
silver for a lampstand and its lamps, according to
the use of each in the service, 16 the weight of gold
for each table for the rows of bread, the silver for
the silver tables, 17 and pure gold for the forks, the
basins, and the cups; for the golden bowls and
the weight of each; for the silver bowls and the
weight of each; 18 for the altar of incense made of
refined gold, and its weight; also his plan for the
golden chariot of the cherubim that spread their
wings and covered the ark of the covenant of the
LORD.

19 "All this, in writing at the LORD's direction,
he made clear to me—the plan of all the works."

20 David said further to his son Solomon,
"Be strong and of good courage, and act. Do not
be afraid or dismayed; for the LORD God, my
God, is with you. He will not fail you or forsake
you, until all the work for the service of the house
of the LORD is finished. 21 Here are the divisions
of the priests and the Levites for all the service of
the house of God; and with you in all the work
will be every volunteer who has skill for any kind
of service; also the officers and all the people will
be wholly at your command."

29 King David said to the whole assembly,
"My son Solomon, whom alone God
has chosen, is young and inexperienced, and
the work is great; for the temple[a] will not be for
mortals but for the LORD God. 2 So I have provided for the house of my God, so far as I was
able, the gold for the things of gold, the silver for
the things of silver, and the bronze for the things
of bronze, the iron for the things of iron, and
wood for the things of wood, besides great quantities of onyx and stones for setting, antimony,
colored stones, all sorts of precious stones, and
marble in abundance. 3 Moreover, in addition to
all that I have provided for the holy house, I have
a treasure of my own of gold and silver, and because of my devotion to the house of my God I
give it to the house of my God: 4 three thousand
talents of gold, of the gold of Ophir, and seven
thousand talents of refined silver, for overlaying
the walls of the house, 5 and for all the work to
be done by artisans, gold for the things of gold
and silver for the things of silver. Who then will
offer willingly, consecrating themselves today to
the LORD?"

6 Then the leaders of ancestral houses made
their freewill offerings, as did also the leaders of
the tribes, the commanders of the thousands and
of the hundreds, and the officers over the king's
work. 7 They gave for the service of the house
of God five thousand talents and ten thousand
darics of gold, ten thousand talents of silver,
eighteen thousand talents of bronze, and one
hundred thousand talents of iron. 8 Whoever had
precious stones gave them to the treasury of the
house of the LORD, into the care of Jehiel the
Gershonite. 9 Then the people rejoiced because
these had given willingly, for with single mind
they had offered freely to the LORD; King David
also rejoiced greatly.

10 Then David blessed the LORD in the presence of all the assembly; David said: "Blessed are
you, O LORD, the God of our ancestor Israel, forever and ever. 11 Yours, O LORD, are the greatness,
the power, the glory, the victory, and the majesty;
for all that is in the heavens and on the earth is
yours; yours is the kingdom, O LORD, and you
are exalted as head above all. 12 Riches and honor
come from you, and you rule over all. In your
hand are power and might; and it is in your hand
to make great and to give strength to all. 13 And
now, our God, we give thanks to you and praise
your glorious name.

14 "But who am I, and what is my people, that
we should be able to make this freewill offering?
For all things come from you, and of your own
have we given you. 15 For we are aliens and tran-
sients before you, as were all our ancestors; our
days on the earth are like a shadow, and there is
no hope. 16 O LORD our God, all this abundance

[a] Heb *fortress*

that we have provided for building you a house
for your holy name comes from your hand and is
all your own. 17 I know, my God, that you search
the heart, and take pleasure in uprightness; in the
uprightness of my heart I have freely offered all
these things, and now I have seen your people,
who are present here, offering freely and joyously
to you. 18 O LORD, the God of Abraham, Isaac,
and Israel, our ancestors, keep forever such purposes and thoughts in the hearts of your people,
and direct their hearts toward you. 19 Grant to my
son Solomon that with single mind he may keep
your commandments, your decrees, and your
statutes, performing all of them, and that he may
build the temple[a] for which I have made provision."

20 Then David said to the whole assembly,
"Bless the LORD your God." And all the assembly blessed the LORD, the God of their ancestors,
and bowed their heads and prostrated themselves before the LORD and the king. 21 On the
next day they offered sacrifices and burnt offerings to the LORD, a thousand bulls, a thousand
rams, and a thousand lambs, with their libations,
and sacrifices in abundance for all Israel; 22 and
they ate and drank before the LORD on that day
with great joy.

They made David's son Solomon king a second time; they anointed him as the LORD's
prince, and Zadok as priest. 23 Then Solomon sat
on the throne of the LORD, succeeding his father
David as king; he prospered, and all Israel obeyed
him. 24 All the leaders and the mighty warriors,
and also all the sons of King David, pledged their
allegiance to King Solomon. 25 The LORD highly
exalted Solomon in the sight of all Israel, and bestowed upon him such royal majesty as had not
been on any king before him in Israel.

26 Thus David son of Jesse reigned over all Israel. 27 The period that he reigned over Israel was
forty years; he reigned seven years in Hebron,
and thirty-three years in Jerusalem. 28 He died in a
good old age, full of days, riches, and honor; and
his son Solomon succeeded him. 29 Now the acts
of King David, from first to last, are written in the
records of the seer Samuel, and in the records of
the prophet Nathan, and in the records of the seer
Gad, 30 with accounts of all his rule and his might
and of the events that befell him and Israel and all
the kingdoms of the earth.

[a] Heb *fortress*

1 Chronicles 29:26-30

David's last days and Solomon's succession are presented in terms of unalloyed glory and prosperity. Both are approved by God and the people, who pledge their loyalty, and the most important institutions in Israel's common life—the Aaronic priesthood and the temple—are well established. The author knows, of course, that the end of this story includes the nation's defeat by a hostile empire. From the serenity afforded by the temple's restoration after the exile, however, the narrator affirms that "the events that befell [David] and Israel and all the kingdoms of the earth" (v. 30) are in God's hands.

—NE

2 Chronicles

THIS BOOK CONTINUES the narrative begun in 1 Chronicles (see the introduction to that book). First comes a rather idealized account of the reign of Solomon (chs. 1–9), and then an account of the subsequent kings of Judah (chs. 10–36). Very little attention is given to the kings of the Northern Kingdom.

How readers respond to these two books depends, first, on how they view the historical record. In other words, what counts as history? What justifies a particular interpretation of history? If we remove these texts from their Diaspora context and treat them in isolation from the conditions of their emergence, it is easy for them to appear inconsistent and to lack historical value. Nevertheless, when the collective memory of displaced people is in fragments, members often resort to creative forms of re-creating their collective memory. As Martha Chew-Sánchez has argued in *Corridors in Migrant Memory*, these peoples may look elsewhere for new images to fill the gaps where the original collective memory was destroyed.

Our response also depends on where we stand. As someone who identifies himself as a Mexican American from the U.S. Southwest—a land where we find at the margins the lived experiences of those today who face internal colonialism—I am drawn to the marginalized stories of colonization and Diaspora in the Hebrew Bible. Even more tragic than this internal colonialism, however, is the dismissed experience of the displaced, an experience captured within marginal texts that are usually concealed from the fashioned histories of the ruling order. I read 2 Chronicles as an effort to affirm the text of the Other. Perhaps 1 and 2 Chronicles provide a helpful example of how such collective remembering may take place among contemporary peoples as well.

— ***Gregory Lee Cuéllar***

1 Solomon son of David established himself
in his kingdom; the LORD his God was with
him and made him exceedingly great.
2 Solomon summoned all Israel, the commanders of the thousands and of the hundreds,
the judges, and all the leaders of all Israel, the
heads of families. 3 Then Solomon, and the whole
assembly with him, went to the high place that
was at Gibeon; for God's tent of meeting, which
Moses the servant of the LORD had made in the
wilderness, was there. 4 (But David had brought
the ark of God up from Kiriath-jearim to the place

that David had prepared for it; for he had pitched
a tent for it in Jerusalem.) 5 Moreover the bronze
altar that Bezalel son of Uri, son of Hur, had
made, was there in front of the tabernacle of the
LORD. And Solomon and the assembly inquired
at it. 6 Solomon went up there to the bronze altar
before the LORD, which was at the tent of meeting, and offered a thousand burnt offerings on it.
7 That night God appeared to Solomon, and
said to him, "Ask what I should give you." 8 Solomon said to God, "You have shown great and
steadfast love to my father David, and have made
me succeed him as king. 9 O LORD God, let your
promise to my father David now be fulfilled, for
you have made me king over a people as numerous as the dust of the earth. 10 Give me now wisdom and knowledge to go out and come in before
this people, for who can rule this great people of
yours?" 11 God answered Solomon, "Because this
was in your heart, and you have not asked for possessions, wealth, honor, or the life of those who
hate you, and have not even asked for long life,
but have asked for wisdom and knowledge for
yourself that you may rule my people over whom
I have made you king, 12 wisdom and knowledge
are granted to you. I will also give you riches,
possessions, and honor, such as none of the kings
had who were before you, and none after you
shall have the like." 13 So Solomon came from[a] the
high place at Gibeon, from the tent of meeting, to
Jerusalem. And he reigned over Israel.
14 Solomon gathered together chariots and
horses; he had fourteen hundred chariots and
twelve thousand horses, which he stationed in
the chariot cities and with the king in Jerusalem.
15 The king made silver and gold as common in Jerusalem as stone, and he made cedar as plentiful
as the sycamore of the Shephelah. 16 Solomon's
horses were imported from Egypt and Kue; the
king's traders received them from Kue at the prevailing price. 17 They imported from Egypt, and
then exported, a chariot for six hundred shekels
of silver, and a horse for one hundred fifty; so
through them these were exported to all the kings
of the Hittites and the kings of Aram.

2 [b] Solomon decided to build a temple for the
name of the LORD, and a royal palace for
himself. 2 [c] Solomon conscripted seventy thousand
laborers and eighty thousand stonecutters in the
hill country, with three thousand six hundred to
oversee them.
3 Solomon sent word to King Huram of
Tyre: "Once you dealt with my father David and
sent him cedar to build himself a house to live in.
4 I am now about to build a house for the name
of the LORD my God and dedicate it to him for
offering fragrant incense before him, and for the
regular offering of the rows of bread, and for burnt
offerings morning and evening, on the sabbaths
and the new moons and the appointed festivals
of the LORD our God, as ordained forever for Israel. 5 The house that I am about to build will be
great, for our God is greater than other gods. 6 But
who is able to build him a house, since heaven,
even highest heaven, cannot contain him? Who
am I to build a house for him, except as a place
to make offerings before him? 7 So now send me
an artisan skilled to work in gold, silver, bronze,
and iron, and in purple, crimson, and blue fabrics, trained also in engraving, to join the skilled
workers who are with me in Judah and Jerusalem,
whom my father David provided. 8 Send me also
cedar, cypress, and algum timber from Lebanon,
for I know that your servants are skilled in cutting
Lebanon timber. My servants will work with your
servants 9 to prepare timber for me in abundance,
for the house I am about to build will be great
and wonderful. 10 I will provide for your servants,
those who cut the timber, twenty thousand cors
of crushed wheat, twenty thousand cors of barley, twenty thousand baths[d] of wine, and twenty
thousand baths of oil."
11 Then King Huram of Tyre answered in a
letter that he sent to Solomon, "Because the LORD
loves his people he has made you king over them."
12 Huram also said, "Blessed be the LORD God of
Israel, who made heaven and earth, who has given
King David a wise son, endowed with discretion
and understanding, who will build a temple for
the LORD, and a royal palace for himself.

[a] Gk Vg: Heb *to* [b] Ch 1.18 in Heb [c] Ch 2.1 in Heb [d] A Hebrew measure of volume

13 "I have dispatched Huram-abi, a skilled
artisan, endowed with understanding, 14the son
of one of the Danite women, his father a Tyrian.
He is trained to work in gold, silver, bronze, iron,
stone, and wood, and in purple, blue, and crimson fabrics and fine linen, and to do all sorts of
engraving and execute any design that may be assigned him, with your artisans, the artisans of my
lord, your father David. 15Now, as for the wheat,
barley, oil, and wine, of which my lord has spoken, let him send them to his servants. 16We will
cut whatever timber you need from Lebanon, and
bring it to you as rafts by sea to Joppa; you will
take it up to Jerusalem."

17 Then Solomon took a census of all the
aliens who were residing in the land of Israel,
after the census that his father David had taken;
and there were found to be one hundred fifty-
three thousand six hundred. 18Seventy thousand
of them he assigned as laborers, eighty thousand
as stonecutters in the hill country, and three thousand six hundred as overseers to make the people
work.

3 Solomon began to build the house of the
LORD in Jerusalem on Mount Moriah, where
the LORD had appeared to his father David, at the
place that David had designated, on the threshing
floor of Ornan the Jebusite. 2He began to build on
the second day of the second month of the fourth
year of his reign. 3These are Solomon's measurements[a] for building the house of God: the length,
in cubits of the old standard, was sixty cubits, and
the width twenty cubits. 4The vestibule in front
of the nave of the house was twenty cubits long,
across the width of the house;[b] and its height was
one hundred twenty cubits. He overlaid it on the
inside with pure gold. 5The nave he lined with cypress, covered it with fine gold, and made palms
and chains on it. 6He adorned the house with settings of precious stones. The gold was gold from
Parvaim. 7So he lined the house with gold—its
beams, its thresholds, its walls, and its doors; and
he carved cherubim on the walls.

8 He made the most holy place; its length,
corresponding to the width of the house, was
twenty cubits, and its width was twenty cubits;
he overlaid it with six hundred talents of fine
gold. 9The weight of the nails was fifty shekels of
gold. He overlaid the upper chambers with gold.

10 In the most holy place he made two carved
cherubim and overlaid[c] them with gold. 11The
wings of the cherubim together extended twenty
cubits: one wing of the one, five cubits long,
touched the wall of the house, and its other wing,
five cubits long, touched the wing of the other
cherub; 12and of this cherub, one wing, five cubits
long, touched the wall of the house, and the other
wing, also five cubits long, was joined to the wing
of the first cherub. 13The wings of these cherubim
extended twenty cubits; the cherubim[d] stood on
their feet, facing the nave. 14And Solomon[e] made
the curtain of blue and purple and crimson fabrics and fine linen, and worked cherubim into it.

15 In front of the house he made two pillars
thirty-five cubits high, with a capital of five cubits
on the top of each. 16He made encircling[f] chains
and put them on the tops of the pillars; and he
made one hundred pomegranates, and put them
on the chains. 17He set up the pillars in front of
the temple, one on the right, the other on the left;
the one on the right he called Jachin, and the one
on the left, Boaz.

4 He made an altar of bronze, twenty cubits
long, twenty cubits wide, and ten cubits high.
2Then he made the molten sea; it was round, ten
cubits from rim to rim, and five cubits high. A
line of thirty cubits would encircle it completely.
3Under it were panels all around, each of ten cubits, surrounding the sea; there were two rows of
panels, cast when it was cast. 4It stood on twelve
oxen, three facing north, three facing west, three
facing south, and three facing east; the sea was set
on them. The hindquarters of each were toward
the inside. 5Its thickness was a handbreadth; its
rim was made like the rim of a cup, like the flower
of a lily; it held three thousand baths.[g] 6He also
made ten basins in which to wash, and set five on
the right side, and five on the left. In these they

[a] Syr: Heb *foundations* [b] Compare 1 Kings 6.3: Meaning of Heb uncertain [c] Heb *they overlaid* [d] Heb *they* [e] Heb *he* [f] Cn: Heb *in the inner sanctuary* [g] A Hebrew measure of volume

were to rinse what was used for the burnt offering. The sea was for the priests to wash in.
7 He made ten golden lampstands as prescribed, and set them in the temple, five on the
south side and five on the north. 8 He also made
ten tables and placed them in the temple, five on
the right side and five on the left. And he made
one hundred basins of gold. 9 He made the court
of the priests, and the great court, and doors for
the court; he overlaid their doors with bronze.
10 He set the sea at the southeast corner of the
house.
11 And Huram made the pots, the shovels,
and the basins. Thus Huram finished the work
that he did for King Solomon on the house of
God: 12 the two pillars, the bowls, and the two
capitals on the top of the pillars; and the two
latticeworks to cover the two bowls of the capitals that were on the top of the pillars; 13 the four
hundred pomegranates for the two latticeworks,
two rows of pomegranates for each latticework,
to cover the two bowls of the capitals that were
on the pillars. 14 He made the stands, the basins
on the stands, 15 the one sea, and the twelve oxen
underneath it. 16 The pots, the shovels, the forks,
and all the equipment for these Huram-abi made
of burnished bronze for King Solomon for the
house of the LORD. 17 In the plain of the Jordan
the king cast them, in the clay ground between
Succoth and Zeredah. 18 Solomon made all these
things in great quantities, so that the weight of
the bronze was not determined.
19 So Solomon made all the things that were
in the house of God: the golden altar, the tables
for the bread of the Presence, 20 the lampstands
and their lamps of pure gold to burn before the
inner sanctuary, as prescribed; 21 the flowers, the
lamps, and the tongs, of purest gold; 22 the snuffers, basins, ladles, and firepans, of pure gold. As
for the entrance to the temple: the inner doors to
the most holy place and the doors of the nave of
the temple were of gold.

5 Thus all the work that Solomon did for the
house of the LORD was finished. Solomon
brought in the things that his father David
had dedicated, and stored the silver, the gold,
and all the vessels in the treasuries of the house
of God.
2 Then Solomon assembled the elders of Israel and all the heads of the tribes, the leaders of
the ancestral houses of the people of Israel, in Jerusalem, to bring up the ark of the covenant of
the LORD out of the city of David, which is Zion.
3 And all the Israelites assembled before the king
at the festival that is in the seventh month. 4 And
all the elders of Israel came, and the Levites carried the ark. 5 So they brought up the ark, the tent
of meeting, and all the holy vessels that were in
the tent; the priests and the Levites brought them
up. 6 King Solomon and all the congregation of
Israel, who had assembled before him, were before the ark, sacrificing so many sheep and oxen
that they could not be numbered or counted.
7 Then the priests brought the ark of the covenant
of the LORD to its place, in the inner sanctuary of
the house, in the most holy place, underneath the
wings of the cherubim. 8 For the cherubim spread
out their wings over the place of the ark, so that
the cherubim made a covering above the ark and
its poles. 9 The poles were so long that the ends of
the poles were seen from the holy place in front of
the inner sanctuary; but they could not be seen
from outside; they are there to this day. 10 There
was nothing in the ark except the two tablets that
Moses put there at Horeb, where the LORD made
a covenant[a] with the people of Israel after they
came out of Egypt.
11 Now when the priests came out of the
holy place (for all the priests who were present
had sanctified themselves, without regard to their
divisions), 12 all the levitical singers, Asaph, Heman, and Jeduthun, their sons and kindred, arrayed in fine linen, with cymbals, harps, and lyres,
stood east of the altar with one hundred twenty
priests who were trumpeters. 13 It was the duty of
the trumpeters and singers to make themselves
heard in unison in praise and thanksgiving to the
LORD, and when the song was raised, with trumpets and cymbals and other musical instruments,
in praise to the LORD,

[a] Heb lacks *a covenant*

"For he is good,
for his steadfast love endures forever,"

the house, the house of the LORD, was filled with a cloud, 14so that the priests could not stand to minister because of the cloud; for the glory of the LORD filled the house of God.

6 Then Solomon said, "The LORD has said that he would reside in thick darkness. 2I have built you an exalted house, a place for you to reside in forever."

3 Then the king turned around and blessed all the assembly of Israel, while all the assembly of Israel stood. 4And he said, "Blessed be the LORD, the God of Israel, who with his hand has fulfilled what he promised with his mouth to my father David, saying, 5'Since the day that I brought my people out of the land of Egypt, I have not chosen a city from any of the tribes of Israel in which to build a house, so that my name might be there, and I chose no one as ruler over my people Israel; 6but I have chosen Jerusalem in order that my name may be there, and I have chosen David to be over my people Israel.' 7My father David had it in mind to build a house for the name of the LORD, the God of Israel. 8But the LORD said to my father David, 'You did well to consider building a house for my name; 9nevertheless you shall not build the house, but your son who shall be born to you shall build the house for my name.' 10Now the LORD has fulfilled his promise that he made; for I have succeeded my father David, and sit on the throne of Israel, as the LORD promised, and have built the house for the name of the LORD, the God of Israel. 11There I have set the ark, in which is the covenant of the LORD that he made with the people of Israel."

12 Then Solomon[a] stood before the altar of the LORD in the presence of the whole assembly of Israel, and spread out his hands. 13Solomon had made a bronze platform five cubits long, five cubits wide, and three cubits high, and had set it in the court; and he stood on it. Then he knelt on his knees in the presence of the whole assembly of Israel, and spread out his hands toward heaven. 14He said, "O LORD, God of Israel, there is no God like you, in heaven or on earth, keeping covenant in steadfast love with your servants who walk before you with all their heart— 15you who have kept for your servant, my father David, what you promised to him. Indeed, you promised with your mouth and this day have fulfilled with your hand. 16Therefore, O LORD, God of Israel, keep for your servant, my father David, that which you promised him, saying, 'There shall never fail you a successor before me to sit on the throne of Israel, if only your children keep to their way, to walk in my law as you have walked before me.' 17Therefore, O LORD, God of Israel, let your word be confirmed, which you promised to your servant David.

18 "But will God indeed reside with mortals on earth? Even heaven and the highest heaven cannot contain you, how much less this house that I have built! 19Regard your servant's prayer and his plea, O LORD my God, heeding the cry and the prayer that your servant prays to you. 20May your eyes be open day and night toward this house, the place where you promised to set your name, and may you heed the prayer that your servant prays toward this place. 21And hear the plea of your servant and of your people Israel, when they pray toward this place; may you hear from heaven your dwelling place; hear and forgive.

22 "If someone sins against another and is required to take an oath and comes and swears before your altar in this house, 23may you hear from heaven, and act, and judge your servants, repaying the guilty by bringing their conduct on their own head, and vindicating those who are in the right by rewarding them in accordance with their righteousness.

24 "When your people Israel, having sinned against you, are defeated before an enemy but turn again to you, confess your name, pray and plead with you in this house, 25may you hear from heaven, and forgive the sin of your people Israel, and bring them again to the land that you gave to them and to their ancestors.

26 "When heaven is shut up and there is no rain because they have sinned against you, and

[a] Heb *he*

then they pray toward this place, confess your
name, and turn from their sin, because you punish them, 27may you hear in heaven, forgive the
sin of your servants, your people Israel, when you
teach them the good way in which they should
walk; and send down rain upon your land, which
you have given to your people as an inheritance.

28 "If there is famine in the land, if there is
plague, blight, mildew, locust, or caterpillar; if
their enemies besiege them in any of the settlements of the lands; whatever suffering, whatever
sickness there is; 29whatever prayer, whatever
plea from any individual or from all your people
Israel, all knowing their own suffering and their
own sorrows so that they stretch out their hands
toward this house; 30may you hear from heaven,
your dwelling place, forgive, and render to all
whose heart you know, according to all their
ways, for only you know the human heart. 31Thus
may they fear you and walk in your ways all the
days that they live in the land that you gave to our
ancestors.

32 "Likewise when foreigners, who are not of
your people Israel, come from a distant land because of your great name, and your mighty hand,
and your outstretched arm, when they come and
pray toward this house, 33may you hear from
heaven your dwelling place, and do whatever the
foreigners ask of you, in order that all the peoples
of the earth may know your name and fear you,
as do your people Israel, and that they may know
that your name has been invoked on this house
that I have built.

34 "If your people go out to battle against
their enemies, by whatever way you shall send
them, and they pray to you toward this city that
you have chosen and the house that I have built
for your name, 35then hear from heaven their
prayer and their plea, and maintain their cause.

36 "If they sin against you—for there is no
one who does not sin—and you are angry with
them and give them to an enemy, so that they are
carried away captive to a land far or near; 37then
if they come to their senses in the land to which
they have been taken captive, and repent, and
plead with you in the land of their captivity, saying, 'We have sinned, and have done wrong; we
have acted wickedly'; 38if they repent with all
their heart and soul in the land of their captivity, to which they were taken captive, and pray
toward their land, which you gave to their ancestors, the city that you have chosen, and the house
that I have built for your name, 39then hear from
heaven your dwelling place their prayer and their
pleas, maintain their cause and forgive your people who have sinned against you. 40Now, O my
God, let your eyes be open and your ears attentive to prayer from this place.

41 "Now rise up, O LORD God, and go to your
resting place,
you and the ark of your might.
Let your priests, O LORD God, be clothed
with salvation,
and let your faithful rejoice in your
goodness.
42 O LORD God, do not reject your anointed
one.
Remember your steadfast love for your
servant David."

7 When Solomon had ended his prayer, fire
came down from heaven and consumed the
burnt offering and the sacrifices; and the glory of
the LORD filled the temple. 2The priests could not
enter the house of the LORD, because the glory
of the LORD filled the LORD's house. 3When all
the people of Israel saw the fire come down and
the glory of the LORD on the temple, they bowed
down on the pavement with their faces to the
ground, and worshiped and gave thanks to the
LORD, saying,

"For he is good,
for his steadfast love endures forever."

4 Then the king and all the people offered
sacrifice before the LORD. 5King Solomon offered
as a sacrifice twenty-two thousand oxen and one
hundred twenty thousand sheep. So the king and
all the people dedicated the house of God. 6The
priests stood at their posts; the Levites also, with
the instruments for music to the LORD that King
David had made for giving thanks to the LORD—
for his steadfast love endures forever—whenever
David offered praises by their ministry. Opposite
them the priests sounded trumpets; and all Israel
stood.

7 Solomon consecrated the middle of the
court that was in front of the house of the LORD;
for there he offered the burnt offerings and the fat
of the offerings of well-being because the bronze
altar Solomon had made could not hold the burnt
offering and the grain offering and the fat parts.
8 At that time Solomon held the festival for
seven days, and all Israel with him, a very great
congregation, from Lebo-hamath to the Wadi of
Egypt. 9On the eighth day they held a solemn assembly; for they had observed the dedication of
the altar seven days and the festival seven days.
10On the twenty-third day of the seventh month
he sent the people away to their homes, joyful
and in good spirits because of the goodness that
the LORD had shown to David and to Solomon
and to his people Israel.
11 Thus Solomon finished the house of the
LORD and the king's house; all that Solomon had
planned to do in the house of the LORD and in his
own house he successfully accomplished.
12 Then the LORD appeared to Solomon in
the night and said to him: "I have heard your
prayer, and have chosen this place for myself as a
house of sacrifice. 13When I shut up the heavens
so that there is no rain, or command the locust
to devour the land, or send pestilence among
my people, 14if my people who are called by my
name humble themselves, pray, seek my face,
and turn from their wicked ways, then I will hear
from heaven, and will forgive their sin and heal
their land. 15Now my eyes will be open and my
ears attentive to the prayer that is made in this
place. 16For now I have chosen and consecrated
this house so that my name may be there forever;
my eyes and my heart will be there for all time.
17As for you, if you walk before me, as your father David walked, doing according to all that I
have commanded you and keeping my statutes
and my ordinances, 18then I will establish your
royal throne, as I made covenant with your father
David saying, 'You shall never lack a successor to
rule over Israel.'
19 "But if you[a] turn aside and forsake my
statutes and my commandments that I have set
before you, and go and serve other gods and worship them, 20then I will pluck you[b] up from the
land that I have given you;[b] and this house, which
I have consecrated for my name, I will cast out of
my sight, and will make it a proverb and a byword
among all peoples. 21And regarding this house,
now exalted, everyone passing by will be astonished, and say, 'Why has the LORD done such a
thing to this land and to this house?' 22Then they
will say, 'Because they abandoned the LORD the
God of their ancestors who brought them out of
the land of Egypt, and they adopted other gods,
and worshiped them and served them; therefore
he has brought all this calamity upon them.'"

8 At the end of twenty years, during which Solomon had built the house of the LORD and
his own house, 2Solomon rebuilt the cities that
Huram had given to him, and settled the people
of Israel in them.
3 Solomon went to Hamath-zobah, and captured it. 4He built Tadmor in the wilderness and
all the storage towns that he built in Hamath.
5He also built Upper Beth-horon and Lower
Beth-horon, fortified cities, with walls, gates, and
bars, 6and Baalath, as well as all Solomon's storage towns, and all the towns for his chariots, the
towns for his cavalry, and whatever Solomon desired to build, in Jerusalem, in Lebanon, and in
all the land of his dominion. 7All the people who
were left of the Hittites, the Amorites, the Perizzites, the Hivites, and the Jebusites, who were not
of Israel, 8from their descendants who were still
left in the land, whom the people of Israel had not
destroyed—these Solomon conscripted for forced
labor, as is still the case today. 9But of the people
of Israel Solomon made no slaves for his work;
they were soldiers, and his officers, the commanders of his chariotry and cavalry. 10These were the
chief officers of King Solomon, two hundred fifty
of them, who exercised authority over the people.
11 Solomon brought Pharaoh's daughter
from the city of David to the house that he had
built for her, for he said, "My wife shall not live in
the house of King David of Israel, for the places to
which the ark of the LORD has come are holy."

[a] The word *you* in this verse is plural [b] Heb *them*

12 Then Solomon offered up burnt offerings
to the LORD on the altar of the LORD that he had
built in front of the vestibule, 13as the duty of
each day required, offering according to the commandment of Moses for the sabbaths, the new
moons, and the three annual festivals—the festival of unleavened bread, the festival of weeks, and
the festival of booths. 14According to the ordinance of his father David, he appointed the divisions of the priests for their service, and the
Levites for their offices of praise and ministry
alongside the priests as the duty of each day required, and the gatekeepers in their divisions for
the several gates; for so David the man of God
had commanded. 15They did not turn away from
what the king had commanded the priests and
Levites regarding anything at all, or regarding the
treasuries.

16 Thus all the work of Solomon was accomplished from[a] the day the foundation of the house
of the LORD was laid until the house of the LORD
was finished completely.

17 Then Solomon went to Ezion-geber and
Eloth on the shore of the sea, in the land of
Edom. 18Huram sent him, in the care of his ser-
vants, ships and servants familiar with the sea.
They went to Ophir, together with the servants
of Solomon, and imported from there four hun-
dred fifty talents of gold and brought it to King
Solomon.

9 When the queen of Sheba heard of the fame
of Solomon, she came to Jerusalem to test
him with hard questions, having a very great retinue and camels bearing spices and very much gold
and precious stones. When she came to Solomon,
she discussed with him all that was on her mind.
2Solomon answered all her questions; there was
nothing hidden from Solomon that he could not
explain to her. 3When the queen of Sheba had observed the wisdom of Solomon, the house that he
had built, 4the food of his table, the seating of his
officials, and the attendance of his servants, and
their clothing, his valets, and their clothing, and
his burnt offerings[b] that he offered at the house of
the LORD, there was no more spirit left in her.

5 So she said to the king, "The report was
true that I heard in my own land of your accomplishments and of your wisdom, 6but I did not
believe the[c] reports until I came and my own
eyes saw it. Not even half of the greatness of your
wisdom had been told to me; you far surpass the
report that I had heard. 7Happy are your people!
Happy are these your servants, who continually
attend you and hear your wisdom! 8Blessed be
the LORD your God, who has delighted in you
and set you on his throne as king for the LORD
your God. Because your God loved Israel and
would establish them forever, he has made you
king over them, that you may execute justice
and righteousness." 9Then she gave the king one
hundred twenty talents of gold, a very great quantity of spices, and precious stones: there were no
spices such as those that the queen of Sheba gave
to King Solomon.

10 Moreover the servants of Huram and the
servants of Solomon who brought gold from
Ophir brought algum wood and precious stones.
11From the algum wood, the king made steps[d] for
the house of the LORD and for the king's house,
lyres also and harps for the singers; there never
was seen the like of them before in the land of
Judah.

12 Meanwhile King Solomon granted the
queen of Sheba every desire that she expressed,
well beyond what she had brought to the king.
Then she returned to her own land, with her servants.

13 The weight of gold that came to Solomon
in one year was six hundred sixty-six talents of
gold, 14besides that which the traders and merchants brought; and all the kings of Arabia and
the governors of the land brought gold and silver
to Solomon. 15King Solomon made two hundred
large shields of beaten gold; six hundred shekels
of beaten gold went into each large shield. 16He
made three hundred shields of beaten gold;
three hundred shekels of gold went into each
shield; and the king put them in the House of
the Forest of Lebanon. 17The king also made a
great ivory throne, and overlaid it with pure gold.

[a] Gk Syr Vg: Heb *to* [b] Gk Syr Vg 1 Kings 10.5: Heb *ascent* [c] Heb *their* [d] Gk Vg: Meaning of Heb uncertain

18The throne had six steps and a footstool of
gold, which were attached to the throne, and on
each side of the seat were arm rests and two lions
standing beside the arm rests, 19while twelve lions were standing, one on each end of a step on
the six steps. The like of it was never made in any
kingdom. 20All King Solomon's drinking vessels
were of gold, and all the vessels of the House of
the Forest of Lebanon were of pure gold; silver
was not considered as anything in the days of
Solomon. 21For the king's ships went to Tarshish
with the servants of Huram; once every three
years the ships of Tarshish used to come bringing
gold, silver, ivory, apes, and peacocks.[a]

22 Thus King Solomon excelled all the kings
of the earth in riches and in wisdom. 23All the
kings of the earth sought the presence of Solomon to hear his wisdom, which God had put into
his mind. 24Every one of them brought a present,
objects of silver and gold, garments, weaponry,
spices, horses, and mules, so much year by year.
25Solomon had four thousand stalls for horses
and chariots, and twelve thousand horses, which
he stationed in the chariot cities and with the
king in Jerusalem. 26He ruled over all the kings
from the Euphrates to the land of the Philistines,
and to the border of Egypt. 27The king made silver as common in Jerusalem as stone, and cedar
as plentiful as the sycamore of the Shephelah.
28Horses were imported for Solomon from Egypt
and from all lands.

29 Now the rest of the acts of Solomon, from
first to last, are they not written in the history of
the prophet Nathan, and in the prophecy of Ahijah the Shilonite, and in the visions of the seer
Iddo concerning Jeroboam son of Nebat? 30Sol-
omon reigned in Jerusalem over all Israel forty
years. 31Solomon slept with his ancestors and
was buried in the city of his father David; and his
son Rehoboam succeeded him.

10 Rehoboam went to Shechem, for all Israel had come to Shechem to make him
king. 2When Jeroboam son of Nebat heard of it
(for he was in Egypt, where he had fled from King
Solomon), then Jeroboam returned from Egypt.
3They sent and called him; and Jeroboam and all
Israel came and said to Rehoboam, 4"Your father
made our yoke heavy. Now therefore lighten the
hard service of your father and his heavy yoke
that he placed on us, and we will serve you." 5He
said to them, "Come to me again in three days."
So the people went away.

6 Then King Rehoboam took counsel with
the older men who had attended his father Solomon while he was still alive, saying, "How do
you advise me to answer this people?" 7They
answered him, "If you will be kind to this people
and please them, and speak good words to them,
then they will be your servants forever." 8But he
rejected the advice that the older men gave him,
and consulted the young men who had grown
up with him and now attended him. 9He said to
them, "What do you advise that we answer this
people who have said to me, 'Lighten the yoke
that your father put on us'?" 10The young men
who had grown up with him said to him, "Thus
should you speak to the people who said to you,
'Your father made our yoke heavy, but you must
lighten it for us'; tell them, 'My little finger is
thicker than my father's loins. 11Now, whereas my
father laid on you a heavy yoke, I will add to your
yoke. My father disciplined you with whips, but I
will discipline you with scorpions.' "

12 So Jeroboam and all the people came to
Rehoboam the third day, as the king had said,
"Come to me again the third day." 13The king answered them harshly. King Rehoboam rejected
the advice of the older men; 14he spoke to them
in accordance with the advice of the young men,
"My father made your yoke heavy, but I will add
to it; my father disciplined you with whips, but I
will discipline you with scorpions." 15So the king
did not listen to the people, because it was a turn
of affairs brought about by God so that the LORD
might fulfill his word, which he had spoken by
Ahijah the Shilonite to Jeroboam son of Nebat.

16 When all Israel saw that the king would
not listen to them, the people answered the king,

"What share do we have in David?
We have no inheritance in the son of Jesse.

[a] Or *baboons*

Each of you to your tents, O Israel!
Look now to your own house, O David."
So all Israel departed to their tents. 17But Rehoboam reigned over the people of Israel who were
living in the cities of Judah. 18When King Rehoboam sent Hadoram, who was taskmaster over
the forced labor, the people of Israel stoned him
to death. King Rehoboam hurriedly mounted
his chariot to flee to Jerusalem. 19So Israel has
been in rebellion against the house of David to
this day.

11 When Rehoboam came to Jerusalem, he
assembled one hundred eighty thousand
chosen troops of the house of Judah and Benjamin to fight against Israel, to restore the kingdom
to Rehoboam. 2But the word of the LORD came
to Shemaiah the man of God: 3Say to King Rehoboam of Judah, son of Solomon, and to all Israel in
Judah and Benjamin, 4"Thus says the LORD: You
shall not go up or fight against your kindred. Let
everyone return home, for this thing is from me."
So they heeded the word of the LORD and turned
back from the expedition against Jeroboam.

5 Rehoboam resided in Jerusalem, and he
built cities for defense in Judah. 6He built up
Bethlehem, Etam, Tekoa, 7Beth-zur, Soco, Adullam, 8Gath, Mareshah, Ziph, 9Adoraim, Lachish,
Azekah, 10Zorah, Aijalon, and Hebron, fortified
cities that are in Judah and in Benjamin. 11He
made the fortresses strong, and put commanders
in them, and stores of food, oil, and wine. 12He
also put large shields and spears in all the cities,
and made them very strong. So he held Judah and
Benjamin.

13 The priests and the Levites who were in all
Israel presented themselves to him from all their
territories. 14The Levites had left their common
lands and their holdings and had come to Judah
and Jerusalem, because Jeroboam and his sons
had prevented them from serving as priests of
the LORD, 15and had appointed his own priests
for the high places, and for the goat-demons, and
for the calves that he had made. 16Those who had
set their hearts to seek the LORD God of Israel
came after them from all the tribes of Israel to Jerusalem to sacrifice to the LORD, the God of their
ancestors. 17They strengthened the kingdom of
Judah, and for three years they made Rehoboam
son of Solomon secure, for they walked for three
years in the way of David and Solomon.

18 Rehoboam took as his wife Mahalath
daughter of Jerimoth son of David, and of Abihail daughter of Eliab son of Jesse. 19She bore him
sons: Jeush, Shemariah, and Zaham. 20After her
he took Maacah daughter of Absalom, who bore
him Abijah, Attai, Ziza, and Shelomith. 21Reho-
boam loved Maacah daughter of Absalom more
than all his other wives and concubines (he took
eighteen wives and sixty concubines, and became the father of twenty-eight sons and sixty
daughters). 22Rehoboam appointed Abijah son
of Maacah as chief prince among his brothers, for
he intended to make him king. 23He dealt wisely,
and distributed some of his sons through all the
districts of Judah and Benjamin, in all the fortified cities; he gave them abundant provisions,
and found many wives for them.

12 When the rule of Rehoboam was established and he grew strong, he abandoned
the law of the LORD, he and all Israel with him.
2In the fifth year of King Rehoboam, because they
had been unfaithful to the LORD, King Shishak of
Egypt came up against Jerusalem 3with twelve
hundred chariots and sixty thousand cavalry. A
countless army came with him from Egypt—
Libyans, Sukkiim, and Ethiopians.[a] 4He took
the fortified cities of Judah and came as far as
Jerusalem. 5Then the prophet Shemaiah came to
Rehoboam and to the officers of Judah, who had
gathered at Jerusalem because of Shishak, and
said to them, "Thus says the LORD: You abandoned me, so I have abandoned you to the hand
of Shishak." 6Then the officers of Israel and the
king humbled themselves and said, "The LORD
is in the right." 7When the LORD saw that they
humbled themselves, the word of the LORD came
to Shemaiah, saying: "They have humbled themselves; I will not destroy them, but I will grant
them some deliverance, and my wrath shall not be
poured out on Jerusalem by the hand of Shishak.

[a] Or *Nubians*; Heb *Cushites*

8 Nevertheless they shall be his servants, so that
they may know the difference between serving
me and serving the kingdoms of other lands."
9 So King Shishak of Egypt came up against
Jerusalem; he took away the treasures of the
house of the LORD and the treasures of the king's
house; he took everything. He also took away the
shields of gold that Solomon had made; 10 but
King Rehoboam made in place of them shields
of bronze, and committed them to the hands of
the officers of the guard, who kept the door of the
king's house. 11 Whenever the king went into the
house of the LORD, the guard would come along
bearing them, and would then bring them back
to the guardroom. 12 Because he humbled himself
the wrath of the LORD turned from him, so as not
to destroy them completely; moreover, conditions were good in Judah.
13 So King Rehoboam established himself in
Jerusalem and reigned. Rehoboam was forty-one
years old when he began to reign; he reigned seventeen years in Jerusalem, the city that the LORD
had chosen out of all the tribes of Israel to put his
name there. His mother's name was Naamah the
Ammonite. 14 He did evil, for he did not set his
heart to seek the LORD.
15 Now the acts of Rehoboam, from first to
last, are they not written in the records of the
prophet Shemaiah and of the seer Iddo, recorded
by genealogy? There were continual wars between Rehoboam and Jeroboam. 16 Rehoboam
slept with his ancestors and was buried in the city
of David; and his son Abijah succeeded him.

13 In the eighteenth year of King Jeroboam,
Abijah began to reign over Judah. 2 He
reigned for three years in Jerusalem. His mother's
name was Micaiah daughter of Uriel of Gibeah.

Now there was war between Abijah and Jeroboam. 3 Abijah engaged in battle, having an army
of valiant warriors, four hundred thousand picked
men; and Jeroboam drew up his line of battle
against him with eight hundred thousand picked
mighty warriors. 4 Then Abijah stood on the slope
of Mount Zemaraim that is in the hill country of
Ephraim, and said, "Listen to me, Jeroboam and
all Israel! 5 Do you not know that the LORD God
of Israel gave the kingship over Israel forever to
David and his sons by a covenant of salt? 6 Yet
Jeroboam son of Nebat, a servant of Solomon
son of David, rose up and rebelled against his
lord; 7 and certain worthless scoundrels gathered
around him and defied Rehoboam son of Solomon, when Rehoboam was young and irresolute
and could not withstand them.
8 "And now you think that you can withstand
the kingdom of the LORD in the hand of the sons
of David, because you are a great multitude and
have with you the golden calves that Jeroboam
made as gods for you. 9 Have you not driven out
the priests of the LORD, the descendants of Aaron,
and the Levites, and made priests for yourselves
like the peoples of other lands? Whoever comes
to be consecrated with a young bull or seven rams
becomes a priest of what are no gods. 10 But as for
us, the LORD is our God, and we have not abandoned him. We have priests ministering to the
LORD who are descendants of Aaron, and Levites
for their service. 11 They offer to the LORD every
morning and every evening burnt offerings and
fragrant incense, set out the rows of bread on the
table of pure gold, and care for the golden lampstand so that its lamps may burn every evening;
for we keep the charge of the LORD our God, but
you have abandoned him. 12 See, God is with us at
our head, and his priests have their battle trumpets to sound the call to battle against you. O Israelites, do not fight against the LORD, the God of
your ancestors; for you cannot succeed."
13 Jeroboam had sent an ambush around
to come on them from behind; thus his troops[a]
were in front of Judah, and the ambush was behind them. 14 When Judah turned, the battle was
in front of them and behind them. They cried
out to the LORD, and the priests blew the trumpets. 15 Then the people of Judah raised the battle
shout. And when the people of Judah shouted,
God defeated Jeroboam and all Israel before Abijah and Judah. 16 The Israelites fled before Judah,
and God gave them into their hands. 17 Abijah and
his army defeated them with great slaughter; five

[a] Heb *they*

hundred thousand picked men of Israel fell slain.
18Thus the Israelites were subdued at that time,
and the people of Judah prevailed, because they
relied on the LORD, the God of their ancestors.
19Abijah pursued Jeroboam, and took cities from
him: Bethel with its villages and Jeshanah with its
villages and Ephron[a] with its villages. 20Jeroboam
did not recover his power in the days of Abijah;
the LORD struck him down, and he died. 21But
Abijah grew strong. He took fourteen wives, and
became the father of twenty-two sons and sixteen
daughters. 22The rest of the acts of Abijah, his behavior and his deeds, are written in the story of
the prophet Iddo.

14 [b] So Abijah slept with his ancestors, and
they buried him in the city of David. His
son Asa succeeded him. In his days the land had
rest for ten years. 2[c]Asa did what was good and
right in the sight of the LORD his God. 3He took
away the foreign altars and the high places, broke
down the pillars, hewed down the sacred poles,[d]
4and commanded Judah to seek the LORD, the
God of their ancestors, and to keep the law and
the commandment. 5He also removed from all
the cities of Judah the high places and the incense
altars. And the kingdom had rest under him. 6He
built fortified cities in Judah while the land had
rest. He had no war in those years, for the LORD
gave him peace. 7He said to Judah, "Let us build
these cities, and surround them with walls and
towers, gates and bars; the land is still ours because we have sought the LORD our God; we
have sought him, and he has given us peace on
every side." So they built and prospered. 8Asa
had an army of three hundred thousand from
Judah, armed with large shields and spears, and
two hundred eighty thousand troops from Benjamin who carried shields and drew bows; all these
were mighty warriors.

9 Zerah the Ethiopian[e] came out against them
with an army of a million men and three hundred
chariots, and came as far as Mareshah. 10Asa went
out to meet him, and they drew up their lines of
battle in the valley of Zephathah at Mareshah.
11Asa cried to the LORD his God, "O LORD, there
is no difference for you between helping the
mighty and the weak. Help us, O LORD our God,
for we rely on you, and in your name we have
come against this multitude. O LORD, you are our
God; let no mortal prevail against you." 12So the
LORD defeated the Ethiopians[f] before Asa and
before Judah, and the Ethiopians[f] fled. 13Asa and
the army with him pursued them as far as Gerar,
and the Ethiopians[f] fell until no one remained
alive; for they were broken before the LORD and
his army. The people of Judah[g] carried away a
great quantity of booty. 14They defeated all the
cities around Gerar, for the fear of the LORD was
on them. They plundered all the cities; for there
was much plunder in them. 15They also attacked
the tents of those who had livestock,[h] and carried
away sheep and goats in abundance, and camels.
Then they returned to Jerusalem.

15 The spirit of God came upon Azariah
son of Oded. 2He went out to meet Asa
and said to him, "Hear me, Asa, and all Judah
and Benjamin: The LORD is with you, while you
are with him. If you seek him, he will be found
by you, but if you abandon him, he will abandon
you. 3For a long time Israel was without the true
God, and without a teaching priest, and without
law; 4but when in their distress they turned to the
LORD, the God of Israel, and sought him, he was
found by them. 5In those times it was not safe for
anyone to go or come, for great disturbances afflicted all the inhabitants of the lands. 6They were
broken in pieces, nation against nation and city
against city, for God troubled them with every
sort of distress. 7But you, take courage! Do not
let your hands be weak, for your work shall be
rewarded."

8 When Asa heard these words, the prophecy of Azariah son of Oded,[i] he took courage, and
put away the abominable idols from all the land
of Judah and Benjamin and from the towns that
he had taken in the hill country of Ephraim. He

[a] Another reading is *Ephrain* [b] Ch 13.23 in Heb [c] Ch 14.1 in Heb [d] Heb *Asherim* [e] Or *Nubian*; Heb *Cushite*
[f] Or *Nubians*; Heb *Cushites* [g] Heb *They* [h] Meaning of Heb uncertain
[i] Compare Syr Vg: Heb *the prophecy, the prophet Obed*

repaired the altar of the LORD that was in front of the vestibule of the house of the LORD.[a] 9 He gathered all Judah and Benjamin, and those from Ephraim, Manasseh, and Simeon who were residing as aliens with them, for great numbers had deserted to him from Israel when they saw that the LORD his God was with him. 10 They were gathered at Jerusalem in the third month of the fifteenth year of the reign of Asa. 11 They sacrificed to the LORD on that day, from the booty that they had brought, seven hundred oxen and seven thousand sheep. 12 They entered into a covenant to seek the LORD, the God of their ancestors, with all their heart and with all their soul. 13 Whoever would not seek the LORD, the God of Israel, should be put to death, whether young or old, man or woman. 14 They took an oath to the LORD with a loud voice, and with shouting, and with trumpets, and with horns. 15 All Judah rejoiced over the oath; for they had sworn with all their heart, and had sought him with their whole desire, and he was found by them, and the LORD gave them rest all around.

16 King Asa even removed his mother Maacah from being queen mother because she had made an abominable image for Asherah. Asa cut down her image, crushed it, and burned it at the Wadi Kidron. 17 But the high places were not taken out of Israel. Nevertheless the heart of Asa was true all his days. 18 He brought into the house of God the votive gifts of his father and his own votive gifts—silver, gold, and utensils. 19 And there was no more war until the thirty-fifth year of the reign of Asa.

16 In the thirty-sixth year of the reign of Asa, King Baasha of Israel went up against Judah, and built Ramah, to prevent anyone from going out or coming into the territory of[b] King Asa of Judah. 2 Then Asa took silver and gold from the treasures of the house of the LORD and the king's house, and sent them to King Ben-hadad of Aram, who resided in Damascus, saying, 3 "Let there be an alliance between me and you, like that between my father and your father; I am sending to you silver and gold; go, break your alliance with King Baasha of Israel, so that he may withdraw from me." 4 Ben-hadad listened to King Asa, and sent the commanders of his armies against the cities of Israel. They conquered Ijon, Dan, Abel-maim, and all the store-cities of Naphtali. 5 When Baasha heard of it, he stopped building Ramah, and let his work cease. 6 Then King Asa brought all Judah, and they carried away the stones of Ramah and its timber, with which Baasha had been building, and with them he built up Geba and Mizpah.

7 At that time the seer Hanani came to King Asa of Judah, and said to him, "Because you relied on the king of Aram, and did not rely on the LORD your God, the army of the king of Aram has escaped you. 8 Were not the Ethiopians[c] and the Libyans a huge army with exceedingly many chariots and cavalry? Yet because you relied on the LORD, he gave them into your hand. 9 For the eyes of the LORD range throughout the entire earth, to strengthen those whose heart is true to him. You have done foolishly in this; for from now on you will have wars." 10 Then Asa was angry with the seer, and put him in the stocks, in prison, for he was in a rage with him because of this. And Asa inflicted cruelties on some of the people at the same time.

11 The acts of Asa, from first to last, are written in the Book of the Kings of Judah and Israel. 12 In the thirty-ninth year of his reign Asa was diseased in his feet, and his disease became severe; yet even in his disease he did not seek the LORD, but sought help from physicians. 13 Then Asa slept with his ancestors, dying in the forty-first year of his reign. 14 They buried him in the tomb that he had hewn out for himself in the city of David. They laid him on a bier that had been filled with various kinds of spices prepared by the perfumer's art; and they made a very great fire in his honor.

17 His son Jehoshaphat succeeded him, and strengthened himself against Israel. 2 He placed forces in all the fortified cities of Judah, and set garrisons in the land of Judah, and in the cities of Ephraim that his father Asa had taken.

[a] Heb *the vestibule of the* LORD [b] Heb lacks *the territory of* [c] Or *Nubians*; Heb *Cushites*

3The LORD was with Jehoshaphat, because he
walked in the earlier ways of his father;[a] he did
not seek the Baals, 4but sought the God of his
father and walked in his commandments, and
not according to the ways of Israel. 5Therefore
the LORD established the kingdom in his hand.
All Judah brought tribute to Jehoshaphat, and he
had great riches and honor. 6His heart was courageous in the ways of the LORD; and furthermore
he removed the high places and the sacred poles[b]
from Judah.

7 In the third year of his reign he sent his officials, Ben-hail, Obadiah, Zechariah, Nethanel,
and Micaiah, to teach in the cities of Judah. 8With
them were the Levites, Shemaiah, Nethaniah,
Zebadiah, Asahel, Shemiramoth, Jehonathan,
Adonijah, Tobijah, and Tob-adonijah; and with
these Levites, the priests Elishama and Jehoram.
9They taught in Judah, having the book of the
law of the LORD with them; they went around
through all the cities of Judah and taught among
the people.

10 The fear of the LORD fell on all the kingdoms of the lands around Judah, and they did not
make war against Jehoshaphat. 11Some of the Philistines brought Jehoshaphat presents, and silver
for tribute; and the Arabs also brought him seven
thousand seven hundred rams and seven thousand seven hundred male goats. 12Jehoshaphat
grew steadily greater. He built fortresses and storage cities in Judah. 13He carried out great works in
the cities of Judah. He had soldiers, mighty warriors, in Jerusalem. 14This was the muster of them
by ancestral houses: Of Judah, the commanders
of the thousands: Adnah the commander, with
three hundred thousand mighty warriors, 15and
next to him Jehohanan the commander, with
two hundred eighty thousand, 16and next to him
Amasiah son of Zichri, a volunteer for the service
of the LORD, with two hundred thousand mighty
warriors. 17Of Benjamin: Eliada, a mighty warrior, with two hundred thousand armed with bow
and shield, 18and next to him Jehozabad with one
hundred eighty thousand armed for war. 19These
were in the service of the king, besides those
whom the king had placed in the fortified cities
throughout all Judah.

18 Now Jehoshaphat had great riches and
honor; and he made a marriage alliance
with Ahab. 2After some years he went down to
Ahab in Samaria. Ahab slaughtered an abundance
of sheep and oxen for him and for the people who
were with him, and induced him to go up against
Ramoth-gilead. 3King Ahab of Israel said to King
Jehoshaphat of Judah, "Will you go with me to
Ramoth-gilead?" He answered him, "I am with
you, my people are your people. We will be with
you in the war."

4 But Jehoshaphat also said to the king of
Israel, "Inquire first for the word of the LORD."
5Then the king of Israel gathered the prophets
together, four hundred of them, and said to them,
"Shall we go to battle against Ramoth-gilead, or
shall I refrain?" They said, "Go up; for God will
give it into the hand of the king." 6But Jehoshaphat said, "Is there no other prophet of the
LORD here of whom we may inquire?" 7The king
of Israel said to Jehoshaphat, "There is still one
other by whom we may inquire of the LORD, Micaiah son of Imlah; but I hate him, for he never
prophesies anything favorable about me, but only
disaster." Jehoshaphat said, "Let the king not say
such a thing." 8Then the king of Israel summoned
an officer and said, "Bring quickly Micaiah son
of Imlah." 9Now the king of Israel and King Jehoshaphat of Judah were sitting on their thrones,
arrayed in their robes; and they were sitting at
the threshing floor at the entrance of the gate of
Samaria; and all the prophets were prophesying before them. 10Zedekiah son of Chenaanah
made for himself horns of iron, and he said,
"Thus says the LORD: With these you shall gore
the Arameans until they are destroyed." 11All the
prophets were prophesying the same and saying,
"Go up to Ramoth-gilead and triumph; the LORD
will give it into the hand of the king."

12 The messenger who had gone to summon Micaiah said to him, "Look, the words of
the prophets with one accord are favorable to
the king; let your word be like the word of one

[a] Another reading is *his father David* [b] Heb *Asherim*

of them, and speak favorably." 13But Micaiah said,
"As the LORD lives, whatever my God says, that I
will speak."
14 When he had come to the king, the king
said to him, "Micaiah, shall we go to Ramoth-
gilead to battle, or shall I refrain?" He answered,
"Go up and triumph; they will be given into your
hand." 15But the king said to him, "How many
times must I make you swear to tell me nothing
but the truth in the name of the LORD?" 16Then
Micaiah[a] said, "I saw all Israel scattered on the
mountains, like sheep without a shepherd; and
the LORD said, 'These have no master; let each
one go home in peace.'" 17The king of Israel said
to Jehoshaphat, "Did I not tell you that he would
not prophesy anything favorable about me, but
only disaster?"
18 Then Micaiah[a] said, "Therefore hear the
word of the LORD: I saw the LORD sitting on his
throne, with all the host of heaven standing to the
right and to the left of him. 19And the LORD said,
'Who will entice King Ahab of Israel, so that he
may go up and fall at Ramoth-gilead?' Then one
said one thing, and another said another, 20until
a spirit came forward and stood before the LORD,
saying, 'I will entice him.' The LORD asked him,
'How?' 21He replied, 'I will go out and be a lying spirit in the mouth of all his prophets.' Then
the LORD[a] said, 'You are to entice him, and you
shall succeed; go out and do it.' 22So you see, the
LORD has put a lying spirit in the mouth of these
your prophets; the LORD has decreed disaster for
you."
23 Then Zedekiah son of Chenaanah came
up to Micaiah, slapped him on the cheek, and
said, "Which way did the spirit of the LORD pass
from me to speak to you?" 24Micaiah replied,
"You will find out on that day when you go in to
hide in an inner chamber." 25The king of Israel
then ordered, "Take Micaiah, and return him to
Amon the governor of the city and to Joash the
king's son; 26and say, 'Thus says the king: Put
this fellow in prison, and feed him on reduced rations of bread and water until I return in peace.'"
27Micaiah said, "If you return in peace, the LORD
has not spoken by me." And he said, "Hear, you
peoples, all of you!"
28 So the king of Israel and King Jehoshaphat
of Judah went up to Ramoth-gilead. 29The king
of Israel said to Jehoshaphat, "I will disguise myself and go into battle, but you wear your robes."
So the king of Israel disguised himself, and they
went into battle. 30Now the king of Aram had
commanded the captains of his chariots, "Fight
with no one small or great, but only with the king
of Israel." 31When the captains of the chariots saw
Jehoshaphat, they said, "It is the king of Israel." So
they turned to fight against him; and Jehoshaphat
cried out, and the LORD helped him. God drew
them away from him, 32for when the captains of
the chariots saw that it was not the king of Israel,
they turned back from pursuing him. 33But a certain man drew his bow and unknowingly struck
the king of Israel between the scale armor and the
breastplate; so he said to the driver of his chariot,
"Turn around, and carry me out of the battle, for
I am wounded." 34The battle grew hot that day,
and the king of Israel propped himself up in his
chariot facing the Arameans until evening; then
at sunset he died.

19 King Jehoshaphat of Judah returned in
safety to his house in Jerusalem. 2Jehu
son of Hanani the seer went out to meet him and
said to King Jehoshaphat, "Should you help the
wicked and love those who hate the LORD? Because of this, wrath has gone out against you from
the LORD. 3Nevertheless, some good is found in
you, for you destroyed the sacred poles[b] out of
the land, and have set your heart to seek God."
4 Jehoshaphat resided at Jerusalem; then he
went out again among the people, from Beer-
sheba to the hill country of Ephraim, and brought
them back to the LORD, the God of their ancestors. 5He appointed judges in the land in all the
fortified cities of Judah, city by city, 6and said to
the judges, "Consider what you are doing, for you
judge not on behalf of human beings but on the
LORD's behalf; he is with you in giving judgment.
7Now, let the fear of the LORD be upon you; take
care what you do, for there is no perversion of

[a] Heb *he* [b] Heb *Asheroth*

justice with the LORD our God, or partiality, or
taking of bribes."
8 Moreover in Jerusalem Jehoshaphat appointed certain Levites and priests and heads of
families of Israel, to give judgment for the LORD
and to decide disputed cases. They had their seat
at Jerusalem. 9He charged them: "This is how
you shall act: in the fear of the LORD, in faithfulness, and with your whole heart; 10whenever a
case comes to you from your kindred who live in
their cities, concerning bloodshed, law or commandment, statutes or ordinances, then you shall
instruct them, so that they may not incur guilt
before the LORD and wrath may not come on you
and your kindred. Do so, and you will not incur
guilt. 11See, Amariah the chief priest is over you
in all matters of the LORD; and Zebadiah son of
Ishmael, the governor of the house of Judah, in all
the king's matters; and the Levites will serve you
as officers. Deal courageously, and may the LORD
be with the good!"

20 After this the Moabites and Ammonites,
and with them some of the Meunites,[a]
came against Jehoshaphat for battle. 2Messengers[b]
came and told Jehoshaphat, "A great multitude is
coming against you from Edom,[c] from beyond
the sea; already they are at Hazazon-tamar" (that
is, En-gedi). 3Jehoshaphat was afraid; he set
himself to seek the LORD, and proclaimed a fast
throughout all Judah. 4Judah assembled to seek
help from the LORD; from all the towns of Judah
they came to seek the LORD.
5 Jehoshaphat stood in the assembly of Judah
and Jerusalem, in the house of the LORD, before
the new court, 6and said, "O LORD, God of our
ancestors, are you not God in heaven? Do you
not rule over all the kingdoms of the nations? In
your hand are power and might, so that no one is
able to withstand you. 7Did you not, O our God,
drive out the inhabitants of this land before your
people Israel, and give it forever to the descendants of your friend Abraham? 8They have lived
in it, and in it have built you a sanctuary for your
name, saying, 9'If disaster comes upon us, the
sword, judgment,[d] or pestilence, or famine, we
will stand before this house, and before you, for
your name is in this house, and cry to you in our
distress, and you will hear and save.' 10See now,
the people of Ammon, Moab, and Mount Seir,
whom you would not let Israel invade when they
came from the land of Egypt, and whom they
avoided and did not destroy— 11they reward us
by coming to drive us out of your possession that
you have given us to inherit. 12O our God, will
you not execute judgment upon them? For we
are powerless against this great multitude that is
coming against us. We do not know what to do,
but our eyes are on you."
13 Meanwhile all Judah stood before the
LORD, with their little ones, their wives, and their
children. 14Then the spirit of the LORD came
upon Jahaziel son of Zechariah, son of Benaiah,
son of Jeiel, son of Mattaniah, a Levite of the sons
of Asaph, in the middle of the assembly. 15He
said, "Listen, all Judah and inhabitants of Jerusalem, and King Jehoshaphat: Thus says the LORD
to you: 'Do not fear or be dismayed at this great
multitude; for the battle is not yours but God's.
16Tomorrow go down against them; they will
come up by the ascent of Ziz; you will find them
at the end of the valley, before the wilderness of
Jeruel. 17This battle is not for you to fight; take
your position, stand still, and see the victory of
the LORD on your behalf, O Judah and Jerusalem.'
Do not fear or be dismayed; tomorrow go out
against them, and the LORD will be with you."
18 Then Jehoshaphat bowed down with his
face to the ground, and all Judah and the inhabitants of Jerusalem fell down before the LORD,
worshiping the LORD. 19And the Levites, of the
Kohathites and the Korahites, stood up to praise
the LORD, the God of Israel, with a very loud
voice.
20 They rose early in the morning and went
out into the wilderness of Tekoa; and as they went
out, Jehoshaphat stood and said, "Listen to me,
O Judah and inhabitants of Jerusalem! Believe in
the LORD your God and you will be established;
believe his prophets." 21When he had taken counsel with the people, he appointed those who were

[a] Compare 26.7: Heb *Ammonites* [b] Heb *They* [c] One Ms: MT *Aram* [d] Or *the sword of judgment*

to sing to the LORD and praise him in holy splendor, as they went before the army, saying,
“Give thanks to the LORD,
for his steadfast love endures forever.”
22 As they began to sing and praise, the LORD set
an ambush against the Ammonites, Moab, and
Mount Seir, who had come against Judah, so
that they were routed. 23 For the Ammonites and
Moab attacked the inhabitants of Mount Seir, destroying them utterly; and when they had made
an end of the inhabitants of Seir, they all helped
to destroy one another.
24 When Judah came to the watchtower of
the wilderness, they looked toward the multitude; they were corpses lying on the ground; no
one had escaped. 25 When Jehoshaphat and his
people came to take the booty from them, they
found livestock[a] in great numbers, goods, clothing, and precious things, which they took for
themselves until they could carry no more. They
spent three days taking the booty, because of its
abundance. 26 On the fourth day they assembled
in the Valley of Beracah, for there they blessed
the LORD; therefore that place has been called
the Valley of Beracah[b] to this day. 27 Then all the
people of Judah and Jerusalem, with Jehoshaphat
at their head, returned to Jerusalem with joy, for
the LORD had enabled them to rejoice over their
enemies. 28 They came to Jerusalem, with harps
and lyres and trumpets, to the house of the LORD.
29 The fear of God came on all the kingdoms of
the countries when they heard that the LORD had
fought against the enemies of Israel. 30 And the
realm of Jehoshaphat was quiet, for his God gave
him rest all around.
31 So Jehoshaphat reigned over Judah. He
was thirty-five years old when he began to reign;
he reigned twenty-five years in Jerusalem. His
mother’s name was Azubah daughter of Shilhi.
32 He walked in the way of his father Asa and did
not turn aside from it, doing what was right in the
sight of the LORD. 33 Yet the high places were not
removed; the people had not yet set their hearts
upon the God of their ancestors.
34 Now the rest of the acts of Jehoshaphat,
from first to last, are written in the Annals of Jehu
son of Hanani, which are recorded in the Book of
the Kings of Israel.
35 After this King Jehoshaphat of Judah
joined with King Ahaziah of Israel, who did wickedly. 36 He joined him in building ships to go to
Tarshish; they built the ships in Ezion-geber.
37 Then Eliezer son of Dodavahu of Mareshah
prophesied against Jehoshaphat, saying, “Because
you have joined with Ahaziah, the LORD will destroy what you have made.” And the ships were
wrecked and were not able to go to Tarshish.

21 Jehoshaphat slept with his ancestors and
was buried with his ancestors in the city
of David; his son Jehoram succeeded him. 2 He
had brothers, the sons of Jehoshaphat: Azariah,
Jehiel, Zechariah, Azariah, Michael, and Shephatiah; all these were the sons of King Jehoshaphat
of Judah.[c] 3 Their father gave them many gifts, of
silver, gold, and valuable possessions, together
with fortified cities in Judah; but he gave the kingdom to Jehoram, because he was the firstborn.
4 When Jehoram had ascended the throne of his
father and was established, he put all his brothers to the sword, and also some of the officials of
Israel. 5 Jehoram was thirty-two years old when he
began to reign; he reigned eight years in Jerusalem. 6 He walked in the way of the kings of Israel,
as the house of Ahab had done; for the daughter
of Ahab was his wife. He did what was evil in the
sight of the LORD. 7 Yet the LORD would not destroy the house of David because of the covenant
that he had made with David, and since he had
promised to give a lamp to him and to his descendants forever.
8 In his days Edom revolted against the rule
of Judah and set up a king of their own. 9 Then Jehoram crossed over with his commanders and all
his chariots. He set out by night and attacked the
Edomites, who had surrounded him and his chariot commanders. 10 So Edom has been in revolt
against the rule of Judah to this day. At that time
Libnah also revolted against his rule, because he
had forsaken the LORD, the God of his ancestors.
11 Moreover he made high places in the hill

[a] Gk: Heb *among them* [b] That is *Blessing* [c] Gk Syr: Heb *Israel*

country of Judah, and led the inhabitants of Jerusalem into unfaithfulness, and made Judah go
astray. 12 A letter came to him from the prophet
Elijah, saying: "Thus says the LORD, the God of
your father David: Because you have not walked
in the ways of your father Jehoshaphat or in the
ways of King Asa of Judah, 13 but have walked in
the way of the kings of Israel, and have led Judah
and the inhabitants of Jerusalem into unfaithfulness, as the house of Ahab led Israel into unfaithfulness, and because you also have killed your
brothers, members of your father's house, who
were better than yourself, 14 see, the LORD will
bring a great plague on your people, your children, your wives, and all your possessions, 15 and
you yourself will have a severe sickness with a disease of your bowels, until your bowels come out,
day after day, because of the disease."

16 The LORD aroused against Jehoram the
anger of the Philistines and of the Arabs who
are near the Ethiopians.[a] 17 They came up against
Judah, invaded it, and carried away all the possessions they found that belonged to the king's
house, along with his sons and his wives, so
that no son was left to him except Jehoahaz, his
youngest son.

18 After all this the LORD struck him in his
bowels with an incurable disease. 19 In course of
time, at the end of two years, his bowels came out
because of the disease, and he died in great agony.
His people made no fire in his honor, like the fires
made for his ancestors. 20 He was thirty-two years
old when he began to reign; he reigned eight
years in Jerusalem. He departed with no one's regret. They buried him in the city of David, but not
in the tombs of the kings.

22 The inhabitants of Jerusalem made his
youngest son Ahaziah king as his successor; for the troops who came with the Arabs to
the camp had killed all the older sons. So Ahaziah son of Jehoram reigned as king of Judah.
2 Ahaziah was forty-two years old when he began
to reign; he reigned one year in Jerusalem. His
mother's name was Athaliah, a granddaughter of
Omri. 3 He also walked in the ways of the house
of Ahab, for his mother was his counselor in doing wickedly. 4 He did what was evil in the sight
of the LORD, as the house of Ahab had done; for
after the death of his father they were his counselors, to his ruin. 5 He even followed their advice,
and went with Jehoram son of King Ahab of Israel to make war against King Hazael of Aram at
Ramoth-gilead. The Arameans wounded Joram,
6 and he returned to be healed in Jezreel of the
wounds that he had received at Ramah, when he
fought King Hazael of Aram. And Ahaziah son of
King Jehoram of Judah went down to see Joram
son of Ahab in Jezreel, because he was sick.

7 But it was ordained by God that the downfall of Ahaziah should come about through his
going to visit Joram. For when he came there he
went out with Jehoram to meet Jehu son of Nimshi, whom the LORD had anointed to destroy
the house of Ahab. 8 When Jehu was executing
judgment on the house of Ahab, he met the officials of Judah and the sons of Ahaziah's brothers,
who attended Ahaziah, and he killed them. 9 He
searched for Ahaziah, who was captured while
hiding in Samaria and was brought to Jehu, and
put to death. They buried him, for they said, "He
is the grandson of Jehoshaphat, who sought the
LORD with all his heart." And the house of Ahaziah had no one able to rule the kingdom.

10 Now when Athaliah, Ahaziah's mother,
saw that her son was dead, she set about to destroy all the royal family of the house of Judah.
11 But Jehoshabeath, the king's daughter, took
Joash son of Ahaziah, and stole him away from
among the king's children who were about to be
killed; she put him and his nurse in a bedroom.
Thus Jehoshabeath, daughter of King Jehoram
and wife of the priest Jehoiada—because she
was a sister of Ahaziah—hid him from Athaliah,
so that she did not kill him; 12 he remained with
them six years, hidden in the house of God, while
Athaliah reigned over the land.

23 But in the seventh year Jehoiada took
courage, and entered into a compact with
the commanders of the hundreds, Azariah son of
Jeroham, Ishmael son of Jehohanan, Azariah son

[a] Or *Nubians*; Heb *Cushites*

of Obed, Maaseiah son of Adaiah, and Elishaphat
son of Zichri. 2They went around through Judah
and gathered the Levites from all the towns of Judah, and the heads of families of Israel, and they
came to Jerusalem. 3Then the whole assembly
made a covenant with the king in the house of
God. Jehoiada[a] said to them, "Here is the king's
son! Let him reign, as the LORD promised concerning the sons of David. 4This is what you are
to do: one-third of you, priests and Levites, who
come on duty on the sabbath, shall be gatekeepers, 5one-third shall be at the king's house,
and one-third at the Gate of the Foundation; and
all the people shall be in the courts of the house
of the LORD. 6Do not let anyone enter the house
of the LORD except the priests and ministering
Levites; they may enter, for they are holy, but all
the other[b] people shall observe the instructions
of the LORD. 7The Levites shall surround the
king, each with his weapons in his hand; and
whoever enters the house shall be killed. Stay
with the king in his comings and goings."

8 The Levites and all Judah did according
to all that the priest Jehoiada commanded; each
brought his men, who were to come on duty on
the sabbath, with those who were to go off duty
on the sabbath; for the priest Jehoiada did not dismiss the divisions. 9The priest Jehoiada delivered
to the captains the spears and the large and small
shields that had been King David's, which were
in the house of God; 10and he set all the people
as a guard for the king, everyone with weapon
in hand, from the south side of the house to the
north side of the house, around the altar and the
house. 11Then he brought out the king's son, put
the crown on him, and gave him the covenant;[c]
they proclaimed him king, and Jehoiada and his
sons anointed him; and they shouted, "Long live
the king!"

12 When Athaliah heard the noise of the
people running and praising the king, she went
into the house of the LORD to the people; 13and
when she looked, there was the king standing by
his pillar at the entrance, and the captains and the
trumpeters beside the king, and all the people
of the land rejoicing and blowing trumpets, and
the singers with their musical instruments leading in the celebration. Athaliah tore her clothes,
and cried, "Treason! Treason!" 14Then the priest
Jehoiada brought out the captains who were set
over the army, saying to them, "Bring her out between the ranks; anyone who follows her is to be
put to the sword." For the priest said, "Do not put
her to death in the house of the LORD." 15So they
laid hands on her; she went into the entrance of
the Horse Gate of the king's house, and there they
put her to death.

16 Jehoiada made a covenant between himself and all the people and the king that they
should be the LORD's people. 17Then all the people went to the house of Baal, and tore it down;
his altars and his images they broke in pieces, and
they killed Mattan, the priest of Baal, in front
of the altars. 18Jehoiada assigned the care of the
house of the LORD to the levitical priests whom
David had organized to be in charge of the house
of the LORD, to offer burnt offerings to the LORD,
as it is written in the law of Moses, with rejoicing
and with singing, according to the order of David.
19He stationed the gatekeepers at the gates of the
house of the LORD so that no one should enter
who was in any way unclean. 20And he took the
captains, the nobles, the governors of the people,
and all the people of the land, and they brought
the king down from the house of the LORD,
marching through the upper gate to the king's
house. They set the king on the royal throne. 21So
all the people of the land rejoiced, and the city
was quiet after Athaliah had been killed with the
sword.

24 Joash was seven years old when he began
to reign; he reigned forty years in Jerusalem; his mother's name was Zibiah of Beer-sheba.
2Joash did what was right in the sight of the LORD
all the days of the priest Jehoiada. 3Jehoiada got
two wives for him, and he became the father of
sons and daughters.

4 Some time afterward Joash decided to restore the house of the LORD. 5He assembled the
priests and the Levites and said to them, "Go out

[a] Heb *He* [b] Heb lacks *other* [c] Or *treaty*, or *testimony*; Heb *eduth*

to the cities of Judah and gather money from all
Israel to repair the house of your God, year by
year; and see that you act quickly." But the Levites
did not act quickly. 6So the king summoned Jehoiada the chief, and said to him, "Why have you
not required the Levites to bring in from Judah
and Jerusalem the tax levied by Moses, the servant of the LORD, on[a] the congregation of Israel
for the tent of the covenant?"[b] 7For the children
of Athaliah, that wicked woman, had broken
into the house of God, and had even used all the
dedicated things of the house of the LORD for
the Baals.

8 So the king gave command, and they made
a chest, and set it outside the gate of the house of
the LORD. 9A proclamation was made throughout
Judah and Jerusalem to bring in for the LORD the
tax that Moses the servant of God laid on Israel in
the wilderness. 10All the leaders and all the people
rejoiced and brought their tax and dropped it into
the chest until it was full. 11Whenever the chest
was brought to the king's officers by the Levites,
when they saw that there was a large amount of
money in it, the king's secretary and the officer of
the chief priest would come and empty the chest
and take it and return it to its place. So they did
day after day, and collected money in abundance.
12The king and Jehoiada gave it to those who had
charge of the work of the house of the LORD,
and they hired masons and carpenters to restore
the house of the LORD, and also workers in iron
and bronze to repair the house of the LORD. 13So
those who were engaged in the work labored, and
the repairing went forward at their hands, and
they restored the house of God to its proper condition and strengthened it. 14When they had finished, they brought the rest of the money to the
king and Jehoiada, and with it were made utensils
for the house of the LORD, utensils for the service
and for the burnt offerings, and ladles, and vessels
of gold and silver. They offered burnt offerings in
the house of the LORD regularly all the days of
Jehoiada.

15 But Jehoiada grew old and full of days, and
died; he was one hundred thirty years old at his
death. 16And they buried him in the city of David
among the kings, because he had done good in
Israel, and for God and his house.

17 Now after the death of Jehoiada the officials of Judah came and did obeisance to the king;
then the king listened to them. 18They abandoned
the house of the LORD, the God of their ancestors, and served the sacred poles[c] and the idols.
And wrath came upon Judah and Jerusalem for
this guilt of theirs. 19Yet he sent prophets among
them to bring them back to the LORD; they testified against them, but they would not listen.

20 Then the spirit of God took possession of[d]
Zechariah son of the priest Jehoiada; he stood
above the people and said to them, "Thus says
God: Why do you transgress the commandments
of the LORD, so that you cannot prosper? Because
you have forsaken the LORD, he has also forsaken
you." 21But they conspired against him, and by
command of the king they stoned him to death in
the court of the house of the LORD. 22King Joash
did not remember the kindness that Jehoiada,
Zechariah's father, had shown him, but killed his
son. As he was dying, he said, "May the LORD see
and avenge!"

23 At the end of the year the army of Aram
came up against Joash. They came to Judah and
Jerusalem, and destroyed all the officials of the
people from among them, and sent all the booty
they took to the king of Damascus. 24Although
the army of Aram had come with few men, the
LORD delivered into their hand a very great army,
because they had abandoned the LORD, the God
of their ancestors. Thus they executed judgment
on Joash.

25 When they had withdrawn, leaving him
severely wounded, his servants conspired against
him because of the blood of the son[e] of the priest
Jehoiada, and they killed him on his bed. So he
died; and they buried him in the city of David, but
they did not bury him in the tombs of the kings.
26Those who conspired against him were Zabad
son of Shimeath the Ammonite, and Jehozabad

[a] Compare Vg: Heb *and* [b] Or *treaty*, or *testimony*; Heb *eduth* [c] Heb *Asherim* [d] Heb *clothed itself with*
[e] Gk Vg: Heb *sons*

son of Shimrith the Moabite. 27Accounts of his
sons, and of the many oracles against him, and of
the rebuilding[a] of the house of God are written in
the Commentary on the Book of the Kings. And
his son Amaziah succeeded him.

25 Amaziah was twenty-five years old when
he began to reign, and he reigned twenty-
nine years in Jerusalem. His mother's name was
Jehoaddan of Jerusalem. 2He did what was right
in the sight of the LORD, yet not with a true heart.
3As soon as the royal power was firmly in his
hand he killed his servants who had murdered
his father the king. 4But he did not put their children to death, according to what is written in the
law, in the book of Moses, where the LORD commanded, "The parents shall not be put to death
for the children, or the children be put to death
for the parents; but all shall be put to death for
their own sins."

5 Amaziah assembled the people of Judah,
and set them by ancestral houses under commanders of the thousands and of the hundreds
for all Judah and Benjamin. He mustered those
twenty years old and upward, and found that they
were three hundred thousand picked troops fit
for war, able to handle spear and shield. 6He also
hired one hundred thousand mighty warriors
from Israel for one hundred talents of silver. 7But
a man of God came to him and said, "O king,
do not let the army of Israel go with you, for the
LORD is not with Israel—all these Ephraimites.
8Rather, go by yourself and act; be strong in
battle, or God will fling you down before the enemy; for God has power to help or to overthrow."
9Amaziah said to the man of God, "But what shall
we do about the hundred talents that I have given
to the army of Israel?" The man of God answered,
"The LORD is able to give you much more than
this." 10Then Amaziah discharged the army that
had come to him from Ephraim, letting them go
home again. But they became very angry with Judah, and returned home in fierce anger.

11 Amaziah took courage, and led out his
people; he went to the Valley of Salt, and struck
down ten thousand men of Seir. 12The people
of Judah captured another ten thousand alive,
took them to the top of Sela, and threw them
down from the top of Sela, so that all of them
were dashed to pieces. 13But the men of the army
whom Amaziah sent back, not letting them go
with him to battle, fell on the cities of Judah from
Samaria to Beth-horon; they killed three thousand people in them, and took much booty.

14 Now after Amaziah came from the slaughter of the Edomites, he brought the gods of the
people of Seir, set them up as his gods, and worshiped them, making offerings to them. 15The
LORD was angry with Amaziah and sent to him a
prophet, who said to him, "Why have you resorted
to a people's gods who could not deliver their
own people from your hand?" 16But as he was
speaking the king[b] said to him, "Have we made
you a royal counselor? Stop! Why should you be
put to death?" So the prophet stopped, but said,
"I know that God has determined to destroy you,
because you have done this and have not listened
to my advice."

17 Then King Amaziah of Judah took counsel and sent to King Joash son of Jehoahaz son
of Jehu of Israel, saying, "Come, let us look one
another in the face." 18King Joash of Israel sent
word to King Amaziah of Judah, "A thornbush
on Lebanon sent to a cedar on Lebanon, saying,
'Give your daughter to my son for a wife'; but a
wild animal of Lebanon passed by and trampled
down the thornbush. 19You say, 'See, I have defeated Edom,' and your heart has lifted you up in
boastfulness. Now stay at home; why should you
provoke trouble so that you fall, you and Judah
with you?"

20 But Amaziah would not listen—it was
God's doing, in order to hand them over, because
they had sought the gods of Edom. 21So King
Joash of Israel went up; he and King Amaziah
of Judah faced one another in battle at Beth-
shemesh, which belongs to Judah. 22Judah was
defeated by Israel; everyone fled home. 23King
Joash of Israel captured King Amaziah of Judah,
son of Joash, son of Ahaziah, at Beth-shemesh; he
brought him to Jerusalem, and broke down the

[a] Heb *founding* [b] Heb *he*

wall of Jerusalem from the Ephraim Gate to the
Corner Gate, a distance of four hundred cubits.
24 He seized all the gold and silver, and all the
vessels that were found in the house of God, and
Obed-edom with them; he seized also the treasuries of the king's house, also hostages; then he
returned to Samaria.

25 King Amaziah son of Joash of Judah, lived
fifteen years after the death of King Joash son of
Jehoahaz of Israel. 26 Now the rest of the deeds
of Amaziah, from first to last, are they not written in the Book of the Kings of Judah and Israel?
27 From the time that Amaziah turned away from
the LORD they made a conspiracy against him in
Jerusalem, and he fled to Lachish. But they sent
after him to Lachish, and killed him there. 28 They
brought him back on horses; he was buried with
his ancestors in the city of David.

26 Then all the people of Judah took Uzziah,
who was sixteen years old, and made him
king to succeed his father Amaziah. 2 He rebuilt
Eloth and restored it to Judah, after the king slept
with his ancestors. 3 Uzziah was sixteen years old
when he began to reign, and he reigned fifty-two
years in Jerusalem. His mother's name was Jecoliah of Jerusalem. 4 He did what was right in the
sight of the LORD, just as his father Amaziah had
done. 5 He set himself to seek God in the days
of Zechariah, who instructed him in the fear of
God; and as long as he sought the LORD, God
made him prosper.

6 He went out and made war against the Philistines, and broke down the wall of Gath and the
wall of Jabneh and the wall of Ashdod; he built
cities in the territory of Ashdod and elsewhere
among the Philistines. 7 God helped him against
the Philistines, against the Arabs who lived in Gur-
baal, and against the Meunites. 8 The Ammonites paid tribute to Uzziah, and his fame spread
even to the border of Egypt, for he became very
strong. 9 Moreover Uzziah built towers in Jerusalem at the Corner Gate, at the Valley Gate, and at
the Angle, and fortified them. 10 He built towers
in the wilderness and hewed out many cisterns,
for he had large herds, both in the Shephelah and
in the plain, and he had farmers and vinedressers
in the hills and in the fertile lands, for he loved
the soil. 11 Moreover Uzziah had an army of soldiers, fit for war, in divisions according to the
numbers in the muster made by the secretary
Jeiel and the officer Maaseiah, under the direction of Hananiah, one of the king's commanders.
12 The whole number of the heads of ancestral
houses of mighty warriors was two thousand six
hundred. 13 Under their command was an army of
three hundred seven thousand five hundred, who
could make war with mighty power, to help the
king against the enemy. 14 Uzziah provided for
all the army the shields, spears, helmets, coats of
mail, bows, and stones for slinging. 15 In Jerusalem
he set up machines, invented by skilled workers,
on the towers and the corners for shooting arrows
and large stones. And his fame spread far, for he
was marvelously helped until he became strong.

16 But when he had become strong he grew
proud, to his destruction. For he was false to the
LORD his God, and entered the temple of the
LORD to make offering on the altar of incense.
17 But the priest Azariah went in after him, with
eighty priests of the LORD who were men of
valor; 18 they withstood King Uzziah, and said to
him, "It is not for you, Uzziah, to make offering to
the LORD, but for the priests the descendants of
Aaron, who are consecrated to make offering. Go
out of the sanctuary; for you have done wrong,
and it will bring you no honor from the LORD
God." 19 Then Uzziah was angry. Now he had a
censer in his hand to make offering, and when he
became angry with the priests a leprous[a] disease
broke out on his forehead, in the presence of the
priests in the house of the LORD, by the altar of
incense. 20 When the chief priest Azariah, and all
the priests, looked at him, he was leprous[a] in his
forehead. They hurried him out, and he himself
hurried to get out, because the LORD had struck
him. 21 King Uzziah was leprous[a] to the day of
his death, and being leprous[a] lived in a separate
house, for he was excluded from the house of the
LORD. His son Jotham was in charge of the palace
of the king, governing the people of the land.

[a] A term for several skin diseases; precise meaning uncertain

22 Now the rest of the acts of Uzziah, from first to last, the prophet Isaiah son of Amoz wrote. 23 Uzziah slept with his ancestors; they buried him near his ancestors in the burial field that belonged to the kings, for they said, "He is leprous."[a] His son Jotham succeeded him.

27 Jotham was twenty-five years old when he began to reign; he reigned sixteen years in Jerusalem. His mother's name was Jerushah daughter of Zadok. 2 He did what was right in the sight of the LORD just as his father Uzziah had done—only he did not invade the temple of the LORD. But the people still followed corrupt practices. 3 He built the upper gate of the house of the LORD, and did extensive building on the wall of Ophel. 4 Moreover he built cities in the hill country of Judah, and forts and towers on the wooded hills. 5 He fought with the king of the Ammonites and prevailed against them. The Ammonites gave him that year one hundred talents of silver, ten thousand cors of wheat and ten thousand of barley. The Ammonites paid him the same amount in the second and the third years. 6 So Jotham became strong because he ordered his ways before the LORD his God. 7 Now the rest of the acts of Jotham, and all his wars and his ways, are written in the Book of the Kings of Israel and Judah. 8 He was twenty-five years old when he began to reign; he reigned sixteen years in Jerusalem. 9 Jotham slept with his ancestors, and they buried him in the city of David; and his son Ahaz succeeded him.

28 Ahaz was twenty years old when he began to reign; he reigned sixteen years in Jerusalem. He did not do what was right in the sight of the LORD, as his ancestor David had done, 2 but he walked in the ways of the kings of Israel. He even made cast images for the Baals; 3 and he made offerings in the valley of the son of Hinnom, and made his sons pass through fire, according to the abominable practices of the nations whom the LORD drove out before the people of Israel. 4 He sacrificed and made offerings on the high places, on the hills, and under every green tree.

5 Therefore the LORD his God gave him into the hand of the king of Aram, who defeated him and took captive a great number of his people and brought them to Damascus. He was also given into the hand of the king of Israel, who defeated him with great slaughter. 6 Pekah son of Remaliah killed one hundred twenty thousand in Judah in one day, all of them valiant warriors, because they had abandoned the LORD, the God of their ancestors. 7 And Zichri, a mighty warrior of Ephraim, killed the king's son Maaseiah, Azrikam the commander of the palace, and Elkanah the next in authority to the king.

8 The people of Israel took captive two hundred thousand of their kin, women, sons, and daughters; they also took much booty from them and brought the booty to Samaria. 9 But a prophet of the LORD was there, whose name was Oded; he went out to meet the army that came to Samaria, and said to them, "Because the LORD, the God of your ancestors, was angry with Judah, he gave them into your hand, but you have killed them in a rage that has reached up to heaven. 10 Now you intend to subjugate the people of Judah and Jerusalem, male and female, as your slaves. But what have you except sins against the LORD your God? 11 Now hear me, and send back the captives whom you have taken from your kindred, for the fierce wrath of the LORD is upon you." 12 Moreover, certain chiefs of the Ephraimites, Azariah son of Johanan, Berechiah son of Meshillemoth, Jehizkiah son of Shallum, and Amasa son of Hadlai, stood up against those who were coming from the war, 13 and said to them, "You shall not bring the captives in here, for you propose to bring on us guilt against the LORD in addition to our present sins and guilt. For our guilt is already great, and there is fierce wrath against Israel." 14 So the warriors left the captives and the booty before the officials and all the assembly. 15 Then those who were mentioned by name got up and took the captives, and with the booty they clothed all that were naked among them; they clothed them, gave them sandals, provided them with food and drink, and anointed them; and carrying all the feeble among them on donkeys, they brought

[a] A term for several skin diseases; precise meaning uncertain

them to their kindred at Jericho, the city of palm trees. Then they returned to Samaria.

16 At that time King Ahaz sent to the king[a] of Assyria for help. 17 For the Edomites had again invaded and defeated Judah, and carried away captives. 18 And the Philistines had made raids on the cities in the Shephelah and the Negeb of Judah, and had taken Beth-shemesh, Aijalon, Gederoth, Soco with its villages, Timnah with its villages, and Gimzo with its villages; and they settled there. 19 For the LORD brought Judah low because of King Ahaz of Israel, for he had behaved without restraint in Judah and had been faithless to the LORD. 20 So King Tilgath-pilneser of Assyria came against him, and oppressed him instead of strengthening him. 21 For Ahaz plundered the house of the LORD and the houses of the king and of the officials, and gave tribute to the king of Assyria; but it did not help him.

22 In the time of his distress he became yet more faithless to the LORD—this same King Ahaz. 23 For he sacrificed to the gods of Damascus, which had defeated him, and said, "Because the gods of the kings of Aram helped them, I will sacrifice to them so that they may help me." But they were the ruin of him, and of all Israel. 24 Ahaz gathered together the utensils of the house of God, and cut in pieces the utensils of the house of God. He shut up the doors of the house of the LORD and made himself altars in every corner of Jerusalem. 25 In every city of Judah he made high places to make offerings to other gods, provoking to anger the LORD, the God of his ancestors. 26 Now the rest of his acts and all his ways, from first to last, are written in the Book of the Kings of Judah and Israel. 27 Ahaz slept with his ancestors, and they buried him in the city, in Jerusalem; but they did not bring him into the tombs of the kings of Israel. His son Hezekiah succeeded him.

29 Hezekiah began to reign when he was twenty-five years old; he reigned twenty-nine years in Jerusalem. His mother's name was Abijah daughter of Zechariah. 2 He did what was right in the sight of the LORD, just as his ancestor David had done.

3 In the first year of his reign, in the first month, he opened the doors of the house of the LORD and repaired them. 4 He brought in the priests and the Levites and assembled them in the square on the east. 5 He said to them, "Listen to me, Levites! Sanctify yourselves, and sanctify the house of the LORD, the God of your ancestors, and carry out the filth from the holy place. 6 For our ancestors have been unfaithful and have done what was evil in the sight of the LORD our God; they have forsaken him, and have turned away their faces from the dwelling of the LORD, and turned their backs. 7 They also shut the doors of the vestibule and put out the lamps, and have not offered incense or made burnt offerings in the holy place to the God of Israel. 8 Therefore the wrath of the LORD came upon Judah and Jerusalem, and he has made them an object of horror, of astonishment, and of hissing, as you see with your own eyes. 9 Our fathers have fallen by the sword and our sons and our daughters and our wives are in captivity for this. 10 Now it is in my heart to make a covenant with the LORD, the God of Israel, so that his fierce anger may turn away from us. 11 My sons, do not now be negligent, for the LORD has chosen you to stand in his presence to minister to him, and to be his ministers and make offerings to him."

12 Then the Levites arose, Mahath son of Amasai, and Joel son of Azariah, of the sons of the Kohathites; and of the sons of Merari, Kish son of Abdi, and Azariah son of Jehallelel; and of the Gershonites, Joah son of Zimmah, and Eden son of Joah; 13 and of the sons of Elizaphan, Shimri and Jeuel; and of the sons of Asaph, Zechariah and Mattaniah; 14 and of the sons of Heman, Jehuel and Shimei; and of the sons of Jeduthun, Shemaiah and Uzziel. 15 They gathered their brothers, sanctified themselves, and went in as the king had commanded, by the words of the LORD, to cleanse the house of the LORD. 16 The priests went into the inner part of the house of the LORD to cleanse it, and they brought out all the unclean things that they found in the temple of the LORD into the court of the house of the

[a] Gk Syr Vg Compare 2 Kings 16.7: Heb *kings*

LORD; and the Levites took them and carried
them out to the Wadi Kidron. 17They began to
sanctify on the first day of the first month, and on
the eighth day of the month they came to the vestibule of the LORD; then for eight days they sanctified the house of the LORD, and on the sixteenth
day of the first month they finished. 18Then they
went inside to King Hezekiah and said, "We have
cleansed all the house of the LORD, the altar of
burnt offering and all its utensils, and the table
for the rows of bread and all its utensils. 19All
the utensils that King Ahaz repudiated during his
reign when he was faithless, we have made ready
and sanctified; see, they are in front of the altar
of the LORD."

20 Then King Hezekiah rose early, assembled
the officials of the city, and went up to the house
of the LORD. 21They brought seven bulls, seven
rams, seven lambs, and seven male goats for a sin
offering for the kingdom and for the sanctuary
and for Judah. He commanded the priests the
descendants of Aaron to offer them on the altar
of the LORD. 22So they slaughtered the bulls,
and the priests received the blood and dashed it
against the altar; they slaughtered the rams and
their blood was dashed against the altar; they
also slaughtered the lambs and their blood was
dashed against the altar. 23Then the male goats
for the sin offering were brought to the king and
the assembly; they laid their hands on them,
24and the priests slaughtered them and made a
sin offering with their blood at the altar, to make
atonement for all Israel. For the king commanded
that the burnt offering and the sin offering should
be made for all Israel.

25 He stationed the Levites in the house of
the LORD with cymbals, harps, and lyres, according to the commandment of David and of Gad
the king's seer and of the prophet Nathan, for the
commandment was from the LORD through his
prophets. 26The Levites stood with the instruments of David, and the priests with the trumpets. 27Then Hezekiah commanded that the
burnt offering be offered on the altar. When the
burnt offering began, the song to the LORD began also, and the trumpets, accompanied by the
instruments of King David of Israel. 28The whole
assembly worshiped, the singers sang, and the
trumpeters sounded; all this continued until the
burnt offering was finished. 29When the offering
was finished, the king and all who were present
with him bowed down and worshiped. 30King
Hezekiah and the officials commanded the Levites to sing praises to the LORD with the words
of David and of the seer Asaph. They sang praises
with gladness, and they bowed down and worshiped.

31 Then Hezekiah said, "You have now consecrated yourselves to the LORD; come near,
bring sacrifices and thank offerings to the house
of the LORD." The assembly brought sacrifices
and thank offerings; and all who were of a willing heart brought burnt offerings. 32The number
of the burnt offerings that the assembly brought
was seventy bulls, one hundred rams, and two
hundred lambs; all these were for a burnt offering to the LORD. 33The consecrated offerings
were six hundred bulls and three thousand sheep.
34But the priests were too few and could not skin
all the burnt offerings, so, until other priests had
sanctified themselves, their kindred, the Levites,
helped them until the work was finished—for
the Levites were more conscientious[a] than the
priests in sanctifying themselves. 35Besides the
great number of burnt offerings there was the fat
of the offerings of well-being, and there were the
drink offerings for the burnt offerings. Thus the
service of the house of the LORD was restored.
36And Hezekiah and all the people rejoiced because of what God had done for the people; for
the thing had come about suddenly.

30 Hezekiah sent word to all Israel and Judah,
and wrote letters also to Ephraim and Manasseh, that they should come to the house of the
LORD at Jerusalem, to keep the passover to the
LORD the God of Israel. 2For the king and his officials and all the assembly in Jerusalem had taken
counsel to keep the passover in the second month
3(for they could not keep it at its proper time because the priests had not sanctified themselves in

[a] Heb *upright in heart*

sufficient number, nor had the people assembled in Jerusalem). [4]The plan seemed right to the king and all the assembly. [5]So they decreed to make a proclamation throughout all Israel, from Beer-sheba to Dan, that the people should come and keep the passover to the LORD the God of Israel, at Jerusalem; for they had not kept it in great numbers as prescribed. [6]So couriers went throughout all Israel and Judah with letters from the king and his officials, as the king had commanded, saying, "O people of Israel, return to the LORD, the God of Abraham, Isaac, and Israel, so that he may turn again to the remnant of you who have escaped from the hand of the kings of Assyria. [7]Do not be like your ancestors and your kindred, who were faithless to the LORD God of their ancestors, so that he made them a desolation, as you see. [8]Do not now be stiff-necked as your ancestors were, but yield yourselves to the LORD and come to his sanctuary, which he has sanctified forever, and serve the LORD your God, so that his fierce anger may turn away from you. [9]For as you return to the LORD, your kindred and your children will find compassion with their captors, and return to this land. For the LORD your God is gracious and merciful, and will not turn away his face from you, if you return to him."

10 So the couriers went from city to city through the country of Ephraim and Manasseh, and as far as Zebulun; but they laughed them to scorn, and mocked them. [11]Only a few from Asher, Manasseh, and Zebulun humbled themselves and came to Jerusalem. [12]The hand of God was also on Judah to give them one heart to do what the king and the officials commanded by the word of the LORD.

13 Many people came together in Jerusalem to keep the festival of unleavened bread in the second month, a very large assembly. [14]They set to work and removed the altars that were in Jerusalem, and all the altars for offering incense they took away and threw into the Wadi Kidron. [15]They slaughtered the passover lamb on the fourteenth day of the second month. The priests and the Levites were ashamed, and they sanctified themselves and brought burnt offerings into the house of the LORD. [16]They took their accustomed posts according to the law of Moses the man of God; the priests dashed the blood that they received[a] from the hands of the Levites. [17]For there were many in the assembly who had not sanctified themselves; therefore the Levites had to slaughter the passover lamb for everyone who was not clean, to make it holy to the LORD. [18]For a multitude of the people, many of them from Ephraim, Manasseh, Issachar, and Zebulun, had not cleansed themselves, yet they ate the passover otherwise than as prescribed. But Hezekiah prayed for them, saying, "The good LORD pardon all [19]who set their hearts to seek God, the LORD the God of their ancestors, even though not in accordance with the sanctuary's rules of cleanness." [20]The LORD heard Hezekiah, and healed the people. [21]The people of Israel who were present at Jerusalem kept the festival of unleavened bread seven days with great gladness; and the Levites and the priests praised the LORD day by day, accompanied by loud instruments for the LORD. [22]Hezekiah spoke encouragingly to all the Levites who showed good skill in the service of the LORD. So the people ate the food of the festival for seven days, sacrificing offerings of well-being and giving thanks to the LORD the God of their ancestors.

23 Then the whole assembly agreed together to keep the festival for another seven days; so they kept it for another seven days with gladness. [24]For King Hezekiah of Judah gave the assembly a thousand bulls and seven thousand sheep for offerings, and the officials gave the assembly a thousand bulls and ten thousand sheep. The priests sanctified themselves in great numbers. [25]The whole assembly of Judah, the priests and the Levites, and the whole assembly that came out of Israel, and the resident aliens who came out of the land of Israel, and the resident aliens who lived in Judah, rejoiced. [26]There was great joy in Jerusalem, for since the time of Solomon son of King David of Israel there had been nothing like this in Jerusalem. [27]Then the priests and

[a] Heb lacks *that they received*

the Levites stood up and blessed the people, and their voice was heard; their prayer came to his holy dwelling in heaven.

31 Now when all this was finished, all Israel who were present went out to the cities of Judah and broke down the pillars, hewed down the sacred poles,[a] and pulled down the high places and the altars throughout all Judah and Benjamin, and in Ephraim and Manasseh, until they had destroyed them all. Then all the people of Israel returned to their cities, all to their individual properties.

2 Hezekiah appointed the divisions of the priests and of the Levites, division by division, everyone according to his service, the priests and the Levites, for burnt offerings and offerings of well-being, to minister in the gates of the camp of the LORD and to give thanks and praise. 3 The contribution of the king from his own possessions was for the burnt offerings: the burnt offerings of morning and evening, and the burnt offerings for the sabbaths, the new moons, and the appointed festivals, as it is written in the law of the LORD. 4 He commanded the people who lived in Jerusalem to give the portion due to the priests and the Levites, so that they might devote themselves to the law of the LORD. 5 As soon as the word spread, the people of Israel gave in abundance the first fruits of grain, wine, oil, honey, and of all the produce of the field; and they brought in abundantly the tithe of everything. 6 The people of Israel and Judah who lived in the cities of Judah also brought in the tithe of cattle and sheep, and the tithe of the dedicated things that had been consecrated to the LORD their God, and laid them in heaps. 7 In the third month they began to pile up the heaps, and finished them in the seventh month. 8 When Hezekiah and the officials came and saw the heaps, they blessed the LORD and his people Israel. 9 Hezekiah questioned the priests and the Levites about the heaps. 10 The chief priest Azariah, who was of the house of Zadok, answered him, "Since they began to bring the contributions into the house of the LORD, we have had enough to eat and have plenty to spare; for the LORD has blessed his people, so that we have this great supply left over."

11 Then Hezekiah commanded them to prepare store-chambers in the house of the LORD; and they prepared them. 12 Faithfully they brought in the contributions, the tithes and the dedicated things. The chief officer in charge of them was Conaniah the Levite, with his brother Shimei as second; 13 while Jehiel, Azaziah, Nahath, Asahel, Jerimoth, Jozabad, Eliel, Ismachiah, Mahath, and Benaiah were overseers assisting Conaniah and his brother Shimei, by the appointment of King Hezekiah and of Azariah the chief officer of the house of God. 14 Kore son of Imnah the Levite, keeper of the east gate, was in charge of the freewill offerings to God, to apportion the contribution reserved for the LORD and the most holy offerings. 15 Eden, Miniamin, Jeshua, Shemaiah, Amariah, and Shecaniah were faithfully assisting him in the cities of the priests, to distribute the portions to their kindred, old and young alike, by divisions, 16 except those enrolled by genealogy, males from three years old and upwards, all who entered the house of the LORD as the duty of each day required, for their service according to their offices, by their divisions. 17 The enrollment of the priests was according to their ancestral houses; that of the Levites from twenty years old and upwards was according to their offices, by their divisions. 18 The priests were enrolled with all their little children, their wives, their sons, and their daughters, the whole multitude; for they were faithful in keeping themselves holy. 19 And for the descendants of Aaron, the priests, who were in the fields of common land belonging to their towns, town by town, the people designated by name were to distribute portions to every male among the priests and to everyone among the Levites who was enrolled.

20 Hezekiah did this throughout all Judah; he did what was good and right and faithful before the LORD his God. 21 And every work that he undertook in the service of the house of God, and in accordance with the law and the command-

[a] Heb *Asherim*

ments, to seek his God, he did with all his heart;
and he prospered.

32 After these things and these acts of faithfulness, King Sennacherib of Assyria
came and invaded Judah and encamped against
the fortified cities, thinking to win them for himself. 2When Hezekiah saw that Sennacherib had
come and intended to fight against Jerusalem, 3he
planned with his officers and his warriors to stop
the flow of the springs that were outside the city;
and they helped him. 4A great many people were
gathered, and they stopped all the springs and the
wadi that flowed through the land, saying, "Why
should the Assyrian kings come and find water in
abundance?" 5Hezekiah[a] set to work resolutely
and built up the entire wall that was broken down,
and raised towers on it,[b] and outside it he built another wall; he also strengthened the Millo in the
city of David, and made weapons and shields in
abundance. 6He appointed combat commanders
over the people, and gathered them together to
him in the square at the gate of the city and spoke
encouragingly to them, saying, 7"Be strong and
of good courage. Do not be afraid or dismayed
before the king of Assyria and all the horde that
is with him; for there is one greater with us than
with him. 8With him is an arm of flesh; but with
us is the LORD our God, to help us and to fight
our battles." The people were encouraged by the
words of King Hezekiah of Judah.

9 After this, while King Sennacherib of Assyria was at Lachish with all his forces, he sent his
servants to Jerusalem to King Hezekiah of Judah
and to all the people of Judah that were in Jerusalem, saying, 10"Thus says King Sennacherib of
Assyria: On what are you relying, that you undergo the siege of Jerusalem? 11Is not Hezekiah
misleading you, handing you over to die by famine and by thirst, when he tells you, 'The LORD
our God will save us from the hand of the king
of Assyria'? 12Was it not this same Hezekiah who
took away his high places and his altars and commanded Judah and Jerusalem, saying, 'Before
one altar you shall worship, and upon it you shall
make your offerings'? 13Do you not know what
I and my ancestors have done to all the peoples
of other lands? Were the gods of the nations of
those lands at all able to save their lands out of
my hand? 14Who among all the gods of those nations that my ancestors utterly destroyed was able
to save his people from my hand, that your God
should be able to save you from my hand? 15Now
therefore do not let Hezekiah deceive you or mislead you in this fashion, and do not believe him,
for no god of any nation or kingdom has been
able to save his people from my hand or from the
hand of my ancestors. How much less will your
God save you out of my hand!"

16 His servants said still more against the
Lord GOD and against his servant Hezekiah.
17He also wrote letters to throw contempt on the
LORD the God of Israel and to speak against him,
saying, "Just as the gods of the nations in other
lands did not rescue their people from my hands,
so the God of Hezekiah will not rescue his people
from my hand." 18They shouted it with a loud
voice in the language of Judah to the people of
Jerusalem who were on the wall, to frighten and
terrify them, in order that they might take the
city. 19They spoke of the God of Jerusalem as if
he were like the gods of the peoples of the earth,
which are the work of human hands.

20 Then King Hezekiah and the prophet Isaiah son of Amoz prayed because of this and cried
to heaven. 21And the LORD sent an angel who cut
off all the mighty warriors and commanders and
officers in the camp of the king of Assyria. So he
returned in disgrace to his own land. When he
came into the house of his god, some of his own
sons struck him down there with the sword. 22So
the LORD saved Hezekiah and the inhabitants of
Jerusalem from the hand of King Sennacherib of
Assyria and from the hand of all his enemies; he
gave them rest[c] on every side. 23Many brought
gifts to the LORD in Jerusalem and precious
things to King Hezekiah of Judah, so that he was
exalted in the sight of all nations from that time
onward.

24 In those days Hezekiah became sick and
was at the point of death. He prayed to the LORD,

[a] Heb *He* [b] Vg: Heb *and raised on the towers* [c] Gk Vg: Heb *guided them*

and he answered him and gave him a sign. 25 But
Hezekiah did not respond according to the benefit done to him, for his heart was proud. Therefore wrath came upon him and upon Judah and
Jerusalem. 26 Then Hezekiah humbled himself for
the pride of his heart, both he and the inhabitants
of Jerusalem, so that the wrath of the LORD did
not come upon them in the days of Hezekiah.

27 Hezekiah had very great riches and honor;
and he made for himself treasuries for silver, for
gold, for precious stones, for spices, for shields,
and for all kinds of costly objects; 28 storehouses
also for the yield of grain, wine, and oil; and stalls
for all kinds of cattle, and sheepfolds.[a] 29 He likewise provided cities for himself, and flocks and
herds in abundance; for God had given him very
great possessions. 30 This same Hezekiah closed
the upper outlet of the waters of Gihon and directed them down to the west side of the city of
David. Hezekiah prospered in all his works. 31 So
also in the matter of the envoys of the officials of
Babylon, who had been sent to him to inquire
about the sign that had been done in the land,
God left him to himself, in order to test him and
to know all that was in his heart.

32 Now the rest of the acts of Hezekiah, and
his good deeds, are written in the vision of the
prophet Isaiah son of Amoz in the Book of the
Kings of Judah and Israel. 33 Hezekiah slept with
his ancestors, and they buried him on the ascent
to the tombs of the descendants of David; and all
Judah and the inhabitants of Jerusalem did him
honor at his death. His son Manasseh succeeded
him.

33 Manasseh was twelve years old when he
began to reign; he reigned fifty-five years
in Jerusalem. 2 He did what was evil in the sight of
the LORD, according to the abominable practices
of the nations whom the LORD drove out before
the people of Israel. 3 For he rebuilt the high places
that his father Hezekiah had pulled down, and
erected altars to the Baals, made sacred poles,[b]
worshiped all the host of heaven, and served
them. 4 He built altars in the house of the LORD,
of which the LORD had said, "In Jerusalem shall
my name be forever." 5 He built altars for all the
host of heaven in the two courts of the house of
the LORD. 6 He made his son pass through fire in
the valley of the son of Hinnom, practiced soothsaying and augury and sorcery, and dealt with
mediums and with wizards. He did much evil in
the sight of the LORD, provoking him to anger.
7 The carved image of the idol that he had made
he set in the house of God, of which God said to
David and to his son Solomon, "In this house, and
in Jerusalem, which I have chosen out of all the
tribes of Israel, I will put my name forever; 8 I will
never again remove the feet of Israel from the land
that I appointed for your ancestors, if only they
will be careful to do all that I have commanded
them, all the law, the statutes, and the ordinances
given through Moses." 9 Manasseh misled Judah
and the inhabitants of Jerusalem, so that they did
more evil than the nations whom the LORD had
destroyed before the people of Israel.

10 The LORD spoke to Manasseh and to his
people, but they gave no heed. 11 Therefore the
LORD brought against them the commanders of
the army of the king of Assyria, who took Manasseh captive in manacles, bound him with fetters, and brought him to Babylon. 12 While he was
in distress he entreated the favor of the LORD his
God and humbled himself greatly before the God
of his ancestors. 13 He prayed to him, and God received his entreaty, heard his plea, and restored
him again to Jerusalem and to his kingdom. Then
Manasseh knew that the LORD indeed was God.

14 Afterward he built an outer wall for the
city of David west of Gihon, in the valley, reaching the entrance at the Fish Gate; he carried it
around Ophel, and raised it to a very great height.
He also put commanders of the army in all the
fortified cities in Judah. 15 He took away the foreign gods and the idol from the house of the
LORD, and all the altars that he had built on the
mountain of the house of the LORD and in Jerusalem, and he threw them out of the city. 16 He
also restored the altar of the LORD and offered
on it sacrifices of well-being and of thanksgiving;
and he commanded Judah to serve the LORD the

[a] Gk Vg: Heb *flocks for folds* [b] Heb *Asheroth*

God of Israel. 17 The people, however, still sacrificed at the high places, but only to the LORD
their God.

18 Now the rest of the acts of Manasseh, his
prayer to his God, and the words of the seers who
spoke to him in the name of the LORD God of Israel, these are in the Annals of the Kings of Israel.
19 His prayer, and how God received his entreaty,
all his sin and his faithlessness, the sites on which
he built high places and set up the sacred poles[a]
and the images, before he humbled himself, these
are written in the records of the seers.[b] 20 So Manasseh slept with his ancestors, and they buried
him in his house. His son Amon succeeded him.

21 Amon was twenty-two years old when he
began to reign; he reigned two years in Jerusalem.
22 He did what was evil in the sight of the LORD,
as his father Manasseh had done. Amon sacrificed to all the images that his father Manasseh
had made, and served them. 23 He did not humble
himself before the LORD, as his father Manasseh
had humbled himself, but this Amon incurred
more and more guilt. 24 His servants conspired
against him and killed him in his house. 25 But the
people of the land killed all those who had conspired against King Amon; and the people of the
land made his son Josiah king to succeed him.

34 Josiah was eight years old when he began
to reign; he reigned thirty-one years in
Jerusalem. 2 He did what was right in the sight of
the LORD, and walked in the ways of his ancestor David; he did not turn aside to the right or
to the left. 3 For in the eighth year of his reign,
while he was still a boy, he began to seek the God
of his ancestor David, and in the twelfth year he
began to purge Judah and Jerusalem of the high
places, the sacred poles,[a] and the carved and the
cast images. 4 In his presence they pulled down
the altars of the Baals; he demolished the incense
altars that stood above them. He broke down the
sacred poles[a] and the carved and the cast images;
he made dust of them and scattered it over the
graves of those who had sacrificed to them. 5 He
also burned the bones of the priests on their altars, and purged Judah and Jerusalem. 6 In the
towns of Manasseh, Ephraim, and Simeon, and
as far as Naphtali, in their ruins[c] all around, 7 he
broke down the altars, beat the sacred poles[a] and
the images into powder, and demolished all the
incense altars throughout all the land of Israel.
Then he returned to Jerusalem.

8 In the eighteenth year of his reign, when
he had purged the land and the house, he sent
Shaphan son of Azaliah, Maaseiah the governor
of the city, and Joah son of Joahaz, the recorder,
to repair the house of the LORD his God. 9 They
came to the high priest Hilkiah and delivered the
money that had been brought into the house of
God, which the Levites, the keepers of the threshold, had collected from Manasseh and Ephraim
and from all the remnant of Israel and from all
Judah and Benjamin and from the inhabitants of
Jerusalem. 10 They delivered it to the workers who
had the oversight of the house of the LORD, and
the workers who were working in the house of the
LORD gave it for repairing and restoring the house.
11 They gave it to the carpenters and the builders
to buy quarried stone, and timber for binders,
and beams for the buildings that the kings of Judah had let go to ruin. 12 The people did the work
faithfully. Over them were appointed the Levites
Jahath and Obadiah, of the sons of Merari, along
with Zechariah and Meshullam, of the sons of the
Kohathites, to have oversight. Other Levites, all
skillful with instruments of music, 13 were over
the burden bearers and directed all who did work
in every kind of service; and some of the Levites
were scribes, and officials, and gatekeepers.

14 While they were bringing out the money
that had been brought into the house of the
LORD, the priest Hilkiah found the book of the
law of the LORD given through Moses. 15 Hilkiah
said to the secretary Shaphan, "I have found the
book of the law in the house of the LORD"; and
Hilkiah gave the book to Shaphan. 16 Shaphan
brought the book to the king, and further reported to the king, "All that was committed to
your servants they are doing. 17 They have emptied out the money that was found in the house
of the LORD and have delivered it into the hand

[a] Heb *Asherim* [b] One Ms Gk: MT *of Hozai* [c] Meaning of Heb uncertain

of the overseers and the workers." 18 The secretary Shaphan informed the king, "The priest Hilkiah has given me a book." Shaphan then read it aloud to the king.

19 When the king heard the words of the law he tore his clothes. 20 Then the king commanded Hilkiah, Ahikam son of Shaphan, Abdon son of Micah, the secretary Shaphan, and the king's servant Asaiah: 21 "Go, inquire of the LORD for me and for those who are left in Israel and in Judah, concerning the words of the book that has been found; for the wrath of the LORD that is poured out on us is great, because our ancestors did not keep the word of the LORD, to act in accordance with all that is written in this book."

22 So Hilkiah and those whom the king had sent went to the prophet Huldah, the wife of Shallum son of Tokhath son of Hasrah, keeper of the wardrobe (who lived in Jerusalem in the Second Quarter) and spoke to her to that effect. 23 She declared to them, "Thus says the LORD, the God of Israel: Tell the man who sent you to me, 24 Thus says the LORD: I will indeed bring disaster upon this place and upon its inhabitants, all the curses that are written in the book that was read before the king of Judah. 25 Because they have forsaken me and have made offerings to other gods, so that they have provoked me to anger with all the works of their hands, my wrath will be poured out on this place and will not be quenched. 26 But as to the king of Judah, who sent you to inquire of the LORD, thus shall you say to him: Thus says the LORD, the God of Israel: Regarding the words that you have heard, 27 because your heart was penitent and you humbled yourself before God when you heard his words against this place and its inhabitants, and you have humbled yourself before me, and have torn your clothes and wept before me, I also have heard you, says the LORD. 28 I will gather you to your ancestors and you shall be gathered to your grave in peace; your eyes shall not see all the disaster that I will bring on this place and its inhabitants." They took the message back to the king.

29 Then the king sent word and gathered together all the elders of Judah and Jerusalem. 30 The king went up to the house of the LORD, with all the people of Judah, the inhabitants of Jerusalem, the priests and the Levites, all the people both great and small; he read in their hearing all the words of the book of the covenant that had been found in the house of the LORD. 31 The king stood in his place and made a covenant before the LORD, to follow the LORD, keeping his commandments, his decrees, and his statutes, with all his heart and all his soul, to perform the words of the covenant that were written in this book. 32 Then he made all who were present in Jerusalem and in Benjamin pledge themselves to it. And the inhabitants of Jerusalem acted according to the covenant of God,

2 Chronicles 34:14-28

When a scroll of Moses (probably some form of Deuteronomy) was discovered during temple renovations during the reign of the young king, Josiah (639–609 BCE), the first person to be consulted about the discovery was a woman prophet named Huldah. She was married to Shallum, the "keeper of the [royal] wardrobe," but was obviously a person of authority in her own right. The discovery of this old scroll and Huldah's prophesy of impending destruction led Josiah to initiate extensive religious reforms. Katherine Doob Sakenfeld comments,

> [R]eading a text as it stands may even help us to discover a historical reality (not just an authorial reality) that we had heretofore supposed to be nonexistent. What if ancient Israel really believed that God did not want women to be subordinated to men?... What if women prophets were quite ordinary?... Imagination and the discipline of historical reconstruction need to work in tandem to help us examine all of our presuppositions about the character of an ancient patriarchal and androcentric culture. In some respects the culture may turn out to be more patriarchal than we have feared, but in others it may be less so.[26]

— *DB*

the God of their ancestors. 33 Josiah took away all
the abominations from all the territory that belonged to the people of Israel, and made all who
were in Israel worship the LORD their God. All his
days they did not turn away from following the
LORD the God of their ancestors.

35 Josiah kept a passover to the LORD in Jerusalem; they slaughtered the passover
lamb on the fourteenth day of the first month.
2 He appointed the priests to their offices and
encouraged them in the service of the house of
the LORD. 3 He said to the Levites who taught all
Israel and who were holy to the LORD, "Put the
holy ark in the house that Solomon son of David,
king of Israel, built; you need no longer carry it
on your shoulders. Now serve the LORD your
God and his people Israel. 4 Make preparations by
your ancestral houses by your divisions, following
the written directions of King David of Israel and
the written directions of his son Solomon. 5 Take
position in the holy place according to the groupings of the ancestral houses of your kindred the
people, and let there be Levites for each division
of an ancestral house.[a] 6 Slaughter the passover
lamb, sanctify yourselves, and on behalf of your
kindred make preparations, acting according to
the word of the LORD by Moses."

7 Then Josiah contributed to the people, as
passover offerings for all that were present, lambs
and kids from the flock to the number of thirty
thousand, and three thousand bulls; these were
from the king's possessions. 8 His officials contributed willingly to the people, to the priests,
and to the Levites. Hilkiah, Zechariah, and Jehiel,
the chief officers of the house of God, gave to the
priests for the passover offerings two thousand six
hundred lambs and kids and three hundred bulls.
9 Conaniah also, and his brothers Shemaiah and
Nethanel, and Hashabiah and Jeiel and Jozabad,
the chiefs of the Levites, gave to the Levites for
the passover offerings five thousand lambs and
kids and five hundred bulls.

10 When the service had been prepared for,
the priests stood in their place, and the Levites in
their divisions according to the king's command.
11 They slaughtered the passover lamb, and the
priests dashed the blood that they received[b] from
them, while the Levites did the skinning. 12 They
set aside the burnt offerings so that they might
distribute them according to the groupings of
the ancestral houses of the people, to offer to the
LORD, as it is written in the book of Moses. And
they did the same with the bulls. 13 They roasted
the passover lamb with fire according to the ordinance; and they boiled the holy offerings in pots,
in caldrons, and in pans, and carried them quickly
to all the people. 14 Afterward they made preparations for themselves and for the priests, because
the priests the descendants of Aaron were occupied in offering the burnt offerings and the
fat parts until night; so the Levites made preparations for themselves and for the priests, the
descendants of Aaron. 15 The singers, the descendants of Asaph, were in their place according to
the command of David, and Asaph, and Heman,
and the king's seer Jeduthun. The gatekeepers
were at each gate; they did not need to interrupt
their service, for their kindred the Levites made
preparations for them.

16 So all the service of the LORD was prepared that day, to keep the passover and to offer
burnt offerings on the altar of the LORD, according to the command of King Josiah. 17 The people
of Israel who were present kept the passover at
that time, and the festival of unleavened bread
seven days. 18 No passover like it had been kept in
Israel since the days of the prophet Samuel; none
of the kings of Israel had kept such a passover as
was kept by Josiah, by the priests and the Levites,
by all Judah and Israel who were present, and by
the inhabitants of Jerusalem. 19 In the eighteenth
year of the reign of Josiah this passover was kept.

20 After all this, when Josiah had set the
temple in order, King Neco of Egypt went up to
fight at Carchemish on the Euphrates, and Josiah
went out against him. 21 But Neco[c] sent envoys to
him, saying, "What have I to do with you, king
of Judah? I am not coming against you today,
but against the house with which I am at war;
and God has commanded me to hurry. Cease

[a] Meaning of Heb uncertain
[b] Heb lacks *that they received*
[c] Heb *he*

opposing God, who is with me, so that he will not destroy you." 22But Josiah would not turn away from him, but disguised himself in order to fight with him. He did not listen to the words of Neco from the mouth of God, but joined battle in the plain of Megiddo. 23The archers shot King Josiah; and the king said to his servants, "Take me away, for I am badly wounded." 24So his servants took him out of the chariot and carried him in his second chariot[a] and brought him to Jerusalem. There he died, and was buried in the tombs of his ancestors. All Judah and Jerusalem mourned for Josiah. 25Jeremiah also uttered a lament for Josiah, and all the singing men and singing women have spoken of Josiah in their laments to this day. They made these a custom in Israel; they are recorded in the Laments. 26Now the rest of the acts of Josiah and his faithful deeds in accordance with what is written in the law of the LORD, 27and his acts, first and last, are written in the Book of the Kings of Israel and Judah.

36 The people of the land took Jehoahaz son of Josiah and made him king to succeed his father in Jerusalem. 2Jehoahaz was twenty-three years old when he began to reign; he reigned three months in Jerusalem. 3Then the king of Egypt deposed him in Jerusalem and laid on the land a tribute of one hundred talents of silver and one talent of gold. 4The king of Egypt made his brother Eliakim king over Judah and Jerusalem, and changed his name to Jehoiakim; but Neco took his brother Jehoahaz and carried him to Egypt.

5 Jehoiakim was twenty-five years old when he began to reign; he reigned eleven years in Jerusalem. He did what was evil in the sight of the LORD his God. 6Against him King Nebuchadnezzar of Babylon came up, and bound him with fetters to take him to Babylon. 7Nebuchadnezzar also carried some of the vessels of the house of the LORD to Babylon and put them in his palace in Babylon. 8Now the rest of the acts of Jehoiakim, and the abominations that he did, and what was found against him, are written in the Book of the Kings of Israel and Judah; and his son Jehoiachin succeeded him.

9 Jehoiachin was eight years old when he began to reign; he reigned three months and ten days in Jerusalem. He did what was evil in the sight of the LORD. 10In the spring of the year King Nebuchadnezzar sent and brought him to Babylon, along with the precious vessels of the house of the LORD, and made his brother Zedekiah king over Judah and Jerusalem.

11 Zedekiah was twenty-one years old when he began to reign; he reigned eleven years in Jerusalem. 12He did what was evil in the sight of the LORD his God. He did not humble himself before the prophet Jeremiah who spoke from the mouth of the LORD. 13He also rebelled against King Nebuchadnezzar, who had made him swear by God; he stiffened his neck and hardened his heart against turning to the LORD, the God of Israel. 14All the leading priests and the people also were exceedingly unfaithful, following all the abominations of the nations; and they polluted the house of the LORD that he had consecrated in Jerusalem.

15 The LORD, the God of their ancestors, sent persistently to them by his messengers, because he had compassion on his people and on his dwelling place; 16but they kept mocking the messengers of God, despising his words, and scoffing at his prophets, until the wrath of the LORD against his people became so great that there was no remedy.

17 Therefore he brought up against them the king of the Chaldeans, who killed their youths with the sword in the house of their sanctuary, and had no compassion on young man or young woman, the aged or the feeble; he gave them all into his hand. 18All the vessels of the house of God, large and small, and the treasures of the house of the LORD, and the treasures of the king and of his officials, all these he brought to Babylon. 19They burned the house of God, broke down the wall of Jerusalem, burned all its palaces with fire, and destroyed all its precious vessels. 20He took into exile in Babylon those who had escaped from the sword, and they became servants to him and to his sons until the establishment of the kingdom

[a] Or *the chariot of his deputy*

of Persia, 21 to fulfill the word of the LORD by the
mouth of Jeremiah, until the land had made up
for its sabbaths. All the days that it lay desolate it
kept sabbath, to fulfill seventy years.

22 In the first year of King Cyrus of Persia,
in fulfillment of the word of the LORD spoken by
Jeremiah, the LORD stirred up the spirit of King
Cyrus of Persia so that he sent a herald throughout all his kingdom and also declared in a written edict: 23 "Thus says King Cyrus of Persia: The
LORD, the God of heaven, has given me all the
kingdoms of the earth, and he has charged me to
build him a house at Jerusalem, which is in Judah.
Whoever is among you of all his people, may the
LORD his God be with him! Let him go up."

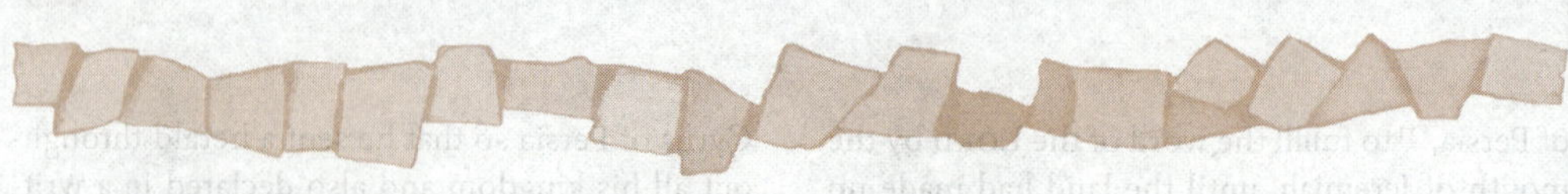

Ezra

The book of Ezra is part of a composition that also includes the book of Nehemiah. Origen and Jerome, two early Christian scholars, separated Ezra-Nehemiah into two books, but only after the fifteenth century did the books appear as separated compositions in Hebrew Bibles. The two books were unanimously accepted by Judaism and Western Christianity as belonging to the biblical canon, but they were rejected as such by the Syrian Church. In the Hebrew Bible, Ezra-Nehemiah are placed at the end of the Writings, after 1 and 2 Chronicles. The books were probably written in the land of Israel in the first quarter of the fourth century BCE.

The book of Ezra continues the story told in 1 and 2 Chronicles, beginning with Israel's return from exile in Babylon and the rebuilding of the temple in Jerusalem (chs. 1–6). It continues with an Aramaic section that includes the incidents with Rehum, Shimshai, Tattenai, and Shethar-bozenai (4:8—6:15) and the dedication of the second temple (Ezra 6:16-18). The narrative proceeds in Hebrew with the completion of the temple and the Passover celebration (6:19-22), and a narrative about the initial work of Ezra (chs. 7–10), which includes a letter written in Aramaic (Ezra 7:12-26). Ezra concludes with a third-person narrative about the resolution to send away foreign wives and children (ch. 10).

In 538 the Persian Cyrus, whom 2 Isaiah calls God's shepherd and Messiah (Isa 44:28; 45:1), issued a decree liberating the exiles. The return from the Babylonian exile and the rebuilding of the Jerusalem Temple mark the beginning of the second temple period in the history of the Jewish people. This was a crucial time for the religious definition of Judaism, and Ezra played a pivotal role in its shaping. The destruction of Jerusalem and its Temple by the Babylonians in 586 BCE and the subsequent captivity was one of the most devastating experiences for the people of God. Hope was proclaimed again in Babylon by prophets like the Second Isaiah (Isaiah 40–55), who promised a new exodus from Babylon (Isa 43:14-21) and a glorious return to the promised land.

In contrast to that glorious vision, the harsh reality of life in Jerusalem after the exile represented a difficult challenge for the faith of the post-exile community. Long gone were the days of national independence and Davidic kings. The people of God, now constituted as a colony under Persian rule, had to redefine their identity around religious institutions and relegate to a future restoration their dreams of political independence. In this context, Ezra's mission is twofold: to appoint magistrates and judges (7:25) who should *apply* God's law; and to teach the law to those who don't know it (for example, in the reforms of King Jehoshaphat discussed in 2 Chr 19:4-11). Ezra will also strictly prohibit marriages to foreign women, a drastic decision but perhaps the only way he could imagine to preserve the integrity and hopes of the (again) liberated community. Thus, the book of Ezra reflects tensions and negotiations in the cultural identity of this early Jewish community upon their return from the exile.

I can resonate quite readily with the tensions in cultural identity raised by this book because they correspond in some ways to my own life experiences. I was born and grew up in Argentina, a few miles south of Buenos Aires. Three of my grandparents had emigrated from Italy and one from Spain, and that European connection set the tone of my childhood. During my high school and early college years, however, my country experienced a bloody right-wing dictatorship that murdered thirty thousand of my people. It was then that I made a conscious decision to side with those who were persecuted and oppressed by the military, most of whom still remain "missing." I understand society as being in constant struggle—more specifically a class struggle—and try my best to be an organic intellectual on behalf of my people. This class consciousness—both of myself as an interpreter, and of the class options made explicit in the texts—conditions my reading of the Bible in general, and the books of Ezra and Nehemiah in particular.

— Alejandro F. Botta

1 In the first year of King Cyrus of Persia, in
order that the word of the LORD by the
mouth of Jeremiah might be accomplished, the
LORD stirred up the spirit of King Cyrus of Persia
so that he sent a herald throughout all his kingdom, and also in a written edict declared:
2 "Thus says King Cyrus of Persia: The LORD,
the God of heaven, has given me all the kingdoms
of the earth, and he has charged me to build him
a house at Jerusalem in Judah. 3 Any of those
among you who are of his people—may their
God be with them!—are now permitted to go up
to Jerusalem in Judah, and rebuild the house of
the LORD, the God of Israel—he is the God who
is in Jerusalem; 4 and let all survivors, in whatever
place they reside, be assisted by the people of
their place with silver and gold, with goods and
with animals, besides freewill offerings for the
house of God in Jerusalem."
5 The heads of the families of Judah and Benjamin, and the priests and the Levites—everyone
whose spirit God had stirred—got ready to go up
and rebuild the house of the LORD in Jerusalem.
6 All their neighbors aided them with silver vessels, with gold, with goods, with animals, and
with valuable gifts, besides all that was freely offered. 7 King Cyrus himself brought out the vessels
of the house of the LORD that Nebuchadnezzar
had carried away from Jerusalem and placed in
the house of his gods. 8 King Cyrus of Persia had
them released into the charge of Mithredath the
treasurer, who counted them out to Sheshbazzar
the prince of Judah. 9 And this was the inventory:
gold basins, thirty; silver basins, one thousand;
knives,[a] twenty-nine; 10 gold bowls, thirty; other
silver bowls, four hundred ten; other vessels, one
thousand; 11 the total of the gold and silver vessels
was five thousand four hundred. All these Sheshbazzar brought up, when the exiles were brought
up from Babylonia to Jerusalem.

2 Now these were the people of the province
who came from those captive exiles whom
King Nebuchadnezzar of Babylon had carried
captive to Babylonia; they returned to Jerusalem
and Judah, all to their own towns. 2 They came
with Zerubbabel, Jeshua, Nehemiah, Seraiah,

[a] Vg: Meaning of Heb uncertain

Reelaiah, Mordecai, Bilshan, Mispar, Bigvai, Rehum, and Baanah.

The number of the Israelite people: [3]the descendants of Parosh, two thousand one hundred seventy-two. [4]Of Shephatiah, three hundred seventy-two. [5]Of Arah, seven hundred seventy-five. [6]Of Pahath-moab, namely the descendants of Jeshua and Joab, two thousand eight hundred twelve. [7]Of Elam, one thousand two hundred fifty-four. [8]Of Zattu, nine hundred forty-five. [9]Of Zaccai, seven hundred sixty. [10]Of Bani, six hundred forty-two. [11]Of Bebai, six hundred twenty-three. [12]Of Azgad, one thousand two hundred twenty-two. [13]Of Adonikam, six hundred sixty-six. [14]Of Bigvai, two thousand fifty-six. [15]Of Adin, four hundred fifty-four. [16]Of Ater, namely of Hezekiah, ninety-eight. [17]Of Bezai, three hundred twenty-three. [18]Of Jorah, one hundred twelve. [19]Of Hashum, two hundred twenty-three. [20]Of Gibbar, ninety-five. [21]Of Bethlehem, one hundred twenty-three. [22]The people of Netophah, fifty-six. [23]Of Anathoth, one hundred twenty-eight. [24]The descendants of Azmaveth, forty-two. [25]Of Kiriatharim, Chephirah, and Beeroth, seven hundred forty-three. [26]Of Ramah and Geba, six hundred twenty-one. [27]The people of Michmas, one hundred twenty-two. [28]Of Bethel and Ai, two hundred twenty-three. [29]The descendants of Nebo, fifty-two. [30]Of Magbish, one hundred fifty-six. [31]Of the other Elam, one thousand two hundred fifty-four. [32]Of Harim, three hundred twenty. [33]Of Lod, Hadid, and Ono, seven hundred twenty-five. [34]Of Jericho, three hundred forty-five. [35]Of Senaah, three thousand six hundred thirty.

36 The priests: the descendants of Jedaiah, of the house of Jeshua, nine hundred seventy-three. [37]Of Immer, one thousand fifty-two. [38]Of Pashhur, one thousand two hundred forty-seven. [39]Of Harim, one thousand seventeen.

40 The Levites: the descendants of Jeshua and Kadmiel, of the descendants of Hodaviah, seventy-four. [41]The singers: the descendants of Asaph, one hundred twenty-eight. [42]The descendants of the gatekeepers: of Shallum, of Ater, of Talmon, of Akkub, of Hatita, and of Shobai, in all one hundred thirty-nine.

43 The temple servants: the descendants of Ziha, Hasupha, Tabbaoth, [44]Keros, Siaha, Padon, [45]Lebanah, Hagabah, Akkub, [46]Hagab, Shamlai, Hanan, [47]Giddel, Gahar, Reaiah, [48]Rezin, Nekoda, Gazzam, [49]Uzza, Paseah, Besai, [50]Asnah, Meunim, Nephisim, [51]Bakbuk, Hakupha, Harhur, [52]Bazluth, Mehida, Harsha, [53]Barkos, Sisera, Temah, [54]Neziah, and Hatipha.

55 The descendants of Solomon's servants: Sotai, Hassophereth, Peruda, [56]Jaalah, Darkon, Giddel, [57]Shephatiah, Hattil, Pochereth-hazzebaim, and Ami.

Ezra 2:55

Hidden among the descendants of Solomon that were exiled to Babylon are a female scribe and her disciples. Hassophereth means "the female scribe," and descendants really are *disciples*—in the same way that "sons" or "children" of prophets are their disciples, not their offspring. Female scribes are well known in the ancient world. Among the best known female scribes is Amat-Mamu, whose forty-year career was spent in service to three different kings, including Hammurabi.

— *WG*

58 All the temple servants and the descendants of Solomon's servants were three hundred ninety-two.

59 The following were those who came up from Tel-melah, Tel-harsha, Cherub, Addan, and Immer, though they could not prove their families or their descent, whether they belonged to Israel: [60]the descendants of Delaiah, Tobiah, and Nekoda, six hundred fifty-two. [61]Also, of the descendants of the priests: the descendants of Habaiah, Hakkoz, and Barzillai (who had married one of the daughters of Barzillai the Gileadite, and was called by their name). [62]These looked for their entries in the genealogical records, but they were not found there, and so they were excluded from the priesthood as unclean; [63]the governor told them that they were not to partake of the most holy food, until there should be a priest to consult Urim and Thummim.

64 The whole assembly together was forty-
two thousand three hundred sixty, 65 besides their
male and female servants, of whom there were
seven thousand three hundred thirty-seven; and
they had two hundred male and female singers.
66 They had seven hundred thirty-six horses, two
hundred forty-five mules, 67 four hundred thirty-
five camels, and six thousand seven hundred
twenty donkeys.

68 As soon as they came to the house of the
LORD in Jerusalem, some of the heads of families
made freewill offerings for the house of God, to
erect it on its site. 69 According to their resources
they gave to the building fund sixty-one thousand
darics of gold, five thousand minas of silver, and
one hundred priestly robes.

70 The priests, the Levites, and some of the
people lived in Jerusalem and its vicinity;[a] and
the singers, the gatekeepers, and the temple servants lived in their towns, and all Israel in their
towns.

3 When the seventh month came, and the Israelites were in the towns, the people gathered
together in Jerusalem. 2 Then Jeshua son of Jozadak, with his fellow priests, and Zerubbabel son
of Shealtiel with his kin set out to build the altar
of the God of Israel, to offer burnt offerings on it,
as prescribed in the law of Moses the man of God.
3 They set up the altar on its foundation, because
they were in dread of the neighboring peoples,
and they offered burnt offerings upon it
to the LORD, morning and evening. 4 And they
kept the festival of booths,[b] as prescribed, and offered the daily burnt offerings by number according to the ordinance, as required for each day,
5 and after that the regular burnt offerings, the
offerings at the new moon and at all the sacred
festivals of the LORD, and the offerings of everyone who made a freewill offering to the LORD.
6 From the first day of the seventh month they began to offer burnt offerings to the LORD. But the
foundation of the temple of the LORD was not yet
laid. 7 So they gave money to the masons and the
carpenters, and food, drink, and oil to the Sidonians and the Tyrians to bring cedar trees from
Lebanon to the sea, to Joppa, according to the
grant that they had from King Cyrus of Persia.

8 In the second year after their arrival at the
house of God at Jerusalem, in the second month,
Zerubbabel son of Shealtiel and Jeshua son of
Jozadak made a beginning, together with the rest
of their people, the priests and the Levites and all
who had come to Jerusalem from the captivity.
They appointed the Levites, from twenty years old
and upward, to have the oversight of the work on
the house of the LORD. 9 And Jeshua with his sons
and his kin, and Kadmiel and his sons, Binnui and
Hodaviah[c] along with the sons of Henadad, the
Levites, their sons and kin, together took charge
of the workers in the house of God.

10 When the builders laid the foundation of
the temple of the LORD, the priests in their vestments were stationed to praise the LORD with
trumpets, and the Levites, the sons of Asaph,
with cymbals, according to the directions of King
David of Israel; 11 and they sang responsively,
praising and giving thanks to the LORD,

"For he is good,
for his steadfast love endures forever toward
Israel."

And all the people responded with a great shout
when they praised the LORD, because the foundation of the house of the LORD was laid. 12 But
many of the priests and Levites and heads of
families, old people who had seen the first house
on its foundations, wept with a loud voice when
they saw this house, though many shouted aloud
for joy, 13 so that the people could not distinguish
the sound of the joyful shout from the sound of
the people's weeping, for the people shouted so
loudly that the sound was heard far away.

4 When the adversaries of Judah and Benjamin
heard that the returned exiles were building a
temple to the LORD, the God of Israel, 2 they approached Zerubbabel and the heads of families
and said to them, "Let us build with you, for we
worship your God as you do, and we have been
sacrificing to him ever since the days of King

[a] 1 Esdras 5.46: Heb lacks *lived in Jerusalem and its vicinity*
[b] Or *tabernacles*; Heb *succoth*
[c] Compare 2.40; Neh 7.43; 1 Esdras 5.58: Heb *sons of Judah*

Esar-haddon of Assyria who brought us here."
[3]But Zerubbabel, Jeshua, and the rest of the
heads of families in Israel said to them, "You shall
have no part with us in building a house to our
God; but we alone will build to the LORD, the
God of Israel, as King Cyrus of Persia has commanded us."

> **Ezra 4:1-3**
>
> The struggle over land is told in many ways in the biblical narratives. Here people are called "adversaries" for asking to be included in the temple-building project, even though they worship the same God. Sadly, the temple-builders cannot accept as fellow worshipers folk whose ethnic origin is different from their own. It is only after their rejection that the people who asked to be included in the project sabotage it. No wonder white supremacists like the Ku Klux Klan in the United States have based some of their segregationist rhetoric on Ezra-Nehemiah.
>
> — *WG*

4 Then the people of the land discouraged the
people of Judah, and made them afraid to build,
[5]and they bribed officials to frustrate their plan
throughout the reign of King Cyrus of Persia and
until the reign of King Darius of Persia.

6 In the reign of Ahasuerus, in his accession
year, they wrote an accusation against the inhabitants of Judah and Jerusalem.

7 And in the days of Artaxerxes, Bishlam and
Mithredath and Tabeel and the rest of their associates wrote to King Artaxerxes of Persia; the letter
was written in Aramaic and translated.[a] [8]Rehum
the royal deputy and Shimshai the scribe wrote
a letter against Jerusalem to King Artaxerxes as
follows [9](then Rehum the royal deputy, Shimshai the scribe, and the rest of their associates,
the judges, the envoys, the officials, the Persians,
the people of Erech, the Babylonians, the people
of Susa, that is, the Elamites, [10]and the rest of
the nations whom the great and noble Osnappar deported and settled in the cities of Samaria
and in the rest of the province Beyond the River
wrote—and now [11]this is a copy of the letter that
they sent):

"To King Artaxerxes: Your servants, the people of the province Beyond the River, send greeting. And now [12]may it be known to the king that
the Jews who came up from you to us have gone
to Jerusalem. They are rebuilding that rebellious
and wicked city; they are finishing the walls and
repairing the foundations. [13]Now may it be
known to the king that, if this city is rebuilt and
the walls finished, they will not pay tribute, custom, or toll, and the royal revenue will be reduced. [14]Now because we share the salt of the
palace and it is not fitting for us to witness the
king's dishonor, therefore we send and inform
the king, [15]so that a search may be made in the
annals of your ancestors. You will discover in the
annals that this is a rebellious city, hurtful to kings
and provinces, and that sedition was stirred up in
it from long ago. On that account this city was
laid waste. [16]We make known to the king that, if
this city is rebuilt and its walls finished, you will
then have no possession in the province Beyond
the River."

17 The king sent an answer: "To Rehum the
royal deputy and Shimshai the scribe and the rest
of their associates who live in Samaria and in the
rest of the province Beyond the River, greeting.
And now [18]the letter that you sent to us has been
read in translation before me. [19]So I made a decree, and someone searched and discovered that
this city has risen against kings from long ago, and
that rebellion and sedition have been made in it.
[20]Jerusalem has had mighty kings who ruled over
the whole province Beyond the River, to whom
tribute, custom, and toll were paid. [21]Therefore
issue an order that these people be made to cease,
and that this city not be rebuilt, until I make a decree. [22]Moreover, take care not to be slack in this
matter; why should damage grow to the hurt of
the king?"

[a] Heb adds *in Aramaic,* indicating that 4.8–6.18 is in Aramaic. Another interpretation is *The letter was written in the Aramaic script and set forth in the Aramaic language*

23 Then when the copy of King Artaxerxes'
letter was read before Rehum and the scribe
Shimshai and their associates, they hurried to the
Jews in Jerusalem and by force and power made
them cease. 24At that time the work on the house
of God in Jerusalem stopped and was discontinued until the second year of the reign of King
Darius of Persia.

5 Now the prophets, Haggai[a] and Zechariah
son of Iddo, prophesied to the Jews who were
in Judah and Jerusalem, in the name of the God of
Israel who was over them. 2Then Zerubbabel son
of Shealtiel and Jeshua son of Jozadak set out to
rebuild the house of God in Jerusalem; and with
them were the prophets of God, helping them.

3 At the same time Tattenai the governor
of the province Beyond the River and Shethar-
bozenai and their associates came to them and
spoke to them thus, "Who gave you a decree to
build this house and to finish this structure?"
4They[b] also asked them this, "What are the names
of the men who are building this building?" 5But
the eye of their God was upon the elders of the
Jews, and they did not stop them until a report
reached Darius and then answer was returned by
letter in reply to it.

6 The copy of the letter that Tattenai the
governor of the province Beyond the River and
Shethar-bozenai and his associates the envoys
who were in the province Beyond the River sent
to King Darius; 7they sent him a report, in which
was written as follows: "To Darius the king, all
peace! 8May it be known to the king that we went
to the province of Judah, to the house of the great
God. It is being built of hewn stone, and timber is laid in the walls; this work is being done
diligently and prospers in their hands. 9Then we
spoke to those elders and asked them, 'Who gave
you a decree to build this house and to finish this
structure?' 10We also asked them their names, for
your information, so that we might write down
the names of the men at their head. 11This was
their reply to us: 'We are the servants of the God
of heaven and earth, and we are rebuilding the
house that was built many years ago, which a great
king of Israel built and finished. 12But because
our ancestors had angered the God of heaven, he
gave them into the hand of King Nebuchadnezzar of Babylon, the Chaldean, who destroyed this
house and carried away the people to Babylonia.
13However, King Cyrus of Babylon, in the first
year of his reign, made a decree that this house of
God should be rebuilt. 14Moreover, the gold and
silver vessels of the house of God, which Nebuchadnezzar had taken out of the temple in Jerusalem and had brought into the temple of Babylon,
these King Cyrus took out of the temple of Babylon, and they were delivered to a man named
Sheshbazzar, whom he had made governor. 15He
said to him, "Take these vessels; go and put them
in the temple in Jerusalem, and let the house of
God be rebuilt on its site." 16Then this Sheshbazzar came and laid the foundations of the house of
God in Jerusalem; and from that time until now
it has been under construction, and it is not yet
finished.' 17And now, if it seems good to the king,
have a search made in the royal archives there in
Babylon, to see whether a decree was issued by
King Cyrus for the rebuilding of this house of
God in Jerusalem. Let the king send us his pleasure in this matter."

6 Then King Darius made a decree, and they
searched the archives where the documents
were stored in Babylon. 2But it was in Ecbatana,
the capital in the province of Media, that a scroll
was found on which this was written: "A record.
3In the first year of his reign, King Cyrus issued
a decree: Concerning the house of God at Jerusalem, let the house be rebuilt, the place where
sacrifices are offered and burnt offerings are
brought;[c] its height shall be sixty cubits and its
width sixty cubits, 4with three courses of hewn
stones and one course of timber; let the cost be
paid from the royal treasury. 5Moreover, let the
gold and silver vessels of the house of God, which
Nebuchadnezzar took out of the temple in Jerusalem and brought to Babylon, be restored and
brought back to the temple in Jerusalem, each
to its place; you shall put them in the house of
God."

[a] Aram adds *the prophet* [b] Gk Syr: Aram *We* [c] Meaning of Aram uncertain

6 "Now you, Tattenai, governor of the province Beyond the River, Shethar-bozenai, and you,
their associates, the envoys in the province Beyond the River, keep away; 7let the work on this
house of God alone; let the governor of the Jews
and the elders of the Jews rebuild this house of
God on its site. 8Moreover I make a decree regarding what you shall do for these elders of the
Jews for the rebuilding of this house of God: the
cost is to be paid to these people, in full and without delay, from the royal revenue, the tribute of
the province Beyond the River. 9Whatever is
needed—young bulls, rams, or sheep for burnt
offerings to the God of heaven, wheat, salt, wine,
or oil, as the priests in Jerusalem require—let that
be given to them day by day without fail, 10so that
they may offer pleasing sacrifices to the God of
heaven, and pray for the life of the king and his
children. 11Furthermore I decree that if anyone
alters this edict, a beam shall be pulled out of the
house of the perpetrator, who then shall be impaled on it. The house shall be made a dunghill.
12May the God who has established his name
there overthrow any king or people that shall put
forth a hand to alter this, or to destroy this house
of God in Jerusalem. I, Darius, make a decree; let
it be done with all diligence."

13 Then, according to the word sent by King
Darius, Tattenai, the governor of the province
Beyond the River, Shethar-bozenai, and their associates did with all diligence what King Darius
had ordered. 14So the elders of the Jews built
and prospered, through the prophesying of the
prophet Haggai and Zechariah son of Iddo. They
finished their building by command of the God
of Israel and by decree of Cyrus, Darius, and King
Artaxerxes of Persia; 15and this house was finished on the third day of the month of Adar, in
the sixth year of the reign of King Darius.

16 The people of Israel, the priests and the
Levites, and the rest of the returned exiles, celebrated the dedication of this house of God with
joy. 17They offered at the dedication of this house
of God one hundred bulls, two hundred rams,
four hundred lambs, and as a sin offering for all
Israel, twelve male goats, according to the number of the tribes of Israel. 18Then they set the
priests in their divisions and the Levites in their
courses for the service of God at Jerusalem, as it
is written in the book of Moses.

19 On the fourteenth day of the first month
the returned exiles kept the passover. 20For both
the priests and the Levites had purified themselves; all of them were clean. So they killed the
passover lamb for all the returned exiles, for their
fellow priests, and for themselves. 21It was eaten
by the people of Israel who had returned from
exile, and also by all who had joined them and
separated themselves from the pollutions of the
nations of the land to worship the LORD, the God
of Israel. 22With joy they celebrated the festival
of unleavened bread seven days; for the LORD
had made them joyful, and had turned the heart
of the king of Assyria to them, so that he aided
them in the work on the house of God, the God
of Israel.

7 After this, in the reign of King Artaxerxes of
Persia, Ezra son of Seraiah, son of Azariah,
son of Hilkiah, 2son of Shallum, son of Zadok, son
of Ahitub, 3son of Amariah, son of Azariah, son of
Meraioth, 4son of Zerahiah, son of Uzzi, son of
Bukki, 5son of Abishua, son of Phinehas, son
of Eleazar, son of the chief priest Aaron— 6this
Ezra went up from Babylonia. He was a scribe
skilled in the law of Moses that the LORD the God
of Israel had given; and the king granted him all
that he asked, for the hand of the LORD his God
was upon him.

7 Some of the people of Israel, and some of
the priests and Levites, the singers and gatekeepers, and the temple servants also went up to Jerusalem, in the seventh year of King Artaxerxes.
8They came to Jerusalem in the fifth month,
which was in the seventh year of the king. 9On
the first day of the first month the journey up
from Babylon was begun, and on the first day of
the fifth month he came to Jerusalem, for the gracious hand of his God was upon him. 10For Ezra
had set his heart to study the law of the LORD,
and to do it, and to teach the statutes and ordinances in Israel.

11 This is a copy of the letter that King Artaxerxes gave to the priest Ezra, the scribe, a scholar
of the text of the commandments of the LORD

and his statutes for Israel: 12“Artaxerxes, king of
kings, to the priest Ezra, the scribe of the law of
the God of heaven: Peace.[a] And now 13I decree
that any of the people of Israel or their priests or
Levites in my kingdom who freely offers to go to
Jerusalem may go with you. 14For you are sent by
the king and his seven counselors to make inqui-
ries about Judah and Jerusalem according to the
law of your God, which is in your hand, 15and
also to convey the silver and gold that the king
and his counselors have freely offered to the God
of Israel, whose dwelling is in Jerusalem, 16with
all the silver and gold that you shall find in the
whole province of Babylonia, and with the freewill offerings of the people and the priests, given
willingly for the house of their God in Jerusalem.
17With this money, then, you shall with all diligence buy bulls, rams, and lambs, and their grain
offerings and their drink offerings, and you shall
offer them on the altar of the house of your God
in Jerusalem. 18Whatever seems good to you and
your colleagues to do with the rest of the silver
and gold, you may do, according to the will of
your God. 19The vessels that have been given you
for the service of the house of your God, you shall
deliver before the God of Jerusalem. 20And whatever else is required for the house of your God,
which you are responsible for providing, you may
provide out of the king’s treasury.

21 “I, King Artaxerxes, decree to all the treasurers in the province Beyond the River: Whatever the priest Ezra, the scribe of the law of the
God of heaven, requires of you, let it be done with
all diligence, 22up to one hundred talents of silver,
one hundred cors of wheat, one hundred baths[b]
of wine, one hundred baths[b] of oil, and unlimited
salt. 23Whatever is commanded by the God of
heaven, let it be done with zeal for the house of
the God of heaven, or wrath will come upon the
realm of the king and his heirs. 24We also notify
you that it shall not be lawful to impose tribute,
custom, or toll on any of the priests, the Levites,
the singers, the doorkeepers, the temple servants,
or other servants of this house of God.

25 “And you, Ezra, according to the God-
given wisdom you possess, appoint magistrates
and judges who may judge all the people in the
province Beyond the River who know the laws of
your God; and you shall teach those who do not
know them. 26All who will not obey the law of
your God and the law of the king, let judgment be
strictly executed on them, whether for death or
for banishment or for confiscation of their goods
or for imprisonment.”

27 Blessed be the Lord, the God of our ancestors, who put such a thing as this into the heart
of the king to glorify the house of the Lord in Jerusalem, 28and who extended to me steadfast love
before the king and his counselors, and before all
the king’s mighty officers. I took courage, for the
hand of the Lord my God was upon me, and I
gathered leaders from Israel to go up with me.

8 These are their family heads, and this is the
genealogy of those who went up with me
from Babylonia, in the reign of King Artaxerxes:
2Of the descendants of Phinehas, Gershom.
Of Ithamar, Daniel. Of David, Hattush, 3of the
descendants of Shecaniah. Of Parosh, Zechariah, with whom were registered one hundred
fifty males. 4Of the descendants of Pahath-moab,
Eliehoenai son of Zerahiah, and with him two
hundred males. 5Of the descendants of Zattu,[c]
Shecaniah son of Jahaziel, and with him three
hundred males. 6Of the descendants of Adin,
Ebed son of Jonathan, and with him fifty males.
7Of the descendants of Elam, Jeshaiah son of Athaliah, and with him seventy males. 8Of the descendants of Shephatiah, Zebadiah son of Michael,
and with him eighty males. 9Of the descendants
of Joab, Obadiah son of Jehiel, and with him two
hundred eighteen males. 10Of the descendants
of Bani,[d] Shelomith son of Josiphiah, and with
him one hundred sixty males. 11Of the descendants of Bebai, Zechariah son of Bebai, and with
him twenty-eight males. 12Of the descendants of
Azgad, Johanan son of Hakkatan, and with him
one hundred ten males. 13Of the descendants of
Adonikam, those who came later, their names

[a] Syr Vg 1 Esdras 8.9: Aram *Perfect*
[b] A Heb measure of volume
[c] Gk 1 Esdras 8.32: Heb lacks *of Zattu*
[d] Gk 1 Esdras 8.36: Heb lacks *Bani*

being Eliphelet, Jeuel, and Shemaiah, and with
them sixty males. 14 Of the descendants of Bigvai,
Uthai and Zaccur, and with them seventy males.

15 I gathered them by the river that runs to
Ahava, and there we camped three days. As I re-
viewed the people and the priests, I found there
none of the descendants of Levi. 16 Then I sent
for Eliezer, Ariel, Shemaiah, Elnathan, Jarib, Elnathan, Nathan, Zechariah, and Meshullam, who
were leaders, and for Joiarib and Elnathan, who
were wise, 17 and sent them to Iddo, the leader
at the place called Casiphia, telling them what
to say to Iddo and his colleagues the temple servants at Casiphia, namely, to send us ministers
for the house of our God. 18 Since the gracious
hand of our God was upon us, they brought us
a man of discretion, of the descendants of Mahli
son of Levi son of Israel, namely Sherebiah, with
his sons and kin, eighteen; 19 also Hashabiah and
with him Jeshaiah of the descendants of Merari,
with his kin and their sons, twenty; 20 besides two
hundred twenty of the temple servants, whom
David and his officials had set apart to attend the
Levites. These were all mentioned by name.

21 Then I proclaimed a fast there, at the
river Ahava, that we might deny ourselves[a] before our God, to seek from him a safe journey for
ourselves, our children, and all our possessions.
22 For I was ashamed to ask the king for a band
of soldiers and cavalry to protect us against the
enemy on our way, since we had told the king that
the hand of our God is gracious to all who seek
him, but his power and his wrath are against all
who forsake him. 23 So we fasted and petitioned
our God for this, and he listened to our entreaty.

24 Then I set apart twelve of the leading
priests: Sherebiah, Hashabiah, and ten of their
kin with them. 25 And I weighed out to them the
silver and the gold and the vessels, the offering for
the house of our God that the king, his counselors, his lords, and all Israel there present had offered; 26 I weighed out into their hand six hundred
fifty talents of silver, and one hundred silver vessels worth . . . talents,[b] and one hundred talents
of gold, 27 twenty gold bowls worth a thousand
darics, and two vessels of fine polished bronze as
precious as gold. 28 And I said to them, "You are
holy to the LORD, and the vessels are holy; and
the silver and the gold are a freewill offering to
the LORD, the God of your ancestors. 29 Guard
them and keep them until you weigh them before
the chief priests and the Levites and the heads of
families in Israel at Jerusalem, within the chambers of the house of the LORD." 30 So the priests
and the Levites took over the silver, the gold, and
the vessels as they were weighed out, to bring
them to Jerusalem, to the house of our God.

31 Then we left the river Ahava on the twelfth
day of the first month, to go to Jerusalem; the
hand of our God was upon us, and he delivered us
from the hand of the enemy and from ambushes
along the way. 32 We came to Jerusalem and remained there three days. 33 On the fourth day,
within the house of our God, the silver, the gold,
and the vessels were weighed into the hands of
the priest Meremoth son of Uriah, and with him
was Eleazar son of Phinehas, and with them were
the Levites, Jozabad son of Jeshua and Noadiah son
of Binnui. 34 The total was counted and weighed,
and the weight of everything was recorded.

35 At that time those who had come from
captivity, the returned exiles, offered burnt offerings to the God of Israel, twelve bulls for all Israel,
ninety-six rams, seventy-seven lambs, and as a sin
offering twelve male goats; all this was a burnt
offering to the LORD. 36 They also delivered the
king's commissions to the king's satraps and to the
governors of the province Beyond the River; and
they supported the people and the house of God.

9 After these things had been done, the officials approached me and said, "The people
of Israel, the priests, and the Levites have not
separated themselves from the peoples of the
lands with their abominations, from the Canaanites, the Hittites, the Perizzites, the Jebusites, the
Ammonites, the Moabites, the Egyptians, and
the Amorites. 2 For they have taken some of their
daughters as wives for themselves and for their
sons. Thus the holy seed has mixed itself with the
peoples of the lands, and in this faithlessness the

[a] Or *might fast* [b] The number of talents is lacking

officials and leaders have led the way." 3When I
heard this, I tore my garment and my mantle, and
pulled hair from my head and beard, and sat appalled. 4Then all who trembled at the words of
the God of Israel, because of the faithlessness of
the returned exiles, gathered around me while I
sat appalled until the evening sacrifice.

5 At the evening sacrifice I got up from my
fasting, with my garments and my mantle torn,
and fell on my knees, spread out my hands to the
LORD my God, 6and said,

"O my God, I am too ashamed and embarrassed to lift my face to you, my God, for our
iniquities have risen higher than our heads, and
our guilt has mounted up to the heavens. 7From
the days of our ancestors to this day we have
been deep in guilt, and for our iniquities we, our
kings, and our priests have been handed over to
the kings of the lands, to the sword, to captivity,
to plundering, and to utter shame, as is now the
case. 8But now for a brief moment favor has been
shown by the LORD our God, who has left us a
remnant, and given us a stake in his holy place,
in order that he[a] may brighten our eyes and grant
us a little sustenance in our slavery. 9For we are
slaves; yet our God has not forsaken us in our
slavery, but has extended to us his steadfast love
before the kings of Persia, to give us new life to set
up the house of our God, to repair its ruins, and
to give us a wall in Judea and Jerusalem.

10 "And now, our God, what shall we say after
this? For we have forsaken your commandments,
11which you commanded by your servants the
prophets, saying, 'The land that you are entering
to possess is a land unclean with the pollutions of
the peoples of the lands, with their abominations.
They have filled it from end to end with their uncleanness. 12Therefore do not give your daughters to their sons, neither take their daughters for
your sons, and never seek their peace or prosperity, so that you may be strong and eat the good
of the land and leave it for an inheritance to your
children forever.' 13After all that has come upon
us for our evil deeds and for our great guilt, seeing that you, our God, have punished us less than
our iniquities deserved and have given us such a
remnant as this, 14shall we break your commandments again and intermarry with the peoples who
practice these abominations? Would you not be
angry with us until you destroy us without remnant or survivor? 15O LORD, God of Israel, you
are just, but we have escaped as a remnant, as is
now the case. Here we are before you in our guilt,
though no one can face you because of this."

10 While Ezra prayed and made confession,
weeping and throwing himself down before the house of God, a very great assembly of
men, women, and children gathered to him out
of Israel; the people also wept bitterly. 2Sheca-
niah son of Jehiel, of the descendants of Elam,
addressed Ezra, saying, "We have broken faith
with our God and have married foreign women
from the peoples of the land, but even now there
is hope for Israel in spite of this. 3So now let us
make a covenant with our God to send away all
these wives and their children, according to the
counsel of my lord and of those who tremble
at the commandment of our God; and let it be
done according to the law. 4Take action, for it is
your duty, and we are with you; be strong, and
do it." 5Then Ezra stood up and made the leading
priests, the Levites, and all Israel swear that they
would do as had been said. So they swore.

6 Then Ezra withdrew from before the house
of God, and went to the chamber of Jehohanan
son of Eliashib, where he spent the night.[b] He did
not eat bread or drink water, for he was mourning
over the faithlessness of the exiles. 7They made a
proclamation throughout Judah and Jerusalem to
all the returned exiles that they should assemble
at Jerusalem, 8and that if any did not come within
three days, by order of the officials and the elders
all their property should be forfeited, and they
themselves banned from the congregation of the
exiles.

9 Then all the people of Judah and Benjamin
assembled at Jerusalem within the three days;
it was the ninth month, on the twentieth day of
the month. All the people sat in the open square
before the house of God, trembling because of this

[a] Heb *our God* [b] 1 Esdras 9.2: Heb *where he went*

matter and because of the heavy rain. 10 Then Ezra
the priest stood up and said to them, "You have
trespassed and married foreign women, and so
increased the guilt of Israel. 11 Now make confession to the LORD the God of your ancestors, and
do his will; separate yourselves from the peoples
of the land and from the foreign wives." 12 Then
all the assembly answered with a loud voice, "It is
so; we must do as you have said. 13 But the people
are many, and it is a time of heavy rain; we cannot
stand in the open. Nor is this a task for one day or
for two, for many of us have transgressed in this
matter. 14 Let our officials represent the whole assembly, and let all in our towns who have taken
foreign wives come at appointed times, and with
them the elders and judges of every town, until
the fierce wrath of our God on this account is
averted from us." 15 Only Jonathan son of Asahel
and Jahzeiah son of Tikvah opposed this, and Meshullam and Shabbethai the Levites supported
them.

16 Then the returned exiles did so. Ezra the
priest selected men,[a] heads of families, according to their families, each of them designated by
name. On the first day of the tenth month they
sat down to examine the matter. 17 By the first day
of the first month they had come to the end of all
the men who had married foreign women.

18 There were found of the descendants of
the priests who had married foreign women, of
the descendants of Jeshua son of Jozadak and his
brothers: Maaseiah, Eliezer, Jarib, and Gedaliah.
19 They pledged themselves to send away their
wives, and their guilt offering was a ram of the
flock for their guilt. 20 Of the descendants of Immer: Hanani and Zebadiah. 21 Of the descendants
of Harim: Maaseiah, Elijah, Shemaiah, Jehiel,
and Uzziah. 22 Of the descendants of Pashhur:
Elioenai, Maaseiah, Ishmael, Nethanel, Jozabad,
and Elasah.

23 Of the Levites: Jozabad, Shimei, Kelaiah
(that is, Kelita), Pethahiah, Judah, and Eliezer.
24 Of the singers: Eliashib. Of the gatekeepers:
Shallum, Telem, and Uri.

25 And of Israel: of the descendants of Parosh: Ramiah, Izziah, Malchijah, Mijamin,
Eleazar, Hashabiah,[b] and Benaiah. 26 Of the descendants of Elam: Mattaniah, Zechariah, Jehiel,
Abdi, Jeremoth, and Elijah. 27 Of the descendants
of Zattu: Elioenai, Eliashib, Mattaniah, Jeremoth,
Zabad, and Aziza. 28 Of the descendants of Bebai: Jehohanan, Hananiah, Zabbai, and Athlai.
29 Of the descendants of Bani: Meshullam, Malluch, Adaiah, Jashub, Sheal, and Jeremoth. 30 Of
the descendants of Pahath-moab: Adna, Chelal,
Benaiah, Maaseiah, Mattaniah, Bezalel, Binnui,
and Manasseh. 31 Of the descendants of Harim:
Eliezer, Isshijah, Malchijah, Shemaiah, Shimeon,
32 Benjamin, Malluch, and Shemariah. 33 Of the
descendants of Hashum: Mattenai, Mattattah,
Zabad, Eliphelet, Jeremai, Manasseh, and Shimei.
34 Of the descendants of Bani: Maadai, Amram,
Uel, 35 Benaiah, Bedeiah, Cheluhi, 36 Vaniah,
Meremoth, Eliashib, 37 Mattaniah, Mattenai, and
Jaasu. 38 Of the descendants of Binnui:[c] Shimei,
39 Shelemiah, Nathan, Adaiah, 40 Machnadebai,
Shashai, Sharai, 41 Azarel, Shelemiah, Shemariah, 42 Shallum, Amariah, and Joseph. 43 Of the
descendants of Nebo: Jeiel, Mattithiah, Zabad,
Zebina, Jaddai, Joel, and Benaiah. 44 All these had
married foreign women, and they sent them away
with their children.[d]

[a] 1 Esdras 9.16: Syr: Heb *And there were selected Ezra,* [b] 1 Esdras 9.26 Gk: Heb *Malchijah* [c] Gk: Heb *Bani, Binnui*
[d] 1 Esdras 9.36; meaning of Heb uncertain

Nehemiah

The book of Nehemiah was originally part of a composition that also included the book of Ezra. Exactly how the chronology of Nehemiah's mission aligns with that of Ezra continues to be a matter of debate, but there is some agreement that "the twentieth year" of Neh 1:1 refers to the reign of Artaxerxes I (445 BCE). The name Nehemiah means "the Lord is compassionate." Appropriately, the book begins with a first-person narrative describing the return of Nehemiah from exile and the rebuilding of the walls of Jerusalem (1:1—7:73a), a clear manifestation of God's compassion for God's people. This section comprises roughly half of the book and tells how Nehemiah—after hearing that Jerusalem's wall had been breached in many places and its gates had been destroyed by fire—mourns, fasts, and offers a confessional prayer (1:4-11). In the prayer, Nehemiah reminds God of the promise that if the people would return to God and keep the commandments "though your outcasts are under the farthest skies, I will gather them from there and bring them to the place at which I have chosen to establish my name" (1:9). The sequence of events shows that God has indeed heard the prayer, and shortly afterward Artaxerxes accepts Nehemiah's request to return to Jerusalem and rebuild its wall (2:1-10).

However, the task does not seem to be without opposition. In Neh 2:11—4:23, we see not only how the work is organized but also how Sanballat, Tobiah, and Geshem opposed Nehemiah. This conflict continues in Neh 6:1-14 until the completion of the wall (6:15-19). The tension within the community is evident in the class conflict described in Neh 5:1-13. The nobles and the officials have allowed an extreme situation of inequality to arise, forcing their fellow Jews into such poverty that to survive they had to force their sons and daughters into slavery. Their claim "Now our flesh is the same as that of our kindred; our children are the same as their children" (5:5) is a demand for a just society where all persons have their needs met. The struggle to bring reality into an approximation of the demand is all too familiar in colonial and postcolonial situations around the world today.

The second part of the book (7:73b—10:39) covers the central event of Ezra's mission in Jerusalem: the public reading of the Torah (7:73b—8:12) and the commitment of the community to observe God's commandments (9:38—10:39). The celebration of Tabernacles follows, a reenactment of the last stage of the exodus experience (see Deut 31:9-13). The book ends with the repopulation of Jerusalem (ch. 11), the dedication of the walls (12:27-47), and Nehemiah's religious reforms (ch. 13). These include the implementation of Sabbath observance and the condemnation of wives taken from Ashdod, Ammon, and Moab.

— ***Alejandro F. Botta***

1 The words of Nehemiah son of Hacaliah. In
the month of Chislev, in the twentieth year,
while I was in Susa the capital, 2 one of my brothers, Hanani, came with certain men from Judah;
and I asked them about the Jews that survived,
those who had escaped the captivity, and about
Jerusalem. 3 They replied, "The survivors there
in the province who escaped captivity are in
great trouble and shame; the wall of Jerusalem is
broken down, and its gates have been destroyed
by fire."

4 When I heard these words I sat down and
wept, and mourned for days, fasting and praying
before the God of heaven. 5 I said, "O LORD God
of heaven, the great and awesome God who keeps
covenant and steadfast love with those who love
him and keep his commandments; 6 let your ear
be attentive and your eyes open to hear the prayer
of your servant that I now pray before you day
and night for your servants, the people of Israel,
confessing the sins of the people of Israel, which
we have sinned against you. Both I and my family have sinned. 7 We have offended you deeply,
failing to keep the commandments, the statutes,
and the ordinances that you commanded your
servant Moses. 8 Remember the word that you
commanded your servant Moses, 'If you are unfaithful, I will scatter you among the peoples; 9 but
if you return to me and keep my commandments
and do them, though your outcasts are under the
farthest skies, I will gather them from there and
bring them to the place at which I have chosen
to establish my name.' 10 They are your servants
and your people, whom you redeemed by your
great power and your strong hand. 11 O Lord, let
your ear be attentive to the prayer of your servant,
and to the prayer of your servants who delight
in revering your name. Give success to your servant today, and grant him mercy in the sight of
this man!"

At the time, I was cupbearer to the king.

2 In the month of Nisan, in the twentieth year
of King Artaxerxes, when wine was served
him, I carried the wine and gave it to the king.
Now, I had never been sad in his presence before.
2 So the king said to me, "Why is your face sad,
since you are not sick? This can only be sadness of
the heart." Then I was very much afraid. 3 I said to
the king, "May the king live forever! Why should
my face not be sad, when the city, the place of my
ancestors' graves, lies waste, and its gates have
been destroyed by fire?" 4 Then the king said to
me, "What do you request?" So I prayed to the
God of heaven. 5 Then I said to the king, "If it
pleases the king, and if your servant has found
favor with you, I ask that you send me to Judah,
to the city of my ancestors' graves, so that I may
rebuild it." 6 The king said to me (the queen also
was sitting beside him), "How long will you be
gone, and when will you return?" So it pleased
the king to send me, and I set him a date. 7 Then
I said to the king, "If it pleases the king, let letters be given me to the governors of the province
Beyond the River, that they may grant me passage
until I arrive in Judah; 8 and a letter to Asaph, the
keeper of the king's forest, directing him to give
me timber to make beams for the gates of the
temple fortress, and for the wall of the city, and
for the house that I shall occupy." And the king
granted me what I asked, for the gracious hand of
my God was upon me.

9 Then I came to the governors of the province Beyond the River, and gave them the king's
letters. Now the king had sent officers of the
army and cavalry with me. 10 When Sanballat
the Horonite and Tobiah the Ammonite official
heard this, it displeased them greatly that someone had come to seek the welfare of the people
of Israel.

11 So I came to Jerusalem and was there for
three days. 12 Then I got up during the night, I and
a few men with me; I told no one what my God
had put into my heart to do for Jerusalem. The
only animal I took was the animal I rode. 13 I went
out by night by the Valley Gate past the Dragon's
Spring and to the Dung Gate, and I inspected the
walls of Jerusalem that had been broken down
and its gates that had been destroyed by fire.
14 Then I went on to the Fountain Gate and to the
King's Pool; but there was no place for the animal
I was riding to continue. 15 So I went up by way of
the valley by night and inspected the wall. Then I
turned back and entered by the Valley Gate, and
so returned. 16 The officials did not know where I

had gone or what I was doing; I had not yet told
the Jews, the priests, the nobles, the officials, and
the rest that were to do the work.

17 Then I said to them, "You see the trouble
we are in, how Jerusalem lies in ruins with its
gates burned. Come, let us rebuild the wall of
Jerusalem, so that we may no longer suffer disgrace." 18 I told them that the hand of my God had
been gracious upon me, and also the words that
the king had spoken to me. Then they said, "Let
us start building!" So they committed themselves
to the common good. 19 But when Sanballat the
Horonite and Tobiah the Ammonite official, and
Geshem the Arab heard of it, they mocked and
ridiculed us, saying, "What is this that you are doing? Are you rebelling against the king?" 20 Then
I replied to them, "The God of heaven is the one
who will give us success, and we his servants are
going to start building; but you have no share or
claim or historic right in Jerusalem."

3 Then the high priest Eliashib set to work with
his fellow priests and rebuilt the Sheep Gate.
They consecrated it and set up its doors; they
consecrated it as far as the Tower of the Hundred
and as far as the Tower of Hananel. 2 And the men
of Jericho built next to him. And next to them[a]
Zaccur son of Imri built.

3 The sons of Hassenaah built the Fish Gate;
they laid its beams and set up its doors, its bolts,
and its bars. 4 Next to them Meremoth son of
Uriah son of Hakkoz made repairs. Next to them
Meshullam son of Berechiah son of Meshezabel
made repairs. Next to them Zadok son of Baana
made repairs. 5 Next to them the Tekoites made
repairs; but their nobles would not put their
shoulders to the work of their Lord.[b]

6 Joiada son of Paseah and Meshullam son
of Besodeiah repaired the Old Gate; they laid its
beams and set up its doors, its bolts, and its bars.
7 Next to them repairs were made by Melatiah the
Gibeonite and Jadon the Meronothite—the men
of Gibeon and of Mizpah—who were under the
jurisdiction of[c] the governor of the province Beyond the River. 8 Next to them Uzziel son of Har-
haiah, one of the goldsmiths, made repairs. Next
to him Hananiah, one of the perfumers, made
repairs; and they restored Jerusalem as far as the
Broad Wall. 9 Next to them Rephaiah son of Hur,
ruler of half the district of[d] Jerusalem, made repairs. 10 Next to them Jedaiah son of Harumaph
made repairs opposite his house; and next to him
Hattush son of Hashabneiah made repairs. 11 Malchijah son of Harim and Hasshub son of Pahath-
moab repaired another section and the Tower of
the Ovens. 12 Next to him Shallum son of Hallo-
hesh, ruler of half the district of[d] Jerusalem, made
repairs, he and his daughters.

13 Hanun and the inhabitants of Zanoah
repaired the Valley Gate; they rebuilt it and set
up its doors, its bolts, and its bars, and repaired
a thousand cubits of the wall, as far as the Dung
Gate.

14 Malchijah son of Rechab, ruler of the
district of[e] Beth-haccherem, repaired the Dung
Gate; he rebuilt it and set up its doors, its bolts,
and its bars.

15 And Shallum son of Col-hozeh, ruler of
the district of[e] Mizpah, repaired the Fountain
Gate; he rebuilt it and covered it and set up its
doors, its bolts, and its bars; and he built the wall
of the Pool of Shelah of the king's garden, as far
as the stairs that go down from the City of David. 16 After him Nehemiah son of Azbuk, ruler
of half the district of[d] Beth-zur, repaired from a
point opposite the graves of David, as far as the
artificial pool and the house of the warriors. 17 After him the Levites made repairs: Rehum son of
Bani; next to him Hashabiah, ruler of half the
district of[d] Keilah, made repairs for his district.
18 After him their kin made repairs: Binnui,[f] son
of Henadad, ruler of half the district of[d] Keilah;
19 next to him Ezer son of Jeshua, ruler[g] of Mizpah, repaired another section opposite the ascent
to the armory at the Angle. 20 After him Baruch
son of Zabbai repaired another section from the
Angle to the door of the house of the high priest
Eliashib. 21 After him Meremoth son of Uriah
son of Hakkoz repaired another section from the

[a] Heb *him* [b] Or *lords* [c] Meaning of Heb uncertain [d] Or *supervisor of half the portion assigned to*
[e] Or *supervisor of the portion assigned to* [f] Gk Syr Compare verse 24, 10.9: Heb *Bavvai* [g] Or *supervisor*

door of the house of Eliashib to the end of the
house of Eliashib. 22After him the priests, the
men of the surrounding area, made repairs. 23Af-
ter them Benjamin and Hasshub made repairs
opposite their house. After them Azariah son of
Maaseiah son of Ananiah made repairs beside his
own house. 24After him Binnui son of Henadad
repaired another section, from the house of Azariah to the Angle and to the corner. 25Palal son of
Uzai repaired opposite the Angle and the tower
projecting from the upper house of the king at
the court of the guard. After him Pedaiah son
of Parosh 26and the temple servants living[a] on
Ophel made repairs up to a point opposite the
Water Gate on the east and the projecting tower.
27After him the Tekoites repaired another section
opposite the great projecting tower as far as the
wall of Ophel.

28 Above the Horse Gate the priests made
repairs, each one opposite his own house. 29After
them Zadok son of Immer made repairs opposite
his own house. After him Shemaiah son of Shecaniah, the keeper of the East Gate, made repairs.
30After him Hananiah son of Shelemiah and Hanun sixth son of Zalaph repaired another section.
After him Meshullam son of Berechiah made
repairs opposite his living quarters. 31After him
Malchijah, one of the goldsmiths, made repairs
as far as the house of the temple servants and of
the merchants, opposite the Muster Gate,[b] and to
the upper room of the corner. 32And between the
upper room of the corner and the Sheep Gate the
goldsmiths and the merchants made repairs.

4[c] Now when Sanballat heard that we were
building the wall, he was angry and greatly
enraged, and he mocked the Jews. 2He said in the
presence of his associates and of the army of Samaria, "What are these feeble Jews doing? Will
they restore things? Will they sacrifice? Will they
finish it in a day? Will they revive the stones out of
the heaps of rubbish—and burned ones at that?"
3Tobiah the Ammonite was beside him, and he
said, "That stone wall they are building—any
fox going up on it would break it down!" 4Hear,
O our God, for we are despised; turn their taunt
back on their own heads, and give them over as
plunder in a land of captivity. 5Do not cover their
guilt, and do not let their sin be blotted out from
your sight; for they have hurled insults in the face
of the builders.

6 So we rebuilt the wall, and all the wall was
joined together to half its height; for the people
had a mind to work.

7[d] But when Sanballat and Tobiah and the
Arabs and the Ammonites and the Ashdodites
heard that the repairing of the walls of Jerusalem
was going forward and the gaps were beginning
to be closed, they were very angry, 8and all plotted together to come and fight against Jerusalem
and to cause confusion in it. 9So we prayed to our
God, and set a guard as a protection against them
day and night.

10 But Judah said, "The strength of the burden bearers is failing, and there is too much rubbish so that we are unable to work on the wall."
11And our enemies said, "They will not know or
see anything before we come upon them and kill
them and stop the work." 12When the Jews who
lived near them came, they said to us ten times,
"From all the places where they live[e] they will
come up against us."[f] 13So in the lowest parts of
the space behind the wall, in open places, I stationed the people according to their families,[g]
with their swords, their spears, and their bows.
14After I looked these things over, I stood up and
said to the nobles and the officials and the rest of
the people, "Do not be afraid of them. Remember the LORD, who is great and awesome, and
fight for your kin, your sons, your daughters, your
wives, and your homes."

15 When our enemies heard that their plot
was known to us, and that God had frustrated
it, we all returned to the wall, each to his work.
16From that day on, half of my servants worked
on construction, and half held the spears, shields,
bows, and body-armor; and the leaders posted
themselves behind the whole house of Judah,
17who were building the wall. The burden bearers

[a] Cn: Heb *were living* [b] Or *Hammiphkad Gate* [c] Ch 3.33 in Heb [d] Ch 4.1 in Heb [e] Cn: Heb *you return*
[f] Compare Gk Syr: Meaning of Heb uncertain [g] Meaning of Heb uncertain

carried their loads in such a way that each labored
on the work with one hand and with the other
held a weapon. 18And each of the builders had his
sword strapped at his side while he built. The man
who sounded the trumpet was beside me. 19And I
said to the nobles, the officials, and the rest of the
people, "The work is great and widely spread out,
and we are separated far from one another on the
wall. 20Rally to us wherever you hear the sound of
the trumpet. Our God will fight for us."
21 So we labored at the work, and half of them
held the spears from break of dawn until the stars
came out. 22I also said to the people at that time,
"Let every man and his servant pass the night inside Jerusalem, so that they may be a guard for us
by night and may labor by day." 23So neither I nor
my brothers nor my servants nor the men of the
guard who followed me ever took off our clothes;
each kept his weapon in his right hand.[a]

5 Now there was a great outcry of the people
and of their wives against their Jewish kin.
2For there were those who said, "With our sons
and our daughters, we are many; we must get
grain, so that we may eat and stay alive." 3There
were also those who said, "We are having to pledge
our fields, our vineyards, and our houses in order
to get grain during the famine." 4And there were
those who said, "We are having to borrow money
on our fields and vineyards to pay the king's tax.
5Now our flesh is the same as that of our kindred;
our children are the same as their children; and
yet we are forcing our sons and daughters to be
slaves, and some of our daughters have been ravished; we are powerless, and our fields and vineyards now belong to others."
6 I was very angry when I heard their outcry
and these complaints. 7After thinking it over, I
brought charges against the nobles and the officials; I said to them, "You are all taking interest
from your own people." And I called a great assembly to deal with them, 8and said to them, "As
far as we were able, we have bought back our Jewish kindred who had been sold to other nations;
but now you are selling your own kin, who must
then be bought back by us!" They were silent, and
could not find a word to say. 9So I said, "The thing
that you are doing is not good. Should you not
walk in the fear of our God, to prevent the taunts
of the nations our enemies? 10Moreover I and my
brothers and my servants are lending them money and grain. Let us stop this taking of interest.
11Restore to them, this very day, their fields, their
vineyards, their olive orchards, and their houses,
and the interest on money, grain, wine, and oil
that you have been exacting from them." 12Then
they said, "We will restore everything and demand nothing more from them. We will do as you
say." And I called the priests, and made them take
an oath to do as they had promised. 13I also shook
out the fold of my garment and said, "So may God
shake out everyone from house and from property who does not perform this promise. Thus may
they be shaken out and emptied." And all the assembly said, "Amen," and praised the LORD. And
the people did as they had promised.
14 Moreover from the time that I was appointed to be their governor in the land of Judah,

Nehemiah 5

Nehemiah's confrontation of the powerful of his nation finds echoes in our own day. A 1994 Religious News Service release stated that Martin Luther King Jr. has continued, more than a quarter century after his assassination, to be a fixture in the national consciousness because he always sought to practice what he preached. Though beset by the moral and ethical contradictions that plague us all, he tried to walk it like he talked it. The fact and manner of his death reveals the apathy of all who seek to invoke his memory without following his example.[27] Trust in God, as King exemplified, is expressed in the freedom to love one's neighbor, all neighbors; to seek the good of the other, the many; to identify with the oppressed and anxious, to work for justice and peace, in spite of the ambiguities and problems inevitably involved; and even to give one's life for others, if so called.

— DB

[a] Cn: Heb *each his weapon the water*

from the twentieth year to the thirty-second year of King Artaxerxes, twelve years, neither I nor my brothers ate the food allowance of the governor. 15 The former governors who were before me laid heavy burdens on the people, and took food and wine from them, besides forty shekels of silver. Even their servants lorded it over the people. But I did not do so, because of the fear of God. 16 Indeed, I devoted myself to the work on this wall, and acquired no land; and all my servants were gathered there for the work. 17 Moreover there were at my table one hundred fifty people, Jews and officials, besides those who came to us from the nations around us. 18 Now that which was prepared for one day was one ox and six choice sheep; also fowls were prepared for me, and every ten days skins of wine in abundance; yet with all this I did not demand the food allowance of the governor, because of the heavy burden of labor on the people. 19 Remember for my good, O my God, all that I have done for this people.

6 Now when it was reported to Sanballat and Tobiah and to Geshem the Arab and to the rest of our enemies that I had built the wall and that there was no gap left in it (though up to that time I had not set up the doors in the gates), 2 Sanballat and Geshem sent to me, saying, "Come and let us meet together in one of the villages in the plain of Ono." But they intended to do me harm. 3 So I sent messengers to them, saying, "I am doing a great work and I cannot come down. Why should the work stop while I leave it to come down to you?" 4 They sent to me four times in this way, and I answered them in the same manner. 5 In the same way Sanballat for the fifth time sent his servant to me with an open letter in his hand. 6 In it was written, "It is reported among the nations—and Geshem[a] also says it—that you and the Jews intend to rebel; that is why you are building the wall; and according to this report you wish to become their king. 7 You have also set up prophets to proclaim in Jerusalem concerning you, 'There is a king in Judah!' And now it will be reported to the king according to these words. So come, therefore, and let us confer together." 8 Then I sent to him, saying, "No such things as you say have been done; you are inventing them out of your own mind" 9 —for they all wanted to frighten us, thinking, "Their hands will drop from the work, and it will not be done." But now, O God, strengthen my hands.

10 One day when I went into the house of Shemaiah son of Delaiah son of Mehetabel, who was confined to his house, he said, "Let us meet together in the house of God, within the temple, and let us close the doors of the temple, for they are coming to kill you; indeed, tonight they are coming to kill you." 11 But I said, "Should a man like me run away? Would a man like me go into the temple to save his life? I will not go in!" 12 Then I perceived and saw that God had not sent him at all, but he had pronounced the prophecy against me because Tobiah and Sanballat had hired him. 13 He was hired for this purpose, to intimidate me and make me sin by acting in this way, and so they could give me a bad name, in order to taunt me. 14 Remember Tobiah and Sanballat, O my God, according to these things that they did, and also the prophetess Noadiah and the rest of the prophets who wanted to make me afraid.

15 So the wall was finished on the twenty-fifth day of the month Elul, in fifty-two days. 16 And when all our enemies heard of it, all the nations around us were afraid[b] and fell greatly in their own esteem; for they perceived that this work had been accomplished with the help of our God. 17 Moreover in those days the nobles of Judah sent many letters to Tobiah, and Tobiah's letters came to them. 18 For many in Judah were bound by oath to him, because he was the son-in-law of Shecaniah son of Arah: and his son Jehohanan had married the daughter of Meshullam son of Berechiah. 19 Also they spoke of his good deeds in my presence, and reported my words to him. And Tobiah sent letters to intimidate me.

7 Now when the wall had been built and I had set up the doors, and the gatekeepers, the singers, and the Levites had been appointed, 2 I gave my brother Hanani charge over Jerusalem, along with Hananiah the commander of the cit-

[a] Heb *Gashmu* [b] Another reading is *saw*

adel—for he was a faithful man and feared God
more than many. 3 And I said to them, "The gates
of Jerusalem are not to be opened until the sun
is hot; while the gatekeepers[a] are still standing
guard, let them shut and bar the doors. Appoint
guards from among the inhabitants of Jerusalem,
some at their watch posts, and others before their
own houses." 4 The city was wide and large, but
the people within it were few and no houses had
been built.

5 Then my God put it into my mind to assemble the nobles and the officials and the people to
be enrolled by genealogy. And I found the book of
the genealogy of those who were the first to come
back, and I found the following written in it:

6 These are the people of the province who
came up out of the captivity of those exiles whom
King Nebuchadnezzar of Babylon had carried
into exile; they returned to Jerusalem and Judah,
each to his town. 7 They came with Zerubbabel,
Jeshua, Nehemiah, Azariah, Raamiah, Nahamani,
Mordecai, Bilshan, Mispereth, Bigvai, Nehum,
Baanah.

The number of the Israelite people: 8 the descendants of Parosh, two thousand one hundred
seventy-two. 9 Of Shephatiah, three hundred
seventy-two. 10 Of Arah, six hundred fifty-two.
11 Of Pahath-moab, namely the descendants of
Jeshua and Joab, two thousand eight hundred
eighteen. 12 Of Elam, one thousand two hundred
fifty-four. 13 Of Zattu, eight hundred forty-five.
14 Of Zaccai, seven hundred sixty. 15 Of Binnui,
six hundred forty-eight. 16 Of Bebai, six hundred
twenty-eight. 17 Of Azgad, two thousand three
hundred twenty-two. 18 Of Adonikam, six hundred
sixty-seven. 19 Of Bigvai, two thousand sixty-seven.
20 Of Adin, six hundred fifty-five. 21 Of Ater, namely
of Hezekiah, ninety-eight. 22 Of Hashum, three
hundred twenty-eight. 23 Of Bezai, three hundred
twenty-four. 24 Of Hariph, one hundred twelve.
25 Of Gibeon, ninety-five. 26 The people of Bethlehem and Netophah, one hundred eighty-eight.
27 Of Anathoth, one hundred twenty-eight. 28 Of
Beth-azmaveth, forty-two. 29 Of Kiriath-jearim,
Chephirah, and Beeroth, seven hundred forty-
three. 30 Of Ramah and Geba, six hundred twenty-
one. 31 Of Michmas, one hundred twenty-two.
32 Of Bethel and Ai, one hundred twenty-three.
33 Of the other Nebo, fifty-two. 34 The descendants
of the other Elam, one thousand two hundred
fifty-four. 35 Of Harim, three hundred twenty. 36 Of
Jericho, three hundred forty-five. 37 Of Lod, Hadid,
and Ono, seven hundred twenty-one. 38 Of Senaah,
three thousand nine hundred thirty.

39 The priests: the descendants of Jedaiah,
namely the house of Jeshua, nine hundred
seventy-three. 40 Of Immer, one thousand fifty-
two. 41 Of Pashhur, one thousand two hundred
forty-seven. 42 Of Harim, one thousand seventeen.

43 The Levites: the descendants of Jeshua,
namely of Kadmiel of the descendants of Hode-
vah, seventy-four. 44 The singers: the descendants
of Asaph, one hundred forty-eight. 45 The gatekeepers: the descendants of Shallum, of Ater, of
Talmon, of Akkub, of Hatita, of Shobai, one hundred thirty-eight.

46 The temple servants: the descendants of
Ziha, of Hasupha, of Tabbaoth, 47 of Keros, of Sia,
of Padon, 48 of Lebana, of Hagaba, of Shalmai,
49 of Hanan, of Giddel, of Gahar, 50 of Reaiah,
of Rezin, of Nekoda, 51 of Gazzam, of Uzza, of
Paseah, 52 of Besai, of Meunim, of Nephushesim,
53 of Bakbuk, of Hakupha, of Harhur, 54 of Bazlith,
of Mehida, of Harsha, 55 of Barkos, of Sisera, of
Temah, 56 of Neziah, of Hatipha.

57 The descendants of Solomon's servants:
of Sotai, of Sophereth, of Perida, 58 of Jaala, of
Darkon, of Giddel, 59 of Shephatiah, of Hattil, of
Pochereth-hazzebaim, of Amon.

60 All the temple servants and the descendants of Solomon's servants were three hundred
ninety-two.

61 The following were those who came up
from Tel-melah, Tel-harsha, Cherub, Addon, and
Immer, but they could not prove their ancestral
houses or their descent, whether they belonged
to Israel: 62 the descendants of Delaiah, of Tobiah,
of Nekoda, six hundred forty-two. 63 Also, of the
priests: the descendants of Hobaiah, of Hakkoz, of
Barzillai (who had married one of the daughters

[a] Heb *while they*

of Barzillai the Gileadite and was called by their name). 64 These sought their registration among those enrolled in the genealogies, but it was not found there, so they were excluded from the priesthood as unclean; 65 the governor told them that they were not to partake of the most holy food, until a priest with Urim and Thummim should come.

66 The whole assembly together was forty-two thousand three hundred sixty, 67 besides their male and female slaves, of whom there were seven thousand three hundred thirty-seven; and they had two hundred forty-five singers, male and female. 68 They had seven hundred thirty-six horses, two hundred forty-five mules,[a] 69 four hundred thirty-five camels, and six thousand seven hundred twenty donkeys.

70 Now some of the heads of ancestral houses contributed to the work. The governor gave to the treasury one thousand darics of gold, fifty basins, and five hundred thirty priestly robes. 71 And some of the heads of ancestral houses gave into the building fund twenty thousand darics of gold and two thousand two hundred minas of silver. 72 And what the rest of the people gave was twenty thousand darics of gold, two thousand minas of silver, and sixty-seven priestly robes.

73 So the priests, the Levites, the gatekeepers, the singers, some of the people, the temple servants, and all Israel settled in their towns.

8 When the seventh month came—the people of Israel being settled in their towns— 1 all the people gathered together into the square before the Water Gate. They told the scribe Ezra to bring the book of the law of Moses, which the LORD had given to Israel. 2 Accordingly, the priest Ezra brought the law before the assembly, both men and women and all who could hear with understanding. This was on the first day of the seventh month. 3 He read from it facing the square before the Water Gate from early morning until midday, in the presence of the men and the women and those who could understand; and the ears of all the people were attentive to the book of the law. 4 The scribe Ezra stood on a wooden platform that had been made for the purpose; and beside him stood Mattithiah, Shema, Anaiah, Uriah, Hilkiah, and Maaseiah on his right hand; and Pedaiah, Mishael, Malchijah, Hashum, Hash-baddanah, Zechariah, and Meshullam on his left hand. 5 And Ezra opened the book in the sight of all the people, for he was standing above all the people; and when he opened it, all the people stood up. 6 Then Ezra blessed the LORD, the great God, and all the people answered, "Amen, Amen," lifting up their hands. Then they bowed their heads and worshiped the LORD with their faces to the ground. 7 Also Jeshua, Bani, Sherebiah, Jamin, Akkub, Shabbethai, Hodiah, Maaseiah, Kelita, Azariah, Jozabad, Hanan, Pelaiah, the Levites,[b] helped the people to understand the law, while the people remained in their places. 8 So they read from the book, from the law of God, with interpretation. They gave the sense, so that the people understood the reading.

9 And Nehemiah, who was the governor, and Ezra the priest and scribe, and the Levites who taught the people said to all the people, "This day is holy to the LORD your God; do not mourn or weep." For all the people wept when they heard the words of the law. 10 Then he said to them, "Go your way, eat the fat and drink sweet wine and send portions of them to those for whom nothing is prepared, for this day is holy to our LORD; and do not be grieved, for the joy of the LORD is your strength." 11 So the Levites stilled all the people, saying, "Be quiet, for this day is holy; do not be grieved." 12 And all the people went their way to eat and drink and to send portions and to make great rejoicing, because they had understood the words that were declared to them.

13 On the second day the heads of ancestral houses of all the people, with the priests and the Levites, came together to the scribe Ezra in order to study the words of the law. 14 And they found it written in the law, which the LORD had commanded by Moses, that the people of Israel should live in booths[c] during the festival of the

[a] Ezra 2.66 and the margins of some Hebrew Mss: MT lacks *They had . . . forty-five mules* [b] 1 Esdras 9.48 Vg: Heb *and the Levites* [c] Or *tabernacles*; Heb *succoth*

seventh month, 15 and that they should publish
and proclaim in all their towns and in Jerusalem
as follows, "Go out to the hills and bring branches
of olive, wild olive, myrtle, palm, and other leafy
trees to make booths,[a] as it is written." 16 So the
people went out and brought them, and made
booths[a] for themselves, each on the roofs of their
houses, and in their courts and in the courts of the
house of God, and in the square at the Water Gate
and in the square at the Gate of Ephraim. 17 And
all the assembly of those who had returned from
the captivity made booths[a] and lived in them; for
from the days of Jeshua son of Nun to that day the
people of Israel had not done so. And there was
very great rejoicing. 18 And day by day, from the
first day to the last day, he read from the book of
the law of God. They kept the festival seven days;
and on the eighth day there was a solemn assembly, according to the ordinance.

9 Now on the twenty-fourth day of this month
the people of Israel were assembled with
fasting and in sackcloth, and with earth on their
heads.[b] 2 Then those of Israelite descent separated
themselves from all foreigners, and stood and confessed their sins and the iniquities of their ancestors. 3 They stood up in their place and read from
the book of the law of the LORD their God for a
fourth part of the day, and for another fourth they
made confession and worshiped the LORD their
God. 4 Then Jeshua, Bani, Kadmiel, Shebaniah,
Bunni, Sherebiah, Bani, and Chenani stood on
the stairs of the Levites and cried out with a loud
voice to the LORD their God. 5 Then the Levites,
Jeshua, Kadmiel, Bani, Hashabneiah, Sherebiah,
Hodiah, Shebaniah, and Pethahiah, said, "Stand
up and bless the LORD your God from everlasting to everlasting. Blessed be your glorious name,
which is exalted above all blessing and praise."

6 And Ezra said:[c] "You are the LORD, you
alone; you have made heaven, the heaven of
heavens, with all their host, the earth and all
that is on it, the seas and all that is in them. To
all of them you give life, and the host of heaven
worships you. 7 You are the LORD, the God who
chose Abram and brought him out of Ur of the
Chaldeans and gave him the name Abraham;
8 and you found his heart faithful before you, and
made with him a covenant to give to his descendants the land of the Canaanite, the Hittite, the
Amorite, the Perizzite, the Jebusite, and the Gir-
gashite; and you have fulfilled your promise, for
you are righteous.

9 "And you saw the distress of our ancestors
in Egypt and heard their cry at the Red Sea.[d]
10 You performed signs and wonders against Pharaoh and all his servants and all the people of
his land, for you knew that they acted insolently
against our ancestors. You made a name for yourself, which remains to this day. 11 And you divided
the sea before them, so that they passed through
the sea on dry land, but you threw their pursuers
into the depths, like a stone into mighty waters.
12 Moreover, you led them by day with a pillar of
cloud, and by night with a pillar of fire, to give
them light on the way in which they should go.
13 You came down also upon Mount Sinai, and
spoke with them from heaven, and gave them right
ordinances and true laws, good statutes and commandments, 14 and you made known your holy
sabbath to them and gave them commandments
and statutes and a law through your servant Moses. 15 For their hunger you gave them bread from
heaven, and for their thirst you brought water for
them out of the rock, and you told them to go in
to possess the land that you swore to give them.

16 "But they and our ancestors acted presumptuously and stiffened their necks and did
not obey your commandments; 17 they refused
to obey, and were not mindful of the wonders
that you performed among them; but they stiffened their necks and determined to return to
their slavery in Egypt. But you are a God ready
to forgive, gracious and merciful, slow to anger
and abounding in steadfast love, and you did
not forsake them. 18 Even when they had cast
an image of a calf for themselves and said, 'This
is your God who brought you up out of Egypt,'
and had committed great blasphemies, 19 you in
your great mercies did not forsake them in the
wilderness; the pillar of cloud that led them in

[a] Or *tabernacles*; Heb *succoth* [b] Heb *on them* [c] Gk: Heb lacks *And Ezra said* [d] Or *Sea of Reeds*

the way did not leave them by day, nor the pillar
of fire by night that gave them light on the way
by which they should go. 20You gave your good
spirit to instruct them, and did not withhold your
manna from their mouths, and gave them water
for their thirst. 21Forty years you sustained them
in the wilderness so that they lacked nothing;
their clothes did not wear out and their feet did
not swell. 22And you gave them kingdoms and
peoples, and allotted to them every corner,[a] so
they took possession of the land of King Sihon
of Heshbon and the land of King Og of Bashan.
23You multiplied their descendants like the stars
of heaven, and brought them into the land that
you had told their ancestors to enter and possess.
24So the descendants went in and possessed the
land, and you subdued before them the inhabitants of the land, the Canaanites, and gave them
into their hands, with their kings and the peoples
of the land, to do with them as they pleased.
25And they captured fortress cities and a rich
land, and took possession of houses filled with
all sorts of goods, hewn cisterns, vineyards, olive
orchards, and fruit trees in abundance; so they
ate, and were filled and became fat, and delighted
themselves in your great goodness.

26 "Nevertheless they were disobedient and
rebelled against you and cast your law behind
their backs and killed your prophets, who had
warned them in order to turn them back to you,
and they committed great blasphemies. 27There-
fore you gave them into the hands of their enemies, who made them suffer. Then in the time
of their suffering they cried out to you and you
heard them from heaven, and according to your
great mercies you gave them saviors who saved
them from the hands of their enemies. 28But after they had rest, they again did evil before you,
and you abandoned them to the hands of their
enemies, so that they had dominion over them;
yet when they turned and cried to you, you heard
from heaven, and many times you rescued them
according to your mercies. 29And you warned
them in order to turn them back to your law. Yet
they acted presumptuously and did not obey
your commandments, but sinned against your
ordinances, by the observance of which a person
shall live. They turned a stubborn shoulder and
stiffened their neck and would not obey. 30Many
years you were patient with them, and warned
them by your spirit through your prophets; yet
they would not listen. Therefore you handed
them over to the peoples of the lands. 31Never-
theless, in your great mercies you did not make
an end of them or forsake them, for you are a gracious and merciful God.

32 "Now therefore, our God—the great and
mighty and awesome God, keeping covenant and
steadfast love—do not treat lightly all the hardship that has come upon us, upon our kings, our
officials, our priests, our prophets, our ancestors,
and all your people, since the time of the kings
of Assyria until today. 33You have been just in all
that has come upon us, for you have dealt faithfully and we have acted wickedly; 34our kings,
our officials, our priests, and our ancestors have
not kept your law or heeded the commandments
and the warnings that you gave them. 35Even in
their own kingdom, and in the great goodness
you bestowed on them, and in the large and rich
land that you set before them, they did not serve
you and did not turn from their wicked works.
36Here we are, slaves to this day—slaves in the
land that you gave to our ancestors to enjoy its
fruit and its good gifts. 37Its rich yield goes to the
kings whom you have set over us because of our
sins; they have power also over our bodies and
over our livestock at their pleasure, and we are in
great distress."

38[b] Because of all this we make a firm agreement in writing, and on that sealed document are
inscribed the names of our officials, our Levites,
and our priests.

10[c] Upon the sealed document are the
names of Nehemiah the governor, son of
Hacaliah, and Zedekiah; 2Seraiah, Azariah, Jeremiah, 3Pashhur, Amariah, Malchijah, 4Hattush,
Shebaniah, Malluch, 5Harim, Meremoth, Obadiah, 6Daniel, Ginnethon, Baruch, 7Meshullam,
Abijah, Mijamin, 8Maaziah, Bilgai, Shemaiah;

[a] Meaning of Heb uncertain [b] Ch 10.1 in Heb [c] Ch 10.2 in Heb

these are the priests. 9And the Levites: Jeshua son
of Azaniah, Binnui of the sons of Henadad, Kadmiel; 10and their associates, Shebaniah, Hodiah,
Kelita, Pelaiah, Hanan, 11Mica, Rehob, Hashabiah, 12Zaccur, Sherebiah, Shebaniah, 13Hodiah,
Bani, Beninu. 14The leaders of the people: Parosh,
Pahath-moab, Elam, Zattu, Bani, 15Bunni, Azgad,
Bebai, 16Adonijah, Bigvai, Adin, 17Ater, Hezekiah, Azzur, 18Hodiah, Hashum, Bezai, 19Hariph,
Anathoth, Nebai, 20Magpiash, Meshullam, Hezir,
21Meshezabel, Zadok, Jaddua, 22Pelatiah, Hanan,
Anaiah, 23Hoshea, Hananiah, Hasshub, 24Hallo-
hesh, Pilha, Shobek, 25Rehum, Hashabnah, Maaseiah, 26Ahiah, Hanan, Anan, 27Malluch, Harim,
and Baanah.

28 The rest of the people, the priests, the
Levites, the gatekeepers, the singers, the temple
servants, and all who have separated themselves
from the peoples of the lands to adhere to the law
of God, their wives, their sons, their daughters, all
who have knowledge and understanding, 29join
with their kin, their nobles, and enter into a curse
and an oath to walk in God's law, which was given
by Moses the servant of God, and to observe and
do all the commandments of the LORD our Lord
and his ordinances and his statutes. 30We will
not give our daughters to the peoples of the land
or take their daughters for our sons; 31and if the
peoples of the land bring in merchandise or any
grain on the sabbath day to sell, we will not buy it
from them on the sabbath or on a holy day; and
we will forego the crops of the seventh year and
the exaction of every debt.

32 We also lay on ourselves the obligation to
charge ourselves yearly one-third of a shekel for
the service of the house of our God: 33for the
rows of bread, the regular grain offering, the regular burnt offering, the sabbaths, the new moons,
the appointed festivals, the sacred donations, and
the sin offerings to make atonement for Israel,
and for all the work of the house of our God. 34We
have also cast lots among the priests, the Levites,
and the people, for the wood offering, to bring it
into the house of our God, by ancestral houses, at
appointed times, year by year, to burn on the altar
of the LORD our God, as it is written in the law.
35We obligate ourselves to bring the first fruits of
our soil and the first fruits of all fruit of every tree,
year by year, to the house of the LORD; 36also to
bring to the house of our God, to the priests who
minister in the house of our God, the firstborn of
our sons and of our livestock, as it is written in
the law, and the firstlings of our herds and of our
flocks; 37and to bring the first of our dough, and
our contributions, the fruit of every tree, the wine
and the oil, to the priests, to the chambers of the
house of our God; and to bring to the Levites
the tithes from our soil, for it is the Levites who

Nehemiah 10:29-30; 13:23-29

Once the wall was constructed and rebuilding the Temple was well underway, the reform continued. Additional directives were announced regarding worship, the responsibilities of the priests, and how the Sabbath and other holy days were to be observed. Then came the final, unexpected and most exacting demand. The people of Judah were ordered by Ezra and Nehemiah to separate themselves "from all foreign peoples" and to send away their "foreign wives" (Ezra 10:11; Neh 10:29-30; 13:23-29). It was an extreme demand occasioned by fear and mistrust.

Why did they go to such extremes? The answer is found in human nature. When the future is uncertain, when people are disoriented, when the symbols of unity and stability have disappeared, and when the survival of the community is perceived to be at risk, the natural propensity is to circle the wagons, build fences, and erect walls.

The measures taken to protect the community during the time of Ezra and Nehemiah "tended to close the community to the dynamic outreach" clearly implied in the Abrahamic covenant: "And through you I will bless all nations" (Gen 12:3).[28]

— Alan Neely

collect the tithes in all our rural towns. 38 And
the priest, the descendant of Aaron, shall be with
the Levites when the Levites receive the tithes;
and the Levites shall bring up a tithe of the tithes
to the house of our God, to the chambers of the
storehouse. 39 For the people of Israel and the
sons of Levi shall bring the contribution of grain,
wine, and oil to the storerooms where the vessels
of the sanctuary are, and where the priests that
minister, and the gatekeepers and the singers are.
We will not neglect the house of our God.

11 Now the leaders of the people lived in
Jerusalem; and the rest of the people cast
lots to bring one out of ten to live in the holy city
Jerusalem, while nine-tenths remained in the
other towns. 2 And the people blessed all those
who willingly offered to live in Jerusalem.

3 These are the leaders of the province who
lived in Jerusalem; but in the towns of Judah all
lived on their property in their towns: Israel, the
priests, the Levites, the temple servants, and the
descendants of Solomon's servants. 4 And in Jerusalem lived some of the Judahites and of the
Benjaminites. Of the Judahites: Athaiah son of
Uzziah son of Zechariah son of Amariah son of
Shephatiah son of Mahalalel, of the descendants
of Perez; 5 and Maaseiah son of Baruch son of
Col-hozeh son of Hazaiah son of Adaiah son of
Joiarib son of Zechariah son of the Shilonite. 6 All
the descendants of Perez who lived in Jerusalem
were four hundred sixty-eight valiant warriors.

7 And these are the Benjaminites: Sallu son
of Meshullam son of Joed son of Pedaiah son of
Kolaiah son of Maaseiah son of Ithiel son of Jeshaiah. 8 And his brothers[a] Gabbai, Sallai: nine
hundred twenty-eight. 9 Joel son of Zichri was
their overseer; and Judah son of Hassenuah was
second in charge of the city.

10 Of the priests: Jedaiah son of Joiarib,
Jachin, 11 Seraiah son of Hilkiah son of Meshullam son of Zadok son of Meraioth son of Ahitub,
officer of the house of God, 12 and their associates who did the work of the house, eight hundred twenty-two; and Adaiah son of Jeroham son
of Pelaliah son of Amzi son of Zechariah son of
Pashhur son of Malchijah, 13 and his associates,
heads of ancestral houses, two hundred forty-
two; and Amashsai son of Azarel son of Ahzai
son of Meshillemoth son of Immer, 14 and their
associates, valiant warriors, one hundred twenty-
eight; their overseer was Zabdiel son of Hagge-
dolim.

15 And of the Levites: Shemaiah son of
Hasshub son of Azrikam son of Hashabiah son
of Bunni; 16 and Shabbethai and Jozabad, of the
leaders of the Levites, who were over the outside
work of the house of God; 17 and Mattaniah son
of Mica son of Zabdi son of Asaph, who was the
leader to begin the thanksgiving in prayer, and
Bakbukiah, the second among his associates; and
Abda son of Shammua son of Galal son of Jeduthun. 18 All the Levites in the holy city were two
hundred eighty-four.

19 The gatekeepers, Akkub, Talmon and their
associates, who kept watch at the gates, were one
hundred seventy-two. 20 And the rest of Israel,
and of the priests and the Levites, were in all the
towns of Judah, all of them in their inheritance.
21 But the temple servants lived on Ophel; and
Ziha and Gishpa were over the temple servants.

22 The overseer of the Levites in Jerusalem
was Uzzi son of Bani son of Hashabiah son of
Mattaniah son of Mica, of the descendants of
Asaph, the singers, in charge of the work of the
house of God. 23 For there was a command from
the king concerning them, and a settled provision
for the singers, as was required every day. 24 And
Pethahiah son of Meshezabel, of the descendants
of Zerah son of Judah, was at the king's hand in all
matters concerning the people.

25 And as for the villages, with their fields,
some of the people of Judah lived in Kiriath-arba
and its villages, and in Dibon and its villages, and
in Jekabzeel and its villages, 26 and in Jeshua and
in Moladah and Beth-pelet, 27 in Hazar-shual, in
Beer-sheba and its villages, 28 in Ziklag, in Meco-
nah and its villages, 29 in En-rimmon, in Zorah,
in Jarmuth, 30 Zanoah, Adullam, and their villages, Lachish and its fields, and Azekah and its
villages. So they camped from Beer-sheba to the

[a] Gk Mss: Heb *And after him*

valley of Hinnom. 31 The people of Benjamin
also lived from Geba onward, at Michmash, Aija,
Bethel and its villages, 32 Anathoth, Nob, Ananiah, 33 Hazor, Ramah, Gittaim, 34 Hadid, Zeboim, Neballat, 35 Lod, and Ono, the valley of
artisans. 36 And certain divisions of the Levites in
Judah were joined to Benjamin.

12 These are the priests and the Levites who
came up with Zerubbabel son of Shealtiel,
and Jeshua: Seraiah, Jeremiah, Ezra, 2 Amariah,
Malluch, Hattush, 3 Shecaniah, Rehum, Meremoth, 4 Iddo, Ginnethoi, Abijah, 5 Mijamin, Maa-
diah, Bilgah, 6 Shemaiah, Joiarib, Jedaiah, 7 Sallu,
Amok, Hilkiah, Jedaiah. These were the leaders
of the priests and of their associates in the days
of Jeshua.

8 And the Levites: Jeshua, Binnui, Kadmiel,
Sherebiah, Judah, and Mattaniah, who with his
associates was in charge of the songs of thanksgiving. 9 And Bakbukiah and Unno their associates stood opposite them in the service. 10 Jeshua
was the father of Joiakim, Joiakim the father of
Eliashib, Eliashib the father of Joiada, 11 Joiada
the father of Jonathan, and Jonathan the father of
Jaddua.

12 In the days of Joiakim the priests, heads of
ancestral houses, were: of Seraiah, Meraiah; of
Jeremiah, Hananiah; 13 of Ezra, Meshullam;
of Amariah, Jehohanan; 14 of Malluchi, Jonathan;
of Shebaniah, Joseph; 15 of Harim, Adna; of
Meraioth, Helkai; 16 of Iddo, Zechariah; of Ginnethon, Meshullam; 17 of Abijah, Zichri; of Miniamin, of Moadiah, Piltai; 18 of Bilgah, Shammua;
of Shemaiah, Jehonathan; 19 of Joiarib, Mattenai;
of Jedaiah, Uzzi; 20 of Sallai, Kallai; of Amok,
Eber; 21 of Hilkiah, Hashabiah; of Jedaiah, Nethanel.

22 As for the Levites, in the days of Eliashib,
Joiada, Johanan, and Jaddua, there were recorded
the heads of ancestral houses; also the priests
until the reign of Darius the Persian. 23 The Levites, heads of ancestral houses, were recorded in
the Book of the Annals until the days of Johanan
son of Eliashib. 24 And the leaders of the Levites:
Hashabiah, Sherebiah, and Jeshua son of Kadmiel,
with their associates over against them, to praise
and to give thanks, according to the commandment of David the man of God, section opposite
to section. 25 Mattaniah, Bakbukiah, Obadiah,
Meshullam, Talmon, and Akkub were gatekeepers standing guard at the storehouses of the gates.
26 These were in the days of Joiakim son of Jeshua
son of Jozadak, and in the days of the governor
Nehemiah and of the priest Ezra, the scribe.

27 Now at the dedication of the wall of Jerusalem they sought out the Levites in all their
places, to bring them to Jerusalem to celebrate
the dedication with rejoicing, with thanksgivings
and with singing, with cymbals, harps, and lyres.
28 The companies of the singers gathered together
from the circuit around Jerusalem and from the
villages of the Netophathites; 29 also from Beth-
gilgal and from the region of Geba and Azmaveth;
for the singers had built for themselves villages
around Jerusalem. 30 And the priests and the Levites purified themselves; and they purified the
people and the gates and the wall.

31 Then I brought the leaders of Judah up
onto the wall, and appointed two great companies that gave thanks and went in procession. One
went to the right on the wall to the Dung Gate;
32 and after them went Hoshaiah and half the officials of Judah, 33 and Azariah, Ezra, Meshullam,
34 Judah, Benjamin, Shemaiah, and Jeremiah,
35 and some of the young priests with trumpets:
Zechariah son of Jonathan son of Shemaiah son
of Mattaniah son of Micaiah son of Zaccur son
of Asaph; 36 and his kindred, Shemaiah, Azarel,
Milalai, Gilalai, Maai, Nethanel, Judah, and Hanani, with the musical instruments of David the
man of God; and the scribe Ezra went in front of
them. 37 At the Fountain Gate, in front of them,
they went straight up by the stairs of the city of
David, at the ascent of the wall, above the house
of David, to the Water Gate on the east.

38 The other company of those who gave
thanks went to the left,[a] and I followed them with
half of the people on the wall, above the Tower
of the Ovens, to the Broad Wall, 39 and above the
Gate of Ephraim, and by the Old Gate, and by the

[a] Cn: Heb *opposite*

Fish Gate and the Tower of Hananel and the Tower of the Hundred, to the Sheep Gate; and they
came to a halt at the Gate of the Guard. 40So both
companies of those who gave thanks stood in the
house of God, and I and half of the officials with
me; 41and the priests Eliakim, Maaseiah, Miniamin, Micaiah, Elioenai, Zechariah, and Hananiah, with trumpets; 42and Maaseiah, Shemaiah,
Eleazar, Uzzi, Jehohanan, Malchijah, Elam, and
Ezer. And the singers sang with Jezrahiah as their
leader. 43They offered great sacrifices that day and
rejoiced, for God had made them rejoice with
great joy; the women and children also rejoiced.
The joy of Jerusalem was heard far away.

44 On that day men were appointed over the
chambers for the stores, the contributions, the
first fruits, and the tithes, to gather into them
the portions required by the law for the priests
and for the Levites from the fields belonging
to the towns; for Judah rejoiced over the priests
and the Levites who ministered. 45They performed the service of their God and the service of
purification, as did the singers and the gatekeepers, according to the command of David and his
son Solomon. 46For in the days of David and
Asaph long ago there was a leader of the singers,
and there were songs of praise and thanksgiving
to God. 47In the days of Zerubbabel and in the
days of Nehemiah all Israel gave the daily portions for the singers and the gatekeepers. They set
apart that which was for the Levites; and the Levites set apart that which was for the descendants
of Aaron.

13 On that day they read from the book of
Moses in the hearing of the people; and
in it was found written that no Ammonite or
Moabite should ever enter the assembly of God,
2because they did not meet the Israelites with
bread and water, but hired Balaam against them
to curse them—yet our God turned the curse
into a blessing. 3When the people heard the law,
they separated from Israel all those of foreign descent.

4 Now before this, the priest Eliashib, who
was appointed over the chambers of the house of
our God, and who was related to Tobiah, 5pre-
pared for Tobiah a large room where they had
previously put the grain offering, the frankincense, the vessels, and the tithes of grain, wine,
and oil, which were given by commandment to
the Levites, singers, and gatekeepers, and the
contributions for the priests. 6While this was taking place I was not in Jerusalem, for in the thirty-
second year of King Artaxerxes of Babylon I went
to the king. After some time I asked leave of the
king 7and returned to Jerusalem. I then discovered the wrong that Eliashib had done on behalf
of Tobiah, preparing a room for him in the courts
of the house of God. 8And I was very angry, and I
threw all the household furniture of Tobiah out
of the room. 9Then I gave orders and they cleansed
the chambers, and I brought back the vessels of
the house of God, with the grain offering and the
frankincense.

10 I also found out that the portions of the
Levites had not been given to them; so that the
Levites and the singers, who had conducted
the service, had gone back to their fields. 11So I
remonstrated with the officials and said, "Why is
the house of God forsaken?" And I gathered them
together and set them in their stations. 12Then all
Judah brought the tithe of the grain, wine, and oil
into the storehouses. 13And I appointed as treasurers over the storehouses the priest Shelemiah,
the scribe Zadok, and Pedaiah of the Levites, and
as their assistant Hanan son of Zaccur son of
Mattaniah, for they were considered faithful; and
their duty was to distribute to their associates.
14Remember me, O my God, concerning this,
and do not wipe out my good deeds that I
have done for the house of my God and for his
service.

15 In those days I saw in Judah people treading wine presses on the sabbath, and bringing in
heaps of grain and loading them on donkeys; and
also wine, grapes, figs, and all kinds of burdens,
which they brought into Jerusalem on the sabbath day; and I warned them at that time against
selling food. 16Tyrians also, who lived in the city,
brought in fish and all kinds of merchandise and
sold them on the sabbath to the people of Judah,
and in Jerusalem. 17Then I remonstrated with
the nobles of Judah and said to them, "What is
this evil thing that you are doing, profaning the

sabbath day? [18]Did not your ancestors act in this
way, and did not our God bring all this disaster on
us and on this city? Yet you bring more wrath on
Israel by profaning the sabbath."

19 When it began to be dark at the gates of
Jerusalem before the sabbath, I commanded that
the doors should be shut and gave orders that
they should not be opened until after the sabbath.
And I set some of my servants over the gates, to
prevent any burden from being brought in on the
sabbath day. [20]Then the merchants and sellers of
all kinds of merchandise spent the night outside
Jerusalem once or twice. [21]But I warned them
and said to them, "Why do you spend the night
in front of the wall? If you do so again, I will lay
hands on you." From that time on they did not
come on the sabbath. [22]And I commanded the
Levites that they should purify themselves and
come and guard the gates, to keep the sabbath
day holy. Remember this also in my favor, O my
God, and spare me according to the greatness of
your steadfast love.

23 In those days also I saw Jews who had
married women of Ashdod, Ammon, and Moab;
[24]and half of their children spoke the language of
Ashdod, and they could not speak the language
of Judah, but spoke the language of various peoples. [25]And I contended with them and cursed
them and beat some of them and pulled out their
hair; and I made them take an oath in the name of
God, saying, "You shall not give your daughters
to their sons, or take their daughters for your sons
or for yourselves. [26]Did not King Solomon of Israel sin on account of such women? Among the
many nations there was no king like him, and he
was beloved by his God, and God made him king
over all Israel; nevertheless, foreign women made
even him to sin. [27]Shall we then listen to you and
do all this great evil and act treacherously against
our God by marrying foreign women?"

28 And one of the sons of Jehoiada, son of
the high priest Eliashib, was the son-in-law of
Sanballat the Horonite; I chased him away from
me. [29]Remember them, O my God, because
they have defiled the priesthood, the covenant
of the priests and the Levites.

30 Thus I cleansed them from everything
foreign, and I established the duties of the
priests and Levites, each in his work; [31]and I
provided for the wood offering, at appointed
times, and for the first fruits. Remember me,
O my God, for good.

Esther

The book of Esther is one of the most powerful and interesting texts in the Hebrew Bible. It is the only book in the Hebrew Bible that makes no overt reference to God. Neither does it mention other significant facets of daily Jewish ritual life. However, the events narrated in the book are the occasion for Purim, the holiday that celebrates the Jewish people's deliverance from government-sanctioned mass destruction. Therefore, despite those just-named omissions, Esther offers an important characterization of God's eternal commitment to and relationship with this people.

The book of Esther, set in a king's court during the Persian (Achaemenid) Era, is dated to c. 400–200 BCE. Many modern scholars have questioned the book's genre, though it was once simply considered historical. For those who continue to view Esther as a type of history, the book is termed a *historical novella*. One counterargument to that characterization relates to confusion about King Ahasuerus's identity. Even though some scholars settle this matter by conflating Ahasuerus with King Xerxes, for others that identification remains problematic. Some scholars propose that Ahasuerus represents an unspecified legendary figure. Assertions that the events narrated here cannot be verified historically in no way detract from the power of the work, nor do they limit the extent to which Esther can convey important general truths about the early Jewish Diaspora.

The rabbis included the ten-chapter book as a part of the Writings, or *Kethuvim*. The book involves an intricate cast of characters and its plot provides insights about the meanings of power, power relations, and liberation. The five principal characters are very different but interconnected. At the outset, the outspoken Queen Vashti is deposed; she has disobeyed her husband, Ahaseurus, and the king responds foolishly by issuing a decree that women must obey their husbands. Due to Vashti's unwillingness to appear before the king and his cronies wearing her crown—and *only* that, explained later rabbinic interpreters!—Vashti is banished. Her misbehavior in court paves the way for Queen Esther and her guardian, Mordecai. Haman, a Persian official, also surfaces early in the narrative, plotting genocide for the Jewish people. Ultimately, this architect of Jewish demise is led to his death by Esther and Mordecai, two purportedly weaker characters. Esther and Mordecai serve as a foil for Haman and the legislative acts of the puppet-king, Ahasuerus. The absurdity of the king's edict points to the unlikelihood that this aspect of the book of Esther, at least, is historical; but perhaps more important for the reader, it reinforces the king's ineptitude.

Based on what scholars know about the historical Achaemenid Empire, the notion that a member of an ethnic minority could become queen of Persia is as absurd as the edict against women (1:19-20). An extensive study of women in the empire makes clear that it is unlikely that anyone other than a Persian woman would have ascended to such a position of royalty. Nevertheless, both

the edict against wives and the beauty pageant in which Esther was selected function in the plot to reveal who had *actual rather than perceived power*. The ultimate demonstration of this power emerges when Mordecai and Esther succeed in devising a plan to undermine the king's presumed authority.

One alternative to viewing the book of Esther as history is to understand it as illustrating Hellenistic comedy or farce. This interpretation is based in part on the ostensibly ludicrous actions of King Ahasuerus but also includes the way Esther is selected as queen. Contemporary humor is often used to broach society's thorniest issues. Indeed, some of the most biting commentary on political matters is delivered through comedic satire. For an ethnic minority to view its relationship to the empire in the fashion expressed in Esther provides for the Jewish Diaspora an opportunity to reckon with its reality. The experiences of being under the Achaemenid Empire—no matter how tolerant of diverse religious traditions the Persians might have been—compounded with the aftermath of the Babylonian exile, which brought the loss of land and other traumas, placed the Jewish Diaspora in an unenviable and vulnerable position. That the genre of Esther may be comparable to Hellenistic comedy does not diminish the serious nature of the book.

The narrative pokes fun at the hapless king. This enhances even more the image of Mordecai, a towering figure of wisdom and strength who outthinks the king and his entourage of advisers at every turn. Esther, a member of the recently scolded gender, circumspectly presents her case to the king. As a representative of Yehud's ethnic minority, Esther is, in fact, doubly strong. She speaks to the king, who had earlier sought to quiet women. Esther thereby provides the means through which Mordecai is able to conduct his strategy to dismantle Haman's plan of genocide. By speaking to the king and *acting womanishly*—as a feminist—Esther obliterates Haman's devised doom for the Jewish people and grants to women of every ethnic background the wisdom to pursue worthy goals by practical means.

The book of Esther's harrowing drama of a people confronted with threats to the viability of its ethnic community, if not genocide, ought to inspire the survivor in all of us. I find inspiration here, not only as a biblical scholar, a spouse, and a mother but as a disabled African American survivor of breast cancer. Like Esther, I grew up without my mother, who died after she turned fifty and I nineteen. But although I missed my mother and best friend, I was far from motherless. The spirit of the woman who birthed me has guided me, and when I needed the gentle embrace of elders, women from the African American community loved and nurtured me. That experience leads me to take seriously a commitment to the welfare of a diminished and tattered African American community, a commitment not unlike Esther's own; my task is to help salvage from utter devastation the spirit that breathed life into me on bitter and difficult days.

— ***Willa E. M. Johnson***

1 This happened in the days of Ahasuerus,
the same Ahasuerus who ruled over one
hundred twenty-seven provinces from India to
Ethiopia.[a] 2 In those days when King Ahasuerus
sat on his royal throne in the citadel of Susa, 3 in
the third year of his reign, he gave a banquet for
all his officials and ministers. The army of Persia
and Media and the nobles and governors of the
provinces were present, 4 while he displayed the
great wealth of his kingdom and the splendor and
pomp of his majesty for many days, one hundred
eighty days in all.

5 When these days were completed, the king
gave for all the people present in the citadel of
Susa, both great and small, a banquet lasting for
seven days, in the court of the garden of the king's
palace. 6 There were white cotton curtains and
blue hangings tied with cords of fine linen and
purple to silver rings[b] and marble pillars. There
were couches of gold and silver on a mosaic pavement of porphyry, marble, mother-of-pearl, and
colored stones. 7 Drinks were served in golden
goblets, goblets of different kinds, and the royal
wine was lavished according to the bounty of the
king. 8 Drinking was by flagons, without restraint;
for the king had given orders to all the officials
of his palace to do as each one desired. 9 Furthermore, Queen Vashti gave a banquet for the women
in the palace of King Ahasuerus.

10 On the seventh day, when the king was
merry with wine, he commanded Mehuman, Biz-
tha, Harbona, Bigtha and Abagtha, Zethar and
Carkas, the seven eunuchs who attended him,
11 to bring Queen Vashti before the king, wearing
the royal crown, in order to show the peoples and
the officials her beauty; for she was fair to behold.
12 But Queen Vashti refused to come at the king's
command conveyed by the eunuchs. At this the
king was enraged, and his anger burned within
him.

13 Then the king consulted the sages who
knew the laws[c] (for this was the king's procedure
toward all who were versed in law and custom,
14 and those next to him were Carshena, Shethar,
Admatha, Tarshish, Meres, Marsena, and Memucan, the seven officials of Persia and Media, who
had access to the king, and sat first in the kingdom): 15 "According to the law, what is to be done
to Queen Vashti because she has not performed
the command of King Ahasuerus conveyed by
the eunuchs?" 16 Then Memucan said in the presence of the king and the officials, "Not only has
Queen Vashti done wrong to the king, but also to
all the officials and all the peoples who are in all
the provinces of King Ahasuerus. 17 For this deed
of the queen will be made known to all women,
causing them to look with contempt on their husbands, since they will say, 'King Ahasuerus commanded Queen Vashti to be brought before him,
and she did not come.' 18 This very day the noble
ladies of Persia and Media who have heard of the
queen's behavior will rebel against[d] the king's officials, and there will be no end of contempt and
wrath! 19 If it pleases the king, let a royal order
go out from him, and let it be written among the
laws of the Persians and the Medes so that it may
not be altered, that Vashti is never again to come
before King Ahasuerus; and let the king give her
royal position to another who is better than she.
20 So when the decree made by the king is proclaimed throughout all his kingdom, vast as it is,
all women will give honor to their husbands, high
and low alike."

21 This advice pleased the king and the officials, and the king did as Memucan proposed;
22 he sent letters to all the royal provinces, to every province in its own script and to every people
in its own language, declaring that every man
should be master in his own house.[e]

2 After these things, when the anger of King
Ahasuerus had abated, he remembered
Vashti and what she had done and what had been
decreed against her. 2 Then the king's servants
who attended him said, "Let beautiful young virgins be sought out for the king. 3 And let the king
appoint commissioners in all the provinces of his
kingdom to gather all the beautiful young virgins
to the harem in the citadel of Susa under custody

[a] Or *Nubia*; Heb *Cush* [b] Or *rods* [c] Cn: Heb *times* [d] Cn: Heb *will tell*
[e] Heb adds *and speak according to the language of his people*

of Hegai, the king's eunuch, who is in charge of
the women; let their cosmetic treatments be
given them. 4 And let the girl who pleases the king
be queen instead of Vashti." This pleased the king,
and he did so.
5 Now there was a Jew in the citadel of Susa
whose name was Mordecai son of Jair son of
Shimei son of Kish, a Benjaminite. 6 Kish[a] had
been carried away from Jerusalem among the
captives carried away with King Jeconiah of Judah, whom King Nebuchadnezzar of Babylon
had carried away. 7 Mordecai[b] had brought up
Hadassah, that is Esther, his cousin, for she had
neither father nor mother; the girl was fair and
beautiful, and when her father and her mother
died, Mordecai adopted her as his own daughter. 8 So when the king's order and his edict were
proclaimed, and when many young women were
gathered in the citadel of Susa in custody of Hegai,
Esther also was taken into the king's palace and
put in custody of Hegai, who had charge of the
women. 9 The girl pleased him and won his favor,
and he quickly provided her with her cosmetic
treatments and her portion of food, and with
seven chosen maids from the king's palace, and
advanced her and her maids to the best place in
the harem. 10 Esther did not reveal her people or
kindred, for Mordecai had charged her not to tell.
11 Every day Mordecai would walk around in front
of the court of the harem, to learn how Esther was
and how she fared.
12 The turn came for each girl to go in to
King Ahasuerus, after being twelve months under the regulations for the women, since this was
the regular period of their cosmetic treatment,
six months with oil of myrrh and six months with
perfumes and cosmetics for women. 13 When the
girl went in to the king she was given whatever
she asked for to take with her from the harem to
the king's palace. 14 In the evening she went in;
then in the morning she came back to the second
harem in custody of Shaashgaz, the king's eunuch,
who was in charge of the concubines; she did not
go in to the king again, unless the king delighted
in her and she was summoned by name.
15 When the turn came for Esther daughter of Abihail the uncle of Mordecai, who had
adopted her as his own daughter, to go in to the
king, she asked for nothing except what Hegai
the king's eunuch, who had charge of the women,
advised. Now Esther was admired by all who saw
her. 16 When Esther was taken to King Ahasuerus
in his royal palace in the tenth month, which is
the month of Tebeth, in the seventh year of his
reign, 17 the king loved Esther more than all the
other women; of all the virgins she won his favor
and devotion, so that he set the royal crown on
her head and made her queen instead of Vashti.
18 Then the king gave a great banquet to all his officials and ministers—"Esther's banquet." He also
granted a holiday[c] to the provinces, and gave gifts
with royal liberality.
19 When the virgins were being gathered together,[d] Mordecai was sitting at the king's gate.
20 Now Esther had not revealed her kindred or her
people, as Mordecai had charged her; for Esther
obeyed Mordecai just as when she was brought
up by him. 21 In those days, while Mordecai was
sitting at the king's gate, Bigthan and Teresh, two
of the king's eunuchs, who guarded the threshold,
became angry and conspired to assassinate[e] King
Ahasuerus. 22 But the matter came to the knowledge of Mordecai, and he told it to Queen Esther,
and Esther told the king in the name of Mordecai.
23 When the affair was investigated and found to
be so, both the men were hanged on the gallows.
It was recorded in the book of the annals in the
presence of the king.

3 After these things King Ahasuerus promoted
Haman son of Hammedatha the Agagite,
and advanced him and set his seat above all the
officials who were with him. 2 And all the king's
servants who were at the king's gate bowed down
and did obeisance to Haman; for the king had
so commanded concerning him. But Mordecai
did not bow down or do obeisance. 3 Then the
king's servants who were at the king's gate said
to Mordecai, "Why do you disobey the king's
command?" 4 When they spoke to him day after
day and he would not listen to them, they told

[a] Heb *a Benjaminite* [6] *who* [b] Heb *He* [c] Or *an amnesty* [d] Heb adds *a second time* [e] Heb *to lay hands on*

Haman, in order to see whether Mordecai's
words would avail; for he had told them that he
was a Jew. 5When Haman saw that Mordecai did
not bow down or do obeisance to him, Haman
was infuriated. 6But he thought it beneath him
to lay hands on Mordecai alone. So, having been
told who Mordecai's people were, Haman plotted
to destroy all the Jews, the people of Mordecai,
throughout the whole kingdom of Ahasuerus.

7 In the first month, which is the month of
Nisan, in the twelfth year of King Ahasuerus,
they cast Pur—which means "the lot"—before
Haman for the day and for the month, and the lot
fell on the thirteenth day[a] of the twelfth month,
which is the month of Adar. 8Then Haman said
to King Ahasuerus, "There is a certain people
scattered and separated among the peoples in
all the provinces of your kingdom; their laws are
different from those of every other people, and
they do not keep the king's laws, so that it is not
appropriate for the king to tolerate them. 9If it
pleases the king, let a decree be issued for their
destruction, and I will pay ten thousand talents
of silver into the hands of those who have charge
of the king's business, so that they may put it into
the king's treasuries." 10So the king took his signet
ring from his hand and gave it to Haman son of
Hammedatha the Agagite, the enemy of the Jews.
11The king said to Haman, "The money is given
to you, and the people as well, to do with them as
it seems good to you."

12 Then the king's secretaries were summoned on the thirteenth day of the first month,
and an edict, according to all that Haman commanded, was written to the king's satraps and to
the governors over all the provinces and to the
officials of all the peoples, to every province in its
own script and every people in its own language;
it was written in the name of King Ahasuerus and
sealed with the king's ring. 13Letters were sent
by couriers to all the king's provinces, giving orders to destroy, to kill, and to annihilate all Jews,
young and old, women and children, in one day,
the thirteenth day of the twelfth month, which is
the month of Adar, and to plunder their goods.
14A copy of the document was to be issued as a
decree in every province by proclamation, calling
on all the peoples to be ready for that day. 15The
couriers went quickly by order of the king, and
the decree was issued in the citadel of Susa. The
king and Haman sat down to drink; but the city
of Susa was thrown into confusion.

4 When Mordecai learned all that had been
done, Mordecai tore his clothes and put on
sackcloth and ashes, and went through the city,
wailing with a loud and bitter cry; 2he went up to
the entrance of the king's gate, for no one might
enter the king's gate clothed with sackcloth. 3In
every province, wherever the king's command
and his decree came, there was great mourning
among the Jews, with fasting and weeping and
lamenting, and most of them lay in sackcloth and
ashes.

4 When Esther's maids and her eunuchs came
and told her, the queen was deeply distressed;
she sent garments to clothe Mordecai, so that he
might take off his sackcloth; but he would not accept them. 5Then Esther called for Hathach, one
of the king's eunuchs, who had been appointed
to attend her, and ordered him to go to Mordecai
to learn what was happening and why. 6Hathach
went out to Mordecai in the open square of the
city in front of the king's gate, 7and Mordecai told
him all that had happened to him, and the exact
sum of money that Haman had promised to pay
into the king's treasuries for the destruction of
the Jews. 8Mordecai also gave him a copy of the
written decree issued in Susa for their destruction, that he might show it to Esther, explain it to
her, and charge her to go to the king to make supplication to him and entreat him for her people.

9 Hathach went and told Esther what Mordecai had said. 10Then Esther spoke to Hathach and
gave him a message for Mordecai, saying, 11"All
the king's servants and the people of the king's
provinces know that if any man or woman goes
to the king inside the inner court without being
called, there is but one law—all alike are to be put
to death. Only if the king holds out the golden
scepter to someone, may that person live. I my-

[a] Cn Compare Gk and verse 13 below: Heb *the twelfth month*

self have not been called to come in to the king
for thirty days." 12When they told Mordecai what
Esther had said, 13Mordecai told them to reply
to Esther, "Do not think that in the king's palace
you will escape any more than all the other Jews.
14For if you keep silence at such a time as this,
relief and deliverance will rise for the Jews from
another quarter, but you and your father's family will perish. Who knows? Perhaps you have
come to royal dignity for just such a time as this."
15Then Esther said in reply to Mordecai, 16"Go,
gather all the Jews to be found in Susa, and hold
a fast on my behalf, and neither eat nor drink for
three days, night or day. I and my maids will also
fast as you do. After that I will go to the king,
though it is against the law; and if I perish, I perish." 17Mordecai then went away and did everything as Esther had ordered him.

Esther 4:13-17

The story of Esther plays on themes of ethnic or racial hostility (compare the note at Exod 1:15-22). Esther is one of a multitude of women gathered from the provinces in an Empire-wide beauty contest. Because she is able to conceal "her people" and her "kindred" (2:10), nothing in her countenance, language, bearing, or practices prevents her being crowned as queen (2:17). Later, King Ahaseurus authorizes Haman to destroy a disobedient people within his empire (3:7-11), without recognizing that Haman is referring to the Jews. Haman is ultimately undone because he presumes the king will perceive all Jews as different from "us" and will believe his false generalizations about them (3:8)—but the king sees instead the loyalty of Mordecai and the courage of Esther, and grants their people the right of self-defense (8:9-14).

—NE

5 On the third day Esther put on her royal robes
and stood in the inner court of the king's palace, opposite the king's hall. The king was sitting
on his royal throne inside the palace opposite the
entrance to the palace. 2As soon as the king saw
Queen Esther standing in the court, she won his
favor and he held out to her the golden scepter
that was in his hand. Then Esther approached and
touched the top of the scepter. 3The king said to
her, "What is it, Queen Esther? What is your request? It shall be given you, even to the half of
my kingdom." 4Then Esther said, "If it pleases
the king, let the king and Haman come today to a
banquet that I have prepared for the king." 5Then
the king said, "Bring Haman quickly, so that we
may do as Esther desires." So the king and Haman
came to the banquet that Esther had prepared.
6While they were drinking wine, the king said to
Esther, "What is your petition? It shall be granted
you. And what is your request? Even to the half
of my kingdom, it shall be fulfilled." 7Then Esther
said, "This is my petition and request: 8If I have
won the king's favor, and if it pleases the king to
grant my petition and fulfill my request, let the
king and Haman come tomorrow to the banquet
that I will prepare for them, and then I will do as
the king has said."
9 Haman went out that day happy and in
good spirits. But when Haman saw Mordecai
in the king's gate, and observed that he neither
rose nor trembled before him, he was infuriated
with Mordecai; 10nevertheless Haman restrained
himself and went home. Then he sent and called
for his friends and his wife Zeresh, 11and Haman
recounted to them the splendor of his riches,
the number of his sons, all the promotions with
which the king had honored him, and how he had
advanced him above the officials and the ministers of the king. 12Haman added, "Even Queen
Esther let no one but myself come with the king
to the banquet that she prepared. Tomorrow also
I am invited by her, together with the king. 13Yet
all this does me no good so long as I see the Jew
Mordecai sitting at the king's gate." 14Then his
wife Zeresh and all his friends said to him, "Let
a gallows fifty cubits high be made, and in the
morning tell the king to have Mordecai hanged
on it; then go with the king to the banquet in
good spirits." This advice pleased Haman, and he
had the gallows made.

6 On that night the king could not sleep, and
he gave orders to bring the book of records,

the annals, and they were read to the king. 2It was
found written how Mordecai had told about Big-
thana and Teresh, two of the king's eunuchs, who
guarded the threshold, and who had conspired to
assassinate[a] King Ahasuerus. 3Then the king said,
"What honor or distinction has been bestowed
on Mordecai for this?" The king's servants who
attended him said, "Nothing has been done for
him." 4The king said, "Who is in the court?"
Now Haman had just entered the outer court of
the king's palace to speak to the king about having Mordecai hanged on the gallows that he had
prepared for him. 5So the king's servants told
him, "Haman is there, standing in the court." The
king said, "Let him come in." 6So Haman came
in, and the king said to him, "What shall be done
for the man whom the king wishes to honor?"
Haman said to himself, "Whom would the king
wish to honor more than me?" 7So Haman said
to the king, "For the man whom the king wishes
to honor, 8let royal robes be brought, which
the king has worn, and a horse that the king
has ridden, with a royal crown on its head. 9Let
the robes and the horse be handed over to one
of the king's most noble officials; let him[b] robe
the man whom the king wishes to honor, and let
him[b] conduct the man on horseback through the
open square of the city, proclaiming before him:
'Thus shall it be done for the man whom the king
wishes to honor.'" 10Then the king said to Haman, "Quickly, take the robes and the horse, as
you have said, and do so to the Jew Mordecai who
sits at the king's gate. Leave out nothing that you
have mentioned." 11So Haman took the robes and
the horse and robed Mordecai and led him riding
through the open square of the city, proclaiming,
"Thus shall it be done for the man whom the king
wishes to honor."

12 Then Mordecai returned to the king's gate,
but Haman hurried to his house, mourning and
with his head covered. 13When Haman told his
wife Zeresh and all his friends everything that
had happened to him, his advisers and his wife
Zeresh said to him, "If Mordecai, before whom
your downfall has begun, is of the Jewish people,
you will not prevail against him, but will surely
fall before him."

14 While they were still talking with him, the
king's eunuchs arrived and hurried Haman off to
the banquet that Esther had prepared.

7 1So
the king and Haman went in to feast with
Queen Esther. 2On the second day, as they were
drinking wine, the king again said to Esther,
"What is your petition, Queen Esther? It shall
be granted you. And what is your request? Even
to the half of my kingdom, it shall be fulfilled."
3Then Queen Esther answered, "If I have won
your favor, O king, and if it pleases the king, let
my life be given me—that is my petition—and
the lives of my people—that is my request. 4For
we have been sold, I and my people, to be destroyed, to be killed, and to be annihilated. If we
had been sold merely as slaves, men and women,
I would have held my peace; but no enemy can
compensate for this damage to the king."[c] 5Then
King Ahasuerus said to Queen Esther, "Who is
he, and where is he, who has presumed to do
this?" 6Esther said, "A foe and enemy, this wicked Haman!" Then Haman was terrified before
the king and the queen. 7The king rose from the
feast in wrath and went into the palace garden,
but Haman stayed to beg his life from Queen
Esther, for he saw that the king had determined
to destroy him. 8When the king returned from
the palace garden to the banquet hall, Haman
had thrown himself on the couch where Esther
was reclining; and the king said, "Will he even
assault the queen in my presence, in my own
house?" As the words left the mouth of the king,
they covered Haman's face. 9Then Harbona, one
of the eunuchs in attendance on the king, said,
"Look, the very gallows that Haman has prepared
for Mordecai, whose word saved the king, stands
at Haman's house, fifty cubits high." And the
king said, "Hang him on that." 10So they hanged
Haman on the gallows that he had prepared for
Mordecai. Then the anger of the king abated.

8 On that day King Ahasuerus gave to Queen
Esther the house of Haman, the enemy of the
Jews; and Mordecai came before the king, for Es-

[a] Heb *to lay hands on* [b] Heb *them* [c] Meaning of Heb uncertain

ther had told what he was to her. 2 Then the king
took off his signet ring, which he had taken from
Haman, and gave it to Mordecai. So Esther set
Mordecai over the house of Haman.

3 Then Esther spoke again to the king; she
fell at his feet, weeping and pleading with him to
avert the evil design of Haman the Agagite and
the plot that he had devised against the Jews.
4 The king held out the golden scepter to Esther,
5 and Esther rose and stood before the king. She
said, "If it pleases the king, and if I have won his
favor, and if the thing seems right before the king,
and I have his approval, let an order be written
to revoke the letters devised by Haman son of
Hammedatha the Agagite, which he wrote giving
orders to destroy the Jews who are in all the provinces of the king. 6 For how can I bear to see the
calamity that is coming on my people? Or how
can I bear to see the destruction of my kindred?"
7 Then King Ahasuerus said to Queen Esther and
to the Jew Mordecai, "See, I have given Esther the
house of Haman, and they have hanged him on
the gallows, because he plotted to lay hands on
the Jews. 8 You may write as you please with regard to the Jews, in the name of the king, and seal
it with the king's ring; for an edict written in the
name of the king and sealed with the king's ring
cannot be revoked."

9 The king's secretaries were summoned at
that time, in the third month, which is the month
of Sivan, on the twenty-third day; and an edict
was written, according to all that Mordecai commanded, to the Jews and to the satraps and the
governors and the officials of the provinces from
India to Ethiopia,[a] one hundred twenty-seven
provinces, to every province in its own script and
to every people in its own language, and also to
the Jews in their script and their language. 10 He
wrote letters in the name of King Ahasuerus,
sealed them with the king's ring, and sent them
by mounted couriers riding on fast steeds bred
from the royal herd.[b] 11 By these letters the king
allowed the Jews who were in every city to assemble and defend their lives, to destroy, to kill,
and to annihilate any armed force of any people
or province that might attack them, with their
children and women, and to plunder their goods
12 on a single day throughout all the provinces
of King Ahasuerus, on the thirteenth day of the
twelfth month, which is the month of Adar. 13 A
copy of the writ was to be issued as a decree in every province and published to all peoples, and the
Jews were to be ready on that day to take revenge
on their enemies. 14 So the couriers, mounted on
their swift royal steeds, hurried out, urged by the
king's command. The decree was issued in the
citadel of Susa.

15 Then Mordecai went out from the presence of the king, wearing royal robes of blue and
white, with a great golden crown and a mantle
of fine linen and purple, while the city of Susa
shouted and rejoiced. 16 For the Jews there was
light and gladness, joy and honor. 17 In every
province and in every city, wherever the king's
command and his edict came, there was gladness
and joy among the Jews, a festival and a holiday.
Furthermore, many of the peoples of the country
professed to be Jews, because the fear of the Jews
had fallen upon them.

9 Now in the twelfth month, which is the
month of Adar, on the thirteenth day, when
the king's command and edict were about to be
executed, on the very day when the enemies of
the Jews hoped to gain power over them, but
which had been changed to a day when the Jews
would gain power over their foes, 2 the Jews gathered in their cities throughout all the provinces of
King Ahasuerus to lay hands on those who had
sought their ruin; and no one could withstand
them, because the fear of them had fallen upon
all peoples. 3 All the officials of the provinces, the
satraps and the governors, and the royal officials
were supporting the Jews, because the fear of
Mordecai had fallen upon them. 4 For Mordecai
was powerful in the king's house, and his fame
spread throughout all the provinces as the man
Mordecai grew more and more powerful. 5 So
the Jews struck down all their enemies with the
sword, slaughtering, and destroying them, and
did as they pleased to those who hated them. 6 In

[a] Or *Nubia*; Heb *Cush* [b] Meaning of Heb uncertain

the citadel of Susa the Jews killed and destroyed five hundred people. 7 They killed Parshandatha, Dalphon, Aspatha, 8 Poratha, Adalia, Aridatha, 9 Parmashta, Arisai, Aridai, Vaizatha, 10 the ten sons of Haman son of Hammedatha, the enemy of the Jews; but they did not touch the plunder.

11 That very day the number of those killed in the citadel of Susa was reported to the king. 12 The king said to Queen Esther, "In the citadel of Susa the Jews have killed five hundred people and also the ten sons of Haman. What have they done in the rest of the king's provinces? Now what is your petition? It shall be granted you. And what further is your request? It shall be fulfilled." 13 Esther said, "If it pleases the king, let the Jews who are in Susa be allowed tomorrow also to do according to this day's edict, and let the ten sons of Haman be hanged on the gallows." 14 So the king commanded this to be done; a decree was issued in Susa, and the ten sons of Haman were hanged. 15 The Jews who were in Susa gathered also on the fourteenth day of the month of Adar and they killed three hundred persons in Susa; but they did not touch the plunder.

16 Now the other Jews who were in the king's provinces also gathered to defend their lives, and gained relief from their enemies, and killed seventy-five thousand of those who hated them; but they laid no hands on the plunder. 17 This was on the thirteenth day of the month of Adar, and on the fourteenth day they rested and made that a day of feasting and gladness.

18 But the Jews who were in Susa gathered on the thirteenth day and on the fourteenth, and rested on the fifteenth day, making that a day of feasting and gladness. 19 Therefore the Jews of the villages, who live in the open towns, hold the fourteenth day of the month of Adar as a day for gladness and feasting, a holiday on which they send gifts of food to one another.

20 Mordecai recorded these things, and sent letters to all the Jews who were in all the provinces of King Ahasuerus, both near and far, 21 enjoining them that they should keep the fourteenth day of the month Adar and also the fifteenth day of the same month, year by year, 22 as the days on which the Jews gained relief from their enemies, and as the month that had been turned for them from sorrow into gladness and from mourning into a holiday; that they should make them days of feasting and gladness, days for sending gifts of food to one another and presents to the poor. 23 So the Jews adopted as a custom what they had begun to do, as Mordecai had written to them.

24 Haman son of Hammedatha the Agagite, the enemy of all the Jews, had plotted against the Jews to destroy them, and had cast Pur—that is "the lot"—to crush and destroy them; 25 but when Esther came before the king, he gave orders in writing that the wicked plot that he had devised against the Jews should come upon his own head, and that he and his sons should be hanged on the gallows. 26 Therefore these days are called Purim, from the word Pur. Thus because of all that was written in this letter, and of what they had faced in this matter, and of what had happened to them, 27 the Jews established and accepted as a custom for themselves and their descendants and all who joined them, that without fail they would continue to observe these two days every year, as it was written and at the time appointed. 28 These days should be remembered and kept throughout every generation, in every family, province, and city; and these days of Purim should never fall into disuse among the Jews, nor should the commemoration of these days cease among their descendants.

29 Queen Esther daughter of Abihail, along with the Jew Mordecai, gave full written authority, confirming this second letter about Purim. 30 Letters were sent wishing peace and security to all the Jews, to the one hundred twenty-seven provinces of the kingdom of Ahasuerus, 31 and giving orders that these days of Purim should be observed at their appointed seasons, as the Jew Mordecai and Queen Esther enjoined on the Jews, just as they had laid down for themselves and for their descendants regulations concerning their fasts and their lamentations. 32 The command of Queen Esther fixed these practices of Purim, and it was recorded in writing.

10 King Ahasuerus laid tribute on the land and on the islands of the sea. 2 All the acts of his power and might, and the full account of

the high honor of Mordecai, to which the king advanced him, are they not written in the annals of the kings of Media and Persia?
3 For Mordecai the Jew was next in rank to King Ahasuerus, and he was powerful among the Jews and popular with his many kindred, for he sought the good of his people and interceded for the welfare of all his descendants.

Wisdom and Poetry

INTRODUCTION

Francisco García-Treto

Wisdom and Poetry, understood as terms of artistic form in the literary study of the Bible, can be found in many books of the Hebrew Scriptures, including the prophets—but six (or eight) books traditionally have been regarded as comprising the Wisdom and poetic writings. The Psalms, the Song of Solomon (also called the Song of Songs, or simply Songs), and Lamentations are labeled poetic, and Proverbs, Job, and Ecclesiastes (also called *Qoheleth*) are considered wisdom books. All of these books belong in the third division of the Hebrew canon (the *Kethuvim*, or Writings), where they are joined by others (Ruth, Esther, Daniel, Ezra, Nehemiah, 1 and 2 Chronicles) that in Christian Bibles are placed among the historical or prophetical books. Because the Roman Catholic and Orthodox canons incorporate the books that others call Apocryphal or Deuterocanonical writings in the Old Testament itself, rather than in a separate section, these churches thus add Ecclesiasticus (also known as Sirach) and the Wisdom of Solomon to the list of wisdom or sapiential books.

Poetry

A look at the way modern Bibles set the wisdom books in type is enough to show that they are entirely or in large part in poetic form. Only Ecclesiastes alternates poetry and prose throughout. Job surrounds a long series of poetic dialogues between Job, his friends, and finally YHWH with brief prose portions that serve as introduction and conclusion to the work. We customarily distinguish the books into the two groups mentioned above, wisdom and poetry, but there are nevertheless points of similarity between the two literary categories that go beyond the simple observation that they all have some kind of poetic form. But what *is* poetic form?

Poetry and Song

In the most general terms, poetry uses a variety of means to enhance language to communicate a wide range of emotion. Music is one of the most obvious enhancements available, and it is not surprising that song is among the earliest and most durable forms in which poetry appears in Hebrew literature, as in any other. David, the model king, is also the model singer and poet in 1 and 2 Samuel, from the time he joins Saul's court as a skilled musician (1 Sam 16:14-23), to the powerful scene beginning at 2 Sam 1:17, where the NRSV text says that he "intoned"—that is, sang—the "Song of the Bow," his moving funeral song for Saul and Jonathan. The Psalms are, for the most part, hymns from temple services, and many of them even have editors' notes addressed to the choirmaster, specifying the kinds of instruments to use for accompaniment, or the name of a tune to which the psalm was to be sung. Psalm 150 even lists string, wind, and percussion instruments with which the psalmist entreats the congregation to "Praise the LORD!" Unfortunately, the ancient Hebrews did not develop a system of musical notation, so today we can only guess at how their music sounded; and for most of us, who depend on translations for reading the Bible, even the sound of the Hebrew words themselves is absent. Many characteristic features of Hebrew poetry—for example, the rhythm of accents in a line, the number of syllables in a verse, or the many forms of wordplay based on sound—are available only to the reader of the original language. That is not to say that all is lost; there is much that a good translation can convey.

The Craft of Poetry

Parallelism is the most distinctive and frequently seen feature of biblical Hebrew poetry. At its simplest—and the patterns and techniques of parallelism are a vast subject—it is a reinforcement of an idea or image by repeating it in the same verse using different words, or even by stating it in the opposite way. Psalm 1:5-6 can be used to illustrate both points:

> Therefore the wicked will not stand in the judgment,
>   nor sinners [stand] in the congregation of the righteous;
> for the LORD watches over the way of the righteous,
>   but the way of the wicked will perish.

The ancient Hebrew poets also used devices such as similes and metaphors, universal tools of the poetic craft. Psalm 1, for example, pairs similes to say that those who delight in the law of the LORD are "like trees planted by streams of water, which yield their fruit in its season, and their leaves do not wither," while the wicked "are like chaff that the wind drives away" (Ps 1:3, 4). Perhaps the best-known and loved of the metaphors in the Psalms is the one that begins the Twenty-third Psalm: "The LORD is my shepherd, I shall not want."

Genres

An important issue to take into account when reading any work of literature, poetry in particular, is its genre, that is, the kind of literature it is. A sonnet, for example, differs from a limerick not only in form and range of content but also in the audience's expectations of where and for what purpose it is fitting to use one or the other. That is not to say that creative poets may not displace genres to make powerful statements. The prophet Amos, for example, sings a funeral lament or *qinah* over the nation, as if he were lamenting an individual "maiden Israel" (Amos 5:1). David uses the same genre in his song in 2 Sam 1:17. Not all biblical poetry is of the same genre, nor was it intended for the same setting or purpose.

Psalms, Lamentations, Song of Solomon

The book of Psalms reached its final form after the Babylonian exile, even though its collections of largely cultic poetry include some very ancient songs. By and large, the voices we hear in its 150 poems are those of Israel at worship, with the inclusion at times of the voice of the teachers of wisdom, promoting the study of Torah. Many Psalms can thus be classified as hymns in praise of God, while others are prayers of lament and petition, whether of individuals or of the entire community. Others are royal songs associated with ceremonies such as the enthronement of a king, while yet others are songs for the pilgrimage festivals associated with Jerusalem, and so forth.

Lamentations (1:1) gives voice to the pain of the loss of Jerusalem, ravaged and desecrated by the Babylonians:

How lonely sits the city
    that once was full of people!
How like a widow she has become,
    she that was great among the nations!
She that was a princess among the provinces
    has become a vassal.

In Lam 5:15-16 the poet weeps for the suffering of the inhabitants in images whose power reaches across the gap of time and language and moves us:

The joy of our hearts has ceased;
    our dancing has been turned to mourning.
The crown has fallen from our head;
    woe to us, for we have sinned!

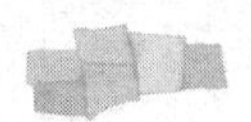

The Song of Solomon represents a totally different genre: it is a cycle of poems celebrating human love and physical beauty, universal and worthy themes of poetry. Placed in the canonical context of Scripture, however, these poems have been read as representing the reciprocal loves of God and Israel, or of Christ and the church, or have been used by Jewish and Christian mystics to convey the soul's desire for union with God.

Wisdom

An important trait shared by the poetic and wisdom books is their openness to international or intercultural influences. This shows in a variety of areas, ranging from form and style to content and scope of interest, where the Hebrew writers apparently knew, or even directly depended upon, the literary heritage of Israel's neighbors. Substantial parallels ranging from Sumerian laments to Babylonian hymns to Egyptian love songs, for example, inform our reading of Lamentations, Psalms, or the Song of Solomon, while the very words of the Instruction of Amenemopet, a well-known Egyptian wisdom text, stand behind the Hebrew text of Prov 22:17—24:22. On the other hand, the grandson of Jesus ben Sirach tells us, in his Greek translation of his grandfather's Hebrew text, that he has translated it "so that by becoming familiar also with his book those who love learning might make even greater progress in living according to the law" (prologue of Ecclesiasticus). In other words, he worked so that Greek-speaking Jews living in Egypt, some with a limited grasp of Hebrew, could read the book his grandfather had written in Jerusalem.

Royal and imperial courts, as well as major religious establishments such as the Temple, needed literate, skilled personnel capable of keeping records and accounts, writing legal documents, and carrying out correspondence—in short, bureaucrats, administrators, and clerks—to conduct their varied affairs. As a class, these people are known as scribes (literally, "writers") because of the basic importance of literacy to what they did. Apparently there were schools and teachers in Israel, as there were in Egypt, Mesopotamia, and Syria, and they provided the likely context for the production of what we know as wisdom literature.

Proverbs is a large collection of texts that praise and recommend the acquisition of wisdom for very practical and this-worldly ends. Religious piety plays an important part in what Proverbs recommends, including that "the fear of the LORD is the beginning of knowledge" (1:7). But what will ultimately lead to success and to the reward of one's good name are human virtues such as prudence, understanding, diligence, honesty, temperance and humility. An extraordinary poem in Proverbs 8 presents Wisdom in the figure of a merchant peddling and advertising her educational wares in the public square and, in verses 22-31, making the remarkable assertion of having been the first of God's creations, fashioned as a "master worker" (v. 30) to aid in the making of the world. The world, therefore, is comprehensible through wisdom. Much of the material in Proverbs is presented in the short genre that gives the book its name; in most cases a single verse in two parts, held together by parallelism:

A slack hand causes poverty,
but the hand of the diligent makes rich. (10:4)

Pride goes before destruction,
and a haughty spirit before a fall. (16:18)

Ecclesiastes and Job represent critiques *from within* of the central claim of the wisdom schools. In the view represented by Proverbs, the faithful practice of piety and virtue—of wisdom—leads to a good name, honor, and a long, prosperous, tranquil life, or at least it should. The writers of Ecclesiastes and Job are clearly among "the wise," but for them the results of wisdom are less rosy. The writer of Job questions the implied judgment on those who suffer—that it must be because of their own sin. Job is a wise and righteous man, at first rich, happy, and honored, who loses everything in a terrible series of events, through no fault of his own. Through the long poetic dialogues that compose the book, he defends his integrity against his wise friends, who encourage him to confess what in their opinion must be some terrible and secret sin. Job's refusal, and his appeal to YHWH—who finally appears, but in the end refuses to answer Job's query—pose the ever-unanswered questions that human suffering raises, and refute the too-easy answer that suffering is always the victim's fault. Ecclesiastes raises an even more universal question: does not the inevitability of death give the lie to any human idea of lasting achievement or accomplishment? A profound weariness sounds in the theme of the book, which goes on to speak of various areas of human effort as amounting to the same thing:

Vanity of vanities, says the Teacher,
vanity of vanities! All is vanity.
What do people gain from all the toil
at which they toil under the sun? (Eccl 1:2-3)

Two works of the later Hellenistic period, Sirach and Wisdom of Solomon, represent the development of the wisdom tradition in, respectively, Jerusalem and in the Diaspora (see the introductions to those books in the Apocrypha).

Being a member of the "Cuban Diaspora," having been a college professor in a department of religion for forty years, and, inevitably, getting old have given me an appreciation of the Wisdom writings and of the poetry of the Hebrew Bible. This appreciation has become deeper

and richer than when I first encountered these texts as a child in church (Presbyterian), and in school (Methodist and Presbyterian), in the Cuba of my youth, or when I learned to read them with all of the historical-critical tools of a graduate education in the United States. I rediscovered these writings only when I became a new teacher, someone who had to come to grips with exile and with treading the thin line that exiles must always negotiate in order to survive, while simultaneously trying to succeed and serve others in a different country than the country of my birth and formation. In this process, I found the wisdom writers and the poets of the Hebrew Bible to be very different than what I had, early in my life, thought them to be. Now I think I understand them better, and because of my own experience, I feel more comfortable in their company.

Job

Job, a poetic drama, asks how it is that evil and injustice seem to be allowed, permitted, or tolerated by God. Theologically, Job's dilemma is about *theodicy* or divine justice (from the Greek *theos*, "God," and *dikē*, "justice"): Why do evil things happen to innocent people? Is an all-powerful God good? Either a just God is not all-powerful, or a just God is not all-beneficent—or else the suffering person cannot really be innocent of wrongdoing and thus has earned retribution rather than beneficence.

The book's prologue (chs. 1–2) opens with God and "the Accuser" or "the adversary"—in Hebrew, *ha-satan*, an angelic figure who will only later develop into the New Testament's "Satan"—placing a wager on righteous Job to test his piety and faithfulness. The rich poetic dialogues that follow (chs. 3–27), filled with legal disputations and logical arguments between Job and his so-called friends, Eliphaz, Bildad, and Zophar, debate the question: Why *is* Job being punished? His friends insist that he must have sinned. They posit that God is and must always be good, right, and just. A poem (ch. 28) suggests that wisdom is only within God. In the monologues that follow (29:1—42:6), Job, Elihu, and God speak in turn. Job says God should not punish innocent people.

Job's friends fail to refute him. Elihu chastises Job for justifying himself and asserts that God can never pervert justice (32–37). Then YHWH appears in a storm theophany (a dramatic in-breaking of the divine) and questions Job, but avoids responding to Job's questions of suffering or divine justice through cosmological and mythological assertions (38:1—42:6). Job extols God's greatness and accepts God's decisions. Amid irony and dissonance, in the epilogue (42:7-17) God is angry with Job's friends, has them offer sacrifice, and has Job pray for them. Then God makes Job prosperous again, and Job dies an old man "full of days" (42:17).

Subjects of Intrigue

The rich, powerful themes within Job stand in tension. Job and his friends authorize their truth claims within different realities. The friends' traditional positions on suffering require authenticating Job's implicit wrongs. Job feels alienated from God, and amid relentless arguments, accuses God of injustice, while others accuse Job of wrongdoing. Job experiences agony, despair, and deep anguish.

Contradictions in the book mirror these tensions. Job's life descends into chaos, which is reflected in the dialogues as conflicting assertions regarding God are made by characters seeking to justify themselves. As the story develops, it presses us to question our own socio-religious and moral assumptions and values, our notions of personal faith and piety, of divine and human relationships, and of human suffering.

I relate to this book as a professor of theology and women's studies and an ordained elder in the Christian Methodist Episcopal Church, but also as the wife of a beloved husband, Mike, who was misdiagnosed with Alzheimer's disease and mistreated for four years. At last, by grace, his malady was found to be a side effect of a common statin drug. We regard this as our own "Job experience"; indeed, Job is a representative figure for all who suffer in spite of all that seems to be right.

Carol Newsom has declared that the book of Job disorients and reorients the reader, offering a drastically different paradigm for God, creation, and human existence. In the story, Job's wife offers insight that shakes Job's presumptions. Regarding authority, his friends rely on common sense and various traditions about God (traditions very reminiscent of the language of Deuteronomy); Job, on the other hand, protests his own integrity. When Job was wealthy, he demonstrated empathy for women and the poor. Now Job expects God to treat him as he treats others in need: by being benevolent, paternal, and just. He and his friends seem to expect God to react to Job's benevolence: Doesn't God follow God's own justice (as later expressed in the Golden Rule) by treating Job as God wishes to be treated by him? But this question never receives a direct answer. Rather, the book implies, humans are made for God, not God for humankind. God seeks to reorient Job, apparently leaving the redress of injustice, oppression, and suffering as a human task.

Seams, Collisions, and Convergences

In the world represented by the book of Job, a chaotic God blesses the wicked and abuses the poor. This God is a tyrant and yet is declared just. René Girard posits that Job, like Jesus, is a popular hero who becomes a communal scapegoat, an innocent person who polarizes the community and attracts universal rejection. The Job of the prologue is a wealthy, popular potentate; but the Job of the dialogues is a victim of an awful reversal of fortunes. His friends' speeches reveal imitative hatred and envy, and truth is not their goal. Amid deception, God's own delay to intervene appears cruel. Job's harshly accusatory language blurs his status as victim. The God described by his persecutors as a providential God stands in tension with the God who stands with the victims. The epilogue offers an incomplete, happily-ever-after scenario that masks the scapegoating dynamic of the story.

Holiness (*qōdesh* in Hebrew, *hagiosynē* in Greek) is an infrequent theme in the wisdom literature, and when it appears there it primarily concerns the fear of the Lord. Yet Job's holiness, and God's, are important. Calvin Samuel argues that Job's experience in the plot casts doubt on God's holiness and righteousness. Job fears God, is blameless and upright, and meets disaster with personal holiness; yet he suffers. Intriguingly, Job is from Uz: God must go outside the people, covenant, and cult of Israel to find this premier example of holiness. Here the sages who produced the wisdom literature have recast holiness to represent a holy, leprous Gentile who lives in an unholy land with unholy people, without cultic access to God's grace. In so doing the sages implicitly question God's holiness and portray God as a bullying, almost demonic caricature. God bestows holiness, yet it must be pursued by humans. The wisdom tradition holds in tension divine sovereignty and human responsibility. Job maintains personal integrity. Ultimately, however, the sages offer no conclusive explanations, and God's ways remain inscrutable.

— ***Cheryl A. Kirk-Duggan***

1 There was once a man in the land of Uz
whose name was Job. That man was blameless and upright, one who feared God and turned
away from evil. 2 There were born to him seven
sons and three daughters. 3 He had seven thousand sheep, three thousand camels, five hundred
yoke of oxen, five hundred donkeys, and very
many servants; so that this man was the greatest of all the people of the east. 4 His sons used
to go and hold feasts in one another's houses in
turn; and they would send and invite their three
sisters to eat and drink with them. 5 And when the
feast days had run their course, Job would send
and sanctify them, and he would rise early in the
morning and offer burnt offerings according to
the number of them all; for Job said, "It may be
that my children have sinned, and cursed God in
their hearts." This is what Job always did.

6 One day the heavenly beings[a] came to present themselves before the LORD, and Satan[b] also
came among them. 7 The LORD said to Satan,[b]
"Where have you come from?" Satan[b] answered
the LORD, "From going to and fro on the earth,
and from walking up and down on it." 8 The LORD
said to Satan,[b] "Have you considered my servant Job? There is no one like him on the earth,
a blameless and upright man who fears God and
turns away from evil." 9 Then Satan[b] answered the
LORD, "Does Job fear God for nothing? 10 Have
you not put a fence around him and his house and
all that he has, on every side? You have blessed
the work of his hands, and his possessions have
increased in the land. 11 But stretch out your hand
now, and touch all that he has, and he will curse
you to your face." 12 The LORD said to Satan,[b]
"Very well, all that he has is in your power; only
do not stretch out your hand against him!" So Satan[b] went out from the presence of the LORD.

13 One day when his sons and daughters
were eating and drinking wine in the eldest
brother's house, 14 a messenger came to Job and
said, "The oxen were plowing and the donkeys
were feeding beside them, 15 and the Sabeans
fell on them and carried them off, and killed the
servants with the edge of the sword; I alone have
escaped to tell you." 16 While he was still speaking, another came and said, "The fire of God fell
from heaven and burned up the sheep and the
servants, and consumed them; I alone have escaped to tell you." 17 While he was still speaking,
another came and said, "The Chaldeans formed
three columns, made a raid on the camels and
carried them off, and killed the servants with
the edge of the sword; I alone have escaped to
tell you." 18 While he was still speaking, another
came and said, "Your sons and daughters were
eating and drinking wine in their eldest brother's
house, 19 and suddenly a great wind came across
the desert, struck the four corners of the house,
and it fell on the young people, and they are dead;
I alone have escaped to tell you."

20 Then Job arose, tore his robe, shaved his
head, and fell on the ground and worshiped. 21 He
said, "Naked I came from my mother's womb, and
naked shall I return there; the LORD gave, and the
LORD has taken away; blessed be the name of the
LORD."

22 In all this Job did not sin or charge God
with wrongdoing.

2 One day the heavenly beings[a] came to present themselves before the LORD, and Satan[b]
also came among them to present himself before
the LORD. 2 The LORD said to Satan,[b] "Where
have you come from?" Satan[b] answered the
LORD, "From going to and fro on the earth, and
from walking up and down on it." 3 The LORD said
to Satan,[b] "Have you considered my servant Job?
There is no one like him on the earth, a blameless and upright man who fears God and turns
away from evil. He still persists in his integrity,
although you incited me against him, to destroy
him for no reason." 4 Then Satan[b] answered the
LORD, "Skin for skin! All that people have they
will give to save their lives.[c] 5 But stretch out your
hand now and touch his bone and his flesh, and
he will curse you to your face." 6 The LORD said
to Satan,[b] "Very well, he is in your power; only
spare his life."

7 So Satan[b] went out from the presence of the
LORD, and inflicted loathsome sores on Job from

[a] Heb *sons of God* [b] Or *the Accuser*; Heb *ha-satan* [c] Or *All that the man has he will give for his life*

the sole of his foot to the crown of his head. 8 Job[a]
took a potsherd with which to scrape himself, and
sat among the ashes.

9 Then his wife said to him, "Do you still persist in your integrity? Curse[b] God, and die." 10 But
he said to her, "You speak as any foolish woman
would speak. Shall we receive the good at the
hand of God, and not receive the bad?" In all this
Job did not sin with his lips.

11 Now when Job's three friends heard of all
these troubles that had come upon him, each of
them set out from his home—Eliphaz the Temanite, Bildad the Shuhite, and Zophar the Naamathite. They met together to go and console and
comfort him. 12 When they saw him from a distance, they did not recognize him, and they raised
their voices and wept aloud; they tore their robes
and threw dust in the air upon their heads. 13 They
sat with him on the ground seven days and seven
nights, and no one spoke a word to him, for they
saw that his suffering was very great.

3 After this Job opened his mouth and cursed
the day of his birth. 2 Job said:

3 "Let the day perish in which I was born,
and the night that said,
'A man-child is conceived.'
4 Let that day be darkness!
May God above not seek it,
or light shine on it.
5 Let gloom and deep darkness claim it.
Let clouds settle upon it;
let the blackness of the day terrify it.
6 That night—let thick darkness seize it!
let it not rejoice among the days of the
year;
let it not come into the number of the
months.
7 Yes, let that night be barren;
let no joyful cry be heard[c] in it.
8 Let those curse it who curse the Sea,[d]
those who are skilled to rouse up
Leviathan.
9 Let the stars of its dawn be dark;
let it hope for light, but have none;
may it not see the eyelids of the
morning—
10 because it did not shut the doors of my
mother's womb,
and hide trouble from my eyes.

11 "Why did I not die at birth,
come forth from the womb and expire?
12 Why were there knees to receive me,
or breasts for me to suck?
13 Now I would be lying down and quiet;
I would be asleep; then I would be at rest
14 with kings and counselors of the earth
who rebuild ruins for themselves,
15 or with princes who have gold,
who fill their houses with silver.
16 Or why was I not buried like a stillborn
child,
like an infant that never sees the light?
17 There the wicked cease from troubling,
and there the weary are at rest.
18 There the prisoners are at ease together;
they do not hear the voice of the
taskmaster.
19 The small and the great are there,
and the slaves are free from their
masters.

20 "Why is light given to one in misery,
and life to the bitter in soul,
21 who long for death, but it does not come,
and dig for it more than for hidden
treasures;
22 who rejoice exceedingly,
and are glad when they find the grave?
23 Why is light given to one who cannot see the
way,
whom God has fenced in?
24 For my sighing comes like[e] my bread,
and my groanings are poured out like
water.
25 Truly the thing that I fear comes upon me,
and what I dread befalls me.
26 I am not at ease, nor am I quiet;
I have no rest; but trouble comes."

[a] Heb *He* [b] Heb *Bless* [c] Heb *come* [d] Cn: Heb *day* [e] Heb *before*

4 Then Eliphaz the Temanite answered:
2 "If one ventures a word with you, will you be offended?
But who can keep from speaking?
3 See, you have instructed many;
you have strengthened the weak hands.
4 Your words have supported those who were stumbling,
and you have made firm the feeble knees.
5 But now it has come to you, and you are impatient;
it touches you, and you are dismayed.
6 Is not your fear of God your confidence,
and the integrity of your ways your hope?

7 "Think now, who that was innocent ever perished?
Or where were the upright cut off?
8 As I have seen, those who plow iniquity
and sow trouble reap the same.
9 By the breath of God they perish,
and by the blast of his anger they are consumed.
10 The roar of the lion, the voice of the fierce lion,
and the teeth of the young lions are broken.
11 The strong lion perishes for lack of prey,
and the whelps of the lioness are scattered.

12 "Now a word came stealing to me,
my ear received the whisper of it.
13 Amid thoughts from visions of the night,
when deep sleep falls on mortals,
14 dread came upon me, and trembling,
which made all my bones shake.
15 A spirit glided past my face;
the hair of my flesh bristled.
16 It stood still,
but I could not discern its appearance.
A form was before my eyes;
there was silence, then I heard a voice:
17 'Can mortals be righteous before[a] God?
Can human beings be pure before[a] their Maker?
18 Even in his servants he puts no trust,
and his angels he charges with error;
19 how much more those who live in houses of clay,
whose foundation is in the dust,
who are crushed like a moth.
20 Between morning and evening they are destroyed;
they perish forever without any regarding it.
21 Their tent-cord is plucked up within them,
and they die devoid of wisdom.'

5 "Call now; is there anyone who will answer you?
To which of the holy ones will you turn?
2 Surely vexation kills the fool,
and jealousy slays the simple.
3 I have seen fools taking root,
but suddenly I cursed their dwelling.
4 Their children are far from safety,
they are crushed in the gate,
and there is no one to deliver them.
5 The hungry eat their harvest,
and they take it even out of the thorns;[b]
and the thirsty[c] pant after their wealth.
6 For misery does not come from the earth,
nor does trouble sprout from the ground;
7 but human beings are born to trouble
just as sparks[d] fly upward.

8 "As for me, I would seek God,
and to God I would commit my cause.
9 He does great things and unsearchable,
marvelous things without number.
10 He gives rain on the earth
and sends waters on the fields;
11 he sets on high those who are lowly,
and those who mourn are lifted to safety.
12 He frustrates the devices of the crafty,
so that their hands achieve no success.
13 He takes the wise in their own craftiness;
and the schemes of the wily are brought to a quick end.
14 They meet with darkness in the daytime,

[a] Or *more than* [b] Meaning of Heb uncertain [c] Aquila Symmachus Syr Vg: Heb *snare*
[d] Or *birds*; Heb *sons of Resheph*

and grope at noonday as in the night.
15 But he saves the needy from the sword of
their mouth,
from the hand of the mighty.
16 So the poor have hope,
and injustice shuts its mouth.

17 "How happy is the one whom God reproves;
therefore do not despise the discipline of
the Almighty.[a]

Job 5:17

There is great danger, and perhaps a perversion of scripture, to state that everything happens for a divine reason, including bad things; or that God has subjected me to a tragedy to make me strong. Such a Nietzschean God is a masochist and demonic. Such a God does not exist.

— CKD

18 For he wounds, but he binds up;
he strikes, but his hands heal.
19 He will deliver you from six troubles;
in seven no harm shall touch you.
20 In famine he will redeem you from death,
and in war from the power of the sword.
21 You shall be hidden from the scourge of the
tongue,
and shall not fear destruction when it
comes.
22 At destruction and famine you shall laugh,
and shall not fear the wild animals of the
earth.
23 For you shall be in league with the stones of
the field,
and the wild animals shall be at peace with
you.
24 You shall know that your tent is safe,
you shall inspect your fold and miss
nothing.
25 You shall know that your descendants will be
many,
and your offspring like the grass of the
earth.
26 You shall come to your grave in ripe old age,
as a shock of grain comes up to the
threshing floor in its season.
27 See, we have searched this out; it is true.
Hear, and know it for yourself."

6 Then Job answered:
2 "O that my vexation were weighed,
and all my calamity laid in the balances!
3 For then it would be heavier than the sand of
the sea;
therefore my words have been rash.
4 For the arrows of the Almighty[a] are in me;
my spirit drinks their poison;
the terrors of God are arrayed against me.
5 Does the wild ass bray over its grass,
or the ox low over its fodder?
6 Can that which is tasteless be eaten without
salt,
or is there any flavor in the juice of
mallows?[b]
7 My appetite refuses to touch them;
they are like food that is loathsome to me.[b]

8 "O that I might have my request,
and that God would grant my desire;
9 that it would please God to crush me,
that he would let loose his hand and cut
me off!
10 This would be my consolation;
I would even exult[b] in unrelenting pain;
for I have not denied the words of the
Holy One.
11 What is my strength, that I should wait?
And what is my end, that I should be
patient?
12 Is my strength the strength of stones,
or is my flesh bronze?
13 In truth I have no help in me,
and any resource is driven from me.

14 "Those who withhold[c] kindness from a friend
forsake the fear of the Almighty.[a]

[a] Traditional rendering of Heb *Shaddai* [b] Meaning of Heb uncertain [c] Syr Vg Compare Tg: Meaning of Heb uncertain

15 My companions are treacherous like a
torrent-bed,
like freshets that pass away,
16 that run dark with ice,
turbid with melting snow.
17 In time of heat they disappear;
when it is hot, they vanish from their
place.
18 The caravans turn aside from their course;
they go up into the waste, and perish.
19 The caravans of Tema look,
the travelers of Sheba hope.
20 They are disappointed because they were
confident;
they come there and are confounded.
21 Such you have now become to me;[a]
you see my calamity, and are afraid.
22 Have I said, 'Make me a gift'?
Or, 'From your wealth offer a bribe for me'?
23 Or, 'Save me from an opponent's hand'?
Or, 'Ransom me from the hand of
oppressors'?

24 "Teach me, and I will be silent;
make me understand how I have gone
wrong.
25 How forceful are honest words!
But your reproof, what does it reprove?
26 Do you think that you can reprove words,
as if the speech of the desperate were
wind?
27 You would even cast lots over the orphan,
and bargain over your friend.

28 "But now, be pleased to look at me;
for I will not lie to your face.
29 Turn, I pray, let no wrong be done.
Turn now, my vindication is at stake.
30 Is there any wrong on my tongue?
Cannot my taste discern calamity?

7 "Do not human beings have a hard service
on earth,
and are not their days like the days of a
laborer?
2 Like a slave who longs for the shadow,
and like laborers who look for their wages,
3 so I am allotted months of emptiness,
and nights of misery are apportioned
to me.
4 When I lie down I say, 'When shall I rise?'
But the night is long,
and I am full of tossing until dawn.
5 My flesh is clothed with worms and dirt;
my skin hardens, then breaks out again.
6 My days are swifter than a weaver's shuttle,
and come to their end without hope.[b]

7 "Remember that my life is a breath;
my eye will never again see good.
8 The eye that beholds me will see me no
more;
while your eyes are upon me, I shall be
gone.
9 As the cloud fades and vanishes,
so those who go down to Sheol do not
come up;
10 they return no more to their houses,
nor do their places know them any more.

11 "Therefore I will not restrain my mouth;
I will speak in the anguish of my spirit;
I will complain in the bitterness of my
soul.
12 Am I the Sea, or the Dragon,
that you set a guard over me?
13 When I say, 'My bed will comfort me,
my couch will ease my complaint,'
14 then you scare me with dreams
and terrify me with visions,
15 so that I would choose strangling
and death rather than this body.
16 I loathe my life; I would not live forever.
Let me alone, for my days are a breath.
17 What are human beings, that you make so
much of them,
that you set your mind on them,
18 visit them every morning,
test them every moment?
19 Will you not look away from me for a while,

[a] Cn Compare Gk Syr: Meaning of Heb uncertain
[b] Or *as the thread runs out*

let me alone until I swallow my spittle?
20 If I sin, what do I do to you, you watcher of
humanity?
Why have you made me your target?
Why have I become a burden to you?
21 Why do you not pardon my transgression
and take away my iniquity?
For now I shall lie in the earth;
you will seek me, but I shall not be."

8 Then Bildad the Shuhite answered:
2 "How long will you say these things,
and the words of your mouth be a great
wind?
3 Does God pervert justice?
Or does the Almighty[a] pervert the right?
4 If your children sinned against him,
he delivered them into the power of their
transgression.
5 If you will seek God
and make supplication to the Almighty,[a]
6 if you are pure and upright,
surely then he will rouse himself for you
and restore to you your rightful place.
7 Though your beginning was small,
your latter days will be very great.

8 "For inquire now of bygone generations,
and consider what their ancestors have
found;
9 for we are but of yesterday, and we know
nothing,
for our days on earth are but a shadow.
10 Will they not teach you and tell you
and utter words out of their
understanding?

11 "Can papyrus grow where there is no marsh?
Can reeds flourish where there is no
water?
12 While yet in flower and not cut down,
they wither before any other plant.
13 Such are the paths of all who forget God;
the hope of the godless shall perish.
14 Their confidence is gossamer,
a spider's house their trust.
15 If one leans against its house, it will not
stand;
if one lays hold of it, it will not endure.
16 The wicked thrive[b] before the sun,
and their shoots spread over the garden.
17 Their roots twine around the stoneheap;
they live among the rocks.[c]
18 If they are destroyed from their place,
then it will deny them, saying, 'I have
never seen you.'
19 See, these are their happy ways,[d]
and out of the earth still others will spring.

20 "See, God will not reject a blameless person,
nor take the hand of evildoers.
21 He will yet fill your mouth with laughter,
and your lips with shouts of joy.
22 Those who hate you will be clothed with
shame,
and the tent of the wicked will be no
more."

9 Then Job answered:
2 "Indeed I know that this is so;
but how can a mortal be just before God?
3 If one wished to contend with him,
one could not answer him once in a
thousand.
4 He is wise in heart, and mighty in strength
—who has resisted him, and succeeded?—
5 he who removes mountains, and they do not
know it,
when he overturns them in his anger;
6 who shakes the earth out of its place,
and its pillars tremble;
7 who commands the sun, and it does not rise;
who seals up the stars;
8 who alone stretched out the heavens
and trampled the waves of the Sea;[e]
9 who made the Bear and Orion,
the Pleiades and the chambers of the
south;

[a] Traditional rendering of Heb *Shaddai* [b] Heb *He thrives* [c] Gk Vg: Meaning of Heb uncertain [d] Meaning of Heb uncertain [e] Or *trampled the back of the sea dragon*

10 who does great things beyond understanding,
and marvelous things without number.
11 Look, he passes by me, and I do not see him;
he moves on, but I do not perceive him.
12 He snatches away; who can stop him?
Who will say to him, 'What are you doing?'

13 "God will not turn back his anger;
the helpers of Rahab bowed beneath him.
14 How then can I answer him,
choosing my words with him?
15 Though I am innocent, I cannot answer him;
I must appeal for mercy to my accuser.[a]
16 If I summoned him and he answered me,
I do not believe that he would listen to my voice.
17 For he crushes me with a tempest,
and multiplies my wounds without cause;
18 he will not let me get my breath,
but fills me with bitterness.
19 If it is a contest of strength, he is the strong one!
If it is a matter of justice, who can summon him?[b]
20 Though I am innocent, my own mouth would condemn me;
though I am blameless, he would prove me perverse.
21 I am blameless; I do not know myself;
I loathe my life.
22 It is all one; therefore I say,
he destroys both the blameless and the wicked.
23 When disaster brings sudden death,
he mocks at the calamity[c] of the innocent.
24 The earth is given into the hand of the wicked;
he covers the eyes of its judges—
if it is not he, who then is it?

25 "My days are swifter than a runner;
they flee away, they see no good.
26 They go by like skiffs of reed,
like an eagle swooping on the prey.
27 If I say, 'I will forget my complaint;
I will put off my sad countenance and be of good cheer,'
28 I become afraid of all my suffering,
for I know you will not hold me innocent.
29 I shall be condemned;
why then do I labor in vain?
30 If I wash myself with soap
and cleanse my hands with lye,
31 yet you will plunge me into filth,
and my own clothes will abhor me.
32 For he is not a mortal, as I am, that I might answer him,
that we should come to trial together.
33 There is no umpire[d] between us,
who might lay his hand on us both.
34 If he would take his rod away from me,
and not let dread of him terrify me,
35 then I would speak without fear of him,
for I know I am not what I am thought to be.[e]

10 "I loathe my life;
I will give free utterance to my complaint;
I will speak in the bitterness of my soul.
2 I will say to God, Do not condemn me;
let me know why you contend against me.
3 Does it seem good to you to oppress,
to despise the work of your hands
and favor the schemes of the wicked?
4 Do you have eyes of flesh?
Do you see as humans see?
5 Are your days like the days of mortals,
or your years like human years,
6 that you seek out my iniquity
and search for my sin,
7 although you know that I am not guilty,
and there is no one to deliver out of your hand?
8 Your hands fashioned and made me;
and now you turn and destroy me.[f]
9 Remember that you fashioned me like clay;

[a] Or *for my right* [b] Compare Gk: Heb *me* [c] Meaning of Heb uncertain [d] Another reading is *Would that there were an umpire* [e] Cn: Heb *for I am not so in myself* [f] Cn Compare Gk Syr: Heb *made me together all around, and you destroy me*

and will you turn me to dust again?
10 Did you not pour me out like milk
and curdle me like cheese?
11 You clothed me with skin and flesh,
and knit me together with bones and sinews.
12 You have granted me life and steadfast love,
and your care has preserved my spirit.
13 Yet these things you hid in your heart;
I know that this was your purpose.
14 If I sin, you watch me,
and do not acquit me of my iniquity.
15 If I am wicked, woe to me!
If I am righteous, I cannot lift up my head,
for I am filled with disgrace
and look upon my affliction.
16 Bold as a lion you hunt me;
you repeat your exploits against me.
17 You renew your witnesses against me,
and increase your vexation toward me;
you bring fresh troops against me.[a]

18 "Why did you bring me forth from the womb?
Would that I had died before any eye had seen me,
19 and were as though I had not been,
carried from the womb to the grave.
20 Are not the days of my life few?[b]
Let me alone, that I may find a little comfort[c]
21 before I go, never to return,
to the land of gloom and deep darkness,
22 the land of gloom[d] and chaos,
where light is like darkness."

11 Then Zophar the Naamathite answered:
2 "Should a multitude of words go unanswered,
and should one full of talk be vindicated?
3 Should your babble put others to silence,
and when you mock, shall no one shame you?
4 For you say, 'My conduct[e] is pure,
and I am clean in God's[f] sight.'
5 But O that God would speak,
and open his lips to you,
6 and that he would tell you the secrets of wisdom!
For wisdom is many-sided.[g]
Know then that God exacts of you less than your guilt deserves.

7 "Can you find out the deep things of God?
Can you find out the limit of the Almighty?[h]
8 It is higher than heaven[i]—what can you do?
Deeper than Sheol—what can you know?
9 Its measure is longer than the earth,
and broader than the sea.
10 If he passes through, and imprisons,
and assembles for judgment, who can hinder him?
11 For he knows those who are worthless;
when he sees iniquity, will he not consider it?
12 But a stupid person will get understanding,
when a wild ass is born human.[g]

13 "If you direct your heart rightly,
you will stretch out your hands toward him.
14 If iniquity is in your hand, put it far away,
and do not let wickedness reside in your tents.
15 Surely then you will lift up your face without blemish;
you will be secure, and will not fear.
16 You will forget your misery;
you will remember it as waters that have passed away.
17 And your life will be brighter than the noonday;
its darkness will be like the morning.
18 And you will have confidence, because there is hope;

[a] Cn Compare Gk: Heb *toward me; changes and a troop are with me* [b] Cn Compare Gk Syr: Heb *Are not my days few? Let him cease!* [c] Heb *that I may brighten up a little* [d] Heb *gloom as darkness, deep darkness* [e] Gk: Heb *teaching* [f] Heb *your* [g] Meaning of Heb uncertain [h] Traditional rendering of Heb *Shaddai* [i] Heb *The heights of heaven*

you will be protected[a] and take your rest
in safety.
19 You will lie down, and no one will make you
afraid;
many will entreat your favor.
20 But the eyes of the wicked will fail;
all way of escape will be lost to them,
and their hope is to breathe their last."

12 Then Job answered:
2 "No doubt you are the people,
and wisdom will die with you.
3 But I have understanding as well as you;
I am not inferior to you.
Who does not know such things as these?
4 I am a laughingstock to my friends;
I, who called upon God and he
answered me,
a just and blameless man, I am a
laughingstock.
5 Those at ease have contempt for misfortune,[b]
but it is ready for those whose feet are
unstable.
6 The tents of robbers are at peace,
and those who provoke God are secure,
who bring their god in their hands.[c]

7 "But ask the animals, and they will teach you;
the birds of the air, and they will tell you;
8 ask the plants of the earth,[d] and they will
teach you;
and the fish of the sea will declare to you.
9 Who among all these does not know
that the hand of the LORD has done this?
10 In his hand is the life of every living thing
and the breath of every human being.
11 Does not the ear test words
as the palate tastes food?
12 Is wisdom with the aged,
and understanding in length of days?

13 "With God[e] are wisdom and strength;
he has counsel and understanding.
14 If he tears down, no one can rebuild;
if he shuts someone in, no one can
open up.
15 If he withholds the waters, they dry up;
if he sends them out, they overwhelm the
land.
16 With him are strength and wisdom;
the deceived and the deceiver are his.
17 He leads counselors away stripped,
and makes fools of judges.
18 He looses the sash of kings,
and binds a waistcloth on their loins.
19 He leads priests away stripped,
and overthrows the mighty.
20 He deprives of speech those who are trusted,
and takes away the discernment of the
elders.
21 He pours contempt on princes,
and looses the belt of the strong.
22 He uncovers the deeps out of darkness,
and brings deep darkness to light.
23 He makes nations great, then destroys them;
he enlarges nations, then leads them away.
24 He strips understanding from the leaders[f] of
the earth,
and makes them wander in a pathless
waste.
25 They grope in the dark without light;
he makes them stagger like a drunkard.

13 "Look, my eye has seen all this,
my ear has heard and understood it.
2 What you know, I also know;
I am not inferior to you.
3 But I would speak to the Almighty,[g]
and I desire to argue my case with God.
4 As for you, you whitewash with lies;
all of you are worthless physicians.
5 If you would only keep silent,
that would be your wisdom!
6 Hear now my reasoning,
and listen to the pleadings of my lips.
7 Will you speak falsely for God,
and speak deceitfully for him?
8 Will you show partiality toward him,

[a] Or *you will look around* [b] Meaning of Heb uncertain [c] Or *whom God brought forth by his hand*; Meaning of Heb uncertain [d] Or *speak to the earth* [e] Heb *him* [f] Heb adds *of the people* [g] Traditional rendering of Heb *Shaddai*

will you plead the case for God?
9 Will it be well with you when he searches you out?
Or can you deceive him, as one person deceives another?
10 He will surely rebuke you
if in secret you show partiality.
11 Will not his majesty terrify you,
and the dread of him fall upon you?
12 Your maxims are proverbs of ashes,
your defenses are defenses of clay.

13 "Let me have silence, and I will speak,
and let come on me what may.
14 I will take my flesh in my teeth,
and put my life in my hand.[a]
15 See, he will kill me; I have no hope;[b]
but I will defend my ways to his face.
16 This will be my salvation,
that the godless shall not come before him.
17 Listen carefully to my words,
and let my declaration be in your ears.
18 I have indeed prepared my case;
I know that I shall be vindicated.
19 Who is there that will contend with me?
For then I would be silent and die.
20 Only grant two things to me,
then I will not hide myself from your face:
21 withdraw your hand far from me,
and do not let dread of you terrify me.
22 Then call, and I will answer;
or let me speak, and you reply to me.
23 How many are my iniquities and my sins?
Make me know my transgression and my sin.
24 Why do you hide your face,
and count me as your enemy?
25 Will you frighten a windblown leaf
and pursue dry chaff?
26 For you write bitter things against me,
and make me reap[c] the iniquities of my youth.
27 You put my feet in the stocks,
and watch all my paths;
you set a bound to the soles of my feet.
28 One wastes away like a rotten thing,
like a garment that is moth-eaten.

14 "A mortal, born of woman, few of days
and full of trouble,
2 comes up like a flower and withers,
flees like a shadow and does not last.
3 Do you fix your eyes on such a one?
Do you bring me into judgment with you?
4 Who can bring a clean thing out of an unclean?
No one can.
5 Since their days are determined,
and the number of their months is known to you,
and you have appointed the bounds that they cannot pass,
6 look away from them, and desist,[d]
that they may enjoy, like laborers, their days.

7 "For there is hope for a tree,
if it is cut down, that it will sprout again,
and that its shoots will not cease.
8 Though its root grows old in the earth,
and its stump dies in the ground,
9 yet at the scent of water it will bud
and put forth branches like a young plant.
10 But mortals die, and are laid low;
humans expire, and where are they?
11 As waters fail from a lake,
and a river wastes away and dries up,
12 so mortals lie down and do not rise again;
until the heavens are no more, they will not awake
or be roused out of their sleep.
13 O that you would hide me in Sheol,
that you would conceal me until your wrath is past,
that you would appoint me a set time, and remember me!
14 If mortals die, will they live again?
All the days of my service I would wait

[a] Gk: Heb *Why should I take . . . in my hand?* [b] Or *Though he kill me, yet I will trust in him* [c] Heb *inherit*
[d] Cn: Heb *that they may desist*

until my release should come.
15 You would call, and I would answer you;
you would long for the work of your
hands.
16 For then you would not[a] number my steps,
you would not keep watch over my sin;
17 my transgression would be sealed up in a bag,
and you would cover over my iniquity.

18 "But the mountain falls and crumbles away,
and the rock is removed from its place;
19 the waters wear away the stones;
the torrents wash away the soil of the
earth;
so you destroy the hope of mortals.
20 You prevail forever against them, and they
pass away;
you change their countenance, and send
them away.
21 Their children come to honor, and they do
not know it;
they are brought low, and it goes
unnoticed.
22 They feel only the pain of their own bodies,
and mourn only for themselves."

15 Then Eliphaz the Temanite answered:
2 "Should the wise answer with windy
knowledge,
and fill themselves with the east wind?
3 Should they argue in unprofitable talk,
or in words with which they can do no
good?
4 But you are doing away with the fear of God,
and hindering meditation before God.
5 For your iniquity teaches your mouth,
and you choose the tongue of the crafty.
6 Your own mouth condemns you, and not I;
your own lips testify against you.

7 "Are you the firstborn of the human race?
Were you brought forth before the hills?
8 Have you listened in the council of God?
And do you limit wisdom to yourself?
9 What do you know that we do not know?
What do you understand that is not clear
to us?
10 The gray-haired and the aged are on our side,
those older than your father.
11 Are the consolations of God too small for
you,
or the word that deals gently with you?
12 Why does your heart carry you away,
and why do your eyes flash,[b]
13 so that you turn your spirit against God,
and let such words go out of your mouth?
14 What are mortals, that they can be clean?
Or those born of woman, that they can be
righteous?
15 God puts no trust even in his holy ones,
and the heavens are not clean in his sight;
16 how much less one who is abominable and
corrupt,
one who drinks iniquity like water!

17 "I will show you; listen to me;
what I have seen I will declare—
18 what sages have told,
and their ancestors have not hidden,
19 to whom alone the land was given,
and no stranger passed among them.
20 The wicked writhe in pain all their days,
through all the years that are laid up for
the ruthless.
21 Terrifying sounds are in their ears;
in prosperity the destroyer will come upon
them.
22 They despair of returning from darkness,
and they are destined for the sword.
23 They wander abroad for bread, saying,
'Where is it?'
They know that a day of darkness is ready
at hand;
24 distress and anguish terrify them;
they prevail against them, like a king
prepared for battle.
25 Because they stretched out their hands
against God,
and bid defiance to the Almighty,[c]
26 running stubbornly against him

[a] Syr: Heb lacks *not* [b] Meaning of Heb uncertain [c] Traditional rendering of Heb *Shaddai*

with a thick-bossed shield;
27 because they have covered their faces with their fat,
and gathered fat upon their loins,
28 they will live in desolate cities,
in houses that no one should inhabit,
houses destined to become heaps of ruins;
29 they will not be rich, and their wealth will not endure,
nor will they strike root in the earth;[a]
30 they will not escape from darkness;
the flame will dry up their shoots,
and their blossom[b] will be swept away[c] by the wind.
31 Let them not trust in emptiness, deceiving themselves;
for emptiness will be their recompense.
32 It will be paid in full before their time,
and their branch will not be green.
33 They will shake off their unripe grape, like the vine,
and cast off their blossoms, like the olive tree.
34 For the company of the godless is barren,
and fire consumes the tents of bribery.
35 They conceive mischief and bring forth evil
and their heart prepares deceit."

16 Then Job answered:
2 "I have heard many such things;
miserable comforters are you all.
3 Have windy words no limit?
Or what provokes you that you keep on talking?
4 I also could talk as you do,
if you were in my place;
I could join words together against you,
and shake my head at you.
5 I could encourage you with my mouth,
and the solace of my lips would assuage your pain.

6 "If I speak, my pain is not assuaged,
and if I forbear, how much of it leaves me?
7 Surely now God has worn me out;
he has[d] made desolate all my company.
8 And he has[d] shriveled me up,
which is a witness against me;
my leanness has risen up against me,
and it testifies to my face.
9 He has torn me in his wrath, and hated me;
he has gnashed his teeth at me;
my adversary sharpens his eyes against me.
10 They have gaped at me with their mouths;
they have struck me insolently on the cheek;
they mass themselves together against me.
11 God gives me up to the ungodly,
and casts me into the hands of the wicked.
12 I was at ease, and he broke me in two;
he seized me by the neck and dashed me to pieces;
he set me up as his target;
13 his archers surround me.
He slashes open my kidneys, and shows no mercy;
he pours out my gall on the ground.
14 He bursts upon me again and again;
he rushes at me like a warrior.
15 I have sewed sackcloth upon my skin,
and have laid my strength in the dust.
16 My face is red with weeping,
and deep darkness is on my eyelids,
17 though there is no violence in my hands,
and my prayer is pure.

18 "O earth, do not cover my blood;
let my outcry find no resting place.
19 Even now, in fact, my witness is in heaven,
and he that vouches for me is on high.
20 My friends scorn me;
my eye pours out tears to God,
21 that he would maintain the right of a mortal with God,
as[e] one does for a neighbor.
22 For when a few years have come,
I shall go the way from which I shall not return.

17 My spirit is broken, my days are extinct,
the grave is ready for me.

[a] Vg: Meaning of Heb uncertain [b] Gk: Heb *mouth* [c] Cn: Heb *will depart* [d] Heb *you have* [e] Syr Vg Tg: Heb *and*

2 Surely there are mockers around me,
and my eye dwells on their provocation.

3 "Lay down a pledge for me with yourself;
who is there that will give surety for me?
4 Since you have closed their minds to
understanding,
therefore you will not let them triumph.
5 Those who denounce friends for reward—
the eyes of their children will fail.

6 "He has made me a byword of the peoples,
and I am one before whom people spit.
7 My eye has grown dim from grief,
and all my members are like a shadow.
8 The upright are appalled at this,
and the innocent stir themselves up
against the godless.
9 Yet the righteous hold to their way,
and they that have clean hands grow
stronger and stronger.
10 But you, come back now, all of you,
and I shall not find a sensible person
among you.
11 My days are past, my plans are broken off,
the desires of my heart.
12 They make night into day;
'The light,' they say, 'is near to the
darkness.'[a]
13 If I look for Sheol as my house,
if I spread my couch in darkness,
14 if I say to the Pit, 'You are my father,'
and to the worm, 'My mother,' or 'My
sister,'
15 where then is my hope?
Who will see my hope?
16 Will it go down to the bars of Sheol?
Shall we descend together into the dust?"

18 Then Bildad the Shuhite answered:
2 "How long will you hunt for words?
Consider, and then we shall speak.
3 Why are we counted as cattle?
Why are we stupid in your sight?
4 You who tear yourself in your anger—
shall the earth be forsaken because of you,
or the rock be removed out of its place?

5 "Surely the light of the wicked is put out,
and the flame of their fire does not shine.
6 The light is dark in their tent,
and the lamp above them is put out.
7 Their strong steps are shortened,
and their own schemes throw them down.
8 For they are thrust into a net by their own
feet,
and they walk into a pitfall.
9 A trap seizes them by the heel;
a snare lays hold of them.
10 A rope is hid for them in the ground,
a trap for them in the path.
11 Terrors frighten them on every side,
and chase them at their heels.
12 Their strength is consumed by hunger,[b]
and calamity is ready for their stumbling.
13 By disease their skin is consumed,[c]
the firstborn of Death consumes their
limbs.
14 They are torn from the tent in which they
trusted,
and are brought to the king of terrors.
15 In their tents nothing remains;
sulfur is scattered upon their habitations.
16 Their roots dry up beneath,
and their branches wither above.
17 Their memory perishes from the earth,
and they have no name in the street.
18 They are thrust from light into darkness,
and driven out of the world.
19 They have no offspring or descendant among
their people,
and no survivor where they used to live.
20 They of the west are appalled at their fate,
and horror seizes those of the east.
21 Surely such are the dwellings of the ungodly,
such is the place of those who do not
know God."

19 Then Job answered:
2 "How long will you torment me,

[a] Meaning of Heb uncertain [b] Or *Disaster is hungry for them* [c] Cn: Heb *It consumes the limbs of his skin*

and break me in pieces with words?
3 These ten times you have cast reproach
upon me;
are you not ashamed to wrong me?
4 And even if it is true that I have erred,
my error remains with me.
5 If indeed you magnify yourselves against me,
and make my humiliation an argument
against me,
6 know then that God has put me in the wrong,
and closed his net around me.
7 Even when I cry out, 'Violence!' I am not
answered;
I call aloud, but there is no justice.
8 He has walled up my way so that I cannot
pass,
and he has set darkness upon my paths.
9 He has stripped my glory from me,
and taken the crown from my head.
10 He breaks me down on every side, and I am
gone,
he has uprooted my hope like a tree.
11 He has kindled his wrath against me,
and counts me as his adversary.
12 His troops come on together;
they have thrown up siegeworks[a]
against me,
and encamp around my tent.

13 "He has put my family far from me,
and my acquaintances are wholly
estranged from me.
14 My relatives and my close friends have
failed me;
15 the guests in my house have forgotten me;
my serving girls count me as a stranger;
I have become an alien in their eyes.
16 I call to my servant, but he gives me no
answer;
I must myself plead with him.
17 My breath is repulsive to my wife;
I am loathsome to my own family.
18 Even young children despise me;
when I rise, they talk against me.
19 All my intimate friends abhor me,
and those whom I loved have turned
against me.
20 My bones cling to my skin and to my flesh,
and I have escaped by the skin of my
teeth.
21 Have pity on me, have pity on me, O you my
friends,
for the hand of God has touched me!
22 Why do you, like God, pursue me,
never satisfied with my flesh?

23 "O that my words were written down!
O that they were inscribed in a book!
24 O that with an iron pen and with lead
they were engraved on a rock forever!
25 For I know that my Redeemer[b] lives,
and that at the last he[c] will stand upon the
earth;[d]
26 and after my skin has been thus destroyed,
then in[e] my flesh I shall see God,[f]
27 whom I shall see on my side,[g]
and my eyes shall behold, and not another.
My heart faints within me!
28 If you say, 'How we will persecute him!'
and, 'The root of the matter is found in
him';
29 be afraid of the sword,
for wrath brings the punishment of the
sword,
so that you may know there is a judgment."

20 Then Zophar the Naamathite answered:
2 "Pay attention! My thoughts urge me
to answer,
because of the agitation within me.
3 I hear censure that insults me,
and a spirit beyond my understanding
answers me.
4 Do you not know this from of old,
ever since mortals were placed on earth,
5 that the exulting of the wicked is short,
and the joy of the godless is but for a
moment?

[a] Cn: Heb *their way* [b] Or *Vindicator* [c] Or *that he the Last* [d] Heb *dust* [e] Or *without* [f] Meaning of Heb of this verse uncertain [g] Or *for myself*

6 Even though they mount up high as the heavens,
and their head reaches to the clouds,
7 they will perish forever like their own dung;
those who have seen them will say, 'Where are they?'
8 They will fly away like a dream, and not be found;
they will be chased away like a vision of the night.
9 The eye that saw them will see them no more,
nor will their place behold them any longer.
10 Their children will seek the favor of the poor,
and their hands will give back their wealth.
11 Their bodies, once full of youth,
will lie down in the dust with them.

12 "Though wickedness is sweet in their mouth,
though they hide it under their tongues,
13 though they are loath to let it go,
and hold it in their mouths,
14 yet their food is turned in their stomachs;
it is the venom of asps within them.
15 They swallow down riches and vomit them up again;
God casts them out of their bellies.
16 They will suck the poison of asps;
the tongue of a viper will kill them.
17 They will not look on the rivers,
the streams flowing with honey and curds.
18 They will give back the fruit of their toil,
and will not swallow it down;
from the profit of their trading
they will get no enjoyment.
19 For they have crushed and abandoned the poor,
they have seized a house that they did not build.

20 "They knew no quiet in their bellies;
in their greed they let nothing escape.
21 There was nothing left after they had eaten;
therefore their prosperity will not endure.
22 In full sufficiency they will be in distress;
all the force of misery will come upon them.
23 To fill their belly to the full
God[a] will send his fierce anger into them,
and rain it upon them as their food.[b]
24 They will flee from an iron weapon;
a bronze arrow will strike them through.
25 It is drawn forth and comes out of their body,
and the glittering point comes out of their gall;
terrors come upon them.
26 Utter darkness is laid up for their treasures;
a fire fanned by no one will devour them;
what is left in their tent will be consumed.
27 The heavens will reveal their iniquity,
and the earth will rise up against them.
28 The possessions of their house will be carried away,
dragged off in the day of God's[c] wrath.
29 This is the portion of the wicked from God,
the heritage decreed for them by God."

21 Then Job answered:
2 "Listen carefully to my words,
and let this be your consolation.
3 Bear with me, and I will speak;
then after I have spoken, mock on.
4 As for me, is my complaint addressed to mortals?
Why should I not be impatient?
5 Look at me, and be appalled,
and lay your hand upon your mouth.
6 When I think of it I am dismayed,
and shuddering seizes my flesh.
7 Why do the wicked live on,
reach old age, and grow mighty in power?
8 Their children are established in their presence,
and their offspring before their eyes.
9 Their houses are safe from fear,
and no rod of God is upon them.
10 Their bull breeds without fail;
their cow calves and never miscarries.
11 They send out their little ones like a flock,
and their children dance around.

[a] Heb *he* [b] Cn: Meaning of Heb uncertain [c] Heb *his*

12 They sing to the tambourine and the lyre,
and rejoice to the sound of the pipe.
13 They spend their days in prosperity,
and in peace they go down to Sheol.
14 They say to God, 'Leave us alone!
We do not desire to know your ways.
15 What is the Almighty,[a] that we should serve him?
And what profit do we get if we pray to him?'
16 Is not their prosperity indeed their own achievement?[b]
The plans of the wicked are repugnant to me.

17 "How often is the lamp of the wicked put out?
How often does calamity come upon them?
How often does God[c] distribute pains in his anger?
18 How often are they like straw before the wind,
and like chaff that the storm carries away?
19 You say, 'God stores up their iniquity for their children.'
Let it be paid back to them, so that they may know it.
20 Let their own eyes see their destruction,
and let them drink of the wrath of the Almighty.[a]
21 For what do they care for their household after them,
when the number of their months is cut off?
22 Will any teach God knowledge,
seeing that he judges those that are on high?
23 One dies in full prosperity,
being wholly at ease and secure,
24 his loins full of milk
and the marrow of his bones moist.
25 Another dies in bitterness of soul,
never having tasted of good.
26 They lie down alike in the dust,
and the worms cover them.

27 "Oh, I know your thoughts,
and your schemes to wrong me.
28 For you say, 'Where is the house of the prince?
Where is the tent in which the wicked lived?'
29 Have you not asked those who travel the roads,
and do you not accept their testimony,
30 that the wicked are spared in the day of calamity,
and are rescued in the day of wrath?
31 Who declares their way to their face,
and who repays them for what they have done?
32 When they are carried to the grave,
a watch is kept over their tomb.
33 The clods of the valley are sweet to them;
everyone will follow after,
and those who went before are innumerable.
34 How then will you comfort me with empty nothings?
There is nothing left of your answers but falsehood."

22 Then Eliphaz the Temanite answered:
2 "Can a mortal be of use to God?
Can even the wisest be of service to him?
3 Is it any pleasure to the Almighty[a] if you are righteous,
or is it gain to him if you make your ways blameless?
4 Is it for your piety that he reproves you,
and enters into judgment with you?
5 Is not your wickedness great?
There is no end to your iniquities.
6 For you have exacted pledges from your family for no reason,
and stripped the naked of their clothing.
7 You have given no water to the weary to drink,
and you have withheld bread from the hungry.
8 The powerful possess the land,

[a] Traditional rendering of Heb *Shaddai* [b] Heb *in their hand* [c] Heb *he*

and the favored live in it.
9 You have sent widows away empty-handed,
and the arms of the orphans you have crushed.[a]
10 Therefore snares are around you,
and sudden terror overwhelms you,
11 or darkness so that you cannot see;
a flood of water covers you.

12 "Is not God high in the heavens?
See the highest stars, how lofty they are!
13 Therefore you say, 'What does God know?
Can he judge through the deep darkness?
14 Thick clouds enwrap him, so that he does not see,
and he walks on the dome of heaven.'
15 Will you keep to the old way
that the wicked have trod?
16 They were snatched away before their time;
their foundation was washed away by a flood.
17 They said to God, 'Leave us alone,'
and 'What can the Almighty[b] do to us?'[c]
18 Yet he filled their houses with good things—
but the plans of the wicked are repugnant to me.
19 The righteous see it and are glad;
the innocent laugh them to scorn,
20 saying, 'Surely our adversaries are cut off,
and what they left, the fire has consumed.'

21 "Agree with God,[d] and be at peace;
in this way good will come to you.
22 Receive instruction from his mouth,
and lay up his words in your heart.
23 If you return to the Almighty,[b] you will be restored,
if you remove unrighteousness from your tents,
24 if you treat gold like dust,
and gold of Ophir like the stones of the torrent-bed,
25 and if the Almighty[b] is your gold
and your precious silver,
26 then you will delight yourself in the Almighty,[b]
and lift up your face to God.
27 You will pray to him, and he will hear you,
and you will pay your vows.
28 You will decide on a matter, and it will be established for you,
and light will shine on your ways.
29 When others are humiliated, you say it is pride;
for he saves the humble.
30 He will deliver even those who are guilty;
they will escape because of the cleanness of your hands."[e]

23 Then Job answered:
2 "Today also my complaint is bitter;[f]
his[g] hand is heavy despite my groaning.
3 Oh, that I knew where I might find him,
that I might come even to his dwelling!
4 I would lay my case before him,
and fill my mouth with arguments.
5 I would learn what he would answer me,
and understand what he would say to me.
6 Would he contend with me in the greatness of his power?
No; but he would give heed to me.
7 There an upright person could reason with him,
and I should be acquitted forever by my judge.

8 "If I go forward, he is not there;
or backward, I cannot perceive him;
9 on the left he hides, and I cannot behold him;
I turn[h] to the right, but I cannot see him.
10 But he knows the way that I take;
when he has tested me, I shall come out like gold.
11 My foot has held fast to his steps;
I have kept his way and have not turned aside.
12 I have not departed from the commandment of his lips;

[a] Gk Syr Tg Vg: Heb *were crushed* [b] Traditional rendering of Heb *Shaddai* [c] Gk Syr: Heb *them* [d] Heb *him* [e] Meaning of Heb uncertain [f] Syr Vg Tg: Heb *rebellious* [g] Gk Syr: Heb *my* [h] Syr Vg: Heb *he turns*

I have treasured in[a] my bosom the words
of his mouth.
13 But he stands alone and who can dissuade
him?
What he desires, that he does.
14 For he will complete what he appoints
for me;
and many such things are in his mind.
15 Therefore I am terrified at his presence;
when I consider, I am in dread of him.
16 God has made my heart faint;
the Almighty[b] has terrified me;
17 If only I could vanish in darkness,
and thick darkness would cover my face![c]

24 "Why are times not kept by the
Almighty,[b]
and why do those who know him never see
his days?
2 The wicked[d] remove landmarks;
they seize flocks and pasture them.
3 They drive away the donkey of the orphan;
they take the widow's ox for a pledge.
4 They thrust the needy off the road;
the poor of the earth all hide themselves.
5 Like wild asses in the desert
they go out to their toil,
scavenging in the wasteland
food for their young.
6 They reap in a field not their own
and they glean in the vineyard of the
wicked.
7 They lie all night naked, without clothing,
and have no covering in the cold.
8 They are wet with the rain of the mountains,
and cling to the rock for want of shelter.

9 "There are those who snatch the orphan child
from the breast,
and take as a pledge the infant of the poor.
10 They go about naked, without clothing;
though hungry, they carry the sheaves;
11 between their terraces[e] they press out oil;
they tread the wine presses, but suffer
thirst.
12 From the city the dying groan,
and the throat of the wounded cries for
help;
yet God pays no attention to their prayer.

13 "There are those who rebel against the light,
who are not acquainted with its ways,

[a] Gk Vg: Heb *from* [b] Traditional rendering of Heb *Shaddai* [c] Or *But I am not destroyed by the darkness; he has concealed the thick darkness from me* [d] Gk: Heb *they* [e] Meaning of Heb uncertain

Job 24:1-12

What is justice? What is injustice? It may help to ask the second question first, because for those who are homeless or without adequate food or… other basic necessities of life the situation is not merely unfortunate. It is unfair; it is unjust. And those of us who benefit from social injustice… are naturally less capable of understanding its real character than those who suffer from it.

It is important, therefore, that we listen to the voices of those who are being oppressed—among them the blacks of South Africa, children living in poverty in the United States, the landless of Latin America, and poor women around the world—and especially that we give ear to their experience of God,… [for] the faith journey of the oppressed can differ markedly from that of the oppressor.

Justice begins in response to injustice. Justice begins with the correction of injustice.… [We should look] at justice, not as rights to be asserted one against the other but as the right relationship of human beings with each other and with the Lord of creation.[29]

— Barbara Jurgensen

and do not stay in its paths.
14 The murderer rises at dusk
to kill the poor and needy,
and in the night is like a thief.
15 The eye of the adulterer also waits for the twilight,
saying, 'No eye will see me';
and he disguises his face.
16 In the dark they dig through houses;
by day they shut themselves up;
they do not know the light.
17 For deep darkness is morning to all of them;
for they are friends with the terrors of deep darkness.

18 "Swift are they on the face of the waters;
their portion in the land is cursed;
no treader turns toward their vineyards.
19 Drought and heat snatch away the snow waters;
so does Sheol those who have sinned.
20 The womb forgets them;
the worm finds them sweet;
they are no longer remembered;
so wickedness is broken like a tree.

21 "They harm[a] the childless woman,
and do no good to the widow.
22 Yet God[b] prolongs the life of the mighty by his power;
they rise up when they despair of life.
23 He gives them security, and they are supported;
his eyes are upon their ways.
24 They are exalted a little while, and then are gone;
they wither and fade like the mallow;[c]
they are cut off like the heads of grain.
25 If it is not so, who will prove me a liar,
and show that there is nothing in what I say?"

25 Then Bildad the Shuhite answered:
2 "Dominion and fear are with God;[d]
he makes peace in his high heaven.
3 Is there any number to his armies?
Upon whom does his light not arise?
4 How then can a mortal be righteous before God?
How can one born of woman be pure?
5 If even the moon is not bright
and the stars are not pure in his sight,
6 how much less a mortal, who is a maggot,
and a human being, who is a worm!"

26 Then Job answered:
2 "How you have helped one who has no power!
How you have assisted the arm that has no strength!
3 How you have counseled one who has no wisdom,
and given much good advice!
4 With whose help have you uttered words,
and whose spirit has come forth from you?
5 The shades below tremble,
the waters and their inhabitants.
6 Sheol is naked before God,
and Abaddon has no covering.
7 He stretches out Zaphon[e] over the void,
and hangs the earth upon nothing.
8 He binds up the waters in his thick clouds,
and the cloud is not torn open by them.
9 He covers the face of the full moon,
and spreads over it his cloud.
10 He has described a circle on the face of the waters,
at the boundary between light and darkness.
11 The pillars of heaven tremble,
and are astounded at his rebuke.
12 By his power he stilled the Sea;
by his understanding he struck down Rahab.
13 By his wind the heavens were made fair;
his hand pierced the fleeing serpent.
14 These are indeed but the outskirts of his ways;
and how small a whisper do we hear of him!

[a] Gk Tg: Heb *feed on or associate with* [b] Heb *he* [c] Gk: Heb *like all others* [d] Heb *him* [e] Or *the North*

But the thunder of his power who can
understand?"

27 Job again took up his discourse and said:
2 "As God lives, who has taken away my
right,
and the Almighty,[a] who has made my soul
bitter,
3 as long as my breath is in me
and the spirit of God is in my nostrils,
4 my lips will not speak falsehood,
and my tongue will not utter deceit.
5 Far be it from me to say that you are right;
until I die I will not put away my integrity
from me.
6 I hold fast my righteousness, and will not let
it go;
my heart does not reproach me for any of
my days.

7 "May my enemy be like the wicked,
and may my opponent be like the
unrighteous.
8 For what is the hope of the godless when
God cuts them off,
when God takes away their lives?
9 Will God hear their cry
when trouble comes upon them?
10 Will they take delight in the Almighty?[a]
Will they call upon God at all times?
11 I will teach you concerning the hand of God;
that which is with the Almighty[a] I will not
conceal.
12 All of you have seen it yourselves;
why then have you become altogether
vain?

13 "This is the portion of the wicked with God,
and the heritage that oppressors receive
from the Almighty:[a]
14 If their children are multiplied, it is for the
sword;
and their offspring have not enough to eat.
15 Those who survive them the pestilence
buries,
and their widows make no lamentation.
16 Though they heap up silver like dust,
and pile up clothing like clay—
17 they may pile it up, but the just will wear it,
and the innocent will divide the silver.
18 They build their houses like nests,
like booths made by sentinels of the
vineyard.
19 They go to bed with wealth, but will do so no
more;
they open their eyes, and it is gone.
20 Terrors overtake them like a flood;
in the night a whirlwind carries them off.
21 The east wind lifts them up and they are
gone;
it sweeps them out of their place.
22 It[b] hurls at them without pity;
they flee from its[c] power in headlong flight.
23 It[b] claps its[c] hands at them,
and hisses at them from its[c] place.

28 "Surely there is a mine for silver,
and a place for gold to be refined.
2 Iron is taken out of the earth,
and copper is smelted from ore.
3 Miners put[d] an end to darkness,
and search out to the farthest bound
the ore in gloom and deep darkness.
4 They open shafts in a valley away from human
habitation;
they are forgotten by travelers,
they sway suspended, remote from people.
5 As for the earth, out of it comes bread;
but underneath it is turned up as by fire.
6 Its stones are the place of sapphires,[e]
and its dust contains gold.

7 "That path no bird of prey knows,
and the falcon's eye has not seen it.
8 The proud wild animals have not trodden it;
the lion has not passed over it.

9 "They put their hand to the flinty rock,
and overturn mountains by the roots.
10 They cut out channels in the rocks,

[a] Traditional rendering of Heb *Shaddai* [b] Or *He* (that is God) [c] Or *his* [d] Heb *He puts* [e] Or *lapis lazuli*

and their eyes see every precious thing.
11 The sources of the rivers they probe;[a]
hidden things they bring to light.

12 "But where shall wisdom be found?
And where is the place of understanding?
13 Mortals do not know the way to it,[b]
and it is not found in the land of the living.
14 The deep says, 'It is not in me,'
and the sea says, 'It is not with me.'
15 It cannot be gotten for gold,
and silver cannot be weighed out as its price.
16 It cannot be valued in the gold of Ophir,
in precious onyx or sapphire.[c]
17 Gold and glass cannot equal it,
nor can it be exchanged for jewels of fine gold.
18 No mention shall be made of coral or of crystal;
the price of wisdom is above pearls.
19 The chrysolite of Ethiopia[d] cannot compare with it,
nor can it be valued in pure gold.

20 "Where then does wisdom come from?
And where is the place of understanding?
21 It is hidden from the eyes of all living,
and concealed from the birds of the air.
22 Abaddon and Death say,
'We have heard a rumor of it with our ears.'

23 "God understands the way to it,
and he knows its place.
24 For he looks to the ends of the earth,
and sees everything under the heavens.
25 When he gave to the wind its weight,
and apportioned out the waters by measure;
26 when he made a decree for the rain,
and a way for the thunderbolt;
27 then he saw it and declared it;
he established it, and searched it out.
28 And he said to humankind,
'Truly, the fear of the Lord, that is wisdom;
and to depart from evil is understanding.' "

29 Job again took up his discourse and said:
2 "O that I were as in the months of old,
as in the days when God watched over me;
3 when his lamp shone over my head,
and by his light I walked through darkness;
4 when I was in my prime,
when the friendship of God was upon my tent;
5 when the Almighty[e] was still with me,
when my children were around me;
6 when my steps were washed with milk,
and the rock poured out for me streams of oil!
7 When I went out to the gate of the city,
when I took my seat in the square,
8 the young men saw me and withdrew,
and the aged rose up and stood;
9 the nobles refrained from talking,
and laid their hands on their mouths;
10 the voices of princes were hushed,
and their tongues stuck to the roof of their mouths.
11 When the ear heard, it commended me,
and when the eye saw, it approved;
12 because I delivered the poor who cried,
and the orphan who had no helper.
13 The blessing of the wretched came upon me,
and I caused the widow's heart to sing for joy.
14 I put on righteousness, and it clothed me;
my justice was like a robe and a turban.
15 I was eyes to the blind,
and feet to the lame.
16 I was a father to the needy,
and I championed the cause of the stranger.
17 I broke the fangs of the unrighteous,
and made them drop their prey from their teeth.
18 Then I thought, 'I shall die in my nest,

[a] Gk Vg: Heb *bind* [b] Gk: Heb *its price* [c] Or *lapis lazuli* [d] Or *Nubia*; Heb *Cush*
[e] Traditional rendering of Heb *Shaddai*

Job 29

Job realizes that his own situation is that of the poor. Where, then, is God in the midst of it all? Will God be deaf to the prayer of the poor? This time, Job's cry is not simply for himself, for he knows that he is part of the world of the poor. It is in that setting that he asks his question, and it carries with it the questions of all those whom he has just recognized as his fellows in misfortune.[30]

— ***Gustavo Gutiérrez***

and I shall multiply my days like the
phoenix;[a]
19 my roots spread out to the waters,
with the dew all night on my branches;
20 my glory was fresh with me,
and my bow ever new in my hand.'

21 "They listened to me, and waited,
and kept silence for my counsel.
22 After I spoke they did not speak again,
and my word dropped upon them like
dew.[b]
23 They waited for me as for the rain;
they opened their mouths as for the spring
rain.
24 I smiled on them when they had no
confidence;
and the light of my countenance they did
not extinguish.[c]
25 I chose their way, and sat as chief,
and I lived like a king among his troops,
like one who comforts mourners.

30 "But now they make sport of me,
those who are younger than I,
whose fathers I would have disdained
to set with the dogs of my flock.
2 What could I gain from the strength of their
hands?
All their vigor is gone.
3 Through want and hard hunger
they gnaw the dry and desolate ground,
4 they pick mallow and the leaves of bushes,
and to warm themselves the roots of
broom.
5 They are driven out from society;
people shout after them as after a thief.
6 In the gullies of wadis they must live,
in holes in the ground, and in the rocks.
7 Among the bushes they bray;
under the nettles they huddle together.
8 A senseless, disreputable brood,
they have been whipped out of the land.

9 "And now they mock me in song;
I am a byword to them.
10 They abhor me, they keep aloof from me;
they do not hesitate to spit at the sight
of me.
11 Because God has loosed my bowstring and
humbled me,
they have cast off restraint in my presence.
12 On my right hand the rabble rise up;
they send me sprawling,
and build roads for my ruin.
13 They break up my path,
they promote my calamity;
no one restrains[d] them.
14 As through a wide breach they come;
amid the crash they roll on.
15 Terrors are turned upon me;
my honor is pursued as by the wind,
and my prosperity has passed away like a
cloud.

16 "And now my soul is poured out within me;
days of affliction have taken hold of me.
17 The night racks my bones,
and the pain that gnaws me takes no rest.
18 With violence he seizes my garment;[e]
he grasps me by[f] the collar of my tunic.
19 He has cast me into the mire,
and I have become like dust and ashes.
20 I cry to you and you do not answer me;

[a] Or *like sand* [b] Heb lacks *like dew* [c] Meaning of Heb uncertain [d] Cn: Heb *helps* [e] Gk: Heb *my garment is disfigured* [f] Heb *like*

I stand, and you merely look at me.
21 You have turned cruel to me;
with the might of your hand you persecute me.
22 You lift me up on the wind, you make me ride on it,
and you toss me about in the roar of the storm.
23 I know that you will bring me to death,
and to the house appointed for all living.

24 "Surely one does not turn against the needy,[a]
when in disaster they cry for help.[b]
25 Did I not weep for those whose day was hard?
Was not my soul grieved for the poor?
26 But when I looked for good, evil came;
and when I waited for light, darkness came.
27 My inward parts are in turmoil, and are never still;
days of affliction come to meet me.
28 I go about in sunless gloom;
I stand up in the assembly and cry for help.
29 I am a brother of jackals,
and a companion of ostriches.
30 My skin turns black and falls from me,
and my bones burn with heat.
31 My lyre is turned to mourning,
and my pipe to the voice of those who weep.

31 "I have made a covenant with my eyes;
how then could I look upon a virgin?
2 What would be my portion from God above,
and my heritage from the Almighty[c] on high?
3 Does not calamity befall the unrighteous,
and disaster the workers of iniquity?
4 Does he not see my ways,
and number all my steps?

5 "If I have walked with falsehood,
and my foot has hurried to deceit—
6 let me be weighed in a just balance,
and let God know my integrity!—
7 if my step has turned aside from the way,
and my heart has followed my eyes,
and if any spot has clung to my hands;
8 then let me sow, and another eat;
and let what grows for me be rooted out.

9 "If my heart has been enticed by a woman,
and I have lain in wait at my neighbor's door;
10 then let my wife grind for another,
and let other men kneel over her.
11 For that would be a heinous crime;
that would be a criminal offense;
12 for that would be a fire consuming down to Abaddon,
and it would burn to the root all my harvest.

13 "If I have rejected the cause of my male or female slaves,
when they brought a complaint against me;
14 what then shall I do when God rises up?
When he makes inquiry, what shall I answer him?
15 Did not he who made me in the womb make them?
And did not one fashion us in the womb?

16 "If I have withheld anything that the poor desired,
or have caused the eyes of the widow to fail,
17 or have eaten my morsel alone,
and the orphan has not eaten from it—
18 for from my youth I reared the orphan[d] like a father,
and from my mother's womb I guided the widow[e]—
19 if I have seen anyone perish for lack of clothing,
or a poor person without covering,
20 whose loins have not blessed me,
and who was not warmed with the fleece of my sheep;

[a] Heb *ruin* [b] Cn: Meaning of Heb uncertain [c] Traditional rendering of Heb *Shaddai* [d] Heb *him* [e] Heb *her*

21 if I have raised my hand against the orphan,
because I saw I had supporters at the gate;
22 then let my shoulder blade fall from my shoulder,
and let my arm be broken from its socket.
23 For I was in terror of calamity from God,
and I could not have faced his majesty.

24 "If I have made gold my trust,
or called fine gold my confidence;
25 if I have rejoiced because my wealth was great,
or because my hand had gotten much;
26 if I have looked at the sun[a] when it shone,
or the moon moving in splendor,
27 and my heart has been secretly enticed,
and my mouth has kissed my hand;
28 this also would be an iniquity to be punished by the judges,
for I should have been false to God above.

29 "If I have rejoiced at the ruin of those who hated me,
or exulted when evil overtook them—
30 I have not let my mouth sin
by asking for their lives with a curse—
31 if those of my tent ever said,
'O that we might be sated with his flesh!'[b]—
32 the stranger has not lodged in the street;
I have opened my doors to the traveler—
33 if I have concealed my transgressions as others do,[c]
by hiding my iniquity in my bosom,
34 because I stood in great fear of the multitude,
and the contempt of families terrified me,
so that I kept silence, and did not go out of doors—
35 O that I had one to hear me!
(Here is my signature! Let the Almighty[d] answer me!)
O that I had the indictment written by my adversary!
36 Surely I would carry it on my shoulder;
I would bind it on me like a crown;
37 I would give him an account of all my steps;
like a prince I would approach him.

38 "If my land has cried out against me,
and its furrows have wept together;
39 if I have eaten its yield without payment,
and caused the death of its owners;
40 let thorns grow instead of wheat,
and foul weeds instead of barley."

The words of Job are ended.

32 So these three men ceased to answer Job,
because he was righteous in his own eyes.
2 Then Elihu son of Barachel the Buzite, of the
family of Ram, became angry. He was angry at Job
because he justified himself rather than God; 3 he
was angry also at Job's three friends because they
had found no answer, though they had declared
Job to be in the wrong.[e] 4 Now Elihu had waited
to speak to Job, because they were older than he.
5 But when Elihu saw that there was no answer in
the mouths of these three men, he became angry.

6 Elihu son of Barachel the Buzite answered:
"I am young in years,
and you are aged;
therefore I was timid and afraid
to declare my opinion to you.
7 I said, 'Let days speak,
and many years teach wisdom.'
8 But truly it is the spirit in a mortal,
the breath of the Almighty,[d] that makes for understanding.
9 It is not the old[f] that are wise,
nor the aged that understand what is right.
10 Therefore I say, 'Listen to me;
let me also declare my opinion.'

11 "See, I waited for your words,
I listened for your wise sayings,
while you searched out what to say.
12 I gave you my attention,

[a] Heb *the light* [b] Meaning of Heb uncertain [c] Or *as Adam did* [d] Traditional rendering of Heb *Shaddai*
[e] Another ancient tradition reads *answer, and had put God in the wrong* [f] Gk Syr Vg: Heb *many*

but there was in fact no one that confuted
Job,
no one among you that answered his
words.
13 Yet do not say, 'We have found wisdom;
God may vanquish him, not a human.'
14 He has not directed his words against me,
and I will not answer him with your
speeches.

15 "They are dismayed, they answer no more;
they have not a word to say.
16 And am I to wait, because they do not speak,
because they stand there, and answer no
more?
17 I also will give my answer;
I also will declare my opinion.
18 For I am full of words;
the spirit within me constrains me.
19 My heart is indeed like wine that has no vent;
like new wineskins, it is ready to burst.
20 I must speak, so that I may find relief;
I must open my lips and answer.
21 I will not show partiality to any person
or use flattery toward anyone.
22 For I do not know how to flatter—
or my Maker would soon put an end
to me!

33 "But now, hear my speech, O Job,
and listen to all my words.
2 See, I open my mouth;
the tongue in my mouth speaks.
3 My words declare the uprightness of my
heart,
and what my lips know they speak
sincerely.
4 The spirit of God has made me,
and the breath of the Almighty[a] gives me
life.
5 Answer me, if you can;
set your words in order before me; take
your stand.
6 See, before God I am as you are;
I too was formed from a piece of clay.
7 No fear of me need terrify you;
my pressure will not be heavy on you.

8 "Surely, you have spoken in my hearing,
and I have heard the sound of your words.
9 You say, 'I am clean, without transgression;
I am pure, and there is no iniquity in me.
10 Look, he finds occasions against me,
he counts me as his enemy;
11 he puts my feet in the stocks,
and watches all my paths.'

12 "But in this you are not right. I will answer
you:
God is greater than any mortal.
13 Why do you contend against him,
saying, 'He will answer none of my[b]
words'?
14 For God speaks in one way,
and in two, though people do not
perceive it.
15 In a dream, in a vision of the night,
when deep sleep falls on mortals,
while they slumber on their beds,
16 then he opens their ears,
and terrifies them with warnings,
17 that he may turn them aside from their deeds,
and keep them from pride,
18 to spare their souls from the Pit,
their lives from traversing the River.
19 They are also chastened with pain upon their
beds,
and with continual strife in their bones,
20 so that their lives loathe bread,
and their appetites dainty food.
21 Their flesh is so wasted away that it cannot be
seen;
and their bones, once invisible, now stick
out.
22 Their souls draw near the Pit,
and their lives to those who bring death.
23 Then, if there should be for one of them an
angel,
a mediator, one of a thousand,
one who declares a person upright,

[a] Traditional rendering of Heb *Shaddai* [b] Compare Gk: Heb *his*

24 and he is gracious to that person, and says,
'Deliver him from going down into the Pit;
I have found a ransom;
25 let his flesh become fresh with youth;
let him return to the days of his youthful vigor';
26 then he prays to God, and is accepted by him,
he comes into his presence with joy,
and God[a] repays him for his righteousness.
27 That person sings to others and says,
'I sinned, and perverted what was right,
and it was not paid back to me.
28 He has redeemed my soul from going down to the Pit,
and my life shall see the light.'

29 "God indeed does all these things,
twice, three times, with mortals,
30 to bring back their souls from the Pit,
so that they may see the light of life.[b]
31 Pay heed, Job, listen to me;
be silent, and I will speak.
32 If you have anything to say, answer me;
speak, for I desire to justify you.
33 If not, listen to me;
be silent, and I will teach you wisdom."

34 Then Elihu continued and said:
2 "Hear my words, you wise men,
and give ear to me, you who know;
3 for the ear tests words
as the palate tastes food.
4 Let us choose what is right;
let us determine among ourselves what is good.
5 For Job has said, 'I am innocent,
and God has taken away my right;
6 in spite of being right I am counted a liar;
my wound is incurable, though I am without transgression.'
7 Who is there like Job,
who drinks up scoffing like water,
8 who goes in company with evildoers
and walks with the wicked?
9 For he has said, 'It profits one nothing
to take delight in God.'

10 "Therefore, hear me, you who have sense,
far be it from God that he should do wickedness,
and from the Almighty[c] that he should do wrong.
11 For according to their deeds he will repay them,
and according to their ways he will make it befall them.
12 Of a truth, God will not do wickedly,
and the Almighty[c] will not pervert justice.
13 Who gave him charge over the earth
and who laid on him[d] the whole world?
14 If he should take back his spirit[e] to himself,
and gather to himself his breath,
15 all flesh would perish together,
and all mortals return to dust.

16 "If you have understanding, hear this;
listen to what I say.
17 Shall one who hates justice govern?
Will you condemn one who is righteous and mighty,
18 who says to a king, 'You scoundrel!'
and to princes, 'You wicked men!';
19 who shows no partiality to nobles,
nor regards the rich more than the poor,
for they are all the work of his hands?
20 In a moment they die;
at midnight the people are shaken and pass away,
and the mighty are taken away by no human hand.

21 "For his eyes are upon the ways of mortals,
and he sees all their steps.
22 There is no gloom or deep darkness
where evildoers may hide themselves.
23 For he has not appointed a time[f] for anyone
to go before God in judgment.
24 He shatters the mighty without investigation,

[a] Heb *he* [b] Syr: Heb *to be lighted with the light of life* [c] Traditional rendering of Heb *Shaddai* [d] Heb lacks *on him* [e] Heb *his heart his spirit* [f] Cn: Heb *yet*

and sets others in their place.
25 Thus, knowing their works,
he overturns them in the night, and they are crushed.
26 He strikes them for their wickedness
while others look on,
27 because they turned aside from following him,
and had no regard for any of his ways,
28 so that they caused the cry of the poor to come to him,
and he heard the cry of the afflicted—
29 When he is quiet, who can condemn?
When he hides his face, who can behold him,
whether it be a nation or an individual?—
30 so that the godless should not reign,
or those who ensnare the people.

31 "For has anyone said to God,
'I have endured punishment; I will not offend any more;
32 teach me what I do not see;
if I have done iniquity, I will do it no more'?
33 Will he then pay back to suit you,
because you reject it?
For you must choose, and not I;
therefore declare what you know.[a]
34 Those who have sense will say to me,
and the wise who hear me will say,
35 'Job speaks without knowledge,
his words are without insight.'
36 Would that Job were tried to the limit,
because his answers are those of the wicked.
37 For he adds rebellion to his sin;
he claps his hands among us,
and multiplies his words against God."

35 Elihu continued and said:
2 "Do you think this to be just?
You say, 'I am in the right before God.'
3 If you ask, 'What advantage have I?
How am I better off than if I had sinned?'
4 I will answer you
and your friends with you.
5 Look at the heavens and see;
observe the clouds, which are higher than you.
6 If you have sinned, what do you accomplish against him?
And if your transgressions are multiplied, what do you do to him?
7 If you are righteous, what do you give to him;
or what does he receive from your hand?
8 Your wickedness affects others like you,
and your righteousness, other human beings.

9 "Because of the multitude of oppressions people cry out;
they call for help because of the arm of the mighty.
10 But no one says, 'Where is God my Maker,
who gives strength in the night,
11 who teaches us more than the animals of the earth,
and makes us wiser than the birds of the air?'
12 There they cry out, but he does not answer,
because of the pride of evildoers.
13 Surely God does not hear an empty cry,
nor does the Almighty[b] regard it.
14 How much less when you say that you do not see him,
that the case is before him, and you are waiting for him!
15 And now, because his anger does not punish,
and he does not greatly heed transgression,[c]
16 Job opens his mouth in empty talk,
he multiplies words without knowledge."

36 Elihu continued and said:
2 "Bear with me a little, and I will show you,

[a] Meaning of Heb of verses 29–33 uncertain [b] Traditional rendering of Heb *Shaddai*
[c] Theodotion Symmachus Compare Vg: Meaning of Heb uncertain

for I have yet something to say on God's
behalf.
3 I will bring my knowledge from far away,
and ascribe righteousness to my Maker.
4 For truly my words are not false;
one who is perfect in knowledge is with
you.

5 "Surely God is mighty and does not despise
any;
he is mighty in strength of understanding.
6 He does not keep the wicked alive,
but gives the afflicted their right.
7 He does not withdraw his eyes from the
righteous,
but with kings on the throne
he sets them forever, and they are
exalted.
8 And if they are bound in fetters
and caught in the cords of affliction,
9 then he declares to them their work
and their transgressions, that they are
behaving arrogantly.
10 He opens their ears to instruction,
and commands that they return from
iniquity.
11 If they listen, and serve him,
they complete their days in prosperity,
and their years in pleasantness.
12 But if they do not listen, they shall perish by
the sword,
and die without knowledge.

13 "The godless in heart cherish anger;
they do not cry for help when he binds
them.
14 They die in their youth,
and their life ends in shame.[a]
15 He delivers the afflicted by their affliction,
and opens their ear by adversity.
16 He also allured you out of distress
into a broad place where there was no
constraint,
and what was set on your table was full of
fatness.

17 "But you are obsessed with the case of the
wicked;
judgment and justice seize you.
18 Beware that wrath does not entice you into
scoffing,
and do not let the greatness of the ransom
turn you aside.
19 Will your cry avail to keep you from distress,
or will all the force of your strength?
20 Do not long for the night,
when peoples are cut off in their place.
21 Beware! Do not turn to iniquity;
because of that you have been tried by
affliction.
22 See, God is exalted in his power;
who is a teacher like him?
23 Who has prescribed for him his way,
or who can say, 'You have done wrong'?

24 "Remember to extol his work,
of which mortals have sung.
25 All people have looked on it;
everyone watches it from far away.
26 Surely God is great, and we do not know
him;
the number of his years is unsearchable.
27 For he draws up the drops of water;
he distills[b] his mist in rain,
28 which the skies pour down
and drop upon mortals abundantly.
29 Can anyone understand the spreading of the
clouds,
the thunderings of his pavilion?
30 See, he scatters his lightning around him
and covers the roots of the sea.
31 For by these he governs peoples;
he gives food in abundance.
32 He covers his hands with the lightning,
and commands it to strike the mark.
33 Its crashing[c] tells about him;
he is jealous[c] with anger against iniquity.

37 "At this also my heart trembles,
and leaps out of its place.
2 Listen, listen to the thunder of his voice

[a] Heb *ends among the temple prostitutes* [b] Cn: Heb *they distill* [c] Meaning of Heb uncertain

and the rumbling that comes from his
mouth.
3 Under the whole heaven he lets it loose,
and his lightning to the corners of the
earth.
4 After it his voice roars;
he thunders with his majestic voice
and he does not restrain the lightnings[a]
when his voice is heard.
5 God thunders wondrously with his voice;
he does great things that we cannot
comprehend.
6 For to the snow he says, 'Fall on the earth';
and the shower of rain, his heavy shower
of rain,
7 serves as a sign on everyone's hand,
so that all whom he has made may
know it.[b]
8 Then the animals go into their lairs
and remain in their dens.
9 From its chamber comes the whirlwind,
and cold from the scattering winds.
10 By the breath of God ice is given,
and the broad waters are frozen fast.
11 He loads the thick cloud with moisture;
the clouds scatter his lightning.
12 They turn round and round by his guidance,
to accomplish all that he commands them
on the face of the habitable world.
13 Whether for correction, or for his land,
or for love, he causes it to happen.

14 "Hear this, O Job;
stop and consider the wondrous works of
God.
15 Do you know how God lays his command
upon them,
and causes the lightning of his cloud to
shine?
16 Do you know the balancings of the clouds,
the wondrous works of the one whose
knowledge is perfect,
17 you whose garments are hot
when the earth is still because of the south
wind?
18 Can you, like him, spread out the skies,
hard as a molten mirror?
19 Teach us what we shall say to him;
we cannot draw up our case because of
darkness.
20 Should he be told that I want to speak?
Did anyone ever wish to be swallowed up?
21 Now, no one can look on the light
when it is bright in the skies,
when the wind has passed and cleared
them.
22 Out of the north comes golden splendor;
around God is awesome majesty.
23 The Almighty[c]—we cannot find him;
he is great in power and justice,
and abundant righteousness he will not
violate.
24 Therefore mortals fear him;
he does not regard any who are wise in
their own conceit."

38 Then the LORD answered Job out of the
whirlwind:
2 "Who is this that darkens counsel by words
without knowledge?
3 Gird up your loins like a man,
I will question you, and you shall declare
to me.

4 "Where were you when I laid the foundation
of the earth?
Tell me, if you have understanding.
5 Who determined its measurements—surely
you know!
Or who stretched the line upon it?
6 On what were its bases sunk,
or who laid its cornerstone
7 when the morning stars sang together
and all the heavenly beings[d] shouted for
joy?

8 "Or who shut in the sea with doors
when it burst out from the womb?—
9 when I made the clouds its garment,
and thick darkness its swaddling band,

[a] Heb *them* [b] Meaning of Heb of verse 7 uncertain [c] Traditional rendering of Heb *Shaddai* [d] Heb *sons of God*

10 and prescribed bounds for it,
and set bars and doors,
11 and said, 'Thus far shall you come, and no farther,
and here shall your proud waves be stopped'?

12 "Have you commanded the morning since your days began,
and caused the dawn to know its place,
13 so that it might take hold of the skirts of the earth,
and the wicked be shaken out of it?
14 It is changed like clay under the seal,
and it is dyed[a] like a garment.
15 Light is withheld from the wicked,
and their uplifted arm is broken.

16 "Have you entered into the springs of the sea,
or walked in the recesses of the deep?
17 Have the gates of death been revealed to you,
or have you seen the gates of deep darkness?
18 Have you comprehended the expanse of the earth?
Declare, if you know all this.

19 "Where is the way to the dwelling of light,
and where is the place of darkness,
20 that you may take it to its territory
and that you may discern the paths to its home?
21 Surely you know, for you were born then,
and the number of your days is great!

22 "Have you entered the storehouses of the snow,
or have you seen the storehouses of the hail,
23 which I have reserved for the time of trouble,
for the day of battle and war?
24 What is the way to the place where the light is distributed,
or where the east wind is scattered upon the earth?

Job 38–41

In his play *J.B.*, based on the book of Job, Archibald MacLeish explores human and divine justice. People generally try to justify suffering and injustice in the aftermath of tragedy. In *J.B.* the title character recognizes that he is not God, human beings are weak and fallible, and we can only repent. The play does not fully restore J.B., and, biblically speaking, innocent suffering occurs. God does not answer the question *why?* but rather implies *why not?*

— *CKD*

25 "Who has cut a channel for the torrents of rain,
and a way for the thunderbolt,
26 to bring rain on a land where no one lives,
on the desert, which is empty of human life,
27 to satisfy the waste and desolate land,
and to make the ground put forth grass?

28 "Has the rain a father,
or who has begotten the drops of dew?
29 From whose womb did the ice come forth,
and who has given birth to the hoarfrost of heaven?
30 The waters become hard like stone,
and the face of the deep is frozen.

31 "Can you bind the chains of the Pleiades,
or loose the cords of Orion?
32 Can you lead forth the Mazzaroth in their season,
or can you guide the Bear with its children?
33 Do you know the ordinances of the heavens?
Can you establish their rule on the earth?

34 "Can you lift up your voice to the clouds,
so that a flood of waters may cover you?

[a] Cn: Heb *and they stand forth*

35 Can you send forth lightnings, so that they may go
and say to you, 'Here we are'?
36 Who has put wisdom in the inward parts,[a]
or given understanding to the mind?[a]
37 Who has the wisdom to number the clouds?
Or who can tilt the waterskins of the heavens,
38 when the dust runs into a mass
and the clods cling together?

39 "Can you hunt the prey for the lion,
or satisfy the appetite of the young lions,
40 when they crouch in their dens,
or lie in wait in their covert?
41 Who provides for the raven its prey,
when its young ones cry to God,
and wander about for lack of food?

39 "Do you know when the mountain goats give birth?
Do you observe the calving of the deer?
2 Can you number the months that they fulfill,
and do you know the time when they give birth,
3 when they crouch to give birth to their offspring,
and are delivered of their young?
4 Their young ones become strong, they grow up in the open;
they go forth, and do not return to them.

5 "Who has let the wild ass go free?
Who has loosed the bonds of the swift ass,
6 to which I have given the steppe for its home,
the salt land for its dwelling place?
7 It scorns the tumult of the city;
it does not hear the shouts of the driver.
8 It ranges the mountains as its pasture,
and it searches after every green thing.

9 "Is the wild ox willing to serve you?
Will it spend the night at your crib?
10 Can you tie it in the furrow with ropes,
or will it harrow the valleys after you?
11 Will you depend on it because its strength is great,
and will you hand over your labor to it?
12 Do you have faith in it that it will return,
and bring your grain to your threshing floor?[b]

13 "The ostrich's wings flap wildly,
though its pinions lack plumage.[a]
14 For it leaves its eggs to the earth,
and lets them be warmed on the ground,
15 forgetting that a foot may crush them,
and that a wild animal may trample them.
16 It deals cruelly with its young, as if they were not its own;
though its labor should be in vain, yet it has no fear;
17 because God has made it forget wisdom,
and given it no share in understanding.
18 When it spreads its plumes aloft,[a]
it laughs at the horse and its rider.

19 "Do you give the horse its might?
Do you clothe its neck with mane?
20 Do you make it leap like the locust?
Its majestic snorting is terrible.
21 It paws[c] violently, exults mightily;
it goes out to meet the weapons.
22 It laughs at fear, and is not dismayed;
it does not turn back from the sword.
23 Upon it rattle the quiver,
the flashing spear, and the javelin.
24 With fierceness and rage it swallows the ground;
it cannot stand still at the sound of the trumpet.
25 When the trumpet sounds, it says 'Aha!'
From a distance it smells the battle,
the thunder of the captains, and the shouting.

26 "Is it by your wisdom that the hawk soars,
and spreads its wings toward the south?
27 Is it at your command that the eagle mounts up

[a] Meaning of Heb uncertain [b] Heb *your grain and your threshing floor* [c] Gk Syr Vg: Heb *they dig*

and makes its nest on high?
28 It lives on the rock and makes its home
in the fastness of the rocky crag.
29 From there it spies the prey;
its eyes see it from far away.
30 Its young ones suck up blood;
and where the slain are, there it is."

40 And the LORD said to Job:
2 "Shall a faultfinder contend with the
Almighty?[a]
Anyone who argues with God must
respond."

3 Then Job answered the LORD:
4 "See, I am of small account; what shall I
answer you?
I lay my hand on my mouth.
5 I have spoken once, and I will not answer;
twice, but will proceed no further."

6 Then the LORD answered Job out of the
whirlwind:
7 "Gird up your loins like a man;
I will question you, and you declare to me.
8 Will you even put me in the wrong?
Will you condemn me that you may be
justified?
9 Have you an arm like God,
and can you thunder with a voice like his?

10 "Deck yourself with majesty and dignity;
clothe yourself with glory and splendor.
11 Pour out the overflowings of your anger,
and look on all who are proud, and abase
them.
12 Look on all who are proud, and bring them
low;
tread down the wicked where they stand.
13 Hide them all in the dust together;
bind their faces in the world below.[b]
14 Then I will also acknowledge to you
that your own right hand can give you
victory.

15 "Look at Behemoth,
which I made just as I made you;
it eats grass like an ox.
16 Its strength is in its loins,
and its power in the muscles of its belly.
17 It makes its tail stiff like a cedar;
the sinews of its thighs are knit together.
18 Its bones are tubes of bronze,
its limbs like bars of iron.

19 "It is the first of the great acts of God—
only its Maker can approach it with the
sword.
20 For the mountains yield food for it
where all the wild animals play.
21 Under the lotus plants it lies,
in the covert of the reeds and in the marsh.
22 The lotus trees cover it for shade;
the willows of the wadi surround it.
23 Even if the river is turbulent, it is not
frightened;
it is confident though Jordan rushes
against its mouth.
24 Can one take it with hooks[c]
or pierce its nose with a snare?

41 [d] "Can you draw out Leviathan[e] with a
fishhook,
or press down its tongue with a cord?
2 Can you put a rope in its nose,
or pierce its jaw with a hook?
3 Will it make many supplications to you?
Will it speak soft words to you?
4 Will it make a covenant with you
to be taken as your servant forever?
5 Will you play with it as with a bird,
or will you put it on leash for your girls?
6 Will traders bargain over it?
Will they divide it up among the
merchants?
7 Can you fill its skin with harpoons,
or its head with fishing spears?
8 Lay hands on it;
think of the battle; you will not do it again!

[a] Traditional rendering of Heb *Shaddai* [b] Heb *the hidden place* [c] Cn: Heb *in his eyes* [d] Ch 40.25 in Heb
[e] Or *the crocodile*

9[a] Any hope of capturing it[b] will be
disappointed;
were not even the gods[c] overwhelmed at
the sight of it?
10 No one is so fierce as to dare to stir it up.
Who can stand before it?[d]
11 Who can confront it[d] and be safe?[e]
—under the whole heaven, who?[f]

12 "I will not keep silence concerning its limbs,
or its mighty strength, or its splendid
frame.
13 Who can strip off its outer garment?
Who can penetrate its double coat of
mail?[g]
14 Who can open the doors of its face?
There is terror all around its teeth.
15 Its back[h] is made of shields in rows,
shut up closely as with a seal.
16 One is so near to another
that no air can come between them.
17 They are joined one to another;
they clasp each other and cannot be
separated.
18 Its sneezes flash forth light,
and its eyes are like the eyelids of the
dawn.
19 From its mouth go flaming torches;
sparks of fire leap out.
20 Out of its nostrils comes smoke,
as from a boiling pot and burning rushes.
21 Its breath kindles coals,
and a flame comes out of its mouth.
22 In its neck abides strength,
and terror dances before it.
23 The folds of its flesh cling together;
it is firmly cast and immovable.
24 Its heart is as hard as stone,
as hard as the lower millstone.
25 When it raises itself up the gods are afraid;
at the crashing they are beside themselves.
26 Though the sword reaches it, it does not avail,
nor does the spear, the dart, or the javelin.
27 It counts iron as straw,
and bronze as rotten wood.
28 The arrow cannot make it flee;
slingstones, for it, are turned to chaff.
29 Clubs are counted as chaff;
it laughs at the rattle of javelins.
30 Its underparts are like sharp potsherds;
it spreads itself like a threshing sledge on
the mire.
31 It makes the deep boil like a pot;
it makes the sea like a pot of ointment.
32 It leaves a shining wake behind it;
one would think the deep to be white-
haired.
33 On earth it has no equal,
a creature without fear.
34 It surveys everything that is lofty;
it is king over all that are proud."

42 Then Job answered the LORD:
2 "I know that you can do all things,
and that no purpose of yours can be
thwarted.
3 'Who is this that hides counsel without
knowledge?'
Therefore I have uttered what I did not
understand,
things too wonderful for me, which I did
not know.
4 'Hear, and I will speak;
I will question you, and you declare to me.'
5 I had heard of you by the hearing of the ear,
but now my eye sees you;
6 therefore I despise myself,
and repent in dust and ashes."

7 After the LORD had spoken these words to
Job, the LORD said to Eliphaz the Temanite: "My
wrath is kindled against you and against your
two friends; for you have not spoken of me what
is right, as my servant Job has. 8 Now therefore
take seven bulls and seven rams, and go to my
servant Job, and offer up for yourselves a burnt
offering; and my servant Job shall pray for you,
for I will accept his prayer not to deal with you

[a] Ch 41.1 in Heb [b] Heb *of it* [c] Cn Compare Symmachus Syr: Heb *one is* [d] Heb *me* [e] Gk: Heb *that I shall repay*
[f] Heb *to me* [g] Gk: Heb *bridle* [h] Cn Compare Gk Vg: Heb *pride*

according to your folly; for you have not spoken
of me what is right, as my servant Job has done."
9So Eliphaz the Temanite and Bildad the Shuhite
and Zophar the Naamathite went and did what
the LORD had told them; and the LORD accepted
Job's prayer.

10 And the LORD restored the fortunes of
Job when he had prayed for his friends; and the
LORD gave Job twice as much as he had before.

Job 42:10

The God of Job, an enigma, is absent at Job's worst moments. While Job regains his health, sociocultural status, a wife and children, this story is not redemptive for Job's dead sons and daughters.

— *CKD*

11Then there came to him all his brothers and sisters and all who had known him before, and they
ate bread with him in his house; they showed him
sympathy and comforted him for all the evil that
the LORD had brought upon him; and each of
them gave him a piece of money[a] and a gold ring.
12The LORD blessed the latter days of Job more
than his beginning; and he had fourteen thousand sheep, six thousand camels, a thousand yoke
of oxen, and a thousand donkeys. 13He also had
seven sons and three daughters. 14He named the
first Jemimah, the second Keziah, and the third
Keren-happuch. 15In all the land there were no
women so beautiful as Job's daughters; and their
father gave them an inheritance along with their
brothers. 16After this Job lived one hundred and
forty years, and saw his children, and his children's children, four generations. 17And Job died,
old and full of days.

[a] Heb *a qesitah*

The Psalms

The book of Psalms is a polyphony of song. It has voices from different times; its texts span five centuries. Moreover, the many historical contexts of different psalms reflect the needs of different locations and peoples, and help explain the diverse qualities of the poetry. Sometimes, if a piece of poetry is to retain its power, it requires alteration. This poetic reconstrual may involve a transformation from one culture to another. For example, a Canaanite storm image became part of a hymn to YHWH in Psalm 29, one of the oldest psalms. Most importantly, the social dislocation of exile and the postexilic context required new songs, such as Psalm 137.

The Psalms remind today's readers of the *plasticity* of great texts, that is, their ability to address different contexts simultaneously. These psalms originally came from a number of regions and historical periods; most were written from the perspective of the Southern Kingdom of Judah, but several psalms, including 80 and 81, came from the Northern Kingdom prior to its fall in 722 BCE. In the process of their being repeated, adapted, and inevitably reconstrued, the songs again and again became part of a new entity and developed new meaning for generations yet to come—in similar and, sometimes, in quite diverse settings and situations. The book of Psalms has several literary genres, but two dominate: laments and hymns. The Hebrew title of the book of Psalms, *tehillim* (praises), testifies to the importance of the hymn genre. This genre emphasizes God, while the laments focus more on the request of the speaker. The hymn has three sections: a call to praise; testimony about God; and a conclusion that expresses some prayer, wish, or blessing. The deity is typically depicted in these testimonies as creator (8, 19, 104) and redeemer (66, 98).

The laments comprise approximately one-third of the psalms. The structure of the lament is complex, often using seven elements: address to God; description of distress; plea for redemption; statement of confidence; confession of sin or affirmation of innocence; pledge or vow; and a conclusion. A lament is often part of a cultural response by which people seek to negotiate a changing social context. The lament psalms both reflect the specific culture from which they emerge and are able to be translated to serve in other historical contexts and situations.

In general, the book of Psalms addresses the complicated nuances of power and privilege as matters of *election*. The royal psalms (2, 18, 20, 21, 45, 72, 91, 101, 110, 144) and the songs of Zion (46, 48, 76, 87, 125) indicate the community's efforts to negotiate a responsible position in society through the images of God's choosing of king and city. The psalms of ascent (120–134) are probably a collection of pilgrim psalms sung as persons made their way to Jerusalem for worship. Overall, the prayers and songs create a poetry of particularity, but the breadth of the psalms nevertheless still evokes attention to the disenfranchisement evident at the margins.

The book of Psalms also includes a range of pieties. The debate on the social origins of the

psalms reminds us that a religion lives not only in the priestly precincts but also in the so-called lay movements. The Psalter provides the best evidence for the coexistence of official religion (24, 95) and expressions of local lay piety (127, 131).

Finally, the book of Psalms is a collection of collections. The collections within the Psalter reflect different entities in the emerging religions of ancient Israel. The superscriptions—the historical notes that appear before many of the psalms—provide significant evidence of multiple groups or guilds, perhaps groups or families of Levitical priests: see, for example, the psalms ascribed to Asaph (50, 73–83) and the Korahites (42, 44–49, 84). Moreover, a preponderance of Yahwistic psalms, identifying the deity through the divine name YHWH, stands side by side with the Elohistic psalms, which name God as Elohim. The final form of the Psalter mediates these cultural differences within a fivefold structure (1–41, 42–72, 73–89, 90–106, 107–150), providing a parallel with the five books of Moses.

I read the psalms with music playing in the background, but this is more than an aesthetic preference. I grew up in an African American home, raised by parents who had suffered the loss of their own parents, in mid-twentieth-century Ohio, where de facto segregation gave to life a contingent, syncopated quality. The poetic rhythms and thematic counter-melodies in the psalms evoke for me both the wonder and the precariousness of life.

— ***Stephen Breck Reid***

BOOK I

PSALM 1

1 Happy are those
who do not follow the advice of the wicked,
or take the path that sinners tread,
or sit in the seat of scoffers;
2 but their delight is in the law of the Lord,
and on his law they meditate day and night.
3 They are like trees
planted by streams of water,
which yield their fruit in its season,
and their leaves do not wither.
In all that they do, they prosper.
4 The wicked are not so,
but are like chaff that the wind drives away.
5 Therefore the wicked will not stand in the judgment,
nor sinners in the congregation of the righteous;
6 for the Lord watches over the way of the righteous,
but the way of the wicked will perish.

PSALM 2

1 Why do the nations conspire,
and the peoples plot in vain?
2 The kings of the earth set themselves,
and the rulers take counsel together,
against the Lord and his anointed, saying,
3 "Let us burst their bonds asunder,
and cast their cords from us."

4 He who sits in the heavens laughs;
the LORD has them in derision.
5 Then he will speak to them in his wrath,
and terrify them in his fury, saying,
6 "I have set my king on Zion, my holy hill."

7 I will tell of the decree of the LORD:
He said to me, "You are my son;
today I have begotten you.
8 Ask of me, and I will make the nations your heritage,
and the ends of the earth your possession.
9 You shall break them with a rod of iron,
and dash them in pieces like a potter's vessel."

10 Now therefore, O kings, be wise;
be warned, O rulers of the earth.
11 Serve the LORD with fear,
with trembling 12kiss his feet,[a]
or he will be angry, and you will perish in the way;
for his wrath is quickly kindled.

Happy are all who take refuge in him.

PSALM 3

A Psalm of David, when he fled from his son Absalom.

1 O LORD, how many are my foes!
Many are rising against me;
2 many are saying to me,
"There is no help for you[b] in God." *Selah*

3 But you, O LORD, are a shield around me,
my glory, and the one who lifts up my head.
4 I cry aloud to the LORD,
and he answers me from his holy hill. *Selah*

5 I lie down and sleep;
I wake again, for the LORD sustains me.
6 I am not afraid of ten thousands of people
who have set themselves against me all around.

7 Rise up, O LORD!
Deliver me, O my God!
For you strike all my enemies on the cheek;
you break the teeth of the wicked.

8 Deliverance belongs to the LORD;
may your blessing be on your people! *Selah*

PSALM 4

To the leader: with stringed instruments. A Psalm of David.

1 Answer me when I call, O God of my right!
You gave me room when I was in distress.
Be gracious to me, and hear my prayer.

2 How long, you people, shall my honor suffer shame?
How long will you love vain words, and seek after lies? *Selah*
3 But know that the LORD has set apart the faithful for himself;
the LORD hears when I call to him.

4 When you are disturbed,[c] do not sin;
ponder it on your beds, and be silent. *Selah*
5 Offer right sacrifices,
and put your trust in the LORD.

6 There are many who say, "O that we might see some good!
Let the light of your face shine on us, O LORD!"
7 You have put gladness in my heart
more than when their grain and wine abound.

8 I will both lie down and sleep in peace;
for you alone, O LORD, make me lie down in safety.

[a] Cn: Meaning of Heb of verses 11b and 12a is uncertain [b] Syr: Heb *him* [c] Or *are angry*

PSALM 5

To the leader: for the flutes. A Psalm of David.

1 Give ear to my words, O Lord;
give heed to my sighing.
2 Listen to the sound of my cry,
my King and my God,
for to you I pray.
3 O Lord, in the morning you hear my voice;
in the morning I plead my case to you, and watch.

4 For you are not a God who delights in wickedness;
evil will not sojourn with you.
5 The boastful will not stand before your eyes;
you hate all evildoers.
6 You destroy those who speak lies;
the Lord abhors the bloodthirsty and deceitful.

7 But I, through the abundance of your steadfast love,
will enter your house,
I will bow down toward your holy temple
in awe of you.
8 Lead me, O Lord, in your righteousness
because of my enemies;
make your way straight before me.

9 For there is no truth in their mouths;
their hearts are destruction;
their throats are open graves;
they flatter with their tongues.
10 Make them bear their guilt, O God;
let them fall by their own counsels;
because of their many transgressions cast them out,
for they have rebelled against you.

11 But let all who take refuge in you rejoice;
let them ever sing for joy.
Spread your protection over them,
so that those who love your name may exult in you.
12 For you bless the righteous, O Lord;
you cover them with favor as with a shield.

PSALM 6

To the leader: with stringed instruments; according to The Sheminith. A Psalm of David.

1 O Lord, do not rebuke me in your anger,
or discipline me in your wrath.
2 Be gracious to me, O Lord, for I am languishing;
O Lord, heal me, for my bones are shaking with terror.
3 My soul also is struck with terror,
while you, O Lord—how long?

4 Turn, O Lord, save my life;
deliver me for the sake of your steadfast love.
5 For in death there is no remembrance of you;
in Sheol who can give you praise?

6 I am weary with my moaning;
every night I flood my bed with tears;
I drench my couch with my weeping.
7 My eyes waste away because of grief;
they grow weak because of all my foes.

8 Depart from me, all you workers of evil,
for the Lord has heard the sound of my weeping.
9 The Lord has heard my supplication;
the Lord accepts my prayer.
10 All my enemies shall be ashamed and struck with terror;
they shall turn back, and in a moment be put to shame.

PSALM 7

A Shiggaion of David, which he sang to the Lord concerning Cush, a Benjaminite.

1 O Lord my God, in you I take refuge;
save me from all my pursuers, and deliver me,
2 or like a lion they will tear me apart;
they will drag me away, with no one to rescue.

3 O Lord my God, if I have done this,
if there is wrong in my hands,

4 if I have repaid my ally with harm
or plundered my foe without cause,
5 then let the enemy pursue and overtake me,
trample my life to the ground,
and lay my soul in the dust. *Selah*

6 Rise up, O Lord, in your anger;
lift yourself up against the fury of my enemies;
awake, O my God;[a] you have appointed a judgment.
7 Let the assembly of the peoples be gathered around you,
and over it take your seat[b] on high.
8 The Lord judges the peoples;
judge me, O Lord, according to my righteousness
and according to the integrity that is in me.

9 O let the evil of the wicked come to an end,
but establish the righteous,
you who test the minds and hearts,
O righteous God.
10 God is my shield,
who saves the upright in heart.
11 God is a righteous judge,
and a God who has indignation every day.

12 If one does not repent, God[c] will whet his sword;
he has bent and strung his bow;
13 he has prepared his deadly weapons,
making his arrows fiery shafts.
14 See how they conceive evil,
and are pregnant with mischief,
and bring forth lies.
15 They make a pit, digging it out,
and fall into the hole that they have made.
16 Their mischief returns upon their own heads,
and on their own heads their violence descends.

17 I will give to the Lord the thanks due to his righteousness,
and sing praise to the name of the Lord, the Most High.

PSALM 8

To the leader: according to The Gittith. A Psalm of David.

1 O Lord, our Sovereign,
how majestic is your name in all the earth!
You have set your glory above the heavens.
2 Out of the mouths of babes and infants
you have founded a bulwark because of your foes,
to silence the enemy and the avenger.
3 When I look at your heavens, the work of your fingers,
the moon and the stars that you have established;
4 what are human beings that you are mindful of them,
mortals[d] that you care for them?

5 Yet you have made them a little lower than God,[e]
and crowned them with glory and honor.
6 You have given them dominion over the works of your hands;
you have put all things under their feet,
7 all sheep and oxen,
and also the beasts of the field,
8 the birds of the air, and the fish of the sea,
whatever passes along the paths of the seas.

9 O Lord, our Sovereign,
how majestic is your name in all the earth!

PSALM 9

To the leader: according to Muth-labben. A Psalm of David.

1 I will give thanks to the Lord with my whole heart;

[a] Or *awake for me* [b] Cn: Heb *return* [c] Heb *he* [d] Heb *ben adam*, lit. *son of man*
[e] Or *than the divine beings* or *angels*: Heb *elohim*

I will tell of all your wonderful deeds.
2 I will be glad and exult in you;
I will sing praise to your name, O Most High.

3 When my enemies turned back,
they stumbled and perished before you.
4 For you have maintained my just cause;
you have sat on the throne giving righteous judgment.

5 You have rebuked the nations, you have destroyed the wicked;
you have blotted out their name forever and ever.
6 The enemies have vanished in everlasting ruins;
their cities you have rooted out;
the very memory of them has perished.

7 But the LORD sits enthroned forever,
he has established his throne for judgment.
8 He judges the world with righteousness;
he judges the peoples with equity.

9 The LORD is a stronghold for the oppressed,
a stronghold in times of trouble.
10 And those who know your name put their trust in you,
for you, O LORD, have not forsaken those who seek you.

11 Sing praises to the LORD, who dwells in Zion.
Declare his deeds among the peoples.
12 For he who avenges blood is mindful of them;
he does not forget the cry of the afflicted.

13 Be gracious to me, O LORD.
See what I suffer from those who hate me;
you are the one who lifts me up from the gates of death,
14 so that I may recount all your praises,
and, in the gates of daughter Zion,
rejoice in your deliverance.

15 The nations have sunk in the pit that they made;
in the net that they hid has their own foot been caught.
16 The LORD has made himself known, he has executed judgment;
the wicked are snared in the work of their own hands. *Higgaion. Selah*

17 The wicked shall depart to Sheol,
all the nations that forget God.

18 For the needy shall not always be forgotten,
nor the hope of the poor perish forever.

19 Rise up, O LORD! Do not let mortals prevail;
let the nations be judged before you.
20 Put them in fear, O LORD;
let the nations know that they are only human. *Selah*

PSALM 10

1 Why, O LORD, do you stand far off?
Why do you hide yourself in times of trouble?
2 In arrogance the wicked persecute the poor—
let them be caught in the schemes they have devised.

3 For the wicked boast of the desires of their heart,
those greedy for gain curse and renounce the LORD.
4 In the pride of their countenance the wicked say, "God will not seek it out";
all their thoughts are, "There is no God."

5 Their ways prosper at all times;
your judgments are on high, out of their sight;
as for their foes, they scoff at them.
6 They think in their heart, "We shall not be moved;
throughout all generations we shall not meet adversity."

7 Their mouths are filled with cursing and
deceit and oppression;
under their tongues are mischief and
iniquity.
8 They sit in ambush in the villages;
in hiding places they murder the innocent.

Their eyes stealthily watch for the helpless;
9 they lurk in secret like a lion in its covert;
they lurk that they may seize the poor;
they seize the poor and drag them off in
their net.

10 They stoop, they crouch,
and the helpless fall by their might.
11 They think in their heart, "God has forgotten,
he has hidden his face, he will never see it."

12 Rise up, O LORD; O God, lift up your hand;
do not forget the oppressed.
13 Why do the wicked renounce God,
and say in their hearts, "You will not call
us to account"?

14 But you do see! Indeed you note trouble and
grief,
that you may take it into your hands;
the helpless commit themselves to you;
you have been the helper of the orphan.

15 Break the arm of the wicked and evildoers;
seek out their wickedness until you find
none.
16 The LORD is king forever and ever;
the nations shall perish from his land.

17 O LORD, you will hear the desire of the
meek;
you will strengthen their heart, you will
incline your ear
18 to do justice for the orphan and the
oppressed,
so that those from earth may strike terror
no more.[a]

Psalm 10

Although the contemporary language of "equal opportunity" suggests that present economic arrangements are perfectly fair and that how each person fares is the result of their own effort (or lack of it), the Bible usually gives voice to the poor who have been *impoverished*. That is, they have been *made* poor, reduced to misery by the calculated treachery and greed of the powerful. In the Psalms, the poor and oppressed are described—or speak for themselves—as those who have no resources and can rely on no one but YHWH. And YHWH is known as the one who *will* hear their cries and act on their behalf (vv. 16-18).

—***NE***

PSALM 11

To the leader. Of David.

1 In the LORD I take refuge; how can you say
to me,
"Flee like a bird to the mountains;[b]
2 for look, the wicked bend the bow,
they have fitted their arrow to the string,
to shoot in the dark at the upright in heart.
3 If the foundations are destroyed,
what can the righteous do?"

4 The LORD is in his holy temple;
the LORD's throne is in heaven.
His eyes behold, his gaze examines
humankind.
5 The LORD tests the righteous and the wicked,
and his soul hates the lover of violence.
6 On the wicked he will rain coals of fire and
sulfur;
a scorching wind shall be the portion of
their cup.
7 For the LORD is righteous;
he loves righteous deeds;
the upright shall behold his face.

[a] Meaning of Heb uncertain [b] Gk Syr Jerome Tg: Heb *flee to your mountain, O bird*

PSALM 12

To the leader: according to The Sheminith. A Psalm of David.

1 Help, O LORD, for there is no longer anyone
who is godly;
the faithful have disappeared from
humankind.
2 They utter lies to each other;
with flattering lips and a double heart they
speak.

3 May the LORD cut off all flattering lips,
the tongue that makes great boasts,
4 those who say, "With our tongues we will
prevail;
our lips are our own—who is our master?"

5 "Because the poor are despoiled, because the
needy groan,
I will now rise up," says the LORD;
"I will place them in the safety for which
they long."
6 The promises of the LORD are promises that
are pure,
silver refined in a furnace on the ground,
purified seven times.

7 You, O LORD, will protect us;
you will guard us from this generation
forever.
8 On every side the wicked prowl,
as vileness is exalted among humankind.

PSALM 13

To the leader. A Psalm of David.

1 How long, O LORD? Will you forget me
forever?
How long will you hide your face
from me?
2 How long must I bear pain[a] in my soul,
and have sorrow in my heart all day long?
How long shall my enemy be exalted
over me?

3 Consider and answer me, O LORD my God!
Give light to my eyes, or I will sleep the
sleep of death,
4 and my enemy will say, "I have prevailed";
my foes will rejoice because I am shaken.

5 But I trusted in your steadfast love;
my heart shall rejoice in your salvation.
6 I will sing to the LORD,
because he has dealt bountifully with me.

PSALM 14

To the leader. Of David.

1 Fools say in their hearts, "There is no God."
They are corrupt, they do abominable
deeds;
there is no one who does good.

2 The LORD looks down from heaven on
humankind
to see if there are any who are wise,
who seek after God.

3 They have all gone astray, they are all alike
perverse;
there is no one who does good,
no, not one.

4 Have they no knowledge, all the evildoers
who eat up my people as they eat bread,
and do not call upon the LORD?

5 There they shall be in great terror,
for God is with the company of the
righteous.
6 You would confound the plans of the poor,
but the LORD is their refuge.

7 O that deliverance for Israel would come
from Zion!
When the LORD restores the fortunes of
his people,
Jacob will rejoice; Israel will be glad.

[a] Syr: Heb *hold counsels*

PSALM 15

A Psalm of David.

1 O LORD, who may abide in your tent?
Who may dwell on your holy hill?

2 Those who walk blamelessly, and do what is right,
and speak the truth from their heart;
3 who do not slander with their tongue,
and do no evil to their friends,
nor take up a reproach against their neighbors;
4 in whose eyes the wicked are despised,
but who honor those who fear the LORD;
who stand by their oath even to their hurt;
5 who do not lend money at interest,
and do not take a bribe against the innocent.

Those who do these things shall never be moved.

PSALM 16

A Miktam of David.

1 Protect me, O God, for in you I take refuge.
2 I say to the LORD, "You are my Lord;
I have no good apart from you."[a]

3 As for the holy ones in the land, they are the noble,
in whom is all my delight.

4 Those who choose another god multiply their sorrows;[b]
their drink offerings of blood I will not pour out
or take their names upon my lips.

5 The LORD is my chosen portion and my cup;
you hold my lot.
6 The boundary lines have fallen for me in pleasant places;
I have a goodly heritage.

7 I bless the LORD who gives me counsel;
in the night also my heart instructs me.
8 I keep the LORD always before me;
because he is at my right hand, I shall not be moved.

9 Therefore my heart is glad, and my soul rejoices;
my body also rests secure.
10 For you do not give me up to Sheol,
or let your faithful one see the Pit.

11 You show me the path of life.
In your presence there is fullness of joy;
in your right hand are pleasures forevermore.

PSALM 17

A Prayer of David.

1 Hear a just cause, O LORD; attend to my cry;
give ear to my prayer from lips free of deceit.
2 From you let my vindication come;
let your eyes see the right.

3 If you try my heart, if you visit me by night,
if you test me, you will find no wickedness in me;
my mouth does not transgress.
4 As for what others do, by the word of your lips
I have avoided the ways of the violent.
5 My steps have held fast to your paths;
my feet have not slipped.

6 I call upon you, for you will answer me, O God;
incline your ear to me, hear my words.
7 Wondrously show your steadfast love,
O savior of those who seek refuge
from their adversaries at your right hand.

8 Guard me as the apple of the eye;
hide me in the shadow of your wings,
9 from the wicked who despoil me,

[a] Jerome Tg: Meaning of Heb uncertain [b] Cn: Meaning of Heb uncertain

my deadly enemies who surround me.
10 They close their hearts to pity;
with their mouths they speak arrogantly.
11 They track me down;[a] now they surround me;
they set their eyes to cast me to the ground.
12 They are like a lion eager to tear,
like a young lion lurking in ambush.

13 Rise up, O LORD, confront them, overthrow them!
By your sword deliver my life from the wicked,
14 from mortals—by your hand, O LORD—
from mortals whose portion in life is in this world.
May their bellies be filled with what you have stored up for them;
may their children have more than enough;
may they leave something over to their little ones.

15 As for me, I shall behold your face in righteousness;
when I awake I shall be satisfied, beholding your likeness.

PSALM 18

To the leader. A Psalm of David the servant of the LORD, who addressed the words of this song to the LORD on the day when the LORD delivered him from the hand of all his enemies, and from the hand of Saul. He said:

1 I love you, O LORD, my strength.
2 The LORD is my rock, my fortress, and my deliverer,
my God, my rock in whom I take refuge,
my shield, and the horn of my salvation, my stronghold.
3 I call upon the LORD, who is worthy to be praised,
so I shall be saved from my enemies.

4 The cords of death encompassed me;
the torrents of perdition assailed me;
5 the cords of Sheol entangled me;
the snares of death confronted me.

6 In my distress I called upon the LORD;
to my God I cried for help.
From his temple he heard my voice,
and my cry to him reached his ears.

7 Then the earth reeled and rocked;
the foundations also of the mountains trembled
and quaked, because he was angry.
8 Smoke went up from his nostrils,
and devouring fire from his mouth;
glowing coals flamed forth from him.
9 He bowed the heavens, and came down;
thick darkness was under his feet.
10 He rode on a cherub, and flew;
he came swiftly upon the wings of the wind.
11 He made darkness his covering around him,

Psalm 18

Here, as so often in the Psalms, the language of theophany—the terrifying irruption of God's power in fire, smoke, earthquake, and darkness—is invoked to describe an individual's deliverance. The superscription attributes these verses to David when he escaped Saul's hands, but like all the Psalms these words have been recited by countless individuals and communities to describe the tremendous experience of relief and exhilaration on escape from the destructive grasp of evildoers.

Those who lived through the long years of the civil rights struggle in the United States or the struggle against apartheid in South Africa can attest to the thrill, deep in the heart, when justice is at last in the air, is glimpsed, is touched—moments that Barbara Ehrenreich has called the experience of "political ecstasy." The Bible understands them as encounters with God.[31]

—NE

[a] One Ms Compare Syr: MT *Our steps*

his canopy thick clouds dark with water.
12 Out of the brightness before him
there broke through his clouds
hailstones and coals of fire.
13 The LORD also thundered in the heavens,
and the Most High uttered his voice.[a]
14 And he sent out his arrows, and scattered
them;
he flashed forth lightnings, and routed
them.
15 Then the channels of the sea were seen,
and the foundations of the world were laid
bare
at your rebuke, O LORD,
at the blast of the breath of your nostrils.

16 He reached down from on high, he took me;
he drew me out of mighty waters.
17 He delivered me from my strong enemy,
and from those who hated me;
for they were too mighty for me.
18 They confronted me in the day of my
calamity;
but the LORD was my support.
19 He brought me out into a broad place;
he delivered me, because he delighted
in me.

20 The LORD rewarded me according to my
righteousness;
according to the cleanness of my hands he
recompensed me.
21 For I have kept the ways of the LORD,
and have not wickedly departed from my
God.
22 For all his ordinances were before me,
and his statutes I did not put away
from me.
23 I was blameless before him,
and I kept myself from guilt.
24 Therefore the LORD has recompensed me
according to my righteousness,
according to the cleanness of my hands in
his sight.

25 With the loyal you show yourself loyal;
with the blameless you show yourself
blameless;
26 with the pure you show yourself pure;
and with the crooked you show yourself
perverse.
27 For you deliver a humble people,
but the haughty eyes you bring down.
28 It is you who light my lamp;
the LORD, my God, lights up my darkness.
29 By you I can crush a troop,
and by my God I can leap over a wall.
30 This God—his way is perfect;
the promise of the LORD proves true;
he is a shield for all who take refuge
in him.

31 For who is God except the LORD?
And who is a rock besides our God?—
32 the God who girded me with strength,
and made my way safe.
33 He made my feet like the feet of a deer,
and set me secure on the heights.
34 He trains my hands for war,
so that my arms can bend a bow of
bronze.
35 You have given me the shield of your
salvation,
and your right hand has supported me;
your help[b] has made me great.
36 You gave me a wide place for my steps
under me,
and my feet did not slip.
37 I pursued my enemies and overtook them;
and did not turn back until they were
consumed.
38 I struck them down, so that they were not
able to rise;
they fell under my feet.
39 For you girded me with strength for the
battle;
you made my assailants sink under me.
40 You made my enemies turn their backs
to me,
and those who hated me I destroyed.

[a] Gk See 2 Sam 22.14: Heb adds *hailstones and coals of fire*

[b] Or *gentleness*

41 They cried for help, but there was no one to save them;
they cried to the LORD, but he did not answer them.
42 I beat them fine, like dust before the wind;
I cast them out like the mire of the streets.

43 You delivered me from strife with the peoples;[a]
you made me head of the nations;
people whom I had not known served me.
44 As soon as they heard of me they obeyed me;
foreigners came cringing to me.
45 Foreigners lost heart,
and came trembling out of their strongholds.

46 The LORD lives! Blessed be my rock,
and exalted be the God of my salvation,
47 the God who gave me vengeance
and subdued peoples under me;
48 who delivered me from my enemies;
indeed, you exalted me above my adversaries;
you delivered me from the violent.

49 For this I will extol you, O LORD, among the nations,
and sing praises to your name.
50 Great triumphs he gives to his king,
and shows steadfast love to his anointed,
to David and his descendants forever.

PSALM 19

To the leader. A Psalm of David.

1 The heavens are telling the glory of God;
and the firmament[b] proclaims his handiwork.
2 Day to day pours forth speech,
and night to night declares knowledge.
3 There is no speech, nor are there words;
their voice is not heard;
4 yet their voice[c] goes out through all the earth,
and their words to the end of the world.

In the heavens[d] he has set a tent for the sun,
5 which comes out like a bridegroom from his wedding canopy,
and like a strong man runs its course with joy.
6 Its rising is from the end of the heavens,
and its circuit to the end of them;
and nothing is hid from its heat.

7 The law of the LORD is perfect,
reviving the soul;
the decrees of the LORD are sure,
making wise the simple;
8 the precepts of the LORD are right,
rejoicing the heart;
the commandment of the LORD is clear,
enlightening the eyes;
9 the fear of the LORD is pure,
enduring forever;
the ordinances of the LORD are true
and righteous altogether.
10 More to be desired are they than gold,
even much fine gold;
sweeter also than honey,
and drippings of the honeycomb.

11 Moreover by them is your servant warned;
in keeping them there is great reward.
12 But who can detect their errors?
Clear me from hidden faults.
13 Keep back your servant also from the insolent;[e]
do not let them have dominion over me.
Then I shall be blameless,
and innocent of great transgression.

14 Let the words of my mouth and the meditation of my heart
be acceptable to you,
O LORD, my rock and my redeemer.

PSALM 20

To the leader. A Psalm of David.

1 The LORD answer you in the day of trouble!

[a] Gk Tg: Heb *people* [b] Or *dome* [c] Gk Jerome Compare Syr: Heb *line* [d] Heb *In them* [e] Or *from proud thoughts*

The name of the God of Jacob protect you!
2 May he send you help from the sanctuary,
and give you support from Zion.
3 May he remember all your offerings,
and regard with favor your burnt sacrifices. *Selah*

4 May he grant you your heart's desire,
and fulfill all your plans.
5 May we shout for joy over your victory,
and in the name of our God set up our banners.
May the LORD fulfill all your petitions.

6 Now I know that the LORD will help his anointed;
he will answer him from his holy heaven
with mighty victories by his right hand.
7 Some take pride in chariots, and some in horses,
but our pride is in the name of the LORD our God.
8 They will collapse and fall,
but we shall rise and stand upright.

9 Give victory to the king, O LORD;
answer us when we call.[a]

PSALM 21

To the leader. A Psalm of David.

1 In your strength the king rejoices, O LORD,
and in your help how greatly he exults!
2 You have given him his heart's desire,
and have not withheld the request of his lips. *Selah*
3 For you meet him with rich blessings;
you set a crown of fine gold on his head.
4 He asked you for life; you gave it to him—
length of days forever and ever.
5 His glory is great through your help;
splendor and majesty you bestow on him.
6 You bestow on him blessings forever;
you make him glad with the joy of your presence.

7 For the king trusts in the LORD,
and through the steadfast love of the Most High he shall not be moved.

8 Your hand will find out all your enemies;
your right hand will find out those who hate you.
9 You will make them like a fiery furnace
when you appear.
The LORD will swallow them up in his wrath,
and fire will consume them.
10 You will destroy their offspring from the earth,
and their children from among humankind.
11 If they plan evil against you,
if they devise mischief, they will not succeed.
12 For you will put them to flight;
you will aim at their faces with your bows.

13 Be exalted, O LORD, in your strength!
We will sing and praise your power.

PSALM 22

To the leader: according to The Deer of the Dawn.
A Psalm of David.

1 My God, my God, why have you forsaken me?
Why are you so far from helping me, from the words of my groaning?
2 O my God, I cry by day, but you do not answer;
and by night, but find no rest.

3 Yet you are holy,
enthroned on the praises of Israel.
4 In you our ancestors trusted;
they trusted, and you delivered them.
5 To you they cried, and were saved;
in you they trusted, and were not put to shame.

6 But I am a worm, and not human;
scorned by others, and despised by the people.

[a] Gk: Heb *give victory, O LORD; let the King answer us when we call*

Psalm 22

This lament psalm will seem especially familiar to Christian readers because phrases from it are woven into the narratives of Jesus' crucifixion in the Gospels. His last cry from the cross in Matthew and Mark is the first verse of this psalm (suggesting to some that he might have been reciting this psalm in his dying moments). He was scorned and mocked (see vv. 6 and 7), he was thirsty (v. 15); those who crucified him divided his clothes among them (see v. 18). The Gospel writers may have meant to imply by these echoes that the way Jesus died was a fulfillment of prophecy. Psalm 22 is not a literal prophecy, however. None of these phrases appears in the future tense. And the psalmist describes other torments—being surrounded by bulls (v. 12), dogs (v. 16), threatened by lions and wild oxen (v. 21)—that play no role in the Gospel stories. Rather, like other lament psalms, this psalm has given anguished, yet faithful voice to generations of men and women caught up in suffering and grief. Jesus' own death can be seen as a part of that greater story.

— *NE*

7 All who see me mock at me;
they make mouths at me, they shake their heads;
8 "Commit your cause to the LORD; let him deliver—
let him rescue the one in whom he delights!"

9 Yet it was you who took me from the womb;
you kept me safe on my mother's breast.
10 On you I was cast from my birth,
and since my mother bore me you have been my God.
11 Do not be far from me,
for trouble is near
and there is no one to help.

12 Many bulls encircle me,
strong bulls of Bashan surround me;
13 they open wide their mouths at me,
like a ravening and roaring lion.

14 I am poured out like water,
and all my bones are out of joint;
my heart is like wax;
it is melted within my breast;
15 my mouth[a] is dried up like a potsherd,
and my tongue sticks to my jaws;
you lay me in the dust of death.

16 For dogs are all around me;
a company of evildoers encircles me.
My hands and feet have shriveled;[b]
17 I can count all my bones.
They stare and gloat over me;
18 they divide my clothes among themselves,
and for my clothing they cast lots.

19 But you, O LORD, do not be far away!
O my help, come quickly to my aid!
20 Deliver my soul from the sword,
my life[c] from the power of the dog!
21 Save me from the mouth of the lion!

From the horns of the wild oxen you have rescued[d] me.
22 I will tell of your name to my brothers and sisters;[e]
in the midst of the congregation I will praise you:
23 You who fear the LORD, praise him!
All you offspring of Jacob, glorify him;
stand in awe of him, all you offspring of Israel!
24 For he did not despise or abhor
the affliction of the afflicted;
he did not hide his face from me,[f]
but heard when I[g] cried to him.

25 From you comes my praise in the great congregation;
my vows I will pay before those who fear him.

[a] Cn: Heb *strength* [b] Meaning of Heb uncertain [c] Heb *my only one* [d] Heb *answered* [e] Or *kindred* [f] Heb *him* [g] Heb *he*

26 The poor[a] shall eat and be satisfied;
those who seek him shall praise the LORD.
May your hearts live forever!

27 All the ends of the earth shall remember
and turn to the LORD;
and all the families of the nations
shall worship before him.[b]
28 For dominion belongs to the LORD,
and he rules over the nations.

29 To him,[c] indeed, shall all who sleep in[d] the
earth bow down;
before him shall bow all who go down to
the dust,
and I shall live for him.[e]
30 Posterity will serve him;
future generations will be told about the
Lord,
31 and[f] proclaim his deliverance to a people yet
unborn,
saying that he has done it.

PSALM 23

A Psalm of David.

1 The LORD is my shepherd, I shall not want.
2 He makes me lie down in green pastures;
he leads me beside still waters;[g]
3 he restores my soul.[h]
He leads me in right paths[i]
for his name's sake.

4 Even though I walk through the darkest valley,[j]
I fear no evil;
for you are with me;
your rod and your staff—
they comfort me.

5 You prepare a table before me
in the presence of my enemies;
you anoint my head with oil;
my cup overflows.
6 Surely[k] goodness and mercy[l] shall follow me
all the days of my life,
and I shall dwell in the house of the LORD
my whole life long.[m]

PSALM 24

Of David. A Psalm.

1 The earth is the LORD's and all that is in it,
the world, and those who live in it;
2 for he has founded it on the seas,
and established it on the rivers.

3 Who shall ascend the hill of the LORD?
And who shall stand in his holy place?
4 Those who have clean hands and pure hearts,
who do not lift up their souls to what is false,
and do not swear deceitfully.
5 They will receive blessing from the LORD,
and vindication from the God of their
salvation.
6 Such is the company of those who seek him,
who seek the face of the God of Jacob.[n]
Selah

7 Lift up your heads, O gates!
and be lifted up, O ancient doors!
that the King of glory may come in.
8 Who is the King of glory?
The LORD, strong and mighty,
the LORD, mighty in battle.
9 Lift up your heads, O gates!
and be lifted up, O ancient doors!
that the King of glory may come in.
10 Who is this King of glory?
The LORD of hosts,
he is the King of glory. *Selah*

PSALM 25

Of David.

1 To you, O LORD, I lift up my soul.

[a] Or *afflicted* [b] Gk Syr Jerome: Heb *you* [c] Cn: Heb *They have eaten and* [d] Cn: Heb *all the fat ones* [e] Compare Gk Syr Vg: Heb *and he who cannot keep himself alive* [f] Compare Gk: Heb *it will be told about the Lord to the generation, [31] they will come and* [g] Heb *waters of rest* [h] Or *life* [i] Or *paths of righteousness* [j] Or *the valley of the shadow of death* [k] Or *Only* [l] Or *kindness* [m] Heb *for length of days* [n] Gk Syr: Heb *your face, O Jacob*

2 O my God, in you I trust;
do not let me be put to shame;
do not let my enemies exult over me.
3 Do not let those who wait for you be put to shame;
let them be ashamed who are wantonly treacherous.

4 Make me to know your ways, O LORD;
teach me your paths.
5 Lead me in your truth, and teach me,
for you are the God of my salvation;
for you I wait all day long.

6 Be mindful of your mercy, O LORD, and of your steadfast love,
for they have been from of old.
7 Do not remember the sins of my youth or my transgressions;
according to your steadfast love remember me,
for your goodness' sake, O LORD!

8 Good and upright is the LORD;
therefore he instructs sinners in the way.
9 He leads the humble in what is right,
and teaches the humble his way.
10 All the paths of the LORD are steadfast love and faithfulness,
for those who keep his covenant and his decrees.

11 For your name's sake, O LORD,
pardon my guilt, for it is great.
12 Who are they that fear the LORD?
He will teach them the way that they should choose.

13 They will abide in prosperity,
and their children shall possess the land.
14 The friendship of the LORD is for those who fear him,
and he makes his covenant known to them.
15 My eyes are ever toward the LORD,
for he will pluck my feet out of the net.

16 Turn to me and be gracious to me,
for I am lonely and afflicted.
17 Relieve the troubles of my heart,
and bring me[a] out of my distress.
18 Consider my affliction and my trouble,
and forgive all my sins.

19 Consider how many are my foes,
and with what violent hatred they hate me.
20 O guard my life, and deliver me;
do not let me be put to shame, for I take refuge in you.
21 May integrity and uprightness preserve me,
for I wait for you.

22 Redeem Israel, O God,
out of all its troubles.

PSALM 26

Of David.

1 Vindicate me, O LORD,
for I have walked in my integrity,
and I have trusted in the LORD without wavering.
2 Prove me, O LORD, and try me;
test my heart and mind.
3 For your steadfast love is before my eyes,
and I walk in faithfulness to you.[b]

4 I do not sit with the worthless,
nor do I consort with hypocrites;
5 I hate the company of evildoers,
and will not sit with the wicked.

6 I wash my hands in innocence,
and go around your altar, O LORD,
7 singing aloud a song of thanksgiving,
and telling all your wondrous deeds.

8 O LORD, I love the house in which you dwell,
and the place where your glory abides.
9 Do not sweep me away with sinners,
nor my life with the bloodthirsty,

[a] Or *The troubles of my heart are enlarged; bring me* [b] Or *in your faithfulness*

10 those in whose hands are evil devices,
and whose right hands are full of bribes.

11 But as for me, I walk in my integrity;
redeem me, and be gracious to me.
12 My foot stands on level ground;
in the great congregation I will bless the
LORD.

PSALM 27

Of David.

1 The LORD is my light and my salvation;
whom shall I fear?
The LORD is the stronghold[a] of my life;
of whom shall I be afraid?

2 When evildoers assail me
to devour my flesh—
my adversaries and foes—
they shall stumble and fall.

3 Though an army encamp against me,
my heart shall not fear;
though war rise up against me,
yet I will be confident.

4 One thing I asked of the LORD,
that will I seek after:
to live in the house of the LORD
all the days of my life,
to behold the beauty of the LORD,
and to inquire in his temple.

5 For he will hide me in his shelter
in the day of trouble;
he will conceal me under the cover of his
tent;
he will set me high on a rock.

6 Now my head is lifted up
above my enemies all around me,
and I will offer in his tent
sacrifices with shouts of joy;
I will sing and make melody to the LORD.

7 Hear, O LORD, when I cry aloud,
be gracious to me and answer me!
8 "Come," my heart says, "seek his face!"
Your face, LORD, do I seek.
9 Do not hide your face from me.

Do not turn your servant away in anger,
you who have been my help.
Do not cast me off, do not forsake me,
O God of my salvation!
10 If my father and mother forsake me,
the LORD will take me up.

11 Teach me your way, O LORD,
and lead me on a level path
because of my enemies.
12 Do not give me up to the will of my
adversaries,
for false witnesses have risen against me,
and they are breathing out violence.

13 I believe that I shall see the goodness of the
LORD
in the land of the living.
14 Wait for the LORD;
be strong, and let your heart take courage;
wait for the LORD!

PSALM 28

Of David.

1 To you, O LORD, I call;
my rock, do not refuse to hear me,
for if you are silent to me,
I shall be like those who go down to the
Pit.
2 Hear the voice of my supplication,
as I cry to you for help,
as I lift up my hands
toward your most holy sanctuary.[b]

3 Do not drag me away with the wicked,
with those who are workers of evil,
who speak peace with their neighbors,
while mischief is in their hearts.

[a] Or *refuge* [b] Heb *your innermost sanctuary*

4 Repay them according to their work,
and according to the evil of their deeds;
repay them according to the work of their hands;
render them their due reward.
5 Because they do not regard the works of the LORD,
or the work of his hands,
he will break them down and build them up no more.

6 Blessed be the LORD,
for he has heard the sound of my pleadings.
7 The LORD is my strength and my shield;
in him my heart trusts;
so I am helped, and my heart exults,
and with my song I give thanks to him.

8 The LORD is the strength of his people;
he is the saving refuge of his anointed.
9 O save your people, and bless your heritage;
be their shepherd, and carry them forever.

PSALM 29

A Psalm of David.

1 Ascribe to the LORD, O heavenly beings,[a]
ascribe to the LORD glory and strength.
2 Ascribe to the LORD the glory of his name;
worship the LORD in holy splendor.

3 The voice of the LORD is over the waters;
the God of glory thunders,
the LORD, over mighty waters.
4 The voice of the LORD is powerful;
the voice of the LORD is full of majesty.

5 The voice of the LORD breaks the cedars;
the LORD breaks the cedars of Lebanon.
6 He makes Lebanon skip like a calf,
and Sirion like a young wild ox.

7 The voice of the LORD flashes forth flames of fire.
8 The voice of the LORD shakes the wilderness;
the LORD shakes the wilderness of Kadesh.

9 The voice of the LORD causes the oaks to whirl,[b]
and strips the forest bare;
and in his temple all say, "Glory!"

10 The LORD sits enthroned over the flood;
the LORD sits enthroned as king forever.
11 May the LORD give strength to his people!
May the LORD bless his people with peace!

PSALM 30

A Psalm. A Song at the dedication of the temple. Of David.

1 I will extol you, O LORD, for you have drawn me up,
and did not let my foes rejoice over me.
2 O LORD my God, I cried to you for help,
and you have healed me.
3 O LORD, you brought up my soul from Sheol,
restored me to life from among those gone down to the Pit.[c]

4 Sing praises to the LORD, O you his faithful ones,
and give thanks to his holy name.
5 For his anger is but for a moment;
his favor is for a lifetime.
Weeping may linger for the night,
but joy comes with the morning.

6 As for me, I said in my prosperity,
"I shall never be moved."
7 By your favor, O LORD,
you had established me as a strong mountain;
you hid your face;
I was dismayed.

8 To you, O LORD, I cried,
and to the LORD I made supplication:

[a] Heb *sons of gods* [b] Or *causes the deer to calve* [c] Or *that I should not go down to the Pit*

9 "What profit is there in my death,
if I go down to the Pit?
Will the dust praise you?
Will it tell of your faithfulness?
10 Hear, O LORD, and be gracious to me!
O LORD, be my helper!"

11 You have turned my mourning into dancing;
you have taken off my sackcloth
and clothed me with joy,
12 so that my soul[a] may praise you and not be silent.
O LORD my God, I will give thanks to you forever.

PSALM 31

To the leader. A Psalm of David.

1 In you, O LORD, I seek refuge;
do not let me ever be put to shame;
in your righteousness deliver me.
2 Incline your ear to me;
rescue me speedily.
Be a rock of refuge for me,
a strong fortress to save me.

3 You are indeed my rock and my fortress;
for your name's sake lead me and guide me,
4 take me out of the net that is hidden for me,
for you are my refuge.
5 Into your hand I commit my spirit;
you have redeemed me, O LORD, faithful God.

6 You hate[b] those who pay regard to worthless idols,
but I trust in the LORD.
7 I will exult and rejoice in your steadfast love,
because you have seen my affliction;
you have taken heed of my adversities,
8 and have not delivered me into the hand of the enemy;
you have set my feet in a broad place.

9 Be gracious to me, O LORD, for I am in distress;
my eye wastes away from grief,
my soul and body also.
10 For my life is spent with sorrow,
and my years with sighing;
my strength fails because of my misery,[c]
and my bones waste away.

11 I am the scorn of all my adversaries,
a horror[d] to my neighbors,
an object of dread to my acquaintances;
those who see me in the street flee from me.
12 I have passed out of mind like one who is dead;
I have become like a broken vessel.
13 For I hear the whispering of many—
terror all around!—
as they scheme together against me,
as they plot to take my life.

14 But I trust in you, O LORD;
I say, "You are my God."
15 My times are in your hand;
deliver me from the hand of my enemies and persecutors.
16 Let your face shine upon your servant;
save me in your steadfast love.
17 Do not let me be put to shame, O LORD,
for I call on you;
let the wicked be put to shame;
let them go dumbfounded to Sheol.
18 Let the lying lips be stilled
that speak insolently against the righteous
with pride and contempt.

19 O how abundant is your goodness
that you have laid up for those who fear you,
and accomplished for those who take refuge in you,
in the sight of everyone!
20 In the shelter of your presence you hide them
from human plots;

[a] Heb *that glory* [b] One Heb Ms Gk Syr Jerome: MT *I hate* [c] Gk Syr: Heb *my iniquity* [d] Cn: Heb *exceedingly*

you hold them safe under your shelter
from contentious tongues.

21 Blessed be the LORD,
for he has wondrously shown his steadfast love to me
when I was beset as a city under siege.
22 I had said in my alarm,
"I am driven far[a] from your sight."
But you heard my supplications
when I cried out to you for help.

23 Love the LORD, all you his saints.
The LORD preserves the faithful,
but abundantly repays the one who acts haughtily.
24 Be strong, and let your heart take courage,
all you who wait for the LORD.

PSALM 32

Of David. A Maskil.

1 Happy are those whose transgression is forgiven,
whose sin is covered.
2 Happy are those to whom the LORD imputes no iniquity,
and in whose spirit there is no deceit.

3 While I kept silence, my body wasted away
through my groaning all day long.
4 For day and night your hand was heavy upon me;
my strength was dried up[b] as by the heat of summer. *Selah*

5 Then I acknowledged my sin to you,
and I did not hide my iniquity;
I said, "I will confess my transgressions to the LORD,"
and you forgave the guilt of my sin. *Selah*

6 Therefore let all who are faithful
offer prayer to you;
at a time of distress,[c] the rush of mighty waters
shall not reach them.
7 You are a hiding place for me;
you preserve me from trouble;
you surround me with glad cries of deliverance. *Selah*

8 I will instruct you and teach you the way you should go;
I will counsel you with my eye upon you.
9 Do not be like a horse or a mule, without understanding,
whose temper must be curbed with bit and bridle,
else it will not stay near you.

10 Many are the torments of the wicked,
but steadfast love surrounds those who trust in the LORD.
11 Be glad in the LORD and rejoice, O righteous,
and shout for joy, all you upright in heart.

PSALM 33

1 Rejoice in the LORD, O you righteous.
Praise befits the upright.
2 Praise the LORD with the lyre;
make melody to him with the harp of ten strings.
3 Sing to him a new song;
play skillfully on the strings, with loud shouts.

4 For the word of the LORD is upright,
and all his work is done in faithfulness.
5 He loves righteousness and justice;
the earth is full of the steadfast love of the LORD.

6 By the word of the LORD the heavens were made,
and all their host by the breath of his mouth.
7 He gathered the waters of the sea as in a bottle;
he put the deeps in storehouses.

[a] Another reading is *cut off* [b] Meaning of Heb uncertain [c] Cn: Heb *at a time of finding only*

8 Let all the earth fear the LORD;
let all the inhabitants of the world stand in awe of him.
9 For he spoke, and it came to be;
he commanded, and it stood firm.

10 The LORD brings the counsel of the nations to nothing;
he frustrates the plans of the peoples.
11 The counsel of the LORD stands forever,
the thoughts of his heart to all generations.
12 Happy is the nation whose God is the LORD,
the people whom he has chosen as his heritage.

13 The LORD looks down from heaven;
he sees all humankind.
14 From where he sits enthroned he watches
all the inhabitants of the earth—
15 he who fashions the hearts of them all,
and observes all their deeds.
16 A king is not saved by his great army;
a warrior is not delivered by his great strength.
17 The war horse is a vain hope for victory,
and by its great might it cannot save.

18 Truly the eye of the LORD is on those who fear him,
on those who hope in his steadfast love,
19 to deliver their soul from death,
and to keep them alive in famine.

20 Our soul waits for the LORD;
he is our help and shield.
21 Our heart is glad in him,
because we trust in his holy name.
22 Let your steadfast love, O LORD, be upon us,
even as we hope in you.

PSALM 34

Of David, when he feigned madness before Abimelech, so that he drove him out, and he went away.

1 I will bless the LORD at all times;
his praise shall continually be in my mouth.
2 My soul makes its boast in the LORD;
let the humble hear and be glad.
3 O magnify the LORD with me,
and let us exalt his name together.

4 I sought the LORD, and he answered me,
and delivered me from all my fears.
5 Look to him, and be radiant;
so your[a] faces shall never be ashamed.
6 This poor soul cried, and was heard by the LORD,
and was saved from every trouble.
7 The angel of the LORD encamps
around those who fear him, and delivers them.
8 O taste and see that the LORD is good;
happy are those who take refuge in him.
9 O fear the LORD, you his holy ones,
for those who fear him have no want.
10 The young lions suffer want and hunger,
but those who seek the LORD lack no good thing.

11 Come, O children, listen to me;
I will teach you the fear of the LORD.
12 Which of you desires life,
and covets many days to enjoy good?
13 Keep your tongue from evil,
and your lips from speaking deceit.
14 Depart from evil, and do good;
seek peace, and pursue it.

15 The eyes of the LORD are on the righteous,
and his ears are open to their cry.
16 The face of the LORD is against evildoers,
to cut off the remembrance of them from the earth.
17 When the righteous cry for help, the LORD hears,
and rescues them from all their troubles.
18 The LORD is near to the brokenhearted,
and saves the crushed in spirit.

[a] Gk Syr Jerome: Heb *their*

19 Many are the afflictions of the righteous,
but the LORD rescues them from them all.
20 He keeps all their bones;
not one of them will be broken.
21 Evil brings death to the wicked,
and those who hate the righteous will be condemned.
22 The LORD redeems the life of his servants;
none of those who take refuge in him will be condemned.

PSALM 35

Of David.

1 Contend, O LORD, with those who contend with me;
fight against those who fight against me!
2 Take hold of shield and buckler,
and rise up to help me!
3 Draw the spear and javelin
against my pursuers;
say to my soul,
"I am your salvation."

4 Let them be put to shame and dishonor
who seek after my life.
Let them be turned back and confounded
who devise evil against me.
5 Let them be like chaff before the wind,
with the angel of the LORD driving them on.
6 Let their way be dark and slippery,
with the angel of the LORD pursuing them.

7 For without cause they hid their net[a] for me;
without cause they dug a pit[b] for my life.
8 Let ruin come on them unawares.
And let the net that they hid ensnare them;
let them fall in it—to their ruin.

9 Then my soul shall rejoice in the LORD,
exulting in his deliverance.
10 All my bones shall say,
"O LORD, who is like you?
You deliver the weak
from those too strong for them,
the weak and needy from those who despoil them."

11 Malicious witnesses rise up;
they ask me about things I do not know.
12 They repay me evil for good;
my soul is forlorn.
13 But as for me, when they were sick,
I wore sackcloth;
I afflicted myself with fasting.
I prayed with head bowed[c] on my bosom,
14 as though I grieved for a friend or a brother;
I went about as one who laments for a mother,
bowed down and in mourning.

15 But at my stumbling they gathered in glee,
they gathered together against me;
ruffians whom I did not know
tore at me without ceasing;

Psalm 35

[T]o the modern reader, the psalms can seem impenetrable: how in the world can we read, let alone pray, these angry and often violent poems from an ancient warrior culture? At a glance, they seem overwhelmingly patriarchal, ill-tempered, moralistic, vengeful, and often seem to reflect precisely what is wrong with our world. And that's the point, or part of it. As one reads the psalms every day, it becomes clear that the world they depict is not really so different from our own; the fourth-century monk Athanasius wrote that the psalms "become like a mirror to the person singing them," and this is as true now as when he wrote it. The psalms remind us that the way we judge each other, with harsh words and acts of vengeance, constitutes injustice, and they remind us that it is the powerless in society who are overwhelmed when injustice becomes institutionalized. Psalm 35, like many psalms, laments God's absence in our unjust world, even to the point of crying, "How long, O LORD, will you look on?" (v. 17).[32]

— Kathleen Norris

[a] Heb *a pit, their net* [b] The word *pit* is transposed from the preceding line [c] Or *My prayer turned back*

16 they impiously mocked more and more,[a]
gnashing at me with their teeth.

17 How long, O LORD, will you look on?
Rescue me from their ravages,
my life from the lions!
18 Then I will thank you in the great congregation;
in the mighty throng I will praise you.

19 Do not let my treacherous enemies rejoice over me,
or those who hate me without cause wink the eye.
20 For they do not speak peace,
but they conceive deceitful words
against those who are quiet in the land.
21 They open wide their mouths against me;
they say, "Aha, Aha,
our eyes have seen it."

22 You have seen, O LORD; do not be silent!
O Lord, do not be far from me!
23 Wake up! Bestir yourself for my defense,
for my cause, my God and my Lord!
24 Vindicate me, O LORD, my God,
according to your righteousness,
and do not let them rejoice over me.
25 Do not let them say to themselves,
"Aha, we have our heart's desire."
Do not let them say, "We have swallowed you[b] up."

26 Let all those who rejoice at my calamity
be put to shame and confusion;
let those who exalt themselves against me
be clothed with shame and dishonor.

27 Let those who desire my vindication
shout for joy and be glad,
and say evermore,
"Great is the LORD,
who delights in the welfare of his servant."
28 Then my tongue shall tell of your righteousness
and of your praise all day long.

PSALM 36

To the leader. Of David, the servant of the LORD.

1 Transgression speaks to the wicked
deep in their hearts;
there is no fear of God
before their eyes.
2 For they flatter themselves in their own eyes
that their iniquity cannot be found out and hated.
3 The words of their mouths are mischief and deceit;
they have ceased to act wisely and do good.
4 They plot mischief while on their beds;
they are set on a way that is not good;
they do not reject evil.

5 Your steadfast love, O LORD, extends to the heavens,
your faithfulness to the clouds.
6 Your righteousness is like the mighty mountains,
your judgments are like the great deep;
you save humans and animals alike,
O LORD.

7 How precious is your steadfast love, O God!
All people may take refuge in the shadow of your wings.
8 They feast on the abundance of your house,
and you give them drink from the river of your delights.
9 For with you is the fountain of life;
in your light we see light.

10 O continue your steadfast love to those who know you,
and your salvation to the upright of heart!
11 Do not let the foot of the arrogant tread on me,
or the hand of the wicked drive me away.

[a] Cn Compare Gk: Heb *like the profanest of mockers of a cake* [b] Heb *him*

12 There the evildoers lie prostrate;
they are thrust down, unable to rise.

PSALM 37

Of David.

1 Do not fret because of the wicked;
do not be envious of wrongdoers,
2 for they will soon fade like the grass,
and wither like the green herb.

3 Trust in the LORD, and do good;
so you will live in the land, and enjoy security.
4 Take delight in the LORD,
and he will give you the desires of your heart.

5 Commit your way to the LORD;
trust in him, and he will act.
6 He will make your vindication shine like the light,
and the justice of your cause like the noonday.

7 Be still before the LORD, and wait patiently for him;
do not fret over those who prosper in their way,
over those who carry out evil devices.

8 Refrain from anger, and forsake wrath.
Do not fret—it leads only to evil.
9 For the wicked shall be cut off,
but those who wait for the LORD shall inherit the land.

10 Yet a little while, and the wicked will be no more;
though you look diligently for their place,
they will not be there.
11 But the meek shall inherit the land,
and delight themselves in abundant prosperity.

12 The wicked plot against the righteous,
and gnash their teeth at them;
13 but the LORD laughs at the wicked,
for he sees that their day is coming.

14 The wicked draw the sword and bend their bows
to bring down the poor and needy,
to kill those who walk uprightly;
15 their sword shall enter their own heart,
and their bows shall be broken.

16 Better is a little that the righteous person has
than the abundance of many wicked.
17 For the arms of the wicked shall be broken,
but the LORD upholds the righteous.

18 The LORD knows the days of the blameless,
and their heritage will abide forever;
19 they are not put to shame in evil times,
in the days of famine they have abundance.

20 But the wicked perish,
and the enemies of the LORD are like the glory of the pastures;
they vanish—like smoke they vanish away.

21 The wicked borrow, and do not pay back,
but the righteous are generous and keep giving;
22 for those blessed by the LORD shall inherit the land,
but those cursed by him shall be cut off.

23 Our steps[a] are made firm by the LORD,
when he delights in our[b] way;
24 though we stumble,[c] we[d] shall not fall headlong,
for the LORD holds us[e] by the hand.

25 I have been young, and now am old,
yet I have not seen the righteous forsaken
or their children begging bread.
26 They are ever giving liberally and lending,
and their children become a blessing.

[a] Heb *A man's steps* [b] Heb *his* [c] Heb *he stumbles* [d] Heb *he* [e] Heb *him*

27 Depart from evil, and do good;
so you shall abide forever.
28 For the LORD loves justice;
he will not forsake his faithful ones.

The righteous shall be kept safe forever,
but the children of the wicked shall be cut off.
29 The righteous shall inherit the land,
and live in it forever.

30 The mouths of the righteous utter wisdom,
and their tongues speak justice.
31 The law of their God is in their hearts;
their steps do not slip.

32 The wicked watch for the righteous,
and seek to kill them.
33 The LORD will not abandon them to their power,
or let them be condemned when they are brought to trial.

34 Wait for the LORD, and keep to his way,
and he will exalt you to inherit the land;
you will look on the destruction of the wicked.

35 I have seen the wicked oppressing,
and towering like a cedar of Lebanon.[a]
36 Again I[b] passed by, and they were no more;
though I sought them, they could not be found.

37 Mark the blameless, and behold the upright,
for there is posterity for the peaceable.
38 But transgressors shall be altogether destroyed;
the posterity of the wicked shall be cut off.

39 The salvation of the righteous is from the LORD;
he is their refuge in the time of trouble.
40 The LORD helps them and rescues them;
he rescues them from the wicked, and saves them,
because they take refuge in him.

PSALM 38

A Psalm of David, for the memorial offering.

1 O LORD, do not rebuke me in your anger,
or discipline me in your wrath.
2 For your arrows have sunk into me,
and your hand has come down on me.

3 There is no soundness in my flesh
because of your indignation;
there is no health in my bones
because of my sin.
4 For my iniquities have gone over my head;
they weigh like a burden too heavy for me.

5 My wounds grow foul and fester
because of my foolishness;
6 I am utterly bowed down and prostrate;
all day long I go around mourning.
7 For my loins are filled with burning,
and there is no soundness in my flesh.
8 I am utterly spent and crushed;
I groan because of the tumult of my heart.

9 O Lord, all my longing is known to you;
my sighing is not hidden from you.
10 My heart throbs, my strength fails me;
as for the light of my eyes—it also has gone from me.
11 My friends and companions stand aloof from my affliction,
and my neighbors stand far off.

12 Those who seek my life lay their snares;
those who seek to hurt me speak of ruin,
and meditate treachery all day long.

13 But I am like the deaf, I do not hear;
like the mute, who cannot speak.
14 Truly, I am like one who does not hear,
and in whose mouth is no retort.

[a] Gk: Meaning of Heb uncertain [b] Gk Syr Jerome: Heb *he*

15 But it is for you, O LORD, that I wait;
it is you, O Lord my God, who will answer.
16 For I pray, "Only do not let them rejoice over me,
those who boast against me when my foot slips."

17 For I am ready to fall,
and my pain is ever with me.
18 I confess my iniquity;
I am sorry for my sin.
19 Those who are my foes without cause[a] are mighty,
and many are those who hate me wrongfully.
20 Those who render me evil for good
are my adversaries because I follow after good.

21 Do not forsake me, O LORD;
O my God, do not be far from me;
22 make haste to help me,
O Lord, my salvation.

PSALM 39

To the leader: to Jeduthun. A Psalm of David.

1 I said, "I will guard my ways
that I may not sin with my tongue;
I will keep a muzzle on my mouth
as long as the wicked are in my presence."
2 I was silent and still;
I held my peace to no avail;
my distress grew worse,
3 my heart became hot within me.
While I mused, the fire burned;
then I spoke with my tongue:

4 "LORD, let me know my end,
and what is the measure of my days;
let me know how fleeting my life is.
5 You have made my days a few handbreadths,
and my lifetime is as nothing in your sight.
Surely everyone stands as a mere breath. *Selah*
6 Surely everyone goes about like a shadow.
Surely for nothing they are in turmoil;
they heap up, and do not know who will gather.

7 "And now, O Lord, what do I wait for?
My hope is in you.
8 Deliver me from all my transgressions.
Do not make me the scorn of the fool.
9 I am silent; I do not open my mouth,
for it is you who have done it.
10 Remove your stroke from me;
I am worn down by the blows[b] of your hand.

11 "You chastise mortals
in punishment for sin,
consuming like a moth what is dear to them;
surely everyone is a mere breath. *Selah*

12 "Hear my prayer, O LORD,
and give ear to my cry;
do not hold your peace at my tears.
For I am your passing guest,
an alien, like all my forebears.
13 Turn your gaze away from me, that I may smile again,
before I depart and am no more."

PSALM 40

To the leader. Of David. A Psalm.

1 I waited patiently for the LORD;
he inclined to me and heard my cry.
2 He drew me up from the desolate pit,[c]
out of the miry bog,
and set my feet upon a rock,
making my steps secure.
3 He put a new song in my mouth,
a song of praise to our God.
Many will see and fear,
and put their trust in the LORD.

4 Happy are those who make
the LORD their trust,

[a] Q Ms: MT *my living foes* [b] Heb *hostility* [c] Cn: Heb *pit of tumult*

who do not turn to the proud,
to those who go astray after false gods.
5 You have multiplied, O LORD my God,
your wondrous deeds and your thoughts toward us;
none can compare with you.
Were I to proclaim and tell of them,
they would be more than can be counted.

6 Sacrifice and offering you do not desire,
but you have given me an open ear.[a]
Burnt offering and sin offering
you have not required.
7 Then I said, "Here I am;
in the scroll of the book it is written of me.[b]
8 I delight to do your will, O my God;
your law is within my heart."

9 I have told the glad news of deliverance
in the great congregation;
see, I have not restrained my lips,
as you know, O LORD.
10 I have not hidden your saving help within my heart,
I have spoken of your faithfulness and your salvation;
I have not concealed your steadfast love and your faithfulness
from the great congregation.

11 Do not, O LORD, withhold
your mercy from me;
let your steadfast love and your faithfulness
keep me safe forever.
12 For evils have encompassed me
without number;
my iniquities have overtaken me,
until I cannot see;
they are more than the hairs of my head,
and my heart fails me.

13 Be pleased, O LORD, to deliver me;
O LORD, make haste to help me.
14 Let all those be put to shame and confusion
who seek to snatch away my life;
let those be turned back and brought to dishonor
who desire my hurt.
15 Let those be appalled because of their shame
who say to me, "Aha, Aha!"

16 But may all who seek you
rejoice and be glad in you;
may those who love your salvation
say continually, "Great is the LORD!"
17 As for me, I am poor and needy,
but the Lord takes thought for me.
You are my help and my deliverer;
do not delay, O my God.

PSALM 41

To the leader. A Psalm of David.

1 Happy are those who consider the poor;[c]
the LORD delivers them in the day of trouble.
2 The LORD protects them and keeps them alive;
they are called happy in the land.
You do not give them up to the will of their enemies.
3 The LORD sustains them on their sickbed;
in their illness you heal all their infirmities.[d]

4 As for me, I said, "O LORD, be gracious to me;
heal me, for I have sinned against you."
5 My enemies wonder in malice
when I will die, and my name perish.
6 And when they come to see me, they utter empty words,
while their hearts gather mischief;
when they go out, they tell it abroad.
7 All who hate me whisper together about me;
they imagine the worst for me.

8 They think that a deadly thing has fastened on me,
that I will not rise again from where I lie.

[a] Heb *ears you have dug for me* [b] Meaning of Heb uncertain [c] Or *weak* [d] Heb *you change all his bed*

9 Even my bosom friend in whom I trusted,
who ate of my bread, has lifted the heel against me.
10 But you, O LORD, be gracious to me,
and raise me up, that I may repay them.

11 By this I know that you are pleased with me;
because my enemy has not triumphed over me.
12 But you have upheld me because of my integrity,
and set me in your presence forever.

13 Blessed be the LORD, the God of Israel,
from everlasting to everlasting.
Amen and Amen.

BOOK II

PSALM 42

To the leader. A Maskil of the Korahites.

1 As a deer longs for flowing streams,
so my soul longs for you, O God.
2 My soul thirsts for God,
for the living God.
When shall I come and behold
the face of God?
3 My tears have been my food
day and night,
while people say to me continually,
"Where is your God?"

4 These things I remember,
as I pour out my soul:
how I went with the throng,[a]
and led them in procession to the house of God,
with glad shouts and songs of thanksgiving,
a multitude keeping festival.
5 Why are you cast down, O my soul,
and why are you disquieted within me?
Hope in God; for I shall again praise him,
my help 6and my God.

My soul is cast down within me;
therefore I remember you
from the land of Jordan and of Hermon,
from Mount Mizar.
7 Deep calls to deep
at the thunder of your cataracts;
all your waves and your billows
have gone over me.
8 By day the LORD commands his steadfast love,
and at night his song is with me,
a prayer to the God of my life.

9 I say to God, my rock,
"Why have you forgotten me?
Why must I walk about mournfully
because the enemy oppresses me?"
10 As with a deadly wound in my body,
my adversaries taunt me,
while they say to me continually,
"Where is your God?"

11 Why are you cast down, O my soul,
and why are you disquieted within me?
Hope in God; for I shall again praise him,
my help and my God.

PSALM 43

1 Vindicate me, O God, and defend my cause
against an ungodly people;
from those who are deceitful and unjust
deliver me!
2 For you are the God in whom I take refuge;
why have you cast me off?
Why must I walk about mournfully
because of the oppression of the enemy?

3 O send out your light and your truth;
let them lead me;
let them bring me to your holy hill
and to your dwelling.
4 Then I will go to the altar of God,
to God my exceeding joy;
and I will praise you with the harp,
O God, my God.

[a] Meaning of Heb uncertain

5 Why are you cast down, O my soul,
and why are you disquieted within me?
Hope in God; for I shall again praise him,
my help and my God.

PSALM 44

To the leader. Of the Korahites. A Maskil.

1 We have heard with our ears, O God,
our ancestors have told us,
what deeds you performed in their days,
in the days of old:
2 you with your own hand drove out the
nations,
but them you planted;
you afflicted the peoples,
but them you set free;
3 for not by their own sword did they win the
land,
nor did their own arm give them victory;
but your right hand, and your arm,
and the light of your countenance,
for you delighted in them.

4 You are my King and my God;
you command[a] victories for Jacob.
5 Through you we push down our foes;
through your name we tread down our
assailants.
6 For not in my bow do I trust,
nor can my sword save me.
7 But you have saved us from our foes,
and have put to confusion those who
hate us.
8 In God we have boasted continually,
and we will give thanks to your name
forever. *Selah*

9 Yet you have rejected us and abased us,
and have not gone out with our armies.
10 You made us turn back from the foe,
and our enemies have gotten spoil.
11 You have made us like sheep for slaughter,
and have scattered us among the nations.
12 You have sold your people for a trifle,
demanding no high price for them.

13 You have made us the taunt of our
neighbors,
the derision and scorn of those around us.
14 You have made us a byword among the
nations,
a laughingstock[b] among the peoples.
15 All day long my disgrace is before me,
and shame has covered my face
16 at the words of the taunters and revilers,
at the sight of the enemy and the avenger.

17 All this has come upon us,
yet we have not forgotten you,
or been false to your covenant.
18 Our heart has not turned back,
nor have our steps departed from your
way,

[a] Gk Syr: Heb *You are my King, O God; command* [b] Heb *a shaking of the head*

Psalm 44

Of the prayers and songs in the book of Psalms, individual and community laments are by far the most numerous. We find a similar form of prayer in the Korean American tong-sung-ki-do. Tong-sung-ki-do, which literally means 'praying together out loud,' is a unique Korean/Korean American practice of faith.… On the one hand, this prayer is a way of laying down the burden of the agony, emotional displacement, oppression, discrimination, and frustration of immigrant life. On the other hand, this practice is an empowering synergy of different tones and voices and distinct intentions. Pray-ers may come together for tong-sung-ki-do for a variety of reasons: some to lament, some for emotional catharsis, some for discernment, some to confess, and some to demand God's intervention in their lives.[33]

— Su Yon Pak, Unzu Lee, Jung Ha Kim, and Myung Ji Cho

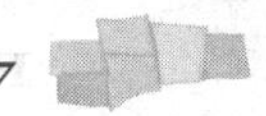

19 yet you have broken us in the haunt of
jackals,
and covered us with deep darkness.

20 If we had forgotten the name of our God,
or spread out our hands to a strange god,
21 would not God discover this?
For he knows the secrets of the heart.
22 Because of you we are being killed all day
long,
and accounted as sheep for the slaughter.

23 Rouse yourself! Why do you sleep, O Lord?
Awake, do not cast us off forever!
24 Why do you hide your face?
Why do you forget our affliction and
oppression?
25 For we sink down to the dust;
our bodies cling to the ground.
26 Rise up, come to our help.
Redeem us for the sake of your steadfast
love.

PSALM 45

To the leader: according to Lilies. Of the Korahites. A Maskil. A love song.

1 My heart overflows with a goodly theme;
I address my verses to the king;
my tongue is like the pen of a ready
scribe.

2 You are the most handsome of men;
grace is poured upon your lips;
therefore God has blessed you forever.
3 Gird your sword on your thigh, O mighty
one,
in your glory and majesty.

4 In your majesty ride on victoriously
for the cause of truth and to defend[a] the
right;
let your right hand teach you dread deeds.
5 Your arrows are sharp
in the heart of the king's enemies;
the peoples fall under you.

6 Your throne, O God,[b] endures forever and
ever.
Your royal scepter is a scepter of equity;
7 you love righteousness and hate
wickedness.
Therefore God, your God, has anointed you
with the oil of gladness beyond your
companions;
8 your robes are all fragrant with myrrh and
aloes and cassia.
From ivory palaces stringed instruments
make you glad;
9 daughters of kings are among your ladies
of honor;
at your right hand stands the queen in gold
of Ophir.

10 Hear, O daughter, consider and incline your
ear;
forget your people and your father's
house,
11 and the king will desire your beauty.
Since he is your lord, bow to him;
12 the people[c] of Tyre will seek your favor
with gifts,
the richest of the people 13with all kinds
of wealth.

The princess is decked in her chamber with
gold-woven robes;[d]
14 in many-colored robes she is led to the king;
behind her the virgins, her companions,
follow.
15 With joy and gladness they are led along
as they enter the palace of the king.

16 In the place of ancestors you, O king,[e] shall
have sons;
you will make them princes in all the earth.
17 I will cause your name to be celebrated in all
generations;

[a] Cn: Heb *and the meekness of* [b] Or *Your throne is a throne of God, it* [c] Heb *daughter* [d] Or *people.* 13*All glorious is the princess within, gold embroidery is her clothing* [e] Heb lacks *O king*

therefore the peoples will praise you
forever and ever.

PSALM 46

To the leader. Of the Korahites. According to Alamoth. A Song.

1 God is our refuge and strength,
a very present[a] help in trouble.
2 Therefore we will not fear, though the earth should change,
though the mountains shake in the heart of the sea;
3 though its waters roar and foam,
though the mountains tremble with its tumult. *Selah*

4 There is a river whose streams make glad the city of God,
the holy habitation of the Most High.
5 God is in the midst of the city;[b] it shall not be moved;
God will help it when the morning dawns.
6 The nations are in an uproar, the kingdoms totter;
he utters his voice, the earth melts.
7 The LORD of hosts is with us;
the God of Jacob is our refuge.[c] *Selah*

8 Come, behold the works of the LORD;
see what desolations he has brought on the earth.
9 He makes wars cease to the end of the earth;
he breaks the bow, and shatters the spear;
he burns the shields with fire.
10 "Be still, and know that I am God!
I am exalted among the nations,
I am exalted in the earth."
11 The LORD of hosts is with us;
the God of Jacob is our refuge.[c] *Selah*

PSALM 47

To the leader. Of the Korahites. A Psalm.

1 Clap your hands, all you peoples;
shout to God with loud songs of joy.
2 For the LORD, the Most High, is awesome,
a great king over all the earth.
3 He subdued peoples under us,
and nations under our feet.
4 He chose our heritage for us,
the pride of Jacob whom he loves. *Selah*

5 God has gone up with a shout,
the LORD with the sound of a trumpet.
6 Sing praises to God, sing praises;
sing praises to our King, sing praises.
7 For God is the king of all the earth;
sing praises with a psalm.[d]

8 God is king over the nations;
God sits on his holy throne.
9 The princes of the peoples gather
as the people of the God of Abraham.
For the shields of the earth belong to God;
he is highly exalted.

PSALM 48

A Song. A Psalm of the Korahites.

1 Great is the LORD and greatly to be praised
in the city of our God.
His holy mountain, 2 beautiful in elevation,
is the joy of all the earth,
Mount Zion, in the far north,
the city of the great King.
3 Within its citadels God
has shown himself a sure defense.

4 Then the kings assembled,
they came on together.
5 As soon as they saw it, they were astounded;
they were in panic, they took to flight;
6 trembling took hold of them there,
pains as of a woman in labor,
7 as when an east wind shatters
the ships of Tarshish.
8 As we have heard, so have we seen
in the city of the LORD of hosts,
in the city of our God,
which God establishes forever. *Selah*

[a] Or *well proved* [b] Heb *of it* [c] Or *fortress* [d] Heb *Maskil*

9 We ponder your steadfast love, O God,
in the midst of your temple.
10 Your name, O God, like your praise,
reaches to the ends of the earth.
Your right hand is filled with victory.
11 Let Mount Zion be glad,
let the towns[a] of Judah rejoice
because of your judgments.

12 Walk about Zion, go all around it,
count its towers,
13 consider well its ramparts;
go through its citadels,
that you may tell the next generation
14 that this is God,
our God forever and ever.
He will be our guide forever.

PSALM 49

To the leader. Of the Korahites. A Psalm.

1 Hear this, all you peoples;
give ear, all inhabitants of the world,
2 both low and high,
rich and poor together.
3 My mouth shall speak wisdom;
the meditation of my heart shall be understanding.
4 I will incline my ear to a proverb;
I will solve my riddle to the music of the harp.

5 Why should I fear in times of trouble,
when the iniquity of my persecutors surrounds me,
6 those who trust in their wealth
and boast of the abundance of their riches?
7 Truly, no ransom avails for one's life,[b]
there is no price one can give to God for it.
8 For the ransom of life is costly,
and can never suffice,
9 that one should live on forever
and never see the grave.[c]

10 When we look at the wise, they die;
fool and dolt perish together
and leave their wealth to others.
11 Their graves[d] are their homes forever,
their dwelling places to all generations,
though they named lands their own.
12 Mortals cannot abide in their pomp;
they are like the animals that perish.

13 Such is the fate of the foolhardy,
the end of those[e] who are pleased with their lot. *Selah*
14 Like sheep they are appointed for Sheol;
Death shall be their shepherd;
straight to the grave they descend,[f]
and their form shall waste away;
Sheol shall be their home.[g]
15 But God will ransom my soul from the power of Sheol,
for he will receive me. *Selah*

16 Do not be afraid when some become rich,
when the wealth of their houses increases.
17 For when they die they will carry nothing away;
their wealth will not go down after them.
18 Though in their lifetime they count themselves happy
—for you are praised when you do well for yourself—
19 they[h] will go to the company of their ancestors,
who will never again see the light.
20 Mortals cannot abide in their pomp;
they are like the animals that perish.

PSALM 50

A Psalm of Asaph.

1 The mighty one, God the Lord,
speaks and summons the earth
from the rising of the sun to its setting.

[a] Heb *daughters* [b] Another reading is *no one can ransom a brother* [c] Heb *the pit* [d] Gk Syr Compare Tg: Heb *their inward* (thought) [e] Tg: Heb *after them* [f] Cn: Heb *the upright shall have dominion over them in the morning* [g] Meaning of Heb uncertain [h] Cn: Heb *you*

2 Out of Zion, the perfection of beauty,
God shines forth.

3 Our God comes and does not keep silence,
before him is a devouring fire,
and a mighty tempest all around him.
4 He calls to the heavens above
and to the earth, that he may judge his people:
5 "Gather to me my faithful ones,
who made a covenant with me by sacrifice!"
6 The heavens declare his righteousness,
for God himself is judge. *Selah*

7 "Hear, O my people, and I will speak,
O Israel, I will testify against you.
I am God, your God.
8 Not for your sacrifices do I rebuke you;
your burnt offerings are continually before me.
9 I will not accept a bull from your house,
or goats from your folds.
10 For every wild animal of the forest is mine,
the cattle on a thousand hills.
11 I know all the birds of the air,[a]
and all that moves in the field is mine.

12 "If I were hungry, I would not tell you,
for the world and all that is in it is mine.
13 Do I eat the flesh of bulls,
or drink the blood of goats?
14 Offer to God a sacrifice of thanksgiving,[b]
and pay your vows to the Most High.
15 Call on me in the day of trouble;
I will deliver you, and you shall glorify me."

16 But to the wicked God says:
"What right have you to recite my statutes,
or take my covenant on your lips?
17 For you hate discipline,
and you cast my words behind you.
18 You make friends with a thief when you see one,
and you keep company with adulterers.

19 "You give your mouth free rein for evil,
and your tongue frames deceit.
20 You sit and speak against your kin;
you slander your own mother's child.
21 These things you have done and I have been silent;
you thought that I was one just like yourself.
But now I rebuke you, and lay the charge before you.

22 "Mark this, then, you who forget God,
or I will tear you apart, and there will be no one to deliver.
23 Those who bring thanksgiving as their sacrifice honor me;
to those who go the right way[c]
I will show the salvation of God."

PSALM 51

To the leader. A Psalm of David, when the prophet Nathan came to him, after he had gone in to Bathsheba.

1 Have mercy on me, O God,
according to your steadfast love;
according to your abundant mercy
blot out my transgressions.
2 Wash me thoroughly from my iniquity,
and cleanse me from my sin.

3 For I know my transgressions,
and my sin is ever before me.
4 Against you, you alone, have I sinned,
and done what is evil in your sight,
so that you are justified in your sentence
and blameless when you pass judgment.
5 Indeed, I was born guilty,
a sinner when my mother conceived me.

6 You desire truth in the inward being;[d]
therefore teach me wisdom in my secret heart.
7 Purge me with hyssop, and I shall be clean;

[a] Gk Syr Tg: Heb *mountains* [b] Or *make thanksgiving your sacrifice to God* [c] Heb *who set a way*
[d] Meaning of Heb uncertain

wash me, and I shall be whiter than snow.
8 Let me hear joy and gladness;
let the bones that you have crushed rejoice.
9 Hide your face from my sins,
and blot out all my iniquities.

10 Create in me a clean heart, O God,
and put a new and right[a] spirit within me.
11 Do not cast me away from your presence,
and do not take your holy spirit from me.
12 Restore to me the joy of your salvation,
and sustain in me a willing[b] spirit.

13 Then I will teach transgressors your ways,
and sinners will return to you.
14 Deliver me from bloodshed, O God,
O God of my salvation,
and my tongue will sing aloud of your deliverance.

15 O Lord, open my lips,
and my mouth will declare your praise.
16 For you have no delight in sacrifice;
if I were to give a burnt offering, you would not be pleased.
17 The sacrifice acceptable to God[c] is a broken spirit;
a broken and contrite heart, O God, you will not despise.

18 Do good to Zion in your good pleasure;
rebuild the walls of Jerusalem,
19 then you will delight in right sacrifices,
in burnt offerings and whole burnt offerings;
then bulls will be offered on your altar.

PSALM 52

To the leader. A Maskil of David, when Doeg the Edomite came to Saul and said to him, "David has come to the house of Ahimelech."

1 Why do you boast, O mighty one,
of mischief done against the godly?[d]
All day long 2 you are plotting destruction.
Your tongue is like a sharp razor,
you worker of treachery.
3 You love evil more than good,
and lying more than speaking the truth. *Selah*

4 You love all words that devour,
O deceitful tongue.

5 But God will break you down forever;
he will snatch and tear you from your tent;
he will uproot you from the land of the living. *Selah*
6 The righteous will see, and fear,
and will laugh at the evildoer,[e] saying,
7 "See the one who would not take refuge in God,
but trusted in abundant riches,
and sought refuge in wealth!"[f]

8 But I am like a green olive tree
in the house of God.
I trust in the steadfast love of God
forever and ever.
9 I will thank you forever,
because of what you have done.
In the presence of the faithful
I will proclaim[g] your name, for it is good.

PSALM 53

To the leader: according to Mahalath. A Maskil of David.

1 Fools say in their hearts, "There is no God."
They are corrupt, they commit abominable acts;
there is no one who does good.

2 God looks down from heaven on humankind
to see if there are any who are wise,
who seek after God.

3 They have all fallen away, they are all alike perverse;

[a] Or *steadfast* [b] Or *generous* [c] Or *My sacrifice, O God,* [d] Cn Compare Syr: Heb *the kindness of God* [e] Heb *him*
[f] Syr Tg: Heb *in his destruction* [g] Cn: Heb *wait for*

there is no one who does good,
no, not one.

4 Have they no knowledge, those evildoers,
who eat up my people as they eat bread,
and do not call upon God?

5 There they shall be in great terror,
in terror such as has not been.
For God will scatter the bones of the ungodly;[a]
they will be put to shame,[b] for God has rejected them.

6 O that deliverance for Israel would come from Zion!
When God restores the fortunes of his people,
Jacob will rejoice; Israel will be glad.

PSALM 54

To the leader: with stringed instruments. A Maskil of David, when the Ziphites went and told Saul, "David is in hiding among us."

1 Save me, O God, by your name,
and vindicate me by your might.
2 Hear my prayer, O God;
give ear to the words of my mouth.

3 For the insolent have risen against me,
the ruthless seek my life;
they do not set God before them. *Selah*

4 But surely, God is my helper;
the Lord is the upholder of[c] my life.
5 He will repay my enemies for their evil.
In your faithfulness, put an end to them.

6 With a freewill offering I will sacrifice to you;
I will give thanks to your name, O LORD,
for it is good.
7 For he has delivered me from every trouble,
and my eye has looked in triumph on my enemies.

PSALM 55

To the leader: with stringed instruments. A Maskil of David.

1 Give ear to my prayer, O God;
do not hide yourself from my supplication.
2 Attend to me, and answer me;
I am troubled in my complaint.
I am distraught 3by the noise of the enemy,
because of the clamor of the wicked.
For they bring[d] trouble upon me,
and in anger they cherish enmity against me.

4 My heart is in anguish within me,
the terrors of death have fallen upon me.
5 Fear and trembling come upon me,
and horror overwhelms me.
6 And I say, "O that I had wings like a dove!
I would fly away and be at rest;
7 truly, I would flee far away;
I would lodge in the wilderness; *Selah*
8 I would hurry to find a shelter for myself
from the raging wind and tempest."

9 Confuse, O Lord, confound their speech;
for I see violence and strife in the city.
10 Day and night they go around it
on its walls,
and iniquity and trouble are within it;
11 ruin is in its midst;
oppression and fraud
do not depart from its marketplace.

12 It is not enemies who taunt me—
I could bear that;
it is not adversaries who deal insolently with me—
I could hide from them.
13 But it is you, my equal,
my companion, my familiar friend,
14 with whom I kept pleasant company;
we walked in the house of God with the throng.

[a] Cn Compare Gk Syr: Heb *him who encamps against you* [b] Gk: Heb *you have put (them) to shame* [c] Gk Syr Jerome: Heb *is of those who uphold* or *is with those who uphold* [d] Cn Compare Gk: Heb *they cause to totter*

15 Let death come upon them;
let them go down alive to Sheol;
for evil is in their homes and in their hearts.

16 But I call upon God,
and the LORD will save me.
17 Evening and morning and at noon
I utter my complaint and moan,
and he will hear my voice.
18 He will redeem me unharmed
from the battle that I wage,
for many are arrayed against me.
19 God, who is enthroned from of old, *Selah*
will hear, and will humble them—
because they do not change,
and do not fear God.

20 My companion laid hands on a friend
and violated a covenant with me[a]
21 with speech smoother than butter,
but with a heart set on war;
with words that were softer than oil,
but in fact were drawn swords.

22 Cast your burden[b] on the LORD,
and he will sustain you;
he will never permit
the righteous to be moved.

23 But you, O God, will cast them down
into the lowest pit;
the bloodthirsty and treacherous
shall not live out half their days.
But I will trust in you.

PSALM 56

To the leader: according to The Dove on Far-off Terebinths. Of David. A Miktam, when the Philistines seized him in Gath.

1 Be gracious to me, O God, for people trample on me;
all day long foes oppress me;
2 my enemies trample on me all day long,
for many fight against me.
O Most High, 3when I am afraid,
I put my trust in you.
4 In God, whose word I praise,
in God I trust; I am not afraid;
what can flesh do to me?

5 All day long they seek to injure my cause;
all their thoughts are against me for evil.
6 They stir up strife, they lurk,
they watch my steps.
As they hoped to have my life,
7 so repay[c] them for their crime;
in wrath cast down the peoples, O God!

8 You have kept count of my tossings;
put my tears in your bottle.
Are they not in your record?
9 Then my enemies will retreat
in the day when I call.
This I know, that[d] God is for me.
10 In God, whose word I praise,
in the LORD, whose word I praise,
11 in God I trust; I am not afraid.
What can a mere mortal do to me?

12 My vows to you I must perform, O God;
I will render thank offerings to you.
13 For you have delivered my soul from death,
and my feet from falling,
so that I may walk before God
in the light of life.

PSALM 57

To the leader: Do Not Destroy. Of David. A Miktam, when he fled from Saul, in the cave.

1 Be merciful to me, O God, be merciful to me,
for in you my soul takes refuge;
in the shadow of your wings I will take refuge,
until the destroying storms pass by.
2 I cry to God Most High,
to God who fulfills his purpose for me.
3 He will send from heaven and save me,

[a] Heb lacks *with me* [b] Or *Cast what he has given you* [c] Cn: Heb *rescue* [d] Or *because*

he will put to shame those who trample
on me. *Selah*
God will send forth his steadfast love and his
faithfulness.

4 I lie down among lions
that greedily devour[a] human prey;
their teeth are spears and arrows,
their tongues sharp swords.

5 Be exalted, O God, above the heavens.
Let your glory be over all the earth.

6 They set a net for my steps;
my soul was bowed down.
They dug a pit in my path,
but they have fallen into it themselves.
Selah

7 My heart is steadfast, O God,
my heart is steadfast.
I will sing and make melody.
8 Awake, my soul!
Awake, O harp and lyre!
I will awake the dawn.
9 I will give thanks to you, O Lord, among the
peoples;
I will sing praises to you among the
nations.
10 For your steadfast love is as high as the
heavens;
your faithfulness extends to the clouds.

11 Be exalted, O God, above the heavens.
Let your glory be over all the earth.

PSALM 58

To the leader: Do Not Destroy.
Of David. A Miktam.

1 Do you indeed decree what is right, you
gods?[b]
Do you judge people fairly?
2 No, in your hearts you devise wrongs;
your hands deal out violence on
earth.
3 The wicked go astray from the womb;
they err from their birth, speaking lies.
4 They have venom like the venom of a serpent,
like the deaf adder that stops its ear,
5 so that it does not hear the voice of charmers
or of the cunning enchanter.

6 O God, break the teeth in their mouths;
tear out the fangs of the young lions,
O LORD!
7 Let them vanish like water that runs away;
like grass let them be trodden down[c] and
wither.
8 Let them be like the snail that dissolves into
slime;
like the untimely birth that never sees the
sun.
9 Sooner than your pots can feel the heat of
thorns,
whether green or ablaze, may he sweep
them away!

10 The righteous will rejoice when they see
vengeance done;
they will bathe their feet in the blood of
the wicked.
11 People will say, "Surely there is a reward for
the righteous;
surely there is a God who judges on earth."

PSALM 59

To the leader: Do Not Destroy. Of David.
A Miktam, when Saul ordered his house
to be watched in order to kill him.

1 Deliver me from my enemies, O my God;
protect me from those who rise up
against me.
2 Deliver me from those who work evil;
from the bloodthirsty save me.

3 Even now they lie in wait for my life;
the mighty stir up strife against me.
For no transgression or sin of mine,
O LORD,

[a] Cn: Heb *are aflame for* [b] Or *mighty lords* [c] Cn: Meaning of Heb uncertain

4 for no fault of mine, they run and make ready.

Rouse yourself, come to my help and see!
5 You, LORD God of hosts, are God of Israel.
Awake to punish all the nations;
spare none of those who treacherously plot evil. *Selah*

6 Each evening they come back,
howling like dogs
and prowling about the city.
7 There they are, bellowing with their mouths,
with sharp words[a] on their lips—
for "Who," they think,[b] "will hear us?"

8 But you laugh at them, O LORD;
you hold all the nations in derision.
9 O my strength, I will watch for you;
for you, O God, are my fortress.
10 My God in his steadfast love will meet me;
my God will let me look in triumph on my enemies.

11 Do not kill them, or my people may forget;
make them totter by your power, and bring them down,
O Lord, our shield.
12 For the sin of their mouths, the words of their lips,
let them be trapped in their pride.
For the cursing and lies that they utter,
13 consume them in wrath;
consume them until they are no more.
Then it will be known to the ends of the earth
that God rules over Jacob. *Selah*

14 Each evening they come back,
howling like dogs
and prowling about the city.
15 They roam about for food,
and growl if they do not get their fill.

16 But I will sing of your might;
I will sing aloud of your steadfast love in the morning.
For you have been a fortress for me
and a refuge in the day of my distress.
17 O my strength, I will sing praises to you,
for you, O God, are my fortress,
the God who shows me steadfast love.

PSALM 60

To the leader: according to the Lily of the Covenant. A Miktam of David; for instruction; when he struggled with Aram-naharaim and with Aram-zobah, and when Joab on his return killed twelve thousand Edomites in the Valley of Salt.

1 O God, you have rejected us, broken our defenses;
you have been angry; now restore us!
2 You have caused the land to quake; you have torn it open;
repair the cracks in it, for it is tottering.
3 You have made your people suffer hard things;
you have given us wine to drink that made us reel.

4 You have set up a banner for those who fear you,
to rally to it out of bowshot.[c] *Selah*
5 Give victory with your right hand, and answer us,[d]
so that those whom you love may be rescued.

6 God has promised in his sanctuary:[e]
"With exultation I will divide up Shechem,
and portion out the Vale of Succoth.
7 Gilead is mine, and Manasseh is mine;
Ephraim is my helmet;
Judah is my scepter.
8 Moab is my washbasin;
on Edom I hurl my shoe;
over Philistia I shout in triumph."

[a] Heb *with swords* [b] Heb lacks *they think* [c] Gk Syr Jerome: Heb *because of the truth* [d] Another reading is *me*
[e] Or *by his holiness*

9 Who will bring me to the fortified city?
Who will lead me to Edom?
10 Have you not rejected us, O God?
You do not go out, O God, with our armies.
11 O grant us help against the foe,
for human help is worthless.
12 With God we shall do valiantly;
it is he who will tread down our foes.

PSALM 61

To the leader: with stringed instruments. Of David.

1 Hear my cry, O God;
listen to my prayer.
2 From the end of the earth I call to you,
when my heart is faint.

Lead me to the rock
that is higher than I;
3 for you are my refuge,
a strong tower against the enemy.

4 Let me abide in your tent forever,
find refuge under the shelter of your wings. *Selah*
5 For you, O God, have heard my vows;
you have given me the heritage of those who fear your name.

6 Prolong the life of the king;
may his years endure to all generations!
7 May he be enthroned forever before God;
appoint steadfast love and faithfulness to watch over him!

8 So I will always sing praises to your name,
as I pay my vows day after day.

PSALM 62

To the leader: according to Jeduthun. A Psalm of David.

1 For God alone my soul waits in silence;
from him comes my salvation.
2 He alone is my rock and my salvation,
my fortress; I shall never be shaken.

3 How long will you assail a person,
will you batter your victim, all of you,
as you would a leaning wall, a tottering fence?
4 Their only plan is to bring down a person of prominence.
They take pleasure in falsehood;
they bless with their mouths,
but inwardly they curse. *Selah*

5 For God alone my soul waits in silence,
for my hope is from him.
6 He alone is my rock and my salvation,
my fortress; I shall not be shaken.
7 On God rests my deliverance and my honor;
my mighty rock, my refuge is in God.

8 Trust in him at all times, O people;
pour out your heart before him;
God is a refuge for us. *Selah*

9 Those of low estate are but a breath,
those of high estate are a delusion;
in the balances they go up;
they are together lighter than a breath.
10 Put no confidence in extortion,
and set no vain hopes on robbery;
if riches increase, do not set your heart on them.

11 Once God has spoken;
twice have I heard this:
that power belongs to God,
12 and steadfast love belongs to you, O Lord.
For you repay to all
according to their work.

PSALM 63

A Psalm of David, when he was in the Wilderness of Judah.

1 O God, you are my God, I seek you,
my soul thirsts for you;
my flesh faints for you,
as in a dry and weary land where there is no water.
2 So I have looked upon you in the sanctuary,

beholding your power and glory.
3 Because your steadfast love is better than life,
my lips will praise you.
4 So I will bless you as long as I live;
I will lift up my hands and call on your name.

5 My soul is satisfied as with a rich feast,[a]
and my mouth praises you with joyful lips
6 when I think of you on my bed,
and meditate on you in the watches of the night;
7 for you have been my help,
and in the shadow of your wings I sing for joy.
8 My soul clings to you;
your right hand upholds me.

9 But those who seek to destroy my life
shall go down into the depths of the earth;
10 they shall be given over to the power of the sword,
they shall be prey for jackals.
11 But the king shall rejoice in God;
all who swear by him shall exult,
for the mouths of liars will be stopped.

PSALM 64

To the leader. A Psalm of David.

1 Hear my voice, O God, in my complaint;
preserve my life from the dread enemy.
2 Hide me from the secret plots of the wicked,
from the scheming of evildoers,
3 who whet their tongues like swords,
who aim bitter words like arrows,
4 shooting from ambush at the blameless;
they shoot suddenly and without fear.
5 They hold fast to their evil purpose;
they talk of laying snares secretly,
thinking, "Who can see us?[b]
6 Who can search out our crimes?[c]
We have thought out a cunningly conceived plot."
For the human heart and mind are deep.

7 But God will shoot his arrow at them;
they will be wounded suddenly.
8 Because of their tongue he will bring them to ruin;[d]
all who see them will shake with horror.
9 Then everyone will fear;
they will tell what God has brought about,
and ponder what he has done.

10 Let the righteous rejoice in the LORD
and take refuge in him.
Let all the upright in heart glory.

PSALM 65

To the leader. A Psalm of David. A Song.

1 Praise is due to you,
O God, in Zion;
and to you shall vows be performed,
2 O you who answer prayer!
To you all flesh shall come.
3 When deeds of iniquity overwhelm us,
you forgive our transgressions.
4 Happy are those whom you choose and bring near
to live in your courts.
We shall be satisfied with the goodness of your house,
your holy temple.

5 By awesome deeds you answer us with deliverance,
O God of our salvation;
you are the hope of all the ends of the earth
and of the farthest seas.
6 By your[e] strength you established the mountains;
you are girded with might.
7 You silence the roaring of the seas,
the roaring of their waves,

[a] Heb *with fat and fatness* [b] Syr: Heb *them* [c] Cn: Heb *They search out crimes* [d] Cn: Heb *They will bring him to ruin, their tongue being against them* [e] Gk Jerome: Heb *his*

the tumult of the peoples.
8 Those who live at earth's farthest bounds are
awed by your signs;
you make the gateways of the morning and
the evening shout for joy.

9 You visit the earth and water it,
you greatly enrich it;
the river of God is full of water;
you provide the people with grain,
for so you have prepared it.
10 You water its furrows abundantly,
settling its ridges,
softening it with showers,
and blessing its growth.
11 You crown the year with your bounty;
your wagon tracks overflow with richness.
12 The pastures of the wilderness overflow,
the hills gird themselves with joy,
13 the meadows clothe themselves with flocks,
the valleys deck themselves with grain,
they shout and sing together for joy.

PSALM 66

To the leader. A Song. A Psalm.

1 Make a joyful noise to God, all the earth;
2 sing the glory of his name;
give to him glorious praise.
3 Say to God, "How awesome are your deeds!
Because of your great power, your enemies
cringe before you.
4 All the earth worships you;
they sing praises to you,
sing praises to your name." *Selah*

5 Come and see what God has done:
he is awesome in his deeds among mortals.
6 He turned the sea into dry land;
they passed through the river on foot.
There we rejoiced in him,
7 who rules by his might forever,
whose eyes keep watch on the nations—
let the rebellious not exalt themselves.
Selah

8 Bless our God, O peoples,
let the sound of his praise be heard,
9 who has kept us among the living,
and has not let our feet slip.
10 For you, O God, have tested us;
you have tried us as silver is tried.
11 You brought us into the net;
you laid burdens on our backs;
12 you let people ride over our heads;
we went through fire and through water;
yet you have brought us out to a spacious
place.[a]

13 I will come into your house with burnt
offerings;
I will pay you my vows,
14 those that my lips uttered
and my mouth promised when I was in
trouble.
15 I will offer to you burnt offerings of fatlings,
with the smoke of the sacrifice of rams;
I will make an offering of bulls and goats.
Selah

16 Come and hear, all you who fear God,
and I will tell what he has done for me.
17 I cried aloud to him,
and he was extolled with my tongue.
18 If I had cherished iniquity in my heart,
the Lord would not have listened.
19 But truly God has listened;
he has given heed to the words of my
prayer.

20 Blessed be God,
because he has not rejected my prayer
or removed his steadfast love from me.

PSALM 67

To the leader: with stringed instruments.
A Psalm. A Song.

1 May God be gracious to us and bless us
and make his face to shine upon us, *Selah*
2 that your way may be known upon earth,

[a] Cn Compare Gk Syr Jerome Tg: Heb *to a saturation*

your saving power among all nations.
3 Let the peoples praise you, O God;
let all the peoples praise you.

4 Let the nations be glad and sing for joy,
for you judge the peoples with equity
and guide the nations upon earth. *Selah*
5 Let the peoples praise you, O God;
let all the peoples praise you.

6 The earth has yielded its increase;
God, our God, has blessed us.
7 May God continue to bless us;
let all the ends of the earth revere him.

PSALM 68

To the leader. Of David. A Psalm. A Song.

1 Let God rise up, let his enemies be scattered;
let those who hate him flee before him.
2 As smoke is driven away, so drive them away;
as wax melts before the fire,
let the wicked perish before God.
3 But let the righteous be joyful;
let them exult before God;
let them be jubilant with joy.

4 Sing to God, sing praises to his name;
lift up a song to him who rides upon the clouds[a]—
his name is the LORD—
be exultant before him.

5 Father of orphans and protector of widows
is God in his holy habitation.
6 God gives the desolate a home to live in;
he leads out the prisoners to prosperity,
but the rebellious live in a parched land.

7 O God, when you went out before your people,
when you marched through the wilderness, *Selah*
8 the earth quaked, the heavens poured down rain
at the presence of God, the God of Sinai,
at the presence of God, the God of Israel.
9 Rain in abundance, O God, you showered abroad;
you restored your heritage when it languished;
10 your flock found a dwelling in it;
in your goodness, O God, you provided for the needy.

11 The Lord gives the command;
great is the company of those[b] who bore the tidings:
12 "The kings of the armies, they flee, they flee!"
The women at home divide the spoil,
13 though they stay among the sheepfolds—
the wings of a dove covered with silver,
its pinions with green gold.
14 When the Almighty[c] scattered kings there,
snow fell on Zalmon.

15 O mighty mountain, mountain of Bashan;
O many-peaked mountain, mountain of Bashan!
16 Why do you look with envy, O many-peaked mountain,
at the mount that God desired for his abode,
where the LORD will reside forever?

17 With mighty chariotry, twice ten thousand,
thousands upon thousands,
the Lord came from Sinai into the holy place.[d]
18 You ascended the high mount,
leading captives in your train
and receiving gifts from people,
even from those who rebel against the LORD God's abiding there.
19 Blessed be the Lord,
who daily bears us up;

[a] Or *cast up a highway for him who rides through the deserts* [b] Or *company of the women* [c] Traditional rendering of Heb *Shaddai* [d] Cn: Heb *The Lord among them Sinai in the holy* (place)

God is our salvation. *Selah*
20 Our God is a God of salvation,
and to GOD, the Lord, belongs escape
from death.
21 But God will shatter the heads of his
enemies,
the hairy crown of those who walk in their
guilty ways.
22 The Lord said,
"I will bring them back from Bashan,
I will bring them back from the depths of the
sea,
23 so that you may bathe[a] your feet in blood,
so that the tongues of your dogs may have
their share from the foe."

24 Your solemn processions are seen,[b] O God,
the processions of my God, my King, into
the sanctuary—
25 the singers in front, the musicians last,
between them girls playing tambourines:
26 "Bless God in the great congregation,
the LORD, O you who are of Israel's
fountain!"
27 There is Benjamin, the least of them, in the
lead,
the princes of Judah in a body,
the princes of Zebulun, the princes of
Naphtali.

28 Summon your might, O God;
show your strength, O God, as you have
done for us before.
29 Because of your temple at Jerusalem
kings bear gifts to you.
30 Rebuke the wild animals that live among the
reeds,
the herd of bulls with the calves of the
peoples.
Trample[c] under foot those who lust after
tribute;
scatter the peoples who delight in war.[d]
31 Let bronze be brought from Egypt;
let Ethiopia[e] hasten to stretch out its hands
to God.

32 Sing to God, O kingdoms of the earth;
sing praises to the Lord, *Selah*
33 O rider in the heavens, the ancient heavens;
listen, he sends out his voice, his mighty
voice.
34 Ascribe power to God,
whose majesty is over Israel;
and whose power is in the skies.
35 Awesome is God in his[f] sanctuary,
the God of Israel;
he gives power and strength to his people.

Blessed be God!

PSALM 69

To the leader: according to Lilies. Of David.

1 Save me, O God,
for the waters have come up to my neck.
2 I sink in deep mire,
where there is no foothold;
I have come into deep waters,
and the flood sweeps over me.
3 I am weary with my crying;
my throat is parched.
My eyes grow dim
with waiting for my God.

4 More in number than the hairs of my head
are those who hate me without cause;
many are those who would destroy me,
my enemies who accuse me falsely.
What I did not steal
must I now restore?
5 O God, you know my folly;
the wrongs I have done are not hidden
from you.

6 Do not let those who hope in you be put to
shame because of me,
O Lord GOD of hosts;

[a] Gk Syr Tg: Heb *shatter* [b] Or *have been seen* [c] Cn: Heb *Trampling* [d] Meaning of Heb of verse 30 is uncertain
[e] Or *Nubia*; Heb *Cush* [f] Gk: Heb *from your*

do not let those who seek you be dishonored
because of me,
O God of Israel.
7 It is for your sake that I have borne reproach,
that shame has covered my face.
8 I have become a stranger to my kindred,
an alien to my mother's children.

9 It is zeal for your house that has consumed
me;
the insults of those who insult you have
fallen on me.
10 When I humbled my soul with fasting,[a]
they insulted me for doing so.
11 When I made sackcloth my clothing,
I became a byword to them.
12 I am the subject of gossip for those who sit in
the gate,
and the drunkards make songs about me.

13 But as for me, my prayer is to you, O LORD.
At an acceptable time, O God,
in the abundance of your steadfast love,
answer me.
With your faithful help 14rescue me
from sinking in the mire;
let me be delivered from my enemies
and from the deep waters.
15 Do not let the flood sweep over me,
or the deep swallow me up,
or the Pit close its mouth over me.

16 Answer me, O LORD, for your steadfast love
is good;
according to your abundant mercy, turn
to me.
17 Do not hide your face from your servant,
for I am in distress—make haste to
answer me.
18 Draw near to me, redeem me,
set me free because of my enemies.

19 You know the insults I receive,
and my shame and dishonor;
my foes are all known to you.
20 Insults have broken my heart,
so that I am in despair.
I looked for pity, but there was none;
and for comforters, but I found none.
21 They gave me poison for food,
and for my thirst they gave me vinegar to
drink.

22 Let their table be a trap for them,
a snare for their allies.
23 Let their eyes be darkened so that they
cannot see,
and make their loins tremble continually.
24 Pour out your indignation upon them,
and let your burning anger overtake them.
25 May their camp be a desolation;
let no one live in their tents.
26 For they persecute those whom you have
struck down,
and those whom you have wounded, they
attack still more.[b]
27 Add guilt to their guilt;
may they have no acquittal from you.
28 Let them be blotted out of the book of the
living;
let them not be enrolled among the
righteous.
29 But I am lowly and in pain;
let your salvation, O God, protect me.

30 I will praise the name of God with a song;
I will magnify him with thanksgiving.
31 This will please the LORD more than an ox
or a bull with horns and hoofs.
32 Let the oppressed see it and be glad;
you who seek God, let your hearts revive.
33 For the LORD hears the needy,
and does not despise his own that are in
bonds.

34 Let heaven and earth praise him,
the seas and everything that moves in
them.
35 For God will save Zion
and rebuild the cities of Judah;

[a] Gk Syr: Heb *I wept, with fasting my soul,* or *I made my soul mourn with fasting* [b] Gk Syr: Heb *recount the pain of*

and his servants shall live[a] there and
possess it;
36 the children of his servants shall inherit it,
and those who love his name shall live
in it.

PSALM 70

To the leader. Of David, for the memorial offering.

1 Be pleased, O God, to deliver me.
O LORD, make haste to help me!
2 Let those be put to shame and confusion
who seek my life.
Let those be turned back and brought to
dishonor
who desire to hurt me.
3 Let those who say, "Aha, Aha!"
turn back because of their shame.

4 Let all who seek you
rejoice and be glad in you.
Let those who love your salvation
say evermore, "God is great!"
5 But I am poor and needy;
hasten to me, O God!
You are my help and my deliverer;
O LORD, do not delay!

PSALM 71

1 In you, O LORD, I take refuge;
let me never be put to shame.
2 In your righteousness deliver me and
rescue me;
incline your ear to me and save me.
3 Be to me a rock of refuge,
a strong fortress,[b] to save me,
for you are my rock and my fortress.

4 Rescue me, O my God, from the hand of the
wicked,
from the grasp of the unjust and cruel.
5 For you, O Lord, are my hope,
my trust, O LORD, from my youth.
6 Upon you I have leaned from my birth;
it was you who took me from my mother's
womb.
My praise is continually of you.

7 I have been like a portent to many,
but you are my strong refuge.
8 My mouth is filled with your praise,
and with your glory all day long.
9 Do not cast me off in the time of old age;
do not forsake me when my strength is
spent.
10 For my enemies speak concerning me,
and those who watch for my life consult
together.
11 They say, "Pursue and seize that person
whom God has forsaken,
for there is no one to deliver."

12 O God, do not be far from me;
O my God, make haste to help me!
13 Let my accusers be put to shame and
consumed;
let those who seek to hurt me
be covered with scorn and disgrace.
14 But I will hope continually,
and will praise you yet more and more.
15 My mouth will tell of your righteous acts,
of your deeds of salvation all day long,
though their number is past my
knowledge.
16 I will come praising the mighty deeds of the
Lord GOD,
I will praise your righteousness, yours
alone.

17 O God, from my youth you have taught me,
and I still proclaim your wondrous deeds.
18 So even to old age and gray hairs,
O God, do not forsake me,
until I proclaim your might
to all the generations to come.[c]
Your power 19 and your righteousness,
O God,
reach the high heavens.

[a] Syr: Heb *and they shall live* [b] Gk Compare 31.3: Heb *to come continually you have commanded*
[c] Gk Compare Syr: Heb *to a generation, to all that come*

You who have done great things,
O God, who is like you?
20 You who have made me see many troubles
and calamities
will revive me again;
from the depths of the earth
you will bring me up again.
21 You will increase my honor,
and comfort me once again.

22 I will also praise you with the harp
for your faithfulness, O my God;
I will sing praises to you with the lyre,
O Holy One of Israel.
23 My lips will shout for joy
when I sing praises to you;
my soul also, which you have rescued.
24 All day long my tongue will talk of your
righteous help,
for those who tried to do me harm
have been put to shame, and disgraced.

PSALM 72

Of Solomon.

1 Give the king your justice, O God,
and your righteousness to a king's son.
2 May he judge your people with
righteousness,
and your poor with justice.
3 May the mountains yield prosperity for the
people,
and the hills, in righteousness.
4 May he defend the cause of the poor of the
people,
give deliverance to the needy,
and crush the oppressor.

5 May he live[a] while the sun endures,
and as long as the moon, throughout all
generations.
6 May he be like rain that falls on the mown
grass,
like showers that water the earth.
7 In his days may righteousness flourish
and peace abound, until the moon is no
more.
8 May he have dominion from sea to sea,
and from the River to the ends of the earth.
9 May his foes[b] bow down before him,
and his enemies lick the dust.
10 May the kings of Tarshish and of the isles
render him tribute,
may the kings of Sheba and Seba
bring gifts.
11 May all kings fall down before him,
all nations give him service.

12 For he delivers the needy when they call,
the poor and those who have no helper.
13 He has pity on the weak and the needy,
and saves the lives of the needy.
14 From oppression and violence he redeems
their life;
and precious is their blood in his sight.

15 Long may he live!
May gold of Sheba be given to him.

Psalm 72

Although in many psalms the poor and oppressed cry out directly to the Lord for vindication, in this psalm the king is imagined as the instrument of God's justice. There is no illusion that whatever the king wills is blessed by God. The standard of justice is clear: it is the welfare of the poor. Rather than further the interests of the aristocracy, this idealized king will "give deliverance to the needy and crush the oppressor" (v. 4). Like the Lord himself, he is the first resort of the needy who have no other resource. Not surprisingly, this psalm became a classic messianic text in early Judaism and Christianity alike. But it speaks as urgently to parliamentary democracies in our own day: do they answer primarily to the vested interests of property and capital or to the welfare of the poor that is alone the biblical measure of justice?

— *NE*

[a] Gk: Heb *may they fear you* [b] Cn: Heb *those who live in the wilderness*

May prayer be made for him continually,
and blessings invoked for him all day long.
16 May there be abundance of grain in the land;
may it wave on the tops of the mountains;
may its fruit be like Lebanon;
and may people blossom in the cities
like the grass of the field.
17 May his name endure forever,
his fame continue as long as the sun.
May all nations be blessed in him;[a]
may they pronounce him happy.

18 Blessed be the LORD, the God of Israel,
who alone does wondrous things.
19 Blessed be his glorious name forever;
may his glory fill the whole earth.
Amen and Amen.

20 The prayers of David son of Jesse are ended.

BOOK III

PSALM 73

A Psalm of Asaph.

1 Truly God is good to the upright,[b]
to those who are pure in heart.
2 But as for me, my feet had almost stumbled;
my steps had nearly slipped.
3 For I was envious of the arrogant;
I saw the prosperity of the wicked.

4 For they have no pain;
their bodies are sound and sleek.
5 They are not in trouble as others are;
they are not plagued like other people.
6 Therefore pride is their necklace;
violence covers them like a garment.
7 Their eyes swell out with fatness;
their hearts overflow with follies.
8 They scoff and speak with malice;
loftily they threaten oppression.
9 They set their mouths against heaven,
and their tongues range over the earth.
10 Therefore the people turn and praise them,[c]
and find no fault in them.[d]
11 And they say, "How can God know?
Is there knowledge in the Most High?"
12 Such are the wicked;
always at ease, they increase in riches.
13 All in vain I have kept my heart clean
and washed my hands in innocence.
14 For all day long I have been plagued,
and am punished every morning.

15 If I had said, "I will talk on in this way,"
I would have been untrue to the circle of
your children.
16 But when I thought how to understand this,
it seemed to me a wearisome task,
17 until I went into the sanctuary of God;
then I perceived their end.
18 Truly you set them in slippery places;
you make them fall to ruin.
19 How they are destroyed in a moment,
swept away utterly by terrors!
20 They are[e] like a dream when one awakes;
on awaking you despise their
phantoms.

21 When my soul was embittered,
when I was pricked in heart,
22 I was stupid and ignorant;
I was like a brute beast toward you.
23 Nevertheless I am continually with you;
you hold my right hand.
24 You guide me with your counsel,
and afterward you will receive me with
honor.[f]
25 Whom have I in heaven but you?
And there is nothing on earth that I desire
other than you.
26 My flesh and my heart may fail,
but God is the strength[g] of my heart and
my portion forever.

27 Indeed, those who are far from you will
perish;

[a] Or *bless themselves by him* [b] Or *good to Israel* [c] Cn: Heb *his people return here* [d] Cn: Heb *abundant waters are drained by them* [e] Cn: Heb *Lord* [f] Or *to glory* [g] Heb *rock*

you put an end to those who are false to you.
28 But for me it is good to be near God;
I have made the Lord GOD my refuge,
to tell of all your works.

PSALM 74

A Maskil of Asaph.

1 O God, why do you cast us off forever?
Why does your anger smoke against the sheep of your pasture?
2 Remember your congregation, which you acquired long ago,
which you redeemed to be the tribe of your heritage.
Remember Mount Zion, where you came to dwell.
3 Direct your steps to the perpetual ruins;
the enemy has destroyed everything in the sanctuary.

4 Your foes have roared within your holy place;
they set up their emblems there.
5 At the upper entrance they hacked
the wooden trellis with axes.[a]
6 And then, with hatchets and hammers,
they smashed all its carved work.
7 They set your sanctuary on fire;
they desecrated the dwelling place of your name,
bringing it to the ground.
8 They said to themselves, "We will utterly subdue them";
they burned all the meeting places of God in the land.

9 We do not see our emblems;
there is no longer any prophet,
and there is no one among us who knows how long.
10 How long, O God, is the foe to scoff?
Is the enemy to revile your name forever?
11 Why do you hold back your hand;
why do you keep your hand in[b] your bosom?

12 Yet God my King is from of old,
working salvation in the earth.
13 You divided the sea by your might;
you broke the heads of the dragons in the waters.
14 You crushed the heads of Leviathan;
you gave him as food[c] for the creatures of the wilderness.
15 You cut openings for springs and torrents;
you dried up ever-flowing streams.
16 Yours is the day, yours also the night;
you established the luminaries[d] and the sun.
17 You have fixed all the bounds of the earth;
you made summer and winter.

18 Remember this, O LORD, how the enemy scoffs,
and an impious people reviles your name.
19 Do not deliver the soul of your dove to the wild animals;
do not forget the life of your poor forever.

20 Have regard for your[e] covenant,
for the dark places of the land are full of the haunts of violence.
21 Do not let the downtrodden be put to shame;
let the poor and needy praise your name.
22 Rise up, O God, plead your cause;
remember how the impious scoff at you all day long.
23 Do not forget the clamor of your foes,
the uproar of your adversaries that goes up continually.

PSALM 75

To the leader: Do Not Destroy.
A Psalm of Asaph. A Song.

1 We give thanks to you, O God;
we give thanks; your name is near.
People tell of your wondrous deeds.

[a] Cn Compare Gk Syr: Meaning of Heb uncertain [b] Cn: Heb *do you consume your right hand from* [c] Heb *food for the people* [d] Or *moon;* Heb *light* [e] Gk Syr: Heb *the*

2 At the set time that I appoint
I will judge with equity.
3 When the earth totters, with all its inhabitants,
it is I who keep its pillars steady. *Selah*
4 I say to the boastful, "Do not boast,"
and to the wicked, "Do not lift up your horn;
5 do not lift up your horn on high,
or speak with insolent neck."

6 For not from the east or from the west
and not from the wilderness comes lifting up;
7 but it is God who executes judgment,
putting down one and lifting up another.
8 For in the hand of the LORD there is a cup
with foaming wine, well mixed;
he will pour a draught from it,
and all the wicked of the earth
shall drain it down to the dregs.
9 But I will rejoice[a] forever;
I will sing praises to the God of Jacob.

10 All the horns of the wicked I will cut off,
but the horns of the righteous shall be exalted.

PSALM 76

To the leader: with stringed instruments.
A Psalm of Asaph. A Song.

1 In Judah God is known,
his name is great in Israel.
2 His abode has been established in Salem,
his dwelling place in Zion.
3 There he broke the flashing arrows,
the shield, the sword, and the weapons of war. *Selah*

4 Glorious are you, more majestic
than the everlasting mountains.[b]
5 The stouthearted were stripped of their spoil;
they sank into sleep;
none of the troops
was able to lift a hand.
6 At your rebuke, O God of Jacob,
both rider and horse lay stunned.

7 But you indeed are awesome!
Who can stand before you
when once your anger is roused?
8 From the heavens you uttered judgment;
the earth feared and was still
9 when God rose up to establish judgment,
to save all the oppressed of the earth. *Selah*

10 Human wrath serves only to praise you,
when you bind the last bit of your[c] wrath around you.
11 Make vows to the LORD your God, and perform them;
let all who are around him bring gifts
to the one who is awesome,
12 who cuts off the spirit of princes,
who inspires fear in the kings of the earth.

PSALM 77

To the leader: according to Jeduthun.
Of Asaph. A Psalm.

1 I cry aloud to God,
aloud to God, that he may hear me.
2 In the day of my trouble I seek the Lord;
in the night my hand is stretched out without wearying;
my soul refuses to be comforted.
3 I think of God, and I moan;
I meditate, and my spirit faints. *Selah*

4 You keep my eyelids from closing;
I am so troubled that I cannot speak.
5 I consider the days of old,
and remember the years of long ago.
6 I commune[d] with my heart in the night;
I meditate and search my spirit:[e]
7 "Will the Lord spurn forever,
and never again be favorable?

[a] Gk: Heb *declare* [b] Gk: Heb *the mountains of prey* [c] Heb lacks *your* [d] Gk Syr: Heb *My music*
[e] Syr Jerome: Heb *my spirit searches*

8 Has his steadfast love ceased forever?
Are his promises at an end for all time?
9 Has God forgotten to be gracious?
Has he in anger shut up his compassion?"
Selah
10 And I say, "It is my grief
that the right hand of the Most High has changed."

11 I will call to mind the deeds of the LORD;
I will remember your wonders of old.
12 I will meditate on all your work,
and muse on your mighty deeds.
13 Your way, O God, is holy.
What god is so great as our God?
14 You are the God who works wonders;
you have displayed your might among the peoples.
15 With your strong arm you redeemed your people,
the descendants of Jacob and Joseph. *Selah*

16 When the waters saw you, O God,
when the waters saw you, they were afraid;
the very deep trembled.
17 The clouds poured out water;
the skies thundered;
your arrows flashed on every side.
18 The crash of your thunder was in the whirlwind;
your lightnings lit up the world;
the earth trembled and shook.
19 Your way was through the sea,
your path, through the mighty waters;
yet your footprints were unseen.
20 You led your people like a flock
by the hand of Moses and Aaron.

PSALM 78

A Maskil of Asaph.

1 Give ear, O my people, to my teaching;
incline your ears to the words of my mouth.
2 I will open my mouth in a parable;
I will utter dark sayings from of old,
3 things that we have heard and known,
that our ancestors have told us.
4 We will not hide them from their children;
we will tell to the coming generation
the glorious deeds of the LORD, and his might,
and the wonders that he has done.

5 He established a decree in Jacob,
and appointed a law in Israel,
which he commanded our ancestors
to teach to their children;
6 that the next generation might know them,
the children yet unborn,
and rise up and tell them to their children,
7 so that they should set their hope in God,
and not forget the works of God,
but keep his commandments;
8 and that they should not be like their ancestors,
a stubborn and rebellious generation,
a generation whose heart was not steadfast,
whose spirit was not faithful to God.

9 The Ephraimites, armed with[a] the bow,
turned back on the day of battle.
10 They did not keep God's covenant,
but refused to walk according to his law.
11 They forgot what he had done,
and the miracles that he had shown them.
12 In the sight of their ancestors he worked marvels
in the land of Egypt, in the fields of Zoan.
13 He divided the sea and let them pass through it,
and made the waters stand like a heap.
14 In the daytime he led them with a cloud,
and all night long with a fiery light.
15 He split rocks open in the wilderness,
and gave them drink abundantly as from the deep.
16 He made streams come out of the rock,
and caused waters to flow down like rivers.

[a] Heb *armed with shooting*

17 Yet they sinned still more against him,
rebelling against the Most High in the desert.
18 They tested God in their heart
by demanding the food they craved.
19 They spoke against God, saying,
"Can God spread a table in the wilderness?
20 Even though he struck the rock so that water gushed out
and torrents overflowed,
can he also give bread,
or provide meat for his people?"

21 Therefore, when the LORD heard, he was full of rage;
a fire was kindled against Jacob,
his anger mounted against Israel,
22 because they had no faith in God,
and did not trust his saving power.
23 Yet he commanded the skies above,
and opened the doors of heaven;
24 he rained down on them manna to eat,
and gave them the grain of heaven.
25 Mortals ate of the bread of angels;
he sent them food in abundance.
26 He caused the east wind to blow in the heavens,
and by his power he led out the south wind;
27 he rained flesh upon them like dust,
winged birds like the sand of the seas;
28 he let them fall within their camp,
all around their dwellings.
29 And they ate and were well filled,
for he gave them what they craved.
30 But before they had satisfied their craving,
while the food was still in their mouths,
31 the anger of God rose against them
and he killed the strongest of them,
and laid low the flower of Israel.

32 In spite of all this they still sinned;
they did not believe in his wonders.
33 So he made their days vanish like a breath,
and their years in terror.
34 When he killed them, they sought for him;
they repented and sought God earnestly.
35 They remembered that God was their rock,
the Most High God their redeemer.
36 But they flattered him with their mouths;
they lied to him with their tongues.
37 Their heart was not steadfast toward him;
they were not true to his covenant.
38 Yet he, being compassionate,
forgave their iniquity,
and did not destroy them;
often he restrained his anger,
and did not stir up all his wrath.
39 He remembered that they were but flesh,
a wind that passes and does not come again.
40 How often they rebelled against him in the wilderness
and grieved him in the desert!
41 They tested God again and again,
and provoked the Holy One of Israel.
42 They did not keep in mind his power,
or the day when he redeemed them from the foe;
43 when he displayed his signs in Egypt,
and his miracles in the fields of Zoan.
44 He turned their rivers to blood,
so that they could not drink of their streams.
45 He sent among them swarms of flies, which devoured them,
and frogs, which destroyed them.
46 He gave their crops to the caterpillar,
and the fruit of their labor to the locust.
47 He destroyed their vines with hail,
and their sycamores with frost.
48 He gave over their cattle to the hail,
and their flocks to thunderbolts.
49 He let loose on them his fierce anger,
wrath, indignation, and distress,
a company of destroying angels.
50 He made a path for his anger;
he did not spare them from death,
but gave their lives over to the plague.
51 He struck all the firstborn in Egypt,
the first issue of their strength in the tents of Ham.
52 Then he led out his people like sheep,

and guided them in the wilderness like a
flock.
53 He led them in safety, so that they were not
afraid;
but the sea overwhelmed their enemies.
54 And he brought them to his holy hill,
to the mountain that his right hand had
won.

Psalm 78:52-54

Martin Luther King, Jr., was not born a prophet, but he stood in the prophetic tradition. He sounded like people felt. By sounding like they felt he could move them beyond their feelings to embrace new solutions to old problems.

Martin Luther King, Jr., … [also] stood in the priestly tradition of the Old Testament. He decided to suffer with his people and on their behalf.… He was willing to risk his life for his people. Time after time, he engaged in campaign after campaign for no ostensibly selfish, profit-making reasons. He himself said, "I've been to the mountain top." The people gave Martin power (and a sense of themselves as a people) because he gave them his life. His life was not his own. He walked, talked, and marched for freedom.… "Nothing matters to me now, I've been to the mountain top."[34]

— Willie K. Smith

55 He drove out nations before them;
he apportioned them for a possession
and settled the tribes of Israel in their
tents.

56 Yet they tested the Most High God,
and rebelled against him.
They did not observe his decrees,
57 but turned away and were faithless like their
ancestors;
they twisted like a treacherous bow.
58 For they provoked him to anger with their
high places;
they moved him to jealousy with their
idols.
59 When God heard, he was full of wrath,
and he utterly rejected Israel.
60 He abandoned his dwelling at Shiloh,
the tent where he dwelt among mortals,
61 and delivered his power to captivity,
his glory to the hand of the foe.
62 He gave his people to the sword,
and vented his wrath on his heritage.
63 Fire devoured their young men,
and their girls had no marriage song.
64 Their priests fell by the sword,
and their widows made no lamentation.
65 Then the Lord awoke as from sleep,
like a warrior shouting because of wine.
66 He put his adversaries to rout;
he put them to everlasting disgrace.

67 He rejected the tent of Joseph,
he did not choose the tribe of Ephraim;
68 but he chose the tribe of Judah,
Mount Zion, which he loves.
69 He built his sanctuary like the high heavens,
like the earth, which he has founded
forever.
70 He chose his servant David,
and took him from the sheepfolds;
71 from tending the nursing ewes he brought him
to be the shepherd of his people Jacob,
of Israel, his inheritance.
72 With upright heart he tended them,
and guided them with skillful hand.

PSALM 79

A Psalm of Asaph.

1 O God, the nations have come into your
inheritance;
they have defiled your holy temple;
they have laid Jerusalem in ruins.
2 They have given the bodies of your servants
to the birds of the air for food,
the flesh of your faithful to the wild
animals of the earth.
3 They have poured out their blood like water
all around Jerusalem,
and there was no one to bury them.
4 We have become a taunt to our neighbors,
mocked and derided by those around us.

5 How long, O LORD? Will you be angry
forever?
Will your jealous wrath burn like fire?
6 Pour out your anger on the nations
that do not know you,
and on the kingdoms
that do not call on your name.
7 For they have devoured Jacob
and laid waste his habitation.

8 Do not remember against us the iniquities of
our ancestors;
let your compassion come speedily to
meet us,
for we are brought very low.
9 Help us, O God of our salvation,
for the glory of your name;
deliver us, and forgive our sins,
for your name's sake.
10 Why should the nations say,
"Where is their God?"
Let the avenging of the outpoured blood of
your servants
be known among the nations before our
eyes.

11 Let the groans of the prisoners come before
you;
according to your great power preserve
those doomed to die.
12 Return sevenfold into the bosom of our
neighbors
the taunts with which they taunted you,
O Lord!
13 Then we your people, the flock of your
pasture,
will give thanks to you forever;
from generation to generation we will
recount your praise.

PSALM 80

To the leader: on Lilies, a Covenant. Of Asaph. A Psalm.

1 Give ear, O Shepherd of Israel,
you who lead Joseph like a flock!
You who are enthroned upon the cherubim,
shine forth
2 before Ephraim and Benjamin and
Manasseh.
Stir up your might,
and come to save us!

3 Restore us, O God;
let your face shine, that we may be saved.

4 O LORD God of hosts,
how long will you be angry with your
people's prayers?
5 You have fed them with the bread of tears,
and given them tears to drink in full
measure.
6 You make us the scorn[a] of our neighbors;
our enemies laugh among themselves.

7 Restore us, O God of hosts;
let your face shine, that we may be saved.

8 You brought a vine out of Egypt;
you drove out the nations and planted it.
9 You cleared the ground for it;
it took deep root and filled the land.
10 The mountains were covered with its shade,
the mighty cedars with its branches;
11 it sent out its branches to the sea,
and its shoots to the River.
12 Why then have you broken down its walls,
so that all who pass along the way pluck
its fruit?
13 The boar from the forest ravages it,
and all that move in the field feed on it.

14 Turn again, O God of hosts;
look down from heaven, and see;
have regard for this vine,
15 the stock that your right hand planted.[b]
16 They have burned it with fire, they have cut it
down;[c]
may they perish at the rebuke of your
countenance.

[a] Syr: Heb *strife* [b] Heb adds from verse 17 *and upon the one whom you made strong for yourself* [c] Cn: Heb *it is cut down*

17 But let your hand be upon the one at your
right hand,
the one whom you made strong for
yourself.
18 Then we will never turn back from you;
give us life, and we will call on your name.

19 Restore us, O LORD God of hosts;
let your face shine, that we may be saved.

PSALM 81

To the leader: according to The Gittith. Of Asaph.

1 Sing aloud to God our strength;
shout for joy to the God of Jacob.
2 Raise a song, sound the tambourine,
the sweet lyre with the harp.
3 Blow the trumpet at the new moon,
at the full moon, on our festal day.
4 For it is a statute for Israel,
an ordinance of the God of Jacob.
5 He made it a decree in Joseph,
when he went out over[a] the land of Egypt.

I hear a voice I had not known:
6 "I relieved your[b] shoulder of the burden;
your[b] hands were freed from the basket.
7 In distress you called, and I rescued you;
I answered you in the secret place of
thunder;
I tested you at the waters of Meribah. *Selah*
8 Hear, O my people, while I admonish you;
O Israel, if you would but listen to me!
9 There shall be no strange god among you;
you shall not bow down to a foreign god.
10 I am the LORD your God,
who brought you up out of the land of
Egypt.
Open your mouth wide and I will fill it.

11 "But my people did not listen to my voice;
Israel would not submit to me.
12 So I gave them over to their stubborn hearts,
to follow their own counsels.
13 O that my people would listen to me,
that Israel would walk in my ways!
14 Then I would quickly subdue their enemies,
and turn my hand against their foes.
15 Those who hate the LORD would cringe
before him,
and their doom would last forever.
16 I would feed you[c] with the finest of the wheat,
and with honey from the rock I would
satisfy you."

PSALM 82

A Psalm of Asaph.

1 God has taken his place in the divine council;
in the midst of the gods he holds
judgment:
2 "How long will you judge unjustly
and show partiality to the wicked? *Selah*
3 Give justice to the weak and the orphan;
maintain the right of the lowly and the
destitute.

Psalm 82:2-4

By growing up in the black church among the so-called middle-class blacks and the poor and the rest, Martin [Luther King Jr.] knew... that black people had a common destiny. Black people, regardless of class, status, or honor, accepted their destiny. God was in charge! Only luck and education separated the highly affluent from the lowly. They placed their future in the hands of God. Their destiny was God's destiny. Thus, what the black community believed about God and his activities in the world greatly influenced how they interpreted their conditions, past, present, and future. Black people have never been without a history, a faith, and a hope. They viewed themselves as a collectivity, tied together by at least one friend, God, and by at least one enemy, segregation. Day after day, week after week, year after year, they cried out to [God] in groanings, murmurings, and whispers, "Oh Lord, how long? How long? How long?" Black churches and their preachers helped to find an answer.[35]

— Willie K. Smith

[a] Or *against* [b] Heb *his* [c] Cn Compare verse 16b: Heb *he would feed him*

4 Rescue the weak and the needy;
deliver them from the hand of the wicked."

5 They have neither knowledge nor understanding,
they walk around in darkness;
all the foundations of the earth are shaken.

6 I say, "You are gods,
children of the Most High, all of you;
7 nevertheless, you shall die like mortals,
and fall like any prince."[a]

8 Rise up, O God, judge the earth;
for all the nations belong to you!

PSALM 83

A Song. A Psalm of Asaph.

1 O God, do not keep silence;
do not hold your peace or be still, O God!
2 Even now your enemies are in tumult;
those who hate you have raised their heads.
3 They lay crafty plans against your people;
they consult together against those you protect.
4 They say, "Come, let us wipe them out as a nation;
let the name of Israel be remembered no more."
5 They conspire with one accord;
against you they make a covenant—
6 the tents of Edom and the Ishmaelites,
Moab and the Hagrites,
7 Gebal and Ammon and Amalek,
Philistia with the inhabitants of Tyre;
8 Assyria also has joined them;
they are the strong arm of the children of Lot. *Selah*

9 Do to them as you did to Midian,
as to Sisera and Jabin at the Wadi Kishon,
10 who were destroyed at En-dor,
who became dung for the ground.
11 Make their nobles like Oreb and Zeeb,
all their princes like Zebah and Zalmunna,
12 who said, "Let us take the pastures of God
for our own possession."

13 O my God, make them like whirling dust,[b]
like chaff before the wind.
14 As fire consumes the forest,
as the flame sets the mountains ablaze,
15 so pursue them with your tempest
and terrify them with your hurricane.
16 Fill their faces with shame,
so that they may seek your name, O LORD.
17 Let them be put to shame and dismayed forever;
let them perish in disgrace.
18 Let them know that you alone,
whose name is the LORD,
are the Most High over all the earth.

PSALM 84

To the leader: according to The Gittith.
Of the Korahites. A Psalm.

1 How lovely is your dwelling place,
O LORD of hosts!
2 My soul longs, indeed it faints
for the courts of the LORD;
my heart and my flesh sing for joy
to the living God.

3 Even the sparrow finds a home,
and the swallow a nest for herself,
where she may lay her young,
at your altars, O LORD of hosts,
my King and my God.
4 Happy are those who live in your house,
ever singing your praise. *Selah*

5 Happy are those whose strength is in you,
in whose heart are the highways to Zion.[c]
6 As they go through the valley of Baca
they make it a place of springs;
the early rain also covers it with pools.
7 They go from strength to strength;
the God of gods will be seen in Zion.

[a] Or *fall as one man, O princes* [b] Or *a tumbleweed* [c] Heb lacks *to Zion*

8 O LORD God of hosts, hear my prayer;
give ear, O God of Jacob! *Selah*
9 Behold our shield, O God;
look on the face of your anointed.

10 For a day in your courts is better
than a thousand elsewhere.
I would rather be a doorkeeper in the house
of my God
than live in the tents of wickedness.
11 For the LORD God is a sun and shield;
he bestows favor and honor.
No good thing does the LORD withhold
from those who walk uprightly.
12 O LORD of hosts,
happy is everyone who trusts in you.

PSALM 85

To the leader. Of the Korahites. A Psalm.

1 LORD, you were favorable to your land;
you restored the fortunes of Jacob.
2 You forgave the iniquity of your people;
you pardoned all their sin. *Selah*
3 You withdrew all your wrath;
you turned from your hot anger.

4 Restore us again, O God of our salvation,
and put away your indignation
toward us.
5 Will you be angry with us forever?
Will you prolong your anger to all
generations?
6 Will you not revive us again,
so that your people may rejoice in you?
7 Show us your steadfast love, O LORD,
and grant us your salvation.

8 Let me hear what God the LORD will speak,
for he will speak peace to his people,
to his faithful, to those who turn to him in
their hearts.[a]
9 Surely his salvation is at hand for those who
fear him,
that his glory may dwell in our land.

10 Steadfast love and faithfulness will meet;
righteousness and peace will kiss each
other.
11 Faithfulness will spring up from the ground,
and righteousness will look down from
the sky.
12 The LORD will give what is good,
and our land will yield its increase.
13 Righteousness will go before him,
and will make a path for his steps.

PSALM 86

A Prayer of David.

1 Incline your ear, O LORD, and answer me,
for I am poor and needy.
2 Preserve my life, for I am devoted to you;
save your servant who trusts in you.
You are my God; 3be gracious to me, O Lord,
for to you do I cry all day long.
4 Gladden the soul of your servant,
for to you, O Lord, I lift up my soul.
5 For you, O Lord, are good and forgiving,
abounding in steadfast love to all who call
on you.
6 Give ear, O LORD, to my prayer;
listen to my cry of supplication.
7 In the day of my trouble I call on you,
for you will answer me.

8 There is none like you among the gods,
O Lord,
nor are there any works like yours.
9 All the nations you have made shall come
and bow down before you, O Lord,
and shall glorify your name.
10 For you are great and do wondrous things;
you alone are God.
11 Teach me your way, O LORD,
that I may walk in your truth;
give me an undivided heart to revere your
name.
12 I give thanks to you, O Lord my God, with
my whole heart,
and I will glorify your name forever.

[a] Gk: Heb *but let them not turn back to folly*

13 For great is your steadfast love toward me;
you have delivered my soul from the depths of Sheol.

14 O God, the insolent rise up against me;
a band of ruffians seeks my life,
and they do not set you before them.
15 But you, O Lord, are a God merciful and gracious,
slow to anger and abounding in steadfast love and faithfulness.
16 Turn to me and be gracious to me;
give your strength to your servant;
save the child of your serving girl.
17 Show me a sign of your favor,
so that those who hate me may see it and be put to shame,
because you, LORD, have helped me and comforted me.

PSALM 87

Of the Korahites. A Psalm. A Song.

1 On the holy mount stands the city he founded;
2 the LORD loves the gates of Zion
more than all the dwellings of Jacob.
3 Glorious things are spoken of you,
O city of God. *Selah*

4 Among those who know me I mention Rahab and Babylon;
Philistia too, and Tyre, with Ethiopia[a]—
"This one was born there," they say.

5 And of Zion it shall be said,
"This one and that one were born in it";
for the Most High himself will establish it.
6 The LORD records, as he registers the peoples,
"This one was born there." *Selah*

7 Singers and dancers alike say,
"All my springs are in you."

PSALM 88

A Song. A Psalm of the Korahites. To the leader: according to Mahalath Leannoth. A Maskil of Heman the Ezrahite.

1 O LORD, God of my salvation,
when, at night, I cry out in your presence,
2 let my prayer come before you;
incline your ear to my cry.

3 For my soul is full of troubles,
and my life draws near to Sheol.
4 I am counted among those who go down to the Pit;
I am like those who have no help,
5 like those forsaken among the dead,
like the slain that lie in the grave,
like those whom you remember no more,
for they are cut off from your hand.
6 You have put me in the depths of the Pit,
in the regions dark and deep.
7 Your wrath lies heavy upon me,
and you overwhelm me with all your waves. *Selah*

8 You have caused my companions to shun me;
you have made me a thing of horror to them.
I am shut in so that I cannot escape;
9 my eye grows dim through sorrow.
Every day I call on you, O LORD;
I spread out my hands to you.
10 Do you work wonders for the dead?
Do the shades rise up to praise you? *Selah*
11 Is your steadfast love declared in the grave,
or your faithfulness in Abaddon?
12 Are your wonders known in the darkness,
or your saving help in the land of forgetfulness?

13 But I, O LORD, cry out to you;
in the morning my prayer comes before you.
14 O LORD, why do you cast me off?
Why do you hide your face from me?

[a] Or *Nubia*; Heb *Cush*

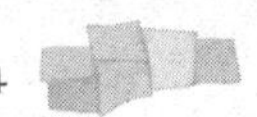

15 Wretched and close to death from my youth up,
I suffer your terrors; I am desperate.[a]
16 Your wrath has swept over me;
your dread assaults destroy me.
17 They surround me like a flood all day long;
from all sides they close in on me.
18 You have caused friend and neighbor to shun me;
my companions are in darkness.

PSALM 89

A Maskil of Ethan the Ezrahite.

1 I will sing of your steadfast love, O LORD,[b] forever;
with my mouth I will proclaim your faithfulness to all generations.
2 I declare that your steadfast love is established forever;
your faithfulness is as firm as the heavens.

3 You said, "I have made a covenant with my chosen one,
I have sworn to my servant David:
4 'I will establish your descendants forever,
and build your throne for all generations.'"
Selah

5 Let the heavens praise your wonders, O LORD,
your faithfulness in the assembly of the holy ones.
6 For who in the skies can be compared to the LORD?
Who among the heavenly beings is like the LORD,
7 a God feared in the council of the holy ones,
great and awesome[c] above all that are around him?
8 O LORD God of hosts,
who is as mighty as you, O LORD?
Your faithfulness surrounds you.
9 You rule the raging of the sea;
when its waves rise, you still them.
10 You crushed Rahab like a carcass;
you scattered your enemies with your mighty arm.
11 The heavens are yours, the earth also is yours;
the world and all that is in it—you have founded them.
12 The north and the south[d]—you created them;
Tabor and Hermon joyously praise your name.
13 You have a mighty arm;
strong is your hand, high your right hand.
14 Righteousness and justice are the foundation of your throne;
steadfast love and faithfulness go before you.
15 Happy are the people who know the festal shout,
who walk, O LORD, in the light of your countenance;
16 they exult in your name all day long,
and extol[e] your righteousness.
17 For you are the glory of their strength;
by your favor our horn is exalted.
18 For our shield belongs to the LORD,
our king to the Holy One of Israel.

19 Then you spoke in a vision to your faithful one, and said:
"I have set the crown[f] on one who is mighty,
I have exalted one chosen from the people.
20 I have found my servant David;
with my holy oil I have anointed him;
21 my hand shall always remain with him;
my arm also shall strengthen him.
22 The enemy shall not outwit him,
the wicked shall not humble him.
23 I will crush his foes before him
and strike down those who hate him.
24 My faithfulness and steadfast love shall be with him;
and in my name his horn shall be exalted.

[a] Meaning of Heb uncertain [b] Gk: Heb *the steadfast love of the LORD* [c] Gk Syr: Heb *greatly awesome*
[d] Or *Zaphon and Yamin* [e] Cn: Heb *are exalted in* [f] Cn: Heb *help*

25 I will set his hand on the sea
and his right hand on the rivers.
26 He shall cry to me, 'You are my Father,
my God, and the Rock of my salvation!'
27 I will make him the firstborn,
the highest of the kings of the earth.
28 Forever I will keep my steadfast love for him,
and my covenant with him will stand firm.
29 I will establish his line forever,
and his throne as long as the heavens
endure.
30 If his children forsake my law
and do not walk according to my
ordinances,
31 if they violate my statutes
and do not keep my commandments,
32 then I will punish their transgression with
the rod
and their iniquity with scourges;
33 but I will not remove from him my steadfast
love,
or be false to my faithfulness.
34 I will not violate my covenant,
or alter the word that went forth from my
lips.
35 Once and for all I have sworn by my holiness;
I will not lie to David.
36 His line shall continue forever,
and his throne endure before me like the
sun.
37 It shall be established forever like the moon,
an enduring witness in the skies." *Selah*

38 But now you have spurned and rejected him;
you are full of wrath against your anointed.
39 You have renounced the covenant with your
servant;
you have defiled his crown in the dust.
40 You have broken through all his walls;
you have laid his strongholds in ruins.
41 All who pass by plunder him;
he has become the scorn of his neighbors.
42 You have exalted the right hand of his foes;
you have made all his enemies rejoice.
43 Moreover, you have turned back the edge of
his sword,
and you have not supported him in battle.
44 You have removed the scepter from his hand,[a]
and hurled his throne to the ground.
45 You have cut short the days of his youth;
you have covered him with shame. *Selah*

46 How long, O LORD? Will you hide yourself
forever?
How long will your wrath burn like fire?
47 Remember how short my time is—[b]
for what vanity you have created all
mortals!
48 Who can live and never see death?
Who can escape the power of Sheol?
Selah

49 Lord, where is your steadfast love of old,
which by your faithfulness you swore to
David?
50 Remember, O Lord, how your servant is
taunted;
how I bear in my bosom the insults of the
peoples,[c]
51 with which your enemies taunt, O LORD,
with which they taunted the footsteps of
your anointed.

52 Blessed be the LORD forever.
Amen and Amen.

BOOK IV

PSALM 90

A Prayer of Moses, the man of God.

1 Lord, you have been our dwelling place[d]
in all generations.
2 Before the mountains were brought forth,
or ever you had formed the earth and the
world,
from everlasting to everlasting you are God.

[a] Cn: Heb *removed his cleanness* [b] Meaning of Heb uncertain [c] Cn: Heb *bosom all of many peoples*
[d] Another reading is *our refuge*

3 You turn us[a] back to dust,
and say, "Turn back, you mortals."
4 For a thousand years in your sight
are like yesterday when it is past,
or like a watch in the night.

5 You sweep them away; they are like a dream,
like grass that is renewed in the morning;
6 in the morning it flourishes and is renewed;
in the evening it fades and withers.

7 For we are consumed by your anger;
by your wrath we are overwhelmed.
8 You have set our iniquities before you,
our secret sins in the light of your countenance.

9 For all our days pass away under your wrath;
our years come to an end[b] like a sigh.
10 The days of our life are seventy years,
or perhaps eighty, if we are strong;
even then their span[c] is only toil and trouble;
they are soon gone, and we fly away.

11 Who considers the power of your anger?
Your wrath is as great as the fear that is due you.
12 So teach us to count our days
that we may gain a wise heart.

13 Turn, O LORD! How long?
Have compassion on your servants!
14 Satisfy us in the morning with your steadfast love,
so that we may rejoice and be glad all our days.
15 Make us glad as many days as you have afflicted us,
and as many years as we have seen evil.
16 Let your work be manifest to your servants,
and your glorious power to their children.
17 Let the favor of the Lord our God be upon us,
and prosper for us the work of our hands—
O prosper the work of our hands!

PSALM 91

1 You who live in the shelter of the Most High,
who abide in the shadow of the Almighty,[d]
2 will say to the LORD, "My refuge and my fortress;
my God, in whom I trust."
3 For he will deliver you from the snare of the fowler
and from the deadly pestilence;
4 he will cover you with his pinions,
and under his wings you will find refuge;
his faithfulness is a shield and buckler.
5 You will not fear the terror of the night,
or the arrow that flies by day,
6 or the pestilence that stalks in darkness,
or the destruction that wastes at noonday.

7 A thousand may fall at your side,
ten thousand at your right hand,
but it will not come near you.
8 You will only look with your eyes
and see the punishment of the wicked.

9 Because you have made the LORD your refuge,[e]
the Most High your dwelling place,
10 no evil shall befall you,
no scourge come near your tent.

11 For he will command his angels concerning you
to guard you in all your ways.
12 On their hands they will bear you up,
so that you will not dash your foot against a stone.
13 You will tread on the lion and the adder,
the young lion and the serpent you will trample under foot.

14 Those who love me, I will deliver;
I will protect those who know my name.

[a] Heb *humankind* [b] Syr: Heb *we bring our years to an end* [c] Cn Compare Gk Syr Jerome Tg: Heb *pride* [d] Traditional rendering of Heb *Shaddai* [e] Cn: Heb *Because you, LORD, are my refuge; you have made*

15 When they call to me, I will answer them;
I will be with them in trouble,
I will rescue them and honor them.
16 With long life I will satisfy them,
and show them my salvation.

PSALM 92

A Psalm. A Song for the Sabbath Day.

1 It is good to give thanks to the LORD,
to sing praises to your name, O Most High;
2 to declare your steadfast love in the morning,
and your faithfulness by night,
3 to the music of the lute and the harp,
to the melody of the lyre.
4 For you, O LORD, have made me glad by your work;
at the works of your hands I sing for joy.

5 How great are your works, O LORD!
Your thoughts are very deep!
6 The dullard cannot know,
the stupid cannot understand this:
7 though the wicked sprout like grass
and all evildoers flourish,
they are doomed to destruction forever,
8 but you, O LORD, are on high forever.
9 For your enemies, O LORD,
for your enemies shall perish;
all evildoers shall be scattered.

10 But you have exalted my horn like that of the wild ox;
you have poured over me[a] fresh oil.
11 My eyes have seen the downfall of my enemies;
my ears have heard the doom of my evil assailants.

12 The righteous flourish like the palm tree,
and grow like a cedar in Lebanon.
13 They are planted in the house of the LORD;
they flourish in the courts of our God.
14 In old age they still produce fruit;
they are always green and full of sap,
15 showing that the LORD is upright;
he is my rock, and there is no unrighteousness in him.

PSALM 93

1 The LORD is king, he is robed in majesty;
the LORD is robed, he is girded with strength.
He has established the world; it shall never be moved;
2 your throne is established from of old;
you are from everlasting.

3 The floods have lifted up, O LORD,
the floods have lifted up their voice;
the floods lift up their roaring.
4 More majestic than the thunders of mighty waters,
more majestic than the waves[b] of the sea,
majestic on high is the LORD!

5 Your decrees are very sure;
holiness befits your house,
O LORD, forevermore.

PSALM 94

1 O LORD, you God of vengeance,
you God of vengeance, shine forth!
2 Rise up, O judge of the earth;
give to the proud what they deserve!
3 O LORD, how long shall the wicked,
how long shall the wicked exult?
4 They pour out their arrogant words;
all the evildoers boast.
5 They crush your people, O LORD,
and afflict your heritage.
6 They kill the widow and the stranger,
they murder the orphan,
7 and they say, "The LORD does not see;
the God of Jacob does not perceive."

8 Understand, O dullest of the people;
fools, when will you be wise?

[a] Syr: Meaning of Heb uncertain [b] Cn: Heb *majestic are the waves*

Psalm 94

When the wretched of the earth awake, their first challenge is not to religion but to the social... order oppressing them and to the ideology supporting it,... and since religious elements are present in these ideologies, religion must be criticized.... Given that fact, the first question cannot be... how are we to talk about God in a world come of age, but how are we to tell people who are scarcely human that God's love makes us one family?[36]

— ***Gustavo Gutiérrez***

9 He who planted the ear, does he not hear?
He who formed the eye, does he not see?
10 He who disciplines the nations,
he who teaches knowledge to humankind,
does he not chastise?
11 The LORD knows our thoughts,[a]
that they are but an empty breath.

12 Happy are those whom you discipline,
O LORD,
and whom you teach out of your law,
13 giving them respite from days of trouble,
until a pit is dug for the wicked.
14 For the LORD will not forsake his people;
he will not abandon his heritage;
15 for justice will return to the righteous,
and all the upright in heart will follow it.

16 Who rises up for me against the wicked?
Who stands up for me against evildoers?
17 If the LORD had not been my help,
my soul would soon have lived in the land
of silence.
18 When I thought, "My foot is slipping,"
your steadfast love, O LORD, held
me up.
19 When the cares of my heart are many,
your consolations cheer my soul.
20 Can wicked rulers be allied with you,
those who contrive mischief by statute?
21 They band together against the life of the
righteous,
and condemn the innocent to death.
22 But the LORD has become my stronghold,
and my God the rock of my refuge.
23 He will repay them for their iniquity
and wipe them out for their wickedness;
the LORD our God will wipe them out.

PSALM 95

1 O come, let us sing to the LORD;
let us make a joyful noise to the rock of
our salvation!
2 Let us come into his presence with
thanksgiving;
let us make a joyful noise to him with
songs of praise!
3 For the LORD is a great God,
and a great King above all gods.
4 In his hand are the depths of the earth;
the heights of the mountains are his also.
5 The sea is his, for he made it,
and the dry land, which his hands have
formed.

6 O come, let us worship and bow down,
let us kneel before the LORD, our Maker!
7 For he is our God,
and we are the people of his pasture,
and the sheep of his hand.

O that today you would listen to his voice!
8 Do not harden your hearts, as at Meribah,
as on the day at Massah in the wilderness,
9 when your ancestors tested me,
and put me to the proof, though they had
seen my work.
10 For forty years I loathed that generation
and said, "They are a people whose hearts
go astray,
and they do not regard my ways."
11 Therefore in my anger I swore,
"They shall not enter my rest."

[a] Heb *the thoughts of humankind*

PSALM 96

1 O sing to the LORD a new song;
sing to the LORD, all the earth.
2 Sing to the LORD, bless his name;
tell of his salvation from day to day.
3 Declare his glory among the nations,
his marvelous works among all the peoples.
4 For great is the LORD, and greatly to be praised;
he is to be revered above all gods.
5 For all the gods of the peoples are idols,
but the LORD made the heavens.
6 Honor and majesty are before him;
strength and beauty are in his sanctuary.

7 Ascribe to the LORD, O families of the peoples,
ascribe to the LORD glory and strength.
8 Ascribe to the LORD the glory due his name;
bring an offering, and come into his courts.
9 Worship the LORD in holy splendor;
tremble before him, all the earth.

10 Say among the nations, "The LORD is king!
The world is firmly established; it shall never be moved.
He will judge the peoples with equity."
11 Let the heavens be glad, and let the earth rejoice;
let the sea roar, and all that fills it;
12 let the field exult, and everything in it.
Then shall all the trees of the forest sing for joy
13 before the LORD; for he is coming,
for he is coming to judge the earth.
He will judge the world with righteousness,
and the peoples with his truth.

PSALM 97

1 The LORD is king! Let the earth rejoice;
let the many coastlands be glad!
2 Clouds and thick darkness are all around him;
righteousness and justice are the foundation of his throne.
3 Fire goes before him,
and consumes his adversaries on every side.
4 His lightnings light up the world;
the earth sees and trembles.
5 The mountains melt like wax before the LORD,
before the Lord of all the earth.

6 The heavens proclaim his righteousness;
and all the peoples behold his glory.
7 All worshipers of images are put to shame,
those who make their boast in worthless idols;
all gods bow down before him.
8 Zion hears and is glad,
and the towns[a] of Judah rejoice,
because of your judgments, O God.
9 For you, O LORD, are most high over all the earth;
you are exalted far above all gods.

10 The LORD loves those who hate[b] evil;
he guards the lives of his faithful;
he rescues them from the hand of the wicked.
11 Light dawns[c] for the righteous,
and joy for the upright in heart.
12 Rejoice in the LORD, O you righteous,
and give thanks to his holy name!

PSALM 98

A Psalm.

1 O sing to the LORD a new song,
for he has done marvelous things.
His right hand and his holy arm
have gotten him victory.
2 The LORD has made known his victory;
he has revealed his vindication in the sight of the nations.

[a] Heb *daughters* [b] Cn: Heb *You who love the LORD hate* [c] Gk Syr Jerome: Heb *is sown*

3 He has remembered his steadfast love and
faithfulness
to the house of Israel.
All the ends of the earth have seen
the victory of our God.

4 Make a joyful noise to the LORD, all the earth;
break forth into joyous song and sing
praises.
5 Sing praises to the LORD with the lyre,
with the lyre and the sound of melody.
6 With trumpets and the sound of the horn
make a joyful noise before the King, the
LORD.

7 Let the sea roar, and all that fills it;
the world and those who live in it.
8 Let the floods clap their hands;
let the hills sing together for joy
9 at the presence of the LORD, for he is coming
to judge the earth.
He will judge the world with righteousness,
and the peoples with equity.

PSALM 99

1 The LORD is king; let the peoples tremble!
He sits enthroned upon the cherubim; let
the earth quake!
2 The LORD is great in Zion;
he is exalted over all the peoples.
3 Let them praise your great and awesome
name.
Holy is he!
4 Mighty King,[a] lover of justice,
you have established equity;
you have executed justice
and righteousness in Jacob.
5 Extol the LORD our God;
worship at his footstool.
Holy is he!

6 Moses and Aaron were among his priests,
Samuel also was among those who called
on his name.
They cried to the LORD, and he answered
them.
7 He spoke to them in the pillar of cloud;
they kept his decrees,
and the statutes that he gave them.

8 O LORD our God, you answered them;
you were a forgiving God to them,
but an avenger of their wrongdoings.
9 Extol the LORD our God,
and worship at his holy mountain;
for the LORD our God is holy.

PSALM 100

A Psalm of thanksgiving.

1 Make a joyful noise to the LORD, all the earth.
2 Worship the LORD with gladness;
come into his presence with singing.

3 Know that the LORD is God.
It is he that made us, and we are his;[b]
we are his people, and the sheep of his
pasture.

4 Enter his gates with thanksgiving,
and his courts with praise.
Give thanks to him, bless his name.

5 For the LORD is good;
his steadfast love endures forever,
and his faithfulness to all generations.

PSALM 101

Of David. A Psalm.

1 I will sing of loyalty and of justice;
to you, O LORD, I will sing.
2 I will study the way that is blameless.
When shall I attain it?

I will walk with integrity of heart
within my house;
3 I will not set before my eyes
anything that is base.

[a] Cn: Heb *And a king's strength* [b] Another reading is *and not we ourselves*

I hate the work of those who fall away;
it shall not cling to me.
4 Perverseness of heart shall be far from me;
I will know nothing of evil.

5 One who secretly slanders a neighbor
I will destroy.
A haughty look and an arrogant heart
I will not tolerate.

6 I will look with favor on the faithful in the land,
so that they may live with me;
whoever walks in the way that is blameless
shall minister to me.

7 No one who practices deceit
shall remain in my house;
no one who utters lies
shall continue in my presence.

8 Morning by morning I will destroy
all the wicked in the land,
cutting off all evildoers
from the city of the LORD.

PSALM 102

A prayer of one afflicted, when faint and pleading before the LORD.

1 Hear my prayer, O LORD;
let my cry come to you.
2 Do not hide your face from me
in the day of my distress.
Incline your ear to me;
answer me speedily in the day when I call.

3 For my days pass away like smoke,
and my bones burn like a furnace.
4 My heart is stricken and withered like grass;
I am too wasted to eat my bread.
5 Because of my loud groaning
my bones cling to my skin.
6 I am like an owl of the wilderness,
like a little owl of the waste places.
7 I lie awake;
I am like a lonely bird on the housetop.
8 All day long my enemies taunt me;
those who deride me use my name for a curse.
9 For I eat ashes like bread,
and mingle tears with my drink,
10 because of your indignation and anger;
for you have lifted me up and thrown me aside.
11 My days are like an evening shadow;
I wither away like grass.

12 But you, O LORD, are enthroned forever;
your name endures to all generations.
13 You will rise up and have compassion on Zion,
for it is time to favor it;
the appointed time has come.
14 For your servants hold its stones dear,
and have pity on its dust.
15 The nations will fear the name of the LORD,
and all the kings of the earth your glory.
16 For the LORD will build up Zion;
he will appear in his glory.
17 He will regard the prayer of the destitute,
and will not despise their prayer.

18 Let this be recorded for a generation to come,
so that a people yet unborn may praise the LORD:
19 that he looked down from his holy height,
from heaven the LORD looked at the earth,
20 to hear the groans of the prisoners,
to set free those who were doomed to die;
21 so that the name of the LORD may be declared in Zion,
and his praise in Jerusalem,
22 when peoples gather together,
and kingdoms, to worship the LORD.

23 He has broken my strength in midcourse;
he has shortened my days.
24 "O my God," I say, "do not take me away
at the midpoint of my life,
you whose years endure
throughout all generations."

25 Long ago you laid the foundation of the earth,
and the heavens are the work of your hands.
26 They will perish, but you endure;
they will all wear out like a garment.
You change them like clothing, and they pass away;
27 but you are the same, and your years have no end.
28 The children of your servants shall live secure;
their offspring shall be established in your presence.

PSALM 103

Of David.

1 Bless the LORD, O my soul,
and all that is within me,
bless his holy name.
2 Bless the LORD, O my soul,
and do not forget all his benefits—
3 who forgives all your iniquity,
who heals all your diseases,
4 who redeems your life from the Pit,
who crowns you with steadfast love and mercy,
5 who satisfies you with good as long as you live[a]
so that your youth is renewed like the eagle's.

6 The LORD works vindication
and justice for all who are oppressed.
7 He made known his ways to Moses,
his acts to the people of Israel.
8 The LORD is merciful and gracious,
slow to anger and abounding in steadfast love.
9 He will not always accuse,
nor will he keep his anger forever.
10 He does not deal with us according to our sins,
nor repay us according to our iniquities.

Psalm 103:6

When we search the Bible for a message about oppression we discover, as others throughout the world are discovering, that oppression is a central theme that runs right through the Old and New Testaments.... Moreover, the description of oppression in the Bible is concrete and vivid. The Bible describes oppression as the experience of being crushed, degraded, humiliated, exploited, impoverished, defrauded, deceived and enslaved. And the oppressors are described as cruel, ruthless, arrogant, greedy, violent and tyrannical and as the enemy. Such descriptions could only have been written originally by people who had had a long and painful experience of what it means to be oppressed.... Throughout the Bible God appears as the liberator of the oppressed. He is not neutral. He does not attempt to reconcile Moses and Pharaoh, to reconcile the Hebrew slaves with their Egyptian oppressors, or to reconcile the Jewish people with any of their later oppressors. Oppression is sin and it cannot be compromised with; it must be done away with. God takes sides with the oppressed. As we read in Psalm 103:6 (JB), "God, who does what is right, is always on the side of the oppressed."[37]

— ***The Kairos Document* (1985)**

11 For as the heavens are high above the earth,
so great is his steadfast love toward those who fear him;
12 as far as the east is from the west,
so far he removes our transgressions from us.
13 As a father has compassion for his children,
so the LORD has compassion for those who fear him.
14 For he knows how we were made;
he remembers that we are dust.

15 As for mortals, their days are like grass;
they flourish like a flower of the field;
16 for the wind passes over it, and it is gone,
and its place knows it no more.

[a] Meaning of Heb uncertain

17 But the steadfast love of the LORD is from
everlasting to everlasting
on those who fear him,
and his righteousness to children's
children,
18 to those who keep his covenant
and remember to do his commandments.

19 The LORD has established his throne in the
heavens,
and his kingdom rules over all.
20 Bless the LORD, O you his angels,
you mighty ones who do his bidding,
obedient to his spoken word.
21 Bless the LORD, all his hosts,
his ministers that do his will.
22 Bless the LORD, all his works,
in all places of his dominion.
Bless the LORD, O my soul.

PSALM 104

1 Bless the LORD, O my soul.
O LORD my God, you are very great.
You are clothed with honor and majesty,
2 wrapped in light as with a garment.
You stretch out the heavens like a tent,
3 you set the beams of your[a] chambers on
the waters,
you make the clouds your[a] chariot,
you ride on the wings of the wind,
4 you make the winds your[a] messengers,
fire and flame your[a] ministers.

5 You set the earth on its foundations,
so that it shall never be shaken.
6 You cover it with the deep as with a garment;
the waters stood above the mountains.
7 At your rebuke they flee;
at the sound of your thunder they take to
flight.
8 They rose up to the mountains, ran down to
the valleys
to the place that you appointed for them.
9 You set a boundary that they may not pass,
so that they might not again cover the
earth.

10 You make springs gush forth in the valleys;
they flow between the hills,
11 giving drink to every wild animal;
the wild asses quench their thirst.
12 By the streams[b] the birds of the air have their
habitation;
they sing among the branches.
13 From your lofty abode you water the
mountains;
the earth is satisfied with the fruit of your
work.

14 You cause the grass to grow for the cattle,
and plants for people to use,[c]
to bring forth food from the earth,
15 and wine to gladden the human heart,
oil to make the face shine,
and bread to strengthen the human heart.
16 The trees of the LORD are watered
abundantly,
the cedars of Lebanon that he planted.
17 In them the birds build their nests;
the stork has its home in the fir trees.
18 The high mountains are for the wild goats;
the rocks are a refuge for the coneys.
19 You have made the moon to mark the
seasons;
the sun knows its time for setting.
20 You make darkness, and it is night,
when all the animals of the forest come
creeping out.
21 The young lions roar for their prey,
seeking their food from God.
22 When the sun rises, they withdraw
and lie down in their dens.
23 People go out to their work
and to their labor until the evening.

24 O LORD, how manifold are your works!
In wisdom you have made them all;
the earth is full of your creatures.
25 Yonder is the sea, great and wide,

[a] Heb *his* [b] Heb *By them* [c] Or *to cultivate*

creeping things innumerable are there,
living things both small and great.
26 There go the ships,
and Leviathan that you formed to sport in it.

27 These all look to you
to give them their food in due season;
28 when you give to them, they gather it up;
when you open your hand, they are filled with good things.
29 When you hide your face, they are dismayed;
when you take away their breath, they die
and return to their dust.
30 When you send forth your spirit,[a] they are created;
and you renew the face of the ground.

31 May the glory of the LORD endure forever;
may the LORD rejoice in his works—
32 who looks on the earth and it trembles,
who touches the mountains and they smoke.
33 I will sing to the LORD as long as I live;
I will sing praise to my God while I have being.
34 May my meditation be pleasing to him,
for I rejoice in the LORD.
35 Let sinners be consumed from the earth,
and let the wicked be no more.
Bless the LORD, O my soul.
Praise the LORD!

PSALM 105

1 O give thanks to the LORD, call on his name,
make known his deeds among the peoples.
2 Sing to him, sing praises to him;
tell of all his wonderful works.
3 Glory in his holy name;
let the hearts of those who seek the LORD rejoice.
4 Seek the LORD and his strength;
seek his presence continually.
5 Remember the wonderful works he has done,
his miracles, and the judgments he has uttered,
6 O offspring of his servant Abraham,[b]
children of Jacob, his chosen ones.

7 He is the LORD our God;
his judgments are in all the earth.
8 He is mindful of his covenant forever,
of the word that he commanded, for a thousand generations,
9 the covenant that he made with Abraham,
his sworn promise to Isaac,
10 which he confirmed to Jacob as a statute,
to Israel as an everlasting covenant,
11 saying, "To you I will give the land of Canaan
as your portion for an inheritance."

12 When they were few in number,
of little account, and strangers in it,
13 wandering from nation to nation,
from one kingdom to another people,
14 he allowed no one to oppress them;
he rebuked kings on their account,
15 saying, "Do not touch my anointed ones;
do my prophets no harm."

16 When he summoned famine against the land,
and broke every staff of bread,
17 he had sent a man ahead of them,
Joseph, who was sold as a slave.
18 His feet were hurt with fetters,
his neck was put in a collar of iron;
19 until what he had said came to pass,
the word of the LORD kept testing him.
20 The king sent and released him;
the ruler of the peoples set him free.
21 He made him lord of his house,
and ruler of all his possessions,
22 to instruct[c] his officials at his pleasure,
and to teach his elders wisdom.

23 Then Israel came to Egypt;
Jacob lived as an alien in the land of Ham.
24 And the LORD made his people very fruitful,
and made them stronger than their foes,

[a] Or *your breath* [b] Another reading is *Israel* (compare 1 Chr 16.13) [c] Gk Syr Jerome: Heb *to bind*

25 whose hearts he then turned to hate his
people,
to deal craftily with his servants.

26 He sent his servant Moses,
and Aaron whom he had chosen.
27 They performed his signs among them,
and miracles in the land of Ham.
28 He sent darkness, and made the land dark;
they rebelled[a] against his words.
29 He turned their waters into blood,
and caused their fish to die.
30 Their land swarmed with frogs,
even in the chambers of their kings.
31 He spoke, and there came swarms of flies,
and gnats throughout their country.
32 He gave them hail for rain,
and lightning that flashed through their
land.
33 He struck their vines and fig trees,
and shattered the trees of their country.
34 He spoke, and the locusts came,
and young locusts without number;
35 they devoured all the vegetation in their land,
and ate up the fruit of their ground.
36 He struck down all the firstborn in their
land,
the first issue of all their strength.

37 Then he brought Israel[b] out with silver and
gold,
and there was no one among their tribes
who stumbled.
38 Egypt was glad when they departed,
for dread of them had fallen upon it.
39 He spread a cloud for a covering,
and fire to give light by night.
40 They asked, and he brought quails,
and gave them food from heaven in
abundance.
41 He opened the rock, and water gushed out;
it flowed through the desert like a river.
42 For he remembered his holy promise,
and Abraham, his servant.

43 So he brought his people out with joy,
his chosen ones with singing.
44 He gave them the lands of the nations,
and they took possession of the wealth of
the peoples,
45 that they might keep his statutes
and observe his laws.
Praise the LORD!

PSALM 106

1 Praise the LORD!
O give thanks to the LORD, for he is good;
for his steadfast love endures forever.
2 Who can utter the mighty doings of the
LORD,
or declare all his praise?
3 Happy are those who observe justice,
who do righteousness at all times.

4 Remember me, O LORD, when you show
favor to your people;
help me when you deliver them;
5 that I may see the prosperity of your chosen
ones,
that I may rejoice in the gladness of your
nation,
that I may glory in your heritage.

6 Both we and our ancestors have sinned;
we have committed iniquity, have done
wickedly.
7 Our ancestors, when they were in Egypt,
did not consider your wonderful works;
they did not remember the abundance of
your steadfast love,
but rebelled against the Most High[c] at the
Red Sea.[d]
8 Yet he saved them for his name's sake,
so that he might make known his mighty
power.
9 He rebuked the Red Sea,[d] and it became dry;
he led them through the deep as through
a desert.

[a] Cn Compare Gk Syr: Heb *they did not rebel* [b] Heb *them* [c] Cn Compare 78.17, 56: Heb *rebelled at the sea*
[d] Or *Sea of Reeds*

Psalm 106:7

If we do not remember, we do not live. Rather we fall into rebellion (Ps 106:7). They did not remember the abundance of your steadfast love, but rebelled against the Most High at the Red Sea (Ps 106:7b, NRSV). On the other hand, if we do remember, we must wrestle with the ghosts of memory. . . . The dominant culture in contemporary North America has exchanged the life of re-memory for a death-dealing drug, a falsely managed past. This dominant culture vacillates from amnesia to narcotic nostalgia. Such a position allows us to escape the responsibility of history by flattening history in favor of a valorization or demonization of the past.[38]

— Stephen Breck Reid

10 So he saved them from the hand of the foe,
and delivered them from the hand of the enemy.
11 The waters covered their adversaries;
not one of them was left.
12 Then they believed his words;
they sang his praise.

13 But they soon forgot his works;
they did not wait for his counsel.
14 But they had a wanton craving in the wilderness,
and put God to the test in the desert;
15 he gave them what they asked,
but sent a wasting disease among them.

16 They were jealous of Moses in the camp,
and of Aaron, the holy one of the LORD.
17 The earth opened and swallowed up Dathan,
and covered the faction of Abiram.
18 Fire also broke out in their company;
the flame burned up the wicked.

19 They made a calf at Horeb
and worshiped a cast image.
20 They exchanged the glory of God[a]
for the image of an ox that eats grass.
21 They forgot God, their Savior,
who had done great things in Egypt,
22 wondrous works in the land of Ham,
and awesome deeds by the Red Sea.[b]
23 Therefore he said he would destroy them—
had not Moses, his chosen one,
stood in the breach before him,
to turn away his wrath from destroying them.

24 Then they despised the pleasant land,
having no faith in his promise.
25 They grumbled in their tents,
and did not obey the voice of the LORD.
26 Therefore he raised his hand and swore to them
that he would make them fall in the wilderness,
27 and would disperse[c] their descendants among the nations,
scattering them over the lands.

28 Then they attached themselves to the Baal of Peor,
and ate sacrifices offered to the dead;
29 they provoked the LORD to anger with their deeds,
and a plague broke out among them.
30 Then Phinehas stood up and interceded,
and the plague was stopped.
31 And that has been reckoned to him as righteousness
from generation to generation forever.

32 They angered the LORD[d] at the waters of Meribah,
and it went ill with Moses on their account;
33 for they made his spirit bitter,
and he spoke words that were rash.

34 They did not destroy the peoples,
as the LORD commanded them,

[a] Compare Gk Mss: Heb *exchanged their glory* [b] Or *Sea of Reeds* [c] Syr Compare Ezek 20.23: Heb *cause to fall*
[d] Heb *him*

35 but they mingled with the nations
and learned to do as they did.
36 They served their idols,
which became a snare to them.
37 They sacrificed their sons
and their daughters to the demons;
38 they poured out innocent blood,
the blood of their sons and daughters,
whom they sacrificed to the idols of Canaan;
and the land was polluted with blood.
39 Thus they became unclean by their acts,
and prostituted themselves in their doings.

40 Then the anger of the Lord was kindled against his people,
and he abhorred his heritage;
41 he gave them into the hand of the nations,
so that those who hated them ruled over them.
42 Their enemies oppressed them,
and they were brought into subjection under their power.
43 Many times he delivered them,
but they were rebellious in their purposes,
and were brought low through their iniquity.
44 Nevertheless he regarded their distress
when he heard their cry.
45 For their sake he remembered his covenant,
and showed compassion according to the abundance of his steadfast love.
46 He caused them to be pitied
by all who held them captive.

47 Save us, O Lord our God,
and gather us from among the nations,
that we may give thanks to your holy name
and glory in your praise.

48 Blessed be the Lord, the God of Israel,
from everlasting to everlasting.
And let all the people say, "Amen."
Praise the Lord!

BOOK V

PSALM 107

1 O give thanks to the Lord, for he is good;
for his steadfast love endures forever.
2 Let the redeemed of the Lord say so,
those he redeemed from trouble
3 and gathered in from the lands,
from the east and from the west,
from the north and from the south.[a]

4 Some wandered in desert wastes,
finding no way to an inhabited town;
5 hungry and thirsty,
their soul fainted within them.
6 Then they cried to the Lord in their trouble,
and he delivered them from their distress;
7 he led them by a straight way,
until they reached an inhabited town.
8 Let them thank the Lord for his steadfast love,
for his wonderful works to humankind.
9 For he satisfies the thirsty,
and the hungry he fills with good things.

10 Some sat in darkness and in gloom,
prisoners in misery and in irons,
11 for they had rebelled against the words of God,
and spurned the counsel of the Most High.
12 Their hearts were bowed down with hard labor;
they fell down, with no one to help.
13 Then they cried to the Lord in their trouble,
and he saved them from their distress;
14 he brought them out of darkness and gloom,
and broke their bonds asunder.
15 Let them thank the Lord for his steadfast love,
for his wonderful works to humankind.
16 For he shatters the doors of bronze,
and cuts in two the bars of iron.

[a] Cn: Heb *sea*

17 Some were sick[a] through their sinful ways,
and because of their iniquities endured affliction;
18 they loathed any kind of food,
and they drew near to the gates of death.
19 Then they cried to the LORD in their trouble,
and he saved them from their distress;
20 he sent out his word and healed them,
and delivered them from destruction.
21 Let them thank the LORD for his steadfast love,
for his wonderful works to humankind.
22 And let them offer thanksgiving sacrifices,
and tell of his deeds with songs of joy.

23 Some went down to the sea in ships,
doing business on the mighty waters;
24 they saw the deeds of the LORD,
his wondrous works in the deep.
25 For he commanded and raised the stormy wind,
which lifted up the waves of the sea.
26 They mounted up to heaven, they went down to the depths;
their courage melted away in their calamity;
27 they reeled and staggered like drunkards,
and were at their wits' end.
28 Then they cried to the LORD in their trouble,
and he brought them out from their distress;
29 he made the storm be still,
and the waves of the sea were hushed.
30 Then they were glad because they had quiet,
and he brought them to their desired haven.
31 Let them thank the LORD for his steadfast love,
for his wonderful works to humankind.
32 Let them extol him in the congregation of the people,
and praise him in the assembly of the elders.

33 He turns rivers into a desert,
springs of water into thirsty ground,
34 a fruitful land into a salty waste,
because of the wickedness of its inhabitants.
35 He turns a desert into pools of water,
a parched land into springs of water.
36 And there he lets the hungry live,
and they establish a town to live in;
37 they sow fields, and plant vineyards,
and get a fruitful yield.
38 By his blessing they multiply greatly,
and he does not let their cattle decrease.

39 When they are diminished and brought low
through oppression, trouble, and sorrow,
40 he pours contempt on princes
and makes them wander in trackless wastes;
41 but he raises up the needy out of distress,
and makes their families like flocks.
42 The upright see it and are glad;
and all wickedness stops its mouth.
43 Let those who are wise give heed to these things,
and consider the steadfast love of the LORD.

PSALM 108

A Song. A Psalm of David.

1 My heart is steadfast, O God, my heart is steadfast;[b]
I will sing and make melody.
Awake, my soul![c]
2 Awake, O harp and lyre!
I will awake the dawn.
3 I will give thanks to you, O LORD, among the peoples,
and I will sing praises to you among the nations.
4 For your steadfast love is higher than the heavens,
and your faithfulness reaches to the clouds.

5 Be exalted, O God, above the heavens,
and let your glory be over all the earth.

[a] Cn: Heb *fools* [b] Heb Mss Gk Syr: MT lacks *my heart is steadfast* [c] Compare 57.8: Heb *also my soul*

6 Give victory with your right hand, and
answer me,
so that those whom you love may be
rescued.

7 God has promised in his sanctuary:[a]
"With exultation I will divide up Shechem,
and portion out the Vale of Succoth.
8 Gilead is mine; Manasseh is mine;
Ephraim is my helmet;
Judah is my scepter.
9 Moab is my washbasin;
on Edom I hurl my shoe;
over Philistia I shout in triumph."

10 Who will bring me to the fortified city?
Who will lead me to Edom?
11 Have you not rejected us, O God?
You do not go out, O God, with our
armies.
12 O grant us help against the foe,
for human help is worthless.
13 With God we shall do valiantly;
it is he who will tread down our foes.

PSALM 109

To the leader. Of David. A Psalm.

1 Do not be silent, O God of my praise.
2 For wicked and deceitful mouths are opened
against me,
speaking against me with lying tongues.
3 They beset me with words of hate,
and attack me without cause.
4 In return for my love they accuse me,
even while I make prayer for them.[b]
5 So they reward me evil for good,
and hatred for my love.

6 They say,[c] "Appoint a wicked man against
him;
let an accuser stand on his right.
7 When he is tried, let him be found guilty;
let his prayer be counted as sin.
8 May his days be few;
may another seize his position.
9 May his children be orphans,
and his wife a widow.
10 May his children wander about and beg;
may they be driven out of[d] the ruins they
inhabit.
11 May the creditor seize all that he has;
may strangers plunder the fruits of his toil.
12 May there be no one to do him a kindness,
nor anyone to pity his orphaned children.
13 May his posterity be cut off;
may his name be blotted out in the second
generation.
14 May the iniquity of his father[e] be
remembered before the LORD,
and do not let the sin of his mother be
blotted out.
15 Let them be before the LORD continually,
and may his[f] memory be cut off from the
earth.
16 For he did not remember to show kindness,
but pursued the poor and needy
and the brokenhearted to their death.
17 He loved to curse; let curses come on him.
He did not like blessing; may it be far from
him.
18 He clothed himself with cursing as his coat,
may it soak into his body like water,
like oil into his bones.
19 May it be like a garment that he wraps around
himself,
like a belt that he wears every day."

20 May that be the reward of my accusers from
the LORD,
of those who speak evil against my life.
21 But you, O LORD my Lord,
act on my behalf for your name's sake;
because your steadfast love is good,
deliver me.
22 For I am poor and needy,
and my heart is pierced within me.
23 I am gone like a shadow at evening;

[a] Or *by his holiness* [b] Syr: Heb *I prayer* [c] Heb lacks *They say* [d] Gk: Heb *and seek* [e] Cn: Heb *fathers*
[f] Gk: Heb *their*

I am shaken off like a locust.
24 My knees are weak through fasting;
my body has become gaunt.
25 I am an object of scorn to my accusers;
when they see me, they shake their heads.

26 Help me, O LORD my God!
Save me according to your steadfast love.
27 Let them know that this is your hand;
you, O LORD, have done it.
28 Let them curse, but you will bless.
Let my assailants be put to shame;[a] may
your servant be glad.
29 May my accusers be clothed with dishonor;
may they be wrapped in their own shame
as in a mantle.
30 With my mouth I will give great thanks to the
LORD;
I will praise him in the midst of the
throng.
31 For he stands at the right hand of the
needy,
to save them from those who would
condemn them to death.

PSALM 110

Of David. A Psalm.

1 The LORD says to my lord,
"Sit at my right hand
until I make your enemies your footstool."

2 The LORD sends out from Zion
your mighty scepter.
Rule in the midst of your foes.
3 Your people will offer themselves willingly
on the day you lead your forces
on the holy mountains.[b]
From the womb of the morning,
like dew, your youth[c] will come to you.
4 The LORD has sworn and will not change his
mind,
"You are a priest forever according to the
order of Melchizedek."[d]

5 The Lord is at your right hand;
he will shatter kings on the day of his
wrath.
6 He will execute judgment among the nations,
filling them with corpses;
he will shatter heads
over the wide earth.
7 He will drink from the stream by the path;
therefore he will lift up his head.

PSALM 111

1 Praise the LORD!
I will give thanks to the LORD with my whole
heart,
in the company of the upright, in the
congregation.
2 Great are the works of the LORD,
studied by all who delight in them.
3 Full of honor and majesty is his work,
and his righteousness endures forever.
4 He has gained renown by his wonderful
deeds;
the LORD is gracious and merciful.
5 He provides food for those who fear him;
he is ever mindful of his covenant.
6 He has shown his people the power of his
works,
in giving them the heritage of the
nations.
7 The works of his hands are faithful and just;
all his precepts are trustworthy.
8 They are established forever and ever,
to be performed with faithfulness and
uprightness.
9 He sent redemption to his people;
he has commanded his covenant forever.
Holy and awesome is his name.
10 The fear of the LORD is the beginning of
wisdom;
all those who practice it[e] have a good
understanding.
His praise endures forever.

[a] Gk: Heb *They have risen up and have been put to shame* [b] Another reading is *in holy splendor* [c] Cn: Heb *the dew of your youth* [d] Or *forever, a rightful king by my edict* [e] Gk Syr: Heb *them*

PSALM 112

1 Praise the LORD!
Happy are those who fear the LORD,
who greatly delight in his commandments.
2 Their descendants will be mighty in the land;
the generation of the upright will be blessed.
3 Wealth and riches are in their houses,
and their righteousness endures forever.
4 They rise in the darkness as a light for the upright;
they are gracious, merciful, and righteous.
5 It is well with those who deal generously and lend,
who conduct their affairs with justice.
6 For the righteous will never be moved;
they will be remembered forever.
7 They are not afraid of evil tidings;
their hearts are firm, secure in the LORD.
8 Their hearts are steady, they will not be afraid;
in the end they will look in triumph on their foes.
9 They have distributed freely, they have given to the poor;
their righteousness endures forever;
their horn is exalted in honor.
10 The wicked see it and are angry;
they gnash their teeth and melt away;
the desire of the wicked comes to nothing.

PSALM 113

1 Praise the LORD!
Praise, O servants of the LORD;
praise the name of the LORD.

2 Blessed be the name of the LORD
from this time on and forevermore.
3 From the rising of the sun to its setting
the name of the LORD is to be praised.
4 The LORD is high above all nations,
and his glory above the heavens.

5 Who is like the LORD our God,
who is seated on high,
6 who looks far down
on the heavens and the earth?
7 He raises the poor from the dust,
and lifts the needy from the ash heap,
8 to make them sit with princes,
with the princes of his people.
9 He gives the barren woman a home,
making her the joyous mother of children.
Praise the LORD!

PSALM 114

1 When Israel went out from Egypt,
the house of Jacob from a people of strange language,
2 Judah became God's[a] sanctuary,
Israel his dominion.

3 The sea looked and fled;
Jordan turned back.
4 The mountains skipped like rams,
the hills like lambs.

5 Why is it, O sea, that you flee?
O Jordan, that you turn back?
6 O mountains, that you skip like rams?
O hills, like lambs?

7 Tremble, O earth, at the presence of the LORD,
at the presence of the God of Jacob,
8 who turns the rock into a pool of water,
the flint into a spring of water.

PSALM 115

1 Not to us, O LORD, not to us, but to your name give glory,
for the sake of your steadfast love and your faithfulness.
2 Why should the nations say,
"Where is their God?"
3 Our God is in the heavens;
he does whatever he pleases.

[a] Heb *his*

4 Their idols are silver and gold,
the work of human hands.
5 They have mouths, but do not speak;
eyes, but do not see.
6 They have ears, but do not hear;
noses, but do not smell.
7 They have hands, but do not feel;
feet, but do not walk;
they make no sound in their throats.
8 Those who make them are like them;
so are all who trust in them.

9 O Israel, trust in the LORD!
He is their help and their shield.
10 O house of Aaron, trust in the LORD!
He is their help and their shield.
11 You who fear the LORD, trust in the LORD!
He is their help and their shield.

12 The LORD has been mindful of us; he will bless us;
he will bless the house of Israel;
he will bless the house of Aaron;
13 he will bless those who fear the LORD,
both small and great.

14 May the LORD give you increase,
both you and your children.
15 May you be blessed by the LORD,
who made heaven and earth.

16 The heavens are the LORD's heavens,
but the earth he has given to human beings.
17 The dead do not praise the LORD,
nor do any that go down into silence.
18 But we will bless the LORD
from this time on and forevermore.
Praise the LORD!

PSALM 116

1 I love the LORD, because he has heard
my voice and my supplications.
2 Because he inclined his ear to me,
therefore I will call on him as long as I live.
3 The snares of death encompassed me;
the pangs of Sheol laid hold on me;
I suffered distress and anguish.
4 Then I called on the name of the LORD:
"O LORD, I pray, save my life!"

5 Gracious is the LORD, and righteous;
our God is merciful.
6 The LORD protects the simple;
when I was brought low, he saved me.
7 Return, O my soul, to your rest,
for the LORD has dealt bountifully with you.

8 For you have delivered my soul from death,
my eyes from tears,

Psalm 115:16

The biblical axiom that "the world is given to all" was decisive for the social teaching of the early church. It fueled Ambrose of Milan (337–97 CE) in his furious condemnation of the oppressive rich and his advocacy of the dignity of the poor. To the rich he exclaimed, "How far will you push your frenzied greed? Are you alone to dwell on the earth? Why do you cast out [others] who are fellow-creatures and claim all creation as your own? Earth at its beginning was for all in common.... What right have you to monopolize the soil?" Ambrose excoriated especially the complacent rich who filled his church but did nothing to alleviate the suffering of the poor. They showed off their contracts and deeds, but, he exclaimed, "I pronounce the words of God's law.... You say: 'I will pull down my barns.' The Lord says: 'Rather let all the store in them be turned to the service of poor and needy.'... How can you ask that God should hear you favorably when to God himself you give no hearing?"[39]

—NE

my feet from stumbling.
9 I walk before the LORD
in the land of the living.
10 I kept my faith, even when I said,
"I am greatly afflicted";
11 I said in my consternation,
"Everyone is a liar."

12 What shall I return to the LORD
for all his bounty to me?
13 I will lift up the cup of salvation
and call on the name of the LORD,
14 I will pay my vows to the LORD
in the presence of all his people.
15 Precious in the sight of the LORD
is the death of his faithful ones.
16 O LORD, I am your servant;
I am your servant, the child of your serving girl.
You have loosed my bonds.
17 I will offer to you a thanksgiving sacrifice
and call on the name of the LORD.
18 I will pay my vows to the LORD
in the presence of all his people,
19 in the courts of the house of the LORD,
in your midst, O Jerusalem.
Praise the LORD!

PSALM 117

1 Praise the LORD, all you nations!
Extol him, all you peoples!
2 For great is his steadfast love toward us,
and the faithfulness of the LORD endures forever.
Praise the LORD!

PSALM 118

1 O give thanks to the LORD, for he is good;
his steadfast love endures forever!

2 Let Israel say,
"His steadfast love endures forever."
3 Let the house of Aaron say,
"His steadfast love endures forever."
4 Let those who fear the LORD say,
"His steadfast love endures forever."

5 Out of my distress I called on the LORD;
the LORD answered me and set me in a broad place.
6 With the LORD on my side I do not fear.
What can mortals do to me?
7 The LORD is on my side to help me;
I shall look in triumph on those who hate me.
8 It is better to take refuge in the LORD
than to put confidence in mortals.
9 It is better to take refuge in the LORD
than to put confidence in princes.

10 All nations surrounded me;
in the name of the LORD I cut them off!
11 They surrounded me, surrounded me on every side;
in the name of the LORD I cut them off!
12 They surrounded me like bees;
they blazed[a] like a fire of thorns;
in the name of the LORD I cut them off!
13 I was pushed hard,[b] so that I was falling,
but the LORD helped me.
14 The LORD is my strength and my might;
he has become my salvation.

15 There are glad songs of victory in the tents of the righteous:
"The right hand of the LORD does valiantly;
16 the right hand of the LORD is exalted;
the right hand of the LORD does valiantly."
17 I shall not die, but I shall live,
and recount the deeds of the LORD.
18 The LORD has punished me severely,
but he did not give me over to death.

19 Open to me the gates of righteousness,
that I may enter through them
and give thanks to the LORD.

20 This is the gate of the LORD;
the righteous shall enter through it.

[a] Gk: Heb *were extinguished* [b] Gk Syr Jerome: Heb *You pushed me hard*

Psalm 118:22

"The stone the builders rejected has become the chief cornerstone."... Many of us knowingly nod our heads when we hear of the builders rejecting stones.... We murmur to ourselves, "Not me, Lord, I'm not a builder, especially that kind of builder." Guess again! All of us are builders.

Women and blacks are rejected simply because of their gender or race. In the West they are oppressed in a world defined and controlled by the white male. In other parts of the world women are oppressed in a world defined and controlled by the male, regardless of color. In every place they are victims of controlled economies and political systems. In modern America... [b]lacks struggle in a system which denies them access to the things of success (education, jobs, housing, health care, etc.) and then blames them for their dependent status and points to their unsuccesses as justification for prejudicial stereotypes. Their cries for acceptance are met with hostility, indifference, condescension, and fear while the white, male-dominated culture continues with its building projects, glibly rejecting stones which do not meet its specifications.[40]

— **Robert C. Fulton**

21 I thank you that you have answered me
and have become my salvation.
22 The stone that the builders rejected
has become the chief cornerstone.
23 This is the LORD's doing;
it is marvelous in our eyes.
24 This is the day that the LORD has made;
let us rejoice and be glad in it.[a]
25 Save us, we beseech you, O LORD!
O LORD, we beseech you, give us
success!

26 Blessed is the one who comes in the name of
the LORD.[b]
We bless you from the house of the
LORD.
27 The LORD is God,
and he has given us light.
Bind the festal procession with branches,
up to the horns of the altar.[c]

28 You are my God, and I will give thanks to
you;
you are my God, I will extol you.

29 O give thanks to the LORD, for he is
good,
for his steadfast love endures forever.

PSALM 119

1 Happy are those whose way is blameless,
who walk in the law of the LORD.
2 Happy are those who keep his decrees,
who seek him with their whole heart,
3 who also do no wrong,
but walk in his ways.
4 You have commanded your precepts
to be kept diligently.
5 O that my ways may be steadfast
in keeping your statutes!
6 Then I shall not be put to shame,
having my eyes fixed on all your
commandments.
7 I will praise you with an upright heart,
when I learn your righteous ordinances.
8 I will observe your statutes;
do not utterly forsake me.

9 How can young people keep their way pure?
By guarding it according to your word.
10 With my whole heart I seek you;
do not let me stray from your
commandments.
11 I treasure your word in my heart,
so that I may not sin against you.
12 Blessed are you, O LORD;

[a] Or *in him* [b] Or *Blessed in the name of the LORD is the one who comes* [c] Meaning of Heb uncertain

teach me your statutes.
13 With my lips I declare
all the ordinances of your mouth.
14 I delight in the way of your decrees
as much as in all riches.
15 I will meditate on your precepts,
and fix my eyes on your ways.
16 I will delight in your statutes;
I will not forget your word.

17 Deal bountifully with your servant,
so that I may live and observe your word.
18 Open my eyes, so that I may behold
wondrous things out of your law.
19 I live as an alien in the land;
do not hide your commandments
from me.
20 My soul is consumed with longing
for your ordinances at all times.
21 You rebuke the insolent, accursed ones,
who wander from your commandments;
22 take away from me their scorn and contempt,
for I have kept your decrees.
23 Even though princes sit plotting against me,
your servant will meditate on your
statutes.
24 Your decrees are my delight,
they are my counselors.

25 My soul clings to the dust;
revive me according to your word.
26 When I told of my ways, you answered me;
teach me your statutes.
27 Make me understand the way of your
precepts,
and I will meditate on your wondrous
works.
28 My soul melts away for sorrow;
strengthen me according to your word.
29 Put false ways far from me;
and graciously teach me your law.
30 I have chosen the way of faithfulness;
I set your ordinances before me.
31 I cling to your decrees, O LORD;
let me not be put to shame.
32 I run the way of your commandments,
for you enlarge my understanding.

33 Teach me, O LORD, the way of your statutes,
and I will observe it to the end.
34 Give me understanding, that I may keep your
law
and observe it with my whole heart.
35 Lead me in the path of your commandments,
for I delight in it.
36 Turn my heart to your decrees,
and not to selfish gain.
37 Turn my eyes from looking at vanities;
give me life in your ways.
38 Confirm to your servant your promise,
which is for those who fear you.
39 Turn away the disgrace that I dread,
for your ordinances are good.
40 See, I have longed for your precepts;
in your righteousness give me life.

41 Let your steadfast love come to me, O LORD,
your salvation according to your promise.
42 Then I shall have an answer for those who
taunt me,
for I trust in your word.
43 Do not take the word of truth utterly out of
my mouth,
for my hope is in your ordinances.
44 I will keep your law continually,
forever and ever.
45 I shall walk at liberty,
for I have sought your precepts.
46 I will also speak of your decrees before kings,
and shall not be put to shame;
47 I find my delight in your commandments,
because I love them.
48 I revere your commandments, which I love,
and I will meditate on your statutes.

49 Remember your word to your servant,
in which you have made me hope.
50 This is my comfort in my distress,
that your promise gives me life.
51 The arrogant utterly deride me,
but I do not turn away from your law.
52 When I think of your ordinances from of old,
I take comfort, O LORD.
53 Hot indignation seizes me because of the
wicked,

those who forsake your law.
54 Your statutes have been my songs
wherever I make my home.
55 I remember your name in the night, O LORD,
and keep your law.
56 This blessing has fallen to me,
for I have kept your precepts.

57 The LORD is my portion;
I promise to keep your words.
58 I implore your favor with all my heart;
be gracious to me according to your promise.
59 When I think of your ways,
I turn my feet to your decrees;
60 I hurry and do not delay
to keep your commandments.
61 Though the cords of the wicked ensnare me,
I do not forget your law.
62 At midnight I rise to praise you,
because of your righteous ordinances.
63 I am a companion of all who fear you,
of those who keep your precepts.
64 The earth, O LORD, is full of your steadfast
love;
teach me your statutes.

65 You have dealt well with your servant,
O LORD, according to your word.
66 Teach me good judgment and knowledge,
for I believe in your commandments.
67 Before I was humbled I went astray,
but now I keep your word.
68 You are good and do good;
teach me your statutes.
69 The arrogant smear me with lies,
but with my whole heart I keep your
precepts.
70 Their hearts are fat and gross,
but I delight in your law.
71 It is good for me that I was humbled,
so that I might learn your statutes.
72 The law of your mouth is better to me
than thousands of gold and silver pieces.

73 Your hands have made and fashioned me;
give me understanding that I may learn
your commandments.
74 Those who fear you shall see me and rejoice,
because I have hoped in your word.
75 I know, O LORD, that your judgments are
right,
and that in faithfulness you have
humbled me.
76 Let your steadfast love become my comfort
according to your promise to your servant.
77 Let your mercy come to me, that I may live;
for your law is my delight.
78 Let the arrogant be put to shame,
because they have subverted me with guile;
as for me, I will meditate on your precepts.
79 Let those who fear you turn to me,
so that they may know your decrees.
80 May my heart be blameless in your statutes,
so that I may not be put to shame.

81 My soul languishes for your salvation;
I hope in your word.
82 My eyes fail with watching for your promise;
I ask, "When will you comfort me?"
83 For I have become like a wineskin in the
smoke,
yet I have not forgotten your statutes.
84 How long must your servant endure?
When will you judge those who
persecute me?
85 The arrogant have dug pitfalls for me;
they flout your law.
86 All your commandments are enduring;
I am persecuted without cause; help me!
87 They have almost made an end of me on
earth;
but I have not forsaken your precepts.
88 In your steadfast love spare my life,
so that I may keep the decrees of your
mouth.

89 The LORD exists forever;
your word is firmly fixed in heaven.
90 Your faithfulness endures to all generations;
you have established the earth, and it
stands fast.
91 By your appointment they stand today,
for all things are your servants.
92 If your law had not been my delight,

I would have perished in my misery.
93 I will never forget your precepts,
for by them you have given me life.
94 I am yours; save me,
for I have sought your precepts.
95 The wicked lie in wait to destroy me,
but I consider your decrees.
96 I have seen a limit to all perfection,
but your commandment is exceedingly
broad.

97 Oh, how I love your law!
It is my meditation all day long.
98 Your commandment makes me wiser than
my enemies,
for it is always with me.
99 I have more understanding than all my
teachers,
for your decrees are my meditation.
100 I understand more than the aged,
for I keep your precepts.
101 I hold back my feet from every evil way,
in order to keep your word.
102 I do not turn away from your ordinances,
for you have taught me.
103 How sweet are your words to my taste,
sweeter than honey to my mouth!
104 Through your precepts I get understanding;
therefore I hate every false way.

105 Your word is a lamp to my feet
and a light to my path.
106 I have sworn an oath and confirmed it,
to observe your righteous ordinances.
107 I am severely afflicted;
give me life, O Lord, according to your
word.
108 Accept my offerings of praise, O Lord,
and teach me your ordinances.
109 I hold my life in my hand continually,
but I do not forget your law.
110 The wicked have laid a snare for me,
but I do not stray from your precepts.
111 Your decrees are my heritage forever;
they are the joy of my heart.
112 I incline my heart to perform your statutes
forever, to the end.

113 I hate the double-minded,
but I love your law.

Psalm 119:113

The U.S. Catholic Bishops warned in their pastoral letter *Economic Justice for All* (1986) against "a tragic separation between faith and everyday life" and the presumption that economic matters were somehow immune from moral judgment. In place of such "double-mindedness" they called for conversion to six biblical principles: 1. Every economic decision and institution must be judged in light of whether it protects or undermines the dignity of the human person. 2. Human dignity can be realized and protected only in community. 3. All people have a right to participate in the economic life of society. 4. All members of society have a special obligation to the poor and vulnerable; . . . the justice of a society is tested by the treatment of the poor. 5. Human rights are the minimum conditions for life in community. 6. Society as a whole, acting through public and private institutions, has the moral responsibility to enhance human dignity and protect human rights.[41]

— *NE*

114 You are my hiding place and my shield;
I hope in your word.
115 Go away from me, you evildoers,
that I may keep the commandments of my
God.
116 Uphold me according to your promise, that I
may live,
and let me not be put to shame in my hope.
117 Hold me up, that I may be safe
and have regard for your statutes
continually.
118 You spurn all who go astray from your statutes;
for their cunning is in vain.
119 All the wicked of the earth you count as dross;
therefore I love your decrees.
120 My flesh trembles for fear of you,
and I am afraid of your judgments.

121 I have done what is just and right;
do not leave me to my oppressors.

122 Guarantee your servant's well-being;
do not let the godless oppress me.
123 My eyes fail from watching for your salvation,
and for the fulfillment of your righteous promise.
124 Deal with your servant according to your steadfast love,
and teach me your statutes.
125 I am your servant; give me understanding,
so that I may know your decrees.
126 It is time for the LORD to act,
for your law has been broken.
127 Truly I love your commandments
more than gold, more than fine gold.
128 Truly I direct my steps by all your precepts;[a]
I hate every false way.

129 Your decrees are wonderful;
therefore my soul keeps them.
130 The unfolding of your words gives light;
it imparts understanding to the simple.
131 With open mouth I pant,
because I long for your commandments.
132 Turn to me and be gracious to me,
as is your custom toward those who love your name.
133 Keep my steps steady according to your promise,
and never let iniquity have dominion over me.
134 Redeem me from human oppression,
that I may keep your precepts.
135 Make your face shine upon your servant,
and teach me your statutes.
136 My eyes shed streams of tears
because your law is not kept.

137 You are righteous, O LORD,
and your judgments are right.
138 You have appointed your decrees in righteousness
and in all faithfulness.
139 My zeal consumes me
because my foes forget your words.
140 Your promise is well tried,
and your servant loves it.
141 I am small and despised,
yet I do not forget your precepts.
142 Your righteousness is an everlasting righteousness,
and your law is the truth.
143 Trouble and anguish have come upon me,
but your commandments are my delight.
144 Your decrees are righteous forever;
give me understanding that I may live.

145 With my whole heart I cry; answer me, O LORD.
I will keep your statutes.
146 I cry to you; save me,
that I may observe your decrees.
147 I rise before dawn and cry for help;
I put my hope in your words.
148 My eyes are awake before each watch of the night,
that I may meditate on your promise.
149 In your steadfast love hear my voice;
O LORD, in your justice preserve my life.
150 Those who persecute me with evil purpose draw near;
they are far from your law.
151 Yet you are near, O LORD,
and all your commandments are true.
152 Long ago I learned from your decrees
that you have established them forever.

153 Look on my misery and rescue me,
for I do not forget your law.
154 Plead my cause and redeem me;
give me life according to your promise.
155 Salvation is far from the wicked,
for they do not seek your statutes.
156 Great is your mercy, O LORD;
give me life according to your justice.
157 Many are my persecutors and my adversaries,
yet I do not swerve from your decrees.
158 I look at the faithless with disgust,
because they do not keep your commands.
159 Consider how I love your precepts;

[a] Gk Jerome: Meaning of Heb uncertain

preserve my life according to your
steadfast love.
160 The sum of your word is truth;
and every one of your righteous
ordinances endures forever.

161 Princes persecute me without cause,
but my heart stands in awe of your words.
162 I rejoice at your word
like one who finds great spoil.
163 I hate and abhor falsehood,
but I love your law.
164 Seven times a day I praise you
for your righteous ordinances.
165 Great peace have those who love your law;
nothing can make them stumble.
166 I hope for your salvation, O Lord,
and I fulfill your commandments.
167 My soul keeps your decrees;
I love them exceedingly.
168 I keep your precepts and decrees,
for all my ways are before you.

169 Let my cry come before you, O Lord;
give me understanding according to your
word.
170 Let my supplication come before you;
deliver me according to your promise.
171 My lips will pour forth praise,
because you teach me your statutes.
172 My tongue will sing of your promise,
for all your commandments are right.
173 Let your hand be ready to help me,
for I have chosen your precepts.
174 I long for your salvation, O Lord,
and your law is my delight.
175 Let me live that I may praise you,
and let your ordinances help me.
176 I have gone astray like a lost sheep; seek out
your servant,
for I do not forget your commandments.

PSALM 120

A Song of Ascents.

1 In my distress I cry to the Lord,
that he may answer me:
2 "Deliver me, O Lord,
from lying lips,
from a deceitful tongue."

3 What shall be given to you?
And what more shall be done to you,
you deceitful tongue?
4 A warrior's sharp arrows,
with glowing coals of the broom tree!

5 Woe is me, that I am an alien in Meshech,
that I must live among the tents of Kedar.
6 Too long have I had my dwelling
among those who hate peace.
7 I am for peace;
but when I speak,
they are for war.

PSALM 121

A Song of Ascents.

1 I lift up my eyes to the hills—
from where will my help come?
2 My help comes from the Lord,
who made heaven and earth.

3 He will not let your foot be moved;
he who keeps you will not slumber.
4 He who keeps Israel
will neither slumber nor sleep.

5 The Lord is your keeper;
the Lord is your shade at your right
hand.
6 The sun shall not strike you by day,
nor the moon by night.

7 The Lord will keep you from all evil;
he will keep your life.
8 The Lord will keep
your going out and your coming in
from this time on and forevermore.

PSALM 122

A Song of Ascents. Of David.

1 I was glad when they said to me,
"Let us go to the house of the Lord!"

2 Our feet are standing
within your gates, O Jerusalem.

3 Jerusalem—built as a city
that is bound firmly together.
4 To it the tribes go up,
the tribes of the LORD,
as was decreed for Israel,
to give thanks to the name of the LORD.
5 For there the thrones for judgment were set up,
the thrones of the house of David.

6 Pray for the peace of Jerusalem:
"May they prosper who love you.
7 Peace be within your walls,
and security within your towers."
8 For the sake of my relatives and friends
I will say, "Peace be within you."
9 For the sake of the house of the LORD our God,
I will seek your good.

PSALM 123

A Song of Ascents.

1 To you I lift up my eyes,
O you who are enthroned in the heavens!
2 As the eyes of servants
look to the hand of their master,
as the eyes of a maid
to the hand of her mistress,
so our eyes look to the LORD our God,
until he has mercy upon us.

3 Have mercy upon us, O LORD, have mercy upon us,
for we have had more than enough of contempt.
4 Our soul has had more than its fill
of the scorn of those who are at ease,
of the contempt of the proud.

PSALM 124

A Song of Ascents. Of David.

1 If it had not been the LORD who was on our side
—let Israel now say—
2 if it had not been the LORD who was on our side,
when our enemies attacked us,
3 then they would have swallowed us up alive,
when their anger was kindled against us;
4 then the flood would have swept us away,
the torrent would have gone over us;
5 then over us would have gone
the raging waters.

6 Blessed be the LORD,
who has not given us
as prey to their teeth.
7 We have escaped like a bird
from the snare of the fowlers;
the snare is broken,
and we have escaped.

8 Our help is in the name of the LORD,
who made heaven and earth.

PSALM 125

A Song of Ascents.

1 Those who trust in the LORD are like Mount Zion,
which cannot be moved, but abides forever.
2 As the mountains surround Jerusalem,
so the LORD surrounds his people,
from this time on and forevermore.
3 For the scepter of wickedness shall not rest
on the land allotted to the righteous,
so that the righteous might not stretch out
their hands to do wrong.
4 Do good, O LORD, to those who are good,
and to those who are upright in their hearts.
5 But those who turn aside to their own crooked ways
the LORD will lead away with evildoers.
Peace be upon Israel!

PSALM 126

A Song of Ascents.

1 When the LORD restored the fortunes of
Zion,[a]
we were like those who dream.
2 Then our mouth was filled with laughter,
and our tongue with shouts of joy;
then it was said among the nations,
"The LORD has done great things for
them."
3 The LORD has done great things for us,
and we rejoiced.

4 Restore our fortunes, O LORD,
like the watercourses in the Negeb.
5 May those who sow in tears
reap with shouts of joy.
6 Those who go out weeping,
bearing the seed for sowing,
shall come home with shouts of joy,
carrying their sheaves.

PSALM 127

A Song of Ascents. Of Solomon.

1 Unless the LORD builds the house,
those who build it labor in vain.
Unless the LORD guards the city,
the guard keeps watch in vain.
2 It is in vain that you rise up early
and go late to rest,
eating the bread of anxious toil;
for he gives sleep to his beloved.[b]

3 Sons are indeed a heritage from the LORD,
the fruit of the womb a reward.
4 Like arrows in the hand of a warrior
are the sons of one's youth.
5 Happy is the man who has
his quiver full of them.
He shall not be put to shame
when he speaks with his enemies in the
gate.

PSALM 128

A Song of Ascents.

1 Happy is everyone who fears the LORD,
who walks in his ways.
2 You shall eat the fruit of the labor of your
hands;
you shall be happy, and it shall go well
with you.

3 Your wife will be like a fruitful vine
within your house;
your children will be like olive shoots
around your table.
4 Thus shall the man be blessed
who fears the LORD.

5 The LORD bless you from Zion.
May you see the prosperity of Jerusalem
all the days of your life.
6 May you see your children's children.
Peace be upon Israel!

PSALM 129

A Song of Ascents.

1 "Often have they attacked me from my
youth"
—let Israel now say—
2 "often have they attacked me from my youth,
yet they have not prevailed against me.
3 The plowers plowed on my back;
they made their furrows long."
4 The LORD is righteous;
he has cut the cords of the wicked.
5 May all who hate Zion
be put to shame and turned backward.
6 Let them be like the grass on the housetops
that withers before it grows up,
7 with which reapers do not fill their hands
or binders of sheaves their arms,
8 while those who pass by do not say,
"The blessing of the LORD be upon you!
We bless you in the name of the LORD!"

[a] Or *brought back those who returned to Zion* [b] Or *for he provides for his beloved during sleep*

PSALM 130

A Song of Ascents.

1 Out of the depths I cry to you, O LORD.
2 Lord, hear my voice!
Let your ears be attentive
to the voice of my supplications!

3 If you, O LORD, should mark iniquities,
Lord, who could stand?
4 But there is forgiveness with you,
so that you may be revered.

5 I wait for the LORD, my soul waits,
and in his word I hope;
6 my soul waits for the Lord
more than those who watch for the morning,
more than those who watch for the morning.

7 O Israel, hope in the LORD!
For with the LORD there is steadfast love,
and with him is great power to redeem.
8 It is he who will redeem Israel
from all its iniquities.

Psalm 130

Though many readers turn to the Bible to discern "what God says," the Psalms are usually speech—or cries from the heart—to God. The psalmist, or rather, every human being who resorts to the Psalms in a time of anguish, confusion, grief, or doubt, cries "out of the depths" to God. Yet this psalm does not speak from a distance, as if one had turned away in shame or withdrawn in fear of God. It is a psalm *of ascent*, of approach, spoken by one who anticipates that God will hear, must hear, and respond.

— *NE*

PSALM 131

A Song of Ascents. Of David.

1 O LORD, my heart is not lifted up,
my eyes are not raised too high;
I do not occupy myself with things
too great and too marvelous for me.
2 But I have calmed and quieted my soul,
like a weaned child with its mother;
my soul is like the weaned child that is with me.[a]

3 O Israel, hope in the LORD
from this time on and forevermore.

PSALM 132

A Song of Ascents.

1 O LORD, remember in David's favor
all the hardships he endured;
2 how he swore to the LORD
and vowed to the Mighty One of Jacob,
3 "I will not enter my house
or get into my bed;
4 I will not give sleep to my eyes
or slumber to my eyelids,
5 until I find a place for the LORD,
a dwelling place for the Mighty One of Jacob."

6 We heard of it in Ephrathah;
we found it in the fields of Jaar.
7 "Let us go to his dwelling place;
let us worship at his footstool."

8 Rise up, O LORD, and go to your resting place,
you and the ark of your might.
9 Let your priests be clothed with righteousness,
and let your faithful shout for joy.
10 For your servant David's sake

[a] Or *my soul within me is like a weaned child*

do not turn away the face of your anointed
one.

11 The LORD swore to David a sure oath
from which he will not turn back:
"One of the sons of your body
I will set on your throne.
12 If your sons keep my covenant
and my decrees that I shall teach them,
their sons also, forevermore,
shall sit on your throne."

13 For the LORD has chosen Zion;
he has desired it for his habitation:
14 "This is my resting place forever;
here I will reside, for I have desired it.
15 I will abundantly bless its provisions;
I will satisfy its poor with bread.
16 Its priests I will clothe with salvation,
and its faithful will shout for joy.
17 There I will cause a horn to sprout up for
David;
I have prepared a lamp for my anointed
one.
18 His enemies I will clothe with disgrace,
but on him, his crown will gleam."

PSALM 133

A Song of Ascents.

1 How very good and pleasant it is
when kindred live together in unity!
2 It is like the precious oil on the head,
running down upon the beard,
on the beard of Aaron,
running down over the collar of his robes.
3 It is like the dew of Hermon,
which falls on the mountains of Zion.
For there the LORD ordained his blessing,
life forevermore.

PSALM 134

A Song of Ascents.

1 Come, bless the LORD, all you servants of the
LORD,
who stand by night in the house of the
LORD!
2 Lift up your hands to the holy place,
and bless the LORD.

3 May the LORD, maker of heaven and earth,
bless you from Zion.

PSALM 135

1 Praise the LORD!
Praise the name of the LORD;
give praise, O servants of the LORD,
2 you that stand in the house of the LORD,
in the courts of the house of our God.
3 Praise the LORD, for the LORD is good;
sing to his name, for he is gracious.
4 For the LORD has chosen Jacob for
himself,
Israel as his own possession.

5 For I know that the LORD is great;
our Lord is above all gods.
6 Whatever the LORD pleases he does,
in heaven and on earth,
in the seas and all deeps.
7 He it is who makes the clouds rise at the end
of the earth;
he makes lightnings for the rain
and brings out the wind from his
storehouses.

8 He it was who struck down the firstborn of
Egypt,
both human beings and animals;
9 he sent signs and wonders
into your midst, O Egypt,
against Pharaoh and all his servants.
10 He struck down many nations
and killed mighty kings—
11 Sihon, king of the Amorites,
and Og, king of Bashan,
and all the kingdoms of Canaan—
12 and gave their land as a heritage,
a heritage to his people Israel.

13 Your name, O LORD, endures forever,
your renown, O LORD, throughout all
ages.

14 For the LORD will vindicate his people,
and have compassion on his servants.

15 The idols of the nations are silver and gold,
the work of human hands.
16 They have mouths, but they do not speak;
they have eyes, but they do not see;
17 they have ears, but they do not hear,
and there is no breath in their mouths.
18 Those who make them
and all who trust them
shall become like them.

19 O house of Israel, bless the LORD!
O house of Aaron, bless the LORD!
20 O house of Levi, bless the LORD!
You that fear the LORD, bless the LORD!
21 Blessed be the LORD from Zion,
he who resides in Jerusalem.
Praise the LORD!

PSALM 136

1 O give thanks to the LORD, for he is good,
for his steadfast love endures forever.
2 O give thanks to the God of gods,
for his steadfast love endures forever.
3 O give thanks to the Lord of lords,
for his steadfast love endures forever;

4 who alone does great wonders,
for his steadfast love endures forever;
5 who by understanding made the heavens,
for his steadfast love endures forever;
6 who spread out the earth on the waters,
for his steadfast love endures forever;
7 who made the great lights,
for his steadfast love endures forever;
8 the sun to rule over the day,
for his steadfast love endures forever;
9 the moon and stars to rule over the night,
for his steadfast love endures forever;

10 who struck Egypt through their firstborn,
for his steadfast love endures forever;
11 and brought Israel out from among them,
for his steadfast love endures forever;
12 with a strong hand and an outstretched arm,
for his steadfast love endures forever;
13 who divided the Red Sea[a] in two,
for his steadfast love endures forever;
14 and made Israel pass through the midst of it,
for his steadfast love endures forever;
15 but overthrew Pharaoh and his army in the Red Sea,[a]
for his steadfast love endures forever;
16 who led his people through the wilderness,
for his steadfast love endures forever;
17 who struck down great kings,
for his steadfast love endures forever;
18 and killed famous kings,
for his steadfast love endures forever;
19 Sihon, king of the Amorites,
for his steadfast love endures forever;
20 and Og, king of Bashan,
for his steadfast love endures forever;
21 and gave their land as a heritage,
for his steadfast love endures forever;
22 a heritage to his servant Israel,
for his steadfast love endures forever.

23 It is he who remembered us in our low estate,
for his steadfast love endures forever;
24 and rescued us from our foes,
for his steadfast love endures forever;
25 who gives food to all flesh,
for his steadfast love endures forever.

26 O give thanks to the God of heaven,
for his steadfast love endures forever.

PSALM 137

1 By the rivers of Babylon—
there we sat down and there we wept
when we remembered Zion.
2 On the willows[b] there
we hung up our harps.
3 For there our captors
asked us for songs,

[a] Or *Sea of Reeds* [b] Or *poplars*

and our tormentors asked for mirth, saying,
"Sing us one of the songs of Zion!"

4 How could we sing the LORD's song
in a foreign land?
5 If I forget you, O Jerusalem,
let my right hand wither!
6 Let my tongue cling to the roof of my mouth,
if I do not remember you,
if I do not set Jerusalem
above my highest joy.

7 Remember, O LORD, against the Edomites
the day of Jerusalem's fall,
how they said, "Tear it down! Tear it down!
Down to its foundations!"
8 O daughter Babylon, you devastator![a]
Happy shall they be who pay you back
what you have done to us!
9 Happy shall they be who take your little ones
and dash them against the rock!

Psalm 137

This well-known psalm depicts the realities of exile. Throughout history hostile empires have displaced other peoples. In this case the Babylonians have forced the people of Judah into exile. I am two generations removed from a different type of exile. On February 19, 1942, President Franklin Delano Roosevelt signed Executive Order 9066, which ordered the internment of more than 120,000 Japanese and Japanese Americans, predominantly from the West Coast. Though Psalm 137 describes a specific historical reality with a particular set of culturally determined responses (in this case an angry lament against enemies), the ethos of exile extends to other displaced communities. It has become a prominent theological lens through which people understand their diasporic identities.

— *FY*

PSALM 138

Of David.

1 I give you thanks, O LORD, with my whole heart;
before the gods I sing your praise;
2 I bow down toward your holy temple
and give thanks to your name for your steadfast love and your faithfulness;
for you have exalted your name and your word
above everything.[b]
3 On the day I called, you answered me,
you increased my strength of soul.[c]

4 All the kings of the earth shall praise you, O LORD,
for they have heard the words of your mouth.
5 They shall sing of the ways of the LORD,
for great is the glory of the LORD.
6 For though the LORD is high, he regards the lowly;
but the haughty he perceives from far away.

7 Though I walk in the midst of trouble,
you preserve me against the wrath of my enemies;
you stretch out your hand,
and your right hand delivers me.
8 The LORD will fulfill his purpose for me;
your steadfast love, O LORD, endures forever.
Do not forsake the work of your hands.

PSALM 139

To the leader. Of David. A Psalm.

1 O LORD, you have searched me and known me.
2 You know when I sit down and when I rise up;
you discern my thoughts from far away.

[a] Or *you who are devastated* [b] Cn: Heb *you have exalted your word above all your name*
[c] Syr Compare Gk Tg: Heb *you made me arrogant in my soul with strength*

3 You search out my path and my lying down,
and are acquainted with all my ways.
4 Even before a word is on my tongue,
O LORD, you know it completely.
5 You hem me in, behind and before,
and lay your hand upon me.
6 Such knowledge is too wonderful for me;
it is so high that I cannot attain it.

7 Where can I go from your spirit?
Or where can I flee from your presence?
8 If I ascend to heaven, you are there;
if I make my bed in Sheol, you are there.
9 If I take the wings of the morning
and settle at the farthest limits of the sea,
10 even there your hand shall lead me,
and your right hand shall hold me fast.
11 If I say, "Surely the darkness shall cover me,
and the light around me become night,"
12 even the darkness is not dark to you;
the night is as bright as the day,
for darkness is as light to you.

13 For it was you who formed my inward parts;
you knit me together in my mother's
womb.
14 I praise you, for I am fearfully and
wonderfully made.
Wonderful are your works;
that I know very well.
15 My frame was not hidden from you,
when I was being made in secret,
intricately woven in the depths of the
earth.
16 Your eyes beheld my unformed substance.
In your book were written
all the days that were formed for me,
when none of them as yet existed.
17 How weighty to me are your thoughts,
O God!
How vast is the sum of them!
18 I try to count them—they are more than the
sand;
I come to the end[a]—I am still with you.

19 O that you would kill the wicked, O God,
and that the bloodthirsty would depart
from me—
20 those who speak of you maliciously,
and lift themselves up against you for
evil![b]
21 Do I not hate those who hate you,
O LORD?
And do I not loathe those who rise up
against you?
22 I hate them with perfect hatred;
I count them my enemies.
23 Search me, O God, and know my heart;
test me and know my thoughts.
24 See if there is any wicked[c] way in me,
and lead me in the way everlasting.[d]

PSALM 140

To the leader. A Psalm of David.

1 Deliver me, O LORD, from evildoers;
protect me from those who are violent,
2 who plan evil things in their minds
and stir up wars continually.
3 They make their tongue sharp as a snake's,
and under their lips is the venom of vipers.
Selah

4 Guard me, O LORD, from the hands of the
wicked;
protect me from the violent
who have planned my downfall.
5 The arrogant have hidden a trap for me,
and with cords they have spread a net,[e]
along the road they have set snares for me.
Selah

6 I say to the LORD, "You are my God;
give ear, O LORD, to the voice of my
supplications."
7 O LORD, my Lord, my strong deliverer,
you have covered my head in the day of
battle.

[a] Or *I awake* [b] Cn: Meaning of Heb uncertain [c] Heb *hurtful* [d] Or *the ancient way*. Compare Jer 6.16
[e] Or *they have spread cords as a net*

8 Do not grant, O LORD, the desires of the wicked;
do not further their evil plot.[a] *Selah*
9 Those who surround me lift up their heads;[b]
let the mischief of their lips overwhelm them!
10 Let burning coals fall on them!
Let them be flung into pits, no more to rise!
11 Do not let the slanderer be established in the land;
let evil speedily hunt down the violent!

12 I know that the LORD maintains the cause of the needy,
and executes justice for the poor.
13 Surely the righteous shall give thanks to your name;
the upright shall live in your presence.

PSALM 141

A Psalm of David.

1 I call upon you, O LORD; come quickly to me;
give ear to my voice when I call to you.
2 Let my prayer be counted as incense before you,
and the lifting up of my hands as an evening sacrifice.

3 Set a guard over my mouth, O LORD;
keep watch over the door of my lips.
4 Do not turn my heart to any evil,
to busy myself with wicked deeds
in company with those who work iniquity;
do not let me eat of their delicacies.

5 Let the righteous strike me;
let the faithful correct me.
Never let the oil of the wicked anoint my head,[c]
for my prayer is continually[d] against their wicked deeds.
6 When they are given over to those who shall condemn them,
then they shall learn that my words were pleasant.
7 Like a rock that one breaks apart and shatters on the land,
so shall their bones be strewn at the mouth of Sheol.[e]

8 But my eyes are turned toward you, O GOD, my Lord;
in you I seek refuge; do not leave me defenseless.
9 Keep me from the trap that they have laid for me,
and from the snares of evildoers.
10 Let the wicked fall into their own nets,
while I alone escape.

PSALM 142

A Maskil of David. When he was in the cave. A Prayer.

1 With my voice I cry to the LORD;
with my voice I make supplication to the LORD.
2 I pour out my complaint before him;
I tell my trouble before him.
3 When my spirit is faint,
you know my way.

In the path where I walk
they have hidden a trap for me.
4 Look on my right hand and see—
there is no one who takes notice of me;
no refuge remains to me;
no one cares for me.

5 I cry to you, O LORD;
I say, "You are my refuge,
my portion in the land of the living."
6 Give heed to my cry,
for I am brought very low.

[a] Heb adds *they are exalted* [b] Cn Compare Gk: Heb *those who surround me are uplifted in head;* Heb divides verses 8 and 9 differently [c] Gk: Meaning of Heb uncertain [d] Cn: Heb *for continually and my prayer*
[e] Meaning of Heb of verses 5–7 is uncertain

Save me from my persecutors,
for they are too strong for me.
7 Bring me out of prison,
so that I may give thanks to your name.
The righteous will surround me,
for you will deal bountifully with me.

PSALM 143

A Psalm of David.

1 Hear my prayer, O LORD;
give ear to my supplications in your faithfulness;
answer me in your righteousness.
2 Do not enter into judgment with your servant,
for no one living is righteous before you.

3 For the enemy has pursued me,
crushing my life to the ground,
making me sit in darkness like those long dead.
4 Therefore my spirit faints within me;
my heart within me is appalled.

5 I remember the days of old,
I think about all your deeds,
I meditate on the works of your hands.
6 I stretch out my hands to you;
my soul thirsts for you like a parched land. *Selah*

7 Answer me quickly, O LORD;
my spirit fails.
Do not hide your face from me,
or I shall be like those who go down to the Pit.
8 Let me hear of your steadfast love in the morning,
for in you I put my trust.
Teach me the way I should go,
for to you I lift up my soul.

9 Save me, O LORD, from my enemies;
I have fled to you for refuge.[a]

10 Teach me to do your will,
for you are my God.
Let your good spirit lead me
on a level path.

11 For your name's sake, O LORD, preserve my life.
In your righteousness bring me out of trouble.
12 In your steadfast love cut off my enemies,
and destroy all my adversaries,
for I am your servant.

PSALM 144

Of David.

1 Blessed be the LORD, my rock,
who trains my hands for war, and my fingers for battle;
2 my rock[b] and my fortress,
my stronghold and my deliverer,
my shield, in whom I take refuge,
who subdues the peoples[c] under me.

3 O LORD, what are human beings that you regard them,
or mortals that you think of them?
4 They are like a breath;
their days are like a passing shadow.

5 Bow your heavens, O LORD, and come down;
touch the mountains so that they smoke.
6 Make the lightning flash and scatter them;
send out your arrows and rout them.
7 Stretch out your hand from on high;
set me free and rescue me from the mighty waters,
from the hand of aliens,
8 whose mouths speak lies,
and whose right hands are false.

[a] One Heb Ms Gk: MT *to you I have hidden* [b] With 18.2 and 2 Sam 22.2: Heb *my steadfast love*
[c] Heb Mss Syr Aquila Jerome: MT *my people*

9 I will sing a new song to you, O God;
upon a ten-stringed harp I will play to you,
10 the one who gives victory to kings,
who rescues his servant David.
11 Rescue me from the cruel sword,
and deliver me from the hand of aliens,
whose mouths speak lies,
and whose right hands are false.

12 May our sons in their youth
be like plants full grown,
our daughters like corner pillars,
cut for the building of a palace.
13 May our barns be filled,
with produce of every kind;
may our sheep increase by thousands,
by tens of thousands in our fields,
14 and may our cattle be heavy with young.
May there be no breach in the walls,[a] no exile,
and no cry of distress in our streets.

15 Happy are the people to whom such blessings fall;
happy are the people whose God is the LORD.

PSALM 145

Praise. Of David.

1 I will extol you, my God and King,
and bless your name forever and ever.
2 Every day I will bless you,
and praise your name forever and ever.
3 Great is the LORD, and greatly to be praised;
his greatness is unsearchable.
4 One generation shall laud your works to another,
and shall declare your mighty acts.
5 On the glorious splendor of your majesty,
and on your wondrous works, I will meditate.
6 The might of your awesome deeds shall be proclaimed,
and I will declare your greatness.
7 They shall celebrate the fame of your abundant goodness,
and shall sing aloud of your righteousness.
8 The LORD is gracious and merciful,
slow to anger and abounding in steadfast love.
9 The LORD is good to all,
and his compassion is over all that he has made.

10 All your works shall give thanks to you, O LORD,
and all your faithful shall bless you.
11 They shall speak of the glory of your kingdom,
and tell of your power,
12 to make known to all people your[b] mighty deeds,
and the glorious splendor of your[c] kingdom.
13 Your kingdom is an everlasting kingdom,
and your dominion endures throughout all generations.

The LORD is faithful in all his words,
and gracious in all his deeds.[d]
14 The LORD upholds all who are falling,
and raises up all who are bowed down.
15 The eyes of all look to you,
and you give them their food in due season.
16 You open your hand,
satisfying the desire of every living thing.
17 The LORD is just in all his ways,
and kind in all his doings.
18 The LORD is near to all who call on him,
to all who call on him in truth.
19 He fulfills the desire of all who fear him;
he also hears their cry, and saves them.
20 The LORD watches over all who love him,
but all the wicked he will destroy.

[a] Heb lacks *in the walls* [b] Gk Jerome Syr: Heb *his* [c] Heb *his* [d] These two lines supplied by Q Ms Gk Syr

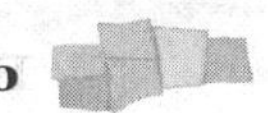

21 My mouth will speak the praise of the LORD,
and all flesh will bless his holy name
forever and ever.

PSALM 146

1 Praise the LORD!
Praise the LORD, O my soul!
2 I will praise the LORD as long as I live;
I will sing praises to my God all my life long.

3 Do not put your trust in princes,
in mortals, in whom there is no help.
4 When their breath departs, they return to the earth;
on that very day their plans perish.

5 Happy are those whose help is the God of Jacob,
whose hope is in the LORD their God,
6 who made heaven and earth,
the sea, and all that is in them;
who keeps faith forever;
7 who executes justice for the oppressed;
who gives food to the hungry.

The LORD sets the prisoners free;
8 the LORD opens the eyes of the blind.
The LORD lifts up those who are bowed down;
the LORD loves the righteous.
9 The LORD watches over the strangers;
he upholds the orphan and the widow,
but the way of the wicked he brings to ruin.

10 The LORD will reign forever,
your God, O Zion, for all generations.
Praise the LORD!

PSALM 147

1 Praise the LORD!
How good it is to sing praises to our God;
for he is gracious, and a song of praise is fitting.
2 The LORD builds up Jerusalem;
he gathers the outcasts of Israel.
3 He heals the brokenhearted,
and binds up their wounds.
4 He determines the number of the stars;
he gives to all of them their names.
5 Great is our Lord, and abundant in power;
his understanding is beyond measure.
6 The LORD lifts up the downtrodden;
he casts the wicked to the ground.

7 Sing to the LORD with thanksgiving;
make melody to our God on the lyre.
8 He covers the heavens with clouds,
prepares rain for the earth,
makes grass grow on the hills.
9 He gives to the animals their food,
and to the young ravens when they cry.
10 His delight is not in the strength of the horse,
nor his pleasure in the speed of a runner;[a]
11 but the LORD takes pleasure in those who fear him,
in those who hope in his steadfast love.

12 Praise the LORD, O Jerusalem!
Praise your God, O Zion!
13 For he strengthens the bars of your gates;
he blesses your children within you.
14 He grants peace[b] within your borders;
he fills you with the finest of wheat.
15 He sends out his command to the earth;
his word runs swiftly.
16 He gives snow like wool;
he scatters frost like ashes.
17 He hurls down hail like crumbs—
who can stand before his cold?
18 He sends out his word, and melts them;
he makes his wind blow, and the waters flow.
19 He declares his word to Jacob,
his statutes and ordinances to Israel.
20 He has not dealt thus with any other nation;
they do not know his ordinances.
Praise the LORD!

[a] Heb *legs of a person* [b] Or *prosperity*

PSALM 148

1 Praise the LORD!
Praise the LORD from the heavens;
praise him in the heights!
2 Praise him, all his angels;
praise him, all his host!

3 Praise him, sun and moon;
praise him, all you shining stars!
4 Praise him, you highest heavens,
and you waters above the heavens!

5 Let them praise the name of the LORD,
for he commanded and they were created.
6 He established them forever and ever;
he fixed their bounds, which cannot be passed.[a]

7 Praise the LORD from the earth,
you sea monsters and all deeps,
8 fire and hail, snow and frost,
stormy wind fulfilling his command!

9 Mountains and all hills,
fruit trees and all cedars!
10 Wild animals and all cattle,
creeping things and flying birds!

11 Kings of the earth and all peoples,
princes and all rulers of the earth!
12 Young men and women alike,
old and young together!

13 Let them praise the name of the LORD,
for his name alone is exalted;
his glory is above earth and heaven.
14 He has raised up a horn for his people,
praise for all his faithful,
for the people of Israel who are close to him.
Praise the LORD!

PSALM 149

1 Praise the LORD!
Sing to the LORD a new song,
his praise in the assembly of the faithful.
2 Let Israel be glad in its Maker;
let the children of Zion rejoice in their King.
3 Let them praise his name with dancing,
making melody to him with tambourine and lyre.
4 For the LORD takes pleasure in his people;
he adorns the humble with victory.
5 Let the faithful exult in glory;
let them sing for joy on their couches.
6 Let the high praises of God be in their throats
and two-edged swords in their hands,
7 to execute vengeance on the nations
and punishment on the peoples,
8 to bind their kings with fetters
and their nobles with chains of iron,
9 to execute on them the judgment decreed.
This is glory for all his faithful ones.
Praise the LORD!

PSALM 150

1 Praise the LORD!
Praise God in his sanctuary;
praise him in his mighty firmament![b]
2 Praise him for his mighty deeds;
praise him according to his surpassing greatness!

3 Praise him with trumpet sound;
praise him with lute and harp!
4 Praise him with tambourine and dance;
praise him with strings and pipe!
5 Praise him with clanging cymbals;
praise him with loud clashing cymbals!
6 Let everything that breathes praise the LORD!
Praise the LORD!

[a] Or *he set a law that cannot pass away* [b] Or *dome*

Proverbs

A "PROVERB" IS A SHORT SAYING that summarizes some truth about life. Knowing and practicing such truths constitutes wisdom—the ability to navigate human relationships and realities. A literary collection of proverbs is thus intended to communicate wisdom. The biblical book of Proverbs is presented as such a collection: "The proverbs of Solomon son of David, king of Israel" (1:1). The book's title is, obviously, derived from this opening line. Similar phrases are found throughout Proverbs. These titles suggest two important points about this book: it is a collection of other, smaller collections, and it was collected by scribes.

Proverbs is comprised of six sections: 1:1—9:18; 10:1—22:16; 22:17—24:22; 24:23-34; 25:1—29:27; and 30:1—31:31. The first nine chapters introduce the book as a whole. The prologue (1:1-7) gives the book's purpose. It explains that these proverbs enable the learner to obtain wisdom and understanding (1:2). Learning to live wisely means practicing righteousness, justice, and equity (1:3). Such learning matures the naïve and deepens the wisdom of those already astute (1:4-6). This learning begins with "the fear of the LORD" (1:7). The prologue's paradigmatic introduction provides key concepts for the entire book.

Only the first section addresses its audience as "child" or "children," a common stylistic feature in ancient Near Eastern instruction especially for young men preparing for service in royal courts (1:8; 2:1; 3:1, 21; 4:1, 10; 5:1; 6:1, 20; 7:1). Besides the use of "father" and "son" in the original Hebrew (but see the unusual "mother" in 1:8; 4:3), this orientation is evident in the warnings against the Strange Woman (2:16-19; 5:1-23; 6:20-35; 7:1-27). In conjunction with counsel against the wicked (2:12-15; 3:31-32; 4:10-19), these denunciations present the Strange Woman as a femme fatale—a woman who seduces the innocent, unassuming male. This figure certainly promotes a caricature of women and displaces onto the woman the man's responsibility for the attraction he feels. Accordingly, any appropriation of this language today must creatively reimagine it in ways that do not perpetuate its potential for misogyny.

To counter the attraction of the Strange Woman, the author personifies the book's teachings as Woman Wisdom (1:20-33; 3:13-20; 8:1-36; 9:1-18). Wisdom, often capitalized (though not in the NRSV translation) because she speaks for herself, describes herself as the first creation, delighting the LORD and rejoicing in humanity (8:22-31). Because of her heavenly stature, she and her words are more valuable than precious stones. In a word, she is priceless (3:13-18; 8:17-21). Thus, those who seek to be wise must enter her house and dine with her, resisting the allure of the forbidden woman (9:1-6, 13-18).

Having chosen wisdom over foolishness, the learner passes from the parental guidance of chapters 1–9 to the various collections of 10–31. Here one must select the right counsel for the appropriate situation. Some situations require silence to avoid foolishness, while others require instruction about speech (26:4-5). Also, wealth may be viewed as a reward for righteousness (10:15, 22) or as the illegitimate possession of oppressors (15:27; 22:16, 22-29). Likewise, poverty can be spoken of as a consequence of laziness (10:4; 13:18; 14:23; 19:15) or as a condition created by the wickedness of others (14:31; 15:16-17; 16:8, 19:1; 20:10). Given the nature of any individual saying as well as the function of a collection of such sayings, this instructional variety seems appropriately balanced: such variety corresponds to life's genuine complexities.

The title of each section suggests that various scribes edited Proverbs over several centuries. Indeed, many of these proverbs are attributed to Solomon (1:1; 10:1; 25:1). Smaller sections are attributed to "the wise" (22:17; 24:23), and the final sections mention the otherwise unknown Agur and Lemuel (30:1; 31:1). Critical scholars have concluded that the attribution to Solomon is due more to the traditional practice of naming an important figure as author than to an actual literary history. As Moses is the lawgiver and source of the Pentateuch, and David the songwriter and composer of many psalms, Solomon is presented here as the paradigmatic wise man (described elsewhere as the author of three thousand proverbs: see 1 Kgs 3:16-28; 4:29-34).

Given the limits of ancient literacy, high-ranking government scribes probably composed and edited Proverbs, the book reaching its final form after the exile, in the fifth or fourth century BCE. The social status of these scribes is consistent with what we know from similar ancient Egyptian wisdom literature. It is likely that this literature was first used to instruct the apprentices of these scribes, and some may have been actual sons. In its original setting, the book was a means of transferring the privileges of the scribal position. It was the exclusive possession of the literate elite. Only with increased literacy in later Judaism and Christianity did the book become accessible to a wider audience.

Investigating the original context for this book creates interesting connections for me as an African American scholar. It reminds me of how education can be a means of exclusion or an instrument of liberation. African Americans have long viewed education as a primary means of freedom, the path by which one secures the ability to flourish. Yet education is perhaps the resource most often denied to those without socioeconomic status. Education is often cited as a key indicator of the distance between the privileged and the poor. The content and context of Proverbs reminds me that education can be a means of social mobility, on the one hand, or a tool for maintaining the status quo on the other.

— ***Joseph F. Scrivner***

1 The proverbs of Solomon son of David, king of Israel:

2 For learning about wisdom and instruction,
for understanding words of insight,
3 for gaining instruction in wise dealing,
righteousness, justice, and equity;
4 to teach shrewdness to the simple,
knowledge and prudence to the young—
5 let the wise also hear and gain in learning,
and the discerning acquire skill,
6 to understand a proverb and a figure,
the words of the wise and their riddles.

7 The fear of the LORD is the beginning of knowledge;
fools despise wisdom and instruction.

8 Hear, my child, your father's instruction,
and do not reject your mother's teaching;
9 for they are a fair garland for your head,
and pendants for your neck.
10 My child, if sinners entice you,
do not consent.
11 If they say, "Come with us, let us lie in wait for blood;
let us wantonly ambush the innocent;
12 like Sheol let us swallow them alive
and whole, like those who go down to the Pit.
13 We shall find all kinds of costly things;
we shall fill our houses with booty.
14 Throw in your lot among us;
we will all have one purse"—
15 my child, do not walk in their way,
keep your foot from their paths;
16 for their feet run to evil,
and they hurry to shed blood.
17 For in vain is the net baited
while the bird is looking on;
18 yet they lie in wait—to kill themselves!
and set an ambush—for their own lives!
19 Such is the end[a] of all who are greedy for gain;
it takes away the life of its possessors.

20 Wisdom cries out in the street;
in the squares she raises her voice.
21 At the busiest corner she cries out;
at the entrance of the city gates she speaks:
22 "How long, O simple ones, will you love being simple?
How long will scoffers delight in their scoffing
and fools hate knowledge?
23 Give heed to my reproof;
I will pour out my thoughts to you;
I will make my words known to you.
24 Because I have called and you refused,
have stretched out my hand and no one heeded,
25 and because you have ignored all my counsel
and would have none of my reproof,
26 I also will laugh at your calamity;
I will mock when panic strikes you,
27 when panic strikes you like a storm,
and your calamity comes like a whirlwind,
when distress and anguish come upon you.
28 Then they will call upon me, but I will not answer;
they will seek me diligently, but will not find me.
29 Because they hated knowledge
and did not choose the fear of the LORD,
30 would have none of my counsel,
and despised all my reproof,
31 therefore they shall eat the fruit of their way
and be sated with their own devices.
32 For waywardness kills the simple,
and the complacency of fools destroys them;
33 but those who listen to me will be secure
and will live at ease, without dread of disaster."

2 My child, if you accept my words
and treasure up my commandments within you,
2 making your ear attentive to wisdom
and inclining your heart to understanding;
3 if you indeed cry out for insight,

[a] Gk: Heb *are the ways*

and raise your voice for understanding;
4 if you seek it like silver,
and search for it as for hidden treasures—
5 then you will understand the fear of the LORD
and find the knowledge of God.
6 For the LORD gives wisdom;
from his mouth come knowledge and understanding;
7 he stores up sound wisdom for the upright;
he is a shield to those who walk blamelessly,
8 guarding the paths of justice
and preserving the way of his faithful ones.
9 Then you will understand righteousness and justice
and equity, every good path;
10 for wisdom will come into your heart,
and knowledge will be pleasant to your soul;
11 prudence will watch over you;
and understanding will guard you.
12 It will save you from the way of evil,
from those who speak perversely,
13 who forsake the paths of uprightness
to walk in the ways of darkness,
14 who rejoice in doing evil
and delight in the perverseness of evil;
15 those whose paths are crooked,
and who are devious in their ways.

16 You will be saved from the loose[a] woman,
from the adulteress with her smooth words,
17 who forsakes the partner of her youth
and forgets her sacred covenant;
18 for her way[b] leads down to death,
and her paths to the shades;
19 those who go to her never come back,
nor do they regain the paths of life.

20 Therefore walk in the way of the good,
and keep to the paths of the just.
21 For the upright will abide in the land,
and the innocent will remain in it;
22 but the wicked will be cut off from the land,
and the treacherous will be rooted out of it.

3 My child, do not forget my teaching,
but let your heart keep my commandments;
2 for length of days and years of life
and abundant welfare they will give you.

3 Do not let loyalty and faithfulness forsake you;
bind them around your neck,
write them on the tablet of your heart.
4 So you will find favor and good repute
in the sight of God and of people.

5 Trust in the LORD with all your heart,
and do not rely on your own insight.
6 In all your ways acknowledge him,
and he will make straight your paths.
7 Do not be wise in your own eyes;
fear the LORD, and turn away from evil.
8 It will be a healing for your flesh
and a refreshment for your body.

9 Honor the LORD with your substance
and with the first fruits of all your produce;
10 then your barns will be filled with plenty,
and your vats will be bursting with wine.

11 My child, do not despise the LORD's discipline
or be weary of his reproof,
12 for the LORD reproves the one he loves,
as a father the son in whom he delights.

13 Happy are those who find wisdom,
and those who get understanding,
14 for her income is better than silver,
and her revenue better than gold.
15 She is more precious than jewels,
and nothing you desire can compare with her.
16 Long life is in her right hand;
in her left hand are riches and honor.

[a] Heb *strange* [b] Cn: Heb *house*

17 Her ways are ways of pleasantness,
and all her paths are peace.
18 She is a tree of life to those who lay hold of her;
those who hold her fast are called happy.

19 The LORD by wisdom founded the earth;
by understanding he established the heavens;
20 by his knowledge the deeps broke open,
and the clouds drop down the dew.
21 My child, do not let these escape from your sight:
keep sound wisdom and prudence,
22 and they will be life for your soul
and adornment for your neck.
23 Then you will walk on your way securely
and your foot will not stumble.
24 If you sit down,[a] you will not be afraid;
when you lie down, your sleep will be sweet.
25 Do not be afraid of sudden panic,
or of the storm that strikes the wicked;
26 for the LORD will be your confidence
and will keep your foot from being caught.

27 Do not withhold good from those to whom it is due,[b]
when it is in your power to do it.
28 Do not say to your neighbor, "Go, and come again,
tomorrow I will give it"—when you have it with you.
29 Do not plan harm against your neighbor
who lives trustingly beside you.
30 Do not quarrel with anyone without cause,
when no harm has been done to you.
31 Do not envy the violent
and do not choose any of their ways;
32 for the perverse are an abomination to the LORD,
but the upright are in his confidence.
33 The LORD's curse is on the house of the wicked,
but he blesses the abode of the righteous.
34 Toward the scorners he is scornful,
but to the humble he shows favor.
35 The wise will inherit honor,
but stubborn fools, disgrace.

4 Listen, children, to a father's instruction,
and be attentive, that you may gain[c] insight;
2 for I give you good precepts:
do not forsake my teaching.
3 When I was a son with my father,
tender, and my mother's favorite,
4 he taught me, and said to me,
"Let your heart hold fast my words;
keep my commandments, and live.
5 Get wisdom; get insight: do not forget, nor turn away
from the words of my mouth.
6 Do not forsake her, and she will keep you;
love her, and she will guard you.
7 The beginning of wisdom is this: Get wisdom,
and whatever else you get, get insight.
8 Prize her highly, and she will exalt you;
she will honor you if you embrace her.
9 She will place on your head a fair garland;
she will bestow on you a beautiful crown."

10 Hear, my child, and accept my words,
that the years of your life may be many.
11 I have taught you the way of wisdom;
I have led you in the paths of uprightness.
12 When you walk, your step will not be hampered;
and if you run, you will not stumble.
13 Keep hold of instruction; do not let go;
guard her, for she is your life.
14 Do not enter the path of the wicked,
and do not walk in the way of evildoers.
15 Avoid it; do not go on it;
turn away from it and pass on.
16 For they cannot sleep unless they have done wrong;
they are robbed of sleep unless they have made someone stumble.

[a] Gk: Heb *lie down* [b] Heb *from its owners* [c] Heb *know*

17 For they eat the bread of wickedness
and drink the wine of violence.
18 But the path of the righteous is like the light
of dawn,
which shines brighter and brighter until
full day.
19 The way of the wicked is like deep darkness;
they do not know what they stumble over.
20 My child, be attentive to my words;
incline your ear to my sayings.
21 Do not let them escape from your sight;
keep them within your heart.
22 For they are life to those who find them,
and healing to all their flesh.
23 Keep your heart with all vigilance,
for from it flow the springs of life.
24 Put away from you crooked speech,
and put devious talk far from you.
25 Let your eyes look directly forward,
and your gaze be straight before you.
26 Keep straight the path of your feet,
and all your ways will be sure.
27 Do not swerve to the right or to the left;
turn your foot away from evil.

5 My child, be attentive to my wisdom;
incline your ear to my understanding,
2 so that you may hold on to prudence,
and your lips may guard knowledge.
3 For the lips of a loose[a] woman drip honey,
and her speech is smoother than oil;
4 but in the end she is bitter as wormwood,
sharp as a two-edged sword.
5 Her feet go down to death;
her steps follow the path to Sheol.
6 She does not keep straight to the path of life;
her ways wander, and she does not
know it.

7 And now, my child,[b] listen to me,
and do not depart from the words of my
mouth.
8 Keep your way far from her,
and do not go near the door of her house;
9 or you will give your honor to others,
and your years to the merciless,
10 and strangers will take their fill of your
wealth,
and your labors will go to the house of an
alien;
11 and at the end of your life you will groan,
when your flesh and body are consumed,
12 and you say, "Oh, how I hated discipline,
and my heart despised reproof!
13 I did not listen to the voice of my teachers
or incline my ear to my instructors.

[a] Heb *strange* [b] Gk Vg: Heb *children*

Proverbs 5

As the women's movement has developed in the religions, something akin to a spiritual uprising is taking place. Women are experiencing themselves as beloved of God. We are being converted from trivializing ourselves to honoring ourselves as genuinely equal images of God.

This has ramifications for women's well-being all over the world. As United Nations figures report, women, who form one-half of the world's population, do two-thirds of the world's work, receive one-tenth of the world's salary, own one-hundredth of the world's land, constitute two-thirds of illiterate adults, and, together with their starving children, are three-fourths of the world's starving people. To make a dark picture even bleaker, women are bodily and sexually exploited, physically abused, raped, battered, and murdered by men to a degree that is not mutual.... Factoring in racism, classism, heterosexism, ageism, colonialism, militarism, and supremacy over the earth, structures that interlock in diverse ways to shape women's lives, makes clear the complexity of oppressions against which women struggle for fullness of life.[42]

— Elizabeth A. Johnson

14 Now I am at the point of utter ruin
in the public assembly."

15 Drink water from your own cistern,
flowing water from your own well.
16 Should your springs be scattered abroad,
streams of water in the streets?
17 Let them be for yourself alone,
and not for sharing with strangers.
18 Let your fountain be blessed,
and rejoice in the wife of your youth,
19 a lovely deer, a graceful doe.
May her breasts satisfy you at all times;
may you be intoxicated always by her love.
20 Why should you be intoxicated, my son, by
another woman
and embrace the bosom of an adulteress?
21 For human ways are under the eyes of the
LORD,
and he examines all their paths.
22 The iniquities of the wicked ensnare them,
and they are caught in the toils of their sin.
23 They die for lack of discipline,
and because of their great folly they are
lost.

6 My child, if you have given your pledge to
your neighbor,
if you have bound yourself to another,[a]
2 you are snared by the utterance of your lips,[b]
caught by the words of your mouth.
3 So do this, my child, and save yourself,
for you have come into your neighbor's
power:
go, hurry,[c] and plead with your neighbor.
4 Give your eyes no sleep
and your eyelids no slumber;
5 save yourself like a gazelle from the hunter,[d]
like a bird from the hand of the fowler.

6 Go to the ant, you lazybones;
consider its ways, and be wise.
7 Without having any chief
or officer or ruler,
8 it prepares its food in summer,
and gathers its sustenance in harvest.
9 How long will you lie there, O lazybones?
When will you rise from your sleep?
10 A little sleep, a little slumber,
a little folding of the hands to rest,
11 and poverty will come upon you like a
robber,
and want, like an armed warrior.

12 A scoundrel and a villain
goes around with crooked speech,
13 winking the eyes, shuffling the feet,
pointing the fingers,
14 with perverted mind devising evil,
continually sowing discord;
15 on such a one calamity will descend
suddenly;
in a moment, damage beyond repair.

16 There are six things that the LORD hates,
seven that are an abomination to him:
17 haughty eyes, a lying tongue,
and hands that shed innocent blood,
18 a heart that devises wicked plans,
feet that hurry to run to evil,
19 a lying witness who testifies falsely,
and one who sows discord in a family.

20 My child, keep your father's commandment,
and do not forsake your mother's teaching.
21 Bind them upon your heart always;
tie them around your neck.
22 When you walk, they[e] will lead you;
when you lie down, they[e] will watch over
you;
and when you awake, they[e] will talk with
you.
23 For the commandment is a lamp and the
teaching a light,
and the reproofs of discipline are the way
of life,
24 to preserve you from the wife of another,[f]
from the smooth tongue of the adulteress.
25 Do not desire her beauty in your heart,

[a] Or *a stranger* [b] Cn Compare Gk Syr: Heb *the words of your mouth* [c] Or *humble yourself* [d] Cn: Heb *from the hand*
[e] Heb *it* [f] Gk: MT *the evil woman*

and do not let her capture you with her
eyelashes;
26 for a prostitute's fee is only a loaf of bread,[a]
but the wife of another stalks a man's very
life.
27 Can fire be carried in the bosom
without burning one's clothes?
28 Or can one walk on hot coals
without scorching the feet?
29 So is he who sleeps with his neighbor's wife;
no one who touches her will go
unpunished.
30 Thieves are not despised who steal only
to satisfy their appetite when they are
hungry.
31 Yet if they are caught, they will pay sevenfold;
they will forfeit all the goods of their
house.
32 But he who commits adultery has no sense;
he who does it destroys himself.
33 He will get wounds and dishonor,
and his disgrace will not be wiped away.
34 For jealousy arouses a husband's fury,
and he shows no restraint when he takes
revenge.
35 He will accept no compensation,
and refuses a bribe no matter how great.

7 My child, keep my words
and store up my commandments with
you;
2 keep my commandments and live,
keep my teachings as the apple of your eye;
3 bind them on your fingers,
write them on the tablet of your heart.
4 Say to wisdom, "You are my sister,"
and call insight your intimate friend,
5 that they may keep you from the loose[b]
woman,
from the adulteress with her smooth
words.

6 For at the window of my house
I looked out through my lattice,
7 and I saw among the simple ones,
I observed among the youths,
a young man without sense,
8 passing along the street near her corner,
taking the road to her house
9 in the twilight, in the evening,
at the time of night and darkness.

10 Then a woman comes toward him,
decked out like a prostitute, wily of heart.[c]
11 She is loud and wayward;
her feet do not stay at home;
12 now in the street, now in the squares,
and at every corner she lies in wait.
13 She seizes him and kisses him,
and with impudent face she says to him:
14 "I had to offer sacrifices,
and today I have paid my vows;
15 so now I have come out to meet you,
to seek you eagerly, and I have found you!
16 I have decked my couch with coverings,
colored spreads of Egyptian linen;
17 I have perfumed my bed with myrrh,
aloes, and cinnamon.
18 Come, let us take our fill of love until
morning;
let us delight ourselves with love.
19 For my husband is not at home;
he has gone on a long journey.
20 He took a bag of money with him;
he will not come home until full moon."

21 With much seductive speech she persuades
him;
with her smooth talk she compels him.
22 Right away he follows her,
and goes like an ox to the slaughter,
or bounds like a stag toward the trap[d]
23 until an arrow pierces its entrails.
He is like a bird rushing into a snare,
not knowing that it will cost him his life.

24 And now, my children, listen to me,
and be attentive to the words of my mouth.

[a] Cn Compare Gk Syr Vg Tg: Heb *for because of a harlot to a piece of bread* [b] Heb *strange* [c] Meaning of Heb uncertain
[d] Cn Compare Gk: Meaning of Heb uncertain

25 Do not let your hearts turn aside to her ways;
do not stray into her paths.
26 For many are those she has laid low,
and numerous are her victims.
27 Her house is the way to Sheol,
going down to the chambers of death.

8 Does not wisdom call,
and does not understanding raise her voice?
2 On the heights, beside the way,
at the crossroads she takes her stand;
3 beside the gates in front of the town,
at the entrance of the portals she cries out:
4 "To you, O people, I call,
and my cry is to all that live.
5 O simple ones, learn prudence;
acquire intelligence, you who lack it.
6 Hear, for I will speak noble things,
and from my lips will come what is right;
7 for my mouth will utter truth;
wickedness is an abomination to my lips.
8 All the words of my mouth are righteous;
there is nothing twisted or crooked in them.
9 They are all straight to one who understands
and right to those who find knowledge.
10 Take my instruction instead of silver,
and knowledge rather than choice gold;
11 for wisdom is better than jewels,
and all that you may desire cannot compare with her.
12 I, wisdom, live with prudence,[a]
and I attain knowledge and discretion.
13 The fear of the LORD is hatred of evil.
Pride and arrogance and the way of evil
and perverted speech I hate.
14 I have good advice and sound wisdom;
I have insight, I have strength.
15 By me kings reign,
and rulers decree what is just;
16 by me rulers rule,
and nobles, all who govern rightly.
17 I love those who love me,
and those who seek me diligently find me.
18 Riches and honor are with me,
enduring wealth and prosperity.
19 My fruit is better than gold, even fine gold,
and my yield than choice silver.
20 I walk in the way of righteousness,
along the paths of justice,
21 endowing with wealth those who love me,
and filling their treasuries.
22 The LORD created me at the beginning[b] of his work,[c]
the first of his acts of long ago.
23 Ages ago I was set up,
at the first, before the beginning of the earth.
24 When there were no depths I was brought forth,
when there were no springs abounding with water.
25 Before the mountains had been shaped,
before the hills, I was brought forth—
26 when he had not yet made earth and fields,[a]
or the world's first bits of soil.
27 When he established the heavens, I was there,
when he drew a circle on the face of the deep,
28 when he made firm the skies above,
when he established the fountains of the deep,
29 when he assigned to the sea its limit,
so that the waters might not transgress his command,
when he marked out the foundations of the earth,
30 then I was beside him, like a master worker;[d]
and I was daily his[e] delight,
rejoicing before him always,
31 rejoicing in his inhabited world
and delighting in the human race.

32 "And now, my children, listen to me:
happy are those who keep my ways.
33 Hear instruction and be wise,

[a] Meaning of Heb uncertain [b] Or *me as the beginning* [c] Heb *way* [d] Another reading is *little child*
[e] Gk: Heb lacks *his*

and do not neglect it.
34 Happy is the one who listens to me,
watching daily at my gates,
waiting beside my doors.
35 For whoever finds me finds life
and obtains favor from the LORD;
36 but those who miss me injure themselves;
all who hate me love death."

9 Wisdom has built her house,
she has hewn her seven pillars.
2 She has slaughtered her animals, she has
mixed her wine,
she has also set her table.
3 She has sent out her servant-girls, she calls
from the highest places in the town,
4 "You that are simple, turn in here!"
To those without sense she says,
5 "Come, eat of my bread
and drink of the wine I have mixed.
6 Lay aside immaturity,[a] and live,
and walk in the way of insight."

7 Whoever corrects a scoffer wins abuse;
whoever rebukes the wicked gets hurt.
8 A scoffer who is rebuked will only hate you;
the wise, when rebuked, will love you.
9 Give instruction[b] to the wise, and they will
become wiser still;
teach the righteous and they will gain in
learning.
10 The fear of the LORD is the beginning of
wisdom,
and the knowledge of the Holy One is
insight.
11 For by me your days will be multiplied,
and years will be added to your life.
12 If you are wise, you are wise for yourself;
if you scoff, you alone will bear it.

13 The foolish woman is loud;
she is ignorant and knows nothing.
14 She sits at the door of her house,
on a seat at the high places of the town,
15 calling to those who pass by,
who are going straight on their way,
16 "You who are simple, turn in here!"
And to those without sense she says,
17 "Stolen water is sweet,
and bread eaten in secret is pleasant."
18 But they do not know that the dead[c] are
there,
that her guests are in the depths of Sheol.

10 The proverbs of Solomon.

A wise child makes a glad father,
but a foolish child is a mother's grief.
2 Treasures gained by wickedness do not
profit,
but righteousness delivers from death.
3 The LORD does not let the righteous go
hungry,
but he thwarts the craving of the wicked.
4 A slack hand causes poverty,
but the hand of the diligent makes rich.
5 A child who gathers in summer is prudent,
but a child who sleeps in harvest brings
shame.
6 Blessings are on the head of the righteous,
but the mouth of the wicked conceals
violence.
7 The memory of the righteous is a blessing,
but the name of the wicked will rot.
8 The wise of heart will heed commandments,
but a babbling fool will come to ruin.
9 Whoever walks in integrity walks securely,
but whoever follows perverse ways will be
found out.
10 Whoever winks the eye causes trouble,
but the one who rebukes boldly makes
peace.[d]
11 The mouth of the righteous is a fountain of
life,
but the mouth of the wicked conceals
violence.
12 Hatred stirs up strife,
but love covers all offenses.
13 On the lips of one who has understanding
wisdom is found,

[a] Or *simpleness* [b] Heb lacks *instruction* [c] Heb *shades* [d] Gk: Heb *but a babbling fool will come to ruin*

but a rod is for the back of one who lacks
sense.
14 The wise lay up knowledge,
but the babbling of a fool brings ruin near.
15 The wealth of the rich is their fortress;
the poverty of the poor is their ruin.
16 The wage of the righteous leads to life,
the gain of the wicked to sin.
17 Whoever heeds instruction is on the path to
life,
but one who rejects a rebuke goes astray.
18 Lying lips conceal hatred,
and whoever utters slander is a fool.
19 When words are many, transgression is not
lacking,
but the prudent are restrained in speech.
20 The tongue of the righteous is choice silver;
the mind of the wicked is of little worth.
21 The lips of the righteous feed many,
but fools die for lack of sense.
22 The blessing of the LORD makes rich,
and he adds no sorrow with it.[a]
23 Doing wrong is like sport to a fool,
but wise conduct is pleasure to a person of
understanding.
24 What the wicked dread will come upon
them,

Proverbs 10:19-21

The 20th century has so politicized reality that we listen to other worldviews only with difficulty, hesitation or derision. Our tendency to manipulate tradition only deepens our enslavement to modern categories, questions and assumptions. As long as we cling to our own categories we cannot hear the voices of our tradition that speak about the importance of poverty and silence, that talk about the benefits of unjust suffering, . . . that depict human struggle in terms of solitude and self-abnegation, that speak of freedom in terms of self-denial and asceticism, and that perceive wisdom in terms of detachment and transcendence.[43]

— *Susan E. Schreiner*

but the desire of the righteous will be
granted.
25 When the tempest passes, the wicked are no
more,
but the righteous are established forever.
26 Like vinegar to the teeth, and smoke to the
eyes,
so are the lazy to their employers.
27 The fear of the LORD prolongs life,
but the years of the wicked will be short.
28 The hope of the righteous ends in gladness,
but the expectation of the wicked comes
to nothing.
29 The way of the LORD is a stronghold for the
upright,
but destruction for evildoers.
30 The righteous will never be removed,
but the wicked will not remain in the land.
31 The mouth of the righteous brings forth
wisdom,
but the perverse tongue will be cut off.
32 The lips of the righteous know what is
acceptable,
but the mouth of the wicked what is
perverse.

11 A false balance is an abomination to the
LORD,
but an accurate weight is his delight.
2 When pride comes, then comes disgrace;
but wisdom is with the humble.
3 The integrity of the upright guides them,
but the crookedness of the treacherous
destroys them.
4 Riches do not profit in the day of wrath,
but righteousness delivers from death.
5 The righteousness of the blameless keeps
their ways straight,
but the wicked fall by their own
wickedness.
6 The righteousness of the upright saves them,
but the treacherous are taken captive by
their schemes.
7 When the wicked die, their hope perishes,
and the expectation of the godless comes
to nothing.

[a] *Or and toil adds nothing to it*

8 The righteous are delivered from trouble,
and the wicked get into it instead.
9 With their mouths the godless would destroy their neighbors,
but by knowledge the righteous are delivered.
10 When it goes well with the righteous, the city rejoices;
and when the wicked perish, there is jubilation.
11 By the blessing of the upright a city is exalted,
but it is overthrown by the mouth of the wicked.
12 Whoever belittles another lacks sense,
but an intelligent person remains silent.
13 A gossip goes about telling secrets,
but one who is trustworthy in spirit keeps a confidence.
14 Where there is no guidance, a nation[a] falls,
but in an abundance of counselors there is safety.
15 To guarantee loans for a stranger brings trouble,
but there is safety in refusing to do so.
16 A gracious woman gets honor,
but she who hates virtue is covered with shame.[b]
The timid become destitute,[c]
but the aggressive gain riches.
17 Those who are kind reward themselves,
but the cruel do themselves harm.
18 The wicked earn no real gain,
but those who sow righteousness get a true reward.
19 Whoever is steadfast in righteousness will live,
but whoever pursues evil will die.
20 Crooked minds are an abomination to the Lord,
but those of blameless ways are his delight.
21 Be assured, the wicked will not go unpunished,
but those who are righteous will escape.
22 Like a gold ring in a pig's snout
is a beautiful woman without good sense.
23 The desire of the righteous ends only in good;
the expectation of the wicked in wrath.
24 Some give freely, yet grow all the richer;
others withhold what is due, and only suffer want.
25 A generous person will be enriched,
and one who gives water will get water.
26 The people curse those who hold back grain,
but a blessing is on the head of those who sell it.
27 Whoever diligently seeks good seeks favor,
but evil comes to the one who searches for it.
28 Those who trust in their riches will wither,[d]
but the righteous will flourish like green leaves.
29 Those who trouble their households will inherit wind,
and the fool will be servant to the wise.
30 The fruit of the righteous is a tree of life,
but violence[e] takes lives away.
31 If the righteous are repaid on earth,
how much more the wicked and the sinner!

12 Whoever loves discipline loves knowledge,
but those who hate to be rebuked are stupid.
2 The good obtain favor from the Lord,
but those who devise evil he condemns.
3 No one finds security by wickedness,
but the root of the righteous will never be moved.
4 A good wife is the crown of her husband,
but she who brings shame is like rottenness in his bones.
5 The thoughts of the righteous are just;
the advice of the wicked is treacherous.
6 The words of the wicked are a deadly ambush,
but the speech of the upright delivers them.

[a] Or *an army* [b] Compare Gk Syr: Heb lacks *but she . . . shame* [c] Gk: Heb lacks *The timid . . . destitute* [d] Cn: Heb *fall*
[e] Cn Compare Gk Syr: Heb *a wise man*

7 The wicked are overthrown and are no more,
but the house of the righteous will stand.
8 One is commended for good sense,
but a perverse mind is despised.
9 Better to be despised and have a servant,
than to be self-important and lack food.
10 The righteous know the needs of their animals,
but the mercy of the wicked is cruel.
11 Those who till their land will have plenty of food,
but those who follow worthless pursuits have no sense.
12 The wicked covet the proceeds of wickedness,[a]
but the root of the righteous bears fruit.
13 The evil are ensnared by the transgression of their lips,
but the righteous escape from trouble.
14 From the fruit of the mouth one is filled with good things,
and manual labor has its reward.
15 Fools think their own way is right,
but the wise listen to advice.
16 Fools show their anger at once,
but the prudent ignore an insult.
17 Whoever speaks the truth gives honest evidence,
but a false witness speaks deceitfully.
18 Rash words are like sword thrusts,
but the tongue of the wise brings healing.
19 Truthful lips endure forever,
but a lying tongue lasts only a moment.
20 Deceit is in the mind of those who plan evil,
but those who counsel peace have joy.
21 No harm happens to the righteous,
but the wicked are filled with trouble.
22 Lying lips are an abomination to the LORD,
but those who act faithfully are his delight.
23 One who is clever conceals knowledge,
but the mind of a fool[b] broadcasts folly.
24 The hand of the diligent will rule,
while the lazy will be put to forced labor.
25 Anxiety weighs down the human heart,
but a good word cheers it up.
26 The righteous gives good advice to friends,[c]
but the way of the wicked leads astray.
27 The lazy do not roast[d] their game,
but the diligent obtain precious wealth.[d]
28 In the path of righteousness there is life,
in walking its path there is no death.

13 A wise child loves discipline,[e]
but a scoffer does not listen to rebuke.
2 From the fruit of their words good persons eat good things,
but the desire of the treacherous is for wrongdoing.
3 Those who guard their mouths preserve their lives;
those who open wide their lips come to ruin.
4 The appetite of the lazy craves, and gets nothing,
while the appetite of the diligent is richly supplied.
5 The righteous hate falsehood,
but the wicked act shamefully and disgracefully.
6 Righteousness guards one whose way is upright,
but sin overthrows the wicked.
7 Some pretend to be rich, yet have nothing;
others pretend to be poor, yet have great wealth.
8 Wealth is a ransom for a person's life,
but the poor get no threats.
9 The light of the righteous rejoices,
but the lamp of the wicked goes out.
10 By insolence the heedless make strife,
but wisdom is with those who take advice.
11 Wealth hastily gotten[f] will dwindle,
but those who gather little by little will increase it.
12 Hope deferred makes the heart sick,
but a desire fulfilled is a tree of life.
13 Those who despise the word bring destruction on themselves,

[a] Or *covet the catch of the wicked* [b] Heb *the heart of fools* [c] Syr: Meaning of Heb uncertain [d] Meaning of Heb uncertain [e] Cn:Heb *A wise child the discipline of his father* [f] Gk Vg: Heb *from vanity*

but those who respect the commandment
will be rewarded.
14 The teaching of the wise is a fountain of life,
so that one may avoid the snares of death.
15 Good sense wins favor,
but the way of the faithless is their ruin.[a]
16 The clever do all things intelligently,
but the fool displays folly.
17 A bad messenger brings trouble,
but a faithful envoy, healing.
18 Poverty and disgrace are for the one who
ignores instruction,
but one who heeds reproof is honored.
19 A desire realized is sweet to the soul,
but to turn away from evil is an
abomination to fools.
20 Whoever walks with the wise becomes wise,
but the companion of fools suffers harm.
21 Misfortune pursues sinners,
but prosperity rewards the righteous.
22 The good leave an inheritance to their
children's children,
but the sinner's wealth is laid up for the
righteous.
23 The field of the poor may yield much food,
but it is swept away through injustice.
24 Those who spare the rod hate their children,
but those who love them are diligent to
discipline them.
25 The righteous have enough to satisfy their
appetite,
but the belly of the wicked is empty.

14 The wise woman[b] builds her house,
but the foolish tears it down with her
own hands.
2 Those who walk uprightly fear the LORD,
but one who is devious in conduct
despises him.
3 The talk of fools is a rod for their backs,[c]
but the lips of the wise preserve them.
4 Where there are no oxen, there is no grain;
abundant crops come by the strength of
the ox.
5 A faithful witness does not lie,
but a false witness breathes out lies.
6 A scoffer seeks wisdom in vain,
but knowledge is easy for one who
understands.
7 Leave the presence of a fool,
for there you do not find words of
knowledge.
8 It is the wisdom of the clever to understand
where they go,
but the folly of fools misleads.
9 Fools mock at the guilt offering,[d]
but the upright enjoy God's favor.
10 The heart knows its own bitterness,
and no stranger shares its joy.

[a] Cn Compare Gk Syr Vg Tg: Heb *is enduring* [b] Heb *Wisdom of women* [c] Cn: Heb *a rod of pride*
[d] Meaning of Heb uncertain

Proverbs 13:23

In the Middle Ages poverty was often viewed as an "estate," a human condition which providentially provided the rich with an occasion for charity. In the Bible, on the other hand, being poor is always the result of oppression. It is not a fact of life but a result of the sin of the powerful, a cause for God's wrath, and God uses the poor to judge the rich. This means that accepting poverty as "natural" is a form of unfaith. It is exactly the fatalistic "kismet" idea which conversion to the biblical perspective calls into question.

There is another essential quality to "being poor." It is the recognition that being poor is not a matter of individual shortcomings or lack of personal gumption. Being poor means being a member of a class or race that has been made poor as an entity. This awareness of the collective quality of poverty and of its structural causes is also integral to being poor.[44]

— ***Harvey Cox***

11 The house of the wicked is destroyed,
but the tent of the upright flourishes.
12 There is a way that seems right to a person,
but its end is the way to death.[a]
13 Even in laughter the heart is sad,
and the end of joy is grief.
14 The perverse get what their ways deserve,
and the good, what their deeds deserve.[b]
15 The simple believe everything,
but the clever consider their steps.
16 The wise are cautious and turn away from evil,
but the fool throws off restraint and is careless.
17 One who is quick-tempered acts foolishly,
and the schemer is hated.
18 The simple are adorned with[c] folly,
but the clever are crowned with knowledge.
19 The evil bow down before the good,
the wicked at the gates of the righteous.
20 The poor are disliked even by their neighbors,
but the rich have many friends.
21 Those who despise their neighbors are sinners,
but happy are those who are kind to the poor.
22 Do they not err that plan evil?
Those who plan good find loyalty and faithfulness.
23 In all toil there is profit,
but mere talk leads only to poverty.
24 The crown of the wise is their wisdom,[d]
but folly is the garland[e] of fools.
25 A truthful witness saves lives,
but one who utters lies is a betrayer.
26 In the fear of the LORD one has strong confidence,
and one's children will have a refuge.
27 The fear of the LORD is a fountain of life,
so that one may avoid the snares of death.
28 The glory of a king is a multitude of people;
without people a prince is ruined.
29 Whoever is slow to anger has great understanding,
but one who has a hasty temper exalts folly.
30 A tranquil mind gives life to the flesh,
but passion makes the bones rot.
31 Those who oppress the poor insult their Maker,
but those who are kind to the needy honor him.
32 The wicked are overthrown by their evildoing,
but the righteous find a refuge in their integrity.[f]
33 Wisdom is at home in the mind of one who has understanding,
but it is not[g] known in the heart of fools.
34 Righteousness exalts a nation,
but sin is a reproach to any people.
35 A servant who deals wisely has the king's favor,
but his wrath falls on one who acts shamefully.

15 A soft answer turns away wrath,
but a harsh word stirs up anger.
2 The tongue of the wise dispenses knowledge,[h]
but the mouths of fools pour out folly.
3 The eyes of the LORD are in every place,
keeping watch on the evil and the good.
4 A gentle tongue is a tree of life,
but perverseness in it breaks the spirit.
5 A fool despises a parent's instruction,
but the one who heeds admonition is prudent.
6 In the house of the righteous there is much treasure,
but trouble befalls the income of the wicked.
7 The lips of the wise spread knowledge;
not so the minds of fools.
8 The sacrifice of the wicked is an abomination to the LORD,
but the prayer of the upright is his delight.

[a] Heb *ways of death* [b] Cn: Heb *from upon him* [c] Or *inherit* [d] Cn Compare Gk: Heb *riches* [e] Cn: Heb *is the folly* [f] Gk Syr: Heb *in their death* [g] Gk Syr: Heb lacks *not* [h] Cn: Heb *makes knowledge good*

9 The way of the wicked is an abomination to the LORD,
but he loves the one who pursues righteousness.
10 There is severe discipline for one who forsakes the way,
but one who hates a rebuke will die.
11 Sheol and Abaddon lie open before the LORD,
how much more human hearts!
12 Scoffers do not like to be rebuked;
they will not go to the wise.
13 A glad heart makes a cheerful countenance,
but by sorrow of heart the spirit is broken.
14 The mind of one who has understanding seeks knowledge,
but the mouths of fools feed on folly.
15 All the days of the poor are hard,
but a cheerful heart has a continual feast.
16 Better is a little with the fear of the LORD
than great treasure and trouble with it.
17 Better is a dinner of vegetables where love is
than a fatted ox and hatred with it.
18 Those who are hot-tempered stir up strife,
but those who are slow to anger calm contention.
19 The way of the lazy is overgrown with thorns,
but the path of the upright is a level highway.
20 A wise child makes a glad father,
but the foolish despise their mothers.
21 Folly is a joy to one who has no sense,
but a person of understanding walks straight ahead.
22 Without counsel, plans go wrong,
but with many advisers they succeed.
23 To make an apt answer is a joy to anyone,
and a word in season, how good it is!
24 For the wise the path of life leads upward,
in order to avoid Sheol below.
25 The LORD tears down the house of the proud,
but maintains the widow's boundaries.
26 Evil plans are an abomination to the LORD,
but gracious words are pure.
27 Those who are greedy for unjust gain make trouble for their households,
but those who hate bribes will live.
28 The mind of the righteous ponders how to answer,
but the mouth of the wicked pours out evil.
29 The LORD is far from the wicked,
but he hears the prayer of the righteous.
30 The light of the eyes rejoices the heart,
and good news refreshes the body.
31 The ear that heeds wholesome admonition
will lodge among the wise.
32 Those who ignore instruction despise themselves,
but those who heed admonition gain understanding.
33 The fear of the LORD is instruction in wisdom,
and humility goes before honor.

16 The plans of the mind belong to mortals,
but the answer of the tongue is from the LORD.
2 All one's ways may be pure in one's own eyes,
but the LORD weighs the spirit.
3 Commit your work to the LORD,
and your plans will be established.
4 The LORD has made everything for its purpose,
even the wicked for the day of trouble.
5 All those who are arrogant are an abomination to the LORD;
be assured, they will not go unpunished.
6 By loyalty and faithfulness iniquity is atoned for,
and by the fear of the LORD one avoids evil.
7 When the ways of people please the LORD,
he causes even their enemies to be at peace with them.
8 Better is a little with righteousness
than large income with injustice.
9 The human mind plans the way,
but the LORD directs the steps.
10 Inspired decisions are on the lips of a king;
his mouth does not sin in judgment.
11 Honest balances and scales are the LORD's;
all the weights in the bag are his work.
12 It is an abomination to kings to do evil,

for the throne is established by
righteousness.
13 Righteous lips are the delight of a king,
and he loves those who speak what is right.
14 A king's wrath is a messenger of death,
and whoever is wise will appease it.
15 In the light of a king's face there is life,
and his favor is like the clouds that bring
the spring rain.
16 How much better to get wisdom than gold!
To get understanding is to be chosen
rather than silver.
17 The highway of the upright avoids evil;
those who guard their way preserve their
lives.
18 Pride goes before destruction,
and a haughty spirit before a fall.
19 It is better to be of a lowly spirit among the
poor
than to divide the spoil with the proud.
20 Those who are attentive to a matter will
prosper,
and happy are those who trust in the
LORD.
21 The wise of heart is called perceptive,
and pleasant speech increases
persuasiveness.
22 Wisdom is a fountain of life to one who has it,
but folly is the punishment of fools.
23 The mind of the wise makes their speech
judicious,
and adds persuasiveness to their lips.
24 Pleasant words are like a honeycomb,
sweetness to the soul and health to the
body.
25 Sometimes there is a way that seems to be
right,
but in the end it is the way to death.
26 The appetite of workers works for them;
their hunger urges them on.
27 Scoundrels concoct evil,
and their speech is like a scorching fire.
28 A perverse person spreads strife,
and a whisperer separates close friends.
29 The violent entice their neighbors,
and lead them in a way that is not good.
30 One who winks the eyes plans[a] perverse
things;
one who compresses the lips brings evil
to pass.
31 Gray hair is a crown of glory;
it is gained in a righteous life.
32 One who is slow to anger is better than the
mighty,
and one whose temper is controlled than
one who captures a city.
33 The lot is cast into the lap,
but the decision is the LORD's alone.

17 Better is a dry morsel with quiet
than a house full of feasting with strife.
2 A slave who deals wisely will rule over a child
who acts shamefully,
and will share the inheritance as one of the
family.
3 The crucible is for silver, and the furnace is
for gold,
but the LORD tests the heart.
4 An evildoer listens to wicked lips;

Proverbs 17:5

Elaborating the thought of martyred Salvadoran theologian Ignacio Ellacuría, Jon Sobrino observes that in the contemporary world the poor are usually treated not with outright mockery so much as a dehumanizing silence. The global reality that John Paul II called "the war of the powerful against the weak" is abetted by contempt on the part of the powerful for the will of the majority of humankind. But this reality "continues to sink into oblivion and silence." The world's richest democracies show little concern to oppose the lies that replace it. "And very few of the churches dare to take their prophetic duty seriously." The "most radical dehumanization of all," Sobrino writes, "is to keep living normally in this world *etsi pauperes non darentur*"—as if the poor did not exist.[45]

— *NE*

[a] Gk Syr Vg Tg: Heb *to plan*

and a liar gives heed to a mischievous
tongue.
5 Those who mock the poor insult their
Maker;
those who are glad at calamity will not go
unpunished.
6 Grandchildren are the crown of the aged,
and the glory of children is their parents.
7 Fine speech is not becoming to a fool;
still less is false speech to a ruler.[a]
8 A bribe is like a magic stone in the eyes of
those who give it;
wherever they turn they prosper.
9 One who forgives an affront fosters
friendship,
but one who dwells on disputes will
alienate a friend.
10 A rebuke strikes deeper into a discerning
person
than a hundred blows into a fool.
11 Evil people seek only rebellion,
but a cruel messenger will be sent against
them.
12 Better to meet a she-bear robbed of its cubs
than to confront a fool immersed in folly.
13 Evil will not depart from the house
of one who returns evil for good.
14 The beginning of strife is like letting out
water;
so stop before the quarrel breaks out.
15 One who justifies the wicked and one who
condemns the righteous
are both alike an abomination to the
LORD.
16 Why should fools have a price in hand
to buy wisdom, when they have no mind
to learn?
17 A friend loves at all times,
and kinsfolk are born to share adversity.
18 It is senseless to give a pledge,
to become surety for a neighbor.
19 One who loves transgression loves strife;
one who builds a high threshold invites
broken bones.
20 The crooked of mind do not prosper,
and the perverse of tongue fall into
calamity.
21 The one who begets a fool gets trouble;
the parent of a fool has no joy.
22 A cheerful heart is a good medicine,
but a downcast spirit dries up the bones.
23 The wicked accept a concealed bribe
to pervert the ways of justice.
24 The discerning person looks to wisdom,
but the eyes of a fool to the ends of the
earth.
25 Foolish children are a grief to their father
and bitterness to her who bore them.
26 To impose a fine on the innocent is not
right,
or to flog the noble for their integrity.
27 One who spares words is knowledgeable;
one who is cool in spirit has
understanding.
28 Even fools who keep silent are considered
wise;
when they close their lips, they are
deemed intelligent.

18 The one who lives alone is self-indulgent,
showing contempt for all who have
sound judgment.[b]
2 A fool takes no pleasure in understanding,
but only in expressing personal opinion.
3 When wickedness comes, contempt comes
also;
and with dishonor comes disgrace.
4 The words of the mouth are deep waters;
the fountain of wisdom is a gushing
stream.
5 It is not right to be partial to the guilty,
or to subvert the innocent in judgment.
6 A fool's lips bring strife,
and a fool's mouth invites a flogging.
7 The mouths of fools are their ruin,
and their lips a snare to themselves.
8 The words of a whisperer are like delicious
morsels;
they go down into the inner parts of the
body.
9 One who is slack in work

[a] Or *a noble person* [b] Meaning of Heb uncertain

is close kin to a vandal.
10 The name of the LORD is a strong tower;
the righteous run into it and are safe.
11 The wealth of the rich is their strong city;
in their imagination it is like a high wall.
12 Before destruction one's heart is haughty,
but humility goes before honor.
13 If one gives answer before hearing,
it is folly and shame.
14 The human spirit will endure sickness;
but a broken spirit—who can bear?
15 An intelligent mind acquires knowledge,
and the ear of the wise seeks knowledge.
16 A gift opens doors;
it gives access to the great.
17 The one who first states a case seems right,
until the other comes and cross-examines.
18 Casting the lot puts an end to disputes
and decides between powerful contenders.
19 An ally offended is stronger than a city;[a]
such quarreling is like the bars of a castle.
20 From the fruit of the mouth one's stomach is satisfied;
the yield of the lips brings satisfaction.
21 Death and life are in the power of the tongue,
and those who love it will eat its fruits.
22 He who finds a wife finds a good thing,
and obtains favor from the LORD.
23 The poor use entreaties,
but the rich answer roughly.
24 Some[b] friends play at friendship[c]
but a true friend sticks closer than one's nearest kin.

19 Better the poor walking in integrity
than one perverse of speech who is a fool.
2 Desire without knowledge is not good,
and one who moves too hurriedly misses the way.
3 One's own folly leads to ruin,
yet the heart rages against the LORD.
4 Wealth brings many friends,
but the poor are left friendless.
5 A false witness will not go unpunished,
and a liar will not escape.
6 Many seek the favor of the generous,
and everyone is a friend to a giver of gifts.
7 If the poor are hated even by their kin,
how much more are they shunned by their friends!
When they call after them, they are not there.[d]
8 To get wisdom is to love oneself;
to keep understanding is to prosper.
9 A false witness will not go unpunished,
and the liar will perish.
10 It is not fitting for a fool to live in luxury,
much less for a slave to rule over princes.
11 Those with good sense are slow to anger,
and it is their glory to overlook an offense.
12 A king's anger is like the growling of a lion,
but his favor is like dew on the grass.
13 A stupid child is ruin to a father,
and a wife's quarreling is a continual dripping of rain.
14 House and wealth are inherited from parents,
but a prudent wife is from the LORD.
15 Laziness brings on deep sleep;
an idle person will suffer hunger.
16 Those who keep the commandment will live;
those who are heedless of their ways will die.
17 Whoever is kind to the poor lends to the LORD,
and will be repaid in full.
18 Discipline your children while there is hope;
do not set your heart on their destruction.
19 A violent tempered person will pay the penalty;
if you effect a rescue, you will only have to do it again.[d]
20 Listen to advice and accept instruction,
that you may gain wisdom for the future.
21 The human mind may devise many plans,

[a] Gk Syr Vg Tg: Meaning of Heb uncertain [b] Syr Tg: Heb *A man of* [c] Cn Compare Syr Vg Tg: Meaning of Heb uncertain
[d] Meaning of Heb uncertain

but it is the purpose of the LORD that will
be established.
22 What is desirable in a person is loyalty,
and it is better to be poor than a liar.
23 The fear of the LORD is life indeed;
filled with it one rests secure
and suffers no harm.
24 The lazy person buries a hand in the dish,
and will not even bring it back to the
mouth.
25 Strike a scoffer, and the simple will learn
prudence;
reprove the intelligent, and they will gain
knowledge.
26 Those who do violence to their father and
chase away their mother
are children who cause shame and bring
reproach.
27 Cease straying, my child, from the words of
knowledge,
in order that you may hear instruction.
28 A worthless witness mocks at justice,
and the mouth of the wicked devours
iniquity.
29 Condemnation is ready for scoffers,
and flogging for the backs of fools.

20 Wine is a mocker, strong drink a brawler,
and whoever is led astray by it is not
wise.
2 The dread anger of a king is like the growling
of a lion;
anyone who provokes him to anger forfeits
life itself.
3 It is honorable to refrain from strife,
but every fool is quick to quarrel.
4 The lazy person does not plow in season;
harvest comes, and there is nothing to be
found.
5 The purposes in the human mind are like
deep water,
but the intelligent will draw them out.
6 Many proclaim themselves loyal,
but who can find one worthy of trust?
7 The righteous walk in integrity—
happy are the children who follow them!
8 A king who sits on the throne of judgment
winnows all evil with his eyes.
9 Who can say, "I have made my heart clean;
I am pure from my sin"?
10 Diverse weights and diverse measures
are both alike an abomination to the
LORD.
11 Even children make themselves known by
their acts,
by whether what they do is pure and right.
12 The hearing ear and the seeing eye—
the LORD has made them both.
13 Do not love sleep, or else you will come to
poverty;
open your eyes, and you will have plenty
of bread.
14 "Bad, bad," says the buyer,
then goes away and boasts.
15 There is gold, and abundance of costly
stones;
but the lips informed by knowledge are a
precious jewel.
16 Take the garment of one who has given
surety for a stranger;
seize the pledge given as surety for
foreigners.
17 Bread gained by deceit is sweet,
but afterward the mouth will be full of
gravel.
18 Plans are established by taking advice;
wage war by following wise guidance.
19 A gossip reveals secrets;
therefore do not associate with a babbler.
20 If you curse father or mother,
your lamp will go out in utter darkness.
21 An estate quickly acquired in the beginning
will not be blessed in the end.
22 Do not say, "I will repay evil";
wait for the LORD, and he will help you.
23 Differing weights are an abomination to the
LORD,
and false scales are not good.
24 All our steps are ordered by the LORD;
how then can we understand our own
ways?
25 It is a snare for one to say rashly, "It is holy,"
and begin to reflect only after making a
vow.
26 A wise king winnows the wicked,

and drives the wheel over them.
27 The human spirit is the lamp of the LORD,
searching every inmost part.
28 Loyalty and faithfulness preserve the king,
and his throne is upheld by righteousness.[a]
29 The glory of youths is their strength,
but the beauty of the aged is their gray
hair.
30 Blows that wound cleanse away evil;
beatings make clean the innermost parts.

21 The king's heart is a stream of water in
the hand of the LORD;
he turns it wherever he will.
2 All deeds are right in the sight of the doer,
but the LORD weighs the heart.
3 To do righteousness and justice
is more acceptable to the LORD than
sacrifice.
4 Haughty eyes and a proud heart—
the lamp of the wicked—are sin.
5 The plans of the diligent lead surely to
abundance,
but everyone who is hasty comes only to
want.
6 The getting of treasures by a lying tongue
is a fleeting vapor and a snare[b] of death.
7 The violence of the wicked will sweep them
away,
because they refuse to do what is just.
8 The way of the guilty is crooked,
but the conduct of the pure is right.
9 It is better to live in a corner of the housetop
than in a house shared with a contentious
wife.
10 The souls of the wicked desire evil;
their neighbors find no mercy in their
eyes.
11 When a scoffer is punished, the simple
become wiser;
when the wise are instructed, they increase
in knowledge.
12 The Righteous One observes the house of the
wicked;
he casts the wicked down to ruin.
13 If you close your ear to the cry of the poor,
you will cry out and not be heard.
14 A gift in secret averts anger;
and a concealed bribe in the bosom, strong
wrath.
15 When justice is done, it is a joy to the
righteous,
but dismay to evildoers.
16 Whoever wanders from the way of
understanding
will rest in the assembly of the dead.
17 Whoever loves pleasure will suffer want;
whoever loves wine and oil will not be
rich.
18 The wicked is a ransom for the righteous,
and the faithless for the upright.
19 It is better to live in a desert land
than with a contentious and fretful wife.
20 Precious treasure remains[c] in the house of the
wise,
but the fool devours it.
21 Whoever pursues righteousness and kindness
will find life[d] and honor.
22 One wise person went up against a city of
warriors
and brought down the stronghold in
which they trusted.
23 To watch over mouth and tongue
is to keep out of trouble.
24 The proud, haughty person, named "Scoffer,"
acts with arrogant pride.
25 The craving of the lazy person is fatal,
for lazy hands refuse to labor.
26 All day long the wicked covet,[e]
but the righteous give and do not hold
back.
27 The sacrifice of the wicked is an abomination;
how much more when brought with evil
intent.
28 A false witness will perish,
but a good listener will testify successfully.
29 The wicked put on a bold face,
but the upright give thought to[f] their ways.
30 No wisdom, no understanding, no counsel,

[a] Gk: Heb *loyalty* [b] Gk: Heb *seekers* [c] Gk: Heb *and oil* [d] Gk: Heb *life and righteousness* [e] Gk: Heb *all day long one covets covetously* [f] Another reading is *establish*

can avail against the LORD.
31 The horse is made ready for the day of battle,
but the victory belongs to the LORD.

22 A good name is to be chosen rather than great riches,
and favor is better than silver or gold.
2 The rich and the poor have this in common:
the LORD is the maker of them all.
3 The clever see danger and hide;
but the simple go on, and suffer for it.
4 The reward for humility and fear of the LORD
is riches and honor and life.
5 Thorns and snares are in the way of the perverse;
the cautious will keep far from them.
6 Train children in the right way,
and when old, they will not stray.
7 The rich rule over the poor,
and the borrower is the slave of the lender.
8 Whoever sows injustice will reap calamity,
and the rod of anger will fail.
9 Those who are generous are blessed,
for they share their bread with the poor.
10 Drive out a scoffer, and strife goes out;
quarreling and abuse will cease.
11 Those who love a pure heart and are gracious in speech
will have the king as a friend.
12 The eyes of the LORD keep watch over knowledge,
but he overthrows the words of the faithless.
13 The lazy person says, "There is a lion outside!
I shall be killed in the streets!"
14 The mouth of a loose[a] woman is a deep pit;
he with whom the LORD is angry falls into it.
15 Folly is bound up in the heart of a boy,
but the rod of discipline drives it far away.
16 Oppressing the poor in order to enrich oneself,
and giving to the rich, will lead only to loss.

17 The words of the wise:
Incline your ear and hear my words,[b]
and apply your mind to my teaching;
18 for it will be pleasant if you keep them within you,
if all of them are ready on your lips.
19 So that your trust may be in the LORD,
I have made them known to you today—yes, to you.
20 Have I not written for you thirty sayings
of admonition and knowledge,
21 to show you what is right and true,
so that you may give a true answer to those who sent you?

22 Do not rob the poor because they are poor,
or crush the afflicted at the gate;
23 for the LORD pleads their cause
and despoils of life those who despoil them.

24 Make no friends with those given to anger,

Proverbs 22:22-23

The ancient Israelites had a strong communal and egalitarian tradition, valuing each human life, rich or poor, as integrally a part of the commonwealth. A major influence is the deep cultural memory that "we were once slaves in the land of Egypt." The *Shema,* the great commandment (Deut 6:4-5) to love God with all one's heart and soul and might, assumed that this serving God is at the same time serving the common good—that is, loving one's neighbor as oneself. But the Torah and the Wisdom literature are realistic and do not envision a time when poverty would be eliminated or of the ways of the wealthy and powerful, which often "crush the afflicted," would disappear. The assumption is that there will always be rich and poor and the agonizing dichotomy between them. However, the consistent warning is that God, taking the side of the poor, "pleads their cause and despoils of life those who despoil them." Thus, the societal goal was to seek balance toward improving the life of the poor.

— DB

[a] Heb *strange* [b] Cn Compare Gk: Heb *Incline your ear, and hear the words of the wise*

and do not associate with hotheads,
25 or you may learn their ways
and entangle yourself in a snare.
26 Do not be one of those who give pledges,
who become surety for debts.
27 If you have nothing with which to pay,
why should your bed be taken from under you?
28 Do not remove the ancient landmark
that your ancestors set up.
29 Do you see those who are skillful in their work?
They will serve kings;
they will not serve common people.

23 When you sit down to eat with a ruler,
observe carefully what[a] is before you,
2 and put a knife to your throat
if you have a big appetite.
3 Do not desire the ruler's[b] delicacies,
for they are deceptive food.
4 Do not wear yourself out to get rich;
be wise enough to desist.
5 When your eyes light upon it, it is gone;
for suddenly it takes wings to itself,
flying like an eagle toward heaven.
6 Do not eat the bread of the stingy;
do not desire their delicacies;
7 for like a hair in the throat, so are they.[c]
"Eat and drink!" they say to you;
but they do not mean it.
8 You will vomit up the little you have eaten,
and you will waste your pleasant words.
9 Do not speak in the hearing of a fool,
who will only despise the wisdom of your words.
10 Do not remove an ancient landmark
or encroach on the fields of orphans,
11 for their redeemer is strong;
he will plead their cause against you.
12 Apply your mind to instruction
and your ear to words of knowledge.
13 Do not withhold discipline from your children;
if you beat them with a rod, they will not die.
14 If you beat them with the rod,
you will save their lives from Sheol.
15 My child, if your heart is wise,
my heart too will be glad.
16 My soul will rejoice
when your lips speak what is right.
17 Do not let your heart envy sinners,
but always continue in the fear of the LORD.
18 Surely there is a future,
and your hope will not be cut off.

19 Hear, my child, and be wise,
and direct your mind in the way.
20 Do not be among winebibbers,
or among gluttonous eaters of meat;
21 for the drunkard and the glutton will come to poverty,
and drowsiness will clothe them with rags.

22 Listen to your father who begot you,
and do not despise your mother when she is old.
23 Buy truth, and do not sell it;
buy wisdom, instruction, and understanding.
24 The father of the righteous will greatly rejoice;
he who begets a wise son will be glad in him.
25 Let your father and mother be glad;
let her who bore you rejoice.

26 My child, give me your heart,
and let your eyes observe[d] my ways.
27 For a prostitute is a deep pit;
an adulteress[e] is a narrow well.
28 She lies in wait like a robber
and increases the number of the faithless.

29 Who has woe? Who has sorrow?
Who has strife? Who has complaining?
Who has wounds without cause?

[a] Or *who* [b] Heb *his* [c] Meaning of Heb uncertain [d] Another reading is *delight in* [e] Heb *an alien woman*

Who has redness of eyes?
30 Those who linger late over wine,
those who keep trying mixed wines.
31 Do not look at wine when it is red,
when it sparkles in the cup
and goes down smoothly.
32 At the last it bites like a serpent,
and stings like an adder.
33 Your eyes will see strange things,
and your mind utter perverse things.
34 You will be like one who lies down in the
midst of the sea,
like one who lies on the top of a mast.[a]
35 "They struck me," you will say,[b] "but I was
not hurt;
they beat me, but I did not feel it.
When shall I awake?
I will seek another drink."

24 Do not envy the wicked,
nor desire to be with them;
2 for their minds devise violence,
and their lips talk of mischief.

3 By wisdom a house is built,
and by understanding it is established;
4 by knowledge the rooms are filled
with all precious and pleasant riches.
5 Wise warriors are mightier than strong ones,[c]
and those who have knowledge than those
who have strength;
6 for by wise guidance you can wage your war,
and in abundance of counselors there is
victory.
7 Wisdom is too high for fools;
in the gate they do not open their
mouths.

8 Whoever plans to do evil
will be called a mischief-maker.
9 The devising of folly is sin,
and the scoffer is an abomination to all.

10 If you faint in the day of adversity,
your strength being small;
11 if you hold back from rescuing those taken
away to death,
those who go staggering to the slaughter;
12 if you say, "Look, we did not know this"—
does not he who weighs the heart
perceive it?
Does not he who keeps watch over your soul
know it?
And will he not repay all according to their
deeds?

13 My child, eat honey, for it is good,
and the drippings of the honeycomb are
sweet to your taste.
14 Know that wisdom is such to your soul;
if you find it, you will find a future,
and your hope will not be cut off.

15 Do not lie in wait like an outlaw against the
home of the righteous;
do no violence to the place where the
righteous live;
16 for though they fall seven times, they will rise
again;
but the wicked are overthrown by
calamity.

17 Do not rejoice when your enemies fall,
and do not let your heart be glad when
they stumble,
18 or else the LORD will see it and be
displeased,
and turn away his anger from them.

19 Do not fret because of evildoers.
Do not envy the wicked;
20 for the evil have no future;
the lamp of the wicked will go out.

21 My child, fear the LORD and the king,
and do not disobey either of them;[d]
22 for disaster comes from them suddenly,
and who knows the ruin that both can
bring?

[a] Meaning of Heb uncertain [b] Gk Syr Vg Tg: Heb lacks *you will say* [c] Gk Compare Syr Tg: Heb *A wise man is strength*
[d] Gk: Heb *do not associate with those who change*

23 These also are sayings of the wise:

Partiality in judging is not good.
24 Whoever says to the wicked, "You are innocent,"
will be cursed by peoples, abhorred by nations;
25 but those who rebuke the wicked will have delight,
and a good blessing will come upon them.
26 One who gives an honest answer
gives a kiss on the lips.
27 Prepare your work outside,
get everything ready for you in the field;
and after that build your house.

28 Do not be a witness against your neighbor without cause,
and do not deceive with your lips.
29 Do not say, "I will do to others as they have done to me;
I will pay them back for what they have done."

30 I passed by the field of one who was lazy,
by the vineyard of a stupid person;
31 and see, it was all overgrown with thorns;
the ground was covered with nettles,
and its stone wall was broken down.
32 Then I saw and considered it;
I looked and received instruction.
33 A little sleep, a little slumber,
a little folding of the hands to rest,
34 and poverty will come upon you like a robber,
and want, like an armed warrior.

25 These are other proverbs of Solomon that the officials of King Hezekiah of Judah copied.

2 It is the glory of God to conceal things,
but the glory of kings is to search things out.
3 Like the heavens for height, like the earth for depth,
so the mind of kings is unsearchable.
4 Take away the dross from the silver,
and the smith has material for a vessel;
5 take away the wicked from the presence of the king,
and his throne will be established in righteousness.
6 Do not put yourself forward in the king's presence
or stand in the place of the great;
7 for it is better to be told, "Come up here,"
than to be put lower in the presence of a noble.

What your eyes have seen
8 do not hastily bring into court;
for[a] what will you do in the end,
when your neighbor puts you to shame?
9 Argue your case with your neighbor directly,
and do not disclose another's secret;
10 or else someone who hears you will bring shame upon you,
and your ill repute will have no end.

11 A word fitly spoken
is like apples of gold in a setting of silver.
12 Like a gold ring or an ornament of gold
is a wise rebuke to a listening ear.
13 Like the cold of snow in the time of harvest
are faithful messengers to those who send them;
they refresh the spirit of their masters.
14 Like clouds and wind without rain
is one who boasts of a gift never given.
15 With patience a ruler may be persuaded,
and a soft tongue can break bones.
16 If you have found honey, eat only enough for you,
or else, having too much, you will vomit it.
17 Let your foot be seldom in your neighbor's house,
otherwise the neighbor will become weary of you and hate you.

[a] Cn: Heb *or else*

18 Like a war club, a sword, or a sharp arrow
is one who bears false witness against a neighbor.
19 Like a bad tooth or a lame foot
is trust in a faithless person in time of trouble.
20 Like vinegar on a wound[a]
is one who sings songs to a heavy heart.
Like a moth in clothing or a worm in wood,
sorrow gnaws at the human heart.[b]
21 If your enemies are hungry, give them bread to eat;
and if they are thirsty, give them water to drink;
22 for you will heap coals of fire on their heads,
and the LORD will reward you.
23 The north wind produces rain,
and a backbiting tongue, angry looks.
24 It is better to live in a corner of the housetop
than in a house shared with a contentious wife.
25 Like cold water to a thirsty soul,
so is good news from a far country.
26 Like a muddied spring or a polluted fountain
are the righteous who give way before the wicked.
27 It is not good to eat much honey,
or to seek honor on top of honor.
28 Like a city breached, without walls,
is one who lacks self-control.

26 Like snow in summer or rain in harvest,
so honor is not fitting for a fool.
2 Like a sparrow in its flitting, like a swallow in its flying,
an undeserved curse goes nowhere.
3 A whip for the horse, a bridle for the donkey,
and a rod for the back of fools.
4 Do not answer fools according to their folly,
or you will be a fool yourself.
5 Answer fools according to their folly,
or they will be wise in their own eyes.
6 It is like cutting off one's foot and drinking down violence,
to send a message by a fool.
7 The legs of a disabled person hang limp;
so does a proverb in the mouth of a fool.
8 It is like binding a stone in a sling
to give honor to a fool.
9 Like a thornbush brandished by the hand of a drunkard
is a proverb in the mouth of a fool.
10 Like an archer who wounds everybody
is one who hires a passing fool or drunkard.[c]
11 Like a dog that returns to its vomit
is a fool who reverts to his folly.
12 Do you see persons wise in their own eyes?
There is more hope for fools than for them.
13 The lazy person says, "There is a lion in the road!
There is a lion in the streets!"
14 As a door turns on its hinges,
so does a lazy person in bed.
15 The lazy person buries a hand in the dish,
and is too tired to bring it back to the mouth.
16 The lazy person is wiser in self-esteem
than seven who can answer discreetly.
17 Like somebody who takes a passing dog by the ears
is one who meddles in the quarrel of another.
18 Like a maniac who shoots deadly firebrands and arrows,
19 so is one who deceives a neighbor
and says, "I am only joking!"
20 For lack of wood the fire goes out,
and where there is no whisperer, quarreling ceases.
21 As charcoal is to hot embers and wood to fire,
so is a quarrelsome person for kindling strife.
22 The words of a whisperer are like delicious morsels;
they go down into the inner parts of the body.
23 Like the glaze[d] covering an earthen vessel

[a] Gk: Heb *Like one who takes off a garment on a cold day, like vinegar on lye* [b] Gk Syr Tg: Heb lacks *Like a moth . . . human heart* [c] Meaning of Heb uncertain [d] Cn: Heb *silver of dross*

are smooth[a] lips with an evil heart.
24 An enemy dissembles in speaking
while harboring deceit within;
25 when an enemy speaks graciously, do not
believe it,
for there are seven abominations
concealed within;
26 though hatred is covered with guile,
the enemy's wickedness will be exposed in
the assembly.
27 Whoever digs a pit will fall into it,
and a stone will come back on the one
who starts it rolling.
28 A lying tongue hates its victims,
and a flattering mouth works ruin.

27 Do not boast about tomorrow,
for you do not know what a day may
bring.
2 Let another praise you, and not your own
mouth—
a stranger, and not your own lips.
3 A stone is heavy, and sand is weighty,
but a fool's provocation is heavier than
both.
4 Wrath is cruel, anger is overwhelming,
but who is able to stand before jealousy?
5 Better is open rebuke
than hidden love.
6 Well meant are the wounds a friend inflicts,
but profuse are the kisses of an enemy.
7 The sated appetite spurns honey,
but to a ravenous appetite even the bitter
is sweet.
8 Like a bird that strays from its nest
is one who strays from home.
9 Perfume and incense make the heart glad,
but the soul is torn by trouble.[b]
10 Do not forsake your friend or the friend of
your parent;
do not go to the house of your kindred in
the day of your calamity.
Better is a neighbor who is nearby
than kindred who are far away.
11 Be wise, my child, and make my heart glad,
so that I may answer whoever
reproaches me.
12 The clever see danger and hide;
but the simple go on, and suffer for it.
13 Take the garment of one who has given
surety for a stranger;
seize the pledge given as surety for
foreigners.[c]
14 Whoever blesses a neighbor with a loud voice,
rising early in the morning,
will be counted as cursing.
15 A continual dripping on a rainy day
and a contentious wife are alike;
16 to restrain her is to restrain the wind
or to grasp oil in the right hand.[d]
17 Iron sharpens iron,
and one person sharpens the wits[e] of
another.
18 Anyone who tends a fig tree will eat its fruit,
and anyone who takes care of a master will
be honored.
19 Just as water reflects the face,
so one human heart reflects another.
20 Sheol and Abaddon are never satisfied,
and human eyes are never satisfied.
21 The crucible is for silver, and the furnace is
for gold,
so a person is tested[f] by being praised.
22 Crush a fool in a mortar with a pestle
along with crushed grain,
but the folly will not be driven out.
23 Know well the condition of your flocks,
and give attention to your herds;
24 for riches do not last forever,
nor a crown for all generations.
25 When the grass is gone, and new growth
appears,
and the herbage of the mountains is
gathered,
26 the lambs will provide your clothing,
and the goats the price of a field;
27 there will be enough goats' milk for your
food,

[a] Gk: Heb *burning* [b] Gk: Heb *the sweetness of a friend is better than one's own counsel* [c] Vg and 20.16: Heb *for a foreign woman* [d] Meaning of Heb uncertain [e] Heb *face* [f] Heb lacks *is tested*

for the food of your household
and nourishment for your servant-girls.

28 The wicked flee when no one pursues,
but the righteous are as bold as a lion.
2 When a land rebels
it has many rulers;
but with an intelligent ruler
there is lasting order.[a]
3 A ruler[b] who oppresses the poor
is a beating rain that leaves no food.
4 Those who forsake the law praise the wicked,
but those who keep the law struggle against them.
5 The evil do not understand justice,
but those who seek the LORD understand it completely.
6 Better to be poor and walk in integrity
than to be crooked in one's ways even though rich.
7 Those who keep the law are wise children,
but companions of gluttons shame their parents.
8 One who augments wealth by exorbitant interest
gathers it for another who is kind to the poor.
9 When one will not listen to the law,
even one's prayers are an abomination.
10 Those who mislead the upright into evil ways
will fall into pits of their own making,
but the blameless will have a goodly inheritance.
11 The rich is wise in self-esteem,
but an intelligent poor person sees through the pose.
12 When the righteous triumph, there is great glory,
but when the wicked prevail, people go into hiding.
13 No one who conceals transgressions will prosper,
but one who confesses and forsakes them will obtain mercy.
14 Happy is the one who is never without fear,
but one who is hard-hearted will fall into calamity.
15 Like a roaring lion or a charging bear
is a wicked ruler over a poor people.
16 A ruler who lacks understanding is a cruel oppressor;
but one who hates unjust gain will enjoy a long life.
17 If someone is burdened with the blood of another,
let that killer be a fugitive until death;
let no one offer assistance.
18 One who walks in integrity will be safe,
but whoever follows crooked ways will fall into the Pit.[c]
19 Anyone who tills the land will have plenty of bread,
but one who follows worthless pursuits will have plenty of poverty.
20 The faithful will abound with blessings,
but one who is in a hurry to be rich will not go unpunished.
21 To show partiality is not good—
yet for a piece of bread a person may do wrong.
22 The miser is in a hurry to get rich
and does not know that loss is sure to come.
23 Whoever rebukes a person will afterward find more favor
than one who flatters with the tongue.
24 Anyone who robs father or mother
and says, "That is no crime,"
is partner to a thug.
25 The greedy person stirs up strife,
but whoever trusts in the LORD will be enriched.
26 Those who trust in their own wits are fools;
but those who walk in wisdom come through safely.
27 Whoever gives to the poor will lack nothing,
but one who turns a blind eye will get many a curse.
28 When the wicked prevail, people go into hiding;

[a] Meaning of Heb uncertain [b] Cn: Heb *A poor person* [c] Syr: Heb *fall all at once*

but when they perish, the righteous
increase.

29 One who is often reproved, yet remains
stubborn,
will suddenly be broken beyond healing.
2 When the righteous are in authority, the
people rejoice;
but when the wicked rule, the people
groan.
3 A child who loves wisdom makes a parent
glad,
but to keep company with prostitutes is to
squander one's substance.
4 By justice a king gives stability to the land,
but one who makes heavy exactions ruins it.
5 Whoever flatters a neighbor
is spreading a net for the neighbor's feet.
6 In the transgression of the evil there is a
snare,
but the righteous sing and rejoice.
7 The righteous know the rights of the poor;
the wicked have no such understanding.
8 Scoffers set a city aflame,
but the wise turn away wrath.
9 If the wise go to law with fools,
there is ranting and ridicule without relief.
10 The bloodthirsty hate the blameless,
and they seek the life of the upright.
11 A fool gives full vent to anger,
but the wise quietly holds it back.
12 If a ruler listens to falsehood,
all his officials will be wicked.
13 The poor and the oppressor have this in
common:
the LORD gives light to the eyes of both.
14 If a king judges the poor with equity,
his throne will be established forever.
15 The rod and reproof give wisdom,
but a mother is disgraced by a neglected
child.
16 When the wicked are in authority,
transgression increases,
but the righteous will look upon their
downfall.
17 Discipline your children, and they will give
you rest;
they will give delight to your heart.
18 Where there is no prophecy, the people cast
off restraint,
but happy are those who keep the law.
19 By mere words servants are not disciplined,
for though they understand, they will not
give heed.
20 Do you see someone who is hasty in speech?
There is more hope for a fool than for
anyone like that.
21 A slave pampered from childhood
will come to a bad end.[a]
22 One given to anger stirs up strife,
and the hothead causes much
transgression.
23 A person's pride will bring humiliation,
but one who is lowly in spirit will obtain
honor.
24 To be a partner of a thief is to hate one's own
life;
one hears the victim's curse, but discloses
nothing.[b]
25 The fear of others[c] lays a snare,
but one who trusts in the LORD is secure.
26 Many seek the favor of a ruler,
but it is from the LORD that one gets
justice.
27 The unjust are an abomination to the
righteous,
but the upright are an abomination to the
wicked.

30 The words of Agur son of Jakeh. An oracle.

Thus says the man: I am weary, O God,
I am weary, O God. How can I prevail?[d]
2 Surely I am too stupid to be human;
I do not have human understanding.
3 I have not learned wisdom,
nor have I knowledge of the holy ones.[e]
4 Who has ascended to heaven and come
down?

[a] Vg: Meaning of Heb uncertain [b] Meaning of Heb uncertain [c] Or *human fear* [d] Or *I am spent*. Meaning of Heb uncertain [e] Or *Holy One*

Who has gathered the wind in the hollow
of the hand?
Who has wrapped up the waters in a
garment?
Who has established all the ends of the
earth?
What is the person's name?
And what is the name of the person's child?
Surely you know!

5 Every word of God proves true;
he is a shield to those who take refuge in
him.
6 Do not add to his words,
or else he will rebuke you, and you will be
found a liar.

7 Two things I ask of you;
do not deny them to me before I die:
8 Remove far from me falsehood and lying;
give me neither poverty nor riches;
feed me with the food that I need,
9 or I shall be full, and deny you,
and say, "Who is the LORD?"
or I shall be poor, and steal,
and profane the name of my God.

10 Do not slander a servant to a master,
or the servant will curse you, and you will
be held guilty.

11 There are those who curse their fathers
and do not bless their mothers.
12 There are those who are pure in their own
eyes
yet are not cleansed of their filthiness.
13 There are those—how lofty are their eyes,
how high their eyelids lift!—
14 there are those whose teeth are swords,
whose teeth are knives,
to devour the poor from off the earth,
the needy from among mortals.

15 The leech[a] has two daughters;
"Give, give," they cry.
Three things are never satisfied;
four never say, "Enough":
16 Sheol, the barren womb,
the earth ever thirsty for water,
and the fire that never says, "Enough."[a]

17 The eye that mocks a father
and scorns to obey a mother
will be pecked out by the ravens of the valley
and eaten by the vultures.

18 Three things are too wonderful for me;
four I do not understand:
19 the way of an eagle in the sky,
the way of a snake on a rock,
the way of a ship on the high seas,
and the way of a man with a girl.

20 This is the way of an adulteress:
she eats, and wipes her mouth,
and says, "I have done no wrong."

21 Under three things the earth trembles;
under four it cannot bear up:
22 a slave when he becomes king,
and a fool when glutted with food;
23 an unloved woman when she gets a husband,
and a maid when she succeeds her
mistress.

24 Four things on earth are small,
yet they are exceedingly wise:
25 the ants are a people without strength,
yet they provide their food in the summer;
26 the badgers are a people without power,
yet they make their homes in the rocks;
27 the locusts have no king,
yet all of them march in rank;
28 the lizard[b] can be grasped in the hand,
yet it is found in kings' palaces.

29 Three things are stately in their stride;
four are stately in their gait:
30 the lion, which is mightiest among wild
animals

[a] Meaning of Heb uncertain   [b] Or *spider*

and does not turn back before any;
31 the strutting rooster,[a] the he-goat,
and a king striding before[b] his people.

32 If you have been foolish, exalting yourself,
or if you have been devising evil,
put your hand on your mouth.
33 For as pressing milk produces curds,
and pressing the nose produces blood,
so pressing anger produces strife.

31 The words of King Lemuel. An oracle that his mother taught him:

2 No, my son! No, son of my womb!
No, son of my vows!
3 Do not give your strength to women,
your ways to those who destroy kings.
4 It is not for kings, O Lemuel,
it is not for kings to drink wine,
or for rulers to desire[c] strong drink;
5 or else they will drink and forget what has been decreed,
and will pervert the rights of all the afflicted.
6 Give strong drink to one who is perishing,
and wine to those in bitter distress;
7 let them drink and forget their poverty,
and remember their misery no more.
8 Speak out for those who cannot speak,
for the rights of all the destitute.[d]
9 Speak out, judge righteously,
defend the rights of the poor and needy.

10 A capable wife who can find?
She is far more precious than jewels.
11 The heart of her husband trusts in her,
and he will have no lack of gain.
12 She does him good, and not harm,
all the days of her life.
13 She seeks wool and flax,
and works with willing hands.
14 She is like the ships of the merchant,
she brings her food from far away.

Proverbs 31:8-9

*[W]hat is at the core of Desmond Tutu's ubuntu theology is that human beings were created in the image of God (*imago Dei*), therefore no race is superior over another. This stands in direct contradistinction with Afrikaner theology in South Africa which asserts that Afrikaners are an elite race, chosen by God, and that racial identities are hierarchies from God [and with] the western materialistic understanding of human identity and value which is dependent on the production of goods.... Tutu's ubuntu theology asserts that individuals have unique gifts, that none will ever be self-sufficient, and that God has made us so that we need each other.*

Tutu's ubuntu theology has a conciliatory tone. It is a theology that is borne in the midst of oppression of the black people in South Africa, yet it does not seek [vengeance] against the white oppressors but to free the oppressed as well as reconcile all races, since all people are made in the image of God and God loves all.[46]

— ***Thulisiwe Ndelu Beresford***

15 She rises while it is still night
and provides food for her household
and tasks for her servant-girls.
16 She considers a field and buys it;
with the fruit of her hands she plants a vineyard.
17 She girds herself with strength,
and makes her arms strong.
18 She perceives that her merchandise is profitable.
Her lamp does not go out at night.
19 She puts her hands to the distaff,
and her hands hold the spindle.
20 She opens her hand to the poor,
and reaches out her hands to the needy.
21 She is not afraid for her household when it snows,

[a] Gk Syr Tg Compare Vg: Meaning of Heb uncertain [b] Meaning of Heb uncertain [c] Cn: Heb *where*
[d] Heb *all children of passing away*

for all her household are clothed in
crimson.
22 She makes herself coverings;
her clothing is fine linen and purple.
23 Her husband is known in the city gates,
taking his seat among the elders of the land.
24 She makes linen garments and sells them;
she supplies the merchant with sashes.
25 Strength and dignity are her clothing,
and she laughs at the time to come.
26 She opens her mouth with wisdom,
and the teaching of kindness is on her
tongue.
27 She looks well to the ways of her
household,
and does not eat the bread of idleness.
28 Her children rise up and call her happy;
her husband too, and he praises her:
29 "Many women have done excellently,
but you surpass them all."
30 Charm is deceitful, and beauty is vain,
but a woman who fears the LORD is to be
praised.
31 Give her a share in the fruit of her hands,
and let her works praise her in the city
gates.

Ecclesiastes

THE AUTHOR OF ECCLESIASTES IS COPING with a reality that most human beings either face directly or try to avoid: the reality and imminence of one's own death. As death approaches, the twelve chapters of Ecclesiastes are sprinkled with resignation. "All is vanity" (1:2)…"Look, the tears of the oppressed—with no one to comfort them!…I thought the dead…more fortunate than the living!" (4:1-2)…"The fate of humans and the fate of animals is the same; as one dies, so dies the other" (3:19)…"The lover of money will not be satisfied with money; nor the lover of wealth, with gain" (5:10; 5:9 in Hebrew)…"The day of death [is better] than the day of birth" (7:1)…"It is better to go to the house of mourning than to go to the house of feasting; for this is the end of everyone" (7:2).

At some point during an encounter with death, as in the book of Ecclesiastes, most believers struggle with the meaning of life. At those times, Ecclesiastes may be a source of comfort. Well-wishers during rough times tend to sugarcoat the gravity of life, but the author of Ecclesiastes allows the reader to accept the bitter pill of life for what it is—bitter.

In Hebrew this book is known as Qoheleth, "The Teacher." The title Ecclesiastes is an anglicized form of the book's Greek title, which is a translation of *Qoheleth*. The book's content is most likely the product of an assembly of sages who instructed one another in wisdom schools. One might think it odd for a teacher who presumes the existence of God to be so thoroughly pessimistic, so decidedly negative, and so coolly logical; yet it is precisely the author's irreverence toward human effort that makes his fundamental claims holy, sacred, and wise. The subtext of his theological musing becomes the key to understanding: "when considering one's own mortality, be joyful in the day of prosperity, and in the day of adversity, consider God" (7:14, my translation). When all is said and done, the knowledge of God alone is sufficient. A wise person can eat, drink, enjoy life, and face death if she or he has wisdom and the knowledge of God (2:26; 3:14, 17; 5:7, 18; 8:12, 13; 12:1).

My reading of the Hebrew Scriptures is strongly shaped by my social location as an African American woman. For seven years, while pursuing degrees in business and divinity, I stood in solidarity with homeless people as they trained me for the ministry. The transformative power of instruction from the lives of the homeless has shaped my soul and revealed my strident classism and unexamined hypocrisy. The persistent threat of death that homeless people face forces them daily to grapple with end-of-life questions similar to those raised by the author of Ecclesiastes.

— ***Madeline McClenney-Sadler***

1 The words of the Teacher,[a] the son of David,
king in Jerusalem.

2 Vanity of vanities, says the Teacher,[a]
vanity of vanities! All is vanity.
3 What do people gain from all the toil
at which they toil under the sun?
4 A generation goes, and a generation
comes,
but the earth remains forever.
5 The sun rises and the sun goes down,
and hurries to the place where it rises.
6 The wind blows to the south,
and goes around to the north;
round and round goes the wind,
and on its circuits the wind returns.
7 All streams run to the sea,
but the sea is not full;
to the place where the streams flow,
there they continue to flow.
8 All things[b] are wearisome;
more than one can express;
the eye is not satisfied with seeing,
or the ear filled with hearing.
9 What has been is what will be,
and what has been done is what will be
done;
there is nothing new under the sun.
10 Is there a thing of which it is said,
"See, this is new"?
It has already been,
in the ages before us.
11 The people of long ago are not
remembered,
nor will there be any remembrance
of people yet to come
by those who come after them.

12 I, the Teacher,[a] when king over Israel in Jerusalem, 13 applied my mind to seek and to search
out by wisdom all that is done under heaven; it is
an unhappy business that God has given to human beings to be busy with. 14 I saw all the deeds
that are done under the sun; and see, all is vanity
and a chasing after wind.[c]
15 What is crooked cannot be made straight,
and what is lacking cannot be counted.

16 I said to myself, "I have acquired great
wisdom, surpassing all who were over Jerusalem
before me; and my mind has had great experience
of wisdom and knowledge." 17 And I applied my
mind to know wisdom and to know madness and
folly. I perceived that this also is but a chasing after wind.[c]
18 For in much wisdom is much vexation,
and those who increase knowledge increase
sorrow.

2 I said to myself, "Come now, I will make a
test of pleasure; enjoy yourself." But again,
this also was vanity. 2 I said of laughter, "It is mad,"
and of pleasure, "What use is it?" 3 I searched with
my mind how to cheer my body with wine—my
mind still guiding me with wisdom—and how
to lay hold on folly, until I might see what was
good for mortals to do under heaven during
the few days of their life. 4 I made great works; I
built houses and planted vineyards for myself; 5 I
made myself gardens and parks, and planted in
them all kinds of fruit trees. 6 I made myself pools
from which to water the forest of growing trees.
7 I bought male and female slaves, and had slaves
who were born in my house; I also had great possessions of herds and flocks, more than any who
had been before me in Jerusalem. 8 I also gathered for myself silver and gold and the treasure
of kings and of the provinces; I got singers, both
men and women, and delights of the flesh, and
many concubines.[d]

9 So I became great and surpassed all who
were before me in Jerusalem; also my wisdom
remained with me. 10 Whatever my eyes desired
I did not keep from them; I kept my heart from
no pleasure, for my heart found pleasure in all
my toil, and this was my reward for all my toil.
11 Then I considered all that my hands had done
and the toil I had spent in doing it, and again, all
was vanity and a chasing after wind,[c] and there
was nothing to be gained under the sun.

12 So I turned to consider wisdom and madness and folly; for what can the one do who comes

[a] Heb *Qoheleth,* traditionally rendered *Preacher* [b] Or *words* [c] Or *a feeding on wind.* See Hos 12.1
[d] Meaning of Heb uncertain

after the king? Only what has already been done.
13 Then I saw that wisdom excels folly as light excels darkness.

14 The wise have eyes in their head,
 but fools walk in darkness.

Yet I perceived that the same fate befalls all of
them. 15 Then I said to myself, "What happens to
the fool will happen to me also; why then have
I been so very wise?" And I said to myself that
this also is vanity. 16 For there is no enduring remembrance of the wise or of fools, seeing that in
the days to come all will have been long forgotten. How can the wise die just like fools? 17 So I
hated life, because what is done under the sun
was grievous to me; for all is vanity and a chasing
after wind.[a]

18 I hated all my toil in which I had toiled
under the sun, seeing that I must leave it to those
who come after me 19 —and who knows whether
they will be wise or foolish? Yet they will be master of all for which I toiled and used my wisdom
under the sun. This also is vanity. 20 So I turned
and gave my heart up to despair concerning all
the toil of my labors under the sun, 21 because
sometimes one who has toiled with wisdom and
knowledge and skill must leave all to be enjoyed
by another who did not toil for it. This also is vanity and a great evil. 22 What do mortals get from
all the toil and strain with which they toil under
the sun? 23 For all their days are full of pain, and
their work is a vexation; even at night their minds
do not rest. This also is vanity.

24 There is nothing better for mortals than
to eat and drink, and find enjoyment in their toil.
This also, I saw, is from the hand of God; 25 for
apart from him[b] who can eat or who can have enjoyment? 26 For to the one who pleases him God
gives wisdom and knowledge and joy; but to the
sinner he gives the work of gathering and heaping, only to give to one who pleases God. This
also is vanity and a chasing after wind.[a]

3 For everything there is a season, and a time
for every matter under heaven:

2 a time to be born, and a time to die;
 a time to plant, and a time to pluck up what
 is planted;
3 a time to kill, and a time to heal;
 a time to break down, and a time to build up;
4 a time to weep, and a time to laugh;
 a time to mourn, and a time to dance;
5 a time to throw away stones, and a time to
 gather stones together;
 a time to embrace, and a time to refrain from
 embracing;
6 a time to seek, and a time to lose;
 a time to keep, and a time to throw away;
7 a time to tear, and a time to sew;
 a time to keep silence, and a time to speak;
8 a time to love, and a time to hate;
 a time for war, and a time for peace.

9 What gain have the workers from their toil?
10 I have seen the business that God has given to
everyone to be busy with. 11 He has made everything suitable for its time; moreover he has put
a sense of past and future into their minds, yet
they cannot find out what God has done from
the beginning to the end. 12 I know that there is
nothing better for them than to be happy and enjoy themselves as long as they live; 13 moreover, it
is God's gift that all should eat and drink and take
pleasure in all their toil. 14 I know that whatever
God does endures forever; nothing can be added
to it, nor anything taken from it; God has done
this, so that all should stand in awe before him.
15 That which is, already has been; that which is
to be, already is; and God seeks out what has
gone by.[c]

16 Moreover I saw under the sun that in the
place of justice, wickedness was there, and in the
place of righteousness, wickedness was there as
well. 17 I said in my heart, God will judge the righteous and the wicked, for he has appointed a time
for every matter, and for every work. 18 I said in
my heart with regard to human beings that God
is testing them to show that they are but animals.
19 For the fate of humans and the fate of animals
is the same; as one dies, so dies the other. They
all have the same breath, and humans have no advantage over the animals; for all is vanity. 20 All go

[a] Or *a feeding on wind*. See Hos 12.1 [b] Gk Syr: Heb *apart from me* [c] Heb *what is pursued*

Ecclesiastes 3:16-22

As a Japanese American, my experience and beliefs are shaped by many overlapping and conflicting influences from the West and East: my upbringing in a nominally Buddhist home; existentialism; Rudolf Bultmann; Jacques Derrida; and Christianity. For Qoheleth, the teacher in Ecclesiastes, death is the great leveler—where the poor and rich, the wise and the foolish, the righteous and the wicked all share the same fate. The teacher does not despair, however, but provides the following words: "So I saw that there is nothing better than that all should enjoy their work, for that is their lot" (3:22). This is not escapism, naïve optimism, or a heroic call to live life under the banner "carpe diem." For Qoheleth, living a life of wisdom includes an uncompromising realism, of facing the finitude of human experience—the inability of humans to transcend the limitations of life and death. It is only with such a realization that one can live authentically and joyfully in the face of one's death.

— FY

to one place; all are from the dust, and all turn
to dust again. 21 Who knows whether the human
spirit goes upward and the spirit of animals goes
downward to the earth? 22 So I saw that there is
nothing better than that all should enjoy their
work, for that is their lot; who can bring them to
see what will be after them?

4 Again I saw all the oppressions that are practiced under the sun. Look, the tears of the
oppressed—with no one to comfort them! On
the side of their oppressors there was power—
with no one to comfort them. 2 And I thought
the dead, who have already died, more fortunate
than the living, who are still alive; 3 but better
than both is the one who has not yet been, and
has not seen the evil deeds that are done under
the sun.

4 Then I saw that all toil and all skill in work
come from one person's envy of another. This
also is vanity and a chasing after wind.[a]

5 Fools fold their hands
and consume their own flesh.
6 Better is a handful with quiet
than two handfuls with toil,
and a chasing after wind.[a]

7 Again, I saw vanity under the sun: 8 the case
of solitary individuals, without sons or brothers;
yet there is no end to all their toil, and their eyes
are never satisfied with riches. "For whom am
I toiling," they ask, "and depriving myself of pleasure?" This also is vanity and an unhappy business.

9 Two are better than one, because they have
a good reward for their toil. 10 For if they fall,
one will lift up the other; but woe to one who is
alone and falls and does not have another to help.
11 Again, if two lie together, they keep warm; but
how can one keep warm alone? 12 And though one
might prevail against another, two will withstand
one. A threefold cord is not quickly broken.

13 Better is a poor but wise youth than an
old but foolish king, who will no longer take
advice. 14 One can indeed come out of prison to
reign, even though born poor in the kingdom. 15 I
saw all the living who, moving about under the
sun, follow that[b] youth who replaced the king;[c]
16 there was no end to all those people whom he
led. Yet those who come later will not rejoice in
him. Surely this also is vanity and a chasing after
wind.[a]

5 [d] Guard your steps when you go to the house
of God; to draw near to listen is better than
the sacrifice offered by fools; for they do not
know how to keep from doing evil.[e] 2 [f] Never be
rash with your mouth, nor let your heart be quick
to utter a word before God, for God is in heaven,
and you upon earth; therefore let your words be
few.

3 For dreams come with many cares, and a
fool's voice with many words.

4 When you make a vow to God, do not delay
fulfilling it; for he has no pleasure in fools. Fulfill

[a] Or *a feeding on wind.* See Hos 12.1 [b] Heb *the second* [c] Heb *him* [d] Ch 4.17 in Heb [e] Cn: Heb *they do not know how to do evil* [f] Ch 5.1 in Heb

what you vow. 5 It is better that you should not
vow than that you should vow and not fulfill it.
6 Do not let your mouth lead you into sin, and do
not say before the messenger that it was a mistake; why should God be angry at your words,
and destroy the work of your hands?

7 With many dreams come vanities and a
multitude of words;[a] but fear God.

8 If you see in a province the oppression of
the poor and the violation of justice and right, do
not be amazed at the matter; for the high official
is watched by a higher, and there are yet higher
ones over them. 9 But all things considered, this
is an advantage for a land: a king for a plowed
field.[a]

10 The lover of money will not be satisfied
with money; nor the lover of wealth, with gain.
This also is vanity.

11 When goods increase, those who eat them
increase; and what gain has their owner but to see
them with his eyes?

12 Sweet is the sleep of laborers, whether
they eat little or much; but the surfeit of the rich
will not let them sleep.

13 There is a grievous ill that I have seen under the sun: riches were kept by their owners to
their hurt, 14 and those riches were lost in a bad
venture; though they are parents of children, they
have nothing in their hands. 15 As they came from
their mother's womb, so they shall go again, naked as they came; they shall take nothing for their
toil, which they may carry away with their hands.
16 This also is a grievous ill: just as they came, so
shall they go; and what gain do they have from
toiling for the wind? 17 Besides, all their days they
eat in darkness, in much vexation and sickness
and resentment.

18 This is what I have seen to be good: it is
fitting to eat and drink and find enjoyment in all
the toil with which one toils under the sun the
few days of the life God gives us; for this is our
lot. 19 Likewise all to whom God gives wealth
and possessions and whom he enables to enjoy
them, and to accept their lot and find enjoyment
in their toil—this is the gift of God. 20 For they
will scarcely brood over the days of their lives,
because God keeps them occupied with the joy
of their hearts.

6 There is an evil that I have seen under the sun,
and it lies heavy upon humankind: 2 those to
whom God gives wealth, possessions, and honor,
so that they lack nothing of all that they desire,
yet God does not enable them to enjoy these
things, but a stranger enjoys them. This is vanity;
it is a grievous ill. 3 A man may beget a hundred
children, and live many years; but however many
are the days of his years, if he does not enjoy life's
good things, or has no burial, I say that a stillborn
child is better off than he. 4 For it comes into vanity and goes into darkness, and in darkness its
name is covered; 5 moreover it has not seen the
sun or known anything; yet it finds rest rather
than he. 6 Even though he should live a thousand
years twice over, yet enjoy no good—do not all
go to one place?

7 All human toil is for the mouth, yet the appetite is not satisfied. 8 For what advantage have
the wise over fools? And what do the poor have
who know how to conduct themselves before the
living? 9 Better is the sight of the eyes than the
wandering of desire; this also is vanity and a chasing after wind.[b]

10 Whatever has come to be has already been
named, and it is known what human beings are,
and that they are not able to dispute with those
who are stronger. 11 The more words, the more
vanity, so how is one the better? 12 For who knows
what is good for mortals while they live the few
days of their vain life, which they pass like a
shadow? For who can tell them what will be after
them under the sun?

7 A good name is better than precious
ointment,
and the day of death, than the day of
birth.
2 It is better to go to the house of mourning
than to go to the house of feasting;
for this is the end of everyone,
and the living will lay it to heart.
3 Sorrow is better than laughter,

[a] Meaning of Heb uncertain [b] Or *a feeding on wind.* See Hos 12.1

for by sadness of countenance the heart is
made glad.
4 The heart of the wise is in the house of
mourning;
but the heart of fools is in the house of
mirth.
5 It is better to hear the rebuke of the wise
than to hear the song of fools.
6 For like the crackling of thorns under a pot,
so is the laughter of fools;
this also is vanity.
7 Surely oppression makes the wise foolish,
and a bribe corrupts the heart.
8 Better is the end of a thing than its beginning;
the patient in spirit are better than the
proud in spirit.
9 Do not be quick to anger,
for anger lodges in the bosom of fools.
10 Do not say, "Why were the former days better
than these?"
For it is not from wisdom that you ask this.
11 Wisdom is as good as an inheritance,
an advantage to those who see the sun.
12 For the protection of wisdom is like the
protection of money,
and the advantage of knowledge is that
wisdom gives life to the one who
possesses it.
13 Consider the work of God;
who can make straight what he has made
crooked?

14 In the day of prosperity be joyful, and in
the day of adversity consider; God has made the
one as well as the other, so that mortals may not
find out anything that will come after them.

15 In my vain life I have seen everything;
there are righteous people who perish in their
righteousness, and there are wicked people who
prolong their life in their evildoing. 16 Do not be
too righteous, and do not act too wise; why should
you destroy yourself? 17 Do not be too wicked,
and do not be a fool; why should you die before
your time? 18 It is good that you should take hold
of the one, without letting go of the other; for the
one who fears God shall succeed with both.

19 Wisdom gives strength to the wise more
than ten rulers that are in a city.

20 Surely there is no one on earth so righteous as to do good without ever sinning.

21 Do not give heed to everything that people say, or you may hear your servant cursing you;
22 your heart knows that many times you have
yourself cursed others.

23 All this I have tested by wisdom; I said,
"I will be wise," but it was far from me. 24 That
which is, is far off, and deep, very deep; who can
find it out? 25 I turned my mind to know and to
search out and to seek wisdom and the sum of
things, and to know that wickedness is folly and
that foolishness is madness. 26 I found more bitter
than death the woman who is a trap, whose heart
is snares and nets, whose hands are fetters; one
who pleases God escapes her, but the sinner is
taken by her. 27 See, this is what I found, says the
Teacher,[a] adding one thing to another to find the
sum, 28 which my mind has sought repeatedly, but
I have not found. One man among a thousand I
found, but a woman among all these I have not
found. 29 See, this alone I found, that God made
human beings straightforward, but they have devised many schemes.

8 Who is like the wise man?
And who knows the interpretation of a
thing?
Wisdom makes one's face shine,
and the hardness of one's countenance is
changed.

2 Keep[b] the king's command because of your
sacred oath. 3 Do not be terrified; go from his
presence, do not delay when the matter is unpleasant, for he does whatever he pleases. 4 For
the word of the king is powerful, and who can say
to him, "What are you doing?" 5 Whoever obeys a
command will meet no harm, and the wise mind
will know the time and way. 6 For every matter has
its time and way, although the troubles of mortals
lie heavy upon them. 7 Indeed, they do not know
what is to be, for who can tell them how it will be?
8 No one has power over the wind[c] to restrain the
wind,[c] or power over the day of death; there is no

[a] *Qoheleth,* traditionally rendered *Preacher* [b] Heb *I keep* [c] Or *breath*

Ecclesiastes 8:9

The "preferential option for the poor," in the words of Latin American Christians, is crucial. It means that the needs of the poor should have priority over the wants of the rich in any decision-making process. But it also means that the first task in confronting issues of development is to listen to the poor and unemployed, to get their perspectives on the issues and options, and to include them in the decision-making process. Certainly we know that it makes a world of difference whose experience guides our thinking on social matters.... We have learned to recognize that the God of the Hebrew and Christian Scriptures was revealed first and primarily among the oppressed, the slaves in Egypt and the poor and oppressed of first-century Palestine dominated by the Roman empire, and is present today among similar groups struggling for justice.[47]

— Lee Cormie

discharge from the battle, nor does wickedness deliver those who practice it. 9 All this I observed, applying my mind to all that is done under the sun, while one person exercises authority over another to the other's hurt.

10 Then I saw the wicked buried; they used to go in and out of the holy place, and were praised in the city where they had done such things.[a] This also is vanity. 11 Because sentence against an evil deed is not executed speedily, the human heart is fully set to do evil. 12 Though sinners do evil a hundred times and prolong their lives, yet I know that it will be well with those who fear God, because they stand in fear before him, 13 but it will not be well with the wicked, neither will they prolong their days like a shadow, because they do not stand in fear before God.

14 There is a vanity that takes place on earth, that there are righteous people who are treated according to the conduct of the wicked, and there are wicked people who are treated according to the conduct of the righteous. I said that this also is vanity. 15 So I commend enjoyment, for there is nothing better for people under the sun than to eat, and drink, and enjoy themselves, for this will go with them in their toil through the days of life that God gives them under the sun.

16 When I applied my mind to know wisdom, and to see the business that is done on earth, how one's eyes see sleep neither day nor night, 17 then I saw all the work of God, that no one can find out what is happening under the sun. However much they may toil in seeking, they will not find it out; even though those who are wise claim to know, they cannot find it out.

9 All this I laid to heart, examining it all, how the righteous and the wise and their deeds are in the hand of God; whether it is love or hate one does not know. Everything that confronts them 2 is vanity,[b] since the same fate comes to all, to the righteous and the wicked, to the good and the evil,[c] to the clean and the unclean, to those who sacrifice and those who do not sacrifice. As are the good, so are the sinners; those who swear are like those who shun an oath. 3 This is an evil in all that happens under the sun, that the same fate comes to everyone. Moreover, the hearts of all are full of evil; madness is in their hearts while they live, and after that they go to the dead. 4 But whoever is joined with all the living has hope, for a living dog is better than a dead lion. 5 The living know that they will die, but the dead know nothing; they have no more reward, and even the memory of them is lost. 6 Their love and their hate and their envy have already perished; never again will they have any share in all that happens under the sun.

7 Go, eat your bread with enjoyment, and drink your wine with a merry heart; for God has long ago approved what you do. 8 Let your garments always be white; do not let oil be lacking on your head. 9 Enjoy life with the wife whom you love, all the days of your vain life that are given you under the sun, because that is your portion in life and in your toil at which you toil under the sun. 10 Whatever your hand finds to do, do with

[a] Meaning of Heb uncertain [b] Syr Compare Gk: Heb *Everything that confronts them* [2]*is everything*
[c] Gk Syr Vg: Heb lacks *and the evil*

your might; for there is no work or thought or
knowledge or wisdom in Sheol, to which you are
going.
11 Again I saw that under the sun the race is
not to the swift, nor the battle to the strong, nor
bread to the wise, nor riches to the intelligent,
nor favor to the skillful; but time and chance happen to them all. 12For no one can anticipate the
time of disaster. Like fish taken in a cruel net, and
like birds caught in a snare, so mortals are snared
at a time of calamity, when it suddenly falls upon
them.
13 I have also seen this example of wisdom
under the sun, and it seemed great to me. 14There
was a little city with few people in it. A great king
came against it and besieged it, building great
siegeworks against it. 15Now there was found in it
a poor wise man, and he by his wisdom delivered
the city. Yet no one remembered that poor man.
16So I said, "Wisdom is better than might; yet the
poor man's wisdom is despised, and his words are
not heeded."

17 The quiet words of the wise are more to be
heeded
than the shouting of a ruler among fools.
18 Wisdom is better than weapons of war,
but one bungler destroys much good.

10 Dead flies make the perfumer's ointment
give off a foul odor;
so a little folly outweighs wisdom and
honor.
2 The heart of the wise inclines to the right,
but the heart of a fool to the left.
3 Even when fools walk on the road, they lack
sense,
and show to everyone that they are fools.
4 If the anger of the ruler rises against you, do
not leave your post,
for calmness will undo great offenses.

5 There is an evil that I have seen under
the sun, as great an error as if it proceeded from
the ruler: 6folly is set in many high places, and the
rich sit in a low place. 7I have seen slaves on horseback, and princes walking on foot like slaves.

8 Whoever digs a pit will fall into it;
and whoever breaks through a wall will be
bitten by a snake.
9 Whoever quarries stones will be hurt by
them;
and whoever splits logs will be endangered
by them.
10 If the iron is blunt, and one does not whet the
edge,
then more strength must be exerted;
but wisdom helps one to succeed.
11 If the snake bites before it is charmed,
there is no advantage in a charmer.
12 Words spoken by the wise bring them favor,
but the lips of fools consume them.
13 The words of their mouths begin in
foolishness,
and their talk ends in wicked madness;
14 yet fools talk on and on.
No one knows what is to happen,
and who can tell anyone what the future
holds?
15 The toil of fools wears them out,
for they do not even know the way to
town.
16 Alas for you, O land, when your king is a
servant,[a]
and your princes feast in the morning!
17 Happy are you, O land, when your king is a
nobleman,
and your princes feast at the proper
time—
for strength, and not for drunkenness!
18 Through sloth the roof sinks in,
and through indolence the house leaks.
19 Feasts are made for laughter;
wine gladdens life,
and money meets every need.
20 Do not curse the king, even in your thoughts,
or curse the rich, even in your bedroom;
for a bird of the air may carry your voice,
or some winged creature tell the matter.

11 Send out your bread upon the waters,
for after many days you will get it back.

[a] Or *a child*

2 Divide your means seven ways, or even eight,
for you do not know what disaster may
happen on earth.
3 When clouds are full,
they empty rain on the earth;
whether a tree falls to the south or to the
north,
in the place where the tree falls, there it
will lie.
4 Whoever observes the wind will not sow;
and whoever regards the clouds will not
reap.

5 Just as you do not know how the breath
comes to the bones in the mother's womb, so you
do not know the work of God, who makes everything.
6 In the morning sow your seed, and at evening do not let your hands be idle; for you do not
know which will prosper, this or that, or whether
both alike will be good.
7 Light is sweet, and it is pleasant for the eyes
to see the sun.
8 Even those who live many years should rejoice in them all; yet let them remember that the
days of darkness will be many. All that comes is
vanity.
9 Rejoice, young man, while you are young,
and let your heart cheer you in the days of your
youth. Follow the inclination of your heart and
the desire of your eyes, but know that for all these
things God will bring you into judgment.
10 Banish anxiety from your mind, and put
away pain from your body; for youth and the
dawn of life are vanity.

12 Remember your creator in the days of
your youth, before the days of trouble
come, and the years draw near when you will say,
"I have no pleasure in them"; 2before the sun and
the light and the moon and the stars are darkened
and the clouds return with[a] the rain; 3in the day
when the guards of the house tremble, and the
strong men are bent, and the women who grind
cease working because they are few, and those
who look through the windows see dimly; 4when
the doors on the street are shut, and the sound
of the grinding is low, and one rises up at the
sound of a bird, and all the daughters of song are
brought low; 5when one is afraid of heights, and
terrors are in the road; the almond tree blossoms,
the grasshopper drags itself along[b] and desire
fails; because all must go to their eternal home,
and the mourners will go about the streets; 6be-
fore the silver cord is snapped,[c] and the golden
bowl is broken, and the pitcher is broken at the
fountain, and the wheel broken at the cistern,
7and the dust returns to the earth as it was, and
the breath[d] returns to God who gave it. 8Vanity of
vanities, says the Teacher;[e] all is vanity.
9 Besides being wise, the Teacher[e] also taught
the people knowledge, weighing and studying and
arranging many proverbs. 10The Teacher[e] sought
to find pleasing words, and he wrote words of
truth plainly.
11 The sayings of the wise are like goads, and
like nails firmly fixed are the collected sayings
that are given by one shepherd.[f] 12Of anything
beyond these, my child, beware. Of making many
books there is no end, and much study is a weariness of the flesh.
13 The end of the matter; all has been heard.
Fear God, and keep his commandments; for that
is the whole duty of everyone. 14For God will
bring every deed into judgment, including[g] every
secret thing, whether good or evil.

[a] Or *after*; Heb *'ahar* [b] Or *is a burden* [c] Syr Vg Compare Gk: Heb *is removed* [d] Or *the spirit* [e] *Qoheleth*, traditionally rendered *Preacher* [f] Meaning of Heb uncertain [g] Or *into the judgment on*

The Song of Solomon

The Song of Solomon or Song of Songs—meaning, the most magnificent of all songs—demonstrates, perhaps more clearly than any other biblical material, the multivalent complexity and beauty of the Bible. On the face of it, the book—often called simply the Song—seems to have no religious connection, never mentioning God. Yet the book explores love—intimate, life-giving, provocative, mutual, erotic, dynamic, engaging, complex, longing, passionate love—and perhaps reveals that fully intimate relationships are a way of experiencing God, at once both immanent and transcendent.

Ancient writings were often attributed to people whose legendary name might lend the book credibility, and the Song is no exception: its authorship is traditionally ascribed to Solomon. The book's enigmatic form has led readers to make various suggestions about its genre, some seeing it as a series of love songs akin to Egyptian love poetry, others seeing it as including songs for recital at a religious ceremony such as a fertility festival or a marriage celebration. Earlier Christian interpreters read the book as allegory, revealing God's love for Israel or Christ's love for the Christian church. The book continues to be used liturgically, read by some contemporary Jewish congregations at the end of the festival of Passover and by others prior to Sabbath.

Today's Western, Eurocentric philosophical way of reading often creates expectations for linear, documentary narratives that disclose characters involved in, and controlled by, a singular plot and clear imagery. The Song demands more from its readers, however. It portrays robust passion between clandestine lovers, often desperate to spend time together despite societal pressures. The book moves among a variety of speakers. The female lover speaks most often, answered by her male lover or by a chorus of females, daughters of Jerusalem, who encourage, cajole, voice concern, and celebrate with the female lover. Shifting in mood, intensity, theme, and setting, the Song craftily calls for examination of societal structures and still offers glimpses into the most intimate moments between the lovers. Innuendos—vineyards, clefts, gardens, locks, and hanging fruit, to name a few—permeate the Song. Many of the metaphors and allusions are inaccessible to today's readers, creating wonder over the apparent literary artistry of the writer.

The Song gives voice to females in a way unlike other portions of the Bible, which often reflect successful attempts to silence or control female expression. The speech and thoughts of women dominate the book. For example, while most biblical references to going to one's parents' home literally translate as "my father's house," the Song twice finds the woman speaking of going to "my mother's house."

The Song also seems to be countercultural in other ways. The Song addresses a wide variety of what we today consider justice issues. What are the implications of having dark skin? The woman

proclaims, "I am black and beautiful" (1:5), and her lover agrees wholeheartedly. Who and what is considered beautiful? The woman defends the appearance of her small breasts against the teasing of her brothers, and her male lover continually extols her incomparable beauty. Does society have the right to decide who can love each other? The lovers often find themselves seeking each other but thwarted by interruptions. Even their supporters, the daughters of Jerusalem, sometime succumb to society's notions of appropriateness. The lovers must meet in private, even though the woman longs to have a public relationship. And the Song reveals possible undercurrents of class struggle. Perhaps a young man from among the elite has fallen in love with a poorer, less privileged young woman. In this way, the Song could be interpreted as a form of resistance literature. Other evidences of oppression appear throughout the book. The sentinels question, beat, and perhaps even rape the woman as she wanders the city streets at night searching for her lover. Concurrently, the Song magnificently displays the complexity of human life, both individual and communal, for even as the female's voice is freely heard, society seeks to control intimacy, social interaction, and notions of beauty.

Near the end of the Song, readers get a glimpse at the intended conclusion, if there is one, in 8:6-7, from which all can take courage in the face of oppression. Love is as strong as death; passion is as fierce as the grave. Love rages as flame. Water cannot quench it, floods cannot drown it, money cannot buy it. In the end, nothing matters but love.

I am a white, Protestant, upper-middle class, straight female who has been privileged with opportunities and choices. My social location with regard to race and ethnicity often goes unlabeled and, perhaps even more often, is considered normative. My racial context as privileged and unlabeled leave me, I believe, an extra responsibility to name contexts around me. Issues of gender remain omnipresent for me as I struggle to give voice to assumptions and values that often silence women. Recognizing my own context and the contexts around me feeds my interpretation of the Song of Songs.

— *Alice Hunt*

1 The Song of Songs, which is Solomon's.

2 Let him kiss me with the kisses of his mouth!
For your love is better than wine,
3 your anointing oils are fragrant,
your name is perfume poured out;
therefore the maidens love you.
4 Draw me after you, let us make haste.
The king has brought me into his chambers.
We will exult and rejoice in you;
we will extol your love more than wine;
rightly do they love you.

5 I am black and beautiful,
O daughters of Jerusalem,
like the tents of Kedar,
like the curtains of Solomon.
6 Do not gaze at me because I am dark,
because the sun has gazed on me.

Song of Solomon 1:5

The old saying goes, "beauty is in the eye of the beholder." In Western-European culture, white is used as a standard for beauty. Within this mentality of the colonizer, dark skin is often viewed as secondary, inferior, foreign, at best exotic. In some translations of Song 1:5, the verse reads, "I am dark—*but* lovely" (NIV) or "I am black *but* lovely" (NASB). Translating the Hebrew conjunction *waw* as "but" is grammatically possible, but betrays an ideological bias—as if one cannot be black *and* beautiful. The NRSV provides a translation that is equally valid grammatically but less biased culturally: "I am black and beautiful." Beauty is in the eye of the beholder; and translation is always interpretation.

— *FY*

My mother's sons were angry with me;
they made me keeper of the vineyards,
but my own vineyard I have not kept!
7 Tell me, you whom my soul loves,
where you pasture your flock,
where you make it lie down at noon;
for why should I be like one who is veiled
beside the flocks of your companions?

8 If you do not know,
O fairest among women,
follow the tracks of the flock,
and pasture your kids
beside the shepherds' tents.

9 I compare you, my love,
to a mare among Pharaoh's chariots.
10 Your cheeks are comely with ornaments,
your neck with strings of jewels.
11 We will make you ornaments of gold,
studded with silver.

12 While the king was on his couch,
my nard gave forth its fragrance.
13 My beloved is to me a bag of myrrh
that lies between my breasts.
14 My beloved is to me a cluster of henna
blossoms
in the vineyards of En-gedi.

15 Ah, you are beautiful, my love;
ah, you are beautiful;
your eyes are doves.
16 Ah, you are beautiful, my beloved,
truly lovely.
Our couch is green;
17 the beams of our house are cedar,
our rafters[a] are pine.

2 I am a rose[b] of Sharon,
a lily of the valleys.

2 As a lily among brambles,
so is my love among maidens.

3 As an apple tree among the trees of the wood,
so is my beloved among young men.
With great delight I sat in his shadow,
and his fruit was sweet to my taste.
4 He brought me to the banqueting house,
and his intention toward me was love.
5 Sustain me with raisins,
refresh me with apples;
for I am faint with love.
6 O that his left hand were under my head,
and that his right hand embraced me!
7 I adjure you, O daughters of Jerusalem,
by the gazelles or the wild does:
do not stir up or awaken love
until it is ready!

8 The voice of my beloved!
Look, he comes,
leaping upon the mountains,
bounding over the hills.
9 My beloved is like a gazelle
or a young stag.
Look, there he stands
behind our wall,
gazing in at the windows,

[a] Meaning of Heb uncertain [b] Heb *crocus*

looking through the lattice.
10 My beloved speaks and says to me:
"Arise, my love, my fair one,
and come away;
11 for now the winter is past,
the rain is over and gone.
12 The flowers appear on the earth;
the time of singing has come,
and the voice of the turtledove
is heard in our land.
13 The fig tree puts forth its figs,
and the vines are in blossom;
they give forth fragrance.
Arise, my love, my fair one,
and come away.
14 O my dove, in the clefts of the rock,
in the covert of the cliff,
let me see your face,
let me hear your voice;
for your voice is sweet,
and your face is lovely.
15 Catch us the foxes,
the little foxes,
that ruin the vineyards--
for our vineyards are in blossom."

16 My beloved is mine and I am his;
he pastures his flock among the lilies.
17 Until the day breathes
and the shadows flee,
turn, my beloved, be like a gazelle
or a young stag on the cleft mountains.[a]

3 Upon my bed at night
I sought him whom my soul loves;
I sought him, but found him not;
I called him, but he gave no answer.[b]
2 "I will rise now and go about the city,
in the streets and in the squares;
I will seek him whom my soul loves."
I sought him, but found him not.
3 The sentinels found me,
as they went about in the city.
"Have you seen him whom my soul loves?"
4 Scarcely had I passed them,
when I found him whom my soul loves.
I held him, and would not let him go
until I brought him into my mother's
house,
and into the chamber of her that
conceived me.
5 I adjure you, O daughters of Jerusalem,
by the gazelles or the wild does:
do not stir up or awaken love
until it is ready!

6 What is that coming up from the wilderness,
like a column of smoke,
perfumed with myrrh and frankincense,
with all the fragrant powders of the
merchant?
7 Look, it is the litter of Solomon!
Around it are sixty mighty men
of the mighty men of Israel,
8 all equipped with swords
and expert in war,
each with his sword at his thigh
because of alarms by night.
9 King Solomon made himself a palanquin
from the wood of Lebanon.
10 He made its posts of silver,
its back of gold, its seat of purple;
its interior was inlaid with love.[c]
Daughters of Jerusalem,
11 come out.
Look, O daughters of Zion,
at King Solomon,
at the crown with which his mother crowned
him
on the day of his wedding,
on the day of the gladness of his heart.

4 How beautiful you are, my love,
how very beautiful!
Your eyes are doves
behind your veil.
Your hair is like a flock of goats,
moving down the slopes of Gilead.
2 Your teeth are like a flock of shorn ewes
that have come up from the washing,

[a] Or *on the mountains of Bether*; meaning of Heb uncertain [b] Gk: Heb lacks this line [c] Meaning of Heb uncertain

all of which bear twins,
and not one among them is bereaved.
3 Your lips are like a crimson thread,
and your mouth is lovely.
Your cheeks are like halves of a pomegranate
behind your veil.
4 Your neck is like the tower of David,
built in courses;
on it hang a thousand bucklers,
all of them shields of warriors.
5 Your two breasts are like two fawns,
twins of a gazelle,
that feed among the lilies.
6 Until the day breathes
and the shadows flee,
I will hasten to the mountain of myrrh
and the hill of frankincense.
7 You are altogether beautiful, my love;
there is no flaw in you.
8 Come with me from Lebanon, my bride;
come with me from Lebanon.
Depart[a] from the peak of Amana,
from the peak of Senir and Hermon,
from the dens of lions,
from the mountains of leopards.

9 You have ravished my heart, my sister, my
bride,
you have ravished my heart with a glance
of your eyes,
with one jewel of your necklace.
10 How sweet is your love, my sister, my bride!
how much better is your love than wine,
and the fragrance of your oils than any
spice!
11 Your lips distill nectar, my bride;
honey and milk are under your tongue;
the scent of your garments is like the scent
of Lebanon.
12 A garden locked is my sister, my bride,
a garden locked, a fountain sealed.
13 Your channel[b] is an orchard of pomegranates
with all choicest fruits,
henna with nard,
14 nard and saffron, calamus and cinnamon,
with all trees of frankincense,
myrrh and aloes,
with all chief spices--
15 a garden fountain, a well of living water,
and flowing streams from Lebanon.

16 Awake, O north wind,
and come, O south wind!
Blow upon my garden
that its fragrance may be wafted abroad.
Let my beloved come to his garden,
and eat its choicest fruits.

5 I come to my garden, my sister, my bride;
I gather my myrrh with my spice,
I eat my honeycomb with my honey,
I drink my wine with my milk.

Eat, friends, drink,
and be drunk with love.

2 I slept, but my heart was awake.
Listen! my beloved is knocking.
"Open to me, my sister, my love,
my dove, my perfect one;
for my head is wet with dew,
my locks with the drops of the night."
3 I had put off my garment;
how could I put it on again?
I had bathed my feet;
how could I soil them?
4 My beloved thrust his hand into the opening,
and my inmost being yearned for him.
5 I arose to open to my beloved,
and my hands dripped with myrrh,
my fingers with liquid myrrh,
upon the handles of the bolt.
6 I opened to my beloved,
but my beloved had turned and was
gone.
My soul failed me when he spoke.
I sought him, but did not find him;
I called him, but he gave no answer.
7 Making their rounds in the city
the sentinels found me;

[a] Or *Look* [b] Meaning of Heb uncertain

they beat me, they wounded me,
they took away my mantle,
those sentinels of the walls.
8 I adjure you, O daughters of Jerusalem,
if you find my beloved,
tell him this:
I am faint with love.

9 What is your beloved more than another beloved,
O fairest among women?
What is your beloved more than another beloved,
that you thus adjure us?

10 My beloved is all radiant and ruddy,
distinguished among ten thousand.
11 His head is the finest gold;
his locks are wavy,
black as a raven.
12 His eyes are like doves
beside springs of water,
bathed in milk,
fitly set.[a]
13 His cheeks are like beds of spices,
yielding fragrance.
His lips are lilies,
distilling liquid myrrh.
14 His arms are rounded gold,
set with jewels.
His body is ivory work,[a]
encrusted with sapphires.[b]
15 His legs are alabaster columns,
set upon bases of gold.
His appearance is like Lebanon,
choice as the cedars.
16 His speech is most sweet,
and he is altogether desirable.
This is my beloved and this is my friend,
O daughters of Jerusalem.

6 Where has your beloved gone,
O fairest among women?
Which way has your beloved turned,
that we may seek him with you?

2 My beloved has gone down to his garden,
to the beds of spices,
to pasture his flock in the gardens,
and to gather lilies.
3 I am my beloved's and my beloved is mine;
he pastures his flock among the lilies.

4 You are beautiful as Tirzah, my love,
comely as Jerusalem,
terrible as an army with banners.
5 Turn away your eyes from me,
for they overwhelm me!
Your hair is like a flock of goats,
moving down the slopes of Gilead.
6 Your teeth are like a flock of ewes,
that have come up from the washing;
all of them bear twins,
and not one among them is bereaved.
7 Your cheeks are like halves of a pomegranate
behind your veil.
8 There are sixty queens and eighty concubines,
and maidens without number.
9 My dove, my perfect one, is the only one,
the darling of her mother,
flawless to her that bore her.
The maidens saw her and called her happy;
the queens and concubines also, and they praised her.
10 "Who is this that looks forth like the dawn,
fair as the moon, bright as the sun,
terrible as an army with banners?"

11 I went down to the nut orchard,
to look at the blossoms of the valley,
to see whether the vines had budded,
whether the pomegranates were in bloom.
12 Before I was aware, my fancy set me
in a chariot beside my prince.[c]

13[d] Return, return, O Shulammite!
Return, return, that we may look upon you.

[a] Meaning of Heb uncertain [b] Heb *lapis lazuli* [c] Cn: Meaning of Heb uncertain [d] Ch 7.1 in Heb

Why should you look upon the Shulammite,
as upon a dance before two armies?[a]

7 How graceful are your feet in sandals,
O queenly maiden!
Your rounded thighs are like jewels,
the work of a master hand.
2 Your navel is a rounded bowl
that never lacks mixed wine.
Your belly is a heap of wheat,
encircled with lilies.
3 Your two breasts are like two fawns,
twins of a gazelle.
4 Your neck is like an ivory tower.
Your eyes are pools in Heshbon,
by the gate of Bath-rabbim.
Your nose is like a tower of Lebanon,
overlooking Damascus.
5 Your head crowns you like Carmel,
and your flowing locks are like purple;
a king is held captive in the tresses.[b]

6 How fair and pleasant you are,
O loved one, delectable maiden![c]
7 You are stately[d] as a palm tree,
and your breasts are like its clusters.
8 I say I will climb the palm tree
and lay hold of its branches.
O may your breasts be like clusters of the vine,
and the scent of your breath like apples,
9 and your kisses[e] like the best wine
that goes down[f] smoothly,
gliding over lips and teeth.[g]

10 I am my beloved's,
and his desire is for me.
11 Come, my beloved,
let us go forth into the fields,
and lodge in the villages;
12 let us go out early to the vineyards,
and see whether the vines have budded,
whether the grape blossoms have opened
and the pomegranates are in bloom.
There I will give you my love.
13 The mandrakes give forth fragrance,
and over our doors are all choice fruits,
new as well as old,
which I have laid up for you, O my
beloved.

8 O that you were like a brother to me,
who nursed at my mother's breast!
If I met you outside, I would kiss you,
and no one would despise me.
2 I would lead you and bring you
into the house of my mother,
and into the chamber of the one who
bore me.[h]
I would give you spiced wine to drink,
the juice of my pomegranates.
3 O that his left hand were under my head,
and that his right hand embraced me!
4 I adjure you, O daughters of Jerusalem,
do not stir up or awaken love
until it is ready!

5 Who is that coming up from the wilderness,
leaning upon her beloved?

Under the apple tree I awakened you.
There your mother was in labor with you;
there she who bore you was in labor.

6 Set me as a seal upon your heart,
as a seal upon your arm;
for love is strong as death,
passion fierce as the grave.
Its flashes are flashes of fire,
a raging flame.
7 Many waters cannot quench love,
neither can floods drown it.
If one offered for love
all the wealth of one's house,
it would be utterly scorned.

8 We have a little sister,
and she has no breasts.

[a] Or *dance of Mahanaim* [b] Meaning of Heb uncertain [c] Syr: Heb *in delights* [d] Heb *This your stature is*
[e] Heb *palate* [f] Heb *down for my lover* [g] Gk Syr Vg: Heb *lips of sleepers*
[h] Gk Syr: Heb *my mother; she* (or *you*) *will teach me*

What shall we do for our sister,
on the day when she is spoken for?
9 If she is a wall,
we will build upon her a battlement of silver;
but if she is a door,
we will enclose her with boards of cedar.
10 I was a wall,
and my breasts were like towers;
then I was in his eyes
as one who brings[a] peace.
11 Solomon had a vineyard at Baal-hamon;
he entrusted the vineyard to keepers;
each one was to bring for its fruit a thousand pieces of silver.
12 My vineyard, my very own, is for myself;
you, O Solomon, may have the thousand,
and the keepers of the fruit two hundred!

13 O you who dwell in the gardens,
my companions are listening for your voice;
let me hear it.

14 Make haste, my beloved,
and be like a gazelle
or a young stag
upon the mountains of spices!

[a] Or *finds*

The Prophets

INTRODUCTION

Lai Ling Elizabeth Ngan

The Christian Bible differs from the Hebrew Bible in its ordering of Scriptures. The second section of the Hebrew Bible is known as *Nevi'im*, "the Prophets." It consists of two subdivisions: the "Former Prophets," including Joshua, Judges, 1 and 2 Samuel, and 1 and 2 Kings (which in Christian Bibles and in *The Peoples' Bible* are numbered among a separate set of writings, the "Historical Books": see the introduction on p. 340), and the "Latter Prophets," including Isaiah, Jeremiah, Ezekiel, and the Book of the Twelve (Hosea–Malachi), which in Christian Bibles are simply labeled "The Prophets." These books follow here.

Prophecy and divination were common phenomena throughout the ancient Near East. While Israel shared in these experiences with its neighbors, the Hebrew Bible condemns diviners from outside Israel, but accepts prophets as divine messengers—even when they were associated with divination. (Divination—an umbrella category for a number of Hebrew words—is hard to define, but generally involves trying to determine the future by manipulating sacred things.) The Hebrew Bible further distinguishes "true" from "false" prophets in Israel, and tends to represent the former as a distinct minority (see, for example, 1 Kings 22)—even opposing the prevailing religion of the nation (as in the book of Jeremiah, for example, 1:18-19).

According to the Bible, the messages the (true) prophets delivered grew out of an intimate relationship with God. In *The Prophets*, Abraham J. Heschel wrote that a prophet was in "communion with the divine consciousness which comes through the prophet's reflection

of, or participation in, the divine pathos." Prophets delivered words of indictment, judgment, comfort, and hope to their audiences; they also presented controversies to God and pleaded for the people.

A prominent theme in both the Former and Latter Prophets is the relationship between prophecy (or promise) and fulfillment. According to Deut 18:20-22, the words of a true prophet must come true. The stories and pronouncements of the prophets in the Hebrew Bible were likely preserved because what they said came true, and the people ultimately found their stories and sayings to be meaningful and formative for their understanding of YHWH and the LORD's activities in the history of Israel.

Another prominent theme is God's covenant faithfulness, which is often contrasted with Israel's infidelity and idolatry. The prophets preached the exclusive worship of YHWH, but the Israelites struggled throughout their history to determine who this YHWH they worshiped was. The prophetic books also present an ethical norm consistent with the teaching of the Torah: caring for the vulnerable of society, justice in every facet of life, and mutuality are expected of God's people.

The Former Prophets

In Christian Bibles, the Former Prophets are considered part of the Historical Books because they purport to recount the history of ancient Israel, beginning where Deuteronomy left off. Because they present that history from the perspective of Deuteronomy, scholars have named them together the Deuteronomistic History. This history tells the stories of Israel from the time of Joshua to the end of Judah in early sixth century BCE.

These so-called Historical Books are not historical as most twenty-first century readers understand that word. The stories in them are not the result of the objective, sequential reporting of events. Their stories were selected and written to describe and emphasize God's activity in Israel's history, and they reflect the writers' social contexts, theology, and intentions. These stories and traditions went through a long history of transmission and editing. Most scholars agree that the Babylonian exile was the crisis that precipitated the formation of the Torah and much of the Prophets. As *prophetic* books, Joshua, Judges, 1 and 2 Samuel, and 1 and 2 Kings invite readers to reflect upon the messages they contain (Josh 1:8).

The stories and traditions were collected from many sources: tribes, clans, and families; royal archives and annuals; books of poetry; and songs such as the Book of Jashar (2 Sam 1:18), the Song of Deborah, and the Song of Hannah. The scholar Martin Noth was the first person to recognize that the editors of the Former Prophets were telling Israel's story within a Deuteronomic framework, and therafter these four books have also been called the Deuteronomistic History.

The Deuteronomistic History provided an explanation to readers in the exilic and postexilic periods for their predicament in the Diaspora and served as a resource for theological reflection.

Latter Prophets

While the respective "Former Prophets" (the prophets who appear in the Deuteronomistic History) were portrayed through stories depicting their personal encounters and miracle-making, little is known about the stories of their counterparts among the Latter Prophets. The superscriptions introducing the following books provide some of the clues to the historical contexts in which these prophets served as YHWH's messengers.

The prophets' scrolls contain collections of oracles associated with the prophets for whom the books were named, but these are not stories about the respective prophets. The book of Jonah is the sole exception. It is a story about the prophet and includes only one oracle, of five Hebrew words (Jonah 3:4). To gain the most understanding of these texts, readers need to correlate the messages of the Latter Prophets with the stories and historical context provided in the Former Prophets. The Latter Prophets were addressing issues of their day, and their messages will be better understood when readers understand the historical contexts.

The Latter Prophets consist of four books: Isaiah, Jeremiah, Ezekiel, and the Book of the Twelve, also called the "Minor Prophets." The book of Daniel follows in Christian Bibles and *The Peoples' Bible*, but is not in this section of the Hebrew Bible, but in the third section, the "Writings." The books of the Latter Prophets are designated as major or minor, based on their length, not their relative importance. The oracles are primarily in poetic form; they were first spoken by the prophets, then later collected and arranged by their disciples and associates. The ministries of the Latter Prophets ranged from the eighth century to the fourth century BCE, but the collection and editing of these books into their final form came even later.

The prophets used common life experiences and expressions to communicate the messages of God. The oracles often used a "messenger formula" that begins an oracle with "thus says the LORD" and ends with "utterance of YHWH," to show that the message had a divine origin. Some oracles are presented in the form of the *rib*, or covenant lawsuit, where God, through the prophet, takes Israel to court. These oracles may borrow their form from cultic pronouncements, blessings and curses, oaths, funerals, dirges and lamentations, and wisdom sayings. A feature common in many oracles is the use of "therefore" as a pivot on which words of indictment turn to words of judgment. The prophet's task was not only to announce condemnation; a major concern was to achieve the repentance of the people so that divine judgment could perhaps be diverted. The prophets often proffered the possibilities of hope and restoration.

The prophets whose oracles were collected into the books of the Latter Prophets were considered authentic messengers of YHWH, in some cases because what they said happened within a relatively short time. When Isaiah said to Ahaz that the threat posed by Rezin and Pekah will disappear in two or three years, it happened (Isa 7:1-9). When Micah and Jeremiah preached that Jerusalem itself would be destroyed, it happened. In other cases, the reader is given no reason why a prophet is recognized as authentic. It is clear, however, that the veracity of the prophets depended on the veracity of their words. The New Testament writers claim some of the prophets' sayings as messianic prophecies pertaining to Jesus of Nazareth. For example, Matthew appropriated the oracles in Isaiah 7–9 to refer to Jesus (Matt 1:23). Contemporary historians recognize that Isaiah's prophecies originally related to an immediate situation, the Syro-Ephraimitic crisis in 734–733; but this judgment has not prevented some readers from understanding that the words of the prophets may have had levels of meaning that the original prophets and their contemporaries may not have recognized. The prophets, both Former and Latter, were concerned about covenant faithfulness to God; they were equally concerned about justice and equity for all people. The relationship with God is reflected in the relationship with neighbors, especially the poor, the weak, and the vulnerable. *Orthodoxy* (right thinking or right belief) and *orthopraxis* (right practice) cannot be separated; they are two sides of the same coin. In a world filled with injustice and inequity, where the poor and hungry are ignored, where racial equality remains a still unfulfilled dream, where women are discriminated against and belittled, where all kinds of -isms are deeply entrenched, the words of the Hebrew prophets call us to judgment. How well would those who consider themselves righteous measure up to the indictments in these books?

As a Chinese American woman, I have experienced discrimination because of my race and gender. I am aware of the difficulty of fitting seamlessly into a predominately white society where Asian Americans are considered "perpetual foreigners." The ancient Israelites had similar experiences, as outsiders in Babylon and other locations of exile. I am aware of my privileged position as an academic who has had the luxury of studying the Bible and of my participation as a U.S. consumer in the exploitation of low-wage laborers to bring me cheap goods from around the world. The prophets preached against the rich who exploited the poor, and against the powerful elites who abused power and distorted justice. These indictments still ring true.

After 586 BCE, the Israelites came to live in diaspora, just as I and many other immigrants live in diaspora in the United States. Where, in the contemporary world, is compassion and understanding for those who are so far from home and struggling to survive? The prophets' words continue to be relevant for our time.

Isaiah

ISAIAH IS ONE OF THE LONGEST BOOKS in the Hebrew Bible and one of the most quoted books in the New Testament. Its main content includes prophetic warnings against Israel and Judah (chs. 1–12), oracles against the nations (13–23), visions of apocalyptic victory (24–27), woe-oracles alongside the announcement of a righteous ruler (28–33), hope for restoration (34–35), and excerpts from 2 Kgs 18–20 (36–39); and from a later time, an announcement of restoration and homecoming (40–55), and a call for reform in a rebuilt community (56–66).

This lengthy collection of literature covers a wide range of historical events, including the end of King Uzziah's fifty-two-year reign (see 2 Kgs 15:1-7; 2 Chronicles 26), the Syro-Ephraimite war (735–732 BCE), the Assyrian King Sennacherib's siege of Jerusalem (701), the Babylonian destruction of Judah (587), the demise of Babylon culminating in the edict of the Persian king Cyrus (539), and the rebuilding of Jerusalem (450). For contemporary readers, the book is a crossroads of different but interconnected historical settings and texts, from the oracles of eighth-century Judean prophet Isaiah to anonymous prophetic messages from the post-exilic age (which scholars call Second Isaiah, chs. 40–55, and Third Isaiah, chs. 56–66).

One case of cultural clash between the prophetic vision and the prophet's people is the *call narrative* (ch. 6), which highlights the contrasts between the holiness of YHWH and the sinfulness of the people, between the corruption of the nobles and the cleansing power of YHWH. The historical setting refers back to the death of King Uzziah, the conclusion of whose long reign could signify an end of relative stability and a beginning of turmoil. In this sociopolitical situation—the anticipation of a new king—the prophet receives the divine call. The threefold chant of "holy" describing the divine presence emphasizes a cultural clash with the people of "unclean lips" (6:5). The moral corruption of the people, from the highest to the lowliest, is exposed (see 1:4, 6, 21). It is no wonder that they cannot truly "see" or "hear" the word of YHWH. A leading motif in Isaiah is humanity's inability to see or hear. Careful readers will find numerous occurrences of this motif throughout the book. Thus the nobles of Israel, in the north, are called mere drunkards whose vision is intoxicated and to whom YHWH's word sounds only as gibberish (28:7-13). The accusation is also applied to those who govern the southern nation, Judah, who are blinded in their own stupidity (29:9-10). Even the prophet himself had to be cleansed of his iniquity so as to hear the divine commissioning (6:7-8). Likewise, the qualifications of a new king include righteousness and the fear of YHWH rather than what is customary to his eyes and ears (11:3-4). In the end, it is YHWH alone who can open the eyes of the blind and the ears of the deaf (35:5; 42:18).

Near the middle of Isaiah is a narrative associated with King Hezekiah (chs. 36–39) that is almost identical to 2 Kgs 18:13—20:19. Scholars have identified the significant role these chapters

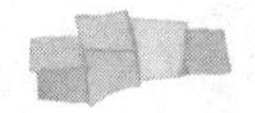

play as a bridge between two seemingly disconnected portions of the book. Furthermore, the name Hezekiah in Hebrew means "YHWH has strengthened." This pun-name came to denote YHWH's strength united with the king's human faith as exemplified in Hezekiah's life and prayers. Hezekiah's firm faith contrasts sharply with that of King Ahaz, who opted instead for a political alliance with Assyria during the crisis of the Syro-Ephraimite war (7:9). Ahaz's decision demonstrated the influence of the prevailing culture, where military weaponry and the plans of superpowers were considered more powerful and appealing than any cry for prayer and for trust in God. This contrast in perspective continues in subsequent chapters, where the artisan's action of "strengthening" idols with nails is ridiculed by the prophet (41:6-7). In today's culture, the prophet's call to repent (6:10, 13; 66:2) collides with the pursuit of military supremacy, just as the poet's mockery resounds loudly against modern idolatries: economic pride, which comes at the cost of exploitation; progress at the expense of ecological decay; and social systems that disenfranchise many.

In reading Isaiah, I am often reminded of my social history and location. As a Korean Christian, I recall the hardship Koreans had to endure during colonization and occupation in the first half of the twentieth century. One of Isaiah's theologically most difficult themes surfaces in the call narrative, when the prophet is ordered to harden the hearts of the people (6:10). The notion that YHWH would whistle to the northern army, sending it to invade YHWH's own people, does show that giant empires are mere tools of YHWH. However, it also presents the challenging question of *theodicy*—the notion that God's goodness and justice will be vindicated (10:5-6, 12-14). Was Korea's hardship a divine chastisement? Was the imperial colonizer a divine instrument? If we turn to YHWH's divine pathos in rebuking the corrupt leaders and masses and listen to the message to the broken-hearted, "Comfort, O comfort" (40:1), the text offers a profound message: Isaiah's God is neither immobilized by nor indifferent to historical and sociopolitical wrongdoings. This God does interrupt and disturb wrongful affairs with divine indignation. But if we carelessly moralize instead, applying this notion to the misfortunes of others, we fall into interpretive misuse.

Such misuse parallels the way the powerful notion of the righteous servant's vicarious suffering (52:13—53:12) has been wrongfully abused in certain Christian interpretations of the passage, in which the servant is identified exclusively with Jesus, and his assailants identified narrowly with Jewish antagonists. Such interpretation leans toward anti-Semitism and fails to recognize potential continuity between the fate of Jesus and the prophet's vision of a righteous servant in the suffering people themselves.

The social settings of the final form of the book would be close to the settings of the so-called Third Isaiah (chs. 56–66), in the postexilic time of rebuilding during the Persian period. Unlike the hopes and dreams of the glorious return to Zion (43:3; 49:23), the rebuilding process became an ongoing experience of confusion, disappointment, and dissension (57:1-2; 59:5-8; 66:22-24). Many exiles lived as a diaspora of small ethnic groups, displaced to the margins yet essential parts of the dominating empires that oppressed them. To those who long to truly see and hear, Isaiah's cry resonates powerfully: "How long, O Lord?" (6:11). As an Asian American, my experiences of the English language barrier converge with the motif, throughout Isaiah, of the inability to see and hear. I wonder how often we see and hear but do not understand (43:8) the silences and voices of fellow aliens, sisters and brothers, in the marginalized locations of a multicultural world. Perhaps, in the prophet's cry "How long, O Lord?" and in a humble effort toward solidarity (1:16-17; 58:6-7), we too can hope to be like the ox and donkey who know their owners (1:3), acknowledging our Maker of weal and woe, darkness and light (40:27-31; 45:7).

— *Hyun Chul Paul Kim*

1 The vision of Isaiah son of Amoz, which he saw concerning Judah and Jerusalem in the days of Uzziah, Jotham, Ahaz, and Hezekiah, kings of Judah.

2 Hear, O heavens, and listen, O earth;
for the LORD has spoken:
I reared children and brought them up,
but they have rebelled against me.
3 The ox knows its owner,
and the donkey its master's crib;
but Israel does not know,
my people do not understand.

4 Ah, sinful nation,
people laden with iniquity,
offspring who do evil,
children who deal corruptly,
who have forsaken the LORD,
who have despised the Holy One of Israel,
who are utterly estranged!

5 Why do you seek further beatings?
Why do you continue to rebel?
The whole head is sick,
and the whole heart faint.
6 From the sole of the foot even to the head,
there is no soundness in it,
but bruises and sores
and bleeding wounds;
they have not been drained, or bound up,
or softened with oil.
7 Your country lies desolate,
your cities are burned with fire;
in your very presence
aliens devour your land;
it is desolate, as overthrown by foreigners.
8 And daughter Zion is left
like a booth in a vineyard,
like a shelter in a cucumber field,
like a besieged city.
9 If the LORD of hosts
had not left us a few survivors,
we would have been like Sodom,
and become like Gomorrah.

10 Hear the word of the LORD,
you rulers of Sodom!
Listen to the teaching of our God,
you people of Gomorrah!
11 What to me is the multitude of your sacrifices?
says the LORD;
I have had enough of burnt offerings of rams
and the fat of fed beasts;
I do not delight in the blood of bulls,
or of lambs, or of goats.

12 When you come to appear before me,[a]
who asked this from your hand?
Trample my courts no more;
13 bringing offerings is futile;
incense is an abomination to me.
New moon and sabbath and calling of convocation—

[a] Or see *my face*

I cannot endure solemn assemblies with
iniquity.
14 Your new moons and your appointed festivals
my soul hates;
they have become a burden to me,
I am weary of bearing them.
15 When you stretch out your hands,
I will hide my eyes from you;
even though you make many prayers,
I will not listen;
your hands are full of blood.
16 Wash yourselves; make yourselves clean;
remove the evil of your doings
from before my eyes;
cease to do evil,
17 learn to do good;
seek justice,
rescue the oppressed,
defend the orphan,
plead for the widow.

18 Come now, let us argue it out,
says the LORD:
though your sins are like scarlet,
they shall be like snow;
though they are red like crimson,
they shall become like wool.
19 If you are willing and obedient,
you shall eat the good of the land;
20 but if you refuse and rebel,
you shall be devoured by the sword;
for the mouth of the LORD has spoken.

21 How the faithful city
has become a whore!
She that was full of justice,
righteousness lodged in her—
but now murderers!
22 Your silver has become dross,
your wine is mixed with water.
23 Your princes are rebels
and companions of thieves.
Everyone loves a bribe
and runs after gifts.
They do not defend the orphan,
and the widow's cause does not come
before them.

24 Therefore says the Sovereign, the LORD of
hosts, the Mighty One of Israel:
Ah, I will pour out my wrath on my enemies,
and avenge myself on my foes!
25 I will turn my hand against you;
I will smelt away your dross as with lye
and remove all your alloy.
26 And I will restore your judges as at the first,
and your counselors as at the beginning.
Afterward you shall be called the city of
righteousness,
the faithful city.

27 Zion shall be redeemed by justice,
and those in her who repent, by
righteousness.
28 But rebels and sinners shall be destroyed
together,
and those who forsake the LORD shall be
consumed.
29 For you shall be ashamed of the oaks
in which you delighted;
and you shall blush for the gardens
that you have chosen.
30 For you shall be like an oak
whose leaf withers,
and like a garden without water.
31 The strong shall become like tinder,
and their work[a] like a spark;
they and their work shall burn together,
with no one to quench them.

2 The word that Isaiah son of Amoz saw concerning Judah and Jerusalem.

2 In days to come
the mountain of the LORD's house
shall be established as the highest of the
mountains,
and shall be raised above the hills;
all the nations shall stream to it.
3 Many peoples shall come and say,

[a] Or *its makers*

"Come, let us go up to the mountain of the
LORD,
to the house of the God of Jacob;
that he may teach us his ways
and that we may walk in his paths."
For out of Zion shall go forth instruction,
and the word of the LORD from Jerusalem.
4 He shall judge between the nations,
and shall arbitrate for many peoples;
they shall beat their swords into plowshares,
and their spears into pruning hooks;
nation shall not lift up sword against nation,
neither shall they learn war any more.

5 O house of Jacob,
come, let us walk
in the light of the LORD!
6 For you have forsaken the ways of[a] your
people,
O house of Jacob.
Indeed they are full of diviners[b] from the east
and of soothsayers like the Philistines,
and they clasp hands with foreigners.
7 Their land is filled with silver and gold,
and there is no end to their treasures;
their land is filled with horses,
and there is no end to their chariots.
8 Their land is filled with idols;
they bow down to the work of their hands,
to what their own fingers have made.
9 And so people are humbled,
and everyone is brought low—
do not forgive them!
10 Enter into the rock,
and hide in the dust
from the terror of the LORD,
and from the glory of his majesty.
11 The haughty eyes of people shall be brought
low,
and the pride of everyone shall be
humbled;
and the LORD alone will be exalted on that
day.
12 For the LORD of hosts has a day
against all that is proud and lofty,
against all that is lifted up and high;[c]
13 against all the cedars of Lebanon,
lofty and lifted up;
and against all the oaks of Bashan;
14 against all the high mountains,
and against all the lofty hills;
15 against every high tower,
and against every fortified wall;
16 against all the ships of Tarshish,
and against all the beautiful craft.[d]
17 The haughtiness of people shall be humbled,
and the pride of everyone shall be brought
low;
and the LORD alone will be exalted on that
day.
18 The idols shall utterly pass away.
19 Enter the caves of the rocks
and the holes of the ground,
from the terror of the LORD,
and from the glory of his majesty,
when he rises to terrify the earth.
20 On that day people will throw away
to the moles and to the bats
their idols of silver and their idols of gold,
which they made for themselves to
worship,
21 to enter the caverns of the rocks
and the clefts in the crags,
from the terror of the LORD,
and from the glory of his majesty,
when he rises to terrify the earth.
22 Turn away from mortals,
who have only breath in their nostrils,
for of what account are they?

3 For now the Sovereign, the LORD of hosts,
is taking away from Jerusalem and from
Judah
support and staff—
all support of bread,
and all support of water—
2 warrior and soldier,
judge and prophet,
diviner and elder,

[a] Heb lacks *the ways of* [b] Cn: Heb lacks *of diviners* [c] Cn Compare Gk: Heb *low*
[d] Compare Gk: Meaning of Heb uncertain

3 captain of fifty
and dignitary,
counselor and skillful magician
and expert enchanter.
4 And I will make boys their princes,
and babes shall rule over them.
5 The people will be oppressed,
everyone by another
and everyone by a neighbor;
the youth will be insolent to the elder,
and the base to the honorable.

6 Someone will even seize a relative,
a member of the clan, saying,
"You have a cloak;
you shall be our leader,
and this heap of ruins
shall be under your rule."
7 But the other will cry out on that day, saying,
"I will not be a healer;
in my house there is neither bread nor
cloak;
you shall not make me
leader of the people."
8 For Jerusalem has stumbled
and Judah has fallen,
because their speech and their deeds are
against the LORD,
defying his glorious presence.

9 The look on their faces bears witness against
them;
they proclaim their sin like Sodom,
they do not hide it.
Woe to them!
For they have brought evil on themselves.
10 Tell the innocent how fortunate they are,
for they shall eat the fruit of their labors.
11 Woe to the guilty! How unfortunate they are,
for what their hands have done shall be
done to them.
12 My people—children are their oppressors,
and women rule over them.
O my people, your leaders mislead you,
and confuse the course of your paths.

13 The LORD rises to argue his case;
he stands to judge the peoples.
14 The LORD enters into judgment
with the elders and princes of his
people:
It is you who have devoured the vineyard;
the spoil of the poor is in your houses.
15 What do you mean by crushing my people,
by grinding the face of the poor? says the
Lord GOD of hosts.

16 The LORD said:
Because the daughters of Zion are haughty
and walk with outstretched necks,
glancing wantonly with their eyes,
mincing along as they go,
tinkling with their feet;
17 the Lord will afflict with scabs
the heads of the daughters of Zion,
and the LORD will lay bare their secret
parts.

18 In that day the Lord will take away the finery of the anklets, the headbands, and the crescents; 19the pendants, the bracelets, and the
scarfs; 20the headdresses, the armlets, the sashes,
the perfume boxes, and the amulets; 21the signet
rings and nose rings; 22the festal robes, the man-
tles, the cloaks, and the handbags; 23the garments
of gauze, the linen garments, the turbans, and the
veils.
24 Instead of perfume there will be a stench;
and instead of a sash, a rope;
and instead of well-set hair, baldness;
and instead of a rich robe, a binding of
sackcloth;
instead of beauty, shame.[a]
25 Your men shall fall by the sword
and your warriors in battle.
26 And her gates shall lament and mourn;
ravaged, she shall sit upon the ground.

4 Seven women shall take hold of one man in
that day, saying,
"We will eat our own bread and wear our
own clothes;

[a] Q Ms: MT lacks *shame*

just let us be called by your name;
take away our disgrace."

2 On that day the branch of the LORD shall
be beautiful and glorious, and the fruit of the
land shall be the pride and glory of the survivors
of Israel. 3 Whoever is left in Zion and remains in
Jerusalem will be called holy, everyone who has
been recorded for life in Jerusalem, 4 once the
Lord has washed away the filth of the daughters
of Zion and cleansed the bloodstains of Jerusalem from its midst by a spirit of judgment and by
a spirit of burning. 5 Then the LORD will create
over the whole site of Mount Zion and over its
places of assembly a cloud by day and smoke and
the shining of a flaming fire by night. Indeed over
all the glory there will be a canopy. 6 It will serve
as a pavilion, a shade by day from the heat, and a
refuge and a shelter from the storm and rain.

5 Let me sing for my beloved
my love-song concerning his vineyard:
My beloved had a vineyard
on a very fertile hill.
2 He dug it and cleared it of stones,
and planted it with choice vines;
he built a watchtower in the midst of it,
and hewed out a wine vat in it;
he expected it to yield grapes,
but it yielded wild grapes.

3 And now, inhabitants of Jerusalem
and people of Judah,
judge between me
and my vineyard.
4 What more was there to do for my vineyard
that I have not done in it?
When I expected it to yield grapes,
why did it yield wild grapes?

5 And now I will tell you
what I will do to my vineyard.
I will remove its hedge,
and it shall be devoured;
I will break down its wall,
and it shall be trampled down.
6 I will make it a waste;
it shall not be pruned or hoed,
and it shall be overgrown with briers and thorns;
I will also command the clouds
that they rain no rain upon it.

7 For the vineyard of the LORD of hosts
is the house of Israel,
and the people of Judah
are his pleasant planting;
he expected justice,
but saw bloodshed;
righteousness,
but heard a cry!
8 Ah, you who join house to house,
who add field to field,
until there is room for no one but you,
and you are left to live alone
in the midst of the land!
9 The LORD of hosts has sworn in my hearing:
Surely many houses shall be desolate,
large and beautiful houses, without inhabitant.
10 For ten acres of vineyard shall yield but one bath,
and a homer of seed shall yield a mere ephah.[a]

11 Ah, you who rise early in the morning
in pursuit of strong drink,
who linger in the evening
to be inflamed by wine,
12 whose feasts consist of lyre and harp,
tambourine and flute and wine,
but who do not regard the deeds of the LORD,
or see the work of his hands!
13 Therefore my people go into exile without knowledge;
their nobles are dying of hunger,
and their multitude is parched with thirst.

[a] The Heb *bath, homer,* and *ephah* are measures of quantity

14 Therefore Sheol has enlarged its appetite
and opened its mouth beyond measure;
the nobility of Jerusalem[a] and her multitude
go down,
her throng and all who exult in her.
15 People are bowed down, everyone is brought
low,
and the eyes of the haughty are humbled.
16 But the LORD of hosts is exalted by justice,
and the Holy God shows himself holy by
righteousness.
17 Then the lambs shall graze as in their pasture,
fatlings and kids[b] shall feed among the
ruins.

18 Ah, you who drag iniquity along with cords
of falsehood,
who drag sin along as with cart ropes,
19 who say, "Let him make haste,
let him speed his work
that we may see it;
let the plan of the Holy One of Israel hasten
to fulfillment,
that we may know it!"
20 Ah, you who call evil good
and good evil,
who put darkness for light
and light for darkness,
who put bitter for sweet
and sweet for bitter!
21 Ah, you who are wise in your own eyes,
and shrewd in your own sight!
22 Ah, you who are heroes in drinking wine
and valiant at mixing drink,
23 who acquit the guilty for a bribe,
and deprive the innocent of their rights!
24 Therefore, as the tongue of fire devours the
stubble,
and as dry grass sinks down in the flame,
so their root will become rotten,
and their blossom go up like dust;
for they have rejected the instruction of the
LORD of hosts,
and have despised the word of the Holy
One of Israel.

25 Therefore the anger of the LORD was kindled
against his people,
and he stretched out his hand against them
and struck them;
the mountains quaked,
and their corpses were like refuse
in the streets.
For all this his anger has not turned away,
and his hand is stretched out still.

26 He will raise a signal for a nation far away,
and whistle for a people at the ends of the
earth;
Here they come, swiftly, speedily!
27 None of them is weary, none stumbles,
none slumbers or sleeps,
not a loincloth is loose,
not a sandal-thong broken;
28 their arrows are sharp,
all their bows bent,
their horses' hoofs seem like flint,
and their wheels like the whirlwind.
29 Their roaring is like a lion,
like young lions they roar;
they growl and seize their prey,
they carry it off, and no one can
rescue.
30 They will roar over it on that day,
like the roaring of the sea.
And if one look to the land—
only darkness and distress;
and the light grows dark with clouds.

6 In the year that King Uzziah died, I saw the
Lord sitting on a throne, high and lofty; and
the hem of his robe filled the temple. 2Seraphs
were in attendance above him; each had six wings:
with two they covered their faces, and with two
they covered their feet, and with two they flew.
3And one called to another and said:
"Holy, holy, holy is the LORD of hosts;
the whole earth is full of his glory."
4The pivots[c] on the thresholds shook at the
voices of those who called, and the house filled
with smoke. 5And I said: "Woe is me! I am lost,

[a] Heb *her nobility* [b] Cn Compare Gk: Heb *aliens* [c] Meaning of Heb uncertain

for I am a man of unclean lips, and I live among a
people of unclean lips; yet my eyes have seen the
King, the LORD of hosts!"
6 Then one of the seraphs flew to me, holding
a live coal that had been taken from the altar with
a pair of tongs. 7 The seraph[a] touched my mouth
with it and said: "Now that this has touched your
lips, your guilt has departed and your sin is blotted out." 8 Then I heard the voice of the Lord saying, "Whom shall I send, and who will go for us?"
And I said, "Here am I; send me!" 9 And he said,
"Go and say to this people:

'Keep listening, but do not comprehend;
keep looking, but do not understand.'
10 Make the mind of this people dull,
and stop their ears,
and shut their eyes,
so that they may not look with their eyes,
and listen with their ears,
and comprehend with their minds,
and turn and be healed."
11 Then I said, "How long, O Lord?" And he said:
"Until cities lie waste
without inhabitant,
and houses without people,
and the land is utterly desolate;
12 until the LORD sends everyone far away,
and vast is the emptiness in the midst of the land.
13 Even if a tenth part remain in it,
it will be burned again,
like a terebinth or an oak
whose stump remains standing
when it is felled."[b]
The holy seed is its stump.

7 In the days of Ahaz son of Jotham son of Uzziah, king of Judah, King Rezin of Aram and
King Pekah son of Remaliah of Israel went up to
attack Jerusalem, but could not mount an attack
against it. 2 When the house of David heard that
Aram had allied itself with Ephraim, the heart of
Ahaz[c] and the heart of his people shook as the
trees of the forest shake before the wind.
3 Then the LORD said to Isaiah, Go out to
meet Ahaz, you and your son Shear-jashub,[d] at
the end of the conduit of the upper pool on the
highway to the Fuller's Field, 4 and say to him,
Take heed, be quiet, do not fear, and do not let
your heart be faint because of these two smoldering stumps of firebrands, because of the fierce anger of Rezin and Aram and the son of Remaliah.
5 Because Aram—with Ephraim and the son of
Remaliah—has plotted evil against you, saying,
6 Let us go up against Judah and cut off Jerusalem[e]
and conquer it for ourselves and make the son of
Tabeel king in it; 7 therefore thus says the Lord
GOD:

It shall not stand,
and it shall not come to pass.
8 For the head of Aram is Damascus,
and the head of Damascus is Rezin.
(Within sixty-five years Ephraim will be shattered, no longer a people.)
9 The head of Ephraim is Samaria,
and the head of Samaria is the son of Remaliah.

Isaiah 6:1-13

Neither truth nor love tends to flow freely when we are comfortably in the middle of society, successful in society's terms, profiting from the way things are arranged. Certain crucial truths about our lives are more easily seen when we are on the edge, at the margin, when we are poor or sick or hungry or in prison—and these truths can break the heart open to compassion. When we live on the edge, or take the view of those who do, we can more easily see our world and what the Lord requires. 48

— ***Parker J. Palmer***

[a] Heb *He* [b] Meaning of Heb uncertain [c] Heb *his heart* [d] That is *A remnant shall return* [e] Heb *cut it off*

If you do not stand firm in faith,
you shall not stand at all.
10 Again the LORD spoke to Ahaz, saying,
11Ask a sign of the LORD your God; let it be deep
as Sheol or high as heaven. 12But Ahaz said, I will
not ask, and I will not put the LORD to the test.
13Then Isaiah[a] said: "Hear then, O house of David!
Is it too little for you to weary mortals, that you
weary my God also? 14Therefore the Lord himself
will give you a sign. Look, the young woman[b] is
with child and shall bear a son, and shall name him
Immanuel.[c] 15He shall eat curds and honey by the
time he knows how to refuse the evil and choose
the good. 16For before the child knows how to refuse the evil and choose the good, the land before
whose two kings you are in dread will be deserted.
17The LORD will bring on you and on your people
and on your ancestral house such days as have not
come since the day that Ephraim departed from
Judah—the king of Assyria."
18 On that day the LORD will whistle for the
fly that is at the sources of the streams of Egypt,
and for the bee that is in the land of Assyria.
19And they will all come and settle in the steep
ravines, and in the clefts of the rocks, and on all
the thornbushes, and on all the pastures.
20 On that day the Lord will shave with a
razor hired beyond the River—with the king of
Assyria—the head and the hair of the feet, and it
will take off the beard as well.
21 On that day one will keep alive a young
cow and two sheep, 22and will eat curds because
of the abundance of milk that they give; for everyone that is left in the land shall eat curds and
honey.
23 On that day every place where there used
to be a thousand vines, worth a thousand shekels
of silver, will become briers and thorns. 24With
bow and arrows one will go there, for all the land
will be briers and thorns; 25and as for all the hills
that used to be hoed with a hoe, you will not go
there for fear of briers and thorns; but they will
become a place where cattle are let loose and
where sheep tread.

8 Then the LORD said to me, Take a large tablet and write on it in common characters,
"Belonging to Maher-shalal-hash-baz,"[d] 2and
have it attested[e] for me by reliable witnesses, the
priest Uriah and Zechariah son of Jeberechiah.
3And I went to the prophetess, and she conceived
and bore a son. Then the LORD said to me, Name
him Maher-shalal-hash-baz; 4for before the child
knows how to call "My father" or "My mother,"
the wealth of Damascus and the spoil of Samaria
will be carried away by the king of Assyria.
5 The LORD spoke to me again: 6Because this
people has refused the waters of Shiloah that flow
gently, and melt in fear before[f] Rezin and the son
of Remaliah; 7therefore, the Lord is bringing up
against it the mighty flood waters of the River, the
king of Assyria and all his glory; it will rise above
all its channels and overflow all its banks; 8it will
sweep on into Judah as a flood, and, pouring over,
it will reach up to the neck; and its outspread
wings will fill the breadth of your land, O Immanuel.

9 Band together, you peoples, and be
dismayed;
listen, all you far countries;
gird yourselves and be dismayed;
gird yourselves and be dismayed!
10 Take counsel together, but it shall be brought
to naught;
speak a word, but it will not stand,
for God is with us.[g]

11 For the LORD spoke thus to me while his
hand was strong upon me, and warned me not
to walk in the way of this people, saying: 12Do
not call conspiracy all that this people calls conspiracy, and do not fear what it fears, or be in
dread. 13But the LORD of hosts, him you shall
regard as holy; let him be your fear, and let him
be your dread. 14He will become a sanctuary, a
stone one strikes against; for both houses of Israel he will become a rock one stumbles over—a
trap and a snare for the inhabitants of Jerusalem.
15And many among them shall stumble; they

[a] Heb *he* [b] Gk *the virgin* [c] That is *God is with us* [d] That is *The spoil speeds, the prey hastens* [e] Q Ms Gk Syr: MT *and I caused to be attested* [f] Cn: Meaning of Heb uncertain [g] Heb *immanu el*

shall fall and be broken; they shall be snared and
taken.
16 Bind up the testimony, seal the teaching
among my disciples. 17 I will wait for the LORD,
who is hiding his face from the house of Jacob,
and I will hope in him. 18 See, I and the children
whom the LORD has given me are signs and
portents in Israel from the LORD of hosts, who
dwells on Mount Zion. 19 Now if people say to
you, "Consult the ghosts and the familiar spirits
that chirp and mutter; should not a people consult their gods, the dead on behalf of the living,
20 for teaching and for instruction?" surely, those
who speak like this will have no dawn! 21 They
will pass through the land,[a] greatly distressed
and hungry; when they are hungry, they will be
enraged and will curse[b] their king and their gods.
They will turn their faces upward, 22 or they will
look to the earth, but will see only distress and
darkness, the gloom of anguish; and they will be
thrust into thick darkness.[c]

9 [d] But there will be no gloom for those who
were in anguish. In the former time he
brought into contempt the land of Zebulun and
the land of Naphtali, but in the latter time he will
make glorious the way of the sea, the land beyond
the Jordan, Galilee of the nations.

2[e] The people who walked in darkness
have seen a great light;
those who lived in a land of deep darkness—
on them light has shined.
3 You have multiplied the nation,
you have increased its joy;
they rejoice before you
as with joy at the harvest,
as people exult when dividing plunder.
4 For the yoke of their burden,
and the bar across their shoulders,
the rod of their oppressor,
you have broken as on the day of Midian.
5 For all the boots of the tramping warriors
and all the garments rolled in blood
shall be burned as fuel for the fire.
6 For a child has been born for us,
a son given to us;
authority rests upon his shoulders;
and he is named
Wonderful Counselor, Mighty God,
Everlasting Father, Prince of Peace.
7 His authority shall grow continually,
and there shall be endless peace
for the throne of David and his kingdom.
He will establish and uphold it
with justice and with righteousness
from this time onward and forevermore.
The zeal of the LORD of hosts will do this.

8 The Lord sent a word against Jacob,
and it fell on Israel;
9 and all the people knew it—
Ephraim and the inhabitants of Samaria—
but in pride and arrogance of heart they
said:
10 "The bricks have fallen,
but we will build with dressed stones;
the sycamores have been cut down,
but we will put cedars in their place."
11 So the LORD raised adversaries[f] against
them,
and stirred up their enemies,
12 the Arameans on the east and the Philistines
on the west,

Isaiah 9:2-7

The stirring arias of Handel's *Messiah* have made these verses some of the most familiar in the Bible to the general public. Yet Handel had to select his texts carefully to craft the impression that they pointed prophetically to Jesus of Nazareth. The climactic verses 4 and 5 speak of the removal of the oppressor and an end to conquest and war, realities still too dismally evident today. Isaiah's words are stirring pointers to a future for which we still long and toward which we must work.

—NE

[a] Heb *it* [b] Or *curse by* [c] Meaning of Heb uncertain [d] Ch 8.23 in Heb [e] Ch 9.1 in Heb
[f] Cn: Heb *the adversaries of Rezin*

and they devoured Israel with open
mouth.
For all this his anger has not turned away;
his hand is stretched out still.

13 The people did not turn to him who struck
them,
or seek the LORD of hosts.
14 So the LORD cut off from Israel head and tail,
palm branch and reed in one day—
15 elders and dignitaries are the head,
and prophets who teach lies are the tail;
16 for those who led this people led them
astray,
and those who were led by them were left
in confusion.
17 That is why the Lord did not have pity on[a]
their young people,
or compassion on their orphans and
widows;
for everyone was godless and an evildoer,
and every mouth spoke folly.
For all this his anger has not turned away;
his hand is stretched out still.

18 For wickedness burned like a fire,
consuming briers and thorns;
it kindled the thickets of the forest,
and they swirled upward in a column of
smoke.
19 Through the wrath of the LORD of hosts
the land was burned,
and the people became like fuel for the fire;
no one spared another.
20 They gorged on the right, but still were
hungry,
and they devoured on the left, but were
not satisfied;
they devoured the flesh of their own
kindred;[b]
21 Manasseh devoured Ephraim, and Ephraim
Manasseh,
and together they were against Judah.
For all this his anger has not turned away;
his hand is stretched out still.

10 Ah, you who make iniquitous decrees,
who write oppressive statutes,
2 to turn aside the needy from justice
and to rob the poor of my people of their
right,
that widows may be your spoil,
and that you may make the orphans your
prey!
3 What will you do on the day of punishment,
in the calamity that will come from far
away?
To whom will you flee for help,
and where will you leave your wealth,
4 so as not to crouch among the prisoners
or fall among the slain?
For all this his anger has not turned away;
his hand is stretched out still.

5 Ah, Assyria, the rod of my anger—
the club in their hands is my fury!
6 Against a godless nation I send him,
and against the people of my wrath I
command him,
to take spoil and seize plunder,
and to tread them down like the mire of
the streets.
7 But this is not what he intends,
nor does he have this in mind;
but it is in his heart to destroy,
and to cut off nations not a few.
8 For he says:
"Are not my commanders all kings?
9 Is not Calno like Carchemish?
Is not Hamath like Arpad?
Is not Samaria like Damascus?
10 As my hand has reached to the kingdoms of
the idols
whose images were greater than those of
Jerusalem and Samaria,
11 shall I not do to Jerusalem and her idols
what I have done to Samaria and her
images?"

12 When the Lord has finished all his work
on Mount Zion and on Jerusalem, he[c] will punish

[a] Q Ms: MT *rejoice over* [b] Or *arm* [c] Heb *I*

the arrogant boasting of the king of Assyria and
his haughty pride. 13For he says:

"By the strength of my hand I have done it,
and by my wisdom, for I have understanding;
I have removed the boundaries of peoples,
and have plundered their treasures;
like a bull I have brought down those who sat on thrones.
14 My hand has found, like a nest,
the wealth of the peoples;
and as one gathers eggs that have been forsaken,
so I have gathered all the earth;
and there was none that moved a wing,
or opened its mouth, or chirped."

15 Shall the ax vaunt itself over the one who wields it,
or the saw magnify itself against the one who handles it?
As if a rod should raise the one who lifts it up,
or as if a staff should lift the one who is not wood!
16 Therefore the Sovereign, the LORD of hosts,
will send wasting sickness among his stout warriors,
and under his glory a burning will be kindled,
like the burning of fire.
17 The light of Israel will become a fire,
and his Holy One a flame;
and it will burn and devour
his thorns and briers in one day.
18 The glory of his forest and his fruitful land
the LORD will destroy, both soul and body,
and it will be as when an invalid wastes away.
19 The remnant of the trees of his forest will be so few
that a child can write them down.

20 On that day the remnant of Israel and
the survivors of the house of Jacob will no more
lean on the one who struck them, but will lean
on the LORD, the Holy One of Israel, in truth.
21A remnant will return, the remnant of Jacob, to
the mighty God. 22For though your people Israel
were like the sand of the sea, only a remnant of
them will return. Destruction is decreed, overflowing with righteousness. 23For the Lord GOD
of hosts will make a full end, as decreed, in all the
earth.[a]

24 Therefore thus says the Lord GOD of hosts:
O my people, who live in Zion, do not be afraid of
the Assyrians when they beat you with a rod and
lift up their staff against you as the Egyptians did.
25For in a very little while my indignation will
come to an end, and my anger will be directed to
their destruction. 26The LORD of hosts will wield
a whip against them, as when he struck Midian at
the rock of Oreb; his staff will be over the sea, and
he will lift it as he did in Egypt. 27On that day his
burden will be removed from your shoulder, and
his yoke will be destroyed from your neck.

He has gone up from Rimmon,[b]
28 he has come to Aiath;
he has passed through Migron,
at Michmash he stores his baggage;
29 they have crossed over the pass,
at Geba they lodge for the night;
Ramah trembles,
Gibeah of Saul has fled.
30 Cry aloud, O daughter Gallim!
Listen, O Laishah!
Answer her, O Anathoth!
31 Madmenah is in flight,
the inhabitants of Gebim flee for safety.
32 This very day he will halt at Nob,
he will shake his fist
at the mount of daughter Zion,
the hill of Jerusalem.

33 Look, the Sovereign, the LORD of hosts,
will lop the boughs with terrifying power;
the tallest trees will be cut down,
and the lofty will be brought low.
34 He will hack down the thickets of the forest
with an ax,

[a] Or *land* [b] Cn: Heb *and his yoke from your neck, and a yoke will be destroyed because of fatness*

and Lebanon with its majestic trees[a] will
fall.

11 A shoot shall come out from the stump
of Jesse,
and a branch shall grow out of his roots.
2 The spirit of the LORD shall rest on him,
the spirit of wisdom and understanding,
the spirit of counsel and might,
the spirit of knowledge and the fear of the
LORD.
3 His delight shall be in the fear of the LORD.

He shall not judge by what his eyes see,
or decide by what his ears hear;
4 but with righteousness he shall judge the poor,
and decide with equity for the meek of the
earth;
he shall strike the earth with the rod of his
mouth,
and with the breath of his lips he shall kill
the wicked.
5 Righteousness shall be the belt around his
waist,
and faithfulness the belt around his loins.

6 The wolf shall live with the lamb,
the leopard shall lie down with the kid,
the calf and the lion and the fatling together,
and a little child shall lead them.
7 The cow and the bear shall graze,
their young shall lie down together;
and the lion shall eat straw like the ox.
8 The nursing child shall play over the hole of
the asp,
and the weaned child shall put its hand on
the adder's den.
9 They will not hurt or destroy
on all my holy mountain;
for the earth will be full of the knowledge of
the LORD
as the waters cover the sea.

10 On that day the root of Jesse shall stand as
a signal to the peoples; the nations shall inquire
of him, and his dwelling shall be glorious.

11 On that day the Lord will extend his hand
yet a second time to recover the remnant that is
left of his people, from Assyria, from Egypt, from
Pathros, from Ethiopia,[b] from Elam, from Shinar,
from Hamath, and from the coastlands of the sea.
12 He will raise a signal for the nations,
and will assemble the outcasts of Israel,
and gather the dispersed of Judah
from the four corners of the earth.
13 The jealousy of Ephraim shall depart,
the hostility of Judah shall be cut off;
Ephraim shall not be jealous of Judah,
and Judah shall not be hostile towards
Ephraim.
14 But they shall swoop down on the backs of
the Philistines in the west,
together they shall plunder the people of
the east.
They shall put forth their hand against Edom
and Moab,
and the Ammonites shall obey them.
15 And the LORD will utterly destroy
the tongue of the sea of Egypt;
and will wave his hand over the River
with his scorching wind;
and will split it into seven channels,
and make a way to cross on foot;
16 so there shall be a highway from Assyria
for the remnant that is left of his
people,
as there was for Israel
when they came up from the land of
Egypt.

12 You will say in that day:
I will give thanks to you, O LORD,
for though you were angry with me,
your anger turned away,
and you comforted me.

2 Surely God is my salvation;
I will trust, and will not be afraid,
for the LORD GOD[c] is my strength and my
might;
he has become my salvation.

[a] Cn Compare Gk Vg: Heb *with a majestic one* [b] Or *Nubia*; Heb *Cush* [c] Heb *for Yah, the LORD*

3 With joy you will draw water from the wells
of salvation. 4And you will say in that day:
Give thanks to the LORD,
call on his name;
make known his deeds among the nations;
proclaim that his name is exalted.

5 Sing praises to the LORD, for he has done gloriously;
let this be known[a] in all the earth.
6 Shout aloud and sing for joy, O royal[b] Zion,
for great in your midst is the Holy One of Israel.

13 The oracle concerning Babylon that Isaiah son of Amoz saw.

2 On a bare hill raise a signal,
cry aloud to them;
wave the hand for them to enter
the gates of the nobles.
3 I myself have commanded my consecrated ones,
have summoned my warriors, my proudly exulting ones,
to execute my anger.

4 Listen, a tumult on the mountains
as of a great multitude!
Listen, an uproar of kingdoms,
of nations gathering together!
The LORD of hosts is mustering
an army for battle.
5 They come from a distant land,
from the end of the heavens,
the LORD and the weapons of his indignation,
to destroy the whole earth.

6 Wail, for the day of the LORD is near;
it will come like destruction from the Almighty![c]
7 Therefore all hands will be feeble,
and every human heart will melt,
8 and they will be dismayed.
Pangs and agony will seize them;
they will be in anguish like a woman in labor.
They will look aghast at one another;
their faces will be aflame.
9 See, the day of the LORD comes,
cruel, with wrath and fierce anger,
to make the earth a desolation,
and to destroy its sinners from it.
10 For the stars of the heavens and their constellations
will not give their light;
the sun will be dark at its rising,
and the moon will not shed its light.
11 I will punish the world for its evil,
and the wicked for their iniquity;
I will put an end to the pride of the arrogant,
and lay low the insolence of tyrants.
12 I will make mortals more rare than fine gold,
and humans than the gold of Ophir.
13 Therefore I will make the heavens tremble,
and the earth will be shaken out of its place,
at the wrath of the LORD of hosts
in the day of his fierce anger.
14 Like a hunted gazelle,
or like sheep with no one to gather them,
all will turn to their own people,
and all will flee to their own lands.
15 Whoever is found will be thrust through,
and whoever is caught will fall by the sword.
16 Their infants will be dashed to pieces
before their eyes;
their houses will be plundered,
and their wives ravished.
17 See, I am stirring up the Medes against them,
who have no regard for silver
and do not delight in gold.
18 Their bows will slaughter the young men;
they will have no mercy on the fruit of the womb;
their eyes will not pity children.
19 And Babylon, the glory of kingdoms,
the splendor and pride of the Chaldeans,

[a] Or *this is made known* [b] Or *O inhabitant of* [c] Traditional rendering of Heb *Shaddai*

will be like Sodom and Gomorrah
when God overthrew them.
20 It will never be inhabited
or lived in for all generations;
Arabs will not pitch their tents there,
shepherds will not make their flocks lie down there.
21 But wild animals will lie down there,
and its houses will be full of howling creatures;
there ostriches will live,
and there goat-demons will dance.
22 Hyenas will cry in its towers,
and jackals in the pleasant palaces;
its time is close at hand,
and its days will not be prolonged.

14 But the LORD will have compassion on
Jacob and will again choose Israel, and
will set them in their own land; and aliens will
join them and attach themselves to the house of
Jacob. 2And the nations will take them and bring
them to their place, and the house of Israel will
possess the nations[a] as male and female slaves in
the LORD's land; they will take captive those who
were their captors, and rule over those who oppressed them.

3 When the LORD has given you rest from
your pain and turmoil and the hard service with
which you were made to serve, 4you will take up
this taunt against the king of Babylon:
How the oppressor has ceased!
How his insolence[b] has ceased!
5 The LORD has broken the staff of the wicked,
the scepter of rulers,
6 that struck down the peoples in wrath
with unceasing blows,
that ruled the nations in anger
with unrelenting persecution.
7 The whole earth is at rest and quiet;
they break forth into singing.
8 The cypresses exult over you,
the cedars of Lebanon, saying,
"Since you were laid low,
no one comes to cut us down."
9 Sheol beneath is stirred up
to meet you when you come;
it rouses the shades to greet you,
all who were leaders of the earth;
it raises from their thrones
all who were kings of the nations.
10 All of them will speak
and say to you:
"You too have become as weak as we!
You have become like us!"
11 Your pomp is brought down to Sheol,
and the sound of your harps;
maggots are the bed beneath you,
and worms are your covering.

12 How you are fallen from heaven,
O Day Star, son of Dawn!
How you are cut down to the ground,
you who laid the nations low!
13 You said in your heart,
"I will ascend to heaven;
I will raise my throne
above the stars of God;
I will sit on the mount of assembly
on the heights of Zaphon;[c]
14 I will ascend to the tops of the clouds,
I will make myself like the Most High."
15 But you are brought down to Sheol,
to the depths of the Pit.
16 Those who see you will stare at you,
and ponder over you:
"Is this the man who made the earth tremble,
who shook kingdoms,
17 who made the world like a desert
and overthrew its cities,
who would not let his prisoners go home?"
18 All the kings of the nations lie in glory,
each in his own tomb;
19 but you are cast out, away from your grave,
like loathsome carrion,[d]
clothed with the dead, those pierced by the sword,
who go down to the stones of the Pit,
like a corpse trampled underfoot.

[a] Heb *them* [b] Q Ms Compare Gk Syr Vg: Meaning of MT uncertain [c] Or *assembly in the far north*
[d] Cn Compare Gk: Heb *like a loathed branch*

20 You will not be joined with them in burial,
because you have destroyed your land,
you have killed your people.

May the descendants of evildoers
nevermore be named!
21 Prepare slaughter for his sons
because of the guilt of their father.[a]
Let them never rise to possess the earth
or cover the face of the world with cities.

22 I will rise up against them, says the LORD
of hosts, and will cut off from Babylon name and
remnant, offspring and posterity, says the LORD.
23 And I will make it a possession of the hedgehog,
and pools of water, and I will sweep it with the
broom of destruction, says the LORD of hosts.

24 The LORD of hosts has sworn:
As I have designed,
so shall it be;
and as I have planned,
so shall it come to pass:
25 I will break the Assyrian in my land,
and on my mountains trample him under foot;
his yoke shall be removed from them,
and his burden from their shoulders.
26 This is the plan that is planned
concerning the whole earth;
and this is the hand that is stretched out
over all the nations.
27 For the LORD of hosts has planned,
and who will annul it?
His hand is stretched out,
and who will turn it back?

28 In the year that King Ahaz died this oracle
came:

29 Do not rejoice, all you Philistines,
that the rod that struck you is broken,
for from the root of the snake will come forth
an adder,
and its fruit will be a flying fiery serpent.
30 The firstborn of the poor will graze,
and the needy lie down in safety;
but I will make your root die of famine,
and your remnant I[b] will kill.
31 Wail, O gate; cry, O city;
melt in fear, O Philistia, all of you!
For smoke comes out of the north,
and there is no straggler in its ranks.

32 What will one answer the messengers of the nation?
"The LORD has founded Zion,
and the needy among his people
will find refuge in her."

15

An oracle concerning Moab.

Because Ar is laid waste in a night,
Moab is undone;
because Kir is laid waste in a night,
Moab is undone.
2 Dibon[c] has gone up to the temple,
to the high places to weep;
over Nebo and over Medeba
Moab wails.
On every head is baldness,
every beard is shorn;
3 in the streets they bind on sackcloth;
on the housetops and in the squares
everyone wails and melts in tears.
4 Heshbon and Elealeh cry out,
their voices are heard as far as Jahaz;
therefore the loins of Moab quiver;[d]
his soul trembles.
5 My heart cries out for Moab;
his fugitives flee to Zoar,
to Eglath-shelishiyah.
For at the ascent of Luhith
they go up weeping;
on the road to Horonaim
they raise a cry of destruction;
6 the waters of Nimrim
are a desolation;

[a] Syr Compare Gk: Heb *fathers* [b] Q Ms Vg: MT *he* [c] Cn: Heb *the house and Dibon*
[d] Cn Compare Gk Syr: Heb *the armed men of Moab cry aloud*

the grass is withered, the new growth fails,
the verdure is no more.
7 Therefore the abundance they have gained
and what they have laid up
they carry away
over the Wadi of the Willows.
8 For a cry has gone
around the land of Moab;
the wailing reaches to Eglaim,
the wailing reaches to Beer-elim.
9 For the waters of Dibon[a] are full of blood;
yet I will bring upon Dibon[a] even more—
a lion for those of Moab who escape,
for the remnant of the land.

16 Send lambs
to the ruler of the land,
from Sela, by way of the desert,
to the mount of daughter Zion.
2 Like fluttering birds,
like scattered nestlings,
so are the daughters of Moab
at the fords of the Arnon.
3 "Give counsel,
grant justice;
make your shade like night
at the height of noon;
hide the outcasts,
do not betray the fugitive;
4 let the outcasts of Moab
settle among you;
be a refuge to them
from the destroyer."

When the oppressor is no more,
and destruction has ceased,
and marauders have vanished from the land,
5 then a throne shall be established in steadfast love
in the tent of David,
and on it shall sit in faithfulness
a ruler who seeks justice
and is swift to do what is right.

6 We have heard of the pride of Moab
—how proud he is!—
of his arrogance, his pride, and his insolence;
his boasts are false.
7 Therefore let Moab wail,
let everyone wail for Moab.
Mourn, utterly stricken,
for the raisin cakes of Kir-hareseth.

8 For the fields of Heshbon languish,
and the vines of Sibmah,
whose clusters once made drunk
the lords of the nations,
reached to Jazer
and strayed to the desert;
their shoots once spread abroad
and crossed over the sea.
9 Therefore I weep with the weeping of Jazer
for the vines of Sibmah;
I drench you with my tears,
O Heshbon and Elealeh;
for the shout over your fruit harvest
and your grain harvest has ceased.
10 Joy and gladness are taken away
from the fruitful field;
and in the vineyards no songs are sung,
no shouts are raised;
no treader treads out wine in the presses;
the vintage-shout is hushed.[b]
11 Therefore my heart throbs like a harp for Moab,
and my very soul for Kir-heres.

12 When Moab presents himself, when he
wearies himself upon the high place, when he
comes to his sanctuary to pray, he will not prevail.
13 This was the word that the LORD spoke
concerning Moab in the past. 14 But now the
LORD says, In three years, like the years of a hired
worker, the glory of Moab will be brought into
contempt, in spite of all its great multitude; and
those who survive will be very few and feeble.

17 An oracle concerning Damascus.

See, Damascus will cease to be a city,
and will become a heap of ruins.

[a] Q Ms Vg Compare Syr: MT *Dimon* [b] Gk: Heb *I have hushed*

2 Her towns will be deserted forever;[a]
they will be places for flocks,
which will lie down, and no one will make
them afraid.
3 The fortress will disappear from Ephraim,
and the kingdom from Damascus;
and the remnant of Aram will be
like the glory of the children of Israel,
says the LORD of hosts.

4 On that day
the glory of Jacob will be brought low,
and the fat of his flesh will grow lean.
5 And it shall be as when reapers gather
standing grain
and their arms harvest the ears,
and as when one gleans the ears of grain
in the Valley of Rephaim.
6 Gleanings will be left in it,
as when an olive tree is beaten—
two or three berries
in the top of the highest bough,
four or five
on the branches of a fruit tree,
says the LORD God of Israel.

7 On that day people will regard their Maker,
and their eyes will look to the Holy One of Israel;
8 they will not have regard for the altars, the work
of their hands, and they will not look to what their
own fingers have made, either the sacred poles[b] or
the altars of incense.
9 On that day their strong cities will be like
the deserted places of the Hivites and the Amorites,[c] which they deserted because of the children of Israel, and there will be desolation.

10 For you have forgotten the God of your
salvation,
and have not remembered the Rock of
your refuge;
therefore, though you plant pleasant
plants
and set out slips of an alien god,
11 though you make them grow on the day that
you plant them,
and make them blossom in the morning
that you sow;
yet the harvest will flee away
in a day of grief and incurable pain.

12 Ah, the thunder of many peoples,
they thunder like the thundering of the sea!
Ah, the roar of nations,
they roar like the roaring of mighty waters!
13 The nations roar like the roaring of many
waters,
but he will rebuke them, and they will flee
far away,
chased like chaff on the mountains before the
wind
and whirling dust before the storm.
14 At evening time, lo, terror!
Before morning, they are no more.
This is the fate of those who despoil us,
and the lot of those who plunder us.

18 Ah, land of whirring wings
beyond the rivers of Ethiopia,[d]
2 sending ambassadors by the Nile
in vessels of papyrus on the waters!
Go, you swift messengers,
to a nation tall and smooth,
to a people feared near and far,
a nation mighty and conquering,
whose land the rivers divide.

3 All you inhabitants of the world,
you who live on the earth,
when a signal is raised on the mountains,
look!
When a trumpet is blown, listen!
4 For thus the LORD said to me:
I will quietly look from my dwelling
like clear heat in sunshine,
like a cloud of dew in the heat of harvest.
5 For before the harvest, when the blossom is
over

[a] Cn Compare Gk: Heb *the cities of Aroer are deserted* [b] Heb *Asherim* [c] Cn Compare Gk: Heb *places of the wood and the highest bough* [d] Or *Nubia*; Heb *Cush*

and the flower becomes a ripening grape,
he will cut off the shoots with pruning hooks,
and the spreading branches he will hew
away.
6 They shall all be left
to the birds of prey of the mountains
and to the animals of the earth.
And the birds of prey will summer on them,
and all the animals of the earth will winter
on them.

7 At that time gifts will be brought to the
LORD of hosts from[a] a people tall and smooth,
from a people feared near and far, a nation mighty
and conquering, whose land the rivers divide, to
Mount Zion, the place of the name of the LORD
of hosts.

19 An oracle concerning Egypt.

See, the LORD is riding on a swift cloud
and comes to Egypt;
the idols of Egypt will tremble at his
presence,
and the heart of the Egyptians will melt
within them.
2 I will stir up Egyptians against Egyptians,
and they will fight, one against the other,
neighbor against neighbor,
city against city, kingdom against
kingdom;
3 the spirit of the Egyptians within them will
be emptied out,
and I will confound their plans;
they will consult the idols and the spirits of
the dead
and the ghosts and the familiar spirits;
4 I will deliver the Egyptians
into the hand of a hard master;
a fierce king will rule over them,
says the Sovereign, the LORD of hosts.

5 The waters of the Nile will be dried up,
and the river will be parched and dry;
6 its canals will become foul,
and the branches of Egypt's Nile will
diminish and dry up,
reeds and rushes will rot away.
7 There will be bare places by the Nile,
on the brink of the Nile;
and all that is sown by the Nile will dry up,
be driven away, and be no more.
8 Those who fish will mourn;
all who cast hooks in the Nile will lament,
and those who spread nets on the water
will languish.
9 The workers in flax will be in despair,
and the carders and those at the loom will
grow pale.
10 Its weavers will be dismayed,
and all who work for wages will be
grieved.

11 The princes of Zoan are utterly foolish;
the wise counselors of Pharaoh give stupid
counsel.
How can you say to Pharaoh,
"I am one of the sages,
a descendant of ancient kings"?
12 Where now are your sages?
Let them tell you and make known
what the LORD of hosts has planned
against Egypt.
13 The princes of Zoan have become fools,
and the princes of Memphis are deluded;
those who are the cornerstones of its tribes
have led Egypt astray.
14 The LORD has poured into them[b]
a spirit of confusion;
and they have made Egypt stagger in all its
doings
as a drunkard staggers around in vomit.
15 Neither head nor tail, palm branch or reed,
will be able to do anything for Egypt.

16 On that day the Egyptians will be like
women, and tremble with fear before the hand
that the LORD of hosts raises against them. 17 And
the land of Judah will become a terror to the
Egyptians; everyone to whom it is mentioned

[a] Q Ms Gk Vg: MT *of* [b] Gk Compare Tg: Heb *it*

will fear because of the plan that the LORD of
hosts is planning against them.
18 On that day there will be five cities in the
land of Egypt that speak the language of Canaan
and swear allegiance to the LORD of hosts. One of
these will be called the City of the Sun.
19 On that day there will be an altar to the
LORD in the center of the land of Egypt, and a
pillar to the LORD at its border. 20 It will be a sign
and a witness to the LORD of hosts in the land
of Egypt; when they cry to the LORD because of
oppressors, he will send them a savior, and will
defend and deliver them. 21 The LORD will make
himself known to the Egyptians; and the Egyptians will know the LORD on that day, and will
worship with sacrifice and burnt offering, and
they will make vows to the LORD and perform
them. 22 The LORD will strike Egypt, striking and
healing; they will return to the LORD, and he will
listen to their supplications and heal them.
23 On that day there will be a highway from
Egypt to Assyria, and the Assyrian will come
into Egypt, and the Egyptian into Assyria, and
the Egyptians will worship with the Assyrians.
24 On that day Israel will be the third with
Egypt and Assyria, a blessing in the midst of the
earth, 25 whom the LORD of hosts has blessed,
saying, "Blessed be Egypt my people, and Assyria
the work of my hands, and Israel my heritage."

20 In the year that the commander-in-chief,
who was sent by King Sargon of Assyria,
came to Ashdod and fought against it and took
it— 2 at that time the LORD had spoken to Isaiah
son of Amoz, saying, "Go, and loose the sackcloth from your loins and take your sandals off
your feet," and he had done so, walking naked
and barefoot. 3 Then the LORD said, "Just as my
servant Isaiah has walked naked and barefoot for
three years as a sign and a portent against Egypt
and Ethiopia,[a] 4 so shall the king of Assyria lead
away the Egyptians as captives and the Ethiopians[b] as exiles, both the young and the old, naked
and barefoot, with buttocks uncovered, to the
shame of Egypt. 5 And they shall be dismayed
and confounded because of Ethiopia[a] their hope
and of Egypt their boast. 6 In that day the inhabitants of this coastland will say, 'See, this is what
has happened to those in whom we hoped and to
whom we fled for help and deliverance from the
king of Assyria! And we, how shall we escape?'"

21 The oracle concerning the wilderness of
the sea.

As whirlwinds in the Negeb sweep on,
  it comes from the desert,
  from a terrible land.
2 A stern vision is told to me;
  the betrayer betrays,
  and the destroyer destroys.
Go up, O Elam,
  lay siege, O Media;
all the sighing she has caused
  I bring to an end.
3 Therefore my loins are filled with anguish;
  pangs have seized me,
  like the pangs of a woman in labor;
I am bowed down so that I cannot hear,
  I am dismayed so that I cannot see.
4 My mind reels, horror has appalled me;
  the twilight I longed for
  has been turned for me into trembling.
5 They prepare the table,
  they spread the rugs,
  they eat, they drink.
Rise up, commanders,
  oil the shield!
6 For thus the Lord said to me:
"Go, post a lookout,
  let him announce what he sees.
7 When he sees riders, horsemen in pairs,
  riders on donkeys, riders on camels,
let him listen diligently,
  very diligently."
8 Then the watcher[c] called out:
"Upon a watchtower I stand, O Lord,
  continually by day,
and at my post I am stationed
  throughout the night.

[a] Or *Nubia*; Heb *Cush* [b] Or *Nubians*; Heb *Cushites* [c] Q Ms: MT *a lion*

9 Look, there they come, riders,
horsemen in pairs!"
Then he responded,
"Fallen, fallen is Babylon;
and all the images of her gods
lie shattered on the ground."
10 O my threshed and winnowed one,
what I have heard from the LORD of hosts,
the God of Israel, I announce to you.

11 The oracle concerning Dumah.

One is calling to me from Seir,
"Sentinel, what of the night?
Sentinel, what of the night?"
12 The sentinel says:
"Morning comes, and also the night.
If you will inquire, inquire;
come back again."

13 The oracle concerning the desert plain.

In the scrub of the desert plain you will lodge,
O caravans of Dedanites.
14 Bring water to the thirsty,
meet the fugitive with bread,
O inhabitants of the land of Tema.
15 For they have fled from the swords,
from the drawn sword,
from the bent bow,
and from the stress of battle.

16 For thus the Lord said to me: Within a
year, according to the years of a hired worker, all
the glory of Kedar will come to an end; 17 and the
remaining bows of Kedar's warriors will be few;
for the LORD, the God of Israel, has spoken.

22 The oracle concerning the valley of vision.

What do you mean that you have gone up,
all of you, to the housetops,
2 you that are full of shoutings,
tumultuous city, exultant town?
Your slain are not slain by the sword,
nor are they dead in battle.
3 Your rulers have all fled together;
they were captured without the use of a bow.[a]
All of you who were found were captured,
though they had fled far away.[b]
4 Therefore I said:
Look away from me,
let me weep bitter tears;
do not try to comfort me
for the destruction of my beloved people.

5 For the Lord GOD of hosts has a day
of tumult and trampling and confusion
in the valley of vision,
a battering down of walls
and a cry for help to the mountains.
6 Elam bore the quiver
with chariots and cavalry,[c]
and Kir uncovered the shield.
7 Your choicest valleys were full of chariots,
and the cavalry took their stand at the gates.
8 He has taken away the covering of Judah.

On that day you looked to the weapons of the
House of the Forest, 9 and you saw that there were
many breaches in the city of David, and you collected the waters of the lower pool. 10 You counted
the houses of Jerusalem, and you broke down the
houses to fortify the wall. 11 You made a reservoir
between the two walls for the water of the old
pool. But you did not look to him who did it, or
have regard for him who planned it long ago.

12 In that day the Lord GOD of hosts
called to weeping and mourning,
to baldness and putting on sackcloth;
13 but instead there was joy and festivity,
killing oxen and slaughtering sheep,
eating meat and drinking wine.
"Let us eat and drink,
for tomorrow we die."
14 The LORD of hosts has revealed himself in my ears:

[a] Or *without their bows* [b] Gk Syr Vg: Heb *fled from far away* [c] Meaning of Heb uncertain

Surely this iniquity will not be forgiven you
until you die,
says the Lord GOD of hosts.
15 Thus says the Lord GOD of hosts: Come,
go to this steward, to Shebna, who is master of
the household, and say to him: 16 What right do
you have here? Who are your relatives here, that
you have cut out a tomb here for yourself, cutting
a tomb on the height, and carving a habitation for
yourself in the rock? 17 The LORD is about to hurl
you away violently, my fellow. He will seize firm
hold on you, 18 whirl you round and round, and
throw you like a ball into a wide land; there you
shall die, and there your splendid chariots shall
lie, O you disgrace to your master's house! 19 I
will thrust you from your office, and you will be
pulled down from your post.
20 On that day I will call my servant Eliakim
son of Hilkiah, 21 and will clothe him with your
robe and bind your sash on him. I will commit
your authority to his hand, and he shall be a father
to the inhabitants of Jerusalem and to the house of
Judah. 22 I will place on his shoulder the key of the
house of David; he shall open, and no one shall
shut; he shall shut, and no one shall open. 23 I will
fasten him like a peg in a secure place, and he will
become a throne of honor to his ancestral house.
24 And they will hang on him the whole weight of
his ancestral house, the offspring and issue, every
small vessel, from the cups to all the flagons. 25 On
that day, says the LORD of hosts, the peg that was
fastened in a secure place will give way; it will be
cut down and fall, and the load that was on it will
perish, for the LORD has spoken.

23 The oracle concerning Tyre.

Wail, O ships of Tarshish,
for your fortress is destroyed.[a]
When they came in from Cyprus
they learned of it.
2 Be still, O inhabitants of the coast,
O merchants of Sidon,
your messengers crossed over the sea[b]
3 and were on the mighty waters;
your revenue was the grain of Shihor,
the harvest of the Nile;
you were the merchant of the nations.
4 Be ashamed, O Sidon, for the sea has
spoken,
the fortress of the sea, saying:
"I have neither labored nor given birth,
I have neither reared young men
nor brought up young women."
5 When the report comes to Egypt,
they will be in anguish over the report
about Tyre.
6 Cross over to Tarshish—
wail, O inhabitants of the coast!
7 Is this your exultant city
whose origin is from days of old,
whose feet carried her
to settle far away?
8 Who has planned this
against Tyre, the bestower of crowns,
whose merchants were princes,
whose traders were the honored of the
earth?
9 The LORD of hosts has planned it—
to defile the pride of all glory,
to shame all the honored of the earth.
10 Cross over to your own land,
O ships of[c] Tarshish;
this is a harbor[d] no more.
11 He has stretched out his hand over the sea,
he has shaken the kingdoms;
the LORD has given command concerning
Canaan
to destroy its fortresses.
12 He said:
You will exult no longer,
O oppressed virgin daughter Sidon;
rise, cross over to Cyprus—
even there you will have no rest.

13 Look at the land of the Chaldeans! This
is the people; it was not Assyria. They destined
Tyre for wild animals. They erected their siege

[a] Cn Compare verse 14: Heb *for it is destroyed, without houses*
[b] Q Ms: MT *crossing over the sea, they replenished you*
[c] Cn Compare Gk: Heb *like the Nile, daughter*
[d] Cn: Heb *restraint*

towers, they tore down her palaces, they made her a ruin.[a]

14 Wail, O ships of Tarshish,
for your fortress is destroyed.

15 From that day Tyre will be forgotten for seventy years, the lifetime of one king. At the end
of seventy years, it will happen to Tyre as in the
song about the prostitute:

16 Take a harp,
go about the city,
you forgotten prostitute!
Make sweet melody,
sing many songs,
that you may be remembered.

17 At the end of seventy years, the LORD will visit
Tyre, and she will return to her trade, and will
prostitute herself with all the kingdoms of the
world on the face of the earth. 18 Her merchandise and her wages will be dedicated to the LORD;
her profits[b] will not be stored or hoarded, but her
merchandise will supply abundant food and fine
clothing for those who live in the presence of the
LORD.

24

Now the LORD is about to lay waste the earth and make it desolate,
and he will twist its surface and scatter its inhabitants.
2 And it shall be, as with the people, so with the priest;
as with the slave, so with his master;
as with the maid, so with her mistress;
as with the buyer, so with the seller;
as with the lender, so with the borrower;
as with the creditor, so with the debtor.
3 The earth shall be utterly laid waste and utterly despoiled;
for the LORD has spoken this word.

4 The earth dries up and withers,
the world languishes and withers;
the heavens languish together with the earth.
5 The earth lies polluted
under its inhabitants;
for they have transgressed laws,
violated the statutes,
broken the everlasting covenant.
6 Therefore a curse devours the earth,
and its inhabitants suffer for their guilt;
therefore the inhabitants of the earth dwindled,
and few people are left.
7 The wine dries up,
the vine languishes,
all the merry-hearted sigh.
8 The mirth of the timbrels is stilled,
the noise of the jubilant has ceased,
the mirth of the lyre is stilled.
9 No longer do they drink wine with singing;
strong drink is bitter to those who drink it.
10 The city of chaos is broken down,
every house is shut up so that no one can enter.
11 There is an outcry in the streets for lack of wine;
all joy has reached its eventide;
the gladness of the earth is banished.
12 Desolation is left in the city,
the gates are battered into ruins.
13 For thus it shall be on the earth
and among the nations,
as when an olive tree is beaten,
as at the gleaning when the grape harvest is ended.

14 They lift up their voices, they sing for joy;
they shout from the west over the majesty of the LORD.
15 Therefore in the east give glory to the LORD;
in the coastlands of the sea glorify the name of the LORD, the God of Israel.
16 From the ends of the earth we hear songs of praise,
of glory to the Righteous One.
But I say, I pine away,
I pine away. Woe is me!
For the treacherous deal treacherously,
the treacherous deal very treacherously.

[a] Meaning of Heb uncertain [b] Heb *it*

17 Terror, and the pit, and the snare
are upon you, O inhabitant of the earth!
18 Whoever flees at the sound of the terror
shall fall into the pit;
and whoever climbs out of the pit
shall be caught in the snare.
For the windows of heaven are opened,
and the foundations of the earth tremble.
19 The earth is utterly broken,
the earth is torn asunder,
the earth is violently shaken.
20 The earth staggers like a drunkard,
it sways like a hut;
its transgression lies heavy upon it,
and it falls, and will not rise again.

21 On that day the LORD will punish
the host of heaven in heaven,
and on earth the kings of the earth.
22 They will be gathered together
like prisoners in a pit;
they will be shut up in a prison,
and after many days they will be punished.
23 Then the moon will be abashed,
and the sun ashamed;
for the LORD of hosts will reign
on Mount Zion and in Jerusalem,
and before his elders he will manifest his
glory.

25 O LORD, you are my God;
I will exalt you, I will praise your name;
for you have done wonderful things,
plans formed of old, faithful and sure.
2 For you have made the city a heap,
the fortified city a ruin;
the palace of aliens is a city no more,
it will never be rebuilt.
3 Therefore strong peoples will glorify you;
cities of ruthless nations will fear you.
4 For you have been a refuge to the poor,
a refuge to the needy in their distress,
a shelter from the rainstorm and a shade
from the heat.
When the blast of the ruthless was like a
winter rainstorm,
5 the noise of aliens like heat in a dry place,
you subdued the heat with the shade of
clouds;
the song of the ruthless was stilled.

6 On this mountain the LORD of hosts will
make for all peoples
a feast of rich food, a feast of well-aged
wines,
of rich food filled with marrow, of well-
aged wines strained clear.
7 And he will destroy on this mountain
the shroud that is cast over all peoples,
the sheet that is spread over all nations;
8 he will swallow up death forever.
Then the Lord GOD will wipe away the tears
from all faces,
and the disgrace of his people he will take
away from all the earth,
for the LORD has spoken.
9 It will be said on that day,
Lo, this is our God; we have waited for
him, so that he might save us.
This is the LORD for whom we have
waited;
let us be glad and rejoice in his
salvation.

Isaiah 25:6-10

One of the most important rediscoveries of the liturgical movement in the 1960s and 1970s was the wealth of biblical imagery concerning meals, imagery that came to be incorporated into the eucharistic prayers of many churches. Of these images, one of the most important is Isaiah's vision of the peoples of the earth gathered for a rich feast upon God's mountain, free of the pall of death and disgrace that has so distorted human history. Perhaps more than any other, this vision has lifted Christian eyes from the congregation's table to the horizon of the world and of God's future. In a time when neoliberal policies have undermined local markets and jeopardized the food security of peoples around the world, Isaiah's vision is more urgent than ever.

— NE

10 For the hand of the LORD will rest on this mountain.

The Moabites shall be trodden down in their place
as straw is trodden down in a dung-pit.
11 Though they spread out their hands in the midst of it,
as swimmers spread out their hands to swim,
their pride will be laid low despite the struggle[a] of their hands.
12 The high fortifications of his walls will be brought down,
laid low, cast to the ground, even to the dust.

26 On that day this song will be sung in the land of Judah:
We have a strong city;
he sets up victory
like walls and bulwarks.
2 Open the gates,
so that the righteous nation that keeps faith
may enter in.
3 Those of steadfast mind you keep in peace—
in peace because they trust in you.
4 Trust in the LORD forever,
for in the LORD GOD[b]
you have an everlasting rock.
5 For he has brought low
the inhabitants of the height;
the lofty city he lays low.
He lays it low to the ground,
casts it to the dust.
6 The foot tramples it,
the feet of the poor,
the steps of the needy.

7 The way of the righteous is level;
O Just One, you make smooth the path of the righteous.
8 In the path of your judgments,
O LORD, we wait for you;
your name and your renown
are the soul's desire.
9 My soul yearns for you in the night,
my spirit within me earnestly seeks you.
For when your judgments are in the earth,
the inhabitants of the world learn righteousness.
10 If favor is shown to the wicked,
they do not learn righteousness;
in the land of uprightness they deal perversely
and do not see the majesty of the LORD.
11 O LORD, your hand is lifted up,
but they do not see it.
Let them see your zeal for your people, and be ashamed.
Let the fire for your adversaries consume them.
12 O LORD, you will ordain peace for us,
for indeed, all that we have done, you have done for us.
13 O LORD our God,
other lords besides you have ruled over us,
but we acknowledge your name alone.
14 The dead do not live;
shades do not rise—
because you have punished and destroyed them,
and wiped out all memory of them.
15 But you have increased the nation, O LORD,
you have increased the nation; you are glorified;
you have enlarged all the borders of the land.

16 O LORD, in distress they sought you,
they poured out a prayer[a]
when your chastening was on them.
17 Like a woman with child,
who writhes and cries out in her pangs
when she is near her time,
so were we because of you, O LORD;
18 we were with child, we writhed,
but we gave birth only to wind.
We have won no victories on earth,

[a] Meaning of Heb uncertain [b] Heb *in Yah, the LORD*

and no one is born to inhabit the world.
19 Your dead shall live, their corpses[a] shall rise.
O dwellers in the dust, awake and sing for joy!
For your dew is a radiant dew,
and the earth will give birth to those long dead.[b]

20 Come, my people, enter your chambers,
and shut your doors behind you;
hide yourselves for a little while
until the wrath is past.
21 For the LORD comes out from his place
to punish the inhabitants of the earth for their iniquity;
the earth will disclose the blood shed on it,
and will no longer cover its slain.

27 On that day the LORD with his cruel and great and strong sword will punish Leviathan the fleeing serpent, Leviathan the twisting serpent, and he will kill the dragon that is in the sea.

2 On that day:
A pleasant vineyard, sing about it!
3 I, the LORD, am its keeper;
every moment I water it.
I guard it night and day
so that no one can harm it;
4 I have no wrath.
If it gives me thorns and briers,
I will march to battle against it.
I will burn it up.
5 Or else let it cling to me for protection,
let it make peace with me,
let it make peace with me.

6 In days to come[c] Jacob shall take root,
Israel shall blossom and put forth shoots,
and fill the whole world with fruit.

7 Has he struck them down as he struck down those who struck them?
Or have they been killed as their killers were killed?
8 By expulsion,[d] by exile you struggled against them;
with his fierce blast he removed them in the day of the east wind.
9 Therefore by this the guilt of Jacob will be expiated,
and this will be the full fruit of the removal of his sin:
when he makes all the stones of the altars
like chalkstones crushed to pieces,
no sacred poles[e] or incense altars will remain standing.
10 For the fortified city is solitary,
a habitation deserted and forsaken, like the wilderness;
the calves graze there,
there they lie down, and strip its branches.
11 When its boughs are dry, they are broken;
women come and make a fire of them.
For this is a people without understanding;
therefore he that made them will not have compassion on them,
he that formed them will show them no favor.

12 On that day the LORD will thresh from the
channel of the Euphrates to the Wadi of Egypt,
and you will be gathered one by one, O people of
Israel. 13 And on that day a great trumpet will be
blown, and those who were lost in the land of Assyria and those who were driven out to the land
of Egypt will come and worship the LORD on the
holy mountain at Jerusalem.

28 Ah, the proud garland of the drunkards of Ephraim,
and the fading flower of its glorious beauty,
which is on the head of those bloated with rich food, of those overcome with wine!

[a] Cn Compare Syr Tg: Heb *my corpse* [b] Heb *to the shades* [c] Heb *Those to come* [d] Meaning of Heb uncertain
[e] Heb *Asherim*

2 See, the Lord has one who is mighty and
strong;
like a storm of hail, a destroying tempest,
like a storm of mighty, overflowing waters;
with his hand he will hurl them down to
the earth.
3 Trampled under foot will be
the proud garland of the drunkards of
Ephraim.
4 And the fading flower of its glorious beauty,
which is on the head of those bloated with
rich food,
will be like a first-ripe fig before the
summer;
whoever sees it, eats it up
as soon as it comes to hand.

5 In that day the LORD of hosts will be a
garland of glory,
and a diadem of beauty, to the remnant of
his people;
6 and a spirit of justice to the one who sits in
judgment,
and strength to those who turn back the
battle at the gate.

7 These also reel with wine
and stagger with strong drink;
the priest and the prophet reel with strong
drink,
they are confused with wine,
they stagger with strong drink;
they err in vision,
they stumble in giving judgment.
8 All tables are covered with filthy vomit;
no place is clean.

9 "Whom will he teach knowledge,
and to whom will he explain the message?
Those who are weaned from milk,
those taken from the breast?
10 For it is precept upon precept, precept upon
precept,
line upon line, line upon line,
here a little, there a little."[a]

11 Truly, with stammering lip
and with alien tongue
he will speak to this people,
12 to whom he has said,
"This is rest;
give rest to the weary;
and this is repose";
yet they would not hear.
13 Therefore the word of the LORD will be to
them,
"Precept upon precept, precept upon
precept,
line upon line, line upon line,
here a little, there a little;"[a]
in order that they may go, and fall backward,
and be broken, and snared, and taken.

14 Therefore hear the word of the LORD, you
scoffers
who rule this people in Jerusalem.
15 Because you have said, "We have made a
covenant with death,
and with Sheol we have an agreement;
when the overwhelming scourge passes
through
it will not come to us;
for we have made lies our refuge,
and in falsehood we have taken shelter";
16 therefore thus says the Lord GOD,
See, I am laying in Zion a foundation stone,
a tested stone,
a precious cornerstone, a sure foundation:
"One who trusts will not panic."
17 And I will make justice the line,
and righteousness the plummet;
hail will sweep away the refuge of lies,
and waters will overwhelm the shelter.
18 Then your covenant with death will be
annulled,
and your agreement with Sheol will not
stand;
when the overwhelming scourge passes
through
you will be beaten down by it.
19 As often as it passes through, it will take you;

[a] Meaning of Heb of this verse uncertain

for morning by morning it will pass
through,
by day and by night;
and it will be sheer terror to understand the
message.
20 For the bed is too short to stretch oneself
on it,
and the covering too narrow to wrap
oneself in it.
21 For the LORD will rise up as on Mount
Perazim,
he will rage as in the valley of Gibeon
to do his deed—strange is his deed!—
and to work his work—alien is his
work!
22 Now therefore do not scoff,
or your bonds will be made stronger;
for I have heard a decree of destruction
from the Lord GOD of hosts upon the
whole land.

23 Listen, and hear my voice;
Pay attention, and hear my speech.
24 Do those who plow for sowing plow
continually?
Do they continually open and harrow their
ground?
25 When they have leveled its surface,
do they not scatter dill, sow cummin,
and plant wheat in rows
and barley in its proper place,
and spelt as the border?
26 For they are well instructed;
their God teaches them.

27 Dill is not threshed with a threshing sledge,
nor is a cart wheel rolled over cummin;
but dill is beaten out with a stick,
and cummin with a rod.
28 Grain is crushed for bread,
but one does not thresh it forever;
one drives the cart wheel and horses over it,
but does not pulverize it.
29 This also comes from the LORD of hosts;
he is wonderful in counsel,
and excellent in wisdom.

29 Ah, Ariel, Ariel,
the city where David encamped!
Add year to year;
let the festivals run their round.
2 Yet I will distress Ariel,
and there shall be moaning and
lamentation,
and Jerusalem[a] shall be to me like an
Ariel.[b]
3 And like David[c] I will encamp against you;
I will besiege you with towers
and raise siegeworks against you.
4 Then deep from the earth you shall speak,
from low in the dust your words shall
come;
your voice shall come from the ground like
the voice of a ghost,
and your speech shall whisper out of the
dust.

5 But the multitude of your foes[d] shall be like
small dust,
and the multitude of tyrants like flying
chaff.
And in an instant, suddenly,
6 you will be visited by the LORD of hosts
with thunder and earthquake and great noise,
with whirlwind and tempest, and the flame
of a devouring fire.
7 And the multitude of all the nations that fight
against Ariel,
all that fight against her and her
stronghold, and who distress her,
shall be like a dream, a vision of the night.
8 Just as when a hungry person dreams of
eating
and wakes up still hungry,
or a thirsty person dreams of drinking
and wakes up faint, still thirsty,
so shall the multitude of all the nations be
that fight against Mount Zion.

[a] Heb *she* [b] Probable meaning, *altar hearth*; compare Ezek 43.15 [c] Gk: Meaning of Heb uncertain
[d] Cn: Heb *strangers*

9 Stupefy yourselves and be in a stupor,
blind yourselves and be blind!
Be drunk, but not from wine;
stagger, but not from strong drink!
10 For the LORD has poured out upon you
a spirit of deep sleep;
he has closed your eyes, you prophets,
and covered your heads, you seers.
11 The vision of all this has become for you
like the words of a sealed document. If it is given
to those who can read, with the command, "Read
this," they say, "We cannot, for it is sealed." 12 And
if it is given to those who cannot read, saying,
"Read this," they say, "We cannot read."

13 The Lord said:
Because these people draw near with their
mouths
and honor me with their lips,
while their hearts are far from me,
and their worship of me is a human
commandment learned by rote;
14 so I will again do
amazing things with this people,
shocking and amazing.
The wisdom of their wise shall perish,
and the discernment of the discerning
shall be hidden.

15 Ha! You who hide a plan too deep for the
LORD,
whose deeds are in the dark,
and who say, "Who sees us? Who
knows us?"
16 You turn things upside down!
Shall the potter be regarded as the clay?
Shall the thing made say of its maker,
"He did not make me";
or the thing formed say of the one who
formed it,
"He has no understanding"?

17 Shall not Lebanon in a very little while
become a fruitful field,
and the fruitful field be regarded as a
forest?
18 On that day the deaf shall hear
the words of a scroll,
and out of their gloom and darkness
the eyes of the blind shall see.
19 The meek shall obtain fresh joy in the LORD,
and the neediest people shall exult in the
Holy One of Israel.
20 For the tyrant shall be no more,
and the scoffer shall cease to be;
all those alert to do evil shall be cut off—
21 those who cause a person to lose a lawsuit,
who set a trap for the arbiter in the gate,
and without grounds deny justice to the
one in the right.

22 Therefore thus says the LORD, who redeemed Abraham, concerning the house of
Jacob:
No longer shall Jacob be ashamed,
no longer shall his face grow pale.
23 For when he sees his children,
the work of my hands, in his midst,
they will sanctify my name;
they will sanctify the Holy One of Jacob,
and will stand in awe of the God of Israel.
24 And those who err in spirit will come to
understanding,
and those who grumble will accept
instruction.

30 Oh, rebellious children, says the LORD,
who carry out a plan, but not mine;
who make an alliance, but against my will,
adding sin to sin;
2 who set out to go down to Egypt
without asking for my counsel,
to take refuge in the protection of Pharaoh,
and to seek shelter in the shadow of Egypt;
3 Therefore the protection of Pharaoh shall
become your shame,
and the shelter in the shadow of Egypt
your humiliation.
4 For though his officials are at Zoan
and his envoys reach Hanes,
5 everyone comes to shame
through a people that cannot profit them,
that brings neither help nor profit,
but shame and disgrace.

6 An oracle concerning the animals of the Negeb.

Through a land of trouble and distress,
of lioness and roaring[a] lion,
of viper and flying serpent,
they carry their riches on the backs of donkeys,
and their treasures on the humps of camels,
to a people that cannot profit them.
7 For Egypt's help is worthless and empty,
therefore I have called her,
"Rahab who sits still."[b]

8 Go now, write it before them on a tablet,
and inscribe it in a book,
so that it may be for the time to come
as a witness forever.
9 For they are a rebellious people,
faithless children,
children who will not hear
the instruction of the LORD;
10 who say to the seers, "Do not see";
and to the prophets, "Do not prophesy to us what is right;
speak to us smooth things,
prophesy illusions,
11 leave the way, turn aside from the path,
let us hear no more about the Holy One of Israel."
12 Therefore thus says the Holy One of Israel:
Because you reject this word,
and put your trust in oppression and deceit,
and rely on them;
13 therefore this iniquity shall become for you
like a break in a high wall, bulging out, and about to collapse,
whose crash comes suddenly, in an instant;
14 its breaking is like that of a potter's vessel
that is smashed so ruthlessly
that among its fragments not a sherd is found
for taking fire from the hearth,
or dipping water out of the cistern.

[a] Cn: Heb *from them* [b] Meaning of Heb uncertain

15 For thus said the Lord GOD, the Holy One of Israel:
In returning and rest you shall be saved;
in quietness and in trust shall be your strength.
But you refused 16 and said,
"No! We will flee upon horses"—
therefore you shall flee!
and, "We will ride upon swift steeds"—
therefore your pursuers shall be swift!
17 A thousand shall flee at the threat of one,
at the threat of five you shall flee,
until you are left
like a flagstaff on the top of a mountain,
like a signal on a hill.

18 Therefore the LORD waits to be gracious to you;
therefore he will rise up to show mercy to you.
For the LORD is a God of justice;
blessed are all those who wait for him.

19 Truly, O people in Zion, inhabitants of Jerusalem, you shall weep no more. He will surely
be gracious to you at the sound of your cry; when
he hears it, he will answer you. 20 Though the
Lord may give you the bread of adversity and
the water of affliction, yet your Teacher will not
hide himself any more, but your eyes shall see
your Teacher. 21 And when you turn to the right
or when you turn to the left, your ears shall hear
a word behind you, saying, "This is the way; walk
in it." 22 Then you will defile your silver-covered
idols and your gold-plated images. You will scatter them like filthy rags; you will say to them,
"Away with you!"

23 He will give rain for the seed with which
you sow the ground, and grain, the produce of
the ground, which will be rich and plenteous. On
that day your cattle will graze in broad pastures;
24 and the oxen and donkeys that till the ground
will eat silage, which has been winnowed with
shovel and fork. 25 On every lofty mountain and
every high hill there will be brooks running with
water—on a day of the great slaughter, when the

towers fall. 26Moreover the light of the moon will
be like the light of the sun, and the light of the
sun will be sevenfold, like the light of seven days,
on the day when the LORD binds up the injuries
of his people, and heals the wounds inflicted by
his blow.

27 See, the name of the LORD comes from far
away,
burning with his anger, and in thick rising
smoke;[a]
his lips are full of indignation,
and his tongue is like a devouring fire;
28 his breath is like an overflowing stream
that reaches up to the neck—
to sift the nations with the sieve of
destruction,
and to place on the jaws of the peoples a
bridle that leads them astray.

29 You shall have a song as in the night when
a holy festival is kept; and gladness of heart, as
when one sets out to the sound of the flute to go
to the mountain of the LORD, to the Rock of Israel. 30And the LORD will cause his majestic voice
to be heard and the descending blow of his arm to
be seen, in furious anger and a flame of devouring
fire, with a cloudburst and tempest and hailstones.
31The Assyrian will be terror-stricken at the voice
of the LORD, when he strikes with his rod. 32And
every stroke of the staff of punishment that the
LORD lays upon him will be to the sound of timbrels and lyres; battling with brandished arm he
will fight with him. 33For his burning place[b] has
long been prepared; truly it is made ready for the
king,[c] its pyre made deep and wide, with fire and
wood in abundance; the breath of the LORD, like
a stream of sulfur, kindles it.

31 Alas for those who go down to Egypt for
help
and who rely on horses,
who trust in chariots because they are many
and in horsemen because they are very
strong,
but do not look to the Holy One of Israel
or consult the LORD!
2 Yet he too is wise and brings disaster;
he does not call back his words,
but will rise against the house of the
evildoers,
and against the helpers of those who work
iniquity.
3 The Egyptians are human, and not God;
their horses are flesh, and not spirit.
When the LORD stretches out his hand,
the helper will stumble, and the one
helped will fall,
and they will all perish together.

4 For thus the LORD said to me,
As a lion or a young lion growls over its prey,
and—when a band of shepherds is called
out against it—
is not terrified by their shouting
or daunted at their noise,
so the LORD of hosts will come down
to fight upon Mount Zion and upon its
hill.
5 Like birds hovering overhead, so the LORD of
hosts
will protect Jerusalem;
he will protect and deliver it,
he will spare and rescue it.

6 Turn back to him whom you[d] have deeply
betrayed, O people of Israel. 7For on that day all

Isaiah 31:1-5

No prophet is more strident in denouncing the search for security in military alliances than Isaiah of Jerusalem, who regards them as nothing but a "covenant with death" (28:15). Are his words even comprehensible in an age when "national security" is practically synonymous with the doctrine of overwhelming military supremacy?

—NE

[a] Meaning of Heb uncertain [b] Or *Topheth* [c] Or *Molech* [d] Heb *they*

of you shall throw away your idols of silver and idols of gold, which your hands have sinfully made for you.

8 "Then the Assyrian shall fall by a sword, not of mortals;
and a sword, not of humans, shall devour him;
he shall flee from the sword,
and his young men shall be put to forced labor.
9 His rock shall pass away in terror,
and his officers desert the standard in panic,"
says the LORD, whose fire is in Zion,
and whose furnace is in Jerusalem.

32 See, a king will reign in righteousness,
and princes will rule with justice.
2 Each will be like a hiding place from the wind,
a covert from the tempest,
like streams of water in a dry place,
like the shade of a great rock in a weary land.
3 Then the eyes of those who have sight will not be closed,
and the ears of those who have hearing will listen.
4 The minds of the rash will have good judgment,
and the tongues of stammerers will speak readily and distinctly.
5 A fool will no longer be called noble,
nor a villain said to be honorable.
6 For fools speak folly,
and their minds plot iniquity:
to practice ungodliness,
to utter error concerning the LORD,
to leave the craving of the hungry unsatisfied,
and to deprive the thirsty of drink.
7 The villainies of villains are evil;
they devise wicked devices
to ruin the poor with lying words,
even when the plea of the needy is right.
8 But those who are noble plan noble things,
and by noble things they stand.

9 Rise up, you women who are at ease, hear my voice;
you complacent daughters, listen to my speech.
10 In little more than a year
you will shudder, you complacent ones;
for the vintage will fail,
the fruit harvest will not come.
11 Tremble, you women who are at ease,
shudder, you complacent ones;
strip, and make yourselves bare,
and put sackcloth on your loins.
12 Beat your breasts for the pleasant fields,
for the fruitful vine,
13 for the soil of my people
growing up in thorns and briers;
yes, for all the joyous houses
in the jubilant city.
14 For the palace will be forsaken,
the populous city deserted;
the hill and the watchtower
will become dens forever,
the joy of wild asses,
a pasture for flocks;
15 until a spirit from on high is poured out on us,
and the wilderness becomes a fruitful field,
and the fruitful field is deemed a forest.
16 Then justice will dwell in the wilderness,
and righteousness abide in the fruitful field.
17 The effect of righteousness will be peace,
and the result of righteousness, quietness and trust forever.
18 My people will abide in a peaceful habitation,
in secure dwellings, and in quiet resting places.
19 The forest will disappear completely,[a]
and the city will be utterly laid low.
20 Happy will you be who sow beside every stream,
who let the ox and the donkey range freely.

[a] Cn: Heb *And it will hail when the forest comes down*

33

Ah, you destroyer,
who yourself have not been destroyed;
you treacherous one,
with whom no one has dealt
treacherously!
When you have ceased to destroy,
you will be destroyed;
and when you have stopped dealing
treacherously,
you will be dealt with treacherously.

2 O LORD, be gracious to us; we wait for you.
Be our arm every morning,
our salvation in the time of trouble.
3 At the sound of tumult, peoples fled;
before your majesty, nations scattered.
4 Spoil was gathered as the caterpillar gathers;
as locusts leap, they leaped[a] upon it.
5 The LORD is exalted, he dwells on high;
he filled Zion with justice and
righteousness;
6 he will be the stability of your times,
abundance of salvation, wisdom, and
knowledge;
the fear of the LORD is Zion's treasure.[b]

7 Listen! the valiant[a] cry in the streets;
the envoys of peace weep bitterly.
8 The highways are deserted,
travelers have quit the road.
The treaty is broken,
its oaths[c] are despised,
its obligation[d] is disregarded.
9 The land mourns and languishes;
Lebanon is confounded and withers away;
Sharon is like a desert;
and Bashan and Carmel shake off their
leaves.

10 "Now I will arise," says the LORD,
"now I will lift myself up;
now I will be exalted.
11 You conceive chaff, you bring forth stubble;
your breath is a fire that will consume you.
12 And the peoples will be as if burned to lime,
like thorns cut down, that are burned in
the fire."

13 Hear, you who are far away, what I have done;
and you who are near, acknowledge my
might.
14 The sinners in Zion are afraid;
trembling has seized the godless:
"Who among us can live with the devouring
fire?
Who among us can live with everlasting
flames?"
15 Those who walk righteously and speak
uprightly,
who despise the gain of oppression,
who wave away a bribe instead of accepting it,
who stop their ears from hearing of
bloodshed
and shut their eyes from looking on evil,
16 they will live on the heights;
their refuge will be the fortresses of rocks;
their food will be supplied, their water
assured.

17 Your eyes will see the king in his beauty;
they will behold a land that stretches far
away.
18 Your mind will muse on the terror:
"Where is the one who counted?
Where is the one who weighed the
tribute?
Where is the one who counted the towers?"
19 No longer will you see the insolent people,
the people of an obscure speech that you
cannot comprehend,
stammering in a language that you cannot
understand.
20 Look on Zion, the city of our appointed
festivals!
Your eyes will see Jerusalem,
a quiet habitation, an immovable tent,
whose stakes will never be pulled up,
and none of whose ropes will be broken.
21 But there the LORD in majesty will be for us
a place of broad rivers and streams,

[a] Meaning of Heb uncertain [b] Heb *his treasure*; meaning of Heb uncertain [c] Q Ms: MT *cities* [d] Or *everyone*

where no galley with oars can go,
nor stately ship can pass.
22 For the Lord is our judge, the Lord is our ruler,
the Lord is our king; he will save us.

23 Your rigging hangs loose;
it cannot hold the mast firm in its place,
or keep the sail spread out.

Then prey and spoil in abundance will be divided;
even the lame will fall to plundering.
24 And no inhabitant will say, "I am sick";
the people who live there will be forgiven their iniquity.

34 Draw near, O nations, to hear;
O peoples, give heed!
Let the earth hear, and all that fills it;
the world, and all that comes from it.
2 For the Lord is enraged against all the nations,
and furious against all their hordes;
he has doomed them, has given them over for slaughter.
3 Their slain shall be cast out,
and the stench of their corpses shall rise;
the mountains shall flow with their blood.
4 All the host of heaven shall rot away,
and the skies roll up like a scroll.
All their host shall wither
like a leaf withering on a vine,
or fruit withering on a fig tree.

5 When my sword has drunk its fill in the heavens,
lo, it will descend upon Edom,
upon the people I have doomed to judgment.
6 The Lord has a sword; it is sated with blood,
it is gorged with fat,
with the blood of lambs and goats,
with the fat of the kidneys of rams.
For the Lord has a sacrifice in Bozrah,
a great slaughter in the land of Edom.
7 Wild oxen shall fall with them,
and young steers with the mighty bulls.
Their land shall be soaked with blood,
and their soil made rich with fat.

8 For the Lord has a day of vengeance,
a year of vindication by Zion's cause.[a]
9 And the streams of Edom[b] shall be turned into pitch,
and her soil into sulfur;
her land shall become burning pitch.
10 Night and day it shall not be quenched;
its smoke shall go up forever.
From generation to generation it shall lie waste;
no one shall pass through it forever and ever.
11 But the hawk[c] and the hedgehog[c] shall possess it;
the owl[c] and the raven shall live in it.
He shall stretch the line of confusion over it,
and the plummet of chaos over[d] its nobles.
12 They shall name it No Kingdom There,
and all its princes shall be nothing.
13 Thorns shall grow over its strongholds,
nettles and thistles in its fortresses.
It shall be the haunt of jackals,
an abode for ostriches.
14 Wildcats shall meet with hyenas,
goat-demons shall call to each other;
there too Lilith shall repose,
and find a place to rest.

Isaiah 34:14

Lilith is the Hebrew version of Sumerian and Babylonian night-stalking creatures understood to attack pregnant women and infants. In later mythology, Lilith became Adam's fiercely independent first wife who left him rather than submit to him; in still later stories she is identified as the mother of all vampires, borrowing from her ancient origins.

— *WG*

[a] Or *of recompense by Zion's defender* [b] Heb *her streams* [c] Identification uncertain [d] Heb lacks *over*

15 There shall the owl nest
and lay and hatch and brood in its shadow;
there too the buzzards shall gather,
each one with its mate.
16 Seek and read from the book of the LORD:
Not one of these shall be missing;
none shall be without its mate.
For the mouth of the LORD has commanded,
and his spirit has gathered them.
17 He has cast the lot for them,
his hand has portioned it out to them with the line;
they shall possess it forever,
from generation to generation they shall live in it.

35 The wilderness and the dry land shall be glad,
the desert shall rejoice and blossom;
like the crocus 2 it shall blossom abundantly,
and rejoice with joy and singing.
The glory of Lebanon shall be given to it,
the majesty of Carmel and Sharon.
They shall see the glory of the LORD,
the majesty of our God.

3 Strengthen the weak hands,
and make firm the feeble knees.
4 Say to those who are of a fearful heart,
"Be strong, do not fear!
Here is your God.
He will come with vengeance,
with terrible recompense.
He will come and save you."

5 Then the eyes of the blind shall be opened,
and the ears of the deaf unstopped;
6 then the lame shall leap like a deer,
and the tongue of the speechless sing for joy.
For waters shall break forth in the wilderness,
and streams in the desert;
7 the burning sand shall become a pool,
and the thirsty ground springs of water;
the haunt of jackals shall become a swamp,[a]
the grass shall become reeds and rushes.
8 A highway shall be there,
and it shall be called the Holy Way;
the unclean shall not travel on it,[b]
but it shall be for God's people;[c]
no traveler, not even fools, shall go astray.
9 No lion shall be there,
nor shall any ravenous beast come up on it;
they shall not be found there,
but the redeemed shall walk there.
10 And the ransomed of the LORD shall return,
and come to Zion with singing;
everlasting joy shall be upon their heads;
they shall obtain joy and gladness,
and sorrow and sighing shall flee away.

36 In the fourteenth year of King Hezekiah, King Sennacherib of Assyria came
up against all the fortified cities of Judah and
captured them. 2 The king of Assyria sent the
Rabshakeh from Lachish to King Hezekiah at
Jerusalem, with a great army. He stood by the
conduit of the upper pool on the highway to the
Fuller's Field. 3 And there came out to him Eliakim son of Hilkiah, who was in charge of the
palace, and Shebna the secretary, and Joah son of
Asaph, the recorder.
4 The Rabshakeh said to them, "Say to Hezekiah: Thus says the great king, the king of Assyria:
On what do you base this confidence of yours?
5 Do you think that mere words are strategy and
power for war? On whom do you now rely, that
you have rebelled against me? 6 See, you are relying on Egypt, that broken reed of a staff, which
will pierce the hand of anyone who leans on it.
Such is Pharaoh king of Egypt to all who rely on
him. 7 But if you say to me, 'We rely on the LORD
our God,' is it not he whose high places and altars
Hezekiah has removed, saying to Judah and to
Jerusalem, 'You shall worship before this altar'?
8 Come now, make a wager with my master the
king of Assyria: I will give you two thousand
horses, if you are able on your part to set riders
on them. 9 How then can you repulse a single captain among the least of my master's servants, when
you rely on Egypt for chariots and for horsemen?

[a] Cn: Heb *in the haunt of jackals is her resting place* [b] Or *pass it by* [c] Cn: Heb *for them*

10 Moreover, is it without the LORD that I have
come up against this land to destroy it? The LORD
said to me, Go up against this land, and destroy it."
11 Then Eliakim, Shebna, and Joah said to
the Rabshakeh, "Please speak to your servants
in Aramaic, for we understand it; do not speak
to us in the language of Judah within the hearing of the people who are on the wall." 12 But the
Rabshakeh said, "Has my master sent me to speak
these words to your master and to you, and not to
the people sitting on the wall, who are doomed
with you to eat their own dung and drink their
own urine?"
13 Then the Rabshakeh stood and called out
in a loud voice in the language of Judah, "Hear
the words of the great king, the king of Assyria!
14 Thus says the king: 'Do not let Hezekiah deceive you, for he will not be able to deliver you.
15 Do not let Hezekiah make you rely on the
LORD by saying, The LORD will surely deliver
us; this city will not be given into the hand of the
king of Assyria.' 16 Do not listen to Hezekiah; for
thus says the king of Assyria: 'Make your peace
with me and come out to me; then every one of
you will eat from your own vine and your own
fig tree and drink water from your own cistern,
17 until I come and take you away to a land like
your own land, a land of grain and wine, a land of
bread and vineyards. 18 Do not let Hezekiah mislead you by saying, The LORD will save us. Has
any of the gods of the nations saved their land
out of the hand of the king of Assyria? 19 Where
are the gods of Hamath and Arpad? Where are
the gods of Sepharvaim? Have they delivered Samaria out of my hand? 20 Who among all the gods
of these countries have saved their countries out
of my hand, that the LORD should save Jerusalem
out of my hand?'"
21 But they were silent and answered him
not a word, for the king's command was, "Do not
answer him." 22 Then Eliakim son of Hilkiah, who
was in charge of the palace, and Shebna the secretary, and Joah son of Asaph, the recorder, came
to Hezekiah with their clothes torn, and told him
the words of the Rabshakeh.

37 When King Hezekiah heard it, he tore his
clothes, covered himself with sackcloth,
and went into the house of the LORD. 2 And he
sent Eliakim, who was in charge of the palace, and
Shebna the secretary, and the senior priests, covered with sackcloth, to the prophet Isaiah son of
Amoz. 3 They said to him, "Thus says Hezekiah,
This day is a day of distress, of rebuke, and of disgrace; children have come to the birth, and there
is no strength to bring them forth. 4 It may be
that the LORD your God heard the words of the
Rabshakeh, whom his master the king of Assyria
has sent to mock the living God, and will rebuke
the words that the LORD your God has heard;
therefore lift up your prayer for the remnant that
is left."
5 When the servants of King Hezekiah came
to Isaiah, 6 Isaiah said to them, "Say to your master, 'Thus says the LORD: Do not be afraid because
of the words that you have heard, with which the
servants of the king of Assyria have reviled me. 7 I
myself will put a spirit in him, so that he shall hear
a rumor, and return to his own land; I will cause
him to fall by the sword in his own land.'"
8 The Rabshakeh returned, and found the
king of Assyria fighting against Libnah; for he had
heard that the king had left Lachish. 9 Now the
king[a] heard concerning King Tirhakah of Ethiopia,[b] "He has set out to fight against you." When
he heard it, he sent messengers to Hezekiah, saying, 10 "Thus shall you speak to King Hezekiah of
Judah: Do not let your God on whom you rely deceive you by promising that Jerusalem will not be
given into the hand of the king of Assyria. 11 See,
you have heard what the kings of Assyria have
done to all lands, destroying them utterly. Shall
you be delivered? 12 Have the gods of the nations
delivered them, the nations that my predecessors destroyed, Gozan, Haran, Rezeph, and the
people of Eden who were in Telassar? 13 Where is
the king of Hamath, the king of Arpad, the king of
the city of Sepharvaim, the king of Hena, or the
king of Ivvah?"
14 Hezekiah received the letter from the hand
of the messengers and read it; then Hezekiah went

[a] Heb *he* [b] Or *Nubia*; Heb *Cush*

up to the house of the LORD and spread it before
the LORD. 15 And Hezekiah prayed to the LORD,
saying: 16 "O LORD of hosts, God of Israel, who
are enthroned above the cherubim, you are God,
you alone, of all the kingdoms of the earth; you
have made heaven and earth. 17 Incline your ear,
O LORD, and hear; open your eyes, O LORD, and
see; hear all the words of Sennacherib, which he
has sent to mock the living God. 18 Truly, O LORD,
the kings of Assyria have laid waste all the nations
and their lands, 19 and have hurled their gods into
the fire, though they were no gods, but the work
of human hands—wood and stone—and so they
were destroyed. 20 So now, O LORD our God, save
us from his hand, so that all the kingdoms of the
earth may know that you alone are the LORD."

21 Then Isaiah son of Amoz sent to Hezekiah,
saying: "Thus says the LORD, the God of Israel:
Because you have prayed to me concerning King
Sennacherib of Assyria, 22 this is the word that the
LORD has spoken concerning him:

She despises you, she scorns you—
virgin daughter Zion;
she tosses her head—behind your back,
daughter Jerusalem.

23 "Whom have you mocked and reviled?
Against whom have you raised your voice
and haughtily lifted your eyes?
Against the Holy One of Israel!
24 By your servants you have mocked the Lord,
and you have said, 'With my many chariots
I have gone up the heights of the mountains,
to the far recesses of Lebanon;
I felled its tallest cedars,
its choicest cypresses;
I came to its remotest height,
its densest forest.
25 I dug wells
and drank waters,
I dried up with the sole of my foot
all the streams of Egypt.'

26 "Have you not heard
that I determined it long ago?
I planned from days of old
what now I bring to pass,
that you should make fortified cities
crash into heaps of ruins,
27 while their inhabitants, shorn of strength,
are dismayed and confounded;
they have become like plants of the field
and like tender grass,
like grass on the housetops,
blighted[a] before it is grown.

28 "I know your rising up[b] and your sitting down,
your going out and coming in,
and your raging against me.
29 Because you have raged against me
and your arrogance has come to my ears,
I will put my hook in your nose
and my bit in your mouth;
I will turn you back on the way
by which you came.

30 "And this shall be the sign for you: This
year eat what grows of itself, and in the second
year what springs from that; then in the third year
sow, reap, plant vineyards, and eat their fruit.
31 The surviving remnant of the house of Judah
shall again take root downward, and bear fruit upward; 32 for from Jerusalem a remnant shall go
out, and from Mount Zion a band of survivors.
The zeal of the LORD of hosts will do this.

33 "Therefore thus says the LORD concerning
the king of Assyria: He shall not come into this
city, shoot an arrow there, come before it with a
shield, or cast up a siege ramp against it. 34 By the
way that he came, by the same he shall return; he
shall not come into this city, says the LORD. 35 For
I will defend this city to save it, for my own sake
and for the sake of my servant David."

36 Then the angel of the LORD set out and
struck down one hundred eighty-five thousand
in the camp of the Assyrians; when morning
dawned, they were all dead bodies. 37 Then King
Sennacherib of Assyria left, went home, and lived
at Nineveh. 38 As he was worshiping in the house

[a] With 2 Kings 19.26: Heb *field* [b] Q Ms Gk: MT lacks *your rising up*

of his god Nisroch, his sons Adrammelech and
Sharezer killed him with the sword, and they
escaped into the land of Ararat. His son Esar-
haddon succeeded him.

38 In those days Hezekiah became sick and
was at the point of death. The prophet
Isaiah son of Amoz came to him, and said to him,
"Thus says the LORD: Set your house in order, for
you shall die; you shall not recover." 2 Then Hezekiah turned his face to the wall, and prayed to
the LORD: 3 "Remember now, O LORD, I implore
you, how I have walked before you in faithfulness
with a whole heart, and have done what is good in
your sight." And Hezekiah wept bitterly.

4 Then the word of the LORD came to Isaiah:
5 "Go and say to Hezekiah, Thus says the LORD,
the God of your ancestor David: I have heard
your prayer, I have seen your tears; I will add fifteen years to your life. 6 I will deliver you and this
city out of the hand of the king of Assyria, and
defend this city.

7 "This is the sign to you from the LORD, that
the LORD will do this thing that he has promised:
8 See, I will make the shadow cast by the declining
sun on the dial of Ahaz turn back ten steps." So
the sun turned back on the dial the ten steps by
which it had declined.[a]

9 A writing of King Hezekiah of Judah, after
he had been sick and had recovered from his sickness:

10 I said: In the noontide of my days
I must depart;
I am consigned to the gates of Sheol
for the rest of my years.
11 I said, I shall not see the LORD
in the land of the living;
I shall look upon mortals no more
among the inhabitants of the world.
12 My dwelling is plucked up and removed
from me
like a shepherd's tent;
like a weaver I have rolled up my life;
he cuts me off from the loom;
from day to night you bring me to an end;[a]
13 I cry for help[b] until morning;
like a lion he breaks all my bones;
from day to night you bring me to an end.[a]

14 Like a swallow or a crane[a] I clamor,
I moan like a dove.
My eyes are weary with looking upward.
O Lord, I am oppressed; be my security!
15 But what can I say? For he has spoken to me,
and he himself has done it.
All my sleep has fled[c]
because of the bitterness of my soul.

16 O Lord, by these things people live,
and in all these is the life of my spirit.[a]
Oh, restore me to health and make me live!
17 Surely it was for my welfare
that I had great bitterness;
but you have held back[d] my life
from the pit of destruction,
for you have cast all my sins
behind your back.
18 For Sheol cannot thank you,
death cannot praise you;
those who go down to the Pit cannot hope
for your faithfulness.
19 The living, the living, they thank you,
as I do this day;
fathers make known to children
your faithfulness.

20 The LORD will save me,
and we will sing to stringed instruments[e]
all the days of our lives,
at the house of the LORD.

21 Now Isaiah had said, "Let them take a
lump of figs, and apply it to the boil, so that he
may recover." 22 Hezekiah also had said, "What
is the sign that I shall go up to the house of the
LORD?"

39 At that time King Merodach-baladan
son of Baladan of Babylon sent envoys

[a] Meaning of Heb uncertain [b] Cn: Meaning of Heb uncertain [c] Cn Compare Syr: Heb *I will walk slowly all my years*
[d] Cn Compare Gk Vg: Heb *loved* [e] Heb *my stringed instruments*

with letters and a present to Hezekiah, for he
heard that he had been sick and had recovered.
2 Hezekiah welcomed them; he showed them his
treasure house, the silver, the gold, the spices,
the precious oil, his whole armory, all that was
found in his storehouses. There was nothing in
his house or in all his realm that Hezekiah did
not show them. 3 Then the prophet Isaiah came
to King Hezekiah and said to him, "What did
these men say? From where did they come to
you?" Hezekiah answered, "They have come to
me from a far country, from Babylon." 4 He said,
"What have they seen in your house?" Hezekiah
answered, "They have seen all that is in my house;
there is nothing in my storehouses that I did not
show them."

5 Then Isaiah said to Hezekiah, "Hear the
word of the LORD of hosts: 6 Days are coming
when all that is in your house, and that which
your ancestors have stored up until this day, shall
be carried to Babylon; nothing shall be left, says
the LORD. 7 Some of your own sons who are born
to you shall be taken away; they shall be eunuchs
in the palace of the king of Babylon." 8 Then Hezekiah said to Isaiah, "The word of the LORD that
you have spoken is good." For he thought, "There
will be peace and security in my days."

40 Comfort, O comfort my people,
says your God.
2 Speak tenderly to Jerusalem,
and cry to her
that she has served her term,
that her penalty is paid,
that she has received from the LORD's hand
double for all her sins.

3 A voice cries out:
"In the wilderness prepare the way of the
LORD,
make straight in the desert a highway for
our God.
4 Every valley shall be lifted up,
and every mountain and hill be made low;
the uneven ground shall become level,
and the rough places a plain.
5 Then the glory of the LORD shall be
revealed,
and all people shall see it together,
for the mouth of the LORD has spoken."

6 A voice says, "Cry out!"
And I said, "What shall I cry?"
All people are grass,
their constancy is like the flower of the
field.
7 The grass withers, the flower fades,
when the breath of the LORD blows upon it;
surely the people are grass.
8 The grass withers, the flower fades;
but the word of our God will stand forever.
9 Get you up to a high mountain,
O Zion, herald of good tidings;[a]
lift up your voice with strength,
O Jerusalem, herald of good tidings,[b]
lift it up, do not fear;
say to the cities of Judah,
"Here is your God!"
10 See, the Lord GOD comes with might,
and his arm rules for him;
his reward is with him,
and his recompense before him.
11 He will feed his flock like a shepherd;
he will gather the lambs in his arms,
and carry them in his bosom,
and gently lead the mother sheep.

12 Who has measured the waters in the hollow
of his hand
and marked off the heavens with a span,
enclosed the dust of the earth in a measure,
and weighed the mountains in scales
and the hills in a balance?
13 Who has directed the spirit of the LORD,
or as his counselor has instructed him?
14 Whom did he consult for his enlightenment,
and who taught him the path of justice?
Who taught him knowledge,
and showed him the way of
understanding?

[a] Or *O herald of good tidings to Zion* [b] Or *O herald of good tidings to Jerusalem*

15 Even the nations are like a drop from a bucket,
and are accounted as dust on the scales;
see, he takes up the isles like fine dust.
16 Lebanon would not provide fuel enough,
nor are its animals enough for a burnt offering.
17 All the nations are as nothing before him;
they are accounted by him as less than nothing and emptiness.

18 To whom then will you liken God,
or what likeness compare with him?
19 An idol? —A workman casts it,
and a goldsmith overlays it with gold,
and casts for it silver chains.
20 As a gift one chooses mulberry wood[a]
—wood that will not rot—
then seeks out a skilled artisan
to set up an image that will not topple.

21 Have you not known? Have you not heard?
Has it not been told you from the beginning?
Have you not understood from the foundations of the earth?
22 It is he who sits above the circle of the earth,
and its inhabitants are like grasshoppers;
who stretches out the heavens like a curtain,
and spreads them like a tent to live in;
23 who brings princes to naught,
and makes the rulers of the earth as nothing.

24 Scarcely are they planted, scarcely sown,
scarcely has their stem taken root in the earth,
when he blows upon them, and they wither,
and the tempest carries them off like stubble.

25 To whom then will you compare me,
or who is my equal? says the Holy One.
26 Lift up your eyes on high and see:
Who created these?
He who brings out their host and numbers them,
calling them all by name;
because he is great in strength,
mighty in power,
not one is missing.

27 Why do you say, O Jacob,
and speak, O Israel,
"My way is hidden from the LORD,
and my right is disregarded by my God"?
28 Have you not known? Have you not heard?
The LORD is the everlasting God,
the Creator of the ends of the earth.
He does not faint or grow weary;
his understanding is unsearchable.
29 He gives power to the faint,
and strengthens the powerless.
30 Even youths will faint and be weary,
and the young will fall exhausted;
31 but those who wait for the LORD shall renew their strength,
they shall mount up with wings like eagles,
they shall run and not be weary,
they shall walk and not faint.

41 Listen to me in silence, O coastlands;
let the peoples renew their strength;
let them approach, then let them speak;
let us together draw near for judgment.

2 Who has roused a victor from the east,
summoned him to his service?
He delivers up nations to him,
and tramples kings under foot;
he makes them like dust with his sword,
like driven stubble with his bow.
3 He pursues them and passes on safely,
scarcely touching the path with his feet.
4 Who has performed and done this,
calling the generations from the beginning?
I, the LORD, am first,
and will be with the last.
5 The coastlands have seen and are afraid,
the ends of the earth tremble;

[a] Meaning of Heb uncertain

they have drawn near and come.
6 Each one helps the other,
saying to one another, "Take courage!"
7 The artisan encourages the goldsmith,
and the one who smooths with the hammer encourages the one who strikes the anvil,
saying of the soldering, "It is good";
and they fasten it with nails so that it cannot be moved.
8 But you, Israel, my servant,
Jacob, whom I have chosen,
the offspring of Abraham, my friend;
9 you whom I took from the ends of the earth,
and called from its farthest corners,
saying to you, "You are my servant,
I have chosen you and not cast you off";
10 do not fear, for I am with you,
do not be afraid, for I am your God;
I will strengthen you, I will help you,
I will uphold you with my victorious right hand.

11 Yes, all who are incensed against you
shall be ashamed and disgraced;
those who strive against you
shall be as nothing and shall perish.
12 You shall seek those who contend with you,
but you shall not find them;
those who war against you
shall be as nothing at all.
13 For I, the LORD your God,
hold your right hand;
it is I who say to you, "Do not fear,
I will help you."

14 Do not fear, you worm Jacob,
you insect[a] Israel!
I will help you, says the LORD;
your Redeemer is the Holy One of Israel.
15 Now, I will make of you a threshing sledge,
sharp, new, and having teeth;
you shall thresh the mountains and crush them,
and you shall make the hills like chaff.
16 You shall winnow them and the wind shall carry them away,
and the tempest shall scatter them.
Then you shall rejoice in the LORD;
in the Holy One of Israel you shall glory.

17 When the poor and needy seek water,
and there is none,
and their tongue is parched with thirst,
I the LORD will answer them,
I the God of Israel will not forsake them.
18 I will open rivers on the bare heights,[b]
and fountains in the midst of the valleys;
I will make the wilderness a pool of water,
and the dry land springs of water.
19 I will put in the wilderness the cedar,
the acacia, the myrtle, and the olive;
I will set in the desert the cypress,
the plane and the pine together,
20 so that all may see and know,
all may consider and understand,
that the hand of the LORD has done this,
the Holy One of Israel has created it.

21 Set forth your case, says the LORD;
bring your proofs, says the King of Jacob.
22 Let them bring them, and tell us
what is to happen.
Tell us the former things, what they are,
so that we may consider them,
and that we may know their outcome;
or declare to us the things to come.
23 Tell us what is to come hereafter,
that we may know that you are gods;
do good, or do harm,
that we may be afraid and terrified.
24 You, indeed, are nothing
and your work is nothing at all;
whoever chooses you is an abomination.

25 I stirred up one from the north, and he has come,
from the rising of the sun he was summoned by name.[c]
He shall trample[d] on rulers as on mortar,

[a] Syr: Heb *men of* [b] Or *trails* [c] Cn Compare Q Ms Gk: MT *and he shall call on my name* [d] Cn: Heb *come*

as the potter treads clay.
26 Who declared it from the beginning, so that
we might know,
and beforehand, so that we might say, "He
is right"?
There was no one who declared it, none who
proclaimed,
none who heard your words.
27 I first have declared it to Zion,[a]
and I give to Jerusalem a herald of good
tidings.
28 But when I look there is no one;
among these there is no counselor
who, when I ask, gives an answer.
29 No, they are all a delusion;
their works are nothing;
their images are empty wind.

42 Here is my servant, whom I uphold,
my chosen, in whom my soul delights;
I have put my spirit upon him;
he will bring forth justice to the nations.
2 He will not cry or lift up his voice,
or make it heard in the street;
3 a bruised reed he will not break,
and a dimly burning wick he will not
quench;
he will faithfully bring forth justice.
4 He will not grow faint or be crushed
until he has established justice in the earth;
and the coastlands wait for his teaching.

5 Thus says God, the LORD,
who created the heavens and stretched
them out,
who spread out the earth and what comes
from it,
who gives breath to the people upon it
and spirit to those who walk in it:
6 I am the LORD, I have called you in
righteousness,
I have taken you by the hand and kept you;
I have given you as a covenant to the people,[b]
a light to the nations,
7 to open the eyes that are blind,
to bring out the prisoners from the dungeon,
from the prison those who sit in darkness.
8 I am the LORD, that is my name;
my glory I give to no other,
nor my praise to idols.
9 See, the former things have come to pass,
and new things I now declare;
before they spring forth,
I tell you of them.

10 Sing to the LORD a new song,
his praise from the end of the earth!
Let the sea roar[c] and all that fills it,
the coastlands and their inhabitants.
11 Let the desert and its towns lift up their voice,
the villages that Kedar inhabits;
let the inhabitants of Sela sing for joy,
let them shout from the tops of the
mountains.
12 Let them give glory to the LORD,
and declare his praise in the coastlands.
13 The LORD goes forth like a soldier,
like a warrior he stirs up his fury;
he cries out, he shouts aloud,
he shows himself mighty against his foes.

14 For a long time I have held my peace,
I have kept still and restrained myself;
now I will cry out like a woman in labor,
I will gasp and pant.
15 I will lay waste mountains and hills,
and dry up all their herbage;
I will turn the rivers into islands,
and dry up the pools.
16 I will lead the blind
by a road they do not know,
by paths they have not known
I will guide them.
I will turn the darkness before them into
light,
the rough places into level ground.
These are the things I will do,
and I will not forsake them.

[a] Cn: Heb *First to Zion—Behold, behold them* [b] Meaning of Heb uncertain
[c] Cn Compare Ps 96.11; 98.7: Heb *Those who go down to the sea*

17 They shall be turned back and utterly put to
shame—
those who trust in carved images,
who say to cast images,
"You are our gods."

18 Listen, you that are deaf;
and you that are blind, look up and see!
19 Who is blind but my servant,
or deaf like my messenger whom I send?
Who is blind like my dedicated one,
or blind like the servant of the LORD?
20 He sees many things, but does[a] not observe
them;
his ears are open, but he does not hear.
21 The LORD was pleased, for the sake of his
righteousness,
to magnify his teaching and make it
glorious.
22 But this is a people robbed and plundered,
all of them are trapped in holes
and hidden in prisons;
they have become a prey with no one to
rescue,
a spoil with no one to say, "Restore!"
23 Who among you will give heed to this,
who will attend and listen for the time to
come?
24 Who gave up Jacob to the spoiler,
and Israel to the robbers?
Was it not the LORD, against whom we have
sinned,
in whose ways they would not walk,
and whose law they would not obey?
25 So he poured upon him the heat of his anger
and the fury of war;
it set him on fire all around, but he did not
understand;
it burned him, but he did not take it to
heart.

43 But now thus says the LORD,
he who created you, O Jacob,
he who formed you, O Israel:
Do not fear, for I have redeemed you;
I have called you by name, you are mine.
2 When you pass through the waters, I will be
with you;
and through the rivers, they shall not
overwhelm you;
when you walk through fire you shall not be
burned,
and the flame shall not consume you.
3 For I am the LORD your God,
the Holy One of Israel, your Savior.
I give Egypt as your ransom,
Ethiopia[b] and Seba in exchange for you.
4 Because you are precious in my sight,
and honored, and I love you,
I give people in return for you,
nations in exchange for your life.
5 Do not fear, for I am with you;
I will bring your offspring from the east,
and from the west I will gather you;
6 I will say to the north, "Give them up,"
and to the south, "Do not withhold;
bring my sons from far away
and my daughters from the end of the
earth—
7 everyone who is called by my name,
whom I created for my glory,
whom I formed and made."

8 Bring forth the people who are blind, yet
have eyes,
who are deaf, yet have ears!
9 Let all the nations gather together,
and let the peoples assemble.
Who among them declared this,
and foretold to us the former things?
Let them bring their witnesses to justify
them,
and let them hear and say, "It is true."
10 You are my witnesses, says the LORD,
and my servant whom I have chosen,
so that you may know and believe me
and understand that I am he.
Before me no god was formed,
nor shall there be any after me.
11 I, I am the LORD,

[a] Heb *You see many things but do* [b] Or *Nubia*; Heb *Cush*

and besides me there is no savior.
12 I declared and saved and proclaimed,
when there was no strange god among you;
and you are my witnesses, says the LORD.
13 I am God, and also henceforth I am He;
there is no one who can deliver from my hand;
I work and who can hinder it?

14 Thus says the LORD,
your Redeemer, the Holy One of Israel:
For your sake I will send to Babylon
and break down all the bars,
and the shouting of the Chaldeans will be turned to lamentation.[a]
15 I am the LORD, your Holy One,
the Creator of Israel, your King.
16 Thus says the LORD,
who makes a way in the sea,
a path in the mighty waters,
17 who brings out chariot and horse,
army and warrior;
they lie down, they cannot rise,
they are extinguished, quenched like a wick:
18 Do not remember the former things,
or consider the things of old.
19 I am about to do a new thing;
now it springs forth, do you not perceive it?
I will make a way in the wilderness
and rivers in the desert.
20 The wild animals will honor me,
the jackals and the ostriches;
for I give water in the wilderness,
rivers in the desert,
to give drink to my chosen people,
21 the people whom I formed for myself
so that they might declare my praise.

22 Yet you did not call upon me, O Jacob;
but you have been weary of me, O Israel!
23 You have not brought me your sheep for burnt offerings,
or honored me with your sacrifices.
I have not burdened you with offerings,
or wearied you with frankincense.
24 You have not bought me sweet cane with money,
or satisfied me with the fat of your sacrifices.
But you have burdened me with your sins;
you have wearied me with your iniquities.

25 I, I am He
who blots out your transgressions for my own sake,
and I will not remember your sins.
26 Accuse me, let us go to trial;
set forth your case, so that you may be proved right.
27 Your first ancestor sinned,
and your interpreters transgressed against me.
28 Therefore I profaned the princes of the sanctuary,
I delivered Jacob to utter destruction,
and Israel to reviling.

44 But now hear, O Jacob my servant,
Israel whom I have chosen!
2 Thus says the LORD who made you,
who formed you in the womb and will help you:
Do not fear, O Jacob my servant,
Jeshurun whom I have chosen.
3 For I will pour water on the thirsty land,
and streams on the dry ground;
I will pour my spirit upon your descendants,
and my blessing on your offspring.
4 They shall spring up like a green tamarisk,
like willows by flowing streams.
5 This one will say, "I am the LORD's,"
another will be called by the name of Jacob,
yet another will write on the hand, "The LORD's,"
and adopt the name of Israel.

6 Thus says the LORD, the King of Israel,
and his Redeemer, the LORD of hosts:

[a] Meaning of Heb uncertain

I am the first and I am the last;
besides me there is no god.
7 Who is like me? Let them proclaim it,
let them declare and set it forth before me.
Who has announced from of old the things
to come?[a]
Let them tell us[b] what is yet to be.
8 Do not fear, or be afraid;
have I not told you from of old and
declared it?
You are my witnesses!
Is there any god besides me?
There is no other rock; I know not one.

9 All who make idols are nothing, and the
things they delight in do not profit; their witnesses neither see nor know. And so they will be put
to shame. 10 Who would fashion a god or cast an
image that can do no good? 11 Look, all its devo-
tees shall be put to shame; the artisans too are
merely human. Let them all assemble, let them
stand up; they shall be terrified, they shall all be
put to shame.
12 The ironsmith fashions it[c] and works it
over the coals, shaping it with hammers, and
forging it with his strong arm; he becomes hungry and his strength fails, he drinks no water and
is faint. 13 The carpenter stretches a line, marks
it out with a stylus, fashions it with planes, and
marks it with a compass; he makes it in human
form, with human beauty, to be set up in a shrine.
14 He cuts down cedars or chooses a holm tree or
an oak and lets it grow strong among the trees of
the forest. He plants a cedar and the rain nourishes it. 15 Then it can be used as fuel. Part of it
he takes and warms himself; he kindles a fire and
bakes bread. Then he makes a god and worships
it, makes it a carved image and bows down before
it. 16 Half of it he burns in the fire; over this half he
roasts meat, eats it and is satisfied. He also warms
himself and says, "Ah, I am warm, I can feel the
fire!" 17 The rest of it he makes into a god, his idol,
bows down to it and worships it; he prays to it
and says, "Save me, for you are my god!"
18 They do not know, nor do they comprehend; for their eyes are shut, so that they cannot
see, and their minds as well, so that they cannot
understand. 19 No one considers, nor is there
knowledge or discernment to say, "Half of it I
burned in the fire; I also baked bread on its coals,
I roasted meat and have eaten. Now shall I make
the rest of it an abomination? Shall I fall down
before a block of wood?" 20 He feeds on ashes; a
deluded mind has led him astray, and he cannot
save himself or say, "Is not this thing in my right
hand a fraud?"

21 Remember these things, O Jacob,
and Israel, for you are my servant;
I formed you, you are my servant;
O Israel, you will not be forgotten by me.
22 I have swept away your transgressions like a
cloud,
and your sins like mist;
return to me, for I have redeemed you.

23 Sing, O heavens, for the LORD has done it;
shout, O depths of the earth;
break forth into singing, O mountains,
O forest, and every tree in it!
For the LORD has redeemed Jacob,
and will be glorified in Israel.

24 Thus says the LORD, your Redeemer,
who formed you in the womb:
I am the LORD, who made all things,
who alone stretched out the heavens,
who by myself spread out the earth;
25 who frustrates the omens of liars,
and makes fools of diviners;
who turns back the wise,
and makes their knowledge foolish;
26 who confirms the word of his servant,
and fulfills the prediction of his
messengers;
who says of Jerusalem, "It shall be inhabited,"
and of the cities of Judah, "They shall be
rebuilt,
and I will raise up their ruins";
27 who says to the deep, "Be dry—

[a] Cn: Heb *from my placing an eternal people and things to come* [b] Tg: Heb *them* [c] Cn: Heb *an ax*

I will dry up your rivers";
28 who says of Cyrus, "He is my shepherd,
and he shall carry out all my purpose";
and who says of Jerusalem, "It shall be rebuilt,"
and of the temple, "Your foundation shall be laid."

45

Thus says the LORD to his anointed, to Cyrus,
whose right hand I have grasped
to subdue nations before him
and strip kings of their robes,
to open doors before him—
and the gates shall not be closed:
2 I will go before you
and level the mountains,[a]
I will break in pieces the doors of bronze
and cut through the bars of iron,
3 I will give you the treasures of darkness
and riches hidden in secret places,
so that you may know that it is I, the LORD,
the God of Israel, who call you by your name.
4 For the sake of my servant Jacob,
and Israel my chosen,
I call you by your name,
I surname you, though you do not know me.
5 I am the LORD, and there is no other;
besides me there is no god.
I arm you, though you do not know me,
6 so that they may know, from the rising of the sun
and from the west, that there is no one besides me;
I am the LORD, and there is no other.
7 I form light and create darkness,
I make weal and create woe;
I the LORD do all these things.

8 Shower, O heavens, from above,
and let the skies rain down righteousness;
let the earth open, that salvation may spring up,[b]
and let it cause righteousness to sprout up also;
I the LORD have created it.

9 Woe to you who strive with your Maker,
earthen vessels with the potter![c]
Does the clay say to the one who fashions it,
"What are you making"?
or "Your work has no handles"?
10 Woe to anyone who says to a father, "What are you begetting?"
or to a woman, "With what are you in labor?"
11 Thus says the LORD,
the Holy One of Israel, and its Maker:
Will you question me[d] about my children,
or command me concerning the work of my hands?
12 I made the earth,
and created humankind upon it;
it was my hands that stretched out the heavens,
and I commanded all their host.
13 I have aroused Cyrus[e] in righteousness,
and I will make all his paths straight;
he shall build my city
and set my exiles free,
not for price or reward,
says the LORD of hosts.
14 Thus says the LORD:
The wealth of Egypt and the merchandise of Ethiopia,[f]
and the Sabeans, tall of stature,
shall come over to you and be yours,
they shall follow you;
they shall come over in chains and bow down to you.
They will make supplication to you, saying,
"God is with you alone, and there is no other;
there is no god besides him."
15 Truly, you are a God who hides himself,

[a] Q Ms Gk: MT *the swellings* [b] Q Ms: MT *that they may bring forth salvation* [c] Cn: Heb *with the potsherds,* or *with the potters* [d] Cn: Heb *Ask me of things to come* [e] Heb *him* [f] Or *Nubia;* Heb *Cush*

O God of Israel, the Savior.
16 All of them are put to shame and
confounded,
the makers of idols go in confusion
together.
17 But Israel is saved by the LORD
with everlasting salvation;
you shall not be put to shame or confounded
to all eternity.

18 For thus says the LORD,
who created the heavens
(he is God!),
who formed the earth and made it
(he established it;
he did not create it a chaos,
he formed it to be inhabited!):
I am the LORD, and there is no other.
19 I did not speak in secret,
in a land of darkness;
I did not say to the offspring of Jacob,
"Seek me in chaos."
I the LORD speak the truth,
I declare what is right.

20 Assemble yourselves and come together,
draw near, you survivors of the nations!
They have no knowledge—
those who carry about their wooden
idols,
and keep on praying to a god
that cannot save.
21 Declare and present your case;
let them take counsel together!
Who told this long ago?
Who declared it of old?
Was it not I, the LORD?
There is no other god besides me,
a righteous God and a Savior;
there is no one besides me.

22 Turn to me and be saved,
all the ends of the earth!
For I am God, and there is no other.
23 By myself I have sworn,
from my mouth has gone forth in
righteousness
a word that shall not return:
"To me every knee shall bow,
every tongue shall swear."

24 Only in the LORD, it shall be said of me,
are righteousness and strength;
all who were incensed against him
shall come to him and be ashamed.
25 In the LORD all the offspring of Israel
shall triumph and glory.

46 Bel bows down, Nebo stoops,
their idols are on beasts and cattle;
these things you carry are loaded
as burdens on weary animals.
2 They stoop, they bow down together;
they cannot save the burden,
but themselves go into captivity.

3 Listen to me, O house of Jacob,
all the remnant of the house of Israel,
who have been borne by me from your birth,
carried from the womb;
4 even to your old age I am he,
even when you turn gray I will carry you.
I have made, and I will bear;
I will carry and will save.

5 To whom will you liken me and make me
equal,
and compare me, as though we were alike?
6 Those who lavish gold from the purse,
and weigh out silver in the scales—
they hire a goldsmith, who makes it into a god;
then they fall down and worship!
7 They lift it to their shoulders, they carry it,
they set it in its place, and it stands there;
it cannot move from its place.
If one cries out to it, it does not answer
or save anyone from trouble.

8 Remember this and consider,[a]
recall it to mind, you transgressors,

[a] Meaning of Heb uncertain

9 remember the former things of old;
for I am God, and there is no other;
I am God, and there is no one like me,
10 declaring the end from the beginning
and from ancient times things not yet
done,
saying, "My purpose shall stand,
and I will fulfill my intention,"
11 calling a bird of prey from the east,
the man for my purpose from a far
country.
I have spoken, and I will bring it to pass;
I have planned, and I will do it.

12 Listen to me, you stubborn of heart,
you who are far from deliverance:
13 I bring near my deliverance, it is not far off,
and my salvation will not tarry;
I will put salvation in Zion,
for Israel my glory.

47 Come down and sit in the dust,
virgin daughter Babylon!
Sit on the ground without a throne,
daughter Chaldea!
For you shall no more be called
tender and delicate.
2 Take the millstones and grind meal,
remove your veil,
strip off your robe, uncover your legs,
pass through the rivers.
3 Your nakedness shall be uncovered,
and your shame shall be seen.
I will take vengeance,
and I will spare no one.
4 Our Redeemer—the LORD of hosts is his
name—
is the Holy One of Israel.

5 Sit in silence, and go into darkness,
daughter Chaldea!
For you shall no more be called
the mistress of kingdoms.
6 I was angry with my people,
I profaned my heritage;
I gave them into your hand,
you showed them no mercy;
on the aged you made your yoke
exceedingly heavy.
7 You said, "I shall be mistress forever,"
so that you did not lay these things to
heart
or remember their end.

8 Now therefore hear this, you lover of
pleasures,
who sit securely,
who say in your heart,
"I am, and there is no one besides me;
I shall not sit as a widow
or know the loss of children"—
9 both these things shall come upon you
in a moment, in one day:
the loss of children and widowhood
shall come upon you in full measure,
in spite of your many sorceries
and the great power of your enchantments.

10 You felt secure in your wickedness;
you said, "No one sees me."
Your wisdom and your knowledge
led you astray,
and you said in your heart,
"I am, and there is no one besides me."
11 But evil shall come upon you,
which you cannot charm away;
disaster shall fall upon you,
which you will not be able to ward off;
and ruin shall come on you suddenly,
of which you know nothing.

12 Stand fast in your enchantments
and your many sorceries,
with which you have labored from your
youth;
perhaps you may be able to succeed,
perhaps you may inspire terror.
13 You are wearied with your many
consultations;
let those who study[a] the heavens

[a] Meaning of Heb uncertain

stand up and save you,
those who gaze at the stars,
and at each new moon predict
what[a] shall befall you.

14 See, they are like stubble,
the fire consumes them;
they cannot deliver themselves
from the power of the flame.
No coal for warming oneself is this,
no fire to sit before!
15 Such to you are those with whom you have labored,
who have trafficked with you from your youth;
they all wander about in their own paths;
there is no one to save you.

48 Hear this, O house of Jacob,
who are called by the name of Israel,
and who came forth from the loins[b] of Judah;
who swear by the name of the LORD,
and invoke the God of Israel,
but not in truth or right.
2 For they call themselves after the holy city,
and lean on the God of Israel;
the LORD of hosts is his name.

3 The former things I declared long ago,
they went out from my mouth and I made them known;
then suddenly I did them and they came to pass.
4 Because I know that you are obstinate,
and your neck is an iron sinew
and your forehead brass,
5 I declared them to you from long ago,
before they came to pass I announced them to you,
so that you would not say, "My idol did them,
my carved image and my cast image commanded them."
6 You have heard; now see all this;
and will you not declare it?
From this time forward I make you hear new things,
hidden things that you have not known.
7 They are created now, not long ago;
before today you have never heard of them,
so that you could not say, "I already knew them."
8 You have never heard, you have never known,
from of old your ear has not been opened.
For I knew that you would deal very treacherously,
and that from birth you were called a rebel.

9 For my name's sake I defer my anger,
for the sake of my praise I restrain it for you,
so that I may not cut you off.
10 See, I have refined you, but not like[c] silver;
I have tested you in the furnace of adversity.
11 For my own sake, for my own sake, I do it,
for why should my name[d] be profaned?
My glory I will not give to another.

12 Listen to me, O Jacob,
and Israel, whom I called:
I am He; I am the first,
and I am the last.
13 My hand laid the foundation of the earth,
and my right hand spread out the heavens;
when I summon them,
they stand at attention.

14 Assemble, all of you, and hear!
Who among them has declared these things?
The LORD loves him;
he shall perform his purpose on Babylon,
and his arm shall be against the Chaldeans.
15 I, even I, have spoken and called him,
I have brought him, and he will prosper in his way.

[a] Gk Syr Compare Vg: Heb *from what* [b] Cn: Heb *waters* [c] Cn: Heb *with* [d] Gk Old Latin: Heb *for why should it*

16 Draw near to me, hear this!
From the beginning I have not spoken in secret,
from the time it came to be I have been there.
And now the Lord GOD has sent me and his spirit.

17 Thus says the LORD,
your Redeemer, the Holy One of Israel:
I am the LORD your God,
who teaches you for your own good,
who leads you in the way you should go.
18 O that you had paid attention to my commandments!
Then your prosperity would have been like a river,
and your success like the waves of the sea;
19 your offspring would have been like the sand,
and your descendants like its grains;
their name would never be cut off
or destroyed from before me.

20 Go out from Babylon, flee from Chaldea,
declare this with a shout of joy, proclaim it,
send it forth to the end of the earth;
say, "The LORD has redeemed his servant Jacob!"
21 They did not thirst when he led them through the deserts;
he made water flow for them from the rock;
he split open the rock and the water gushed out.

22 "There is no peace," says the LORD, "for the wicked."

49 Listen to me, O coastlands,
pay attention, you peoples from far away!
The LORD called me before I was born,
while I was in my mother's womb he named me.
2 He made my mouth like a sharp sword,
in the shadow of his hand he hid me;
he made me a polished arrow,
in his quiver he hid me away.
3 And he said to me, "You are my servant,
Israel, in whom I will be glorified."
4 But I said, "I have labored in vain,
I have spent my strength for nothing and vanity;
yet surely my cause is with the LORD,
and my reward with my God."

5 And now the LORD says,
who formed me in the womb to be his servant,
to bring Jacob back to him,
and that Israel might be gathered to him,
for I am honored in the sight of the LORD,
and my God has become my strength—
6 he says,
"It is too light a thing that you should be my servant
to raise up the tribes of Jacob
and to restore the survivors of Israel;
I will give you as a light to the nations,
that my salvation may reach to the end of the earth."

7 Thus says the LORD,
the Redeemer of Israel and his Holy One,
to one deeply despised, abhorred by the nations,
the slave of rulers,
"Kings shall see and stand up,
princes, and they shall prostrate themselves,
because of the LORD, who is faithful,
the Holy One of Israel, who has chosen you."

8 Thus says the LORD:
In a time of favor I have answered you,
on a day of salvation I have helped you;
I have kept you and given you
as a covenant to the people,[a]
to establish the land,
to apportion the desolate heritages;

[a] Meaning of Heb uncertain

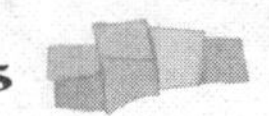

9 saying to the prisoners, "Come out,"
to those who are in darkness, "Show yourselves."
They shall feed along the ways,
on all the bare heights[a] shall be their pasture;
10 they shall not hunger or thirst,
neither scorching wind nor sun shall strike them down,
for he who has pity on them will lead them,
and by springs of water will guide them.
11 And I will turn all my mountains into a road,
and my highways shall be raised up.
12 Lo, these shall come from far away,
and lo, these from the north and from the west,
and these from the land of Syene.[b]

13 Sing for joy, O heavens, and exult, O earth;
break forth, O mountains, into singing!
For the LORD has comforted his people,
and will have compassion on his suffering ones.

14 But Zion said, "The LORD has forsaken me,
my Lord has forgotten me."
15 Can a woman forget her nursing child,
or show no compassion for the child of her womb?
Even these may forget,
yet I will not forget you.
16 See, I have inscribed you on the palms of my hands;
your walls are continually before me.
17 Your builders outdo your destroyers,[c]
and those who laid you waste go away from you.
18 Lift up your eyes all around and see;
they all gather, they come to you.
As I live, says the LORD,
you shall put all of them on like an ornament,
and like a bride you shall bind them on.
19 Surely your waste and your desolate places
and your devastated land—
surely now you will be too crowded for your inhabitants,
and those who swallowed you up will be far away.
20 The children born in the time of your bereavement
will yet say in your hearing:
"The place is too crowded for me;
make room for me to settle."
21 Then you will say in your heart,
"Who has borne me these?
I was bereaved and barren,
exiled and put away—
so who has reared these?
I was left all alone—
where then have these come from?"

22 Thus says the Lord GOD:
I will soon lift up my hand to the nations,
and raise my signal to the peoples;
and they shall bring your sons in their bosom,
and your daughters shall be carried on their shoulders.
23 Kings shall be your foster fathers,
and their queens your nursing mothers.
With their faces to the ground they shall bow down to you,
and lick the dust of your feet.
Then you will know that I am the LORD;
those who wait for me shall not be put to shame.

24 Can the prey be taken from the mighty,
or the captives of a tyrant[d] be rescued?
25 But thus says the LORD:
Even the captives of the mighty shall be taken,
and the prey of the tyrant be rescued;
for I will contend with those who contend with you,
and I will save your children.

[a] Or *the trails* [b] Q Ms: MT *Sinim* [c] Or *Your children come swiftly; your destroyers*
[d] Q Ms Syr Vg: MT *of a righteous person*

26 I will make your oppressors eat their own
flesh,
and they shall be drunk with their own
blood as with wine.
Then all flesh shall know
that I am the LORD your Savior,
and your Redeemer, the Mighty One of
Jacob.

50 Thus says the LORD:
Where is your mother's bill of divorce
with which I put her away?
Or which of my creditors is it
to whom I have sold you?
No, because of your sins you were sold,
and for your transgressions your mother
was put away.
2 Why was no one there when I came?
Why did no one answer when I
called?
Is my hand shortened, that it cannot
redeem?
Or have I no power to deliver?
By my rebuke I dry up the sea,
I make the rivers a desert;
their fish stink for lack of water,
and die of thirst.[a]
3 I clothe the heavens with blackness,
and make sackcloth their covering.

4 The Lord GOD has given me
the tongue of a teacher,[b]
that I may know how to sustain
the weary with a word.
Morning by morning he wakens—
wakens my ear
to listen as those who are taught.
5 The Lord GOD has opened my ear,
and I was not rebellious,
I did not turn backward.
6 I gave my back to those who struck me,
and my cheeks to those who pulled out the
beard;
I did not hide my face
from insult and spitting.

7 The Lord GOD helps me;
therefore I have not been disgraced;
therefore I have set my face like flint,
and I know that I shall not be put to
shame;
8 he who vindicates me is near.
Who will contend with me?
Let us stand up together.
Who are my adversaries?
Let them confront me.
9 It is the Lord GOD who helps me;
who will declare me guilty?
All of them will wear out like a garment;
the moth will eat them up.

10 Who among you fears the LORD
and obeys the voice of his servant,
who walks in darkness
and has no light,
yet trusts in the name of the LORD
and relies upon his God?
11 But all of you are kindlers of fire,
lighters of firebrands.[c]
Walk in the flame of your fire,
and among the brands that you have
kindled!
This is what you shall have from my hand:
you shall lie down in torment.

51 Listen to me, you that pursue
righteousness,
you that seek the LORD.
Look to the rock from which you were hewn,
and to the quarry from which you were
dug.
2 Look to Abraham your father
and to Sarah who bore you;
for he was but one when I called him,
but I blessed him and made him many.
3 For the LORD will comfort Zion;
he will comfort all her waste places,
and will make her wilderness like Eden,
her desert like the garden of the LORD;
joy and gladness will be found in her,
thanksgiving and the voice of song.

[a] Or *die on the thirsty ground* [b] Cn: Heb *of those who are taught* [c] Syr: Heb *you gird yourselves with firebrands*

4 Listen to me, my people,
and give heed to me, my nation;
for a teaching will go out from me,
and my justice for a light to the peoples.
5 I will bring near my deliverance swiftly,
my salvation has gone out
and my arms will rule the peoples;
the coastlands wait for me,
and for my arm they hope.
6 Lift up your eyes to the heavens,
and look at the earth beneath;
for the heavens will vanish like smoke,
the earth will wear out like a garment,
and those who live on it will die like
gnats;[a]
but my salvation will be forever,
and my deliverance will never be ended.

7 Listen to me, you who know righteousness,
you people who have my teaching in your
hearts;
do not fear the reproach of others,
and do not be dismayed when they revile
you.
8 For the moth will eat them up like a garment,
and the worm will eat them like wool;
but my deliverance will be forever,
and my salvation to all generations.

9 Awake, awake, put on strength,
O arm of the LORD!
Awake, as in days of old,
the generations of long ago!
Was it not you who cut Rahab in pieces,
who pierced the dragon?
10 Was it not you who dried up the sea,
the waters of the great deep;
who made the depths of the sea a way
for the redeemed to cross over?
11 So the ransomed of the LORD shall return,
and come to Zion with singing;
everlasting joy shall be upon their heads;
they shall obtain joy and gladness,
and sorrow and sighing shall flee away.

12 I, I am he who comforts you;
why then are you afraid of a mere mortal
who must die,
a human being who fades like grass?
13 You have forgotten the LORD, your Maker,
who stretched out the heavens
and laid the foundations of the earth.
You fear continually all day long
because of the fury of the oppressor,
who is bent on destruction.
But where is the fury of the oppressor?
14 The oppressed shall speedily be released;
they shall not die and go down to the Pit,
nor shall they lack bread.
15 For I am the LORD your God,
who stirs up the sea so that its waves
roar—
the LORD of hosts is his name.
16 I have put my words in your mouth,
and hidden you in the shadow of my
hand,
stretching out[b] the heavens

Isaiah 51:1-8

Following centuries of repressive Assyrian and Babylonian policies toward minority peoples throughout the ancient Near East, it was suddenly the policy of Cyrus to allow the peoples to return to their homelands. He granted them authority to rebuild ruined cities and temples. Isaiah's words here are startling. Strange as it may seem, God is working through Cyrus and the Persian government to bring about release from exile and restoration of Jerusalem and the Judean homeland. In Isa 45:1, this prophet even calls Cyrus God's "messiah" (in Hebrew; "christ" in Greek, translated "anointed" in the NRSV)—a specially appointed agent who will bring about God's will. Isaiah says this is God at work in the events of human history, and God can at any time bring startling change for the oppressed and marginalized.

— DB

[a] Or *in like manner* [b] Syr: Heb *planting*

and laying the foundations of the earth,
and saying to Zion, "You are my people."

17 Rouse yourself, rouse yourself!
Stand up, O Jerusalem,
you who have drunk at the hand of the LORD
the cup of his wrath,
who have drunk to the dregs
the bowl of staggering.
18 There is no one to guide her
among all the children she has borne;
there is no one to take her by the hand
among all the children she has brought up.
19 These two things have befallen you
—who will grieve with you?—
devastation and destruction, famine and
sword—
who will comfort you?[a]
20 Your children have fainted,
they lie at the head of every street
like an antelope in a net;
they are full of the wrath of the LORD,
the rebuke of your God.

21 Therefore hear this, you who are wounded,[b]
who are drunk, but not with wine:
22 Thus says your Sovereign, the LORD,
your God who pleads the cause of his
people:
See, I have taken from your hand the cup of
staggering;
you shall drink no more
from the bowl of my wrath.
23 And I will put it into the hand of your
tormentors,
who have said to you,
"Bow down, that we may walk on you";
and you have made your back like the ground
and like the street for them to walk on.

52 Awake, awake,
put on your strength, O Zion!
Put on your beautiful garments,
O Jerusalem, the holy city;
for the uncircumcised and the unclean
shall enter you no more.
2 Shake yourself from the dust, rise up,
O captive[c] Jerusalem;
loose the bonds from your neck,
O captive daughter Zion!

3 For thus says the LORD: You were sold
for nothing, and you shall be redeemed without
money. 4 For thus says the Lord GOD: Long ago,
my people went down into Egypt to reside there
as aliens; the Assyrian, too, has oppressed them
without cause. 5 Now therefore what am I doing
here, says the LORD, seeing that my people are
taken away without cause? Their rulers howl, says
the LORD, and continually, all day long, my name
is despised. 6 Therefore my people shall know my
name; therefore in that day they shall know that
it is I who speak; here am I.

7 How beautiful upon the mountains
are the feet of the messenger who
announces peace,
who brings good news,
who announces salvation,
who says to Zion, "Your God reigns."
8 Listen! Your sentinels lift up their voices,
together they sing for joy;
for in plain sight they see
the return of the LORD to Zion.
9 Break forth together into singing,
you ruins of Jerusalem;
for the LORD has comforted his people,
he has redeemed Jerusalem.
10 The LORD has bared his holy arm
before the eyes of all the nations;
and all the ends of the earth shall see
the salvation of our God.

11 Depart, depart, go out from there!
Touch no unclean thing;
go out from the midst of it, purify yourselves,
you who carry the vessels of the LORD.
12 For you shall not go out in haste,
and you shall not go in flight;
for the LORD will go before you,

[a] Q Ms Gk Syr Vg: MT *how may I comfort you?* [b] Or *humbled* [c] Cn: Heb *rise up, sit*

and the God of Israel will be your rear
guard.

13 See, my servant shall prosper;
he shall be exalted and lifted up,
and shall be very high.
14 Just as there were many who were astonished
at him[a]
—so marred was his appearance, beyond
human semblance,
and his form beyond that of mortals—
15 so he shall startle[b] many nations;
kings shall shut their mouths because of
him;
for that which had not been told them they
shall see,
and that which they had not heard they
shall contemplate.

53 Who has believed what we have heard?
And to whom has the arm of the LORD
been revealed?
2 For he grew up before him like a young plant,
and like a root out of dry ground;
he had no form or majesty that we should
look at him,
nothing in his appearance that we should
desire him.
3 He was despised and rejected by others;
a man of suffering[c] and acquainted with
infirmity;
and as one from whom others hide their faces[d]
he was despised, and we held him of no
account.

4 Surely he has borne our infirmities
and carried our diseases;
yet we accounted him stricken,
struck down by God, and afflicted.
5 But he was wounded for our transgressions,
crushed for our iniquities;
upon him was the punishment that made us
whole,
and by his bruises we are healed.
6 All we like sheep have gone astray;
we have all turned to our own way,
and the LORD has laid on him
the iniquity of us all.

7 He was oppressed, and he was afflicted,
yet he did not open his mouth;
like a lamb that is led to the slaughter,
and like a sheep that before its shearers is
silent,
so he did not open his mouth.
8 By a perversion of justice he was taken away.
Who could have imagined his future?
For he was cut off from the land of the living,
stricken for the transgression of my
people.
9 They made his grave with the wicked
and his tomb[e] with the rich,[f]
although he had done no violence,
and there was no deceit in his mouth.

10 Yet it was the will of the LORD to crush him
with pain.[g]

Isaiah 53:7, 11-12

It is obvious that the historical conflict that has existed between the black churches and the larger white society has not resulted in any profound existential estrangement from whites by blacks.... Although they have viewed the Ku Klux Klan as wholly hostile, the race has refrained from viewing all white Americans similarly.... [B]lacks responded to the KKK mainly by avoidance and rarely resorted to violence, even in self-defense. Martin Luther King, Jr., rightly captured the spirit of the black community when he said repeatedly that non-violent resistance is redemptive. While its active dimension fails to compromise evil, its passive side manifests an alternative method of response that keeps the conditions of communication open rather than closed. The availability of such conditions implies the redeemability of the opponent.[49]

— Peter J. Paris

[a] Syr Tg: Heb *you* [b] Meaning of Heb uncertain [c] Or *a man of sorrows* [d] Or *as one who hides his face from us*
[e] Q Ms: MT *and in his death* [f] Cn: Heb *with a rich person* [g] Or *by disease*; meaning of Heb uncertain

When you make his life an offering for sin,[a]
he shall see his offspring, and shall prolong his days;
through him the will of the LORD shall prosper.
11 Out of his anguish he shall see light;[b]
he shall find satisfaction through his knowledge.
The righteous one,[c] my servant, shall make many righteous,
and he shall bear their iniquities.
12 Therefore I will allot him a portion with the great,
and he shall divide the spoil with the strong;
because he poured out himself to death,
and was numbered with the transgressors;
yet he bore the sin of many,
and made intercession for the transgressors.

54 Sing, O barren one who did not bear;
burst into song and shout,
you who have not been in labor!
For the children of the desolate woman will be more
than the children of her that is married,
says the LORD.
2 Enlarge the site of your tent,
and let the curtains of your habitations be stretched out;
do not hold back; lengthen your cords
and strengthen your stakes.
3 For you will spread out to the right and to the left,
and your descendants will possess the nations
and will settle the desolate towns.

4 Do not fear, for you will not be ashamed;
do not be discouraged, for you will not suffer disgrace;
for you will forget the shame of your youth,
and the disgrace of your widowhood you will remember no more.
5 For your Maker is your husband,
the LORD of hosts is his name;
the Holy One of Israel is your Redeemer,
the God of the whole earth he is called.
6 For the LORD has called you
like a wife forsaken and grieved in spirit,
like the wife of a man's youth when she is cast off,
says your God.
7 For a brief moment I abandoned you,
but with great compassion I will gather you.
8 In overflowing wrath for a moment
I hid my face from you,
but with everlasting love I will have compassion on you,
says the LORD, your Redeemer.

9 This is like the days of Noah to me:
Just as I swore that the waters of Noah
would never again go over the earth,
so I have sworn that I will not be angry with you
and will not rebuke you.
10 For the mountains may depart
and the hills be removed,
but my steadfast love shall not depart from you,
and my covenant of peace shall not be removed,
says the LORD, who has compassion on you.

11 O afflicted one, storm-tossed, and not comforted,
I am about to set your stones in antimony,
and lay your foundations with sapphires.[d]
12 I will make your pinnacles of rubies,
your gates of jewels,
and all your wall of precious stones.
13 All your children shall be taught by the LORD,

[a] Meaning of Heb uncertain [b] Q Mss: MT lacks *light* [c] Or *and he shall find satisfaction. Through his knowledge, the righteous one* [d] Or *lapis lazuli*

and great shall be the prosperity of your
children.
14 In righteousness you shall be established;
you shall be far from oppression, for you
shall not fear;
and from terror, for it shall not come near
you.
15 If anyone stirs up strife,
it is not from me;
whoever stirs up strife with you
shall fall because of you.
16 See it is I who have created the smith
who blows the fire of coals,
and produces a weapon fit for its
purpose;
I have also created the ravager to destroy.
17 No weapon that is fashioned against you
shall prosper,
and you shall confute every tongue that
rises against you in judgment.
This is the heritage of the servants of the
LORD
and their vindication from me, says the
LORD.

55 Ho, everyone who thirsts,
come to the waters;
and you that have no money,
come, buy and eat!
Come, buy wine and milk
without money and without price.
2 Why do you spend your money for that
which is not bread,
and your labor for that which does not
satisfy?
Listen carefully to me, and eat what is good,
and delight yourselves in rich food.
3 Incline your ear, and come to me;
listen, so that you may live.
I will make with you an everlasting covenant,
my steadfast, sure love for David.
4 See, I made him a witness to the peoples,
a leader and commander for the peoples.
5 See, you shall call nations that you do not
know,
and nations that do not know you shall run
to you,
because of the LORD your God, the Holy
One of Israel,
for he has glorified you.

6 Seek the LORD while he may be found,
call upon him while he is near;
7 let the wicked forsake their way,
and the unrighteous their thoughts;
let them return to the LORD, that he may
have mercy on them,
and to our God, for he will abundantly
pardon.
8 For my thoughts are not your thoughts,
nor are your ways my ways, says the LORD.
9 For as the heavens are higher than the earth,
so are my ways higher than your ways
and my thoughts than your thoughts.

10 For as the rain and the snow come down
from heaven,
and do not return there until they have
watered the earth,
making it bring forth and sprout,
giving seed to the sower and bread to the
eater,
11 so shall my word be that goes out from my
mouth;
it shall not return to me empty,
but it shall accomplish that which I purpose,
and succeed in the thing for which I sent it.

12 For you shall go out in joy,
and be led back in peace;
the mountains and the hills before you
shall burst into song,
and all the trees of the field shall clap their
hands.
13 Instead of the thorn shall come up the
cypress;
instead of the brier shall come up the
myrtle;
and it shall be to the LORD for a memorial,
for an everlasting sign that shall not be cut
off.

56 Thus says the LORD:
Maintain justice, and do what is right,

for soon my salvation will come,
and my deliverance be revealed.

2 Happy is the mortal who does this,
the one who holds it fast,
who keeps the sabbath, not profaning it,
and refrains from doing any evil.

3 Do not let the foreigner joined to the LORD say,
"The LORD will surely separate me from his people";
and do not let the eunuch say,
"I am just a dry tree."
4 For thus says the LORD:
To the eunuchs who keep my sabbaths,
who choose the things that please me
and hold fast my covenant,
5 I will give, in my house and within my walls,
a monument and a name
better than sons and daughters;
I will give them an everlasting name
that shall not be cut off.

6 And the foreigners who join themselves to the LORD,
to minister to him, to love the name of the LORD,
and to be his servants,
all who keep the sabbath, and do not profane it,
and hold fast my covenant—
7 these I will bring to my holy mountain,
and make them joyful in my house of prayer;
their burnt offerings and their sacrifices
will be accepted on my altar;
for my house shall be called a house of prayer
for all peoples.
8 Thus says the Lord GOD,
who gathers the outcasts of Israel,
I will gather others to them
besides those already gathered.[a]

9 All you wild animals,
all you wild animals in the forest, come to devour!
10 Israel's[b] sentinels are blind,
they are all without knowledge;
they are all silent dogs
that cannot bark;
dreaming, lying down,
loving to slumber.
11 The dogs have a mighty appetite;
they never have enough.
The shepherds also have no understanding;

[a] Heb *besides his gathered ones* [b] Heb *His*

Isaiah 56:6-8

The prophet makes clear that in the time of the restored temple and in the renewed worship after the exile, the all-encompassing breadth of God's universal love will be apparent. Using the examples of "foreigners" (resident aliens or guest workers) and eunuchs, who in the past had been unwelcome (Deut 23:1) and discriminated against, Isaiah declares that in the future reality God's salvation and favor will extend to anyone and everyone who does what is just and right (Isa 56:1), regardless of whether they are eunuchs, foreigners, immigrants, outcasts, or citizens (56:3-4). In 56:7, speaking again for God, Isaiah declares that "my house shall be called a house of prayer for *all* peoples." It is easy to fall into the trap of us-them thinking and assume that God concurs with *our* cultural and social biases. Isaiah sees beyond the comfortable narrowness to which God's people are so susceptible and proclaims instead that God, who loves all human beings, does not discriminate among persons, regardless of class, race, language, power, credentials, status, achievements, or faith! God's people can help radiate that love by their own words and deeds.

— DB

they have all turned to their own way,
to their own gain, one and all.
12 "Come," they say, "let us[a] get wine;
let us fill ourselves with strong drink.
And tomorrow will be like today,
great beyond measure."

57 The righteous perish,
and no one takes it to heart;
the devout are taken away,
while no one understands.
For the righteous are taken away from
calamity,
2 and they enter into peace;
those who walk uprightly
will rest on their couches.
3 But as for you, come here,
you children of a sorceress,
you offspring of an adulterer and a whore.[b]
4 Whom are you mocking?
Against whom do you open your mouth
wide
and stick out your tongue?
Are you not children of transgression,
the offspring of deceit—
5 you that burn with lust among the oaks,
under every green tree;
you that slaughter your children in the
valleys,
under the clefts of the rocks?
6 Among the smooth stones of the valley is
your portion;
they, they, are your lot;
to them you have poured out a drink offering,
you have brought a grain offering.
Shall I be appeased for these things?
7 Upon a high and lofty mountain
you have set your bed,
and there you went up to offer sacrifice.
8 Behind the door and the doorpost
you have set up your symbol;
for, in deserting me,[c] you have uncovered
your bed,
you have gone up to it,
you have made it wide;
and you have made a bargain for yourself
with them,
you have loved their bed,
you have gazed on their nakedness.[d]
9 You journeyed to Molech[e] with oil,
and multiplied your perfumes;
you sent your envoys far away,
and sent down even to Sheol.
10 You grew weary from your many wanderings,
but you did not say, "It is useless."
You found your desire rekindled,
and so you did not weaken.

11 Whom did you dread and fear
so that you lied,
and did not remember me
or give me a thought?
Have I not kept silent and closed my eyes,[f]
and so you do not fear me?
12 I will concede your righteousness and your
works,
but they will not help you.
13 When you cry out, let your collection of idols
deliver you!
The wind will carry them off,
a breath will take them away.
But whoever takes refuge in me shall possess
the land
and inherit my holy mountain.

14 It shall be said,
"Build up, build up, prepare the way,
remove every obstruction from my
people's way."
15 For thus says the high and lofty one
who inhabits eternity, whose name is
Holy:
I dwell in the high and holy place,
and also with those who are contrite and
humble in spirit,
to revive the spirit of the humble,

[a] Q Ms Syr Vg Tg: MT *me* [b] Heb *an adulterer and she plays the whore* [c] Meaning of Heb uncertain [d] Or *their phallus*; Heb *the hand* [e] Or *the king* [f] Gk Vg: Heb *silent even for a long time*

and to revive the heart of the contrite.
16 For I will not continually accuse,
nor will I always be angry;
for then the spirits would grow faint before me,
even the souls that I have made.
17 Because of their wicked covetousness I was
angry;
I struck them, I hid and was angry;
but they kept turning back to their own
ways.
18 I have seen their ways, but I will heal them;
I will lead them and repay them with
comfort,
creating for their mourners the fruit of the
lips.[a]
19 Peace, peace, to the far and the near, says the
LORD;
and I will heal them.
20 But the wicked are like the tossing sea
that cannot keep still;
its waters toss up mire and mud.
21 There is no peace, says my God, for the
wicked.

58 Shout out, do not hold back!
Lift up your voice like a trumpet!
Announce to my people their rebellion,
to the house of Jacob their sins.
2 Yet day after day they seek me
and delight to know my ways,
as if they were a nation that practiced
righteousness
and did not forsake the ordinance of their
God;
they ask of me righteous judgments,
they delight to draw near to God.
3 "Why do we fast, but you do not see?
Why humble ourselves, but you do not
notice?"
Look, you serve your own interest on your
fast day,
and oppress all your workers.
4 Look, you fast only to quarrel and to fight
and to strike with a wicked fist.
Such fasting as you do today
will not make your voice heard on high.
5 Is such the fast that I choose,
a day to humble oneself?
Is it to bow down the head like a bulrush,
and to lie in sackcloth and ashes?
Will you call this a fast,
a day acceptable to the LORD?

6 Is not this the fast that I choose:
to loose the bonds of injustice,
to undo the thongs of the yoke,
to let the oppressed go free,
and to break every yoke?
7 Is it not to share your bread with the hungry,
and bring the homeless poor into your
house;
when you see the naked, to cover them,
and not to hide yourself from your own kin?
8 Then your light shall break forth like the
dawn,
and your healing shall spring up quickly;
your vindicator[b] shall go before you,
the glory of the LORD shall be your rear
guard.
9 Then you shall call, and the LORD will
answer;
you shall cry for help, and he will say, Here
I am.

If you remove the yoke from among you,
the pointing of the finger, the speaking of
evil,
10 if you offer your food to the hungry
and satisfy the needs of the afflicted,
then your light shall rise in the darkness
and your gloom be like the noonday.
11 The LORD will guide you continually,
and satisfy your needs in parched places,
and make your bones strong;
and you shall be like a watered garden,
like a spring of water,
whose waters never fail.
12 Your ancient ruins shall be rebuilt;
you shall raise up the foundations of many
generations;

[a] Meaning of Heb uncertain [b] Or *vindication*

Isaiah 58:6-9

Under the Commerce Street bridge on the west side of downtown San Antonio can be a dark place even in the daytime.... It is a dangerous area, yet it is home for many of San Antonio's citizens who are homeless.... Around 8 p.m. each Friday, members of Camino Real...set up tables in a space under the bridge. The evening begins with Scripture readings, a sermon, sometimes a testimonial from one of the participants, and prayers with the homeless who gather there. A pot of soup is provided each week, along with bread, cold water and sodas. Ralph Gibson, who heads the Friday night ministry for Camino Real, stated: "I was reading the Bible one day and read that the light had come for all, and that the light shines in the darkness.... I felt God called me to take the light to the darkness."

*According to the National Coalition for the Homeless...approximately 3.5 million people, 1.35 million of them children, are likely to experience homelessness in a given year (*National Law Center on Homelessness and Poverty, 2007*).*[50]

— John Dellis

you shall be called the repairer of the breach,
the restorer of streets to live in.

13 If you refrain from trampling the sabbath,
from pursuing your own interests on my holy day;
if you call the sabbath a delight
and the holy day of the LORD honorable;
if you honor it, not going your own ways,
serving your own interests, or pursuing your own affairs;[a]
14 then you shall take delight in the LORD,
and I will make you ride upon the heights of the earth;
I will feed you with the heritage of your ancestor Jacob,
for the mouth of the LORD has spoken.

59 See, the LORD's hand is not too short to save,
nor his ear too dull to hear.
2 Rather, your iniquities have been barriers
between you and your God,
and your sins have hidden his face from you
so that he does not hear.
3 For your hands are defiled with blood,
and your fingers with iniquity;
your lips have spoken lies,
your tongue mutters wickedness.
4 No one brings suit justly,
no one goes to law honestly;
they rely on empty pleas, they speak lies,
conceiving mischief and begetting iniquity.
5 They hatch adders' eggs,
and weave the spider's web;
whoever eats their eggs dies,
and the crushed egg hatches out a viper.
6 Their webs cannot serve as clothing;
they cannot cover themselves with what they make.
Their works are works of iniquity,
and deeds of violence are in their hands.
7 Their feet run to evil,
and they rush to shed innocent blood;
their thoughts are thoughts of iniquity,
desolation and destruction are in their highways.
8 The way of peace they do not know,
and there is no justice in their paths.
Their roads they have made crooked;
no one who walks in them knows peace.

9 Therefore justice is far from us,
and righteousness does not reach us;
we wait for light, and lo! there is darkness;
and for brightness, but we walk in gloom.
10 We grope like the blind along a wall,
groping like those who have no eyes;

[b] Heb *or speaking words*

we stumble at noon as in the twilight,
among the vigorous[a] as though we were dead.
11 We all growl like bears;
like doves we moan mournfully.
We wait for justice, but there is none;
for salvation, but it is far from us.
12 For our transgressions before you are many,
and our sins testify against us.
Our transgressions indeed are with us,
and we know our iniquities:
13 transgressing, and denying the LORD,
and turning away from following our God,
talking oppression and revolt,
conceiving lying words and uttering them from the heart.
14 Justice is turned back,
and righteousness stands at a distance;
for truth stumbles in the public square,
and uprightness cannot enter.
15 Truth is lacking,
and whoever turns from evil is despoiled.

The LORD saw it, and it displeased him
that there was no justice.
16 He saw that there was no one,
and was appalled that there was no one to intervene;
so his own arm brought him victory,
and his righteousness upheld him.
17 He put on righteousness like a breastplate,
and a helmet of salvation on his head;
he put on garments of vengeance for clothing,
and wrapped himself in fury as in a mantle.
18 According to their deeds, so will he repay;
wrath to his adversaries, requital to his enemies;
to the coastlands he will render requital.
19 So those in the west shall fear the name of the LORD,
and those in the east, his glory;
for he will come like a pent-up stream
that the wind of the LORD drives on.
20 And he will come to Zion as Redeemer,
to those in Jacob who turn from transgression, says the LORD.

21 And as for me, this is my covenant with them,
says the LORD: my spirit that is upon you, and my
words that I have put in your mouth, shall not depart out of your mouth, or out of the mouths of
your children, or out of the mouths of your children's children, says the LORD, from now on and
forever.

60 Arise, shine; for your light has come,
and the glory of the LORD has risen upon you.
2 For darkness shall cover the earth,
and thick darkness the peoples;
but the LORD will arise upon you,
and his glory will appear over you.
3 Nations shall come to your light,
and kings to the brightness of your dawn.

4 Lift up your eyes and look around;
they all gather together, they come to you;
your sons shall come from far away,
and your daughters shall be carried on their nurses' arms.
5 Then you shall see and be radiant;
your heart shall thrill and rejoice,[b]
because the abundance of the sea shall be brought to you,
the wealth of the nations shall come to you.
6 A multitude of camels shall cover you,
the young camels of Midian and Ephah;
all those from Sheba shall come.
They shall bring gold and frankincense,
and shall proclaim the praise of the LORD.
7 All the flocks of Kedar shall be gathered to you,
the rams of Nebaioth shall minister to you;
they shall be acceptable on my altar,
and I will glorify my glorious house.

8 Who are these that fly like a cloud,
and like doves to their windows?

[a] Meaning of Heb uncertain [b] Heb *be enlarged*

9 For the coastlands shall wait for me,
the ships of Tarshish first,
to bring your children from far away,
their silver and gold with them,
for the name of the LORD your God,
and for the Holy One of Israel,
because he has glorified you.
10 Foreigners shall build up your walls,
and their kings shall minister to you;
for in my wrath I struck you down,
but in my favor I have had mercy on you.
11 Your gates shall always be open;
day and night they shall not be shut,
so that nations shall bring you their wealth,
with their kings led in procession.
12 For the nation and kingdom
that will not serve you shall perish;
those nations shall be utterly laid waste.
13 The glory of Lebanon shall come to you,
the cypress, the plane, and the pine,
to beautify the place of my sanctuary;
and I will glorify where my feet rest.
14 The descendants of those who oppressed you
shall come bending low to you,
and all who despised you
shall bow down at your feet;
they shall call you the City of the LORD,
the Zion of the Holy One of Israel.
15 Whereas you have been forsaken and hated,
with no one passing through,
I will make you majestic forever,
a joy from age to age.
16 You shall suck the milk of nations,
you shall suck the breasts of kings;
and you shall know that I, the LORD, am your Savior
and your Redeemer, the Mighty One of Jacob.

17 Instead of bronze I will bring gold,
instead of iron I will bring silver;
instead of wood, bronze,
instead of stones, iron.
I will appoint Peace as your overseer
and Righteousness as your taskmaster.
18 Violence shall no more be heard in your land,
devastation or destruction within your borders;
you shall call your walls Salvation,
and your gates Praise.
19 The sun shall no longer be
your light by day,
nor for brightness shall the moon
give light to you by night;[a]
but the LORD will be your everlasting light,
and your God will be your glory.
20 Your sun shall no more go down,
or your moon withdraw itself;
for the LORD will be your everlasting light,
and your days of mourning shall be ended.
21 Your people shall all be righteous;
they shall possess the land forever.
They are the shoot that I planted, the work of my hands,
so that I might be glorified.
22 The least of them shall become a clan,
and the smallest one a mighty nation;
I am the LORD;
in its time I will accomplish it quickly.

61 The spirit of the Lord GOD is upon me,
because the LORD has anointed me;
he has sent me to bring good news to the oppressed,
to bind up the brokenhearted,
to proclaim liberty to the captives,
and release to the prisoners;
2 to proclaim the year of the LORD's favor,
and the day of vengeance of our God;
to comfort all who mourn;
3 to provide for those who mourn in Zion—
to give them a garland instead of ashes,
the oil of gladness instead of mourning,
the mantle of praise instead of a faint spirit.
They will be called oaks of righteousness,
the planting of the LORD, to display his glory.
4 They shall build up the ancient ruins,
they shall raise up the former devastations;

[a] Q Ms Gk Old Latin Tg: MT lacks *by night*

they shall repair the ruined cities,
the devastations of many generations.

5 Strangers shall stand and feed your flocks,
foreigners shall till your land and dress your vines;
6 but you shall be called priests of the LORD,
you shall be named ministers of our God;
you shall enjoy the wealth of the nations,
and in their riches you shall glory.
7 Because their[a] shame was double,
and dishonor was proclaimed as their lot,
therefore they shall possess a double portion;
everlasting joy shall be theirs.

8 For I the LORD love justice,
I hate robbery and wrongdoing;[b]
I will faithfully give them their recompense,
and I will make an everlasting covenant with them.
9 Their descendants shall be known among the nations,
and their offspring among the peoples;
all who see them shall acknowledge
that they are a people whom the LORD has blessed.
10 I will greatly rejoice in the LORD,
my whole being shall exult in my God;
for he has clothed me with the garments of salvation,
he has covered me with the robe of righteousness,
as a bridegroom decks himself with a garland,
and as a bride adorns herself with her jewels.
11 For as the earth brings forth its shoots,
and as a garden causes what is sown in it to spring up,
so the Lord GOD will cause righteousness and praise
to spring up before all the nations.

62 For Zion's sake I will not keep silent,
and for Jerusalem's sake I will not rest,
until her vindication shines out like the dawn,
and her salvation like a burning torch.
2 The nations shall see your vindication,
and all the kings your glory;
and you shall be called by a new name
that the mouth of the LORD will give.
3 You shall be a crown of beauty in the hand of the LORD,
and a royal diadem in the hand of your God.
4 You shall no more be termed Forsaken,[c]
and your land shall no more be termed Desolate;[d]
but you shall be called My Delight Is in Her,[e]
and your land Married;[f]
for the LORD delights in you,
and your land shall be married.
5 For as a young man marries a young woman,
so shall your builder[g] marry you,
and as the bridegroom rejoices over the bride,
so shall your God rejoice over you.

6 Upon your walls, O Jerusalem,
I have posted sentinels;
all day and all night
they shall never be silent.
You who remind the LORD,
take no rest,
7 and give him no rest
until he establishes Jerusalem
and makes it renowned throughout the earth.
8 The LORD has sworn by his right hand
and by his mighty arm:
I will not again give your grain
to be food for your enemies,
and foreigners shall not drink the wine
for which you have labored;
9 but those who garner it shall eat it
and praise the LORD,
and those who gather it shall drink it
in my holy courts.

[a] Heb *your* [b] Or *robbery with a burnt offering* [c] Heb *Azubah* [d] Heb *Shemamah* [e] Heb *Hephzibah* [f] Heb *Beulah* [g] Cn: Heb *your sons*

10 Go through, go through the gates,
prepare the way for the people;
build up, build up the highway,
clear it of stones,
lift up an ensign over the peoples.
11 The LORD has proclaimed
to the end of the earth:
Say to daughter Zion,
"See, your salvation comes;
his reward is with him,
and his recompense before him."
12 They shall be called, "The Holy People,
The Redeemed of the LORD";
and you shall be called, "Sought Out,
A City Not Forsaken."

63 "Who is this that comes from Edom,
from Bozrah in garments stained
crimson?
Who is this so splendidly robed,
marching in his great might?"

"It is I, announcing vindication,
mighty to save."

2 "Why are your robes red,
and your garments like theirs who tread
the wine press?"

3 "I have trodden the wine press alone,
and from the peoples no one was with me;
I trod them in my anger
and trampled them in my wrath;
their juice spattered on my garments,
and stained all my robes.
4 For the day of vengeance was in my heart,
and the year for my redeeming work had
come.
5 I looked, but there was no helper;
I stared, but there was no one to sustain me;
so my own arm brought me victory,
and my wrath sustained me.
6 I trampled down peoples in my anger,
I crushed them in my wrath,
and I poured out their lifeblood on the
earth."

7 I will recount the gracious deeds of the
LORD,
the praiseworthy acts of the LORD,
because of all that the LORD has done for us,
and the great favor to the house of Israel
that he has shown them according to his
mercy,
according to the abundance of his steadfast
love.
8 For he said, "Surely they are my people,
children who will not deal falsely";
and he became their savior
9 in all their distress.
It was no messenger[a] or angel
but his presence that saved them;[b]
in his love and in his pity he redeemed them;
he lifted them up and carried them all the
days of old.

10 But they rebelled
and grieved his holy spirit;
therefore he became their enemy;
he himself fought against them.
11 Then they[c] remembered the days of old,
of Moses his servant.[d]
Where is the one who brought them up out
of the sea
with the shepherds of his flock?
Where is the one who put within them
his holy spirit,
12 who caused his glorious arm
to march at the right hand of Moses,
who divided the waters before them
to make for himself an everlasting name,
13 who led them through the depths?
Like a horse in the desert,
they did not stumble.
14 Like cattle that go down into the valley,
the spirit of the LORD gave them rest.
Thus you led your people,
to make for yourself a glorious name.

[a] Gk: Heb *anguish* [b] Or *savior.* [9] *In all their distress he was distressed; the angel of his presence saved them;* [c] Heb *he*
[d] Cn: Heb *his people*

15 Look down from heaven and see,
from your holy and glorious habitation.
Where are your zeal and your might?
The yearning of your heart and your compassion?
They are withheld from me.
16 For you are our father,
though Abraham does not know us
and Israel does not acknowledge us;
you, O LORD, are our father;
our Redeemer from of old is your name.
17 Why, O LORD, do you make us stray from your ways
and harden our heart, so that we do not fear you?
Turn back for the sake of your servants,
for the sake of the tribes that are your heritage.
18 Your holy people took possession for a little while;
but now our adversaries have trampled down your sanctuary.
19 We have long been like those whom you do not rule,
like those not called by your name.

64 O that you would tear open the heavens and come down,
so that the mountains would quake at your presence—
2[a] as when fire kindles brushwood
and the fire causes water to boil—
to make your name known to your adversaries,
so that the nations might tremble at your presence!
3 When you did awesome deeds that we did not expect,
you came down, the mountains quaked at your presence.
4 From ages past no one has heard,
no ear has perceived,
no eye has seen any God besides you,
who works for those who wait for him.
5 You meet those who gladly do right,
those who remember you in your ways.
But you were angry, and we sinned;
because you hid yourself we transgressed.[b]
6 We have all become like one who is unclean,
and all our righteous deeds are like a filthy cloth.
We all fade like a leaf,
and our iniquities, like the wind, take us away.
7 There is no one who calls on your name,
or attempts to take hold of you;
for you have hidden your face from us,
and have delivered[c] us into the hand of our iniquity.
8 Yet, O LORD, you are our Father;
we are the clay, and you are our potter;
we are all the work of your hand.
9 Do not be exceedingly angry, O LORD,
and do not remember iniquity forever.
Now consider, we are all your people.
10 Your holy cities have become a wilderness,
Zion has become a wilderness,
Jerusalem a desolation.
11 Our holy and beautiful house,
where our ancestors praised you,
has been burned by fire,
and all our pleasant places have become ruins.
12 After all this, will you restrain yourself, O LORD?
Will you keep silent, and punish us so severely?

65 I was ready to be sought out by those who did not ask,
to be found by those who did not seek me.
I said, "Here I am, here I am,"
to a nation that did not call on my name.
2 I held out my hands all day long
to a rebellious people,
who walk in a way that is not good,
following their own devices;
3 a people who provoke me
to my face continually,
sacrificing in gardens

[a] Ch 64.1 in Heb [b] Meaning of Heb uncertain [c] Gk Syr Old Latin Tg: Heb *melted*

and offering incense on bricks;
4 who sit inside tombs,
and spend the night in secret places;
who eat swine's flesh,
with broth of abominable things in their vessels;
5 who say, "Keep to yourself,
do not come near me, for I am too holy for you."
These are a smoke in my nostrils,
a fire that burns all day long.
6 See, it is written before me:
I will not keep silent, but I will repay;
I will indeed repay into their laps
7 their[a] iniquities and their[a] ancestors' iniquities together,
says the LORD;
because they offered incense on the mountains
and reviled me on the hills,
I will measure into their laps
full payment for their actions.
8 Thus says the LORD:
As the wine is found in the cluster,
and they say, "Do not destroy it,
for there is a blessing in it,"
so I will do for my servants' sake,
and not destroy them all.
9 I will bring forth descendants[b] from Jacob,
and from Judah inheritors[c] of my mountains;
my chosen shall inherit it,
and my servants shall settle there.
10 Sharon shall become a pasture for flocks,
and the Valley of Achor a place for herds to lie down,
for my people who have sought me.
11 But you who forsake the LORD,
who forget my holy mountain,
who set a table for Fortune
and fill cups of mixed wine for Destiny;
12 I will destine you to the sword,
and all of you shall bow down to the slaughter;
because, when I called, you did not answer,
when I spoke, you did not listen,
but you did what was evil in my sight,
and chose what I did not delight in.
13 Therefore thus says the Lord GOD:
My servants shall eat,
but you shall be hungry;
my servants shall drink,
but you shall be thirsty;
my servants shall rejoice,
but you shall be put to shame;
14 my servants shall sing for gladness of heart,
but you shall cry out for pain of heart,
and shall wail for anguish of spirit.
15 You shall leave your name to my chosen to use as a curse,
and the Lord GOD will put you to death;
but to his servants he will give a different name.
16 Then whoever invokes a blessing in the land
shall bless by the God of faithfulness,
and whoever takes an oath in the land
shall swear by the God of faithfulness;
because the former troubles are forgotten
and are hidden from my sight.

17 For I am about to create new heavens
and a new earth;
the former things shall not be remembered
or come to mind.
18 But be glad and rejoice forever
in what I am creating;
for I am about to create Jerusalem as a joy,
and its people as a delight.
19 I will rejoice in Jerusalem,
and delight in my people;
no more shall the sound of weeping be heard in it,
or the cry of distress.
20 No more shall there be in it
an infant that lives but a few days,
or an old person who does not live out a lifetime;
for one who dies at a hundred years will be considered a youth,

[a] Gk Syr: Heb *your* [b] Or *a descendant* [c] Or *an inheritor*

and one who falls short of a hundred will
be considered accursed.
21 They shall build houses and inhabit
them;
they shall plant vineyards and eat their
fruit.
22 They shall not build and another inhabit;
they shall not plant and another eat;
for like the days of a tree shall the days of my
people be,
and my chosen shall long enjoy the work
of their hands.
23 They shall not labor in vain,
or bear children for calamity;[a]
for they shall be offspring blessed by the
LORD—
and their descendants as well.
24 Before they call I will answer,
while they are yet speaking I will hear.
25 The wolf and the lamb shall feed together,
the lion shall eat straw like the ox;
but the serpent—its food shall be dust!
They shall not hurt or destroy
on all my holy mountain,
says the LORD.

66 Thus says the LORD:
Heaven is my throne
and the earth is my footstool;
what is the house that you would build
for me,
and what is my resting place?
2 All these things my hand has made,
and so all these things are mine,[b]
says the LORD.
But this is the one to whom I will look,
to the humble and contrite in spirit,
who trembles at my word.

3 Whoever slaughters an ox is like one who
kills a human being;
whoever sacrifices a lamb, like one who
breaks a dog's neck;
whoever presents a grain offering, like one
who offers swine's blood;[c]
whoever makes a memorial offering of
frankincense, like one who blesses
an idol.
These have chosen their own ways,
and in their abominations they take
delight;
4 I also will choose to mock[d] them,
and bring upon them what they fear;
because, when I called, no one answered,
when I spoke, they did not listen;
but they did what was evil in my sight,
and chose what did not please me.
5 Hear the word of the LORD,
you who tremble at his word:
Your own people who hate you
and reject you for my name's sake
have said, "Let the LORD be glorified,
so that we may see your joy";
but it is they who shall be put to shame.

6 Listen, an uproar from the city!
A voice from the temple!
The voice of the LORD,
dealing retribution to his enemies!

7 Before she was in labor
she gave birth;
before her pain came upon her
she delivered a son.
8 Who has heard of such a thing?
Who has seen such things?
Shall a land be born in one day?
Shall a nation be delivered in one
moment?
Yet as soon as Zion was in labor
she delivered her children.
9 Shall I open the womb and not deliver?
says the LORD;
shall I, the one who delivers, shut the womb?
says your God.

10 Rejoice with Jerusalem, and be glad for her,
all you who love her;
rejoice with her in joy,
all you who mourn over her—

[a] Or *sudden terror* [b] Gk Syr: Heb *these things came to be* [c] Meaning of Heb uncertain [d] Or *to punish*

11 that you may nurse and be satisfied
from her consoling breast;
that you may drink deeply with delight
from her glorious bosom.

12 For thus says the LORD:
I will extend prosperity to her like a river,
and the wealth of the nations like an
overflowing stream;
and you shall nurse and be carried on her
arm,
and dandled on her knees.
13 As a mother comforts her child,
so I will comfort you;
you shall be comforted in Jerusalem.
14 You shall see, and your heart shall rejoice;
your bodies[a] shall flourish like the grass;
and it shall be known that the hand of the
LORD is with his servants,
and his indignation is against his enemies.
15 For the LORD will come in fire,
and his chariots like the whirlwind,
to pay back his anger in fury,
and his rebuke in flames of fire.
16 For by fire will the LORD execute judgment,
and by his sword, on all flesh;
and those slain by the LORD shall be many.

17 Those who sanctify and purify themselves
to go into the gardens, following the one in the
center, eating the flesh of pigs, vermin, and ro-
dents, shall come to an end together, says the
LORD.

18 For I know[b] their works and their
thoughts, and I am[c] coming to gather all nations
and tongues; and they shall come and shall see
my glory, 19and I will set a sign among them.
From them I will send survivors to the nations, to
Tarshish, Put,[d] and Lud—which draw the bow—
to Tubal and Javan, to the coastlands far away that
have not heard of my fame or seen my glory; and
they shall declare my glory among the nations.
20They shall bring all your kindred from all the
nations as an offering to the LORD, on horses,
and in chariots, and in litters, and on mules, and
on dromedaries, to my holy mountain Jerusalem,
says the LORD, just as the Israelites bring a grain
offering in a clean vessel to the house of the LORD.
21And I will also take some of them as priests and
as Levites, says the LORD.

22 For as the new heavens and the new earth,
which I will make,
shall remain before me, says the LORD;
so shall your descendants and your name
remain.
23 From new moon to new moon,
and from sabbath to sabbath,
all flesh shall come to worship before me,
says the LORD.

24 And they shall go out and look at the dead
bodies of the people who have rebelled against
me; for their worm shall not die, their fire shall
not be quenched, and they shall be an abhorrence
to all flesh.

[a] Heb *bones* [b] Gk Syr: Heb lacks *know* [c] Gk Syr Vg Tg: Heb *it is* [d] Gk: Heb *Pul*

Jeremiah

The book of Jeremiah comes to us as a collection of laments, proclamations of judgment, and a few powerful eschatological promises, interspersed with stories about the life of the prophet during a time of trials and tribulations for the people of Israel. Located, in its initial layer of voices, in the seventh century BCE in the years leading up to the experiences of dislocation and exile in Babylon, the book warns of an impending disaster, then tells of the actual war and destruction and of the various ways the people and their leaders responded to the crisis. Two later editorial layers offer differing evaluations by the next generation of what had led to the calamities in which the hearers of exilic and postexilic times found themselves, having experienced deportation and disaster in and around Jerusalem.

The book of Jeremiah, like most prophetic literature in the Bible, testifies to the challenges and conflicts among the man Jeremiah, the people of Israel and Judah, and their God, YHWH, who is portrayed mostly as masculine yet sometimes also as feminine. Prophet and people search, together and separately, to make sense of their experiences of war and violence, chaos and attempts at resistance, defeat and daily life. A collection of poetry and prose, the book's fifty-two chapters lack a clear chronological order and offer several repetitions of some historical events. Complicating the interpreter's task is the fact that the Hebrew and Greek versions of Jeremiah differ significantly in length, order, and content.

Issues, Collisions, and Convergences

Biblical scholars have long debated the composition of the book and the identity—or identities—of the prophet Jeremiah. The leading theories on how the book was put together assume three sources and/or authors, posit *two* scrolls that eventually were combined, or propose various editors working at various times. Alternative interpretations have mostly dealt with the book in its final form. Feminist and womanist interpreters focus on the numerous layers of female imagery, on the gendered representations of power dynamics in the book, and on its descriptions of sexual violence. Post-colonial readers emphasize instances of resistance to the empires of the time: Assyria, Babylon, and Persia. Lesbian, gay, bisexual, transgender, and queer (LGBTQ) perspectives highlight the fluidity of gender dynamics in Jeremiah and the sexual connotations in interchanges between God and prophet.

In politics and ideology, Jeremiah portrays a prophet critical of the rulers of his time. He is also angry and dissatisfied with the people for not standing up against the injustices in their midst, and for worshipping in ways that make them feel good rather than honor their God, YHWH, in words and deeds. Resonances to current realities in the United States abound. Jeremiah constantly calls the people to turn back to faithful living laid out in the covenant made with their ancestors at Mount Sinai, meaning to act justly in community and to do God's work in the world. Resonances with the contemporary world suggest the question, Who are prophets today?

As a point of caution, the rhetoric used to express the message of having strayed from God's way is full of powerful and problematic images. Addressed to a predominantly male audience, gendered and racialized metaphors invite the hearers to imagine being raped by divine power and shamed publicly (Jer 13:20-27). Contemporary readers may wonder about the effectiveness of rhetorical strategies that publicly shame their audiences into exhibiting changed behavior by means of misogynous, effeminizing, and racist accusations. Modern psychology has taught us that shaming evokes feelings of inadequacy and inferiority, rejection and powerlessness—the opposite of the strength needed for the challenging work of change. A first-generation immigrant from Germany who identifies as a white, anti-racist, lesbian feminist, I serve as a professor of Bible, culture, and interpretation at a divinity school, where in my teaching and writing I emphasize various aspects of social location (gender, race, sexual identity, etc.) and their interconnectedness in shaping our interpretations. Facing questions about the value of the prophet's rhetorical strategies is for me an inescapable part of our responsibility as interpreters today.

— *Angela Bauer-Levesque*

1 The words of Jeremiah son of Hilkiah, of
the priests who were in Anathoth in the land
of Benjamin, 2to whom the word of the LORD
came in the days of King Josiah son of Amon of
Judah, in the thirteenth year of his reign. 3It came
also in the days of King Jehoiakim son of Josiah
of Judah, and until the end of the eleventh year
of King Zedekiah son of Josiah of Judah, until the
captivity of Jerusalem in the fifth month.

4 Now the word of the LORD came to me
saying,

5 "Before I formed you in the womb I knew
you,
and before you were born I consecrated you;
I appointed you a prophet to the nations."
6Then I said, "Ah, Lord GOD! Truly I do not know
how to speak, for I am only a boy." 7But the LORD
said to me,

"Do not say, 'I am only a boy';
for you shall go to all to whom I send you,
and you shall speak whatever I command
you.
8 Do not be afraid of them,
for I am with you to deliver you,
says the LORD."

Jeremiah 1:4

The call of Jeremiah (1:4-10) portrays God in maternal imagery, calling forth the prophet from the womb and sending forth the prophet to bring messages of doom and hope to the people. Rabbinic interpretation has pointed out that Jeremiah here is modeled after Moses (Exodus 3), who also is reluctant to accept his commission and needs God's assurance for the undoubtedly difficult road ahead.

— *ABL*

9 Then the LORD put out his hand and touched
my mouth; and the LORD said to me,

"Now I have put my words in your mouth.
10 See, today I appoint you over nations and
over kingdoms,
to pluck up and to pull down,
to destroy and to overthrow,
to build and to plant."

11 The word of the LORD came to me, saying,
"Jeremiah, what do you see?" And I said, "I see a
branch of an almond tree."[a] 12 Then the LORD said
to me, "You have seen well, for I am watching[b]
over my word to perform it." 13 The word of the
LORD came to me a second time, saying, "What
do you see?" And I said, "I see a boiling pot, tilted
away from the north."

14 Then the LORD said to me: Out of the
north disaster shall break out on all the inhabitants of the land. 15 For now I am calling all the
tribes of the kingdoms of the north, says the
LORD; and they shall come and all of them shall
set their thrones at the entrance of the gates of
Jerusalem, against all its surrounding walls and
against all the cities of Judah. 16 And I will utter
my judgments against them, for all their wickedness in forsaking me; they have made offerings to
other gods, and worshiped the works of their own
hands. 17 But you, gird up your loins; stand up
and tell them everything that I command you. Do
not break down before them, or I will break you
before them. 18 And I for my part have made you
today a fortified city, an iron pillar, and a bronze
wall, against the whole land—against the kings
of Judah, its princes, its priests, and the people of
the land. 19 They will fight against you; but they
shall not prevail against you, for I am with you,
says the LORD, to deliver you.

2 The word of the LORD came to me, saying:
2 Go and proclaim in the hearing of Jerusalem, Thus says the LORD:

I remember the devotion of your youth,
your love as a bride,
how you followed me in the wilderness,
in a land not sown.
3 Israel was holy to the LORD,
the first fruits of his harvest.
All who ate of it were held guilty;
disaster came upon them,
says the LORD.

4 Hear the word of the LORD, O house of
Jacob, and all the families of the house of Israel.
5 Thus says the LORD:

What wrong did your ancestors find in me
that they went far from me,
and went after worthless things, and became
worthless themselves?
6 They did not say, "Where is the LORD
who brought us up from the land of Egypt,
who led us in the wilderness,
in a land of deserts and pits,
in a land of drought and deep darkness,
in a land that no one passes through,
where no one lives?"
7 I brought you into a plentiful land
to eat its fruits and its good things.
But when you entered you defiled my land,
and made my heritage an abomination.
8 The priests did not say, "Where is the LORD?"
Those who handle the law did not
know me;
the rulers[c] transgressed against me;
the prophets prophesied by Baal,
and went after things that do not profit.

9 Therefore once more I accuse you,
says the LORD,
and I accuse your children's children.
10 Cross to the coasts of Cyprus and look,
send to Kedar and examine with care;
see if there has ever been such a thing.
11 Has a nation changed its gods,
even though they are no gods?
But my people have changed their glory
for something that does not profit.
12 Be appalled, O heavens, at this,
be shocked, be utterly desolate,
says the LORD,
13 for my people have committed two evils:
they have forsaken me,

[a] Heb *shaqed* [b] Heb *shoqed* [c] Heb *shepherds*

the fountain of living water,
and dug out cisterns for themselves,
cracked cisterns
that can hold no water.

14 Is Israel a slave? Is he a homeborn servant?
Why then has he become plunder?
15 The lions have roared against him,
they have roared loudly.
They have made his land a waste;
his cities are in ruins, without inhabitant.
16 Moreover, the people of Memphis and Tahpanhes
have broken the crown of your head.
17 Have you not brought this upon yourself
by forsaking the LORD your God,
while he led you in the way?
18 What then do you gain by going to Egypt,
to drink the waters of the Nile?
Or what do you gain by going to Assyria,
to drink the waters of the Euphrates?
19 Your wickedness will punish you,
and your apostasies will convict you.
Know and see that it is evil and bitter
for you to forsake the LORD your God;
the fear of me is not in you,
says the Lord GOD of hosts.

20 For long ago you broke your yoke
and burst your bonds,
and you said, "I will not serve!"
On every high hill
and under every green tree
you sprawled and played the whore.
21 Yet I planted you as a choice vine,
from the purest stock.
How then did you turn degenerate
and become a wild vine?
22 Though you wash yourself with lye
and use much soap,
the stain of your guilt is still before me,
says the Lord GOD.
23 How can you say, "I am not defiled,
I have not gone after the Baals"?
Look at your way in the valley;
know what you have done—
a restive young camel interlacing her tracks,
24 a wild ass at home in the wilderness,
in her heat sniffing the wind!
Who can restrain her lust?
None who seek her need weary themselves;
in her month they will find her.
25 Keep your feet from going unshod
and your throat from thirst.
But you said, "It is hopeless,
for I have loved strangers,
and after them I will go."

26 As a thief is shamed when caught,
so the house of Israel shall be shamed—
they, their kings, their officials,
their priests, and their prophets,
27 who say to a tree, "You are my father,"
and to a stone, "You gave me birth."
For they have turned their backs to me,
and not their faces.
But in the time of their trouble they say,
"Come and save us!"
28 But where are your gods
that you made for yourself?
Let them come, if they can save you,
in your time of trouble;
for you have as many gods
as you have towns, O Judah.

29 Why do you complain against me?
You have all rebelled against me,
says the LORD.
30 In vain I have struck down your children;
they accepted no correction.
Your own sword devoured your prophets
like a ravening lion.
31 And you, O generation, behold the word of the LORD![a]
Have I been a wilderness to Israel,
or a land of thick darkness?
Why then do my people say, "We are free,
we will come to you no more"?
32 Can a girl forget her ornaments,
or a bride her attire?

[a] Meaning of Heb uncertain

Yet my people have forgotten me,
days without number.

33 How well you direct your course
to seek lovers!
So that even to wicked women
you have taught your ways.
34 Also on your skirts is found
the lifeblood of the innocent poor,
though you did not catch them breaking in.
Yet in spite of all these things[a]
35 you say, "I am innocent;
surely his anger has turned from me."
Now I am bringing you to judgment
for saying, "I have not sinned."
36 How lightly you gad about,
changing your ways!
You shall be put to shame by Egypt
as you were put to shame by Assyria.
37 From there also you will come away
with your hands on your head;
for the LORD has rejected those in whom you
trust,
and you will not prosper through them.

3 If[b] a man divorces his wife
and she goes from him
and becomes another man's wife,
will he return to her?
Would not such a land be greatly polluted?
You have played the whore with many
lovers;
and would you return to me?
says the LORD.
2 Look up to the bare heights,[c] and see!
Where have you not been lain with?
By the waysides you have sat waiting for
lovers,
like a nomad in the wilderness.
You have polluted the land
with your whoring and wickedness.
3 Therefore the showers have been withheld,
and the spring rain has not come;
yet you have the forehead of a whore,
you refuse to be ashamed.
4 Have you not just now called to me,
"My Father, you are the friend of my
youth—
5 will he be angry forever,
will he be indignant to the end?"
This is how you have spoken,
but you have done all the evil that you
could.

6 The LORD said to me in the days of King
Josiah: Have you seen what she did, that faithless
one, Israel, how she went up on every high hill
and under every green tree, and played the whore
there? 7 And I thought, "After she has done all this
she will return to me"; but she did not return,
and her false sister Judah saw it. 8 She[d] saw that
for all the adulteries of that faithless one, Israel,
I had sent her away with a decree of divorce; yet
her false sister Judah did not fear, but she too
went and played the whore. 9 Because she took
her whoredom so lightly, she polluted the land,
committing adultery with stone and tree. 10 Yet
for all this her false sister Judah did not return to
me with her whole heart, but only in pretense,
says the LORD.

11 Then the LORD said to me: Faithless Israel has shown herself less guilty than false Judah.
12 Go, and proclaim these words toward the north,
and say:
Return, faithless Israel,
says the LORD.
I will not look on you in anger,
for I am merciful,
says the LORD;
I will not be angry forever.
13 Only acknowledge your guilt,
that you have rebelled against the LORD
your God,
and scattered your favors among strangers
under every green tree,
and have not obeyed my voice,
says the LORD.
14 Return, O faithless children,
says the LORD,
for I am your master;

[a] Meaning of Heb uncertain [b] Q Ms Gk Syr: MT *Saying, If* [c] Or *the trails* [d] Q Ms Gk Mss Syr: MT *I*

I will take you, one from a city and two from
a family,
and I will bring you to Zion.

15 I will give you shepherds after my own
heart, who will feed you with knowledge and
understanding. 16 And when you have multiplied
and increased in the land, in those days, says
the LORD, they shall no longer say, "The ark of
the covenant of the LORD." It shall not come to
mind, or be remembered, or missed; nor shall
another one be made. 17 At that time Jerusalem
shall be called the throne of the LORD, and all
nations shall gather to it, to the presence of the
LORD in Jerusalem, and they shall no longer stubbornly follow their own evil will. 18 In those days
the house of Judah shall join the house of Israel,
and together they shall come from the land of the
north to the land that I gave your ancestors for a
heritage.

19 I thought
how I would set you among my children,
and give you a pleasant land,
the most beautiful heritage of all the
nations.
And I thought you would call me, My Father,
and would not turn from following me.
20 Instead, as a faithless wife leaves her husband,
so you have been faithless to me, O house
of Israel,
says the LORD.

21 A voice on the bare heights[a] is heard,
the plaintive weeping of Israel's children,
because they have perverted their way,
they have forgotten the LORD their God:
22 Return, O faithless children,
I will heal your faithlessness.

"Here we come to you;
for you are the LORD our God.
23 Truly the hills are[b] a delusion,
the orgies on the mountains.
Truly in the LORD our God
is the salvation of Israel.

24 "But from our youth the shameful thing
has devoured all for which our ancestors had labored, their flocks and their herds, their sons and
their daughters. 25 Let us lie down in our shame,
and let our dishonor cover us; for we have sinned
against the LORD our God, we and our ancestors,
from our youth even to this day; and we have not
obeyed the voice of the LORD our God."

4 If you return, O Israel,
says the LORD,
if you return to me,
if you remove your abominations from my
presence,
and do not waver,
2 and if you swear, "As the LORD lives!"
in truth, in justice, and in uprightness,
then nations shall be blessed[c] by him,
and by him they shall boast.

3 For thus says the LORD to the people of
Judah and to the inhabitants of Jerusalem:
Break up your fallow ground,
and do not sow among thorns.
4 Circumcise yourselves to the LORD,
remove the foreskin of your hearts,
O people of Judah and inhabitants of
Jerusalem,
or else my wrath will go forth like fire,
and burn with no one to quench it,
because of the evil of your doings.

5 Declare in Judah, and proclaim in Jerusalem, and say:
Blow the trumpet through the land;
shout aloud[d] and say,
"Gather together, and let us go
into the fortified cities!"
6 Raise a standard toward Zion,
flee for safety, do not delay,
for I am bringing evil from the north,
and a great destruction.
7 A lion has gone up from its thicket,

[a] Or *the trails* [b] Gk Syr Vg: Heb *Truly from the hills is* [c] Or *shall bless themselves*
[d] Or *shout, take your weapons*: Heb *shout, fill* (your hand)

a destroyer of nations has set out;
he has gone out from his place
to make your land a waste;
your cities will be ruins
without inhabitant.
8 Because of this put on sackcloth,
lament and wail:
"The fierce anger of the LORD
has not turned away from us."

9On that day, says the LORD, courage shall fail
the king and the officials; the priests shall be appalled and the prophets astounded. 10Then I said,
"Ah, Lord GOD, how utterly you have deceived
this people and Jerusalem, saying, 'It shall be well
with you,' even while the sword is at the throat!"

11 At that time it will be said to this people
and to Jerusalem: A hot wind comes from me out
of the bare heights[a] in the desert toward my poor
people, not to winnow or cleanse—12a wind too
strong for that. Now it is I who speak in judgment
against them.
13 Look! He comes up like clouds,
his chariots like the whirlwind;
his horses are swifter than eagles—
woe to us, for we are ruined!
14 O Jerusalem, wash your heart clean of
wickedness
so that you may be saved.
How long shall your evil schemes
lodge within you?
15 For a voice declares from Dan
and proclaims disaster from Mount
Ephraim.
16 Tell the nations, "Here they are!"
Proclaim against Jerusalem,
"Besiegers come from a distant land;
they shout against the cities of Judah.
17 They have closed in around her like watchers
of a field,
because she has rebelled against me,
says the LORD.
18 Your ways and your doings
have brought this upon you.
This is your doom; how bitter it is!
It has reached your very heart."

19 My anguish, my anguish! I writhe in pain!
Oh, the walls of my heart!
My heart is beating wildly;
I cannot keep silent;
for I[b] hear the sound of the trumpet,
the alarm of war.
20 Disaster overtakes disaster,
the whole land is laid waste.
Suddenly my tents are destroyed,
my curtains in a moment.
21 How long must I see the standard,
and hear the sound of the trumpet?
22 "For my people are foolish,
they do not know me;
they are stupid children,
they have no understanding.
They are skilled in doing evil,
but do not know how to do good."

23 I looked on the earth, and lo, it was waste and
void;
and to the heavens, and they had no light.
24 I looked on the mountains, and lo, they were
quaking,
and all the hills moved to and fro.
25 I looked, and lo, there was no one at all,
and all the birds of the air had fled.
26 I looked, and lo, the fruitful land was a desert,
and all its cities were laid in ruins
before the LORD, before his fierce anger.

27 For thus says the LORD: The whole land
shall be a desolation; yet I will not make a full
end.
28 Because of this the earth shall mourn,
and the heavens above grow black;
for I have spoken, I have purposed;
I have not relented nor will I turn back.

29 At the noise of horseman and archer
every town takes to flight;
they enter thickets; they climb among rocks;
all the towns are forsaken,

[a] Or *the trails* [b] Another reading is *for you, O my soul,*

and no one lives in them.
30 And you, O desolate one,
what do you mean that you dress in crimson,
that you deck yourself with ornaments of gold,
that you enlarge your eyes with paint?
In vain you beautify yourself.
Your lovers despise you;
they seek your life.
31 For I heard a cry as of a woman in labor,
anguish as of one bringing forth her first child,
the cry of daughter Zion gasping for breath,
stretching out her hands,
"Woe is me! I am fainting before killers!"

5 Run to and fro through the streets of Jerusalem,
look around and take note!
Search its squares and see
if you can find one person
who acts justly
and seeks truth—
so that I may pardon Jerusalem.[a]
2 Although they say, "As the LORD lives,"
yet they swear falsely.
3 O LORD, do your eyes not look for truth?
You have struck them,
but they felt no anguish;
you have consumed them,
but they refused to take correction.
They have made their faces harder than rock;
they have refused to turn back.

4 Then I said, "These are only the poor,
they have no sense;
for they do not know the way of the LORD,
the law of their God.
5 Let me go to the rich[b]
and speak to them;
surely they know the way of the LORD,
the law of their God."
But they all alike had broken the yoke,
they had burst the bonds.
6 Therefore a lion from the forest shall kill them,
a wolf from the desert shall destroy them.
A leopard is watching against their cities;
everyone who goes out of them shall be torn in pieces—
because their transgressions are many,
their apostasies are great.

7 How can I pardon you?
Your children have forsaken me,
and have sworn by those who are no gods.
When I fed them to the full,
they committed adultery
and trooped to the houses of prostitutes.
8 They were well-fed lusty stallions,
each neighing for his neighbor's wife.
9 Shall I not punish them for these things?
says the LORD;
and shall I not bring retribution
on a nation such as this?

10 Go up through her vine-rows and destroy,
but do not make a full end;
strip away her branches,
for they are not the LORD's.
11 For the house of Israel and the house of Judah
have been utterly faithless to me,
says the LORD.
12 They have spoken falsely of the LORD,
and have said, "He will do nothing.
No evil will come upon us,
and we shall not see sword or famine."
13 The prophets are nothing but wind,
for the word is not in them.
Thus shall it be done to them!

14 Therefore thus says the LORD, the God of hosts:
Because they[c] have spoken this word,
I am now making my words in your mouth a fire,
and this people wood, and the fire shall devour them.

[a] Heb *it* [b] Or *the great* [c] Heb *you*

15 I am going to bring upon you
a nation from far away, O house of Israel,
says the LORD.
It is an enduring nation,
it is an ancient nation,
a nation whose language you do not know,
nor can you understand what they say.
16 Their quiver is like an open tomb;
all of them are mighty warriors.
17 They shall eat up your harvest and your food;
they shall eat up your sons and your daughters;
they shall eat up your flocks and your herds;
they shall eat up your vines and your fig trees;
they shall destroy with the sword
your fortified cities in which you trust.

18 But even in those days, says the LORD, I
will not make a full end of you. 19 And when your
people say, "Why has the LORD our God done all
these things to us?" you shall say to them, "As you
have forsaken me and served foreign gods in your
land, so you shall serve strangers in a land that is
not yours."

20 Declare this in the house of Jacob,
proclaim it in Judah:
21 Hear this, O foolish and senseless people,
who have eyes, but do not see,
who have ears, but do not hear.
22 Do you not fear me? says the LORD;
Do you not tremble before me?
I placed the sand as a boundary for the sea,
a perpetual barrier that it cannot pass;
though the waves toss, they cannot prevail,
though they roar, they cannot pass over it.
23 But this people has a stubborn and rebellious heart;
they have turned aside and gone away.
24 They do not say in their hearts,
"Let us fear the LORD our God,
who gives the rain in its season,
the autumn rain and the spring rain,
and keeps for us
the weeks appointed for the harvest."
25 Your iniquities have turned these away,
and your sins have deprived you of good.
26 For scoundrels are found among my people;
they take over the goods of others.
Like fowlers they set a trap;[a]
they catch human beings.
27 Like a cage full of birds,
their houses are full of treachery;
therefore they have become great and rich,
28 they have grown fat and sleek.
They know no limits in deeds of wickedness;
they do not judge with justice
the cause of the orphan, to make it prosper,
and they do not defend the rights of the needy.
29 Shall I not punish them for these things?
says the LORD,
and shall I not bring retribution
on a nation such as this?

30 An appalling and horrible thing
has happened in the land:
31 the prophets prophesy falsely,
and the priests rule as the prophets direct;[b]
my people love to have it so,
but what will you do when the end comes?

6 Flee for safety, O children of Benjamin,
from the midst of Jerusalem!
Blow the trumpet in Tekoa,
and raise a signal on Beth-haccherem;
for evil looms out of the north,
and great destruction.
2 I have likened daughter Zion
to the loveliest pasture.[c]
3 Shepherds with their flocks shall come against her.
They shall pitch their tents around her;
they shall pasture, all in their places.
4 "Prepare war against her;
up, and let us attack at noon!"
"Woe to us, for the day declines,
the shadows of evening lengthen!"
5 "Up, and let us attack by night,

[a] Meaning of Heb uncertain [b] Or *rule by their own authority* [c] Or *I will destroy daughter Zion, the loveliest pasture*

and destroy her palaces!"
6 For thus says the LORD of hosts:
Cut down her trees;
cast up a siege ramp against Jerusalem.
This is the city that must be punished;[a]
there is nothing but oppression within her.
7 As a well keeps its water fresh,
so she keeps fresh her wickedness;
violence and destruction are heard within her;
sickness and wounds are ever before me.
8 Take warning, O Jerusalem,
or I shall turn from you in disgust,
and make you a desolation,
an uninhabited land.

9 Thus says the LORD of hosts:
Glean[b] thoroughly as a vine
the remnant of Israel;
like a grape-gatherer, pass your hand again
over its branches.

10 To whom shall I speak and give warning,
that they may hear?
See, their ears are closed,[c]
they cannot listen.
The word of the LORD is to them an object of scorn;
they take no pleasure in it.
11 But I am full of the wrath of the LORD;
I am weary of holding it in.

Pour it out on the children in the street,
and on the gatherings of young men as well;
both husband and wife shall be taken,
the old folk and the very aged.
12 Their houses shall be turned over to others,
their fields and wives together;
for I will stretch out my hand
against the inhabitants of the land,
says the LORD.

13 For from the least to the greatest of them,
everyone is greedy for unjust gain;
and from prophet to priest,
everyone deals falsely.
14 They have treated the wound of my people carelessly,
saying, "Peace, peace,"
when there is no peace.
15 They acted shamefully, they committed abomination;
yet they were not ashamed,
they did not know how to blush.
Therefore they shall fall among those who fall;
at the time that I punish them, they shall be overthrown,
says the LORD.

16 Thus says the LORD:
Stand at the crossroads, and look,
and ask for the ancient paths,
where the good way lies; and walk in it,
and find rest for your souls.
But they said, "We will not walk in it."
17 Also I raised up sentinels for you:
"Give heed to the sound of the trumpet!"
But they said, "We will not give heed."
18 Therefore hear, O nations,
and know, O congregation, what will happen to them.
19 Hear, O earth; I am going to bring disaster on this people,
the fruit of their schemes,
because they have not given heed to my words;
and as for my teaching, they have rejected it.
20 Of what use to me is frankincense that comes from Sheba,
or sweet cane from a distant land?
Your burnt offerings are not acceptable,
nor are your sacrifices pleasing to me.
21 Therefore thus says the LORD:
See, I am laying before this people
stumbling blocks against which they shall stumble;
parents and children together,
neighbor and friend shall perish.

[a] Or *the city of license* [b] Cn: Heb *They shall glean* [c] Heb *are uncircumcised*

22 Thus says the LORD:
See, a people is coming from the land of the north,
a great nation is stirring from the farthest parts of the earth.
23 They grasp the bow and the javelin,
they are cruel and have no mercy,
their sound is like the roaring sea;
they ride on horses,
equipped like a warrior for battle,
against you, O daughter Zion!

24 "We have heard news of them,
our hands fall helpless;
anguish has taken hold of us,
pain as of a woman in labor.
25 Do not go out into the field,
or walk on the road;
for the enemy has a sword,
terror is on every side."

26 O my poor people, put on sackcloth,
and roll in ashes;
make mourning as for an only child,
most bitter lamentation:
for suddenly the destroyer
will come upon us.

27 I have made you a tester and a refiner[a] among my people
so that you may know and test their ways.
28 They are all stubbornly rebellious,
going about with slanders;
they are bronze and iron,
all of them act corruptly.
29 The bellows blow fiercely,
the lead is consumed by the fire;
in vain the refining goes on,
for the wicked are not removed.
30 They are called "rejected silver,"
for the LORD has rejected them.

7 The word that came to Jeremiah from the
LORD: 2Stand in the gate of the LORD's house,
and proclaim there this word, and say, Hear the
word of the LORD, all you people of Judah, you
that enter these gates to worship the LORD. 3Thus
says the LORD of hosts, the God of Israel: Amend
your ways and your doings, and let me dwell with
you[b] in this place. 4Do not trust in these deceptive words: "This is[c] the temple of the LORD, the
temple of the LORD, the temple of the LORD."

5 For if you truly amend your ways and your
doings, if you truly act justly one with another,
6if you do not oppress the alien, the orphan, and
the widow, or shed innocent blood in this place,
and if you do not go after other gods to your own
hurt, 7then I will dwell with you in this place, in
the land that I gave of old to your ancestors forever and ever.

8 Here you are, trusting in deceptive words to
no avail. 9Will you steal, murder, commit adultery,
swear falsely, make offerings to Baal, and go after
other gods that you have not known, 10and then
come and stand before me in this house, which is

Jeremiah 7:1-10

In the classical era of biblical Israel, women were still legally subordinate (depending on their age) to either their fathers or husbands. It is not insignificant that "woman" (translated "wife" here, although there is no separate Hebrew word for wife) is listed in the commandment forbidding coveting, along with house, servants, and animals, as part of the usual "property" of a man. Youth as well had no particular status; they were valued for their economic contribution to the family but not seen as having a voice or ideas to be heard. But because husbandless women and orphaned youth were the most vulnerable persons in that society—having no societal safety net if family did not care for them—they are declared in the Torah and in the Prophets to be of special concern to God; therefore care for their well-being should be a primary human mercy exercised by all. The argument is one from the greater to the lesser: if God cares so much for them, so should we.

— ***DB***

[a] Or *a fortress* [b] Or *and I will let you dwell* [c] Heb *They are*

called by my name, and say, "We are safe!"—only to go on doing all these abominations? 11 Has this house, which is called by my name, become a den of robbers in your sight? You know, I too am watching, says the LORD. 12 Go now to my place that was in Shiloh, where I made my name dwell at first, and see what I did to it for the wickedness of my people Israel. 13 And now, because you have done all these things, says the LORD, and when I spoke to you persistently, you did not listen, and when I called you, you did not answer, 14 therefore I will do to the house that is called by my name, in which you trust, and to the place that I gave to you and to your ancestors, just what I did to Shiloh. 15 And I will cast you out of my sight, just as I cast out all your kinsfolk, all the offspring of Ephraim.

16 As for you, do not pray for this people, do not raise a cry or prayer on their behalf, and do not intercede with me, for I will not hear you. 17 Do you not see what they are doing in the towns of Judah and in the streets of Jerusalem? 18 The children gather wood, the fathers kindle fire, and the women knead dough, to make cakes for the queen of heaven; and they pour out drink offerings to other gods, to provoke me to anger. 19 Is it I whom they provoke? says the LORD. Is it not themselves, to their own hurt? 20 Therefore thus says the Lord GOD: My anger and my wrath shall be poured out on this place, on human beings and animals, on the trees of the field and the fruit of the ground; it will burn and not be quenched.

21 Thus says the LORD of hosts, the God of Israel: Add your burnt offerings to your sacrifices, and eat the flesh. 22 For in the day that I brought your ancestors out of the land of Egypt, I did not speak to them or command them concerning burnt offerings and sacrifices. 23 But this command I gave them, "Obey my voice, and I will be your God, and you shall be my people; and walk only in the way that I command you, so that it may be well with you." 24 Yet they did not obey or incline their ear, but, in the stubbornness of their evil will, they walked in their own counsels, and looked backward rather than forward. 25 From the day that your ancestors came out of the land of Egypt until this day, I have persistently sent all my servants the prophets to them, day after day; 26 yet they did not listen to me, or pay attention, but they stiffened their necks. They did worse than their ancestors did.

27 So you shall speak all these words to them, but they will not listen to you. You shall call to them, but they will not answer you. 28 You shall say to them: This is the nation that did not obey the voice of the LORD their God, and did not accept discipline; truth has perished; it is cut off from their lips.

29 Cut off your hair and throw it away;
raise a lamentation on the bare heights,[a]
for the LORD has rejected and forsaken
the generation that provoked his wrath.

30 For the people of Judah have done evil in my sight, says the LORD; they have set their abominations in the house that is called by my name, defiling it. 31 And they go on building the high place[b] of Topheth, which is in the valley of the son of Hinnom, to burn their sons and their daughters in the fire—which I did not command, nor did it come into my mind. 32 Therefore, the days are surely coming, says the LORD, when it will no more be called Topheth, or the valley of the son of Hinnom, but the valley of Slaughter: for they will bury in Topheth until there is no more room. 33 The corpses of this people will be food for the birds of the air, and for the animals of the earth; and no one will frighten them away. 34 And I will bring to an end the sound of mirth and gladness, the voice of the bride and bridegroom in the cities of Judah and in the streets of Jerusalem; for the land shall become a waste.

8 At that time, says the LORD, the bones of the kings of Judah, the bones of its officials, the bones of the priests, the bones of the prophets, and the bones of the inhabitants of Jerusalem shall be brought out of their tombs; 2 and they shall be spread before the sun and the moon and all the host of heaven, which they have loved and served, which they have followed, and which they have inquired of and worshiped; and they shall not be

[a] Or *the trails* [b] Gk Tg: Heb *high places*

gathered or buried; they shall be like dung on the
surface of the ground. 3 Death shall be preferred
to life by all the remnant that remains of this evil
family in all the places where I have driven them,
says the LORD of hosts.

4 You shall say to them, Thus says the LORD:
When people fall, do they not get up again?
If they go astray, do they not turn back?
5 Why then has this people[a] turned away
in perpetual backsliding?
They have held fast to deceit,
they have refused to return.
6 I have given heed and listened,
but they do not speak honestly;
no one repents of wickedness,
saying, "What have I done!"
All of them turn to their own course,
like a horse plunging headlong into battle.
7 Even the stork in the heavens
knows its times;
and the turtledove, swallow, and crane[b]
observe the time of their coming;
but my people do not know
the ordinance of the LORD.

8 How can you say, "We are wise,
and the law of the LORD is with us,"
when, in fact, the false pen of the scribes
has made it into a lie?
9 The wise shall be put to shame,
they shall be dismayed and taken;
since they have rejected the word of the LORD,
what wisdom is in them?
10 Therefore I will give their wives to others
and their fields to conquerors,
because from the least to the greatest
everyone is greedy for unjust gain;
from prophet to priest
everyone deals falsely.
11 They have treated the wound of my people carelessly,
saying, "Peace, peace,"
when there is no peace.
12 They acted shamefully, they committed abomination;
yet they were not at all ashamed,
they did not know how to blush.
Therefore they shall fall among those who fall;
at the time when I punish them, they shall be overthrown,
says the LORD.
13 When I wanted to gather them, says the LORD,
there are[c] no grapes on the vine,
nor figs on the fig tree;
even the leaves are withered,
and what I gave them has passed away from them.[b]

14 Why do we sit still?
Gather together, let us go into the fortified cities
and perish there;
for the LORD our God has doomed us to perish,
and has given us poisoned water to drink,
because we have sinned against the LORD.
15 We look for peace, but find no good,
for a time of healing, but there is terror instead.

16 The snorting of their horses is heard from Dan;
at the sound of the neighing of their stallions
the whole land quakes.
They come and devour the land and all that fills it,
the city and those who live in it.
17 See, I am letting snakes loose among you,
adders that cannot be charmed,
and they shall bite you,
says the LORD.

[a] One Ms Gk: MT *this people, Jerusalem,* [b] Meaning of Heb uncertain
[c] Or *I will make an end of them, says the LORD. There are*

Jeremiah 8:18-22

The African-American spiritual "There Is a Balm in Gilead" builds on Jer 8:18-22. The encouragement that enslaved people of African descent have drawn from singing it joins with the songs of communal lament and yearning for hope in other settings of powerlessness and oppression (see also the singing, mourning women in Jer 9:17-22).

— *ABL*

18 My joy is gone, grief is upon me,
my heart is sick.
19 Hark, the cry of my poor people
from far and wide in the land:
"Is the LORD not in Zion?
Is her King not in her?"
("Why have they provoked me to anger with
their images,
with their foreign idols?")
20 "The harvest is past, the summer is ended,
and we are not saved."
21 For the hurt of my poor people I am hurt,
I mourn, and dismay has taken hold of me.

22 Is there no balm in Gilead?
Is there no physician there?
Why then has the health of my poor
people
not been restored?

9[a] O that my head were a spring of water,
and my eyes a fountain of tears,
so that I might weep day and night
for the slain of my poor people!
2[b] O that I had in the desert
a traveler's lodging place,
that I might leave my people
and go away from them!
For they are all adulterers,
a band of traitors.
3 They bend their tongues like bows;
they have grown strong in the land for
falsehood, and not for truth;
for they proceed from evil to evil,
and they do not know me, says the LORD.

4 Beware of your neighbors,
and put no trust in any of your kin;[c]
for all your kin[d] are supplanters,
and every neighbor goes around like a
slanderer.
5 They all deceive their neighbors,
and no one speaks the truth;
they have taught their tongues to speak lies;
they commit iniquity and are too weary to
repent.[e]
6 Oppression upon oppression, deceit[f] upon
deceit!
They refuse to know me, says the LORD.

7 Therefore thus says the LORD of hosts:
I will now refine and test them,
for what else can I do with my sinful
people?[g]
8 Their tongue is a deadly arrow;
it speaks deceit through the mouth.
They all speak friendly words to their
neighbors,
but inwardly are planning to lay an
ambush.
9 Shall I not punish them for these things? says
the LORD;
and shall I not bring retribution
on a nation such as this?

10 Take up[h] weeping and wailing for the
mountains,
and a lamentation for the pastures of the
wilderness,
because they are laid waste so that no one
passes through,
and the lowing of cattle is not heard;
both the birds of the air and the animals
have fled and are gone.

[a] Ch 8.23 in Heb [b] Ch 9.1 in Heb [c] Heb *in a brother* [d] Heb *for every brother* [e] Cn Compare Gk: Heb *they weary themselves with iniquity.* [6]*Your dwelling* [f] Cn: Heb *Your dwelling in the midst of deceit* [g] Or *my poor people* [h] Gk Syr: Heb *I will take up*

11 I will make Jerusalem a heap of ruins,
a lair of jackals;
and I will make the towns of Judah a
desolation,
without inhabitant.

12 Who is wise enough to understand this?
To whom has the mouth of the LORD spoken, so
that they may declare it? Why is the land ruined
and laid waste like a wilderness, so that no one
passes through? 13And the LORD says: Because
they have forsaken my law that I set before them,
and have not obeyed my voice, or walked in accordance with it, 14but have stubbornly followed
their own hearts and have gone after the Baals,
as their ancestors taught them. 15Therefore thus
says the LORD of hosts, the God of Israel: I am
feeding this people with wormwood, and giving
them poisonous water to drink. 16I will scatter
them among nations that neither they nor their
ancestors have known; and I will send the sword
after them, until I have consumed them.

17 Thus says the LORD of hosts:
Consider, and call for the mourning women
to come;
send for the skilled women to come;
18 let them quickly raise a dirge over us,
so that our eyes may run down with tears,
and our eyelids flow with water.
19 For a sound of wailing is heard from Zion:
"How we are ruined!
We are utterly shamed,
because we have left the land,
because they have cast down our dwellings."

20 Hear, O women, the word of the LORD,
and let your ears receive the word of his
mouth;
teach to your daughters a dirge,
and each to her neighbor a lament.
21 "Death has come up into our windows,
it has entered our palaces,
to cut off the children from the streets
and the young men from the squares."
22 Speak! Thus says the LORD:
"Human corpses shall fall
like dung upon the open field,
like sheaves behind the reaper,
and no one shall gather them."

23 Thus says the LORD: Do not let the wise
boast in their wisdom, do not let the mighty
boast in their might, do not let the wealthy boast
in their wealth; 24but let those who boast boast
in this, that they understand and know me, that
I am the LORD; I act with steadfast love, justice,
and righteousness in the earth, for in these things
I delight, says the LORD.

Jeremiah 9:23-24

[Activist Bryant] Myers... believes that the "dichotomies of the modern worldview" inhibit even well-intentioned attempts to aid the poor, and he calls for change in the attitudes and practices of those who work in impoverished and traditional communities. Myers describes in some detail what he terms "the marred identity of the poor" and the harmful "god-complexes of the non-poor" who want to help them. Drawing on the insights of both First and Third World practitioners of development and integrating these with the studies of sociologists, anthropologists, and economists, the author urges the inauguration of projects which rely on the full participation of the poor, are sustainable into the future, and which have the potential to change existing relationships and practices.... [The poor are] subjects,... persons with their own history and hopes and possibilities.[51]

— ***Wayne Stumme***

25 The days are surely coming, says the LORD,
when I will attend to all those who are circumcised only in the foreskin: 26Egypt, Judah, Edom,
the Ammonites, Moab, and all those with shaven
temples who live in the desert. For all these nations are uncircumcised, and all the house of Israel is uncircumcised in heart.

10 Hear the word that the LORD speaks to
you, O house of Israel. 2Thus says the
LORD:

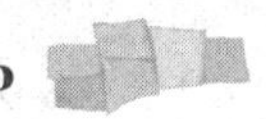

Do not learn the way of the nations,
or be dismayed at the signs of the heavens;
for the nations are dismayed at them.
3 For the customs of the peoples are false:
a tree from the forest is cut down,
and worked with an ax by the hands of an artisan;
4 people deck it with silver and gold;
they fasten it with hammer and nails
so that it cannot move.
5 Their idols[a] are like scarecrows in a cucumber field,
and they cannot speak;
they have to be carried,
for they cannot walk.
Do not be afraid of them,
for they cannot do evil,
nor is it in them to do good.

6 There is none like you, O LORD;
you are great, and your name is great in might.
7 Who would not fear you, O King of the nations?
For that is your due;
among all the wise ones of the nations
and in all their kingdoms
there is no one like you.
8 They are both stupid and foolish;
the instruction given by idols
is no better than wood![b]
9 Beaten silver is brought from Tarshish,
and gold from Uphaz.
They are the work of the artisan and of the hands of the goldsmith;
their clothing is blue and purple;
they are all the product of skilled workers.
10 But the LORD is the true God;
he is the living God and the everlasting King.
At his wrath the earth quakes,
and the nations cannot endure his indignation.

11 Thus shall you say to them: The gods who
did not make the heavens and the earth shall perish from the earth and from under the heavens.[c]

12 It is he who made the earth by his power,
who established the world by his wisdom,
and by his understanding stretched out the heavens.
13 When he utters his voice, there is a tumult of waters in the heavens,
and he makes the mist rise from the ends of the earth.
He makes lightnings for the rain,
and he brings out the wind from his storehouses.
14 Everyone is stupid and without knowledge;
goldsmiths are all put to shame by their idols;
for their images are false,
and there is no breath in them.
15 They are worthless, a work of delusion;
at the time of their punishment they shall perish.
16 Not like these is the LORD,[d] the portion of Jacob,
for he is the one who formed all things,
and Israel is the tribe of his inheritance;
the LORD of hosts is his name.

17 Gather up your bundle from the ground,
O you who live under siege!
18 For thus says the LORD:
I am going to sling out the inhabitants of the land
at this time,
and I will bring distress on them,
so that they shall feel it.

19 Woe is me because of my hurt!
My wound is severe.
But I said, "Truly this is my punishment,
and I must bear it."
20 My tent is destroyed,
and all my cords are broken;

[a] Heb *They* [b] Meaning of Heb uncertain [c] This verse is in Aramaic [d] Heb lacks *the LORD*

my children have gone from me,
    and they are no more;
there is no one to spread my tent again,
    and to set up my curtains.
21 For the shepherds are stupid,
    and do not inquire of the LORD;
therefore they have not prospered,
    and all their flock is scattered.

22 Hear, a noise! Listen, it is coming—
    a great commotion from the land of the
        north
to make the cities of Judah a desolation,
    a lair of jackals.

23 I know, O LORD, that the way of human
        beings is not in their control,
    that mortals as they walk cannot direct
        their steps.
24 Correct me, O LORD, but in just measure;
    not in your anger, or you will bring me to
        nothing.

25 Pour out your wrath on the nations that do
        not know you,
    and on the peoples that do not call on your
        name;
for they have devoured Jacob;
    they have devoured him and consumed
        him,
    and have laid waste his habitation.

11 The word that came to Jeremiah from
the LORD: 2Hear the words of this covenant, and speak to the people of Judah and the
inhabitants of Jerusalem. 3You shall say to them,
Thus says the LORD, the God of Israel: Cursed
be anyone who does not heed the words of this
covenant, 4which I commanded your ancestors
when I brought them out of the land of Egypt,
from the iron-smelter, saying, Listen to my voice,
and do all that I command you. So shall you be
my people, and I will be your God, 5that I may
perform the oath that I swore to your ancestors,
to give them a land flowing with milk and honey,
as at this day. Then I answered, "So be it, LORD."
6 And the LORD said to me: Proclaim all
these words in the cities of Judah, and in the
streets of Jerusalem: Hear the words of this covenant and do them. 7For I solemnly warned your
ancestors when I brought them up out of the land
of Egypt, warning them persistently, even to this
day, saying, Obey my voice. 8Yet they did not
obey or incline their ear, but everyone walked
in the stubbornness of an evil will. So I brought
upon them all the words of this covenant, which I
commanded them to do, but they did not.

Jeremiah 11:8

Jeremiah is known for what in the nineteenth century CE was named his "Confessions," six presumably autobiographical poems of lament in first-person speech, complaining about the burdens of being a prophet and beseeching God to intervene (11:18—12:6; 15:10-21; 17:14-18; 18:18-23; 20:7-13; 20:14-18).

— ABL

9 And the LORD said to me: Conspiracy exists among the people of Judah and the inhabitants of Jerusalem. 10They have turned back to the
iniquities of their ancestors of old, who refused to
heed my words; they have gone after other gods
to serve them; the house of Israel and the house of
Judah have broken the covenant that I made with
their ancestors. 11Therefore, thus says the LORD,
assuredly I am going to bring disaster upon them
that they cannot escape; though they cry out to
me, I will not listen to them. 12Then the cities of
Judah and the inhabitants of Jerusalem will go
and cry out to the gods to whom they make offerings, but they will never save them in the time of
their trouble. 13For your gods have become as
many as your towns, O Judah; and as many as the
streets of Jerusalem are the altars to shame you
have set up, altars to make offerings to Baal.
14 As for you, do not pray for this people,
or lift up a cry or prayer on their behalf, for I
will not listen when they call to me in the time
of their trouble. 15What right has my beloved in
my house, when she has done vile deeds? Can

vows[a] and sacrificial flesh avert your doom? Can
you then exult? 16The LORD once called you, "A
green olive tree, fair with goodly fruit"; but with
the roar of a great tempest he will set fire to it,
and its branches will be consumed. 17The LORD
of hosts, who planted you, has pronounced evil
against you, because of the evil that the house of
Israel and the house of Judah have done, provoking me to anger by making offerings to Baal.

18 It was the LORD who made it known to me,
and I knew;
then you showed me their evil deeds.
19 But I was like a gentle lamb
led to the slaughter.
And I did not know it was against me
that they devised schemes, saying,
"Let us destroy the tree with its fruit,
let us cut him off from the land of the living,
so that his name will no longer be remembered!"
20 But you, O LORD of hosts, who judge righteously,
who try the heart and the mind,
let me see your retribution upon them,
for to you I have committed my cause.

21 Therefore thus says the LORD concerning
the people of Anathoth, who seek your life, and
say, "You shall not prophesy in the name of the
LORD, or you will die by our hand"— 22therefore
thus says the LORD of hosts: I am going to punish them; the young men shall die by the sword;
their sons and their daughters shall die by famine;
23and not even a remnant shall be left of them.
For I will bring disaster upon the people of Anathoth, the year of their punishment.

12 You will be in the right, O LORD,
when I lay charges against you;
but let me put my case to you.
Why does the way of the guilty prosper?
Why do all who are treacherous thrive?
2 You plant them, and they take root;
they grow and bring forth fruit;
you are near in their mouths
yet far from their hearts.
3 But you, O LORD, know me;
You see me and test me—my heart is with you.
Pull them out like sheep for the slaughter,
and set them apart for the day of slaughter.
4 How long will the land mourn,
and the grass of every field wither?
For the wickedness of those who live in it
the animals and the birds are swept away,
and because people said, "He is blind to our ways."[b]

5 If you have raced with foot-runners and they have wearied you,
how will you compete with horses?
And if in a safe land you fall down,
how will you fare in the thickets of the Jordan?
6 For even your kinsfolk and your own family,
even they have dealt treacherously with you;
they are in full cry after you;
do not believe them,
though they speak friendly words to you.

7 I have forsaken my house,
I have abandoned my heritage;
I have given the beloved of my heart
into the hands of her enemies.
8 My heritage has become to me
like a lion in the forest;
she has lifted up her voice against me—
therefore I hate her.
9 Is the hyena greedy[c] for my heritage at my command?
Are the birds of prey all around her?
Go, assemble all the wild animals;
bring them to devour her.
10 Many shepherds have destroyed my vineyard,
they have trampled down my portion,
they have made my pleasant portion
a desolate wilderness.
11 They have made it a desolation;

[a] Gk: Heb *Can many* [b] Gk: Heb *to our future* [c] Cn: Heb *Is the hyena, the bird of prey*

desolate, it mourns to me.
The whole land is made desolate,
but no one lays it to heart.
12 Upon all the bare heights[a] in the desert
spoilers have come;
for the sword of the LORD devours
from one end of the land to the other;
no one shall be safe.
13 They have sown wheat and have reaped
thorns,
they have tired themselves out but profit
nothing.
They shall be ashamed of their[b] harvests
because of the fierce anger of the LORD.

14 Thus says the LORD concerning all my
evil neighbors who touch the heritage that I have
given my people Israel to inherit: I am about to
pluck them up from their land, and I will pluck
up the house of Judah from among them. 15And
after I have plucked them up, I will again have
compassion on them, and I will bring them again
to their heritage and to their land, every one of
them. 16And then, if they will diligently learn the
ways of my people, to swear by my name, "As the
LORD lives," as they taught my people to swear
by Baal, then they shall be built up in the midst
of my people. 17But if any nation will not listen,
then I will completely uproot it and destroy it,
says the LORD.

13 Thus said the LORD to me, "Go and buy
yourself a linen loincloth, and put it on
your loins, but do not dip it in water." 2So I bought
a loincloth according to the word of the LORD,
and put it on my loins. 3And the word of the
LORD came to me a second time, saying, 4"Take
the loincloth that you bought and are wearing,
and go now to the Euphrates,[c] and hide it there
in a cleft of the rock." 5So I went, and hid it by the
Euphrates,[c] as the LORD commanded me. 6And
after many days the LORD said to me, "Go now
to the Euphrates,[c] and take from there the loincloth that I commanded you to hide there." 7Then
I went to the Euphrates,[c] and dug, and I took the
loincloth from the place where I had hidden it.
But now the loincloth was ruined; it was good for
nothing.
8 Then the word of the LORD came to me:
9Thus says the LORD: Just so I will ruin the pride
of Judah and the great pride of Jerusalem. 10This
evil people, who refuse to hear my words, who
stubbornly follow their own will and have gone
after other gods to serve them and worship them,
shall be like this loincloth, which is good for nothing. 11For as the loincloth clings to one's loins, so
I made the whole house of Israel and the whole
house of Judah cling to me, says the LORD, in order that they might be for me a people, a name, a
praise, and a glory. But they would not listen.

12 You shall speak to them this word: Thus
says the LORD, the God of Israel: Every wine-jar
should be filled with wine. And they will say to
you, "Do you think we do not know that every
wine-jar should be filled with wine?" 13Then you
shall say to them: Thus says the LORD: I am about
to fill all the inhabitants of this land—the kings
who sit on David's throne, the priests, the prophets, and all the inhabitants of Jerusalem—with
drunkenness. 14And I will dash them one against
another, parents and children together, says the
LORD. I will not pity or spare or have compassion
when I destroy them.

15 Hear and give ear; do not be haughty,
for the LORD has spoken.
16 Give glory to the LORD your God
before he brings darkness,
and before your feet stumble
on the mountains at twilight;
while you look for light,
he turns it into gloom
and makes it deep darkness.
17 But if you will not listen,
my soul will weep in secret for your pride;
my eyes will weep bitterly and run down with
tears,
because the LORD's flock has been taken
captive.

[a] Or *the trails* [b] Heb *your* [c] Or *to Parah*; Heb *perath*

18 Say to the king and the queen mother:
"Take a lowly seat,
for your beautiful crown
has come down from your head."[a]
19 The towns of the Negeb are shut up
with no one to open them;
all Judah is taken into exile,
wholly taken into exile.

20 Lift up your eyes and see
those who come from the north.
Where is the flock that was given you,
your beautiful flock?
21 What will you say when they set as head over
you
those whom you have trained
to be your allies?
Will not pangs take hold of you,
like those of a woman in labor?
22 And if you say in your heart,
"Why have these things come upon me?"
it is for the greatness of your iniquity
that your skirts are lifted up,
and you are violated.
23 Can Ethiopians[b] change their skin
or leopards their spots?
Then also you can do good
who are accustomed to do evil.
24 I will scatter you[c] like chaff
driven by the wind from the desert.
25 This is your lot,
the portion I have measured out to you,
says the LORD,
because you have forgotten me
and trusted in lies.
26 I myself will lift up your skirts over your
face,
and your shame will be seen.
27 I have seen your abominations,
your adulteries and neighings, your
shameless prostitutions
on the hills of the countryside.
Woe to you, O Jerusalem!
How long will it be
before you are made clean?

14 The word of the LORD that came to Jeremiah concerning the drought:
2 Judah mourns
and her gates languish;
they lie in gloom on the ground,
and the cry of Jerusalem goes up.
3 Her nobles send their servants for water;
they come to the cisterns,
they find no water,
they return with their vessels empty.
They are ashamed and dismayed
and cover their heads,
4 because the ground is cracked.
Because there has been no rain on the land
the farmers are dismayed;
they cover their heads.
5 Even the doe in the field forsakes her
newborn fawn
because there is no grass.
6 The wild asses stand on the bare heights,[d]
they pant for air like jackals;
their eyes fail
because there is no herbage.

7 Although our iniquities testify against us,
act, O LORD, for your name's sake;
our apostasies indeed are many,
and we have sinned against you.
8 O hope of Israel,
its savior in time of trouble,
why should you be like a stranger in the land,
like a traveler turning aside for the night?
9 Why should you be like someone confused,
like a mighty warrior who cannot give
help?
Yet you, O LORD, are in the midst of us,
and we are called by your name;
do not forsake us!

10 Thus says the LORD concerning this people:
Truly they have loved to wander,
they have not restrained their feet;
therefore the LORD does not accept them,
now he will remember their iniquity
and punish their sins.

[a] Gk Syr Vg: Meaning of Heb uncertain [b] Or *Nubians*; Heb *Cushites* [c] Heb *them* [d] Or *the trails*

11 The LORD said to me: Do not pray for the
welfare of this people. 12 Although they fast, I do
not hear their cry, and although they offer burnt
offering and grain offering, I do not accept them;
but by the sword, by famine, and by pestilence I
consume them.

13 Then I said: "Ah, Lord GOD! Here are the
prophets saying to them, 'You shall not see the
sword, nor shall you have famine, but I will give
you true peace in this place.'" 14 And the LORD
said to me: The prophets are prophesying lies in
my name; I did not send them, nor did I command them or speak to them. They are prophesying to you a lying vision, worthless divination,
and the deceit of their own minds. 15 Therefore
thus says the LORD concerning the prophets
who prophesy in my name though I did not send
them, and who say, "Sword and famine shall not
come on this land": By sword and famine those
prophets shall be consumed. 16 And the people to
whom they prophesy shall be thrown out into the
streets of Jerusalem, victims of famine and sword.
There shall be no one to bury them—themselves,
their wives, their sons, and their daughters. For I
will pour out their wickedness upon them.

17 You shall say to them this word:
Let my eyes run down with tears night and day,
and let them not cease,
for the virgin daughter—my people—is struck down with a crushing blow,
with a very grievous wound.
18 If I go out into the field,
look—those killed by the sword!
And if I enter the city,
look—those sick with[a] famine!
For both prophet and priest ply their trade throughout the land,
and have no knowledge.

19 Have you completely rejected Judah?
Does your heart loathe Zion?
Why have you struck us down
so that there is no healing for us?
We look for peace, but find no good;
for a time of healing, but there is terror instead.
20 We acknowledge our wickedness, O LORD,
the iniquity of our ancestors,
for we have sinned against you.
21 Do not spurn us, for your name's sake;
do not dishonor your glorious throne;
remember and do not break your covenant with us.
22 Can any idols of the nations bring rain?
Or can the heavens give showers?
Is it not you, O LORD our God?
We set our hope on you,
for it is you who do all this.

15 Then the LORD said to me: Though Moses
and Samuel stood before me, yet my heart
would not turn toward this people. Send them
out of my sight, and let them go! 2 And when they
say to you, "Where shall we go?" you shall say to
them: Thus says the LORD:
Those destined for pestilence, to pestilence,
and those destined for the sword, to the sword;
those destined for famine, to famine,
and those destined for captivity, to captivity.

3 And I will appoint over them four kinds of
destroyers, says the LORD: the sword to kill, the
dogs to drag away, and the birds of the air and the
wild animals of the earth to devour and destroy.
4 I will make them a horror to all the kingdoms of
the earth because of what King Manasseh son of
Hezekiah of Judah did in Jerusalem.

5 Who will have pity on you, O Jerusalem,
or who will bemoan you?
Who will turn aside
to ask about your welfare?
6 You have rejected me, says the LORD,
you are going backward;
so I have stretched out my hand against you and destroyed you—
I am weary of relenting.

[a] Heb *look—the sicknesses of*

7 I have winnowed them with a winnowing
fork
in the gates of the land;
I have bereaved them, I have destroyed my
people;
they did not turn from their ways.
8 Their widows became more numerous
than the sand of the seas;
I have brought against the mothers of youths
a destroyer at noonday;
I have made anguish and terror
fall upon her suddenly.
9 She who bore seven has languished;
she has swooned away;
her sun went down while it was yet day;
she has been shamed and disgraced.
And the rest of them I will give to the sword
before their enemies,
says the LORD.

10 Woe is me, my mother, that you ever bore
me, a man of strife and contention to the whole
land! I have not lent, nor have I borrowed, yet all
of them curse me. 11The LORD said: Surely I have
intervened in your life[a] for good, surely I have imposed enemies on you in a time of trouble and in
a time of distress.[b] 12Can iron and bronze break
iron from the north?
13 Your wealth and your treasures I will
give as plunder, without price, for all your sins,
throughout all your territory. 14I will make you
serve your enemies in a land that you do not
know, for in my anger a fire is kindled that shall
burn forever.
15 O LORD, you know;
remember me and visit me,
and bring down retribution for me on my
persecutors.
In your forbearance do not take me away;
know that on your account I suffer insult.
16 Your words were found, and I ate them,
and your words became to me a joy
and the delight of my heart;
for I am called by your name,
O LORD, God of hosts.

17 I did not sit in the company of merrymakers,
nor did I rejoice;
under the weight of your hand I sat alone,
for you had filled me with indignation.
18 Why is my pain unceasing,
my wound incurable,
refusing to be healed?
Truly, you are to me like a deceitful brook,
like waters that fail.

19 Therefore thus says the LORD:
If you turn back, I will take you back,
and you shall stand before me.
If you utter what is precious, and not what is
worthless,
you shall serve as my mouth.
It is they who will turn to you,
not you who will turn to them.
20 And I will make you to this people
a fortified wall of bronze;
they will fight against you,
but they shall not prevail over you,
for I am with you
to save you and deliver you,
says the LORD.
21 I will deliver you out of the hand of the
wicked,
and redeem you from the grasp of the
ruthless.

16 The word of the LORD came to me: 2You
shall not take a wife, nor shall you have
sons or daughters in this place. 3For thus says the
LORD concerning the sons and daughters who are
born in this place, and concerning the mothers
who bear them and the fathers who beget them
in this land: 4They shall die of deadly diseases.
They shall not be lamented, nor shall they be buried; they shall become like dung on the surface of
the ground. They shall perish by the sword and by
famine, and their dead bodies shall become food
for the birds of the air and for the wild animals of
the earth.
5 For thus says the LORD: Do not enter the
house of mourning, or go to lament, or bemoan
them; for I have taken away my peace from this

[a] Heb *intervened with you* [b] Meaning of Heb uncertain

people, says the LORD, my steadfast love and
mercy. 6Both great and small shall die in this land;
they shall not be buried, and no one shall lament
for them; there shall be no gashing, no shaving of
the head for them. 7No one shall break bread[a] for
the mourner, to offer comfort for the dead; nor
shall anyone give them the cup of consolation to
drink for their fathers or their mothers. 8You shall
not go into the house of feasting to sit with them,
to eat and drink. 9For thus says the LORD of hosts,
the God of Israel: I am going to banish from this
place, in your days and before your eyes, the voice
of mirth and the voice of gladness, the voice of
the bridegroom and the voice of the bride.

10 And when you tell this people all these
words, and they say to you, "Why has the LORD
pronounced all this great evil against us? What is
our iniquity? What is the sin that we have committed against the LORD our God?" 11then you
shall say to them: It is because your ancestors
have forsaken me, says the LORD, and have gone
after other gods and have served and worshiped
them, and have forsaken me and have not kept
my law; 12and because you have behaved worse
than your ancestors, for here you are, every one of
you, following your stubborn evil will, refusing to
listen to me. 13Therefore I will hurl you out of this
land into a land that neither you nor your ancestors have known, and there you shall serve other
gods day and night, for I will show you no favor.

14 Therefore, the days are surely coming,
says the LORD, when it shall no longer be said,
"As the LORD lives who brought the people of Israel up out of the land of Egypt," 15but "As the
LORD lives who brought the people of Israel up
out of the land of the north and out of all the
lands where he had driven them." For I will bring
them back to their own land that I gave to their
ancestors.

16 I am now sending for many fishermen,
says the LORD, and they shall catch them; and
afterward I will send for many hunters, and they
shall hunt them from every mountain and every
hill, and out of the clefts of the rocks. 17For my
eyes are on all their ways; they are not hidden
from my presence, nor is their iniquity concealed
from my sight. 18And[b] I will doubly repay their
iniquity and their sin, because they have polluted
my land with the carcasses of their detestable
idols, and have filled my inheritance with their
abominations.

19 O LORD, my strength and my stronghold,
my refuge in the day of trouble,
to you shall the nations come
from the ends of the earth and say:
Our ancestors have inherited nothing but
lies,
worthless things in which there is no
profit.
20 Can mortals make for themselves gods?
Such are no gods!

21 "Therefore I am surely going to teach
them, this time I am going to teach them my
power and my might, and they shall know that
my name is the LORD."

17 The sin of Judah is written with an iron
pen; with a diamond point it is engraved
on the tablet of their hearts, and on the horns of
their altars, 2while their children remember their
altars and their sacred poles,[c] beside every green
tree, and on the high hills, 3on the mountains in
the open country. Your wealth and all your treasures I will give for spoil as the price of your sin[d]
throughout all your territory. 4By your own act
you shall lose the heritage that I gave you, and I
will make you serve your enemies in a land that
you do not know, for in my anger a fire is kindled[e]
that shall burn forever.

5 Thus says the LORD:
Cursed are those who trust in mere mortals
and make mere flesh their strength,
whose hearts turn away from the LORD.
6 They shall be like a shrub in the desert,
and shall not see when relief comes.

[a] Two Mss Gk: MT *break for them* [b] Gk: Heb *And first* [c] Heb *Asherim* [d] Cn: Heb *spoil your high places for sin*
[e] Two Mss Theodotion: *you kindled*

 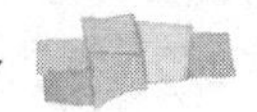

They shall live in the parched places of the
wilderness,
in an uninhabited salt land.

7 Blessed are those who trust in the LORD,
whose trust is the LORD.
8 They shall be like a tree planted by water,
sending out its roots by the stream.
It shall not fear when heat comes,
and its leaves shall stay green;
in the year of drought it is not anxious,
and it does not cease to bear fruit.

9 The heart is devious above all else;
it is perverse—
who can understand it?
10 I the LORD test the mind
and search the heart,
to give to all according to their ways,
according to the fruit of their doings.

11 Like the partridge hatching what it did not
lay,
so are all who amass wealth unjustly;
in mid-life it will leave them,
and at their end they will prove to be fools.

12 O glorious throne, exalted from the
beginning,
shrine of our sanctuary!
13 O hope of Israel! O LORD!
All who forsake you shall be put to shame;
those who turn away from you[a] shall be
recorded in the underworld,[b]
for they have forsaken the fountain of
living water, the LORD.

14 Heal me, O LORD, and I shall be healed;
save me, and I shall be saved;
for you are my praise.
15 See how they say to me,
"Where is the word of the LORD?
Let it come!"
16 But I have not run away from being a
shepherd[c] in your service,
nor have I desired the fatal day.
You know what came from my lips;
it was before your face.
17 Do not become a terror to me;
you are my refuge in the day of disaster;
18 Let my persecutors be shamed,
but do not let me be shamed;
let them be dismayed,
but do not let me be dismayed;
bring on them the day of disaster;
destroy them with double destruction!

19 Thus said the LORD to me: Go and stand
in the People's Gate, by which the kings of Judah
enter and by which they go out, and in all the gates
of Jerusalem, 20 and say to them: Hear the word
of the LORD, you kings of Judah, and all Judah,
and all the inhabitants of Jerusalem, who enter by
these gates. 21 Thus says the LORD: For the sake
of your lives, take care that you do not bear a burden on the sabbath day or bring it in by the gates
of Jerusalem. 22 And do not carry a burden out of
your houses on the sabbath or do any work, but
keep the sabbath day holy, as I commanded your
ancestors. 23 Yet they did not listen or incline their
ear; they stiffened their necks and would not hear
or receive instruction.
24 But if you listen to me, says the LORD, and
bring in no burden by the gates of this city on the
sabbath day, but keep the sabbath day holy and
do no work on it, 25 then there shall enter by the
gates of this city kings[d] who sit on the throne of
David, riding in chariots and on horses, they and
their officials, the people of Judah and the inhabitants of Jerusalem; and this city shall be inhabited forever. 26 And people shall come from the
towns of Judah and the places around Jerusalem,
from the land of Benjamin, from the Shephelah,
from the hill country, and from the Negeb, bringing burnt offerings and sacrifices, grain offerings
and frankincense, and bringing thank offerings to
the house of the LORD. 27 But if you do not listen to me, to keep the sabbath day holy, and to
carry in no burden through the gates of Jerusalem
on the sabbath day, then I will kindle a fire in its

[a] Heb *me* [b] Or *in the earth* [c] Meaning of Heb uncertain [d] Cn: Heb *kings and officials*

gates; it shall devour the palaces of Jerusalem and
shall not be quenched.

18 The word that came to Jeremiah from the
LORD: 2"Come, go down to the potter's
house, and there I will let you hear my words."
3So I went down to the potter's house, and there
he was working at his wheel. 4The vessel he was
making of clay was spoiled in the potter's hand,
and he reworked it into another vessel, as seemed
good to him.

5 Then the word of the LORD came to me:
6Can I not do with you, O house of Israel, just
as this potter has done? says the LORD. Just like
the clay in the potter's hand, so are you in my
hand, O house of Israel. 7At one moment I may
declare concerning a nation or a kingdom, that I
will pluck up and break down and destroy it, 8but
if that nation, concerning which I have spoken,
turns from its evil, I will change my mind about
the disaster that I intended to bring on it. 9And at
another moment I may declare concerning a nation or a kingdom that I will build and plant it,
10but if it does evil in my sight, not listening to
my voice, then I will change my mind about the
good that I had intended to do to it. 11Now, therefore, say to the people of Judah and the inhabitants of Jerusalem: Thus says the LORD: Look, I
am a potter shaping evil against you and devising
a plan against you. Turn now, all of you from your
evil way, and amend your ways and your doings.

12 But they say, "It is no use! We will follow
our own plans, and each of us will act according
to the stubbornness of our evil will."

13 Therefore thus says the LORD:
Ask among the nations:
Who has heard the like of this?
The virgin Israel has done
a most horrible thing.
14 Does the snow of Lebanon leave
the crags of Sirion?[a]
Do the mountain[b] waters run dry,[c]
the cold flowing streams?
15 But my people have forgotten me,
they burn offerings to a delusion;
they have stumbled[d] in their ways,
in the ancient roads,
and have gone into bypaths,
not the highway,
16 making their land a horror,
a thing to be hissed at forever.
All who pass by it are horrified
and shake their heads.
17 Like the wind from the east,
I will scatter them before the enemy.
I will show them my back, not my face,
in the day of their calamity.

18 Then they said, "Come, let us make plots against Jeremiah—for instruction shall not perish from the priest, nor counsel from the wise, nor the word from the prophet. Come, let us bring charges against him,[e] and let us not heed any of his words."

19 Give heed to me, O LORD,
and listen to what my adversaries say!
20 Is evil a recompense for good?
Yet they have dug a pit for my life.
Remember how I stood before you
to speak good for them,
to turn away your wrath from them.
21 Therefore give their children over to famine;
hurl them out to the power of the sword,
let their wives become childless and
widowed.
May their men meet death by pestilence,
their youths be slain by the sword in battle.
22 May a cry be heard from their houses,
when you bring the marauder suddenly
upon them!
For they have dug a pit to catch me,
and laid snares for my feet.
23 Yet you, O LORD, know
all their plotting to kill me.
Do not forgive their iniquity,
do not blot out their sin from your sight.

[a] Cn: Heb *of the field* [b] Cn: Heb *foreign* [c] Cn: Heb *Are . . . plucked up?* [d] Gk Syr Vg: Heb *they made them stumble*
[e] Heb *strike him with the tongue*

Let them be tripped up before you;
deal with them while you are angry.

19 Thus said the LORD: Go and buy a potter's earthenware jug. Take with you[a]
some of the elders of the people and some of the
senior priests, 2and go out to the valley of the son
of Hinnom at the entry of the Potsherd Gate, and
proclaim there the words that I tell you. 3You
shall say: Hear the word of the LORD, O kings of
Judah and inhabitants of Jerusalem. Thus says the
LORD of hosts, the God of Israel: I am going to
bring such disaster upon this place that the ears
of everyone who hears of it will tingle. 4Because
the people have forsaken me, and have profaned
this place by making offerings in it to other gods
whom neither they nor their ancestors nor the
kings of Judah have known, and because they have
filled this place with the blood of the innocent,
5and gone on building the high places of Baal to
burn their children in the fire as burnt offerings to
Baal, which I did not command or decree, nor did
it enter my mind; 6therefore the days are surely
coming, says the LORD, when this place shall no
more be called Topheth, or the valley of the son
of Hinnom, but the valley of Slaughter. 7And in
this place I will make void the plans of Judah and
Jerusalem, and will make them fall by the sword
before their enemies, and by the hand of those
who seek their life. I will give their dead bodies for
food to the birds of the air and to the wild animals
of the earth. 8And I will make this city a horror,
a thing to be hissed at; everyone who passes by
it will be horrified and will hiss because of all its
disasters. 9And I will make them eat the flesh of
their sons and the flesh of their daughters, and all
shall eat the flesh of their neighbors in the siege,
and in the distress with which their enemies and
those who seek their life afflict them.

10 Then you shall break the jug in the sight of
those who go with you, 11and shall say to them:
Thus says the LORD of hosts: So will I break this
people and this city, as one breaks a potter's vessel, so that it can never be mended. In Topheth
they shall bury until there is no more room
to bury. 12Thus will I do to this place, says the
LORD, and to its inhabitants, making this city like
Topheth. 13And the houses of Jerusalem and the
houses of the kings of Judah shall be defiled like
the place of Topheth—all the houses upon whose
roofs offerings have been made to the whole host
of heaven, and libations have been poured out to
other gods.

14 When Jeremiah came from Topheth,
where the LORD had sent him to prophesy, he
stood in the court of the LORD's house and said
to all the people: 15Thus says the LORD of hosts,
the God of Israel: I am now bringing upon this
city and upon all its towns all the disaster that I
have pronounced against it, because they have
stiffened their necks, refusing to hear my words.

20 Now the priest Pashhur son of Immer,
who was chief officer in the house of the
LORD, heard Jeremiah prophesying these things.
2Then Pashhur struck the prophet Jeremiah, and
put him in the stocks that were in the upper Benjamin Gate of the house of the LORD. 3The next
morning when Pashhur released Jeremiah from
the stocks, Jeremiah said to him, The LORD has
named you not Pashhur but "Terror-all-around."
4For thus says the LORD: I am making you a terror to yourself and to all your friends; and they
shall fall by the sword of their enemies while you
look on. And I will give all Judah into the hand of
the king of Babylon; he shall carry them captive
to Babylon, and shall kill them with the sword.
5I will give all the wealth of this city, all its gains,
all its prized belongings, and all the treasures of
the kings of Judah into the hand of their enemies,
who shall plunder them, and seize them, and
carry them to Babylon. 6And you, Pashhur, and
all who live in your house, shall go into captivity,
and to Babylon you shall go; there you shall die,
and there you shall be buried, you and all your
friends, to whom you have prophesied falsely.

7 O LORD, you have enticed me,
and I was enticed;
you have overpowered me,
and you have prevailed.
I have become a laughingstock all day long;

[a] Syr Tg Compare Gk: Heb lacks *take with you*

everyone mocks me.
8 For whenever I speak, I must cry out,
I must shout, "Violence and destruction!"
For the word of the LORD has become for me
a reproach and derision all day long.
9 If I say, "I will not mention him,
or speak any more in his name,"
then within me there is something like a burning fire
shut up in my bones;
I am weary with holding it in,
and I cannot.
10 For I hear many whispering:
"Terror is all around!
Denounce him! Let us denounce him!"
All my close friends
are watching for me to stumble.
"Perhaps he can be enticed,
and we can prevail against him,
and take our revenge on him."

Jeremiah 20:7-10

Jeremiah's agonized protest is a far cry from the self-satisfied enthusiasm of many a self-styled prophet, in his day and our own. In contrast to the abundant proliferation of printed Bibles in our day, Jeremiah suggests that a genuine encounter with the Word of God is as rare an event as it will be unwelcome.

— *NE*

11 But the LORD is with me like a dread warrior;
therefore my persecutors will stumble,
and they will not prevail.
They will be greatly shamed,
for they will not succeed.
Their eternal dishonor
will never be forgotten.
12 O LORD of hosts, you test the righteous,
you see the heart and the mind;
let me see your retribution upon them,
for to you I have committed my cause.
13 Sing to the LORD;
praise the LORD!
For he has delivered the life of the needy
from the hands of evildoers.
14 Cursed be the day
on which I was born!
The day when my mother bore me,
let it not be blessed!
15 Cursed be the man
who brought the news to my father, saying,
"A child is born to you, a son,"
making him very glad.
16 Let that man be like the cities
that the LORD overthrew without pity;
let him hear a cry in the morning
and an alarm at noon,
17 because he did not kill me in the womb;
so my mother would have been my grave,
and her womb forever great.
18 Why did I come forth from the womb
to see toil and sorrow,
and spend my days in shame?

21 This is the word that came to Jeremiah
from the LORD, when King Zedekiah sent
to him Pashhur son of Malchiah and the priest
Zephaniah son of Maaseiah, saying, 2"Please inquire of the LORD on our behalf, for King Nebuchadrezzar of Babylon is making war against us;
perhaps the LORD will perform a wonderful deed
for us, as he has often done, and will make him
withdraw from us."
3 Then Jeremiah said to them: 4Thus you
shall say to Zedekiah: Thus says the LORD, the
God of Israel: I am going to turn back the weapons of war that are in your hands and with which
you are fighting against the king of Babylon and
against the Chaldeans who are besieging you outside the walls; and I will bring them together into
the center of this city. 5I myself will fight against
you with outstretched hand and mighty arm,
in anger, in fury, and in great wrath. 6And I will
strike down the inhabitants of this city, both human beings and animals; they shall die of a great
pestilence. 7Afterward, says the LORD, I will give

King Zedekiah of Judah, and his servants, and the
people in this city—those who survive the pestilence, sword, and famine—into the hands of
King Nebuchadrezzar of Babylon, into the hands
of their enemies, into the hands of those who
seek their lives. He shall strike them down with
the edge of the sword; he shall not pity them, or
spare them, or have compassion.
8 And to this people you shall say: Thus says
the LORD: See, I am setting before you the way
of life and the way of death. 9Those who stay in
this city shall die by the sword, by famine, and by
pestilence; but those who go out and surrender
to the Chaldeans who are besieging you shall live
and shall have their lives as a prize of war. 10For I
have set my face against this city for evil and not
for good, says the LORD: it shall be given into the
hands of the king of Babylon, and he shall burn
it with fire.
11 To the house of the king of Judah say:
Hear the word of the LORD, 12O house of David!
Thus says the LORD:

Execute justice in the morning,
  and deliver from the hand of the oppressor
  anyone who has been robbed,
or else my wrath will go forth like fire,
  and burn, with no one to quench it,
  because of your evil doings.

13 See, I am against you, O inhabitant of the
    valley,
  O rock of the plain,
        says the LORD;
you who say, "Who can come down
    against us,
  or who can enter our places of refuge?"
14 I will punish you according to the fruit of
    your doings,
        says the LORD;
  I will kindle a fire in its forest,
  and it shall devour all that is around it.

22 Thus says the LORD: Go down to the
house of the king of Judah, and speak
there this word, 2and say: Hear the word of the
LORD, O King of Judah sitting on the throne of
David—you, and your servants, and your people
who enter these gates. 3Thus says the LORD: Act
with justice and righteousness, and deliver from
the hand of the oppressor anyone who has been
robbed. And do no wrong or violence to the
alien, the orphan, and the widow, or shed innocent blood in this place. 4For if you will indeed
obey this word, then through the gates of this
house shall enter kings who sit on the throne of
David, riding in chariots and on horses, they, and
their servants, and their people. 5But if you will
not heed these words, I swear by myself, says the
LORD, that this house shall become a desolation.
6For thus says the LORD concerning the house of
the king of Judah:

You are like Gilead to me,
  like the summit of Lebanon;
but I swear that I will make you a desert,
  an uninhabited city.[a]
7 I will prepare destroyers against you,
  all with their weapons;
they shall cut down your choicest cedars
  and cast them into the fire.

8 And many nations will pass by this city, and
all of them will say one to another, "Why has the
LORD dealt in this way with that great city?" 9And
they will answer, "Because they abandoned the
covenant of the LORD their God, and worshiped
other gods and served them."

10 Do not weep for him who is dead,
  nor bemoan him;
weep rather for him who goes away,
  for he shall return no more
  to see his native land.

11 For thus says the LORD concerning Shallum son of King Josiah of Judah, who succeeded
his father Josiah, and who went away from this
place: He shall return here no more, 12but in the
place where they have carried him captive he shall
die, and he shall never see this land again.

13 Woe to him who builds his house by
    unrighteousness,

[a] Cn: Heb *uninhabited cities*

and his upper rooms by injustice;
who makes his neighbors work for nothing,
and does not give them their wages;
14 who says, "I will build myself a spacious house
with large upper rooms,"
and who cuts out windows for it,
paneling it with cedar,
and painting it with vermilion.
15 Are you a king
because you compete in cedar?
Did not your father eat and drink
and do justice and righteousness?
Then it was well with him.
16 He judged the cause of the poor and needy;
then it was well.
Is not this to know me?
says the LORD.
17 But your eyes and heart
are only on your dishonest gain,
for shedding innocent blood,
and for practicing oppression and violence.

18 Therefore thus says the LORD concerning
King Jehoiakim son of Josiah of Judah:
They shall not lament for him, saying,
"Alas, my brother!" or "Alas, sister!"
They shall not lament for him, saying,
"Alas, lord!" or "Alas, his majesty!"
19 With the burial of a donkey he shall be buried—
dragged off and thrown out beyond the gates of Jerusalem.

20 Go up to Lebanon, and cry out,
and lift up your voice in Bashan;
cry out from Abarim,
for all your lovers are crushed.
21 I spoke to you in your prosperity,
but you said, "I will not listen."
This has been your way from your youth,
for you have not obeyed my voice.
22 The wind shall shepherd all your shepherds,
and your lovers shall go into captivity;
then you will be ashamed and dismayed
because of all your wickedness.
23 O inhabitant of Lebanon,
nested among the cedars,
how you will groan[a] when pangs come upon you,
pain as of a woman in labor!

24 As I live, says the LORD, even if King Coniah son of Jehoiakim of Judah were the signet
ring on my right hand, even from there I would
tear you off 25 and give you into the hands of
those who seek your life, into the hands of those
of whom you are afraid, even into the hands of
King Nebuchadrezzar of Babylon and into the
hands of the Chaldeans. 26 I will hurl you and
the mother who bore you into another country,
where you were not born, and there you shall die.
27 But they shall not return to the land to which
they long to return.
28 Is this man Coniah a despised broken pot,
a vessel no one wants?
Why are he and his offspring hurled out
and cast away in a land that they do not know?
29 O land, land, land,
hear the word of the LORD!
30 Thus says the LORD:
Record this man as childless,
a man who shall not succeed in his days;
for none of his offspring shall succeed
in sitting on the throne of David,
and ruling again in Judah.

23 Woe to the shepherds who destroy and
scatter the sheep of my pasture! says the
LORD. 2 Therefore thus says the LORD, the God
of Israel, concerning the shepherds who shepherd my people: It is you who have scattered my
flock, and have driven them away, and you have
not attended to them. So I will attend to you for
your evil doings, says the LORD. 3 Then I myself
will gather the remnant of my flock out of all the
lands where I have driven them, and I will bring
them back to their fold, and they shall be fruitful
and multiply. 4 I will raise up shepherds over them

[a] Gk Vg Syr: Heb *will be pitied*

who will shepherd them, and they shall not fear
any longer, or be dismayed, nor shall any be missing, says the LORD.
5 The days are surely coming, says the LORD,
when I will raise up for David a righteous Branch,
and he shall reign as king and deal wisely, and shall
execute justice and righteousness in the land. 6In
his days Judah will be saved and Israel will live in
safety. And this is the name by which he will be
called: "The LORD is our righteousness."
7 Therefore, the days are surely coming, says
the LORD, when it shall no longer be said, "As
the LORD lives who brought the people of Israel
up out of the land of Egypt," 8but "As the LORD
lives who brought out and led the offspring of the
house of Israel out of the land of the north and
out of all the lands where he[a] had driven them."
Then they shall live in their own land.

9 Concerning the prophets:
My heart is crushed within me,
all my bones shake;
I have become like a drunkard,
like one overcome by wine,
because of the LORD
and because of his holy words.
10 For the land is full of adulterers;
because of the curse the land mourns,
and the pastures of the wilderness are
dried up.
Their course has been evil,
and their might is not right.
11 Both prophet and priest are ungodly;
even in my house I have found their
wickedness,
says the LORD.
12 Therefore their way shall be to them
like slippery paths in the darkness,
into which they shall be driven and fall;
for I will bring disaster upon them
in the year of their punishment,
says the LORD.
13 In the prophets of Samaria
I saw a disgusting thing:
they prophesied by Baal
and led my people Israel astray.
14 But in the prophets of Jerusalem
I have seen a more shocking thing:
they commit adultery and walk in lies;
they strengthen the hands of evildoers,
so that no one turns from wickedness;
all of them have become like Sodom to me,
and its inhabitants like Gomorrah.
15 Therefore thus says the LORD of hosts
concerning the prophets:
"I am going to make them eat wormwood,
and give them poisoned water to drink;
for from the prophets of Jerusalem
ungodliness has spread throughout the
land."

16 Thus says the LORD of hosts: Do not listen to the words of the prophets who prophesy
to you; they are deluding you. They speak visions
of their own minds, not from the mouth of the
LORD. 17They keep saying to those who despise
the word of the LORD, "It shall be well with you";
and to all who stubbornly follow their own stubborn hearts, they say, "No calamity shall come
upon you."

18 For who has stood in the council of the LORD
so as to see and to hear his word?
Who has given heed to his word so as to
proclaim it?
19 Look, the storm of the LORD!
Wrath has gone forth,
a whirling tempest;
it will burst upon the head of the wicked.
20 The anger of the LORD will not turn back
until he has executed and accomplished
the intents of his mind.
In the latter days you will understand it
clearly.

21 I did not send the prophets,
yet they ran;
I did not speak to them,
yet they prophesied.
22 But if they had stood in my council,

[a] Gk: Heb *I*

then they would have proclaimed my
words to my people,
and they would have turned them from their
evil way,
and from the evil of their doings.

23 Am I a God near by, says the LORD, and not a God far off? 24Who can hide in secret places so that I cannot see them? says the LORD. Do I not fill heaven and earth? says the LORD. 25I have heard what the prophets have said who prophesy lies in my name, saying, "I have dreamed, I have dreamed!" 26How long? Will the hearts of the prophets ever turn back—those who prophesy lies, and who prophesy the deceit of their own heart? 27They plan to make my people forget my name by their dreams that they tell one another, just as their ancestors forgot my name for Baal. 28Let the prophet who has a dream tell the dream, but let the one who has my word speak my word faithfully. What has straw in common with wheat? says the LORD. 29Is not my word like fire, says the LORD, and like a hammer that breaks a rock in pieces? 30See, therefore, I am against the prophets, says the LORD, who steal my words from one another. 31See, I am against the prophets, says the LORD, who use their own tongues and say, "Says the LORD." 32See, I am against those who prophesy lying dreams, says the LORD, and who tell them, and who lead my people astray by their lies and their recklessness, when I did not send them or appoint them; so they do not profit this people at all, says the LORD.

33 When this people, or a prophet, or a priest asks you, "What is the burden of the LORD?" you shall say to them, "You are the burden,[a] and I will cast you off, says the LORD." 34And as for the prophet, priest, or the people who say, "The burden of the LORD," I will punish them and their households. 35Thus shall you say to one another, among yourselves, "What has the LORD answered?" or "What has the LORD spoken?" 36But "the burden of the LORD" you shall mention no more, for the burden is everyone's own word, and so you pervert the words of the living God, the LORD of hosts, our God. 37Thus you shall ask the prophet, "What has the LORD answered you?" or "What has the LORD spoken?" 38But if you say, "the burden of the LORD," thus says the LORD: Because you have said these words, "the burden of the LORD," when I sent to you, saying, You shall not say, "the burden of the LORD," 39therefore, I will surely lift you up[b] and cast you away from my presence, you and the city that I gave to you and your ancestors. 40And I will bring upon you everlasting disgrace and perpetual shame, which shall not be forgotten.

24 The LORD showed me two baskets of figs placed before the temple of the LORD. This was after King Nebuchadrezzar of Babylon had taken into exile from Jerusalem King Jeconiah son of Jehoiakim of Judah, together with the officials of Judah, the artisans, and the smiths, and had brought them to Babylon. 2One basket had very good figs, like first-ripe figs, but the other basket had very bad figs, so bad that they could not be eaten. 3And the LORD said to me, "What do you see, Jeremiah?" I said, "Figs, the good figs very good, and the bad figs very bad, so bad that they cannot be eaten."

4 Then the word of the LORD came to me: 5Thus says the LORD, the God of Israel: Like these good figs, so I will regard as good the exiles from Judah, whom I have sent away from this place to the land of the Chaldeans. 6I will set my eyes upon them for good, and I will bring them back to this land. I will build them up, and not tear them down; I will plant them, and not pluck them up. 7I will give them a heart to know that I am the LORD; and they shall be my people and I will be their God, for they shall return to me with their whole heart.

8 But thus says the LORD: Like the bad figs that are so bad they cannot be eaten, so will I treat King Zedekiah of Judah, his officials, the remnant of Jerusalem who remain in this land, and those who live in the land of Egypt. 9I will make them a horror, an evil thing, to all the kingdoms of the earth—a disgrace, a byword, a taunt, and a curse

[a] Gk Vg: Heb *What burden* [b] Heb Mss Gk Vg: MT *forget you*

in all the places where I shall drive them. 10 And
I will send sword, famine, and pestilence upon
them, until they are utterly destroyed from the
land that I gave to them and their ancestors.

25 The word that came to Jeremiah concerning all the people of Judah, in the fourth
year of King Jehoiakim son of Josiah of Judah
(that was the first year of King Nebuchadrezzar
of Babylon), 2 which the prophet Jeremiah spoke
to all the people of Judah and all the inhabitants
of Jerusalem: 3 For twenty-three years, from the
thirteenth year of King Josiah son of Amon of Judah, to this day, the word of the LORD has come
to me, and I have spoken persistently to you, but
you have not listened. 4 And though the LORD
persistently sent you all his servants the prophets,
you have neither listened nor inclined your ears
to hear 5 when they said, "Turn now, every one of
you, from your evil way and wicked doings, and
you will remain upon the land that the LORD has
given to you and your ancestors from of old and
forever; 6 do not go after other gods to serve and
worship them, and do not provoke me to anger
with the work of your hands. Then I will do you
no harm." 7 Yet you did not listen to me, says the
LORD, and so you have provoked me to anger
with the work of your hands to your own harm.

8 Therefore thus says the LORD of hosts: Because you have not obeyed my words, 9 I am going to send for all the tribes of the north, says the
LORD, even for King Nebuchadrezzar of Babylon,
my servant, and I will bring them against this land
and its inhabitants, and against all these nations
around; I will utterly destroy them, and make
them an object of horror and of hissing, and an
everlasting disgrace.[a] 10 And I will banish from
them the sound of mirth and the sound of gladness, the voice of the bridegroom and the voice
of the bride, the sound of the millstones and the
light of the lamp. 11 This whole land shall become
a ruin and a waste, and these nations shall serve
the king of Babylon seventy years. 12 Then after
seventy years are completed, I will punish the
king of Babylon and that nation, the land of the
Chaldeans, for their iniquity, says the LORD, making the land an everlasting waste. 13 I will bring
upon that land all the words that I have uttered
against it, everything written in this book, which
Jeremiah prophesied against all the nations. 14 For
many nations and great kings shall make slaves of
them also; and I will repay them according to
their deeds and the work of their hands.

15 For thus the LORD, the God of Israel, said
to me: Take from my hand this cup of the wine of
wrath, and make all the nations to whom I send
you drink it. 16 They shall drink and stagger and
go out of their minds because of the sword that I
am sending among them.

17 So I took the cup from the LORD's hand,
and made all the nations to whom the LORD sent
me drink it: 18 Jerusalem and the towns of Judah,
its kings and officials, to make them a desolation
and a waste, an object of hissing and of cursing,
as they are today; 19 Pharaoh king of Egypt, his
servants, his officials, and all his people; 20 all the
mixed people;[b] all the kings of the land of Uz; all
the kings of the land of the Philistines—Ashkelon, Gaza, Ekron, and the remnant of Ashdod;
21 Edom, Moab, and the Ammonites; 22 all the
kings of Tyre, all the kings of Sidon, and the kings
of the coastland across the sea; 23 Dedan, Tema,
Buz, and all who have shaven temples; 24 all the
kings of Arabia and all the kings of the mixed
peoples[b] that live in the desert; 25 all the kings of
Zimri, all the kings of Elam, and all the kings of
Media; 26 all the kings of the north, far and near,
one after another, and all the kingdoms of the
world that are on the face of the earth. And after
them the king of Sheshach[c] shall drink.

27 Then you shall say to them, Thus says
the LORD of hosts, the God of Israel: Drink, get
drunk and vomit, fall and rise no more, because
of the sword that I am sending among you.

28 And if they refuse to accept the cup from
your hand to drink, then you shall say to them:
Thus says the LORD of hosts: You must drink!
29 See, I am beginning to bring disaster on the
city that is called by my name, and how can you

[a] Gk Compare Syr: Heb *and everlasting desolations* [b] Meaning of Heb uncertain
[c] *Sheshach* is a cryptogram for *Babel*, Babylon

possibly avoid punishment? You shall not go unpunished, for I am summoning a sword against
all the inhabitants of the earth, says the LORD of
hosts.
30 You, therefore, shall prophesy against them
all these words, and say to them:

The LORD will roar from on high,
and from his holy habitation utter his
voice;
he will roar mightily against his fold,
and shout, like those who tread grapes,
against all the inhabitants of the earth.
31 The clamor will resound to the ends of the
earth,
for the LORD has an indictment against the
nations;
he is entering into judgment with all flesh,
and the guilty he will put to the sword,
says the LORD.

32 Thus says the LORD of hosts:
See, disaster is spreading
from nation to nation,
and a great tempest is stirring
from the farthest parts of the earth!

33 Those slain by the LORD on that day shall
extend from one end of the earth to the other.
They shall not be lamented, or gathered, or buried; they shall become dung on the surface of the
ground.

34 Wail, you shepherds, and cry out;
roll in ashes, you lords of the flock,
for the days of your slaughter have come—
and your dispersions,[a]
and you shall fall like a choice vessel.
35 Flight shall fail the shepherds,
and there shall be no escape for the lords
of the flock.
36 Hark! the cry of the shepherds,
and the wail of the lords of the flock!
For the LORD is despoiling their pasture,
37 and the peaceful folds are devastated,
because of the fierce anger of the LORD.
38 Like a lion he has left his covert;
for their land has become a waste
because of the cruel sword,
and because of his fierce anger.

26 At the beginning of the reign of King Jehoiakim son of Josiah of Judah, this word
came from the LORD: 2 Thus says the LORD: Stand
in the court of the LORD's house, and speak to all
the cities of Judah that come to worship in the
house of the LORD; speak to them all the words
that I command you; do not hold back a word. 3 It
may be that they will listen, all of them, and will
turn from their evil way, that I may change my
mind about the disaster that I intend to bring on
them because of their evil doings. 4 You shall say
to them: Thus says the LORD: If you will not listen to me, to walk in my law that I have set before
you, 5 and to heed the words of my servants the
prophets whom I send to you urgently—though
you have not heeded— 6 then I will make this
house like Shiloh, and I will make this city a curse
for all the nations of the earth.
7 The priests and the prophets and all the
people heard Jeremiah speaking these words in
the house of the LORD. 8 And when Jeremiah had
finished speaking all that the LORD had commanded him to speak to all the people, then the
priests and the prophets and all the people laid
hold of him, saying, "You shall die! 9 Why have
you prophesied in the name of the LORD, saying,
'This house shall be like Shiloh, and this city shall
be desolate, without inhabitant'?" And all the
people gathered around Jeremiah in the house of
the LORD.
10 When the officials of Judah heard these
things, they came up from the king's house to the
house of the LORD and took their seat in the entry of the New Gate of the house of the LORD.
11 Then the priests and the prophets said to the
officials and to all the people, "This man deserves
the sentence of death because he has prophesied
against this city, as you have heard with your own
ears."
12 Then Jeremiah spoke to all the officials
and all the people, saying, "It is the LORD who
sent me to prophesy against this house and this

[a] Meaning of Heb uncertain

city all the words you have heard. 13Now therefore amend your ways and your doings, and obey
the voice of the LORD your God, and the LORD
will change his mind about the disaster that he
has pronounced against you. 14But as for me, here
I am in your hands. Do with me as seems good
and right to you. 15Only know for certain that
if you put me to death, you will be bringing innocent blood upon yourselves and upon this city
and its inhabitants, for in truth the LORD sent me
to you to speak all these words in your ears."

16 Then the officials and all the people said to
the priests and the prophets, "This man does not
deserve the sentence of death, for he has spoken
to us in the name of the LORD our God." 17And
some of the elders of the land arose and said to
all the assembled people, 18"Micah of Moresheth,
who prophesied during the days of King Hezekiah of Judah, said to all the people of Judah:
'Thus says the LORD of hosts,

Zion shall be plowed as a field;
  Jerusalem shall become a heap of ruins,
  and the mountain of the house a wooded
    height.'

19Did King Hezekiah of Judah and all Judah actually put him to death? Did he not fear the LORD
and entreat the favor of the LORD, and did not the
LORD change his mind about the disaster that he
had pronounced against them? But we are about
to bring great disaster on ourselves!"

20 There was another man prophesying in
the name of the LORD, Uriah son of Shemaiah
from Kiriath-jearim. He prophesied against this
city and against this land in words exactly like
those of Jeremiah. 21And when King Jehoiakim,
with all his warriors and all the officials, heard
his words, the king sought to put him to death;
but when Uriah heard of it, he was afraid and fled
and escaped to Egypt. 22Then King Jehoiakim
sent[a] Elnathan son of Achbor and men with him
to Egypt, 23and they took Uriah from Egypt and
brought him to King Jehoiakim, who struck him
down with the sword and threw his dead body
into the burial place of the common people.

24 But the hand of Ahikam son of Shaphan
was with Jeremiah so that he was not given over
into the hands of the people to be put to death.

27 In the beginning of the reign of King
Zedekiah[b] son of Josiah of Judah, this
word came to Jeremiah from the LORD. 2Thus the
LORD said to me: Make yourself a yoke of straps
and bars, and put them on your neck. 3Send word[c]
to the king of Edom, the king of Moab, the king of
the Ammonites, the king of Tyre, and the king of
Sidon by the hand of the envoys who have come
to Jerusalem to King Zedekiah of Judah. 4Give
them this charge for their masters: Thus says the
LORD of hosts, the God of Israel: This is what
you shall say to your masters: 5It is I who by my
great power and my outstretched arm have made
the earth, with the people and animals that are
on the earth, and I give it to whomever I please.
6Now I have given all these lands into the hand
of King Nebuchadnezzar of Babylon, my servant,
and I have given him even the wild animals of the
field to serve him. 7All the nations shall serve him
and his son and his grandson, until the time of
his own land comes; then many nations and great
kings shall make him their slave.

8 But if any nation or kingdom will not serve
this king, Nebuchadnezzar of Babylon, and put its
neck under the yoke of the king of Babylon, then
I will punish that nation with the sword, with
famine, and with pestilence, says the LORD, until I have completed its[d] destruction by his hand.
9You, therefore, must not listen to your prophets,
your diviners, your dreamers,[e] your soothsayers,
or your sorcerers, who are saying to you, "You
shall not serve the king of Babylon." 10For they
are prophesying a lie to you, with the result that
you will be removed far from your land; I will
drive you out, and you will perish. 11But any nation that will bring its neck under the yoke of the
king of Babylon and serve him, I will leave on its
own land, says the LORD, to till it and live there.

12 I spoke to King Zedekiah of Judah in the
same way: Bring your necks under the yoke of the

[a] Heb adds *men to Egypt* [b] Another reading is *Jehoiakim* [c] Cn: Heb *send them* [d] Heb *their*
[e] Gk Syr Vg: Heb *dreams*

king of Babylon, and serve him and his people,
and live. 13 Why should you and your people die
by the sword, by famine, and by pestilence, as the
LORD has spoken concerning any nation that will
not serve the king of Babylon? 14 Do not listen to
the words of the prophets who are telling you not
to serve the king of Babylon, for they are prophesying a lie to you. 15 I have not sent them, says
the LORD, but they are prophesying falsely in my
name, with the result that I will drive you out and
you will perish, you and the prophets who are
prophesying to you.
16 Then I spoke to the priests and to all this
people, saying, Thus says the LORD: Do not listen to the words of your prophets who are prophesying to you, saying, "The vessels of the LORD's
house will soon be brought back from Babylon,"
for they are prophesying a lie to you. 17 Do not
listen to them; serve the king of Babylon and
live. Why should this city become a desolation?
18 If indeed they are prophets, and if the word of
the LORD is with them, then let them intercede
with the LORD of hosts, that the vessels left in the
house of the LORD, in the house of the king of
Judah, and in Jerusalem may not go to Babylon.
19 For thus says the LORD of hosts concerning the
pillars, the sea, the stands, and the rest of the vessels that are left in this city, 20 which King Nebuchadnezzar of Babylon did not take away when
he took into exile from Jerusalem to Babylon
King Jeconiah son of Jehoiakim of Judah, and all
the nobles of Judah and Jerusalem— 21 thus says
the LORD of hosts, the God of Israel, concerning the vessels left in the house of the LORD, in
the house of the king of Judah, and in Jerusalem:
22 They shall be carried to Babylon, and there they
shall stay, until the day when I give attention to
them, says the LORD. Then I will bring them up
and restore them to this place.

28 In that same year, at the beginning of the
reign of King Zedekiah of Judah, in the
fifth month of the fourth year, the prophet Hananiah son of Azzur, from Gibeon, spoke to me
in the house of the LORD, in the presence of the
priests and all the people, saying, 2 "Thus says the
LORD of hosts, the God of Israel: I have broken
the yoke of the king of Babylon. 3 Within two
years I will bring back to this place all the vessels
of the LORD's house, which King Nebuchadnezzar of Babylon took away from this place and
carried to Babylon. 4 I will also bring back to this
place King Jeconiah son of Jehoiakim of Judah,
and all the exiles from Judah who went to Babylon, says the LORD, for I will break the yoke of
the king of Babylon."
5 Then the prophet Jeremiah spoke to the
prophet Hananiah in the presence of the priests
and all the people who were standing in the house
of the LORD; 6 and the prophet Jeremiah said,
"Amen! May the LORD do so; may the LORD fulfill the words that you have prophesied, and bring
back to this place from Babylon the vessels of the
house of the LORD, and all the exiles. 7 But listen
now to this word that I speak in your hearing and
in the hearing of all the people. 8 The prophets
who preceded you and me from ancient times
prophesied war, famine, and pestilence against
many countries and great kingdoms. 9 As for the
prophet who prophesies peace, when the word of
that prophet comes true, then it will be known
that the LORD has truly sent the prophet."
10 Then the prophet Hananiah took the yoke
from the neck of the prophet Jeremiah, and broke
it. 11 And Hananiah spoke in the presence of all
the people, saying, "Thus says the LORD: This is
how I will break the yoke of King Nebuchadnezzar of Babylon from the neck of all the nations
within two years." At this, the prophet Jeremiah
went his way.
12 Sometime after the prophet Hananiah had
broken the yoke from the neck of the prophet Jeremiah, the word of the LORD came to Jeremiah:
13 Go, tell Hananiah, Thus says the LORD: You
have broken wooden bars only to forge iron bars
in place of them! 14 For thus says the LORD of
hosts, the God of Israel: I have put an iron yoke
on the neck of all these nations so that they may
serve King Nebuchadnezzar of Babylon, and they
shall indeed serve him; I have even given him the
wild animals. 15 And the prophet Jeremiah said
to the prophet Hananiah, "Listen, Hananiah, the
LORD has not sent you, and you made this people
trust in a lie. 16 Therefore thus says the LORD: I
am going to send you off the face of the earth.

Within this year you will be dead, because you
have spoken rebellion against the LORD."
17 In that same year, in the seventh month,
the prophet Hananiah died.

29 These are the words of the letter that the
prophet Jeremiah sent from Jerusalem to
the remaining elders among the exiles, and to the
priests, the prophets, and all the people, whom
Nebuchadnezzar had taken into exile from Jerusalem to Babylon. 2This was after King Jeconiah, and the queen mother, the court officials,
the leaders of Judah and Jerusalem, the artisans,
and the smiths had departed from Jerusalem.
3The letter was sent by the hand of Elasah son of
Shaphan and Gemariah son of Hilkiah, whom
King Zedekiah of Judah sent to Babylon to King
Nebuchadnezzar of Babylon. It said: 4Thus says
the LORD of hosts, the God of Israel, to all the
exiles whom I have sent into exile from Jerusalem
to Babylon: 5Build houses and live in them; plant
gardens and eat what they produce. 6Take wives
and have sons and daughters; take wives for your
sons, and give your daughters in marriage, that
they may bear sons and daughters; multiply there,
and do not decrease. 7But seek the welfare of the
city where I have sent you into exile, and pray
to the LORD on its behalf, for in its welfare you
will find your welfare. 8For thus says the LORD of
hosts, the God of Israel: Do not let the prophets
and the diviners who are among you deceive you,
and do not listen to the dreams that they dream,[a]
9for it is a lie that they are prophesying to you in
my name; I did not send them, says the LORD.
10 For thus says the LORD: Only when Babylon's seventy years are completed will I visit you,
and I will fulfill to you my promise and bring you
back to this place. 11For surely I know the plans I
have for you, says the LORD, plans for your welfare and not for harm, to give you a future with
hope. 12Then when you call upon me and come
and pray to me, I will hear you. 13When you
search for me, you will find me; if you seek me
with all your heart, 14I will let you find me, says
the LORD, and I will restore your fortunes and
gather you from all the nations and all the places
where I have driven you, says the LORD, and I will
bring you back to the place from which I sent you
into exile.
15 Because you have said, "The LORD has
raised up prophets for us in Babylon,"— 16Thus
says the LORD concerning the king who sits on
the throne of David, and concerning all the people who live in this city, your kinsfolk who did not
go out with you into exile: 17Thus says the LORD
of hosts, I am going to let loose on them sword,
famine, and pestilence, and I will make them like
rotten figs that are so bad they cannot be eaten.
18I will pursue them with the sword, with famine,
and with pestilence, and will make them a horror
to all the kingdoms of the earth, to be an object of

[a] Cn: Heb *your dreams that you cause to dream*

Jeremiah 29:11

The penultimate note of African-American faith and religious discourse—and a characteristic feature of its legacy—is the note of hope. Continually drawing upon its own resources to survive, and struggling ever to excel, African-American Christians, inspired by a conviction that a sovereign God will continue to act within the course of human events and human history to achieve God's divine purposes for all humankind, stand in partnership with those who seek to live as members of God's new creation. The African-American religious heritage… reminds us that we are all charged with the task of bridging the chasm between what we claim to be and what we are,… between parochial, monocultural visions of community, and more inclusive and pluralistic communities. We are called to transform the selective, restrictive use of power to benefit the few to a use of power which will serve the purposes of love and fulfill justice, and so lead to a fuller realization of the highest human values and ideals—personal, social, and institutional.[52]

— *Clarice J. Martin*

cursing, and horror, and hissing, and a derision
among all the nations where I have driven them,
19because they did not heed my words, says the
LORD, when I persistently sent to you my servants
the prophets, but they[a] would not listen, says the
LORD. 20But now, all you exiles whom I sent away
from Jerusalem to Babylon, hear the word of the
LORD: 21Thus says the LORD of hosts, the God
of Israel, concerning Ahab son of Kolaiah and
Zedekiah son of Maaseiah, who are prophesying a lie to you in my name: I am going to deliver
them into the hand of King Nebuchadrezzar of
Babylon, and he shall kill them before your eyes.
22And on account of them this curse shall be used
by all the exiles from Judah in Babylon: "The
LORD make you like Zedekiah and Ahab, whom
the king of Babylon roasted in the fire," 23because
they have perpetrated outrage in Israel and have
committed adultery with their neighbors' wives,
and have spoken in my name lying words that I
did not command them; I am the one who knows
and bears witness, says the LORD.

24 To Shemaiah of Nehelam you shall say:
25Thus says the LORD of hosts, the God of Israel: In your own name you sent a letter to all the
people who are in Jerusalem, and to the priest
Zephaniah son of Maaseiah, and to all the priests,
saying, 26The LORD himself has made you priest
instead of the priest Jehoiada, so that there may
be officers in the house of the LORD to control
any madman who plays the prophet, to put him
in the stocks and the collar. 27So now why have
you not rebuked Jeremiah of Anathoth who plays
the prophet for you? 28For he has actually sent
to us in Babylon, saying, "It will be a long time;
build houses and live in them, and plant gardens
and eat what they produce."

29 The priest Zephaniah read this letter in
the hearing of the prophet Jeremiah. 30Then the
word of the LORD came to Jeremiah: 31Send to all
the exiles, saying, Thus says the LORD concerning Shemaiah of Nehelam: Because Shemaiah has
prophesied to you, though I did not send him,
and has led you to trust in a lie, 32therefore thus
says the LORD: I am going to punish Shemaiah of
Nehelam and his descendants; he shall not have
anyone living among this people to see[b] the good
that I am going to do to my people, says the LORD,
for he has spoken rebellion against the LORD.

30 The word that came to Jeremiah from the
LORD: 2Thus says the LORD, the God of
Israel: Write in a book all the words that I have
spoken to you. 3For the days are surely coming,
says the LORD, when I will restore the fortunes of
my people, Israel and Judah, says the LORD, and I
will bring them back to the land that I gave to their
ancestors and they shall take possession of it.

4 These are the words that the LORD spoke
concerning Israel and Judah:

5 Thus says the LORD:
We have heard a cry of panic,
of terror, and no peace.
6 Ask now, and see,
can a man bear a child?
Why then do I see every man
with his hands on his loins like a woman
in labor?
Why has every face turned pale?
7 Alas! that day is so great
there is none like it;
it is a time of distress for Jacob;
yet he shall be rescued from it.

8 On that day, says the LORD of hosts, I will
break the yoke from off his[c] neck, and I will burst
his[c] bonds, and strangers shall no more make a
servant of him. 9But they shall serve the LORD
their God and David their king, whom I will raise
up for them.

10 But as for you, have no fear, my servant Jacob,
says the LORD,
and do not be dismayed, O Israel;
for I am going to save you from far away,
and your offspring from the land of their
captivity.
Jacob shall return and have quiet and ease,
and no one shall make him afraid.
11 For I am with you, says the LORD, to save you;
I will make an end of all the nations

[a] Syr: Heb *you* [b] Gk: Heb *and he shall not see* [c] Cn: Heb *your*

among which I scattered you,
but of you I will not make an end.
I will chastise you in just measure,
and I will by no means leave you
unpunished.

12 For thus says the LORD:
Your hurt is incurable,
your wound is grievous.
13 There is no one to uphold your cause,
no medicine for your wound,
no healing for you.
14 All your lovers have forgotten you;
they care nothing for you;
for I have dealt you the blow of an enemy,
the punishment of a merciless foe,
because your guilt is great,
because your sins are so numerous.
15 Why do you cry out over your hurt?
Your pain is incurable.
Because your guilt is great,
because your sins are so numerous,
I have done these things to you.
16 Therefore all who devour you shall be
devoured,
and all your foes, every one of them, shall
go into captivity;
those who plunder you shall be plundered,
and all who prey on you I will make a prey.
17 For I will restore health to you,
and your wounds I will heal,
says the LORD,
because they have called you an outcast:
"It is Zion; no one cares for her!"

18 Thus says the LORD:
I am going to restore the fortunes of the tents
of Jacob,
and have compassion on his dwellings;
the city shall be rebuilt upon its mound,
and the citadel set on its rightful site.
19 Out of them shall come thanksgiving,
and the sound of merrymakers.
I will make them many, and they shall not be
few;
I will make them honored, and they shall
not be disdained.
20 Their children shall be as of old,
their congregation shall be established
before me;
and I will punish all who oppress them.
21 Their prince shall be one of their own,
their ruler shall come from their midst;
I will bring him near, and he shall approach me,
for who would otherwise dare to
approach me?
says the LORD.
22 And you shall be my people,
and I will be your God.

23 Look, the storm of the LORD!
Wrath has gone forth,
a whirling[a] tempest;
it will burst upon the head of the wicked.
24 The fierce anger of the LORD will not turn
back
until he has executed and accomplished
the intents of his mind.
In the latter days you will understand this.

31 At that time, says the LORD, I will be the
God of all the families of Israel, and they
shall be my people.
2 Thus says the LORD:
The people who survived the sword
found grace in the wilderness;
when Israel sought for rest,
3 the LORD appeared to him[b] from far away.[c]
I have loved you with an everlasting love;
therefore I have continued my faithfulness
to you.
4 Again I will build you, and you shall be built,
O virgin Israel!
Again you shall take[d] your tambourines,
and go forth in the dance of the merrymakers.
5 Again you shall plant vineyards
on the mountains of Samaria;
the planters shall plant,
and shall enjoy the fruit.
6 For there shall be a day when sentinels will
call

[a] One Ms: Meaning of MT uncertain [b] Gk: Heb *me* [c] Or *to him long ago* [d] Or *adorn yourself with*

in the hill country of Ephraim:
"Come, let us go up to Zion,
to the LORD our God."

7 For thus says the LORD:
Sing aloud with gladness for Jacob,
and raise shouts for the chief of the nations;
proclaim, give praise, and say,
"Save, O LORD, your people,
the remnant of Israel."
8 See, I am going to bring them from the land
of the north,
and gather them from the farthest parts of
the earth,
among them the blind and the lame,
those with child and those in labor,
together;
a great company, they shall return here.
9 With weeping they shall come,
and with consolations[a] I will lead them
back,
I will let them walk by brooks of water,
in a straight path in which they shall not
stumble;
for I have become a father to Israel,
and Ephraim is my firstborn.

10 Hear the word of the LORD, O nations,
and declare it in the coastlands far away;
say, "He who scattered Israel will gather him,
and will keep him as a shepherd a flock."
11 For the LORD has ransomed Jacob,
and has redeemed him from hands too
strong for him.
12 They shall come and sing aloud on the height
of Zion,
and they shall be radiant over the
goodness of the LORD,
over the grain, the wine, and the oil,
and over the young of the flock and the
herd;
their life shall become like a watered garden,
and they shall never languish again.
13 Then shall the young women rejoice in the
dance,
and the young men and the old shall be
merry.
I will turn their mourning into joy,
I will comfort them, and give them
gladness for sorrow.
14 I will give the priests their fill of fatness,
and my people shall be satisfied with my
bounty,
says the LORD.

15 Thus says the LORD:
A voice is heard in Ramah,
lamentation and bitter weeping.

[a] Gk Compare Vg Tg: Heb *supplications*

Jeremiah 31:15

The humor of [Margaret Atwood's 1986 novel The Handmaid's Tale*] is dark, and its vision harrowing [in a futuristic "Republic of Gilead" women must ever keep silent], yet it also contains a kind of celebration, a gathering of a vast sisterhood in the Everywoman's voice narrating the tale. Just as Rachel resisting false comfort for her children symbolizes the nation in Jeremiah 31:15, so this Everywoman tells everyone's story. Among those gathered here in her modern voice (through scriptural images, verbal echoes, parallel situations) are women whose stories have been muffled in the Bible's tradition—Hagar, Bilhah, Zilpah, Mary, the Lord's "handmaiden," Sarah, Rachel, Leah, Rebekah, Ruth, Puah and Shiphrah (the Hebrew midwives in Egypt), Jael, Jephthah's daughter, the "Jezebel" of Revelation, and other, unnamed ancestresses, "missing persons" without textual authority. . . . [The novel] does suggest the complexity of their inner lives as well as the trickiness of their textual words that we do have to ponder—discourse rarely simple, since historically women have had to express themselves indirectly, within the suppressive language of patriarchy.*[53]

— ***Janet K. Larson***

Rachel is weeping for her children;
she refuses to be comforted for her children,
because they are no more.

16 Thus says the LORD:
Keep your voice from weeping,
and your eyes from tears;
for there is a reward for your work,
says the LORD:
they shall come back from the land of the enemy;
17 there is hope for your future,
says the LORD:
your children shall come back to their own country.

18 Indeed I heard Ephraim pleading:
"You disciplined me, and I took the discipline;
I was like a calf untrained.
Bring me back, let me come back,
for you are the LORD my God.
19 For after I had turned away I repented;
and after I was discovered, I struck my thigh;
I was ashamed, and I was dismayed
because I bore the disgrace of my youth."
20 Is Ephraim my dear son?
Is he the child I delight in?
As often as I speak against him,
I still remember him.
Therefore I am deeply moved for him;
I will surely have mercy on him,
says the LORD.

21 Set up road markers for yourself,
make yourself signposts;
consider well the highway,
the road by which you went.
Return, O virgin Israel,
return to these your cities.
22 How long will you waver,
O faithless daughter?
For the LORD has created a new thing on the earth:
a woman encompasses[a] a man.

23 Thus says the LORD of hosts, the God of
Israel: Once more they shall use these words in
the land of Judah and in its towns when I restore
their fortunes:

"The LORD bless you, O abode of righteousness,
O holy hill!"

24 And Judah and all its towns shall live there together, and the farmers and those who wander[b]
with their flocks.

25 I will satisfy the weary,
and all who are faint I will replenish.

26 Thereupon I awoke and looked, and my
sleep was pleasant to me.
27 The days are surely coming, says the LORD,
when I will sow the house of Israel and the house
of Judah with the seed of humans and the seed of
animals. 28 And just as I have watched over them
to pluck up and break down, to overthrow, destroy, and bring evil, so I will watch over them to
build and to plant, says the LORD. 29 In those days
they shall no longer say:

"The parents have eaten sour grapes,
and the children's teeth are set on edge."

30 But all shall die for their own sins; the teeth
of everyone who eats sour grapes shall be set on
edge.
31 The days are surely coming, says the
LORD, when I will make a new covenant with the
house of Israel and the house of Judah. 32 It will
not be like the covenant that I made with their
ancestors when I took them by the hand to bring
them out of the land of Egypt—a covenant that
they broke, though I was their husband,[c] says the
LORD. 33 But this is the covenant that I will make
with the house of Israel after those days, says the
LORD: I will put my law within them, and I will
write it on their hearts; and I will be their God,
and they shall be my people. 34 No longer shall
they teach one another, or say to each other,
"Know the LORD," for they shall all know me,
from the least of them to the greatest, says the
LORD; for I will forgive their iniquity, and remember their sin no more.

[a] Meaning of Heb uncertain [b] Cn Compare Syr Vg Tg: Heb *and they shall wander* [c] Or *master*

35 Thus says the LORD,
who gives the sun for light by day
and the fixed order of the moon and the
stars for light by night,
who stirs up the sea so that its waves roar—
the LORD of hosts is his name:
36 If this fixed order were ever to cease
from my presence, says the LORD,
then also the offspring of Israel would cease
to be a nation before me forever.

37 Thus says the LORD:
If the heavens above can be measured,
and the foundations of the earth below can
be explored,
then I will reject all the offspring of Israel
because of all they have done,
says the LORD.

38 The days are surely coming, says the LORD,
when the city shall be rebuilt for the LORD from
the tower of Hananel to the Corner Gate. 39 And
the measuring line shall go out farther, straight to
the hill Gareb, and shall then turn to Goah. 40 The
whole valley of the dead bodies and the ashes,
and all the fields as far as the Wadi Kidron, to the
corner of the Horse Gate toward the east, shall
be sacred to the LORD. It shall never again be uprooted or overthrown.

32 The word that came to Jeremiah from
the LORD in the tenth year of King Zedekiah of Judah, which was the eighteenth year of
Nebuchadrezzar. 2 At that time the army of the
king of Babylon was besieging Jerusalem, and
the prophet Jeremiah was confined in the court
of the guard that was in the palace of the king
of Judah, 3 where King Zedekiah of Judah had
confined him. Zedekiah had said, "Why do you
prophesy and say: Thus says the LORD: I am going to give this city into the hand of the king of
Babylon, and he shall take it; 4 King Zedekiah of
Judah shall not escape out of the hands of the
Chaldeans, but shall surely be given into the
hands of the king of Babylon, and shall speak
with him face to face and see him eye to eye; 5 and
he shall take Zedekiah to Babylon, and there he
shall remain until I attend to him, says the LORD;
though you fight against the Chaldeans, you shall
not succeed?"

6 Jeremiah said, The word of the LORD came
to me: 7 Hanamel son of your uncle Shallum is going to come to you and say, "Buy my field that is
at Anathoth, for the right of redemption by purchase is yours." 8 Then my cousin Hanamel came
to me in the court of the guard, in accordance
with the word of the LORD, and said to me, "Buy
my field that is at Anathoth in the land of Benjamin, for the right of possession and redemption
is yours; buy it for yourself." Then I knew that this
was the word of the LORD.

9 And I bought the field at Anathoth from
my cousin Hanamel, and weighed out the money
to him, seventeen shekels of silver. 10 I signed the
deed, sealed it, got witnesses, and weighed the
money on scales. 11 Then I took the sealed deed
of purchase, containing the terms and conditions,
and the open copy; 12 and I gave the deed of purchase to Baruch son of Neriah son of Mahseiah,
in the presence of my cousin Hanamel, in the
presence of the witnesses who signed the deed of
purchase, and in the presence of all the Judeans
who were sitting in the court of the guard. 13 In
their presence I charged Baruch, saying, 14 Thus
says the LORD of hosts, the God of Israel: Take
these deeds, both this sealed deed of purchase
and this open deed, and put them in an earthenware jar, in order that they may last for a long
time. 15 For thus says the LORD of hosts, the God
of Israel: Houses and fields and vineyards shall
again be bought in this land.

16 After I had given the deed of purchase
to Baruch son of Neriah, I prayed to the LORD,
saying: 17 Ah Lord GOD! It is you who made the
heavens and the earth by your great power and by
your outstretched arm! Nothing is too hard for
you. 18 You show steadfast love to the thousandth
generation,[a] but repay the guilt of parents into
the laps of their children after them, O great and
mighty God whose name is the LORD of hosts,

[a] Or *to thousands*

19great in counsel and mighty in deed; whose
eyes are open to all the ways of mortals, rewarding all according to their ways and according to
the fruit of their doings. 20You showed signs and
wonders in the land of Egypt, and to this day in
Israel and among all humankind, and have made
yourself a name that continues to this very day.
21You brought your people Israel out of the land
of Egypt with signs and wonders, with a strong
hand and outstretched arm, and with great terror; 22and you gave them this land, which you
swore to their ancestors to give them, a land flowing with milk and honey; 23and they entered and
took possession of it. But they did not obey your
voice or follow your law; of all you commanded
them to do, they did nothing. Therefore you have
made all these disasters come upon them. 24See,
the siege ramps have been cast up against the city
to take it, and the city, faced with sword, famine,
and pestilence, has been given into the hands of
the Chaldeans who are fighting against it. What
you spoke has happened, as you yourself can see.
25Yet you, O Lord GOD, have said to me, "Buy
the field for money and get witnesses"—though
the city has been given into the hands of the
Chaldeans.

26 The word of the LORD came to Jeremiah: 27See, I am the LORD, the God of all flesh;
is anything too hard for me? 28Therefore, thus
says the LORD: I am going to give this city into
the hands of the Chaldeans and into the hand
of King Nebuchadrezzar of Babylon, and he
shall take it. 29The Chaldeans who are fighting
against this city shall come, set it on fire, and
burn it, with the houses on whose roofs offerings have been made to Baal and libations have
been poured out to other gods, to provoke me to
anger. 30For the people of Israel and the people
of Judah have done nothing but evil in my sight
from their youth; the people of Israel have done
nothing but provoke me to anger by the work
of their hands, says the LORD. 31This city has
aroused my anger and wrath, from the day it was
built until this day, so that I will remove it from
my sight 32because of all the evil of the people
of Israel and the people of Judah that they did to
provoke me to anger—they, their kings and their
officials, their priests and their prophets, the citizens of Judah and the inhabitants of Jerusalem.
33They have turned their backs to me, not their
faces; though I have taught them persistently,
they would not listen and accept correction.
34They set up their abominations in the house
that bears my name, and defiled it. 35They built
the high places of Baal in the valley of the son of
Hinnom, to offer up their sons and daughters to
Molech, though I did not command them, nor
did it enter my mind that they should do this
abomination, causing Judah to sin.

36 Now therefore thus says the LORD, the
God of Israel, concerning this city of which you
say, "It is being given into the hand of the king of
Babylon by the sword, by famine, and by pestilence": 37See, I am going to gather them from all
the lands to which I drove them in my anger and
my wrath and in great indignation; I will bring
them back to this place, and I will settle them in
safety. 38They shall be my people, and I will be
their God. 39I will give them one heart and one
way, that they may fear me for all time, for their
own good and the good of their children after
them. 40I will make an everlasting covenant with
them, never to draw back from doing good
to them; and I will put the fear of me in their
hearts, so that they may not turn from me. 41I will
rejoice in doing good to them, and I will plant
them in this land in faithfulness, with all my heart
and all my soul.

42 For thus says the LORD: Just as I have
brought all this great disaster upon this people, so
I will bring upon them all the good fortune that
I now promise them. 43Fields shall be bought in
this land of which you are saying, It is a desolation, without human beings or animals; it has
been given into the hands of the Chaldeans.
44Fields shall be bought for money, and deeds
shall be signed and sealed and witnessed, in the
land of Benjamin, in the places around Jerusalem,
and in the cities of Judah, of the hill country, of
the Shephelah, and of the Negeb; for I will restore
their fortunes, says the LORD.

33 The word of the LORD came to Jeremiah
a second time, while he was still confined
in the court of the guard: 2Thus says the LORD

who made the earth,[a] the LORD who formed it
to establish it—the LORD is his name: 3Call to
me and I will answer you, and will tell you great
and hidden things that you have not known. 4For
thus says the LORD, the God of Israel, concerning
the houses of this city and the houses of the kings
of Judah that were torn down to make a defense
against the siege ramps and before the sword:[b]
5The Chaldeans are coming in to fight[c] and to
fill them with the dead bodies of those whom I
shall strike down in my anger and my wrath, for I
have hidden my face from this city because of all
their wickedness. 6I am going to bring it recovery
and healing; I will heal them and reveal to them
abundance[b] of prosperity and security. 7I will restore the fortunes of Judah and the fortunes of Israel, and rebuild them as they were at first. 8I will
cleanse them from all the guilt of their sin against
me, and I will forgive all the guilt of their sin and
rebellion against me. 9And this city[d] shall be to
me a name of joy, a praise and a glory before all
the nations of the earth who shall hear of all the
good that I do for them; they shall fear and tremble because of all the good and all the prosperity
I provide for it.

10 Thus says the LORD: In this place of which
you say, "It is a waste without human beings or
animals," in the towns of Judah and the streets of
Jerusalem that are desolate, without inhabitants,
human or animal, there shall once more be heard
11the voice of mirth and the voice of gladness,
the voice of the bridegroom and the voice of the
bride, the voices of those who sing, as they bring
thank offerings to the house of the LORD:

"Give thanks to the LORD of hosts,
for the LORD is good,
for his steadfast love endures forever!"

For I will restore the fortunes of the land as at
first, says the LORD.

12 Thus says the LORD of hosts: In this place
that is waste, without human beings or animals,
and in all its towns there shall again be pasture
for shepherds resting their flocks. 13In the towns
of the hill country, of the Shephelah, and of the
Negeb, in the land of Benjamin, the places around
Jerusalem, and in the towns of Judah, flocks shall
again pass under the hands of the one who counts
them, says the LORD.

14 The days are surely coming, says the LORD,
when I will fulfill the promise I made to the house
of Israel and the house of Judah. 15In those days
and at that time I will cause a righteous Branch to
spring up for David; and he shall execute justice
and righteousness in the land. 16In those days Judah will be saved and Jerusalem will live in safety.
And this is the name by which it will be called:
"The LORD is our righteousness."

17 For thus says the LORD: David shall never
lack a man to sit on the throne of the house of Israel, 18and the levitical priests shall never lack a man
in my presence to offer burnt offerings, to make
grain offerings, and to make sacrifices for all time.

19 The word of the LORD came to Jeremiah:
20Thus says the LORD: If any of you could break
my covenant with the day and my covenant with
the night, so that day and night would not come at
their appointed time, 21only then could my covenant with my servant David be broken, so that
he would not have a son to reign on his throne,
and my covenant with my ministers the Levites.
22Just as the host of heaven cannot be numbered
and the sands of the sea cannot be measured, so
I will increase the offspring of my servant David,
and the Levites who minister to me.

23 The word of the LORD came to Jeremiah:
24Have you not observed how these people say,
"The two families that the LORD chose have been
rejected by him," and how they hold my people in
such contempt that they no longer regard them
as a nation? 25Thus says the LORD: Only if I had
not established my covenant with day and night
and the ordinances of heaven and earth, 26would
I reject the offspring of Jacob and of my servant
David and not choose any of his descendants as
rulers over the offspring of Abraham, Isaac, and
Jacob. For I will restore their fortunes, and will
have mercy upon them.

34 The word that came to Jeremiah from the
LORD, when King Nebuchadrezzar of

[a] Gk: Heb *it* [b] Meaning of Heb uncertain [c] Cn: Heb *They are coming in to fight against the Chaldeans* [d] Heb *And it*

Babylon and all his army and all the kingdoms of
the earth and all the peoples under his dominion
were fighting against Jerusalem and all its cities:
2 Thus says the LORD, the God of Israel: Go and
speak to King Zedekiah of Judah and say to him:
Thus says the LORD: I am going to give this city
into the hand of the king of Babylon, and he shall
burn it with fire. 3 And you yourself shall not escape from his hand, but shall surely be captured
and handed over to him; you shall see the king
of Babylon eye to eye and speak with him face to
face; and you shall go to Babylon. 4 Yet hear the
word of the LORD, O King Zedekiah of Judah!
Thus says the LORD concerning you: You shall
not die by the sword; 5 you shall die in peace.
And as spices were burned[a] for your ancestors,
the earlier kings who preceded you, so they shall
burn spices[b] for you and lament for you, saying,
"Alas, lord!" For I have spoken the word, says the
LORD.

6 Then the prophet Jeremiah spoke all these
words to Zedekiah king of Judah, in Jerusalem,
7 when the army of the king of Babylon was fighting against Jerusalem and against all the cities
of Judah that were left, Lachish and Azekah; for
these were the only fortified cities of Judah that
remained.

8 The word that came to Jeremiah from the
LORD, after King Zedekiah had made a covenant
with all the people in Jerusalem to make a proclamation of liberty to them— 9 that all should
set free their Hebrew slaves, male and female, so
that no one should hold another Judean in slavery. 10 And they obeyed, all the officials and all
the people who had entered into the covenant
that all would set free their slaves, male or female, so that they would not be enslaved again;
they obeyed and set them free. 11 But afterward
they turned around and took back the male and
female slaves they had set free, and brought them
again into subjection as slaves. 12 The word of the
LORD came to Jeremiah from the LORD: 13 Thus
says the LORD, the God of Israel: I myself made
a covenant with your ancestors when I brought
them out of the land of Egypt, out of the house of
slavery, saying, 14 "Every seventh year each of you
must set free any Hebrews who have been sold
to you and have served you six years; you must
set them free from your service." But your ancestors did not listen to me or incline their ears to
me. 15 You yourselves recently repented and did
what was right in my sight by proclaiming liberty
to one another, and you made a covenant before
me in the house that is called by my name; 16 but
then you turned around and profaned my name
when each of you took back your male and female
slaves, whom you had set free according to their
desire, and you brought them again into subjection to be your slaves. 17 Therefore, thus says the
LORD: You have not obeyed me by granting a
release to your neighbors and friends; I am going to grant a release to you, says the LORD—a
release to the sword, to pestilence, and to famine.
I will make you a horror to all the kingdoms of
the earth. 18 And those who transgressed my covenant and did not keep the terms of the covenant
that they made before me, I will make like[c] the calf
when they cut it in two and passed between its
parts: 19 the officials of Judah, the officials of Jerusalem, the eunuchs, the priests, and all the people
of the land who passed between the parts of the
calf 20 shall be handed over to their enemies and
to those who seek their lives. Their corpses shall
become food for the birds of the air and the wild
animals of the earth. 21 And as for King Zedekiah
of Judah and his officials, I will hand them over to
their enemies and to those who seek their lives, to
the army of the king of Babylon, which has withdrawn from you. 22 I am going to command, says
the LORD, and will bring them back to this city;
and they will fight against it, and take it, and burn
it with fire. The towns of Judah I will make a desolation without inhabitant.

35 The word that came to Jeremiah from
the LORD in the days of King Jehoiakim
son of Josiah of Judah: 2 Go to the house of the
Rechabites, and speak with them, and bring them
to the house of the LORD, into one of the chambers; then offer them wine to drink. 3 So I took

[a] Heb *as there was burning* [b] Heb *shall burn* [c] Cn: Heb lacks *like*

Jaazaniah son of Jeremiah son of Habazziniah,
and his brothers, and all his sons, and the whole
house of the Rechabites. 4I brought them to the
house of the LORD into the chamber of the sons
of Hanan son of Igdaliah, the man of God, which
was near the chamber of the officials, above the
chamber of Maaseiah son of Shallum, keeper of
the threshold. 5Then I set before the Rechabites
pitchers full of wine, and cups; and I said to them,
"Have some wine." 6But they answered, "We will
drink no wine, for our ancestor Jonadab son of
Rechab commanded us, 'You shall never drink
wine, neither you nor your children; 7nor shall
you ever build a house, or sow seed; nor shall
you plant a vineyard, or even own one; but you
shall live in tents all your days, that you may live
many days in the land where you reside.' 8We have
obeyed the charge of our ancestor Jonadab son of
Rechab in all that he commanded us, to drink no
wine all our days, ourselves, our wives, our sons,
or our daughters, 9and not to build houses to live
in. We have no vineyard or field or seed; 10but we
have lived in tents, and have obeyed and done all
that our ancestor Jonadab commanded us. 11But
when King Nebuchadrezzar of Babylon came up
against the land, we said, 'Come, and let us go to
Jerusalem for fear of the army of the Chaldeans
and the army of the Arameans.' That is why we are
living in Jerusalem."

12 Then the word of the LORD came to Jeremiah: 13Thus says the LORD of hosts, the God
of Israel: Go and say to the people of Judah and
the inhabitants of Jerusalem, Can you not learn a
lesson and obey my words? says the LORD. 14The
command has been carried out that Jonadab son
of Rechab gave to his descendants to drink no
wine; and they drink none to this day, for they
have obeyed their ancestor's command. But I
myself have spoken to you persistently, and you
have not obeyed me. 15I have sent to you all my
servants the prophets, sending them persistently,
saying, "Turn now every one of you from your
evil way, and amend your doings, and do not go
after other gods to serve them, and then you shall
live in the land that I gave to you and your ancestors." But you did not incline your ear or obey
me. 16The descendants of Jonadab son of Rechab
have carried out the command that their ancestor gave them, but this people has not obeyed
me. 17Therefore, thus says the LORD, the God of
hosts, the God of Israel: I am going to bring on
Judah and on all the inhabitants of Jerusalem every disaster that I have pronounced against them;
because I have spoken to them and they have not
listened, I have called to them and they have not
answered.

18 But to the house of the Rechabites Jeremiah said: Thus says the LORD of hosts, the God
of Israel: Because you have obeyed the command of your ancestor Jonadab, and kept all his
precepts, and done all that he commanded you,
19therefore thus says the LORD of hosts, the God
of Israel: Jonadab son of Rechab shall not lack a
descendant to stand before me for all time.

36 In the fourth year of King Jehoiakim son
of Josiah of Judah, this word came to Jeremiah from the LORD: 2Take a scroll and write on
it all the words that I have spoken to you against
Israel and Judah and all the nations, from the day
I spoke to you, from the days of Josiah until today.
3It may be that when the house of Judah hears of
all the disasters that I intend to do to them, all of
them may turn from their evil ways, so that I may
forgive their iniquity and their sin.

4 Then Jeremiah called Baruch son of Neriah,
and Baruch wrote on a scroll at Jeremiah's dictation all the words of the LORD that he had spoken
to him. 5And Jeremiah ordered Baruch, saying,
"I am prevented from entering the house of the
LORD; 6so you go yourself, and on a fast day in
the hearing of the people in the LORD's house you
shall read the words of the LORD from the scroll
that you have written at my dictation. You shall
read them also in the hearing of all the people of
Judah who come up from their towns. 7It may be
that their plea will come before the LORD, and
that all of them will turn from their evil ways, for
great is the anger and wrath that the LORD has
pronounced against this people." 8And Baruch
son of Neriah did all that the prophet Jeremiah
ordered him about reading from the scroll the
words of the LORD in the LORD's house.

9 In the fifth year of King Jehoiakim son of

Josiah of Judah, in the ninth month, all the people
in Jerusalem and all the people who came from
the towns of Judah to Jerusalem proclaimed a fast
before the LORD. 10 Then, in the hearing of all the
people, Baruch read the words of Jeremiah from
the scroll, in the house of the LORD, in the chamber of Gemariah son of Shaphan the secretary,
which was in the upper court, at the entry of the
New Gate of the LORD's house.
11 When Micaiah son of Gemariah son of
Shaphan heard all the words of the LORD from
the scroll, 12 he went down to the king's house,
into the secretary's chamber; and all the officials were sitting there: Elishama the secretary,
Delaiah son of Shemaiah, Elnathan son of Achbor, Gemariah son of Shaphan, Zedekiah son of
Hananiah, and all the officials. 13 And Micaiah
told them all the words that he had heard, when
Baruch read the scroll in the hearing of the people. 14 Then all the officials sent Jehudi son of
Nethaniah son of Shelemiah son of Cushi to say
to Baruch, "Bring the scroll that you read in the
hearing of the people, and come." So Baruch son
of Neriah took the scroll in his hand and came to
them. 15 And they said to him, "Sit down and read
it to us." So Baruch read it to them. 16 When they
heard all the words, they turned to one another
in alarm, and said to Baruch, "We certainly must
report all these words to the king." 17 Then they
questioned Baruch, "Tell us now, how did you
write all these words? Was it at his dictation?"
18 Baruch answered them, "He dictated all these
words to me, and I wrote them with ink on the
scroll." 19 Then the officials said to Baruch, "Go
and hide, you and Jeremiah, and let no one know
where you are."
20 Leaving the scroll in the chamber of Elishama the secretary, they went to the court of the
king; and they reported all the words to the king.
21 Then the king sent Jehudi to get the scroll, and
he took it from the chamber of Elishama the secretary; and Jehudi read it to the king and all the
officials who stood beside the king. 22 Now the
king was sitting in his winter apartment (it was
the ninth month), and there was a fire burning in
the brazier before him. 23 As Jehudi read three or
four columns, the king[a] would cut them off with
a penknife and throw them into the fire in the
brazier, until the entire scroll was consumed in
the fire that was in the brazier. 24 Yet neither the
king, nor any of his servants who heard all these
words, was alarmed, nor did they tear their garments. 25 Even when Elnathan and Delaiah and
Gemariah urged the king not to burn the scroll,
he would not listen to them. 26 And the king commanded Jerahmeel the king's son and Seraiah son
of Azriel and Shelemiah son of Abdeel to arrest
the secretary Baruch and the prophet Jeremiah.
But the LORD hid them.
27 Now, after the king had burned the scroll
with the words that Baruch wrote at Jeremiah's
dictation, the word of the LORD came to Jeremiah: 28 Take another scroll and write on it all the
former words that were in the first scroll, which
King Jehoiakim of Judah has burned. 29 And concerning King Jehoiakim of Judah you shall say:
Thus says the LORD, You have dared to burn this
scroll, saying, Why have you written in it that the
king of Babylon will certainly come and destroy
this land, and will cut off from it human beings
and animals? 30 Therefore thus says the LORD
concerning King Jehoiakim of Judah: He shall
have no one to sit upon the throne of David, and
his dead body shall be cast out to the heat by day
and the frost by night. 31 And I will punish him
and his offspring and his servants for their iniquity; I will bring on them, and on the inhabitants
of Jerusalem, and on the people of Judah, all the
disasters with which I have threatened them—
but they would not listen.
32 Then Jeremiah took another scroll and
gave it to the secretary Baruch son of Neriah, who
wrote on it at Jeremiah's dictation all the words
of the scroll that King Jehoiakim of Judah had
burned in the fire; and many similar words were
added to them.

37 Zedekiah son of Josiah, whom King
Nebuchadrezzar of Babylon made king
in the land of Judah, succeeded Coniah son of

[a] Heb *he*

Jehoiakim. 2But neither he nor his servants nor
the people of the land listened to the words of
the LORD that he spoke through the prophet Jeremiah.
3 King Zedekiah sent Jehucal son of Shelemiah and the priest Zephaniah son of Maaseiah
to the prophet Jeremiah saying, "Please pray for
us to the LORD our God." 4Now Jeremiah was still
going in and out among the people, for he had
not yet been put in prison. 5Meanwhile, the army
of Pharaoh had come out of Egypt; and when the
Chaldeans who were besieging Jerusalem heard
news of them, they withdrew from Jerusalem.
6 Then the word of the LORD came to the
prophet Jeremiah: 7Thus says the LORD, God of
Israel: This is what the two of you shall say to the
king of Judah, who sent you to me to inquire of
me: Pharaoh's army, which set out to help you, is
going to return to its own land, to Egypt. 8And
the Chaldeans shall return and fight against this
city; they shall take it and burn it with fire. 9Thus
says the LORD: Do not deceive yourselves, saying, "The Chaldeans will surely go away from us,"
for they will not go away. 10Even if you defeated
the whole army of Chaldeans who are fighting
against you, and there remained of them only
wounded men in their tents, they would rise up
and burn this city with fire.
11 Now when the Chaldean army had withdrawn from Jerusalem at the approach of Pharaoh's
army, 12Jeremiah set out from Jerusalem to go to
the land of Benjamin to receive his share of property[a] among the people there. 13When he reached
the Benjamin Gate, a sentinel there named Irijah
son of Shelemiah son of Hananiah arrested the
prophet Jeremiah saying, "You are deserting to
the Chaldeans." 14And Jeremiah said, "That is a
lie; I am not deserting to the Chaldeans." But Irijah would not listen to him, and arrested Jeremiah
and brought him to the officials. 15The officials
were enraged at Jeremiah, and they beat him and
imprisoned him in the house of the secretary
Jonathan, for it had been made a prison. 16Thus
Jeremiah was put in the cistern house, in the cells,
and remained there many days.
17 Then King Zedekiah sent for him, and
received him. The king questioned him secretly
in his house, and said, "Is there any word from
the LORD?" Jeremiah said, "There is!" Then he
said, "You shall be handed over to the king of
Babylon." 18Jeremiah also said to King Zedekiah,
"What wrong have I done to you or your servants
or this people, that you have put me in prison?
19Where are your prophets who prophesied to
you, saying, 'The king of Babylon will not come
against you and against this land'? 20Now please
hear me, my lord king: be good enough to listen
to my plea, and do not send me back to the house
of the secretary Jonathan to die there." 21So King
Zedekiah gave orders, and they committed Jeremiah to the court of the guard; and a loaf of bread
was given him daily from the bakers' street, until
all the bread of the city was gone. So Jeremiah remained in the court of the guard.

38 Now Shephatiah son of Mattan, Gedaliah
son of Pashhur, Jucal son of Shelemiah,
and Pashhur son of Malchiah heard the words
that Jeremiah was saying to all the people, 2Thus
says the LORD, Those who stay in this city shall
die by the sword, by famine, and by pestilence;
but those who go out to the Chaldeans shall live;
they shall have their lives as a prize of war, and
live. 3Thus says the LORD, This city shall surely be
handed over to the army of the king of Babylon
and be taken. 4Then the officials said to the king,
"This man ought to be put to death, because he
is discouraging the soldiers who are left in this
city, and all the people, by speaking such words
to them. For this man is not seeking the welfare
of this people, but their harm." 5King Zedekiah
said, "Here he is; he is in your hands; for the king
is powerless against you." 6So they took Jeremiah
and threw him into the cistern of Malchiah, the
king's son, which was in the court of the guard,
letting Jeremiah down by ropes. Now there was
no water in the cistern, but only mud, and Jeremiah sank in the mud.
7 Ebed-melech the Ethiopian,[b] a eunuch in
the king's house, heard that they had put Jeremiah into the cistern. The king happened to be

[a] Meaning of Heb uncertain
[b] Or *Nubian*; Heb *Cushite*

sitting at the Benjamin Gate, [8] So Ebed-melech
left the king's house and spoke to the king, [9] "My
lord king, these men have acted wickedly in
all they did to the prophet Jeremiah by throwing him into the cistern to die there of hunger,
for there is no bread left in the city." [10] Then the
king commanded Ebed-melech the Ethiopian,[a]
"Take three men with you from here, and pull the
prophet Jeremiah up from the cistern before he
dies." [11] So Ebed-melech took the men with him
and went to the house of the king, to a wardrobe
of[b] the storehouse, and took from there old rags
and worn-out clothes, which he let down to Jeremiah in the cistern by ropes. [12] Then Ebed-melech
the Ethiopian[a] said to Jeremiah, "Just put the rags
and clothes between your armpits and the ropes."
Jeremiah did so. [13] Then they drew Jeremiah up by
the ropes and pulled him out of the cistern. And
Jeremiah remained in the court of the guard.

14 King Zedekiah sent for the prophet Jeremiah and received him at the third entrance
of the temple of the LORD. The king said to Jeremiah, "I have something to ask you; do not hide
anything from me." [15] Jeremiah said to Zedekiah,
"If I tell you, you will put me to death, will you
not? And if I give you advice, you will not listen
to me." [16] So King Zedekiah swore an oath in secret to Jeremiah, "As the LORD lives, who gave us
our lives, I will not put you to death or hand you
over to these men who seek your life."

17 Then Jeremiah said to Zedekiah, "Thus
says the LORD, the God of hosts, the God of Israel, If you will only surrender to the officials of
the king of Babylon, then your life shall be spared,
and this city shall not be burned with fire, and you
and your house shall live. [18] But if you do not surrender to the officials of the king of Babylon, then
this city shall be handed over to the Chaldeans,
and they shall burn it with fire, and you yourself
shall not escape from their hand." [19] King Zedekiah said to Jeremiah, "I am afraid of the Judeans
who have deserted to the Chaldeans, for I might
be handed over to them and they would abuse
me." [20] Jeremiah said, "That will not happen. Just
obey the voice of the LORD in what I say to you,
and it shall go well with you, and your life shall be
spared. [21] But if you are determined not to surrender, this is what the LORD has shown me— [22] a
vision of all the women remaining in the house of
the king of Judah being led out to the officials of
the king of Babylon and saying,

'Your trusted friends have seduced you
and have overcome you;
Now that your feet are stuck in the mud,
they desert you.'

[23] All your wives and your children shall be led
out to the Chaldeans, and you yourself shall not
escape from their hand, but shall be seized by the
king of Babylon; and this city shall be burned
with fire."

24 Then Zedekiah said to Jeremiah, "Do not
let anyone else know of this conversation, or you
will die. [25] If the officials should hear that I have
spoken with you, and they should come and say
to you, 'Just tell us what you said to the king;
do not conceal it from us, or we will put you to
death. What did the king say to you?' [26] then you
shall say to them, 'I was presenting my plea to the
king not to send me back to the house of Jonathan to die there.'" [27] All the officials did come to
Jeremiah and questioned him; and he answered
them in the very words the king had commanded.
So they stopped questioning him, for the conversation had not been overheard. [28] And Jeremiah
remained in the court of the guard until the day
that Jerusalem was taken.

39 In the ninth year of King Zedekiah of Ju-
dah, in the tenth month, King Nebucha-
drezzar of Babylon and all his army came against
Jerusalem and besieged it; [2] in the eleventh year of
Zedekiah, in the fourth month, on the ninth day of
the month, a breach was made in the city. [3] When
Jerusalem was taken,[c] all the officials of the king of
Babylon came and sat in the middle gate: Nergal-
sharezer, Samgar-nebo, Sarsechim the Rabsaris,
Nergal-sharezer the Rabmag, with all the rest of
the officials of the king of Babylon. [4] When King
Zedekiah of Judah and all the soldiers saw them,
they fled, going out of the city at night by way of
the king's garden through the gate between the

[a] Or *Nubian*; Heb *Cushite* [b] Cn: Heb *to under* [c] This clause has been transposed from 38.28

two walls; and they went toward the Arabah. 5But
the army of the Chaldeans pursued them, and
overtook Zedekiah in the plains of Jericho; and
when they had taken him, they brought him up
to King Nebuchadrezzar of Babylon, at Riblah, in
the land of Hamath; and he passed sentence on
him. 6The king of Babylon slaughtered the sons of
Zedekiah at Riblah before his eyes; also the king
of Babylon slaughtered all the nobles of Judah.
7He put out the eyes of Zedekiah, and bound him
in fetters to take him to Babylon. 8The Chaldeans
burned the king's house and the houses of the
people, and broke down the walls of Jerusalem.
9Then Nebuzaradan the captain of the guard exiled to Babylon the rest of the people who were
left in the city, those who had deserted to him,
and the people who remained. 10Nebuzaradan the
captain of the guard left in the land of Judah some
of the poor people who owned nothing, and gave
them vineyards and fields at the same time.

11 King Nebuchadrezzar of Babylon gave
command concerning Jeremiah through Nebuzaradan, the captain of the guard, saying, 12"Take
him, look after him well and do him no harm, but
deal with him as he may ask you." 13So Nebuzaradan the captain of the guard, Nebushazban
the Rabsaris, Nergal-sharezer the Rabmag, and
all the chief officers of the king of Babylon sent
14and took Jeremiah from the court of the guard.
They entrusted him to Gedaliah son of Ahikam
son of Shaphan to be brought home. So he stayed
with his own people.

15 The word of the LORD came to Jeremiah
while he was confined in the court of the guard:
16Go and say to Ebed-melech the Ethiopian:[a]
Thus says the LORD of hosts, the God of Israel:
I am going to fulfill my words against this city
for evil and not for good, and they shall be accomplished in your presence on that day. 17But
I will save you on that day, says the LORD, and
you shall not be handed over to those whom you
dread. 18For I will surely save you, and you shall
not fall by the sword; but you shall have your life
as a prize of war, because you have trusted in me,
says the LORD.

40 The word that came to Jeremiah from
the LORD after Nebuzaradan the captain
of the guard had let him go from Ramah, when
he took him bound in fetters along with all the
captives of Jerusalem and Judah who were being exiled to Babylon. 2The captain of the guard
took Jeremiah and said to him, "The LORD your
God threatened this place with this disaster; 3and
now the LORD has brought it about, and has done
as he said, because all of you sinned against the
LORD and did not obey his voice. Therefore this
thing has come upon you. 4Now look, I have just
released you today from the fetters on your hands.
If you wish to come with me to Babylon, come,
and I will take good care of you; but if you do
not wish to come with me to Babylon, you need
not come. See, the whole land is before you; go
wherever you think it good and right to go. 5If you
remain,[b] then return to Gedaliah son of Ahikam
son of Shaphan, whom the king of Babylon appointed governor of the towns of Judah, and stay
with him among the people; or go wherever you
think it right to go." So the captain of the guard
gave him an allowance of food and a present, and
let him go. 6Then Jeremiah went to Gedaliah son
of Ahikam at Mizpah, and stayed with him among
the people who were left in the land.

7 When all the leaders of the forces in the
open country and their troops heard that the
king of Babylon had appointed Gedaliah son of
Ahikam governor in the land, and had committed to him men, women, and children, those of
the poorest of the land who had not been taken
into exile to Babylon, 8they went to Gedaliah at
Mizpah—Ishmael son of Nethaniah, Johanan son
of Kareah, Seraiah son of Tanhumeth, the sons of
Ephai the Netophathite, Jezaniah son of the Maacathite, they and their troops. 9Gedaliah son of
Ahikam son of Shaphan swore to them and their
troops, saying, "Do not be afraid to serve the
Chaldeans. Stay in the land and serve the king
of Babylon, and it shall go well with you. 10As
for me, I am staying at Mizpah to represent you
before the Chaldeans who come to us; but as for
you, gather wine and summer fruits and oil, and

[a] Or *Nubian*; Heb *Cushite* [b] Syr: Meaning of Heb uncertain

store them in your vessels, and live in the towns
that you have taken over." 11 Likewise, when all
the Judeans who were in Moab and among the
Ammonites and in Edom and in other lands heard
that the king of Babylon had left a remnant in Judah and had appointed Gedaliah son of Ahikam
son of Shaphan as governor over them, 12 then all
the Judeans returned from all the places to which
they had been scattered and came to the land of
Judah, to Gedaliah at Mizpah; and they gathered
wine and summer fruits in great abundance.

13 Now Johanan son of Kareah and all the
leaders of the forces in the open country came to
Gedaliah at Mizpah 14 and said to him, "Are you
at all aware that Baalis king of the Ammonites has
sent Ishmael son of Nethaniah to take your life?"
But Gedaliah son of Ahikam would not believe
them. 15 Then Johanan son of Kareah spoke secretly to Gedaliah at Mizpah, "Please let me go
and kill Ishmael son of Nethaniah, and no one
else will know. Why should he take your life, so
that all the Judeans who are gathered around you
would be scattered, and the remnant of Judah
would perish?" 16 But Gedaliah son of Ahikam
said to Johanan son of Kareah, "Do not do such a
thing, for you are telling a lie about Ishmael."

41 In the seventh month, Ishmael son of
Nethaniah son of Elishama, of the royal
family, one of the chief officers of the king, came
with ten men to Gedaliah son of Ahikam, at Mizpah. As they ate bread together there at Mizpah,
2 Ishmael son of Nethaniah and the ten men with
him got up and struck down Gedaliah son of
Ahikam son of Shaphan with the sword and killed
him, because the king of Babylon had appointed
him governor in the land. 3 Ishmael also killed all
the Judeans who were with Gedaliah at Mizpah,
and the Chaldean soldiers who happened to be
there.

4 On the day after the murder of Gedaliah,
before anyone knew of it, 5 eighty men arrived
from Shechem and Shiloh and Samaria, with
their beards shaved and their clothes torn, and
their bodies gashed, bringing grain offerings and
incense to present at the temple of the LORD.
6 And Ishmael son of Nethaniah came out from
Mizpah to meet them, weeping as he came. As he
met them, he said to them, "Come to Gedaliah
son of Ahikam." 7 When they reached the middle
of the city, Ishmael son of Nethaniah and the men
with him slaughtered them, and threw them[a] into
a cistern. 8 But there were ten men among them
who said to Ishmael, "Do not kill us, for we have
stores of wheat, barley, oil, and honey hidden in
the fields." So he refrained, and did not kill them
along with their companions.

9 Now the cistern into which Ishmael had
thrown all the bodies of the men whom he had
struck down was the large cistern[b] that King Asa
had made for defense against King Baasha of Israel; Ishmael son of Nethaniah filled that cistern
with those whom he had killed. 10 Then Ishmael
took captive all the rest of the people who were
in Mizpah, the king's daughters and all the people
who were left at Mizpah, whom Nebuzaradan,
the captain of the guard, had committed to Gedaliah son of Ahikam. Ishmael son of Nethaniah
took them captive and set out to cross over to the
Ammonites.

11 But when Johanan son of Kareah and all
the leaders of the forces with him heard of all the
crimes that Ishmael son of Nethaniah had done,
12 they took all their men and went to fight against
Ishmael son of Nethaniah. They came upon him
at the great pool that is in Gibeon. 13 And when all
the people who were with Ishmael saw Johanan
son of Kareah and all the leaders of the forces with
him, they were glad. 14 So all the people whom
Ishmael had carried away captive from Mizpah
turned around and came back, and went to Johanan son of Kareah. 15 But Ishmael son of Nethaniah escaped from Johanan with eight men, and
went to the Ammonites. 16 Then Johanan son of
Kareah and all the leaders of the forces with him
took all the rest of the people whom Ishmael son
of Nethaniah had carried away captive[c] from Mizpah after he had slain Gedaliah son of Ahikam—
soldiers, women, children, and eunuchs, whom

[a] Syr: Heb lacks *and threw them*; compare verse 9 [b] Gk: Heb *whom he had killed by the hand of Gedaliah*
[c] Cn: Heb *whom he recovered from Ishmael son of Nethaniah*

Johanan brought back from Gibeon.[a] 17And they set out, and stopped at Geruth Chimham near Bethlehem, intending to go to Egypt 18because of the Chaldeans; for they were afraid of them, because Ishmael son of Nethaniah had killed Gedaliah son of Ahikam, whom the king of Babylon had made governor over the land.

42 Then all the commanders of the forces, and Johanan son of Kareah and Azariah[b] son of Hoshaiah, and all the people from the least to the greatest, approached 2the prophet Jeremiah and said, "Be good enough to listen to our plea, and pray to the LORD your God for us—for all this remnant. For there are only a few of us left out of many, as your eyes can see. 3Let the LORD your God show us where we should go and what we should do." 4The prophet Jeremiah said to them, "Very well: I am going to pray to the LORD your God as you request, and whatever the LORD answers you I will tell you; I will keep nothing back from you." 5They in their turn said to Jeremiah, "May the LORD be a true and faithful witness against us if we do not act according to everything that the LORD your God sends us through you. 6Whether it is good or bad, we will obey the voice of the LORD our God to whom we are sending you, in order that it may go well with us when we obey the voice of the LORD our God."

7 At the end of ten days the word of the LORD came to Jeremiah. 8Then he summoned Johanan son of Kareah and all the commanders of the forces who were with him, and all the people from the least to the greatest, 9and said to them, "Thus says the LORD, the God of Israel, to whom you sent me to present your plea before him: 10If you will only remain in this land, then I will build you up and not pull you down; I will plant you, and not pluck you up; for I am sorry for the disaster that I have brought upon you. 11Do not be afraid of the king of Babylon, as you have been; do not be afraid of him, says the LORD, for I am with you, to save you and to rescue you from his hand. 12I will grant you mercy, and he will have mercy on you and restore you to your native soil. 13But if you continue to say, 'We will not stay in this land,' thus disobeying the voice of the LORD your God 14and saying, 'No, we will go to the land of Egypt, where we shall not see war, or hear the sound of the trumpet, or be hungry for bread, and there we will stay,' 15then hear the word of the LORD, O remnant of Judah. Thus says the LORD of hosts, the God of Israel: If you are determined to enter Egypt and go to settle there, 16then the sword that you fear shall overtake you there, in the land of Egypt; and the famine that you dread shall follow close after you into Egypt; and there you shall die. 17All the people who have determined to go to Egypt to settle there shall die by the sword, by famine, and by pestilence; they shall have no remnant or survivor from the disaster that I am bringing upon them.

18 "For thus says the LORD of hosts, the God of Israel: Just as my anger and my wrath were poured out on the inhabitants of Jerusalem, so my wrath will be poured out on you when you go to Egypt. You shall become an object of execration and horror, of cursing and ridicule. You shall see this place no more. 19The LORD has said to you, O remnant of Judah, Do not go to Egypt. Be well aware that I have warned you today 20that you have made a fatal mistake. For you yourselves sent me to the LORD your God, saying, 'Pray for us to the LORD our God, and whatever the LORD our God says, tell us and we will do it.' 21So I have told you today, but you have not obeyed the voice of the LORD your God in anything that he sent me to tell you. 22Be well aware, then, that you shall die by the sword, by famine, and by pestilence in the place where you desire to go and settle."

43 When Jeremiah finished speaking to all the people all these words of the LORD their God, with which the LORD their God had sent him to them, 2Azariah son of Hoshaiah and Johanan son of Kareah and all the other insolent men said to Jeremiah, "You are telling a lie. The LORD our God did not send you to say, 'Do not go to Egypt to settle there'; 3but Baruch son of Neriah is inciting you against us, to hand us over to the Chaldeans, in order that they may kill us

[a] Meaning of Heb uncertain [b] Gk: Heb *Jezaniah*

or take us into exile in Babylon." 4So Johanan son
of Kareah and all the commanders of the forces
and all the people did not obey the voice of the
LORD, to stay in the land of Judah. 5But Johanan
son of Kareah and all the commanders of the
forces took all the remnant of Judah who had returned to settle in the land of Judah from all the
nations to which they had been driven— 6the
men, the women, the children, the princesses,
and everyone whom Nebuzaradan the captain of
the guard had left with Gedaliah son of Ahikam
son of Shaphan; also the prophet Jeremiah and
Baruch son of Neriah. 7And they came into the
land of Egypt, for they did not obey the voice of
the LORD. And they arrived at Tahpanhes.

8 Then the word of the LORD came to Jeremiah in Tahpanhes: 9Take some large stones in
your hands, and bury them in the clay pavement[a]
that is at the entrance to Pharaoh's palace in Tahpanhes. Let the Judeans see you do it, 10and say to
them, Thus says the LORD of hosts, the God of Israel: I am going to send and take my servant King
Nebuchadrezzar of Babylon, and he[b] will set his
throne above these stones that I have buried, and
he will spread his royal canopy over them. 11He
shall come and ravage the land of Egypt, giving

those who are destined for pestilence, to
pestilence,
and those who are destined for captivity,
to captivity,
and those who are destined for the sword,
to the sword.

12He[c] shall kindle a fire in the temples of the gods
of Egypt; and he shall burn them and carry them
away captive; and he shall pick clean the land of
Egypt, as a shepherd picks his cloak clean of vermin; and he shall depart from there safely. 13He
shall break the obelisks of Heliopolis, which is in
the land of Egypt; and the temples of the gods of
Egypt he shall burn with fire.

44 The word that came to Jeremiah for all
the Judeans living in the land of Egypt,
at Migdol, at Tahpanhes, at Memphis, and in the
land of Pathros, 2Thus says the LORD of hosts, the
God of Israel: You yourselves have seen all the
disaster that I have brought on Jerusalem and on
all the towns of Judah. Look at them; today they
are a desolation, without an inhabitant in them,
3because of the wickedness that they committed,
provoking me to anger, in that they went to make
offerings and serve other gods that they had not
known, neither they, nor you, nor your ancestors.
4Yet I persistently sent to you all my servants the
prophets, saying, "I beg you not to do this abominable thing that I hate!" 5But they did not listen
or incline their ear, to turn from their wickedness and make no offerings to other gods. 6So my
wrath and my anger were poured out and kindled
in the towns of Judah and in the streets of Jerusalem; and they became a waste and a desolation,
as they still are today. 7And now thus says the
LORD God of hosts, the God of Israel: Why are
you doing such great harm to yourselves, to cut
off man and woman, child and infant, from the
midst of Judah, leaving yourselves without a remnant? 8Why do you provoke me to anger with the
works of your hands, making offerings to other
gods in the land of Egypt where you have come to
settle? Will you be cut off and become an object
of cursing and ridicule among all the nations of
the earth? 9Have you forgotten the crimes of your
ancestors, of the kings of Judah, of their[d] wives,
your own crimes and those of your wives, which
they committed in the land of Judah and in the
streets of Jerusalem? 10They have shown no con-
trition or fear to this day, nor have they walked in
my law and my statutes that I set before you and
before your ancestors.

11 Therefore thus says the LORD of hosts, the
God of Israel: I am determined to bring disaster
on you, to bring all Judah to an end. 12I will take
the remnant of Judah who are determined to
come to the land of Egypt to settle, and they shall
perish, everyone; in the land of Egypt they shall
fall; by the sword and by famine they shall perish;
from the least to the greatest, they shall die by the
sword and by famine; and they shall become an
object of execration and horror, of cursing and
ridicule. 13I will punish those who live in the land

[a] Meaning of Heb uncertain [b] Gk Syr: Heb *I* [c] Gk Syr Vg: Heb *I* [d] Heb *his*

of Egypt, as I have punished Jerusalem, with the sword, with famine, and with pestilence, 14so that none of the remnant of Judah who have come to settle in the land of Egypt shall escape or survive or return to the land of Judah. Although they long to go back to live there, they shall not go back, except some fugitives.

15 Then all the men who were aware that their wives had been making offerings to other gods, and all the women who stood by, a great assembly, all the people who lived in Pathros in the land of Egypt, answered Jeremiah: 16"As for the word that you have spoken to us in the name of the LORD, we are not going to listen to you. 17Instead, we will do everything that we have vowed, make offerings to the queen of heaven and pour out libations to her, just as we and our ancestors, our kings and our officials, used to do in the towns of Judah and in the streets of Jerusalem. We used to have plenty of food, and prospered, and saw no misfortune. 18But from the time we stopped making offerings to the queen of heaven and pouring out libations to her, we have lacked everything and have perished by the sword and by famine." 19And the women said,[a] "Indeed we will go on making offerings to the queen of heaven and pouring out libations to her; do you think that we made cakes for her, marked with her image, and poured out libations to her without our husbands' being involved?"

20 Then Jeremiah said to all the people, men and women, all the people who were giving him this answer: 21"As for the offerings that you made in the towns of Judah and in the streets of Jerusalem, you and your ancestors, your kings and your officials, and the people of the land, did not the LORD remember them? Did it not come into his mind? 22The LORD could no longer bear the sight of your evil doings, the abominations that you committed; therefore your land became a desolation and a waste and a curse, without inhabitant, as it is to this day. 23It is because you burned offerings, and because you sinned against the LORD and did not obey the voice of the LORD or walk in his law and in his statutes and in his decrees, that this disaster has befallen you, as is still evident today."

24 Jeremiah said to all the people and all the women, "Hear the word of the LORD, all you Judeans who are in the land of Egypt, 25Thus says the LORD of hosts, the God of Israel: You and your wives have accomplished in deeds what you declared in words, saying, 'We are determined to perform the vows that we have made, to make offerings to the queen of heaven and to pour out libations to her.' By all means, keep your vows and make your libations! 26Therefore hear the word of the LORD, all you Judeans who live in the land of Egypt: Lo, I swear by my great name, says the LORD, that my name shall no longer be pronounced on the lips of any of the people of Judah in all the land of Egypt, saying, 'As the Lord GOD lives.' 27I am going to watch over them for harm and not for good; all the people of Judah who are in the land of Egypt shall perish by the sword and by famine, until not one is left. 28And those who escape the sword shall return from the land of Egypt to the land of Judah, few in number; and all the remnant of Judah, who have come to the land of Egypt to settle, shall know whose words will stand, mine or theirs! 29This shall be the sign to you, says the LORD, that I am going to punish you in this place, in order that you may know that my words against you will surely be carried out: 30Thus says the LORD, I am going to give Pharaoh Hophra, king of Egypt, into the hands of his enemies, those who seek his life, just as I gave King Zedekiah of Judah into the hand of King Nebuchadrezzar of Babylon, his enemy who sought his life."

45

The word that the prophet Jeremiah spoke to Baruch son of Neriah, when he wrote these words in a scroll at the dictation of Jeremiah, in the fourth year of King Jehoiakim son of Josiah of Judah: 2Thus says the LORD, the God of Israel, to you, O Baruch: 3You said, "Woe is me! The LORD has added sorrow to my pain; I am weary with my groaning, and I find no rest." 4Thus you shall say to him, "Thus says the LORD:

[a] Compare Syr: Heb lacks *And the women said*

I am going to break down what I have built, and
pluck up what I have planted—that is, the whole
land. 5 And you, do you seek great things for yourself? Do not seek them; for I am going to bring
disaster upon all flesh, says the LORD; but I will
give you your life as a prize of war in every place
to which you may go."

46 The word of the LORD that came to the prophet Jeremiah concerning the nations.

2 Concerning Egypt, about the army of Pharaoh Neco, king of Egypt, which was by the river Euphrates at Carchemish and which King Nebuchadrezzar of Babylon defeated in the fourth year of King Jehoiakim son of Josiah of Judah:

3 Prepare buckler and shield,
and advance for battle!
4 Harness the horses;
mount the steeds!
Take your stations with your helmets,
whet your lances,
put on your coats of mail!
5 Why do I see them terrified?
They have fallen back;
their warriors are beaten down,
and have fled in haste.
They do not look back—
terror is all around!
says the LORD.
6 The swift cannot flee away,
nor can the warrior escape;
in the north by the river Euphrates
they have stumbled and fallen.

7 Who is this, rising like the Nile,
like rivers whose waters surge?
8 Egypt rises like the Nile,
like rivers whose waters surge.
It said, Let me rise, let me cover the earth,
let me destroy cities and their inhabitants.
9 Advance, O horses,
and dash madly, O chariots!
Let the warriors go forth:
Ethiopia[a] and Put who carry the shield,
the Ludim, who draw[b] the bow.
10 That day is the day of the Lord GOD of hosts,
a day of retribution,
to gain vindication from his foes.
The sword shall devour and be sated,
and drink its fill of their blood.
For the Lord GOD of hosts holds a sacrifice
in the land of the north by the river
Euphrates.
11 Go up to Gilead, and take balm,
O virgin daughter Egypt!
In vain you have used many medicines;
there is no healing for you.
12 The nations have heard of your shame,
and the earth is full of your cry;
for warrior has stumbled against warrior;
both have fallen together.

13 The word that the LORD spoke to the prophet Jeremiah about the coming of King Nebuchadrezzar of Babylon to attack the land of Egypt:

14 Declare in Egypt, and proclaim in Migdol;
proclaim in Memphis and Tahpanhes;
Say, "Take your stations and be ready,
for the sword shall devour those around
you."
15 Why has Apis fled?[c]
Why did your bull not stand?
—because the LORD thrust him down.
16 Your multitude stumbled[d] and fell,
and one said to another,[e]
"Come, let us go back to our own people
and to the land of our birth,
because of the destroying sword."
17 Give Pharaoh, king of Egypt, the name
"Braggart who missed his chance."

18 As I live, says the King,
whose name is the LORD of hosts,
one is coming
like Tabor among the mountains,
and like Carmel by the sea.

[a] Or *Nubia*; Heb *Cush* [b] Cn: Heb *who grasp, who draw* [c] Gk: Heb *Why was it swept away* [d] Gk: Meaning of Heb uncertain [e] Gk: Heb *and fell one to another and they said*

19 Pack your bags for exile,
sheltered daughter Egypt!
For Memphis shall become a waste,
a ruin, without inhabitant.

20 A beautiful heifer is Egypt—
a gadfly from the north lights upon her.
21 Even her mercenaries in her midst
are like fatted calves;
they too have turned and fled together,
they did not stand;
for the day of their calamity has come upon
them,
the time of their punishment.

22 She makes a sound like a snake gliding away;
for her enemies march in force,
and come against her with axes,
like those who fell trees.
23 They shall cut down her forest,
says the LORD,
though it is impenetrable,
because they are more numerous
than locusts;
they are without number.
24 Daughter Egypt shall be put to shame;
she shall be handed over to a people from
the north.

25 The LORD of hosts, the God of Israel,
said: See, I am bringing punishment upon Amon
of Thebes, and Pharaoh, and Egypt and her gods
and her kings, upon Pharaoh and those who trust
in him. 26 I will hand them over to those who seek
their life, to King Nebuchadrezzar of Babylon and
his officers. Afterward Egypt shall be inhabited as
in the days of old, says the LORD.

27 But as for you, have no fear, my servant Jacob,
and do not be dismayed, O Israel;
for I am going to save you from far away,
and your offspring from the land of their
captivity.
Jacob shall return and have quiet and ease,
and no one shall make him afraid.
28 As for you, have no fear, my servant Jacob,
says the LORD,
for I am with you.
I will make an end of all the nations
among which I have banished you,
but I will not make an end of you!
I will chastise you in just measure,
and I will by no means leave you
unpunished.

47 The word of the LORD that came to the
prophet Jeremiah concerning the Philistines, before Pharaoh attacked Gaza:
2 Thus says the LORD:
See, waters are rising out of the north
and shall become an overflowing torrent;
they shall overflow the land and all that
fills it,
the city and those who live in it.
People shall cry out,
and all the inhabitants of the land shall
wail.
3 At the noise of the stamping of the hoofs of
his stallions,
at the clatter of his chariots, at the
rumbling of their wheels,
parents do not turn back for children,
so feeble are their hands,
4 because of the day that is coming
to destroy all the Philistines,
to cut off from Tyre and Sidon
every helper that remains.
For the LORD is destroying the Philistines,
the remnant of the coastland of
Caphtor.
5 Baldness has come upon Gaza,
Ashkelon is silenced.
O remnant of their power![a]
How long will you gash yourselves?
6 Ah, sword of the LORD!
How long until you are quiet?
Put yourself into your scabbard,
rest and be still!
7 How can it[b] be quiet,
when the LORD has given it an order?

[a] Gk: Heb *their valley* [b] Gk Vg: Heb *you*

Against Ashkelon and against the
seashore—
there he has appointed it.

48 Concerning Moab.

Thus says the LORD of hosts, the God of Israel:
Alas for Nebo, it is laid waste!
Kiriathaim is put to shame, it is taken;
the fortress is put to shame and broken
down;
2 the renown of Moab is no more.
In Heshbon they planned evil against her:
"Come, let us cut her off from being a
nation!"
You also, O Madmen, shall be brought to
silence;[a]
the sword shall pursue you.

3 Hark! a cry from Horonaim,
"Desolation and great destruction!"
4 "Moab is destroyed!"
her little ones cry out.
5 For at the ascent of Luhith
they go[b] up weeping bitterly;
for at the descent of Horonaim
they have heard the distressing cry of
anguish.
6 Flee! Save yourselves!
Be like a wild ass[c] in the desert!
7 Surely, because you trusted in your
strongholds[d] and your treasures,
you also shall be taken;
Chemosh shall go out into exile,
with his priests and his attendants.
8 The destroyer shall come upon every town,
and no town shall escape;
the valley shall perish,
and the plain shall be destroyed,
as the LORD has spoken.

9 Set aside salt for Moab,
for she will surely fall;
her towns shall become a desolation,
with no inhabitant in them.

10 Accursed is the one who is slack in doing
the work of the LORD; and accursed is the one
who keeps back the sword from bloodshed.

11 Moab has been at ease from his youth,
settled like wine[e] on its dregs;
he has not been emptied from vessel to
vessel,
nor has he gone into exile;
therefore his flavor has remained
and his aroma is unspoiled.
12 Therefore, the time is surely coming, says
the LORD, when I shall send to him decanters to
decant him, and empty his vessels, and break his[f]
jars in pieces. 13 Then Moab shall be ashamed of
Chemosh, as the house of Israel was ashamed of
Bethel, their confidence.

14 How can you say, "We are heroes
and mighty warriors"?
15 The destroyer of Moab and his towns has
come up,
and the choicest of his young men have
gone down to slaughter,
says the King, whose name is the LORD of
hosts.
16 The calamity of Moab is near at hand
and his doom approaches swiftly.
17 Mourn over him, all you his neighbors,
and all who know his name;
say, "How the mighty scepter is broken,
the glorious staff!"

18 Come down from glory,
and sit on the parched ground,
enthroned daughter Dibon!
For the destroyer of Moab has come up
against you;
he has destroyed your strongholds.
19 Stand by the road and watch,
you inhabitant of Aroer!

[a] The place-name *Madmen* sounds like the Hebrew verb *to be silent* [b] Cn: Heb *he goes* [c] Gk Aquila: Heb *like Aroer*
[d] Gk: Heb *works* [e] Heb lacks *like wine* [f] Gk Aquila: Heb *their*

Ask the man fleeing and the woman
escaping;
say, "What has happened?"
20 Moab is put to shame, for it is broken down;
wail and cry!
Tell it by the Arnon,
that Moab is laid waste.

21 Judgment has come upon the tableland,
upon Holon, and Jahzah, and Mephaath, 22 and
Dibon, and Nebo, and Beth-diblathaim, 23 and
Kiriathaim, and Beth-gamul, and Beth-meon,
24 and Kerioth, and Bozrah, and all the towns of
the land of Moab, far and near. 25 The horn of
Moab is cut off, and his arm is broken, says the
LORD.

26 Make him drunk, because he magnified
himself against the LORD; let Moab wallow in
his vomit; he too shall become a laughingstock.
27 Israel was a laughingstock for you, though he
was not caught among thieves; but whenever you
spoke of him you shook your head!

28 Leave the towns, and live on the rock,
O inhabitants of Moab!
Be like the dove that nests
on the sides of the mouth of a gorge.
29 We have heard of the pride of Moab—
he is very proud—
of his loftiness, his pride, and his arrogance,
and the haughtiness of his heart.
30 I myself know his insolence, says the LORD;
his boasts are false,
his deeds are false.
31 Therefore I wail for Moab;
I cry out for all Moab;
for the people of Kir-heres I mourn.
32 More than for Jazer I weep for you,
O vine of Sibmah!
Your branches crossed over the sea,
reached as far as Jazer;[a]
upon your summer fruits and your vintage
the destroyer has fallen.
33 Gladness and joy have been taken away
from the fruitful land of Moab;
I have stopped the wine from the wine
presses;
no one treads them with shouts of joy;
the shouting is not the shout of joy.

34 Heshbon and Elealeh cry out;[b] as far as Jahaz they utter their voice, from Zoar to Horonaim
and Eglath-shelishiyah. For even the waters of
Nimrim have become desolate. 35 And I will bring
to an end in Moab, says the LORD, those who offer sacrifice at a high place and make offerings to
their gods. 36 Therefore my heart moans for Moab
like a flute, and my heart moans like a flute for
the people of Kir-heres; for the riches they gained
have perished.

37 For every head is shaved and every beard
cut off; on all the hands there are gashes, and on
the loins sackcloth. 38 On all the housetops of
Moab and in the squares there is nothing but lamentation; for I have broken Moab like a vessel that
no one wants, says the LORD. 39 How it is broken!
How they wail! How Moab has turned his back
in shame! So Moab has become a derision and a
horror to all his neighbors.
40 For thus says the LORD:
Look, he shall swoop down like an eagle,
and spread his wings against Moab;
41 the towns[c] shall be taken
and the strongholds seized.
The hearts of the warriors of Moab, on that
day,
shall be like the heart of a woman in labor.
42 Moab shall be destroyed as a people,
because he magnified himself against the
LORD.
43 Terror, pit, and trap
are before you, O inhabitants of Moab!
says the LORD.
44 Everyone who flees from the terror
shall fall into the pit,
and everyone who climbs out of the pit
shall be caught in the trap.
For I will bring these things[d] upon Moab

[a] Two Mss and Isa 16.8: MT *the sea of Jazer* [b] Cn: Heb *From the cry of Heshbon to Elealeh* [c] Or *Kerioth*
[d] Gk Syr: Heb *bring upon it*

in the year of their punishment,
says the LORD.

45 In the shadow of Heshbon
fugitives stop exhausted;
for a fire has gone out from Heshbon,
a flame from the house of Sihon;
it has destroyed the forehead of Moab,
the scalp of the people of tumult.[a]
46 Woe to you, O Moab!
The people of Chemosh have perished,
for your sons have been taken captive,
and your daughters into captivity.
47 Yet I will restore the fortunes of Moab
in the latter days, says the LORD.
Thus far is the judgment on Moab.

49 Concerning the Ammonites.

Thus says the LORD:
Has Israel no sons?
Has he no heir?
Why then has Milcom dispossessed Gad,
and his people settled in its towns?
2 Therefore, the time is surely coming,
says the LORD,
when I will sound the battle alarm
against Rabbah of the Ammonites;
it shall become a desolate mound,
and its villages shall be burned with fire;
then Israel shall dispossess those who
dispossessed him,
says the LORD.

3 Wail, O Heshbon, for Ai is laid waste!
Cry out, O daughters[b] of Rabbah!
Put on sackcloth,
lament, and slash yourselves with whips![c]
For Milcom shall go into exile,
with his priests and his attendants.
4 Why do you boast in your strength?
Your strength is ebbing,
O faithless daughter.
You trusted in your treasures, saying,
"Who will attack me?"

5 I am going to bring terror upon you,
says the Lord GOD of hosts,
from all your neighbors,
and you will be scattered, each headlong,
with no one to gather the fugitives.
6 But afterward I will restore the fortunes of
the Ammonites, says the LORD.

7 Concerning Edom.

Thus says the LORD of hosts:
Is there no longer wisdom in Teman?
Has counsel perished from the prudent?
Has their wisdom vanished?
8 Flee, turn back, get down low,
inhabitants of Dedan!
For I will bring the calamity of Esau upon
him,
the time when I punish him.
9 If grape-gatherers came to you,
would they not leave gleanings?
If thieves came by night,
even they would pillage only what they
wanted.
10 But as for me, I have stripped Esau bare,
I have uncovered his hiding places,
and he is not able to conceal himself.
His offspring are destroyed, his kinsfolk
and his neighbors; and he is no more.
11 Leave your orphans, I will keep them alive;
and let your widows trust in me.
12 For thus says the LORD: If those who do
not deserve to drink the cup still have to drink it,
shall you be the one to go unpunished? You shall
not go unpunished; you must drink it. 13 For by
myself I have sworn, says the LORD, that Bozrah
shall become an object of horror and ridicule, a
waste, and an object of cursing; and all her towns
shall be perpetual wastes.
14 I have heard tidings from the LORD,
and a messenger has been sent among the
nations:
"Gather yourselves together and come
against her,
and rise up for battle!"

[a] Or *of Shaon* [b] Or *villages* [c] Cn: Meaning of Heb uncertain

15 For I will make you least among the nations,
despised by humankind.
16 The terror you inspire
and the pride of your heart have deceived
you,
you who live in the clefts of the rock,[a]
who hold the height of the hill.
Although you make your nest as high as the
eagle's,
from there I will bring you down,
says the LORD.

17 Edom shall become an object of horror;
everyone who passes by it will be horrified and
will hiss because of all its disasters. 18 As when
Sodom and Gomorrah and their neighbors were
overthrown, says the LORD, no one shall live
there, nor shall anyone settle in it. 19 Like a lion
coming up from the thickets of the Jordan against
a perennial pasture, I will suddenly chase Edom[b]
away from it; and I will appoint over it whomever
I choose.[c] For who is like me? Who can summon
me? Who is the shepherd who can stand before
me? 20 Therefore hear the plan that the LORD has
made against Edom and the purposes that he has
formed against the inhabitants of Teman: Surely
the little ones of the flock shall be dragged away;
surely their fold shall be appalled at their fate. 21 At
the sound of their fall the earth shall tremble; the
sound of their cry shall be heard at the Red Sea.[d]
22 Look, he shall mount up and swoop down like
an eagle, and spread his wings against Bozrah,
and the heart of the warriors of Edom in that day
shall be like the heart of a woman in labor.

23 Concerning Damascus.

Hamath and Arpad are confounded,
for they have heard bad news;
they melt in fear, they are troubled like the sea[e]
that cannot be quiet.
24 Damascus has become feeble, she turned to
flee,
and panic seized her;
anguish and sorrows have taken hold of her,
as of a woman in labor.
25 How the famous city is forsaken,[f]
the joyful town![g]
26 Therefore her young men shall fall in her
squares,
and all her soldiers shall be destroyed in
that day,
says the LORD of hosts.
27 And I will kindle a fire at the wall of
Damascus,
and it shall devour the strongholds of
Ben-hadad.

28 Concerning Kedar and the kingdoms of
Hazor that King Nebuchadrezzar of Babylon defeated.

Thus says the LORD:
Rise up, advance against Kedar!
Destroy the people of the east!
29 Take their tents and their flocks,
their curtains and all their goods;
carry off their camels for yourselves,
and a cry shall go up: "Terror is all
around!"
30 Flee, wander far away, hide in deep places,
O inhabitants of Hazor!
says the LORD.
For King Nebuchadrezzar of Babylon
has made a plan against you
and formed a purpose against you.

31 Rise up, advance against a nation at ease,
that lives secure,
says the LORD,
that has no gates or bars,
that lives alone.
32 Their camels shall become booty,
their herds of cattle a spoil.
I will scatter to every wind
those who have shaven temples,
and I will bring calamity
against them from every side,
says the LORD.

[a] Or *of Sela* [b] Heb *him* [c] Or *and I will single out the choicest of his rams*: Meaning of Heb uncertain [d] Or *Sea of Reeds*
[e] Cn: Heb *there is trouble in the sea* [f] Vg: Heb *is not forsaken* [g] Syr Vg Tg: Heb *the town of my joy*

33 Hazor shall become a lair of jackals,
an everlasting waste;
no one shall live there,
nor shall anyone settle in it.

34 The word of the LORD that came to the
prophet Jeremiah concerning Elam, at the beginning of the reign of King Zedekiah of Judah.
35 Thus says the LORD of hosts: I am going
to break the bow of Elam, the mainstay of their
might; 36and I will bring upon Elam the four
winds from the four quarters of heaven; and I will
scatter them to all these winds, and there shall be
no nation to which the exiles from Elam shall not
come. 37I will terrify Elam before their enemies,
and before those who seek their life; I will bring
disaster upon them, my fierce anger, says the
LORD. I will send the sword after them, until I
have consumed them; 38and I will set my throne
in Elam, and destroy their king and officials, says
the LORD.
39 But in the latter days I will restore the fortunes of Elam, says the LORD.

50 The word that the LORD spoke concerning Babylon, concerning the land of the
Chaldeans, by the prophet Jeremiah:

2 Declare among the nations and proclaim,
set up a banner and proclaim,
do not conceal it, say:
Babylon is taken,
Bel is put to shame,
Merodach is dismayed.
Her images are put to shame,
her idols are dismayed.

3 For out of the north a nation has come up
against her; it shall make her land a desolation,
and no one shall live in it; both human beings and
animals shall flee away.

4 In those days and in that time, says the
LORD, the people of Israel shall come, they and
the people of Judah together; they shall come
weeping as they seek the LORD their God. 5They
shall ask the way to Zion, with faces turned toward it, and they shall come and join[a] themselves
to the LORD by an everlasting covenant that will
never be forgotten.

6 My people have been lost sheep; their shepherds have led them astray, turning them away on
the mountains; from mountain to hill they have
gone, they have forgotten their fold. 7All who
found them have devoured them, and their enemies have said, "We are not guilty, because they
have sinned against the LORD, the true pasture,
the LORD, the hope of their ancestors."

8 Flee from Babylon, and go out of the land of
the Chaldeans, and be like male goats leading the
flock. 9For I am going to stir up and bring against
Babylon a company of great nations from the
land of the north; and they shall array themselves
against her; from there she shall be taken. Their
arrows are like the arrows of a skilled warrior who
does not return empty-handed. 10Chaldea shall
be plundered; all who plunder her shall be sated,
says the LORD.

11 Though you rejoice, though you exult,
O plunderers of my heritage,
though you frisk about like a heifer on the
grass,
and neigh like stallions,
12 your mother shall be utterly shamed,
and she who bore you shall be disgraced.
Lo, she shall be the last of the nations,
a wilderness, dry land, and a desert.
13 Because of the wrath of the LORD she shall
not be inhabited,
but shall be an utter desolation;
everyone who passes by Babylon shall be
appalled
and hiss because of all her wounds.
14 Take up your positions around Babylon,
all you that bend the bow;
shoot at her, spare no arrows,
for she has sinned against the LORD.
15 Raise a shout against her from all sides,
"She has surrendered;

[a] Gk: Heb *toward it. Come! They shall join*

her bulwarks have fallen,
her walls are thrown down."
For this is the vengeance of the LORD:
take vengeance on her,
do to her as she has done.
16 Cut off from Babylon the sower,
and the wielder of the sickle in time of harvest;
because of the destroying sword
all of them shall return to their own people,
and all of them shall flee to their own land.

17 Israel is a hunted sheep driven away by
lions. First the king of Assyria devoured it, and
now at the end King Nebuchadrezzar of Babylon
has gnawed its bones. 18 Therefore, thus says the
LORD of hosts, the God of Israel: I am going to
punish the king of Babylon and his land, as I punished the king of Assyria. 19 I will restore Israel
to its pasture, and it shall feed on Carmel and in
Bashan, and on the hills of Ephraim and in Gilead
its hunger shall be satisfied. 20 In those days and
at that time, says the LORD, the iniquity of Israel
shall be sought, and there shall be none; and the
sins of Judah, and none shall be found; for I will
pardon the remnant that I have spared.

21 Go up to the land of Merathaim;[a]
go up against her,
and attack the inhabitants of Pekod[b]
and utterly destroy the last of them,[c]
says the LORD;
do all that I have commanded you.
22 The noise of battle is in the land,
and great destruction!
23 How the hammer of the whole earth
is cut down and broken!
How Babylon has become
a horror among the nations!
24 You set a snare for yourself and you were caught, O Babylon,
but you did not know it;
you were discovered and seized,
because you challenged the LORD.
25 The LORD has opened his armory,
and brought out the weapons of his wrath,
for the Lord GOD of hosts has a task to do
in the land of the Chaldeans.
26 Come against her from every quarter;
open her granaries;
pile her up like heaps of grain, and destroy her utterly;
let nothing be left of her.
27 Kill all her bulls,
let them go down to the slaughter.
Alas for them, their day has come,
the time of their punishment!

28 Listen! Fugitives and refugees from the land of Babylon are coming to declare in Zion the vengeance of the LORD our God, vengeance for his temple.

29 Summon archers against Babylon, all who
bend the bow. Encamp all around her; let no one
escape. Repay her according to her deeds; just as
she has done, do to her—for she has arrogantly
defied the LORD, the Holy One of Israel. 30 Therefore her young men shall fall in her squares, and
all her soldiers shall be destroyed on that day, says
the LORD.

31 I am against you, O arrogant one,
says the Lord GOD of hosts;
for your day has come,
the time when I will punish you.
32 The arrogant one shall stumble and fall,
with no one to raise him up,
and I will kindle a fire in his cities,
and it will devour everything around him.

33 Thus says the LORD of hosts: The people
of Israel are oppressed, and so too are the people
of Judah; all their captors have held them fast and
refuse to let them go. 34 Their Redeemer is strong;
the LORD of hosts is his name. He will surely plead
their cause, that he may give rest to the earth, but
unrest to the inhabitants of Babylon.

[a] Or *of Double Rebellion* [b] Or *of Punishment* [c] Tg: Heb *destroy after them*

35 A sword against the Chaldeans, says the
LORD,
and against the inhabitants of Babylon,
and against her officials and her sages!
36 A sword against the diviners,
so that they may become fools!
A sword against her warriors,
so that they may be destroyed!
37 A sword against her[a] horses and against her[a]
chariots,
and against all the foreign troops in her
midst,
so that they may become women!
A sword against all her treasures,
that they may be plundered!
38 A drought[b] against her waters,
that they may be dried up!
For it is a land of images,
and they go mad over idols.

39 Therefore wild animals shall live with hyenas in Babylon,[c] and ostriches shall inhabit her;
she shall never again be peopled, or inhabited for
all generations. 40 As when God overthrew Sodom and Gomorrah and their neighbors, says the
LORD, so no one shall live there, nor shall anyone
settle in her.

41 Look, a people is coming from the north;
a mighty nation and many kings
are stirring from the farthest parts of the
earth.
42 They wield bow and spear,
they are cruel and have no mercy.
The sound of them is like the roaring sea;
they ride upon horses,
set in array as a warrior for battle,
against you, O daughter Babylon!

43 The king of Babylon heard news of them,
and his hands fell helpless;
anguish seized him,
pain like that of a woman in labor.

44 Like a lion coming up from the thickets
of the Jordan against a perennial pasture, I will
suddenly chase them away from her; and I will
appoint over her whomever I choose.[d] For who is
like me? Who can summon me? Who is the shepherd who can stand before me? 45 Therefore hear
the plan that the LORD has made against Babylon, and the purposes that he has formed against
the land of the Chaldeans: Surely the little ones
of the flock shall be dragged away; surely their[e]
fold shall be appalled at their fate. 46 At the sound
of the capture of Babylon the earth shall tremble,
and her cry shall be heard among the nations.

51 Thus says the LORD:
I am going to stir up a destructive wind[f]
against Babylon
and against the inhabitants of Leb-qamai;[g]
2 and I will send winnowers to Babylon,
and they shall winnow her.
They shall empty her land
when they come against her from every
side
on the day of trouble.
3 Let not the archer bend his bow,
and let him not array himself in his coat
of mail.
Do not spare her young men;
utterly destroy her entire army.
4 They shall fall down slain in the land of the
Chaldeans,
and wounded in her streets.
5 Israel and Judah have not been forsaken
by their God, the LORD of hosts,
though their land is full of guilt
before the Holy One of Israel.

6 Flee from the midst of Babylon,
save your lives, each of you!
Do not perish because of her guilt,
for this is the time of the LORD's
vengeance;
he is repaying her what is due.

[a] Cn: Heb *his* [b] Another reading is *A sword* [c] Heb lacks *in Babylon* [d] Or *and I will single out the choicest of her rams:* Meaning of Heb uncertain [e] Syr Gk Tg Compare 49.20: Heb lacks *their* [f] Or *stir up the spirit of a destroyer* [g] *Leb-qamai* is a cryptogram for *Kasdim*, Chaldea

7 Babylon was a golden cup in the LORD's hand,
making all the earth drunken;
the nations drank of her wine,
and so the nations went mad.
8 Suddenly Babylon has fallen and is shattered;
wail for her!
Bring balm for her wound;
perhaps she may be healed.
9 We tried to heal Babylon,
but she could not be healed.
Forsake her, and let each of us go
to our own country;
for her judgment has reached up to heaven
and has been lifted up even to the skies.
10 The LORD has brought forth our vindication;
come, let us declare in Zion
the work of the LORD our God.

11 Sharpen the arrows!
Fill the quivers!
The LORD has stirred up the spirit of the kings
of the Medes, because his purpose concerning
Babylon is to destroy it, for that is the vengeance
of the LORD, vengeance for his temple.
12 Raise a standard against the walls of Babylon;
make the watch strong;
post sentinels;
prepare the ambushes;
for the LORD has both planned and done
what he spoke concerning the inhabitants
of Babylon.
13 You who live by mighty waters,
rich in treasures,
your end has come,
the thread of your life is cut.
14 The LORD of hosts has sworn by himself:
Surely I will fill you with troops like a swarm
of locusts,
and they shall raise a shout of victory over
you.

15 It is he who made the earth by his power,
who established the world by his wisdom,
and by his understanding stretched out the
heavens.
16 When he utters his voice there is a tumult of
waters in the heavens,
and he makes the mist rise from the ends
of the earth.
He makes lightnings for the rain,
and he brings out the wind from his
storehouses.
17 Everyone is stupid and without knowledge;
goldsmiths are all put to shame by their
idols;
for their images are false,
and there is no breath in them.
18 They are worthless, a work of delusion;
at the time of their punishment they shall
perish.
19 Not like these is the LORD,[a] the portion of
Jacob,
for he is the one who formed all things,
and Israel is the tribe of his inheritance;
the LORD of hosts is his name.

20 You are my war club, my weapon of battle:
with you I smash nations;
with you I destroy kingdoms;
21 with you I smash the horse and its rider;
with you I smash the chariot and the
charioteer;
22 with you I smash man and woman;
with you I smash the old man and the boy;
with you I smash the young man and the girl;
23 with you I smash shepherds and their
flocks;
with you I smash farmers and their teams;
with you I smash governors and deputies.

24 I will repay Babylon and all the inhabitants
of Chaldea before your very eyes for all the wrong
that they have done in Zion, says the LORD.

25 I am against you, O destroying mountain,
says the LORD,
that destroys the whole earth;
I will stretch out my hand against you,
and roll you down from the crags,
and make you a burned-out mountain.

[a] Heb lacks *the LORD*

26 No stone shall be taken from you for a corner
and no stone for a foundation,
but you shall be a perpetual waste,
says the LORD.

27 Raise a standard in the land,
blow the trumpet among the nations;
prepare the nations for war against her,
summon against her the kingdoms,
Ararat, Minni, and Ashkenaz;
appoint a marshal against her,
bring up horses like bristling locusts.
28 Prepare the nations for war against her,
the kings of the Medes, with their
governors and deputies,
and every land under their dominion.
29 The land trembles and writhes,
for the LORD's purposes against Babylon
stand,
to make the land of Babylon a desolation,
without inhabitant.
30 The warriors of Babylon have given up
fighting,
they remain in their strongholds;
their strength has failed,
they have become women;
her buildings are set on fire,
her bars are broken.
31 One runner runs to meet another,
and one messenger to meet another,
to tell the king of Babylon
that his city is taken from end to end:
32 the fords have been seized,
the marshes have been burned with fire,
and the soldiers are in panic.
33 For thus says the LORD of hosts, the God of
Israel:
Daughter Babylon is like a threshing floor
at the time when it is trodden;
yet a little while
and the time of her harvest will come.

34 "King Nebuchadrezzar of Babylon has
devoured me,
he has crushed me;
he has made me an empty vessel,
he has swallowed me like a monster;
he has filled his belly with my delicacies,
he has spewed me out.
35 May my torn flesh be avenged on Babylon,"
the inhabitants of Zion shall say.
"May my blood be avenged on the
inhabitants of Chaldea,"
Jerusalem shall say.
36 Therefore thus says the LORD:
I am going to defend your cause
and take vengeance for you.
I will dry up her sea
and make her fountain dry;
37 and Babylon shall become a heap of ruins,
a den of jackals,
an object of horror and of hissing,
without inhabitant.

38 Like lions they shall roar together;
they shall growl like lions' whelps.
39 When they are inflamed, I will set out their
drink
and make them drunk, until they become
merry
and then sleep a perpetual sleep
and never wake, says the LORD.
40 I will bring them down like lambs to the
slaughter,
like rams and goats.

41 How Sheshach[a] is taken,
the pride of the whole earth seized!
How Babylon has become
an object of horror among the nations!
42 The sea has risen over Babylon;
she has been covered by its tumultuous
waves.
43 Her cities have become an object of horror,
a land of drought and a desert,
a land in which no one lives,
and through which no mortal passes.
44 I will punish Bel in Babylon,
and make him disgorge what he has
swallowed.

[a] *Sheshach* is a cryptogram for *Babel,* Babylon

The nations shall no longer stream to him;
the wall of Babylon has fallen.

45 Come out of her, my people!
Save your lives, each of you,
from the fierce anger of the LORD!
46 Do not be fainthearted or fearful
at the rumors heard in the land—
one year one rumor comes,
the next year another,
rumors of violence in the land
and of ruler against ruler.

47 Assuredly, the days are coming
when I will punish the images of Babylon;
her whole land shall be put to shame,
and all her slain shall fall in her midst.
48 Then the heavens and the earth,
and all that is in them,
shall shout for joy over Babylon;
for the destroyers shall come against them
out of the north,
says the LORD.
49 Babylon must fall for the slain of Israel,
as the slain of all the earth have fallen
because of Babylon.

50 You survivors of the sword,
go, do not linger!
Remember the LORD in a distant land,
and let Jerusalem come into your mind:
51 We are put to shame, for we have heard
insults;
dishonor has covered our face,
for aliens have come
into the holy places of the LORD's house.

52 Therefore the time is surely coming, says the
LORD,
when I will punish her idols,
and through all her land
the wounded shall groan.
53 Though Babylon should mount up to heaven,
and though she should fortify her strong
height,
from me destroyers would come upon her,
says the LORD.

54 Listen!—a cry from Babylon!
A great crashing from the land of the
Chaldeans!
55 For the LORD is laying Babylon waste,
and stilling her loud clamor.
Their waves roar like mighty waters,
the sound of their clamor resounds;
56 for a destroyer has come against her,
against Babylon;
her warriors are taken,
their bows are broken;
for the LORD is a God of recompense,
he will repay in full.
57 I will make her officials and her sages drunk,
also her governors, her deputies, and her
warriors;
they shall sleep a perpetual sleep and never
wake,
says the King, whose name is the LORD of
hosts.

58 Thus says the LORD of hosts:
The broad wall of Babylon
shall be leveled to the ground,
and her high gates
shall be burned with fire.
The peoples exhaust themselves for nothing,
and the nations weary themselves only for
fire.[a]

59 The word that the prophet Jeremiah commanded Seraiah son of Neriah son of Mahseiah,
when he went with King Zedekiah of Judah to
Babylon, in the fourth year of his reign. Seraiah
was the quartermaster. 60 Jeremiah wrote in a[b]
scroll all the disasters that would come on Babylon, all these words that are written concerning
Babylon. 61 And Jeremiah said to Seraiah: "When
you come to Babylon, see that you read all these
words, 62 and say, 'O LORD, you yourself threatened to destroy this place so that neither human
beings nor animals shall live in it, and it shall be

[a] Gk Syr Compare Hab 2.13: Heb *and the nations for fire, and they are weary* [b] Or *one*

desolate forever.' 63When you finish reading this
scroll, tie a stone to it, and throw it into the middle of the Euphrates, 64and say, 'Thus shall Babylon sink, to rise no more, because of the disasters that I am bringing on her.' "[a]
Thus far are the words of Jeremiah.

52 Zedekiah was twenty-one years old when
he began to reign; he reigned eleven years
in Jerusalem. His mother's name was Hamutal
daughter of Jeremiah of Libnah. 2He did what
was evil in the sight of the LORD, just as Jehoiakim had done. 3Indeed, Jerusalem and Judah so
angered the LORD that he expelled them from his
presence.
Zedekiah rebelled against the king of Babylon.
4And in the ninth year of his reign, in the tenth
month, on the tenth day of the month, King
Nebuchadrezzar of Babylon came with all his
army against Jerusalem, and they laid siege to it;
they built siegeworks against it all around. 5So the
city was besieged until the eleventh year of King
Zedekiah. 6On the ninth day of the fourth month
the famine became so severe in the city that there
was no food for the people of the land. 7Then
a breach was made in the city wall;[b] and all the
soldiers fled and went out from the city by night
by the way of the gate between the two walls, by
the king's garden, though the Chaldeans were all
around the city. They went in the direction of the
Arabah. 8But the army of the Chaldeans pursued
the king, and overtook Zedekiah in the plains of
Jericho; and all his army was scattered, deserting
him. 9Then they captured the king, and brought
him up to the king of Babylon at Riblah in the
land of Hamath, and he passed sentence on him.
10The king of Babylon killed the sons of Zedekiah
before his eyes, and also killed all the officers of
Judah at Riblah. 11He put out the eyes of Zedekiah, and bound him in fetters, and the king of
Babylon took him to Babylon, and put him in
prison until the day of his death.
12 In the fifth month, on the tenth day of the
month—which was the nineteenth year of King
Nebuchadrezzar, king of Babylon—Nebuzaradan
the captain of the bodyguard who served the king
of Babylon, entered Jerusalem. 13He burned the
house of the LORD, the king's house, and all the
houses of Jerusalem; every great house he burned
down. 14All the army of the Chaldeans, who were
with the captain of the guard, broke down all the
walls around Jerusalem. 15Nebuzaradan the captain of the guard carried into exile some of the
poorest of the people and the rest of the people
who were left in the city and the deserters who
had defected to the king of Babylon, together
with the rest of the artisans. 16But Nebuzaradan
the captain of the guard left some of the poorest
people of the land to be vinedressers and tillers
of the soil.
17 The pillars of bronze that were in the
house of the LORD, and the stands and the bronze
sea that were in the house of the LORD, the
Chaldeans broke in pieces, and carried all the
bronze to Babylon. 18They took away the pots,
the shovels, the snuffers, the basins, the ladles,
and all the vessels of bronze used in the temple
service. 19The captain of the guard took away the
small bowls also, the firepans, the basins, the pots,
the lampstands, the ladles, and the bowls for libation, both those of gold and those of silver. 20As
for the two pillars, the one sea, the twelve bronze
bulls that were under the sea, and the stands,[c]
which King Solomon had made for the house of
the LORD, the bronze of all these vessels was beyond weighing. 21As for the pillars, the height of
the one pillar was eighteen cubits, its circumference was twelve cubits; it was hollow and its
thickness was four fingers. 22Upon it was a capital
of bronze; the height of the capital was five cubits; latticework and pomegranates, all of bronze,
encircled the top of the capital. And the second
pillar had the same, with pomegranates. 23There
were ninety-six pomegranates on the sides; all
the pomegranates encircling the latticework
numbered one hundred.
24 The captain of the guard took the chief
priest Seraiah, the second priest Zephaniah,
and the three guardians of the threshold; 25and
from the city he took an officer who had been in

[a] Gk: Heb *on her. And they shall weary themselves* [b] Heb lacks *wall* [c] Cn: Heb *that were under the stands*

command of the soldiers, and seven men of the
king's council who were found in the city; the
secretary of the commander of the army who
mustered the people of the land; and sixty men
of the people of the land who were found inside
the city. 26Then Nebuzaradan the captain of the
guard took them, and brought them to the king
of Babylon at Riblah. 27And the king of Babylon
struck them down, and put them to death at Riblah in the land of Hamath. So Judah went into exile out of its land.

28 This is the number of the people whom
Nebuchadrezzar took into exile: in the seventh
year, three thousand twenty-three Judeans; 29in
the eighteenth year of Nebuchadrezzar he took
into exile from Jerusalem eight hundred thirty-
two persons; 30in the twenty-third year of Nebuchadrezzar, Nebuzaradan the captain of the guard
took into exile of the Judeans seven hundred
forty-five persons; all the persons were four thousand six hundred.

31 In the thirty-seventh year of the exile of
King Jehoiachin of Judah, in the twelfth month,
on the twenty-fifth day of the month, King Evil-
merodach of Babylon, in the year he began to
reign, showed favor to King Jehoiachin of Judah
and brought him out of prison; 32he spoke kindly
to him, and gave him a seat above the seats of the
other kings who were with him in Babylon. 33So
Jehoiachin put aside his prison clothes, and every
day of his life he dined regularly at the king's table.
34For his allowance, a regular daily allowance was
given him by the king of Babylon, as long as he
lived, up to the day of his death.

Lamentations

LAMENTS — POETIC LITURGIES OF PAIN AND ANGUISH — evoke individual and communal agony over horrific loss. As passionate prayers of complaint, protest, rage, and grief over tragedy, they request divine deliverance. Some laments chronicle themes of funeral dirges, of weeping and wailing for the dead. In the company of God's faithful people, laments presume that God will intercede on their behalf. Whether concerning destruction of the city or the temple, the end of its rites, or the trauma of Babylonian exile, the book of Lamentations dramatizes visceral, catastrophic grief and tragedy and helps contemporary audiences as well to name and experience comparable realities, to grieve, and ultimately to heal.

The five laments of this book exude power and ambiguity, as they arise from difficult life dramas. Except for the third lament, each of the others contains twenty-two verses, forming an acrostic in which each line begins with a letter of the Hebrew alphabet sequentially. This use of acrostics unites diverse, often contradictory, voices, complex relationships, and tragic themes—from the slaughter of people to starving mothers reduced to cannibalism, to exile, and to the end of worship. Daughter Zion, represented as woman, princess, widow, lover, daughter, and/or mother, personifies Jerusalem, YHWH's punished spouse. Ancient societies viewed cities as the divine wives of the relevant god. Lamentations, a magnificent, artistic matrix, concretizes the community's suffering.

Issues Then and Now

Throughout history, people have needed to express loss and to respond to death. Mozart, Verdi, Brahms, Fauré, and many others have written requiems, musical masses for the dead, featuring voices and orchestra. The blues—bad times captured in song form, originating from African American folk songs at the turn of the twentieth century—are responsorial, empathetic, and cosmological; they rely on a distinctive twelve-bar vocal melody form based upon a five-tone scale, with instrumental accompaniment. These songs are poignant, provocative laments reflecting the spectrum of daily life, from melancholy to complaint to celebration framed by thanks.

Emilie Townes, a womanist social ethicist, reminds us that lament precedes healing. Lament asks for deliverance, moving from crisis and tragedy to deliverance, and praising God. Lament, central to divine-human relations, is our cry for help. After exhausting human ingenuity and purpose, we become victims of our own arrogance. We begin actions we cannot contain and have to cry out to God, in anguish, for succor. Communal laments are forums for communal complaint, grief, and sorrow over physical or sociocultural devastation. Naming the pain makes it bearable. A lament helps us to be in covenant with God, to practice faith responsibly, to seek justice, and to anticipate God's salvific deliverance.

Intersections of collisions and convergences

The book of Lamentations includes imagery biased against women. Daughter Zion is the spokesperson for the community's grief and sorrow and later is an adversary against the divine to challenge mistreatment by God. Women and their suffering are valued as metaphors for communal pain. Yet Lamentations portrays the daughter as catalyst and collaborator in her own abuse; as inferior and subordinate to the divine male. As a menstruating woman, her body symbolizes humiliation and shame (1:8-11). Daughter Zion experiences bitter lament and reflects today's battered spouse: she experiences torture, abuse, and beatings (1:12-22).

Hebrew Bible scholar Linda Day reminds us that unwarranted and inexplicable suffering often triggers lament; victims are frequently blamed for the violence done to them. The suffering of the most vulnerable people problematizes the notion that suffering is necessary: Why, Lord? Jerusalem's ancient suffering and much suffering today cannot be redemptive. If we suggest that all suffering is redemptive, at what cost do we make that assertion? Amid great pain and agony, powerful questions arise: Where is God? Ancient times and the twenty-first century come together in the experiences of abandonment, violence, suffering, death, and helplessness. The book of Lamentations testifies to past pain, signals survival, and artistically renders suffering as classic poetry while questioning *theodicy*, God's justice. What happens when God, hope, or compassion seem absent? How do those who are privileged (rather than oppressed) know suffering?

Lament is not a resource for moments of grief alone. I am a professor of theology and women's studies at a divinity school and an ordained elder in the Christian Methodist Episcopal Church; I am also an athlete and a musician, on a quest for a healthy, holistic, spiritual life. The Lamentations remind us that we, with our limited anthropological categories, wrestle throughout our lives to address an inexplicable, mysterious God, and that as community we must take time to grieve if we are to move toward healing.

— ***Cheryl A. Kirk-Duggan***

1 How lonely sits the city
that once was full of people!
How like a widow she has become,
she that was great among the nations!
She that was a princess among the provinces
has become a vassal.

2 She weeps bitterly in the night,
with tears on her cheeks;
among all her lovers
she has no one to comfort her;
all her friends have dealt treacherously
with her,
they have become her enemies.

3 Judah has gone into exile with suffering
and hard servitude;
she lives now among the nations,

and finds no resting place;
her pursuers have all overtaken her
in the midst of her distress.

4 The roads to Zion mourn,
for no one comes to the festivals;
all her gates are desolate,
her priests groan;
her young girls grieve,[a]
and her lot is bitter.

5 Her foes have become the masters,
her enemies prosper,
because the LORD has made her suffer
for the multitude of her transgressions;
her children have gone away,
captives before the foe.

6 From daughter Zion has departed
all her majesty.
Her princes have become like stags
that find no pasture;
they fled without strength
before the pursuer.

7 Jerusalem remembers,
in the days of her affliction and wandering,
all the precious things
that were hers in days of old.
When her people fell into the hand of the foe,
and there was no one to help her,
the foe looked on mocking
over her downfall.

8 Jerusalem sinned grievously,
so she has become a mockery;
all who honored her despise her,
for they have seen her nakedness;
she herself groans,
and turns her face away.

9 Her uncleanness was in her skirts;
she took no thought of her future;
her downfall was appalling,
with none to comfort her.
"O LORD, look at my affliction,
for the enemy has triumphed!"

10 Enemies have stretched out their hands
over all her precious things;
she has even seen the nations
invade her sanctuary,
those whom you forbade
to enter your congregation.

11 All her people groan
as they search for bread;
they trade their treasures for food

[a] Meaning of Heb uncertain

Lamentations 1:3-7

I remembered the story of a young missionary priest sent to a small village in South America. He was just out of seminary, full of enthusiasm, idealism, and energy. Well trained and well meaning, he worked endless hours among the poor. He petitioned bishops and banks, argued with bureaucrats and held meetings in farmyards. As months passed he remained untiring, unwavering and eminently unsuccessful.

Finally, bludgeoned to the point of hopelessness, he began to pack his few belongings to leave.... [H]is housekeeper asked, "Padre, where are you going?" "Away," he told her, "because I am totally powerless to help. As God is my witness I tried but it cannot be done. In this village there are always more mouths to feed and less food. Promises of help remain promises. I am defeated, angry and resigned. And powerless to change things." To this, the woman replied, "But Padre, now that you are one of us, why are you leaving?"[54]

— ***Richard McCall***

to revive their strength.
Look, O LORD, and see
how worthless I have become.

12 Is it nothing to you,[a] all you who pass by?
Look and see
if there is any sorrow like my sorrow,
which was brought upon me,
which the LORD inflicted
on the day of his fierce anger.

13 From on high he sent fire;
it went deep into my bones;
he spread a net for my feet;
he turned me back;
he has left me stunned,
faint all day long.

14 My transgressions were bound[a] into a yoke;
by his hand they were fastened together;
they weigh on my neck,
sapping my strength;
the Lord handed me over
to those whom I cannot withstand.

15 The LORD has rejected
all my warriors in the midst of me;
he proclaimed a time against me
to crush my young men;
the Lord has trodden as in a wine press
the virgin daughter Judah.

16 For these things I weep;
my eyes flow with tears;
for a comforter is far from me,
one to revive my courage;
my children are desolate,
for the enemy has prevailed.

17 Zion stretches out her hands,
but there is no one to comfort her;
the LORD has commanded against Jacob
that his neighbors should become his foes;
Jerusalem has become
a filthy thing among them.

18 The LORD is in the right,
for I have rebelled against his word;
but hear, all you peoples,
and behold my suffering;
my young women and young men
have gone into captivity.

19 I called to my lovers
but they deceived me;
my priests and elders
perished in the city
while seeking food
to revive their strength.

20 See, O LORD, how distressed I am;
my stomach churns,
my heart is wrung within me,
because I have been very rebellious.
In the street the sword bereaves;
in the house it is like death.

21 They heard how I was groaning,
with no one to comfort me.
All my enemies heard of my trouble;
they are glad that you have done it.
Bring on the day you have announced,
and let them be as I am.

22 Let all their evil doing come before you;
and deal with them
as you have dealt with me
because of all my transgressions;
for my groans are many
and my heart is faint.

2 How the Lord in his anger
has humiliated[a] daughter Zion!
He has thrown down from heaven to earth
the splendor of Israel;
he has not remembered his footstool
in the day of his anger.

2 The Lord has destroyed without mercy
all the dwellings of Jacob;
in his wrath he has broken down

[a] Meaning of Heb uncertain

the strongholds of daughter Judah;
he has brought down to the ground in dishonor
the kingdom and its rulers.

3 He has cut down in fierce anger
all the might of Israel;
he has withdrawn his right hand from them
in the face of the enemy;
he has burned like a flaming fire in Jacob,
consuming all around.

4 He has bent his bow like an enemy,
with his right hand set like a foe;
he has killed all in whom we took pride
in the tent of daughter Zion;
he has poured out his fury like fire.

5 The Lord has become like an enemy;
he has destroyed Israel.
He has destroyed all its palaces,
laid in ruins its strongholds,
and multiplied in daughter Judah
mourning and lamentation.

6 He has broken down his booth like a garden,
he has destroyed his tabernacle;
the LORD has abolished in Zion
festival and sabbath,
and in his fierce indignation has spurned
king and priest.

7 The Lord has scorned his altar,
disowned his sanctuary;
he has delivered into the hand of the enemy
the walls of her palaces;
a clamor was raised in the house of the LORD
as on a day of festival.

8 The LORD determined to lay in ruins
the wall of daughter Zion;
he stretched the line;
he did not withhold his hand from destroying;
he caused rampart and wall to lament;
they languish together.

9 Her gates have sunk into the ground;
he has ruined and broken her bars;
her king and princes are among the nations;
guidance is no more,
and her prophets obtain
no vision from the LORD.

10 The elders of daughter Zion
sit on the ground in silence;
they have thrown dust on their heads
and put on sackcloth;
the young girls of Jerusalem
have bowed their heads to the ground.

11 My eyes are spent with weeping;
my stomach churns;
my bile is poured out on the ground
because of the destruction of my people,
because infants and babes faint
in the streets of the city.

12 They cry to their mothers,
"Where is bread and wine?"
as they faint like the wounded
in the streets of the city,
as their life is poured out
on their mothers' bosom.

13 What can I say for you, to what compare you,
O daughter Jerusalem?
To what can I liken you, that I may comfort you,
O virgin daughter Zion?
For vast as the sea is your ruin;
who can heal you?

14 Your prophets have seen for you
false and deceptive visions;
they have not exposed your iniquity
to restore your fortunes,
but have seen oracles for you
that are false and misleading.

15 All who pass along the way
clap their hands at you;
they hiss and wag their heads
at daughter Jerusalem;

"Is this the city that was called
the perfection of beauty,
the joy of all the earth?"

16 All your enemies
open their mouths against you;
they hiss, they gnash their teeth,
they cry: "We have devoured her!
Ah, this is the day we longed for;
at last we have seen it!"

17 The LORD has done what he purposed,
he has carried out his threat;
as he ordained long ago,
he has demolished without pity;
he has made the enemy rejoice over you,
and exalted the might of your foes.

18 Cry aloud[a] to the Lord!
O wall of daughter Zion!
Let tears stream down like a torrent
day and night!
Give yourself no rest,
your eyes no respite!

19 Arise, cry out in the night,
at the beginning of the watches!
Pour out your heart like water
before the presence of the Lord!
Lift your hands to him
for the lives of your children,
who faint for hunger
at the head of every street.

20 Look, O LORD, and consider!
To whom have you done this?
Should women eat their offspring,
the children they have borne?
Should priest and prophet be killed
in the sanctuary of the Lord?

21 The young and the old are lying
on the ground in the streets;
my young women and my young men
have fallen by the sword;
in the day of your anger you have killed them,
slaughtering without mercy.

22 You invited my enemies from all around
as if for a day of festival;
and on the day of the anger of the LORD
no one escaped or survived;
those whom I bore and reared
my enemy has destroyed.

3 I am one who has seen affliction
under the rod of God's[b] wrath;
2 he has driven and brought me
into darkness without any light;
3 against me alone he turns his hand,
again and again, all day long.

4 He has made my flesh and my skin waste away,
and broken my bones;
5 he has besieged and enveloped me
with bitterness and tribulation;
6 he has made me sit in darkness
like the dead of long ago.

7 He has walled me about so that I cannot escape;
he has put heavy chains on me;
8 though I call and cry for help,
he shuts out my prayer;
9 he has blocked my ways with hewn stones,
he has made my paths crooked.

10 He is a bear lying in wait for me,
a lion in hiding;
11 he led me off my way and tore me to pieces;
he has made me desolate;
12 he bent his bow and set me
as a mark for his arrow.

13 He shot into my vitals
the arrows of his quiver;
14 I have become the laughingstock of all my people,
the object of their taunt-songs all day long.

[a] Cn: Heb *Their heart cried* [b] Heb *his*

15 He has filled me with bitterness,
he has sated me with wormwood.

16 He has made my teeth grind on gravel,
and made me cower in ashes;
17 my soul is bereft of peace;
I have forgotten what happiness is;
18 so I say, "Gone is my glory,
and all that I had hoped for from the
LORD."

19 The thought of my affliction and my
homelessness
is wormwood and gall!
20 My soul continually thinks of it
and is bowed down within me.
21 But this I call to mind,
and therefore I have hope:

22 The steadfast love of the LORD never ceases,[a]
his mercies never come to an end;
23 they are new every morning;
great is your faithfulness.
24 "The LORD is my portion," says my soul,
"therefore I will hope in him."

25 The LORD is good to those who wait for him,
to the soul that seeks him.
26 It is good that one should wait quietly
for the salvation of the LORD.
27 It is good for one to bear
the yoke in youth,
28 to sit alone in silence
when the Lord has imposed it,
29 to put one's mouth to the dust
(there may yet be hope),
30 to give one's cheek to the smiter,
and be filled with insults.

31 For the Lord will not
reject forever.
32 Although he causes grief, he will have
compassion
according to the abundance of his steadfast
love;
33 for he does not willingly afflict
or grieve anyone.

34 When all the prisoners of the land
are crushed under foot,
35 when human rights are perverted
in the presence of the Most High,
36 when one's case is subverted
—does the Lord not see it?

37 Who can command and have it done,
if the Lord has not ordained it?
38 Is it not from the mouth of the Most High

[a] Syr Tg: Heb *LORD, we are not cut off*

Lamentations 3:34-36

Any community which can at tolerable expense eliminate human distress but refrains from doing so must either believe that it benefits from unemployment and poverty, or that the poor and unemployed are inferior people, or that other important values will be threatened by efforts to assist the lower orders—or all of these statements.

[A]s Herbert Gans has eloquently argued, poverty serves numerous functions for the non-poor. The poor do the community's dirty work. The poor lighten the tax burden of the affluent by paying higher percentages of their meager earnings to the revenue agents than their financial betters.

When the rich contemplate the poor, they can cope the more readily with their own failures of intelligence and character. Because the poor are politically infirm, they, in Gans' words, can "conveniently absorb the political, economic and social costs of change and growth."[55]

— Robert Lekachman

that good and bad come?
39 Why should any who draw breath complain
about the punishment of their sins?

40 Let us test and examine our ways,
and return to the LORD.
41 Let us lift up our hearts as well as our hands
to God in heaven.
42 We have transgressed and rebelled,
and you have not forgiven.

43 You have wrapped yourself with anger and pursued us,
killing without pity;
44 you have wrapped yourself with a cloud
so that no prayer can pass through.
45 You have made us filth and rubbish
among the peoples.

46 All our enemies
have opened their mouths against us;
47 panic and pitfall have come upon us,
devastation and destruction.
48 My eyes flow with rivers of tears
because of the destruction of my people.

49 My eyes will flow without ceasing,
without respite,
50 until the LORD from heaven
looks down and sees.
51 My eyes cause me grief
at the fate of all the young women in my city.

52 Those who were my enemies without cause
have hunted me like a bird;
53 they flung me alive into a pit
and hurled stones on me;
54 water closed over my head;
I said, "I am lost."

55 I called on your name, O LORD,
from the depths of the pit;
56 you heard my plea, "Do not close your ear
to my cry for help, but give me relief!"
57 You came near when I called on you;
you said, "Do not fear!"

58 You have taken up my cause, O Lord,
you have redeemed my life.
59 You have seen the wrong done to me, O LORD;
judge my cause.
60 You have seen all their malice,
all their plots against me.

61 You have heard their taunts, O LORD,
all their plots against me.
62 The whispers and murmurs of my assailants
are against me all day long.
63 Whether they sit or rise—see,
I am the object of their taunt-songs.

64 Pay them back for their deeds, O LORD,
according to the work of their hands!
65 Give them anguish of heart;
your curse be on them!
66 Pursue them in anger and destroy them
from under the LORD's heavens.

4 How the gold has grown dim,
how the pure gold is changed!
The sacred stones lie scattered
at the head of every street.

2 The precious children of Zion,
worth their weight in fine gold—
how they are reckoned as earthen pots,
the work of a potter's hands!

3 Even the jackals offer the breast
and nurse their young,
but my people has become cruel,
like the ostriches in the wilderness.

4 The tongue of the infant sticks
to the roof of its mouth for thirst;
the children beg for food,
but no one gives them anything.

5 Those who feasted on delicacies
perish in the streets;
those who were brought up in purple
cling to ash heaps.

Lamentations 4:4

Fifteen to 20 million people die each year of hunger related diseases brought on by lowered resistance due to malnutrition. Three out of every four of these are children. Over 40 percent of all deaths in poor countries occur among children under five years old.

There is no one whose life is not connected to the lives of the hungry. It has long been a meaningful religious sentiment to say we are "members one of another," indeed members of the same body. But in our time it is factually true as well, and with undeniable force. It is true for better or for worse. Our lives are bundled together. This being the case, there is no one, young or old, educated or not, of whatever race, sex, creed, and gifted with whatever natural or acquired skills and "know-how," who does not have some piece of some part of the ached-for answer to the petition for daily bread.[56]

— ***Larry Rasmussen***

6 For the chastisement[a] of my people has
been greater
than the punishment[b] of Sodom,
which was overthrown in a moment,
though no hand was laid on it.[c]

7 Her princes were purer than snow,
whiter than milk;
their bodies were more ruddy than coral,
their hair[c] like sapphire.[d]

8 Now their visage is blacker than soot;
they are not recognized in the streets.
Their skin has shriveled on their bones;
it has become as dry as wood.

9 Happier were those pierced by the sword
than those pierced by hunger,
whose life drains away, deprived
of the produce of the field.

10 The hands of compassionate women
have boiled their own children;
they became their food
in the destruction of my people.

11 The LORD gave full vent to his wrath;
he poured out his hot anger,
and kindled a fire in Zion
that consumed its foundations.

12 The kings of the earth did not believe,
nor did any of the inhabitants of the world,
that foe or enemy could enter
the gates of Jerusalem.

13 It was for the sins of her prophets
and the iniquities of her priests,
who shed the blood of the righteous
in the midst of her.

14 Blindly they wandered through the streets,
so defiled with blood
that no one was able
to touch their garments.

15 "Away! Unclean!" people shouted at them;
"Away! Away! Do not touch!"
So they became fugitives and wanderers;
it was said among the nations,
"They shall stay here no longer."

16 The LORD himself has scattered them,
he will regard them no more;
no honor was shown to the priests,
no favor to the elders.

17 Our eyes failed, ever watching
vainly for help;
we were watching eagerly
for a nation that could not save.

[a] Or *iniquity* [b] Or *sin* [c] Meaning of Heb uncertain [d] Or *lapis lazuli*

18 They dogged our steps
so that we could not walk in our streets;
our end drew near; our days were numbered;
for our end had come.

19 Our pursuers were swifter
than the eagles in the heavens;
they chased us on the mountains,
they lay in wait for us in the wilderness.

20 The LORD's anointed, the breath of our life,
was taken in their pits—
the one of whom we said, "Under his shadow
we shall live among the nations."

21 Rejoice and be glad, O daughter Edom,
you that live in the land of Uz;
but to you also the cup shall pass;
you shall become drunk and strip yourself
bare.

22 The punishment of your iniquity, O daughter
Zion, is accomplished,
he will keep you in exile no longer;
but your iniquity, O daughter Edom, he will
punish,
he will uncover your sins.

5 Remember, O LORD, what has befallen us;
look, and see our disgrace!
2 Our inheritance has been turned over to
strangers,
our homes to aliens.
3 We have become orphans, fatherless;
our mothers are like widows.
4 We must pay for the water we drink;
the wood we get must be bought.
5 With a yoke[a] on our necks we are hard
driven;
we are weary, we are given no rest.
6 We have made a pact with[b] Egypt and
Assyria,
to get enough bread.
7 Our ancestors sinned; they are no more,
and we bear their iniquities.
8 Slaves rule over us;
there is no one to deliver us from their
hand.
9 We get our bread at the peril of our lives,
because of the sword in the wilderness.
10 Our skin is black as an oven
from the scorching heat of famine.
11 Women are raped in Zion,
virgins in the towns of Judah.
12 Princes are hung up by their hands;
no respect is shown to the elders.
13 Young men are compelled to grind,
and boys stagger under loads of wood.
14 The old men have left the city gate,
the young men their music.
15 The joy of our hearts has ceased;
our dancing has been turned to mourning.
16 The crown has fallen from our head;
woe to us, for we have sinned!
17 Because of this our hearts are sick,
because of these things our eyes have
grown dim:
18 because of Mount Zion, which lies desolate;
jackals prowl over it.

19 But you, O LORD, reign forever;
your throne endures to all generations.
20 Why have you forgotten us completely?
Why have you forsaken us these many
days?
21 Restore us to yourself, O LORD, that we may
be restored;
renew our days as of old—
22 unless you have utterly rejected us,
and are angry with us beyond measure.

[a] Symmachus: Heb lacks *With a yoke* [b] Heb *have given the hand to*

Ezekiel

Reading Ezekiel is a "trip" in more ways than one. The prophet was part of the first group forcibly exiled from Jerusalem and taken to Babylonia in 597 BCE. In his trance journeys, he is spirited back and forth, often violently, between the two places. Some scholars have wondered, in all seriousness, whether Ezekiel was having a hallucinogenic trip. He sees fantastic visions and performs bizarre symbolic acts. He speaks in strange parables and vivid allegories, some of which are pornographic. Others have thought he was mad or perhaps suffering from some type of paranoid schizophrenia. The extraordinary vision in Ezekiel 1 of God's chariot—with its exotic creatures, wheels within wheels and eyes in its rims—has even been interpreted as an encounter with a UFO!

Ezekiel's eccentricity can be explained, at least in part, by the traumatic context in which he lived. He was part of the priestly class that served in the great temple that Solomon built in Jerusalem. His was a turbulent period in Judah's history, a time of foreign colonization and conquest by the great superpower Babylonia under King Nebuchadrezzar (also spelled Nebuchadnezzar, as in NRSV). Babylonian foreign policy dictated the exile of the upper-class leaders of a conquered nation, cutting off its "head" so that the rest of the land could be more easily controlled. Ezekiel was thus one of the first to go into exile in 597, along with many from the ruling, military, and artisan classes (2 Kings 24). Several years later, Nebuchadrezzar conquered Jerusalem, sacked the temple of its enormous wealth, and burned it (2 Kings 25). A second elite group was deported in 587. Many of the exiles became unpaid laborers for Babylon's numerous building projects or were resettled as farmers in undeveloped parts of the empire. Ezekiel was probably among the latter, suffering not only deportation to a strange land but also a loss of status and prestige while forced to work like a peasant for his conquerors.

The book can be structured roughly into three parts:

1–24	Oracles against Judah and Jerusalem prior to 587 BCE
25–32	Oracles against the foreign nations
33–48	Oracles of hope and restoration for Judah

The first section details Ezekiel's prophetic words and visions of doom against the nation and city for their idolatry and faithlessness. The extraordinary vision of God's glorious chariot is a significant theological theme throughout. At the beginning of the book, the vision and his commission to prophesy leave Ezekiel literally speechless (chs. 1–3). He then performs a series of sign-acts that symbolize the state and the dismal future of the nation. (They are not unlike the street theater performed with a decidedly political edge in India today.) Because of the presence of foreign gods in the temple, God decides to quit the temple, leaving Jerusalem open to the invading Babylonians. Chapters 10–11 vividly describe God's glory as the fabulous chariot departs the temple and Jerusalem in three dramatic stages. God will not return in his chariot to the temple until chapter 43, after Ezekiel has a vision of the new temple in Jerusalem.

The second section begins with oracles against nations that are in close proximity to Israel: Ammon, Moab, and Edom (ch. 25). The oracles then shift to coastal nations and their monarchs (26–28). The section ends with diatribes against Egypt, Israel's historical and ancestral foe.

The third section of the book offers hope to a traumatized people. Chapter 34 foretells a new leader, a good shepherd, who will restore the exiles in Judah. Chapter 36 proclaims that the exiles' heart of stone will be replaced by a heart of flesh and a new spirit within them. Chapter 37 describes Ezekiel's famous vision of the dry bones, the inspiration for the Negro spiritual "Dem bones, dem bones, dem dry bones."

The book of Ezekiel will resonate with readers who have left their homelands, especially those forcibly wrenched from them. Their trauma is Ezekiel's. We recall only some of them: Native Americans sequestered on reservations after the seizure of their sacred lands; Africans packed onto slave ships bound for cotton fields in the American South; Jews taken from their homes in Europe and sent to concentration camps; Japanese Americans put in internment camps; black Africans dumped into Bantustans in South Africa. Even more millions leave their mother countries because of famine, poverty, unemployment, war, or natural disasters. My own family left the destitution of southern China to better their lives in Gold Mountain, the Chinese term for the United States.

The book of Ezekiel ends in hope: the hope of a people restored to their lands, of a rebuilt temple, and a new society of peace and prosperity. We must offer this same hope to the exiles and refugees of our time and work for justice in their name.

— *Gale A. Yee*

1 In the thirtieth year, in the fourth month, on
the fifth day of the month, as I was among
the exiles by the river Chebar, the heavens were
opened, and I saw visions of God. 2 On the fifth
day of the month (it was the fifth year of the exile
of King Jehoiachin), 3 the word of the LORD came
to the priest Ezekiel son of Buzi, in the land of the
Chaldeans by the river Chebar; and the hand of
the LORD was on him there.

4 As I looked, a stormy wind came out of the
north: a great cloud with brightness around it and
fire flashing forth continually, and in the middle
of the fire, something like gleaming amber. 5 In the
middle of it was something like four living creatures.
This was their appearance: they were of human
form. 6 Each had four faces, and each of them
had four wings. 7 Their legs were straight, and the
soles of their feet were like the sole of a calf's foot;
and they sparkled like burnished bronze. 8 Under
their wings on their four sides they had human
hands. And the four had their faces and their wings
thus: 9 their wings touched one another; each of

them moved straight ahead, without turning as
they moved. 10As for the appearance of their faces:
the four had the face of a human being, the face
of a lion on the right side, the face of an ox on the
left side, and the face of an eagle; 11such were their
faces. Their wings were spread out above; each
creature had two wings, each of which touched
the wing of another, while two covered their bodies. 12Each moved straight ahead; wherever the
spirit would go, they went, without turning as they
went. 13In the middle of[a] the living creatures there
was something that looked like burning coals of
fire, like torches moving to and fro among the living creatures; the fire was bright, and lightning issued from the fire. 14The living creatures darted to
and fro, like a flash of lightning.

15 As I looked at the living creatures, I saw
a wheel on the earth beside the living creatures,
one for each of the four of them.[b] 16As for the appearance of the wheels and their construction:
their appearance was like the gleaming of beryl;
and the four had the same form, their construction being something like a wheel within a wheel.
17When they moved, they moved in any of the
four directions without veering as they moved.
18Their rims were tall and awesome, for the rims
of all four were full of eyes all around. 19When
the living creatures moved, the wheels moved
beside them; and when the living creatures rose
from the earth, the wheels rose. 20Wherever the
spirit would go, they went, and the wheels rose
along with them; for the spirit of the living creatures was in the wheels. 21When they moved, the
others moved; when they stopped, the others
stopped; and when they rose from the earth, the
wheels rose along with them; for the spirit of the
living creatures was in the wheels.

22 Over the heads of the living creatures
there was something like a dome, shining like
crystal,[c] spread out above their heads. 23Under
the dome their wings were stretched out straight,
one toward another; and each of the creatures
had two wings covering its body. 24When they
moved, I heard the sound of their wings like the
sound of mighty waters, like the thunder of the
Almighty,[d] a sound of tumult like the sound of
an army; when they stopped, they let down their
wings. 25And there came a voice from above the
dome over their heads; when they stopped, they
let down their wings.

26 And above the dome over their heads
there was something like a throne, in appearance
like sapphire;[e] and seated above the likeness of a
throne was something that seemed like a human
form. 27Upward from what appeared like the
loins I saw something like gleaming amber, something that looked like fire enclosed all around;
and downward from what looked like the loins I
saw something that looked like fire, and there was
a splendor all around. 28Like the bow in a cloud
on a rainy day, such was the appearance of the
splendor all around. This was the appearance of
the likeness of the glory of the LORD.

When I saw it, I fell on my face, and I heard
the voice of someone speaking.

2 He said to me: O mortal,[f] stand up on your
feet, and I will speak with you. 2And when
he spoke to me, a spirit entered into me and set
me on my feet; and I heard him speaking to me.
3He said to me, Mortal, I am sending you to the
people of Israel, to a nation[g] of rebels who have
rebelled against me; they and their ancestors have
transgressed against me to this very day. 4The descendants are impudent and stubborn. I am sending you to them, and you shall say to them, "Thus
says the Lord GOD." 5Whether they hear or refuse
to hear (for they are a rebellious house), they shall
know that there has been a prophet among them.
6And you, O mortal, do not be afraid of them, and
do not be afraid of their words, though briers and
thorns surround you and you live among scorpions; do not be afraid of their words, and do not
be dismayed at their looks, for they are a rebellious house. 7You shall speak my words to them,
whether they hear or refuse to hear; for they are a
rebellious house.

[a] Gk OL: Heb *And the appearance of* [b] Heb *of their faces* [c] Gk: Heb *like the awesome crystal* [d] Traditional rendering of Heb *Shaddai* [e] Or *lapis lazuli* [f] Or *son of man*; Heb *ben adam* (and so throughout the book when Ezekiel is addressed) [g] Syr: Heb *to nations*

8 But you, mortal, hear what I say to you; do not be rebellious like that rebellious house; open your mouth and eat what I give you. 9I looked, and a hand was stretched out to me, and a written scroll was in it. 10He spread it before me; it had writing on the front and on the back, and written on it were words of lamentation and mourning and woe.

3 He said to me, O mortal, eat what is offered to you; eat this scroll, and go, speak to the house of Israel. 2So I opened my mouth, and he gave me the scroll to eat. 3He said to me, Mortal, eat this scroll that I give you and fill your stomach with it. Then I ate it; and in my mouth it was as sweet as honey.

4 He said to me: Mortal, go to the house of Israel and speak my very words to them. 5For you are not sent to a people of obscure speech and difficult language, but to the house of Israel— 6not to many peoples of obscure speech and difficult language, whose words you cannot understand. Surely, if I sent you to them, they would listen to you. 7But the house of Israel will not listen to you, for they are not willing to listen to me; because all the house of Israel have a hard forehead and a stubborn heart. 8See, I have made your face hard against their faces, and your forehead hard against their foreheads. 9Like the hardest stone, harder than flint, I have made your forehead; do not fear them or be dismayed at their looks, for they are a rebellious house. 10He said to me: Mortal, all my words that I shall speak to you receive in your heart and hear with your ears; 11then go to the exiles, to your people, and speak to them. Say to them, "Thus says the Lord GOD"; whether they hear or refuse to hear.

12 Then the spirit lifted me up, and as the glory of the LORD rose[a] from its place, I heard behind me the sound of loud rumbling; 13it was the sound of the wings of the living creatures brushing against one another, and the sound of the wheels beside them, that sounded like a loud rumbling. 14The spirit lifted me up and bore me away; I went in bitterness in the heat of my spirit, the hand of the LORD being strong upon me. 15I came to the exiles at Tel-abib, who lived by the river Chebar.[b] And I sat there among them, stunned, for seven days.

16 At the end of seven days, the word of the LORD came to me: 17Mortal, I have made you a sentinel for the house of Israel; whenever you hear a word from my mouth, you shall give them warning from me. 18If I say to the wicked, "You shall surely die," and you give them no warning, or speak to warn the wicked from their wicked way, in order to save their life, those wicked persons shall die for their iniquity; but their blood I will require at your hand. 19But if you warn the wicked, and they do not turn from their wickedness, or from their wicked way, they shall die for their iniquity; but you will have saved your life. 20Again, if the righteous turn from their righteousness and commit iniquity, and I lay a stumbling block before them, they shall die; because you have not warned them, they shall die for their sin, and their righteous deeds that they have done shall not be remembered; but their blood I will require at your hand. 21If, however, you warn the righteous not to sin, and they do not sin, they shall surely live, because they took warning; and you will have saved your life.

22 Then the hand of the LORD was upon me there; and he said to me, Rise up, go out into the valley, and there I will speak with you. 23So I rose up and went out into the valley; and the glory of the LORD stood there, like the glory that I had seen by the river Chebar; and I fell on my face. 24The spirit entered into me, and set me on my feet; and he spoke with me and said to me: Go, shut yourself inside your house. 25As for you, mortal, cords shall be placed on you, and you shall be bound with them, so that you cannot go out among the people; 26and I will make your tongue cling to the roof of your mouth, so that you shall be speechless and unable to reprove them; for they are a rebellious house. 27But when I speak with you, I will open your mouth, and you shall say to them, "Thus says the Lord GOD"; let those

[a] Cn: Heb *and blessed be the glory of the LORD*

[b] Two Mss Syr: Heb *Chebar, and to where they lived.* Another reading is *Chebar, and I sat where they sat*

who will hear, hear; and let those who refuse to
hear, refuse; for they are a rebellious house.

4 And you, O mortal, take a brick and set it before you. On it portray a city, Jerusalem; 2and
put siegeworks against it, and build a siege wall
against it, and cast up a ramp against it; set camps
also against it, and plant battering rams against
it all around. 3Then take an iron plate and place
it as an iron wall between you and the city; set
your face toward it, and let it be in a state of siege,
and press the siege against it. This is a sign for the
house of Israel.

4 Then lie on your left side, and place the
punishment of the house of Israel upon it; you
shall bear their punishment for the number of
the days that you lie there. 5For I assign to you
a number of days, three hundred ninety days,
equal to the number of the years of their punishment; and so you shall bear the punishment of
the house of Israel. 6When you have completed
these, you shall lie down a second time, but on
your right side, and bear the punishment of the
house of Judah; forty days I assign you, one day
for each year. 7You shall set your face toward the
siege of Jerusalem, and with your arm bared you
shall prophesy against it. 8See, I am putting cords
on you so that you cannot turn from one side to
the other until you have completed the days of
your siege.

9 And you, take wheat and barley, beans and
lentils, millet and spelt; put them into one vessel,
and make bread for yourself. During the number
of days that you lie on your side, three hundred
ninety days, you shall eat it. 10The food that you
eat shall be twenty shekels a day by weight; at
fixed times you shall eat it. 11And you shall drink
water by measure, one-sixth of a hin; at fixed
times you shall drink. 12You shall eat it as a barley-
cake, baking it in their sight on human dung.
13The LORD said, "Thus shall the people of Israel
eat their bread, unclean, among the nations to
which I will drive them." 14Then I said, "Ah Lord
GOD! I have never defiled myself; from my youth
up until now I have never eaten what died of itself or was torn by animals, nor has carrion flesh
come into my mouth." 15Then he said to me, "See,
I will let you have cow's dung instead of human
dung, on which you may prepare your bread."

16 Then he said to me, Mortal, I am going to
break the staff of bread in Jerusalem; they shall
eat bread by weight and with fearfulness; and
they shall drink water by measure and in dismay.
17Lacking bread and water, they will look at one
another in dismay, and waste away under their
punishment.

5 And you, O mortal, take a sharp sword; use it
as a barber's razor and run it over your head
and your beard; then take balances for weighing,
and divide the hair. 2One third of the hair you
shall burn in the fire inside the city, when the
days of the siege are completed; one third you
shall take and strike with the sword all around
the city;[a] and one third you shall scatter to the
wind, and I will unsheathe the sword after them.
3Then you shall take from these a small number,
and bind them in the skirts of your robe. 4From
these, again, you shall take some, throw them into
the fire and burn them up; from there a fire will
come out against all the house of Israel.

5 Thus says the Lord GOD: This is Jerusalem;
I have set her in the center of the nations, with
countries all around her. 6But she has rebelled
against my ordinances and my statutes, becoming
more wicked than the nations and the countries
all around her, rejecting my ordinances and not
following my statutes. 7Therefore thus says the
Lord GOD: Because you are more turbulent than
the nations that are all around you, and have not
followed my statutes or kept my ordinances, but
have acted according to the ordinances of the nations that are all around you; 8therefore thus says
the Lord GOD: I, I myself, am coming against you;
I will execute judgments among you in the sight
of the nations. 9And because of all your abominations, I will do to you what I have never yet
done, and the like of which I will never do again.
10Surely, parents shall eat their children in your
midst, and children shall eat their parents; I will
execute judgments on you, and any of you who
survive I will scatter to every wind. 11Therefore,

[a] Heb *it*

as I live, says the Lord GOD, surely, because you
have defiled my sanctuary with all your detestable
things and with all your abominations—therefore
I will cut you down;[a] my eye will not spare, and
I will have no pity. 12 One third of you shall die
of pestilence or be consumed by famine among
you; one third shall fall by the sword around you;
and one third I will scatter to every wind and will
unsheathe the sword after them.

13 My anger shall spend itself, and I will vent
my fury on them and satisfy myself; and they
shall know that I, the LORD, have spoken in my
jealousy, when I spend my fury on them. 14 Moreover I will make you a desolation and an object
of mocking among the nations around you, in the
sight of all that pass by. 15 You shall be[b] a mockery
and a taunt, a warning and a horror, to the nations
around you, when I execute judgments on you in
anger and fury, and with furious punishments—I,
the LORD, have spoken— 16 when I loose against
you[c] my deadly arrows of famine, arrows for destruction, which I will let loose to destroy you, and
when I bring more and more famine upon you,
and break your staff of bread. 17 I will send famine
and wild animals against you, and they will rob
you of your children; pestilence and bloodshed
shall pass through you; and I will bring the sword
upon you. I, the LORD, have spoken.

6 The word of the LORD came to me: 2 O mortal, set your face toward the mountains of
Israel, and prophesy against them, 3 and say, You
mountains of Israel, hear the word of the Lord
GOD! Thus says the Lord GOD to the mountains
and the hills, to the ravines and the valleys: I, I
myself will bring a sword upon you, and I will
destroy your high places. 4 Your altars shall become desolate, and your incense stands shall
be broken; and I will throw down your slain in
front of your idols. 5 I will lay the corpses of the
people of Israel in front of their idols; and I will
scatter your bones around your altars. 6 Wherever
you live, your towns shall be waste and your high
places ruined, so that your altars will be waste and
ruined,[d] your idols broken and destroyed, your
incense stands cut down, and your works wiped
out. 7 The slain shall fall in your midst; then you
shall know that I am the LORD.

8 But I will spare some. Some of you shall
escape the sword among the nations and be scattered through the countries. 9 Those of you who
escape shall remember me among the nations
where they are carried captive, how I was crushed
by their wanton heart that turned away from me,
and their wanton eyes that turned after their idols.
Then they will be loathsome in their own sight for
the evils that they have committed, for all their
abominations. 10 And they shall know that I am
the LORD; I did not threaten in vain to bring this
disaster upon them.

11 Thus says the Lord GOD: Clap your hands
and stamp your foot, and say, Alas for all the vile
abominations of the house of Israel! For they
shall fall by the sword, by famine, and by pestilence. 12 Those far off shall die of pestilence; those
nearby shall fall by the sword; and any who are
left and are spared shall die of famine. Thus I will
spend my fury upon them. 13 And you shall know
that I am the LORD, when their slain lie among
their idols around their altars, on every high hill,
on all the mountain tops, under every green tree,
and under every leafy oak, wherever they offered
pleasing odor to all their idols. 14 I will stretch out
my hand against them, and make the land desolate and waste, throughout all their settlements,
from the wilderness to Riblah.[e] Then they shall
know that I am the LORD.

7 The word of the LORD came to me: 2 You,
O mortal, thus says the Lord GOD to the land
of Israel:

An end! The end has come
upon the four corners of the land.
3 Now the end is upon you,
I will let loose my anger upon you;
I will judge you according to your ways,
I will punish you for all your
abominations.
4 My eye will not spare you, I will have no pity.

[a] Another reading is *I will withdraw* [b] Gk Syr Vg Tg: Heb *It shall be* [c] Heb *them* [d] Syr Vg Tg: Heb *and be made guilty* [e] Another reading is *Diblah*

I will punish you for your ways,
while your abominations are among you.
Then you shall know that I am the LORD.
5 Thus says the Lord GOD:
Disaster after disaster! See, it comes.
6 An end has come, the end has come.
It has awakened against you; see, it comes!
7 Your doom[a] has come to you,
O inhabitant of the land.
The time has come, the day is near—
of tumult, not of reveling on the
mountains.
8 Soon now I will pour out my wrath upon
you;
I will spend my anger against you.
I will judge you according to your ways,
and punish you for all your abominations.
9 My eye will not spare; I will have no pity.
I will punish you according to your ways,
while your abominations are among you.
Then you shall know that it is I the LORD who strike.
10 See, the day! See, it comes!
Your doom[a] has gone out.
The rod has blossomed, pride has budded.
11 Violence has grown into a rod of
wickedness.
None of them shall remain,
not their abundance, not their wealth;
no pre-eminence among them.[a]
12 The time has come, the day draws near;
let not the buyer rejoice, nor the seller
mourn,
for wrath is upon all their multitude.
13 For the sellers shall not return to what has
been sold as long as they remain alive. For the vision concerns all their multitude; it shall not be
revoked. Because of their iniquity, they cannot
maintain their lives.[a]
14 They have blown the horn and made
everything ready;
but no one goes to battle,
for my wrath is upon all their multitude.
15 The sword is outside, pestilence and famine
are inside;
those in the field die by the sword;
those in the city—famine and pestilence
devour them.
16 If any survivors escape,
they shall be found on the mountains
like doves of the valleys,
all of them moaning over their iniquity.
17 All hands shall grow feeble,
all knees turn to water.
18 They shall put on sackcloth,
horror shall cover them.
Shame shall be on all faces,
baldness on all their heads.
19 They shall fling their silver into the streets,
their gold shall be treated as unclean.
Their silver and gold cannot save them on the day
of the wrath of the LORD. They shall not satisfy
their hunger or fill their stomachs with it. For it
was the stumbling block of their iniquity.
20 From
their[b] beautiful ornament, in which they took
pride, they made their abominable images, their
detestable things; therefore I will make of it an
unclean thing to them.
21 I will hand it over to strangers as booty,
to the wicked of the earth as plunder;
they shall profane it.
22 I will avert my face from them,
so that they may profane my treasured[c]
place;
the violent shall enter it,
they shall profane it.
23 Make a chain![a]
For the land is full of bloody crimes;
the city is full of violence.
24 I will bring the worst of the nations
to take possession of their houses.
I will put an end to the arrogance of the
strong,
and their holy places shall be profaned.
25 When anguish comes, they will seek peace,
but there shall be none.
26 Disaster comes upon disaster,
rumor follows rumor;
they shall keep seeking a vision from the
prophet;

[a] Meaning of Heb uncertain [b] Syr Symmachus: Heb *its* [c] Or *secret*

instruction shall perish from the priest,
and counsel from the elders.
27 The king shall mourn,
the prince shall be wrapped in despair,
and the hands of the people of the land
shall tremble.
According to their way I will deal with them;
according to their own judgments I will
judge them.
And they shall know that I am the LORD.

8 In the sixth year, in the sixth month, on the
fifth day of the month, as I sat in my house,
with the elders of Judah sitting before me, the
hand of the Lord GOD fell upon me there. 2 I
looked, and there was a figure that looked like
a human being;[a] below what appeared to be its
loins it was fire, and above the loins it was like the
appearance of brightness, like gleaming amber.
3 It stretched out the form of a hand, and took me
by a lock of my head; and the spirit lifted me up
between earth and heaven, and brought me in visions of God to Jerusalem, to the entrance of the
gateway of the inner court that faces north, to the
seat of the image of jealousy, which provokes to
jealousy. 4 And the glory of the God of Israel was
there, like the vision that I had seen in the valley.

5 Then God[b] said to me, "O mortal, lift up
your eyes now in the direction of the north." So
I lifted up my eyes toward the north, and there,
north of the altar gate, in the entrance, was this
image of jealousy. 6 He said to me, "Mortal, do
you see what they are doing, the great abominations that the house of Israel are committing here,
to drive me far from my sanctuary? Yet you will
see still greater abominations."

7 And he brought me to the entrance of the
court; I looked, and there was a hole in the wall.
8 Then he said to me, "Mortal, dig through the
wall"; and when I dug through the wall, there
was an entrance. 9 He said to me, "Go in, and see
the vile abominations that they are committing
here." 10 So I went in and looked; there, portrayed
on the wall all around, were all kinds of creeping things, and loathsome animals, and all the
idols of the house of Israel. 11 Before them stood
seventy of the elders of the house of Israel, with
Jaazaniah son of Shaphan standing among them.
Each had his censer in his hand, and the fragrant
cloud of incense was ascending. 12 Then he said
to me, "Mortal, have you seen what the elders of
the house of Israel are doing in the dark, each in
his room of images? For they say, 'The LORD does
not see us, the LORD has forsaken the land.'" 13 He
said also to me, "You will see still greater abominations that they are committing."

14 Then he brought me to the entrance of
the north gate of the house of the LORD; women
were sitting there weeping for Tammuz. 15 Then
he said to me, "Have you seen this, O mortal? You
will see still greater abominations than these."

16 And he brought me into the inner court
of the house of the LORD; there, at the entrance of
the temple of the LORD, between the porch and
the altar, were about twenty-five men, with their
backs to the temple of the LORD, and their faces
toward the east, prostrating themselves to the sun
toward the east. 17 Then he said to me, "Have you
seen this, O mortal? Is it not bad enough that the
house of Judah commits the abominations done
here? Must they fill the land with violence, and
provoke my anger still further? See, they are putting the branch to their nose! 18 Therefore I will
act in wrath; my eye will not spare, nor will I have
pity; and though they cry in my hearing with a
loud voice, I will not listen to them."

9 Then he cried in my hearing with a loud
voice, saying, "Draw near, you executioners
of the city, each with his destroying weapon in his
hand." 2 And six men came from the direction of
the upper gate, which faces north, each with his
weapon for slaughter in his hand; among them
was a man clothed in linen, with a writing case
at his side. They went in and stood beside the
bronze altar.

3 Now the glory of the God of Israel had
gone up from the cherub on which it rested to the
threshold of the house. The LORD called to the
man clothed in linen, who had the writing case
at his side; 4 and said to him, "Go through the
city, through Jerusalem, and put a mark on the

[a] Gk: Heb *like fire* [b] Heb *he*

foreheads of those who sigh and groan over all
the abominations that are committed in it." 5 To
the others he said in my hearing, "Pass through the
city after him, and kill; your eye shall not spare,
and you shall show no pity. 6 Cut down old men,
young men and young women, little children and
women, but touch no one who has the mark. And
begin at my sanctuary." So they began with the
elders who were in front of the house. 7 Then he
said to them, "Defile the house, and fill the courts
with the slain. Go!" So they went out and killed
in the city. 8 While they were killing, and I was left
alone, I fell prostrate on my face and cried out,
"Ah Lord GOD! will you destroy all who remain
of Israel as you pour out your wrath upon Jerusalem?" 9 He said to me, "The guilt of the house of
Israel and Judah is exceedingly great; the land is
full of bloodshed and the city full of perversity;
for they say, 'The LORD has forsaken the land,
and the LORD does not see.' 10 As for me, my eye
will not spare, nor will I have pity, but I will bring
down their deeds upon their heads."

11 Then the man clothed in linen, with the
writing case at his side, brought back word, saying, "I have done as you commanded me."

10 Then I looked, and above the dome that
was over the heads of the cherubim there
appeared above them something like a sapphire,[a]
in form resembling a throne. 2 He said to the man
clothed in linen, "Go within the wheelwork underneath the cherubim; fill your hands with burning coals from among the cherubim, and scatter
them over the city." He went in as I looked on.
3 Now the cherubim were standing on the south
side of the house when the man went in; and a
cloud filled the inner court. 4 Then the glory of
the LORD rose up from the cherub to the threshold of the house; the house was filled with the
cloud, and the court was full of the brightness of
the glory of the LORD. 5 The sound of the wings of
the cherubim was heard as far as the outer court,
like the voice of God Almighty[b] when he speaks.

6 When he commanded the man clothed
in linen, "Take fire from within the wheelwork,
from among the cherubim," he went in and stood
beside a wheel. 7 And a cherub stretched out his
hand from among the cherubim to the fire that
was among the cherubim, took some of it and put
it into the hands of the man clothed in linen, who
took it and went out. 8 The cherubim appeared
to have the form of a human hand under their
wings.

9 I looked, and there were four wheels beside the cherubim, one beside each cherub; and
the appearance of the wheels was like gleaming
beryl. 10 And as for their appearance, the four
looked alike, something like a wheel within a
wheel. 11 When they moved, they moved in any
of the four directions without veering as they
moved; but in whatever direction the front wheel
faced, the others followed without veering as
they moved. 12 Their entire body, their rims, their
spokes, their wings, and the wheels—the wheels
of the four of them—were full of eyes all around.
13 As for the wheels, they were called in my hearing "the wheelwork." 14 Each one had four faces:
the first face was that of the cherub, the second
face was that of a human being, the third that of a
lion, and the fourth that of an eagle.

15 The cherubim rose up. These were the
living creatures that I saw by the river Chebar.
16 When the cherubim moved, the wheels moved
beside them; and when the cherubim lifted up
their wings to rise up from the earth, the wheels
at their side did not veer. 17 When they stopped,
the others stopped, and when they rose up, the
others rose up with them; for the spirit of the living creatures was in them.

18 Then the glory of the LORD went out from
the threshold of the house and stopped above
the cherubim. 19 The cherubim lifted up their
wings and rose up from the earth in my sight as
they went out with the wheels beside them. They
stopped at the entrance of the east gate of the
house of the LORD; and the glory of the God of
Israel was above them.

20 These were the living creatures that I saw
underneath the God of Israel by the river Chebar;
and I knew that they were cherubim. 21 Each had
four faces, each four wings, and underneath their

[a] Or *lapis lazuli* [b] Traditional rendering of Heb *El Shaddai*

wings something like human hands. 22 As for
what their faces were like, they were the same
faces whose appearance I had seen by the river
Chebar. Each one moved straight ahead.

11 The spirit lifted me up and brought me
to the east gate of the house of the LORD,
which faces east. There, at the entrance of the
gateway, were twenty-five men; among them I
saw Jaazaniah son of Azzur, and Pelatiah son of
Benaiah, officials of the people. 2 He said to me,
"Mortal, these are the men who devise iniquity
and who give wicked counsel in this city; 3 they
say, 'The time is not near to build houses; this
city is the pot, and we are the meat.' 4 Therefore
prophesy against them; prophesy, O mortal."

5 Then the spirit of the LORD fell upon me,
and he said to me, "Say, Thus says the LORD: This
is what you think, O house of Israel; I know the
things that come into your mind. 6 You have killed
many in this city, and have filled its streets with
the slain. 7 Therefore thus says the Lord GOD: The
slain whom you have placed within it are the meat,
and this city is the pot; but you shall be taken out
of it. 8 You have feared the sword; and I will bring
the sword upon you, says the Lord GOD. 9 I will
take you out of it and give you over to the hands
of foreigners, and execute judgments upon you.
10 You shall fall by the sword; I will judge you at
the border of Israel. And you shall know that I am
the LORD. 11 This city shall not be your pot, and
you shall not be the meat inside it; I will judge
you at the border of Israel. 12 Then you shall know
that I am the LORD, whose statutes you have not
followed, and whose ordinances you have not
kept, but you have acted according to the ordinances of the nations that are around you."

13 Now, while I was prophesying, Pelatiah
son of Benaiah died. Then I fell down on my
face, cried with a loud voice, and said, "Ah Lord
GOD! will you make a full end of the remnant of
Israel?"

14 Then the word of the LORD came to me:
15 Mortal, your kinsfolk, your own kin, your fellow exiles,[a] the whole house of Israel, all of them,
are those of whom the inhabitants of Jerusalem
have said, "They have gone far from the LORD; to
us this land is given for a possession." 16 Therefore
say: Thus says the Lord GOD: Though I removed
them far away among the nations, and though I
scattered them among the countries, yet I have
been a sanctuary to them for a little while[b] in the
countries where they have gone. 17 Therefore say:
Thus says the Lord GOD: I will gather you from
the peoples, and assemble you out of the countries where you have been scattered, and I will
give you the land of Israel. 18 When they come
there, they will remove from it all its detestable
things and all its abominations. 19 I will give them

[a] Gk Syr: Heb *people of your kindred* [b] Or *to some extent*

Ezekiel 11:1-12

"The claim to and the struggle for human rights represents a struggle against human abuses and dehumanizing structures and situations" (Daniel Jenkins). In former times this abuse was not taken notice of within the church, because based on an individualized understanding of sin, the coming of the Kingdom of God was understood as salvation of the individual from his/her sins. The impetus of the Kingdom of God was no longer seen in the direction of saving the world.

Evil can no longer be considered as the sin of the individual. To us it is now recognizable that evil can step out of humanity to settle quasi anonymously in "evil" structures. It is not only the bad will of single human beings that prevents the coming of the Kingdom of God,... it is also the unjust structures that keep me a prisoner and do not let me participate in the struggle for the coming of the Kingdom of God. Therefore, the struggle for human rights is today necessarily a struggle against structures which make me an accomplice of injustice.[57]

— Helmut Frenz

one[a] heart, and put a new spirit within them; I
will remove the heart of stone from their flesh
and give them a heart of flesh, 20so that they may
follow my statutes and keep my ordinances and
obey them. Then they shall be my people, and I
will be their God. 21But as for those whose heart
goes after their detestable things and their abominations,[b] I will bring their deeds upon their own
heads, says the Lord GOD.
22 Then the cherubim lifted up their wings,
with the wheels beside them; and the glory of
the God of Israel was above them. 23And the
glory of the LORD ascended from the middle of
the city, and stopped on the mountain east of
the city. 24The spirit lifted me up and brought
me in a vision by the spirit of God into Chaldea,
to the exiles. Then the vision that I had seen left
me. 25And I told the exiles all the things that the
LORD had shown me.

12 The word of the LORD came to me: 2Mor-
tal, you are living in the midst of a rebellious house, who have eyes to see but do not see,
who have ears to hear but do not hear; 3for they
are a rebellious house. Therefore, mortal, prepare
for yourself an exile's baggage, and go into exile by
day in their sight; you shall go like an exile from
your place to another place in their sight. Perhaps
they will understand, though they are a rebellious
house. 4You shall bring out your baggage by day in
their sight, as baggage for exile; and you shall go
out yourself at evening in their sight, as those do
who go into exile. 5Dig through the wall in their
sight, and carry the baggage through it. 6In their
sight you shall lift the baggage on your shoulder,
and carry it out in the dark; you shall cover your
face, so that you may not see the land; for I have
made you a sign for the house of Israel.
7 I did just as I was commanded. I brought
out my baggage by day, as baggage for exile, and
in the evening I dug through the wall with my
own hands; I brought it out in the dark, carrying
it on my shoulder in their sight.
8 In the morning the word of the LORD came
to me: 9Mortal, has not the house of Israel, the
rebellious house, said to you, "What are you doing?" 10Say to them, "Thus says the Lord GOD:
This oracle concerns the prince in Jerusalem and
all the house of Israel in it." 11Say, "I am a sign for
you: as I have done, so shall it be done to them;
they shall go into exile, into captivity." 12And the
prince who is among them shall lift his baggage
on his shoulder in the dark, and shall go out; he[c]
shall dig through the wall and carry it through; he
shall cover his face, so that he may not see the land
with his eyes. 13I will spread my net over him, and
he shall be caught in my snare; and I will bring
him to Babylon, the land of the Chaldeans, yet
he shall not see it; and he shall die there. 14I will
scatter to every wind all who are around him, his
helpers and all his troops; and I will unsheathe
the sword behind them. 15And they shall know
that I am the LORD, when I disperse them among
the nations and scatter them through the countries. 16But I will let a few of them escape from
the sword, from famine and pestilence, so that
they may tell of all their abominations among the
nations where they go; then they shall know that
I am the LORD.
17 The word of the LORD came to me: 18Mor-
tal, eat your bread with quaking, and drink your
water with trembling and with fearfulness; 19and
say to the people of the land, Thus says the Lord
GOD concerning the inhabitants of Jerusalem in
the land of Israel: They shall eat their bread with
fearfulness, and drink their water in dismay, because their land shall be stripped of all it contains,
on account of the violence of all those who live in
it. 20The inhabited cities shall be laid waste, and
the land shall become a desolation; and you shall
know that I am the LORD.
21 The word of the LORD came to me: 22Mor-
tal, what is this proverb of yours about the land
of Israel, which says, "The days are prolonged,
and every vision comes to nothing"? 23Tell them
therefore, "Thus says the Lord GOD: I will put an
end to this proverb, and they shall use it no more
as a proverb in Israel." But say to them, The days

[a] Another reading is *a new* [b] Cn: Heb *And to the heart of their detestable things and their abominations their heart goes*
[c] Gk Syr: Heb *they*

are near, and the fulfillment of every vision. 24For there shall no longer be any false vision or flattering divination within the house of Israel. 25But I the LORD will speak the word that I speak, and it will be fulfilled. It will no longer be delayed; but in your days, O rebellious house, I will speak the word and fulfill it, says the Lord GOD.

26 The word of the LORD came to me: 27Mortal, the house of Israel is saying, "The vision that he sees is for many years ahead; he prophesies for distant times." 28Therefore say to them, Thus says the Lord GOD: None of my words will be delayed any longer, but the word that I speak will be fulfilled, says the Lord GOD.

13 The word of the LORD came to me: 2Mortal, prophesy against the prophets of Israel who are prophesying; say to those who prophesy out of their own imagination: "Hear the word of the LORD!" 3Thus says the Lord GOD, Alas for the senseless prophets who follow their own spirit, and have seen nothing! 4Your prophets have been like jackals among ruins, O Israel. 5You have not gone up into the breaches, or repaired a wall for the house of Israel, so that it might stand in battle on the day of the LORD. 6They have envisioned falsehood and lying divination; they say, "Says the LORD," when the LORD has not sent them, and yet they wait for the fulfillment of their word! 7Have you not seen a false vision or uttered a lying divination, when you have said, "Says the LORD," even though I did not speak?

8 Therefore thus says the Lord GOD: Because you have uttered falsehood and envisioned lies, I am against you, says the Lord GOD. 9My hand will be against the prophets who see false visions and utter lying divinations; they shall not be in the council of my people, nor be enrolled in the register of the house of Israel, nor shall they enter the land of Israel; and you shall know that I am the Lord GOD. 10Because, in truth, because they have misled my people, saying, "Peace," when there is no peace; and because, when the people build a wall, these prophets[a] smear whitewash on it. 11Say to those who smear whitewash on it that it shall fall. There will be a deluge of rain,[b] great hailstones will fall, and a stormy wind will break out. 12When the wall falls, will it not be said to you, "Where is the whitewash you smeared on it?" 13Therefore thus says the Lord GOD: In my wrath I will make a stormy wind break out, and in my anger there shall be a deluge of rain, and hailstones in wrath to destroy it. 14I will break down the wall that you have smeared with whitewash, and bring it to the ground, so that its foundation will be laid bare; when it falls, you shall perish within it; and you shall know that I am the LORD. 15Thus I will spend my wrath upon the wall, and upon those who have smeared it with whitewash; and I will say to you, The wall is no more, nor those who smeared it— 16the prophets of Israel who prophesied concerning Jerusalem and saw visions of peace for it, when there was no peace, says the Lord GOD.

17 As for you, mortal, set your face against the daughters of your people, who prophesy out of their own imagination; prophesy against them 18and say, Thus says the Lord GOD: Woe to the women who sew bands on all wrists, and make veils for the heads of persons of every height, in the hunt for human lives! Will you hunt down lives among my people, and maintain your own lives? 19You have profaned me among my people for handfuls of barley and for pieces of bread, putting to death persons who should not die and keeping alive persons who should not live, by your lies to my people, who listen to lies.

20 Therefore thus says the Lord GOD: I am against your bands with which you hunt lives;[c] I will tear them from your arms, and let the lives go free, the lives that you hunt down like birds. 21I will tear off your veils, and save my people from your hands; they shall no longer be prey in your hands; and you shall know that I am the LORD. 22Because you have disheartened the righteous falsely, although I have not disheartened them, and you have encouraged the wicked not to turn from their wicked way and save their lives; 23therefore you shall no longer see false visions or practice divination; I will save my people from your hand. Then you will know that I am the LORD.

[a] Heb *they*   [b] Heb *rain and you*   [c] Gk Syr: Heb *lives for birds*

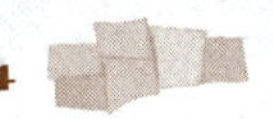

14 Certain elders of Israel came to me and
sat down before me. 2And the word of the
LORD came to me: 3Mortal, these men have taken
their idols into their hearts, and placed their iniquity as a stumbling block before them; shall I let
myself be consulted by them? 4Therefore speak to
them, and say to them, Thus says the Lord GOD:
Any of those of the house of Israel who take their
idols into their hearts and place their iniquity as
a stumbling block before them, and yet come to
the prophet—I the LORD will answer those who
come with the multitude of their idols, 5in order
that I may take hold of the hearts of the house of
Israel, all of whom are estranged from me through
their idols.

6 Therefore say to the house of Israel, Thus
says the Lord GOD: Repent and turn away from
your idols; and turn away your faces from all your
abominations. 7For any of those of the house of
Israel, or of the aliens who reside in Israel, who
separate themselves from me, taking their idols
into their hearts and placing their iniquity as a
stumbling block before them, and yet come to a
prophet to inquire of me by him, I the LORD will
answer them myself. 8I will set my face against
them; I will make them a sign and a byword and
cut them off from the midst of my people; and
you shall know that I am the LORD.

9 If a prophet is deceived and speaks a word,
I, the LORD, have deceived that prophet, and I
will stretch out my hand against him, and will
destroy him from the midst of my people Israel.
10And they shall bear their punishment—the
punishment of the inquirer and the punishment
of the prophet shall be the same— 11so that the
house of Israel may no longer go astray from me,
nor defile themselves any more with all their
transgressions. Then they shall be my people, and
I will be their God, says the Lord GOD.

12 The word of the LORD came to me:
13Mortal, when a land sins against me by acting
faithlessly, and I stretch out my hand against it,
and break its staff of bread and send famine upon
it, and cut off from it human beings and animals,
14even if Noah, Daniel,[a] and Job, these three,
were in it, they would save only their own lives
by their righteousness, says the Lord GOD. 15If I
send wild animals through the land to ravage it,
so that it is made desolate, and no one may pass
through because of the animals; 16even if these
three men were in it, as I live, says the Lord GOD,
they would save neither sons nor daughters; they
alone would be saved, but the land would be desolate. 17Or if I bring a sword upon that land and
say, "Let a sword pass through the land," and I cut
off human beings and animals from it; 18though
these three men were in it, as I live, says the Lord
GOD, they would save neither sons nor daughters, but they alone would be saved. 19Or if I send
a pestilence into that land, and pour out my wrath
upon it with blood, to cut off humans and animals
from it; 20even if Noah, Daniel,[a] and Job were in
it, as I live, says the Lord GOD, they would save
neither son nor daughter; they would save only
their own lives by their righteousness.

21 For thus says the Lord GOD: How much
more when I send upon Jerusalem my four deadly
acts of judgment, sword, famine, wild animals,
and pestilence, to cut off humans and animals
from it! 22Yet, survivors shall be left in it, sons
and daughters who will be brought out; they will
come out to you. When you see their ways and
their deeds, you will be consoled for the evil that
I have brought upon Jerusalem, for all that I have
brought upon it. 23They shall console you, when
you see their ways and their deeds; and you shall
know that it was not without cause that I did all
that I have done in it, says the Lord GOD.

15 The word of the LORD came to me:
2 O mortal, how does the wood of the
vine surpass all other wood—
the vine branch that is among the trees of
the forest?
3 Is wood taken from it to make anything?
Does one take a peg from it on which to
hang any object?
4 It is put in the fire for fuel;
when the fire has consumed both ends of it
and the middle of it is charred,
is it useful for anything?

[a] Or, as otherwise read, *Danel*

5 When it was whole it was used for nothing;
how much less—when the fire has
consumed it,
and it is charred—
can it ever be used for anything!

6 Therefore thus says the Lord GOD: Like
the wood of the vine among the trees of the forest, which I have given to the fire for fuel, so I will
give up the inhabitants of Jerusalem. 7I will set
my face against them; although they escape from
the fire, the fire shall still consume them; and
you shall know that I am the LORD, when I set
my face against them. 8And I will make the land
desolate, because they have acted faithlessly, says
the Lord GOD.

16 The word of the LORD came to me:
2Mortal, make known to Jerusalem her
abominations, 3and say, Thus says the Lord GOD
to Jerusalem: Your origin and your birth were in
the land of the Canaanites; your father was an
Amorite, and your mother a Hittite. 4As for your
birth, on the day you were born your navel cord
was not cut, nor were you washed with water to
cleanse you, nor rubbed with salt, nor wrapped
in cloths. 5No eye pitied you, to do any of these
things for you out of compassion for you; but you
were thrown out in the open field, for you were
abhorred on the day you were born.

6 I passed by you, and saw you flailing about
in your blood. As you lay in your blood, I said
to you, "Live! 7and grow up[a] like a plant of the
field." You grew up and became tall and arrived
at full womanhood;[b] your breasts were formed,
and your hair had grown; yet you were naked and
bare.

8 I passed by you again and looked on you;
you were at the age for love. I spread the edge
of my cloak over you, and covered your nakedness: I pledged myself to you and entered into a
covenant with you, says the Lord GOD, and you
became mine. 9Then I bathed you with water and
washed off the blood from you, and anointed you
with oil. 10I clothed you with embroidered cloth
and with sandals of fine leather; I bound you in
fine linen and covered you with rich fabric.[c] 11I
adorned you with ornaments: I put bracelets
on your arms, a chain on your neck, 12a ring on
your nose, earrings in your ears, and a beautiful crown upon your head. 13You were adorned
with gold and silver, while your clothing was of
fine linen, rich fabric,[c] and embroidered cloth.
You had choice flour and honey and oil for food.
You grew exceedingly beautiful, fit to be a queen.
14Your fame spread among the nations on account of your beauty, for it was perfect because
of my splendor that I had bestowed on you, says
the Lord GOD.

Ezekiel 16

Chapters 16 and 24 in Ezekiel are among the most explicitly sexually violent texts in the Scriptures. In both passages God disciplines wicked women who represent Jerusalem (and Samaria) by sexually humiliating them—publicly stripping them—and leaving them vulnerable to sexual assault. Ironically, the rhetorical strategy underlying the text is to shame and humiliate the male leadership of Jerusalem by verbally emasculating them. The prophet is making those men experience the lot of Iron Age women. To be clear, the prophet does not condemn the physical or sexual abuse of women. He accepts it as normative.
Texts like these leave readers with a number of questions, perhaps chief among them: Do violent texts like these reveal divine or human misogyny?

— *WG*

15 But you trusted in your beauty, and played
the whore because of your fame, and lavished your
whorings on any passer-by.[d] 16You took some of
your garments, and made for yourself colorful
shrines, and on them played the whore; nothing
like this has ever been or ever shall be.[c] 17You also
took your beautiful jewels of my gold and my silver that I had given you, and made for yourself
male images, and with them played the whore;

[a] Gk Syr: Heb *Live! I made you a myriad* [b] Cn: Heb *ornament of ornaments* [c] Meaning of Heb uncertain
[d] Heb adds *let it be his*

18and you took your embroidered garments to
cover them, and set my oil and my incense before
them. 19Also my bread that I gave you—I fed you
with choice flour and oil and honey—you set it
before them as a pleasing odor; and so it was, says
the Lord God. 20You took your sons and your
daughters, whom you had borne to me, and these
you sacrificed to them to be devoured. As if your
whorings were not enough! 21You slaughtered
my children and delivered them up as an offering to them. 22And in all your abominations and
your whorings you did not remember the days of
your youth, when you were naked and bare, flailing about in your blood.

23 After all your wickedness (woe, woe to
you! says the Lord God), 24you built yourself a
platform and made yourself a lofty place in every
square; 25at the head of every street you built your
lofty place and prostituted your beauty, offering
yourself to every passer-by, and multiplying your
whoring. 26You played the whore with the Egyptians, your lustful neighbors, multiplying your
whoring, to provoke me to anger. 27Therefore I
stretched out my hand against you, reduced your
rations, and gave you up to the will of your enemies, the daughters of the Philistines, who were
ashamed of your lewd behavior. 28You played the
whore with the Assyrians, because you were insatiable; you played the whore with them, and
still you were not satisfied. 29You multiplied your
whoring with Chaldea, the land of merchants;
and even with this you were not satisfied.

30 How sick is your heart, says the Lord God,
that you did all these things, the deeds of a brazen
whore; 31building your platform at the head of
every street, and making your lofty place in every
square! Yet you were not like a whore, because
you scorned payment. 32Adulterous wife, who
receives strangers instead of her husband! 33Gifts
are given to all whores; but you gave your gifts
to all your lovers, bribing them to come to you
from all around for your whorings. 34So you were
different from other women in your whorings: no
one solicited you to play the whore; and you gave
payment, while no payment was given to you;
you were different.

35 Therefore, O whore, hear the word of the
Lord: 36Thus says the Lord God, Because your
lust was poured out and your nakedness uncovered in your whoring with your lovers, and because of all your abominable idols, and because of
the blood of your children that you gave to them,
37therefore, I will gather all your lovers, with
whom you took pleasure, all those you loved and
all those you hated; I will gather them against you
from all around, and will uncover your nakedness
to them, so that they may see all your nakedness.
38I will judge you as women who commit adultery and shed blood are judged, and bring blood
upon you in wrath and jealousy. 39I will deliver
you into their hands, and they shall throw down
your platform and break down your lofty places;
they shall strip you of your clothes and take your
beautiful objects and leave you naked and bare.
40They shall bring up a mob against you, and
they shall stone you and cut you to pieces with
their swords. 41They shall burn your houses and
execute judgments on you in the sight of many
women; I will stop you from playing the whore,
and you shall also make no more payments. 42So I
will satisfy my fury on you, and my jealousy shall
turn away from you; I will be calm, and will be
angry no longer. 43Because you have not remembered the days of your youth, but have enraged me
with all these things; therefore, I have returned
your deeds upon your head, says the Lord God.

Have you not committed lewdness beyond
all your abominations? 44See, everyone who uses
proverbs will use this proverb about you, "Like
mother, like daughter." 45You are the daughter of
your mother, who loathed her husband and her
children; and you are the sister of your sisters,
who loathed their husbands and their children.
Your mother was a Hittite and your father an
Amorite. 46Your elder sister is Samaria, who lived
with her daughters to the north of you; and your
younger sister, who lived to the south of you, is
Sodom with her daughters. 47You not only followed their ways, and acted according to their
abominations; within a very little time you were
more corrupt than they in all your ways. 48As I
live, says the Lord God, your sister Sodom and
her daughters have not done as you and your
daughters have done. 49This was the guilt of your

sister Sodom: she and her daughters had pride,
excess of food, and prosperous ease, but did not
aid the poor and needy. 50They were haughty,
and did abominable things before me; therefore
I removed them when I saw it. 51Samaria has not
committed half your sins; you have committed
more abominations than they, and have made
your sisters appear righteous by all the abominations that you have committed. 52Bear your disgrace, you also, for you have brought about for
your sisters a more favorable judgment; because
of your sins in which you acted more abominably
than they, they are more in the right than you. So
be ashamed, you also, and bear your disgrace, for
you have made your sisters appear righteous.

53 I will restore their fortunes, the fortunes
of Sodom and her daughters and the fortunes
of Samaria and her daughters, and I will restore
your own fortunes along with theirs, 54in order
that you may bear your disgrace and be ashamed
of all that you have done, becoming a consolation to them. 55As for your sisters, Sodom and
her daughters shall return to their former state,
Samaria and her daughters shall return to their
former state, and you and your daughters shall
return to your former state. 56Was not your
sister Sodom a byword in your mouth in the
day of your pride, 57before your wickedness
was uncovered? Now you are a mockery to the
daughters of Aram[a] and all her neighbors, and to
the daughters of the Philistines, those all around
who despise you. 58You must bear the penalty
of your lewdness and your abominations, says
the LORD.

59 Yes, thus says the Lord GOD: I will deal
with you as you have done, you who have despised the oath, breaking the covenant; 60yet I
will remember my covenant with you in the days
of your youth, and I will establish with you an
everlasting covenant. 61Then you will remember
your ways, and be ashamed when I[b] take your sisters, both your elder and your younger, and give
them to you as daughters, but not on account of
my[c] covenant with you. 62I will establish my covenant with you, and you shall know that I am the
LORD, 63in order that you may remember and be
confounded, and never open your mouth again
because of your shame, when I forgive you all that
you have done, says the Lord GOD.

17 The word of the LORD came to me:
2O mortal, propound a riddle, and speak
an allegory to the house of Israel. 3Say: Thus says
the Lord GOD:

A great eagle, with great wings and long
    pinions,
  rich in plumage of many colors,
  came to the Lebanon.
He took the top of the cedar,
4 broke off its topmost shoot;
he carried it to a land of trade,
  set it in a city of merchants.
5 Then he took a seed from the land,
  placed it in fertile soil;
a plant[d] by abundant waters,
  he set it like a willow twig.
6 It sprouted and became a vine
  spreading out, but low;
its branches turned toward him,
  its roots remained where it stood.
So it became a vine;
  it brought forth branches,
  put forth foliage.

7 There was another great eagle,
  with great wings and much plumage.
And see! This vine stretched out
  its roots toward him;
it shot out its branches toward him,
  so that he might water it.
From the bed where it was planted
8 it was transplanted
to good soil by abundant waters,
  so that it might produce branches
  and bear fruit
  and become a noble vine.
9Say: Thus says the Lord GOD:
Will it prosper?
Will he not pull up its roots,
  cause its fruit to rot[d] and wither,
  its fresh sprouting leaves to fade?

[a] Another reading is *Edom* [b] Syr: Heb *you* [c] Heb lacks *my* [d] Meaning of Heb uncertain

No strong arm or mighty army will be needed
to pull it from its roots.
10 When it is transplanted, will it thrive?
When the east wind strikes it,
will it not utterly wither,
wither on the bed where it grew?

11 Then the word of the LORD came to me:
12 Say now to the rebellious house: Do you not
know what these things mean? Tell them: The
king of Babylon came to Jerusalem, took its king
and its officials, and brought them back with him
to Babylon. 13 He took one of the royal offspring
and made a covenant with him, putting him under oath (he had taken away the chief men of the
land), 14 so that the kingdom might be humble and
not lift itself up, and that by keeping his covenant
it might stand. 15 But he rebelled against him by
sending ambassadors to Egypt, in order that they
might give him horses and a large army. Will he
succeed? Can one escape who does such things?
Can he break the covenant and yet escape? 16 As I
live, says the Lord GOD, surely in the place where
the king resides who made him king, whose oath
he despised, and whose covenant with him he
broke—in Babylon he shall die. 17 Pharaoh with
his mighty army and great company will not help
him in war, when ramps are cast up and siege walls
built to cut off many lives. 18 Because he despised
the oath and broke the covenant, because he gave
his hand and yet did all these things, he shall not
escape. 19 Therefore thus says the Lord GOD: As
I live, I will surely return upon his head my oath
that he despised, and my covenant that he broke.
20 I will spread my net over him, and he shall be
caught in my snare; I will bring him to Babylon
and enter into judgment with him there for the
treason he has committed against me. 21 All the
pick[a] of his troops shall fall by the sword, and
the survivors shall be scattered to every wind; and
you shall know that I, the LORD, have spoken.

22 Thus says the Lord GOD:
I myself will take a sprig
from the lofty top of a cedar;
I will set it out.
I will break off a tender one
from the topmost of its young twigs;
I myself will plant it
on a high and lofty mountain.
23 On the mountain height of Israel
I will plant it,
in order that it may produce boughs and bear
fruit,
and become a noble cedar.
Under it every kind of bird will live;
in the shade of its branches will nest
winged creatures of every kind.
24 All the trees of the field shall know
that I am the LORD.
I bring low the high tree,
I make high the low tree;
I dry up the green tree
and make the dry tree flourish.
I the LORD have spoken;
I will accomplish it.

18 The word of the LORD came to me: 2 What
do you mean by repeating this proverb
concerning the land of Israel, "The parents have
eaten sour grapes, and the children's teeth are set
on edge"? 3 As I live, says the Lord GOD, this proverb shall no more be used by you in Israel. 4 Know
that all lives are mine; the life of the parent as well
as the life of the child is mine: it is only the person
who sins that shall die.

5 If a man is righteous and does what is lawful
and right— 6 if he does not eat upon the mountains or lift up his eyes to the idols of the house
of Israel, does not defile his neighbor's wife or
approach a woman during her menstrual period,
7 does not oppress anyone, but restores to the
debtor his pledge, commits no robbery, gives his
bread to the hungry and covers the naked with
a garment, 8 does not take advance or accrued
interest, withholds his hand from iniquity, executes true justice between contending parties,
9 follows my statutes, and is careful to observe my
ordinances, acting faithfully—such a one is righteous; he shall surely live, says the Lord GOD.

10 If he has a son who is violent, a shedder
of blood, 11 who does any of these things (though
his father[b] does none of them), who eats upon

[a] Another reading is *fugitives* [b] Heb *he*

the mountains, defiles his neighbor's wife, 12 oppresses the poor and needy, commits robbery,
does not restore the pledge, lifts up his eyes to the
idols, commits abomination, 13 takes advance or
accrued interest; shall he then live? He shall not.
He has done all these abominable things; he shall
surely die; his blood shall be upon himself.

14 But if this man has a son who sees all
the sins that his father has done, considers, and
does not do likewise, 15 who does not eat upon
the mountains or lift up his eyes to the idols of
the house of Israel, does not defile his neighbor's wife, 16 does not wrong anyone, exacts no
pledge, commits no robbery, but gives his bread
to the hungry and covers the naked with a garment, 17 withholds his hand from iniquity,[a] takes
no advance or accrued interest, observes my ordinances, and follows my statutes; he shall not
die for his father's iniquity; he shall surely live.
18 As for his father, because he practiced extortion, robbed his brother, and did what is not good
among his people, he dies for his iniquity.

19 Yet you say, "Why should not the son suffer for the iniquity of the father?" When the son
has done what is lawful and right, and has been
careful to observe all my statutes, he shall surely
live. 20 The person who sins shall die. A child shall
not suffer for the iniquity of a parent, nor a parent
suffer for the iniquity of a child; the righteousness
of the righteous shall be his own, and the wickedness of the wicked shall be his own.

21 But if the wicked turn away from all their
sins that they have committed and keep all my
statutes and do what is lawful and right, they
shall surely live; they shall not die. 22 None of the
transgressions that they have committed shall be
remembered against them; for the righteousness
that they have done they shall live. 23 Have I any
pleasure in the death of the wicked, says the Lord
GOD, and not rather that they should turn from
their ways and live? 24 But when the righteous
turn away from their righteousness and commit
iniquity and do the same abominable things that
the wicked do, shall they live? None of the righteous deeds that they have done shall be remembered; for the treachery of which they are guilty
and the sin they have committed, they shall die.

25 Yet you say, "The way of the Lord is unfair." Hear now, O house of Israel: Is my way unfair? Is it not your ways that are unfair? 26 When
the righteous turn away from their righteousness
and commit iniquity, they shall die for it; for the
iniquity that they have committed they shall die.
27 Again, when the wicked turn away from the
wickedness they have committed and do what is
lawful and right, they shall save their life. 28 Because they considered and turned away from
all the transgressions that they had committed,
they shall surely live; they shall not die. 29 Yet the
house of Israel says, "The way of the Lord is unfair." O house of Israel, are my ways unfair? Is it
not your ways that are unfair?

30 Therefore I will judge you, O house of Israel, all of you according to your ways, says the
Lord GOD. Repent and turn from all your transgressions; otherwise iniquity will be your ruin.[b]
31 Cast away from you all the transgressions that
you have committed against me, and get yourselves a new heart and a new spirit! Why will you
die, O house of Israel? 32 For I have no pleasure
in the death of anyone, says the Lord GOD. Turn,
then, and live.

19 As for you, raise up a lamentation for the
princes of Israel, 2 and say:

What a lioness was your mother
among lions!
She lay down among young lions,
rearing her cubs.
3 She raised up one of her cubs;
he became a young lion,
and he learned to catch prey;
he devoured humans.
4 The nations sounded an alarm against him;
he was caught in their pit;
and they brought him with hooks
to the land of Egypt.
5 When she saw that she was thwarted,
that her hope was lost,
she took another of her cubs
and made him a young lion.

[a] Gk: Heb *the poor* [b] Or *so that they shall not be a stumbling block of iniquity to you*

6 He prowled among the lions;
he became a young lion,
and he learned to catch prey;
he devoured people.
7 And he ravaged their strongholds,[a]
and laid waste their towns;
the land was appalled, and all in it,
at the sound of his roaring.
8 The nations set upon him
from the provinces all around;
they spread their net over him;
he was caught in their pit.
9 With hooks they put him in a cage,
and brought him to the king of Babylon;
they brought him into custody,
so that his voice should be heard no more
on the mountains of Israel.
10 Your mother was like a vine in a vineyard[b]
transplanted by the water,
fruitful and full of branches
from abundant water.
11 Its strongest stem became
a ruler's scepter;[c]
it towered aloft
among the thick boughs;
it stood out in its height
with its mass of branches.
12 But it was plucked up in fury,
cast down to the ground;
the east wind dried it up;
its fruit was stripped off,
its strong stem was withered;
the fire consumed it.
13 Now it is transplanted into the wilderness,
into a dry and thirsty land.
14 And fire has gone out from its stem,
has consumed its branches and fruit,
so that there remains in it no strong stem,
no scepter for ruling.

This is a lamentation, and it is used as a lamentation.

20 In the seventh year, in the fifth month, on
the tenth day of the month, certain elders
of Israel came to consult the LORD, and sat down
before me. 2And the word of the LORD came to
me: 3Mortal, speak to the elders of Israel, and say
to them: Thus says the Lord GOD: Why are you
coming? To consult me? As I live, says the Lord
GOD, I will not be consulted by you. 4Will you
judge them, mortal, will you judge them? Then
let them know the abominations of their ancestors, 5and say to them: Thus says the Lord GOD:
On the day when I chose Israel, I swore to the
offspring of the house of Jacob—making myself
known to them in the land of Egypt—I swore
to them, saying, I am the LORD your God. 6On
that day I swore to them that I would bring them
out of the land of Egypt into a land that I had
searched out for them, a land flowing with milk
and honey, the most glorious of all lands. 7And
I said to them, Cast away the detestable things
your eyes feast on, every one of you, and do not
defile yourselves with the idols of Egypt; I am the
LORD your God. 8But they rebelled against me
and would not listen to me; not one of them cast
away the detestable things their eyes feasted on,
nor did they forsake the idols of Egypt.

Then I thought I would pour out my wrath
upon them and spend my anger against them in
the midst of the land of Egypt. 9But I acted for
the sake of my name, that it should not be profaned in the sight of the nations among whom
they lived, in whose sight I made myself known to
them in bringing them out of the land of Egypt.
10So I led them out of the land of Egypt and
brought them into the wilderness. 11I gave them
my statutes and showed them my ordinances, by
whose observance everyone shall live. 12Moreover I gave them my sabbaths, as a sign between
me and them, so that they might know that I the
LORD sanctify them. 13But the house of Israel rebelled against me in the wilderness; they did not
observe my statutes but rejected my ordinances,
by whose observance everyone shall live; and my
sabbaths they greatly profaned.

Then I thought I would pour out my wrath
upon them in the wilderness, to make an end of
them. 14But I acted for the sake of my name, so
that it should not be profaned in the sight of the

[a] Heb *his widows* [b] Cn: Heb *in your blood* [c] Heb *Its strongest stems became rulers' scepters*

nations, in whose sight I had brought them out. 15 Moreover I swore to them in the wilderness that I would not bring them into the land that I had given them, a land flowing with milk and honey, the most glorious of all lands, 16 because they rejected my ordinances and did not observe my statutes, and profaned my sabbaths; for their heart went after their idols. 17 Nevertheless my eye spared them, and I did not destroy them or make an end of them in the wilderness.

18 I said to their children in the wilderness, Do not follow the statutes of your parents, nor observe their ordinances, nor defile yourselves with their idols. 19 I the LORD am your God; follow my statutes, and be careful to observe my ordinances, 20 and hallow my sabbaths that they may be a sign between me and you, so that you may know that I the LORD am your God. 21 But the children rebelled against me; they did not follow my statutes, and were not careful to observe my ordinances, by whose observance everyone shall live; they profaned my sabbaths.

Then I thought I would pour out my wrath upon them and spend my anger against them in the wilderness. 22 But I withheld my hand, and acted for the sake of my name, so that it should not be profaned in the sight of the nations, in whose sight I had brought them out. 23 Moreover I swore to them in the wilderness that I would scatter them among the nations and disperse them through the countries, 24 because they had not executed my ordinances, but had rejected my statutes and profaned my sabbaths, and their eyes were set on their ancestors' idols. 25 Moreover I gave them statutes that were not good and ordinances by which they could not live. 26 I defiled them through their very gifts, in their offering up all their firstborn, in order that I might horrify them, so that they might know that I am the LORD.

27 Therefore, mortal, speak to the house of Israel and say to them, Thus says the Lord GOD: In this again your ancestors blasphemed me, by dealing treacherously with me. 28 For when I had brought them into the land that I swore to give them, then wherever they saw any high hill or any leafy tree, there they offered their sacrifices and presented the provocation of their offering; there they sent up their pleasing odors, and there they poured out their drink offerings. 29 (I said to them, What is the high place to which you go? So it is called Bamah[a] to this day.) 30 Therefore say to the house of Israel, Thus says the Lord GOD: Will you defile yourselves after the manner of your ancestors and go astray after their detestable things? 31 When you offer your gifts and make your children pass through the fire, you defile yourselves with all your idols to this day. And shall I be consulted by you, O house of Israel? As I live, says the Lord GOD, I will not be consulted by you.

32 What is in your mind shall never happen—the thought, "Let us be like the nations, like the tribes of the countries, and worship wood and stone."

33 As I live, says the Lord GOD, surely with a mighty hand and an outstretched arm, and with wrath poured out, I will be king over you. 34 I will bring you out from the peoples and gather you out of the countries where you are scattered, with a mighty hand and an outstretched arm, and with wrath poured out; 35 and I will bring you into the wilderness of the peoples, and there I will enter into judgment with you face to face. 36 As I entered into judgment with your ancestors in the wilderness of the land of Egypt, so I will enter into judgment with you, says the Lord GOD. 37 I will make you pass under the staff, and will bring you within the bond of the covenant. 38 I will purge out the rebels among you, and those who transgress against me; I will bring them out of the land where they reside as aliens, but they shall not enter the land of Israel. Then you shall know that I am the LORD.

39 As for you, O house of Israel, thus says the Lord GOD: Go serve your idols, every one of you now and hereafter, if you will not listen to me; but my holy name you shall no more profane with your gifts and your idols.

40 For on my holy mountain, the mountain height of Israel, says the Lord GOD, there all the house of Israel, all of them, shall serve me in the

[a] That is *High Place*

land; there I will accept them, and there I will require your contributions and the choicest of your
gifts, with all your sacred things. 41As a pleasing
odor I will accept you, when I bring you out from
the peoples, and gather you out of the countries
where you have been scattered; and I will manifest my holiness among you in the sight of the
nations. 42You shall know that I am the LORD,
when I bring you into the land of Israel, the country that I swore to give to your ancestors. 43There
you shall remember your ways and all the deeds
by which you have polluted yourselves; and you
shall loathe yourselves for all the evils that you
have committed. 44And you shall know that I am
the LORD, when I deal with you for my name's
sake, not according to your evil ways, or corrupt
deeds, O house of Israel, says the Lord GOD.

45[a] The word of the LORD came to me:
46Mortal, set your face toward the south, preach
against the south, and prophesy against the forest land in the Negeb; 47say to the forest of the
Negeb, Hear the word of the LORD: Thus says the
Lord GOD, I will kindle a fire in you, and it shall
devour every green tree in you and every dry tree;
the blazing flame shall not be quenched, and all
faces from south to north shall be scorched by it.
48All flesh shall see that I the LORD have kindled
it; it shall not be quenched. 49Then I said, "Ah
Lord GOD! they are saying of me, 'Is he not a
maker of allegories?' "

21 [b] The word of the LORD came to me:
2Mortal, set your face toward Jerusalem
and preach against the sanctuaries; prophesy
against the land of Israel 3and say to the land of
Israel, Thus says the LORD: I am coming against
you, and will draw my sword out of its sheath, and
will cut off from you both righteous and wicked.
4Because I will cut off from you both righteous
and wicked, therefore my sword shall go out of
its sheath against all flesh from south to north;
5and all flesh shall know that I the LORD have
drawn my sword out of its sheath; it shall not be
sheathed again. 6Moan therefore, mortal; moan
with breaking heart and bitter grief before their
eyes. 7And when they say to you, "Why do you
moan?" you shall say, "Because of the news that
has come. Every heart will melt and all hands will
be feeble, every spirit will faint and all knees will
turn to water. See, it comes and it will be fulfilled,"
says the Lord GOD.

8 And the word of the LORD came to me:
9Mortal, prophesy and say: Thus says the Lord;
Say:

A sword, a sword is sharpened,
  it is also polished;
10 it is sharpened for slaughter,
  honed to flash like lightning!
How can we make merry?
  You have despised the rod,
  and all discipline.[c]
11 The sword[d] is given to be polished,
  to be grasped in the hand;
it is sharpened, the sword is polished,
  to be placed in the slayer's hand.
12 Cry and wail, O mortal,
  for it is against my people;
it is against all Israel's princes;
  they are thrown to the sword,
  together with my people.
  Ah! Strike the thigh!
13For consider: What! If you despise the rod, will
it not happen?[c] says the Lord GOD.
14 And you, mortal, prophesy;
  strike hand to hand.
Let the sword fall twice, thrice;
  it is a sword for killing.
A sword for great slaughter—
  it surrounds them;
15 therefore hearts melt
  and many stumble.
At all their gates I have set
  the point[c] of the sword.
Ah! It is made for flashing,
  it is polished[e] for slaughter.
16 Attack to the right!
  Engage to the left!
  —wherever your edge is directed.
17 I too will strike hand to hand,
  I will satisfy my fury;
  I the LORD have spoken.

[a] Ch 21.1 in Heb [b] Ch 21.6 in Heb [c] Meaning of Heb uncertain [d] Heb *It* [e] Tg: Heb *wrapped up*

18 The word of the LORD came to me:
19 Mortal, mark out two roads for the sword of the
king of Babylon to come; both of them shall issue
from the same land. And make a signpost, make
it for a fork in the road leading to a city; 20 mark
out the road for the sword to come to Rabbah of
the Ammonites or to Judah and to[a] Jerusalem the
fortified. 21 For the king of Babylon stands at the
parting of the way, at the fork in the two roads, to
use divination; he shakes the arrows, he consults
the teraphim,[b] he inspects the liver. 22 Into his
right hand comes the lot for Jerusalem, to set battering rams, to call out for slaughter, for raising the
battle cry, to set battering rams against the gates,
to cast up ramps, to build siege towers. 23 But to
them it will seem like a false divination; they have
sworn solemn oaths; but he brings their guilt to
remembrance, bringing about their capture.

24 Therefore thus says the Lord GOD: Because you have brought your guilt to remembrance, in that your transgressions are uncovered,
so that in all your deeds your sins appear—because you have come to remembrance, you shall
be taken in hand.[c]

25 As for you, vile, wicked prince of Israel,
you whose day has come,
the time of final punishment,
26 thus says the Lord GOD:
Remove the turban, take off the crown;
things shall not remain as they are.
Exalt that which is low,
abase that which is high.
27 A ruin, a ruin, a ruin—
I will make it!
(Such has never occurred.)
Until he comes whose right it is;
to him I will give it.

28 As for you, mortal, prophesy, and say,
Thus says the Lord GOD concerning the Ammonites, and concerning their reproach; say:

A sword, a sword! Drawn for slaughter,
polished to consume,[d] to flash like
lightning.
29 Offering false visions for you,
divining lies for you,
they place you over the necks
of the vile, wicked ones—
those whose day has come,
the time of final punishment.
30 Return it to its sheath!
In the place where you were created,
in the land of your origin,
I will judge you.
31 I will pour out my indignation upon you,
with the fire of my wrath
I will blow upon you.
I will deliver you into brutish hands,
those skillful to destroy.
32 You shall be fuel for the fire,
your blood shall enter the earth;
you shall be remembered no more,
for I the LORD have spoken.

22 The word of the LORD came to me: 2 You,
mortal, will you judge, will you judge the
bloody city? Then declare to it all its abominable
deeds. 3 You shall say, Thus says the Lord GOD:
A city! Shedding blood within itself; its time has
come; making its idols, defiling itself. 4 You have
become guilty by the blood that you have shed,
and defiled by the idols that you have made; you
have brought your day near, the appointed time
of your years has come. Therefore I have made
you a disgrace before the nations, and a mockery to all the countries. 5 Those who are near and
those who are far from you will mock you, you
infamous one, full of tumult.

6 The princes of Israel in you, everyone according to his power, have been bent on shedding blood. 7 Father and mother are treated with
contempt in you; the alien residing within you
suffers extortion; the orphan and the widow are
wronged in you. 8 You have despised my holy
things, and profaned my sabbaths. 9 In you are
those who slander to shed blood, those in you
who eat upon the mountains, who commit lewdness in your midst. 10 In you they uncover their
fathers' nakedness; in you they violate women in
their menstrual periods. 11 One commits abomination with his neighbor's wife; another lewdly
defiles his daughter-in-law; another in you defiles

[a] Gk Syr: Heb *Judah in* [b] Or *the household gods* [c] Or *be taken captive* [d] Cn: Heb *to contain*

his sister, his father's daughter. 12In you, they take
bribes to shed blood; you take both advance interest and accrued interest, and make gain of your
neighbors by extortion; and you have forgotten
me, says the Lord GOD.

13 See, I strike my hands together at the
dishonest gain you have made, and at the blood
that has been shed within you. 14Can your courage endure, or can your hands remain strong in
the days when I shall deal with you? I the LORD
have spoken, and I will do it. 15I will scatter you
among the nations and disperse you through the
countries, and I will purge your filthiness out of
you. 16And I[a] shall be profaned through you in
the sight of the nations; and you shall know that
I am the LORD.

17 The word of the LORD came to me: 18Mor-
tal, the house of Israel has become dross to me; all
of them, silver,[b] bronze, tin, iron, and lead. In the
smelter they have become dross. 19Therefore thus
says the Lord GOD: Because you have all become
dross, I will gather you into the midst of Jerusalem. 20As one gathers silver, bronze, iron, lead,
and tin into a smelter, to blow the fire upon them
in order to melt them; so I will gather you in my
anger and in my wrath, and I will put you in and
melt you. 21I will gather you and blow upon you
with the fire of my wrath, and you shall be melted
within it. 22As silver is melted in a smelter, so you
shall be melted in it; and you shall know that I the
LORD have poured out my wrath upon you.

23 The word of the LORD came to me: 24Mor-
tal, say to it: You are a land that is not cleansed,
not rained upon in the day of indignation. 25Its
princes[c] within it are like a roaring lion tearing
the prey; they have devoured human lives; they
have taken treasure and precious things; they have
made many widows within it. 26Its priests have
done violence to my teaching and have profaned
my holy things; they have made no distinction
between the holy and the common, neither have
they taught the difference between the unclean
and the clean, and they have disregarded my sabbaths, so that I am profaned among them. 27Its
officials within it are like wolves tearing the prey,
shedding blood, destroying lives to get dishonest
gain. 28Its prophets have smeared whitewash on
their behalf, seeing false visions and divining lies
for them, saying, "Thus says the Lord GOD," when
the LORD has not spoken. 29The people of the land
have practiced extortion and committed robbery;
they have oppressed the poor and needy, and have
extorted from the alien without redress. 30And I
sought for anyone among them who would repair
the wall and stand in the breach before me on behalf of the land, so that I would not destroy it; but
I found no one. 31Therefore I have poured out my
indignation upon them; I have consumed them
with the fire of my wrath; I have returned their
conduct upon their heads, says the Lord GOD.

23 The word of the LORD came to me: 2Mor-
tal, there were two women, the daughters
of one mother; 3they played the whore in Egypt;
they played the whore in their youth; their breasts
were caressed there, and their virgin bosoms were
fondled. 4Oholah was the name of the elder and
Oholibah the name of her sister. They became
mine, and they bore sons and daughters. As for
their names, Oholah is Samaria, and Oholibah is
Jerusalem.

5 Oholah played the whore while she was
mine; she lusted after her lovers the Assyrians,
warriors[d] 6clothed in blue, governors and commanders, all of them handsome young men,
mounted horsemen. 7She bestowed her favors
upon them, the choicest men of Assyria all of
them; and she defiled herself with all the idols
of everyone for whom she lusted. 8She did not
give up her whorings that she had practiced since
Egypt; for in her youth men had lain with her and
fondled her virgin bosom and poured out their
lust upon her. 9Therefore I delivered her into the
hands of her lovers, into the hands of the Assyrians, for whom she lusted. 10These uncovered her
nakedness; they seized her sons and her daughters; and they killed her with the sword. Judgment was executed upon her, and she became a
byword among women.

[a] Gk Syr Vg: Heb *you* [b] Transposed from the end of the verse; compare verse 20 [c] Gk: Heb *indignation.* [25]*A conspiracy of its prophets* [d] Meaning of Heb uncertain

11 Her sister Oholibah saw this, yet she was
more corrupt than she in her lusting and in her
whorings, which were worse than those of her
sister. 12She lusted after the Assyrians, governors
and commanders, warriors[a] clothed in full armor, mounted horsemen, all of them handsome
young men. 13And I saw that she was defiled;
they both took the same way. 14But she carried
her whorings further; she saw male figures carved
on the wall, images of the Chaldeans portrayed
in vermilion, 15with belts around their waists,
with flowing turbans on their heads, all of them
looking like officers—a picture of Babylonians
whose native land was Chaldea. 16When she saw
them she lusted after them, and sent messengers
to them in Chaldea. 17And the Babylonians came
to her into the bed of love, and they defiled her
with their lust; and after she defiled herself with
them, she turned from them in disgust. 18When
she carried on her whorings so openly and
flaunted her nakedness, I turned in disgust from
her, as I had turned from her sister. 19Yet she increased her whorings, remembering the days of
her youth, when she played the whore in the land
of Egypt 20and lusted after her paramours there,
whose members were like those of donkeys, and
whose emission was like that of stallions. 21Thus
you longed for the lewdness of your youth, when
the Egyptians[b] fondled your bosom and caressed[c]
your young breasts.

22 Therefore, O Oholibah, thus says the Lord
GOD: I will rouse against you your lovers from
whom you turned in disgust, and I will bring
them against you from every side: 23the Babylonians and all the Chaldeans, Pekod and Shoa and
Koa, and all the Assyrians with them, handsome
young men, governors and commanders all of
them, officers and warriors,[d] all of them riding on
horses. 24They shall come against you from the
north[a] with chariots and wagons and a host of
peoples; they shall set themselves against you on
every side with buckler, shield, and helmet, and I
will commit the judgment to them, and they shall
judge you according to their ordinances. 25I will
direct my indignation against you, in order that
they may deal with you in fury. They shall cut off
your nose and your ears, and your survivors shall
fall by the sword. They shall seize your sons and
your daughters, and your survivors shall be devoured by fire. 26They shall also strip you of your
clothes and take away your fine jewels. 27So I will
put an end to your lewdness and your whoring
brought from the land of Egypt; you shall not
long for them, or remember Egypt any more.
28For thus says the Lord GOD: I will deliver you
into the hands of those whom you hate, into the
hands of those from whom you turned in disgust;
29and they shall deal with you in hatred, and take
away all the fruit of your labor, and leave you naked and bare, and the nakedness of your whorings
shall be exposed. Your lewdness and your whorings 30have brought this upon you, because you
played the whore with the nations, and polluted
yourself with their idols. 31You have gone the way
of your sister; therefore I will give her cup into
your hand. 32Thus says the Lord GOD:

You shall drink your sister's cup,
deep and wide;
you shall be scorned and derided,
it holds so much.
33 You shall be filled with drunkenness and
sorrow.
A cup of horror and desolation
is the cup of your sister Samaria;
34 you shall drink it and drain it out,
and gnaw its sherds,
and tear out your breasts;

for I have spoken, says the Lord GOD. 35There-
fore thus says the Lord GOD: Because you have
forgotten me and cast me behind your back,
therefore bear the consequences of your lewdness and whorings.

36 The LORD said to me: Mortal, will you
judge Oholah and Oholibah? Then declare to
them their abominable deeds. 37For they have
committed adultery, and blood is on their hands;
with their idols they have committed adultery;
and they have even offered up to them for food

[a] Meaning of Heb uncertain [b] Two Mss: MT *from Egypt* [c] Cn: Heb *for the sake of*
[d] Compare verses 6 and 12: Heb *officers and called ones*

the children whom they had borne to me. 38More-
over this they have done to me: they have defiled
my sanctuary on the same day and profaned my
sabbaths. 39For when they had slaughtered their
children for their idols, on the same day they
came into my sanctuary to profane it. This is what
they did in my house.

40 They even sent for men to come from far
away, to whom a messenger was sent, and they
came. For them you bathed yourself, painted your
eyes, and decked yourself with ornaments; 41you
sat on a stately couch, with a table spread before it
on which you had placed my incense and my oil.
42The sound of a raucous multitude was around
her, with many of the rabble brought in drunken
from the wilderness; and they put bracelets on
the arms[a] of the women, and beautiful crowns
upon their heads.

43 Then I said, Ah, she is worn out with adulteries, but they carry on their sexual acts with
her. 44For they have gone in to her, as one goes
in to a whore. Thus they went in to Oholah and
to Oholibah, wanton women. 45But righteous
judges shall declare them guilty of adultery and
of bloodshed; because they are adulteresses and
blood is on their hands.

46 For thus says the Lord GOD: Bring up an
assembly against them, and make them an object
of terror and of plunder. 47The assembly shall
stone them and with their swords they shall cut
them down; they shall kill their sons and their
daughters, and burn up their houses. 48Thus will
I put an end to lewdness in the land, so that all
women may take warning and not commit lewdness as you have done. 49They shall repay you for
your lewdness, and you shall bear the penalty for
your sinful idolatry; and you shall know that I am
the Lord GOD.

24 In the ninth year, in the tenth month, on
the tenth day of the month, the word of
the LORD came to me: 2Mortal, write down the
name of this day, this very day. The king of Babylon has laid siege to Jerusalem this very day.
3And utter an allegory to the rebellious house and
say to them, Thus says the Lord GOD:

Set on the pot, set it on,
pour in water also;
4 put in it the pieces,
all the good pieces, the thigh and the
shoulder;
fill it with choice bones.
5 Take the choicest one of the flock,
pile the logs[b] under it;
boil its pieces,[c]
seethe[d] also its bones in it.

6 Therefore thus says the Lord GOD:
Woe to the bloody city,
the pot whose rust is in it,
whose rust has not gone out of it!
Empty it piece by piece,
making no choice at all.[e]
7 For the blood she shed is inside it;
she placed it on a bare rock;
she did not pour it out on the ground,
to cover it with earth.
8 To rouse my wrath, to take vengeance,
I have placed the blood she shed
on a bare rock,
so that it may not be covered.
9Therefore thus says the Lord GOD:
Woe to the bloody city!
I will even make the pile great.
10 Heap up the logs, kindle the fire;
boil the meat well, mix in the spices,
let the bones be burned.
11 Stand it empty upon the coals,
so that it may become hot, its copper glow,
its filth melt in it, its rust be consumed.
12 In vain I have wearied myself;[f]
its thick rust does not depart.
To the fire with its rust![g]
13 Yet, when I cleansed you in your filthy
lewdness,
you did not become clean from your filth;
you shall not again be cleansed
until I have satisfied my fury upon you.
14I the LORD have spoken; the time is coming,

[a] Heb *hands* [b] Compare verse 10: Heb *the bones* [c] Two Mss: Heb *its boilings* [d] Cn: Heb *its bones seethe*
[e] Heb *piece, no lot has fallen on it* [f] Cn: Meaning of Heb uncertain [g] Meaning of Heb uncertain

I will act. I will not refrain, I will not spare, I will
not relent. According to your ways and your doings I will judge you, says the Lord GOD.

15 The word of the LORD came to me: 16Mor-
tal, with one blow I am about to take away from
you the delight of your eyes; yet you shall not
mourn or weep, nor shall your tears run down.
17Sigh, but not aloud; make no mourning for the
dead. Bind on your turban, and put your sandals
on your feet; do not cover your upper lip or eat
the bread of mourners.[a] 18So I spoke to the people
in the morning, and at evening my wife died. And
on the next morning I did as I was commanded.

19 Then the people said to me, "Will you not
tell us what these things mean for us, that you are
acting this way?" 20Then I said to them: The word
of the LORD came to me: 21Say to the house of
Israel, Thus says the Lord GOD: I will profane my
sanctuary, the pride of your power, the delight of
your eyes, and your heart's desire; and your sons
and your daughters whom you left behind shall
fall by the sword. 22And you shall do as I have
done; you shall not cover your upper lip or eat
the bread of mourners.[a] 23Your turbans shall be
on your heads and your sandals on your feet;
you shall not mourn or weep, but you shall pine
away in your iniquities and groan to one another.
24Thus Ezekiel shall be a sign to you; you shall do
just as he has done. When this comes, then you
shall know that I am the Lord GOD.

25 And you, mortal, on the day when I take
from them their stronghold, their joy and glory,
the delight of their eyes and their heart's affection,
and also[b] their sons and their daughters, 26on that
day, one who has escaped will come to you to report to you the news. 27On that day your mouth
shall be opened to the one who has escaped, and
you shall speak and no longer be silent. So you
shall be a sign to them; and they shall know that
I am the LORD.

25 The word of the LORD came to me: 2Mor-
tal, set your face toward the Ammonites
and prophesy against them. 3Say to the Ammonites, Hear the word of the Lord GOD: Thus says
the Lord GOD, Because you said, "Aha!" over my
sanctuary when it was profaned, and over the land
of Israel when it was made desolate, and over the
house of Judah when it went into exile; 4therefore
I am handing you over to the people of the east for
a possession. They shall set their encampments
among you and pitch their tents in your midst;
they shall eat your fruit, and they shall drink your
milk. 5I will make Rabbah a pasture for camels
and Ammon a fold for flocks. Then you shall
know that I am the LORD. 6For thus says the Lord
GOD: Because you have clapped your hands and
stamped your feet and rejoiced with all the malice
within you against the land of Israel, 7therefore I
have stretched out my hand against you, and will
hand you over as plunder to the nations. I will cut
you off from the peoples and will make you perish out of the countries; I will destroy you. Then
you shall know that I am the LORD.

8 Thus says the Lord GOD: Because Moab[c]
said, The house of Judah is like all the other nations, 9therefore I will lay open the flank of Moab
from the towns[d] on its frontier, the glory of the
country, Beth-jeshimoth, Baal-meon, and Kiriathaim. 10I will give it along with Ammon to the
people of the east as a possession. Thus Ammon
shall be remembered no more among the nations,
11and I will execute judgments upon Moab. Then
they shall know that I am the LORD.

12 Thus says the Lord GOD: Because Edom
acted revengefully against the house of Judah
and has grievously offended in taking vengeance
upon them, 13therefore thus says the Lord GOD,
I will stretch out my hand against Edom, and cut
off from it humans and animals, and I will make
it desolate; from Teman even to Dedan they shall
fall by the sword. 14I will lay my vengeance upon
Edom by the hand of my people Israel; and they
shall act in Edom according to my anger and according to my wrath; and they shall know my
vengeance, says the Lord GOD.

15 Thus says the Lord GOD: Because with
unending hostilities the Philistines acted in vengeance, and with malice of heart took revenge in
destruction; 16therefore thus says the Lord GOD,

[a] Vg Tg: Heb *of men* [b] Heb lacks *and also* [c] Gk Old Latin: Heb *Moab and Seir* [d] Heb *towns from its towns*

I will stretch out my hand against the Philistines, cut off the Cherethites, and destroy the rest of the seacoast. 17 I will execute great vengeance on them with wrathful punishments. Then they shall know that I am the LORD, when I lay my vengeance on them.

26 In the eleventh year, on the first day of the month, the word of the LORD came to me: 2 Mortal, because Tyre said concerning Jerusalem,

"Aha, broken is the gateway of the peoples;
it has swung open to me;
I shall be replenished,
now that it is wasted,"
3 therefore, thus says the Lord GOD:
See, I am against you, O Tyre!
I will hurl many nations against you,
as the sea hurls its waves.
4 They shall destroy the walls of Tyre
and break down its towers.
I will scrape its soil from it
and make it a bare rock.
5 It shall become, in the midst of the sea,
a place for spreading nets.
I have spoken, says the Lord GOD.
It shall become plunder for the nations,
6 and its daughter-towns in the country
shall be killed by the sword.
Then they shall know that I am the LORD.

7 For thus says the Lord GOD: I will bring
against Tyre from the north King Nebuchadrezzar of Babylon, king of kings, together with
horses, chariots, cavalry, and a great and powerful
army.

8 Your daughter-towns in the country
he shall put to the sword.
He shall set up a siege wall against you,
cast up a ramp against you,
and raise a roof of shields against you.
9 He shall direct the shock of his battering rams
against your walls
and break down your towers with his axes.
10 His horses shall be so many
that their dust shall cover you.
At the noise of cavalry, wheels, and chariots
your very walls shall shake,
when he enters your gates
like those entering a breached city.
11 With the hoofs of his horses
he shall trample all your streets.
He shall put your people to the sword,
and your strong pillars shall fall to the ground.
12 They will plunder your riches
and loot your merchandise;
they shall break down your walls
and destroy your fine houses.
Your stones and timber and soil
they shall cast into the water.
13 I will silence the music of your songs;
the sound of your lyres shall be heard no more.
14 I will make you a bare rock;
you shall be a place for spreading nets.
You shall never again be rebuilt,
for I the LORD have spoken,
says the Lord GOD.

15 Thus says the Lord GOD to Tyre: Shall
not the coastlands shake at the sound of your fall,
when the wounded groan, when slaughter goes
on within you? 16 Then all the princes of the sea
shall step down from their thrones; they shall remove their robes and strip off their embroidered
garments. They shall clothe themselves with
trembling, and shall sit on the ground; they shall
tremble every moment, and be appalled at you.
17 And they shall raise a lamentation over you,
and say to you:

How you have vanished[a] from the seas,
O city renowned,
once mighty on the sea,
you and your inhabitants,[b]
who imposed your[c] terror
on all the mainland![d]
18 Now the coastlands tremble
on the day of your fall;
the coastlands by the sea
are dismayed at your passing.

[a] Gk OL Aquila: Heb *have vanished, O inhabited one,* [b] Heb *it and its inhabitants* [c] Heb *their*
[d] Cn: Heb *its inhabitants*

19 For thus says the Lord GOD: When I make
you a city laid waste, like cities that are not inhabited, when I bring up the deep over you, and the
great waters cover you, 20 then I will thrust you
down with those who descend into the Pit, to the
people of long ago, and I will make you live in the
world below, among primeval ruins, with those
who go down to the Pit, so that you will not be
inhabited or have a place[a] in the land of the living.
21 I will bring you to a dreadful end, and you shall
be no more; though sought for, you will never be
found again, says the Lord GOD.

27 The word of the LORD came to me: 2 Now
you, mortal, raise a lamentation over Tyre,
3 and say to Tyre, which sits at the entrance to the
sea, merchant of the peoples on many coastlands,
Thus says the Lord GOD:

O Tyre, you have said,
"I am perfect in beauty."
4 Your borders are in the heart of the seas;
your builders made perfect your beauty.
5 They made all your planks
of fir trees from Senir;
they took a cedar from Lebanon
to make a mast for you.
6 From oaks of Bashan
they made your oars;
they made your deck of pines[b]
from the coasts of Cyprus,
inlaid with ivory.
7 Of fine embroidered linen from Egypt
was your sail,
serving as your ensign;
blue and purple from the coasts of Elishah
was your awning.
8 The inhabitants of Sidon and Arvad
were your rowers;
skilled men of Zemer[c] were within you,
they were your pilots.
9 The elders of Gebal and its artisans were
within you,
caulking your seams;
all the ships of the sea with their mariners
were within you,
to barter for your wares.
10 Paras[d] and Lud and Put
were in your army,
your mighty warriors;
they hung shield and helmet in you;
they gave you splendor.
11 Men of Arvad and Helech[e]
were on your walls all around;
men of Gamad were at your towers.
They hung their quivers all around your
walls;
they made perfect your beauty.

12 Tarshish did business with you out of the
abundance of your great wealth; silver, iron, tin,
and lead they exchanged for your wares. 13 Javan, Tubal, and Meshech traded with you; they
exchanged human beings and vessels of bronze
for your merchandise. 14 Beth-togarmah exchanged for your wares horses, war horses, and
mules. 15 The Rhodians[f] traded with you; many
coastlands were your own special markets; they
brought you in payment ivory tusks and ebony.
16 Edom[g] did business with you because of your
abundant goods; they exchanged for your wares
turquoise, purple, embroidered work, fine linen,
coral, and rubies. 17 Judah and the land of Israel
traded with you; they exchanged for your merchandise wheat from Minnith, millet,[h] honey, oil,
and balm. 18 Damascus traded with you for your
abundant goods—because of your great wealth
of every kind—wine of Helbon, and white wool.
19 Vedan and Javan from Uzal[h] entered into trade
for your wares; wrought iron, cassia, and sweet
cane were bartered for your merchandise. 20 Dedan traded with you in saddlecloths for riding.
21 Arabia and all the princes of Kedar were your
favored dealers in lambs, rams, and goats; in these
they did business with you. 22 The merchants of
Sheba and Raamah traded with you; they exchanged for your wares the best of all kinds of
spices, and all precious stones, and gold. 23 Haran,
Canneh, Eden, the merchants of Sheba, Asshur,
and Chilmad traded with you. 24 These traded
with you in choice garments, in clothes of blue

[a] Gk: Heb *I will give beauty* [b] Or *boxwood* [c] Cn Compare Gen 10.18: Heb *your skilled men, O Tyre* [d] Or *Persia*
[e] Or *and your army* [f] Gk: Heb *The Dedanites* [g] Another reading is *Aram* [h] Meaning of Heb uncertain

and embroidered work, and in carpets of colored
material, bound with cords and made secure; in
these they traded with you.[a] 25The ships of Tarshish traveled for you in your trade.

So you were filled and heavily laden
in the heart of the seas.
26 Your rowers have brought you
into the high seas.
The east wind has wrecked you
in the heart of the seas.
27 Your riches, your wares, your merchandise,
your mariners and your pilots,
your caulkers, your dealers in merchandise,
and all your warriors within you,
with all the company
that is with you,
sink into the heart of the seas
on the day of your ruin.
28 At the sound of the cry of your pilots
the countryside shakes,
29 and down from their ships
come all that handle the oar.
The mariners and all the pilots of the sea
stand on the shore
30 and wail aloud over you,
and cry bitterly.
They throw dust on their heads
and wallow in ashes;
31 they make themselves bald for you,
and put on sackcloth,
and they weep over you in bitterness of soul,
with bitter mourning.
32 In their wailing they raise a lamentation for
you,
and lament over you:
"Who was ever destroyed[b] like Tyre
in the midst of the sea?
33 When your wares came from the seas,
you satisfied many peoples;
with your abundant wealth and merchandise
you enriched the kings of the earth.
34 Now you are wrecked by the seas,
in the depths of the waters;
your merchandise and all your crew
have sunk with you.
35 All the inhabitants of the coastlands
are appalled at you;
and their kings are horribly afraid,
their faces are convulsed.
36 The merchants among the peoples hiss at
you;
you have come to a dreadful end
and shall be no more forever."

28 The word of the LORD came to me: 2Mor-
tal, say to the prince of Tyre, Thus says
the Lord GOD:

Because your heart is proud
and you have said, "I am a god;
I sit in the seat of the gods,
in the heart of the seas,"
yet you are but a mortal, and no god,
though you compare your mind
with the mind of a god.
3 You are indeed wiser than Daniel;[c]
no secret is hidden from you;
4 by your wisdom and your understanding
you have amassed wealth for yourself,
and have gathered gold and silver
into your treasuries.
5 By your great wisdom in trade
you have increased your wealth,
and your heart has become proud in your
wealth.
6 Therefore thus says the Lord GOD:
Because you compare your mind
with the mind of a god,
7 therefore, I will bring strangers against you,
the most terrible of the nations;
they shall draw their swords against the
beauty of your wisdom
and defile your splendor.
8 They shall thrust you down to the Pit,
and you shall die a violent death
in the heart of the seas.
9 Will you still say, "I am a god,"
in the presence of those who kill you,
though you are but a mortal, and no god,
in the hands of those who wound you?
10 You shall die the death of the uncircumcised
by the hand of foreigners;

[a] Cn: Heb *in your market* [b] Tg Vg: Heb *like silence* [c] Or, as otherwise read, *Danel*

for I have spoken, says the Lord GOD.
11 Moreover the word of the LORD came to
me: 12 Mortal, raise a lamentation over the king of
Tyre, and say to him, Thus says the Lord GOD:
You were the signet of perfection,[a]
full of wisdom and perfect in beauty.
13 You were in Eden, the garden of God;
every precious stone was your covering,
carnelian, chrysolite, and moonstone,
beryl, onyx, and jasper,
sapphire,[b] turquoise, and emerald;
and worked in gold were your settings
and your engravings.[a]
On the day that you were created
they were prepared.
14 With an anointed cherub as guardian I placed
you;[a]
you were on the holy mountain of God;
you walked among the stones of fire.
15 You were blameless in your ways
from the day that you were created,
until iniquity was found in you.
16 In the abundance of your trade
you were filled with violence, and you
sinned;
so I cast you as a profane thing from the
mountain of God,
and the guardian cherub drove you out
from among the stones of fire.
17 Your heart was proud because of your beauty;
you corrupted your wisdom for the sake of
your splendor.
I cast you to the ground;
I exposed you before kings,
to feast their eyes on you.
18 By the multitude of your iniquities,
in the unrighteousness of your trade,
you profaned your sanctuaries.
So I brought out fire from within you;
it consumed you,
and I turned you to ashes on the earth
in the sight of all who saw you.
19 All who know you among the peoples
are appalled at you;
you have come to a dreadful end
and shall be no more forever.
20 The word of the LORD came to me: 21 Mortal, set your face toward Sidon, and prophesy
against it, 22 and say, Thus says the Lord GOD:
I am against you, O Sidon,
and I will gain glory in your midst.
They shall know that I am the LORD
when I execute judgments in it,
and manifest my holiness in it;
23 for I will send pestilence into it,
and bloodshed into its streets;
and the dead shall fall in its midst,
by the sword that is against it on every side.
And they shall know that I am the LORD.
24 The house of Israel shall no longer find a
pricking brier or a piercing thorn among all their
neighbors who have treated them with contempt.
And they shall know that I am the Lord GOD.
25 Thus says the Lord GOD: When I gather
the house of Israel from the peoples among
whom they are scattered, and manifest my holiness in them in the sight of the nations, then they
shall settle on their own soil that I gave to my
servant Jacob. 26 They shall live in safety in it, and
shall build houses and plant vineyards. They shall
live in safety, when I execute judgments upon all
their neighbors who have treated them with contempt. And they shall know that I am the LORD
their God.

29 In the tenth year, in the tenth month, on
the twelfth day of the month, the word
of the LORD came to me: 2 Mortal, set your face
against Pharaoh king of Egypt, and prophesy
against him and against all Egypt; 3 speak, and say,
Thus says the Lord GOD:
I am against you,
Pharaoh king of Egypt,
the great dragon sprawling
in the midst of its channels,
saying, "My Nile is my own;
I made it for myself."
4 I will put hooks in your jaws,
and make the fish of your channels stick to
your scales.
I will draw you up from your channels,

[a] Meaning of Heb uncertain [b] Or *lapis lazuli*

with all the fish of your channels
sticking to your scales.
5 I will fling you into the wilderness,
you and all the fish of your channels;
you shall fall in the open field,
and not be gathered and buried.
To the animals of the earth and to the birds
of the air
I have given you as food.
6 Then all the inhabitants of Egypt shall know
that I am the LORD
because you[a] were a staff of reed
to the house of Israel;
7 when they grasped you with the hand, you
broke,
and tore all their shoulders;
and when they leaned on you, you broke,
and made all their legs unsteady.[b]

8 Therefore, thus says the Lord GOD: I will
bring a sword upon you, and will cut off from you
human being and animal; 9and the land of Egypt
shall be a desolation and a waste. Then they shall
know that I am the LORD.

Because you[c] said, "The Nile is mine, and
I made it," 10therefore, I am against you, and
against your channels, and I will make the land of
Egypt an utter waste and desolation, from Migdol
to Syene, as far as the border of Ethiopia.[d] 11No
human foot shall pass through it, and no animal
foot shall pass through it; it shall be uninhabited forty years. 12I will make the land of Egypt
a desolation among desolated countries; and her
cities shall be a desolation forty years among cities that are laid waste. I will scatter the Egyptians
among the nations, and disperse them among the
countries.

13 Further, thus says the Lord GOD: At the
end of forty years I will gather the Egyptians
from the peoples among whom they were scattered; 14and I will restore the fortunes of Egypt,
and bring them back to the land of Pathros, the
land of their origin; and there they shall be a
lowly kingdom. 15It shall be the most lowly of
the kingdoms, and never again exalt itself above
the nations; and I will make them so small that
they will never again rule over the nations. 16The
Egyptians[e] shall never again be the reliance of
the house of Israel; they will recall their iniquity,
when they turned to them for aid. Then they shall
know that I am the Lord GOD.

17 In the twenty-seventh year, in the first
month, on the first day of the month, the word
of the LORD came to me: 18Mortal, King Nebuchadrezzar of Babylon made his army labor hard
against Tyre; every head was made bald and every
shoulder was rubbed bare; yet neither he nor his
army got anything from Tyre to pay for the labor
that he had expended against it. 19Therefore thus
says the Lord GOD: I will give the land of Egypt
to King Nebuchadrezzar of Babylon; and he shall
carry off its wealth and despoil it and plunder it;
and it shall be the wages for his army. 20I have
given him the land of Egypt as his payment for
which he labored, because they worked for me,
says the Lord GOD.

21 On that day I will cause a horn to sprout
up for the house of Israel, and I will open your
lips among them. Then they shall know that I am
the LORD.

30 The word of the LORD came to me: 2Mor-
tal, prophesy, and say, Thus says the Lord
GOD:

Wail, "Alas for the day!"
3 For a day is near,
the day of the LORD is near;
it will be a day of clouds,
a time of doom[f] for the nations.
4 A sword shall come upon Egypt,
and anguish shall be in Ethiopia,[d]
when the slain fall in Egypt,
and its wealth is carried away,
and its foundations are torn down.

5Ethiopia,[d] and Put, and Lud, and all Arabia, and
Libya,[g] and the people of the allied land[h] shall fall
with them by the sword.

6 Thus says the LORD:
Those who support Egypt shall fall,

[a] Gk Syr Vg: Heb *they* [b] Syr: Heb *stand* [c] Gk Syr Vg: Heb *he* [d] Or *Nubia*; Heb *Cush* [e] Heb *It* [f] Heb lacks *of doom* [g] Compare Gk Syr Vg: Heb *Cub* [h] Meaning of Heb uncertain

and its proud might shall come down;
from Migdol to Syene
they shall fall within it by the sword,
says the Lord GOD.
7 They shall be desolated among other
desolated countries,
and their cities shall lie among cities laid
waste.
8 Then they shall know that I am the LORD,
when I have set fire to Egypt,
and all who help it are broken.

9 On that day, messengers shall go out from
me in ships to terrify the unsuspecting Ethiopians;[a] and anguish shall come upon them on the
day of Egypt's doom;[b] for it is coming!

10 Thus says the Lord GOD:
I will put an end to the hordes of Egypt,
by the hand of King Nebuchadrezzar of
Babylon.
11 He and his people with him, the most terrible
of the nations,
shall be brought in to destroy the land;
and they shall draw their swords against
Egypt,
and fill the land with the slain.
12 I will dry up the channels,
and will sell the land into the hand of
evildoers;
I will bring desolation upon the land and
everything in it
by the hand of foreigners;
I the LORD have spoken.

13 Thus says the Lord GOD:
I will destroy the idols
and put an end to the images in Memphis;
there shall no longer be a prince in the land
of Egypt;
so I will put fear in the land of Egypt.
14 I will make Pathros a desolation,
and will set fire to Zoan,
and will execute acts of judgment on
Thebes.
15 I will pour my wrath upon Pelusium,
the stronghold of Egypt,
and cut off the hordes of Thebes.
16 I will set fire to Egypt;
Pelusium shall be in great agony;
Thebes shall be breached,
and Memphis face adversaries by day.
17 The young men of On and of Pi-beseth shall
fall by the sword;
and the cities themselves[c] shall go into
captivity.
18 At Tehaphnehes the day shall be dark,
when I break there the dominion of Egypt,
and its proud might shall come to an end;
the city[d] shall be covered by a cloud,
and its daughter-towns shall go into
captivity.
19 Thus I will execute acts of judgment on
Egypt.
Then they shall know that I am the LORD.

20 In the eleventh year, in the first month,
on the seventh day of the month, the word of the
LORD came to me: 21 Mortal, I have broken the
arm of Pharaoh king of Egypt; it has not been
bound up for healing or wrapped with a bandage,
so that it may become strong to wield the sword.
22 Therefore thus says the Lord GOD: I am against
Pharaoh king of Egypt, and will break his arms,
both the strong arm and the one that was broken;
and I will make the sword fall from his hand. 23 I
will scatter the Egyptians among the nations,
and disperse them throughout the lands. 24 I will
strengthen the arms of the king of Babylon, and
put my sword in his hand; but I will break the
arms of Pharaoh, and he will groan before him
with the groans of one mortally wounded. 25 I
will strengthen the arms of the king of Babylon,
but the arms of Pharaoh shall fall. And they shall
know that I am the LORD, when I put my sword
into the hand of the king of Babylon. He shall
stretch it out against the land of Egypt, 26 and I
will scatter the Egyptians among the nations and
disperse them throughout the countries. Then
they shall know that I am the LORD.

31 In the eleventh year, in the third month,
on the first day of the month, the word of

[a] Or *Nubians*; Heb *Cush* [b] Heb *the day of Egypt* [c] Heb *and they* [d] Heb *she*

the LORD came to me: 2Mortal, say to Pharaoh
king of Egypt and to his hordes:

Whom are you like in your greatness?
3 Consider Assyria, a cedar of Lebanon,
with fair branches and forest shade,
and of great height,
its top among the clouds.[a]
4 The waters nourished it,
the deep made it grow tall,
making its rivers flow[b]
around the place it was planted,
sending forth its streams
to all the trees of the field.
5 So it towered high
above all the trees of the field;
its boughs grew large
and its branches long,
from abundant water in its shoots.
6 All the birds of the air
made their nests in its boughs;
under its branches all the animals of the field
gave birth to their young;
and in its shade
all great nations lived.
7 It was beautiful in its greatness,
in the length of its branches;
for its roots went down
to abundant water.
8 The cedars in the garden of God could not
rival it,
nor the fir trees equal its boughs;
the plane trees were as nothing
compared with its branches;
no tree in the garden of God
was like it in beauty.
9 I made it beautiful
with its mass of branches,
the envy of all the trees of Eden
that were in the garden of God.

10 Therefore thus says the Lord GOD: Because it[c] towered high and set its top among the
clouds,[a] and its heart was proud of its height, 11I
gave it into the hand of the prince of the nations;
he has dealt with it as its wickedness deserves. I
have cast it out. 12Foreigners from the most terrible of the nations have cut it down and left it. On
the mountains and in all the valleys its branches
have fallen, and its boughs lie broken in all the
watercourses of the land; and all the peoples of
the earth went away from its shade and left it.
13 On its fallen trunk settle
all the birds of the air,
and among its boughs lodge
all the wild animals.
14All this is in order that no trees by the waters
may grow to lofty height or set their tops among
the clouds,[a] and that no trees that drink water
may reach up to them in height.

For all of them are handed over to death,
to the world below;
along with all mortals,
with those who go down to the Pit.

15 Thus says the Lord GOD: On the day it
went down to Sheol I closed the deep over it and
covered it; I restrained its rivers, and its mighty
waters were checked. I clothed Lebanon in gloom
for it, and all the trees of the field fainted because
of it. 16I made the nations quake at the sound of
its fall, when I cast it down to Sheol with those
who go down to the Pit; and all the trees of Eden,
the choice and best of Lebanon, all that were
well watered, were consoled in the world below.
17They also went down to Sheol with it, to those
killed by the sword, along with its allies,[d] those
who lived in its shade among the nations.

18 Which among the trees of Eden was like
you in glory and in greatness? Now you shall be
brought down with the trees of Eden to the world
below; you shall lie among the uncircumcised,
with those who are killed by the sword. This is
Pharaoh and all his horde, says the Lord GOD.

32 In the twelfth year, in the twelfth month,
on the first day of the month, the word of
the LORD came to me: 2Mortal, raise a lamentation over Pharaoh king of Egypt, and say to him:

You consider yourself a lion among the
nations,
but you are like a dragon in the seas;
you thrash about in your streams,
trouble the water with your feet,

[a] Gk: Heb *thick boughs* [b] Gk: Heb *rivers going* [c] Syr Vg: Heb *you* [d] Heb *its arms*

and foul your[a] streams.
3 Thus says the Lord GOD:
In an assembly of many peoples
I will throw my net over you;
and I[b] will haul you up in my dragnet.
4 I will throw you on the ground,
on the open field I will fling you,
and will cause all the birds of the air to settle
on you,
and I will let the wild animals of the whole
earth gorge themselves with you.
5 I will strew your flesh on the mountains,
and fill the valleys with your carcass.[c]
6 I will drench the land with your flowing
blood
up to the mountains,
and the watercourses will be filled with
you.
7 When I blot you out, I will cover the heavens,
and make their stars dark;
I will cover the sun with a cloud,
and the moon shall not give its light.
8 All the shining lights of the heavens
I will darken above you,
and put darkness on your land,
says the Lord GOD.
9 I will trouble the hearts of many peoples,
as I carry you captive[d] among the nations,
into countries you have not known.
10 I will make many peoples appalled at you;
their kings shall shudder because of you.
When I brandish my sword before them,
they shall tremble every moment
for their lives, each one of them,
on the day of your downfall.
11 For thus says the Lord GOD:
The sword of the king of Babylon shall come
against you.
12 I will cause your hordes to fall
by the swords of mighty ones,
all of them most terrible among the
nations.
They shall bring to ruin the pride of Egypt,
and all its hordes shall perish.
13 I will destroy all its livestock
from beside abundant waters;
and no human foot shall trouble them any
more,
nor shall the hoofs of cattle trouble them.
14 Then I will make their waters clear,
and cause their streams to run like oil, says
the Lord GOD.
15 When I make the land of Egypt desolate
and when the land is stripped of all that
fills it,
when I strike down all who live in it,
then they shall know that I am the LORD.
16 This is a lamentation; it shall be chanted.
The women of the nations shall chant it.
Over Egypt and all its hordes they shall
chant it,
says the Lord GOD.

17 In the twelfth year, in the first month,[e] on
the fifteenth day of the month, the word of the
LORD came to me:
18 Mortal, wail over the hordes of Egypt,
and send them down,
with Egypt[f] and the daughters of majestic
nations,
to the world below,
with those who go down to the Pit.
19 "Whom do you surpass in beauty?
Go down! Be laid to rest with the
uncircumcised!"
20 They shall fall among those who are killed by
the sword. Egypt[g] has been handed over to the
sword; carry away both it and its hordes. 21 The
mighty chiefs shall speak of them, with their helpers, out of the midst of Sheol: "They have come
down, they lie still, the uncircumcised, killed by
the sword."

22 Assyria is there, and all its company, their
graves all around it, all of them killed, fallen by
the sword. 23 Their graves are set in the uttermost
parts of the Pit. Its company is all around its grave,
all of them killed, fallen by the sword, who spread
terror in the land of the living.

24 Elam is there, and all its hordes around its

[a] Heb *their* [b] Gk Vg: Heb *they* [c] Symmachus Syr Vg: Heb *your height* [d] Gk: Heb *bring your destruction*
[e] Gk: Heb lacks *in the first month* [f] Heb *it* [g] Heb *It*

grave; all of them killed, fallen by the sword, who
went down uncircumcised into the world below,
who spread terror in the land of the living. They
bear their shame with those who go down to the
Pit. 25 They have made Elam[a] a bed among the
slain with all its hordes, their graves all around it,
all of them uncircumcised, killed by the sword;
for terror of them was spread in the land of the
living, and they bear their shame with those who
go down to the Pit; they are placed among the
slain.

26 Meshech and Tubal are there, and all
their multitude, their graves all around them, all
of them uncircumcised, killed by the sword; for
they spread terror in the land of the living. 27 And
they do not lie with the fallen warriors of long
ago[b] who went down to Sheol with their weapons
of war, whose swords were laid under their heads,
and whose shields[c] are upon their bones; for the
terror of the warriors was in the land of the living. 28 So you shall be broken and lie among the
uncircumcised, with those who are killed by the
sword.

29 Edom is there, its kings and all its princes,
who for all their might are laid with those who are
killed by the sword; they lie with the uncircumcised, with those who go down to the Pit.

30 The princes of the north are there, all of
them, and all the Sidonians, who have gone down
in shame with the slain, for all the terror that they
caused by their might; they lie uncircumcised
with those who are killed by the sword, and bear
their shame with those who go down to the Pit.

31 When Pharaoh sees them, he will be consoled for all his hordes—Pharaoh and all his army,
killed by the sword, says the Lord God. 32 For he[d]
spread terror in the land of the living; therefore
he shall be laid to rest among the uncircumcised,
with those who are slain by the sword—Pharaoh
and all his multitude, says the Lord God.

33 The word of the Lord came to me:
2 O Mortal, speak to your people and say
to them, If I bring the sword upon a land, and
the people of the land take one of their number
as their sentinel; 3 and if the sentinel sees the
sword coming upon the land and blows the trumpet and warns the people; 4 then if any who hear
the sound of the trumpet do not take warning,
and the sword comes and takes them away, their
blood shall be upon their own heads. 5 They heard
the sound of the trumpet and did not take warning; their blood shall be upon themselves. But if
they had taken warning, they would have saved
their lives. 6 But if the sentinel sees the sword
coming and does not blow the trumpet, so that
the people are not warned, and the sword comes
and takes any of them, they are taken away in
their iniquity, but their blood I will require at the
sentinel's hand.

7 So you, mortal, I have made a sentinel for
the house of Israel; whenever you hear a word
from my mouth, you shall give them warning from me. 8 If I say to the wicked, "O wicked
ones, you shall surely die," and you do not speak
to warn the wicked to turn from their ways, the
wicked shall die in their iniquity, but their blood
I will require at your hand. 9 But if you warn the
wicked to turn from their ways, and they do not
turn from their ways, the wicked shall die in their
iniquity, but you will have saved your life.

10 Now you, mortal, say to the house of Israel,
Thus you have said: "Our transgressions and our
sins weigh upon us, and we waste away because
of them; how then can we live?" 11 Say to them,
As I live, says the Lord God, I have no pleasure
in the death of the wicked, but that the wicked
turn from their ways and live; turn back, turn
back from your evil ways; for why will you die,
O house of Israel? 12 And you, mortal, say to your
people, The righteousness of the righteous shall
not save them when they transgress; and as for
the wickedness of the wicked, it shall not make
them stumble when they turn from their wickedness; and the righteous shall not be able to live
by their righteousness[e] when they sin. 13 Though
I say to the righteous that they shall surely live,
yet if they trust in their righteousness and commit iniquity, none of their righteous deeds shall
be remembered; but in the iniquity that they have
committed they shall die. 14 Again, though I say to

[a] Heb *it* [b] Gk Old Latin: Heb *of the uncircumcised* [c] Cn: Heb *iniquities* [d] Cn: Heb *I* [e] Heb *by it*

the wicked, "You shall surely die," yet if they turn
from their sin and do what is lawful and right—
15if the wicked restore the pledge, give back what
they have taken by robbery, and walk in the statutes of life, committing no iniquity—they shall
surely live, they shall not die. 16None of the sins
that they have committed shall be remembered
against them; they have done what is lawful and
right, they shall surely live.

17 Yet your people say, "The way of the Lord
is not just," when it is their own way that is not
just. 18When the righteous turn from their righteousness, and commit iniquity, they shall die for
it.[a] 19And when the wicked turn from their wickedness, and do what is lawful and right, they shall
live by it.[a] 20Yet you say, "The way of the Lord is
not just." O house of Israel, I will judge all of you
according to your ways!

21 In the twelfth year of our exile, in the tenth
month, on the fifth day of the month, someone
who had escaped from Jerusalem came to me and
said, "The city has fallen." 22Now the hand of the
LORD had been upon me the evening before the
fugitive came; but he had opened my mouth by
the time the fugitive came to me in the morning;
so my mouth was opened, and I was no longer
unable to speak.

23 The word of the LORD came to me:
24Mortal, the inhabitants of these waste places
in the land of Israel keep saying, "Abraham was
only one man, yet he got possession of the land;
but we are many; the land is surely given us to
possess." 25Therefore say to them, Thus says the
Lord GOD: You eat flesh with the blood, and lift
up your eyes to your idols, and shed blood; shall
you then possess the land? 26You depend on your
swords, you commit abominations, and each of
you defiles his neighbor's wife; shall you then
possess the land? 27Say this to them, Thus says
the Lord GOD: As I live, surely those who are in
the waste places shall fall by the sword; and those
who are in the open field I will give to the wild
animals to be devoured; and those who are in
strongholds and in caves shall die by pestilence.
28I will make the land a desolation and a waste,
and its proud might shall come to an end; and
the mountains of Israel shall be so desolate that
no one will pass through. 29Then they shall know
that I am the LORD, when I have made the land a
desolation and a waste because of all their abominations that they have committed.

30 As for you, mortal, your people who talk
together about you by the walls, and at the doors
of the houses, say to one another, each to a neighbor, "Come and hear what the word is that comes
from the LORD." 31They come to you as people
come, and they sit before you as my people, and
they hear your words, but they will not obey
them. For flattery is on their lips, but their heart
is set on their gain. 32To them you are like a singer
of love songs,[b] one who has a beautiful voice and
plays well on an instrument; they hear what you
say, but they will not do it. 33When this comes—
and come it will!—then they shall know that a
prophet has been among them.

34 The word of the LORD came to me: 2Mor-
tal, prophesy against the shepherds of
Israel: prophesy, and say to them—to the shepherds: Thus says the Lord GOD: Ah, you shepherds of Israel who have been feeding yourselves!
Should not shepherds feed the sheep? 3You eat
the fat, you clothe yourselves with the wool, you
slaughter the fatlings; but you do not feed the
sheep. 4You have not strengthened the weak, you
have not healed the sick, you have not bound up
the injured, you have not brought back the strayed,
you have not sought the lost, but with force and
harshness you have ruled them. 5So they were
scattered, because there was no shepherd; and
scattered, they became food for all the wild animals. 6My sheep were scattered, they wandered
over all the mountains and on every high hill; my
sheep were scattered over all the face of the earth,
with no one to search or seek for them.

7 Therefore, you shepherds, hear the word of
the LORD: 8As I live, says the Lord GOD, because
my sheep have become a prey, and my sheep have
become food for all the wild animals, since there
was no shepherd; and because my shepherds have
not searched for my sheep, but the shepherds

[a] Heb *them* [b] Cn: Heb *like a love song*

have fed themselves, and have not fed my sheep;
9therefore, you shepherds, hear the word of the
LORD: 10Thus says the Lord GOD, I am against
the shepherds; and I will demand my sheep at
their hand, and put a stop to their feeding the
sheep; no longer shall the shepherds feed themselves. I will rescue my sheep from their mouths,
so that they may not be food for them.

11 For thus says the Lord GOD: I myself will
search for my sheep, and will seek them out. 12As
shepherds seek out their flocks when they are
among their scattered sheep, so I will seek out my
sheep. I will rescue them from all the places to
which they have been scattered on a day of clouds
and thick darkness. 13I will bring them out from
the peoples and gather them from the countries,
and will bring them into their own land; and I
will feed them on the mountains of Israel, by the
watercourses, and in all the inhabited parts of the
land. 14I will feed them with good pasture, and
the mountain heights of Israel shall be their pasture; there they shall lie down in good grazing
land, and they shall feed on rich pasture on the
mountains of Israel. 15I myself will be the shepherd of my sheep, and I will make them lie down,
says the Lord GOD. 16I will seek the lost, and I
will bring back the strayed, and I will bind up the
injured, and I will strengthen the weak, but the
fat and the strong I will destroy. I will feed them
with justice.

17 As for you, my flock, thus says the Lord
GOD: I shall judge between sheep and sheep, between rams and goats: 18Is it not enough for you
to feed on the good pasture, but you must tread
down with your feet the rest of your pasture?
When you drink of clear water, must you foul
the rest with your feet? 19And must my sheep eat
what you have trodden with your feet, and drink
what you have fouled with your feet?

20 Therefore, thus says the Lord GOD to
them: I myself will judge between the fat sheep
and the lean sheep. 21Because you pushed with
flank and shoulder, and butted at all the weak animals with your horns until you scattered them far
and wide, 22I will save my flock, and they shall no
longer be ravaged; and I will judge between sheep
and sheep.

23 I will set up over them one shepherd, my
servant David, and he shall feed them: he shall
feed them and be their shepherd. 24And I, the
LORD, will be their God, and my servant David
shall be prince among them; I, the LORD, have
spoken.

25 I will make with them a covenant of peace
and banish wild animals from the land, so that
they may live in the wild and sleep in the woods
securely. 26I will make them and the region
around my hill a blessing; and I will send down
the showers in their season; they shall be showers of blessing. 27The trees of the field shall yield
their fruit, and the earth shall yield its increase.
They shall be secure on their soil; and they shall

Ezekiel 34:21

North Americans—and Christians are not an outstanding exception—are continuing to consume the products of earth at indefensibly high rates and appear to be firmly set on reaching even higher levels, at the very time when it is a matter of public record that unaccounted millions are seriously malnourished and even starving.... The fact that we control a disproportionately large share of the world's real wealth is partly due to our domination of "world trade," a new economic colonialism by which we have repatriated large profits from countries which have only some basic raw material to sell and a large supply of cheap labor. In every way they are disadvantaged in relation to our superior economic leverage and technical development. We are rather like the fat sheep in Ezekiel's pathetic picture, which "push and thrust at the weak until they are scattered abroad" (Ezek 34:21). We, the wealthy six percent of the world's population, cluster around the well of the earth's resources and drink deeply from it, while the vast majority of peoples are shunted aside lapping up the trickles that spill from our cups.[58]

— *Clark Pinnock*

know that I am the LORD, when I break the bars
of their yoke, and save them from the hands of
those who enslaved them. 28They shall no more
be plunder for the nations, nor shall the animals
of the land devour them; they shall live in safety,
and no one shall make them afraid. 29I will provide for them a splendid vegetation so that they
shall no more be consumed with hunger in the
land, and no longer suffer the insults of the nations. 30They shall know that I, the LORD their
God, am with them, and that they, the house of
Israel, are my people, says the Lord GOD. 31You
are my sheep, the sheep of my pasture[a] and I am
your God, says the Lord GOD.

35 The word of the LORD came to me: 2Mor-
tal, set your face against Mount Seir, and
prophesy against it, 3and say to it, Thus says the
Lord GOD:

I am against you, Mount Seir;
  I stretch out my hand against you
  to make you a desolation and a waste.
4 I lay your towns in ruins;
  you shall become a desolation,
  and you shall know that I am the LORD.

5Because you cherished an ancient enmity, and
gave over the people of Israel to the power of the
sword at the time of their calamity, at the time of
their final punishment; 6therefore, as I live, says
the Lord GOD, I will prepare you for blood, and
blood shall pursue you; since you did not hate
bloodshed, bloodshed shall pursue you. 7I will
make Mount Seir a waste and a desolation; and
I will cut off from it all who come and go. 8I will
fill its mountains with the slain; on your hills and
in your valleys and in all your watercourses those
killed with the sword shall fall. 9I will make you
a perpetual desolation, and your cities shall never
be inhabited. Then you shall know that I am the
LORD.

10 Because you said, "These two nations and
these two countries shall be mine, and we will
take possession of them,"—although the LORD
was there— 11therefore, as I live, says the Lord
GOD, I will deal with you according to the anger
and envy that you showed because of your hatred against them; and I will make myself known
among you,[b] when I judge you. 12You shall know
that I, the LORD, have heard all the abusive speech
that you uttered against the mountains of Israel,
saying, "They are laid desolate, they are given
us to devour." 13And you magnified yourselves
against me with your mouth, and multiplied your
words against me; I heard it. 14Thus says the Lord
GOD: As the whole earth rejoices, I will make you
desolate. 15As you rejoiced over the inheritance
of the house of Israel, because it was desolate, so
I will deal with you; you shall be desolate, Mount
Seir, and all Edom, all of it. Then they shall know
that I am the LORD.

36 And you, mortal, prophesy to the mountains of Israel, and say: O mountains of
Israel, hear the word of the LORD. 2Thus says
the Lord GOD: Because the enemy said of you,
"Aha!" and, "The ancient heights have become
our possession," 3therefore prophesy, and say:
Thus says the Lord GOD: Because they made
you desolate indeed, and crushed you from all
sides, so that you became the possession of the
rest of the nations, and you became an object of
gossip and slander among the people; 4therefore,
O mountains of Israel, hear the word of the Lord
GOD: Thus says the Lord GOD to the mountains
and the hills, the watercourses and the valleys,
the desolate wastes and the deserted towns,
which have become a source of plunder and an
object of derision to the rest of the nations all
around; 5therefore thus says the Lord GOD: I
am speaking in my hot jealousy against the rest
of the nations, and against all Edom, who, with
wholehearted joy and utter contempt, took my
land as their possession, because of its pasture,
to plunder it. 6Therefore prophesy concerning the land of Israel, and say to the mountains
and hills, to the watercourses and valleys, Thus
says the Lord GOD: I am speaking in my jealous
wrath, because you have suffered the insults of
the nations; 7therefore thus says the Lord GOD:
I swear that the nations that are all around you
shall themselves suffer insults.

8 But you, O mountains of Israel, shall shoot

[a] Gk OL: Heb *pasture, you are people* [b] Gk: Heb *them*

out your branches, and yield your fruit to my
people Israel; for they shall soon come home.
9 See now, I am for you; I will turn to you, and
you shall be tilled and sown; 10 and I will multiply your population, the whole house of Israel, all
of it; the towns shall be inhabited and the waste
places rebuilt; 11 and I will multiply human beings
and animals upon you. They shall increase and be
fruitful; and I will cause you to be inhabited as
in your former times, and will do more good to
you than ever before. Then you shall know that I
am the LORD. 12 I will lead people upon you—my
people Israel—and they shall possess you, and
you shall be their inheritance. No longer shall you
bereave them of children.

13 Thus says the Lord GOD: Because they
say to you, "You devour people, and you bereave
your nation of children," 14 therefore you shall no
longer devour people and no longer bereave your
nation of children, says the Lord GOD; 15 and no
longer will I let you hear the insults of the nations, no longer shall you bear the disgrace of the
peoples; and no longer shall you cause your nation to stumble, says the Lord GOD.

16 The word of the LORD came to me:
17 Mortal, when the house of Israel lived on their
own soil, they defiled it with their ways and their
deeds; their conduct in my sight was like the uncleanness of a woman in her menstrual period.
18 So I poured out my wrath upon them for the
blood that they had shed upon the land, and for
the idols with which they had defiled it. 19 I scattered them among the nations, and they were
dispersed through the countries; in accordance
with their conduct and their deeds I judged them.
20 But when they came to the nations, wherever
they came, they profaned my holy name, in that
it was said of them, "These are the people of the
LORD, and yet they had to go out of his land."
21 But I had concern for my holy name, which the
house of Israel had profaned among the nations
to which they came.

22 Therefore say to the house of Israel, Thus
says the Lord GOD: It is not for your sake, O house
of Israel, that I am about to act, but for the sake of
my holy name, which you have profaned among
the nations to which you came. 23 I will sanctify
my great name, which has been profaned among
the nations, and which you have profaned among
them; and the nations shall know that I am the
LORD, says the Lord GOD, when through you I
display my holiness before their eyes. 24 I will take
you from the nations, and gather you from all the
countries, and bring you into your own land. 25 I
will sprinkle clean water upon you, and you shall
be clean from all your uncleannesses, and from
all your idols I will cleanse you. 26 A new heart I
will give you, and a new spirit I will put within
you; and I will remove from your body the heart
of stone and give you a heart of flesh. 27 I will put
my spirit within you, and make you follow my
statutes and be careful to observe my ordinances.
28 Then you shall live in the land that I gave to
your ancestors; and you shall be my people, and
I will be your God. 29 I will save you from all your
uncleannesses, and I will summon the grain and
make it abundant and lay no famine upon you. 30 I
will make the fruit of the tree and the produce of
the field abundant, so that you may never again
suffer the disgrace of famine among the nations.
31 Then you shall remember your evil ways, and
your dealings that were not good; and you shall
loathe yourselves for your iniquities and your
abominable deeds. 32 It is not for your sake that
I will act, says the Lord GOD; let that be known
to you. Be ashamed and dismayed for your ways,
O house of Israel.

33 Thus says the Lord GOD: On the day
that I cleanse you from all your iniquities, I will
cause the towns to be inhabited, and the waste
places shall be rebuilt. 34 The land that was desolate shall be tilled, instead of being the desolation that it was in the sight of all who passed by.
35 And they will say, "This land that was desolate
has become like the garden of Eden; and the
waste and desolate and ruined towns are now
inhabited and fortified." 36 Then the nations
that are left all around you shall know that I,
the LORD, have rebuilt the ruined places, and
replanted that which was desolate; I, the LORD,
have spoken, and I will do it.

37 Thus says the Lord GOD: I will also let
the house of Israel ask me to do this for them: to
increase their population like a flock. 38 Like the

flock for sacrifices,[a] like the flock at Jerusalem
during her appointed festivals, so shall the ruined
towns be filled with flocks of people. Then they
shall know that I am the LORD.

37 The hand of the LORD came upon me,
and he brought me out by the spirit of the
LORD and set me down in the middle of a valley; it was full of bones. 2He led me all around
them; there were very many lying in the valley,
and they were very dry. 3He said to me, "Mortal,
can these bones live?" I answered, "O Lord GOD,
you know." 4Then he said to me, "Prophesy to
these bones, and say to them: O dry bones, hear
the word of the LORD. 5Thus says the Lord GOD
to these bones: I will cause breath[b] to enter you,
and you shall live. 6I will lay sinews on you, and
will cause flesh to come upon you, and cover you
with skin, and put breath[b] in you, and you shall
live; and you shall know that I am the LORD."

7 So I prophesied as I had been commanded;
and as I prophesied, suddenly there was a noise, a
rattling, and the bones came together, bone to its
bone. 8I looked, and there were sinews on them,
and flesh had come upon them, and skin had
covered them; but there was no breath in them.
9Then he said to me, "Prophesy to the breath,
prophesy, mortal, and say to the breath:[c] Thus
says the Lord GOD: Come from the four winds,
O breath,[c] and breathe upon these slain, that they
may live." 10I prophesied as he commanded me,
and the breath came into them, and they lived,
and stood on their feet, a vast multitude.

11 Then he said to me, "Mortal, these bones
are the whole house of Israel. They say, 'Our
bones are dried up, and our hope is lost; we are
cut off completely.' 12Therefore prophesy, and say
to them, Thus says the Lord GOD: I am going to
open your graves, and bring you up from your
graves, O my people; and I will bring you back
to the land of Israel. 13And you shall know that I
am the LORD, when I open your graves, and bring
you up from your graves, O my people. 14I will
put my spirit within you, and you shall live, and
I will place you on your own soil; then you shall
know that I, the LORD, have spoken and will act,
says the LORD."

15 The word of the LORD came to me: 16Mor-
tal, take a stick and write on it, "For Judah, and
the Israelites associated with it"; then take another stick and write on it, "For Joseph (the stick
of Ephraim) and all the house of Israel associated
with it"; 17and join them together into one stick,
so that they may become one in your hand. 18And
when your people say to you, "Will you not show
us what you mean by these?" 19say to them, Thus
says the Lord GOD: I am about to take the stick of
Joseph (which is in the hand of Ephraim) and the
tribes of Israel associated with it; and I will put
the stick of Judah upon it,[d] and make them one
stick, in order that they may be one in my hand.
20When the sticks on which you write are in your
hand before their eyes, 21then say to them, Thus
says the Lord GOD: I will take the people of Israel from the nations among which they have
gone, and will gather them from every quarter,
and bring them to their own land. 22I will make
them one nation in the land, on the mountains of
Israel; and one king shall be king over them all.
Never again shall they be two nations, and never
again shall they be divided into two kingdoms.
23They shall never again defile themselves with
their idols and their detestable things, or with any
of their transgressions. I will save them from all
the apostasies into which they have fallen,[e] and
will cleanse them. Then they shall be my people,
and I will be their God.

24 My servant David shall be king over them;
and they shall all have one shepherd. They shall
follow my ordinances and be careful to observe
my statutes. 25They shall live in the land that I
gave to my servant Jacob, in which your ancestors
lived; they and their children and their children's
children shall live there forever; and my servant
David shall be their prince forever. 26I will make
a covenant of peace with them; it shall be an everlasting covenant with them; and I will bless[f] them
and multiply them, and will set my sanctuary

[a] Heb *flock of holy things* [b] Or *spirit* [c] Or *wind* or *spirit* [d] Heb *I will put them upon it* [e] Another reading is *from all the settlements in which they have sinned* [f] Tg: Heb *give*

among them forevermore. 27My dwelling place
shall be with them; and I will be their God, and
they shall be my people. 28Then the nations shall
know that I the LORD sanctify Israel, when my
sanctuary is among them forevermore.

38 The word of the LORD came to me: 2Mor-
tal, set your face toward Gog, of the land
of Magog, the chief prince of Meshech and Tubal. Prophesy against him 3and say: Thus says the
Lord GOD: I am against you, O Gog, chief prince
of Meshech and Tubal; 4I will turn you around
and put hooks into your jaws, and I will lead you
out with all your army, horses and horsemen, all
of them clothed in full armor, a great company, all
of them with shield and buckler, wielding swords.
5Persia, Ethiopia,[a] and Put are with them, all of
them with buckler and helmet; 6Gomer and all its
troops; Beth-togarmah from the remotest parts
of the north with all its troops—many peoples
are with you.

7 Be ready and keep ready, you and all the
companies that are assembled around you, and
hold yourselves in reserve for them. 8After many
days you shall be mustered; in the latter years you
shall go against a land restored from war, a land
where people were gathered from many nations
on the mountains of Israel, which had long lain
waste; its people were brought out from the nations and now are living in safety, all of them.
9You shall advance, coming on like a storm; you
shall be like a cloud covering the land, you and all
your troops, and many peoples with you.

10 Thus says the Lord GOD: On that day
thoughts will come into your mind, and you will
devise an evil scheme. 11You will say, "I will go
up against the land of unwalled villages; I will fall
upon the quiet people who live in safety, all of
them living without walls, and having no bars or
gates"; 12to seize spoil and carry off plunder; to
assail the waste places that are now inhabited, and
the people who were gathered from the nations,
who are acquiring cattle and goods, who live at
the center[b] of the earth. 13Sheba and Dedan and
the merchants of Tarshish and all its young warriors[c] will say to you, "Have you come to seize
spoil? Have you assembled your horde to carry
off plunder, to carry away silver and gold, to take
away cattle and goods, to seize a great amount of
booty?"

14 Therefore, mortal, prophesy, and say to
Gog: Thus says the Lord GOD: On that day when
my people Israel are living securely, you will
rouse yourself[d] 15and come from your place out
of the remotest parts of the north, you and many
peoples with you, all of them riding on horses, a
great horde, a mighty army; 16you will come up
against my people Israel, like a cloud covering the
earth. In the latter days I will bring you against
my land, so that the nations may know me, when
through you, O Gog, I display my holiness before
their eyes.

17 Thus says the Lord GOD: Are you he of
whom I spoke in former days by my servants the
prophets of Israel, who in those days prophesied
for years that I would bring you against them?
18On that day, when Gog comes against the land
of Israel, says the Lord GOD, my wrath shall be
aroused. 19For in my jealousy and in my blazing
wrath I declare: On that day there shall be a great
shaking in the land of Israel; 20the fish of the sea,
and the birds of the air, and the animals of the
field, and all creeping things that creep on the
ground, and all human beings that are on the face
of the earth, shall quake at my presence, and the
mountains shall be thrown down, and the cliffs
shall fall, and every wall shall tumble to the
ground. 21I will summon the sword against Gog[e]
in[f] all my mountains, says the Lord GOD; the
swords of all will be against their comrades. 22With
pestilence and bloodshed I will enter into judgment with him; and I will pour down torrential
rains and hailstones, fire and sulfur, upon him and
his troops and the many peoples that are with him.
23So I will display my greatness and my holiness
and make myself known in the eyes of many nations. Then they shall know that I am the LORD.

39 And you, mortal, prophesy against Gog,
and say: Thus says the Lord GOD: I am

[a] Or *Nubia;* Heb *Cush* [b] Heb *navel* [c] Heb *young lions* [d] Gk: Heb *will you not know?* [e] Heb *him*
[f] Heb *to* or *for*

against you, O Gog, chief prince of Meshech and
Tubal! 2I will turn you around and drive you forward, and bring you up from the remotest parts of
the north, and lead you against the mountains of
Israel. 3I will strike your bow from your left hand,
and will make your arrows drop out of your right
hand. 4You shall fall on the mountains of Israel,
you and all your troops and the peoples that are
with you; I will give you to birds of prey of every kind and to the wild animals to be devoured.
5You shall fall in the open field; for I have spoken,
says the Lord GOD. 6I will send fire on Magog and
on those who live securely in the coastlands; and
they shall know that I am the LORD.

7 My holy name I will make known among
my people Israel; and I will not let my holy name
be profaned any more; and the nations shall know
that I am the LORD, the Holy One in Israel. 8It
has come! It has happened, says the Lord GOD.
This is the day of which I have spoken.

9 Then those who live in the towns of Israel
will go out and make fires of the weapons and
burn them—bucklers and shields, bows and arrows, handpikes and spears—and they will make
fires of them for seven years. 10They will not need
to take wood out of the field or cut down any trees
in the forests, for they will make their fires of the
weapons; they will despoil those who despoiled
them, and plunder those who plundered them,
says the Lord GOD.

11 On that day I will give to Gog a place for
burial in Israel, the Valley of the Travelers[a] east
of the sea; it shall block the path of the travelers,
for there Gog and all his horde will be buried; it
shall be called the Valley of Hamon-gog.[b] 12Seven
months the house of Israel shall spend burying
them, in order to cleanse the land. 13All the people of the land shall bury them; and it will bring
them honor on the day that I show my glory, says
the Lord GOD. 14They will set apart men to pass
through the land regularly and bury any invaders[c] who remain on the face of the land, so as to
cleanse it; for seven months they shall make their
search. 15As the searchers[c] pass through the land,
anyone who sees a human bone shall set up a sign
by it, until the buriers have buried it in the Valley of Hamon-gog.[b] 16(A city Hamonah[d] is there
also.) Thus they shall cleanse the land.

17 As for you, mortal, thus says the Lord
GOD: Speak to the birds of every kind and to all
the wild animals: Assemble and come, gather
from all around to the sacrificial feast that I am
preparing for you, a great sacrificial feast on
the mountains of Israel, and you shall eat flesh
and drink blood. 18You shall eat the flesh of the
mighty, and drink the blood of the princes of the
earth—of rams, of lambs, and of goats, of bulls,
all of them fatlings of Bashan. 19You shall eat fat
until you are filled, and drink blood until you are
drunk, at the sacrificial feast that I am preparing
for you. 20And you shall be filled at my table with
horses and charioteers,[e] with warriors and all
kinds of soldiers, says the Lord GOD.

21 I will display my glory among the nations;
and all the nations shall see my judgment that I
have executed, and my hand that I have laid on
them. 22The house of Israel shall know that I
am the LORD their God, from that day forward.
23And the nations shall know that the house of
Israel went into captivity for their iniquity, because they dealt treacherously with me. So I hid
my face from them and gave them into the hand
of their adversaries, and they all fell by the sword.
24I dealt with them according to their uncleanness and their transgressions, and hid my face
from them.

25 Therefore thus says the Lord GOD: Now I
will restore the fortunes of Jacob, and have mercy
on the whole house of Israel; and I will be jealous for my holy name. 26They shall forget[f] their
shame, and all the treachery they have practiced
against me, when they live securely in their land
with no one to make them afraid, 27when I have
brought them back from the peoples and gathered them from their enemies' lands, and through
them have displayed my holiness in the sight of
many nations. 28Then they shall know that I am
the LORD their God because I sent them into ex-

[a] Or *of the Abarim* [b] That is, *the Horde of Gog* [c] Heb *travelers* [d] That is *The Horde* [e] Heb *chariots*
[f] Another reading is *They shall bear*

ile among the nations, and then gathered them
into their own land. I will leave none of them behind; 29and I will never again hide my face from
them, when I pour out my spirit upon the house
of Israel, says the Lord GOD.

40 In the twenty-fifth year of our exile, at the
beginning of the year, on the tenth day of
the month, in the fourteenth year after the city
was struck down, on that very day, the hand of
the LORD was upon me, and he brought me there.
2He brought me, in visions of God, to the land of
Israel, and set me down upon a very high mountain, on which was a structure like a city to the
south. 3When he brought me there, a man was
there, whose appearance shone like bronze, with
a linen cord and a measuring reed in his hand;
and he was standing in the gateway. 4The man
said to me, "Mortal, look closely and listen attentively, and set your mind upon all that I shall
show you, for you were brought here in order that
I might show it to you; declare all that you see to
the house of Israel."

5 Now there was a wall all around the outside
of the temple area. The length of the measuring
reed in the man's hand was six long cubits, each
being a cubit and a handbreadth in length; so he
measured the thickness of the wall, one reed; and
the height, one reed. 6Then he went into the gateway facing east, going up its steps, and measured
the threshold of the gate, one reed deep.[a] There
were 7recesses, and each recess was one reed wide
and one reed deep; and the space between the recesses, five cubits; and the threshold of the gate
by the vestibule of the gate at the inner end was
one reed deep. 8Then he measured the inner vestibule of the gateway, one cubit. 9Then he measured the vestibule of the gateway, eight cubits;
and its pilasters, two cubits; and the vestibule of
the gate was at the inner end. 10There were three
recesses on either side of the east gate; the three
were of the same size; and the pilasters on either
side were of the same size. 11Then he measured
the width of the opening of the gateway, ten cubits; and the width of the gateway, thirteen cubits.
12There was a barrier before the recesses, one cubit on either side; and the recesses were six cubits
on either side. 13Then he measured the gate from
the back[b] of the one recess to the back[b] of the
other, a width of twenty-five cubits, from wall to
wall.[c] 14He measured[d] also the vestibule, twenty
cubits; and the gate next to the pilaster on every
side of the court.[e] 15From the front of the gate at
the entrance to the end of the inner vestibule of
the gate was fifty cubits. 16The recesses and their
pilasters had windows, with shutters[e] on the inside of the gateway all around, and the vestibules
also had windows on the inside all around; and
on the pilasters were palm trees.

17 Then he brought me into the outer court;
there were chambers there, and a pavement, all
around the court; thirty chambers fronted on
the pavement. 18The pavement ran along the
side of the gates, corresponding to the length of
the gates; this was the lower pavement. 19Then
he measured the distance from the inner front
of[f] the lower gate to the outer front of the inner
court, one hundred cubits.[g]

20 Then he measured the gate of the outer
court that faced north—its depth and width. 21Its
recesses, three on either side, and its pilasters and
its vestibule were of the same size as those of the
first gate; its depth was fifty cubits, and its width
twenty-five cubits. 22Its windows, its vestibule,
and its palm trees were of the same size as those
of the gate that faced toward the east. Seven steps
led up to it; and its vestibule was on the inside.[h]
23Opposite the gate on the north, as on the east,
was a gate to the inner court; he measured from
gate to gate, one hundred cubits.

24 Then he led me toward the south, and
there was a gate on the south; and he measured
its pilasters and its vestibule; they had the same
dimensions as the others. 25There were windows
all around in it and in its vestibule, like the windows of the others; its depth was fifty cubits, and
its width twenty-five cubits. 26There were seven
steps leading up to it; its vestibule was on the

[a] Heb *deep, and one threshold, one reed deep* [b] Gk: Heb *roof* [c] Heb *opening facing opening* [d] Heb *made* [e] Meaning of Heb uncertain [f] Compare Gk: Heb *from before* [g] Heb adds *the east and the north* [h] Gk: Heb *before them*

inside.[a] It had palm trees on its pilasters, one on
either side. 27There was a gate on the south of the
inner court; and he measured from gate to gate
toward the south, one hundred cubits.
28 Then he brought me to the inner court by
the south gate, and he measured the south gate;
it was of the same dimensions as the others. 29Its
recesses, its pilasters, and its vestibule were of
the same size as the others; and there were windows all around in it and in its vestibule; its depth
was fifty cubits, and its width twenty-five cubits.
30There were vestibules all around, twenty-five
cubits deep and five cubits wide. 31Its vestibule
faced the outer court, and palm trees were on its
pilasters, and its stairway had eight steps.
32 Then he brought me to the inner court on
the east side, and he measured the gate; it was of
the same size as the others. 33Its recesses, its pilasters, and its vestibule were of the same dimensions as the others; and there were windows all
around in it and in its vestibule; its depth was fifty
cubits, and its width twenty-five cubits. 34Its vestibule faced the outer court, and it had palm trees
on its pilasters, on either side; and its stairway
had eight steps.
35 Then he brought me to the north gate,
and he measured it; it had the same dimensions
as the others. 36Its recesses, its pilasters, and its
vestibule were of the same size as the others;[b] and
it had windows all around. Its depth was fifty cubits, and its width twenty-five cubits. 37Its vestibule[c] faced the outer court, and it had palm trees
on its pilasters, on either side; and its stairway
had eight steps.
38 There was a chamber with its door in the
vestibule of the gate,[d] where the burnt offering
was to be washed. 39And in the vestibule of the
gate were two tables on either side, on which the
burnt offering and the sin offering and the guilt
offering were to be slaughtered. 40On the outside
of the vestibule[e] at the entrance of the north gate
were two tables; and on the other side of the vestibule of the gate were two tables. 41Four tables
were on the inside, and four tables on the outside
of the side of the gate, eight tables, on which the
sacrifices were to be slaughtered. 42There were
also four tables of hewn stone for the burnt offering, a cubit and a half long, and one cubit and a
half wide, and one cubit high, on which the instruments were to be laid with which the burnt
offerings and the sacrifices were slaughtered.
43There were pegs, one handbreadth long, fastened all around the inside. And on the tables the
flesh of the offering was to be laid.
44 On the outside of the inner gateway there
were chambers for the singers in the inner court,
one[f] at the side of the north gate facing south,
the other at the side of the east gate facing north.
45He said to me, "This chamber that faces south
is for the priests who have charge of the temple,
46and the chamber that faces north is for the
priests who have charge of the altar; these are the
descendants of Zadok, who alone among the descendants of Levi may come near to the LORD to
minister to him." 47He measured the court, one
hundred cubits deep, and one hundred cubits
wide, a square; and the altar was in front of the
temple.
48 Then he brought me to the vestibule of
the temple and measured the pilasters of the vestibule, five cubits on either side; and the width of
the gate was fourteen cubits; and the sidewalls of
the gate were three cubits[g] on either side. 49The
depth of the vestibule was twenty cubits, and the
width twelve[h] cubits; ten steps led up[i] to it; and
there were pillars beside the pilasters on either
side.

41 Then he brought me to the nave, and
measured the pilasters; on each side six
cubits was the width of the pilasters.[j] 2The width
of the entrance was ten cubits; and the sidewalls
of the entrance were five cubits on either side.
He measured the length of the nave, forty cubits, and its width, twenty cubits. 3Then he went

[a] Gk: Heb *before them* [b] One Ms: Compare verses 29 and 33: MT lacks *were of the same size as the others* [c] Gk Vg Compare verses 26, 31, 34: Heb *pilasters* [d] Cn: Heb *at the pilasters of the gates* [e] Cn: Heb *to him who goes up* [f] Heb lacks *one* [g] Gk: Heb *and the width of the gate was three cubits* [h] Gk: Heb *eleven* [i] Gk: Heb *and by steps that went up* [j] Compare Gk: Heb *tent*

into the inner room and measured the pilasters
of the entrance, two cubits; and the width of the
entrance, six cubits; and the sidewalls[a] of the entrance, seven cubits. 4He measured the depth of
the room, twenty cubits, and its width, twenty
cubits, beyond the nave. And he said to me, This
is the most holy place.

5 Then he measured the wall of the temple,
six cubits thick; and the width of the side chambers, four cubits, all around the temple. 6The side
chambers were in three stories, one over another,
thirty in each story. There were offsets[b] all around
the wall of the temple to serve as supports for the
side chambers, so that they should not be supported by the wall of the temple. 7The passage-
way[c] of the side chambers widened from story to
story; for the structure was supplied with a stairway all around the temple. For this reason the
structure became wider from story to story. One
ascended from the bottom story to the uppermost story by way of the middle one. 8I saw also
that the temple had a raised platform all around;
the foundations of the side chambers measured a
full reed of six long cubits. 9The thickness of the
outer wall of the side chambers was five cubits;
and the free space between the side chambers of
the temple 10and the chambers of the court was a
width of twenty cubits all around the temple on
every side. 11The side chambers opened onto the
area left free, one door toward the north, and another door toward the south; and the width of the
part that was left free was five cubits all around.

12 The building that was facing the temple
yard on the west side was seventy cubits wide;
and the wall of the building was five cubits thick
all around, and its depth ninety cubits.

13 Then he measured the temple, one hundred cubits deep; and the yard and the building
with its walls, one hundred cubits deep; 14also
the width of the east front of the temple and the
yard, one hundred cubits.

15 Then he measured the depth of the building facing the yard at the west, together with its
galleries[d] on either side, one hundred cubits.

The nave of the temple and the inner room
and the outer[e] vestibule 16were paneled,[f] and,
all around, all three had windows with recessed[g]
frames. Facing the threshold the temple was paneled with wood all around, from the floor up to
the windows (now the windows were covered),
17to the space above the door, even to the inner
room, and on the outside. And on all the walls all
around in the inner room and the nave there was
a pattern.[h] 18It was formed of cherubim and palm
trees, a palm tree between cherub and cherub.
Each cherub had two faces: 19a human face
turned toward the palm tree on the one side, and
the face of a young lion turned toward the palm
tree on the other side. They were carved on the
whole temple all around; 20from the floor to the
area above the door, cherubim and palm trees
were carved on the wall.[i]

21 The doorposts of the nave were square. In
front of the holy place was something resembling
22an altar of wood, three cubits high, two cubits
long, and two cubits wide;[j] its corners, its base,[k]
and its walls were of wood. He said to me, "This
is the table that stands before the LORD." 23The
nave and the holy place had each a double door.
24The doors had two leaves apiece, two swinging
leaves for each door. 25On the doors of the nave
were carved cherubim and palm trees, such as
were carved on the walls; and there was a canopy
of wood in front of the vestibule outside. 26And
there were recessed windows and palm trees on
either side, on the sidewalls of the vestibule.[l]

42 Then he led me out into the outer court,
toward the north, and he brought me to
the chambers that were opposite the temple yard
and opposite the building on the north. 2The
length of the building that was on the north side[m]
was[n] one hundred cubits, and the width fifty

[a] Gk: Heb *width* [b] Gk Compare 1 Kings 6.6: Heb *they entered* [c] Cn: Heb *it was surrounded* [d] Cn: Meaning of Heb uncertain [e] Gk: Heb *of the court* [f] Gk: Heb *the thresholds* [g] Cn Compare Gk 1 Kings 6.4: Meaning of Heb uncertain [h] Heb *measures* [i] Cn Compare verse 25: Heb *and the wall* [j] Gk: Heb lacks *two cubits wide* [k] Gk: Heb *length* [l] Cn: Heb *vestibule. And the side chambers of the temple and the canopies* [m] Gk: Heb *door* [n] Gk: Heb *before the length*

cubits. 3Across the twenty cubits that belonged to the inner court, and facing the pavement that belonged to the outer court, the chambers rose[a] gallery[b] by gallery[b] in three stories. 4In front of the chambers was a passage on the inner side, ten cubits wide and one hundred cubits deep,[c] and its[d] entrances were on the north. 5Now the upper chambers were narrower, for the galleries[b] took more away from them than from the lower and middle chambers in the building. 6For they were in three stories, and they had no pillars like the pillars of the outer[e] court; for this reason the upper chambers were set back from the ground more than the lower and the middle ones. 7There was a wall outside parallel to the chambers, toward the outer court, opposite the chambers, fifty cubits long. 8For the chambers on the outer court were fifty cubits long, while those opposite the temple were one hundred cubits long. 9At the foot of these chambers ran a passage that one entered from the east in order to enter them from the outer court. 10The width of the passage[f] was fixed by the wall of the court.

On the south[g] also, opposite the vacant area and opposite the building, there were chambers 11with a passage in front of them; they were similar to the chambers on the north, of the same length and width, with the same exits[h] and arrangements and doors. 12So the entrances of the chambers to the south were entered through the entrance at the head of the corresponding passage, from the east, along the matching wall.[b]

13 Then he said to me, "The north chambers and the south chambers opposite the vacant area are the holy chambers, where the priests who approach the LORD shall eat the most holy offerings; there they shall deposit the most holy offerings—the grain offering, the sin offering, and the guilt offering—for the place is holy. 14When the priests enter the holy place, they shall not go out of it into the outer court without laying there the vestments in which they minister, for these are holy; they shall put on other garments before they go near to the area open to the people."

15 When he had finished measuring the interior of the temple area, he led me out by the gate that faces east, and measured the temple area all around. 16He measured the east side with the measuring reed, five hundred cubits by the measuring reed. 17Then he turned and measured[i] the north side, five hundred cubits by the measuring reed. 18Then he turned and measured[i] the south side, five hundred cubits by the measuring reed. 19Then he turned to the west side and measured, five hundred cubits by the measuring reed. 20He measured it on the four sides. It had a wall around it, five hundred cubits long and five hundred cubits wide, to make a separation between the holy and the common.

43 Then he brought me to the gate, the gate facing east. 2And there, the glory of the God of Israel was coming from the east; the sound was like the sound of mighty waters; and the earth shone with his glory. 3The[j] vision I saw was like the vision that I had seen when he came to destroy the city, and[k] like the vision that I had seen by the river Chebar; and I fell upon my face. 4As the glory of the LORD entered the temple by the gate facing east, 5the spirit lifted me up, and brought me into the inner court; and the glory of the LORD filled the temple.

6 While the man was standing beside me, I heard someone speaking to me out of the temple. 7He said to me: Mortal, this is the place of my throne and the place for the soles of my feet, where I will reside among the people of Israel forever. The house of Israel shall no more defile my holy name, neither they nor their kings, by their whoring, and by the corpses of their kings at their death.[l] 8When they placed their threshold by my threshold and their doorposts beside my doorposts, with only a wall between me and them, they were defiling my holy name by their abominations that they committed; therefore I have consumed them in my anger. 9Now let them

[a] Heb lacks *the chambers rose* [b] Meaning of Heb uncertain [c] Gk Syr: Heb *a way of one cubit* [d] Heb *their* [e] Gk: Heb lacks *outer* [f] Heb lacks *of the passage* [g] Gk: Heb *east* [h] Heb *and all their exits* [i] Gk: Heb *measuring reed all around. He measured* [j] Gk: Heb *Like the vision* [k] Syr: Heb *and the visions* [l] Or *on their high places*

put away their idolatry and the corpses of their
kings far from me, and I will reside among them
forever.

10 As for you, mortal, describe the temple to
the house of Israel, and let them measure the pattern; and let them be ashamed of their iniquities.
11 When they are ashamed of all that they have
done, make known to them the plan of the temple, its arrangement, its exits and its entrances,
and its whole form—all its ordinances and its entire plan and all its laws; and write it down in their
sight, so that they may observe and follow the entire plan and all its ordinances. 12 This is the law of
the temple: the whole territory on the top of the
mountain all around shall be most holy. This is
the law of the temple.

13 These are the dimensions of the altar by
cubits (the cubit being one cubit and a handbreadth): its base shall be one cubit high,[a] and
one cubit wide, with a rim of one span around its
edge. This shall be the height of the altar: 14 From
the base on the ground to the lower ledge, two
cubits, with a width of one cubit; and from the
smaller ledge to the larger ledge, four cubits,
with a width of one cubit; 15 and the altar hearth,
four cubits; and from the altar hearth projecting
upward, four horns. 16 The altar hearth shall be
square, twelve cubits long by twelve wide. 17 The
ledge also shall be square, fourteen cubits long
by fourteen wide, with a rim around it half a cubit wide, and its surrounding base, one cubit. Its
steps shall face east.

18 Then he said to me: Mortal, thus says
the Lord GOD: These are the ordinances for the
altar: On the day when it is erected for offering
burnt offerings upon it and for dashing blood
against it, 19 you shall give to the levitical priests
of the family of Zadok, who draw near to me to
minister to me, says the Lord GOD, a bull for
a sin offering. 20 And you shall take some of its
blood, and put it on the four horns of the altar,
and on the four corners of the ledge, and upon
the rim all around; thus you shall purify it and
make atonement for it. 21 You shall also take the
bull of the sin offering, and it shall be burnt in
the appointed place belonging to the temple,
outside the sacred area.

22 On the second day you shall offer a male
goat without blemish for a sin offering; and the altar shall be purified, as it was purified with the bull.
23 When you have finished purifying it, you shall
offer a bull without blemish and a ram from the
flock without blemish. 24 You shall present them
before the LORD, and the priests shall throw salt on
them and offer them up as a burnt offering to the
LORD. 25 For seven days you shall provide daily a
goat for a sin offering; also a bull and a ram from
the flock, without blemish, shall be provided.
26 Seven days shall they make atonement for the
altar and cleanse it, and so consecrate it. 27 When
these days are over, then from the eighth day onward the priests shall offer upon the altar your
burnt offerings and your offerings of well-being;
and I will accept you, says the Lord GOD.

44 Then he brought me back to the outer
gate of the sanctuary, which faces east;
and it was shut. 2 The LORD said to me: This gate
shall remain shut; it shall not be opened, and no
one shall enter by it; for the LORD, the God of
Israel, has entered by it; therefore it shall remain
shut. 3 Only the prince, because he is a prince,
may sit in it to eat food before the LORD; he shall
enter by way of the vestibule of the gate, and shall
go out by the same way.

4 Then he brought me by way of the north
gate to the front of the temple; and I looked, and
lo! the glory of the LORD filled the temple of the
LORD; and I fell upon my face. 5 The LORD said
to me: Mortal, mark well, look closely, and listen
attentively to all that I shall tell you concerning all
the ordinances of the temple of the LORD and all
its laws; and mark well those who may be admitted to[b] the temple and all those who are to be excluded from the sanctuary. 6 Say to the rebellious
house,[c] to the house of Israel, Thus says the Lord
GOD: O house of Israel, let there be an end to all
your abominations 7 in admitting foreigners, uncircumcised in heart and flesh, to be in my sanctuary, profaning my temple when you offer to me
my food, the fat and the blood. You[d] have broken

[a] Gk: Heb lacks *high* [b] Cn: Heb *the entrance of* [c] Gk: Heb lacks *house* [d] Gk Syr Vg: Heb *They*

my covenant with all your abominations. 8And
you have not kept charge of my sacred offerings;
but you have appointed foreigners[a] to act for you
in keeping my charge in my sanctuary.
9 Thus says the Lord GOD: No foreigner, uncircumcised in heart and flesh, of all the foreigners
who are among the people of Israel, shall enter my
sanctuary. 10But the Levites who went far from
me, going astray from me after their idols when
Israel went astray, shall bear their punishment.
11They shall be ministers in my sanctuary, having oversight at the gates of the temple, and serving in the temple; they shall slaughter the burnt
offering and the sacrifice for the people, and they
shall attend on them and serve them. 12Because
they ministered to them before their idols and
made the house of Israel stumble into iniquity,
therefore I have sworn concerning them, says the
Lord GOD, that they shall bear their punishment.
13They shall not come near to me, to serve me as
priest, nor come near any of my sacred offerings,
the things that are most sacred; but they shall bear
their shame, and the consequences of the abominations that they have committed. 14Yet I will appoint them to keep charge of the temple, to do all
its chores, all that is to be done in it.
15 But the levitical priests, the descendants
of Zadok, who kept the charge of my sanctuary
when the people of Israel went astray from me,
shall come near to me to minister to me; and they
shall attend me to offer me the fat and the blood,
says the Lord GOD. 16It is they who shall enter my
sanctuary, it is they who shall approach my table,
to minister to me, and they shall keep my charge.
17When they enter the gates of the inner court,
they shall wear linen vestments; they shall have
nothing of wool on them, while they minister at
the gates of the inner court, and within. 18They
shall have linen turbans on their heads, and
linen undergarments on their loins; they shall not
bind themselves with anything that causes sweat.
19When they go out into the outer court to the
people, they shall remove the vestments in which
they have been ministering, and lay them in the
holy chambers; and they shall put on other garments, so that they may not communicate holiness to the people with their vestments. 20They
shall not shave their heads or let their locks grow
long; they shall only trim the hair of their heads.
21No priest shall drink wine when he enters the
inner court. 22They shall not marry a widow, or a
divorced woman, but only a virgin of the stock of
the house of Israel, or a widow who is the widow
of a priest. 23They shall teach my people the difference between the holy and the common, and
show them how to distinguish between the unclean and the clean. 24In a controversy they shall
act as judges, and they shall decide it according to
my judgments. They shall keep my laws and my
statutes regarding all my appointed festivals, and
they shall keep my sabbaths holy. 25They shall
not defile themselves by going near to a dead person; for father or mother, however, and for son
or daughter, and for brother or unmarried sister
they may defile themselves. 26After he has become clean, they shall count seven days for him.
27On the day that he goes into the holy place, into
the inner court, to minister in the holy place, he
shall offer his sin offering, says the Lord GOD.
28 This shall be their inheritance: I am their
inheritance; and you shall give them no holding
in Israel; I am their holding. 29They shall eat the
grain offering, the sin offering, and the guilt offering; and every devoted thing in Israel shall be
theirs. 30The first of all the first fruits of all kinds,
and every offering of all kinds from all your offerings, shall belong to the priests; you shall also give
to the priests the first of your dough, in order that
a blessing may rest on your house. 31The priests
shall not eat of anything, whether bird or animal,
that died of itself or was torn by animals.

45 When you allot the land as an inheritance,
you shall set aside for the LORD a portion
of the land as a holy district, twenty-five thousand
cubits long and twenty[b] thousand cubits wide;
it shall be holy throughout its entire extent. 2Of
this, a square plot of five hundred by five hundred
cubits shall be for the sanctuary, with fifty cubits
for an open space around it. 3In the holy district
you shall measure off a section twenty-five thou-

[a] Heb lacks *foreigners* [b] Gk: Heb *ten*

sand cubits long and ten thousand wide, in which
shall be the sanctuary, the most holy place. 4It
shall be a holy portion of the land; it shall be for
the priests, who minister in the sanctuary and approach the LORD to minister to him; and it shall
be both a place for their houses and a holy place
for the sanctuary. 5Another section, twenty-five
thousand cubits long and ten thousand cubits
wide, shall be for the Levites who minister at the
temple, as their holding for cities to live in.[a]

6 Alongside the portion set apart as the holy
district you shall assign as a holding for the city
an area five thousand cubits wide, and twenty-
five thousand cubits long; it shall belong to the
whole house of Israel.

7 And to the prince shall belong the land on
both sides of the holy district and the holding of
the city, alongside the holy district and the holding of the city, on the west and on the east, corresponding in length to one of the tribal portions,
and extending from the western to the eastern
boundary 8of the land. It is to be his property in
Israel. And my princes shall no longer oppress my
people; but they shall let the house of Israel have
the land according to their tribes.

9 Thus says the Lord GOD: Enough, O princes
of Israel! Put away violence and oppression, and
do what is just and right. Cease your evictions of
my people, says the Lord GOD.

10 You shall have honest balances, an honest
ephah, and an honest bath.[b] 11The ephah and the
bath shall be of the same measure, the bath containing one-tenth of a homer, and the ephah one-
tenth of a homer; the homer shall be the standard
measure. 12The shekel shall be twenty gerahs.
Twenty shekels, twenty-five shekels, and fifteen
shekels shall make a mina for you.

13 This is the offering that you shall make:
one-sixth of an ephah from each homer of wheat,
and one-sixth of an ephah from each homer of
barley, 14and as the fixed portion of oil,[c] one-tenth
of a bath from each cor (the cor,[d] like the homer,
contains ten baths); 15and one sheep from every
flock of two hundred, from the pastures of Israel.
This is the offering for grain offerings, burnt offerings, and offerings of well-being, to make atonement for them, says the Lord GOD. 16All the
people of the land shall join with the prince in
Israel in making this offering. 17But this shall be
the obligation of the prince regarding the burnt
offerings, grain offerings, and drink offerings, at
the festivals, the new moons, and the sabbaths, all
the appointed festivals of the house of Israel: he
shall provide the sin offerings, grain offerings, the
burnt offerings, and the offerings of well-being, to
make atonement for the house of Israel.

18 Thus says the Lord GOD: In the first
month, on the first day of the month, you shall
take a young bull without blemish, and purify
the sanctuary. 19The priest shall take some of the
blood of the sin offering and put it on the doorposts of the temple, the four corners of the ledge
of the altar, and the posts of the gate of the inner
court. 20You shall do the same on the seventh day
of the month for anyone who has sinned through
error or ignorance; so you shall make atonement
for the temple.

21 In the first month, on the fourteenth day
of the month, you shall celebrate the festival of
the passover, and for seven days unleavened
bread shall be eaten. 22On that day the prince
shall provide for himself and all the people of the
land a young bull for a sin offering. 23And during
the seven days of the festival he shall provide as a
burnt offering to the LORD seven young bulls and
seven rams without blemish, on each of the seven
days; and a male goat daily for a sin offering. 24He
shall provide as a grain offering an ephah for each
bull, an ephah for each ram, and a hin of oil to
each ephah. 25In the seventh month, on the fifteenth day of the month and for the seven days of
the festival, he shall make the same provision for
sin offerings, burnt offerings, and grain offerings,
and for the oil.

46 Thus says the Lord GOD: The gate of the
inner court that faces east shall remain
closed on the six working days; but on the sabbath
day it shall be opened and on the day of the new

[a] Gk: Heb *as their holding, twenty chambers* [b] A Heb measure of volume [c] Cn: Heb *oil, the bath the oil*
[d] Vg: Heb *homer*

moon it shall be opened. 2The prince shall enter
by the vestibule of the gate from outside, and shall
take his stand by the post of the gate. The priests
shall offer his burnt offering and his offerings of
well-being, and he shall bow down at the threshold
of the gate. Then he shall go out, but the gate shall
not be closed until evening. 3The people of the
land shall bow down at the entrance of that gate
before the LORD on the sabbaths and on the new
moons. 4The burnt offering that the prince offers
to the LORD on the sabbath day shall be six lambs
without blemish and a ram without blemish; 5and
the grain offering with the ram shall be an ephah,
and the grain offering with the lambs shall be as
much as he wishes to give, together with a hin of
oil to each ephah. 6On the day of the new moon
he shall offer a young bull without blemish, and
six lambs and a ram, which shall be without blemish; 7as a grain offering he shall provide an ephah
with the bull and an ephah with the ram, and with
the lambs as much as he wishes, together with a
hin of oil to each ephah. 8When the prince enters,
he shall come in by the vestibule of the gate, and
he shall go out by the same way.

9 When the people of the land come before
the LORD at the appointed festivals, whoever enters by the north gate to worship shall go out by
the south gate; and whoever enters by the south
gate shall go out by the north gate: they shall not
return by way of the gate by which they entered,
but shall go out straight ahead. 10When they
come in, the prince shall come in with them; and
when they go out, he shall go out.

11 At the festivals and the appointed seasons
the grain offering with a young bull shall be an
ephah, and with a ram an ephah, and with the
lambs as much as one wishes to give, together
with a hin of oil to an ephah. 12When the prince
provides a freewill offering, either a burnt offering or offerings of well-being as a freewill offering
to the LORD, the gate facing east shall be opened
for him; and he shall offer his burnt offering or his
offerings of well-being as he does on the sabbath
day. Then he shall go out, and after he has gone
out the gate shall be closed.

13 He shall provide a lamb, a yearling, without blemish, for a burnt offering to the LORD
daily; morning by morning he shall provide it.
14And he shall provide a grain offering with it
morning by morning regularly, one-sixth of an
ephah, and one-third of a hin of oil to moisten the
choice flour, as a grain offering to the LORD; this
is the ordinance for all time. 15Thus the lamb and
the grain offering and the oil shall be provided,
morning by morning, as a regular burnt offering.

16 Thus says the Lord GOD: If the prince
makes a gift to any of his sons out of his inheritance,[a] it shall belong to his sons, it is their holding by inheritance. 17But if he makes a gift out of
his inheritance to one of his servants, it shall be
his to the year of liberty; then it shall revert to the
prince; only his sons may keep a gift from his inheritance. 18The prince shall not take any of the
inheritance of the people, thrusting them out of
their holding; he shall give his sons their inheritance out of his own holding, so that none of my
people shall be dispossessed of their holding.

19 Then he brought me through the entrance, which was at the side of the gate, to the
north row of the holy chambers for the priests;
and there I saw a place at the extreme western end
of them. 20He said to me, "This is the place where
the priests shall boil the guilt offering and the
sin offering, and where they shall bake the grain
offering, in order not to bring them out into the
outer court and so communicate holiness to the
people."

21 Then he brought me out to the outer
court, and led me past the four corners of the
court; and in each corner of the court there was
a court— 22in the four corners of the court were
small[b] courts, forty cubits long and thirty wide;
the four were of the same size. 23On the inside,
around each of the four courts[c] was a row of ma-
sonry, with hearths made at the bottom of the
rows all around. 24Then he said to me, "These are
the kitchens where those who serve at the temple
shall boil the sacrifices of the people."

47 Then he brought me back to the entrance
of the temple; there, water was flowing

[a] Gk: Heb *it is his inheritance* [b] Gk Syr Vg: Meaning of Heb uncertain [c] Heb *the four of them*

from below the threshold of the temple toward
the east (for the temple faced east); and the water was flowing down from below the south end
of the threshold of the temple, south of the altar.
2Then he brought me out by way of the north
gate, and led me around on the outside to the
outer gate that faces toward the east;[a] and the water was coming out on the south side.

3 Going on eastward with a cord in his hand,
the man measured one thousand cubits, and then
led me through the water; and it was ankle-deep.
4Again he measured one thousand, and led me
through the water; and it was knee-deep. Again
he measured one thousand, and led me through
the water; and it was up to the waist. 5Again he
measured one thousand, and it was a river that I
could not cross, for the water had risen; it was deep
enough to swim in, a river that could not be crossed.
6He said to me, "Mortal, have you seen this?"

Then he led me back along the bank of the
river. 7As I came back, I saw on the bank of the
river a great many trees on the one side and on the
other. 8He said to me, "This water flows toward
the eastern region and goes down into the Arabah; and when it enters the sea, the sea of stagnant
waters, the water will become fresh. 9Wherever
the river goes,[b] every living creature that swarms
will live, and there will be very many fish, once
these waters reach there. It will become fresh; and
everything will live where the river goes. 10People
will stand fishing beside the sea[c] from En-gedi
to En-eglaim; it will be a place for the spreading
of nets; its fish will be of a great many kinds, like
the fish of the Great Sea. 11But its swamps and
marshes will not become fresh; they are to be left
for salt. 12On the banks, on both sides of the river,
there will grow all kinds of trees for food. Their
leaves will not wither nor their fruit fail, but they
will bear fresh fruit every month, because the water for them flows from the sanctuary. Their fruit
will be for food, and their leaves for healing."

13 Thus says the Lord GOD: These are the
boundaries by which you shall divide the land for
inheritance among the twelve tribes of Israel. Joseph shall have two portions. 14You shall divide it
equally; I swore to give it to your ancestors, and
this land shall fall to you as your inheritance.

15 This shall be the boundary of the land:
On the north side, from the Great Sea by way
of Hethlon to Lebo-hamath, and on to Zedad,[d]
16Berothah, Sibraim (which lies between the
border of Damascus and the border of Hamath),
as far as Hazer-hatticon, which is on the border
of Hauran. 17So the boundary shall run from the
sea to Hazar-enon, which is north of the border
of Damascus, with the border of Hamath to the
north.[a] This shall be the north side.

18 On the east side, between Hauran and
Damascus; along the Jordan between Gilead and
the land of Israel; to the eastern sea and as far as
Tamar.[e] This shall be the east side.

19 On the south side, it shall run from Tamar
as far as the waters of Meribath-kadesh, from
there along the Wadi of Egypt[f] to the Great Sea.
This shall be the south side.

20 On the west side, the Great Sea shall be
the boundary to a point opposite Lebo-hamath.
This shall be the west side.

21 So you shall divide this land among you
according to the tribes of Israel. 22You shall allot it as an inheritance for yourselves and for the
aliens who reside among you and have begotten
children among you. They shall be to you as citizens of Israel; with you they shall be allotted an
inheritance among the tribes of Israel. 23In whatever tribe aliens reside, there you shall assign
them their inheritance, says the Lord GOD.

48 These are the names of the tribes: Beginning at the northern border, on the
Hethlon road,[g] from Lebo-hamath, as far as Hazar-
enon (which is on the border of Damascus, with
Hamath to the north), and[h] extending from the
east side to the west,[i] Dan, one portion. 2Adjoin-
ing the territory of Dan, from the east side to the
west, Asher, one portion. 3Adjoining the territory
of Asher, from the east side to the west, Naphtali,

[a] Meaning of Heb uncertain [b] Gk Syr Vg Tg: Heb *the two rivers go* [c] Heb *it* [d] Gk: Heb *Lebo-zedad, 16Hamath* [e] Compare Syr: Heb *you shall measure* [f] Heb lacks *of Egypt* [g] Compare 47.15: Heb *by the side of the way* [h] Cn: Heb *and they shall be his* [i] Gk Compare verses 2–8: Heb *the east side the west*

one portion. 4Adjoining the territory of Naphtali, from the east side to the west, Manasseh, one portion. 5Adjoining the territory of Manasseh, from the east side to the west, Ephraim, one portion. 6Adjoining the territory of Ephraim, from the east side to the west, Reuben, one portion. 7Adjoining the territory of Reuben, from the east side to the west, Judah, one portion.

8 Adjoining the territory of Judah, from the east side to the west, shall be the portion that you shall set apart, twenty-five thousand cubits in width, and in length equal to one of the tribal portions, from the east side to the west, with the sanctuary in the middle of it. 9The portion that you shall set apart for the LORD shall be twenty-five thousand cubits in length, and twenty[a] thousand in width. 10These shall be the allotments of the holy portion: the priests shall have an allotment measuring twenty-five thousand cubits on the northern side, ten thousand cubits in width on the western side, ten thousand in width on the eastern side, and twenty-five thousand in length on the southern side, with the sanctuary of the LORD in the middle of it. 11This shall be for the consecrated priests, the descendants[b] of Zadok, who kept my charge, who did not go astray when the people of Israel went astray, as the Levites did. 12It shall belong to them as a special portion from the holy portion of the land, a most holy place, adjoining the territory of the Levites. 13Alongside the territory of the priests, the Levites shall have an allotment twenty-five thousand cubits in length and ten thousand in width. The whole length shall be twenty-five thousand cubits and the width twenty[c] thousand. 14They shall not sell or exchange any of it; they shall not transfer this choice portion of the land, for it is holy to the LORD.

15 The remainder, five thousand cubits in width and twenty-five thousand in length, shall be for ordinary use for the city, for dwellings and for open country. In the middle of it shall be the city; 16and these shall be its dimensions: the north side four thousand five hundred cubits, the south side four thousand five hundred, the east side four thousand five hundred, and the west side four thousand five hundred. 17The city shall have open land: on the north two hundred fifty cubits, on the south two hundred fifty, on the east two hundred fifty, on the west two hundred fifty. 18The remainder of the length alongside the holy portion shall be ten thousand cubits to the east, and ten thousand to the west, and it shall be alongside the holy portion. Its produce shall be food for the workers of the city. 19The workers of the city, from all the tribes of Israel, shall cultivate it. 20The whole portion that you shall set apart shall be twenty-five thousand cubits square, that is, the holy portion together with the property of the city.

21 What remains on both sides of the holy portion and of the property of the city shall belong to the prince. Extending from the twenty-five thousand cubits of the holy portion to the east border, and westward from the twenty-five thousand cubits to the west border, parallel to the tribal portions, it shall belong to the prince. The holy portion with the sanctuary of the temple in the middle of it, 22and the property of the Levites and of the city, shall be in the middle of that which belongs to the prince. The portion of the prince shall lie between the territory of Judah and the territory of Benjamin.

23 As for the rest of the tribes: from the east side to the west, Benjamin, one portion. 24Adjoining the territory of Benjamin, from the east side to the west, Simeon, one portion. 25Adjoining the territory of Simeon, from the east side to the west, Issachar, one portion. 26Adjoining the territory of Issachar, from the east side to the west, Zebulun, one portion. 27Adjoining the territory of Zebulun, from the east side to the west, Gad, one portion. 28And adjoining the territory of Gad to the south, the boundary shall run from Tamar to the waters of Meribath-kadesh, from there along the Wadi of Egypt[d] to the Great Sea. 29This is the land that you shall allot as an inheritance among the tribes of Israel, and these are their portions, says the Lord GOD.

30 These shall be the exits of the city: On the north side, which is to be four thousand five hun-

[a] Compare 45.1: Heb *ten* [b] One Ms Gk: Heb *of the descendants* [c] Gk: Heb *ten* [d] Heb lacks *of Egypt*

dred cubits by measure, [31]three gates, the gate of
Reuben, the gate of Judah, and the gate of Levi,
the gates of the city being named after the tribes
of Israel. [32]On the east side, which is to be four
thousand five hundred cubits, three gates, the
gate of Joseph, the gate of Benjamin, and the gate
of Dan. [33]On the south side, which is to be four
thousand five hundred cubits by measure, three
gates, the gate of Simeon, the gate of Issachar, and
the gate of Zebulun. [34]On the west side, which
is to be four thousand five hundred cubits, three
gates,[a] the gate of Gad, the gate of Asher, and the
gate of Naphtali. [35]The circumference of the city
shall be eighteen thousand cubits. And the name
of the city from that time on shall be, The LORD
is There.

[a] One Ms Gk Syr: MT *their gates three*

Daniel

Daniel is a book that includes six Diaspora stories (chs. 1–6) and four visions (7:1-28; 8:1-27; 9:20-27; 10:1—12:13), all set within a textual framework that extends over three empires: Babylonian, Median-Persian, and Greek. The book contains some of the best-known tales in the Bible, including the stories of Daniel's interpretation of Nebuchadnezzar's dreams (ch. 2) and "the writing on the wall" (ch. 5), Daniel's miraculous deliverance from a den of lions (ch. 6), and the courageous counter-Babylonian resistance of the three friends, Shadrach, Meshach, and Abednego (ch. 3). Within the Hebrew Bible, Daniel also contains the only full-fledged example of apocalyptic literature—a literary genre with a particular interest in revealing heavenly secrets to a visionary through dreams, visions, or angelic beings. The book was written in two languages (2:4b—7:28 in Aramaic, the rest in Hebrew) within a narrative framework based on the exilic experience and visions of a pious exile named Daniel.

I engage the text of Daniel as a first-generation Chinese Canadian and as a minority person in my profession. I see significant juxtapositions between Daniel's "captive" experience and my own experience. The Chinese individual "I" (small self) is situated within the collective "we" (big self). Within this perspective, reading and hearing the "I" voice of Daniel in chapters 7–12 allows for a sense of identification with him.

Text and Culture

Daniel is a text surrounded by people of diverse cultures. Daniel's social world is unpleasant and difficult because of foreign rule. Perseverance and the ability to adapt are necessary tools for survival. If we read Daniel as a success story, the overall stance of the narratives in chapters 1–6 is one of loyalty, optimism, and accommodation towards the ruling power. Crossing borders between the home and the host culture, immigrant families today have to go through the same journey of alienation, adaptation, assimilation, and, for some, reorientation. As in Daniel, pleasure or pain and success or failure are among the possibilities of this border-crossing experience in the Diaspora. Likewise, remaining in a borderland existence or negotiating an ever-expanding "in-between space" are among the options in the life of an immigrant. Daniel exemplifies an individual's breaking away from a captive status to become an aspiring sage in an adopted culture. Failing to perceive this possibility in life, we would remain perpetual captives in a free land.

Text and Community

As a profoundly pastoral book, Daniel is a text for people of different faith communities. It was written at a time of great national peril to encourage faithful Jews that God is still in control, despite

their current situations. Within my own interpretive communities, Daniel has been heavily employed, reflected upon, and critiqued among many postcolonial discourses. In my own culture-specific faith community, the book has been strategically appropriated in helping members come to terms with the new world realities after the tragedy of September 11, 2001. The world of Daniel is full of conflicts and turbulence, as well as the rise and fall of kings and kingdoms in the course of human history and beyond.

I am in the prime of my life, with a ministry among my privileged peers—well-educated, middle-class professionals, Chinese and non-Chinese baby boomers. Within this context, one reality persistently disturbs the community of baby boomers: Our collective Canadian culture, our professional lives, and our social and economic status cannot adequately provide answers to our inquiry into the magnitude and intensity of human suffering. As in the case of Daniel, we look into the future with a high degree of uncertainty but glimpses of hope.

Text and Contextualization

Daniel is a text that often is appropriated by people who discover that it speaks to the contexts in which they find themselves. In 9:2, Daniel himself turns to a book—Jeremiah—as he seeks to understand his present situation. In doing so, he mirrors our own search for meaning and significance in our contexts. Daniel can be read as a manual for survival—and even success—under a hostile and dominating empire. Yet the means for resisting kings and empires as reflected in chapters 1–6 is the creative use of satire and humor, as David Valeta has argued. This may have profound implications for coping strategies on the part of minorities today, particularly in the academic religious or theological disciplines. The sharp contrast between the public Daniel as an aspiring sage (chs. 1–6) and the private Daniel as a dysfunctional seer (who speaks as "I" in chs. 7–12), suggests a degree of cognitive dissonance which contemporary minority students and scholars of the Bible may recognize.

— ***Barbara M. Leung Lai***

1 In the third year of the reign of King Jehoiakim of Judah, King Nebuchadnezzar of Babylon came to Jerusalem and besieged it. 2 The Lord let King Jehoiakim of Judah fall into his power, as well as some of the vessels of the house of God. These he brought to the land of Shinar,[a] and placed the vessels in the treasury of his gods.

3 Then the king commanded his palace master Ashpenaz to bring some of the Israelites of the royal family and of the nobility, 4 young men without physical defect and handsome, versed in every branch of wisdom, endowed with knowledge and insight, and competent to serve in the king's palace; they were to be taught the literature and language of the Chaldeans. 5 The king assigned them a daily portion of the royal rations of

[a] Gk Theodotion: Heb adds *to the house of his own gods*

food and wine. They were to be educated for three years, so that at the end of that time they could be stationed in the king's court. 6 Among them were Daniel, Hananiah, Mishael, and Azariah, from the tribe of Judah. 7 The palace master gave them other names: Daniel he called Belteshazzar, Hananiah he called Shadrach, Mishael he called Meshach, and Azariah he called Abednego.

8 But Daniel resolved that he would not defile himself with the royal rations of food and wine; so he asked the palace master to allow him not to defile himself. 9 Now God allowed Daniel to receive favor and compassion from the palace master. 10 The palace master said to Daniel, "I am afraid of my lord the king; he has appointed your food and your drink. If he should see you in poorer condition than the other young men of your own age, you would endanger my head with the king." 11 Then Daniel asked the guard whom the palace master had appointed over Daniel, Hananiah, Mishael, and Azariah: 12 "Please test your servants for ten days. Let us be given vegetables to eat and water to drink. 13 You can then compare our appearance with the appearance of the young men who eat the royal rations, and deal with your servants according to what you observe." 14 So he agreed to this proposal and tested them for ten days. 15 At the end of ten days it was observed that they appeared better and fatter than all the young men who had been eating the royal rations. 16 So the guard continued to withdraw their royal rations and the wine they were to drink, and gave them vegetables. 17 To these four young men God gave knowledge and skill in every aspect of literature and wisdom; Daniel also had insight into all visions and dreams.

18 At the end of the time that the king had set for them to be brought in, the palace master brought them into the presence of Nebuchadnezzar, 19 and the king spoke with them. And among them all, no one was found to compare with Daniel, Hananiah, Mishael, and Azariah; therefore they were stationed in the king's court. 20 In every matter of wisdom and understanding concerning which the king inquired of them, he found them ten times better than all the magicians and enchanters in his whole kingdom. 21 And Daniel continued there until the first year of King Cyrus.

2 In the second year of Nebuchadnezzar's reign, Nebuchadnezzar dreamed such dreams that his spirit was troubled and his sleep left him. 2 So the king commanded that the magicians, the enchanters, the sorcerers, and the Chaldeans be summoned to tell the king his dreams. When they came in and stood before the king, 3 he said to them, "I have had such a dream that my spirit is troubled by the desire to understand it." 4 The Chaldeans said to the king (in Aramaic),[a] "O king, live forever! Tell your servants the dream, and we will reveal the interpretation." 5 The king answered the Chaldeans, "This is a public decree: if you do not tell me both the dream and its interpretation, you shall be torn limb from limb, and your houses shall be laid in ruins. 6 But if you do tell me the dream and its interpretation, you shall receive from me gifts and rewards and great honor. Therefore tell me the dream and its interpretation." 7 They answered a second time, "Let the king first tell his servants the dream, then we can give its interpretation." 8 The king answered, "I know with certainty that you are trying to gain time, because you see I have firmly decreed: 9 if you do not tell me the dream, there is but one verdict for you. You have agreed to speak lying and misleading words to me until things take a turn. Therefore, tell me the dream, and I shall know that you can give me its interpretation." 10 The Chaldeans answered the king, "There is no one on earth who can reveal what the king demands! In fact no king, however great and powerful, has ever asked such a thing of any magician or enchanter or Chaldean. 11 The thing that the king is asking is too difficult, and no one can reveal it to the king except the gods, whose dwelling is not with mortals."

12 Because of this the king flew into a violent rage and commanded that all the wise men of Babylon be destroyed. 13 The decree was issued,

[a] The text from this point to the end of chapter 7 is in Aramaic

and the wise men were about to be executed;
and they looked for Daniel and his companions,
to execute them. 14 Then Daniel responded with
prudence and discretion to Arioch, the king's
chief executioner, who had gone out to execute
the wise men of Babylon; 15 he asked Arioch, the
royal official, "Why is the decree of the king so
urgent?" Arioch then explained the matter to
Daniel. 16 So Daniel went in and requested that
the king give him time and he would tell the king
the interpretation.

17 Then Daniel went to his home and informed his companions, Hananiah, Mishael, and
Azariah, 18 and told them to seek mercy from the
God of heaven concerning this mystery, so that
Daniel and his companions with the rest of the
wise men of Babylon might not perish. 19 Then
the mystery was revealed to Daniel in a vision of
the night, and Daniel blessed the God of heaven.

20 Daniel said:
"Blessed be the name of God from age to age,
for wisdom and power are his.
21 He changes times and seasons,
deposes kings and sets up kings;
he gives wisdom to the wise
and knowledge to those who have
understanding.
22 He reveals deep and hidden things;
he knows what is in the darkness,
and light dwells with him.
23 To you, O God of my ancestors,
I give thanks and praise,
for you have given me wisdom and
power,
and have now revealed to me what we
asked of you,
for you have revealed to us what the king
ordered."

24 Therefore Daniel went to Arioch, whom
the king had appointed to destroy the wise men
of Babylon, and said to him, "Do not destroy the
wise men of Babylon; bring me in before the king,
and I will give the king the interpretation."

25 Then Arioch quickly brought Daniel
before the king and said to him: "I have found
among the exiles from Judah a man who can tell
the king the interpretation." 26 The king said to
Daniel, whose name was Belteshazzar, "Are you
able to tell me the dream that I have seen and its
interpretation?" 27 Daniel answered the king, "No
wise men, enchanters, magicians, or diviners can
show to the king the mystery that the king is asking, 28 but there is a God in heaven who reveals
mysteries, and he has disclosed to King Nebuchadnezzar what will happen at the end of days.
Your dream and the visions of your head as you
lay in bed were these: 29 To you, O king, as you lay
in bed, came thoughts of what would be hereafter, and the revealer of mysteries disclosed to you
what is to be. 30 But as for me, this mystery has not
been revealed to me because of any wisdom that I
have more than any other living being, but in order that the interpretation may be known to the
king and that you may understand the thoughts
of your mind.

31 "You were looking, O king, and lo! there
was a great statue. This statue was huge, its brilliance extraordinary; it was standing before you,
and its appearance was frightening. 32 The head of
that statue was of fine gold, its chest and arms of
silver, its middle and thighs of bronze, 33 its legs
of iron, its feet partly of iron and partly of clay.
34 As you looked on, a stone was cut out, not by
human hands, and it struck the statue on its feet
of iron and clay and broke them in pieces. 35 Then
the iron, the clay, the bronze, the silver, and the
gold, were all broken in pieces and became like
the chaff of the summer threshing floors; and the
wind carried them away, so that not a trace of
them could be found. But the stone that struck
the statue became a great mountain and filled the
whole earth.

36 "This was the dream; now we will tell the
king its interpretation. 37 You, O king, the king
of kings—to whom the God of heaven has given
the kingdom, the power, the might, and the glory,
38 into whose hand he has given human beings,
wherever they live, the wild animals of the field,
and the birds of the air, and whom he has established as ruler over them all—you are the head of
gold. 39 After you shall arise another kingdom inferior to yours, and yet a third kingdom of bronze,
which shall rule over the whole earth. 40 And there
shall be a fourth kingdom, strong as iron; just as

iron crushes and smashes everything,[a] it shall
crush and shatter all these. 41As you saw the feet
and toes partly of potter's clay and partly of iron,
it shall be a divided kingdom; but some of the
strength of iron shall be in it, as you saw the iron
mixed with the clay. 42As the toes of the feet were
part iron and part clay, so the kingdom shall be
partly strong and partly brittle. 43As you saw the
iron mixed with clay, so will they mix with one
another in marriage,[b] but they will not hold together, just as iron does not mix with clay. 44And
in the days of those kings the God of heaven will
set up a kingdom that shall never be destroyed,
nor shall this kingdom be left to another people.
It shall crush all these kingdoms and bring them
to an end, and it shall stand forever; 45just as you
saw that a stone was cut from the mountain not
by hands, and that it crushed the iron, the bronze,
the clay, the silver, and the gold. The great God
has informed the king what shall be hereafter.
The dream is certain, and its interpretation trustworthy."
46 Then King Nebuchadnezzar fell on his
face, worshiped Daniel, and commanded that
a grain offering and incense be offered to him.
47The king said to Daniel, "Truly, your God is
God of gods and Lord of kings and a revealer of
mysteries, for you have been able to reveal this
mystery!" 48Then the king promoted Daniel, gave
him many great gifts, and made him ruler over
the whole province of Babylon and chief prefect
over all the wise men of Babylon. 49Daniel made
a request of the king, and he appointed Shadrach,
Meshach, and Abednego over the affairs of the
province of Babylon. But Daniel remained at the
king's court.

3 King Nebuchadnezzar made a golden statue
whose height was sixty cubits and whose
width was six cubits; he set it up on the plain of
Dura in the province of Babylon. 2Then King
Nebuchadnezzar sent for the satraps, the prefects,
and the governors, the counselors, the treasurers,
the justices, the magistrates, and all the officials
of the provinces, to assemble and come to the
dedication of the statue that King Nebuchadnezzar had set up. 3So the satraps, the prefects, and
the governors, the counselors, the treasurers, the
justices, the magistrates, and all the officials of
the provinces, assembled for the dedication of
the statue that King Nebuchadnezzar had set up.
When they were standing before the statue that
Nebuchadnezzar had set up, 4the herald proclaimed aloud, "You are commanded, O peoples,
nations, and languages, 5that when you hear the
sound of the horn, pipe, lyre, trigon, harp, drum,
and entire musical ensemble, you are to fall down
and worship the golden statue that King Nebuchadnezzar has set up. 6Whoever does not fall
down and worship shall immediately be thrown
into a furnace of blazing fire." 7Therefore, as soon
as all the peoples heard the sound of the horn,
pipe, lyre, trigon, harp, drum, and entire musical
ensemble, all the peoples, nations, and languages
fell down and worshiped the golden statue that
King Nebuchadnezzar had set up.
8 Accordingly, at this time certain Chaldeans
came forward and denounced the Jews. 9They
said to King Nebuchadnezzar, "O king, live forever! 10You, O king, have made a decree, that
everyone who hears the sound of the horn, pipe,
lyre, trigon, harp, drum, and entire musical ensemble, shall fall down and worship the golden
statue, 11and whoever does not fall down and
worship shall be thrown into a furnace of blazing
fire. 12There are certain Jews whom you have appointed over the affairs of the province of Babylon: Shadrach, Meshach, and Abednego. These
pay no heed to you, O king. They do not serve
your gods and they do not worship the golden
statue that you have set up."
13 Then Nebuchadnezzar in furious rage
commanded that Shadrach, Meshach, and Abednego be brought in; so they brought those men
before the king. 14Nebuchadnezzar said to them,
"Is it true, O Shadrach, Meshach, and Abednego,
that you do not serve my gods and you do not
worship the golden statue that I have set up?
15Now if you are ready when you hear the sound
of the horn, pipe, lyre, trigon, harp, drum, and entire musical ensemble to fall down and worship

[a] Gk Theodotion Syr Vg: Aram adds *and like iron that crushes*

[b] Aram *by human seed*

the statue that I have made, well and good.[a] But
if you do not worship, you shall immediately be
thrown into a furnace of blazing fire, and who is
the god that will deliver you out of my hands?"
16 Shadrach, Meshach, and Abednego answered the king, "O Nebuchadnezzar, we have no
need to present a defense to you in this matter.
17 If our God whom we serve is able to deliver us
from the furnace of blazing fire and out of your
hand, O king, let him deliver us.[b] 18 But if not, be
it known to you, O king, that we will not serve
your gods and we will not worship the golden
statue that you have set up."
19 Then Nebuchadnezzar was so filled with
rage against Shadrach, Meshach, and Abednego
that his face was distorted. He ordered the furnace
heated up seven times more than was customary,
20 and ordered some of the strongest guards in his
army to bind Shadrach, Meshach, and Abednego
and to throw them into the furnace of blazing
fire. 21 So the men were bound, still wearing their
tunics,[c] their trousers,[c] their hats, and their other
garments, and they were thrown into the furnace
of blazing fire. 22 Because the king's command was
urgent and the furnace was so overheated, the
raging flames killed the men who lifted Shadrach,
Meshach, and Abednego. 23 But the three men,
Shadrach, Meshach, and Abednego, fell down,
bound, into the furnace of blazing fire.
24 Then King Nebuchadnezzar was astonished and rose up quickly. He said to his counselors, "Was it not three men that we threw bound
into the fire?" They answered the king, "True,
O king." 25 He replied, "But I see four men un-
bound, walking in the middle of the fire, and they
are not hurt; and the fourth has the appearance
of a god."[d] 26 Nebuchadnezzar then approached
the door of the furnace of blazing fire and said,
"Shadrach, Meshach, and Abednego, servants
of the Most High God, come out! Come here!"
So Shadrach, Meshach, and Abednego came out
from the fire. 27 And the satraps, the prefects, the
governors, and the king's counselors gathered
together and saw that the fire had not had any
power over the bodies of those men; the hair of
their heads was not singed, their tunics[c] were not
harmed, and not even the smell of fire came from
them. 28 Nebuchadnezzar said, "Blessed be the
God of Shadrach, Meshach, and Abednego, who
has sent his angel and delivered his servants who
trusted in him. They disobeyed the king's command and yielded up their bodies rather than
serve and worship any god except their own God.
29 Therefore I make a decree: Any people, nation,
or language that utters blasphemy against the
God of Shadrach, Meshach, and Abednego shall
be torn limb from limb, and their houses laid in
ruins; for there is no other god who is able to
deliver in this way." 30 Then the king promoted
Shadrach, Meshach, and Abednego in the province of Babylon.

4[e] King Nebuchadnezzar to all peoples, nations, and languages that live throughout the
earth: May you have abundant prosperity! 2 The
signs and wonders that the Most High God has
worked for me I am pleased to recount.

3 How great are his signs,
how mighty his wonders!
His kingdom is an everlasting kingdom,
and his sovereignty is from generation to
generation.

4[f] I, Nebuchadnezzar, was living at ease in
my home and prospering in my palace. 5 I saw a
dream that frightened me; my fantasies in bed and
the visions of my head terrified me. 6 So I made a
decree that all the wise men of Babylon should
be brought before me, in order that they might
tell me the interpretation of the dream. 7 Then the
magicians, the enchanters, the Chaldeans, and the
diviners came in, and I told them the dream, but
they could not tell me its interpretation. 8 At last
Daniel came in before me—he who was named
Belteshazzar after the name of my god, and who
is endowed with a spirit of the holy gods[g]—and
I told him the dream: 9 "O Belteshazzar, chief of
the magicians, I know that you are endowed with

[a] Aram lacks *well and good* [b] Or *If our God whom we serve is able to deliver us, he will deliver us from the furnace of blazing fire and out of your hand, O king.* [c] Meaning of Aram word uncertain [d] Aram *a son of the gods* [e] Ch 3.31 in Aram [f] Ch 4.1 in Aram [g] Or *a holy, divine spirit*

a spirit of the holy gods[a] and that no mystery is
too difficult for you. Hear[b] the dream that I saw;
tell me its interpretation.

10[c] Upon my bed this is what I saw;
there was a tree at the center of the earth,
and its height was great.
11 The tree grew great and strong,
its top reached to heaven,
and it was visible to the ends of the whole
earth.
12 Its foliage was beautiful,
its fruit abundant,
and it provided food for all.
The animals of the field found shade under it,
the birds of the air nested in its branches,
and from it all living beings were fed.

13 "I continued looking, in the visions of my
head as I lay in bed, and there was a holy watcher,
coming down from heaven. 14He cried aloud and
said:

'Cut down the tree and chop off its branches,
strip off its foliage and scatter its fruit.
Let the animals flee from beneath it
and the birds from its branches.
15 But leave its stump and roots in the ground,
with a band of iron and bronze,
in the tender grass of the field.
Let him be bathed with the dew of heaven,
and let his lot be with the animals of the
field
in the grass of the earth.
16 Let his mind be changed from that of a
human,
and let the mind of an animal be given to
him.
And let seven times pass over him.
17 The sentence is rendered by decree of the
watchers,
the decision is given by order of the holy
ones,
in order that all who live may know
that the Most High is sovereign over the
kingdom of mortals;
he gives it to whom he will
and sets over it the lowliest of human
beings.'

18 "This is the dream that I, King Nebuchadnezzar, saw. Now you, Belteshazzar, declare
the interpretation, since all the wise men of my
kingdom are unable to tell me the interpretation.
You are able, however, for you are endowed with
a spirit of the holy gods."[a]

19 Then Daniel, who was called Belteshazzar,
was severely distressed for a while. His thoughts
terrified him. The king said, "Belteshazzar, do not
let the dream or the interpretation terrify you."
Belteshazzar answered, "My lord, may the dream
be for those who hate you, and its interpretation
for your enemies! 20The tree that you saw, which
grew great and strong, so that its top reached to
heaven and was visible to the end of the whole
earth, 21whose foliage was beautiful and its fruit
abundant, and which provided food for all, under which animals of the field lived, and in whose
branches the birds of the air had nests— 22it is you,
O king! You have grown great and strong. Your
greatness has increased and reaches to heaven,
and your sovereignty to the ends of the earth.
23And whereas the king saw a holy watcher coming down from heaven and saying, 'Cut down the
tree and destroy it, but leave its stump and roots
in the ground, with a band of iron and bronze, in
the grass of the field; and let him be bathed with
the dew of heaven, and let his lot be with the
animals of the field, until seven times pass over
him'— 24this is the interpretation, O king, and it
is a decree of the Most High that has come upon
my lord the king: 25You shall be driven away from
human society, and your dwelling shall be with
the wild animals. You shall be made to eat grass
like oxen, you shall be bathed with the dew of
heaven, and seven times shall pass over you, until
you have learned that the Most High has sovereignty over the kingdom of mortals, and gives it
to whom he will. 26As it was commanded to leave
the stump and roots of the tree, your kingdom

[a] Or *a holy, divine spirit* [b] Theodotion: Aram *The visions of*
[c] Theodotion Syr Compare Gk: Aram adds *The visions of my head*

shall be re-established for you from the time that
you learn that Heaven is sovereign. 27Therefore,
O king, may my counsel be acceptable to you:
atone for[a] your sins with righteousness, and your
iniquities with mercy to the oppressed, so that
your prosperity may be prolonged."

28 All this came upon King Nebuchadnezzar.
29At the end of twelve months he was walking on
the roof of the royal palace of Babylon, 30and the
king said, "Is this not magnificent Babylon, which
I have built as a royal capital by my mighty power
and for my glorious majesty?" 31While the words
were still in the king's mouth, a voice came from
heaven: "O King Nebuchadnezzar, to you it is
declared: The kingdom has departed from you!
32You shall be driven away from human society,
and your dwelling shall be with the animals of the
field. You shall be made to eat grass like oxen, and
seven times shall pass over you, until you have
learned that the Most High has sovereignty over
the kingdom of mortals and gives it to whom he
will." 33Immediately the sentence was fulfilled
against Nebuchadnezzar. He was driven away
from human society, ate grass like oxen, and his
body was bathed with the dew of heaven, until his
hair grew as long as eagles' feathers and his nails
became like birds' claws.

34 When that period was over, I, Nebuchadnezzar, lifted my eyes to heaven, and my reason
returned to me.

I blessed the Most High,
  and praised and honored the one who lives
    forever.
For his sovereignty is an everlasting
    sovereignty,
  and his kingdom endures from generation
    to generation.
35 All the inhabitants of the earth are accounted
    as nothing,
  and he does what he wills with the host of
    heaven
  and the inhabitants of the earth.
There is no one who can stay his hand
  or say to him, "What are you doing?"

36At that time my reason returned to me; and
my majesty and splendor were restored to me for
the glory of my kingdom. My counselors and my
lords sought me out, I was re-established over my
kingdom, and still more greatness was added to
me. 37Now I, Nebuchadnezzar, praise and extol
and honor the King of heaven,

for all his works are truth,
  and his ways are justice;
and he is able to bring low
  those who walk in pride.

5 King Belshazzar made a great festival for a
thousand of his lords, and he was drinking
wine in the presence of the thousand.

2 Under the influence of the wine, Belshazzar
commanded that they bring in the vessels of gold
and silver that his father Nebuchadnezzar had
taken out of the temple in Jerusalem, so that the
king and his lords, his wives, and his concubines
might drink from them. 3So they brought in the
vessels of gold and silver[b] that had been taken out
of the temple, the house of God in Jerusalem, and
the king and his lords, his wives, and his concubines drank from them. 4They drank the wine
and praised the gods of gold and silver, bronze,
iron, wood, and stone.

5 Immediately the fingers of a human hand
appeared and began writing on the plaster of the
wall of the royal palace, next to the lampstand.
The king was watching the hand as it wrote. 6Then
the king's face turned pale, and his thoughts terrified him. His limbs gave way, and his knees
knocked together. 7The king cried aloud to bring
in the enchanters, the Chaldeans, and the diviners; and the king said to the wise men of Babylon,
"Whoever can read this writing and tell me its
interpretation shall be clothed in purple, have a
chain of gold around his neck, and rank third in
the kingdom." 8Then all the king's wise men came
in, but they could not read the writing or tell the
king the interpretation. 9Then King Belshazzar
became greatly terrified and his face turned pale,
and his lords were perplexed.

10 The queen, when she heard the discussion
of the king and his lords, came into the banqueting

[a] Aram *break off* [b] Theodotion Vg: Aram lacks *and silver*

hall. The queen said, "O king, live forever! Do
not let your thoughts terrify you or your face
grow pale. [11]There is a man in your kingdom
who is endowed with a spirit of the holy gods.[a]
In the days of your father he was found to have
enlightenment, understanding, and wisdom like
the wisdom of the gods. Your father, King Nebuchadnezzar, made him chief of the magicians, enchanters, Chaldeans, and diviners,[b] [12]because an
excellent spirit, knowledge, and understanding to
interpret dreams, explain riddles, and solve problems were found in this Daniel, whom the king
named Belteshazzar. Now let Daniel be called,
and he will give the interpretation."

13 Then Daniel was brought in before the
king. The king said to Daniel, "So you are Daniel, one of the exiles of Judah, whom my father
the king brought from Judah? [14]I have heard of
you that a spirit of the gods[c] is in you, and that
enlightenment, understanding, and excellent
wisdom are found in you. [15]Now the wise men,
the enchanters, have been brought in before me
to read this writing and tell me its interpretation,
but they were not able to give the interpretation
of the matter. [16]But I have heard that you can give
interpretations and solve problems. Now if you
are able to read the writing and tell me its interpretation, you shall be clothed in purple, have a
chain of gold around your neck, and rank third in
the kingdom."

17 Then Daniel answered in the presence of
the king, "Let your gifts be for yourself, or give
your rewards to someone else! Nevertheless I will
read the writing to the king and let him know the
interpretation. [18]O king, the Most High God gave
your father Nebuchadnezzar kingship, greatness,
glory, and majesty. [19]And because of the greatness that he gave him, all peoples, nations, and
languages trembled and feared before him. He
killed those he wanted to kill, kept alive those he
wanted to keep alive, honored those he wanted to
honor, and degraded those he wanted to degrade.
[20]But when his heart was lifted up and his spirit
was hardened so that he acted proudly, he was deposed from his kingly throne, and his glory was
stripped from him. [21]He was driven from human
society, and his mind was made like that of an animal. His dwelling was with the wild asses, he was
fed grass like oxen, and his body was bathed with
the dew of heaven, until he learned that the Most
High God has sovereignty over the kingdom of
mortals, and sets over it whomever he will. [22]And
you, Belshazzar his son, have not humbled your
heart, even though you knew all this! [23]You have
exalted yourself against the Lord of heaven! The
vessels of his temple have been brought in before
you, and you and your lords, your wives and your
concubines have been drinking wine from them.
You have praised the gods of silver and gold, of
bronze, iron, wood, and stone, which do not see
or hear or know; but the God in whose power is
your very breath, and to whom belong all your
ways, you have not honored.

24 "So from his presence the hand was sent
and this writing was inscribed. [25]And this is the
writing that was inscribed: MENE, MENE, TEKEL,
AND PARSIN. [26]This is the interpretation of the
matter: MENE, God has numbered the days of[d]
your kingdom and brought it to an end; [27]TEKEL,
you have been weighed on the scales and found
wanting; [28]PERES,[e] your kingdom is divided and
given to the Medes and Persians."

29 Then Belshazzar gave the command, and
Daniel was clothed in purple, a chain of gold was
put around his neck, and a proclamation was
made concerning him that he should rank third
in the kingdom.

30 That very night Belshazzar, the Chaldean
king, was killed. [31][f] And Darius the Mede received
the kingdom, being about sixty-two years old.

6 It pleased Darius to set over the kingdom one
hundred twenty satraps, stationed throughout the whole kingdom, [2]and over them three
presidents, including Daniel; to these the satraps
gave account, so that the king might suffer no
loss. [3]Soon Daniel distinguished himself above
all the other presidents and satraps because an
excellent spirit was in him, and the king planned

[a] Or *a holy, divine spirit*
[b] Aram adds *the king your father*
[c] Or *a divine spirit*
[d] Aram lacks *the days of*
[e] The singular of *Parsin*
[f] Ch 6.1 in Aram

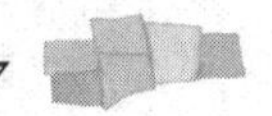

to appoint him over the whole kingdom. 4So the
presidents and the satraps tried to find grounds
for complaint against Daniel in connection with
the kingdom. But they could find no grounds
for complaint or any corruption, because he was
faithful, and no negligence or corruption could
be found in him. 5The men said, "We shall not
find any ground for complaint against this Daniel
unless we find it in connection with the law of his
God."

6 So the presidents and satraps conspired
and came to the king and said to him, "O King
Darius, live forever! 7All the presidents of the
kingdom, the prefects and the satraps, the counselors and the governors are agreed that the king
should establish an ordinance and enforce an interdict, that whoever prays to anyone, divine or
human, for thirty days, except to you, O king,
shall be thrown into a den of lions. 8Now, O king,
establish the interdict and sign the document, so
that it cannot be changed, according to the law of
the Medes and the Persians, which cannot be revoked." 9Therefore King Darius signed the document and interdict.

10 Although Daniel knew that the document had been signed, he continued to go to his
house, which had windows in its upper room
open toward Jerusalem, and to get down on his
knees three times a day to pray to his God and
praise him, just as he had done previously. 11The
conspirators came and found Daniel praying and
seeking mercy before his God. 12Then they approached the king and said concerning the interdict, "O king! Did you not sign an interdict, that
anyone who prays to anyone, divine or human,
within thirty days except to you, O king, shall be
thrown into a den of lions?" The king answered,
"The thing stands fast, according to the law of the
Medes and Persians, which cannot be revoked."
13Then they responded to the king, "Daniel, one
of the exiles from Judah, pays no attention to you,
O king, or to the interdict you have signed, but he
is saying his prayers three times a day."

14 When the king heard the charge, he was
very much distressed. He was determined to save
Daniel, and until the sun went down he made every effort to rescue him. 15Then the conspirators
came to the king and said to him, "Know, O king,
that it is a law of the Medes and Persians that no
interdict or ordinance that the king establishes
can be changed."

16 Then the king gave the command, and
Daniel was brought and thrown into the den of
lions. The king said to Daniel, "May your God,
whom you faithfully serve, deliver you!" 17A
stone was brought and laid on the mouth of the
den, and the king sealed it with his own signet
and with the signet of his lords, so that nothing
might be changed concerning Daniel. 18Then the
king went to his palace and spent the night fasting; no food was brought to him, and sleep fled
from him.

19 Then, at break of day, the king got up and
hurried to the den of lions. 20When he came near
the den where Daniel was, he cried out anxiously
to Daniel, "O Daniel, servant of the living God,
has your God whom you faithfully serve been
able to deliver you from the lions?" 21Daniel
then said to the king, "O king, live forever! 22My
God sent his angel and shut the lions' mouths
so that they would not hurt me, because I was
found blameless before him; and also before
you, O king, I have done no wrong." 23Then the
king was exceedingly glad and commanded that
Daniel be taken up out of the den. So Daniel was
taken up out of the den, and no kind of harm was
found on him, because he had trusted in his God.
24The king gave a command, and those who had
accused Daniel were brought and thrown into
the den of lions—they, their children, and their
wives. Before they reached the bottom of the den
the lions overpowered them and broke all their
bones in pieces.

25 Then King Darius wrote to all peoples and
nations of every language throughout the whole
world: "May you have abundant prosperity! 26I
make a decree, that in all my royal dominion
people should tremble and fear before the God
of Daniel:

For he is the living God,
  enduring forever.
His kingdom shall never be destroyed,
  and his dominion has no end.
27 He delivers and rescues,

he works signs and wonders in heaven and
on earth;
for he has saved Daniel
from the power of the lions."
28 So this Daniel prospered during the reign of
Darius and the reign of Cyrus the Persian.
7 In the first year of King Belshazzar of Babylon, Daniel had a dream and visions of his
head as he lay in bed. Then he wrote down the
dream:[a] 2 I,[b] Daniel, saw in my vision by night the
four winds of heaven stirring up the great sea,
3 and four great beasts came up out of the sea,
different from one another. 4 The first was like a
lion and had eagles' wings. Then, as I watched, its
wings were plucked off, and it was lifted up from
the ground and made to stand on two feet like a
human being; and a human mind was given to
it. 5 Another beast appeared, a second one, that
looked like a bear. It was raised up on one side,
had three tusks[c] in its mouth among its teeth and
was told, "Arise, devour many bodies!" 6 After this,
as I watched, another appeared, like a leopard.
The beast had four wings of a bird on its back and
four heads; and dominion was given to it. 7 After
this I saw in the visions by night a fourth beast,
terrifying and dreadful and exceedingly strong.
It had great iron teeth and was devouring, breaking in pieces, and stamping what was left with its
feet. It was different from all the beasts that preceded it, and it had ten horns. 8 I was considering
the horns, when another horn appeared, a little
one coming up among them; to make room for
it, three of the earlier horns were plucked up by
the roots. There were eyes like human eyes in this
horn, and a mouth speaking arrogantly.
9 As I watched,
thrones were set in place,
and an Ancient One[d] took his throne,
his clothing was white as snow,
and the hair of his head like pure wool;
his throne was fiery flames,
and its wheels were burning fire.
10 A stream of fire issued
and flowed out from his presence.
A thousand thousands served him,
and ten thousand times ten thousand
stood attending him.
The court sat in judgment,
and the books were opened.
11 I watched then because of the noise of the arrogant words that the horn was speaking. And as I
watched, the beast was put to death, and its body
destroyed and given over to be burned with fire.
12 As for the rest of the beasts, their dominion was
taken away, but their lives were prolonged for a
season and a time. 13 As I watched in the night visions,
I saw one like a human being[e]
coming with the clouds of heaven.
And he came to the Ancient One[f]
and was presented before him.
14 To him was given dominion
and glory and kingship,
that all peoples, nations, and languages
should serve him.
His dominion is an everlasting dominion
that shall not pass away,
and his kingship is one
that shall never be destroyed.
15 As for me, Daniel, my spirit was troubled
within me,[g] and the visions of my head terrified
me. 16 I approached one of the attendants to ask
him the truth concerning all this. So he said that
he would disclose to me the interpretation of
the matter: 17 "As for these four great beasts, four
kings shall arise out of the earth. 18 But the holy
ones of the Most High shall receive the kingdom
and possess the kingdom forever—forever and
ever."
19 Then I desired to know the truth concerning the fourth beast, which was different from all
the rest, exceedingly terrifying, with its teeth of
iron and claws of bronze, and which devoured
and broke in pieces, and stamped what was left
with its feet; 20 and concerning the ten horns that
were on its head, and concerning the other horn,

[a] Q Ms Theodotion: MT adds *the beginning of the words; he said* [b] Theodotion: Aram *Daniel answered and said, I*
[c] Or *ribs* [d] Aram *an Ancient of Days* [e] Aram *one like a son of man* [f] Aram *the Ancient of Days*
[g] Aram *troubled in its sheath*

which came up and to make room for which three
of them fell out—the horn that had eyes and a
mouth that spoke arrogantly, and that seemed
greater than the others. 21 As I looked, this horn
made war with the holy ones and was prevailing
over them, 22 until the Ancient One[a] came; then
judgment was given for the holy ones of the Most
High, and the time arrived when the holy ones
gained possession of the kingdom.

23 This is what he said: "As for the fourth
beast,

there shall be a fourth kingdom on earth
that shall be different from all the other
kingdoms;
it shall devour the whole earth,
and trample it down, and break it to
pieces.

24 As for the ten horns,
out of this kingdom ten kings shall arise,
and another shall arise after them.
This one shall be different from the former
ones,
and shall put down three kings.

25 He shall speak words against the Most High,
shall wear out the holy ones of the Most
High,
and shall attempt to change the sacred
seasons and the law;
and they shall be given into his power
for a time, two times,[b] and half a time.

26 Then the court shall sit in judgment,
and his dominion shall be taken away,
to be consumed and totally destroyed.

27 The kingship and dominion
and the greatness of the kingdoms under
the whole heaven
shall be given to the people of the holy
ones of the Most High;
their kingdom shall be an everlasting
kingdom,
and all dominions shall serve and obey
them."

28 Here the account ends. As for me, Daniel, my thoughts greatly terrified me, and my face
turned pale; but I kept the matter in my mind.

8 In the third year of the reign of King Belshazzar a vision appeared to me, Daniel, after the
one that had appeared to me at first. 2 In the vision
I was looking and saw myself in Susa the capital,
in the province of Elam,[c] and I was by the river
Ulai.[d] 3 I looked up and saw a ram standing beside the river.[e] It had two horns. Both horns were
long, but one was longer than the other, and the
longer one came up second. 4 I saw the ram charging westward and northward and southward. All
beasts were powerless to withstand it, and no one
could rescue from its power; it did as it pleased
and became strong.

5 As I was watching, a male goat appeared
from the west, coming across the face of the whole
earth without touching the ground. The goat had
a horn[f] between its eyes. 6 It came toward the ram
with the two horns that I had seen standing beside the river,[e] and it ran at it with savage force. 7 I
saw it approaching the ram. It was enraged against
it and struck the ram, breaking its two horns. The
ram did not have power to withstand it; it threw
the ram down to the ground and trampled upon
it, and there was no one who could rescue the
ram from its power. 8 Then the male goat grew
exceedingly great; but at the height of its power,
the great horn was broken, and in its place there
came up four prominent horns toward the four
winds of heaven.

9 Out of one of them came another[g] horn, a
little one, which grew exceedingly great toward
the south, toward the east, and toward the beautiful land. 10 It grew as high as the host of heaven.
It threw down to the earth some of the host and
some of the stars, and trampled on them. 11 Even
against the prince of the host it acted arrogantly;
it took the regular burnt offering away from him
and overthrew the place of his sanctuary. 12 Because of wickedness, the host was given over to
it together with the regular burnt offering;[h] it
cast truth to the ground, and kept prospering in

[a] Aram *the Ancient of Days* [b] Aram *a time, times* [c] Gk Theodotion: MT Q Ms repeat *in the vision I was looking*
[d] Or *the Ulai Gate* [e] Or *gate* [f] Theodotion: Gk *one horn*; Heb *a horn of vision* [g] Cn Compare 7.8: Heb *one*
[h] Meaning of Heb uncertain

what it did. 13Then I heard a holy one speaking,
and another holy one said to the one that spoke,
"For how long is this vision concerning the regular burnt offering, the transgression that makes
desolate, and the giving over of the sanctuary and
host to be trampled?"[a] 14And he answered him,[b]
"For two thousand three hundred evenings and
mornings; then the sanctuary shall be restored to
its rightful state."

15 When I, Daniel, had seen the vision, I tried
to understand it. Then someone appeared standing before me, having the appearance of a man,
16and I heard a human voice by the Ulai, calling,
"Gabriel, help this man understand the vision."
17So he came near where I stood; and when he
came, I became frightened and fell prostrate. But
he said to me, "Understand, O mortal,[c] that the
vision is for the time of the end."

Daniel 8:16

Gabriel and Michael are understood as angels (literally "messengers" in Hebrew) in post-biblical Jewish and Christian tradition. Both appear in Daniel, but neither is called an "angel." Gabriel has no title in 8:16 and is called "the man Gabriel" in 9:21. Michael is called a "prince" or "chief" in 10:13, 21; 12:1. Most of contemporary Jewish and Christian lore about angels has its basis in the extra-biblical book of Enoch in which angels abound.

— *WG*

18 As he was speaking to me, I fell into a
trance, face to the ground; then he touched me
and set me on my feet. 19He said, "Listen, and I
will tell you what will take place later in the period of wrath; for it refers to the appointed time
of the end. 20As for the ram that you saw with the
two horns, these are the kings of Media and Persia. 21The male goat[d] is the king of Greece, and the
great horn between its eyes is the first king. 22As
for the horn that was broken, in place of which
four others arose, four kingdoms shall arise from
his[e] nation, but not with his power.

23 At the end of their rule,
when the transgressions have reached their full measure,
a king of bold countenance shall arise,
skilled in intrigue.
24 He shall grow strong in power,[f]
shall cause fearful destruction,
and shall succeed in what he does.
He shall destroy the powerful
and the people of the holy ones.
25 By his cunning
he shall make deceit prosper under his hand,
and in his own mind he shall be great.
Without warning he shall destroy many
and shall even rise up against the Prince of princes.
But he shall be broken, and not by human hands.

26The vision of the evenings and the mornings
that has been told is true. As for you, seal up the
vision, for it refers to many days from now."

27 So I, Daniel, was overcome and lay sick for
some days; then I arose and went about the king's
business. But I was dismayed by the vision and
did not understand it.

9 In the first year of Darius son of Ahasuerus,
by birth a Mede, who became king over the
realm of the Chaldeans— 2in the first year of his
reign, I, Daniel, perceived in the books the number of years that, according to the word of the
LORD to the prophet Jeremiah, must be fulfilled
for the devastation of Jerusalem, namely, seventy
years.

3 Then I turned to the Lord God, to seek an
answer by prayer and supplication with fasting
and sackcloth and ashes. 4I prayed to the LORD
my God and made confession, saying,

"Ah, Lord, great and awesome God, keeping
covenant and steadfast love with those who love
you and keep your commandments, 5we have

[a] Meaning of Heb uncertain [b] Gk Theodotion Syr Vg: Heb *me* [c] Heb *son of man* [d] Or *shaggy male goat*
[e] Gk Theodotion Vg: Heb *the* [f] Theodotion and one Gk Ms: Heb repeats (from 8.22) *but not with his power*

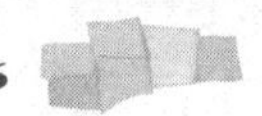

sinned and done wrong, acted wickedly and rebelled, turning aside from your commandments
and ordinances. 6We have not listened to your
servants the prophets, who spoke in your name
to our kings, our princes, and our ancestors, and
to all the people of the land.

7 "Righteousness is on your side, O Lord, but
open shame, as at this day, falls on us, the people
of Judah, the inhabitants of Jerusalem, and all
Israel, those who are near and those who are far
away, in all the lands to which you have driven
them, because of the treachery that they have
committed against you. 8Open shame, O LORD,
falls on us, our kings, our officials, and our ancestors, because we have sinned against you. 9To
the Lord our God belong mercy and forgiveness,
for we have rebelled against him, 10and have not
obeyed the voice of the LORD our God by following his laws, which he set before us by his servants
the prophets.

11 "All Israel has transgressed your law and
turned aside, refusing to obey your voice. So the
curse and the oath written in the law of Moses,
the servant of God, have been poured out upon
us, because we have sinned against you. 12He has
confirmed his words, which he spoke against us
and against our rulers, by bringing upon us a calamity so great that what has been done against
Jerusalem has never before been done under the
whole heaven. 13Just as it is written in the law of
Moses, all this calamity has come upon us. We
did not entreat the favor of the LORD our God,
turning from our iniquities and reflecting on his[a]
fidelity. 14So the LORD kept watch over this calamity until he brought it upon us. Indeed, the
LORD our God is right in all that he has done; for
we have disobeyed his voice.

15 "And now, O Lord our God, who brought
your people out of the land of Egypt with a
mighty hand and made your name renowned
even to this day—we have sinned, we have done
wickedly. 16O Lord, in view of all your righteous
acts, let your anger and wrath, we pray, turn away
from your city Jerusalem, your holy mountain;
because of our sins and the iniquities of our ancestors, Jerusalem and your people have become
a disgrace among all our neighbors. 17Now therefore, O our God, listen to the prayer of your servant and to his supplication, and for your own
sake, Lord,[b] let your face shine upon your desolated sanctuary. 18Incline your ear, O my God,
and hear. Open your eyes and look at our desolation and the city that bears your name. We do not
present our supplication before you on the
ground of our righteousness, but on the ground
of your great mercies. 19O Lord, hear; O Lord,
forgive; O Lord, listen and act and do not delay!
For your own sake, O my God, because your city
and your people bear your name!"

20 While I was speaking, and was praying
and confessing my sin and the sin of my people
Israel, and presenting my supplication before the
LORD my God on behalf of the holy mountain of
my God— 21while I was speaking in prayer, the
man Gabriel, whom I had seen before in a vision,
came to me in swift flight at the time of the evening sacrifice. 22He came[c] and said to me, "Daniel, I have now come out to give you wisdom and
understanding. 23At the beginning of your supplications a word went out, and I have come to
declare it, for you are greatly beloved. So consider
the word and understand the vision:

24 "Seventy weeks are decreed for your people and your holy city: to finish the transgression,
to put an end to sin, and to atone for iniquity, to
bring in everlasting righteousness, to seal both
vision and prophet, and to anoint a most holy
place.[d] 25Know therefore and understand: from
the time that the word went out to restore and
rebuild Jerusalem until the time of an anointed
prince, there shall be seven weeks; and for sixty-
two weeks it shall be built again with streets and
moat, but in a troubled time. 26After the sixty-
two weeks, an anointed one shall be cut off and
shall have nothing, and the troops of the prince
who is to come shall destroy the city and the
sanctuary. Its[e] end shall come with a flood, and
to the end there shall be war. Desolations are

[a] Heb *your* [b] Theodotion Vg Compare Syr: Heb *for the Lord's sake* [c] Gk Syr: Heb *He made to understand*
[d] Or *thing* or *one* [e] Or *His*

decreed. 27He shall make a strong covenant with
many for one week, and for half of the week he
shall make sacrifice and offering cease; and in
their place[a] shall be an abomination that desolates, until the decreed end is poured out upon
the desolator."

10 In the third year of King Cyrus of Persia
a word was revealed to Daniel, who was
named Belteshazzar. The word was true, and it
concerned a great conflict. He understood the
word, having received understanding in the vision.

2 At that time I, Daniel, had been mourning
for three weeks. 3I had eaten no rich food, no
meat or wine had entered my mouth, and I had
not anointed myself at all, for the full three weeks.
4On the twenty-fourth day of the first month, as
I was standing on the bank of the great river (that
is, the Tigris), 5I looked up and saw a man clothed
in linen, with a belt of gold from Uphaz around
his waist. 6His body was like beryl, his face like
lightning, his eyes like flaming torches, his arms
and legs like the gleam of burnished bronze, and
the sound of his words like the roar of a multitude. 7I, Daniel, alone saw the vision; the people
who were with me did not see the vision, though
a great trembling fell upon them, and they fled
and hid themselves. 8So I was left alone to see
this great vision. My strength left me, and my
complexion grew deathly pale, and I retained no
strength. 9Then I heard the sound of his words;
and when I heard the sound of his words, I fell
into a trance, face to the ground.

10 But then a hand touched me and roused me
to my hands and knees. 11He said to me, "Daniel,
greatly beloved, pay attention to the words that
I am going to speak to you. Stand on your feet,
for I have now been sent to you." So while he was
speaking this word to me, I stood up trembling.
12He said to me, "Do not fear, Daniel, for from
the first day that you set your mind to gain understanding and to humble yourself before your
God, your words have been heard, and I have
come because of your words. 13But the prince of
the kingdom of Persia opposed me twenty-one
days. So Michael, one of the chief princes, came
to help me, and I left him there with the prince of
the kingdom of Persia,[b] 14and have come to help
you understand what is to happen to your people
at the end of days. For there is a further vision for
those days."

15 While he was speaking these words to
me, I turned my face toward the ground and was
speechless. 16Then one in human form touched
my lips, and I opened my mouth to speak, and
said to the one who stood before me, "My lord,
because of the vision such pains have come upon
me that I retain no strength. 17How can my lord's
servant talk with my lord? For I am shaking,[c]
no strength remains in me, and no breath is left
in me."

18 Again one in human form touched me
and strengthened me. 19He said, "Do not fear,
greatly beloved, you are safe. Be strong and courageous!" When he spoke to me, I was strengthened and said, "Let my lord speak, for you have
strengthened me." 20Then he said, "Do you know
why I have come to you? Now I must return to
fight against the prince of Persia, and when I
am through with him, the prince of Greece will
come. 21But I am to tell you what is inscribed in
the book of truth. There is no one with me who
contends against these princes except Michael,

11 your prince. 1As for me, in the first year
of Darius the Mede, I stood up to support
and strengthen him.

2 "Now I will announce the truth to you.
Three more kings shall arise in Persia. The fourth
shall be far richer than all of them, and when he
has become strong through his riches, he shall stir
up all against the kingdom of Greece. 3Then a warrior king shall arise, who shall rule with great dominion and take action as he pleases. 4And while
still rising in power, his kingdom shall be broken
and divided toward the four winds of heaven, but
not to his posterity, nor according to the dominion with which he ruled; for his kingdom shall be
uprooted and go to others besides these.

5 "Then the king of the south shall grow
strong, but one of his officers shall grow stron-

[a] Cn: Meaning of Heb uncertain [b] Gk Theodotion: Heb *I was left there with the kings of Persia* [c] Gk: Heb *from now*

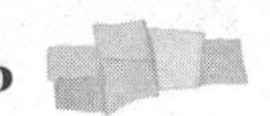

ger than he and shall rule a realm greater than his
own realm. 6After some years they shall make an
alliance, and the daughter of the king of the south
shall come to the king of the north to ratify the
agreement. But she shall not retain her power,
and his offspring shall not endure. She shall be
given up, she and her attendants and her child
and the one who supported her.

"In those times 7a branch from her roots shall
rise up in his place. He shall come against the army
and enter the fortress of the king of the north,
and he shall take action against them and prevail.
8Even their gods, with their idols and with their
precious vessels of silver and gold, he shall carry
off to Egypt as spoils of war. For some years he
shall refrain from attacking the king of the north;
9then the latter shall invade the realm of the king
of the south, but will return to his own land.

10 "His sons shall wage war and assemble a
multitude of great forces, which shall advance like
a flood and pass through, and again shall carry
the war as far as his fortress. 11Moved with rage,
the king of the south shall go out and do battle
against the king of the north, who shall muster
a great multitude, which shall, however, be defeated by his enemy. 12When the multitude has
been carried off, his heart shall be exalted, and he
shall overthrow tens of thousands, but he shall
not prevail. 13For the king of the north shall again
raise a multitude, larger than the former, and after
some years[a] he shall advance with a great army
and abundant supplies.

14 "In those times many shall rise against the
king of the south. The lawless among your own
people shall lift themselves up in order to fulfill
the vision, but they shall fail. 15Then the king of
the north shall come and throw up siegeworks,
and take a well-fortified city. And the forces of the
south shall not stand, not even his picked troops,
for there shall be no strength to resist. 16But he
who comes against him shall take the actions he
pleases, and no one shall withstand him. He shall
take a position in the beautiful land, and all of it
shall be in his power. 17He shall set his mind to
come with the strength of his whole kingdom, and
he shall bring terms of peace[b] and perform them.
In order to destroy the kingdom,[c] he shall give
him a woman in marriage; but it shall not succeed
or be to his advantage. 18Afterward he shall turn
to the coastlands, and shall capture many. But a
commander shall put an end to his insolence; indeed,[d] he shall turn his insolence back upon him.
19Then he shall turn back toward the fortresses of
his own land, but he shall stumble and fall, and
shall not be found.

20 "Then shall arise in his place one who shall
send an official for the glory of the kingdom; but
within a few days he shall be broken, though not
in anger or in battle. 21In his place shall arise a
contemptible person on whom royal majesty
had not been conferred; he shall come in without warning and obtain the kingdom through
intrigue. 22Armies shall be utterly swept away
and broken before him, and the prince of the covenant as well. 23And after an alliance is made with
him, he shall act deceitfully and become strong
with a small party. 24Without warning he shall
come into the richest parts[e] of the province and
do what none of his predecessors had ever done,
lavishing plunder, spoil, and wealth on them. He
shall devise plans against strongholds, but only
for a time. 25He shall stir up his power and determination against the king of the south with a
great army, and the king of the south shall wage
war with a much greater and stronger army. But
he shall not succeed, for plots shall be devised
against him 26by those who eat of the royal rations. They shall break him, his army shall be
swept away, and many shall fall slain. 27The two
kings, their minds bent on evil, shall sit at one table and exchange lies. But it shall not succeed, for
there remains an end at the time appointed. 28He
shall return to his land with great wealth, but his
heart shall be set against the holy covenant. He
shall work his will, and return to his own land.

29 "At the time appointed he shall return and
come into the south, but this time it shall not be
as it was before. 30For ships of Kittim shall come

[a] Heb *and at the end of the times years* [b] Gk: Heb *kingdom, and upright ones with him* [c] Heb *it* [d] Meaning of Heb uncertain [e] Or *among the richest men*

against him, and he shall lose heart and withdraw.
He shall be enraged and take action against the
holy covenant. He shall turn back and pay heed
to those who forsake the holy covenant. 31 Forces
sent by him shall occupy and profane the temple
and fortress. They shall abolish the regular burnt
offering and set up the abomination that makes
desolate. 32 He shall seduce with intrigue those
who violate the covenant; but the people who
are loyal to their God shall stand firm and take
action. 33 The wise among the people shall give
understanding to many; for some days, however,
they shall fall by sword and flame, and suffer captivity and plunder. 34 When they fall victim, they
shall receive a little help, and many shall join
them insincerely. 35 Some of the wise shall fall, so
that they may be refined, purified, and cleansed,[a]
until the time of the end, for there is still an interval until the time appointed.

36 "The king shall act as he pleases. He shall
exalt himself and consider himself greater than
any god, and shall speak horrendous things
against the God of gods. He shall prosper until
the period of wrath is completed, for what is determined shall be done. 37 He shall pay no respect
to the gods of his ancestors, or to the one beloved
by women; he shall pay no respect to any other
god, for he shall consider himself greater than all.
38 He shall honor the god of fortresses instead of
these; a god whom his ancestors did not know he
shall honor with gold and silver, with precious
stones and costly gifts. 39 He shall deal with the
strongest fortresses by the help of a foreign god.
Those who acknowledge him he shall make more
wealthy, and shall appoint them as rulers over
many, and shall distribute the land for a price.

40 "At the time of the end the king of the
south shall attack him. But the king of the north
shall rush upon him like a whirlwind, with chariots and horsemen, and with many ships. He shall
advance against countries and pass through like
a flood. 41 He shall come into the beautiful land,
and tens of thousands shall fall victim, but Edom
and Moab and the main part of the Ammonites
shall escape from his power. 42 He shall stretch
out his hand against the countries, and the land
of Egypt shall not escape. 43 He shall become
ruler of the treasures of gold and of silver, and
all the riches of Egypt; and the Libyans and the
Ethiopians[b] shall follow in his train. 44 But reports
from the east and the north shall alarm him, and
he shall go out with great fury to bring ruin and
complete destruction to many. 45 He shall pitch
his palatial tents between the sea and the beautiful holy mountain. Yet he shall come to his end,
with no one to help him.

12 "At that time Michael, the great prince,
the protector of your people, shall arise.
There shall be a time of anguish, such as has never
occurred since nations first came into existence.
But at that time your people shall be delivered,
everyone who is found written in the book.
2 Many of those who sleep in the dust of the earth[c]
shall awake, some to everlasting life, and some to
shame and everlasting contempt. 3 Those who are
wise shall shine like the brightness of the sky,[d]
and those who lead many to righteousness, like
the stars forever and ever. 4 But you, Daniel, keep
the words secret and the book sealed until the
time of the end. Many shall be running back and
forth, and evil[e] shall increase."

5 Then I, Daniel, looked, and two others appeared, one standing on this bank of the stream
and one on the other. 6 One of them said to the
man clothed in linen, who was upstream, "How
long shall it be until the end of these wonders?"
7 The man clothed in linen, who was upstream,
raised his right hand and his left hand toward
heaven. And I heard him swear by the one who
lives forever that it would be for a time, two times,
and half a time,[f] and that when the shattering of
the power of the holy people comes to an end, all
these things would be accomplished. 8 I heard but
could not understand; so I said, "My lord, what
shall be the outcome of these things?" 9 He said,
"Go your way, Daniel, for the words are to remain secret and sealed until the time of the end.
10 Many shall be purified, cleansed, and refined,

[a] Heb *made them white* [b] Or *Nubians*; Heb *Cushites* [c] Or *the land of dust* [d] Or *dome* [e] Cn Compare Gk: Heb *knowledge* [f] Heb *a time, times, and a half*

but the wicked shall continue to act wickedly.
None of the wicked shall understand, but those
who are wise shall understand. 11 From the time
that the regular burnt offering is taken away and
the abomination that desolates is set up, there
shall be one thousand two hundred ninety days.
12 Happy are those who persevere and attain the
thousand three hundred thirty-five days. 13 But
you, go your way,[a] and rest; you shall rise for your
reward at the end of the days."

[a] Gk Theodotion: Heb adds *to the end*

Hosea

Hosea was an eighth-century BCE prophet, a Northerner, who brought YHWH's words to his own people in Israel. He prophesied roughly from 740 to 724, from the death of Jereboam II to the fall of Samaria to the Assyrians. Therefore, Hosea saw the decline and social political upheaval of the last years of the Northern Kingdom. Hosea apparently experienced turmoil in his family life and, through it, realized God's deep love for Israel and deep pain for the people's infidelity to the covenant relationship.

A major theme in Hosea is *hesed*, "steadfast love" or "covenant loyalty," a concept that was meant to be reality in all relationships in life. God's desire for Israel was hesed and the knowledge of God—that is, to have an intimate relationship with YHWH (Hos 6:6). Hosea was the first to proclaim (2:16-17) that YHWH wanted to be called "husband" (or "man," Hebrew *ish*) and not *baal*—a word that means "master" or "lord," and was also the name of a rival Canaanite deity. (The English word Lord, when written in capital and small-capital letters in the NRSV, represents the Hebrew YHWH, the proper name of Israel's God.)

Hosea spoke of Israel's experience in the wilderness as a positive period in which the people were wholly devoted to YHWH. He used spousal and parent-child relationships as metaphors to describe the relationship between God and Israel. His view of covenant fidelity as marriage and the wilderness sojourn as honeymoon influenced later prophets, especially Jeremiah.

The book of Hosea consists of three sections. Hosea 1–3 tells of the prophet's marriage to Gomer, described as a "wife of whoredom," and the naming of the three children. "Whoredom" is a plural, abstract noun that refers to a personal quality or tendency, and not to the activities of prostitution. The Hebrew phrase might be better translated as "promiscuous woman."

The language of "whoredom" has led interpreters to debate whether Gomer was in fact a prostitute or whether she became one after she married Hosea. A prior question—and a more pressing issue—concerns prostitution in ancient Israel in general. While the prescribed roles for women were either as virgins in their fathers' houses or as son-bearing wives in their husbands' homes, prostitutes were accepted as a part of the social fabric. A woman who did not have male relatives to support her would have no recourse but to turn to prostitution to survive; she often had no other choice. Prostitution was thus a profession of last resort. Prostitutes were sexual playthings that men could use without fear of offending another male in the community. The association of females, more than males, with sexual promiscuity and evil continues to haunt us today. Ultimately, the point of Hosea's metaphor is that Gomer was like everyone else in Israel who did not remain faithful to covenant commitment with YHWH. Hosea's entire life and family thus became signs of God's judgment on Israel.

Hosea 4–12 consists of messages of indictment and judgment in the form of a *rib*, or covenant lawsuit. The leaders, especially the priests and kings, were called to account because they led the people into idolatry. Israel was pronounced guilty. This portion of Hosea offers glimpses of the frantic political activities in the last years of Israel, when wars and assassinations were frequent occurrences. Nevertheless, Hosea 14, the book's final chapter, provides words of hope. It urges the Israelites to turn back to YHWH, who would restore them like a beautiful, well-watered garden.

As a Chinese American and Christian woman, I am pained by the plight of women in Hosea's day. Their valuation as inferior to men and their powerlessness and lack of self-determination are issues that today's readers must address. Their experiences can be judged as inappropriate then and now. Today's readers need to consider carefully some of the expressions and ideas in Hosea. Gomer is described negatively as an unfaithful wife, but she is not given a voice to respond to the charges against her. The juxtaposition of male prophet, male God, and faithfulness over against promiscuous wife, female, and unfaithfulness gives the mistaken impression that male represents what is good and female represents what is evil. In a patriarchy such as ancient Israel, the female was frequently described in simplistic, clichéd ways to satisfy the expectations of a primarily male audience. The fact is that both males and females are equally capable of good and evil. A negative valuation of females continues to disadvantage women in today's society, not least in the church.

A third issue is the language of violent punishment that the husband (God) was going to mete out to the incorrigible wife (Israel, ch. 2). The correlations of husband and punisher, wife and punished can be misused as a justification for spousal abuse. Some men have claimed for themselves the right to "discipline" their wives through physical and sexual assaults, just as God punished wayward Israel. Even the wooing back of Hosea's wife (and Israel) in 2:14-23 sounds eerily similar to comforting words that many abusive husbands offer after severe attacks. The book of Hosea speaks clearly about the unwavering love of God for God's people, but like all other books in the Bible, it requires prayerful reflection and interpretation.

— Lai Ling Elizabeth Ngan

1 The word of the LORD that came to Hosea son of Beeri, in the days of Kings Uzziah, Jotham, Ahaz, and Hezekiah of Judah, and in the days of King Jeroboam son of Joash of Israel.

2 When the LORD first spoke through Hosea, the LORD said to Hosea, "Go, take for yourself a wife of whoredom and have children of whoredom, for the land commits great whoredom by forsaking the LORD."
3 So he went and took Gomer daughter of Diblaim, and she conceived and bore him a son.

4 And the LORD said to him, "Name him Jezreel;[a] for in a little while I will punish the house of Jehu for the blood of Jezreel, and I will put an

[a] That is *God sows*

end to the kingdom of the house of Israel. 5On
that day I will break the bow of Israel in the valley
of Jezreel."

6 She conceived again and bore a daughter. Then the LORD said to him, "Name her Lo-
ruhamah,[a] for I will no longer have pity on the
house of Israel or forgive them. 7But I will have
pity on the house of Judah, and I will save them
by the LORD their God; I will not save them by
bow, or by sword, or by war, or by horses, or by
horsemen."

8 When she had weaned Lo-ruhamah, she
conceived and bore a son. 9Then the LORD said,
"Name him Lo-ammi,[b] for you are not my people
and I am not your God."[c]

10[d] Yet the number of the people of Israel
shall be like the sand of the sea, which can be
neither measured nor numbered; and in the place
where it was said to them, "You are not my people," it shall be said to them, "Children of the living God." 11The people of Judah and the people
of Israel shall be gathered together, and they shall
appoint for themselves one head; and they shall
take possession of[e] the land, for great shall be the
day of Jezreel.

2[f] Say to your brother,[g] Ammi,[h] and to your sister,[i] Ruhamah.[j]

2 Plead with your mother, plead—
for she is not my wife,
and I am not her husband—
that she put away her whoring from her face,
and her adultery from between her breasts,
3 or I will strip her naked
and expose her as in the day she was born,
and make her like a wilderness,
and turn her into a parched land,
and kill her with thirst.
4 Upon her children also I will have no pity,
because they are children of whoredom.
5 For their mother has played the whore;
she who conceived them has acted shamefully.
For she said, "I will go after my lovers;
they give me my bread and my water,
my wool and my flax, my oil and my drink."
6 Therefore I will hedge up her[k] way with thorns;
and I will build a wall against her,
so that she cannot find her paths.
7 She shall pursue her lovers,
but not overtake them;
and she shall seek them,
but shall not find them.
Then she shall say, "I will go
and return to my first husband,
for it was better with me then than now."
8 She did not know
that it was I who gave her
the grain, the wine, and the oil,
and who lavished upon her silver
and gold that they used for Baal.
9 Therefore I will take back
my grain in its time,
and my wine in its season;
and I will take away my wool and my flax,
which were to cover her nakedness.
10 Now I will uncover her shame
in the sight of her lovers,
and no one shall rescue her out of my hand.
11 I will put an end to all her mirth,
her festivals, her new moons, her sabbaths,
and all her appointed festivals.
12 I will lay waste her vines and her fig trees,
of which she said,
"These are my pay,
which my lovers have given me."
I will make them a forest,
and the wild animals shall devour them.
13 I will punish her for the festival days of the Baals,
when she offered incense to them
and decked herself with her ring and jewelry,
and went after her lovers,
and forgot me, says the LORD.
14 Therefore, I will now allure her,
and bring her into the wilderness,

[a] That is *Not pitied* [b] That is *Not my people* [c] Heb *I am not yours* [d] Ch 2.1 in Heb [e] Heb *rise up from* [f] Ch 2.3 in Heb [g] Gk: Heb *brothers* [h] That is *My people* [i] Gk Vg: Heb *sisters* [j] That is *Pitied* [k] Gk Syr: Heb *your*

and speak tenderly to her.
15 From there I will give her her vineyards,
and make the Valley of Achor a door of hope.
There she shall respond as in the days of her youth,
as at the time when she came out of the land of Egypt.

16 On that day, says the LORD, you will call me,
"My husband," and no longer will you call me,
"My Baal."[a] 17 For I will remove the names of the
Baals from her mouth, and they shall be mentioned by name no more. 18 I will make for you[b]
a covenant on that day with the wild animals, the
birds of the air, and the creeping things of the
ground; and I will abolish[c] the bow, the sword,
and war from the land; and I will make you lie
down in safety. 19 And I will take you for my wife
forever; I will take you for my wife in righteousness and in justice, in steadfast love, and in mercy.
20 I will take you for my wife in faithfulness; and
you shall know the LORD.

Hosea 2:20

Hosea uses two relational metaphors to describe God: In chapters 1–2, particularly in 2:20, God is Israel's husband. In Hosea 11, particularly in 11:4, God is Israel's breast-feeding mother. By using masculine *and* feminine imagery for God in the same book, Hosea provides a model for how we can speak of God today.

— *WG*

21 On that day I will answer, says the LORD,
I will answer the heavens
and they shall answer the earth;
22 and the earth shall answer the grain, the wine, and the oil,
and they shall answer Jezreel;[d]
23 and I will sow him[e] for myself in the land.
And I will have pity on Lo-ruhamah,[f]
and I will say to Lo-ammi,[g] "You are my people";
and he shall say, "You are my God."

3 The LORD said to me again, "Go, love a woman
who has a lover and is an adulteress, just as
the LORD loves the people of Israel, though they
turn to other gods and love raisin cakes." 2 So I
bought her for fifteen shekels of silver and a homer of barley and a measure of wine.[h] 3 And I said
to her, "You must remain as mine for many days;
you shall not play the whore, you shall not have
intercourse with a man, nor I with you." 4 For the
Israelites shall remain many days without king or
prince, without sacrifice or pillar, without ephod
or teraphim. 5 Afterward the Israelites shall return
and seek the LORD their God, and David their
king; they shall come in awe to the LORD and to
his goodness in the latter days.

4 Hear the word of the LORD, O people of Israel;
for the LORD has an indictment against the inhabitants of the land.
There is no faithfulness or loyalty,
and no knowledge of God in the land.
2 Swearing, lying, and murder,
and stealing and adultery break out;
bloodshed follows bloodshed.
3 Therefore the land mourns,
and all who live in it languish;
together with the wild animals
and the birds of the air,
even the fish of the sea are perishing.

4 Yet let no one contend,
and let none accuse,
for with you is my contention, O priest.[i]
5 You shall stumble by day;
the prophet also shall stumble with you by night,
and I will destroy your mother.
6 My people are destroyed for lack of knowledge;
because you have rejected knowledge,
I reject you from being a priest to me.

[a] That is, *"My master"* [b] Heb *them* [c] Heb *break* [d] That is *God sows* [e] Cn: Heb *her* [f] That is *Not pitied*
[g] That is *Not my people* [h] Gk: Heb *a homer of barley and a lethech of barley* [i] Cn: Meaning of Heb uncertain

And since you have forgotten the law of your
God,
I also will forget your children.

7 The more they increased,
the more they sinned against me;
they changed[a] their glory into shame.
8 They feed on the sin of my people;
they are greedy for their iniquity.
9 And it shall be like people, like priest;
I will punish them for their ways,
and repay them for their deeds.
10 They shall eat, but not be satisfied;
they shall play the whore, but not
multiply;
because they have forsaken the LORD
to devote themselves to 11 whoredom.

Wine and new wine
take away the understanding.
12 My people consult a piece of wood,
and their divining rod gives them oracles.
For a spirit of whoredom has led them astray,
and they have played the whore, forsaking
their God.
13 They sacrifice on the tops of the mountains,
and make offerings upon the hills,
under oak, poplar, and terebinth,
because their shade is good.

Therefore your daughters play the whore,
and your daughters-in-law commit
adultery.
14 I will not punish your daughters when they
play the whore,
nor your daughters-in-law when they
commit adultery;
for the men themselves go aside with whores,
and sacrifice with temple prostitutes;
thus a people without understanding comes
to ruin.

15 Though you play the whore, O Israel,
do not let Judah become guilty.
Do not enter into Gilgal,
or go up to Beth-aven,
and do not swear, "As the LORD lives."
16 Like a stubborn heifer,
Israel is stubborn;
can the LORD now feed them
like a lamb in a broad pasture?

17 Ephraim is joined to idols—
let him alone.
18 When their drinking is ended, they indulge in
sexual orgies;
they love lewdness more than their glory.[b]
19 A wind has wrapped them[c] in its wings,
and they shall be ashamed because of their
altars.[d]

5 Hear this, O priests!
Give heed, O house of Israel!
Listen, O house of the king!
For the judgment pertains to you;
for you have been a snare at Mizpah,
and a net spread upon Tabor,
2 and a pit dug deep in Shittim;[e]
but I will punish all of them.

3 I know Ephraim,
and Israel is not hidden from me;
for now, O Ephraim, you have played the
whore;
Israel is defiled.
4 Their deeds do not permit them
to return to their God.
For the spirit of whoredom is within them,
and they do not know the LORD.

5 Israel's pride testifies against him;
Ephraim[f] stumbles in his guilt;
Judah also stumbles with them.
6 With their flocks and herds they shall go
to seek the LORD,
but they will not find him;
he has withdrawn from them.
7 They have dealt faithlessly with the LORD;

[a] Ancient Heb tradition: MT *I will change* [b] Cn Compare Gk: Meaning of Heb uncertain [c] Heb *her* [d] Gk Syr: Heb *sacrifices* [e] Cn: Meaning of Heb uncertain [f] Heb *Israel and Ephraim*

for they have borne illegitimate children.
Now the new moon shall devour them
along with their fields.

8 Blow the horn in Gibeah,
the trumpet in Ramah.
Sound the alarm at Beth-aven;
look behind you, Benjamin!
9 Ephraim shall become a desolation
in the day of punishment;
among the tribes of Israel
I declare what is sure.
10 The princes of Judah have become
like those who remove the landmark;
on them I will pour out
my wrath like water.
11 Ephraim is oppressed, crushed in judgment,
because he was determined to go after
vanity.[a]
12 Therefore I am like maggots to Ephraim,
and like rottenness to the house of
Judah.
13 When Ephraim saw his sickness,
and Judah his wound,
then Ephraim went to Assyria,
and sent to the great king.[b]
But he is not able to cure you
or heal your wound.
14 For I will be like a lion to Ephraim,
and like a young lion to the house of
Judah.
I myself will tear and go away;
I will carry off, and no one shall rescue.
15 I will return again to my place
until they acknowledge their guilt and seek
my face.
In their distress they will beg my favor:

6 "Come, let us return to the LORD;
for it is he who has torn, and he will
heal us;
he has struck down, and he will bind us up.
2 After two days he will revive us;
on the third day he will raise us up,
that we may live before him.
3 Let us know, let us press on to know the
LORD;
his appearing is as sure as the dawn;
he will come to us like the showers,
like the spring rains that water the earth."
4 What shall I do with you, O Ephraim?
What shall I do with you, O Judah?
Your love is like a morning cloud,
like the dew that goes away early.
5 Therefore I have hewn them by the prophets,
I have killed them by the words of my
mouth,
and my[c] judgment goes forth as the light.
6 For I desire steadfast love and not sacrifice,
the knowledge of God rather than burnt
offerings.

7 But at[d] Adam they transgressed the covenant;
there they dealt faithlessly with me.
8 Gilead is a city of evildoers,
tracked with blood.
9 As robbers lie in wait[e] for someone,
so the priests are banded together;[f]
they murder on the road to Shechem,
they commit a monstrous crime.
10 In the house of Israel I have seen a horrible
thing;
Ephraim's whoredom is there, Israel is
defiled.

11 For you also, O Judah, a harvest is appointed.

When I would restore the fortunes of my
people,

7 1 when I would heal Israel,
the corruption of Ephraim is revealed,
and the wicked deeds of Samaria;
for they deal falsely,
the thief breaks in,
and the bandits raid outside.
2 But they do not consider
that I remember all their wickedness.
Now their deeds surround them,
they are before my face.

[a] Gk: Meaning of Heb uncertain [b] Cn: Heb *to a king who will contend* [c] Gk Syr: Heb *your* [d] Cn: Heb *like*
[e] Cn: Meaning of Heb uncertain [f] Syr: Heb *are a company*

3 By their wickedness they make the king
glad,
and the officials by their treachery.
4 They are all adulterers;
they are like a heated oven,
whose baker does not need to stir the fire,
from the kneading of the dough until it is
leavened.
5 On the day of our king the officials
became sick with the heat of wine;
he stretched out his hand with mockers.
6 For they are kindled[a] like an oven, their heart
burns within them;
all night their anger smolders;
in the morning it blazes like a flaming fire.
7 All of them are hot as an oven,
and they devour their rulers.
All their kings have fallen;
none of them calls upon me.

8 Ephraim mixes himself with the peoples;
Ephraim is a cake not turned.
9 Foreigners devour his strength,
but he does not know it;
gray hairs are sprinkled upon him,
but he does not know it.
10 Israel's pride testifies against[b] him;
yet they do not return to the LORD their
God,
or seek him, for all this.

11 Ephraim has become like a dove,
silly and without sense;
they call upon Egypt, they go to Assyria.
12 As they go, I will cast my net over them;
I will bring them down like birds of the
air;
I will discipline them according to the
report made to their assembly.[c]
13 Woe to them, for they have strayed from me!
Destruction to them, for they have
rebelled against me!
I would redeem them,
but they speak lies against me.
14 They do not cry to me from the heart,
but they wail upon their beds;
they gash themselves for grain and wine;
they rebel against me.
15 It was I who trained and strengthened their
arms,
yet they plot evil against me.
16 They turn to that which does not profit;[d]
they have become like a defective bow;
their officials shall fall by the sword
because of the rage of their tongue.
So much for their babbling in the land of
Egypt.

8 Set the trumpet to your lips!
One like a vulture[c] is over the house of the
LORD,
because they have broken my covenant,
and transgressed my law.
2 Israel cries to me,
"My God, we—Israel—know you!"
3 Israel has spurned the good;
the enemy shall pursue him.

4 They made kings, but not through me;
they set up princes, but without my
knowledge.
With their silver and gold they made idols
for their own destruction.
5 Your calf is rejected, O Samaria.
My anger burns against them.
How long will they be incapable of
innocence?
6 For it is from Israel,
an artisan made it;
it is not God.
The calf of Samaria
shall be broken to pieces.[e]

7 For they sow the wind,
and they shall reap the whirlwind.
The standing grain has no heads,
it shall yield no meal;
if it were to yield,

[a] Gk Syr: Heb *brought near* [b] Or *humbles* [c] Meaning of Heb uncertain [d] Cn: Meaning of Heb uncertain
[e] Or *shall go up in flames*

foreigners would devour it.
8 Israel is swallowed up;
now they are among the nations
as a useless vessel.
9 For they have gone up to Assyria,
a wild ass wandering alone;
Ephraim has bargained for lovers.
10 Though they bargain with the nations,
I will now gather them up.
They shall soon writhe
under the burden of kings and princes.

11 When Ephraim multiplied altars to expiate sin,
they became to him altars for sinning.
12 Though I write for him the multitude of my instructions,
they are regarded as a strange thing.
13 Though they offer choice sacrifices,[a]
though they eat flesh,
the LORD does not accept them.
Now he will remember their iniquity,
and punish their sins;
they shall return to Egypt.
14 Israel has forgotten his Maker,
and built palaces;
and Judah has multiplied fortified cities;
but I will send a fire upon his cities,
and it shall devour his strongholds.

9 Do not rejoice, O Israel!
Do not exult[b] as other nations do;
for you have played the whore, departing from your God.
You have loved a prostitute's pay
on all threshing floors.
2 Threshing floor and wine vat shall not feed them,
and the new wine shall fail them.
3 They shall not remain in the land of the LORD;
but Ephraim shall return to Egypt,
and in Assyria they shall eat unclean food.
4 They shall not pour drink offerings of wine to the LORD,
and their sacrifices shall not please him.
Such sacrifices shall be like mourners' bread;
all who eat of it shall be defiled;
for their bread shall be for their hunger only;
it shall not come to the house of the LORD.

5 What will you do on the day of appointed festival,
and on the day of the festival of the LORD?
6 For even if they escape destruction,
Egypt shall gather them,
Memphis shall bury them.
Nettles shall possess their precious things of silver;[c]
thorns shall be in their tents.

7 The days of punishment have come,
the days of recompense have come;
Israel cries,[d]
"The prophet is a fool,
the man of the spirit is mad!"
Because of your great iniquity,
your hostility is great.
8 The prophet is a sentinel for my God over Ephraim,
yet a fowler's snare is on all his ways,
and hostility in the house of his God.
9 They have deeply corrupted themselves
as in the days of Gibeah;
he will remember their iniquity,
he will punish their sins.

10 Like grapes in the wilderness,
I found Israel.
Like the first fruit on the fig tree,
in its first season,
I saw your ancestors.
But they came to Baal-peor,
and consecrated themselves to a thing of shame,
and became detestable like the thing they loved.

[a] Cn: Meaning of Heb uncertain [b] Gk: Heb *To exultation* [c] Meaning of Heb uncertain
[d] Cn Compare Gk: Heb *shall know*

11 Ephraim's glory shall fly away like a
bird—
no birth, no pregnancy, no conception!
12 Even if they bring up children,
I will bereave them until no one is left.
Woe to them indeed
when I depart from them!
13 Once I saw Ephraim as a young palm planted
in a lovely meadow,[a]
but now Ephraim must lead out his
children for slaughter.
14 Give them, O LORD—
what will you give?
Give them a miscarrying womb
and dry breasts.

15 Every evil of theirs began at Gilgal;
there I came to hate them.
Because of the wickedness of their deeds
I will drive them out of my house.
I will love them no more;
all their officials are rebels.

16 Ephraim is stricken,
their root is dried up,
they shall bear no fruit.
Even though they give birth,
I will kill the cherished offspring of their
womb.
17 Because they have not listened to him,
my God will reject them;
they shall become wanderers among the
nations.

10 Israel is a luxuriant vine
that yields its fruit.
The more his fruit increased
the more altars he built;
as his country improved,
he improved his pillars.
2 Their heart is false;
now they must bear their guilt.
The LORD[b] will break down their altars,
and destroy their pillars.

3 For now they will say:
"We have no king,
for we do not fear the LORD,
and a king—what could he do for us?"
4 They utter mere words;
with empty oaths they make covenants;
so litigation springs up like poisonous weeds
in the furrows of the field.
5 The inhabitants of Samaria tremble
for the calf[c] of Beth-aven.
Its people shall mourn for it,
and its idolatrous priests shall wail[d] over it,
over its glory that has departed from it.
6 The thing itself shall be carried to Assyria
as tribute to the great king.[e]
Ephraim shall be put to shame,
and Israel shall be ashamed of his idol.[f]

7 Samaria's king shall perish
like a chip on the face of the waters.
8 The high places of Aven, the sin of Israel,
shall be destroyed.
Thorn and thistle shall grow up
on their altars.
They shall say to the mountains, Cover us,
and to the hills, Fall on us.

9 Since the days of Gibeah you have sinned,
O Israel;
there they have continued.
Shall not war overtake them in Gibeah?
10 I will come[g] against the wayward people to
punish them;
and nations shall be gathered against them
when they are punished[h] for their double
iniquity.

11 Ephraim was a trained heifer
that loved to thresh,
and I spared her fair neck;
but I will make Ephraim break the ground;
Judah must plow;
Jacob must harrow for himself.
12 Sow for yourselves righteousness;

[a] Meaning of Heb uncertain [b] Heb *he* [c] Gk Syr: Heb *calves* [d] Cn: Heb *exult* [e] Cn: Heb *to a king who will contend* [f] Cn: Heb *counsel* [g] Cn Compare Gk: Heb *In my desire* [h] Gk: Heb *bound*

reap steadfast love;
break up your fallow ground;
for it is time to seek the LORD,
that he may come and rain righteousness upon you.

13 You have plowed wickedness,
you have reaped injustice,
you have eaten the fruit of lies.
Because you have trusted in your power
and in the multitude of your warriors,
14 therefore the tumult of war shall rise against your people,
and all your fortresses shall be destroyed,
as Shalman destroyed Beth-arbel on the day of battle
when mothers were dashed in pieces with their children.
15 Thus it shall be done to you, O Bethel,
because of your great wickedness.

Hosea 11:1-4

In this chapter God is portrayed as the female parent of Israel: God taught the toddler, Israel called Ephraim, how to walk. God holds the infant up and nuzzles the baby's cheeks. God also bends down to feed the child whenever he is hungry. All of these images reflect maternal love in the time of the text and in our own. In ancient Israel, women were the primary caretakers of children, largely because women were the only ones biologically equipped to feed infants. In Hosea 11, God is Israel's mother. The notion of God as a nursing mother endures into the Christian Scriptures where young Christians are urged to desire the milk of the gospel in 1 Peter 2:2; God is of course the source of the gospel. The presence of both these images of God, male and female, mother and husband indicate how flexible was the ancient Israelite understanding of gender, particularly when applied to God.

— *WG*

At dawn the king of Israel
shall be utterly cut off.

11 When Israel was a child, I loved him,
and out of Egypt I called my son.
2 The more I[a] called them,
the more they went from me;[b]
they kept sacrificing to the Baals,
and offering incense to idols.

3 Yet it was I who taught Ephraim to walk,
I took them up in my[c] arms;
but they did not know that I healed them.
4 I led them with cords of human kindness,
with bands of love.
I was to them like those
who lift infants to their cheeks.[d]
I bent down to them and fed them.

5 They shall return to the land of Egypt,
and Assyria shall be their king,
because they have refused to return to me.
6 The sword rages in their cities,
it consumes their oracle-priests,
and devours because of their schemes.
7 My people are bent on turning away from me.
To the Most High they call,
but he does not raise them up at all.[e]

8 How can I give you up, Ephraim?
How can I hand you over, O Israel?
How can I make you like Admah?
How can I treat you like Zeboiim?
My heart recoils within me;
my compassion grows warm and tender.
9 I will not execute my fierce anger;
I will not again destroy Ephraim;
for I am God and no mortal,
the Holy One in your midst,
and I will not come in wrath.[e]

10 They shall go after the LORD,
who roars like a lion;
when he roars,

[a] Gk: Heb *they* [b] Gk: Heb *them* [c] Gk Syr Vg: Heb *his* [d] Or *who ease the yoke on their jaws*
[e] Meaning of Heb uncertain

his children shall come trembling from the
west.
11 They shall come trembling like birds from
Egypt,
and like doves from the land of Assyria;
and I will return them to their homes, says
the LORD.

12[a] Ephraim has surrounded me with lies,
and the house of Israel with deceit;
but Judah still walks[b] with God,
and is faithful to the Holy One.
12 Ephraim herds the wind,
and pursues the east wind all day long;
they multiply falsehood and violence;
they make a treaty with Assyria,
and oil is carried to Egypt.

2 The LORD has an indictment against Judah,
and will punish Jacob according to his
ways,
and repay him according to his deeds.
3 In the womb he tried to supplant his
brother,
and in his manhood he strove with God.
4 He strove with the angel and prevailed,
he wept and sought his favor;
he met him at Bethel,
and there he spoke with him.[c]
5 The LORD the God of hosts,
the LORD is his name!
6 But as for you, return to your God,
hold fast to love and justice,
and wait continually for your God.

7 A trader, in whose hands are false balances,
he loves to oppress.
8 Ephraim has said, "Ah, I am rich,
I have gained wealth for myself;
in all of my gain
no offense has been found in me
that would be sin."[d]
9 I am the LORD your God
from the land of Egypt;
I will make you live in tents again,
as in the days of the appointed festival.

10 I spoke to the prophets;
it was I who multiplied visions,
and through the prophets I will bring
destruction.
11 In Gilead[e] there is iniquity,
they shall surely come to nothing.
In Gilgal they sacrifice bulls,
so their altars shall be like stone heaps
on the furrows of the field.
12 Jacob fled to the land of Aram,
there Israel served for a wife,
and for a wife he guarded sheep.[f]
13 By a prophet the LORD brought Israel up
from Egypt,
and by a prophet he was guarded.
14 Ephraim has given bitter offense,
so his Lord will bring his crimes down on
him
and pay him back for his insults.

13 When Ephraim spoke, there was
trembling;
he was exalted in Israel;
but he incurred guilt through Baal and
died.
2 And now they keep on sinning
and make a cast image for themselves,
idols of silver made according to their
understanding,
all of them the work of artisans.
"Sacrifice to these," they say.[g]
People are kissing calves!
3 Therefore they shall be like the morning mist
or like the dew that goes away early,
like chaff that swirls from the threshing floor
or like smoke from a window.

4 Yet I have been the LORD your God
ever since the land of Egypt;
you know no God but me,
and besides me there is no savior.
5 It was I who fed[h] you in the wilderness,

[a] Ch 12.1 in Heb [b] Heb *roams* or *rules* [c] Gk Syr: Heb *us* [d] Meaning of Heb uncertain [e] Compare Syr: Heb *Gilead* [f] Heb lacks *sheep* [g] Cn Compare Gk: Heb *To these they say sacrifices of people* [h] Gk Syr: Heb *knew*

in the land of drought.
6 When I fed[a] them, they were satisfied;
they were satisfied, and their heart was proud;
therefore they forgot me.
7 So I will become like a lion to them,
like a leopard I will lurk beside the way.
8 I will fall upon them like a bear robbed of her cubs,
and will tear open the covering of their heart;
there I will devour them like a lion,
as a wild animal would mangle them.

9 I will destroy you, O Israel;
who can help you?[b]
10 Where now is[c] your king, that he may save you?
Where in all your cities are your rulers,
of whom you said,
"Give me a king and rulers"?
11 I gave you a king in my anger,
and I took him away in my wrath.

12 Ephraim's iniquity is bound up;
his sin is kept in store.
13 The pangs of childbirth come for him,
but he is an unwise son;
for at the proper time he does not present himself
at the mouth of the womb.

14 Shall I ransom them from the power of Sheol?
Shall I redeem them from Death?
O Death, where are[d] your plagues?
O Sheol, where is[d] your destruction?
Compassion is hidden from my eyes.

15 Although he may flourish among rushes,[e]
the east wind shall come, a blast from the LORD,
rising from the wilderness;
and his fountain shall dry up,
his spring shall be parched.
It shall strip his treasury
of every precious thing.
16[f] Samaria shall bear her guilt,
because she has rebelled against her God;
they shall fall by the sword,
their little ones shall be dashed in pieces,
and their pregnant women ripped open.

14 Return, O Israel, to the LORD your God,
for you have stumbled because of your iniquity.
2 Take words with you
and return to the LORD;
say to him,
"Take away all guilt;
accept that which is good,
and we will offer
the fruit[g] of our lips.
3 Assyria shall not save us;
we will not ride upon horses;
we will say no more, 'Our God,'
to the work of our hands.
In you the orphan finds mercy."

4 I will heal their disloyalty;
I will love them freely,
for my anger has turned from them.
5 I will be like the dew to Israel;
he shall blossom like the lily,
he shall strike root like the forests of Lebanon.[h]
6 His shoots shall spread out;
his beauty shall be like the olive tree,
and his fragrance like that of Lebanon.
7 They shall again live beneath my[i] shadow,
they shall flourish as a garden;[j]
they shall blossom like the vine,
their fragrance shall be like the wine of Lebanon.

8 O Ephraim, what have I[k] to do with idols?
It is I who answer and look after you.[l]

[a] Cn: Heb *according to their pasture* [b] Gk Syr: Heb *for in me is your help* [c] Gk Syr Vg: Heb *I will be* [d] Gk Syr: Heb *I will be* [e] Or *among brothers* [f] Ch 14.1 in Heb [g] Gk Syr: Heb *bulls* [h] Cn: Heb *like Lebanon* [i] Heb *his* [j] Cn: Heb *they shall grow grain* [k] Or *What more has Ephraim* [l] Heb *him*

I am like an evergreen cypress;
your faithfulness[a] comes from me.
9 Those who are wise understand these things;
those who are discerning know them.
For the ways of the LORD are right,
and the upright walk in them,
but transgressors stumble in them.

[a] Heb *your fruit*

Joel

The book of Joel is the second in the collection of prophetic books known as the Minor Prophets in the Christian Bible and the second book in the scroll of the Twelve Prophets in the Hebrew Bible. Although the name Joel is common in the Bible, the book does not provide any personal information about the prophet or the historical circumstances of his ministry. The introduction of the book identifies Joel as the son of Pethuel (1:1). His name means "The Lord is God." Unlike the other prophetic books of the Old Testament, no historical information establishes the date when the book was written.

Internal evidence provides an approximate date for the historical setting of Joel's ministry. The book seems to indicate that Joel lived in Judah during the Persian period. It mentions the restored temple (1:13-14) and the rebuilt walls of Jerusalem (2:9), the role of the priests in assembling the people (1:14; 2:15-16), the exile of Judah (3:2-3 [in Hebrew 4:2-3]), and the slave trade by the Ionians (Greeks) (3:6 [Heb 4:6]). The absence of the Assyrians, Babylonians, and Persians, the lack of reference to a king, and the apocalyptic imagery used by the prophet indicate that the book probably was written late in the postexilic period, roughly 500–400 BCE. Joel quotes from earlier prophets including Amos, Isaiah, Ezekiel, Zephaniah, and Obadiah.

In the Hebrew Bible, Joel has four chapters. The Septuagint and the Vulgate combined chapters 3 and 4 into one chapter; the Septuagint also includes as 2:28-32 what is 3:1-5 in Hebrew. English translations follow the Septuagint.

The prophet Joel used the devastation brought by a plague of locusts to announce the coming of the Day of the Lord as a day of judgment for the nations and of ultimate salvation for Jerusalem. The prophet used the plague and the drought that followed to call the people in Jerusalem to fast and to repent. Joel's graphic account of the locust invasion becomes a representation of the attack of the nations against Jerusalem and the final battle on the Day of YHWH.

The book begins with a vivid description of the plague of locusts and its consequences. Locust infestations have occurred in many parts of the world, including Africa, Syria, and Palestine. They can quickly leave fields, orchards, and vineyards stripped bare, bringing disaster to people who depend on the land and its produce for survival. As a Brazilian whose parents were born and grew up on a farm, I can sympathize with the plight of farmers confronted with plagues and drought. Many Brazilians live on small farms and have to work hard to earn a living. When plagues destroy their crops, they, like the people in the days of Joel, pray to God and seek divine assistance.

The locust plague was a national crisis and a test of Israel's faith, and the prophet used it to summon the people to repent of their sins and petition the Lord for assistance. The prophet demanded genuine brokenness of heart and issued a call to the people to fast, weep, and mourn.

The advance of the locust is compared to the advance of an army prepared for battle. Joel uses the plague to portray the events preceding the coming Day of the LORD. It will be a day of gloom and darkness and will be accompanied by the outpouring of God's Spirit, portents in the skies of the final battle, the judgment of the nations in the Valley of Jehoshaphat, and the manifestation of YHWH to restore the fortunes of Israel.

Joel is divided into two main sections, outlined below. The first deals with the locust plague and its aftermath. The second describes the events related to the Day of the LORD and the judgment of the nations.

The coming of the locust, 1:2—2:17
The locust plague, 1:2-12
A call to prayer, 1:13-20
The Day of the LORD, 2:1-11
Repentance and restoration, 2:12-27
The outpouring of God's Spirit, 2:28-32
The judgment of the nations, 3:1-21
A summons to judgment, 3:1-8
A call to war, 3:9-16
The restoration of Israel, 3:17-21

— ***Claude F. Mariottini***

1 The word of the LORD that came to Joel son of Pethuel:

2 Hear this, O elders,
give ear, all inhabitants of the land!
Has such a thing happened in your days,
or in the days of your ancestors?
3 Tell your children of it,
and let your children tell their children,
and their children another generation.

4 What the cutting locust left,
the swarming locust has eaten.
What the swarming locust left,
the hopping locust has eaten,
and what the hopping locust left,
the destroying locust has eaten.

5 Wake up, you drunkards, and weep;
and wail, all you wine-drinkers,
over the sweet wine,
for it is cut off from your mouth.
6 For a nation has invaded my land,
powerful and innumerable;
its teeth are lions' teeth,
and it has the fangs of a lioness.
7 It has laid waste my vines,
and splintered my fig trees;
it has stripped off their bark and thrown it down;
their branches have turned white.

8 Lament like a virgin dressed in sackcloth
for the husband of her youth.

9 The grain offering and the drink offering are
cut off
from the house of the LORD.
The priests mourn,
the ministers of the LORD.
10 The fields are devastated,
the ground mourns;
for the grain is destroyed,
the wine dries up,
the oil fails.

11 Be dismayed, you farmers,
wail, you vinedressers,
over the wheat and the barley;
for the crops of the field are ruined.
12 The vine withers,
the fig tree droops.
Pomegranate, palm, and apple—
all the trees of the field are dried up;
surely, joy withers away
among the people.

13 Put on sackcloth and lament, you priests;
wail, you ministers of the altar.
Come, pass the night in sackcloth,
you ministers of my God!
Grain offering and drink offering
are withheld from the house of your God.

14 Sanctify a fast,
call a solemn assembly.
Gather the elders
and all the inhabitants of the land
to the house of the LORD your God,
and cry out to the LORD.

15 Alas for the day!
For the day of the LORD is near,
and as destruction from the Almighty[a] it
comes.
16 Is not the food cut off
before our eyes,
joy and gladness
from the house of our God?

17 The seed shrivels under the clods,[b]
the storehouses are desolate;
the granaries are ruined
because the grain has failed.
18 How the animals groan!
The herds of cattle wander about
because there is no pasture for them;
even the flocks of sheep are dazed.[c]

19 To you, O LORD, I cry.
For fire has devoured
the pastures of the wilderness,
and flames have burned
all the trees of the field.
20 Even the wild animals cry to you
because the watercourses are dried up,
and fire has devoured
the pastures of the wilderness.

2 Blow the trumpet in Zion;
sound the alarm on my holy mountain!
Let all the inhabitants of the land tremble,
for the day of the LORD is coming, it is
near—
2 a day of darkness and gloom,
a day of clouds and thick darkness!
Like blackness spread upon the mountains
a great and powerful army comes;
their like has never been from of old,
nor will be again after them
in ages to come.

3 Fire devours in front of them,
and behind them a flame burns.
Before them the land is like the garden of
Eden,
but after them a desolate wilderness,
and nothing escapes them.

4 They have the appearance of horses,
and like war-horses they charge.
5 As with the rumbling of chariots,
they leap on the tops of the mountains,
like the crackling of a flame of fire

[a] Traditional rendering of Heb *Shaddai* [b] Meaning of Heb uncertain
[c] Compare Gk Syr Vg: Meaning of Heb uncertain

devouring the stubble,
like a powerful army
drawn up for battle.

6 Before them peoples are in anguish,
all faces grow pale.[a]
7 Like warriors they charge,
like soldiers they scale the wall.
Each keeps to its own course,
they do not swerve from[b] their paths.
8 They do not jostle one another,
each keeps to its own track;
they burst through the weapons
and are not halted.
9 They leap upon the city,
they run upon the walls;
they climb up into the houses,
they enter through the windows like a thief.

10 The earth quakes before them,
the heavens tremble.
The sun and the moon are darkened,
and the stars withdraw their shining.
11 The LORD utters his voice
at the head of his army;
how vast is his host!
Numberless are those who obey his command.
Truly the day of the LORD is great;
terrible indeed—who can endure it?

12 Yet even now, says the LORD,
return to me with all your heart,
with fasting, with weeping, and with mourning;
13 rend your hearts and not your clothing.
Return to the LORD, your God,
for he is gracious and merciful,
slow to anger, and abounding in steadfast love,
and relents from punishing.
14 Who knows whether he will not turn and relent,
and leave a blessing behind him,
a grain offering and a drink offering
for the LORD, your God?

15 Blow the trumpet in Zion;
sanctify a fast;
call a solemn assembly;
16 gather the people.
Sanctify the congregation;
assemble the aged;
gather the children,
even infants at the breast.
Let the bridegroom leave his room,
and the bride her canopy.

17 Between the vestibule and the altar
let the priests, the ministers of the LORD, weep.
Let them say, "Spare your people, O LORD,
and do not make your heritage a mockery,
a byword among the nations.
Why should it be said among the peoples,
'Where is their God?' "

18 Then the LORD became jealous for his land,
and had pity on his people.
19 In response to his people the LORD said:
I am sending you
grain, wine, and oil,
and you will be satisfied;
and I will no more make you
a mockery among the nations.

20 I will remove the northern army far from you,
and drive it into a parched and desolate land,
its front into the eastern sea,
and its rear into the western sea;
its stench and foul smell will rise up.
Surely he has done great things!

21 Do not fear, O soil;
be glad and rejoice,
for the LORD has done great things!
22 Do not fear, you animals of the field,

[a] Meaning of Heb uncertain [b] Gk Syr Vg: Heb *they do not take a pledge along*

for the pastures of the wilderness are
green;
the tree bears its fruit,
the fig tree and vine give their full yield.

23 O children of Zion, be glad
and rejoice in the LORD your God;
for he has given the early rain[a] for your
vindication,
he has poured down for you abundant
rain,
the early and the later rain, as before.
24 The threshing floors shall be full of grain,
the vats shall overflow with wine
and oil.

25 I will repay you for the years
that the swarming locust has eaten,
the hopper, the destroyer, and the cutter,
my great army, which I sent against you.

26 You shall eat in plenty and be satisfied,
and praise the name of the LORD your
God,
who has dealt wondrously with you.
And my people shall never again be put to
shame.
27 You shall know that I am in the midst of
Israel,
and that I, the LORD, am your God and
there is no other.
And my people shall never again be put to
shame.

28[b] Then afterward
I will pour out my spirit on all flesh;
your sons and your daughters shall prophesy,
your old men shall dream dreams,
and your young men shall see visions.
29 Even on the male and female slaves,
in those days, I will pour out my spirit.

30 I will show portents in the heavens and on
the earth, blood and fire and columns of smoke.
31 The sun shall be turned to darkness, and the
moon to blood, before the great and terrible day
of the LORD comes. 32 Then everyone who calls
on the name of the LORD shall be saved; for in
Mount Zion and in Jerusalem there shall be those
who escape, as the LORD has said, and among the
survivors shall be those whom the LORD calls.

3[c] For then, in those days and at that time, when
I restore the fortunes of Judah and Jerusalem, 2 I will gather all the nations and bring them
down to the valley of Jehoshaphat, and I will enter into judgment with them there, on account of
my people and my heritage Israel, because they
have scattered them among the nations. They

[a] Meaning of Heb uncertain [b] Ch 3.1 in Heb [c] Ch 4.1 in Heb

Joel 2:28

Young persons in biblical times, as now, had ideas and viewpoints. They just weren't given much opportunity to express them. They were capable, in the prophet Joel's words, of prophecy and visions, but their views were rarely valued. The Sri Lankan theologian Tissa Balasuriya observes:

> Youth today has a greater awareness of and concern for justice than perhaps ever in the past. They are particularly sensitive to the needs of social justice.... They want more respect for the human person and for his or her rights. They are more aware of the communitarian aspect of justice. They see the absence of effective sharing despite protestations of good will, aid and charity by the affluent.... The media of communications make them aware that the world has the means to remedy such problems as malnutrition and hunger almost overnight if only the people of the world were prepared to share their goods with those in need.... Youth want actions that are related to problems and not mere ideological postures.[59]

— DB

have divided my land, [3]and cast lots for my people, and traded boys for prostitutes, and sold girls
for wine, and drunk it down.
4 What are you to me, O Tyre and Sidon,
and all the regions of Philistia? Are you paying
me back for something? If you are paying me
back, I will turn your deeds back upon your own
heads swiftly and speedily. [5]For you have taken
my silver and my gold, and have carried my rich
treasures into your temples.[a] [6]You have sold the
people of Judah and Jerusalem to the Greeks,
removing them far from their own border. [7]But
now I will rouse them to leave the places to which
you have sold them, and I will turn your deeds
back upon your own heads. [8]I will sell your sons
and your daughters into the hand of the people of
Judah, and they will sell them to the Sabeans, to a
nation far away; for the LORD has spoken.

9 Proclaim this among the nations:
Prepare war,[b]
  stir up the warriors.
Let all the soldiers draw near,
  let them come up.
10 Beat your plowshares into swords,
  and your pruning hooks into spears;
  let the weakling say, "I am a warrior."

11 Come quickly,[c]
  all you nations all around,
  gather yourselves there.
Bring down your warriors, O LORD.
12 Let the nations rouse themselves,
  and come up to the valley of
    Jehoshaphat;
for there I will sit to judge
  all the neighboring nations.

13 Put in the sickle,
  for the harvest is ripe.
Go in, tread,
  for the wine press is full.
The vats overflow,
  for their wickedness is great.

14 Multitudes, multitudes,
  in the valley of decision!
For the day of the LORD is near
  in the valley of decision.
15 The sun and the moon are darkened,
  and the stars withdraw their shining.

16 The LORD roars from Zion,
  and utters his voice from Jerusalem,
  and the heavens and the earth shake.
But the LORD is a refuge for his people,
  a stronghold for the people of Israel.

17 So you shall know that I, the LORD your God,
  dwell in Zion, my holy mountain.
And Jerusalem shall be holy,
  and strangers shall never again pass
    through it.

18 In that day
the mountains shall drip sweet wine,
  the hills shall flow with milk,
and all the stream beds of Judah
  shall flow with water;
a fountain shall come forth from the house of
  the LORD
  and water the Wadi Shittim.

19 Egypt shall become a desolation
  and Edom a desolate wilderness,
because of the violence done to the people
  of Judah,
  in whose land they have shed innocent
  blood.
20 But Judah shall be inhabited forever,
  and Jerusalem to all generations.
21 I will avenge their blood, and I will not clear
  the guilty,[d]
  for the LORD dwells in Zion.

[a] Or *palaces* [b] Heb *sanctify war* [c] Meaning of Heb uncertain
[d] Gk Syr: Heb *I will hold innocent their blood that I have not held innocent*

Amos

My grandfather, Kempis McKinney, was a well-respected gentleman farmer and a deacon in his Baptist congregation. People knew he was "a praying man." His business allowed him to interact with wealthy and poor people alike. He was a fair-skinned black man, which made it easier for him to interact with whites in the Jim Crow South. He fiercely defended those he perceived were vulnerable because they were uneducated, without means, or ill. I think often of my grandfather when reading about the persona and message recorded in Amos.

Amos came from Tekoa (1:1) in Judah, a city that we know had at least one famous wise woman (2 Sam 14:1-10). He may have been familiar with the banter and storytelling of the wisdom guilds, known for exposing the absurdity of life, the exploits of the wealthy, and the dishonest governmental behavior that affects people with little or no power. Amos, a person of means, got to see up close the self-centeredness of those with access to resources. He was a dresser of sycamore and fig trees and a "sheep breeder" (translated "herdsman" in 7:14-15 in the NRSV; compare 2 Kgs 3:4), suggesting he owned flocks. According to his testimony, Amos was not a prophet (7:14-15), nor a member of a prophets' guild (not "a prophet's son"), a collection of people who kept alive the words of prophets or who surrounded prophets to practice discerning what ordinary, daily signs meant from a spiritual perspective (cf. 1 Kgs 20:35; 2 Kgs 2:3).

Using a rhetoric of entrapment, the book of Amos draws listeners into position as the prophet elicits their agreement about the punishment of Israel's enemies. Slowly, however, the prophetic words turn on Israel and Judah, the presumed chosen people. Their status as chosen people (3:2) ultimately is repudiated as they learn that they are "like the Ethiopians" to the deity, who is God of all (9:7). Amos's poetic pronouncements against Israel were heightened by his day-to-day marketplace contacts. As a trader, he paid close attention to the ways merchants bargained or put extra weight on a scale in an effort to cheat. He noticed the plight of widows, children, and their vulnerability as he plied his own wares of wine, sheepskins, milk, and meat. He stood in city gates where officials meted out justice, listened to city elders give favor to the wealthy, abuse the poor, and take financial kickbacks. Amos was very conscious of the plight of poor people and decided to align himself, under God's influence, as a spokesman on their behalf.

Though attuned to the marketplace, Amos used primarily agrarian language that people would recognize: God's voice as lion's roar (1:1-2; 3:3-8); nature as testament to the name and character of Israel's God (4:13; 5:8; 9:5-6). His words are specific to his times; yet as he lifts up injustice done by powerful people against vulnerable ones, his words continue to speak today.

The book tackles corruption on three fronts: the courts, wealthy people's lifestyles, and sanctuary worship in Bethel and Gilgal. The terms "justice" and "righteousness" are Amos' linchpins for what constitutes a rightly ordered society; these two words are coupled at 5:7, 5:24, and 6:12 (see also 2:6-7; 5:12, and 5:15). He favors a rightly ordered society over worship (compare Isa 1:10-17; Mic 6:6-8; Hos 6:6). He condemns the nations, and ancient Israel, for their unjust practices.

Amos aims at those entrenched in power and wealth. Like leaders during South Africa's days of apartheid, for example, they did not easily relinquish power, clothing it instead in religious language. The prophet provides a scathing indictment, noting that their worship is tainted by greed, sexual impropriety, and disregard for the poor (2:6-8). They rush through worship, or at least long for it to end, so they may return to their corrupt business practices (8:4-7). Amos mocks the call to worship and excoriates people for being pious without justice (4:4-5). His attacks on this manner of worship resemble those of his near contemporary, Hosea (8:11-14). As they have oppressed the poor, God will raise a nation to oppress them (6:14).

God's power is evident in the drama of the cosmos. God's identity as a warrior is revealed in nature, in the wind, the changing of night to day, the stars, the seas and rivers; indeed, God's palace may be in heaven, but its foundations are upon the earth (4:13, 5:8, and 9:5-6). In Amos, readers understand that Israel expected "the Day of the LORD" (5:18) to be an ultimate blessing for Israel. But Amos assures them that the day will be nothing like they imagine. It will be as if, trying to escape a lion, one runs into a bear, then, escaping the bear, is killed by a poisonous snake in the supposed safety of one's home (5:18-20). The answer for their plight is to "seek the LORD and live" (in various forms, 5:4, 6, 14). The repetition and doing of this phrase is the antidote for what ails them.

Like other prophets, Amos relies on attitudes toward women to make his point. He lays oppressive practices on the beds of women, "you cows of Bashan" (4:1). When the priest Amaziah challenges him, Amos declares that Amaziah's wife will become a prostitute or a spoil of war (7:17). Using women as scapegoats or in a pejorative way is a common biblical phenomenon (see Num 5:11-32; Ezekiel 16; Proverbs 5 and 7; Judges 16; 1 Kings 21).

Amos's visions for the Northern Kingdom were so powerful that Jeremiah later referred to them to make his own case toward Judah.

— Valerie Bridgeman

1 The words of Amos, who was among the shepherds of Tekoa, which he saw concerning Israel in the days of King Uzziah of Judah and in the days of King Jeroboam son of Joash of Israel, two years[a] before the earthquake.

2 And he said:
The LORD roars from Zion,
and utters his voice from Jerusalem;
the pastures of the shepherds wither,
and the top of Carmel dries up.

[a] Or *during two years*

3 Thus says the LORD:
For three transgressions of Damascus,
and for four, I will not revoke the punishment;[a]
because they have threshed Gilead
with threshing sledges of iron.
4 So I will send a fire on the house of Hazael,
and it shall devour the strongholds of Ben-hadad.
5 I will break the gate bars of Damascus,
and cut off the inhabitants from the Valley of Aven,
and the one who holds the scepter from Beth-eden;
and the people of Aram shall go into exile to Kir,
says the LORD.

6 Thus says the LORD:
For three transgressions of Gaza,
and for four, I will not revoke the punishment;[a]
because they carried into exile entire communities,
to hand them over to Edom.
7 So I will send a fire on the wall of Gaza,
fire that shall devour its strongholds.
8 I will cut off the inhabitants from Ashdod,
and the one who holds the scepter from Ashkelon;
I will turn my hand against Ekron,
and the remnant of the Philistines shall perish,
says the Lord GOD.

9 Thus says the LORD:
For three transgressions of Tyre,
and for four, I will not revoke the punishment;[a]
because they delivered entire communities over to Edom,
and did not remember the covenant of kinship.
10 So I will send a fire on the wall of Tyre,
fire that shall devour its strongholds.

11 Thus says the LORD:
For three transgressions of Edom,
and for four, I will not revoke the punishment;[a]
because he pursued his brother with the sword
and cast off all pity;
he maintained his anger perpetually,[b]
and kept his wrath[c] forever.
12 So I will send a fire on Teman,
and it shall devour the strongholds of Bozrah.

13 Thus says the LORD:
For three transgressions of the Ammonites,
and for four, I will not revoke the punishment;[a]
because they have ripped open pregnant women in Gilead
in order to enlarge their territory.
14 So I will kindle a fire against the wall of Rabbah,
fire that shall devour its strongholds,
with shouting on the day of battle,
with a storm on the day of the whirlwind;
15 then their king shall go into exile,
he and his officials together,
says the LORD.

2 Thus says the LORD:
For three transgressions of Moab,
and for four, I will not revoke the punishment;[a]
because he burned to lime
the bones of the king of Edom.
2 So I will send a fire on Moab,
and it shall devour the strongholds of Kerioth,
and Moab shall die amid uproar,
amid shouting and the sound of the trumpet;
3 I will cut off the ruler from its midst,
and will kill all its officials with him,
says the LORD.

[a] Heb *cause it to return* [b] Syr Vg: Heb *and his anger tore perpetually* [c] Gk Syr Vg: Heb *and his wrath kept*

4 Thus says the LORD:
For three transgressions of Judah,
and for four, I will not revoke the punishment;[a]
because they have rejected the law of the LORD,
and have not kept his statutes,
but they have been led astray by the same lies
after which their ancestors walked.
5 So I will send a fire on Judah,
and it shall devour the strongholds of Jerusalem.

6 Thus says the LORD:
For three transgressions of Israel,
and for four, I will not revoke the punishment;[a]
because they sell the righteous for silver,
and the needy for a pair of sandals—
7 they who trample the head of the poor into the dust of the earth,
and push the afflicted out of the way;
father and son go in to the same girl,
so that my holy name is profaned;
8 they lay themselves down beside every altar
on garments taken in pledge;
and in the house of their God they drink
wine bought with fines they imposed.

9 Yet I destroyed the Amorite before them,
whose height was like the height of cedars,
and who was as strong as oaks;
I destroyed his fruit above,
and his roots beneath.
10 Also I brought you up out of the land of Egypt,
and led you forty years in the wilderness,
to possess the land of the Amorite.
11 And I raised up some of your children to be prophets
and some of your youths to be nazirites.[b]
Is it not indeed so, O people of Israel?
says the LORD.

12 But you made the nazirites[b] drink wine,
and commanded the prophets,
saying, "You shall not prophesy."

13 So, I will press you down in your place,
just as a cart presses down
when it is full of sheaves.[c]
14 Flight shall perish from the swift,
and the strong shall not retain their strength,
nor shall the mighty save their lives;
15 those who handle the bow shall not stand,
and those who are swift of foot shall not save themselves,

[a] Heb *cause it to return* [b] That is, *those separated* or *those consecrated* [c] Meaning of Heb uncertain

Amos 2:6-8

Despite the noble ideal of ancient Israel—that the land is a gift of God's grace, that all have a right to own land, and that the wealthy will share their bounty with the poor—there were abuses of power. Amos denounced those newly rich Israelites who flouted this ideal in their rampant greed, saying that they "trample the head of the poor" and would not hesitate to sell some poor debtor into slavery for the mere price of a pair of sandals. In those days small landowners were vulnerable to famines or bad decisions and could be forced to sell themselves into slavery because of insurmountable debts. The powerful were eager to grab more land for themselves, but even with more land their interest was not in producing staples for the poor. For Amos this pattern is against the commands of God to help the poor and needy in their distress. This pattern of greed by society's powerful is against the common good and the basic understanding of community, which seeks the best interest of all persons in society, rich or poor. Amos condemns this social injustice—and he sees looming on the eastern horizon the coming end of this unjust system in the specter of an advancing Assyrian army.

— DB

nor shall those who ride horses save their lives;
16 and those who are stout of heart among the mighty
shall flee away naked in that day,
says the LORD.

3

Hear this word that the LORD has spoken
against you, O people of Israel, against the
whole family that I brought up out of the land of
Egypt:
2 You only have I known
of all the families of the earth;
therefore I will punish you
for all your iniquities.

3 Do two walk together
unless they have made an appointment?
4 Does a lion roar in the forest,
when it has no prey?
Does a young lion cry out from its den,
if it has caught nothing?
5 Does a bird fall into a snare on the earth,
when there is no trap for it?
Does a snare spring up from the ground,
when it has taken nothing?
6 Is a trumpet blown in a city,
and the people are not afraid?
Does disaster befall a city,
unless the LORD has done it?
7 Surely the Lord GOD does nothing,
without revealing his secret
to his servants the prophets.
8 The lion has roared;
who will not fear?
The Lord GOD has spoken;
who can but prophesy?

9 Proclaim to the strongholds in Ashdod,
and to the strongholds in the land of Egypt,
and say, "Assemble yourselves on Mount[a] Samaria,
and see what great tumults are within it,
and what oppressions are in its midst."
10 They do not know how to do right, says the LORD,
those who store up violence and robbery
in their strongholds.
11 Therefore thus says the Lord GOD:
An adversary shall surround the land,
and strip you of your defense;
and your strongholds shall be plundered.

12 Thus says the LORD: As the shepherd
rescues from the mouth of the lion two legs, or
a piece of an ear, so shall the people of Israel who
live in Samaria be rescued, with the corner of a
couch and part[b] of a bed.

13 Hear, and testify against the house of Jacob,
says the Lord GOD, the God of hosts:
14 On the day I punish Israel for its transgressions,
I will punish the altars of Bethel,
and the horns of the altar shall be cut off
and fall to the ground.
15 I will tear down the winter house as well as the summer house;
and the houses of ivory shall perish,
and the great houses[c] shall come to an end,
says the LORD.

4

Hear this word, you cows of Bashan
who are on Mount Samaria,
who oppress the poor, who crush the needy,
who say to their husbands, "Bring something to drink!"
2 The Lord GOD has sworn by his holiness:
The time is surely coming upon you,
when they shall take you away with hooks,
even the last of you with fishhooks.
3 Through breaches in the wall you shall leave,
each one straight ahead;
and you shall be flung out into Harmon,[b]
says the LORD.
4 Come to Bethel—and transgress;
to Gilgal—and multiply transgression;
bring your sacrifices every morning,
your tithes every three days;

[a] Gk Syr: Heb *the mountains of* [b] Meaning of Heb uncertain [c] Or *many houses*

5 bring a thank offering of leavened bread,
and proclaim freewill offerings, publish them;
for so you love to do, O people of Israel!
says the Lord GOD.

6 I gave you cleanness of teeth in all your cities,
and lack of bread in all your places,
yet you did not return to me,
says the LORD.

7 And I also withheld the rain from you
when there were still three months to the harvest;
I would send rain on one city,
and send no rain on another city;
one field would be rained upon,
and the field on which it did not rain withered;
8 so two or three towns wandered to one town
to drink water, and were not satisfied;
yet you did not return to me,
says the LORD.

9 I struck you with blight and mildew;
I laid waste[a] your gardens and your vineyards;
the locust devoured your fig trees and your olive trees;
yet you did not return to me,
says the LORD.

10 I sent among you a pestilence after the manner of Egypt;
I killed your young men with the sword;
I carried away your horses;[b]
and I made the stench of your camp go up into your nostrils;
yet you did not return to me,
says the LORD.

11 I overthrew some of you,
as when God overthrew Sodom and Gomorrah,
and you were like a brand snatched from the fire;
yet you did not return to me,
says the LORD.

12 Therefore thus I will do to you, O Israel;
because I will do this to you,
prepare to meet your God, O Israel!

13 For lo, the one who forms the mountains,
creates the wind,
reveals his thoughts to mortals,
makes the morning darkness,
and treads on the heights of the earth—
the LORD, the God of hosts, is his name!

5 Hear this word that I take up over you in lamentation, O house of Israel:
2 Fallen, no more to rise,
is maiden Israel;
forsaken on her land,
with no one to raise her up.

3 For thus says the Lord GOD:
The city that marched out a thousand
shall have a hundred left,
and that which marched out a hundred
shall have ten left.[c]

4 For thus says the LORD to the house of Israel:
Seek me and live;
5 but do not seek Bethel,
and do not enter into Gilgal
or cross over to Beer-sheba;
for Gilgal shall surely go into exile,
and Bethel shall come to nothing.

6 Seek the LORD and live,
or he will break out against the house of Joseph like fire,
and it will devour Bethel, with no one to quench it.
7 Ah, you that turn justice to wormwood,
and bring righteousness to the ground!

[a] Cn: Heb *the multitude of* [b] Heb *with the captivity of your horses* [c] Heb adds *to the house of Israel*

8 The one who made the Pleiades and Orion,
and turns deep darkness into the morning,
and darkens the day into night,
who calls for the waters of the sea,
and pours them out on the surface of the earth,
the LORD is his name,
9 who makes destruction flash out against the strong,
so that destruction comes upon the fortress.

10 They hate the one who reproves in the gate,
and they abhor the one who speaks the truth.
11 Therefore because you trample on the poor
and take from them levies of grain,
you have built houses of hewn stone,
but you shall not live in them;
you have planted pleasant vineyards,
but you shall not drink their wine.
12 For I know how many are your transgressions,
and how great are your sins—
you who afflict the righteous, who take a bribe,
and push aside the needy in the gate.
13 Therefore the prudent will keep silent in such a time;
for it is an evil time.

14 Seek good and not evil,
that you may live;
and so the LORD, the God of hosts, will be with you,
just as you have said.
15 Hate evil and love good,
and establish justice in the gate;
it may be that the LORD, the God of hosts,
will be gracious to the remnant of Joseph.

16 Therefore thus says the LORD, the God of hosts, the Lord:
In all the squares there shall be wailing;
and in all the streets they shall say, "Alas! alas!"
They shall call the farmers to mourning,
and those skilled in lamentation, to wailing;
17 in all the vineyards there shall be wailing,
for I will pass through the midst of you,
says the LORD.

18 Alas for you who desire the day of the LORD!
Why do you want the day of the LORD?
It is darkness, not light;
19 as if someone fled from a lion,
and was met by a bear;
or went into the house and rested a hand against the wall,
and was bitten by a snake.

Amos 5:10-15

After quoting several texts from the prophetic tradition of the Old Testament to refute those who might deny an integral relationship between religion and politics, Bishop [Reverdy C.] Ransom . . . proceeded to admonish the church to become engaged deliberately and forthrightly in specific actions aimed at social justice:

> *The world has little interest in us or concern about us as to what we do or what we say here. To them we are just a group of Negroes here legislating and voting on matters that concern our Church. But once let us take up in the name of a just and righteous God, the conditions that confront our people in this country; and the newspapers and every other public influence will immediately spring to attention. [For t]he sharecroppers of the South whose present conditions are but little removed from slavery. . . . What have we done, what will we do, to help them secure industrial and economic justice?*[60]

— Peter J. Paris

20 Is not the day of the LORD darkness, not
light,
and gloom with no brightness in it?

21 I hate, I despise your festivals,
and I take no delight in your solemn
assemblies.
22 Even though you offer me your burnt
offerings and grain offerings,
I will not accept them;
and the offerings of well-being of your fatted
animals
I will not look upon.
23 Take away from me the noise of your songs;
I will not listen to the melody of your
harps.
24 But let justice roll down like waters,
and righteousness like an ever-flowing
stream.

25 Did you bring to me sacrifices and offerings the forty years in the wilderness, O house
of Israel? 26 You shall take up Sakkuth your king,
and Kaiwan your star-god, your images,[a] which
you made for yourselves; 27 therefore I will take
you into exile beyond Damascus, says the LORD,
whose name is the God of hosts.

6 Alas for those who are at ease in Zion,
and for those who feel secure on Mount
Samaria,
the notables of the first of the nations,
to whom the house of Israel resorts!
2 Cross over to Calneh, and see;
from there go to Hamath the great;
then go down to Gath of the Philistines.
Are you better[b] than these kingdoms?
Or is your[c] territory greater than their[d]
territory,
3 O you that put far away the evil day,
and bring near a reign of violence?

4 Alas for those who lie on beds of ivory,
and lounge on their couches,
and eat lambs from the flock,
and calves from the stall;
5 who sing idle songs to the sound of the harp,
and like David improvise on instruments
of music;
6 who drink wine from bowls,
and anoint themselves with the finest oils,
but are not grieved over the ruin of Joseph!
7 Therefore they shall now be the first to go
into exile,
and the revelry of the loungers shall pass
away.

8 The Lord GOD has sworn by himself
(says the LORD, the God of hosts):
I abhor the pride of Jacob
and hate his strongholds;
and I will deliver up the city and all that
is in it.

9 If ten people remain in one house, they
shall die. 10 And if a relative, one who burns the
dead,[e] shall take up the body to bring it out of the
house, and shall say to someone in the innermost
parts of the house, "Is anyone else with you?" the
answer will come, "No." Then the relative[f] shall
say, "Hush! We must not mention the name of
the LORD."

11 See, the LORD commands,
and the great house shall be shattered to
bits,
and the little house to pieces.
12 Do horses run on rocks?
Does one plow the sea with oxen?[g]
But you have turned justice into poison
and the fruit of righteousness into
wormwood—
13 you who rejoice in Lo-debar,[h]
who say, "Have we not by our own strength
taken Karnaim[i] for ourselves?"
14 Indeed, I am raising up against you a nation,
O house of Israel, says the LORD, the God
of hosts,

[a] Heb *your images, your star-god* [b] Or *Are they better* [c] Heb *their* [d] Heb *your* [e] Or *who makes a burning for him*
[f] Heb *he* [g] Or *Does one plow them with oxen* [h] Or *in a thing of nothingness* [i] Or *horns*

and they shall oppress you from
Lebo-hamath
to the Wadi Arabah.

7 This is what the Lord God showed me: he
was forming locusts at the time the latter
growth began to sprout (it was the latter growth
after the king's mowings). 2When they had finished eating the grass of the land, I said,
"O Lord God, forgive, I beg you!
How can Jacob stand?
He is so small!"
3 The Lord relented concerning this;
"It shall not be," said the Lord.

4 This is what the Lord God showed me: the
Lord God was calling for a shower of fire,[a] and
it devoured the great deep and was eating up the
land. 5Then I said,
"O Lord God, cease, I beg you!
How can Jacob stand?
He is so small!"
6 The Lord relented concerning this;
"This also shall not be," said the Lord God.

7 This is what he showed me: the Lord was
standing beside a wall built with a plumb line,
with a plumb line in his hand. 8And the Lord
said to me, "Amos, what do you see?" And I said,
"A plumb line." Then the Lord said,
"See, I am setting a plumb line
in the midst of my people Israel;
I will never again pass them by;
9 the high places of Isaac shall be made
desolate,
and the sanctuaries of Israel shall be laid
waste,
and I will rise against the house of
Jeroboam with the sword."

10 Then Amaziah, the priest of Bethel, sent to
King Jeroboam of Israel, saying, "Amos has conspired against you in the very center of the house
of Israel; the land is not able to bear all his words.
11For thus Amos has said,
'Jeroboam shall die by the sword,
and Israel must go into exile
away from his land.'"
12And Amaziah said to Amos, "O seer, go, flee
away to the land of Judah, earn your bread there,
and prophesy there; 13but never again prophesy
at Bethel, for it is the king's sanctuary, and it is a
temple of the kingdom."

14 Then Amos answered Amaziah, "I am[b] no
prophet, nor a prophet's son; but I am[b] a herdsman, and a dresser of sycamore trees, 15and the
Lord took me from following the flock, and the
Lord said to me, 'Go, prophesy to my people
Israel.'
16 "Now therefore hear the word of the Lord.
You say, 'Do not prophesy against Israel,
and do not preach against the house of
Isaac.'
17 Therefore thus says the Lord:
'Your wife shall become a prostitute in the
city,
and your sons and your daughters shall fall
by the sword,
and your land shall be parceled out by line;
you yourself shall die in an unclean land,
and Israel shall surely go into exile away
from its land.'"

Amos 7:1-17

It is characteristic of Amos's vision that God's mercy is constrained by God's justice—the "plumb line" by which all society is measured (vv. 7-9). It is characteristic of the national religion of his time—and of other times and other nations in history—that calling for that justice is deemed an intolerable threat to the public order.

— NE

8 This is what the Lord God showed me—a
basket of summer fruit.[c] 2He said, "Amos,
what do you see?" And I said, "A basket of summer fruit."[c] Then the Lord said to me,

[a] Or *for a judgment by fire* [b] Or *was* [c] Heb *qayits*

"The end[a] has come upon my people Israel;
I will never again pass them by.
3 The songs of the temple[b] shall become
wailings in that day,"
says the Lord GOD;
"the dead bodies shall be many,
cast out in every place. Be silent!"

4 Hear this, you that trample on the needy,
and bring to ruin the poor of the land,
5 saying, "When will the new moon be over
so that we may sell grain;
and the sabbath,
so that we may offer wheat for sale?
We will make the ephah small and the shekel
great,
and practice deceit with false balances,
6 buying the poor for silver
and the needy for a pair of sandals,
and selling the sweepings of the wheat."

7 The LORD has sworn by the pride of Jacob:
Surely I will never forget any of their deeds.
8 Shall not the land tremble on this account,
and everyone mourn who lives in it,
and all of it rise like the Nile,
and be tossed about and sink again, like
the Nile of Egypt?

9 On that day, says the Lord GOD,
I will make the sun go down at noon,
and darken the earth in broad daylight.
10 I will turn your feasts into mourning,
and all your songs into lamentation;
I will bring sackcloth on all loins,
and baldness on every head;
I will make it like the mourning for an only
son,
and the end of it like a bitter day.

11 The time is surely coming, says the Lord
GOD,
when I will send a famine on the land;
not a famine of bread, or a thirst for water,
but of hearing the words of the LORD.
12 They shall wander from sea to sea,
and from north to east;
they shall run to and fro, seeking the word of
the LORD,
but they shall not find it.

13 In that day the beautiful young women and
the young men
shall faint for thirst.
14 Those who swear by Ashimah of Samaria,
and say, "As your god lives, O Dan,"
and, "As the way of Beer-sheba lives"—
they shall fall, and never rise again.

9 I saw the LORD standing beside[c] the altar,
and he said:
Strike the capitals until the thresholds shake,
and shatter them on the heads of all the
people;[d]
and those who are left I will kill with the
sword;
not one of them shall flee away,
not one of them shall escape.

2 Though they dig into Sheol,
from there shall my hand take them;
though they climb up to heaven,
from there I will bring them down.
3 Though they hide themselves on the top of
Carmel,
from there I will search out and take them;
and though they hide from my sight at the
bottom of the sea,
there I will command the sea-serpent, and
it shall bite them.
4 And though they go into captivity in front of
their enemies,
there I will command the sword, and it
shall kill them;
and I will fix my eyes on them
for harm and not for good.

5 The Lord, GOD of hosts,
he who touches the earth and it melts,
and all who live in it mourn,

[a] Heb *qets* [b] Or *palace* [c] Or *on* [d] Heb *all of them*

and all of it rises like the Nile,
and sinks again, like the Nile of Egypt;
6 who builds his upper chambers in the heavens,
and founds his vault upon the earth;
who calls for the waters of the sea,
and pours them out upon the surface of the earth—
the LORD is his name.

7 Are you not like the Ethiopians[a] to me,
O people of Israel? says the LORD.
Did I not bring Israel up from the land of Egypt,
and the Philistines from Caphtor and the Arameans from Kir?
8 The eyes of the Lord GOD are upon the sinful kingdom,
and I will destroy it from the face of the earth
—except that I will not utterly destroy the house of Jacob,
says the LORD.

9 For lo, I will command,
and shake the house of Israel among all the nations
as one shakes with a sieve,
but no pebble shall fall to the ground.
10 All the sinners of my people shall die by the sword,
who say, "Evil shall not overtake or meet us."

11 On that day I will raise up
the booth of David that is fallen,
and repair its[b] breaches,
and raise up its[c] ruins,
and rebuild it as in the days of old;
12 in order that they may possess the remnant of Edom
and all the nations who are called by my name,
says the LORD who does this.

13 The time is surely coming, says the LORD,
when the one who plows shall overtake the one who reaps,
and the treader of grapes the one who sows the seed;
the mountains shall drip sweet wine,
and all the hills shall flow with it.
14 I will restore the fortunes of my people Israel,
and they shall rebuild the ruined cities and inhabit them;

[a] Or *Nubians*; Heb *Cushites* [b] Gk: Heb *their* [c] Gk: Heb *his*

Amos 9:7

To be the "chosen people" is, from the time of the Sinai covenant, a matter of *responsibility*—to serve God and, in Isaiah's words, to be a light to the nations. But the human tendency is to see this as a matter of *privilege*. And when this calling is seen as privileged, the next easy step is to become chauvinistic, to look down on other peoples and cultures and to regard them as less than equals. Prophets such as Amos challenged this thinking. In Amos 1–2 this northern prophet speaks judgments against six nearby kingdoms and against Israel and Judah as well. His charges largely concern inhumanity and barbarousness, including cruelty, slave trading, dishonoring the dead, and idolatry. For Amos, who speaks for God, there is no difference between the chosen people and other nations. His climactic conclusion at 9:7, "Are you not like the Ethiopians to me?" demonstrates our common humanity from the divine perspective.

The sheer breadth of Amos's view of God's doings must have been shocking at the time. He denies the concept of privileged people and calls all peoples to responsible living, especially across cultural and national borders.

— DB

they shall plant vineyards and drink their
wine,
and they shall make gardens and eat their
fruit.

15 I will plant them upon their land,
and they shall never again be plucked up
out of the land that I have given them,
says the Lord your God.

Obadiah

The name Obadiah means "servant of YHWH." Historically, the background to the book of Obadiah is the second forced migration, or exile, from Judah in 587 BCE. During this time, Nebuzaradan, the commander in charge of Nebuchadnezzar's Babylonian army, attacked, seized, and burned the palace, the temple, and all other major edifices in Jerusalem. Judah had been annexed ten years earlier, in 597, when Jehoiachin relinquished his throne and was taken to Babylon along with a first wave of Judean royal officials, elites, priests, and other noble and skilled workers for Babylonian economic gain. This second displacement of Judeans to Babylon was a further devastating blow to a vassal nation that was already broken. To add to this painful fracture, the Edomites—a geographical neighbor and related by blood as descendents of Esau—joined in on the pillage (v. 6) and slaughter (v. 10) and cut off the men, women, and children fleeing for their lives by handing them over to the Babylonians (v. 14). Obadiah, the shortest book in the Old Testament, speaks volumes about betrayal and the desire for revenge against a neighbor, one's own brother.

A neighbor's or relative's ill action becomes a source for a curse in Psalm 137:7-9. The motif of malediction against the Edomites has a unique role in the Hebrew Bible (Isa 34:5; Jer 49:7; Lam 4:21; Ezek 25:12; Joel 3:19; Amos 1:6; Mal 1:4). The atrocious action of one's enemy is understood; however, being trapped, deceived, and plundered by a neighbor or relative is a very different situation. The fact that one neighbor has turned away from another neighbor, relative has turned against relative, is seen as something that requires more than the standard reprimand. Throughout the twenty-one verses of Obadiah, issues of betrayal and desire for vengeance cut across the text.

We know that families and religious communities *should* be among the last places that exhibit this betrayal-vengeance pattern. But ironically, where neighbors and sisters and brothers gather, we witness these traits. I am a second-generation Korean American and a third-generation Christian. My maternal grandmother was one of the first women to be educated by missionaries from the United States. For her generation, education was generally only for men and boys. She once noted that she was both grateful and embarrassed to be literate. She grew up in what we now call North Korea. After hearing and embracing the gospel, she was baptized, trained, and became an itinerant preacher. She went from village to village sharing the gospel. But for her in-laws and others in her immediate community, she was betraying the traditional religions of ancient Korea. She was ostracized by her own family. When her husband died, she was seen as the source of his death. She was left with nothing except her two young children. Her escape to South Korea is a modern-day tale like that of Harriet Tubman. She and her children escaped by hiding by day and traveling on foot at night.

North Koreans and South Koreans are brothers and sisters. However, betrayal and the persistent desire for revenge, or the threat of judgment and war, is constantly at bay. Both North and South Koreans see themselves as the victim and the other as aggressor—like Edom. With warriors (v. 9) on each side, and the North ready to pillage, "All your allies have deceived you, they have driven you to the border; your confederates have prevailed against you; those who ate your bread have set a trap for you—there is no understanding of it" (v. 7). Those *seem* not the ancient words of the sixth century BCE but words that describe some conflicts and hatreds of the twentieth and twenty-first centuries.

There is an important lesson to be learned, however. If one seeks judgment upon a brother or sister, be prepared to have it also fall upon oneself. In the oracles against the nations and Edom, Judah is also included (v. 18). In the end, however, those in forced migrations will be restored. "Those who have been saved shall go up to Mount Zion" to be one unified kingdom under the LORD.

— John J. Ahn

1 The vision of Obadiah.

Thus says the Lord GOD concerning Edom:
We have heard a report from the LORD,
and a messenger has been sent among the nations:
"Rise up! Let us rise against it for battle!"
2 I will surely make you least among the nations;
you shall be utterly despised.
3 Your proud heart has deceived you,
you that live in the clefts of the rock,[a]
whose dwelling is in the heights.
You say in your heart,
"Who will bring me down to the ground?"
4 Though you soar aloft like the eagle,
though your nest is set among the stars,
from there I will bring you down,
says the LORD.

5 If thieves came to you,
if plunderers by night
—how you have been destroyed!—
would they not steal only what they wanted?
If grape-gatherers came to you,
would they not leave gleanings?
6 How Esau has been pillaged,
his treasures searched out!
7 All your allies have deceived you,
they have driven you to the border;
your confederates have prevailed against you;
those who ate[b] your bread have set a trap for you—
there is no understanding of it.
8 On that day, says the LORD,
I will destroy the wise out of Edom,
and understanding out of Mount Esau.
9 Your warriors shall be shattered, O Teman,
so that everyone from Mount Esau will be cut off.
10 For the slaughter and violence done to your brother Jacob,
shame shall cover you,

[a] Or *clefts of Sela* [b] Cn: Heb lacks *those who ate*

and you shall be cut off forever.
11 On the day that you stood aside,
on the day that strangers carried off his wealth,
and foreigners entered his gates
and cast lots for Jerusalem,
you too were like one of them.
12 But you should not have gloated[a] over[b] your brother
on the day of his misfortune;
you should not have rejoiced over the people of Judah
on the day of their ruin;
you should not have boasted
on the day of distress.
13 You should not have entered the gate of my people
on the day of their calamity;
you should not have joined in the gloating over Judah's[c] disaster
on the day of his calamity;
you should not have looted his goods
on the day of his calamity.
14 You should not have stood at the crossings
to cut off his fugitives;
you should not have handed over his survivors
on the day of distress.

15 For the day of the LORD is near against all the nations.
As you have done, it shall be done to you;
your deeds shall return on your own head.
16 For as you have drunk on my holy mountain,
all the nations around you shall drink;
they shall drink and gulp down,[d]
and shall be as though they had never been.
17 But on Mount Zion there shall be those that escape,
and it shall be holy;
and the house of Jacob shall take possession of those who dispossessed them.
18 The house of Jacob shall be a fire,
the house of Joseph a flame,
and the house of Esau stubble;
they shall burn them and consume them,
and there shall be no survivor of the house of Esau;
for the LORD has spoken.
19 Those of the Negeb shall possess Mount Esau,
and those of the Shephelah the land of the Philistines;
they shall possess the land of Ephraim and the land of Samaria,
and Benjamin shall possess Gilead.
20 The exiles of the Israelites who are in Halah[e]
shall possess[f] Phoenicia as far as Zarephath;
and the exiles of Jerusalem who are in Sepharad
shall possess the towns of the Negeb.
21 Those who have been saved[g] shall go up to Mount Zion
to rule Mount Esau;
and the kingdom shall be the LORD's.

Obadiah 11-14

Verses 11-14 of the brief prophecy of Obadiah are powerfully evocative of a firsthand account of tragedy. Ten times in four verses, Edom is castigated for their role in the fall of Judah and Jerusalem. Tiny Edom does not compare in military might to the juggernaut Babylon, yet they are equally culpable (v. 11). Edom is guilty for celebrating the demise of Jerusalem (v. 12), participating in looting the city (v. 13), and preventing Judean fugitives from escaping the carnage (v. 14). Verse 14 also evokes memories of the immediate aftermath of Hurricane Katrina, when those fleeing from the carnage of the storm were turned back from safety at gunpoint: "You should not have stood at the crossings to cut off [the] fugitives."

— *WG*

[a] Heb *But do not gloat* (and similarly through verse 14) [b] Heb *on the day of* [c] Heb *his* [d] Meaning of Heb uncertain
[e] Cn: Heb *in this army* [f] Cn: Meaning of Heb uncertain [g] Or *Saviors*

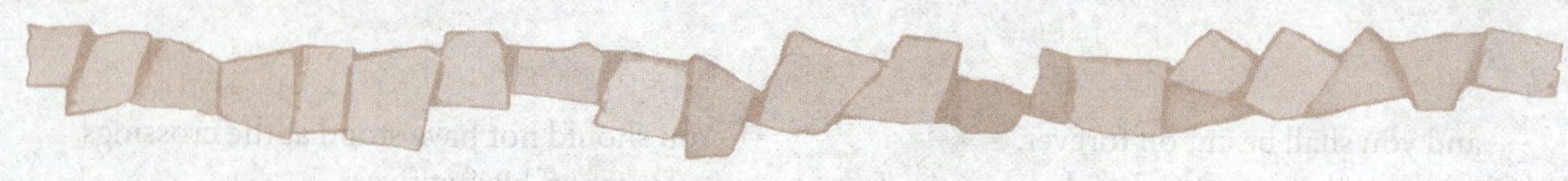

Jonah

The book of Jonah is different from other prophetic books in the Old Testament. It is not a collection of prophetic oracles but a short story about an eighth-century prophet of the same name. It includes only one brief message proclaimed by Jonah.

The main character of the book is identified with the prophet Jonah, the son of Amittai (2 Kgs 14:25), who prophesied during the reign of Jeroboam II, king of Israel (786–746 BCE), that the borders of the Northern Kingdom would be expanded. The prophet Jonah was born in Gath-hepher, a village that belonged to the tribe of Zebulun (Josh 19:10, 13). His name means "Dove."

The traditional view assigns the composition of the book to Jonah himself, writing in the eighth century BCE. However, internal evidence suggests that the book was written not by Jonah but by an anonymous writer who lived in the later postexilic community, probably in the fifth century BCE. There are several reasons to date the book in the late postexilic period. Its language contains Aramaic expressions current in the Persian period. The implication that Nineveh was the capital of the Assyrian empire places it no earlier than late in the eighth century; and the title "king of Nineveh" (3:6) is never used of the king of Assyria in biblical literature outside Jonah.

There is some debate about the literary characteristics of the book. Does it refer to a historical event, or is it a prophetic novel, a didactic story, an allegory, or a parable? The content of the book is loosely related to historical events, and the book includes a didactic story that seems designed to teach about God's concern for people who lived outside the covenant community.

The story begins as Jonah receives a divine commission to go to Nineveh and announce the coming of God's judgment against the city. But instead of going to Nineveh, Jonah flees to Tarshish, a city probably located in southern Spain, thus representing about the farthest place Jonah could flee from the Lord. En route, a storm threatens to destroy Jonah and the sailors who, to save their lives, threw Jonah into the sea. The Lord prepares a great fish to rescue Jonah. After Jonah is saved, the Lord commissions him a second time to go to Nineveh. Jonah goes, warns the citizens that the city will be destroyed in forty days, and the Ninevites repent and the judgment is averted. Jonah complains to God and sulks because the city's conversion moved God to suspend the judgment. God rebukes him and declares his concern for people and animals.

The story in Jonah may reflect a conflict of cultural values in postexilic Israel. The book's message is a criticism of the narrow nationalism of the people returning from exile. Some Jews believed that divine grace included the acceptance of Gentiles, while others, in the interest of self-preservation, held strong nationalistic views that excluded Gentiles from their community.

Some scholars believe Jonah was written as a protest against this exclusivist policy. Like Jonah, some Jews were not willing to share their faith with Gentiles, preferring that they be destroyed rather than saved. The author of the book wanted to show that the God of Israel is "a gracious God and merciful, slow to anger, and abounding in steadfast love, and ready to relent from punishing" (Jonah 4:2). The message of the book teaches about the Lord's desire to redeem people, forgive their sins, and honor their conversion. In presenting Jonah as a rebellious prophet, the writer was calling Israel back to its mission in the world.

Like Israel, the church has a mission to the world. God's desire to redeem people is manifested in the lives of thousands of immigrants who experience the grace of God in the fellowship of other believers. As a pastor of a church that includes people from South and Central America, I can testify that the gospel transcends culture and nationality. The message of hope that Jonah failed to proclaim is being proclaimed in multicultural churches all over our nation.

The book may be outlined as follows:

Jonah's flight from God, 1:1-17
Jonah's song of thanksgiving, 2:1-10
Jonah's mission to Nineveh, 3:1-10
Jonah's struggle with God, 4:1-11

— Claude F. Mariottini

1 Now the word of the LORD came to Jonah
son of Amittai, saying, 2"Go at once to Nineveh, that great city, and cry out against it; for
their wickedness has come up before me." 3But
Jonah set out to flee to Tarshish from the presence of the LORD. He went down to Joppa and
found a ship going to Tarshish; so he paid his fare
and went on board, to go with them to Tarshish,
away from the presence of the LORD.
4 But the LORD hurled a great wind upon
the sea, and such a mighty storm came upon the
sea that the ship threatened to break up. 5Then
the mariners were afraid, and each cried to his
god. They threw the cargo that was in the ship
into the sea, to lighten it for them. Jonah, meanwhile, had gone down into the hold of the ship
and had lain down, and was fast asleep. 6The captain came and said to him, "What are you doing
sound asleep? Get up, call on your god! Perhaps

Jonah 1:2

The reluctance of Jonah to preach to Nineveh is particularly striking in the current age when one realizes that Nineveh is in Iraq. Then again, one might imagine that Jonah would be excited to tell the enemies of his people that God was going to destroy them. Jonah knows (4:2) that God is "a gracious God and merciful, slow to anger, and abounding in steadfast love, and ready to relent from punishing." The reason that Jonah does not want to preach to the Ninevites is that he knows they might repent and God might forgive them. Jonah is afraid both of having egg on his face when Nineveh *is not* overthrown and of living in a world where his God forgives his enemies.

— WG

Jonah 1, 3–4

The irony in the story of Jonah is that it is not the Israelite prophet, but others who respond in faith to Jonah's God. While Jonah tries to get away from God's call and sleeps on board ship during the terrible storm, it is the sailors who pray to their gods and eventually offer sacrifice to Jonah's God whom they believe has stilled the storm. Not Jews, but Ninevites, their feared enemies, respond to Jonah's call to repentance. Much to Jonah's surprise and disappointment, God forgives the enemies of Jonah's people. Why does it surprise us to discover that God's mercy and love can and do include those who are different from us, or even those who may have done us harm?

— *ST*

the god will spare us a thought so that we do not
perish."
7 The sailors[a] said to one another, "Come, let
us cast lots, so that we may know on whose account this calamity has come upon us." So they
cast lots, and the lot fell on Jonah. 8Then they
said to him, "Tell us why this calamity has come
upon us. What is your occupation? Where do you
come from? What is your country? And of what
people are you?" 9"I am a Hebrew," he replied. "I
worship the LORD, the God of heaven, who made
the sea and the dry land." 10Then the men were
even more afraid, and said to him, "What is this
that you have done!" For the men knew that he
was fleeing from the presence of the LORD, because he had told them so.
11 Then they said to him, "What shall we do
to you, that the sea may quiet down for us?" For
the sea was growing more and more tempestu-
ous. 12He said to them, "Pick me up and throw
me into the sea; then the sea will quiet down for
you; for I know it is because of me that this great
storm has come upon you." 13Nevertheless the
men rowed hard to bring the ship back to land,
but they could not, for the sea grew more and
more stormy against them. 14Then they cried
out to the LORD, "Please, O LORD, we pray, do
not let us perish on account of this man's life. Do
not make us guilty of innocent blood; for you,
O LORD, have done as it pleased you." 15So they
picked Jonah up and threw him into the sea; and
the sea ceased from its raging. 16Then the men
feared the LORD even more, and they offered a
sacrifice to the LORD and made vows.
17[b] But the LORD provided a large fish to
swallow up Jonah; and Jonah was in the belly of
the fish three days and three nights.

2 Then Jonah prayed to the LORD his God
from the belly of the fish, 2saying,

"I called to the LORD out of my
distress,
and he answered me;
out of the belly of Sheol I cried,
and you heard my voice.
3 You cast me into the deep,
into the heart of the seas,
and the flood surrounded me;
all your waves and your billows
passed over me.
4 Then I said, 'I am driven away
from your sight;
how[c] shall I look again
upon your holy temple?'
5 The waters closed in over me;
the deep surrounded me;
weeds were wrapped around my head
6 at the roots of the mountains.
I went down to the land
whose bars closed upon me forever;
yet you brought up my life from the Pit,
O LORD my God.
7 As my life was ebbing away,
I remembered the LORD;
and my prayer came to you,
into your holy temple.
8 Those who worship vain idols
forsake their true loyalty.
9 But I with the voice of thanksgiving
will sacrifice to you;
what I have vowed I will pay.
Deliverance belongs to the LORD!"

[a] Heb *They* [b] Ch 2.1 in Heb [c] Theodotion: Heb *surely*

10 Then the LORD spoke to the fish, and it spewed
Jonah out upon the dry land.

3 The word of the LORD came to Jonah a second time, saying, 2 "Get up, go to Nineveh, that
great city, and proclaim to it the message that I tell
you." 3 So Jonah set out and went to Nineveh, according to the word of the LORD. Now Nineveh
was an exceedingly large city, a three days' walk
across. 4 Jonah began to go into the city, going a
day's walk. And he cried out, "Forty days more, and
Nineveh shall be overthrown!" 5 And the people of
Nineveh believed God; they proclaimed a fast, and
everyone, great and small, put on sackcloth.

6 When the news reached the king of Nineveh, he rose from his throne, removed his robe,
covered himself with sackcloth, and sat in ashes.
7 Then he had a proclamation made in Nineveh:
"By the decree of the king and his nobles: No human being or animal, no herd or flock, shall taste
anything. They shall not feed, nor shall they drink
water. 8 Human beings and animals shall be covered with sackcloth, and they shall cry mightily to
God. All shall turn from their evil ways and from
the violence that is in their hands. 9 Who knows?
God may relent and change his mind; he may turn
from his fierce anger, so that we do not perish."

10 When God saw what they did, how they
turned from their evil ways, God changed his
mind about the calamity that he had said he
would bring upon them; and he did not do it.

4 But this was very displeasing to Jonah, and
he became angry. 2 He prayed to the LORD
and said, "O LORD! Is not this what I said while I
was still in my own country? That is why I fled to
Tarshish at the beginning; for I knew that you are
a gracious God and merciful, slow to anger, and
abounding in steadfast love, and ready to relent
from punishing. 3 And now, O LORD, please take
my life from me, for it is better for me to die than
to live." 4 And the LORD said, "Is it right for you to
be angry?" 5 Then Jonah went out of the city and
sat down east of the city, and made a booth for
himself there. He sat under it in the shade, waiting to see what would become of the city.

6 The LORD God appointed a bush,[a] and
made it come up over Jonah, to give shade over
his head, to save him from his discomfort; so Jonah was very happy about the bush. 7 But when
dawn came up the next day, God appointed a
worm that attacked the bush, so that it withered.
8 When the sun rose, God prepared a sultry east
wind, and the sun beat down on the head of Jonah
so that he was faint and asked that he might die.
He said, "It is better for me to die than to live."

9 But God said to Jonah, "Is it right for you
to be angry about the bush?" And he said, "Yes,
angry enough to die." 10 Then the LORD said,
"You are concerned about the bush, for which
you did not labor and which you did not grow; it
came into being in a night and perished in a night.
11 And should I not be concerned about Nineveh,
that great city, in which there are more than a
hundred and twenty thousand persons who do
not know their right hand from their left, and also
many animals?"

[a] Heb *qiqayon*, possibly *the castor bean plant*

Micah

THE BOOK OF MICAH IS NORMALLY DIVIDED into three sections, chapters 1–3, 4–5, and 6–7, with only the first section definitively attributed to the sayings of the historical Micah. The first section can be dated at the end of the eighth century BCE, either anticipating or reflecting on the devastations of Assyrian campaigns in Samaria in 722 or attacks in Judah in 701 under Sennacherib. An apparent reference to Babylon and the exile (4:10) suggests that the second and third sections must be additions to the older chapters 1–3, made after 587 BCE. These additions may have been written or compiled by those who considered themselves students or followers of the prophet Micah, since the famous "swords into plowshares" passage of 4:1-5 has clear associations with Micah's rural imagery in chapters 1–3.

We know little about the prophet Micah other than the notable reference to his words in the later book of Jeremiah, quoted to defend Jeremiah from charges of treason, suggesting that Micah was well known (Jer 26:16-18).

Micah's village of Moresheth is located southwest of Jerusalem. It was among the smaller agricultural settlements that were under threat from invading armies that would have a far more difficult time making a successful assault on the walled city of Jerusalem, where the elite lived or sought refuge. And Jerusalem depended on the villages for both supplies and soldiers. Thus, in Micah we hear echoes of rural versus urban and workers versus elites.

As a Quaker reader of biblical texts, I am particularly attentive to the use and abuse of religious arguments as a defense of violence and privilege. Micah is a significant example of a prophet who resisted warfare as a crude means of exploiting the rural agricultural workers and village economies that formed the vast majority of Hebrew society. A Quaker-informed abolitionist reading of the Bible allows one to imagine a modern Micah complaining about the constant drain of local resources that militarism always creates, whether in developed or developing societies.

The angry judgments of Micah relate directly to the social and economic context of both Israelite and Judean policies as well as the pressures of Assyrian domination in the entire region. Micah, like many other prophets, angrily denounces the abuses suffered by the population of his agriculturally-based village at the hands of elite city dwellers, including rulers, landowners, military leaders, and priests.

Micah's angry judgments are more understandable if we note that Israel's land-owning class was at the time consolidating its hold over both land and workers, with the cooperation of the nation's central institutions of religion and monarchy. This development was expressed in more detail by Micah's contemporary, Isaiah (see, for example, Isaiah 5).

Micah expresses the farmers' profound anger over the injustices they are suffering:

The punishment of the two capital cities, Jerusalem and Samaria, is that their lands would be returned to arable, useful land—"a place for planting vineyards" (1:6) and "plowed as a field" (3:12).

Warfare is resented for diverting usable farmers' tools into weapons; correspondingly, peace is represented as the people being free to pursue their farming, with the accompanying hope that nations would meet to settle their differences as rural households must do (4:3-4).

The abuses by the elite who "covet fields, and seize them; houses, and take them away" (2:2), and "eat the flesh of my people" (3:1-3) should be condemned.

True piety is described as living a just life rather than making many sacrifices of one's farm produce, which chiefly benefits the urban priests and other elites (6:6-8).

Next, Micah turns his attention to the larger empires that have designs on the smaller nations and communities. The Babylonian conquest of Jerusalem early in the sixth century BCE is alluded to in 4:10. Micah expresses the hope of God's judgment on the war machines of all the nations in 5:7-15, with the assurance that the Hebrew people will finally be left alone.

The book returns to judgment in the final section, chapters 6–7, with a warning not to follow "the statutes of Omri and all the works of the house of Ahab" (6:16)—two rulers whose legacy in the Northern Kingdom (1 Kings 17–19) resulted in the disenfranchisement of rural agricultural workers like Naboth. In the end, the Israelite peoples are condemned for their economic corruption (7:2-3), but the bigger nations are warned not to take advantage of this; they too will come to repent of their ravenous violence on the smaller nations: "The nations shall see and be ashamed of all their might" (7:16).

A careful reading of Micah raises questions about internal solidarity in the face of outside aggression—and about the fact that such aggression is often used to deflect attention from the seriousness of internal injustice. Too often internal corruption is tolerated in the name of loyalty to cultural or national liberation. But Micah condemns the corrupt exploitation of the peasant farmers (a majority of the population) by the Israelite elite who tax and conscript the workers to increase their own economic advantages *and* the threats posed by the larger imperial powers, Assyria and Babylon.

The book may be outlined as follows:

1:1-5	Introduction—Samaria and Judah on trial
1:6-7	Punishment for false ideology
1:8-16	Lamentation at the fate of Judah and Samaria
2:1-2	The injustice of the elite against the poor
2:3-5	The promise of punishment for oppression
2:6	Protest from the judged: "Don't talk like that!"
2:7-13	Affirmation of the judgment from Micah
3:1-12	Systematic accusations against leaders (3:1-4, against heads of households; 3:5-8, against false prophets; 3:9-12, against rulers and priests)

4:1-5 Judgment on militarism and its oppression of the poor
4:6-13 Reversal of fortune: the poor and '"lame" will benefit

5:1-15 Promise of deliverance from the foreign oppressor

6:1-5 God resumes the trial
6:6-8 Justice is better than sacrifice
6:7-16 Words against Judean policies of oppression

7:1-7 Social instability after God's judgment
7:8-20 Hope for future restoration

— Daniel L. Smith-Christopher

1 The word of the LORD that came to Micah
of Moresheth in the days of Kings Jotham,
Ahaz, and Hezekiah of Judah, which he saw concerning Samaria and Jerusalem.

2 Hear, you peoples, all of you;
listen, O earth, and all that is in it;
and let the Lord GOD be a witness against you,
the Lord from his holy temple.
3 For lo, the LORD is coming out of his place,
and will come down and tread upon the high places of the earth.
4 Then the mountains will melt under him
and the valleys will burst open,
like wax near the fire,
like waters poured down a steep place.
5 All this is for the transgression of Jacob
and for the sins of the house of Israel.
What is the transgression of Jacob?
Is it not Samaria?
And what is the high place[a] of Judah?
Is it not Jerusalem?
6 Therefore I will make Samaria a heap in the open country,
a place for planting vineyards.
I will pour down her stones into the valley,
and uncover her foundations.
7 All her images shall be beaten to pieces,
all her wages shall be burned with fire,
and all her idols I will lay waste;
for as the wages of a prostitute she gathered them,
and as the wages of a prostitute they shall again be used.

8 For this I will lament and wail;
I will go barefoot and naked;
I will make lamentation like the jackals,
and mourning like the ostriches.
9 For her wound[b] is incurable.
It has come to Judah;
it has reached to the gate of my people,
to Jerusalem.

[a] Heb *what are the high places* [b] Gk Syr Vg: Heb *wounds*

10 Tell it not in Gath,
weep not at all;
in Beth-leaphrah
roll yourselves in the dust.
11 Pass on your way,
inhabitants of Shaphir,
in nakedness and shame;
the inhabitants of Zaanan
do not come forth;
Beth-ezel is wailing
and shall remove its support from you.
12 For the inhabitants of Maroth
wait anxiously for good,
yet disaster has come down from the LORD
to the gate of Jerusalem.
13 Harness the steeds to the chariots,
inhabitants of Lachish;
it was the beginning of sin
to daughter Zion,
for in you were found
the transgressions of Israel.
14 Therefore you shall give parting gifts
to Moresheth-gath;
the houses of Achzib shall be a deception
to the kings of Israel.
15 I will again bring a conqueror upon you,
inhabitants of Mareshah;
the glory of Israel
shall come to Adullam.
16 Make yourselves bald and cut off your hair
for your pampered children;
make yourselves as bald as the eagle,
for they have gone from you into exile.

2 Alas for those who devise wickedness
and evil deeds[a] on their beds!
When the morning dawns, they perform it,
because it is in their power.
2 They covet fields, and seize them;
houses, and take them away;
they oppress householder and house,
people and their inheritance.
3 Therefore thus says the LORD:
Now, I am devising against this family an
evil

Micah 2:1-3

The middle of the night. The little lights
of the dispossessed shine on the shores.
Their tearful reflections.
Far, far away laugh the lights of Rio de Janiero
and the lights of Brasilia.

How shall they possess the earth if the earth is
owned
by landowners?

Unproductive, prized only for land
speculation and fat loans from the Bank of Brazil.
There He is always sold for Thirty Dollars
on the River of the Dead.
The price of a peon. In spite of
2,000 years of inflation.[61]

— ***Ernesto Cardenal***

from which you cannot remove your
necks;
and you shall not walk haughtily,
for it will be an evil time.
4 On that day they shall take up a taunt song
against you,
and wail with bitter lamentation,
and say, "We are utterly ruined;
the LORD[b] alters the inheritance of my
people;
how he removes it from me!
Among our captors[c] he parcels out our
fields."
5 Therefore you will have no one to cast the
line by lot
in the assembly of the LORD.

6 "Do not preach"—thus they preach—
"one should not preach of such things;
disgrace will not overtake us."
7 Should this be said, O house of Jacob?
Is the LORD's patience exhausted?
Are these his doings?
Do not my words do good

[a] Cn: Heb *work evil* [b] Heb *he* [c] Cn: Heb *the rebellious*

to one who walks uprightly?
8 But you rise up against my people[a] as an
enemy;
you strip the robe from the peaceful,[b]
from those who pass by trustingly
with no thought of war.
9 The women of my people you drive out
from their pleasant houses;
from their young children you take away
my glory forever.
10 Arise and go;
for this is no place to rest,
because of uncleanness that destroys
with a grievous destruction.[c]
11 If someone were to go about uttering empty
falsehoods,
saying, "I will preach to you of wine and
strong drink,"
such a one would be the preacher for this
people!

12 I will surely gather all of you, O Jacob,
I will gather the survivors of Israel;
I will set them together
like sheep in a fold,
like a flock in its pasture;
it will resound with people.
13 The one who breaks out will go up before
them;
they will break through and pass the gate,
going out by it.
Their king will pass on before them,
the LORD at their head.

3 And I said:
Listen, you heads of Jacob
and rulers of the house of Israel!
Should you not know justice?—
2 you who hate the good and love the evil,
who tear the skin off my people,[d]
and the flesh off their bones;
3 who eat the flesh of my people,
flay their skin off them,
break their bones in pieces,
and chop them up like meat[e] in a kettle,
like flesh in a caldron.

4 Then they will cry to the LORD,
but he will not answer them;
he will hide his face from them at that time,
because they have acted wickedly.

5 Thus says the LORD concerning the prophets
who lead my people astray,
who cry "Peace"
when they have something to eat,
but declare war against those
who put nothing into their mouths.
6 Therefore it shall be night to you, without
vision,
and darkness to you, without revelation.
The sun shall go down upon the prophets,
and the day shall be black over them;
7 the seers shall be disgraced,
and the diviners put to shame;
they shall all cover their lips,
for there is no answer from God.
8 But as for me, I am filled with power,
with the spirit of the LORD,
and with justice and might,
to declare to Jacob his transgression
and to Israel his sin.

9 Hear this, you rulers of the house of Jacob
and chiefs of the house of Israel,
who abhor justice
and pervert all equity,
10 who build Zion with blood
and Jerusalem with wrong!
11 Its rulers give judgment for a bribe,
its priests teach for a price,
its prophets give oracles for money;
yet they lean upon the LORD and say,
"Surely the LORD is with us!
No harm shall come upon us."
12 Therefore because of you
Zion shall be plowed as a field;
Jerusalem shall become a heap of ruins,

[a] Cn: Heb *But yesterday my people rose* [b] Cn: Heb *from before a garment* [c] Meaning of Heb uncertain
[d] Heb *from them* [e] Gk: Heb *as*

and the mountain of the house a wooded
height.

4 In days to come
the mountain of the LORD's house
shall be established as the highest of the
mountains,
and shall be raised up above the hills.
Peoples shall stream to it,
2 and many nations shall come and say:
"Come, let us go up to the mountain of the
LORD,
to the house of the God of Jacob;
that he may teach us his ways
and that we may walk in his paths."
For out of Zion shall go forth instruction,
and the word of the LORD from Jerusalem.
3 He shall judge between many peoples,
and shall arbitrate between strong nations
far away;
they shall beat their swords into plowshares,
and their spears into pruning hooks;
nation shall not lift up sword against nation,
neither shall they learn war any more;
4 but they shall all sit under their own vines
and under their own fig trees,
and no one shall make them afraid;
for the mouth of the LORD of hosts has
spoken.

5 For all the peoples walk,
each in the name of its god,
but we will walk in the name of the LORD our
God
forever and ever.

6 In that day, says the LORD,
I will assemble the lame
and gather those who have been driven
away,
and those whom I have afflicted.
7 The lame I will make the remnant,
and those who were cast off, a strong
nation;
and the LORD will reign over them in Mount
Zion
now and forevermore.

8 And you, O tower of the flock,
hill of daughter Zion,
to you it shall come,
the former dominion shall come,
the sovereignty of daughter Jerusalem.

9 Now why do you cry aloud?
Is there no king in you?
Has your counselor perished,
that pangs have seized you like a woman
in labor?
10 Writhe and groan,[a] O daughter Zion,
like a woman in labor;
for now you shall go forth from the city
and camp in the open country;
you shall go to Babylon.
There you shall be rescued,
there the LORD will redeem you
from the hands of your enemies.

11 Now many nations
are assembled against you,
saying, "Let her be profaned,
and let our eyes gaze upon Zion."
12 But they do not know
the thoughts of the LORD;
they do not understand his plan,
that he has gathered them as sheaves to the
threshing floor.
13 Arise and thresh,
O daughter Zion,
for I will make your horn iron
and your hoofs bronze;
you shall beat in pieces many peoples,
and shall[b] devote their gain to the LORD,
their wealth to the Lord of the whole
earth.

5 [c] Now you are walled around with a wall;[d]
siege is laid against us;

[a] Meaning of Heb uncertain [b] Gk Syr Tg: Heb *and I will* [c] Ch 4.14 in Heb
[d] Cn Compare Gk: Meaning of Heb uncertain

with a rod they strike the ruler of Israel
upon the cheek.

2[a] But you, O Bethlehem of Ephrathah,
who are one of the little clans of Judah,
from you shall come forth for me
one who is to rule in Israel,
whose origin is from of old,
from ancient days.
3 Therefore he shall give them up until the time
when she who is in labor has brought
forth;
then the rest of his kindred shall return
to the people of Israel.
4 And he shall stand and feed his flock in the
strength of the LORD,
in the majesty of the name of the LORD
his God.
And they shall live secure, for now he shall
be great
to the ends of the earth;
5 and he shall be the one of peace.

If the Assyrians come into our land
and tread upon our soil,[b]
we will raise against them seven shepherds
and eight installed as rulers.
6 They shall rule the land of Assyria with the
sword,
and the land of Nimrod with the drawn
sword;[c]
they[d] shall rescue us from the Assyrians
if they come into our land
or tread within our border.

7 Then the remnant of Jacob,
surrounded by many peoples,
shall be like dew from the LORD,
like showers on the grass,
which do not depend upon people
or wait for any mortal.
8 And among the nations the remnant of Jacob,
surrounded by many peoples,
shall be like a lion among the animals of the
forest,
like a young lion among the flocks of
sheep,
which, when it goes through, treads down
and tears in pieces, with no one to deliver.
9 Your hand shall be lifted up over your
adversaries,
and all your enemies shall be cut off.

10 In that day, says the LORD,
I will cut off your horses from among you
and will destroy your chariots;
11 and I will cut off the cities of your land
and throw down all your strongholds;
12 and I will cut off sorceries from your hand,
and you shall have no more soothsayers;
13 and I will cut off your images
and your pillars from among you,
and you shall bow down no more
to the work of your hands;
14 and I will uproot your sacred poles[e] from
among you
and destroy your towns.
15 And in anger and wrath I will execute
vengeance
on the nations that did not obey.

6 Hear what the LORD says:
Rise, plead your case before the
mountains,
and let the hills hear your voice.
2 Hear, you mountains, the controversy of the
LORD,
and you enduring foundations of the
earth;
for the LORD has a controversy with his
people,
and he will contend with Israel.

3 "O my people, what have I done to you?
In what have I wearied you? Answer me!
4 For I brought you up from the land of Egypt,
and redeemed you from the house of
slavery;
and I sent before you Moses,
Aaron, and Miriam.

[a] Ch 5.1 in Heb [b] Gk: Heb *in our palaces* [c] Cn: Heb *in its entrances* [d] Heb *he* [e] Heb *Asherim*

5 O my people, remember now what King
Balak of Moab devised,
what Balaam son of Beor answered him,
and what happened from Shittim to Gilgal,
that you may know the saving acts of the
LORD."

6 "With what shall I come before the LORD,
and bow myself before God on high?
Shall I come before him with burnt offerings,
with calves a year old?
7 Will the LORD be pleased with thousands of
rams,
with ten thousands of rivers of oil?
Shall I give my firstborn for my transgression,
the fruit of my body for the sin of my
soul?"
8 He has told you, O mortal, what is good;
and what does the LORD require of you
but to do justice, and to love kindness,
and to walk humbly with your God?

9 The voice of the LORD cries to the city
(it is sound wisdom to fear your name):
Hear, O tribe and assembly of the city![a]
10 Can I forget[b] the treasures of wickedness
in the house of the wicked,
and the scant measure that is accursed?
11 Can I tolerate wicked scales
and a bag of dishonest weights?
12 Your[c] wealthy are full of violence;
your[d] inhabitants speak lies,
with tongues of deceit in their mouths.
13 Therefore I have begun[e] to strike you down,
making you desolate because of your sins.
14 You shall eat, but not be satisfied,
and there shall be a gnawing hunger within
you;
you shall put away, but not save,
and what you save, I will hand over to the
sword.
15 You shall sow, but not reap;
you shall tread olives, but not anoint
yourselves with oil;

Micah 6:9-15

"The voice of the LORD cries to the city.... Can I tolerate wicked scales and a bag of dishonest weights? Your wealthy are full of violence; your inhabitants speak lies." This is so true today of the exploiters in the big metropolises. We have developed economically, but are barbaric in our relationships with each other. Hence there is deep unrest in our times. The oppressed are unhappy because of their misery. The oppressing one-third of humanity are dehumanized in their ill-gotten affluence.

[The LORD] shows what is the way of true righteousness: "He has told you, O mortal, what is good; and what does the LORD require of you but to do justice, and to love kindness, and to walk humbly with your God?"[62]

— ***Tissa Balasuriya***

you shall tread grapes, but not drink wine.
16 For you have kept the statutes of Omri[f]
and all the works of the house of Ahab,
and you have followed their counsels.
Therefore I will make you a desolation,
and your[g] inhabitants an object of
hissing;
so you shall bear the scorn of my people.

7 Woe is me! For I have become like one
who,
after the summer fruit has been gathered,
after the vintage has been gleaned,
finds no cluster to eat;
there is no first-ripe fig for which I
hunger.
2 The faithful have disappeared from the land,
and there is no one left who is upright;
they all lie in wait for blood,
and they hunt each other with nets.
3 Their hands are skilled to do evil;
the official and the judge ask for a bribe,
and the powerful dictate what they desire;

[a] Cn Compare Gk: Heb *tribe, and who has appointed it yet?* [b] Cn: Meaning of Heb uncertain [c] Heb *Whose* [d] Heb *whose* [e] Gk Syr Vg: Heb *have made sick* [f] Gk Syr Vg Tg: Heb *the statutes of Omri are kept* [g] Heb *its*

thus they pervert justice.[a]
4 The best of them is like a brier,
the most upright of them a thorn hedge.
The day of their[b] sentinels, of their[b]
punishment, has come;
now their confusion is at hand.
5 Put no trust in a friend,
have no confidence in a loved one;
guard the doors of your mouth
from her who lies in your embrace;
6 for the son treats the father with contempt,
the daughter rises up against her mother,
the daughter-in-law against her
mother-in-law;
your enemies are members of your own
household.
7 But as for me, I will look to the LORD,
I will wait for the God of my salvation;
my God will hear me.

8 Do not rejoice over me, O my enemy;
when I fall, I shall rise;
when I sit in darkness,
the LORD will be a light to me.
9 I must bear the indignation of the LORD,
because I have sinned against him,
until he takes my side
and executes judgment for me.
He will bring me out to the light;
I shall see his vindication.
10 Then my enemy will see,
and shame will cover her who said to me,
"Where is the LORD your God?"
My eyes will see her downfall;[c]
now she will be trodden down
like the mire of the streets.

11 A day for the building of your walls!
In that day the boundary shall be far
extended.
12 In that day they will come to you
from Assyria to[d] Egypt,
and from Egypt to the River,
from sea to sea and from mountain to
mountain.
13 But the earth will be desolate
because of its inhabitants,
for the fruit of their doings.

14 Shepherd your people with your staff,
the flock that belongs to you,
which lives alone in a forest
in the midst of a garden land;
let them feed in Bashan and Gilead
as in the days of old.
15 As in the days when you came out of the land
of Egypt,
show us[e] marvelous things.
16 The nations shall see and be ashamed
of all their might;
they shall lay their hands on their mouths;
their ears shall be deaf;
17 they shall lick dust like a snake,
like the crawling things of the earth;
they shall come trembling out of their
fortresses;
they shall turn in dread to the LORD our
God,
and they shall stand in fear of you.

18 Who is a God like you, pardoning iniquity
and passing over the transgression
of the remnant of your[f] possession?
He does not retain his anger forever,
because he delights in showing
clemency.
19 He will again have compassion upon us;
he will tread our iniquities under foot.
You will cast all our[g] sins
into the depths of the sea.
20 You will show faithfulness to Jacob
and unswerving loyalty to Abraham,
as you have sworn to our ancestors
from the days of old.

[a] Cn: Heb *they weave it* [b] Heb *your* [c] Heb lacks *downfall* [d] One Ms: MT *Assyria and cities of* [e] Cn: Heb *I will show him* [f] Heb *his* [g] Gk Syr Vg Tg: Heb *their*

Nahum

The book of Nahum has only forty-seven verses and a single theme: the punishment of the Assyrian Empire. It offers no internal critique of the behavior of either the Israelites or the Judeans, and its apparent nationalist sentiment creates unease in many contemporary readers and commentators. As a Quaker reader of the Bible, however, I am particularly interested in understanding the context of violent rhetoric, especially when expressed by those who have suffered military threat or domination. Can one be *informed* by the rhetoric of anger, acknowledging the useful attention it can bring to real injustices, and yet refuse to *endorse* the hastily advocated violence that often accompanies such rhetoric? Paying attention to contemporary debates among minority cultures or small nation-states, especially with regard to the role of nationalism or internationalism as a positive or negative step in self-determination, allows us to read Nahum with greater appreciation, especially when it is brought into dialogue with Jonah or others among the Twelve Prophets. If, on the one hand, Jonah holds out the possibilities of positive change among enemies, Nahum reflects vengeful anger on the other.

The book is often divided into smaller sections that separate oracles (for example 1:12-15 and 3:1-7) and taunt songs (3: 8-13 and again in 3:14-17). But some scholars are correct in pointing out two main sections that divide at 1:15 and 2:1. The first part focuses on the appearance and description of God as divine Judge and avenger, often drawing on Canaanite cosmic battle imagery, as in 1:3-4. The second part focuses on—and almost relishes—the destruction of Assyria, to be lamented by none (3:7). That this destruction has not yet happened suggests that the writings we call Nahum was completed before the final destruction of Nineveh in 612 BCE at the hands of the Medes, in alliance with the Babylonians, who then rose in power themselves.

We know next to nothing about Nahum himself because all attention is focused on Nineveh, the major city of the late Neo-Assyrian Empire. (That empire was radically and efficiently reorganized under Tiglath-Pileser III in 744–727, called Pul in 2 Kings 15.) But Israel suffered its most significant attacks under Shalmaneser V (726–722) or Sargan II (721–705), and Judah was brutally attacked by Sennacherib (704–681) when Jerusalem only escaped when Hezekiah sued for terms (even though the Bible also says that God defended Jerusalem, 2 Kgs 19:32-34).

Assyrian inscriptions are notorious for bravado and brutality, and while historians are certain of their exaggeration of that nation's accomplishments, including booty taken and enemy killed, the sheer cruelty of Assyrian imperial design is striking. Nahum cannot be understood apart from some familiarity with these writings and the social and economic suffering they represent for Assyria's opponents (see "bloodshed" and "booty," 3:1). Not without reason was Assyria famous for its militarism and economic exploitation. Nahum's rhetoric expresses horrified familiarity with many of the details of Assyrian hegemony, including the armaments of invading armies (2:3-5; 3:3); enslavement (2:7); the numbers of dead (3:3b); and stolen wealth (2:9; 3:16).

Nahum and Jonah represent an interesting dialogue between Nahum—with its unrelenting and indiscriminate judgment on all things Assyrian as evil—and Jonah's sense that there may be Assyrians worth saving after all and his implied criticism of Judean resistance to God's intentions for foreigners other than destruction.

The book may be outlined as follows:

1:1-8	Announcement of God's coming in judgment
1:9-11	Accusations against Nineveh
1:12-14	The coming punishments of Nineveh
1:15/2:1(Hebrew)–2:9	Announcement of attack on Nineveh
2:10-13	Nineveh compared to lion's prey
3:1-15	Like other oppressive empires, Nineveh will fall
3:16-19	Nobody will mourn Assyria's fall

A Postcolonial Reading of Nahum's Anger

Nahum's rhetoric can be appreciated on a number of levels. While it may be disturbing in its unrelenting and indiscriminate judgment of national opponents, modern readers must reckon with the reality of angry rhetoric and actions that can result directly from real social and political exploitation. Thus, one way to read Nahum's anger is not so much with a sense of offended propriety (often a luxury of the privileged and powerful) as much as a discerning and compassionate understanding of the kinds of social, economic, and political subordination that inevitably—and often appropriately—provoke this kind of furious response. Who are the *modern* Assyrian Empires whose policies have nurtured such theologies of angry hatred among subordinated and exploited peoples? Whether one takes modern offense at Nahum's angry celebration of Assyria's fall can depend entirely on one's point of view! Nahum's rhetoric can thus be helpfully compared to the angry rhetoric of movements such as the Black Panthers in the United States or the indigenous Maori (New Zealand/Aotearoa) *Hikoi* movements for social change and for justice long delayed.

— ***Daniel L. Smith-Christopher***

1 An oracle concerning Nineveh. The book of the vision of Nahum of Elkosh.

Nahum 1:1

The New Testament city Capernaum may well be named for the prophet Nahum. In Hebrew the name of the city is *Kephar Nachum*, or Town of Nachum. (The Greek has trouble with the Hebrew letter *het* and simply dropped it.) There is no other identifiable "Nahum" as prominent as the prophet who left us this small book after whom the town could be named.

— *WG*

2 A jealous and avenging God is the LORD,
the LORD is avenging and wrathful;
the LORD takes vengeance on his adversaries
and rages against his enemies.
3 The LORD is slow to anger but great in power,
and the LORD will by no means clear the guilty.

His way is in whirlwind and storm,
and the clouds are the dust of his feet.
4 He rebukes the sea and makes it dry,
and he dries up all the rivers;
Bashan and Carmel wither,
and the bloom of Lebanon fades.
5 The mountains quake before him,
and the hills melt;
the earth heaves before him,
the world and all who live in it.

6 Who can stand before his indignation?
Who can endure the heat of his anger?
His wrath is poured out like fire,
and by him the rocks are broken in pieces.
7 The LORD is good,
a stronghold in a day of trouble;
he protects those who take refuge in him,
8 even in a rushing flood.
He will make a full end of his adversaries,[a]
and will pursue his enemies into darkness.
9 Why do you plot against the LORD?
He will make an end;
no adversary will rise up twice.
10 Like thorns they are entangled,
like drunkards they are drunk;
they are consumed like dry straw.
11 From you one has gone out
who plots evil against the LORD,
one who counsels wickedness.

12 Thus says the LORD,
"Though they are at full strength and many,[b]
they will be cut off and pass away.
Though I have afflicted you,
I will afflict you no more.
13 And now I will break off his yoke from you
and snap the bonds that bind you."

14 The LORD has commanded concerning you:
"Your name shall be perpetuated no longer;
from the house of your gods I will cut off
the carved image and the cast image.
I will make your grave, for you are worthless."

15[c] Look! On the mountains the feet of one
who brings good tidings,
who proclaims peace!
Celebrate your festivals, O Judah,
fulfill your vows,
for never again shall the wicked invade you;
they are utterly cut off.

2 A shatterer[d] has come up against you.
Guard the ramparts;
watch the road;
gird your loins;
collect all your strength.

2 (For the LORD is restoring the majesty of Jacob,
as well as the majesty of Israel,
though ravagers have ravaged them
and ruined their branches.)

[a] Gk: Heb *of her place* [b] Meaning of Heb uncertain [c] Ch 2.1 in Heb [d] Cn:Heb *scatterer*

3 The shields of his warriors are red;
his soldiers are clothed in crimson.
The metal on the chariots flashes
on the day when he musters them;
the chargers[a] prance.
4 The chariots race madly through the
streets,
they rush to and fro through the
squares;
their appearance is like torches,
they dart like lightning.
5 He calls his officers;
they stumble as they come forward;
they hasten to the wall,
and the mantelet[b] is set up.
6 The river gates are opened,
the palace trembles.
7 It is decreed[b] that the city[c] be exiled,
its slave women led away,
moaning like doves
and beating their breasts.
8 Nineveh is like a pool
whose waters[d] run away.
"Halt! Halt!"—
but no one turns back.
9 "Plunder the silver,
plunder the gold!
There is no end of treasure!
An abundance of every precious thing!"

10 Devastation, desolation, and destruction!
Hearts faint and knees tremble,
all loins quake,
all faces grow pale!
11 What became of the lions' den,
the cave[e] of the young lions,
where the lion goes,
and the lion's cubs, with no one to disturb
them?
12 The lion has torn enough for his whelps
and strangled prey for his lionesses;
he has filled his caves with prey
and his dens with torn flesh.

13 See, I am against you, says the LORD of
hosts, and I will burn your[f] chariots in smoke, and
the sword shall devour your young lions; I will
cut off your prey from the earth, and the voice of
your messengers shall be heard no more.

3 Ah! City of bloodshed,
utterly deceitful, full of booty—
no end to the plunder!
2 The crack of whip and rumble of wheel,
galloping horse and bounding chariot!
3 Horsemen charging,
flashing sword and glittering spear,
piles of dead,
heaps of corpses,
dead bodies without end—
they stumble over the bodies!
4 Because of the countless debaucheries of the
prostitute,
gracefully alluring, mistress of sorcery,
who enslaves[g] nations through her
debaucheries,
and peoples through her sorcery,
5 I am against you,
says the LORD of hosts,
and will lift up your skirts over your face;
and I will let nations look on your
nakedness
and kingdoms on your shame.
6 I will throw filth at you
and treat you with contempt,
and make you a spectacle.
7 Then all who see you will shrink from you
and say,
"Nineveh is devastated; who will bemoan
her?"
Where shall I seek comforters for you?

8 Are you better than Thebes[h]
that sat by the Nile,
with water around her,
her rampart a sea,
water her wall?
9 Ethiopia[i] was her strength,

[a] Cn Compare Gk Syr: Heb *cypresses* [b] Meaning of Heb uncertain [c] Heb *it* [d] Cn Compare Gk: Heb *a pool, from the days that she has become, and they* [e] Cn: Heb *pasture* [f] Heb *her* [g] Heb *sells* [h] Heb *No-amon* [i] Or *Nubia*; Heb *Cush*

Egypt too, and that without limit;
Put and the Libyans were her[a] helpers.

10 Yet she became an exile,
she went into captivity;
even her infants were dashed in pieces
at the head of every street;
lots were cast for her nobles,
all her dignitaries were bound in fetters.
11 You also will be drunken,
you will go into hiding;[b]
you will seek
a refuge from the enemy.
12 All your fortresses are like fig trees
with first-ripe figs—
if shaken they fall
into the mouth of the eater.
13 Look at your troops:
they are women in your midst.
The gates of your land
are wide open to your foes;
fire has devoured the bars of your gates.

14 Draw water for the siege,
strengthen your forts;
trample the clay,
tread the mortar,
take hold of the brick mold!
15 There the fire will devour you,
the sword will cut you off.
It will devour you like the locust.

Multiply yourselves like the locust,
multiply like the grasshopper!
16 You increased your merchants
more than the stars of the heavens.
The locust sheds its skin and flies away.
17 Your guards are like grasshoppers,
your scribes like swarms[b] of locusts
settling on the fences
on a cold day—
when the sun rises, they fly away;
no one knows where they have gone.

18 Your shepherds are asleep,
O king of Assyria;
your nobles slumber.
Your people are scattered on the
mountains
with no one to gather them.
19 There is no assuaging your hurt,
your wound is mortal.
All who hear the news about you
clap their hands over you.
For who has ever escaped
your endless cruelty?

[a] Gk: Heb *your* [b] Meaning of Heb uncertain

Nahum 3:18-19

The book of Nahum provides an interesting series of contrasts when read in conjunction with other prophetic books. In Jonah, God calls for the destruction of Nineveh, but they are spared when they repent: in Nahum, Nineveh is destroyed. In Obadiah, Edom is denounced for rejoicing in Jerusalem's downfall: in Nahum, Israel rejoices over the downfall of Nineveh.

— *WG*

Habakkuk

I GREW UP FORTY MILES SOUTHEAST of Bull Connor's Birmingham, a place where dogs were loosed on children, where water hoses were turned on teenagers, and where some people were called "pickaninny." Faith played a pivotal role in the lives of those who willingly resisted oppressive and dangerous racism. It is from that history that I read Habakkuk. *How does one watch God watch evil?* That is the dilemma Habakkuk faced. It also is the question asked by enslaved people, by sexually abused people, and by those who ponder the reality of the mid-twentieth-century Holocaust and the plight of the dispossessed in the two-thirds world.

The book of Habakkuk addresses issues of violence, corruption, foreign occupation, and poverty. Habakkuk was probably written as Judah's existence as a nation-state came to an end, between 609 BCE, when it became a vassal state, and 586, when the inhabitants were forced into exile. Judeans were living under the brutal occupation of the Chaldeans and a corrupt government of puppet leaders. Using ancient lament and complaint forms, Habakkuk calls God to the witness stand, demanding to know how a just and holy God can allow destruction and violence to persist. Pairing the Hebrew words "destruction and violence" (1:3) connotes a legal phrase used to describe physical, political, and economic violence leveled against vulnerable people (compare Prov 13:2; Jer 20:8; Amos 3:10; Ezek 45:9). In the presence of that violence, Habakkuk raised persistent questions of *theodicy*: where is God when evil is rampant? Why is God silent? Habakkuk puts the question in distinctly theological language. Those reading or, perhaps, hearing the prophet's complaint no doubt experienced shock when Habakkuk accused God of complicity in violence. Habakkuk does not question God's power. For the prophet the problem is rather why God is willing to allow evil to continue, and even to participate with evil, since God is "pure" (1:13). God supported, even stirred up, Chaldean violence, using it to punish wickedness (1:5-11). Habakkuk rebuts the deity by saying that violence does not stem violence. The deity promises that violent culprits will get their comeuppance in the end.

The prophet takes a stand in order to be able to see how God will answer the controversy. He invokes priests who stood watch, suggesting that Habakkuk confronts God in a liturgical setting. He accuses God, who replies by instructing the prophet to "write the vision" that "will surely come" (2:1-3). YHWH tells Habakkuk to expect a messenger. The message will be so plain that runners will be able to read it. God's answer (2:4), that "the righteous live by their faith" (or faithfulness), is so compelling that it later becomes one of the cornerstones of Paul's theology of justification (Rom 1:17; Gal 3:11; compare also Heb 10:38-39).

Habakkuk's concern is especially the way in which justice is perverted or "broken." For ancient Israelite and Judean prophets, justice was not an abstract concept. It was intimately tied to the

lives of the defenseless. Injustices "cry out," even from the walls (2:11), indicating just how systemic broken justice was. Broken justice is supported by "the proud," whose appetite for wealth is treacherous and, like death, cannot be satiated (2:4-5; compare Prov 30:15-16). In the marketplace people become debt-slaves, booty for those with means (2:6). The prophet declares that all created order suffers. Animal cruelty and ecological mayhem (2:17) result from this violence and human bloodshed. Whole cities are established by violence, and streets are filled with blood (2:8, 12). This violent, dehumanizing life is sanctioned by the religious world, represented by the icons of their gods, plated with gold and silver (2:19-20). The only possible dam against the flood of blood will be the future flood of "knowledge of the glory of the Lord," which will be as significant as Noah's flood (2:14; 3:3).

The prophetic words shift from liturgical lament and prosecutorial complaint against the deity to taunts against the enemy (2:6-19). The doxology in 2:20, "But the Lord is in his holy temple; let all the earth keep silence before him!" serves as prelude to the hymn of faith in chapter 3, where the prophet prays (3:1-2), experiences a theophany (3:3-16), then declares unwavering and steadfast faith, even in the face of evil and violence (3:17-19). The prophet appropriates metaphors, typically used to describe the Canaanite storm-god, Baal, to describe a theophany of YHWH.

Habakkuk begs God to remember mercy, because God is so wrathful (3:2, 8). The prophet knows what happens when the deity gets angry. The theophany is overwhelming, destructive, awe-inspiring, and frightening. In response, the prophet's heart pounds, lips quiver, bones began to decay, and legs tremble (3:16) at the thought of this impending doom. The concluding verses of Habakkuk proclaim faith and trust in God in the midst of dire circumstances that suggested abandonment by God. Habakkuk rejoices and exults in a God who often seems inscrutable (compare Job 42:1-3). All that people need to survive—fig trees, grapevines, olive branches, crops, and livestock—is at jeopardy. Habakkuk's is a vision of stark nothingness. Yet, in the face of this dearth and desolation, the prophet declares he will rejoice in YHWH, who saves. He finds hope in God in withering times, much like the rabbis of Auschwitz, in spite of the evidence.

—Valerie Bridgeman

1 The oracle that the prophet Habakkuk saw.

2 O Lord, how long shall I cry for help,
and you will not listen?
Or cry to you "Violence!"
and you will not save?
3 Why do you make me see wrongdoing
and look at trouble?
Destruction and violence are before me;
strife and contention arise.
4 So the law becomes slack
and justice never prevails.
The wicked surround the righteous—
therefore judgment comes forth perverted.

5 Look at the nations, and see!
Be astonished! Be astounded!
For a work is being done in your days
that you would not believe if you were told.

Habakkuk 1:5

More shocking than Habakkuk's accusation is God's response. God does not deny complicity.

— *VB*

6 For I am rousing the Chaldeans,
that fierce and impetuous nation,
who march through the breadth of the earth
to seize dwellings not their own.
7 Dread and fearsome are they;
their justice and dignity proceed from themselves.
8 Their horses are swifter than leopards,
more menacing than wolves at dusk;
their horses charge.
Their horsemen come from far away;
they fly like an eagle swift to devour.
9 They all come for violence,
with faces pressing[a] forward;
they gather captives like sand.
10 At kings they scoff,
and of rulers they make sport.
They laugh at every fortress,
and heap up earth to take it.
11 Then they sweep by like the wind;
they transgress and become guilty;
their own might is their god!

12 Are you not from of old,
O LORD my God, my Holy One?
You[b] shall not die.
O LORD, you have marked them for judgment;
and you, O Rock, have established them for punishment.
13 Your eyes are too pure to behold evil,
and you cannot look on wrongdoing;
why do you look on the treacherous,
and are silent when the wicked swallow those more righteous than they?
14 You have made people like the fish of the sea,
like crawling things that have no ruler.
15 The enemy[c] brings all of them up with a hook;
he drags them out with his net,
he gathers them in his seine;
so he rejoices and exults.
16 Therefore he sacrifices to his net
and makes offerings to his seine;
for by them his portion is lavish,
and his food is rich.
17 Is he then to keep on emptying his net,
and destroying nations without mercy?

2 I will stand at my watchpost,
and station myself on the rampart;
I will keep watch to see what he will say to me,
and what he[d] will answer concerning my complaint.
2 Then the LORD answered me and said:
Write the vision;
make it plain on tablets,
so that a runner may read it.
3 For there is still a vision for the appointed time;
it speaks of the end, and does not lie.
If it seems to tarry, wait for it;
it will surely come, it will not delay.
4 Look at the proud!
Their spirit is not right in them,
but the righteous live by their faith.[e]
5 Moreover, wealth[f] is treacherous;
the arrogant do not endure.
They open their throats wide as Sheol;
like Death they never have enough.
They gather all nations for themselves,
and collect all peoples as their own.

[a] Meaning of Heb uncertain [b] Ancient Heb tradition: MT *We* [c] Heb *He* [d] Syr: Heb *I* [e] Or *faithfulness*
[f] Other Heb Mss read *wine*

6 Shall not everyone taunt such people and,
with mocking riddles, say about them,
"Alas for you who heap up what is not your
own!"
How long will you load yourselves with
goods taken in pledge?
7 Will not your own creditors suddenly rise,
and those who make you tremble wake up?
Then you will be booty for them.
8 Because you have plundered many nations,
all that survive of the peoples shall plunder
you—
because of human bloodshed, and violence to
the earth,
to cities and all who live in them.

9 "Alas for you who get evil gain for your house,
setting your nest on high
to be safe from the reach of harm!"
10 You have devised shame for your house
by cutting off many peoples;
you have forfeited your life.
11 The very stones will cry out from the wall,
and the plaster[a] will respond from the
woodwork.

Habakkuk 2:11

Violence was so pervasive and virulent that society faced perverted and broken justice. It was so systemic that even the physical structures seemed to cry out.

— *VB*

12 "Alas for you who build a town by bloodshed,
and found a city on iniquity!"
13 Is it not from the LORD of hosts
that peoples labor only to feed the flames,
and nations weary themselves for nothing?
14 But the earth will be filled
with the knowledge of the glory of the
LORD,
as the waters cover the sea.

15 "Alas for you who make your neighbors
drink,
pouring out your wrath[b] until they are
drunk,
in order to gaze on their nakedness!"
16 You will be sated with contempt instead of
glory.
Drink, you yourself, and stagger![c]
The cup in the LORD's right hand
will come around to you,
and shame will come upon your glory!
17 For the violence done to Lebanon will
overwhelm you;
the destruction of the animals will terrify
you—[d]
because of human bloodshed and violence to
the earth,
to cities and all who live in them.

18 What use is an idol
once its maker has shaped it—
a cast image, a teacher of lies?
For its maker trusts in what has been made,
though the product is only an idol that
cannot speak!
19 Alas for you who say to the wood,
"Wake up!"
to silent stone, "Rouse yourself!"
Can it teach?
See, it is gold and silver plated,
and there is no breath in it at all.

20 But the LORD is in his holy temple;
let all the earth keep silence before him!

3 A prayer of the prophet Habakkuk according
to Shigionoth.

2 O LORD, I have heard of your renown,
and I stand in awe, O LORD, of your work.
In our own time revive it;
in our own time make it known;
in wrath may you remember mercy.
3 God came from Teman,
the Holy One from Mount Paran. *Selah*

[a] Or *beam* [b] Or *poison* [c] Q Ms Gk: MT *be uncircumcised* [d] Gk Syr: Meaning of Heb uncertain

His glory covered the heavens,
and the earth was full of his praise.
4 The brightness was like the sun;
rays came forth from his hand,
where his power lay hidden.
5 Before him went pestilence,
and plague followed close behind.
6 He stopped and shook the earth;
he looked and made the nations tremble.
The eternal mountains were shattered;
along his ancient pathways
the everlasting hills sank low.
7 I saw the tents of Cushan under affliction;
the tent-curtains of the land of Midian
trembled.
8 Was your wrath against the rivers,[a] O LORD?
Or your anger against the rivers,[a]
or your rage against the sea,[b]
when you drove your horses,
your chariots to victory?
9 You brandished your naked bow,
sated[c] were the arrows at your command.[d]
Selah
You split the earth with rivers.
10 The mountains saw you, and writhed;
a torrent of water swept by;
the deep gave forth its voice.
The sun[e] raised high its hands;
11 the moon[f] stood still in its exalted place,
at the light of your arrows speeding by,
at the gleam of your flashing spear.
12 In fury you trod the earth,
in anger you trampled nations.

13 You came forth to save your people,
to save your anointed.
You crushed the head of the wicked house,
laying it bare from foundation to roof.[d]
Selah
14 You pierced with their[g] own arrows the head[h]
of his warriors,[i]
who came like a whirlwind to scatter us,[j]
gloating as if ready to devour the poor who
were in hiding.
15 You trampled the sea with your horses,
churning the mighty waters.

16 I hear, and I tremble within;
my lips quiver at the sound.
Rottenness enters into my bones,
and my steps tremble[k] beneath me.
I wait quietly for the day of calamity
to come upon the people who attack us.

17 Though the fig tree does not blossom,
and no fruit is on the vines;
though the produce of the olive fails,
and the fields yield no food;
though the flock is cut off from the fold,
and there is no herd in the stalls,
18 yet I will rejoice in the LORD;
I will exult in the God of my salvation.
19 GOD, the Lord, is my strength;
he makes my feet like the feet of a deer,
and makes me tread upon the heights.[l]

To the leader: with stringed[m] instruments.

[a] Or *against River* [b] Or *against Sea* [c] Cn: Heb *oaths* [d] Meaning of Heb uncertain [e] Heb *It* [f] Heb *sun, moon* [g] Heb *his* [h] Or *leader* [i] Vg Compare Gk Syr: Meaning of Heb uncertain [j] Heb *me* [k] Cn Compare Gk: Meaning of Heb uncertain [l] Heb *my heights* [m] Heb *my stringed*

Zephaniah

THE CENTRAL MESSAGE of the book of Zephaniah is God's impending judgment on Judah. The book begins with a superscription (1:1). Judgment on Judah and Jerusalem is found in 1:2—2:3. A transitory section about oracles against the foreign nations is found in 2:4-15. Then, final judgment is transformed to salvation in 3:1-20. In its final, canonical shape, the book ends on a beautiful note of home, gathering, and praise for Judah (3:20).

Between the eighth-century BCE prophet Isaiah, son of Amoz, and the sixth-century prophet Jeremiah stands Zephaniah, son of Cushi, the most influential voice among the prophets of the intervening seventh century. For years, biblical scholars have suggested that Zephaniah may have been a disciple of Isaiah, heavily influenced by Isaiah's thought and preaching, and especially "Isaiah's Memoir" in Isa 6:1—9:6. Like Isaiah, Zephaniah too walked in the midst of the powerful inner circle (Zeph 1:1).

Isaiah of Jerusalem had two central means of transmitting judgment, using variations of the expression "the LORD's hand" (Isa 5:25; 9:12, 17, 21; 14:26-27; 23:11; 31:3; 40:2), and "on that day" (Isa 7:18, 20, 21, 23; also in Amos and Micah). In the book of Zephaniah, we hear both of these expressions. The theme "I will stretch out my hand against Judah" is found in the opening of the book at 1:4 and again at 2:13. Isaiah's fourfold "On that day" also is found in Zephaniah, beginning at 1:9-10 and continuing and concluding at 3:11, 16. But in the latter chapter Zephaniah gives the phrase a fascinating positive turn. Rather than the expected words of injunction, we hear a song of redemption and celebration. Here is a return to the original use of "On that day"—when it was employed as a celebration near the end of the grape harvest (Feast of Tabernacles or Succoth; compare the Song of the Vineyard, Isa 5:1-7). The image of crushed grapes became the impetus for words of judgment. Now a second-generation disciple preserves and employs his teacher's teaching, yet adapts it to promise hope and redemption for daughter Zion.

In Zephaniah we can also detect Deuteronomic or Jeremiah-like concerns that speak out against the worship of Baal and pronounce judgment against officials, judges, prophets, and priests for misconduct (Zeph 3:3-5). The only individual missing from the list is the king! Here is a prophet who indeed bridges the traditions of Isaiah and Jeremiah.

The name Zephaniah means "the Lord hides." As Zephaniah links the two great prophets, he also bridges the two great kings of Judah. Counting King Hezekiah as the first generation, and the first who attempted centralization and reform, Zephaniah is a direct fifth-generation descendent of this royal lineage. He prophesied during the reign of King Josiah (640–609 BCE). Josiah was only the second king of Judah who attempted and then actually advanced Judah's reformation. It is this "hidden one," Zephaniah, a prophet, not a king, who links these two great reformers of Judah.

Every generation has amazing stories to share and tell. The social philosopher Karl Mannheim, in his 1928 essay "On the Problem of Generations," was the first to systematically examine the impact of generational experiences on groups separated by geography, class, and other factors. Korean Americans and other immigrant groups in the United States (and, globally, Russian Israelis, Vietnamese Australians, and others) share some of the same generational divides. In "generation 1.5" are those who were pulled from their homelands and arrived in a new context as adolescents.

In the Korean-American church, we continue to live out generational issues, concerns, and tensions. Members of the first generation often seem quicker to criticize the second generation's lack of proficiency in Korean than to improve their own proficiency in English. In the first-generation context, one is expected to bow and speak in honorifics, showing deference; but the typical second-generation teen simply and directly asks, "Whassup, Elder Kim?" Attitudes and relationships among first- and second-generation Korean Americans can become complex.

My entry point into the book of Zephaniah is the role of bridge maker—between Isaiah and Jeremiah, and Hezekiah and Josiah. The role of a transitional generation must be visionary. It must go beyond its own context and see the concerns of those who stand before and those who will come after. In the case of the Korean American church, the church must prepare for the third generation. However, without the second generation, there is no third generation. But all of this is entirely dependent on the first generation. Generation 1.5 has a special responsibility to help the first generation see things from a different perspective, because they are culturally closer to that generation. The second generation must respect and preserve cherished and functional traditions, but must adapt and amend them in ways that benefit ensuing generations.

— *John J. Ahn*

1 The word of the LORD that came to Zephaniah son of Cushi son of Gedaliah son of Amariah son of Hezekiah, in the days of King Josiah
son of Amon of Judah.

2 I will utterly sweep away everything
from the face of the earth, says the LORD.
3 I will sweep away humans and animals;
I will sweep away the birds of the air
and the fish of the sea.
I will make the wicked stumble.[a]
I will cut off humanity
from the face of the earth, says the LORD.
4 I will stretch out my hand against Judah,
and against all the inhabitants of Jerusalem;
and I will cut off from this place every
remnant of Baal
and the name of the idolatrous priests;[b]
5 those who bow down on the roofs
to the host of the heavens;
those who bow down and swear to the LORD,
but also swear by Milcom;[c]

[a] Cn: Heb *sea, and those who cause the wicked to stumble* [b] Compare Gk: Heb *the idolatrous priests with the priests* [c] Gk Mss Syr Vg: Heb *Malcam* (or, *their king*)

6 those who have turned back from following
the LORD,
who have not sought the LORD or inquired
of him.

7 Be silent before the Lord GOD!
For the day of the LORD is at hand;
the LORD has prepared a sacrifice,
he has consecrated his guests.
8 And on the day of the LORD's sacrifice
I will punish the officials and the king's sons
and all who dress themselves in foreign
attire.
9 On that day I will punish
all who leap over the threshold,
who fill their master's house
with violence and fraud.

10 On that day, says the LORD,
a cry will be heard from the Fish Gate,
a wail from the Second Quarter,
a loud crash from the hills.
11 The inhabitants of the Mortar wail,
for all the traders have perished;
all who weigh out silver are cut off.
12 At that time I will search Jerusalem with
lamps,
and I will punish the people
who rest complacently[a] on their dregs,
those who say in their hearts,
"The LORD will not do good,
nor will he do harm."
13 Their wealth shall be plundered,
and their houses laid waste.
Though they build houses,
they shall not inhabit them;
though they plant vineyards,
they shall not drink wine from them.

14 The great day of the LORD is near,
near and hastening fast;
the sound of the day of the LORD is bitter,
the warrior cries aloud there.
15 That day will be a day of wrath,
a day of distress and anguish,
a day of ruin and devastation,
a day of darkness and gloom,
a day of clouds and thick darkness,
16 a day of trumpet blast and battle cry
against the fortified cities
and against the lofty battlements.

17 I will bring such distress upon people
that they shall walk like the blind;
because they have sinned against the
LORD,
their blood shall be poured out like dust,
and their flesh like dung.
18 Neither their silver nor their gold
will be able to save them
on the day of the LORD's wrath;
in the fire of his passion
the whole earth shall be consumed;
for a full, a terrible end
he will make of all the inhabitants of the
earth.

2 Gather together, gather,
O shameless nation,
2 before you are driven away
like the drifting chaff,[b]
before there comes upon you
the fierce anger of the LORD,
before there comes upon you
the day of the LORD's wrath.
3 Seek the LORD, all you humble of the land,
who do his commands;
seek righteousness, seek humility;
perhaps you may be hidden
on the day of the LORD's wrath.
4 For Gaza shall be deserted,
and Ashkelon shall become a desolation;
Ashdod's people shall be driven out at
noon,
and Ekron shall be uprooted.

5 Ah, inhabitants of the seacoast,
you nation of the Cherethites!
The word of the LORD is against you,
O Canaan, land of the Philistines;

[a] Heb *who thicken* [b] Cn Compare Gk Syr: Heb *before a decree is born; like chaff a day has passed away*

and I will destroy you until no inhabitant
is left.
6 And you, O seacoast, shall be pastures,
meadows for shepherds
and folds for flocks.
7 The seacoast shall become the possession
of the remnant of the house of Judah,
on which they shall pasture,
and in the houses of Ashkelon
they shall lie down at evening.
For the LORD their God will be mindful of
them
and restore their fortunes.

8 I have heard the taunts of Moab
and the revilings of the Ammonites,
how they have taunted my people
and made boasts against their territory.
9 Therefore, as I live, says the LORD of hosts,
the God of Israel,
Moab shall become like Sodom
and the Ammonites like Gomorrah,
a land possessed by nettles and salt pits,
and a waste forever.
The remnant of my people shall plunder
them,
and the survivors of my nation shall
possess them.
10 This shall be their lot in return for their pride,
because they scoffed and boasted
against the people of the LORD of hosts.
11 The LORD will be terrible against them;
he will shrivel all the gods of the earth,
and to him shall bow down,
each in its place,
all the coasts and islands of the nations.

12 You also, O Ethiopians,[a]
shall be killed by my sword.

13 And he will stretch out his hand against the
north,
and destroy Assyria;
and he will make Nineveh a desolation,
a dry waste like the desert.
14 Herds shall lie down in it,
every wild animal;[b]
the desert owl[c] and the screech owl[c]
shall lodge on its capitals;
the owl[d] shall hoot at the window,
the raven[e] croak on the threshold;
for its cedar work will be laid bare.
15 Is this the exultant city
that lived secure,
that said to itself,
"I am, and there is no one else"?
What a desolation it has become,
a lair for wild animals!
Everyone who passes by it
hisses and shakes the fist.

3 Ah, soiled, defiled,
oppressing city!
2 It has listened to no voice;
it has accepted no correction.
It has not trusted in the LORD;
it has not drawn near to its God.

3 The officials within it
are roaring lions;
its judges are evening wolves
that leave nothing until the morning.
4 Its prophets are reckless,
faithless persons;
its priests have profaned what is sacred,
they have done violence to the law.
5 The LORD within it is righteous;
he does no wrong.
Every morning he renders his judgment,
each dawn without fail;
but the unjust knows no shame.

6 I have cut off nations;
their battlements are in ruins;
I have laid waste their streets
so that no one walks in them;
their cities have been made desolate,
without people, without inhabitants.

[a] Or *Nubians*; Heb *Cushites* [b] Tg Compare Gk: Heb *nation* [c] Meaning of Heb uncertain [d] Cn: Heb *a voice*
[e] Gk Vg: Heb *desolation*

7 I said, "Surely the city[a] will fear me,
it will accept correction;
it will not lose sight[b]
of all that I have brought upon it."
But they were the more eager
to make all their deeds corrupt.

8 Therefore wait for me, says the LORD,
for the day when I arise as a witness.
For my decision is to gather nations,
to assemble kingdoms,
to pour out upon them my indignation,
all the heat of my anger;
for in the fire of my passion
all the earth shall be consumed.

9 At that time I will change the speech of the peoples
to a pure speech,
that all of them may call on the name of the LORD
and serve him with one accord.
10 From beyond the rivers of Ethiopia[c]
my suppliants, my scattered ones,
shall bring my offering.

11 On that day you shall not be put to shame
because of all the deeds by which you have rebelled against me;
for then I will remove from your midst
your proudly exultant ones,
and you shall no longer be haughty
in my holy mountain.
12 For I will leave in the midst of you
a people humble and lowly.
They shall seek refuge in the name of the LORD—
13 the remnant of Israel;
they shall do no wrong
and utter no lies,
nor shall a deceitful tongue
be found in their mouths.
Then they will pasture and lie down,
and no one shall make them afraid.

14 Sing aloud, O daughter Zion;
shout, O Israel!
Rejoice and exult with all your heart,
O daughter Jerusalem!
15 The LORD has taken away the judgments against you,
he has turned away your enemies.
The king of Israel, the LORD, is in your midst;
you shall fear disaster no more.
16 On that day it shall be said to Jerusalem:
Do not fear, O Zion;
do not let your hands grow weak.

[a] Heb *it* [b] Gk Syr: Heb *its dwelling will not be cut off* [c] Or *Nubia*; Heb *Cush*

Zephaniah 3:14-20

The title "Daughter Zion" (*bat Tzion* in Hebrew) can be translated as "daughter of Zion" and refer to an individual woman or a community (a city or a nation) addressed metaphorically as a woman. We can never know, but might imagine how individual women may have heard certain texts. Imagine Mary of Nazareth hearing this text: Would she have been comforted by the words in verse 15, "The LORD has taken away the judgments against you"? Would she have taken the words "The LORD, your God, is in your midst" literally? As a Christian reader, I imagine that at the end of her life she may well have been able to relate the words in verse 19, "I will save the lame and gather the outcast," to the ministry of the One who was indeed in her midst. And, as an Episcopalian, I hear the words in verse 20, "At that time I will bring you home," through the tradition of the Assumption of the Blessed Virgin, the teaching that she did not die, but was rather received bodily into heaven like Enoch and Elijah. This type of reading is in part inspired by the readings of New Testament authors who regularly read the prophets through the lens of the story of Jesus.

— WG

17 The LORD, your God, is in your midst,
a warrior who gives victory;
he will rejoice over you with gladness,
he will renew you[a] in his love;
he will exult over you with loud singing
18 as on a day of festival.[b]
I will remove disaster from you,[c]
so that you will not bear reproach for it.
19 I will deal with all your oppressors
at that time.
And I will save the lame
and gather the outcast,
and I will change their shame into praise
and renown in all the earth.
20 At that time I will bring you home,
at the time when I gather you;
for I will make you renowned and praised
among all the peoples of the earth,
when I restore your fortunes
before your eyes, says the LORD.

[a] Gk Syr: Heb *he will be silent* [b] Gk Syr: Meaning of Heb uncertain [c] Cn: Heb *I will remove from you; they were*

Haggai

The book of Haggai provides some of the most reliable dating available in the Bible. Offering leadership during the reconstruction of the temple, the prophet Haggai dates his visions from August to December in 520 BCE, early in the reign of the Persian king Darius. The repeated formula (1:1; 2:1, 10) that consistently includes the name of Darius supplies both historical exactness and names the period in terms of imperial history.

Persian imperialism enabled deported Judeans to return to their homeland and provided resources to rebuild the temple. However, these measures alone did not result in economic prosperity or even communal cohesion. The book opens with a prophetic rebuke to a dispirited community accepting their fate (1:2) as imperial subjects in an economically ruined province. Details about Haggai's life are lacking, so it is not clear whether he returned to Jerusalem from Babylon. This uncertainty, though, eliminates arguments about his ethnic authenticity and helps focus greater attention on his message.

I read Haggai from the context of growing up in a recently independent country, Trinidad and Tobago, which achieved independence in 1962, but where several marks of colonialism remain in place. My formative years were developed against the background of a country trying to find its identity and unique place in the world.

Haggai communicates four visions from God (1:1-11; 2:1-9; 2:10-19; 2:20-23) that detail the value of a rebuilt temple. He begins by rebuking the residents of the city for their unwillingness to rebuild the temple (1:2). Their reluctance to work on the temple appears to be partly a result of poor economic conditions and partly the failure to establish a sense of community. A sense of scarcity had created among the residents a drive to take care of their individual needs to the neglect of the temple, the center of community life and identity. Haggai argues that as long as the temple is in ruins, the city's economic fortunes and the prosperity of the residents will remain bleak. He points out that drought conditions (1:9-11) and the futility of the efforts of the residents to eke out a living (1:6) results from the ruined temple. When eventually work had begun on the temple, he would ask the people to notice how their fortunes changed since the completion of its foundation (2:18-19).

Haggai's argument for the necessity of the temple lies not so much in its ritual and cultic functions as in its economic benefits to the people. Although he acknowledges that the completed temple would render the people ritually clean (2:10-18), Haggai argues that ritual cleanliness results in economic benefits, sharing the commonly held ancient worldview that the building of a temple guaranteed economic prosperity. Haggai helps the city see the temple as its central and focal point, but more importantly as the symbol of their identity as a people. The text constantly reminds the readers that Darius, the Persian, is king. The rebuilt temple serves to answer that reality with the statement of God's power and God's restoration of God's people to their land.

Haggai's fourth vision (2:20-23) pulls together the theme of restoration, but with a focus on a Davidic figure. This vision, exclusively delivered to Zerubbabel, the Persian provincial governor, contains promises in language reminiscent of early kings—"my servant," "signet ring," and "I have chosen you" (2:23). Throughout the book, the words of the prophet affirm the leadership of both Zerubbabel and Joshua, the high priest. Although the prophecy's concern remains the temple, civic leadership receives in the last vision a focus that underlines a future role for Zerubbabel in partnership with God. Yet on that day Zerubbabel plays no role but merely stands by as a spectator of God's power. The centrality of the temple does not assume a central leader that accumulates power to himself. Both Joshua and Zerubbabel are subject to God's prophecy and are seen to obey the instructions of the prophet (1:12). This vision places God in opposition to other powers ("throne of kingdoms," "kingdoms of the nations," 2:22), without specifically naming any opponent. While the reader would expect this kind of judgment against the Babylonians or even the Persians, the vision offers a generic threat to all kingdoms. This vision offers a trans-historical perspective that shows a time when even the imperial powers will no longer exist. The prophet's message to the community in Jerusalem during the reign of Darius encouraged the rebuilding of the temple—the symbol of the presence of God and of the power of God in the face of empire, and a vision that outlasts temporal powers.

— ***Steed Vernyl Davidson***

1 In the second year of King Darius, in the sixth
month, on the first day of the month, the
word of the LORD came by the prophet Haggai to
Zerubbabel son of Shealtiel, governor of Judah,
and to Joshua son of Jehozadak, the high priest:
2 Thus says the LORD of hosts: These people say
the time has not yet come to rebuild the LORD's
house. 3 Then the word of the LORD came by the
prophet Haggai, saying: 4 Is it a time for you yourselves to live in your paneled houses, while this
house lies in ruins? 5 Now therefore thus says the
LORD of hosts: Consider how you have fared.
6 You have sown much, and harvested little; you
eat, but you never have enough; you drink, but
you never have your fill; you clothe yourselves,
but no one is warm; and you that earn wages earn
wages to put them into a bag with holes.

7 Thus says the LORD of hosts: Consider
how you have fared. 8 Go up to the hills and bring
wood and build the house, so that I may take pleasure in it and be honored, says the LORD. 9 You
have looked for much, and, lo, it came to little;
and when you brought it home, I blew it away.
Why? says the LORD of hosts. Because my house
lies in ruins, while all of you hurry off to your own
houses. 10 Therefore the heavens above you have
withheld the dew, and the earth has withheld its
produce. 11 And I have called for a drought on the
land and the hills, on the grain, the new wine, the
oil, on what the soil produces, on human beings
and animals, and on all their labors.

12 Then Zerubbabel son of Shealtiel, and
Joshua son of Jehozadak, the high priest, with all
the remnant of the people, obeyed the voice of the

Lord their God, and the words of the prophet
Haggai, as the Lord their God had sent him; and
the people feared the Lord. [13]Then Haggai, the
messenger of the Lord, spoke to the people with
the Lord's message, saying, I am with you, says
the Lord. [14]And the Lord stirred up the spirit
of Zerubbabel son of Shealtiel, governor of Judah, and the spirit of Joshua son of Jehozadak, the
high priest, and the spirit of all the remnant of the
people; and they came and worked on the house
of the Lord of hosts, their God, [15]on the twenty-
fourth day of the month, in the sixth month.

Haggai 2:1

Haggai's dating system differs markedly from what we see in earlier prophets or even in the books of Kings and Chronicles. In those books, time is marked by reference to the reigning king of Israel and the king of Judah. Now, under Persian occupation, the province of Yehud replaced the independent kingdom of Judah at the end of the Babylonian Empire. Imperial powers tend to remake territories in their own image, imposing their own culture, currency, power structure, language, and systems on indigenous peoples. Haggai's repeated use of the year of Darius's reign for dating his prophecies serves as a reminder of his imperial realities and the necessity to construct the temple as a marker of Judean identity.

— SVD

2 In the second year of King Darius, [1]in the
seventh month, on the twenty-first day of
the month, the word of the Lord came by the
prophet Haggai, saying: [2]Speak now to Zerubbabel son of Shealtiel, governor of Judah, and
to Joshua son of Jehozadak, the high priest, and
to the remnant of the people, and say, [3]Who is
left among you that saw this house in its former
glory? How does it look to you now? Is it not
in your sight as nothing? [4]Yet now take courage, O Zerubbabel, says the Lord; take courage, O Joshua, son of Jehozadak, the high priest;
take courage, all you people of the land, says the
Lord; work, for I am with you, says the Lord of
hosts, [5]according to the promise that I made you
when you came out of Egypt. My spirit abides
among you; do not fear. [6]For thus says the Lord
of hosts: Once again, in a little while, I will shake
the heavens and the earth and the sea and the dry
land; [7]and I will shake all the nations, so that the
treasure of all nations shall come, and I will fill
this house with splendor, says the Lord of hosts.
[8]The silver is mine, and the gold is mine, says the
Lord of hosts. [9]The latter splendor of this house
shall be greater than the former, says the Lord of
hosts; and in this place I will give prosperity, says
the Lord of hosts.

10 On the twenty-fourth day of the ninth
month, in the second year of Darius, the word of
the Lord came by the prophet Haggai, saying:
[11]Thus says the Lord of hosts: Ask the priests for
a ruling: [12]If one carries consecrated meat in the
fold of one's garment, and with the fold touches
bread, or stew, or wine, or oil, or any kind of food,
does it become holy? The priests answered, "No."
[13]Then Haggai said, "If one who is unclean by contact with a dead body touches any of these, does
it become unclean?" The priests answered, "Yes,
it becomes unclean." [14]Haggai then said, So is it
with this people, and with this nation before me,
says the Lord; and so with every work of their
hands; and what they offer there is unclean. [15]But
now, consider what will come to pass from this
day on. Before a stone was placed upon a stone
in the Lord's temple, [16]how did you fare?[a] When
one came to a heap of twenty measures, there
were but ten; when one came to the wine vat to
draw fifty measures, there were but twenty. [17]I
struck you and all the products of your toil with
blight and mildew and hail; yet you did not return to me, says the Lord. [18]Consider from this
day on, from the twenty-fourth day of the ninth
month. Since the day that the foundation of the
Lord's temple was laid, consider: [19]Is there any
seed left in the barn? Do the vine, the fig tree,
the pomegranate, and the olive tree still yield
nothing? From this day on I will bless you.

[a] Gk: Heb *since they were*

Haggai 2:18

The first task of those returning to Jerusalem from Babylon in 539 was to work on restoring the foundations of the temple. The work of the prophets Haggai and Zechariah helped push forward stalled efforts at reconstruction, leading to the completion of the Second Temple in 515. This temple underwent various renovations and extensions and stood until its destruction by the Romans in 70 CE. Like other destroyed national symbols that have been rebuilt as a sign of defiance, the second temple stands in the text of Haggai as a sign of triumph over enemy empires. The same is true of the reconstruction of the World Trade Center in New York after the terrorist attacks of September 11, 2001.

— SVD

20 The word of the LORD came a second
time to Haggai on the twenty-fourth day of the
month: [21]Speak to Zerubbabel, governor of
Judah, saying, I am about to shake the heavens
and the earth, [22]and to overthrow the throne of
kingdoms; I am about to destroy the strength
of the kingdoms of the nations, and overthrow
the chariots and their riders; and the horses and
their riders shall fall, every one by the sword
of a comrade. [23]On that day, says the LORD of
hosts, I will take you, O Zerubbabel my servant,
son of Shealtiel, says the LORD, and make you
like a signet ring; for I have chosen you, says the
LORD of hosts.

Haggai 2:23

While it may appear that the Persians courted trouble by making Zerubbabel governor, the move probably was a means of garnering support for Persian rule through the use of a favored local leader. Haggai sees in Zerubbabel the promise of a restored monarchy (2:23). These aspirations reflect the desire of colonized peoples not only to have their own leaders but to have leaders that mirror their indigenous needs and culture. Haggai's vision for Zerubbabel appears to be for him to serve not in the interests of the Persians but in the traditions of God's kings—like David.

— SVD

Zechariah

I READ ZECHARIAH AS AN IMMIGRANT who was living in New York City during the attacks on the World Trade Center in 2001. I heard and felt the outrage of native New Yorkers towards such an insult to their national pride, and I also heard and felt the fear and pain of the rest of the world with regards to the responses to those attacks. In my reading of Zechariah, this context of double-vision that sees the whole emerges.

New Orleans will always remember Katrina not merely as the hurricane of 2005 but as a cataclysmic event that resulted in the deportation of vast numbers of the population. In its aftermath, many blamed the failure of government agencies to provide leadership necessary to prevent the scattering of people. Others blamed the disaster on the perceived permissive culture and lifestyle of the Big Easy.

Tensions over the deportation of Judeans to Babylon in the sixth century BCE are evident in the text of the book of Zechariah. The book can easily be divided into two sections: chapters 1–8 represent an optimistic prophecy of a time of restoration, guaranteed by the rebuilt temple and the consecrated leadership of Zerubbabel, the governor, and Joshua, the high priest. Chapters 9–14 angrily chastise other nations and various leaders of Judah for the population expulsion and call for faith in God to guarantee a secure future.

The prophet named Zechariah receives eight visions (chs. 1–7) that require angelic interpretation. In these visions, mostly relating to Jerusalem, he sees the restoration of the city (2:1-5), symbolic fixtures in the temple (4:1-7), the removal of idolatry from the city (5:5-11), and the affirmation of the leadership of Joshua (3:1-10; 6:9-15). All this sets the stage for the completion of the temple, built with the help of those from far away (6:15). As in Haggai, the reconstructed temple provides prosperity to the community (8:9-13).

Unlike Haggai, however, the primary leadership lies here with the priest Joshua, who receives purification and a mandate (3:3-10), a crown (6:11), and the messianic title Branch (6:12) to confirm the centrality of the temple and its priesthood in the restored community. The disaster that fell on the city as a result of the failure to heed Torah obligations (7:8-14) can be avoided by a commitment to keep these obligations (8:14-17). While Zerubbabel receives attention in Zechariah as the builder of the temple (4:8-10), this happens without him receiving the title "governor," and he is counseled on the superiority of the spirit of God over military might (4:6). The hoped-for future projected onto the restored temple envisages a community of people so attractive that they will compel the world to the temple by their presence (8:20-23).

This version of restoration in 1–8 contrasts markedly with the rest of the book, which takes on a heated tone in chapter 9. In these sections no prophet is named and some of the normal prophetic forms disappear. These chapters find little confidence in the institutions and leadership of Judah and blame them for the disaster. The priests, prophets, diviners, monarchs, and even the house of David receive strong criticism and find credibility only with divine forgiveness and cleansing. Perhaps reflecting the thoughts of someone outside the establishment, this section envisions that leadership of the people will rest firmly with God (11:7; 14:9). The center of the restored community lies in the city itself, not the temple (14:10-11). Foreign nations get blame and punishment for their part in the scattering of the people (9:1-8). The idyllic picture of universalism of the first part turns coercive as foreigners are compelled to participate in the festival of booths (14:16-19). All this comes with the renewed confidence that Jerusalem would never again be destroyed (14:12-14).

The reader may not find it necessary to arbitrate between these two different visions of renewal, as may be the case in real-life situations. Certainly, they continue, side by side, unresolved in the Bible. The main difference between the two sections of this book lies in their *anthropology* rather than in their theology. The first manifests a confidence in institutions and systems to work as they are designed. It sees the disaster as a result of the failure of the community to heed the law and believes that with another chance from God, a new start can be made for a repopulated and prosperous city. The second section lacks this optimistic view of institutions and pays attention to their flawed nature. While including strong mention of David (12:7-10), there is an acknowledgement that even this great dynasty remains defective and can only function from a strong theocentric focus. Such is the pessimism regarding institutions that the second section envisages its universalism not in human categories but in personified nations. Its reliance on God to effect the future restoration and prevention of more disasters distinguishes it from the first. Yet the first section presents a much starker picture of desolation in the passages relating to God's punishment (7:13-14), suggesting a recognition of the harshness of the experience of disaster and the abiding hope that someone—perhaps named Joshua—leading an institution like the temple can help the community work to prevent another disaster. The reader who comes to this book having experienced a disaster is unlikely to make any choice at all between these two perspectives.

— ***Steed Vernyl Davidson***

1 In the eighth month, in the second year of
Darius, the word of the LORD came to the
prophet Zechariah son of Berechiah son of Iddo,
saying: 2The LORD was very angry with your
ancestors. 3Therefore say to them, Thus says the
LORD of hosts: Return to me, says the LORD of
hosts, and I will return to you, says the LORD of
hosts. 4Do not be like your ancestors, to whom
the former prophets proclaimed, "Thus says the
LORD of hosts, Return from your evil ways and
from your evil deeds." But they did not hear or
heed me, says the LORD. 5Your ancestors, where

are they? And the prophets, do they live forever?
6But my words and my statutes, which I commanded my servants the prophets, did they not
overtake your ancestors? So they repented and
said, "The LORD of hosts has dealt with us according to our ways and deeds, just as he planned
to do."

7 On the twenty-fourth day of the eleventh
month, the month of Shebat, in the second year
of Darius, the word of the LORD came to the
prophet Zechariah son of Berechiah son of Iddo;
and Zechariah[a] said, 8In the night I saw a man
riding on a red horse! He was standing among
the myrtle trees in the glen; and behind him
were red, sorrel, and white horses. 9Then I said,
"What are these, my lord?" The angel who talked
with me said to me, "I will show you what they
are." 10So the man who was standing among the
myrtle trees answered, "They are those whom the
LORD has sent to patrol the earth." 11Then they
spoke to the angel of the LORD who was standing
among the myrtle trees, "We have patrolled the
earth, and lo, the whole earth remains at peace."
12Then the angel of the LORD said, "O LORD of
hosts, how long will you withhold mercy from
Jerusalem and the cities of Judah, with which you
have been angry these seventy years?" 13Then
the LORD replied with gracious and comforting
words to the angel who talked with me. 14So the
angel who talked with me said to me, Proclaim
this message: Thus says the LORD of hosts; I am
very jealous for Jerusalem and for Zion. 15And I
am extremely angry with the nations that are at
ease; for while I was only a little angry, they made
the disaster worse. 16Therefore, thus says the
LORD, I have returned to Jerusalem with compassion; my house shall be built in it, says the LORD
of hosts, and the measuring line shall be stretched
out over Jerusalem. 17Proclaim further: Thus says
the LORD of hosts: My cities shall again overflow
with prosperity; the LORD will again comfort
Zion and again choose Jerusalem.

18[b] And I looked up and saw four horns.
19I asked the angel who talked with me, "What
are these?" And he answered me, "These are the
horns that have scattered Judah, Israel, and Jerusalem." 20Then the LORD showed me four black-
smiths. 21And I asked, "What are they coming to
do?" He answered, "These are the horns that scattered Judah, so that no head could be raised; but
these have come to terrify them, to strike down
the horns of the nations that lifted up their horns
against the land of Judah to scatter its people."[c]

2 [d] I looked up and saw a man with a measuring line in his hand. 2Then I asked, "Where
are you going?" He answered me, "To measure
Jerusalem, to see what is its width and what is
its length." 3Then the angel who talked with me
came forward, and another angel came forward
to meet him, 4and said to him, "Run, say to that
young man: Jerusalem shall be inhabited like villages without walls, because of the multitude of
people and animals in it. 5For I will be a wall of
fire all around it, says the LORD, and I will be the
glory within it."

6 Up, up! Flee from the land of the north,
says the LORD; for I have spread you abroad like
the four winds of heaven, says the LORD. 7Up! Escape to Zion, you that live with daughter Babylon.

Zechariah 2:6-12

Today many people live away from their homeland because of direct political expulsion or as a result of economic, social, or political necessity. Ancient Judeans living in Egypt, Babylon, and other places where they were scattered envisioned a time of return as seen in 2:6-12. Those who leave their homeland tend to take with them their productive capacities, so a time of return is seen as a period of prosperity. While Jerusalem was never completely depopulated, the image of a city of children and old men and women of "great age" after the return of the exiles appears in 8:4-8. Refugees living in camps around the world share a similar dream of return to their homeland and the time when their land will blossom in prosperity.

— *SVD*

[a] Heb *and he* [b] Ch 2.1 in Heb [c] Heb *it* [d] Ch 2.5 in Heb

8For thus said the LORD of hosts (after his glory[a] sent me) regarding the nations that plundered you: Truly, one who touches you touches the apple of my eye.[b] 9See now, I am going to raise[c] my hand against them, and they shall become plunder for their own slaves. Then you will know that the LORD of hosts has sent me. 10Sing and rejoice, O daughter Zion! For lo, I will come and dwell in your midst, says the LORD. 11Many nations shall join themselves to the LORD on that day, and shall be my people; and I will dwell in your midst. And you shall know that the LORD of hosts has sent me to you. 12The LORD will inherit Judah as his portion in the holy land, and will again choose Jerusalem.

13 Be silent, all people, before the LORD; for he has roused himself from his holy dwelling.

3 Then he showed me the high priest Joshua standing before the angel of the LORD, and Satan[d] standing at his right hand to accuse him. 2And the LORD said to Satan,[d] "The LORD rebuke you, O Satan![d] The LORD who has chosen Jerusalem rebuke you! Is not this man a brand plucked from the fire?" 3Now Joshua was dressed with filthy clothes as he stood before the angel. 4The angel said to those who were standing before him, "Take off his filthy clothes." And to him he said, "See, I have taken your guilt away from you, and I will clothe you with festal apparel." 5And I said, "Let them put a clean turban on his head." So they put a clean turban on his head and clothed him with the apparel; and the angel of the LORD was standing by.

6 Then the angel of the LORD assured Joshua, saying 7"Thus says the LORD of hosts: If you will walk in my ways and keep my requirements, then you shall rule my house and have charge of my courts, and I will give you the right of access among those who are standing here. 8Now listen, Joshua, high priest, you and your colleagues who sit before you! For they are an omen of things to come: I am going to bring my servant the Branch. 9For on the stone that I have set before Joshua, on a single stone with seven facets, I will engrave its inscription, says the LORD of hosts, and I will

Zechariah 3:6

The picture of God in Zechariah includes God as the head with a number of heavenly creatures serving in royal court. Monotheism does not always mean a single deity; at times it includes lesser beings with active roles. Zechariah is helped by different angels to understand the visions he receives. A being named the "angel of the LORD" mediates the divine word to Zechariah (3:6). The two female creatures that remove the basket of idolatry (5:9) are described as having wings. Satan also appears as part of the heavenly court, not as a malevolent being but as the one to validate Joshua in his role. Many people already understand God as leading a number of lesser beings performing specific roles. This idea adds depth to their understanding of God as one who has limitless resources available. While drawn from the ancient world of kings and courts, this idea finds resonance in today's world in the entourage, the posse, or even in joint leadership of communities.

— SVD

remove the guilt of this land in a single day. 10On that day, says the LORD of hosts, you shall invite each other to come under your vine and fig tree."

4 The angel who talked with me came again, and wakened me, as one is wakened from sleep. 2He said to me, "What do you see?" And I said, "I see a lampstand all of gold, with a bowl on the top of it; there are seven lamps on it, with seven lips on each of the lamps that are on the top of it. 3And by it there are two olive trees, one on the right of the bowl and the other on its left." 4I said to the angel who talked with me, "What are these, my lord?" 5Then the angel who talked with me answered me, "Do you not know what these are?" I said, "No, my lord." 6He said to me, "This is the word of the LORD to Zerubbabel: Not by might, nor by power, but by my spirit, says the LORD of hosts. 7What are you, O great mountain? Before Zerubbabel you shall become a plain; and

[a] Cn: Heb *after glory he* [b] Heb *his eye* [c] Or *wave* [d] Or *the Accuser*; Heb *the Adversary*

he shall bring out the top stone amid shouts of
'Grace, grace to it!'"
8 Moreover the word of the LORD came to
me, saying, 9"The hands of Zerubbabel have laid
the foundation of this house; his hands shall also
complete it. Then you will know that the LORD
of hosts has sent me to you. 10For whoever has
despised the day of small things shall rejoice,
and shall see the plummet in the hand of Zerubbabel.
"These seven are the eyes of the LORD, which
range through the whole earth." 11Then I said to
him, "What are these two olive trees on the right
and the left of the lampstand?" 12And a second
time I said to him, "What are these two branches
of the olive trees, which pour out the oil[a] through
the two golden pipes?" 13He said to me, "Do you
not know what these are?" I said, "No, my lord."
14Then he said, "These are the two anointed ones
who stand by the Lord of the whole earth."

5 Again I looked up and saw a flying scroll.
2And he said to me, "What do you see?" I answered, "I see a flying scroll; its length is twenty
cubits, and its width ten cubits." 3Then he said to
me, "This is the curse that goes out over the face
of the whole land; for everyone who steals shall
be cut off according to the writing on one side,
and everyone who swears falsely[b] shall be cut off
according to the writing on the other side. 4I have
sent it out, says the LORD of hosts, and it shall
enter the house of the thief, and the house of anyone who swears falsely by my name; and it shall
abide in that house and consume it, both timber
and stones."
5 Then the angel who talked with me came
forward and said to me, "Look up and see what
this is that is coming out." 6I said, "What is it?"
He said, "This is a basket[c] coming out." And he
said, "This is their iniquity[d] in all the land." 7Then
a leaden cover was lifted, and there was a woman
sitting in the basket![c] 8And he said, "This is Wickedness." So he thrust her back into the basket,[c]
and pressed the leaden weight down on its mouth.
9Then I looked up and saw two women coming
forward. The wind was in their wings; they had
wings like the wings of a stork, and they lifted up
the basket[c] between earth and sky. 10Then I said
to the angel who talked with me, "Where are they
taking the basket?"[c] 11He said to me, "To the land
of Shinar, to build a house for it; and when this
is prepared, they will set the basket[c] down there
on its base."

6 And again I looked up and saw four chariots
coming out from between two mountains—
mountains of bronze. 2The first chariot had red
horses, the second chariot black horses, 3the third
chariot white horses, and the fourth chariot dappled gray[e] horses. 4Then I said to the angel who
talked with me, "What are these, my lord?" 5The
angel answered me, "These are the four winds[f] of
heaven going out, after presenting themselves before the Lord of all the earth. 6The chariot with
the black horses goes toward the north country,
the white ones go toward the west country,[g] and
the dappled ones go toward the south country."
7When the steeds came out, they were impatient
to get off and patrol the earth. And he said, "Go,
patrol the earth." So they patrolled the earth.
8Then he cried out to me, "Lo, those who go toward the north country have set my spirit at rest
in the north country."
9 The word of the LORD came to me: 10Col-
lect silver and gold[h] from the exiles—from Heldai, Tobijah, and Jedaiah—who have arrived
from Babylon; and go the same day to the house
of Josiah son of Zephaniah. 11Take the silver and
gold and make a crown,[i] and set it on the head
of the high priest Joshua son of Jehozadak; 12say
to him: Thus says the LORD of hosts: Here is a
man whose name is Branch: for he shall branch
out in his place, and he shall build the temple of
the LORD. 13It is he that shall build the temple of
the LORD; he shall bear royal honor, and shall sit
upon his throne and rule. There shall be a priest
by his throne, with peaceful understanding between the two of them. 14And the crown[j] shall

[a] Cn: Heb *gold* [b] The word *falsely* added from verse 4 [c] Heb *ephah* [d] Gk Compare Syr: Heb *their eye* [e] Compare Gk: Meaning of Heb uncertain [f] Or *spirits* [g] Cn: Heb *go after them* [h] Cn Compare verse 11: Heb lacks *silver and gold* [i] Gk Mss Syr Tg: Heb *crowns* [j] Gk Syr: Heb *crowns*

Zechariah 6:12

In words directed to Joshua the priest, we read about a futuristic person called "Branch" (3:8; 6:12) whose role will largely be to inaugurate a new era starting with the rebuilding of the temple. This usage of future leader by the name "Branch" links with similar ideas in Jeremiah of a righteous branch (Jer 23:5-6; 33:15-16). In Jeremiah, "Branch" will be a descendant of David playing a restoring role to ensure the reign of justice. In the same way, Isaiah speaks of the "shoot" from Jesse that grows a branch endowed with various spiritual gifts (Isa 11:1-2). Messianic hopes were attached to Davidic descendants who may restore the monarchy and rule with justice. While Zechariah does not speak of "Branch" as a descendant of David, he does picture him as a ruler in keeping with the character of the messiah.

— SVD

be in the care of Heldai,[a] Tobijah, Jedaiah, and
Josiah[b] son of Zephaniah, as a memorial in the
temple of the LORD.
15 Those who are far off shall come and help
to build the temple of the LORD; and you shall
know that the LORD of hosts has sent me to you.
This will happen if you diligently obey the voice
of the LORD your God.
7 In the fourth year of King Darius, the word of
the LORD came to Zechariah on the fourth day
of the ninth month, which is Chislev. 2 Now the
people of Bethel had sent Sharezer and Regem-
melech and their men, to entreat the favor of the
LORD, 3 and to ask the priests of the house of the
LORD of hosts and the prophets, "Should I mourn
and practice abstinence in the fifth month, as I
have done for so many years?" 4 Then the word
of the LORD of hosts came to me: 5 Say to all the
people of the land and the priests: When you
fasted and lamented in the fifth month and in the
seventh, for these seventy years, was it for me that
you fasted? 6 And when you eat and when you
drink, do you not eat and drink only for yourselves? 7 Were not these the words that the LORD
proclaimed by the former prophets, when Jerusalem was inhabited and in prosperity, along with
the towns around it, and when the Negeb and the
Shephelah were inhabited?
8 The word of the LORD came to Zechariah,
saying: 9 Thus says the LORD of hosts: Render
true judgments, show kindness and mercy to
one another; 10 do not oppress the widow, the
orphan, the alien, or the poor; and do not devise
evil in your hearts against one another. 11 But they
refused to listen, and turned a stubborn shoulder, and stopped their ears in order not to hear.
12 They made their hearts adamant in order not to
hear the law and the words that the LORD of hosts
had sent by his spirit through the former prophets. Therefore great wrath came from the LORD
of hosts. 13 Just as, when I[c] called, they would not
hear, so, when they called, I would not hear, says
the LORD of hosts, 14 and I scattered them with
a whirlwind among all the nations that they had
not known. Thus the land they left was desolate,
so that no one went to and fro, and a pleasant land
was made desolate.
8 The word of the LORD of hosts came to me,
saying: 2 Thus says the LORD of hosts: I am
jealous for Zion with great jealousy, and I am jealous for her with great wrath. 3 Thus says the LORD:
I will return to Zion, and will dwell in the midst
of Jerusalem; Jerusalem shall be called the faithful
city, and the mountain of the LORD of hosts shall
be called the holy mountain. 4 Thus says the LORD
of hosts: Old men and old women shall again
sit in the streets of Jerusalem, each with staff in
hand because of their great age. 5 And the streets
of the city shall be full of boys and girls playing
in its streets. 6 Thus says the LORD of hosts: Even
though it seems impossible to the remnant of this
people in these days, should it also seem impossible to me, says the LORD of hosts? 7 Thus says
the LORD of hosts: I will save my people from the
east country and from the west country; 8 and I
will bring them to live in Jerusalem. They shall be
my people and I will be their God, in faithfulness
and in righteousness.

[a] Syr Compare verse 10: Heb *Helem* [b] Syr Compare verse 10: Heb *Hen* [c] Heb *he*

9 Thus says the LORD of hosts: Let your hands
be strong—you that have recently been hearing
these words from the mouths of the prophets
who were present when the foundation was laid
for the rebuilding of the temple, the house of the
LORD of hosts. 10 For before those days there were
no wages for people or for animals, nor was there
any safety from the foe for those who went out or
came in, and I set them all against one another.
11 But now I will not deal with the remnant of this
people as in the former days, says the LORD of
hosts. 12 For there shall be a sowing of peace; the
vine shall yield its fruit, the ground shall give its
produce, and the skies shall give their dew; and I
will cause the remnant of this people to possess
all these things. 13 Just as you have been a cursing among the nations, O house of Judah and
house of Israel, so I will save you and you shall
be a blessing. Do not be afraid, but let your hands
be strong.

14 For thus says the LORD of hosts: Just as I
purposed to bring disaster upon you, when your
ancestors provoked me to wrath, and I did not relent, says the LORD of hosts, 15 so again I have purposed in these days to do good to Jerusalem and
to the house of Judah; do not be afraid. 16 These
are the things that you shall do: Speak the truth
to one another, render in your gates judgments
that are true and make for peace, 17 do not devise
evil in your hearts against one another, and love
no false oath; for all these are things that I hate,
says the LORD.

18 The word of the LORD of hosts came to
me, saying: 19 Thus says the LORD of hosts: The
fast of the fourth month, and the fast of the fifth,
and the fast of the seventh, and the fast of the
tenth, shall be seasons of joy and gladness, and
cheerful festivals for the house of Judah: therefore love truth and peace.

20 Thus says the LORD of hosts: Peoples shall
yet come, the inhabitants of many cities; 21 the
inhabitants of one city shall go to another, saying, "Come, let us go to entreat the favor of the
LORD, and to seek the LORD of hosts; I myself am
going." 22 Many peoples and strong nations shall
come to seek the LORD of hosts in Jerusalem, and
to entreat the favor of the LORD. 23 Thus says the
LORD of hosts: In those days ten men from nations of every language shall take hold of a Jew,
grasping his garment and saying, "Let us go with
you, for we have heard that God is with you."

9

An Oracle.

The word of the LORD is against the land of
Hadrach
and will rest upon Damascus.
For to the LORD belongs the capital[a] of Aram,[b]
as do all the tribes of Israel;
2 Hamath also, which borders on it,
Tyre and Sidon, though they are very wise.
3 Tyre has built itself a rampart,
and heaped up silver like dust,
and gold like the dirt of the streets.
4 But now, the Lord will strip it of its
possessions
and hurl its wealth into the sea,
and it shall be devoured by fire.

5 Ashkelon shall see it and be afraid;
Gaza too, and shall writhe in anguish;
Ekron also, because its hopes are withered.
The king shall perish from Gaza;
Ashkelon shall be uninhabited;
6 a mongrel people shall settle in Ashdod,
and I will make an end of the pride of
Philistia.
7 I will take away its blood from its mouth,
and its abominations from between its
teeth;
it too shall be a remnant for our God;
it shall be like a clan in Judah,
and Ekron shall be like the Jebusites.
8 Then I will encamp at my house as a guard,
so that no one shall march to and fro;
no oppressor shall again overrun them,
for now I have seen with my own eyes.

9 Rejoice greatly, O daughter Zion!
Shout aloud, O daughter Jerusalem!

[a] Heb *eye* [b] Cn: Heb *of Adam* (or *of humankind*)

Lo, your king comes to you;
triumphant and victorious is he,
humble and riding on a donkey,
on a colt, the foal of a donkey.
10 He[a] will cut off the chariot from Ephraim
and the war-horse from Jerusalem;
and the battle bow shall be cut off,
and he shall command peace to the nations;
his dominion shall be from sea to sea,
and from the River to the ends of the earth.

11 As for you also, because of the blood of my covenant with you,
I will set your prisoners free from the waterless pit.
12 Return to your stronghold, O prisoners of hope;
today I declare that I will restore to you double.
13 For I have bent Judah as my bow;
I have made Ephraim its arrow.
I will arouse your sons, O Zion,
against your sons, O Greece,
and wield you like a warrior's sword.

14 Then the LORD will appear over them,
and his arrow go forth like lightning;
the Lord GOD will sound the trumpet
and march forth in the whirlwinds of the south.
15 The LORD of hosts will protect them,
and they shall devour and tread down the slingers;[b]
they shall drink their blood[c] like wine,
and be full like a bowl,
drenched like the corners of the altar.

16 On that day the LORD their God will save them
for they are the flock of his people;
for like the jewels of a crown
they shall shine on his land.
17 For what goodness and beauty are his!
Grain shall make the young men flourish,
and new wine the young women.

10 Ask rain from the LORD
in the season of the spring rain,
from the LORD who makes the storm clouds,
who gives showers of rain to you,[d]
the vegetation in the field to everyone.
2 For the teraphim[e] utter nonsense,
and the diviners see lies;
the dreamers tell false dreams,
and give empty consolation.
Therefore the people wander like sheep;
they suffer for lack of a shepherd.

3 My anger is hot against the shepherds,
and I will punish the leaders;[f]

[a] Gk: Heb *I* [b] Cn: Heb *the slingstones* [c] Gk: Heb *shall drink* [d] Heb *them* [e] Or *household gods* [f] Or *male goats*

Zechariah 10:2-3

As seen in other parts of the Bible, Zechariah uses the image of the shepherd to refer to the leaders of the community such as the king. This usage is also found in other ancient Near Eastern cultures and reflects the idea of leadership and formation of the people into a community. While many connect this notion of the shepherd-leader with David in the Bible, a more powerful connection can be seen with Moses. African Americans view Moses as the paradigm of a national leader who formed a people out of oppression and led them to freedom. For her work on the Underground Railroad, Harriet Tubman was called Moses. Martin Luther King Jr. was called Moses for his leadership in the civil rights movement of the 1960s. Imagine leaders like these failing their roles and you get a sense of the disappointment in Zechariah.

— *SVD*

for the LORD of hosts cares for his flock, the
house of Judah,
and will make them like his proud
war-horse.
4 Out of them shall come the cornerstone,
out of them the tent peg,
out of them the battle bow,
out of them every commander.
5 Together they shall be like warriors in battle,
trampling the foe in the mud of the streets;
they shall fight, for the LORD is with them,
and they shall put to shame the riders on
horses.

6 I will strengthen the house of Judah,
and I will save the house of Joseph.
I will bring them back because I have
compassion on them,
and they shall be as though I had not
rejected them;
for I am the LORD their God and I will
answer them.
7 Then the people of Ephraim shall become
like warriors,
and their hearts shall be glad as with wine.
Their children shall see it and rejoice,
their hearts shall exult in the LORD.

8 I will signal for them and gather them in,
for I have redeemed them,
and they shall be as numerous as they were
before.
9 Though I scattered them among the nations,
yet in far countries they shall remember me,
and they shall rear their children and
return.
10 I will bring them home from the land of
Egypt,
and gather them from Assyria;
I will bring them to the land of Gilead and to
Lebanon,
until there is no room for them.
11 They[a] shall pass through the sea of distress,
and the waves of the sea shall be struck
down,
and all the depths of the Nile dried up.
The pride of Assyria shall be laid low,
and the scepter of Egypt shall depart.
12 I will make them strong in the LORD,
and they shall walk in his name,
says the LORD.

11 Open your doors, O Lebanon,
so that fire may devour your cedars!
2 Wail, O cypress, for the cedar has fallen,
for the glorious trees are ruined!
Wail, oaks of Bashan,
for the thick forest has been felled!
3 Listen, the wail of the shepherds,
for their glory is despoiled!
Listen, the roar of the lions,
for the thickets of the Jordan are
destroyed!

4 Thus said the LORD my God: Be a shepherd
of the flock doomed to slaughter. 5Those who buy
them kill them and go unpunished; and those
who sell them say, "Blessed be the LORD, for I
have become rich"; and their own shepherds have
no pity on them. 6For I will no longer have pity
on the inhabitants of the earth, says the LORD. I
will cause them, every one, to fall each into the
hand of a neighbor, and each into the hand of the
king; and they shall devastate the earth, and I will
deliver no one from their hand.
7 So, on behalf of the sheep merchants, I
became the shepherd of the flock doomed to
slaughter. I took two staffs; one I named Favor,
the other I named Unity, and I tended the sheep.
8In one month I disposed of the three shepherds,
for I had become impatient with them, and they
also detested me. 9So I said, "I will not be your
shepherd. What is to die, let it die; what is to be
destroyed, let it be destroyed; and let those that
are left devour the flesh of one another!" 10I took
my staff Favor and broke it, annulling the covenant that I had made with all the peoples. 11So
it was annulled on that day, and the sheep merchants, who were watching me, knew that it was
the word of the LORD. 12I then said to them, "If it

[a] Gk: Heb *He*

seems right to you, give me my wages; but if not,
keep them." So they weighed out as my wages
thirty shekels of silver. 13 Then the LORD said to
me, "Throw it into the treasury"[a]—this lordly
price at which I was valued by them. So I took
the thirty shekels of silver and threw them into
the treasury[a] in the house of the LORD. 14 Then I
broke my second staff Unity, annulling the family
ties between Judah and Israel.

15 Then the LORD said to me: Take once
more the implements of a worthless shepherd.
16 For I am now raising up in the land a shepherd
who does not care for the perishing, or seek the
wandering,[b] or heal the maimed, or nourish the
healthy,[c] but devours the flesh of the fat ones,
tearing off even their hoofs.

17 Oh, my worthless shepherd,
who deserts the flock!
May the sword strike his arm
and his right eye!
Let his arm be completely withered,
his right eye utterly blinded!

12

An Oracle.

The word of the LORD concerning Israel: Thus
says the LORD, who stretched out the heavens
and founded the earth and formed the human
spirit within: 2 See, I am about to make Jerusalem
a cup of reeling for all the surrounding peoples; it
will be against Judah also in the siege against Jerusalem. 3 On that day I will make Jerusalem a heavy
stone for all the peoples; all who lift it shall grievously hurt themselves. And all the nations of the
earth shall come together against it. 4 On that day,
says the LORD, I will strike every horse with panic,
and its rider with madness. But on the house of
Judah I will keep a watchful eye, when I strike
every horse of the peoples with blindness. 5 Then
the clans of Judah shall say to themselves, "The
inhabitants of Jerusalem have strength through
the LORD of hosts, their God."

6 On that day I will make the clans of Judah
like a blazing pot on a pile of wood, like a flaming torch among sheaves; and they shall devour
to the right and to the left all the surrounding
peoples, while Jerusalem shall again be inhabited
in its place, in Jerusalem.

7 And the LORD will give victory to the tents
of Judah first, that the glory of the house of David
and the glory of the inhabitants of Jerusalem may
not be exalted over that of Judah. 8 On that day
the LORD will shield the inhabitants of Jerusalem so that the feeblest among them on that day
shall be like David, and the house of David shall
be like God, like the angel of the LORD, at their
head. 9 And on that day I will seek to destroy all
the nations that come against Jerusalem.

10 And I will pour out a spirit of compassion and supplication on the house of David and
the inhabitants of Jerusalem, so that, when they
look on the one[d] whom they have pierced, they
shall mourn for him, as one mourns for an only
child, and weep bitterly over him, as one weeps
over a firstborn. 11 On that day the mourning in
Jerusalem will be as great as the mourning for
Hadad-rimmon in the plain of Megiddo. 12 The
land shall mourn, each family by itself; the family
of the house of David by itself, and their wives by

Zechariah 12:12-14

Zechariah presents a list of families that will mourn for the pierced one. This list is further separated to give attention to women mourners. While this may indicate a special role for women in mourning in the ancient world and some cultures, it also suggests the unequal burden carried by women for the stability of the community. Some think that as bearers of children, women feel the pain of death much more closely than men and the loss this implies for the community. In frontier communities women take on the task of ensuring the growth of more members and therefore become critically involved in the experience of death, even when it is not their own child. In these communities women's leadership remains valued and critical.

— SVD

[a] Syr: Heb *it to the potter* [b] Syr Compare Gk Vg: Heb *the youth* [c] Meaning of Heb uncertain [d] Heb *on me*

themselves; the family of the house of Nathan by
itself, and their wives by themselves; 13 the family
of the house of Levi by itself, and their wives by
themselves; the family of the Shimeites by itself,
and their wives by themselves; 14 and all the families that are left, each by itself, and their wives by
themselves.

13 On that day a fountain shall be opened
for the house of David and the inhabitants of Jerusalem, to cleanse them from sin and
impurity.

2 On that day, says the LORD of hosts, I will
cut off the names of the idols from the land, so
that they shall be remembered no more; and also
I will remove from the land the prophets and the
unclean spirit. 3 And if any prophets appear again,
their fathers and mothers who bore them will say
to them, "You shall not live, for you speak lies
in the name of the LORD"; and their fathers and
their mothers who bore them shall pierce them
through when they prophesy. 4 On that day the
prophets will be ashamed, every one, of their visions when they prophesy; they will not put on
a hairy mantle in order to deceive, 5 but each of
them will say, "I am no prophet, I am a tiller of the
soil; for the land has been my possession[a] since
my youth." 6 And if anyone asks them, "What are
these wounds on your chest?"[b] the answer will
be "The wounds I received in the house of my
friends."

7 "Awake, O sword, against my shepherd,
against the man who is my associate,"
says the LORD of hosts.
Strike the shepherd, that the sheep may be
scattered;
I will turn my hand against the little ones.
8 In the whole land, says the LORD,
two-thirds shall be cut off and perish,
and one-third shall be left alive.
9 And I will put this third into the fire,
refine them as one refines silver,
and test them as gold is tested.
They will call on my name,
and I will answer them.
I will say, "They are my people";
and they will say, "The LORD is our God."

14 See, a day is coming for the LORD, when
the plunder taken from you will be divided in your midst. 2 For I will gather all the
nations against Jerusalem to battle, and the city
shall be taken and the houses looted and the
women raped; half the city shall go into exile, but
the rest of the people shall not be cut off from
the city. 3 Then the LORD will go forth and fight
against those nations as when he fights on a day
of battle. 4 On that day his feet shall stand on the
Mount of Olives, which lies before Jerusalem on
the east; and the Mount of Olives shall be split
in two from east to west by a very wide valley; so
that one half of the Mount shall withdraw northward, and the other half southward. 5 And you
shall flee by the valley of the LORD's mountain,[c]
for the valley between the mountains shall reach
to Azal;[d] and you shall flee as you fled from the
earthquake in the days of King Uzziah of Judah.
Then the LORD my God will come, and all the
holy ones with him.

6 On that day there shall not be[e] either cold
or frost.[f] 7 And there shall be continuous day (it is
known to the LORD), not day and not night, for at
evening time there shall be light.

8 On that day living waters shall flow out
from Jerusalem, half of them to the eastern sea
and half of them to the western sea; it shall continue in summer as in winter.

9 And the LORD will become king over all the
earth; on that day the LORD will be one and his
name one.

10 The whole land shall be turned into a
plain from Geba to Rimmon south of Jerusalem.
But Jerusalem shall remain aloft on its site from
the Gate of Benjamin to the place of the former
gate, to the Corner Gate, and from the Tower of
Hananel to the king's wine presses. 11 And it shall
be inhabited, for never again shall it be doomed
to destruction; Jerusalem shall abide in security.

[a] Cn: Heb *for humankind has caused me to possess* [b] Heb *wounds between your hands* [c] Heb *my mountains* [d] Meaning of Heb uncertain [e] Cn: Heb *there shall not be light* [f] Compare Gk Syr Vg Tg: Meaning of Heb uncertain

12 This shall be the plague with which the
LORD will strike all the peoples that wage war
against Jerusalem: their flesh shall rot while
they are still on their feet; their eyes shall rot in
their sockets, and their tongues shall rot in their
mouths. 13 On that day a great panic from the
LORD shall fall on them, so that each will seize the
hand of a neighbor, and the hand of the one will
be raised against the hand of the other; 14 even Judah will fight at Jerusalem. And the wealth of all
the surrounding nations shall be collected—gold,
silver, and garments in great abundance. 15 And
a plague like this plague shall fall on the horses,
the mules, the camels, the donkeys, and whatever
animals may be in those camps.

16 Then all who survive of the nations that
have come against Jerusalem shall go up year after year to worship the King, the LORD of hosts,
and to keep the festival of booths.[a] 17 If any of the
families of the earth do not go up to Jerusalem
to worship the King, the LORD of hosts, there
will be no rain upon them. 18 And if the family of
Egypt do not go up and present themselves, then
on them shall[b] come the plague that the LORD
inflicts on the nations that do not go up to keep
the festival of booths.[a] 19 Such shall be the punishment of Egypt and the punishment of all the
nations that do not go up to keep the festival of
booths.[a]

20 On that day there shall be inscribed on the
bells of the horses, "Holy to the LORD." And the
cooking pots in the house of the LORD shall be
as holy as[c] the bowls in front of the altar; 21 and
every cooking pot in Jerusalem and Judah shall be
sacred to the LORD of hosts, so that all who sacrifice may come and use them to boil the flesh of
the sacrifice. And there shall no longer be traders[d]
in the house of the LORD of hosts on that day.

[a] Or *tabernacles*; Heb *succoth* [b] Gk Syr: Heb *shall not* [c] Heb *shall be like* [d] Or *Canaanites*

Malachi

The Book of Malachi is the last of the twelve Minor Prophets (Hosea–Malachi) in the Christian Bible, called simply the Book of the Twelve in the Hebrew Bible. It was most probably written after the reconstruction of the Temple in 516 BCE and before or during the time of the reforms of Ezra and Nehemiah around 450. One reason for this dating is that the word "governor" in 1:8 seems to indicate the postexilic Persian period and is also used in Hag 1:1, 14; 2:2, 21 and Neh 5:14, which were also written during this period. Another is the reference to the degeneration of temple worship, which seems to imply that the system must have been in place for a while. A third reason is that Malachi shares some common themes with Ezra-Nehemiah, namely, intermarriage with foreign women, tithing, and social injustices.

The name Malachi means "my [God's] messenger." And, more than a proper name, it may represent an anonymous prophet who speaks in the name of YHWH, the God of Israel. Therefore, the message is more important than the messenger.

The book begins: "An oracle. The word of the LORD to Israel by Malachi" (1:1). It ends with the announcement of the coming of the day of the LORD (4:1-3). That is followed by two postscripts (4:4, 5-6) that were perhaps added by the book's final editor. Most of the book consists of six oracles (1:1-5; 1:6—2:9; 2:10-16; 2:17—3:5; 3:6-12; and 3:13—4:3) in the form of disputations between God on the one hand and the priests and people on the other. Each disputation consists of a question that is misunderstood by the ones being addressed. This in turn leads to a divine answer to the original question. This answer includes a rebuke and a promise of judgment.

Malachi is written for a postexilic community experiencing deep divisions. Those in charge of the leadership—priests and powerful people—are forgetting their responsibilities and acting in ways that advance their own agendas. The priests are accepting sacrifices of lesser quality and perhaps using the good animals for their own benefit (1:7-8). The rich and affluent are divorcing their Jewish wives and entering into marital agreements with the leading families of the surrounding territories for economic self-aggrandizement (2:10-16). People are holding back their tithes, jeopardizing the temple's function as a center of redistribution of food for the poor (3:8-10). In the process, laborers are defrauded of their wages, widows and orphans are being oppressed, aliens are deprived of justice (3:5), and women are the objects of violence through unjust divorces (2:16). And the most astonishing thing is that the leaders of the people are surprised when God disputes with them and accuses them of all these things. They even wonder where the God of justice is (2:17). Therefore the prophet announces a day of retribution and judgment when God will come to the temple to purify the priesthood and make sure that the people will bring the appropriate offerings. On that day God will also secure a group of faithful ones who revere the LORD's name. The new age, which will dawn after God's coming, will be anticipated by the coming of the prophet Elijah. This text became important for the writers of the New Testament, who saw in John the Baptist the fulfillment of this prophecy.

The first readers of this text were imperial subjects of Persia. Judah was ruled by a governor, appointed by the Persian Empire, who extracted tribute from the people (1:8). At the same time the temple system required sacrifices and tithes. People were caught between two loyalties, the empire and the God of Israel. Some, the priests and the powerful, skirted their covenantal responsibilities by trying to shortchange God. The rest of the people, perhaps the majority, were the victims of this game of trying to please two masters. But God takes the side of these oppressed men and women and promises to come in judgment (3:5).

The book of Malachi presents a big challenge for today's readers: how can one fulfill one's responsibilities toward God and neighbor when one lives in the midst of an empire that demands total allegiance? Is it possible to live in the empire and at the same time be faithful to God? The Bible offers us positive examples of people who were able to do that, such as Daniel, Jesus, and Paul. The book of Malachi represents a negative example, for the people being indicted here were unable to remain faithful to God. It should serve the reader as a warning and a challenge.

I was born in Argentina and now live and teach in the United States. I live daily the tension between allegiance to God and to the society I have chosen. It is a difficult task, for I many times find myself doing the same things the priests and people of Malachi's community did. Like many of us, I tend to accommodate, and to break faith with God and with those to whom I am accountable. The book of Malachi serves as a powerful reminder of what God expects of us. It announces with a clear voice that the consequence of being unfaithful to God is that innocent people suffer. My faithfulness, or lack of it, has social repercussions.

— ***Osvaldo D. Vena***

1 An oracle. The word of the LORD to Israel by
Malachi.[a]

2 I have loved you, says the LORD. But you
say, "How have you loved us?" Is not Esau Jacob's
brother? says the LORD. Yet I have loved Jacob
3 but I have hated Esau; I have made his hill country
a desolation and his heritage a desert for jackals.
4 If Edom says, "We are shattered but we will
rebuild the ruins," the LORD of hosts says: They
may build, but I will tear down, until they are
called the wicked country, the people with whom
the LORD is angry forever.
5 Your own eyes shall
see this, and you shall say, "Great is the LORD beyond
the borders of Israel!"

6 A son honors his father, and servants their
master. If then I am a father, where is the honor
due me? And if I am a master, where is the respect
due me? says the LORD of hosts to you,
O priests, who despise my name. You say, "How

[a] Or *by my messenger*

have we despised your name?” 7By offering polluted food on my altar. And you say, “How have
we polluted it?”[a] By thinking that the LORD’s
table may be despised. 8When you offer blind
animals in sacrifice, is that not wrong? And when
you offer those that are lame or sick, is that not
wrong? Try presenting that to your governor; will
he be pleased with you or show you favor? says
the LORD of hosts. 9And now implore the favor
of God, that he may be gracious to us. The fault
is yours. Will he show favor to any of you? says
the LORD of hosts. 10Oh, that someone among
you would shut the temple[b] doors, so that you
would not kindle fire on my altar in vain! I have
no pleasure in you, says the LORD of hosts, and I
will not accept an offering from your hands. 11For
from the rising of the sun to its setting my name
is great among the nations, and in every place incense is offered to my name, and a pure offering;
for my name is great among the nations, says the
LORD of hosts. 12But you profane it when you say
that the Lord’s table is polluted, and the food for
it[c] may be despised. 13“What a weariness this is,”
you say, and you sniff at me,[d] says the LORD of
hosts. You bring what has been taken by violence
or is lame or sick, and this you bring as your offering! Shall I accept that from your hand? says the
LORD. 14Cursed be the cheat who has a male in
the flock and vows to give it, and yet sacrifices to
the Lord what is blemished; for I am a great King,
says the LORD of hosts, and my name is rever-
enced among the nations.

2 And now, O priests, this command is for you.
2If you will not listen, if you will not lay it to
heart to give glory to my name, says the LORD of
hosts, then I will send the curse on you and I will
curse your blessings; indeed I have already cursed
them,[e] because you do not lay it to heart. 3I will
rebuke your offspring, and spread dung on your
faces, the dung of your offerings, and I will put
you out of my presence.[f]

4 Know, then, that I have sent this command
to you, that my covenant with Levi may hold, says
the LORD of hosts. 5My covenant with him was a
covenant of life and well-being, which I gave him;
this called for reverence, and he revered me and
stood in awe of my name. 6True instruction was in
his mouth, and no wrong was found on his lips. He
walked with me in integrity and uprightness, and
he turned many from iniquity. 7For the lips of a
priest should guard knowledge, and people should
seek instruction from his mouth, for he is the messenger of the LORD of hosts. 8But you have turned
aside from the way; you have caused many to
stumble by your instruction; you have corrupted
the covenant of Levi, says the LORD of hosts, 9and
so I make you despised and abased before all the
people, inasmuch as you have not kept my ways
but have shown partiality in your instruction.

10 Have we not all one father? Has not one
God created us? Why then are we faithless to one
another, profaning the covenant of our ancestors?
11Judah has been faithless, and abomination has
been committed in Israel and in Jerusalem; for
Judah has profaned the sanctuary of the LORD,
which he loves, and has married the daughter of
a foreign god. 12May the LORD cut off from the
tents of Jacob anyone who does this—any to
witness[g] or answer, or to bring an offering to the
LORD of hosts.

13 And this you do as well: You cover the
LORD’s altar with tears, with weeping and groaning because he no longer regards the offering
or accepts it with favor at your hand. 14You ask,
“Why does he not?” Because the LORD was a witness between you and the wife of your youth, to
whom you have been faithless, though she is your
companion and your wife by covenant. 15Did not
one God make her?[h] Both flesh and spirit are his.[i]
And what does the one God[j] desire? Godly offspring. So look to yourselves, and do not let anyone be faithless to the wife of his youth. 16For I
hate[k] divorce, says the LORD, the God of Israel,
and covering one’s garment with violence, says
the LORD of hosts. So take heed to yourselves and
do not be faithless.

[a] Gk: Heb *you* [b] Heb lacks *temple* [c] Compare Syr Tg: Heb *its fruit, its food* [d] Another reading is *at it* [e] Heb *it*
[f] Cn Compare Gk Syr: Heb *and he shall bear you to it* [g] Cn Compare Gk: Heb *arouse* [h] Or *Has not he made one?*
[i] Cn: Heb *and a remnant of spirit was his* [j] Heb *he* [k] Cn: Heb *he hates*

17 You have wearied the LORD with your
words. Yet you say, "How have we wearied him?"
By saying, "All who do evil are good in the sight of
the LORD, and he delights in them." Or by asking,
"Where is the God of justice?"

3 See, I am sending my messenger to prepare
the way before me, and the Lord whom you
seek will suddenly come to his temple. The messenger of the covenant in whom you delight—indeed, he is coming, says the LORD of hosts. 2But
who can endure the day of his coming, and who
can stand when he appears?

For he is like a refiner's fire and like fullers'
soap; 3he will sit as a refiner and purifier of silver,
and he will purify the descendants of Levi and refine them like gold and silver, until they present
offerings to the LORD in righteousness.[a] 4Then
the offering of Judah and Jerusalem will be pleasing to the LORD as in the days of old and as in
former years.

5 Then I will draw near to you for judgment; I
will be swift to bear witness against the sorcerers,
against the adulterers, against those who swear
falsely, against those who oppress the hired workers in their wages, the widow and the orphan,
against those who thrust aside the alien, and do
not fear me, says the LORD of hosts.

6 For I the LORD do not change; therefore
you, O children of Jacob, have not perished.
7Ever since the days of your ancestors you have
turned aside from my statutes and have not kept
them. Return to me, and I will return to you, says
the LORD of hosts. But you say, "How shall we
return?"

8 Will anyone rob God? Yet you are robbing
me! But you say, "How are we robbing you?" In
your tithes and offerings! 9You are cursed with a
curse, for you are robbing me—the whole nation
of you! 10Bring the full tithe into the storehouse,
so that there may be food in my house, and thus
put me to the test, says the LORD of hosts; see if I
will not open the windows of heaven for you and
pour down for you an overflowing blessing. 11I
will rebuke the locust[b] for you, so that it will not
destroy the produce of your soil; and your vine
in the field shall not be barren, says the LORD of
hosts. 12Then all nations will count you happy,
for you will be a land of delight, says the LORD
of hosts.

13 You have spoken harsh words against me,
says the LORD. Yet you say, "How have we spoken
against you?" 14You have said, "It is vain to serve
God. What do we profit by keeping his command
or by going about as mourners before the LORD
of hosts? 15Now we count the arrogant happy;
evildoers not only prosper, but when they put
God to the test they escape."

16 Then those who revered the LORD spoke
with one another. The LORD took note and listened, and a book of remembrance was written
before him of those who revered the LORD and
thought on his name. 17They shall be mine, says
the LORD of hosts, my special possession on the
day when I act, and I will spare them as parents
spare their children who serve them. 18Then
once more you shall see the difference between

Malachi 3:5

Since the beginning of the Anglo-American conquest, the Mexicans have been systematically insulted, dehumanised, exploited, segregated, abused, oppressed and massacred.... All the institutions, including the United States churches, have worked together to systematically discredit and destroy anything Mexican. Popular literature has continually portrayed the Mexican as a lazy, drunken, dumb, good-for-nothing subhuman race. The churches have strengthened this negative view by looking upon the faith expressions of the people as uninformed, superstitious and childish.... Economic institutions have exploited the Mexican American workers and political institutions have kept the people from participation.... The sweat, broken backs and lives of the exploited Mexican workers have been the life-source of much of the wealth of this country. Yet the very powers which have exploited the people and become rich through their work, have discredited them as lazy, unreliable and irresponsible.[63]

— ***Virgil Elizondo***

[a] Or *right offerings to the LORD* [b] Heb *devourer*

the righteous and the wicked, between one who
serves God and one who does not serve him.

4 [a] See, the day is coming, burning like an oven,
when all the arrogant and all evildoers will
be stubble; the day that comes shall burn them
up, says the LORD of hosts, so that it will leave
them neither root nor branch. 2 But for you who
revere my name the sun of righteousness shall
rise, with healing in its wings. You shall go out
leaping like calves from the stall. 3 And you shall
tread down the wicked, for they will be ashes under the soles of your feet, on the day when I act,
says the LORD of hosts.

4 Remember the teaching of my servant
Moses, the statutes and ordinances that I commanded him at Horeb for all Israel.

5 Lo, I will send you the prophet Elijah
before the great and terrible day of the LORD
comes. 6 He will turn the hearts of parents to
their children and the hearts of children to their
parents, so that I will not come and strike the
land with a curse.[b]

[a] Ch 4.1–6 are Ch 3.19–24 in Heb [b] Or *a ban of utter destruction*

Gallery

The Bible at the Crossroads of Cultures

In the 1960s and 70s, the Biblical Theology and narrative theology movements proposed reading the Bible as the ongoing story of "the people of God." The Liturgical Movement in Europe and North America reshaped worship in many Christian churches around themes of this people's journey through history.

In this same period, however, biblical scholars drew critical attention to thematic disagreements, breaks, and dislocations in the biblical narratives. The Christian presumption to inherit the legacy of "the people of God" was challenged by Jews and Christians alike in the wake of the Shoah (or Holocaust). And other theological voices—including feminist, Black and Latin-American liberation theologians, Asian and Native American theologians, and postcolonial critics from outside Europe and North America—questioned the construct of a single unified "people of God." What did it mean—what can it mean—to speak of "the people of God" given disparities of wealth, power, and privilege among the world's peoples today? The images presented here serve not to answer that question but to bring its various dimensions into sharper focus.

(detail)

Fig. 1

Ethnicity in the ancient world. Differences among peoples were recognized and emphasized in the ancient near east. In these details from an Egyptian mural from the Middle Kingdom (nineteenth century BCE), a variety of peoples request entry into Egypt for trade and food. The artisans, hunters, and herders depicted in brightly colored robes are variously identified today as "Semitic," "Asiatic," or "Hebrew" immigrants from Palestine, seeking Egyptian grain: compare the biblical accounts of Abraham (Gen. 12:10-11) and Joseph and his brothers (41:53–42:5).

Fig. 2

Ethnic differences were emphasized by empires concerned to catalog the variety of peoples subservient to them or dependent on them. Here a Nubian and an Asiatic prisoner are painted on the soles of a pair of sandals crafted in the Egyptian New Kingdom. The person who wore these sandals might have imagined the figures looking at each other in consternation; others might have seen a glance of recognition and solidarity.

Christian mission and evangelization have often gone hand in hand with European colonization of other lands and slavery in the Americas. This has meant that the Bible has often been introduced to a people—or imposed upon them—as if it were the possession of the colonizing or enslaving power. It is all the more remarkable, therefore, that characters, episodes, and themes in the Bible have been embraced by so many peoples as part of their own experience and heritage, as the following images show.

Fig. 3

Pictorial Bible Quilt, 1898. Born a slave in Georgia in 1837, Harriet Powers depicts scenes from the Bible in this piece. Powers's quilts are among the best known and best preserved examples of the quilting tradition in the U.S. South.

The Finding of Moses, 2004. Chinese artist He Qi renders the discovery of the future deliverer of Hebrew slaves as a moment of serenity and stately elegance in Pharaoh's court.

Fig. 4

Grapes of Canaan, 1983, by Sadao Watanabe (1913–1996), whose father converted to Christianity in the face of government persecution, mastered traditional Japanese printmaking in order to convey biblical narratives—here, the story of the Hebrew spies returning from Canaan (Joshua 2)—in indigenous Japanese style.

Fig. 5

Fig. 6

Sheba and Solomon. As the Book of Acts makes clear, Jesus' apostles traveled south, to Africa, as well as west, across the Mediterranean to Europe. But Ethiopia's biblical heritage is much more ancient. Here the meeting of Solomon and the Queen of Sheba is illustrated on pages from an illuminated nineteenth century manuscript of "The History of the Queen of Sheba" (Ge'ez and Amharic).

Song of Solomon, 2004. The amorous poetry of the Song of Solomon, addressed by an anonymous lover to his beloved, attracts contemporary interest as well. Interestingly, Chinese artist He Qi depicts the male lover as darker-skinned, though in the text it is the woman who declares "I am black and beautiful" (1:5).

Fig. 7

Nativity, 1993, by Chinese artist Lu Lan. As events in the life of Jesus have been portrayed through many eyes, Jesus and his family have been depicted as members of many cultures. Of course, the "classical" Christian art of medieval Europe did nothing less.

Fig. 8

Feeding of the 5,000, 1999. Of Antiguan heritage, New York artist Laura James incorporates motifs and styles from Ethiopian art and iconography into her work.

Fig. 9

The Last Supper, 1973. Sadao Watanabe understood the social world of biblical cultures but used Japanese images—sushi at the last supper, for example—to indigenize biblical episodes. Here Jesus and his disciples eat while seated on the floor, in traditional Japanese style (and as Jesus and his disciples likely did as well).

Fig. 10

Peter Repentant. An African Peter feels remorse for his denial of Christ; an African Mary and John look on, in an illustration from a late-seventeenth-century manuscript of the Gospels and other scriptures from Gondar in Ethiopia.

Fig. 11

Mount Calvary, 1944. William H. Johnson (1901–1970) developed a "folk" style to represent the distinctive intensity of African American religious experience.

Fig. 12

Golgotha, 1945, by one of the leading artists of the Harlem Renaissance, Romare Bearden (1911–1988), bristles with weapons that echo the angular lines of cross and crucified.

Fig. 13

Mother and Son, 2001, by Jamaican-born Michael Escoffery, offers a realistic portrait of a black Christ and his mother. The style of some of Escoffery's other works is sometimes compared with that of Amedeo Modigliani—whose modernist style owed much in turn to the European and North American discovery of traditional African art.

Fig. 14

Fig. 15

Pieta, c. 1912, by German artist Käthe Kollwitz (1867–1945). Though the genre of the Pieta usually depicts a grieving Mary holding the body of her dead son, this Pieta is one of a number of Kollwitz's sculptures and paintings depicting parents holding their dead children—here, a daughter. A large replica of another of Kollwitz's sculptures, *Mother with Her Dead Son,* is featured in Berlin's Neue Wache, a monument "to Victims of War and Tyranny."

Fig. 16

An Ethnic Jesus. Perhaps the best known and widely reproduced image of Jesus in the twentieth century, with over one billion reproductions mass-marketed around the world, Warner Sallman's *Head of Christ* (1940) depicts a serene Jesus with light skin, blue eyes, fair hair, and decidedly northern-European features. When Sallman painted more contemporary versions in the 1960s, he was concerned (as were his critics) that the portrait of Jesus not look too "feminine."[64] For a discussion of this and the following images see the article "Jesus and Cultures."

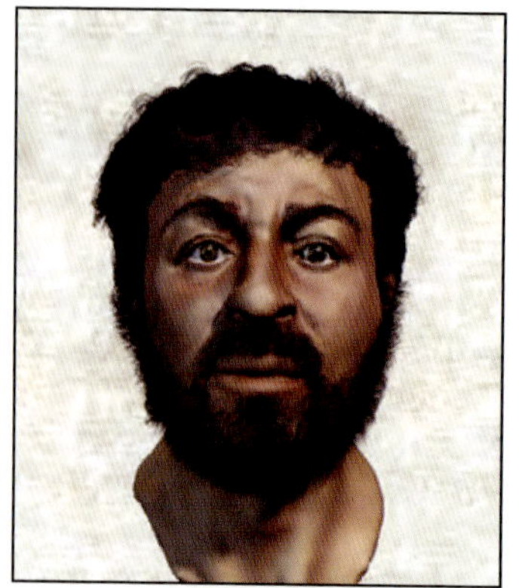

Fig. 17

A Scientific Reconstruction. The December 2002 issue of *Popular Mechanics* offered a portrait of Jesus created by forensic anthropologist Richard Neave, in its article "The Real Face of Jesus." Neave sought to base his image of Jesus on an objective, scientific basis rather than on the cultural predispositions of artists' imaginations. He relied on archaeological discoveries of Galilean skeletons from the first century CE, since according to the Gospels, Jesus' appearance was so similar to that of his disciples that he had to be singled out by Judas Iscariot (Matt. 26:48-50 and parallels).

Fig. 18

Jesus of the People, 1999. Artist Janet McKenzie sought in her portrait to depict a Jesus widely representative of the world's people, especially the poor. The image incorporates symbols from Asian and Native American cultures; the model was an African-American woman. "The essence of the work," McKenzie declared, "is that Jesus is all of us." The portrait won the National Catholic Reporter Jesus 2000 competition; the judge wrote, "this is a haunting image of a peasant Jesus—dark, thick-lipped, looking out on us with ineffable dignity, with sadness but with confidence."

Fig. 19

The earliest pictures of Jesus were very different from the images to which we are accustomed today. In a typical portrait from a fresco in the Roman catacomb of St. Priscilla (first to third century CE), Jesus is portrayed as a beardless youth surrounded by sheep. The portrait depicts Jesus as the Good Shepherd of John 8:11, but similar frescos showing Jesus with a lyre may allude as well to the biblical image of David—or to Orpheus, a figure from Greek mythology associated with the afterlife.

Fig. 20

Still beardless, Jesus is depicted in this third-century mosaic in St. Peter's Basilica, Rome, driving his chariot across the sky, in the figure of the sun god Apollo.

Fig. 21

The style of portrait with which we are more familiar today—a bearded Jesus with long dark hair, parted in the center, seated on a heavenly throne and wielding a scepter as *Pantocrator* ("all-ruler")—first arose in the Christian Byzantine Empire, and reflects the fashion of the Byzantine court; Pantocrator was originally one of the titles of the Roman Emperor. This sixth-century mosaic is from the Church of St. Apollinare Nuovo, Ravenna.

Fig. 22

Devon Cunningham's *Black Jesus* (1995) features a Black Christ as the heavenly Pantocrator ("All-Ruler") of Byzantine art. Mural at St. Cecilia's Catholic Church, Detroit.

Although it is often easy for those who enjoy privilege and power to read the Bible as depicting a distant, ancient time, the peoples who make up the world's majority readily recognize biblical themes—such as crucifixion—as names for the historical realities they have themselves experienced. The following images depict such historical events. Can we understand the Bible differently by trying to see through the eyes of others?

Migration. Judaism, Christianity, and Islam find their shared ancestor in Abraham, described in the Bible as a "wandering Aramean" (Deut 26:5) who, in faith, left his family home in Ur and crossed national boundaries in search of a new home (Gen 12:1-4). Though historical migrations are often triggered by natural calamities (earthquake, famine) or political ones (war, economic deprivation, political oppression)—or, often, both—those who strike out, leaving homes and families behind, inevitably do so in hope that a better future lies ahead.

Here families who have lost their land to drought and bank foreclosure flee the Dust Bowl of the Midwest to travel westward (1939).

Fig. 23

During and after so-called counterinsurgency wars in Central America in the 1970s and 1980s and the economic hardship that followed, many Mexican and Central American men and women migrated to the United States, where they took work at low wages that many U.S. citizens disdained. Here Mexican migrant workers sort vegetables in California.

Fig. 24

Exile. The exile of much of the population of Judah following the Babylonian conquest of Jerusalem was one of most traumatic events in Israel's history, and one of the most formative for its traditions. Contemporary peoples also remember, and have been shaped by, specific experiences of Exile. How do these experiences shape their reading of the Bible?

Fig. 25

Cherokee Trail of Tears, 2001, by Cherokee artist John Guthrie. The Trail of Tears was a forced march in which the U.S. Army displaced the Cherokee from their native lands in the state of Georgia to the Oklahoma Territory in 1838. Some five thousand men, women, and children died on the Trail.

During World War II, Japanese-American families and individuals were compelled to board buses headed for forced internment camps in California and (here) Washington.

Fig. 26

Crucifixion. Images of those who have suffered abuse, torture, and death at the hands of military powers have for many people become contemporary icons of justice denied.

In 1917, Charlemagne Peralte, leader of the Haitian resistance to the U.S. invasion of Haiti, was killed by a Marine officer who came to his camp under guise of seeking to negotiate a truce; the Marines distributed photographs of his body tied to a door as a warning to others. The image of "Peralte crucified" instead became a rallying symbol of Haitian independence.

Fig. 27

On March 24, 1980, Salvadoran Archbishop Oscar Romero was assassinated while celebrating the Eucharist. Weeks earlier he had written an open letter to U.S. President Jimmy Carter asking that the flow of weapons to the Salvadoran military be cut off. Days before his death, he had called on the members of the armed forces to "stop the repression" of their brothers and sisters. Nine years later, Salvadoran theologian Ignacio Ellacuría and several of his Jesuit brothers were assassinated by a unit of the Salvadoran National Guard on November 16, 1989. Like Archbishop Oscar Romero before them, their deaths—but more importantly, their lives—came to symbolize the shared destiny of the Salvadoran people.

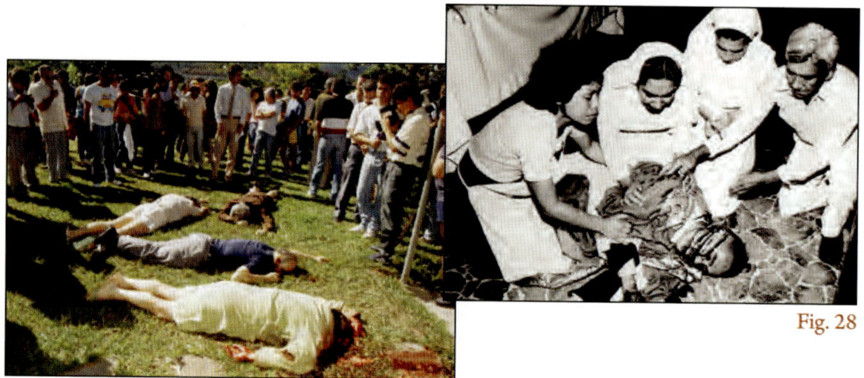

Fig. 28

Fig. 29

Shortly before his death, Ellacuría wrote:

If we are to understand what the people of God is, it is very important that we open our eyes to the reality around us. . . . This reality is simply the existence of a vast portion of humankind, which is literally and actually crucified by natural oppressions and especially by historical and personal oppressions. . . . The historically crucified people which remains constant although the historical forms of crucifixion are different . . . is the historical continuation of the servant of Yahweh, whose humanity is still being disfigured by the sin of the world, whom the powers of this world are still stripping of everything, taking away everything including his life, especially his life.[65]

Deliverance. Despite the energy with which slave owners in the southern U.S. sought to indoctrinate their slaves with the Christian duty to obey their masters, slaves heard another message in the Bible: that the God of the Exodus opposed slavery and willed the freedom of all people. Participants in the "underground railroad"—depicted here in a contemporary engraving—understood their efforts as a participation in a new Exodus.

Fig. 30

Fig. 31

Following World War II, the partition of Berlin into Western and Eastern sectors was for decades an occasion of misery. Even after the Wall was erected, East Germans attempted to flee to the West; refugees were often discovered, arrested, and even killed at the border. If they succeeded, their first stop was one of West Germany's refugee camps, as for this family of eight in 1962.

The wall's destruction in November 1989 was an event of public celebration around the world.

Fig. 32

Hope. One of the most enduring messages in the Bible is of hope for the human future.

Another episode of what Barbara Ehrenreich describes as the long history of "collective joy"[66] at moments of deliverance was the first election in South Africa in which blacks could vote, in 1994. The election ended decades of racial apartheid in that country.

Fig. 33

Jesus' last supper with his disciples and the theme of his self-sacrificial action are at the heart of much Christian memory and practice. The language of sacrifice has often been used harmfully, however, to elicit self-denial and renunciation from those from whom much has already been taken. Historians, theologians, and worship leaders point to a deeper wealth of symbolism surrounding the Lord's Supper or Eucharist: Israel's remembrance of liberation in the Passover meal; the miraculous provision of food—manna in the wilderness; bread and meal for a widow and her son in the days of Elijah; Isaiah's vision of the world's peoples gathered for a feast on a sacred mountain; and Jesus' own presence at wedding feasts and at the tables of those considered outcasts or notorious sinners.

Fig. 34

In *The First Supper*, 1989, Jane Evershed depicts a dinner gathering of diverse women—Native American, African, Asian, Chicano, Latino, Muslim and Jew—brought together by compassion, respect for the earth, and mutual empowerment. The painting accompanies a poem that reads, in part, "It is not too late for us to make a new world together."

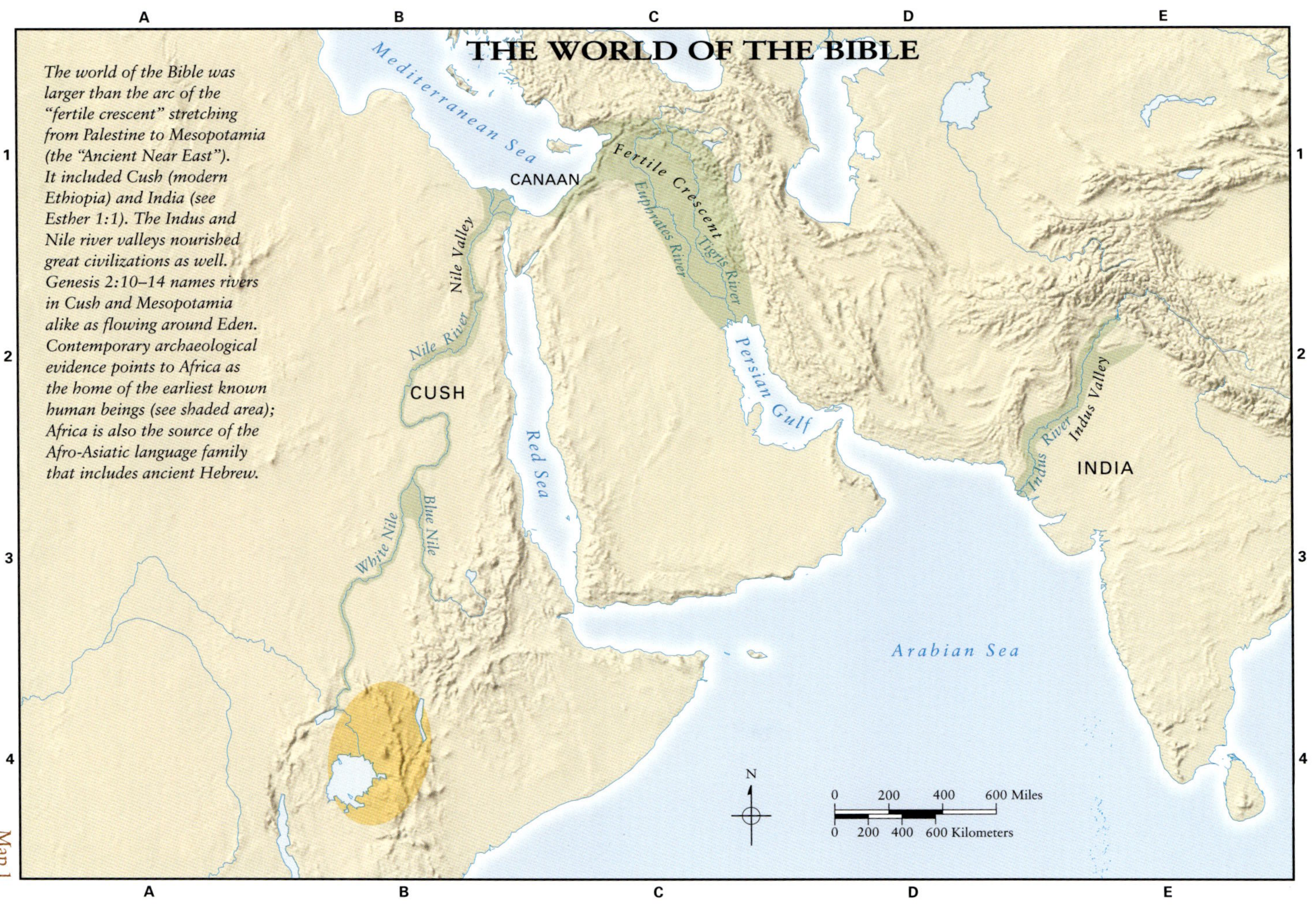
THE WORLD OF THE BIBLE
The world of the Bible was larger than the arc of the "fertile crescent" stretching from Palestine to Mesopotamia (the "Ancient Near East"). It included Cush (modern Ethiopia) and India (see Esther 1:1). The Indus and Nile river valleys nourished great civilizations as well. Genesis 2:10–14 names rivers in Cush and Mesopotamia alike as flowing around Eden. Contemporary archaeological evidence points to Africa as the home of the earliest known human beings (see shaded area); Africa is also the source of the Afro-Asiatic language family that includes ancient Hebrew.
A
B
C
D
E
1
2
3
4
Mediterranean Sea
CANAAN
Fertile Crescent
Euphrates River
Tigris River
Persian Gulf
Red Sea
Nile Valley
Nile River
CUSH
White Nile
Blue Nile
Arabian Sea
Indus Valley
Indus River
INDIA
N
0
200
400
600 Miles
0
200
400
600 Kilometers

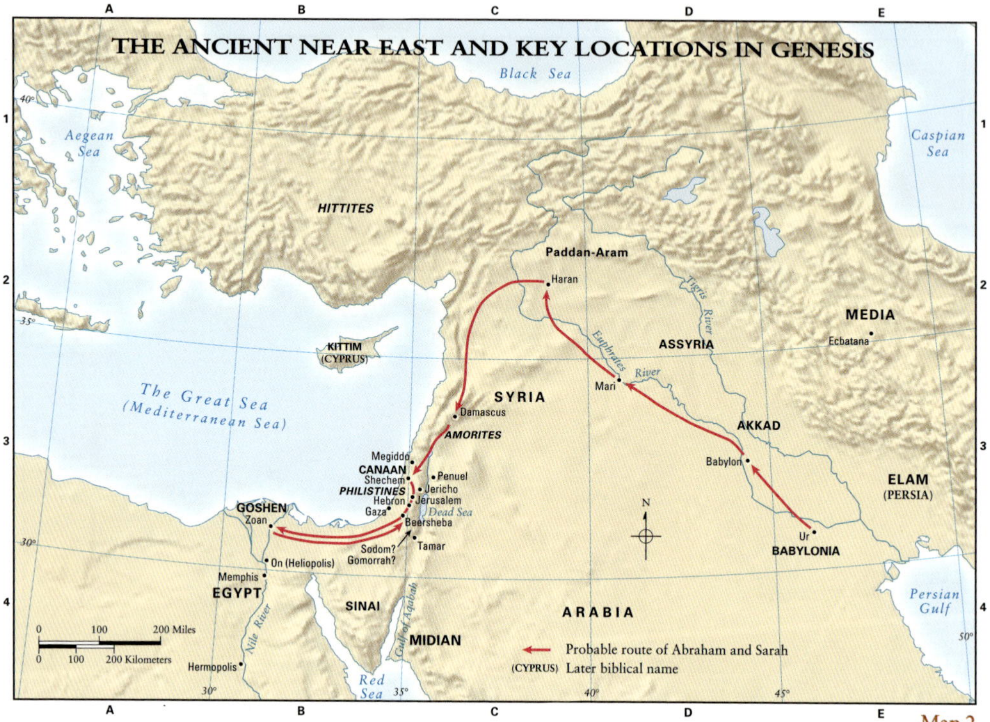
THE ANCIENT NEAR EAST AND KEY LOCATIONS IN GENESIS
A
B
C
D
E
1
2
3
4
Black Sea
Aegean Sea
Caspian Sea
HITTITES
Paddan-Aram
Haran
Tigris River
MEDIA
Ecbatana
ASSYRIA
Euphrates River
KITTIM (CYPRUS)
The Great Sea (Mediterranean Sea)
Mari
SYRIA
Damascus
AMORITES
AKKAD
Megiddo
CANAAN
Shechem
PHILISTINES
Hebron
Gaza
Penuel
Jericho
Jerusalem
Dead Sea
Beersheba
Babylon
ELAM (PERSIA)
GOSHEN
Zoan
Sodom? Gomorrah?
Tamar
On (Heliopolis)
Memphis
EGYPT
Ur
BABYLONIA
N
SINAI
ARABIA
Persian Gulf
MIDIAN
Gulf of Aqabah
Nile River
Hermopolis
Red Sea
0 100 200 Miles
0 100 200 Kilometers
Probable route of Abraham and Sarah
(CYPRUS) Later biblical name
40°
35°
30°
50°
45°

Map 2

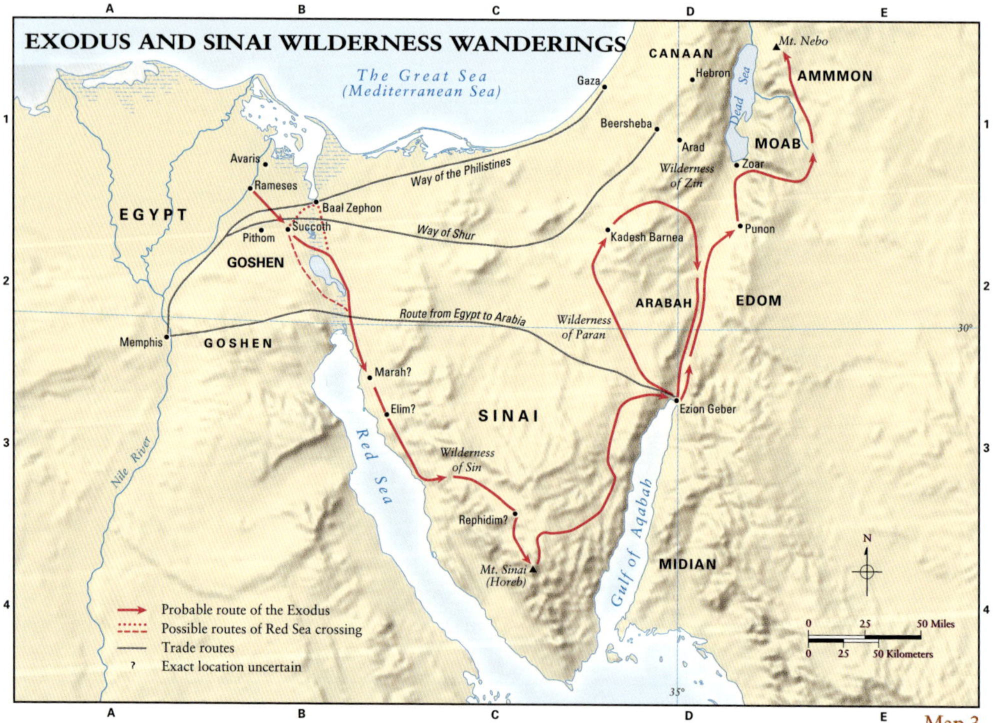
EXODUS AND SINAI WILDERNESS WANDERINGS
A
B
C
D
E
1
2
3
4
CANAAN
Mt. Nebo
The Great Sea (Mediterranean Sea)
Gaza
Hebron
Dead Sea
AMMMON
Beersheba
Arad
MOAB
Avaris
Zoar
Wilderness of Zin
Way of the Philistines
Rameses
EGYPT
Baal Zephon
Succoth
Pithom
Way of Shur
Kadesh Barnea
Punon
GOSHEN
ARABAH
EDOM
Route from Egypt to Arabia
Wilderness of Paran
Memphis
GOSHEN
30°
Marah?
Ezion Geber
Elim?
SINAI
Red Sea
Nile River
Wilderness of Sin
Rephidim?
Mt. Sinai (Horeb)
Gulf of Aqabah
MIDIAN
N
Probable route of the Exodus
Possible routes of Red Sea crossing
Trade routes
? Exact location uncertain
0 25 50 Miles
0 25 50 Kilometers
35°

Map 3

CANAAN AND KEY LOCATIONS IN JOSHUA AND JUDGES
The Great Sea (Mediterranean Sea)
PHOENICIANS
ARAM
ASHER
NAPHTALI
ZEBULUN
ISSACHAR
GESHUR
MANASSEH
BASHAN
HAVVOTH-JAIR
BETH REHOB
EPHRAIM
DAN
BENJAMIN
GAD
AMMON
REUBEN
JUDAH
PHILISTINES
CHERETHITES
SIMEON
KENITES
MOAB
EDOM
SEIR
Sea of Chinnereth
Jordan River
Dead Sea
Mt. Hermon
Mt. Carmel
Mt. Tabor
Mt. Ebal
Mt. Gerizim
Mt. Halak
Sidon
Zarephath
Ahlab
Tyre
Kanah
Misrephoth-maim
Achzib
Acco
Achshaph
Aphek
Cabul
Nahalol
Kitron
Helkath
Harosheth-ha-goiim
Bethlehem
Ophrah
Dor
Megiddo
Beth-anath
Ramah
Rimmon
Gath-hepher
Shimron
Japhia
Sarid
Daberath
Chesulloth
Shunem
Remeth
Jezreel
Harod
Rehob
En-gannim
Beth-shean
Mizpeh
Dan
Kedesh
Shimron-meron
Hazor
Merom
Chinnereth
Madon
Rakkath
Aphek
Golan
Ashtaroth
Nobah
Edrei
Ephraim
Ramoth-gilead
Socoh
Thebez
Tirzah
Abel-meholah
Hepher
Shechem
Pirathon
Zaphon
Penuel
Succoth
Mahanaim
Janoah
Taanath-shiloh
Aphek
Tappuah
Lebonah
Shiloh
Adam
Mizpeh
Gilead
Bene-berak
Ono
Jehud
Timnath-serah
Bethel
Ephraim
Rimmon
Beeroth
Jazer
Abel-Keramim
Betonim
Beth-nimrah
Minnith
Heshbon
Jabneel
Eltekeh
Gibbethon
Gezer
Beth-huron
Aijalon
Gibeon
Geba
Ai
Ramah
Gilgal
Jericho
Beth-arabah
Beth-hoglah
Beth-jeshimoth
Jabneh
Eshtaol
Zorah
Ekron
Kiriath-jearim
Gibeah
Jerusalem
Ashdod
Timnah
Beth-shemesh
Libnah
Jarmuth
Azekah
Bethlehem
Ashkelon
Socoh
Adullam
Etam
Keilah
Gath
Makkedah
Beth-zur
Halhul
Lachish
Hebron
Eglon
Gaza
Ziph
Debir
En-gedi
Eshtemoa
Carmel
Maon
Anab
Zanoah
Ziklag
Jattir
Arad
Ataroth
Almon
Kiriathaim
Dibon
Aroer
Beer-sheba
Hormah
Aroer
DAN Hebrew Tribes
Indefinite boundaries
0 10 20 Miles
0 10 20 Kilometers
N
A B C D E
1 2 3 4 5 6 7 8

THE TWELVE TRIBES OF ISRAEL, 1200–1030 BCE
A
B
C
D
1
2
3
4
5
The Great Sea
(Mediterranean Sea)
Damascus
Mt. Hermon
Ijon
Tyre
Dan
ARAM
ASHER
NAPHTALI
Kedesh
Hazor
Merom
Acco
Cabul
Sea of Galilee
Ashtaroth
Rimmon
Golan
ZEBULUN
MANASSEH
Mt. Tabor
Edrei
Dor
Mt. Moreh
Megiddo
ISSACHAR
Jezreel
Ramoth Gilead
Taanach
Beth Shan
Jabesh Gilead
MANASSEH
Samaria
Tirzah
Mt. Ebal
Shechem
Succoth
Mahanaim
Mt. Gerizim
Aphek
Shiloh
GAD
Joppa
EPHRAIM
Jordan River
Jazer
DAN
Bethel
Rabbah
Mizpah
Gilgal
Gezer
Jericho
AMMON
Gibeon
BENJAMIN
Kiriath Jearim
Heshbon
Ashdod
Ekron
Bezer
Jerusalem
Beth Shemesh
Mt. Nebo
Ashkelon
Gath
Bethlehem
REUBEN
Lachish
Hebron
Dibon
Gaza
Eglon
JUDAH
En-gedi
Dead Sea
Aroer
N
Gerar
Ziklag
Beersheba
Hormah
MOAB
SIMEON
Cities of refuge
Other cities
EDOM
0 10 20 30 Miles
0 10 20 30 Kilometers

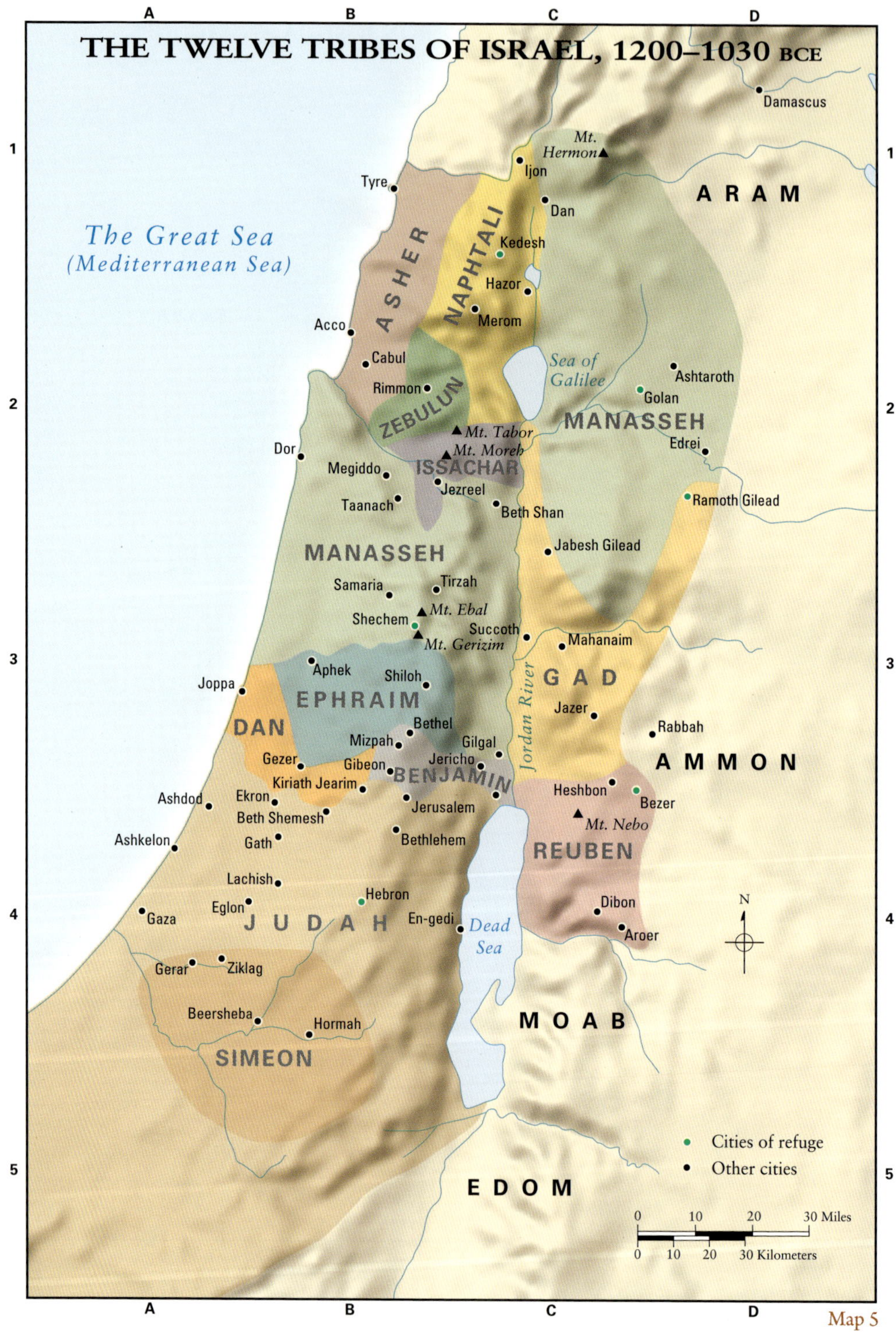

Map 5

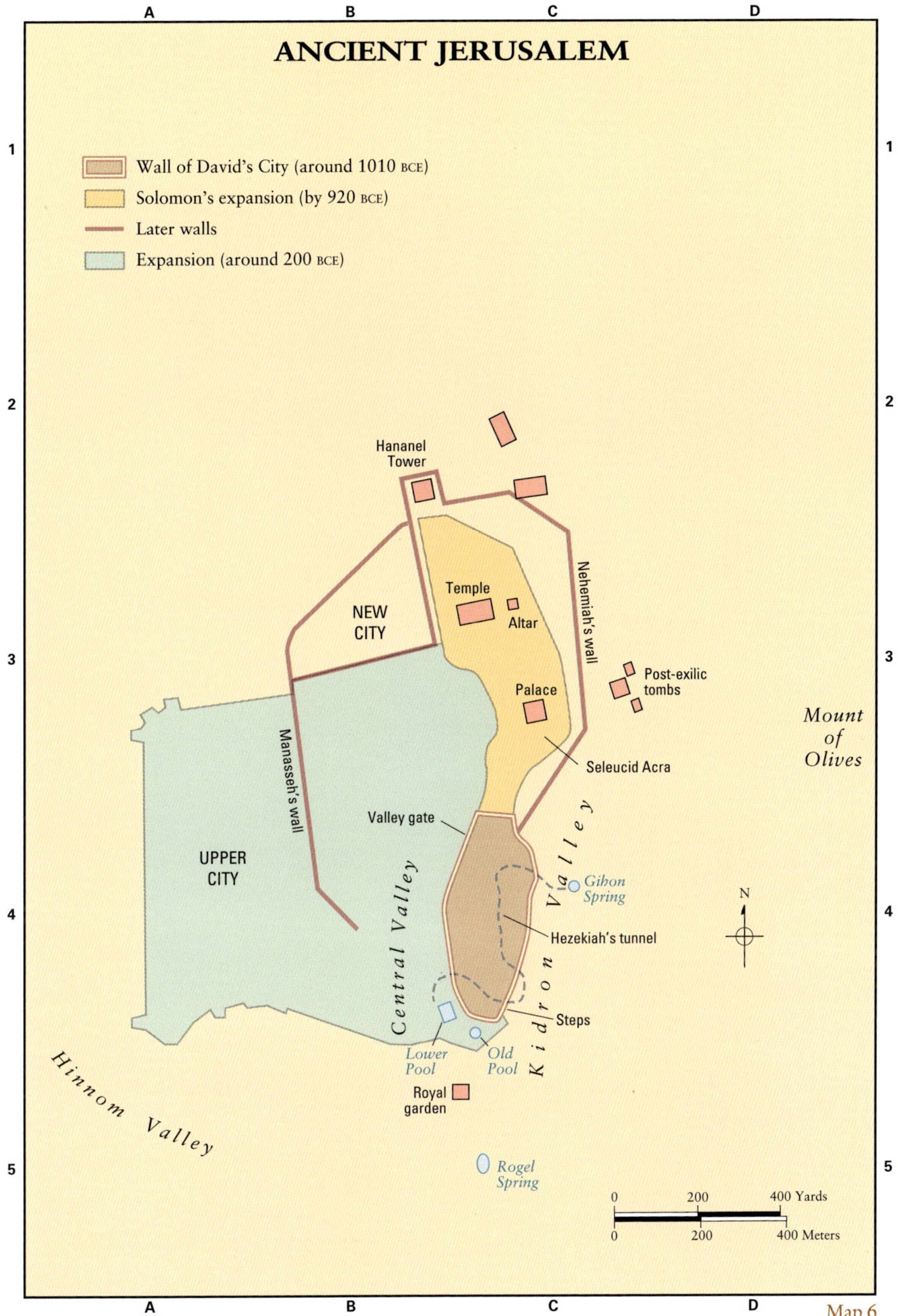

A
B
C
D
ANCIENT JERUSALEM
1
2
3
4
5
Wall of David's City (around 1010 BCE)
Solomon's expansion (by 920 BCE)
Later walls
Expansion (around 200 BCE)
Hananel Tower
Temple
Altar
NEW CITY
Nehemiah's wall
Post-exilic tombs
Palace
Mount of Olives
Seleucid Acra
Manasseh's wall
Valley gate
UPPER CITY
Central Valley
Gibon Spring
Hezekiah's tunnel
Kidron Valley
N
Steps
Lower Pool
Old Pool
Royal garden
Hinnom Valley
Rogel Spring
0
200
400 Yards
0
200
400 Meters

UNITED KINGDOM OF ISRAEL, 1000–924 BCE
A
B
C
D
1
2
3
4
5
Aleppo
Euphrates River
Tipsah
HAMATH
Hamath
Qatna
Kittim (Cyprus)
Arvad
Kadesh
Tadmor
Gebal
Berothai
PHOENICIA
The Great Sea (Mediterranean Sea)
Aramean Desert
Sidon
Damascus
Mt. Hermon
Tyre
ARAM
Dan
Kedesh
Hazor
Acco
Sea of Galilee
Ashtaroth
Edrei
Megiddo
Taanach
Beth Shan
Mt. Gilboa
Ramoth Gilead
Jordan River
Mahanaim
Shechem
AMMON
Joppa
Gezer
Gibeah
Rabbah
Ashdod
Jerusalem
PHILISTIA
Gath
Medeba
Dead Sea
Eastern Desert
Gaza
Hebron
Ziklag
Kir Hareseth
Beersheba
MOAB
Tamar
Kadesh Barnea
EDOM
N
0 20 40 60 Miles
0 20 40 60 Kilometers
Saul's kingdom
David and Solomon's kingdom
Territory under Solomon's control
Ezion Geber
Sinai
Gulf of Aqabah

THE MONARCHIES OF ISRAEL AND JUDAH, 924–722 BCE
A
B
C
D
1
2
3
4
5
ARAM (SYRIA)
Damascus
Sidon
Zarephath
PHOENICIA
Mt. Hermon
Tyre
The Great Sea (Mediterranean Sea)
Kedesh
Hazor
BASHAN
GALILEE
Sea of Galilee
Mt. Carmel
Yarmuk River
Edrei
Shunem
Megiddo
Jezreel
Ramoth
Mt. Gilboa
River
GILEAD
ISRAEL
Samaria
Penuel
Jabbok River
Shechem
Succoth
Mahanaim
AMMON
Joppa
Shiloh
Jordan
Bethel
Gilgal
Rabbah
Geba
Jericho
Ashdod
Ekron
Heshbon
Jerusalem
Ashkelon
Bethlehem
PHILISTIA
Libnah
Lachish
Gath
Gaza
Hebron
Dead Sea
Arnon River
Gath
JUDAH
Kir-Hareseth
Beersheba
N
MOAB
0 10 20 30 Miles
0 10 20 30 Kilometers
EDOM
Zered River

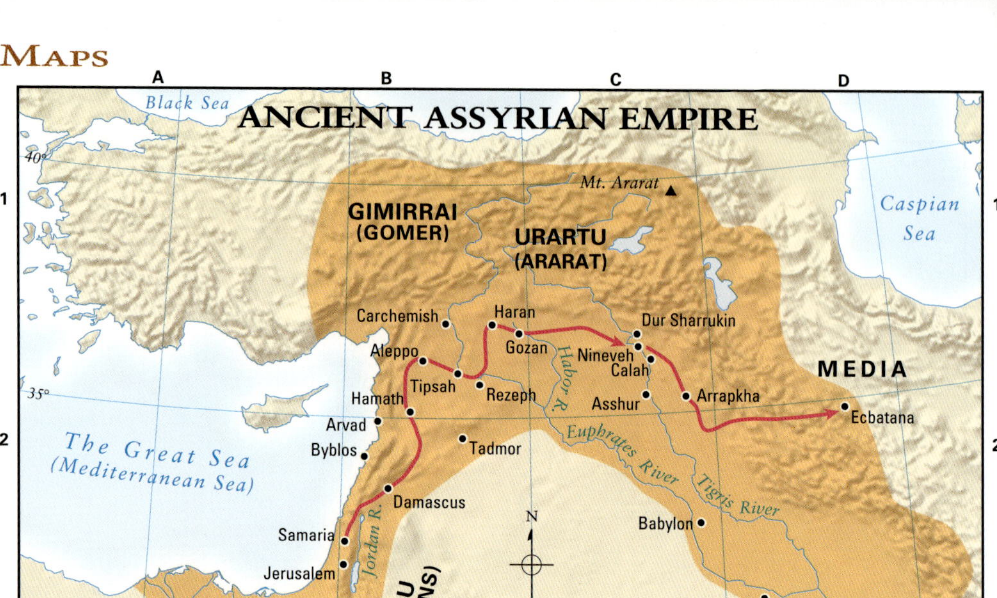

Map 9

ANCIENT BABYLONIAN EMPIRE

Black Sea
Caspian Sea
The Great Sea (Mediterranean Sea)
Red Sea
Persian Gulf
Mt. Ararat
URARTU (ARARAT)
MEDIA
EGYPT
Carchemish
Haran
Gozan
Nineveh
Aleppo
Rezeph
Habor R.
Hamath
Asshur
Arvad
Riblah
Byblos
Tadmor
Euphrates River
Tigris River
Damascus
Mizpah
Jerusalem
Jordan R.
Babylon
Nippur
Susa
Erech
Ur
Memphis

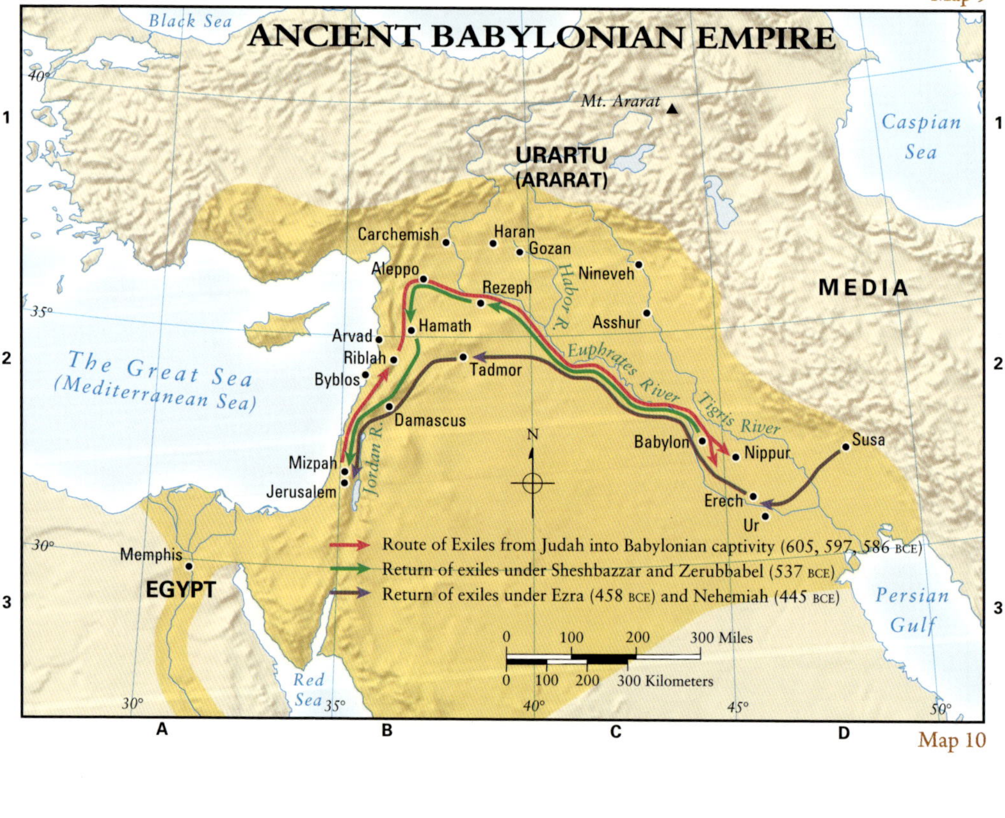

Route of Exiles from Judah into Babylonian captivity (605, 597, 586 BCE)
Return of exiles under Sheshbazzar and Zerubbabel (537 BCE)
Return of exiles under Ezra (458 BCE) and Nehemiah (445 BCE)

0 100 200 300 Miles
0 100 200 300 Kilometers

A B C D
1 2 3
40° 35° 30° 45° 50°

Map 10

ANCIENT PERSIAN KINGDOM

Black Sea
Caspian Sea
Mediterranean Sea
Red Sea
Persian Gulf
THRACE
IONIA
LUD
CAPPADOCIA
SCYTHIANS
ARMENIA
SOGDIANA
BACTRIA
MEDIA
PARTHIA
ARIA
SAGARTIA
GANDHARA
ARACHOSIA
INDIA
MAKA
ISLES OF THE SEA
ATHURA
BABYLONIA
SHUSHAN
ARABIA
LIBYA
EGYPT
ETHIOPIA (CUSH)
Athens
Sparta
Ephesus
Crete
Cyprus
Tarsus
Aleppo
Rezeph
Nineveh
Asshur
Ecbatana
Tadmor
Damascus
Babylon
Nippur
Susa
Ur
Persepolis
Jerusalem
Tahpanhes
Memphis
Cyrene
Euphrates River
Tigris River
Nile River

Persian homeland under Cyrus before 550 BCE
Kingdom of Medes, 550–525 BCE
Empire of Darius and Xerxes
Probable route of Exiles, 538–515 BCE
Probable route of Exiles, 457–428 BCE

0 100 200 300 Miles
0 100 200 300 Kilometers

Map 11

THE GREEK EMPIRE

Black Sea
Caspian Sea
Aegean Sea
Mediterranean Sea
Red Sea
Persian Gulf
THRACE
MACEDONIA
EPIRUS
THESSALY
AETOLIA
ACHAEA
IONIA
PHRYGIA
BITHYNIA
PAPHLAGONIA
PONTUS
GALATIA
CAPPADOCIA
PISIDIA
CILICIA
ARMENIA
ATROPATENE
MEDIA
SELEUCID KINGDOM
SYRIA
BABYLONIA
ARABIA
CYPRUS
CRETE
EGYPT
PTOLEMAIC KINGDOM
Philippi
Pella
Thessalonica
Byzantium
Calchedon
Lysimachia
Nicaea
Heraclea
Sinope
Trapezus
Ilium (Troy)
Dascylium
Delphi
Thebes
Corinth
Athens
Olympia
Sparta
Mytilene
Pergamum
Magnesia
Sardis
Ephesus
Samos
Miletus
Didyma
Halicarnassus
Rhodes
Xanthus
Phaselis
Perga
Ipsus
Apamea (Celaenae)
Gordium (Gordion)
Ancyra
Preria?
Tyana
Melitene
Soli
Tarsus
Issus
Alexandria
Antioch
Aleppo
Carchemish
Nisibis
Gaugamela
Arbela
Rages (Rhagae)
Ecbatana
Cydonia
Knossos
Gortyna
Salamis
Citium
Paphos
Laodicea
Marathus
Tripolis
Biblos
Berytus
Sidon
Tyre
Ptolemais
Dora
Samaria
Azotus
Gaza
Raphia
Emesa
Dura-Europus
Palmyra
Damascus
Paneas
Antioch (Cerasa)
Philadelphia
Jerusalem
Petra
Ctesiphon
Seleucia
Babylon
Nippur
Uruk
Susa
Gabae
Parsagarda
Persepolis
Cyrene
Paraetonium
Alexandria
Sais
Pelusium
Bubastis
Heliopolis
Memphis
Arsinoe
Crocodilopolis
Hermopolis
Lycopolis
Ptolemais
Nag Hammadi
Thebes
Euphrates River
Tigris River
Nile River

0 100 200 Miles
0 100 200 Kilometers

Map 12

PALESTINE IN THE TIME OF THE MACCABEES, 175–63 BCE
Judea, 166 BCE
Conquests, 134 BCE
Total Maccabean conquests, 76 BCE
Major roads
Mediterranean Sea
PHOENICIA
SYRIA
Sidon
Damascus
Mt. Hermon
Tyre
Kedesh
Hazor
Seleucia
Ptolemais (Acco)
Baskama
Sea of Galilee
GALILEE
Karnaim
Mt. Carmel
Mt. Tabor
Yarmuk River
Edrei
Dor
Gadara
Ephron
Beth-Shan (Scythopolis)
SAMARIA
GILEAD
Jordan River
Samaria
Gerasa
Apollonia
Jabbok River
AMMON
Joppa
Lydda
Beth-Horon
Ephraim
Berea
Modein
Tyrus
Philadelphia (Rabbah)
Jabneel
Mizpah
Jericho
Gezer
Heshbon
Emmaus
Ashdod (Azotus)
Ekron
JUDEA
Jerusalem
Medeba
Ashkelon
PHILISTIA
Beth Zechariah
Bethbasi
Marisa
Beth-Zur
Gaza
Hebron
Dead Sea
Arnon River
NABATEA
IDUMEA
Masada
Raphia
Beersheba
0 10 20 30 Miles
0 10 20 30 Kilometers
Zered River
N
A B C D
1 2 3 4 5

PALESTINE IN JESUS' TIME, 6–30 CE
A
B
C
D
1
2
3
4
5
Mediterranean Sea
Sidon
Zarephath
PHOENICIA
Abila
ABILENE
Damascus
SYRIA
Mt. Hermon
Tyre
ITURAEA
Caesarea Philippi
BATANEA
BASHAN
Ptolemais (Acco)
Chorazin
Capernaum
GALILEE
Sea of Galilee
Magadan
Tiberias
AURANITIS
Cana
Hippos
Dion
Mt. Carmel
Nazareth
Mt. Tabor
Yarmuk River
Nain
Gadara
Mt. Moreh
Dor
Caesarea
Scythopolis
DECAPOLIS
Pella
River
SAMARIA
Salim
Aenon
GILEAD
Samaria
Gerasa
Mt. Ebal
Sychar
Mt. Gerizim
Jabbok River
PEREA
Jordan
Joppa
Arimathea
Lydda
Ephraim
Philadelphia
Jericho
Jabneel
Emmaus
Jerusalem
Ashdod (Azotus)
Bethany
Qumran
Bethlehem
Ascalon
JUDEA
Gaza
Hebron
Dead Sea
Arnon River
Raphia
IDUMEA
NABATEA
Beersheba
0 10 20 30 Miles
0 10 20 30 Kilometers
N
Zered River

THE RO

A B

1 2 3 4

BRITAIN
London
German Sea
Atlantic Ocean
Cologna
GERMANY
Mainz
GAUL
Lyons
SPAIN
ILLYRI
Solona
Adriatic Sea
Corsica
ITALY
Rome
Sardinia
Puteoli
Tyrrhenian Sea
Sicily
Carthage
Syracuse
MAURETANIA
AFRICA
Mediterra

- Roman Empire by the time of Julius Caesar, 44 BCE
- Territory added by Augustus Caesar, 14 BCE
- Territory added by Trajan, 117 BCE
- Territory temporarily annexed by Rome

N

0° 10°

A B

D
E
MPIRE
0
200
400
600 Miles
0
200
400
600 Kilometers
50°
1
SARMATIA
Caspian Sea
2
CIA
Black Sea
OESIA
40°
THRACE
Byzantium
BITHYNIA & PONTUS
ARMENIA
Philippi
GALATIA
MYSIA
CAPPADOCIA
Aegean Sea
Pergamum
PARTHIA
PHRYGIA
Edessa
Tigris River
Athens
Ephesus
CILICIA
MESOPOTAMIA
3
Derbe
Tarsus
Euphrates River
Antioch
SYRIA
Dura-Europos
Cyprus
Sidon
Damascus
Crete
Tyre
JUDEA
Pella
NABATEA
30°
Jerusalem
Alexandria
4
E
Memphis
Arabian Desert
Nile River
Antinoe
Red Sea
EGYPT
30°
55°
40°
D
E

A B

PAUL'S MISSIONARY JOU

DALMATIA
ITALY
Adriatic Sea
Corsica
Rome
Forum of Appius
Three Taverns
Puteoli
MACEDO
Thessalonic
Berea
Sardinia
EPIRUS
Tyrrhenian Sea
Delp
Rhegium
Cor
Sicily
Cench
ACH
Syracuse
AFRICA
Malta
Mediterranean S
TRIPOLITANIA

First missionary journey (46–48 CE)
Second missionary journey (49–52 CE)
Third missionary journey (53–57 CE)
Trip to Rome (59–60 CE)

N

0
0 100

10° 20°

1 2 3 4

A B

D
E
ACCORDING TO ACTS
Black Sea
IA
THRACE
BITHYNIA & PONTUS
GALATIA
1
2
3
4
40°
30°
Troas
MYSIA
Pergamum
Mitylene
ASIA
Smyrna
LYDIA
Ephesus
Miletus
PHRYGIA
Laodicea
Pisidian Antioch
LYCAONIA
CAPPADOCIA
COMMAGENE
Iconium
Lystra
Derbe
CILICIA
Tarsus
Issus
Antioch
Seleucia
Euphrates River
Perga
Attalia
Cnidus
Patara
Rhodes
Myra
Cyprus
Salamis
Paphos
SYRIA
PHOENICIA
ABILENE
Sidon
Tyre
Damascus
Ptolemais
Caesarea
JUDEA
Jerusalem
ARABIA
EGYPT
Nile River
Red Sea
300 Miles
ometers
30°
D
E

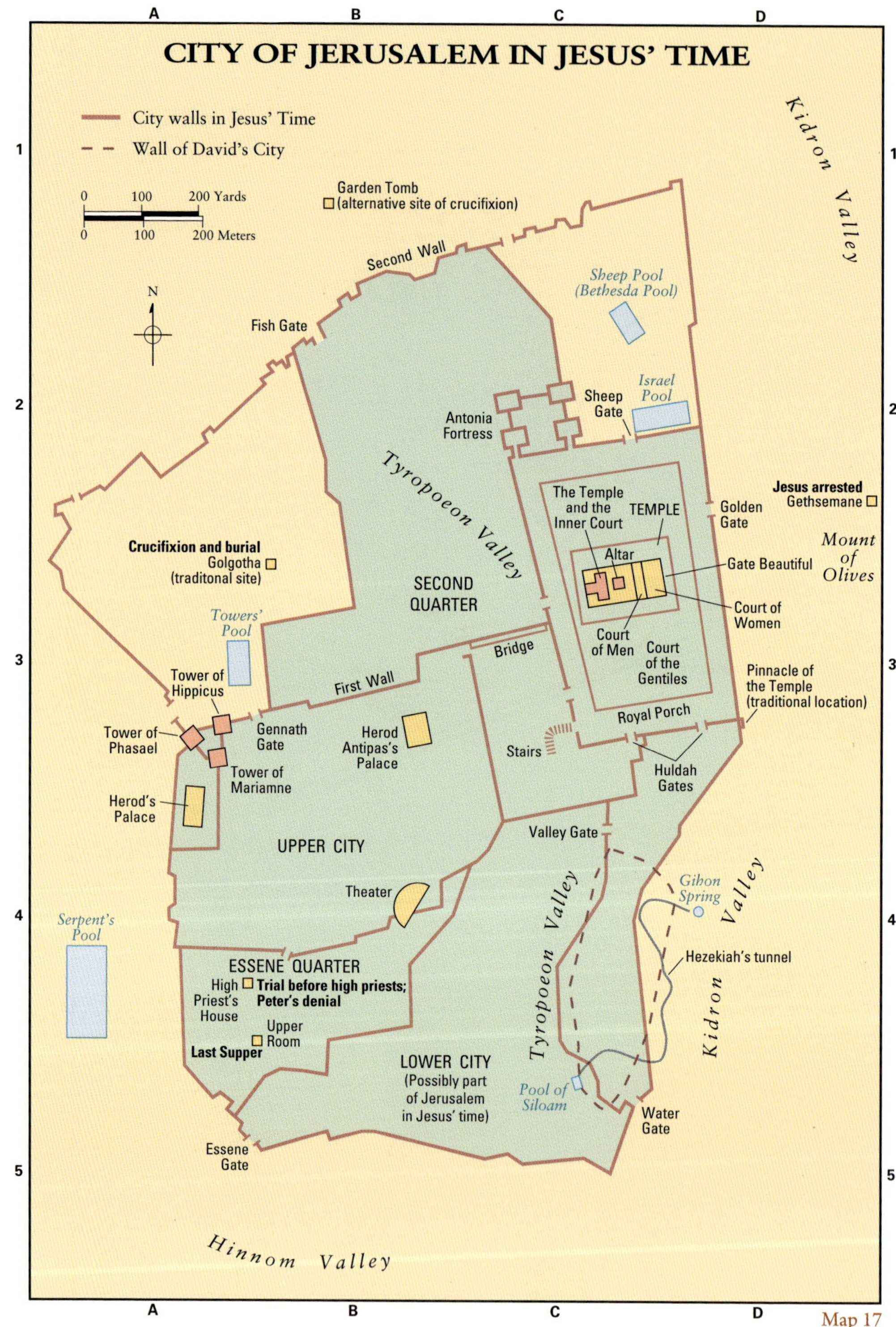

CITY OF JERUSALEM IN JESUS' TIME
City walls in Jesus' Time
Wall of David's City
0 100 200 Yards
0 100 200 Meters
N
A B C D
1 2 3 4 5
Kidron Valley
Garden Tomb (alternative site of crucifixion)
Second Wall
Sheep Pool (Bethesda Pool)
Fish Gate
Israel Pool
Sheep Gate
Antonia Fortress
Tyropoeon Valley
The Temple and the Inner Court
TEMPLE
Jesus arrested Gethsemane
Golden Gate
Mount of Olives
Altar
Gate Beautiful
Crucifixion and burial
Golgotha (traditonal site)
SECOND QUARTER
Court of Women
Towers' Pool
Court of Men
Court of the Gentiles
Bridge
Tower of Hippicus
First Wall
Pinnacle of the Temple (traditional location)
Royal Porch
Tower of Phasael
Gennath Gate
Herod Antipas's Palace
Stairs
Huldah Gates
Tower of Mariamne
Herod's Palace
Valley Gate
UPPER CITY
Gihon Spring
Theater
Serpent's Pool
Hezekiah's tunnel
ESSENE QUARTER
High Priest's House
Trial before high priests; Peter's denial
Upper Room
Last Supper
LOWER CITY (Possibly part of Jerusalem in Jesus' time)
Pool of Siloam
Water Gate
Essene Gate
Hinnom Valley

The Apocryphal/ Deuterocanonical Books

Apocryphal/ Deuterocanonical Books

INTRODUCTION

Wilda C. Gafney

More than any other division of Scripture, the Apocrypha (or Deuterocanonical writings) push readers to think about what they mean by Scripture. The very name we use for this literature stakes a claim. In my personal reading practices, I embrace a wide-open canon, recognizing, with respect, all Jewish and Christian canons as valid, from the five-book (Genesis–Deuteronomy) Samaritan Jewish canon to the not-quite-closed Ethiopian Orthodox canon that holds about eighty books, including *1* and *2 Enoch* and *1* and *2 Jubilees.* (I say "about" because the Ethiopian Orthodox have never published an official list or edition of the Bible.)

How do we categorize these books? Are they apocryphal (literally "hidden": compare 1 Macc 1:23) or deuterocanonical (a "secondary" or later canon)? *The Peoples' Bible* uses the NRSV translation of the Bible, which identifies these writings as *Apocrypha* and places them in a special section between the testaments. Use of the term *Apocrypha* is not meant to disparage the value of these writings (as the common use of the term "apocryphal" might imply), or that their meaning is somehow "hidden" (as a particular kind of Protestant interpretation presumes). The editors of *The Peoples' Bible* come from largely Protestant contexts, and so we have chosen to present these texts as they are understood from a broadly Protestant perspective.

Of course, not all Christians are Protestant. A majority of Christians on the planet—Roman Catholic, Orthodox (in many configurations), and Anglican—read these texts as deuterocanonical, literally as a second canon that is interwoven with the texts that virtually all Christians regard as primary in the First Testament. As an Episcopalian, part of the worldwide Anglican communion, I understand myself to be both catholic and Protestant. (Some Anglicans would go further and say that we are both Protestant and catholic and neither Protestant nor catholic!) We read this material as both deuterocanonical (as it is printed in Bibles such as the *New Jerusalem Bible*) and as Apocrypha (as printed in *The Peoples' Bible*, which uses the NRSV).

But neither are all readers of this book Christians, and so *The Peoples' Bible* is designed to be a resource for all people interested in the Bible.

At issue for readers is the question, What is scripture? There is no single answer, as indicated by the number of different canons (or authorized lists of contents) for Jews and Christians around the world.

The ancient Israelites, exiled from their homeland by the Babylonians, produced two versions of the Scriptures, one including the texts now called apocryphal or deuterocanonical. The community deported to Babylon produced in Hebrew the books that are called the "Hebrew Bible" and that appear in Protestant Bibles, albeit in a different sequence, as the Old Testament. The community exiled in Egypt produced in Greek a version called the Septuagint, which includes the books that are in Catholic, Orthodox, and Anglican Bibles. (Earlier biblical scholars taught that the Septuagint was a translation, expansion, and revision of a standard Hebrew Bible, but we now regard the two versions as somewhat independent of each other.) Some deuterocanonical or apocryphal material has been identified as a series of additions to the Hebrew Bible, particularly in the books of Esther and Daniel.

The discovery of the Dead Sea Scrolls changed the way many biblical scholars had thought about this material. Researchers discovered Hebrew scrolls that corresponded both to the previously known Hebrew versions of biblical books and to the Greek versions of biblical books, demonstrating that the Septuagint translators were faithful in translating the Scriptures they knew.

As a reader of African descent, I am reluctant to assign the Scriptures treasured by North African Jews to secondary status. As a Christian reader, I am interested in the use of the Septuagint and the Hebrew Bible in the Christian New Testament, where both are cited regularly. And as an Episcopalian teaching at a Lutheran seminary, I am interested in the manner in which Martin Luther understood these books and the ways that Lutherans have received them.

These texts generally date from 300 BCE to 70 CE. They are preserved in early Greek manuscripts (Codices Vaticanus, Sinaiticus, and Alexandrinus). Sirach, also called The Wisdom of Jesus Son of Sirach), chapter six of Baruch (also known as The Letter of Jeremiah), and Tobit were found in Hebrew among the Dead Sea Scrolls at Qumran. Most scholars believe that the majority of these works were composed in Hebrew or Aramaic and subsequently translated into Greek; Wisdom of Solomon and 2 Maccabees were most likely composed in Greek. These Jewish texts were initially understood as sacred, particularly in North Africa.

Eventually only those texts composed in Hebrew and collected by the earliest rabbinic authorities in the Babylonian diaspora became canonical, therefore authorized for all Jews in subsequent generations. How this happened is not clear. The story of a rabbinic council meeting at Jabneh and voting on the books of the Bible has been discredited. On the other hand, it is clear that early Greek-speaking Christians received the deuterocanonical books as Scripture. (Codices Sinaiticus, Alexandrinus, and Vaticanus all included the Greek New Testament as well as so-called New Testament apocryphal works: the *Epistle of Barnabas,* the *Shepherd of Hermas,* and the *Epistles of Clement*).

As already mentioned, the reception of these texts into the Christian canon has been uneven. In the fourth century, Jerome excluded them from the canon because he considered authoritative only the Hebrew manuscripts then available. In the sixteenth century, Martin Luther translated these texts and included them in his Bible, writing introductions to many of them, and designating them as apocryphal, along with the Epistle of James and the Apocalypse (or Revelation) of John. In response, the Council of Trent declared the Apocrypha to be deuterocanonical. This position is still held by the Roman Catholic Church.

The deuterocanonical or apocryphal literature can be divided into two categories. There are, first, distinct versions of books that also occur in Hebrew, such as Daniel and Esther:

Greek Esther. The differences between Greek and Hebrew Esther are centered in a few chapters that only exist in Greek. These unique portions of Esther include dreams and their fulfillment, prayers, plots and counter-plots. One significant aspect of the Greek version is that the piety of the main characters is affirmed by mentioning God, who is not mentioned in the Hebrew version, some fifty times.

Greek Daniel. Several narratives in the Greek version of Daniel are not in the standard text of the Hebrew Bible, called the Masoretic Text. The Prayer of Azariah and the Song of the Three Jews are both psalms set in the midst of the fiery furnace. The stories of Susanna, which with

Bel and the Dragon at one time served as the introduction to the book of Daniel, highlights Daniel's gifts as a wise and discerning judge.

Second, the vast majority of the apocryphal books are not included in the Hebrew canon. These texts, in the order of the Christian canon, are:

Tobit is the story of a Jewish man, his wife, Anna, and their son Tobias, who are in exile after the first Assyrian deportation. The story also turns on a young woman named Sarah, whose seven husbands have been killed by a demon before any of their marriages were consummated. The angel Raphael enables Tobias to drive off the demon so he can marry Sarah and heals Tobit, who had become blind.

Judith tells the story of a series of battles in the war between Israel and Assyria. The story's pious heroine saves the day by assassinating the enemy general, who has tried but failed to seduce her.

Wisdom is a collection of proverbial sayings attributed to Solomon. Similarities between Wisdom and Proverbs include the feminine personification of Wisdom and dependence on Egyptian and Greek philosophies.

Sirach is another collection of proverbial material, also called the Wisdom of Jesus Son of Sirach and, from its Latin name, Ecclesiasticus. Sirach venerates core Jewish values: the one God, the Torah, and the temple. It offers powerful critiques to Gentile culture and religion. Ben Sira, as the corpus is also known, employs strong language lamenting the birth of daughters and demeaning women in general.

Baruch offers reflections attributed to Jeremiah's scribe, Baruch ben Neriah. It includes practical advice for surviving Babylonian exile and a critique of idol worship. Its sixth and last chapter has circulated independently as the Epistle of Jeremiah.

First and Second Maccabees, books intended to look like the double books Samuel, Kings, and Chronicles, are in fact two separate works. First Maccabees tells the story of Judas Maccabeaus and his family as they lead their people, the Judeans under Syrian oppression, to revolt and then restore Jewish worship in Jerusalem. Antiochus (IV) Epiphanes was determined to forcibly Hellenize the Jews by slaughtering a number of men on Shabbat and by executing any who had been circumcised, had performed circumcisions, or possessed Torah scrolls. Antiochus also sacrificed a pig on the altar of the temple, desecrating it. Restoration

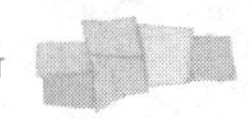

and rededication of the temple is celebrated in the festival of Hanukkah (see John 10:22 for its observance in the New Testament).

Second Maccabees is a theological treatise that includes the only surviving excerpt of a historical text by the Jewish historian Jason of Cyrene. Second Maccabees advocates Jewish religious values, such as celebrating Hanukkah, and makes theological arguments for resurrection, divine revelation, miracles, and martyrdom.

First Esdras is a theological reflection on biblical history from the reforms of the prophet Huldah and King Josiah in 2 Kings 22–23 through the reforms of Ezra. The book of Ezra is known as 1 Esdras (and Nehemiah as 2 Esdras) in some Greek and Slavonic bibles, which designate our deuterocanonical/apocryphal 1 Esdras as 3 Esdras. This 1 Esdras/3 Esdras shares with Ezra, Nehemiah, Haggai, and Zechariah a preoccupation with the temple and the character Zerubbabel.

The Prayer of Manasseh presents a prayer of lament attributed to King Manasseh of Judah, who though regarded as an apostate (2 Kgs 21:1-16; 2 Chr 33:1-9), was depicted as being repentant in the Chronicles account, (33:12-13).

Third Maccabees doesn't mention the exploits of the Maccabees but recounts a somewhat parallel situation, with its own dangerous monarch, the Egyptian Ptolemy IV (Philopater), who profanes the temple with his presence. After being struck by God, he attempts to take his revenge on the Jews but is thwarted by God.

Second Esdras is a collection of seven apocalyptic visions concerning Jerusalem. The visionary is Ezra, the biblical scribe, who receives visions directly and is privy to an angelic apparition. He is ultimately assumed bodily into heaven, as were Enoch and Elijah.

Fourth Maccabees is set roughly in the Maccabean period but has little connection to the other Maccabean writings. Like the other literature that bears this name, the story turns on persecution and martyrdoms, in this case of the righteous Eleazar the sage, an elderly Jewish woman, and her seven sons. Here the antagonists are the Greeks.

While the full collection of these books varies significantly in reception and use by religious readers, all were at one time or another considered inspired and/or authoritative by some ancient Jewish and Christian communities. The preservation of these texts as Scripture, even in the most marginal sense, reminds us of Scripture's complexity and, ultimately, of its mystery.

Tobit

In 722 BCE, the army of mighty Assyria destroyed the Northern Kingdom of Israel, as the prophet Amos had foretold. Survivors were taken captive and resettled throughout the Assyrian empire. Deportation ripped families apart, tearing the Israelite people from the land of their inheritance and from one another. So began the first Diaspora, or scattering, of the Israelites. For centuries and even millennia to come, Jews in the Diaspora continually negotiated their identity in relation to one another and to the people around them. How would they live as a minority people? Should they preserve their laws, stories, customs, religious practices and beliefs—and if so, how? Should they embrace the culture that now surrounded them? Even as they coped with the loss of homeland and kindred, they faced the dangers and difficulties of living in alien environments under foreign rule. They also built lives and formed families, prospered, and found joy.

This is the setting for the book of Tobit, a novella, or short romance, written around 200 BCE. The story is as fantastic as it is down to earth. An apocalypse enters the household: a demon haunts the bridal chamber while an angel plays matchmaker. The book's stunning revelation is that God answers prayer, is present with and within the family, and heals those who suffer. The book locates identity in the bonds of family, in religious praxis, in memory, and above all in acts of charity. By caring for members of the Israelite community in Diaspora, specifically by feeding the hungry, clothing the naked, burying the dead, and giving alms to the poor, the heroes of the book ensure the community's survival and welfare and free themselves from the bonds of death.

As a captive in Assyria, Tobit of Naphtali sets himself apart by abstaining from "the food of the Gentiles" (1:10), keeping the commands taught him by his grandmother Deborah, and marrying Anna, a woman from his own tribe (1:8-9). When his people suffer, he cares for them; he buries the Israelite dead at the risk of his own life (1:16-18). Tobit's fortunes rise and fall with the succession of kings: under one he conducts the king's business; under another he is a fugitive; under a third he is restored (1:13, 19-20; 2:1).

Yet sorrow lies ahead. Tobit suffers blindness (2:10). His nephew cares for him and his wife supports him, but he longs for death (2:10—3:6). Miles away in Ecbatana, Sarah, daughter of Edna and Raguel, also prays for death: the virgin bride has seen seven husbands strangled by the demon who loves her; she despairs of marriage and of life (3:7-15). God hears their prayers and sends the angel Raphael to heal them both (3:16-17). Disguised in human form, the angel leads Tobit's son Tobiah to Ecbatana (ch. 6). On the way, Tobiah conquers a fish (6:4). From its body he gains not only nourishment but also the means to banish Sarah's demon and heal his father's blindness (6:7-9).

Another happy ending is in store: the very day Tobiah arrives at Ecbatana, he marries his cousin Sarah (7:1—8:8). Raphael wrestles the demon (8:3); he also travels on to Rages, in Media,

to retrieve a fortune Tobit had stored there in his days of prosperity (9:1-5). Finally, after much feasting, Tobiah, Sarah, and Raphael return to Nineveh, where Tobiah heals his father's blindness (11:1-13). Tobit sees his family and rejoices (11:13-15).

The book's recognition of suffering, message of comfort, and assurance of God's providence holds out a happy ending, not only for righteous individuals but for the people of Israel as a whole. In his testament before his death, Tobit warns his son of the destruction of Nineveh as well as Jerusalem (14:3-4). But he also foretells the ingathering of the scattered Israelites, the glorious restoration of the holy city and temple, and the conversion of all nations to true worship of the God of Israel (14:6). There is one exception to this vision of universal blessing: at the end of the book, Tobit's son, Tobiah, rejoices in the destruction of the people of Nineveh (14:15).

I read Tobit as a white woman in the United States who has received many privileges at the expense of others: I may more closely resemble the Assyrian than the Israelite. These verses, like the psalms of imprecation (for example, Psalm 137), challenge me to reckon with the anger of the oppressed, to acknowledge my part in oppression, and to promote healing for all God's people.

— ***Anathea E. Portier-Young***

1 This book tells the story of Tobit son of
Tobiel son of Hananiel son of Aduel son of
Gabael son of Raphael son of Raguel of the descendants[a] of Asiel, of the tribe of Naphtali, 2 who
in the days of King Shalmaneser[b] of the Assyrians
was taken into captivity from Thisbe, which is
to the south of Kedesh Naphtali in Upper Galilee, above Asher toward the west, and north of
Phogor.
3 I, Tobit, walked in the ways of truth and
righteousness all the days of my life. I performed
many acts of charity for my kindred and my people who had gone with me in exile to Nineveh
in the land of the Assyrians. 4 When I was in my
own country, in the land of Israel, while I was
still a young man, the whole tribe of my ancestor
Naphtali deserted the house of David and Jerusalem. This city had been chosen from among all
the tribes of Israel, where all the tribes of Israel
should offer sacrifice and where the temple, the
dwelling of God, had been consecrated and established for all generations forever.
5 All my kindred and our ancestral house of
Naphtali sacrificed to the calf[c] that King Jeroboam of Israel had erected in Dan and on all the
mountains of Galilee. 6 But I alone went often to
Jerusalem for the festivals, as it is prescribed for
all Israel by an everlasting decree. I would hurry
off to Jerusalem with the first fruits of the crops
and the firstlings of the flock, the tithes of the cattle, and the first shearings of the sheep. 7 I would
give these to the priests, the sons of Aaron, at the
altar; likewise the tenth of the grain, wine, olive
oil, pomegranates, figs, and the rest of the fruits
to the sons of Levi who ministered at Jerusalem.
Also for six years I would save up a second tenth
in money and go and distribute it in Jerusalem.
8 A third tenth[d] I would give to the orphans and

[a] Other ancient authorities lack *of Raphael son of Raguel of the descendants* [b] Gk *Enemessaros* [c] Other ancient authorities read *heifer* [d] *A third tenth* added from other ancient authorities

widows and to the converts who had attached
themselves to Israel. I would bring it and give it to
them in the third year, and we would eat it according to the ordinance decreed concerning it in the
law of Moses and according to the instructions of
Deborah, the mother of my father Tobiel,[a] for my
father had died and left me an orphan. 9 When I
became a man I married a woman,[b] a member of
our own family, and by her I became the father of
a son whom I named Tobias.

> **Tobit 1:8**
>
> Deborah of Naphtali, mother of Tobiel, raised her orphaned grandson Tobit and taught him the commandments of the Torah. Tobit honors her commands by celebrating the pilgrimage festivals and bringing tithes to Jerusalem. These tithes supported the priests, Levites, widows, orphans, and converts.
>
> — *APY*

10 After I was carried away captive to Assyria and came as a captive to Nineveh, everyone
of my kindred and my people ate the food of the
Gentiles, 11 but I kept myself from eating the food
of the Gentiles. 12 Because I was mindful of God
with all my heart, 13 the Most High gave me favor and good standing with Shalmaneser,[c] and
I used to buy everything he needed. 14 Until his
death I used to go into Media, and buy for him
there. While in the country of Media I left bags of
silver worth ten talents in trust with Gabael, the
brother of Gabri. 15 But when Shalmaneser[c] died,
and his son Sennacherib reigned in his place, the
highways into Media became unsafe and I could
no longer go there.

16 In the days of Shalmaneser[c] I performed
many acts of charity to my kindred, those of my
tribe. 17 I would give my food to the hungry and
my clothing to the naked; and if I saw the dead
body of any of my people thrown out behind the
wall of Nineveh, I would bury it. 18 I also buried
any whom King Sennacherib put to death when
he came fleeing from Judea in those days of judgment that the king of heaven executed upon him
because of his blasphemies. For in his anger he
put to death many Israelites; but I would secretly
remove the bodies and bury them. So when Sennacherib looked for them he could not find them.
19 Then one of the Ninevites went and informed
the king about me, that I was burying them; so I
hid myself. But when I realized that the king knew
about me and that I was being searched for to be
put to death, I was afraid and ran away. 20 Then all
my property was confiscated; nothing was left to
me that was not taken into the royal treasury except my wife Anna and my son Tobias.

21 But not forty[d] days passed before two of
Sennacherib's[e] sons killed him, and they fled to
the mountains of Ararat, and his son Esar-haddon[f]
reigned after him. He appointed Ahikar, the son
of my brother Hanael[g] over all the accounts of
his kingdom, and he had authority over the entire administration. 22 Ahikar interceded for me,
and I returned to Nineveh. Now Ahikar was chief
cupbearer, keeper of the signet, and in charge of
administration of the accounts under King Sennacherib of Assyria; so Esar-haddon[f] reappointed
him. He was my nephew and so a close relative.

2 Then during the reign of Esar-haddon[f] I returned home, and my wife Anna and my son
Tobias were restored to me. At our festival of
Pentecost, which is the sacred festival of weeks, a
good dinner was prepared for me and I reclined to
eat. 2 When the table was set for me and an abundance of food placed before me, I said to my son
Tobias, "Go, my child, and bring whatever poor
person you may find of our people among the exiles in Nineveh, who is wholeheartedly mindful
of God,[h] and he shall eat together with me. I will
wait for you, until you come back." 3 So Tobias
went to look for some poor person of our people.
When he had returned he said, "Father!" And I
replied, "Here I am, my child." Then he went on
to say, "Look, father, one of our own people has

[a] Lat: Gk *Hananiel* [b] Other ancient authorities add *Anna* [c] Gk *Enemessaros* [d] Other ancient authorities read either *forty-five* or *fifty* [e] Gk *his* [f] Gk *Sacherdonos* [g] Other authorities read *Hananael* [h] Lat: Gk *wholeheartedly mindful*

been murdered and thrown into the market place,
and now he lies there strangled." 4Then I sprang
up, left the dinner before even tasting it, and removed the body[a] from the square[b] and laid it[a] in
one of the rooms until sunset when I might bury
it.[a] 5When I returned, I washed myself and ate my
food in sorrow. 6Then I remembered the prophecy of Amos, how he said against Bethel,[c]

"Your festivals shall be turned into
mourning,
and all your songs into lamentation."

And I wept.

7 When the sun had set, I went and dug
a grave and buried him. 8And my neighbors
laughed and said, "Is he still not afraid? He has
already been hunted down to be put to death for
doing this, and he ran away; yet here he is again
burying the dead!" 9That same night I washed
myself and went into my courtyard and slept by
the wall of the courtyard; and my face was uncovered because of the heat. 10I did not know that
there were sparrows on the wall; their fresh drop-
pings fell into my eyes and produced white films.
I went to physicians to be healed, but the more
they treated me with ointments the more my vision was obscured by the white films, until I became completely blind. For four years I remained
unable to see. All my kindred were sorry for me,
and Ahikar took care of me for two years before
he went to Elymais.

11 At that time, also, my wife Anna earned
money at women's work. 12She used to send what
she made to the owners and they would pay wages
to her. One day, the seventh of Dystrus, when she
cut off a piece she had woven and sent it to the
owners, they paid her full wages and also gave her
a young goat for a meal. 13When she returned to
me, the goat began to bleat. So I called her and
said, "Where did you get this goat? It is surely not
stolen, is it? Return it to the owners; for we have
no right to eat anything stolen." 14But she said to
me, "It was given to me as a gift in addition to my
wages." But I did not believe her, and told her to
return it to the owners. I became flushed with anger against her over this. Then she replied to me,
"Where are your acts of charity? Where are your
righteous deeds? These things are known about
you!"[d]

3 Then with much grief and anguish of heart I
wept, and with groaning began to pray:

2 "You are righteous, O Lord,
and all your deeds are just;
all your ways are mercy and truth;
you judge the world.[e]
3 And now, O Lord, remember me
and look favorably upon me.
Do not punish me for my sins
and for my unwitting offenses
and those that my ancestors committed
before you.
They sinned against you,
4 and disobeyed your commandments.
So you gave us over to plunder, exile, and
death,
to become the talk, the byword, and an
object of reproach
among all the nations among whom you
have dispersed us.
5 And now your many judgments are true
in exacting penalty from me for my
sins.
For we have not kept your commandments
and have not walked in accordance with
truth before you.
6 So now deal with me as you will;
command my spirit to be taken from me,
so that I may be released from the face of
the earth and become dust.
For it is better for me to die than to live,
because I have had to listen to undeserved
insults,
and great is the sorrow within me.
Command, O Lord, that I be released from
this distress;
release me to go to the eternal home,
and do not, O Lord, turn your face away
from me.
For it is better for me to die

[a] Gk *him* [b] Other ancient authorities lack *from the square* [c] Other ancient authorities read *against Bethlehem*
[d] Or *to you;* Gk *with you* [e] Other ancient authorities read *you render true and righteous judgment forever*

than to see so much distress in my life
and to listen to insults."

7 On the same day, at Ecbatana in Media, it
also happened that Sarah, the daughter of Raguel,
was reproached by one of her father's maids. 8 For
she had been married to seven husbands, and
the wicked demon Asmodeus had killed each
of them before they had been with her as is customary for wives. So the maid said to her, "You
are the one who kills[a] your husbands! See, you
have already been married to seven husbands and
have not borne the name of[b] a single one of them.
9 Why do you beat us? Because your husbands are
dead? Go with them! May we never see a son or
daughter of yours!"

10 On that day she was grieved in spirit and
wept. When she had gone up to her father's upper room, she intended to hang herself. But she
thought it over and said, "Never shall they reproach my father, saying to him, 'You had only
one beloved daughter but she hanged herself
because of her distress.' And I shall bring my father in his old age down in sorrow to Hades. It
is better for me not to hang myself, but to pray
the Lord that I may die and not listen to these
reproaches anymore." 11 At that same time, with
hands outstretched toward the window, she
prayed and said,

"Blessed are you, merciful God!
Blessed is your name forever;
let all your works praise you forever.
12 And now, Lord,[c] I turn my face to you,
and raise my eyes toward you.
13 Command that I be released from the earth
and not listen to such reproaches any more.
14 You know, O Master, that I am innocent
of any defilement with a man,
15 and that I have not disgraced my name
or the name of my father in the land of my
exile.
I am my father's only child;
he has no other child to be his heir;
and he has no close relative or other kindred
for whom I should keep myself as wife.
Already seven husbands of mine have died.
Why should I still live?
But if it is not pleasing to you, O Lord, to
take my life,
hear me in my disgrace."

16 At that very moment, the prayers of both
of them were heard in the glorious presence of
God. 17 So Raphael was sent to heal both of them:
Tobit, by removing the white films from his eyes,
so that he might see God's light with his eyes; and
Sarah, daughter of Raguel, by giving her in marriage to Tobias son of Tobit, and by setting her
free from the wicked demon Asmodeus. For Tobias was entitled to have her before all others who
had desired to marry her. At the same time that
Tobit returned from the courtyard into his house,
Sarah daughter of Raguel came down from her
upper room.

4 That same day Tobit remembered the money
that he had left in trust with Gabael at Rages
in Media, 2 and he said to himself, "Now I have
asked for death. Why do I not call my son Tobias and explain to him about the money before I die?" 3 Then he called his son Tobias, and
when he came to him he said, "My son, when I
die,[d] give me a proper burial. Honor your mother
and do not abandon her all the days of her life.
Do whatever pleases her, and do not grieve her in
anything. 4 Remember her, my son, because she
faced many dangers for you while you were in her
womb. And when she dies, bury her beside me in
the same grave.

5 "Revere the Lord all your days, my son, and
refuse to sin or to transgress his commandments.
Live uprightly all the days of your life, and do
not walk in the ways of wrongdoing; 6 for those
who act in accordance with truth will prosper in
all their activities. To all those who practice righteousness[e] 7 give alms from your possessions, and

[a] Other ancient authorities read *strangles* [b] Other ancient authorities read *have had no benefit from* [c] Other ancient authorities lack *Lord* [d] Lat [e] The text of codex Sinaiticus goes directly from verse 6 to verse 19, reading *To those who practice righteousness* [19] *the Lord will give good counsel.* In order to fill the lacuna verses 7 to 18 are derived from other ancient authorities

do not let your eye begrudge the gift when you
make it. Do not turn your face away from anyone who is poor, and the face of God will not be
turned away from you. 8 If you have many possessions, make your gift from them in proportion;
if few, do not be afraid to give according to the
little you have. 9 So you will be laying up a good
treasure for yourself against the day of necessity.
10 For almsgiving delivers from death and keeps
you from going into the Darkness. 11 Indeed,
almsgiving, for all who practice it, is an excellent
offering in the presence of the Most High.

12 "Beware, my son, of every kind of fornication. First of all, marry a woman from among the
descendants of your ancestors; do not marry a
foreign woman, who is not of your father's tribe;
for we are the descendants of the prophets. Remember, my son, that Noah, Abraham, Isaac, and
Jacob, our ancestors of old, all took wives from
among their kindred. They were blessed in their
children, and their posterity will inherit the land.
13 So now, my son, love your kindred, and in your
heart do not disdain your kindred, the sons and
daughters of your people, by refusing to take a
wife for yourself from among them. For in pride
there is ruin and great confusion. And in idleness
there is loss and dire poverty, because idleness is
the mother of famine.

14 "Do not keep over until the next day the
wages of those who work for you, but pay them at
once. If you serve God you will receive payment.
Watch yourself, my son, in everything you do,
and discipline yourself in all your conduct. 15 And
what you hate, do not do to anyone. Do not drink
wine to excess or let drunkenness go with you on
your way. 16 Give some of your food to the hungry, and some of your clothing to the naked. Give
all your surplus as alms, and do not let your eye
begrudge your giving of alms. 17 Place your bread
on the grave of the righteous, but give none to
sinners. 18 Seek advice from every wise person
and do not despise any useful counsel. 19 At all
times bless the Lord God, and ask him that your
ways may be made straight and that all your paths
and plans may prosper. For none of the nations
has understanding, but the Lord himself will give
them good counsel; but if he chooses otherwise,
he casts down to deepest Hades. So now, my
child, remember these commandments, and do
not let them be erased from your heart.

20 "And now, my son, let me explain to you
that I left ten talents of silver in trust with Gabael
son of Gabrias, at Rages in Media. 21 Do not be
afraid, my son, because we have become poor.
You have great wealth if you fear God and flee
from every sin and do what is good in the sight of
the Lord your God."

5 Then Tobias answered his father Tobit, "I will
do everything that you have commanded me,
father; 2 but how can I obtain the money[a] from
him, since he does not know me and I do not
know him? What evidence[b] am I to give him so
that he will recognize and trust me, and give me
the money? Also, I do not know the roads to Media, or how to get there." 3 Then Tobit answered
his son Tobias, "He gave me his bond and I gave
him my bond. I[c] divided his in two; we each took
one part, and I put one with the money. And now
twenty years have passed since I left this money
in trust. So now, my son, find yourself a trustworthy man to go with you, and we will pay him
wages until you return. But get back the money
from Gabael."[d]

4 So Tobias went out to look for a man to go
with him to Media, someone who was acquainted
with the way. He went out and found the angel
Raphael standing in front of him; but he did not
perceive that he was an angel of God. 5 Tobias[e]
said to him, "Where do you come from, young
man?" "From your kindred, the Israelites," he
replied, "and I have come here to work." Then
Tobias[f] said to him, "Do you know the way to go
to Media?" 6 "Yes," he replied, "I have been there
many times; I am acquainted with it and know
all the roads. I have often traveled to Media, and
would stay with our kinsman Gabael who lives
in Rages of Media. It is a journey of two days
from Ecbatana to Rages; for it lies in a mountain-
ous area, while Ecbatana is in the middle of the
plain." 7 Then Tobias said to him, "Wait for me,

[a] Gk *it* [b] Gk *sign* [c] Other authorities read *He* [d] Gk *from him* [e] Gk *He* [f] Gk *he*

young man, until I go in and tell my father; for I
do need you to travel with me, and I will pay you
your wages." 8He replied, "All right, I will wait;
but do not take too long."
9 So Tobias[a] went in to tell his father Tobit
and said to him, "I have just found a man who
is one of our own Israelite kindred!" He replied,
"Call the man in, my son, so that I may learn
about his family and to what tribe he belongs,
and whether he is trustworthy enough to go
with you."
10 Then Tobias went out and called him, and
said, "Young man, my father is calling for you." So
he went in to him, and Tobit greeted him first. He
replied, "Joyous greetings to you!" But Tobit re-
torted, "What joy is left for me any more? I am
a man without eyesight; I cannot see the light of
heaven, but I lie in darkness like the dead who
no longer see the light. Although still alive, I am
among the dead. I hear people but I cannot see
them." But the young man[a] said, "Take courage;
the time is near for God to heal you; take courage." Then Tobit said to him, "My son Tobias
wishes to go to Media. Can you accompany him
and guide him? I will pay your wages, brother."
He answered, "I can go with him and I know all
the roads, for I have often gone to Media and have
crossed all its plains, and I am familiar with its
mountains and all of its roads."
11 Then Tobit[a] said to him, "Brother, of
what family are you and from what tribe? Tell
me, brother." 12He replied, "Why do you need
to know my tribe?" But Tobit[a] said, "I want to be
sure, brother, whose son you are and what your
name is." 13He replied, "I am Azariah, the son of
the great Hananiah, one of your relatives." 14Then
Tobit said to him, "Welcome! God save you,
brother. Do not feel bitter toward me, brother,
because I wanted to be sure about your ancestry.
It turns out that you are a kinsman, and of good
and noble lineage. For I knew Hananiah and Nathan,[b] the two sons of Shemeliah,[c] and they used
to go with me to Jerusalem and worshiped with
me there, and were not led astray. Your kindred
are good people; you come of good stock. Hearty
welcome!"
15 Then he added, "I will pay you a drachma
a day as wages, as well as expenses for yourself
and my son. So go with my son, 16and[d] I will add
something to your wages." Raphael[e] answered, "I
will go with him; so do not fear. We shall leave
in good health and return to you in good health,
because the way is safe." 17So Tobit[a] said to him,
"Blessings be upon you, brother."

Then he called his son and said to him, "Son,
prepare supplies for the journey and set out with
your brother. May God in heaven bring you safely
there and return you in good health to me; and
may his angel, my son, accompany you both for
your safety."

Before he went out to start his journey, he
kissed his father and mother. Tobit then said to
him, "Have a safe journey."
18 But his mother[f] began to weep, and said to
Tobit, "Why is it that you have sent my child away?
Is he not the staff of our hand as he goes in and out
before us? 19Do not heap money upon money, but
let it be a ransom for our child. 20For the life that is
given to us by the Lord is enough for us." 21Tobit[e]
said to her, "Do not worry; our child will leave in
good health and return to us in good health. Your
eyes will see him on the day when he returns to
you in good health. Say no more! Do not fear for
them, my sister. 22For a good angel will accompany him; his journey will be successful, and he
will come back in good health." 1So she
stopped weeping.

6

The young man went out and the angel went
with him; 2and the dog came out with him and
went along with them. So they both journeyed
along, and when the first night overtook them
they camped by the Tigris river. 3Then the young
man went down to wash his feet in the Tigris
river. Suddenly a large fish leaped up from the
water and tried to swallow the young man's foot,
and he cried out. 4But the angel said to the young
man, "Catch hold of the fish and hang on to it!"

[a] Gk *he* [b] Other ancient authorities read *Jathan* or *Nathaniah* [c] Other ancient authorities read *Shemaiah*
[d] Other ancient authorities add *when you return safely* [e] Gk *He* [f] Other ancient authorities add *Anna*

So the young man grasped the fish and drew it up on the land. 5 Then the angel said to him, "Cut open the fish and take out its gall, heart, and liver. Keep them with you, but throw away the intestines. For its gall, heart, and liver are useful as medicine." 6 So after cutting open the fish the young man gathered together the gall, heart, and liver; then he roasted and ate some of the fish, and kept some to be salted.

The two continued on their way together until they were near Media.[a] 7 Then the young man questioned the angel and said to him, "Brother Azariah, what medicinal value is there in the fish's heart and liver, and in the gall?" 8 He replied, "As for the fish's heart and liver, you must burn them to make a smoke in the presence of a man or woman afflicted by a demon or evil spirit, and every affliction will flee away and never remain with that person any longer. 9 And as for the gall, anoint a person's eyes where white films have appeared on them; blow upon them, upon the white films, and the eyes[b] will be healed."

10 When he entered Media and already was approaching Ecbatana,[c] 11 Raphael said to the young man, "Brother Tobias." "Here I am," he answered. Then Raphael[d] said to him, "We must stay this night in the home of Raguel. He is your relative, and he has a daughter named Sarah. 12 He has no male heir and no daughter except Sarah only, and you, as next of kin to her, have before all other men a hereditary claim on her. Also it is right for you to inherit her father's possessions. Moreover, the girl is sensible, brave, and very beautiful, and her father is a good man." 13 He continued, "You have every right to take her in marriage. So listen to me, brother; tonight I will speak to her father about the girl, so that we may take her to be your bride. When we return from Rages we will celebrate her marriage. For I know that Raguel can by no means keep her from you or promise her to another man without incurring the penalty of death according to the decree of the book of Moses. Indeed he knows that you, rather than any other man, are entitled to marry his daughter. So now listen to me, brother, and tonight we shall speak concerning the girl and arrange her engagement to you. And when we return from Rages we will take her and bring her back with us to your house."

14 Then Tobias said in answer to Raphael, "Brother Azariah, I have heard that she already has been married to seven husbands and that they died in the bridal chamber. On the night when they went in to her, they would die. I have heard people saying that it was a demon that killed them. 15 It does not harm her, but it kills anyone who desires to approach her. So now, since I am the only son my father has, I am afraid that I may die and bring my father's and mother's life down to their grave, grieving for me—and they have no other son to bury them."

16 But Raphael[d] said to him, "Do you not remember your father's orders when he commanded you to take a wife from your father's house? Now listen to me, brother, and say no more about this demon. Take her. I know that this very night she will be given to you in marriage. 17 When you enter the bridal chamber, take some of the fish's liver and heart, and put them on the embers of the incense. An odor will be given off; 18 the demon will smell it and flee, and will never be seen near her any more. Now when you are about to go to bed with her, both of you must first stand up and pray, imploring the Lord of heaven that mercy and safety may be granted to you. Do not

Tobit 6:16

Family is a key to identity in Tobit. Like Abraham, Tobit wants his son to marry within their kinship group (4:12; see Gen 24:4). Known as endogamy, marriage to kin was a way to preserve religious, cultural, and material heritage and to strengthen social bonds within the extended family group. The moment he learns of their kinship, Tobit falls in love with Sarah and determines to marry her despite the dangers he must face.

— *APY*

[a] Other ancient authorities read *Ecbatana* [b] Gk *they* [c] Other ancient authorities read *Rages* [d] Gk *he*

be afraid, for she was set apart for you before the
world was made. You will save her, and she will
go with you. I presume that you will have children
by her, and they will be as brothers to you. Now
say no more!" When Tobias heard the words of
Raphael and learned that she was his kinswoman,[a]
related through his father's lineage, he loved her
very much, and his heart was drawn to her.

7 Now when they[b] entered Ecbatana, Tobias[c] said to him, "Brother Azariah, take me
straight to our brother Raguel." So he took him
to Raguel's house, where they found him sitting
beside the courtyard door. They greeted him first,
and he replied, "Joyous greetings, brothers; welcome and good health!" Then he brought them
into his house. 2 He said to his wife Edna, "How
much the young man resembles my kinsman
Tobit!" 3 Then Edna questioned them, saying,
"Where are you from, brothers?" They answered,
"We belong to the descendants of Naphtali who
are exiles in Nineveh." 4 She said to them, "Do
you know our kinsman Tobit?" And they replied,
"Yes, we know him." Then she asked them, "Is he[d]
in good health?" 5 They replied, "He is alive and
in good health." And Tobias added, "He is my
father!" 6 At that Raguel jumped up and kissed
him and wept. 7 He also spoke to him as follows,
"Blessings on you, my child, son of a good and
noble father![e] O most miserable of calamities
that such an upright and beneficent man has become blind!" He then embraced his kinsman Tobias and wept. 8 His wife Edna also wept for him,
and their daughter Sarah likewise wept. 9 Then
Raguel[c] slaughtered a ram from the flock and received them very warmly.

When they had bathed and washed themselves and had reclined to dine, Tobias said to
Raphael, "Brother Azariah, ask Raguel to give me
my kinswoman[a] Sarah." 10 But Raguel overheard it
and said to the lad, "Eat and drink, and be merry
tonight. For no one except you, brother, has the
right to marry my daughter Sarah. Likewise I am
not at liberty to give her to any other man than
yourself, because you are my nearest relative.
But let me explain to you the true situation more
fully, my child. 11 I have given her to seven men of
our kinsmen, and all died on the night when they
went in to her. But now, my child, eat and drink,
and the Lord will act on behalf of you both." But
Tobias said, "I will neither eat nor drink anything
until you settle the things that pertain to me." So
Raguel said, "I will do so. She is given to you in
accordance with the decree in the book of Moses,
and it has been decreed from heaven that she be
given to you. Take your kinswoman;[a] from now
on you are her brother and she is your sister. She
is given to you from today and forever. May the
Lord of heaven, my child, guide and prosper you
both this night and grant you mercy and peace."
12 Then Raguel summoned his daughter Sarah.
When she came to him he took her by the hand
and gave her to Tobias,[f] saying, "Take her to be
your wife in accordance with the law and decree written in the book of Moses. Take her and
bring her safely to your father. And may the God
of heaven prosper your journey with his peace."
13 Then he called her mother and told her to bring
writing material; and he wrote out a copy of a
marriage contract, to the effect that he gave her to
him as wife according to the decree of the law of
Moses. 14 Then they began to eat and drink.

15 Raguel called his wife Edna and said to
her, "Sister, get the other room ready, and take
her there." 16 So she went and made the bed in
the room as he had told her, and brought Sarah[g]
there. She wept for her daughter.[g] Then, wiping
away the tears,[h] she said to her, "Take courage,
my daughter; the Lord of heaven grant you joy[i] in
place of your sorrow. Take courage, my daughter."
Then she went out.

8 When they had finished eating and drinking
they wanted to retire; so they took the young
man and brought him into the bedroom. 2 Then
Tobias remembered the words of Raphael, and
he took the fish's liver and heart out of the bag

[a] Gk *sister* [b] Other ancient authorities read *he* [c] Gk *he* [d] Other ancient authorities add *alive and*
[e] Other ancient authorities add *When he heard that Tobit had lost his sight, he was stricken with grief and wept. Then he said,*
[f] Gk *him* [g] Gk *her* [h] Other ancient authorities read *the tears of her daughter* [i] Other ancient authorities read *favor*

where he had them and put them on the embers
of the incense. 3 The odor of the fish so repelled
the demon that he fled to the remotest parts[a] of
Egypt. But Raphael followed him, and at once
bound him there hand and foot.

4 When the parents[b] had gone out and shut
the door of the room, Tobias got out of bed and
said to Sarah,[c] "Sister, get up, and let us pray
and implore our Lord that he grant us mercy and
safety." 5 So she got up, and they began to pray and
implore that they might be kept safe. Tobias[d] began by saying,

"Blessed are you, O God of our ancestors,
and blessed is your name in all generations
forever.
Let the heavens and the whole creation bless
you forever.
6 You made Adam, and for him you made his
wife Eve
as a helper and support.
From the two of them the human race has
sprung.
You said, 'It is not good that the man should
be alone;
let us make a helper for him like himself.'
7 I now am taking this kinswoman of mine,
not because of lust,
but with sincerity.
Grant that she and I may find mercy
and that we may grow old together."

8 And they both said, "Amen, Amen." 9 Then they
went to sleep for the night.

But Raguel arose and called his servants to
him, and they went and dug a grave, 10 for he said,
"It is possible that he will die and we will become
an object of ridicule and derision." 11 When they
had finished digging the grave, Raguel went into
his house and called his wife, 12 saying, "Send one
of the maids and have her go in to see if he is alive.
But if he is dead, let us bury him without anyone
knowing it." 13 So they sent the maid, lit a lamp,
and opened the door; and she went in and found
them sound asleep together. 14 Then the maid
came out and informed them that he was alive
and that nothing was wrong. 15 So they blessed
the God of heaven, and Raguel[b] said,

"Blessed are you, O God, with every pure
blessing;
let all your chosen ones bless you.[e]
Let them bless you forever.
16 Blessed are you because you have made me
glad.
It has not turned out as I expected,
but you have dealt with us according to
your great mercy.
17 Blessed are you because you had compassion
on two only children.
Be merciful to them, O Master, and keep
them safe;
bring their lives to fulfillment
in happiness and mercy."

18 Then he ordered his servants to fill in the grave
before daybreak.

19 After this he asked his wife to bake many
loaves of bread; and he went out to the herd and
brought two steers and four rams and ordered
them to be slaughtered. So they began to make
preparations. 20 Then he called for Tobias and
swore on oath to him in these words:[f] "You shall
not leave here for fourteen days, but shall stay
here eating and drinking with me; and you shall
cheer up my daughter, who has been depressed.
21 Take at once half of what I own and return in
safety to your father; the other half will be yours
when my wife and I die. Take courage, my child. I
am your father and Edna is your mother, and we
belong to you as well as to your wife[g] now and
forever. Take courage, my child."

9 Then Tobias called Raphael and said to him,
2 "Brother Azariah, take four servants and
two camels with you and travel to Rages. Go to
the home of Gabael, give him the bond, get the
money, and then bring him with you to the wedding celebration. 4 For you know that my father
must be counting the days, and if I delay even
one day I will upset him very much. 3 You are
witness to the oath Raguel has sworn, and I cannot violate his oath."[h] 5 So Raphael with the four

[a] Or *fled through the air to the parts* [b] Gk *they* [c] Gk *her* [d] Gk *He* [e] Other ancient authorities lack this line
[f] Other ancient authorities read *Tobias and said to him* [g] Gk *sister* [h] In other ancient authorities verse 3 precedes verse 4

servants and two camels went to Rages in Media
and stayed with Gabael. Raphael[a] gave him the
bond and informed him that Tobit's son Tobias
had married and was inviting him to the wedding
celebration. So Gabael[b] got up and counted out to
him the money bags, with their seals intact; then
they loaded them on the camels.[c] 6 In the morning
they both got up early and went to the wedding
celebration. When they came into Raguel's house
they found Tobias reclining at table. He sprang
up and greeted Gabael,[d] who wept and blessed
him with the words, "Good and noble son of a father good and noble, upright and generous! May
the Lord grant the blessing of heaven to you and
your wife, and to your wife's father and mother.
Blessed be God, for I see in Tobias the very image
of my cousin Tobit."

10 Now, day by day, Tobit kept counting
how many days Tobias[b] would need for
going and for returning. And when the days had
passed and his son did not appear, 2 he said, "Is
it possible that he has been detained? Or that
Gabael has died, and there is no one to give him
the money?" 3 And he began to worry. 4 His wife
Anna said, "My child has perished and is no
longer among the living." And she began to weep
and mourn for her son, saying, 5 "Woe to me, my
child, the light of my eyes, that I let you make the
journey." 6 But Tobit kept saying to her, "Be quiet
and stop worrying, my dear;[e] he is all right. Probably something unexpected has happened there.
The man who went with him is trustworthy and
is one of our own kin. Do not grieve for him, my
dear;[e] he will soon be here." 7 She answered him,
"Be quiet yourself! Stop trying to deceive me!
My child has perished." She would rush out every
day and watch the road her son had taken, and
would heed no one.[f] When the sun had set she
would go in and mourn and weep all night long,
getting no sleep at all.

Now when the fourteen days of the wedding
celebration had ended that Raguel had sworn to
observe for his daughter, Tobias came to him and
said, "Send me back, for I know that my father and
mother do not believe that they will see me again.
So I beg of you, father, to let me go so that I may
return to my own father. I have already explained
to you how I left him." 8 But Raguel said to Tobias,
"Stay, my child, stay with me; I will send messengers to your father Tobit and they will inform him
about you." 9 But he said, "No! I beg you to send
me back to my father." 10 So Raguel promptly
gave Tobias his wife Sarah, as well as half of all
his property: male and female slaves, oxen and
sheep, donkeys and camels, clothing, money,
and household goods. 11 Then he saw them safely
off; he embraced Tobias[d] and said, "Farewell, my
child; have a safe journey. The Lord of heaven
prosper you and your wife Sarah, and may I see
children of yours before I die." 12 Then he kissed
his daughter Sarah and said to her, "My daughter, honor your father-in-law and your mother-in-
law,[g] since from now on they are as much your
parents as those who gave you birth. Go in peace,
daughter, and may I hear a good report about you
as long as I live." Then he bade them farewell and
let them go. Then Edna said to Tobias, "My child
and dear brother, the Lord of heaven bring you
back safely, and may I live long enough to see
children of you and of my daughter Sarah before
I die. In the sight of the Lord I entrust my daughter to you; do nothing to grieve her all the days of
your life. Go in peace, my child. From now on I
am your mother and Sarah is your beloved wife.[e]
May we all prosper together all the days of our
lives." Then she kissed them both and saw them
safely off. 13 Tobias parted from Raguel with happiness and joy, praising the Lord of heaven and
earth, King over all, because he had made his
journey a success. Finally, he blessed Raguel and
his wife Edna, and said, "I have been commanded
by the Lord to honor you all the days of my life."[h]

11 When they came near to Kaserin, which
is opposite Nineveh, Raphael said, 2 "You
are aware of how we left your father. 3 Let us run

[a] Gk *He* [b] Gk *he* [c] Other ancient authorities lack *on the camels* [d] Gk *him* [e] Gk *sister* [f] Other ancient authorities read *and she would eat nothing* [g] Other ancient authorities lack parts of *Then . . . mother-in-law*
[h] Lat: Meaning of Gk uncertain

ahead of your wife and prepare the house while
they are still on the way." 4 As they went on together Raphael[a] said to him, "Have the gall ready."
And the dog[b] went along behind them.

5 Meanwhile Anna sat looking intently down
the road by which her son would come. 6 When
she caught sight of him coming, she said to his
father, "Look, your son is coming, and the man
who went with him!"

7 Raphael said to Tobias, before he had approached his father, "I know that his eyes will be
opened. 8 Smear the gall of the fish on his eyes;
the medicine will make the white films shrink
and peel off from his eyes, and your father will regain his sight and see the light."

9 Then Anna ran up to her son and threw
her arms around him, saying, "Now that I have
seen you, my child, I am ready to die." And she
wept. 10 Then Tobit got up and came stumbling
out through the courtyard door. Tobias went up
to him, 11 with the gall of the fish in his hand, and
holding him firmly, he blew into his eyes, saying,
"Take courage, father." With this he applied the
medicine on his eyes, 12 and it made them smart.[c]
13 Next, with both his hands he peeled off the
white films from the corners of his eyes. Then Tobit[a] saw his son and[d] threw his arms around him,
14 and he wept and said to him, "I see you, my son,
the light of my eyes!" Then he said,

"Blessed be God,
    and blessed be his great name,
    and blessed be all his holy angels.
May his holy name be blessed[e]
    throughout all the ages.
15 Though he afflicted me,
    he has had mercy upon me.[f]
    Now I see my son Tobias!"

So Tobit went in rejoicing and praising God at
the top of his voice. Tobias reported to his father
that his journey had been successful, that he had
brought the money, that he had married Raguel's
daughter Sarah, and that she was, indeed, on her
way there, very near to the gate of Nineveh.

16 Then Tobit, rejoicing and praising God,
went out to meet his daughter-in-law at the gate
of Nineveh. When the people of Nineveh saw
him coming, walking along in full vigor and with
no one leading him, they were amazed. 17 Before
them all, Tobit acknowledged that God had been
merciful to him and had restored his sight. When
Tobit met Sarah the wife of his son Tobias, he
blessed her saying, "Come in, my daughter, and
welcome. Blessed be your God who has brought
you to us, my daughter. Blessed be your father
and your mother, blessed be my son Tobias, and
blessed be you, my daughter. Come in now to
your home, and welcome, with blessing and joy.
Come in, my daughter." So on that day there was
rejoicing among all the Jews who were in Nineveh. 18 Ahikar and his nephew Nadab were also
present to share Tobit's joy. With merriment they
celebrated Tobias's wedding feast for seven days,
and many gifts were given to him.[g]

12 When the wedding celebration was
ended, Tobit called his son Tobias and
said to him, "My child, see to paying the wages of
the man who went with you, and give him a bonus as well." 2 He replied, "Father, how much shall
I pay him? It would do no harm to give him half
of the possessions brought back with me. 3 For
he has led me back to you safely, he cured my
wife, he brought the money back with me, and
he healed you. How much extra shall I give him
as a bonus?" 4 Tobit said, "He deserves, my child,
to receive half of all that he brought back." 5 So
Tobias[a] called him and said, "Take for your wages
half of all that you brought back, and farewell."

6 Then Raphael[a] called the two of them
privately and said to them, "Bless God and acknowledge him in the presence of all the living
for the good things he has done for you. Bless
and sing praise to his name. With fitting honor
declare to all people the deeds[h] of God. Do not
be slow to acknowledge him. 7 It is good to conceal the secret of a king, but to acknowledge and

[a] Gk *he* [b] Codex Sinaiticus reads *And the Lord* [c] Lat: Meaning of Gk uncertain [d] Other ancient authorities lack *saw his son and* [e] Codex Sinaiticus reads *May his great name be upon us and blessed be all the angels* [f] Lat: Gk lacks this line [g] Other ancient authorities lack parts of this sentence [h] Gk *words*; other ancient authorities read *words of the deeds*

reveal the works of God, and with fitting honor
to acknowledge him. Do good and evil will not
overtake you. 8Prayer with fasting[a] is good, but
better than both is almsgiving with righteousness. A little with righteousness is better than
wealth with wrongdoing.[b] It is better to give
alms than to lay up gold. 9For almsgiving saves
from death and purges away every sin. Those
who give alms will enjoy a full life, 10but those
who commit sin and do wrong are their own
worst enemies.

11 "I will now declare the whole truth to
you and will conceal nothing from you. Already
I have declared it to you when I said, 'It is good
to conceal the secret of a king, but to reveal with
due honor the works of God.' 12So now when you
and Sarah prayed, it was I who brought and read[c]
the record of your prayer before the glory of the
Lord, and likewise whenever you would bury the
dead. 13And that time when you did not hesitate
to get up and leave your dinner to go and bury
the dead, 14I was sent to you to test you. And at
the same time God sent me to heal you and Sarah
your daughter-in-law. 15I am Raphael, one of the
seven angels who stand ready and enter before
the glory of the Lord."

16 The two of them were shaken; they fell
face down, for they were afraid. 17But he said
to them, "Do not be afraid; peace be with you.
Bless God forevermore. 18As for me, when I was
with you, I was not acting on my own will, but
by the will of God. Bless him each and every day;
sing his praises. 19Although you were watching
me, I really did not eat or drink anything—but
what you saw was a vision. 20So now get up from
the ground,[d] and acknowledge God. See, I am
ascending to him who sent me. Write down all
these things that have happened to you." And he
ascended. 21Then they stood up, and could see
him no more. 22They kept blessing God and singing his praises, and they acknowledged God for
these marvelous deeds of his, when an angel of
God had appeared to them.

13 Then Tobit[e] said:
"Blessed be God who lives forever,
because his kingdom[f] lasts throughout all ages.
2 For he afflicts, and he shows mercy;
he leads down to Hades in the lowest regions of the earth,
and he brings up from the great abyss,[g]
and there is nothing that can escape his hand.
3 Acknowledge him before the nations,
O children of Israel;
for he has scattered you among them.
4 He has shown you his greatness even there.
Exalt him in the presence of every living being,
because he is our Lord and he is our God;
he is our Father and he is God forever.
5 He will afflict[h] you for your iniquities,
but he will again show mercy on all of you.
He will gather you from all the nations
among whom you have been scattered.
6 If you turn to him with all your heart and with all your soul,
to do what is true before him,
then he will turn to you
and will no longer hide his face from you.
So now see what he has done for you;
acknowledge him at the top of your voice.
Bless the Lord of righteousness,
and exalt the King of the ages.[i]
In the land of my exile I acknowledge him,
and show his power and majesty to a nation of sinners:
'Turn back, you sinners, and do what is right before him;
perhaps he may look with favor upon you
and show you mercy.'
7 As for me, I exalt my God,
and my soul rejoices in the King of heaven.
8 Let all people speak of his majesty,
and acknowledge him in Jerusalem.
9 O Jerusalem, the holy city,

[a] Codex Sinaiticus *with sincerity* [b] Lat [c] Lat: Gk lacks *and read* [d] Other ancient authorities read *now bless the Lord on earth* [e] Gk *he* [f] Other ancient authorities read *forever, and his kingdom* [g] Gk *from destruction* [h] Other ancient authorities read *He afflicted* [i] The lacuna in codex Sinaiticus, verses 6b to 10a, is filled in from other ancient authorities

he afflicted[a] you for the deeds of your
hands,[b]
but will again have mercy on the children
of the righteous.
10 Acknowledge the Lord, for he is good,[c]
and bless the King of the ages,
so that his tent[d] may be rebuilt in you in joy.
May he cheer all those within you who are
captives,
and love all those within you who are
distressed,
to all generations forever.
11 A bright light will shine to all the ends of the
earth;
many nations will come to you from far
away,
the inhabitants of the remotest parts of the
earth to your holy name,
bearing gifts in their hands for the King of
heaven.
Generation after generation will give joyful
praise in you;
the name of the chosen city will endure
forever.
12 Cursed are all who speak a harsh word against
you;
cursed are all who conquer you
and pull down your walls,
all who overthrow your towers
and set your homes on fire.
But blessed forever will be all who revere
you.[e]
13 Go, then, and rejoice over the children of the
righteous,
for they will be gathered together
and will praise the Lord of the ages.
14 Happy are those who love you,
and happy are those who rejoice in your
prosperity.
Happy also are all people who grieve with
you
because of your afflictions;
for they will rejoice with you
and witness all your glory forever.
15 My soul blesses[f] the Lord, the great King!
16 For Jerusalem will be built[g] as his house
for all ages.
How happy I will be if a remnant of my
descendants should survive
to see your glory and acknowledge the
King of heaven.
The gates of Jerusalem will be built with
sapphire and emerald,
and all your walls with precious stones.
The towers of Jerusalem will be built with
gold,
and their battlements with pure gold.
The streets of Jerusalem will be paved
with ruby and with stones of Ophir.
17 The gates of Jerusalem will sing hymns of joy,
and all her houses will cry, 'Hallelujah!
Blessed be the God of Israel!'
and the blessed will bless the holy name
forever and ever."

14 So ended Tobit's words of praise.
2 Tobit[h] died in peace when he was one
hundred twelve years old, and was buried with
great honor in Nineveh. He was sixty-two[i] years
old when he lost his eyesight, and after regain-
ing it he lived in prosperity, giving alms and continually blessing God and acknowledging God's
majesty.
3 When he was about to die, he called his son
Tobias and the seven sons of Tobias[j] and gave
this command: "My son, take your children 4and
hurry off to Media, for I believe the word of God
that Nahum spoke about Nineveh, that all these
things will take place and overtake Assyria and
Nineveh. Indeed, everything that was spoken by
the prophets of Israel, whom God sent, will occur. None of all their words will fail, but all will
come true at their appointed times. So it will be
safer in Media than in Assyria and Babylon. For I
know and believe that whatever God has said will

[a] Other ancient authorities read *will afflict* [b] Other ancient authorities read *your children* [c] Other ancient authorities read *Lord worthily* [d] Or *tabernacle* [e] Other ancient authorities read *who build you up* [f] Or *O my soul, bless* [g] Other ancient authorities add *for a city* [h] Gk *He* [i] Other ancient authorities read *fifty-eight* [j] Lat: Gk lacks *and the seven sons of Tobias*

be fulfilled and will come true; not a single word
of the prophecies will fail. All of our kindred, inhabitants of the land of Israel, will be scattered
and taken as captives from the good land; and the
whole land of Israel will be desolate, even Samaria
and Jerusalem will be desolate. And the temple of
God in it will be burned to the ground, and it will
be desolate for a while.[a]

5 "But God will again have mercy on them,
and God will bring them back into the land of
Israel; and they will rebuild the temple of God,
but not like the first one until the period when
the times of fulfillment shall come. After this they
all will return from their exile and will rebuild
Jerusalem in splendor; and in it the temple of
God will be rebuilt, just as the prophets of Israel
have said concerning it. 6 Then the nations in the
whole world will all be converted and worship
God in truth. They will all abandon their idols,
which deceitfully have led them into their error;
7 and in righteousness they will praise the eternal
God. All the Israelites who are saved in those days
and are truly mindful of God will be gathered
together; they will go to Jerusalem and live in
safety forever in the land of Abraham, and it will
be given over to them. Those who sincerely love
God will rejoice, but those who commit sin and
injustice will vanish from all the earth. 8,9 So now,
my children, I command you, serve God faithfully and do what is pleasing in his sight. Your
children are also to be commanded to do what is
right and to give alms, and to be mindful of God
and to bless his name at all times with sincerity
and with all their strength. So now, my son, leave
Nineveh; do not remain here. 10 On whatever day
you bury your mother beside me, do not stay
overnight within the confines of the city. For I see
that there is much wickedness within it, and that
much deceit is practiced within it, while the people are without shame. See, my son, what Nadab
did to Ahikar who had reared him. Was he not,
while still alive, brought down into the earth? For
God repaid him to his face for this shameful treatment. Ahikar came out into the light, but Nadab
went into the eternal darkness, because he tried
to kill Ahikar. Because he gave alms, Ahikar[b] escaped the fatal trap that Nadab had set for him,
but Nadab fell into it himself, and was destroyed.
11 So now, my children, see what almsgiving accomplishes, and what injustice does—it brings
death! But now my breath fails me."

Then they laid him on his bed, and he died;
and he received an honorable funeral. 12 When
Tobias's mother died, he buried her beside his father. Then he and his wife and children[c] returned
to Media and settled in Ecbatana with Raguel his
father-in-law. 13 He treated his parents-in-law[d]
with great respect in their old age, and buried
them in Ecbatana of Media. He inherited both
the property of Raguel and that of his father Tobit. 14 He died highly respected at the age of one
hundred seventeen[e] years. 15 Before he died he
heard[f] of the destruction of Nineveh, and he saw
its prisoners being led into Media, those whom
King Cyaxares[g] of Media had taken captive. Tobias[h] praised God for all he had done to the people of Nineveh and Assyria; before he died he
rejoiced over Nineveh, and he blessed the Lord
God forever and ever. Amen.[i]

Tobit 14:12-13

Tobit teaches what it means to honor mother and father through example and instruction. Anticipating his death, Tobit instructs his son to honor his mother, Anna, remaining mindful of her trials in childbearing (4:3-4). Throughout the story, Tobiah and Sarah act to ensure their parents' health and well-being and care for them in their old age. Tobiah provides honorable burial for Tobit, Anna, Raguel, and Edna.

—APY

[a] Lat: Other ancient authorities read *of God will be in distress and will be burned for a while* [b] Gk *he*; other ancient authorities read *Manasses* [c] Codex Sinaiticus lacks *and children* [d] Gk *them* [e] Other authorities read other numbers [f] Codex Sinaiticus reads *saw and heard* [g] Cn: Codex Sinaiticus *Ahikar*; other ancient authorities read *Nebuchadnezzar and Ahasuerus* [h] Gk *He* [i] Other ancient authorities lack *Amen*

Judith

Judith has been celebrated in works of art as a Jewish and Christian example of piety, fidelity, courage, godliness, and celibacy, even though the book was not part of the Hebrew or Protestant canons. My interest in Judith stems from its canonical status in my church, my preference for feminist readings of the biblical text, and from my regular participation in Reconstructionist Jewish liturgy. Judith is one of the most active and vocal women in the canon, comparable to Rebekah (Gen 24:15-67). Like Deborah and Jael (Judges 4–5), she is (or becomes) a warrior and psalmist, and, like Jael (Judg 5:28-30), she is a defender of raped women. In addition, Judith contains one of the few biblical references to rape from a woman's perspective.

The text is full of historical inaccuracies, leading many scholars to classify it as fiction. Nebuchadnezzar is depicted as ruling from Nineveh, even though it was destroyed before he ascended to the throne. Babylon is never mentioned, even though Nebuchadnezzar ruled Babylon, not Assyria. The temple is described as being rebuilt, although that would not happen until nearly fifty years after his death. In addition, Judith's hometown of Bethulia is unknown. It is depicted as being in Samaria, but this is problematic given the setting at a time when Samaritans were reviled and not recognized by Judeans as legitimate worshippers of YHWH. The conversion to Judaism of Achior the Ammonite at the end of the story is also a challenge to reading the text literally, because the Ammonites were perhaps more reviled than Samaritans. Holofernes, Nebuchadnezzar's general, is otherwise unknown, and the Persian form of his name makes it unlikely for an Assyrian (or Babylonian). While the exact date of Judith's composition is unknown, it must be dated no later than the first century CE because of Clement's discussion of the text. A likely period is 76–67 BCE, which would make Judith a celebration of the widowed and pious Queen Salome Alexandra.

Even though the book bears the name of its heroine, the first seven chapters do not mention her. The book opens with a long description, set in the time of Nebuchadnezzar, of the hostilities between Israel and Assyria. When Judith is introduced in chapter 8, she is presented with the longest genealogy of any character in the First Testament (Hebrew or Greek), and, with the exception of Jesus, any character in the Christian New Testament. It is hard for some scholars, myself among them, to accept the whole of Judith's lengthy genealogy as fictionalized, so perhaps the text should be understood as historical fiction. A number of Judith's most distant ancestors, Simeon, Shelumiel and Zurishaddai, are mentioned in several other places (Num 1:6, 2:12, 7:36, 7:41, and 10:19).

In the story, Israel is besieged by the Assyrians and the people blame their leaders, particularly Uzziah the magistrate, for failing to capitulate to the Assyrians. He urges the people to wait five days for God to intervene, promising that if nothing happens he will surrender on their behalf. The people cry out to God in 7:29 in despair and defeat; Judith responds to the people's distress by summoning the leaders of the magistrates and exhorting them in 8:11-27. She will not demand that God perform on a human timetable, nor will she countenance surrender. Judith will become the vessel of God's deliverance; she is blessed by the leaders and people, even though they cannot know what she will do.

In chapter 9 Judith prays the longest prayer, thirteen verses, attributed to any woman in the Bible. Judith's prayer begins with the certainties that women will be raped in the coming war and that their rape is contrary to the will of God (v. 2). This aspect of the text leads some feminists to believe that Judith was composed in part by a woman. However, Judith also ascribes to God the practice of the abduction and rape of enemy women and girls, seeing that as God's justice (vv. 3-4).

In chapter 10, Judith rides off with her unnamed woman-servant on the adventure of her life. She Judith dresses herself to display her beauty (10:3-4) and offers herself as an informant to Holofernes. Maintaining her piety by eating only her own kosher food (12:2), she dines with Holofernes as he gets drunk. Judith's virtue is suspect—and was condemned by Victorian readers—because she does not keep her servant with her (12:15). For his part, Holofernes intends to seduce her (12:12). But he passes out "dead drunk" before he can do the deed (13:2). With two blows, Judith decapitates Holofernes with his own sword (13:7-8). She puts his head in her now-empty food bag, and we must presume that no one notices a blood trail as she leaves the enemy camp to rejoin her people, as though she were just going for prayer (13:10-11).

When Judith arrives home, she proclaims (echoing Deborah) that Holofernes was struck down by the hand of a woman and (perhaps in opposition to Jael) that God had kept Holofernes from molesting her (13:16). Judith is then blessed in words given to Jael and Mary of Nazareth: "you are blessed by the Most High God above all other women on earth" (13:18). With the head of Holofernes on the wall (14:1, 11), Judith offers a psalm (16:1-17). She then returns to her widowhood, refusing all suitors, and lives to the age of 105, setting her servant free and giving away her substantial possessions before her death (16:21-24). Her epitaph is verse 25: "No one ever again spread terror among the Israelites during the lifetime of Judith, or for a long time after her death."

— ***Wilda C. Gafney***

1 It was the twelfth year of the reign of Nebuchadnezzar, who ruled over the Assyrians in
the great city of Nineveh. In those days Arphaxad
ruled over the Medes in Ecbatana. 2 He built walls
around Ecbatana with hewn stones three cubits
thick and six cubits long; he made the walls seventy cubits high and fifty cubits wide. 3 At its
gates he raised towers one hundred cubits high
and sixty cubits wide at the foundations. 4 He
made its gates seventy cubits high and forty cubits wide to allow his armies to march out in
force and his infantry to form their ranks. 5 Then
King Nebuchadnezzar made war against King
Arphaxad in the great plain that is on the borders
of Ragau. 6 There rallied to him all the people of
the hill country and all those who lived along the

Judith 1:1

Some Western or Ashkenazic Jewish feminists have adopted an Eastern or Sephardic practice of associating the book of Judith with the festival of Hanukkah, celebrating Judith and Judah Maccabee as saviors of Israel. In Episcopal and other Anglican churches, a reading from Judith is used for the Feast of Saint Mary Magdalene.

— *WG*

Euphrates, the Tigris, and the Hydaspes, and, on
the plain, Arioch, king of the Elymeans. Thus,
many nations joined the forces of the Chaldeans.[a]
7 Then Nebuchadnezzar, king of the Assyrians, sent messengers to all who lived in Persia
and to all who lived in the west, those who lived
in Cilicia and Damascus, Lebanon and Antileba-
non, and all who lived along the seacoast, 8and
those among the nations of Carmel and Gilead,
and Upper Galilee and the great plain of Esdraelon, 9and all who were in Samaria and its towns,
and beyond the Jordan as far as Jerusalem and
Bethany and Chelous and Kadesh and the river
of Egypt, and Tahpanhes and Raamses and the
whole land of Goshen, 10even beyond Tanis and
Memphis, and all who lived in Egypt as far as the
borders of Ethiopia. 11But all who lived in the
whole region disregarded the summons of Nebuchadnezzar, king of the Assyrians, and refused
to join him in the war; for they were not afraid
of him, but regarded him as only one man.[b] So
they sent back his messengers empty-handed and
in disgrace.
12 Then Nebuchadnezzar became very angry
with this whole region, and swore by his throne
and kingdom that he would take revenge on the
whole territory of Cilicia and Damascus and
Syria, that he would kill with his sword also all
the inhabitants of the land of Moab, and the people of Ammon, and all Judea, and every one in
Egypt, as far as the coasts of the two seas.
13 In the seventeenth year he led his forces
against King Arphaxad and defeated him in battle, overthrowing the whole army of Arphaxad
and all his cavalry and all his chariots. 14Thus he
took possession of his towns and came to Ecbatana, captured its towers, plundered its markets,
and turned its glory into disgrace. 15He captured
Arphaxad in the mountains of Ragau and struck
him down with his spears, thus destroying him
once and for all. 16Then he returned to Nineveh, he and all his combined forces, a vast body
of troops; and there he and his forces rested and
feasted for one hundred twenty days.
2 In the eighteenth year, on the twenty-second
day of the first month, there was talk in the
palace of Nebuchadnezzar, king of the Assyrians,
about carrying out his revenge on the whole region, just as he had said. 2He summoned all his
ministers and all his nobles and set before them
his secret plan and recounted fully, with his own
lips, all the wickedness of the region.[c] 3They decided that every one who had not obeyed his
command should be destroyed.
4 When he had completed his plan, Nebuchadnezzar, king of the Assyrians, called Holofernes, the chief general of his army, second only
to himself, and said to him, 5"Thus says the Great
King, the lord of the whole earth: Leave my presence and take with you men confident in their
strength, one hundred twenty thousand foot soldiers and twelve thousand cavalry. 6March out
against all the land to the west, because they disobeyed my orders. 7Tell them to prepare earth
and water, for I am coming against them in my
anger, and will cover the whole face of the earth
with the feet of my troops, to whom I will hand
them over to be plundered. 8Their wounded shall
fill their ravines and gullies, and the swelling river
shall be filled with their dead. 9I will lead them
away captive to the ends of the whole earth.
10You shall go and seize all their territory for me
in advance. They must yield themselves to you,
and you shall hold them for me until the day of
their punishment. 11But to those who resist show
no mercy, but hand them over to slaughter and

[a] Syr: Gk *Cheleoudites* [b] Or *a man* [c] Meaning of Gk uncertain

plunder throughout your whole region. 12For as I live, and by the power of my kingdom, what I have spoken I will accomplish by my own hand. 13And you—take care not to transgress any of your lord's commands, but carry them out exactly as I have ordered you; do it without delay."

14 So Holofernes left the presence of his lord, and summoned all the commanders, generals, and officers of the Assyrian army. 15He mustered the picked troops by divisions as his lord had ordered him to do, one hundred twenty thousand of them, together with twelve thousand archers on horseback, 16and he organized them as a great army is marshaled for a campaign. 17He took along a vast number of camels and donkeys and mules for transport, and innumerable sheep and oxen and goats for food; 18also ample rations for everyone, and a huge amount of gold and silver from the royal palace.

19 Then he set out with his whole army, to go ahead of King Nebuchadnezzar and to cover the whole face of the earth to the west with their chariots and cavalry and picked foot soldiers. 20Along with them went a mixed crowd like a swarm of locusts, like the dust[a] of the earth—a multitude that could not be counted.

21 They marched for three days from Nineveh to the plain of Bectileth, and camped opposite Bectileth near the mountain that is to the north of Upper Cilicia. 22From there Holofernes[b] took his whole army, the infantry, cavalry, and chariots, and went up into the hill country. 23He ravaged Put and Lud, and plundered all the Rassisites and the Ishmaelites on the border of the desert, south of the country of the Chelleans. 24Then he followed[c] the Euphrates and passed through Mesopotamia and destroyed all the fortified towns along the brook Abron, as far as the sea. 25He also seized the territory of Cilicia, and killed everyone who resisted him. Then he came to the southern borders of Japheth, facing Arabia. 26He surrounded all the Midianites, and burned their tents and plundered their sheepfolds. 27Then he went down into the plain of Damascus during the wheat harvest, and burned all their fields and destroyed their flocks and herds and sacked their towns and ravaged their lands and put all their young men to the sword.

28 So fear and dread of him fell upon all the people who lived along the seacoast, at Sidon and Tyre, and those who lived in Sur and Ocina and all who lived in Jamnia. Those who lived in Azotus and Ascalon feared him greatly.

3 They therefore sent messengers to him to sue for peace in these words: 2"We, the servants of Nebuchadnezzar, the Great King, lie prostrate before you. Do with us whatever you will. 3See, our buildings and all our land and all our wheat fields and our flocks and herds and all our encampments[d] lie before you; do with them as you please. 4Our towns and their inhabitants are also your slaves; come and deal with them as you see fit."

5 The men came to Holofernes and told him all this. 6Then he went down to the seacoast with his army and stationed garrisons in the fortified towns and took picked men from them as auxiliaries. 7These people and all in the countryside welcomed him with garlands and dances and tambourines. 8Yet he demolished all their shrines[e] and cut down their sacred groves; for he had been commissioned to destroy all the gods of the land, so that all nations should worship Nebuchadnezzar alone, and that all their dialects and tribes should call upon him as a god.

9 Then he came toward Esdraelon, near Dothan, facing the great ridge of Judea; 10he camped between Geba and Scythopolis, and remained for a whole month in order to collect all the supplies for his army.

4 When the Israelites living in Judea heard of everything that Holofernes, the general of Nebuchadnezzar, the king of the Assyrians, had done to the nations, and how he had plundered and destroyed all their temples, 2they were therefore greatly terrified at his approach; they were alarmed both for Jerusalem and for the temple of the Lord their God. 3For they had only recently returned from exile, and all the people of Judea had just now gathered together, and the sacred vessels and the altar and the temple had been

[a] Gk *sand* [b] Gk *he* [c] Or *crossed* [d] Gk *all the sheepfolds of our tents* [e] Syr: Gk *borders*

consecrated after their profanation. 4So they sent
word to every district of Samaria, and to Kona,
Beth-horon, Belmain, and Jericho, and to Choba
and Aesora, and the valley of Salem. 5They immediately seized all the high hilltops and fortified
the villages on them and stored up food in preparation for war—since their fields had recently
been harvested.

6 The high priest, Joakim, who was in Jerusalem at the time, wrote to the people of Bethulia
and Betomesthaim, which faces Esdraelon opposite the plain near Dothan, 7ordering them to
seize the mountain passes, since by them Judea
could be invaded; and it would be easy to stop
any who tried to enter, for the approach was narrow, wide enough for only two at a time to pass.

8 So the Israelites did as they had been ordered by the high priest Joakim and the senate
of the whole people of Israel, in session at Jerusalem. 9And every man of Israel cried out to God
with great fervor, and they humbled themselves
with much fasting. 10They and their wives and
their children and their cattle and every resident
alien and hired laborer and purchased slave—
they all put sackcloth around their waists. 11And
all the Israelite men, women, and children living
at Jerusalem prostrated themselves before the
temple and put ashes on their heads and spread
out their sackcloth before the Lord. 12They even
draped the altar with sackcloth and cried out in
unison, praying fervently to the God of Israel not
to allow their infants to be carried off and their
wives to be taken as booty, and the towns they
had inherited to be destroyed, and the sanctuary
to be profaned and desecrated to the malicious
joy of the Gentiles.

13 The Lord heard their prayers and had regard for their distress; for the people fasted many
days throughout Judea and in Jerusalem before
the sanctuary of the Lord Almighty. 14The high
priest Joakim and all the priests who stood before
the Lord and ministered to the Lord, with sackcloth around their loins, offered the daily burnt
offerings, the votive offerings, and freewill offerings of the people. 15With ashes on their turbans,
they cried out to the Lord with all their might to
look with favor on the whole house of Israel.

5 It was reported to Holofernes, the general of
the Assyrian army, that the people of Israel
had prepared for war and had closed the mountain passes and fortified all the high hilltops and
set up barricades in the plains. 2In great anger he
called together all the princes of Moab and the
commanders of Ammon and all the governors of
the coastland, 3and said to them, "Tell me, you
Canaanites, what people is this that lives in the
hill country? What towns do they inhabit? How
large is their army, and in what does their power
and strength consist? Who rules over them as
king and leads their army? 4And why have they
alone, of all who live in the west, refused to come
out and meet me?"

5 Then Achior, the leader of all the Ammonites, said to him, "May my lord please listen to a
report from the mouth of your servant, and I will
tell you the truth about this people that lives in
the mountain district near you. No falsehood shall
come from your servant's mouth. 6These people
are descended from the Chaldeans. 7At one time
they lived in Mesopotamia, because they did not
wish to follow the gods of their ancestors who
were in Chaldea. 8Since they had abandoned the
ways of their ancestors, and worshiped the God
of heaven, the God they had come to know, their
ancestors[a] drove them out from the presence of
their gods. So they fled to Mesopotamia, and
lived there for a long time. 9Then their God commanded them to leave the place where they were
living and go to the land of Canaan. There they
settled, and grew very prosperous in gold and silver and very much livestock. 10When a famine
spread over the land of Canaan they went down
to Egypt and lived there as long as they had food.
There they became so great a multitude that their
race could not be counted. 11So the king of Egypt
became hostile to them; he exploited them and
forced them to make bricks. 12They cried out
to their God, and he afflicted the whole land of
Egypt with incurable plagues. So the Egyptians
drove them out of their sight. 13Then God dried

[a] Gk *they*

up the Red Sea before them, 14 and he led them by
the way of Sinai and Kadesh-barnea. They drove
out all the people of the desert, 15 and took up residence in the land of the Amorites, and by their
might destroyed all the inhabitants of Heshbon;
and crossing over the Jordan they took possession
of all the hill country. 16 They drove out before
them the Canaanites, the Perizzites, the Jebusites,
the Shechemites, and all the Gergesites, and lived
there a long time.

17 "As long as they did not sin against their
God they prospered, for the God who hates iniquity is with them. 18 But when they departed from
the way he had prescribed for them, they were utterly defeated in many battles and were led away
captive to a foreign land. The temple of their God
was razed to the ground, and their towns were
occupied by their enemies. 19 But now they have
returned to their God, and have come back from
the places where they were scattered, and have
occupied Jerusalem, where their sanctuary is, and
have settled in the hill country, because it was uninhabited.

20 "So now, my master and lord, if there is any
oversight in this people and they sin against their
God and we find out their offense, then we can go
up and defeat them. 21 But if they are not a guilty
nation, then let my lord pass them by; for their
Lord and God will defend them, and we shall become the laughingstock of the whole world."

22 When Achior had finished saying these
things, all the people standing around the tent began to complain; Holofernes' officers and all the
inhabitants of the seacoast and Moab insisted that
he should be cut to pieces. 23 They said, "We are
not afraid of the Israelites; they are a people with
no strength or power for making war. 24 Therefore
let us go ahead, Lord Holofernes, and your vast
army will swallow them up."

6 When the disturbance made by the people
outside the council had died down, Holofernes, the commander of the Assyrian army,
said to Achior[a] in the presence of all the foreign
contingents:

2 "Who are you, Achior and you mercenaries
of Ephraim, to prophesy among us as you have
done today and tell us not to make war against
the people of Israel because their God will defend them? What god is there except Nebuchadnezzar? He will send his forces and destroy them
from the face of the earth. Their God will not save
them; 3 we the king's[b] servants will destroy them
as one man. They cannot resist the might of our
cavalry. 4 We will overwhelm them;[c] their mountains will be drunk with their blood, and their
fields will be full of their dead. Not even their
footprints will survive our attack; they will utterly perish. So says King Nebuchadnezzar, lord
of the whole earth. For he has spoken; none of his
words shall be in vain.

5 "As for you, Achior, you Ammonite mercenary, you have said these words in a moment of
perversity; you shall not see my face again from
this day until I take revenge on this race that
came out of Egypt. 6 Then at my return the sword
of my army and the spear[d] of my servants shall
pierce your sides, and you shall fall among their
wounded. 7 Now my slaves are going to take you
back into the hill country and put you in one of
the towns beside the passes. 8 You will not die until you perish along with them. 9 If you really hope
in your heart that they will not be taken, then do
not look downcast! I have spoken, and none of
my words shall fail to come true."

10 Then Holofernes ordered his slaves, who
waited on him in his tent, to seize Achior and take
him away to Bethulia and hand him over to the
Israelites. 11 So the slaves took him and led him
out of the camp into the plain, and from the plain
they went up into the hill country and came to
the springs below Bethulia. 12 When the men of
the town saw them,[e] they seized their weapons
and ran out of the town to the top of the hill,
and all the slingers kept them from coming up by
throwing stones at them. 13 So having taken shelter below the hill, they bound Achior and left him
lying at the foot of the hill, and returned to their
master.

[a] Other ancient authorities add *and to all the Moabites* [b] Gk *his* [c] Other ancient authorities add *with it* [d] Lat Syr: Gk *people* [e] Other ancient authorities add *on the top of the hill*

14 Then the Israelites came down from their town and found him; they untied him and brought him into Bethulia and placed him before the magistrates of their town, 15 who in those days were Uzziah son of Micah, of the tribe of Simeon, and Chabris son of Gothoniel, and Charmis son of Melchiel. 16 They called together all the elders of the town, and all their young men and women ran to the assembly. They set Achior in the midst of all their people, and Uzziah questioned him about what had happened. 17 He answered and told them what had taken place at the council of Holofernes, and all that he had said in the presence of the Assyrian leaders, and all that Holofernes had boasted he would do against the house of Israel. 18 Then the people fell down and worshiped God, and cried out:

19 "O Lord God of heaven, see their arrogance, and have pity on our people in their humiliation, and look kindly today on the faces of those who are consecrated to you."

20 Then they reassured Achior, and praised him highly. 21 Uzziah took him from the assembly to his own house and gave a banquet for the elders; and all that night they called on the God of Israel for help.

7 The next day Holofernes ordered his whole army, and all the allies who had joined him, to break camp and move against Bethulia, and to seize the passes up into the hill country and make war on the Israelites. 2 So all their warriors marched off that day; their fighting forces numbered one hundred seventy thousand infantry and twelve thousand cavalry, not counting the baggage and the foot soldiers handling it, a very great multitude. 3 They encamped in the valley near Bethulia, beside the spring, and they spread out in breadth over Dothan as far as Balbaim and in length from Bethulia to Cyamon, which faces Esdraelon.

4 When the Israelites saw their vast numbers, they were greatly terrified and said to one another, "They will now strip clean the whole land; neither the high mountains nor the valleys nor the hills will bear their weight." 5 Yet they all seized their weapons, and when they had kindled fires on their towers, they remained on guard all that night.

6 On the second day Holofernes led out all his cavalry in full view of the Israelites in Bethulia. 7 He reconnoitered the approaches to their town, and visited the springs that supplied their water; he seized them and set guards of soldiers over them, and then returned to his army.

8 Then all the chieftains of the Edomites and all the leaders of the Moabites and the commanders of the coastland came to him and said, 9 "Listen to what we have to say, my lord, and your army will suffer no losses. 10 This people, the Israelites, do not rely on their spears but on the height of the mountains where they live, for it is not easy to reach the tops of their mountains. 11 Therefore, my lord, do not fight against them in regular formation, and not a man of your army will fall. 12 Remain in your camp, and keep all the men in your forces with you; let your servants take possession of the spring of water that flows from the foot of the mountain, 13 for this is where all the people of Bethulia get their water. So thirst will destroy them, and they will surrender their town. Meanwhile, we and our people will go up to the tops of the nearby mountains and camp there to keep watch to see that no one gets out of the town. 14 They and their wives and children will waste away with famine, and before the sword reaches them they will be strewn about in the streets where they live. 15 Thus you will pay them back with evil, because they rebelled and did not receive you peaceably."

16 These words pleased Holofernes and all his attendants, and he gave orders to do as they had said. 17 So the army of the Ammonites moved forward, together with five thousand Assyrians, and they encamped in the valley and seized the water supply and the springs of the Israelites. 18 And the Edomites and Ammonites went up and encamped in the hill country opposite Dothan; and they sent some of their men toward the south and the east, toward Egrebeh, which is near Chusi beside the Wadi Mochmur. The rest of the Assyrian army encamped in the plain, and covered the whole face of the land. Their tents and supply trains spread out in great number, and they formed a vast multitude.

19 The Israelites then cried out to the Lord

their God, for their courage failed, because all their enemies had surrounded them, and there was no way of escape from them. [20]The whole Assyrian army, their infantry, chariots, and cavalry, surrounded them for thirty-four days, until all the water containers of every inhabitant of Bethulia were empty; [21]their cisterns were going dry, and on no day did they have enough water to drink, for their drinking water was rationed. [22]Their children were listless, and the women and young men fainted from thirst and were collapsing in the streets of the town and in the gateways; they no longer had any strength.

23 Then all the people, the young men, the women, and the children, gathered around Uzziah and the rulers of the town and cried out with a loud voice, and said before all the elders, [24]"Let God judge between you and us! You have done us a great injury in not making peace with the Assyrians. [25]For now we have no one to help us; God has sold us into their hands, to be strewn before them in thirst and exhaustion. [26]Now summon them and surrender the whole town as booty to the army of Holofernes and to all his forces. [27]For it would be better for us to be captured by them.[a] We shall indeed become slaves, but our lives will be spared, and we shall not witness our little ones dying before our eyes, and our wives and children drawing their last breath. [28]We call to witness against you heaven and earth and our God, the Lord of our ancestors, who punishes us for our sins and the sins of our ancestors; do today the things that we have described!"

29 Then great and general lamentation arose throughout the assembly, and they cried out to the Lord God with a loud voice. [30]But Uzziah said to them, "Courage, my brothers and sisters![b] Let us hold out for five days more; by that time the Lord our God will turn his mercy to us again, for he will not forsake us utterly. [31]But if these days pass by, and no help comes for us, I will do as you say."

32 Then he dismissed the people to their various posts, and they went up on the walls and towers of their town. The women and children he sent home. In the town they were in great misery.

8 Now in those days Judith heard about these things: she was the daughter of Merari son of Ox son of Joseph son of Oziel son of Elkiah son of Ananias son of Gideon son of Raphain son of Ahitub son of Elijah son of Hilkiah son of Eliab son of Nathanael son of Salamiel son of Sarasadai son of Israel. [2]Her husband Manasseh, who belonged to her tribe and family, had died during the barley harvest. [3]For as he stood overseeing those who were binding sheaves in the field, he was overcome by the burning heat, and took to his bed and died in his town Bethulia. So they buried him with his ancestors in the field between Dothan and Balamon. [4]Judith remained as a widow for three years and four months [5]at home where she set up a tent for herself on the roof of her house. She put sackcloth around her waist and dressed in widow's clothing. [6]She fasted all the days of her widowhood, except the day before the sabbath and the sabbath itself, the day before the new moon and the day of the new moon, and the festivals and days of rejoicing of the house of Israel. [7]She was beautiful in appearance, and was very lovely to behold. Her husband Manasseh had left her gold and silver, men and women slaves, livestock, and fields; and she maintained this estate. [8]No one spoke ill of her, for she feared God with great devotion.

9 When Judith heard the harsh words spoken by the people against the ruler, because they were

Judith 8:4

There are parallels between Judith and the prophet Anna in Luke 2:36-38. Both are widows known for their piety, as signaled by their prayer and fasting. And both are associated with the salvation of Israel, Judith by her own hand and Anna through Jesus of Nazareth about whom she prophesied.

— *WG*

[a] Other ancient authorities add *than to die of thirst* [b] Gk *Courage, brothers*

faint for lack of water, and when she heard all that
Uzziah said to them, and how he promised them
under oath to surrender the town to the Assyrians after five days, 10 she sent her maid, who was
in charge of all she possessed, to summon Uzziah
and[a] Chabris and Charmis, the elders of her town.
11 They came to her, and she said to them:

"Listen to me, rulers of the people of Bethulia!
What you have said to the people today is not
right; you have even sworn and pronounced this
oath between God and you, promising to surrender the town to our enemies unless the Lord turns
and helps us within so many days. 12 Who are you
to put God to the test today, and to set yourselves
up in the place of[b] God in human affairs? 13 You
are putting the Lord Almighty to the test, but you
will never learn anything! 14 You cannot plumb
the depths of the human heart or understand the
workings of the human mind; how do you expect
to search out God, who made all these things, and
find out his mind or comprehend his thought?
No, my brothers, do not anger the Lord our God.
15 For if he does not choose to help us within
these five days, he has power to protect us within
any time he pleases, or even to destroy us in the
presence of our enemies. 16 Do not try to bind the
purposes of the Lord our God; for God is not like
a human being, to be threatened, or like a mere
mortal, to be won over by pleading. 17 Therefore,
while we wait for his deliverance, let us call upon
him to help us, and he will hear our voice, if it
pleases him.

18 "For never in our generation, nor in these
present days, has there been any tribe or family or
people or town of ours that worships gods made
with hands, as was done in days gone by. 19 That
was why our ancestors were handed over to the
sword and to pillage, and so they suffered a great
catastrophe before our enemies. 20 But we know
no other god but him, and so we hope that he will
not disdain us or any of our nation. 21 For if we
are captured, all Judea will be captured and our
sanctuary will be plundered; and he will make
us pay for its desecration with our blood. 22 The
slaughter of our kindred and the captivity of the
land and the desolation of our inheritance—all
this he will bring on our heads among the Gentiles, wherever we serve as slaves; and we shall
be an offense and a disgrace in the eyes of those
who acquire us. 23 For our slavery will not bring
us into favor, but the Lord our God will turn it
to dishonor.

24 "Therefore, my brothers, let us set an example for our kindred, for their lives depend upon
us, and the sanctuary—both the temple and the
altar—rests upon us. 25 In spite of everything let
us give thanks to the Lord our God, who is putting us to the test as he did our ancestors. 26 Remember what he did with Abraham, and how he
tested Isaac, and what happened to Jacob in Syrian Mesopotamia, while he was tending the sheep
of Laban, his mother's brother. 27 For he has not
tried us with fire, as he did them, to search their
hearts, nor has he taken vengeance on us; but the
Lord scourges those who are close to him in order to admonish them."

28 Then Uzziah said to her, "All that you have
said was spoken out of a true heart, and there
is no one who can deny your words. 29 Today is
not the first time your wisdom has been shown,
but from the beginning of your life all the people have recognized your understanding, for your
heart's disposition is right. 30 But the people were
so thirsty that they compelled us to do for them
what we have promised, and made us take an oath
that we cannot break. 31 Now since you are a God-
fearing woman, pray for us, so that the Lord may
send us rain to fill our cisterns. Then we will no
longer feel faint from thirst."

32 Then Judith said to them, "Listen to me.
I am about to do something that will go down
through all generations of our descendants.
33 Stand at the town gate tonight so that I may
go out with my maid; and within the days after
which you have promised to surrender the town
to our enemies, the Lord will deliver Israel by my
hand. 34 Only, do not try to find out what I am
doing; for I will not tell you until I have finished
what I am about to do."

35 Uzziah and the rulers said to her, "Go in

[a] Other ancient authorities lack *Uzziah and* (see verses 28 and 35) [b] Or *above*

peace, and may the Lord God go before you, to take vengeance on our enemies." 36So they returned from the tent and went to their posts.

9 Then Judith prostrated herself, put ashes on her head, and uncovered the sackcloth she was wearing. At the very time when the evening incense was being offered in the house of God in Jerusalem, Judith cried out to the Lord with a loud voice, and said,

> **Judith 9:1**
>
> Other extended women's prayers in the Scriptures, like Hannah's in 1 Samuel 2 and Mary's prayer in Luke 1, provoke divine response to save God's people.
>
> — *WG*

2 "O Lord God of my ancestor Simeon, to whom you gave a sword to take revenge on those strangers who had torn off a virgin's clothing[a] to defile her, and exposed her thighs to put her to shame, and polluted her womb to disgrace her; for you said, 'It shall not be done'—yet they did it; 3so you gave up their rulers to be killed, and their bed, which was ashamed of the deceit they had practiced, was stained with blood, and you struck down slaves along with princes, and princes on their thrones. 4You gave up their wives for booty and their daughters to captivity, and all their booty to be divided among your beloved children who burned with zeal for you and abhorred the pollution of their blood and called on you for help. O God, my God, hear me also, a widow.

5 "For you have done these things and those that went before and those that followed. You have designed the things that are now, and those that are to come. What you had in mind has happened; 6the things you decided on presented themselves and said, 'Here we are!' For all your ways are prepared in advance, and your judgment is with foreknowledge.

7 "Here now are the Assyrians, a greatly increased force, priding themselves in their horses and riders, boasting in the strength of their foot soldiers, and trusting in shield and spear, in bow and sling. They do not know that you are the Lord who crushes wars; the Lord is your name. 8Break their strength by your might, and bring down their power in your anger; for they intend to defile your sanctuary, and to pollute the tabernacle where your glorious name resides, and to break off the horns[b] of your altar with the sword. 9Look at their pride, and send your wrath upon their heads. Give to me, a widow, the strong hand to do what I plan. 10By the deceit of my lips strike down the slave with the prince and the prince with his servant; crush their arrogance by the hand of a woman.

11 "For your strength does not depend on numbers, nor your might on the powerful. But you are the God of the lowly, helper of the oppressed, upholder of the weak, protector of the forsaken, savior of those without hope. 12Please, please, God of my father, God of the heritage of Israel, Lord of heaven and earth, Creator of the waters, King of all your creation, hear my prayer! 13Make my deceitful words bring wound and bruise on those who have planned cruel things against your covenant, and against your sacred house, and against Mount Zion, and against the house your children possess. 14Let your whole nation and every tribe know and understand that you are God, the God of all power and might, and that there is no other who protects the people of Israel but you alone!"

10 When Judith[c] had stopped crying out to the God of Israel, and had ended all these words, 2she rose from where she lay prostrate. She called her maid and went down into the house where she lived on sabbaths and on her festal days. 3She removed the sackcloth she had been wearing, took off her widow's garments, bathed her body with water, and anointed herself with precious ointment. She combed her hair, put on a tiara, and dressed herself in the festive attire that she used to wear while her husband Manasseh was living. 4She put sandals on her feet, and

[a] Cn: Gk *loosed her womb* [b] Syr: Gk *horn* [c] Gk *she*

put on her anklets, bracelets, rings, earrings, and
all her other jewelry. Thus she made herself very
beautiful, to entice the eyes of all the men who
might see her. 5 She gave her maid a skin of wine
and a flask of oil, and filled a bag with roasted
grain, dried fig cakes, and fine bread;[a] then she
wrapped up all her dishes and gave them to her
to carry.
6 Then they went out to the town gate of
Bethulia and found Uzziah standing there with
the elders of the town, Chabris and Charmis.
7 When they saw her transformed in appearance
and dressed differently, they were very greatly astounded at her beauty and said to her, 8 “May the
God of our ancestors grant you favor and fulfill
your plans, so that the people of Israel may glory
and Jerusalem may be exalted.” She bowed down
to God.
9 Then she said to them, “Order the gate of
the town to be opened for me so that I may go out
and accomplish the things you have just said to
me.” So they ordered the young men to open the
gate for her, as she requested. 10 When they had
done this, Judith went out, accompanied by her
maid. The men of the town watched her until she
had gone down the mountain and passed through
the valley, where they lost sight of her.
11 As the women[b] were going straight on
through the valley, an Assyrian patrol met her
12 and took her into custody. They asked her, “To
what people do you belong, and where are you
coming from, and where are you going?” She replied, “I am a daughter of the Hebrews, but I am
fleeing from them, for they are about to be handed
over to you to be devoured. 13 I am on my way to
see Holofernes the commander of your army, to
give him a true report; I will show him a way by
which he can go and capture all the hill country
without losing one of his men, captured or slain.”
14 When the men heard her words, and observed her face—she was in their eyes marvelously
beautiful—they said to her, 15 “You have saved
your life by hurrying down to see our lord. Go at
once to his tent; some of us will escort you and
hand you over to him. 16 When you stand before
him, have no fear in your heart, but tell him what
you have just said, and he will treat you well.”
17 They chose from their number a hundred
men to accompany her and her maid, and they
brought them to the tent of Holofernes. 18 There
was great excitement in the whole camp, for her
arrival was reported from tent to tent. They came
and gathered around her as she stood outside the
tent of Holofernes, waiting until they told him
about her. 19 They marveled at her beauty and
admired the Israelites, judging them by her. They
said to one another, “Who can despise these people, who have women like this among them? It is
not wise to leave one of their men alive, for if we
let them go they will be able to beguile the whole
world!”
20 Then the guards of Holofernes and all
his servants came out and led her into the tent.
21 Holofernes was resting on his bed under a canopy that was woven with purple and gold, emer-
alds and other precious stones. 22 When they told
him of her, he came to the front of the tent, with
silver lamps carried before him. 23 When Judith
came into the presence of Holofernes[c] and his
servants, they all marveled at the beauty of her
face. She prostrated herself and did obeisance to
him, but his slaves raised her up.

11 Then Holofernes said to her, “Take courage, woman, and do not be afraid in your
heart, for I have never hurt anyone who chose
to serve Nebuchadnezzar, king of all the earth.
2 Even now, if your people who live in the hill
country had not slighted me, I would never have
lifted my spear against them. They have brought
this on themselves. 3 But now tell me why you
have fled from them and have come over to us. In
any event, you have come to safety. Take courage!
You will live tonight and ever after. 4 No one will
hurt you. Rather, all will treat you well, as they do
the servants of my lord King Nebuchadnezzar.”
5 Judith answered him, “Accept the words of
your slave, and let your servant speak in your presence. I will say nothing false to my lord this night.
6 If you follow out the words of your servant, God
will accomplish something through you, and my

[a] Other ancient authorities add *and cheese* [b] Gk *they* [c] Gk *him*

lord will not fail to achieve his purposes. 7By the life of Nebuchadnezzar, king of the whole earth, and by the power of him who has sent you to direct every living being! Not only do human beings serve him because of you, but also the animals of the field and the cattle and the birds of the air will live, because of your power, under Nebuchadnezzar and all his house. 8For we have heard of your wisdom and skill, and it is reported throughout the whole world that you alone are the best in the whole kingdom, the most informed and the most astounding in military strategy.

9 "Now as for Achior's speech in your council, we have heard his words, for the people of Bethulia spared him and he told them all he had said to you. 10Therefore, lord and master, do not disregard what he said, but keep it in your mind, for it is true. Indeed our nation cannot be punished, nor can the sword prevail against them, unless they sin against their God.

11 "But now, in order that my lord may not be defeated and his purpose frustrated, death will fall upon them, for a sin has overtaken them by which they are about to provoke their God to anger when they do what is wrong. 12Since their food supply is exhausted and their water has almost given out, they have planned to kill their livestock and have determined to use all that God by his laws has forbidden them to eat. 13They have decided to consume the first fruits of the grain and the tithes of the wine and oil, which they had consecrated and set aside for the priests who minister in the presence of our God in Jerusalem—things it is not lawful for any of the people even to touch with their hands. 14Since even the people in Jerusalem have been doing this, they have sent messengers there in order to bring back permission from the council of the elders. 15When the response reaches them and they act upon it, on that very day they will be handed over to you to be destroyed.

16 "So when I, your slave, learned all this, I fled from them. God has sent me to accomplish with you things that will astonish the whole world wherever people shall hear about them. 17Your servant is indeed God-fearing and serves the God of heaven night and day. So, my lord, I will remain with you; but every night your servant will go out into the valley and pray to God. He will tell me when they have committed their sins. 18Then I will come and tell you, so that you may go out with your whole army, and not one of them will be able to withstand you. 19Then I will lead you through Judea, until you come to Jerusalem; there I will set your throne.[a] You will drive them like sheep that have no shepherd, and no dog will so much as growl at you. For this was told me to give me foreknowledge; it was announced to me, and I was sent to tell you."

20 Her words pleased Holofernes and all his servants. They marveled at her wisdom and said, 21"No other woman from one end of the earth to the other looks so beautiful or speaks so wisely!" 22Then Holofernes said to her, "God has done well to send you ahead of the people, to strengthen our hands and bring destruction on those who have despised my lord. 23You are not only beautiful in appearance, but wise in speech. If you do as you have said, your God shall be my God, and you shall live in the palace of King Nebuchadnezzar and be renowned throughout the whole world."

12 Then he commanded them to bring her in where his silver dinnerware was kept, and ordered them to set a table for her with some of his own delicacies, and with some of his own wine to drink. 2But Judith said, "I cannot partake of them, or it will be an offense; but I will have enough with the things I brought with me." 3Holofernes said to her, "If your supply runs out, where can we get you more of the same? For none of your people are here with us." 4Judith replied, "As surely as you live, my lord, your servant will not use up the supplies I have with me before the Lord carries out by my hand what he has determined."

5 Then the servants of Holofernes brought her into the tent, and she slept until midnight. Toward the morning watch she got up 6and sent this message to Holofernes: "Let my lord now give

[a] Or *chariot*

orders to allow your servant to go out and pray." 7So Holofernes commanded his guards not to hinder her. She remained in the camp three days. She went out each night to the valley of Bethulia, and bathed at the spring in the camp.[a] 8After bathing, she prayed the Lord God of Israel to direct her way for the triumph of his[b] people. 9Then she returned purified and stayed in the tent until she ate her food toward evening.

10 On the fourth day Holofernes held a banquet for his personal attendants only, and did not invite any of his officers. 11He said to Bagoas, the eunuch who had charge of his personal affairs, "Go and persuade the Hebrew woman who is in your care to join us and to eat and drink with us. 12For it would be a disgrace if we let such a woman go without having intercourse with her. If we do not seduce her, she will laugh at us."

13 So Bagoas left the presence of Holofernes, and approached her and said, "Let this pretty girl not hesitate to come to my lord to be honored in his presence, and to enjoy drinking wine with us, and to become today like one of the Assyrian women who serve in the palace of Nebuchadnezzar." 14Judith replied, "Who am I to refuse my lord? Whatever pleases him I will do at once, and it will be a joy to me until the day of my death." 15So she proceeded to dress herself in all her woman's finery. Her maid went ahead and spread for her on the ground before Holofernes the lambskins she had received from Bagoas for her daily use in reclining.

16 Then Judith came in and lay down. Holofernes' heart was ravished with her and his passion was aroused, for he had been waiting for an opportunity to seduce her from the day he first saw her. 17So Holofernes said to her, "Have a drink and be merry with us!" 18Judith said, "I will gladly drink, my lord, because today is the greatest day in my whole life." 19Then she took what her maid had prepared and ate and drank before him. 20Holofernes was greatly pleased with her, and drank a great quantity of wine, much more than he had ever drunk in any one day since he was born.

13 When evening came, his slaves quickly withdrew. Bagoas closed the tent from outside and shut out the attendants from his master's presence. They went to bed, for they all were weary because the banquet had lasted so long. 2But Judith was left alone in the tent, with Holofernes stretched out on his bed, for he was dead drunk.

3 Now Judith had told her maid to stand outside the bedchamber and to wait for her to come out, as she did on the other days; for she said she would be going out for her prayers. She had said the same thing to Bagoas. 4So everyone went out, and no one, either small or great, was left in the bedchamber. Then Judith, standing beside his bed, said in her heart, "O Lord God of all might, look in this hour on the work of my hands for the exaltation of Jerusalem. 5Now indeed is the time to help your heritage and to carry out my design to destroy the enemies who have risen up against us."

6 She went up to the bedpost near Holofernes' head, and took down his sword that hung there. 7She came close to his bed, took hold of the hair of his head, and said, "Give me strength today, O Lord God of Israel!" 8Then she struck his neck twice with all her might, and cut off his head. 9Next she rolled his body off the bed and pulled down the canopy from the posts. Soon afterward she went out and gave Holofernes' head to her maid, 10who placed it in her food bag.

Then the two of them went out together, as they were accustomed to do for prayer. They passed through the camp, circled around the valley, and went up the mountain to Bethulia, and came to its gates. 11From a distance Judith called out to the sentries at the gates, "Open, open the gate! God, our God, is with us, still showing his power in Israel and his strength against our enemies, as he has done today!"

12 When the people of her town heard her voice, they hurried down to the town gate and summoned the elders of the town. 13They all ran together, both small and great, for it seemed unbelievable that she had returned. They opened

[a] Other ancient authorities lack *in the camp* [b] Other ancient authorities read *her*

the gate and welcomed them. Then they lit a fire
to give light, and gathered around them. 14 Then
she said to them with a loud voice, "Praise
God, O praise him! Praise God, who has not
withdrawn his mercy from the house of Israel,
but has destroyed our enemies by my hand this
very night!"

15 Then she pulled the head out of the bag
and showed it to them, and said, "See here, the
head of Holofernes, the commander of the Assyrian army, and here is the canopy beneath which
he lay in his drunken stupor. The Lord has struck
him down by the hand of a woman. 16 As the Lord
lives, who has protected me in the way I went, I
swear that it was my face that seduced him to his
destruction, and that he committed no sin with
me, to defile and shame me."

17 All the people were greatly astonished.
They bowed down and worshiped God, and said
with one accord, "Blessed are you our God, who
have this day humiliated the enemies of your
people."

18 Then Uzziah said to her, "O daughter, you
are blessed by the Most High God above all other
women on earth; and blessed be the Lord God,
who created the heavens and the earth, who has
guided you to cut off the head of the leader of our
enemies. 19 Your praise[a] will never depart from
the hearts of those who remember the power
of God. 20 May God grant this to be a perpetual
honor to you, and may he reward you with blessings, because you risked your own life when our
nation was brought low, and you averted our ruin,
walking in the straight path before our God." And
all the people said, "Amen. Amen."

14 Then Judith said to them, "Listen to me,
my friends. Take this head and hang it
upon the parapet of your wall. 2 As soon as day
breaks and the sun rises on the earth, each of you
take up your weapons, and let every able-bodied
man go out of the town; set a captain over them,
as if you were going down to the plain against the
Assyrian outpost; only do not go down. 3 Then
they will seize their arms and go into the camp
and rouse the officers of the Assyrian army. They
will rush into the tent of Holofernes and will not
find him. Then panic will come over them, and
they will flee before you. 4 Then you and all who
live within the borders of Israel will pursue them
and cut them down in their tracks. 5 But before
you do all this, bring Achior the Ammonite to me
so that he may see and recognize the man who
despised the house of Israel and sent him to us as
if to his death."

6 So they summoned Achior from the house
of Uzziah. When he came and saw the head of
Holofernes in the hand of one of the men in the
assembly of the people, he fell down on his face in
a faint. 7 When they raised him up he threw himself at Judith's feet, and did obeisance to her, and
said, "Blessed are you in every tent of Judah! In
every nation those who hear your name will be
alarmed. 8 Now tell me what you have done during these days."

So Judith told him in the presence of the people all that she had done, from the day she left
until the moment she began speaking to them.
9 When she had finished, the people raised a great
shout and made a joyful noise in their town.
10 When Achior saw all that the God of Israel had
done, he believed firmly in God. So he was circumcised, and joined the house of Israel, remaining so to this day.

11 As soon as it was dawn they hung the head
of Holofernes on the wall. Then they all took
their weapons, and they went out in companies to
the mountain passes. 12 When the Assyrians saw
them they sent word to their commanders, who
then went to the generals and the captains and
to all their other officers. 13 They came to Holofernes' tent and said to the steward in charge of
all his personal affairs, "Wake up our lord, for the
slaves have been so bold as to come down against
us to give battle, to their utter destruction."

14 So Bagoas went in and knocked at the entry of the tent, for he supposed that he was sleeping with Judith. 15 But when no one answered,
he opened it and went into the bedchamber and
found him sprawled on the floor dead, with his
head missing. 16 He cried out with a loud voice

[a] Other ancient authorities read *hope*

and wept and groaned and shouted, and tore his
clothes. 17 Then he went to the tent where Judith had stayed, and when he did not find her,
he rushed out to the people and shouted, 18 "The
slaves have tricked us! One Hebrew woman has
brought disgrace on the house of King Nebuchadnezzar. Look, Holofernes is lying on the
ground, and his head is missing!"

19 When the leaders of the Assyrian army
heard this, they tore their tunics and were greatly
dismayed, and their loud cries and shouts rose up
throughout the camp.

15 When the men in the tents heard it, they
were amazed at what had happened.
2 Overcome with fear and trembling, they did
not wait for one another, but with one impulse
all rushed out and fled by every path across the
plain and through the hill country. 3 Those who
had camped in the hills around Bethulia also took
to flight. Then the Israelites, everyone that was a
soldier, rushed out upon them. 4 Uzziah sent men
to Betomasthaim[a] and Choba and Kola, and to
all the frontiers of Israel, to tell what had taken
place and to urge all to rush out upon the enemy
to destroy them. 5 When the Israelites heard it,
with one accord they fell upon the enemy,[b] and
cut them down as far as Choba. Those in Jerusalem and all the hill country also came, for they
were told what had happened in the camp of the
enemy. The men in Gilead and in Galilee outflanked them with great slaughter, even beyond
Damascus and its borders. 6 The rest of the people of Bethulia fell upon the Assyrian camp and
plundered it, acquiring great riches. 7 And the
Israelites, when they returned from the slaughter, took possession of what remained. Even the
villages and towns in the hill country and in the
plain got a great amount of booty, since there was
a vast quantity of it.

8 Then the high priest Joakim and the elders
of the Israelites who lived in Jerusalem came to
witness the good things that the Lord had done
for Israel, and to see Judith and to wish her well.
9 When they met her, they all blessed her with
one accord and said to her, "You are the glory of
Jerusalem, you are the great boast of Israel, you
are the great pride of our nation! 10 You have done
all this with your own hand; you have done great
good to Israel, and God is well pleased with it.
May the Almighty Lord bless you forever!" And
all the people said, "Amen."

11 All the people plundered the camp for
thirty days. They gave Judith the tent of Holofernes and all his silver dinnerware, his beds, his
bowls, and all his furniture. She took them and
loaded her mules and hitched up her carts and
piled the things on them.

12 All the women of Israel gathered to see her,
and blessed her, and some of them performed a
dance in her honor. She took ivy-wreathed wands
in her hands and distributed them to the women
who were with her; 13 and she and those who were
with her crowned themselves with olive wreaths.
She went before all the people in the dance, leading all the women, while all the men of Israel followed, bearing their arms and wearing garlands
and singing hymns.

14 Judith began this thanksgiving before all
Israel, and all the people loudly sang this song of
16 praise. 1 And Judith said,

Begin a song to my God with
tambourines,
sing to my Lord with cymbals.
Raise to him a new psalm;[c]
exalt him, and call upon his name.
2 For the Lord is a God who crushes wars;
he sets up his camp among his people;
he delivered me from the hands of my
pursuers.
3 The Assyrian came down from the mountains
of the north;
he came with myriads of his warriors;
their numbers blocked up the wadis,
and their cavalry covered the hills.
4 He boasted that he would burn up my
territory,
and kill my young men with the sword,
and dash my infants to the ground,
and seize my children as booty,
and take my virgins as spoil.

[a] Other ancient authorities add *and Bebai* [b] Gk *them* [c] Other ancient authorities read *a psalm and praise*

5 But the Lord Almighty has foiled them
by the hand of a woman.[a]
6 For their mighty one did not fall by the hands of the young men,
nor did the sons of the Titans strike him down,
nor did tall giants set upon him;
but Judith daughter of Merari
with the beauty of her countenance undid him.

7 For she put away her widow's clothing
to exalt the oppressed in Israel.
She anointed her face with perfume;
8 she fastened her hair with a tiara
and put on a linen gown to beguile him.
9 Her sandal ravished his eyes,
her beauty captivated his mind,
and the sword severed his neck!
10 The Persians trembled at her boldness,
the Medes were daunted at her daring.

11 Then my oppressed people shouted;
my weak people cried out,[b] and the enemy[c] trembled;
they lifted up their voices, and the enemy[c] were turned back.
12 Sons of slave-girls pierced them through
and wounded them like the children of fugitives;
they perished before the army of my Lord.

13 I will sing to my God a new song:
O Lord, you are great and glorious,
wonderful in strength, invincible.
14 Let all your creatures serve you,
for you spoke, and they were made.
You sent forth your spirit,[d] and it formed them;[e]
there is none that can resist your voice.
15 For the mountains shall be shaken to their foundations with the waters;
before your glance the rocks shall melt like wax.
But to those who fear you
you show mercy.
16 For every sacrifice as a fragrant offering is a small thing,
and the fat of all whole burnt offerings to you is a very little thing;
but whoever fears the Lord is great forever.

17 Woe to the nations that rise up against my people!
The Lord Almighty will take vengeance on them in the day of judgment;
he will send fire and worms into their flesh;
they shall weep in pain forever.

18 When they arrived at Jerusalem, they worshiped God. As soon as the people were purified,
they offered their burnt offerings, their freewill
offerings, and their gifts. 19 Judith also dedicated
to God all the possessions of Holofernes, which
the people had given her; and the canopy that she
had taken for herself from his bedchamber she
gave as a votive offering. 20 For three months the
people continued feasting in Jerusalem before the
sanctuary, and Judith remained with them.
21 After this they all returned home to their
own inheritances. Judith went to Bethulia, and
remained on her estate. For the rest of her life
she was honored throughout the whole country.
22 Many desired to marry her, but she gave herself
to no man all the days of her life after her husband
Manasseh died and was gathered to his people.
23 She became more and more famous, and grew

Judith 16:23

Judith joins the few women whose death and burials are mentioned in the Scriptures: Sarah in Gen 23:1-20, Deborah the nurse of Rebekah in Gen 35:8, and Rachel in Gen 35:18.

— *WG*

[a] Other ancient authorities add *he has confounded them* [b] Other ancient authorities read *feared* [c] Gk *they*
[d] Or *breath* [e] Other ancient authorities read *they were created*

old in her husband's house, reaching the age of
one hundred five. She set her maid free. She died
in Bethulia, and they buried her in the cave of
her husband Manasseh;
24and the house of Israel
mourned her for seven days. Before she died she
distributed her property to all those who were
next of kin to her husband Manasseh, and to her
own nearest kindred.
25No one ever again spread
terror among the Israelites during the lifetime of
Judith, or for a long time after her death.

Esther
(The Greek Version Containing the Additional Chapters)

THE GREEK ACCOUNT OF ESTHER is significantly expanded, by more than 100 unique verses, beyond the Hebrew. It appeared with the Septuagint, the Greek version of the Hebrew Bible, at a time when Greek had become the most commonly spoken language of the Jewish Diaspora and of the Roman Empire, between 300 and 200 BCE. Within Judaism, the Greek account of Esther was recognized early on as a retelling and interpretation of the Hebrew text. Along with other books written in Greek and included in the Septuagint, the Greek version of Esther was accepted as Scripture in the formation of the Christian canon, only to be dismissed in favor of the Hebrew text by Protestant reformers when they defined the canon for themselves. It continues nevertheless to be accepted as the canonical version of Esther by the Roman Catholic and Orthodox Churches and by the Anglican Communion, including the Episcopal Church in the United States.

The two commonly cited texts of the Greek version of Esther are known as the *A* text, also known as the *Lucian* text, and the *B* text. Though they differ in some respects, both texts make two overall changes to the story as we have it in the Hebrew. First, references to God that are completely lacking in the Hebrew book have been added, and the hero's piety is enhanced. Second, Mordecai's role is extended in the Greek version, creating resonance between his character and endangered biblical wise men such as Joseph and Daniel. Both sets of changes point to a desire on the part of translators to bring the story into line with the readers' expectations of Scripture, most likely because the canonical status of the Hebrew version was often questioned.

Significantly, the Greek version of the story begins not with Vashti's rebellion and the gender issue it raises but with Mordecai having an apocalyptic dream in which "the whole righteous nation" (11:9) narrowly avoids a vague but terrible destruction. Mordecai's discovery and report of an assassination plot against the king, an act that brings Mordecai to honor and power, occurs in detail before any woman enters the scene. In the *A* text the court's panicked response to Vashti's rebellion does not occur. Thus, the gender tension in the Hebrew account of that event is diffused, indeed all but erased in the Greek. Here the story is solely concerned with the conflict of Jew versus Persian (or Greek, as Haman becomes a Macedonian in translation), and God's preservation of the former. Other significant additions in the Greek include a lengthy prayer by Mordecai and one by Esther in which she makes a point of forswearing sex with Gentiles (this despite her marriage to the Persian king).

As an American Protestant, I first encountered the Greek version of Esther in a graduate-school classroom rather than in a faith context. As the only Bibles I knew growing up were the King James and Revised Standard Versions, I had not until seminary known that version of Esther's story. To me, a feminist and a Protestant, the Greek versions of Esther seem to obscure, rather than expand upon, the story of Esther herself. She was a girl born into an ethnic minority and torn between the

survival strategies of assimilation on the one hand and advocacy for her people on the other. She was pushed by circumstance into exploiting her own sexuality to save her own life, Mordecai's, and those of the Jews. In place of that story, the Greek version tells the story of yet another "great man" (11:3), as the Greek refers to Mordecai, and the great man's interaction with God. The Greek version is valuable for me because it tells a story about the stories we tell. That is, it is a classic example and written record of one intriguing, maverick story—the Hebrew Esther—that through translation and retelling was pulled back within the limits of patriarchy and theological orthodoxy.

— Nicole Wilkinson Duran

ADDITION A

11[a] 2In the second year of the reign of Artaxerxes the Great, on the first day of Nisan,
Mordecai son of Jair son of Shimei[b] son of Kish,
of the tribe of Benjamin, had a dream. 3He was a
Jew living in the city of Susa, a great man, serving in the court of the king. 4He was one of the
captives whom King Nebuchadnezzar of Babylon
had brought from Jerusalem with King Jeconiah
of Judea. And this was his dream: 5Noises[c] and
confusion, thunders and earthquake, tumult on
the earth! 6Then two great dragons came forward, both ready to fight, and they roared terribly.
7At their roaring every nation prepared for war, to
fight against the righteous nation. 8It was a day of
darkness and gloom, of tribulation and distress,
affliction and great tumult on the earth! 9And the
whole righteous nation was troubled; they feared
the evils that threatened them,[d] and were ready to
perish. 10Then they cried out to God; and at their
outcry, as though from a tiny spring, there came
a great river, with abundant water; 11light came,
and the sun rose, and the lowly were exalted and
devoured those held in honor.
12 Mordecai saw in this dream what God had
determined to do, and after he awoke he had it
on his mind, seeking all day to understand it in
every detail.

12 Now Mordecai took his rest in the courtyard with Gabatha and Tharra, the two eunuchs of the king who kept watch in the courtyard.
2He overheard their conversation and inquired
into their purposes, and learned that they were
preparing to lay hands on King Artaxerxes; and
he informed the king concerning them. 3Then the
king examined the two eunuchs, and after they had
confessed it, they were led away to execution. 4The
king made a permanent record of these things, and
Mordecai wrote an account of them. 5And the
king ordered Mordecai to serve in the court, and
rewarded him for these things. 6But Haman son of
Hammedatha, a Bougean, who was in great honor
with the king, determined to injure Mordecai and
his people because of the two eunuchs of the king.

END OF ADDITION A

---

1 It was after this that the following things happened in the days of Artaxerxes, the same
Artaxerxes who ruled over one hundred twenty-
seven provinces from India to Ethiopia.[e] 2In those

[a] Chapters 11.2—12.6 correspond to chapter A 1–17 in some translations. [b] Gk *Semeios* [c] Or *Voices* [d] Gk *their own evils* [e] Other ancient authorities lack *to Ethiopia*

days, when King Artaxerxes was enthroned in the
city of Susa, 3in the third year of his reign, he gave
a banquet for his Friends and other persons of
various nations, the Persians and Median nobles,
and the governors of the provinces. 4After this,
when he had displayed to them the riches of his
kingdom and the splendor of his bountiful celebration during the course of one hundred eighty
days, 5at the end of the festivity[a] the king gave a
drinking party for the people of various nations
who lived in the city. This was held for six days
in the courtyard of the royal palace, 6which was
adorned with curtains of fine linen and cotton,
held by cords of purple linen attached to gold
and silver blocks on pillars of marble and other
stones. Gold and silver couches were placed on
a mosaic floor of emerald, mother-of-pearl, and
marble. There were coverings of gauze, embroidered in various colors, with roses arranged
around them. 7The cups were of gold and silver,
and a miniature cup was displayed, made of ruby,
worth thirty thousand talents. There was abundant sweet wine, such as the king himself drank.
8The drinking was not according to a fixed rule;
but the king wished to have it so, and he commanded his stewards to comply with his pleasure
and with that of the guests.

9 Meanwhile, Queen Vashti[b] gave a drinking
party for the women in the palace where King
Artaxerxes was.

10 On the seventh day, when the king was
in good humor, he told Haman, Bazan, Tharra,
Boraze, Zatholtha, Abataza, and Tharaba, the
seven eunuchs who served King Artaxerxes, 11to
escort the queen to him in order to proclaim her
as queen and to place the diadem on her head, and
to have her display her beauty to all the governors
and the people of various nations, for she was indeed a beautiful woman. 12But Queen Vashti[b] refused to obey him and would not come with the
eunuchs. This offended the king and he became
furious. 13He said to his Friends, "This is how
Vashti[b] has answered me.[c] Give therefore your
ruling and judgment on this matter." 14Arkesaeus,
Sarsathaeus, and Malesear, then the governors of
the Persians and Medes who were closest to the
king—Arkesaeus, Sarsathaeus, and Malesear,
who sat beside him in the chief seats—came to
him 15and told him what must be done to Queen
Vashti[b] for not obeying the order that the king had
sent her by the eunuchs. 16Then Muchaeus said
to the king and the governors, "Queen Vashti[b] has
insulted not only the king but also all the king's
governors and officials" 17(for he had reported to
them what the queen had said and how she had
defied the king). "And just as she defied King
Artaxerxes, 18so now the other ladies who are
wives of the Persian and Median governors, on
hearing what she has said to the king, will likewise dare to insult their husbands. 19If therefore
it pleases the king, let him issue a royal decree, inscribed in accordance with the laws of the Medes
and Persians so that it may not be altered, that the
queen may no longer come into his presence; but
let the king give her royal rank to a woman better
than she. 20Let whatever law the king enacts be
proclaimed in his kingdom, and thus all women
will give honor to their husbands, rich and poor
alike." 21This speech pleased the king and the governors, and the king did as Muchaeus had recommended. 22The king sent the decree into all his
kingdom, to every province in its own language,
so that in every house respect would be shown to
every husband.

2 After these things, the king's anger abated,
and he no longer was concerned about
Vashti[b] or remembered what he had said and how
he had condemned her. 2Then the king's servants
said, "Let beautiful and virtuous girls be sought
out for the king. 3The king shall appoint officers
in all the provinces of his kingdom, and they shall
select beautiful young virgins to be brought to
the harem in Susa, the capital. Let them be entrusted to the king's eunuch who is in charge of
the women, and let ointments and whatever else
they need be given them. 4And the woman who
pleases the king shall be queen instead of Vashti."[b]
This pleased the king, and he did so.

5 Now there was a Jew in Susa the capital whose name was Mordecai son of Jair son of

[a] Gk *marriage feast* [b] Gk *Astin* [c] Gk *Astin has said thus and so*

Shimei[a] son of Kish, of the tribe of Benjamin; 6he
had been taken captive from Jerusalem among
those whom King Nebuchadnezzar of Babylon had
captured. 7And he had a foster child, the daughter
of his father's brother, Aminadab, and her name
was Esther. When her parents died, he brought her
up to womanhood as his own. The girl was beautiful in appearance. 8So, when the decree of the
king was proclaimed, and many girls were gathered in Susa the capital in custody of Gai, Esther
also was brought to Gai, who had custody of the
women. 9The girl pleased him and won his favor,
and he quickly provided her with ointments and
her portion of food,[b] as well as seven maids chosen from the palace; he treated her and her maids
with special favor in the harem. 10Now Esther had
not disclosed her people or country, for Mordecai
had commanded her not to make it known. 11And
every day Mordecai walked in the courtyard of the
harem, to see what would happen to Esther.

12 Now the period after which a girl was to
go to the king was twelve months. During this
time the days of beautification are completed—
six months while they are anointing themselves
with oil of myrrh, and six months with spices and
ointments for women. 13Then she goes in to the
king; she is handed to the person appointed, and
goes with him from the harem to the king's palace. 14In the evening she enters and in the morning she departs to the second harem, where Gai
the king's eunuch is in charge of the women; and
she does not go in to the king again unless she is
summoned by name.

15 When the time was fulfilled for Esther
daughter of Aminadab, the brother of Mordecai's
father, to go in to the king, she neglected none
of the things that Gai, the eunuch in charge of
the women, had commanded. Now Esther found
favor in the eyes of all who saw her. 16So Esther
went in to King Artaxerxes in the twelfth month,
which is Adar, in the seventh year of his reign.
17And the king loved Esther and she found favor
beyond all the other virgins, so he put on her the
queen's diadem. 18Then the king gave a banquet
lasting seven days for all his Friends and the officers to celebrate his marriage to Esther; and he
granted a remission of taxes to those who were
under his rule.

19 Meanwhile Mordecai was serving in the
courtyard. 20Esther had not disclosed her country—such were the instructions of Mordecai; but
she was to fear God and keep his laws, just as she
had done when she was with him. So Esther did
not change her mode of life.

21 Now the king's eunuchs, who were chief
bodyguards, were angry because of Mordecai's
advancement, and they plotted to kill King Artaxerxes. 22The matter became known to Mordecai,
and he warned Esther, who in turn revealed the
plot to the king. 23He investigated the two eunuchs and hanged them. Then the king ordered a
memorandum to be deposited in the royal library
in praise of the goodwill shown by Mordecai.

3 After these events King Artaxerxes promoted
Haman son of Hammedatha, a Bougean, advancing him and granting him precedence over
all the king's[c] Friends. 2So all who were at court
used to do obeisance to Haman,[d] for so the king
had commanded to be done. Mordecai, however,
did not do obeisance. 3Then the king's courtiers
said to Mordecai, "Mordecai, why do you disobey
the king's command?" 4Day after day they spoke
to him, but he would not listen to them. Then
they informed Haman that Mordecai was resisting the king's command. Mordecai had told them
that he was a Jew. 5So when Haman learned that
Mordecai was not doing obeisance to him, he became furiously angry, 6and plotted to destroy all
the Jews under Artaxerxes' rule.

7 In the twelfth year of King Artaxerxes Haman[e] came to a decision by casting lots, taking the
days and the months one by one, to fix on one day
to destroy the whole race of Mordecai. The lot fell
on the fourteenth[f] day of the month of Adar.

8 Then Haman[e] said to King Artaxerxes,
"There is a certain nation scattered among the
other nations in all your kingdom; their laws are
different from those of every other nation, and

[a] Gk *Semeios* [b] Gk lacks *of food* [c] Gk *all his* [d] Gk *him* [e] Gk *he*
[f] Other ancient witnesses read *thirteenth*; see 8.12

they do not keep the laws of the king. It is not ex-
pedient for the king to tolerate them. 9 If it pleases
the king, let it be decreed that they are to be destroyed, and I will pay ten thousand talents of silver into the king's treasury." 10 So the king took off
his signet ring and gave it to Haman to seal the
decree[a] that was to be written against the Jews.
11 The king told Haman, "Keep the money, and do
whatever you want with that nation."

12 So on the thirteenth day of the first month
the king's secretaries were summoned, and in accordance with Haman's instructions they wrote
in the name of King Artaxerxes to the magistrates
and the governors in every province from India
to Ethiopia. There were one hundred twenty-
seven provinces in all, and the governors were addressed each in his own language. 13 Instructions
were sent by couriers throughout all the empire
of Artaxerxes to destroy the Jewish people on a
given day of the twelfth month, which is Adar,
and to plunder their goods.

Addition B

13 [b] This is a copy of the letter: "The Great
King, Artaxerxes, writes the following to
the governors of the hundred twenty-seven provinces from India to Ethiopia and to the officials
under them:

2 "Having become ruler of many nations and
master of the whole world (not elated with presumption of authority but always acting reason-
ably and with kindness), I have determined to
settle the lives of my subjects in lasting tranquility
and, in order to make my kingdom peaceable and
open to travel throughout all its extent, to restore
the peace desired by all people.

3 "When I asked my counselors how this
might be accomplished, Haman—who excels
among us in sound judgment, and is distinguished for his unchanging goodwill and steadfast fidelity, and has attained the second place in
the kingdom— 4 pointed out to us that among all
the nations in the world there is scattered a certain hostile people, who have laws contrary to
those of every nation and continually disregard
the ordinances of kings, so that the unifying of
the kingdom that we honorably intend cannot be
brought about. 5 We understand that this people,
and it alone, stands constantly in opposition to
every nation, perversely following a strange manner of life and laws, and is ill-disposed to our government, doing all the harm they can so that our
kingdom may not attain stability.

6 "Therefore we have decreed that those indicated to you in the letters written by Haman,
who is in charge of affairs and is our second father, shall all—wives and children included—be
utterly destroyed by the swords of their enemies,
without pity or restraint, on the fourteenth day
of the twelfth month, Adar, of this present year,
7 so that those who have long been hostile and remain so may in a single day go down in violence
to Hades, and leave our government completely
secure and untroubled hereafter."

End of Addition B

3 14 Copies of the document were posted in
every province, and all the nations were ordered to be prepared for that day. 15 The matter
was expedited also in Susa. And while the king
and Haman caroused together, the city of Susa[c]
was thrown into confusion.

4 When Mordecai learned of all that had been
done, he tore his clothes, put on sackcloth,
and sprinkled himself with ashes; then he rushed
through the street of the city, shouting loudly:
"An innocent nation is being destroyed!" 2 He got
as far as the king's gate, and there he stopped, because no one was allowed to enter the courtyard
clothed in sackcloth and ashes. 3 And in every
province where the king's proclamation had been
posted there was a loud cry of mourning and lamentation among the Jews, and they put on sackcloth and ashes. 4 When the queen's[d] maids and

[a] Gk lacks *the decree* [b] Chapter 13.1–7 corresponds to chapter B 1–7 in some translations. [c] Gk *the city*
[d] Gk *When her*

eunuchs came and told her, she was deeply troubled by what she heard had happened, and sent
some clothes to Mordecai to put on instead of
sackcloth; but he would not consent. 5Then Esther summoned Hachratheus, the eunuch who
attended her, and ordered him to get accurate information for her from Mordecai.[a]
7 So Mordecai told him what had happened
and how Haman had promised to pay ten thousand talents into the royal treasury to bring about
the destruction of the Jews. 8He also gave him a
copy of what had been posted in Susa for their destruction, to show to Esther; and he told him to
charge her to go in to the king and plead for his favor in behalf of the people. "Remember," he said,
"the days when you were an ordinary person,
being brought up under my care—for Haman,
who stands next to the king, has spoken against
us and demands our death. Call upon the Lord;
then speak to the king in our behalf, and save us
from death."
9 Hachratheus went in and told Esther all
these things. 10And she said to him, "Go to Mordecai and say, 11'All nations of the empire know
that if any man or woman goes to the king inside
the inner court without being called, there is no
escape for that person. Only the one to whom the
king stretches out the golden scepter is safe—and
it is now thirty days since I was called to go to
the king.'"
12 When Hachratheus delivered her entire
message to Mordecai, 13Mordecai told him to go
back and say to her, "Esther, do not say to yourself that you alone among all the Jews will escape
alive. 14For if you keep quiet at such a time as this,
help and protection will come to the Jews from
another quarter, but you and your father's family
will perish. Yet, who knows whether it was not for
such a time as this that you were made queen?"
15Then Esther gave the messenger this answer to
take back to Mordecai: 16"Go and gather all the
Jews who are in Susa and fast on my behalf; for
three days and nights do not eat or drink, and my
maids and I will also go without food. After that
I will go to the king, contrary to the law, even if I
must die." 17So Mordecai went away and did what
Esther had told him to do.

Addition C

13 8[b]Then Mordecai[c] prayed to the Lord,
calling to remembrance all the works of
the Lord.
9 He said, "O Lord, Lord, you rule as King
over all things, for the universe is in your power
and there is no one who can oppose you when
it is your will to save Israel, 10for you have made
heaven and earth and every wonderful thing under heaven. 11You are Lord of all, and there is no
one who can resist you, the Lord. 12You know
all things; you know, O Lord, that it was not in
insolence or pride or for any love of glory that I
did this, and refused to bow down to this proud
Haman; 13for I would have been willing to kiss
the soles of his feet to save Israel! 14But I did this
so that I might not set human glory above the
glory of God, and I will not bow down to anyone but you, who are my Lord; and I will not do
these things in pride. 15And now, O Lord God
and King, God of Abraham, spare your people;
for the eyes of our foes are upon us[d] to annihilate
us, and they desire to destroy the inheritance that
has been yours from the beginning. 16Do not neglect your portion, which you redeemed for yourself out of the land of Egypt. 17Hear my prayer,
and have mercy upon your inheritance; turn our
mourning into feasting that we may live and sing
praise to your name, O Lord; do not destroy the
lips[e] of those who praise you."
18 And all Israel cried out mightily, for their
death was before their eyes.

14 Then Queen Esther, seized with deadly
anxiety, fled to the Lord. 2She took off
her splendid apparel and put on the garments
of distress and mourning, and instead of costly

[a] Other ancient witnesses add 6*So Hachratheus went out to Mordecai in the street of the city opposite the city gate.*

[b] Chapters 13.8—15.16 correspond to chapters C 1–30 and D 1–16 in some translations. [c] Gk *he* [d] Gk *for they are eying us* [e] Gk *mouth*

perfumes she covered her head with ashes and
dung, and she utterly humbled her body; every
part that she loved to adorn she covered with her
tangled hair. 3 She prayed to the Lord God of Israel, and said: "O my Lord, you only are our king;
help me, who am alone and have no helper but
you, 4 for my danger is in my hand. 5 Ever since
I was born I have heard in the tribe of my family that you, O Lord, took Israel out of all the
nations, and our ancestors from among all their
forebears, for an everlasting inheritance, and that
you did for them all that you promised. 6 And now
we have sinned before you, and you have handed
us over to our enemies 7 because we glorified their
gods. You are righteous, O Lord! 8 And now they
are not satisfied that we are in bitter slavery, but
they have covenanted with their idols 9 to abolish
what your mouth has ordained, and to destroy
your inheritance, to stop the mouths of those
who praise you and to quench your altar and the
glory of your house, 10 to open the mouths of the
nations for the praise of vain idols, and to magnify forever a mortal king.

11 "O Lord, do not surrender your scepter to what has no being; and do not let them
laugh at our downfall; but turn their plan against
them, and make an example of him who began
this against us. 12 Remember, O Lord; make
yourself known in this time of our affliction,
and give me courage, O King of the gods and
Master of all dominion! 13 Put eloquent speech
in my mouth before the lion, and turn his heart
to hate the man who is fighting against us, so
that there may be an end of him and those who
agree with him. 14 But save us by your hand,
and help me, who am alone and have no helper
but you, O Lord. 15 You have knowledge of all
things, and you know that I hate the splendor
of the wicked and abhor the bed of the uncircumcised and of any alien. 16 You know my
necessity—that I abhor the sign of my proud
position, which is upon my head on days when I
appear in public. I abhor it like a filthy rag, and I
do not wear it on the days when I am at leisure.
17 And your servant has not eaten at Haman's
table, and I have not honored the king's feast or
drunk the wine of libations. 18 Your servant has
had no joy since the day that I was brought here
until now, except in you, O Lord God of Abraham. 19 O God, whose might is over all, hear the
voice of the despairing, and save us from the
hands of evildoers. And save me from my fear!"

End of Addition C

Addition D

15 On the third day, when she ended her
prayer, she took off the garments in which
she had worshiped, and arrayed herself in splendid attire. 2 Then, majestically adorned, after in-
voking the aid of the all-seeing God and Savior,
she took two maids with her; 3 on one she leaned
gently for support, 4 while the other followed,
carrying her train. 5 She was radiant with perfect
beauty, and she looked happy, as if beloved, but
her heart was frozen with fear. 6 When she had
gone through all the doors, she stood before the
king. He was seated on his royal throne, clothed in
the full array of his majesty, all covered with gold
and precious stones. He was most terrifying.

7 Lifting his face, flushed with splendor, he
looked at her in fierce anger. The queen faltered,
and turned pale and faint, and collapsed on the
head of the maid who went in front of her. 8 Then
God changed the spirit of the king to gentleness,
and in alarm he sprang from his throne and took
her in his arms until she came to herself. He comforted her with soothing words, and said to her,
9 "What is it, Esther? I am your husband.[a] Take
courage; 10 You shall not die, for our law applies
only to our subjects.[b] Come near."

11 Then he raised the golden scepter and
touched her neck with it; 12 he embraced her, and
said, "Speak to me." 13 She said to him, "I saw you,
my lord, like an angel of God, and my heart was
shaken with fear at your glory. 14 For you are wonderful, my lord, and your countenance is full of
grace." 15 And while she was speaking, she fainted

[a] Gk *brother* [b] Meaning of Gk uncertain

and fell. 16 Then the king was agitated, and all his
servants tried to comfort her.

END OF ADDITION D

---

5 [a] 3 The king said to her, "What do you wish,
Esther? What is your request? It shall be
given you, even to half of my kingdom." 4 And
Esther said, "Today is a special day for me. If it
pleases the king, let him and Haman come to the
dinner that I shall prepare today." 5 Then the king
said, "Bring Haman quickly, so that we may do as
Esther desires." So they both came to the dinner
that Esther had spoken about. 6 While they were
drinking wine, the king said to Esther, "What is it,
Queen Esther? It shall be granted you." 7 She said,
"My petition and request is: 8 if I have found favor
in the sight of the king, let the king and Haman
come to the dinner that I shall prepare them, and
tomorrow I will do as I have done today."

9 So Haman went out from the king joyful
and glad of heart. But when he saw Mordecai the
Jew in the courtyard, he was filled with anger.
10 Nevertheless, he went home and summoned
his friends and his wife Zosara. 11 And he told
them about his riches and the honor that the king
had bestowed on him, and how he had advanced
him to be the first in the kingdom. 12 And Haman
said, "The queen did not invite anyone to the dinner with the king except me; and I am invited
again tomorrow. 13 But these things give me no
pleasure as long as I see Mordecai the Jew in the
courtyard." 14 His wife Zosara and his friends said
to him, "Let a gallows be made, fifty cubits high,
and in the morning tell the king to have Mordecai
hanged on it. Then, go merrily with the king to
the dinner." This advice pleased Haman, and so
the gallows was prepared.

6 That night the Lord took sleep from the king,
so he gave orders to his secretary to bring the
book of daily records, and to read to him. 2 He
found the words written about Mordecai, how
he had told the king about the two royal eunuchs
who were on guard and sought to lay hands on
King Artaxerxes. 3 The king said, "What honor or
dignity did we bestow on Mordecai?" The king's
servants said, "You have not done anything for
him." 4 While the king was inquiring about the
goodwill shown by Mordecai, Haman was in
the courtyard. The king asked, "Who is in the
courtyard?" Now Haman had come to speak to
the king about hanging Mordecai on the gallows
that he had prepared. 5 The servants of the king
answered, "Haman is standing in the courtyard."
And the king said, "Summon him." 6 Then the
king said to Haman, "What shall I do for the person whom I wish to honor?" And Haman said to
himself, "Whom would the king wish to honor
more than me?" 7 So he said to the king, "For a
person whom the king wishes to honor, 8 let the
king's servants bring out the fine linen robe that
the king has worn, and the horse on which the
king rides, 9 and let both be given to one of the
king's honored Friends, and let him robe the person whom the king loves and mount him on the
horse, and let it be proclaimed through the open
square of the city, saying, 'Thus shall it be done
to everyone whom the king honors.'" 10 Then the
king said to Haman, "You have made an excellent
suggestion! Do just as you have said for Mordecai the Jew, who is on duty in the courtyard. And
let nothing be omitted from what you have proposed." 11 So Haman got the robe and the horse;
he put the robe on Mordecai and made him ride
through the open square of the city, proclaiming, "Thus shall it be done to everyone whom the
king wishes to honor." 12 Then Mordecai returned
to the courtyard, and Haman hurried back to
his house, mourning and with his head covered.
13 Haman told his wife Zosara and his friends
what had befallen him. His friends and his wife
said to him, "If Mordecai is of the Jewish people,
and you have begun to be humiliated before him,
you will surely fall. You will not be able to defend
yourself, because the living God is with him."

14 While they were still talking, the eunuchs
arrived and hurriedly brought Haman to the ban-
7 quet that Esther had prepared. 1 So the king
and Haman went in to drink with the queen.

[a] In Greek, Chapter D replaces verses 1 and 2 in Hebrew.

2 And the second day, as they were drinking wine,
the king said, "What is it, Queen Esther? What is
your petition and what is your request? It shall be
granted to you, even to half of my kingdom." 3 She
answered and said, "If I have found favor with the
king, let my life be granted me at my petition, and
my people at my request. 4 For we have been sold,
I and my people, to be destroyed, plundered,
and made slaves—we and our children—male
and female slaves. This has come to my knowledge. Our antagonist brings shame on[a] the king's
court." 5 Then the king said, "Who is the person
that would dare to do this thing?" 6 Esther said,
"Our enemy is this evil man Haman!" At this, Haman was terrified in the presence of the king and
queen.
7 The king rose from the banquet and went
into the garden, and Haman began to beg for his
life from the queen, for he saw that he was in serious trouble. 8 When the king returned from the
garden, Haman had thrown himself on the couch,
pleading with the queen. The king said, "Will he
dare even assault my wife in my own house?" Haman, when he heard, turned away his face. 9 Then
Bugathan, one of the eunuchs, said to the king,
"Look, Haman has even prepared a gallows for
Mordecai, who gave information of concern to
the king; it is standing at Haman's house, a gallows fifty cubits high." So the king said, "Let Haman be hanged on that." 10 So Haman was hanged
on the gallows he had prepared for Mordecai.
With that the anger of the king abated.

8 On that very day King Artaxerxes granted to
Esther all the property of the persecutor[b] Haman. Mordecai was summoned by the king, for
Esther had told the king[c] that he was related to
her. 2 The king took the ring that had been taken
from Haman, and gave it to Mordecai; and Esther set Mordecai over everything that had been
Haman's.
3 Then she spoke once again to the king and,
falling at his feet, she asked him to avert all the
evil that Haman had planned against the Jews.
4 The king extended his golden scepter to Esther,
and she rose and stood before the king. 5 Esther said, "If it pleases you, and if I have found
favor, let an order be sent rescinding the letters
that Haman wrote and sent to destroy the Jews
in your kingdom. 6 How can I look on the ruin
of my people? How can I be safe if my ancestral
nation[d] is destroyed?" 7 The king said to Esther,
"Now that I[e] have granted all of Haman's property
to you and have hanged him on a tree because he
acted against the Jews, what else do you request?
8 Write in my name what you think best and seal it
with my ring; for whatever is written at the king's
command and sealed with my ring cannot be
contravened."
9 The secretaries were summoned on the
twenty-third day of the first month, that is, Nisan,
in the same year; and all that he commanded with
respect to the Jews was given in writing to the
administrators and governors of the provinces
from India to Ethiopia, one hundred twenty-
seven provinces, to each province in its own language. 10 The edict was written[f] with the king's
authority and sealed with his ring, and sent out
by couriers. 11 He ordered the Jews in every city
to observe their own laws, to defend themselves,
and to act as they wished against their opponents
and enemies 12 on a certain day, the thirteenth of
the twelfth month, which is Adar, throughout all
the kingdom of Artaxerxes.

Addition E

16 [g] The following is a copy of this letter:
"The Great King, Artaxerxes, to the governors of the provinces from India to Ethiopia,
one hundred twenty-seven provinces, and to
those who are loyal to our government, greetings.
2 "Many people, the more they are honored
with the most generous kindness of their benefactors, the more proud do they become, 3 and
not only seek to injure our subjects, but in their
inability to stand prosperity, they even undertake

[a] Gk *is not worthy of* [b] Gk *slanderer* [c] Gk *him* [d] Gk *country* [e] Gk *If I* [f] Gk *It was written*
[g] Chapter 16.1–24 corresponds to chapter E 1–24 in some translations.

to scheme against their own benefactors. 4They
not only take away thankfulness from others, but,
carried away by the boasts of those who know
nothing of goodness, they even assume that they
will escape the evil-hating justice of God, who always sees everything. 5And often many of those
who are set in places of authority have been made
in part responsible for the shedding of innocent
blood, and have been involved in irremediable
calamities, by the persuasion of friends who have
been entrusted with the administration of public
affairs, 6when these persons by the false trickery
of their evil natures beguile the sincere goodwill
of their sovereigns.
7 "What has been wickedly accomplished
through the pestilent behavior of those who exercise authority unworthily can be seen, not so
much from the more ancient records that we
hand on, as from investigation of matters close
at hand.[a] 8In the future we will take care to render our kingdom quiet and peaceable for all, 9by
changing our methods and always judging what
comes before our eyes with more equitable consideration. 10For Haman son of Hammedatha, a
Macedonian (really an alien to the Persian blood,
and quite devoid of our kindliness), having become our guest, 11enjoyed so fully the goodwill
that we have for every nation that he was called
our father and was continually bowed down to
by all as the person second to the royal throne.
12But, unable to restrain his arrogance, he undertook to deprive us of our kingdom and our
life,[b] 13and with intricate craft and deceit asked
for the destruction of Mordecai, our savior and
perpetual benefactor, and of Esther, the blameless partner of our kingdom, together with their
whole nation. 14He thought that by these methods he would catch us undefended and would
transfer the kingdom of the Persians to the Macedonians.
15 "But we find that the Jews, who were consigned to annihilation by this thrice-accursed
man, are not evildoers, but are governed by most
righteous laws 16and are children of the living
God, most high, most mighty,[c] who has directed
the kingdom both for us and for our ancestors in
the most excellent order.
17 "You will therefore do well not to put
in execution the letters sent by Haman son of
Hammedatha, 18since he, the one who did these
things, has been hanged at the gate of Susa with
all his household—for God, who rules over all
things, has speedily inflicted on him the punishment that he deserved.
19 "Therefore post a copy of this letter publicly in every place, and permit the Jews to live
under their own laws. 20And give them reinforce-
ments, so that on the thirteenth day of the twelfth
month, Adar, on that very day, they may defend
themselves against those who attack them at the
time of oppression. 21For God, who rules over
all things, has made this day to be a joy for his
chosen people instead of a day of destruction for
them.
22 "Therefore you shall observe this with all
good cheer as a notable day among your com-
memorative festivals, 23so that both now and
hereafter it may represent deliverance for you[d] and
the loyal Persians, but that it may be a reminder of
destruction for those who plot against us.
24 "Every city and country, without exception, that does not act accordingly shall be destroyed in wrath with spear and fire. It shall be
made not only impassable for human beings, but
also most hateful to wild animals and birds for
all time.

End of Addition E

---

8 13"Let copies of the decree be posted conspicuously in all the kingdom, and let all the
Jews be ready on that day to fight against their
enemies."
14 So the messengers on horseback set out
with all speed to perform what the king had commanded; and the decree was published also in
Susa. 15Mordecai went out dressed in the royal
robe and wearing a gold crown and a turban of
purple linen. The people in Susa rejoiced on seeing

[a] Gk *matters beside* (your) *feet* [b] Gk *our spirit* [c] Gk *greatest* [d] Other ancient authorities read *for us*

him. 16And the Jews had light and gladness 17in
every city and province wherever the decree was
published; wherever the proclamation was made,
the Jews had joy and gladness, a banquet and a
holiday. And many of the Gentiles were circumcised and became Jews out of fear of the Jews.

9 Now on the thirteenth day of the twelfth
month, which is Adar, the decree written
by the king arrived. 2On that same day the enemies of the Jews perished; no one resisted, because they feared them. 3The chief provincial
governors, the princes, and the royal secretaries
were paying honor to the Jews, because fear of
Mordecai weighed upon them. 4The king's decree required that Mordecai's name be held in
honor throughout the kingdom.[a] 6Now in the
city of Susa the Jews killed five hundred people,
7including Pharsannestain, Delphon, Phasga,
8Pharadatha, Barea, Sarbacha, 9Marmasima, Aru-
phaeus, Arsaeus, Zabutheus, 10the ten sons of
Haman son of Hammedatha, the Bougean, the
enemy of the Jews—and they indulged[b] themselves in plunder.

11 That very day the number of those killed
in Susa was reported to the king. 12The king said
to Esther, "In Susa, the capital, the Jews have
destroyed five hundred people. What do you
suppose they have done in the surrounding countryside? Whatever more you ask will be done for
you." 13And Esther said to the king, "Let the Jews
be allowed to do the same tomorrow. Also, hang
up the bodies of Haman's ten sons." 14So he permitted this to be done, and handed over to the
Jews of the city the bodies of Haman's sons to
hang up. 15The Jews who were in Susa gathered
on the fourteenth and killed three hundred people, but took no plunder.

16 Now the other Jews in the kingdom gathered to defend themselves, and got relief from
their enemies. They destroyed fifteen thousand
of them, but did not engage in plunder. 17On the
fourteenth day they rested and made that same
day a day of rest, celebrating it with joy and gladness. 18The Jews who were in Susa, the capital,
came together also on the fourteenth, but did
not rest. They celebrated the fifteenth with joy
and gladness. 19On this account then the Jews
who are scattered around the country outside
Susa keep the fourteenth of Adar as a joyful holiday, and send presents of food to one another,
while those who live in the large cities keep the
fifteenth day of Adar as their joyful holiday, also
sending presents to one another.

20 Mordecai recorded these things in a book,
and sent it to the Jews in the kingdom of Artaxerxes both near and far, 21telling them that they
should keep the fourteenth and fifteenth days of
Adar, 22for on these days the Jews got relief from
their enemies. The whole month (namely, Adar),
in which their condition had been changed from
sorrow into gladness and from a time of distress
to a holiday, was to be celebrated as a time for
feasting[c] and gladness and for sending presents of
food to their friends and to the poor.

23 So the Jews accepted what Mordecai
had written to them 24—how Haman son of
Hammedatha, the Macedonian,[d] fought against
them, how he made a decree and cast lots[e] to destroy them, 25and how he went in to the king,
telling him to hang Mordecai; but the wicked
plot he had devised against the Jews came back
upon himself, and he and his sons were hanged.
26Therefore these days were called "Purim," because of the lots (for in their language this is the
word that means "lots"). And so, because of what
was written in this letter, and because of what
they had experienced in this affair and what had
befallen them, Mordecai established this festival,[f]
27and the Jews took upon themselves, upon their
descendants, and upon all who would join them,
to observe it without fail.[g] These days of Purim
should be a memorial and kept from generation
to generation, in every city, family, and country.
28These days of Purim were to be observed for all

[a] Meaning of Gk uncertain. Some ancient authorities add verse 5, *So the Jews struck down all their enemies with the sword, killing and destroying them, and they did as they pleased to those who hated them.* [b] Other ancient authorities read *did not indulge* [c] Gk *of weddings* [d] Other ancient witnesses read *the Bougean* [e] Gk *a lot* [f] Gk *he established* (it) [g] Meaning of Gk uncertain

time, and the commemoration of them was never
to cease among their descendants.
29 Then Queen Esther daughter of Aminadab along with Mordecai the Jew wrote down
what they had done, and gave full authority to the
letter about Purim.[a] 31 And Mordecai and Queen
Esther established this decision on their own responsibility, pledging their own well-being to the
plan.[b] 32 Esther established it by a decree forever,
and it was written for a memorial.

10 The king levied a tax upon his kingdom
both by land and sea. 2 And as for his
power and bravery, and the wealth and glory of
his kingdom, they were recorded in the annals of
the kings of the Persians and the Medes. 3 Mordecai acted with authority on behalf of King Artaxerxes and was great in the kingdom, as well as
honored by the Jews. His way of life was such as
to make him beloved to his whole nation.

Addition F

4[c] And Mordecai said, "These things have
come from God; 5 for I remember the dream
that I had concerning these matters, and none of
them has failed to be fulfilled. 6 There was the little spring that became a river, and there was light
and sun and abundant water—the river is Esther,
whom the king married and made queen. 7 The
two dragons are Haman and myself. 8 The nations
are those that gathered to destroy the name of the
Jews. 9 And my nation, this is Israel, who cried
out to God and was saved. The Lord has saved
his people; the Lord has rescued us from all these
evils; God has done great signs and wonders,
wonders that have never happened among the
nations. 10 For this purpose he made two lots, one
for the people of God and one for all the nations,
11 and these two lots came to the hour and moment and day of decision before God and among
all the nations. 12 And God remembered his people and vindicated his inheritance. 13 So they will
observe these days in the month of Adar, on the
fourteenth and fifteenth[d] of that month, with
an assembly and joy and gladness before God,
from generation to generation forever among his
people Israel."

11 1 In the fourth year of the
reign of Ptolemy and Cleopatra, Dositheus, who said that he was a priest and a Levite,[e]
and his son Ptolemy brought to Egypt[f] the preceding Letter about Purim, which they said
was authentic and had been translated by Lysimachus son of Ptolemy, one of the residents of Jerusalem.

End of Addition F

---

[a] Verse 30 in Heb is lacking in Gk: *Letters were sent to all the Jews, to the one hundred twenty-seven provinces of the kingdom of Ahasuerus, in words of peace and truth.* [b] Meaning of Gk uncertain [c] Chapter 10.4–13 and 11.1 correspond to chapter F 1–11 in some translations. [d] Other ancient authorities lack *and fifteenth* [e] Or *priest, and Levitas*
[f] Cn: Gk *brought in*

The Wisdom of Solomon

Although the Wisdom of Solomon mentions Israel's wise king in the title and is written as though Solomon were speaking, the book was probably written many centuries after Solomon lived. (It was not uncommon in the ancient world for writers to credit well-known and well-respected figures from the past. This type of writing is called *pseudepigrapha*; other examples include apocalypses and testaments of Israel's Patriarchs and prophets such as the books of *Enoch.* Since Solomon was well known for being very wise, it is not surprising that the writer uses his name in a book that focuses on the meaning of true wisdom.

Some scholars have suggested that the book was written originally in Hebrew and translated into Greek, but no such Hebrew original has been discovered. This has led others to conclude that the language and style of the book point to a Jewish author who wrote in Greek and was very familiar with Greek thought. The Wisdom of Solomon was not included in the Jewish Scriptures but is placed between Job and Ecclesiastes in the Greek Septuagint.

The author probably wrote Wisdom to encourage the Jews living in Alexandria, Egypt, in the first or second century BCE to be faithful to God. Some had abandoned the Jewish religion and adopted Greek religions or turned to worshiping Egyptian gods. The author wanted to show fellow Jews that the wisdom of God was better than any Greek philosophy or Egyptian religion. To do this, the author also had to deal with a theme that appears in earlier books of Hebrew wisdom (Job, for example), namely, why evil people are sometimes successful while good people suffer. The author states that God will bring about justice when God judges all people after death. The wicked will be punished, but those who were faithful to God will live with God forever.

The author describes wisdom as "a breath of the power of God" (7:25), which is similar to the way earlier books describe wisdom as being present with God at creation (see Prov 8:22-31; Job 28:12-28). But a number of descriptions of wisdom in the book are similar to Greek understandings of wisdom. This likely reflects the author's Greek background in a city of Greek culture and language. For example, the author uses phrases such as "a pure emanation of the glory of the Almighty" (7:25) and as "a spotless mirror of the working of God" (7:26).

When the author quotes Scripture, he quotes from the Greek Septuagint, which tradition says seventy-two translators completed in Egypt shortly after 250 BCE. The author understands Jewish thought and knows Jewish history, but also is very familiar with Greek philosophy. Some scholars believe the book was written before the time of the Jewish philosopher Philo of Alexandria, who lived from 20 BCE to 54 CE. The author does not seem to quote from Philo's work, and Philo doesn't

mention the Wisdom of Solomon in his writings. It has also been suggested, however, that the anti-Jewish riots that took place in Alexandria in 38 CE could be the background for the strong vision of judgment against the enemies of God's people found in 5:15-23 and for the strong anti-Egyptian tone of the book (see chs. 10–19).

These theories cannot be proved, but it is probably safe to say that Wisdom is one of the latest, if not the latest, book in the Greek Septuagint. In fact, in one early listing of books considered to be canonical, the Muratorian Canon, which dates from the late second century CE, the Wisdom of Solomon is listed as a book of the New Testament.

It is difficult for one who grew up in a Scandinavian Lutheran enclave to understand what it means to live in a hostile or unwelcoming environment—the kind of environment the Jews living in Egypt may have experienced and the sort of environment racial or religious minorities face on a daily basis. For me, the wisdom of God resided in the elders, including pastors and teachers, who attended the majority church in town, a place where most people seemed to look the same and most had names ending in -son. Prejudice and fear of others unlike us existed, but this was also an environment that taught me remarkable openness and tolerance. We imagined that God's light surely shined on us, as it had shined on the people of Israel. But we also learned that God's wisdom and God's grace were meant for all people.

— ***Scott Tunseth***

1 Love righteousness, you rulers of the earth,
think of the Lord in goodness
and seek him with sincerity of heart;
2 because he is found by those who do not put him to the test,
and manifests himself to those who do not distrust him.
3 For perverse thoughts separate people from God,
and when his power is tested, it exposes the foolish;
4 because wisdom will not enter a deceitful soul,
or dwell in a body enslaved to sin.
5 For a holy and disciplined spirit will flee from deceit,
and will leave foolish thoughts behind,
and will be ashamed at the approach of unrighteousness.
6 For wisdom is a kindly spirit,
but will not free blasphemers from the guilt of their words;
because God is witness of their inmost feelings,
and a true observer of their hearts, and a hearer of their tongues.
7 Because the spirit of the Lord has filled the world,
and that which holds all things together knows what is said,
8 therefore those who utter unrighteous things will not escape notice,
and justice, when it punishes, will not pass them by.

9 For inquiry will be made into the counsels of
the ungodly,
and a report of their words will come to the
Lord,
to convict them of their lawless deeds;
10 because a jealous ear hears all things,
and the sound of grumbling does not go
unheard.
11 Beware then of useless grumbling,
and keep your tongue from slander;
because no secret word is without result,[a]
and a lying mouth destroys the soul.

Wisdom 1:10—2:10

The reasoning of the ungodly is a theme throughout Wisdom. The author attributes their iniquity to the belief that "we were born by mere chance" and that after death "we shall be as though we had never been" (2:2). They are hostile to the righteous whose testimony of holy living is an affront to them.

—NE

12 Do not invite death by the error of your life,
or bring on destruction by the works of your
hands;
13 because God did not make death,
and he does not delight in the death of the
living.
14 For he created all things so that they might
exist;
the generative forces[b] of the world are
wholesome,
and there is no destructive poison in them,
and the dominion[c] of Hades is not on earth.
15 For righteousness is immortal.

16 But the ungodly by their words and deeds
summoned death;[d]
considering him a friend, they pined away
and made a covenant with him,
because they are fit to belong to his company.

2 For they reasoned unsoundly, saying to
themselves,
"Short and sorrowful is our life,
and there is no remedy when a life comes to
its end,
and no one has been known to return from
Hades.
2 For we were born by mere chance,
and hereafter we shall be as though we had
never been,
for the breath in our nostrils is smoke,
and reason is a spark kindled by the beating
of our hearts;
3 when it is extinguished, the body will turn to
ashes,
and the spirit will dissolve like empty air.
4 Our name will be forgotten in time,
and no one will remember our works;
our life will pass away like the traces of a
cloud,
and be scattered like mist
that is chased by the rays of the sun
and overcome by its heat.
5 For our allotted time is the passing of a
shadow,
and there is no return from our death,
because it is sealed up and no one turns back.

6 "Come, therefore, let us enjoy the good
things that exist,
and make use of the creation to the full as in
youth.
7 Let us take our fill of costly wine and
perfumes,
and let no flower of spring pass us by.
8 Let us crown ourselves with rosebuds before
they wither.
9 Let none of us fail to share in our revelry;
everywhere let us leave signs of enjoyment,
because this is our portion, and this our lot.
10 Let us oppress the righteous poor man;
let us not spare the widow
or regard the gray hairs of the aged.
11 But let our might be our law of right,
for what is weak proves itself to be useless.

[a] Or *will go unpunished* [b] Or *the creatures* [c] Or *palace* [d] Gk *him*

12 "Let us lie in wait for the righteous man,
because he is inconvenient to us and opposes our actions;
he reproaches us for sins against the law,
and accuses us of sins against our training.
13 He professes to have knowledge of God,
and calls himself a child[a] of the Lord.
14 He became to us a reproof of our thoughts;
15 the very sight of him is a burden to us,
because his manner of life is unlike that of others,
and his ways are strange.
16 We are considered by him as something base,
and he avoids our ways as unclean;
he calls the last end of the righteous happy,
and boasts that God is his father.
17 Let us see if his words are true,
and let us test what will happen at the end of his life;
18 for if the righteous man is God's child, he will help him,
and will deliver him from the hand of his adversaries.
19 Let us test him with insult and torture,
so that we may find out how gentle he is,
and make trial of his forbearance.
20 Let us condemn him to a shameful death,
for, according to what he says, he will be protected."

21 Thus they reasoned, but they were led astray,
for their wickedness blinded them,
22 and they did not know the secret purposes of God,
nor hoped for the wages of holiness,
nor discerned the prize for blameless souls;
23 for God created us for incorruption,
and made us in the image of his own eternity,[b]
24 but through the devil's envy death entered the world,
and those who belong to his company experience it.

3 But the souls of the righteous are in the hand of God,
and no torment will ever touch them.
2 In the eyes of the foolish they seemed to have died,
and their departure was thought to be a disaster,
3 and their going from us to be their destruction;
but they are at peace.
4 For though in the sight of others they were punished,
their hope is full of immortality.
5 Having been disciplined a little, they will receive great good,
because God tested them and found them worthy of himself;
6 like gold in the furnace he tried them,
and like a sacrificial burnt offering he accepted them.
7 In the time of their visitation they will shine forth,
and will run like sparks through the stubble.
8 They will govern nations and rule over peoples,
and the Lord will reign over them forever.
9 Those who trust in him will understand truth,
and the faithful will abide with him in love,
because grace and mercy are upon his holy ones,
and he watches over his elect.[c]

10 But the ungodly will be punished as their reasoning deserves,
those who disregarded the righteous[d]
and rebelled against the Lord;
11 for those who despise wisdom and instruction are miserable.
Their hope is vain, their labors are unprofitable,
and their works are useless.
12 Their wives are foolish, and their children evil;

[a] Or *servant* [b] Other ancient authorities read *nature* [c] Text of this line uncertain; omitted by some ancient authorities. Compare 4.15 [d] Or *what is right*

13 their offspring are accursed.
For blessed is the barren woman who is undefiled,
who has not entered into a sinful union;
she will have fruit when God examines souls.
14 Blessed also is the eunuch whose hands have done no lawless deed,
and who has not devised wicked things against the Lord;
for special favor will be shown him for his faithfulness,
and a place of great delight in the temple of the Lord.
15 For the fruit of good labors is renowned,
and the root of understanding does not fail.
16 But children of adulterers will not come to maturity,
and the offspring of an unlawful union will perish.
17 Even if they live long they will be held of no account,
and finally their old age will be without honor.
18 If they die young, they will have no hope
and no consolation on the day of judgment.
19 For the end of an unrighteous generation is grievous.

4 Better than this is childlessness with virtue,
for in the memory of virtue[a] is immortality,
because it is known both by God and by mortals.
2 When it is present, people imitate[b] it,
and they long for it when it has gone;
throughout all time it marches, crowned in triumph,
victor in the contest for prizes that are undefiled.
3 But the prolific brood of the ungodly will be of no use,
and none of their illegitimate seedlings will strike a deep root
or take a firm hold.
4 For even if they put forth boughs for a while,
standing insecurely they will be shaken by the wind,
and by the violence of the winds they will be uprooted.
5 The branches will be broken off before they come to maturity,
and their fruit will be useless,
not ripe enough to eat, and good for nothing.
6 For children born of unlawful unions
are witnesses of evil against their parents when God examines them.[c]
7 But the righteous, though they die early, will be at rest.
8 For old age is not honored for length of time,
or measured by number of years;
9 but understanding is gray hair for anyone,
and a blameless life is ripe old age.
10 There were some who pleased God and were loved by him,
and while living among sinners were taken up.
11 They were caught up so that evil might not change their understanding
or guile deceive their souls.
12 For the fascination of wickedness obscures what is good,
and roving desire perverts the innocent mind.
13 Being perfected in a short time, they fulfilled long years;
14 for their souls were pleasing to the Lord,
therefore he took them quickly from the midst of wickedness.
15 Yet the peoples saw and did not understand,
or take such a thing to heart,
that God's grace and mercy are with his elect,
and that he watches over his holy ones.

16 The righteous who have died will condemn the ungodly who are living,
and youth that is quickly perfected[d] will condemn the prolonged old age of the unrighteous.
17 For they will see the end of the wise,

[a] Gk *it* [b] Other ancient authorities read *honor* [c] Gk *at their examination* [d] Or *ended*

and will not understand what the Lord
purposed for them,
and for what he kept them safe.
18 The unrighteous[a] will see, and will have
contempt for them,
but the Lord will laugh them to scorn.
After this they will become dishonored
corpses,
and an outrage among the dead forever;
19 because he will dash them speechless to the
ground,
and shake them from the foundations;
they will be left utterly dry and barren,
and they will suffer anguish,
and the memory of them will perish.

20 They will come with dread when their sins
are reckoned up,
and their lawless deeds will convict them to
their face.

5 Then the righteous will stand with great
confidence
in the presence of those who have oppressed
them
and those who make light of their labors.
2 When the unrighteous[b] see them, they will be
shaken with dreadful fear,
and they will be amazed at the unexpected
salvation of the righteous.
3 They will speak to one another in repentance,
and in anguish of spirit they will groan, and
say,
4 "These are persons whom we once held in
derision
and made a byword of reproach—fools that
we were!
We thought that their lives were madness
and that their end was without honor.
5 Why have they been numbered among the
children of God?
And why is their lot among the saints?
6 So it was we who strayed from the way of
truth,
and the light of righteousness did not shine
on us,
and the sun did not rise upon us.
7 We took our fill of the paths of lawlessness
and destruction,
and we journeyed through trackless deserts,
but the way of the Lord we have not known.
8 What has our arrogance profited us?
And what good has our boasted wealth
brought us?

9 "All those things have vanished like a shadow,
and like a rumor that passes by;
10 like a ship that sails through the billowy
water,
and when it has passed no trace can be found,
no track of its keel in the waves;
11 or as, when a bird flies through the air,
no evidence of its passage is found;
the light air, lashed by the beat of its pinions
and pierced by the force of its rushing flight,
is traversed by the movement of its wings,
and afterward no sign of its coming is found
there;
12 or as, when an arrow is shot at a target,
the air, thus divided, comes together at once,
so that no one knows its pathway.
13 So we also, as soon as we were born, ceased
to be,
and we had no sign of virtue to show,
but were consumed in our wickedness."
14 Because the hope of the ungodly is like
thistledown[c] carried by the wind,
and like a light frost[d] driven away by a storm;
it is dispersed like smoke before the wind,
and it passes like the remembrance of a guest
who stays but a day.

15 But the righteous live forever,
and their reward is with the Lord;
the Most High takes care of them.
16 Therefore they will receive a glorious crown
and a beautiful diadem from the hand of the
Lord,
because with his right hand he will cover
them,
and with his arm he will shield them.

[a] Gk *They* [b] Gk *they* [c] Other ancient authorities read *dust* [d] Other ancient authorities read *spider's web*

17 The Lord[a] will take his zeal as his whole
armor,
and will arm all creation to repel[b] his enemies;
18 he will put on righteousness as a breastplate,
and wear impartial justice as a helmet;
19 he will take holiness as an invincible shield,
20 and sharpen stern wrath for a sword,
and creation will join with him to fight
against his frenzied foes.
21 Shafts of lightning will fly with true aim,
and will leap from the clouds to the target, as
from a well-drawn bow,
22 and hailstones full of wrath will be hurled as
from a catapult;
the water of the sea will rage against them,
and rivers will relentlessly overwhelm them;
23 a mighty wind will rise against them,
and like a tempest it will winnow them away.
Lawlessness will lay waste the whole earth,
and evildoing will overturn the thrones of
rulers.

6 Listen therefore, O kings, and understand;
learn, O judges of the ends of the earth.
2 Give ear, you that rule over multitudes,
and boast of many nations.
3 For your dominion was given you from the
Lord,
and your sovereignty from the Most High;
he will search out your works and inquire
into your plans.
4 Because as servants of his kingdom you did
not rule rightly,
or keep the law,
or walk according to the purpose of God,
5 he will come upon you terribly and swiftly,
because severe judgment falls on those in
high places.
6 For the lowliest may be pardoned in mercy,
but the mighty will be mightily tested.
7 For the Lord of all will not stand in awe of
anyone,
or show deference to greatness;
because he himself made both small and
great,
and he takes thought for all alike.
8 But a strict inquiry is in store for the mighty.
9 To you then, O monarchs, my words are
directed,
so that you may learn wisdom and not
transgress.
10 For they will be made holy who observe holy
things in holiness,
and those who have been taught them will
find a defense.
11 Therefore set your desire on my words;
long for them, and you will be instructed.

12 Wisdom is radiant and unfading,
and she is easily discerned by those who love
her,
and is found by those who seek her.
13 She hastens to make herself known to those
who desire her.
14 One who rises early to seek her will have no
difficulty,
for she will be found sitting at the gate.
15 To fix one's thought on her is perfect
understanding,
and one who is vigilant on her account will
soon be free from care,
16 because she goes about seeking those worthy
of her,
and she graciously appears to them in their
paths,
and meets them in every thought.

17 The beginning of wisdom[c] is the most sincere
desire for instruction,
and concern for instruction is love of her,
18 and love of her is the keeping of her laws,
and giving heed to her laws is assurance of
immortality,
19 and immortality brings one near to God;
20 so the desire for wisdom leads to a kingdom.

21 Therefore if you delight in thrones and
scepters, O monarchs over the
peoples,
honor wisdom, so that you may reign forever.

[a] Gk *He* [b] Or *punish* [c] Gk *Her beginning*

22 I will tell you what wisdom is and how she
came to be,
and I will hide no secrets from you,
but I will trace her course from the beginning
of creation,
and make knowledge of her clear,
and I will not pass by the truth;
23 nor will I travel in the company of sickly envy,
for envy[a] does not associate with wisdom.
24 The multitude of the wise is the salvation of
the world,
and a sensible king is the stability of any
people.
25 Therefore be instructed by my words, and
you will profit.

7 I also am mortal, like everyone else,
a descendant of the first-formed child of
earth;
and in the womb of a mother I was molded
into flesh,
2 within the period of ten months, compacted
with blood,
from the seed of a man and the pleasure of
marriage.
3 And when I was born, I began to breathe the
common air,
and fell upon the kindred earth;
my first sound was a cry, as is true of all.
4 I was nursed with care in swaddling cloths.
5 For no king has had a different beginning of
existence;
6 there is for all one entrance into life, and one
way out.
7 Therefore I prayed, and understanding was
given me;
I called on God, and the spirit of wisdom
came to me.
8 I preferred her to scepters and thrones,
and I accounted wealth as nothing in
comparison with her.
9 Neither did I liken to her any priceless
gem,
because all gold is but a little sand in her
sight,
and silver will be accounted as clay before
her.
10 I loved her more than health and beauty,
and I chose to have her rather than light,
because her radiance never ceases.
11 All good things came to me along with her,
and in her hands uncounted wealth.
12 I rejoiced in them all, because wisdom leads
them;
but I did not know that she was their
mother.
13 I learned without guile and I impart without
grudging;
I do not hide her wealth,
14 for it is an unfailing treasure for mortals;
those who get it obtain friendship with God,
commended for the gifts that come from
instruction.

15 May God grant me to speak with judgment,
and to have thoughts worthy of what I have
received;
for he is the guide even of wisdom
and the corrector of the wise.
16 For both we and our words are in his hand,
as are all understanding and skill in crafts.
17 For it is he who gave me unerring knowledge
of what exists,
to know the structure of the world and the
activity of the elements;
18 the beginning and end and middle of times,
the alternations of the solstices and the
changes of the seasons,
19 the cycles of the year and the constellations
of the stars,
20 the natures of animals and the tempers of
wild animals,
the powers of spirits[b] and the thoughts of
human beings,
the varieties of plants and the virtues of
roots;
21 I learned both what is secret and what is
manifest,
22 for wisdom, the fashioner of all things,
taught me.

[a] Gk *this* [b] Or *winds*

Wisdom 7:22

Wisdom—*Hokmah* in Hebrew, *Sophia* in the Greek of this writing—is "the fashioner of all things" (7:22) who "orders all things well" (8:1) and who was present when God made the world (9:9). Wisdom is even identified with God's "holy spirit" (9:17). Later Christian teaching about Jesus Christ being present with God and active in creation (Col 1:15-20), eternally present with God as the Word (John 1), and sharing in the divine nature with the Holy Spirit (the language of the Nicene Creed) have antecedents in a long tradition of Jewish teaching about divine Wisdom.

—NE

There is in her a spirit that is intelligent, holy,
unique, manifold, subtle,
mobile, clear, unpolluted,
distinct, invulnerable, loving the good, keen,
irresistible, 23beneficent, humane,
steadfast, sure, free from anxiety,
all-powerful, overseeing all,
and penetrating through all spirits
that are intelligent, pure, and altogether subtle.
24 For wisdom is more mobile than any motion;
because of her pureness she pervades and penetrates all things.
25 For she is a breath of the power of God,
and a pure emanation of the glory of the Almighty;
therefore nothing defiled gains entrance into her.
26 For she is a reflection of eternal light,
a spotless mirror of the working of God,
and an image of his goodness.
27 Although she is but one, she can do all things,
and while remaining in herself, she renews all things;
in every generation she passes into holy souls
and makes them friends of God, and prophets;
28 for God loves nothing so much as the person who lives with wisdom.
29 She is more beautiful than the sun,
and excels every constellation of the stars.
Compared with the light she is found to be superior,
30 for it is succeeded by the night,
but against wisdom evil does not prevail.

8 She reaches mightily from one end of the earth to the other,
and she orders all things well.
2 I loved her and sought her from my youth;
I desired to take her for my bride,
and became enamored of her beauty.
3 She glorifies her noble birth by living with God,
and the Lord of all loves her.
4 For she is an initiate in the knowledge of God,
and an associate in his works.
5 If riches are a desirable possession in life,
what is richer than wisdom, the active cause of all things?
6 And if understanding is effective,
who more than she is fashioner of what exists?
7 And if anyone loves righteousness,
her labors are virtues;
for she teaches self-control and prudence,
justice and courage;
nothing in life is more profitable for mortals than these.
8 And if anyone longs for wide experience,
she knows the things of old, and infers the things to come;
she understands turns of speech and the solutions of riddles;
she has foreknowledge of signs and wonders
and of the outcome of seasons and times.
9 Therefore I determined to take her to live with me,
knowing that she would give me good counsel
and encouragement in cares and grief.
10 Because of her I shall have glory among the multitudes
and honor in the presence of the elders, though I am young.
11 I shall be found keen in judgment,

and in the sight of rulers I shall be admired.
12 When I am silent they will wait for me,
and when I speak they will give heed;
if I speak at greater length,
they will put their hands on their mouths.
13 Because of her I shall have immortality,
and leave an everlasting remembrance to those who come after me.
14 I shall govern peoples,
and nations will be subject to me;
15 dread monarchs will be afraid of me when they hear of me;
among the people I shall show myself capable, and courageous in war.
16 When I enter my house, I shall find rest with her;
for companionship with her has no bitterness,
and life with her has no pain, but gladness and joy.
17 When I considered these things inwardly,
and pondered in my heart
that in kinship with wisdom there is immortality,
18 and in friendship with her, pure delight,
and in the labors of her hands, unfailing wealth,
and in the experience of her company, understanding,
and renown in sharing her words,
I went about seeking how to get her for myself.
19 As a child I was naturally gifted,
and a good soul fell to my lot;
20 or rather, being good, I entered an undefiled body.
21 But I perceived that I would not possess wisdom unless God gave her to me—
and it was a mark of insight to know whose gift she was—
so I appealed to the Lord and implored him,
and with my whole heart I said:

9 "O God of my ancestors and Lord of mercy,
who have made all things by your word,
2 and by your wisdom have formed humankind
to have dominion over the creatures you have made,
3 and rule the world in holiness and righteousness,
and pronounce judgment in uprightness of soul,
4 give me the wisdom that sits by your throne,
and do not reject me from among your servants.
5 For I am your servant[a] the son of your serving girl,
a man who is weak and short-lived,
with little understanding of judgment and laws;
6 for even one who is perfect among human beings
will be regarded as nothing without the wisdom that comes from you.
7 You have chosen me to be king of your people
and to be judge over your sons and daughters.
8 You have given command to build a temple on your holy mountain,
and an altar in the city of your habitation,
a copy of the holy tent that you prepared from the beginning.
9 With you is wisdom, she who knows your works
and was present when you made the world;
she understands what is pleasing in your sight
and what is right according to your commandments.
10 Send her forth from the holy heavens,
and from the throne of your glory send her,
that she may labor at my side,
and that I may learn what is pleasing to you.
11 For she knows and understands all things,
and she will guide me wisely in my actions
and guard me with her glory.
12 Then my works will be acceptable,
and I shall judge your people justly,
and shall be worthy of the throne[b] of my father.
13 For who can learn the counsel of God?
Or who can discern what the Lord wills?

[a] Gk *slave* [b] Gk *thrones*

14 For the reasoning of mortals is worthless,
and our designs are likely to fail;
15 for a perishable body weighs down the soul,
and this earthy tent burdens the thoughtful[a] mind.
16 We can hardly guess at what is on earth,
and what is at hand we find with labor;
but who has traced out what is in the heavens?
17 Who has learned your counsel,
unless you have given wisdom
and sent your holy spirit from on high?
18 And thus the paths of those on earth were set right,
and people were taught what pleases you,
and were saved by wisdom."

10 Wisdom[b] protected the first-formed father of the world, when he alone had been created;
she delivered him from his transgression,

Wisdom 10:1

The "first-formed father of the world" is, of course, Adam. Here the author begins a long recitation of human and Israelite history in terms of the constant intervention and guidance of Wisdom, whose purpose is always to reclaim and restore a fallen humanity—beginning already with the restoration of Adam.

—*NE*

2 and gave him strength to rule all things.
3 But when an unrighteous man departed from her in his anger,
he perished because in rage he killed his brother.
4 When the earth was flooded because of him,
wisdom again saved it,
steering the righteous man by a paltry piece of wood.
5 Wisdom[b] also, when the nations in wicked agreement had been put to confusion,
recognized the righteous man and preserved him blameless before God,
and kept him strong in the face of his compassion for his child.
6 Wisdom[b] rescued a righteous man when the ungodly were perishing;
he escaped the fire that descended on the Five Cities.[c]
7 Evidence of their wickedness still remains:
a continually smoking wasteland,
plants bearing fruit that does not ripen,
and a pillar of salt standing as a monument to an unbelieving soul.
8 For because they passed wisdom by,
they not only were hindered from recognizing the good,
but also left for humankind a reminder of their folly,
so that their failures could never go unnoticed.
9 Wisdom rescued from troubles those who served her.
10 When a righteous man fled from his brother's wrath,
she guided him on straight paths;
she showed him the kingdom of God,
and gave him knowledge of holy things;
she prospered him in his labors,
and increased the fruit of his toil.
11 When his oppressors were covetous,
she stood by him and made him rich.
12 She protected him from his enemies,
and kept him safe from those who lay in wait for him;
in his arduous contest she gave him the victory,
so that he might learn that godliness is more powerful than anything else.
13 When a righteous man was sold, wisdom[d] did not desert him,

[a] Or *anxious* [b] Gk *She* [c] Or *on Pentapolis* [d] Gk *she*

but delivered him from sin.
She descended with him into the dungeon,
14 and when he was in prison she did not leave him,
until she brought him the scepter of a kingdom
and authority over his masters.
Those who accused him she showed to be false,
and she gave him everlasting honor.

15 A holy people and blameless race
wisdom delivered from a nation of oppressors.
16 She entered the soul of a servant of the Lord,
and withstood dread kings with wonders and signs.
17 She gave to holy people the reward of their labors;
she guided them along a marvelous way,
and became a shelter to them by day,
and a starry flame through the night.
18 She brought them over the Red Sea,
and led them through deep waters;
19 but she drowned their enemies,
and cast them up from the depth of the sea.
20 Therefore the righteous plundered the ungodly;
they sang hymns, O Lord, to your holy name,
and praised with one accord your defending hand;
21 for wisdom opened the mouths of those who were mute,
and made the tongues of infants speak clearly.

11 Wisdom[a] prospered their works by the hand of a holy prophet.
2 They journeyed through an uninhabited wilderness,
and pitched their tents in untrodden places.
3 They withstood their enemies and fought off their foes.
4 When they were thirsty, they called upon you,
and water was given them out of flinty rock,
and from hard stone a remedy for their thirst.
5 For through the very things by which their enemies were punished,
they themselves received benefit in their need.
6 Instead of the fountain of an ever-flowing river,
stirred up and defiled with blood
7 in rebuke for the decree to kill the infants,
you gave them abundant water unexpectedly,
8 showing by their thirst at that time
how you punished their enemies.
9 For when they were tried, though they were being disciplined in mercy,
they learned how the ungodly were tormented when judged in wrath.
10 For you tested them as a parent[b] does in warning,
but you examined the ungodly[c] as a stern king does in condemnation.
11 Whether absent or present, they were equally distressed,
12 for a twofold grief possessed them,
and a groaning at the memory of what had occurred.
13 For when they heard that through their own punishments
the righteous[d] had received benefit, they perceived it was the Lord's doing.
14 For though they had mockingly rejected him who long before had been cast out and exposed,
at the end of the events they marveled at him,
when they felt thirst in a different way from the righteous.

15 In return for their foolish and wicked thoughts,
which led them astray to worship irrational serpents and worthless animals,
you sent upon them a multitude of irrational creatures to punish them,
16 so that they might learn that one is punished by the very things by which one sins.
17 For your all-powerful hand,

[a] Gk *She* [b] Gk *a father* [c] Gk *those* [d] Gk *they*

which created the world out of formless
matter,
did not lack the means to send upon them a
multitude of bears, or bold lions,
18 or newly-created unknown beasts full of rage,
or such as breathe out fiery breath,
or belch forth a thick pall of smoke,
or flash terrible sparks from their eyes;
19 not only could the harm they did destroy
people,[a]
but the mere sight of them could kill by
fright.
20 Even apart from these, people[b] could fall at a
single breath
when pursued by justice
and scattered by the breath of your power.
But you have arranged all things by measure
and number and weight.

21 For it is always in your power to show great
strength,
and who can withstand the might of your arm?
22 Because the whole world before you is like a
speck that tips the scales,
and like a drop of morning dew that falls on
the ground.
23 But you are merciful to all, for you can do all
things,
and you overlook people's sins, so that they
may repent.
24 For you love all things that exist,
and detest none of the things that you have
made,
for you would not have made anything if you
had hated it.
25 How would anything have endured if you had
not willed it?
Or how would anything not called forth by
you have been preserved?
26 You spare all things, for they are yours,
O Lord, you who love the living.

12 For your immortal spirit is in all things.
2 Therefore you correct little by little
those who trespass,
and you remind and warn them of the things
through which they sin,
so that they may be freed from wickedness
and put their trust in you, O Lord.

3 Those who lived long ago in your holy land
4 you hated for their detestable practices,
their works of sorcery and unholy rites,
5 their merciless slaughter[c] of children,
and their sacrificial feasting on human flesh
and blood.
These initiates from the midst of a heathen
cult,[d]
6 these parents who murder helpless lives,
you willed to destroy by the hands of our
ancestors,
7 so that the land most precious of all to you
might receive a worthy colony of the
servants[e] of God.
8 But even these you spared, since they were
but mortals,
and sent wasps[f] as forerunners of your army

[a] Gk *them* [b] Gk *they* [c] Gk *slaughterers* [d] Meaning of Gk uncertain [e] Or *children* [f] Or *hornets*

Wisdom 12:3-11

In a dramatic departure from the "conquest" narrative in Joshua and Judges, *Wisdom* asserts that God showed mercy on the Canaanites, "judging them little by little" in order to give them "an opportunity to repent" (v. 10). The author's point is not sympathy with the Canaanites, however, who are still regarded as "an accursed race" incapable of change (v. 11), but emphasis on divine forbearance. Even the Jews of Alexandria, sorely abused by their neighbors, are to understand that God's tolerance of the wicked springs from both divine sovereignty and divine mercy.

— *NE*

to destroy them little by little,
9 though you were not unable to give the
ungodly into the hands of the
righteous in battle,
or to destroy them at one blow by dread wild
animals or your stern word.
10 But judging them little by little you gave them
an opportunity to repent,
though you were not unaware that their
origin[a] was evil
and their wickedness inborn,
and that their way of thinking would never
change.
11 For they were an accursed race from the
beginning,
and it was not through fear of anyone that
you left them unpunished for their
sins.

12 For who will say, "What have you done?"
or will resist your judgment?
Who will accuse you for the destruction of
nations that you made?
Or who will come before you to plead as an
advocate for the unrighteous?
13 For neither is there any god besides you,
whose care is for all people,[b]
to whom you should prove that you have not
judged unjustly;
14 nor can any king or monarch confront
you about those whom you have
punished.
15 You are righteous and you rule all things
righteously,
deeming it alien to your power
to condemn anyone who does not deserve to
be punished.
16 For your strength is the source of
righteousness,
and your sovereignty over all causes you to
spare all.
17 For you show your strength when people
doubt the completeness of your
power,
and you rebuke any insolence among those
who know it.[c]
18 Although you are sovereign in strength, you
judge with mildness,
and with great forbearance you govern us;
for you have power to act whenever you
choose.

19 Through such works you have taught your
people
that the righteous must be kind,
and you have filled your children with good
hope,
because you give repentance for sins.
20 For if you punished with such great care and
indulgence[d]
the enemies of your servants[e] and those
deserving of death,
granting them time and opportunity to give
up their wickedness,
21 with what strictness you have judged your
children,
to whose ancestors you gave oaths and
covenants full of good promises!
22 So while chastening us you scourge our
enemies ten thousand times more,
so that, when we judge, we may meditate
upon your goodness,
and when we are judged, we may expect
mercy.

23 Therefore those who lived unrighteously, in a
life of folly,
you tormented through their own
abominations.
24 For they went far astray on the paths of error,
accepting as gods those animals that even
their enemies[f] despised;
they were deceived like foolish infants.
25 Therefore, as though to children who cannot
reason,
you sent your judgment to mock them.
26 But those who have not heeded the warning
of mild rebukes

[a] Or *nature* [b] Or *all things* [c] Meaning of Gk uncertain [d] Other ancient authorities lack *and indulgence*; others read *and entreaty* [e] Or *children* [f] Gk *they*

will experience the deserved judgment of
God.
27 For when in their suffering they became
incensed
at those creatures that they had thought to
be gods, being punished by means of
them,
they saw and recognized as the true God the
one whom they had before refused
to know.
Therefore the utmost condemnation came
upon them.

13 For all people who were ignorant of God
were foolish by nature;
and they were unable from the good things
that are seen to know the one who
exists,
nor did they recognize the artisan while
paying heed to his works;
2 but they supposed that either fire or wind or
swift air,
or the circle of the stars, or turbulent water,
or the luminaries of heaven were the gods
that rule the world.
3 If through delight in the beauty of these
things people assumed them to be
gods,
let them know how much better than these is
their Lord,
for the author of beauty created them.
4 And if people[a] were amazed at their power
and working,
let them perceive from them
how much more powerful is the one who
formed them.
5 For from the greatness and beauty of created
things
comes a corresponding perception of their
Creator.
6 Yet these people are little to be blamed,
for perhaps they go astray
while seeking God and desiring to find him.
7 For while they live among his works, they
keep searching,
and they trust in what they see, because the
things that are seen are beautiful.
8 Yet again, not even they are to be excused;
9 for if they had the power to know so much
that they could investigate the world,
how did they fail to find sooner the Lord of
these things?

10 But miserable, with their hopes set on dead
things, are those
who give the name "gods" to the works of
human hands,
gold and silver fashioned with skill,
and likenesses of animals,
or a useless stone, the work of an ancient
hand.
11 A skilled woodcutter may saw down a tree
easy to handle
and skillfully strip off all its bark,
and then with pleasing workmanship
make a useful vessel that serves life's needs,
12 and burn the cast-off pieces of his work
to prepare his food, and eat his fill.
13 But a cast-off piece from among them, useful
for nothing,
a stick crooked and full of knots,
he takes and carves with care in his leisure,
and shapes it with skill gained in idleness;[b]
he forms it in the likeness of a human being,
14 or makes it like some worthless animal,
giving it a coat of red paint and coloring its
surface red
and covering every blemish in it with paint;
15 then he makes a suitable niche for it,
and sets it in the wall, and fastens it there
with iron.
16 He takes thought for it, so that it may not
fall,
because he knows that it cannot help itself,
for it is only an image and has need of help.
17 When he prays about possessions and his
marriage and children,
he is not ashamed to address a lifeless thing.
18 For health he appeals to a thing that is weak;
for life he prays to a thing that is dead;

[a] Gk *they* [b] Other ancient authorities read *with intelligent skill*

for aid he entreats a thing that is utterly
inexperienced;
for a prosperous journey, a thing that cannot
take a step;
19 for money-making and work and success with
his hands
he asks strength of a thing whose hands have
no strength.

14 Again, one preparing to sail and about to
voyage over raging waves
calls upon a piece of wood more fragile than
the ship that carries him.
2 For it was desire for gain that planned that
vessel,
and wisdom was the artisan who built it;
3 but it is your providence, O Father, that steers
its course,
because you have given it a path in the sea,
and a safe way through the waves,
4 showing that you can save from every danger,
so that even a person who lacks skill may put
to sea.
5 It is your will that works of your wisdom
should not be without effect;
therefore people trust their lives even to the
smallest piece of wood,
and passing through the billows on a raft they
come safely to land.
6 For even in the beginning, when arrogant
giants were perishing,
the hope of the world took refuge on a raft,
and guided by your hand left to the world the
seed of a new generation.
7 For blessed is the wood by which
righteousness comes.

8 But the idol made with hands is accursed,
and so is the one who made it—
he for having made it, and the perishable
thing because it was named a god.
9 For equally hateful to God are the ungodly
and their ungodliness;
10 for what was done will be punished together
with the one who did it.

11 Therefore there will be a visitation also upon
the heathen idols,
because, though part of what God created,
they became an abomination,
snares for human souls
and a trap for the feet of the foolish.

12 For the idea of making idols was the
beginning of fornication,
and the invention of them was the corruption
of life;
13 for they did not exist from the beginning,
nor will they last forever.
14 For through human vanity they entered the
world,
and therefore their speedy end has been
planned.

15 For a father, consumed with grief at an
untimely bereavement,
made an image of his child, who had been
suddenly taken from him;
he now honored as a god what was once a
dead human being,
and handed on to his dependents secret rites
and initiations.
16 Then the ungodly custom, grown strong with
time, was kept as a law,
and at the command of monarchs carved
images were worshiped.
17 When people could not honor monarchs[a] in
their presence, since they lived at a
distance,
they imagined their appearance far away,
and made a visible image of the king whom
they honored,
so that by their zeal they might flatter the
absent one as though present.

18 Then the ambition of the artisan impelled
even those who did not know the king to
intensify their worship.
19 For he, perhaps wishing to please his ruler,
skillfully forced the likeness to take more
beautiful form,

[a] Gk *them*

20 and the multitude, attracted by the charm of
his work,
now regarded as an object of worship the
one whom shortly before they had
honored as a human being.
21 And this became a hidden trap for
humankind,
because people, in bondage to misfortune or
to royal authority,
bestowed on objects of stone or wood the
name that ought not to be shared.

22 Then it was not enough for them to err about
the knowledge of God,
but though living in great strife due to
ignorance,
they call such great evils peace.
23 For whether they kill children in their
initiations, or celebrate secret
mysteries,
or hold frenzied revels with strange customs,
24 they no longer keep either their lives or their
marriages pure,
but they either treacherously kill one another,
or grieve one another by adultery,
25 and all is a raging riot of blood and murder,
theft and deceit, corruption,
faithlessness, tumult, perjury,
26 confusion over what is good, forgetfulness of
favors,
defiling of souls, sexual perversion,
disorder in marriages, adultery, and
debauchery.
27 For the worship of idols not to be named
is the beginning and cause and end of every
evil.
28 For their worshipers[a] either rave in
exultation,
or prophesy lies, or live unrighteously, or
readily commit perjury;
29 for because they trust in lifeless idols
they swear wicked oaths and expect to suffer
no harm.
30 But just penalties will overtake them on two
counts:
because they thought wrongly about God in
devoting themselves to idols,
and because in deceit they swore
unrighteously through contempt for
holiness.
31 For it is not the power of the things by which
people swear,[b]
but the just penalty for those who sin,
that always pursues the transgression of the
unrighteous.

15 But you, our God, are kind and true,
patient, and ruling all things[c] in mercy.
2 For even if we sin we are yours, knowing your
power;
but we will not sin, because we know that you
acknowledge us as yours.
3 For to know you is complete righteousness,
and to know your power is the root of
immortality.
4 For neither has the evil intent of human art
misled us,
nor the fruitless toil of painters,
a figure stained with varied colors,
5 whose appearance arouses yearning in fools,
so that they desire[d] the lifeless form of a dead
image.
6 Lovers of evil things and fit for such objects
of hope[e]
are those who either make or desire or
worship them.

7 A potter kneads the soft earth
and laboriously molds each vessel for our
service,
fashioning out of the same clay
both the vessels that serve clean uses
and those for contrary uses, making all
alike;
but which shall be the use of each of them
the worker in clay decides.
8 With misspent toil, these workers form a
futile god from the same clay—
these mortals who were made of earth a short
time before

[a] Gk *they* [b] Or *of the oaths people swear* [c] Or *ruling the universe* [d] Gk *and he desires* [e] Gk *such hopes*

and after a little while go to the earth from
which all mortals are taken,
when the time comes to return the souls that
were borrowed.
9 But the workers are not concerned that
mortals are destined to die
or that their life is brief,
but they compete with workers in gold and
silver,
and imitate workers in copper;
and they count it a glorious thing to mold
counterfeit gods.
10 Their heart is ashes, their hope is cheaper
than dirt,
and their lives are of less worth than clay,
11 because they failed to know the one who
formed them
and inspired them with active souls
and breathed a living spirit into them.
12 But they considered our existence an idle game,
and life a festival held for profit,
for they say one must get money however
one can, even by base means.
13 For these persons, more than all others, know
that they sin
when they make from earthy matter fragile
vessels and carved images.

14 But most foolish, and more miserable than an
infant,
are all the enemies who oppressed your
people.
15 For they thought that all their heathen idols
were gods,
though these have neither the use of their
eyes to see with,
nor nostrils with which to draw breath,
nor ears with which to hear,
nor fingers to feel with,
and their feet are of no use for walking.
16 For a human being made them,
and one whose spirit is borrowed formed
them;
for none can form gods that are like
themselves.
17 People are mortal, and what they make with
lawless hands is dead;
for they are better than the objects they
worship,
since[a] they have life, but the idols[b] never had.

18 Moreover, they worship even the most
hateful animals,
which are worse than all others when judged
by their lack of intelligence;
19 and even as animals they are not so beautiful
in appearance that one would desire
them,
but they have escaped both the praise of God
and his blessing.

16 Therefore those people[c] were deservedly
punished through such creatures,
and were tormented by a multitude of
animals.
2 Instead of this punishment you showed
kindness to your people,
and you prepared quails to eat,
a delicacy to satisfy the desire of appetite;
3 in order that those people, when they desired
food,
might lose the least remnant of appetite[d]
because of the odious creatures sent to
them,
while your people,[c] after suffering want a
short time,
might partake of delicacies.
4 For it was necessary that upon those
oppressors inescapable want should
come,
while to these others it was merely shown
how their enemies were being
tormented.

5 For when the terrible rage of wild animals
came upon your people[e]
and they were being destroyed by the bites of
writhing serpents,
your wrath did not continue to the end;
6 they were troubled for a little while as a
warning,

[a] Other ancient authorities read *of which* [b] Gk *but they* [c] Gk *they* [d] Gk *loathed the necessary appetite* [e] Gk *them*

and received a symbol of deliverance to
remind them of your law's command.
7 For the one who turned toward it was saved,
not by the thing that was beheld,
but by you, the Savior of all.
8 And by this also you convinced our
enemies
that it is you who deliver from every evil.
9 For they were killed by the bites of locusts
and flies,
and no healing was found for them,
because they deserved to be punished by
such things.
10 But your children were not conquered even
by the fangs of venomous serpents,
for your mercy came to their help and healed
them.
11 To remind them of your oracles they were
bitten,
and then were quickly delivered,
so that they would not fall into deep
forgetfulness
and become unresponsive[a] to your kindness.
12 For neither herb nor poultice cured them,
but it was your word, O Lord, that heals all
people.
13 For you have power over life and death;
you lead mortals down to the gates of Hades
and back again.
14 A person in wickedness kills another,
but cannot bring back the departed spirit,
or set free the imprisoned soul.

15 To escape from your hand is impossible;
16 for the ungodly, refusing to know you,
were flogged by the strength of your arm,
pursued by unusual rains and hail and
relentless storms,
and utterly consumed by fire.
17 For—most incredible of all—in water, which
quenches all things,
the fire had still greater effect,
for the universe defends the righteous.
18 At one time the flame was restrained,
so that it might not consume the creatures
sent against the ungodly,
but that seeing this they might know
that they were being pursued by the
judgment of God;
19 and at another time even in the midst of
water it burned more intensely than
fire,
to destroy the crops of the unrighteous land.
20 Instead of these things you gave your people
food of angels,
and without their toil you supplied them
from heaven with bread ready to eat,
providing every pleasure and suited to every
taste.
21 For your sustenance manifested your
sweetness toward your children;
and the bread, ministering[b] to the desire of
the one who took it,
was changed to suit everyone's liking.
22 Snow and ice withstood fire without melting,
so that they might know that the crops of
their enemies
were being destroyed by the fire that blazed
in the hail
and flashed in the showers of rain;
23 whereas the fire,[c] in order that the righteous
might be fed,
even forgot its native power.

24 For creation, serving you who made it,
exerts itself to punish the unrighteous,
and in kindness relaxes on behalf of those
who trust in you.
25 Therefore at that time also, changed into all
forms,
it served your all-nourishing bounty,
according to the desire of those who had
need,[d]
26 so that your children, whom you loved,
O Lord, might learn
that it is not the production of crops that
feeds humankind
but that your word sustains those who trust
in you.

[a] Meaning of Gk uncertain [b] Gk *and it, ministering* [c] Gk *this* [d] Or *who made supplication*

27 For what was not destroyed by fire
was melted when simply warmed by a
fleeting ray of the sun,
28 to make it known that one must rise before
the sun to give you thanks,
and must pray to you at the dawning of the
light;
29 for the hope of an ungrateful person will melt
like wintry frost,
and flow away like waste water.

17 Great are your judgments and hard to
describe;
therefore uninstructed souls have gone astray.
2 For when lawless people supposed that they
held the holy nation in their power,
they themselves lay as captives of darkness
and prisoners of long night,
shut in under their roofs, exiles from eternal
providence.
3 For thinking that in their secret sins they
were unobserved
behind a dark curtain of forgetfulness,
they were scattered, terribly[a] alarmed,
and appalled by specters.
4 For not even the inner chamber that held
them protected them from fear,
but terrifying sounds rang out around them,
and dismal phantoms with gloomy faces
appeared.
5 And no power of fire was able to give light,
nor did the brilliant flames of the stars
avail to illumine that hateful night.
6 Nothing was shining through to them
except a dreadful, self-kindled fire,
and in terror they deemed the things that
they saw
to be worse than that unseen appearance.
7 The delusions of their magic art lay humbled,
and their boasted wisdom was scornfully
rebuked.
8 For those who promised to drive off the fears
and disorders of a sick soul
were sick themselves with ridiculous fear.
9 For even if nothing disturbing frightened
them,
yet, scared by the passing of wild animals and
the hissing of snakes
10 they perished in trembling fear,
refusing to look even at the air, though it
nowhere could be avoided.
11 For wickedness is a cowardly thing,
condemned by its own testimony;[b]
distressed by conscience, it has always
exaggerated[c] the difficulties.
12 For fear is nothing but a giving up of the
helps that come from reason;
13 and hope, defeated by this inward weakness,
prefers ignorance of what causes the torment.
14 But throughout the night, which was really
powerless
and which came upon them from the recesses
of powerless Hades,
they all slept the same sleep,
15 and now were driven by monstrous specters,
and now were paralyzed by their souls'
surrender;
for sudden and unexpected fear overwhelmed
them.
16 And whoever was there fell down,
and thus was kept shut up in a prison not
made of iron;
17 for whether they were farmers or shepherds
or workers who toiled in the wilderness,
they were seized, and endured the
inescapable fate;
for with one chain of darkness they all were
bound.
18 Whether there came a whistling wind,
or a melodious sound of birds in wide-
spreading branches,
or the rhythm of violently rushing water,
19 or the harsh crash of rocks hurled down,
or the unseen running of leaping animals,
or the sound of the most savage roaring
beasts,
or an echo thrown back from a hollow of the
mountains,

[a] Other ancient authorities read *unobserved, they were darkened behind a dark curtain of forgetfulness, terribly* [b] Meaning of Gk uncertain [c] Other ancient authorities read *anticipated*

it paralyzed them with terror.
20 For the whole world was illumined with brilliant light,
and went about its work unhindered,
21 while over those people alone heavy night was spread,
an image of the darkness that was destined to receive them;
but still heavier than darkness were they to themselves.

18 But for your holy ones there was very great light.
Their enemies[a] heard their voices but did not see their forms,
and counted them happy for not having suffered,
2 and were thankful that your holy ones,[b] though previously wronged, were doing them no injury;
and they begged their pardon for having been at variance with them.[b]
3 Therefore you provided a flaming pillar of fire
as a guide for your people's[c] unknown journey,
and a harmless sun for their glorious wandering.
4 For their enemies[d] deserved to be deprived of light and imprisoned in darkness,
those who had kept your children imprisoned,
through whom the imperishable light of the law was to be given to the world.

5 When they had resolved to kill the infants of your holy ones,
and one child had been abandoned and rescued,
you in punishment took away a multitude of their children;
and you destroyed them all together by a mighty flood.
6 That night was made known beforehand to our ancestors,
so that they might rejoice in sure knowledge of the oaths in which they trusted.
7 The deliverance of the righteous and the destruction of their enemies
were expected by your people.
8 For by the same means by which you punished our enemies
you called us to yourself and glorified us.
9 For in secret the holy children of good people offered sacrifices,
and with one accord agreed to the divine law,
so that the saints would share alike the same things,
both blessings and dangers;
and already they were singing the praises of the ancestors.[e]
10 But the discordant cry of their enemies echoed back,
and their piteous lament for their children was spread abroad.
11 The slave was punished with the same penalty as the master,
and the commoner suffered the same loss as the king;
12 and they all together, by the one form[f] of death,
had corpses too many to count.
For the living were not sufficient even to bury them,
since in one instant their most valued children had been destroyed.
13 For though they had disbelieved everything because of their magic arts,
yet, when their firstborn were destroyed,
they acknowledged your people to be God's child.
14 For while gentle silence enveloped all things,
and night in its swift course was now half gone,
15 your all-powerful word leaped from heaven, from the royal throne,
into the midst of the land that was doomed,
a stern warrior

[a] Gk *They* [b] Meaning of Gk uncertain [c] Gk *their* [d] Gk *those persons* [e] Other ancient authorities read *dangers, the ancestors already leading the songs of praise* [f] Gk *name*

16 carrying the sharp sword of your authentic
command,
and stood and filled all things with death,
and touched heaven while standing on the
earth.
17 Then at once apparitions in dreadful dreams
greatly troubled them,
and unexpected fears assailed them;
18 and one here and another there, hurled down
half dead,
made known why they were dying;
19 for the dreams that disturbed them
forewarned them of this,
so that they might not perish without
knowing why they suffered.

20 The experience of death touched also the
righteous,
and a plague came upon the multitude in the
desert,
but the wrath did not long continue.
21 For a blameless man was quick to act as their
champion;
he brought forward the shield of his ministry,
prayer and propitiation by incense;
he withstood the anger and put an end to the
disaster,
showing that he was your servant.
22 He conquered the wrath[a] not by strength of
body,
not by force of arms,
but by his word he subdued the avenger,
appealing to the oaths and covenants given to
our ancestors.
23 For when the dead had already fallen on one
another in heaps,
he intervened and held back the wrath,
and cut off its way to the living.
24 For on his long robe the whole world was
depicted,
and the glories of the ancestors were
engraved on the four rows of stones,
and your majesty was on the diadem upon
his head.
25 To these the destroyer yielded, these he[b]
feared;
for merely to test the wrath was enough.

19 But the ungodly were assailed to the end
by pitiless anger,
for God[c] knew in advance even their future
actions:
2 how, though they themselves had permitted[d]
your people to depart
and hastily sent them out,
they would change their minds and pursue
them.
3 For while they were still engaged in
mourning,
and were lamenting at the graves of their
dead,
they reached another foolish decision,
and pursued as fugitives those whom they
had begged and compelled to leave.
4 For the fate they deserved drew them on to
this end,
and made them forget what had happened,
in order that they might fill up the
punishment that their torments still
lacked,
5 and that your people might experience[e] an
incredible journey,
but they themselves might meet a strange
death.

6 For the whole creation in its nature was
fashioned anew,
complying with your commands,
so that your children[f] might be kept
unharmed.
7 The cloud was seen overshadowing the camp,
and dry land emerging where water had
stood before,
an unhindered way out of the Red Sea,
and a grassy plain out of the raging waves,
8 where those protected by your hand passed
through as one nation,
after gazing on marvelous wonders.

[a] Cn: Gk *multitude* [b] Other ancient authorities read *they* [c] Gk *he* [d] Other ancient authorities read *had changed their minds to permit* [e] Other ancient authorities read *accomplish* [f] Or *servants*

9 For they ranged like horses,
and leaped like lambs,
praising you, O Lord, who delivered them.
10 For they still recalled the events of their sojourn,
how instead of producing animals the earth brought forth gnats,
and instead of fish the river spewed out vast numbers of frogs.
11 Afterward they saw also a new kind[a] of birds,
when desire led them to ask for luxurious food;
12 for, to give them relief, quails came up from the sea.

13 The punishments did not come upon the sinners
without prior signs in the violence of thunder,
for they justly suffered because of their wicked acts;
for they practiced a more bitter hatred of strangers.
14 Others had refused to receive strangers when they came to them,
but these made slaves of guests who were their benefactors.
15 And not only so—but, while punishment of some sort will come upon the former
for having received strangers with hostility,
16 the latter, having first received them with festal celebrations,
afterward afflicted with terrible sufferings
those who had already shared the same rights.
17 They were stricken also with loss of sight—
just as were those at the door of the righteous man—
when, surrounded by yawning darkness,
all of them tried to find the way through their own doors.

18 For the elements changed[b] places with one another,
as on a harp the notes vary the nature of the rhythm,
while each note remains the same.[c]
This may be clearly inferred from the sight of what took place.
19 For land animals were transformed into water creatures,
and creatures that swim moved over to the land.
20 Fire even in water retained its normal power,
and water forgot its fire-quenching nature.
21 Flames, on the contrary, failed to consume
the flesh of perishable creatures that walked among them,
nor did they melt[d] the crystalline, quick-melting kind of heavenly food.

22 For in everything, O Lord, you have exalted and glorified your people,
and you have not neglected to help them at all times and in all places.

[a] Or *production* [b] Gk *changing* [c] Meaning of Gk uncertain [d] Cn: Gk *nor could be melted*

Ecclesiasticus, or the Wisdom of Jesus Son of

Sirach

The book of Sirach was written by one who described himself as a student of the law of the Most High (see 39:1-11) and as one who taught others (51:23). That writer was Jesus son of Eleazar son of Sirach (50:27). He is often also identified by the shortened Hebrew form of the name, Jesus Ben Sira (*Sirach* is the Greek for *Sira*). The author's grandson wrote the prologue and translated the book into Greek sometime after 132 BCE, "in the thirty-eighth year of the reign of Euergetes" (the latter a Greek-speaking Egyptian monarch from the Ptolemy dynasty: Ptolemy VIII Euergetes II Physcon, 145–116 BCE). Based on 50:1-24, Jesus son of Sirach likely wrote the book after the time Simon son of Onias was high priest in Jerusalem (219–196 BCE) and before the Maccabean-led revolts began, after 180 BCE.

The book of Sirach can be described as the class notes of a teacher of Hebrew wisdom who was seeking to help students learn the art of living well under the guidance of the Lord, the source of all wisdom (1:1). Sirach's notes contain many different kinds of literature, including prayers (23:1-6; 51:1-12), hymns (39:12-35), etiquette (32:1-13), numerical lists (25:1-2, 7-11), and poems honoring Israel's past heroes (chs. 44–50). But the book is primarily made up of typical wisdom sayings of the kind found in other wisdom books, such as Proverbs and the Wisdom of Solomon.

Themes in Sirach are also consistent with themes found in Hebrew wisdom. These include the importance of fearing (respecting) the Lord, proper use of wealth and the giving of alms to the poor, being honest and taking care not to use words to slander or lie, choosing friends wisely, practicing self-control, and raising children properly. Sirach also has specific advice for particular types of workers and for rulers (9:10—10:18; 38:1-15). Sirach does speak about facing suffering (2:1-6; 4:1-10), but the book holds to the belief common in earlier Hebrew wisdom that in this life good is rewarded and evil punished. The book does not raise the possibility of life after death.

I find that the attitude toward women depicted in Sirach is at times even more strident and unsympathetic than other biblical literature (see especially chs. 25–26), and this is troubling to me as a male reader. These words in particular are a reminder of the challenge we all face in hearing the text as *wisdom* for today. Again we recognize the difficulty of reading the Bible as God's Word when those words are presented through the lenses of a particular ancient cultural perspective. And yet compare those words to Sirach's more compassionate plea to avoid judging others by appearances (11:1-4). Reading the Bible is an exercise in wise discernment, in which we discern not only texts but also people, including ourselves.

No matter what vocational hat I wear—pastor, educator, editor, parent, spouse—Sirach challenges me not only to *seek* the Lord's wisdom but to be a channel for it as well. Yet, I do well to recognize that the channel does not flow in a single direction only, as if, being wise or powerful or privileged, one can simply own and dispense it. True wisdom, it seems, always runs in both directions. The Scriptures themselves invite us all into this sacred dialog.

— ***Scott Tunseth***

The Prologue

Many great teachings have been given to us through the Law and the Prophets and the others[a] that followed them, and for these we should praise Israel for instruction and wisdom. Now, those who read the scriptures must not only themselves understand them, but must also as lovers of learning be able through the spoken and written word to help the outsiders. So my grandfather Jesus, who had devoted himself especially to the reading of the Law and the Prophets and the other books of our ancestors, and had acquired considerable proficiency in them, was himself also led to write something pertaining to instruction and wisdom, so that by becoming familiar also with his book[b] those who love learning might make even greater progress in living according to the law.

You are invited therefore to read it with goodwill and attention, and to be indulgent in cases where, despite our diligent labor in translating, we may seem to have rendered some phrases imperfectly. For what was originally expressed in Hebrew does not have exactly the same sense when translated into another language. Not only this book, but even the Law itself, the Prophecies, and the rest of the books differ not a little when read in the original.

When I came to Egypt in the thirty-eighth year of the reign of Euergetes and stayed for some time, I found opportunity for no little instruction.[c] It seemed highly necessary that I should myself devote some diligence and labor to the translation of this book. During that time I have applied my skill day and night to complete and publish the book for those living abroad who wished to gain learning and are disposed to live according to the law.

1 All wisdom is from the Lord,
and with him it remains forever.
2 The sand of the sea, the drops of rain,
and the days of eternity—who can count them?
3 The height of heaven, the breadth of the earth,
the abyss, and wisdom[d]—who can search them out?
4 Wisdom was created before all other things,
and prudent understanding from eternity.[e]
6 The root of wisdom—to whom has it been revealed?
Her subtleties—who knows them?[f]
8 There is but one who is wise, greatly to be feared,
seated upon his throne—the Lord.
9 It is he who created her;
he saw her and took her measure;
he poured her out upon all his works,

[a] Or *other books* [b] Gk *with these things* [c] Other ancient authorities read *I found a copy affording no little instruction* [d] Other ancient authorities read *the depth of the abyss* [e] Other ancient authorities add as verse 5, *The source of wisdom is God's word in the highest heaven, and her ways are the eternal commandments.* [f] Other ancient authorities add as verse 7, *The knowledge of wisdom—to whom was it manifested? And her abundant experience—who has understood it?*

10 upon all the living according to his gift;
he lavished her upon those who love him.[a]
11 The fear of the Lord is glory and exultation,
and gladness and a crown of rejoicing.
12 The fear of the Lord delights the heart,
and gives gladness and joy and long life.[b]
13 Those who fear the Lord will have a happy end;
on the day of their death they will be blessed.

14 To fear the Lord is the beginning of wisdom;
she is created with the faithful in the womb.
15 She made[c] among human beings an eternal foundation,
and among their descendants she will abide faithfully.
16 To fear the Lord is fullness of wisdom;
she inebriates mortals with her fruits;
17 she fills their[d] whole house with desirable goods,
and their[d] storehouses with her produce.
18 The fear of the Lord is the crown of wisdom,
making peace and perfect health to flourish.[e]
19 She rained down knowledge and discerning comprehension,
and she heightened the glory of those who held her fast.
20 To fear the Lord is the root of wisdom,
and her branches are long life.[f]

22 Unjust anger cannot be justified,
for anger tips the scale to one's ruin.
23 Those who are patient stay calm until the right moment,
and then cheerfulness comes back to them.
24 They hold back their words until the right moment;
then the lips of many tell of their good sense.

25 In the treasuries of wisdom are wise sayings,
but godliness is an abomination to a sinner.
26 If you desire wisdom, keep the commandments,
and the Lord will lavish her upon you.
27 For the fear of the Lord is wisdom and discipline,
fidelity and humility are his delight.

28 Do not disobey the fear of the Lord;
do not approach him with a divided mind.
29 Do not be a hypocrite before others,
and keep watch over your lips.
30 Do not exalt yourself, or you may fall
and bring dishonor upon yourself.
The Lord will reveal your secrets
and overthrow you before the whole congregation,
because you did not come in the fear of the Lord,
and your heart was full of deceit.

2 My child, when you come to serve the Lord,
prepare yourself for testing.[g]
2 Set your heart right and be steadfast,
and do not be impetuous in time of calamity.
3 Cling to him and do not depart,
so that your last days may be prosperous.
4 Accept whatever befalls you,
and in times of humiliation be patient.
5 For gold is tested in the fire,
and those found acceptable, in the furnace of humiliation.[h]

[a] Other ancient authorities add *Love of the Lord is glorious wisdom; to those to whom he appears he apportions her, that they may see him.* [b] Other ancient authorities add *The fear of the Lord is a gift from the Lord; also for love he makes firm paths.* [c] Gk *made as a nest* [d] Other ancient authorities read *her* [e] Other ancient authorities add *Both are gifts of God for peace; glory opens out for those who love him. He saw her and took her measure.* [f] Other ancient authorities add as verse 21, *The fear of the Lord drives away sins; and where it abides, it will turn away all anger.* [g] Or *trials*
[h] Other ancient authorities add *in sickness and poverty put your trust in him*

6 Trust in him, and he will help you;
make your ways straight, and hope in him.
7 You who fear the Lord, wait for his mercy;
do not stray, or else you may fall.
8 You who fear the Lord, trust in him,
and your reward will not be lost.
9 You who fear the Lord, hope for good things,
for lasting joy and mercy.[a]
10 Consider the generations of old and see:
has anyone trusted in the Lord and been disappointed?
Or has anyone persevered in the fear of the Lord[b] and been forsaken?
Or has anyone called upon him and been neglected?
11 For the Lord is compassionate and merciful;
he forgives sins and saves in time of distress.

12 Woe to timid hearts and to slack hands,
and to the sinner who walks a double path!
13 Woe to the fainthearted who have no trust!
Therefore they will have no shelter.
14 Woe to you who have lost your nerve!
What will you do when the Lord's reckoning comes?

15 Those who fear the Lord do not disobey his words,
and those who love him keep his ways.
16 Those who fear the Lord seek to please him,
and those who love him are filled with his law.
17 Those who fear the Lord prepare their hearts,
and humble themselves before him.
18 Let us fall into the hands of the Lord,
but not into the hands of mortals;
for equal to his majesty is his mercy,
and equal to his name are his works.[c]

3 Listen to me your father, O children;
act accordingly, that you may be kept in safety.
2 For the Lord honors a father above his children,
and he confirms a mother's right over her children.
3 Those who honor their father atone for sins,
4 and those who respect their mother are like those who lay up treasure.
5 Those who honor their father will have joy in their own children,
and when they pray they will be heard.
6 Those who respect their father will have long life,
and those who honor[d] their mother obey the Lord;
7 they will serve their parents as their masters.[e]
8 Honor your father by word and deed,
that his blessing may come upon you.
9 For a father's blessing strengthens the houses of the children,
but a mother's curse uproots their foundations.
10 Do not glorify yourself by dishonoring your father,
for your father's dishonor is no glory to you.
11 The glory of one's father is one's own glory,
and it is a disgrace for children not to respect their mother.

12 My child, help your father in his old age,
and do not grieve him as long as he lives;
13 even if his mind fails, be patient with him;
because you have all your faculties do not despise him.
14 For kindness to a father will not be forgotten,
and will be credited to you against your sins;
15 in the day of your distress it will be remembered in your favor;
like frost in fair weather, your sins will melt away.

[a] Other ancient authorities add *For his reward is an everlasting gift with joy.* [b] Gk *of him*
[c] Syr: Gk lacks this line [d] Heb: Other ancient authorities read *comfort*
[e] In other ancient authorities this line is preceded by *Those who fear the Lord honor their father,*

16 Whoever forsakes a father is like a
blasphemer,
and whoever angers a mother is cursed by
the Lord.

17 My child, perform your tasks with humility;[a]
then you will be loved by those whom
God accepts.
18 The greater you are, the more you must
humble yourself;
so you will find favor in the sight of the
Lord.[b]
20 For great is the might of the Lord;
but by the humble he is glorified.
21 Neither seek what is too difficult for you,
nor investigate what is beyond your power.
22 Reflect upon what you have been
commanded,
for what is hidden is not your concern.
23 Do not meddle in matters that are beyond
you,
for more than you can understand has
been shown you.
24 For their conceit has led many astray,
and wrong opinion has impaired their
judgment.

25 Without eyes there is no light;
without knowledge there is no wisdom.[c]
26 A stubborn mind will fare badly at the end,
and whoever loves danger will perish in it.
27 A stubborn mind will be burdened by
troubles,
and the sinner adds sin to sins.
28 When calamity befalls the proud, there is no
healing,
for an evil plant has taken root in him.
29 The mind of the intelligent appreciates
proverbs,
and an attentive ear is the desire of the
wise.

30 As water extinguishes a blazing fire,
so almsgiving atones for sin.

31 Those who repay favors give thought to the
future;
when they fall they will find support.

4 My child, do not cheat the poor of their
living,
and do not keep needy eyes waiting.
2 Do not grieve the hungry,
or anger one in need.
3 Do not add to the troubles of the desperate,
or delay giving to the needy.
4 Do not reject a suppliant in distress,
or turn your face away from the poor.
5 Do not avert your eye from the needy,
and give no one reason to curse you;
6 for if in bitterness of soul some should curse
you,
their Creator will hear their prayer.

7 Endear yourself to the congregation;
bow your head low to the great.
8 Give a hearing to the poor,
and return their greeting politely.
9 Rescue the oppressed from the oppressor;
and do not be hesitant in giving a verdict.
10 Be a father to orphans,
and be like a husband to their mother;
you will then be like a son of the Most High,
and he will love you more than does your
mother.

11 Wisdom teaches[d] her children
and gives help to those who seek her.
12 Whoever loves her loves life,
and those who seek her from early
morning are filled with joy.
13 Whoever holds her fast inherits glory,
and the Lord blesses the place she[e] enters.
14 Those who serve her minister to the Holy
One;
the Lord loves those who love her.
15 Those who obey her will judge the nations,
and all who listen to her will live secure.
16 If they remain faithful, they will inherit her;
their descendants will also obtain her.

[a] Heb: Gk *meekness* [b] Other ancient authorities add as verse 19, *Many are lofty and renowned, but to the humble he reveals his secrets.* [c] Heb: Other ancient authorities lack verse 25 [d] Heb Syr: Gk *exalts* [e] Or *he*

17 For at first she will walk with them on
tortuous paths;
she will bring fear and dread upon them,
and will torment them by her discipline
until she trusts them,[a]
and she will test them with her ordinances.
18 Then she will come straight back to them
again and gladden them,
and will reveal her secrets to them.
19 If they go astray she will forsake them,
and hand them over to their ruin.

20 Watch for the opportune time, and beware of
evil,
and do not be ashamed to be yourself.
21 For there is a shame that leads to sin,
and there is a shame that is glory and favor.
22 Do not show partiality, to your own harm,
or deference, to your downfall.
23 Do not refrain from speaking at the proper
moment,[b]
and do not hide your wisdom.[c]
24 For wisdom becomes known through
speech,
and education through the words of the
tongue.
25 Never speak against the truth,
but be ashamed of your ignorance.
26 Do not be ashamed to confess your sins,
and do not try to stop the current of a
river.
27 Do not subject yourself to a fool,
or show partiality to a ruler.
28 Fight to the death for truth,
and the Lord God will fight for you.

29 Do not be reckless in your speech,
or sluggish and remiss in your deeds.
30 Do not be like a lion in your home,
or suspicious of your servants.
31 Do not let your hand be stretched out to
receive
and closed when it is time to give.

5 Do not rely on your wealth,
or say, "I have enough."
2 Do not follow your inclination and strength
in pursuing the desires of your heart.
3 Do not say, "Who can have power over me?"
for the Lord will surely punish you.

4 Do not say, "I sinned, yet what has happened
to me?"
for the Lord is slow to anger.
5 Do not be so confident of forgiveness[d]
that you add sin to sin.
6 Do not say, "His mercy is great,
he will forgive[e] the multitude of my sins,"
for both mercy and wrath are with him,
and his anger will rest on sinners.
7 Do not delay to turn back to the Lord,
and do not postpone it from day to day;
for suddenly the wrath of the Lord will come
upon you,
and at the time of punishment you will
perish.
8 Do not depend on dishonest wealth,
for it will not benefit you on the day of
calamity.

9 Do not winnow in every wind,
or follow every path.[f]
10 Stand firm for what you know,
and let your speech be consistent.
11 Be quick to hear,
but deliberate in answering.
12 If you know what to say, answer your
neighbor;
but if not, put your hand over your
mouth.
13 Honor and dishonor come from speaking,
and the tongue of mortals may be their
downfall.
14 Do not be called double-tongued[g]
and do not lay traps with your tongue;
for shame comes to the thief,

[a] Or *until they remain faithful in their heart* [b] Heb: Gk *at a time of salvation* [c] So some Gk Mss and Heb Syr Lat: Other Gk Mss lack *and do not hide your wisdom* [d] Heb: Gk *atonement* [e] Heb: Gk *he* (or *it*) *will atone for* [f] Gk adds *so it is with the double-tongued sinner* (see 6.1) [g] Heb: Gk *a slanderer*

and severe condemnation to the double-tongued.
15 In great and small matters cause no harm,[a]
6 1 and do not become an enemy instead of a friend;
for a bad name incurs shame and reproach;
so it is with the double-tongued sinner.

2 Do not fall into the grip of passion,[b]
or you may be torn apart as by a bull.[c]
3 Your leaves will be devoured and your fruit destroyed,
and you will be left like a withered tree.
4 Evil passion destroys those who have it,
and makes them the laughingstock of their enemies.

5 Pleasant speech multiplies friends,
and a gracious tongue multiplies courtesies.
6 Let those who are friendly with you be many,
but let your advisers be one in a thousand.
7 When you gain friends, gain them through testing,
and do not trust them hastily.
8 For there are friends who are such when it suits them,
but they will not stand by you in time of trouble.
9 And there are friends who change into enemies,
and tell of the quarrel to your disgrace.
10 And there are friends who sit at your table,
but they will not stand by you in time of trouble.
11 When you are prosperous, they become your second self,
and lord it over your servants;
12 but if you are brought low, they turn against you,
and hide themselves from you.
13 Keep away from your enemies,
and be on guard with your friends.

14 Faithful friends are a sturdy shelter:
whoever finds one has found a treasure.
15 Faithful friends are beyond price;
no amount can balance their worth.
16 Faithful friends are life-saving medicine;
and those who fear the Lord will find them.
17 Those who fear the Lord direct their friendship aright,
for as they are, so are their neighbors also.

18 My child, from your youth choose discipline,
and when you have gray hair you will still find wisdom.
19 Come to her like one who plows and sows,
and wait for her good harvest.
For when you cultivate her you will toil but little,
and soon you will eat of her produce.
20 She seems very harsh to the undisciplined;
fools cannot remain with her.
21 She will be like a heavy stone to test them,
and they will not delay in casting her aside.
22 For wisdom is like her name;
she is not readily perceived by many.

23 Listen, my child, and accept my judgment;
do not reject my counsel.
24 Put your feet into her fetters,
and your neck into her collar.
25 Bend your shoulders and carry her,
and do not fret under her bonds.
26 Come to her with all your soul,
and keep her ways with all your might.
27 Search out and seek, and she will become known to you;
and when you get hold of her, do not let her go.
28 For at last you will find the rest she gives,
and she will be changed into joy for you.
29 Then her fetters will become for you a strong defense,
and her collar a glorious robe.
30 Her yoke[d] is a golden ornament,
and her bonds a purple cord.

[a] Heb Syr: Gk *be ignorant* [b] Heb: Meaning of Gk uncertain [c] Meaning of Gk uncertain [d] Heb: Gk *Upon her*

31 You will wear her like a glorious robe,
and put her on like a splendid crown.[a]
32 If you are willing, my child, you can be disciplined,
and if you apply yourself you will become clever.
33 If you love to listen you will gain knowledge,
and if you pay attention you will become wise.
34 Stand in the company of the elders.
Who is wise? Attach yourself to such a one.
35 Be ready to listen to every godly discourse,
and let no wise proverbs escape you.
36 If you see an intelligent person, rise early to visit him;
let your foot wear out his doorstep.
37 Reflect on the statutes of the Lord,
and meditate at all times on his commandments.
It is he who will give insight to[b] your mind,
and your desire for wisdom will be granted.

7 Do no evil, and evil will never overtake you.
2 Stay away from wrong, and it will turn away from you.
3 Do[c] not sow in the furrows of injustice,
and you will not reap a sevenfold crop.

4 Do not seek from the Lord high office,
or the seat of honor from the king.
5 Do not assert your righteousness before the Lord,
or display your wisdom before the king.
6 Do not seek to become a judge,
or you may be unable to root out injustice;
you may be partial to the powerful,
and so mar your integrity.
7 Commit no offense against the public,
and do not disgrace yourself among the people.
8 Do not commit a sin twice;
not even for one will you go unpunished.
9 Do not say, "He will consider the great number of my gifts,
and when I make an offering to the Most High God, he will accept it."
10 Do not grow weary when you pray;
do not neglect to give alms.
11 Do not ridicule a person who is embittered in spirit,
for there is One who humbles and exalts.
12 Do not devise[d] a lie against your brother,
or do the same to a friend.
13 Refuse to utter any lie,
for it is a habit that results in no good.
14 Do not babble in the assembly of the elders,
and do not repeat yourself when you pray.

15 Do not hate hard labor
or farm work, which was created by the Most High.
16 Do not enroll in the ranks of sinners;
remember that retribution does not delay.
17 Humble yourself to the utmost,
for the punishment of the ungodly is fire and worms.[e]

18 Do not exchange a friend for money,
or a real brother for the gold of Ophir.
19 Do not dismiss[f] a wise and good wife,
for her charm is worth more than gold.
20 Do not abuse slaves who work faithfully,
or hired laborers who devote themselves to their task.
21 Let your soul love intelligent slaves;[g]
do not withhold from them their freedom.

22 Do you have cattle? Look after them;
if they are profitable to you, keep them.
23 Do you have children? Discipline them,
and make them obedient[h] from their youth.

[a] Heb: Gk *crown of gladness* [b] Heb: Gk *will confirm* [c] Gk *My child, do* [d] Heb: Gk *plow* [e] Heb *for the expectation of mortals is worms* [f] Heb: Gk *deprive yourself of* [g] Heb *Love a wise slave as yourself* [h] Gk *bend their necks*

24 Do you have daughters? Be concerned for
their chastity,[a]
and do not show yourself too indulgent
with them.
25 Give a daughter in marriage, and you
complete a great task;
but give her to a sensible man.
26 Do you have a wife who pleases you?[b] Do not
divorce her;
but do not trust yourself to one whom you
detest.

27 With all your heart honor your father,
and do not forget the birth pangs of your
mother.
28 Remember that it was of your parents[c] you
were born;
how can you repay what they have given
to you?

29 With all your soul fear the Lord,
and revere his priests.
30 With all your might love your Maker,
and do not neglect his ministers.
31 Fear the Lord and honor the priest,
and give him his portion, as you have been
commanded:
the first fruits, the guilt offering, the gift of
the shoulders,
the sacrifice of sanctification, and the first
fruits of the holy things.

32 Stretch out your hand to the poor,
so that your blessing may be complete.
33 Give graciously to all the living;
do not withhold kindness even from the
dead.
34 Do not avoid those who weep,
but mourn with those who mourn.
35 Do not hesitate to visit the sick,
because for such deeds you will be
loved.
36 In all you do, remember the end of your
life,
and then you will never sin.

8 Do not contend with the powerful,
or you may fall into their hands.
2 Do not quarrel with the rich,
in case their resources outweigh yours;
for gold has ruined many,
and has perverted the minds of kings.
3 Do not argue with the loud of mouth,
and do not heap wood on their fire.

4 Do not make fun of one who is ill-bred,
or your ancestors may be insulted.
5 Do not reproach one who is turning away
from sin;
remember that we all deserve punishment.
6 Do not disdain one who is old,
for some of us are also growing old.
7 Do not rejoice over anyone's death;
remember that we must all die.

8 Do not slight the discourse of the sages,
but busy yourself with their maxims;
because from them you will learn discipline
and how to serve princes.
9 Do not ignore the discourse of the aged,
for they themselves learned from their
parents;[d]
from them you learn how to understand
and to give an answer when the need
arises.

10 Do not kindle the coals of sinners,
or you may be burned in their flaming fire.
11 Do not let the insolent bring you to your feet,
or they may lie in ambush against your
words.
12 Do not lend to one who is stronger than you;
but if you do lend anything, count it as a
loss.
13 Do not give surety beyond your means;
but if you give surety, be prepared to pay.

14 Do not go to law against a judge,
for the decision will favor him because of
his standing.
15 Do not go traveling with the reckless,

[a] Gk *body* [b] Heb Syr lack *who pleases you* [c] Gk *them* [d] Or *ancestors*

or they will be burdensome to you;
for they will act as they please,
and through their folly you will perish with them.
16 Do not pick a fight with the quick-tempered,
and do not journey with them through lonely country,
because bloodshed means nothing to them,
and where no help is at hand, they will strike you down.
17 Do not consult with fools,
for they cannot keep a secret.
18 In the presence of strangers do nothing that is to be kept secret,
for you do not know what they will divulge.[a]
19 Do not reveal your thoughts to anyone,
or you may drive away your happiness.[b]

9 Do not be jealous of the wife of your bosom,
or you will teach her an evil lesson to your own hurt.
2 Do not give yourself to a woman
and let her trample down your strength.
3 Do not go near a loose woman,
or you will fall into her snares.
4 Do not dally with a singing girl,
or you will be caught by her tricks.
5 Do not look intently at a virgin,
or you may stumble and incur penalties for her.
6 Do not give yourself to prostitutes,
or you may lose your inheritance.
7 Do not look around in the streets of a city,
or wander about in its deserted sections.
8 Turn away your eyes from a shapely woman,
and do not gaze at beauty belonging to another;
many have been seduced by a woman's beauty,
and by it passion is kindled like a fire.
9 Never dine with another man's wife,
or revel with her at wine;
or your heart may turn aside to her,
and in blood[c] you may be plunged into destruction.
10 Do not abandon old friends,
for new ones cannot equal them.
A new friend is like new wine;
when it has aged, you can drink it with pleasure.
11 Do not envy the success of sinners,
for you do not know what their end will be like.
12 Do not delight in what pleases the ungodly;
remember that they will not be held guiltless all their lives.
13 Keep far from those who have power to kill,
and you will not be haunted by the fear of death.
But if you approach them, make no misstep,
or they may rob you of your life.
Know that you are stepping among snares,
and that you are walking on the city battlements.
14 As much as you can, aim to know your neighbors,
and consult with the wise.
15 Let your conversation be with intelligent people,
and let all your discussion be about the law of the Most High.
16 Let the righteous be your dinner companions,
and let your glory be in the fear of the Lord.
17 A work is praised for the skill of the artisan;
so a people's leader is proved wise by his words.
18 The loud of mouth are feared in their city,
and the one who is reckless in speech is hated.

10 A wise magistrate educates his people,
and the rule of an intelligent person is well ordered.
2 As the people's judge is, so are his officials;

[a] Or *it will bring forth* [b] Heb: Gk *and let him not return a favor to you* [c] Heb: Gk *by your spirit*

as the ruler of the city is, so are all its
inhabitants.
3 An undisciplined king ruins his people,
but a city becomes fit to live in through the
understanding of its rulers.
4 The government of the earth is in the hand of
the Lord,
and over it he will raise up the right leader
for the time.
5 Human success is in the hand of the Lord,
and it is he who confers honor upon the
lawgiver.[a]

6 Do not get angry with your neighbor for
every injury,
and do not resort to acts of insolence.
7 Arrogance is hateful to the Lord and to
mortals,
and injustice is outrageous to both.
8 Sovereignty passes from nation to nation
on account of injustice and insolence and
wealth.[b]
9 How can dust and ashes be proud?
Even in life the human body decays.[c]
10 A long illness baffles the physician;[d]
the king of today will die tomorrow.
11 For when one is dead
he inherits maggots and vermin[e] and
worms.
12 The beginning of human pride is to forsake
the Lord;
the heart has withdrawn from its Maker.
13 For the beginning of pride is sin,
and the one who clings to it pours out
abominations.
Therefore the Lord brings upon them
unheard-of calamities,
and destroys them completely.
14 The Lord overthrows the thrones of rulers,
and enthrones the lowly in their place.
15 The Lord plucks up the roots of the nations,[f]
and plants the humble in their place.
16 The Lord lays waste the lands of the nations,
and destroys them to the foundations of
the earth.
17 He removes some of them and destroys
them,
and erases the memory of them from the
earth.
18 Pride was not created for human beings,
or violent anger for those born of women.

19 Whose offspring are worthy of honor?
Human offspring.
Whose offspring are worthy of honor?
Those who fear the Lord.
Whose offspring are unworthy of honor?
Human offspring.
Whose offspring are unworthy of honor?
Those who break the commandments.
20 Among family members their leader is
worthy of honor,
but those who fear the Lord are worthy of
honor in his eyes.[g]
22 The rich, and the eminent, and the poor—
their glory is the fear of the Lord.
23 It is not right to despise one who is intelligent
but poor,
and it is not proper to honor one who is
sinful.
24 The prince and the judge and the ruler are
honored,
but none of them is greater than the one
who fears the Lord.
25 Free citizens will serve a wise servant,
and an intelligent person will not
complain.

26 Do not make a display of your wisdom when
you do your work,
and do not boast when you are in need.
27 Better is the worker who has goods in
plenty
than the boaster who lacks bread.

[a] Heb: Gk *scribe* [b] Other ancient authorities add here or after verse 9a, *Nothing is more wicked than one who loves money, for such a person puts his own soul up for sale.* [c] Heb: Meaning of Gk uncertain [d] Heb Lat: Meaning of Gk uncertain [e] Heb: Gk *wild animals* [f] Other ancient authorities read *proud nations* [g] Other ancient authorities add as verse 21, *The fear of the Lord is the beginning of acceptance; obduracy and pride are the beginning of rejection.*

28 My child, honor yourself with humility,
and give yourself the esteem you deserve.
29 Who will acquit those who condemn[a]
themselves?
And who will honor those who dishonor
themselves?[b]
30 The poor are honored for their knowledge,
while the rich are honored for their wealth.
31 One who is honored in poverty, how much
more in wealth!
And one dishonored in wealth, how much
more in poverty!

11 The wisdom of the humble lifts their
heads high,
and seats them among the great.
2 Do not praise individuals for their good
looks,
or loathe anyone because of appearance
alone.
3 The bee is small among flying creatures,
but what it produces is the best of sweet
things.
4 Do not boast about wearing fine clothes,
and do not exalt yourself when you are
honored;
for the works of the Lord are wonderful,
and his works are concealed from
humankind.
5 Many kings have had to sit on the ground,
but one who was never thought of has
worn a crown.
6 Many rulers have been utterly disgraced,
and the honored have been handed over
to others.

7 Do not find fault before you investigate;
examine first, and then criticize.
8 Do not answer before you listen,
and do not interrupt when another is
speaking.
9 Do not argue about a matter that does not
concern you,
and do not sit with sinners when they
judge a case.

10 My child, do not busy yourself with many
matters;
if you multiply activities, you will not be
held blameless.
If you pursue, you will not overtake,
and by fleeing you will not escape.
11 There are those who work and struggle and
hurry,
but are so much the more in want.
12 There are others who are slow and need help,
who lack strength and abound in poverty;
but the eyes of the Lord look kindly upon
them;
he lifts them out of their lowly condition
13 and raises up their heads
to the amazement of the many.

14 Good things and bad, life and death,
poverty and wealth, come from the Lord.[c]
17 The Lord's gift remains with the devout,
and his favor brings lasting success.
18 One becomes rich through diligence and
self-denial,
and the reward allotted to him is this:
19 when he says, "I have found rest,
and now I shall feast on my goods!"
he does not know how long it will be
until he leaves them to others and dies.

20 Stand by your agreement and attend to it,
and grow old in your work.
21 Do not wonder at the works of a sinner,
but trust in the Lord and keep at your job;
for it is easy in the sight of the Lord
to make the poor rich suddenly, in an
instant.
22 The blessing of the Lord is[d] the reward of the
pious,
and quickly God causes his blessing to
flourish.

[a] Heb: Gk *sin against* [b] Heb Lat: Gk *their own life* [c] Other ancient authorities add as verses 15 and 16, [15] *Wisdom, understanding, and knowledge of the law come from the Lord; affection and the ways of good works come from him.* [16] *Error and darkness were created with sinners; evil grows old with those who take pride in malice.* [d] Heb: Gk *is in*

23 Do not say, "What do I need,
and what further benefit can be mine?"
24 Do not say, "I have enough,
and what harm can come to me now?"
25 In the day of prosperity, adversity is forgotten,
and in the day of adversity, prosperity is not remembered.
26 For it is easy for the Lord on the day of death
to reward individuals according to their conduct.
27 An hour's misery makes one forget past delights,
and at the close of one's life one's deeds are revealed.
28 Call no one happy before his death;
by how he ends, a person becomes known.[a]

29 Do not invite everyone into your home,
for many are the tricks of the crafty.
30 Like a decoy partridge in a cage, so is the mind of the proud,
and like spies they observe your weakness;[b]
31 for they lie in wait, turning good into evil,
and to worthy actions they attach blame.
32 From a spark many coals are kindled,
and a sinner lies in wait to shed blood.
33 Beware of scoundrels, for they devise evil,
and they may ruin your reputation forever.
34 Receive strangers into your home and they will stir up trouble for you,
and will make you a stranger to your own family.

12 If you do good, know to whom you do it,
and you will be thanked for your good deeds.
2 Do good to the devout, and you will be repaid—
if not by them, certainly by the Most High.
3 No good comes to one who persists in evil
or to one who does not give alms.
4 Give to the devout, but do not help the sinner.
5 Do good to the humble, but do not give to the ungodly;
hold back their bread, and do not give it to them,
for by means of it they might subdue you;
then you will receive twice as much evil
for all the good you have done to them.
6 For the Most High also hates sinners
and will inflict punishment on the ungodly.[c]
7 Give to the one who is good, but do not help the sinner.
8 A friend is not known[d] in prosperity,
nor is an enemy hidden in adversity.
9 One's enemies are friendly[e] when one prospers,
but in adversity even one's friend disappears.
10 Never trust your enemy,
for like corrosion in copper, so is his wickedness.
11 Even if he humbles himself and walks bowed down,
take care to be on your guard against him.
Be to him like one who polishes a mirror,
to be sure it does not become completely tarnished.
12 Do not put him next to you,
or he may overthrow you and take your place.
Do not let him sit at your right hand,
or else he may try to take your own seat,
and at last you will realize the truth of my words,
and be stung by what I have said.

13 Who pities a snake charmer when he is bitten,
or all those who go near wild animals?
14 So no one pities a person who associates with a sinner
and becomes involved in the other's sins.

[a] Heb: Gk *and through his children a person becomes known* [b] Heb: Gk *downfall* [c] Other ancient authorities add *and he is keeping them for the day of their punishment* [d] Other ancient authorities read *punished* [e] Heb: Gk *grieved*

15 He stands by you for a while,
but if you falter, he will not be there.
16 An enemy speaks sweetly with his lips,
but in his heart he plans to throw you into a pit;
an enemy may have tears in his eyes,
but if he finds an opportunity he will never have enough of your blood.
17 If evil comes upon you, you will find him there ahead of you;
pretending to help, he will trip you up.
18 Then he will shake his head, and clap his hands,
and whisper much, and show his true face.

13 Whoever touches pitch gets dirty,
and whoever associates with a proud person becomes like him.
2 Do not lift a weight too heavy for you,
or associate with one mightier and richer than you.
How can the clay pot associate with the iron kettle?
The pot will strike against it and be smashed.
3 A rich person does wrong, and even adds insults;
a poor person suffers wrong, and must add apologies.
4 A rich person[a] will exploit you if you can be of use to him,
but if you are in need he will abandon you.
5 If you own something, he will live with you;
he will drain your resources without a qualm.
6 When he needs you he will deceive you,
and will smile at you and encourage you;
he will speak to you kindly and say, "What do you need?"
7 He will embarrass you with his delicacies,
until he has drained you two or three times,
and finally he will laugh at you.
Should he see you afterwards, he will pass you by
and shake his head at you.
8 Take care not to be led astray
and humiliated when you are enjoying yourself.[b]
9 When an influential person invites you, be reserved,
and he will invite you more insistently.
10 Do not be forward, or you may be rebuffed;
do not stand aloof, or you will be forgotten.
11 Do not try to treat him as an equal,
or trust his lengthy conversations;
for he will test you by prolonged talk,
and while he smiles he will be examining you.
12 Cruel are those who do not keep your secrets;
they will not spare you harm or imprisonment.
13 Be on your guard and very careful,
for you are walking about with your own downfall.[c]
15 Every creature loves its like,
and every person the neighbor.
16 All living beings associate with their own kind,
and people stick close to those like themselves.
17 What does a wolf have in common with a lamb?
No more has a sinner with the devout.
18 What peace is there between a hyena and a dog?
And what peace between the rich and the poor?
19 Wild asses in the wilderness are the prey of lions;
likewise the poor are feeding grounds for the rich.
20 Humility is an abomination to the proud;

[a] Gk *He* [b] Other ancient authorities read *in your folly* [c] Other ancient authorities add as verse 14, *When you hear these things in your sleep, wake up! During all your life love the Lord, and call on him for your salvation.*

likewise the poor are an abomination to
the rich.

21 When the rich person totters, he is supported
by friends,
but when the humble[a] falls, he is pushed
away even by friends.
22 If the rich person slips, many come to the
rescue;
he speaks unseemly words, but they justify
him.
If the humble person slips, they even criticize
him;
he talks sense, but is not given a hearing.
23 The rich person speaks and all are silent;
they extol to the clouds what he says.
The poor person speaks and they say, "Who
is this fellow?"
And should he stumble, they even push
him down.
24 Riches are good if they are free from sin;
poverty is evil only in the opinion of the
ungodly.
25 The heart changes the countenance,
either for good or for evil.[b]
26 The sign of a happy heart is a cheerful face,
but to devise proverbs requires painful
thinking.

14 Happy are those who do not blunder
with their lips,
and need not suffer remorse for sin.
2 Happy are those whose hearts do not
condemn them,
and who have not given up their hope.
3 Riches are inappropriate for a small-minded
person;
and of what use is wealth to a miser?
4 What he denies himself he collects for others;
and others will live in luxury on his goods.
5 If one is mean to himself, to whom will he be
generous?
He will not enjoy his own riches.
6 No one is worse than one who is grudging to
himself;
this is the punishment for his meanness.
7 If ever he does good, it is by mistake;
and in the end he reveals his meanness.
8 The miser is an evil person;
he turns away and disregards people.
9 The eye of the greedy person is not satisfied
with his share;
greedy injustice withers the soul.
10 A miser begrudges bread,
and it is lacking at his table.
11 My child, treat yourself well, according to
your means,
and present worthy offerings to the Lord.
12 Remember that death does not tarry,
and the decree[c] of Hades has not been
shown to you.
13 Do good to friends before you die,
and reach out and give to them as much as
you can.
14 Do not deprive yourself of a day's
enjoyment;
do not let your share of desired good pass
by you.
15 Will you not leave the fruit of your labors to
another,
and what you acquired by toil to be
divided by lot?
16 Give, and take, and indulge yourself,
because in Hades one cannot look for
luxury.
17 All living beings become old like a
garment,
for the decree[d] from of old is, "You must
die!"
18 Like abundant leaves on a spreading tree
that sheds some and puts forth others,
so are the generations of flesh and blood:
one dies and another is born.
19 Every work decays and ceases to exist,
and the one who made it will pass away
with it.

[a] Other ancient authorities read *poor* [b] Other ancient authorities add *and a glad heart makes a cheerful countenance*
[c] Heb Syr: Gk *covenant* [d] Heb: Gk *covenant*

20 Happy is the person who meditates on[a]
wisdom
and reasons intelligently,
21 who[b] reflects in his heart on her ways
and ponders her secrets,
22 pursuing her like a hunter,
and lying in wait on her paths;
23 who peers through her windows
and listens at her doors;
24 who camps near her house
and fastens his tent peg to her walls;
25 who pitches his tent near her,
and so occupies an excellent lodging
place;
26 who places his children under her shelter,
and lodges under her boughs;
27 who is sheltered by her from the heat,
and dwells in the midst of her glory.

15 Whoever fears the Lord will do this,
and whoever holds to the law will obtain
wisdom.[c]
2 She will come to meet him like a mother,
and like a young bride she will welcome
him.
3 She will feed him with the bread of learning,
and give him the water of wisdom to
drink.
4 He will lean on her and not fall,
and he will rely on her and not be put to
shame.
5 She will exalt him above his neighbors,
and will open his mouth in the midst of
the assembly.
6 He will find gladness and a crown of
rejoicing,
and will inherit an everlasting name.
7 The foolish will not obtain her,
and sinners will not see her.
8 She is far from arrogance,
and liars will never think of her.
9 Praise is unseemly on the lips of a sinner,
for it has not been sent from the Lord.
10 For in wisdom must praise be uttered,
and the Lord will make it prosper.

11 Do not say, "It was the Lord's doing that I fell
away";
for he does not do[d] what he hates.
12 Do not say, "It was he who led me astray";
for he has no need of the sinful.
13 The Lord hates all abominations;
such things are not loved by those who
fear him.
14 It was he who created humankind in the
beginning,
and he left them in the power of their own
free choice.
15 If you choose, you can keep the
commandments,
and to act faithfully is a matter of your own
choice.
16 He has placed before you fire and water;
stretch out your hand for whichever you
choose.
17 Before each person are life and death,
and whichever one chooses will be given.
18 For great is the wisdom of the Lord;
he is mighty in power and sees everything;
19 his eyes are on those who fear him,
and he knows every human action.
20 He has not commanded anyone to be
wicked,
and he has not given anyone permission
to sin.

16 Do not desire a multitude of worthless[e]
children,
and do not rejoice in ungodly offspring.
2 If they multiply, do not rejoice in them,
unless the fear of the Lord is in them.
3 Do not trust in their survival,
or rely on their numbers;[f]
for one can be better than a thousand,
and to die childless is better than to have
ungodly children.

[a] Other ancient authorities read *dies in* [b] The structure adopted in verses 21–27 follows the Heb
[c] Gk *her* [d] Heb: Gk *you ought not to do* [e] Heb: Gk *unprofitable*
[f] Other ancient authorities add *For you will groan in untimely mourning, and will know of their sudden end.*

4 For through one intelligent person a city can
be filled with people,
but through a clan of outlaws it becomes
desolate.

5 Many such things my eye has seen,
and my ear has heard things more striking
than these.
6 In an assembly of sinners a fire is kindled,
and in a disobedient nation wrath
blazes up.
7 He did not forgive the ancient giants
who revolted in their might.
8 He did not spare the neighbors of Lot,
whom he loathed on account of their
arrogance.
9 He showed no pity on the doomed nation,
on those dispossessed because of their
sins;[a]
10 or on the six hundred thousand foot soldiers
who assembled in their stubbornness.[b]
11 Even if there were only one stiff-necked
person,
it would be a wonder if he remained
unpunished.
For mercy and wrath are with the Lord;[c]
he is mighty to forgive—but he also pours
out wrath.
12 Great as is his mercy, so also is his
chastisement;
he judges a person according to his or her
deeds.
13 The sinner will not escape with plunder,
and the patience of the godly will not be
frustrated.
14 He makes room for every act of mercy;
everyone receives in accordance with his
or her deeds.[d]

17 Do not say, "I am hidden from the Lord,
and who from on high has me in mind?
Among so many people I am unknown,
for what am I in a boundless creation?
18 Lo, heaven and the highest heaven,
the abyss and the earth, tremble at his
visitation![e]
19 The very mountains and the foundations of
the earth
quiver and quake when he looks upon
them.
20 But no human mind can grasp this,
and who can comprehend his ways?
21 Like a tempest that no one can see,
so most of his works are concealed.[f]
22 Who is to announce his acts of justice?
Or who can await them? For his decree[g] is
far off."[h]
23 Such are the thoughts of one devoid of
understanding;
a senseless and misguided person thinks
foolishly.

24 Listen to me, my child, and acquire
knowledge,
and pay close attention to my words.
25 I will impart discipline precisely[i]
and declare knowledge accurately.

26 When the Lord created[j] his works from the
beginning,
and, in making them, determined their
boundaries,
27 he arranged his works in an eternal order,
and their dominion[k] for all generations.
They neither hunger nor grow weary,
and they do not abandon their tasks.
28 They do not crowd one another,

[a] Other ancient authorities add *All these things he did to the hard-hearted nations, and by the multitude of his holy ones he was not appeased.* [b] Other ancient authorities add *Chastising, showing mercy, striking, healing, the Lord persisted in mercy and discipline.* [c] Gk *him* [d] Other ancient authorities add *15 The Lord hardened Pharaoh so that he did not recognize him, in order that his works might be known under heaven. 16 His mercy is manifest to the whole of creation, and he divided his light and darkness with a plumb line.* [e] Other ancient authorities add *The whole world past and present is in his will.* [f] Meaning of Gk uncertain: Heb Syr *If I sin, no eye can see me, and if I am disloyal all in secret, who is to know?* [g] Heb *the decree*: Gk *the covenant* [h] Other ancient authorities add *and a scrutiny for all comes at the end* [i] Gk *by weight* [j] Heb: Gk *judged* [k] Or *elements*

and they never disobey his word.
29 Then the Lord looked upon the earth,
and filled it with his good things.
30 With all kinds of living beings he covered its surface,
and into it they must return.

17 The Lord created human beings out of earth,
and makes them return to it again.
2 He gave them a fixed number of days,
but granted them authority over everything on the earth.[a]
3 He endowed them with strength like his own,[b]
and made them in his own image.
4 He put the fear of them[c] in all living beings,
and gave them dominion over beasts and birds.[d]
6 Discretion and tongue and eyes,
ears and a mind for thinking he gave them.
7 He filled them with knowledge and understanding,
and showed them good and evil.
8 He put the fear of him into[e] their hearts
to show them the majesty of his works.[f]
10 And they will praise his holy name,
9 to proclaim the grandeur of his works.
11 He bestowed knowledge upon them,
and allotted to them the law of life.[g]
12 He established with them an eternal covenant,
and revealed to them his decrees.
13 Their eyes saw his glorious majesty,
and their ears heard the glory of his voice.
14 He said to them, "Beware of all evil."
And he gave commandment to each of them concerning the neighbor.
15 Their ways are always known to him;
they will not be hid from his eyes.[h]
17 He appointed a ruler for every nation,
but Israel is the Lord's own portion.[i]
19 All their works are as clear as the sun before him,
and his eyes are ever upon their ways.
20 Their iniquities are not hidden from him,
and all their sins are before the Lord.[j]
22 One's almsgiving is like a signet ring with the Lord,[k]
and he will keep a person's kindness like the apple of his eye.[l]
23 Afterward he will rise up and repay them,
and he will bring their recompense on their heads.
24 Yet to those who repent he grants a return,
and he encourages those who are losing hope.

25 Turn back to the Lord and forsake your sins;
pray in his presence and lessen your offense.
26 Return to the Most High and turn away from iniquity,[m]
and hate intensely what he abhors.
27 Who will sing praises to the Most High in Hades
in place of the living who give thanks?
28 From the dead, as from one who does not exist, thanksgiving has ceased;
those who are alive and well sing the Lord's praises.
29 How great is the mercy of the Lord,

[a] Lat: Gk *it* [b] Lat: Gk *proper to them* [c] Syr: Gk *him* [d] Other ancient authorities add as verse 5, *They obtained the use of the five faculties of the Lord; as sixth he distributed to them the gift of mind, and as seventh, reason, the interpreter of one's faculties.* [e] Other ancient authorities read *He set his eye upon* [f] Other ancient authorities add *and he gave them to boast of his marvels forever* [g] Other ancient authorities add *so that they may know that they who are alive now are mortal* [h] Other ancient authorities add [16]*Their ways from youth tend toward evil, and they are unable to make for themselves hearts of flesh in place of their stony hearts.* [17]*For in the division of the nations of the whole earth, he appointed* [i] Other ancient authorities add as verse 18, *whom, being his firstborn, he brings up with discipline, and allotting to him the light of his love, he does not neglect him.* [j] Other ancient authorities add as verse 21, *But the Lord, who is gracious and knows how they are formed, has neither left them nor abandoned them, but has spared them.* [k] Gk *him* [l] Other ancient authorities add *apportioning repentance to his sons and daughters* [m] Other ancient authorities add *for he will lead you out of darkness to the light of health.*

and his forgiveness for those who return
to him!
30 For not everything is within human
capability,
since human beings are not immortal.
31 What is brighter than the sun? Yet it can be
eclipsed.
So flesh and blood devise evil.
32 He marshals the host of the height of heaven;
but all human beings are dust and ashes.

18 He who lives forever created the whole
universe;
2 the Lord alone is just.[a]
4 To none has he given power to proclaim his
works;
and who can search out his mighty
deeds?
5 Who can measure his majestic power?
And who can fully recount his mercies?
6 It is not possible to diminish or increase
them,
nor is it possible to fathom the wonders of
the Lord.
7 When human beings have finished, they are
just beginning,
and when they stop, they are still
perplexed.
8 What are human beings, and of what use are
they?
What is good in them, and what is evil?
9 The number of days in their life is great if
they reach one hundred years.[b]
10 Like a drop of water from the sea and a grain
of sand,
so are a few years among the days of
eternity.
11 That is why the Lord is patient with them
and pours out his mercy upon them.
12 He sees and recognizes that their end is
miserable;
therefore he grants them forgiveness all
the more.
13 The compassion of human beings is for their
neighbors,
but the compassion of the Lord is for
every living thing.
He rebukes and trains and teaches them,
and turns them back, as a shepherd his
flock.
14 He has compassion on those who accept his
discipline
and who are eager for his precepts.

15 My child, do not mix reproach with your
good deeds,
or spoil your gift by harsh words.
16 Does not the dew give relief from the
scorching heat?
So a word is better than a gift.
17 Indeed, does not a word surpass a good gift?
Both are to be found in a gracious person.
18 A fool is ungracious and abusive,
and the gift of a grudging giver makes the
eyes dim.

19 Before you speak, learn;
and before you fall ill, take care of your
health.
20 Before judgment comes, examine yourself;
and at the time of scrutiny you will find
forgiveness.
21 Before falling ill, humble yourself;
and when you have sinned, repent.
22 Let nothing hinder you from paying a vow
promptly,
and do not wait until death to be released
from it.
23 Before making a vow, prepare yourself;
do not be like one who puts the Lord to
the test.
24 Think of his wrath on the day of death,
and of the moment of vengeance when he
turns away his face.
25 In the time of plenty think of the time of
hunger;

[a] Other ancient authorities add *and there is no other beside him;* [3]*he steers the world with the span of his hand, and all things obey his will; for he is king of all things by his power, separating among them the holy things from the profane.*
[b] Other ancient authorities add *but the death of each one is beyond the calculation of all*

in days of wealth think of poverty and
need.
26 From morning to evening conditions
change;
all things move swiftly before the Lord.

27 One who is wise is cautious in everything;
when sin is all around, one guards against
wrongdoing.
28 Every intelligent person knows wisdom,
and praises the one who finds her.
29 Those who are skilled in words become wise
themselves,
and pour forth apt proverbs.[a]

SELF-CONTROL[b]

30 Do not follow your base desires,
but restrain your appetites.
31 If you allow your soul to take pleasure in base
desire,
it will make you the laughingstock of your
enemies.
32 Do not revel in great luxury,
or you may become impoverished by its
expense.
33 Do not become a beggar by feasting with
borrowed money,
when you have nothing in your purse.[c]

19 The one who does this[d] will not become
rich;
one who despises small things will fail
little by little.
2 Wine and women lead intelligent men
astray,
and the man who consorts with prostitutes
is reckless.
3 Decay and worms will take possession of
him,
and the reckless person will be snatched
away.
4 One who trusts others too quickly has a
shallow mind,
and one who sins does wrong to
himself.
5 One who rejoices in wickedness[e] will be
condemned,[f]
6 but one who hates gossip has less evil.
7 Never repeat a conversation,
and you will lose nothing at all.
8 With friend or foe do not report it,
and unless it would be a sin for you, do not
reveal it;
9 for someone may have heard you and
watched you,
and in time will hate you.
10 Have you heard something? Let it die with
you.
Be brave, it will not make you burst!
11 Having heard something, the fool suffers
birth pangs
like a woman in labor with a child.
12 Like an arrow stuck in a person's thigh,
so is gossip inside a fool.

13 Question a friend; perhaps he did not do it;
or if he did, so that he may not do it
again.
14 Question a neighbor; perhaps he did not
say it;
or if he said it, so that he may not
repeat it.
15 Question a friend, for often it is slander;
so do not believe everything you hear.
16 A person may make a slip without
intending it.
Who has not sinned with his tongue?
17 Question your neighbor before you threaten
him;
and let the law of the Most High take its
course.[g]

[a] Other ancient authorities add *Better is confidence in the one Lord than clinging with a dead heart to a dead one.* [b] This heading is included in the Gk text. [c] Other ancient authorities add *for you will be plotting against your own life* [d] Heb: Gk *A worker who is a drunkard* [e] Other ancient authorities read *heart* [f] Other ancient authorities add *but one who withstands pleasures crowns his life.* [6]*One who controls the tongue will live without strife,* [g] Other ancient authorities add *and do not be angry.* [18]*The fear of the Lord is the beginning of acceptance, and wisdom obtains his love.* [19]*The knowledge of the Lord's commandments is life-giving discipline; and those who do what is pleasing to him enjoy the fruit of the tree of immortality.*

20 The whole of wisdom is fear of the Lord,
and in all wisdom there is the fulfillment
of the law.[a]
22 The knowledge of wickedness is not wisdom,
nor is there prudence in the counsel of
sinners.
23 There is a cleverness that is detestable,
and there is a fool who merely lacks
wisdom.
24 Better are the God-fearing who lack
understanding
than the highly intelligent who transgress
the law.
25 There is a cleverness that is exact but unjust,
and there are people who abuse favors to
gain a verdict.
26 There is the villain bowed down in mourning,
but inwardly he is full of deceit.
27 He hides his face and pretends not to hear,
but when no one notices, he will take
advantage of you.
28 Even if lack of strength keeps him from
sinning,
he will nevertheless do evil when he finds
the opportunity.
29 A person is known by his appearance,
and a sensible person is known when first
met, face to face.
30 A person's attire and hearty laughter,
and the way he walks, show what he is.

20 There is a rebuke that is untimely,
and there is the person who is wise
enough to keep silent.
2 How much better it is to rebuke than to fume!
3 And the one who admits his fault will be kept
from failure.
4 Like a eunuch lusting to violate a girl
is the person who does right under
compulsion.
5 Some people keep silent and are thought to
be wise,
while others are detested for being
talkative.
6 Some people keep silent because they have
nothing to say,
while others keep silent because they
know when to speak.
7 The wise remain silent until the right
moment,
but a boasting fool misses the right
moment.
8 Whoever talks too much is detested,
and whoever pretends to authority is
hated.[b]

9 There may be good fortune for a person in
adversity,
and a windfall may result in a loss.
10 There is the gift that profits you nothing,
and the gift to be paid back double.
11 There are losses for the sake of glory,
and there are some who have raised their
heads from humble circumstances.
12 Some buy much for little,
but pay for it seven times over.
13 The wise make themselves beloved by only
few words,[c]
but the courtesies of fools are wasted.
14 A fool's gift will profit you nothing,[d]
for he looks for recompense sevenfold.[e]
15 He gives little and upbraids much;
he opens his mouth like a town crier.
Today he lends and tomorrow he asks it
back;
such a one is hateful to God and humans.[f]
16 The fool says, "I have no friends,
and I get no thanks for my good deeds.
Those who eat my bread are evil-tongued."
17 How many will ridicule him, and how often![g]

[a] Other ancient authorities add *and the knowledge of his omnipotence.* [21] *When a slave says to his master, "I will not act as you wish," even if later he does it, he angers the one who supports him.* [b] Other ancient authorities add *How good it is to show repentance when you are reproved, for so you will escape deliberate sin!* [c] Heb: Gk *by words* [d] Other ancient authorities add *so it is with the envious who give under compulsion* [e] Syr: Gk *he has many eyes instead of one* [f] Other ancient authorities lack *to God and humans*
[g] Other ancient authorities add *for he has not honestly received what he has, and what he does not have is unimportant to him*

18 A slip on the pavement is better than a slip of
the tongue;
the downfall of the wicked will occur just
as speedily.
19 A coarse person is like an inappropriate story,
continually on the lips of the ignorant.
20 A proverb from a fool's lips will be rejected,
for he does not tell it at the proper time.

21 One may be prevented from sinning by
poverty;
so when he rests he feels no remorse.
22 One may lose his life through shame,
or lose it because of human respect.[a]
23 Another out of shame makes promises to a
friend,
and so makes an enemy for nothing.

24 A lie is an ugly blot on a person;
it is continually on the lips of the ignorant.
25 A thief is preferable to a habitual liar,
but the lot of both is ruin.
26 A liar's way leads to disgrace,
and his shame is ever with him.

Proverbial Sayings[b]

27 The wise person advances himself by his
words,
and one who is sensible pleases the great.
28 Those who cultivate the soil heap up their
harvest,
and those who please the great atone for
injustice.
29 Favors and gifts blind the eyes of the wise;
like a muzzle on the mouth they stop
reproofs.
30 Hidden wisdom and unseen treasure,
of what value is either?
31 Better are those who hide their folly
than those who hide their wisdom.[c]

21 Have you sinned, my child? Do so no
more,
but ask forgiveness for your past sins.
2 Flee from sin as from a snake;
for if you approach sin, it will bite you.
Its teeth are lion's teeth,
and can destroy human lives.
3 All lawlessness is like a two-edged sword;
there is no healing for the wound it
inflicts.

4 Panic and insolence will waste away riches;
thus the house of the proud will be laid
waste.[d]
5 The prayer of the poor goes from their lips to
the ears of God,[e]
and his judgment comes speedily.
6 Those who hate reproof walk in the sinner's
steps,
but those who fear the Lord repent in their
heart.
7 The mighty in speech are widely known;
when they slip, the sensible person
knows it.

8 Whoever builds his house with other people's
money
is like one who gathers stones for his burial
mound.[f]
9 An assembly of the wicked is like a bundle of
tow,
and their end is a blazing fire.
10 The way of sinners is paved with smooth
stones,
but at its end is the pit of Hades.

11 Whoever keeps the law controls his thoughts,
and the fulfillment of the fear of the Lord
is wisdom.
12 The one who is not clever cannot be taught,
but there is a cleverness that increases
bitterness.
13 The knowledge of the wise will increase like a
flood,
and their counsel like a life-giving spring.

[a] Other ancient authorities read *his foolish look* [b] This heading is included in the Gk text. [c] Other ancient authorities add [32] *Unwearied endurance in seeking the Lord is better than a masterless charioteer of one's own life.* [d] Other ancient authorities read *uprooted* [e] Gk *his ears* [f] Other ancient authorities read *for the winter*

14 The mind[a] of a fool is like a broken jar;
it can hold no knowledge.

15 When an intelligent person hears a wise saying,
he praises it and adds to it;
when a fool[b] hears it, he laughs at[c] it
and throws it behind his back.
16 A fool's chatter is like a burden on a journey,
but delight is found in the speech of the intelligent.
17 The utterance of a sensible person is sought in the assembly,
and they ponder his words in their minds.

18 Like a house in ruins is wisdom to a fool,
and to the ignorant, knowledge is talk that has no meaning.
19 To a senseless person education is fetters on his feet,
and like manacles on his right hand.
20 A fool raises his voice when he laughs,
but the wise[d] smile quietly.
21 To the sensible person education is like a golden ornament,
and like a bracelet on the right arm.

22 The foot of a fool rushes into a house,
but an experienced person waits respectfully outside.
23 A boor peers into the house from the door,
but a cultivated person remains outside.
24 It is ill-mannered for a person to listen at a door;
the discreet would be grieved by the disgrace.

25 The lips of babblers speak of what is not their concern,[e]
but the words of the prudent are weighed in the balance.
26 The mind of fools is in their mouth,
but the mouth of the wise is in[f] their mind.
27 When an ungodly person curses an adversary,[g]
he curses himself.
28 A whisperer degrades himself
and is hated in his neighborhood.

22 The idler is like a filthy stone,
and every one hisses at his disgrace.
2 The idler is like the filth of dunghills;
anyone that picks it up will shake it off his hand.

3 It is a disgrace to be the father of an undisciplined son,
and the birth of a daughter is a loss.
4 A sensible daughter obtains a husband of her own,
but one who acts shamefully is a grief to her father.
5 An impudent daughter disgraces father and husband,
and is despised by both.
6 Like music in time of mourning is ill-timed conversation,
but a thrashing and discipline are at all times wisdom.[h]

9 Whoever teaches a fool is like one who glues potsherds together,
or who rouses a sleeper from deep slumber.
10 Whoever tells a story to a fool tells it to a drowsy man;
and at the end he will say, "What is it?"
11 Weep for the dead, for he has left the light behind;
and weep for the fool, for he has left intelligence behind.
Weep less bitterly for the dead, for he is at rest;
but the life of the fool is worse than death.
12 Mourning for the dead lasts seven days,

[a] Syr Lat: Gk *entrails* [b] Syr: Gk *reveler* [c] Syr: Gk *dislikes* [d] Syr Lat: Gk *clever* [e] Other ancient authorities read *of strangers speak of these things* [f] Other ancient authorities omit *in* [g] Or *curses Satan*
[h] Other ancient authorities add [7]*Children who are brought up in a good life, conceal the lowly birth of their parents.* [8]*Children who are disdainfully and boorishly haughty stain the nobility of their kindred.*

but for the foolish or the ungodly it lasts
all the days of their lives.

13 Do not talk much with a senseless person
or visit an unintelligent person.[a]
Stay clear of him, or you may have trouble,
and be spattered when he shakes himself
off.
Avoid him and you will find rest,
and you will never be wearied by his lack
of sense.
14 What is heavier than lead?
And what is its name except "Fool"?
15 Sand, salt, and a piece of iron
are easier to bear than a stupid person.

16 A wooden beam firmly bonded into a
building
is not loosened by an earthquake;
so the mind firmly resolved after due
reflection
will not be afraid in a crisis.
17 A mind settled on an intelligent thought
is like stucco decoration that makes a wall
smooth.
18 Fences[b] set on a high place
will not stand firm against the wind;
so a timid mind with a fool's resolve
will not stand firm against any fear.

19 One who pricks the eye brings tears,
and one who pricks the heart makes clear
its feelings.
20 One who throws a stone at birds scares them
away,
and one who reviles a friend destroys a
friendship.
21 Even if you draw your sword against a
friend,
do not despair, for there is a way back.
22 If you open your mouth against your friend,
do not worry, for reconciliation is
possible.
But as for reviling, arrogance, disclosure of
secrets, or a treacherous blow—
in these cases any friend will take to
flight.

23 Gain the trust of your neighbor in his
poverty,
so that you may rejoice with him in his
prosperity.
Stand by him in time of distress,
so that you may share with him in his
inheritance.[c]
24 The vapor and smoke of the furnace precede
the fire;
so insults precede bloodshed.
25 I am not ashamed to shelter a friend,
and I will not hide from him.
26 But if harm should come to me because of
him,
whoever hears of it will beware of him.

27 Who will set a guard over my mouth,
and an effective seal upon my lips,
so that I may not fall because of them,
and my tongue may not destroy me?

23 O Lord, Father and Master of my life,
do not abandon me to their designs,
and do not let me fall because of them!
2 Who will set whips over my thoughts,
and the discipline of wisdom over my
mind,
so as not to spare me in my errors,
and not overlook my[d] sins?
3 Otherwise my mistakes may be multiplied,
and my sins may abound,
and I may fall before my adversaries,
and my enemy may rejoice over me.[e]
4 O Lord, Father and God of my life,
do not give me haughty eyes,
5 and remove evil desire from me.
6 Let neither gluttony nor lust overcome me,
and do not give me over to shameless
passion.

[a] Other ancient authorities add *For being without sense he will despise everything about you* [b] Other ancient authorities read *Pebbles* [c] Other ancient authorities add *For one should not always despise restricted circumstances, or admire a rich person who is stupid.* [d] Gk *their* [e] Other ancient authorities add *From them the hope of your mercy is remote*

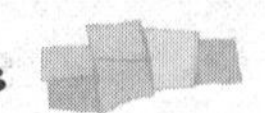

Discipline of the Tongue[a]

7 Listen, my children, to instruction
concerning the mouth;
the one who observes it will never be
caught.
8 Sinners are overtaken through their lips;
by them the reviler and the arrogant are
tripped up.
9 Do not accustom your mouth to oaths,
nor habitually utter the name of the Holy
One;
10 for as a servant who is constantly under
scrutiny
will not lack bruises,
so also the person who always swears and
utters the Name
will never be cleansed[b] from sin.
11 The one who swears many oaths is full of
iniquity,
and the scourge will not leave his house.
If he swears in error, his sin remains on him,
and if he disregards it, he sins doubly;
if he swears a false oath, he will not be
justified,
for his house will be filled with calamities.

12 There is a manner of speaking comparable to
death;[c]
may it never be found in the inheritance
of Jacob!
Such conduct will be far from the godly,
and they will not wallow in sins.
13 Do not accustom your mouth to coarse, foul
language,
for it involves sinful speech.
14 Remember your father and mother
when you sit among the great,
or you may forget yourself in their
presence,
and behave like a fool through bad habit;
then you will wish that you had never been
born,
and you will curse the day of your birth.
15 Those who are accustomed to using abusive
language
will never become disciplined as long as
they live.

16 Two kinds of individuals multiply sins,
and a third incurs wrath.
Hot passion that blazes like a fire
will not be quenched until it burns itself
out;
one who commits fornication with his near
of kin
will never cease until the fire burns him up.
17 To a fornicator all bread is sweet;
he will never weary until he dies.
18 The one who sins against his marriage bed
says to himself, "Who can see me?
Darkness surrounds me, the walls hide me,
and no one sees me. Why should I worry?
The Most High will not remember sins."
19 His fear is confined to human eyes
and he does not realize that the eyes of the
Lord
are ten thousand times brighter than the
sun;
they look upon every aspect of human
behavior
and see into hidden corners.
20 Before the universe was created, it was known
to him,
and so it is since its completion.
21 This man will be punished in the streets of
the city,
and where he least suspects it, he will be
seized.

22 So it is with a woman who leaves her husband
and presents him with an heir by another
man.
23 For first of all, she has disobeyed the law of
the Most High;
second, she has committed an offense
against her husband;
and third, through her fornication she has
committed adultery
and brought forth children by another
man.

[a] This heading is included in the Gk text. [b] Syr *be free* [c] Other ancient authorities read *clothed about with death*

24 She herself will be brought before the
assembly,
and her punishment will extend to her
children.
25 Her children will not take root,
and her branches will not bear fruit.
26 She will leave behind an accursed memory
and her disgrace will never be blotted
out.
27 Those who survive her will recognize
that nothing is better than the fear of the
Lord,
and nothing sweeter than to heed the
commandments of the Lord.[a]

The Praise of Wisdom[b]

24 Wisdom praises herself,
and tells of her glory in the midst of her
people.
2 In the assembly of the Most High she opens
her mouth,
and in the presence of his hosts she tells of
her glory:
3 "I came forth from the mouth of the Most
High,
and covered the earth like a mist.
4 I dwelt in the highest heavens,
and my throne was in a pillar of cloud.
5 Alone I compassed the vault of heaven
and traversed the depths of the abyss.
6 Over waves of the sea, over all the earth,
and over every people and nation I have
held sway.[c]
7 Among all these I sought a resting place;
in whose territory should I abide?
8 "Then the Creator of all things gave me a
command,
and my Creator chose the place for my
tent.
He said, 'Make your dwelling in Jacob,
and in Israel receive your inheritance.'
9 Before the ages, in the beginning, he
created me,
and for all the ages I shall not cease to be.
10 In the holy tent I ministered before him,
and so I was established in Zion.
11 Thus in the beloved city he gave me a resting
place,
and in Jerusalem was my domain.
12 I took root in an honored people,
in the portion of the Lord, his heritage.
13 "I grew tall like a cedar in Lebanon,
and like a cypress on the heights of
Hermon.

[a] Other ancient authorities add as verse 28, *It is a great honor to follow God, and to be received by him is long life.*
[b] This heading is included in the Gk text. [c] Other ancient authorities read *I have acquired a possession*

Sirach 24:1-12

Earlier Israelite speculation on heavenly Wisdom (Proverbs 8–9; Wisdom 7–9) continues here. Wisdom was present at the beginning of creation, hovering over the waters as did the Spirit of God in Genesis 1. Wisdom "sought a resting place" on the earth (24:7), just as the dove that Noah sent out from the ark sought a place to set its foot after the great flood (Gen 8:6-12). Could this tradition have informed the Gospels' portrayal of the Spirit of God descending on Jesus after his baptism "like a dove" (Matt 3:16; Luke 3:22)?

Here Wisdom is sent to dwell in Israel (vv. 8-12). Some time later, however, *1 Enoch* declared that Wisdom could find no place on the earth to dwell, and had to return to heaven (42:1-2); the Son of Man would reveal wisdom only to the righteous (48:1-7). Still later, the Gospel of John spoke in similar terms of the Word, who "came to what was his own" but was rejected, but nevertheless gave power "to all who received him" to become children of God (1:10-13).

—*NE*

14 I grew tall like a palm tree in En-gedi,[a]
and like rosebushes in Jericho;
like a fair olive tree in the field,
and like a plane tree beside water[b] I grew
tall.
15 Like cassia and camel's thorn I gave forth
perfume,
and like choice myrrh I spread my
fragrance,
like galbanum, onycha, and stacte,
and like the odor of incense in the tent.
16 Like a terebinth I spread out my branches,
and my branches are glorious and graceful.
17 Like the vine I bud forth delights,
and my blossoms become glorious and
abundant fruit.[c]

19 "Come to me, you who desire me,
and eat your fill of my fruits.
20 For the memory of me is sweeter than honey,
and the possession of me sweeter than the
honeycomb.
21 Those who eat of me will hunger for more,
and those who drink of me will thirst for
more.
22 Whoever obeys me will not be put to shame,
and those who work with me will not sin."

23 All this is the book of the covenant of the
Most High God,
the law that Moses commanded us
as an inheritance for the congregations of
Jacob.[d]
25 It overflows, like the Pishon, with wisdom,
and like the Tigris at the time of the first
fruits.
26 It runs over, like the Euphrates, with
understanding,
and like the Jordan at harvest time.
27 It pours forth instruction like the Nile,[e]
like the Gihon at the time of vintage.
28 The first man did not know wisdom[f] fully,
nor will the last one fathom her.
29 For her thoughts are more abundant than
the sea,
and her counsel deeper than the great
abyss.

30 As for me, I was like a canal from a river,
like a water channel into a garden.
31 I said, "I will water my garden
and drench my flower-beds."
And lo, my canal became a river,
and my river a sea.
32 I will again make instruction shine forth like
the dawn,
and I will make it clear from far away.
33 I will again pour out teaching like prophecy,
and leave it to all future generations.
34 Observe that I have not labored for myself
alone,
but for all who seek wisdom.[f]

25 I take pleasure in three things,
and they are beautiful in the sight of God
and of mortals:[g]
agreement among brothers and sisters,
friendship among neighbors,
and a wife and a husband who live in
harmony.
2 I hate three kinds of people,
and I loathe their manner of life:
a pauper who boasts, a rich person who lies,
and an old fool who commits adultery.

3 If you gathered nothing in your youth,
how can you find anything in your old age?
4 How attractive is sound judgment in the
gray-haired,
and for the aged to possess good counsel!

[a] Other ancient authorities read *on the beaches* [b] Other ancient authorities omit *beside water* [c] Other ancient authorities add as verse 18, *I am the mother of beautiful love, of fear, of knowledge, and of holy hope; being eternal, I am given to all my children, to those who are named by him.* [d] Other ancient authorities add as verse 24, *"Do not cease to be strong in the Lord, cling to him so that he may strengthen you; the Lord Almighty alone is God, and besides him there is no savior."*
[e] Syr: Gk *It makes instruction shine forth like light* [f] Gk *her*
[g] Syr Lat: Gk *In three things I was beautiful and I stood in beauty before the Lord and mortals.*

5 How attractive is wisdom in the aged,
and understanding and counsel in the venerable!
6 Rich experience is the crown of the aged,
and their boast is the fear of the Lord.

7 I can think of nine whom I would call blessed,
and a tenth my tongue proclaims:
a man who can rejoice in his children;
a man who lives to see the downfall of his foes.
8 Happy the man who lives with a sensible wife,
and the one who does not plow with ox and ass together.[a]
Happy is the one who does not sin with the tongue,
and the one who has not served an inferior.
9 Happy is the one who finds a friend,[b]
and the one who speaks to attentive listeners.
10 How great is the one who finds wisdom!
But none is superior to the one who fears the Lord.
11 Fear of the Lord surpasses everything;
to whom can we compare the one who has it?[c]

13 Any wound, but not a wound of the heart!
Any wickedness, but not the wickedness of a woman!
14 Any suffering, but not suffering from those who hate!
And any vengeance, but not the vengeance of enemies!
15 There is no venom[d] worse than a snake's venom,[d]
and no anger worse than a woman's[e] wrath.

16 I would rather live with a lion and a dragon
than live with an evil woman.
17 A woman's wickedness changes her appearance,
and darkens her face like that of a bear.
18 Her husband sits[f] among the neighbors,
and he cannot help sighing[g] bitterly.
19 Any iniquity is small compared to a woman's iniquity;
may a sinner's lot befall her!
20 A sandy ascent for the feet of the aged—
such is a garrulous wife to a quiet husband.
21 Do not be ensnared by a woman's beauty,
and do not desire a woman for her possessions.[h]
22 There is wrath and impudence and great disgrace
when a wife supports her husband.
23 Dejected mind, gloomy face,
and wounded heart come from an evil wife.
Drooping hands and weak knees
come from the wife who does not make her husband happy.
24 From a woman sin had its beginning,
and because of her we all die.
25 Allow no outlet to water,
and no boldness of speech to an evil wife.
26 If she does not go as you direct,
separate her from yourself.

26 Happy is the husband of a good wife;
the number of his days will be doubled.
2 A loyal wife brings joy to her husband,
and he will complete his years in peace.
3 A good wife is a great blessing;
she will be granted among the blessings of the man who fears the Lord.
4 Whether rich or poor, his heart is content,
and at all times his face is cheerful.
5 Of three things my heart is frightened,
and of a fourth I am in great fear:[i]
Slander in the city, the gathering of a mob,

[a] Heb Syr: Gk lacks *and the one who does not plow with ox and ass together* [b] Lat Syr: Gk *good sense* [c] Other ancient authorities add as verse 12, *The fear of the Lord is the beginning of love for him, and faith is the beginning of clinging to him.* [d] Syr: Gk *head* [e] Other ancient authorities read *an enemy's* [f] Heb Syr: Gk *loses heart* [g] Other ancient authorities read *and listening he sighs* [h] Heb Syr: Other Gk authorities read *for her beauty* [i] Syr: Meaning of Gk uncertain

and false accusation—all these are worse
than death.
6 But it is heartache and sorrow when a wife is
jealous of a rival,
and a tongue-lashing makes it known to all.
7 A bad wife is a chafing yoke;
taking hold of her is like grasping a scorpion.
8 A drunken wife arouses great anger;
she cannot hide her shame.
9 The haughty stare betrays an unchaste wife;
her eyelids give her away.

10 Keep strict watch over a headstrong daughter,
or else, when she finds liberty, she will
make use of it.
11 Be on guard against her impudent eye,
and do not be surprised if she sins against
you.
12 As a thirsty traveler opens his mouth
and drinks from any water near him,
so she will sit in front of every tent peg
and open her quiver to the arrow.

13 A wife's charm delights her husband,
and her skill puts flesh on his bones.
14 A silent wife is a gift from the Lord,
and nothing is so precious as her
self-discipline.
15 A modest wife adds charm to charm,
and no scales can weigh the value of her
chastity.
16 Like the sun rising in the heights of the Lord,
so is the beauty of a good wife in her well-
ordered home.
17 Like the shining lamp on the holy lampstand,
so is a beautiful face on a stately figure.
18 Like golden pillars on silver bases,
so are shapely legs and steadfast feet.

Other ancient authorities add verses 19–27:

19 *My child, keep sound the bloom of your youth,*
and do not give your strength to strangers.
20 *Seek a fertile field within the whole plain,*
and sow it with your own seed, trusting in
your fine stock.
21 *So your offspring will prosper,*
and, having confidence in their good descent,
will grow great.
22 *A prostitute is regarded as spittle,*
and a married woman as a tower of death to
her lovers.
23 *A godless wife is given as a portion to a lawless*
man,
but a pious wife is given to the man who fears
the Lord.
24 *A shameless woman constantly acts disgracefully,*
but a modest daughter will even be
embarrassed before her husband.
25 *A headstrong wife is regarded as a dog,*
but one who has a sense of shame will fear
the Lord.
26 *A wife honoring her husband will seem wise to all,*
but if she dishonors him in her pride she will
be known to all as ungodly.
Happy is the husband of a good wife;
for the number of his years will be doubled.
27 *A loud-voiced and garrulous wife is like a*
trumpet sounding the charge,
and every person like this lives in the anarchy
of war.

---

28 At two things my heart is grieved,
and because of a third anger comes
over me:
a warrior in want through poverty,
intelligent men who are treated
contemptuously,
and a man who turns back from
righteousness to sin—
the Lord will prepare him for the sword!

29 A merchant can hardly keep from
wrongdoing,
nor is a tradesman innocent of sin.
27 Many have committed sin for gain,[a]
and those who seek to get rich will avert
their eyes.

[a] Other ancient authorities read *a trifle*

2 As a stake is driven firmly into a fissure
between stones,
so sin is wedged in between selling and
buying.
3 If a person is not steadfast in the fear of the
Lord,
his house will be quickly overthrown.

4 When a sieve is shaken, the refuse appears;
so do a person's faults when he speaks.
5 The kiln tests the potter's vessels;
so the test of a person is in his
conversation.
6 Its fruit discloses the cultivation of a tree;
so a person's speech discloses the
cultivation of his mind.
7 Do not praise anyone before he speaks,
for this is the way people are tested.

8 If you pursue justice, you will attain it
and wear it like a glorious robe.
9 Birds roost with their own kind,
so honesty comes home to those who
practice it.
10 A lion lies in wait for prey;
so does sin for evildoers.

11 The conversation of the godly is always wise,
but the fool changes like the moon.
12 Among stupid people limit your time,
but among thoughtful people linger on.
13 The talk of fools is offensive,
and their laughter is wantonly sinful.
14 Their cursing and swearing make one's hair
stand on end,
and their quarrels make others stop their
ears.
15 The strife of the proud leads to bloodshed,
and their abuse is grievous to hear.

16 Whoever betrays secrets destroys
confidence,
and will never find a congenial friend.
17 Love your friend and keep faith with him;
but if you betray his secrets, do not follow
after him.
18 For as a person destroys his enemy,
so you have destroyed the friendship of
your neighbor.
19 And as you allow a bird to escape from your
hand,
so you have let your neighbor go, and will
not catch him again.
20 Do not go after him, for he is too far off,
and has escaped like a gazelle from a
snare.
21 For a wound may be bandaged,
and there is reconciliation after abuse,
but whoever has betrayed secrets is
without hope.

22 Whoever winks the eye plots mischief,
and those who know him will keep their
distance.
23 In your presence his mouth is all sweetness,
and he admires your words;
but later he will twist his speech
and with your own words he will trip
you up.
24 I have hated many things, but him above all;
even the Lord hates him.
25 Whoever throws a stone straight up throws it
on his own head,
and a treacherous blow opens up many
wounds.
26 Whoever digs a pit will fall into it,
and whoever sets a snare will be caught
in it.
27 If a person does evil, it will roll back upon
him,
and he will not know where it came from.
28 Mockery and abuse issue from the proud,
but vengeance lies in wait for them like a
lion.
29 Those who rejoice in the fall of the godly will
be caught in a snare,
and pain will consume them before their
death.

30 Anger and wrath, these also are
abominations,
yet a sinner holds on to them.

28 The vengeful will face the Lord's
vengeance,

for he keeps a strict account of[a] their sins.
2 Forgive your neighbor the wrong he has
done,
and then your sins will be pardoned when
you pray.
3 Does anyone harbor anger against another,
and expect healing from the Lord?
4 If one has no mercy toward another like
himself,
can he then seek pardon for his own sins?
5 If a mere mortal harbors wrath,
who will make an atoning sacrifice for his
sins?
6 Remember the end of your life, and set
enmity aside;
remember corruption and death, and be
true to the commandments.
7 Remember the commandments, and do not
be angry with your neighbor;
remember the covenant of the Most High,
and overlook faults.

8 Refrain from strife, and your sins will be
fewer;
for the hot-tempered kindle strife,
9 and the sinner disrupts friendships
and sows discord among those who are at
peace.
10 In proportion to the fuel, so will the fire burn,
and in proportion to the obstinacy, so will
strife increase;[b]
in proportion to a person's strength will be
his anger,
and in proportion to his wealth he will
increase his wrath.
11 A hasty quarrel kindles a fire,
and a hasty dispute sheds blood.
12 If you blow on a spark, it will glow;
if you spit on it, it will be put out;
yet both come out of your mouth.

13 Curse the gossips and the double-tongued,
for they destroy the peace of many.
14 Slander[c] has shaken many,
and scattered them from nation to nation;
it has destroyed strong cities,
and overturned the houses of the great.
15 Slander[c] has driven virtuous women from
their homes,
and deprived them of the fruit of their toil.
16 Those who pay heed to slander[d] will not find
rest,
nor will they settle down in peace.
17 The blow of a whip raises a welt,
but a blow of the tongue crushes the
bones.
18 Many have fallen by the edge of the sword,
but not as many as have fallen because of
the tongue.
19 Happy is the one who is protected from it,
who has not been exposed to its anger,
who has not borne its yoke,
and has not been bound with its fetters.
20 For its yoke is a yoke of iron,
and its fetters are fetters of bronze;
21 its death is an evil death,
and Hades is preferable to it.
22 It has no power over the godly;
they will not be burned in its flame.
23 Those who forsake the Lord will fall into its
power;
it will burn among them and will not be
put out.
It will be sent out against them like a lion;
like a leopard it will mangle them.
24a As you fence in your property with thorns,
25b so make a door and a bolt for your mouth.
24b As you lock up your silver and gold,
25a so make balances and scales for your
words.
26 Take care not to err with your tongue,[e]
and fall victim to one lying in wait.

29 The merciful lend to their neighbors;
by holding out a helping hand they keep
the commandments.
2 Lend to your neighbor in his time of need;
repay your neighbor when a loan falls due.

[a] Other ancient authorities read *for he firmly establishes* [b] Other ancient authorities read *burn* [c] Gk *A third tongue* [d] Gk *it* [e] Gk *with it*

3 Keep your promise and be honest with him,
and on every occasion you will find what you need.
4 Many regard a loan as a windfall,
and cause trouble to those who help them.
5 One kisses another's hands until he gets a loan,
and is deferential in speaking of his neighbor's money;
but at the time for repayment he delays,
and pays back with empty promises,
and finds fault with the time.
6 If he can pay, his creditor[a] will hardly get back half,
and will regard that as a windfall.
If he cannot pay, the borrower[a] has robbed the other of his money,
and he has needlessly made him an enemy;
he will repay him with curses and reproaches,
and instead of glory will repay him with dishonor.
7 Many refuse to lend, not because of meanness,
but from fear[b] of being defrauded needlessly.

8 Nevertheless, be patient with someone in humble circumstances,
and do not keep him waiting for your alms.
9 Help the poor for the commandment's sake,
and in their need do not send them away empty-handed.
10 Lose your silver for the sake of a brother or a friend,
and do not let it rust under a stone and be lost.
11 Lay up your treasure according to the commandments of the Most High,
and it will profit you more than gold.
12 Store up almsgiving in your treasury,
and it will rescue you from every disaster;
13 better than a stout shield and a sturdy spear,
it will fight for you against the enemy.

14 A good person will be surety for his neighbor,
but the one who has lost all sense of shame will fail him.
15 Do not forget the kindness of your guarantor,
for he has given his life for you.
16 A sinner wastes the property of his guarantor,
17 and the ungrateful person abandons his rescuer.
18 Being surety has ruined many who were prosperous,
and has tossed them about like waves of the sea;
it has driven the influential into exile,
and they have wandered among foreign nations.
19 The sinner comes to grief through surety;
his pursuit of gain involves him in lawsuits.
20 Assist your neighbor to the best of your ability,
but be careful not to fall yourself.

21 The necessities of life are water, bread, and clothing,
and also a house to assure privacy.
22 Better is the life of the poor under their own crude roof
than sumptuous food in the house of others.
23 Be content with little or much,
and you will hear no reproach for being a guest.[c]
24 It is a miserable life to go from house to house;
as a guest you should not open your mouth;
25 you will play the host and provide drink without being thanked,
and besides this you will hear rude words like these:
26 "Come here, stranger, prepare the table;
let me eat what you have there."
27 "Be off, stranger, for an honored guest is here;
my brother has come for a visit, and I need the guest-room."

[a] Gk *he* [b] Other ancient authorities read *many refuse to lend, therefore, because of such meanness; they are afraid*
[c] Lat: Gk *reproach from your family*; other ancient authorities lack this line

28 It is hard for a sensible person to bear
scolding about lodging[a] and the insults of
the moneylender.

Concerning Children[b]

30 He who loves his son will whip him
often,
so that he may rejoice at the way he turns
out.
2 He who disciplines his son will profit by him,
and will boast of him among
acquaintances.
3 He who teaches his son will make his
enemies envious,
and will glory in him among his friends.
4 When the father dies he will not seem to be
dead,
for he has left behind him one like
himself,
5 whom in his life he looked upon with joy
and at death, without grief.
6 He has left behind him an avenger against his
enemies,
and one to repay the kindness of his
friends.

7 Whoever spoils his son will bind up his
wounds,
and will suffer heartache at every cry.
8 An unbroken horse turns out stubborn,
and an unchecked son turns out
headstrong.
9 Pamper a child, and he will terrorize you;
play with him, and he will grieve you.
10 Do not laugh with him, or you will have
sorrow with him,
and in the end you will gnash your teeth.
11 Give him no freedom in his youth,
and do not ignore his errors.
12 Bow down his neck in his youth,[c]
and beat his sides while he is young,
or else he will become stubborn and disobey
you,
and you will have sorrow of soul from
him.[d]
13 Discipline your son and make his yoke
heavy,[e]
so that you may not be offended by his
shamelessness.

14 Better off poor, healthy, and fit
than rich and afflicted in body.
15 Health and fitness are better than any gold,
and a robust body than countless riches.
16 There is no wealth better than health of body,
and no gladness above joy of heart.
17 Death is better than a life of misery,
and eternal sleep[f] than chronic sickness.

Concerning Foods[g]

18 Good things poured out upon a mouth that is
closed
are like offerings of food placed upon a
grave.
19 Of what use to an idol is a sacrifice?
For it can neither eat nor smell.
So is the one punished by the Lord;
20 he sees with his eyes and groans
as a eunuch groans when embracing a girl.[h]

21 Do not give yourself over to sorrow,
and do not distress yourself deliberately.
22 A joyful heart is life itself,
and rejoicing lengthens one's life span.
23 Indulge yourself[i] and take comfort,
and remove sorrow far from you,
for sorrow has destroyed many,
and no advantage ever comes from it.
24 Jealousy and anger shorten life,
and anxiety brings on premature old age.
25 Those who are cheerful and merry at table
will benefit from their food.

[a] Or *scolding from the household* [b] This heading is included in the Gk text. [c] Other ancient authorities lack this line and the preceding line [d] Other ancient authorities lack this line [e] Heb: Gk *take pains with him* [f] Other ancient authorities lack *eternal sleep* [g] This heading is included in the Gk text; other ancient authorities place the heading before verse 16 [h] Other ancient authorities add *So is the person who does right under compulsion*
[i] Other ancient authorities read *Beguile yourself*

31 Wakefulness over wealth wastes away
one's flesh,
and anxiety about it drives away sleep.
2 Wakeful anxiety prevents slumber,
and a severe illness carries off sleep.[a]
3 The rich person toils to amass a fortune,
and when he rests he fills himself with his
dainties.
4 The poor person toils to make a meager
living,
and if ever he rests he becomes needy.
5 One who loves gold will not be justified;
one who pursues money will be led astray[b]
by it.
6 Many have come to ruin because of gold,
and their destruction has met them face
to face.
7 It is a stumbling block to those who are avid
for it,
and every fool will be taken captive by it.
8 Blessed is the rich person who is found
blameless,
and who does not go after gold.
9 Who is he, that we may praise him?
For he has done wonders among his people.
10 Who has been tested by it and been found
perfect?
Let it be for him a ground for boasting.
Who has had the power to transgress and did
not transgress,
and to do evil and did not do it?
11 His prosperity will be established,[c]
and the assembly will proclaim his acts of
charity.

12 Are you seated at the table of the great?[d]
Do not be greedy at it,
and do not say, "How much food there is
here!"
13 Remember that a greedy eye is a bad thing.
What has been created more greedy than
the eye?
Therefore it sheds tears for any reason.
14 Do not reach out your hand for everything
you see,
and do not crowd your neighbor[e] at the
dish.
15 Judge your neighbor's feelings by your own,
and in every matter be thoughtful.
16 Eat what is set before you like a well brought-
up person,[f]
and do not chew greedily, or you will give
offense.
17 Be the first to stop, as befits good manners,
and do not be insatiable, or you will give
offense.
18 If you are seated among many persons,
do not help yourself[g] before they do.
19 How ample a little is for a well-disciplined
person!
He does not breathe heavily when in bed.
20 Healthy sleep depends on moderate eating;
he rises early, and feels fit.
The distress of sleeplessness and of nausea
and colic are with the glutton.
21 If you are overstuffed with food,
get up to vomit, and you will have relief.
22 Listen to me, my child, and do not
disregard me,
and in the end you will appreciate my
words.
In everything you do be moderate,[h]
and no sickness will overtake you.
23 People bless the one who is liberal with food,
and their testimony to his generosity is
trustworthy.
24 The city complains of the one who is stingy
with food,
and their testimony to his stinginess is
accurate.

25 Do not try to prove your strength by
wine-drinking,
for wine has destroyed many.

[a] Other ancient authorities read *sleep carries off a severe illness* [b] Heb Syr: Gk *pursues destruction will be filled* [c] Other ancient authorities add *because of this* [d] Heb Syr: Gk *at a great table* [e] Gk *him* [f] Heb: Gk *like a human being* [g] Gk *reach out your hand* [h] Heb Syr: Gk *industrious*

26 As the furnace tests the work of the smith,[a]
so wine tests hearts when the insolent
quarrel.
27 Wine is very life to human beings
if taken in moderation.
What is life to one who is without wine?
It has been created to make people happy.
28 Wine drunk at the proper time and in
moderation
is rejoicing of heart and gladness of soul.
29 Wine drunk to excess leads to bitterness of
spirit,
to quarrels and stumbling.
30 Drunkenness increases the anger of a fool to
his own hurt,
reducing his strength and adding wounds.
31 Do not reprove your neighbor at a banquet of
wine,
and do not despise him in his
merrymaking;
speak no word of reproach to him,
and do not distress him by making
demands of him.

32 If they make you master of the feast, do
not exalt yourself;
be among them as one of their number.
Take care of them first and then sit down;
2 when you have fulfilled all your duties,
take your place,
so that you may be merry along with them
and receive a wreath for your excellent
leadership.

3 Speak, you who are older, for it is your
right,
but with accurate knowledge, and do not
interrupt the music.
4 Where there is entertainment, do not pour
out talk;
do not display your cleverness at the
wrong time.
5 A ruby seal in a setting of gold
is a concert of music at a banquet of wine.
6 A seal of emerald in a rich setting of gold
is the melody of music with good wine.

7 Speak, you who are young, if you are
obliged to,
but no more than twice, and only if asked.
8 Be brief; say much in few words;
be as one who knows and can still hold his
tongue.
9 Among the great do not act as their equal;
and when another is speaking, do not
babble.

10 Lightning travels ahead of the thunder,
and approval goes before one who is
modest.
11 Leave in good time and do not be the last;
go home quickly and do not linger.
12 Amuse yourself there to your heart's content,
but do not sin through proud speech.
13 But above all bless your Maker,
who fills you with his good gifts.

14 The one who seeks God[b] will accept his
discipline,
and those who rise early to seek him[c] will
find favor.
15 The one who seeks the law will be filled
with it,
but the hypocrite will stumble at it.
16 Those who fear the Lord will form true
judgments,
and they will kindle righteous deeds like
a light.
17 The sinner will shun reproof,
and will find a decision according to his
liking.

18 A sensible person will not overlook a
thoughtful suggestion;
an insolent[d] and proud person will not be
deterred by fear.[e]
19 Do nothing without deliberation,

[a] Heb: Gk *tests the hardening of steel by dipping* [b] Heb: Gk *who fears the Lord*
[c] Other ancient authorities lack *to seek him* [d] Heb: Gk *alien*
[e] Meaning of Gk uncertain. Other ancient authorities add *and after acting, with him, without deliberation*

but when you have acted, do not regret it.
20 Do not go on a path full of hazards,
and do not stumble at an obstacle twice.[a]
21 Do not be overconfident on a smooth[b] road,
22 and give good heed to your paths.[c]
23 Guard[d] yourself in every act,
for this is the keeping of the commandments.

24 The one who keeps the law preserves himself,[e]
and the one who trusts the Lord will not suffer loss.

33 No evil will befall the one who fears the Lord,
but in trials such a one will be rescued again and again.
2 The wise will not hate the law,
but the one who is hypocritical about it is like a boat in a storm.
3 The sensible person will trust in the law;
for such a one the law is as dependable as a divine oracle.

4 Prepare what to say, and then you will be listened to;
draw upon your training, and give your answer.
5 The heart of a fool is like a cart wheel,
and his thoughts like a turning axle.
6 A mocking friend is like a stallion
that neighs no matter who the rider is.

7 Why is one day more important than another,
when all the daylight in the year is from the sun?
8 By the Lord's wisdom they were distinguished,
and he appointed the different seasons and festivals.
9 Some days he exalted and hallowed,
and some he made ordinary days.
10 All human beings come from the ground,
and humankind[f] was created out of the dust.
11 In the fullness of his knowledge the Lord distinguished them
and appointed their different ways.
12 Some he blessed and exalted,
and some he made holy and brought near to himself;
but some he cursed and brought low,
and turned them out of their place.
13 Like clay in the hand of the potter,
to be molded as he pleases,
so all are in the hand of their Maker,
to be given whatever he decides.

14 Good is the opposite of evil,
and life the opposite of death;
so the sinner is the opposite of the godly.
15 Look at all the works of the Most High;
they come in pairs, one the opposite of the other.

16 Now I was the last to keep vigil;
I was like a gleaner following the grape-pickers;
17 by the blessing of the Lord I arrived first,
and like a grape-picker I filled my wine press.
18 Consider that I have not labored for myself alone,
but for all who seek instruction.
19 Hear me, you who are great among the people,
and you leaders of the congregation, pay heed!

20 To son or wife, to brother or friend,
do not give power over yourself, as long as you live;
and do not give your property to another,
in case you change your mind and must ask for it.
21 While you are still alive and have breath in you,

[a] Heb: Gk *stumble on stony ground* [b] Or *an unexplored* [c] Heb Syr: Gk *and beware of your children* [d] Heb Syr: Gk *Trust* [e] Heb: Gk *who believes the law heeds the commandments* [f] Heb: Gk *Adam*

do not let anyone take your place.
22 For it is better that your children should ask
from you
than that you should look to the hand of
your children.
23 Excel in all that you do;
bring no stain upon your honor.
24 At the time when you end the days of your
life,
in the hour of death, distribute your
inheritance.

25 Fodder and a stick and burdens for a donkey;
bread and discipline and work for a slave.
26 Set your slave to work, and you will find rest;
leave his hands idle, and he will seek
liberty.
27 Yoke and thong will bow the neck,
and for a wicked slave there are racks and
tortures.
28 Put him to work, in order that he may not be
idle,
29 for idleness teaches much evil.
30 Set him to work, as is fitting for him,
and if he does not obey, make his fetters
heavy.
Do not be overbearing toward anyone,
and do nothing unjust.

31 If you have but one slave, treat him like
yourself,
because you have bought him with blood.
If you have but one slave, treat him like a
brother,
for you will need him as you need your life.
32 If you ill-treat him, and he leaves you and
runs away,
33 which way will you go to seek him?

34 The senseless have vain and false hopes,
and dreams give wings to fools.
2 As one who catches at a shadow and pursues
the wind,
so is anyone who believes in[a] dreams.
3 What is seen in dreams is but a reflection,
the likeness of a face looking at itself.
4 From an unclean thing what can be clean?
And from something false what can be
true?
5 Divinations and omens and dreams are
unreal,
and like a woman in labor, the mind has
fantasies.
6 Unless they are sent by intervention from the
Most High,
pay no attention to them.
7 For dreams have deceived many,
and those who put their hope in them have
perished.
8 Without such deceptions the law will be
fulfilled,
and wisdom is complete in the mouth of
the faithful.

9 An educated[b] person knows many things,
and one with much experience knows
what he is talking about.
10 An inexperienced person knows few things,
11 but he that has traveled acquires much
cleverness.
12 I have seen many things in my travels,
and I understand more than I can express.
13 I have often been in danger of death,
but have escaped because of these
experiences.

14 The spirit of those who fear the Lord will live,
15 for their hope is in him who saves them.
16 Those who fear the Lord will not be timid,
or play the coward, for he is their hope.
17 Happy is the soul that fears the Lord!
18 To whom does he look? And who is his
support?
19 The eyes of the Lord are on those who love
him,
a mighty shield and strong support,
a shelter from scorching wind and a shade
from noonday sun,
a guard against stumbling and a help
against falling.

[a] Syr: Gk *pays heed to* [b] Other ancient authorities read *A traveled*

20 He lifts up the soul and makes the eyes
sparkle;
he gives health and life and blessing.

21 If one sacrifices ill-gotten goods, the offering
is blemished;[a]
22 the gifts[b] of the lawless are not acceptable.
23 The Most High is not pleased with the
offerings of the ungodly,
nor for a multitude of sacrifices does he
forgive sins.
24 Like one who kills a son before his father's
eyes
is the person who offers a sacrifice from
the property of the poor.
25 The bread of the needy is the life of the poor;
whoever deprives them of it is a murderer.
26 To take away a neighbor's living is to commit
murder;
27 to deprive an employee of wages is to shed
blood.

28 When one builds and another tears down,
what do they gain but hard work?
29 When one prays and another curses,
to whose voice will the Lord listen?
30 If one washes after touching a corpse, and
touches it again,
what has been gained by washing?
31 So if one fasts for his sins,
and goes again and does the same things,
who will listen to his prayer?
And what has he gained by humbling
himself?

35 The one who keeps the law makes many
offerings;
2 one who heeds the commandments makes
an offering of well-being.
3 The one who returns a kindness offers choice
flour,
4 and one who gives alms sacrifices a thank
offering.
5 To keep from wickedness is pleasing to the
Lord,
and to forsake unrighteousness is an
atonement.
6 Do not appear before the Lord
empty-handed,
7 for all that you offer is in fulfillment of the
commandment.
8 The offering of the righteous enriches the
altar,
and its pleasing odor rises before the Most
High.
9 The sacrifice of the righteous is acceptable,
and it will never be forgotten.
10 Be generous when you worship the Lord,
and do not stint the first fruits of your
hands.
11 With every gift show a cheerful face,
and dedicate your tithe with gladness.
12 Give to the Most High as he has given to you,
and as generously as you can afford.
13 For the Lord is the one who repays,
and he will repay you sevenfold.
14 Do not offer him a bribe, for he will not
accept it;
15 and do not rely on a dishonest sacrifice;
for the Lord is the judge,
and with him there is no partiality.
16 He will not show partiality to the poor;
but he will listen to the prayer of one who
is wronged.
17 He will not ignore the supplication of the
orphan,
or the widow when she pours out her
complaint.
18 Do not the tears of the widow run down her
cheek
19 as she cries out against the one who causes
them to fall?
20 The one whose service is pleasing to the Lord
will be accepted,
and his prayer will reach to the clouds.
21 The prayer of the humble pierces the clouds,
and it will not rest until it reaches its
goal;
it will not desist until the Most High
responds

[a] Other ancient authorities read *is made in mockery* [b] Other ancient authorities read *mockeries*

22 and does justice for the righteous, and
executes judgment.
Indeed, the Lord will not delay,
and like a warrior[a] will not be patient
until he crushes the loins of the unmerciful
23 and repays vengeance on the nations;
until he destroys the multitude of the
insolent,
and breaks the scepters of the unrighteous;
24 until he repays mortals according to their
deeds,
and the works of all according to their
thoughts;
25 until he judges the case of his people
and makes them rejoice in his mercy.
26 His mercy is as welcome in time of distress
as clouds of rain in time of drought.

36 Have mercy upon us, O God[b] of all,
2 and put all the nations in fear of you.
3 Lift up your hand against foreign nations
and let them see your might.
4 As you have used us to show your holiness to
them,
so use them to show your glory to us.
5 Then they will know,[c] as we have known,
that there is no God but you, O Lord.
6 Give new signs, and work other wonders;
7 make your hand and right arm glorious.
8 Rouse your anger and pour out your wrath;
9 destroy the adversary and wipe out the
enemy.
10 Hasten the day, and remember the appointed
time,[d]
and let people recount your mighty deeds.
11 Let survivors be consumed in the fiery wrath,
and may those who harm your people
meet destruction.
12 Crush the heads of hostile rulers
who say, "There is no one but ourselves."
13 Gather all the tribes of Jacob,[e]
16 and give them their inheritance, as at the
beginning.
17 Have mercy, O Lord, on the people called by
your name,
on Israel, whom you have named[f] your
firstborn,
18 Have pity on the city of your sanctuary,[g]
Jerusalem, the place of your dwelling.[h]
19 Fill Zion with your majesty,[i]
and your temple[j] with your glory.
20 Bear witness to those whom you created in
the beginning,
and fulfill the prophecies spoken in your
name.
21 Reward those who wait for you
and let your prophets be found
trustworthy.
22 Hear, O Lord, the prayer of your servants,
according to your goodwill toward[k]
your people,
and all who are on the earth will know
that you are the Lord, the God of the ages.

23 The stomach will take any food,
yet one food is better than another.
24 As the palate tastes the kinds of game,
so an intelligent mind detects false words.
25 A perverse mind will cause grief,
but a person with experience will pay him
back.
26 A woman will accept any man as a husband,
but one girl is preferable to another.
27 A woman's beauty lights up a man's face,
and there is nothing he desires more.
28 If kindness and humility mark her speech,
her husband is more fortunate than other
men.
29 He who acquires a wife gets his best
possession,[l]

[a] Heb: Gk *and with them* [b] Heb: Gk *O Master, the God* [c] Heb: Gk *And let them know you* [d] Other ancient authorities read *remember your oath* [e] Owing to a dislocation in the Greek Mss of Sirach, the verse numbers 14 and 15 are not used in chapter 36, though no text is missing. [f] Other ancient authorities read *you have likened to* [g] Or *on your holy city* [h] Heb: Gk *your rest* [i] Heb Syr: Gk *the celebration of your wondrous deeds* [j] Heb Syr: Gk Lat *people* [k] Heb and two Gk witnesses: Lat and most Gk witnesses read *according to the blessing of Aaron for* [l] Heb: Gk *enters upon a possession*

a helper fit for him and a pillar of support.[a]
30 Where there is no fence, the property will be plundered;
and where there is no wife, a man will become a fugitive and a wanderer.[b]
31 For who will trust a nimble robber
that skips from city to city?
So who will trust a man that has no nest,
but lodges wherever night overtakes him?

37 Every friend says, "I too am a friend";
but some friends are friends only in name.
2 Is it not a sorrow like that for death itself
when a dear friend turns into an enemy?
3 O inclination to evil, why were you formed
to cover the land with deceit?
4 Some companions rejoice in the happiness of a friend,
but in time of trouble they are against him.
5 Some companions help a friend for their stomachs' sake,
yet in battle they will carry his shield.
6 Do not forget a friend during the battle,[c]
and do not be unmindful of him when you distribute your spoils.[d]

7 All counselors praise the counsel they give,
but some give counsel in their own interest.
8 Be wary of a counselor,
and learn first what is his interest,
for he will take thought for himself.
He may cast the lot against you
9 and tell you, "Your way is good,"
and then stand aside to see what happens to you.
10 Do not consult the one who regards you with suspicion;
hide your intentions from those who are jealous of you.
11 Do not consult with a woman about her rival
or with a coward about war,
with a merchant about business
or with a buyer about selling,
with a miser about generosity[e]
or with the merciless about kindness,
with an idler about any work
or with a seasonal laborer about completing his work,
with a lazy servant about a big task—
pay no attention to any advice they give.
12 But associate with a godly person
whom you know to be a keeper of the commandments,
who is like-minded with yourself,
and who will grieve with you if you fail.
13 And heed[f] the counsel of your own heart,
for no one is more faithful to you than it is.
14 For our own mind sometimes keeps us better informed
than seven sentinels sitting high on a watchtower.
15 But above all pray to the Most High
that he may direct your way in truth.

16 Discussion is the beginning of every work,
and counsel precedes every undertaking.
17 The mind is the root of all conduct;
18 it sprouts four branches,[g]
good and evil, life and death;
and it is the tongue that continually rules them.
19 Some people may be clever enough to teach many,
and yet be useless to themselves.
20 A skillful speaker may be hated;
he will be destitute of all food,
21 for the Lord has withheld the gift of charm,
since he is lacking in all wisdom.
22 If a person is wise to his own advantage,
the fruits of his good sense will be praiseworthy.[h]
23 A wise person instructs his own people,
and the fruits of his good sense will endure.

[a] Heb: Gk *rest* [b] Heb: Gk *wander about and sigh* [c] Heb: Gk *in your heart* [d] Heb: Gk *him in your wealth*
[e] Heb: Gk *gratitude* [f] Heb: Gk *establish* [g] Heb: Gk *As a clue to changes of heart four kinds of destiny appear*
[h] Other ancient witnesses read *trustworthy*

24 A wise person will have praise heaped upon him,
and all who see him will call him happy.
25 The days of a person's life are numbered,
but the days of Israel are without number.
26 One who is wise among his people will inherit honor,[a]
and his name will live forever.

27 My child, test yourself while you live;
see what is bad for you and do not give in to it.
28 For not everything is good for everyone,
and no one enjoys everything.
29 Do not be greedy for every delicacy,
and do not eat without restraint;
30 for overeating brings sickness,
and gluttony leads to nausea.
31 Many have died of gluttony,
but the one who guards against it prolongs his life.

38 Honor physicians for their services,
for the Lord created them;
2 for their gift of healing comes from the Most High,
and they are rewarded by the king.
3 The skill of physicians makes them distinguished,
and in the presence of the great they are admired.
4 The Lord created medicines out of the earth,
and the sensible will not despise them.
5 Was not water made sweet with a tree
in order that its[b] power might be known?
6 And he gave skill to human beings
that he[c] might be glorified in his marvelous works.
7 By them the physician[d] heals and takes away pain;
8 the pharmacist makes a mixture from them.
God's[e] works will never be finished;
and from him health[f] spreads over all the earth.

9 My child, when you are ill, do not delay,
but pray to the Lord, and he will heal you.
10 Give up your faults and direct your hands rightly,
and cleanse your heart from all sin.
11 Offer a sweet-smelling sacrifice, and a memorial portion of choice flour,
and pour oil on your offering, as much as you can afford.[g]
12 Then give the physician his place, for the Lord created him;
do not let him leave you, for you need him.
13 There may come a time when recovery lies in the hands of physicians,[h]
14 for they too pray to the Lord
that he grant them success in diagnosis[i]
and in healing, for the sake of preserving life.
15 He who sins against his Maker,
will be defiant toward the physician.[j]

16 My child, let your tears fall for the dead,
and as one in great pain begin the lament.
Lay out the body with due ceremony,
and do not neglect the burial.
17 Let your weeping be bitter and your wailing fervent;
make your mourning worthy of the departed,
for one day, or two, to avoid criticism;
then be comforted for your grief.
18 For grief may result in death,
and a sorrowful heart saps one's strength.
19 When a person is taken away, sorrow is over;
but the life of the poor weighs down the heart.
20 Do not give your heart to grief;
drive it away, and remember your own end.
21 Do not forget, there is no coming back;

[a] Other ancient authorities read *confidence* [b] Or *his* [c] Or *they* [d] Heb: Gk *he* [e] Gk *His* [f] Or *peace*
[g] Heb: Lat lacks *as much as you can afford*; Meaning of Gk uncertain [h] Gk *in their hands* [i] Heb: Gk *rest*
[j] Heb: Gk *may he fall into the hands of the physician*

you do the dead[a] no good, and you injure
yourself.
22 Remember his[b] fate, for yours is like it;
yesterday it was his,[c] and today it is yours.
23 When the dead is at rest, let his remembrance
rest too,
and be comforted for him when his spirit
has departed.

24 The wisdom of the scribe depends on the
opportunity of leisure;
only the one who has little business can
become wise.
25 How can one become wise who handles the
plow,
and who glories in the shaft of a goad,
who drives oxen and is occupied with their
work,
and whose talk is about bulls?
26 He sets his heart on plowing furrows,
and he is careful about fodder for the
heifers.
27 So it is with every artisan and master artisan
who labors by night as well as by day;
those who cut the signets of seals,
each is diligent in making a great variety;
they set their heart on painting a lifelike
image,
and they are careful to finish their work.
28 So it is with the smith, sitting by the anvil,
intent on his iron-work;
the breath of the fire melts his flesh,
and he struggles with the heat of the
furnace;
the sound of the hammer deafens his ears,[d]
and his eyes are on the pattern of the
object.
He sets his heart on finishing his handiwork,
and he is careful to complete its
decoration.
29 So it is with the potter sitting at his work
and turning the wheel with his feet;
he is always deeply concerned over his
products,
and he produces them in quantity.
30 He molds the clay with his arm
and makes it pliable with his feet;
he sets his heart to finish the glazing,
and he takes care in firing[e] the kiln.

31 All these rely on their hands,
and all are skillful in their own work.
32 Without them no city can be inhabited,
and wherever they live, they will not go
hungry.[f]
Yet they are not sought out for the council of
the people,[g]
33 nor do they attain eminence in the public
assembly.
They do not sit in the judge's seat,
nor do they understand the decisions of
the courts;
they cannot expound discipline or judgment,
and they are not found among the rulers.[h]
34 But they maintain the fabric of the world,
and their concern is for[i] the exercise of
their trade.

How different the one who devotes himself
to the study of the law of the Most High!
39 He seeks out the wisdom of all the
ancients,
and is concerned with prophecies;
2 he preserves the sayings of the famous
and penetrates the subtleties of parables;
3 he seeks out the hidden meanings of proverbs
and is at home with the obscurities of
parables.
4 He serves among the great
and appears before rulers;
he travels in foreign lands
and learns what is good and evil in the
human lot.
5 He sets his heart to rise early
to seek the Lord who made him,
and to petition the Most High;
he opens his mouth in prayer
and asks pardon for his sins.

[a] Gk *him* [b] Heb: Gk *my* [c] Heb: Gk *mine* [d] Cn: Gk *renews his ear* [e] Cn: Gk *cleaning* [f] Syr: Gk *and people can neither live nor walk there* [g] Most ancient authorities lack this line [h] Cn: Gk *among parables* [i] Syr: Gk *prayer is in*

 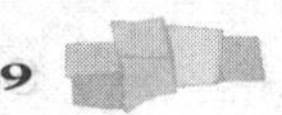

6 If the great Lord is willing,
he will be filled with the spirit of understanding;
he will pour forth words of wisdom of his own
and give thanks to the Lord in prayer.
7 The Lord[a] will direct his counsel and knowledge,
as he meditates on his mysteries.
8 He will show the wisdom of what he has learned,
and will glory in the law of the Lord's covenant.
9 Many will praise his understanding;
it will never be blotted out.
His memory will not disappear,
and his name will live through all generations.
10 Nations will speak of his wisdom,
and the congregation will proclaim his praise.
11 If he lives long, he will leave a name greater than a thousand,
and if he goes to rest, it is enough[b] for him.

12 I have more on my mind to express;
I am full like the full moon.
13 Listen to me, my faithful children, and blossom
like a rose growing by a stream of water.
14 Send out fragrance like incense,
and put forth blossoms like a lily.
Scatter the fragrance, and sing a hymn of praise;
bless the Lord for all his works.
15 Ascribe majesty to his name
and give thanks to him with praise,
with songs on your lips, and with harps;
this is what you shall say in thanksgiving:

16 "All the works of the Lord are very good,
and whatever he commands will be done at the appointed time.
17 No one can say, 'What is this?' or 'Why is that?'—
for at the appointed time all such questions will be answered.
At his word the waters stood in a heap,
and the reservoirs of water at the word of his mouth.
18 When he commands, his every purpose is fulfilled,
and none can limit his saving power.
19 The works of all are before him,
and nothing can be hidden from his eyes.
20 From the beginning to the end of time he can see everything,
and nothing is too marvelous for him.
21 No one can say, 'What is this?' or 'Why is that?'—
for everything has been created for its own purpose.

22 "His blessing covers the dry land like a river,
and drenches it like a flood.
23 But his wrath drives out the nations,
as when he turned a watered land into salt.
24 To the faithful his ways are straight,
but full of pitfalls for the wicked.
25 From the beginning good things were created for the good,
but for sinners good things and bad.[c]
26 The basic necessities of human life
are water and fire and iron and salt
and wheat flour and milk and honey,
the blood of the grape and oil and clothing.
27 All these are good for the godly,
but for sinners they turn into evils.

28 "There are winds created for vengeance,
and in their anger they can dislodge mountains;[d]
on the day of reckoning they will pour out their strength
and calm the anger of their Maker.
29 Fire and hail and famine and pestilence,

[a] Gk *He himself* [b] Cn: Meaning of Gk uncertain [c] Heb Lat: Gk *sinners bad things*
[d] Heb Syr: Gk *can scourge mightily*

all these have been created for vengeance;
30 the fangs of wild animals and scorpions and vipers,
and the sword that punishes the ungodly with destruction.
31 They take delight in doing his bidding,
always ready for his service on earth;
and when their time comes they never disobey his command."

32 So from the beginning I have been convinced of all this
and have thought it out and left it in writing:
33 All the works of the Lord are good,
and he will supply every need in its time.
34 No one can say, "This is not as good as that,"
for everything proves good in its appointed time.
35 So now sing praise with all your heart and voice,
and bless the name of the Lord.

40 Hard work was created for everyone,
and a heavy yoke is laid on the children of Adam,
from the day they come forth from their mother's womb
until the day they return to[a] the mother of all the living.[b]
2 Perplexities and fear of heart are theirs,
and anxious thought of the day of their death.
3 From the one who sits on a splendid throne
to the one who grovels in dust and ashes,
4 from the one who wears purple and a crown
to the one who is clothed in burlap,
5 there is anger and envy and trouble and unrest,
and fear of death, and fury and strife.
And when one rests upon his bed,
his sleep at night confuses his mind.
6 He gets little or no rest;
he struggles in his sleep as he did by day.[c]
He is troubled by the visions of his mind
like one who has escaped from the battlefield.
7 At the moment he reaches safety he wakes up,
astonished that his fears were groundless.
8 To all creatures, human and animal,
but to sinners seven times more,
9 come death and bloodshed and strife and sword,
calamities and famine and ruin and plague.
10 All these were created for the wicked,
and on their account the flood came.
11 All that is of earth returns to earth,
and what is from above returns above.[d]

12 All bribery and injustice will be blotted out,
but good faith will last forever.
13 The wealth of the unjust will dry up like a river,
and crash like a loud clap of thunder in a storm.
14 As a generous person has cause to rejoice,
so lawbreakers will utterly fail.
15 The children of the ungodly put out few branches;
they are unhealthy roots on sheer rock.
16 The reeds by any water or river bank
are plucked up before any grass;
17 but kindness is like a garden of blessings,
and almsgiving endures forever.

18 Wealth and wages make life sweet,[e]
but better than either is finding a treasure.
19 Children and the building of a city establish one's name,
but better than either is the one who finds wisdom.
Cattle and orchards make one prosperous;[f]
but a blameless wife is accounted better than either.
20 Wine and music gladden the heart,

[a] Other Gk and Lat authorities read *are buried in* [b] Heb: Gk *of all* [c] Arm: Meaning of Gk uncertain [d] Heb Syr: Gk Lat *from the waters returns to the sea* [e] Heb: Gk *Life is sweet for the self-reliant worker*
[f] Heb Syr: Gk lacks *but better . . . prosperous*

but the love of friends[a] is better than
either.
21 The flute and the harp make sweet melody,
but a pleasant voice is better than either.
22 The eye desires grace and beauty,
but the green shoots of grain more than
either.
23 A friend or companion is always welcome,
but a sensible wife[b] is better than either.
24 Kindred and helpers are for a time of trouble,
but almsgiving rescues better than either.
25 Gold and silver make one stand firm,
but good counsel is esteemed more than
either.
26 Riches and strength build up confidence,
but the fear of the Lord is better than
either.
There is no want in the fear of the Lord,
and with it there is no need to seek for help.
27 The fear of the Lord is like a garden of
blessing,
and covers a person better than any glory.

28 My child, do not lead the life of a beggar;
it is better to die than to beg.
29 When one looks to the table of another,
one's way of life cannot be considered a
life.
One loses self-respect with another person's
food,
but one who is intelligent and well
instructed guards against that.
30 In the mouth of the shameless begging is
sweet,
but it kindles a fire inside him.

41 O death, how bitter is the thought of you
to the one at peace among possessions,
who has nothing to worry about and is
prosperous in everything,
and still is vigorous enough to enjoy food!
2 O death, how welcome is your sentence
to one who is needy and failing in
strength,
worn down by age and anxious about
everything;
to one who is contrary, and has lost all
patience!
3 Do not fear death's decree for you;
remember those who went before you and
those who will come after.
4 This is the Lord's decree for all flesh;
why then should you reject the will of the
Most High?
Whether life lasts for ten years or a hundred
or a thousand,
there are no questions asked in Hades.

5 The children of sinners are abominable
children,
and they frequent the haunts of the
ungodly.
6 The inheritance of the children of sinners will
perish,
and on their offspring will be a perpetual
disgrace.
7 Children will blame an ungodly father,
for they suffer disgrace because of him.
8 Woe to you, the ungodly,
who have forsaken the law of the Most
High God!
9 If you have children, calamity will be theirs;
you will beget them only for groaning.
When you stumble, there is lasting joy;[c]
and when you die, a curse is your lot.
10 Whatever comes from earth returns to
earth;
so the ungodly go from curse to
destruction.

11 The human body is a fleeting thing,
but a virtuous name will never be blotted
out.[d]
12 Have regard for your name, since it will
outlive you
longer than a thousand hoards of gold.
13 The days of a good life are numbered,
but a good name lasts forever.

[a] Heb: Gk *wisdom* [b] Heb Compare Syr: Gk *wife with her husband* [c] Heb: Meaning of Gk uncertain
[d] Heb: Gk *People grieve over the death of the body, but the bad name of sinners will be blotted out*

14 My children, be true to your training and be
at peace;
hidden wisdom and unseen treasure—
of what value is either?
15 Better are those who hide their folly
than those who hide their wisdom.
16 Therefore show respect for my words;
for it is not good to feel shame in every
circumstance,
nor is every kind of abashment to be
approved.[a]

17 Be ashamed of sexual immorality, before your
father or mother;
and of a lie, before a prince or a ruler;
18 of a crime, before a judge or magistrate;
and of a breach of the law, before the
congregation and the people;
of unjust dealing, before your partner or your
friend;
19 and of theft, in the place where you live.
Be ashamed of breaking an oath or agreement,[b]
and of leaning on your elbow at meals;
of surliness in receiving or giving,
20 and of silence, before those who greet you;
of looking at a prostitute,
21 and of rejecting the appeal of a relative;
of taking away someone's portion or gift,
and of gazing at another man's wife;
22 of meddling with his servant-girl—
and do not approach her bed;
of abusive words, before friends—
and do not be insulting after making a gift.
42 Be ashamed of repeating what you hear,
and of betraying secrets.
Then you will show proper shame,
and will find favor with everyone.

Of the following things do not be ashamed,
and do not sin to save face:
2 Do not be ashamed of the law of the Most
High and his covenant,
and of rendering judgment to acquit the
ungodly;
3 of keeping accounts with a partner or with
traveling companions,
and of dividing the inheritance of friends;
4 of accuracy with scales and weights,
and of acquiring much or little;
5 of profit from dealing with merchants,
and of frequent disciplining of children,
and of drawing blood from the back of a
wicked slave.
6 Where there is an untrustworthy wife, a seal
is a good thing;
and where there are many hands, lock
things up.
7 When you make a deposit, be sure it is
counted and weighed,
and when you give or receive, put it all in
writing.
8 Do not be ashamed to correct the stupid or
foolish
or the aged who are guilty of sexual
immorality.
Then you will show your sound training,
and will be approved by all.

9 A daughter is a secret anxiety to her father,
and worry over her robs him of sleep;
when she is young, for fear she may not
marry,
or if married, for fear she may be disliked;
10 while a virgin, for fear she may be seduced
and become pregnant in her father's
house;
or having a husband, for fear she may go
astray,
or, though married, for fear she may be
barren.
11 Keep strict watch over a headstrong daughter,
or she may make you a laughingstock to
your enemies,
a byword in the city and the assembly of[c] the
people,
and put you to shame in public
gatherings.[d]
See that there is no lattice in her room,

[a] Heb: Gk *and not everything is confidently esteemed by everyone* [b] Heb: Gk *before the truth of God and the covenant*
[c] Heb: Meaning of Gk uncertain [d] Heb: Gk *to shame before the great multitude*

no spot that overlooks the approaches to
the house.[a]
12 Do not let her parade her beauty before any
man,
or spend her time among married
women;[b]
13 for from garments comes the moth,
and from a woman comes woman's
wickedness.
14 Better is the wickedness of a man than a
woman who does good;
it is woman who brings shame and
disgrace.

15 I will now call to mind the works of the Lord,
and will declare what I have seen.
By the word of the Lord his works are made;
and all his creatures do his will.[c]
16 The sun looks down on everything with its
light,
and the work of the Lord is full of his
glory.
17 The Lord has not empowered even his holy
ones
to recount all his marvelous works,
which the Lord the Almighty has established
so that the universe may stand firm in his
glory.
18 He searches out the abyss and the human
heart;
he understands their innermost secrets.
For the Most High knows all that may be
known;
he sees from of old the things that are to
come.[d]
19 He discloses what has been and what is to be,
and he reveals the traces of hidden things.
20 No thought escapes him,
and nothing is hidden from him.
21 He has set in order the splendors of his
wisdom;
he is from all eternity one and the same.
Nothing can be added or taken away,
and he needs no one to be his counselor.
22 How desirable are all his works,
and how sparkling they are to see![e]
23 All these things live and remain forever;
each creature is preserved to meet a
particular need.[f]
24 All things come in pairs, one opposite the
other,
and he has made nothing incomplete.
25 Each supplements the virtues of the other.
Who could ever tire of seeing his glory?

43 The pride of the higher realms is the clear
vault of the sky,
as glorious to behold as the sight of the
heavens.
2 The sun, when it appears, proclaims as it rises
what a marvelous instrument it is, the
work of the Most High.
3 At noon it parches the land,
and who can withstand its burning heat?
4 A man tending[g] a furnace works in burning
heat,
but three times as hot is the sun scorching
the mountains;
it breathes out fiery vapors,
and its bright rays blind the eyes.
5 Great is the Lord who made it;
at his orders it hurries on its course.

6 It is the moon that marks the changing
seasons,[b]
governing the times, their everlasting
sign.
7 From the moon comes the sign for festal
days,
a light that wanes when it completes its
course.
8 The new moon, as its name suggests, renews
itself;[h]
how marvelous it is in this change,
a beacon to the hosts on high,
shining in the vault of the heavens!

[a] Heb: Gk lacks *See . . . house* [b] Heb: Meaning of Gk uncertain [c] Syr Compare Heb: most Gk witnesses lack *and all . . . will* [d] Heb: Gk *he sees the sign(s) of the age* [e] Meaning of Gk uncertain [f] Heb: Gk *forever for every need, and all are obedient* [g] Other ancient authorities read *blowing upon* [h] Heb: Gk *The month is named after the moon*

9 The glory of the stars is the beauty of heaven,
a glittering array in the heights of the Lord.
10 On the orders of the Holy One they stand in their appointed places;
they never relax in their watches.
11 Look at the rainbow, and praise him who made it;
it is exceedingly beautiful in its brightness.
12 It encircles the sky with its glorious arc;
the hands of the Most High have stretched it out.

13 By his command he sends the driving snow
and speeds the lightnings of his judgment.
14 Therefore the storehouses are opened,
and the clouds fly out like birds.
15 In his majesty he gives the clouds their strength,
and the hailstones are broken in pieces.
17a The voice of his thunder rebukes the earth;
16 when he appears, the mountains shake.
At his will the south wind blows;
17b so do the storm from the north and the whirlwind.
He scatters the snow like birds flying down,
and its descent is like locusts alighting.
18 The eye is dazzled by the beauty of its whiteness,
and the mind is amazed as it falls.
19 He pours frost over the earth like salt,
and icicles form like pointed thorns.
20 The cold north wind blows,
and ice freezes on the water;
it settles on every pool of water,
and the water puts it on like a breastplate.
21 He consumes the mountains and burns up the wilderness,
and withers the tender grass like fire.
22 A mist quickly heals all things;
the falling dew gives refreshment from the heat.

23 By his plan he stilled the deep
and planted islands in it.
24 Those who sail the sea tell of its dangers,
and we marvel at what we hear.
25 In it are strange and marvelous creatures,
all kinds of living things, and huge sea-monsters.
26 Because of him each of his messengers succeeds,
and by his word all things hold together.

27 We could say more but could never say enough;
let the final word be: "He is the all."
28 Where can we find the strength to praise him?
For he is greater than all his works.
29 Awesome is the Lord and very great,
and marvelous is his power.
30 Glorify the Lord and exalt him as much as you can,
for he surpasses even that.
When you exalt him, summon all your strength,
and do not grow weary, for you cannot praise him enough.
31 Who has seen him and can describe him?
Or who can extol him as he is?
32 Many things greater than these lie hidden,
for I[a] have seen but few of his works.
33 For the Lord has made all things,
and to the godly he has given wisdom.

Hymn in Honor of Our Ancestors[b]

44 Let us now sing the praises of famous men,
our ancestors in their generations.
2 The Lord apportioned to them[c] great glory,
his majesty from the beginning.
3 There were those who ruled in their kingdoms,
and made a name for themselves by their valor;
those who gave counsel because they were intelligent;
those who spoke in prophetic oracles;
4 those who led the people by their counsels

[a] Heb: Gk *we* [b] This title is included in the Gk text. [c] Heb: Gk *created*

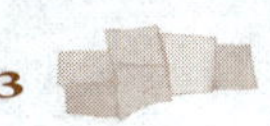

and by their knowledge of the people's
lore;
they were wise in their words of
instruction;
5 those who composed musical tunes,
or put verses in writing;
6 rich men endowed with resources,
living peacefully in their homes—
7 all these were honored in their generations,
and were the pride of their times.
8 Some of them have left behind a name,
so that others declare their praise.
9 But of others there is no memory;
they have perished as though they had
never existed;
they have become as though they had never
been born,
they and their children after them.
10 But these also were godly men,
whose righteous deeds have not been
forgotten;
11 their wealth will remain with their
descendants,
and their inheritance with their children's
children.[a]
12 Their descendants stand by the covenants;
their children also, for their sake.
13 Their offspring will continue forever,
and their glory will never be blotted out.
14 Their bodies are buried in peace,
but their name lives on generation after
generation.
15 The assembly declares[b] their wisdom,
and the congregation proclaims their
praise.

16 Enoch pleased the Lord and was taken up,
an example of repentance to all
generations.

17 Noah was found perfect and righteous;
in the time of wrath he kept the race alive;[c]
therefore a remnant was left on the earth
when the flood came.
18 Everlasting covenants were made with him
that all flesh should never again be blotted
out by a flood.

19 Abraham was the great father of a multitude
of nations,
and no one has been found like him in
glory.
20 He kept the law of the Most High,
and entered into a covenant with him;
he certified the covenant in his flesh,
and when he was tested he proved faithful.
21 Therefore the Lord[d] assured him with an
oath
that the nations would be blessed through
his offspring;
that he would make him as numerous as the
dust of the earth,
and exalt his offspring like the stars,
and give them an inheritance from sea to sea
and from the Euphrates[e] to the ends of the
earth.
22 To Isaac also he gave the same assurance
for the sake of his father Abraham.
The blessing of all people and the covenant
23 he made to rest on the head of Jacob;
he acknowledged him with his blessings,
and gave him his inheritance;
he divided his portions,
and distributed them among twelve tribes.

From his descendants the Lord[d] brought
forth a godly man,
who found favor in the sight of all
45 [1]and was beloved by God and people,
Moses, whose memory is blessed.
2 He made him equal in glory to the holy ones,
and made him great, to the terror of his
enemies.
3 By his words he performed swift miracles;[f]
the Lord[d] glorified him in the presence of
kings.
He gave him commandments for his people,
and revealed to him his glory.

[a] Heb Compare Lat Syr: Meaning of Gk uncertain [b] Heb: Gk *Peoples declare* [c] Heb: Gk *was taken in exchange*
[d] Gk *he* [e] Syr: Heb Gk *River* [f] Heb: Gk *caused signs to cease*

4 For his faithfulness and meekness he
consecrated him,
choosing him out of all humankind.
5 He allowed him to hear his voice,
and led him into the dark cloud,
and gave him the commandments face to
face,
the law of life and knowledge,
so that he might teach Jacob the covenant,
and Israel his decrees.

6 He exalted Aaron, a holy man like Moses[a]
who was his brother, of the tribe of Levi.
7 He made an everlasting covenant with him,
and gave him the priesthood of the people.
He blessed him with stateliness,
and put a glorious robe on him.
8 He clothed him in perfect splendor,
and strengthened him with the symbols of
authority,
the linen undergarments, the long robe,
and the ephod.
9 And he encircled him with pomegranates,
with many golden bells all around,
to send forth a sound as he walked,
to make their ringing heard in the temple
as a reminder to his people;
10 with the sacred vestment, of gold and violet
and purple, the work of an embroiderer;
with the oracle of judgment, Urim and
Thummim;
11 with twisted crimson, the work of an
artisan;
with precious stones engraved like seals,
in a setting of gold, the work of a jeweler,
to commemorate in engraved letters
each of the tribes of Israel;
12 with a gold crown upon his turban,
inscribed like a seal with "Holiness,"
a distinction to be prized, the work of an
expert,
a delight to the eyes, richly adorned.
13 Before him such beautiful things did not
exist.
No outsider ever put them on,
but only his sons
and his descendants in perpetuity.
14 His sacrifices shall be wholly burned
twice every day continually.
15 Moses ordained him,
and anointed him with holy oil;
it was an everlasting covenant for him
and for his descendants as long as the
heavens endure,
to minister to the Lord[a] and serve as priest
and bless his people in his name.
16 He chose him out of all the living
to offer sacrifice to the Lord,
incense and a pleasing odor as a memorial
portion,
to make atonement for the[b] people.
17 In his commandments he gave him
authority and statutes and[c] judgments,
to teach Jacob the testimonies,
and to enlighten Israel with his law.
18 Outsiders conspired against him,
and envied him in the wilderness,
Dathan and Abiram and their followers
and the company of Korah, in wrath and
anger.
19 The Lord saw it and was not pleased,
and in the heat of his anger they were
destroyed;
he performed wonders against them
to consume them in flaming fire.
20 He added glory to Aaron
and gave him a heritage;
he allotted to him the best of the first fruits,
and prepared bread of first fruits in
abundance;
21 for they eat the sacrifices of the Lord,
which he gave to him and his descendants.
22 But in the land of the people he has no
inheritance,
and he has no portion among the
people;
for the Lord[d] himself is his[e] portion and
inheritance.

[a] Gk *him* [b] Other ancient authorities read *his* or *your* [c] Heb: Gk *authority in covenants of* [d] Gk *he*
[e] Other ancient authorities read *your*

23 Phinehas son of Eleazar ranks third in glory
for being zealous in the fear of the Lord,
and standing firm, when the people turned away,
in the noble courage of his soul;
and he made atonement for Israel.
24 Therefore a covenant of friendship was established with him,
that he should be leader of the sanctuary and of his people,
that he and his descendants should have
the dignity of the priesthood forever.
25 Just as a covenant was established with David
son of Jesse of the tribe of Judah,
that the king's heritage passes only from son to son,
so the heritage of Aaron is for his descendants alone.

26 And now bless the Lord
who has crowned you with glory.[a]
May the Lord[b] grant you wisdom of mind
to judge his people with justice,
so that their prosperity may not vanish,
and that their glory may endure through all their generations.

46 Joshua son of Nun was mighty in war,
and was the successor of Moses in the prophetic office.
He became, as his name implies,
a great savior of God's[c] elect,
to take vengeance on the enemies that rose against them,
so that he might give Israel its inheritance.
2 How glorious he was when he lifted his hands
and brandished his sword against the cities!
3 Who before him ever stood so firm?
For he waged the wars of the Lord.
4 Was it not through him that the sun stood still
and one day became as long as two?
5 He called upon the Most High, the Mighty One,
when enemies pressed him on every side,
and the great Lord answered him
with hailstones of mighty power.
6 He overwhelmed that nation in battle,
and on the slope he destroyed his opponents,
so that the nations might know his armament,
that he was fighting in the sight of the Lord;
for he was a devoted follower of the Mighty One.
7 And in the days of Moses he proved his loyalty,
he and Caleb son of Jephunneh:
they opposed the congregation,[d]
restrained the people from sin,
and stilled their wicked grumbling.
8 And these two alone were spared
out of six hundred thousand infantry,
to lead the people[e] into their inheritance,
the land flowing with milk and honey.
9 The Lord gave Caleb strength,
which remained with him in his old age,
so that he went up to the hill country,
and his children obtained it for an inheritance,
10 so that all the Israelites might see
how good it is to follow the Lord.

11 The judges also, with their respective names,
whose hearts did not fall into idolatry
and who did not turn away from the Lord—
may their memory be blessed!
12 May their bones send forth new life from where they lie,
and may the names of those who have been honored
live again in their children!

13 Samuel was beloved by his Lord;
a prophet of the Lord, he established the kingdom
and anointed rulers over his people.

[a] Heb: Gk lacks *And . . . glory* [b] Gk *he* [c] Gk *his* [d] Other ancient authorities read *the enemy* [e] Gk *them*

14 By the law of the Lord he judged the
congregation,
and the Lord watched over Jacob.
15 By his faithfulness he was proved to be a
prophet,
and by his words he became known as a
trustworthy seer.
16 He called upon the Lord, the Mighty One,
when his enemies pressed him on every
side,
and he offered in sacrifice a suckling lamb.
17 Then the Lord thundered from heaven,
and made his voice heard with a mighty
sound;
18 he subdued the leaders of the enemy[a]
and all the rulers of the Philistines.
19 Before the time of his eternal sleep,
Samuel[b] bore witness before the Lord and
his anointed:
"No property, not so much as a pair of shoes,
have I taken from anyone!"
And no one accused him.
20 Even after he had fallen asleep, he prophesied
and made known to the king his death,
and lifted up his voice from the ground
in prophecy, to blot out the wickedness of
the people.

47 After him Nathan rose up
to prophesy in the days of David.
2 As the fat is set apart from the offering of
well-being,
so David was set apart from the Israelites.
3 He played with lions as though they were
young goats,
and with bears as though they were lambs
of the flock.
4 In his youth did he not kill a giant,
and take away the people's disgrace,
when he whirled the stone in the sling
and struck down the boasting Goliath?
5 For he called on the Lord, the Most High,
and he gave strength to his right arm
to strike down a mighty warrior,
and to exalt the power[c] of his people.
6 So they glorified him for the tens of
thousands he conquered,
and praised him for the blessings bestowed
by the Lord,
when the glorious diadem was given to
him.
7 For he wiped out his enemies on every side,
and annihilated his adversaries the
Philistines;
he crushed their power[c] to our own day.
8 In all that he did he gave thanks
to the Holy One, the Most High,
proclaiming his glory;
he sang praise with all his heart,
and he loved his Maker.
9 He placed singers before the altar,
to make sweet melody with their voices.[d]
10 He gave beauty to the festivals,
and arranged their times throughout the
year,[e]
while they praised God's[f] holy name,
and the sanctuary resounded from early
morning.
11 The Lord took away his sins,
and exalted his power[c] forever;
he gave him a covenant of kingship
and a glorious throne in Israel.
12 After him a wise son rose up
who because of him lived in security:[g]
13 Solomon reigned in an age of peace,
because God made all his borders tranquil,
so that he might build a house in his name
and provide a sanctuary to stand forever.
14 How wise you were when you were young!
You overflowed like the Nile[h] with
understanding.
15 Your influence spread throughout the earth,
and you filled it with proverbs having deep
meaning.
16 Your fame reached to far-off islands,
and you were loved for your peaceful
reign.

[a] Heb: Gk *leaders of the people of Tyre* [b] Gk *he* [c] Gk *horn* [d] Other ancient authorities add *and daily they sing his praises* [e] Gk *to completion* [f] Gk *his* [g] Heb: Gk *in a broad place* [h] Heb: Gk *a river*

17 Your songs, proverbs, and parables,
and the answers you gave astounded the nations.
18 In the name of the Lord God,
who is called the God of Israel,
you gathered gold like tin
and amassed silver like lead.
19 But you brought in women to lie at your side,
and through your body you were brought into subjection.
20 You stained your honor,
and defiled your family line,
so that you brought wrath upon your children,
and they were grieved[a] at your folly,
21 because the sovereignty was divided
and a rebel kingdom arose out of Ephraim.
22 But the Lord will never give up his mercy,
or cause any of his works to perish;
he will never blot out the descendants of his chosen one,
or destroy the family line of him who loved him.
So he gave a remnant to Jacob,
and to David a root from his own family.

23 Solomon rested with his ancestors,
and left behind him one of his sons,
broad in[b] folly and lacking in sense,
Rehoboam, whose policy drove the people to revolt.
Then Jeroboam son of Nebat led Israel into sin
and started Ephraim on its sinful ways.
24 Their sins increased more and more,
until they were exiled from their land.
25 For they sought out every kind of wickedness,
until vengeance came upon them.

48 Then Elijah arose, a prophet like fire,
and his word burned like a torch.
2 He brought a famine upon them,
and by his zeal he made them few in number.
3 By the word of the Lord he shut up the heavens,
and also three times brought down fire.
4 How glorious you were, Elijah, in your wondrous deeds!
Whose glory is equal to yours?
5 You raised a corpse from death
and from Hades, by the word of the Most High.
6 You sent kings down to destruction,
and famous men, from their sickbeds.
7 You heard rebuke at Sinai
and judgments of vengeance at Horeb.
8 You anointed kings to inflict retribution,
and prophets to succeed you.[c]
9 You were taken up by a whirlwind of fire,
in a chariot with horses of fire.
10 At the appointed time, it is written, you are destined[d]
to calm the wrath of God before it breaks out in fury,
to turn the hearts of parents to their children,
and to restore the tribes of Jacob.
11 Happy are those who saw you
and were adorned[e] with your love!
For we also shall surely live.[f]

12 When Elijah was enveloped in the whirlwind,
Elisha was filled with his spirit.
He performed twice as many signs,
and marvels with every utterance of his mouth.[g]
Never in his lifetime did he tremble before any ruler,
nor could anyone intimidate him at all.
13 Nothing was too hard for him,
and when he was dead, his body prophesied.
14 In his life he did wonders,
and in death his deeds were marvelous.

[a] Other ancient authorities read *I was grieved* [b] Heb (with a play on the name Rehoboam) Syr: Gk *the people's* [c] Heb: Gk *him* [d] Heb: Gk *are for reproofs* [e] Other ancient authorities read *and have died* [f] Text and meaning of Gk uncertain [g] Heb: Gk lacks *He performed . . . mouth*

15 Despite all this the people did not repent,
nor did they forsake their sins,
until they were carried off as plunder from their land,
and were scattered over all the earth.
The people were left very few in number,
but with a ruler from the house of David.
16 Some of them did what was right,
but others sinned more and more.

17 Hezekiah fortified his city,
and brought water into its midst;
he tunneled the rock with iron tools,
and built cisterns for the water.
18 In his days Sennacherib invaded the country;
he sent his commander[a] and departed;
he shook his fist against Zion,
and made great boasts in his arrogance.
19 Then their hearts were shaken and their hands trembled,
and they were in anguish, like women in labor.
20 But they called upon the Lord who is merciful,
spreading out their hands toward him.
The Holy One quickly heard them from heaven,
and delivered them through Isaiah.
21 The Lord[b] struck down the camp of the Assyrians,
and his angel wiped them out.
22 For Hezekiah did what was pleasing to the Lord,
and he kept firmly to the ways of his ancestor David,
as he was commanded by the prophet Isaiah,
who was great and trustworthy in his visions.
23 In Isaiah's[c] days the sun went backward,
and he prolonged the life of the king.
24 By his dauntless spirit he saw the future,
and comforted the mourners in Zion.
25 He revealed what was to occur to the end of time,
and the hidden things before they happened.

49 The name[d] of Josiah is like blended incense
prepared by the skill of the perfumer;
his memory[e] is as sweet as honey to every mouth,
and like music at a banquet of wine.
2 He did what was right by reforming the people,
and removing the wicked abominations.
3 He kept his heart fixed on the Lord;
in lawless times he made godliness prevail.

4 Except for David and Hezekiah and Josiah,
all of them were great sinners,
for they abandoned the law of the Most High;
the kings of Judah came to an end.
5 They[f] gave their power to others,
and their glory to a foreign nation,
6 who set fire to the chosen city of the sanctuary,
and made its streets desolate,
as Jeremiah had foretold.[g]
7 For they had mistreated him,
who even in the womb had been consecrated a prophet,
to pluck up and ruin and destroy,
and likewise to build and to plant.

8 It was Ezekiel who saw the vision of glory,
which God[b] showed him above the chariot of the cherubim.
9 For God[h] also mentioned Job
who held fast to all the ways of justice.[i]
10 May the bones of the Twelve Prophets
send forth new life from where they lie,
for they comforted the people of Jacob
and delivered them with confident hope.

11 How shall we magnify Zerubbabel?
He was like a signet ring on the right hand,
12 and so was Jeshua son of Jozadak;

[a] Other ancient authorities add *from Lachish* [b] Gk *He* [c] Gk *his* [d] Heb: Gk *memory* [e] Heb: Gk *it* [f] Heb: *He* [g] Gk *by the hand of Jeremiah* [h] Gk *he* [i] Heb Compare Syr: Meaning of Gk uncertain

in their days they built the house
and raised a temple[a] holy to the Lord,
destined for everlasting glory.
13 The memory of Nehemiah also is lasting;
he raised our fallen walls,
and set up gates and bars,
and rebuilt our ruined houses.

14 Few have[b] ever been created on earth like Enoch,
for he was taken up from the earth.
15 Nor was anyone ever born like Joseph;[c]
even his bones were cared for.
16 Shem and Seth and Enosh were honored,[d]
but above every other created living being was Adam.

50 The leader of his brothers and the pride of his people[e]
was the high priest, Simon son of Onias,
who in his life repaired the house,
and in his time fortified the temple.
2 He laid the foundations for the high double walls,
the high retaining walls for the temple enclosure.
3 In his days a water cistern was dug,[f]
a reservoir like the sea in circumference.
4 He considered how to save his people from ruin,
and fortified the city against siege.
5 How glorious he was, surrounded by the people,
as he came out of the house of the curtain.
6 Like the morning star among the clouds,
like the full moon at the festal season;[f]
7 like the sun shining on the temple of the Most High,
like the rainbow gleaming in splendid clouds;
8 like roses in the days of first fruits,
like lilies by a spring of water,
like a green shoot on Lebanon on a summer day;
9 like fire and incense in the censer,
like a vessel of hammered gold
studded with all kinds of precious stones;
10 like an olive tree laden with fruit,
and like a cypress towering in the clouds.
11 When he put on his glorious robe
and clothed himself in perfect splendor,
when he went up to the holy altar,
he made the court of the sanctuary glorious.

12 When he received the portions from the hands of the priests,
as he stood by the hearth of the altar
with a garland of brothers around him,
he was like a young cedar on Lebanon
surrounded by the trunks of palm trees.
13 All the sons of Aaron in their splendor
held the Lord's offering in their hands
before the whole congregation of Israel.
14 Finishing the service at the altars,[g]
and arranging the offering to the Most High, the Almighty,
15 he held out his hand for the cup
and poured a drink offering of the blood of the grape;
he poured it out at the foot of the altar,
a pleasing odor to the Most High, the king of all.
16 Then the sons of Aaron shouted;
they blew their trumpets of hammered metal;
they sounded a mighty fanfare
as a reminder before the Most High.
17 Then all the people together quickly
fell to the ground on their faces
to worship their Lord,
the Almighty, God Most High.

18 Then the singers praised him with their voices

[a] Other ancient authorities read *people* [b] Heb Syr: Gk *No one has* [c] Heb Syr: Gk adds *the leader of his brothers, the support of the people* [d] Heb: Gk *Shem and Seth were honored by people* [e] Heb Syr: Gk lacks this line. Compare 49.15 [f] Heb: Meaning of Gk uncertain [g] Other ancient authorities read *altar*

in sweet and full-toned melody.[a]
19 And the people of the Lord Most High offered
their prayers before the Merciful One,
until the order of worship of the Lord was ended,
and they completed his ritual.
20 Then Simon[b] came down and raised his hands
over the whole congregation of Israelites,
to pronounce the blessing of the Lord with his lips,
and to glory in his name;
21 and they bowed down in worship a second time,
to receive the blessing from the Most High.
22 And now bless the God of all,
who everywhere works great wonders,
who fosters our growth from birth,
and deals with us according to his mercy.
23 May he give us[c] gladness of heart,
and may there be peace in our[d] days
in Israel, as in the days of old.
24 May he entrust to us his mercy,
and may he deliver us in our[e] days!

25 Two nations my soul detests,
and the third is not even a people:
26 Those who live in Seir,[f] and the Philistines,
and the foolish people that live in Shechem.

27 Instruction in understanding and knowledge
I have written in this book,
Jesus son of Eleazar son of Sirach[g] of Jerusalem,
whose mind poured forth wisdom.
28 Happy are those who concern themselves with these things,
and those who lay them to heart will become wise.
29 For if they put them into practice, they will be equal to anything,
for the fear[h] of the Lord is their path.

Prayer of Jesus Son of Sirach[i]

51 I give you thanks, O Lord and King,
and praise you, O God my Savior.
I give thanks to your name,
2 for you have been my protector and helper
and have delivered me from destruction
and from the trap laid by a slanderous tongue,
from lips that fabricate lies.
In the face of my adversaries
you have been my helper 3 and delivered me,
in the greatness of your mercy and of your name,
from grinding teeth about to devour me,
from the hand of those seeking my life,
from the many troubles I endured,
4 from choking fire on every side,
and from the midst of fire that I had not kindled,
5 from the deep belly of Hades,
from an unclean tongue and lying words—
6 the slander of an unrighteous tongue to the king.
My soul drew near to death,
and my life was on the brink of Hades below.
7 They surrounded me on every side,
and there was no one to help me;
I looked for human assistance,
and there was none.
8 Then I remembered your mercy, O Lord,
and your kindness[j] from of old,
for you rescue those who wait for you
and save them from the hand of their enemies.

[a] Other ancient authorities read *in sweet melody throughout the house* [b] Gk *he* [c] Other ancient authorities read *you* [d] Other ancient authorities read *your* [e] Other ancient authorities read *his* [f] Heb Compare Lat: Gk *on the mountain of Samaria* [g] Heb: Meaning of Gk uncertain [h] Heb: Other ancient authorities read *light* [i] This title is included in the Gk text. [j] Other ancient authorities read *work*

9 And I sent up my prayer from the earth,
and begged for rescue from death.
10 I cried out, "Lord, you are my Father;[a]
do not forsake me in the days of trouble,
when there is no help against the proud.
11 I will praise your name continually,
and will sing hymns of thanksgiving."
My prayer was heard,
12 for you saved me from destruction
and rescued me in time of trouble.
For this reason I thank you and praise you,
and I bless the name of the Lord.

Heb adds:

Give thanks to the LORD, for he is good,
for his steadfast love endures forever;

Give thanks to the God of praises,
for his steadfast love endures forever;

Give thanks to the guardian of Israel,
for his steadfast love endures forever;

Give thanks to him who formed all things,
for his steadfast love endures forever;

Give thanks to the redeemer of Israel,
for his steadfast love endures forever;

Give thanks to him who gathers the dispersed of Israel,
for his steadfast love endures forever;

Give thanks to him who rebuilt his city and his sanctuary,
for his steadfast love endures forever;

Give thanks to him who makes a horn to sprout for the house of David,
for his steadfast love endures forever;

Give thanks to him who has chosen the sons of Zadok to be priests,
for his steadfast love endures forever;

Give thanks to the shield of Abraham,
for his steadfast love endures forever;

Give thanks to the rock of Isaac,
for his steadfast love endures forever;

Give thanks to the mighty one of Jacob,
for his steadfast love endures forever;

Give thanks to him who has chosen Zion,
for his steadfast love endures forever;

Give thanks to the King of the kings of kings,
for his steadfast love endures forever;

He has raised up a horn for his people,
praise for all his loyal ones.

For the children of Israel, the people close to him.
Praise the LORD!

---

13 While I was still young, before I went on my travels,
I sought wisdom openly in my prayer.
14 Before the temple I asked for her,
and I will search for her until the end.

15 From the first blossom to the ripening grape
my heart delighted in her;
my foot walked on the straight path;
from my youth I followed her steps.

16 I inclined my ear a little and received her,
and I found for myself much instruction.
17 I made progress in her;
to him who gives wisdom I will give glory.

18 For I resolved to live according to wisdom,[b]
and I was zealous for the good,
and I shall never be disappointed.
19 My soul grappled with wisdom,[b]
and in my conduct I was strict;[c]

[a] Heb: Gk *the Father of my lord* [b] Gk *her* [c] Meaning of Gk uncertain

I spread out my hands to the heavens,
and lamented my ignorance of her.
20 I directed my soul to her,
and in purity I found her.
With her I gained understanding from the first;
therefore I will never be forsaken.
21 My heart was stirred to seek her;
therefore I have gained a prize possession.
22 The Lord gave me my tongue as a reward,
and I will praise him with it.

23 Draw near to me, you who are uneducated,
and lodge in the house of instruction.
24 Why do you say you are lacking in these things,[a]
and why do you endure such great thirst?
25 I opened my mouth and said,
Acquire wisdom[b] for yourselves without money.
26 Put your neck under her[c] yoke,
and let your souls receive instruction;
it is to be found close by.
27 See with your own eyes that I have labored but little
and found for myself much serenity.
28 Hear but a little of my instruction,
and through me you will acquire silver and gold.[d]

29 May your soul rejoice in God's[e] mercy,
and may you never be ashamed to praise him.
30 Do your work in good time,
and in his own time God[f] will give you your reward.

[a] Cn Compare Heb Syr: Meaning of Gk uncertain [b] Heb: Gk lacks *wisdom* [c] Heb: other ancient authorities read *the* [d] Syr Compare Heb: Gk *Get instruction with a large sum of silver, and you will gain by it much gold.* [e] Gk *his* [f] Gk *he*

Baruch

IN TIMES OF PERSECUTION AND DISTRESS, people look for hope. They want to remember that other people have previously survived calamity. They need to know that even though their community and its leaders have sinned and broken covenant with God, God does not and will not abandon God's people.

The book of Baruch first recalls the year 597 BCE (1:1-14). Baruch, who had been the friend and scribe of the prophet Jeremiah, was, we are told, now with the exiles in Babylon. Learning of the destruction of Jerusalem, Baruch sought to console and lead the people to confess their sins. After he read his book to King Jeconiah (called Coniah in Jer 22:24, 28 and by his royal name, Jehoiachin, in 2 Kgs 24:6) and to the rest of the exiles, the people wept, fasted, and prayed. Then they sent Baruch with his book, temple vessels, and other offerings to Jerusalem. The confession of sins of the exiles in Babylon (1:15—2:10) is similar to one found in Daniel 9; both are based in a Deuteronomic theology. Then comes a heartfelt prayer for deliverance (2:11-26), followed by a recollection of God's promise to restore and "make an everlasting covenant" with "my people" (2:27-35), and concluding with further prayer to the eternal God of mercy and might (3:1-8).

The second major section of the book (3:9—4:4) is a poetic praise of Wisdom and contemplation of her ways. While at first glance this may seem an interpolation into the book of Baruch, it was chosen to be an integral part of his message, again using language and themes found elsewhere in Scripture. The people are in the mess they are in because they have failed to follow the ways of Wisdom that are, indeed, God's ways and those of Torah (see Sirach 24). Although the fullness of Wisdom is mysterious, and God's ways can never be fully known (see Job 28), those who seek to follow Wisdom will find life and peace (see also Proverbs 1–7).

In its third and final section, the book of Baruch concludes (4:5—5:9) with words of encouragement and promise not unlike the prophetic hope offered in Isaiah 40–66. In four odes—each beginning "Take courage!"—and a psalm (much like Psalm 11 in the *Psalms of Solomon*), we hear that, yes, Israel has sinned, but a new day is coming. Through the prophet, and in the voice of mother Zion, God tells of deliverance and the end of exile. "Take courage.... Arise.... Look towards the east, O Jerusalem.... Take off the garment of your sorrow and affliction.... [E]very high mountain and the everlasting hills [will] be made low and the valleys filled up.... God will lead Israel with joy in the light of his glory" (4:30—5:9).

Now fast-forward to a time around the year 167 BCE, shortly after Antiochus IV came roaring out of Syria with his strong army, sacking Jerusalem, despoiling the temple, and forbidding the worship of the Lord and study of Torah. Once again God's ways and Wisdom may seem mysterious, but again there may be hope, and God's promises can be heard. Perhaps it was in this decade, or during some other time of difficulty and challenge, that the author of Baruch brought some disparate writings together into a message, similar in several ways to the overall message of the prophet Jeremiah, that speaks to oppressed people in every time and circumstance.

As a white, well-educated male who has been a university dean of chapel and professor, a divinity school professor and head, and a bishop, I have had to learn the ways that I am a person of considerable privilege. I have had to learn the "hermeneutics of suspicion" and how to try to listen to the voices of many others when interpreting Scripture. Baruch writes, "Take courage!" Those who confess their sins and trust again in God's ways and Wisdom will know a God of restoration, deliverance, and everlasting promise.

*— **Frederick Houk Borsch***

1 These are the words of the book that Baruch
son of Neriah son of Mahseiah son of Zedekiah son of Hasadiah son of Hilkiah wrote in
Babylon, 2in the fifth year, on the seventh day of
the month, at the time when the Chaldeans took
Jerusalem and burned it with fire.

3 Baruch read the words of this book to Jeconiah son of Jehoiakim, king of Judah, and to all
the people who came to hear the book, 4and to
the nobles and the princes, and to the elders, and
to all the people, small and great, all who lived in
Babylon by the river Sud.

5 Then they wept, and fasted, and prayed before the Lord; 6they collected as much money
as each could give, 7and sent it to Jerusalem to
the high priest[a] Jehoiakim son of Hilkiah son of
Shallum, and to the priests, and to all the people who were present with him in Jerusalem. 8At
the same time, on the tenth day of Sivan, Baruch[b] took the vessels of the house of the Lord,
which had been carried away from the temple, to
return them to the land of Judah—the silver vessels that Zedekiah son of Josiah, king of Judah,
had made, 9after King Nebuchadnezzar of Babylon had carried away from Jerusalem Jeconiah
and the princes and the prisoners and the nobles
and the people of the land, and brought them to
Babylon.

10 They said: Here we send you money; so
buy with the money burnt offerings and sin offerings and incense, and prepare a grain offering, and
offer them on the altar of the Lord our God; 11and
pray for the life of King Nebuchadnezzar of Babylon, and for the life of his son Belshazzar, so that
their days on earth may be like the days of heaven.
12The Lord will give us strength, and light to our
eyes; we shall live under the protection[c] of King
Nebuchadnezzar of Babylon, and under the protection of his son Belshazzar, and we shall serve
them many days and find favor in their sight.
13Pray also for us to the Lord our God, for we
have sinned against the Lord our God, and to this
day the anger of the Lord and his wrath have not
turned away from us. 14And you shall read aloud
this scroll that we are sending you, to make your
confession in the house of the Lord on the days of
the festivals and at appointed seasons.

15 And you shall say: The Lord our God is in
the right, but there is open shame on us today, on
the people of Judah, on the inhabitants of Jerusalem, 16and on our kings, our rulers, our priests,
our prophets, and our ancestors, 17because we

[a] Gk *the priest* [b] Gk *he* [c] Gk *in the shadow*

have sinned before the Lord. 18We have disobeyed him, and have not heeded the voice of the
Lord our God, to walk in the statutes of the Lord
that he set before us. 19From the time when the
Lord brought our ancestors out of the land of
Egypt until today, we have been disobedient to
the Lord our God, and we have been negligent, in
not heeding his voice. 20So to this day there have
clung to us the calamities and the curse that the
Lord declared through his servant Moses at the
time when he brought our ancestors out of
the land of Egypt to give to us a land flowing with
milk and honey. 21We did not listen to the voice
of the Lord our God in all the words of the prophets whom he sent to us, 22but all of us followed
the intent of our own wicked hearts by serving
other gods and doing what is evil in the sight of
the Lord our God.

2 So the Lord carried out the threat he spoke
against us: against our judges who ruled Israel, and against our kings and our rulers and the
people of Israel and Judah. 2Under the whole
heaven there has not been done the like of what
he has done in Jerusalem, in accordance with the
threats that were[a] written in the law of Moses.
3Some of us ate the flesh of their sons and others
the flesh of their daughters. 4He made them subject to all the kingdoms around us, to be an object
of scorn and a desolation among all the surrounding peoples, where the Lord has scattered them.
5They were brought down and not raised up,
because our nation[b] sinned against the Lord our
God, in not heeding his voice.

6 The Lord our God is in the right, but there
is open shame on us and our ancestors this very
day. 7All those calamities with which the Lord
threatened us have come upon us. 8Yet we have
not entreated the favor of the Lord by turning
away, each of us, from the thoughts of our wicked
hearts. 9And the Lord has kept the calamities
ready, and the Lord has brought them upon us,
for the Lord is just in all the works that he has
commanded us to do. 10Yet we have not obeyed
his voice, to walk in the statutes of the Lord that
he set before us.

11 And now, O Lord God of Israel, who
brought your people out of the land of Egypt
with a mighty hand and with signs and wonders
and with great power and outstretched arm, and
made yourself a name that continues to this day,
12we have sinned, we have been ungodly, we have
done wrong, O Lord our God, against all your
ordinances. 13Let your anger turn away from us,
for we are left, few in number, among the nations
where you have scattered us. 14Hear, O Lord, our
prayer and our supplication, and for your own
sake deliver us, and grant us favor in the sight of
those who have carried us into exile; 15so that all
the earth may know that you are the Lord our
God, for Israel and his descendants are called by
your name.

16 O Lord, look down from your holy dwelling, and consider us. Incline your ear, O Lord,
and hear; 17open your eyes, O Lord, and see, for
the dead who are in Hades, whose spirit has been
taken from their bodies, will not ascribe glory
or justice to the Lord; 18but the person who is
deeply grieved, who walks bowed and feeble,
with failing eyes and famished soul, will declare
your glory and righteousness, O Lord.

19 For it is not because of any righteous deeds
of our ancestors or our kings that we bring before
you our prayer for mercy, O Lord our God. 20For
you have sent your anger and your wrath upon
us, as you declared by your servants the prophets,
saying: 21Thus says the Lord: Bend your shoulders and serve the king of Babylon, and you will
remain in the land that I gave to your ancestors.
22But if you will not obey the voice of the Lord
and will not serve the king of Babylon, 23I will
make to cease from the towns of Judah and from
the region around Jerusalem the voice of mirth
and the voice of gladness, the voice of the bridegroom and the voice of the bride, and the whole
land will be a desolation without inhabitants.

24 But we did not obey your voice, to serve
the king of Babylon; and you have carried out
your threats, which you spoke by your servants
the prophets, that the bones of our kings and the
bones of our ancestors would be brought out of

[a] Gk *in accordance with what is* [b] Gk *because we*

their resting place; 25 and indeed they have been
thrown out to the heat of day and the frost of
night. They perished in great misery, by famine
and sword and pestilence. 26 And the house that is
called by your name you have made as it is today,
because of the wickedness of the house of Israel
and the house of Judah.

27 Yet you have dealt with us, O Lord our
God, in all your kindness and in all your great
compassion, 28 as you spoke by your servant Moses on the day when you commanded him to
write your law in the presence of the people of Israel, saying, 29 "If you will not obey my voice, this
very great multitude will surely turn into a small
number among the nations, where I will scatter
them. 30 For I know that they will not obey me,
for they are a stiff-necked people. But in the land
of their exile they will come to themselves 31 and
know that I am the Lord their God. I will give
them a heart that obeys and ears that hear; 32 they
will praise me in the land of their exile, and will
remember my name 33 and turn from their stubbornness and their wicked deeds; for they will remember the ways of their ancestors, who sinned
before the Lord. 34 I will bring them again into
the land that I swore to give to their ancestors, to
Abraham, Isaac, and Jacob, and they will rule over
it; and I will increase them, and they will not be
diminished. 35 I will make an everlasting covenant
with them to be their God and they shall be my
people; and I will never again remove my people
Israel from the land that I have given them."

3 O Lord Almighty, God of Israel, the soul
in anguish and the wearied spirit cry out
to you. 2 Hear, O Lord, and have mercy, for we
have sinned before you. 3 For you are enthroned
forever, and we are perishing forever. 4 O Lord
Almighty, God of Israel, hear now the prayer of
the people[a] of Israel, the children of those who
sinned before you, who did not heed the voice
of the Lord their God, so that calamities have
clung to us. 5 Do not remember the iniquities of
our ancestors, but in this crisis remember your
power and your name. 6 For you are the Lord our
God, and it is you, O Lord, whom we will praise.
7 For you have put the fear of you in our hearts so
that we would call upon your name; and we will
praise you in our exile, for we have put away from
our hearts all the iniquity of our ancestors who
sinned against you. 8 See, we are today in our exile where you have scattered us, to be reproached
and cursed and punished for all the iniquities of
our ancestors, who forsook the Lord our God.

9 Hear the commandments of life, O Israel;
give ear, and learn wisdom!
10 Why is it, O Israel, why is it that you are in
the land of your enemies,
that you are growing old in a foreign
country,
that you are defiled with the dead,
11 that you are counted among those in
Hades?
12 You have forsaken the fountain of wisdom.
13 If you had walked in the way of God,
you would be living in peace forever.
14 Learn where there is wisdom,
where there is strength,
where there is understanding,
so that you may at the same time discern
where there is length of days, and life,
where there is light for the eyes, and peace.
15 Who has found her place?
And who has entered her storehouses?
16 Where are the rulers of the nations,
and those who lorded it over the animals
on earth;
17 those who made sport of the birds of the air,
and who hoarded up silver and gold
in which people trust,
and there is no end to their getting;
18 those who schemed to get silver, and were
anxious,
but there is no trace of their works?
19 They have vanished and gone down to Hades,
and others have arisen in their place.
20 Later generations have seen the light of day,
and have lived upon the earth;

[a] Gk *dead*

but they have not learned the way to
knowledge,
nor understood her paths,
nor laid hold of her.
21 Their descendants have strayed far from her[a]
way.
22 She has not been heard of in Canaan,
or seen in Teman;
23 the descendants of Hagar, who seek for
understanding on the earth,
the merchants of Merran and Teman,
the story-tellers and the seekers for
understanding,
have not learned the way to wisdom,
or given thought to her paths.

24 O Israel, how great is the house of God,
how vast the territory that he possesses!
25 It is great and has no bounds;
it is high and immeasurable.
26 The giants were born there, who were famous
of old,
great in stature, expert in war.
27 God did not choose them,
or give them the way to knowledge;
28 so they perished because they had no
wisdom,
they perished through their folly.

29 Who has gone up into heaven, and taken
her,
and brought her down from the clouds?
30 Who has gone over the sea, and found her,
and will buy her for pure gold?
31 No one knows the way to her,
or is concerned about the path to her.
32 But the one who knows all things knows her,
he found her by his understanding.
The one who prepared the earth for all time
filled it with four-footed creatures;
33 the one who sends forth the light, and it
goes;
he called it, and it obeyed him, trembling;
34 the stars shone in their watches, and were
glad;
he called them, and they said, "Here we
are!"
They shone with gladness for him who
made them.
35 This is our God;
no other can be compared to him.
36 He found the whole way to knowledge,
and gave her to his servant Jacob
and to Israel, whom he loved.
37 Afterward she appeared on earth
and lived with humankind.

4 She is the book of the commandments of
God,
the law that endures forever.
All who hold her fast will live,
and those who forsake her will die.
2 Turn, O Jacob, and take her;
walk toward the shining of her light.
3 Do not give your glory to another,
or your advantages to an alien people.
4 Happy are we, O Israel,
for we know what is pleasing to God.

5 Take courage, my people,
who perpetuate Israel's name!
6 It was not for destruction
that you were sold to the nations,
but you were handed over to your enemies
because you angered God.
7 For you provoked the one who made you
by sacrificing to demons and not to God.
8 You forgot the everlasting God, who brought
you up,
and you grieved Jerusalem, who reared
you.
9 For she saw the wrath that came upon you
from God,
and she said:
Listen, you neighbors of Zion,
God has brought great sorrow upon me;
10 for I have seen the exile of my sons and
daughters,
which the Everlasting brought upon them.
11 With joy I nurtured them,

[a] Other ancient authorities read *their*

but I sent them away with weeping and
sorrow.
12 Let no one rejoice over me, a widow
and bereaved of many;
I was left desolate because of the sins of my
children,
because they turned away from the law of
God.
13 They had no regard for his statutes;
they did not walk in the ways of God's
commandments,
or tread the paths his righteousness
showed them.
14 Let the neighbors of Zion come;
remember the capture of my sons and
daughters,
which the Everlasting brought upon them.
15 For he brought a distant nation against them,
a nation ruthless and of a strange language,
which had no respect for the aged
and no pity for a child.
16 They led away the widow's beloved sons,
and bereaved the lonely woman of her
daughters.

17 But I, how can I help you?
18 For he who brought these calamities upon
you
will deliver you from the hand of your
enemies.
19 Go, my children, go;
for I have been left desolate.
20 I have taken off the robe of peace
and put on sackcloth for my supplication;
I will cry to the Everlasting all my days.

21 Take courage, my children, cry to God,
and he will deliver you from the power and
hand of the enemy.
22 For I have put my hope in the Everlasting to
save you,
and joy has come to me from the Holy
One,
because of the mercy that will soon come to
you
from your everlasting savior.[a]
23 For I sent you out with sorrow and weeping,
but God will give you back to me with joy
and gladness forever.
24 For as the neighbors of Zion have now seen
your capture,
so they soon will see your salvation by God,
which will come to you with great glory
and with the splendor of the Everlasting.
25 My children, endure with patience the wrath
that has come upon you from God.
Your enemy has overtaken you,
but you will soon see their destruction
and will tread upon their necks.
26 My pampered children have traveled rough
roads;
they were taken away like a flock carried
off by the enemy.

27 Take courage, my children, and cry to God,
for you will be remembered by the one
who brought this upon you.
28 For just as you were disposed to go astray
from God,
return with tenfold zeal to seek him.
29 For the one who brought these calamities
upon you
will bring you everlasting joy with your
salvation.

30 Take courage, O Jerusalem,
for the one who named you will comfort
you.
31 Wretched will be those who mistreated you
and who rejoiced at your fall.
32 Wretched will be the cities that your children
served as slaves;
wretched will be the city that received
your offspring.
33 For just as she rejoiced at your fall
and was glad for your ruin,
so she will be grieved at her own
desolation.
34 I will take away her pride in her great
population,

[a] Or *from the Everlasting, your savior*

and her insolence will be turned to grief.
35 For fire will come upon her from the
Everlasting for many days,
and for a long time she will be inhabited
by demons.

36 Look toward the east, O Jerusalem,
and see the joy that is coming to you from
God.
37 Look, your children are coming, whom you
sent away;
they are coming, gathered from east and
west,
at the word of the Holy One,
rejoicing in the glory of God.

5 Take off the garment of your sorrow and
affliction, O Jerusalem,
and put on forever the beauty of the glory
from God.
2 Put on the robe of the righteousness that
comes from God;
put on your head the diadem of the glory
of the Everlasting;
3 for God will show your splendor everywhere
under heaven.
4 For God will give you evermore the name,
"Righteous Peace, Godly Glory."

5 Arise, O Jerusalem, stand upon the height;
look toward the east,
and see your children gathered from west and
east
at the word of the Holy One,
rejoicing that God has remembered them.
6 For they went out from you on foot,
led away by their enemies;
but God will bring them back to you,
carried in glory, as on a royal throne.
7 For God has ordered that every high
mountain and the everlasting hills be
made low
and the valleys filled up, to make level
ground,
so that Israel may walk safely in the glory
of God.
8 The woods and every fragrant tree
have shaded Israel at God's command.
9 For God will lead Israel with joy,
in the light of his glory,
with the mercy and righteousness that
come from him.

The Letter of Jeremiah

The Letter of Jeremiah, a warning against idol worship, was perhaps first drafted in the fourth century BCE. It claims to be a letter from Jeremiah and bears resemblance to similar warnings found in Jer 10:2-16. The letter's first verses recall Jer 29:1-23, which advises that the exile in Babylon will last a long time (seventy years), but the letter now extends that time to "up to seven generations" (v. 3). A further historical link is made by reference (vv. 2-4) to the "gods made of silver and gold and wood" that the Jewish exiles will see being carried about in Babylon. The first nine warnings in the letter end in a refrain asking why anyone would think idols are gods, or declaring that "they are not gods; so do not fear them." Probably written originally in Hebrew or Aramaic, the letter likely received alteration and amendment during several centuries. A Greek version is found in the Dead Sea Scrolls.

In early Greek manuscripts the letter of Jeremiah was placed as a separate writing following the books of Baruch and Lamentations and in this manner was linked to the book of Jeremiah (there was a tradition that Jeremiah was also the author of Lamentations). Its scriptural placement, however, has never been secure, and in the Latin Vulgate and then in the King James Version of the Bible the "Letter of Jeremy" is attached to the book of Baruch as chapter 6.

While valued for its reinforcement of the dangers of idolatry, the argument is a rehearsal of the warnings found in other biblical passages (Ps 115:1-8; Isa 44:9-20; 46:1-12, 5-7). The popularity of such admonitions can also be seen in the Greek version of Daniel, the story of Bel and the Dragon, and is found in later legends, both Jewish and Muslim. Such parodies were in one sense easy to make. Lifeless idols are helpless; they cannot defend themselves. They cannot even wipe away the dust and soot that gets in their eyes and on their faces. They have to be carried about. More important, they cannot bring healing or wealth. However, one might at least sympathize with desperate people who pray to idols of one form or another. Foolish it may be, but humans often display a tendency to domesticate their deities and try to gain some power over their favors by paying obeisance, whether the idols be made of wood, stone, or precious metals or are other representations of the powers of this world.

Jesus warned that one cannot serve God and the god "Mammon" or wealth. We may want to laugh, but there are those today who demonstrate a near-religious reverence for obedience to, for example, the "invisible hand" of market forces that goes beyond mere economic theory, or call for obeisance to a flag or another symbol that goes beyond true patriotism. Seen in this light, the people of God perhaps always need something like the satire and ridicule of lifeless idols

that we encounter here as reminders of their call to worship and serve the living God of justice and mercy.

As a white male who has enjoyed considerable privilege, I hear behind all such warnings the second of the commandments in the Decalogue: "You shall not make for yourself an idol, whether in the form of anything that is in heaven above, or that is on the earth beneath, or that is in the water under the earth. You shall not bow down to them or worship them" (Exod 20:3-5; Deut 5:7-9).

— ***Frederick Houk Borsch***

6[a] A copy of a letter that Jeremiah sent to those
who were to be taken to Babylon as exiles
by the king of the Babylonians, to give them the
message that God had commanded him.
2 Because of the sins that you have committed
before God, you will be taken to Babylon as exiles by Nebuchadnezzar, king of the Babylonians.
3 Therefore when you have come to Babylon you
will remain there for many years, for a long time,
up to seven generations; after that I will bring you
away from there in peace. 4 Now in Babylon you
will see gods made of silver and gold and wood,
which people carry on their shoulders, and which
cause the heathen to fear. 5 So beware of becoming at all like the foreigners or of letting fear for
these gods[b] possess you 6 when you see the multitude before and behind them worshiping them.
But say in your heart, "It is you, O Lord, whom
we must worship." 7 For my angel is with you, and
he is watching over your lives.
8 Their tongues are smoothed by the carpenter, and they themselves are overlaid with gold
and silver; but they are false and cannot speak.
9 People[c] take gold and make crowns for the heads
of their gods, as they might for a girl who loves
ornaments. 10 Sometimes the priests secretly take
gold and silver from their gods and spend it on
themselves, 11 or even give some of it to the prostitutes on the terrace. They deck their gods[d] out
with garments like human beings—these gods
of silver and gold and wood 12 that cannot save
themselves from rust and corrosion. When they
have been dressed in purple robes, 13 their faces
are wiped because of the dust from the temple,
which is thick upon them. 14 One of them holds a
scepter, like a district judge, but is unable to destroy anyone who offends it. 15 Another has a dag-
ger in its right hand, and an ax, but cannot defend
itself from war and robbers. 16 From this it is evident that they are not gods; so do not fear them.
17 For just as someone's dish is useless when
it is broken, 18 so are their gods when they have
been set up in the temples. Their eyes are full of
the dust raised by the feet of those who enter.
And just as the gates are shut on every side against
anyone who has offended a king, as though under
sentence of death, so the priests make their temples secure with doors and locks and bars, in order that they may not be plundered by robbers.
19 They light more lamps for them than they light
for themselves, though their gods[e] can see none
of them. 20 They are[f] just like a beam of the temple, but their hearts, it is said, are eaten away
when crawling creatures from the earth devour

[a] The King James Version (like the Latin Vulgate) prints The Letter of Jeremiah as Chapter 6 of the Book of Baruch, and the chapter and verse numbers are here retained. In the Greek Septuagint, the Letter is separated from Baruch by the Book of Lamentations. [b] Gk *for them* [c] Gk *They* [d] Gk *them* [e] Gk *they* [f] Gk *It is*

them and their robes. They do not notice 21when
their faces have been blackened by the smoke
of the temple. 22Bats, swallows, and birds alight
on their bodies and heads; and so do cats. 23From
this you will know that they are not gods; so do
not fear them.

24 As for the gold that they wear for beauty—
it[a] will not shine unless someone wipes off the
tarnish; for even when they were being cast, they
did not feel it. 25They are bought without regard
to cost, but there is no breath in them. 26Having
no feet, they are carried on the shoulders of others, revealing to humankind their worthlessness.
And those who serve them are put to shame 27because, if any of these gods falls[b] to the ground,
they themselves must pick it up. If anyone sets it
upright, it cannot move itself; and if it is tipped
over, it cannot straighten itself. Gifts are placed
before them just as before the dead. 28The priests
sell the sacrifices that are offered to these gods[c]
and use the money themselves. Likewise their
wives preserve some of the meat[d] with salt, but
give none to the poor or helpless. 29Sacrifices to
them may even be touched by women in their periods or at childbirth. Since you know by these
things that they are not gods, do not fear them.

30 For how can they be called gods? Women
serve meals for gods of silver and gold and wood;
31and in their temples the priests sit with their
clothes torn, their heads and beards shaved, and
their heads uncovered. 32They howl and shout
before their gods as some do at a funeral banquet. 33The priests take some of the clothing of
their gods[e] to clothe their wives and children.
34Whether one does evil to them or good, they
will not be able to repay it. They cannot set up a
king or depose one. 35Likewise they are not able
to give either wealth or money; if one makes a
vow to them and does not keep it, they will not
require it. 36They cannot save anyone from death
or rescue the weak from the strong. 37They cannot restore sight to the blind; they cannot rescue
one who is in distress. 38They cannot take pity
on a widow or do good to an orphan. 39These
things that are made of wood and overlaid with
gold and silver are like stones from the mountain,
and those who serve them will be put to shame.
40Why then must anyone think that they are
gods, or call them gods?

Besides, even the Chaldeans themselves dishonor them; for when they see someone who cannot speak, they bring Bel and pray that the mute
may speak, as though Bel[f] were able to understand! 41Yet they themselves cannot perceive this
and abandon them, for they have no sense. 42And
the women, with cords around them, sit along the
passageways, burning bran for incense. 43When
one of them is led off by one of the passersby and is taken to bed by him, she derides the
woman next to her, because she was not as attractive as herself and her cord was not broken.
44Whatever is done for these idols[g] is false. Why
then must anyone think that they are gods, or call
them gods?

45 They are made by carpenters and goldsmiths; they can be nothing but what the artisans
wish them to be. 46Those who make them will
certainly not live very long themselves; 47how
then can the things that are made by them be
gods? They have left only lies and reproach for
those who come after. 48For when war or calamity comes upon them, the priests consult together
as to where they can hide themselves and their
gods.[g] 49How then can one fail to see that these
are not gods, for they cannot save themselves
from war or calamity? 50Since they are made of
wood and overlaid with gold and silver, it will afterward be known that they are false. 51It will be
manifest to all the nations and kings that they are
not gods but the work of human hands, and that
there is no work of God in them. 52Who then can
fail to know that they are not gods?[h]

53 For they cannot set up a king over a country or give rain to people. 54They cannot judge
their own cause or deliver one who is wronged,
for they have no power; 55they are like crows between heaven and earth. When fire breaks out in
a temple of wooden gods overlaid with gold or

[a] Lat Syr: Gk *they* [b] Gk *if they fall* [c] Gk *to them* [d] Gk *of them* [e] Gk *some of their clothing* [f] Gk *he*
[g] Gk *them* [h] Meaning of Gk uncertain

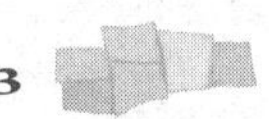

silver, their priests will flee and escape, but the
gods[a] will be burned up like timbers. 56 Besides,
they can offer no resistance to king or enemy.
Why then must anyone admit or think that they
are gods?

57 Gods made of wood and overlaid with silver and gold are unable to save themselves from
thieves or robbers. 58 Anyone who can will strip
them of their gold and silver and of the robes they
wear, and go off with this booty, and they will not
be able to help themselves. 59 So it is better to be a
king who shows his courage, or a household uten-
sil that serves its owner's need, than to be these
false gods; better even the door of a house that
protects its contents, than these false gods; better
also a wooden pillar in a palace, than these false
gods.

60 For sun and moon and stars are bright,
and when sent to do a service, they are obedient.
61 So also the lightning, when it flashes, is widely
seen; and the wind likewise blows in every land.
62 When God commands the clouds to go over the
whole world, they carry out his command. 63 And
the fire sent from above to consume mountains
and woods does what it is ordered. But these
idols[b] are not to be compared with them in appearance or power. 64 Therefore one must not
think that they are gods, nor call them gods, for
they are not able either to decide a case or to do
good to anyone. 65 Since you know then that they
are not gods, do not fear them.

66 They can neither curse nor bless kings;
67 they cannot show signs in the heavens for the
nations, or shine like the sun or give light like the
moon. 68 The wild animals are better than they
are, for they can flee to shelter and help themselves. 69 So we have no evidence whatever that
they are gods; therefore do not fear them.

70 Like a scarecrow in a cucumber bed, which
guards nothing, so are their gods of wood, overlaid with gold and silver. 71 In the same way, their
gods of wood, overlaid with gold and silver, are
like a thornbush in a garden on which every bird
perches; or like a corpse thrown out in the darkness. 72 From the purple and linen[c] that rot upon
them you will know that they are not gods; and
they will finally be consumed themselves, and
be a reproach in the land. 73 Better, therefore, is
someone upright who has no idols; such a person
will be far above reproach.

[a] Gk *they* [b] Gk *these things* [c] Cn: Gk *marble*, Syr *silk*

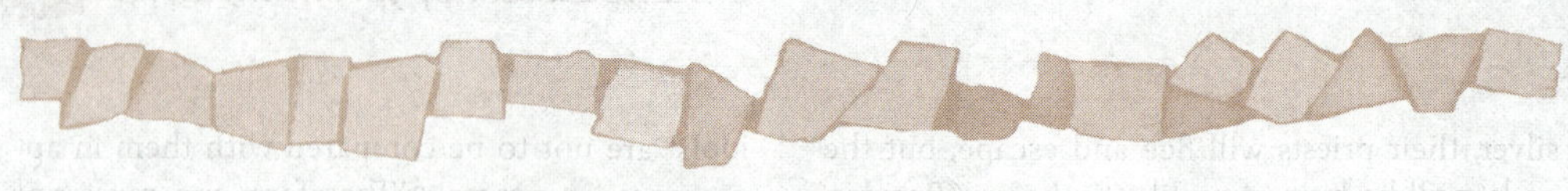

The Prayer of Azariah and the Song of the Three Jews

THE GREEK VERSION OF DANIEL preserved in the Septuagint provides a fuller, richer account of the events found in the Hebrew version of Daniel. In many ways, the Greek version answers questions left unanswered by the Hebrew text, even when those questions are not apparent.

The character Daniel is a revered sage whose exploits were known to Greek and Hebrew writers long before the composition of either version of scripture (see Ezek 28:3, "are you wiser than Daniel?"). The earliest stories of Daniel, known as *Dnil* and *Danel* in other Semitic literature, date from more than a thousand years before the setting of the stories about Daniel recounted in the Hebrew and Greek Scriptures. Because Daniel was a revered figure (in Ezek 14:14 he is listed as one of the righteous generation of Noah and Job), stories about Daniel abounded in the Ancient Near East. A number of those stories are preserved in the Greek version of Daniel.

Two units of Greek scripture not present in the Hebrew book of Daniel are prayer hymns: The Prayer of Azariah and the Song of the Three Jews. These prayers are set in the scene in which Nebuchadnezzar throws the renamed Hananiah (Shadrach), Mishael (Meshach) and Azariah (Aved-Nego) into the fiery furnace for refusing to worship him.

In 3:23 the three Hebrew boys are thrown into the fiery furnace. The Greek account tells us what happens next. Azariah, whose name is usually listed last indicating that he has the least status (perhaps he is the youngest, or the smallest), prays for twenty-one verses. His prayer is a prayer of confession on behalf of his nation: it is because of their corporate sin that they have been deported. In the Greek version (3:46), it is in response to Azariah's prayer that the furnace is heated seven times hotter than usual. It is also in response to Azariah's prayer that God's angel joins them in the fire and "made the inside of the furnace as if a moist breeze were whistling through" (3:49-50). In response to their divine deliverance, the three of them sing praises to God together, calling on all creation to join them in verses 52-90.

After the young men finish their song, Nebuchadnezzar sees a divine presence in the fire and discovers that Hananiah, Mishael, and Azariah are untouched by the flames. The Hebrew and Greek texts merge after the hymn, with 3:24-30 in Hebrew corresponding to 3:91-97 in Greek.

— ***Wilda C. Gafney***

(Additions to Daniel, inserted between 3.23 and 3.24)

1 They[a] walked around in the midst of the
flames, singing hymns to God and blessing the
Lord. 2 Then Azariah stood still in the fire and
prayed aloud:

3 "Blessed are you, O Lord, God of our
ancestors, and worthy of praise;
and glorious is your name forever!
4 For you are just in all you have done;
all your works are true and your ways
right,
and all your judgments are true.
5 You have executed true judgments in all you
have brought upon us
and upon Jerusalem, the holy city of our
ancestors;
by a true judgment you have brought all
this upon us because of our sins.
6 For we have sinned and broken your law in
turning away from you;
in all matters we have sinned grievously.
7 We have not obeyed your commandments,
we have not kept them or done what you
have commanded us for our own
good.
8 So all that you have brought upon us,
and all that you have done to us,
you have done by a true judgment.
9 You have handed us over to our enemies,
lawless and hateful rebels,
and to an unjust king, the most wicked in
all the world.
10 And now we cannot open our mouths;
we, your servants who worship you, have
become a shame and a reproach.
11 For your name's sake do not give us up
forever,
and do not annul your covenant.
12 Do not withdraw your mercy from us,
for the sake of Abraham your beloved
and for the sake of your servant Isaac
and Israel your holy one,
13 to whom you promised
to multiply their descendants like the stars
of heaven
and like the sand on the shore of the sea.
14 For we, O Lord, have become fewer than any
other nation,
and are brought low this day in all the
world because of our sins.
15 In our day we have no ruler, or prophet, or
leader,
no burnt offering, or sacrifice, or oblation,
or incense,
no place to make an offering before you
and to find mercy.
16 Yet with a contrite heart and a humble spirit
may we be accepted,
17 as though it were with burnt offerings of
rams and bulls,
or with tens of thousands of fat lambs;
such may our sacrifice be in your sight
today,
and may we unreservedly follow you,[b]
for no shame will come to those who trust
in you.
18 And now with all our heart we follow you;
we fear you and seek your presence.
19 Do not put us to shame,
but deal with us in your patience
and in your abundant mercy.
20 Deliver us in accordance with your marvelous
works,
and bring glory to your name, O Lord.
21 Let all who do harm to your servants be put
to shame;
let them be disgraced and deprived of all
power,
and let their strength be broken.
22 Let them know that you alone are the Lord
God,
glorious over the whole world."

23 Now the king's servants who threw them
in kept stoking the furnace with naphtha, pitch,
tow, and brushwood. 24 And the flames poured
out above the furnace forty-nine cubits, 25 and

[a] That is, Hananiah, Mishael, and Azariah (Dan 2.17), the original names of Shadrach, Meshach, and Abednego (Dan 1.6–7)
[b] Meaning of Gk uncertain

spread out and burned those Chaldeans who
were caught near the furnace. 26 But the angel of
the Lord came down into the furnace to be with
Azariah and his companions, and drove the fiery
flame out of the furnace, 27 and made the inside
of the furnace as though a moist wind were whistling through it. The fire did not touch them at all
and caused them no pain or distress.

28 Then the three with one voice praised and
glorified and blessed God in the furnace:

29 "Blessed are you, O Lord, God of our
ancestors,
and to be praised and highly exalted
forever;
30 And blessed is your glorious, holy name,
and to be highly praised and highly exalted
forever.
31 Blessed are you in the temple of your holy
glory,
and to be extolled and highly glorified
forever.
32 Blessed are you who look into the depths
from your throne on the cherubim,
and to be praised and highly exalted
forever.
33 Blessed are you on the throne of your
kingdom,
and to be extolled and highly exalted
forever.
34 Blessed are you in the firmament of heaven,
and to be sung and glorified forever.

35 "Bless the Lord, all you works of the Lord;
sing praise to him and highly exalt him
forever.
36 Bless the Lord, you heavens;
sing praise to him and highly exalt him
forever.
37 Bless the Lord, you angels of the Lord;
sing praise to him and highly exalt him
forever.
38 Bless the Lord, all you waters above the
heavens;
sing praise to him and highly exalt him
forever.
39 Bless the Lord, all you powers of the
Lord;
sing praise to him and highly exalt him
forever.
40 Bless the Lord, sun and moon;
sing praise to him and highly exalt him
forever.
41 Bless the Lord, stars of heaven;
sing praise to him and highly exalt him
forever.

42 "Bless the Lord, all rain and dew;
sing praise to him and highly exalt him
forever.
43 Bless the Lord, all you winds;
sing praise to him and highly exalt him
forever.
44 Bless the Lord, fire and heat;
sing praise to him and highly exalt him
forever.
45 Bless the Lord, winter cold and summer heat;
sing praise to him and highly exalt him
forever.
46 Bless the Lord, dews and falling snow;
sing praise to him and highly exalt him
forever.
47 Bless the Lord, nights and days;
sing praise to him and highly exalt him
forever.
48 Bless the Lord, light and darkness;
sing praise to him and highly exalt him
forever.
49 Bless the Lord, ice and cold;
sing praise to him and highly exalt him
forever.
50 Bless the Lord, frosts and snows;
sing praise to him and highly exalt him
forever.
51 Bless the Lord, lightnings and clouds;
sing praise to him and highly exalt him
forever.

52 "Let the earth bless the Lord;
let it sing praise to him and highly exalt
him forever.
53 Bless the Lord, mountains and hills;
sing praise to him and highly exalt him
forever.
54 Bless the Lord, all that grows in the ground;

Azariah (Greek Daniel) 3:52

This thirty-eight-verse hymn is a responsive psalm, similar to Psalm 136. Selections from this canticle are used in the Easter Vigil of the Evangelical Lutheran Church of America and in the Daily Office prayer cycle of the Episcopal Church in the United States.

— *WG*

sing praise to him and highly exalt him
forever.
55 Bless the Lord, seas and rivers;
sing praise to him and highly exalt him
forever.
56 Bless the Lord, you springs;
sing praise to him and highly exalt him
forever.
57 Bless the Lord, you whales and all that swim
in the waters;
sing praise to him and highly exalt him
forever.
58 Bless the Lord, all birds of the air;
sing praise to him and highly exalt him
forever.
59 Bless the Lord, all wild animals and cattle;
sing praise to him and highly exalt him
forever.

60 "Bless the Lord, all people on earth;
sing praise to him and highly exalt him
forever.
61 Bless the Lord, O Israel;
sing praise to him and highly exalt him
forever.
62 Bless the Lord, you priests of the Lord;
sing praise to him and highly exalt him
forever.
63 Bless the Lord, you servants of the Lord;
sing praise to him and highly exalt him
forever.
64 Bless the Lord, spirits and souls of the
righteous;
sing praise to him and highly exalt him
forever.
65 Bless the Lord, you who are holy and humble
in heart;
sing praise to him and highly exalt him
forever.

66 "Bless the Lord, Hananiah, Azariah, and
Mishael;
sing praise to him and highly exalt him
forever.
For he has rescued us from Hades and saved
us from the power[a] of death,
and delivered us from the midst of the
burning fiery furnace;
from the midst of the fire he has
delivered us.
67 Give thanks to the Lord, for he is good,
for his mercy endures forever.
68 All who worship the Lord, bless the God of
gods,
sing praise to him and give thanks to him,
for his mercy endures forever."

[a] Gk *hand*

Susanna

(Chapter 13 of the Greek Version of Daniel)

The story of Susanna, now in chapter 13 of the Greek version of the book of Daniel (see the introduction to The Prayer of Azariah and the Song of the Three Jews), both circulated independently of biblical Daniel and as the prologue to the Greek version. In that narrative, a very young Daniel, whose name means either "God is my Judge" or "God's Judge," demonstrates his sagacity by saving the life of a virtuous woman falsely accused of adultery. This story demonstrates that Daniel is a sage from his youth; therefore it is not surprise that he is able to interpret dreams in the later story. Here Daniel separates the two rejected would-be lovers of Susanna and questions them separately. Their stories do not agree, they are proved to be liars, and Susanna is vindicated.

— ***Wilda C. Gafney***

1 There was a man living in Babylon whose
name was Joakim. 2He married the daughter of
Hilkiah, named Susanna, a very beautiful woman
and one who feared the Lord. 3Her parents were
righteous, and had trained their daughter according to the law of Moses. 4Joakim was very rich,
and had a fine garden adjoining his house; the Jews used to come to him because he was the most honored of them all.

5 That year two elders from the people were appointed as judges. Concerning them the Lord had said: "Wickedness came forth from Babylon, from elders who were judges, who were supposed to govern the people."
6These men were
frequently at Joakim's house, and all who had a case to be tried came to them there.

7 When the people left at noon, Susanna would go into her husband's garden to walk.
8Every day the two elders used to see her, going in and walking about, and they began to lust
for her. 9They suppressed their consciences and turned away their eyes from looking to Heaven or remembering their duty to administer justice.
10Both were overwhelmed with passion for her, but they did not tell each other of their distress,
11for they were ashamed to disclose their lustful
desire to seduce her. 12Day after day they watched
eagerly to see her.

13 One day they said to each other, "Let us go home, for it is time for lunch." So they both left
and parted from each other. 14But turning back,
they met again; and when each pressed the other for the reason, they confessed their lust. Then together they arranged for a time when they could find her alone.

15 Once, while they were watching for an opportune day, she went in as before with only two maids, and wished to bathe in the garden, for

it was a hot day. [16]No one was there except the
two elders, who had hidden themselves and were
watching her. [17]She said to her maids, "Bring
me olive oil and ointments, and shut the garden
doors so that I can bathe." [18]They did as she told
them: they shut the doors of the garden and went
out by the side doors to bring what they had been
commanded; they did not see the elders, because
they were hiding.

19 When the maids had gone out, the two elders got up and ran to her. [20]They said, "Look, the
garden doors are shut, and no one can see us. We
are burning with desire for you; so give your consent, and lie with us. [21]If you refuse, we will testify against you that a young man was with you,
and this was why you sent your maids away."

22 Susanna groaned and said, "I am completely trapped. For if I do this, it will mean death
for me; if I do not, I cannot escape your hands.
[23]I choose not to do it; I will fall into your hands,
rather than sin in the sight of the Lord."

24 Then Susanna cried out with a loud voice,
and the two elders shouted against her. [25]And
one of them ran and opened the garden doors.
[26]When the people in the house heard the shouting in the garden, they rushed in at the side door
to see what had happened to her. [27]And when the
elders told their story, the servants felt very much
ashamed, for nothing like this had ever been said
about Susanna.

28 The next day, when the people gathered at
the house of her husband Joakim, the two elders
came, full of their wicked plot to have Susanna
put to death. In the presence of the people they
said, [29]"Send for Susanna daughter of Hilkiah,
the wife of Joakim." [30]So they sent for her. And
she came with her parents, her children, and all
her relatives.

31 Now Susanna was a woman of great re-
finement and beautiful in appearance. [32]As she
was veiled, the scoundrels ordered her to be unveiled, so that they might feast their eyes on her
beauty. [33]Those who were with her and all who
saw her were weeping.

34 Then the two elders stood up before
the people and laid their hands on her head.
[35]Through her tears she looked up toward
Heaven, for her heart trusted in the Lord. [36]The
elders said, "While we were walking in the garden alone, this woman came in with two maids,
shut the garden doors, and dismissed the maids.
[37]Then a young man, who was hiding there, came
to her and lay with her. [38]We were in a corner of
the garden, and when we saw this wickedness we
ran to them. [39]Although we saw them embracing,
we could not hold the man, because he was stronger than we, and he opened the doors and got
away. [40]We did, however, seize this woman and
asked who the young man was, [41]but she would
not tell us. These things we testify."

Because they were elders of the people and
judges, the assembly believed them and condemned her to death.

42 Then Susanna cried out with a loud voice,
and said, "O eternal God, you know what is secret
and are aware of all things before they come to
be; [43]you know that these men have given false
evidence against me. And now I am to die, though
I have done none of the wicked things that they
have charged against me!"

44 The Lord heard her cry. [45]Just as she was
being led off to execution, God stirred up the
holy spirit of a young lad named Daniel, [46]and
he shouted with a loud voice, "I want no part in
shedding this woman's blood!"

47 All the people turned to him and asked,
"What is this you are saying?" [48]Taking his stand
among them he said, "Are you such fools, O Israelites, as to condemn a daughter of Israel without examination and without learning the facts?
[49]Return to court, for these men have given false
evidence against her."

50 So all the people hurried back. And the
rest of the[a] elders said to him, "Come, sit among
us and inform us, for God has given you the
standing of an elder." [51]Daniel said to them, "Separate them far from each other, and I will examine
them."

52 When they were separated from each
other, he summoned one of them and said to

[a] Gk lacks *rest of the*

Susanna (Greek Daniel) 13:51

Daniel's wisdom in the Susanna story stands in marked contrast with that of Solomon, who famously threatened to cut a baby in half in order to identify its mother.

— *WG*

him, "You old relic of wicked days, your sins have now come home, which you have committed in the past, 53pronouncing unjust judgments, condemning the innocent and acquitting the guilty, though the Lord said, 'You shall not put an innocent and righteous person to death.' 54Now then, if you really saw this woman, tell me this: Under what tree did you see them being intimate with each other?" He answered, "Under a mastic tree."[a] 55And Daniel said, "Very well! This lie has cost you your head, for the angel of God has received the sentence from God and will immediately cut[a] you in two."

56 Then, putting him to one side, he ordered them to bring the other. And he said to him, "You offspring of Canaan and not of Judah, beauty has beguiled you and lust has perverted your heart. 57This is how you have been treating the daughters of Israel, and they were intimate with you through fear; but a daughter of Judah would not tolerate your wickedness. 58Now then, tell me: Under what tree did you catch them being intimate with each other?" He answered, "Under an evergreen oak."[b] 59Daniel said to him, "Very well! This lie has cost you also your head, for the angel of God is waiting with his sword to split[b] you in two, so as to destroy you both."

60 Then the whole assembly raised a great shout and blessed God, who saves those who hope in him. 61And they took action against the two elders, because out of their own mouths Daniel had convicted them of bearing false witness; they did to them as they had wickedly planned to do to their neighbor. 62Acting in accordance with the law of Moses, they put them to death. Thus innocent blood was spared that day.

63 Hilkiah and his wife praised God for their daughter Susanna, and so did her husband Joakim and all her relatives, because she was found innocent of a shameful deed. 64And from that day onward Daniel had a great reputation among the people.

[a] The Greek words for *mastic tree* and *cut* are similar, thus forming an ironic wordplay [b] The Greek words for *evergreen oak* and *split* are similar, thus forming an ironic wordplay

Bel and the Dragon

(Chapter 14 of the Greek Version of Daniel)

The third section of Daniel unique to the Greek version (see the introduction to The Prayer of Azariah and the Song of the Three Jews) is also a double unit: the stories of *Bel*, a Babylonian god, and *the Dragon*, a live dragon, which Daniel kills. In the first story, the temple of Bel is unmasked as a fraud in which human attendants take away the food offerings so it appears as if the idol eats them. In a familiar display of sagacity, Daniel outwits the attendants by sprinkling ashes on the floor to record their surreptitious footprints (14:14-21). In the second narrative (14:23), people are worshipping a living dragon. In order to promote the worship of the one God, Daniel kills the dragon with a potion largely consisting of a magic hairball, "pitch and fat and hair" (14:27). Both of these stories are attributed to the biblical prophet Habakkuk (14:1).

I have an appreciation for dragon lore and am sorry that the dragons of Scripture, especially this one, fare so poorly. As an Episcopalian for whom Greek Daniel is canonical, I prefer the Greek text to the Hebrew one. I find it to be fuller and richer. It is for me most meaningful when read sequentially as an integrated text, as in the *New American* or *New Jerusalem* Bibles.

— ***Wilda C. Gafney***

1 When King Astyages was laid to rest with his ancestors, Cyrus the Persian succeeded to his kingdom. 2Daniel was a companion of the king, and was the most honored of all his Friends.

3 Now the Babylonians had an idol called Bel, and every day they provided for it twelve bushels of choice flour and forty sheep and six measures[a] of wine. 4The king revered it and went every day to worship it. But Daniel worshiped his own God.

So the king said to him, "Why do you not worship Bel?" 5He answered, "Because I do not revere idols made with hands, but the living God, who created heaven and earth and has dominion over all living creatures."

6 The king said to him, "Do you not think that Bel is a living god? Do you not see how much he eats and drinks every day?" 7And Daniel laughed, and said, "Do not be deceived, O king, for this thing is only clay inside and bronze outside, and it never ate or drank anything."

8 Then the king was angry and called the

[a] A little more than fifty gallons

priests of Bel[a] and said to them, "If you do not tell
me who is eating these provisions, you shall die.
9 But if you prove that Bel is eating them, Daniel shall die, because he has spoken blasphemy
against Bel." Daniel said to the king, "Let it be
done as you have said."

10 Now there were seventy priests of Bel, besides their wives and children. So the king went
with Daniel into the temple of Bel. 11 The priests
of Bel said, "See, we are now going outside; you
yourself, O king, set out the food and prepare the
wine, and shut the door and seal it with your signet. 12 When you return in the morning, if you do
not find that Bel has eaten it all, we will die; otherwise Daniel will, who is telling lies about us."
13 They were unconcerned, for beneath the table
they had made a hidden entrance, through which
they used to go in regularly and consume the provisions. 14 After they had gone out, the king set out
the food for Bel. Then Daniel ordered his servants
to bring ashes, and they scattered them throughout
the whole temple in the presence of the king alone.
Then they went out, shut the door and sealed it
with the king's signet, and departed. 15 During the
night the priests came as usual, with their wives
and children, and they ate and drank everything.

16 Early in the morning the king rose and
came, and Daniel with him. 17 The king said, "Are
the seals unbroken, Daniel?" He answered, "They
are unbroken, O king." 18 As soon as the doors
were opened, the king looked at the table, and
shouted in a loud voice, "You are great, O Bel,
and in you there is no deceit at all!"

19 But Daniel laughed and restrained the
king from going in. "Look at the floor," he said,
"and notice whose footprints these are." 20 The
king said, "I see the footprints of men and women
and children."

21 Then the king was enraged, and he arrested the priests and their wives and children.
They showed him the secret doors through which
they used to enter to consume what was on the
table. 22 Therefore the king put them to death, and
gave Bel over to Daniel, who destroyed it and its
temple.

23 Now in that place[b] there was a great dragon, which the Babylonians revered. 24 The king
said to Daniel, "You cannot deny that this is a living god; so worship him." 25 Daniel said, "I worship the Lord my God, for he is the living God.
26 But give me permission, O king, and I will kill
the dragon without sword or club." The king said,
"I give you permission."

Bel and the Dragon (Greek Daniel) 14:23

The Greek word *drakon* can also be translated "serpent"; see Revelation 12, however, where it is consistently translated *dragon*.

— *WG*

27 Then Daniel took pitch, fat, and hair, and
boiled them together and made cakes, which he
fed to the dragon. The dragon ate them, and burst
open. Then Daniel said, "See what you have been
worshiping!"

28 When the Babylonians heard about it,
they were very indignant and conspired against
the king, saying, "The king has become a Jew;
he has destroyed Bel, and killed the dragon, and
slaughtered the priests." 29 Going to the king, they
said, "Hand Daniel over to us, or else we will kill
you and your household." 30 The king saw that
they were pressing him hard, and under compulsion he handed Daniel over to them.

31 They threw Daniel into the lions' den, and
he was there for six days. 32 There were seven lions in the den, and every day they had been given
two human bodies and two sheep; but now they
were given nothing, so that they would devour
Daniel.

33 Now the prophet Habakkuk was in Judea;
he had made a stew and had broken bread into
a bowl, and was going into the field to take it
to the reapers. 34 But the angel of the Lord said
to Habakkuk, "Take the food that you have to
Babylon, to Daniel, in the lions' den." 35 Habak-

[a] Gk *his priests* [b] Other ancient authorities lack *in that place*

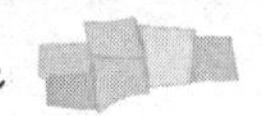

kuk said, "Sir, I have never seen Babylon, and I know nothing about the den." 36 Then the angel of the Lord took him by the crown of his head and carried him by his hair; with the speed of the wind[a] he set him down in Babylon, right over the den.

37 Then Habakkuk shouted, "Daniel, Daniel! Take the food that God has sent you." 38 Daniel said, "You have remembered me, O God, and have not forsaken those who love you." 39 So Daniel got up and ate. And the angel of God immediately returned Habakkuk to his own place.

40 On the seventh day the king came to mourn for Daniel. When he came to the den he looked in, and there sat Daniel! 41 The king shouted with a loud voice, "You are great, O Lord, the God of Daniel, and there is no other besides you!" 42 Then he pulled Daniel[b] out, and threw into the den those who had attempted his destruction, and they were instantly eaten before his eyes.

[a] Or *by the power of his spirit* [b] Gk *him*

1 Maccabees

Written about 100 BCE, the national history of 1 Maccabees conveyed to its first readers a common identity and values in order to unite them as one people, liberated and led by the Hasmoneans. The book also solidified and defended the claims of the Hasmonean dynasty to the high priesthood and kingship of Judea.

Empire is the stage for the drama that unfolds in this book. The Hellenistic kings exploited their subject peoples through conquest, plunder, and slavery as well as systems of patronage and tribute. Under their rule, Judeans were compelled to serve two masters: God and empire.

Israel's covenant with God commanded circumcision, worship of YHWH alone, and adherence to the laws of Torah. It called Israel to be a people set apart from other nations. Their temple, their laws, and their practices symbolized their distinctive identity as God's own people. According to 1 Maccabees 1, around the year 175 BCE "certain renegades" (1:11) or "lawless" people in Israel (9:58) abandoned the covenant with God in order to "make a covenant with the Gentiles." This group of elite Judeans sought permission from the Seleucid king Antiochus IV Epiphanes, ruler of the Seleucid Empire and, by extension, of Judea, to "observe the ordinances of the Gentiles" (1:13). They built a gymnasium—the hallmark of Greek education and culture—and they "removed the marks of circumcision," masking the bodily sign of their covenant with God (1:15).

Before long, the same king who authorized the building of the gymnasium plundered the Jerusalem temple (1:21-24). Two years later his army plundered and set fire to the holy city, ripped down its houses and walls, and established a military garrison in its heart (1:29-40). In 167 he decreed a religious persecution of the Judeans under the pretense that "all should be one people" (1:41). Torah scrolls were burned (1:56). Judeans were commanded to eat pork, sacrifice to idols, defile their sacred space, and profane their sacred times (1:45-47). Antiochus erected a "desolating sacrilege" upon the altar of YHWH (1:54). Circumcised infants were killed and hung from their mothers' necks, and their families were killed (1:60-61). The king punished covenant obedience with death (1:50, 57, 63). Many acquiesced to save their lives (1:43-52) and many died as martyrs (1:63; 2:38). Others fled (1:53; 2:28-29). Some, spurred by the leadership of the Hasmonean priest Mattathias, chose to fight (ch. 2).

The story of revolt and liberation follows. It is also a story of the Hasmonean rise to power. As Mattathias was dying, he appointed his son Judas commander of the newly formed guerrilla army (2:66). The longest section of 1 Maccabees (3:1—9:22) tells of Judas's military victories as well as the purification and rededication of the defiled temple, an event commemorated today in the Jewish feast of Hanukkah. The next section (9:23—12:53) describes the savvy leadership of Jonathan, his brother, who became high priest and governor after Judas's death. Chapters 13–16 portray the

idyllic rule of their brother Simon, who succeeded Jonathan and in 142 finally ended the occupation of Jerusalem and liberated the Judeans from Seleucid rule. At Simon's death his son John Hyrcanus assumed the high priesthood and Judean kingship, establishing a dynasty that would last until the rule of Herod the Great in 37 BCE.

The book begins with a collision: covenant identity clashes with the culture of "the Gentiles" (1:11). But by the book's end we see this as a deceptively simple—and indeed false—opposition. References to "the Gentiles" and "foreigners" were a rhetorical device designed to evoke feelings of national unity and even to justify policies of expansion (for example, 11:68 and 13:6). The Hasmoneans were brutal to their near neighbors in Azotus and Gaza and ruthlessly rooted out the "lawless" within the ranks of Israel (2:44; 5:68; 10:84; 11:61). But if they condemned those who "made a covenant with the Gentiles," the Hasmoneans themselves sought alliances with Rome and Sparta, whom they identified as "brethren" (8:1-32; 12:12-13; 14:20). They resisted the persecutor Antiochus IV, but allied themselves with his successors (14:38). Like their "lawless" enemies, they secured power within a system of imperial patronage and adopted symbols of power from their "Gentile" patrons (10:20).

I read this book as a Catholic, a white woman, and a pacifist. For Catholics as for believers in the Orthodox traditions, including Anglicans, 1 Maccabees has the status of inspired Scripture. For me, this means that the Spirit uncovers through this sacred text the myth of false universalism, the injustice of religious intolerance, the rapacity of empires, the brutality of war, and the deceptive and destructive power of racial rhetoric. Such stories shape our understanding of ourselves and of one another.

— Anathea E. Portier-Young

1 After Alexander son of Philip, the Macedonian, who came from the land of Kittim, had
defeated[a] King Darius of the Persians and the
Medes, he succeeded him as king. (He had previously become king of Greece.) 2He fought many
battles, conquered strongholds, and put to death
the kings of the earth. 3He advanced to the ends of
the earth, and plundered many nations. When the
earth became quiet before him, he was exalted,
and his heart was lifted up. 4He gathered a very
strong army and ruled over countries, nations,
and princes, and they became tributary to him.

5 After this he fell sick and perceived that he
was dying. 6So he summoned his most honored
officers, who had been brought up with him from
youth, and divided his kingdom among them
while he was still alive. 7And after Alexander had
reigned twelve years, he died.

8 Then his officers began to rule, each in his
own place. 9They all put on crowns after his death,
and so did their descendants after them for many
years; and they caused many evils on the earth.

10 From them came forth a sinful root, Antiochus Epiphanes, son of King Antiochus; he had

[a] Gk adds *and he defeated*

been a hostage in Rome. He began to reign in the
one hundred thirty-seventh year of the kingdom
of the Greeks.[a]

11 In those days certain renegades came out
from Israel and misled many, saying, "Let us go
and make a covenant with the Gentiles around
us, for since we separated from them many disasters have come upon us." 12 This proposal pleased
them, 13 and some of the people eagerly went to
the king, who authorized them to observe the ordinances of the Gentiles. 14 So they built a gymnasium in Jerusalem, according to Gentile custom,
15 and removed the marks of circumcision, and
abandoned the holy covenant. They joined with
the Gentiles and sold themselves to do evil.

16 When Antiochus saw that his kingdom
was established, he determined to become king
of the land of Egypt, in order that he might reign
over both kingdoms. 17 So he invaded Egypt with
a strong force, with chariots and elephants and
cavalry and with a large fleet. 18 He engaged King
Ptolemy of Egypt in battle, and Ptolemy turned
and fled before him, and many were wounded
and fell. 19 They captured the fortified cities in
the land of Egypt, and he plundered the land of
Egypt.

20 After subduing Egypt, Antiochus returned
in the one hundred forty-third year.[b] He went up
against Israel and came to Jerusalem with a strong
force. 21 He arrogantly entered the sanctuary and
took the golden altar, the lampstand for the light,
and all its utensils. 22 He took also the table for the
bread of the Presence, the cups for drink offerings, the bowls, the golden censers, the curtain,
the crowns, and the gold decoration on the front
of the temple; he stripped it all off. 23 He took the
silver and the gold, and the costly vessels; he took
also the hidden treasures that he found. 24 Taking
them all, he went into his own land.

He shed much blood,
and spoke with great arrogance.
25 Israel mourned deeply in every community,
26 rulers and elders groaned,
young women and young men became faint,
the beauty of the women faded.
27 Every bridegroom took up the lament;
she who sat in the bridal chamber was
mourning.
28 Even the land trembled for its inhabitants,
and all the house of Jacob was clothed
with shame.

29 Two years later the king sent to the cities
of Judah a chief collector of tribute, and he came
to Jerusalem with a large force. 30 Deceitfully he
spoke peaceable words to them, and they believed
him; but he suddenly fell upon the city, dealt it a
severe blow, and destroyed many people of Israel.
31 He plundered the city, burned it with fire, and
tore down its houses and its surrounding walls.
32 They took captive the women and children, and
seized the livestock. 33 Then they fortified the city
of David with a great strong wall and strong towers, and it became their citadel. 34 They stationed
there a sinful people, men who were renegades.
These strengthened their position; 35 they stored
up arms and food, and collecting the spoils of Jerusalem they stored them there, and became a
great menace,
36 for the citadel[c] became an ambush against the
sanctuary,
an evil adversary of Israel at all times.
37 On every side of the sanctuary they shed
innocent blood;
they even defiled the sanctuary.
38 Because of them the residents of Jerusalem
fled;
she became a dwelling of strangers;
she became strange to her offspring,
and her children forsook her.
39 Her sanctuary became desolate like a desert;
her feasts were turned into mourning,
her sabbaths into a reproach,
her honor into contempt.
40 Her dishonor now grew as great as her glory;
her exaltation was turned into mourning.

41 Then the king wrote to his whole kingdom
that all should be one people, 42 and that all should
give up their particular customs. 43 All the Gentiles
accepted the command of the king. Many even
from Israel gladly adopted his religion; they sac-

[a] 175 B.C. [b] 169 B.C. [c] Gk *it*

rificed to idols and profaned the sabbath. 44 And
the king sent letters by messengers to Jerusalem
and the towns of Judah; he directed them to follow customs strange to the land, 45 to forbid burnt
offerings and sacrifices and drink offerings in the
sanctuary, to profane sabbaths and festivals, 46 to
defile the sanctuary and the priests, 47 to build altars and sacred precincts and shrines for idols, to
sacrifice swine and other unclean animals, 48 and
to leave their sons uncircumcised. They were to
make themselves abominable by everything unclean and profane, 49 so that they would forget the
law and change all the ordinances. 50 He added,[a]
"And whoever does not obey the command of the
king shall die."

51 In such words he wrote to his whole kingdom. He appointed inspectors over all the people and commanded the towns of Judah to offer
sacrifice, town by town. 52 Many of the people,
everyone who forsook the law, joined them, and
they did evil in the land; 53 they drove Israel into
hiding in every place of refuge they had.

54 Now on the fifteenth day of Chislev, in
the one hundred forty-fifth year,[b] they erected a
desolating sacrilege on the altar of burnt offering.
They also built altars in the surrounding towns of
Judah, 55 and offered incense at the doors of the
houses and in the streets. 56 The books of the law
that they found they tore to pieces and burned
with fire. 57 Anyone found possessing the book of
the covenant, or anyone who adhered to the law,
was condemned to death by decree of the king.
58 They kept using violence against Israel, against
those who were found month after month in the
towns. 59 On the twenty-fifth day of the month
they offered sacrifice on the altar that was on top
of the altar of burnt offering. 60 According to the
decree, they put to death the women who had
their children circumcised, 61 and their families
and those who circumcised them; and they hung
the infants from their mothers' necks.

62 But many in Israel stood firm and were
resolved in their hearts not to eat unclean food.
63 They chose to die rather than to be defiled by
food or to profane the holy covenant; and they
did die. 64 Very great wrath came upon Israel.

2 In those days Mattathias son of John son
of Simeon, a priest of the family of Joarib,
moved from Jerusalem and settled in Modein.
2 He had five sons, John surnamed Gaddi, 3 Simon
called Thassi, 4 Judas called Maccabeus, 5 Eleazar
called Avaran, and Jonathan called Apphus. 6 He
saw the blasphemies being committed in Judah
and Jerusalem, 7 and said,

"Alas! Why was I born to see this,
the ruin of my people, the ruin of the holy city,
and to live there when it was given over to the enemy,
the sanctuary given over to aliens?
8 Her temple has become like a person without honor;[c]
9 her glorious vessels have been carried into exile.
Her infants have been killed in her streets,
her youths by the sword of the foe.
10 What nation has not inherited her palaces[d]
and has not seized her spoils?
11 All her adornment has been taken away;
no longer free, she has become a slave.
12 And see, our holy place, our beauty,
and our glory have been laid waste;
the Gentiles have profaned them.
13 Why should we live any longer?"

14 Then Mattathias and his sons tore their
clothes, put on sackcloth, and mourned greatly.

15 The king's officers who were enforcing the
apostasy came to the town of Modein to make
them offer sacrifice. 16 Many from Israel came to
them; and Mattathias and his sons were assembled. 17 Then the king's officers spoke to Mattathias as follows: "You are a leader, honored and
great in this town, and supported by sons and
brothers. 18 Now be the first to come and do what
the king commands, as all the Gentiles and the
people of Judah and those that are left in Jerusalem have done. Then you and your sons will be
numbered among the Friends of the king, and

[a] Gk lacks *He added* [b] 167 B.C. [c] Meaning of Gk uncertain
[d] Other ancient authorities read *has not had a part in her kingdom*

you and your sons will be honored with silver and
gold and many gifts."
19 But Mattathias answered and said in a
loud voice: "Even if all the nations that live under
the rule of the king obey him, and have chosen
to obey his commandments, every one of them
abandoning the religion of their ancestors, 20 I
and my sons and my brothers will continue to live
by the covenant of our ancestors. 21 Far be it from
us to desert the law and the ordinances. 22 We will
not obey the king's words by turning aside from
our religion to the right hand or to the left."
23 When he had finished speaking these
words, a Jew came forward in the sight of all to
offer sacrifice on the altar in Modein, according
to the king's command. 24 When Mattathias saw
it, he burned with zeal and his heart was stirred.
He gave vent to righteous anger; he ran and killed
him on the altar. 25 At the same time he killed the
king's officer who was forcing them to sacrifice,
and he tore down the altar. 26 Thus he burned
with zeal for the law, just as Phinehas did against
Zimri son of Salu.
27 Then Mattathias cried out in the town with
a loud voice, saying: "Let every one who is zealous for the law and supports the covenant come
out with me!" 28 Then he and his sons fled to the
hills and left all that they had in the town.
29 At that time many who were seeking righteousness and justice went down to the wilderness
to live there, 30 they, their sons, their wives, and
their livestock, because troubles pressed heavily
upon them. 31 And it was reported to the king's
officers, and to the troops in Jerusalem the city
of David, that those who had rejected the king's
command had gone down to the hiding places in
the wilderness. 32 Many pursued them, and overtook them; they encamped opposite them and
prepared for battle against them on the sabbath
day. 33 They said to them, "Enough of this! Come
out and do what the king commands, and you will
live." 34 But they said, "We will not come out, nor
will we do what the king commands and so profane the sabbath day." 35 Then the enemy[a] quickly
attacked them. 36 But they did not answer them
or hurl a stone at them or block up their hiding
places, 37 for they said, "Let us all die in our innocence; heaven and earth testify for us that you are
killing us unjustly." 38 So they attacked them on
the sabbath, and they died, with their wives and
children and livestock, to the number of a thousand persons.
39 When Mattathias and his friends learned
of it, they mourned for them deeply. 40 And all
said to their neighbors: "If we all do as our kindred have done and refuse to fight with the Gentiles for our lives and for our ordinances, they
will quickly destroy us from the earth." 41 So they
made this decision that day: "Let us fight against
anyone who comes to attack us on the sabbath
day; let us not all die as our kindred died in their
hiding places."
42 Then there united with them a company
of Hasideans, mighty warriors of Israel, all who
offered themselves willingly for the law. 43 And
all who became fugitives to escape their troubles
joined them and reinforced them. 44 They organized an army, and struck down sinners in their
anger and renegades in their wrath; the survivors
fled to the Gentiles for safety. 45 And Mattathias
and his friends went around and tore down the
altars; 46 they forcibly circumcised all the uncircumcised boys that they found within the borders of Israel. 47 They hunted down the arrogant,
and the work prospered in their hands. 48 They
rescued the law out of the hands of the Gentiles
and kings, and they never let the sinner gain the
upper hand.
49 Now the days drew near for Mattathias to
die, and he said to his sons: "Arrogance and scorn
have now become strong; it is a time of ruin and
furious anger. 50 Now, my children, show zeal for
the law, and give your lives for the covenant of
our ancestors.
51 "Remember the deeds of the ancestors,
which they did in their generations; and you
will receive great honor and an everlasting name.
52 Was not Abraham found faithful when tested,
and it was reckoned to him as righteousness?
53 Joseph in the time of his distress kept the com-

[a] Gk *they*

mandment, and became lord of Egypt. 54 Phinehas our ancestor, because he was deeply zealous,
received the covenant of everlasting priesthood.
55 Joshua, because he fulfilled the command, became a judge in Israel. 56 Caleb, because he testified in the assembly, received an inheritance in
the land. 57 David, because he was merciful, inherited the throne of the kingdom forever. 58 Elijah, because of great zeal for the law, was taken up
into heaven. 59 Hananiah, Azariah, and Mishael
believed and were saved from the flame. 60 Daniel, because of his innocence, was delivered from
the mouth of the lions.

61 "And so observe, from generation to generation, that none of those who put their trust in
him will lack strength. 62 Do not fear the words of
sinners, for their splendor will turn into dung and
worms. 63 Today they will be exalted, but tomorrow they will not be found, because they will have
returned to the dust, and their plans will have
perished. 64 My children, be courageous and grow
strong in the law, for by it you will gain honor.

65 "Here is your brother Simeon who, I
know, is wise in counsel; always listen to him; he
shall be your father. 66 Judas Maccabeus has been
a mighty warrior from his youth; he shall command the army for you and fight the battle against
the peoples.[a] 67 You shall rally around you all who
observe the law, and avenge the wrong done to
your people. 68 Pay back the Gentiles in full, and
obey the commands of the law."

69 Then he blessed them, and was gathered
to his ancestors. 70 He died in the one hundred
forty-sixth year[b] and was buried in the tomb of
his ancestors at Modein. And all Israel mourned
for him with great lamentation.

3 Then his son Judas, who was called Maccabeus, took command in his place. 2 All his
brothers and all who had joined his father helped
him; they gladly fought for Israel.

3 He extended the glory of his people.
Like a giant he put on his breastplate;
he bound on his armor of war and waged
battles,
protecting the camp by his sword.

4 He was like a lion in his deeds,
like a lion's cub roaring for prey.

5 He searched out and pursued those who
broke the law;
he burned those who troubled his people.

6 Lawbreakers shrank back for fear of him;
all the evildoers were confounded;
and deliverance prospered by his hand.

7 He embittered many kings,
but he made Jacob glad by his deeds,
and his memory is blessed forever.

8 He went through the cities of Judah;
he destroyed the ungodly out of the land;[c]
thus he turned away wrath from Israel.

9 He was renowned to the ends of the earth;
he gathered in those who were perishing.

10 Apollonius now gathered together Gentiles and a large force from Samaria to fight against
Israel. 11 When Judas learned of it, he went out to
meet him, and he defeated and killed him. Many
were wounded and fell, and the rest fled. 12 Then
they seized their spoils; and Judas took the sword
of Apollonius, and used it in battle the rest of
his life.

13 When Seron, the commander of the Syrian army, heard that Judas had gathered a large
company, including a body of faithful soldiers
who stayed with him and went out to battle,
14 he said, "I will make a name for myself and win
honor in the kingdom. I will make war on Judas
and his companions, who scorn the king's command." 15 Once again a strong army of godless
men went up with him to help him, to take vengeance on the Israelites.

16 When he approached the ascent of Beth-
horon, Judas went out to meet him with a small
company. 17 But when they saw the army coming
to meet them, they said to Judas, "How can we,
few as we are, fight against so great and so strong
a multitude? And we are faint, for we have eaten
nothing today." 18 Judas replied, "It is easy for
many to be hemmed in by few, for in the sight of
Heaven there is no difference between saving by
many or by few. 19 It is not on the size of the army
that victory in battle depends, but strength comes

[a] Or *of the people* [b] 166 B.C. [c] Gk *it*

from Heaven. 20They come against us in great insolence and lawlessness to destroy us and our
wives and our children, and to despoil us; 21but
we fight for our lives and our laws. 22He himself
will crush them before us; as for you, do not be
afraid of them."

23 When he finished speaking, he rushed suddenly against Seron and his army, and they were
crushed before him. 24They pursued them[a] down
the descent of Beth-horon to the plain; eight hundred of them fell, and the rest fled into the land
of the Philistines. 25Then Judas and his brothers
began to be feared, and terror fell on the Gentiles
all around them. 26His fame reached the king, and
the Gentiles talked of the battles of Judas.

27 When King Antiochus heard these reports, he was greatly angered; and he sent and
gathered all the forces of his kingdom, a very
strong army. 28He opened his coffers and gave a
year's pay to his forces, and ordered them to be
ready for any need. 29Then he saw that the money
in the treasury was exhausted, and that the revenues from the country were small because of the
dissension and disaster that he had caused in the
land by abolishing the laws that had existed from
the earliest days. 30He feared that he might not
have such funds as he had before for his expenses
and for the gifts that he used to give more lavishly
than preceding kings. 31He was greatly perplexed
in mind; then he determined to go to Persia and
collect the revenues from those regions and raise
a large fund.

32 He left Lysias, a distinguished man of royal
lineage, in charge of the king's affairs from the
river Euphrates to the borders of Egypt. 33Lys-
ias was also to take care of his son Antiochus until he returned. 34And he turned over to Lysias[b]
half of his forces and the elephants, and gave him
orders about all that he wanted done. As for the
residents of Judea and Jerusalem, 35Lysias was to
send a force against them to wipe out and destroy
the strength of Israel and the remnant of Jerusalem; he was to banish the memory of them from
the place, 36settle aliens in all their territory, and
distribute their land by lot. 37Then the king took
the remaining half of his forces and left Antioch
his capital in the one hundred and forty-seventh
year.[c] He crossed the Euphrates river and went
through the upper provinces.

38 Lysias chose Ptolemy son of Dorymenes,
and Nicanor and Gorgias, able men among the
Friends of the king, 39and sent with them forty
thousand infantry and seven thousand cavalry to
go into the land of Judah and destroy it, as the
king had commanded. 40So they set out with
their entire force, and when they arrived they encamped near Emmaus in the plain. 41When the
traders of the region heard what was said to them,
they took silver and gold in immense amounts,
and fetters,[d] and went to the camp to get the Israelites for slaves. And forces from Syria and the
land of the Philistines joined with them.

42 Now Judas and his brothers saw that misfortunes had increased and that the forces were
encamped in their territory. They also learned
what the king had commanded to do to the people to cause their final destruction. 43But they
said to one another, "Let us restore the ruins
of our people, and fight for our people and the
sanctuary." 44So the congregation assembled to
be ready for battle, and to pray and ask for mercy
and compassion.

45 Jerusalem was uninhabited like a
 wilderness;
 not one of her children went in or out.
The sanctuary was trampled down,
 and aliens held the citadel;
 it was a lodging place for the Gentiles.
Joy was taken from Jacob;
 the flute and the harp ceased to play.

46 Then they gathered together and went to
Mizpah, opposite Jerusalem, because Israel formerly had a place of prayer in Mizpah. 47They
fasted that day, put on sackcloth and sprinkled
ashes on their heads, and tore their clothes.
48And they opened the book of the law to inquire
into those matters about which the Gentiles consulted the likenesses of their gods. 49They also
brought the vestments of the priesthood and the
first fruits and the tithes, and they stirred up the

[a] Other ancient authorities read *him* [b] Gk *him* [c] 165 B.C. [d] Syr: Gk Mss, Vg *slaves*

nazirites[a] who had completed their days; 50and
they cried aloud to Heaven, saying,

"What shall we do with these?
Where shall we take them?
51 Your sanctuary is trampled down and
profaned,
and your priests mourn in humiliation.
52 Here the Gentiles are assembled against us to
destroy us;
you know what they plot against us.
53 How will we be able to withstand them,
if you do not help us?"

54 Then they sounded the trumpets and gave
a loud shout. 55After this Judas appointed leaders of the people, in charge of thousands and
hundreds and fifties and tens. 56Those who were
building houses, or were about to be married, or
were planting a vineyard, or were fainthearted,
he told to go home again, according to the law.
57Then the army marched out and encamped to
the south of Emmaus.

58 And Judas said, "Arm yourselves and be
courageous. Be ready early in the morning to fight
with these Gentiles who have assembled against
us to destroy us and our sanctuary. 59It is better
for us to die in battle than to see the misfortunes
of our nation and of the sanctuary. 60But as his
will in heaven may be, so shall he do."

4 Now Gorgias took five thousand infantry and
one thousand picked cavalry, and this division moved out by night 2to fall upon the camp of
the Jews and attack them suddenly. Men from the
citadel were his guides. 3But Judas heard of it, and
he and his warriors moved out to attack the king's
force in Emmaus 4while the division was still absent from the camp. 5When Gorgias entered the
camp of Judas by night, he found no one there, so
he looked for them in the hills, because he said,
"These men are running away from us."

6 At daybreak Judas appeared in the plain
with three thousand men, but they did not have
armor and swords such as they desired. 7And
they saw the camp of the Gentiles, strong and fortified, with cavalry all around it; and these men
were trained in war. 8But Judas said to those who
were with him, "Do not fear their numbers or be
afraid when they charge. 9Remember how our
ancestors were saved at the Red Sea, when Pharaoh with his forces pursued them. 10And now,
let us cry to Heaven, to see whether he will favor
us and remember his covenant with our ancestors
and crush this army before us today. 11Then all
the Gentiles will know that there is one who redeems and saves Israel."

12 When the foreigners looked up and saw
them coming against them, 13they went out
from their camp to battle. Then the men with
Judas blew their trumpets 14and engaged in battle. The Gentiles were crushed, and fled into the
plain, 15and all those in the rear fell by the sword.
They pursued them to Gazara, and to the plains
of Idumea, and to Azotus and Jamnia; and three
thousand of them fell. 16Then Judas and his force
turned back from pursuing them, 17and he said
to the people, "Do not be greedy for plunder, for
there is a battle before us; 18Gorgias and his force
are near us in the hills. But stand now against our
enemies and fight them, and afterward seize the
plunder boldly."

19 Just as Judas was finishing this speech, a
detachment appeared, coming out of the hills.
20They saw that their army[b] had been put to flight,
and that the Jews[b] were burning the camp, for the
smoke that was seen showed what had happened.
21When they perceived this, they were greatly
frightened, and when they also saw the army of
Judas drawn up in the plain for battle, 22they all
fled into the land of the Philistines. 23Then Judas
returned to plunder the camp, and they seized a
great amount of gold and silver, and cloth dyed
blue and sea purple, and great riches. 24On their
return they sang hymns and praises to Heaven—
"For he is good, for his mercy endures forever."
25Thus Israel had a great deliverance that day.

26 Those of the foreigners who escaped went
and reported to Lysias all that had happened.
27When he heard it, he was perplexed and discouraged, for things had not happened to Israel as
he had intended, nor had they turned out as the
king had ordered. 28But the next year he mustered

[a] That is *those separated* or *those consecrated*   [b] Gk *they*

sixty thousand picked infantry and five thousand
cavalry to subdue them. 29They came into Idumea and encamped at Beth-zur, and Judas met
them with ten thousand men.

30 When he saw that their army was strong,
he prayed, saying, "Blessed are you, O Savior of
Israel, who crushed the attack of the mighty warrior by the hand of your servant David, and gave
the camp of the Philistines into the hands of Jonathan son of Saul, and of the man who carried his
armor. 31Hem in this army by the hand of your
people Israel, and let them be ashamed of their
troops and their cavalry. 32Fill them with cowardice; melt the boldness of their strength; let them
tremble in their destruction. 33Strike them down
with the sword of those who love you, and let all
who know your name praise you with hymns."

34 Then both sides attacked, and there fell of
the army of Lysias five thousand men; they fell in
action.[a] 35When Lysias saw the rout of his troops
and observed the boldness that inspired those of
Judas, and how ready they were either to live or
to die nobly, he withdrew to Antioch and enlisted
mercenaries in order to invade Judea again with
an even larger army.

36 Then Judas and his brothers said, "See,
our enemies are crushed; let us go up to cleanse
the sanctuary and dedicate it." 37So all the army
assembled and went up to Mount Zion. 38There
they saw the sanctuary desolate, the altar profaned, and the gates burned. In the courts they
saw bushes sprung up as in a thicket, or as on one
of the mountains. They saw also the chambers of
the priests in ruins. 39Then they tore their clothes
and mourned with great lamentation; they sprinkled themselves with ashes 40and fell face down
on the ground. And when the signal was given
with the trumpets, they cried out to Heaven.

41 Then Judas detailed men to fight against
those in the citadel until he had cleansed the
sanctuary. 42He chose blameless priests devoted
to the law, 43and they cleansed the sanctuary and
removed the defiled stones to an unclean place.
44They deliberated what to do about the altar of
burnt offering, which had been profaned. 45And
they thought it best to tear it down, so that it
would not be a lasting shame to them that the
Gentiles had defiled it. So they tore down the altar, 46and stored the stones in a convenient place
on the temple hill until a prophet should come
to tell what to do with them. 47Then they took
unhewn[b] stones, as the law directs, and built a
new altar like the former one. 48They also rebuilt
the sanctuary and the interior of the temple, and
consecrated the courts. 49They made new holy
vessels, and brought the lampstand, the altar of
incense, and the table into the temple. 50Then
they offered incense on the altar and lit the lamps
on the lampstand, and these gave light in the
temple. 51They placed the bread on the table and
hung up the curtains. Thus they finished all the
work they had undertaken.

52 Early in the morning on the twenty-fifth
day of the ninth month, which is the month of
Chislev, in the one hundred forty-eighth year,[c]
53they rose and offered sacrifice, as the law directs, on the new altar of burnt offering that they
had built. 54At the very season and on the very day
that the Gentiles had profaned it, it was dedicated
with songs and harps and lutes and cymbals. 55All
the people fell on their faces and worshiped and
blessed Heaven, who had prospered them. 56So
they celebrated the dedication of the altar for
eight days, and joyfully offered burnt offerings;
they offered a sacrifice of well-being and a thanksgiving offering. 57They decorated the front of the
temple with golden crowns and small shields;
they restored the gates and the chambers for the
priests, and fitted them with doors. 58There was
very great joy among the people, and the disgrace
brought by the Gentiles was removed.

59 Then Judas and his brothers and all the assembly of Israel determined that every year at that
season the days of dedication of the altar should
be observed with joy and gladness for eight days,
beginning with the twenty-fifth day of the month
of Chislev.

60 At that time they fortified Mount Zion
with high walls and strong towers all around, to
keep the Gentiles from coming and trampling

[a] Or *and some fell on the opposite side* [b] Gk *whole* [c] 164 B.C.

them down as they had done before. 61 Judas[a] stationed a garrison there to guard it; he also fortified Beth-zur to guard it, so that the people might have a stronghold that faced Idumea.

5 When the Gentiles all around heard that the altar had been rebuilt and the sanctuary dedicated as it was before, they became very angry, 2 and they determined to destroy the descendants of Jacob who lived among them. So they began to kill and destroy among the people. 3 But Judas made war on the descendants of Esau in Idumea, at Akrabattene, because they kept lying in wait for Israel. He dealt them a heavy blow and humbled them and despoiled them. 4 He also remembered the wickedness of the sons of Baean, who were a trap and a snare to the people and ambushed them on the highways. 5 They were shut up by him in their[b] towers; and he encamped against them, vowed their complete destruction, and burned with fire their towers and all who were in them. 6 Then he crossed over to attack the Ammonites, where he found a strong band and many people, with Timothy as their leader. 7 He engaged in many battles with them, and they were crushed before him; he struck them down. 8 He also took Jazer and its villages; then he returned to Judea.

9 Now the Gentiles in Gilead gathered together against the Israelites who lived in their territory, and planned to destroy them. But they fled to the stronghold of Dathema, 10 and sent to Judas and his brothers a letter that said, "The Gentiles around us have gathered together to destroy us. 11 They are preparing to come and capture the stronghold to which we have fled, and Timothy is leading their forces. 12 Now then, come and rescue us from their hands, for many of us have fallen, 13 and all our kindred who were in the land of Tob have been killed; the enemy[c] have captured their wives and children and goods, and have destroyed about a thousand persons there."

14 While the letter was still being read, other messengers, with their garments torn, came from Galilee and made a similar report; 15 they said that the people of Ptolemais and Tyre and Sidon, and all Galilee of the Gentiles,[d] had gathered together against them "to annihilate us." 16 When Judas and the people heard these messages, a great assembly was called to determine what they should do for their kindred who were in distress and were being attacked by enemies.[e] 17 Then Judas said to his brother Simon, "Choose your men and go and rescue your kindred in Galilee; Jonathan my brother and I will go to Gilead." 18 But he left Joseph, son of Zechariah, and Azariah, a leader of the people, with the rest of the forces, in Judea to guard it; 19 and he gave them this command, "Take charge of this people, but do not engage in battle with the Gentiles until we return." 20 Then three thousand men were assigned to Simon to go to Galilee, and eight thousand to Judas for Gilead.

21 So Simon went to Galilee and fought many battles against the Gentiles, and the Gentiles were crushed before him. 22 He pursued them to the gate of Ptolemais; as many as three thousand of the Gentiles fell, and he despoiled them. 23 Then he took the Jews[f] of Galilee and Arbatta, with their wives and children, and all they possessed, and led them to Judea with great rejoicing.

24 Judas Maccabeus and his brother Jonathan crossed the Jordan and made three days' journey into the wilderness. 25 They encountered the Nabateans, who met them peaceably and told them all that had happened to their kindred in Gilead: 26 "Many of them have been shut up in Bozrah and Bosor, in Alema and Chaspho, Maked and Carnaim"—all these towns were strong and large— 27 "and some have been shut up in the other towns of Gilead; the enemy[c] are getting ready to attack the strongholds tomorrow and capture and destroy all these people in a single day."

28 Then Judas and his army quickly turned back by the wilderness road to Bozrah; and he took the town, and killed every male by the edge of the sword; then he seized all its spoils and burned it with fire. 29 He left the place at night, and they went all the way to the stronghold of Dathema.[g] 30 At dawn they looked out and saw a large company, which could not be counted, carrying

[a] Gk *He* [b] Gk *her* [c] Gk *they* [d] Gk *aliens* [e] Gk *them* [f] Gk *those* [g] Gk lacks *of Dathema*. See verse 9

ladders and engines of war to capture the stronghold, and attacking the Jews within.[a] 31 So Judas saw that the battle had begun and that the cry of the town went up to Heaven, with trumpets and loud shouts, 32 and he said to the men of his forces, "Fight today for your kindred!" 33 Then he came up behind them in three companies, who sounded their trumpets and cried aloud in prayer. 34 And when the army of Timothy realized that it was Maccabeus, they fled before him, and he dealt them a heavy blow. As many as eight thousand of them fell that day.

35 Next he turned aside to Maapha,[b] and fought against it and took it; and he killed every male in it, plundered it, and burned it with fire. 36 From there he marched on and took Chaspho, Maked, and Bosor, and the other towns of Gilead.

37 After these things Timothy gathered another army and encamped opposite Raphon, on the other side of the stream. 38 Judas sent men to spy out the camp, and they reported to him, "All the Gentiles around us have gathered to him; it is a very large force. 39 They also have hired Arabs to help them, and they are encamped across the stream, ready to come and fight against you." And Judas went to meet them.

40 Now as Judas and his army drew near to the stream of water, Timothy said to the officers of his forces, "If he crosses over to us first, we will not be able to resist him, for he will surely defeat us. 41 But if he shows fear and camps on the other side of the river, we will cross over to him and defeat him." 42 When Judas approached the stream of water, he stationed the officers[c] of the army at the stream and gave them this command, "Permit no one to encamp, but make them all enter the battle." 43 Then he crossed over against them first, and the whole army followed him. All the Gentiles were defeated before him, and they threw away their arms and fled into the sacred precincts at Carnaim. 44 But he took the town and burned the sacred precincts with fire, together with all who were in them. Thus Carnaim was conquered; they could stand before Judas no longer.

45 Then Judas gathered together all the Israelites in Gilead, the small and the great, with their wives and children and goods, a very large company, to go to the land of Judah. 46 So they came to Ephron. This was a large and very strong town on the road, and they could not go around it to the right or to the left; they had to go through it. 47 But the people of the town shut them out and blocked up the gates with stones.

48 Judas sent them this friendly message, "Let us pass through your land to get to our land. No one will do you harm; we will simply pass by on foot." But they refused to open to him. 49 Then Judas ordered proclamation to be made to the army that all should encamp where they were. 50 So the men of the forces encamped, and he fought against the town all that day and all the night, and the town was delivered into his hands. 51 He destroyed every male by the edge of the sword, and razed and plundered the town. Then he passed through the town over the bodies of the dead.

52 Then they crossed the Jordan into the large plain before Beth-shan. 53 Judas kept rallying the laggards and encouraging the people all the way until he came to the land of Judah. 54 So they went up to Mount Zion with joy and gladness, and offered burnt offerings, because they had returned in safety; not one of them had fallen.

55 Now while Judas and Jonathan were in Gilead and their[d] brother Simon was in Galilee before Ptolemais, 56 Joseph son of Zechariah, and Azariah, the commanders of the forces, heard of their brave deeds and of the heroic war they had fought. 57 So they said, "Let us also make a name for ourselves; let us go and make war on the Gentiles around us." 58 So they issued orders to the men of the forces that were with them and marched against Jamnia. 59 Gorgias and his men came out of the town to meet them in battle. 60 Then Joseph and Azariah were routed, and were pursued to the borders of Judea; as many as two thousand of the people of Israel fell that day. 61 Thus the people suffered a great rout because, thinking to do a brave deed, they did not listen to Judas and his brothers. 62 But they did not belong

[a] Gk *and they were attacking them* [b] Other ancient authorities read *Alema* [c] Or *scribes* [d] Gk *his*

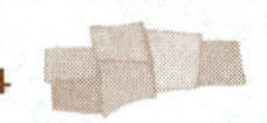

to the family of those men through whom deliverance was given to Israel.
63 The man Judas and his brothers were
greatly honored in all Israel and among all the
Gentiles, wherever their name was heard. 64 People gathered to them and praised them.
65 Then Judas and his brothers went out and
fought the descendants of Esau in the land to the
south. He struck Hebron and its villages and tore
down its strongholds and burned its towers on all
sides. 66 Then he marched off to go into the land
of the Philistines, and passed through Marisa.[a]
67 On that day some priests, who wished to do
a brave deed, fell in battle, for they went out to
battle unwisely. 68 But Judas turned aside to Azotus in the land of the Philistines; he tore down
their altars, and the carved images of their gods
he burned with fire; he plundered the towns and
returned to the land of Judah.

6 King Antiochus was going through the upper provinces when he heard that Elymais in
Persia was a city famed for its wealth in silver and
gold. 2 Its temple was very rich, containing golden
shields, breastplates, and weapons left there by
Alexander son of Philip, the Macedonian king
who first reigned over the Greeks. 3 So he came
and tried to take the city and plunder it, but he
could not because his plan had become known to
the citizens 4 and they withstood him in battle. So
he fled and in great disappointment left there to
return to Babylon.
5 Then someone came to him in Persia and reported that the armies that had gone into the land
of Judah had been routed; 6 that Lysias had gone
first with a strong force, but had turned and fled
before the Jews;[b] that the Jews[c] had grown strong
from the arms, supplies, and abundant spoils
that they had taken from the armies they had cut
down; 7 that they had torn down the abomination
that he had erected on the altar in Jerusalem; and
that they had surrounded the sanctuary with high
walls as before, and also Beth-zur, his town.
8 When the king heard this news, he was astounded and badly shaken. He took to his bed
and became sick from disappointment, because
things had not turned out for him as he had
planned. 9 He lay there for many days, because
deep disappointment continually gripped him,
and he realized that he was dying. 10 So he called
all his Friends and said to them, "Sleep has departed from my eyes and I am downhearted
with worry. 11 I said to myself, 'To what distress
I have come! And into what a great flood I now
am plunged! For I was kind and beloved in my
power.' 12 But now I remember the wrong I did in
Jerusalem. I seized all its vessels of silver and gold,
and I sent to destroy the inhabitants of Judah
without good reason. 13 I know that it is because
of this that these misfortunes have come upon
me; here I am, perishing of bitter disappointment
in a strange land."
14 Then he called for Philip, one of his
Friends, and made him ruler over all his kingdom. 15 He gave him the crown and his robe and
the signet, so that he might guide his son Antiochus and bring him up to be king. 16 Thus King
Antiochus died there in the one hundred forty-
ninth year.[d] 17 When Lysias learned that the king
was dead, he set up Antiochus the king's[e] son to
reign. Lysias[f] had brought him up from boyhood;
he named him Eupator.
18 Meanwhile the garrison in the citadel
kept hemming Israel in around the sanctuary.
They were trying in every way to harm them
and strengthen the Gentiles. 19 Judas therefore
resolved to destroy them, and assembled all the
people to besiege them. 20 They gathered together
and besieged the citadel[g] in the one hundred fiftieth year;[h] and he built siege towers and other
engines of war. 21 But some of the garrison escaped from the siege and some of the ungodly
Israelites joined them. 22 They went to the king
and said, "How long will you fail to do justice and
to avenge our kindred? 23 We were happy to serve
your father, to live by what he said, and to follow
his commands. 24 For this reason the sons of our
people besieged the citadel[i] and became hostile
to us; moreover, they have put to death as many

[a] Other ancient authorities read *Samaria* [b] Gk *them* [c] Gk *they* [d] 163 B.C. [e] Gk *his* [f] Gk *He* [g] Gk *it*
[h] 162 B.C. [i] Meaning of Gk uncertain

of us as they have caught, and they have seized
our inheritances. 25 It is not against us alone that
they have stretched out their hands; they have
also attacked all the lands on their borders. 26 And
see, today they have encamped against the citadel
in Jerusalem to take it; they have fortified both
the sanctuary and Beth-zur; 27 unless you quickly
prevent them, they will do still greater things, and
you will not be able to stop them."

28 The king was enraged when he heard this.
He assembled all his Friends, the commanders of
his forces and those in authority.[a] 29 Mercenary
forces also came to him from other kingdoms
and from islands of the seas. 30 The number of his
forces was one hundred thousand foot soldiers,
twenty thousand horsemen, and thirty-two elephants accustomed to war. 31 They came through
Idumea and encamped against Beth-zur, and for
many days they fought and built engines of war;
but the Jews[b] sallied out and burned these with
fire, and fought courageously.

32 Then Judas marched away from the citadel and encamped at Beth-zechariah, opposite
the camp of the king. 33 Early in the morning the
king set out and took his army by a forced march
along the road to Beth-zechariah, and his troops
made ready for battle and sounded their trumpets. 34 They offered the elephants the juice of
grapes and mulberries, to arouse them for battle. 35 They distributed the animals among the
phalanxes; with each elephant they stationed a
thousand men armed with coats of mail, and with
brass helmets on their heads; and five hundred
picked horsemen were assigned to each beast.
36 These took their position beforehand wherever the animal was; wherever it went, they went
with it, and they never left it. 37 On the elephants[c]
were wooden towers, strong and covered; they
were fastened on each animal by special harness,
and on each were four[d] armed men who fought
from there, and also its Indian driver. 38 The rest
of the cavalry were stationed on either side, on
the two flanks of the army, to harass the enemy
while being themselves protected by the phalanxes. 39 When the sun shone on the shields of
gold and brass, the hills were ablaze with them
and gleamed like flaming torches.

1 Maccabees 6:37

The elephants of the Seleucid army came from India. According to Strabo, Seleucus I first acquired 500 war elephants from Chandragupta Maurya, founder of the Mauryan Empire in India, in exchange for contested territories, including modern-day Afghanistan. The elephants inspired terror on the battlefield. Their presence in this story, along with the Indian mahouts who drive them, testifies to the ambitions, reach, and limits of empire in the ancient world.

— ***APY***

40 Now a part of the king's army was spread
out on the high hills, and some troops were on
the plain, and they advanced steadily and in good
order. 41 All who heard the noise made by their
multitude, by the marching of the multitude and
the clanking of their arms, trembled, for the army
was very large and strong. 42 But Judas and his
army advanced to the battle, and six hundred of
the king's army fell. 43 Now Eleazar, called Avaran, saw that one of the animals was equipped
with royal armor. It was taller than all the others, and he supposed that the king was on it. 44 So
he gave his life to save his people and to win for
himself an everlasting name. 45 He courageously
ran into the midst of the phalanx to reach it; he
killed men right and left, and they parted before
him on both sides. 46 He got under the elephant,
stabbed it from beneath, and killed it; but it fell
to the ground upon him and he died. 47 When the
Jews[b] saw the royal might and the fierce attack of
the forces, they turned away in flight.

48 The soldiers of the king's army went up to
Jerusalem against them, and the king encamped
in Judea and at Mount Zion. 49 He made peace
with the people of Beth-zur, and they evacuated
the town because they had no provisions there
to withstand a siege, since it was a sabbatical year

[a] Gk *those over the reins* [b] Gk *they* [c] Gk *them* [d] Cn: Some authorities read *thirty*; others *thirty-two*

for the land. 50So the king took Beth-zur and
stationed a guard there to hold it. 51Then he encamped before the sanctuary for many days. He
set up siege towers, engines of war to throw fire
and stones, machines to shoot arrows, and catapults. 52The Jews[a] also made engines of war to
match theirs, and fought for many days. 53But
they had no food in storage,[b] because it was the
seventh year; those who had found safety in Judea from the Gentiles had consumed the last of
the stores. 54Only a few men were left in the sanctuary; the rest scattered to their own homes, for
the famine proved too much for them.

55 Then Lysias heard that Philip, whom
King Antiochus while still living had appointed
to bring up his son Antiochus to be king, 56had
returned from Persia and Media with the forces
that had gone with the king, and that he was trying to seize control of the government. 57So he
quickly gave orders to withdraw, and said to the
king, to the commanders of the forces, and to the
troops, "Daily we grow weaker, our food supply
is scant, the place against which we are fighting
is strong, and the affairs of the kingdom press
urgently on us. 58Now then let us come to terms
with these people, and make peace with them and
with all their nation. 59Let us agree to let them
live by their laws as they did before; for it was on
account of their laws that we abolished that they
became angry and did all these things."

60 The speech pleased the king and the commanders, and he sent to the Jews[c] an offer of
peace, and they accepted it. 61So the king and the
commanders gave them their oath. On these conditions the Jews[a] evacuated the stronghold. 62But
when the king entered Mount Zion and saw what
a strong fortress the place was, he broke the oath
he had sworn and gave orders to tear down the
wall all around. 63Then he set off in haste and returned to Antioch. He found Philip in control of
the city, but he fought against him, and took the
city by force.

7 In the one hundred fifty-first year[d] Demetrius
son of Seleucus set out from Rome, sailed
with a few men to a town by the sea, and there
began to reign. 2As he was entering the royal palace of his ancestors, the army seized Antiochus
and Lysias to bring them to him. 3But when this
act became known to him, he said, "Do not let
me see their faces!" 4So the army killed them,
and Demetrius took his seat on the throne of his
kingdom.

5 Then there came to him all the renegade
and godless men of Israel; they were led by Alcimus, who wanted to be high priest. 6They brought
to the king this accusation against the people:
"Judas and his brothers have destroyed all your
Friends, and have driven us out of our land. 7Now
then send a man whom you trust; let him go and
see all the ruin that Judas[e] has brought on us and
on the land of the king, and let him punish them
and all who help them."

8 So the king chose Bacchides, one of the
king's Friends, governor of the province Beyond
the River; he was a great man in the kingdom and
was faithful to the king. 9He sent him, and with
him he sent the ungodly Alcimus, whom he made
high priest; and he commanded him to take vengeance on the Israelites. 10So they marched away
and came with a large force into the land of Judah;
and he sent messengers to Judas and his brothers
with peaceable but treacherous words. 11But they
paid no attention to their words, for they saw that
they had come with a large force.

12 Then a group of scribes appeared in a
body before Alcimus and Bacchides to ask for
just terms. 13The Hasideans were first among the
Israelites to seek peace from them, 14for they said,
"A priest of the line of Aaron has come with the
army, and he will not harm us." 15Alcimus[f] spoke
peaceable words to them and swore this oath to
them, "We will not seek to injure you or your
friends." 16So they trusted him; but he seized
sixty of them and killed them in one day, in accordance with the word that was written,

17 "The flesh of your faithful ones and their
blood
they poured out all around Jerusalem,
and there was no one to bury them."

18Then the fear and dread of them fell on all the

[a] Gk *they* [b] Other ancient authorities read *in the sanctuary* [c] Gk *them* [d] 161 B.C. [e] Gk *he* [f] Gk *He*

people, for they said, "There is no truth or justice in them, for they have violated the agreement and the oath that they swore."

19 Then Bacchides withdrew from Jerusalem and encamped in Beth-zaith. And he sent and seized many of the men who had deserted to him,[a] and some of the people, and killed them and threw them into a great pit. 20 He placed Alcimus in charge of the country and left with him a force to help him; then Bacchides went back to the king.

21 Alcimus struggled to maintain his high priesthood, 22 and all who were troubling their people joined him. They gained control of the land of Judah and did great damage in Israel. 23 And Judas saw all the wrongs that Alcimus and those with him had done among the Israelites; it was more than the Gentiles had done. 24 So Judas[b] went out into all the surrounding parts of Judea, taking vengeance on those who had deserted and preventing those in the city[c] from going out into the country. 25 When Alcimus saw that Judas and those with him had grown strong, and realized that he could not withstand them, he returned to the king and brought malicious charges against them.

26 Then the king sent Nicanor, one of his honored princes, who hated and detested Israel, and he commanded him to destroy the people. 27 So Nicanor came to Jerusalem with a large force, and treacherously sent to Judas and his brothers this peaceable message, 28 "Let there be no fighting between you and me; I shall come with a few men to see you face to face in peace."

29 So he came to Judas, and they greeted one another peaceably; but the enemy were preparing to kidnap Judas. 30 It became known to Judas that Nicanor[b] had come to him with treacherous intent, and he was afraid of him and would not meet him again. 31 When Nicanor learned that his plan had been disclosed, he went out to meet Judas in battle near Caphar-salama. 32 About five hundred of the army of Nicanor fell, and the rest[d] fled into the city of David.

33 After these events Nicanor went up to Mount Zion. Some of the priests from the sanctuary and some of the elders of the people came out to greet him peaceably and to show him the burnt offering that was being offered for the king. 34 But he mocked them and derided them and defiled them and spoke arrogantly, 35 and in anger he swore this oath, "Unless Judas and his army are delivered into my hands this time, then if I return safely I will burn up this house." And he went out in great anger. 36 At this the priests went in and stood before the altar and the temple; they wept and said,

37 "You chose this house to be called by your
 name,
 and to be for your people a house of prayer
 and supplication.
38 Take vengeance on this man and on his army,
 and let them fall by the sword;
 remember their blasphemies,
 and let them live no longer."

39 Now Nicanor went out from Jerusalem and encamped in Beth-horon, and the Syrian army joined him. 40 Judas encamped in Adasa with three thousand men. Then Judas prayed and said, 41 "When the messengers from the king spoke blasphemy, your angel went out and struck down one hundred eighty-five thousand of the Assyrians.[e] 42 So also crush this army before us today; let the rest learn that Nicanor[b] has spoken wickedly against the sanctuary, and judge him according to this wickedness."

43 So the armies met in battle on the thirteenth day of the month of Adar. The army of Nicanor was crushed, and he himself was the first to fall in the battle. 44 When his army saw that Nicanor had fallen, they threw down their arms and fled. 45 The Jews[d] pursued them a day's journey, from Adasa as far as Gazara, and as they followed they kept sounding the battle call on the trumpets. 46 People came out of all the surrounding villages of Judea, and they outflanked the enemy[f] and drove them back to their pursuers,[g] so that they all fell by the sword; not even one of them

[a] Or *many of his men who had deserted* [b] Gk *he* [c] Gk *and they were prevented* [d] Gk *they* [e] Gk *of them* [f] Gk *them* [g] Gk *these*

was left. 47Then the Jews[a] seized the spoils and
the plunder; they cut off Nicanor's head and the
right hand that he had so arrogantly stretched
out, and brought them and displayed them just
outside Jerusalem. 48The people rejoiced greatly
and celebrated that day as a day of great gladness.
49They decreed that this day should be celebrated
each year on the thirteenth day of Adar. 50So the
land of Judah had rest for a few days.

8 Now Judas heard of the fame of the Romans,
that they were very strong and were well-
disposed toward all who made an alliance with
them, that they pledged friendship to those who
came to them, 2and that they were very strong.
He had been told of their wars and of the brave
deeds that they were doing among the Gauls, how
they had defeated them and forced them to pay
tribute, 3and what they had done in the land of
Spain to get control of the silver and gold mines
there, 4and how they had gained control of the
whole region by their planning and patience, even
though the place was far distant from them. They
also subdued the kings who came against them
from the ends of the earth, until they crushed
them and inflicted great disaster on them; the rest
paid them tribute every year. 5They had crushed
in battle and conquered Philip, and King Perseus
of the Macedonians,[b] and the others who rose up
against them. 6They also had defeated Antiochus
the Great, king of Asia, who went to fight against
them with one hundred twenty elephants and
with cavalry and chariots and a very large army.
He was crushed by them; 7they took him alive
and decreed that he and those who would reign
after him should pay a heavy tribute and give hostages and surrender some of their best provinces,
8the countries of India, Media, and Lydia. These
they took from him and gave to King Eumenes.
9The Greeks planned to come and destroy them,
10but this became known to them, and they sent
a general against the Greeks[c] and attacked them.
Many of them were wounded and fell, and the Romans[a] took captive their wives and children; they
plundered them, conquered the land, tore down
their strongholds, and enslaved them to this day.
11The remaining kingdoms and islands, as many
as ever opposed them, they destroyed and enslaved; 12but with their friends and those who
rely on them they have kept friendship. They have
subdued kings far and near, and as many as have
heard of their fame have feared them. 13Those
whom they wish to help and to make kings, they
make kings, and those whom they wish they depose; and they have been greatly exalted. 14Yet
for all this not one of them has put on a crown or
worn purple as a mark of pride, 15but they have
built for themselves a senate chamber, and every
day three hundred twenty senators constantly
deliberate concerning the people, to govern them
well. 16They trust one man each year to rule over
them and to control all their land; they all heed
the one man, and there is no envy or jealousy
among them.

17 So Judas chose Eupolemus son of John
son of Accos, and Jason son of Eleazar, and sent
them to Rome to establish friendship and alliance, 18and to free themselves from the yoke; for
they saw that the kingdom of the Greeks was enslaving Israel completely. 19They went to Rome,
a very long journey; and they entered the senate
chamber and spoke as follows: 20"Judas, who is
also called Maccabeus, and his brothers and the
people of the Jews have sent us to you to establish alliance and peace with you, so that we may
be enrolled as your allies and friends." 21The proposal pleased them, 22and this is a copy of the letter that they wrote in reply, on bronze tablets, and
sent to Jerusalem to remain with them there as a
memorial of peace and alliance:

23 "May all go well with the Romans and
with the nation of the Jews at sea and on land
forever, and may sword and enemy be far from
them. 24If war comes first to Rome or to any of
their allies in all their dominion, 25the nation of
the Jews shall act as their allies wholeheartedly,
as the occasion may indicate to them. 26To the
enemy that makes war they shall not give or supply grain, arms, money, or ships, just as Rome
has decided; and they shall keep their obligations
without receiving any return. 27In the same way,

[a] Gk *they* [b] Or *Kittim* [c] Gk *them*

if war comes first to the nation of the Jews, the
Romans shall willingly act as their allies, as the
occasion may indicate to them. 28 And to their enemies there shall not be given grain, arms, money,
or ships, just as Rome has decided; and they shall
keep these obligations and do so without deceit.
29 Thus on these terms the Romans make a treaty
with the Jewish people. 30 If after these terms are
in effect both parties shall determine to add or
delete anything, they shall do so at their discretion, and any addition or deletion that they may
make shall be valid.

31 "Concerning the wrongs that King Demetrius is doing to them, we have written to him as
follows, 'Why have you made your yoke heavy
on our friends and allies the Jews? 32 If now they
appeal again for help against you, we will defend
their rights and fight you on sea and on land.'"

9 When Demetrius heard that Nicanor and
his army had fallen in battle, he sent Bacchides and Alcimus into the land of Judah a second
time, and with them the right wing of the army.
2 They went by the road that leads to Gilgal and
encamped against Mesaloth in Arbela, and they
took it and killed many people. 3 In the first
month of the one hundred fifty-second year[a] they
encamped against Jerusalem; 4 then they marched
off and went to Berea with twenty thousand foot
soldiers and two thousand cavalry.

5 Now Judas was encamped in Elasa, and
with him were three thousand picked men.
6 When they saw the huge number of the enemy
forces, they were greatly frightened, and many
slipped away from the camp, until no more than
eight hundred of them were left.

7 When Judas saw that his army had slipped
away and the battle was imminent, he was crushed
in spirit, for he had no time to assemble them.
8 He became faint, but he said to those who were
left, "Let us get up and go against our enemies.
We may have the strength to fight them." 9 But
they tried to dissuade him, saying, "We do not
have the strength. Let us rather save our own lives
now, and let us come back with our kindred and
fight them; we are too few." 10 But Judas said, "Far
be it from us to do such a thing as to flee from
them. If our time has come, let us die bravely for
our kindred, and leave no cause to question our
honor."

11 Then the army of Bacchides[b] marched out
from the camp and took its stand for the encounter. The cavalry was divided into two companies,
and the slingers and the archers went ahead of the
army, as did all the chief warriors. 12 Bacchides
was on the right wing. Flanked by the two companies, the phalanx advanced to the sound of the
trumpets; and the men with Judas also blew their
trumpets. 13 The earth was shaken by the noise
of the armies, and the battle raged from morning
until evening.

14 Judas saw that Bacchides and the strength
of his army were on the right; then all the stouthearted men went with him, 15 and they crushed
the right wing, and he pursued them as far as
Mount Azotus. 16 When those on the left wing
saw that the right wing was crushed, they turned
and followed close behind Judas and his men.
17 The battle became desperate, and many on both
sides were wounded and fell. 18 Judas also fell, and
the rest fled.

19 Then Jonathan and Simon took their
brother Judas and buried him in the tomb of their
ancestors at Modein, 20 and wept for him. All Israel made great lamentation for him; they
mourned many days and said,

21 "How is the mighty fallen,
the savior of Israel!"

22 Now the rest of the acts of Judas, and his wars
and the brave deeds that he did, and his greatness, have not been recorded, but they were very
many.

23 After the death of Judas, the renegades
emerged in all parts of Israel; all the wrongdoers
reappeared. 24 In those days a very great famine
occurred, and the country went over to their side.
25 Bacchides chose the godless and put them in
charge of the country. 26 They made inquiry and
searched for the friends of Judas, and brought
them to Bacchides, who took vengeance on them
and made sport of them. 27 So there was great dis-

[a] 160 B.C. [b] Gk lacks *of Bacchides*

tress in Israel, such as had not been since the time
that prophets ceased to appear among them.

28 Then all the friends of Judas assembled
and said to Jonathan, 29"Since the death of your
brother Judas there has been no one like him to
go against our enemies and Bacchides, and to
deal with those of our nation who hate us. 30Now
therefore we have chosen you today to take his
place as our ruler and leader, to fight our battle."
31So Jonathan accepted the leadership at that
time in place of his brother Judas.

32 When Bacchides learned of this, he tried
to kill him. 33But Jonathan and his brother Simon
and all who were with him heard of it, and they
fled into the wilderness of Tekoa and camped
by the water of the pool of Asphar. 34Bacchides
found this out on the sabbath day, and he with all
his army crossed the Jordan.

35 So Jonathan[a] sent his brother as leader of
the multitude and begged the Nabateans, who
were his friends, for permission to store with
them the great amount of baggage that they had.
36But the family of Jambri from Medeba came
out and seized John and all that he had, and left
with it.

37 After these things it was reported to Jonathan and his brother Simon, "The family of
Jambri are celebrating a great wedding, and are
conducting the bride, a daughter of one of the
great nobles of Canaan, from Nadabath with a
large escort." 38Remembering how their brother
John had been killed, they went up and hid under cover of the mountain. 39They looked out and
saw a tumultuous procession with a great amount
of baggage; and the bridegroom came out with
his friends and his brothers to meet them with
tambourines and musicians and many weapons.
40Then they rushed on them from the ambush
and began killing them. Many were wounded and
fell, and the rest fled to the mountain; and the
Jews[b] took all their goods. 41So the wedding was
turned into mourning and the voice of their musicians into a funeral dirge. 42After they had fully
avenged the blood of their brother, they returned
to the marshes of the Jordan.

43 When Bacchides heard of this, he came
with a large force on the sabbath day to the banks
of the Jordan. 44And Jonathan said to those with
him, "Let us get up now and fight for our lives,
for today things are not as they were before. 45For
look! the battle is in front of us and behind us;
the water of the Jordan is on this side and on that,
with marsh and thicket; there is no place to turn.
46Cry out now to Heaven that you may be delivered from the hands of our enemies." 47So the
battle began, and Jonathan stretched out his hand
to strike Bacchides, but he eluded him and went
to the rear. 48Then Jonathan and the men with
him leaped into the Jordan and swam across to
the other side, and the enemy[b] did not cross the
Jordan to attack them. 49And about one thousand
of Bacchides' men fell that day.

50 Then Bacchides[a] returned to Jerusalem
and built strong cities in Judea: the fortress in Jericho, and Emmaus, and Beth-horon, and Bethel,
and Timnath, and[c] Pharathon, and Tephon, with
high walls and gates and bars. 51And he placed
garrisons in them to harass Israel. 52He also fortified the town of Beth-zur, and Gazara, and the
citadel, and in them he put troops and stores of
food. 53And he took the sons of the leading men
of the land as hostages and put them under guard
in the citadel at Jerusalem.

54 In the one hundred and fifty-third year,[d]
in the second month, Alcimus gave orders to tear
down the wall of the inner court of the sanctuary.
He tore down the work of the prophets! 55But he
only began to tear it down, for at that time Alcimus was stricken and his work was hindered; his
mouth was stopped and he was paralyzed, so that
he could no longer say a word or give commands
concerning his house. 56And Alcimus died at that
time in great agony. 57When Bacchides saw that
Alcimus was dead, he returned to the king, and
the land of Judah had rest for two years.

58 Then all the lawless plotted and said, "See!
Jonathan and his men are living in quiet and
confidence. So now let us bring Bacchides back,
and he will capture them all in one night." 59And
they went and consulted with him. 60He started

[a] Gk *he* [b] Gk *they* [c] Some authorities omit *and* [d] 159 B.C.

to come with a large force, and secretly sent letters to all his allies in Judea, telling them to seize
Jonathan and his men; but they were unable to
do it, because their plan became known. 61And
Jonathan's men[a] seized about fifty of the men of
the country who were leaders in this treachery,
and killed them.
62 Then Jonathan with his men, and Simon,
withdrew to Bethbasi in the wilderness; he rebuilt the parts of it that had been demolished,
and they fortified it. 63When Bacchides learned
of this, he assembled all his forces, and sent orders to the men of Judea. 64Then he came and encamped against Bethbasi; he fought against it for
many days and made machines of war.
65 But Jonathan left his brother Simon in the
town, while he went out into the country; and
he went with only a few men. 66He struck down
Odomera and his kindred and the people of Phas-
iron in their tents. 67Then he[b] began to attack and
went into battle with his forces; and Simon and
his men sallied out from the town and set fire to
the machines of war. 68They fought with Bacchides, and he was crushed by them. They pressed
him very hard, for his plan and his expedition had
been in vain. 69So he was very angry at the renegades who had counseled him to come into the
country, and he killed many of them. Then he decided to go back to his own land.
70 When Jonathan learned of this, he sent
ambassadors to him to make peace with him and
obtain release of the captives. 71He agreed, and
did as he said; and he swore to Jonathan[c] that he
would not try to harm him as long as he lived.
72He restored to him the captives whom he had
taken previously from the land of Judah; then he
turned and went back to his own land, and did not
come again into their territory. 73Thus the sword
ceased from Israel. Jonathan settled in Michmash
and began to judge the people; and he destroyed
the godless out of Israel.

10 In the one hundred sixtieth year[d] Alexander Epiphanes, son of Antiochus, landed
and occupied Ptolemais. They welcomed him,
and there he began to reign. 2When King Demetrius heard of it, he assembled a very large army
and marched out to meet him in battle. 3Deme-
trius sent Jonathan a letter in peaceable words
to honor him; 4for he said to himself, "Let us act
first to make peace with him[e] before he makes
peace with Alexander against us, 5for he will remember all the wrongs that we did to him and to
his brothers and his nation." 6So Demetrius[f] gave
him authority to recruit troops, to equip them
with arms, and to become his ally; and he commanded that the hostages in the citadel should be
released to him.
7 Then Jonathan came to Jerusalem and read
the letter in the hearing of all the people and of
those in the citadel. 8They were greatly alarmed
when they heard that the king had given him authority to recruit troops. 9But those in the citadel released the hostages to Jonathan, and he
returned them to their parents.
10 And Jonathan took up residence in Jerusalem and began to rebuild and restore the city.
11He directed those who were doing the work
to build the walls and encircle Mount Zion with
squared stones, for better fortification; and they
did so.
12 Then the foreigners who were in the
strongholds that Bacchides had built fled; 13all of
them left their places and went back to their own
lands. 14Only in Beth-zur did some remain who
had forsaken the law and the commandments, for
it served as a place of refuge.
15 Now King Alexander heard of all the
promises that Demetrius had sent to Jonathan,
and he heard of the battles that Jonathan[f] and his
brothers had fought, of the brave deeds that they
had done, and of the troubles that they had endured. 16So he said, "Shall we find another such
man? Come now, we will make him our friend
and ally." 17And he wrote a letter and sent it to
him, in the following words:
18 "King Alexander to his brother Jonathan,
greetings. 19We have heard about you, that you
are a mighty warrior and worthy to be our friend.
20And so we have appointed you today to be the
high priest of your nation; you are to be called

[a] Gk *they* [b] Other ancient authorities read *they* [c] Gk *him* [d] 152 B.C. [e] Gk *them* [f] Gk *he*

the king's Friend and you are to take our side and keep friendship with us." He also sent him a purple robe and a golden crown.

21 So Jonathan put on the sacred vestments in the seventh month of the one hundred sixtieth year,[a] at the festival of booths,[b] and he recruited troops and equipped them with arms in abundance. 22 When Demetrius heard of these things he was distressed and said, 23 "What is this that we have done? Alexander has gotten ahead of us in forming a friendship with the Jews to strengthen himself. 24 I also will write them words of encouragement and promise them honor and gifts, so that I may have their help." 25 So he sent a message to them in the following words:

"King Demetrius to the nation of the Jews, greetings. 26 Since you have kept your agreement with us and have continued your friendship with us, and have not sided with our enemies, we have heard of it and rejoiced. 27 Now continue still to keep faith with us, and we will repay you with good for what you do for us. 28 We will grant you many immunities and give you gifts.

29 "I now free you and exempt all the Jews from payment of tribute and salt tax and crown levies, 30 and instead of collecting the third of the grain and the half of the fruit of the trees that I should receive, I release them from this day and henceforth. I will not collect them from the land of Judah or from the three districts added to it from Samaria and Galilee, from this day and for all time. 31 Jerusalem and its environs, its tithes and its revenues, shall be holy and free from tax. 32 I release also my control of the citadel in Jerusalem and give it to the high priest, so that he may station in it men of his own choice to guard it. 33 And everyone of the Jews taken as a captive from the land of Judah into any part of my kingdom, I set free without payment; and let all officials cancel also the taxes on their livestock.

34 "All the festivals and sabbaths and new moons and appointed days, and the three days before a festival and the three after a festival—let them all be days of immunity and release for all the Jews who are in my kingdom. 35 No one shall have authority to exact anything from them or annoy any of them about any matter.

36 "Let Jews be enrolled in the king's forces to the number of thirty thousand men, and let the maintenance be given them that is due to all the forces of the king. 37 Let some of them be stationed in the great strongholds of the king, and let some of them be put in positions of trust in the kingdom. Let their officers and leaders be of their own number, and let them live by their own laws, just as the king has commanded in the land of Judah.

38 "As for the three districts that have been added to Judea from the country of Samaria, let them be annexed to Judea so that they may be considered to be under one ruler and obey no other authority than the high priest. 39 Ptolemais and the land adjoining it I have given as a gift to the sanctuary in Jerusalem, to meet the necessary expenses of the sanctuary. 40 I also grant fifteen thousand shekels of silver yearly out of the king's revenues from appropriate places. 41 And all the additional funds that the government officials have not paid as they did in the first years,[c] they shall give from now on for the service of the temple.[d] 42 Moreover, the five thousand shekels of silver that my officials[e] have received every year from the income of the services of the temple, this too is canceled, because it belongs to the priests who minister there. 43 And all who take refuge at the temple in Jerusalem, or in any of its precincts, because they owe money to the king or are in debt, let them be released and receive back all their property in my kingdom.

44 "Let the cost of rebuilding and restoring the structures of the sanctuary be paid from the revenues of the king. 45 And let the cost of rebuilding the walls of Jerusalem and fortifying it all around, and the cost of rebuilding the walls in Judea, also be paid from the revenues of the king."

46 When Jonathan and the people heard these words, they did not believe or accept them, because they remembered the great wrongs that Demetrius[f] had done in Israel and how much he

[a] 152 B.C. [b] Or *tabernacles* [c] Meaning of Gk uncertain [d] Gk *house* [e] Gk *they* [f] Gk *he*

had oppressed them. 47 They favored Alexander,
because he had been the first to speak peaceable
words to them, and they remained his allies all his
days.
48 Now King Alexander assembled large
forces and encamped opposite Demetrius. 49 The
two kings met in battle, and the army of Demetrius fled, and Alexander[a] pursued him and defeated them. 50 He pressed the battle strongly
until the sun set, and on that day Demetrius fell.
51 Then Alexander sent ambassadors to
Ptolemy king of Egypt with the following message: 52 "Since I have returned to my kingdom and
have taken my seat on the throne of my ancestors,
and established my rule—for I crushed Demetrius and gained control of our country; 53 I met
him in battle, and he and his army were crushed
by us, and we have taken our seat on the throne
of his kingdom— 54 now therefore let us establish
friendship with one another; give me now your
daughter as my wife, and I will become your son-
in-law, and will make gifts to you and to her in
keeping with your position."
55 Ptolemy the king replied and said, "Happy
was the day on which you returned to the land of
your ancestors and took your seat on the throne
of their kingdom. 56 And now I will do for you
as you wrote, but meet me at Ptolemais, so that
we may see one another, and I will become your
father-in-law, as you have said."
57 So Ptolemy set out from Egypt, he and his
daughter Cleopatra, and came to Ptolemais in the
one hundred sixty-second year.[b] 58 King Alexander met him, and Ptolemy[c] gave him his daughter
Cleopatra in marriage, and celebrated her wedding at Ptolemais with great pomp, as kings do.
59 Then King Alexander wrote to Jonathan
to come and meet him. 60 So he went with pomp
to Ptolemais and met the two kings; he gave them
and their Friends silver and gold and many gifts,
and found favor with them. 61 A group of malcontents from Israel, renegades, gathered together
against him to accuse him; but the king paid no
attention to them. 62 The king gave orders to take
off Jonathan's garments and to clothe him in purple, and they did so. 63 The king also seated him at
his side; and he said to his officers, "Go out with
him into the middle of the city and proclaim that
no one is to bring charges against him about any
matter, and let no one annoy him for any reason."
64 When his accusers saw the honor that was paid
him, in accord with the proclamation, and saw
him clothed in purple, they all fled. 65 Thus the
king honored him and enrolled him among his
chief[d] Friends, and made him general and governor of the province. 66 And Jonathan returned to
Jerusalem in peace and gladness.
67 In the one hundred sixty-fifth year[e] Demetrius son of Demetrius came from Crete to the
land of his ancestors. 68 When King Alexander
heard of it, he was greatly distressed and returned
to Antioch. 69 And Demetrius appointed Apollonius the governor of Coelesyria, and he assembled a large force and encamped against Jamnia.
Then he sent the following message to the high
priest Jonathan:

[a] Other ancient authorities read *Alexander fled, and Demetrius*

[b] 150 B.C.

[c] Gk *he*

[d] Gk *first*

[e] 147 B.C.

1 Maccabees 10:54-58

This passage describes the marriage of Ptolemaic Princess Cleopatra Thea Eueteria (her name means Cleopatra, Goddess of Prosperity) to the Seleucid king Alexander Balas. Ancient coins celebrated their union with a double portrait of the king and queen. As daughter of the Egyptian king Ptolemy VI and great-granddaughter of the Seleucid king Antiochus III, Cleopatra bridged two dynasties and two empires. She was married to three kings, and gave birth to four. As queen, she was sole ruler of the Seleucid Empire in the years 126–125 BCE and ruled as co-regent with her young son 125–121. Coins bearing her sole image portrayed a horn of plenty on the reverse.

— *APY*

70 "You are the only one to rise up against us,
and I have fallen into ridicule and disgrace because
of you. Why do you assume authority against us
in the hill country? 71 If you now have confidence
in your forces, come down to the plain to meet us,
and let us match strength with each other there,
for I have with me the power of the cities. 72 Ask
and learn who I am and who the others are that
are helping us. People will tell you that you cannot stand before us, for your ancestors were twice
put to flight in their own land. 73 And now you
will not be able to withstand my cavalry and such
an army in the plain, where there is no stone or
pebble, or place to flee."

74 When Jonathan heard the words of Apollonius, his spirit was aroused. He chose ten thousand men and set out from Jerusalem, and his
brother Simon met him to help him. 75 He encamped before Joppa, but the people of the city
closed its gates, for Apollonius had a garrison in
Joppa. 76 So they fought against it, and the people
of the city became afraid and opened the gates,
and Jonathan gained possession of Joppa.

77 When Apollonius heard of it, he mustered
three thousand cavalry and a large army, and went
to Azotus as though he were going farther. At the
same time he advanced into the plain, for he had
a large troop of cavalry and put confidence in it.
78 Jonathan[a] pursued him to Azotus, and the armies engaged in battle. 79 Now Apollonius had
secretly left a thousand cavalry behind them.
80 Jonathan learned that there was an ambush behind him, for they surrounded his army and shot
arrows at his men from early morning until late afternoon. 81 But his men stood fast, as Jonathan had
commanded, and the enemy's[b] horses grew tired.

82 Then Simon brought forward his force and
engaged the phalanx in battle (for the cavalry was
exhausted); they were overwhelmed by him and
fled, 83 and the cavalry was dispersed in the plain.
They fled to Azotus and entered Beth-dagon, the
temple of their idol, for safety. 84 But Jonathan
burned Azotus and the surrounding towns and
plundered them; and the temple of Dagon, and
those who had taken refuge in it, he burned with
fire. 85 The number of those who fell by the sword,
with those burned alive, came to eight thousand.

86 Then Jonathan left there and encamped
against Askalon, and the people of the city came
out to meet him with great pomp.

87 He and those with him then returned to
Jerusalem with a large amount of booty. 88 When
King Alexander heard of these things, he honored Jonathan still more; 89 and he sent to him a
golden buckle, such as it is the custom to give to
the King's Kinsmen. He also gave him Ekron and
all its environs as his possession.

11 Then the king of Egypt gathered great
forces, like the sand by the seashore, and
many ships; and he tried to get possession of Alexander's kingdom by trickery and add it to his
own kingdom. 2 He set out for Syria with peaceable words, and the people of the towns opened
their gates to him and went to meet him, for King
Alexander had commanded them to meet him,
since he was Alexander's[c] father-in-law. 3 But
when Ptolemy entered the towns he stationed
forces as a garrison in each town.

4 When he[d] approached Azotus, they showed
him the burnt-out temple of Dagon, and Azotus
and its suburbs destroyed, and the corpses lying
about, and the charred bodies of those whom Jonathan[a] had burned in the war, for they had piled
them in heaps along his route. 5 They also told the
king what Jonathan had done, to throw blame on
him; but the king kept silent. 6 Jonathan met the
king at Joppa with pomp, and they greeted one
another and spent the night there. 7 And Jonathan went with the king as far as the river called
Eleutherus; then he returned to Jerusalem.

8 So King Ptolemy gained control of the
coastal cities as far as Seleucia by the sea, and
he kept devising wicked designs against Alexander. 9 He sent envoys to King Demetrius, saying,
"Come, let us make a covenant with each other,
and I will give you in marriage my daughter
who was Alexander's wife, and you shall reign
over your father's kingdom. 10 I now regret that
I gave him my daughter, for he has tried to kill
me." 11 He threw blame on Alexander[e] because he

[a] Gk *he* [b] Gk *their* [c] Gk *his* [d] Other ancient authorities read *they* [e] Gk *him*

coveted his kingdom. 12 So he took his daughter
away from him and gave her to Demetrius. He
was estranged from Alexander, and their enmity
became manifest.

13 Then Ptolemy entered Antioch and put
on the crown of Asia. Thus he put two crowns
on his head, the crown of Egypt and that of Asia.
14 Now King Alexander was in Cilicia at that time,
because the people of that region were in revolt.
15 When Alexander heard of it, he came against
him in battle. Ptolemy marched out and met him
with a strong force, and put him to flight. 16 So
Alexander fled into Arabia to find protection
there, and King Ptolemy was triumphant. 17 Zabdiel the Arab cut off the head of Alexander and
sent it to Ptolemy. 18 But King Ptolemy died three
days later, and his troops in the strongholds were
killed by the inhabitants of the strongholds. 19 So
Demetrius became king in the one hundred sixty-
seventh year.[a]

20 In those days Jonathan assembled the
Judeans to attack the citadel in Jerusalem, and he
built many engines of war to use against it. 21 But
certain renegades who hated their nation went to
the king and reported to him that Jonathan was
besieging the citadel. 22 When he heard this he
was angry, and as soon as he heard it he set out
and came to Ptolemais; and he wrote Jonathan
not to continue the siege, but to meet him for a
conference at Ptolemais as quickly as possible.

23 When Jonathan heard this, he gave orders
to continue the siege. He chose some of the elders
of Israel and some of the priests, and put himself
in danger, 24 for he went to the king at Ptolemais,
taking silver and gold and clothing and numerous other gifts. And he won his favor. 25 Although
certain renegades of his nation kept making
complaints against him, 26 the king treated him
as his predecessors had treated him; he exalted
him in the presence of all his Friends. 27 He confirmed him in the high priesthood and in as many
other honors as he had formerly had, and caused
him to be reckoned among his chief[b] Friends.
28 Then Jonathan asked the king to free Judea and
the three districts of Samaria[c] from tribute, and
promised him three hundred talents. 29 The king
consented, and wrote a letter to Jonathan about
all these things; its contents were as follows:

30 "King Demetrius to his brother Jonathan
and to the nation of the Jews, greetings. 31 This
copy of the letter that we wrote concerning you to
our kinsman Lasthenes we have written to you
also, so that you may know what it says. 32 'King
Demetrius to his father Lasthenes, greetings.
33 We have determined to do good to the nation
of the Jews, who are our friends and fulfill their
obligations to us, because of the goodwill they
show toward us. 34 We have confirmed as their
possession both the territory of Judea and the
three districts of Aphairema and Lydda and
Rathamin; the latter, with all the region bordering them, were added to Judea from Samaria. To
all those who offer sacrifice in Jerusalem we have
granted release from[d] the royal taxes that the king
formerly received from them each year, from the
crops of the land and the fruit of the trees. 35 And
the other payments henceforth due to us of the
tithes, and the taxes due to us, and the salt pits
and the crown taxes due to us—from all these we
shall grant them release. 36 And not one of these
grants shall be canceled from this time on forever.
37 Now therefore take care to make a copy of this,
and let it be given to Jonathan and put up in a
conspicuous place on the holy mountain.'"

38 When King Demetrius saw that the land
was quiet before him and that there was no opposition to him, he dismissed all his troops, all
of them to their own homes, except the foreign
troops that he had recruited from the islands of
the nations. So all the troops who had served
under his predecessors hated him. 39 A certain
Trypho had formerly been one of Alexander's
supporters; he saw that all the troops were grumbling against Demetrius. So he went to Imalkue
the Arab, who was bringing up Antiochus, the
young son of Alexander, 40 and insistently urged
him to hand Antiochus[e] over to him, to become
king in place of his father. He also reported to

[a] 145 B.C. [b] Gk *first* [c] Cn: Gk *the three districts and Samaria* [d] Or *Samaria, for all those who offer sacrifice in Jerusalem, in place of* [e] Gk *him*

Imalkue[a] what Demetrius had done and told of the hatred that the troops of Demetrius[b] had for him; and he stayed there many days.

41 Now Jonathan sent to King Demetrius the request that he remove the troops of the citadel from Jerusalem, and the troops in the strongholds; for they kept fighting against Israel. 42And Demetrius sent this message back to Jonathan: "Not only will I do these things for you and your nation, but I will confer great honor on you and your nation, if I find an opportunity. 43Now then you will do well to send me men who will help me, for all my troops have revolted." 44So Jonathan sent three thousand stalwart men to him at Antioch, and when they came to the king, the king rejoiced at their arrival.

45 Then the people of the city assembled within the city, to the number of a hundred and twenty thousand, and they wanted to kill the king. 46But the king fled into the palace. Then the people of the city seized the main streets of the city and began to fight. 47So the king called the Jews to his aid, and they all rallied around him and then spread out through the city; and they killed on that day about one hundred thousand. 48They set fire to the city and seized a large amount of spoil on that day, and saved the king. 49When the people of the city saw that the Jews had gained control of the city as they pleased, their courage failed and they cried out to the king with this entreaty: 50"Grant us peace, and make the Jews stop fighting against us and our city." 51And they threw down their arms and made peace. So the Jews gained glory in the sight of the king and of all the people in his kingdom, and they returned to Jerusalem with a large amount of spoil.

52 So King Demetrius sat on the throne of his kingdom, and the land was quiet before him. 53But he broke his word about all that he had promised; he became estranged from Jonathan and did not repay the favors that Jonathan[c] had done him, but treated him very harshly.

54 After this Trypho returned, and with him the young boy Antiochus who began to reign and put on the crown. 55All the troops that Demetrius had discharged gathered around him; they fought against Demetrius,[a] and he fled and was routed. 56Trypho captured the elephants[d] and gained control of Antioch. 57Then the young Antiochus wrote to Jonathan, saying, "I confirm you in the high priesthood and set you over the four districts and make you one of the king's Friends." 58He also sent him gold plates and a table service, and granted him the right to drink from gold cups and dress in purple and wear a gold buckle. 59He appointed Jonathan's[e] brother Simon governor from the Ladder of Tyre to the borders of Egypt.

60 Then Jonathan set out and traveled beyond the river and among the towns, and all the army of Syria gathered to him as allies. When he came to Askalon, the people of the city met him and paid him honor. 61From there he went to Gaza, but the people of Gaza shut him out. So he besieged it and burned its suburbs with fire and plundered them. 62Then the people of Gaza pleaded with Jonathan, and he made peace with them, and took the sons of their rulers as hostages and sent them to Jerusalem. And he passed through the country as far as Damascus.

63 Then Jonathan heard that the officers of Demetrius had come to Kadesh in Galilee with a large army, intending to remove him from office. 64He went to meet them, but left his brother Simon in the country. 65Simon encamped before Beth-zur and fought against it for many days and hemmed it in. 66Then they asked him to grant them terms of peace, and he did so. He removed them from there, took possession of the town, and set a garrison over it.

67 Jonathan and his army encamped by the waters of Gennesaret. Early in the morning they marched to the plain of Hazor, 68and there in the plain the army of the foreigners met him; they had set an ambush against him in the mountains, but they themselves met him face to face. 69Then the men in ambush emerged from their places and joined battle. 70All the men with Jonathan fled; not one of them was left except Mattathias son of Absalom and Judas son of Chalphi, commanders of the forces of the army. 71Jonathan tore his

[a] Gk *him* [b] Gk *his troops* [c] Gk *he* [d] Gk *animals* [e] Gk *his*

clothes, put dust on his head, and prayed. 72Then
he turned back to the battle against the enemy[a]
and routed them, and they fled. 73When his men
who were fleeing saw this, they returned to him
and joined him in the pursuit as far as Kadesh, to
their camp, and there they encamped. 74As many
as three thousand of the foreigners fell that day.
And Jonathan returned to Jerusalem.

12 Now when Jonathan saw that the time
was favorable for him, he chose men and
sent them to Rome to confirm and renew the
friendship with them. 2He also sent letters to the
same effect to the Spartans and to other places.
3So they went to Rome and entered the senate
chamber and said, "The high priest Jonathan and
the Jewish nation have sent us to renew the former friendship and alliance with them." 4And the
Romans[b] gave them letters to the people in every
place, asking them to provide for the envoys[a] safe
conduct to the land of Judah.

5 This is a copy of the letter that Jonathan
wrote to the Spartans: 6"The high priest Jonathan,
the senate of the nation, the priests, and the rest
of the Jewish people to their brothers the Spartans, greetings. 7Already in time past a letter was
sent to the high priest Onias from Arius,[c] who was
king among you, stating that you are our brothers,
as the appended copy shows. 8Onias welcomed
the envoy with honor, and received the letter,
which contained a clear declaration of alliance
and friendship. 9Therefore, though we have no
need of these things, since we have as encouragement the holy books that are in our hands, 10we
have undertaken to send to renew our family ties
and friendship with you, so that we may not become estranged from you, for considerable time
has passed since you sent your letter to us. 11We
therefore remember you constantly on every occasion, both at our festivals and on other appropriate days, at the sacrifices that we offer and in
our prayers, as it is right and proper to remember
brothers. 12And we rejoice in your glory. 13But as
for ourselves, many trials and many wars have encircled us; the kings around us have waged war
against us. 14We were unwilling to annoy you and
our other allies and friends with these wars, 15for
we have the help that comes from Heaven for our
aid, and so we were delivered from our enemies,
and our enemies were humbled. 16We therefore
have chosen Numenius son of Antiochus and Antipater son of Jason, and have sent them to Rome
to renew our former friendship and alliance with
them. 17We have commanded them to go also to
you and greet you and deliver to you this letter
from us concerning the renewal of our family ties.
18And now please send us a reply to this."

19 This is a copy of the letter that they sent
to Onias: 20"King Arius of the Spartans, to the
high priest Onias, greetings. 21It has been found
in writing concerning the Spartans and the Jews
that they are brothers and are of the family of
Abraham. 22And now that we have learned this,
please write us concerning your welfare; 23we on
our part write to you that your livestock and your
property belong to us, and ours belong to you.
We therefore command that our envoys[b] report
to you accordingly."

24 Now Jonathan heard that the commanders of Demetrius had returned, with a larger force
than before, to wage war against him. 25So he
marched away from Jerusalem and met them in
the region of Hamath, for he gave them no opportunity to invade his own country. 26He sent
spies to their camp, and they returned and reported to him that the enemy[b] were being drawn
up in formation to attack the Jews[a] by night. 27So
when the sun had set, Jonathan commanded his
troops to be alert and to keep their arms at hand
so as to be ready all night for battle, and he stationed outposts around the camp. 28When the
enemy heard that Jonathan and his troops were
prepared for battle, they were afraid and were terrified at heart; so they kindled fires in their camp
and withdrew.[d] 29But Jonathan and his troops
did not know it until morning, for they saw the
fires burning. 30Then Jonathan pursued them, but
he did not overtake them, for they had crossed
the Eleutherus river. 31So Jonathan turned aside
against the Arabs who are called Zabadeans, and
he crushed them and plundered them. 32Then he

[a] Gk *them* [b] Gk *they* [c] Vg Compare verse 20: Gk *Darius* [d] Other ancient authorities omit *and withdrew*

broke camp and went to Damascus, and marched
through all that region.
33 Simon also went out and marched through
the country as far as Askalon and the neighboring
strongholds. He turned aside to Joppa and took
it by surprise, [34]for he had heard that they were
ready to hand over the stronghold to those whom
Demetrius had sent. And he stationed a garrison
there to guard it.
35 When Jonathan returned he convened the
elders of the people and planned with them to
build strongholds in Judea, [36]to build the walls
of Jerusalem still higher, and to erect a high barrier between the citadel and the city to separate
it from the city, in order to isolate it so that its
garrison[a] could neither buy nor sell. [37]So they
gathered together to rebuild the city; part of the
wall on the valley to the east had fallen, and he repaired the section called Chaphenatha. [38]Simon
also built Adida in the Shephelah; he fortified it
and installed gates with bolts.
39 Then Trypho attempted to become king in
Asia and put on the crown, and to raise his hand
against King Antiochus. [40]He feared that Jonathan might not permit him to do so, but might
make war on him, so he kept seeking to seize and
kill him, and he marched out and came to Beth-
shan. [41]Jonathan went out to meet him with forty
thousand picked warriors, and he came to Beth-
shan. [42]When Trypho saw that he had come with
a large army, he was afraid to raise his hand against
him. [43]So he received him with honor and commended him to all his Friends, and he gave him
gifts and commanded his Friends and his troops
to obey him as they would himself. [44]Then he said
to Jonathan, "Why have you put all these people to so much trouble when we are not at war?
[45]Dismiss them now to their homes and choose
for yourself a few men to stay with you, and come
with me to Ptolemais. I will hand it over to you as
well as the other strongholds and the remaining
troops and all the officials, and will turn around
and go home. For that is why I am here."
46 Jonathan[b] trusted him and did as he said;
he sent away the troops, and they returned to the
land of Judah. [47]He kept with himself three thousand men, two thousand of whom he left in Galilee, while one thousand accompanied him. [48]But
when Jonathan entered Ptolemais, the people of
Ptolemais closed the gates and seized him, and
they killed with the sword all who had entered
with him.
49 Then Trypho sent troops and cavalry into
Galilee and the Great Plain to destroy all Jonathan's soldiers. [50]But they realized that Jonathan
had been seized and had perished along with
his men, and they encouraged one another and
kept marching in close formation, ready for battle. [51]When their pursuers saw that they would
fight for their lives, they turned back. [52]So they
all reached the land of Judah safely, and they
mourned for Jonathan and his companions and
were in great fear; and all Israel mourned deeply.
[53]All the nations around them tried to destroy
them, for they said, "They have no leader or
helper. Now therefore let us make war on them
and blot out the memory of them from humankind."

13 Simon heard that Trypho had assembled
a large army to invade the land of Judah
and destroy it, [2]and he saw that the people were
trembling with fear. So he went up to Jerusalem, and gathering the people together [3]he encouraged them, saying to them, "You yourselves
know what great things my brothers and I and the
house of my father have done for the laws and the
sanctuary; you know also the wars and the difficulties that my brothers and I have seen. [4]By reason of this all my brothers have perished for the
sake of Israel, and I alone am left. [5]And now, far
be it from me to spare my life in any time of distress, for I am not better than my brothers. [6]But I
will avenge my nation and the sanctuary and your
wives and children, for all the nations have gathered together out of hatred to destroy us."
7 The spirit of the people was rekindled when
they heard these words, [8]and they answered in a
loud voice, "You are our leader in place of Judas
and your brother Jonathan. [9]Fight our battles,
and all that you say to us we will do." [10]So he

[a] Gk *they* [b] Gk *he*

assembled all the warriors and hurried to complete the walls of Jerusalem, and he fortified it on every side. 11 He sent Jonathan son of Absalom to Joppa, and with him a considerable army; he drove out its occupants and remained there.

12 Then Trypho left Ptolemais with a large army to invade the land of Judah, and Jonathan was with him under guard. 13 Simon encamped in Adida, facing the plain. 14 Trypho learned that Simon had risen up in place of his brother Jonathan, and that he was about to join battle with him, so he sent envoys to him and said, 15 "It is for the money that your brother Jonathan owed the royal treasury, in connection with the offices he held, that we are detaining him. 16 Send now one hundred talents of silver and two of his sons as hostages, so that when released he will not revolt against us, and we will release him."

17 Simon knew that they were speaking deceitfully to him, but he sent to get the money and the sons, so that he would not arouse great hostility among the people, who might say, 18 "It was because Simon[a] did not send him the money and the sons, that Jonathan[b] perished." 19 So he sent the sons and the hundred talents, but Trypho[b] broke his word and did not release Jonathan.

20 After this Trypho came to invade the country and destroy it, and he circled around by the way to Adora. But Simon and his army kept marching along opposite him to every place he went. 21 Now the men in the citadel kept sending envoys to Trypho urging him to come to them by way of the wilderness and to send them food. 22 So Trypho got all his cavalry ready to go, but that night a very heavy snow fell, and he did not go because of the snow. He marched off and went into the land of Gilead. 23 When he approached Baskama, he killed Jonathan, and he was buried there. 24 Then Trypho turned and went back to his own land.

25 Simon sent and took the bones of his brother Jonathan, and buried him in Modein, the city of his ancestors. 26 All Israel bewailed him with great lamentation, and mourned for him many days. 27 And Simon built a monument over the tomb of his father and his brothers; he made it high so that it might be seen, with polished stone at the front and back. 28 He also erected seven pyramids, opposite one another, for his father and mother and four brothers. 29 For the pyramids[c] he devised an elaborate setting, erecting about them great columns, and on the columns he put suits of armor for a permanent memorial, and beside the suits of armor he carved ships, so that they could be seen by all who sail the sea. 30 This is the tomb that he built in Modein; it remains to this day.

31 Trypho dealt treacherously with the young King Antiochus; he killed him 32 and became king in his place, putting on the crown of Asia; and he brought great calamity on the land. 33 But Simon built up the strongholds of Judea and walled them all around, with high towers and great walls and gates and bolts, and he stored food in the strongholds. 34 Simon also chose emissaries and sent them to King Demetrius with a request to grant relief to the country, for all that Trypho did was to plunder. 35 King Demetrius sent him a favorable reply to this request, and wrote him a letter as follows, 36 "King Demetrius to Simon, the high priest and friend of kings, and to the elders and nation of the Jews, greetings. 37 We have received the gold crown and the palm branch that you[d] sent, and we are ready to make a general peace with you and to write to our officials to grant you release from tribute. 38 All the grants that we have made to you remain valid, and let the strongholds that you have built be your possession. 39 We pardon any errors and offenses committed to this day, and cancel the crown tax that you owe; and whatever other tax has been collected in Jerusalem shall be collected no longer. 40 And if any of you are qualified to be enrolled in our bodyguard,[e] let them be enrolled, and let there be peace between us."

41 In the one hundred seventieth year[f] the yoke of the Gentiles was removed from Israel, 42 and the people began to write in their documents and contracts, "In the first year of Simon the great high priest and commander and leader of the Jews."

[a] Gk *I* [b] Gk *he* [c] Gk *For these* [d] The word *you* in verses 37–40 is plural [e] Or *court* [f] 142 B.C.

43 In those days Simon[a] encamped against
Gazara[b] and surrounded it with troops. He made
a siege engine, brought it up to the city, and battered and captured one tower. 44 The men in the
siege engine leaped out into the city, and a great
tumult arose in the city. 45 The men in the city,
with their wives and children, went up on the wall
with their clothes torn, and they cried out with
a loud voice, asking Simon to make peace with
them; 46 they said, "Do not treat us according to
our wicked acts but according to your mercy."
47 So Simon reached an agreement with them and
stopped fighting against them. But he expelled
them from the city and cleansed the houses in
which the idols were located, and then entered it
with hymns and praise. 48 He removed all uncleanness from it, and settled in it those who observed
the law. He also strengthened its fortifications and
built in it a house for himself.

1 Maccabees 13:45-47

This book repeatedly reminds us that women and children are the victims of war. They are killed (2:38), taken captive (5:13), sold into slavery (8:10), and surrendered as hostages (9:53; 13:19). Here the women, children, and men of Gazara take action during the siege of their city: they stand on the city walls, rend their clothes, and beg for mercy. Their lives are spared, but they are driven out from their homes and from their city.

— APY

49 Those who were in the citadel at Jerusalem were prevented from going in and out to buy
and sell in the country. So they were very hungry,
and many of them perished from famine. 50 Then
they cried to Simon to make peace with them,
and he did so. But he expelled them from there
and cleansed the citadel from its pollutions. 51 On
the twenty-third day of the second month, in the
one hundred seventy-first year,[c] the Jews[d] entered
it with praise and palm branches, and with harps
and cymbals and stringed instruments, and with
hymns and songs, because a great enemy had
been crushed and removed from Israel. 52 Simon[e]
decreed that every year they should celebrate this
day with rejoicing. He strengthened the fortifications of the temple hill alongside the citadel, and
he and his men lived there. 53 Simon saw that his
son John had reached manhood, and so he made
him commander of all the forces; and he lived at
Gazara.

14 In the one hundred seventy-second year[f]
King Demetrius assembled his forces and
marched into Media to obtain help, so that he
could make war against Trypho. 2 When King Arsaces of Persia and Media heard that Demetrius
had invaded his territory, he sent one of his generals to take him alive. 3 The general[e] went and defeated the army of Demetrius, and seized him and
took him to Arsaces, who put him under guard.

4 The land[g] had rest all the days of Simon.
He sought the good of his nation;
his rule was pleasing to them,
as was the honor shown him, all his days.
5 To crown all his honors he took Joppa for a harbor,
and opened a way to the isles of the sea.
6 He extended the borders of his nation,
and gained full control of the country.
7 He gathered a host of captives;
he ruled over Gazara and Beth-zur and the citadel,
and he removed its uncleanness from it;
and there was none to oppose him.
8 They tilled their land in peace;
the ground gave its increase,
and the trees of the plains their fruit.
9 Old men sat in the streets;
they all talked together of good things,
and the youths put on splendid military attire.
10 He supplied the towns with food,

[a] Gk *he* [b] Cn: Gk *Gaza* [c] 141 B.C. [d] Gk *they* [e] Gk *He* [f] 140 B.C.
[g] Other ancient authorities add *of Judah*

and furnished them with the means of defense,
until his renown spread to the ends of the earth.
11 He established peace in the land,
and Israel rejoiced with great joy.
12 All the people sat under their own vines and fig trees,
and there was none to make them afraid.
13 No one was left in the land to fight them,
and the kings were crushed in those days.
14 He gave help to all the humble among his people;
he sought out the law,
and did away with all the renegades and outlaws.
15 He made the sanctuary glorious,
and added to the vessels of the sanctuary.

16 It was heard in Rome, and as far away as
Sparta, that Jonathan had died, and they were
deeply grieved. 17When they heard that his
brother Simon had become high priest in his
stead, and that he was ruling over the country and
the towns in it, 18they wrote to him on bronze
tablets to renew with him the friendship and alliance that they had established with his brothers
Judas and Jonathan. 19And these were read before
the assembly in Jerusalem.

20 This is a copy of the letter that the Spartans sent:

"The rulers and the city of the Spartans to
the high priest Simon and to the elders and the
priests and the rest of the Jewish people, our
brothers, greetings. 21The envoys who were sent
to our people have told us about your glory and
honor, and we rejoiced at their coming. 22We
have recorded what they said in our public decrees, as follows, 'Numenius son of Antiochus
and Antipater son of Jason, envoys of the Jews,
have come to us to renew their friendship with us.
23It has pleased our people to receive these men
with honor and to put a copy of their words in the
public archives, so that the people of the Spartans
may have a record of them. And they have sent a
copy of this to the high priest Simon.' "

24 After this Simon sent Numenius to Rome
with a large gold shield weighing one thousand
minas, to confirm the alliance with the Romans.[a]

25 When the people heard these things they
said, "How shall we thank Simon and his sons?
26For he and his brothers and the house of his
father have stood firm; they have fought and repulsed Israel's enemies and established its freedom." 27So they made a record on bronze tablets
and put it on pillars on Mount Zion.

This is a copy of what they wrote: "On the
eighteenth day of Elul, in the one hundred
seventy-second year,[b] which is the third year of
the great high priest Simon, 28in Asaramel,[c] in
the great assembly of the priests and the people
and the rulers of the nation and the elders of the
country, the following was proclaimed to us:

29 "Since wars often occurred in the country,
Simon son of Mattathias, a priest of the sons[d] of
Joarib, and his brothers, exposed themselves to
danger and resisted the enemies of their nation,
in order that their sanctuary and the law might be
preserved; and they brought great glory to their
nation. 30Jonathan rallied the[e] nation, became
their high priest, and was gathered to his people.
31When their enemies decided to invade their
country and lay hands on their sanctuary, 32then
Simon rose up and fought for his nation. He spent
great sums of his own money; he armed the soldiers of his nation and paid them wages. 33He fortified the towns of Judea, and Beth-zur on the
borders of Judea, where formerly the arms of the
enemy had been stored, and he placed there a garrison of Jews. 34He also fortified Joppa, which is
by the sea, and Gazara, which is on the borders of
Azotus, where the enemy formerly lived. He settled Jews there, and provided in those towns[a]
whatever was necessary for their restoration.

35 "The people saw Simon's faithfulness[f] and
the glory that he had resolved to win for his nation, and they made him their leader and high
priest, because he had done all these things and

[a] Gk *them* [b] 140 B.C. [c] This word resembles the Hebrew words for *the court of the people of God* or *the prince of the people of God* [d] Meaning of Gk uncertain [e] Gk *their* [f] Other ancient authorities read *conduct*

because of the justice and loyalty that he had
maintained toward his nation. He sought in every
way to exalt his people. 36In his days things prospered in his hands, so that the Gentiles were put
out of the[a] country, as were also those in the city
of David in Jerusalem, who had built themselves
a citadel from which they used to sally forth and
defile the environs of the sanctuary, doing great
damage to its purity. 37He settled Jews in it and
fortified it for the safety of the country and of the
city, and built the walls of Jerusalem higher.

38 "In view of these things King Demetrius
confirmed him in the high priesthood, 39made
him one of his Friends, and paid him high honors.
40For he had heard that the Jews were addressed
by the Romans as friends and allies and brothers,
and that the Romans[b] had received the envoys of
Simon with honor.

41 "The Jews and their priests have resolved
that Simon should be their leader and high priest
forever, until a trustworthy prophet should arise,
42and that he should be governor over them
and that he should take charge of the sanctuary
and appoint officials over its tasks and over the
country and the weapons and the strongholds,
and that he should take charge of the sanctuary,
43and that he should be obeyed by all, and that
all contracts in the country should be written in
his name, and that he should be clothed in purple
and wear gold.

44 "None of the people or priests shall be
permitted to nullify any of these decisions or to
oppose what he says, or to convene an assembly
in the country without his permission, or to be
clothed in purple or put on a gold buckle. 45Who-
ever acts contrary to these decisions or rejects any
of them shall be liable to punishment."

46 All the people agreed to grant Simon the
right to act in accordance with these decisions.
47So Simon accepted and agreed to be high priest,
to be commander and ethnarch of the Jews and
priests, and to be protector of them all.[c] 48And
they gave orders to inscribe this decree on bronze
tablets, to put them up in a conspicuous place in
the precincts of the sanctuary, 49and to deposit
copies of them in the treasury, so that Simon and
his sons might have them.

15 Antiochus, son of King Demetrius, sent
a letter from the islands of the sea to Simon, the priest and ethnarch of the Jews, and
to all the nation; 2its contents were as follows:
"King Antiochus to Simon the high priest and
ethnarch and to the nation of the Jews, greetings. 3Whereas certain scoundrels have gained
control of the kingdom of our ancestors, and I
intend to lay claim to the kingdom so that I may
restore it as it formerly was, and have recruited
a host of mercenary troops and have equipped
warships, 4and intend to make a landing in the
country so that I may proceed against those who
have destroyed our country and those who have
devastated many cities in my kingdom, 5now
therefore I confirm to you all the tax remissions
that the kings before me have granted you, and a
release from all the other payments from which
they have released you. 6I permit you to mint
your own coinage as money for your country,
7and I grant freedom to Jerusalem and the sanctuary. All the weapons that you have prepared
and the strongholds that you have built and now
hold shall remain yours. 8Every debt you owe to
the royal treasury and any such future debts shall
be canceled for you from henceforth and for all
time. 9When we gain control of our kingdom, we
will bestow great honor on you and your nation
and the temple, so that your glory will become
manifest in all the earth."

10 In the one hundred seventy-fourth year[d]
Antiochus set out and invaded the land of his ancestors. All the troops rallied to him, so that there
were only a few with Trypho. 11Antiochus pursued
him, and Trypho[e] came in his flight to Dor, which
is by the sea; 12for he knew that troubles had con-
verged on him, and his troops had deserted him.
13So Antiochus encamped against Dor, and with
him were one hundred twenty thousand warriors
and eight thousand cavalry. 14He surrounded the
town, and the ships joined battle from the sea; he
pressed the town hard from land and sea, and permitted no one to leave or enter it.

[a] Gk *their* [b] Gk *they* [c] Or *to preside over them all* [d] 138 B.C. [e] Gk *he*

15 Then Numenius and his companions arrived from Rome, with letters to the kings and
countries, in which the following was written:
16“Lucius, consul of the Romans, to King Ptolemy, greetings. 17The envoys of the Jews have
come to us as our friends and allies to renew our
ancient friendship and alliance. They had been
sent by the high priest Simon and by the Jewish
people 18and have brought a gold shield weighing one thousand minas. 19We therefore have decided to write to the kings and countries that they
should not seek their harm or make war against
them and their cities and their country, or make
alliance with those who war against them. 20And
it has seemed good to us to accept the shield from
them. 21Therefore if any scoundrels have fled to
you from their country, hand them over to the
high priest Simon, so that he may punish them
according to their law.”

22 The consul[a] wrote the same thing to King
Demetrius and to Attalus and Ariarathes and
Arsaces, 23and to all the countries, and to Samp-
sames,[b] and to the Spartans, and to Delos, and to
Myndos, and to Sicyon, and to Caria, and to Sa-
mos, and to Pamphylia, and to Lycia, and to Hali-
carnassus, and to Rhodes, and to Phaselis, and to
Cos, and to Side, and to Aradus and Gortyna and
Cnidus and Cyprus and Cyrene. 24They also sent
a copy of these things to the high priest Simon.

25 King Antiochus besieged Dor for the second time, continually throwing his forces against
it and making engines of war; and he shut Trypho up and kept him from going out or in. 26And
Simon sent to Antiochus[c] two thousand picked
troops, to fight for him, and silver and gold and
a large amount of military equipment. 27But he
refused to receive them, and broke all the agreements he formerly had made with Simon, and
became estranged from him. 28He sent to him
Athenobius, one of his Friends, to confer with
him, saying, “You hold control of Joppa and
Gazara and the citadel in Jerusalem; they are cities of my kingdom. 29You have devastated their
territory, you have done great damage in the land,
and you have taken possession of many places
in my kingdom. 30Now then, hand over the cities that you have seized and the tribute money of
the places that you have conquered outside the
borders of Judea; 31or else pay me five hundred
talents of silver for the destruction that you have
caused and five hundred talents more for the tribute money of the cities. Otherwise we will come
and make war on you.”

32 So Athenobius, the king’s Friend, came to
Jerusalem, and when he saw the splendor of Simon, and the sideboard with its gold and silver
plate, and his great magnificence, he was amazed.
When he reported to him the king’s message,
33Simon said to him in reply: “We have neither
taken foreign land nor seized foreign property,
but only the inheritance of our ancestors, which
at one time had been unjustly taken by our enemies. 34Now that we have the opportunity, we are
firmly holding the inheritance of our ancestors.
35As for Joppa and Gazara, which you demand,
they were causing great damage among the people and to our land; for them we will give you one
hundred talents.”

Athenobius[a] did not answer him a word, 36but
returned in wrath to the king and reported to him
these words, and also the splendor of Simon and
all that he had seen. And the king was very angry.

37 Meanwhile Trypho embarked on a ship
and escaped to Orthosia. 38Then the king made
Cendebeus commander-in-chief of the coastal
country, and gave him troops of infantry and cavalry. 39He commanded him to encamp against Judea, to build up Kedron and fortify its gates, and
to make war on the people; but the king pursued
Trypho. 40So Cendebeus came to Jamnia and began to provoke the people and invade Judea and
take the people captive and kill them. 41He built
up Kedron and stationed horsemen and troops
there, so that they might go out and make raids
along the highways of Judea, as the king had ordered him.

16 John went up from Gazara and reported
to his father Simon what Cendebeus had
done. 2And Simon called in his two eldest sons
Judas and John, and said to them: “My brothers

[a] Gk *He* [b] The name is uncertain [c] Gk *him*

and I and my father's house have fought the wars
of Israel from our youth until this day, and things
have prospered in our hands so that we have delivered Israel many times. 3But now I have grown
old, and you by Heaven's[a] mercy are mature in
years. Take my place and my brother's, and go out
and fight for our nation, and may the help that
comes from Heaven be with you."

4 So John[b] chose out of the country twenty
thousand warriors and cavalry, and they marched
against Cendebeus and camped for the night in
Modein. 5Early in the morning they started out
and marched into the plain, where a large force
of infantry and cavalry was coming to meet them;
and a stream lay between them. 6Then he and
his army lined up against them. He saw that the
soldiers were afraid to cross the stream, so he
crossed over first; and when his troops saw him,
they crossed over after him. 7Then he divided the
army and placed the cavalry in the center of the
infantry, for the cavalry of the enemy were very
numerous. 8They sounded the trumpets, and
Cendebeus and his army were put to flight; many
of them fell wounded and the rest fled into the
stronghold. 9At that time Judas the brother of
John was wounded, but John pursued them until
Cendebeus[c] reached Kedron, which he had built.
10They also fled into the towers that were in the
fields of Azotus, and John[c] burned it with fire,
and about two thousand of them fell. He then returned to Judea safely.

11 Now Ptolemy son of Abubus had been
appointed governor over the plain of Jericho; he
had a large store of silver and gold, 12for he was
son-in-law of the high priest. 13His heart was
lifted up; he determined to get control of the
country, and made treacherous plans against Simon and his sons, to do away with them. 14Now
Simon was visiting the towns of the country and
attending to their needs, and he went down to
Jericho with his sons Mattathias and Judas, in the
one hundred seventy-seventh year,[d] in the eleventh month, which is the month of Shebat. 15The
son of Abubus received them treacherously in the
little stronghold called Dok, which he had built;
he gave them a great banquet, and hid men there.
16When Simon and his sons were drunk, Ptolemy
and his men rose up, took their weapons, rushed
in against Simon in the banquet hall and killed
him and his two sons, as well as some of his servants. 17So he committed an act of great treachery and returned evil for good.

18 Then Ptolemy wrote a report about these
things and sent it to the king, asking him to send
troops to aid him and to turn over to him the
towns and the country. 19He sent other troops
to Gazara to do away with John; he sent letters
to the captains asking them to come to him so
that he might give them silver and gold and gifts;
20and he sent other troops to take possession of
Jerusalem and the temple hill. 21But someone
ran ahead and reported to John at Gazara that his
father and brothers had perished, and that "he
has sent men to kill you also." 22When he heard
this, he was greatly shocked; he seized the men
who came to destroy him and killed them, for
he had found out that they were seeking to destroy him.

23 The rest of the acts of John and his wars
and the brave deeds that he did, and the building
of the walls that he completed, and his achievements, 24are written in the annals of his high
priesthood, from the time that he became high
priest after his father.

[a] Gk *his* [b] Other ancient authorities read *he* [c] Gk *he* [d] 134 B.C.

2 Maccabees

At the center of 2 Maccabees stands the Jerusalem temple. This sacred space provides a fundamental point of orientation for Jews in Judea and scattered in Diaspora. It is the place of worship, directing all attention to God. It is the chosen place through which God's presence is mediated to all God's people, ensuring their welfare. The temple links past and present, reaching back before the time of subjugation to foreign empires, before the exile and dispersion, to the days of Solomon and David, and even to the time of Moses when the tabernacle accompanied the people from their wilderness wanderings into the promised land.

Like 1 Maccabees, 2 Maccabees relates events leading up to the persecution of Jews by Antiochus IV Epiphanes in the year 167 BCE, the persecution itself, and the story of Jewish resistance. The story in 2 Maccabees is one of repeated threats to the Jerusalem temple—some of them realized. In this story, God and God's heavenly armies fought together with the faithful to protect and free it. Unlike 1 Maccabees, 2 Maccabees expresses belief in miracles and in resurrection (ch. 7). The book nuances its Deuteronomic theology of sin and punishment with the belief that suffering in this life can serve to discipline the faithful in preparation for life in the world to come (6:12-16; 7:18). Belief in bodily resurrection gave hope to those who suffered for their faith, enabling them to die for the law and for the temple in the hope of receiving the breath of life again (7:9-23).

The story of an unnamed mother of seven sons (later traditions will name her Hannah and Miryam) forms the heart and hinge of the book (ch. 7). As a mother and a Catholic raised in the traditions of the martyrs, I am drawn to her story. This mother and her sons were taken captive, tortured, and brought before the persecutor, Antiochus, who tried to make them eat pork (7:1). They refused. Six brothers suffered torture, spoke eloquently in defense of the law, proclaimed their faith in the resurrection and their belief in the justice of God, and so refused to defile themselves. Six brothers died (7:2-19).

Yet we are told that their mother excelled them all in courage, hope, and nobility (7:20). Speaking in their ancestral language, she encouraged each son (7:21). She related the mystery and miracle of gestation and childbirth to that of resurrection (7:22). The God who formed her children so mysteriously in her womb would by equal mystery give them the breath of life again (7:23). By their uncompromising faithfulness she and her sons would help to accomplish the work and plan of God for the redemption of Israel (7:37-38).

Antiochus asked her to intercede with her seventh son, to convince him to yield (7:25). He could not understand the words she had spoken in the ancestral language and did not know that she was exhorting her children to stand firm in their faith (7:24). She now instructed her youngest son to consider God's creation and so understand the providence in which they had their hope

(7:27-29). Like the others, this seventh son made his choice freely (7:30-37). He prayed that the deaths of the martyrs would turn away God's anger from the Jewish people so that salvation might come (7:37-38). He died "in his integrity," placing all trust in God (7:39). The mother died last of all, having witnessed the sufferings of all her children (7:41). Immediately following the story of the mother and her sons, the narrator tells us that the faithful rallied together, asking God to hear the cry of the martyrs' blood (8:1-4). God's anger changed to mercy (8:5).

The sacrifice of the mother and her seven sons effected a turning point in Judas's revolt and in the fate of their people, atoning for the sins of a nation. She was confident that each one would receive back from God the life they gave so freely for the law. She did not try to stop them, but encouraged them, and watched and listened as each one made his choice, spoke, suffered, and died. Her story is one of incredible faith, a faith that she clearly instilled in her children as their first and most influential teacher. She did not speak for her children nor choose for them, but neither did she turn away in their time of greatest suffering. She offered them encouragement, perspective, presence, and hope.

— ***Anathea E. Portier-Young***

1 The Jews in Jerusalem and those in the land
of Judea,
To their Jewish kindred in Egypt,
Greetings and true peace.
2 May God do good to you, and may he remember his covenant with Abraham and Isaac
and Jacob, his faithful servants. 3May he give you
all a heart to worship him and to do his will with
a strong heart and a willing spirit. 4May he open
your heart to his law and his commandments, and
may he bring peace. 5May he hear your prayers and
be reconciled to you, and may he not forsake you
in time of evil. 6We are now praying for you here.
7 In the reign of Demetrius, in the one hundred sixty-ninth year,[a] we Jews wrote to you, in
the critical distress that came upon us in those
years after Jason and his company revolted from
the holy land and the kingdom 8and burned the
gate and shed innocent blood. We prayed to the
Lord and were heard, and we offered sacrifice and
grain offering, and we lit the lamps and set out
the loaves. 9And now see that you keep the festival of booths in the month of Chislev, in the one
hundred eighty-eighth year.[b]

[a] 143 B.C. [b] 124 B.C.

2 Maccabees 1:1

The letters that form the preface of this book articulate the belief that common worship would unite the Jewish people, regardless of their location. They are also united by their kinship, by their shared cultural memory, by their ancestral covenant, and by the act of praying for one another (1:1—2:18).

— *APY*

10 The people of Jerusalem and of Judea and
the senate and Judas,

To Aristobulus, who is of the family of the
anointed priests, teacher of King Ptolemy, and to
the Jews in Egypt,

Greetings and good health.

11 Having been saved by God out of grave
dangers we thank him greatly for taking our side
against the king,[a] 12for he drove out those who
fought against the holy city. 13When the leader
reached Persia with a force that seemed irresistible,
they were cut to pieces in the temple of Nanea by a
deception employed by the priests of the goddess[b]
Nanea. 14On the pretext of intending to marry
her, Antiochus came to the place together with his
Friends, to secure most of its treasures as a dowry.
15When the priests of the temple of Nanea had set
out the treasures and Antiochus had come with
a few men inside the wall of the sacred precinct,
they closed the temple as soon as he entered it.
16Opening a secret door in the ceiling, they threw
stones and struck down the leader and his men;
they dismembered them and cut off their heads
and threw them to the people outside. 17Blessed
in every way be our God, who has brought judgment on those who have behaved impiously.

18 Since on the twenty-fifth day of Chislev we
shall celebrate the purification of the temple, we
thought it necessary to notify you, in order that
you also may celebrate the festival of booths and
the festival of the fire given when Nehemiah, who
built the temple and the altar, offered sacrifices.

19 For when our ancestors were being led
captive to Persia, the pious priests of that time
took some of the fire of the altar and secretly hid
it in the hollow of a dry cistern, where they took
such precautions that the place was unknown to
anyone. 20But after many years had passed, when
it pleased God, Nehemiah, having been commissioned by the king of Persia, sent the descendants
of the priests who had hidden the fire to get it.
And when they reported to us that they had not
found fire but only a thick liquid, he ordered them
to dip it out and bring it. 21When the materials for
the sacrifices were presented, Nehemiah ordered
the priests to sprinkle the liquid on the wood and
on the things laid upon it. 22When this had been
done and some time had passed, and when the
sun, which had been clouded over, shone out, a
great fire blazed up, so that all marveled. 23And
while the sacrifice was being consumed, the
priests offered prayer—the priests and everyone.
Jonathan led, and the rest responded, as did Nehemiah. 24The prayer was to this effect:

"O Lord, Lord God, Creator of all things, you
are awe-inspiring and strong and just and merciful, you alone are king and are kind, 25you alone
are bountiful, you alone are just and almighty and
eternal. You rescue Israel from every evil; you
chose the ancestors and consecrated them. 26Ac-
cept this sacrifice on behalf of all your people Israel and preserve your portion and make it holy.
27Gather together our scattered people, set free
those who are slaves among the Gentiles, look on
those who are rejected and despised, and let the
Gentiles know that you are our God. 28Punish
those who oppress and are insolent with pride.
29Plant your people in your holy place, as Moses
promised."

30 Then the priests sang the hymns. 31After
the materials of the sacrifice had been consumed,
Nehemiah ordered that the liquid that was left
should be poured on large stones. 32When this
was done, a flame blazed up; but when the light
from the altar shone back, it went out. 33When
this matter became known, and it was reported
to the king of the Persians that, in the place
where the exiled priests had hidden the fire, the
liquid had appeared with which Nehemiah and
his associates had burned the materials of the
sacrifice, 34the king investigated the matter, and
enclosed the place and made it sacred. 35And
with those persons whom the king favored he
exchanged many excellent gifts. 36Nehemiah
and his associates called this "nephthar," which
means purification, but by most people it is called
naphtha.[c]

2 One finds in the records that the prophet Jeremiah ordered those who were being deported
to take some of the fire, as has been mentioned,

[a] Cn: Gk *as those who array themselves against a king* [b] Gk lacks *the goddess* [c] Gk *nephthai*

[2]and that the prophet, after giving them the law, instructed those who were being deported not to forget the commandments of the Lord, or to be led astray in their thoughts on seeing the gold and silver statues and their adornment. [3]And with other similar words he exhorted them that the law should not depart from their hearts.

4 It was also in the same document that the prophet, having received an oracle, ordered that the tent and the ark should follow with him, and that he went out to the mountain where Moses had gone up and had seen the inheritance of God. [5]Jeremiah came and found a cave-dwelling, and he brought there the tent and the ark and the altar of incense; then he sealed up the entrance. [6]Some of those who followed him came up intending to mark the way, but could not find it. [7]When Jeremiah learned of it, he rebuked them and declared: "The place shall remain unknown until God gathers his people together again and shows his mercy. [8]Then the Lord will disclose these things, and the glory of the Lord and the cloud will appear, as they were shown in the case of Moses, and as Solomon asked that the place should be specially consecrated."

9 It was also made clear that being possessed of wisdom Solomon[a] offered sacrifice for the dedication and completion of the temple. [10]Just as Moses prayed to the Lord, and fire came down from heaven and consumed the sacrifices, so also Solomon prayed, and the fire came down and consumed the whole burnt offerings. [11]And Moses said, "They were consumed because the sin offering had not been eaten." [12]Likewise Solomon also kept the eight days.

13 The same things are reported in the records and in the memoirs of Nehemiah, and also that he founded a library and collected the books about the kings and prophets, and the writings of David, and letters of kings about votive offerings. [14]In the same way Judas also collected all the books that had been lost on account of the war that had come upon us, and they are in our possession. [15]So if you have need of them, send people to get them for you.

16 Since, therefore, we are about to celebrate the purification, we write to you. Will you therefore please keep the days? [17]It is God who has saved all his people, and has returned the inheritance to all, and the kingship and the priesthood and the consecration, [18]as he promised through the law. We have hope in God that he will soon have mercy on us and will gather us from everywhere under heaven into his holy place, for he has rescued us from great evils and has purified the place.

19 The story of Judas Maccabeus and his brothers, and the purification of the great temple, and the dedication of the altar, [20]and further the wars against Antiochus Epiphanes and his son Eupator, [21]and the appearances that came from heaven to those who fought bravely for Judaism, so that though few in number they seized the whole land and pursued the barbarian hordes, [22]and regained possession of the temple famous throughout the world, and liberated the city, and re-established the laws that were about to be abolished, while the Lord with great kindness became gracious to them— [23]all this, which has been set forth by Jason of Cyrene in five volumes, we shall attempt to condense into a single book. [24]For considering the flood of statistics involved and the difficulty there is for those who wish to enter upon the narratives of history because of the mass of material, [25]we have aimed to please those who wish to read, to make it easy for those who are inclined to memorize, and to profit all readers. [26]For us who have undertaken the toil of abbreviating, it is no light matter but calls for sweat and loss of sleep, [27]just as it is not easy for one who prepares a banquet and seeks the benefit of others. Nevertheless, to secure the gratitude of many we will gladly endure the uncomfortable toil, [28]leaving the responsibility for exact details to the compiler, while devoting our effort to arriving at the outlines of the condensation. [29]For as the master builder of a new house must be concerned with the whole construction, while the one who undertakes its painting and decoration has to consider only what is suitable for its

[a] Gk *he*

adornment, such in my judgment is the case with us. 30It is the duty of the original historian to occupy the ground, to discuss matters from every side, and to take trouble with details, 31but the one who recasts the narrative should be allowed to strive for brevity of expression and to forego exhaustive treatment. 32At this point therefore let us begin our narrative, without adding any more to what has already been said; for it would be foolish to lengthen the preface while cutting short the history itself.

3 While the holy city was inhabited in unbroken peace and the laws were strictly observed because of the piety of the high priest Onias and his hatred of wickedness, 2it came about that the kings themselves honored the place and glorified the temple with the finest presents, 3even to the extent that King Seleucus of Asia defrayed from his own revenues all the expenses connected with the service of the sacrifices.

4 But a man named Simon, of the tribe of Benjamin, who had been made captain of the temple, had a disagreement with the high priest about the administration of the city market. 5Since he could not prevail over Onias, he went to Apollonius of Tarsus,[a] who at that time was governor of Coelesyria and Phoenicia, 6and reported to him that the treasury in Jerusalem was full of untold sums of money, so that the amount of the funds could not be reckoned, and that they did not belong to the account of the sacrifices, but that it was possible for them to fall under the control of the king. 7When Apollonius met the king, he told him of the money about which he had been informed. The king[b] chose Heliodorus, who was in charge of his affairs, and sent him with commands to effect the removal of the reported wealth. 8Heliodorus at once set out on his journey, ostensibly to make a tour of inspection of the cities of Coelesyria and Phoenicia, but in fact to carry out the king's purpose.

9 When he had arrived at Jerusalem and had been kindly welcomed by the high priest of[c] the city, he told about the disclosure that had been made and stated why he had come, and he inquired whether this really was the situation. 10The high priest explained that there were some deposits belonging to widows and orphans, 11and also some money of Hyrcanus son of Tobias, a man of very prominent position, and that it totaled in all four hundred talents of silver and two hundred of gold. To such an extent the impious Simon had misrepresented the facts. 12And he said that it was utterly impossible that wrong should be done to those people who had trusted in the holiness of the place and in the sanctity and inviolability of the temple that is honored throughout the whole world.

13 But Heliodorus, because of the orders he had from the king, said that this money must in any case be confiscated for the king's treasury. 14So he set a day and went in to direct the inspection of these funds.

There was no little distress throughout the whole city. 15The priests prostrated themselves before the altar in their priestly vestments and called toward heaven upon him who had given the law about deposits, that he should keep them safe for those who had deposited them. 16To see the appearance of the high priest was to be wounded at heart, for his face and the change in his color disclosed the anguish of his soul. 17For terror and bodily trembling had come over the man, which plainly showed to those who looked at him the pain lodged in his heart. 18People also hurried out of their houses in crowds to make a general supplication because the holy place was about to be brought into dishonor. 19Women, girded with sackcloth under their breasts, thronged the streets. Some of the young women who were kept indoors ran together to the gates, and some to the walls, while others peered out of the windows. 20And holding up their hands to heaven, they all made supplication. 21There was something pitiable in the prostration of the whole populace and the anxiety of the high priest in his great anguish.

22 While they were calling upon the Almighty Lord that he would keep what had been entrusted safe and secure for those who had

[a] Gk *Apollonius son of Tharseas* [b] Gk *He* [c] Other ancient authorities read *and*

entrusted it, 23 Heliodorus went on with what
had been decided. 24 But when he arrived at the
treasury with his bodyguard, then and there the
Sovereign of spirits and of all authority caused
so great a manifestation that all who had been
so bold as to accompany him were astounded by
the power of God, and became faint with terror.
25 For there appeared to them a magnificently ca-
parisoned horse, with a rider of frightening mien;
it rushed furiously at Heliodorus and struck at
him with its front hoofs. Its rider was seen to
have armor and weapons of gold. 26 Two young
men also appeared to him, remarkably strong,
gloriously beautiful and splendidly dressed, who
stood on either side of him and flogged him continuously, inflicting many blows on him. 27 When
he suddenly fell to the ground and deep darkness
came over him, his men took him up, put him on
a stretcher, 28 and carried him away—this man
who had just entered the aforesaid treasury with
a great retinue and all his bodyguard but was now
unable to help himself. They recognized clearly
the sovereign power of God.

29 While he lay prostrate, speechless because
of the divine intervention and deprived of any
hope of recovery, 30 they praised the Lord who
had acted marvelously for his own place. And the
temple, which a little while before was full of fear
and disturbance, was filled with joy and gladness,
now that the Almighty Lord had appeared.

31 Some of Heliodorus's friends quickly
begged Onias to call upon the Most High to grant
life to one who was lying quite at his last breath.
32 So the high priest, fearing that the king might
get the notion that some foul play had been perpetrated by the Jews with regard to Heliodorus,
offered sacrifice for the man's recovery. 33 While
the high priest was making an atonement, the
same young men appeared again to Heliodorus
dressed in the same clothing, and they stood and
said, "Be very grateful to the high priest Onias,
since for his sake the Lord has granted you your
life. 34 And see that you, who have been flogged by
heaven, report to all people the majestic power of
God." Having said this they vanished.

35 Then Heliodorus offered sacrifice to the
Lord and made very great vows to the Savior of
his life, and having bidden Onias farewell, he
marched off with his forces to the king. 36 He bore
testimony to all concerning the deeds of the supreme God, which he had seen with his own eyes.
37 When the king asked Heliodorus what sort of
person would be suitable to send on another mission to Jerusalem, he replied, 38 "If you have any
enemy or plotter against your government, send
him there, for you will get him back thoroughly
flogged, if he survives at all; for there is certainly
some power of God about the place. 39 For he
who has his dwelling in heaven watches over that
place himself and brings it aid, and he strikes and
destroys those who come to do it injury." 40 This
was the outcome of the episode of Heliodorus
and the protection of the treasury.

4 The previously mentioned Simon, who had
informed about the money against[a] his own
country, slandered Onias, saying that it was he
who had incited Heliodorus and had been the
real cause of the misfortune. 2 He dared to designate as a plotter against the government the man
who was the benefactor of the city, the protector of his compatriots, and a zealot for the laws.
3 When his hatred progressed to such a degree
that even murders were committed by one of Simon's approved agents, 4 Onias recognized that
the rivalry was serious and that Apollonius son
of Menestheus,[b] and governor of Coelesyria and
Phoenicia, was intensifying the malice of Simon.
5 So he appealed to the king, not accusing his
compatriots but having in view the welfare, both
public and private, of all the people. 6 For he saw
that without the king's attention public affairs
could not again reach a peaceful settlement, and
that Simon would not stop his folly.

7 When Seleucus died and Antiochus, who
was called Epiphanes, succeeded to the kingdom,
Jason the brother of Onias obtained the high priesthood by corruption, 8 promising the king at an interview[c] three hundred sixty talents of silver, and
from another source of revenue eighty talents. 9 In
addition to this he promised to pay one hundred

[a] Gk *and* [b] Vg Compare verse 21: Meaning of Gk uncertain [c] Or *by a petition*

fifty more if permission were given to establish by
his authority a gymnasium and a body of youth
for it, and to enroll the people of Jerusalem as citizens of Antioch. 10 When the king assented and
Jason[a] came to office, he at once shifted his compatriots over to the Greek way of life.

11 He set aside the existing royal concessions
to the Jews, secured through John the father of
Eupolemus, who went on the mission to establish friendship and alliance with the Romans;
and he destroyed the lawful ways of living and introduced new customs contrary to the law. 12 He
took delight in establishing a gymnasium right
under the citadel, and he induced the noblest of
the young men to wear the Greek hat. 13 There was
such an extreme of Hellenization and increase in
the adoption of foreign ways because of the surpassing wickedness of Jason, who was ungodly
and no true[b] high priest, 14 that the priests were
no longer intent upon their service at the altar.
Despising the sanctuary and neglecting the sacrifices, they hurried to take part in the unlawful
proceedings in the wrestling arena after the signal
for the discus-throwing, 15 disdaining the honors
prized by their ancestors and putting the highest
value upon Greek forms of prestige. 16 For this
reason heavy disaster overtook them, and those
whose ways of living they admired and wished
to imitate completely became their enemies and
punished them. 17 It is no light thing to show irreverence to the divine laws—a fact that later
events will make clear.

18 When the quadrennial games were being
held at Tyre and the king was present, 19 the vile
Jason sent envoys, chosen as being Antiochian
citizens from Jerusalem, to carry three hundred
silver drachmas for the sacrifice to Hercules.
Those who carried the money, however, thought
best not to use it for sacrifice, because that was
inappropriate, but to expend it for another purpose. 20 So this money was intended by the sender
for the sacrifice to Hercules, but by the decision
of its carriers it was applied to the construction
of triremes.

21 When Apollonius son of Menestheus was
sent to Egypt for the coronation[c] of Philometor
as king, Antiochus learned that Philometor[a] had
become hostile to his government, and he took
measures for his own security. Therefore upon
arriving at Joppa he proceeded to Jerusalem.
22 He was welcomed magnificently by Jason and
the city, and ushered in with a blaze of torches
and with shouts. Then he marched his army into
Phoenicia.

23 After a period of three years Jason sent
Menelaus, the brother of the previously mentioned Simon, to carry the money to the king
and to complete the records of essential business.
24 But he, when presented to the king, extolled
him with an air of authority, and secured the high
priesthood for himself, outbidding Jason by three
hundred talents of silver. 25 After receiving the
king's orders he returned, possessing no qualification for the high priesthood, but having the hot
temper of a cruel tyrant and the rage of a savage
wild beast. 26 So Jason, who after supplanting his
own brother was supplanted by another man, was
driven as a fugitive into the land of Ammon. 27 Although Menelaus continued to hold the office, he
did not pay regularly any of the money promised
to the king. 28 When Sostratus the captain of the
citadel kept requesting payment—for the collection of the revenue was his responsibility—the
two of them were summoned by the king on
account of this issue. 29 Menelaus left his own
brother Lysimachus as deputy in the high priesthood, while Sostratus left Crates, the commander
of the Cyprian troops.

30 While such was the state of affairs, it happened that the people of Tarsus and of Mallus
revolted because their cities had been given as a
present to Antiochis, the king's concubine. 31 So
the king went hurriedly to settle the trouble, leaving Andronicus, a man of high rank, to act as his
deputy. 32 But Menelaus, thinking he had obtained
a suitable opportunity, stole some of the gold
vessels of the temple and gave them to Andronicus; other vessels, as it happened, he had sold to
Tyre and the neighboring cities. 33 When Onias
became fully aware of these acts, he publicly ex-

[a] Gk *he* [b] Gk lacks *true* [c] Meaning of Gk uncertain

posed them, having first withdrawn to a place of
sanctuary at Daphne near Antioch. 34Therefore
Menelaus, taking Andronicus aside, urged him
to kill Onias. Andronicus[a] came to Onias, and
resorting to treachery, offered him sworn pledges
and gave him his right hand; he persuaded him,
though still suspicious, to come out from the
place of sanctuary; then, with no regard for justice, he immediately put him out of the way.

35 For this reason not only Jews, but many
also of other nations, were grieved and displeased
at the unjust murder of the man. 36When the king
returned from the region of Cilicia, the Jews in
the city[b] appealed to him with regard to the unreasonable murder of Onias, and the Greeks shared
their hatred of the crime. 37Therefore Antiochus
was grieved at heart and filled with pity, and wept
because of the moderation and good conduct of
the deceased. 38Inflamed with anger, he immediately stripped off the purple robe from Andronicus, tore off his clothes, and led him around the
whole city to that very place where he had committed the outrage against Onias, and there he
dispatched the bloodthirsty fellow. The Lord thus
repaid him with the punishment he deserved.

39 When many acts of sacrilege had been
committed in the city by Lysimachus with the
connivance of Menelaus, and when report of
them had spread abroad, the populace gathered against Lysimachus, because many of the
gold vessels had already been stolen. 40Since the
crowds were becoming aroused and filled with
anger, Lysimachus armed about three thousand
men and launched an unjust attack, under the
leadership of a certain Auranus, a man advanced
in years and no less advanced in folly. 41But when
the Jews[c] became aware that Lysimachus was
attacking them, some picked up stones, some
blocks of wood, and others took handfuls of the
ashes that were lying around, and threw them in
wild confusion at Lysimachus and his men. 42As
a result, they wounded many of them, and killed
some, and put all the rest to flight; the temple
robber himself they killed close by the treasury.

43 Charges were brought against Menelaus
about this incident. 44When the king came to
Tyre, three men sent by the senate presented the
case before him. 45But Menelaus, already as good
as beaten, promised a substantial bribe to Ptolemy
son of Dorymenes to win over the king. 46There-
fore Ptolemy, taking the king aside into a colonnade as if for refreshment, induced the king to
change his mind. 47Menelaus, the cause of all the
trouble, he acquitted of the charges against him,
while he sentenced to death those unfortunate
men, who would have been freed uncondemned
if they had pleaded even before Scythians. 48And
so those who had spoken for the city and the villages[d] and the holy vessels quickly suffered the
unjust penalty. 49Therefore even the Tyrians,
showing their hatred of the crime, provided magnificently for their funeral. 50But Menelaus, because of the greed of those in power, remained in
office, growing in wickedness, having become the
chief plotter against his compatriots.

5 About this time Antiochus made his second
invasion of Egypt. 2And it happened that, for
almost forty days, there appeared over all the city
golden-clad cavalry charging through the air, in
companies fully armed with lances and drawn
swords— 3troops of cavalry drawn up, attacks
and counterattacks made on this side and on that,
brandishing of shields, massing of spears, hurling
of missiles, the flash of golden trappings, and armor of all kinds. 4Therefore everyone prayed that
the apparition might prove to have been a good
omen.

5 When a false rumor arose that Antiochus
was dead, Jason took no fewer than a thousand
men and suddenly made an assault on the city.
When the troops on the wall had been forced
back and at last the city was being taken, Menelaus took refuge in the citadel. 6But Jason kept
relentlessly slaughtering his compatriots, not realizing that success at the cost of one's kindred is
the greatest misfortune, but imagining that he was
setting up trophies of victory over enemies and
not over compatriots. 7He did not, however, gain
control of the government; in the end he got only

[a] Gk *He* [b] Or *in each city* [c] Gk *they* [d] Other ancient authorities read *the people*

disgrace from his conspiracy, and fled again into
the country of the Ammonites. 8 Finally he met a
miserable end. Accused[a] before Aretas the ruler
of the Arabs, fleeing from city to city, pursued by
everyone, hated as a rebel against the laws, and
abhorred as the executioner of his country and
his compatriots, he was cast ashore in Egypt.
9 There he who had driven many from their own
country into exile died in exile, having embarked
to go to the Lacedaemonians in hope of finding
protection because of their kinship. 10 He who
had cast out many to lie unburied had no one to
mourn for him; he had no funeral of any sort and
no place in the tomb of his ancestors.

11 When news of what had happened reached
the king, he took it to mean that Judea was in revolt. So, raging inwardly, he left Egypt and took
the city by storm. 12 He commanded his soldiers
to cut down relentlessly everyone they met and
to kill those who went into their houses. 13 Then
there was massacre of young and old, destruction of boys, women, and children, and slaughter
of young girls and infants. 14 Within the total of
three days eighty thousand were destroyed, forty
thousand in hand-to-hand fighting, and as many
were sold into slavery as were killed.

15 Not content with this, Antiochus[b] dared
to enter the most holy temple in all the world,
guided by Menelaus, who had become a traitor
both to the laws and to his country. 16 He took the
holy vessels with his polluted hands, and swept
away with profane hands the votive offerings that
other kings had made to enhance the glory and
honor of the place. 17 Antiochus was elated in
spirit, and did not perceive that the Lord was angered for a little while because of the sins of those
who lived in the city, and that this was the reason he was disregarding the holy place. 18 But if
it had not happened that they were involved in
many sins, this man would have been flogged and
turned back from his rash act as soon as he came
forward, just as Heliodorus had been, whom
King Seleucus sent to inspect the treasury. 19 But
the Lord did not choose the nation for the sake
of the holy place, but the place for the sake of the
nation. 20 Therefore the place itself shared in the
misfortunes that befell the nation and afterward
participated in its benefits; and what was forsaken in the wrath of the Almighty was restored
again in all its glory when the great Lord became
reconciled.

21 So Antiochus carried off eighteen hundred talents from the temple, and hurried away to
Antioch, thinking in his arrogance that he could
sail on the land and walk on the sea, because
his mind was elated. 22 He left governors to oppress the people: at Jerusalem, Philip, by birth a
Phrygian and in character more barbarous than
the man who appointed him; 23 and at Gerizim,
Andronicus; and besides these Menelaus, who
lorded it over his compatriots worse than the others did. In his malice toward the Jewish citizens,[c]
24 Antiochus[b] sent Apollonius, the captain of the
Mysians, with an army of twenty-two thousand,
and commanded him to kill all the grown men
and to sell the women and boys as slaves. 25 When
this man arrived in Jerusalem, he pretended to
be peaceably disposed and waited until the holy
sabbath day; then, finding the Jews not at work,
he ordered his troops to parade under arms. 26 He
put to the sword all those who came out to see
them, then rushed into the city with his armed
warriors and killed great numbers of people.

27 But Judas Maccabeus, with about nine
others, got away to the wilderness, and kept himself and his companions alive in the mountains as
wild animals do; they continued to live on what
grew wild, so that they might not share in the defilement.

6 Not long after this, the king sent an Athenian[d] senator[e] to compel the Jews to forsake
the laws of their ancestors and no longer to live
by the laws of God; 2 also to pollute the temple in
Jerusalem and to call it the temple of Olympian
Zeus, and to call the one in Gerizim the temple of
Zeus-the-Friend-of-Strangers, as did the people
who lived in that place.

[a] Cn: Gk *Imprisoned* [b] Gk *he* [c] Or *worse than the others did in his malice toward the Jewish citizens* [d] Other ancient authorities read *Antiochian* [e] Or *Geron an Athenian*

 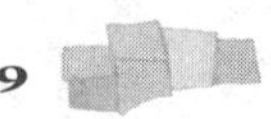

3 Harsh and utterly grievous was the on-
slaught of evil. 4For the temple was filled with
debauchery and reveling by the Gentiles, who
dallied with prostitutes and had intercourse with
women within the sacred precincts, and besides
brought in things for sacrifice that were unfit.
5The altar was covered with abominable offerings
that were forbidden by the laws. 6People could
neither keep the sabbath, nor observe the festivals of their ancestors, nor so much as confess
themselves to be Jews.

7 On the monthly celebration of the king's
birthday, the Jews[a] were taken, under bitter constraint, to partake of the sacrifices; and when a
festival of Dionysus was celebrated, they were
compelled to wear wreaths of ivy and to walk in
the procession in honor of Dionysus. 8At the suggestion of the people of Ptolemais[b] a decree was
issued to the neighboring Greek cities that they
should adopt the same policy toward the Jews
and make them partake of the sacrifices, 9and
should kill those who did not choose to change
over to Greek customs. One could see, therefore,
the misery that had come upon them. 10For example, two women were brought in for having
circumcised their children. They publicly pa-
raded them around the city, with their babies
hanging at their breasts, and then hurled them
down headlong from the wall. 11Others who had
assembled in the caves nearby, in order to observe
the seventh day secretly, were betrayed to Philip
and were all burned together, because their piety
kept them from defending themselves, in view of
their regard for that most holy day.

12 Now I urge those who read this book not
to be depressed by such calamities, but to recognize that these punishments were designed not
to destroy but to discipline our people. 13In fact,
it is a sign of great kindness not to let the impious alone for long, but to punish them immediately. 14For in the case of the other nations the
Lord waits patiently to punish them until they
have reached the full measure of their sins; but he
does not deal in this way with us, 15in order that
he may not take vengeance on us afterward when
our sins have reached their height. 16Therefore he
never withdraws his mercy from us. Although he
disciplines us with calamities, he does not forsake
his own people. 17Let what we have said serve as a
reminder; we must go on briefly with the story.

18 Eleazar, one of the scribes in high position, a man now advanced in age and of noble
presence, was being forced to open his mouth to
eat swine's flesh. 19But he, welcoming death with
honor rather than life with pollution, went up to
the rack of his own accord, spitting out the flesh,
20as all ought to go who have the courage to refuse things that it is not right to taste, even for the
natural love of life.

21 Those who were in charge of that unlawful
sacrifice took the man aside because of their long
acquaintance with him, and privately urged him
to bring meat of his own providing, proper for
him to use, and to pretend that he was eating the
flesh of the sacrificial meal that had been commanded by the king, 22so that by doing this he
might be saved from death, and be treated kindly
on account of his old friendship with them. 23But
making a high resolve, worthy of his years and the
dignity of his old age and the gray hairs that he
had reached with distinction and his excellent life
even from childhood, and moreover according
to the holy God-given law, he declared himself
quickly, telling them to send him to Hades.

24 "Such pretense is not worthy of our time
of life," he said, "for many of the young might suppose that Eleazar in his ninetieth year had gone
over to an alien religion, 25and through my pretense, for the sake of living a brief moment longer,
they would be led astray because of me, while I
defile and disgrace my old age. 26Even if for the
present I would avoid the punishment of mortals, yet whether I live or die I will not escape the
hands of the Almighty. 27Therefore, by bravely
giving up my life now, I will show myself worthy
of my old age 28and leave to the young a noble
example of how to die a good death willingly and
nobly for the revered and holy laws."

When he had said this, he went[c] at once to
the rack. 29Those who a little before had acted

[a] Gk *they* [b] Cn: Gk *suggestion of the Ptolemies* (or *of Ptolemy*) [c] Other ancient authorities read *was dragged*

toward him with goodwill now changed to ill will,
because the words he had uttered were in their
opinion sheer madness.[a] 30When he was about to
die under the blows, he groaned aloud and said:
"It is clear to the Lord in his holy knowledge that,
though I might have been saved from death, I am
enduring terrible sufferings in my body under
this beating, but in my soul I am glad to suffer
these things because I fear him."
31 So in this way he died, leaving in his death
an example of nobility and a memorial of courage, not only to the young but to the great body
of his nation.

7 It happened also that seven brothers and
their mother were arrested and were being
compelled by the king, under torture with whips
and thongs, to partake of unlawful swine's flesh.
2One of them, acting as their spokesman, said,
"What do you intend to ask and learn from us?
For we are ready to die rather than transgress the
laws of our ancestors."
3 The king fell into a rage, and gave orders
to have pans and caldrons heated. 4These were
heated immediately, and he commanded that the
tongue of their spokesman be cut out and that
they scalp him and cut off his hands and feet,
while the rest of the brothers and the mother
looked on. 5When he was utterly helpless, the
king[b] ordered them to take him to the fire, still
breathing, and to fry him in a pan. The smoke
from the pan spread widely, but the brothers[c]
and their mother encouraged one another to die
nobly, saying, 6"The Lord God is watching over
us and in truth has compassion on us, as Moses
declared in his song that bore witness against the
people to their faces, when he said, 'And he will
have compassion on his servants.'"[d]
7 After the first brother had died in this way,
they brought forward the second for their sport.
They tore off the skin of his head with the hair,
and asked him, "Will you eat rather than have
your body punished limb by limb?" 8He replied
in the language of his ancestors and said to them,
"No." Therefore he in turn underwent tortures
as the first brother had done. 9And when he was
at his last breath, he said, "You accursed wretch,
you dismiss us from this present life, but the
King of the universe will raise us up to an everlasting renewal of life, because we have died for
his laws."
10 After him, the third was the victim of their
sport. When it was demanded, he quickly put out
his tongue and courageously stretched forth his
hands, 11and said nobly, "I got these from Heaven,
and because of his laws I disdain them, and from
him I hope to get them back again." 12As a result
the king himself and those with him were astonished at the young man's spirit, for he regarded
his sufferings as nothing.
13 After he too had died, they maltreated and
tortured the fourth in the same way. 14When he
was near death, he said, "One cannot but choose
to die at the hands of mortals and to cherish the
hope God gives of being raised again by him. But
for you there will be no resurrection to life!"
15 Next they brought forward the fifth and
maltreated him. 16But he looked at the king,[e] and
said, "Because you have authority among mortals, though you also are mortal, you do what you
please. But do not think that God has forsaken
our people. 17Keep on, and see how his mighty
power will torture you and your descendants!"
18 After him they brought forward the sixth.
And when he was about to die, he said, "Do not
deceive yourself in vain. For we are suffering
these things on our own account, because of our
sins against our own God. Therefore[f] astounding
things have happened. 19But do not think that
you will go unpunished for having tried to fight
against God!"
20 The mother was especially admirable and
worthy of honorable memory. Although she saw
her seven sons perish within a single day, she
bore it with good courage because of her hope
in the Lord. 21She encouraged each of them in
the language of their ancestors. Filled with a noble spirit, she reinforced her woman's reasoning

[a] Meaning of Gk uncertain [b] Gk *he* [c] Gk *they* [d] Gk *slaves* [e] Gk *at him*
[f] Lat: Other ancient authorities lack *Therefore*

with a man's courage, and said to them, 22“I do
not know how you came into being in my womb.
It was not I who gave you life and breath, nor I
who set in order the elements within each of you.
23Therefore the Creator of the world, who shaped
the beginning of humankind and devised the origin of all things, will in his mercy give life and
breath back to you again, since you now forget
yourselves for the sake of his laws.”

24 Antiochus felt that he was being treated
with contempt, and he was suspicious of her re-
proachful tone. The youngest brother being still
alive, Antiochus[a] not only appealed to him in
words, but promised with oaths that he would
make him rich and enviable if he would turn from
the ways of his ancestors, and that he would take
him for his Friend and entrust him with public
affairs. 25Since the young man would not listen
to him at all, the king called the mother to him
and urged her to advise the youth to save himself. 26After much urging on his part, she undertook to persuade her son. 27But, leaning close to
him, she spoke in their native language as follows,
deriding the cruel tyrant: “My son, have pity on
me. I carried you nine months in my womb, and
nursed you for three years, and have reared you
and brought you up to this point in your life, and
have taken care of you.[b] 28I beg you, my child, to
look at the heaven and the earth and see everything that is in them, and recognize that God did
not make them out of things that existed.[c] And
in the same way the human race came into being. 29Do not fear this butcher, but prove worthy
of your brothers. Accept death, so that in God's
mercy I may get you back again along with your
brothers.”

30 While she was still speaking, the young
man said, “What are you[d] waiting for? I will not
obey the king's command, but I obey the command of the law that was given to our ancestors
through Moses. 31But you,[e] who have contrived
all sorts of evil against the Hebrews, will certainly
not escape the hands of God. 32For we are suffering because of our own sins. 33And if our living Lord is angry for a little while, to rebuke and
discipline us, he will again be reconciled with his
own servants.[f] 34But you, unholy wretch, you
most defiled of all mortals, do not be elated in
vain and puffed up by uncertain hopes, when you
raise your hand against the children of heaven.
35You have not yet escaped the judgment of the
almighty, all-seeing God. 36For our brothers after enduring a brief suffering have drunk[g] of ever-
flowing life, under God's covenant; but you, by
the judgment of God, will receive just punishment for your arrogance. 37I, like my brothers,
give up body and life for the laws of our ancestors, appealing to God to show mercy soon to
our nation and by trials and plagues to make you
confess that he alone is God, 38and through me
and my brothers to bring to an end the wrath of
the Almighty that has justly fallen on our whole
nation.”

39 The king fell into a rage, and handled him
worse than the others, being exasperated at his
scorn. 40So he died in his integrity, putting his
whole trust in the Lord.

41 Last of all, the mother died, after her
sons.

42 Let this be enough, then, about the eating
of sacrifices and the extreme tortures.

8 Meanwhile Judas, who was also called Maccabeus, and his companions secretly entered
the villages and summoned their kindred and
enlisted those who had continued in the Jewish
faith, and so they gathered about six thousand.
2They implored the Lord to look upon the people who were oppressed by all; and to have pity
on the temple that had been profaned by the godless; 3to have mercy on the city that was being
destroyed and about to be leveled to the ground;
to hearken to the blood that cried out to him; 4to
remember also the lawless destruction of the innocent babies and the blasphemies committed
against his name; and to show his hatred of evil.

5 As soon as Maccabeus got his army organized, the Gentiles could not withstand him, for

[a] Gk *he* [b] Or *have borne the burden of your education* [c] Or *God made them out of things that did not exist* [d] The Gk here for *you* is plural [e] The Gk here for *you* is singular [f] Gk *slaves* [g] Cn: Gk *fallen*

the wrath of the Lord had turned to mercy. 6Com-
ing without warning, he would set fire to towns
and villages. He captured strategic positions and
put to flight not a few of the enemy. 7He found
the nights most advantageous for such attacks.
And talk of his valor spread everywhere.

8 When Philip saw that the man was gaining
ground little by little, and that he was pushing
ahead with more frequent successes, he wrote to
Ptolemy, the governor of Coelesyria and Phoenicia, to come to the aid of the king's government.
9Then Ptolemy[a] promptly appointed Nicanor son
of Patroclus, one of the king's chief[b] Friends, and
sent him, in command of no fewer than twenty
thousand Gentiles of all nations, to wipe out the
whole race of Judea. He associated with him Gorgias, a general and a man of experience in military
service. 10Nicanor determined to make up for the
king the tribute due to the Romans, two thousand talents, by selling the captured Jews into
slavery. 11So he immediately sent to the towns on
the seacoast, inviting them to buy Jewish slaves
and promising to hand over ninety slaves for a
talent, not expecting the judgment from the Almighty that was about to overtake him.

12 Word came to Judas concerning Nicanor's
invasion; and when he told his companions of the
arrival of the army, 13those who were cowardly
and distrustful of God's justice ran off and got
away. 14Others sold all their remaining property,
and at the same time implored the Lord to rescue
those who had been sold by the ungodly Nicanor
before he ever met them, 15if not for their own
sake, then for the sake of the covenants made
with their ancestors, and because he had called
them by his holy and glorious name. 16But Maccabeus gathered his forces together, to the number six thousand, and exhorted them not to be
frightened by the enemy and not to fear the great
multitude of Gentiles who were wickedly coming
against them, but to fight nobly, 17keeping before
their eyes the lawless outrage that the Gentiles[c]
had committed against the holy place, and the
torture of the derided city, and besides, the overthrow of their ancestral way of life. 18"For they
trust to arms and acts of daring," he said, "but
we trust in the Almighty God, who is able with
a single nod to strike down those who are coming against us, and even, if necessary, the whole
world."

19 Moreover, he told them of the occasions
when help came to their ancestors; how, in the
time of Sennacherib, when one hundred eighty-
five thousand perished, 20and the time of the
battle against the Galatians that took place in Babylonia, when eight thousand Jews[d] fought along
with four thousand Macedonians; yet when the
Macedonians were hard pressed, the eight thousand, by the help that came to them from heaven,
destroyed one hundred twenty thousand Galatians[e] and took a great amount of booty.

21 With these words he filled them with courage and made them ready to die for their laws and
their country; then he divided his army into four
parts. 22He appointed his brothers also, Simon
and Joseph and Jonathan, each to command a division, putting fifteen hundred men under each.
23Besides, he appointed Eleazar to read aloud[f]
from the holy book, and gave the watchword,
"The help of God"; then, leading the first division
himself, he joined battle with Nicanor.

24 With the Almighty as their ally, they killed
more than nine thousand of the enemy, and
wounded and disabled most of Nicanor's army,
and forced them all to flee. 25They captured the
money of those who had come to buy them as
slaves. After pursuing them for some distance,
they were obliged to return because the hour
was late. 26It was the day before the sabbath, and
for that reason they did not continue their pursuit. 27When they had collected the arms of the
enemy and stripped them of their spoils, they
kept the sabbath, giving great praise and thanks
to the Lord, who had preserved them for that day
and allotted it to them as the beginning of mercy.
28After the sabbath they gave some of the spoils
to those who had been tortured and to the widows and orphans, and distributed the rest among
themselves and their children. 29When they had
done this, they made common supplication and

[a] Gk *he* [b] Gk *one of the first* [c] Gk *they* [d] Gk lacks *Jews* [e] Gk lacks *Galatians* [f] Meaning of Gk uncertain

implored the merciful Lord to be wholly reconciled with his servants.[a]

30 In encounters with the forces of Timothy and Bacchides they killed more than twenty thousand of them and got possession of some exceedingly high strongholds, and they divided a very large amount of plunder, giving to those who had been tortured and to the orphans and widows, and also to the aged, shares equal to their own.
31They collected the arms of the enemy,[b] and carefully stored all of them in strategic places; the rest of the spoils they carried to Jerusalem. 32They killed the commander of Timothy's forces, a most wicked man, and one who had greatly troubled the Jews. 33While they were celebrating the victory in the city of their ancestors, they burned those who had set fire to the sacred gates, Callisthenes and some others, who had fled into one little house; so these received the proper reward for their impiety.[c]

34 The thrice-accursed Nicanor, who had brought the thousand merchants to buy the Jews,
35having been humbled with the help of the Lord by opponents whom he regarded as of the least account, took off his splendid uniform and made his way alone like a runaway slave across the country until he reached Antioch, having succeeded chiefly in the destruction of his own army! 36So he who had undertaken to secure tribute for the Romans by the capture of the people of Jerusalem proclaimed that the Jews had a Defender, and that therefore the Jews were invulnerable, because they followed the laws ordained by him.

9 About that time, as it happened, Antiochus had retreated in disorder from the region of Persia. 2He had entered the city called Persepolis and attempted to rob the temples and control the city. Therefore the people rushed to the rescue with arms, and Antiochus and his army were defeated,[d] with the result that Antiochus was put to flight by the inhabitants and beat a shameful retreat. 3While he was in Ecbatana, news came to him of what had happened to Nicanor and the forces of Timothy. 4Transported with rage, he conceived the idea of turning upon the Jews the injury done by those who had put him to flight; so he ordered his charioteer to drive without stopping until he completed the journey. But the judgment of heaven rode with him! For in his arrogance he said, "When I get there I will make Jerusalem a cemetery of Jews."

5 But the all-seeing Lord, the God of Israel, struck him with an incurable and invisible blow. As soon as he stopped speaking he was seized with a pain in his bowels, for which there was no relief, and with sharp internal tortures— 6and that very justly, for he had tortured the bowels of others with many and strange inflictions. 7Yet he did not in any way stop his insolence, but was even more filled with arrogance, breathing fire in his rage against the Jews, and giving orders to drive even faster. And so it came about that he fell out of his chariot as it was rushing along, and the fall was so hard as to torture every limb of his body. 8Thus he who only a little while before had thought in his superhuman arrogance that he could command the waves of the sea, and had imagined that he could weigh the high mountains in a balance, was brought down to earth and carried in a litter, making the power of God manifest to all. 9And so the ungodly man's body swarmed with worms, and while he was still living in anguish and pain, his flesh rotted away, and because of the stench the whole army felt revulsion at his decay. 10Because of his intolerable stench no one was able to carry the man who a little while before had thought that he could touch the stars of heaven. 11Then it was that, broken in spirit, he began to lose much of his arrogance and to come to his senses under the scourge of God, for he was tortured with pain every moment. 12And when he could not endure his own stench, he uttered these words, "It is right to be subject to God; mortals should not think that they are equal to God."[e]

13 Then the abominable fellow made a vow to the Lord, who would no longer have mercy on him, stating 14that the holy city, which he was

[a] Gk *slaves* [b] Gk *their arms* [c] Meaning of Gk uncertain [d] Gk *they were defeated*
[e] Or *not think thoughts proper only to God*

hurrying to level to the ground and to make a
cemetery, he was now declaring to be free; 15 and
the Jews, whom he had not considered worth
burying but had planned to throw out with their
children for the wild animals and for the birds
to eat, he would make, all of them, equal to citizens of Athens; 16 and the holy sanctuary, which
he had formerly plundered, he would adorn with
the finest offerings; and all the holy vessels he
would give back, many times over; and the expenses incurred for the sacrifices he would provide from his own revenues; 17 and in addition to
all this he also would become a Jew and would
visit every inhabited place to proclaim the power
of God. 18 But when his sufferings did not in any
way abate, for the judgment of God had justly
come upon him, he gave up all hope for himself
and wrote to the Jews the following letter, in the
form of a supplication. This was its content:

19 "To his worthy Jewish citizens, Antiochus
their king and general sends hearty greetings and
good wishes for their health and prosperity. 20 If
you and your children are well and your affairs are
as you wish, I am glad. As my hope is in heaven, 21 I
remember with affection your esteem and goodwill. On my way back from the region of Persia I
suffered an annoying illness, and I have deemed
it necessary to take thought for the general security of all. 22 I do not despair of my condition, for
I have good hope of recovering from my illness,
23 but I observed that my father, on the occasions
when he made expeditions into the upper country, appointed his successor, 24 so that, if anything
unexpected happened or any unwelcome news
came, the people throughout the realm would
not be troubled, for they would know to whom
the government was left. 25 Moreover, I understand how the princes along the borders and the
neighbors of my kingdom keep watching for opportunities and waiting to see what will happen.
So I have appointed my son Antiochus to be king,
whom I have often entrusted and commended to
most of you when I hurried off to the upper provinces; and I have written to him what is written
here. 26 I therefore urge and beg you to remember
the public and private services rendered to you
and to maintain your present goodwill, each of
you, toward me and my son. 27 For I am sure that
he will follow my policy and will treat you with
moderation and kindness."

28 So the murderer and blasphemer, having
endured the more intense suffering, such as he
had inflicted on others, came to the end of his life
by a most pitiable fate, among the mountains in
a strange land. 29 And Philip, one of his courtiers,
took his body home; then, fearing the son of Antiochus, he withdrew to Ptolemy Philometor in
Egypt.

10 Now Maccabeus and his followers, the
Lord leading them on, recovered the temple and the city; 2 they tore down the altars that
had been built in the public square by the foreigners, and also destroyed the sacred precincts.
3 They purified the sanctuary, and made another
altar of sacrifice; then, striking fire out of flint,
they offered sacrifices, after a lapse of two years,
and they offered incense and lighted lamps and
set out the bread of the Presence. 4 When they
had done this, they fell prostrate and implored
the Lord that they might never again fall into such
misfortunes, but that, if they should ever sin, they
might be disciplined by him with forbearance and
not be handed over to blasphemous and barbarous nations. 5 It happened that on the same day
on which the sanctuary had been profaned by the
foreigners, the purification of the sanctuary took
place, that is, on the twenty-fifth day of the same
month, which was Chislev. 6 They celebrated it
for eight days with rejoicing, in the manner of
the festival of booths, remembering how not long
before, during the festival of booths, they had
been wandering in the mountains and caves like
wild animals. 7 Therefore, carrying ivy-wreathed
wands and beautiful branches and also fronds of
palm, they offered hymns of thanksgiving to him
who had given success to the purifying of his own
holy place. 8 They decreed by public edict, ratified
by vote, that the whole nation of the Jews should
observe these days every year.

9 Such then was the end of Antiochus, who
was called Epiphanes.

10 Now we will tell what took place under
Antiochus Eupator, who was the son of that un-

godly man, and will give a brief summary of the principal calamities of the wars. [11]This man, when he succeeded to the kingdom, appointed one Lysias to have charge of the government and to be chief governor of Coelesyria and Phoenicia. [12]Ptolemy, who was called Macron, took the lead in showing justice to the Jews because of the wrong that had been done to them, and attempted to maintain peaceful relations with them. [13]As a result he was accused before Eupator by the king's Friends. He heard himself called a traitor at every turn, because he had abandoned Cyprus, which Philometor had entrusted to him, and had gone over to Antiochus Epiphanes. Unable to command the respect due his office,[a] he took poison and ended his life.

14 When Gorgias became governor of the region, he maintained a force of mercenaries, and at every turn kept attacking the Jews. [15]Besides this, the Idumeans, who had control of important strongholds, were harassing the Jews; they received those who were banished from Jerusalem, and endeavored to keep up the war. [16]But Maccabeus and his forces, after making solemn supplication and imploring God to fight on their side, rushed to the strongholds of the Idumeans. [17]Attacking them vigorously, they gained possession of the places, and beat off all who fought upon the wall, and slaughtered those whom they encountered, killing no fewer than twenty thousand.

18 When at least nine thousand took refuge in two very strong towers well equipped to withstand a siege, [19]Maccabeus left Simon and Joseph, and also Zacchaeus and his troops, a force sufficient to besiege them; and he himself set off for places where he was more urgently needed. [20]But those with Simon, who were money-hungry, were bribed by some of those who were in the towers, and on receiving seventy thousand drachmas let some of them slip away. [21]When word of what had happened came to Maccabeus, he gathered the leaders of the people, and accused these men of having sold their kindred for money by setting their enemies free to fight against them. [22]Then he killed these men who had turned traitor, and immediately captured the two towers. [23]Having success at arms in everything he undertook, he destroyed more than twenty thousand in the two strongholds.

24 Now Timothy, who had been defeated by the Jews before, gathered a tremendous force of mercenaries and collected the cavalry from Asia in no small number. He came on, intending to take Judea by storm. [25]As he drew near, Maccabeus and his men sprinkled dust on their heads and girded their loins with sackcloth, in supplication to God. [26]Falling upon the steps before the altar, they implored him to be gracious to them and to be an enemy to their enemies and an adversary to their adversaries, as the law declares. [27]And rising from their prayer they took up their arms and advanced a considerable distance from the city; and when they came near the enemy they halted. [28]Just as dawn was breaking, the two armies joined battle, the one having as pledge of success and victory not only their valor but also their reliance on the Lord, while the other made rage their leader in the fight.

29 When the battle became fierce, there appeared to the enemy from heaven five resplendent men on horses with golden bridles, and they were leading the Jews. [30]Two of them took Maccabeus between them, and shielding him with their own armor and weapons, they kept him from being wounded. They showered arrows and thunderbolts on the enemy, so that, confused and blinded, they were thrown into disorder and cut to pieces. [31]Twenty thousand five hundred were slaughtered, besides six hundred cavalry.

32 Timothy himself fled to a stronghold called Gazara, especially well garrisoned, where Chaereas was commander. [33]Then Maccabeus and his men were glad, and they besieged the fort for four days. [34]The men within, relying on the strength of the place, kept blaspheming terribly and uttering wicked words. [35]But at dawn of the fifth day, twenty young men in the army of Maccabeus, fired with anger because of the blasphemies, bravely stormed the wall and with savage fury cut down everyone they met. [36]Others who

[a] Cn: Meaning of Gk uncertain

came up in the same way wheeled around against
the defenders and set fire to the towers; they kindled fires and burned the blasphemers alive. Others broke open the gates and let in the rest of the
force, and they occupied the city. 37They killed
Timothy, who was hiding in a cistern, and his
brother Chaereas, and Apollophanes. 38When
they had accomplished these things, with hymns
and thanksgivings they blessed the Lord who
shows great kindness to Israel and gives them the
victory.

11 Very soon after this, Lysias, the king's
guardian and kinsman, who was in charge
of the government, being vexed at what had happened, 2gathered about eighty thousand infantry
and all his cavalry and came against the Jews. He
intended to make the city a home for Greeks,
3and to levy tribute on the temple as he did on
the sacred places of the other nations, and to put
up the high priesthood for sale every year. 4He
took no account whatever of the power of God,
but was elated with his ten thousands of infantry, and his thousands of cavalry, and his eighty
elephants. 5Invading Judea, he approached Beth-
zur, which was a fortified place about five stadia[a]
from Jerusalem, and pressed it hard.

6 When Maccabeus and his men got word
that Lysias[b] was besieging the strongholds, they
and all the people, with lamentations and tears,
prayed the Lord to send a good angel to save Israel. 7Maccabeus himself was the first to take up
arms, and he urged the others to risk their lives
with him to aid their kindred. Then they eagerly
rushed off together. 8And there, while they were
still near Jerusalem, a horseman appeared at their
head, clothed in white and brandishing weapons of gold. 9And together they all praised the
merciful God, and were strengthened in heart,
ready to assail not only humans but the wildest
animals or walls of iron. 10They advanced in battle order, having their heavenly ally, for the Lord
had mercy on them. 11They hurled themselves
like lions against the enemy, and laid low eleven
thousand of them and sixteen hundred cavalry,
and forced all the rest to flee. 12Most of them got
away stripped and wounded, and Lysias himself
escaped by disgraceful flight.

13 As he was not without intelligence, he
pondered over the defeat that had befallen him,
and realized that the Hebrews were invincible
because the mighty God fought on their side. So
he sent to them 14and persuaded them to settle
everything on just terms, promising that he would
persuade the king, constraining him to be their
friend.[a] 15Maccabeus, having regard for the common good, agreed to all that Lysias urged. For the
king granted every request in behalf of the Jews
which Maccabeus delivered to Lysias in writing.

16 The letter written to the Jews by Lysias
was to this effect:

"Lysias to the people of the Jews, greetings.
17John and Absalom, who were sent by you, have
delivered your signed communication and have
asked about the matters indicated in it. 18I have informed the king of everything that needed to be
brought before him, and he has agreed to what
was possible. 19If you will maintain your goodwill toward the government, I will endeavor in
the future to help promote your welfare. 20And
concerning such matters and their details, I have
ordered these men and my representatives to confer with you. 21Farewell. The one hundred forty-
eighth year,[c] Dioscorinthius twenty-fourth."

22 The king's letter ran thus:

"King Antiochus to his brother Lysias, greetings. 23Now that our father has gone on to the
gods, we desire that the subjects of the kingdom
be undisturbed in caring for their own affairs.
24We have heard that the Jews do not consent to
our father's change to Greek customs, but prefer
their own way of living and ask that their own
customs be allowed them. 25Accordingly, since
we choose that this nation also should be free
from disturbance, our decision is that their temple be restored to them and that they shall live according to the customs of their ancestors. 26You
will do well, therefore, to send word to them and
give them pledges of friendship, so that they may
know our policy and be of good cheer and go on
happily in the conduct of their own affairs."

[a] Meaning of Gk uncertain [b] Gk *he* [c] 164 B.C.

27 To the nation the king's letter was as follows:
"King Antiochus to the senate of the Jews and
to the other Jews, greetings. 28If you are well, it is
as we desire. We also are in good health. 29Mene-
laus has informed us that you wish to return home
and look after your own affairs. 30Therefore those
who go home by the thirtieth of Xanthicus will
have our pledge of friendship and full permission
31for the Jews to enjoy their own food and laws,
just as formerly, and none of them shall be mo-
lested in any way for what may have been done
in ignorance. 32And I have also sent Menelaus
to encourage you. 33Farewell. The one hundred
forty-eighth year,[a] Xanthicus fifteenth."
34 The Romans also sent them a letter, which
read thus:
"Quintus Memmius and Titus Manius, envoys
of the Romans, to the people of the Jews, greetings. 35With regard to what Lysias the kinsman of
the king has granted you, we also give consent.
36But as to the matters that he decided are to be
referred to the king, as soon as you have considered them, send some one promptly so that we
may make proposals appropriate for you. For we
are on our way to Antioch. 37Therefore make haste
and send messengers so that we may have your
judgment. 38Farewell. The one hundred forty-
eighth year,[a] Xanthicus fifteenth."

12 When this agreement had been reached,
Lysias returned to the king, and the Jews
went about their farming.
2 But some of the governors in various places,
Timothy and Apollonius son of Gennaeus, as well
as Hieronymus and Demophon, and in addition
to these Nicanor the governor of Cyprus, would
not let them live quietly and in peace. 3And the
people of Joppa did so ungodly a deed as this:
they invited the Jews who lived among them to
embark, with their wives and children, on boats
that they had provided, as though there were no
ill will to the Jews;[b] 4and this was done by public vote of the city. When they accepted, because
they wished to live peaceably and suspected
nothing, the people of Joppa[c] took them out to
sea and drowned them, at least two hundred.
5When Judas heard of the cruelty visited on his
compatriots, he gave orders to his men 6and, calling upon God, the righteous judge, attacked the
murderers of his kindred. He set fire to the harbor
by night, burned the boats, and massacred those
who had taken refuge there. 7Then, because the
city's gates were closed, he withdrew, intending
to come again and root out the whole community
of Joppa. 8But learning that the people in Jamnia
meant in the same way to wipe out the Jews who
were living among them, 9he attacked the Jam-
nites by night and set fire to the harbor and the
fleet, so that the glow of the light was seen in Jerusalem, thirty miles[d] distant.
10 When they had gone more than a mile[e]
from there, on their march against Timothy, at
least five thousand Arabs with five hundred cavalry attacked them. 11After a hard fight, Judas and
his companions, with God's help, were victorious. The defeated nomads begged Judas to grant
them pledges of friendship, promising to give
him livestock and to help his people[f] in all other
ways. 12Judas, realizing that they might indeed be
useful in many ways, agreed to make peace with
them; and after receiving his pledges they went
back to their tents.
13 He also attacked a certain town that was
strongly fortified with earthworks[g] and walls, and
inhabited by all sorts of Gentiles. Its name was
Caspin. 14Those who were within, relying on the
strength of the walls and on their supply of provisions, behaved most insolently toward Judas and
his men, railing at them and even blaspheming and
saying unholy things. 15But Judas and his men,
calling upon the great Sovereign of the world, who
without battering rams or engines of war overthrew Jericho in the days of Joshua, rushed furiously upon the walls. 16They took the town by the
will of God, and slaughtered untold numbers, so
that the adjoining lake, a quarter of a mile[h] wide,
appeared to be running over with blood.

[a] 164 B.C. [b] Gk *to them* [c] Gk *they* [d] Gk *two hundred forty stadia* [e] Gk *nine stadia* [f] Gk *them* [g] Meaning of Gk uncertain [h] Gk *two stadia*

17 When they had gone ninety-five miles[a]
from there, they came to Charax, to the Jews who
are called Toubiani. 18 They did not find Timothy
in that region, for he had by then left there without accomplishing anything, though in one place
he had left a very strong garrison. 19 Dositheus
and Sosipater, who were captains under Maccabeus, marched out and destroyed those whom
Timothy had left in the stronghold, more than
ten thousand men. 20 But Maccabeus arranged his
army in divisions, set men[b] in command of the divisions, and hurried after Timothy, who had with
him one hundred twenty thousand infantry and
two thousand five hundred cavalry. 21 When Timothy learned of the approach of Judas, he sent off
the women and the children and also the baggage
to a place called Carnaim; for that place was hard
to besiege and difficult of access because of the
narrowness of all the approaches. 22 But when Judas's first division appeared, terror and fear came
over the enemy at the manifestation to them of
him who sees all things. In their flight they rushed
headlong in every direction, so that often they
were injured by their own men and pierced by
the points of their own swords. 23 Judas pressed
the pursuit with the utmost vigor, putting the
sinners to the sword, and destroyed as many as
thirty thousand.

24 Timothy himself fell into the hands of
Dositheus and Sosipater and their men. With
great guile he begged them to let him go in safety,
because he held the parents of most of them, and
the brothers of some, to whom no consideration
would be shown. 25 And when with many words
he had confirmed his solemn promise to restore
them unharmed, they let him go, for the sake of
saving their kindred.

26 Then Judas[c] marched against Carnaim
and the temple of Atargatis, and slaughtered
twenty-five thousand people. 27 After the rout
and destruction of these, he marched also against
Ephron, a fortified town where Lysias lived with
multitudes of people of all nationalities.[d] Stalwart
young men took their stand before the walls and
made a vigorous defense; and great stores of war
engines and missiles were there. 28 But the Jews[e]
called upon the Sovereign who with power shatters the might of his enemies, and they got the
town into their hands, and killed as many as
twenty-five thousand of those who were in it.

29 Setting out from there, they hastened to
Scythopolis, which is seventy-five miles[f] from
Jerusalem. 30 But when the Jews who lived there
bore witness to the goodwill that the people of
Scythopolis had shown them and their kind
treatment of them in times of misfortune, 31 they
thanked them and exhorted them to be well disposed to their race in the future also. Then they
went up to Jerusalem, as the festival of weeks was
close at hand.

32 After the festival called Pentecost, they
hurried against Gorgias, the governor of Idumea,
33 who came out with three thousand infantry and
four hundred cavalry. 34 When they joined battle,
it happened that a few of the Jews fell. 35 But a certain Dositheus, one of Bacenor's men, who was
on horseback and was a strong man, caught hold
of Gorgias, and grasping his cloak was dragging
him off by main strength, wishing to take the accursed man alive, when one of the Thracian cavalry bore down on him and cut off his arm; so
Gorgias escaped and reached Marisa.

36 As Esdris and his men had been fighting
for a long time and were weary, Judas called upon
the Lord to show himself their ally and leader in
the battle. 37 In the language of their ancestors he
raised the battle cry, with hymns; then he charged
against Gorgias's troops when they were not expecting it, and put them to flight.

38 Then Judas assembled his army and went
to the city of Adullam. As the seventh day was
coming on, they purified themselves according to
the custom, and kept the sabbath there.

39 On the next day, as had now become necessary, Judas and his men went to take up the
bodies of the fallen and to bring them back to
lie with their kindred in the sepulchres of their
ancestors. 40 Then under the tunic of each one of

[a] Gk *seven hundred fifty stadia* [b] Gk *them* [c] Gk *he* [d] Meaning of Gk uncertain [e] Gk *they*
[f] Gk *six hundred stadia*

the dead they found sacred tokens of the idols of
Jamnia, which the law forbids the Jews to wear.
And it became clear to all that this was the reason these men had fallen. 41 So they all blessed the
ways of the Lord, the righteous judge, who reveals
the things that are hidden; 42 and they turned to
supplication, praying that the sin that had been
committed might be wholly blotted out. The noble Judas exhorted the people to keep themselves
free from sin, for they had seen with their own
eyes what had happened as the result of the sin
of those who had fallen. 43 He also took up a collection, man by man, to the amount of two thousand drachmas of silver, and sent it to Jerusalem
to provide for a sin offering. In doing this he acted
very well and honorably, taking account of the
resurrection. 44 For if he were not expecting that
those who had fallen would rise again, it would
have been superfluous and foolish to pray for the
dead. 45 But if he was looking to the splendid reward that is laid up for those who fall asleep in
godliness, it was a holy and pious thought. Therefore he made atonement for the dead, so that they
might be delivered from their sin.

13 In the one hundred forty-ninth year[a]
word came to Judas and his men that Antiochus Eupator was coming with a great army
against Judea, 2 and with him Lysias, his guardian,
who had charge of the government. Each of them
had a Greek force of one hundred ten thousand
infantry, five thousand three hundred cavalry,
twenty-two elephants, and three hundred chariots armed with scythes.

3 Menelaus also joined them and with utter
hypocrisy urged Antiochus on, not for the sake of
his country's welfare, but because he thought that
he would be established in office. 4 But the King
of kings aroused the anger of Antiochus against
the scoundrel; and when Lysias informed him
that this man was to blame for all the trouble, he
ordered them to take him to Beroea and to put
him to death by the method that is customary in
that place. 5 For there is a tower there, fifty cubits
high, full of ashes, and it has a rim running around
it that on all sides inclines precipitously into the
ashes. 6 There they all push to destruction anyone
guilty of sacrilege or notorious for other crimes.
7 By such a fate it came about that Menelaus the
lawbreaker died, without even burial in the earth.
8 And this was eminently just; because he had
committed many sins against the altar whose fire
and ashes were holy, he met his death in ashes.

9 The king with barbarous arrogance was
coming to show the Jews things far worse than
those that had been done[b] in his father's time.
10 But when Judas heard of this, he ordered the
people to call upon the Lord day and night, now
if ever to help those who were on the point of being deprived of the law and their country and the
holy temple, 11 and not to let the people who had
just begun to revive fall into the hands of the blasphemous Gentiles. 12 When they had all joined in
the same petition and had implored the merciful
Lord with weeping and fasting and lying prostrate
for three days without ceasing, Judas exhorted
them and ordered them to stand ready.

13 After consulting privately with the elders,
he determined to march out and decide the matter
by the help of God before the king's army could
enter Judea and get possession of the city. 14 So,
committing the decision to the Creator of the
world and exhorting his troops to fight bravely to
the death for the laws, temple, city, country, and
commonwealth, he pitched his camp near Modein. 15 He gave his troops the watchword, "God's
victory," and with a picked force of the bravest
young men, he attacked the king's pavilion at
night and killed as many as two thousand men in
the camp. He stabbed[c] the leading elephant and
its rider. 16 In the end they filled the camp with
terror and confusion and withdrew in triumph.
17 This happened, just as day was dawning, because the Lord's help protected him.

18 The king, having had a taste of the daring
of the Jews, tried strategy in attacking their positions. 19 He advanced against Beth-zur, a strong
fortress of the Jews, was turned back, attacked
again,[d] and was defeated. 20 Judas sent in to the
garrison whatever was necessary. 21 But Rhodocus,

[a] 163 B.C. [b] Or *the worst of the things that had been done* [c] Meaning of Gk uncertain [d] Or *faltered*

a man from the ranks of the Jews, gave secret
information to the enemy; he was sought for,
caught, and put in prison. 22 The king negotiated
a second time with the people in Beth-zur, gave
pledges, received theirs, withdrew, attacked Judas
and his men, was defeated; 23 he got word that
Philip, who had been left in charge of the government, had revolted in Antioch; he was dismayed,
called in the Jews, yielded and swore to observe
all their rights, settled with them and offered sacrifice, honored the sanctuary and showed generosity to the holy place. 24 He received Maccabeus,
left Hegemonides as governor from Ptolemais to
Gerar, 25 and went to Ptolemais. The people of
Ptolemais were indignant over the treaty; in fact
they were so angry that they wanted to annul its
terms.[a] 26 Lysias took the public platform, made
the best possible defense, convinced them, appeased them, gained their goodwill, and set out
for Antioch. This is how the king's attack and
withdrawal turned out.

14 Three years later, word came to Judas and
his men that Demetrius son of Seleucus
had sailed into the harbor of Tripolis with a strong
army and a fleet, 2 and had taken possession of the
country, having made away with Antiochus and
his guardian Lysias.

3 Now a certain Alcimus, who had formerly
been high priest but had willfully defiled himself
in the times of separation,[b] realized that there was
no way for him to be safe or to have access again
to the holy altar, 4 and went to King Demetrius in
about the one hundred fifty-first year,[c] presenting to him a crown of gold and a palm, and besides these some of the customary olive branches
from the temple. During that day he kept quiet.
5 But he found an opportunity that furthered his
mad purpose when he was invited by Demetrius
to a meeting of the council and was asked about
the attitude and intentions of the Jews. He answered:

6 "Those of the Jews who are called Hasideans, whose leader is Judas Maccabeus, are keeping up war and stirring up sedition, and will not
let the kingdom attain tranquility. 7 Therefore I
have laid aside my ancestral glory—I mean the
high priesthood—and have now come here, 8 first
because I am genuinely concerned for the interests of the king, and second because I have regard
also for my compatriots. For through the folly of
those whom I have mentioned our whole nation
is now in no small misfortune. 9 Since you are acquainted, O king, with the details of this matter,
may it please you to take thought for our country and our hard-pressed nation with the gracious
kindness that you show to all. 10 For as long as Judas lives, it is impossible for the government to
find peace." 11 When he had said this, the rest of
the king's Friends,[d] who were hostile to Judas,
quickly inflamed Demetrius still more. 12 He immediately chose Nicanor, who had been in command of the elephants, appointed him governor
of Judea, and sent him off 13 with orders to kill
Judas and scatter his troops, and to install Alcimus as high priest of the great[e] temple. 14 And the
Gentiles throughout Judea, who had fled before[a]
Judas, flocked to join Nicanor, thinking that the
misfortunes and calamities of the Jews would
mean prosperity for themselves.

15 When the Jews[f] heard of Nicanor's coming and the gathering of the Gentiles, they sprinkled dust on their heads and prayed to him who
established his own people forever and always
upholds his own heritage by manifesting himself. 16 At the command of the leader, they[g] set
out from there immediately and engaged them
in battle at a village called Dessau.[a] 17 Simon, the
brother of Judas, had encountered Nicanor, but
had been temporarily[h] checked because of the
sudden consternation created by the enemy.

18 Nevertheless Nicanor, hearing of the valor
of Judas and his troops and their courage in battle
for their country, shrank from deciding the issue
by bloodshed. 19 Therefore he sent Posidonius,
Theodotus, and Mattathias to give and receive
pledges of friendship. 20 When the terms had been
fully considered, and the leader had informed the

[a] Meaning of Gk uncertain [b] Other ancient authorities read *of mixing* [c] 161 B.C. [d] Gk *of the Friends*
[e] Gk *greatest* [f] Gk *they* [g] Gk *he* [h] Other ancient authorities read *slowly*

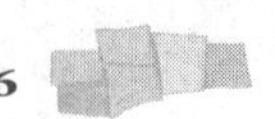

people, and it had appeared that they were of one mind, they agreed to the covenant. 21 The leaders[a] set a day on which to meet by themselves. A chariot came forward from each army; seats of honor were set in place; 22 Judas posted armed men in readiness at key places to prevent sudden treachery on the part of the enemy; so they duly held the consultation.

23 Nicanor stayed on in Jerusalem and did nothing out of the way, but dismissed the flocks of people that had gathered. 24 And he kept Judas always in his presence; he was warmly attached to the man. 25 He urged him to marry and have children; so Judas[b] married, settled down, and shared the common life.

26 But when Alcimus noticed their goodwill for one another, he took the covenant that had been made and went to Demetrius. He told him that Nicanor was disloyal to the government, since he had appointed that conspirator against the kingdom, Judas, to be his successor. 27 The king became excited and, provoked by the false accusations of that depraved man, wrote to Nicanor, stating that he was displeased with the covenant and commanding him to send Maccabeus to Antioch as a prisoner without delay.

28 When this message came to Nicanor, he was troubled and grieved that he had to annul their agreement when the man had done no wrong. 29 Since it was not possible to oppose the king, he watched for an opportunity to accomplish this by a stratagem. 30 But Maccabeus, noticing that Nicanor was more austere in his dealings with him and was meeting him more rudely than had been his custom, concluded that this austerity did not spring from the best motives. So he gathered not a few of his men, and went into hiding from Nicanor. 31 When the latter became aware that he had been cleverly outwitted by the man, he went to the great[c] and holy temple while the priests were offering the customary sacrifices, and commanded them to hand the man over. 32 When they declared on oath that they did not know where the man was whom he wanted, 33 he stretched out his right hand toward the sanctuary, and swore this oath: "If you do not hand Judas over to me as a prisoner, I will level this shrine of God to the ground and tear down the altar, and build here a splendid temple to Dionysus."

34 Having said this, he went away. Then the priests stretched out their hands toward heaven and called upon the constant Defender of our nation, in these words: 35 "O Lord of all, though you have need of nothing, you were pleased that there should be a temple for your habitation among us; 36 so now, O holy One, Lord of all holiness, keep undefiled forever this house that has been so recently purified."

37 A certain Razis, one of the elders of Jerusalem, was denounced to Nicanor as a man who loved his compatriots and was very well thought of and for his goodwill was called father of the Jews. 38 In former times, when there was no mingling with the Gentiles, he had been accused of Judaism, and he had most zealously risked body and life for Judaism. 39 Nicanor, wishing to exhibit the enmity that he had for the Jews, sent more than five hundred soldiers to arrest him; 40 for he thought that by arresting[d] him he would do them an injury. 41 When the troops were about to capture the tower and were forcing the door of the courtyard, they ordered that fire be brought and the doors burned. Being surrounded, Razis[b] fell upon his own sword, 42 preferring to die nobly rather than to fall into the hands of sinners and suffer outrages unworthy of his noble birth. 43 But in the heat of the struggle he did not hit exactly, and the crowd was now rushing in through the doors. He courageously ran up on the wall, and bravely threw himself down into the crowd. 44 But as they quickly drew back, a space opened and he fell in the middle of the empty space. 45 Still alive and aflame with anger, he rose, and though his blood gushed forth and his wounds were severe he ran through the crowd; and standing upon a steep rock, 46 with his blood now completely drained from him, he tore out his entrails, took them in both hands and hurled them at the crowd, calling upon the Lord of life and spirit to give them back to him again. This was the manner of his death.

[a] Gk *They* [b] Gk *he* [c] Gk *greatest* [d] Meaning of Gk uncertain

15 When Nicanor heard that Judas and his
troops were in the region of Samaria, he
made plans to attack them with complete safety
on the day of rest. 2When the Jews who were
compelled to follow him said, "Do not destroy so
savagely and barbarously, but show respect for the
day that he who sees all things has honored and
hallowed above other days," 3the thrice-accursed
wretch asked if there were a sovereign in heaven
who had commanded the keeping of the sabbath
day. 4When they declared, "It is the living Lord
himself, the Sovereign in heaven, who ordered us
to observe the seventh day," 5he replied, "But I am
a sovereign also, on earth, and I command you to
take up arms and finish the king's business." Nevertheless, he did not succeed in carrying out his
abominable design.

6 This Nicanor in his utter boastfulness and
arrogance had determined to erect a public monument of victory over Judas and his forces. 7But
Maccabeus did not cease to trust with all confidence that he would get help from the Lord. 8He
exhorted his troops not to fear the attack of the
Gentiles, but to keep in mind the former times
when help had come to them from heaven, and so
to look for the victory that the Almighty would
give them. 9Encouraging them from the law and
the prophets, and reminding them also of the
struggles they had won, he made them the more
eager. 10When he had aroused their courage, he
issued his orders, at the same time pointing out
the perfidy of the Gentiles and their violation of
oaths. 11He armed each of them not so much with
confidence in shields and spears as with the inspiration of brave words, and he cheered them all by
relating a dream, a sort of vision,[a] which was worthy of belief.

12 What he saw was this: Onias, who had
been high priest, a noble and good man, of modest bearing and gentle manner, one who spoke fit-
tingly and had been trained from childhood in all
that belongs to excellence, was praying with outstretched hands for the whole body of the Jews.
13Then in the same fashion another appeared,
distinguished by his gray hair and dignity, and of
marvelous majesty and authority. 14And Onias
spoke, saying, "This is a man who loves the family of Israel and prays much for the people and
the holy city—Jeremiah, the prophet of God."
15Jeremiah stretched out his right hand and gave
to Judas a golden sword, and as he gave it he addressed him thus: 16"Take this holy sword, a gift
from God, with which you will strike down your
adversaries."

17 Encouraged by the words of Judas, so noble and so effective in arousing valor and awaking
courage in the souls of the young, they determined
not to carry on a campaign[b] but to attack bravely,
and to decide the matter by fighting hand to hand
with all courage, because the city and the sanctuary and the temple were in danger. 18Their concern
for wives and children, and also for brothers and
sisters[c] and relatives, lay upon them less heavily;
their greatest and first fear was for the consecrated
sanctuary. 19And those who had to remain in the
city were in no little distress, being anxious over
the encounter in the open country.

20 When all were now looking forward to the
coming issue, and the enemy was already close at
hand with their army drawn up for battle, the elephants[d] strategically stationed and the cavalry de-
ployed on the flanks, 21Maccabeus, observing the
masses that were in front of him and the varied
supply of arms and the savagery of the elephants,
stretched out his hands toward heaven and called
upon the Lord who works wonders; for he knew
that it is not by arms, but as the Lord[e] decides,
that he gains the victory for those who deserve it.
22He called upon him in these words: "O Lord,
you sent your angel in the time of King Hezekiah
of Judea, and he killed fully one hundred eighty-
five thousand in the camp of Sennacherib. 23So
now, O Sovereign of the heavens, send a good
angel to spread terror and trembling before us.
24By the might of your arm may these blasphemers who come against your holy people be struck
down." With these words he ended his prayer.

25 Nicanor and his troops advanced with
trumpets and battle songs, 26but Judas and his
troops met the enemy in battle with invocations

[a] Meaning of Gk uncertain [b] Or *to remain in camp* [c] Gk *for brothers* [d] Gk *animals* [e] Gk *he*

to God and prayers. 27 So, fighting with their hands and praying to God in their hearts, they laid low at least thirty-five thousand, and were greatly gladdened by God's manifestation.

28 When the action was over and they were returning with joy, they recognized Nicanor, lying dead, in full armor. 29 Then there was shouting and tumult, and they blessed the Sovereign Lord in the language of their ancestors. 30 Then the man who was ever in body and soul the defender of his people, the man who maintained his youthful goodwill toward his compatriots, ordered them to cut off Nicanor's head and arm and carry them to Jerusalem. 31 When he arrived there and had called his compatriots together and stationed the priests before the altar, he sent for those who were in the citadel. 32 He showed them the vile Nicanor's head and that profane man's arm, which had been boastfully stretched out against the holy house of the Almighty. 33 He cut out the tongue of the ungodly Nicanor and said that he would feed it piecemeal to the birds and would hang up these rewards of his folly opposite the sanctuary. 34 And they all, looking to heaven, blessed the Lord who had manifested himself, saying, "Blessed is he who has kept his own place undefiled!" 35 Judas[a] hung Nicanor's head from the citadel, a clear and conspicuous sign to everyone of the help of the Lord. 36 And they all decreed by public vote never to let this day go unobserved, but to celebrate the thirteenth day of the twelfth month—which is called Adar in the Aramaic language—the day before Mordecai's day.

37 This, then, is how matters turned out with Nicanor, and from that time the city has been in the possession of the Hebrews. So I will here end my story.

38 If it is well told and to the point, that is what I myself desired; if it is poorly done and mediocre, that was the best I could do. 39 For just as it is harmful to drink wine alone, or, again, to drink water alone, while wine mixed with water is sweet and delicious and enhances one's enjoyment, so also the style of the story delights the ears of those who read the work. And here will be the end.

[a] Gk *He*

1 Esdras

The titles of 1 and 2 Esdras suggest that they are connected, but that is not the case. First Esdras, found in Greek and Russian Orthodox Bibles, is a second-century BCE narrative that retells the story of life after the Babylonian exile (587/586–539 BCE) as also described in 2 Chronicles, Ezra, and Nehemiah. The book's only original section is 1 Esd 3:1—5:6, an account of a contest between three bodyguards about which is the strongest element on earth. The winner of the contest is Zerubbabel, the faithful Israelite, and his reward is authorization to rebuild the Jerusalem temple. Historically, this addition is unlikely, and it does not fit comfortably within the larger narrative.

I was raised as a Pentecostal Christian, so none of the apocryphal texts is canonical for me. However, graduate school, teaching, and personal devotion have introduced me to these books. Being an African American woman raised by a feminist makes it difficult for me to read 1 Esdras as anything other than problematic. My father was an Air Force sergeant for the first seventeen years of my life, so my mother was the one who kept the family together when he was away, which was frequently. As a result, I grew up seeing a woman who handled business not through charm or beauty but through brains and persistence.

As a feminist I am particularly interested in what 1 Esdras teaches about gender and in the construction of gender from a religious perspective both when the book was written and now. Zerubbabel, the governor of Yehud (the remnant of Judah), who figures prominently in Haggai, Zechariah, Ezra, and Nehemiah, claims that "women are strongest, but above all things truth is victor" (3:12). His argument adheres to the patriarchy common in the ancient world: women are powerful because they are mothers (4:15-16), homemakers (4:17), and inciters of heterosexual lust, which may lead to marriage (4:18-31). Zerubbabel concludes that when a man, even a king, is smitten, he behaves as follows: "If she smiles at him, he laughs; if she loses her temper with him, he flatters her, so that she may be reconciled to him" (4:31). Contemporary with 1 Esdras, the biblical (Apocrypha) book of Sirach warns men against falling for women's sexual charms (9:1-9).

Feminists challenge the claim that women are powerful only insofar as they can manipulate men either through their seductive beauty or their chaste conduct. One of the first women to do so was Mary Wollstonecraft. In *A Vindication of the Rights of Woman* (1792), she insisted that the "power" Zerubbabel described was a false one that enslaved women by making them dependent upon their physical appearance and manners in order to gain male protection and thus survive. Freedom for women would come through equal educational opportunities for both sexes. Anyone reading 1 Esdras, regardless of religious belief or political philosophy, should wrestle with the sexism inherent in Zerubbabel's argument and what power meant then and means now.

— ***Stacy Davis***

1 Josiah kept the passover to his Lord in Jerusalem; he killed the passover lamb on the fourteenth day of the first month, 2 having placed the priests according to their divisions, arrayed in their vestments, in the temple of the Lord. 3 He told the Levites, the temple servants of Israel, that they should sanctify themselves to the Lord and put the holy ark of the Lord in the house that King Solomon, son of David, had built; 4 and he said, "You need no longer carry it on your shoulders. Now worship the Lord your God and serve his people Israel; prepare yourselves by your families and kindred, 5 in accordance with the directions of King David of Israel and the magnificence of his son Solomon. Stand in order in the temple according to the groupings of the ancestral houses of you Levites, who minister before your kindred the people of Israel, 6 and kill the passover lamb and prepare the sacrifices for your kindred, and keep the passover according to the commandment of the Lord that was given to Moses."

7 To the people who were present Josiah gave thirty thousand lambs and kids, and three thousand calves; these were given from the king's possessions, as he promised, to the people and the priests and Levites. 8 Hilkiah, Zechariah, and Jehiel,[a] the chief officers of the temple, gave to the priests for the passover two thousand six hundred sheep and three hundred calves. 9 And Jeconiah and Shemaiah and his brother Nethanel, and Hashabiah and Ochiel and Joram, captains over thousands, gave the Levites for the passover five thousand sheep and seven hundred calves.

10 This is what took place. The priests and the Levites, having the unleavened bread, stood in proper order according to kindred 11 and the grouping of the ancestral houses, before the people, to make the offering to the Lord as it is written in the book of Moses; this they did in the morning. 12 They roasted the passover lamb with fire, as required; and they boiled the sacrifices in bronze pots and caldrons, with a pleasing odor, 13 and carried them to all the people. Afterward they prepared the passover for themselves and for their kindred the priests, the sons of Aaron, 14 because the priests were offering the fat until nightfall; so the Levites prepared it for themselves and for their kindred the priests, the sons of Aaron. 15 The temple singers, the sons of Asaph, were in their place according to the arrangement made by David, and also Asaph, Zechariah, and Eddinus, who represented the king. 16 The gatekeepers were at each gate; no one needed to interrupt his daily duties, for their kindred the Levites prepared the passover for them.

17 So the things that had to do with the sacrifices to the Lord were accomplished that day: the passover was kept 18 and the sacrifices were offered on the altar of the Lord, according to the command of King Josiah. 19 And the people of Israel who were present at that time kept the passover and the festival of unleavened bread seven days. 20 No passover like it had been kept in Israel since the times of the prophet Samuel; 21 none of the kings of Israel had kept such a passover as was kept by Josiah and the priests and Levites and the people of Judah and all of Israel who were living in Jerusalem. 22 In the eighteenth year of the reign of Josiah this passover was kept.

23 And the deeds of Josiah were upright in the sight of the Lord, for his heart was full of godliness. 24 In ancient times the events of his reign have been recorded—concerning those who sinned and acted wickedly toward the Lord beyond any other people or kingdom, and how they grieved the Lord[b] deeply, so that the words of the Lord fell upon Israel.

25 After all these acts of Josiah, it happened that Pharaoh, king of Egypt, went to make war at Carchemish on the Euphrates, and Josiah went out against him. 26 And the king of Egypt sent word to him saying, "What have we to do with each other, O king of Judea? 27 I was not sent against you by the Lord God, for my war is at the Euphrates. And now the Lord is with me! The Lord is with me, urging me on! Stand aside, and do not oppose the Lord."

28 Josiah, however, did not turn back to his chariot, but tried to fight with him, and did not heed the words of the prophet Jeremiah from the

[a] Gk *Esyelus* [b] Gk *him*

mouth of the Lord. 29 He joined battle with him in the plain of Megiddo, and the commanders came down against King Josiah. 30 The king said to his servants, "Take me away from the battle, for I am very weak." And immediately his servants took him out of the line of battle. 31 He got into his second chariot; and after he was brought back to Jerusalem he died, and was buried in the tomb of his ancestors.

32 In all Judea they mourned for Josiah. The prophet Jeremiah lamented for Josiah, and the principal men, with the women,[a] have made lamentation for him to this day; it was ordained that this should always be done throughout the whole nation of Israel. 33 These things are written in the book of the histories of the kings of Judea; and every one of the acts of Josiah, and his splendor, and his understanding of the law of the Lord, and the things that he had done before, and these that are now told, are recorded in the book of the kings of Israel and Judah.

34 The men of the nation took Jeconiah[b] son of Josiah, who was twenty-three years old, and made him king in succession to his father Josiah. 35 He reigned three months in Judah and Jerusalem. Then the king of Egypt deposed him from reigning in Jerusalem, 36 and fined the nation one hundred talents of silver and one talent of gold. 37 The king of Egypt made his brother Jehoiakim king of Judea and Jerusalem. 38 Jehoiakim put the nobles in prison, and seized his brother Zarius and brought him back from Egypt.

39 Jehoiakim was twenty-five years old when he began to reign in Judea and Jerusalem; he did what was evil in the sight of the Lord. 40 King Nebuchadnezzar of Babylon came up against him; he bound him with a chain of bronze and took him away to Babylon. 41 Nebuchadnezzar also took some holy vessels of the Lord, and carried them away, and stored them in his temple in Babylon. 42 But the things that are reported about Jehoiakim,[c] and his uncleanness and impiety, are written in the annals of the kings.

43 His son Jehoiachin[d] became king in his place; when he was made king he was eighteen years old, 44 and he reigned three months and ten days in Jerusalem. He did what was evil in the sight of the Lord. 45 A year later Nebuchadnezzar sent and removed him to Babylon, with the holy vessels of the Lord, 46 and made Zedekiah king of Judea and Jerusalem.

Zedekiah was twenty-one years old, and he reigned eleven years. 47 He also did what was evil in the sight of the Lord, and did not heed the words that were spoken by the prophet Jeremiah from the mouth of the Lord. 48 Although King Nebuchadnezzar had made him swear by the name of the Lord, he broke his oath and rebelled; he stiffened his neck and hardened his heart and transgressed the laws of the Lord, the God of Israel. 49 Even the leaders of the people and of the priests committed many acts of sacrilege and lawlessness beyond all the unclean deeds of all the nations, and polluted the temple of the Lord in Jerusalem—the temple that God had made holy. 50 The God of their ancestors sent his messenger to call them back, because he would have spared them and his dwelling place. 51 But they mocked his messengers, and whenever the Lord spoke, they scoffed at his prophets, 52 until in his anger against his people because of their ungodly acts he gave command to bring against them the kings of the Chaldeans. 53 These killed their young men with the sword around their holy temple, and did not spare young man or young woman,[e] old man or child, for he gave them all into their hands. 54 They took all the holy vessels of the Lord, great and small, the treasure chests of the Lord, and the royal stores, and carried them away to Babylon. 55 They burned the house of the Lord, broke down the walls of Jerusalem, burned their towers with fire, 56 and utterly destroyed all its glorious things. The survivors he led away to Babylon with the sword, 57 and they were servants to him and to his sons until the Persians began to reign, in fulfillment of the word of the Lord by the mouth of Jeremiah, 58 saying, "Until the land has enjoyed its sabbaths, it shall keep sabbath all the time of its desolation until the completion of seventy years."

[a] Or *their wives* [b] 2 Kings 23.30; 2 Chr 36.1 *Jehoahaz* [c] Gk *him* [d] Gk *Jehoiakim* [e] Gk *virgin*

2 In the first year of Cyrus as king of the Persians, so that the word of the Lord by the
mouth of Jeremiah might be accomplished—
2the Lord stirred up the spirit of King Cyrus of
the Persians, and he made a proclamation throughout all his kingdom and also put it in writing:
3 "Thus says Cyrus king of the Persians: The
Lord of Israel, the Lord Most High, has made me
king of the world, 4and he has commanded me to
build him a house at Jerusalem, which is in Judea.
5If any of you, therefore, are of his people, may
your Lord be with you; go up to Jerusalem, which
is in Judea, and build the house of the Lord of
Israel—he is the Lord who dwells in Jerusalem—
6and let each of you, wherever you may live, be
helped by the people of your place with gold and
silver, 7with gifts and with horses and cattle, besides the other things added as votive offerings
for the temple of the Lord that is in Jerusalem."
8 Then arose the heads of families of the tribes
of Judah and Benjamin, and the priests and the
Levites, and all whose spirit the Lord had stirred
to go up to build the house in Jerusalem for the
Lord; 9their neighbors helped them with everything, with silver and gold, with horses and cattle,
and with a very great number of votive offerings from many whose hearts were stirred.
10 King Cyrus also brought out the holy vessels of the Lord that Nebuchadnezzar had carried
away from Jerusalem and stored in his temple
of idols. 11When King Cyrus of the Persians
brought these out, he gave them to Mithridates,
his treasurer, 12and by him they were given to
Sheshbazzar,[a] the governor of Judea. 13The number of these was: one thousand gold cups, one
thousand silver cups, twenty-nine silver censers,
thirty gold bowls, two thousand four hundred
ten silver bowls, and one thousand other vessels.
14All the vessels were handed over, gold and silver, five thousand four hundred sixty-nine, 15and
they were carried back by Sheshbazzar with the
returning exiles from Babylon to Jerusalem.
16 In the time of King Artaxerxes of the
Persians, Bishlam, Mithridates, Tabeel, Rehum,
Beltethmus, the scribe Shimshai, and the rest
of their associates, living in Samaria and other
places, wrote him the following letter, against
those who were living in Judea and Jerusalem:
17 "To King Artaxerxes our lord, your servants the recorder Rehum and the scribe Shimshai and the other members of their council, and
the judges in Coelesyria and Phoenicia: 18Let it
now be known to our lord the king that the Jews
who came up from you to us have gone to Jerusalem and are building that rebellious and wicked
city, repairing its market places and walls and
laying the foundations for a temple. 19Now if
this city is built and the walls finished, they will
not only refuse to pay tribute but will even resist
kings. 20Since the building of the temple is now
going on, we think it best not to neglect such a
matter, 21but to speak to our lord the king, in order that, if it seems good to you, search may be
made in the records of your ancestors. 22You will
find in the annals what has been written about
them, and will learn that this city was rebellious,
troubling both kings and other cities, 23and that
the Jews were rebels and kept setting up block-
ades in it from of old. That is why this city was
laid waste. 24Therefore we now make known to
you, O lord and king, that if this city is built and
its walls finished, you will no longer have access
to Coelesyria and Phoenicia."
25 Then the king, in reply to the recorder Rehum, Beltethmus, the scribe Shimshai, and the
others associated with them and living in Samaria
and Syria and Phoenicia, wrote as follows:
26 "I have read the letter that you sent me. So
I ordered search to be made, and it has been found
that this city from of old has fought against kings,
27that the people in it were given to rebellion and
war, and that mighty and cruel kings ruled in Jerusalem and exacted tribute from Coelesyria and
Phoenicia. 28Therefore I have now issued orders
to prevent these people from building the city
and to take care that nothing more be done 29and
that such wicked proceedings go no further to the
annoyance of kings."
30 Then, when the letter from King Artaxerxes was read, Rehum and the scribe Shimshai

[a] Gk *Sanabassaros*

and their associates went quickly to Jerusalem,
with cavalry and a large number of armed troops,
and began to hinder the builders. And the building of the temple in Jerusalem stopped until the
second year of the reign of King Darius of the
Persians.

3 Now King Darius gave a great banquet for
all that were under him, all that were born in
his house, and all the nobles of Media and Persia,
2and all the satraps and generals and governors
that were under him in the hundred twenty-seven
satrapies from India to Ethiopia. 3They ate and
drank, and when they were satisfied they went
away, and King Darius went to his bedroom; he
went to sleep, but woke up again.

4 Then the three young men of the bodyguard, who kept guard over the person of the
king, said to one another, 5"Let each of us state
what one thing is strongest; and to the one whose
statement seems wisest, King Darius will give
rich gifts and great honors of victory. 6He shall be
clothed in purple, and drink from gold cups, and
sleep on a gold bed,[a] and have a chariot with gold
bridles, and a turban of fine linen, and a necklace
around his neck; 7and because of his wisdom he
shall sit next to Darius and shall be called Kinsman of Darius."

8 Then each wrote his own statement, and
they sealed them and put them under the pillow
of King Darius, 9and said, "When the king wakes,
they will give him the writing; and to the one
whose statement the king and the three nobles of
Persia judge to be wisest the victory shall be given
according to what is written." 10The first wrote,
"Wine is strongest." 11The second wrote, "The
king is strongest." 12The third wrote, "Women are
strongest, but above all things truth is victor."[b]

13 When the king awoke, they took the writing and gave it to him, and he read it. 14Then he
sent and summoned all the nobles of Persia and
Media and the satraps and generals and governors
and prefects, 15and he took his seat in the council
chamber, and the writing was read in their presence. 16He said, "Call the young men, and they
shall explain their statements." So they were summoned, and came in. 17They said to them, "Explain to us what you have written."

Then the first, who had spoken of the strength
of wine, began and said: 18"Gentlemen, how is
wine the strongest? It leads astray the minds of
all who drink it. 19It makes equal the mind of the
king and the orphan, of the slave and the free, of
the poor and the rich. 20It turns every thought
to feasting and mirth, and forgets all sorrow and
debt. 21It makes all hearts feel rich, forgets kings
and satraps, and makes everyone talk in millions.[c]
22When people drink they forget to be friendly
with friends and kindred, and before long they
draw their swords. 23And when they recover from
the wine, they do not remember what they have
done. 24Gentlemen, is not wine the strongest,
since it forces people to do these things?" When
he had said this, he stopped speaking.

4 Then the second, who had spoken of the
strength of the king, began to speak: 2"Gentlemen, are not men strongest, who rule over land
and sea and all that is in them? 3But the king is
stronger; he is their lord and master, and whatever he says to them they obey. 4If he tells them
to make war on one another, they do it; and if he
sends them out against the enemy, they go, and
conquer mountains, walls, and towers. 5They kill
and are killed, and do not disobey the king's command; if they win the victory, they bring everything to the king—whatever spoil they take and
everything else. 6Likewise those who do not
serve in the army or make war but till the soil;
whenever they sow and reap, they bring some
to the king; and they compel one another to pay
taxes to the king. 7And yet he is only one man! If
he tells them to kill, they kill; if he tells them to
release, they release; 8if he tells them to attack,
they attack; if he tells them to lay waste, they lay
waste; if he tells them to build, they build; 9if he
tells them to cut down, they cut down; if he tells
them to plant, they plant. 10All his people and
his armies obey him. Furthermore, he reclines,
he eats and drinks and sleeps, 11but they keep
watch around him, and no one may go away to attend to his own affairs, nor do they disobey him.

[a] Gk *on gold* [b] Or *but truth is victor over all things* [c] Gk *talents*

 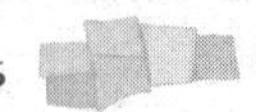

[12]Gentlemen, why is not the king the strongest, since he is to be obeyed in this fashion?" And he stopped speaking.

13 Then the third, who had spoken of women and truth (and this was Zerubbabel), began to speak: [14]"Gentlemen, is not the king great, and are not men many, and is not wine strong? Who is it, then, that rules them, or has the mastery over them? Is it not women? [15]Women gave birth to the king and to every people that rules over sea and land. [16]From women they came; and women brought up the very men who plant the vineyards from which comes wine. [17]Women make men's clothes; they bring men glory; men cannot exist without women. [18]If men gather gold and silver or any other beautiful thing, and then see a woman lovely in appearance and beauty, [19]they let all those things go, and gape at her, and with open mouths stare at her, and all prefer her to gold or silver or any other beautiful thing. [20]A man leaves his own father, who brought him up, and his own country, and clings to his wife. [21]With his wife he ends his days, with no thought of his father or his mother or his country. [22]Therefore you must realize that women rule over you!

"Do you not labor and toil, and bring everything and give it to women? [23]A man takes his sword, and goes out to travel and rob and steal and to sail the sea and rivers; [24]he faces lions, and he walks in darkness, and when he steals and robs and plunders, he brings it back to the woman he loves. [25]A man loves his wife more than his father or his mother. [26]Many men have lost their minds because of women, and have become slaves because of them. [27]Many have perished, or stumbled, or sinned because of women. [28]And now do you not believe me?

"Is not the king great in his power? Do not all lands fear to touch him? [29]Yet I have seen him with Apame, the king's concubine, the daughter of the illustrious Bartacus; she would sit at the king's right hand [30]and take the crown from the king's head and put it on her own, and slap the king with her left hand. [31]At this the king would gaze at her with mouth agape. If she smiles at him, he laughs; if she loses her temper with him, he flatters her, so that she may be reconciled to him. [32]Gentlemen, why are not women strong, since they do such things?"

33 Then the king and the nobles looked at one another; and he began to speak about truth: [34]"Gentlemen, are not women strong? The earth is vast, and heaven is high, and the sun is swift in its course, for it makes the circuit of the heavens and returns to its place in one day. [35]Is not the one who does these things great? But truth is great, and stronger than all things. [36]The whole earth calls upon truth, and heaven blesses it. All God's works[a] quake and tremble, and with him there is nothing unrighteous. [37]Wine is unrighteous, the king is unrighteous, women are unrighteous, all human beings are unrighteous, all their works are unrighteous, and all such things. There is no truth in them and in their unrighteousness they will perish. [38]But truth endures and is strong forever, and lives and prevails forever and ever. [39]With it there is no partiality or preference, but it does what is righteous instead of anything that is unrighteous or wicked. Everyone approves its deeds, [40]and there is nothing unrighteous in its judgment. To it belongs the strength and the kingship and the power and the majesty of all the ages. Blessed be the God of truth!" [41]When he stopped speaking, all the people shouted and said, "Great is truth, and strongest of all!"

42 Then the king said to him, "Ask what you wish, even beyond what is written, and we will give it to you, for you have been found to be the wisest. You shall sit next to me, and be called my Kinsman." [43]Then he said to the king, "Remember the vow that you made on the day when you became king, to build Jerusalem, [44]and to send back all the vessels that were taken from Jerusalem, which Cyrus set apart when he began[b] to destroy Babylon, and vowed to send them back there. [45]You also vowed to build the temple, which the Edomites burned when Judea was laid waste by the Chaldeans. [46]And now, O lord the king, this is what I ask and request of you, and this befits your greatness. I pray therefore that

[a] Gk *All the works* [b] Cn: Gk *vowed*

you fulfill the vow whose fulfillment you vowed
to the King of heaven with your own lips."
47 Then King Darius got up and kissed him,
and wrote letters for him to all the treasurers and
governors and generals and satraps, that they
should give safe conduct to him and to all who
were going up with him to build Jerusalem. 48 And
he wrote letters to all the governors in Coelesyria
and Phoenicia and to those in Lebanon, to bring
cedar timber from Lebanon to Jerusalem, and to
help him build the city. 49 He wrote in behalf of all
the Jews who were going up from his kingdom to
Judea, in the interest of their freedom, that no officer or satrap or governor or treasurer should forcibly enter their doors; 50 that all the country that
they would occupy should be theirs without tribute; that the Idumeans should give up the villages
of the Jews that they held; 51 that twenty talents a
year should be given for the building of the temple
until it was completed, 52 and an additional ten talents a year for burnt offerings to be offered on the
altar every day, in accordance with the commandment to make seventeen offerings; 53 and that all
who came from Babylonia to build the city should
have their freedom, they and their children and all
the priests who came. 54 He wrote also concerning
their support and the priests' vestments in which[a]
they were to minister. 55 He wrote that the support
for the Levites should be provided until the day
when the temple would be finished and Jerusalem
built. 56 He wrote that land and wages should be
provided for all who guarded the city. 57 And he
sent back from Babylon all the vessels that Cyrus
had set apart; everything that Cyrus had ordered
to be done, he also commanded to be done and to
be sent to Jerusalem.
58 When the young man went out, he lifted
up his face to heaven toward Jerusalem, and
praised the King of heaven, saying, 59 "From you
comes the victory; from you comes wisdom, and
yours is the glory. I am your servant. 60 Blessed
are you, who have given me wisdom; I give you
thanks, O Lord of our ancestors."
61 So he took the letters, and went to Babylon and told this to all his kindred. 62 And they
praised the God of their ancestors, because he
had given them release and permission 63 to go up
and build Jerusalem and the temple that is called
by his name; and they feasted, with music and rejoicing, for seven days.

5 After this the heads of ancestral houses were
chosen to go up, according to their tribes,
with their wives and sons and daughters, and
their male and female servants, and their livestock. 2 And Darius sent with them a thousand
cavalry to take them back to Jerusalem in safety,
with the music of drums and flutes; 3 all their kindred were making merry. And he made them go
up with them.
4 These are the names of the men who went
up, according to their ancestral houses in the
tribes, over their groups: 5 the priests, the descendants of Phinehas son of Aaron; Jeshua son of
Jozadak son of Seraiah and Joakim son of Zerubbabel son of Shealtiel, of the house of David, of
the lineage of Phares, of the tribe of Judah, 6 who
spoke wise words before King Darius of the Persians, in the second year of his reign, in the month
of Nisan, the first month.
7 These are the Judeans who came up out of
their sojourn in exile, whom King Nebuchadnezzar of Babylon had carried away to Babylon 8 and
who returned to Jerusalem and the rest of Judea,
each to his own town. They came with Zerubbabel and Jeshua, Nehemiah, Seraiah, Resaiah, Ene-
neus, Mordecai, Beelsarus, Aspharasus, Reeliah,
Rehum, and Baanah, their leaders.
9 The number of those of the nation and their
leaders: the descendants of Parosh, two thousand
one hundred seventy-two. The descendants of
Shephatiah, four hundred seventy-two. 10 The descendants of Arah, seven hundred fifty-six. 11 The
descendants of Pahath-moab, of the descendants
of Jeshua and Joab, two thousand eight hundred
twelve. 12 The descendants of Elam, one thousand two hundred fifty-four. The descendants of
Zattu, nine hundred forty-five. The descendants
of Chorbe, seven hundred five. The descendants
of Bani, six hundred forty-eight. 13 The descendants of Bebai, six hundred twenty-three. The de-

[a] Gk *in what priestly vestments*

scendants of Azgad, one thousand three hundred twenty-two. [14]The descendants of Adonikam, six hundred sixty-seven. The descendants of Bigvai, two thousand sixty-six. The descendants of Adin, four hundred fifty-four. [15]The descendants of Ater, namely of Hezekiah, ninety-two. The descendants of Kilan and Azetas, sixty-seven. The descendants of Azaru, four hundred thirty-two. [16]The descendants of Annias, one hundred one. The descendants of Arom. The descendants of Bezai, three hundred twenty-three. The descendants of Arsiphurith, one hundred twelve. [17]The descendants of Baiterus, three thousand five. The descendants of Bethlomon, one hundred twenty-three. [18]Those from Netophah, fifty-five. Those from Anathoth, one hundred fifty-eight. Those from Bethasmoth, forty-two. [19]Those from Kiriatharim, twenty-five. Those from Chephirah and Beeroth, seven hundred forty-three. [20]The Chadiasans and Ammidians, four hundred twenty-two. Those from Kirama and Geba, six hundred twenty-one. [21]Those from Macalon, one hundred twenty-two. Those from Betolio, fifty-two. The descendants of Niphish, one hundred fifty-six. [22]The descendants of the other Calamolalus and Ono, seven hundred twenty-five. The descendants of Jerechus, three hundred forty-five. [23]The descendants of Senaah, three thousand three hundred thirty.

24 The priests: the descendants of Jedaiah son of Jeshua, of the descendants of Anasib, nine hundred seventy-two. The descendants of Immer, one thousand and fifty-two. [25]The descendants of Pashhur, one thousand two hundred forty-seven. The descendants of Charme, one thousand seventeen.

26 The Levites: the descendants of Jeshua and Kadmiel and Bannas and Sudias, seventy-four. [27]The temple singers: the descendants of Asaph, one hundred twenty-eight. [28]The gatekeepers: the descendants of Shallum, the descendants of Ater, the descendants of Talmon, the descendants of Akkub, the descendants of Hatita, the descendants of Shobai, in all one hundred thirty-nine.

29 The temple servants: the descendants of Esau, the descendants of Hasupha, the descendants of Tabbaoth, the descendants of Keros, the descendants of Sua, the descendants of Padon, the descendants of Lebanah, the descendants of Hagabah, [30]the descendants of Akkub, the descendants of Uthai, the descendants of Ketab, the descendants of Hagab, the descendants of Subai, the descendants of Hana, the descendants of Cathua, the descendants of Geddur, [31]the descendants of Jairus, the descendants of Daisan, the descendants of Noeba, the descendants of Chezib, the descendants of Gazera, the descendants of Uzza, the descendants of Phinoe, the descendants of Hasrah, the descendants of Basthai, the descendants of Asnah, the descendants of Maani, the descendants of Nephisim, the descendants of Acuph,[a] the descendants of Hakupha, the descendants of Asur, the descendants of Pharakim, the descendants of Bazluth, [32]the descendants of Mehida, the descendants of Cutha, the descendants of Charea, the descendants of Barkos, the descendants of Serar, the descendants of Temah, the descendants of Neziah, the descendants of Hatipha.

33 The descendants of Solomon's servants: the descendants of Assaphioth, the descendants of Peruda, the descendants of Jaalah, the descendants of Lozon, the descendants of Isdael, the descendants of Shephatiah, [34]the descendants of Agia, the descendants of Pochereth-hazzebaim, the descendants of Sarothie, the descendants of Masiah, the descendants of Gas, the descendants of Addus, the descendants of Subas, the descendants of Apherra, the descendants of Barodis, the descendants of Shaphat, the descendants of Allon.

35 All the temple servants and the descendants of Solomon's servants were three hundred seventy-two.

36 The following are those who came up from Tel-melah and Tel-harsha, under the leadership of Cherub, Addan, and Immer, [37]though they could not prove by their ancestral houses or lineage that they belonged to Israel: the descendants

[a] Other ancient authorities read *Acub* or *Acum*

of Delaiah son of Tobiah, and the descendants of
Nekoda, six hundred fifty-two.
38 Of the priests the following had assumed
the priesthood but were not found registered:
the descendants of Habaiah, the descendants of
Hakkoz, and the descendants of Jaddus who had
married Agia, one of the daughters of Barzillai,
and was called by his name. 39 When a search was
made in the register and the genealogy of these
men was not found, they were excluded from
serving as priests. 40 And Nehemiah and Atthar-
ias[a] told them not to share in the holy things until a high priest should appear wearing Urim and
Thummim.[b]
41 All those of Israel, twelve or more years of
age, besides male and female servants, were forty-
two thousand three hundred sixty; 42 their male
and female servants were seven thousand three
hundred thirty-seven; there were two hundred
forty-five musicians and singers. 43 There were
four hundred thirty-five camels, and seven thousand thirty-six horses, two hundred forty-five
mules, and five thousand five hundred twenty-
five donkeys.
44 Some of the heads of families, when they
came to the temple of God that is in Jerusalem,
vowed that, to the best of their ability, they would
erect the house on its site, 45 and that they would
give to the sacred treasury for the work a thousand minas of gold, five thousand minas of silver,
and one hundred priests' vestments.
46 The priests, the Levites, and some of the
people[c] settled in Jerusalem and its vicinity; and
the temple singers, the gatekeepers, and all Israel
in their towns.

47 When the seventh month came, and the
Israelites were all in their own homes, they gathered with a single purpose in the square before
the first gate toward the east. 48 Then Jeshua son
of Jozadak, with his fellow priests, and Zerubbabel son of Shealtiel, with his kinsmen, took their
places and prepared the altar of the God of Israel,
49 to offer burnt offerings upon it, in accordance
with the directions in the book of Moses the man
of God. 50 And some joined them from the other
peoples of the land. And they erected the altar
in its place, for all the peoples of the land were
hostile to them and were stronger than they; and
they offered sacrifices at the proper times and
burnt offerings to the Lord morning and evening. 51 They kept the festival of booths, as it is
commanded in the law, and offered the proper
sacrifices every day, 52 and thereafter the regular
offerings and sacrifices on sabbaths and at new
moons and at all the consecrated feasts. 53 And
all who had made any vow to God began to offer
sacrifices to God, from the new moon of the seventh month, though the temple of God was not
yet built. 54 They gave money to the masons and
the carpenters, and food and drink 55 and carts[d]
to the Sidonians and the Tyrians, to bring cedar
logs from Lebanon and convey them in rafts to
the harbor of Joppa, according to the decree that
they had in writing from King Cyrus of the Persians.
56 In the second year after their coming to
the temple of God in Jerusalem, in the second
month, Zerubbabel son of Shealtiel and Jeshua
son of Jozadak made a beginning, together with
their kindred and the levitical priests and all who
had come back to Jerusalem from exile; 57 and
they laid the foundation of the temple of God on
the new moon of the second month in the second year after they came to Judea and Jerusalem.
58 They appointed the Levites who were twenty
or more years of age to have charge of the work
of the Lord. And Jeshua arose, and his sons and
kindred and his brother Kadmiel and the sons of
Jeshua Emadabun and the sons of Joda son of Ili-
adun, with their sons and kindred, all the Levites,
pressing forward the work on the house of God
with a single purpose.
So the builders built the temple of the Lord.
59 And the priests stood arrayed in their vestments, with musical instruments and trumpets,
and the Levites, the sons of Asaph, with cymbals,
60 praising the Lord and blessing him, according
to the directions of King David of Israel; 61 they
sang hymns, giving thanks to the Lord, "For his

[a] Or *the governor* [b] Gk *Manifestation and Truth* [c] Or *those who were of the people* [d] Meaning of Gk uncertain

goodness and his glory are forever upon all Israel." 62And all the people sounded trumpets and
shouted with a great shout, praising the Lord for
the erection of the house of the Lord. 63Some of
the levitical priests and heads of ancestral houses,
old men who had seen the former house, came
to the building of this one with outcries and loud
weeping, 64while many came with trumpets and
a joyful noise, 65so that the people could not
hear the trumpets because of the weeping of the
people.

For the multitude sounded the trumpets loudly,
so that the sound was heard far away; 66and when
the enemies of the tribe of Judah and Benjamin
heard it, they came to find out what the sound of
the trumpets meant. 67They learned that those
who had returned from exile were building the
temple for the Lord God of Israel. 68So they approached Zerubbabel and Jeshua and the heads
of the ancestral houses and said to them, "We will
build with you. 69For we obey your Lord just as
you do and we have been sacrificing to him ever
since the days of King Esar-haddon[a] of the Assyrians, who brought us here." 70But Zerubbabel
and Jeshua and the heads of the ancestral houses
in Israel said to them, "You have nothing to do
with us in building the house for the Lord our
God, 71for we alone will build it for the Lord of
Israel, as Cyrus, the king of the Persians, has commanded us." 72But the peoples of the land pressed
hard[b] upon those in Judea, cut off their supplies,
and hindered their building; 73and by plots and
demagoguery and uprisings they prevented the
completion of the building as long as King Cyrus
lived. They were kept from building for two years,
until the reign of Darius.

6 Now in the second year of the reign of Darius, the prophets Haggai and Zechariah son
of Iddo prophesied to the Jews who were in Judea and Jerusalem; they prophesied to them in
the name of the Lord God of Israel. 2Then Zerubbabel son of Shealtiel and Jeshua son of Jozadak began to build the house of the Lord that is
in Jerusalem, with the help of the prophets of the
Lord who were with them.

3 At the same time Sisinnes the governor of
Syria and Phoenicia and Sathrabuzanes and their
associates came to them and said, 4"By whose
order are you building this house and this roof
and finishing all the other things? And who are
the builders that are finishing these things?" 5Yet
the elders of the Jews were dealt with kindly,
for the providence of the Lord was over the captives; 6they were not prevented from building until word could be sent to Darius concerning them
and a report made.

7 A copy of the letter that Sisinnes the governor of Syria and Phoenicia, and Sathrabuzanes,
and their associates the local rulers in Syria and
Phoenicia, wrote and sent to Darius:

8 "To King Darius, greetings. Let it be fully
known to our lord the king that, when we went to
the country of Judea and entered the city of Jerusalem, we found the elders of the Jews, who had
been in exile, 9building in the city of Jerusalem a
great new house for the Lord, of hewn stone, with
costly timber laid in the walls. 10These operations
are going on rapidly, and the work is prospering in their hands and being completed with all
splendor and care. 11Then we asked these elders,
'At whose command are you building this house
and laying the foundations of this structure?' 12In
order that we might inform you in writing who
the leaders are, we questioned them and asked
them for a list of the names of those who are at
their head. 13They answered us, 'We are the servants of the Lord who created the heaven and the
earth. 14The house was built many years ago by a
king of Israel who was great and strong, and it was
finished. 15But when our ancestors sinned against
the Lord of Israel who is in heaven, and provoked
him, he gave them over into the hands of King
Nebuchadnezzar of Babylon, king of the Chaldeans; 16and they pulled down the house, and
burned it, and carried the people away captive to
Babylon. 17But in the first year that Cyrus reigned
over the country of Babylonia, King Cyrus wrote
that this house should be rebuilt. 18And the holy
vessels of gold and of silver, which Nebuchadnezzar had taken out of the house in Jerusalem

[a] Gk *Asbasareth* [b] Meaning of Gk uncertain

and stored in his own temple, these King Cyrus
took out again from the temple in Babylon, and
they were delivered to Zerubbabel and Sheshbazzar[a] the governor 19 with the command that he
should take all these vessels back and put them in
the temple at Jerusalem, and that this temple of
the Lord should be rebuilt on its site. 20 Then this
Sheshbazzar, after coming here, laid the foundations of the house of the Lord that is in Jerusalem.
Although it has been in process of construction
from that time until now, it has not yet reached
completion.' 21 Now therefore, O king, if it seems
wise to do so, let search be made in the royal archives of our lord[b] the king that are in Babylon;
22 if it is found that the building of the house of
the Lord in Jerusalem was done with the consent
of King Cyrus, and if it is approved by our lord
the king, let him send us directions concerning
these things."

23 Then Darius commanded that search be
made in the royal archives that were deposited
in Babylon. And in Ecbatana, the fortress that is
in the country of Media, a scroll[c] was found in
which this was recorded: 24 "In the first year of
the reign of King Cyrus, he ordered the building
of the house of the Lord in Jerusalem, where they
sacrifice with perpetual fire; 25 its height to be
sixty cubits and its width sixty cubits, with three
courses of hewn stone and one course of new
native timber; the cost to be paid from the treasury of King Cyrus; 26 and that the holy vessels of
the house of the Lord, both of gold and of silver,
which Nebuchadnezzar took out of the house in
Jerusalem and carried away to Babylon, should be
restored to the house in Jerusalem, to be placed
where they had been."

27 So Darius[d] commanded Sisinnes the
governor of Syria and Phoenicia, and Sathrabuzanes, and their associates, and those who were
appointed as local rulers in Syria and Phoenicia,
to keep away from the place, and to permit Zerubbabel, the servant of the Lord and governor
of Judea, and the elders of the Jews to build this
house of the Lord on its site. 28 "And I command
that it be built completely, and that full effort be
made to help those who have returned from the
exile of Judea, until the house of the Lord is finished; 29 and that out of the tribute of Coelesyria
and Phoenicia a portion be scrupulously given to
these men, that is, to Zerubbabel the governor,
for sacrifices to the Lord, for bulls and rams and
lambs, 30 and likewise wheat and salt and wine
and oil, regularly every year, without quibbling,
for daily use as the priests in Jerusalem may indicate, 31 in order that libations may be made to the
Most High God for the king and his children, and
prayers be offered for their lives."

32 He commanded that if anyone should
transgress or nullify any of the things herein written,[e] a beam should be taken out of the house
of the perpetrator, who then should be impaled
upon it, and all property forfeited to the king.

33 "Therefore may the Lord, whose name
is there called upon, destroy every king and nation that shall stretch out their hands to hinder or
damage that house of the Lord in Jerusalem.

34 "I, King Darius, have decreed that it be
done with all diligence as here prescribed."

7 Then Sisinnes the governor of Coelesyria
and Phoenicia, and Sathrabuzanes, and their
associates, following the orders of King Darius,
2 supervised the holy work with very great care, assisting the elders of the Jews and the chief officers
of the temple. 3 The holy work prospered, while
the prophets Haggai and Zechariah prophesied;
4 and they completed it by the command of the
Lord God of Israel. So with the consent of Cyrus
and Darius and Artaxerxes, kings of the Persians,
5 the holy house was finished by the twenty-third
day of the month of Adar, in the sixth year of King
Darius. 6 And the people of Israel, the priests, the
Levites, and the rest of those who returned from
exile who joined them, did according to what
was written in the book of Moses. 7 They offered
at the dedication of the temple of the Lord one
hundred bulls, two hundred rams, four hundred
lambs, 8 and twelve male goats for the sin of all Israel, according to the number of the twelve lead-

[a] Gk *Sanabassarus* [b] Other ancient authorities read *of Cyrus* [c] Other authorities read *passage* [d] Gk *he*
[e] Other authorities read *stated above* or *added in writing*

ers of the tribes of Israel; 9 and the priests and the
Levites stood arrayed in their vestments, according to kindred, for the services of the Lord God of
Israel in accordance with the book of Moses; and
the gatekeepers were at each gate.
10 The people of Israel who came from exile
kept the passover on the fourteenth day of the first
month, after the priests and the Levites were purified together. 11 Not all of the returned captives
were purified, but the Levites were all purified together,[a] 12 and they sacrificed the passover lamb
for all the returned captives and for their kindred
the priests and for themselves. 13 The people of Israel who had returned from exile ate it, all those
who had separated themselves from the abominations of the peoples of the land and sought the
Lord. 14 They also kept the festival of unleavened
bread seven days, rejoicing before the Lord, 15 because he had changed the will of the king of the
Assyrians concerning them, to strengthen their
hands for the service of the Lord God of Israel.
8 After these things, when Artaxerxes, the king
of the Persians, was reigning, Ezra came, the
son of Seraiah, son of Azariah, son of Hilkiah, son
of Shallum, 2 son of Zadok, son of Ahitub, son
of Amariah, son of Uzzi, son of Bukki, son of
Abishua, son of Phineas, son of Eleazar, son of
Aaron the high[b] priest. 3 This Ezra came up from
Babylon as a scribe skilled in the law of Moses,
which was given by the God of Israel; 4 and the
king showed him honor, for he found favor before
the king[c] in all his requests. 5 There came up with
him to Jerusalem some of the people of Israel and
some of the priests and Levites and temple singers and gatekeepers and temple servants, 6 in the
seventh year of the reign of Artaxerxes, in the fifth
month (this was the king's seventh year); for they
left Babylon on the new moon of the first month
and arrived in Jerusalem on the new moon of the
fifth month, by the prosperous journey that the
Lord gave them.[d] 7 For Ezra possessed great
knowledge, so that he omitted nothing from the
law of the Lord or the commandments, but taught
all Israel all the ordinances and judgments.
8 The following is a copy of the written commission from King Artaxerxes that was delivered
to Ezra the priest and reader of the law of the
Lord:
9 "King Artaxerxes to Ezra the priest and
reader of the law of the Lord, greeting. 10 In accordance with my gracious decision, I have given
orders that those of the Jewish nation and of the
priests and Levites and others in our realm, those
who freely choose to do so, may go with you
to Jerusalem. 11 Let as many as are so disposed,
therefore, leave with you, just as I and the seven
Friends who are my counselors have decided,
12 in order to look into matters in Judea and Jerusalem, in accordance with what is in the law
of the Lord, 13 and to carry to Jerusalem the gifts
for the Lord of Israel that I and my Friends have
vowed, and to collect for the Lord in Jerusalem all
the gold and silver that may be found in the country of Babylonia, 14 together with what is given by
the nation for the temple of their Lord that is in
Jerusalem, both gold and silver for bulls and rams
and lambs and what goes with them, 15 so as to
offer sacrifices on the altar of their Lord that is in
Jerusalem. 16 Whatever you and your kindred are
minded to do with the gold and silver, perform
it in accordance with the will of your God; 17 deliver the holy vessels of the Lord that are given
you for the use of the temple of your God that is
in Jerusalem. 18 And whatever else occurs to you
as necessary for the temple of your God, you may
provide out of the royal treasury.
19 "I, King Artaxerxes, have commanded
the treasurers of Syria and Phoenicia that whatever Ezra the priest and reader of the law of the
Most High God sends for, they shall take care to
give him, 20 up to a hundred talents of silver, and
likewise up to a hundred cors of wheat, a hundred baths of wine, and salt in abundance. 21 Let
all things prescribed in the law of God be scrupulously fulfilled for the Most High God, so that
wrath may not come upon the kingdom of the
king and his sons. 22 You are also informed that
no tribute or any other tax is to be laid on any of
the priests or Levites or temple singers or gatekeepers or temple servants or persons employed

[a] Meaning of Gk uncertain [b] Gk *the first* [c] Gk *him* [d] Other authorities add *for him* or *upon him*

in this temple, and that no one has authority to impose any tax on them.

23 "And you, Ezra, according to the wisdom of God, appoint judges and justices to judge all those who know the law of your God, throughout all Syria and Phoenicia; and you shall teach it to those who do not know it. 24All who transgress the law of your God or the law of the kingdom shall be strictly punished, whether by death or some other punishment, either fine or imprisonment."

25 Then Ezra the scribe said,[a] "Blessed be the Lord alone, who put this into the heart of the king, to glorify his house that is in Jerusalem, 26and who honored me in the sight of the king and his counselors and all his Friends and nobles. 27I was encouraged by the help of the Lord my God, and I gathered men from Israel to go up with me."

28 These are the leaders, according to their ancestral houses and their groups, who went up with me from Babylon, in the reign of King Artaxerxes: 29Of the descendants of Phineas, Gershom. Of the descendants of Ithamar, Gamael. Of the descendants of David, Hattush son of Shecaniah. 30Of the descendants of Parosh, Zechariah, and with him a hundred fifty men enrolled. 31Of the descendants of Pahath-moab, Eliehoenai son of Zerahiah, and with him two hundred men. 32Of the descendants of Zattu, Shecaniah son of Jahaziel, and with him three hundred men. Of the descendants of Adin, Obed son of Jonathan, and with him two hundred fifty men. 33Of the descendants of Elam, Jeshaiah son of Gotholiah, and with him seventy men. 34Of the descendants of Shephatiah, Zeraiah son of Michael, and with him seventy men. 35Of the descendants of Joab, Obadiah son of Jehiel, and with him two hundred twelve men. 36Of the descendants of Bani, Shelomith son of Josiphiah, and with him a hundred sixty men. 37Of the descendants of Bebai, Zechariah son of Bebai, and with him twenty-eight men. 38Of the descendants of Azgad, Johanan son of Hakkatan, and with him a hundred ten men. 39Of the descendants of Adonikam, the last ones, their names being Eliphelet, Jeuel, and Shemaiah, and with them seventy men. 40Of the descendants of Bigvai, Uthai son of Istalcurus, and with him seventy men.

41 I assembled them at the river called Theras, and we encamped there three days, and I inspected them. 42When I found there none of the descendants of the priests or of the Levites, 43I sent word to Eliezar, Iduel, Maasmas, 44Elnathan, Shemaiah, Jarib, Nathan, Elnathan, Zechariah, and Meshullam, who were leaders and men of understanding; 45I told them to go to Iddo, who was the leading man at the place of the treasury, 46and ordered them to tell Iddo and his kindred and the treasurers at that place to send us men to serve as priests in the house of our Lord. 47And by the mighty hand of our Lord they brought us competent men of the descendants of Mahli son of Levi, son of Israel, namely Sherebiah[b] with his descendants and kinsmen, eighteen; 48also Hashabiah and Annunus and his brother Jeshaiah, of the descendants of Hananiah, and their descendants, twenty men; 49and of the temple servants, whom David and the leaders had given for the service of the Levites, two hundred twenty temple servants; the list of all their names was reported.

50 There I proclaimed a fast for the young men before our Lord, to seek from him a prosperous journey for ourselves and for our children and the livestock that were with us. 51For I was ashamed to ask the king for foot soldiers and cavalry and an escort to keep us safe from our adversaries; 52for we had said to the king, "The power of our Lord will be with those who seek him, and will support them in every way." 53And again we prayed to our Lord about these things, and we found him very merciful.

54 Then I set apart twelve of the leaders of the priests, Sherebiah and Hashabiah, and ten of their kinsmen with them; 55and I weighed out to them the silver and the gold and the holy vessels of the house of our Lord, which the king himself and his counselors and the nobles and all Israel had given. 56I weighed and gave to them six hundred fifty talents of silver, and silver vessels

[a] Other ancient authorities lack *Then Ezra the scribe said* [b] Gk *Asbebias*

worth a hundred talents, and a hundred talents of gold, 57 and twenty golden bowls, and twelve bronze vessels of fine bronze that glittered like gold. 58 And I said to them, "You are holy to the Lord, and the vessels are holy, and the silver and the gold are vowed to the Lord, the Lord of our ancestors. 59 Be watchful and on guard until you deliver them to the leaders of the priests and the Levites, and to the heads of the ancestral houses of Israel, in Jerusalem, in the chambers of the house of our Lord." 60 So the priests and the Levites who took the silver and the gold and the vessels that had been in Jerusalem carried them to the temple of the Lord.

61 We left the river Theras on the twelfth day of the first month; and we arrived in Jerusalem by the mighty hand of our Lord, which was upon us; he delivered us from every enemy on the way, and so we came to Jerusalem. 62 When we had been there three days, the silver and the gold were weighed and delivered in the house of our Lord to the priest Meremoth son of Uriah; 63 with him was Eleazar son of Phinehas, and with them were Jozabad son of Jeshua and Moeth son of Binnui,[a] the Levites. 64 The whole was counted and weighed, and the weight of everything was recorded at that very time. 65 And those who had returned from exile offered sacrifices to the Lord, the God of Israel, twelve bulls for all Israel, ninety-six rams, 66 seventy-two lambs, and as a thank offering twelve male goats—all as a sacrifice to the Lord. 67 They delivered the king's orders to the royal stewards and to the governors of Coelesyria and Phoenicia; and these officials[b] honored the people and the temple of the Lord.

68 After these things had been done, the leaders came to me and said, 69 "The people of Israel and the rulers and the priests and the Levites have not put away from themselves the alien peoples of the land and their pollutions, the Canaanites, the Hittites, the Perizzites, the Jebusites, the Moabites, the Egyptians, and the Edomites. 70 For they and their descendants have married the daughters of these people,[c] and the holy race has been mixed with the alien peoples of the land; and from the beginning of this matter the leaders and the nobles have been sharing in this iniquity."

71 As soon as I heard these things I tore my garments and my holy mantle, and pulled out hair from my head and beard, and sat down in anxiety and grief. 72 And all who were ever moved at[d] the word of the Lord of Israel gathered around me, as I mourned over this iniquity, and I sat grief-stricken until the evening sacrifice. 73 Then I rose from my fast, with my garments and my holy mantle torn, and kneeling down and stretching out my hands to the Lord 74 I said,

"O Lord, I am ashamed and confused before your face. 75 For our sins have risen higher than our heads, and our mistakes have mounted up to heaven 76 from the times of our ancestors, and we are in great sin to this day. 77 Because of our sins and the sins of our ancestors, we with our kindred and our kings and our priests were given over to the kings of the earth, to the sword and exile and plundering, in shame until this day. 78 And now in some measure mercy has come to us from you, O Lord, to leave to us a root and a name in your holy place, 79 and to uncover a light for us in the house of the Lord our God, and to give us food in the time of our servitude. 80 Even in our bondage we were not forsaken by our Lord, but he brought us into favor with the kings of the Persians, so that they have given us food 81 and glorified the temple of our Lord, and raised Zion from desolation, to give us a stronghold in Judea and Jerusalem.

82 "And now, O Lord, what shall we say, when we have these things? For we have transgressed your commandments, which you gave by your servants the prophets, saying, 83 'The land that you are entering to take possession of is a land polluted with the pollution of the aliens of the land, and they have filled it with their uncleanness. 84 Therefore do not give your daughters in marriage to their descendants, and do not take their daughters for your descendants; 85 do not seek ever to have peace with them, so that you may be strong and eat the good things of the

[a] Gk *Sabannus* [b] Gk *they* [c] Gk *their daughters* [d] Or *zealous for*

land and leave it for an inheritance to your children forever.' 86And all that has happened to us
has come about because of our evil deeds and our
great sins. For you, O Lord, lifted the burden of
our sins 87and gave us such a root as this; but we
turned back again to transgress your law by mixing with the uncleanness of the peoples of the
land. 88Were you not angry enough with us to destroy us without leaving a root or seed or name?
89O Lord of Israel, you are faithful; for we are left
as a root to this day. 90See, we are now before you
in our iniquities; for we can no longer stand in
your presence because of these things."

91 While Ezra was praying and making his
confession, weeping and lying on the ground before the temple, there gathered around him a very
great crowd of men and women and youths from
Jerusalem; for there was great weeping among the
multitude. 92Then Shecaniah son of Jehiel, one
of the men of Israel, called out, and said to Ezra,
"We have sinned against the Lord, and have married foreign women from the peoples of the land;
but even now there is hope for Israel. 93Let us take
an oath to the Lord about this, that we will put
away all our foreign wives, with their children,
94as seems good to you and to all who obey the
law of the Lord. 95Rise up[a] and take action, for it is
your task, and we are with you to take strong measures." 96Then Ezra rose up and made the leaders
of the priests and Levites of all Israel swear that
they would do this. And they swore to it.

9 Then Ezra set out and went from the court of
the temple to the chamber of Jehohanan son
of Eliashib, 2and spent the night there; and he did
not eat bread or drink water, for he was mourning
over the great iniquities of the multitude. 3And a
proclamation was made throughout Judea and Jerusalem to all who had returned from exile that
they should assemble at Jerusalem, 4and that if
any did not meet there within two or three days, in
accordance with the decision of the ruling elders,
their livestock would be seized for sacrifice and
the men themselves[b] expelled from the multitude
of those who had returned from the captivity.

5 Then the men of the tribe of Judah and
Benjamin assembled at Jerusalem within three
days; this was the ninth month, on the twentieth
day of the month. 6All the multitude sat in the
open square before the temple, shivering because
of the bad weather that prevailed. 7Then Ezra
stood up and said to them, "You have broken the
law and married foreign women, and so have increased the sin of Israel. 8Now then make confession and give glory to the Lord the God of our
ancestors, 9and do his will; separate yourselves
from the peoples of the land and from your foreign wives."

10 Then all the multitude shouted and said
with a loud voice, "We will do as you have said.
11But the multitude is great and it is winter, and
we are not able to stand in the open air. This is
not a work we can do in one day or two, for we
have sinned too much in these things. 12So let the
leaders of the multitude stay, and let all those in
our settlements who have foreign wives come at
the time appointed, 13with the elders and judges
of each place, until we are freed from the wrath of
the Lord over this matter."

14 Jonathan son of Asahel and Jahzeiah son of
Tikvah[c] undertook the matter on these terms, and
Meshullam and Levi and Shabbethai served with
them as judges. 15And those who had returned
from exile acted in accordance with all this.

16 Ezra the priest chose for himself the leading men of their ancestral houses, all of them by
name; and on the new moon of the tenth month
they began their sessions to investigate the matter. 17And the cases of the men who had foreign
wives were brought to an end by the new moon
of the first month.

18 Of the priests, those who were brought
in and found to have foreign wives were: 19of the
descendants of Jeshua son of Jozadak and his kindred, Maaseiah, Eliezar, Jarib, and Jodan. 20They
pledged themselves to put away their wives, and
to offer rams in expiation of their error. 21Of the
descendants of Immer: Hanani and Zebadiah and
Maaseiah and Shemaiah and Jehiel and Azariah.

[a] Other ancient authorities read *as seems good to you." And all who obeyed the law of the Lord rose and said to Ezra, 95"Rise up*
[b] Gk *he himself* [c] Gk *Thocanos*

22 Of the descendants of Pashhur: Elioenai, Maaseiah, Ishmael, and Nathanael, and Gedaliah, and
Salthas.

23 And of the Levites: Jozabad and Shimei
and Kelaiah, who was Kelita, and Pethahiah and
Judah and Jonah. 24 Of the temple singers: Eliashib and Zaccur.[a] 25 Of the gatekeepers: Shallum
and Telem.[b]

26 Of Israel: of the descendants of Parosh:
Ramiah, Izziah, Malchijah, Mijamin, and Eleazar,
and Asibias, and Benaiah. 27 Of the descendants
of Elam: Mattaniah and Zechariah, Jezrielus and
Abdi, and Jeremoth and Elijah. 28 Of the descendants of Zamoth: Eliadas, Eliashib, Othoniah,
Jeremoth, and Zabad and Zerdaiah. 29 Of the
descendants of Bebai: Jehohanan and Hananiah
and Zabbai and Emathis. 30 Of the descendants
of Mani: Olamus, Mamuchus, Adaiah, Jashub,
and Sheal and Jeremoth. 31 Of the descendants of
Addi: Naathus and Moossias, Laccunus and Nai-
dus, and Bescaspasmys and Sesthel, and Belnuus
and Manasseas. 32 Of the descendants of Annan,
Elionas and Asaias and Melchias and Sabbaias
and Simon Chosamaeus. 33 Of the descendants
of Hashum: Mattenai and Mattattah and Zabad
and Eliphelet and Manasseh and Shimei. 34 Of the
descendants of Bani: Jeremai, Momdius, Maerus,
Joel, Mamdai and Bedeiah and Vaniah, Caraba-
sion and Eliashib and Mamitanemus, Eliasis, Binnui, Elialis, Shimei, Shelemiah, Nethaniah. Of
the descendants of Ezora: Shashai, Azarel, Azael,
Samatus, Zambris, Joseph. 35 Of the descendants
of Nooma: Mazitias, Zabad, Iddo, Joel, Benaiah.
36 All these had married foreign women, and they
put them away together with their children.

37 The priests and the Levites and the Israelites settled in Jerusalem and in the country. On
the new moon of the seventh month, when the
people of Israel were in their settlements, 38 the
whole multitude gathered with one accord in
the open square before the east gate of the temple; 39 they told Ezra the chief priest and reader
to bring the law of Moses that had been given by
the Lord God of Israel. 40 So Ezra the chief priest
brought the law, for all the multitude, men and
women, and all the priests to hear the law, on the
new moon of the seventh month. 41 He read aloud
in the open square before the gate of the temple
from early morning until midday, in the presence
of both men and women; and all the multitude
gave attention to the law. 42 Ezra the priest and
reader of the law stood on the wooden platform
that had been prepared; 43 and beside him stood
Mattathiah, Shema, Ananias, Azariah, Uriah,
Hezekiah, and Baalsamus on his right, 44 and on
his left Pedaiah, Mishael, Malchijah, Lothasubus,
Nabariah, and Zechariah. 45 Then Ezra took up
the book of the law in the sight of the multitude, for he had the place of honor in the presence of all. 46 When he opened the law, they all
stood erect. And Ezra blessed the Lord God Most
High, the God of hosts, the Almighty, 47 and the
multitude answered, "Amen." They lifted up their
hands, and fell to the ground and worshiped the
Lord. 48 Jeshua and Anniuth and Sherebiah, Jadi-
nus, Akkub, Shabbethai, Hodiah, Maiannas and
Kelita, Azariah and Jozabad, Hanan, Pelaiah, the
Levites, taught the law of the Lord,[c] at the same
time explaining what was read.

49 Then Attharates[d] said to Ezra the chief
priest and reader, and to the Levites who were
teaching the multitude, and to all, 50 "This day is
holy to the Lord"—now they were all weeping as
they heard the law— 51 "so go your way, eat the fat
and drink the sweet, and send portions to those
who have none; 52 for the day is holy to the Lord;
and do not be sorrowful, for the Lord will exalt
you." 53 The Levites commanded all the people,
saying, "This day is holy; do not be sorrowful."
54 Then they all went their way, to eat and drink
and enjoy themselves, and to give portions to
those who had none, and to make great rejoicing;
55 because they were inspired by the words which
they had been taught. And they came together.[e]

[a] Gk *Bacchurus* [b] Gk *Tolbanes* [c] Other ancient authorities add *and read the law of the Lord to the multitude*
[d] Or *the governor* [e] The Greek text ends abruptly: compare Neh 8.13

The Prayer of Manasseh

I encounter the Prayer of Manasseh regularly when I pray the midnight office. I use Phyllis Trickle's *The Night Offices*, based on the Book of Common Prayer (Episcopal Church, 1979), for evening prayers. Manasseh's plea to God is not part of the Protestant Bible that represents my canon as a Pentecostal Christian, nor is it included in the Anglican-Episcopal canon; yet it forms part of that community's practice of prayer, and now my own. The Greek and Russian Orthodox communities do consider this short prayer to be Scripture.

This text purports to be a prayer of Manasseh, a seventh-century king of Judah, who in 2 Kgs 21:1-18 is described as the worst possible king. He is idolatrous, unrepentant, and partially responsible for Judah's fall to Babylon. In contrast, 2 Chron 33:10-17 describes the king as disobedient but later remorseful. The Prayer of Manasseh is a late first-century BCE expansion of the earlier view in 2 Chronicles.

The prayer's argument that God acknowledges and forgives the repentant was a common theme in Judaism, both before and after the exile in 587/586. This theme appears in the texts read today for Yom Kippur, the Jewish Day of Atonement, and for Roman Catholic and mainline Protestant Ash Wednesday services.

— *Stacy Davis*

1 O Lord Almighty,
God of our ancestors,
of Abraham and Isaac and Jacob
and of their righteous offspring;
2 you who made heaven and earth
with all their order;
3 who shackled the sea by your word of command,
who confined the deep
and sealed it with your terrible and glorious name;
4 at whom all things shudder,
and tremble before your power,
5 for your glorious splendor cannot be borne,
and the wrath of your threat to sinners is unendurable;
6 yet immeasurable and unsearchable
is your promised mercy,

7 for you are the Lord Most High,
of great compassion, long-suffering, and very merciful,
and you relent at human suffering.
O Lord, according to your great goodness
you have promised repentance and forgiveness
to those who have sinned against you,
and in the multitude of your mercies
you have appointed repentance for sinners,
so that they may be saved.[a]
8 Therefore you, O Lord, God of the righteous,
have not appointed repentance for the righteous,
for Abraham and Isaac and Jacob, who did not sin against you,
but you have appointed repentance for me, who am a sinner.
9 For the sins I have committed are more in number than the sand of the sea;
my transgressions are multiplied, O Lord, they are multiplied!
I am not worthy to look up and see the height of heaven
because of the multitude of my iniquities.
10 I am weighted down with many an iron fetter,
so that I am rejected[b] because of my sins,
and I have no relief;
for I have provoked your wrath
and have done what is evil in your sight,
setting up abominations and multiplying offenses.
11 And now I bend the knee of my heart,
imploring you for your kindness.
12 I have sinned, O Lord, I have sinned,
and I acknowledge my transgressions.
13 I earnestly implore you,
forgive me, O Lord, forgive me!
Do not destroy me with my transgressions!
Do not be angry with me forever or store up evil for me;
do not condemn me to the depths of the earth.
For you, O Lord, are the God of those who repent,
14 and in me you will manifest your goodness;
for, unworthy as I am, you will save me according to your great mercy,
15 and I will praise you continually all the days of my life.
For all the host of heaven sings your praise,
and yours is the glory forever. Amen.

[a] Other ancient authorities lack *O Lord, according . . . be saved*
[b] Other ancient authorities read *so that I cannot lift up my head*

Psalm 151

People loved to reminisce and romanticize about David. Dead Sea scroll 11QPs[a] includes several extra-biblical psalms and also a notice that claims that King David composed 3,600 psalms and 450 songs. That is a great deal of composition and adds to the ascription to David of seventy-three of the 150 biblical psalms. For all his faults (his relationship with Bathsheba and betraying his loyal soldier, Uriah, to death), David remained a hero in Jewish lore. He was chosen and favored by God, and during his lifetime his kingdom and the people generally flourished. Michelangelo's statue of the handsome young David is a later expression of that love of heroes.

It makes sense, then, that there was a long tradition that added a 151st psalm to the Hebrew Psalter, recounting two important events in David's life. This short psalm served as a coda to the Psalter. Psalm 151 is preserved in most manuscripts of the Septuagint (LXX) and is found in other ancient biblical traditions; the Russian and Greek Orthodox churches include it in their authoritative scriptures.

Psalm 151 is evidently a compressed version of two earlier psalms that are found—the second only in part—in Dead Sea scroll 11QPs[a]. It appears that as early as the third century BCE an imaginative editor hit upon the idea of concluding the Psalter with the voice of David himself recalling these great moments in his life. These are great moments because they are also significant events in the story of God coming to the aid of God's people. The first is the anointing of David ("I was small among my brothers, and the youngest in my father's house") to be king. Noted also are his musical skills that in the tradition made him such a fine composer of psalms and songs. The last two verses of the psalm recall his victory over the giant warrior Goliath, Israel's great enemy and oppressor.

As a white, well-educated male who has served in positions of great privilege (as a university dean of chapel and professor, a divinity school professor and head, and a bishop), I have had to learn to listen to the voices of many others when interpreting Scripture. In the saga of his people, David was the underdog. His victories showed that God was with him. His victories on behalf of his people showed that God is on the side of the lesser and the oppressed. Psalm 151 ends some versions of the Psalter with this encomium to David, the composer of many psalms and the underdog chosen by God, in order to bring further encouragement and courage to God's people.

— ***Frederick Houk Borsch***

This psalm is ascribed to David as his own composition (though it is outside the number[a]), after he had fought in single combat with Goliath.

1 I was small among my brothers,
and the youngest in my father's house;
I tended my father's sheep.

2 My hands made a harp;
my fingers fashioned a lyre.

3 And who will tell my Lord?
The Lord himself; it is he who hears.[b]

4 It was he who sent his messenger[c]
and took me from my father's sheep,
and anointed me with his anointing oil.

5 My brothers were handsome and tall,
but the Lord was not pleased with them.

6 I went out to meet the Philistine,[d]
and he cursed me by his idols.

7 But I drew his own sword;
I beheaded him, and took away disgrace
from the people of Israel.

[a] Other ancient authorities add *of the one hundred fifty* (psalms) [b] Other ancient authorities add *everything*; others add *me*; others read *who will hear me* [c] Or *angel* [d] Or *foreigner*

3 Maccabees

THE SUBJECT OF 3 AND 4 MACCABEES is the same—religious persecution. Only their responses differ. Unlike 4 Maccabees, 3 Maccabees does not discuss the Maccabean Revolt, in which Israel's Jews successfully rebelled against Greek rule in the 160s BCE. Third Maccabees describes both faithfulness and unfaithfulness to Judaism, while 4 Maccabees emphasizes faithfulness to the point of martyrdom.

Classified as sacred Scripture in the Greek and Russian Orthodox communities, 3 Maccabees describes a third-century BCE conflict between Alexandrian Jews and their Egyptian rulers. For the Russian Orthodox who lived through waves of persecution and repression during the twentieth-century Communist era, 3 Maccabees would sound eerily like their own recent history. While the demise of Communism ended their struggle, the Jewish community in 3 Maccabees was rescued from extermination because God answered their prayers for deliverance. The book accurately describes the tension between the dominant Gentile culture and the minority Jewish one. Gentiles perceived Jews as haters of humankind because of their monotheism and dietary restrictions (2:27-30; 3:2-8). Writing in the first century CE, the Jewish historian Josephus repeated the critique. In *Against Apion*, he remarked that Jews are seen "as the very vilest of [humankind]" (2:236). In rebuttal, however, both the author of 3 Maccabees and Josephus insist that Jews should not be criticized or persecuted, because they are loyal citizens of the empire (3 Macc 6:26; *Against Apion* 2:225–35).

But 3 Maccabees' description of Jews who decide to obey the command of the emperor to worship foreign gods (2:31) is distinctive. Josephus later insisted upon the necessity of Jewish faithfulness to the Torah, which creates good citizens (*Against Apion* 2:144, 146, 291). The author of 3 Maccabees takes that a step further; once the threat of extermination has passed, those Jews who remained faithful receive state permission to kill the Jews who fell away (7:10-16).

The problem of what to do with apostates—those who abandon the faith—reappeared in early Christianity. In the mid-third century, Cyprian of Carthage responded to a time of persecution in which some Christians, under torture or fear, sacrificed to other deities. He concluded that those who had been tortured should without question be forgiven; all others must repent before being accepted back into communion with the church (*De Lapsis* 13, 16, 23, 29, 33, 35). There was no talk of killing the unfaithful, as in 3 Maccabees. This suggests that different communities can and do respond to apostasy in different ways, depending upon their context.

I have no personal or family experience of religious persecution. However, I am descended from African American slaves on both sides of my family. My family's history is shaped by slavery and its aftermath, including legal segregation in the South on my mother's side and the Great Migration to cities in the North on my father's. In both cases, my family's determination to build a

better life for themselves against the odds enables me to respect the determination displayed by the communities described in both 3 and 4 Maccabees. As an African-American Christian, my religious and my ethnic context have suffering and persecution imbedded in them. These writings pose to me and to every reader this question: For what, if anything, are we prepared to die?

— *Stacy Davis*

1 When Philopator learned from those who returned that the regions that he had controlled
had been seized by Antiochus, he gave orders to
all his forces, both infantry and cavalry, took with
him his sister Arsinoë, and marched out to the region near Raphia, where the army of Antiochus
was encamped. 2 But a certain Theodotus, determined to carry out the plot he had devised, took
with him the best of the Ptolemaic arms that had
been previously issued to him,[a] and crossed over
by night to the tent of Ptolemy, intending single-
handed to kill him and thereby end the war. 3 But
Dositheus, known as the son of Drimylus, a Jew
by birth who later changed his religion and apos-
tatized from the ancestral traditions, had led the
king away and arranged that a certain insignificant
man should sleep in the tent; and so it turned out
that this man incurred the vengeance meant for
the king.[b] 4 When a bitter fight resulted, and matters were turning out rather in favor of Antiochus,
Arsinoë went to the troops with wailing and tears,
her locks all disheveled, and exhorted them to
defend themselves and their children and wives
bravely, promising to give them each two minas
of gold if they won the battle. 5 And so it came
about that the enemy was routed in the action,
and many captives also were taken. 6 Now that
he had foiled the plot, Ptolemy[c] decided to visit
the neighboring cities and encourage them. 7 By
doing this, and by endowing their sacred enclo-
sures with gifts, he strengthened the morale of
his subjects.

8 Since the Jews had sent some of their council and elders to greet him, to bring him gifts of
welcome, and to congratulate him on what had
happened, he was all the more eager to visit them
as soon as possible. 9 After he had arrived in Jerusalem, he offered sacrifice to the supreme God[d]
and made thank offerings and did what was fitting for the holy place.[e] Then, upon entering the
place and being impressed by its excellence and
its beauty, 10 he marveled at the good order of
the temple, and conceived a desire to enter the
sanctuary. 11 When they said that this was not
permitted, because not even members of their
own nation were allowed to enter, not even all
of the priests, but only the high priest who was
pre-eminent over all—and he only once a year—
the king was by no means persuaded. 12 Even after
the law had been read to him, he did not cease to
maintain that he ought to enter, saying, "Even if
those men are deprived of this honor, I ought not
to be." 13 And he inquired why, when he entered
every other temple,[f] no one there had stopped
him. 14 And someone answered thoughtlessly
that it was wrong to take that as a portent.[g] 15 "But
since this has happened," the king[c] said, "why
should not I at least enter, whether they wish it
or not?"

16 Then the priests in all their vestments

[a] *Or the best of the Ptolemaic soldiers previously put under his command* [b] *Gk that one* [c] *Gk he* [d] *Gk the greatest God* [e] *Gk the place* [f] *Or entered the temple precincts* [g] *Or to boast of this*

prostrated themselves and entreated the supreme
God[a] to aid in the present situation and to avert
the violence of this evil design, and they filled
the temple with cries and tears; 17those who remained behind in the city were agitated and hurried out, supposing that something mysterious
was occurring. 18Young women who had been
secluded in their chambers rushed out with their
mothers, sprinkled their hair with dust,[b] and filled
the streets with groans and lamentations. 19Those
women who had recently been arrayed for marriage abandoned the bridal chambers[c] prepared
for wedded union, and, neglecting proper modesty, in a disorderly rush flocked together in the
city. 20Mothers and nurses abandoned even newborn children here and there, some in houses and
some in the streets, and without a backward look
they crowded together at the most high temple.
21Various were the supplications of those gathered there because of what the king was profanely
plotting. 22In addition, the bolder of the citizens
would not tolerate the completion of his plans or
the fulfillment of his intended purpose. 23They
shouted to their compatriots to take arms and die
courageously for the ancestral law, and created a
considerable disturbance in the holy place;[d] and
being barely restrained by the old men and the
elders,[e] they resorted to the same posture of supplication as the others. 24Meanwhile the crowd,
as before, was engaged in prayer, 25while the elders near the king tried in various ways to change
his arrogant mind from the plan that he had
conceived. 26But he, in his arrogance, took heed
of nothing, and began now to approach, determined to bring the aforesaid plan to a conclusion.
27When those who were around him observed
this, they turned, together with our people, to call
upon him who has all power to defend them in the
present trouble and not to overlook this unlawful
and haughty deed. 28The continuous, vehement,
and concerted cry of the crowds[f] resulted in an
immense uproar; 29for it seemed that not only
the people but also the walls and the whole earth
around echoed, because indeed all at that time[g]
preferred death to the profanation of the place.

2 Then the high priest Simon, facing the sanctuary, bending his knees and extending his
hands with calm dignity, prayed as follows:[h]
2"Lord, Lord, king of the heavens, and sovereign
of all creation, holy among the holy ones, the
only ruler, almighty, give attention to us who are
suffering grievously from an impious and profane
man, puffed up in his audacity and power. 3For
you, the creator of all things and the governor
of all, are a just Ruler, and you judge those who
have done anything in insolence and arrogance.
4You destroyed those who in the past committed injustice, among whom were even giants who
trusted in their strength and boldness, whom you
destroyed by bringing on them a boundless flood.
5You consumed with fire and sulfur the people of
Sodom who acted arrogantly, who were notorious
for their vices;[i] and you made them an example
to those who should come afterward. 6You made
known your mighty power by inflicting many and
varied punishments on the audacious Pharaoh
who had enslaved your holy people Israel. 7And
when he pursued them with chariots and a mass
of troops, you overwhelmed him in the depths of
the sea, but carried through safely those who had
put their confidence in you, the Ruler over the
whole creation. 8And when they had seen works
of your hands, they praised you, the Almighty.
9You, O King, when you had created the boundless and immeasurable earth, chose this city and
sanctified this place for your name, though you
have no need of anything; and when you had glorified it by your magnificent manifestation,[j] you
made it a firm foundation for the glory of your
great and honored name. 10And because you
love the house of Israel, you promised that if we
should have reverses and tribulation should overtake us, you would listen to our petition when we
come to this place and pray. 11And indeed you are

[a] Gk *the greatest God* [b] Other ancient authorities add *and ashes* [c] Or *the canopies* [d] Gk *the place* [e] Other ancient authorities read *priests* [f] Other ancient authorities read *vehement cry of the assembled crowds* [g] Other ancient authorities lack *at that time* [h] Other ancient authorities lack verse 1 [i] Other ancient authorities read *secret in their vices* [j] Or *epiphany*

faithful and true. 12 And because oftentimes when our fathers were oppressed you helped them in their humiliation, and rescued them from great evils, 13 see now, O holy King, that because of our many and great sins we are crushed with suffering, subjected to our enemies, and overtaken by helplessness. 14 In our downfall this audacious and profane man undertakes to violate the holy place on earth dedicated to your glorious name. 15 For your dwelling is the heaven of heavens, unapproachable by human beings. 16 But because you graciously bestowed your glory on your people Israel, you sanctified this place. 17 Do not punish us for the defilement committed by these men, or call us to account for this profanation, otherwise the transgressors will boast in their wrath and exult in the arrogance of their tongue, saying, 18 'We have trampled down the house of the sanctuary as the houses of the abominations are trampled down.' 19 Wipe away our sins and disperse our errors, and reveal your mercy at this hour. 20 Speedily let your mercies overtake us, and put praises in the mouth of those who are downcast and broken in spirit, and give us peace."

21 Thereupon God, who oversees all things, the first Father of all, holy among the holy ones, having heard the lawful supplication, scourged him who had exalted himself in insolence and audacity. 22 He shook him on this side and that as a reed is shaken by the wind, so that he lay helpless on the ground and, besides being paralyzed in his limbs, was unable even to speak, since he was smitten[a] by a righteous judgment. 23 Then both friends and bodyguards, seeing the severe punishment that had overtaken him, and fearing that he would lose his life, quickly dragged him out, panic-stricken in their exceedingly great fear. 24 After a while he recovered, and though he had been punished, he by no means repented, but went away uttering bitter threats.

25 When he arrived in Egypt, he increased in his deeds of malice, abetted by the previously mentioned drinking companions and comrades, who were strangers to everything just. 26 He was not content with his uncounted licentious deeds, but even continued with such audacity that he framed evil reports in the various localities; and many of his friends, intently observing the king's purpose, themselves also followed his will. 27 He proposed to inflict public disgrace on the Jewish community,[b] and he set up a stone[c] on the tower in the courtyard with this inscription: 28 "None of those who do not sacrifice shall enter their sanctuaries, and all Jews shall be subjected to a registration involving poll tax and to the status of slaves. Those who object to this are to be taken by force and put to death; 29 those who are registered are also to be branded on their bodies by fire with the ivy-leaf symbol of Dionysus, and they shall also be reduced to their former limited status." 30 In order that he might not appear to be an enemy of all, he inscribed below: "But if any of them prefer to join those who have been initiated into the mysteries, they shall have equal citizenship with the Alexandrians."

31 Now some, however, with an obvious abhorrence of the price to be exacted for maintaining the religion of their city,[d] readily gave themselves up, since they expected to enhance their reputation by their future association with the king. 32 But the majority acted firmly with a courageous spirit and did not abandon their religion; and by paying money in exchange for life they confidently attempted to save themselves from the registration. 33 They remained resolutely hopeful of obtaining help, and they abhorred those who separated themselves from them, considering them to be enemies of the Jewish nation,[b] and depriving them of companionship and mutual help.

3 When the impious king comprehended this situation, he became so infuriated that not only was he enraged against those Jews who lived in Alexandria, but was still more bitterly hostile toward those in the countryside; and he ordered that all should promptly be gathered into one place, and put to death by the most cruel means. 2 While these matters were being arranged, a hostile rumor was circulated against the Jewish nation by some who conspired to do them ill,

[a] Other ancient authorities read *pierced* [b] Gk *the nation* [c] Gk *stele* [d] Meaning of Gk uncertain

a pretext being given by a report that they hindered others[a] from the observance of their customs. 3The Jews, however, continued to maintain goodwill and unswerving loyalty toward the dynasty; 4but because they worshiped God and conducted themselves by his law, they kept their separateness with respect to foods. For this reason they appeared hateful to some; 5but since they adorned their style of life with the good deeds of upright people, they were established in good repute with everyone. 6Nevertheless those of other races paid no heed to their good service to their nation, which was common talk among all; 7instead they gossiped about the differences in worship and foods, alleging that these people were loyal neither to the king nor to his authorities, but were hostile and greatly opposed to his government. So they attached no ordinary reproach to them.

8 The Greeks in the city, though wronged in no way, when they saw an unexpected tumult around these people and the crowds that suddenly were forming, were not strong enough to help them, for they lived under tyranny. They did try to console them, being grieved at the situation, and expected that matters would change; 9for such a great community ought not be left to its fate when it had committed no offense. 10And already some of their neighbors and friends and business associates had taken some of them aside privately and were pledging to protect them and to exert more earnest efforts for their assistance.

11 Then the king, boastful of his present good fortune, and not considering the might of the supreme God,[b] but assuming that he would persevere constantly in his same purpose, wrote this letter against them:

12 "King Ptolemy Philopator to his generals and soldiers in Egypt and all its districts, greetings and good health:

13 "I myself and our government are faring well. 14When our expedition took place in Asia, as you yourselves know, it was brought to conclusion, according to plan, by the gods' deliberate alliance with us in battle, 15and we considered that we should not rule the nations inhabiting Coelesyria and Phoenicia by the power of the spear, but should cherish them with clemency and great benevolence, gladly treating them well. 16And when we had granted very great revenues to the temples in the cities, we came on to Jerusalem also, and went up to honor the temple of those wicked people, who never cease from their folly. 17They accepted our presence by word, but insincerely by deed, because when we proposed to enter their inner temple and honor it with magnificent and most beautiful offerings, 18they were carried away by their traditional arrogance, and excluded us from entering; but they were spared the exercise of our power because of the benevolence that we have toward all. 19By maintaining their manifest ill-will toward us, they become the only people among all nations who hold their heads high in defiance of kings and their own benefactors, and are unwilling to regard any action as sincere.

20 "But we, when we arrived in Egypt victorious, accommodated ourselves to their folly and did as was proper, since we treat all nations with benevolence. 21Among other things, we made known to all our amnesty toward their compatriots here, both because of their alliance with us and the myriad affairs liberally entrusted to them from the beginning; and we ventured to make a change, by deciding both to deem them worthy of Alexandrian citizenship and to make them participants in our regular religious rites.[c] 22But in their innate malice they took this in a contrary spirit, and disdained what is good. Since they incline constantly to evil, 23they not only spurn the priceless citizenship, but also both by speech and by silence they abominate those few among them who are sincerely disposed toward us; in every situation, in accordance with their infamous way of life, they secretly suspect that we may soon alter our policy. 24Therefore, fully convinced by these indications that they are ill-disposed toward us in every way, we have taken precautions so that, if a sudden disorder later arises against us, we shall not have these impious people behind our backs as traitors and barbarous enemies.

[a] Gk *them* [b] Gk *the greatest God* [c] Other ancient authorities read *partners of our regular priests*

25Therefore we have given orders that, as soon
as this letter arrives, you are to send to us those
who live among you, together with their wives
and children, with insulting and harsh treatment,
and bound securely with iron fetters, to suffer
the sure and shameful death that befits enemies.
26For when all of these have been punished, we
are sure that for the remaining time the government will be established for ourselves in good order and in the best state. 27But those who shelter
any of the Jews, whether old people or children
or even infants, will be tortured to death with the
most hateful torments, together with their families. 28Any who are willing to give information
will receive the property of those who incur the
punishment, and also two thousand drachmas
from the royal treasury, and will be awarded their
freedom.[a] 29Every place detected sheltering a Jew
is to be made unapproachable and burned with
fire, and shall become useless for all time to any
mortal creature." 30The letter was written in the
above form.

4 In every place, then, where this decree arrived, a feast at public expense was arranged
for the Gentiles with shouts and gladness, for the
inveterate enmity that had long ago been in their
minds was now made evident and outspoken.
2But among the Jews there was incessant mourning, lamentation, and tearful cries; everywhere
their hearts were burning, and they groaned because of the unexpected destruction that had
suddenly been decreed for them. 3What district
or city, or what habitable place at all, or what
streets were not filled with mourning and wailing for them? 4For with such a harsh and ruthless
spirit were they being sent off, all together, by the
generals in the several cities, that at the sight of
their unusual punishments, even some of their
enemies, perceiving the common object of pity
before their eyes, reflected on the uncertainty of
life and shed tears at the most miserable expulsion of these people. 5For a multitude of gray-
headed old men, sluggish and bent with age, was
being led away, forced to march at a swift pace by
the violence with which they were driven in such
a shameful manner. 6And young women who had
just entered the bridal chamber[b] to share married life exchanged joy for wailing, their myrrh-
perfumed hair sprinkled with ashes, and were
carried away unveiled, all together raising a lament instead of a wedding song, as they were torn
by the harsh treatment of the heathen.[c] 7In bonds
and in public view they were violently dragged
along as far as the place of embarkation. 8Their
husbands, in the prime of youth, their necks encircled with ropes instead of garlands, spent the
remaining days of their marriage festival in lamentations instead of good cheer and youthful
revelry, seeing death immediately before them.[d]
9They were brought on board like wild animals,
driven under the constraint of iron bonds; some
were fastened by the neck to the benches of the
boats, others had their feet secured by unbreak-
able fetters, 10and in addition they were confined
under a solid deck, so that, with their eyes in total
darkness, they would undergo treatment befitting
traitors during the whole voyage.

11 When these people had been brought to
the place called Schedia, and the voyage was concluded as the king had decreed, he commanded
that they should be enclosed in the hippodrome
that had been built with a monstrous perimeter
wall in front of the city, and that was well suited
to make them an obvious spectacle to all coming
back into the city and to those from the city[e] going out into the country, so that they could neither communicate with the king's forces nor in
any way claim to be inside the circuit of the city.[f]
12And when this had happened, the king, hearing that the Jews' compatriots from the city frequently went out in secret to lament bitterly the
ignoble misfortune of their kindred, 13ordered
in his rage that these people be dealt with in precisely the same fashion as the others, not omit-
ting any detail of their punishment. 14The entire
race was to be registered individually, not for the

[a] Gk *crowned with freedom* [b] Or *the canopy* [c] Other ancient authorities read *as though torn by heathen whelps*
[d] Gk *seeing Hades already lying at their feet* [e] Gk *those of them*
[f] Or *claim protection of the walls*; meaning of Gk uncertain

hard labor that has been briefly mentioned before, but to be tortured with the outrages that he
had ordered, and at the end to be destroyed in the
space of a single day. 15 The registration of these
people was therefore conducted with bitter haste
and zealous intensity from the rising of the sun
until its setting, coming to an end after forty days
but still uncompleted.

16 The king was greatly and continually filled
with joy, organizing feasts in honor of all his
idols, with a mind alienated from truth and with
a profane mouth, praising speechless things that
are not able even to communicate or to come to
one's help, and uttering improper words against
the supreme God.[a] 17 But after the previously
mentioned interval of time the scribes declared
to the king that they were no longer able to take
the census of the Jews because of their immense
number, 18 though most of them were still in the
country, some still residing in their homes, and
some at the place;[b] the task was impossible for all
the generals in Egypt. 19 After he had threatened
them severely, charging that they had been bribed
to contrive a means of escape, he was clearly convinced about the matter 20 when they said and
proved that both the paper[c] and the pens they
used for writing had already given out. 21 But this
was an act of the invincible providence of him
who was aiding the Jews from heaven.

5 Then the king, completely inflexible, was
filled with overpowering anger and wrath; so
he summoned Hermon, keeper of the elephants,
2 and ordered him on the following day to drug all
the elephants—five hundred in number—with
large handfuls of frankincense and plenty of unmixed wine, and to drive them in, maddened by
the lavish abundance of drink, so that the Jews
might meet their doom. 3 When he had given
these orders he returned to his feasting, together
with those of his Friends and of the army who
were especially hostile toward the Jews. 4 And
Hermon, keeper of the elephants, proceeded
faithfully to carry out the orders. 5 The servants in
charge of the Jews[d] went out in the evening and
bound the hands of the wretched people and arranged for their continued custody through the
night, convinced that the whole nation would experience its final destruction. 6 For to the Gentiles
it appeared that the Jews were left without any
aid, 7 because in their bonds they were forcibly
confined on every side. But with tears and a voice
hard to silence they all called upon the Almighty
Lord and Ruler of all power, their merciful God
and Father, praying 8 that he avert with vengeance
the evil plot against them and in a glorious manifestation rescue them from the fate now prepared
for them. 9 So their entreaty ascended fervently to
heaven.

10 Hermon, however, when he had drugged
the pitiless elephants until they had been filled
with a great abundance of wine and satiated with
frankincense, presented himself at the courtyard
early in the morning to report to the king about
these preparations. 11 But the Lord[e] sent upon the
king a portion of sleep, that beneficence that from
the beginning, night and day, is bestowed by him
who grants it to whomever he wishes. 12 And by
the action of the Lord he was overcome by so
pleasant and deep a sleep[f] that he quite failed in
his lawless purpose and was completely frustrated
in his inflexible plan. 13 Then the Jews, since they
had escaped the appointed hour, praised their
holy God and again implored him who is easily
reconciled to show the might of his all-powerful
hand to the arrogant Gentiles.

14 But now, since it was nearly the middle
of the tenth hour, the person who was in charge
of the invitations, seeing that the guests were assembled, approached the king and nudged him.
15 And when he had with difficulty roused him,
he pointed out that the hour of the banquet
was already slipping by, and he gave him an account of the situation. 16 The king, after considering this, returned to his drinking, and ordered
those present for the banquet to recline opposite
him. 17 When this was done he urged them to
give themselves over to revelry and to make the
present[g] portion of the banquet joyful by cele-

[a] Gk *the greatest God* [b] Other ancient authorities read *on the way* [c] Or *paper factory* [d] Gk *them* [e] Gk *he*
[f] Other ancient authorities add *from evening until the ninth hour* [g] Other ancient authorities read *delayed* (Gk *untimely*)

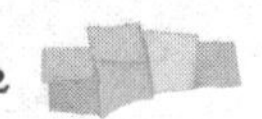

brating all the more. 18 After the party had been going on for some time, the king summoned Hermon and with sharp threats demanded to know why the Jews had been allowed to remain alive through the present day. 19 But when he, with the corroboration of the king's[a] Friends, pointed out that while it was still night he had carried out completely the order given him, 20 the king,[b] possessed by a savagery worse than that of Phalaris, said that the Jews[c] were benefited by today's sleep, "but," he added, "tomorrow without delay prepare the elephants in the same way for the destruction of the lawless Jews!" 21 When the king had spoken, all those present readily and joyfully with one accord gave their approval, and all went to their own homes. 22 But they did not so much employ the duration of the night in sleep as in devising all sorts of insults for those they thought to be doomed.

23 Then, as soon as the cock had crowed in the early morning, Hermon, having equipped[d] the animals, began to move them along in the great colonnade. 24 The crowds of the city had been assembled for this most pitiful spectacle and they were eagerly waiting for daybreak. 25 But the Jews, at their last gasp—since the time had run out—stretched their hands toward heaven and with most tearful supplication and mournful dirges implored the supreme God[e] to help them again at once. 26 The rays of the sun were not yet shed abroad, and while the king was receiving his Friends, Hermon arrived and invited him to come out, indicating that what the king desired was ready for action. 27 But he, on receiving the report and being struck by the unusual invitation to come out—since he had been completely overcome by incomprehension—inquired what the matter was for which this had been so zealously completed for him. 28 This was the act of God who rules over all things, for he had implanted in the king's mind a forgetfulness of the things he had previously devised. 29 Then Hermon and all the king's Friends[f] pointed out that the animals and the armed forces were ready, "O king, according to your eager purpose."[g] 30 But at these words he was filled with an overpowering wrath, because by the providence of God his whole mind had been deranged concerning these matters; and with a threatening look he said, 31 "If your parents or children were present, I would have prepared them to be a rich feast for the savage animals instead of the Jews, who give me no ground for complaint and have exhibited to an extraordinary degree a full and firm loyalty to my ancestors. 32 In fact you would have been deprived of life instead of these, if it were not for an affection arising from our nurture in common and your usefulness." 33 So Hermon suffered an unexpected and dangerous threat, and his eyes wavered and his face fell. 34 The king's Friends one by one sullenly slipped away and dismissed[h] the assembled people to their own occupations. 35 Then the Jews, on hearing what the king had said, praised the manifest Lord God, King of kings, since this also was his aid that they had received.

36 The king, however, reconvened the party in the same manner and urged the guests to return to their celebrating. 37 After summoning Hermon he said in a threatening tone, "How many times, you poor wretch, must I give you orders about these things? 38 Equip[i] the elephants now once more for the destruction of the Jews tomorrow!" 39 But the officials who were at table with him, wondering at his instability of mind, remonstrated as follows: 40 "O king, how long will you put us to the test, as though we are idiots, ordering now for a third time that they be destroyed, and again revoking your decree in the matter?[j] 41 As a result the city is in a tumult because of its expectation; it is crowded with masses of people, and also in constant danger of being plundered."

42 At this the king, a Phalaris in everything and filled with madness, took no account of the changes of mind that had come about within him for the protection of the Jews, and he firmly swore an irrevocable oath that he would send

[a] Gk *his* [b] Gk *he* [c] Gk *they* [d] Or *armed* [e] Gk *the greatest God* [f] Gk *all the Friends* [g] Other ancient authorities read *pointed to the beasts and the armed forces, saying, "They are ready, O king, according to your eager purpose."* [h] Other ancient authorities read *he dismissed* [i] Or *Arm* [j] Other ancient authorities read *when the matter is in hand*

them to death[a] without delay, mangled by the knees and feet of the animals, 43 and would also march against Judea and rapidly level it to the ground with fire and spear, and by burning to the ground the temple inaccessible to him[b] would quickly render it forever empty of those who offered sacrifices there. 44 Then the Friends and officers departed with great joy, and they confidently posted the armed forces at the places in the city most favorable for keeping guard.

45 Now when the animals had been brought virtually to a state of madness, so to speak, by the very fragrant draughts of wine mixed with frankincense and had been equipped with frightful devices, the elephant keeper 46 entered at about dawn into the courtyard—the city now being filled with countless masses of people crowding their way into the hippodrome—and urged the king on to the matter at hand. 47 So he, when he had filled his impious mind with a deep rage, rushed out in full force along with the animals, wishing to witness, with invulnerable heart and with his own eyes, the grievous and pitiful destruction of the aforementioned people.

48 When the Jews saw the dust raised by the elephants going out at the gate and by the following armed forces, as well as by the trampling of the crowd, and heard the loud and tumultuous noise, 49 they thought that this was their last moment of life, the end of their most miserable suspense, and giving way to lamentation and groans they kissed each other, embracing relatives and falling into one another's arms[c]—parents and children, mothers and daughters, and others with babies at their breasts who were drawing their last milk. 50 Not only this, but when they considered the help that they had received before from heaven, they prostrated themselves with one accord on the ground, removing the babies from their breasts, 51 and cried out in a very loud voice, imploring the Ruler over every power to manifest himself and be merciful to them, as they stood now at the gates of death.[a]

6 Then a certain Eleazar, famous among the priests of the country, who had attained a ripe old age and throughout his life had been adorned with every virtue, directed the elders around him to stop calling upon the holy God, and he prayed as follows: 2 "King of great power, Almighty God Most High, governing all creation with mercy, 3 look upon the descendants of Abraham, O Father, upon the children of the sainted Jacob, a people of your consecrated portion who are perishing as foreigners in a foreign land. 4 Pharaoh with his abundance of chariots, the former ruler of this Egypt, exalted with lawless insolence and boastful tongue, you destroyed together with his arrogant army by drowning them in the sea, manifesting the light of your mercy on the nation of Israel. 5 Sennacherib exulting in his countless forces, oppressive king of the Assyrians, who had already gained control of the whole world by the spear and was lifted up against your holy city, speaking grievous words with boasting and insolence, you, O Lord, broke in pieces, showing your power to many nations. 6 The three companions in Babylon who had voluntarily surrendered their lives to the flames so as not to serve vain things, you rescued unharmed, even to a hair, moistening the fiery furnace with dew and turning the flame against all their enemies. 7 Daniel, who through envious slanders was thrown down into the ground to lions as food for wild animals, you brought up to the light unharmed. 8 And Jonah, wasting away in the belly of a huge, sea-born monster, you, Father, watched over and restored[d] unharmed to all his family. 9 And now, you who hate insolence, all-merciful and protector of all, reveal yourself quickly to those of the nation of Israel[e]—who are being outrageously treated by the abominable and lawless Gentiles.

10 "Even if our lives have become entangled in impieties in our exile, rescue us from the hand of the enemy, and destroy us, Lord, by whatever fate you choose. 11 Let not the vain-minded praise their vanities[f] at the destruction of your beloved people, saying, 'Not even their god has rescued them.' 12 But you, O Eternal One, who have all might and all power, watch over us now and have

[a] Gk *Hades* [b] Gk *us* [c] Gk *falling upon their necks* [d] Other ancient authorities read *rescued and restored*; others, *mercifully restored* [e] Other ancient authorities read *to the saints of Israel* [f] Or *bless their vain gods*

 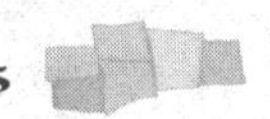

mercy on us who by the senseless insolence of the lawless are being deprived of life in the manner of traitors. 13 And let the Gentiles cower today in fear of your invincible might, O honored One, who have power to save the nation of Jacob. 14 The whole throng of infants and their parents entreat you with tears. 15 Let it be shown to all the Gentiles that you are with us, O Lord, and have not turned your face from us; but just as you have said, 'Not even when they were in the land of their enemies did I neglect them,' so accomplish it, O Lord."

16 Just as Eleazar was ending his prayer, the king arrived at the hippodrome with the animals and all the arrogance of his forces. 17 And when the Jews observed this they raised great cries to heaven so that even the nearby valleys resounded with them and brought an uncontrollable terror upon the army. 18 Then the most glorious, almighty, and true God revealed his holy face and opened the heavenly gates, from which two glorious angels of fearful aspect descended, visible to all but the Jews. 19 They opposed the forces of the enemy and filled them with confusion and terror, binding them with immovable shackles. 20 Even the king began to shudder bodily, and he forgot his sullen insolence. 21 The animals turned back upon the armed forces following them and began trampling and destroying them.

22 Then the king's anger was turned to pity and tears because of the things that he had devised beforehand. 23 For when he heard the shouting and saw them all fallen headlong to destruction, he wept and angrily threatened his Friends, saying, 24 "You are committing treason and surpassing tyrants in cruelty; and even me, your benefactor, you are now attempting to deprive of dominion and life by secretly devising acts of no advantage to the kingdom. 25 Who has driven from their homes those who faithfully kept our country's fortresses, and foolishly gathered every one of them here? 26 Who is it that has so lawlessly encompassed with outrageous treatment those who from the beginning differed from[a] all nations in their goodwill toward us and often have accepted willingly the worst of human dangers? 27 Loose and untie their unjust bonds! Send them back to their homes in peace, begging pardon for your former actions![b] 28 Release the children of the almighty and living God of heaven, who from the time of our ancestors until now has granted an unimpeded and notable stability to our government." 29 These then were the things he said; and the Jews, immediately released, praised their holy God and Savior, since they now had escaped death.

30 Then the king, when he had returned to the city, summoned the official in charge of the revenues and ordered him to provide to the Jews both wines and everything else needed for a festival of seven days, deciding that they should celebrate their rescue with all joyfulness in that same place in which they had expected to meet their destruction. 31 Accordingly those disgracefully treated and near to death,[c] or rather, who stood at its gates, arranged for a banquet of deliverance instead of a bitter and lamentable death, and full of joy they apportioned to celebrants the place that had been prepared for their destruction and burial. 32 They stopped their chanting of dirges and took up the song of their ancestors, praising God, their Savior and worker of wonders.[d] Putting an end to all mourning and wailing, they formed choruses[e] as a sign of peaceful joy. 33 Likewise also the king, after convening a great banquet to celebrate these events, gave thanks to heaven unceasingly and lavishly for the unexpected rescue that he[f] had experienced. 34 Those who had previously believed that the Jews would be destroyed and become food for birds, and had joyfully registered them, groaned as they themselves were overcome by disgrace, and their fire-breathing boldness was ignominiously[g] quenched.

35 The Jews, as we have said before, arranged the aforementioned choral group[h] and passed the time in feasting to the accompaniment of joyous

[a] Or *excelled above* [b] Other ancient authorities read *revoking your former commands* [c] Gk *Hades* [d] Other ancient authorities read *praising Israel and the wonder-working God*; or *praising Israel's Savior, the wonder-working God* [e] Or *dances* [f] Other ancient authorities read *they* [g] Other ancient authorities read *completely* [h] Or *dance*

thanksgiving and psalms. 36 And when they had
ordained a public rite for these things in their
whole community and for their descendants, they
instituted the observance of the aforesaid days as
a festival, not for drinking and gluttony, but because of the deliverance that had come to them
through God. 37 Then they petitioned the king,
asking for dismissal to their homes. 38 So their
registration was carried out from the twenty-fifth
of Pachon to the fourth of Epeiph,[a] for forty days;
and their destruction was set for the fifth to the
seventh of Epeiph,[b] the three days 39 on which the
Lord of all most gloriously revealed his mercy and
rescued them all together and unharmed. 40 Then
they feasted, being provided with everything by
the king, until the fourteenth day,[c] on which also
they made the petition for their dismissal. 41 The
king granted their request at once and wrote the
following letter for them to the generals in the cities, magnanimously expressing his concern:

7 "King Ptolemy Philopator to the generals in
Egypt and all in authority in his government,
greetings and good health:

2 "We ourselves and our children are faring
well, the great God guiding our affairs according
to our desire. 3 Certain of our friends, frequently
urging us with malicious intent, persuaded us
to gather together the Jews of the kingdom in a
body and to punish them with barbarous penalties as traitors; 4 for they declared that our government would never be firmly established until
this was accomplished, because of the ill-will that
these people had toward all nations. 5 They also
led them out with harsh treatment as slaves, or
rather as traitors, and, girding themselves with
a cruelty more savage than that of Scythian custom, they tried without any inquiry or examination to put them to death. 6 But we very severely
threatened them for these acts, and in accordance
with the clemency that we have toward all people
we barely spared their lives. Since we have come
to realize that the God of heaven surely defends
the Jews, always taking their part as a father does
for his children, 7 and since we have taken into
account the friendly and firm goodwill that they
had toward us and our ancestors, we justly have
acquitted them of every charge of whatever kind.
8 We also have ordered all people to return to their
own homes, with no one in any place[d] doing them
harm at all or reproaching them for the irrational
things that have happened. 9 For you should know
that if we devise any evil against them or cause
them any grief at all, we always shall have not a
mortal but the Ruler over every power, the Most
High God, in everything and inescapably as an
antagonist to avenge such acts. Farewell."

3 Maccabees 7:2-9

The king's letter addresses a common charge in Hellenistic and, later, Roman antiquity that the distinctiveness of Jewish community life constituted "ill-will . . . toward all nations" (v. 4). The letter serves clear apologetic interests for the author: having been made aware of the "friendly and firm goodwill" the Jews hold toward all people, the king "justly [has] acquitted them of every charge of whatever kind" (v. 7). The dark irony of the Greek vision of a "universal" culture here is that it could only be achieved through violent and terrible suppression of another culture, Judaism.

— *NE*

10 On receiving this letter the Jews[e] did not
immediately hurry to make their departure, but
they requested of the king that at their own hands
those of the Jewish nation who had willfully transgressed against the holy God and the law of God
should receive the punishment they deserved.
11 They declared that those who for the belly's
sake had transgressed the divine commandments
would never be favorably disposed toward the
king's government. 12 The king[f] then, admitting
and approving the truth of what they said, granted
them a general license so that freely, and without
royal authority or supervision, they might destroy those everywhere in his kingdom who had
transgressed the law of God. 13 When they had
applauded him in fitting manner, their priests and

[a] July 7—August 15 [b] August 16—18 [c] August 25 [d] Other ancient authorities read *way* [e] Gk *they* [f] Gk *He*

the whole multitude shouted the Hallelujah and joyfully departed. 14 And so on their way they punished and put to a public and shameful death any whom they met of their compatriots who had become defiled. 15 In that day they put to death more than three hundred men; and they kept the day as a joyful festival, since they had destroyed the profaners. 16 But those who had held fast to God even to death and had received the full enjoyment of deliverance began their departure from the city, crowned with all sorts of very fragrant flowers, joyfully and loudly giving thanks to the one God of their ancestors, the eternal Savior[a] of Israel, in words of praise and all kinds of melodious songs.

17 When they had arrived at Ptolemais, called "rose-bearing" because of a characteristic of the place, the fleet waited for them, in accordance with the common desire, for seven days. 18 There they celebrated their deliverance,[b] for the king had generously provided all things to them for their journey until all of them arrived at their own houses. 19 And when they had all landed in peace with appropriate thanksgiving, there too in like manner they decided to observe these days as a joyous festival during the time of their stay. 20 Then, after inscribing them as holy on a pillar and dedicating a place of prayer at the site of the festival, they departed unharmed, free, and overjoyed, since at the king's command they had all of them been brought safely by land and sea and river to their own homes. 21 They also possessed greater prestige among their enemies, being held in honor and awe; and they were not subject at all to confiscation of their belongings by anyone. 22 Besides, they all recovered all of their property, in accordance with the registration, so that those who held any of it restored it to them with extreme fear.[c] So the supreme God perfectly performed great deeds for their deliverance. 23 Blessed be the Deliverer of Israel through all times! Amen.

[a] Other ancient authorities read *the holy Savior*; others, *the holy one* [b] Gk *they made a cup of deliverance*
[c] Other ancient authorities read *with a very large supplement*

2 Esdras

Second Esdras appears only in the Slavonic Bible and in Coptic Christian manuscripts, two traditions that give less attention to precise definitions of what is sacred Scripture than others do. The book was assembled from three parts that circulated in early Christian circles under other names:

CHAPTERS	ALSO CALLED	ORIGIN
1–2	5 Ezra	Written by Christians in second century
3–14	4 Ezra	A Jewish apocalypse from late first century CE
15–16	6 Ezra	Written by Christians in third century

The first part of the book (5 Ezra) argues that Christians have replaced Jews as God's chosen people. The last part (6 Ezra) warns Christians of impending judgment and encourages them to remain faithful. As a whole, 2 Esdras gives a Jewish and a Christian response to the fall of the Jerusalem temple in 70 CE.

The Jewish approach in the core of the writing (4 Ezra) is one of *theodicy*, a questioning of God's justice, of which the book of Job is a fine example. The author of 4 Ezra mourns both the loss of the temple and the mystery inherent in the world, but the grieving protagonist finds peace through an understanding that bad things sometimes just happen and that one day the Messiah will come (4:21-25; 11:5-24; 12:31-34).

The Christian approach in other parts of the book, however, blames Jewish unbelief in Jesus for the temple's destruction and rejoices in the devastation (1:24-35). This view was all too common in early Christian theology. Melito of Sardis, contemporary with 5 Ezra, blames Jews for the loss of their temple in the Roman-Jewish War (66–73 CE). Jews killed Jesus and deserve what happened to them (*Pevi Pascha* [*On the Passover*] 72–82, 86–90). "You smashed the Lord to the ground; you were razed to the ground" (*Pevi Pascha* 99).

Historically, both Jews and Christians suffered persecution at Roman imperial hands. Christians, however, did not see Jewish communities as their siblings enduring a common oppression but rather as their enemies. Writing about the educational challenges faced by oppressed peasants in South America, Paulo Freire observes in *Pedagogy of the Oppressed*: "But almost always, during the initial stage of the struggle, the oppressed, instead of striving for liberation, tend themselves to become oppressors, or 'sub-oppressors.'" Christian anti-Judaism was born in a context of imperial persecution but long outlived it, and became an often harmful force in its own right. Only after the mid-twentieth-century Holocaust did Christians seriously consider the theological consequences of their caricature of Judaism. Modern readers of 2 Esdras will confront those troubling images.

As a feminist and a scholar and teacher of Judaism, 1 and 2 Esdras are distasteful to me; nevertheless, their ancient views on gender relations and inter-religious dialogue exist in modern times and cannot be ignored.

— *Stacy Davis*

Comprising what is sometimes called
5 Ezra (chapters 1–2), 4 Ezra (chapters 3–14),
and 6 Ezra (chapters 15–16)

1 The book[a] of the prophet Ezra son of Seraiah, son of Azariah, son of Hilkiah, son of
Shallum, son of Zadok, son of Ahitub, 2son of
Ahijah, son of Phinehas, son of Eli, son of Amariah, son of Azariah, son of Meraimoth, son of
Arna, son of Uzzi, son of Borith, son of Abishua,
son of Phinehas, son of Eleazar, 3son of Aaron, of
the tribe of Levi, who was a captive in the country of the Medes in the reign of Artaxerxes, king
of the Persians.[b]
4 The word of the Lord came to me, saying,
5"Go, declare to my people their evil deeds, and
to their children the iniquities that they have committed against me, so that they may tell[c] their children's children 6that the sins of their parents have
increased in them, for they have forgotten me and
have offered sacrifices to strange gods. 7Was it not
I who brought them out of the land of Egypt, out
of the house of bondage? But they have angered
me and despised my counsels. 8Now you, pull
out the hair of your head and hurl[d] all evils upon
them, for they have not obeyed my law—they
are a rebellious people. 9How long shall I endure
them, on whom I have bestowed such great benefits? 10For their sake I have overthrown many
kings; I struck down Pharaoh with his servants
and all his army. 11I destroyed all nations before
them, and scattered in the east the peoples of
two provinces,[e] Tyre and Sidon; I killed all their
enemies.
12 "But speak to them and say, Thus says the
Lord: 13Surely it was I who brought you through
the sea, and made safe highways for you where
there was no road; I gave you Moses as leader and
Aaron as priest; 14I provided light for you from a
pillar of fire, and did great wonders among you.
Yet you have forgotten me, says the Lord.
15 "Thus says the Lord Almighty:[f] The quails
were a sign to you; I gave you camps for your
protection, and in them you complained. 16You
have not exulted in my name at the destruction of
your enemies, but to this day you still complain.[g]
17Where are the benefits that I bestowed on you?
When you were hungry and thirsty in the wilderness, did you not cry out to me, 18saying, 'Why
have you led us into this wilderness to kill us? It
would have been better for us to serve the Egyptians than to die in this wilderness.' 19I pitied your
groanings and gave you manna for food; you ate
the bread of angels. 20When you were thirsty,
did I not split the rock so that waters flowed in
abundance? Because of the heat I clothed you
with the leaves of trees.[h] 21I divided fertile lands

[a] Other ancient authorities read *The second book* [b] Other ancient authorities, which place chapters 1 and 2 after 16.78, lack verses 1–3 and begin the chapter: *The word of the Lord that came to Ezra son of Chusi in the days of King Nebuchadnezzar, saying, "Go,* [c] Other ancient authorities read *nourish* [d] Other ancient authorities read *and shake out* [e] Other ancient authorities read *Did I not destroy the city of Bethsaida because of you, and to the south burn two cities . . . ?* [f] Other ancient authorities lack *Almighty* [g] Other ancient authorities read verse 16, *Your pursuer with his army I sank in the sea, but still the people complain also concerning their own destruction.* [h] Other ancient authorities read *I made for you trees with leaves*

among you; I drove out the Canaanites, the Perizzites, and the Philistines[a] before you. What more
can I do for you? says the Lord. 22 Thus says the
Lord Almighty:[b] When you were in the wilderness, at the bitter stream, thirsty and blaspheming
my name, 23 I did not send fire on you for your
blasphemies, but threw a tree into the water and
made the stream sweet.

24 "What shall I do to you, O Jacob? You,
Judah, would not obey me. I will turn to other nations and will give them my name, so that they
may keep my statutes. 25 Because you have forsaken me, I also will forsake you. When you beg
mercy of me, I will show you no mercy. 26 When
you call to me, I will not listen to you; for you
have defiled your hands with blood, and your feet
are swift to commit murder. 27 It is not as though
you had forsaken me; you have forsaken yourselves, says the Lord.

28 "Thus says the Lord Almighty: Have I
not entreated you as a father entreats his sons or
a mother her daughters or a nurse her children,
29 so that you should be my people and I should
be your God, and that you should be my children
and I should be your father? 30 I gathered you as a
hen gathers her chicks under her wings. But now,
what shall I do to you? I will cast you out from
my presence. 31 When you offer oblations to me,
I will turn my face from you; for I have rejected
your[c] festal days, and new moons, and circumcisions of the flesh.[d] 32 I sent you my servants the
prophets, but you have taken and killed them and
torn their bodies[e] in pieces; I will require their
blood of you, says the Lord.[f]

33 "Thus says the Lord Almighty: Your
house is desolate; I will drive you out as the
wind drives straw; 34 and your sons will have no
children, because with you[g] they have neglected
my commandment and have done what is evil in
my sight. 35 I will give your houses to a people
that will come, who without having heard me
will believe. Those to whom I have shown no
signs will do what I have commanded. 36 They
have seen no prophets, yet will recall their former state.[h] 37 I call to witness the gratitude of the
people that is to come, whose children rejoice
with gladness;[i] though they do not see me with
bodily eyes, yet with the spirit they will believe
the things I have said.

38 "And now, father,[j] look with pride and see
the people coming from the east; 39 to them I will
give as leaders Abraham, Isaac, and Jacob, and
Hosea and Amos and Micah and Joel and Obadiah and Jonah 40 and Nahum and Habakkuk,
Zephaniah, Haggai, Zechariah and Malachi, who
is also called the messenger of the Lord.[k]

2 "Thus says the Lord: I brought this people
out of bondage, and I gave them commandments through my servants the prophets; but they
would not listen to them, and made my counsels
void. 2 The mother who bore them[l] says to them,
'Go, my children, because I am a widow and forsaken. 3 I brought you up with gladness; but with
mourning and sorrow I have lost you, because
you have sinned before the Lord God and have
done what is evil in my sight.[m] 4 But now what can
I do for you? For I am a widow and forsaken. Go,
my children, and ask for mercy from the Lord.'

[a] Other ancient authorities read *Perizzites and their children* [b] Other ancient authorities lack *Almighty* [c] Other ancient authorities read *I have not commanded for you* [d] Other ancient authorities lack *of the flesh* [e] Other ancient authorities read *the bodies of the apostles* [f] Other ancient authorities add *Thus says the Lord Almighty: Recently you also laid hands on me, crying out before the judge's seat for him to deliver me to you. You took me as a sinner, not as a father who freed you from slavery, and you delivered me to death by hanging me on the tree; these are the things you have done. Therefore, says the Lord, let my Father and his angels return and judge between you and me; if I have not kept the commandment of the Father, if I have not nourished you, if I have not done the things my Father commanded, I will contend in judgment with you, says the Lord.* [g] Other ancient authorities lack *with you* [h] Other ancient authorities read *their iniquities* [i] Other ancient authorities read *The apostles bear witness to the coming people with joy* [j] Other ancient authorities read *brother* [k] Other ancient authorities read *and Jacob, Elijah and Enoch, Zechariah and Hosea, Amos, Joel, Micah, Obadiah, Zephaniah, [40]Nahum, Jonah, Mattia* (or *Mattathias*), *Habakkuk, and twelve angels with flowers* [l] Other ancient authorities read *They begat for themselves a mother who* [m] Other ancient authorities read *in his sight*

5 Now I call upon you, father, as a witness in addition to the mother of the children, because they
would not keep my covenant, 6 so that you may
bring confusion on them and bring their mother
to ruin, so that they may have no offspring. 7 Let
them be scattered among the nations; let their
names be blotted out from the earth, because
they have despised my covenant.
8 "Woe to you, Assyria, who conceal the unrighteous within you! O wicked nation, remember what I did to Sodom and Gomorrah, 9 whose
land lies in lumps of pitch and heaps of ashes.[a]
That is what I will do to those who have not listened to me, says the Lord Almighty."
10 Thus says the Lord to Ezra: "Tell my
people that I will give them the kingdom of Jerusalem, which I was going to give to Israel.
11 Moreover, I will take back to myself their glory,
and will give to these others the everlasting habitations, which I had prepared for Israel.[b] 12 The
tree of life shall give them fragrant perfume, and
they shall neither toil nor become weary. 13 Go[c]
and you will receive; pray that your days may be
few, that they may be shortened. The kingdom
is already prepared for you; be on the watch!
14 Call, O call heaven and earth to witness: I set
aside evil and created good; for I am the Living
One, says the Lord.
15 "Mother, embrace your children; bring
them up with gladness, as does a dove; strengthen
their feet, because I have chosen you, says the
Lord. 16 And I will raise up the dead from their
places, and bring them out from their tombs, because I recognize my name in them. 17 Do not fear,
mother of children, for I have chosen you, says the
Lord. 18 I will send you help, my servants Isaiah
and Jeremiah. According to their counsel I have
consecrated and prepared for you twelve trees
loaded with various fruits, 19 and the same number
of springs flowing with milk and honey, and seven
mighty mountains on which roses and lilies grow;
by these I will fill your children with joy.
20 "Guard the rights of the widow, secure justice for the ward, give to the needy, defend the
orphan, clothe the naked, 21 care for the injured
and the weak, do not ridicule the lame, protect
the maimed, and let the blind have a vision of my
splendor. 22 Protect the old and the young within
your walls. 23 When you find any who are dead,
commit them to the grave and mark it,[d] and I
will give you the first place in my resurrection.
24 Pause and be quiet, my people, because your
rest will come.
25 "Good nurse, nourish your children;
strengthen their feet. 26 Not one of the servants[e]
whom I have given you will perish, for I will require them from among your number. 27 Do not
be anxious, for when the day of tribulation and
anguish comes, others shall weep and be sorrowful, but you shall rejoice and have abundance.
28 The nations shall envy you, but they shall not
be able to do anything against you, says the Lord.
29 My power will protect[f] you, so that your children may not see hell.[g]
30 "Rejoice, O mother, with your children,
because I will deliver you, says the Lord. 31 Remember your children that sleep, because I will
bring them out of the hiding places of the earth,
and will show mercy to them; for I am merciful,
says the Lord Almighty. 32 Embrace your children until I come, and proclaim mercy to them;
because my springs run over, and my grace will
not fail."

33 I, Ezra, received a command from the
Lord on Mount Horeb to go to Israel. When I
came to them they rejected me and refused the
Lord's commandment. 34 Therefore I say to you,
O nations that hear and understand, "Wait for
your shepherd; he will give you everlasting rest,
because he who will come at the end of the age
is close at hand. 35 Be ready for the rewards of
the kingdom, because perpetual light will shine
on you forevermore. 36 Flee from the shadow of
this age, receive the joy of your glory; I publicly
call on my savior to witness.[h] 37 Receive what the

[a] Other ancient authorities read *Gomorrah, whose land descends to hell* [b] Lat *for those* [c] Other ancient authorities read *Seek* [d] Or *seal it*; or *mark them and commit them to the grave* [e] Or *slaves* [f] Lat *hands will cover* [g] Lat *Gehenna* [h] Other ancient authorities read *I testify that my savior has been commissioned by the Lord*

Lord has entrusted to you and be joyful, giving
thanks to him who has called you to the celestial
kingdoms. 38 Rise, stand erect and see the number of those who have been sealed at the feast of
the Lord. 39 Those who have departed from the
shadow of this age have received glorious garments from the Lord. 40 Take again your full number, O Zion, and close the list of your people who
are clothed in white, who have fulfilled the law of
the Lord. 41 The number of your children, whom
you desired, is now complete; implore the Lord's
authority that your people, who have been called
from the beginning, may be made holy."

42 I, Ezra, saw on Mount Zion a great multitude that I could not number, and they all were
praising the Lord with songs. 43 In their midst was
a young man of great stature, taller than any of the
others, and on the head of each of them he placed
a crown, but he was more exalted than they. And
I was held spellbound. 44 Then I asked an angel,
"Who are these, my lord?" 45 He answered and
said to me, "These are they who have put off
mortal clothing and have put on the immortal,
and have confessed the name of God. Now they
are being crowned, and receive palms." 46 Then I
said to the angel, "Who is that young man who
is placing crowns on them and putting palms in
their hands?" 47 He answered and said to me, "He
is the Son of God, whom they confessed in the
world." So I began to praise those who had stood
valiantly for the name of the Lord.[a] 48 Then the
angel said to me, "Go, tell my people how great
and how many are the wonders of the Lord God
that you have seen."

---

3 In the thirtieth year after the destruction of
the city, I was in Babylon—I, Salathiel, who
am also called Ezra. I was troubled as I lay on my
bed, and my thoughts welled up in my heart, 2 because I saw the desolation of Zion and the wealth
of those who lived in Babylon. 3 My spirit was
greatly agitated, and I began to speak anxious
words to the Most High, and said, 4 "O sovereign
Lord, did you not speak at the beginning when
you planted[b] the earth—and that without help—
and commanded the dust[c] 5 and it gave you Adam,
a lifeless body? Yet he was the creation of your
hands, and you breathed into him the breath of
life, and he was made alive in your presence. 6 And
you led him into the garden that your right hand
had planted before the earth appeared. 7 And
you laid upon him one commandment of yours;
but he transgressed it, and immediately you appointed death for him and for his descendants.
From him there sprang nations and tribes, peoples and clans without number. 8 And every nation walked after its own will; they did ungodly
things in your sight and rejected your commands,
and you did not hinder them. 9 But again, in its
time you brought the flood upon the inhabitants
of the world and destroyed them. 10 And the same
fate befell all of them: just as death came upon
Adam, so the flood upon them. 11 But you left one
of them, Noah with his household, and all the
righteous who have descended from him.

12 "When those who lived on earth began to
multiply, they produced children and peoples and
many nations, and again they began to be more
ungodly than were their ancestors. 13 And when
they were committing iniquity in your sight, you
chose for yourself one of them, whose name was
Abraham; 14 you loved him, and to him alone you
revealed the end of the times, secretly by night.
15 You made an everlasting covenant with him,
and promised him that you would never forsake
his descendants; and you gave him Isaac, and to
Isaac you gave Jacob and Esau. 16 You set apart Jacob for yourself, but Esau you rejected; and Jacob became a great multitude. 17 And when you
led his descendants out of Egypt, you brought
them to Mount Sinai. 18 You bent down the heavens and shook[d] the earth, and moved the world,
and caused the depths to tremble, and troubled
the times. 19 Your glory passed through the four
gates of fire and earthquake and wind and ice, to
give the law to the descendants of Jacob, and your
commandment to the posterity of Israel.

[a] Other ancient authorities read *to praise and glorify the Lord* [b] Other ancient authorities read *formed* [c] Syr Ethiop: Lat *people* or *world* [d] Syr Ethiop Arab 1 Georg: Lat *set fast*

20 "Yet you did not take away their evil heart
from them, so that your law might produce fruit in
them. 21 For the first Adam, burdened with an evil
heart, transgressed and was overcome, as were also
all who were descended from him. 22 Thus the disease became permanent; the law was in the hearts
of the people along with the evil root; but what
was good departed, and the evil remained. 23 So
the times passed and the years were completed,
and you raised up for yourself a servant, named
David. 24 You commanded him to build a city for
your name, and there to offer you oblations from
what is yours. 25 This was done for many years; but
the inhabitants of the city transgressed, 26 in everything doing just as Adam and all his descendants
had done, for they also had the evil heart. 27 So you
handed over your city to your enemies.

28 "Then I said in my heart, Are the deeds of
those who inhabit Babylon any better? Is that why
it has gained dominion over Zion? 29 For when I
came here I saw ungodly deeds without number,
and my soul has seen many sinners during these
thirty years.[a] And my heart failed me, 30 because
I have seen how you endure those who sin, and
have spared those who act wickedly, and have destroyed your people, and protected your enemies,
31 and have not shown to anyone how your way
may be comprehended.[b] Are the deeds of Babylon better than those of Zion? 32 Or has another
nation known you besides Israel? Or what tribes
have so believed the covenants as these tribes of
Jacob? 33 Yet their reward has not appeared and
their labor has borne no fruit. For I have traveled
widely among the nations and have seen that they
abound in wealth, though they are unmindful of
your commandments. 34 Now therefore weigh in
a balance our iniquities and those of the inhabitants of the world; and it will be found which way
the turn of the scale will incline. 35 When have the
inhabitants of the earth not sinned in your sight?
Or what nation has kept your commandments
so well? 36 You may indeed find individuals who
have kept your commandments, but nations you
will not find."

4 Then the angel that had been sent to me,
whose name was Uriel, answered 2 and said
to me, "Your understanding has utterly failed
regarding this world, and do you think you can
comprehend the way of the Most High?" 3 Then I
said, "Yes, my lord." And he replied to me, "I have
been sent to show you three ways, and to put before you three problems. 4 If you can solve one of
them for me, then I will show you the way you
desire to see, and will teach you why the heart is
evil."

> **2 *Esdras* 4:1**
>
> While 1 and 2 Esdras are not canonical in most Christian bodies, the traditional identification of the four archangels (as celebrated, for example, in the Anglican Feast of St. Michael and the Angels on September 29) includes the angel Uriel, named in 2 Esdras 4:1, 5:20, and 10:28.
>
> — *WG*

5 I said, "Speak, my lord."
And he said to me, "Go, weigh for me the
weight of fire, or measure for me a blast[c] of wind,
or call back for me the day that is past."
6 I answered and said, "Who of those that
have been born can do that, that you should ask
me about such things?"
7 And he said to me, "If I had asked you, 'How
many dwellings are in the heart of the sea, or how
many streams are at the source of the deep, or
how many streams are above the firmament, or
which are the exits of Hades, or which are the entrances[d] of paradise?' 8 perhaps you would have
said to me, 'I never went down into the deep, nor
as yet into Hades, neither did I ever ascend into
heaven.' 9 But now I have asked you only about
fire and wind and the day—things that you have
experienced and from which you cannot be separated, and you have given me no answer about
them." 10 He said to me, "You cannot understand

[a] Ethiop Arab 1 Arm: Lat Syr *in this thirtieth year* [b] Syr; compare Ethiop: Lat *how this way should be forsaken* [c] Syr Ethiop Arab 1 Arab 2 Georg *a measure* [d] Syr Compare Ethiop Arab 2 Arm: Lat lacks *of Hades, or which are the entrances*

the things with which you have grown up; 11 how then can your mind comprehend the way of the Most High? And how can one who is already worn out[a] by the corrupt world understand incorruption?"[b] When I heard this, I fell on my face[c] 12 and said to him, "It would have been better for us not to be here than to come here and live in ungodliness, and to suffer and not understand why."

13 He answered me and said, "I went into a forest of trees of the plain, and they made a plan 14 and said, 'Come, let us go and make war against the sea, so that it may recede before us and so that we may make for ourselves more forests.' 15 In like manner the waves of the sea also made a plan and said, 'Come, let us go up and subdue the forest of the plain so that there also we may gain more territory for ourselves.' 16 But the plan of the forest was in vain, for the fire came and consumed it; 17 likewise also the plan of the waves of the sea was in vain,[d] for the sand stood firm and blocked it. 18 If now you were a judge between them, which would you undertake to justify, and which to condemn?"

19 I answered and said, "Each made a foolish plan, for the land has been assigned to the forest, and the locale of the sea a place to carry its waves."

20 He answered me and said, "You have judged rightly, but why have you not judged so in your own case? 21 For as the land has been assigned to the forest and the sea to its waves, so also those who inhabit the earth can understand only what is on the earth, and he who is[e] above the heavens can understand what is above the height of the heavens."

22 Then I answered and said, "I implore you, my lord, why[f] have I been endowed with the power of understanding? 23 For I did not wish to inquire about the ways above, but about those things that we daily experience: why Israel has been given over to the Gentiles in disgrace; why the people whom you loved has been given over to godless tribes, and the law of our ancestors has been brought to destruction and the written covenants no longer exist. 24 We pass from the world like locusts, and our life is like a mist,[g] and we are not worthy to obtain mercy. 25 But what will he do for his[h] name that is invoked over us? It is about these things that I have asked."

26 He answered me and said, "If you are alive, you will see, and if you live long,[i] you will often marvel, because the age is hurrying swiftly to its end. 27 It will not be able to bring the things that have been promised to the righteous in their appointed times, because this age is full of sadness and infirmities. 28 For the evil about which[j] you ask me has been sown, but the harvest of it has not yet come. 29 If therefore that which has been sown is not reaped, and if the place where the evil has been sown does not pass away, the field where the good has been sown will not come. 30 For a grain of evil seed was sown in Adam's heart from the beginning, and how much ungodliness it has produced until now—and will produce until the time of threshing comes! 31 Consider now for yourself how much fruit of ungodliness a grain of evil seed has produced. 32 When heads of grain without number are sown, how great a threshing floor they will fill!"

33 Then I answered and said, "How long?[j] When will these things be? Why are our years few and evil?" 34 He answered me and said, "Do not be in a greater hurry than the Most High. You, indeed, are in a hurry for yourself,[k] but the Highest is in a hurry on behalf of many. 35 Did not the souls of the righteous in their chambers ask about these matters, saying, 'How long are we to remain here?[l] And when will the harvest of our reward come?' 36 And the archangel Jeremiel answered and said, 'When the number of those like yourselves is completed;[m] for he has weighed the age

[a] Meaning of Lat uncertain [b] Syr Ethiop *the way of the incorruptible?* [c] Syr Ethiop Arab 1: Meaning of Lat uncertain [d] Lat lacks *was in vain* [e] Or *those who are* [f] Syr Ethiop Arm: Meaning of Lat uncertain [g] Syr Ethiop Arab Georg: Lat *a trembling* [h] Ethiop adds *holy* [i] Syr: Lat *live* [j] Syr Ethiop: Meaning of Lat uncertain [k] Syr Ethiop Arab Arm: Meaning of Lat uncertain [l] Syr Ethiop Arab 2 Georg: Lat *How long do I hope thus?* [m] Syr Ethiop Arab 2: Lat *number of seeds is completed for you*

in the balance, 37 and measured the times by measure, and numbered the times by number; and he
will not move or arouse them until that measure
is fulfilled.' "
38 Then I answered and said, "But, O sovereign Lord, all of us also are full of ungodliness.
39 It is perhaps on account of us that the time of
threshing is delayed for the righteous—on account of the sins of those who inhabit the earth."
40 He answered me and said, "Go and ask a
pregnant woman whether, when her nine months
have been completed, her womb can keep the fe-
tus within her any longer."
41 And I said, "No, lord, it cannot."
He said to me, "In Hades the chambers of the
souls are like the womb. 42 For just as a woman
who is in labor makes haste to escape the pangs of
birth, so also do these places hasten to give back
those things that were committed to them from
the beginning. 43 Then the things that you desire
to see will be disclosed to you."
44 I answered and said, "If I have found favor in your sight, and if it is possible, and if I am
worthy, 45 show me this also: whether more time
is to come than has passed, or whether for us the
greater part has gone by. 46 For I know what has
gone by, but I do not know what is to come."
47 And he said to me, "Stand at my right
side, and I will show you the interpretation of a
parable."
48 So I stood and looked, and lo, a flaming furnace passed by before me, and when the
flame had gone by I looked, and lo, the smoke
remained. 49 And after this a cloud full of water
passed before me and poured down a heavy and
violent rain, and when the violent rainstorm had
passed, drops still remained in the cloud.[a]
50 He said to me, "Consider it for yourself;
for just as the rain is more than the drops, and the
fire is greater than the smoke, so the quantity that
passed was far greater; but drops and smoke remained."
51 Then I prayed and said, "Do you think that
I shall live until those days? Or who will be alive
in those days?"
52 He answered me and said, "Concerning
the signs about which you ask me, I can tell you
in part; but I was not sent to tell you concerning
your life, for I do not know.

5 "Now concerning the signs: lo, the days are
coming when those who inhabit the earth
shall be seized with great terror,[b] and the way of
truth shall be hidden, and the land shall be barren
of faith. 2 Unrighteousness shall be increased beyond what you yourself see, and beyond what you
heard of formerly. 3 And the land that you now see
ruling shall be a trackless waste, and people shall
see it desolate. 4 But if the Most High grants that
you live, you shall see it thrown into confusion
after the third period;[c]

and the sun shall suddenly begin to shine at
night,
and the moon during the day.
5 Blood shall drip from wood,
and the stone shall utter its voice;
the peoples shall be troubled,
and the stars shall fall.[d]

6 And one shall reign whom those who inhabit
the earth do not expect, and the birds shall fly
away together; 7 and the Dead Sea[e] shall cast up
fish; and one whom the many do not know shall
make his voice heard by night, and all shall hear
his voice.[f] 8 There shall be chaos also in many
places, fire shall often break out, the wild animals
shall roam beyond their haunts, and menstruous
women shall bring forth monsters. 9 Salt waters
shall be found in the sweet, and all friends shall
conquer one another; then shall reason hide itself, and wisdom shall withdraw into its chamber,
10 and it shall be sought by many but shall not
be found, and unrighteousness and unrestraint
shall increase on earth. 11 One country shall ask
its neighbor, 'Has righteousness, or anyone who
does right, passed through you?' And it will answer, 'No.' 12 At that time people shall hope but
not obtain; they shall labor, but their ways shall

[a] Lat *in it* [b] Syr Ethiop: Meaning of Lat uncertain [c] Literally *after the third*; Ethiop *after three months*; Arm *after the third vision*; Georg *after the third day* [d] Ethiop Compare Syr and Arab: Meaning of Lat uncertain [e] Lat *Sea of Sodom*
[f] Cn: Lat *fish; and it shall make its voice heard by night, which the many have not known, but all shall hear its voice.*

not prosper. 13 These are the signs that I am permitted to tell you, and if you pray again, and weep
as you do now, and fast for seven days, you shall
hear yet greater things than these."
14 Then I woke up, and my body shuddered
violently, and my soul was so troubled that it
fainted. 15 But the angel who had come and talked
with me held me and strengthened me and set me
on my feet.
16 Now on the second night Phaltiel, a chief
of the people, came to me and said, "Where have
you been? And why is your face sad? 17 Or do you
not know that Israel has been entrusted to you in
the land of their exile? 18 Rise therefore and eat
some bread, and do not forsake us, like a shepherd who leaves the flock in the power of savage
wolves."
19 Then I said to him, "Go away from me and
do not come near me for seven days; then you
may come to me."
He heard what I said and left me. 20 So I fasted
seven days, mourning and weeping, as the angel
Uriel had commanded me.
21 After seven days the thoughts of my heart
were very grievous to me again. 22 Then my soul
recovered the spirit of understanding, and I began once more to speak words in the presence of
the Most High. 23 I said, "O sovereign Lord, from
every forest of the earth and from all its trees you
have chosen one vine, 24 and from all the lands of
the world you have chosen for yourself one region,[a] and from all the flowers of the world you
have chosen for yourself one lily, 25 and from all
the depths of the sea you have filled for yourself
one river, and from all the cities that have been
built you have consecrated Zion for yourself,
26 and from all the birds that have been created
you have named for yourself one dove, and from
all the flocks that have been made you have provided for yourself one sheep, 27 and from all the
multitude of peoples you have gotten for yourself
one people; and to this people, whom you have
loved, you have given the law that is approved by
all. 28 And now, O Lord, why have you handed the
one over to the many, and dishonored[b] the one root
beyond the others, and scattered your only one
among the many? 29 And those who opposed your
promises have trampled on those who believed
your covenants. 30 If you really hate your people,
they should be punished at your own hands."
31 When I had spoken these words, the angel
who had come to me on a previous night was sent
to me. 32 He said to me, "Listen to me, and I will
instruct you; pay attention to me, and I will tell
you more."
33 Then I said, "Speak, my lord." And he said
to me, "Are you greatly disturbed in mind over
Israel? Or do you love him more than his Maker
does?"
34 I said, "No, my lord, but because of my
grief I have spoken; for every hour I suffer agonies of heart, while I strive to understand the way
of the Most High and to search out some part of
his judgment."
35 He said to me, "You cannot." And I said,
"Why not, my lord? Why then was I born? Or
why did not my mother's womb become my
grave, so that I would not see the travail of Jacob
and the exhaustion of the people of Israel?"
36 He said to me, "Count up for me those
who have not yet come, and gather for me the
scattered raindrops, and make the withered flowers bloom again for me; 37 open for me the closed
chambers, and bring out for me the winds shut
up in them, or show me the picture of a voice;
and then I will explain to you the travail that you
ask to understand."[c]
38 I said, "O sovereign Lord, who is able to
know these things except him whose dwelling is
not with mortals? 39 As for me, I am without wisdom, and how can I speak concerning the things
that you have asked me?"
40 He said to me, "Just as you cannot do one
of the things that were mentioned, so you cannot
discover my judgment, or the goal of the love that
I have promised to my people."
41 I said, "Yet, O Lord, you have charge of
those who are alive at the end, but what will those
do who lived before me, or we, ourselves, or those
who come after us?"

[a] Ethiop: Lat *pit* [b] Syr Ethiop Arab: Lat *prepared* [c] Lat *see*

42 He said to me, "I shall liken my judgment
to a circle;[a] just as for those who are last there is
no slowness, so for those who are first there is no
haste."
43 Then I answered and said, "Could you not
have created at one time those who have been
and those who are and those who will be, so that
you might show your judgment the sooner?"
44 He replied to me and said, "The creation
cannot move faster than the Creator, nor can the
world hold at one time those who have been created in it."
45 I said, "How have you said to your servant
that you[b] will certainly give life at one time to
your creation? If therefore all creatures will live
at one time[c] and the creation will sustain them,
it might even now be able to support all of them
present at one time."
46 He said to me, "Ask a woman's womb, and
say to it, 'If you bear ten[d] children, why one after
another?' Request it therefore to produce ten at
one time."
47 I said, "Of course it cannot, but only each
in its own time."
48 He said to me, "Even so I have given the
womb of the earth to those who from time to
time are sown in it. 49 For as an infant does not
bring forth, and a woman who has become old
does not bring forth any longer, so I have made
the same rule for the world that I created."
50 Then I inquired and said, "Since you have
now given me the opportunity, let me speak
before you. Is our mother, of whom you have
told me, still young? Or is she now approaching
old age?"
51 He replied to me, "Ask a woman who
bears children, and she will tell you. 52 Say to
her, 'Why are those whom you have borne recently not like those whom you bore before, but
smaller in stature?' 53 And she herself will answer
you, 'Those born in the strength of youth are different from those born during the time of old
age, when the womb is failing.' 54 Therefore you
also should consider that you and your contemporaries are smaller in stature than those who
were before you, 55 and those who come after you
will be smaller than you, as born of a creation
that already is aging and passing the strength of
youth."
56 I said, "I implore you, O Lord, if I have
found favor in your sight, show your servant
through whom you will visit your creation."

6 He said to me, "At the beginning of the circle of the earth, before[e] the portals of the
world were in place, and before the assembled
winds blew, 2 and before the rumblings of thunder sounded, and before the flashes of lightning
shone, and before the foundations of paradise
were laid, 3 and before the beautiful flowers were
seen, and before the powers of movements[f] were
established, and before the innumerable hosts of
angels were gathered together, 4 and before the
heights of the air were lifted up, and before the
measures of the firmaments were named, and before the footstool of Zion was established, 5 and
before the present years were reckoned and before the imaginations of those who now sin were
estranged, and before those who stored up treasures of faith were sealed— 6 then I planned these
things, and they were made through me alone and
not through another; just as the end shall come
through me alone and not through another."
7 I answered and said, "What will be the dividing of the times? Or when will be the end of
the first age and the beginning of the age that follows?"
8 He said to me, "From Abraham to Isaac,[g]
because from him were born Jacob and Esau, for
Jacob's hand held Esau's heel from the beginning.
9 Now Esau is the end of this age, and Jacob is
the beginning of the age that follows. 10 The beginning of a person is the hand, and the end of

[a] Or *crown* [b] Syr Ethiop Arab 1: Meaning of Lat uncertain [c] Lat lacks *If . . . one time* [d] Syr Ethiop Arab 2 Arm: Meaning of Lat uncertain [e] Meaning of Lat uncertain: Compare Syr *The beginning by the hand of humankind, but the end by my own hands. For as before the land of the world existed there, and before*; Ethiop: *At first by the Son of Man, and afterwards I myself. For before the earth and the lands were created, and before* [f] Or *earthquakes*
[g] Other ancient authorities read *to Abraham*

a person is the heel;[a] seek for nothing else, Ezra,
between the heel and the hand, Ezra!"
11 I answered and said, "O sovereign Lord, if
I have found favor in your sight, 12show your servant the last of your signs of which you showed
me a part on a previous night."
13 He answered and said to me, "Rise to your
feet and you will hear a full, resounding voice.
14And if the place where you are standing is
greatly shaken 15while the voice is speaking, do
not be terrified; because the word concerns the
end, and the foundations of the earth will understand 16that the speech concerns them. They will
tremble and be shaken, for they know that their
end must be changed."
17 When I heard this, I got to my feet and
listened; a voice was speaking, and its sound was
like the sound of mighty[b] waters. 18It said, "The
days are coming when I draw near to visit the inhabitants of the earth, 19and when I require from
the doers of iniquity the penalty of their iniquity, and when the humiliation of Zion is complete. 20When the seal is placed upon the age
that is about to pass away, then I will show these
signs: the books shall be opened before the face
of the firmament, and all shall see my judgment[c]
together. 21Children a year old shall speak with
their voices, and pregnant women shall give birth
to premature children at three and four months,
and these shall live and leap about. 22Sown places
shall suddenly appear unsown, and full storehouses shall suddenly be found to be empty;
23the trumpet shall sound aloud, and when all
hear it, they shall suddenly be terrified. 24At that
time friends shall make war on friends like enemies, the earth and those who inhabit it shall be
terrified, and the springs of the fountains shall
stand still, so that for three hours they shall not
flow.
25 "It shall be that whoever remains after all
that I have foretold to you shall be saved and shall
see my salvation and the end of my world. 26And
they shall see those who were taken up, who from
their birth have not tasted death; and the heart
of the earth's[d] inhabitants shall be changed and
converted to a different spirit. 27For evil shall
be blotted out, and deceit shall be quenched;
28faithfulness shall flourish, and corruption shall
be overcome, and the truth, which has been so
long without fruit, shall be revealed."
29 While he spoke to me, little by little the
place where I was standing began to rock to and
fro.[e] 30And he said to me, "I have come to show
you these things this night.[f] 31If therefore you
will pray again and fast again for seven days, I will
again declare to you greater things than these,[g]
32because your voice has surely been heard by
the Most High; for the Mighty One has seen your
uprightness and has also observed the purity that
you have maintained from your youth. 33There-
fore he sent me to show you all these things, and
to say to you: 'Believe and do not be afraid! 34Do
not be quick to think vain thoughts concerning
the former times; then you will not act hastily in
the last times.'"
35 Now after this I wept again and fasted seven
days in the same way as before, in order to complete the three weeks that had been prescribed
for me. 36Then on the eighth night my heart was
troubled within me again, and I began to speak in
the presence of the Most High. 37My spirit was
greatly aroused, and my soul was in distress.
38 I said, "O Lord, you spoke at the beginning
of creation, and said on the first day, 'Let heaven
and earth be made,' and your word accomplished
the work. 39Then the spirit was blowing, and
darkness and silence embraced everything; the
sound of human voices was not yet there.[h] 40Then
you commanded a ray of light to be brought out
from your store-chambers, so that your works
could be seen.
41 "Again, on the second day, you created
the spirit of the firmament, and commanded it to
divide and separate the waters, so that one part
might move upward and the other part remain
beneath.

[a] Syr: Meaning of Lat uncertain [b] Lat *many* [c] Syr: Lat lacks *my judgment* [d] Syr Compare Ethiop Arab 1 Arm: Lat lacks *earth's* [e] Syr Ethiop Compare Arab Arm: Meaning of Lat uncertain [f] Syr Compare Ethiop: Meaning of Lat uncertain [g] Syr Ethiop Arab 1 Arm: Lat adds *by day* [h] Syr Ethiop: Lat *was not yet from you*

42 "On the third day you commanded the
waters to be gathered together in a seventh part of
the earth; six parts you dried up and kept so that
some of them might be planted and cultivated
and be of service before you. 43For your word
went forth, and at once the work was done. 44Im-
mediately fruit came forth in endless abundance
and of varied appeal to the taste, and flowers of
inimitable color, and odors of inexpressible fragrance. These were made on the third day.

45 "On the fourth day you commanded the
brightness of the sun, the light of the moon, and
the arrangement of the stars to come into being;
46and you commanded them to serve humankind, about to be formed.

47 "On the fifth day you commanded the
seventh part, where the water had been gathered
together, to bring forth living creatures, birds,
and fishes; and so it was done. 48The dumb and
lifeless water produced living creatures, as it was
commanded, so that therefore the nations might
declare your wondrous works.

49 "Then you kept in existence two living
creatures;[a] the one you called Behemoth[b] and the
name of the other Leviathan. 50And you separated
one from the other, for the seventh part where the
water had been gathered together could not hold
them both. 51And you gave Behemoth[b] one of the
parts that had been dried up on the third day, to
live in it, where there are a thousand mountains;
52but to Leviathan you gave the seventh part, the
watery part; and you have kept them to be eaten
by whom you wish, and when you wish.

53 "On the sixth day you commanded the
earth to bring forth before you cattle, wild animals, and creeping things; 54and over these you
placed Adam, as ruler over all the works that you
had made; and from him we have all come, the
people whom you have chosen.

55 "All this I have spoken before you, O Lord,
because you have said that it was for us that you
created this world.[c] 56As for the other nations
that have descended from Adam, you have said
that they are nothing, and that they are like spittle, and you have compared their abundance to
a drop from a bucket. 57And now, O Lord, these
nations, which are reputed to be as nothing, dom-
ineer over us and devour us. 58But we your people, whom you have called your firstborn, only
begotten, zealous for you,[d] and most dear, have
been given into their hands. 59If the world has indeed been created for us, why do we not possess
our world as an inheritance? How long will this
be so?"

7 When I had finished speaking these words,
the angel who had been sent to me on the former nights was sent to me again. 2He said to me,
"Rise, Ezra, and listen to the words that I have
come to speak to you."

3 I said, "Speak, my lord." And he said to
me, "There is a sea set in a wide expanse so that
it is deep and vast, 4but it has an entrance set in
a narrow place, so that it is like a river. 5If there
are those who wish to reach the sea, to look at it
or to navigate it, how can they come to the broad
part unless they pass through the narrow part?
6Another example: There is a city built and set on
a plain, and it is full of all good things; 7but the
entrance to it is narrow and set in a precipitous
place, so that there is fire on the right hand and
deep water on the left. 8There is only one path lying between them, that is, between the fire and
the water, so that only one person can walk on the
path. 9If now the city is given to someone as an
inheritance, how will the heir receive the inheritance unless by passing through the appointed
danger?"

10 I said, "That is right, lord." He said to me,
"So also is Israel's portion. 11For I made the world
for their sake, and when Adam transgressed my
statutes, what had been made was judged. 12And
so the entrances of this world were made narrow
and sorrowful and toilsome; they are few and
evil, full of dangers and involved in great hardships. 13But the entrances of the greater world are
broad and safe, and yield the fruit of immortality. 14Therefore unless the living pass through the
difficult and futile experiences, they can never

[a] Syr Ethiop: Lat *two souls* [b] Other Lat authorities read *Enoch* [c] Syr Ethiop Arab 2: Lat *the firstborn world* Compare Arab 1 *first world* [d] Meaning of Lat uncertain

receive those things that have been reserved for them. 15Now therefore why are you disturbed, seeing that you are to perish? Why are you moved, seeing that you are mortal? 16Why have you not considered in your mind what is to come, rather than what is now present?"

17 Then I answered and said, "O sovereign Lord, you have ordained in your law that the righteous shall inherit these things, but that the ungodly shall perish. 18The righteous, therefore, can endure difficult circumstances while hoping for easier ones; but those who have done wickedly have suffered the difficult circumstances and will never see the easier ones."

19 He said to me, "You are not a better judge than the Lord,[a] or wiser than the Most High! 20Let many perish who are now living, rather than that the law of God that is set before them be disregarded! 21For the Lord[b] strictly commanded those who came into the world, when they came, what they should do to live, and what they should observe to avoid punishment. 22Nevertheless they were not obedient, and spoke against him;

they devised for themselves vain thoughts,
23 and proposed to themselves wicked
frauds;
they even declared that the Most High does
not exist,
and they ignored his ways.
24 They scorned his law,
and denied his covenants;
they have been unfaithful to his statutes,
and have not performed his works.

25That is the reason, Ezra, that empty things are for the empty, and full things are for the full.

26 "For indeed the time will come, when the signs that I have foretold to you will come to pass, that the city that now is not seen shall appear,[c] and the land that now is hidden shall be disclosed. 27Everyone who has been delivered from the evils that I have foretold shall see my wonders. 28For my son the Messiah[d] shall be revealed with those who are with him, and those who remain shall rejoice four hundred years. 29After those years my son the Messiah shall die, and all who draw human breath.[e] 30Then the world shall be turned back to primeval silence for seven days, as it was at the first beginnings, so that no one shall be left. 31After seven days the world that is not yet awake shall be roused, and that which is corruptible shall perish. 32The earth shall give up those who are asleep in it, and the dust those who rest there in silence; and the chambers shall give up the souls that have been committed to them. 33The Most High shall be revealed on the seat of judgment, and compassion shall pass away, and patience shall be withdrawn.[f] 34Only judgment shall remain, truth shall stand, and faithfulness shall grow strong. 35Recompense shall follow, and the reward shall be manifested; righteous deeds shall awake, and unrighteous deeds shall not sleep.[g] 36The pit[h] of torment shall appear, and opposite it shall be the place of rest; and the furnace of hell[i] shall be disclosed, and opposite it the paradise of delight. 37Then the Most High will say to the nations that have been raised from the dead, 'Look now, and understand whom you have denied, whom you have not served, whose commandments you have despised. 38Look on this side and on that; here are delight and rest, and there are fire and torments.' Thus he will[j] speak to them on the day of judgment— 39a day that has no sun or moon or stars, *40*or cloud or thunder or lightning, or wind or water or air, or darkness or evening or morning, *41*or summer or spring or heat or winter[k] or frost or cold, or hail or rain or dew, *42*or noon or night, or dawn or shining or brightness or light, but only the splendor of the glory of the Most High, by which all shall see what has been destined. *43*It will last as though for a week of years. *44*This is my judgment and its prescribed order; and to you alone I have shown these things."

[a] Other ancient authorities read *God*; Ethiop Georg *the only One* [b] Other ancient authorities read *God* [c] Arm: Lat Syr *that the bride shall appear, even the city appearing* [d] Syr Arab 1: Ethiop *my Messiah*; Arab 2 *the Messiah*; Arm *the Messiah of God*; Lat *my son Jesus* [e] Arm *all who have continued in faith and in patience* [f] Lat *shall gather together* [g] The passage from verse *36* to verse *105*, formerly missing, has been restored to the text [h] Syr Ethiop: Lat *place* [i] Lat Syr Ethiop *Gehenna* [j] Syr Ethiop Arab 1: Lat *you shall* [k] Or *storm*

45 I answered and said, "O sovereign Lord,
I said then and[a] I say now: Blessed are those
who are alive and keep your commandments!
46 But what of those for whom I prayed? For who
among the living is there that has not sinned, or
who is there among mortals that has not transgressed your covenant? 47 And now I see that
the world to come will bring delight to few, but
torments to many. 48 For an evil heart has grown
up in us, which has alienated us from God,[b] and
has brought us into corruption and the ways
of death, and has shown us the paths of perdition and removed us far from life—and that
not merely for a few but for almost all who have
been created."

49 He answered me and said, "Listen to me,
Ezra,[c] and I will instruct you, and will admonish
you once more. 50 For this reason the Most High
has made not one world but two. 51 Inasmuch as
you have said that the righteous are not many but
few, while the ungodly abound, hear the explanation for this.

52 "If you have just a few precious stones, will
you add to them lead and clay?"[d] 53 I said, "Lord,
how could that be?" 54 And he said to me, "Not
only that, but ask the earth and she will tell you;
defer to her, and she will declare it to you. 55 Say
to her, 'You produce gold and silver and bronze,
and also iron and lead and clay; 56 but silver is
more abundant than gold, and bronze than silver, and iron than bronze, and lead than iron, and
clay than lead.' 57 Judge therefore which things are
precious and desirable, those that are abundant
or those that are rare?"

58 I said, "O sovereign Lord, what is plentiful is of less worth, for what is more rare is more
precious."

59 He answered me and said, "Consider
within yourself[e] what you have thought, for the
person who has what is hard to get rejoices more
than the person who has what is plentiful. 60 So
also will be the judgment[f] that I have promised;
for I will rejoice over the few who shall be saved,
because it is they who have made my glory to prevail now, and through them my name has now
been honored. 61 I will not grieve over the great
number of those who perish; for it is they who
are now like a mist, and are similar to a flame and
smoke—they are set on fire and burn hotly, and
are extinguished."

62 I replied and said, "O earth, what have you
brought forth, if the mind is made out of the dust
like the other created things? 63 For it would have
been better if the dust itself had not been born, so
that the mind might not have been made from it.
64 But now the mind grows with us, and therefore
we are tormented, because we perish and we know
it. 65 Let the human race lament, but let the wild
animals of the field be glad; let all who have been
born lament, but let the cattle and the flocks rejoice. 66 It is much better with them than with us;
for they do not look for a judgment, and they do
not know of any torment or salvation promised to
them after death. 67 What does it profit us that we
shall be preserved alive but cruelly tormented?
68 For all who have been born are entangled in[g]
iniquities, and are full of sins and burdened with
transgressions. 69 And if after death we were not
to come into judgment, perhaps it would have
been better for us."

70 He answered me and said, "When the
Most High made the world and Adam and all who
have come from him, he first prepared the judgment and the things that pertain to the judgment.
71 But now, understand from your own words—
for you have said that the mind grows with us.
72 For this reason, therefore, those who live on
earth shall be tormented, because though they
had understanding, they committed iniquity;
and though they received the commandments,
they did not keep them; and though they obtained the law, they dealt unfaithfully with what
they received. 73 What, then, will they have to say
in the judgment, or how will they answer in the
last times? 74 How long the Most High has been
patient with those who inhabit the world!—and

[a] Syr: Lat *And I answered, "I said then, O Lord, and* [b] Cn: Lat Syr Ethiop *from these* [c] Syr Arab 1 Georg: Lat Ethiop lack *Ezra* [d] Arab 1: Meaning of Lat Syr Ethiop uncertain [e] Syr Ethiop Arab 1: Meaning of Lat uncertain [f] Syr Arab 1: Lat *creation* [g] Syr *defiled with*

not for their sake, but because of the times that he
has foreordained."

75 I answered and said, "If I have found favor
in your sight, O Lord, show this also to your servant: whether after death, as soon as everyone of
us yields up the soul, we shall be kept in rest until
those times come when you will renew the creation, or whether we shall be tormented at once?"

76 He answered me and said, "I will show
you that also, but do not include yourself with
those who have shown scorn, or number yourself among those who are tormented. 77 For you
have a treasure of works stored up with the Most
High, but it will not be shown to you until the
last times. 78 Now concerning death, the teaching
is: When the decisive decree has gone out from
the Most High that a person shall die, as the spirit
leaves the body to return again to him who gave
it, first of all it adores the glory of the Most High.
79 If it is one of those who have shown scorn and
have not kept the way of the Most High, who
have despised his law and hated those who fear
God— 80 such spirits shall not enter into habitations, but shall immediately wander about in torments, always grieving and sad, in seven ways.
81 The first way, because they have scorned the
law of the Most High. 82 The second way, because
they cannot now make a good repentance so that
they may live. 83 The third way, they shall see the
reward laid up for those who have trusted the
covenants of the Most High. 84 The fourth way,
they shall consider the torment laid up for themselves in the last days. 85 The fifth way, they shall
see how the habitations of the others are guarded
by angels in profound quiet. 86 The sixth way, they
shall see how some of them will cross over[a] into
torments. 87 The seventh way, which is worse[b]
than all the ways that have been mentioned, because they shall utterly waste away in confusion
and be consumed with shame,[c] and shall wither
with fear at seeing the glory of the Most High
in whose presence they sinned while they were
alive, and in whose presence they are to be judged
in the last times.

88 "Now this is the order of those who have
kept the ways of the Most High, when they shall
be separated from their mortal body.[d] 89 During
the time that they lived in it,[e] they laboriously
served the Most High, and withstood danger
every hour so that they might keep the law of the
Lawgiver perfectly. 90 Therefore this is the teaching concerning them: 91 First of all, they shall
see with great joy the glory of him who receives
them, for they shall have rest in seven orders.
92 The first order, because they have striven with
great effort to overcome the evil thought that was
formed with them, so that it might not lead them
astray from life into death. 93 The second order,
because they see the perplexity in which the souls
of the ungodly wander and the punishment that
awaits them. 94 The third order, they see the witness that he who formed them bears concerning
them, that throughout their life they kept the law
with which they were entrusted. 95 The fourth order, they understand the rest that they now enjoy,
being gathered into their chambers and guarded
by angels in profound quiet, and the glory waiting for them in the last days. 96 The fifth order,
they rejoice that they have now escaped what is
corruptible and shall inherit what is to come; and
besides they see the straits and toil[e] from which
they have been delivered, and the spacious liberty
that they are to receive and enjoy in immortality.
97 The sixth order, when it is shown them how
their face is to shine like the sun, and how they
are to be made like the light of the stars, being
incorruptible from then on. 98 The seventh order, which is greater than all that have been mentioned, because they shall rejoice with boldness,
and shall be confident without confusion, and
shall be glad without fear, for they press forward
to see the face of him whom they served in life
and from whom they are to receive their reward
when glorified. 99 This is the order of the souls of
the righteous, as henceforth is announced;[f] and
the previously mentioned are the ways of torment that those who would not give heed shall
suffer hereafter."

[a] Cn: Meaning of Lat uncertain [b] Lat Syr Ethiop *greater* [c] Syr Ethiop: Meaning of Lat uncertain [d] Lat *the corruptible vessel* [e] Syr Ethiop: Lat *fullness* [f] Syr: Meaning of Lat uncertain

100 Then I answered and said, "Will time
therefore be given to the souls, after they have
been separated from the bodies, to see what you
have described to me?"

101 He said to me, "They shall have freedom
for seven days, so that during these seven days
they may see the things of which you have been
told, and afterwards they shall be gathered in
their habitations."

102 I answered and said, "If I have found
favor in your sight, show further to me, your
servant, whether on the day of judgment the righteous will be able to intercede for the ungodly or
to entreat the Most High for them— *103* fathers
for sons or sons for parents, brothers for brothers, relatives for their kindred, or friends for those
who are most dear."

104 He answered me and said, "Since you
have found favor in my sight, I will show you this
also. The day of judgment is decisive[a] and displays
to all the seal of truth. Just as now a father does
not send his son, or a son his father, or a master
his servant, or a friend his dearest friend, to be ill[b]
or sleep or eat or be healed in his place, *105* so no
one shall ever pray for another on that day, neither shall anyone lay a burden on another;[c] for
then all shall bear their own righteousness and
unrighteousness."

36 *106* I answered and said, "How then do
we find that first Abraham prayed for the people of Sodom, and Moses for our ancestors who
sinned in the desert, 37 *107* and Joshua after him
for Israel in the days of Achan, 38 *108* and Samuel
in the days of Saul,[d] and David for the plague, and
Solomon for those at the dedication, 39 *109* and
Elijah for those who received the rain, and for the
one who was dead, that he might live, 40 *110* and
Hezekiah for the people in the days of Sennacherib, and many others prayed for many? 41 *111* So
if now, when corruption has increased and unrighteousness has multiplied, the righteous have
prayed for the ungodly, why will it not be so then
as well?"

42 *112* He answered me and said, "This
present world is not the end; the full glory does
not[e] remain in it;[f] therefore those who were
strong prayed for the weak. 43 *113* But the day of
judgment will be the end of this age and the beginning[g] of the immortal age to come, in which
corruption has passed away, 44 *114* sinful indulgence has come to an end, unbelief has been cut
off, and righteousness has increased and truth
has appeared. 45 *115* Therefore no one will then
be able to have mercy on someone who has been
condemned in the judgment, or to harm[h] someone who is victorious."

46 *116* I answered and said, "This is my
first and last comment: it would have been better if the earth had not produced Adam, or else,
when it had produced him, had restrained him
from sinning. 47 *117* For what good is it to all that
they live in sorrow now and expect punishment
after death? 48 *118* O Adam, what have you done?
For though it was you who sinned, the fall was
not yours alone, but ours also who are your descendants. 49 *119* For what good is it to us, if an
immortal time has been promised to us, but we
have done deeds that bring death? 50 *120* And
what good is it that an everlasting hope has been
promised to us, but we have miserably failed?
51 *121* Or that safe and healthful habitations have
been reserved for us, but we have lived wickedly?
52 *122* Or that the glory of the Most High will defend those who have led a pure life, but we have
walked in the most wicked ways? 53 *123* Or that a
paradise shall be revealed, whose fruit remains
unspoiled and in which are abundance and healing, but we shall not enter it 54 *124* because we have
lived in perverse ways?[i] 55 *125* Or that the faces of
those who practiced self-control shall shine more
than the stars, but our faces shall be blacker than
darkness? 56 *126* For while we lived and committed
iniquity we did not consider what we should suffer after death."

57 *127* He answered and said, "This is the
significance of the contest that all who are born

[a] Lat *bold* [b] Syr Ethiop Arm: Lat *to understand* [c] Syr Ethiop: Lat lacks *on that . . . another* [d] Syr Ethiop Arab 1: Lat Arab 2 Arm lack *in the days of Saul* [e] Lat lacks *not* [f] Or *the glory does not continuously abide in it* [g] Syr Ethiop: Lat lacks *the beginning* [h] Syr Ethiop: Lat *overwhelm* [i] Cn: Lat Syr *places*

on earth shall wage: 58 128if they are defeated
they shall suffer what you have said, but if they
are victorious they shall receive what I have said.[a]
59 129For this is the way of which Moses, while
he was alive, spoke to the people, saying, 'Choose
life for yourself, so that you may live!' 60 130But
they did not believe him or the prophets after
him, or even myself who have spoken to them.
61 131Therefore there shall not be[b] grief at their
destruction, so much as joy over those to whom
salvation is assured."

62 132 I answered and said, "I know, O Lord,
that the Most High is now called merciful, because he has mercy on those who have not yet
come into the world; 63 133and gracious, because
he is gracious to those who turn in repentance
to his law; 64 134and patient, because he shows
patience toward those who have sinned, since
they are his own creatures; 65 135and bountiful,
because he would rather give than take away;[c]
66 136and abundant in compassion, because he
makes his compassions abound more and more to
those now living and to those who are gone and
to those yet to come— 67 137for if he did not make
them abound, the world with those who inhabit
it would not have life— 68 138and he is called the
giver, because if he did not give out of his goodness so that those who have committed iniquities
might be relieved of them, not one ten-thousandth
of humankind could have life; 69 139and the judge,
because if he did not pardon those who were created by his word and blot out the multitude of
their sins,[d] 70 140there would probably be left only
very few of the innumerable multitude."

8 He answered me and said, "The Most High
made this world for the sake of many, but the
world to come for the sake of only a few. 2But
I tell you a parable, Ezra. Just as, when you ask
the earth, it will tell you that it provides a large
amount of clay from which earthenware is made,
but only a little dust from which gold comes, so is
the course of the present world. 3Many have been
created, but only a few shall be saved."

4 I answered and said, "Then drink your fill
of understanding,[e] O my soul, and drink wisdom,
O my heart. 5For not of your own will did you
come into the world,[f] and against your will you
depart, for you have been given only a short time
to live. 6O Lord above us, grant to your servant
that we may pray before you, and give us a seed
for our heart and cultivation of our understanding so that fruit may be produced, by which every
mortal who bears the likeness[g] of a human being
may be able to live. 7For you alone exist, and we
are a work of your hands, as you have declared.
8And because you give life to the body that is now
fashioned in the womb, and furnish it with members, what you have created is preserved amid
fire and water, and for nine months the womb[h]
endures your creature that has been created in it.
9But that which keeps and that which is kept shall
both be kept by your keeping.[f] And when the
womb gives up again what has been created in it,
10you have commanded that from the members
themselves (that is, from the breasts) milk, the
fruit of the breasts, should be supplied, 11so that
what has been fashioned may be nourished for a
time; and afterwards you will still guide it in your
mercy. 12You have nurtured it in your righteousness, and instructed it in your law, and reproved
it in your wisdom. 13You put it to death as your
creation, and make it live as your work. 14If then
you will suddenly and quickly[i] destroy what with
so great labor was fashioned by your command,
to what purpose was it made? 15And now I will
speak out: About all humankind you know best;
but I will speak about your people, for whom I
am grieved, 16and about your inheritance, for
whom I lament, and about Israel, for whom I
am sad, and about the seed of Jacob, for whom
I am troubled. 17Therefore I will pray before you
for myself and for them, for I see the failings of
us who inhabit the earth; 18and now also[j] I have
heard of the swiftness of the judgment that is to
come. 19Therefore hear my voice and understand
my words, and I will speak before you."

[a] Syr Ethiop Arab 1: Lat *what I say* [b] Syr: Lat *there was not* [c] Or *he is ready to give according to requests* [d] Lat *contempts* [e] Syr: Lat *Then release understanding* [f] Syr: Meaning of Lat uncertain [g] Syr: Lat *place* [h] Lat *what you have formed* [i] Syr: Lat *will with a light command* [j] Syr: Lat *but*

The beginning of the words of Ezra's prayer,[a]
before he was taken up. He said: 20"O Lord, you
who inhabit eternity,[b] whose eyes are exalted[c] and
whose upper chambers are in the air, 21whose
throne is beyond measure and whose glory is beyond comprehension, before whom the hosts of
angels stand trembling 22and at whose command
they are changed to wind and fire,[d] whose word
is sure and whose utterances are certain, whose
command is strong and whose ordinance is terrible, 23whose look dries up the depths and whose
indignation makes the mountains melt away,
and whose truth is established[e] forever— 24hear,
O Lord, the prayer of your servant, and give ear
to the petition of your creature; attend to my
words. 25For as long as I live I will speak, and as
long as I have understanding I will answer. 26O do
not look on the sins of your people, but on those
who serve you in truth. 27Do not take note of the
endeavors of those who act wickedly, but of the
endeavors of those who have kept your covenants
amid afflictions. 28Do not think of those who have
lived wickedly in your sight, but remember those
who have willingly acknowledged that you are to
be feared. 29Do not will the destruction of those
who have the ways of cattle, but regard those who
have gloriously taught your law.[f] 30Do not be angry with those who are deemed worse than wild
animals, but love those who have always put their
trust in your glory. 31For we and our ancestors
have passed our lives in ways that bring death;[g]
but it is because of us sinners that you are called
merciful. 32For if you have desired to have pity on
us, who have no works of righteousness, then you
will be called merciful. 33For the righteous, who
have many works laid up with you, shall receive
their reward in consequence of their own deeds.
34But what are mortals, that you are angry with
them; or what is a corruptible race, that you are
so bitter against it? 35For in truth there is no one
among those who have been born who has not
acted wickedly; among those who have existed[h]
there is no one who has not done wrong. 36For
in this, O Lord, your righteousness and goodness
will be declared, when you are merciful to those
who have no store of good works."

37 He answered me and said, "Some things
you have spoken rightly, and it will turn out according to your words. 38For indeed I will not
concern myself about the fashioning of those
who have sinned, or about their death, their
judgment, or their destruction; 39but I will rejoice over the creation of the righteous, over
their pilgrimage also, and their salvation, and
their receiving their reward. 40As I have spoken,
therefore, so it shall be.

41 "For just as the farmer sows many seeds in
the ground and plants a multitude of seedlings,
and yet not all that have been sown will come up[i]
in due season, and not all that were planted will
take root; so also those who have been sown in
the world will not all be saved."

42 I answered and said, "If I have found favor
in your sight, let me speak. 43If the farmer's seed
does not come up, because it has not received
your rain in due season, or if it has been ruined
by too much rain, it perishes.[j] 44But people, who
have been formed by your hands and are called
your own image because they are made like you,
and for whose sake you have formed all things—
have you also made them like the farmer's seed?
45Surely not, O Lord[k] above! But spare your people and have mercy on your inheritance, for you
have mercy on your own creation."

46 He answered me and said, "Things that
are present are for those who live now, and things
that are future are for those who will live hereafter. 47For you come far short of being able to
love my creation more than I love it. But you have
often compared yourself[l] to the unrighteous.
Never do so! 48But even in this respect you will
be praiseworthy before the Most High, 49because

[a] Syr Ethiop; Lat *beginning of Ezra's words* [b] Or *you who abide forever* [c] Another Lat text reads *whose are the highest heavens* [d] Syr: Lat *they whose service takes the form of wind and fire* [e] Arab 2: Other authorities read *truth bears witness* [f] Syr *have received the brightness of your law* [g] Syr Ethiop: Meaning of Lat uncertain [h] Syr: Meaning of Lat uncertain [i] Syr Ethiop *will live*; Lat *will be saved* [j] Cn: Compare Syr Arab 1 Arm Georg 2: Meaning of Lat uncertain [k] Ethiop Arab Compare Syr: Lat lacks *O Lord* [l] Syr Ethiop: Lat *brought yourself near*

you have humbled yourself, as is becoming for
you, and have not considered yourself to be
among the righteous. You will receive the greatest glory, 50 for many miseries will affect those
who inhabit the world in the last times, because
they have walked in great pride. 51 But think of
your own case, and inquire concerning the glory
of those who are like yourself, 52 because it is for
you that paradise is opened, the tree of life is
planted, the age to come is prepared, plenty is
provided, a city is built, rest is appointed,[a] goodness is established and wisdom perfected beforehand. 53 The root of evil[b] is sealed up from you,
illness is banished from you, and death[c] is hidden; Hades has fled and corruption has been forgotten;[d] 54 sorrows have passed away, and in the
end the treasure of immortality is made manifest.
55 Therefore do not ask any more questions about
the great number of those who perish. 56 For
when they had opportunity to choose, they despised the Most High, and were contemptuous
of his law, and abandoned his ways. 57 Moreover,
they have even trampled on his righteous ones,
58 and said in their hearts that there is no God—
though they knew well that they must die. 59 For
just as the things that I have predicted await[e] you,
so the thirst and torment that are prepared await
them. For the Most High did not intend that anyone should be destroyed; 60 but those who were
created have themselves defiled the name of him
who made them, and have been ungrateful to
him who prepared life for them now. 61 Therefore
my judgment is now drawing near; 62 I have not
shown this to all people, but only to you and a
few like you."

Then I answered and said, 63 "O Lord, you
have already shown me a great number of the
signs that you will do in the last times, but you
have not shown me when you will do them."

9 He answered me and said, "Measure carefully in your mind, and when you see that
some of the predicted signs have occurred, 2 then
you will know that it is the very time when the
Most High is about to visit the world that he has
made. 3 So when there shall appear in the world
earthquakes, tumult of peoples, intrigues of nations, wavering of leaders, confusion of princes,
4 then you will know that it was of these that the
Most High spoke from the days that were of old,
from the beginning. 5 For just as with everything
that has occurred in the world, the beginning is
evident,[f] and the end manifest; 6 so also are the
times of the Most High: the beginnings are manifest in wonders and mighty works, and the end in
penalties[g] and in signs.

7 "It shall be that all who will be saved and
will be able to escape on account of their works,
or on account of the faith by which they have believed, 8 will survive the dangers that have been
predicted, and will see my salvation in my land
and within my borders, which I have sanctified
for myself from the beginning. 9 Then those who
have now abused my ways shall be amazed, and
those who have rejected them with contempt
shall live in torments. 10 For as many as did not
acknowledge me in their lifetime, though they received my benefits, 11 and as many as scorned my
law while they still had freedom, and did not understand but despised it[h] while an opportunity of
repentance was still open to them, 12 these must
in torment acknowledge it[h] after death. 13 Therefore, do not continue to be curious about how the
ungodly will be punished; but inquire how the
righteous will be saved, those to whom the age
belongs and for whose sake the age was made."[i]

14 I answered and said, 15 "I said before, and I
say now, and will say it again: there are more who
perish than those who will be saved, 16 as a wave
is greater than a drop of water."

17 He answered me and said, "As is the field,
so is the seed; and as are the flowers, so are the
colors; and as is the work, so is the product; and
as is the farmer, so is the threshing floor. 18 For
there was a time in this age when I was prepar-

[a] Syr Ethiop: Lat *allowed* [b] Lat lacks *of evil* [c] Syr Ethiop Arm: Lat lacks *death* [d] Syr: Lat *Hades and corruption have fled into oblivion*; or *corruption has fled into Hades to be forgotten* [e] Syr: Lat *will receive* [f] Syr: Ethiop *is in the word;* Meaning of Lat uncertain [g] Syr: Lat Ethiop *in effects* [h] Or *me*
[i] Syr: Lat *saved, and whose is the age and for whose sake the age was made and when*

ing for those who now exist, before the world was
made for them to live in, and no one opposed me
then, for no one existed; 19but now those who
have been created in this world, which is supplied
both with an unfailing table and an inexhaustible
pasture,[a] have become corrupt in their ways. 20So
I considered my world, and saw that it was lost. I
saw that my earth was in peril because of the devices of those who[b] had come into it. 21And I saw
and spared some[c] with great difficulty, and saved
for myself one grape out of a cluster, and one
plant out of a great forest.[d] 22So let the multitude
perish that has been born in vain, but let my grape
and my plant be saved, because with much labor I
have perfected them.

23 "Now, if you will let seven days more
pass—do not, however, fast during them, 24but
go into a field of flowers where no house has been
built, and eat only of the flowers of the field, and
taste no meat and drink no wine, but eat only
flowers— 25and pray to the Most High continually, then I will come and talk with you."

26 So I went, as he directed me, into the field
that is called Ardat;[e] there I sat among the flowers
and ate of the plants of the field, and the nourishment they afforded satisfied me. 27After seven
days, while I lay on the grass, my heart was troubled again as it was before. 28Then my mouth was
opened, and I began to speak before the Most
High, and said, 29"O Lord, you showed yourself among us, to our ancestors in the wilderness
when they came out from Egypt and when they
came into the untrodden and unfruitful wilderness; 30and you said, 'Hear me, O Israel, and give
heed to my words, O descendants of Jacob. 31For
I sow my law in you, and it shall bring forth fruit
in you, and you shall be glorified through it forever.' 32But though our ancestors received the law,
they did not keep it and did not observe the[f] statutes; yet the fruit of the law did not perish—for it
could not, because it was yours. 33Yet those who
received it perished, because they did not keep
what had been sown in them. 34Now this is the
general rule that, when the ground has received
seed, or the sea a ship, or any dish food or drink,
and when it comes about that what was sown
or what was launched or what was put in is destroyed, 35they are destroyed, but the things that
held them remain; yet with us it has not been so.
36For we who have received the law and sinned
will perish, as well as our hearts that received it;
37the law, however, does not perish but survives
in its glory."

38 When I said these things in my heart, I
looked around,[g] and on my right I saw a woman;
she was mourning and weeping with a loud voice,
and was deeply grieved at heart; her clothes were
torn, and there were ashes on her head. 39Then
I dismissed the thoughts with which I had been
engaged, and turned to her 40and said to her,
"Why are you weeping, and why are you grieved
at heart?"

41 She said to me, "Let me alone, my lord,
so that I may weep for myself and continue to
mourn, for I am greatly embittered in spirit and
deeply distressed."

42 I said to her, "What has happened to you?
Tell me."

43 And she said to me, "Your servant was
barren and had no child, though I lived with my
husband for thirty years. 44Every hour and every
day during those thirty years I prayed to the Most
High, night and day. 45And after thirty years God
heard your servant, and looked upon my low estate, and considered my distress, and gave me a
son. I rejoiced greatly over him, I and my husband and all my neighbors;[h] and we gave great
glory to the Mighty One. 46And I brought him
up with much care. 47So when he grew up and I
came to take a wife for him, I set a day for the
marriage feast.

10 "But it happened that when my son entered his wedding chamber, he fell down
and died. 2So all of us put out our lamps, and all
my neighbors[h] attempted to console me; I remained quiet until the evening of the second day.
3But when all of them had stopped consoling me,
encouraging me to be quiet, I got up in the night

[a] Cn: Lat *law* [b] Cn: Lat *devices that* [c] Lat *them* [d] Syr Ethiop Arab 1: Lat *tribe* [e] Syr Ethiop *Arpad*; Arm *Ardab*
[f] Lat *my* [g] Syr Arab Arm: Lat *I looked about me with my eyes* [h] Literally *all my citizens*

and fled, and I came to this field, as you see. 4And
now I intend not to return to the town, but to stay
here; I will neither eat nor drink, but will mourn
and fast continually until I die."

5 Then I broke off the reflections with which
I was still engaged, and answered her in anger
and said, 6"You most foolish of women, do you
not see our mourning, and what has happened
to us? 7For Zion, the mother of us all, is in deep
grief and great distress. 8It is most appropriate to
mourn now, because we are all mourning, and to
be sorrowful, because we are all sorrowing; you
are sorrowing for one son, but we, the whole
world, for our mother.[a] 9Now ask the earth, and
she will tell you that it is she who ought to mourn
over so many who have come into being upon
her. 10From the beginning all have been born of
her, and others will come; and, lo, almost all go[b]
to perdition, and a multitude of them will come
to doom. 11Who then ought to mourn the more,
she who lost so great a multitude, or you who are
grieving for one alone? 12But if you say to me,
'My lamentation is not like the earth's, for I have
lost the fruit of my womb, which I brought forth
in pain and bore in sorrow; 13but it is with the
earth according to the way of the earth—the multitude that is now in it goes as it came'; 14then I
say to you, 'Just as you brought forth in sorrow,
so the earth also has from the beginning given
her fruit, that is, humankind, to him who made
her.' 15Now, therefore, keep your sorrow to yourself, and bear bravely the troubles that have come
upon you. 16For if you acknowledge the decree
of God to be just, you will receive your son back
in due time, and will be praised among women.
17Therefore go into the town to your husband."

18 She said to me, "I will not do so; I will not
go into the city, but I will die here."

19 So I spoke again to her, and said, 20"Do not
do that, but let yourself be persuaded—for how
many are the adversities of Zion?—and be consoled because of the sorrow of Jerusalem. 21For
you see how our sanctuary has been laid waste,
our altar thrown down, our temple destroyed;
22our harp has been laid low, our song has been
silenced, and our rejoicing has been ended; the
light of our lampstand has been put out, the ark of
our covenant has been plundered, our holy things
have been polluted, and the name by which we
are called has been almost profaned; our children[c] have suffered abuse, our priests have been
burned to death, our Levites have gone into exile,
our virgins have been defiled, and our wives have
been ravished; our righteous men[d] have been carried off, our little ones have been cast out, our
young men have been enslaved and our strong
men made powerless. 23And, worst of all, the seal
of Zion has been deprived of its glory, and given
over into the hands of those that hate us. 24There-
fore shake off your great sadness and lay aside
your many sorrows, so that the Mighty One may
be merciful to you again, and the Most High may
give you rest, a respite from your troubles."

25 While I was talking to her, her face suddenly began to shine exceedingly; her countenance flashed like lightning, so that I was too
frightened to approach her, and my heart was terrified. While[e] I was wondering what this meant,
26she suddenly uttered a loud and fearful cry,
so that the earth shook at the sound. 27When I
looked up, the woman was no longer visible to
me, but a city was being built,[f] and a place of huge
foundations showed itself. I was afraid, and cried
with a loud voice and said, 28"Where is the angel
Uriel, who came to me at first? For it was he who
brought me into this overpowering bewilderment; my end has become corruption, and my
prayer a reproach."

29 While I was speaking these words, the angel who had come to me at first came to me, and
when he saw me 30lying there like a corpse, deprived of my understanding, he grasped my right
hand and strengthened me and set me on my feet,
and said to me, 31"What is the matter with you?
And why are you troubled? And why are your understanding and the thoughts of your mind troubled?"

32 I said, "It was because you abandoned me.

[a] Compare Syr: Meaning of Lat uncertain [b] Literally *walk* [c] Ethiop *free men* [d] Syr *our seers* [e] Syr Ethiop Arab 1: Lat lacks *I was too . . . terrified. While* [f] Lat: Syr Ethiop Arab 1 Arab 2 Arm *but there was an established city*

I did as you directed, and went out into the field,
and lo, what I have seen and can still see, I am unable to explain."
33 He said to me, "Stand up like a man, and I
will instruct you."
34 I said, "Speak, my lord; only do not forsake me, so that I may not die before my time.[a]
35 For I have seen what I did not know, and I hear[b]
what I do not understand 36—or is my mind deceived, and my soul dreaming? 37 Now therefore
I beg you to give your servant an explanation of
this bewildering vision."
38 He answered me and said, "Listen to
me, and I will teach you, and tell you about the
things that you fear; for the Most High has revealed many secrets to you. 39 He has seen your
righteous conduct, and that you have sorrowed
continually for your people and mourned greatly
over Zion. 40 This therefore is the meaning of the
vision. 41 The woman who appeared to you a little
while ago, whom you saw mourning and whom
you began to console 42 (you do not now see the
form of a woman, but there appeared to you a
city being built)[c] 43 and who told you about the
misfortune of her son—this is the interpretation:
44 The woman whom you saw is Zion, which you
now behold as a city being built.[d] 45 And as for her
telling you that she was barren for thirty years, the
reason is that there were three thousand[e] years in
the world before any offering was offered in it.[f]
46 And after three thousand[g] years Solomon built
the city, and offered offerings; then it was that the
barren woman bore a son. 47 And as for her telling
you that she brought him up with much care, that
was the period of residence in Jerusalem. 48 And
as for her saying to you, 'My son died as he entered his wedding chamber,' and that misfortune
had overtaken her,[h] this was the destruction that
befell Jerusalem. 49 So you saw her likeness, how
she mourned for her son, and you began to console her for what had happened.[i] 50 For now the
Most High, seeing that you are sincerely grieved
and profoundly distressed for her, has shown you
the brilliance of her glory, and the loveliness of
her beauty. 51 Therefore I told you to remain in the
field where no house had been built, 52 for I knew
that the Most High would reveal these things to
you. 53 Therefore I told you to go into the field
where there was no foundation of any building,
54 because no work of human construction could
endure in a place where the city of the Most High
was to be revealed.
55 "Therefore do not be afraid, and do not
let your heart be terrified; but go in and see the
splendor or[j] the vastness of the building, as far as
it is possible for your eyes to see it, 56 and afterward you will hear as much as your ears can hear.
57 For you are more blessed than many, and you
have been called to be with[k] the Most High as few
have been. 58 But tomorrow night you shall remain here, 59 and the Most High will show you in
those dream visions what the Most High will do
to those who inhabit the earth in the last days."
So I slept that night and the following one, as
he had told me.

11 On the second night I had a dream: I
saw rising from the sea an eagle that had
twelve feathered wings and three heads. 2 I saw it
spread its wings over[l] the whole earth, and all the
winds of heaven blew upon it, and the clouds were
gathered around it.[m] 3 I saw that out of its wings
there grew opposing wings; but they became little, puny wings. 4 But its heads were at rest; the
middle head was larger than the other heads, but
it too was at rest with them. 5 Then I saw that the
eagle flew with its wings, and it reigned over the
earth and over those who inhabit it. 6 And I saw
how all things under heaven were subjected to it,
and no one spoke against it—not a single creature
that was on the earth. 7 Then I saw the eagle rise
upon its talons, and it uttered a cry to its wings,
saying, 8 "Do not all watch at the same time; let

[a] Syr Ethiop Arab: Lat *die to no purpose* [b] Other ancient authorities read *have heard* [c] Lat: Syr Ethiop Arab 1 Arab 2 Arm *an established city* [d] Cn: Lat *an established city* [e] Most Lat Mss read *three* [f] Cn: Lat Syr Arab Arm *her* [g] Syr Ethiop Arab Arm: Lat *three* [h] Or *him* [i] Most Lat Mss and Arab 1 add *These were the things to be opened to you* [j] Other ancient authorities read *and* [k] Or *been named by* [l] Arab 2 Arm: Lat Syr Ethiop *in* [m] Syr: Compare Ethiop Arab: Lat lacks *the clouds* and *around it*

each sleep in its own place, and watch in its turn;
9 but let the heads be reserved for the last."

10 I looked again and saw that the voice did not come from its heads, but from the middle of its body. 11 I counted its rival wings, and there were eight of them. 12 As I watched, one wing on the right side rose up, and it reigned over all the earth. 13 And after a time its reign came to an end, and it disappeared, so that even its place was no longer visible. Then the next wing rose up and reigned, and it continued to reign a long time. 14 While it was reigning its end came also, so that it disappeared like the first. 15 And a voice sounded, saying to it, 16 "Listen to me, you who have ruled the earth all this time; I announce this to you before you disappear. 17 After you no one shall rule as long as you have ruled, not even half as long."

18 Then the third wing raised itself up, and held the rule as the earlier ones had done, and it also disappeared. 19 And so it went with all the wings; they wielded power one after another and then were never seen again. 20 I kept looking, and in due time the wings that followed[a] also rose up on the right[b] side, in order to rule. There were some of them that ruled, yet disappeared suddenly; 21 and others of them rose up, but did not hold the rule.

22 And after this I looked and saw that the twelve wings and the two little wings had disappeared, 23 and nothing remained on the eagle's body except the three heads that were at rest and six little wings.

24 As I kept looking I saw that two little wings separated from the six and remained under the head that was on the right side; but four remained in their place. 25 Then I saw that these little wings[c] planned to set themselves up and hold the rule. 26 As I kept looking, one was set up, but suddenly disappeared; 27 a second also, and this disappeared more quickly than the first. 28 While I continued to look the two that remained were planning between themselves to reign together; 29 and while they were planning, one of the heads that were at rest (the one that was in the middle) suddenly awoke; it was greater than the other two heads. 30 And I saw how it allied the two heads with itself, 31 and how the head turned with those that were with it and devoured the two little wings[c] that were planning to reign. 32 Moreover this head gained control of the whole earth, and with much oppression dominated its inhabitants; it had greater power over the world than all the wings that had gone before.

33 After this I looked again and saw the head in the middle suddenly disappear, just as the wings had done. 34 But the two heads remained, which also in like manner ruled over the earth and its inhabitants. 35 And while I looked, I saw the head on the right side devour the one on the left.

36 Then I heard a voice saying to me, "Look in front of you and consider what you see." 37 When I looked, I saw what seemed to be a lion roused from the forest, roaring; and I heard how it uttered a human voice to the eagle, and spoke, saying, 38 "Listen and I will speak to you. The Most High says to you, 39 'Are you not the one that remains of the four beasts that I had made to reign in my world, so that the end of my times might come through them? 40 You, the fourth that has come, have conquered all the beasts that have gone before; and you have held sway over the world with great terror, and over all the earth with grievous oppression; and for so long you have lived on the earth with deceit.[d] 41 You have judged the earth, but not with truth, 42 for you have oppressed the meek and injured the peaceable; you have hated those who tell the truth, and have loved liars; you have destroyed the homes of those who brought forth fruit, and have laid low the walls of those who did you no harm. 43 Your insolence has come up before the Most High, and your pride to the Mighty One. 44 The Most High has looked at his times; now they have ended, and his ages have reached completion. 45 Therefore you, eagle, will surely disappear, you and your terrifying wings, your most evil little wings, your malicious heads, your most evil talons, and your whole worthless

[a] Syr Arab 2 *the little wings* [b] Some Ethiop Mss read *left* [c] Syr: Lat *underwings*
[d] Syr Arab Arm: Lat Ethiop *The fourth came, however, and conquered . . . and held sway . . . and for so long lived*

body, 46so that the whole earth, freed from your
violence, may be refreshed and relieved, and may
hope for the judgment and mercy of him who
made it.'"

12 While the lion was saying these words
to the eagle, I looked 2and saw that the
remaining head had disappeared. The two wings
that had gone over to it rose up and[a] set themselves up to reign, and their reign was brief and
full of tumult. 3When I looked again, they were
already vanishing. The whole body of the eagle
was burned, and the earth was exceedingly terrified.

Then I woke up in great perplexity of mind
and great fear, and I said to my spirit, 4"You have
brought this upon me, because you search out the
ways of the Most High. 5I am still weary in mind
and very weak in my spirit, and not even a little
strength is left in me, because of the great fear
with which I have been terrified tonight. 6There-
fore I will now entreat the Most High that he may
strengthen me to the end."

7 Then I said, "O sovereign Lord, if I have
found favor in your sight, and if I have been accounted righteous before you beyond many others, and if my prayer has indeed come up before
your face, 8strengthen me and show me, your
servant, the interpretation and meaning of this
terrifying vision so that you may fully comfort
my soul. 9For you have judged me worthy to be
shown the end of the times and the last events of
the times."

10 He said to me, "This is the interpretation
of this vision that you have seen: 11The eagle that
you saw coming up from the sea is the fourth
kingdom that appeared in a vision to your brother
Daniel. 12But it was not explained to him as I now
explain to you or have explained it. 13The days are
coming when a kingdom shall rise on earth, and
it shall be more terrifying than all the kingdoms
that have been before it. 14And twelve kings shall
reign in it, one after another. 15But the second
that is to reign shall hold sway for a longer time
than any other one of the twelve. 16This is the interpretation of the twelve wings that you saw.

17 "As for your hearing a voice that spoke,
coming not from the eagle's[b] heads but from the
midst of its body, this is the interpretation: 18In
the midst of[c] the time of that kingdom great
struggles shall arise, and it shall be in danger of
falling; nevertheless it shall not fall then, but
shall regain its former power.[d] 19As for your seeing eight little wings[e] clinging to its wings, this is
the interpretation: 20Eight kings shall arise in it,
whose times shall be short and their years swift;
21two of them shall perish when the middle of its
time draws near; and four shall be kept for the
time when its end approaches, but two shall be
kept until the end.

22 "As for your seeing three heads at rest, this
is the interpretation: 23In its last days the Most
High will raise up three kings,[f] and they[g] shall
renew many things in it, and shall rule the earth
24and its inhabitants more oppressively than all
who were before them. Therefore they are called
the heads of the eagle, 25because it is they who
shall sum up his wickedness and perform his last
actions. 26As for your seeing that the large head
disappeared, one of the kings[h] shall die in his bed,
but in agonies. 27But as for the two who remained,
the sword shall devour them. 28For the sword of
one shall devour him who was with him; but he
also shall fall by the sword in the last days.

29 "As for your seeing two little wings[i] passing over to[j] the head which was on the right side,
30this is the interpretation: It is these whom the
Most High has kept for the eagle's[b] end; this was
the reign which was brief and full of tumult, as
you have seen.

31 "And as for the lion whom you saw rousing
up out of the forest and roaring and speaking to
the eagle and reproving him for his unrighteousness, and as for all his words that you have heard,
32this is the Messiah[k] whom the Most High has
kept until the end of days, who will arise from the
offspring of David, and will come and speak[l] with

[a] Ethiop: Lat lacks *rose up and* [b] Lat *his* [c] Syr Arm: Lat *After* [d] Ethiop Arab 1 Arm: Lat Syr *its beginning* [e] Syr: Lat *underwings* [f] Syr Ethiop Arab Arm: Lat *kingdoms* [g] Syr Ethiop Arm: Lat *he* [h] Lat *them* [i] Arab 1: Lat *underwings* [j] Syr Ethiop: Lat lacks *to* [k] Literally *anointed one* [l] Syr: Lat lacks *of days . . . and speak*

them. He will denounce them for their ungodliness and for their wickedness, and will display
before them their contemptuous dealings. 33For
first he will bring them alive before his judgment
seat, and when he has reproved them, then he will
destroy them. 34But in mercy he will set free the
remnant of my people, those who have been saved
throughout my borders, and he will make them
joyful until the end comes, the day of judgment,
of which I spoke to you at the beginning. 35This
is the dream that you saw, and this is its interpretation. 36And you alone were worthy to learn this
secret of the Most High. 37Therefore write all
these things that you have seen in a book, put it[a]
in a hidden place; 38and you shall teach them to
the wise among your people, whose hearts you
know are able to comprehend and keep these secrets. 39But as for you, wait here seven days more,
so that you may be shown whatever it pleases the
Most High to show you." Then he left me.

40 When all the people heard that the seven
days were past and I had not returned to the city,
they all gathered together, from the least to the
greatest, and came to me and spoke to me, saying,
41"How have we offended you, and what harm
have we done you, that you have forsaken us and
sit in this place? 42For of all the prophets you
alone are left to us, like a cluster of grapes from
the vintage, and like a lamp in a dark place, and
like a haven for a ship saved from a storm. 43Are
not the disasters that have befallen us enough?
44Therefore if you forsake us, how much better it
would have been for us if we also had been consumed in the burning of Zion. 45For we are no
better than those who died there." And they wept
with a loud voice.

Then I answered them and said, 46"Take courage, O Israel; and do not be sorrowful, O house
of Jacob; 47for the Most High has you in remembrance, and the Mighty One has not forgotten
you in your struggle. 48As for me, I have neither
forsaken you nor withdrawn from you; but I have
come to this place to pray on account of the desolation of Zion, and to seek mercy on account
of the humiliation of our[b] sanctuary. 49Now go
to your homes, every one of you, and after these
days I will come to you." 50So the people went
into the city, as I told them to do. 51But I sat in the
field seven days, as the angel[c] had commanded
me; and I ate only of the flowers of the field, and
my food was of plants during those days.

13 After seven days I dreamed a dream in the
night. 2And lo, a wind arose from the sea
and stirred up[d] all its waves. 3As I kept looking
the wind made something like the figure of a man
come up out of the heart of the sea. And I saw[e]
that this man flew[f] with the clouds of heaven; and
wherever he turned his face to look, everything
under his gaze trembled, 4and whenever his voice
issued from his mouth, all who heard his voice
melted as wax melts[g] when it feels the fire.

5 After this I looked and saw that an innumerable multitude of people were gathered together from the four winds of heaven to make war
against the man who came up out of the sea. 6And
I looked and saw that he carved out for himself a
great mountain, and flew up on to it. 7And I tried
to see the region or place from which the mountain was carved, but I could not.

8 After this I looked and saw that all who had
gathered together against him, to wage war with
him, were filled with fear, and yet they dared to
fight. 9When he saw the onrush of the approaching multitude, he neither lifted his hand nor held
a spear or any weapon of war; 10but I saw only
how he sent forth from his mouth something
like a stream of fire, and from his lips a flaming
breath, and from his tongue he shot forth a storm
of sparks.[h] 11All these were mingled together, the
stream of fire and the flaming breath and the great
storm, and fell on the onrushing multitude that
was prepared to fight, and burned up all of them,
so that suddenly nothing was seen of the innumerable multitude but only the dust of ashes and
the smell of smoke. When I saw it, I was amazed.

12 After this I saw the same man come down

[a] Ethiop Arab 1 Arab 2 Arm: Lat Syr *them* [b] Syr Ethiop: Lat *your* [c] Literally *he* [d] Other ancient authorities read *I saw a wind arise from the sea and stir up* [e] Syr: Lat lacks *the wind . . . I saw* [f] Syr Ethiop Arab Arm: Lat *grew strong* [g] Syr: Lat *burned as the earth rests* [h] Meaning of Lat uncertain

 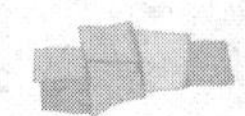

from the mountain and call to himself another
multitude that was peaceable. 13 Then many people[a] came to him, some of whom were joyful and
some sorrowful; some of them were bound, and
some were bringing others as offerings.

Then I woke up in great terror, and prayed to
the Most High, and said, 14 "From the beginning
you have shown your servant these wonders, and
have deemed me worthy to have my prayer heard
by you; 15 now show me the interpretation of this
dream also. 16 For as I consider it in my mind, alas
for those who will be left in those days! And still
more, alas for those who are not left! 17 For those
who are not left will be sad 18 because they understand the things that are reserved for the last days,
but cannot attain them. 19 But alas for those also
who are left, and for that very reason! For they
shall see great dangers and much distress, as these
dreams show. 20 Yet it is better[b] to come into these
things,[c] though incurring peril, than to pass from
the world like a cloud, and not to see what will
happen in the last days."

He answered me and said, 21 "I will tell you the
interpretation of the vision, and I will also explain
to you the things that you have mentioned. 22 As
for what you said about those who survive, and
concerning those who do not survive,[d] this is the
interpretation: 23 The one who brings the peril at
that time will protect those who fall into peril,
who have works and faith toward the Almighty.
24 Understand therefore that those who are left
are more blessed than those who have died.

25 "This is the interpretation of the vision:
As for your seeing a man come up from the heart
of the sea, 26 this is he whom the Most High has
been keeping for many ages, who will himself deliver his creation; and he will direct those who are
left. 27 And as for your seeing wind and fire and a
storm coming out of his mouth, 28 and as for his
not holding a spear or weapon of war, yet destroying the onrushing multitude that came to conquer
him, this is the interpretation: 29 The days are
coming when the Most High will deliver those
who are on the earth. 30 And bewilderment of
mind shall come over those who inhabit the earth.
31 They shall plan to make war against one another, city against city, place against place, people
against people, and kingdom against kingdom.
32 When these things take place and the signs occur that I showed you before, then my Son will
be revealed, whom you saw as a man coming up
from the sea.[e]

33 "Then, when all the nations hear his voice,
all the nations shall leave their own lands and the
warfare that they have against one another; 34 and
an innumerable multitude shall be gathered together, as you saw, wishing to come and conquer
him. 35 But he shall stand on the top of Mount
Zion. 36 And Zion shall come and be made manifest to all people, prepared and built, as you saw
the mountain carved out without hands. 37 Then
he, my Son, will reprove the assembled nations
for their ungodliness (this was symbolized by
the storm), 38 and will reproach them to their
face with their evil thoughts and the torments
with which they are to be tortured (which were
symbolized by the flames), and will destroy them
without effort by means of the law[f] (which was
symbolized by the fire).

39 "And as for your seeing him gather to himself another multitude that was peaceable, 40 these
are the nine[g] tribes that were taken away from
their own land into exile in the days of King Hoshea, whom Shalmaneser, king of the Assyrians,
made captives; he took them across the river, and
they were taken into another land. 41 But they
formed this plan for themselves, that they would
leave the multitude of the nations and go to a
more distant region, where no human beings had
ever lived, 42 so that there at least they might keep
their statutes that they had not kept in their own
land. 43 And they went in by the narrow passages
of the Euphrates river. 44 For at that time the Most
High performed signs for them, and stopped the
channels of the river until they had crossed over.
45 Through that region there was a long way to go,

[a] Lat Syr Arab 2 literally *the faces of many people* [b] Ethiop Compare Arab 2: Lat *easier* [c] Syr: Lat *this* [d] Syr Arab 1: Lat lacks *and . . . not survive* [e] Syr and most Lat Mss lack *from the sea* [f] Syr: Lat *effort and the law*
[g] Other Lat Mss *ten*; Syr Ethiop Arab 1 Arm *nine and a half*

a journey of a year and a half; and that country is
called Arzareth.[a]
46 "Then they lived there until the last times;
and now, when they are about to come again,
47the Most High will stop[b] the channels of the
river again, so that they may be able to cross over.
Therefore you saw the multitude gathered together
in peace. 48But those who are left of your people,
who are found within my holy borders, shall be
saved.[c] 49Therefore when he destroys the multitude of the nations that are gathered together, he
will defend the people who remain. 50And then he
will show them very many wonders."
51 I said, "O sovereign Lord, explain this to
me: Why did I see the man coming up from the
heart of the sea?"
52 He said to me, "Just as no one can explore
or know what is in the depths of the sea, so no
one on earth can see my Son or those who are
with him, except in the time of his day.[d] 53This
is the interpretation of the dream that you saw.
And you alone have been enlightened about this,
54because you have forsaken your own ways and
have applied yourself to mine, and have searched
out my law; 55for you have devoted your life to
wisdom, and called understanding your mother.
56Therefore I have shown you these things; for
there is a reward laid up with the Most High. For
it will be that after three more days I will tell you
other things, and explain weighty and wondrous
matters to you."
57 Then I got up and walked in the field, giving great glory and praise to the Most High for
the wonders that he does[e] from time to time,
58and because he governs the times and whatever
things come to pass in their seasons. And I stayed
there three days.

14 On the third day, while I was sitting under an oak, suddenly a voice came out of
a bush opposite me and said, "Ezra, Ezra!" 2And
I answered, "Here I am, Lord," and I rose to my
feet. 3Then he said to me, "I revealed myself in a
bush and spoke to Moses when my people were
in bondage in Egypt; 4and I sent him and led[f] my
people out of Egypt; and I led him up on Mount
Sinai, where I kept him with me many days. 5I
told him many wondrous things, and showed him
the secrets of the times and declared to him[g] the
end of the times. Then I commanded him, saying,
6'These words you shall publish openly, and these
you shall keep secret.' 7And now I say to you: 8Lay
up in your heart the signs that I have shown you,
the dreams that you have seen, and the interpretations that you have heard; 9for you shall be taken
up from among humankind, and henceforth you
shall live with my Son and with those who are like
you, until the times are ended. 10The age has lost
its youth, and the times begin to grow old. 11For
the age is divided into twelve parts, and nine[h] of
its parts have already passed, 12as well as half of
the tenth part; so two of its parts remain, besides
half of the tenth part.[i] 13Now therefore, set your
house in order, and reprove your people; comfort
the lowly among them, and instruct those that are
wise.[j] And now renounce the life that is corruptible, 14and put away from you mortal thoughts;
cast away from you the burdens of humankind,
and divest yourself now of your weak nature;
15lay to one side the thoughts that are most grievous to you, and hurry to escape from these times.
16For evils worse than those that you have now
seen happen shall take place hereafter. 17For the
weaker the world becomes through old age, the
more shall evils be increased upon its inhabitants.
18Truth shall go farther away, and falsehood shall
come near. For the eagle[k] that you saw in the vision is already hurrying to come."
19 Then I answered and said, "Let me speak[l]
in your presence, Lord. 20For I will go, as you have
commanded me, and I will reprove the people who
are now living; but who will warn those who will
be born hereafter? For the world lies in darkness,

[a] That is *Another Land* [b] Syr: Lat *stops* [c] Syr: Lat lacks *shall be saved* [d] Syr: Ethiop *except when his time and his day have come*. Lat lacks *his* [e] Lat *did* [f] Syr Arab 1 Arab 2 *he led* [g] Syr Ethiop Arab Arm: Lat lacks *declared to him* [h] Cn: Lat Ethiop *ten* [i] Syr lacks verses 11, 12: Ethiop *For the world is divided into ten parts, and has come to the tenth, and half of the tenth remains. Now . . .* [j] Lat lacks *and . . . wise* [k] Syr Ethiop Arab Arm: Meaning of Lat uncertain [l] Most Lat Mss lack *Let me speak*

and its inhabitants are without light. 21For your
law has been burned, and so no one knows the
things which have been done or will be done by
you. 22If then I have found favor with you, send the
holy spirit into me, and I will write everything that
has happened in the world from the beginning, the
things that were written in your law, so that people
may be able to find the path, and that those who
want to live in the last days may do so."

23 He answered me and said, "Go and gather
the people, and tell them not to seek you for forty
days. 24But prepare for yourself many writing
tablets, and take with you Sarea, Dabria, Selemia,
Ethanus, and Asiel—these five, who are trained
to write rapidly; 25and you shall come here, and
I will light in your heart the lamp of understanding, which shall not be put out until what you are
about to write is finished. 26And when you have
finished, some things you shall make public, and
some you shall deliver in secret to the wise; tomorrow at this hour you shall begin to write."

27 Then I went as he commanded me, and I
gathered all the people together, and said, 28"Hear
these words, O Israel. 29At first our ancestors lived
as aliens in Egypt, and they were liberated from
there 30and received the law of life, which they
did not keep, which you also have transgressed
after them. 31Then land was given to you for a
possession in the land of Zion; but you and your
ancestors committed iniquity and did not keep
the ways that the Most High commanded you.
32And since he is a righteous judge, in due time
he took from you what he had given. 33And now
you are here, and your people[a] are farther in the
interior.[b] 34If you, then, will rule over your minds
and discipline your hearts, you shall be kept alive,
and after death you shall obtain mercy. 35For after
death the judgment will come, when we shall live
again; and then the names of the righteous shall
become manifest, and the deeds of the ungodly
shall be disclosed. 36But let no one come to me
now, and let no one seek me for forty days."

37 So I took the five men, as he commanded
me, and we proceeded to the field, and remained
there. 38And on the next day a voice called me,
saying, "Ezra, open your mouth and drink what I
give you to drink." 39So I opened my mouth, and
a full cup was offered to me; it was full of something like water, but its color was like fire. 40I
took it and drank; and when I had drunk it, my
heart poured forth understanding, and wisdom
increased in my breast, for my spirit retained its
memory, 41and my mouth was opened and was
no longer closed. 42Moreover, the Most High
gave understanding to the five men, and by turns
they wrote what was dictated, using characters
that they did not know.[c] They sat forty days; they
wrote during the daytime, and ate their bread at
night. 43But as for me, I spoke in the daytime and
was not silent at night. 44So during the forty days,
ninety-four[d] books were written. 45And when the
forty days were ended, the Most High spoke to
me, saying, "Make public the twenty-four[e] books
that you wrote first, and let the worthy and the
unworthy read them; 46but keep the seventy that
were written last, in order to give them to the wise
among your people. 47For in them is the spring of
understanding, the fountain of wisdom, and the
river of knowledge." 48And I did so.[f]

---

15 [g] Speak in the ears of my people the words
of the prophecy that I will put in your
mouth, says the Lord, 2and cause them to be
written on paper; for they are trustworthy and
true. 3Do not fear the plots against you, and do
not be troubled by the unbelief of those who oppose you. 4For all unbelievers shall die in their
unbelief.[h]

5 Beware, says the Lord, I am bringing evils

[a] Lat *brothers* [b] Syr Ethiop Arm: Lat *are among you* [c] Syr Compare Ethiop Arab 2 Arm: Meaning of Lat uncertain
[d] Syr Ethiop Arab 1 Arm: Meaning of Lat uncertain [e] Syr Arab 1: Lat lacks *twenty-four* [f] Syr adds *in the seventh year of the sixth week, five thousand years and three months and twelve days after creation. At that time Ezra was caught up, and taken to the place of those who are like him, after he had written all these things. And he was called the scribe of the knowledge of the Most High for ever and ever.* Ethiop Arab 1 Arm have a similar ending [g] Chapters 15 and 16 (except 15.57–59, which has been found in Greek) are extant only in Lat [h] Other ancient authorities add *and all who believe shall be saved by their faith*

upon the world, the sword and famine, death and destruction, 6 because iniquity has spread throughout every land, and their harmful doings have reached their limit. 7 Therefore, says the Lord, 8 I will be silent no longer concerning their ungodly acts that they impiously commit, neither will I tolerate their wicked practices. Innocent and righteous blood cries out to me, and the souls of the righteous cry out continually. 9 I will surely avenge them, says the Lord, and will receive to myself all the innocent blood from among them. 10 See, my people are being led like a flock to the slaughter; I will not allow them to live any longer in the land of Egypt, 11 but I will bring them out with a mighty hand and with an uplifted arm, and will strike Egypt with plagues, as before, and will destroy all its land.

12 Let Egypt mourn, and its foundations, because of the plague of chastisement and castigation that the Lord will bring upon it. 13 Let the farmers that till the ground mourn, because their seed shall fail to grow[a] and their trees shall be ruined by blight and hail and by a terrible tempest. 14 Alas for the world and for those who live in it! 15 For the sword and misery draw near them, and nation shall rise up to fight against nation, with swords in their hands. 16 For there shall be unrest among people; growing strong against one another, they shall in their might have no respect for their king or the chief of their leaders. 17 For a person will desire to go into a city, and shall not be able to do so. 18 Because of their pride the cities shall be in confusion, the houses shall be destroyed, and people shall be afraid. 19 People shall have no pity for their neighbors, but shall make an assault upon[b] their houses with the sword, and plunder their goods, because of hunger for bread and because of great tribulation.

20 See how I am calling together all the kings of the earth to turn to me, says God, from the rising sun and from the south, from the east and from Lebanon; to turn and repay what they have given them. 21 Just as they have done to my elect until this day, so I will do, and will repay into their bosom. Thus says the Lord God: 22 My right hand will not spare the sinners, and my sword will not cease from those who shed innocent blood on earth. 23 And a fire went forth from his wrath, and consumed the foundations of the earth and the sinners, like burnt straw. 24 Alas for those who sin and do not observe my commandments, says the Lord;[c] 25 I will not spare them. Depart, you faithless children! Do not pollute my sanctuary. 26 For God[d] knows all who sin against him; therefore he will hand them over to death and slaughter. 27 Already calamities have come upon the whole earth, and you shall remain in them; God[d] will not deliver you, because you have sinned against him.

28 What a terrifying sight, appearing from the east! 29 The nations of the dragons of Arabia shall come out with many chariots, and from the day that they set out, their hissing shall spread over the earth, so that all who hear them will fear and tremble. 30 Also the Carmonians, raging in wrath, shall go forth like wild boars[e] from the forest, and with great power they shall come and engage them in battle, and with their tusks they shall devastate a portion of the land of the Assyrians with their teeth. 31 And then the dragons,[f] remembering their origin, shall become still stronger; and if they combine in great power and turn to pursue them, 32 then these shall be disorganized and silenced by their power, and shall turn and flee.[g] 33 And from the land of the Assyrians an enemy in ambush shall attack them and destroy one of them, and fear and trembling shall come upon their army, and indecision upon their kings.

34 See the clouds from the east, and from the north to the south! Their appearance is exceedingly threatening, full of wrath and storm. 35 They shall clash against one another and shall pour out a heavy tempest on the earth, and their own tempest;[h] and there shall be blood from the sword as high as a horse's belly 36 and a man's thigh and a camel's hock. 37 And there shall be fear and great trembling on the earth; those who see that wrath

[a] Lat lacks *to grow* [b] Cn: Lat *shall empty* [c] Other ancient authorities read *God* [d] Other ancient authorities read *the Lord* [e] Other ancient authorities lack *like wild boars* [f] Cn: Lat *dragon* [g] Other ancient authorities read *turn their face to the north* [h] Meaning of Lat uncertain

shall be horror-stricken, and they shall be seized
with trembling. 38 After that, heavy storm clouds
shall be stirred up from the south, and from the
north, and another part from the west. 39 But the
winds from the east shall prevail over the cloud
that was[a] raised in wrath, and shall dispel it; and
the tempest[b] that was to cause destruction by the
east wind shall be driven violently toward the
south and west. 40 Great and mighty clouds, full
of wrath and tempest, shall rise and destroy all
the earth and its inhabitants, and shall pour out
upon every high and lofty place[c] a terrible tempest, 41 fire and hail and flying swords and floods
of water, so that all the fields and all the streams
shall be filled with the abundance of those waters. 42 They shall destroy cities and walls, mountains and hills, trees of the forests, and grass of
the meadows, and their grain. 43 They shall go on
steadily to Babylon and blot it out. 44 They shall
come to it and surround it; they shall pour out on
it the tempest[b] and all its fury;[d] then the dust and
smoke shall reach the sky, and all who are around
it shall mourn for it. 45 And those who survive
shall serve those who have destroyed it.

46 And you, Asia, who share in the splendor
of Babylon and the glory of her person— 47 woe to
you, miserable wretch! For you have made yourself like her; you have decked out your daughters
for prostitution to please and glory in your lovers, who have always lusted after you. 48 You have
imitated that hateful one in all her deeds and
devices.[e] Therefore God[f] says, 49 I will send evils
upon you: widowhood, poverty, famine, sword,
and pestilence, bringing ruin to your houses,
bringing destruction and death. 50 And the glory
of your strength shall wither like a flower when
the heat shall rise that is sent upon you. 51 You
shall be weakened like a wretched woman who
is beaten and wounded, so that you cannot receive your mighty lovers. 52 Would I have dealt
with you so violently, says the Lord, 53 if you had
not killed my chosen people continually, exulting
and clapping your hands and talking about their
death when you were drunk?

54 Beautify your face! 55 The reward of a
prostitute is in your lap; therefore you shall receive your recompense. 56 As you will do to my
chosen people, says the Lord, so God will do to
you, and will hand you over to adversities. 57 Your
children shall die of hunger, and you shall fall by
the sword; your cities shall be wiped out, and all
your people who are in the open country shall fall
by the sword. 58 Those who are in the mountains
and highlands[g] shall perish of hunger, and they
shall eat their own flesh in hunger for bread and
drink their own blood in thirst for water. 59 Unhappy above all others, you shall come and suffer
fresh miseries. 60 As they pass by they shall crush
the hateful[h] city, and shall destroy a part of your
land and abolish a portion of your glory, when
they return from devastated Babylon. 61 You shall
be broken down by them like stubble,[i] and they
shall be like fire to you. 62 They shall devour you
and your cities, your land and your mountains;
they shall burn with fire all your forests and your
fruitful trees. 63 They shall carry your children
away captive, plunder your wealth, and mar the
glory of your countenance.

16 Woe to you, Babylon and Asia! Woe to
you, Egypt and Syria! 2 Bind on sackcloth
and cloth of goats' hair,[j] and wail for your children, and lament for them; for your destruction is
at hand. 3 The sword has been sent upon you, and
who is there to turn it back? 4 A fire has been sent
upon you, and who is there to quench it? 5 Calamities have been sent upon you, and who is there to
drive them away? 6 Can one drive off a hungry lion
in the forest, or quench a fire in the stubble once
it has started to burn?[k] 7 Can one turn back an arrow shot by a strong archer? 8 The Lord God sends

[a] Literally *that he* [b] Meaning of Lat uncertain [c] Or *eminent person* [d] Other ancient authorities add *until they destroy it to its foundations* [e] Other ancient authorities read *devices, and you have followed after that one about to gratify her magnates and leaders so that you may be made proud and be pleased by her fornications* [f] Other ancient authorities read *the Lord* [g] Gk: Lat omits *and highlands* [h] Another reading is *idle* or *unprofitable* [i] Other ancient authorities read *like dry straw* [j] Other ancient authorities lack *cloth of goats' hair* [k] Other ancient authorities read *fire when dry straw has been set on fire*

calamities, and who will drive them away? 9Fire will go forth from his wrath, and who is there to quench it? 10He will flash lightning, and who will not be afraid? He will thunder, and who will not be terrified? 11The Lord will threaten, and who will not be utterly shattered at his presence? 12The earth and its foundations quake, the sea is churned up from the depths, and its waves and the fish with them shall be troubled at the presence of the Lord and the glory of his power. 13For his right hand that bends the bow is strong, and his arrows that he shoots are sharp and when they are shot to the ends of the world will not miss once. 14Calamities are sent forth and shall not return until they come over the earth. 15The fire is kindled, and shall not be put out until it consumes the foundations of the earth. 16Just as an arrow shot by a mighty archer does not return, so the calamities that are sent upon the earth shall not return. 17Alas for me! Alas for me! Who will deliver me in those days?

18 The beginning of sorrows, when there shall be much lamentation; the beginning of famine, when many shall perish; the beginning of wars, when the powers shall be terrified; the beginning of calamities, when all shall tremble. What shall they do, when the calamities come? 19Famine and plague, tribulation and anguish are sent as scourges for the correction of humankind. 20Yet for all this they will not turn from their iniquities, or ever be mindful of the scourges. 21Indeed, provisions will be so cheap upon earth that people will imagine that peace is assured for them, and then calamities shall spring up on the earth—the sword, famine, and great confusion. 22For many of those who live on the earth shall perish by famine; and those who survive the famine shall die by the sword. 23And the dead shall be thrown out like dung, and there shall be no one to console them; for the earth shall be left desolate, and its cities shall be demolished. 24No one shall be left to cultivate the earth or to sow it. 25The trees shall bear fruit, but who will gather it? 26The grapes shall ripen, but who will tread them? For in all places there shall be great solitude; 27a person will long to see another human being, or even to hear a human voice. 28For ten shall be left out of a city; and two, out of the field, those who have hidden themselves in thick groves and clefts in the rocks. 29Just as in an olive orchard three or four olives may be left on every tree, 30or just as, when a vineyard is gathered, some clusters may be left[a] by those who search carefully through the vineyard, 31so in those days three or four shall be left by those who search their houses with the sword. 32The earth shall be left desolate, and its fields shall be plowed up,[b] and its roads and all its paths shall bring forth thorns, because no sheep will go along them. 33Virgins shall mourn because they have no bridegrooms; women shall mourn because they have no husbands; their daughters shall mourn, because they have no help. 34Their bridegrooms shall be killed in war, and their husbands shall perish of famine.

35 Listen now to these things, and understand them, you who are servants of the Lord. 36This is the word of the Lord; receive it and do not disbelieve what the Lord says.[c] 37The calamities draw near, and are not delayed. 38Just as a pregnant woman, in the ninth month when the time of her delivery draws near, has great pains around her womb for two or three hours beforehand, but when the child comes forth from the womb, there will not be a moment's delay, 39so the calamities will not delay in coming upon the earth, and the world will groan, and pains will seize it on every side.

40 Hear my words, O my people; prepare for battle, and in the midst of the calamities be like strangers on the earth. 41Let the one who sells be like one who will flee; let the one who buys be like one who will lose; 42let the one who does business be like one who will not make a profit; and let the one who builds a house be like one who will not live in it; 43let the one who sows be like one who will not reap; so also the one who prunes the vines, like one who will not gather the grapes; 44those who marry, like those who will have no children; and those who do not marry, like those who are widowed. 45Because of this,

[a] Other ancient authorities read *a cluster may remain exposed*

[b] Other ancient authorities read *be for briers*

[c] Cn: Lat *do not believe the gods of whom the Lord speaks*

those who labor, labor in vain; 46 for strangers
shall gather their fruits, and plunder their goods,
overthrow their houses, and take their children
captive; for in captivity and famine they will produce their children.[a] 47 Those who conduct business, do so only to have it plundered; the more
they adorn their cities, their houses and possessions, and their persons, 48 the more angry I will
be with them for their sins, says the Lord. 49 Just
as a respectable and virtuous woman abhors a
prostitute, 50 so righteousness shall abhor iniquity, when she decks herself out, and shall accuse
her to her face when he comes who will defend
the one who searches out every sin on earth.

51 Therefore do not be like her or her works.
52 For in a very short time iniquity will be removed from the earth, and righteousness will
reign over us. 53 Sinners must not say that they
have not sinned;[b] for God[c] will burn coals of fire
on the head of everyone who says, "I have not
sinned before God and his glory." 54 The Lord[d]
certainly knows everything that people do; he
knows their imaginations and their thoughts and
their hearts. 55 He said, "Let the earth be made,"
and it was made, and "Let the heaven be made,"
and it was made. 56 At his word the stars were
fixed in their places, and he knows the number
of the stars. 57 He searches the abyss and its treasures; he has measured the sea and its contents;
58 he has confined the sea in the midst of the waters;[e] and by his word he has suspended the earth
over the water. 59 He has spread out the heaven
like a dome and made it secure upon the waters; 60 he has put springs of water in the desert,
and pools on the tops of the mountains, so as to
send rivers from the heights to water the earth.
61 He formed human beings and put a heart in the
midst of each body, and gave each person breath
and life and understanding 62 and the spirit[f] of
Almighty God,[g] who surely made all things and
searches out hidden things in hidden places. 63 He
knows your imaginations and what you think in
your hearts! Woe to those who sin and want to
hide their sins! 64 The Lord will strictly examine
all their works, and will make a public spectacle
of all of you. 65 You shall be put to shame when
your sins come out before others, and your own
iniquities shall stand as your accusers on that day.
66 What will you do? Or how will you hide your
sins before the Lord and his glory? 67 Indeed,
God[h] is the judge; fear him! Cease from your sins,
and forget your iniquities, never to commit them
again; so God[h] will lead you forth and deliver you
from all tribulation.

68 The burning wrath of a great multitude
is kindled over you; they shall drag some of you
away and force you to eat what was sacrificed to
idols. 69 And those who consent to eat shall be
held in derision and contempt, and shall be trampled under foot. 70 For in many places[i] and in
neighboring cities there shall be a great uprising
against those who fear the Lord. 71 They shall[j] be
like maniacs, sparing no one, but plundering and
destroying those who continue to fear the Lord.[k]
72 For they shall destroy and plunder their goods,
and drive them out of house and home. 73 Then
the tested quality of my elect shall be manifest,
like gold that is tested by fire.

74 Listen, my elect ones, says the Lord; the
days of tribulation are at hand, but I will deliver
you from them. 75 Do not fear or doubt, for God[h]
is your guide. 76 You who keep my commandments and precepts, says the Lord God, must not
let your sins weigh you down, or your iniquities
prevail over you. 77 Woe to those who are choked
by their sins and overwhelmed by their iniquities! They are like a field choked with underbrush
and its path[l] overwhelmed with thorns, so that no
one can pass through. 78 It is shut off and given up
to be consumed by fire.

[a] Other ancient authorities read *therefore those who are married may know that they will produce children for captivity and famine* [b] Other ancient authorities add *or the unjust done injustice* [c] Lat *for he* [d] Other ancient authorities read *Lord God* [e] Other ancient authorities read *confined the world between the waters and the waters* [f] Or *breath* [g] Other ancient authorities read *of the Lord Almighty* [h] Other ancient authorities read *the Lord* [i] Meaning of Lat uncertain [j] Other ancient authorities read *For people, because of their misfortunes, shall* [k] Other ancient authorities read *fear God* [l] Other ancient authorities read *seed*

4 Maccabees

LIKE 3 MACCABEES, 4 Maccabees is concerned with religious persecution. Written probably in the first century CE, the bulk of the book (3:19—17:24) is a lengthy extension of 2 Maccabees 3–7, which describes the initial persecution and martyrdom that triggered the revolt. But the first chapters of 4 Maccabees outline the author's thesis that the Maccabean martyrs accept torture and death because they virtuously submit to reason and keep the Torah. This claim is summarized in 4 Macc 9:18: "Through all these tortures I will convince you that children of the Hebrews alone are invincible where virtue is concerned." The seven brothers choose death because they hope to "be with God, on whose account we suffer" (9:8). Once again, Josephus, who in this case is contemporary with 4 Maccabees, is useful. He insists that obedience to one's laws is the wisest course of action and that Jews are willing to obey their law to the point of death because of the hope of eternal life (*Against Apion* 2:144, 146).

Fourth Maccabees appears in an appendix to the Greek Bible but has never been explicitly declared Scripture by any church body. Nevertheless, any community that has ever suffered persecution can relate to the agony and courage described in the book. Oscar Romero, the martyred Roman Catholic bishop of El Salvador, speaks eighteen centuries after 4 Maccabees and Josephus in his book *The Violence of Love*. In spite of his different religious and cultural context, his words make the same argument:

> There is a hope. They are a people that march to encounter the Lord. Death is not the end. Death is the opening of eternity's portal. That is why I say: all the blood, all the dead, all the mysteries of iniquity and sin, all the tortures, all those dungeons of our security forces, where unfortunately many persons slowly die, do not mean they are lost forever.

— *Stacy Davis*

1 The subject that I am about to discuss is most
philosophical, that is, whether devout reason
is sovereign over the emotions. So it is right for
me to advise you to pay earnest attention to philosophy. 2 For the subject is essential to everyone
who is seeking knowledge, and in addition it includes the praise of the highest virtue—I mean,
of course, rational judgment. 3 If, then, it is evident that reason rules over those emotions that
hinder self-control, namely, gluttony and lust, 4 it
is also clear that it masters the emotions that hinder one from justice, such as malice, and those
that stand in the way of courage, namely anger,
fear, and pain. 5 Some might perhaps ask, "If reason rules the emotions, why is it not sovereign
over forgetfulness and ignorance?" Their attempt
at argument is ridiculous![a] 6 For reason does not
rule its own emotions, but those that are opposed
to justice, courage, and self-control;[b] and it is not
for the purpose of destroying them, but so that
one may not give way to them.

7 I could prove to you from many and various examples that reason[c] is dominant over the
emotions, 8 but I can demonstrate it best from the
noble bravery of those who died for the sake of
virtue, Eleazar and the seven brothers and their
mother. 9 All of these, by despising sufferings that
bring death, demonstrated that reason controls
the emotions. 10 On this anniversary[d] it is fitting
for me to praise for their virtues those who, with
their mother, died for the sake of nobility and
goodness, but I would also call them blessed
for the honor in which they are held. 11 All people, even their torturers, marveled at their courage and endurance, and they became the cause
of the downfall of tyranny over their nation. By
their endurance they conquered the tyrant, and
thus their native land was purified through them.
12 I shall shortly have an opportunity to speak of
this; but, as my custom is, I shall begin by stating
my main principle, and then I shall turn to their
story, giving glory to the all-wise God.

13 Our inquiry, accordingly, is whether reason is sovereign over the emotions. 14 We shall decide just what reason is and what emotion is, how
many kinds of emotions there are, and whether
reason rules over all these. 15 Now reason is the
mind that with sound logic prefers the life of wisdom. 16 Wisdom, next, is the knowledge of divine and human matters and the causes of these.
17 This, in turn, is education in the law, by which
we learn divine matters reverently and human
affairs to our advantage. 18 Now the kinds of wisdom are rational judgment, justice, courage, and
self-control. 19 Rational judgment is supreme over
all of these, since by means of it reason rules over
the emotions. 20 The two most comprehensive
types[e] of the emotions are pleasure and pain; and
each of these is by nature concerned with both
body and soul. 21 The emotions of both pleasure
and pain have many consequences. 22 Thus desire
precedes pleasure and delight follows it. 23 Fear
precedes pain and sorrow comes after. 24 Anger,
as a person will see by reflecting on this experience, is an emotion embracing pleasure and
pain. 25 In pleasure there exists even a malevolent
tendency, which is the most complex of all the
emotions. 26 In the soul it is boastfulness, covetousness, thirst for honor, rivalry, and malice; 27 in
the body, indiscriminate eating, gluttony, and solitary gormandizing.

28 Just as pleasure and pain are two plants
growing from the body and the soul, so there are
many offshoots of these plants,[f] 29 each of which
the master cultivator, reason, weeds and prunes
and ties up and waters and thoroughly irrigates,
and so tames the jungle of habits and emotions.
30 For reason is the guide of the virtues, but over
the emotions it is sovereign.

Observe now, first of all, that rational judgment is sovereign over the emotions by virtue
of the restraining power of self-control. 31 Self-
control, then, is dominance over the desires.
32 Some desires are mental, others are physical,
and reason obviously rules over both. 33 Otherwise, how is it that when we are attracted to

[a] Or *They are attempting to make my argument ridiculous!* [b] Other ancient authorities add *and rational judgment*
[c] Other ancient authorities read *devout reason* [d] Gk *At this time* [e] Or *sources*
[f] Other ancient authorities read *these emotions*

forbidden foods we abstain from the pleasure to
be had from them? Is it not because reason is able
to rule over appetites? I for one think so. 34There-
fore when we crave seafood and fowl and animals
and all sorts of foods that are forbidden to us by
the law, we abstain because of domination by reason. 35For the emotions of the appetites are restrained, checked by the temperate mind, and all
the impulses of the body are bridled by reason.

2 And why is it amazing that the desires of the
mind for the enjoyment of beauty are rendered powerless? 2It is for this reason, certainly,
that the temperate Joseph is praised, because by
mental effort[a] he overcame sexual desire. 3For
when he was young and in his prime for intercourse, by his reason he nullified the frenzy[b] of
the passions. 4Not only is reason proved to rule
over the frenzied urge of sexual desire, but also
over every desire.[c] 5Thus the law says, "You shall
not covet your neighbor's wife or anything that is
your neighbor's." 6In fact, since the law has told
us not to covet, I could prove to you all the more
that reason is able to control desires.

Just so it is with the emotions that hinder one
from justice. 7Otherwise how could it be that someone who is habitually a solitary gormandizer,
a glutton, or even a drunkard can learn a better
way, unless reason is clearly lord of the emotions?
8Thus, as soon as one adopts a way of life in accordance with the law, even though a lover of money,
one is forced to act contrary to natural ways and
to lend without interest to the needy and to cancel the debt when the seventh year arrives. 9If one
is greedy, one is ruled by the law through reason
so that one neither gleans the harvest nor gathers
the last grapes from the vineyard.

In all other matters we can recognize that reason rules the emotions. 10For the law prevails
even over affection for parents, so that virtue is
not abandoned for their sakes. 11It is superior to
love for one's wife, so that one rebukes her when
she breaks the law. 12It takes precedence over
love for children, so that one punishes them for
misdeeds. 13It is sovereign over the relationship
of friends, so that one rebukes friends when they
act wickedly. 14Do not consider it paradoxical
when reason, through the law, can prevail even
over enmity. The fruit trees of the enemy are not
cut down, but one preserves the property of enemies from marauders and helps raise up what has
fallen.[d]

15 It is evident that reason rules even[e] the
more violent emotions: lust for power, vainglory,
boasting, arrogance, and malice. 16For the temperate mind repels all these malicious emotions,
just as it repels anger—for it is sovereign over even
this. 17When Moses was angry with Dathan and
Abiram, he did nothing against them in anger, but
controlled his anger by reason. 18For, as I have
said, the temperate mind is able to get the better
of the emotions, to correct some, and to render
others powerless. 19Why else did Jacob, our most
wise father, censure the households of Simeon
and Levi for their irrational slaughter of the entire tribe of the Shechemites, saying, "Cursed be
their anger"? 20For if reason could not control anger, he would not have spoken thus. 21Now when
God fashioned human beings, he planted in them
emotions and inclinations, 22but at the same time
he enthroned the mind among the senses as a sacred governor over them all. 23To the mind he
gave the law; and one who lives subject to this
will rule a kingdom that is temperate, just, good,
and courageous.

24 How is it then, one might say, that if reason is master of the emotions, it does not control

3 forgetfulness and ignorance? 1But this argument is entirely ridiculous; for it is evident
that reason rules not over its own emotions, but
over those of the body. 2No one of us[f] can eradicate that kind of desire, but reason can provide a
way for us not to be enslaved by desire. 3No one
of us can eradicate anger from the mind, but reason can help to deal with anger. 4No one of us
can eradicate malice, but reason can fight at our
side so that we are not overcome by malice. 5For
reason does not uproot the emotions but is their
antagonist.

[a] Other ancient authorities add *in reasoning* [b] Or *gadfly* [c] Or *all covetousness* [d] Or *the beasts that have fallen*
[e] Other ancient authorities read *through* [f] Gk *you*

6 Now this can be explained more clearly by
the story of King David's thirst. 7David had been
attacking the Philistines all day long, and together
with the soldiers of his nation had killed many of
them. 8Then when evening fell, he[a] came, sweat-
ing and quite exhausted, to the royal tent, around
which the whole army of our ancestors had encamped. 9Now all the rest were at supper, 10but
the king was extremely thirsty, and though springs
were plentiful there, he could not satisfy his thirst
from them. 11But a certain irrational desire for the
water in the enemy's territory tormented and inflamed him, undid and consumed him. 12When his
guards complained bitterly because of the king's
craving, two staunch young soldiers, respecting[b]
the king's desire, armed themselves fully, and taking a pitcher climbed over the enemy's ramparts.
13Eluding the sentinels at the gates, they went
searching throughout the enemy camp 14and
found the spring, and from it boldly brought the
king a drink. 15But David,[c] though he was burning with thirst, considered it an altogether fearful
danger to his soul to drink what was regarded as
equivalent to blood. 16Therefore, opposing reason
to desire, he poured out the drink as an offering to
God. 17For the temperate mind can conquer the
drives of the emotions and quench the flames of
frenzied desires; 18it can overthrow bodily agonies even when they are extreme, and by nobility
of reason spurn all domination by the emotions.

19 The present occasion now invites us to a
narrative demonstration of temperate reason.

20 At a time when our ancestors were enjoying profound peace because of their observance
of the law and were prospering, so that even
Seleucus Nicanor, king of Asia, had both appropriated money to them for the temple service
and recognized their commonwealth— 21just at
that time certain persons attempted a revolution
against the public harmony and caused many and
various disasters.

4 Now there was a certain Simon, a political
opponent of the noble and good man, Onias,
who then held the high priesthood for life. When
despite all manner of slander he was unable to injure Onias in the eyes of the nation, he fled the
country with the purpose of betraying it. 2So he
came to Apollonius, governor of Syria, Phoenicia,
and Cilicia, and said, 3"I have come here because
I am loyal to the king's government, to report
that in the Jerusalem treasuries there are deposited tens of thousands in private funds, which are
not the property of the temple but belong to King
Seleucus." 4When Apollonius learned the details
of these things, he praised Simon for his service
to the king and went up to Seleucus to inform
him of the rich treasure. 5On receiving authority
to deal with this matter, he proceeded quickly to
our country accompanied by the accursed Simon
and a very strong military force. 6He said that he
had come with the king's authority to seize the
private funds in the treasury. 7The people indig-
nantly protested his words, considering it outrageous that those who had committed deposits to
the sacred treasury should be deprived of them,
and did all that they could to prevent it. 8But, uttering threats, Apollonius went on to the temple.
9While the priests together with women and children were imploring God in the temple to shield
the holy place that was being treated so contemptuously, 10and while Apollonius was going up
with his armed forces to seize the money, angels
on horseback with lightning flashing from their
weapons appeared from heaven, instilling in them
great fear and trembling. 11Then Apollonius fell
down half dead in the temple area that was open
to all, stretched out his hands toward heaven, and
with tears begged the Hebrews to pray for him
and propitiate the wrath of the heavenly army.
12For he said that he had committed a sin deserving of death, and that if he were spared he would
praise the blessedness of the holy place before all
people. 13Moved by these words, the high priest
Onias, although otherwise he had scruples about
doing so, prayed for him so that King Seleucus
would not suppose that Apollonius had been
overcome by human treachery and not by divine justice. 14So Apollonius,[a] having been saved

[a] Other ancient authorities read *he hurried and* [b] Or *embarrassed because of* [c] Gk *he*

beyond all expectations, went away to report to the king what had happened to him.

15 When King Seleucus died, his son Antiochus Epiphanes succeeded to the throne, an arrogant and terrible man, 16who removed Onias from the priesthood and appointed Onias's[b] brother Jason as high priest. 17Jason[c] agreed that if the office were conferred on him he would pay the king three thousand six hundred sixty talents annually. 18So the king appointed him high priest and ruler of the nation. 19Jason[c] changed the nation's way of life and altered its form of government in complete violation of the law, 20so that not only was a gymnasium constructed at the very citadel[d] of our native land, but also the temple service was abolished. 21The divine justice was angered by these acts and caused Antiochus himself to make war on them. 22For when he was warring against Ptolemy in Egypt, he heard that a rumor of his death had spread and that the people of Jerusalem had rejoiced greatly. He speedily marched against them, 23and after he had plundered them he issued a decree that if any of them were found observing the ancestral law they should die. 24When, by means of his decrees, he had not been able in any way to put an end to the people's observance of the law, but saw that all his threats and punishments were being disregarded 25—even to the extent that women, because they had circumcised their sons, were thrown headlong from heights along with their infants, though they had known beforehand that they would suffer this— 26when, I say, his decrees were despised by the people, he himself tried through torture to compel everyone in the nation to eat defiling foods and to renounce Judaism.

5 The tyrant Antiochus, sitting in state with his counselors on a certain high place, and with his armed soldiers standing around him, 2ordered the guards to seize each and every Hebrew and to compel them to eat pork and food sacrificed to idols. 3If any were not willing to eat defiling food, they were to be broken on the wheel and killed. 4When many persons had been rounded up, one man, Eleazar by name, leader of the flock, was brought[e] before the king. He was a man of priestly family, learned in the law, advanced in age, and known to many in the tyrant's court because of his philosophy.[f]

4 Maccabees 5:5

The dialogues between the Greek tyrant and the faithful Jews whom he will torture to death revolve around whether "the religion of the Jews" is reasonable, pious, and appropriate. Repeatedly the king charges that it is neither; repeatedly the martyrs respond that it is the tyrant's idolatrous religion that is irrational, impious, and shameful. Their articulate defiance here helps to define the genre of later Jewish and Christian martyrological literature for centuries to come.

— NE

5 When Antiochus saw him he said, 6"Before I begin to torture you, old man, I would advise you to save yourself by eating pork, 7for I respect your age and your gray hairs. Although you have had them for so long a time, it does not seem to me that you are a philosopher when you observe the religion of the Jews. 8When nature has granted it to us, why should you abhor eating the very excellent meat of this animal? 9It is senseless not to enjoy delicious things that are not shameful, and wrong to spurn the gifts of nature. 10It seems to me that you will do something even more senseless if, by holding a vain opinion concerning the truth, you continue to despise me to your own hurt. 11Will you not awaken from your foolish philosophy, dispel your futile reasonings, adopt a mind appropriate to your years, philosophize according to the truth of what is beneficial, 12and have compassion on your old age by honoring my humane advice? 13For consider this: if there is some power watching over this religion of yours, it will excuse you from any transgression that arises out of compulsion."

[a] Gk *he* [b] Gk *his* [c] Gk *He* [d] Or *high place* [e] Or *was the first of the flock to be brought*
[f] Other ancient authorities read *his advanced age*

14 When the tyrant urged him in this fashion to eat meat unlawfully, Eleazar asked to have
a word. 15When he had received permission to
speak, he began to address the people as follows:
16"We, O Antiochus, who have been persuaded
to govern our lives by the divine law, think that
there is no compulsion more powerful than our
obedience to the law. 17Therefore we consider
that we should not transgress it in any respect.
18Even if, as you suppose, our law were not truly
divine and we had wrongly held it to be divine,
not even so would it be right for us to invalidate
our reputation for piety. 19Therefore do not suppose that it would be a petty sin if we were to eat
defiling food; 20to transgress the law in matters
either small or great is of equal seriousness, 21for
in either case the law is equally despised. 22You
scoff at our philosophy as though living by it were
irrational, 23but it teaches us self-control, so that
we master all pleasures and desires, and it also
trains us in courage, so that we endure any suffering willingly; 24it instructs us in justice, so that in
all our dealings we act impartially,[a] and it teaches
us piety, so that with proper reverence we worship the only living God.

25 "Therefore we do not eat defiling food;
for since we believe that the law was established
by God, we know that in the nature of things
the Creator of the world in giving us the law has
shown sympathy toward us. 26He has permitted
us to eat what will be most suitable for our lives,[b]
but he has forbidden us to eat meats that would
be contrary to this. 27It would be tyrannical for
you to compel us not only to transgress the law,
but also to eat in such a way that you may deride
us for eating defiling foods, which are most hateful to us. 28But you shall have no such occasion
to laugh at me, 29nor will I transgress the sacred
oaths of my ancestors concerning the keeping
of the law, 30not even if you gouge out my eyes
and burn my entrails. 31I am not so old and cowardly as not to be young in reason on behalf of
piety. 32Therefore get your torture wheels ready
and fan the fire more vehemently! 33I do not so
pity my old age as to break the ancestral law by
my own act. 34I will not play false to you, O law
that trained me, nor will I renounce you, beloved
self-control. 35I will not put you to shame, philosophical reason, nor will I reject you, honored
priesthood and knowledge of the law. 36You,
O king,[c] shall not defile the honorable mouth
of my old age, nor my long life lived lawfully.
37My ancestors will receive me as pure, as one
who does not fear your violence even to death.
38You may tyrannize the ungodly, but you shall
not dominate my religious principles, either by
words or through deeds."

6 When Eleazar in this manner had made eloquent response to the exhortations of the
tyrant, the guards who were standing by dragged
him violently to the instruments of torture. 2First
they stripped the old man, though he remained
adorned with the gracefulness of his piety. 3After
they had tied his arms on each side they flogged
him, 4while a herald who faced him cried out,
"Obey the king's commands!" 5But the courageous and noble man, like a true Eleazar, was unmoved, as though being tortured in a dream; 6yet
while the old man's eyes were raised to heaven,
his flesh was being torn by scourges, his blood
flowing, and his sides were being cut to pieces.
7Although he fell to the ground because his body
could not endure the agonies, he kept his reason
upright and unswerving. 8One of the cruel guards
rushed at him and began to kick him in the side to
make him get up again after he fell. 9But he bore
the pains and scorned the punishment and endured the tortures. 10Like a noble athlete the old
man, while being beaten, was victorious over his
torturers; 11in fact, with his face bathed in sweat,
and gasping heavily for breath, he amazed even
his torturers by his courageous spirit.

12 At that point, partly out of pity for his
old age, 13partly out of sympathy from their acquaintance with him, partly out of admiration for
his endurance, some of the king's retinue came
to him and said, 14"Eleazar, why are you so ir-
rationally destroying yourself through these evil
things? 15We will set before you some cooked
meat; save yourself by pretending to eat pork."

[a] Or *so that we hold in balance all our habitual inclinations* [b] Or *souls* [c] Gk lacks *O king*

16 But Eleazar, as though more bitterly tormented by this counsel, cried out: 17“Never may we, the children of Abraham,[a] think so basely that out of cowardice we feign a role unbecoming to us! 18For it would be irrational if having lived in accordance with truth up to old age and having maintained in accordance with law the reputation of such a life, we should now change our course 19and ourselves become a pattern of impiety to the young by setting them an example in the eating of defiling food. 20It would be shameful if we should survive for a little while and during that time be a laughingstock to all for our cowardice, 21and be despised by the tyrant as unmanly by not contending even to death for our divine law. 22Therefore, O children of Abraham, die nobly for your religion! 23And you, guards of the tyrant, why do you delay?”

24 When they saw that he was so courageous in the face of the afflictions, and that he had not been changed by their compassion, the guards brought him to the fire. 25There they burned him with maliciously contrived instruments, threw him down, and poured stinking liquids into his nostrils. 26When he was now burned to his very bones and about to expire, he lifted up his eyes to God and said, 27“You know, O God, that though I might have saved myself, I am dying in burning torments for the sake of the law. 28Be merciful to your people, and let our punishment suffice for them. 29Make my blood their purification, and take my life in exchange for theirs.” 30After he said this, the holy man died nobly in his tortures; even in the tortures of death he resisted, by virtue of reason, for the sake of the law.

31 Admittedly, then, devout reason is sovereign over the emotions. 32For if the emotions had prevailed over reason, we would have testified to their domination. 33But now that reason has conquered the emotions, we properly attribute to it the power to govern. 34It is right for us to acknowledge the dominance of reason when it masters even external agonies. It would be ridiculous to deny it.[b] 35I have proved not only that reason has mastered agonies, but also that it masters pleasures and in no respect yields to them.

7 For like a most skillful pilot, the reason of our father Eleazar steered the ship of religion over the sea of the emotions, 2and though buffeted by the stormings of the tyrant and overwhelmed by the mighty waves of tortures, 3in no way did he turn the rudder of religion until he sailed into the haven of immortal victory. 4No city besieged with many ingenious war machines has ever held out as did that most holy man. Although his sacred life was consumed by tortures and racks, he conquered the besiegers with the shield of his devout reason. 5For in setting his mind firm like a jutting cliff, our father Eleazar broke the maddening waves of the emotions. 6O priest, worthy of the priesthood, you neither defiled your sacred teeth nor profaned your stomach, which had room only for reverence and purity, by eating defiling foods. 7O man in harmony with the law and philosopher of divine life! 8Such should be those who are administrators of the law, shielding it with their own blood and noble sweat in sufferings even to death. 9You, father, strengthened our loyalty to the law through your glorious endurance, and you did not abandon the holiness that you praised, but by your deeds you made your words of divine[c] philosophy credible. 10O aged man, more powerful than tortures; O elder, fiercer than fire; O supreme king over the passions, Eleazar! 11For just as our father Aaron, armed with the censer, ran through the multitude of the people and conquered the fiery[d] angel, 12so the descendant of Aaron, Eleazar, though being consumed by the fire, remained unmoved in his reason. 13Most amazing, indeed, though he was an old man, his body no longer tense and firm,[e] his muscles flabby, his sinews feeble, he became young again 14in spirit through reason; and by reason like that of Isaac he rendered the many-headed rack ineffective. 15O man of blessed age and of venerable gray hair and of law-abiding life, whom the faithful seal of death has perfected!

16 If, therefore, because of piety an aged

[a] Or *O children of Abraham* [b] Syr: Meaning of Gk uncertain [c] Other ancient authorities lack *divine* [d] Other ancient authorities lack *fiery* [e] Gk *the tautness of the body already loosed*

man despised tortures even to death, most certainly devout reason is governor of the emotions. [17]Some perhaps might say, "Not all have full command of their emotions, because not all have prudent reason." [18]But as many as attend to religion with a whole heart, these alone are able to control the passions of the flesh, [19]since they believe that they, like our patriarchs Abraham and Isaac and Jacob, do not die to God, but live to God. [20]No contradiction therefore arises when some persons appear to be dominated by their emotions because of the weakness of their reason. [21]What person who lives as a philosopher by the whole rule of philosophy, and trusts in God, [22]and knows that it is blessed to endure any suffering for the sake of virtue, would not be able to overcome the emotions through godliness? [23]For only the wise and courageous are masters of their emotions.

8 For this is why even the very young, by following a philosophy in accordance with devout reason, have prevailed over the most painful instruments of torture. [2]For when the tyrant was conspicuously defeated in his first attempt, being unable to compel an aged man to eat defiling foods, then in violent rage he commanded that others of the Hebrew captives be brought, and that any who ate defiling food would be freed after eating, but if any were to refuse, they would be tortured even more cruelly.

3 When the tyrant had given these orders, seven brothers—handsome, modest, noble, and accomplished in every way—were brought before him along with their aged mother. [4]When the tyrant saw them, grouped about their mother as though a chorus, he was pleased with them. And struck by their appearance and nobility, he smiled at them, and summoned them nearer and said, [5]"Young men, with favorable feelings I admire each and every one of you, and greatly respect the beauty and the number of such brothers. Not only do I advise you not to display the same madness as that of the old man who has just been tortured, but I also exhort you to yield to me and enjoy my friendship. [6]Just as I am able to punish those who disobey my orders, so I can be a benefactor to those who obey me. [7]Trust me, then, and you will have positions of authority in my government if you will renounce the ancestral tradition of your national life. [8]Enjoy your youth by adopting the Greek way of life and by changing your manner of living. [9]But if by disobedience you rouse my anger, you will compel me to destroy each and every one of you with dreadful punishments through tortures. [10]Therefore take pity on yourselves. Even I, your enemy, have compassion for your youth and handsome appearance. [11]Will you not consider this, that if you disobey, nothing remains for you but to die on the rack?"

12 When he had said these things, he ordered the instruments of torture to be brought forward so as to persuade them out of fear to eat the defiling food. [13]When the guards had placed before them wheels and joint-dislocators, rack and hooks[a] and catapults[b] and caldrons, braziers and thumbscrews and iron claws and wedges and bellows, the tyrant resumed speaking: [14]"Be afraid, young fellows; whatever justice you revere will be merciful to you when you transgress under compulsion."

15 But when they had heard the inducements and saw the dreadful devices, not only were they not afraid, but they also opposed the tyrant with their own philosophy, and by their right reasoning nullified his tyranny. [16]Let us consider, on the other hand, what arguments might have been used if some of them had been cowardly and unmanly. Would they not have been the following? [17]"O wretches that we are and so senseless! Since the king has summoned and exhorted us to accept kind treatment if we obey him, [18]why do we take pleasure in vain resolves and venture upon a disobedience that brings death? [19]O men and brothers, should we not fear the instruments of torture and consider the threats of torments, and give up this vain opinion and this arrogance that threatens to destroy us? [20]Let us take pity on our youth and have compassion on our mother's age; [21]and let us seriously consider that if we disobey

[a] Meaning of Gk uncertain [b] Here and elsewhere in 4 Macc an instrument of torture

we are dead! 22 Also, divine justice will excuse us for fearing the king when we are under compulsion. 23 Why do we banish ourselves from this most pleasant life and deprive ourselves of this delightful world? 24 Let us not struggle against compulsion[a] or take hollow pride in being put to the rack. 25 Not even the law itself would arbitrarily put us to death for fearing the instruments of torture. 26 Why does such contentiousness excite us and such a fatal stubbornness please us, when we can live in peace if we obey the king?"

27 But the youths, though about to be tortured, neither said any of these things nor even seriously considered them. 28 For they were contemptuous of the emotions and sovereign over agonies, 29 so that as soon as the tyrant had ceased counseling them to eat defiling food, all with one voice together, as from one mind, said:

9 "Why do you delay, O tyrant? For we are ready to die rather than transgress our ancestral commandments; 2 we are obviously putting our forebears to shame unless we should practice ready obedience to the law and to Moses[b] our counselor. 3 Tyrant and counselor of lawlessness, in your hatred for us do not pity us more than we pity ourselves.[c] 4 For we consider this pity of yours, which insures our safety through transgression of the law, to be more grievous than death itself. 5 You are trying to terrify us by threatening us with death by torture, as though a short time ago you learned nothing from Eleazar. 6 And if the aged men of the Hebrews because of their religion lived piously[d] while enduring torture, it would be even more fitting that we young men should die despising your coercive tortures, which our aged instructor also overcame. 7 Therefore, tyrant, put us to the test; and if you take our lives because of our religion, do not suppose that you can injure us by torturing us. 8 For we, through this severe suffering and endurance, shall have the prize of virtue and shall be with God, on whose account we suffer; 9 but you, because of your bloodthirstiness toward us, will deservedly undergo from the divine justice eternal torment by fire."

10 When they had said these things, the tyrant was not only indignant, as at those who are disobedient, but also infuriated, as at those who are ungrateful. 11 Then at his command the guards brought forward the eldest, and having torn off his tunic, they bound his hands and arms with thongs on each side. 12 When they had worn themselves out beating him with scourges, without accomplishing anything, they placed him upon the wheel. 13 When the noble youth was stretched out around this, his limbs were dislocated, 14 and with every member disjointed he denounced the tyrant, saying, 15 "Most abominable tyrant, enemy of heavenly justice, savage of mind, you are mangling me in this manner, not because I am a murderer, or as one who acts impiously, but because I protect the divine law." 16 And when the guards said, "Agree to eat so that you may be released from the tortures," 17 he replied, "You abominable lackeys, your wheel is not so powerful as to strangle my reason. Cut my limbs, burn my flesh, and twist my joints; 18 through all these tortures I will convince you that children of the Hebrews alone are invincible where virtue is concerned." 19 While he was saying these things, they spread fire under him, and while fanning the flames[c] they tightened the wheel further. 20 The wheel was completely smeared with blood, and the heap of coals was being quenched by the drippings of gore, and pieces of flesh were falling off the axles of the machine. 21 Although the ligaments joining his bones were already severed, the courageous youth, worthy of Abraham, did not groan, 22 but as though transformed by fire into immortality, he nobly endured the rackings. 23 "Imitate me, brothers," he said. "Do not leave your post in my struggle[e] or renounce our courageous family ties. 24 Fight the sacred and noble battle for religion. Thereby the just Providence of our ancestors may become merciful to our nation and take vengeance on the accursed tyrant." 25 When he had said this, the saintly youth broke the thread of life.

26 While all were marveling at his courageous

[a] Or *fate* [b] Other ancient authorities read *knowledge* [c] Meaning of Gk uncertain [d] Other ancient authorities read *died*
[e] Other ancient authorities read *post forever*

spirit, the guards brought in the next eldest, and
after fitting themselves with iron gauntlets having
sharp hooks, they bound him to the torture machine and catapult. 27Before torturing him, they
inquired if he were willing to eat, and they heard
his noble decision.[a] 28These leopard-like beasts
tore out his sinews with the iron hands, flayed all
his flesh up to his chin, and tore away his scalp.
But he steadfastly endured this agony and said,
29"How sweet is any kind of death for the religion
of our ancestors!" 30To the tyrant he said, "Do
you not think, you most savage tyrant, that you
are being tortured more than I, as you see the arrogant design of your tyranny being defeated by
our endurance for the sake of religion? 31I lighten
my pain by the joys that come from virtue, 32but
you suffer torture by the threats that come from
impiety. You will not escape, you most abominable tyrant, the judgments of the divine wrath."

10 When he too had endured a glorious
death, the third was led in, and many repeatedly urged him to save himself by tasting the
meat. 2But he shouted, "Do you not know that
the same father begot me as well as those who
died, and the same mother bore me, and that I
was brought up on the same teachings? 3I do not
renounce the noble kinship that binds me to my
brothers."[b] 5Enraged by the man's boldness, they
disjointed his hands and feet with their instruments, dismembering him by prying his limbs
from their sockets, 6and breaking his fingers and
arms and legs and elbows. 7Since they were not
able in any way to break his spirit,[c] they abandoned the instruments[d] and scalped him with
their fingernails in a Scythian fashion. 8They immediately brought him to the wheel, and while
his vertebrae were being dislocated by this, he
saw his own flesh torn all around and drops of
blood flowing from his entrails. 9When he was
about to die, he said, 10"We, most abominable
tyrant, are suffering because of our godly training and virtue, 11but you, because of your impiety
and bloodthirstiness, will undergo unceasing torments."

12 When he too had died in a manner worthy
of his brothers, they dragged in the fourth, saying, 13"As for you, do not give way to the same
insanity as your brothers, but obey the king and
save yourself." 14But he said to them, "You do
not have a fire hot enough to make me play the
coward. 15No—by the blessed death of my brothers, by the eternal destruction of the tyrant, and
by the everlasting life of the pious, I will not renounce our noble family ties. 16Contrive tortures, tyrant, so that you may learn from them
that I am a brother to those who have just now
been tortured." 17When he heard this, the bloodthirsty, murderous, and utterly abominable Antiochus gave orders to cut out his tongue. 18But
he said, "Even if you remove my organ of speech,
God hears also those who are mute. 19See, here is
my tongue; cut it off, for in spite of this you will
not make our reason speechless. 20Gladly, for the
sake of God, we let our bodily members be mutilated. 21God will visit you swiftly, for you are cutting out a tongue that has been melodious with
divine hymns."

11 When he too died, after being cruelly tortured, the fifth leaped up, saying, 2"I will
not refuse, tyrant, to be tortured for the sake of
virtue. 3I have come of my own accord, so that by
murdering me you will incur punishment from
the heavenly justice for even more crimes. 4Hater
of virtue, hater of humankind, for what act of ours
are you destroying us in this way? 5Is it because[e]
we revere the Creator of all things and live according to his virtuous law? 6But these deeds deserve
honors, not tortures."[f] 9While he was saying these
things, the guards bound him and dragged him to
the catapult; 10they tied him to it on his knees,
and fitting iron clamps on them, they twisted his
back[g] around the wedge on the wheel,[h] so that he

[a] Other ancient authorities read *having heard his noble decision, they tore him to shreds* [b] Other ancient authorities add verse 4, *So if you have any instrument of torture, apply it to my body; for you cannot touch my soul, even if you wish."* [c] Gk *to strangle him* [d] Other ancient authorities read *they tore off his skin* [e] Other ancient authorities read *Or does it seem evil to you that* [f] Other authorities add verses 7 and 8, 7*If you but understood human feelings and had hope of salvation from God—* 8*but, as it is, you are a stranger to God and persecute those who serve him."* [g] Gk *loins* [h] Meaning of Gk uncertain

was completely curled back like a scorpion, and
all his members were disjointed. 11 In this condition, gasping for breath and in anguish of body,
12 he said, "Tyrant, they are splendid favors that
you grant us against your will, because through
these noble sufferings you give us an opportunity
to show our endurance for the law."

13 When he too had died, the sixth, a mere
boy, was led in. When the tyrant inquired whether
he was willing to eat and be released, he said, 14 "I
am younger in age than my brothers, but I am
their equal in mind. 15 Since to this end we were
born and bred, we ought likewise to die for the
same principles. 16 So if you intend to torture me
for not eating defiling foods, go on torturing!"
17 When he had said this, they led him to the
wheel. 18 He was carefully stretched tight upon
it, his back was broken, and he was roasted[a] from
underneath. 19 To his back they applied sharp
spits that had been heated in the fire, and pierced
his ribs so that his entrails were burned through.
20 While being tortured he said, "O contest befitting holiness, in which so many of us brothers
have been summoned to an arena of sufferings
for religion, and in which we have not been defeated! 21 For religious knowledge, O tyrant, is
invincible. 22 I also, equipped with nobility, will
die with my brothers, 23 and I myself will bring a
great avenger upon you, you inventor of tortures
and enemy of those who are truly devout. 24 We
six boys have paralyzed your tyranny. 25 Since you
have not been able to persuade us to change our
mind or to force us to eat defiling foods, is not
this your downfall? 26 Your fire is cold to us, and
the catapults painless, and your violence powerless. 27 For it is not the guards of the tyrant but
those of the divine law that are set over us; therefore, unconquered, we hold fast to reason."

12 When he too, thrown into the caldron,
had died a blessed death, the seventh
and youngest of all came forward. 2 Even though
the tyrant had been vehemently reproached by
the brothers, he felt strong compassion for this
child when he saw that he was already in fetters.
He summoned him to come nearer and tried to
persuade him, saying, 3 "You see the result of your
brothers' stupidity, for they died in torments because of their disobedience. 4 You too, if you do
not obey, will be miserably tortured and die before your time, 5 but if you yield to persuasion
you will be my friend and a leader in the government of the kingdom." 6 When he had thus
appealed to him, he sent for the boy's mother to
show compassion on her who had been bereaved
of so many sons and to influence her to persuade
the surviving son to obey and save himself. 7 But
when his mother had exhorted him in the Hebrew language, as we shall tell a little later, 8 he
said, "Let me loose, let me speak to the king and
to all his friends that are with him." 9 Extremely
pleased by the boy's declaration, they freed him
at once. 10 Running to the nearest of the braziers,
11 he said, "You profane tyrant, most impious of all
the wicked, since you have received good things
and also your kingdom from God, were you not
ashamed to murder his servants and torture on
the wheel those who practice religion? 12 Because
of this, justice has laid up for you intense and
eternal fire and tortures, and these throughout all
time[b] will never let you go. 13 As a man, were you
not ashamed, you most savage beast, to cut out
the tongues of men who have feelings like yours
and are made of the same elements as you, and to
maltreat and torture them in this way? 14 Surely
they by dying nobly fulfilled their service to God,
but you will wail bitterly for having killed without
cause the contestants for virtue." 15 Then because
he too was about to die, he said, 16 "I do not desert
the excellent example[c] of my brothers, 17 and I call
on the God of our ancestors to be merciful to our
nation;[d] 18 but on you he will take vengeance both
in this present life and when you are dead." 19 After he had uttered these imprecations, he flung
himself into the braziers and so ended his life.[e]

13 Since, then, the seven brothers despised
sufferings even unto death, everyone
must concede that devout reason is sovereign
over the emotions. 2 For if they had been slaves

[a] Other ancient authorities add *by fire* [b] Gk *throughout the whole age* [c] Other ancient authorities read *the witness*
[d] Other ancient authorities read *my race* [e] Gk *and so gave up*; other ancient authorities read *gave up his spirit* or *his soul*

to their emotions and had eaten defiling food, we
would say that they had been conquered by these
emotions. 3 But in fact it was not so. Instead, by
reason, which is praised before God, they prevailed over their emotions. 4 The supremacy of
the mind over these cannot be overlooked, for
the brothers[a] mastered both emotions and pains.
5 How then can one fail to confess the sovereignty of right reason over emotion in those who
were not turned back by fiery agonies? 6 For just
as towers jutting out over harbors hold back the
threatening waves and make it calm for those who
sail into the inner basin, 7 so the seven-towered
right reason of the youths, by fortifying the harbor of religion, conquered the tempest of the
emotions. 8 For they constituted a holy chorus
of religion and encouraged one another, saying,
9 "Brothers, let us die like brothers for the sake of
the law; let us imitate the three youths in Assyria
who despised the same ordeal of the furnace.
10 Let us not be cowardly in the demonstration of
our piety." 11 While one said, "Courage, brother,"
another said, "Bear up nobly," 12 and another reminded them, "Remember whence you came,
and the father by whose hand Isaac would have
submitted to being slain for the sake of religion."
13 Each of them and all of them together looking
at one another, cheerful and undaunted, said,
"Let us with all our hearts consecrate ourselves
to God, who gave us our lives,[b] and let us use our
bodies as a bulwark for the law. 14 Let us not fear
him who thinks he is killing us, 15 for great is the
struggle of the soul and the danger of eternal torment lying before those who transgress the commandment of God. 16 Therefore let us put on the
full armor of self-control, which is divine reason.
17 For if we so die,[c] Abraham and Isaac and Jacob
will welcome us, and all the fathers will praise us."
18 Those who were left behind said to each of the
brothers who were being dragged away, "Do not
put us to shame, brother, or betray the brothers
who have died before us."

19 You are not ignorant of the affection of
family ties, which the divine and all-wise Providence has bequeathed through the fathers to
their descendants and which was implanted in
the mother's womb. 20 There each of the brothers spent the same length of time and was shaped
during the same period of time; and growing
from the same blood and through the same life,
they were brought to the light of day. 21 When they
were born after an equal time of gestation, they
drank milk from the same fountains. From such
embraces brotherly-loving souls are nourished;
22 and they grow stronger from this common
nurture and daily companionship, and from both
general education and our discipline in the law
of God.

23 Therefore, when sympathy and brotherly
affection had been so established, the brothers were the more sympathetic to one another.
24 Since they had been educated by the same law
and trained in the same virtues and brought up in
right living, they loved one another all the more.
25 A common zeal for nobility strengthened their
goodwill toward one another, and their concord,
26 because they could make their brotherly love
more fervent with the aid of their religion. 27 But
although nature and companionship and virtuous habits had augmented the affection of family
ties, those who were left endured for the sake of
religion, while watching their brothers being maltreated and tortured to death.

14 Furthermore, they encouraged them to
face the torture, so that they not only despised their agonies, but also mastered the emotions of brotherly love.

2 O reason,[d] more royal than kings and freer
than the free! 3 O sacred and harmonious concord
of the seven brothers on behalf of religion! 4 None
of the seven youths proved coward or shrank
from death, 5 but all of them, as though running
the course toward immortality, hastened to death
by torture. 6 Just as the hands and feet are moved
in harmony with the guidance of the mind, so
those holy youths, as though moved by an immortal spirit of devotion, agreed to go to death
for its sake. 7 O most holy seven, brothers in harmony! For just as the seven days of creation move
in choral dance around religion, 8 so these youths,

[a] Gk *they* [b] Or *souls* [c] Other ancient authorities read *suffer* [d] Or *O minds*

forming a chorus, encircled the sevenfold fear of
tortures and dissolved it. 9 Even now, we ourselves
shudder as we hear of the suffering of these young
men; they not only saw what was happening, not
only heard the direct word of threat, but also bore
the sufferings patiently, and in agonies of fire at
that. 10 What could be more excruciatingly painful than this? For the power of fire is intense and
swift, and it consumed their bodies quickly.

11 Do not consider it amazing that reason
had full command over these men in their tortures, since the mind of woman despised even
more diverse agonies, 12 for the mother of the
seven young men bore up under the rackings of
each one of her children.

13 Observe how complex is a mother's love
for her children, which draws everything toward
an emotion felt in her inmost parts. 14 Even unreasoning animals, as well as human beings, have
a sympathy and parental love for their offspring.
15 For example, among birds, the ones that are
tame protect their young by building on the
housetops, 16 and the others, by building at the
tops of mountains and the depths of chasms, in
holes of trees, and on tree-tops, hatch the nestlings and ward off the intruder. 17 If they are not
able to keep the intruder[a] away, they do what they
can to help their young by flying in circles around
them in the anguish of love, warning them with
their own calls. 18 And why is it necessary to demonstrate sympathy for children by the example
of unreasoning animals, 19 since even bees at the
time for making honeycombs defend themselves
against intruders and, as though with an iron dart,
sting those who approach their hive and defend it
even to the death? 20 But sympathy for her children did not sway the mother of the young men;
she was of the same mind as Abraham.

15 O reason of the children, tyrant over the
emotions! O religion, more desirable to
the mother than her children! 2 Two courses were
open to this mother, that of religion, and that of
preserving her seven sons for a time, as the tyrant
had promised. 3 She loved religion more, the religion that preserves them for eternal life according to God's promise.[b] 4 In what manner might I
express the emotions of parents who love their
children? We impress upon the character of a
small child a wondrous likeness both of mind
and of form. Especially is this true of mothers,
who because of their birth pangs have a deeper
sympathy toward their offspring than do the fathers. 5 Considering that mothers are the weaker
sex and give birth to many, they are more devoted
to their children.[c] 6 The mother of the seven boys,
more than any other mother, loved her children.
In seven pregnancies she had implanted in herself tender love toward them, 7 and because of the
many pains she suffered with each of them she
had sympathy for them; 8 yet because of the fear
of God she disdained the temporary safety of her
children. 9 Not only so, but also because of the
nobility of her sons and their ready obedience to
the law, she felt a greater tenderness toward them.
10 For they were righteous and self-controlled and
brave and magnanimous, and loved their brothers
and their mother, so that they obeyed her even to
death in keeping the ordinances.

11 Nevertheless, though so many factors influenced the mother to suffer with them out of
love for her children, in the case of none of them
were the various tortures strong enough to pervert her reason. 12 But each child separately and
all of them together the mother urged on to death
for religion's sake. 13 O sacred nature and affection of parental love, yearning of parents toward
offspring, nurture and indomitable suffering by
mothers! 14 This mother, who saw them tortured
and burned one by one, because of religion did
not change her attitude. 15 She watched the flesh
of her children being consumed by fire, their toes
and fingers scattered[d] on the ground, and the flesh
of the head to the chin exposed like masks.

16 O mother, tried now by more bitter pains
than even the birth pangs you suffered for them!
17 O woman, who alone gave birth to such complete devotion! 18 When the firstborn breathed
his last, it did not turn you aside, nor when the

[a] Gk *it* [b] Gk *according to God* [c] Or *For to the degree that mothers are weaker and the more children they bear, the more they are devoted to their children.* [d] Or *quivering*

second in torments looked at you piteously nor
when the third expired; 19 nor did you weep when
you looked at the eyes of each one in his tortures
gazing boldly at the same agonies, and saw in
their nostrils the signs of the approach of death.
20 When you saw the flesh of children burned
upon the flesh of other children, severed hands
upon hands, scalped heads upon heads, and
corpses fallen on other corpses, and when you
saw the place filled with many spectators of the
torturings, you did not shed tears. 21 Neither the
melodies of sirens nor the songs of swans attract
the attention of their hearers as did the voices of
the children in torture calling to their mother.
22 How great and how many torments the mother
then suffered as her sons were tortured on the
wheel and with the hot irons! 23 But devout reason, giving her heart a man's courage in the very
midst of her emotions, strengthened her to disregard, for the time, her parental love.

24 Although she witnessed the destruction
of seven children and the ingenious and various
rackings, this noble mother disregarded all these[a]
because of faith in God. 25 For as in the council
chamber of her own soul she saw mighty advocates—nature, family, parental love, and the rackings of her children— 26 this mother held two
ballots, one bearing death and the other deliverance for her children. 27 She did not approve the
deliverance that would preserve the seven sons
for a short time, 28 but as the daughter of God-
fearing Abraham she remembered his fortitude.

29 O mother of the nation, vindicator of the
law and champion of religion, who carried away
the prize of the contest in your heart! 30 O more
noble than males in steadfastness, and more courageous than men in endurance! 31 Just as Noah's
ark, carrying the world in the universal flood,
stoutly endured the waves, 32 so you, O guardian
of the law, overwhelmed from every side by the
flood of your emotions and the violent winds,
the torture of your sons, endured nobly and withstood the wintry storms that assail religion.

16 If, then, a woman, advanced in years and
mother of seven sons, endured seeing
her children tortured to death, it must be admitted that devout reason is sovereign over the
emotions. 2 Thus I have demonstrated not only
that men have ruled over the emotions, but also
that a woman has despised the fiercest tortures.
3 The lions surrounding Daniel were not so savage, nor was the raging fiery furnace of Mishael so
intensely hot, as was her innate parental love, inflamed as she saw her seven sons tortured in such
varied ways. 4 But the mother quenched so many
and such great emotions by devout reason.

5 Consider this also: If this woman, though
a mother, had been fainthearted, she would have
mourned over them and perhaps spoken as follows: 6 "O how wretched am I and many times
unhappy! After bearing seven children, I am
now the mother of none! 7 O seven childbirths
all in vain, seven profitless pregnancies, fruitless
nurturings and wretched nursings! 8 In vain, my
sons, I endured many birth pangs for you, and the
more grievous anxieties of your upbringing. 9 Alas
for my children, some unmarried, others married
and without offspring.[b] I shall not see your children or have the happiness of being called grandmother. 10 Alas, I who had so many and beautiful
children am a widow and alone, with many sorrows.[c] 11 And when I die, I shall have none of my
sons to bury me."

12 Yet that holy and God-fearing mother did
not wail with such a lament for any of them, nor
did she dissuade any of them from dying, nor did
she grieve as they were dying. 13 On the contrary,
as though having a mind like adamant and giving rebirth for immortality to the whole number
of her sons, she implored them and urged them
on to death for the sake of religion. 14 O mother,
soldier of God in the cause of religion, elder and
woman! By steadfastness you have conquered
even a tyrant, and in word and deed you have
proved more powerful than a man. 15 For when
you and your sons were arrested together, you
stood and watched Eleazar being tortured, and
said to your sons in the Hebrew language, 16 "My
sons, noble is the contest to which you are called
to bear witness for the nation. Fight zealously for

[a] Other ancient authorities read *having bidden them farewell, surrendered them* [b] Gk *without benefit* [c] Or *much to be pitied*

our ancestral law. 17For it would be shameful if, while an aged man endures such agonies for the sake of religion, you young men were to be terrified by tortures. 18Remember that it is through God that you have had a share in the world and have enjoyed life, 19and therefore you ought to endure any suffering for the sake of God. 20For his sake also our father Abraham was zealous to sacrifice his son Isaac, the ancestor of our nation; and when Isaac saw his father's hand wielding a knife[a] and descending upon him, he did not cower. 21Daniel the righteous was thrown to the lions, and Hananiah, Azariah, and Mishael were hurled into the fiery furnace and endured it for the sake of God. 22You too must have the same faith in God and not be grieved. 23It is unreasonable for people who have religious knowledge not to withstand pain."

24 By these words the mother of the seven encouraged and persuaded each of her sons to die rather than violate God's commandment. 25They knew also that those who die for the sake of God live to God, as do Abraham and Isaac and Jacob and all the patriarchs.

17 Some of the guards said that when she also was about to be seized and put to death she threw herself into the flames so that no one might touch her body.

2 O mother, who with your seven sons nullified the violence of the tyrant, frustrated his evil designs, and showed the courage of your faith! 3Nobly set like a roof on the pillars of your sons, you held firm and unswerving against the earthquake of the tortures. 4Take courage, therefore, O holy-minded mother, maintaining firm an enduring hope in God. 5The moon in heaven, with the stars, does not stand so august as you, who, after lighting the way of your star-like seven sons to piety, stand in honor before God and are firmly set in heaven with them. 6For your children were true descendants of father Abraham.[b]

7 If it were possible for us to paint the history of your religion as an artist might, would not those who first beheld it have shuddered as they saw the mother of the seven children enduring their varied tortures to death for the sake of religion? 8Indeed it would be proper to inscribe on their tomb these words as a reminder to the people of our nation:[c]

9 "Here lie buried an aged priest and an aged woman and seven sons, because of the violence of the tyrant who wished to destroy the way of life of the Hebrews. 10They vindicated their nation, looking to God and enduring torture even to death."

11 Truly the contest in which they were engaged was divine, 12for on that day virtue gave the awards and tested them for their endurance. The prize was immortality in endless life. 13Eleazar was the first contestant, the mother of the seven sons entered the competition, and the brothers contended. 14The tyrant was the antagonist, and the world and the human race were the spectators. 15Reverence for God was victor and gave the crown to its own athletes. 16Who did not admire the athletes of the divine[d] legislation? Who were not amazed?

17 The tyrant himself and all his council marveled at their[e] endurance, 18because of which they now stand before the divine throne and live the life of eternal blessedness. 19For Moses says, "All who are consecrated are under your hands." 20These, then, who have been consecrated for the sake of God,[f] are honored, not only with this honor, but also by the fact that because of them our enemies did not rule over our nation, 21the tyrant was punished, and the homeland purified—they having become, as it were, a ransom for the sin of our nation. 22And through the blood of those devout ones and their death as an atoning sacrifice, divine Providence preserved Israel that previously had been mistreated.

23 For the tyrant Antiochus, when he saw the courage of their virtue and their endurance under the tortures, proclaimed them to his soldiers as an example for their own endurance, 24and this

[a] Gk *sword* [b] Gk *For your childbearing was from Abraham the father*; other ancient authorities read *For . . . Abraham the servant* [c] Or *as a memorial to the heroes of our people* [d] Other ancient authorities read *true* [e] Other ancient authorities add *virtue and* [f] Other ancient authorities lack *for the sake of God*

4 Maccabees 17:18-22

The martyrs not only defied the tyrant and demonstrated true philosophy, in the author's view; they also redeemed their homeland through their deaths as an "atoning sacrifice" (v. 22). The Greek word *hilastērion* is later used by New Testament authors to speak of Jesus' atoning death (see Rom 3:25; Heb 9:11-15; 1 Pet 1:19; 1 John 1:7). The antecedent in the story of the Maccabean martyrs suggests that atonement is achieved through the faithful obedience of the righteous (for the New Testament authors, Jesus: see Rom 3:22, where the Greek phrase translated "faith in Jesus Christ" might better be rendered "the faithfulness *of* Jesus Christ.")

— *NE*

made them brave and courageous for infantry battle and siege, and he ravaged and conquered all his enemies.

18 O Israelite children, offspring of the seed of Abraham, obey this law and exercise piety in every way, 2knowing that devout reason is master of all emotions, not only of sufferings from within, but also of those from without.

3 Therefore those who gave over their bodies in suffering for the sake of religion were not only admired by mortals, but also were deemed worthy to share in a divine inheritance. 4Because of them the nation gained peace, and by reviving observance of the law in the homeland they ravaged the enemy. 5The tyrant Antiochus was both punished on earth and is being chastised after his death. Since in no way whatever was he able to compel the Israelites to become pagans and to abandon their ancestral customs, he left Jerusalem and marched against the Persians.

6 The mother of seven sons expressed also these principles to her children: 7"I was a pure virgin and did not go outside my father's house; but I guarded the rib from which woman was made.[a] 8No seducer corrupted me on a desert plain, nor did the destroyer, the deceitful serpent, defile the purity of my virginity. 9In the time of my maturity I remained with my husband, and when these sons had grown up their father died. A happy man was he, who lived out his life with good children, and did not have the grief of bereavement. 10While he was still with you, he taught you the law and the prophets. 11He read to you about Abel slain by Cain, and Isaac who was offered as a burnt offering, and about Joseph in prison. 12He told you of the zeal of Phinehas, and he taught you about Hananiah, Azariah, and Mishael in the fire. 13He praised Daniel in the den of the lions and blessed him. 14He reminded you of the scripture of Isaiah, which says, 'Even though you go through the fire, the flame shall not consume you.' 15He sang to you songs of the psalmist David, who said, 'Many are the afflictions of the righteous.' 16He recounted to you Solomon's proverb, 'There is a tree of life for those who do his will.' 17He confirmed the query of Ezekiel, 'Shall these dry bones live?' 18For he did not forget to teach you the song that Moses taught, which says, 19'I kill and I make alive: this is your life and the length of your days.' "

20 O bitter was that day—and yet not bitter—when that bitter tyrant of the Greeks quenched fire with fire in his cruel caldrons, and in his burning rage brought those seven sons of the daughter of Abraham to the catapult and back again to more[b] tortures, 21pierced the pupils of their eyes and cut out their tongues, and put them to death with various tortures. 22For these crimes divine justice pursued and will pursue the accursed tyrant. 23But the sons of Abraham with their victorious mother are gathered together into the chorus of the fathers, and have received pure and immortal[c] souls from God, 24to whom be glory forever and ever. Amen.

[a] Gk *the rib that was built* [b] Other ancient authorities read *to all his* [c] Other ancient authorities read *victorious*

The New Testament

The Gospels
INTRODUCTION

Cain Hope Felder

If contemporary members of groups who historically have been the most marginalized and exploited in the United States—African Americans, Hispanics, Native Americans, and Asians—were suddenly transported back to the first or second century of the Common Era and brought face to face with Jesus of Nazareth, the central person in the Gospels, they might well be surprised that he was not—as he has so often been portrayed in this nation's history—a mild-mannered spiritual teacher, a virtual priest to the status quo, whose guiding purpose was to rush to Calvary to purge everybody of their sins. Over the centuries, the Jesus of the Gospels has been effectively spiritualized and depoliticized beyond recognition. The stories of his courageous speaking truth to power through his teaching, healing, preaching, and witnessing for righteousness and justice have been greatly muted. The result has been a Jesus with the accent on "Christ," rather than on "Nazareth." Fortunately, thanks to alternative traditions in subordinate communities that have kept alive a different memory of Jesus, the resilience of the original Gospels within the canon allows them still to speak for themselves despite the self-serving, morally skewed agendas that have too often been imposed on them over the centuries.

Scholars designate Matthew, Mark, and Luke the "Synoptic Gospels," because they present the career of Jesus in a similar manner, different from the Johannine Jesus of the Fourth Gospel. In the Synoptic Gospels, Jesus' public ministry essentially progresses from the cities of Galilee in the north to Judea in the south, culminating in the environs of Jerusalem. Jesus' movements are otherwise in the Gospel of John; there he travels back and forth from north to south. The Johannine portrayal of Jesus celebrating three Passovers in Jerusalem has also given rise to the common notion of a three-year framework for Jesus' ministry.

Scholars generally date the composition of the Gospels as follows: Mark, 68–70 CE (that is, during or immediately after the Roman war against Judea, 66–70 CE); Matthew, 80; Luke, 85; and John, 90. In general, the later the date in the first century, the higher the Christology one encounters in a writing. A "low Christology" emphasizes Jesus of Nazareth as prophet, wisdom teacher, preacher, and healer, and allows his human qualities to appear: weariness, self-doubt, and impatience in his journey toward his eventual dying and rising as the Messiah. The Synoptic Gospels generally represent a much lower Christology than that found in the Fourth Gospel, which depicts Jesus as the incarnate Word of God and his identity as virtually one with God's own person. In the course of Christian history, when imperial regimes have claimed the sanction of God and portrayed Christ as a heavenly emperor, this aspect of the Johannine portrayal has seemed to offer little comfort to the men and women victimized by these regimes—and the Jesus portrayed in the Synoptic Gospels has seemed to them more a brother in struggle. But as we shall see, there is more to the Fourth Gospel than this.

Each of the canonical Gospels offers a distinctive version of the Jesus story, and each Gospel becomes more intriguing and even exciting as one discerns the particular community concerns that shaped this particular telling of the story. Although a number of scholars in recent years have sought to challenge the priority of the Gospel of Mark, the majority continue to regard it as the earliest of the four Gospels to reach its final form as a narrative about Jesus. Mark's Gospel presents Jesus of Nazareth as following closely upon the heels of John the Baptist's proclamations about the nearness of the reign of God and about the necessity for persons to repent and undergo public baptism in the Jordan River. Mark describes Jesus as the "Son of Man" who must suffer in order to fulfill his vocation as Messiah and Son of God. For Mark, Jesus is the preeminent miracle worker but one who intentionally hides the true significance of his miracles until he stands before the high priest of Israel. Mark casts Jesus' ministry as part of an urgent apocalyptic drama, because this Gospel evidently was written for a community that faced life and death decisions about either adhering to a boundary-breaking faith or abandoning it.

The Gospel of Matthew is a very appropriate version of the Jesus story to open the New Testament because this Gospel, far more than the others, has the strongest Jewish-Christian tone. Matthew emphasizes the continuity of Jesus' story with prophetic revelations of the Hebrew Bible, which, he claims through many proof-texts, were fulfilled in the ministry of Jesus. For Matthew, Jesus is the son of David who epitomizes a new understanding of the

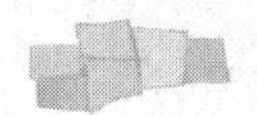

Messiah expected in Judaism. The organization of Jesus' teachings in this Gospel into five main discourses, and the characterization of Jesus as the teacher of a "higher righteousness" who routinely goes up and down mountains, indicate as well Matthew's effort to have his readers find in Jesus a new Moses. If Mark stresses a long list of miracles (Mark 1–11), Matthew has a penchant for Jesus' extraordinary, sustained teachings on themes of justice and mercy. It is clear, on the most widely accepted theory of Synoptic relationships, that Matthew composed his version of the Jesus story by making heavy use of Mark as a source.

The Gospel of Luke is less interested in a new Jewish Messiah than in a universal savior for all people. Luke's Jesus exudes compassion and mercy in his repeated emphasis on role reversals and in his bold ministry to the poor, to those unjustly imprisoned, downcast, or otherwise oppressed. Over the centuries, some scholars have shown a certain discomfort with the Lukan Jesus as he incarnates the Jubilee ideal (Luke 4:18-20; see Leviticus 25). Luke also has used Mark as a source but less than Matthew has. Instead, Luke introduces an extended, theologically distinctive narrative tradition, often called the Journey or Travel Narrative (Luke 9:51—19:27), in which one finds some of the most inspiring and challenging parables and episodes of all the Gospels.

The Gospel of John emerged out of the tense political and religious context of the closing decade of the first century. This unique Gospel raised the stakes for anyone claiming to be Christian. Many scholars believe members of the Johannine community had to cope with the double threats of heightened political and religious tensions with a besieged Judaism on the one hand, and on the other, increasing hostility from an exasperated Roman officialdom that made little distinction between Christians and Jews. Pogroms against the Jews broke out throughout the empire, and the Johannine Christians were being summoned to take their last stand: accept or reject Jesus as the Word of God—the new center of a new religion coming of age—or imperil your very soul! For many interpreters, such threats and stresses make sense of the bold "I am" statements of the Johannine Christ—a new portrayal of Christ as mysteriously and ironically triumphant, even as he goes to the cross; a Christ who (in John 13 and 21) challenges the church to again set its sights on a suffering and oppressed humanity.

I read the Bible as an African American who sees clearly the centrality of the presence and voice of Africans in the Scriptures. As I peruse the Gospels, I cannot miss the fact that Jesus was born a Hebrew, a child of an Afro-Asiatic people. The Afro-Asiatic Jesus was rushed to safety on the continent of Africa shortly after his birth and his cross was carried by an African just before his death. We all need to bring "new eyes" to these first century Gospels and see not just the Greeks and Romans, but also Asians, Africans, and others. We have all been invited by Jesus to the banquet table.

The Gospel According to Matthew

THE GOSPEL ACCORDING TO MATTHEW has been the opening book of the New Testament since the end of the second century, when the formation of the Christian canon began. At that time it was regarded as the first gospel ever written and as the testimony of the apostle Matthew. Now most scholars judge that it was probably not the first gospel—that place belongs to Mark—and that it is an anonymous text, probably written around 85–90 CE. That dating is based in part on the perception in 18:15-20 of a more organized church, which most likely emerged after the year 70. Early church tradition held that Matthew was written in Hebrew, by a Jew writing for a Jewish audience. However, since the gospel was evidently written in Greek, many scholars today point to a Gentile author who valued Jewish tradition and wrote for a Gentile audience familiar with it, or for an audience that included both Jews and Gentiles.

Matthew is considered the most Jewish of the canonical gospels. He outlines Jesus' story as parallel to Israel and depicts him as constantly concerned with upholding the law (see 5:17-20). With more than 100 references to the Hebrew Bible, this gospel presupposes an audience familiar with the Torah and the prophets, to whom Matthew seeks to prove that Jesus came as fulfillment of prophecy. He begins with a long genealogy, establishing Jesus' Jewish ancestry and his royal heritage as the Davidic Messiah. Then, following the literary patterns of ancient Greco-Roman biographies, Matthew offers a classic opening for a hero's life: a miraculous conception, then a sequence of events under constant divine guidance through dreams and angels (the visit to Mary, Joseph, and the child Jesus by wise men from Persia in response to a cosmic invitation, then the flight of the holy family into Egypt to protect Jesus' life, then their return to Nazareth). Some details from this story, including Joseph's dreams and the trip to Egypt, are reminiscent of the dreams of the ancestor Joseph in Exodus as well as of Israel's journey.

Some scholars see in the structure of this gospel another indirect reference to the Torah. Just as the Torah has five books, Matthew has organized Jesus' message in five discourses. The most popular of them the Sermon on the Mount (chs. 5–7). The others are 9:36—11:1; 13:1-53; 18:1—19:1; and 24:3—26:2. This structure seems to present Jesus as a "new Moses" and his teachings as a "new Torah." However, as Jewish as Matthew can be, it is also a very Christian gospel. Besides its particular emphasis on discipleship, it is also the only gospel that writes explicitly about the church (in Greek, *ekklēsia*; see 16:18; 18:17). This tension probably reflects the process by which a Christian group emerging from a larger Jewish community came to identify themselves over against that community. Thus Matthew's references to the synagogue as "their" synagogue uses us-them language that speaks of the strain experienced by the community. Perhaps that strain somehow explains the perceived need of a "new Torah."

In all fairness, however, it is impossible to speak of a clear separation of "Jewish" and "Christian" communities at this stage, or to use distinctive labels such as "Jewish Christians," "Jewish/Gentile Christians," or "Gentile Christians." The people in Matthew's community—including the Gentile converts—most likely considered themselves Jewish, but at the time the gospel was written, things were changing, with new Gentiles coming onto the scene. What we see here is a process of cultural hybridization (mixture) taking place at ideological, religious, and ethnic levels. It is this hybridism, which seems to happen contrary to Matthew's plans, that fascinates me, because it resonates with my personal experience of growing up in a bicultural context. At the end of the gospel, Jesus states that all nations will share in the faith of Israel (28:19-20). But by then non-Jews had already started sharing in the faith (8:5-13; 15:21-28). What was apparently expected to be a two-stage process—first the Jews, then the Gentiles (10:5-6)—never happens, because the Gentiles come to the table before they are invited. The Roman centurion and the Canaanite woman end up sharing the bread intended first for the house of Israel. They come seeking Jesus before they are approached, on their own terms and without being coerced—that is, without being "evangelized" in any imperialistic way.

Ultimately, what comes across as the central message in Matthew is the *inclusiveness* of faith. For me the Gospel of Matthew—and the whole Bible—is about the encounter and dialogue of the divine and the human and how that interaction defined and continues to define both divine and human identities. Perhaps because I grew up in the borderlands between Mexico and the United States, I have seen such divine-human encounters—and all encounters between people and peoples—as constant negotiations of limits. Border-crossing is inevitable, but it needs to be done with respect, avoiding invasion, and acknowledging the inescapable hybridity that occurs in all contact zones, by which we are transformed. All border zones are vulnerable, and people living in them can survive only through interdependency. This and more we can learn from the way borders work in Matthew.

— ***Leticia A. Guardiola-Sáenz***

1 An account of the genealogy[a] of Jesus the
Messiah,[b] the son of David, the son of Abraham.
2 Abraham was the father of Isaac, and Isaac
the father of Jacob, and Jacob the father of Judah and his brothers, 3and Judah the father of
Perez and Zerah by Tamar, and Perez the father
of Hezron, and Hezron the father of Aram, 4and
Aram the father of Aminadab, and Aminadab the
father of Nahshon, and Nahshon the father of
Salmon, 5and Salmon the father of Boaz by Rahab, and Boaz the father of Obed by Ruth, and
Obed the father of Jesse, 6and Jesse the father of
King David.
And David was the father of Solomon by
the wife of Uriah, 7and Solomon the father of

[a] Or *birth* [b] Or *Jesus Christ*

Matthew 1

We are comforted when we read the genealogy of Jesus and find there, not only a Gentile like ourselves, but also incest, and what amounts to David's rape of Bathsheba. The gospel writer did not hide the skeletons in Jesus' closet, but listed them, so that we may know that the Savior has really come to be one of us—not just one of the high and mighty, the aristocratic with impeccable blood lines, but one of us.[67]

— ***Justo L. González***

Rehoboam, and Rehoboam the father of Abijah,
and Abijah the father of Asaph,[a] 8and Asaph[a] the
father of Jehoshaphat, and Jehoshaphat the father
of Joram, and Joram the father of Uzziah, 9and Uzziah the father of Jotham, and Jotham the father
of Ahaz, and Ahaz the father of Hezekiah, 10and
Hezekiah the father of Manasseh, and Manasseh
the father of Amos,[b] and Amos[b] the father of Josiah, 11and Josiah the father of Jechoniah and his
brothers, at the time of the deportation to Babylon.
12 And after the deportation to Babylon:
Jechoniah was the father of Salathiel, and Salathiel
the father of Zerubbabel, 13and Zerubbabel the
father of Abiud, and Abiud the father of Eliakim,
and Eliakim the father of Azor, 14and Azor the
father of Zadok, and Zadok the father of Achim,
and Achim the father of Eliud, 15and Eliud the father of Eleazar, and Eleazar the father of Matthan,
and Matthan the father of Jacob, 16and Jacob the
father of Joseph the husband of Mary, of whom
Jesus was born, who is called the Messiah.[c]
17 So all the generations from Abraham to
David are fourteen generations; and from David
to the deportation to Babylon, fourteen generations; and from the deportation to Babylon to the
Messiah,[c] fourteen generations.

18 Now the birth of Jesus the Messiah[d] took
place in this way. When his mother Mary had
been engaged to Joseph, but before they lived
together, she was found to be with child from
the Holy Spirit. 19Her husband Joseph, being
a righteous man and unwilling to expose her to
public disgrace, planned to dismiss her quietly.
20But just when he had resolved to do this, an angel of the Lord appeared to him in a dream and
said, "Joseph, son of David, do not be afraid to
take Mary as your wife, for the child conceived in
her is from the Holy Spirit. 21She will bear a son,
and you are to name him Jesus, for he will save
his people from their sins." 22All this took place to
fulfill what had been spoken by the Lord through
the prophet:

23 "Look, the virgin shall conceive and bear a son,
and they shall name him Emmanuel,"

which means, "God is with us." 24When Joseph
awoke from sleep, he did as the angel of the Lord
commanded him; he took her as his wife, 25but
had no marital relations with her until she had
borne a son;[e] and he named him Jesus.

2 In the time of King Herod, after Jesus was
born in Bethlehem of Judea, wise men[f] from
the East came to Jerusalem, 2asking, "Where is
the child who has been born king of the Jews? For
we observed his star at its rising,[g] and have come
to pay him homage." 3When King Herod heard
this, he was frightened, and all Jerusalem with
him; 4and calling together all the chief priests and
scribes of the people, he inquired of them where
the Messiah[c] was to be born. 5They told him, "In
Bethlehem of Judea; for so it has been written by
the prophet:

6 'And you, Bethlehem, in the land of Judah,
are by no means least among the rulers of
Judah;
for from you shall come a ruler
who is to shepherd[h] my people Israel.' "

7 Then Herod secretly called for the wise
men[f] and learned from them the exact time when
the star had appeared. 8Then he sent them to
Bethlehem, saying, "Go and search diligently for
the child; and when you have found him, bring
me word so that I may also go and pay him hom-

[a] Other ancient authorities read *Asa* [b] Other ancient authorities read *Amon* [c] Or *the Christ* [d] Or *Jesus Christ*
[e] Other ancient authorities read *her firstborn son* [f] Or *astrologers*; Gk *magi* [g] Or *in the East* [h] Or *rule*

Matthew 2:11

The gifts offered by the wise men echo Isaiah's prophecy that the nations will bring trains of tribute to Israel on the day of its vindication (Isa 60:6). The prophet's vision of a public, international tribute was never fulfilled during Jesus' life; it remained a fervent hope for some early believers, like the apostle Paul. Has Matthew provided a quiet domestic tableau instead?

— NE

age.” 9When they had heard the king, they set out;
and there, ahead of them, went the star that they
had seen at its rising,[a] until it stopped over the
place where the child was. 10When they saw that
the star had stopped,[b] they were overwhelmed
with joy. 11On entering the house, they saw the
child with Mary his mother; and they knelt down
and paid him homage. Then, opening their treasure chests, they offered him gifts of gold, frankincense, and myrrh. 12And having been warned
in a dream not to return to Herod, they left for
their own country by another road.

13 Now after they had left, an angel of the
Lord appeared to Joseph in a dream and said,

Matthew 2:13-15

Fleeing from Herod, Mary and Joseph take Jesus into exile in Egypt, where they are aliens. Perhaps they knew what it meant not to be accepted due to the xenophobia of the dominant culture, which looks down at aliens as those who come to take away jobs and soak up social services. The miracle and lesson of the Gospel is that the Messiah comes not in the form of the temple's high priest or as a client king wielding the authority of Rome's emperor, but rather as the most dispossessed, displaced, and disenfranchised of all humans, the alien in our midst.

— MDLT

“Get up, take the child and his mother, and flee
to Egypt, and remain there until I tell you; for
Herod is about to search for the child, to destroy
him.” 14Then Joseph[c] got up, took the child and
his mother by night, and went to Egypt, 15and remained there until the death of Herod. This was to
fulfill what had been spoken by the Lord through
the prophet, “Out of Egypt I have called my son.”

16 When Herod saw that he had been tricked
by the wise men,[d] he was infuriated, and he sent
and killed all the children in and around Bethlehem who were two years old or under, according
to the time that he had learned from the wise
men.[e] 17Then was fulfilled what had been spoken
through the prophet Jeremiah:

18 “A voice was heard in Ramah,
 wailing and loud lamentation,
Rachel weeping for her children;
 she refused to be consoled, because they
  are no more.”

19 When Herod died, an angel of the Lord
suddenly appeared in a dream to Joseph in
Egypt and said, 20“Get up, take the child and his
mother, and go to the land of Israel, for those who
were seeking the child's life are dead.” 21Then Joseph[c] got up, took the child and his mother, and
went to the land of Israel. 22But when he heard
that Archelaus was ruling over Judea in place of
his father Herod, he was afraid to go there. And
after being warned in a dream, he went away to
the district of Galilee. 23There he made his home
in a town called Nazareth, so that what had been
spoken through the prophets might be fulfilled,
“He will be called a Nazorean.”

3 In those days John the Baptist appeared in
the wilderness of Judea, proclaiming, 2“Repent, for the kingdom of heaven has come near.”[e]
3This is the one of whom the prophet Isaiah
spoke when he said,

“The voice of one crying out in the wilderness:
‘Prepare the way of the Lord,
 make his paths straight.’ ”

4Now John wore clothing of camel's hair with
a leather belt around his waist, and his food was

[a] Or *in the East* [b] Gk *saw the star* [c] Gk *he* [d] Or *astrologers;* Gk *magi* [e] Or *is at hand*

locusts and wild honey. 5Then the people of Jerusalem and all Judea were going out to him, and all the
region along the Jordan, 6and they were baptized
by him in the river Jordan, confessing their sins.

7 But when he saw many Pharisees and Sadducees coming for baptism, he said to them, "You
brood of vipers! Who warned you to flee from the
wrath to come? 8Bear fruit worthy of repentance.
9Do not presume to say to yourselves, 'We have
Abraham as our ancestor'; for I tell you, God is
able from these stones to raise up children to
Abraham. 10Even now the ax is lying at the root of
the trees; every tree therefore that does not bear
good fruit is cut down and thrown into the fire.

11 "I baptize you with[a] water for repentance,
but one who is more powerful than I is coming
after me; I am not worthy to carry his sandals. He
will baptize you with[a] the Holy Spirit and fire.
12His winnowing fork is in his hand, and he will
clear his threshing floor and will gather his wheat
into the granary; but the chaff he will burn with
unquenchable fire."

13 Then Jesus came from Galilee to John at
the Jordan, to be baptized by him. 14John would
have prevented him, saying, "I need to be baptized by you, and do you come to me?" 15But
Jesus answered him, "Let it be so now; for it is
proper for us in this way to fulfill all righteousness." Then he consented. 16And when Jesus had
been baptized, just as he came up from the water,
suddenly the heavens were opened to him and he
saw the Spirit of God descending like a dove and
alighting on him. 17And a voice from heaven said,
"This is my Son, the Beloved,[b] with whom I am
well pleased."

4 Then Jesus was led up by the Spirit into the
wilderness to be tempted by the devil. 2He
fasted forty days and forty nights, and afterwards
he was famished. 3The tempter came and said to
him, "If you are the Son of God, command these
stones to become loaves of bread." 4But he answered, "It is written,

'One does not live by bread alone,
but by every word that comes from the
mouth of God.'"

5 Then the devil took him to the holy city and
placed him on the pinnacle of the temple, 6saying
to him, "If you are the Son of God, throw yourself
down; for it is written,

'He will command his angels concerning you,'
and 'On their hands they will bear you up,
so that you will not dash your foot against a
stone.'"

7Jesus said to him, "Again it is written, 'Do not
put the Lord your God to the test.'"

8 Again, the devil took him to a very high
mountain and showed him all the kingdoms of
the world and their splendor; 9and he said to him,
"All these I will give you, if you will fall down and
worship me." 10Jesus said to him, "Away with you,
Satan! for it is written,

'Worship the Lord your God,
and serve only him.'"

11Then the devil left him, and suddenly angels
came and waited on him.

12 Now when Jesus[c] heard that John had
been arrested, he withdrew to Galilee. 13He left
Nazareth and made his home in Capernaum by
the sea, in the territory of Zebulun and Naphtali, 14so that what had been spoken through the
prophet Isaiah might be fulfilled:

15 "Land of Zebulun, land of Naphtali,
on the road by the sea, across the Jordan,
Galilee of the Gentiles—
16 the people who sat in darkness
have seen a great light,
and for those who sat in the region and
shadow of death
light has dawned."

17From that time Jesus began to proclaim,
"Repent, for the kingdom of heaven has come
near."[d]

18 As he walked by the Sea of Galilee, he saw
two brothers, Simon, who is called Peter, and
Andrew his brother, casting a net into the sea—
for they were fishermen. 19And he said to them,
"Follow me, and I will make you fish for people."
20Immediately they left their nets and followed
him. 21As he went from there, he saw two other

[a] Or *in* [b] Or *my beloved Son* [c] Gk *he* [d] Or *is at hand*

brothers, James son of Zebedee and his brother
John, in the boat with their father Zebedee,
mending their nets, and he called them. 22Im-
mediately they left the boat and their father, and
followed him.

23 Jesus[a] went throughout Galilee, teaching
in their synagogues and proclaiming the good
news[b] of the kingdom and curing every disease and every sickness among the people. 24So
his fame spread throughout all Syria, and they
brought to him all the sick, those who were afflicted with various diseases and pains, demoniacs, epileptics, and paralytics, and he cured them.
25And great crowds followed him from Galilee,
the Decapolis, Jerusalem, Judea, and from beyond the Jordan.

5 When Jesus[c] saw the crowds, he went up the
mountain; and after he sat down, his disciples
came to him. 2Then he began to speak, and taught
them, saying:

3 "Blessed are the poor in spirit, for theirs is
the kingdom of heaven.

4 "Blessed are those who mourn, for they will
be comforted.

5 "Blessed are the meek, for they will inherit
the earth.

6 "Blessed are those who hunger and thirst
for righteousness, for they will be filled.

7 "Blessed are the merciful, for they will receive mercy.

Matthew 5:3

Matthew's form of the blessing on "the poor in spirit" is often compared unfavorably with the version in Luke, which reads simply "blessed are you who are poor" (and is accompanied by a woe against the rich: 6:20, 24). But the phrase "poor in spirit" echoes the language used throughout the Psalms to describe the crushing, incapacitating effect of poverty on the spirit.

— *NE*

8 "Blessed are the pure in heart, for they will
see God.

9 "Blessed are the peacemakers, for they will
be called children of God.

10 "Blessed are those who are persecuted for
righteousness' sake, for theirs is the kingdom of
heaven.

11 "Blessed are you when people revile you
and persecute you and utter all kinds of evil
against you falsely[d] on my account. 12Rejoice and
be glad, for your reward is great in heaven, for in
the same way they persecuted the prophets who
were before you.

13 "You are the salt of the earth; but if salt has
lost its taste, how can its saltiness be restored? It
is no longer good for anything, but is thrown out
and trampled under foot.

14 "You are the light of the world. A city built
on a hill cannot be hid. 15No one after lighting a
lamp puts it under the bushel basket, but on the
lampstand, and it gives light to all in the house.
16In the same way, let your light shine before others, so that they may see your good works and
give glory to your Father in heaven.

17 "Do not think that I have come to abolish
the law or the prophets; I have come not to abolish but to fulfill. 18For truly I tell you, until heav-
en and earth pass away, not one letter,[e] not one
stroke of a letter, will pass from the law until all is
accomplished. 19Therefore, whoever breaks[f] one
of the least of these commandments, and teaches
others to do the same, will be called least in the
kingdom of heaven; but whoever does them and
teaches them will be called great in the kingdom
of heaven. 20For I tell you, unless your righteousness exceeds that of the scribes and Pharisees,
you will never enter the kingdom of heaven.

21 "You have heard that it was said to those of
ancient times, 'You shall not murder'; and 'whoever murders shall be liable to judgment.' 22But I
say to you that if you are angry with a brother or
sister,[g] you will be liable to judgment; and if you
insult[h] a brother or sister,[i] you will be liable to the
council; and if you say, 'You fool,' you will be liable

[a] Gk *He* [b] Gk *gospel* [c] Gk *he* [d] Other ancient authorities lack *falsely* [e] Gk *one iota* [f] Or *annuls* [g] Gk *a brother*; other ancient authorities add *without cause* [h] Gk *say Raca to* (an obscure term of abuse) [i] Gk *a brother*

to the hell[a] of fire. 23So when you are offering
your gift at the altar, if you remember that your
brother or sister[b] has something against you,
24leave your gift there before the altar and go;
first be reconciled to your brother or sister,[b] and
then come and offer your gift. 25Come to terms
quickly with your accuser while you are on the
way to court[c] with him, or your accuser may hand
you over to the judge, and the judge to the guard,
and you will be thrown into prison. 26Truly I tell
you, you will never get out until you have paid the
last penny.

27 "You have heard that it was said, 'You shall
not commit adultery.' 28But I say to you that everyone who looks at a woman with lust has already committed adultery with her in his heart.
29If your right eye causes you to sin, tear it out
and throw it away; it is better for you to lose one
of your members than for your whole body to be
thrown into hell.[d] 30And if your right hand causes
you to sin, cut it off and throw it away; it is better
for you to lose one of your members than for your
whole body to go into hell.[d]

31 "It was also said, 'Whoever divorces his
wife, let him give her a certificate of divorce.'
32But I say to you that anyone who divorces his
wife, except on the ground of unchastity, causes
her to commit adultery; and whoever marries a
divorced woman commits adultery.

33 "Again, you have heard that it was said
to those of ancient times, 'You shall not swear
falsely, but carry out the vows you have made to
the Lord.' 34But I say to you, Do not swear at all,
either by heaven, for it is the throne of God, 35or
by the earth, for it is his footstool, or by Jerusalem, for it is the city of the great King. 36And do
not swear by your head, for you cannot make one
hair white or black. 37Let your word be 'Yes, Yes'
or 'No, No'; anything more than this comes from
the evil one.[e]

38 "You have heard that it was said, 'An eye for
an eye and a tooth for a tooth.' 39But I say to you,
Do not resist an evildoer. But if anyone strikes
you on the right cheek, turn the other also; 40and
if anyone wants to sue you and take your coat,
give your cloak as well; 41and if anyone forces you
to go one mile, go also the second mile. 42Give to
everyone who begs from you, and do not refuse
anyone who wants to borrow from you.

43 "You have heard that it was said, 'You shall
love your neighbor and hate your enemy.' 44But I
say to you, Love your enemies and pray for those
who persecute you, 45so that you may be children
of your Father in heaven; for he makes his sun
rise on the evil and on the good, and sends rain
on the righteous and on the unrighteous. 46For
if you love those who love you, what reward do
you have? Do not even the tax collectors do the
same? 47And if you greet only your brothers and
sisters,[f] what more are you doing than others? Do
not even the Gentiles do the same? 48Be perfect,
therefore, as your heavenly Father is perfect.

6 "Beware of practicing your piety before others in order to be seen by them; for then you
have no reward from your Father in heaven.

2 "So whenever you give alms, do not sound
a trumpet before you, as the hypocrites do in the
synagogues and in the streets, so that they may
be praised by others. Truly I tell you, they have
received their reward. 3But when you give alms,
do not let your left hand know what your right
hand is doing, 4so that your alms may be done
in secret; and your Father who sees in secret will
reward you.[g]

5 "And whenever you pray, do not be like the
hypocrites; for they love to stand and pray in the
synagogues and at the street corners, so that they
may be seen by others. Truly I tell you, they have
received their reward. 6But whenever you pray,
go into your room and shut the door and pray to
your Father who is in secret; and your Father who
sees in secret will reward you.[g]

7 "When you are praying, do not heap up
empty phrases as the Gentiles do; for they think
that they will be heard because of their many
words. 8Do not be like them, for your Father
knows what you need before you ask him.

9 "Pray then in this way:

[a] Gk *Gehenna* [b] Gk *your brother* [c] Gk lacks *to court* [d] Gk *Gehenna* [e] Or *evil* [f] Gk *your brothers*
[g] Other ancient authorities add *openly*

Our Father in heaven,
hallowed be your name.
10 Your kingdom come.
Your will be done,
on earth as it is in heaven.
11 Give us this day our daily bread.[a]
12 And forgive us our debts,
as we also have forgiven our debtors.

Matthew 6:11-12

During the late 1970s, Latin America's foreign debt was having devastating effects on the lives of most people there. According to the Latin American liberation theologian Franz Hinkelammert, it was during this time that some Catholic and Protestant ministers began to change the words of the Lord's Prayer from "Forgive us our debts" to "Forgive us our offenses" or "Forgive us our trespasses." Fear existed that Christians, pauperized by the policies of the World Bank and International Monetary Fund, might take the Lord Prayer's literally and demand that debts be forgiven so that they could have their daily bread.

— MDLT

13 And do not bring us to the time of trial,[b]
but rescue us from the evil one.[c]

14 For if you forgive others their trespasses, your heavenly Father will also forgive you; 15 but if you do not forgive others, neither will your Father forgive your trespasses.

16 "And whenever you fast, do not look dismal, like the hypocrites, for they disfigure their faces so as to show others that they are fasting. Truly I tell you, they have received their reward. 17 But when you fast, put oil on your head and wash your face, 18 so that your fasting may be seen not by others but by your Father who is in secret; and your Father who sees in secret will reward you.[d]

19 "Do not store up for yourselves treasures on earth, where moth and rust[e] consume and where thieves break in and steal; 20 but store up for yourselves treasures in heaven, where neither moth nor rust[e] consumes and where thieves do not break in and steal. 21 For where your treasure is, there your heart will be also.

22 "The eye is the lamp of the body. So, if your eye is healthy, your whole body will be full of light; 23 but if your eye is unhealthy, your whole body will be full of darkness. If then the light in you is darkness, how great is the darkness!

24 "No one can serve two masters; for a slave will either hate the one and love the other, or be devoted to the one and despise the other. You cannot serve God and wealth.[f]

25 "Therefore I tell you, do not worry about your life, what you will eat or what you will drink,[g] or about your body, what you will wear. Is not life more than food, and the body more than clothing? 26 Look at the birds of the air; they neither sow nor reap nor gather into barns, and yet your heavenly Father feeds them. Are you not of more value than they? 27 And can any of you by worrying add a single hour to your span of life?[h] 28 And why do you worry about clothing? Consider the lilies of the field, how they grow; they neither toil nor spin, 29 yet I tell you, even Solomon in all his glory was not clothed like one of these. 30 But if God so clothes the grass of the field, which is alive today and tomorrow is thrown into the oven, will he not much more clothe you—you of little faith? 31 Therefore do not worry, saying, 'What will we eat?' or 'What will we drink?' or 'What will we wear?' 32 For it is the Gentiles who strive for all these things; and indeed your heavenly Father knows that you need all these things. 33 But strive first for the kingdom of God[i] and his[j] righteousness, and all these things will be given to you as well.

34 "So do not worry about tomorrow, for tomorrow will bring worries of its own. Today's trouble is enough for today.

[a] Or *our bread for tomorrow* [b] Or *us into temptation* [c] Or *from evil.* Other ancient authorities add, in some form, *For the kingdom and the power and the glory are yours forever. Amen.* [d] Other ancient authorities add *openly* [e] Gk *eating* [f] Gk *mammon* [g] Other ancient authorities lack *or what you will drink* [h] Or *add one cubit to your height* [i] Other ancient authorities lack *of God* [j] Or *its*

7 "Do not judge, so that you may not be judged.
2 For with the judgment you make you will
be judged, and the measure you give will be the
measure you get. 3 Why do you see the speck in
your neighbor's[a] eye, but do not notice the log
in your own eye? 4 Or how can you say to your
neighbor,[b] 'Let me take the speck out of your eye,'
while the log is in your own eye? 5 You hypocrite,
first take the log out of your own eye, and then
you will see clearly to take the speck out of your
neighbor's[a] eye.

6 "Do not give what is holy to dogs; and do
not throw your pearls before swine, or they will
trample them under foot and turn and maul you.

7 "Ask, and it will be given you; search, and
you will find; knock, and the door will be opened
for you. 8 For everyone who asks receives, and everyone who searches finds, and for everyone who
knocks, the door will be opened. 9 Is there anyone
among you who, if your child asks for bread, will
give a stone? 10 Or if the child asks for a fish, will
give a snake? 11 If you then, who are evil, know
how to give good gifts to your children, how
much more will your Father in heaven give good
things to those who ask him!

12 "In everything do to others as you would
have them do to you; for this is the law and the
prophets.

13 "Enter through the narrow gate; for the
gate is wide and the road is easy[c] that leads to destruction, and there are many who take it. 14 For
the gate is narrow and the road is hard that leads
to life, and there are few who find it.

15 "Beware of false prophets, who come to
you in sheep's clothing but inwardly are ravenous
wolves. 16 You will know them by their fruits. Are
grapes gathered from thorns, or figs from thistles?
17 In the same way, every good tree bears good
fruit, but the bad tree bears bad fruit. 18 A good
tree cannot bear bad fruit, nor can a bad tree bear
good fruit. 19 Every tree that does not bear good
fruit is cut down and thrown into the fire. 20 Thus
you will know them by their fruits.

21 "Not everyone who says to me, 'Lord,
Lord,' will enter the kingdom of heaven, but only
the one who does the will of my Father in heaven.
22 On that day many will say to me, 'Lord, Lord,
did we not prophesy in your name, and cast out
demons in your name, and do many deeds of
power in your name?' 23 Then I will declare to
them, 'I never knew you; go away from me, you
evildoers.'

24 "Everyone then who hears these words of
mine and acts on them will be like a wise man who
built his house on rock. 25 The rain fell, the floods
came, and the winds blew and beat on that house,
but it did not fall, because it had been founded
on rock. 26 And everyone who hears these words
of mine and does not act on them will be like a
foolish man who built his house on sand. 27 The
rain fell, and the floods came, and the winds blew
and beat against that house, and it fell—and great
was its fall!"

28 Now when Jesus had finished saying these
things, the crowds were astounded at his teaching, 29 for he taught them as one having authority,
and not as their scribes.

8 When Jesus[d] had come down from the
mountain, great crowds followed him; 2 and
there was a leper[e] who came to him and knelt
before him, saying, "Lord, if you choose, you
can make me clean." 3 He stretched out his hand
and touched him, saying, "I do choose. Be made
clean!" Immediately his leprosy[e] was cleansed.
4 Then Jesus said to him, "See that you say nothing to anyone; but go, show yourself to the priest,
and offer the gift that Moses commanded, as a
testimony to them."

5 When he entered Capernaum, a centurion came to him, appealing to him 6 and saying,
"Lord, my servant is lying at home paralyzed,
in terrible distress." 7 And he said to him, "I will
come and cure him." 8 The centurion answered,
"Lord, I am not worthy to have you come under
my roof; but only speak the word, and my servant
will be healed. 9 For I also am a man under authority, with soldiers under me; and I say to one,

[a] Gk *brother's* [b] Gk *brother* [c] Other ancient authorities read *for the road is wide and easy* [d] Gk *he*
[e] The terms *leper* and *leprosy* can refer to several diseases

'Go,' and he goes, and to another, 'Come,' and he
comes, and to my slave, 'Do this,' and the slave
does it." 10When Jesus heard him, he was amazed
and said to those who followed him, "Truly I tell
you, in no one[a] in Israel have I found such faith.
11I tell you, many will come from east and west
and will eat with Abraham and Isaac and Jacob in
the kingdom of heaven, 12while the heirs of the
kingdom will be thrown into the outer darkness,
where there will be weeping and gnashing of
teeth." 13And to the centurion Jesus said, "Go; let
it be done for you according to your faith." And
the servant was healed in that hour.

14 When Jesus entered Peter's house, he saw
his mother-in-law lying in bed with a fever; 15he
touched her hand, and the fever left her, and she
got up and began to serve him. 16That evening
they brought to him many who were possessed
with demons; and he cast out the spirits with a
word, and cured all who were sick. 17This was to
fulfill what had been spoken through the prophet
Isaiah, "He took our infirmities and bore our diseases."

18 Now when Jesus saw great crowds around
him, he gave orders to go over to the other side.
19A scribe then approached and said, "Teacher,
I will follow you wherever you go." 20And Jesus
said to him, "Foxes have holes, and birds of the
air have nests; but the Son of Man has nowhere
to lay his head." 21Another of his disciples said to
him, "Lord, first let me go and bury my father."
22But Jesus said to him, "Follow me, and let the
dead bury their own dead."

23 And when he got into the boat, his disciples followed him. 24A windstorm arose on the
sea, so great that the boat was being swamped by
the waves; but he was asleep. 25And they went
and woke him up, saying, "Lord, save us! We are
perishing!" 26And he said to them, "Why are you
afraid, you of little faith?" Then he got up and
rebuked the winds and the sea; and there was a
dead calm. 27They were amazed, saying, "What
sort of man is this, that even the winds and the
sea obey him?"

28 When he came to the other side, to the
country of the Gadarenes,[b] two demoniacs coming out of the tombs met him. They were so fierce
that no one could pass that way. 29Suddenly they
shouted, "What have you to do with us, Son of
God? Have you come here to torment us before
the time?" 30Now a large herd of swine was feeding at some distance from them. 31The demons
begged him, "If you cast us out, send us into the
herd of swine." 32And he said to them, "Go!" So
they came out and entered the swine; and suddenly, the whole herd rushed down the steep
bank into the sea and perished in the water. 33The
swineherds ran off, and on going into the town,
they told the whole story about what had happened to the demoniacs. 34Then the whole town
came out to meet Jesus; and when they saw him,
they begged him to leave their neighborhood.

9 1And after getting into a boat he crossed the
sea and came to his own town.

2 And just then some people were carrying
a paralyzed man lying on a bed. When Jesus saw
their faith, he said to the paralytic, "Take heart,
son; your sins are forgiven." 3Then some of the
scribes said to themselves, "This man is blaspheming." 4But Jesus, perceiving their thoughts,
said, "Why do you think evil in your hearts? 5For
which is easier, to say, 'Your sins are forgiven,' or
to say, 'Stand up and walk'? 6But so that you may
know that the Son of Man has authority on earth
to forgive sins"—he then said to the paralytic—
"Stand up, take your bed and go to your home."
7And he stood up and went to his home. 8When
the crowds saw it, they were filled with awe, and
they glorified God, who had given such authority
to human beings.

9 As Jesus was walking along, he saw a man
called Matthew sitting at the tax booth; and he
said to him, "Follow me." And he got up and followed him.

10 And as he sat at dinner[c] in the house, many
tax collectors and sinners came and were sitting[d]
with him and his disciples. 11When the Pharisees
saw this, they said to his disciples, "Why does

[a] Other ancient authorities read *Truly I tell you, not even* [b] Other ancient authorities read *Gergesenes*; others, *Gerasenes*
[c] Gk *reclined* [d] Gk *were reclining*

your teacher eat with tax collectors and sinners?" 12 But when he heard this, he said, "Those who are well have no need of a physician, but those who are sick. 13 Go and learn what this means, 'I desire mercy, not sacrifice.' For I have come to call not the righteous but sinners."

14 Then the disciples of John came to him, saying, "Why do we and the Pharisees fast often,[a] but your disciples do not fast?" 15 And Jesus said to them, "The wedding guests cannot mourn as long as the bridegroom is with them, can they? The days will come when the bridegroom is taken away from them, and then they will fast. 16 No one sews a piece of unshrunk cloth on an old cloak, for the patch pulls away from the cloak, and a worse tear is made. 17 Neither is new wine put into old wineskins; otherwise, the skins burst, and the wine is spilled, and the skins are destroyed; but new wine is put into fresh wineskins, and so both are preserved."

18 While he was saying these things to them, suddenly a leader of the synagogue[b] came in and knelt before him, saying, "My daughter has just died; but come and lay your hand on her, and she will live." 19 And Jesus got up and followed him, with his disciples. 20 Then suddenly a woman who had been suffering from hemorrhages for twelve years came up behind him and touched the fringe of his cloak, 21 for she said to herself, "If I only touch his cloak, I will be made well." 22 Jesus turned, and seeing her he said, "Take heart, daughter; your faith has made you well." And instantly the woman was made well. 23 When Jesus came to the leader's house and saw the flute players and the crowd making a commotion, 24 he said, "Go away; for the girl is not dead but sleeping." And they laughed at him. 25 But when the crowd had been put outside, he went in and took her by the hand, and the girl got up. 26 And the report of this spread throughout that district.

27 As Jesus went on from there, two blind men followed him, crying loudly, "Have mercy on us, Son of David!" 28 When he entered the house, the blind men came to him; and Jesus said to them, "Do you believe that I am able to do this?" They said to him, "Yes, Lord." 29 Then he touched their eyes and said, "According to your faith let it be done to you." 30 And their eyes were opened. Then Jesus sternly ordered them, "See that no one knows of this." 31 But they went away and spread the news about him throughout that district.

32 After they had gone away, a demoniac who was mute was brought to him. 33 And when the demon had been cast out, the one who had been mute spoke; and the crowds were amazed and said, "Never has anything like this been seen in Israel." 34 But the Pharisees said, "By the ruler of the demons he casts out the demons."[c]

35 Then Jesus went about all the cities and villages, teaching in their synagogues, and proclaiming the good news of the kingdom, and curing every disease and every sickness. 36 When he saw the crowds, he had compassion for them, because they were harassed and helpless, like sheep without a shepherd. 37 Then he said to his disciples, "The harvest is plentiful, but the laborers are few; 38 therefore ask the Lord of the harvest to send out laborers into his harvest."

10 Then Jesus[d] summoned his twelve disciples and gave them authority over unclean spirits, to cast them out, and to cure every disease and every sickness. 2 These are the names of the twelve apostles: first, Simon, also known as Peter, and his brother Andrew; James son of Zebedee, and his brother John; 3 Philip and Bartholomew; Thomas and Matthew the tax collector; James son of Alphaeus, and Thaddaeus;[e] 4 Simon the Cananaean, and Judas Iscariot, the one who betrayed him.

5 These twelve Jesus sent out with the following instructions: "Go nowhere among the Gentiles, and enter no town of the Samaritans, 6 but go rather to the lost sheep of the house of Israel. 7 As you go, proclaim the good news, 'The kingdom of heaven has come near.'[f] 8 Cure the sick, raise the dead, cleanse the lepers,[g] cast out demons.

[a] Other ancient authorities lack *often* [b] Gk lacks *of the synagogue* [c] Other ancient authorities lack this verse
[d] Gk *he* [e] Other ancient authorities read *Lebbaeus,* or *Lebbaeus called Thaddaeus* [f] Or *is at hand*
[g] The terms *leper* and *leprosy* can refer to several diseases

You received without payment; give without payment. 9Take no gold, or silver, or copper in your
belts, 10no bag for your journey, or two tunics, or
sandals, or a staff; for laborers deserve their food.
11Whatever town or village you enter, find out
who in it is worthy, and stay there until you leave.
12As you enter the house, greet it. 13If the house
is worthy, let your peace come upon it; but if it is
not worthy, let your peace return to you. 14If anyone will not welcome you or listen to your words,
shake off the dust from your feet as you leave that
house or town. 15Truly I tell you, it will be more
tolerable for the land of Sodom and Gomorrah
on the day of judgment than for that town.

Matthew 10:14-15

When Jesus sends out his disciples to evangelize the surrounding communities, he tells them that those who refuse to hear the gospel will meet a fate worse than that of Sodom and Gomorrah. For many missionaries in later centuries, infidels were seen as deserving God's wrath unless they accepted the missionaries' beliefs. The destruction of those cultures that chose to continue worshiping the deities of their society was seen as divine judgment. This passage is troublesome, especially to indigenous cultures, because to many it seems to justify genocide on the scale that befell the ancient cities of Sodom and Gomorrah.

— *MDLT*

16 "See, I am sending you out like sheep into
the midst of wolves; so be wise as serpents and
innocent as doves. 17Beware of them, for they
will hand you over to councils and flog you in
their synagogues; 18and you will be dragged before governors and kings because of me, as a testimony to them and the Gentiles. 19When they
hand you over, do not worry about how you are
to speak or what you are to say; for what you are
to say will be given to you at that time; 20for it
is not you who speak, but the Spirit of your Father speaking through you. 21Brother will betray
brother to death, and a father his child, and children will rise against parents and have them put
to death; 22and you will be hated by all because
of my name. But the one who endures to the end
will be saved. 23When they persecute you in one
town, flee to the next; for truly I tell you, you will
not have gone through all the towns of Israel before the Son of Man comes.

24 "A disciple is not above the teacher, nor
a slave above the master; 25it is enough for the
disciple to be like the teacher, and the slave like
the master. If they have called the master of the
house Beelzebul, how much more will they malign those of his household!

26 "So have no fear of them; for nothing is
covered up that will not be uncovered, and nothing secret that will not become known. 27What I
say to you in the dark, tell in the light; and what
you hear whispered, proclaim from the housetops. 28Do not fear those who kill the body but
cannot kill the soul; rather fear him who can destroy both soul and body in hell.[a] 29Are not two
sparrows sold for a penny? Yet not one of them
will fall to the ground apart from your Father.
30And even the hairs of your head are all counted.
31So do not be afraid; you are of more value than
many sparrows.

32 "Everyone therefore who acknowledges
me before others, I also will acknowledge before
my Father in heaven; 33but whoever denies me
before others, I also will deny before my Father
in heaven.

34 "Do not think that I have come to bring
peace to the earth; I have not come to bring
peace, but a sword.

35 For I have come to set a man against his
father,
and a daughter against her mother,
and a daughter-in-law against her mother-in-
law;
36 and one's foes will be members of one's own
household.

37Whoever loves father or mother more than
me is not worthy of me; and whoever loves son
or daughter more than me is not worthy of me;

[a] Gk *Gehenna*

38 and whoever does not take up the cross and
follow me is not worthy of me. 39 Those who find
their life will lose it, and those who lose their life
for my sake will find it.

40 "Whoever welcomes you welcomes me,
and whoever welcomes me welcomes the one
who sent me. 41 Whoever welcomes a prophet
in the name of a prophet will receive a prophet's
reward; and whoever welcomes a righteous person in the name of a righteous person will receive
the reward of the righteous; 42 and whoever gives
even a cup of cold water to one of these little ones
in the name of a disciple—truly I tell you, none of
these will lose their reward."

11 Now when Jesus had finished instructing his twelve disciples, he went on from
there to teach and proclaim his message in their
cities.

2 When John heard in prison what the Messiah[a] was doing, he sent word by his[b] disciples
3 and said to him, "Are you the one who is to come,
or are we to wait for another?" 4 Jesus answered
them, "Go and tell John what you hear and see:
5 the blind receive their sight, the lame walk, the
lepers[c] are cleansed, the deaf hear, the dead are
raised, and the poor have good news brought to
them. 6 And blessed is anyone who takes no offense at me."

7 As they went away, Jesus began to speak to
the crowds about John: "What did you go out
into the wilderness to look at? A reed shaken
by the wind? 8 What then did you go out to see?
Someone[d] dressed in soft robes? Look, those who
wear soft robes are in royal palaces. 9 What then
did you go out to see? A prophet?[e] Yes, I tell you,
and more than a prophet. 10 This is the one about
whom it is written,

'See, I am sending my messenger ahead of
you,
who will prepare your way before you.'

11 Truly I tell you, among those born of women no
one has arisen greater than John the Baptist; yet
the least in the kingdom of heaven is greater than
he. 12 From the days of John the Baptist until now
the kingdom of heaven has suffered violence,[f] and
the violent take it by force. 13 For all the prophets
and the law prophesied until John came; 14 and if
you are willing to accept it, he is Elijah who is to
come. 15 Let anyone with ears[g] listen!

16 "But to what will I compare this generation? It is like children sitting in the marketplaces
and calling to one another,

17 'We played the flute for you, and you did not
dance;
we wailed, and you did not mourn.'

18 For John came neither eating nor drinking, and
they say, 'He has a demon'; 19 the Son of Man
came eating and drinking, and they say, 'Look,
a glutton and a drunkard, a friend of tax collectors and sinners!' Yet wisdom is vindicated by her
deeds."[h]

20 Then he began to reproach the cities
in which most of his deeds of power had been
done, because they did not repent. 21 "Woe to
you, Chorazin! Woe to you, Bethsaida! For if the
deeds of power done in you had been done in
Tyre and Sidon, they would have repented long
ago in sackcloth and ashes. 22 But I tell you, on the
day of judgment it will be more tolerable for Tyre
and Sidon than for you. 23 And you, Capernaum,

will you be exalted to heaven?
No, you will be brought down to Hades.

For if the deeds of power done in you had been
done in Sodom, it would have remained until this
day. 24 But I tell you that on the day of judgment
it will be more tolerable for the land of Sodom
than for you."

25 At that time Jesus said, "I thank[i] you, Father, Lord of heaven and earth, because you have
hidden these things from the wise and the intelligent and have revealed them to infants; 26 yes, Father, for such was your gracious will.[j] 27 All things
have been handed over to me by my Father; and

[a] Or *the Christ* [b] Other ancient authorities read *two of his* [c] The terms *leper* and *leprosy* can refer to several diseases
[d] Or *Why then did you go out? To see someone* [e] Other ancient authorities read *Why then did you go out? To see a prophet?*
[f] Or *has been coming violently* [g] Other ancient authorities add *to hear* [h] Other ancient authorities read *children*
[i] Or *praise* [j] Or *for so it was well-pleasing in your sight*

no one knows the Son except the Father, and no
one knows the Father except the Son and anyone
to whom the Son chooses to reveal him.

28 "Come to me, all you that are weary and
are carrying heavy burdens, and I will give you
rest. 29 Take my yoke upon you, and learn from
me; for I am gentle and humble in heart, and you
will find rest for your souls. 30 For my yoke is easy,
and my burden is light."

Matthew 11:28-30

We often read these verses ("Come to me, all you that are weary…") inscribed on park benches, as if Jesus were enjoining the crowds to take a rest. In the aftermath of John's arrest—a pivotal event in the Gospel—Jesus rallies the poor and promises them relief. The spiritualizing translation "I am gentle and humble in heart" does no justice to the Greek phrase, used throughout the Psalms to describe the poor and oppressed. Jesus is telling the disenfranchised that he is one of them, and takes their part.

— *NE*

12

At that time Jesus went through the grainfields on the sabbath; his disciples were
hungry, and they began to pluck heads of grain
and to eat. 2 When the Pharisees saw it, they said
to him, "Look, your disciples are doing what
is not lawful to do on the sabbath." 3 He said to
them, "Have you not read what David did when
he and his companions were hungry? 4 He entered the house of God and ate the bread of the
Presence, which it was not lawful for him or his
companions to eat, but only for the priests. 5 Or
have you not read in the law that on the sabbath
the priests in the temple break the sabbath and yet
are guiltless? 6 I tell you, something greater than
the temple is here. 7 But if you had known what
this means, 'I desire mercy and not sacrifice,' you
would not have condemned the guiltless. 8 For
the Son of Man is lord of the sabbath."

9 He left that place and entered their synagogue; 10 a man was there with a withered hand,
and they asked him, "Is it lawful to cure on the
sabbath?" so that they might accuse him. 11 He
said to them, "Suppose one of you has only one
sheep and it falls into a pit on the sabbath; will
you not lay hold of it and lift it out? 12 How much
more valuable is a human being than a sheep! So
it is lawful to do good on the sabbath." 13 Then
he said to the man, "Stretch out your hand." He
stretched it out, and it was restored, as sound as
the other. 14 But the Pharisees went out and conspired against him, how to destroy him.

15 When Jesus became aware of this, he
departed. Many crowds[a] followed him, and he
cured all of them, 16 and he ordered them not to
make him known. 17 This was to fulfill what had
been spoken through the prophet Isaiah:

18 "Here is my servant, whom I have chosen,
my beloved, with whom my soul is well pleased.
I will put my Spirit upon him,
and he will proclaim justice to the Gentiles.
19 He will not wrangle or cry aloud,
nor will anyone hear his voice in the streets.
20 He will not break a bruised reed
or quench a smoldering wick
until he brings justice to victory.
21 And in his name the Gentiles will hope."

22 Then they brought to him a demoniac
who was blind and mute; and he cured him, so
that the one who had been mute could speak and
see. 23 All the crowds were amazed and said, "Can
this be the Son of David?" 24 But when the Pharisees heard it, they said, "It is only by Beelzebul,
the ruler of the demons, that this fellow casts out
the demons." 25 He knew what they were thinking and said to them, "Every kingdom divided
against itself is laid waste, and no city or house
divided against itself will stand. 26 If Satan casts
out Satan, he is divided against himself; how then
will his kingdom stand? 27 If I cast out demons by
Beelzebul, by whom do your own exorcists[b] cast
them out? Therefore they will be your judges.

[a] Other ancient authorities lack *crowds* [b] Gk *sons*

28 But if it is by the Spirit of God that I cast out demons, then the kingdom of God has come to you.
29 Or how can one enter a strong man's house and
plunder his property, without first tying up the
strong man? Then indeed the house can be plundered. 30 Whoever is not with me is against me,
and whoever does not gather with me scatters.
31 Therefore I tell you, people will be forgiven for
every sin and blasphemy, but blasphemy against
the Spirit will not be forgiven. 32 Whoever speaks
a word against the Son of Man will be forgiven,
but whoever speaks against the Holy Spirit will
not be forgiven, either in this age or in the age to
come.

33 "Either make the tree good, and its fruit
good; or make the tree bad, and its fruit bad; for
the tree is known by its fruit. 34 You brood of vipers! How can you speak good things, when you
are evil? For out of the abundance of the heart
the mouth speaks. 35 The good person brings
good things out of a good treasure, and the evil
person brings evil things out of an evil treasure.
36 I tell you, on the day of judgment you will have
to give an account for every careless word you utter; 37 for by your words you will be justified, and
by your words you will be condemned."

38 Then some of the scribes and Pharisees
said to him, "Teacher, we wish to see a sign from
you." 39 But he answered them, "An evil and adulterous generation asks for a sign, but no sign will
be given to it except the sign of the prophet Jonah. 40 For just as Jonah was three days and three
nights in the belly of the sea monster, so for three
days and three nights the Son of Man will be in the
heart of the earth. 41 The people of Nineveh will
rise up at the judgment with this generation and
condemn it, because they repented at the proclamation of Jonah, and see, something greater
than Jonah is here! 42 The queen of the South will
rise up at the judgment with this generation and
condemn it, because she came from the ends of
the earth to listen to the wisdom of Solomon, and
see, something greater than Solomon is here!

43 "When the unclean spirit has gone out of
a person, it wanders through waterless regions
looking for a resting place, but it finds none.
44 Then it says, 'I will return to my house from
which I came.' When it comes, it finds it empty,
swept, and put in order. 45 Then it goes and brings
along seven other spirits more evil than itself, and
they enter and live there; and the last state of that
person is worse than the first. So will it be also
with this evil generation."

46 While he was still speaking to the crowds,
his mother and his brothers were standing outside, wanting to speak to him. 47 Someone told
him, "Look, your mother and your brothers are
standing outside, wanting to speak to you."[a] 48 But
to the one who had told him this, Jesus[b] replied,
"Who is my mother, and who are my brothers?"
49 And pointing to his disciples, he said, "Here are
my mother and my brothers! 50 For whoever does
the will of my Father in heaven is my brother and
sister and mother."

13 That same day Jesus went out of the house
and sat beside the sea. 2 Such great crowds
gathered around him that he got into a boat and
sat there, while the whole crowd stood on the
beach. 3 And he told them many things in parables, saying: "Listen! A sower went out to sow.
4 And as he sowed, some seeds fell on the path,
and the birds came and ate them up. 5 Other seeds
fell on rocky ground, where they did not have
much soil, and they sprang up quickly, since they
had no depth of soil. 6 But when the sun rose,
they were scorched; and since they had no root,
they withered away. 7 Other seeds fell among
thorns, and the thorns grew up and choked them.
8 Other seeds fell on good soil and brought forth
grain, some a hundredfold, some sixty, some thirty. 9 Let anyone with ears[c] listen!"

10 Then the disciples came and asked him,
"Why do you speak to them in parables?" 11 He
answered, "To you it has been given to know the
secrets[d] of the kingdom of heaven, but to them
it has not been given. 12 For to those who have,
more will be given, and they will have an abundance; but from those who have nothing, even
what they have will be taken away. 13 The reason

[a] Other ancient authorities lack verse 47 [b] Gk *he* [c] Other ancient authorities add *to hear* [d] Or *mysteries*

Matthew 13

The Gospel of Matthew provides a series of parables framed as prophecies of judgment, where what is good is preserved and what is bad is destroyed: fruitful seed and noxious weed, good and bad fish, an obedient and disobedient son (21:28-31), wise and foolish maidens (25:1-13). Jesus' death is for Matthew a point of division in Israel. For Luke, in contrast, the prospect for reconciliation in Israel is still a lively one, so Luke offers different versions of these same parables.

— *NE*

I speak to them in parables is that 'seeing they do
not perceive, and hearing they do not listen, nor
do they understand.' [14]With them indeed is fulfilled the prophecy of Isaiah that says:

'You will indeed listen, but never
understand,
and you will indeed look, but never
perceive.
15 For this people's heart has grown dull,
and their ears are hard of hearing,
and they have shut their eyes;
so that they might not look with their
eyes,
and listen with their ears,
and understand with their heart and turn—
and I would heal them.'

[16]But blessed are your eyes, for they see, and your
ears, for they hear. [17]Truly I tell you, many prophets and righteous people longed to see what you
see, but did not see it, and to hear what you hear,
but did not hear it.

18 "Hear then the parable of the sower.
[19]When anyone hears the word of the kingdom
and does not understand it, the evil one comes
and snatches away what is sown in the heart;
this is what was sown on the path. [20]As for what
was sown on rocky ground, this is the one who
hears the word and immediately receives it with
joy; [21]yet such a person has no root, but endures
only for a while, and when trouble or persecution
arises on account of the word, that person immediately falls away.[a] [22]As for what was sown among
thorns, this is the one who hears the word, but the
cares of the world and the lure of wealth choke
the word, and it yields nothing. [23]But as for what
was sown on good soil, this is the one who hears
the word and understands it, who indeed bears
fruit and yields, in one case a hundredfold, in another sixty, and in another thirty."

24 He put before them another parable:
"The kingdom of heaven may be compared to
someone who sowed good seed in his field; [25]but
while everybody was asleep, an enemy came and
sowed weeds among the wheat, and then went
away. [26]So when the plants came up and bore
grain, then the weeds appeared as well. [27]And
the slaves of the householder came and said to
him, 'Master, did you not sow good seed in your
field? Where, then, did these weeds come from?'
[28]He answered, 'An enemy has done this.' The
slaves said to him, 'Then do you want us to go and
gather them?' [29]But he replied, 'No; for in gathering the weeds you would uproot the wheat along
with them. [30]Let both of them grow together until the harvest; and at harvest time I will tell the
reapers, Collect the weeds first and bind them in
bundles to be burned, but gather the wheat into
my barn.'"

31 He put before them another parable: "The
kingdom of heaven is like a mustard seed that
someone took and sowed in his field; [32]it is the
smallest of all the seeds, but when it has grown
it is the greatest of shrubs and becomes a tree, so
that the birds of the air come and make nests in
its branches."

33 He told them another parable: "The kingdom of heaven is like yeast that a woman took
and mixed in with[b] three measures of flour until
all of it was leavened."

34 Jesus told the crowds all these things in
parables; without a parable he told them nothing. [35]This was to fulfill what had been spoken
through the prophet:[c]

"I will open my mouth to speak in parables;

[a] Gk *stumbles* [b] Gk *hid in* [c] Other ancient authorities read *the prophet Isaiah*

I will proclaim what has been hidden from
the foundation of the world."[a]

36 Then he left the crowds and went into the
house. And his disciples approached him, saying,
"Explain to us the parable of the weeds of the
field." 37He answered, "The one who sows the
good seed is the Son of Man; 38the field is
the world, and the good seed are the children of
the kingdom; the weeds are the children of the
evil one, 39and the enemy who sowed them is the
devil; the harvest is the end of the age, and
the reapers are angels. 40Just as the weeds are collected and burned up with fire, so will it be at the
end of the age. 41The Son of Man will send his
angels, and they will collect out of his kingdom all
causes of sin and all evildoers, 42and they will
throw them into the furnace of fire, where there
will be weeping and gnashing of teeth. 43Then the
righteous will shine like the sun in the kingdom
of their Father. Let anyone with ears[b] listen!

44 "The kingdom of heaven is like treasure
hidden in a field, which someone found and hid;
then in his joy he goes and sells all that he has and
buys that field.

45 "Again, the kingdom of heaven is like a
merchant in search of fine pearls; 46on finding
one pearl of great value, he went and sold all that
he had and bought it.

47 "Again, the kingdom of heaven is like a
net that was thrown into the sea and caught fish
of every kind; 48when it was full, they drew it
ashore, sat down, and put the good into baskets
but threw out the bad. 49So it will be at the end of
the age. The angels will come out and separate the
evil from the righteous 50and throw them into the
furnace of fire, where there will be weeping and
gnashing of teeth.

51 "Have you understood all this?" They answered, "Yes." 52And he said to them, "Therefore
every scribe who has been trained for the kingdom of heaven is like the master of a household
who brings out of his treasure what is new and
what is old." 53When Jesus had finished these
parables, he left that place.

54 He came to his hometown and began to
teach the people[c] in their synagogue, so that they
were astounded and said, "Where did this man
get this wisdom and these deeds of power? 55Is
not this the carpenter's son? Is not his mother
called Mary? And are not his brothers James and
Joseph and Simon and Judas? 56And are not all
his sisters with us? Where then did this man get
all this?" 57And they took offense at him. But
Jesus said to them, "Prophets are not without
honor except in their own country and in their
own house." 58And he did not do many deeds of
power there, because of their unbelief.

14 At that time Herod the ruler[d] heard reports about Jesus; 2and he said to his
servants, "This is John the Baptist; he has been
raised from the dead, and for this reason these
powers are at work in him." 3For Herod had arrested John, bound him, and put him in prison
on account of Herodias, his brother Philip's wife,[e]
4because John had been telling him, "It is not lawful for you to have her." 5Though Herod[f] wanted
to put him to death, he feared the crowd, because they regarded him as a prophet. 6But when
Herod's birthday came, the daughter of Herodias
danced before the company, and she pleased
Herod 7so much that he promised on oath to
grant her whatever she might ask. 8Prompted
by her mother, she said, "Give me the head of
John the Baptist here on a platter." 9The king was
grieved, yet out of regard for his oaths and for the
guests, he commanded it to be given; 10he sent
and had John beheaded in the prison. 11The head
was brought on a platter and given to the girl,
who brought it to her mother. 12His disciples
came and took the body and buried it; then they
went and told Jesus.

13 Now when Jesus heard this, he withdrew
from there in a boat to a deserted place by himself.
But when the crowds heard it, they followed him
on foot from the towns. 14When he went ashore,
he saw a great crowd; and he had compassion for
them and cured their sick. 15When it was evening,
the disciples came to him and said, "This is a de-

[a] Other ancient authorities lack *of the world* [b] Other ancient authorities add *to hear* [c] Gk *them* [d] Gk *tetrarch*
[e] Other ancient authorities read *his brother's wife* [f] Gk *he*

serted place, and the hour is now late; send the
crowds away so that they may go into the villages
and buy food for themselves." 16 Jesus said to them,
"They need not go away; you give them something
to eat." 17 They replied, "We have nothing here but
five loaves and two fish." 18 And he said, "Bring
them here to me." 19 Then he ordered the crowds to
sit down on the grass. Taking the five loaves and the
two fish, he looked up to heaven, and blessed and
broke the loaves, and gave them to the disciples,
and the disciples gave them to the crowds. 20 And
all ate and were filled; and they took up what was
left over of the broken pieces, twelve baskets full.
21 And those who ate were about five thousand
men, besides women and children.

22 Immediately he made the disciples get
into the boat and go on ahead to the other side,
while he dismissed the crowds. 23 And after he
had dismissed the crowds, he went up the mountain by himself to pray. When evening came, he
was there alone, 24 but by this time the boat, battered by the waves, was far from the land,[a] for
the wind was against them. 25 And early in the
morning he came walking toward them on the
sea. 26 But when the disciples saw him walking on
the sea, they were terrified, saying, "It is a ghost!"
And they cried out in fear. 27 But immediately
Jesus spoke to them and said, "Take heart, it is I;
do not be afraid."

28 Peter answered him, "Lord, if it is you,
command me to come to you on the water."
29 He said, "Come." So Peter got out of the boat,
started walking on the water, and came toward
Jesus. 30 But when he noticed the strong wind,[b]
he became frightened, and beginning to sink, he
cried out, "Lord, save me!" 31 Jesus immediately
reached out his hand and caught him, saying to
him, "You of little faith, why did you doubt?"
32 When they got into the boat, the wind ceased.
33 And those in the boat worshiped him, saying,
"Truly you are the Son of God."

34 When they had crossed over, they came
to land at Gennesaret. 35 After the people of that
place recognized him, they sent word throughout
the region and brought all who were sick to him,
36 and begged him that they might touch even the
fringe of his cloak; and all who touched it were
healed.

15 Then Pharisees and scribes came to Jesus
from Jerusalem and said, 2 "Why do your
disciples break the tradition of the elders? For
they do not wash their hands before they eat."
3 He answered them, "And why do you break the
commandment of God for the sake of your tradition? 4 For God said,[c] 'Honor your father and
your mother,' and, 'Whoever speaks evil of father
or mother must surely die.' 5 But you say that whoever tells father or mother, 'Whatever support
you might have had from me is given to God,'[d]
then that person need not honor the father.[e] 6 So,
for the sake of your tradition, you make void the
word[f] of God. 7 You hypocrites! Isaiah prophesied
rightly about you when he said:

8 'This people honors me with their lips,
but their hearts are far from me;
9 in vain do they worship me,
teaching human precepts as doctrines.' "

10 Then he called the crowd to him and said
to them, "Listen and understand: 11 it is not what
goes into the mouth that defiles a person, but
it is what comes out of the mouth that defiles."
12 Then the disciples approached and said to him,
"Do you know that the Pharisees took offense
when they heard what you said?" 13 He answered,
"Every plant that my heavenly Father has not
planted will be uprooted. 14 Let them alone; they
are blind guides of the blind.[g] And if one blind
person guides another, both will fall into a pit."
15 But Peter said to him, "Explain this parable to
us." 16 Then he said, "Are you also still without
understanding? 17 Do you not see that whatever
goes into the mouth enters the stomach, and goes
out into the sewer? 18 But what comes out of the
mouth proceeds from the heart, and this is what
defiles. 19 For out of the heart come evil intentions,
murder, adultery, fornication, theft, false witness,

[a] Other ancient authorities read *was out on the sea* [b] Other ancient authorities read *the wind* [c] Other ancient authorities read *commanded, saying* [d] Or *is an offering* [e] Other ancient authorities add *or the mother* [f] Other ancient authorities read *law*; others, *commandment* [g] Other ancient authorities lack *of the blind*

slander. 20These are what defile a person, but to eat with unwashed hands does not defile."

21 Jesus left that place and went away to the district of Tyre and Sidon. 22Just then a Canaanite woman from that region came out and started shouting, "Have mercy on me, Lord, Son of David; my daughter is tormented by a demon." 23But he did not answer her at all. And his disciples came and urged him, saying, "Send her away, for she keeps shouting after us." 24He answered, "I was sent only to the lost sheep of the house of Israel." 25But she came and knelt before him, saying, "Lord, help me." 26He answered, "It is not fair to take the children's food and throw it to the dogs." 27She said, "Yes, Lord, yet even the dogs eat the crumbs that fall from their masters' table." 28Then Jesus answered her, "Woman, great is your faith! Let it be done for you as you wish." And her daughter was healed instantly.

29 After Jesus had left that place, he passed along the Sea of Galilee, and he went up the mountain, where he sat down. 30Great crowds came to him, bringing with them the lame, the maimed, the blind, the mute, and many others. They put them at his feet, and he cured them, 31so that the crowd was amazed when they saw the mute speaking, the maimed whole, the lame walking, and the blind seeing. And they praised the God of Israel.

32 Then Jesus called his disciples to him and said, "I have compassion for the crowd, because they have been with me now for three days and have nothing to eat; and I do not want to send them away hungry, for they might faint on the way." 33The disciples said to him, "Where are we to get enough bread in the desert to feed so great a crowd?" 34Jesus asked them, "How many loaves have you?" They said, "Seven, and a few small fish." 35Then ordering the crowd to sit down on the ground, 36he took the seven loaves and the fish; and after giving thanks he broke them and gave them to the disciples, and the disciples gave them to the crowds. 37And all of them ate and were filled; and they took up the broken pieces left over, seven baskets full. 38Those who had eaten were four thousand men, besides women and children. 39After sending away the crowds, he got into the boat and went to the region of Magadan.[a]

16 The Pharisees and Sadducees came, and to test Jesus[b] they asked him to show them a sign from heaven. 2He answered them, "When it is evening, you say, 'It will be fair weather, for the sky is red.' 3And in the morning, 'It will be stormy today, for the sky is red and threatening.' You know how to interpret the appearance of the sky, but you cannot interpret the signs of the times.[c] 4An evil and adulterous generation asks for a sign, but no sign will be given to it except the sign of Jonah." Then he left them and went away.

5 When the disciples reached the other side, they had forgotten to bring any bread. 6Jesus said to them, "Watch out, and beware of the yeast of the Pharisees and Sadducees." 7They said to one another, "It is because we have brought no bread." 8And becoming aware of it, Jesus said, "You of little faith, why are you talking about having no bread? 9Do you still not perceive? Do you not remember the five loaves for the five thousand, and how many baskets you gathered? 10Or the seven loaves for the four thousand, and how many baskets you gathered? 11How could you fail to perceive that I was not speaking about bread? Beware of the yeast of the Pharisees and Sadducees!" 12Then they understood that he had not told them to beware of the yeast of bread, but of the teaching of the Pharisees and Sadducees.

13 Now when Jesus came into the district of Caesarea Philippi, he asked his disciples, "Who do people say that the Son of Man is?" 14And they said, "Some say John the Baptist, but others Elijah, and still others Jeremiah or one of the prophets." 15He said to them, "But who do you say that I am?" 16Simon Peter answered, "You are the Messiah,[d] the Son of the living God." 17And Jesus answered him, "Blessed are you, Simon son of Jonah! For flesh and blood has not revealed

[a] Other ancient authorities read *Magdala* or *Magdalan* [b] Gk *him* [c] Other ancient authorities lack 2*When it is . . . of the times* [d] Or *the Christ*

this to you, but my Father in heaven. 18And I tell you, you are Peter,[a] and on this rock[b] I will build my church, and the gates of Hades will not prevail against it. 19I will give you the keys of the kingdom of heaven, and whatever you bind on earth will be bound in heaven, and whatever you loose on earth will be loosed in heaven." 20Then he sternly ordered the disciples not to tell anyone that he was[c] the Messiah.[d]

21 From that time on, Jesus began to show his disciples that he must go to Jerusalem and undergo great suffering at the hands of the elders and chief priests and scribes, and be killed, and on the third day be raised. 22And Peter took him aside and began to rebuke him, saying, "God forbid it, Lord! This must never happen to you." 23But he turned and said to Peter, "Get behind me, Satan! You are a stumbling block to me; for you are setting your mind not on divine things but on human things."

24 Then Jesus told his disciples, "If any want to become my followers, let them deny themselves and take up their cross and follow me. 25For those who want to save their life will lose it, and those who lose their life for my sake will find it. 26For what will it profit them if they gain the whole world but forfeit their life? Or what will they give in return for their life?

27 "For the Son of Man is to come with his angels in the glory of his Father, and then he will repay everyone for what has been done. 28Truly I tell you, there are some standing here who will not taste death before they see the Son of Man coming in his kingdom."

17 Six days later, Jesus took with him Peter and James and his brother John and led them up a high mountain, by themselves. 2And he was transfigured before them, and his face shone like the sun, and his clothes became dazzling white. 3Suddenly there appeared to them Moses and Elijah, talking with him. 4Then Peter said to Jesus, "Lord, it is good for us to be here; if you wish, I[e] will make three dwellings[f] here, one for you, one for Moses, and one for Elijah." 5While he was still speaking, suddenly a bright cloud overshadowed them, and from the cloud a voice said, "This is my Son, the Beloved;[g] with him I am well pleased; listen to him!" 6When the disciples heard this, they fell to the ground and were overcome by fear. 7But Jesus came and touched them, saying, "Get up and do not be afraid." 8And when they looked up, they saw no one except Jesus himself alone.

9 As they were coming down the mountain, Jesus ordered them, "Tell no one about the vision until after the Son of Man has been raised from the dead." 10And the disciples asked him, "Why, then, do the scribes say that Elijah must come first?" 11He replied, "Elijah is indeed coming and will restore all things; 12but I tell you that Elijah has already come, and they did not recognize him, but they did to him whatever they pleased. So also the Son of Man is about to suffer at their hands." 13Then the disciples understood that he was speaking to them about John the Baptist.

14 When they came to the crowd, a man came to him, knelt before him, 15and said, "Lord, have mercy on my son, for he is an epileptic and he suffers terribly; he often falls into the fire and often into the water. 16And I brought him to your disciples, but they could not cure him." 17Jesus answered, "You faithless and perverse generation, how much longer must I be with you? How much longer must I put up with you? Bring him here to me." 18And Jesus rebuked the demon,[h] and it[i] came out of him, and the boy was cured instantly. 19Then the disciples came to Jesus privately and said, "Why could we not cast it out?" 20He said to them, "Because of your little faith. For truly I tell you, if you have faith the size of a[j] mustard seed, you will say to this mountain, 'Move from here to there,' and it will move; and nothing will be impossible for you."[k]

22 As they were gathering[l] in Galilee, Jesus said to them, "The Son of Man is going to be betrayed into human hands, 23and they will kill

[a] Gk *Petros* [b] Gk *petra* [c] Other ancient authorities add *Jesus* [d] Or *the Christ* [e] Other ancient authorities read *we* [f] Or *tents* [g] Or *my beloved Son* [h] Gk *it* or *him* [i] Gk *the demon* [j] Gk *faith as a grain of* [k] Other ancient authorities add verse 21, *But this kind does not come out except by prayer and fasting* [l] Other ancient authorities read *living*

him, and on the third day he will be raised." And
they were greatly distressed.

24 When they reached Capernaum, the collectors of the temple tax[a] came to Peter and said,
"Does your teacher not pay the temple tax?"[a] 25He
said, "Yes, he does." And when he came home,
Jesus spoke of it first, asking, "What do you think,
Simon? From whom do kings of the earth take
toll or tribute? From their children or from others?" 26When Peter[b] said, "From others," Jesus
said to him, "Then the children are free. 27How-
ever, so that we do not give offense to them, go
to the sea and cast a hook; take the first fish that
comes up; and when you open its mouth, you will
find a coin;[c] take that and give it to them for you
and me."

18 At that time the disciples came to Jesus
and asked, "Who is the greatest in the
kingdom of heaven?" 2He called a child, whom
he put among them, 3and said, "Truly I tell you,
unless you change and become like children, you
will never enter the kingdom of heaven. 4Who-
ever becomes humble like this child is the greatest
in the kingdom of heaven. 5Whoever welcomes
one such child in my name welcomes me.

6 "If any of you put a stumbling block before
one of these little ones who believe in me, it would
be better for you if a great millstone were fastened
around your neck and you were drowned in the
depth of the sea. 7Woe to the world because of
stumbling blocks! Occasions for stumbling are
bound to come, but woe to the one by whom the
stumbling block comes!

8 "If your hand or your foot causes you to
stumble, cut it off and throw it away; it is better
for you to enter life maimed or lame than to have
two hands or two feet and to be thrown into the
eternal fire. 9And if your eye causes you to stumble, tear it out and throw it away; it is better for
you to enter life with one eye than to have two
eyes and to be thrown into the hell[d] of fire.

10 "Take care that you do not despise one
of these little ones; for, I tell you, in heaven their
angels continually see the face of my Father in
heaven.[e] 12What do you think? If a shepherd
has a hundred sheep, and one of them has gone
astray, does he not leave the ninety-nine on the
mountains and go in search of the one that went
astray? 13And if he finds it, truly I tell you, he rejoices over it more than over the ninety-nine that
never went astray. 14So it is not the will of your[f]
Father in heaven that one of these little ones
should be lost.

15 "If another member of the church[g] sins
against you,[h] go and point out the fault when the
two of you are alone. If the member listens to you,
you have regained that one.[i] 16But if you are not
listened to, take one or two others along with you,
so that every word may be confirmed by the evidence of two or three witnesses. 17If the member
refuses to listen to them, tell it to the church; and
if the offender refuses to listen even to the church,
let such a one be to you as a Gentile and a tax collector. 18Truly I tell you, whatever you bind on
earth will be bound in heaven, and whatever you
loose on earth will be loosed in heaven. 19Again,
truly I tell you, if two of you agree on earth about
anything you ask, it will be done for you by my
Father in heaven. 20For where two or three are
gathered in my name, I am there among them."

21 Then Peter came and said to him, "Lord,
if another member of the church[j] sins against me,
how often should I forgive? As many as seven
times?" 22Jesus said to him, "Not seven times,
but, I tell you, seventy-seven[k] times.

23 "For this reason the kingdom of heaven
may be compared to a king who wished to settle
accounts with his slaves. 24When he began the
reckoning, one who owed him ten thousand talents[l] was brought to him; 25and, as he could not
pay, his lord ordered him to be sold, together
with his wife and children and all his posses-

[a] Gk *didrachma* [b] Gk *he* [c] Gk *stater*; the stater was worth two didrachmas [d] Gk *Gehenna* [e] Other ancient authorities add verse 11, *For the Son of Man came to save the lost* [f] Other ancient authorities read *my* [g] Gk *If your brother* [h] Other ancient authorities lack *against you* [i] Gk *the brother* [j] Gk *if my brother* [k] Or *seventy times seven* [l] A talent was worth more than fifteen years' wages of a laborer

sions, and payment to be made. 26So the slave fell
on his knees before him, saying, 'Have patience
with me, and I will pay you everything.' 27And
out of pity for him, the lord of that slave released
him and forgave him the debt. 28But that same
slave, as he went out, came upon one of his fellow slaves who owed him a hundred denarii;[a]
and seizing him by the throat, he said, 'Pay what
you owe.' 29Then his fellow slave fell down and
pleaded with him, 'Have patience with me, and
I will pay you.' 30But he refused; then he went
and threw him into prison until he would pay
the debt. 31When his fellow slaves saw what had
happened, they were greatly distressed, and they
went and reported to their lord all that had taken
place. 32Then his lord summoned him and said
to him, 'You wicked slave! I forgave you all that
debt because you pleaded with me. 33Should you
not have had mercy on your fellow slave, as I had
mercy on you?' 34And in anger his lord handed
him over to be tortured until he would pay his
entire debt. 35So my heavenly Father will also do
to every one of you, if you do not forgive your
brother or sister[b] from your heart."

19 When Jesus had finished saying these
things, he left Galilee and went to the region of Judea beyond the Jordan. 2Large crowds
followed him, and he cured them there.

3 Some Pharisees came to him, and to test
him they asked, "Is it lawful for a man to divorce
his wife for any cause?" 4He answered, "Have you
not read that the one who made them at the beginning 'made them male and female,' 5and said,
'For this reason a man shall leave his father and
mother and be joined to his wife, and the two
shall become one flesh'? 6So they are no longer two, but one flesh. Therefore what God has
joined together, let no one separate." 7They said
to him, "Why then did Moses command us to
give a certificate of dismissal and to divorce her?"
8He said to them, "It was because you were so
hard-hearted that Moses allowed you to divorce
your wives, but from the beginning it was not so.
9And I say to you, whoever divorces his wife, except for unchastity, and marries another commits
adultery."[c]

10 His disciples said to him, "If such is the
case of a man with his wife, it is better not to
marry." 11But he said to them, "Not everyone can
accept this teaching, but only those to whom it is
given. 12For there are eunuchs who have been so
from birth, and there are eunuchs who have been
made eunuchs by others, and there are eunuchs
who have made themselves eunuchs for the sake
of the kingdom of heaven. Let anyone accept this
who can."

13 Then little children were being brought to
him in order that he might lay his hands on them
and pray. The disciples spoke sternly to those
who brought them; 14but Jesus said, "Let the little
children come to me, and do not stop them; for it
is to such as these that the kingdom of heaven
belongs." 15And he laid his hands on them and
went on his way.

16 Then someone came to him and said,
"Teacher, what good deed must I do to have eternal life?" 17And he said to him, "Why do you ask
me about what is good? There is only one who is
good. If you wish to enter into life, keep the commandments." 18He said to him, "Which ones?"
And Jesus said, "You shall not murder; You shall
not commit adultery; You shall not steal; You shall
not bear false witness; 19Honor your father and
mother; also, You shall love your neighbor as yourself." 20The young man said to him, "I have kept all
these;[d] what do I still lack?" 21Jesus said to him, "If
you wish to be perfect, go, sell your possessions,
and give the money[e] to the poor, and you will
have treasure in heaven; then come, follow me."
22When the young man heard this word, he went
away grieving, for he had many possessions.

23 Then Jesus said to his disciples, "Truly I
tell you, it will be hard for a rich person to enter
the kingdom of heaven. 24Again I tell you, it
is easier for a camel to go through the eye of a

[a] The denarius was the usual day's wage for a laborer [b] Gk *brother* [c] Other ancient authorities read *except on the ground of unchastity, causes her to commit adultery*; others add at the end of the verse *and he who marries a divorced woman commits adultery* [d] Other ancient authorities add *from my youth* [e] Gk lacks *the money*

needle than for someone who is rich to enter the
kingdom of God.” 25When the disciples heard
this, they were greatly astounded and said, “Then
who can be saved?” 26But Jesus looked at them
and said, “For mortals it is impossible, but for
God all things are possible.”

27 Then Peter said in reply, “Look, we have
left everything and followed you. What then will
we have?” 28Jesus said to them, “Truly I tell you,
at the renewal of all things, when the Son of Man
is seated on the throne of his glory, you who have
followed me will also sit on twelve thrones, judging the twelve tribes of Israel. 29And everyone
who has left houses or brothers or sisters or father
or mother or children or fields, for my name’s
sake, will receive a hundredfold,[a] and will inherit
eternal life. 30But many who are first will be last,
and the last will be first.

20 “For the kingdom of heaven is like a landowner who went out early in the morning
to hire laborers for his vineyard. 2After agreeing
with the laborers for the usual daily wage,[b] he
sent them into his vineyard. 3When he went out
about nine o’clock, he saw others standing idle in
the marketplace; 4and he said to them, ‘You also
go into the vineyard, and I will pay you whatever
is right.’ So they went. 5When he went out again
about noon and about three o’clock, he did the
same. 6And about five o’clock he went out and
found others standing around; and he said to
them, ‘Why are you standing here idle all day?’
7They said to him, ‘Because no one has hired us.’
He said to them, ‘You also go into the vineyard.’
8When evening came, the owner of the vineyard
said to his manager, ‘Call the laborers and give
them their pay, beginning with the last and then
going to the first.’ 9When those hired about five
o’clock came, each of them received the usual
daily wage.[b] 10Now when the first came, they
thought they would receive more; but each of
them also received the usual daily wage.[b] 11And
when they received it, they grumbled against the
landowner, 12saying, ‘These last worked only one
hour, and you have made them equal to us who
have borne the burden of the day and the scorching heat.’ 13But he replied to one of them, ‘Friend,
I am doing you no wrong; did you not agree with
me for the usual daily wage?[b] 14Take what belongs to you and go; I choose to give to this last
the same as I give to you. 15Am I not allowed to
do what I choose with what belongs to me? Or
are you envious because I am generous?’[c] 16So
the last will be first, and the first will be last.”[d]

17 While Jesus was going up to Jerusalem,
he took the twelve disciples aside by themselves,

[a] Other ancient authorities read *manifold* [b] Gk *a denarius* [c] Gk *is your eye evil because I am good?*
[d] Other ancient authorities add *for many are called but few are chosen*

Matthew 20:1-16

Many interpret the parable of the hired laborers to mean that all who come to Jesus, whether early in life or at one’s deathbed, will receive the same level of grace and blessings in heaven. But what if we take the terms of the parable literally? In a Eurocentric capitalist culture that has normalized the exchange of a worker’s labor for a certain wage, we may hear Jesus suggesting an unfair business practice (though a common one!) that gives greater rewards to the workers who have not put in a full day of work. But today many migrant workers, many of them Latino and Latina, some of them undocumented, read this parable differently. Even when they are ready and able to put in a full day of work, if they are not picked, or are picked to work only a few hours, or are paid low wages, they will not earn enough to feed their family. The lesson Jesus gives workers is to be willing always to give a full day’s work; but to the owners of production, the lesson is that they have a responsibility to their workers to pay each a living wage, regardless of how many hours are actually worked.

— MDLT

and said to them on the way, 18“See, we are going up to Jerusalem, and the Son of Man will be
handed over to the chief priests and scribes, and
they will condemn him to death; 19then they will
hand him over to the Gentiles to be mocked and
flogged and crucified; and on the third day he will
be raised.”

20 Then the mother of the sons of Zebedee
came to him with her sons, and kneeling before
him, she asked a favor of him. 21And he said to
her, “What do you want?” She said to him, “Declare that these two sons of mine will sit, one at
your right hand and one at your left, in your kingdom.” 22But Jesus answered, “You do not know
what you are asking. Are you able to drink the cup
that I am about to drink?”[a] They said to him, “We
are able.” 23He said to them, “You will indeed
drink my cup, but to sit at my right hand and at
my left, this is not mine to grant, but it is for those
for whom it has been prepared by my Father.”

24 When the ten heard it, they were angry
with the two brothers. 25But Jesus called them
to him and said, “You know that the rulers of the
Gentiles lord it over them, and their great ones
are tyrants over them. 26It will not be so among
you; but whoever wishes to be great among you
must be your servant, 27and whoever wishes to be
first among you must be your slave; 28just as the
Son of Man came not to be served but to serve,
and to give his life a ransom for many.”

29 As they were leaving Jericho, a large crowd
followed him. 30There were two blind men sitting
by the roadside. When they heard that Jesus was
passing by, they shouted, “Lord,[b] have mercy
on us, Son of David!” 31The crowd sternly ordered them to be quiet; but they shouted even
more loudly, “Have mercy on us, Lord, Son of
David!” 32Jesus stood still and called them, saying, “What do you want me to do for you?”
33They said to him, “Lord, let our eyes be opened.”
34Moved with compassion, Jesus touched their
eyes. Immediately they regained their sight and
followed him.

21 When they had come near Jerusalem and
had reached Bethphage, at the Mount of
Olives, Jesus sent two disciples, 2saying to them,
“Go into the village ahead of you, and immediately you will find a donkey tied, and a colt with
her; untie them and bring them to me. 3If anyone says anything to you, just say this, ‘The Lord
needs them.’ And he will send them immediately.[c]” 4This took place to fulfill what had been
spoken through the prophet, saying,

5 “Tell the daughter of Zion,
Look, your king is coming to you,
humble, and mounted on a donkey,
and on a colt, the foal of a donkey.”

6The disciples went and did as Jesus had directed
them; 7they brought the donkey and the colt,
and put their cloaks on them, and he sat on them.
8A very large crowd[d] spread their cloaks on the
road, and others cut branches from the trees and
spread them on the road. 9The crowds that went
ahead of him and that followed were shouting,

“Hosanna to the Son of David!
Blessed is the one who comes in the name
of the Lord!
Hosanna in the highest heaven!”

10When he entered Jerusalem, the whole city was
in turmoil, asking, “Who is this?” 11The crowds
were saying, “This is the prophet Jesus from Nazareth in Galilee.”

12 Then Jesus entered the temple[e] and drove
out all who were selling and buying in the temple,
and he overturned the tables of the money changers and the seats of those who sold doves. 13He
said to them, “It is written,

‘My house shall be called a house of
prayer’;
but you are making it a den of robbers.”

14 The blind and the lame came to him in the
temple, and he cured them. 15But when the chief
priests and the scribes saw the amazing things
that he did, and heard[f] the children crying out in
the temple, “Hosanna to the Son of David,” they
became angry 16and said to him, “Do you hear

[a] Other ancient authorities add *or to be baptized with the baptism that I am baptized with?* [b] Other ancient authorities lack *Lord* [c] Or *‘The Lord needs them and will send them back immediately.’* [d] Or *Most of the crowd* [e] Other ancient authorities add *of God* [f] Gk lacks *heard*

what these are saying?" Jesus said to them, "Yes;
have you never read,

'Out of the mouths of infants and nursing
babies
you have prepared praise for yourself'?"

17 He left them, went out of the city to Bethany,
and spent the night there.

18 In the morning, when he returned to the
city, he was hungry. 19 And seeing a fig tree by the
side of the road, he went to it and found nothing
at all on it but leaves. Then he said to it, "May no
fruit ever come from you again!" And the fig tree
withered at once. 20 When the disciples saw it, they
were amazed, saying, "How did the fig tree wither
at once?" 21 Jesus answered them, "Truly I tell you,
if you have faith and do not doubt, not only will
you do what has been done to the fig tree, but
even if you say to this mountain, 'Be lifted up and
thrown into the sea,' it will be done. 22 Whatever
you ask for in prayer with faith, you will receive."

23 When he entered the temple, the chief
priests and the elders of the people came to him as
he was teaching, and said, "By what authority are
you doing these things, and who gave you this authority?" 24 Jesus said to them, "I will also ask you
one question; if you tell me the answer, then I will
also tell you by what authority I do these things.
25 Did the baptism of John come from heaven, or
was it of human origin?" And they argued with
one another, "If we say, 'From heaven,' he will say
to us, 'Why then did you not believe him?' 26 But
if we say, 'Of human origin,' we are afraid of the
crowd; for all regard John as a prophet." 27 So they
answered Jesus, "We do not know." And he said to
them, "Neither will I tell you by what authority I
am doing these things.

28 "What do you think? A man had two sons;
he went to the first and said, 'Son, go and work in
the vineyard today.' 29 He answered, 'I will not';
but later he changed his mind and went. 30 The
father[a] went to the second and said the same;
and he answered, 'I go, sir'; but he did not go.
31 Which of the two did the will of his father?"
They said, "The first." Jesus said to them, "Truly
I tell you, the tax collectors and the prostitutes
are going into the kingdom of God ahead of you.
32 For John came to you in the way of righteousness and you did not believe him, but the tax
collectors and the prostitutes believed him; and
even after you saw it, you did not change your
minds and believe him.

Matthew 21:31

Jesus consistently welcomed those whom his society stigmatized as unclean: the leper, the prostitute, the tax collector, the woman with the constant blood flow, the Gentile. He sought out those whom religious leaders and the so-called pillars of the community saw as outsiders and sinners. He refused to discriminate against them, making a preferential option for the disenfranchised. Which people today are labeled unclean and unworthy by society? Can it be that they, too, are entering heaven ahead of the self-proclaimed righteous and religious leaders?

— MDLT

33 "Listen to another parable. There was a
landowner who planted a vineyard, put a fence
around it, dug a wine press in it, and built a
watchtower. Then he leased it to tenants and went
to another country. 34 When the harvest time had
come, he sent his slaves to the tenants to collect
his produce. 35 But the tenants seized his slaves
and beat one, killed another, and stoned another.
36 Again he sent other slaves, more than the first;
and they treated them in the same way. 37 Finally
he sent his son to them, saying, 'They will respect
my son.' 38 But when the tenants saw the son,
they said to themselves, 'This is the heir; come,
let us kill him and get his inheritance.' 39 So they
seized him, threw him out of the vineyard, and
killed him. 40 Now when the owner of the vineyard comes, what will he do to those tenants?"
41 They said to him, "He will put those wretches
to a miserable death, and lease the vineyard to
other tenants who will give him the produce at
the harvest time."

[a] Gk *He*

42 Jesus said to them, "Have you never read
in the scriptures:
'The stone that the builders rejected
has become the cornerstone;[a]
this was the Lord's doing,
and it is amazing in our eyes'?
43 Therefore I tell you, the kingdom of God will be
taken away from you and given to a people that
produces the fruits of the kingdom.[b] 44 The one
who falls on this stone will be broken to pieces;
and it will crush anyone on whom it falls."[c]
45 When the chief priests and the Pharisees heard his parables, they realized that he was
speaking about them. 46 They wanted to arrest
him, but they feared the crowds, because they regarded him as a prophet.

22 Once more Jesus spoke to them in parables, saying: 2 "The kingdom of heaven
may be compared to a king who gave a wedding
banquet for his son. 3 He sent his slaves to call
those who had been invited to the wedding banquet, but they would not come. 4 Again he sent
other slaves, saying, 'Tell those who have been invited: Look, I have prepared my dinner, my oxen
and my fat calves have been slaughtered, and
everything is ready; come to the wedding banquet.' 5 But they made light of it and went away,
one to his farm, another to his business, 6 while
the rest seized his slaves, mistreated them, and
killed them. 7 The king was enraged. He sent his
troops, destroyed those murderers, and burned
their city. 8 Then he said to his slaves, 'The wedding is ready, but those invited were not worthy.
9 Go therefore into the main streets, and invite everyone you find to the wedding banquet.' 10 Those
slaves went out into the streets and gathered all
whom they found, both good and bad; so the
wedding hall was filled with guests.
11 "But when the king came in to see the
guests, he noticed a man there who was not wearing a wedding robe, 12 and he said to him, 'Friend,
how did you get in here without a wedding robe?'
And he was speechless. 13 Then the king said to the
attendants, 'Bind him hand and foot, and throw
him into the outer darkness, where there will be
weeping and gnashing of teeth.' 14 For many are
called, but few are chosen."
15 Then the Pharisees went and plotted to
entrap him in what he said. 16 So they sent their
disciples to him, along with the Herodians, saying, "Teacher, we know that you are sincere, and
teach the way of God in accordance with truth,
and show deference to no one; for you do not regard people with partiality. 17 Tell us, then, what
you think. Is it lawful to pay taxes to the emperor,
or not?" 18 But Jesus, aware of their malice, said,
"Why are you putting me to the test, you hypocrites? 19 Show me the coin used for the tax." And
they brought him a denarius. 20 Then he said to
them, "Whose head is this, and whose title?"
21 They answered, "The emperor's." Then he said
to them, "Give therefore to the emperor the things
that are the emperor's, and to God the things that
are God's." 22 When they heard this, they were
amazed; and they left him and went away.
23 The same day some Sadducees came to
him, saying there is no resurrection;[d] and they
asked him a question, saying, 24 "Teacher, Moses said, 'If a man dies childless, his brother shall
marry the widow, and raise up children for his
brother.' 25 Now there were seven brothers among
us; the first married, and died childless, leaving
the widow to his brother. 26 The second did the
same, so also the third, down to the seventh.
27 Last of all, the woman herself died. 28 In the resurrection, then, whose wife of the seven will she
be? For all of them had married her."
29 Jesus answered them, "You are wrong,
because you know neither the scriptures nor the
power of God. 30 For in the resurrection they neither marry nor are given in marriage, but are like
angels[e] in heaven. 31 And as for the resurrection of
the dead, have you not read what was said to you
by God, 32 'I am the God of Abraham, the God of
Isaac, and the God of Jacob'? He is God not of the
dead, but of the living." 33 And when the crowd
heard it, they were astounded at his teaching.
34 When the Pharisees heard that he had

[a] Or *keystone* [b] Gk *the fruits of it* [c] Other ancient authorities lack verse 44 [d] Other ancient authorities read *who say that there is no resurrection* [e] Other ancient authorities add *of God*

silenced the Sadducees, they gathered together,
35and one of them, a lawyer, asked him a question
to test him. 36"Teacher, which commandment in
the law is the greatest?" 37He said to him, "'You
shall love the Lord your God with all your heart,
and with all your soul, and with all your mind.'
38This is the greatest and first commandment.
39And a second is like it: 'You shall love your
neighbor as yourself.' 40On these two commandments hang all the law and the prophets."

41 Now while the Pharisees were gathered together, Jesus asked them this question: 42"What
do you think of the Messiah?[a] Whose son is he?"
They said to him, "The son of David." 43He said
to them, "How is it then that David by the Spirit[b]
calls him Lord, saying,

44 'The Lord said to my Lord,
"Sit at my right hand,
until I put your enemies under your
feet" '?

45If David thus calls him Lord, how can he be his
son?" 46No one was able to give him an answer,
nor from that day did anyone dare to ask him any
more questions.

23 Then Jesus said to the crowds and to his
disciples, 2"The scribes and the Pharisees
sit on Moses' seat; 3therefore, do whatever they
teach you and follow it; but do not do as they do,
for they do not practice what they teach. 4They tie
up heavy burdens, hard to bear,[c] and lay them on
the shoulders of others; but they themselves are
unwilling to lift a finger to move them. 5They do
all their deeds to be seen by others; for they make
their phylacteries broad and their fringes long.
6They love to have the place of honor at banquets
and the best seats in the synagogues, 7and to be
greeted with respect in the marketplaces, and to
have people call them rabbi. 8But you are not to
be called rabbi, for you have one teacher, and you
are all students.[d] 9And call no one your father on
earth, for you have one Father—the one in heaven.
10Nor are you to be called instructors, for you
have one instructor, the Messiah.[e] 11The greatest
among you will be your servant. 12All who exalt
themselves will be humbled, and all who humble
themselves will be exalted.

13 "But woe to you, scribes and Pharisees,
hypocrites! For you lock people out of the kingdom of heaven. For you do not go in yourselves,
and when others are going in, you stop them.[f]
15Woe to you, scribes and Pharisees, hypocrites!
For you cross sea and land to make a single convert, and you make the new convert twice as
much a child of hell[g] as yourselves.

16 "Woe to you, blind guides, who say, 'Whoever swears by the sanctuary is bound by nothing,
but whoever swears by the gold of the sanctuary is bound by the oath.' 17You blind fools! For
which is greater, the gold or the sanctuary that
has made the gold sacred? 18And you say, 'Whoever swears by the altar is bound by nothing, but
whoever swears by the gift that is on the altar is
bound by the oath.' 19How blind you are! For
which is greater, the gift or the altar that makes
the gift sacred? 20So whoever swears by the altar,
swears by it and by everything on it; 21and whoever swears by the sanctuary, swears by it and by
the one who dwells in it; 22and whoever swears
by heaven, swears by the throne of God and by
the one who is seated upon it.

23 "Woe to you, scribes and Pharisees, hypocrites! For you tithe mint, dill, and cummin, and
have neglected the weightier matters of the law:
justice and mercy and faith. It is these you ought
to have practiced without neglecting the others.
24You blind guides! You strain out a gnat but
swallow a camel!

25 "Woe to you, scribes and Pharisees, hypocrites! For you clean the outside of the cup and
of the plate, but inside they are full of greed and
self-indulgence. 26You blind Pharisee! First clean
the inside of the cup,[h] so that the outside also may
become clean.

27 "Woe to you, scribes and Pharisees, hyp-

[a] Or *Christ* [b] Gk *in spirit* [c] Other ancient authorities lack *hard to bear* [d] Gk *brothers* [e] Or *the Christ*
[f] Other authorities add here (or after verse 12) verse 14, *Woe to you, scribes and Pharisees, hypocrites! For you devour widows' houses and for the sake of appearance you make long prayers; therefore you will receive the greater condemnation* [g] Gk *Gehenna*
[h] Other ancient authorities add *and of the plate*

ocrites! For you are like whitewashed tombs,
which on the outside look beautiful, but inside
they are full of the bones of the dead and of all
kinds of filth. 28So you also on the outside look
righteous to others, but inside you are full of hypocrisy and lawlessness.

29 "Woe to you, scribes and Pharisees, hypocrites! For you build the tombs of the prophets
and decorate the graves of the righteous, 30and
you say, 'If we had lived in the days of our ancestors, we would not have taken part with them in
shedding the blood of the prophets.' 31Thus you
testify against yourselves that you are descendants of those who murdered the prophets. 32Fill
up, then, the measure of your ancestors. 33You
snakes, you brood of vipers! How can you escape
being sentenced to hell?[a] 34Therefore I send you
prophets, sages, and scribes, some of whom you
will kill and crucify, and some you will flog in
your synagogues and pursue from town to town,
35so that upon you may come all the righteous
blood shed on earth, from the blood of righteous
Abel to the blood of Zechariah son of Barachiah,
whom you murdered between the sanctuary and
the altar. 36Truly I tell you, all this will come upon
this generation.

37 "Jerusalem, Jerusalem, the city that kills
the prophets and stones those who are sent to
it! How often have I desired to gather your children together as a hen gathers her brood under
her wings, and you were not willing! 38See, your
house is left to you, desolate.[b] 39For I tell you, you
will not see me again until you say, 'Blessed is the
one who comes in the name of the Lord.' "

24 As Jesus came out of the temple and was
going away, his disciples came to point
out to him the buildings of the temple. 2Then he
asked them, "You see all these, do you not? Truly
I tell you, not one stone will be left here upon another; all will be thrown down."

3 When he was sitting on the Mount of Olives, the disciples came to him privately, saying,
"Tell us, when will this be, and what will be the
sign of your coming and of the end of the age?"
4Jesus answered them, "Beware that no one leads
you astray. 5For many will come in my name, saying, 'I am the Messiah!'[c] and they will lead many
astray. 6And you will hear of wars and rumors of
wars; see that you are not alarmed; for this must
take place, but the end is not yet. 7For nation will
rise against nation, and kingdom against kingdom, and there will be famines[d] and earthquakes
in various places: 8all this is but the beginning of
the birth pangs.

9 "Then they will hand you over to be tortured and will put you to death, and you will be
hated by all nations because of my name. 10Then
many will fall away,[e] and they will betray one another and hate one another. 11And many false
prophets will arise and lead many astray. 12And
because of the increase of lawlessness, the love of
many will grow cold. 13But the one who endures
to the end will be saved. 14And this good news[f] of
the kingdom will be proclaimed throughout the
world, as a testimony to all the nations; and then
the end will come.

15 "So when you see the desolating sacrilege
standing in the holy place, as was spoken of by
the prophet Daniel (let the reader understand),
16then those in Judea must flee to the mountains;
17the one on the housetop must not go down to
take what is in the house; 18the one in the field
must not turn back to get a coat. 19Woe to those
who are pregnant and to those who are nursing
infants in those days! 20Pray that your flight may
not be in winter or on a sabbath. 21For at that
time there will be great suffering, such as has not
been from the beginning of the world until now,
no, and never will be. 22And if those days had not
been cut short, no one would be saved; but for
the sake of the elect those days will be cut short.
23Then if anyone says to you, 'Look! Here is the
Messiah!'[c] or 'There he is!'—do not believe it.
24For false messiahs[g] and false prophets will appear and produce great signs and omens, to lead
astray, if possible, even the elect. 25Take note, I
have told you beforehand. 26So, if they say to you,

[a] Gk *Gehenna* [b] Other ancient authorities lack *desolate* [c] Or *the Christ* [d] Other ancient authorities add *and pestilences* [e] Or *stumble* [f] Or *gospel* [g] Or *christs*

'Look! He is in the wilderness,' do not go out.
If they say, 'Look! He is in the inner rooms,' do
not believe it. 27 For as the lightning comes from
the east and flashes as far as the west, so will be
the coming of the Son of Man. 28 Wherever the
corpse is, there the vultures will gather.

29 "Immediately after the suffering of those
days

> the sun will be darkened,
>   and the moon will not give its light;
> the stars will fall from heaven,
>   and the powers of heaven will be shaken.

30 Then the sign of the Son of Man will appear in
heaven, and then all the tribes of the earth will
mourn, and they will see 'the Son of Man coming on the clouds of heaven' with power and great
glory. 31 And he will send out his angels with a
loud trumpet call, and they will gather his elect
from the four winds, from one end of heaven to
the other.

32 "From the fig tree learn its lesson: as soon
as its branch becomes tender and puts forth its
leaves, you know that summer is near. 33 So also,
when you see all these things, you know that
he[a] is near, at the very gates. 34 Truly I tell you,
this generation will not pass away until all these
things have taken place. 35 Heaven and earth will
pass away, but my words will not pass away.

36 "But about that day and hour no one
knows, neither the angels of heaven, nor the
Son,[b] but only the Father. 37 For as the days of
Noah were, so will be the coming of the Son of
Man. 38 For as in those days before the flood they
were eating and drinking, marrying and giving
in marriage, until the day Noah entered the ark,
39 and they knew nothing until the flood came
and swept them all away, so too will be the coming of the Son of Man. 40 Then two will be in the
field; one will be taken and one will be left. 41 Two
women will be grinding meal together; one will
be taken and one will be left. 42 Keep awake therefore, for you do not know on what day[c] your Lord
is coming. 43 But understand this: if the owner of
the house had known in what part of the night the
thief was coming, he would have stayed awake
and would not have let his house be broken into.
44 Therefore you also must be ready, for the Son of
Man is coming at an unexpected hour.

45 "Who then is the faithful and wise slave,
whom his master has put in charge of his household, to give the other slaves[d] their allowance of
food at the proper time? 46 Blessed is that slave
whom his master will find at work when he arrives.
47 Truly I tell you, he will put that one in charge of
all his possessions. 48 But if that wicked slave says
to himself, 'My master is delayed,' 49 and he begins
to beat his fellow slaves, and eats and drinks with
drunkards, 50 the master of that slave will come on
a day when he does not expect him and at an hour
that he does not know. 51 He will cut him in pieces[e]
and put him with the hypocrites, where there will
be weeping and gnashing of teeth.

25 "Then the kingdom of heaven will be like
this. Ten bridesmaids[f] took their lamps
and went to meet the bridegroom.[g] 2 Five of them
were foolish, and five were wise. 3 When the foolish took their lamps, they took no oil with them;
4 but the wise took flasks of oil with their lamps.
5 As the bridegroom was delayed, all of them became drowsy and slept. 6 But at midnight there
was a shout, 'Look! Here is the bridegroom!
Come out to meet him.' 7 Then all those bridesmaids[f] got up and trimmed their lamps. 8 The
foolish said to the wise, 'Give us some of your oil,
for our lamps are going out.' 9 But the wise replied,
'No! there will not be enough for you and for us;
you had better go to the dealers and buy some
for yourselves.' 10 And while they went to buy it,
the bridegroom came, and those who were ready
went with him into the wedding banquet; and
the door was shut. 11 Later the other bridesmaids[f]
came also, saying, 'Lord, lord, open to us.' 12 But
he replied, 'Truly I tell you, I do not know you.'
13 Keep awake therefore, for you know neither the
day nor the hour.[h]

14 "For it is as if a man, going on a journey,

[a] Or *it* [b] Other ancient authorities lack *nor the Son* [c] Other ancient authorities read *at what hour*
[d] Gk *to give them* [e] Or *cut him off* [f] Gk *virgins* [g] Other ancient authorities add *and the bride*
[h] Other ancient authorities add *in which the Son of Man is coming*

summoned his slaves and entrusted his property to them; 15 to one he gave five talents,[a] to another two, to another one, to each according to his ability. Then he went away. 16 The one who had received the five talents went off at once and traded with them, and made five more talents. 17 In the same way, the one who had the two talents made two more talents. 18 But the one who had received the one talent went off and dug a hole in the ground and hid his master's money. 19 After a long time the master of those slaves came and settled accounts with them. 20 Then the one who had received the five talents came forward, bringing five more talents, saying, 'Master, you handed over to me five talents; see, I have made five more talents.' 21 His master said to him, 'Well done, good and trustworthy slave; you have been trustworthy in a few things, I will put you in charge of many things; enter into the joy of your master.' 22 And the one with the two talents also came forward, saying, 'Master, you handed over to me two talents; see, I have made two more talents.' 23 His master said to him, 'Well done, good and trustworthy slave; you have been trustworthy in a few things, I will put you in charge of many things; enter into the joy of your master.' 24 Then the one who had received the one talent also came forward, saying, 'Master, I knew that you were a harsh man, reaping where you did not sow, and gathering where you did not scatter seed; 25 so I was afraid, and I went and hid your talent in the ground. Here you have what is yours.' 26 But his master replied, 'You wicked and lazy slave! You knew, did you, that I reap where I did not sow, and gather where I did not scatter? 27 Then you ought to have invested my money with the bankers, and on my return I would have received what was my own with interest. 28 So take the talent from him, and give it to the one with the ten talents. 29 For to all those who have, more will be given, and they will have an abundance; but from those who have nothing, even what they have will be taken away. 30 As for this worthless slave, throw him into the outer darkness, where there will be weeping and gnashing of teeth.'

31 "When the Son of Man comes in his glory, and all the angels with him, then he will sit on the throne of his glory. 32 All the nations will be gathered before him, and he will separate people one from another as a shepherd separates the sheep from the goats, 33 and he will put the sheep at his right hand and the goats at the left. 34 Then the king will say to those at his right hand, 'Come, you that are blessed by my Father, inherit the kingdom prepared for you from the foundation of the world; 35 for I was hungry and you gave me food, I was thirsty and you gave me something to drink, I was a stranger and you welcomed me, 36 I was naked and you gave me clothing, I was sick and you took care of me, I was in prison and you visited me.' 37 Then the righteous will answer him, 'Lord, when was it that we saw you hungry and gave you food, or thirsty and gave you something to drink? 38 And when was it that we saw you a stranger and welcomed you, or naked and gave you clothing? 39 And when was it that we saw you sick or in prison and visited you?' 40 And the king will answer them, 'Truly I tell you, just as you did it to one of the least of these who are members of my family,[b] you did it to me.' 41 Then he will say to those at his left hand, 'You that are accursed, depart from me into the eternal fire prepared for the devil and his angels; 42 for I was hungry and you gave me no food, I was thirsty and you gave me nothing to drink, 43 I was a stranger and

Matthew 25:35-36

Standing where God stands, however, sharing the pain and the destitution of the poor, feeling the pain of their exclusion as well as the burning of their right to inclusion, protects one from the luxury of myth-making. . . . It requires us to soberly assess the situation, not from the comfortable seats of power, but from the depths of the pits where the poor are yearning to be heard. Reconciliation begins truly when the voice from the pit is heard, and when that voice sets the tone.[68]

— ***Allan Boesak***

[a] A talent was worth more than fifteen years' wages of a laborer

[b] Gk *these my brothers*

you did not welcome me, naked and you did not
give me clothing, sick and in prison and you did
not visit me.' 44 Then they also will answer, 'Lord,
when was it that we saw you hungry or thirsty or a
stranger or naked or sick or in prison, and did not
take care of you?' 45 Then he will answer them,
'Truly I tell you, just as you did not do it to one of
the least of these, you did not do it to me.' 46 And
these will go away into eternal punishment, but
the righteous into eternal life."

Matthew 25:44-46

Christians often hear devout exhortations to "see Christ in others." But the point of Jesus' warning is that it is those who spontaneously show mercy to the needy—*without* realizing that they are dealing with the Son of Man—who will be vindicated. I must respond to my neighbor because he or she is in need: that is all. If I wait until I see Christ in them, I delude myself that I can judge who is deserving and who is not—and that, according to Jesus' words, means I have waited too long.

— *NE*

26 When Jesus had finished saying all these
things, he said to his disciples, 2 "You
know that after two days the Passover is coming,
and the Son of Man will be handed over to be
crucified."

3 Then the chief priests and the elders of the
people gathered in the palace of the high priest,
who was called Caiaphas, 4 and they conspired
to arrest Jesus by stealth and kill him. 5 But they
said, "Not during the festival, or there may be a
riot among the people."

6 Now while Jesus was at Bethany in the house
of Simon the leper,[a] 7 a woman came to him with
an alabaster jar of very costly ointment, and she
poured it on his head as he sat at the table. 8 But
when the disciples saw it, they were angry and
said, "Why this waste? 9 For this ointment could
have been sold for a large sum, and the money
given to the poor." 10 But Jesus, aware of this, said
to them, "Why do you trouble the woman? She
has performed a good service for me. 11 For you
always have the poor with you, but you will not
always have me. 12 By pouring this ointment on
my body she has prepared me for burial. 13 Truly I
tell you, wherever this good news[b] is proclaimed
in the whole world, what she has done will be
told in remembrance of her."

14 Then one of the twelve, who was called Judas Iscariot, went to the chief priests 15 and said,
"What will you give me if I betray him to you?"
They paid him thirty pieces of silver. 16 And from
that moment he began to look for an opportunity
to betray him.

17 On the first day of Unleavened Bread the
disciples came to Jesus, saying, "Where do you
want us to make the preparations for you to eat
the Passover?" 18 He said, "Go into the city to a
certain man, and say to him, 'The Teacher says,
My time is near; I will keep the Passover at your
house with my disciples.'" 19 So the disciples did
as Jesus had directed them, and they prepared the
Passover meal.

20 When it was evening, he took his place
with the twelve;[c] 21 and while they were eating,
he said, "Truly I tell you, one of you will betray
me." 22 And they became greatly distressed and
began to say to him one after another, "Surely
not I, Lord?" 23 He answered, "The one who has
dipped his hand into the bowl with me will betray
me. 24 The Son of Man goes as it is written of him,
but woe to that one by whom the Son of Man is
betrayed! It would have been better for that one
not to have been born." 25 Judas, who betrayed
him, said, "Surely not I, Rabbi?" He replied, "You
have said so."

26 While they were eating, Jesus took a loaf
of bread, and after blessing it he broke it, gave it
to the disciples, and said, "Take, eat; this is my
body." 27 Then he took a cup, and after giving
thanks he gave it to them, saying, "Drink from it,
all of you; 28 for this is my blood of the[d] covenant,

[a] The terms *leper* and *leprosy* can refer to several diseases
[b] Or *gospel*
[c] Other ancient authorities add *disciples*
[d] Other ancient authorities add *new*

 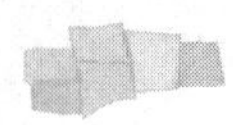

which is poured out for many for the forgiveness
of sins. 29I tell you, I will never again drink of this
fruit of the vine until that day when I drink it new
with you in my Father's kingdom."

30 When they had sung the hymn, they went
out to the Mount of Olives.

31 Then Jesus said to them, "You will all become deserters because of me this night; for it is
written,

'I will strike the shepherd,
and the sheep of the flock will be
scattered.'

32But after I am raised up, I will go ahead of you to
Galilee." 33Peter said to him, "Though all become
deserters because of you, I will never desert you."
34Jesus said to him, "Truly I tell you, this very
night, before the cock crows, you will deny me
three times." 35Peter said to him, "Even though I
must die with you, I will not deny you." And so
said all the disciples.

36 Then Jesus went with them to a place
called Gethsemane; and he said to his disciples,
"Sit here while I go over there and pray." 37He
took with him Peter and the two sons of Zebedee,
and began to be grieved and agitated. 38Then he
said to them, "I am deeply grieved, even to death;
remain here, and stay awake with me." 39And going a little farther, he threw himself on the ground
and prayed, "My Father, if it is possible, let this
cup pass from me; yet not what I want but what
you want." 40Then he came to the disciples and
found them sleeping; and he said to Peter, "So,
could you not stay awake with me one hour?
41Stay awake and pray that you may not come
into the time of trial;[a] the spirit indeed is willing,
but the flesh is weak." 42Again he went away for
the second time and prayed, "My Father, if this
cannot pass unless I drink it, your will be done."
43Again he came and found them sleeping, for
their eyes were heavy. 44So leaving them again, he
went away and prayed for the third time, saying
the same words. 45Then he came to the disciples
and said to them, "Are you still sleeping and taking your rest? See, the hour is at hand, and the
Son of Man is betrayed into the hands of sinners.
46Get up, let us be going. See, my betrayer is at
hand."

47 While he was still speaking, Judas, one of
the twelve, arrived; with him was a large crowd
with swords and clubs, from the chief priests and
the elders of the people. 48Now the betrayer had
given them a sign, saying, "The one I will kiss is
the man; arrest him." 49At once he came up to
Jesus and said, "Greetings, Rabbi!" and kissed
him. 50Jesus said to him, "Friend, do what you
are here to do." Then they came and laid hands on
Jesus and arrested him. 51Suddenly, one of those
with Jesus put his hand on his sword, drew it, and
struck the slave of the high priest, cutting off his
ear. 52Then Jesus said to him, "Put your sword
back into its place; for all who take the sword will
perish by the sword. 53Do you think that I cannot appeal to my Father, and he will at once send
me more than twelve legions of angels? 54But
how then would the scriptures be fulfilled, which
say it must happen in this way?" 55At that hour
Jesus said to the crowds, "Have you come out
with swords and clubs to arrest me as though I
were a bandit? Day after day I sat in the temple
teaching, and you did not arrest me. 56But all
this has taken place, so that the scriptures of the
prophets may be fulfilled." Then all the disciples
deserted him and fled.

57 Those who had arrested Jesus took him
to Caiaphas the high priest, in whose house the
scribes and the elders had gathered. 58But Peter was following him at a distance, as far as the
courtyard of the high priest; and going inside, he
sat with the guards in order to see how this would
end. 59Now the chief priests and the whole council were looking for false testimony against Jesus
so that they might put him to death, 60but they
found none, though many false witnesses came
forward. At last two came forward 61and said,
"This fellow said, 'I am able to destroy the temple
of God and to build it in three days.'" 62The high
priest stood up and said, "Have you no answer?
What is it that they testify against you?" 63But
Jesus was silent. Then the high priest said to him,
"I put you under oath before the living God,

[a] Or *into temptation*

tell us if you are the Messiah,[a] the Son of God."
64 Jesus said to him, "You have said so. But I tell
you,

> From now on you will see the Son of Man
> seated at the right hand of Power
> and coming on the clouds of heaven."

65 Then the high priest tore his clothes and said,
"He has blasphemed! Why do we still need witnesses? You have now heard his blasphemy.
66 What is your verdict?" They answered, "He
deserves death." 67 Then they spat in his face and
struck him; and some slapped him, 68 saying,
"Prophesy to us, you Messiah![a] Who is it that
struck you?"

69 Now Peter was sitting outside in the courtyard. A servant-girl came to him and said, "You
also were with Jesus the Galilean." 70 But he denied
it before all of them, saying, "I do not know what
you are talking about." 71 When he went out to the
porch, another servant-girl saw him, and she said
to the bystanders, "This man was with Jesus of
Nazareth."[b] 72 Again he denied it with an oath, "I
do not know the man." 73 After a little while the bystanders came up and said to Peter, "Certainly you
are also one of them, for your accent betrays you."
74 Then he began to curse, and he swore an oath, "I
do not know the man!" At that moment the cock
crowed. 75 Then Peter remembered what Jesus had
said: "Before the cock crows, you will deny me
three times." And he went out and wept bitterly.

27 When morning came, all the chief priests
and the elders of the people conferred
together against Jesus in order to bring about
his death. 2 They bound him, led him away, and
handed him over to Pilate the governor.

3 When Judas, his betrayer, saw that Jesus[c] was
condemned, he repented and brought back the
thirty pieces of silver to the chief priests and the
elders. 4 He said, "I have sinned by betraying innocent[d] blood." But they said, "What is that to us?
See to it yourself." 5 Throwing down the pieces of
silver in the temple, he departed; and he went and
hanged himself. 6 But the chief priests, taking the
pieces of silver, said, "It is not lawful to put them
into the treasury, since they are blood money."
7 After conferring together, they used them to
buy the potter's field as a place to bury foreigners. 8 For this reason that field has been called
the Field of Blood to this day. 9 Then was fulfilled
what had been spoken through the prophet Jeremiah,[e] "And they took[f] the thirty pieces of silver,
the price of the one on whom a price had been
set,[g] on whom some of the people of Israel had
set a price, 10 and they gave[h] them for the potter's
field, as the Lord commanded me."

11 Now Jesus stood before the governor; and
the governor asked him, "Are you the King of the
Jews?" Jesus said, "You say so." 12 But when he was
accused by the chief priests and elders, he did not
answer. 13 Then Pilate said to him, "Do you not hear
how many accusations they make against you?"
14 But he gave him no answer, not even to a single
charge, so that the governor was greatly amazed.

15 Now at the festival the governor was accustomed to release a prisoner for the crowd,
anyone whom they wanted. 16 At that time they
had a notorious prisoner, called Jesus[i] Barabbas.
17 So after they had gathered, Pilate said to them,
"Whom do you want me to release for you, Jesus[i]
Barabbas or Jesus who is called the Messiah?"[j]
18 For he realized that it was out of jealousy that
they had handed him over. 19 While he was sitting
on the judgment seat, his wife sent word to him,
"Have nothing to do with that innocent man,
for today I have suffered a great deal because of
a dream about him." 20 Now the chief priests and
the elders persuaded the crowds to ask for Barabbas and to have Jesus killed. 21 The governor
again said to them, "Which of the two do you
want me to release for you?" And they said, "Barabbas." 22 Pilate said to them, "Then what should
I do with Jesus who is called the Messiah?"[j] All
of them said, "Let him be crucified!" 23 Then he
asked, "Why, what evil has he done?" But they
shouted all the more, "Let him be crucified!"

24 So when Pilate saw that he could do

[a] Or *Christ* [b] Gk *the Nazorean* [c] Gk *he* [d] Other ancient authorities read *righteous* [e] Other ancient authorities read *Zechariah* or *Isaiah* [f] Or *I took* [g] Or *the price of the precious One* [h] Other ancient authorities read *I gave* [i] Other ancient authorities lack *Jesus* [j] Or *the Christ*

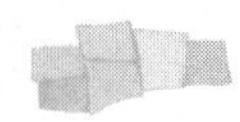

nothing, but rather that a riot was beginning, he took some water and washed his hands before the crowd, saying, "I am innocent of this man's blood;[a] see to it yourselves." 25Then the people as a whole answered, "His blood be on us and on our children!" 26So he released Barabbas for them; and after flogging Jesus, he handed him over to be crucified.

Matthew 27:24-25

The astonishing curse Jesus levels upon the Pharisees and all of "this generation" in 23:35-36 now finds a fateful echo as the people of Jerusalem accept a blood curse on their own heads and those of their children. Many scholars insist that these passages—unique to Matthew—should not be taken as historical; many churches insist that they must not be read as justifying prejudice against Jews as "Christ-killers." We must recognize that the slander has roots in the Gospel itself. Matthew, like other Jewish writers of his day, seeks to explain the destruction of Jerusalem in theological terms; unlike his contemporaries, however, Matthew attributes the city's fate to the murderous will of its population.

— NE

27 Then the soldiers of the governor took
Jesus into the governor's headquarters,[b] and they
gathered the whole cohort around him. 28They
stripped him and put a scarlet robe on him, 29and
after twisting some thorns into a crown, they put
it on his head. They put a reed in his right hand
and knelt before him and mocked him, saying,
"Hail, King of the Jews!" 30They spat on him, and
took the reed and struck him on the head. 31After
mocking him, they stripped him of the robe and
put his own clothes on him. Then they led him
away to crucify him.

32 As they went out, they came upon a man
from Cyrene named Simon; they compelled this
man to carry his cross. 33And when they came to
a place called Golgotha (which means Place of a
Skull), 34they offered him wine to drink, mixed
with gall; but when he tasted it, he would not
drink it. 35And when they had crucified him, they
divided his clothes among themselves by casting
lots;[c] 36then they sat down there and kept watch
over him. 37Over his head they put the charge
against him, which read, "This is Jesus, the King
of the Jews."

38 Then two bandits were crucified with him,
one on his right and one on his left. 39Those who
passed by derided[d] him, shaking their heads 40and
saying, "You who would destroy the temple and
build it in three days, save yourself! If you are the
Son of God, come down from the cross." 41In
the same way the chief priests also, along with the
scribes and elders, were mocking him, saying,
42"He saved others; he cannot save himself.[e] He
is the King of Israel; let him come down from the
cross now, and we will believe in him. 43He trusts
in God; let God deliver him now, if he wants to;
for he said, 'I am God's Son.'" 44The bandits who
were crucified with him also taunted him in the
same way.

45 From noon on, darkness came over the
whole land[f] until three in the afternoon. 46And
about three o'clock Jesus cried with a loud voice,
"Eli, Eli, lema sabachthani?" that is, "My God, my
God, why have you forsaken me?" 47When some
of the bystanders heard it, they said, "This man is
calling for Elijah." 48At once one of them ran and
got a sponge, filled it with sour wine, put it on a
stick, and gave it to him to drink. 49But the others
said, "Wait, let us see whether Elijah will come to
save him."[g] 50Then Jesus cried again with a loud
voice and breathed his last.[h] 51At that moment
the curtain of the temple was torn in two, from
top to bottom. The earth shook, and the rocks

[a] Other ancient authorities read *this righteous blood,* or *this righteous man's blood* [b] Gk *the praetorium* [c] Other ancient authorities add *in order that what had been spoken through the prophet might be fulfilled, "They divided my clothes among themselves, and for my clothing they cast lots."* [d] Or *blasphemed* [e] Or *is he unable to save himself?* [f] Or *earth*
[g] Other ancient authorities add *And another took a spear and pierced his side, and out came water and blood*
[h] Or *gave up his spirit*

were split. 52 The tombs also were opened, and
many bodies of the saints who had fallen asleep
were raised. 53 After his resurrection they came
out of the tombs and entered the holy city and
appeared to many. 54 Now when the centurion
and those with him, who were keeping watch
over Jesus, saw the earthquake and what took
place, they were terrified and said, "Truly this
man was God's Son!"[a]

55 Many women were also there, looking on
from a distance; they had followed Jesus from
Galilee and had provided for him. 56 Among them
were Mary Magdalene, and Mary the mother of
James and Joseph, and the mother of the sons of
Zebedee.

57 When it was evening, there came a rich
man from Arimathea, named Joseph, who was
also a disciple of Jesus. 58 He went to Pilate and
asked for the body of Jesus; then Pilate ordered
it to be given to him. 59 So Joseph took the body
and wrapped it in a clean linen cloth 60 and laid
it in his own new tomb, which he had hewn in
the rock. He then rolled a great stone to the door
of the tomb and went away. 61 Mary Magdalene
and the other Mary were there, sitting opposite
the tomb.

62 The next day, that is, after the day of Preparation, the chief priests and the Pharisees gathered before Pilate 63 and said, "Sir, we remember
what that impostor said while he was still alive,
'After three days I will rise again.' 64 Therefore
command the tomb to be made secure until the
third day; otherwise his disciples may go and steal
him away, and tell the people, 'He has been raised
from the dead,' and the last deception would be
worse than the first." 65 Pilate said to them, "You
have a guard[b] of soldiers; go, make it as secure
as you can."[c] 66 So they went with the guard and
made the tomb secure by sealing the stone.

28 After the sabbath, as the first day of the
week was dawning, Mary Magdalene and
the other Mary went to see the tomb. 2 And suddenly there was a great earthquake; for an angel
of the Lord, descending from heaven, came and
rolled back the stone and sat on it. 3 His appearance was like lightning, and his clothing white
as snow. 4 For fear of him the guards shook and
became like dead men. 5 But the angel said to the
women, "Do not be afraid; I know that you are
looking for Jesus who was crucified. 6 He is not
here; for he has been raised, as he said. Come, see
the place where he[d] lay. 7 Then go quickly and tell
his disciples, 'He has been raised from the dead,[e]
and indeed he is going ahead of you to Galilee;
there you will see him.' This is my message for
you." 8 So they left the tomb quickly with fear
and great joy, and ran to tell his disciples. 9 Suddenly Jesus met them and said, "Greetings!" And
they came to him, took hold of his feet, and worshiped him. 10 Then Jesus said to them, "Do not
be afraid; go and tell my brothers to go to Galilee;
there they will see me."

11 While they were going, some of the guard
went into the city and told the chief priests everything that had happened. 12 After the priests[f] had
assembled with the elders, they devised a plan to
give a large sum of money to the soldiers, 13 telling
them, "You must say, 'His disciples came by night
and stole him away while we were asleep.' 14 If this
comes to the governor's ears, we will satisfy him
and keep you out of trouble." 15 So they took the
money and did as they were directed. And this
story is still told among the Jews to this day.

16 Now the eleven disciples went to Galilee, to the mountain to which Jesus had directed
them. 17 When they saw him, they worshiped him;
but some doubted. 18 And Jesus came and said to
them, "All authority in heaven and on earth has
been given to me. 19 Go therefore and make disciples of all nations, baptizing them in the name of
the Father and of the Son and of the Holy Spirit,
20 and teaching them to obey everything that I
have commanded you. And remember, I am with
you always, to the end of the age."[g]

[a] Or *a son of God* [b] Or *Take a guard* [c] Gk *you know how* [d] Other ancient authorities read *the Lord* [e] Other ancient authorities lack *from the dead* [f] Gk *they* [g] Other ancient authorities add *Amen*

The Gospel According to Mark

Of the written stories of Jesus' mission included in the New Testament, the Gospel of Mark is generally considered to be the earliest. Written outside Palestine, and possibly in Rome, this account is one of the initial writings responsible for carrying the message of the Jesus movement *westward,* toward Italy. The author makes the story of Jesus more suitable for a Latinized or European population. Mark includes a number of stories that highlight Jesus' contact with non-Jewish people. Especially significant among these encounters is one that results in the first *human* confession of Jesus—from the lips of a Roman centurion—as "God's Son" (15:39).

This story begins with Jesus' baptism by that radical countercultural figure John the Baptist. John's life ends when he questions the political activities of King Herod (6:14-29). Jesus' life comes to an abrupt end when he confronts leading Jewish religious figures (11:15-18). His death by crucifixion, a form of execution reserved for slaves or state criminals, suggests the complicity of the religious establishment in Jerusalem with political forces under the authority of Pilate, the Roman procurator.

Mark's message of Jesus' life and actions is bound up with the coming reign of God. This message should be read in light of the author's context, especially the Roman-Jewish War (66–70 CE). How should followers of Jesus live in a world in which Rome and its ruling elite stand in tension with the leaders of the Jews? Whose side should these Jesus followers take? Should they "give to the emperor" or to God? (12:13-17). Jesus' life-giving activity among the villages of Galilee had implications for the early Christian communities of first-century Rome, despite the potential for ethnic tensions between Jews and non-Jews (compare Rom 14:1—15:6).

Most of Mark's story concentrates on Jesus' activities among Jews within the borders of Judea. Yet the author does not avoid the ethnic collision of a Jewish Jesus—from "Nazareth of Galilee" (1:9)—with non-Jews. In fact, the author claims that Jesus also *attracted* non-Jews, from the "region around Tyre and Sidon" (3:8). This attraction leads to the direct confrontation with a Syro-Phoenician woman (7:24-30). Though the story ends well (the woman's request is granted), the author has Jesus reveal an ethnic bias as he implicitly calls the Gentile woman a "dog." Jesus' contacts with persons of other ethnic backgrounds are not uncommon elsewhere in the story: the tomb-bound Gerasene demoniac (5:1-20); the deaf man of the Decapolis (7:31-37); and a large crowd in that same region (8:1-9).

Although archeological evidence of a multiethnic population of Galilee is scarce, the fact that Mark's narrative highlights the encounters of Jesus with several Gentile characters suggests that the author's stories have a larger goal: he wishes to present what could be an ethnically exclusive story in a more inclusive time period and community.

This Gospel, unlike Matthew and Luke, omits a birth narrative with a genealogy or any other intentional Jewish identity markers. Neither does this story conclude with a global agenda comparable to Matt 28:16-20 or Luke 24:45-47. Rather, the story ends with an instruction to the disciples to return to Galilee, implying the development of an inclusive community of disciples (16:7) outside of Jerusalem.

I am part of the first generation of my family born in the United States. My two older siblings were born in the Cayman Islands in the Caribbean, and my two younger siblings were born in the United States. My parents moved to New York City in the early 1960s for economic *and* missionary purposes. Our West Indian American family comfortably receives other ethnic labels—Afro-Caribbean, African American. This mixed racial identity enhances my sensitivity to ethnic hybridity and to differences *and* tensions within the ancient biblical stories, including Mark's story of Jesus.

— Emerson Byron Powery

1 The beginning of the good news[a] of Jesus
Christ, the Son of God.[b]
2 As it is written in the prophet Isaiah,[c]
"See, I am sending my messenger ahead of
you,[d]
who will prepare your way;
3 the voice of one crying out in the wilderness:
'Prepare the way of the Lord,
make his paths straight,' "
4 John the baptizer appeared[e] in the wilderness,
proclaiming a baptism of repentance for the forgiveness of sins. 5 And people from the whole
Judean countryside and all the people of Jerusalem were going out to him, and were baptized
by him in the river Jordan, confessing their sins.
6 Now John was clothed with camel's hair, with a
leather belt around his waist, and he ate locusts
and wild honey. 7 He proclaimed, "The one who
is more powerful than I is coming after me; I am
not worthy to stoop down and untie the thong of
his sandals. 8 I have baptized you with[f] water; but
he will baptize you with[f] the Holy Spirit."
9 In those days Jesus came from Nazareth of
Galilee and was baptized by John in the Jordan.
10 And just as he was coming up out of the water,
he saw the heavens torn apart and the Spirit descending like a dove on him. 11 And a voice came
from heaven, "You are my Son, the Beloved;[g] with
you I am well pleased."
12 And the Spirit immediately drove him out
into the wilderness. 13 He was in the wilderness
forty days, tempted by Satan; and he was with the
wild beasts; and the angels waited on him.
14 Now after John was arrested, Jesus came
to Galilee, proclaiming the good news[a] of God,[h]
15 and saying, "The time is fulfilled, and the kingdom of God has come near;[i] repent, and believe
in the good news."[a]

16 As Jesus passed along the Sea of Galilee,
he saw Simon and his brother Andrew casting a
net into the sea—for they were fishermen. 17 And
Jesus said to them, "Follow me and I will make
you fish for people." 18 And immediately they

[a] Or *gospel* [b] Other ancient authorities lack *the Son of God* [c] Other ancient authorities read *in the prophets* [d] Gk *before your face* [e] Other ancient authorities read *John was baptizing* [f] Or *in* [g] Or *my beloved Son* [h] Other ancient authorities read *of the kingdom* [i] Or *is at hand*

left their nets and followed him. 19As he went a
little farther, he saw James son of Zebedee and
his brother John, who were in their boat mending the nets. 20Immediately he called them; and
they left their father Zebedee in the boat with the
hired men, and followed him.

21 They went to Capernaum; and when the
sabbath came, he entered the synagogue and
taught. 22They were astounded at his teaching,
for he taught them as one having authority, and
not as the scribes. 23Just then there was in their
synagogue a man with an unclean spirit, 24and he
cried out, "What have you to do with us, Jesus of
Nazareth? Have you come to destroy us? I know
who you are, the Holy One of God." 25But Jesus
rebuked him, saying, "Be silent, and come out of
him!" 26And the unclean spirit, convulsing him
and crying with a loud voice, came out of him.
27They were all amazed, and they kept on asking
one another, "What is this? A new teaching—
with authority! He[a] commands even the unclean
spirits, and they obey him." 28At once his fame
began to spread throughout the surrounding region of Galilee.

29 As soon as they[b] left the synagogue, they
entered the house of Simon and Andrew, with
James and John. 30Now Simon's mother-in-law
was in bed with a fever, and they told him about
her at once. 31He came and took her by the hand
and lifted her up. Then the fever left her, and she
began to serve them.

32 That evening, at sunset, they brought to
him all who were sick or possessed with demons.
33And the whole city was gathered around the
door. 34And he cured many who were sick with
various diseases, and cast out many demons; and
he would not permit the demons to speak, because they knew him.

35 In the morning, while it was still very
dark, he got up and went out to a deserted place,
and there he prayed. 36And Simon and his companions hunted for him. 37When they found him,
they said to him, "Everyone is searching for you."
38He answered, "Let us go on to the neighboring towns, so that I may proclaim the message
there also; for that is what I came out to do."
39And he went throughout Galilee, proclaiming
the message in their synagogues and casting out
demons.

40 A leper[c] came to him begging him, and
kneeling[d] he said to him, "If you choose, you
can make me clean." 41Moved with pity,[e] Jesus[f]
stretched out his hand and touched him, and said
to him, "I do choose. Be made clean!" 42Immedi-
ately the leprosy[c] left him, and he was made clean.
43After sternly warning him he sent him away at
once, 44saying to him, "See that you say nothing
to anyone; but go, show yourself to the priest,
and offer for your cleansing what Moses commanded, as a testimony to them." 45But he went
out and began to proclaim it freely, and to spread
the word, so that Jesus[f] could no longer go into a
town openly, but stayed out in the country; and
people came to him from every quarter.

2 When he returned to Capernaum after some
days, it was reported that he was at home. 2So
many gathered around that there was no longer
room for them, not even in front of the door; and
he was speaking the word to them. 3Then some
people[g] came, bringing to him a paralyzed man,
carried by four of them. 4And when they could
not bring him to Jesus because of the crowd, they
removed the roof above him; and after having
dug through it, they let down the mat on which
the paralytic lay. 5When Jesus saw their faith, he
said to the paralytic, "Son, your sins are forgiven."
6Now some of the scribes were sitting there,
questioning in their hearts, 7"Why does this
fellow speak in this way? It is blasphemy! Who
can forgive sins but God alone?" 8At once Jesus
perceived in his spirit that they were discussing
these questions among themselves; and he said to
them, "Why do you raise such questions in your
hearts? 9Which is easier, to say to the paralytic,
'Your sins are forgiven,' or to say, 'Stand up and
take your mat and walk'? 10But so that you may

[a] Or *A new teaching! With authority he* [b] Other ancient authorities read *he* [c] The terms *leper* and *leprosy* can refer to several diseases [d] Other ancient authorities lack *kneeling* [e] Other ancient authorities read *anger* [f] Gk *he* [g] Gk *they*

know that the Son of Man has authority on earth
to forgive sins"—he said to the paralytic— 11"I
say to you, stand up, take your mat and go to your
home." 12And he stood up, and immediately took
the mat and went out before all of them; so that
they were all amazed and glorified God, saying,
"We have never seen anything like this!"

13 Jesus[a] went out again beside the sea;
the whole crowd gathered around him, and he
taught them. 14As he was walking along, he saw
Levi son of Alphaeus sitting at the tax booth, and
he said to him, "Follow me." And he got up and
followed him.

15 And as he sat at dinner[b] in Levi's[c] house,
many tax collectors and sinners were also sitting[d] with Jesus and his disciples—for there were
many who followed him. 16When the scribes of[e]
the Pharisees saw that he was eating with sinners and tax collectors, they said to his disciples,
"Why does he eat[f] with tax collectors and sinners?" 17When Jesus heard this, he said to them,
"Those who are well have no need of a physician,
but those who are sick; I have come to call not the
righteous but sinners."

18 Now John's disciples and the Pharisees
were fasting; and people[g] came and said to him,
"Why do John's disciples and the disciples of the
Pharisees fast, but your disciples do not fast?"
19Jesus said to them, "The wedding guests cannot
fast while the bridegroom is with them, can they?
As long as they have the bridegroom with them,
they cannot fast. 20The days will come when the
bridegroom is taken away from them, and then
they will fast on that day.

21 "No one sews a piece of unshrunk cloth
on an old cloak; otherwise, the patch pulls away
from it, the new from the old, and a worse tear
is made. 22And no one puts new wine into old
wineskins; otherwise, the wine will burst the
skins, and the wine is lost, and so are the skins;
but one puts new wine into fresh wineskins."[h]

23 One sabbath he was going through the
grainfields; and as they made their way his disciples began to pluck heads of grain. 24The Pharisees said to him, "Look, why are they doing what
is not lawful on the sabbath?" 25And he said to
them, "Have you never read what David did when
he and his companions were hungry and in need
of food? 26He entered the house of God, when
Abiathar was high priest, and ate the bread of the
Presence, which it is not lawful for any but the
priests to eat, and he gave some to his companions." 27Then he said to them, "The sabbath was
made for humankind, and not humankind for the
sabbath; 28so the Son of Man is lord even of the
sabbath."

3 Again he entered the synagogue, and a man
was there who had a withered hand. 2They
watched him to see whether he would cure him
on the sabbath, so that they might accuse him.
3And he said to the man who had the withered
hand, "Come forward." 4Then he said to them,
"Is it lawful to do good or to do harm on the sabbath, to save life or to kill?" But they were silent.
5He looked around at them with anger; he was
grieved at their hardness of heart and said to the
man, "Stretch out your hand." He stretched it out,
and his hand was restored. 6The Pharisees went
out and immediately conspired with the Herodians against him, how to destroy him.

7 Jesus departed with his disciples to the sea,
and a great multitude from Galilee followed him;
8hearing all that he was doing, they came to him
in great numbers from Judea, Jerusalem, Idumea,
beyond the Jordan, and the region around Tyre
and Sidon. 9He told his disciples to have a boat
ready for him because of the crowd, so that they
would not crush him; 10for he had cured many,
so that all who had diseases pressed upon him
to touch him. 11Whenever the unclean spirits
saw him, they fell down before him and shouted,
"You are the Son of God!" 12But he sternly ordered them not to make him known.

13 He went up the mountain and called to
him those whom he wanted, and they came to
him. 14And he appointed twelve, whom he also

[a] Gk *He* [b] Gk *reclined* [c] Gk *his* [d] Gk *reclining* [e] Other ancient authorities read *and* [f] Other ancient authorities add *and drink* [g] Gk *they* [h] Other ancient authorities lack *but one puts new wine into fresh wineskins*

Mark 3:12

Jesus' commands to demons "not to make him known," his urging those he has healed to stay silent, his commands to his disciples not to proclaim what they have seen until after his resurrection (9:9), and his declaration that he speaks in parables "in order that" people will not understand him (4:11-12) are peculiar motifs that together scholars call the "Messianic Secret" in Mark. A bright dividing line runs through the Gospel between "those inside," who know the secrets of the kingdom, and those "outside," who are kept from them. One effect of these motifs is to position the readers as more perceptive than the first disciples themselves.

— *NE*

named apostles,[a] to be with him, and to be sent
out to proclaim the message, 15and to have authority to cast out demons. 16So he appointed
the twelve:[b] Simon (to whom he gave the name
Peter); 17James son of Zebedee and John the
brother of James (to whom he gave the name
Boanerges, that is, Sons of Thunder); 18and Andrew, and Philip, and Bartholomew, and Matthew, and Thomas, and James son of Alphaeus,
and Thaddaeus, and Simon the Cananaean, 19and
Judas Iscariot, who betrayed him.

Then he went home; 20and the crowd came
together again, so that they could not even eat.
21When his family heard it, they went out to restrain him, for people were saying, "He has gone
out of his mind." 22And the scribes who came
down from Jerusalem said, "He has Beelzebul, and
by the ruler of the demons he casts out demons."
23And he called them to him, and spoke to them
in parables, "How can Satan cast out Satan? 24If
a kingdom is divided against itself, that kingdom
cannot stand. 25And if a house is divided against
itself, that house will not be able to stand. 26And
if Satan has risen up against himself and is divided,
he cannot stand, but his end has come. 27But no
one can enter a strong man's house and plunder
his property without first tying up the strong man;
then indeed the house can be plundered.

28 "Truly I tell you, people will be forgiven
for their sins and whatever blasphemies they utter; 29but whoever blasphemes against the Holy
Spirit can never have forgiveness, but is guilty of
an eternal sin"— 30for they had said, "He has an
unclean spirit."

31 Then his mother and his brothers came;
and standing outside, they sent to him and called
him. 32A crowd was sitting around him; and they
said to him, "Your mother and your brothers
and sisters[c] are outside, asking for you." 33And
he replied, "Who are my mother and my brothers?" 34And looking at those who sat around him,
he said, "Here are my mother and my brothers!
35Whoever does the will of God is my brother
and sister and mother."

4 Again he began to teach beside the sea. Such
a very large crowd gathered around him that
he got into a boat on the sea and sat there, while
the whole crowd was beside the sea on the land.
2He began to teach them many things in parables,
and in his teaching he said to them: 3"Listen! A
sower went out to sow. 4And as he sowed, some
seed fell on the path, and the birds came and ate it
up. 5Other seed fell on rocky ground, where it did
not have much soil, and it sprang up quickly, since
it had no depth of soil. 6And when the sun rose,
it was scorched; and since it had no root, it withered away. 7Other seed fell among thorns, and the
thorns grew up and choked it, and it yielded no
grain. 8Other seed fell into good soil and brought
forth grain, growing up and increasing and yielding thirty and sixty and a hundredfold." 9And he
said, "Let anyone with ears to hear listen!"

10 When he was alone, those who were
around him along with the twelve asked him
about the parables. 11And he said to them, "To
you has been given the secret[d] of the kingdom of
God, but for those outside, everything comes in
parables; 12in order that

[a] Other ancient authorities lack *whom he also named apostles*
[b] Other ancient authorities lack *So he appointed the twelve*
[c] Other ancient authorities lack *and sisters*
[d] Or *mystery*

'they may indeed look, but not perceive,
and may indeed listen, but not
understand;
so that they may not turn again and be
forgiven.'"
13 And he said to them, "Do you not understand this parable? Then how will you understand all the parables? 14The sower sows the
word. 15These are the ones on the path where the
word is sown: when they hear, Satan immediately
comes and takes away the word that is sown in
them. 16And these are the ones sown on rocky
ground: when they hear the word, they immediately receive it with joy. 17But they have no root,
and endure only for a while; then, when trouble
or persecution arises on account of the word, immediately they fall away.[a] 18And others are those
sown among the thorns: these are the ones who
hear the word, 19but the cares of the world, and
the lure of wealth, and the desire for other things
come in and choke the word, and it yields nothing. 20And these are the ones sown on the good
soil: they hear the word and accept it and bear
fruit, thirty and sixty and a hundredfold."
21 He said to them, "Is a lamp brought in to
be put under the bushel basket, or under the bed,
and not on the lampstand? 22For there is nothing
hidden, except to be disclosed; nor is anything
secret, except to come to light. 23Let anyone with
ears to hear listen!" 24And he said to them, "Pay
attention to what you hear; the measure you give
will be the measure you get, and still more will
be given you. 25For to those who have, more will
be given; and from those who have nothing, even
what they have will be taken away."
26 He also said, "The kingdom of God is as if
someone would scatter seed on the ground, 27and
would sleep and rise night and day, and the seed
would sprout and grow, he does not know how.
28The earth produces of itself, first the stalk, then
the head, then the full grain in the head. 29But
when the grain is ripe, at once he goes in with his
sickle, because the harvest has come."
30 He also said, "With what can we compare
the kingdom of God, or what parable will we use
for it? 31It is like a mustard seed, which, when
sown upon the ground, is the smallest of all the
seeds on earth; 32yet when it is sown it grows up
and becomes the greatest of all shrubs, and puts
forth large branches, so that the birds of the air
can make nests in its shade."
33 With many such parables he spoke the
word to them, as they were able to hear it; 34he
did not speak to them except in parables, but he
explained everything in private to his disciples.

35 On that day, when evening had come, he
said to them, "Let us go across to the other side."
36And leaving the crowd behind, they took him
with them in the boat, just as he was. Other boats
were with him. 37A great windstorm arose, and
the waves beat into the boat, so that the boat was
already being swamped. 38But he was in the stern,
asleep on the cushion; and they woke him up and
said to him, "Teacher, do you not care that we
are perishing?" 39He woke up and rebuked the
wind, and said to the sea, "Peace! Be still!" Then
the wind ceased, and there was a dead calm. 40He
said to them, "Why are you afraid? Have you still
no faith?" 41And they were filled with great awe
and said to one another, "Who then is this, that
even the wind and the sea obey him?"
5 They came to the other side of the sea, to the
country of the Gerasenes.[b] 2And when he
had stepped out of the boat, immediately a man
out of the tombs with an unclean spirit met him.
3He lived among the tombs; and no one could
restrain him any more, even with a chain; 4for he
had often been restrained with shackles and
chains, but the chains he wrenched apart, and the
shackles he broke in pieces; and no one had the
strength to subdue him. 5Night and day among
the tombs and on the mountains he was always
howling and bruising himself with stones. 6When
he saw Jesus from a distance, he ran and bowed
down before him; 7and he shouted at the top of
his voice, "What have you to do with me, Jesus,
Son of the Most High God? I adjure you by God,
do not torment me." 8For he had said to him,
"Come out of the man, you unclean spirit!" 9Then

[a] Or *stumble* [b] Other ancient authorities read *Gergesenes*; others, *Gadarenes*

 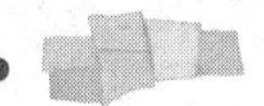

Jesus[a] asked him, "What is your name?" He replied, "My name is Legion; for we are many."
10He begged him earnestly not to send them out
of the country. 11Now there on the hillside a great
herd of swine was feeding; 12and the unclean
spirits[b] begged him, "Send us into the swine; let
us enter them." 13So he gave them permission.
And the unclean spirits came out and entered the
swine; and the herd, numbering about two thousand, rushed down the steep bank into the sea,
and were drowned in the sea.

14 The swineherds ran off and told it in the
city and in the country. Then people came to see
what it was that had happened. 15They came to
Jesus and saw the demoniac sitting there, clothed
and in his right mind, the very man who had had
the legion; and they were afraid. 16Those who had
seen what had happened to the demoniac and to
the swine reported it. 17Then they began to beg
Jesus[c] to leave their neighborhood. 18As he was
getting into the boat, the man who had been possessed by demons begged him that he might be
with him. 19But Jesus[a] refused, and said to him,
"Go home to your friends, and tell them how
much the Lord has done for you, and what mercy
he has shown you." 20And he went away and began to proclaim in the Decapolis how much Jesus
had done for him; and everyone was amazed.

Mark 5:1-20

The evil spirits that possess the man name themselves *Legion.* That is the military term for the principal unit of the Roman Empire's army, comprising 3,000 to 6,000 foot soldiers with cavalry—like the legion that occupies Galilee. Like the Legion possessing the man, the Roman legion occupying the country cannot be bound or controlled. Is the casting out of Legion a subversive message calling for the casting out of Rome's army—and, for that matter, every other empire's army of occupation?

— MDLT

21 When Jesus had crossed again in the boat[d]
to the other side, a great crowd gathered around
him; and he was by the sea. 22Then one of the leaders of the synagogue named Jairus came and, when
he saw him, fell at his feet 23and begged him repeatedly, "My little daughter is at the point of death.
Come and lay your hands on her, so that she may
be made well, and live." 24So he went with him.

And a large crowd followed him and pressed
in on him. 25Now there was a woman who had
been suffering from hemorrhages for twelve
years. 26She had endured much under many physicians, and had spent all that she had; and she
was no better, but rather grew worse. 27She had
heard about Jesus, and came up behind him in
the crowd and touched his cloak, 28for she said,
"If I but touch his clothes, I will be made well."
29Immediately her hemorrhage stopped; and she
felt in her body that she was healed of her disease.
30Immediately aware that power had gone forth
from him, Jesus turned about in the crowd and
said, "Who touched my clothes?" 31And his disciples said to him, "You see the crowd pressing in
on you; how can you say, 'Who touched me?'"
32He looked all around to see who had done it.
33But the woman, knowing what had happened
to her, came in fear and trembling, fell down before him, and told him the whole truth. 34He said
to her, "Daughter, your faith has made you well;
go in peace, and be healed of your disease."

35 While he was still speaking, some people came from the leader's house to say, "Your
daughter is dead. Why trouble the teacher any
further?" 36But overhearing[e] what they said,
Jesus said to the leader of the synagogue, "Do
not fear, only believe." 37He allowed no one to
follow him except Peter, James, and John, the
brother of James. 38When they came to the house
of the leader of the synagogue, he saw a commotion, people weeping and wailing loudly. 39When
he had entered, he said to them, "Why do you
make a commotion and weep? The child is not
dead but sleeping." 40And they laughed at him.
Then he put them all outside, and took the child's

[a] Gk *he* [b] Gk *they* [c] Gk *him* [d] Other ancient authorities lack *in the boat*
[e] Or *ignoring*; other ancient authorities read *hearing*

father and mother and those who were with him,
and went in where the child was. 41 He took her
by the hand and said to her, "Talitha cum," which
means, "Little girl, get up!" 42 And immediately
the girl got up and began to walk about (she was
twelve years of age). At this they were overcome
with amazement. 43 He strictly ordered them that
no one should know this, and told them to give
her something to eat.

6 He left that place and came to his hometown, and his disciples followed him. 2 On
the sabbath he began to teach in the synagogue,
and many who heard him were astounded. They
said, "Where did this man get all this? What is
this wisdom that has been given to him? What
deeds of power are being done by his hands!
3 Is not this the carpenter, the son of Mary[a] and
brother of James and Joses and Judas and Simon,
and are not his sisters here with us?" And they
took offense[b] at him. 4 Then Jesus said to them,
"Prophets are not without honor, except in their
hometown, and among their own kin, and in their
own house." 5 And he could do no deed of power
there, except that he laid his hands on a few sick
people and cured them. 6 And he was amazed at
their unbelief.

Then he went about among the villages teaching. 7 He called the twelve and began to send
them out two by two, and gave them authority
over the unclean spirits. 8 He ordered them to
take nothing for their journey except a staff; no
bread, no bag, no money in their belts; 9 but to
wear sandals and not to put on two tunics. 10 He
said to them, "Wherever you enter a house, stay
there until you leave the place. 11 If any place will
not welcome you and they refuse to hear you, as
you leave, shake off the dust that is on your feet as
a testimony against them." 12 So they went out and
proclaimed that all should repent. 13 They cast out
many demons, and anointed with oil many who
were sick and cured them.

14 King Herod heard of it, for Jesus'[c] name
had become known. Some were[d] saying, "John
the baptizer has been raised from the dead; and
for this reason these powers are at work in him."
15 But others said, "It is Elijah." And others said,
"It is a prophet, like one of the prophets of old."
16 But when Herod heard of it, he said, "John,
whom I beheaded, has been raised."

17 For Herod himself had sent men who arrested John, bound him, and put him in prison
on account of Herodias, his brother Philip's wife,
because Herod[e] had married her. 18 For John had
been telling Herod, "It is not lawful for you to
have your brother's wife." 19 And Herodias had a
grudge against him, and wanted to kill him. But
she could not, 20 for Herod feared John, knowing that he was a righteous and holy man, and
he protected him. When he heard him, he was
greatly perplexed;[f] and yet he liked to listen to
him. 21 But an opportunity came when Herod on
his birthday gave a banquet for his courtiers and
officers and for the leaders of Galilee. 22 When
his daughter Herodias[g] came in and danced, she
pleased Herod and his guests; and the king said to
the girl, "Ask me for whatever you wish, and I will
give it." 23 And he solemnly swore to her, "Whatever you ask me, I will give you, even half of my
kingdom." 24 She went out and said to her mother,
"What should I ask for?" She replied, "The head
of John the baptizer." 25 Immediately she rushed
back to the king and requested, "I want you to
give me at once the head of John the Baptist on a
platter." 26 The king was deeply grieved; yet out of
regard for his oaths and for the guests, he did not
want to refuse her. 27 Immediately the king sent a
soldier of the guard with orders to bring John's[c]
head. He went and beheaded him in the prison,
28 brought his head on a platter, and gave it to the
girl. Then the girl gave it to her mother. 29 When
his disciples heard about it, they came and took
his body, and laid it in a tomb.

30 The apostles gathered around Jesus, and
told him all that they had done and taught. 31 He

[a] Other ancient authorities read *son of the carpenter and of Mary* [b] Or *stumbled* [c] Gk *his* [d] Other ancient authorities read *He was* [e] Gk *he* [f] Other ancient authorities read *he did many things* [g] Other ancient authorities read *the daughter of Herodias herself*

said to them, "Come away to a deserted place all by yourselves and rest a while." For many were coming and going, and they had no leisure even to eat. 32And they went away in the boat to a deserted place by themselves. 33Now many saw them going and recognized them, and they hurried there on foot from all the towns and arrived ahead of them. 34As he went ashore, he saw a great crowd; and he had compassion for them, because they were like sheep without a shepherd; and he began to teach them many things. 35When it grew late, his disciples came to him and said, "This is a deserted place, and the hour is now very late; 36send them away so that they may go into the surrounding country and villages and buy something for themselves to eat." 37But he answered them, "You give them something to eat." They said to him, "Are we to go and buy two hundred denarii[a] worth of bread, and give it to them to eat?" 38And he said to them, "How many loaves have you? Go and see." When they had found out, they said, "Five, and two fish." 39Then he ordered them to get all the people to sit down in groups on the green grass. 40So they sat down in groups of hundreds and of fifties. 41Taking the five loaves and the two fish, he looked up to heaven, and blessed and broke the loaves, and gave them to his disciples to set before the people; and he divided the two fish among them all. 42And all ate and were filled; 43and they took up twelve baskets full of broken pieces and of the fish. 44Those who had eaten the loaves numbered five thousand men.

45 Immediately he made his disciples get into the boat and go on ahead to the other side, to Bethsaida, while he dismissed the crowd. 46After saying farewell to them, he went up on the mountain to pray.

47 When evening came, the boat was out on the sea, and he was alone on the land. 48When he saw that they were straining at the oars against an adverse wind, he came towards them early in the morning, walking on the sea. He intended to pass them by. 49But when they saw him walking on the sea, they thought it was a ghost and cried out; 50for they all saw him and were terrified. But immediately he spoke to them and said, "Take heart, it is I; do not be afraid." 51Then he got into the boat with them and the wind ceased. And they were utterly astounded, 52for they did not understand about the loaves, but their hearts were hardened.

53 When they had crossed over, they came to land at Gennesaret and moored the boat. 54When they got out of the boat, people at once recognized him, 55and rushed about that whole region and began to bring the sick on mats to wherever they heard he was. 56And wherever he went, into villages or cities or farms, they laid the sick in the marketplaces, and begged him that they might touch even the fringe of his cloak; and all who touched it were healed.

7 Now when the Pharisees and some of the scribes who had come from Jerusalem gathered around him, 2they noticed that some of his disciples were eating with defiled hands, that is, without washing them. 3(For the Pharisees, and all the Jews, do not eat unless they thoroughly wash their hands,[b] thus observing the tradition of the elders; 4and they do not eat anything from the market unless they wash it;[c] and there are also many other traditions that they observe, the

Mark 7:3-4

Mark's attempt to explain for his audience the practices of the Pharisees (and indeed of all Jews) relies as much on prejudice as on knowledge: he off-handedly characterizes Judaism as a religion of pots and pans. These lines, and the gloss, unique to Mark, that Jesus' words were intended to declare "all foods clean" (7:19; thus annulling a significant part of the Torah)—as well as the repeated references to "their synagogues"—suggest to some scholars that Mark was written at a considerable cultural and emotional distance from Judaism.

—NE

[a] The denarius was the usual day's wage for a laborer [b] Meaning of Gk uncertain

[c] Other ancient authorities read *and when they come from the marketplace, they do not eat unless they purify themselves*

washing of cups, pots, and bronze kettles.[a]) 5 So
the Pharisees and the scribes asked him, "Why do
your disciples not live[b] according to the tradition
of the elders, but eat with defiled hands?" 6 He
said to them, "Isaiah prophesied rightly about
you hypocrites, as it is written,

'This people honors me with their lips,
but their hearts are far from me;
7 in vain do they worship me,
teaching human precepts as doctrines.'

8 You abandon the commandment of God and
hold to human tradition."

9 Then he said to them, "You have a fine way
of rejecting the commandment of God in order to
keep your tradition! 10 For Moses said, 'Honor your
father and your mother'; and, 'Whoever speaks
evil of father or mother must surely die.' 11 But you
say that if anyone tells father or mother, 'Whatever
support you might have had from me is Corban'
(that is, an offering to God[c])— 12 then you no longer permit doing anything for a father or mother,
13 thus making void the word of God through your
tradition that you have handed on. And you do
many things like this."

14 Then he called the crowd again and said to
them, "Listen to me, all of you, and understand:
15 there is nothing outside a person that by going
in can defile, but the things that come out are
what defile."[d]

17 When he had left the crowd and entered
the house, his disciples asked him about the parable. 18 He said to them, "Then do you also fail to
understand? Do you not see that whatever goes
into a person from outside cannot defile, 19 since
it enters, not the heart but the stomach, and goes
out into the sewer?" (Thus he declared all foods
clean.) 20 And he said, "It is what comes out of a
person that defiles. 21 For it is from within, from
the human heart, that evil intentions come: fornication, theft, murder, 22 adultery, avarice, wickedness, deceit, licentiousness, envy, slander, pride,
folly. 23 All these evil things come from within,
and they defile a person."

24 From there he set out and went away to
the region of Tyre.[e] He entered a house and did
not want anyone to know he was there. Yet he
could not escape notice, 25 but a woman whose
little daughter had an unclean spirit immediately
heard about him, and she came and bowed down
at his feet. 26 Now the woman was a Gentile, of
Syrophoenician origin. She begged him to cast
the demon out of her daughter. 27 He said to her,
"Let the children be fed first, for it is not fair to
take the children's food and throw it to the dogs."
28 But she answered him, "Sir,[f] even the dogs under the table eat the children's crumbs." 29 Then
he said to her, "For saying that, you may go—the
demon has left your daughter." 30 So she went
home, found the child lying on the bed, and the
demon gone.

31 Then he returned from the region of Tyre,
and went by way of Sidon towards the Sea of
Galilee, in the region of the Decapolis. 32 They
brought to him a deaf man who had an impedi-
ment in his speech; and they begged him to lay
his hand on him. 33 He took him aside in private,
away from the crowd, and put his fingers into his
ears, and he spat and touched his tongue. 34 Then
looking up to heaven, he sighed and said to him,
"Ephphatha," that is, "Be opened." 35 And immediately his ears were opened, his tongue was
released, and he spoke plainly. 36 Then Jesus[g] ordered them to tell no one; but the more he ordered them, the more zealously they proclaimed
it. 37 They were astounded beyond measure, saying, "He has done everything well; he even makes
the deaf to hear and the mute to speak."

8 In those days when there was again a great
crowd without anything to eat, he called his
disciples and said to them, 2 "I have compassion
for the crowd, because they have been with me
now for three days and have nothing to eat. 3 If I
send them away hungry to their homes, they will
faint on the way—and some of them have come
from a great distance." 4 His disciples replied, "How
can one feed these people with bread here in the

[a] Other ancient authorities add *and beds* [b] Gk *walk* [c] Gk lacks *to God* [d] Other ancient authorities add verse 16, *"Let anyone with ears to hear listen"* [e] Other ancient authorities add *and Sidon* [f] Or *Lord*; other ancient authorities prefix *Yes* [g] Gk *he*

 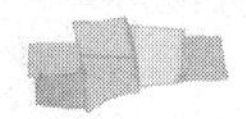

desert?" 5 He asked them, "How many loaves do you have?" They said, "Seven." 6 Then he ordered the crowd to sit down on the ground; and he took the seven loaves, and after giving thanks he broke them and gave them to his disciples to distribute; and they distributed them to the crowd. 7 They had also a few small fish; and after blessing them, he ordered that these too should be distributed. 8 They ate and were filled; and they took up the broken pieces left over, seven baskets full. 9 Now there were about four thousand people. And he sent them away. 10 And immediately he got into the boat with his disciples and went to the district of Dalmanutha.[a]

11 The Pharisees came and began to argue with him, asking him for a sign from heaven, to test him. 12 And he sighed deeply in his spirit and said, "Why does this generation ask for a sign? Truly I tell you, no sign will be given to this generation." 13 And he left them, and getting into the boat again, he went across to the other side.

14 Now the disciples[b] had forgotten to bring any bread; and they had only one loaf with them in the boat. 15 And he cautioned them, saying, "Watch out—beware of the yeast of the Pharisees and the yeast of Herod."[c] 16 They said to one another, "It is because we have no bread." 17 And becoming aware of it, Jesus said to them, "Why are you talking about having no bread? Do you still not perceive or understand? Are your hearts hardened? 18 Do you have eyes, and fail to see? Do you have ears, and fail to hear? And do you not remember? 19 When I broke the five loaves for the five thousand, how many baskets full of broken pieces did you collect?" They said to him, "Twelve." 20 "And the seven for the four thousand, how many baskets full of broken pieces did you collect?" And they said to him, "Seven." 21 Then he said to them, "Do you not yet understand?"

22 They came to Bethsaida. Some people[d] brought a blind man to him and begged him to touch him. 23 He took the blind man by the hand and led him out of the village; and when he had put saliva on his eyes and laid his hands on him, he asked him, "Can you see anything?" 24 And the man[e] looked up and said, "I can see people, but they look like trees, walking." 25 Then Jesus[e] laid his hands on his eyes again; and he looked intently and his sight was restored, and he saw everything clearly. 26 Then he sent him away to his home, saying, "Do not even go into the village."[f]

27 Jesus went on with his disciples to the villages of Caesarea Philippi; and on the way he asked his disciples, "Who do people say that I am?" 28 And they answered him, "John the Baptist; and others, Elijah; and still others, one of the prophets." 29 He asked them, "But who do you say that I am?" Peter answered him, "You are the Messiah."[g] 30 And he sternly ordered them not to tell anyone about him.

31 Then he began to teach them that the Son of Man must undergo great suffering, and be rejected by the elders, the chief priests, and the scribes, and be killed, and after three days rise again. 32 He said all this quite openly. And Peter took him aside and began to rebuke him. 33 But turning and looking at his disciples, he rebuked Peter and said, "Get behind me, Satan! For you are setting your mind not on divine things but on human things."

34 He called the crowd with his disciples, and said to them, "If any want to become my followers, let them deny themselves and take up their cross and follow me. 35 For those who want to save their life will lose it, and those who lose their life for my sake, and for the sake of the gospel,[h] will save it. 36 For what will it profit them to gain the whole world and forfeit their life? 37 Indeed, what can they give in return for their life? 38 Those who are ashamed of me and of my words[i] in this adulterous and sinful generation, of them the Son of Man will also be ashamed when he comes in the glory of his Father with the holy angels."

[a] Other ancient authorities read *Mageda* or *Magdala* [b] Gk *they* [c] Other ancient authorities read *the Herodians* [d] Gk *They* [e] Gk *he* [f] Other ancient authorities add *or tell anyone in the village* [g] Or *the Christ* [h] Other ancient authorities read *lose their life for the sake of the gospel* [i] Other ancient authorities read *and of mine*

9 1And he said to them, "Truly I tell you, there
are some standing here who will not taste
death until they see that the kingdom of God has
come with[a] power."
2 Six days later, Jesus took with him Peter and
James and John, and led them up a high mountain
apart, by themselves. And he was transfigured
before them, 3and his clothes became dazzling
white, such as no one[b] on earth could bleach them.
4And there appeared to them Elijah with Moses,
who were talking with Jesus. 5Then Peter said to
Jesus, "Rabbi, it is good for us to be here; let us
make three dwellings,[c] one for you, one for Moses, and one for Elijah." 6He did not know what
to say, for they were terrified. 7Then a cloud overshadowed them, and from the cloud there came
a voice, "This is my Son, the Beloved;[d] listen to
him!" 8Suddenly when they looked around, they
saw no one with them any more, but only Jesus.
9 As they were coming down the mountain,
he ordered them to tell no one about what they
had seen, until after the Son of Man had risen
from the dead. 10So they kept the matter to themselves, questioning what this rising from the dead
could mean. 11Then they asked him, "Why do the
scribes say that Elijah must come first?" 12He said
to them, "Elijah is indeed coming first to restore
all things. How then is it written about the Son of
Man, that he is to go through many sufferings and
be treated with contempt? 13But I tell you that
Elijah has come, and they did to him whatever
they pleased, as it is written about him."
14 When they came to the disciples, they saw
a great crowd around them, and some scribes arguing with them. 15When the whole crowd saw
him, they were immediately overcome with awe,
and they ran forward to greet him. 16He asked
them, "What are you arguing about with them?"
17Someone from the crowd answered him,
"Teacher, I brought you my son; he has a spirit
that makes him unable to speak; 18and whenever
it seizes him, it dashes him down; and he foams
and grinds his teeth and becomes rigid; and I
asked your disciples to cast it out, but they could
not do so." 19He answered them, "You faithless
generation, how much longer must I be among
you? How much longer must I put up with you?
Bring him to me." 20And they brought the boy[e]
to him. When the spirit saw him, immediately it
convulsed the boy,[e] and he fell on the ground and
rolled about, foaming at the mouth. 21Jesus[f] asked
the father, "How long has this been happening to
him?" And he said, "From childhood. 22It has often cast him into the fire and into the water, to
destroy him; but if you are able to do anything,
have pity on us and help us." 23Jesus said to him,
"If you are able!—All things can be done for the
one who believes." 24Immediately the father of
the child cried out,[g] "I believe; help my unbelief!"
25When Jesus saw that a crowd came running
together, he rebuked the unclean spirit, saying
to it, "You spirit that keeps this boy from speaking and hearing, I command you, come out of
him, and never enter him again!" 26After crying
out and convulsing him terribly, it came out, and
the boy was like a corpse, so that most of them
said, "He is dead." 27But Jesus took him by the
hand and lifted him up, and he was able to stand.
28When he had entered the house, his disciples
asked him privately, "Why could we not cast it
out?" 29He said to them, "This kind can come out
only through prayer."[h]

30 They went on from there and passed
through Galilee. He did not want anyone to know
it; 31for he was teaching his disciples, saying to
them, "The Son of Man is to be betrayed into human hands, and they will kill him, and three days
after being killed, he will rise again." 32But they
did not understand what he was saying and were
afraid to ask him.
33 Then they came to Capernaum; and when
he was in the house he asked them, "What were
you arguing about on the way?" 34But they were
silent, for on the way they had argued with one
another who was the greatest. 35He sat down,
called the twelve, and said to them, "Whoever
wants to be first must be last of all and servant of

[a] Or *in* [b] Gk *no fuller* [c] Or *tents* [d] Or *my beloved Son* [e] Gk *him* [f] Gk *He* [g] Other ancient authorities add *with tears* [h] Other ancient authorities add *and fasting*

all." 36 Then he took a little child and put it among
them; and taking it in his arms, he said to them,
37 "Whoever welcomes one such child in my
name welcomes me, and whoever welcomes me
welcomes not me but the one who sent me."
38 John said to him, "Teacher, we saw someone[a] casting out demons in your name, and we
tried to stop him, because he was not following
us." 39 But Jesus said, "Do not stop him; for no
one who does a deed of power in my name will be
able soon afterward to speak evil of me. 40 Whoever is not against us is for us. 41 For truly I tell
you, whoever gives you a cup of water to drink
because you bear the name of Christ will by no
means lose the reward.
42 "If any of you put a stumbling block before one of these little ones who believe in me,[b] it
would be better for you if a great millstone were
hung around your neck and you were thrown into
the sea. 43 If your hand causes you to stumble, cut
it off; it is better for you to enter life maimed than
to have two hands and to go to hell,[c] to the unquenchable fire.[d] 45 And if your foot causes you to
stumble, cut it off; it is better for you to enter life
lame than to have two feet and to be thrown into
hell.[c,d] 47 And if your eye causes you to stumble,
tear it out; it is better for you to enter the kingdom of God with one eye than to have two eyes
and to be thrown into hell,[c] 48 where their worm
never dies, and the fire is never quenched.
49 "For everyone will be salted with fire.[e]
50 Salt is good; but if salt has lost its saltiness, how
can you season it?[f] Have salt in yourselves, and
be at peace with one another."
10 He left that place and went to the region
of Judea and[g] beyond the Jordan. And
crowds again gathered around him; and, as was
his custom, he again taught them.
2 Some Pharisees came, and to test him they
asked, "Is it lawful for a man to divorce his wife?"
3 He answered them, "What did Moses command
you?" 4 They said, "Moses allowed a man to write a
certificate of dismissal and to divorce her." 5 But
Jesus said to them, "Because of your hardness of
heart he wrote this commandment for you. 6 But
from the beginning of creation, 'God made them
male and female.' 7 'For this reason a man shall
leave his father and mother and be joined to his
wife,[h] 8 and the two shall become one flesh.' So they
are no longer two, but one flesh. 9 Therefore what
God has joined together, let no one separate."
10 Then in the house the disciples asked him
again about this matter. 11 He said to them, "Whoever divorces his wife and marries another commits adultery against her; 12 and if she divorces
her husband and marries another, she commits
adultery."
13 People were bringing little children to him
in order that he might touch them; and the disciples spoke sternly to them. 14 But when Jesus saw
this, he was indignant and said to them, "Let the
little children come to me; do not stop them; for
it is to such as these that the kingdom of God belongs. 15 Truly I tell you, whoever does not receive
the kingdom of God as a little child will never enter it." 16 And he took them up in his arms, laid his
hands on them, and blessed them.
17 As he was setting out on a journey, a man
ran up and knelt before him, and asked him, "Good
Teacher, what must I do to inherit eternal life?"
18 Jesus said to him, "Why do you call me good?
No one is good but God alone. 19 You know the
commandments: 'You shall not murder; You
shall not commit adultery; You shall not steal;
You shall not bear false witness; You shall not defraud; Honor your father and mother.' " 20 He said
to him, "Teacher, I have kept all these since my
youth." 21 Jesus, looking at him, loved him and
said, "You lack one thing; go, sell what you own,
and give the money[i] to the poor, and you will
have treasure in heaven; then come, follow me."
22 When he heard this, he was shocked and went
away grieving, for he had many possessions.
23 Then Jesus looked around and said to his

[a] Other ancient authorities add *who does not follow us* [b] Other ancient authorities lack *in me* [c] Gk *Gehenna*
[d] Verses 44 and 46 (which are identical with verse 48) are lacking in the best ancient authorities [e] Other ancient authorities either add or substitute *and every sacrifice will be salted with salt* [f] Or *how can you restore its saltiness?*
[g] Other ancient authorities lack *and* [h] Other ancient authorities lack *and be joined to his wife* [i] Gk lacks *the money*

disciples, "How hard it will be for those who have
wealth to enter the kingdom of God!" 24And
the disciples were perplexed at these words. But
Jesus said to them again, "Children, how hard it
is[a] to enter the kingdom of God! 25It is easier for
a camel to go through the eye of a needle than
for someone who is rich to enter the kingdom of
God." 26They were greatly astounded and said to
one another,[b] "Then who can be saved?" 27Jesus
looked at them and said, "For mortals it is impossible, but not for God; for God all things are
possible."

Mark 10:17-25

Christians have often reduced salvation to a matter of belief in Jesus' messiahship. Yet in this passage Jesus links salvation for the rich with how they treat the poor. In fact, Jesus calls for a radical redistribution of wealth. Even though this rich young ruler exhibited personal piety through observance of the Commandments, his lack of practices on behalf of the disenfranchised barred him from everlasting life.

— *MDLT*

28 Peter began to say to him, "Look, we have
left everything and followed you." 29Jesus said,
"Truly I tell you, there is no one who has left
house or brothers or sisters or mother or father
or children or fields, for my sake and for the sake
of the good news,[c] 30who will not receive a hundredfold now in this age—houses, brothers and
sisters, mothers and children, and fields, with
persecutions—and in the age to come eternal life.
31But many who are first will be last, and the last
will be first."

32 They were on the road, going up to Jerusalem, and Jesus was walking ahead of them;
they were amazed, and those who followed were
afraid. He took the twelve aside again and began
to tell them what was to happen to him, 33saying,
"See, we are going up to Jerusalem, and the Son
of Man will be handed over to the chief priests
and the scribes, and they will condemn him to
death; then they will hand him over to the Gentiles; 34they will mock him, and spit upon him,
and flog him, and kill him; and after three days he
will rise again."

35 James and John, the sons of Zebedee,
came forward to him and said to him, "Teacher,
we want you to do for us whatever we ask of you."
36And he said to them, "What is it you want me
to do for you?" 37And they said to him, "Grant
us to sit, one at your right hand and one at your
left, in your glory." 38But Jesus said to them, "You
do not know what you are asking. Are you able to
drink the cup that I drink, or be baptized with the
baptism that I am baptized with?" 39They replied,
"We are able." Then Jesus said to them, "The cup
that I drink you will drink; and with the baptism
with which I am baptized, you will be baptized;
40but to sit at my right hand or at my left is not
mine to grant, but it is for those for whom it has
been prepared."

41 When the ten heard this, they began to
be angry with James and John. 42So Jesus called
them and said to them, "You know that among
the Gentiles those whom they recognize as their
rulers lord it over them, and their great ones are
tyrants over them. 43But it is not so among you;
but whoever wishes to become great among you
must be your servant, 44and whoever wishes to
be first among you must be slave of all. 45For the
Son of Man came not to be served but to serve,
and to give his life a ransom for many."

46 They came to Jericho. As he and his disciples and a large crowd were leaving Jericho,
Bartimaeus son of Timaeus, a blind beggar, was
sitting by the roadside. 47When he heard that it
was Jesus of Nazareth, he began to shout out and
say, "Jesus, Son of David, have mercy on me!"
48Many sternly ordered him to be quiet, but he
cried out even more loudly, "Son of David, have
mercy on me!" 49Jesus stood still and said, "Call
him here." And they called the blind man, saying

[a] Other ancient authorities add *for those who trust in riches* [b] Other ancient authorities read *to him* [c] Or *gospel*

to him, "Take heart; get up, he is calling you." 50 So
throwing off his cloak, he sprang up and came to
Jesus. 51 Then Jesus said to him, "What do you
want me to do for you?" The blind man said to
him, "My teacher,[a] let me see again." 52 Jesus said
to him, "Go; your faith has made you well." Immediately he regained his sight and followed him
on the way.

11 When they were approaching Jerusalem, at Bethphage and Bethany, near the
Mount of Olives, he sent two of his disciples 2 and
said to them, "Go into the village ahead of you,
and immediately as you enter it, you will find tied
there a colt that has never been ridden; untie it
and bring it. 3 If anyone says to you, 'Why are you
doing this?' just say this, 'The Lord needs it and
will send it back here immediately.'" 4 They went
away and found a colt tied near a door, outside
in the street. As they were untying it, 5 some of
the bystanders said to them, "What are you doing, untying the colt?" 6 They told them what
Jesus had said; and they allowed them to take it.
7 Then they brought the colt to Jesus and threw
their cloaks on it; and he sat on it. 8 Many people
spread their cloaks on the road, and others spread
leafy branches that they had cut in the fields.
9 Then those who went ahead and those who followed were shouting,

"Hosanna!
Blessed is the one who comes in the name
of the Lord!
10 Blessed is the coming kingdom of our
ancestor David!
Hosanna in the highest heaven!"

11 Then he entered Jerusalem and went into
the temple; and when he had looked around at
everything, as it was already late, he went out to
Bethany with the twelve.

12 On the following day, when they came
from Bethany, he was hungry. 13 Seeing in the
distance a fig tree in leaf, he went to see whether
perhaps he would find anything on it. When he
came to it, he found nothing but leaves, for it was
not the season for figs. 14 He said to it, "May no
one ever eat fruit from you again." And his disciples heard it.

15 Then they came to Jerusalem. And he
entered the temple and began to drive out those
who were selling and those who were buying in
the temple, and he overturned the tables of the
money changers and the seats of those who sold
doves; 16 and he would not allow anyone to carry
anything through the temple. 17 He was teaching
and saying, "Is it not written,

'My house shall be called a house of prayer
for all the nations'?
But you have made it a den of robbers."

18 And when the chief priests and the scribes
heard it, they kept looking for a way to kill him;
for they were afraid of him, because the whole
crowd was spellbound by his teaching. 19 And
when evening came, Jesus and his disciples[b] went
out of the city.

20 In the morning as they passed by, they
saw the fig tree withered away to its roots. 21 Then
Peter remembered and said to him, "Rabbi,
look! The fig tree that you cursed has withered."
22 Jesus answered them, "Have[c] faith in God.
23 Truly I tell you, if you say to this mountain, 'Be
taken up and thrown into the sea,' and if you do
not doubt in your heart, but believe that what you
say will come to pass, it will be done for you. 24 So
I tell you, whatever you ask for in prayer, believe
that you have received[d] it, and it will be yours.

25 "Whenever you stand praying, forgive, if
you have anything against anyone; so that your
Father in heaven may also forgive you your trespasses."[e]

27 Again they came to Jerusalem. As he
was walking in the temple, the chief priests, the
scribes, and the elders came to him 28 and said,
"By what authority are you doing these things?
Who gave you this authority to do them?"
29 Jesus said to them, "I will ask you one question;

[a] Aramaic *Rabbouni* [b] Gk *they*: other ancient authorities read *he*

[c] Other ancient authorities read *"If you have* [d] Other ancient authorities read *are receiving*

[e] Other ancient authorities add verse 26, *"But if you do not forgive, neither will your Father in heaven forgive your trespasses."*

answer me, and I will tell you by what authority I
do these things. [30]Did the baptism of John come
from heaven, or was it of human origin? Answer
me." [31]They argued with one another, "If we say,
'From heaven,' he will say, 'Why then did you
not believe him?' [32]But shall we say, 'Of human
origin'?"—they were afraid of the crowd, for all
regarded John as truly a prophet. [33]So they answered Jesus, "We do not know." And Jesus said
to them, "Neither will I tell you by what authority
I am doing these things."

12 Then he began to speak to them in parables. "A man planted a vineyard, put a
fence around it, dug a pit for the wine press, and
built a watchtower; then he leased it to tenants
and went to another country. [2]When the season
came, he sent a slave to the tenants to collect from
them his share of the produce of the vineyard.
[3]But they seized him, and beat him, and sent him
away empty-handed. [4]And again he sent another
slave to them; this one they beat over the head
and insulted. [5]Then he sent another, and that
one they killed. And so it was with many others;
some they beat, and others they killed. [6]He had
still one other, a beloved son. Finally he sent him
to them, saying, 'They will respect my son.' [7]But
those tenants said to one another, 'This is the
heir; come, let us kill him, and the inheritance
will be ours.' [8]So they seized him, killed him, and
threw him out of the vineyard. [9]What then will
the owner of the vineyard do? He will come and
destroy the tenants and give the vineyard to others. [10]Have you not read this scripture:

'The stone that the builders rejected
has become the cornerstone;[a]
11 this was the Lord's doing,
and it is amazing in our eyes'?"

12 When they realized that he had told this
parable against them, they wanted to arrest him,
but they feared the crowd. So they left him and
went away.

13 Then they sent to him some Pharisees
and some Herodians to trap him in what he said.
[14]And they came and said to him, "Teacher, we
know that you are sincere, and show deference to
no one; for you do not regard people with partiality, but teach the way of God in accordance with
truth. Is it lawful to pay taxes to the emperor, or
not? [15]Should we pay them, or should we not?"
But knowing their hypocrisy, he said to them,
"Why are you putting me to the test? Bring me
a denarius and let me see it." [16]And they brought
one. Then he said to them, "Whose head is this,
and whose title?" They answered, "The emper-
or's." [17]Jesus said to them, "Give to the emperor
the things that are the emperor's, and to God
the things that are God's." And they were utterly
amazed at him.

Mark 12:17

"Rendering to Caesar" has become a slogan for yielding to the civil government's claims; "God and country" has become a battle cry for a sort of patriotism. Since Jesus' time, empires have arisen in his name; "God bless America" is only one of the latest efforts to identify the things of Caesar with the things of God. Yet Jesus will have none of it, clearly delineating between the two. What bears the image of Caesar—the denarius—should be returned to Caesar; but what bears the image of God—all that we are as human beings, created in God's image—should be devoted to God.

— MDLT

18 Some Sadducees, who say there is no resurrection, came to him and asked him a question,
saying, [19]"Teacher, Moses wrote for us that if a
man's brother dies, leaving a wife but no child,
the man[b] shall marry the widow and raise up children for his brother. [20]There were seven brothers;
the first married and, when he died, left no children; [21]and the second married the widow[c] and
died, leaving no children; and the third likewise;
[22]none of the seven left children. Last of all the
woman herself died. [23]In the resurrection[d] whose
wife will she be? For the seven had married her."

24 Jesus said to them, "Is not this the reason

[a] Or *keystone* [b] Gk *his brother* [c] Gk *her* [d] Other ancient authorities add *when they rise*

you are wrong, that you know neither the scriptures nor the power of God? 25 For when they rise
from the dead, they neither marry nor are given
in marriage, but are like angels in heaven. 26 And
as for the dead being raised, have you not read in
the book of Moses, in the story about the bush,
how God said to him, 'I am the God of Abraham,
the God of Isaac, and the God of Jacob'? 27 He is
God not of the dead, but of the living; you are
quite wrong."

28 One of the scribes came near and heard
them disputing with one another, and seeing that
he answered them well, he asked him, "Which
commandment is the first of all?" 29 Jesus answered, "The first is, 'Hear, O Israel: the Lord our
God, the Lord is one; 30 you shall love the Lord
your God with all your heart, and with all your
soul, and with all your mind, and with all your
strength.' 31 The second is this, 'You shall love
your neighbor as yourself.' There is no other commandment greater than these." 32 Then the scribe
said to him, "You are right, Teacher; you have
truly said that 'he is one, and besides him there is
no other'; 33 and 'to love him with all the heart,
and with all the understanding, and with all the
strength,' and 'to love one's neighbor as oneself,'—
this is much more important than all whole burnt
offerings and sacrifices." 34 When Jesus saw that
he answered wisely, he said to him, "You are not
far from the kingdom of God." After that no one
dared to ask him any question.

35 While Jesus was teaching in the temple, he
said, "How can the scribes say that the Messiah[a]
is the son of David? 36 David himself, by the Holy
Spirit, declared,

'The Lord said to my Lord,
"Sit at my right hand,
until I put your enemies under your feet." '

37 David himself calls him Lord; so how can he
be his son?" And the large crowd was listening to
him with delight.

38 As he taught, he said, "Beware of the
scribes, who like to walk around in long robes,
and to be greeted with respect in the marketplaces, 39 and to have the best seats in the synagogues and places of honor at banquets! 40 They
devour widows' houses and for the sake of appearance say long prayers. They will receive the
greater condemnation."

41 He sat down opposite the treasury, and
watched the crowd putting money into the treasury. Many rich people put in large sums. 42 A
poor widow came and put in two small copper
coins, which are worth a penny. 43 Then he called
his disciples and said to them, "Truly I tell you,
this poor widow has put in more than all those
who are contributing to the treasury. 44 For all of
them have contributed out of their abundance;
but she out of her poverty has put in everything
she had, all she had to live on."

13 As he came out of the temple, one of his
disciples said to him, "Look, Teacher,
what large stones and what large buildings!"
2 Then Jesus asked him, "Do you see these great
buildings? Not one stone will be left here upon
another; all will be thrown down."

3 When he was sitting on the Mount of Olives
opposite the temple, Peter, James, John, and Andrew asked him privately, 4 "Tell us, when will this
be, and what will be the sign that all these things
are about to be accomplished?" 5 Then Jesus began to say to them, "Beware that no one leads you
astray. 6 Many will come in my name and say, 'I
am he!'[b] and they will lead many astray. 7 When
you hear of wars and rumors of wars, do not be
alarmed; this must take place, but the end is still
to come. 8 For nation will rise against nation, and
kingdom against kingdom; there will be earthquakes in various places; there will be famines.
This is but the beginning of the birth pangs.

9 "As for yourselves, beware; for they will
hand you over to councils; and you will be beaten
in synagogues; and you will stand before governors and kings because of me, as a testimony to
them. 10 And the good news[c] must first be proclaimed to all nations. 11 When they bring you to
trial and hand you over, do not worry beforehand
about what you are to say; but say whatever is
given you at that time, for it is not you who speak,

[a] Or *the Christ* [b] Gk *I am* [c] Gk *gospel*

but the Holy Spirit. 12Brother will betray brother
to death, and a father his child, and children will
rise against parents and have them put to death;
13and you will be hated by all because of my
name. But the one who endures to the end will
be saved.

14 "But when you see the desolating sacrilege set up where it ought not to be (let the reader
understand), then those in Judea must flee to
the mountains; 15the one on the housetop must
not go down or enter the house to take anything
away; 16the one in the field must not turn back to
get a coat. 17Woe to those who are pregnant and
to those who are nursing infants in those days!
18Pray that it may not be in winter. 19For in those
days there will be suffering, such as has not been
from the beginning of the creation that God created until now, no, and never will be. 20And if the
Lord had not cut short those days, no one would
be saved; but for the sake of the elect, whom
he chose, he has cut short those days. 21And if
anyone says to you at that time, 'Look! Here is
the Messiah!'[a] or 'Look! There he is!'—do not
believe it. 22False messiahs[b] and false prophets
will appear and produce signs and omens, to lead
astray, if possible, the elect. 23But be alert; I have
already told you everything.

24 "But in those days, after that suffering,
the sun will be darkened,
and the moon will not give its light,
25 and the stars will be falling from heaven,
and the powers in the heavens will be
shaken.

26Then they will see 'the Son of Man coming in
clouds' with great power and glory. 27Then he
will send out the angels, and gather his elect from
the four winds, from the ends of the earth to the
ends of heaven.

28 "From the fig tree learn its lesson: as soon
as its branch becomes tender and puts forth its
leaves, you know that summer is near. 29So also,
when you see these things taking place, you know
that he[c] is near, at the very gates. 30Truly I tell
you, this generation will not pass away until all
these things have taken place. 31Heaven and earth
will pass away, but my words will not pass away.

32 "But about that day or hour no one knows,
neither the angels in heaven, nor the Son, but
only the Father. 33Beware, keep alert;[d] for you
do not know when the time will come. 34It is like
a man going on a journey, when he leaves home
and puts his slaves in charge, each with his work,
and commands the doorkeeper to be on the
watch. 35Therefore, keep awake—for you do not
know when the master of the house will come, in
the evening, or at midnight, or at cockcrow, or at
dawn, 36or else he may find you asleep when he
comes suddenly. 37And what I say to you I say to
all: Keep awake."

14 It was two days before the Passover and
the festival of Unleavened Bread. The
chief priests and the scribes were looking for a
way to arrest Jesus[e] by stealth and kill him; 2for
they said, "Not during the festival, or there may
be a riot among the people."

3 While he was at Bethany in the house of
Simon the leper,[f] as he sat at the table, a woman
came with an alabaster jar of very costly ointment
of nard, and she broke open the jar and poured
the ointment on his head. 4But some were there
who said to one another in anger, "Why was the
ointment wasted in this way? 5For this ointment
could have been sold for more than three hundred
denarii,[g] and the money given to the poor." And
they scolded her. 6But Jesus said, "Let her alone;
why do you trouble her? She has performed a
good service for me. 7For you always have the
poor with you, and you can show kindness to
them whenever you wish; but you will not always have me. 8She has done what she could; she
has anointed my body beforehand for its burial.
9Truly I tell you, wherever the good news[h] is proclaimed in the whole world, what she has done
will be told in remembrance of her."

10 Then Judas Iscariot, who was one of the
twelve, went to the chief priests in order to betray
him to them. 11When they heard it, they were

[a] Or *the Christ* [b] Or *christs* [c] Or *it* [d] Other ancient authorities add *and pray* [e] Gk *him* [f] The terms *leper* and *leprosy* can refer to several diseases [g] The denarius was the usual day's wage for a laborer [h] Or *gospel*

Mark 14:3-9

The first words of Jesus' rebuke at the home of Simon, "you always have the poor with you," have often been quoted as a pretext for complacency in the face of social injustice. Why should we spend time, money, or energy to alleviate poverty when Jesus himself said that some people would be perpetually poor? But Jesus' next words are the point: "you can show kindness to them"—literally, you can do good—"whenever you wish." His words echo God's command of Torah: "Since there will never cease to be some in need on the earth, I therefore command you, 'Open your hand to the poor and needy neighbor in your land'" (Deut 15:11).

— *NE*

greatly pleased, and promised to give him money.
So he began to look for an opportunity to betray
him.
12 On the first day of Unleavened Bread,
when the Passover lamb is sacrificed, his disciples
said to him, "Where do you want us to go and
make the preparations for you to eat the Passover?" 13So he sent two of his disciples, saying to
them, "Go into the city, and a man carrying a jar
of water will meet you; follow him, 14and wherever he enters, say to the owner of the house, 'The
Teacher asks, Where is my guest room where I
may eat the Passover with my disciples?' 15He
will show you a large room upstairs, furnished
and ready. Make preparations for us there." 16So
the disciples set out and went to the city, and
found everything as he had told them; and they
prepared the Passover meal.
17 When it was evening, he came with the
twelve. 18And when they had taken their places
and were eating, Jesus said, "Truly I tell you, one
of you will betray me, one who is eating with
me." 19They began to be distressed and to say to
him one after another, "Surely, not I?" 20He said
to them, "It is one of the twelve, one who is dipping bread[a] into the bowl[b] with me. 21For the Son
of Man goes as it is written of him, but woe to
that one by whom the Son of Man is betrayed! It
would have been better for that one not to have
been born."
22 While they were eating, he took a loaf of
bread, and after blessing it he broke it, gave it to
them, and said, "Take; this is my body." 23Then
he took a cup, and after giving thanks he gave it to
them, and all of them drank from it. 24He said to
them, "This is my blood of the[c] covenant, which
is poured out for many. 25Truly I tell you, I will
never again drink of the fruit of the vine until that
day when I drink it new in the kingdom of God."
26 When they had sung the hymn, they went
out to the Mount of Olives. 27And Jesus said to
them, "You will all become deserters; for it is
written,

'I will strike the shepherd,
and the sheep will be scattered.'

28But after I am raised up, I will go before you
to Galilee." 29Peter said to him, "Even though all
become deserters, I will not." 30Jesus said to him,
"Truly I tell you, this day, this very night, before
the cock crows twice, you will deny me three
times." 31But he said vehemently, "Even though I
must die with you, I will not deny you." And all of
them said the same.
32 They went to a place called Gethsemane;
and he said to his disciples, "Sit here while I pray."
33He took with him Peter and James and John,
and began to be distressed and agitated. 34And he
said to them, "I am deeply grieved, even to death;
remain here, and keep awake." 35And going a little farther, he threw himself on the ground and
prayed that, if it were possible, the hour might
pass from him. 36He said, "Abba,[d] Father, for you
all things are possible; remove this cup from me;
yet, not what I want, but what you want." 37He

[a] Gk lacks *bread* [b] Other ancient authorities read *same bowl* [c] Other ancient authorities add *new*
[d] Aramaic for *Father*

came and found them sleeping; and he said to
Peter, "Simon, are you asleep? Could you not keep
awake one hour? 38 Keep awake and pray that you
may not come into the time of trial;[a] the spirit indeed is willing, but the flesh is weak." 39 And again
he went away and prayed, saying the same words.
40 And once more he came and found them sleeping, for their eyes were very heavy; and they did
not know what to say to him. 41 He came a third
time and said to them, "Are you still sleeping and
taking your rest? Enough! The hour has come;
the Son of Man is betrayed into the hands of sinners. 42 Get up, let us be going. See, my betrayer
is at hand."

43 Immediately, while he was still speaking,
Judas, one of the twelve, arrived; and with him
there was a crowd with swords and clubs, from the
chief priests, the scribes, and the elders. 44 Now
the betrayer had given them a sign, saying, "The
one I will kiss is the man; arrest him and lead him
away under guard." 45 So when he came, he went
up to him at once and said, "Rabbi!" and kissed
him. 46 Then they laid hands on him and arrested
him. 47 But one of those who stood near drew his
sword and struck the slave of the high priest, cutting off his ear. 48 Then Jesus said to them, "Have
you come out with swords and clubs to arrest me
as though I were a bandit? 49 Day after day I was
with you in the temple teaching, and you did not
arrest me. But let the scriptures be fulfilled." 50 All
of them deserted him and fled.

51 A certain young man was following him,
wearing nothing but a linen cloth. They caught
hold of him, 52 but he left the linen cloth and ran
off naked.

53 They took Jesus to the high priest; and all
the chief priests, the elders, and the scribes were
assembled. 54 Peter had followed him at a distance, right into the courtyard of the high priest;
and he was sitting with the guards, warming himself at the fire. 55 Now the chief priests and the
whole council were looking for testimony against
Jesus to put him to death; but they found none.
56 For many gave false testimony against him, and
their testimony did not agree. 57 Some stood up
and gave false testimony against him, saying,
58 "We heard him say, 'I will destroy this temple
that is made with hands, and in three days I will
build another, not made with hands.'" 59 But even
on this point their testimony did not agree.
60 Then the high priest stood up before them and
asked Jesus, "Have you no answer? What is it that
they testify against you?" 61 But he was silent and
did not answer. Again the high priest asked him,
"Are you the Messiah,[b] the Son of the Blessed
One?" 62 Jesus said, "I am; and

'you will see the Son of Man
seated at the right hand of the Power,'
and 'coming with the clouds of heaven.'"

63 Then the high priest tore his clothes and said,
"Why do we still need witnesses? 64 You have
heard his blasphemy! What is your decision?"
All of them condemned him as deserving death.
65 Some began to spit on him, to blindfold him,
and to strike him, saying to him, "Prophesy!" The
guards also took him over and beat him.

66 While Peter was below in the courtyard,
one of the servant-girls of the high priest came
by. 67 When she saw Peter warming himself, she
stared at him and said, "You also were with Jesus,
the man from Nazareth." 68 But he denied it, saying, "I do not know or understand what you are
talking about." And he went out into the fore-
court.[c] Then the cock crowed.[d] 69 And the servant-
girl, on seeing him, began again to say to the bystanders, "This man is one of them." 70 But again
he denied it. Then after a little while the bystanders again said to Peter, "Certainly you are one of
them; for you are a Galilean." 71 But he began to
curse, and he swore an oath, "I do not know this
man you are talking about." 72 At that moment the
cock crowed for the second time. Then Peter remembered that Jesus had said to him, "Before the
cock crows twice, you will deny me three times."
And he broke down and wept.

15 As soon as it was morning, the chief
priests held a consultation with the elders
and scribes and the whole council. They bound
Jesus, led him away, and handed him over to
Pilate. 2 Pilate asked him, "Are you the King of the

[a] Or *into temptation* [b] Or *the Christ* [c] Or *gateway* [d] Other ancient authorities lack *Then the cock crowed*

 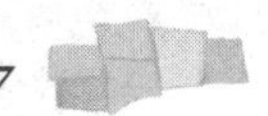

Jews?" He answered him, "You say so." 3Then the chief priests accused him of many things. 4Pilate asked him again, "Have you no answer? See how many charges they bring against you." 5But Jesus made no further reply, so that Pilate was amazed.

6 Now at the festival he used to release a prisoner for them, anyone for whom they asked. 7Now a man called Barabbas was in prison with the rebels who had committed murder during the insurrection. 8So the crowd came and began to ask Pilate to do for them according to his custom. 9Then he answered them, "Do you want me to release for you the King of the Jews?" 10For he realized that it was out of jealousy that the chief priests had handed him over. 11But the chief priests stirred up the crowd to have him release Barabbas for them instead. 12Pilate spoke to them again, "Then what do you wish me to do[a] with the man you call[b] the King of the Jews?" 13They shouted back, "Crucify him!" 14Pilate asked them, "Why, what evil has he done?" But they shouted all the more, "Crucify him!" 15So Pilate, wishing to satisfy the crowd, released Barabbas for them; and after flogging Jesus, he handed him over to be crucified.

16 Then the soldiers led him into the courtyard of the palace (that is, the governor's headquarters[c]); and they called together the whole cohort. 17And they clothed him in a purple cloak; and after twisting some thorns into a crown, they put it on him. 18And they began saluting him, "Hail, King of the Jews!" 19They struck his head with a reed, spat upon him, and knelt down in homage to him. 20After mocking him, they stripped him of the purple cloak and put his own clothes on him. Then they led him out to crucify him.

21 They compelled a passer-by, who was coming in from the country, to carry his cross; it was Simon of Cyrene, the father of Alexander and Rufus. 22Then they brought Jesus[d] to the place called Golgotha (which means the place of a skull). 23And they offered him wine mixed with myrrh; but he did not take it. 24And they crucified him, and divided his clothes among them, casting lots to decide what each should take.

25 It was nine o'clock in the morning when they crucified him. 26The inscription of the charge against him read, "The King of the Jews." 27And with him they crucified two bandits, one on his right and one on his left.[e] 29Those who passed by derided[f] him, shaking their heads and saying, "Aha! You who would destroy the temple and build it in three days, 30save yourself, and come down from the cross!" 31In the same way the chief priests, along with the scribes, were also mocking him among themselves and saying, "He saved others; he cannot save himself. 32Let the Messiah,[g] the King of Israel, come down from the cross now, so that we may see and believe." Those who were crucified with him also taunted him.

33 When it was noon, darkness came over the whole land[h] until three in the afternoon. 34At three o'clock Jesus cried out with a loud voice, "Eloi, Eloi, lema sabachthani?" which means, "My God, my God, why have you forsaken me?"[i] 35When some of the bystanders heard it, they said, "Listen, he is calling for Elijah." 36And someone ran, filled a sponge with sour wine, put it on a stick, and gave it to him to drink, saying, "Wait, let us see whether Elijah will come to take him down." 37Then Jesus gave a loud cry and breathed

Mark 15:17

The crown of thorns has become a symbol of the solidarity of God with the marginalized, the oppressed, and the exploited. It has come to signify the person of Jesus, who makes the groaning of the despised his own cry for liberation. The symbol reveals that God is also suffering with them, while promising their freedom from that oppression.[69]

— ***Kuribayashi Teruo***

[a] Other ancient authorities read *what should I do* [b] Other ancient authorities lack *the man you call* [c] Gk *the praetorium* [d] Gk *him* [e] Other ancient authorities add verse 28, *And the scripture was fulfilled that says, "And he was counted among the lawless."* [f] Or *blasphemed* [g] Or *the Christ* [h] Or *earth* [i] Other ancient authorities read *made me a reproach*

his last. 38 And the curtain of the temple was torn
in two, from top to bottom. 39 Now when the centurion, who stood facing him, saw that in this way
he[a] breathed his last, he said, "Truly this man was
God's Son!"[b]

40 There were also women looking on from
a distance; among them were Mary Magdalene,
and Mary the mother of James the younger and
of Joses, and Salome. 41 These used to follow him
and provided for him when he was in Galilee; and
there were many other women who had come up
with him to Jerusalem.

42 When evening had come, and since it was
the day of Preparation, that is, the day before
the sabbath, 43 Joseph of Arimathea, a respected
member of the council, who was also himself
waiting expectantly for the kingdom of God,
went boldly to Pilate and asked for the body of
Jesus. 44 Then Pilate wondered if he were already
dead; and summoning the centurion, he asked
him whether he had been dead for some time.
45 When he learned from the centurion that he
was dead, he granted the body to Joseph. 46 Then
Joseph[c] bought a linen cloth, and taking down
the body,[d] wrapped it in the linen cloth, and laid
it in a tomb that had been hewn out of the rock.
He then rolled a stone against the door of the
tomb. 47 Mary Magdalene and Mary the mother
of Joses saw where the body[d] was laid.

16 When the sabbath was over, Mary
Magdalene, and Mary the mother of
James, and Salome bought spices, so that they
might go and anoint him. 2 And very early on
the first day of the week, when the sun had risen,
they went to the tomb. 3 They had been saying to
one another, "Who will roll away the stone for
us from the entrance to the tomb?" 4 When they
looked up, they saw that the stone, which was
very large, had already been rolled back. 5 As they
entered the tomb, they saw a young man, dressed
in a white robe, sitting on the right side; and they
were alarmed. 6 But he said to them, "Do not be
alarmed; you are looking for Jesus of Nazareth,
who was crucified. He has been raised; he is not
here. Look, there is the place they laid him. 7 But
go, tell his disciples and Peter that he is going
ahead of you to Galilee; there you will see him,
just as he told you." 8 So they went out and fled
from the tomb, for terror and amazement had
seized them; and they said nothing to anyone, for
they were afraid.[e]

THE SHORTER ENDING OF MARK

⟦And all that had been commanded them they
told briefly to those around Peter. And afterward
Jesus himself sent out through them, from east to
west, the sacred and imperishable proclamation
of eternal salvation.[f]⟧

THE LONGER ENDING OF MARK

9 ⟦Now after he rose early on the first day of
the week, he appeared first to Mary Magdalene,
from whom he had cast out seven demons. 10 She
went out and told those who had been with him,
while they were mourning and weeping. 11 But
when they heard that he was alive and had been
seen by her, they would not believe it.

12 After this he appeared in another form to
two of them, as they were walking into the country. 13 And they went back and told the rest, but
they did not believe them.

14 Later he appeared to the eleven themselves
as they were sitting at the table; and he upbraided
them for their lack of faith and stubbornness, because they had not believed those who saw him
after he had risen.[g] 15 And he said to them, "Go

[a] Other ancient authorities add *cried out and* [b] Or *a son of God* [c] Gk *he* [d] Gk *it* [e] Some of the most ancient authorities bring the book to a close at the end of verse 8. One authority concludes the book with the shorter ending; others include the shorter ending and then continue with verses 9–20. In most authorities verses 9–20 follow immediately after verse 8, though in some of these authorities the passage is marked as being doubtful. [f] Other ancient authorities add *Amen* [g] Other ancient authorities add, in whole or in part, *And they excused themselves, saying, "This age of lawlessness and unbelief is under Satan, who does not allow the truth and power of God to prevail over the unclean things of the spirits. Therefore reveal your righteousness now"—thus they spoke to Christ. And Christ replied to them, "The term of years of Satan's power has been*

into all the world and proclaim the good news[a] to
the whole creation. 16 The one who believes and
is baptized will be saved; but the one who does
not believe will be condemned. 17 And these signs
will accompany those who believe: by using my
name they will cast out demons; they will speak
in new tongues; 18 they will pick up snakes in
their hands,[b] and if they drink any deadly thing,
it will not hurt them; they will lay their hands on
the sick, and they will recover."

19 So then the Lord Jesus, after he had spoken to them, was taken up into heaven and sat
down at the right hand of God. 20 And they went
out and proclaimed the good news everywhere,
while the Lord worked with them and confirmed
the message by the signs that accompanied it.[c]]]

fulfilled, but other terrible things draw near. And for those who have sinned I was handed over to death, that they may return to the truth and sin no more, that they may inherit the spiritual and imperishable glory of righteousness that is in heaven."

[a] Or *gospel*

[b] Other ancient authorities lack *in their hands*

[c] Other ancient authorities add *Amen*

The Gospel According to

Luke

Composed around 80—90 CE, the Gospel of Luke bears the name of a person identified elsewhere in the New Testament as a physician and a companion of the apostle Paul (see Acts 16:10-17, 21:1-18; Col 4:11-14). The author employs a rhetoric of subversion, using a hidden or coded language that speaks against the control and domination of the Roman Empire, the ruling power in Palestine. While addressing the marginalization of the writer's audience, at the same time this secret speech reveals the source of such oppression and exclusion. For Luke's readers, *Pax Romana,* the Peace of Rome, might more accurately be called the pilfering power of Rome.

From the start the author recognizes the power dynamics typical of the imperial society of the time. In dedicating his gospel to his patron, "you, most excellent Theophilus," Luke acknowledges the reality of Roman patron-client relationships and aligns himself with the client side of those relationships, perhaps even with the oppressed (1:1-4). The writer interweaves his narrative with personal experience rather than aesthetically removing himself from the imperialistic background of his "orderly account" (1:3). Nonetheless, the reader can detect a use of code even here, since the literal translation of the Greek *Theophilos* is "god-lover." Thus, this gospel is for any who hear Luke's story who love God and believe in Jesus as God's son.

The Gospel of Luke presents Jesus as a savior accessible to all people. This Jesus transcends not only race and ethnicity but also wealth and poverty. Luke's Jesus confronts the rich so that rich and poor have equal footing (6:24-26; 12:13-21; 16:1-13, 19-31). Women, the lame, the hungry, and those deemed "other" are also at the forefront (4:18-19; 8:1-3). The theology of Luke is grounded in a Jesus who comes not just to offer compassion to those who are wounded but also to speak to the evil of those who wound.

As an African American woman born and nurtured in the South, I have much affinity for this gospel and for Luke's empathy with those on the outskirts. African Americans still occupy an inferior social standing when compared to other races. African American women are at the bottom of the social ladder. There have been some advances against race and gender discrimination, but the ceiling remains. As an ordained Baptist and Disciples of Christ minister, I am joined to other clergywomen who must constantly battle sexism against women in ordained ministry. Those who love God should equally show love for God's people. The portrayal of Jesus in this Gospel as one who releases, sets free, proclaims jubilee, and dialogues with an African (23:26) is quite appealing.

While in structure the Gospel of Luke is similar to Greco-Roman history and biography, its content makes it apparent (on the most widely accepted theory of Gospel relationships) that the writer had access to Mark's Gospel and to another source of "sayings" identified by scholars as "Q," for *Quelle,* the German word for source. Luke also seems to have used a source now called "L,"

because some aspects of Luke are found in neither Mark nor Q and are unique to Luke's work (chs. 22–24).

The Gospel of Luke can be outlined as follows: prologue (1:1-4); infancy narratives (1:5—2:52); preparation for ministry (3:1—4:13); ministry in Galilee (4:14—9:50); journey to Jerusalem (9:51—19:27); Jesus in Jerusalem (19:28—23:56); and leaving Jerusalem behind (ch. 24).

— ***Stephanie Buckhanon Crowder***

1 Since many have undertaken to set down an
orderly account of the events that have been
fulfilled among us, 2 just as they were handed
on to us by those who from the beginning were
eyewitnesses and servants of the word, 3 I too
decided, after investigating everything carefully
from the very first,[a] to write an orderly account
for you, most excellent Theophilus, 4 so that you
may know the truth concerning the things about
which you have been instructed.

5 In the days of King Herod of Judea, there
was a priest named Zechariah, who belonged to
the priestly order of Abijah. His wife was a descendant of Aaron, and her name was Elizabeth.
6 Both of them were righteous before God, living
blamelessly according to all the commandments
and regulations of the Lord. 7 But they had no
children, because Elizabeth was barren, and both
were getting on in years.

8 Once when he was serving as priest before
God and his section was on duty, 9 he was chosen
by lot, according to the custom of the priesthood,
to enter the sanctuary of the Lord and offer incense. 10 Now at the time of the incense offering,
the whole assembly of the people was praying
outside. 11 Then there appeared to him an angel of
the Lord, standing at the right side of the altar of
incense. 12 When Zechariah saw him, he was terrified; and fear overwhelmed him. 13 But the angel
said to him, "Do not be afraid, Zechariah, for your
prayer has been heard. Your wife Elizabeth will
bear you a son, and you will name him John. 14 You
will have joy and gladness, and many will rejoice
at his birth, 15 for he will be great in the sight of the
Lord. He must never drink wine or strong drink;
even before his birth he will be filled with the Holy
Spirit. 16 He will turn many of the people of Israel
to the Lord their God. 17 With the spirit and power
of Elijah he will go before him, to turn the hearts
of parents to their children, and the disobedient
to the wisdom of the righteous, to make ready a
people prepared for the Lord." 18 Zechariah said to
the angel, "How will I know that this is so? For I
am an old man, and my wife is getting on in years."
19 The angel replied, "I am Gabriel. I stand in the
presence of God, and I have been sent to speak to
you and to bring you this good news. 20 But now,
because you did not believe my words, which will
be fulfilled in their time, you will become mute,
unable to speak, until the day these things occur."

21 Meanwhile the people were waiting for
Zechariah, and wondered at his delay in the sanctuary. 22 When he did come out, he could not
speak to them, and they realized that he had seen
a vision in the sanctuary. He kept motioning to
them and remained unable to speak. 23 When his
time of service was ended, he went to his home.

[a] Or *for a long time*

24 After those days his wife Elizabeth conceived, and for five months she remained in se-
clusion. She said, 25"This is what the Lord has
done for me when he looked favorably on me and
took away the disgrace I have endured among my
people."

26 In the sixth month the angel Gabriel was
sent by God to a town in Galilee called Nazareth,
27to a virgin engaged to a man whose name was
Joseph, of the house of David. The virgin's name
was Mary. 28And he came to her and said, "Greetings, favored one! The Lord is with you."[a] 29But
she was much perplexed by his words and pondered what sort of greeting this might be. 30The
angel said to her, "Do not be afraid, Mary, for you
have found favor with God. 31And now, you will
conceive in your womb and bear a son, and you
will name him Jesus. 32He will be great, and will
be called the Son of the Most High, and the Lord
God will give to him the throne of his ancestor
David. 33He will reign over the house of Jacob
forever, and of his kingdom there will be no end."
34Mary said to the angel, "How can this be, since
I am a virgin?"[b] 35The angel said to her, "The Holy
Spirit will come upon you, and the power of the
Most High will overshadow you; therefore the
child to be born[c] will be holy; he will be called
Son of God. 36And now, your relative Elizabeth
in her old age has also conceived a son; and this
is the sixth month for her who was said to be barren. 37For nothing will be impossible with God."
38Then Mary said, "Here am I, the servant of the
Lord; let it be with me according to your word."
Then the angel departed from her.

39 In those days Mary set out and went with
haste to a Judean town in the hill country, 40where
she entered the house of Zechariah and greeted
Elizabeth. 41When Elizabeth heard Mary's greeting, the child leaped in her womb. And Elizabeth
was filled with the Holy Spirit 42and exclaimed
with a loud cry, "Blessed are you among women,
and blessed is the fruit of your womb. 43And why
has this happened to me, that the mother of my
Lord comes to me? 44For as soon as I heard the
sound of your greeting, the child in my womb
leaped for joy. 45And blessed is she who believed
that there would be[d] a fulfillment of what was
spoken to her by the Lord."

46 And Mary[e] said,
"My soul magnifies the Lord,
47 and my spirit rejoices in God my Savior,
48 for he has looked with favor on the lowliness
of his servant.
Surely, from now on all generations will
call me blessed;
49 for the Mighty One has done great things
for me,
and holy is his name.
50 His mercy is for those who fear him
from generation to generation.
51 He has shown strength with his arm;
he has scattered the proud in the thoughts
of their hearts.
52 He has brought down the powerful from
their thrones,
and lifted up the lowly;
53 he has filled the hungry with good things,
and sent the rich away empty.
54 He has helped his servant Israel,
in remembrance of his mercy,
55 according to the promise he made to our
ancestors,
to Abraham and to his descendants
forever."

56 And Mary remained with her about three
months and then returned to her home.

57 Now the time came for Elizabeth to give
birth, and she bore a son. 58Her neighbors and
relatives heard that the Lord had shown his great
mercy to her, and they rejoiced with her.

59 On the eighth day they came to circumcise
the child, and they were going to name him Zechariah after his father. 60But his mother said, "No;
he is to be called John." 61They said to her, "None
of your relatives has this name." 62Then they began motioning to his father to find out what name
he wanted to give him. 63He asked for a writing
tablet and wrote, "His name is John." And all of

[a] Other ancient authorities add *Blessed are you among women* [b] Gk *I do not know a man* [c] Other ancient authorities add *of you* [d] Or *believed, for there will be* [e] Other ancient authorities read *Elizabeth*

them were amazed. 64Immediately his mouth was opened and his tongue freed, and he began to speak, praising God. 65Fear came over all their neighbors, and all these things were talked about throughout the entire hill country of Judea. 66All who heard them pondered them and said, "What then will this child become?" For, indeed, the hand of the Lord was with him.

67 Then his father Zechariah was filled with the Holy Spirit and spoke this prophecy:

68 "Blessed be the Lord God of Israel,
for he has looked favorably on his people
and redeemed them.
69 He has raised up a mighty savior[a] for us
in the house of his servant David,
70 as he spoke through the mouth of his holy
prophets from of old,
71 that we would be saved from our enemies
and from the hand of all who
hate us.
72 Thus he has shown the mercy promised to
our ancestors,
and has remembered his holy covenant,
73 the oath that he swore to our ancestor
Abraham,
to grant us 74that we, being rescued from
the hands of our enemies,
might serve him without fear, 75in holiness
and righteousness
before him all our days.
76 And you, child, will be called the prophet of
the Most High;
for you will go before the Lord to prepare
his ways,
77 to give knowledge of salvation to his people
by the forgiveness of their sins.
78 By the tender mercy of our God,
the dawn from on high will break
upon[b] us,
79 to give light to those who sit in darkness and
in the shadow of death,
to guide our feet into the way of peace."

80 The child grew and became strong in spirit, and he was in the wilderness until the day he appeared publicly to Israel.

2 In those days a decree went out from Emperor Augustus that all the world should be registered. 2This was the first registration and was taken while Quirinius was governor of Syria. 3All went to their own towns to be registered. 4Joseph also went from the town of Nazareth in Galilee to Judea, to the city of David called Bethlehem, because he was descended from the house and family of David. 5He went to be registered with Mary, to whom he was engaged and who was expecting a child. 6While they were there, the time came for her to deliver her child. 7And she gave birth to her firstborn son and wrapped him in bands of cloth, and laid him in a manger, because there was no place for them in the inn.

Luke 2:7

Jesus is born in the conditions of homelessness—in a barn, among animals and the manure they produce. He is placed in a manger, a wooden box or a hole on the cave wall from which horses and cattle ate. The unsanitary conditions of Jesus' birth are not lost on the wretched of the earth, who recognize God's solidarity with them ("to *you* is born...a Savior," v. 11). The slave spirituals bear witness to the link between Jesus and the marginalized, for they would sing "Poor little Jesus boy, Made him to be born in a manger, World treated him so mean, Treats me mean too."

— *MDLT*

8 In that region there were shepherds living in the fields, keeping watch over their flock by night. 9Then an angel of the Lord stood before them, and the glory of the Lord shone around them, and they were terrified. 10But the angel said to them, "Do not be afraid; for see—I am bringing you good news of great joy for all the people: 11to you is born this day in the city of David a Savior, who is the Messiah,[c] the Lord. 12This will be a sign for you: you will find a child wrapped in bands of cloth and lying in a manger." 13And suddenly there was with the angel a

[a] Gk *a horn of salvation* [b] Other ancient authorities read *has broken upon* [c] Or *the Christ*

multitude of the heavenly host,[a] praising God
and saying,
14 "Glory to God in the highest heaven,
and on earth peace among those whom he
favors!"[b]

Luke 2:8-14

When we think of a biblical shepherd we usually imagine someone who is pastoral, tenderly caring for the flock: as the Psalmist reminds us, "The LORD is my shepherd." But in Jesus' time shepherds—especially shepherds hired to watch the flocks of others—had no social status whatsoever; they lived apart from what was considered civilization, among the company of the most miserable outcasts of society. In Luke, the first proclamation of the gospel message is not to the rich and powerful but to society's most disenfranchised group. It is from the margins of privilege that the good news arises.

— *MDLT*

15 When the angels had left them and gone
into heaven, the shepherds said to one another,
"Let us go now to Bethlehem and see this thing
that has taken place, which the Lord has made
known to us." 16 So they went with haste and
found Mary and Joseph, and the child lying in the
manger. 17 When they saw this, they made known
what had been told them about this child; 18 and
all who heard it were amazed at what the shepherds told them. 19 But Mary treasured all these
words and pondered them in her heart. 20 The
shepherds returned, glorifying and praising God
for all they had heard and seen, as it had been told
them.

21 After eight days had passed, it was time to
circumcise the child; and he was called Jesus, the
name given by the angel before he was conceived
in the womb.

22 When the time came for their purification according to the law of Moses, they brought
him up to Jerusalem to present him to the Lord
23 (as it is written in the law of the Lord, "Every
firstborn male shall be designated as holy to the
Lord"), 24 and they offered a sacrifice according
to what is stated in the law of the Lord, "a pair of
turtledoves or two young pigeons."

25 Now there was a man in Jerusalem whose
name was Simeon;[c] this man was righteous and
devout, looking forward to the consolation of Israel, and the Holy Spirit rested on him. 26 It had
been revealed to him by the Holy Spirit that he
would not see death before he had seen the Lord's
Messiah.[d] 27 Guided by the Spirit, Simeon[e] came
into the temple; and when the parents brought in
the child Jesus, to do for him what was customary under the law, 28 Simeon[f] took him in his arms
and praised God, saying,
29 "Master, now you are dismissing your
servant[g] in peace,
according to your word;
30 for my eyes have seen your salvation,
31 which you have prepared in the presence
of all peoples,
32 a light for revelation to the Gentiles
and for glory to your people Israel."

33 And the child's father and mother were
amazed at what was being said about him. 34 Then
Simeon[c] blessed them and said to his mother
Mary, "This child is destined for the falling and
the rising of many in Israel, and to be a sign that
will be opposed 35 so that the inner thoughts of
many will be revealed—and a sword will pierce
your own soul too."

36 There was also a prophet, Anna[h] the
daughter of Phanuel, of the tribe of Asher. She
was of a great age, having lived with her husband
seven years after her marriage, 37 then as a widow
to the age of eighty-four. She never left the temple
but worshiped there with fasting and prayer night
and day. 38 At that moment she came, and began to
praise God and to speak about the child[i] to all who
were looking for the redemption of Jerusalem.

39 When they had finished everything required by the law of the Lord, they returned to

[a] Gk *army* [b] Other ancient authorities read *peace, goodwill among people* [c] Gk *Symeon* [d] Or *the Lord's Christ*
[e] Gk *In the Spirit, he* [f] Gk *he* [g] Gk *slave* [h] Gk *Hanna* [i] Gk *him*

Galilee, to their own town of Nazareth. 40 The
child grew and became strong, filled with wisdom; and the favor of God was upon him.

41 Now every year his parents went to Jerusalem for the festival of the Passover. 42 And when he
was twelve years old, they went up as usual for the
festival. 43 When the festival was ended and they
started to return, the boy Jesus stayed behind in
Jerusalem, but his parents did not know it. 44 Assuming that he was in the group of travelers, they
went a day's journey. Then they started to look for
him among their relatives and friends. 45 When
they did not find him, they returned to Jerusalem
to search for him. 46 After three days they found
him in the temple, sitting among the teachers, listening to them and asking them questions. 47 And
all who heard him were amazed at his understanding and his answers. 48 When his parents[a] saw him
they were astonished; and his mother said to him,
"Child, why have you treated us like this? Look,
your father and I have been searching for you in
great anxiety." 49 He said to them, "Why were you
searching for me? Did you not know that I must
be in my Father's house?"[b] 50 But they did not understand what he said to them. 51 Then he went
down with them and came to Nazareth, and was
obedient to them. His mother treasured all these
things in her heart.

52 And Jesus increased in wisdom and in
years,[c] and in divine and human favor.

3 In the fifteenth year of the reign of Emperor
Tiberius, when Pontius Pilate was governor
of Judea, and Herod was ruler[d] of Galilee, and his
brother Philip ruler[d] of the region of Ituraea and
Trachonitis, and Lysanias ruler[d] of Abilene, 2 during the high priesthood of Annas and Caiaphas,
the word of God came to John son of Zechariah
in the wilderness. 3 He went into all the region
around the Jordan, proclaiming a baptism of
repentance for the forgiveness of sins, 4 as it is
written in the book of the words of the prophet
Isaiah,

"The voice of one crying out in the
wilderness:
'Prepare the way of the Lord,
make his paths straight.
5 Every valley shall be filled,
and every mountain and hill shall be made
low,
and the crooked shall be made straight,
and the rough ways made smooth;
6 and all flesh shall see the salvation of God.' "

7 John said to the crowds that came out to
be baptized by him, "You brood of vipers! Who
warned you to flee from the wrath to come? 8 Bear
fruits worthy of repentance. Do not begin to say
to yourselves, 'We have Abraham as our ancestor'; for I tell you, God is able from these stones
to raise up children to Abraham. 9 Even now the
ax is lying at the root of the trees; every tree therefore that does not bear good fruit is cut down and
thrown into the fire."

10 And the crowds asked him, "What then
should we do?" 11 In reply he said to them, "Whoever has two coats must share with anyone who
has none; and whoever has food must do likewise." 12 Even tax collectors came to be baptized,
and they asked him, "Teacher, what should we
do?" 13 He said to them, "Collect no more than
the amount prescribed for you." 14 Soldiers also
asked him, "And we, what should we do?" He said
to them, "Do not extort money from anyone by
threats or false accusation, and be satisfied with
your wages."

15 As the people were filled with expectation,

Luke 3:9, 14

When soldiers ask John the Baptist what they must do, John responds that they must not use coercion or extortion against anyone. But an empire can only be sustained by its army carrying out violent actions. War, by its very definition, requires violence, and therefore John's response is revolutionary, for if imperial armies cease doing violence, empires will cease to exist.

— MDLT

[a] Gk *they* [b] Or *be about my Father's interests?* [c] Or *in stature* [d] Gk *tetrarch*

and all were questioning in their hearts concerning John, whether he might be the Messiah,[a]
16 John answered all of them by saying, "I baptize
you with water; but one who is more powerful
than I is coming; I am not worthy to untie the
thong of his sandals. He will baptize you with[b]
the Holy Spirit and fire. 17 His winnowing fork
is in his hand, to clear his threshing floor and to
gather the wheat into his granary; but the chaff he
will burn with unquenchable fire."

18 So, with many other exhortations, he proclaimed the good news to the people. 19 But Herod
the ruler,[c] who had been rebuked by him because
of Herodias, his brother's wife, and because of all
the evil things that Herod had done, 20 added to
them all by shutting up John in prison.

21 Now when all the people were baptized,
and when Jesus also had been baptized and was
praying, the heaven was opened, 22 and the Holy
Spirit descended upon him in bodily form like a
dove. And a voice came from heaven, "You are my
Son, the Beloved;[d] with you I am well pleased."[e]

23 Jesus was about thirty years old when he
began his work. He was the son (as was thought)
of Joseph son of Heli, 24 son of Matthat, son of
Levi, son of Melchi, son of Jannai, son of Joseph,
25 son of Mattathias, son of Amos, son of Nahum,
son of Esli, son of Naggai, 26 son of Maath, son
of Mattathias, son of Semein, son of Josech, son
of Joda, 27 son of Joanan, son of Rhesa, son of
Zerubbabel, son of Shealtiel,[f] son of Neri, 28 son
of Melchi, son of Addi, son of Cosam, son of El-
madam, son of Er, 29 son of Joshua, son of Eliezer,
son of Jorim, son of Matthat, son of Levi, 30 son
of Simeon, son of Judah, son of Joseph, son of
Jonam, son of Eliakim, 31 son of Melea, son of
Menna, son of Mattatha, son of Nathan, son
of David, 32 son of Jesse, son of Obed, son of
Boaz, son of Sala,[g] son of Nahshon, 33 son of Amminadab, son of Admin, son of Arni,[h] son of Hezron, son of Perez, son of Judah, 34 son of Jacob,
son of Isaac, son of Abraham, son of Terah, son of
Nahor, 35 son of Serug, son of Reu, son of Peleg,
son of Eber, son of Shelah, 36 son of Cainan, son
of Arphaxad, son of Shem, son of Noah, son of
Lamech, 37 son of Methuselah, son of Enoch, son
of Jared, son of Mahalaleel, son of Cainan, 38 son
of Enos, son of Seth, son of Adam, son of God.

4 Jesus, full of the Holy Spirit, returned from
the Jordan and was led by the Spirit in the
wilderness, 2 where for forty days he was tempted
by the devil. He ate nothing at all during those
days, and when they were over, he was famished.
3 The devil said to him, "If you are the Son of God,
command this stone to become a loaf of bread."
4 Jesus answered him, "It is written, 'One does not
live by bread alone.'"

5 Then the devil[i] led him up and showed him
in an instant all the kingdoms of the world. 6 And
the devil[i] said to him, "To you I will give their
glory and all this authority; for it has been given
over to me, and I give it to anyone I please. 7 If
you, then, will worship me, it will all be yours."
8 Jesus answered him, "It is written,

'Worship the Lord your God,
and serve only him.'"

9 Then the devil[i] took him to Jerusalem, and
placed him on the pinnacle of the temple, saying
to him, "If you are the Son of God, throw yourself
down from here, 10 for it is written,

'He will command his angels concerning you,
to protect you,'

11 and

'On their hands they will bear you up,
so that you will not dash your foot against
a stone.'"

12 Jesus answered him, "It is said, 'Do not put the
Lord your God to the test.'" 13 When the devil
had finished every test, he departed from him until an opportune time.

14 Then Jesus, filled with the power of the
Spirit, returned to Galilee, and a report about
him spread through all the surrounding country.

[a] Or *the Christ* [b] Or *in* [c] Gk *tetrarch* [d] Or *my beloved Son* [e] Other ancient authorities read *You are my Son, today I have begotten you* [f] Gk *Salathiel* [g] Other ancient authorities read *Salmon* [h] Other ancient authorities read *Amminadab, son of Aram*; others vary widely [i] Gk *he*

15He began to teach in their synagogues and was
praised by everyone.
16 When he came to Nazareth, where he had
been brought up, he went to the synagogue on
the sabbath day, as was his custom. He stood up
to read, 17and the scroll of the prophet Isaiah was
given to him. He unrolled the scroll and found
the place where it was written:

18 "The Spirit of the Lord is upon me,
because he has anointed me
to bring good news to the poor.
He has sent me to proclaim release to the captives
and recovery of sight to the blind,
to let the oppressed go free,
19 to proclaim the year of the Lord's favor."

Luke 4:18-19

Jesus' first preached words in Luke resonate with the poor for whom the good news is given; the broken, captives, the wounded, all who hope for the year of Jubilee—the redistribution of wealth to create economic justice. Howard Thurman observed that "the masses of [people] live with their backs constantly against the wall. They are the poor, the disinherited, the dispossessed. What does our religion say to them?... The search for an answer to this question is perhaps the most important religious quest of modern life."[70] But these words are also for all those who refuse to see and need their consciousness raised!

— *MDLT*

20And he rolled up the scroll, gave it back to the attendant, and sat down. The eyes of all in the synagogue were fixed on him. 21Then he began to say
to them, "Today this scripture has been fulfilled
in your hearing." 22All spoke well of him and were
amazed at the gracious words that came from his
mouth. They said, "Is not this Joseph's son?" 23He
said to them, "Doubtless you will quote to me this
proverb, 'Doctor, cure yourself!' And you will say,
'Do here also in your hometown the things that
we have heard you did at Capernaum.'" 24And he
said, "Truly I tell you, no prophet is accepted in the
prophet's hometown. 25But the truth is, there were
many widows in Israel in the time of Elijah, when
the heaven was shut up three years and six months,
and there was a severe famine over all the land;
26yet Elijah was sent to none of them except to a
widow at Zarephath in Sidon. 27There were also
many lepers[a] in Israel in the time of the prophet
Elisha, and none of them was cleansed except Naaman the Syrian." 28When they heard this, all in the
synagogue were filled with rage. 29They got up,
drove him out of the town, and led him to the brow
of the hill on which their town was built, so that
they might hurl him off the cliff. 30But he passed
through the midst of them and went on his way.
31 He went down to Capernaum, a city in
Galilee, and was teaching them on the sabbath.
32They were astounded at his teaching, because
he spoke with authority. 33In the synagogue there
was a man who had the spirit of an unclean demon, and he cried out with a loud voice, 34"Let
us alone! What have you to do with us, Jesus of
Nazareth? Have you come to destroy us? I know
who you are, the Holy One of God." 35But Jesus
rebuked him, saying, "Be silent, and come out of
him!" When the demon had thrown him down
before them, he came out of him without having done him any harm. 36They were all amazed
and kept saying to one another, "What kind of
utterance is this? For with authority and power
he commands the unclean spirits, and out they
come!" 37And a report about him began to reach
every place in the region.
38 After leaving the synagogue he entered
Simon's house. Now Simon's mother-in-law was
suffering from a high fever, and they asked him
about her. 39Then he stood over her and rebuked
the fever, and it left her. Immediately she got up
and began to serve them.
40 As the sun was setting, all those who had
any who were sick with various kinds of diseases
brought them to him; and he laid his hands on
each of them and cured them. 41Demons also
came out of many, shouting, "You are the Son of

[a] The terms *leper* and *leprosy* can refer to several diseases

God!" But he rebuked them and would not allow
them to speak, because they knew that he was the
Messiah.[a]

42 At daybreak he departed and went into a
deserted place. And the crowds were looking for
him; and when they reached him, they wanted to
prevent him from leaving them. 43 But he said to
them, "I must proclaim the good news of the kingdom of God to the other cities also; for I was sent
for this purpose." 44 So he continued proclaiming
the message in the synagogues of Judea.[b]

5 Once while Jesus[c] was standing beside the
lake of Gennesaret, and the crowd was pressing in on him to hear the word of God, 2 he saw
two boats there at the shore of the lake; the fishermen had gone out of them and were washing
their nets. 3 He got into one of the boats, the one
belonging to Simon, and asked him to put out a
little way from the shore. Then he sat down and
taught the crowds from the boat. 4 When he had
finished speaking, he said to Simon, "Put out
into the deep water and let down your nets for
a catch." 5 Simon answered, "Master, we have
worked all night long but have caught nothing.
Yet if you say so, I will let down the nets." 6 When
they had done this, they caught so many fish that
their nets were beginning to break. 7 So they signaled their partners in the other boat to come and
help them. And they came and filled both boats,
so that they began to sink. 8 But when Simon Peter saw it, he fell down at Jesus' knees, saying, "Go
away from me, Lord, for I am a sinful man!" 9 For
he and all who were with him were amazed at the
catch of fish that they had taken; 10 and so also
were James and John, sons of Zebedee, who were
partners with Simon. Then Jesus said to Simon,
"Do not be afraid; from now on you will be catch-
ing people." 11 When they had brought their boats
to shore, they left everything and followed him.

12 Once, when he was in one of the cities,
there was a man covered with leprosy.[d] When he
saw Jesus, he bowed with his face to the ground
and begged him, "Lord, if you choose, you can
make me clean." 13 Then Jesus[c] stretched out his
hand, touched him, and said, "I do choose. Be
made clean." Immediately the leprosy[d] left him.
14 And he ordered him to tell no one. "Go," he said,
"and show yourself to the priest, and, as Moses
commanded, make an offering for your cleansing,
for a testimony to them." 15 But now more than
ever the word about Jesus[e] spread abroad; many
crowds would gather to hear him and to be cured
of their diseases. 16 But he would withdraw to deserted places and pray.

17 One day, while he was teaching, Pharisees and teachers of the law were sitting near by
(they had come from every village of Galilee and
Judea and from Jerusalem); and the power of
the Lord was with him to heal.[f] 18 Just then some
men came, carrying a paralyzed man on a bed.
They were trying to bring him in and lay him before Jesus;[e] 19 but finding no way to bring him in
because of the crowd, they went up on the roof
and let him down with his bed through the tiles
into the middle of the crowd[g] in front of Jesus.
20 When he saw their faith, he said, "Friend,[h] your
sins are forgiven you." 21 Then the scribes and the
Pharisees began to question, "Who is this who
is speaking blasphemies? Who can forgive sins
but God alone?" 22 When Jesus perceived their
questionings, he answered them, "Why do you
raise such questions in your hearts? 23 Which is
easier, to say, 'Your sins are forgiven you,' or to
say, 'Stand up and walk'? 24 But so that you may
know that the Son of Man has authority on earth
to forgive sins"—he said to the one who was paralyzed—"I say to you, stand up and take your bed
and go to your home." 25 Immediately he stood
up before them, took what he had been lying on,
and went to his home, glorifying God. 26 Amazement seized all of them, and they glorified God
and were filled with awe, saying, "We have seen
strange things today."

27 After this he went out and saw a tax collector named Levi, sitting at the tax booth; and
he said to him, "Follow me." 28 And he got up, left
everything, and followed him.

29 Then Levi gave a great banquet for him in

[a] Or *the Christ* [b] Other ancient authorities read *Galilee* [c] Gk *he* [d] The terms *leper* and *leprosy* can refer to several diseases [e] Gk *him* [f] Other ancient authorities read *was present to heal them* [g] Gk *into the midst* [h] Gk *Man*

 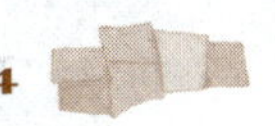

his house; and there was a large crowd of tax collectors and others sitting at the table[a] with them.
30The Pharisees and their scribes were complaining to his disciples, saying, "Why do you eat and
drink with tax collectors and sinners?" 31Jesus
answered, "Those who are well have no need of a
physician, but those who are sick; 32I have come to
call not the righteous but sinners to repentance."

33 Then they said to him, "John's disciples,
like the disciples of the Pharisees, frequently fast
and pray, but your disciples eat and drink." 34Jesus
said to them, "You cannot make wedding guests
fast while the bridegroom is with them, can you?
35The days will come when the bridegroom will
be taken away from them, and then they will fast
in those days." 36He also told them a parable: "No
one tears a piece from a new garment and sews
it on an old garment; otherwise the new will be
torn, and the piece from the new will not match
the old. 37And no one puts new wine into old
wineskins; otherwise the new wine will burst the
skins and will be spilled, and the skins will be destroyed. 38But new wine must be put into fresh
wineskins. 39And no one after drinking old wine
desires new wine, but says, 'The old is good.'"[b]

6 One sabbath[c] while Jesus[d] was going through
the grainfields, his disciples plucked some
heads of grain, rubbed them in their hands, and
ate them. 2But some of the Pharisees said, "Why
are you doing what is not lawful[e] on the sabbath?"
3Jesus answered, "Have you not read what David
did when he and his companions were hungry?
4He entered the house of God and took and ate
the bread of the Presence, which it is not lawful
for any but the priests to eat, and gave some to his
companions?" 5Then he said to them, "The Son
of Man is lord of the sabbath."

6 On another sabbath he entered the synagogue and taught, and there was a man there
whose right hand was withered. 7The scribes
and the Pharisees watched him to see whether
he would cure on the sabbath, so that they might
find an accusation against him. 8Even though he
knew what they were thinking, he said to the man
who had the withered hand, "Come and stand
here." He got up and stood there. 9Then Jesus said
to them, "I ask you, is it lawful to do good or to
do harm on the sabbath, to save life or to destroy
it?" 10After looking around at all of them, he said
to him, "Stretch out your hand." He did so, and
his hand was restored. 11But they were filled with
fury and discussed with one another what they
might do to Jesus.

12 Now during those days he went out to the
mountain to pray; and he spent the night in prayer
to God. 13And when day came, he called his disciples and chose twelve of them, whom he also
named apostles: 14Simon, whom he named Peter,
and his brother Andrew, and James, and John, and
Philip, and Bartholomew, 15and Matthew, and
Thomas, and James son of Alphaeus, and Simon,
who was called the Zealot, 16and Judas son of
James, and Judas Iscariot, who became a traitor.

17 He came down with them and stood on a
level place, with a great crowd of his disciples and
a great multitude of people from all Judea, Jerusalem, and the coast of Tyre and Sidon. 18They
had come to hear him and to be healed of their
diseases; and those who were troubled with unclean spirits were cured. 19And all in the crowd
were trying to touch him, for power came out
from him and healed all of them.

20 Then he looked up at his disciples and
said:

"Blessed are you who are poor,
for yours is the kingdom of God.
21 "Blessed are you who are hungry now,
for you will be filled.
"Blessed are you who weep now,
for you will laugh.

22 "Blessed are you when people hate you,
and when they exclude you, revile you, and de-
fame you[f] on account of the Son of Man. 23Re-
joice in that day and leap for joy, for surely your
reward is great in heaven; for that is what their
ancestors did to the prophets.

24 "But woe to you who are rich,
for you have received your consolation.

[a] Gk *reclining* [b] Other ancient authorities read *better*; others lack verse 39 [c] Other ancient authorities read *On the second first sabbath* [d] Gk *he* [e] Other ancient authorities add *to do* [f] Gk *cast out your name as evil*

25 "Woe to you who are full now,
for you will be hungry.
"Woe to you who are laughing now,
for you will mourn and weep.

26 "Woe to you when all speak well of you,
for that is what their ancestors did to the false
prophets.

27 "But I say to you that listen, Love your
enemies, do good to those who hate you, 28 bless
those who curse you, pray for those who abuse
you. 29 If anyone strikes you on the cheek, offer the
other also; and from anyone who takes away your
coat do not withhold even your shirt. 30 Give to
everyone who begs from you; and if anyone takes
away your goods, do not ask for them again. 31 Do
to others as you would have them do to you.

32 "If you love those who love you, what
credit is that to you? For even sinners love those
who love them. 33 If you do good to those who do
good to you, what credit is that to you? For even
sinners do the same. 34 If you lend to those from
whom you hope to receive, what credit is that to
you? Even sinners lend to sinners, to receive as
much again. 35 But love your enemies, do good,
and lend, expecting nothing in return.[a] Your reward will be great, and you will be children of the
Most High; for he is kind to the ungrateful and
the wicked. 36 Be merciful, just as your Father is
merciful.

37 "Do not judge, and you will not be judged;
do not condemn, and you will not be condemned.
Forgive, and you will be forgiven; 38 give, and it
will be given to you. A good measure, pressed
down, shaken together, running over, will be put
into your lap; for the measure you give will be the
measure you get back."

39 He also told them a parable: "Can a blind
person guide a blind person? Will not both fall
into a pit? 40 A disciple is not above the teacher,
but everyone who is fully qualified will be like
the teacher. 41 Why do you see the speck in your
neighbor's[b] eye, but do not notice the log in your
own eye? 42 Or how can you say to your neighbor,[c]
'Friend,[c] let me take out the speck in your eye,'
when you yourself do not see the log in your own
eye? You hypocrite, first take the log out of your
own eye, and then you will see clearly to take the
speck out of your neighbor's[b] eye.

43 "No good tree bears bad fruit, nor again
does a bad tree bear good fruit; 44 for each tree
is known by its own fruit. Figs are not gathered
from thorns, nor are grapes picked from a bramble bush. 45 The good person out of the good
treasure of the heart produces good, and the evil
person out of evil treasure produces evil; for it is
out of the abundance of the heart that the mouth
speaks.

46 "Why do you call me 'Lord, Lord,' and
do not do what I tell you? 47 I will show you what
someone is like who comes to me, hears my words,
and acts on them. 48 That one is like a man building a house, who dug deeply and laid the foundation on rock; when a flood arose, the river burst
against that house but could not shake it, because
it had been well built.[d] 49 But the one who hears
and does not act is like a man who built a house
on the ground without a foundation. When the
river burst against it, immediately it fell, and great
was the ruin of that house."

7 After Jesus[e] had finished all his sayings in
the hearing of the people, he entered Capernaum. 2 A centurion there had a slave whom he
valued highly, and who was ill and close to death.
3 When he heard about Jesus, he sent some Jewish
elders to him, asking him to come and heal his
slave. 4 When they came to Jesus, they appealed
to him earnestly, saying, "He is worthy of having
you do this for him, 5 for he loves our people, and
it is he who built our synagogue for us." 6 And
Jesus went with them, but when he was not far
from the house, the centurion sent friends to say
to him, "Lord, do not trouble yourself, for I am
not worthy to have you come under my roof;
7 therefore I did not presume to come to you.
But only speak the word, and let my servant be
healed. 8 For I also am a man set under authority,
with soldiers under me; and I say to one, 'Go,' and

[a] Other ancient authorities read *despairing of no one* [b] Gk *brother's* [c] Gk *brother* [d] Other ancient authorities read *founded upon the rock* [e] Gk *he*

 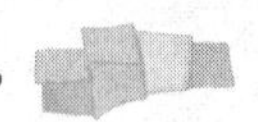

he goes, and to another, 'Come,' and he comes,
and to my slave, 'Do this,' and the slave does it."
9When Jesus heard this he was amazed at him,
and turning to the crowd that followed him, he
said, "I tell you, not even in Israel have I found
such faith." 10When those who had been sent returned to the house, they found the slave in good
health.

11 Soon afterwards[a] he went to a town
called Nain, and his disciples and a large crowd
went with him. 12As he approached the gate of
the town, a man who had died was being carried
out. He was his mother's only son, and she was a
widow; and with her was a large crowd from the
town. 13When the Lord saw her, he had compassion for her and said to her, "Do not weep." 14Then
he came forward and touched the bier, and the
bearers stood still. And he said, "Young man, I say
to you, rise!" 15The dead man sat up and began to
speak, and Jesus[b] gave him to his mother. 16Fear
seized all of them; and they glorified God, saying,
"A great prophet has risen among us!" and "God
has looked favorably on his people!" 17This word
about him spread throughout Judea and all the
surrounding country.

18 The disciples of John reported all these
things to him. So John summoned two of his disciples 19and sent them to the Lord to ask, "Are
you the one who is to come, or are we to wait for
another?" 20When the men had come to him,
they said, "John the Baptist has sent us to you to
ask, 'Are you the one who is to come, or are we to
wait for another?'" 21Jesus[c] had just then cured
many people of diseases, plagues, and evil spirits, and had given sight to many who were blind.
22And he answered them, "Go and tell John what
you have seen and heard: the blind receive their
sight, the lame walk, the lepers[d] are cleansed, the
deaf hear, the dead are raised, the poor have good
news brought to them. 23And blessed is anyone
who takes no offense at me."

24 When John's messengers had gone, Jesus[b]
began to speak to the crowds about John:[e] "What
did you go out into the wilderness to look at? A
reed shaken by the wind? 25What then did you
go out to see? Someone[f] dressed in soft robes?
Look, those who put on fine clothing and live in
luxury are in royal palaces. 26What then did you
go out to see? A prophet? Yes, I tell you, and more
than a prophet. 27This is the one about whom it
is written,

'See, I am sending my messenger ahead of
you,
who will prepare your way before you.'

28I tell you, among those born of women no one
is greater than John; yet the least in the kingdom
of God is greater than he." 29(And all the people
who heard this, including the tax collectors, acknowledged the justice of God,[g] because they
had been baptized with John's baptism. 30But
by refusing to be baptized by him, the Pharisees
and the lawyers rejected God's purpose for themselves.)

31 "To what then will I compare the people
of this generation, and what are they like? 32They
are like children sitting in the marketplace and
calling to one another,

'We played the flute for you, and you did not
dance;
we wailed, and you did not weep.'

33For John the Baptist has come eating no bread
and drinking no wine, and you say, 'He has a
demon'; 34the Son of Man has come eating and
drinking, and you say, 'Look, a glutton and a
drunkard, a friend of tax collectors and sinners!'
35Nevertheless, wisdom is vindicated by all her
children."

36 One of the Pharisees asked Jesus[e] to eat
with him, and he went into the Pharisee's house
and took his place at the table. 37And a woman
in the city, who was a sinner, having learned that
he was eating in the Pharisee's house, brought an
alabaster jar of ointment. 38She stood behind him
at his feet, weeping, and began to bathe his feet
with her tears and to dry them with her hair. Then
she continued kissing his feet and anointing them
with the ointment. 39Now when the Pharisee who
had invited him saw it, he said to himself, "If this

[a] Other ancient authorities read *Next day* [b] Gk *he* [c] Gk *He* [d] The terms *leper* and *leprosy* can refer to several diseases [e] Gk *him* [f] Or *Why then did you go out? To see someone* [g] Or *praised God*

man were a prophet, he would have known who
and what kind of woman this is who is touching
him—that she is a sinner." 40Jesus spoke up and
said to him, "Simon, I have something to say to
you." "Teacher," he replied, "speak." 41"A certain
creditor had two debtors; one owed five hundred
denarii,[a] and the other fifty. 42When they could
not pay, he canceled the debts for both of them.
Now which of them will love him more?" 43Si-
mon answered, "I suppose the one for whom he
canceled the greater debt." And Jesus[b] said to him,
"You have judged rightly." 44Then turning toward
the woman, he said to Simon, "Do you see this
woman? I entered your house; you gave me no
water for my feet, but she has bathed my feet with
her tears and dried them with her hair. 45You gave
me no kiss, but from the time I came in she has
not stopped kissing my feet. 46You did not anoint
my head with oil, but she has anointed my feet
with ointment. 47Therefore, I tell you, her sins,
which were many, have been forgiven; hence she
has shown great love. But the one to whom little is
forgiven, loves little." 48Then he said to her, "Your
sins are forgiven." 49But those who were at the
table with him began to say among themselves,
"Who is this who even forgives sins?" 50And he
said to the woman, "Your faith has saved you; go
in peace."

8 Soon afterwards he went on through cities
and villages, proclaiming and bringing the
good news of the kingdom of God. The twelve
were with him, 2as well as some women who had
been cured of evil spirits and infirmities: Mary,
called Magdalene, from whom seven demons had
gone out, 3and Joanna, the wife of Herod's steward Chuza, and Susanna, and many others, who
provided for them[c] out of their resources.

4 When a great crowd gathered and people
from town after town came to him, he said in a
parable: 5"A sower went out to sow his seed; and
as he sowed, some fell on the path and was trampled on, and the birds of the air ate it up. 6Some
fell on the rock; and as it grew up, it withered for
lack of moisture. 7Some fell among thorns, and
the thorns grew with it and choked it. 8Some fell
into good soil, and when it grew, it produced a
hundredfold." As he said this, he called out, "Let
anyone with ears to hear listen!"

9 Then his disciples asked him what this parable meant. 10He said, "To you it has been given
to know the secrets[d] of the kingdom of God; but
to others I speak[e] in parables, so that

'looking they may not perceive,
and listening they may not understand.'

11 "Now the parable is this: The seed is the
word of God. 12The ones on the path are those
who have heard; then the devil comes and takes
away the word from their hearts, so that they may
not believe and be saved. 13The ones on the rock
are those who, when they hear the word, receive
it with joy. But these have no root; they believe
only for a while and in a time of testing fall away.
14As for what fell among the thorns, these are the
ones who hear; but as they go on their way, they
are choked by the cares and riches and pleasures
of life, and their fruit does not mature. 15But as
for that in the good soil, these are the ones who,
when they hear the word, hold it fast in an honest and good heart, and bear fruit with patient
endurance.

16 "No one after lighting a lamp hides it under a jar, or puts it under a bed, but puts it on a
lampstand, so that those who enter may see the
light. 17For nothing is hidden that will not be disclosed, nor is anything secret that will not become
known and come to light. 18Then pay attention to
how you listen; for to those who have, more will
be given; and from those who do not have, even
what they seem to have will be taken away."

19 Then his mother and his brothers came
to him, but they could not reach him because of
the crowd. 20And he was told, "Your mother and
your brothers are standing outside, wanting to
see you." 21But he said to them, "My mother and
my brothers are those who hear the word of God
and do it."

22 One day he got into a boat with his dis-

[a] The denarius was the usual day's wage for a laborer [b] Gk *he* [c] Other ancient authorities read *him* [d] Or *mysteries*
[e] Gk lacks *I speak*

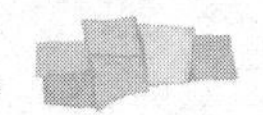

ciples, and he said to them, "Let us go across
to the other side of the lake." So they put out,
23 and while they were sailing he fell asleep. A
windstorm swept down on the lake, and the boat
was filling with water, and they were in danger.
24 They went to him and woke him up, shouting,
"Master, Master, we are perishing!" And he woke
up and rebuked the wind and the raging waves;
they ceased, and there was a calm. 25 He said to
them, "Where is your faith?" They were afraid
and amazed, and said to one another, "Who then
is this, that he commands even the winds and the
water, and they obey him?"

26 Then they arrived at the country of the
Gerasenes,[a] which is opposite Galilee. 27 As he
stepped out on land, a man of the city who had
demons met him. For a long time he had worn[b]
no clothes, and he did not live in a house but in
the tombs. 28 When he saw Jesus, he fell down
before him and shouted at the top of his voice,
"What have you to do with me, Jesus, Son of
the Most High God? I beg you, do not torment
me"— 29 for Jesus[c] had commanded the unclean
spirit to come out of the man. (For many times
it had seized him; he was kept under guard and
bound with chains and shackles, but he would
break the bonds and be driven by the demon into
the wilds.) 30 Jesus then asked him, "What is your
name?" He said, "Legion"; for many demons had
entered him. 31 They begged him not to order
them to go back into the abyss.

32 Now there on the hillside a large herd of
swine was feeding; and the demons[d] begged Jesus[e]
to let them enter these. So he gave them permission. 33 Then the demons came out of the man
and entered the swine, and the herd rushed down
the steep bank into the lake and was drowned.

34 When the swineherds saw what had happened, they ran off and told it in the city and in
the country. 35 Then people came out to see what
had happened, and when they came to Jesus,
they found the man from whom the demons had
gone sitting at the feet of Jesus, clothed and in his
right mind. And they were afraid. 36 Those who
had seen it told them how the one who had been
possessed by demons had been healed. 37 Then
all the people of the surrounding country of the
Gerasenes[a] asked Jesus[e] to leave them; for they
were seized with great fear. So he got into the
boat and returned. 38 The man from whom the
demons had gone begged that he might be with
him; but Jesus[c] sent him away, saying, 39 "Return
to your home, and declare how much God has
done for you." So he went away, proclaiming
throughout the city how much Jesus had done
for him.

40 Now when Jesus returned, the crowd welcomed him, for they were all waiting for him.
41 Just then there came a man named Jairus, a
leader of the synagogue. He fell at Jesus' feet and
begged him to come to his house, 42 for he had an
only daughter, about twelve years old, who was
dying.

As he went, the crowds pressed in on him.
43 Now there was a woman who had been suffering from hemorrhages for twelve years; and
though she had spent all she had on physicians,[f]
no one could cure her. 44 She came up behind him
and touched the fringe of his clothes, and immediately her hemorrhage stopped. 45 Then Jesus
asked, "Who touched me?" When all denied it,
Peter[g] said, "Master, the crowds surround you
and press in on you." 46 But Jesus said, "Someone
touched me; for I noticed that power had gone
out from me." 47 When the woman saw that she
could not remain hidden, she came trembling;
and falling down before him, she declared in the
presence of all the people why she had touched
him, and how she had been immediately healed.
48 He said to her, "Daughter, your faith has made
you well; go in peace."

49 While he was still speaking, someone
came from the leader's house to say, "Your daughter is dead; do not trouble the teacher any longer." 50 When Jesus heard this, he replied, "Do not
fear. Only believe, and she will be saved." 51 When

[a] Other ancient authorities read *Gadarenes*; others, *Gergesenes* [b] Other ancient authorities read *a man of the city who had had demons for a long time met him. He wore* [c] Gk *he* [d] Gk *they* [e] Gk *him* [f] Other ancient authorities lack *and though she had spent all she had on physicians* [g] Other ancient authorities add *and those who were with him*

he came to the house, he did not allow anyone
to enter with him, except Peter, John, and James,
and the child's father and mother. 52They were
all weeping and wailing for her; but he said, "Do
not weep; for she is not dead but sleeping." 53And
they laughed at him, knowing that she was dead.
54But he took her by the hand and called out,
"Child, get up!" 55Her spirit returned, and she
got up at once. Then he directed them to give her
something to eat. 56Her parents were astounded;
but he ordered them to tell no one what had happened.

9 Then Jesus[a] called the twelve together and
gave them power and authority over all demons and to cure diseases, 2and he sent them out
to proclaim the kingdom of God and to heal. 3He
said to them, "Take nothing for your journey, no
staff, nor bag, nor bread, nor money—not even
an extra tunic. 4Whatever house you enter, stay
there, and leave from there. 5Wherever they do
not welcome you, as you are leaving that town
shake the dust off your feet as a testimony against
them." 6They departed and went through the villages, bringing the good news and curing diseases
everywhere.
7 Now Herod the ruler[b] heard about all that
had taken place, and he was perplexed, because it
was said by some that John had been raised from
the dead, 8by some that Elijah had appeared, and
by others that one of the ancient prophets had
arisen. 9Herod said, "John I beheaded; but who
is this about whom I hear such things?" And he
tried to see him.
10 On their return the apostles told Jesus[c] all
they had done. He took them with him and withdrew privately to a city called Bethsaida. 11When
the crowds found out about it, they followed
him; and he welcomed them, and spoke to them
about the kingdom of God, and healed those who
needed to be cured.
12 The day was drawing to a close, and the
twelve came to him and said, "Send the crowd
away, so that they may go into the surrounding
villages and countryside, to lodge and get provisions; for we are here in a deserted place." 13But
he said to them, "You give them something to eat."
They said, "We have no more than five loaves and
two fish—unless we are to go and buy food for all
these people." 14For there were about five thousand men. And he said to his disciples, "Make
them sit down in groups of about fifty each."
15They did so and made them all sit down. 16And
taking the five loaves and the two fish, he looked
up to heaven, and blessed and broke them, and
gave them to the disciples to set before the crowd.
17And all ate and were filled. What was left over
was gathered up, twelve baskets of broken pieces.
18 Once when Jesus[a] was praying alone, with
only the disciples near him, he asked them, "Who
do the crowds say that I am?" 19They answered,
"John the Baptist; but others, Elijah; and still others, that one of the ancient prophets has arisen."
20He said to them, "But who do you say that I
am?" Peter answered, "The Messiah[d] of God."
21 He sternly ordered and commanded them
not to tell anyone, 22saying, "The Son of Man
must undergo great suffering, and be rejected by
the elders, chief priests, and scribes, and be killed,
and on the third day be raised."
23 Then he said to them all, "If any want to
become my followers, let them deny themselves
and take up their cross daily and follow me. 24For
those who want to save their life will lose it, and
those who lose their life for my sake will save it.
25What does it profit them if they gain the whole
world, but lose or forfeit themselves? 26Those
who are ashamed of me and of my words, of them
the Son of Man will be ashamed when he comes
in his glory and the glory of the Father and of the
holy angels. 27But truly I tell you, there are some
standing here who will not taste death before
they see the kingdom of God."
28 Now about eight days after these sayings
Jesus[a] took with him Peter and John and James,
and went up on the mountain to pray. 29And
while he was praying, the appearance of his face
changed, and his clothes became dazzling white.
30Suddenly they saw two men, Moses and Elijah,
talking to him. 31They appeared in glory and were

[a] Gk *he* [b] Gk *tetrarch* [c] Gk *him* [d] Or *The Christ*

speaking of his departure, which he was about to
accomplish at Jerusalem. 32Now Peter and his
companions were weighed down with sleep; but
since they had stayed awake,[a] they saw his glory
and the two men who stood with him. 33Just as
they were leaving him, Peter said to Jesus, "Master, it is good for us to be here; let us make three
dwellings,[b] one for you, one for Moses, and one
for Elijah"—not knowing what he said. 34While he
was saying this, a cloud came and overshadowed
them; and they were terrified as they entered the
cloud. 35Then from the cloud came a voice that
said, "This is my Son, my Chosen;[c] listen to him!"
36When the voice had spoken, Jesus was found
alone. And they kept silent and in those days told
no one any of the things they had seen.

37 On the next day, when they had come
down from the mountain, a great crowd met
him. 38Just then a man from the crowd shouted,
"Teacher, I beg you to look at my son; he is my
only child. 39Suddenly a spirit seizes him, and
all at once he[d] shrieks. It convulses him until he
foams at the mouth; it mauls him and will scarcely
leave him. 40I begged your disciples to cast it out,
but they could not." 41Jesus answered, "You faithless and perverse generation, how much longer
must I be with you and bear with you? Bring your
son here." 42While he was coming, the demon
dashed him to the ground in convulsions. But
Jesus rebuked the unclean spirit, healed the boy,
and gave him back to his father. 43And all were
astounded at the greatness of God.

While everyone was amazed at all that he was
doing, he said to his disciples, 44"Let these words
sink into your ears: The Son of Man is going to
be betrayed into human hands." 45But they did
not understand this saying; its meaning was concealed from them, so that they could not perceive
it. And they were afraid to ask him about this
saying.

46 An argument arose among them as to
which one of them was the greatest. 47But Jesus,
aware of their inner thoughts, took a little child
and put it by his side, 48and said to them, "Whoever welcomes this child in my name welcomes
me, and whoever welcomes me welcomes the one
who sent me; for the least among all of you is the
greatest."

49 John answered, "Master, we saw someone
casting out demons in your name, and we tried
to stop him, because he does not follow with us."
50But Jesus said to him, "Do not stop him; for
whoever is not against you is for you."

51 When the days drew near for him to be
taken up, he set his face to go to Jerusalem. 52And
he sent messengers ahead of him. On their way
they entered a village of the Samaritans to make
ready for him; 53but they did not receive him, because his face was set toward Jerusalem. 54When
his disciples James and John saw it, they said,
"Lord, do you want us to command fire to come
down from heaven and consume them?"[e] 55But
he turned and rebuked them. 56Then[f] they went
on to another village.

Luke 9:51

Only Luke tells us of Jesus resolutely "setting his face" toward Jerusalem. He means to insist that Jesus' eventual fate on the cross is no accident but a consequence Jesus accepted—and enjoined on those who would follow on his way. For Luke this is the beginning of something like a military campaign, except that those Jesus sends ahead of him bring peace (10:1-6). All that Jesus teaches about justice, about the right use of wealth, about prayer and steadfastness in his cause, he teaches as he leads his followers toward a final confrontation in Jerusalem.

— NE

57 As they were going along the road, someone said to him, "I will follow you wherever you
go." 58And Jesus said to him, "Foxes have holes,

[a] Or *but when they were fully awake* [b] Or *tents* [c] Other ancient authorities read *my Beloved* [d] Or *it* [e] Other ancient authorities add *as Elijah did* [f] Other ancient authorities read *rebuked them, and said, "You do not know what spirit you are of, [56]for the Son of Man has not come to destroy the lives of human beings but to save them." Then*

Luke 9:58

Throughout his ministry, Jesus lived in poverty, having "nowhere to lay his head." He traveled without money in his purse, relying on the resources of others (see 8:1-3). Because Jesus chose solidarity with the poor and marginalized, Christians might say that, in Luke's terms, the miracle of the gospel is not that God became *human* (as John describes the incarnation) but that the messiah came as one of the *poor*. Though poverty is often regarded as a thing of shame, attributed to some deficiency in individuals of color, it is rather the product of a society designed to privilege one group over another, usually along racial and ethnic lines. There is nothing romantic about not having enough food to feed your family; but the message of this gospel is that Jesus is on the side of the poor.

— MDLT

and birds of the air have nests; but the Son of
Man has nowhere to lay his head." 59 To another
he said, "Follow me." But he said, "Lord, first let
me go and bury my father." 60 But Jesus[a] said to
him, "Let the dead bury their own dead; but as
for you, go and proclaim the kingdom of God."
61 Another said, "I will follow you, Lord; but let
me first say farewell to those at my home." 62 Jesus
said to him, "No one who puts a hand to the plow
and looks back is fit for the kingdom of God."

10 After this the Lord appointed seventy[b]
others and sent them on ahead of him in
pairs to every town and place where he himself
intended to go. 2 He said to them, "The harvest
is plentiful, but the laborers are few; therefore
ask the Lord of the harvest to send out laborers
into his harvest. 3 Go on your way. See, I am sending you out like lambs into the midst of wolves.
4 Carry no purse, no bag, no sandals; and greet no
one on the road. 5 Whatever house you enter, first
say, 'Peace to this house!' 6 And if anyone is there
who shares in peace, your peace will rest on that
person; but if not, it will return to you. 7 Remain
in the same house, eating and drinking whatever
they provide, for the laborer deserves to be paid.
Do not move about from house to house. 8 Whenever you enter a town and its people welcome
you, eat what is set before you; 9 cure the sick who
are there, and say to them, 'The kingdom of God
has come near to you.'[c] 10 But whenever you enter a town and they do not welcome you, go out
into its streets and say, 11 'Even the dust of your
town that clings to our feet, we wipe off in protest
against you. Yet know this: the kingdom of God
has come near.'[d] 12 I tell you, on that day it will be
more tolerable for Sodom than for that town.

13 "Woe to you, Chorazin! Woe to you, Bethsaida! For if the deeds of power done in you had
been done in Tyre and Sidon, they would have
repented long ago, sitting in sackcloth and ashes.
14 But at the judgment it will be more tolerable for
Tyre and Sidon than for you. 15 And you, Capernaum,

will you be exalted to heaven?

No, you will be brought down to Hades.

16 "Whoever listens to you listens to me, and
whoever rejects you rejects me, and whoever rejects me rejects the one who sent me."

17 The seventy[b] returned with joy, saying,
"Lord, in your name even the demons submit to
us!" 18 He said to them, "I watched Satan fall from
heaven like a flash of lightning. 19 See, I have given
you authority to tread on snakes and scorpions,
and over all the power of the enemy; and nothing will hurt you. 20 Nevertheless, do not rejoice
at this, that the spirits submit to you, but rejoice
that your names are written in heaven."

21 At that same hour Jesus[a] rejoiced in the
Holy Spirit[e] and said, "I thank[f] you, Father, Lord
of heaven and earth, because you have hidden
these things from the wise and the intelligent
and have revealed them to infants; yes, Father,

[a] Gk *he* [b] Other ancient authorities read *seventy-two* [c] Or *is at hand for you* [d] Or *is at hand* [e] Other authorities read *in the spirit* [f] Or *praise*

for such was your gracious will.[a] 22All things have
been handed over to me by my Father; and no
one knows who the Son is except the Father, or
who the Father is except the Son and anyone to
whom the Son chooses to reveal him."

23 Then turning to the disciples, Jesus[b] said
to them privately, "Blessed are the eyes that see
what you see! 24For I tell you that many prophets and kings desired to see what you see, but did
not see it, and to hear what you hear, but did not
hear it."

25 Just then a lawyer stood up to test Jesus.[c]
"Teacher," he said, "what must I do to inherit
eternal life?" 26He said to him, "What is written
in the law? What do you read there?" 27He answered, "You shall love the Lord your God with
all your heart, and with all your soul, and with all
your strength, and with all your mind; and your
neighbor as yourself." 28And he said to him, "You
have given the right answer; do this, and you will
live."

29 But wanting to justify himself, he asked
Jesus, "And who is my neighbor?" 30Jesus replied, "A man was going down from Jerusalem to
Jericho, and fell into the hands of robbers, who
stripped him, beat him, and went away, leaving
him half dead. 31Now by chance a priest was going
down that road; and when he saw him, he passed
by on the other side. 32So likewise a Levite, when
he came to the place and saw him, passed by on
the other side. 33But a Samaritan while traveling
came near him; and when he saw him, he was
moved with pity. 34He went to him and bandaged
his wounds, having poured oil and wine on them.
Then he put him on his own animal, brought him
to an inn, and took care of him. 35The next day he
took out two denarii,[d] gave them to the innkeeper,
and said, 'Take care of him; and when I come
back, I will repay you whatever more you spend.'
36Which of these three, do you think, was a neighbor to the man who fell into the hands of the
robbers?" 37He said, "The one who showed him

Luke 10:30-35

We ordinarily call this parable "The Good Samaritan," yet nowhere in the text is the Samaritan called good. The story plays on the bigoted expectation of its first readers that all other Samaritans are bad. If we tried to recapture the force of Jesus' story in terms of our own day, we might say that a white man was beaten up and left by the side of the road; that one by one, several clergy—all of them privileged white men—walked by and ignored their injured compatriot; and that then an "illegal" alien came along and took care of the injured person. So, contrary to racist expectations that all "illegal" immigrants, specifically those from south of the border, are dirty, lazy, and morally suspect, our story would focus attention on a "Good Illegal."

— MDLT

mercy." Jesus said to him, "Go and do likewise."

38 Now as they went on their way, he entered
a certain village, where a woman named Martha
welcomed him into her home. 39She had a sister
named Mary, who sat at the Lord's feet and listened to what he was saying. 40But Martha was
distracted by her many tasks; so she came to him
and asked, "Lord, do you not care that my sister
has left me to do all the work by myself? Tell her
then to help me." 41But the Lord answered her,
"Martha, Martha, you are worried and distracted
by many things; 42there is need of only one thing.[e]
Mary has chosen the better part, which will not
be taken away from her."

11 He was praying in a certain place, and
after he had finished, one of his disciples
said to him, "Lord, teach us to pray, as John taught
his disciples." 2He said to them, "When you pray,
say:

Father,[f] hallowed be your name.
Your kingdom come.[g]

[a] Or *for so it was well-pleasing in your sight* [b] Gk *he* [c] Gk *him* [d] The denarius was the usual day's wage for a laborer
[e] Other ancient authorities read *few things are necessary, or only one* [f] Other ancient authorities read *Our Father in heaven*
[g] A few ancient authorities read *Your Holy Spirit come upon us and cleanse us.* Other ancient authorities add *Your will be done, on earth as in heaven*

> **Luke 11:2**
>
> Jesus teaches his disciples to pray to God that "Your kingdom come." These words are revolutionary, for to Rome, the superpower of its day, there is only one kingdom, the empire ruled by Caesar. Is it any wonder that Jesus is eventually tried for treason and executed? He puts his disciples on a collision course with the empire by proclaiming a *new* empire to come. Later came empires that clothed themselves as Christian: the Holy Roman Empire, the British Empire, perhaps the present American Empire. How, then, do those who have suffered—or continue to suffer—under such Christian empires say the Lord's Prayer?
>
> — *MDLT*

3 Give us each day our daily bread.[a]
4 And forgive us our sins,
for we ourselves forgive everyone
indebted to us.
And do not bring us to the time of trial."[b]

5 And he said to them, "Suppose one of you
has a friend, and you go to him at midnight and
say to him, 'Friend, lend me three loaves of bread;
6for a friend of mine has arrived, and I have nothing to set before him.' 7And he answers from
within, 'Do not bother me; the door has already
been locked, and my children are with me in bed;
I cannot get up and give you anything.' 8I tell you,
even though he will not get up and give him anything because he is his friend, at least because of
his persistence he will get up and give him whatever he needs.

9 "So I say to you, Ask, and it will be given
you; search, and you will find; knock, and the
door will be opened for you. 10For everyone who
asks receives, and everyone who searches finds,
and for everyone who knocks, the door will be
opened. 11Is there anyone among you who, if
your child asks for[c] a fish, will give a snake instead
of a fish? 12Or if the child asks for an egg, will give
a scorpion? 13If you then, who are evil, know how
to give good gifts to your children, how much
more will the heavenly Father give the Holy Spirit[d] to those who ask him!"

14 Now he was casting out a demon that was
mute; when the demon had gone out, the one
who had been mute spoke, and the crowds were
amazed. 15But some of them said, "He casts out
demons by Beelzebul, the ruler of the demons."
16Others, to test him, kept demanding from him a
sign from heaven. 17But he knew what they were
thinking and said to them, "Every kingdom divided against itself becomes a desert, and house
falls on house. 18If Satan also is divided against
himself, how will his kingdom stand? —for you
say that I cast out the demons by Beelzebul.
19Now if I cast out the demons by Beelzebul, by
whom do your exorcists[e] cast them out? Therefore they will be your judges. 20But if it is by the
finger of God that I cast out the demons, then
the kingdom of God has come to you. 21When
a strong man, fully armed, guards his castle, his
property is safe. 22But when one stronger than he
attacks him and overpowers him, he takes away
his armor in which he trusted and divides his
plunder. 23Whoever is not with me is against me,
and whoever does not gather with me scatters.

24 "When the unclean spirit has gone out of
a person, it wanders through waterless regions
looking for a resting place, but not finding any,
it says, 'I will return to my house from which I
came.' 25When it comes, it finds it swept and put
in order. 26Then it goes and brings seven other
spirits more evil than itself, and they enter and
live there; and the last state of that person is
worse than the first."

27 While he was saying this, a woman in the
crowd raised her voice and said to him, "Blessed
is the womb that bore you and the breasts that
nursed you!" 28But he said, "Blessed rather are
those who hear the word of God and obey it!"

29 When the crowds were increasing, he be-

[a] Or *our bread for tomorrow* [b] Or *us into temptation*. Other ancient authorities add *but rescue us from the evil one* (or *from evil*) [c] Other ancient authorities add *bread, will give a stone; or if your child asks for* [d] Other ancient authorities read *the Father give the Holy Spirit from heaven* [e] Gk *sons*

gan to say, "This generation is an evil generation;
it asks for a sign, but no sign will be given to it except the sign of Jonah. 30For just as Jonah became
a sign to the people of Nineveh, so the Son of
Man will be to this generation. 31The queen of the
South will rise at the judgment with the people of
this generation and condemn them, because she
came from the ends of the earth to listen to the
wisdom of Solomon, and see, something greater
than Solomon is here! 32The people of Nineveh will rise up at the judgment with this generation and condemn it, because they repented
at the proclamation of Jonah, and see, something
greater than Jonah is here!

33 "No one after lighting a lamp puts it in a
cellar,[a] but on the lampstand so that those who
enter may see the light. 34Your eye is the lamp of
your body. If your eye is healthy, your whole body
is full of light; but if it is not healthy, your body
is full of darkness. 35Therefore consider whether
the light in you is not darkness. 36If then your
whole body is full of light, with no part of it in
darkness, it will be as full of light as when a lamp
gives you light with its rays."

37 While he was speaking, a Pharisee invited him to dine with him; so he went in and
took his place at the table. 38The Pharisee was
amazed to see that he did not first wash before
dinner. 39Then the Lord said to him, "Now you
Pharisees clean the outside of the cup and of the
dish, but inside you are full of greed and wickedness. 40You fools! Did not the one who made the
outside make the inside also? 41So give for alms
those things that are within; and see, everything
will be clean for you.

42 "But woe to you Pharisees! For you tithe
mint and rue and herbs of all kinds, and neglect
justice and the love of God; it is these you ought
to have practiced, without neglecting the others.
43Woe to you Pharisees! For you love to have the
seat of honor in the synagogues and to be greeted
with respect in the marketplaces. 44Woe to you!
For you are like unmarked graves, and people
walk over them without realizing it."

45 One of the lawyers answered him, "Teacher,
when you say these things, you insult us too."
46And he said, "Woe also to you lawyers! For you
load people with burdens hard to bear, and you
yourselves do not lift a finger to ease them. 47Woe
to you! For you build the tombs of the prophets
whom your ancestors killed. 48So you are witnesses and approve of the deeds of your ancestors; for they killed them, and you build their
tombs. 49Therefore also the Wisdom of God said,
'I will send them prophets and apostles, some of
whom they will kill and persecute,' 50so that this
generation may be charged with the blood of all
the prophets shed since the foundation of the
world, 51from the blood of Abel to the blood of
Zechariah, who perished between the altar and
the sanctuary. Yes, I tell you, it will be charged
against this generation. 52Woe to you lawyers!
For you have taken away the key of knowledge;
you did not enter yourselves, and you hindered
those who were entering."

53 When he went outside, the scribes and the
Pharisees began to be very hostile toward him
and to cross-examine him about many things,
54lying in wait for him, to catch him in something
he might say.

12 Meanwhile, when the crowd gathered by
the thousands, so that they trampled on
one another, he began to speak first to his disciples, "Beware of the yeast of the Pharisees, that is,
their hypocrisy. 2Nothing is covered up that will
not be uncovered, and nothing secret that will
not become known. 3Therefore whatever you
have said in the dark will be heard in the light,
and what you have whispered behind closed
doors will be proclaimed from the housetops.

4 "I tell you, my friends, do not fear those
who kill the body, and after that can do nothing
more. 5But I will warn you whom to fear: fear him
who, after he has killed, has authority[b] to cast into
hell.[c] Yes, I tell you, fear him! 6Are not five sparrows sold for two pennies? Yet not one of them
is forgotten in God's sight. 7But even the hairs of
your head are all counted. Do not be afraid; you
are of more value than many sparrows.

8 "And I tell you, everyone who acknowledges

[a] Other ancient authorities add *or under the bushel basket* [b] Or *power* [c] Gk *Gehenna*

me before others, the Son of Man also will acknowledge before the angels of God; 9 but whoever denies me before others will be denied
before the angels of God. 10 And everyone who
speaks a word against the Son of Man will be forgiven; but whoever blasphemes against the Holy
Spirit will not be forgiven. 11 When they bring
you before the synagogues, the rulers, and the authorities, do not worry about how[a] you are to defend yourselves or what you are to say; 12 for the
Holy Spirit will teach you at that very hour what
you ought to say."
13 Someone in the crowd said to him,
"Teacher, tell my brother to divide the family inheritance with me." 14 But he said to him, "Friend,
who set me to be a judge or arbitrator over you?"
15 And he said to them, "Take care! Be on your
guard against all kinds of greed; for one's life does
not consist in the abundance of possessions."
16 Then he told them a parable: "The land of a rich
man produced abundantly. 17 And he thought to
himself, 'What should I do, for I have no place to
store my crops?' 18 Then he said, 'I will do this:
I will pull down my barns and build larger ones,
and there I will store all my grain and my goods.
19 And I will say to my soul, Soul, you have ample
goods laid up for many years; relax, eat, drink, be
merry.' 20 But God said to him, 'You fool! This very
night your life is being demanded of you. And the
things you have prepared, whose will they be?'
21 So it is with those who store up treasures for
themselves but are not rich toward God."
22 He said to his disciples, "Therefore I tell
you, do not worry about your life, what you will
eat, or about your body, what you will wear. 23 For
life is more than food, and the body more than
clothing. 24 Consider the ravens: they neither sow
nor reap, they have neither storehouse nor barn,
and yet God feeds them. Of how much more
value are you than the birds! 25 And can any of
you by worrying add a single hour to your span
of life?[b] 26 If then you are not able to do so small
a thing as that, why do you worry about the rest?
27 Consider the lilies, how they grow: they neither
toil nor spin;[c] yet I tell you, even Solomon in all
his glory was not clothed like one of these. 28 But
if God so clothes the grass of the field, which is
alive today and tomorrow is thrown into the
oven, how much more will he clothe you—you
of little faith! 29 And do not keep striving for what
you are to eat and what you are to drink, and do
not keep worrying. 30 For it is the nations of the
world that strive after all these things, and your
Father knows that you need them. 31 Instead,
strive for his[d] kingdom, and these things will be
given to you as well.
32 "Do not be afraid, little flock, for it is your
Father's good pleasure to give you the kingdom.
33 Sell your possessions, and give alms. Make
purses for yourselves that do not wear out, an unfailing treasure in heaven, where no thief comes
near and no moth destroys. 34 For where your
treasure is, there your heart will be also.
35 "Be dressed for action and have your
lamps lit; 36 be like those who are waiting for their
master to return from the wedding banquet, so
that they may open the door for him as soon as
he comes and knocks. 37 Blessed are those slaves
whom the master finds alert when he comes;

Luke 12:16-21

In a capitalist culture, we might normally expect a successful entrepreneur who has a surplus of goods to do what any good businessperson would do—reinvest in capital improvements. The man in Jesus' parable built more warehouses to store his products. Many churches today probably want such a pillar of the community to serve as a deacon or elder, or better yet, as chair of the finance committee or the capital campaign. Yet Jesus denounces this person as a fool, a term he prohibits us from using (Matt 5:22). What our culture holds out as the good life may be a mirage; how we organize our economy may be nothing but foolishness in the eyes of God.

— MDLT

[a] Other ancient authorities add *or what* [b] Or *add a cubit to your stature* [c] Other ancient authorities read *Consider the lilies; they neither spin nor weave* [d] Other ancient authorities read *God's*

truly I tell you, he will fasten his belt and have
them sit down to eat, and he will come and serve
them. 38If he comes during the middle of the
night, or near dawn, and finds them so, blessed
are those slaves.
39 "But know this: if the owner of the house
had known at what hour the thief was coming,
he[a] would not have let his house be broken into.
40You also must be ready, for the Son of Man is
coming at an unexpected hour."
41 Peter said, "Lord, are you telling this parable for us or for everyone?" 42And the Lord said,
"Who then is the faithful and prudent manager
whom his master will put in charge of his slaves,
to give them their allowance of food at the proper
time? 43Blessed is that slave whom his master
will find at work when he arrives. 44Truly I tell
you, he will put that one in charge of all his possessions. 45But if that slave says to himself, 'My
master is delayed in coming,' and if he begins to
beat the other slaves, men and women, and to
eat and drink and get drunk, 46the master of that
slave will come on a day when he does not expect
him and at an hour that he does not know, and
will cut him in pieces,[b] and put him with the unfaithful. 47That slave who knew what his master
wanted, but did not prepare himself or do what
was wanted, will receive a severe beating. 48But
the one who did not know and did what deserved
a beating will receive a light beating. From everyone to whom much has been given, much will be
required; and from the one to whom much has
been entrusted, even more will be demanded.
49 "I came to bring fire to the earth, and how
I wish it were already kindled! 50I have a baptism
with which to be baptized, and what stress I am
under until it is completed! 51Do you think that I
have come to bring peace to the earth? No, I tell
you, but rather division! 52From now on five in
one household will be divided, three against two
and two against three; 53they will be divided:

father against son
  and son against father,
mother against daughter
  and daughter against mother,
mother-in-law against her daughter-in-law
  and daughter-in-law against
    mother-in-law."

54 He also said to the crowds, "When you
see a cloud rising in the west, you immediately
say, 'It is going to rain'; and so it happens. 55And
when you see the south wind blowing, you say,
'There will be scorching heat'; and it happens.
56You hypocrites! You know how to interpret the
appearance of earth and sky, but why do you not
know how to interpret the present time?
57 "And why do you not judge for yourselves
what is right? 58Thus, when you go with your accuser before a magistrate, on the way make an
effort to settle the case,[c] or you may be dragged
before the judge, and the judge hand you over to
the officer, and the officer throw you in prison. 59I
tell you, you will never get out until you have paid
the very last penny."

13 At that very time there were some present
who told him about the Galileans whose
blood Pilate had mingled with their sacrifices.
2He asked them, "Do you think that because these
Galileans suffered in this way they were worse
sinners than all other Galileans? 3No, I tell you;
but unless you repent, you will all perish as they
did. 4Or those eighteen who were killed when the
tower of Siloam fell on them—do you think that
they were worse offenders than all the others living in Jerusalem? 5No, I tell you; but unless you
repent, you will all perish just as they did."
6 Then he told this parable: "A man had a fig
tree planted in his vineyard; and he came looking
for fruit on it and found none. 7So he said to the
gardener, 'See here! For three years I have come
looking for fruit on this fig tree, and still I find
none. Cut it down! Why should it be wasting the
soil?' 8He replied, 'Sir, let it alone for one more
year, until I dig around it and put manure on it. 9If
it bears fruit next year, well and good; but if not,
you can cut it down.' "
10 Now he was teaching in one of the synagogues on the sabbath. 11And just then there appeared a woman with a spirit that had crippled
her for eighteen years. She was bent over and was

[a] Other ancient authorities add *would have watched and* [b] Or *cut him off* [c] Gk *settle with him*

quite unable to stand up straight. [12]When Jesus saw her, he called her over and said, "Woman, you are set free from your ailment." [13]When he laid his hands on her, immediately she stood up straight and began praising God. [14]But the leader of the synagogue, indignant because Jesus had cured on the sabbath, kept saying to the crowd, "There are six days on which work ought to be done; come on those days and be cured, and not on the sabbath day." [15]But the Lord answered him and said, "You hypocrites! Does not each of you on the sabbath untie his ox or his donkey from the manger, and lead it away to give it water? [16]And ought not this woman, a daughter of Abraham whom Satan bound for eighteen long years, be set free from this bondage on the sabbath day?" [17]When he said this, all his opponents were put to shame; and the entire crowd was rejoicing at all the wonderful things that he was doing.

18 He said therefore, "What is the kingdom of God like? And to what should I compare it? [19]It is like a mustard seed that someone took and sowed in the garden; it grew and became a tree, and the birds of the air made nests in its branches."

20 And again he said, "To what should I compare the kingdom of God? [21]It is like yeast that a woman took and mixed in with[a] three measures of flour until all of it was leavened."

22 Jesus[b] went through one town and village after another, teaching as he made his way to Jerusalem. [23]Someone asked him, "Lord, will only a few be saved?" He said to them, [24]"Strive to enter through the narrow door; for many, I tell you, will try to enter and will not be able. [25]When once the owner of the house has got up and shut the door, and you begin to stand outside and to knock at the door, saying, 'Lord, open to us,' then in reply he will say to you, 'I do not know where you come from.' [26]Then you will begin to say, 'We ate and drank with you, and you taught in our streets.' [27]But he will say, 'I do not know where you come from; go away from me, all you evildoers!' [28]There will be weeping and gnashing of teeth when you see Abraham and Isaac and Jacob and all the prophets in the kingdom of God, and you yourselves thrown out. [29]Then people will come from east and west, from north and south, and will eat in the kingdom of God. [30]Indeed, some are last who will be first, and some are first who will be last."

31 At that very hour some Pharisees came and said to him, "Get away from here, for Herod wants to kill you." [32]He said to them, "Go and tell that fox for me,[c] 'Listen, I am casting out demons and performing cures today and tomorrow, and on the third day I finish my work. [33]Yet today, tomorrow, and the next day I must be on my way, because it is impossible for a prophet to be killed outside of Jerusalem.' [34]Jerusalem, Jerusalem, the city that kills the prophets and stones those who are sent to it! How often have I desired to gather your children together as a hen gathers her brood under her wings, and you were not willing! [35]See, your house is left to you. And I tell you, you will not see me until the time comes when[d] you say, 'Blessed is the one who comes in the name of the Lord.' "

14 On one occasion when Jesus[e] was going to the house of a leader of the Pharisees to eat a meal on the sabbath, they were watching him closely. [2]Just then, in front of him, there was a man who had dropsy. [3]And Jesus asked the lawyers and Pharisees, "Is it lawful to cure people on the sabbath, or not?" [4]But they were silent. So Jesus[e] took him and healed him, and sent him away. [5]Then he said to them, "If one of you has a child[f] or an ox that has fallen into a well, will you not immediately pull it out on a sabbath day?" [6]And they could not reply to this.

7 When he noticed how the guests chose the places of honor, he told them a parable. [8]"When you are invited by someone to a wedding banquet, do not sit down at the place of honor, in case someone more distinguished than you has been invited by your host; [9]and the host who invited both of you may come and say to you, 'Give this person your place,' and then in disgrace you would start to take the lowest place. [10]But when

[a] Gk *hid in* [b] Gk *He* [c] Gk lacks *for me* [d] Other ancient authorities lack *the time comes when* [e] Gk *he*
[f] Other ancient authorities read *a donkey*

you are invited, go and sit down at the lowest
place, so that when your host comes, he may say
to you, 'Friend, move up higher'; then you will be
honored in the presence of all who sit at the table
with you. 11 For all who exalt themselves will be
humbled, and those who humble themselves will
be exalted."

12 He said also to the one who had invited
him, "When you give a luncheon or a dinner, do
not invite your friends or your brothers or your
relatives or rich neighbors, in case they may invite you in return, and you would be repaid.
13 But when you give a banquet, invite the poor,
the crippled, the lame, and the blind. 14 And you
will be blessed, because they cannot repay you,
for you will be repaid at the resurrection of the
righteous."

15 One of the dinner guests, on hearing
this, said to him, "Blessed is anyone who will
eat bread in the kingdom of God!" 16 Then Jesus[a]
said to him, "Someone gave a great dinner and invited many. 17 At the time for the dinner he sent
his slave to say to those who had been invited,
'Come; for everything is ready now.' 18 But they
all alike began to make excuses. The first said to
him, 'I have bought a piece of land, and I must
go out and see it; please accept my regrets.' 19 Another said, 'I have bought five yoke of oxen, and
I am going to try them out; please accept my regrets.' 20 Another said, 'I have just been married,
and therefore I cannot come.' 21 So the slave returned and reported this to his master. Then the
owner of the house became angry and said to his
slave, 'Go out at once into the streets and lanes
of the town and bring in the poor, the crippled,
the blind, and the lame.' 22 And the slave said, 'Sir,
what you ordered has been done, and there is still
room.' 23 Then the master said to the slave, 'Go
out into the roads and lanes, and compel people
to come in, so that my house may be filled. 24 For
I tell you,[b] none of those who were invited will
taste my dinner.'"

25 Now large crowds were traveling with
him; and he turned and said to them, 26 "Whoever comes to me and does not hate father and
mother, wife and children, brothers and sisters,
yes, and even life itself, cannot be my disciple.
27 Whoever does not carry the cross and follow me cannot be my disciple. 28 For which of
you, intending to build a tower, does not first sit
down and estimate the cost, to see whether he
has enough to complete it? 29 Otherwise, when
he has laid a foundation and is not able to finish,
all who see it will begin to ridicule him, 30 saying,
'This fellow began to build and was not able to
finish.' 31 Or what king, going out to wage war
against another king, will not sit down first and
consider whether he is able with ten thousand
to oppose the one who comes against him with
twenty thousand? 32 If he cannot, then, while the
other is still far away, he sends a delegation and
asks for the terms of peace. 33 So therefore, none
of you can become my disciple if you do not give
up all your possessions.

34 "Salt is good; but if salt has lost its taste,
how can its saltiness be restored?[c] 35 It is fit neither
for the soil nor for the manure pile; they throw it
away. Let anyone with ears to hear listen!"

15 Now all the tax collectors and sinners
were coming near to listen to him. 2 And
the Pharisees and the scribes were grumbling and
saying, "This fellow welcomes sinners and eats
with them."

3 So he told them this parable: 4 "Which one
of you, having a hundred sheep and losing one
of them, does not leave the ninety-nine in the
wilderness and go after the one that is lost until
he finds it? 5 When he has found it, he lays it on
his shoulders and rejoices. 6 And when he comes
home, he calls together his friends and neighbors,
saying to them, 'Rejoice with me, for I have found
my sheep that was lost.' 7 Just so, I tell you, there
will be more joy in heaven over one sinner who
repents than over ninety-nine righteous persons
who need no repentance.

8 "Or what woman having ten silver coins,[d]
if she loses one of them, does not light a lamp,
sweep the house, and search carefully until she

[a] Gk *he* [b] The Greek word for *you* here is plural [c] Or *how can it be used for seasoning?*
[d] Gk *drachmas,* each worth about a day's wage for a laborer

finds it? 9When she has found it, she calls together her friends and neighbors, saying, 'Rejoice
with me, for I have found the coin that I had lost.'
10Just so, I tell you, there is joy in the presence of
the angels of God over one sinner who repents."
11 Then Jesus[a] said, "There was a man who
had two sons. 12The younger of them said to his
father, 'Father, give me the share of the property
that will belong to me.' So he divided his property
between them. 13A few days later the younger
son gathered all he had and traveled to a distant
country, and there he squandered his property
in dissolute living. 14When he had spent everything, a severe famine took place throughout
that country, and he began to be in need. 15So he
went and hired himself out to one of the citizens
of that country, who sent him to his fields to feed
the pigs. 16He would gladly have filled himself
with[b] the pods that the pigs were eating; and no
one gave him anything. 17But when he came to
himself he said, 'How many of my father's hired
hands have bread enough and to spare, but here I
am dying of hunger! 18I will get up and go to my
father, and I will say to him, "Father, I have sinned
against heaven and before you; 19I am no longer
worthy to be called your son; treat me like one of
your hired hands." ' 20So he set off and went to his
father. But while he was still far off, his father saw
him and was filled with compassion; he ran and
put his arms around him and kissed him. 21Then
the son said to him, 'Father, I have sinned against
heaven and before you; I am no longer worthy
to be called your son.'[c] 22But the father said to
his slaves, 'Quickly, bring out a robe—the best
one—and put it on him; put a ring on his finger
and sandals on his feet. 23And get the fatted calf
and kill it, and let us eat and celebrate; 24for this
son of mine was dead and is alive again; he was
lost and is found!' And they began to celebrate.
25 "Now his elder son was in the field; and
when he came and approached the house, he
heard music and dancing. 26He called one of the
slaves and asked what was going on. 27He replied,
'Your brother has come, and your father has
killed the fatted calf, because he has got him back
safe and sound.' 28Then he became angry and
refused to go in. His father came out and began
to plead with him. 29But he answered his father,
'Listen! For all these years I have been working
like a slave for you, and I have never disobeyed
your command; yet you have never given me
even a young goat so that I might celebrate with
my friends. 30But when this son of yours came
back, who has devoured your property with prostitutes, you killed the fatted calf for him!' 31Then
the father[a] said to him, 'Son, you are always with
me, and all that is mine is yours. 32But we had
to celebrate and rejoice, because this brother of
yours was dead and has come to life; he was lost
and has been found.' "

Luke 15:11-32

The parable of the "lost son" is one of the most poignant narratives of reconciliation in world literature. It stands in dramatic contrast with Matthew's parable about two sons, where Jesus' point is simply that one son obeyed, while the other did not (Matt 21:28-31). While North Americans tend to focus on the moral choices the younger son makes and to judge them, people in other cultures immediately recognize the critical needs caused by "a severe famine" (v. 14), and the necessity of working together to ensure mutual survival.

— *NE*

16 Then Jesus[a] said to the disciples, "There
was a rich man who had a manager, and
charges were brought to him that this man was
squandering his property. 2So he summoned him
and said to him, 'What is this that I hear about
you? Give me an accounting of your management,
because you cannot be my manager any longer.'
3Then the manager said to himself, 'What will
I do, now that my master is taking the position
away from me? I am not strong enough to dig,

[a] Gk *he* [b] Other ancient authorities read *filled his stomach with*
[c] Other ancient authorities add *Treat me like one of your hired servants*

and I am ashamed to beg. [4]I have decided what to do so that, when I am dismissed as manager, people may welcome me into their homes.' [5]So, summoning his master's debtors one by one, he asked the first, 'How much do you owe my master?' [6]He answered, 'A hundred jugs of olive oil.' He said to him, 'Take your bill, sit down quickly, and make it fifty.' [7]Then he asked another, 'And how much do you owe?' He replied, 'A hundred containers of wheat.' He said to him, 'Take your bill and make it eighty.' [8]And his master commended the dishonest manager because he had acted shrewdly; for the children of this age are more shrewd in dealing with their own generation than are the children of light. [9]And I tell you, make friends for yourselves by means of dishonest wealth[a] so that when it is gone, they may welcome you into the eternal homes.[b]

10 "Whoever is faithful in a very little is faithful also in much; and whoever is dishonest in a very little is dishonest also in much. [11]If then you have not been faithful with the dishonest wealth,[a] who will entrust to you the true riches? [12]And if you have not been faithful with what belongs to another, who will give you what is your own? [13]No slave can serve two masters; for a slave will either hate the one and love the other, or be devoted to the one and despise the other. You cannot serve God and wealth."[a]

14 The Pharisees, who were lovers of money, heard all this, and they ridiculed him. [15]So he said to them, "You are those who justify yourselves in the sight of others; but God knows your hearts; for what is prized by human beings is an abomination in the sight of God.

16 "The law and the prophets were in effect until John came; since then the good news of the kingdom of God is proclaimed, and everyone tries to enter it by force.[c] [17]But it is easier for heaven and earth to pass away, than for one stroke of a letter in the law to be dropped.

18 "Anyone who divorces his wife and marries another commits adultery, and whoever marries a woman divorced from her husband commits adultery.

19 "There was a rich man who was dressed in purple and fine linen and who feasted sumptuously every day. [20]And at his gate lay a poor man named Lazarus, covered with sores, [21]who longed to satisfy his hunger with what fell from the rich man's table; even the dogs would come and lick his sores. [22]The poor man died and was carried away by the angels to be with Abraham.[d] The rich man also died and was buried. [23]In Hades, where he was being tormented, he looked up and saw Abraham far away with Lazarus by his side.[e] [24]He called out, 'Father Abraham, have mercy on me, and send Lazarus to dip the tip of his finger in water and cool my tongue; for I am in agony in these flames.' [25]But Abraham said, 'Child, remember that during your lifetime you received your good things, and Lazarus in like manner evil

[a] Gk *mammon* [b] Gk *tents* [c] Or *everyone is strongly urged to enter it* [d] Gk *to Abraham's bosom* [e] Gk *in his bosom*

Luke 16:19-31

Why is it that persons who proclaim eucharistic love and sharing deprive the poor people of the world of food, capital, employment, and even land? Why do they prefer cigarettes and liquor to food and drink for the one-third of humanity that goes hungry to bed each night?

Father Peter Pillai, an ardent apostle of social justice in Sri Lanka, often mentioned with a sense of uneasiness that in Sri Lanka some of the worst slums are in areas… [where] tens of thousands live in terrible squalor and misery in the shadow of monumental churches.… The rich live comfortably like Dives in the Gospel story. The poor eke out a miserable existence in their hovels. And now the luxurious tourist hotels add further contrasts to this sorrowful environment.[71]

— Tissa Balasuriya

things; but now he is comforted here, and you are
in agony. 26 Besides all this, between you and us
a great chasm has been fixed, so that those who
might want to pass from here to you cannot do so,
and no one can cross from there to us.' 27 He said,
'Then, father, I beg you to send him to my father's
house— 28 for I have five brothers—that he may
warn them, so that they will not also come into
this place of torment.' 29 Abraham replied, 'They
have Moses and the prophets; they should listen
to them.' 30 He said, 'No, father Abraham; but if
someone goes to them from the dead, they will
repent.' 31 He said to him, 'If they do not listen to
Moses and the prophets, neither will they be convinced even if someone rises from the dead.' "

17 Jesus[a] said to his disciples, "Occasions for
stumbling are bound to come, but woe to
anyone by whom they come! 2 It would be better for you if a millstone were hung around your
neck and you were thrown into the sea than for
you to cause one of these little ones to stumble.
3 Be on your guard! If another disciple[b] sins, you
must rebuke the offender, and if there is repentance, you must forgive. 4 And if the same person
sins against you seven times a day, and turns back
to you seven times and says, 'I repent,' you must
forgive."

5 The apostles said to the Lord, "Increase our
faith!" 6 The Lord replied, "If you had faith the
size of a[c] mustard seed, you could say to this mulberry tree, 'Be uprooted and planted in the sea,'
and it would obey you.

7 "Who among you would say to your slave
who has just come in from plowing or tending
sheep in the field, 'Come here at once and take
your place at the table'? 8 Would you not rather
say to him, 'Prepare supper for me, put on your
apron and serve me while I eat and drink; later
you may eat and drink'? 9 Do you thank the slave
for doing what was commanded? 10 So you also,
when you have done all that you were ordered to
do, say, 'We are worthless slaves; we have done
only what we ought to have done!' "

11 On the way to Jerusalem Jesus[d] was going
through the region between Samaria and Galilee.
12 As he entered a village, ten lepers[e] approached
him. Keeping their distance, 13 they called out,
saying, "Jesus, Master, have mercy on us!"
14 When he saw them, he said to them, "Go and
show yourselves to the priests." And as they went,
they were made clean. 15 Then one of them, when
he saw that he was healed, turned back, praising
God with a loud voice. 16 He prostrated himself
at Jesus'[f] feet and thanked him. And he was a Samaritan. 17 Then Jesus asked, "Were not ten made
clean? But the other nine, where are they? 18 Was
none of them found to return and give praise to
God except this foreigner?" 19 Then he said to
him, "Get up and go on your way; your faith has
made you well."

20 Once Jesus[d] was asked by the Pharisees
when the kingdom of God was coming, and he
answered, "The kingdom of God is not coming
with things that can be observed; 21 nor will they
say, 'Look, here it is!' or 'There it is!' For, in fact,
the kingdom of God is among[g] you."

22 Then he said to the disciples, "The days
are coming when you will long to see one of the
days of the Son of Man, and you will not see it.
23 They will say to you, 'Look there!' or 'Look
here!' Do not go, do not set off in pursuit. 24 For
as the lightning flashes and lights up the sky from
one side to the other, so will the Son of Man be
in his day.[h] 25 But first he must endure much suffering and be rejected by this generation. 26 Just as
it was in the days of Noah, so too it will be in the
days of the Son of Man. 27 They were eating and
drinking, and marrying and being given in marriage, until the day Noah entered the ark, and the
flood came and destroyed all of them. 28 Likewise,
just as it was in the days of Lot: they were eating
and drinking, buying and selling, planting and
building, 29 but on the day that Lot left Sodom, it
rained fire and sulfur from heaven and destroyed
all of them 30 —it will be like that on the day that
the Son of Man is revealed. 31 On that day, anyone
on the housetop who has belongings in the house
must not come down to take them away; and like-

[a] Gk *He* [b] Gk *your brother* [c] Gk *faith as a grain of* [d] Gk *he* [e] The terms *leper* and *leprosy* can refer to several diseases [f] Gk *his* [g] Or *within* [h] Other ancient authorities lack *in his day*

wise anyone in the field must not turn back. 32 Remember Lot's wife. 33 Those who try to make their
life secure will lose it, but those who lose their life
will keep it. 34 I tell you, on that night there will be
two in one bed; one will be taken and the other
left. 35 There will be two women grinding meal
together; one will be taken and the other left."[a]
37 Then they asked him, "Where, Lord?" He said
to them, "Where the corpse is, there the vultures
will gather."

18 Then Jesus[b] told them a parable about
their need to pray always and not to lose
heart. 2 He said, "In a certain city there was a
judge who neither feared God nor had respect
for people. 3 In that city there was a widow who
kept coming to him and saying, 'Grant me justice
against my opponent.' 4 For a while he refused;
but later he said to himself, 'Though I have no
fear of God and no respect for anyone, 5 yet because this widow keeps bothering me, I will grant
her justice, so that she may not wear me out by
continually coming.' "[c] 6 And the Lord said, "Listen to what the unjust judge says. 7 And will not
God grant justice to his chosen ones who cry to
him day and night? Will he delay long in helping
them? 8 I tell you, he will quickly grant justice to
them. And yet, when the Son of Man comes, will
he find faith on earth?"

9 He also told this parable to some who trusted
in themselves that they were righteous and regarded others with contempt: 10 "Two men went
up to the temple to pray, one a Pharisee and the
other a tax collector. 11 The Pharisee, standing by
himself, was praying thus, 'God, I thank you that I
am not like other people: thieves, rogues, adulterers, or even like this tax collector. 12 I fast twice a
week; I give a tenth of all my income.' 13 But the
tax collector, standing far off, would not even
look up to heaven, but was beating his breast and
saying, 'God, be merciful to me, a sinner!' 14 I tell
you, this man went down to his home justified
rather than the other; for all who exalt themselves
will be humbled, but all who humble themselves
will be exalted."

15 People were bringing even infants to him
that he might touch them; and when the disciples saw it, they sternly ordered them not to
do it. 16 But Jesus called for them and said, "Let
the little children come to me, and do not stop
them; for it is to such as these that the kingdom
of God belongs. 17 Truly I tell you, whoever does
not receive the kingdom of God as a little child
will never enter it."

18 A certain ruler asked him, "Good Teacher,
what must I do to inherit eternal life?" 19 Jesus
said to him, "Why do you call me good? No one
is good but God alone. 20 You know the commandments: 'You shall not commit adultery;
You shall not murder; You shall not steal; You
shall not bear false witness; Honor your father
and mother.' " 21 He replied, "I have kept all these
since my youth." 22 When Jesus heard this, he said
to him, "There is still one thing lacking. Sell all
that you own and distribute the money[d] to the
poor, and you will have treasure in heaven; then
come, follow me." 23 But when he heard this, he
became sad; for he was very rich. 24 Jesus looked
at him and said, "How hard it is for those who
have wealth to enter the kingdom of God! 25 Indeed, it is easier for a camel to go through the eye
of a needle than for someone who is rich to enter
the kingdom of God."

26 Those who heard it said, "Then who can
be saved?" 27 He replied, "What is impossible for
mortals is possible for God."

28 Then Peter said, "Look, we have left our
homes and followed you." 29 And he said to them,
"Truly I tell you, there is no one who has left
house or wife or brothers or parents or children,
for the sake of the kingdom of God, 30 who will
not get back very much more in this age, and in
the age to come eternal life."

31 Then he took the twelve aside and said
to them, "See, we are going up to Jerusalem, and
everything that is written about the Son of Man
by the prophets will be accomplished. 32 For he
will be handed over to the Gentiles; and he will

[a] Other ancient authorities add verse 36, "*Two will be in the field; one will be taken and the other left.*" [b] Gk *he*

[c] Or *so that she may not finally come and slap me in the face* [d] Gk lacks *the money*

be mocked and insulted and spat upon. 33After
they have flogged him, they will kill him, and on
the third day he will rise again." 34But they understood nothing about all these things; in fact, what
he said was hidden from them, and they did not
grasp what was said.
35 As he approached Jericho, a blind man was
sitting by the roadside begging. 36When he heard
a crowd going by, he asked what was happening.
37They told him, "Jesus of Nazareth[a] is passing
by." 38Then he shouted, "Jesus, Son of David,
have mercy on me!" 39Those who were in front
sternly ordered him to be quiet; but he shouted
even more loudly, "Son of David, have mercy on
me!" 40Jesus stood still and ordered the man to be
brought to him; and when he came near, he asked
him, 41"What do you want me to do for you?" He
said, "Lord, let me see again." 42Jesus said to him,
"Receive your sight; your faith has saved you."
43Immediately he regained his sight and followed
him, glorifying God; and all the people, when
they saw it, praised God.
19 He entered Jericho and was passing
through it. 2A man was there named Zacchaeus; he was a chief tax collector and was rich.
3He was trying to see who Jesus was, but on account of the crowd he could not, because he was
short in stature. 4So he ran ahead and climbed a
sycamore tree to see him, because he was going to
pass that way. 5When Jesus came to the place, he
looked up and said to him, "Zacchaeus, hurry and
come down; for I must stay at your house today."
6So he hurried down and was happy to welcome
him. 7All who saw it began to grumble and said,
"He has gone to be the guest of one who is a sinner." 8Zacchaeus stood there and said to the Lord,
"Look, half of my possessions, Lord, I will give to
the poor; and if I have defrauded anyone of anything, I will pay back four times as much." 9Then
Jesus said to him, "Today salvation has come to
this house, because he too is a son of Abraham.
10For the Son of Man came to seek out and to
save the lost."
11 As they were listening to this, he went on to
tell a parable, because he was near Jerusalem, and
because they supposed that the kingdom of God
was to appear immediately. 12So he said, "A nobleman went to a distant country to get royal power
for himself and then return. 13He summoned ten
of his slaves, and gave them ten pounds,[b] and said
to them, 'Do business with these until I come
back.' 14But the citizens of his country hated him
and sent a delegation after him, saying, 'We do
not want this man to rule over us.' 15When he returned, having received royal power, he ordered
these slaves, to whom he had given the money,
to be summoned so that he might find out what
they had gained by trading. 16The first came forward and said, 'Lord, your pound has made ten
more pounds.' 17He said to him, 'Well done, good
slave! Because you have been trustworthy in a
very small thing, take charge of ten cities.' 18Then
the second came, saying, 'Lord, your pound has
made five pounds.' 19He said to him, 'And you,
rule over five cities.' 20Then the other came, saying, 'Lord, here is your pound. I wrapped it up
in a piece of cloth, 21for I was afraid of you, because you are a harsh man; you take what you
did not deposit, and reap what you did not sow.'
22He said to him, 'I will judge you by your own

Luke 19:2-10

When we think of Zacchaeus, we may remember the children's song about a "wee little man" climbing a sycamore tree. But as a senior tax collector for the empire, Zacchaeus was a powerful and very wealthy man—and a traitor to his own people. Jesus shocks everyone, even Zacchaeus, when he says he will dine at his home. Probably for the first time in his life, Zacchaeus regained his humanity by Jesus' acceptance of him. Salvation enters Zacchaeus's house when he dies publicly to the power and privilege that had supported his lifestyle and is moved to act on behalf of the poor. He becomes the first character in Luke's narrative to respond to Jesus' teaching regarding wealth and poverty.

— MDLT

[a] Gk *the Nazorean* [b] The mina, rendered here by *pound*, was about three months' wages for a laborer

words, you wicked slave! You knew, did you, that
I was a harsh man, taking what I did not deposit
and reaping what I did not sow? 23 Why then
did you not put my money into the bank? Then
when I returned, I could have collected it with
interest.' 24 He said to the bystanders, 'Take the
pound from him and give it to the one who has
ten pounds.' 25 (And they said to him, 'Lord, he
has ten pounds!') 26 'I tell you, to all those who
have, more will be given; but from those who
have nothing, even what they have will be taken
away. 27 But as for these enemies of mine who did
not want me to be king over them—bring them
here and slaughter them in my presence.' "

28 After he had said this, he went on ahead,
going up to Jerusalem.

29 When he had come near Bethphage and
Bethany, at the place called the Mount of Olives,
he sent two of the disciples, 30 saying, "Go into the
village ahead of you, and as you enter it you will
find tied there a colt that has never been ridden.
Untie it and bring it here. 31 If anyone asks you,
'Why are you untying it?' just say this, 'The Lord
needs it.' " 32 So those who were sent departed
and found it as he had told them. 33 As they were
untying the colt, its owners asked them, "Why
are you untying the colt?" 34 They said, "The
Lord needs it." 35 Then they brought it to Jesus;
and after throwing their cloaks on the colt, they
set Jesus on it. 36 As he rode along, people kept
spreading their cloaks on the road. 37 As he was
now approaching the path down from the Mount
of Olives, the whole multitude of the disciples began to praise God joyfully with a loud voice for all
the deeds of power that they had seen, 38 saying,

"Blessed is the king
    who comes in the name of the Lord!
Peace in heaven,
    and glory in the highest heaven!"

39 Some of the Pharisees in the crowd said to him,
"Teacher, order your disciples to stop." 40 He answered, "I tell you, if these were silent, the stones
would shout out."

41 As he came near and saw the city, he wept
over it, 42 saying, "If you, even you, had only
recognized on this day the things that make for
peace! But now they are hidden from your eyes.
43 Indeed, the days will come upon you, when
your enemies will set up ramparts around you
and surround you, and hem you in on every side.
44 They will crush you to the ground, you and
your children within you, and they will not leave
within you one stone upon another; because you
did not recognize the time of your visitation from
God."[a]

45 Then he entered the temple and began to
drive out those who were selling things there;
46 and he said, "It is written,

'My house shall be a house of prayer';
    but you have made it a den of robbers."

47 Every day he was teaching in the temple.
The chief priests, the scribes, and the leaders of
the people kept looking for a way to kill him;
48 but they did not find anything they could do,
for all the people were spellbound by what they
heard.

Luke 19:45-48

Though Jesus had often proved a nuisance to those in power, his action in turning over the tables of the money changers at the temple provoked the chief priests to begin to seek a way to eliminate him. Why *this* act? Because these religious leaders were profiting from the business transactions of the money changers. Jesus threatened the source of their power and privilege—their pocketbook. Any détente established between an empire and religious leaders usually carves out a space from which the religious leaders can prosper. This was true during Jesus' time, and it remains true today.

—MDLT

20 One day, as he was teaching the people
in the temple and telling the good news,
the chief priests and the scribes came with the elders 2 and said to him, "Tell us, by what authority
are you doing these things? Who is it who gave

[a] Gk lacks *from God*

you this authority?" 3 He answered them, "I will also ask you a question, and you tell me: 4 Did the baptism of John come from heaven, or was it of human origin?" 5 They discussed it with one another, saying, "If we say, 'From heaven,' he will say, 'Why did you not believe him?' 6 But if we say, 'Of human origin,' all the people will stone us; for they are convinced that John was a prophet." 7 So they answered that they did not know where it came from. 8 Then Jesus said to them, "Neither will I tell you by what authority I am doing these things."

9 He began to tell the people this parable: "A man planted a vineyard, and leased it to tenants, and went to another country for a long time. 10 When the season came, he sent a slave to the tenants in order that they might give him his share of the produce of the vineyard; but the tenants beat him and sent him away empty-handed. 11 Next he sent another slave; that one also they beat and insulted and sent away empty-handed. 12 And he sent still a third; this one also they wounded and threw out. 13 Then the owner of the vineyard said, 'What shall I do? I will send my beloved son; perhaps they will respect him.' 14 But when the tenants saw him, they discussed it among themselves and said, 'This is the heir; let us kill him so that the inheritance may be ours.' 15 So they threw him out of the vineyard and killed him. What then will the owner of the vineyard do to them? 16 He will come and destroy those tenants and give the vineyard to others." When they heard this, they said, "Heaven forbid!" 17 But he looked at them and said, "What then does this text mean:

'The stone that the builders rejected
has become the cornerstone'?[a]

18 Everyone who falls on that stone will be broken to pieces; and it will crush anyone on whom it falls." 19 When the scribes and chief priests realized that he had told this parable against them, they wanted to lay hands on him at that very hour, but they feared the people.

20 So they watched him and sent spies who pretended to be honest, in order to trap him by what he said, so as to hand him over to the jurisdiction and authority of the governor. 21 So they asked him, "Teacher, we know that you are right in what you say and teach, and you show deference to no one, but teach the way of God in accordance with truth. 22 Is it lawful for us to pay taxes to the emperor, or not?" 23 But he perceived their craftiness and said to them, 24 "Show me a denarius. Whose head and whose title does it bear?" They said, "The emperor's." 25 He said to them, "Then give to the emperor the things that are the emperor's, and to God the things that are God's." 26 And they were not able in the presence of the people to trap him by what he said; and being amazed by his answer, they became silent.

27 Some Sadducees, those who say there is no resurrection, came to him 28 and asked him a question, "Teacher, Moses wrote for us that if a man's brother dies, leaving a wife but no children, the man[b] shall marry the widow and raise up children for his brother. 29 Now there were seven brothers; the first married, and died childless; 30 then the second 31 and the third married her, and so in the same way all seven died childless. 32 Finally the woman also died. 33 In the resurrection, therefore, whose wife will the woman be? For the seven had married her."

34 Jesus said to them, "Those who belong to this age marry and are given in marriage; 35 but those who are considered worthy of a place in that age and in the resurrection from the dead neither marry nor are given in marriage. 36 Indeed they cannot die anymore, because they are like angels and are children of God, being children of the resurrection. 37 And the fact that the dead are raised Moses himself showed, in the story about the bush, where he speaks of the Lord as the God of Abraham, the God of Isaac, and the God of Jacob. 38 Now he is God not of the dead, but of the living; for to him all of them are alive." 39 Then some of the scribes answered, "Teacher, you have spoken well." 40 For they no longer dared to ask him another question.

41 Then he said to them, "How can they say that the Messiah[c] is David's son? 42 For David himself says in the book of Psalms,

[a] Or *keystone* [b] Gk *his brother* [c] Or *the Christ*

Luke 20:27-36

Many readers focus on one aspect of this passage—that men and women in their glorified, resurrected bodies will be like angels—and conclude that there is no sex in heaven. But we should read the Sadducees' question as an absurdly hypothetical one. They mean to trap Jesus into admitting that the belief in the resurrection of the dead puts God in the ridiculous place of commanding polygamy. Jesus refutes them from Scripture—but first makes a point about the premises of the Sadducees' argument. They have imagined the law treating a woman as it would treat any man's possession, as if she were the equivalent of a donkey being passed from one brother to another. Jesus' words rebuke the assumptions of a patriarchal order that reduced women to possessions. In heaven, unlike on earth, women are not reduced to commodities that belong to one man until they are passed to another upon death. In heaven, man and woman are not possessor and possession; they are free and equal like the angels.

— MDLT

'The Lord said to my Lord,
"Sit at my right hand,
43 until I make your enemies your
footstool." '
44David thus calls him Lord; so how can he be
his son?"

45 In the hearing of all the people he said to
the[a] disciples, 46"Beware of the scribes, who like to
walk around in long robes, and love to be greeted
with respect in the marketplaces, and to have the
best seats in the synagogues and places of honor
at banquets. 47They devour widows' houses and
for the sake of appearance say long prayers. They
will receive the greater condemnation."

21 He looked up and saw rich people putting
their gifts into the treasury; 2he also saw
a poor widow put in two small copper coins. 3He
said, "Truly I tell you, this poor widow has put in
more than all of them; 4for all of them have contributed out of their abundance, but she out of
her poverty has put in all she had to live on."

5 When some were speaking about the temple, how it was adorned with beautiful stones and
gifts dedicated to God, he said, 6"As for these
things that you see, the days will come when not
one stone will be left upon another; all will be
thrown down."

7 They asked him, "Teacher, when will this
be, and what will be the sign that this is about to
take place?" 8And he said, "Beware that you are
not led astray; for many will come in my name
and say, 'I am he!'[b] and, 'The time is near!'[c] Do
not go after them.

9 "When you hear of wars and insurrections,
do not be terrified; for these things must take
place first, but the end will not follow immediately." 10Then he said to them, "Nation will rise
against nation, and kingdom against kingdom;
11there will be great earthquakes, and in various
places famines and plagues; and there will be
dreadful portents and great signs from heaven.

12 "But before all this occurs, they will arrest
you and persecute you; they will hand you over to
synagogues and prisons, and you will be brought
before kings and governors because of my name.
13This will give you an opportunity to testify.
14So make up your minds not to prepare your
defense in advance; 15for I will give you words[d]
and a wisdom that none of your opponents will
be able to withstand or contradict. 16You will be
betrayed even by parents and brothers, by relatives and friends; and they will put some of you
to death. 17You will be hated by all because of my
name. 18But not a hair of your head will perish.
19By your endurance you will gain your souls.

20 "When you see Jerusalem surrounded by
armies, then know that its desolation has come
near.[e] 21Then those in Judea must flee to the
mountains, and those inside the city must leave
it, and those out in the country must not enter

[a] Other ancient authorities read *his* [b] Gk *I am* [c] Or *at hand* [d] Gk *a mouth* [e] Or *is at hand*

it; 22 for these are days of vengeance, as a fulfillment of all that is written. 23 Woe to those who are
pregnant and to those who are nursing infants in
those days! For there will be great distress on the
earth and wrath against this people; 24 they will
fall by the edge of the sword and be taken away
as captives among all nations; and Jerusalem will
be trampled on by the Gentiles, until the times of
the Gentiles are fulfilled.

25 "There will be signs in the sun, the moon,
and the stars, and on the earth distress among nations confused by the roaring of the sea and the
waves. 26 People will faint from fear and forebod-
ing of what is coming upon the world, for the
powers of the heavens will be shaken. 27 Then they
will see 'the Son of Man coming in a cloud' with
power and great glory. 28 Now when these things
begin to take place, stand up and raise your heads,
because your redemption is drawing near."

29 Then he told them a parable: "Look at the
fig tree and all the trees; 30 as soon as they sprout
leaves you can see for yourselves and know that
summer is already near. 31 So also, when you see
these things taking place, you know that the kingdom of God is near. 32 Truly I tell you, this generation will not pass away until all things have taken
place. 33 Heaven and earth will pass away, but my
words will not pass away.

34 "Be on guard so that your hearts are not
weighed down with dissipation and drunkenness
and the worries of this life, and that day does not
catch you unexpectedly, 35 like a trap. For it will
come upon all who live on the face of the whole
earth. 36 Be alert at all times, praying that you may
have the strength to escape all these things that will
take place, and to stand before the Son of Man."

37 Every day he was teaching in the temple,
and at night he would go out and spend the night
on the Mount of Olives, as it was called. 38 And all
the people would get up early in the morning to
listen to him in the temple.

22 Now the festival of Unleavened Bread,
which is called the Passover, was near.
2 The chief priests and the scribes were looking
for a way to put Jesus[a] to death, for they were
afraid of the people.

3 Then Satan entered into Judas called Iscariot, who was one of the twelve; 4 he went away
and conferred with the chief priests and officers
of the temple police about how he might betray
him to them. 5 They were greatly pleased and
agreed to give him money. 6 So he consented and
began to look for an opportunity to betray him to
them when no crowd was present.

7 Then came the day of Unleavened Bread,
on which the Passover lamb had to be sacrificed.
8 So Jesus[b] sent Peter and John, saying, "Go and
prepare the Passover meal for us that we may eat
it." 9 They asked him, "Where do you want us to
make preparations for it?" 10 "Listen," he said to
them, "when you have entered the city, a man
carrying a jar of water will meet you; follow him
into the house he enters 11 and say to the owner of
the house, 'The teacher asks you, "Where is the
guest room, where I may eat the Passover with
my disciples?"' 12 He will show you a large room
upstairs, already furnished. Make preparations
for us there." 13 So they went and found everything as he had told them; and they prepared the
Passover meal.

14 When the hour came, he took his place at
the table, and the apostles with him. 15 He said to
them, "I have eagerly desired to eat this Passover
with you before I suffer; 16 for I tell you, I will not
eat it[c] until it is fulfilled in the kingdom of God."
17 Then he took a cup, and after giving thanks he
said, "Take this and divide it among yourselves;
18 for I tell you that from now on I will not drink
of the fruit of the vine until the kingdom of God
comes." 19 Then he took a loaf of bread, and when
he had given thanks, he broke it and gave it to
them, saying, "This is my body, which is given for
you. Do this in remembrance of me." 20 And he did
the same with the cup after supper, saying, "This
cup that is poured out for you is the new covenant
in my blood.[d] 21 But see, the one who betrays me
is with me, and his hand is on the table. 22 For the

[a] Gk *him* [b] Gk *he* [c] Other ancient authorities read *never eat it again* [d] Other ancient authorities lack, in whole or in part, verses 19b-20 (*which is given . . . in my blood*)

Son of Man is going as it has been determined,
but woe to that one by whom he is betrayed!"
23Then they began to ask one another which one
of them it could be who would do this.

24 A dispute also arose among them as to
which one of them was to be regarded as the
greatest. 25But he said to them, "The kings of the
Gentiles lord it over them; and those in authority over them are called benefactors. 26But not
so with you; rather the greatest among you must
become like the youngest, and the leader like one
who serves. 27For who is greater, the one who is at
the table or the one who serves? Is it not the one at
the table? But I am among you as one who serves.

28 "You are those who have stood by me in
my trials; 29and I confer on you, just as my Father
has conferred on me, a kingdom, 30so that you
may eat and drink at my table in my kingdom, and
you will sit on thrones judging the twelve tribes
of Israel.

31 "Simon, Simon, listen! Satan has demanded[a] to sift all of you like wheat, 32but I
have prayed for you that your own faith may not
fail; and you, when once you have turned back,
strengthen your brothers." 33And he said to him,
"Lord, I am ready to go with you to prison and to
death!" 34Jesus[b] said, "I tell you, Peter, the cock
will not crow this day, until you have denied three
times that you know me."

35 He said to them, "When I sent you out
without a purse, bag, or sandals, did you lack anything?" They said, "No, not a thing." 36He said to
them, "But now, the one who has a purse must
take it, and likewise a bag. And the one who has
no sword must sell his cloak and buy one. 37For
I tell you, this scripture must be fulfilled in me,
'And he was counted among the lawless'; and indeed what is written about me is being fulfilled."
38They said, "Lord, look, here are two swords."
He replied, "It is enough."

39 He came out and went, as was his custom, to the Mount of Olives; and the disciples
followed him. 40When he reached the place, he
said to them, "Pray that you may not come into
the time of trial."[c] 41Then he withdrew from them

Luke 22:36

These may be some of the most troubling words to come out of Jesus' mouth. Jesus, the Prince of Peace, advises his followers to bring a sword with them as they go out to do his work, indicating that after his death they will face a graver situation than before (compare 10:4). The saying appears as incongruous as if evangelists today were instructed to carry guns. Historically, of course, that is just what occurred as Christian empires conquered other peoples, specifically in the Western Hemisphere, using sword and cannon to proclaim the cross. As an African proverb puts it: "At first we had the land, and the white man had the Bible. When we opened our eyes after praying, we had the Bible and the white man had the land."

— ***MDLT***

about a stone's throw, knelt down, and prayed,
42"Father, if you are willing, remove this cup from
me; yet, not my will but yours be done." ⟦43Then
an angel from heaven appeared to him and gave
him strength. 44In his anguish he prayed more
earnestly, and his sweat became like great drops
of blood falling down on the ground.⟧[d] 45When
he got up from prayer, he came to the disciples
and found them sleeping because of grief, 46and
he said to them, "Why are you sleeping? Get up
and pray that you may not come into the time of
trial."[c]

47 While he was still speaking, suddenly
a crowd came, and the one called Judas, one of
the twelve, was leading them. He approached
Jesus to kiss him; 48but Jesus said to him, "Judas,
is it with a kiss that you are betraying the Son
of Man?" 49When those who were around him
saw what was coming, they asked, "Lord, should
we strike with the sword?" 50Then one of them
struck the slave of the high priest and cut off his
right ear. 51But Jesus said, "No more of this!" And
he touched his ear and healed him. 52Then Jesus
said to the chief priests, the officers of the temple
police, and the elders who had come for him,

[a] Or *has obtained permission* [b] Gk *He* [c] Or *into temptation* [d] Other ancient authorities lack verses 43 and 44

"Have you come out with swords and clubs as
if I were a bandit? 53 When I was with you day
after day in the temple, you did not lay hands
on me. But this is your hour, and the power of
darkness!"

54 Then they seized him and led him away,
bringing him into the high priest's house. But Peter was following at a distance. 55 When they had
kindled a fire in the middle of the courtyard and
sat down together, Peter sat among them. 56 Then
a servant-girl, seeing him in the firelight, stared
at him and said, "This man also was with him."
57 But he denied it, saying, "Woman, I do not
know him." 58 A little later someone else, on seeing him, said, "You also are one of them." But Peter said, "Man, I am not!" 59 Then about an hour
later still another kept insisting, "Surely this man
also was with him; for he is a Galilean." 60 But Peter said, "Man, I do not know what you are talking about!" At that moment, while he was still
speaking, the cock crowed. 61 The Lord turned
and looked at Peter. Then Peter remembered the
word of the Lord, how he had said to him, "Before the cock crows today, you will deny me three
times." 62 And he went out and wept bitterly.

63 Now the men who were holding Jesus began to mock him and beat him; 64 they also blind-
folded him and kept asking him, "Prophesy! Who
is it that struck you?" 65 They kept heaping many
other insults on him.

66 When day came, the assembly of the elders of the people, both chief priests and scribes,
gathered together, and they brought him to their
council. 67 They said, "If you are the Messiah,[a] tell
us." He replied, "If I tell you, you will not believe;
68 and if I question you, you will not answer. 69 But
from now on the Son of Man will be seated at the
right hand of the power of God." 70 All of them
asked, "Are you, then, the Son of God?" He said
to them, "You say that I am." 71 Then they said,
"What further testimony do we need? We have
heard it ourselves from his own lips!"

23 Then the assembly rose as a body and
brought Jesus[b] before Pilate. 2 They began to accuse him, saying, "We found this man
perverting our nation, forbidding us to pay taxes
to the emperor, and saying that he himself is the
Messiah, a king."[c] 3 Then Pilate asked him, "Are
you the king of the Jews?" He answered, "You say
so." 4 Then Pilate said to the chief priests and the
crowds, "I find no basis for an accusation against
this man." 5 But they were insistent and said, "He
stirs up the people by teaching throughout all
Judea, from Galilee where he began even to this
place."

6 When Pilate heard this, he asked whether
the man was a Galilean. 7 And when he learned
that he was under Herod's jurisdiction, he sent
him off to Herod, who was himself in Jerusalem
at that time. 8 When Herod saw Jesus, he was very
glad, for he had been wanting to see him for a
long time, because he had heard about him and
was hoping to see him perform some sign. 9 He
questioned him at some length, but Jesus[d] gave
him no answer. 10 The chief priests and the scribes
stood by, vehemently accusing him. 11 Even
Herod with his soldiers treated him with contempt and mocked him; then he put an elegant
robe on him, and sent him back to Pilate. 12 That
same day Herod and Pilate became friends with
each other; before this they had been enemies.

13 Pilate then called together the chief
priests, the leaders, and the people, 14 and said to
them, "You brought me this man as one who was
perverting the people; and here I have examined
him in your presence and have not found this
man guilty of any of your charges against him.
15 Neither has Herod, for he sent him back to us.
Indeed, he has done nothing to deserve death.
16 I will therefore have him flogged and release
him."[e]

18 Then they all shouted out together, "Away
with this fellow! Release Barabbas for us!" 19 (This
was a man who had been put in prison for an insurrection that had taken place in the city, and
for murder.) 20 Pilate, wanting to release Jesus,
addressed them again; 21 but they kept shouting,
"Crucify, crucify him!" 22 A third time he said to

[a] Or *the Christ* [b] Gk *him* [c] Or *is an anointed king* [d] Gk *he*

[e] Here, or after verse 19, other ancient authorities add verse 17, *Now he was obliged to release someone for them at the festival*

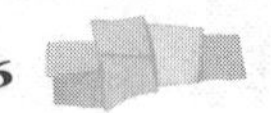

them, "Why, what evil has he done? I have found
in him no ground for the sentence of death; I
will therefore have him flogged and then release
him." 23 But they kept urgently demanding with
loud shouts that he should be crucified; and their
voices prevailed. 24 So Pilate gave his verdict that
their demand should be granted. 25 He released
the man they asked for, the one who had been
put in prison for insurrection and murder, and he
handed Jesus over as they wished.

26 As they led him away, they seized a man,
Simon of Cyrene, who was coming from the
country, and they laid the cross on him, and made
him carry it behind Jesus. 27 A great number of
the people followed him, and among them were
women who were beating their breasts and wailing for him. 28 But Jesus turned to them and said,
"Daughters of Jerusalem, do not weep for me, but
weep for yourselves and for your children. 29 For
the days are surely coming when they will say,
'Blessed are the barren, and the wombs that never
bore, and the breasts that never nursed.' 30 Then
they will begin to say to the mountains, 'Fall on
us'; and to the hills, 'Cover us.' 31 For if they do
this when the wood is green, what will happen
when it is dry?"

32 Two others also, who were criminals, were
led away to be put to death with him. 33 When
they came to the place that is called The Skull,
they crucified Jesus[a] there with the criminals, one
on his right and one on his left. ⟦34 Then Jesus
said, "Father, forgive them; for they do not know
what they are doing."⟧[b] And they cast lots to
divide his clothing. 35 And the people stood by,
watching; but the leaders scoffed at him, saying, "He saved others; let him save himself if he
is the Messiah[c] of God, his chosen one!" 36 The
soldiers also mocked him, coming up and offering him sour wine, 37 and saying, "If you are the
King of the Jews, save yourself!" 38 There was
also an inscription over him,[d] "This is the King of
the Jews."

39 One of the criminals who were hanged
there kept deriding[e] him and saying, "Are you not
the Messiah?[c] Save yourself and us!" 40 But the
other rebuked him, saying, "Do you not fear God,
since you are under the same sentence of condemnation? 41 And we indeed have been condemned
justly, for we are getting what we deserve for our
deeds, but this man has done nothing wrong."
42 Then he said, "Jesus, remember me when you
come into[f] your kingdom." 43 He replied, "Truly I
tell you, today you will be with me in Paradise."

44 It was now about noon, and darkness
came over the whole land[g] until three in the afternoon, 45 while the sun's light failed;[h] and the curtain of the temple was torn in two. 46 Then Jesus,
crying with a loud voice, said, "Father, into your
hands I commend my spirit." Having said this,
he breathed his last. 47 When the centurion saw
what had taken place, he praised God and said,
"Certainly this man was innocent."[i] 48 And when
all the crowds who had gathered there for this
spectacle saw what had taken place, they returned
home, beating their breasts. 49 But all his acquaintances, including the women who had followed
him from Galilee, stood at a distance, watching
these things.

50 Now there was a good and righteous man
named Joseph, who, though a member of the
council, 51 had not agreed to their plan and action.
He came from the Jewish town of Arimathea, and
he was waiting expectantly for the kingdom of
God. 52 This man went to Pilate and asked for the
body of Jesus. 53 Then he took it down, wrapped
it in a linen cloth, and laid it in a rock-hewn tomb
where no one had ever been laid. 54 It was the day
of Preparation, and the sabbath was beginning.[j]
55 The women who had come with him from
Galilee followed, and they saw the tomb and how
his body was laid. 56 Then they returned, and prepared spices and ointments.

On the sabbath they rested according to the
commandment.

[a] Gk *him* [b] Other ancient authorities lack the sentence *Then Jesus . . . what they are doing* [c] Or *the Christ*
[d] Other ancient authorities add *written in Greek and Latin and Hebrew* (that is, *Aramaic*) [e] Or *blaspheming*
[f] Other ancient authorities read *in* [g] Or *earth* [h] Or *the sun was eclipsed*. Other ancient authorities read *the sun was darkened* [i] Or *righteous* [j] Gk *was dawning*

24 But on the first day of the week, at early dawn, they came to the tomb, taking the spices that they had prepared. 2They found the stone rolled away from the tomb, 3but when they went in, they did not find the body.[a] 4While they were perplexed about this, suddenly two men in dazzling clothes stood beside them. 5The women[b] were terrified and bowed their faces to the ground, but the men[c] said to them, "Why do you look for the living among the dead? He is not here, but has risen.[d] 6Remember how he told you, while he was still in Galilee, 7that the Son of Man must be handed over to sinners, and be crucified, and on the third day rise again." 8Then they remembered his words, 9and returning from the tomb, they told all this to the eleven and to all the rest. 10Now it was Mary Magdalene, Joanna, Mary the mother of James, and the other women with them who told this to the apostles. 11But these words seemed to them an idle tale, and they did not believe them. 12But Peter got up and ran to the tomb; stooping and looking in, he saw the linen cloths by themselves; then he went home, amazed at what had happened.[e]

13 Now on that same day two of them were going to a village called Emmaus, about seven miles[f] from Jerusalem, 14and talking with each other about all these things that had happened. 15While they were talking and discussing, Jesus himself came near and went with them, 16but their eyes were kept from recognizing him. 17And he said to them, "What are you discussing with each other while you walk along?" They stood still, looking sad.[g] 18Then one of them, whose name was Cleopas, answered him, "Are you the only stranger in Jerusalem who does not know the things that have taken place there in these days?" 19He asked them, "What things?" They replied, "The things about Jesus of Nazareth,[h] who was a prophet mighty in deed and word before God and all the people, 20and how our chief priests and leaders handed him over to be condemned to death and crucified him. 21But we had hoped that he was the one to redeem Israel.[i] Yes, and besides all this, it is now the third day since these things took place. 22Moreover, some women of our group astounded us. They were at the tomb early this morning, 23and when they did not find his body there, they came back and told us that they had indeed seen a vision of angels who said that he was alive. 24Some of those who were with us went to the tomb and found it just as the women had said; but they did not see him." 25Then he said to them, "Oh, how foolish you are, and how slow of heart to believe all that the prophets have declared! 26Was it not necessary that the Messiah[j] should suffer these things and then enter into his glory?" 27Then beginning with Moses and all the prophets, he interpreted to them the things about himself in all the scriptures.

28 As they came near the village to which they were going, he walked ahead as if he were going on. 29But they urged him strongly, saying, "Stay with us, because it is almost evening and the day is now nearly over." So he went in to stay with them. 30When he was at the table with them, he took bread, blessed and broke it, and gave it to them. 31Then their eyes were opened, and they recognized him; and he vanished from their sight. 32They said to each other, "Were not our hearts burning within us[k] while he was talking to us on the road, while he was opening the scriptures to us?" 33That same hour they got up and returned to Jerusalem; and they found the eleven and their companions gathered together. 34They were saying, "The Lord has risen indeed, and he has appeared to Simon!" 35Then they told what had happened on the road, and how he had been made known to them in the breaking of the bread.

36 While they were talking about this, Jesus himself stood among them and said to them, "Peace be with you."[l] 37They were startled and terrified,

[a] Other ancient authorities add *of the Lord Jesus* [b] Gk *They* [c] Gk *but they* [d] Other ancient authorities lack *He is not here, but has risen* [e] Other ancient authorities lack verse 12 [f] Gk *sixty stadia;* other ancient authorities read *a hundred sixty stadia* [g] Other ancient authorities read *walk along, looking sad?"* [h] Other ancient authorities read *Jesus the Nazorean* [i] Or *to set Israel free* [j] Or *the Christ* [k] Other ancient authorities lack *within us* [l] Other ancient authorities lack *and said to them, "Peace be with you."*

and thought that they were seeing a ghost. 38 He said to them, "Why are you frightened, and why do doubts arise in your hearts? 39 Look at my hands and my feet; see that it is I myself. Touch me and see; for a ghost does not have flesh and bones as you see that I have." 40 And when he had said this, he showed them his hands and his feet.[a] 41 While in their joy they were disbelieving and still wondering, he said to them, "Have you anything here to eat?" 42 They gave him a piece of broiled fish, 43 and he took it and ate in their presence.

44 Then he said to them, "These are my words that I spoke to you while I was still with you—that everything written about me in the law of Moses, the prophets, and the psalms must be fulfilled." 45 Then he opened their minds to understand the scriptures, 46 and he said to them, "Thus it is written, that the Messiah[b] is to suffer and to rise from the dead on the third day, 47 and that repentance and forgiveness of sins is to be proclaimed in his name to all nations, beginning from Jerusalem. 48 You are witnesses[c] of these things. 49 And see, I am sending upon you what my Father promised; so stay here in the city until you have been clothed with power from on high."

50 Then he led them out as far as Bethany, and, lifting up his hands, he blessed them. 51 While he was blessing them, he withdrew from them and was carried up into heaven.[d] 52 And they worshiped him, and[e] returned to Jerusalem with great joy; 53 and they were continually in the temple blessing God.[f]

[a] Other ancient authorities lack verse 40 [b] Or *the Christ* [c] Or *nations. Beginning from Jerusalem* [48]*you are witnesses*
[d] Other ancient authorities lack *and was carried up into heaven* [e] Other ancient authorities lack *worshiped him, and*
[f] Other ancient authorities add *Amen*

The Gospel According to John

Traditionally, the Gospel of John has been attributed to John, the son of Zebedee, associated with the city of Ephesus in Asia Minor, and dated to the final decades of the first century CE. On these points of authorship, place of writing, and time of composition, there has been much debate but no consensus. Given the lack of evidence, the gospel is best approached as a piece written by an anonymous author from an undisclosed location and at an unknown time. The Gospel of John has also been regarded, when compared to the other canonical gospels, as a highly peculiar writing. Scholars have long debated its relationship to the other gospels, arguing for a range of views, from this gospel's creative dependence on the Synoptics, to its connection with the other gospels at an earlier pre-gospel stage, to its complete independence from the other gospels. Despite shifting points of agreement and disagreement in this regard, the distinctive features of the gospel are beyond dispute.

The gospel presents Jesus as the incarnation of the Word of God, a divine figure existing with God before creation and responsible for all creation, and at last sent into the world to make the Father known. The gospel presents two levels of reality that are engaged in conflict: a world "above," the world of "glory" where God rules—marked by life and light, grace and truth; and a world "below," the world of "flesh" where the evil one rules—marked by death and darkness, sin and falsehood. In this portrayal of Jesus' life he is a traveler, on a cosmic journey from the world above into the world below and on a series of geographical journeys up to and down from Jerusalem. Compared with the other gospels, John's devotes much more attention to Jesus' words, the revelation entrusted to him by God, than to his works, the signs given to him by the Father. It depicts Jesus as bringing about a sharp division among all human beings between the "children of God" (1:12; 11:52), those who believe and who are reborn of the Spirit, and those who do not believe, who were "born . . . of the will of the flesh" (1:13). It reduces the expectations (evident in the other gospels) of a coming convulsive end of the world and fulfillment of God's kingdom and instead highlights access to God's kingdom through belief in Jesus.

This gospel raises keen questions about culture and society, both in the social-cultural context in which it was composed and in all subsequent contexts in which it is read, including our own. Fundamental are questions concerning the gospel's depiction of reality in stark either-or terms: a world below, immersed in death and darkness, sin and falsehood; and a world above, in which all who believe are raised to dwell in the household of God, in life and light, grace and truth—but only through the agency of Jesus and his generations of followers. This view of reality has consequences, most important among which are the potential demonization of those individuals and groups who express no belief in Jesus and the divinization of those who do. Most specifically, the collective

character of "the Jews" is singularly marked in negative terms in this gospel, bringing to the fore the question of anti-Judaism, especially in the light of the history of the West toward these internal "Others." At the same time it is clear that where belief is lacking, no group fares any better in this gospel—so we may as well ask about the legacy of this gospel in the history of the Christian West's antagonism toward other non-Christians, what we might call its external Others.

I come to the Gospel of John and its either-or reality as a child of either-or realities in conflict. Born and raised in Cuba, I experienced life first under a right-wing dictatorship, then under a left-wing dictatorship. As someone who emigrated from Latin America to the United States, I experienced life first in the world of the colonized, as a citizen of a dependent country, and then in the world of the colonizer, as a member of what was in the United States a minority ethnic group. As someone who in effect crossed from "East" to "West" at the height of the Cold War, I experienced life first in a socialist state with a centralized economy and an autocratic regime, and then in a capitalist state, with a free-market economy and a liberal regime. All these situations involved variations of either-or contrasts. My whole life has been a reaction against polarization and "othering" and a search for freedom and justice, dignity and well-being. Before the Gospel, I stand in awe of its highly reassuring vision of enlightenment and love—and in fear of its deeply unsettling deployment of either-or rhetoric and ideology. The latter I can only resist; the former I can only admire.

— Fernando F. Segovia

1 In the beginning was the Word, and the Word
was with God, and the Word was God. 2He
was in the beginning with God. 3All things came
into being through him, and without him not one
thing came into being. What has come into being
4in him was life,[a] and the life was the light of all

[a] Or [3]*through him. And without him not one thing came into being that has come into being.* [4]*In him was life*

John 1:1-3

Only the Gospel according to John speaks of Jesus as the incarnation of the eternal Word, and later theological controversies about the incarnation focused tremendous attention on these verses. But John probably was not concerned with the metaphysical questions that preoccupied later Christians. The Word (in Greek, *logos*) is God's active agent in creation, suggesting that theology should reflect this active nature. Hispanic theologians thus understand that theology is something to be *done,* not a word or book to be believed. In Israel's Scriptures the Word is also the active, communicative presence of God: again and again a prophet in Israel proclaimed that "the word of the LORD came to me, saying . . ." The Word burned in Jeremiah's bones like fire (Jer 20:7-9). The gospel declares that Jesus' followers saw it enfleshed in his lived presence.

— NE, MDLT

people. 5The light shines in the darkness, and the
darkness did not overcome it.
6 There was a man sent from God, whose
name was John. 7He came as a witness to testify
to the light, so that all might believe through him.
8He himself was not the light, but he came to testify to the light. 9The true light, which enlightens
everyone, was coming into the world.[a]
10 He was in the world, and the world came
into being through him; yet the world did not
know him. 11He came to what was his own,[b] and
his own people did not accept him. 12But to all
who received him, who believed in his name, he
gave power to become children of God, 13who
were born, not of blood or of the will of the flesh
or of the will of man, but of God.
14 And the Word became flesh and lived
among us, and we have seen his glory, the glory
as of a father's only son,[c] full of grace and truth.
15(John testified to him and cried out, "This was
he of whom I said, 'He who comes after me ranks
ahead of me because he was before me.'") 16From
his fullness we have all received, grace upon grace.
17The law indeed was given through Moses; grace
and truth came through Jesus Christ. 18No one has
ever seen God. It is God the only Son,[d] who is close
to the Father's heart,[e] who has made him known.

19 This is the testimony given by John when
the Jews sent priests and Levites from Jerusalem to
ask him, "Who are you?" 20He confessed and did
not deny it, but confessed, "I am not the Messiah."[f]
21And they asked him, "What then? Are you Elijah?" He said, "I am not." "Are you the prophet?"
He answered, "No." 22Then they said to him, "Who
are you? Let us have an answer for those who sent
us. What do you say about yourself?" 23He said,

"I am the voice of one crying out in the
wilderness,
'Make straight the way of the Lord,' "

as the prophet Isaiah said.
24 Now they had been sent from the Pharisees. 25They asked him, "Why then are you baptizing if you are neither the Messiah,[f] nor Elijah,
nor the prophet?" 26John answered them, "I baptize with water. Among you stands one whom
you do not know, 27the one who is coming after
me; I am not worthy to untie the thong of his
sandal." 28This took place in Bethany across the
Jordan where John was baptizing.
29 The next day he saw Jesus coming toward
him and declared, "Here is the Lamb of God who
takes away the sin of the world! 30This is he of
whom I said, 'After me comes a man who ranks
ahead of me because he was before me.' 31I myself did not know him; but I came baptizing with
water for this reason, that he might be revealed
to Israel." 32And John testified, "I saw the Spirit
descending from heaven like a dove, and it remained on him. 33I myself did not know him, but
the one who sent me to baptize with water said
to me, 'He on whom you see the Spirit descend
and remain is the one who baptizes with the Holy
Spirit.' 34And I myself have seen and have testified that this is the Son of God."[g]
35 The next day John again was standing with
two of his disciples, 36and as he watched Jesus
walk by, he exclaimed, "Look, here is the Lamb
of God!" 37The two disciples heard him say this,
and they followed Jesus. 38When Jesus turned
and saw them following, he said to them, "What
are you looking for?" They said to him, "Rabbi"
(which translated means Teacher), "where are
you staying?" 39He said to them, "Come and see."
They came and saw where he was staying, and
they remained with him that day. It was about
four o'clock in the afternoon. 40One of the two
who heard John speak and followed him was Andrew, Simon Peter's brother. 41He first found his
brother Simon and said to him, "We have found
the Messiah" (which is translated Anointed[h]).
42He brought Simon[i] to Jesus, who looked at him
and said, "You are Simon son of John. You are to
be called Cephas" (which is translated Peter[j]).

[a] Or *He was the true light that enlightens everyone coming into the world* [b] Or *to his own home* [c] Or *the Father's only Son*
[d] Other ancient authorities read *It is an only Son, God,* or *It is the only Son* [e] Gk *bosom* [f] Or *the Christ*
[g] Other ancient authorities read *is God's chosen one* [h] Or *Christ* [i] Gk *him*
[j] From the word for *rock* in Aramaic (*kepha*) and Greek (*petra*), respectively

43 The next day Jesus decided to go to Galilee. He found Philip and said to him, "Follow me."
44 Now Philip was from Bethsaida, the city of Andrew and Peter. 45 Philip found Nathanael and said
to him, "We have found him about whom Moses
in the law and also the prophets wrote, Jesus son
of Joseph from Nazareth." 46 Nathanael said to
him, "Can anything good come out of Nazareth?"
Philip said to him, "Come and see." 47 When Jesus
saw Nathanael coming toward him, he said of him,
"Here is truly an Israelite in whom there is no deceit!" 48 Nathanael asked him, "Where did you get
to know me?" Jesus answered, "I saw you under
the fig tree before Philip called you." 49 Nathanael
replied, "Rabbi, you are the Son of God! You are
the King of Israel!" 50 Jesus answered, "Do you believe because I told you that I saw you under the fig
tree? You will see greater things than these." 51 And
he said to him, "Very truly, I tell you,[a] you will see
heaven opened and the angels of God ascending
and descending upon the Son of Man."

2 On the third day there was a wedding in Cana
of Galilee, and the mother of Jesus was there.
2 Jesus and his disciples had also been invited to the
wedding. 3 When the wine gave out, the mother
of Jesus said to him, "They have no wine." 4 And
Jesus said to her, "Woman, what concern is that to
you and to me? My hour has not yet come." 5 His
mother said to the servants, "Do whatever he tells
you." 6 Now standing there were six stone water
jars for the Jewish rites of purification, each holding twenty or thirty gallons. 7 Jesus said to them,
"Fill the jars with water." And they filled them up
to the brim. 8 He said to them, "Now draw some
out, and take it to the chief steward." So they took
it. 9 When the steward tasted the water that had
become wine, and did not know where it came
from (though the servants who had drawn the
water knew), the steward called the bridegroom
10 and said to him, "Everyone serves the good
wine first, and then the inferior wine after the
guests have become drunk. But you have kept the
good wine until now." 11 Jesus did this, the first
of his signs, in Cana of Galilee, and revealed his
glory; and his disciples believed in him.

12 After this he went down to Capernaum
with his mother, his brothers, and his disciples;
and they remained there a few days.

13 The Passover of the Jews was near, and
Jesus went up to Jerusalem. 14 In the temple he
found people selling cattle, sheep, and doves, and
the money changers seated at their tables. 15 Making a whip of cords, he drove all of them out of
the temple, both the sheep and the cattle. He
also poured out the coins of the money changers
and overturned their tables. 16 He told those who
were selling the doves, "Take these things out of
here! Stop making my Father's house a marketplace!" 17 His disciples remembered that it was
written, "Zeal for your house will consume me."
18 The Jews then said to him, "What sign can you
show us for doing this?" 19 Jesus answered them,
"Destroy this temple, and in three days I will raise
it up." 20 The Jews then said, "This temple has
been under construction for forty-six years, and
will you raise it up in three days?" 21 But he was
speaking of the temple of his body. 22 After he was
raised from the dead, his disciples remembered
that he had said this; and they believed the scripture and the word that Jesus had spoken.

23 When he was in Jerusalem during the
Passover festival, many believed in his name because they saw the signs that he was doing. 24 But
Jesus on his part would not entrust himself to
them, because he knew all people 25 and needed
no one to testify about anyone; for he himself
knew what was in everyone.

3 Now there was a Pharisee named Nicodemus, a leader of the Jews. 2 He came to Jesus[b]
by night and said to him, "Rabbi, we know that
you are a teacher who has come from God; for
no one can do these signs that you do apart from
the presence of God." 3 Jesus answered him, "Very
truly, I tell you, no one can see the kingdom of
God without being born from above."[c] 4 Nicodemus said to him, "How can anyone be born after
having grown old? Can one enter a second time
into the mother's womb and be born?" 5 Jesus answered, "Very truly, I tell you, no one can enter
the kingdom of God without being born of water

[a] Both instances of the Greek word for *you* in this verse are plural [b] Gk *him* [c] Or *born anew*

and Spirit. 6What is born of the flesh is flesh, and what is born of the Spirit is spirit.[a] 7Do not be astonished that I said to you, 'You[b] must be born from above.'[c] 8The wind[a] blows where it chooses, and you hear the sound of it, but you do not know where it comes from or where it goes. So it is with everyone who is born of the Spirit." 9Nicodemus said to him, "How can these things be?" 10Jesus answered him, "Are you a teacher of Israel, and yet you do not understand these things?

11 "Very truly, I tell you, we speak of what we know and testify to what we have seen; yet you[d] do not receive our testimony. 12If I have told you about earthly things and you do not believe, how can you believe if I tell you about heavenly things? 13No one has ascended into heaven except the one who descended from heaven, the Son of Man.[e] 14And just as Moses lifted up the serpent in the wilderness, so must the Son of Man be lifted up, 15that whoever believes in him may have eternal life.[f]

16 "For God so loved the world that he gave his only Son, so that everyone who believes in him may not perish but may have eternal life.

17 "Indeed, God did not send the Son into the world to condemn the world, but in order that the world might be saved through him. 18Those who believe in him are not condemned; but those who do not believe are condemned already, because they have not believed in the name of the only Son of God. 19And this is the judgment, that the light has come into the world, and people loved darkness rather than light because their deeds were evil. 20For all who do evil hate the light and do not come to the light, so that their deeds may not be exposed. 21But those who do what is true come to the light, so that it may be clearly seen that their deeds have been done in God."[f]

22 After this Jesus and his disciples went into the Judean countryside, and he spent some time there with them and baptized. 23John also was baptizing at Aenon near Salim because water was abundant there; and people kept coming and were being baptized 24—John, of course, had not yet been thrown into prison.

25 Now a discussion about purification arose between John's disciples and a Jew.[g] 26They came to John and said to him, "Rabbi, the one who was with you across the Jordan, to whom you testified, here he is baptizing, and all are going to him." 27John answered, "No one can receive anything except what has been given from heaven. 28You yourselves are my witnesses that I said, 'I am not the Messiah,'[h] but I have been sent ahead of him.' 29He who has the bride is the bridegroom. The friend of the bridegroom, who stands and hears him, rejoices greatly at the bridegroom's voice. For this reason my joy has been fulfilled. 30He must increase, but I must decrease."[i]

31 The one who comes from above is above all; the one who is of the earth belongs to the earth and speaks about earthly things. The one who comes from heaven is above all. 32He testifies

John 3:16

God so loved the *world*—God's desire is that neither the earth nor its inhabitants should perish but rather that they may have life. Salvation means that humans have sufficient food and the earth is safeguarded from those who would commodify it for gain. When the few monopolize the earth's resources so that the many cannot be sustained, the gift of salvation is nullified. Christians from industrialized Western nations have interpreted this verse as a call to evangelize the world; but impoverished peoples have responded by pointing out that the capitalist ethos has brought not life but death, as those nations have enriched themselves through extraction and exploitation.

— MDLT

[a] The same Greek word means both *wind* and *spirit* [b] The Greek word for *you* here is plural [c] Or *anew* [d] The Greek word for *you* here and in verse 12 is plural [e] Other ancient authorities add *who is in heaven* [f] Some interpreters hold that the quotation concludes with verse 15 [g] Other ancient authorities read *the Jews* [h] Or *the Christ* [i] Some interpreters hold that the quotation continues through verse 36

to what he has seen and heard, yet no one accepts
his testimony. 33Whoever has accepted his testimony has certified[a] this, that God is true. 34He
whom God has sent speaks the words of God, for
he gives the Spirit without measure. 35The Father loves the Son and has placed all things in his
hands. 36Whoever believes in the Son has eternal
life; whoever disobeys the Son will not see life,
but must endure God's wrath.

4 Now when Jesus[b] learned that the Pharisees
had heard, "Jesus is making and baptizing
more disciples than John" 2—although it was not
Jesus himself but his disciples who baptized—
3he left Judea and started back to Galilee. 4But he
had to go through Samaria. 5So he came to a Samaritan city called Sychar, near the plot of ground
that Jacob had given to his son Joseph. 6Jacob's
well was there, and Jesus, tired out by his journey,
was sitting by the well. It was about noon.

7 A Samaritan woman came to draw water,
and Jesus said to her, "Give me a drink." 8(His
disciples had gone to the city to buy food.) 9The
Samaritan woman said to him, "How is it that
you, a Jew, ask a drink of me, a woman of Samaria?" (Jews do not share things in common
with Samaritans.)[c] 10Jesus answered her, "If you
knew the gift of God, and who it is that is saying to you, 'Give me a drink,' you would have
asked him, and he would have given you living
water." 11The woman said to him, "Sir, you have
no bucket, and the well is deep. Where do you
get that living water? 12Are you greater than our
ancestor Jacob, who gave us the well, and with his
sons and his flocks drank from it?" 13Jesus said to
her, "Everyone who drinks of this water will be
thirsty again, 14but those who drink of the water
that I will give them will never be thirsty. The water that I will give will become in them a spring
of water gushing up to eternal life." 15The woman
said to him, "Sir, give me this water, so that I may
never be thirsty or have to keep coming here to
draw water."

16 Jesus said to her, "Go, call your husband,
and come back." 17The woman answered him,
"I have no husband." Jesus said to her, "You are
right in saying, 'I have no husband'; 18for you
have had five husbands, and the one you have
now is not your husband. What you have said is
true!" 19The woman said to him, "Sir, I see that
you are a prophet. 20Our ancestors worshiped on
this mountain, but you[d] say that the place where
people must worship is in Jerusalem." 21Jesus said
to her, "Woman, believe me, the hour is coming
when you will worship the Father neither on this
mountain nor in Jerusalem. 22You worship what
you do not know; we worship what we know, for
salvation is from the Jews. 23But the hour is coming, and is now here, when the true worshipers
will worship the Father in spirit and truth, for the
Father seeks such as these to worship him. 24God
is spirit, and those who worship him must worship in spirit and truth." 25The woman said to
him, "I know that Messiah is coming" (who is
called Christ). "When he comes, he will proclaim
all things to us." 26Jesus said to her, "I am he,[e] the
one who is speaking to you."

27 Just then his disciples came. They were
astonished that he was speaking with a woman,
but no one said, "What do you want?" or, "Why
are you speaking with her?" 28Then the woman
left her water jar and went back to the city. She
said to the people, 29"Come and see a man who

John 4:1-30

Despite much moralizing commentary about the Samaritan woman's past sexual life, compounded by the supposedly shameful associations of her ethnicity, it is noteworthy that she never responds to Jesus with any expression of guilt or shame; rather the Galilean Jew and the Samaritan engage in what seems a contest of dueling patriotisms. She is at last drawn to his message because he proclaims a coming reign that will not be limited to either Jerusalem or Samaria.

— *NE*

[a] Gk *set a seal to* [b] Other ancient authorities read *the Lord* [c] Other ancient authorities lack this sentence
[d] The Greek word for *you* here and in verses 21 and 22 is plural [e] Gk *I am*

told me everything I have ever done! He cannot
be the Messiah,[a] can he?" 30 They left the city and
were on their way to him.

31 Meanwhile the disciples were urging him,
"Rabbi, eat something." 32 But he said to them,
"I have food to eat that you do not know about."
33 So the disciples said to one another, "Surely no
one has brought him something to eat?" 34 Jesus
said to them, "My food is to do the will of him
who sent me and to complete his work. 35 Do you
not say, 'Four months more, then comes the harvest'? But I tell you, look around you, and see how
the fields are ripe for harvesting. 36 The reaper is
already receiving[b] wages and is gathering fruit for
eternal life, so that sower and reaper may rejoice
together. 37 For here the saying holds true, 'One
sows and another reaps.' 38 I sent you to reap that
for which you did not labor. Others have labored,
and you have entered into their labor."

39 Many Samaritans from that city believed in
him because of the woman's testimony, "He told
me everything I have ever done." 40 So when the
Samaritans came to him, they asked him to stay
with them; and he stayed there two days. 41 And
many more believed because of his word. 42 They
said to the woman, "It is no longer because of
what you said that we believe, for we have heard
for ourselves, and we know that this is truly the
Savior of the world."

43 When the two days were over, he went
from that place to Galilee 44 (for Jesus himself
had testified that a prophet has no honor in the
prophet's own country). 45 When he came to
Galilee, the Galileans welcomed him, since they
had seen all that he had done in Jerusalem at the
festival; for they too had gone to the festival.

46 Then he came again to Cana in Galilee
where he had changed the water into wine. Now
there was a royal official whose son lay ill in Capernaum. 47 When he heard that Jesus had come
from Judea to Galilee, he went and begged him
to come down and heal his son, for he was at the
point of death. 48 Then Jesus said to him, "Unless
you[c] see signs and wonders you will not believe."
49 The official said to him, "Sir, come down before
my little boy dies." 50 Jesus said to him, "Go; your
son will live." The man believed the word that
Jesus spoke to him and started on his way. 51 As he
was going down, his slaves met him and told him
that his child was alive. 52 So he asked them the
hour when he began to recover, and they said to
him, "Yesterday at one in the afternoon the fever
left him." 53 The father realized that this was the
hour when Jesus had said to him, "Your son will
live." So he himself believed, along with his whole
household. 54 Now this was the second sign that
Jesus did after coming from Judea to Galilee.

5 After this there was a festival of the Jews, and
Jesus went up to Jerusalem.

2 Now in Jerusalem by the Sheep Gate there
is a pool, called in Hebrew[d] Beth-zatha,[e] which
has five porticoes. 3 In these lay many invalids—
blind, lame, and paralyzed.[f] 5 One man was there
who had been ill for thirty-eight years. 6 When
Jesus saw him lying there and knew that he had
been there a long time, he said to him, "Do you
want to be made well?" 7 The sick man answered
him, "Sir, I have no one to put me into the pool
when the water is stirred up; and while I am making my way, someone else steps down ahead of
me." 8 Jesus said to him, "Stand up, take your mat
and walk." 9 At once the man was made well, and
he took up his mat and began to walk.

Now that day was a sabbath. 10 So the Jews said
to the man who had been cured, "It is the sabbath; it is not lawful for you to carry your mat."
11 But he answered them, "The man who made
me well said to me, 'Take up your mat and walk.'"
12 They asked him, "Who is the man who said to
you, 'Take it up and walk'?" 13 Now the man who
had been healed did not know who it was, for

[a] Or *the Christ* [b] Or [35]*... the fields are already ripe for harvesting.* [36]*The reaper is receiving* [c] Both instances of the Greek word for *you* in this verse are plural [d] That is, *Aramaic* [e] Other ancient authorities read *Bethesda*, others *Bethsaida*
[f] Other ancient authorities add, wholly or in part, *waiting for the stirring of the water;* [4]*for an angel of the Lord went down at certain seasons into the pool, and stirred up the water; whoever stepped in first after the stirring of the water was made well from whatever disease that person had.*

Jesus had disappeared in[a] the crowd that was there. 14 Later Jesus found him in the temple and said to him, "See, you have been made well! Do not sin any more, so that nothing worse happens to you." 15 The man went away and told the Jews that it was Jesus who had made him well. 16 Therefore the Jews started persecuting Jesus, because he was doing such things on the sabbath. 17 But Jesus answered them, "My Father is still working, and I also am working." 18 For this reason the Jews were seeking all the more to kill him, because he was not only breaking the sabbath, but was also calling God his own Father, thereby making himself equal to God.

19 Jesus said to them, "Very truly, I tell you, the Son can do nothing on his own, but only what he sees the Father doing; for whatever the Father[b] does, the Son does likewise. 20 The Father loves the Son and shows him all that he himself is doing; and he will show him greater works than these, so that you will be astonished. 21 Indeed, just as the Father raises the dead and gives them life, so also the Son gives life to whomever he wishes. 22 The Father judges no one but has given all judgment to the Son, 23 so that all may honor the Son just as they honor the Father. Anyone who does not honor the Son does not honor the Father who sent him. 24 Very truly, I tell you, anyone who hears my word and believes him who sent me has eternal life, and does not come under judgment, but has passed from death to life.

25 "Very truly, I tell you, the hour is coming, and is now here, when the dead will hear the voice of the Son of God, and those who hear will live. 26 For just as the Father has life in himself, so he has granted the Son also to have life in himself; 27 and he has given him authority to execute judgment, because he is the Son of Man. 28 Do not be astonished at this; for the hour is coming when all who are in their graves will hear his voice 29 and will come out—those who have done good, to the resurrection of life, and those who have done evil, to the resurrection of condemnation.

30 "I can do nothing on my own. As I hear, I judge; and my judgment is just, because I seek to do not my own will but the will of him who sent me.

31 "If I testify about myself, my testimony is not true. 32 There is another who testifies on my behalf, and I know that his testimony to me is true. 33 You sent messengers to John, and he testified to the truth. 34 Not that I accept such human testimony, but I say these things so that you may be saved. 35 He was a burning and shining lamp, and you were willing to rejoice for a while in his light. 36 But I have a testimony greater than John's. The works that the Father has given me to complete, the very works that I am doing, testify on my behalf that the Father has sent me. 37 And the Father who sent me has himself testified on my behalf. You have never heard his voice or seen his form, 38 and you do not have his word abiding in you, because you do not believe him whom he has sent.

39 "You search the scriptures because you think that in them you have eternal life; and it is they that testify on my behalf. 40 Yet you refuse to come to me to have life. 41 I do not accept glory from human beings. 42 But I know that you do not have the love of God in[c] you. 43 I have come in my Father's name, and you do not accept me; if another comes in his own name, you will accept him. 44 How can you believe when you accept glory from one another and do not seek the glory that comes from the one who alone is God? 45 Do not think that I will accuse you before the Father; your accuser is Moses, on whom you have set your hope. 46 If you believed Moses, you would believe me, for he wrote about me. 47 But if you do not believe what he wrote, how will you believe what I say?"

6 After this Jesus went to the other side of the Sea of Galilee, also called the Sea of Tiberias.[d] 2 A large crowd kept following him, because they saw the signs that he was doing for the sick. 3 Jesus went up the mountain and sat down there with his disciples. 4 Now the Passover, the festival of the Jews, was near. 5 When he looked up and saw a large crowd coming toward him, Jesus said

[a] Or *had left because of* [b] Gk *that one* [c] Or *among* [d] Gk *of Galilee of Tiberias*

to Philip, “Where are we to buy bread for these
people to eat?” 6 He said this to test him, for he
himself knew what he was going to do. 7 Philip
answered him, “Six months’ wages[a] would not
buy enough bread for each of them to get a little.” 8 One of his disciples, Andrew, Simon Peter’s
brother, said to him, 9 “There is a boy here who
has five barley loaves and two fish. But what are
they among so many people?” 10 Jesus said, “Make
the people sit down.” Now there was a great deal
of grass in the place; so they[b] sat down, about five
thousand in all. 11 Then Jesus took the loaves, and
when he had given thanks, he distributed them to
those who were seated; so also the fish, as much
as they wanted. 12 When they were satisfied, he
told his disciples, “Gather up the fragments left
over, so that nothing may be lost.” 13 So they gathered them up, and from the fragments of the five
barley loaves, left by those who had eaten, they
filled twelve baskets. 14 When the people saw the
sign that he had done, they began to say, “This
is indeed the prophet who is to come into the
world.”

15 When Jesus realized that they were about
to come and take him by force to make him king,
he withdrew again to the mountain by himself.

16 When evening came, his disciples went
down to the sea, 17 got into a boat, and started
across the sea to Capernaum. It was now dark,
and Jesus had not yet come to them. 18 The sea
became rough because a strong wind was blowing. 19 When they had rowed about three or four
miles,[c] they saw Jesus walking on the sea and coming near the boat, and they were terrified. 20 But
he said to them, “It is I;[d] do not be afraid.” 21 Then
they wanted to take him into the boat, and immediately the boat reached the land toward which
they were going.

22 The next day the crowd that had stayed on
the other side of the sea saw that there had been
only one boat there. They also saw that Jesus had
not got into the boat with his disciples, but that
his disciples had gone away alone. 23 Then some
boats from Tiberias came near the place where
they had eaten the bread after the Lord had given
thanks.[e] 24 So when the crowd saw that neither
Jesus nor his disciples were there, they themselves got into the boats and went to Capernaum
looking for Jesus.

25 When they found him on the other side of
the sea, they said to him, “Rabbi, when did you
come here?” 26 Jesus answered them, “Very truly,
I tell you, you are looking for me, not because
you saw signs, but because you ate your fill of the
loaves. 27 Do not work for the food that perishes,
but for the food that endures for eternal life,
which the Son of Man will give you. For it is on
him that God the Father has set his seal.” 28 Then
they said to him, “What must we do to perform
the works of God?” 29 Jesus answered them, “This
is the work of God, that you believe in him whom
he has sent.” 30 So they said to him, “What sign are
you going to give us then, so that we may see it
and believe you? What work are you performing?
31 Our ancestors ate the manna in the wilderness;
as it is written, ‘He gave them bread from heaven
to eat.’ ” 32 Then Jesus said to them, “Very truly, I
tell you, it was not Moses who gave you the bread
from heaven, but it is my Father who gives you
the true bread from heaven. 33 For the bread of
God is that which[f] comes down from heaven and
gives life to the world.” 34 They said to him, “Sir,
give us this bread always.”

35 Jesus said to them, “I am the bread of life.
Whoever comes to me will never be hungry, and
whoever believes in me will never be thirsty. 36 But
I said to you that you have seen me and yet do
not believe. 37 Everything that the Father gives me
will come to me, and anyone who comes to me
I will never drive away; 38 for I have come down
from heaven, not to do my own will, but the will
of him who sent me. 39 And this is the will of him
who sent me, that I should lose nothing of all that
he has given me, but raise it up on the last day.
40 This is indeed the will of my Father, that all who
see the Son and believe in him may have eternal
life; and I will raise them up on the last day.”

41 Then the Jews began to complain about

[a] Gk *Two hundred denarii*; the denarius was the usual day’s wage for a laborer [b] Gk *the men* [c] Gk *about twenty-five or thirty stadia* [d] Gk *I am* [e] Other ancient authorities lack *after the Lord had given thanks* [f] Or *he who*

him because he said, "I am the bread that came down from heaven." 42 They were saying, "Is not this Jesus, the son of Joseph, whose father and mother we know? How can he now say, 'I have come down from heaven'?" 43 Jesus answered them, "Do not complain among yourselves. 44 No one can come to me unless drawn by the Father who sent me; and I will raise that person up on the last day. 45 It is written in the prophets, 'And they shall all be taught by God.' Everyone who has heard and learned from the Father comes to me. 46 Not that anyone has seen the Father except the one who is from God; he has seen the Father. 47 Very truly, I tell you, whoever believes has eternal life. 48 I am the bread of life. 49 Your ancestors ate the manna in the wilderness, and they died. 50 This is the bread that comes down from heaven, so that one may eat of it and not die. 51 I am the living bread that came down from heaven. Whoever eats of this bread will live forever; and the bread that I will give for the life of the world is my flesh."

52 The Jews then disputed among themselves, saying, "How can this man give us his flesh to eat?" 53 So Jesus said to them, "Very truly, I tell you, unless you eat the flesh of the Son of Man and drink his blood, you have no life in you. 54 Those who eat my flesh and drink my blood have eternal life, and I will raise them up on the last day; 55 for my flesh is true food and my blood is true drink. 56 Those who eat my flesh and drink my blood abide in me, and I in them. 57 Just as the living Father sent me, and I live because of the Father, so whoever eats me will live because of me. 58 This is the bread that came down from heaven, not like that which your ancestors ate, and they died. But the one who eats this bread will live forever." 59 He said these things while he was teaching in the synagogue at Capernaum.

60 When many of his disciples heard it, they said, "This teaching is difficult; who can accept it?" 61 But Jesus, being aware that his disciples were complaining about it, said to them, "Does this offend you? 62 Then what if you were to see the Son of Man ascending to where he was before? 63 It is the spirit that gives life; the flesh is useless. The words that I have spoken to you are spirit and life. 64 But among you there are some who do not believe." For Jesus knew from the first who were the ones that did not believe, and who was the one that would betray him. 65 And he said, "For this reason I have told you that no one can come to me unless it is granted by the Father."

66 Because of this many of his disciples turned back and no longer went about with him. 67 So Jesus asked the twelve, "Do you also wish to go away?" 68 Simon Peter answered him, "Lord, to whom can we go? You have the words of eternal life. 69 We have come to believe and know that you are the Holy One of God."[a] 70 Jesus answered them, "Did I not choose you, the twelve? Yet one of you is a devil." 71 He was speaking of Judas son of Simon Iscariot,[b] for he, though one of the twelve, was going to betray him.

7 After this Jesus went about in Galilee. He did not wish[c] to go about in Judea because the Jews were looking for an opportunity to kill him. 2 Now the Jewish festival of Booths[d] was near. 3 So his brothers said to him, "Leave here and go to Judea so that your disciples also may see the works you are doing; 4 for no one who wants[e] to be widely known acts in secret. If you do these things, show yourself to the world." 5 (For not even his brothers believed in him.) 6 Jesus said to them, "My time has not yet come, but your time is always here. 7 The world cannot hate you, but it hates me because I testify against it that its works are evil. 8 Go to the festival yourselves. I am not[f] going to this festival, for my time has not yet fully come." 9 After saying this, he remained in Galilee.

10 But after his brothers had gone to the festival, then he also went, not publicly but as it were[g] in secret. 11 The Jews were looking for him at the

[a] Other ancient authorities read *the Christ, the Son of the living God* [b] Other ancient authorities read *Judas Iscariot son of Simon;* others, *Judas son of Simon from Karyot* (Kerioth) [c] Other ancient authorities read *was not at liberty* [d] Or *Tabernacles* [e] Other ancient authorities read *wants it* [f] Other ancient authorities add *yet* [g] Other ancient authorities lack *as it were*

festival and saying, "Where is he?" 12And there
was considerable complaining about him among
the crowds. While some were saying, "He is a
good man," others were saying, "No, he is deceiving the crowd." 13Yet no one would speak openly
about him for fear of the Jews.

14 About the middle of the festival Jesus went
up into the temple and began to teach. 15The
Jews were astonished at it, saying, "How does
this man have such learning,[a] when he has never
been taught?" 16Then Jesus answered them, "My
teaching is not mine but his who sent me. 17Any-
one who resolves to do the will of God will know
whether the teaching is from God or whether I
am speaking on my own. 18Those who speak on
their own seek their own glory; but the one who
seeks the glory of him who sent him is true, and
there is nothing false in him.

19 "Did not Moses give you the law? Yet
none of you keeps the law. Why are you looking for an opportunity to kill me?" 20The crowd
answered, "You have a demon! Who is trying to
kill you?" 21Jesus answered them, "I performed
one work, and all of you are astonished. 22Moses
gave you circumcision (it is, of course, not from
Moses, but from the patriarchs), and you circumcise a man on the sabbath. 23If a man receives circumcision on the sabbath in order that the law of
Moses may not be broken, are you angry with me
because I healed a man's whole body on the sabbath? 24Do not judge by appearances, but judge
with right judgment."

25 Now some of the people of Jerusalem
were saying, "Is not this the man whom they are
trying to kill? 26And here he is, speaking openly,
but they say nothing to him! Can it be that the
authorities really know that this is the Messiah?[b]
27Yet we know where this man is from; but when
the Messiah[b] comes, no one will know where he
is from." 28Then Jesus cried out as he was teaching in the temple, "You know me, and you know
where I am from. I have not come on my own.
But the one who sent me is true, and you do not
know him. 29I know him, because I am from him,
and he sent me." 30Then they tried to arrest him,
but no one laid hands on him, because his hour
had not yet come. 31Yet many in the crowd believed in him and were saying, "When the Messiah[b] comes, will he do more signs than this man
has done?"[c]

32 The Pharisees heard the crowd muttering
such things about him, and the chief priests and
Pharisees sent temple police to arrest him. 33Jesus
then said, "I will be with you a little while longer,
and then I am going to him who sent me. 34You
will search for me, but you will not find me; and
where I am, you cannot come." 35The Jews said to
one another, "Where does this man intend to go
that we will not find him? Does he intend to go to
the Dispersion among the Greeks and teach the
Greeks? 36What does he mean by saying, 'You
will search for me and you will not find me' and
'Where I am, you cannot come'?"

37 On the last day of the festival, the great
day, while Jesus was standing there, he cried out,
"Let anyone who is thirsty come to me, 38and let
the one who believes in me drink. As[d] the scripture has said, 'Out of the believer's heart[e] shall
flow rivers of living water.'" 39Now he said this
about the Spirit, which believers in him were to
receive; for as yet there was no Spirit,[f] because
Jesus was not yet glorified.

40 When they heard these words, some
in the crowd said, "This is really the prophet."
41Others said, "This is the Messiah."[b] But some
asked, "Surely the Messiah[b] does not come from
Galilee, does he? 42Has not the scripture said that
the Messiah[b] is descended from David and comes
from Bethlehem, the village where David lived?"
43So there was a division in the crowd because of
him. 44Some of them wanted to arrest him, but
no one laid hands on him.

45 Then the temple police went back to the
chief priests and Pharisees, who asked them,
"Why did you not arrest him?" 46The police answered, "Never has anyone spoken like this!"

[a] Or *this man know his letters* [b] Or *the Christ* [c] Other ancient authorities read *is doing*
[d] Or *come to me and drink.* [38]*The one who believes in me, as* [e] Gk *out of his belly*
[f] Other ancient authorities read *for as yet the Spirit* (others, *Holy Spirit*) *had not been given*

 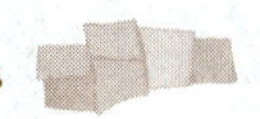

47 Then the Pharisees replied, "Surely you have not been deceived too, have you? 48 Has any one of the authorities or of the Pharisees believed in him? 49 But this crowd, which does not know the law—they are accursed." 50 Nicodemus, who had gone to Jesus[a] before, and who was one of them, asked, 51 "Our law does not judge people without first giving them a hearing to find out what they are doing, does it?" 52 They replied, "Surely you are not also from Galilee, are you? Search and you will see that no prophet is to arise from Galilee."

John 7:52-53

Jesus comes from the "wrong side of the tracks." Nazareth is so insignificant that the Hebrew Bible never mentions it. In Jesus' time, people of privilege looked down on Galileans as uncouth. Thus Nathaniel asks, "Can anything good come out of Nazareth?" (1:46). It is as if today we were to ask if anything good can come out of the *barrio*. Jesus came from what in his time was considered an impure and mixed neighborhood; he experienced the cultural bias of being from the margins of society. Today's inhabitants of ghettos and *barrios* encounter in this gospel a God who understands their social location—because God too came from the wrong, unsafe 'hood.

— *MDLT*

8 ⟦53 Then each of them went home, 1 while Jesus went to the Mount of Olives. 2 Early in the morning he came again to the temple. All the people came to him and he sat down and began to teach them. 3 The scribes and the Pharisees brought a woman who had been caught in adultery; and making her stand before all of them, 4 they said to him, "Teacher, this woman was caught in the very act of committing adultery. 5 Now in the law Moses commanded us to stone such women. Now what do you say?" 6 They said this to test him, so that they might have some charge to bring against him. Jesus bent down and wrote with his finger on the ground. 7 When they kept on questioning him, he straightened up and said to them, "Let anyone among you who is without sin be the first to throw a stone at her." 8 And once again he bent down and wrote on the ground.[b] 9 When they heard it, they went away, one by one, beginning with the elders; and Jesus was left alone with the woman standing before him. 10 Jesus straightened up and said to her, "Woman, where are they? Has no one condemned you?" 11 She said, "No one, sir."[c] And Jesus said, "Neither do I condemn you. Go your way, and from now on do not sin again."⟧[d]

12 Again Jesus spoke to them, saying, "I am the light of the world. Whoever follows me will never walk in darkness but will have the light of life." 13 Then the Pharisees said to him, "You are testifying on your own behalf; your testimony is not valid." 14 Jesus answered, "Even if I testify on my own behalf, my testimony is valid because I know where I have come from and where I am going, but you do not know where I come from or where I am going. 15 You judge by human standards;[e] I judge no one. 16 Yet even if I do judge, my judgment is valid; for it is not I alone who judge, but I and the Father[f] who sent me. 17 In your law it is written that the testimony of two witnesses is valid. 18 I testify on my own behalf, and the Father who sent me testifies on my behalf." 19 Then they said to him, "Where is your Father?" Jesus answered, "You know neither me nor my Father. If you knew me, you would know my Father also." 20 He spoke these words while he was teaching in the treasury of the temple, but no one arrested him, because his hour had not yet come.

21 Again he said to them, "I am going away, and you will search for me, but you will die in your sin. Where I am going, you cannot come." 22 Then the Jews said, "Is he going to kill himself? Is that what he means by saying, 'Where I am going, you cannot come'?" 23 He said to them, "You are from

[a] Gk *him* [b] Other ancient authorities add *the sins of each of them* [c] Or *Lord* [d] The most ancient authorities lack 7.53–8.11; other authorities add the passage here or after 7.36 or after 21.25 or after Luke 21.38, with variations of text; some mark the passage as doubtful. [e] Gk *according to the flesh* [f] Other ancient authorities read *he*

below, I am from above; you are of this world, I
am not of this world. 24I told you that you would
die in your sins, for you will die in your sins unless you believe that I am he."[a] 25They said to him,
"Who are you?" Jesus said to them, "Why do I
speak to you at all?[b] 26I have much to say about
you and much to condemn; but the one who sent
me is true, and I declare to the world what I have
heard from him." 27They did not understand that
he was speaking to them about the Father. 28So
Jesus said, "When you have lifted up the Son of
Man, then you will realize that I am he,[a] and that
I do nothing on my own, but I speak these things
as the Father instructed me. 29And the one who
sent me is with me; he has not left me alone, for
I always do what is pleasing to him." 30As he was
saying these things, many believed in him.

31 Then Jesus said to the Jews who had believed in him, "If you continue in my word, you
are truly my disciples; 32and you will know the
truth, and the truth will make you free." 33They
answered him, "We are descendants of Abraham
and have never been slaves to anyone. What do
you mean by saying, 'You will be made free'?"

34 Jesus answered them, "Very truly, I tell
you, everyone who commits sin is a slave to sin.
35The slave does not have a permanent place in
the household; the son has a place there forever.
36So if the Son makes you free, you will be free indeed. 37I know that you are descendants of Abraham; yet you look for an opportunity to kill me,
because there is no place in you for my word. 38I
declare what I have seen in the Father's presence;
as for you, you should do what you have heard
from the Father."[c]

39 They answered him, "Abraham is our father." Jesus said to them, "If you were Abraham's
children, you would be doing[d] what Abraham
did, 40but now you are trying to kill me, a man
who has told you the truth that I heard from
God. This is not what Abraham did. 41You are indeed doing what your father does." They said to
him, "We are not illegitimate children; we have
one father, God himself." 42Jesus said to them, "If
God were your Father, you would love me, for
I came from God and now I am here. I did not
come on my own, but he sent me. 43Why do you
not understand what I say? It is because you cannot accept my word. 44You are from your father
the devil, and you choose to do your father's desires. He was a murderer from the beginning and
does not stand in the truth, because there is no

John 8:36

These are probably the most revolutionary words found in Scripture. From those held in slavery in the past, to those who today work for slave wages, the promise of the gospel is and always has been *liberation*: Christ comes to make all free. When social structures benefit those in power and enslave the mass of the earth's people, they prevent the gospel from being fulfilled. Even those who call themselves Christians, if they prevent others from living to the full potential to which God has called them, are opposing the liberation that Christ promised.

— MDLT

John 8:39-44

One of the most troubling aspects of the Fourth Gospel is the harshly negative representation of "the Jews" (in Greek, *Ioudaioi*). Jesus often speaks—and the author narrates—as if Jesus himself were not a *Ioudaios.* Scholars increasingly doubt that John means to refer to either an ethnic or a religious identity, which is what we normally mean by "Jew." Rather, they propose that John spoke of *Ioudaioi* meaning a religio-political *class* who had ruled in Judah since their return from Babylonian exile; these *Ioudaioi* looked down with contempt on others (whom *we* would call Jews), who would have included the circle of Jesus and most of his disciples.

— NE

[a] Gk *I am* [b] Or *What I have told you from the beginning* [c] Other ancient authorities read *you do what you have heard from your father* [d] Other ancient authorities read *If you are Abraham's children, then do*

truth in him. When he lies, he speaks according
to his own nature, for he is a liar and the father
of lies. 45But because I tell the truth, you do not
believe me. 46Which of you convicts me of sin?
If I tell the truth, why do you not believe me?
47Whoever is from God hears the words of God.
The reason you do not hear them is that you are
not from God."

48 The Jews answered him, "Are we not right
in saying that you are a Samaritan and have a demon?" 49Jesus answered, "I do not have a demon;
but I honor my Father, and you dishonor me.
50Yet I do not seek my own glory; there is one
who seeks it and he is the judge. 51Very truly, I
tell you, whoever keeps my word will never see
death." 52The Jews said to him, "Now we know
that you have a demon. Abraham died, and so
did the prophets; yet you say, 'Whoever keeps
my word will never taste death.' 53Are you greater
than our father Abraham, who died? The prophets also died. Who do you claim to be?" 54Jesus
answered, "If I glorify myself, my glory is nothing. It is my Father who glorifies me, he of whom
you say, 'He is our God,' 55though you do not
know him. But I know him; if I would say that I
do not know him, I would be a liar like you. But I
do know him and I keep his word. 56Your ancestor Abraham rejoiced that he would see my day;
he saw it and was glad." 57Then the Jews said to
him, "You are not yet fifty years old, and have
you seen Abraham?"[a] 58Jesus said to them, "Very
truly, I tell you, before Abraham was, I am." 59So
they picked up stones to throw at him, but Jesus
hid himself and went out of the temple.

9 As he walked along, he saw a man blind from
birth. 2His disciples asked him, "Rabbi, who
sinned, this man or his parents, that he was born
blind?" 3Jesus answered, "Neither this man nor
his parents sinned; he was born blind so that
God's works might be revealed in him. 4We[b] must
work the works of him who sent me[c] while it is
day; night is coming when no one can work. 5As
long as I am in the world, I am the light of the
world." 6When he had said this, he spat on the
ground and made mud with the saliva and spread
the mud on the man's eyes, 7saying to him, "Go,
wash in the pool of Siloam" (which means Sent).
Then he went and washed and came back able
to see. 8The neighbors and those who had seen
him before as a beggar began to ask, "Is this not
the man who used to sit and beg?" 9Some were
saying, "It is he." Others were saying, "No, but it
is someone like him." He kept saying, "I am the
man." 10But they kept asking him, "Then how
were your eyes opened?" 11He answered, "The
man called Jesus made mud, spread it on my eyes,
and said to me, 'Go to Siloam and wash.' Then I
went and washed and received my sight." 12They
said to him, "Where is he?" He said, "I do not
know."

13 They brought to the Pharisees the man
who had formerly been blind. 14Now it was a sabbath day when Jesus made the mud and opened
his eyes. 15Then the Pharisees also began to ask
him how he had received his sight. He said to
them, "He put mud on my eyes. Then I washed,
and now I see." 16Some of the Pharisees said, "This
man is not from God, for he does not observe the
sabbath." But others said, "How can a man who
is a sinner perform such signs?" And they were
divided. 17So they said again to the blind man,
"What do you say about him? It was your eyes he
opened." He said, "He is a prophet."

18 The Jews did not believe that he had been
blind and had received his sight until they called
the parents of the man who had received his sight
19and asked them, "Is this your son, who you say
was born blind? How then does he now see?"
20His parents answered, "We know that this is
our son, and that he was born blind; 21but we do
not know how it is that now he sees, nor do we
know who opened his eyes. Ask him; he is of age.
He will speak for himself." 22His parents said this
because they were afraid of the Jews; for the Jews
had already agreed that anyone who confessed
Jesus[d] to be the Messiah[e] would be put out of the
synagogue. 23Therefore his parents said, "He is of
age; ask him."

[a] Other ancient authorities read *has Abraham seen you?* [b] Other ancient authorities read *I* [c] Other ancient authorities read *us* [d] Gk *him* [e] Or *the Christ*

24 So for the second time they called the
man who had been blind, and they said to him,
"Give glory to God! We know that this man is a
sinner." 25 He answered, "I do not know whether
he is a sinner. One thing I do know, that though I
was blind, now I see." 26 They said to him, "What
did he do to you? How did he open your eyes?"
27 He answered them, "I have told you already,
and you would not listen. Why do you want to
hear it again? Do you also want to become his disciples?" 28 Then they reviled him, saying, "You are
his disciple, but we are disciples of Moses. 29 We
know that God has spoken to Moses, but as for
this man, we do not know where he comes from."
30 The man answered, "Here is an astonishing
thing! You do not know where he comes from,
and yet he opened my eyes. 31 We know that God
does not listen to sinners, but he does listen to
one who worships him and obeys his will. 32 Never
since the world began has it been heard that anyone opened the eyes of a person born blind. 33 If
this man were not from God, he could do nothing." 34 They answered him, "You were born entirely in sins, and are you trying to teach us?" And
they drove him out.

35 Jesus heard that they had driven him out,
and when he found him, he said, "Do you believe
in the Son of Man?"[a] 36 He answered, "And who
is he, sir?[b] Tell me, so that I may believe in him."
37 Jesus said to him, "You have seen him, and the
one speaking with you is he." 38 He said, "Lord,[b]
I believe." And he worshiped him. 39 Jesus said, "I
came into this world for judgment so that those
who do not see may see, and those who do see
may become blind." 40 Some of the Pharisees near
him heard this and said to him, "Surely we are not
blind, are we?" 41 Jesus said to them, "If you were
blind, you would not have sin. But now that you
say, 'We see,' your sin remains.

10 "Very truly, I tell you, anyone who does
not enter the sheepfold by the gate but
climbs in by another way is a thief and a bandit.
2 The one who enters by the gate is the shepherd
of the sheep. 3 The gatekeeper opens the gate for
him, and the sheep hear his voice. He calls his
own sheep by name and leads them out. 4 When
he has brought out all his own, he goes ahead
of them, and the sheep follow him because they
know his voice. 5 They will not follow a stranger,
but they will run from him because they do not
know the voice of strangers." 6 Jesus used this figure of speech with them, but they did not understand what he was saying to them.

7 So again Jesus said to them, "Very truly,
I tell you, I am the gate for the sheep. 8 All who
came before me are thieves and bandits; but the
sheep did not listen to them. 9 I am the gate. Whoever enters by me will be saved, and will come in
and go out and find pasture. 10 The thief comes
only to steal and kill and destroy. I came that they
may have life, and have it abundantly.

11 "I am the good shepherd. The good shepherd lays down his life for the sheep. 12 The hired
hand, who is not the shepherd and does not own
the sheep, sees the wolf coming and leaves the
sheep and runs away—and the wolf snatches
them and scatters them. 13 The hired hand runs
away because a hired hand does not care for the
sheep. 14 I am the good shepherd. I know my own
and my own know me, 15 just as the Father knows
me and I know the Father. And I lay down my life
for the sheep. 16 I have other sheep that do not belong to this fold. I must bring them also, and they
will listen to my voice. So there will be one flock,
one shepherd. 17 For this reason the Father loves
me, because I lay down my life in order to take
it up again. 18 No one takes[c] it from me, but I lay
it down of my own accord. I have power to lay it
down, and I have power to take it up again. I have
received this command from my Father."

19 Again the Jews were divided because of
these words. 20 Many of them were saying, "He
has a demon and is out of his mind. Why listen
to him?" 21 Others were saying, "These are not
the words of one who has a demon. Can a demon
open the eyes of the blind?"

22 At that time the festival of the Dedication took place in Jerusalem. It was winter, 23 and

[a] Other ancient authorities read *the Son of God*
[b] *Sir* and *Lord* translate the same Greek word
[c] Other ancient authorities read *has taken*

Jesus was walking in the temple, in the portico
of Solomon. 24So the Jews gathered around him
and said to him, "How long will you keep us in
suspense? If you are the Messiah,[a] tell us plainly."
25Jesus answered, "I have told you, and you do
not believe. The works that I do in my Father's
name testify to me; 26but you do not believe, because you do not belong to my sheep. 27My sheep
hear my voice. I know them, and they follow me.
28I give them eternal life, and they will never perish. No one will snatch them out of my hand.
29What my Father has given me is greater than all
else, and no one can snatch it out of the Father's
hand.[b] 30The Father and I are one."

31 The Jews took up stones again to stone him.
32Jesus replied, "I have shown you many good
works from the Father. For which of these are you
going to stone me?" 33The Jews answered, "It is not
for a good work that we are going to stone you, but
for blasphemy, because you, though only a human
being, are making yourself God." 34Jesus answered,
"Is it not written in your law,[c] 'I said, you are gods'?
35If those to whom the word of God came were
called 'gods'—and the scripture cannot be annulled— 36can you say that the one whom the Father has sanctified and sent into the world is
blaspheming because I said, 'I am God's Son'? 37If
I am not doing the works of my Father, then do not
believe me. 38But if I do them, even though you do
not believe me, believe the works, so that you may
know and understand[d] that the Father is in me and
I am in the Father." 39Then they tried to arrest him
again, but he escaped from their hands.

40 He went away again across the Jordan to
the place where John had been baptizing earlier,
and he remained there. 41Many came to him, and
they were saying, "John performed no sign, but
everything that John said about this man was
true." 42And many believed in him there.

11 Now a certain man was ill, Lazarus of
Bethany, the village of Mary and her sister Martha. 2Mary was the one who anointed
the Lord with perfume and wiped his feet with
her hair; her brother Lazarus was ill. 3So the sisters sent a message to Jesus,[e] "Lord, he whom
you love is ill." 4But when Jesus heard it, he said,
"This illness does not lead to death; rather it is
for God's glory, so that the Son of God may be
glorified through it." 5Accordingly, though Jesus
loved Martha and her sister and Lazarus, 6after
having heard that Lazarus[f] was ill, he stayed two
days longer in the place where he was.

7 Then after this he said to the disciples, "Let
us go to Judea again." 8The disciples said to him,
"Rabbi, the Jews were just now trying to stone
you, and are you going there again?" 9Jesus answered, "Are there not twelve hours of daylight?
Those who walk during the day do not stumble,
because they see the light of this world. 10But
those who walk at night stumble, because the
light is not in them." 11After saying this, he told
them, "Our friend Lazarus has fallen asleep, but
I am going there to awaken him." 12The disciples
said to him, "Lord, if he has fallen asleep, he will
be all right." 13Jesus, however, had been speaking about his death, but they thought that he was
referring merely to sleep. 14Then Jesus told them
plainly, "Lazarus is dead. 15For your sake I am
glad I was not there, so that you may believe. But
let us go to him." 16Thomas, who was called the
Twin,[g] said to his fellow disciples, "Let us also go,
that we may die with him."

17 When Jesus arrived, he found that Lazarus[f] had already been in the tomb four days.
18Now Bethany was near Jerusalem, some two
miles[h] away, 19and many of the Jews had come
to Martha and Mary to console them about their
brother. 20When Martha heard that Jesus was
coming, she went and met him, while Mary stayed
at home. 21Martha said to Jesus, "Lord, if you had
been here, my brother would not have died. 22But
even now I know that God will give you whatever you ask of him." 23Jesus said to her, "Your
brother will rise again." 24Martha said to him, "I
know that he will rise again in the resurrection
on the last day." 25Jesus said to her, "I am the

[a] Or *the Christ* [b] Other ancient authorities read *My Father who has given them to me is greater than all, and no one can snatch them out of the Father's hand* [c] Other ancient authorities read *in the law* [d] Other ancient authorities lack *and understand*; others read *and believe* [e] Gk *him* [f] Gk *he* [g] Gk *Didymus* [h] Gk *fifteen stadia*

resurrection and the life.[a] Those who believe in
me, even though they die, will live, 26 and everyone who lives and believes in me will never die.
Do you believe this?" 27 She said to him, "Yes,
Lord, I believe that you are the Messiah,[b] the Son
of God, the one coming into the world."

28 When she had said this, she went back
and called her sister Mary, and told her privately,
"The Teacher is here and is calling for you." 29 And
when she heard it, she got up quickly and went to
him. 30 Now Jesus had not yet come to the village,
but was still at the place where Martha had met
him. 31 The Jews who were with her in the house,
consoling her, saw Mary get up quickly and go
out. They followed her because they thought that
she was going to the tomb to weep there. 32 When
Mary came where Jesus was and saw him, she knelt
at his feet and said to him, "Lord, if you had been
here, my brother would not have died." 33 When
Jesus saw her weeping, and the Jews who came
with her also weeping, he was greatly disturbed in
spirit and deeply moved. 34 He said, "Where have
you laid him?" They said to him, "Lord, come and
see." 35 Jesus began to weep. 36 So the Jews said,
"See how he loved him!" 37 But some of them
said, "Could not he who opened the eyes of the
blind man have kept this man from dying?"

38 Then Jesus, again greatly disturbed, came
to the tomb. It was a cave, and a stone was lying
against it. 39 Jesus said, "Take away the stone." Martha, the sister of the dead man, said to him, "Lord,
already there is a stench because he has been dead
four days." 40 Jesus said to her, "Did I not tell you
that if you believed, you would see the glory of
God?" 41 So they took away the stone. And Jesus
looked upward and said, "Father, I thank you for
having heard me. 42 I knew that you always hear
me, but I have said this for the sake of the crowd
standing here, so that they may believe that you
sent me." 43 When he had said this, he cried with a
loud voice, "Lazarus, come out!" 44 The dead man
came out, his hands and feet bound with strips of
cloth, and his face wrapped in a cloth. Jesus said
to them, "Unbind him, and let him go."

45 Many of the Jews therefore, who had
come with Mary and had seen what Jesus did,
believed in him. 46 But some of them went to the
Pharisees and told them what he had done. 47 So
the chief priests and the Pharisees called a meeting of the council, and said, "What are we to do?
This man is performing many signs. 48 If we let
him go on like this, everyone will believe in him,
and the Romans will come and destroy both our
holy place[c] and our nation." 49 But one of them,
Caiaphas, who was high priest that year, said to
them, "You know nothing at all! 50 You do not
understand that it is better for you to have one
man die for the people than to have the whole nation destroyed." 51 He did not say this on his own,
but being high priest that year he prophesied that
Jesus was about to die for the nation, 52 and not
for the nation only, but to gather into one the
dispersed children of God. 53 So from that day on
they planned to put him to death.

54 Jesus therefore no longer walked about
openly among the Jews, but went from there to a
town called Ephraim in the region near the wilderness; and he remained there with the disciples.

55 Now the Passover of the Jews was near,
and many went up from the country to Jerusalem
before the Passover to purify themselves. 56 They
were looking for Jesus and were asking one another as they stood in the temple, "What do you
think? Surely he will not come to the festival, will
he?" 57 Now the chief priests and the Pharisees
had given orders that anyone who knew where
Jesus[d] was should let them know, so that they
might arrest him.

12 Six days before the Passover Jesus came
to Bethany, the home of Lazarus, whom
he had raised from the dead. 2 There they gave a
dinner for him. Martha served, and Lazarus was
one of those at the table with him. 3 Mary took
a pound of costly perfume made of pure nard,
anointed Jesus' feet, and wiped them[e] with her
hair. The house was filled with the fragrance of
the perfume. 4 But Judas Iscariot, one of his disciples (the one who was about to betray him), said,

[a] Other ancient authorities lack *and the life* [b] Or *the Christ* [c] Or *our temple*; Greek *our place* [d] Gk *he*
[e] Gk *his feet*

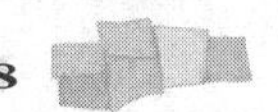

5“Why was this perfume not sold for three hundred denarii[a] and the money given to the poor?”
6(He said this not because he cared about the
poor, but because he was a thief; he kept the common purse and used to steal what was put into it.)
7Jesus said, “Leave her alone. She bought it[b] so
that she might keep it for the day of my burial.
8You always have the poor with you, but you do
not always have me.”

9 When the great crowd of the Jews learned
that he was there, they came not only because of
Jesus but also to see Lazarus, whom he had raised
from the dead. 10So the chief priests planned to
put Lazarus to death as well, 11since it was on account of him that many of the Jews were deserting and were believing in Jesus.

12 The next day the great crowd that had
come to the festival heard that Jesus was coming
to Jerusalem. 13So they took branches of palm
trees and went out to meet him, shouting,

“Hosanna!
Blessed is the one who comes in the name of
the Lord—
the King of Israel!”

14Jesus found a young donkey and sat on it; as it
is written:

15 “Do not be afraid, daughter of Zion.
Look, your king is coming,
sitting on a donkey’s colt!”

16His disciples did not understand these things
at first; but when Jesus was glorified, then they
remembered that these things had been written
of him and had been done to him. 17So the crowd
that had been with him when he called Lazarus
out of the tomb and raised him from the dead
continued to testify.[c] 18It was also because they
heard that he had performed this sign that the
crowd went to meet him. 19The Pharisees then
said to one another, “You see, you can do nothing. Look, the world has gone after him!”

20 Now among those who went up to worship at the festival were some Greeks. 21They
came to Philip, who was from Bethsaida in Galilee, and said to him, “Sir, we wish to see Jesus.”
22Philip went and told Andrew; then Andrew
and Philip went and told Jesus. 23Jesus answered
them, “The hour has come for the Son of Man to
be glorified. 24Very truly, I tell you, unless a grain
of wheat falls into the earth and dies, it remains
just a single grain; but if it dies, it bears much
fruit. 25Those who love their life lose it, and those
who hate their life in this world will keep it for
eternal life. 26Whoever serves me must follow
me, and where I am, there will my servant be also.
Whoever serves me, the Father will honor.

27 “Now my soul is troubled. And what
should I say—‘Father, save me from this hour’?
No, it is for this reason that I have come to this
hour. 28Father, glorify your name.” Then a voice
came from heaven, “I have glorified it, and I will
glorify it again.” 29The crowd standing there heard
it and said that it was thunder. Others said, “An
angel has spoken to him.” 30Jesus answered, “This
voice has come for your sake, not for mine. 31Now
is the judgment of this world; now the ruler
of this world will be driven out. 32And I, when I
am lifted up from the earth, will draw all people[d]
to myself.” 33He said this to indicate the kind of
death he was to die. 34The crowd answered him,
“We have heard from the law that the Messiah[e]
remains forever. How can you say that the Son of
Man must be lifted up? Who is this Son of Man?”
35Jesus said to them, “The light is with you for a
little longer. Walk while you have the light, so that
the darkness may not overtake you. If you walk
in the darkness, you do not know where you are
going. 36While you have the light, believe in the
light, so that you may become children of light.”

After Jesus had said this, he departed and hid
from them. 37Although he had performed so
many signs in their presence, they did not believe
in him. 38This was to fulfill the word spoken by
the prophet Isaiah:

“Lord, who has believed our message,
and to whom has the arm of the Lord been
revealed?”

[a] Three hundred denarii would be nearly a year’s wages for a laborer [b] Gk lacks *She bought it* [c] Other ancient authorities read *with him began to testify that he had called . . . from the dead* [d] Other ancient authorities read *all things* [e] Or *the Christ*

39 And so they could not believe, because Isaiah
also said,
40 "He has blinded their eyes
and hardened their heart,
so that they might not look with their eyes,
and understand with their heart and
turn—
and I would heal them."
41 Isaiah said this because[a] he saw his glory and
spoke about him. 42 Nevertheless many, even of
the authorities, believed in him. But because of
the Pharisees they did not confess it, for fear that
they would be put out of the synagogue; 43 for
they loved human glory more than the glory that
comes from God.
44 Then Jesus cried aloud: "Whoever believes
in me believes not in me but in him who sent me.
45 And whoever sees me sees him who sent me.
46 I have come as light into the world, so that everyone who believes in me should not remain in
the darkness. 47 I do not judge anyone who hears
my words and does not keep them, for I came not
to judge the world, but to save the world. 48 The
one who rejects me and does not receive my word
has a judge; on the last day the word that I have
spoken will serve as judge, 49 for I have not spoken
on my own, but the Father who sent me has himself given me a commandment about what to say
and what to speak. 50 And I know that his commandment is eternal life. What I speak, therefore,
I speak just as the Father has told me."

13 Now before the festival of the Passover,
Jesus knew that his hour had come to depart from this world and go to the Father. Having
loved his own who were in the world, he loved
them to the end. 2 The devil had already put it
into the heart of Judas son of Simon Iscariot to
betray him. And during supper 3 Jesus, knowing
that the Father had given all things into his hands,
and that he had come from God and was going to
God, 4 got up from the table,[b] took off his outer
robe, and tied a towel around himself. 5 Then he
poured water into a basin and began to wash the
disciples' feet and to wipe them with the towel
that was tied around him. 6 He came to Simon Peter, who said to him, "Lord, are you going to wash
my feet?" 7 Jesus answered, "You do not know
now what I am doing, but later you will understand." 8 Peter said to him, "You will never wash
my feet." Jesus answered, "Unless I wash you, you
have no share with me." 9 Simon Peter said to him,
"Lord, not my feet only but also my hands and my
head!" 10 Jesus said to him, "One who has bathed
does not need to wash, except for the feet,[c] but is
entirely clean. And you[d] are clean, though not all
of you." 11 For he knew who was to betray him; for
this reason he said, "Not all of you are clean."
12 After he had washed their feet, had put on
his robe, and had returned to the table, he said to
them, "Do you know what I have done to you?
13 You call me Teacher and Lord—and you are
right, for that is what I am. 14 So if I, your Lord
and Teacher, have washed your feet, you also
ought to wash one another's feet. 15 For I have set
you an example, that you also should do as I have
done to you. 16 Very truly, I tell you, servants[e] are
not greater than their master, nor are messengers
greater than the one who sent them. 17 If you
know these things, you are blessed if you do them.
18 I am not speaking of all of you; I know whom I
have chosen. But it is to fulfill the scripture, 'The
one who ate my bread[f] has lifted his heel against
me.' 19 I tell you this now, before it occurs, so that
when it does occur, you may believe that I am
he.[g] 20 Very truly, I tell you, whoever receives one
whom I send receives me; and whoever receives
me receives him who sent me."
21 After saying this Jesus was troubled in
spirit, and declared, "Very truly, I tell you, one
of you will betray me." 22 The disciples looked at
one another, uncertain of whom he was speaking. 23 One of his disciples—the one whom Jesus
loved—was reclining next to him; 24 Simon Peter
therefore motioned to him to ask Jesus of whom
he was speaking. 25 So while reclining next to
Jesus, he asked him, "Lord, who is it?" 26 Jesus answered, "It is the one to whom I give this piece

[a] Other ancient witnesses read *when* [b] Gk *from supper* [c] Other ancient authorities lack *except for the feet*
[d] The Greek word for *you* here is plural [e] Gk *slaves* [f] Other ancient authorities read *ate bread with me* [g] Gk *I am*

of bread when I have dipped it in the dish."[a] So
when he had dipped the piece of bread, he gave
it to Judas son of Simon Iscariot.[b] 27After he received the piece of bread,[c] Satan entered into
him. Jesus said to him, "Do quickly what you are
going to do." 28Now no one at the table knew why
he said this to him. 29Some thought that, because
Judas had the common purse, Jesus was telling
him, "Buy what we need for the festival"; or, that
he should give something to the poor. 30So, after
receiving the piece of bread, he immediately went
out. And it was night.

John 13:21-30

While all four gospels have Jesus predicting that he will be betrayed, only in John does the betrayer depart from the supper. Only in John is the betrayer the only person to receive food at the table, to his condemnation. Jesus' words over bread and wine are absent; instead, in this gospel it is in a very public scene, on the banks of the Sea of Tiberias, that Jesus speaks of giving his flesh to eat "for the life of the world" (6:51). The First Letter of John indicates a painful separation within the Johannine community. Perhaps in the wake of that separation, it was simply too painful to narrate a last supper where the betrayer received the body and blood of Christ alongside the faithful. The site for Jesus' self-giving is no longer only the community whose interior life has been breached, but is now the whole world.

— NE

31 When he had gone out, Jesus said, "Now
the Son of Man has been glorified, and God has
been glorified in him. 32If God has been glorified in him,[d] God will also glorify him in himself
and will glorify him at once. 33Little children, I
am with you only a little longer. You will look for
me; and as I said to the Jews so now I say to you,
'Where I am going, you cannot come.' 34I give
you a new commandment, that you love one another. Just as I have loved you, you also should
love one another. 35By this everyone will know
that you are my disciples, if you have love for one
another."

36 Simon Peter said to him, "Lord, where are
you going?" Jesus answered, "Where I am going,
you cannot follow me now; but you will follow
afterward." 37Peter said to him, "Lord, why can I
not follow you now? I will lay down my life for
you." 38Jesus answered, "Will you lay down your
life for me? Very truly, I tell you, before the cock
crows, you will have denied me three times.

14 "Do not let your hearts be troubled. Believe[e] in God, believe also in me. 2In my
Father's house there are many dwelling places.
If it were not so, would I have told you that I go
to prepare a place for you?[f] 3And if I go and prepare a place for you, I will come again and will
take you to myself, so that where I am, there you
may be also. 4And you know the way to the place
where I am going."[g] 5Thomas said to him, "Lord,
we do not know where you are going. How can
we know the way?" 6Jesus said to him, "I am the
way, and the truth, and the life. No one comes to
the Father except through me. 7If you know me,
you will know[h] my Father also. From now on you
do know him and have seen him."

8 Philip said to him, "Lord, show us the Father, and we will be satisfied." 9Jesus said to him,
"Have I been with you all this time, Philip, and
you still do not know me? Whoever has seen me
has seen the Father. How can you say, 'Show us
the Father'? 10Do you not believe that I am in the
Father and the Father is in me? The words that I
say to you I do not speak on my own; but the Father who dwells in me does his works. 11Believe
me that I am in the Father and the Father is in me;
but if you do not, then believe me because of the

[a] Gk *dipped it* [b] Other ancient authorities read *Judas Iscariot son of Simon*; others, *Judas son of Simon from Karyot* (Kerioth) [c] Gk *After the piece of bread* [d] Other ancient authorities lack *If God has been glorified in him*
[e] Or *You believe* [f] Or *If it were not so, I would have told you; for I go to prepare a place for you*
[g] Other ancient authorities read *Where I am going you know, and the way you know*
[h] Other ancient authorities read *If you had known me, you would have known*

works themselves. 12 Very truly, I tell you, the one
who believes in me will also do the works that I
do and, in fact, will do greater works than these,
because I am going to the Father. 13 I will do whatever you ask in my name, so that the Father may
be glorified in the Son. 14 If in my name you ask
me[a] for anything, I will do it.

15 "If you love me, you will keep[b] my commandments. 16 And I will ask the Father, and he
will give you another Advocate,[c] to be with you
forever. 17 This is the Spirit of truth, whom the
world cannot receive, because it neither sees him
nor knows him. You know him, because he abides
with you, and he will be in[d] you.

18 "I will not leave you orphaned; I am coming to you. 19 In a little while the world will no
longer see me, but you will see me; because I live,
you also will live. 20 On that day you will know
that I am in my Father, and you in me, and I in
you. 21 They who have my commandments and
keep them are those who love me; and those who
love me will be loved by my Father, and I will love
them and reveal myself to them." 22 Judas (not
Iscariot) said to him, "Lord, how is it that you
will reveal yourself to us, and not to the world?"
23 Jesus answered him, "Those who love me will
keep my word, and my Father will love them,
and we will come to them and make our home
with them. 24 Whoever does not love me does not
keep my words; and the word that you hear is not
mine, but is from the Father who sent me.

25 "I have said these things to you while I
am still with you. 26 But the Advocate,[c] the Holy
Spirit, whom the Father will send in my name,
will teach you everything, and remind you of all
that I have said to you. 27 Peace I leave with you;
my peace I give to you. I do not give to you as the
world gives. Do not let your hearts be troubled,
and do not let them be afraid. 28 You heard me say
to you, 'I am going away, and I am coming to you.'
If you loved me, you would rejoice that I am going
to the Father, because the Father is greater than I.
29 And now I have told you this before it occurs,
so that when it does occur, you may believe. 30 I
will no longer talk much with you, for the ruler of
this world is coming. He has no power over me;
31 but I do as the Father has commanded me, so
that the world may know that I love the Father.
Rise, let us be on our way.

15 "I am the true vine, and my Father is the
vinegrower. 2 He removes every branch in
me that bears no fruit. Every branch that bears
fruit he prunes[e] to make it bear more fruit. 3 You
have already been cleansed[e] by the word that I
have spoken to you. 4 Abide in me as I abide in
you. Just as the branch cannot bear fruit by itself
unless it abides in the vine, neither can you unless you abide in me. 5 I am the vine, you are the
branches. Those who abide in me and I in them
bear much fruit, because apart from me you can
do nothing. 6 Whoever does not abide in me
is thrown away like a branch and withers; such
branches are gathered, thrown into the fire, and
burned. 7 If you abide in me, and my words abide
in you, ask for whatever you wish, and it will be
done for you. 8 My Father is glorified by this, that
you bear much fruit and become[f] my disciples.
9 As the Father has loved me, so I have loved you;
abide in my love. 10 If you keep my commandments, you will abide in my love, just as I have
kept my Father's commandments and abide in
his love. 11 I have said these things to you so that
my joy may be in you, and that your joy may be
complete.

12 "This is my commandment, that you love
one another as I have loved you. 13 No one has
greater love than this, to lay down one's life for
one's friends. 14 You are my friends if you do what
I command you. 15 I do not call you servants[g] any
longer, because the servant[h] does not know what
the master is doing; but I have called you friends,
because I have made known to you everything
that I have heard from my Father. 16 You did not
choose me but I chose you. And I appointed you
to go and bear fruit, fruit that will last, so that the
Father will give you whatever you ask him in my
name. 17 I am giving you these commands so that
you may love one another.

[a] Other ancient authorities lack *me* [b] Other ancient authorities read *me, keep* [c] Or *Helper* [d] Or *among*
[e] The same Greek root refers to pruning and cleansing [f] Or *be* [g] Gk *slaves* [h] Gk *slave*

18 "If the world hates you, be aware that it
hated me before it hated you. 19 If you belonged to
the world,[a] the world would love you as its own.
Because you do not belong to the world, but I
have chosen you out of the world—therefore the
world hates you. 20 Remember the word that I
said to you, 'Servants[b] are not greater than their
master.' If they persecuted me, they will persecute
you; if they kept my word, they will keep yours
also. 21 But they will do all these things to you on
account of my name, because they do not know
him who sent me. 22 If I had not come and spoken
to them, they would not have sin; but now they
have no excuse for their sin. 23 Whoever hates me
hates my Father also. 24 If I had not done among
them the works that no one else did, they would
not have sin. But now they have seen and hated
both me and my Father. 25 It was to fulfill the
word that is written in their law, 'They hated me
without a cause.'

26 "When the Advocate[c] comes, whom I will
send to you from the Father, the Spirit of truth
who comes from the Father, he will testify on my
behalf. 27 You also are to testify because you have
been with me from the beginning.

16 "I have said these things to you to keep
you from stumbling. 2 They will put you
out of the synagogues. Indeed, an hour is coming
when those who kill you will think that by doing
so they are offering worship to God. 3 And they
will do this because they have not known the Father or me. 4 But I have said these things to you so
that when their hour comes you may remember
that I told you about them.

"I did not say these things to you from the beginning, because I was with you. 5 But now I am
going to him who sent me; yet none of you asks
me, 'Where are you going?' 6 But because I have
said these things to you, sorrow has filled your
hearts. 7 Nevertheless I tell you the truth: it is to
your advantage that I go away, for if I do not go
away, the Advocate[c] will not come to you; but if I
go, I will send him to you. 8 And when he comes,
he will prove the world wrong about[d] sin and
righteousness and judgment: 9 about sin, because
they do not believe in me; 10 about righteousness,
because I am going to the Father and you will see
me no longer; 11 about judgment, because the
ruler of this world has been condemned.

12 "I still have many things to say to you, but
you cannot bear them now. 13 When the Spirit of
truth comes, he will guide you into all the truth;
for he will not speak on his own, but will speak
whatever he hears, and he will declare to you the
things that are to come. 14 He will glorify me, because he will take what is mine and declare it to
you. 15 All that the Father has is mine. For this
reason I said that he will take what is mine and
declare it to you.

16 "A little while, and you will no longer see
me, and again a little while, and you will see me."
17 Then some of his disciples said to one another,
"What does he mean by saying to us, 'A little
while, and you will no longer see me, and again
a little while, and you will see me'; and 'Because
I am going to the Father'?" 18 They said, "What
does he mean by this 'a little while'? We do not
know what he is talking about." 19 Jesus knew that
they wanted to ask him, so he said to them, "Are
you discussing among yourselves what I meant
when I said, 'A little while, and you will no longer
see me, and again a little while, and you will see
me'? 20 Very truly, I tell you, you will weep and
mourn, but the world will rejoice; you will have
pain, but your pain will turn into joy. 21 When a
woman is in labor, she has pain, because her hour
has come. But when her child is born, she no longer remembers the anguish because of the joy of
having brought a human being into the world.
22 So you have pain now; but I will see you again,
and your hearts will rejoice, and no one will take
your joy from you. 23 On that day you will ask
nothing of me.[e] Very truly, I tell you, if you ask
anything of the Father in my name, he will give it
to you.[f] 24 Until now you have not asked for anything in my name. Ask and you will receive, so
that your joy may be complete.

25 "I have said these things to you in figures

[a] Gk *were of the world* [b] Gk *Slaves* [c] Or *Helper* [d] Or *convict the world of* [e] Or *will ask me no question*
[f] Other ancient authorities read *Father, he will give it to you in my name*

John 16:16-24

John's Gospel differs from the other Gospel narratives, and the Johannine Jesus is different as well. The focus of the believers' hope is no longer Jesus' eventual return on clouds of glory but Jesus' imminent return—and the giving of the Advocate, the Holy Spirit (15:26)—which will empower the believers for their continued life in the world. It is through their witness, as they do the work Jesus gives them, that he will be made known to the world.

— *NE*

of speech. The hour is coming when I will no longer speak to you in figures, but will tell you plainly
of the Father. 26On that day you will ask in my
name. I do not say to you that I will ask the Father
on your behalf; 27for the Father himself loves you,
because you have loved me and have believed that
I came from God.[a] 28I came from the Father and
have come into the world; again, I am leaving the
world and am going to the Father."

29 His disciples said, "Yes, now you are speaking plainly, not in any figure of speech! 30Now we
know that you know all things, and do not need to
have anyone question you; by this we believe that
you came from God." 31Jesus answered them, "Do
you now believe? 32The hour is coming, indeed it
has come, when you will be scattered, each one to
his home, and you will leave me alone. Yet I am
not alone because the Father is with me. 33I have
said this to you, so that in me you may have peace.
In the world you face persecution. But take courage; I have conquered the world!"

17 After Jesus had spoken these words, he
looked up to heaven and said, "Father,
the hour has come; glorify your Son so that the
Son may glorify you, 2since you have given him
authority over all people,[b] to give eternal life to
all whom you have given him. 3And this is eternal
life, that they may know you, the only true God,
and Jesus Christ whom you have sent. 4I glorified
you on earth by finishing the work that you gave
me to do. 5So now, Father, glorify me in your own
presence with the glory that I had in your presence before the world existed.

6 "I have made your name known to those
whom you gave me from the world. They were
yours, and you gave them to me, and they have
kept your word. 7Now they know that everything
you have given me is from you; 8for the words
that you gave to me I have given to them, and
they have received them and know in truth that I
came from you; and they have believed that you
sent me. 9I am asking on their behalf; I am not
asking on behalf of the world, but on behalf of
those whom you gave me, because they are yours.
10All mine are yours, and yours are mine; and I
have been glorified in them. 11And now I am no
longer in the world, but they are in the world,
and I am coming to you. Holy Father, protect
them in your name that you have given me, so
that they may be one, as we are one. 12While I
was with them, I protected them in your name
that[c] you have given me. I guarded them, and not
one of them was lost except the one destined to
be lost,[d] so that the scripture might be fulfilled.
13But now I am coming to you, and I speak these
things in the world so that they may have my joy
made complete in themselves.[e] 14I have given
them your word, and the world has hated them
because they do not belong to the world, just as
I do not belong to the world. 15I am not asking
you to take them out of the world, but I ask you
to protect them from the evil one.[f] 16They do not
belong to the world, just as I do not belong to the
world. 17Sanctify them in the truth; your word is
truth. 18As you have sent me into the world, so
I have sent them into the world. 19And for their
sakes I sanctify myself, so that they also may be
sanctified in truth.

20 "I ask not only on behalf of these, but also
on behalf of those who will believe in me through
their word, 21that they may all be one. As you,
Father, are in me and I am in you, may they also

[a] Other ancient authorities read *the Father* [b] Gk *flesh* [c] Other ancient authorities read *protected in your name those whom* [d] Gk *except the son of destruction* [e] Or *among themselves* [f] Or *from evil*

be in us,[a] so that the world may believe that you
have sent me. 22 The glory that you have given me
I have given them, so that they may be one, as we
are one, 23 I in them and you in me, that they may
become completely one, so that the world may
know that you have sent me and have loved them
even as you have loved me. 24 Father, I desire that
those also, whom you have given me, may be with
me where I am, to see my glory, which you have
given me because you loved me before the foundation of the world.
25 "Righteous Father, the world does not
know you, but I know you; and these know that
you have sent me. 26 I made your name known to
them, and I will make it known, so that the love
with which you have loved me may be in them,
and I in them."

18 After Jesus had spoken these words, he
went out with his disciples across the
Kidron valley to a place where there was a garden,
which he and his disciples entered. 2 Now Judas,
who betrayed him, also knew the place, because
Jesus often met there with his disciples. 3 So Judas
brought a detachment of soldiers together with
police from the chief priests and the Pharisees,
and they came there with lanterns and torches
and weapons. 4 Then Jesus, knowing all that was
to happen to him, came forward and asked them,
"Whom are you looking for?" 5 They answered,
"Jesus of Nazareth."[b] Jesus replied, "I am he."[c]
Judas, who betrayed him, was standing with
them. 6 When Jesus[d] said to them, "I am he,"[c] they
stepped back and fell to the ground. 7 Again he
asked them, "Whom are you looking for?" And
they said, "Jesus of Nazareth."[b] 8 Jesus answered,
"I told you that I am he.[c] So if you are looking for
me, let these men go." 9 This was to fulfill the word
that he had spoken, "I did not lose a single one of
those whom you gave me." 10 Then Simon Peter,
who had a sword, drew it, struck the high priest's
slave, and cut off his right ear. The slave's name
was Malchus. 11 Jesus said to Peter, "Put your
sword back into its sheath. Am I not to drink the
cup that the Father has given me?"

12 So the soldiers, their officer, and the Jewish police arrested Jesus and bound him. 13 First
they took him to Annas, who was the father-
in-law of Caiaphas, the high priest that year.
14 Caiaphas was the one who had advised the
Jews that it was better to have one person die for
the people.
15 Simon Peter and another disciple followed Jesus. Since that disciple was known to the
high priest, he went with Jesus into the courtyard
of the high priest, 16 but Peter was standing outside at the gate. So the other disciple, who was
known to the high priest, went out, spoke to the
woman who guarded the gate, and brought Peter
in. 17 The woman said to Peter, "You are not also
one of this man's disciples, are you?" He said,
"I am not." 18 Now the slaves and the police had
made a charcoal fire because it was cold, and they
were standing around it and warming themselves.
Peter also was standing with them and warming
himself.
19 Then the high priest questioned Jesus
about his disciples and about his teaching. 20 Jesus
answered, "I have spoken openly to the world; I
have always taught in synagogues and in the
temple, where all the Jews come together. I have
said nothing in secret. 21 Why do you ask me? Ask
those who heard what I said to them; they know
what I said." 22 When he had said this, one of the
police standing nearby struck Jesus on the face,
saying, "Is that how you answer the high priest?"
23 Jesus answered, "If I have spoken wrongly, testify to the wrong. But if I have spoken rightly, why
do you strike me?" 24 Then Annas sent him bound
to Caiaphas the high priest.
25 Now Simon Peter was standing and warming himself. They asked him, "You are not also
one of his disciples, are you?" He denied it and
said, "I am not." 26 One of the slaves of the high
priest, a relative of the man whose ear Peter had
cut off, asked, "Did I not see you in the garden
with him?" 27 Again Peter denied it, and at that
moment the cock crowed.
28 Then they took Jesus from Caiaphas to Pilate's headquarters.[e] It was early in the morning.

[a] Other ancient authorities read *be one in us* [b] Gk *the Nazorean* [c] Gk *I am* [d] Gk *he* [e] Gk *the praetorium*

They themselves did not enter the headquarters,[a] so as to avoid ritual defilement and to be able to eat the Passover. [29]So Pilate went out to them and said, "What accusation do you bring against this man?" [30]They answered, "If this man were not a criminal, we would not have handed him over to you." [31]Pilate said to them, "Take him yourselves and judge him according to your law." The Jews replied, "We are not permitted to put anyone to death." [32](This was to fulfill what Jesus had said when he indicated the kind of death he was to die.)

33 Then Pilate entered the headquarters[a] again, summoned Jesus, and asked him, "Are you the King of the Jews?" [34]Jesus answered, "Do you ask this on your own, or did others tell you about me?" [35]Pilate replied, "I am not a Jew, am I? Your own nation and the chief priests have handed you over to me. What have you done?" [36]Jesus answered, "My kingdom is not from this world. If my kingdom were from this world, my followers would be fighting to keep me from being handed over to the Jews. But as it is, my kingdom is not from here." [37]Pilate asked him, "So you are a king?" Jesus answered, "You say that I am a king. For this I was born, and for this I came into the world, to testify to the truth. Everyone who belongs to the truth listens to my voice." [38]Pilate asked him, "What is truth?"

After he had said this, he went out to the Jews again and told them, "I find no case against him. [39]But you have a custom that I release someone for you at the Passover. Do you want me to release for you the King of the Jews?" [40]They shouted in reply, "Not this man, but Barabbas!" Now Barabbas was a bandit.

19 Then Pilate took Jesus and had him flogged. [2]And the soldiers wove a crown of thorns and put it on his head, and they dressed him in a purple robe. [3]They kept coming up to him, saying, "Hail, King of the Jews!" and striking him on the face. [4]Pilate went out again and said to them, "Look, I am bringing him out to you to let you know that I find no case against him." [5]So Jesus came out, wearing the crown of thorns and the purple robe. Pilate said to them, "Here is the man!" [6]When the chief priests and the police saw him, they shouted, "Crucify him! Crucify him!" Pilate said to them, "Take him yourselves and crucify him; I find no case against him." [7]The Jews answered him, "We have a law, and according to that law he ought to die because he has claimed to be the Son of God."

8 Now when Pilate heard this, he was more afraid than ever. [9]He entered his headquarters[a] again and asked Jesus, "Where are you from?" But Jesus gave him no answer. [10]Pilate therefore said to him, "Do you refuse to speak to me? Do you not know that I have power to release you, and power to crucify you?" [11]Jesus answered him, "You would have no power over me unless it had been given you from above; therefore the one who handed me over to you is guilty of a greater sin." [12]From then on Pilate tried to release him,

[a] Gk *the praetorium*

John 18:33-38

Jesus' appearance before Pilate is loaded with irony, from the ritual scrupulosity of Jesus' enemies that masks their murderous and duplicitous intent (18:28-30) to their obsequious fawning that they "have no king but the emperor" (19:15). Jesus' dialogue with Pilate—absent in the other gospels—lays bare the nakedly pragmatic calculation of imperial power as Pilate asks his banal question, "What is truth?" It is clear that Jesus' followers do not constitute the sort of "kingdom" that will fight to save him from his fate (18:36), but it is also evident that his kingdom is not otherworldly: his followers "do not belong to the world," but Jesus has prepared them nonetheless to expect a long witness in the world (17:14-17).

—NE

but the Jews cried out, "If you release this man, you are no friend of the emperor. Everyone who claims to be a king sets himself against the emperor."

13 When Pilate heard these words, he brought Jesus outside and sat[a] on the judge's bench at a place called The Stone Pavement, or in Hebrew[b] Gabbatha. 14Now it was the day of Preparation for the Passover; and it was about noon. He said to the Jews, "Here is your King!" 15They cried out, "Away with him! Away with him! Crucify him!" Pilate asked them, "Shall I crucify your King?" The chief priests answered, "We have no king but the emperor." 16Then he handed him over to them to be crucified.

So they took Jesus; 17and carrying the cross by himself, he went out to what is called The Place of the Skull, which in Hebrew[b] is called Golgotha. 18There they crucified him, and with him two others, one on either side, with Jesus between them. 19Pilate also had an inscription written and put on the cross. It read, "Jesus of Nazareth,[c] the King of the Jews." 20Many of the Jews read this inscription, because the place where Jesus was crucified was near the city; and it was written in Hebrew,[b] in Latin, and in Greek. 21Then the chief priests of the Jews said to Pilate, "Do not write, 'The King of the Jews,' but, 'This man said, I am King of the Jews.'" 22Pilate answered, "What I have written I have written." 23When the soldiers had crucified Jesus, they took his clothes and divided them into four parts, one for each soldier. They also took his tunic; now the tunic was seamless, woven in one piece from the top. 24So they said to one another, "Let us not tear it, but cast lots for it to see who will get it." This was to fulfill what the scripture says,

"They divided my clothes among themselves,
and for my clothing they cast lots."

25And that is what the soldiers did.

Meanwhile, standing near the cross of Jesus were his mother, and his mother's sister, Mary the wife of Clopas, and Mary Magdalene. 26When Jesus saw his mother and the disciple whom he loved standing beside her, he said to his mother, "Woman, here is your son." 27Then he said to the disciple, "Here is your mother." And from that hour the disciple took her into his own home.

28 After this, when Jesus knew that all was now finished, he said (in order to fulfill the scripture), "I am thirsty." 29A jar full of sour wine was standing there. So they put a sponge full of the wine on a branch of hyssop and held it to his mouth. 30When Jesus had received the wine, he said, "It is finished." Then he bowed his head and gave up his spirit.

31 Since it was the day of Preparation, the Jews did not want the bodies left on the cross during the sabbath, especially because that sabbath was a day of great solemnity. So they asked Pilate to have the legs of the crucified men broken and the bodies removed. 32Then the soldiers came and broke the legs of the first and of the other who had been crucified with him. 33But when they came to Jesus and saw that he was already dead, they did not break his legs. 34Instead, one of the soldiers pierced his side with a spear, and at once blood and water came out. 35(He who saw this has testified so that you also may believe. His testimony is true, and he knows[d] that he tells the truth.) 36These things occurred so that the scripture might be fulfilled, "None of his bones shall be broken." 37And again another passage of scripture says, "They will look on the one whom they have pierced."

38 After these things, Joseph of Arimathea, who was a disciple of Jesus, though a secret one because of his fear of the Jews, asked Pilate to let him take away the body of Jesus. Pilate gave him permission; so he came and removed his body. 39Nicodemus, who had at first come to Jesus by night, also came, bringing a mixture of myrrh and aloes, weighing about a hundred pounds. 40They took the body of Jesus and wrapped it with the spices in linen cloths, according to the burial custom of the Jews. 41Now there was a garden in the place where he was crucified, and in the garden there was a new tomb in which no one had ever been laid. 42And so, because it was the Jewish day of Preparation, and the tomb was nearby, they laid Jesus there.

[a] Or *seated him* [b] That is, *Aramaic* [c] Gk *the Nazorean* [d] Or *there is one who knows*

20 Early on the first day of the week, while
it was still dark, Mary Magdalene came
to the tomb and saw that the stone had been
removed from the tomb. 2So she ran and went
to Simon Peter and the other disciple, the one
whom Jesus loved, and said to them, "They have
taken the Lord out of the tomb, and we do not
know where they have laid him." 3Then Peter and
the other disciple set out and went toward the
tomb. 4The two were running together, but the
other disciple outran Peter and reached the tomb
first. 5He bent down to look in and saw the linen
wrappings lying there, but he did not go in. 6Then
Simon Peter came, following him, and went into
the tomb. He saw the linen wrappings lying there,
7and the cloth that had been on Jesus' head, not
lying with the linen wrappings but rolled up in
a place by itself. 8Then the other disciple, who
reached the tomb first, also went in, and he saw
and believed; 9for as yet they did not understand
the scripture, that he must rise from the dead.
10Then the disciples returned to their homes.

11 But Mary stood weeping outside the
tomb. As she wept, she bent over to look[a] into
the tomb; 12and she saw two angels in white, sitting where the body of Jesus had been lying, one
at the head and the other at the feet. 13They said
to her, "Woman, why are you weeping?" She said
to them, "They have taken away my Lord, and I
do not know where they have laid him." 14When
she had said this, she turned around and saw Jesus
standing there, but she did not know that it was
Jesus. 15Jesus said to her, "Woman, why are you
weeping? Whom are you looking for?" Supposing
him to be the gardener, she said to him, "Sir, if you
have carried him away, tell me where you have laid
him, and I will take him away." 16Jesus said to her,
"Mary!" She turned and said to him in Hebrew,[b]
"Rabbouni!" (which means Teacher). 17Jesus said
to her, "Do not hold on to me, because I have not
yet ascended to the Father. But go to my brothers
and say to them, 'I am ascending to my Father and
your Father, to my God and your God.'" 18Mary
Magdalene went and announced to the disciples,
"I have seen the Lord"; and she told them that he
had said these things to her.

19 When it was evening on that day, the
first day of the week, and the doors of the house
where the disciples had met were locked for fear
of the Jews, Jesus came and stood among them
and said, "Peace be with you." 20After he said this,
he showed them his hands and his side. Then the
disciples rejoiced when they saw the Lord. 21Jesus
said to them again, "Peace be with you. As the Father has sent me, so I send you." 22When he had
said this, he breathed on them and said to them,
"Receive the Holy Spirit. 23If you forgive the sins
of any, they are forgiven them; if you retain the
sins of any, they are retained."

24 But Thomas (who was called the Twin[c]),
one of the twelve, was not with them when Jesus
came. 25So the other disciples told him, "We have
seen the Lord." But he said to them, "Unless I see
the mark of the nails in his hands, and put my finger in the mark of the nails and my hand in his
side, I will not believe."

26 A week later his disciples were again in the
house, and Thomas was with them. Although the
doors were shut, Jesus came and stood among
them and said, "Peace be with you." 27Then he
said to Thomas, "Put your finger here and see my
hands. Reach out your hand and put it in my side.
Do not doubt but believe." 28Thomas answered
him, "My Lord and my God!" 29Jesus said to him,
"Have you believed because you have seen me?
Blessed are those who have not seen and yet have
come to believe."

30 Now Jesus did many other signs in the
presence of his disciples, which are not written
in this book. 31But these are written so that you
may come to believe[d] that Jesus is the Messiah,[e]
the Son of God, and that through believing you
may have life in his name.

21 After these things Jesus showed himself
again to the disciples by the Sea of Tiberias; and he showed himself in this way. 2Gath-
ered there together were Simon Peter, Thomas

[a] Gk lacks *to look* [b] That is, *Aramaic* [c] Gk *Didymus* [d] Other ancient authorities read *may continue to believe*
[e] Or *the Christ*

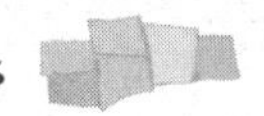

called the Twin,[a] Nathanael of Cana in Galilee,
the sons of Zebedee, and two others of his disciples. 3Simon Peter said to them, "I am going
fishing." They said to him, "We will go with you."
They went out and got into the boat, but that
night they caught nothing.

4 Just after daybreak, Jesus stood on the
beach; but the disciples did not know that it was
Jesus. 5Jesus said to them, "Children, you have no
fish, have you?" They answered him, "No." 6He
said to them, "Cast the net to the right side of
the boat, and you will find some." So they cast it,
and now they were not able to haul it in because
there were so many fish. 7That disciple whom
Jesus loved said to Peter, "It is the Lord!" When
Simon Peter heard that it was the Lord, he put on
some clothes, for he was naked, and jumped into
the sea. 8But the other disciples came in the boat,
dragging the net full of fish, for they were not far
from the land, only about a hundred yards[b] off.

9 When they had gone ashore, they saw a
charcoal fire there, with fish on it, and bread.
10Jesus said to them, "Bring some of the fish that
you have just caught." 11So Simon Peter went
aboard and hauled the net ashore, full of large
fish, a hundred fifty-three of them; and though
there were so many, the net was not torn. 12Jesus
said to them, "Come and have breakfast." Now
none of the disciples dared to ask him, "Who are
you?" because they knew it was the Lord. 13Jesus
came and took the bread and gave it to them, and
did the same with the fish. 14This was now the
third time that Jesus appeared to the disciples after he was raised from the dead.

15 When they had finished breakfast, Jesus
said to Simon Peter, "Simon son of John, do you
love me more than these?" He said to him, "Yes,
Lord; you know that I love you." Jesus said to him,
"Feed my lambs." 16A second time he said to him,
"Simon son of John, do you love me?" He said to
him, "Yes, Lord; you know that I love you." Jesus
said to him, "Tend my sheep." 17He said to him
the third time, "Simon son of John, do you love
me?" Peter felt hurt because he said to him the
third time, "Do you love me?" And he said to him,
"Lord, you know everything; you know that I love
you." Jesus said to him, "Feed my sheep. 18Very
truly, I tell you, when you were younger, you used
to fasten your own belt and to go wherever you
wished. But when you grow old, you will stretch
out your hands, and someone else will fasten a
belt around you and take you where you do not
wish to go." 19(He said this to indicate the kind of
death by which he would glorify God.) After this
he said to him, "Follow me."

20 Peter turned and saw the disciple whom
Jesus loved following them; he was the one who
had reclined next to Jesus at the supper and had
said, "Lord, who is it that is going to betray you?"
21When Peter saw him, he said to Jesus, "Lord,
what about him?" 22Jesus said to him, "If it is my
will that he remain until I come, what is that to
you? Follow me!" 23So the rumor spread in the
community[c] that this disciple would not die. Yet
Jesus did not say to him that he would not die,
but, "If it is my will that he remain until I come,
what is that to you?"[d]

24 This is the disciple who is testifying to
these things and has written them, and we know
that his testimony is true. 25But there are also
many other things that Jesus did; if every one of
them were written down, I suppose that the world
itself could not contain the books that would be
written.

[a] Gk *Didymus* [b] Gk *two hundred cubits* [c] Gk *among the brothers* [d] Other ancient authorities lack *what is that to you*

The Acts of the Apostles

INTRODUCTION

Rubén R. Dupertuis

THE ACTS OF THE APOSTLES STANDS ALONE in the New Testament in telling the story of the spread of Christianity in the first years after Jesus' death and resurrection; it is *the* history of the apostolic period. But Acts is much more and, in some ways, less than that. In part because it follows the conventions of history writing at the time, Acts is selective in what it presents. Peter and particularly Paul—not all of the apostles—dominate the narrative. The picture of Paul that emerges in Acts differs from what can be gathered from Paul's own letters. Acts is far from being a dry reporting of facts and events—it is a narrative that articulates the author's theological perspectives and likely addresses the needs of the author's community at a particular point in time.

Later Christian tradition attributed Acts to a companion of Paul on the basis of sections of the narrative that speak in the first person plural (see 16:10-17; 20:5-15; 21:1-18; and 27:1—28:16). Unfortunately, we know little for certain about the author, his audience, or the circumstances of composition. It is clear that the same person is responsible for Acts and the Gospel of Luke in the forms in which we have them, making Acts part two of a two-volume work. In addition to prologues that address the books to a certain Theophilus, Luke and Acts share similar language, literary styles, and themes. Scholars typically date Acts anywhere from 80 to 125 CE.

The narrative carries out Jesus' charge to the disciples (1:8), describing the spread of the movement from Jerusalem into Gentile areas such as Samaria (chs. 1–9), Asia Minor, Greece, and finally Rome (chs. 10–28). The geographical movement coincides with a shift from a Jewish to a predominantly Gentile mission. In Acts we see a redefining of who and what Israel is and what the boundaries of membership are. The steps toward the inclusion of Gentiles are presented as the result of God's guidance (chs. 10–11) and the fulfillment of prophecy (ch. 15). The largely negative depiction of the Jewish reception of the gospel paves the way for Paul to characterize the Jews as failing to listen and to turn primarily to Gentiles (28:25-28).

Cultural differences and issues of identity surface often. This whirlwind tour of the Mediterranean world plays on contemporary conventions and stereotypes. When narrating scenes that take place in

Jerusalem, the language of Acts strikingly echoes of the Septuagint (the Greek translation of the Old Testament), while in Paul's visit to Athens he looks and sounds remarkably philosophical, even reminiscent of Socrates. The author of Acts can also use and allude to narratives that were probably familiar to his audience. Paul's shipwreck strikingly resembles the shipwrecks of the hero of Homer's *Odyssey*, except that where Odysseus's men drown, Paul's shipmates are all saved. But I see the author of Acts doing something more complex: carving out a space for his community in the cultural landscape of the early Roman Empire. Acts is a kind of apology. The identity the author creates is necessarily made from available materials, but it is nonetheless something new. The true people of God now includes Gentiles for whom the traditional markers of covenant membership do not apply. Gentile Christians are no longer regarded as Greeks, Romans, or anything else in the traditional ways these cultures are understood, in part because they now worship the one true God of Israel. Acts rearranges, bends, and even breaks old cultural and religious boundaries as it lays down new ones.

This cultural complexity and the ambiguity that goes along with it draw me to the study of Acts. I grew up straddling a number of different cultures, and that has always made clear and simple statements of national identity difficult for me. My family is from Argentina, although only my father was born there, and I never lived there. I split most of my childhood between Montemorelos, Mexico, and Michigan, in the United States. From an early age I developed a fairly good sense of the different sets of cultural rules in different places. I identify with several cultures but don't feel I fully belong to any one of them. This is why I am drawn to Acts. I like its complexity and messiness. Even if I can't fully identify with the particular space that Acts tries to carve out for Christians in its time, I can identify with the complex cultural world it presents and with the need to constantly negotiate one's place within it.

1 In the first book, Theophilus, I wrote about all
that Jesus did and taught from the beginning
2 until the day when he was taken up to heaven,
after giving instructions through the Holy Spirit
to the apostles whom he had chosen. 3 After his
suffering he presented himself alive to them by
many convincing proofs, appearing to them during
forty days and speaking about the kingdom
of God. 4 While staying[a] with them, he ordered
them not to leave Jerusalem, but to wait there for
the promise of the Father. "This," he said, "is what
you have heard from me; 5 for John baptized with
water, but you will be baptized with[b] the Holy
Spirit not many days from now."
6 So when they had come together, they
asked him, "Lord, is this the time when you will
restore the kingdom to Israel?" 7 He replied, "It
is not for you to know the times or periods that
the Father has set by his own authority. 8 But you
will receive power when the Holy Spirit has come
upon you; and you will be my witnesses in Jerusalem,
in all Judea and Samaria, and to the ends of
the earth." 9 When he had said this, as they were
watching, he was lifted up, and a cloud took him
out of their sight. 10 While he was going and they
were gazing up toward heaven, suddenly two men
in white robes stood by them. 11 They said, "Men
of Galilee, why do you stand looking up toward
heaven? This Jesus, who has been taken up from
you into heaven, will come in the same way as
you saw him go into heaven."
12 Then they returned to Jerusalem from the

[a] Or *eating* [b] Or *by*

mount called Olivet, which is near Jerusalem, a
sabbath day's journey away. 13When they had
entered the city, they went to the room upstairs
where they were staying, Peter, and John, and
James, and Andrew, Philip and Thomas, Bartholomew and Matthew, James son of Alphaeus,
and Simon the Zealot, and Judas son of[a] James.
14All these were constantly devoting themselves
to prayer, together with certain women, including Mary the mother of Jesus, as well as his
brothers.

15 In those days Peter stood up among the believers[b] (together the crowd numbered about one
hundred twenty persons) and said, 16"Friends,[c]
the scripture had to be fulfilled, which the Holy
Spirit through David foretold concerning Judas, who became a guide for those who arrested
Jesus— 17for he was numbered among us and
was allotted his share in this ministry." 18(Now
this man acquired a field with the reward of his
wickedness; and falling headlong,[d] he burst open
in the middle and all his bowels gushed out.
19This became known to all the residents of Jerusalem, so that the field was called in their language Hakeldama, that is, Field of Blood.) 20"For
it is written in the book of Psalms,

'Let his homestead become desolate,
and let there be no one to live in it';

and

'Let another take his position of overseer.'

21So one of the men who have accompanied us
during all the time that the Lord Jesus went in
and out among us, 22beginning from the baptism
of John until the day when he was taken up from
us—one of these must become a witness with
us to his resurrection." 23So they proposed two,
Joseph called Barsabbas, who was also known
as Justus, and Matthias. 24Then they prayed and
said, "Lord, you know everyone's heart. Show
us which one of these two you have chosen 25to
take the place[e] in this ministry and apostleship
from which Judas turned aside to go to his own
place." 26And they cast lots for them, and the lot
fell on Matthias; and he was added to the eleven
apostles.

Acts 1:21-22

The disciples decide to replace Judas Iscariot, so they put together a job description. They will pick as Judas's replacement someone who has been with Jesus since his baptism by John and has witnessed the resurrection. But only a couple of the apostles themselves had been with Jesus since his baptism! People from communities of color know all too well what is going on with this apostolic job description: The apostles already know who they want to "hire," so they construct a set of employment requirements that excludes certain people—who in today's society are usually applicants of color.

— ***MDLT***

2 When the day of Pentecost had come, they
were all together in one place. 2And suddenly
from heaven there came a sound like the rush of a
violent wind, and it filled the entire house where
they were sitting. 3Divided tongues, as of fire, appeared among them, and a tongue rested on each
of them. 4All of them were filled with the Holy
Spirit and began to speak in other languages, as
the Spirit gave them ability.

5 Now there were devout Jews from every nation under heaven living in Jerusalem. 6And at this
sound the crowd gathered and was bewildered,
because each one heard them speaking in the native language of each. 7Amazed and astonished,
they asked, "Are not all these who are speaking
Galileans? 8And how is it that we hear, each of us,
in our own native language? 9Parthians, Medes,
Elamites, and residents of Mesopotamia, Judea
and Cappadocia, Pontus and Asia, 10Phrygia
and Pamphylia, Egypt and the parts of Libya belonging to Cyrene, and visitors from Rome, both
Jews and proselytes, 11Cretans and Arabs—in
our own languages we hear them speaking about
God's deeds of power." 12All were amazed and
perplexed, saying to one another, "What does
this mean?" 13But others sneered and said, "They
are filled with new wine."

[a] Or *the brother of* [b] Gk *brothers* [c] Gk *Men, brothers* [d] Or *swelling up* [e] Other ancient authorities read *the share*

Acts 2:4-11

Peter, full of the Holy Spirit, addressed the crowd that gathered outside the house where the disciples met. The miracle of Pentecost is not that this multinational crowd understood Peter's language but that each person heard the message in his or her own language. This first Christian assembly was a very multicultural gathering. Now look at your own church. Are the parishioners from every tribe, language, people, and nation? If not, why not? Is homogeneity caused by historical or present racism? If everyone at church looks like you—if the diversity of the body of Christ is not reflected in the body of believers—then the church fails to emulate what it is called to be, because it is either a product or a victim of racism.

— MDLT

14 But Peter, standing with the eleven, raised
his voice and addressed them, "Men of Judea
and all who live in Jerusalem, let this be known
to you, and listen to what I say. 15 Indeed, these
are not drunk, as you suppose, for it is only nine
o'clock in the morning. 16 No, this is what was
spoken through the prophet Joel:

17 'In the last days it will be, God declares,
that I will pour out my Spirit upon all flesh,
and your sons and your daughters shall prophesy,
and your young men shall see visions,
and your old men shall dream dreams.
18 Even upon my slaves, both men and women,
in those days I will pour out my Spirit;
and they shall prophesy.
19 And I will show portents in the heaven above
and signs on the earth below,
blood, and fire, and smoky mist.
20 The sun shall be turned to darkness
and the moon to blood,
before the coming of the Lord's great and glorious day.
21 Then everyone who calls on the name of the Lord shall be saved.'

22 "You that are Israelites,[a] listen to what I
have to say: Jesus of Nazareth,[b] a man attested to
you by God with deeds of power, wonders, and
signs that God did through him among you, as
you yourselves know— 23 this man, handed over
to you according to the definite plan and foreknowledge of God, you crucified and killed by
the hands of those outside the law. 24 But God
raised him up, having freed him from death,[c] because it was impossible for him to be held in its
power. 25 For David says concerning him,

'I saw the Lord always before me,
for he is at my right hand so that I will not be shaken;
26 therefore my heart was glad, and my tongue rejoiced;
moreover my flesh will live in hope.
27 For you will not abandon my soul to Hades,
or let your Holy One experience corruption.
28 You have made known to me the ways of life;
you will make me full of gladness with your presence.'

29 "Fellow Israelites,[d] I may say to you confidently of our ancestor David that he both died
and was buried, and his tomb is with us to this
day. 30 Since he was a prophet, he knew that God
had sworn with an oath to him that he would put
one of his descendants on his throne. 31 Foreseeing this, David[e] spoke of the resurrection of the
Messiah,[f] saying,

'He was not abandoned to Hades,
nor did his flesh experience corruption.'

32 This Jesus God raised up, and of that all of us are
witnesses. 33 Being therefore exalted at[g] the right
hand of God, and having received from the Father
the promise of the Holy Spirit, he has poured out
this that you both see and hear. 34 For David did
not ascend into the heavens, but he himself says,

'The Lord said to my Lord,
"Sit at my right hand,

[a] Gk *Men, Israelites* [b] Gk *the Nazorean* [c] Gk *the pains of death* [d] Gk *Men, brothers* [e] Gk *he* [f] Or *the Christ* [g] Or *by*

35 until I make your enemies your
footstool." '
36 Therefore let the entire house of Israel know
with certainty that God has made him both Lord
and Messiah,[a] this Jesus whom you crucified."
37 Now when they heard this, they were cut
to the heart and said to Peter and to the other
apostles, "Brothers,[b] what should we do?" 38 Peter
said to them, "Repent, and be baptized every one
of you in the name of Jesus Christ so that your
sins may be forgiven; and you will receive the gift
of the Holy Spirit. 39 For the promise is for you,
for your children, and for all who are far away,
everyone whom the Lord our God calls to him."
40 And he testified with many other arguments
and exhorted them, saying, "Save yourselves
from this corrupt generation." 41 So those who
welcomed his message were baptized, and that
day about three thousand persons were added.
42 They devoted themselves to the apostles' teaching and fellowship, to the breaking of bread and
the prayers.

43 Awe came upon everyone, because many
wonders and signs were being done by the apostles. 44 All who believed were together and had all
things in common; 45 they would sell their possessions and goods and distribute the proceeds[c]
to all, as any had need. 46 Day by day, as they spent
much time together in the temple, they broke
bread at home[d] and ate their food with glad and
generous[e] hearts, 47 praising God and having the
goodwill of all the people. And day by day the
Lord added to their number those who were being saved.

3 One day Peter and John were going up to the
temple at the hour of prayer, at three o'clock
in the afternoon. 2 And a man lame from birth
was being carried in. People would lay him daily
at the gate of the temple called the Beautiful Gate
so that he could ask for alms from those entering
the temple. 3 When he saw Peter and John about
to go into the temple, he asked them for alms.
4 Peter looked intently at him, as did John, and
said, "Look at us." 5 And he fixed his attention on
them, expecting to receive something from them.
6 But Peter said, "I have no silver or gold, but what
I have I give you; in the name of Jesus Christ of
Nazareth,[f] stand up and walk." 7 And he took him
by the right hand and raised him up; and immediately his feet and ankles were made strong.
8 Jumping up, he stood and began to walk, and he
entered the temple with them, walking and leaping and praising God. 9 All the people saw him
walking and praising God, 10 and they recognized
him as the one who used to sit and ask for alms at
the Beautiful Gate of the temple; and they were
filled with wonder and amazement at what had
happened to him.

11 While he clung to Peter and John, all the
people ran together to them in the portico called
Solomon's Portico, utterly astonished. 12 When
Peter saw it, he addressed the people, "You Israelites,[g] why do you wonder at this, or why do you
stare at us, as though by our own power or piety
we had made him walk? 13 The God of Abraham,
the God of Isaac, and the God of Jacob, the God
of our ancestors has glorified his servant[h] Jesus,
whom you handed over and rejected in the presence of Pilate, though he had decided to release
him. 14 But you rejected the Holy and Righteous
One and asked to have a murderer given to you,
15 and you killed the Author of life, whom God
raised from the dead. To this we are witnesses.
16 And by faith in his name, his name itself has
made this man strong, whom you see and know;
and the faith that is through Jesus[i] has given him
this perfect health in the presence of all of you.

17 "And now, friends,[j] I know that you acted
in ignorance, as did also your rulers. 18 In this
way God fulfilled what he had foretold through
all the prophets, that his Messiah[k] would suffer.
19 Repent therefore, and turn to God so that your
sins may be wiped out, 20 so that times of refreshing may come from the presence of the Lord,
and that he may send the Messiah[l] appointed for
you, that is, Jesus, 21 who must remain in heaven
until the time of universal restoration that God
announced long ago through his holy prophets.

[a] Or *Christ* [b] Gk *Men, brothers* [c] Gk *them* [d] Or *from house to house* [e] Or *sincere* [f] Gk *the Nazorean*
[g] Gk *Men, Israelites* [h] Or *child* [i] Gk *him* [j] Gk *brothers* [k] Or *his Christ* [l] Or *the Christ*

22 Moses said, 'The Lord your God will raise up
for you from your own people[a] a prophet like me.
You must listen to whatever he tells you. 23 And it
will be that everyone who does not listen to that
prophet will be utterly rooted out of the people.'
24 And all the prophets, as many as have spoken,
from Samuel and those after him, also predicted
these days. 25 You are the descendants of the
prophets and of the covenant that God gave to
your ancestors, saying to Abraham, 'And in your
descendants all the families of the earth shall be
blessed.' 26 When God raised up his servant,[b] he
sent him first to you, to bless you by turning each
of you from your wicked ways."

4 While Peter and John[c] were speaking to the
people, the priests, the captain of the temple,
and the Sadducees came to them, 2 much annoyed because they were teaching the people
and proclaiming that in Jesus there is the resurrection of the dead. 3 So they arrested them and
put them in custody until the next day, for it was
already evening. 4 But many of those who heard
the word believed; and they numbered about five
thousand.

5 The next day their rulers, elders, and scribes
assembled in Jerusalem, 6 with Annas the high
priest, Caiaphas, John,[d] and Alexander, and all
who were of the high-priestly family. 7 When they
had made the prisoners[e] stand in their midst, they
inquired, "By what power or by what name did
you do this?" 8 Then Peter, filled with the Holy
Spirit, said to them, "Rulers of the people and
elders, 9 if we are questioned today because of a
good deed done to someone who was sick and are
asked how this man has been healed, 10 let it be
known to all of you, and to all the people of Israel, that this man is standing before you in good
health by the name of Jesus Christ of Nazareth,[f]
whom you crucified, whom God raised from the
dead. 11 This Jesus[g] is

'the stone that was rejected by you, the
builders;
it has become the cornerstone.'[h]

12 There is salvation in no one else, for there is no
other name under heaven given among mortals
by which we must be saved."

13 Now when they saw the boldness of Peter
and John and realized that they were uneducated
and ordinary men, they were amazed and recognized them as companions of Jesus. 14 When they
saw the man who had been cured standing beside
them, they had nothing to say in opposition. 15 So
they ordered them to leave the council while they
discussed the matter with one another. 16 They
said, "What will we do with them? For it is obvious to all who live in Jerusalem that a notable sign
has been done through them; we cannot deny it.
17 But to keep it from spreading further among
the people, let us warn them to speak no more to
anyone in this name." 18 So they called them and
ordered them not to speak or teach at all in the
name of Jesus. 19 But Peter and John answered
them, "Whether it is right in God's sight to listen
to you rather than to God, you must judge; 20 for
we cannot keep from speaking about what we
have seen and heard." 21 After threatening them
again, they let them go, finding no way to punish them because of the people, for all of them
praised God for what had happened. 22 For the
man on whom this sign of healing had been performed was more than forty years old.

23 After they were released, they went to
their friends[i] and reported what the chief priests
and the elders had said to them. 24 When they
heard it, they raised their voices together to God
and said, "Sovereign Lord, who made the heaven
and the earth, the sea, and everything in them,
25 it is you who said by the Holy Spirit through
our ancestor David, your servant:[b]

'Why did the Gentiles rage,
and the peoples imagine vain things?
26 The kings of the earth took their stand,
and the rulers have gathered together
against the Lord and against his
Messiah.'[j]

27 For in this city, in fact, both Herod and Pontius Pilate, with the Gentiles and the peoples
of Israel, gathered together against your holy

[a] Gk *brothers* [b] Or *child* [c] Gk *While they* [d] Other ancient authorities read *Jonathan* [e] Gk *them*
[f] Gk *the Nazorean* [g] Gk *This* [h] Or *keystone* [i] Gk *their own* [j] Or *his Christ*

servant[a] Jesus, whom you anointed, 28to do whatever your hand and your plan had predestined to
take place. 29And now, Lord, look at their threats,
and grant to your servants[b] to speak your word
with all boldness, 30while you stretch out your
hand to heal, and signs and wonders are performed through the name of your holy servant[a]
Jesus." 31When they had prayed, the place in
which they were gathered together was shaken;
and they were all filled with the Holy Spirit and
spoke the word of God with boldness.

32 Now the whole group of those who believed were of one heart and soul, and no one
claimed private ownership of any possessions,
but everything they owned was held in common. 33With great power the apostles gave their
testimony to the resurrection of the Lord Jesus,
and great grace was upon them all. 34There was
not a needy person among them, for as many as
owned lands or houses sold them and brought
the proceeds of what was sold. 35They laid it at
the apostles' feet, and it was distributed to each
as any had need. 36There was a Levite, a native
of Cyprus, Joseph, to whom the apostles gave the
name Barnabas (which means "son of encouragement"). 37He sold a field that belonged to him,
then brought the money, and laid it at the apostles' feet.

5 But a man named Ananias, with the consent
of his wife Sapphira, sold a piece of property;
2with his wife's knowledge, he kept back some of
the proceeds, and brought only a part and laid
it at the apostles' feet. 3"Ananias," Peter asked,
"why has Satan filled your heart to lie to the Holy
Spirit and to keep back part of the proceeds of
the land? 4While it remained unsold, did it not
remain your own? And after it was sold, were not
the proceeds at your disposal? How is it that you
have contrived this deed in your heart? You did
not lie to us[c] but to God!" 5Now when Ananias
heard these words, he fell down and died. And
great fear seized all who heard of it. 6The young
men came and wrapped up his body,[d] then carried him out and buried him.

7 After an interval of about three hours his
wife came in, not knowing what had happened.
8Peter said to her, "Tell me whether you and your
husband sold the land for such and such a price."
And she said, "Yes, that was the price." 9Then Peter said to her, "How is it that you have agreed
together to put the Spirit of the Lord to the test?
Look, the feet of those who have buried your
husband are at the door, and they will carry you
out." 10Immediately she fell down at his feet and
died. When the young men came in they found
her dead, so they carried her out and buried her
beside her husband. 11And great fear seized the
whole church and all who heard of these things.

12 Now many signs and wonders were done
among the people through the apostles. And they
were all together in Solomon's Portico. 13None of
the rest dared to join them, but the people held
them in high esteem. 14Yet more than ever believers were added to the Lord, great numbers of both
men and women, 15so that they even carried out
the sick into the streets, and laid them on cots and
mats, in order that Peter's shadow might fall on
some of them as he came by. 16A great number of
people would also gather from the towns around
Jerusalem, bringing the sick and those tormented
by unclean spirits, and they were all cured.

17 Then the high priest took action; he and
all who were with him (that is, the sect of the Sadducees), being filled with jealousy, 18arrested the
apostles and put them in the public prison. 19But
during the night an angel of the Lord opened the
prison doors, brought them out, and said, 20"Go,
stand in the temple and tell the people the whole
message about this life." 21When they heard this,
they entered the temple at daybreak and went on
with their teaching.

When the high priest and those with him arrived, they called together the council and the
whole body of the elders of Israel, and sent to
the prison to have them brought. 22But when the
temple police went there, they did not find them
in the prison; so they returned and reported,
23"We found the prison securely locked and
the guards standing at the doors, but when we
opened them, we found no one inside." 24Now

[a] Or *child* [b] Gk *slaves* [c] Gk *to men* [d] Meaning of Gk uncertain

when the captain of the temple and the chief
priests heard these words, they were perplexed
about them, wondering what might be going on.
25 Then someone arrived and announced, "Look,
the men whom you put in prison are standing in
the temple and teaching the people!" 26 Then the
captain went with the temple police and brought
them, but without violence, for they were afraid
of being stoned by the people.

27 When they had brought them, they had
them stand before the council. The high priest
questioned them, 28 saying, "We gave you strict
orders not to teach in this name,[a] yet here you
have filled Jerusalem with your teaching and
you are determined to bring this man's blood on
us." 29 But Peter and the apostles answered, "We
must obey God rather than any human authority.[b] 30 The God of our ancestors raised up Jesus,
whom you had killed by hanging him on a tree.
31 God exalted him at his right hand as Leader
and Savior that he might give repentance to Israel
and forgiveness of sins. 32 And we are witnesses to
these things, and so is the Holy Spirit whom God
has given to those who obey him."

33 When they heard this, they were enraged
and wanted to kill them. 34 But a Pharisee in the
council named Gamaliel, a teacher of the law, respected by all the people, stood up and ordered
the men to be put outside for a short time. 35 Then
he said to them, "Fellow Israelites,[c] consider carefully what you propose to do to these men. 36 For
some time ago Theudas rose up, claiming to be
somebody, and a number of men, about four hundred, joined him; but he was killed, and all who
followed him were dispersed and disappeared.
37 After him Judas the Galilean rose up at the
time of the census and got people to follow him;
he also perished, and all who followed him were
scattered. 38 So in the present case, I tell you, keep
away from these men and let them alone; because
if this plan or this undertaking is of human origin,
it will fail; 39 but if it is of God, you will not be
able to overthrow them—in that case you may
even be found fighting against God!"

They were convinced by him, 40 and when they
had called in the apostles, they had them flogged.
Then they ordered them not to speak in the name
of Jesus, and let them go. 41 As they left the council, they rejoiced that they were considered worthy to suffer dishonor for the sake of the name.
42 And every day in the temple and at home[d] they
did not cease to teach and proclaim Jesus as the
Messiah.[e]

6 Now during those days, when the disciples
were increasing in number, the Hellenists
complained against the Hebrews because their
widows were being neglected in the daily distribution of food. 2 And the twelve called together the
whole community of the disciples and said, "It is
not right that we should neglect the word of God
in order to wait on tables.[f] 3 Therefore, friends,[g]
select from among yourselves seven men of good
standing, full of the Spirit and of wisdom, whom
we may appoint to this task, 4 while we, for our
part, will devote ourselves to prayer and to serving the word." 5 What they said pleased the whole

Acts 6:1-5; 7:2-53

The apostles found themselves distributing food to the needy, which took them away from the more important task of preaching. So they chose seven men to do what they considered the lesser job. What is interesting is that these seven men had Hellenistic, or Greek, names: that is, they were seen as mixed-race, not "pure" Jews. Interestingly, one of them, Stephen, who was called to distribute food, not preach, preaches the longest sermon recorded in Acts. Even though church structures were created to delineate who did the more intellectual work of preaching and who did the more manual work of distributing food, it is often from the church's marginalized spaces—and often in surprising ways—that God's word is proclaimed.

— MDLT

[a] Other ancient authorities read *Did we not give you strict orders not to teach in this name?* [b] Gk *than men*
[c] Gk *Men, Israelites* [d] Or *from house to house* [e] Or *the Christ* [f] Or *keep accounts* [g] Gk *brothers*

community, and they chose Stephen, a man full of faith and the Holy Spirit, together with Philip, Prochorus, Nicanor, Timon, Parmenas, and Nicolaus, a proselyte of Antioch. 6 They had these men stand before the apostles, who prayed and laid their hands on them.

7 The word of God continued to spread; the number of the disciples increased greatly in Jerusalem, and a great many of the priests became obedient to the faith.

8 Stephen, full of grace and power, did great wonders and signs among the people. 9 Then some of those who belonged to the synagogue of the Freedmen (as it was called), Cyrenians, Alexandrians, and others of those from Cilicia and Asia, stood up and argued with Stephen. 10 But they could not withstand the wisdom and the Spirit[a] with which he spoke. 11 Then they secretly instigated some men to say, "We have heard him speak blasphemous words against Moses and God." 12 They stirred up the people as well as the elders and the scribes; then they suddenly confronted him, seized him, and brought him before the council. 13 They set up false witnesses who said, "This man never stops saying things against this holy place and the law; 14 for we have heard him say that this Jesus of Nazareth[b] will destroy this place and will change the customs that Moses handed on to us." 15 And all who sat in the council looked intently at him, and they saw that his face was like the face of an angel.

7 Then the high priest asked him, "Are these things so?" 2 And Stephen replied:

"Brothers[c] and fathers, listen to me. The God of glory appeared to our ancestor Abraham when he was in Mesopotamia, before he lived in Haran, 3 and said to him, 'Leave your country and your relatives and go to the land that I will show you.' 4 Then he left the country of the Chaldeans and settled in Haran. After his father died, God had him move from there to this country in which you are now living. 5 He did not give him any of it as a heritage, not even a foot's length, but promised to give it to him as his possession and to his descendants after him, even though he had no child. 6 And God spoke in these terms, that his descendants would be resident aliens in a country belonging to others, who would enslave them and mistreat them during four hundred years. 7 'But I will judge the nation that they serve,' said God, 'and after that they shall come out and worship me in this place.' 8 Then he gave him the covenant of circumcision. And so Abraham[d] became the father of Isaac and circumcised him on the eighth day; and Isaac became the father of Jacob, and Jacob of the twelve patriarchs.

9 "The patriarchs, jealous of Joseph, sold him into Egypt; but God was with him, 10 and rescued him from all his afflictions, and enabled him to win favor and to show wisdom when he stood before Pharaoh, king of Egypt, who appointed him ruler over Egypt and over all his household. 11 Now there came a famine throughout Egypt and Canaan, and great suffering, and our ancestors could find no food. 12 But when Jacob heard that there was grain in Egypt, he sent our ancestors there on their first visit. 13 On the second visit Joseph made himself known to his brothers, and Joseph's family became known to Pharaoh. 14 Then Joseph sent and invited his father Jacob and all his relatives to come to him, seventy-five in all; 15 so Jacob went down to Egypt. He himself died there as well as our ancestors, 16 and their bodies[e] were brought back to Shechem and laid in the tomb that Abraham had bought for a sum of silver from the sons of Hamor in Shechem.

17 "But as the time drew near for the fulfillment of the promise that God had made to Abraham, our people in Egypt increased and multiplied 18 until another king who had not known Joseph ruled over Egypt. 19 He dealt craftily with our race and forced our ancestors to abandon their infants so that they would die. 20 At this time Moses was born, and he was beautiful before God. For three months he was brought up in his father's house; 21 and when he was abandoned, Pharaoh's daughter adopted him and brought him up as her own son. 22 So Moses was instructed in all the wisdom of the Egyptians and was powerful in his words and deeds.

[a] Or *spirit* [b] Gk *the Nazorean* [c] Gk *Men, brothers* [d] Gk *he* [e] Gk *they*

 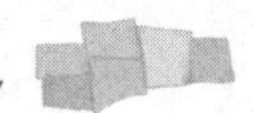

23 "When he was forty years old, it came
into his heart to visit his relatives, the Israelites.[a]
24When he saw one of them being wronged, he
defended the oppressed man and avenged him by
striking down the Egyptian. 25He supposed that
his kinsfolk would understand that God through
him was rescuing them, but they did not understand. 26The next day he came to some of them
as they were quarreling and tried to reconcile
them, saying, 'Men, you are brothers; why do
you wrong each other?' 27But the man who was
wronging his neighbor pushed Moses[b] aside, saying, 'Who made you a ruler and a judge over us?
28Do you want to kill me as you killed the Egyptian yesterday?' 29When he heard this, Moses fled
and became a resident alien in the land of Midian.
There he became the father of two sons.

30 "Now when forty years had passed, an angel appeared to him in the wilderness of Mount
Sinai, in the flame of a burning bush. 31When
Moses saw it, he was amazed at the sight; and as
he approached to look, there came the voice of
the Lord: 32'I am the God of your ancestors, the
God of Abraham, Isaac, and Jacob.' Moses began
to tremble and did not dare to look. 33Then the
Lord said to him, 'Take off the sandals from your
feet, for the place where you are standing is holy
ground. 34I have surely seen the mistreatment of
my people who are in Egypt and have heard their
groaning, and I have come down to rescue them.
Come now, I will send you to Egypt.'

35 "It was this Moses whom they rejected
when they said, 'Who made you a ruler and a
judge?' and whom God now sent as both ruler
and liberator through the angel who appeared to
him in the bush. 36He led them out, having performed wonders and signs in Egypt, at the Red
Sea, and in the wilderness for forty years. 37This
is the Moses who said to the Israelites, 'God will
raise up a prophet for you from your own people[c]
as he raised me up.' 38He is the one who was in
the congregation in the wilderness with the angel
who spoke to him at Mount Sinai, and with our
ancestors; and he received living oracles to give to
us. 39Our ancestors were unwilling to obey him;
instead, they pushed him aside, and in their hearts
they turned back to Egypt, 40saying to Aaron,
'Make gods for us who will lead the way for us;
as for this Moses who led us out from the land
of Egypt, we do not know what has happened to
him.' 41At that time they made a calf, offered a
sacrifice to the idol, and reveled in the works of
their hands. 42But God turned away from them
and handed them over to worship the host of
heaven, as it is written in the book of the prophets:

'Did you offer to me slain victims and
sacrifices
forty years in the wilderness, O house of
Israel?
43 No; you took along the tent of Moloch,
and the star of your god Rephan,
the images that you made to worship;
so I will remove you beyond Babylon.'

44 "Our ancestors had the tent of testimony
in the wilderness, as God[d] directed when he
spoke to Moses, ordering him to make it according to the pattern he had seen. 45Our ancestors in
turn brought it in with Joshua when they dispossessed the nations that God drove out before our
ancestors. And it was there until the time of David, 46who found favor with God and asked that
he might find a dwelling place for the house of
Jacob.[e] 47But it was Solomon who built a house
for him. 48Yet the Most High does not dwell in
houses made with human hands;[f] as the prophet
says,

49 'Heaven is my throne,
and the earth is my footstool.
What kind of house will you build for me,
says the Lord,
or what is the place of my rest?
50 Did not my hand make all these things?'

51 "You stiff-necked people, uncircumcised
in heart and ears, you are forever opposing the
Holy Spirit, just as your ancestors used to do.
52Which of the prophets did your ancestors not
persecute? They killed those who foretold the
coming of the Righteous One, and now you have

[a] Gk *his brothers, the sons of Israel* [b] Gk *him* [c] Gk *your brothers* [d] Gk *he* [e] Other ancient authorities read *for the God of Jacob* [f] Gk *with hands*

become his betrayers and murderers. 53 You are the ones that received the law as ordained by angels, and yet you have not kept it."

54 When they heard these things, they became enraged and ground their teeth at Stephen.[a] 55 But filled with the Holy Spirit, he gazed into heaven and saw the glory of God and Jesus standing at the right hand of God. 56 "Look," he said, "I see the heavens opened and the Son of Man standing at the right hand of God!" 57 But they covered their ears, and with a loud shout all rushed together against him. 58 Then they dragged him out of the city and began to stone him; and the witnesses laid their coats at the feet of a young man named Saul. 59 While they were stoning Stephen, he prayed, "Lord Jesus, receive my spirit." 60 Then he knelt down and cried out in a loud voice, "Lord, do not hold this sin against them." When he had said this, he died.[b]

8 1 And Saul approved of their killing him.

That day a severe persecution began against the church in Jerusalem, and all except the apostles were scattered throughout the countryside of Judea and Samaria. 2 Devout men buried Stephen and made loud lamentation over him. 3 But Saul was ravaging the church by entering house after house; dragging off both men and women, he committed them to prison.

4 Now those who were scattered went from place to place, proclaiming the word. 5 Philip went down to the city[c] of Samaria and proclaimed the Messiah[d] to them. 6 The crowds with one accord listened eagerly to what was said by Philip, hearing and seeing the signs that he did, 7 for unclean spirits, crying with loud shrieks, came out of many who were possessed; and many others who were paralyzed or lame were cured. 8 So there was great joy in that city.

9 Now a certain man named Simon had previously practiced magic in the city and amazed the people of Samaria, saying that he was someone great. 10 All of them, from the least to the greatest, listened to him eagerly, saying, "This man is the power of God that is called Great." 11 And they listened eagerly to him because for a long time he had amazed them with his magic. 12 But when they believed Philip, who was proclaiming the good news about the kingdom of God and the name of Jesus Christ, they were baptized, both men and women. 13 Even Simon himself believed. After being baptized, he stayed constantly with Philip and was amazed when he saw the signs and great miracles that took place.

14 Now when the apostles at Jerusalem heard that Samaria had accepted the word of God, they sent Peter and John to them. 15 The two went down and prayed for them that they might receive the Holy Spirit 16 (for as yet the Spirit had not come[e] upon any of them; they had only been baptized in the name of the Lord Jesus). 17 Then Peter and John[f] laid their hands on them, and they received the Holy Spirit. 18 Now when Simon saw that the Spirit was given through the laying on of the apostles' hands, he offered them money, 19 saying, "Give me also this power so that anyone on whom I lay my hands may receive the Holy Spirit." 20 But Peter said to him, "May your silver perish with you, because you thought you could obtain God's gift with money! 21 You have no part or share in this, for your heart is not right before God. 22 Repent therefore of this wickedness of yours, and pray to the Lord that, if possible, the intent of your heart may be forgiven you. 23 For I see that you are in the gall of bitterness and the chains of wickedness." 24 Simon answered, "Pray for me to the Lord, that nothing of what you[g] have said may happen to me."

25 Now after Peter and John[h] had testified and spoken the word of the Lord, they returned to Jerusalem, proclaiming the good news to many villages of the Samaritans.

26 Then an angel of the Lord said to Philip, "Get up and go toward the south[i] to the road that goes down from Jerusalem to Gaza." (This is a wilderness road.) 27 So he got up and went. Now there was an Ethiopian eunuch, a court official of the Candace, queen of the Ethiopians, in charge of her entire treasury. He had come to Jerusalem

[a] Gk *him* [b] Gk *fell asleep* [c] Other ancient authorities read *a city* [d] Or *the Christ* [e] Gk *fallen* [f] Gk *they*
[g] The Greek word for *you* and the verb *pray* are plural [h] Gk *after they* [i] Or *go at noon*

to worship 28 and was returning home; seated in
his chariot, he was reading the prophet Isaiah.
29 Then the Spirit said to Philip, "Go over to this
chariot and join it." 30 So Philip ran up to it and
heard him reading the prophet Isaiah. He asked,
"Do you understand what you are reading?" 31 He
replied, "How can I, unless someone guides me?"
And he invited Philip to get in and sit beside him.
32 Now the passage of the scripture that he was
reading was this:

"Like a sheep he was led to the slaughter,
and like a lamb silent before its shearer,
so he does not open his mouth.
33 In his humiliation justice was denied him.
Who can describe his generation?
For his life is taken away from the
earth."

34 The eunuch asked Philip, "About whom, may I
ask you, does the prophet say this, about himself
or about someone else?" 35 Then Philip began to
speak, and starting with this scripture, he proclaimed to him the good news about Jesus. 36 As
they were going along the road, they came to
some water; and the eunuch said, "Look, here is
water! What is to prevent me from being baptized?"[a] 38 He commanded the chariot to stop, and
both of them, Philip and the eunuch, went down
into the water, and Philip[b] baptized him. 39 When
they came up out of the water, the Spirit of the
Lord snatched Philip away; the eunuch saw him no
more, and went on his way rejoicing. 40 But Philip
found himself at Azotus, and as he was passing
through the region, he proclaimed the good news
to all the towns until he came to Caesarea.

9 Meanwhile Saul, still breathing threats and
murder against the disciples of the Lord, went
to the high priest 2 and asked him for letters to the
synagogues at Damascus, so that if he found any
who belonged to the Way, men or women, he
might bring them bound to Jerusalem. 3 Now as
he was going along and approaching Damascus,
suddenly a light from heaven flashed around him.
4 He fell to the ground and heard a voice saying to
him, "Saul, Saul, why do you persecute me?" 5 He
asked, "Who are you, Lord?" The reply came, "I
am Jesus, whom you are persecuting. 6 But get up
and enter the city, and you will be told what you
are to do." 7 The men who were traveling with him
stood speechless because they heard the voice
but saw no one. 8 Saul got up from the ground, and
though his eyes were open, he could see nothing;
so they led him by the hand and brought him into
Damascus. 9 For three days he was without sight,
and neither ate nor drank.

10 Now there was a disciple in Damascus
named Ananias. The Lord said to him in a vision,
"Ananias." He answered, "Here I am, Lord." 11 The
Lord said to him, "Get up and go to the street
called Straight, and at the house of Judas look for
a man of Tarsus named Saul. At this moment he
is praying, 12 and he has seen in a vision[c] a man
named Ananias come in and lay his hands on him
so that he might regain his sight." 13 But Ananias
answered, "Lord, I have heard from many about
this man, how much evil he has done to your
saints in Jerusalem; 14 and here he has authority
from the chief priests to bind all who invoke your
name." 15 But the Lord said to him, "Go, for he is
an instrument whom I have chosen to bring my
name before Gentiles and kings and before the
people of Israel; 16 I myself will show him how
much he must suffer for the sake of my name."

Acts 8:26-38

When we think of the gospel message moving beyond the Jews, we usually see the trajectory going toward the center of the empire. Many see the good news as a Eurocentric project that found its fulfillment within the empire. But the first non-Jewish convert to the gospel message was not a European but an *African*, an Ethiopian. Christ's message first goes to the Africans and *after* Africa it makes its way to Europe.

— MDLT

[a] Other ancient authorities add all or most of verse 37, *And Philip said, "If you believe with all your heart, you may." And he replied, "I believe that Jesus Christ is the Son of God."* [b] Gk *he* [c] Other ancient authorities lack *in a vision*

17 So Ananias went and entered the house. He laid his hands on Saul[a] and said, "Brother Saul, the Lord Jesus, who appeared to you on your way here, has sent me so that you may regain your sight and be filled with the Holy Spirit." 18 And immediately something like scales fell from his eyes, and his sight was restored. Then he got up and was baptized, 19 and after taking some food, he regained his strength.

For several days he was with the disciples in Damascus, 20 and immediately he began to proclaim Jesus in the synagogues, saying, "He is the Son of God." 21 All who heard him were amazed and said, "Is not this the man who made havoc in Jerusalem among those who invoked this name? And has he not come here for the purpose of bringing them bound before the chief priests?" 22 Saul became increasingly more powerful and confounded the Jews who lived in Damascus by proving that Jesus[b] was the Messiah.[c]

23 After some time had passed, the Jews plotted to kill him, 24 but their plot became known to Saul. They were watching the gates day and night so that they might kill him; 25 but his disciples took him by night and let him down through an opening in the wall,[d] lowering him in a basket.

26 When he had come to Jerusalem, he attempted to join the disciples; and they were all afraid of him, for they did not believe that he was a disciple. 27 But Barnabas took him, brought him to the apostles, and described for them how on the road he had seen the Lord, who had spoken to him, and how in Damascus he had spoken boldly in the name of Jesus. 28 So he went in and out among them in Jerusalem, speaking boldly in the name of the Lord. 29 He spoke and argued with the Hellenists; but they were attempting to kill him. 30 When the believers[e] learned of it, they brought him down to Caesarea and sent him off to Tarsus.

31 Meanwhile the church throughout Judea, Galilee, and Samaria had peace and was built up. Living in the fear of the Lord and in the comfort of the Holy Spirit, it increased in numbers.

32 Now as Peter went here and there among all the believers,[f] he came down also to the saints living in Lydda. 33 There he found a man named Aeneas, who had been bedridden for eight years, for he was paralyzed. 34 Peter said to him, "Aeneas, Jesus Christ heals you; get up and make your bed!" And immediately he got up. 35 And all the residents of Lydda and Sharon saw him and turned to the Lord.

36 Now in Joppa there was a disciple whose name was Tabitha, which in Greek is Dorcas.[g] She was devoted to good works and acts of charity. 37 At that time she became ill and died. When they had washed her, they laid her in a room upstairs. 38 Since Lydda was near Joppa, the disciples, who heard that Peter was there, sent two men to him with the request, "Please come to us without delay." 39 So Peter got up and went with them; and when he arrived, they took him to the room upstairs. All the widows stood beside him, weeping and showing tunics and other clothing that Dorcas had made while she was with them. 40 Peter put all of them outside, and then he knelt down and prayed. He turned to the body and said, "Tabitha, get up." Then she opened her eyes, and seeing Peter, she sat up. 41 He gave her his hand and helped her up. Then calling the saints and widows, he showed her to be alive. 42 This became known throughout Joppa, and many believed in the Lord. 43 Meanwhile he stayed in Joppa for some time with a certain Simon, a tanner.

10 In Caesarea there was a man named Cornelius, a centurion of the Italian Cohort, as it was called. 2 He was a devout man who feared God with all his household; he gave alms generously to the people and prayed constantly to God. 3 One afternoon at about three o'clock he had a vision in which he clearly saw an angel of God coming in and saying to him, "Cornelius." 4 He stared at him in terror and said, "What is it, Lord?" He answered, "Your prayers and your alms have ascended as a memorial before God. 5 Now send men to Joppa for a certain Simon who is called Peter; 6 he is lodging with Simon, a tanner, whose

[a] Gk *him* [b] Gk *that this* [c] Or *the Christ* [d] Gk *through the wall* [e] Gk *brothers* [f] Gk *all of them*
[g] The name Tabitha in Aramaic and the name Dorcas in Greek mean *a gazelle*

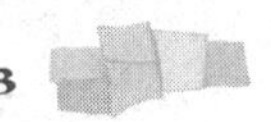

house is by the seaside." 7When the angel who
spoke to him had left, he called two of his slaves
and a devout soldier from the ranks of those who
served him, 8and after telling them everything, he
sent them to Joppa.

9 About noon the next day, as they were on
their journey and approaching the city, Peter
went up on the roof to pray. 10He became hungry
and wanted something to eat; and while it was
being prepared, he fell into a trance. 11He saw the
heaven opened and something like a large sheet
coming down, being lowered to the ground by its
four corners. 12In it were all kinds of four-footed
creatures and reptiles and birds of the air. 13Then
he heard a voice saying, "Get up, Peter; kill and
eat." 14But Peter said, "By no means, Lord; for I
have never eaten anything that is profane or unclean." 15The voice said to him again, a second
time, "What God has made clean, you must not
call profane." 16This happened three times, and
the thing was suddenly taken up to heaven.

17 Now while Peter was greatly puzzled about
what to make of the vision that he had seen, suddenly the men sent by Cornelius appeared. They
were asking for Simon's house and were standing by the gate. 18They called out to ask whether
Simon, who was called Peter, was staying there.
19While Peter was still thinking about the vision,
the Spirit said to him, "Look, three[a] men are
searching for you. 20Now get up, go down, and
go with them without hesitation; for I have sent
them." 21So Peter went down to the men and said,
"I am the one you are looking for; what is the reason for your coming?" 22They answered, "Cornelius, a centurion, an upright and God-fearing
man, who is well spoken of by the whole Jewish
nation, was directed by a holy angel to send for
you to come to his house and to hear what you
have to say." 23So Peter[b] invited them in and gave
them lodging.

The next day he got up and went with them,
and some of the believers[c] from Joppa accompanied him. 24The following day they came to
Caesarea. Cornelius was expecting them and had
called together his relatives and close friends.
25On Peter's arrival Cornelius met him, and falling at his feet, worshiped him. 26But Peter made
him get up, saying, "Stand up; I am only a mortal." 27And as he talked with him, he went in and
found that many had assembled; 28and he said to
them, "You yourselves know that it is unlawful for
a Jew to associate with or to visit a Gentile; but
God has shown me that I should not call anyone
profane or unclean. 29So when I was sent for, I
came without objection. Now may I ask why you
sent for me?"

30 Cornelius replied, "Four days ago at this
very hour, at three o'clock, I was praying in my
house when suddenly a man in dazzling clothes
stood before me. 31He said, 'Cornelius, your
prayer has been heard and your alms have been
remembered before God. 32Send therefore to
Joppa and ask for Simon, who is called Peter; he
is staying in the home of Simon, a tanner, by the
sea.' 33Therefore I sent for you immediately, and
you have been kind enough to come. So now all

[a] One ancient authority reads *two*; others lack the word [b] Gk *he* [c] Gk *brothers*

Acts 10:9-17

Peter's vision is normally read by Christians as a simple allegory: the unclean animals represent "unclean" persons, Gentiles, and the voice from heaven is God, commanding Peter to give up his foolish Jewish scruples. But a Jewish audience would have heard a very different story. The voice from heaven *tempted* Peter to abandon what he knew were the commandments of God, but he refused, faithfully but with some confusion. It is this *faithful* Jew, tested and proven to be law-observant, who subsequently recognizes that it is "kosher" for faithful Gentiles to be welcomed into the church.

— *NE*

of us are here in the presence of God to listen to
all that the Lord has commanded you to say."
34 Then Peter began to speak to them: "I truly
understand that God shows no partiality, 35but
in every nation anyone who fears him and does
what is right is acceptable to him. 36You know the
message he sent to the people of Israel, preaching
peace by Jesus Christ—he is Lord of all. 37That
message spread throughout Judea, beginning in
Galilee after the baptism that John announced:
38how God anointed Jesus of Nazareth with the
Holy Spirit and with power; how he went about
doing good and healing all who were oppressed
by the devil, for God was with him. 39We are witnesses to all that he did both in Judea and in Jerusalem. They put him to death by hanging him on
a tree; 40but God raised him on the third day and
allowed him to appear, 41not to all the people but
to us who were chosen by God as witnesses, and
who ate and drank with him after he rose from
the dead. 42He commanded us to preach to the
people and to testify that he is the one ordained
by God as judge of the living and the dead. 43All
the prophets testify about him that everyone
who believes in him receives forgiveness of sins
through his name."
44 While Peter was still speaking, the Holy
Spirit fell upon all who heard the word. 45The
circumcised believers who had come with Peter
were astounded that the gift of the Holy Spirit
had been poured out even on the Gentiles, 46for
they heard them speaking in tongues and extol-
ling God. Then Peter said, 47"Can anyone withhold the water for baptizing these people who
have received the Holy Spirit just as we have?"
48So he ordered them to be baptized in the name
of Jesus Christ. Then they invited him to stay for
several days.

11 Now the apostles and the believers[a] who
were in Judea heard that the Gentiles had
also accepted the word of God. 2So when Peter
went up to Jerusalem, the circumcised believers[b] criticized him, 3saying, "Why did you go to
uncircumcised men and eat with them?" 4Then
Peter began to explain it to them, step by step,
saying, 5"I was in the city of Joppa praying, and
in a trance I saw a vision. There was something
like a large sheet coming down from heaven, being lowered by its four corners; and it came close
to me. 6As I looked at it closely I saw four-footed
animals, beasts of prey, reptiles, and birds of the
air. 7I also heard a voice saying to me, 'Get up,
Peter; kill and eat.' 8But I replied, 'By no means,
Lord; for nothing profane or unclean has ever entered my mouth.' 9But a second time the voice answered from heaven, 'What God has made clean,
you must not call profane.' 10This happened three
times; then everything was pulled up again to
heaven. 11At that very moment three men, sent to
me from Caesarea, arrived at the house where we
were. 12The Spirit told me to go with them and
not to make a distinction between them and us.[c]
These six brothers also accompanied me, and we
entered the man's house. 13He told us how he had
seen the angel standing in his house and saying,
'Send to Joppa and bring Simon, who is called
Peter; 14he will give you a message by which you
and your entire household will be saved.' 15And as
I began to speak, the Holy Spirit fell upon them
just as it had upon us at the beginning. 16And I
remembered the word of the Lord, how he had
said, 'John baptized with water, but you will be
baptized with the Holy Spirit.' 17If then God gave
them the same gift that he gave us when we believed in the Lord Jesus Christ, who was I that
I could hinder God?" 18When they heard this,
they were silenced. And they praised God, saying, "Then God has given even to the Gentiles the
repentance that leads to life."

19 Now those who were scattered because
of the persecution that took place over Stephen
traveled as far as Phoenicia, Cyprus, and Antioch,
and they spoke the word to no one except Jews.
20But among them were some men of Cyprus
and Cyrene who, on coming to Antioch, spoke
to the Hellenists[d] also, proclaiming the Lord
Jesus. 21The hand of the Lord was with them,
and a great number became believers and turned
to the Lord. 22News of this came to the ears of

[a] Gk *brothers* [b] Gk lacks *believers* [c] Or *not to hesitate* [d] Other ancient authorities read *Greeks*

the church in Jerusalem, and they sent Barnabas
to Antioch. 23 When he came and saw the grace
of God, he rejoiced, and he exhorted them all to
remain faithful to the Lord with steadfast devotion; 24 for he was a good man, full of the Holy
Spirit and of faith. And a great many people were
brought to the Lord. 25 Then Barnabas went to
Tarsus to look for Saul, 26 and when he had found
him, he brought him to Antioch. So it was that
for an entire year they met with[a] the church and
taught a great many people, and it was in Antioch
that the disciples were first called "Christians."

27 At that time prophets came down from
Jerusalem to Antioch. 28 One of them named Agabus stood up and predicted by the Spirit that
there would be a severe famine over all the world;
and this took place during the reign of Claudius.
29 The disciples determined that according to
their ability, each would send relief to the believers[b] living in Judea; 30 this they did, sending it to
the elders by Barnabas and Saul.

12 About that time King Herod laid violent hands upon some who belonged to
the church. 2 He had James, the brother of John,
killed with the sword. 3 After he saw that it pleased
the Jews, he proceeded to arrest Peter also. (This
was during the festival of Unleavened Bread.)
4 When he had seized him, he put him in prison
and handed him over to four squads of soldiers
to guard him, intending to bring him out to the
people after the Passover. 5 While Peter was kept
in prison, the church prayed fervently to God
for him.

6 The very night before Herod was going
to bring him out, Peter, bound with two chains,
was sleeping between two soldiers, while guards
in front of the door were keeping watch over the
prison. 7 Suddenly an angel of the Lord appeared
and a light shone in the cell. He tapped Peter on
the side and woke him, saying, "Get up quickly."
And the chains fell off his wrists. 8 The angel said
to him, "Fasten your belt and put on your sandals." He did so. Then he said to him, "Wrap your
cloak around you and follow me." 9 Peter[c] went
out and followed him; he did not realize that
what was happening with the angel's help was
real; he thought he was seeing a vision. 10 After
they had passed the first and the second guard,
they came before the iron gate leading into the
city. It opened for them of its own accord, and
they went outside and walked along a lane, when
suddenly the angel left him. 11 Then Peter came to
himself and said, "Now I am sure that the Lord
has sent his angel and rescued me from the hands
of Herod and from all that the Jewish people were
expecting."

12 As soon as he realized this, he went to the
house of Mary, the mother of John whose other
name was Mark, where many had gathered and
were praying. 13 When he knocked at the outer
gate, a maid named Rhoda came to answer. 14 On
recognizing Peter's voice, she was so overjoyed
that, instead of opening the gate, she ran in and
announced that Peter was standing at the gate.
15 They said to her, "You are out of your mind!"
But she insisted that it was so. They said, "It is his
angel." 16 Meanwhile Peter continued knocking;
and when they opened the gate, they saw him
and were amazed. 17 He motioned to them with
his hand to be silent, and described for them how
the Lord had brought him out of the prison. And
he added, "Tell this to James and to the believers."[b] Then he left and went to another place.

18 When morning came, there was no small
commotion among the soldiers over what had
become of Peter. 19 When Herod had searched
for him and could not find him, he examined the
guards and ordered them to be put to death. Then
he went down from Judea to Caesarea and stayed
there.

20 Now Herod[d] was angry with the people of
Tyre and Sidon. So they came to him in a body;
and after winning over Blastus, the king's cham-
berlain, they asked for a reconciliation, because
their country depended on the king's country for
food. 21 On an appointed day Herod put on his
royal robes, took his seat on the platform, and
delivered a public address to them. 22 The people
kept shouting, "The voice of a god, and not of
a mortal!" 23 And immediately, because he had

[a] Or *were guests of* [b] Gk *brothers* [c] Gk *He* [d] Gk *he*

not given the glory to God, an angel of the Lord
struck him down, and he was eaten by worms and
died.
24 But the word of God continued to advance and gain adherents. 25 Then after completing their mission Barnabas and Saul returned to[a]
Jerusalem and brought with them John, whose
other name was Mark.

13 Now in the church at Antioch there were
prophets and teachers: Barnabas, Simeon
who was called Niger, Lucius of Cyrene, Manaen
a member of the court of Herod the ruler,[b] and
Saul. 2 While they were worshiping the Lord and
fasting, the Holy Spirit said, "Set apart for me
Barnabas and Saul for the work to which I have
called them." 3 Then after fasting and praying they
laid their hands on them and sent them off.
4 So, being sent out by the Holy Spirit, they
went down to Seleucia; and from there they sailed
to Cyprus. 5 When they arrived at Salamis, they
proclaimed the word of God in the synagogues of
the Jews. And they had John also to assist them.
6 When they had gone through the whole island as
far as Paphos, they met a certain magician, a Jewish false prophet, named Bar-Jesus. 7 He was with
the proconsul, Sergius Paulus, an intelligent man,
who summoned Barnabas and Saul and wanted
to hear the word of God. 8 But the magician Ely-
mas (for that is the translation of his name) opposed them and tried to turn the proconsul away
from the faith. 9 But Saul, also known as Paul,
filled with the Holy Spirit, looked intently at him
10 and said, "You son of the devil, you enemy of all
righteousness, full of all deceit and villainy, will
you not stop making crooked the straight paths
of the Lord? 11 And now listen—the hand of the
Lord is against you, and you will be blind for a
while, unable to see the sun." Immediately mist
and darkness came over him, and he went about
groping for someone to lead him by the hand.
12 When the proconsul saw what had happened,
he believed, for he was astonished at the teaching
about the Lord.
13 Then Paul and his companions set sail
from Paphos and came to Perga in Pamphylia.
John, however, left them and returned to Jerusalem; 14 but they went on from Perga and came to
Antioch in Pisidia. And on the sabbath day they
went into the synagogue and sat down. 15 After
the reading of the law and the prophets, the officials of the synagogue sent them a message,
saying, "Brothers, if you have any word of exhortation for the people, give it." 16 So Paul stood up
and with a gesture began to speak:
"You Israelites,[c] and others who fear God,
listen. 17 The God of this people Israel chose our
ancestors and made the people great during their
stay in the land of Egypt, and with uplifted arm
he led them out of it. 18 For about forty years he
put up with[d] them in the wilderness. 19 After he
had destroyed seven nations in the land of Canaan, he gave them their land as an inheritance
20 for about four hundred fifty years. After that he
gave them judges until the time of the prophet
Samuel. 21 Then they asked for a king; and God
gave them Saul son of Kish, a man of the tribe of
Benjamin, who reigned for forty years. 22 When
he had removed him, he made David their king.
In his testimony about him he said, 'I have found
David, son of Jesse, to be a man after my heart,
who will carry out all my wishes.' 23 Of this man's

Acts 13:9

Saul's other name was Paul. Some insist that Saul becomes Paul with conversion. Change of name accompanies change of person. Yet here, the "saved" Paul is still called Saul. Why? Because like most who live in two cultures, he is forced to hold on to two identities—two different modes of behaving—determined by the cultural context in which he finds himself. He is Saul when operating within his Jewish context, and Paul when operating within the context of the Roman Empire. Even though this story occurred after his conversion, he is stilled called Saul, because he is dealing with the Jewish false prophet Bar-Jesus.

—MDLT

[a] Other ancient authorities read *from* [b] Gk *tetrarch* [c] Gk *Men, Israelites* [d] Other ancient authorities read *cared for*

posterity God has brought to Israel a Savior,
Jesus, as he promised; 24before his coming John
had already proclaimed a baptism of repentance
to all the people of Israel. 25And as John was finishing his work, he said, 'What do you suppose
that I am? I am not he. No, but one is coming after me; I am not worthy to untie the thong of the
sandals[a] on his feet.'

26 "My brothers, you descendants of Abraham's family, and others who fear God, to us[b]
the message of this salvation has been sent. 27Be-
cause the residents of Jerusalem and their leaders
did not recognize him or understand the words
of the prophets that are read every sabbath, they
fulfilled those words by condemning him. 28Even
though they found no cause for a sentence of
death, they asked Pilate to have him killed.
29When they had carried out everything that was
written about him, they took him down from the
tree and laid him in a tomb. 30But God raised him
from the dead; 31and for many days he appeared
to those who came up with him from Galilee to
Jerusalem, and they are now his witnesses to the
people. 32And we bring you the good news that
what God promised to our ancestors 33he has
fulfilled for us, their children, by raising Jesus; as
also it is written in the second psalm,

'You are my Son;
today I have begotten you.'

34As to his raising him from the dead, no more to
return to corruption, he has spoken in this way,

'I will give you the holy promises made to
David.'

35Therefore he has also said in another psalm,

'You will not let your Holy One experience
corruption.'

36For David, after he had served the purpose of
God in his own generation, died,[c] was laid beside his ancestors, and experienced corruption;
37but he whom God raised up experienced no
corruption. 38Let it be known to you therefore,
my brothers, that through this man forgiveness of
sins is proclaimed to you; 39by this Jesus[d] everyone who believes is set free from all those sins[e]
from which you could not be freed by the law of
Moses. 40Beware, therefore, that what the prophets said does not happen to you:

41 'Look, you scoffers!
Be amazed and perish,
for in your days I am doing a work,
a work that you will never believe, even if
someone tells you.'"

42 As Paul and Barnabas[f] were going out, the
people urged them to speak about these things
again the next sabbath. 43When the meeting of
the synagogue broke up, many Jews and devout
converts to Judaism followed Paul and Barnabas,
who spoke to them and urged them to continue
in the grace of God.

44 The next sabbath almost the whole city
gathered to hear the word of the Lord.[g] 45But
when the Jews saw the crowds, they were filled
with jealousy; and blaspheming, they contradicted what was spoken by Paul. 46Then both
Paul and Barnabas spoke out boldly, saying, "It
was necessary that the word of God should be
spoken first to you. Since you reject it and judge
yourselves to be unworthy of eternal life, we are
now turning to the Gentiles. 47For so the Lord
has commanded us, saying,

'I have set you to be a light for the Gentiles,
so that you may bring salvation to the ends
of the earth.'"

48 When the Gentiles heard this, they were
glad and praised the word of the Lord; and as
many as had been destined for eternal life became
believers. 49Thus the word of the Lord spread
throughout the region. 50But the Jews incited
the devout women of high standing and the leading men of the city, and stirred up persecution
against Paul and Barnabas, and drove them out
of their region. 51So they shook the dust off their
feet in protest against them, and went to Iconium.
52And the disciples were filled with joy and with
the Holy Spirit.

14 The same thing occurred in Iconium,
where Paul and Barnabas[f] went into the
Jewish synagogue and spoke in such a way that

[a] Gk *untie the sandals* [b] Other ancient authorities read *you* [c] Gk *fell asleep* [d] Gk *this* [e] Gk *all* [f] Gk *they*
[g] Other ancient authorities read *God*

a great number of both Jews and Greeks became
believers. 2 But the unbelieving Jews stirred up
the Gentiles and poisoned their minds against
the brothers. 3 So they remained for a long time,
speaking boldly for the Lord, who testified to the
word of his grace by granting signs and wonders
to be done through them. 4 But the residents of
the city were divided; some sided with the Jews,
and some with the apostles. 5 And when an attempt was made by both Gentiles and Jews, with
their rulers, to mistreat them and to stone them,
6 the apostles[a] learned of it and fled to Lystra and
Derbe, cities of Lycaonia, and to the surrounding
country; 7 and there they continued proclaiming
the good news.

8 In Lystra there was a man sitting who could
not use his feet and had never walked, for he had
been crippled from birth. 9 He listened to Paul
as he was speaking. And Paul, looking at him intently and seeing that he had faith to be healed,
10 said in a loud voice, "Stand upright on your
feet." And the man[b] sprang up and began to walk.
11 When the crowds saw what Paul had done,
they shouted in the Lycaonian language, "The
gods have come down to us in human form!"
12 Barnabas they called Zeus, and Paul they called
Hermes, because he was the chief speaker. 13 The
priest of Zeus, whose temple was just outside the
city,[c] brought oxen and garlands to the gates; he
and the crowds wanted to offer sacrifice. 14 When
the apostles Barnabas and Paul heard of it, they
tore their clothes and rushed out into the crowd,
shouting, 15 "Friends,[d] why are you doing this? We
are mortals just like you, and we bring you good
news, that you should turn from these worthless
things to the living God, who made the heaven
and the earth and the sea and all that is in them.
16 In past generations he allowed all the nations to
follow their own ways; 17 yet he has not left himself without a witness in doing good—giving you
rains from heaven and fruitful seasons, and filling
you with food and your hearts with joy." 18 Even
with these words, they scarcely restrained the
crowds from offering sacrifice to them.

19 But Jews came there from Antioch and
Iconium and won over the crowds. Then they
stoned Paul and dragged him out of the city, supposing that he was dead. 20 But when the disciples
surrounded him, he got up and went into the
city. The next day he went on with Barnabas to
Derbe.

21 After they had proclaimed the good news
to that city and had made many disciples, they returned to Lystra, then on to Iconium and Antioch.
22 There they strengthened the souls of the disciples and encouraged them to continue in the faith,
saying, "It is through many persecutions that we
must enter the kingdom of God." 23 And after they
had appointed elders for them in each church,
with prayer and fasting they entrusted them to the
Lord in whom they had come to believe.

24 Then they passed through Pisidia and
came to Pamphylia. 25 When they had spoken
the word in Perga, they went down to Attalia.
26 From there they sailed back to Antioch, where
they had been commended to the grace of God
for the work[e] that they had completed. 27 When
they arrived, they called the church together and
related all that God had done with them, and how
he had opened a door of faith for the Gentiles.
28 And they stayed there with the disciples for
some time.

15 Then certain individuals came down from
Judea and were teaching the brothers,
"Unless you are circumcised according to the custom of Moses, you cannot be saved." 2 And after
Paul and Barnabas had no small dissension and
debate with them, Paul and Barnabas and some
of the others were appointed to go up to Jerusalem to discuss this question with the apostles and
the elders. 3 So they were sent on their way by the
church, and as they passed through both Phoenicia and Samaria, they reported the conversion
of the Gentiles, and brought great joy to all the
believers.[f] 4 When they came to Jerusalem, they
were welcomed by the church and the apostles
and the elders, and they reported all that God had
done with them. 5 But some believers who be-

[a] Gk *they* [b] Gk *he* [c] Or *The priest of Zeus-Outside-the-City* [d] Gk *Men* [e] Or *committed in the grace of God to the work*
[f] Gk *brothers*

Acts 15:1-2

The book of Acts has usually been understood as the story of how the church converts the world to Christianity. Yet in reality it is the story of how the early church had to put aside its racism and sexism in order to become faithful to the gospel message. The early Christian church received, among others, a Roman centurion named Cornelius, uncircumcised Gentiles, and women as church leaders. The Latina religious scholar Loida Martell-Otero says it best: "The church is being made to convert, even as it seeks converts."

—MDLT

longed to the sect of the Pharisees stood up and
said, "It is necessary for them to be circumcised
and ordered to keep the law of Moses."

6 The apostles and the elders met together to
consider this matter. 7After there had been much
debate, Peter stood up and said to them, "My
brothers,[a] you know that in the early days God
made a choice among you, that I should be the
one through whom the Gentiles would hear the
message of the good news and become believers.
8And God, who knows the human heart, testified
to them by giving them the Holy Spirit, just as he
did to us; 9and in cleansing their hearts by faith
he has made no distinction between them and us.
10Now therefore why are you putting God to the
test by placing on the neck of the disciples a yoke
that neither our ancestors nor we have been able
to bear? 11On the contrary, we believe that we
will be saved through the grace of the Lord Jesus,
just as they will."

12 The whole assembly kept silence, and listened to Barnabas and Paul as they told of all the
signs and wonders that God had done through
them among the Gentiles. 13After they finished
speaking, James replied, "My brothers,[a] listen to
me. 14Simeon has related how God first looked
favorably on the Gentiles, to take from among
them a people for his name. 15This agrees with
the words of the prophets, as it is written,

16 'After this I will return,
and I will rebuild the dwelling of David,
which has fallen;
from its ruins I will rebuild it,
and I will set it up,
17 so that all other peoples may seek the Lord—
even all the Gentiles over whom my name
has been called.
Thus says the Lord, who has been
making these things 18known from
long ago.'[b]

19Therefore I have reached the decision that we
should not trouble those Gentiles who are turning to God, 20but we should write to them to
abstain only from things polluted by idols and
from fornication and from whatever has been
strangled[c] and from blood. 21For in every city,
for generations past, Moses has had those who
proclaim him, for he has been read aloud every
sabbath in the synagogues."

22 Then the apostles and the elders, with the
consent of the whole church, decided to choose
men from among their members[d] and to send
them to Antioch with Paul and Barnabas. They
sent Judas called Barsabbas, and Silas, leaders
among the brothers, 23with the following letter:
"The brothers, both the apostles and the elders,
to the believers[e] of Gentile origin in Antioch
and Syria and Cilicia, greetings. 24Since we have
heard that certain persons who have gone out
from us, though with no instructions from us,
have said things to disturb you and have unsettled
your minds,[f] 25we have decided unanimously to
choose representatives[g] and send them to you,
along with our beloved Barnabas and Paul, 26who
have risked their lives for the sake of our Lord
Jesus Christ. 27We have therefore sent Judas and
Silas, who themselves will tell you the same things
by word of mouth. 28For it has seemed good to
the Holy Spirit and to us to impose on you no
further burden than these essentials: 29that you

[a] Gk *Men, brothers* [b] Other ancient authorities read *things. 18Known to God from of old are all his works.'*
[c] Other ancient authorities lack *and from whatever has been strangled* [d] Gk *from among them* [e] Gk *brothers*
[f] Other ancient authorities add *saying, 'You must be circumcised and keep the law,'* [g] Gk *men*

abstain from what has been sacrificed to idols and from blood and from what is strangled[a] and from fornication. If you keep yourselves from these, you will do well. Farewell."

30 So they were sent off and went down to Antioch. When they gathered the congregation together, they delivered the letter. 31 When its members[b] read it, they rejoiced at the exhortation. 32 Judas and Silas, who were themselves prophets, said much to encourage and strengthen the believers.[c] 33 After they had been there for some time, they were sent off in peace by the believers[c] to those who had sent them.[d] 35 But Paul and Barnabas remained in Antioch, and there, with many others, they taught and proclaimed the word of the Lord.

36 After some days Paul said to Barnabas, "Come, let us return and visit the believers[c] in every city where we proclaimed the word of the Lord and see how they are doing." 37 Barnabas wanted to take with them John called Mark. 38 But Paul decided not to take with them one who had deserted them in Pamphylia and had not accompanied them in the work. 39 The disagreement became so sharp that they parted company; Barnabas took Mark with him and sailed away to Cyprus. 40 But Paul chose Silas and set out, the believers[c] commending him to the grace of the Lord. 41 He went through Syria and Cilicia, strengthening the churches.

16 Paul[e] went on also to Derbe and to Lystra, where there was a disciple named Timothy, the son of a Jewish woman who was a believer; but his father was a Greek. 2 He was well spoken of by the believers[c] in Lystra and Iconium. 3 Paul wanted Timothy to accompany him; and he took him and had him circumcised because of the Jews who were in those places, for they all knew that his father was a Greek. 4 As they went from town to town, they delivered to them for observance the decisions that had been reached by the apostles and elders who were in Jerusalem. 5 So the churches were strengthened in the faith and increased in numbers daily.

6 They went through the region of Phrygia and Galatia, having been forbidden by the Holy Spirit to speak the word in Asia. 7 When they had come opposite Mysia, they attempted to go into Bithynia, but the Spirit of Jesus did not allow them; 8 so, passing by Mysia, they went down to Troas. 9 During the night Paul had a vision: there stood a man of Macedonia pleading with him and saying, "Come over to Macedonia and help us." 10 When he had seen the vision, we immediately tried to cross over to Macedonia, being convinced that God had called us to proclaim the good news to them.

11 We set sail from Troas and took a straight course to Samothrace, the following day to Neapolis, 12 and from there to Philippi, which is a leading city of the district[f] of Macedonia and a Roman colony. We remained in this city for some days. 13 On the sabbath day we went outside the gate by the river, where we supposed there was a place of prayer; and we sat down and spoke to the women who had gathered there. 14 A certain woman named Lydia, a worshiper of God, was listening to us; she was from the city of Thyatira and a dealer in purple cloth. The Lord opened her heart to listen eagerly to what was said by Paul. 15 When she and her household were baptized, she urged us, saying, "If you have judged me to be faithful to the Lord, come and stay at my home." And she prevailed upon us.

16 One day, as we were going to the place of prayer, we met a slave-girl who had a spirit of divination and brought her owners a great deal of money by fortune-telling. 17 While she followed Paul and us, she would cry out, "These men are slaves of the Most High God, who proclaim to you[g] a way of salvation." 18 She kept doing this for many days. But Paul, very much annoyed, turned and said to the spirit, "I order you in the name of Jesus Christ to come out of her." And it came out that very hour.

[a] Other ancient authorities lack *and from what is strangled* [b] Gk *When they* [c] Gk *brothers* [d] Other ancient authorities add verse 34, *But it seemed good to Silas to remain there* [e] Gk *He* [f] Other authorities read *a city of the first district* [g] Other ancient authorities read *to us*

19 But when her owners saw that their hope
of making money was gone, they seized Paul and
Silas and dragged them into the marketplace before the authorities. 20 When they had brought
them before the magistrates, they said, "These
men are disturbing our city; they are Jews 21 and
are advocating customs that are not lawful for us
as Romans to adopt or observe." 22 The crowd
joined in attacking them, and the magistrates
had them stripped of their clothing and ordered
them to be beaten with rods. 23 After they had
given them a severe flogging, they threw them
into prison and ordered the jailer to keep them
securely. 24 Following these instructions, he put
them in the innermost cell and fastened their feet
in the stocks.

25 About midnight Paul and Silas were praying and singing hymns to God, and the prisoners
were listening to them. 26 Suddenly there was an
earthquake, so violent that the foundations of the
prison were shaken; and immediately all the doors
were opened and everyone's chains were unfas-
tened. 27 When the jailer woke up and saw the
prison doors wide open, he drew his sword and
was about to kill himself, since he supposed that
the prisoners had escaped. 28 But Paul shouted
in a loud voice, "Do not harm yourself, for we are
all here." 29 The jailer[a] called for lights, and rushing
in, he fell down trembling before Paul and Silas.
30 Then he brought them outside and said, "Sirs,
what must I do to be saved?" 31 They answered,
"Believe on the Lord Jesus, and you will be saved,
you and your household." 32 They spoke the word
of the Lord[b] to him and to all who were in his
house. 33 At the same hour of the night he took
them and washed their wounds; then he and his
entire family were baptized without delay. 34 He
brought them up into the house and set food
before them; and he and his entire household rejoiced that he had become a believer in God.

35 When morning came, the magistrates sent
the police, saying, "Let those men go." 36 And
the jailer reported the message to Paul, saying,
"The magistrates sent word to let you go; therefore come out now and go in peace." 37 But Paul
replied, "They have beaten us in public, uncondemned, men who are Roman citizens, and have
thrown us into prison; and now are they going to
discharge us in secret? Certainly not! Let them
come and take us out themselves." 38 The police
reported these words to the magistrates, and they
were afraid when they heard that they were Roman citizens; 39 so they came and apologized to
them. And they took them out and asked them
to leave the city. 40 After leaving the prison they
went to Lydia's home; and when they had seen
and encouraged the brothers and sisters[c] there,
they departed.

17 After Paul and Silas[d] had passed through
Amphipolis and Apollonia, they came to
Thessalonica, where there was a synagogue of the
Jews. 2 And Paul went in, as was his custom, and
on three sabbath days argued with them from the
scriptures, 3 explaining and proving that it was
necessary for the Messiah[e] to suffer and to rise
from the dead, and saying, "This is the Messiah,[e]
Jesus whom I am proclaiming to you." 4 Some of
them were persuaded and joined Paul and Silas,
as did a great many of the devout Greeks and not
a few of the leading women. 5 But the Jews became
jealous, and with the help of some ruffians in the
marketplaces they formed a mob and set the city
in an uproar. While they were searching for Paul
and Silas to bring them out to the assembly, they
attacked Jason's house. 6 When they could not
find them, they dragged Jason and some believers[c] before the city authorities,[f] shouting, "These
people who have been turning the world upside
down have come here also, 7 and Jason has entertained them as guests. They are all acting contrary
to the decrees of the emperor, saying that there is
another king named Jesus." 8 The people and the
city officials were disturbed when they heard this,
9 and after they had taken bail from Jason and the
others, they let them go.

10 That very night the believers[c] sent Paul
and Silas off to Beroea; and when they arrived,
they went to the Jewish synagogue. 11 These Jews
were more receptive than those in Thessalonica,
for they welcomed the message very eagerly and

[a] Gk *He* [b] Other ancient authorities read *word of God* [c] Gk *brothers* [d] Gk *they* [e] Or *the Christ* [f] Gk *politarchs*

examined the scriptures every day to see whether
these things were so. 12 Many of them therefore
believed, including not a few Greek women and
men of high standing. 13 But when the Jews of
Thessalonica learned that the word of God had
been proclaimed by Paul in Beroea as well, they
came there too, to stir up and incite the crowds.
14 Then the believers[a] immediately sent Paul away
to the coast, but Silas and Timothy remained behind. 15 Those who conducted Paul brought him
as far as Athens; and after receiving instructions
to have Silas and Timothy join him as soon as
possible, they left him.

16 While Paul was waiting for them in Athens, he was deeply distressed to see that the city
was full of idols. 17 So he argued in the synagogue
with the Jews and the devout persons, and also in
the marketplace[b] every day with those who happened to be there. 18 Also some Epicurean and
Stoic philosophers debated with him. Some said,
"What does this babbler want to say?" Others
said, "He seems to be a proclaimer of foreign di-
vinities." (This was because he was telling the good
news about Jesus and the resurrection.) 19 So they
took him and brought him to the Areopagus and
asked him, "May we know what this new teaching is that you are presenting? 20 It sounds rather
strange to us, so we would like to know what it
means." 21 Now all the Athenians and the foreigners living there would spend their time in nothing
but telling or hearing something new.

22 Then Paul stood in front of the Areopagus
and said, "Athenians, I see how extremely religious
you are in every way. 23 For as I went through the
city and looked carefully at the objects of your
worship, I found among them an altar with the
inscription, 'To an unknown god.' What therefore
you worship as unknown, this I proclaim to you.
24 The God who made the world and everything
in it, he who is Lord of heaven and earth, does
not live in shrines made by human hands, 25 nor is
he served by human hands, as though he needed
anything, since he himself gives to all mortals life
and breath and all things. 26 From one ancestor[c]
he made all nations to inhabit the whole earth,
and he allotted the times of their existence and
the boundaries of the places where they would
live, 27 so that they would search for God[d] and
perhaps grope for him and find him—though
indeed he is not far from each one of us. 28 For
'In him we live and move and have our being'; as
even some of your own poets have said,

'For we too are his offspring.'

29 Since we are God's offspring, we ought not to
think that the deity is like gold, or silver, or stone,
an image formed by the art and imagination of
mortals. 30 While God has overlooked the times
of human ignorance, now he commands all people everywhere to repent, 31 because he has fixed
a day on which he will have the world judged in
righteousness by a man whom he has appointed,
and of this he has given assurance to all by raising
him from the dead."

32 When they heard of the resurrection of
the dead, some scoffed; but others said, "We will
hear you again about this." 33 At that point Paul
left them. 34 But some of them joined him and
became believers, including Dionysius the Are-
opagite and a woman named Damaris, and others
with them.

18 After this Paul[e] left Athens and went to
Corinth. 2 There he found a Jew named
Aquila, a native of Pontus, who had recently
come from Italy with his wife Priscilla, because
Claudius had ordered all Jews to leave Rome.
Paul[f] went to see them, 3 and, because he was of
the same trade, he stayed with them, and they
worked together—by trade they were tentmakers.
4 Every sabbath he would argue in the synagogue
and would try to convince Jews and Greeks.

5 When Silas and Timothy arrived from
Macedonia, Paul was occupied with proclaiming
the word,[g] testifying to the Jews that the Messiah[h]
was Jesus. 6 When they opposed and reviled him,
in protest he shook the dust from his clothes[i] and
said to them, "Your blood be on your own heads!

[a] Gk *brothers* [b] Or *civic center*; Gk *agora* [c] Gk *From one*; other ancient authorities read *From one blood*
[d] Other ancient authorities read *the Lord* [e] Gk *he* [f] Gk *He* [g] Gk *with the word* [h] Or *the Christ*
[i] Gk *reviled him, he shook out his clothes*

I am innocent. From now on I will go to the Gentiles." 7Then he left the synagogue[a] and went to
the house of a man named Titius[b] Justus, a worshiper of God; his house was next door to the synagogue. 8Crispus, the official of the synagogue,
became a believer in the Lord, together with all
his household; and many of the Corinthians who
heard Paul became believers and were baptized.
9One night the Lord said to Paul in a vision, "Do
not be afraid, but speak and do not be silent; 10for
I am with you, and no one will lay a hand on you
to harm you, for there are many in this city who
are my people." 11He stayed there a year and six
months, teaching the word of God among them.

12 But when Gallio was proconsul of Achaia, the
Jews made a united attack on Paul and brought
him before the tribunal. 13They said, "This man is
persuading people to worship God in ways that
are contrary to the law." 14Just as Paul was about
to speak, Gallio said to the Jews, "If it were a matter of crime or serious villainy, I would be justified in accepting the complaint of you Jews; 15but
since it is a matter of questions about words and
names and your own law, see to it yourselves; I do
not wish to be a judge of these matters." 16And he
dismissed them from the tribunal. 17Then all of
them[c] seized Sosthenes, the official of the syna-

Acts 18:2-17

Luke's apologetic purposes are clear throughout his narrative. Again and again we are told that the Jews who oppose and harass the apostles do so out of jealousy and that their accusations are false. Again and again the Roman magistrates declare—with whatever measure of interest or sympathy—that they find nothing legally objectionable in the apostles' actions. What is not so clear is whether Luke aims this message at what he hopes will be a sympathetic Roman reader, or at a Jewish one.

—NE

gogue, and beat him in front of the tribunal. But
Gallio paid no attention to any of these things.

18 After staying there for a considerable time,
Paul said farewell to the believers[d] and sailed for
Syria, accompanied by Priscilla and Aquila. At
Cenchreae he had his hair cut, for he was under a
vow. 19When they reached Ephesus, he left them
there, but first he himself went into the synagogue
and had a discussion with the Jews. 20When they
asked him to stay longer, he declined; 21but on
taking leave of them, he said, "I[e] will return to
you, if God wills." Then he set sail from Ephesus.

22 When he had landed at Caesarea, he went
up to Jerusalem[f] and greeted the church, and then
went down to Antioch. 23After spending some
time there he departed and went from place to
place through the region of Galatia[g] and Phrygia,
strengthening all the disciples.

24 Now there came to Ephesus a Jew named
Apollos, a native of Alexandria. He was an eloquent man, well-versed in the scriptures. 25He
had been instructed in the Way of the Lord; and
he spoke with burning enthusiasm and taught accurately the things concerning Jesus, though he
knew only the baptism of John. 26He began to
speak boldly in the synagogue; but when Priscilla and Aquila heard him, they took him aside
and explained the Way of God to him more accurately. 27And when he wished to cross over to
Achaia, the believers[d] encouraged him and wrote
to the disciples to welcome him. On his arrival
he greatly helped those who through grace had
become believers, 28for he powerfully refuted the
Jews in public, showing by the scriptures that the
Messiah[h] is Jesus.

19 While Apollos was in Corinth, Paul
passed through the interior regions and
came to Ephesus, where he found some disciples.
2He said to them, "Did you receive the Holy
Spirit when you became believers?" They replied,
"No, we have not even heard that there is a Holy
Spirit." 3Then he said, "Into what then were you
baptized?" They answered, "Into John's baptism."

[a] Gk *left there* [b] Other ancient authorities read *Titus* [c] Other ancient authorities read *all the Greeks* [d] Gk *brothers* [e] Other ancient authorities read *I must at all costs keep the approaching festival in Jerusalem, but I* [f] Gk *went up* [g] Gk *the Galatian region* [h] Or *the Christ*

4Paul said, "John baptized with the baptism of repentance, telling the people to believe in the one
who was to come after him, that is, in Jesus." 5On
hearing this, they were baptized in the name of
the Lord Jesus. 6When Paul had laid his hands on
them, the Holy Spirit came upon them, and they
spoke in tongues and prophesied— 7altogether
there were about twelve of them.

8 He entered the synagogue and for three
months spoke out boldly, and argued persua-
sively about the kingdom of God. 9When some
stubbornly refused to believe and spoke evil of
the Way before the congregation, he left them,
taking the disciples with him, and argued daily
in the lecture hall of Tyrannus.[a] 10This continued
for two years, so that all the residents of Asia, both
Jews and Greeks, heard the word of the Lord.

11 God did extraordinary miracles through
Paul, 12so that when the handkerchiefs or aprons
that had touched his skin were brought to the sick,
their diseases left them, and the evil spirits came
out of them. 13Then some itinerant Jewish exorcists tried to use the name of the Lord Jesus over
those who had evil spirits, saying, "I adjure you by
the Jesus whom Paul proclaims." 14Seven sons of
a Jewish high priest named Sceva were doing this.
15But the evil spirit said to them in reply, "Jesus I
know, and Paul I know; but who are you?" 16Then
the man with the evil spirit leaped on them, mastered them all, and so overpowered them that
they fled out of the house naked and wounded.
17When this became known to all residents of
Ephesus, both Jews and Greeks, everyone was
awestruck; and the name of the Lord Jesus was
praised. 18Also many of those who became believers confessed and disclosed their practices. 19A
number of those who practiced magic collected
their books and burned them publicly; when the
value of these books[b] was calculated, it was found
to come to fifty thousand silver coins. 20So the
word of the Lord grew mightily and prevailed.

21 Now after these things had been accomplished, Paul resolved in the Spirit to go through
Macedonia and Achaia, and then to go on to Jerusalem. He said, "After I have gone there, I must
also see Rome." 22So he sent two of his helpers,
Timothy and Erastus, to Macedonia, while he
himself stayed for some time longer in Asia.

23 About that time no little disturbance
broke out concerning the Way. 24A man named
Demetrius, a silversmith who made silver shrines
of Artemis, brought no little business to the artisans. 25These he gathered together, with the
workers of the same trade, and said, "Men, you
know that we get our wealth from this business.
26You also see and hear that not only in Ephesus
but in almost the whole of Asia this Paul has persuaded and drawn away a considerable number of
people by saying that gods made with hands are
not gods. 27And there is danger not only that this
trade of ours may come into disrepute but also
that the temple of the great goddess Artemis will
be scorned, and she will be deprived of her majesty that brought all Asia and the world to worship her."

28 When they heard this, they were enraged
and shouted, "Great is Artemis of the Ephesians!"
29The city was filled with the confusion; and people[c] rushed together to the theater, dragging with
them Gaius and Aristarchus, Macedonians who
were Paul's travel companions. 30Paul wished to
go into the crowd, but the disciples would not
let him; 31even some officials of the province of
Asia,[d] who were friendly to him, sent him a message urging him not to venture into the theater.
32Meanwhile, some were shouting one thing,
some another; for the assembly was in confusion,
and most of them did not know why they had
come together. 33Some of the crowd gave instructions to Alexander, whom the Jews had pushed
forward. And Alexander motioned for silence
and tried to make a defense before the people.
34But when they recognized that he was a Jew, for
about two hours all of them shouted in unison,
"Great is Artemis of the Ephesians!" 35But when
the town clerk had quieted the crowd, he said,
"Citizens of Ephesus, who is there that does not

[a] Other ancient authorities read *of a certain Tyrannus, from eleven o'clock in the morning to four in the afternoon* [b] Gk *them*
[c] Gk *they* [d] Gk *some of the Asiarchs*

know that the city of the Ephesians is the temple
keeper of the great Artemis and of the statue that
fell from heaven?[a] 36 Since these things cannot
be denied, you ought to be quiet and do nothing
rash. 37 You have brought these men here who are
neither temple robbers nor blasphemers of our[b]
goddess. 38 If therefore Demetrius and the artisans with him have a complaint against anyone,
the courts are open, and there are proconsuls;
let them bring charges there against one another.
39 If there is anything further[c] you want to know,
it must be settled in the regular assembly. 40 For
we are in danger of being charged with rioting
today, since there is no cause that we can give to
justify this commotion." 41 When he had said this,
he dismissed the assembly.

20 After the uproar had ceased, Paul sent for
the disciples; and after encouraging them
and saying farewell, he left for Macedonia. 2 When
he had gone through those regions and had given
the believers[d] much encouragement, he came to
Greece, 3 where he stayed for three months. He
was about to set sail for Syria when a plot was
made against him by the Jews, and so he decided
to return through Macedonia. 4 He was accompanied by Sopater son of Pyrrhus from Beroea, by
Aristarchus and Secundus from Thessalonica, by
Gaius from Derbe, and by Timothy, as well as
by Tychicus and Trophimus from Asia. 5 They
went ahead and were waiting for us in Troas; 6 but
we sailed from Philippi after the days of Unleavened Bread, and in five days we joined them in
Troas, where we stayed for seven days.

7 On the first day of the week, when we
met to break bread, Paul was holding a discussion with them; since he intended to leave the
next day, he continued speaking until midnight.
8 There were many lamps in the room upstairs
where we were meeting. 9 A young man named
Eutychus, who was sitting in the window, began
to sink off into a deep sleep while Paul talked still
longer. Overcome by sleep, he fell to the ground
three floors below and was picked up dead. 10 But
Paul went down, and bending over him took him
in his arms, and said, "Do not be alarmed, for his
life is in him." 11 Then Paul went upstairs, and after he had broken bread and eaten, he continued
to converse with them until dawn; then he left.
12 Meanwhile they had taken the boy away alive
and were not a little comforted.

13 We went ahead to the ship and set sail for
Assos, intending to take Paul on board there; for
he had made this arrangement, intending to go by
land himself. 14 When he met us in Assos, we took
him on board and went to Mitylene. 15 We sailed
from there, and on the following day we arrived
opposite Chios. The next day we touched at Samos, and[e] the day after that we came to Miletus.
16 For Paul had decided to sail past Ephesus, so
that he might not have to spend time in Asia; he
was eager to be in Jerusalem, if possible, on the
day of Pentecost.

17 From Miletus he sent a message to Ephesus, asking the elders of the church to meet him.
18 When they came to him, he said to them:

"You yourselves know how I lived among
you the entire time from the first day that I set
foot in Asia, 19 serving the Lord with all humility and with tears, enduring the trials that came
to me through the plots of the Jews. 20 I did not
shrink from doing anything helpful, proclaiming the message to you and teaching you publicly
and from house to house, 21 as I testified to both
Jews and Greeks about repentance toward God
and faith toward our Lord Jesus. 22 And now, as a
captive to the Spirit,[f] I am on my way to Jerusalem, not knowing what will happen to me there,
23 except that the Holy Spirit testifies to me in
every city that imprisonment and persecutions
are waiting for me. 24 But I do not count my life of
any value to myself, if only I may finish my course
and the ministry that I received from the Lord
Jesus, to testify to the good news of God's grace.

25 "And now I know that none of you,
among whom I have gone about proclaiming the
kingdom, will ever see my face again. 26 Therefore I declare to you this day that I am not responsible for the blood of any of you, 27 for I

[a] Meaning of Gk uncertain [b] Other ancient authorities read *your* [c] Other ancient authorities read *about other matters*
[d] Gk *given them* [e] Other ancient authorities add *after remaining at Trogyllium* [f] Or *And now, bound in the spirit*

did not shrink from declaring to you the whole
purpose of God. 28Keep watch over yourselves
and over all the flock, of which the Holy Spirit
has made you overseers, to shepherd the church
of God[a] that he obtained with the blood of his
own Son.[b] 29I know that after I have gone, savage wolves will come in among you, not sparing
the flock. 30Some even from your own group will
come distorting the truth in order to entice the
disciples to follow them. 31Therefore be alert, remembering that for three years I did not cease
night or day to warn everyone with tears. 32And
now I commend you to God and to the message
of his grace, a message that is able to build you
up and to give you the inheritance among all
who are sanctified. 33I coveted no one's silver or
gold or clothing. 34You know for yourselves that
I worked with my own hands to support myself
and my companions. 35In all this I have given you
an example that by such work we must support
the weak, remembering the words of the Lord
Jesus, for he himself said, 'It is more blessed to
give than to receive.'"

36 When he had finished speaking, he knelt
down with them all and prayed. 37There was
much weeping among them all; they embraced
Paul and kissed him, 38grieving especially because
of what he had said, that they would not see him
again. Then they brought him to the ship.

21 When we had parted from them and set
sail, we came by a straight course to Cos,
and the next day to Rhodes, and from there to
Patara.[c] 2When we found a ship bound for Phoenicia, we went on board and set sail. 3We came
in sight of Cyprus; and leaving it on our left, we
sailed to Syria and landed at Tyre, because the
ship was to unload its cargo there. 4We looked
up the disciples and stayed there for seven days.
Through the Spirit they told Paul not to go on
to Jerusalem. 5When our days there were ended,
we left and proceeded on our journey; and all of
them, with wives and children, escorted us outside the city. There we knelt down on the beach
and prayed 6and said farewell to one another.
Then we went on board the ship, and they returned home.

7 When we had finished[d] the voyage from
Tyre, we arrived at Ptolemais; and we greeted
the believers[e] and stayed with them for one day.
8The next day we left and came to Caesarea; and
we went into the house of Philip the evangelist,
one of the seven, and stayed with him. 9He had
four unmarried daughters[f] who had the gift of
prophecy. 10While we were staying there for several days, a prophet named Agabus came down
from Judea. 11He came to us and took Paul's belt,
bound his own feet and hands with it, and said,
"Thus says the Holy Spirit, 'This is the way the
Jews in Jerusalem will bind the man who owns
this belt and will hand him over to the Gentiles.'"
12When we heard this, we and the people there
urged him not to go up to Jerusalem. 13Then
Paul answered, "What are you doing, weeping
and breaking my heart? For I am ready not only
to be bound but even to die in Jerusalem for the
name of the Lord Jesus." 14Since he would not be
persuaded, we remained silent except to say, "The
Lord's will be done."

15 After these days we got ready and started
to go up to Jerusalem. 16Some of the disciples
from Caesarea also came along and brought us to
the house of Mnason of Cyprus, an early disciple,
with whom we were to stay.

17 When we arrived in Jerusalem, the brothers welcomed us warmly. 18The next day Paul
went with us to visit James; and all the elders
were present. 19After greeting them, he related
one by one the things that God had done among
the Gentiles through his ministry. 20When they
heard it, they praised God. Then they said to him,
"You see, brother, how many thousands of believers there are among the Jews, and they are all zealous for the law. 21They have been told about you
that you teach all the Jews living among the Gentiles to forsake Moses, and that you tell them not
to circumcise their children or observe the customs. 22What then is to be done? They will certainly hear that you have come. 23So do what we

[a] Other ancient authorities read *of the Lord* [b] Or *with his own blood*; Gk *with the blood of his Own* [c] Other ancient authorities add *and Myra* [d] Or *continued* [e] Gk *brothers* [f] Gk *four daughters, virgins,*

tell you. We have four men who are under a vow.
24 Join these men, go through the rite of purification with them, and pay for the shaving of their
heads. Thus all will know that there is nothing in
what they have been told about you, but that you
yourself observe and guard the law. 25 But as for
the Gentiles who have become believers, we have
sent a letter with our judgment that they should
abstain from what has been sacrificed to idols and
from blood and from what is strangled[a] and from
fornication." 26 Then Paul took the men, and the
next day, having purified himself, he entered the
temple with them, making public the completion of the days of purification when the sacrifice
would be made for each of them.

27 When the seven days were almost completed, the Jews from Asia, who had seen him
in the temple, stirred up the whole crowd. They
seized him, 28 shouting, "Fellow Israelites, help!
This is the man who is teaching everyone everywhere against our people, our law, and this place;
more than that, he has actually brought Greeks
into the temple and has defiled this holy place."
29 For they had previously seen Trophimus the
Ephesian with him in the city, and they supposed
that Paul had brought him into the temple. 30 Then
all the city was aroused, and the people rushed together. They seized Paul and dragged him out of
the temple, and immediately the doors were shut.
31 While they were trying to kill him, word came
to the tribune of the cohort that all Jerusalem was
in an uproar. 32 Immediately he took soldiers and
centurions and ran down to them. When they saw
the tribune and the soldiers, they stopped beating Paul. 33 Then the tribune came, arrested him,
and ordered him to be bound with two chains;
he inquired who he was and what he had done.
34 Some in the crowd shouted one thing, some another; and as he could not learn the facts because
of the uproar, he ordered him to be brought into
the barracks. 35 When Paul[b] came to the steps, the
violence of the mob was so great that he had to be
carried by the soldiers. 36 The crowd that followed
kept shouting, "Away with him!"

37 Just as Paul was about to be brought into
the barracks, he said to the tribune, "May I say
something to you?" The tribune[c] replied, "Do
you know Greek? 38 Then you are not the Egyptian who recently stirred up a revolt and led the
four thousand assassins out into the wilderness?"
39 Paul replied, "I am a Jew, from Tarsus in Cilicia, a citizen of an important city; I beg you, let
me speak to the people." 40 When he had given
him permission, Paul stood on the steps and motioned to the people for silence; and when there
was a great hush, he addressed them in the Hebrew[d] language, saying:

22 "Brothers and fathers, listen to the defense that I now make before you."

2 When they heard him addressing them in
Hebrew,[d] they became even more quiet. Then he
said:

3 "I am a Jew, born in Tarsus in Cilicia, but
brought up in this city at the feet of Gamaliel,

[a] Other ancient authorities lack *and from what is strangled* [b] Gk *he* [c] Gk *He* [d] That is, *Aramaic*

Acts 21:17-26

Luke's apologetic purpose is again evident: the Jerusalem apostles recognize that Jewish opponents in the wider Diaspora hold false views of Paul and his companions, but are helpless to counteract those views unless Paul demonstrates his adherence to the law. This Paul is only too eager to do. The clear implication of the following scene is that the charge against Paul—that he violated the sanctity of the barrier preventing Gentiles from entering the temple precinct (21:27-30)—was also false. Whether Luke's narrative was ever effective in convincing Jewish readers of the bona fides of Paul and his coworkers, it was quickly adopted by the Gentile church, which came to read it as a charter of Jewish dispossession and Gentile-Christian supersession.

— *NE*

educated strictly according to our ancestral law,
being zealous for God, just as all of you are today.
4I persecuted this Way up to the point of death
by binding both men and women and putting
them in prison, 5as the high priest and the whole
council of elders can testify about me. From them
I also received letters to the brothers in Damascus, and I went there in order to bind those who
were there and to bring them back to Jerusalem
for punishment.

6 "While I was on my way and approaching
Damascus, about noon a great light from heaven
suddenly shone about me. 7I fell to the ground
and heard a voice saying to me, 'Saul, Saul, why
are you persecuting me?' 8I answered, 'Who
are you, Lord?' Then he said to me, 'I am Jesus
of Nazareth[a] whom you are persecuting.' 9Now
those who were with me saw the light but did not
hear the voice of the one who was speaking to me.
10I asked, 'What am I to do, Lord?' The Lord said
to me, 'Get up and go to Damascus; there you
will be told everything that has been assigned to
you to do.' 11Since I could not see because of the
brightness of that light, those who were with me
took my hand and led me to Damascus.

12 "A certain Ananias, who was a devout man
according to the law and well spoken of by all
the Jews living there, 13came to me; and standing beside me, he said, 'Brother Saul, regain your
sight!' In that very hour I regained my sight and
saw him. 14Then he said, 'The God of our ancestors has chosen you to know his will, to see the
Righteous One and to hear his own voice; 15for
you will be his witness to all the world of what
you have seen and heard. 16And now why do you
delay? Get up, be baptized, and have your sins
washed away, calling on his name.'

17 "After I had returned to Jerusalem and
while I was praying in the temple, I fell into a
trance 18and saw Jesus[b] saying to me, 'Hurry and
get out of Jerusalem quickly, because they will
not accept your testimony about me.' 19And I
said, 'Lord, they themselves know that in every
synagogue I imprisoned and beat those who
believed in you. 20And while the blood of your
witness Stephen was shed, I myself was standing
by, approving and keeping the coats of those who
killed him.' 21Then he said to me, 'Go, for I will
send you far away to the Gentiles.' "

22 Up to this point they listened to him, but
then they shouted, "Away with such a fellow from
the earth! For he should not be allowed to live."
23And while they were shouting, throwing off
their cloaks, and tossing dust into the air, 24the
tribune directed that he was to be brought into
the barracks, and ordered him to be examined
by flogging, to find out the reason for this outcry
against him. 25But when they had tied him up with
thongs,[c] Paul said to the centurion who was standing by, "Is it legal for you to flog a Roman citizen
who is uncondemned?" 26When the centurion
heard that, he went to the tribune and said to him,
"What are you about to do? This man is a Roman
citizen." 27The tribune came and asked Paul,[b] "Tell
me, are you a Roman citizen?" And he said, "Yes."
28The tribune answered, "It cost me a large sum
of money to get my citizenship." Paul said, "But I
was born a citizen." 29Immediately those who were
about to examine him drew back from him; and
the tribune also was afraid, for he realized that Paul
was a Roman citizen and that he had bound him.

30 Since he wanted to find out what Paul[d]
was being accused of by the Jews, the next day
he released him and ordered the chief priests and
the entire council to meet. He brought Paul down
and had him stand before them.

23 While Paul was looking intently at the
council he said, "Brothers,[e] up to this
day I have lived my life with a clear conscience
before God." 2Then the high priest Ananias ordered those standing near him to strike him on
the mouth. 3At this Paul said to him, "God will
strike you, you whitewashed wall! Are you sitting
there to judge me according to the law, and yet in
violation of the law you order me to be struck?"
4Those standing nearby said, "Do you dare to
insult God's high priest?" 5And Paul said, "I did
not realize, brothers, that he was high priest; for
it is written, 'You shall not speak evil of a leader
of your people.' "

[a] Gk *the Nazorean* [b] Gk *him* [c] Or *up for the lashes* [d] Gk *he* [e] Gk *Men, brothers*

6 When Paul noticed that some were Sadducees and others were Pharisees, he called out
in the council, "Brothers, I am a Pharisee, a son
of Pharisees. I am on trial concerning the hope
of the resurrection[a] of the dead." 7 When he said
this, a dissension began between the Pharisees
and the Sadducees, and the assembly was divided.
8 (The Sadducees say that there is no resurrection,
or angel, or spirit; but the Pharisees acknowledge
all three.) 9 Then a great clamor arose, and certain
scribes of the Pharisees' group stood up and contended, "We find nothing wrong with this man.
What if a spirit or an angel has spoken to him?"
10 When the dissension became violent, the tribune, fearing that they would tear Paul to pieces,
ordered the soldiers to go down, take him by
force, and bring him into the barracks.

11 That night the Lord stood near him and
said, "Keep up your courage! For just as you have
testified for me in Jerusalem, so you must bear
witness also in Rome."

12 In the morning the Jews joined in a conspiracy and bound themselves by an oath neither
to eat nor drink until they had killed Paul. 13 There
were more than forty who joined in this conspiracy. 14 They went to the chief priests and elders
and said, "We have strictly bound ourselves by
an oath to taste no food until we have killed Paul.
15 Now then, you and the council must notify the
tribune to bring him down to you, on the pretext
that you want to make a more thorough examination of his case. And we are ready to do away with
him before he arrives."

16 Now the son of Paul's sister heard about
the ambush; so he went and gained entrance to
the barracks and told Paul. 17 Paul called one
of the centurions and said, "Take this young man
to the tribune, for he has something to report to
him." 18 So he took him, brought him to the tribune, and said, "The prisoner Paul called me and
asked me to bring this young man to you; he has
something to tell you." 19 The tribune took him by
the hand, drew him aside privately, and asked,
"What is it that you have to report to me?" 20 He
answered, "The Jews have agreed to ask you to
bring Paul down to the council tomorrow, as
though they were going to inquire more thoroughly into his case. 21 But do not be persuaded
by them, for more than forty of their men are
lying in ambush for him. They have bound themselves by an oath neither to eat nor drink until
they kill him. They are ready now and are waiting
for your consent." 22 So the tribune dismissed the
young man, ordering him, "Tell no one that you
have informed me of this."

23 Then he summoned two of the centurions and said, "Get ready to leave by nine o'clock
tonight for Caesarea with two hundred soldiers,
seventy horsemen, and two hundred spearmen.
24 Also provide mounts for Paul to ride, and take
him safely to Felix the governor." 25 He wrote a
letter to this effect:

26 "Claudius Lysias to his Excellency the governor Felix, greetings. 27 This man was seized by
the Jews and was about to be killed by them, but
when I had learned that he was a Roman citizen,
I came with the guard and rescued him. 28 Since
I wanted to know the charge for which they accused him, I had him brought to their council.
29 I found that he was accused concerning questions of their law, but was charged with nothing
deserving death or imprisonment. 30 When I was
informed that there would be a plot against the
man, I sent him to you at once, ordering his accusers also to state before you what they have
against him.[b]"

31 So the soldiers, according to their instructions, took Paul and brought him during the night
to Antipatris. 32 The next day they let the horsemen go on with him, while they returned to the
barracks. 33 When they came to Caesarea and delivered the letter to the governor, they presented
Paul also before him. 34 On reading the letter, he
asked what province he belonged to, and when he
learned that he was from Cilicia, 35 he said, "I will
give you a hearing when your accusers arrive."
Then he ordered that he be kept under guard in
Herod's headquarters.[c]

24 Five days later the high priest Ananias
came down with some elders and an

[a] Gk *concerning hope and resurrection* [b] Other ancient authorities add *Farewell* [c] Gk *praetorium*

attorney, a certain Tertullus, and they reported
their case against Paul to the governor. 2When
Paul[a] had been summoned, Tertullus began to accuse him, saying:

"Your Excellency,[b] because of you we have
long enjoyed peace, and reforms have been made
for this people because of your foresight. 3We
welcome this in every way and everywhere with
utmost gratitude. 4But, to detain you no further,
I beg you to hear us briefly with your customary
graciousness. 5We have, in fact, found this man
a pestilent fellow, an agitator among all the Jews
throughout the world, and a ringleader of the sect
of the Nazarenes.[c] 6He even tried to profane the
temple, and so we seized him.[d] 8By examining
him yourself you will be able to learn from him
concerning everything of which we accuse him."

9 The Jews also joined in the charge by assert-
ing that all this was true.

10 When the governor motioned to him to
speak, Paul replied:

"I cheerfully make my defense, knowing that
for many years you have been a judge over this
nation. 11As you can find out, it is not more than
twelve days since I went up to worship in Jerusalem. 12They did not find me disputing with anyone in the temple or stirring up a crowd either in
the synagogues or throughout the city. 13Neither
can they prove to you the charge that they now
bring against me. 14But this I admit to you, that
according to the Way, which they call a sect, I worship the God of our ancestors, believing everything laid down according to the law or written
in the prophets. 15I have a hope in God—a hope
that they themselves also accept—that there will
be a resurrection of both[e] the righteous and the
unrighteous. 16Therefore I do my best always to
have a clear conscience toward God and all people. 17Now after some years I came to bring alms
to my nation and to offer sacrifices. 18While I was
doing this, they found me in the temple, completing the rite of purification, without any crowd or
disturbance. 19But there were some Jews from
Asia—they ought to be here before you to make
an accusation, if they have anything against me.
20Or let these men here tell what crime they had
found when I stood before the council, 21unless
it was this one sentence that I called out while
standing before them, 'It is about the resurrection
of the dead that I am on trial before you today.'"

22 But Felix, who was rather well informed
about the Way, adjourned the hearing with the
comment, "When Lysias the tribune comes
down, I will decide your case." 23Then he ordered
the centurion to keep him in custody, but to let
him have some liberty and not to prevent any of
his friends from taking care of his needs.

24 Some days later when Felix came with his
wife Drusilla, who was Jewish, he sent for Paul
and heard him speak concerning faith in Christ
Jesus. 25And as he discussed justice, self-control,
and the coming judgment, Felix became frightened and said, "Go away for the present; when I
have an opportunity, I will send for you." 26At the
same time he hoped that money would be given
him by Paul, and for that reason he used to send
for him very often and converse with him.

27 After two years had passed, Felix was succeeded by Porcius Festus; and since he wanted to
grant the Jews a favor, Felix left Paul in prison.

25 Three days after Festus had arrived in the
province, he went up from Caesarea to Jerusalem 2where the chief priests and the leaders
of the Jews gave him a report against Paul. They
appealed to him 3and requested, as a favor to
them against Paul,[f] to have him transferred to Jerusalem. They were, in fact, planning an ambush
to kill him along the way. 4Festus replied that Paul
was being kept at Caesarea, and that he himself
intended to go there shortly. 5"So," he said, "let
those of you who have the authority come down
with me, and if there is anything wrong about the
man, let them accuse him."

6 After he had stayed among them not more
than eight or ten days, he went down to Caesarea;
the next day he took his seat on the tribunal and

[a] Gk *he* [b] Gk lacks *Your Excellency* [c] Gk *Nazoreans* [d] Other ancient authorities add *and we would have judged him according to our law. 7But the chief captain Lysias came and with great violence took him out of our hands, 8commanding his accusers to come before you.* [e] Other ancient authorities read *of the dead, both of* [f] Gk *him*

ordered Paul to be brought. 7 When he arrived,
the Jews who had gone down from Jerusalem
surrounded him, bringing many serious charges
against him, which they could not prove. 8 Paul
said in his defense, "I have in no way committed
an offense against the law of the Jews, or against
the temple, or against the emperor." 9 But Festus,
wishing to do the Jews a favor, asked Paul, "Do
you wish to go up to Jerusalem and be tried there
before me on these charges?" 10 Paul said, "I am
appealing to the emperor's tribunal; this is where
I should be tried. I have done no wrong to the
Jews, as you very well know. 11 Now if I am in the
wrong and have committed something for which
I deserve to die, I am not trying to escape death;
but if there is nothing to their charges against me,
no one can turn me over to them. I appeal to the
emperor." 12 Then Festus, after he had conferred
with his council, replied, "You have appealed to
the emperor; to the emperor you will go."

13 After several days had passed, King Agrippa
and Bernice arrived at Caesarea to welcome Festus. 14 Since they were staying there several days,
Festus laid Paul's case before the king, saying,
"There is a man here who was left in prison by
Felix. 15 When I was in Jerusalem, the chief priests
and the elders of the Jews informed me about
him and asked for a sentence against him. 16 I told
them that it was not the custom of the Romans
to hand over anyone before the accused had met
the accusers face to face and had been given an
opportunity to make a defense against the charge.
17 So when they met here, I lost no time, but on
the next day took my seat on the tribunal and
ordered the man to be brought. 18 When the accusers stood up, they did not charge him with
any of the crimes[a] that I was expecting. 19 Instead
they had certain points of disagreement with
him about their own religion and about a certain
Jesus, who had died, but whom Paul asserted to
be alive. 20 Since I was at a loss how to investigate
these questions, I asked whether he wished to go
to Jerusalem and be tried there on these charges.[b]
21 But when Paul had appealed to be kept in custody for the decision of his Imperial Majesty, I ordered him to be held until I could send him to the
emperor." 22 Agrippa said to Festus, "I would like
to hear the man myself." "Tomorrow," he said,
"you will hear him."

23 So on the next day Agrippa and Bernice
came with great pomp, and they entered the audience hall with the military tribunes and the
prominent men of the city. Then Festus gave
the order and Paul was brought in. 24 And Festus
said, "King Agrippa and all here present with us,
you see this man about whom the whole Jewish
community petitioned me, both in Jerusalem
and here, shouting that he ought not to live any
longer. 25 But I found that he had done nothing
deserving death; and when he appealed to his Imperial Majesty, I decided to send him. 26 But I have
nothing definite to write to our sovereign about
him. Therefore I have brought him before all of
you, and especially before you, King Agrippa,
so that, after we have examined him, I may have
something to write— 27 for it seems to me unreasonable to send a prisoner without indicating the
charges against him."

26 Agrippa said to Paul, "You have permission
to speak for yourself." Then Paul stretched
out his hand and began to defend himself:

2 "I consider myself fortunate that it is before you, King Agrippa, I am to make my defense
today against all the accusations of the Jews,
3 because you are especially familiar with all the
customs and controversies of the Jews; therefore
I beg of you to listen to me patiently.

4 "All the Jews know my way of life from my
youth, a life spent from the beginning among my
own people and in Jerusalem. 5 They have known
for a long time, if they are willing to testify, that I
have belonged to the strictest sect of our religion
and lived as a Pharisee. 6 And now I stand here
on trial on account of my hope in the promise
made by God to our ancestors, 7 a promise that
our twelve tribes hope to attain, as they earnestly
worship day and night. It is for this hope, your
Excellency,[c] that I am accused by Jews! 8 Why is it
thought incredible by any of you that God raises
the dead?

[a] Other ancient authorities read *with anything* [b] Gk *on them* [c] Gk *O king*

9 "Indeed, I myself was convinced that I
ought to do many things against the name of
Jesus of Nazareth.[a] 10And that is what I did in Jerusalem; with authority received from the chief
priests, I not only locked up many of the saints
in prison, but I also cast my vote against them
when they were being condemned to death. 11By
punishing them often in all the synagogues I tried
to force them to blaspheme; and since I was so
furiously enraged at them, I pursued them even
to foreign cities.

12 "With this in mind, I was traveling to
Damascus with the authority and commission
of the chief priests, 13when at midday along the
road, your Excellency,[b] I saw a light from heaven,
brighter than the sun, shining around me and
my companions. 14When we had all fallen to the
ground, I heard a voice saying to me in the Hebrew[c] language, 'Saul, Saul, why are you persecuting me? It hurts you to kick against the goads.' 15I
asked, 'Who are you, Lord?' The Lord answered,
'I am Jesus whom you are persecuting. 16But get
up and stand on your feet; for I have appeared to
you for this purpose, to appoint you to serve and
testify to the things in which you have seen me[d]
and to those in which I will appear to you. 17I will
rescue you from your people and from the Gentiles—to whom I am sending you 18to open their
eyes so that they may turn from darkness to light
and from the power of Satan to God, so that they
may receive forgiveness of sins and a place among
those who are sanctified by faith in me.'

19 "After that, King Agrippa, I was not disobedient to the heavenly vision, 20but declared
first to those in Damascus, then in Jerusalem and
throughout the countryside of Judea, and also to
the Gentiles, that they should repent and turn to
God and do deeds consistent with repentance.
21For this reason the Jews seized me in the temple and tried to kill me. 22To this day I have had
help from God, and so I stand here, testifying to
both small and great, saying nothing but what the
prophets and Moses said would take place: 23that
the Messiah[e] must suffer, and that, by being the
first to rise from the dead, he would proclaim
light both to our people and to the Gentiles."

24 While he was making this defense, Festus
exclaimed, "You are out of your mind, Paul! Too
much learning is driving you insane!" 25But Paul
said, "I am not out of my mind, most excellent
Festus, but I am speaking the sober truth. 26In-
deed the king knows about these things, and to
him I speak freely; for I am certain that none of
these things has escaped his notice, for this was
not done in a corner. 27King Agrippa, do you
believe the prophets? I know that you believe."
28Agrippa said to Paul, "Are you so quickly persuading me to become a Christian?"[f] 29Paul replied, "Whether quickly or not, I pray to God
that not only you but also all who are listening to
me today might become such as I am—except for
these chains."

30 Then the king got up, and with him the
governor and Bernice and those who had been
seated with them; 31and as they were leaving, they
said to one another, "This man is doing nothing
to deserve death or imprisonment." 32Agrippa
said to Festus, "This man could have been set free
if he had not appealed to the emperor."

27 When it was decided that we were to sail
for Italy, they transferred Paul and some
other prisoners to a centurion of the Augustan
Cohort, named Julius. 2Embarking on a ship of
Adramyttium that was about to set sail to the
ports along the coast of Asia, we put to sea, accompanied by Aristarchus, a Macedonian from
Thessalonica. 3The next day we put in at Sidon;
and Julius treated Paul kindly, and allowed him
to go to his friends to be cared for. 4Putting out
to sea from there, we sailed under the lee of Cyprus, because the winds were against us. 5After
we had sailed across the sea that is off Cilicia and
Pamphylia, we came to Myra in Lycia. 6There the
centurion found an Alexandrian ship bound for
Italy and put us on board. 7We sailed slowly for
a number of days and arrived with difficulty off
Cnidus, and as the wind was against us, we sailed
under the lee of Crete off Salmone. 8Sailing past

[a] Gk *the Nazorean* [b] Gk *O king* [c] That is, *Aramaic* [d] Other ancient authorities read *the things that you have seen* [e] Or *the Christ* [f] Or *Quickly you will persuade me to play the Christian*

it with difficulty, we came to a place called Fair
Havens, near the city of Lasea.
9 Since much time had been lost and sailing
was now dangerous, because even the Fast had already gone by, Paul advised them, 10saying, "Sirs,
I can see that the voyage will be with danger and
much heavy loss, not only of the cargo and the
ship, but also of our lives." 11But the centurion
paid more attention to the pilot and to the owner
of the ship than to what Paul said. 12Since the
harbor was not suitable for spending the winter,
the majority was in favor of putting to sea from
there, on the chance that somehow they could
reach Phoenix, where they could spend the winter. It was a harbor of Crete, facing southwest and
northwest.
13 When a moderate south wind began to
blow, they thought they could achieve their purpose; so they weighed anchor and began to sail
past Crete, close to the shore. 14But soon a violent
wind, called the northeaster, rushed down from
Crete.[a] 15Since the ship was caught and could not
be turned head-on into the wind, we gave way to
it and were driven. 16By running under the lee
of a small island called Cauda[b] we were scarcely
able to get the ship's boat under control. 17After
hoisting it up they took measures[c] to undergird
the ship; then, fearing that they would run on the
Syrtis, they lowered the sea anchor and so were
driven. 18We were being pounded by the storm so
violently that on the next day they began to throw
the cargo overboard, 19and on the third day with
their own hands they threw the ship's tackle overboard. 20When neither sun nor stars appeared for
many days, and no small tempest raged, all hope
of our being saved was at last abandoned.
21 Since they had been without food for a
long time, Paul then stood up among them and
said, "Men, you should have listened to me and
not have set sail from Crete and thereby avoided
this damage and loss. 22I urge you now to keep
up your courage, for there will be no loss of life
among you, but only of the ship. 23For last night
there stood by me an angel of the God to whom
I belong and whom I worship, 24and he said, 'Do
not be afraid, Paul; you must stand before the
emperor; and indeed, God has granted safety to
all those who are sailing with you.' 25So keep up
your courage, men, for I have faith in God that it
will be exactly as I have been told. 26But we will
have to run aground on some island."
27 When the fourteenth night had come, as
we were drifting across the sea of Adria, about
midnight the sailors suspected that they were
nearing land. 28So they took soundings and
found twenty fathoms; a little farther on they
took soundings again and found fifteen fathoms.
29Fearing that we might run on the rocks, they
let down four anchors from the stern and prayed
for day to come. 30But when the sailors tried to
escape from the ship and had lowered the boat
into the sea, on the pretext of putting out anchors
from the bow, 31Paul said to the centurion and
the soldiers, "Unless these men stay in the ship,
you cannot be saved." 32Then the soldiers cut
away the ropes of the boat and set it adrift.
33 Just before daybreak, Paul urged all of
them to take some food, saying, "Today is the
fourteenth day that you have been in suspense
and remaining without food, having eaten nothing. 34Therefore I urge you to take some food, for
it will help you survive; for none of you will lose a
hair from your heads." 35After he had said this, he
took bread; and giving thanks to God in the presence of all, he broke it and began to eat. 36Then all
of them were encouraged and took food for themselves. 37(We were in all two hundred seventy-
six[d] persons in the ship.) 38After they had satisfied
their hunger, they lightened the ship by throwing
the wheat into the sea.
39 In the morning they did not recognize the
land, but they noticed a bay with a beach, on
which they planned to run the ship ashore, if they
could. 40So they cast off the anchors and left them
in the sea. At the same time they loosened the
ropes that tied the steering-oars; then hoisting the
foresail to the wind, they made for the beach.
41But striking a reef,[e] they ran the ship aground;

[a] Gk *it* [b] Other ancient authorities read *Claude* [c] Gk *helps* [d] Other ancient authorities read *seventy-six*; others, *about seventy-six* [e] Gk *place of two seas*

the bow stuck and remained immovable, but the
stern was being broken up by the force of the
waves. 42 The soldiers' plan was to kill the prisoners, so that none might swim away and escape;
43 but the centurion, wishing to save Paul, kept
them from carrying out their plan. He ordered
those who could swim to jump overboard first
and make for the land, 44 and the rest to follow,
some on planks and others on pieces of the ship.
And so it was that all were brought safely to land.

28 After we had reached safety, we then
learned that the island was called Malta.
2 The natives showed us unusual kindness. Since
it had begun to rain and was cold, they kindled a
fire and welcomed all of us around it. 3 Paul had
gathered a bundle of brushwood and was putting
it on the fire, when a viper, driven out by the heat,
fastened itself on his hand. 4 When the natives
saw the creature hanging from his hand, they said
to one another, "This man must be a murderer;
though he has escaped from the sea, justice has
not allowed him to live." 5 He, however, shook off
the creature into the fire and suffered no harm.
6 They were expecting him to swell up or drop
dead, but after they had waited a long time and
saw that nothing unusual had happened to him,
they changed their minds and began to say that
he was a god.

7 Now in the neighborhood of that place were
lands belonging to the leading man of the island,
named Publius, who received us and entertained
us hospitably for three days. 8 It so happened that
the father of Publius lay sick in bed with fever
and dysentery. Paul visited him and cured him
by praying and putting his hands on him. 9 After
this happened, the rest of the people on the island who had diseases also came and were cured.
10 They bestowed many honors on us, and when
we were about to sail, they put on board all the
provisions we needed.

11 Three months later we set sail on a ship that
had wintered at the island, an Alexandrian ship
with the Twin Brothers as its figurehead. 12 We
put in at Syracuse and stayed there for three days;
13 then we weighed anchor and came to Rhegium.
After one day there a south wind sprang up, and
on the second day we came to Puteoli. 14 There
we found believers[a] and were invited to stay with
them for seven days. And so we came to Rome.
15 The believers[a] from there, when they heard of
us, came as far as the Forum of Appius and Three
Taverns to meet us. On seeing them, Paul thanked
God and took courage.

16 When we came into Rome, Paul was allowed to live by himself, with the soldier who was
guarding him.

17 Three days later he called together the local
leaders of the Jews. When they had assembled, he
said to them, "Brothers, though I had done nothing against our people or the customs of our ancestors, yet I was arrested in Jerusalem and handed
over to the Romans. 18 When they had examined
me, the Romans[b] wanted to release me, because
there was no reason for the death penalty in my
case. 19 But when the Jews objected, I was compelled to appeal to the emperor—even though I
had no charge to bring against my nation. 20 For
this reason therefore I have asked to see you and
speak with you,[c] since it is for the sake of the hope
of Israel that I am bound with this chain." 21 They

Acts 28:17-31

Paul's last reported speech, before the Jews of Rome, provokes a division among them that echoes earlier scenes (see 13:46; 18:5-6) and fulfills scripture (Isa 6:9-10; see also Simeon's prophecy that Jesus will be "a sign that will be opposed," Luke 2:34). But the turn to the Gentiles is a rhetorical gesture, not a final verdict: Luke points out that Paul continues to welcome "all who came to him," as he had welcomed responsive Jews and Gentiles alike in previous cities. The narrative significance of the Roman audience is not that they are the last Jews before whom Paul speaks, but that they are the first Diaspora audience that has not been prejudiced by rumors and reports from Paul's opponents (28:21-22).

—NE

[a] Gk *brothers* [b] Gk *they* [c] Or *I have asked you to see me and speak with me*

replied, “We have received no letters from Judea
about you, and none of the brothers coming here
has reported or spoken anything evil about you.
22But we would like to hear from you what you
think, for with regard to this sect we know that
everywhere it is spoken against.”

23 After they had set a day to meet with him,
they came to him at his lodgings in great numbers. From morning until evening he explained
the matter to them, testifying to the kingdom
of God and trying to convince them about
Jesus both from the law of Moses and from the
prophets. 24Some were convinced by what he
had said, while others refused to believe. 25So
they disagreed with each other; and as they were
leaving, Paul made one further statement: “The
Holy Spirit was right in saying to your ancestors
through the prophet Isaiah,

26 ‘Go to this people and say,
You will indeed listen, but never understand,
and you will indeed look, but never
perceive.
27 For this people’s heart has grown dull,
and their ears are hard of hearing,
and they have shut their eyes;
so that they might not look with their
eyes,
and listen with their ears,
and understand with their heart and turn—
and I would heal them.’

28Let it be known to you then that this salvation
of God has been sent to the Gentiles; they will
listen.”[a]

30 He lived there two whole years at his own
expense[b] and welcomed all who came to him,
31proclaiming the kingdom of God and teaching
about the Lord Jesus Christ with all boldness and
without hindrance.

[a] Other ancient authorities add verse 29, *And when he had said these words, the Jews departed, arguing vigorously among themselves* [b] Or *in his own hired dwelling*

The Pauline Letters

INTRODUCTION

Elsa Tamez

Twenty-one of the twenty-seven New Testament writings are letters. We should be amazed by this fact, but we usually do not even notice it because we are accustomed to reading the Bible without thinking about its literary genres. We tend to hear and to study isolated verses, taking them out of their context. But in doing that we lose a great deal of the text's meaning. When reading Paul's writings in particular, we need to keep in mind that they are *letters* he sent to diverse Christian communities, to friends, or to co-workers. This teaches us that Paul's message comes in the midst of everyday life. His letters reflect his own day-to-day life, his thoughts about God from his particular context, and his joys and conflicts in his relationships with Christian communities. From a theological point of view, we who listen for the Word of God in the Bible—and I think especially of our communities in Central America today—may find it easier to understand the message of the biblical texts for us if we remember that God's message comes to us mediated through ancient letters that reflect people's experiences of God in the midst of daily life.

The letter was a common means of communication in antiquity. Archaeologists have found diverse types of ancient letters: personal, official, didactic, and so on. Letters provided a way of communication, mostly among literate people of means. Because the majority of the population were illiterate, those who wrote letters to them needed to ensure that someone would communicate the letter's content orally. That was clearly the case with Paul's letters. In 1 Thess 5:27, Paul asks the recipients of the letter to read it to the whole community.

Thirteen of the twenty-one New Testament letters bear Paul's name as the sender. These letters, often called the "Pauline corpus," were written or dictated either by Paul himself or by others—possibly his disciples—writing under the name of their teacher. (It was a common school practice in antiquity to compose a writing and sign it with the name of an important person, frequently a mentor, and some scholars have suggested that this practice accounts for the writings attributed to Paul that he did not himself write.) This is why there are important differences between the content of some of these letters, for example between Romans and 1 Timothy. Those two letters are dated by most scholars at two very different times: Romans in 57 or 58 CE, 1 Timothy in the 90s or perhaps even after 100. The letters reflect different contexts and the problems of two communities in different locations and different times. Scholars propose three different stages in the Pauline corpus:

Written or dictated by Paul, between 50 and 80: 1 Thessalonians, 1 and 2 Corinthians, Philippians, Philemon, Galatians, Romans

Written by others, circa 80s: Ephesians, Colossians, 2 Thessalonians

Written by others, circa turn of the second century, called Pastoral Epistles: 1–2 Timothy, Titus

Some scholars still debate whether there are more authentic Pauline letters than the seven just identified. But there is wide agreement that what is helpful for understanding any and all of these letters is to read them in their particular context.

The letters follow a structure that was common during Paul's time. Its elements are 1) an introduction that includes the sender's name, the name of the addressee, and a greeting; 2) often, a thanksgiving; 3) the body of the letter, its length and content varying according to the situation of the community or persons to whom Paul is writing; and 4) a closing word.

To the Galatians, who are Gentiles (that is, non-Jews; the Greek word *ethnē* means "nations"), Paul writes urging them to stay away from the false teachers who are demanding obedience to Moses' law through circumcision. He reminds them that God welcomes them by grace, not through circumcision. To the Corinthian community, Paul writes to advise them regarding specific practices that point to deeper theological and moral issues: how to deal with incest, for example, meat offered to idols, order during worship, and faith regarding resurrection. To the communities in Thessalonica and Philippi, he writes to strengthen their faith and to encourage them in their trials. To the Romans he writes, among other things, to clarify his position regarding the law and God's justice, and regarding the inclusion of the Gentiles as children of God. He also hopes the Roman community will sponsor his visit to Spain. To his friend Philemon he extends a personal request—though it was read publicly in the church meeting in his house—to welcome his fugitive slave, Onesimus, and treat him with love as a brother. In all his letters Paul combines exhortation and theological teaching in order to edify the communities and help them conduct themselves within an often hostile Roman society. The theology we have from Paul comes out of these concrete realities.

At the end of the letters comes a closing or final word. It includes, variously, Paul's greetings to particular members of the communities, new exhortations, reference to his personal plans, and often a blessing. Sometimes he also includes a doxology, a word of praise to God, either in the closing or within the body of the letter.

The letter, as a literary genre, was a very useful missionary strategy. It acted as the presence of the apostle even when he was far away. Paul founded communities and then, through his letters, strengthened and exhorted them and clarified some doctrinal issues. We sometimes encounter him discussing unfinished topics or defending himself from those who were attacking him. Sometimes he talks about his personal situation, looking for solidarity and support from the community. We see this when Paul was in prison: he needed the prayers and solidarity of the community in Philippi. He also appealed for the solidarity of the Gentiles when he was collecting the offering for the needy in Jerusalem (Gal 2:10; 2 Cor 8–9). Later, when his relation with the church leaders in Jerusalem was tense, he appealed to the community in Rome for their prayers so that the leaders in Jerusalem would receive the collection (Rom 15:30-32). Paul was a good writer, and despite the clear evidence that he was often opposed, the fact that his letters were collected and circulated among the churches shows that, at least some of the time, members of the churches found his messages persuasive and authoritative.

We know that some of Paul's letters were lost. In 1 Cor 5:9 the apostle speaks of a previous letter he wrote; and in 2 Cor 2:3-4 he speaks of a letter he wrote with "many tears." In Col 4:16 we read of a letter that Paul wrote to the church in Laodicea. Evidently, Paul wrote many more letters, but we have only a few in the New Testament. These survived because little by little they became known and shared among the Christian communities spread all over this part of the Roman Empire. They were copied and in time became a valuable heritage from the first apostle to the Gentiles, worthy of being handed on in the canon of the New Testament.

Many of the main theological concepts in our churches today—including sin, grace, salvation, and justification—come from Paul's theology, although we do not always understand them in exactly the way Paul did. Many of these concepts are expressed in rather abstract terms, which is why many have considered Paul more a theologian than a missionary. However, we should not underestimate his missionary work, since it was through his experience with God in everyday

life, in his missionary work and his relationship with the people of the provinces of the Roman Empire, that his theology emerged. He traveled extensively, by boat and on foot, as we read in Acts. He founded a number of communities and worked with his hands day and night to take care of himself, since he did not want to be a burden on the communities he was evangelizing (1 Thess 2:9). He did not want to accept the support of important people either, because he did not want to lose his freedom. This seems to have been an urgent concern with some people from Corinth (2 Cor 12:13). Paul suffered persecution, imprisonment, whippings, beatings, hunger, cold, danger of death, and shipwrecks. He mentions all this in 2 Cor 6:4-7, in the course of a quarrel with some people he ironically calls the "super-apostles." For Paul, all this suffering was the true mark of his apostleship. Through his letters we see this man inspired by God, passionate about proclaiming as the Son of God, as a *true* Savior and Lord, a Jewish man crucified by the Roman Empire but resurrected by God.

Apostle to the Gentiles

Paul directed his mission to the Gentiles, but—as he explains in Rom 11:13-16—even as "apostle to the Gentiles," he also had the welfare of his fellow Jews at heart. Although he was proud of being a Jew (Phil 3:4b-6), for him the God of Abraham and the Jews was also the God of the Gentiles. What Paul called "my gospel" (Rom 2:16; compare 2 Tim 2:8) had to do with an emphasis on God's grace that encompassed Jews and Gentiles alike, without Gentiles having to follow Moses' law. This is especially the theme of Galatians (Gal 2:7-9). Paul's concern for the Gentiles may be understood in part in light of his experience while growing up in a Gentile city. He was born and reared in Tarsus, a Greek city important for its schools and library. Paul was familiar with Roman culture and law. According to the books of Acts, Paul was a Roman citizen. Having a triple cultural heritage—Jewish, Greek, and Roman—he was interested in bringing all people to participate in God's promise to Abraham and to become part of God's people.

While Jewish, Greek, and Roman traditions imagined all the nations eventually becoming united, though in very different ways, for Paul this was a possibility to be pursued now, in obedience to the crucified and risen Jesus. The novelty of this message brought him trouble, misunderstandings, and conflicts with Roman officials and with the most conservative sector of the Jews, apparently including some from the church in Jerusalem. It was apparently not easy for some Jews to accept as an equal an uncircumcised Gentile who did not follow Moses's law. This cultural clash was not easy to overcome. Paul, on the other hand, urged the Gentile communities to affirm that those baptized in Christ had been made equals, regardless of ethnicity (Jew or Gentile), class (master or slave), or gender, as stated in Gal 3:28.

Through his letters we observe the passionate personality of Paul. He tells how, before becoming a follower of Jesus Christ, he had violently persecuted the churches out of his zeal for his ancestors' traditions (Gal 1:13-14). Later, after the resurrected Christ appeared to him, he changed radically and became just as passionate about the gospel, and particularly about preaching it to the Gentiles. The former persecutor now was persecuted, by Jews and Romans alike. Several times he was imprisoned and faced trials. He spent the last days of his life in prison, in chains. And, according to the church's tradition, he was sentenced to death by the Romans and died a martyr.

The Death and Resurrection of Jesus in Paul's Thought

Paul's letters are the earliest documents that emerged from the Christian movement. The Gospels that speak of Jesus' life were written much later. In Paul's time, Christian communities remembered Jesus' life through oral tradition as they repeated stories about Jesus in their worship. They sang hymns proclaiming Jesus' death as a sacrifice offered for the forgiveness of sins through his blood. According to this interpretation of Jesus' death, neither Jews nor converted Gentiles needed to sacrifice animals in the Temple to be purified or to receive God's forgiveness; rather Jesus' death was enough. In Paul's letters we observe him adopting these themes regarding Jesus' death. But he also *adapted* them, coming to emphasize more Jesus' crucifixion and resurrection. Our present emphasis on the importance of Jesus' crucifixion comes from Paul. It was a key theme for him because it was a way of remembering the historic way Jesus died, and because from it emerged the question of who condemned him to die. Crucifixion was the death penalty imposed by the Roman Empire on slaves and subversives. Jesus was not a slave, but he probably died because he was seen as an insubordinate and dangerously charismatic person (compare John 11:48: "If we let him go on like this, everyone will believe in him…"). Paul declares that Jesus took "the form of a slave" (NRSV "servant"), language that may point to the shameful way Jesus died (Phil 2:7). To proclaim faith in a *crucified* man was crazy in the view of Greek wisdom and a scandal for Jewish culture (1 Cor 1:23). For Paul, however, it signaled God's solidarity with humanity. God was moved to compassion—even in the face of a perverse society that deserves to die for its injustice (Rom 1:18; 3:21-24)—moved enough to offer people a new way of life, modeled by Jesus.

Paul's theological emphasis on the resurrected Christ marks the faith in which this newness of life is possible. We may fairly summarize this aspect of Paul's thought by saying that God's justice was inevitably at odds with what the Roman Empire claimed was justice! (See Introduction to Romans for my thoughts on how my cultural background affects my biblical interpretation.)

— Translated by Leticia A. Guardiola-Sáenz

The Letter of Paul to the Romans

PAUL ADDRESSES THIS LETTER to the Christian believers in Rome, most of whom were Gentiles. He writes from Corinth, as he travels to Jerusalem to deliver a collection for the needy (15:25-28). He dictates the letter to Tertius (16:22) while staying at Gaius's home (16:23), and sends it to Rome with Phoebe (16:1), a leader of the church in Cenchreae. Paul has never visited the church in Rome but now plans to visit them on his way to Spain, where he plans to travel with their help (15:24).

When Paul wrote this letter, around 57–58 CE, he was in a strained relationship with the church of Jerusalem. He had been evangelizing Gentiles without asking them to fulfill the law or get circumcised. For Paul, faith in Jesus as the Messiah was enough. God's grace was equally enough for both Jews and Gentiles, but the tensions described in Galatians 1 suggest that some in the Jerusalem church did not seem to share this idea.

To better understand Paul it is important to read this letter in its context of Roman rule and the customs of the Jewish culture. Otherwise his teachings can sound like dogmas that have nothing to do with real life.

In his letter Paul explains his position regarding the law and how it relates to both Jews and Gentiles (chs. 1–8). He illustrates how Gentiles and Jews have equally sinned, the Jews with their law and the Gentiles without the law, creating unjust and deceiving ways of social life (1:18). Paul calls this social reality, full of injustice, *sin* (3:9)—a major sin that leads everyone to destruction (3:9-20). This situation deserves God's punishment: death. But God's love is so immense that instead of punishing us, God shows us a *new justice* (3:21-26), different from the justice practiced by the Greco-Roman and Jewish societies. God's justice was present in Jesus' life, which moved him to give up his life in solidarity with many as he was crucified by the Roman Empire. The resurrection was then God's approval of Jesus' actions and life. By participating in the way Jesus lived and died, people are forgiven the sin produced through all the injustices committed by Jews and Gentiles. They are freed so that they can live out the justice they have received (6:1-23), like new people in a new creation, not according to selfish interests. This is only possible when people live according to the Spirit (8:1-4).

Paul also deals with the matter of *election*, since speaking of Gentiles as children of God raises the question of Israel as chosen people. He explains (chs. 9–11) that election has always been by grace, through God's mercy (9:16). God rejects exclusion, and out of mercy elects instead those whom society has rejected. God elected Israel, a small nation often oppressed by neighboring empires, in order to liberate it. But when those elected stop following God's paths of justice, the election is suspended and can only be resumed when people return to the paths of justice and make visible God's mercy (11:20-21). That is why Paul warns the Gentiles, using the parable of the olive tree, that they must "not become proud, but stand in awe. For if God did not spare the natural branches, perhaps God will not spare you" (11:20-21).

In the last chapters Paul writes about some issues of everyday life. One has to do with discrimination within the community due to certain dietary practices (14:1—15:7). Some Gentiles, who were the majority, were probably looking down on some people of Jewish background because they were refraining from certain foods and were observing certain days. Paul encourages them not to judge or despise one another because of these minor details, lest they lose sight of the fundamental reason for their gathering, "For the kingdom of God is not food and drink but righteousness and peace and joy in the Holy Spirit" (14:17).

At the end of the letter Paul sends greetings to a number of people, including women (who are eight of the twenty-five people named). Many women were leaders and coworkers with Paul. As he names the people to whom he is sending greetings, he praises them for their work. That is how we know that some women were ministers, teachers, and apostles—and that many of them, including Prisca (16:3-4), risked their lives or, like the apostle Junia (16:7), had been in jail.

Romans can be outlined as follows: greetings and plans (1:1-15); God's justice for all (1:16—4:25); practicing God's justice amid ever-present threats (chs. 5–8); God's election, exclusion, and grace (chs. 9–11); guidance for everyday life (12:1—15:13); and farewell: plans, greetings, and doxology (15:14—16:27).

My reading of Romans is conditioned by my personal and social contexts. I grew up in Monterrey, México—a city marked by dramatic social differences—in a large and poor family where eating meat once in a while and writing with a new pencil represented true happiness. My theological formation happened in Central America during the 1970s and 1980s. That was a context known for social injustice, oppression, and the dictatorships of El Salvador, Guatemala, and Nicaragua, where thousands were tortured, murdered, or disappeared, and people cried out to God for justice. My awareness that 60 percent of Latin America's population—mostly women—live in poverty due to an economic system that mercilessly excludes the weakest has made me denounce the horrors of structural sin. Reading Romans from these realities helps me to see that the letter proclaims good news for all.

— Elsa Tamez

Translated by Leticia A. Guardiola-Sáenz

1 Paul, a servant[a] of Jesus Christ, called to be
an apostle, set apart for the gospel of God,
2 which he promised beforehand through his
prophets in the holy scriptures, 3 the gospel concerning his Son, who was descended from David
according to the flesh 4 and was declared to be
Son of God with power according to the spirit[b] of
holiness by resurrection from the dead, Jesus
Christ our Lord, 5 through whom we have received grace and apostleship to bring about the
obedience of faith among all the Gentiles for
the sake of his name, 6 including yourselves who
are called to belong to Jesus Christ,
7 To all God's beloved in Rome, who are
called to be saints:

Grace to you and peace from God our Father
and the Lord Jesus Christ.

8 First, I thank my God through Jesus Christ
for all of you, because your faith is proclaimed
throughout the world. 9 For God, whom I serve
with my spirit by announcing the gospel[c] of his
Son, is my witness that without ceasing I remember you always in my prayers, 10 asking that
by God's will I may somehow at last succeed in
coming to you. 11 For I am longing to see you so
that I may share with you some spiritual gift to
strengthen you— 12 or rather so that we may be
mutually encouraged by each other's faith, both
yours and mine. 13 I want you to know, brothers
and sisters,[d] that I have often intended to come
to you (but thus far have been prevented), in order that I may reap some harvest among you as
I have among the rest of the Gentiles. 14 I am a
debtor both to Greeks and to barbarians, both to
the wise and to the foolish 15 —hence my eagerness to proclaim the gospel to you also who are
in Rome.
16 For I am not ashamed of the gospel; it is
the power of God for salvation to everyone who
has faith, to the Jew first and also to the Greek.
17 For in it the righteousness of God is revealed
through faith for faith; as it is written, "The one
who is righteous will live by faith."[e]

18 For the wrath of God is revealed from
heaven against all ungodliness and wickedness
of those who by their wickedness suppress the
truth. 19 For what can be known about God is
plain to them, because God has shown it to them.
20 Ever since the creation of the world his eternal
power and divine nature, invisible though they
are, have been understood and seen through the
things he has made. So they are without excuse;
21 for though they knew God, they did not honor
him as God or give thanks to him, but they became futile in their thinking, and their senseless
minds were darkened. 22 Claiming to be wise, they
became fools; 23 and they exchanged the glory of
the immortal God for images resembling a mortal
human being or birds or four-footed animals or
reptiles.
24 Therefore God gave them up in the lusts
of their hearts to impurity, to the degrading of
their bodies among themselves, 25 because they
exchanged the truth about God for a lie and worshiped and served the creature rather than the
Creator, who is blessed forever! Amen.
26 For this reason God gave them up to degrading passions. Their women exchanged natural intercourse for unnatural, 27 and in the same
way also the men, giving up natural intercourse

Romans 1:24-27

Paul rails against the unnatural worship of images instead of the God of all creation. He writes about men who have forsaken "natural intercourse" to be "consumed with passion for one another." On one reading of the passage, his theme is that it is wrong to change one's nature. Heterosexual men should not exchange their nature for homosexual practices (as when heterosexual slaves were forced into homosexual activities such as prostitution). On the same principle, we might infer that homosexuals should not exchange their nature, or orientation, for heterosexual practices.

— MDLT

[a] Gk *slave* [b] Or *Spirit* [c] Gk *my spirit in the gospel* [d] Gk *brothers*
[e] Or *The one who is righteous through faith will live*

with women, were consumed with passion for
one another. Men committed shameless acts with
men and received in their own persons the due
penalty for their error.

28 And since they did not see fit to acknowledge God, God gave them up to a debased mind
and to things that should not be done. 29They
were filled with every kind of wickedness, evil,
covetousness, malice. Full of envy, murder, strife,
deceit, craftiness, they are gossips, 30slanderers,
God-haters,[a] insolent, haughty, boastful, inven-
tors of evil, rebellious toward parents, 31foolish,
faithless, heartless, ruthless. 32They know God's
decree, that those who practice such things deserve to die—yet they not only do them but even
applaud others who practice them.

2 Therefore you have no excuse, whoever you
are, when you judge others; for in passing
judgment on another you condemn yourself,
because you, the judge, are doing the very same
things. 2You say,[b] "We know that God's judgment
on those who do such things is in accordance
with truth." 3Do you imagine, whoever you are,
that when you judge those who do such things
and yet do them yourself, you will escape the
judgment of God? 4Or do you despise the riches
of his kindness and forbearance and patience? Do
you not realize that God's kindness is meant to
lead you to repentance? 5But by your hard and
impenitent heart you are storing up wrath for
yourself on the day of wrath, when God's righteous judgment will be revealed. 6For he will repay according to each one's deeds: 7to those who
by patiently doing good seek for glory and honor
and immortality, he will give eternal life; 8while
for those who are self-seeking and who obey not
the truth but wickedness, there will be wrath and
fury. 9There will be anguish and distress for everyone who does evil, the Jew first and also the
Greek, 10but glory and honor and peace for everyone who does good, the Jew first and also the
Greek. 11For God shows no partiality.

12 All who have sinned apart from the law
will also perish apart from the law, and all who
have sinned under the law will be judged by the
law. 13For it is not the hearers of the law who are
righteous in God's sight, but the doers of the law
who will be justified. 14When Gentiles, who do
not possess the law, do instinctively what the law
requires, these, though not having the law, are
a law to themselves. 15They show that what the
law requires is written on their hearts, to which
their own conscience also bears witness; and
their conflicting thoughts will accuse or perhaps
excuse them 16on the day when, according to my
gospel, God, through Jesus Christ, will judge the
secret thoughts of all.

17 But if you call yourself a Jew and rely on
the law and boast of your relation to God 18and
know his will and determine what is best because
you are instructed in the law, 19and if you are sure
that you are a guide to the blind, a light to those
who are in darkness, 20a corrector of the foolish,
a teacher of children, having in the law the em-
bodiment of knowledge and truth, 21you, then,
that teach others, will you not teach yourself?
While you preach against stealing, do you steal?
22You that forbid adultery, do you commit adultery? You that abhor idols, do you rob temples?
23You that boast in the law, do you dishonor God
by breaking the law? 24For, as it is written, "The
name of God is blasphemed among the Gentiles
because of you."

25 Circumcision indeed is of value if you
obey the law; but if you break the law, your circumcision has become uncircumcision. 26So, if
those who are uncircumcised keep the requirements of the law, will not their uncircumcision be
regarded as circumcision? 27Then those who are
physically uncircumcised but keep the law will
condemn you that have the written code and circumcision but break the law. 28For a person is not
a Jew who is one outwardly, nor is true circumcision something external and physical. 29Rather, a
person is a Jew who is one inwardly, and real circumcision is a matter of the heart—it is spiritual
and not literal. Such a person receives praise not
from others but from God.

3 Then what advantage has the Jew? Or what
is the value of circumcision? 2Much, in every

[a] Or *God-hated* [b] Gk lacks *You say*

way. For in the first place the Jews[a] were entrusted with the oracles of God. 3What if some were
unfaithful? Will their faithlessness nullify the
faithfulness of God? 4By no means! Although
everyone is a liar, let God be proved true, as it is
written,

"So that you may be justified in your words,
and prevail in your judging."[b]

5But if our injustice serves to confirm the justice
of God, what should we say? That God is unjust
to inflict wrath on us? (I speak in a human way.)
6By no means! For then how could God judge
the world? 7But if through my falsehood God's
truthfulness abounds to his glory, why am I still
being condemned as a sinner? 8And why not say
(as some people slander us by saying that we say),
"Let us do evil so that good may come"? Their
condemnation is deserved!

9 What then? Are we any better off?[c] No, not
at all; for we have already charged that all, both
Jews and Greeks, are under the power of sin, 10as
it is written:

"There is no one who is righteous, not even
one;
11 there is no one who has understanding,
there is no one who seeks God.
12 All have turned aside, together they have
become worthless;
there is no one who shows kindness,
there is not even one."
13 "Their throats are opened graves;
they use their tongues to deceive."
"The venom of vipers is under their lips."
14 "Their mouths are full of cursing and
bitterness."
15 "Their feet are swift to shed blood;
16 ruin and misery are in their paths,
17 and the way of peace they have not known."
18 "There is no fear of God before their eyes."

19 Now we know that whatever the law says,
it speaks to those who are under the law, so that
every mouth may be silenced, and the whole
world may be held accountable to God. 20For
"no human being will be justified in his sight" by
deeds prescribed by the law, for through the law
comes the knowledge of sin.

21 But now, apart from law, the righteousness of God has been disclosed, and is attested by
the law and the prophets, 22the righteousness of
God through faith in Jesus Christ[d] for all who believe. For there is no distinction, 23since all have
sinned and fall short of the glory of God; 24they
are now justified by his grace as a gift, through
the redemption that is in Christ Jesus, 25whom
God put forward as a sacrifice of atonement[e] by
his blood, effective through faith. He did this to
show his righteousness, because in his divine forbearance he had passed over the sins previously
committed; 26it was to prove at the present time
that he himself is righteous and that he justifies
the one who has faith in Jesus.[f]

27 Then what becomes of boasting? It is excluded. By what law? By that of works? No, but
by the law of faith. 28For we hold that a person
is justified by faith apart from works prescribed
by the law. 29Or is God the God of Jews only? Is
he not the God of Gentiles also? Yes, of Gentiles
also, 30since God is one; and he will justify the
circumcised on the ground of faith and the uncircumcised through that same faith. 31Do we then
overthrow the law by this faith? By no means! On
the contrary, we uphold the law.

4 What then are we to say was gained by[g]
Abraham, our ancestor according to the
flesh? 2For if Abraham was justified by works, he
has something to boast about, but not before
God. 3For what does the scripture say? "Abraham
believed God, and it was reckoned to him as righteousness." 4Now to one who works, wages are
not reckoned as a gift but as something due. 5But
to one who without works trusts him who justifies the ungodly, such faith is reckoned as righteousness. 6So also David speaks of the
blessedness of those to whom God reckons righteousness apart from works:

7 "Blessed are those whose iniquities are
forgiven,

[a] Gk *they* [b] Gk *when you are being judged* [c] Or *at any disadvantage?* [d] Or *through the faith of Jesus Christ*
[e] Or *a place of atonement* [f] Or *who has the faith of Jesus* [g] Other ancient authorities read *say about*

Romans 4:1

One conventional—but now controversial—way to read the opening chapters of Romans is as a critique of Jewish boasting. The goal in Romans 4, however, is to show that Abraham is the ancestor of *all* the faithful, not just of Jews. That message would have undermined the ethnic presumptions of Greeks and Romans as well. Paul holds out as ancestor for all people an immigrant who left behind a comfortable identity as citizen of what he had come to see as an idolatrous empire in order to follow God into the wilderness.

— *NE*

and whose sins are covered;
8 blessed is the one against whom the Lord will
not reckon sin."
9 Is this blessedness, then, pronounced only
on the circumcised, or also on the uncircumcised? We say, "Faith was reckoned to Abraham
as righteousness." 10How then was it reckoned to
him? Was it before or after he had been circumcised? It was not after, but before he was circumcised. 11He received the sign of circumcision as
a seal of the righteousness that he had by faith
while he was still uncircumcised. The purpose
was to make him the ancestor of all who believe
without being circumcised and who thus have
righteousness reckoned to them, 12and likewise
the ancestor of the circumcised who are not only
circumcised but who also follow the example of
the faith that our ancestor Abraham had before
he was circumcised.
13 For the promise that he would inherit the
world did not come to Abraham or to his descendants through the law but through the righteousness of faith. 14If it is the adherents of the law who
are to be the heirs, faith is null and the promise is
void. 15For the law brings wrath; but where there
is no law, neither is there violation.
16 For this reason it depends on faith, in order that the promise may rest on grace and be
guaranteed to all his descendants, not only to the
adherents of the law but also to those who share
the faith of Abraham (for he is the father of all of
us, 17as it is written, "I have made you the father
of many nations")—in the presence of the God in
whom he believed, who gives life to the dead and
calls into existence the things that do not exist.
18Hoping against hope, he believed that he would
become "the father of many nations," according to
what was said, "So numerous shall your descendants be." 19He did not weaken in faith when he
considered his own body, which was already[a] as
good as dead (for he was about a hundred years
old), or when he considered the barrenness of
Sarah's womb. 20No distrust made him waver concerning the promise of God, but he grew strong in
his faith as he gave glory to God, 21being fully convinced that God was able to do what he had promised. 22Therefore his faith[b] "was reckoned to him
as righteousness." 23Now the words, "it was reckoned to him," were written not for his sake alone,
24but for ours also. It will be reckoned to us who
believe in him who raised Jesus our Lord from the
dead, 25who was handed over to death for our trespasses and was raised for our justification.

5 Therefore, since we are justified by faith, we[c]
have peace with God through our Lord Jesus
Christ, 2through whom we have obtained access[d]
to this grace in which we stand; and we[e] boast in
our hope of sharing the glory of God. 3And not
only that, but we[e] also boast in our sufferings,
knowing that suffering produces endurance, 4and
endurance produces character, and character
produces hope, 5and hope does not disappoint
us, because God's love has been poured into
our hearts through the Holy Spirit that has been
given to us.
6 For while we were still weak, at the right
time Christ died for the ungodly. 7Indeed, rarely
will anyone die for a righteous person—though
perhaps for a good person someone might actually dare to die. 8But God proves his love for us in

[a] Other ancient authorities lack *already* [b] Gk *Therefore it* [c] Other ancient authorities read *let us* [d] Other ancient authorities add *by faith* [e] Or *let us*

that while we still were sinners Christ died for us. 9 Much more surely then, now that we have been justified by his blood, will we be saved through him from the wrath of God.[a] 10 For if while we were enemies, we were reconciled to God through the death of his Son, much more surely, having been reconciled, will we be saved by his life. 11 But more than that, we even boast in God through our Lord Jesus Christ, through whom we have now received reconciliation.

12 Therefore, just as sin came into the world through one man, and death came through sin, and so death spread to all because all have sinned— 13 sin was indeed in the world before the law, but sin is not reckoned when there is no law. 14 Yet death exercised dominion from Adam to Moses, even over those whose sins were not like the transgression of Adam, who is a type of the one who was to come.

15 But the free gift is not like the trespass. For if the many died through the one man's trespass, much more surely have the grace of God and the free gift in the grace of the one man, Jesus Christ, abounded for the many. 16 And the free gift is not like the effect of the one man's sin. For the judgment following one trespass brought condemnation, but the free gift following many trespasses brings justification. 17 If, because of the one man's trespass, death exercised dominion through that one, much more surely will those who receive the abundance of grace and the free gift of righteousness exercise dominion in life through the one man, Jesus Christ.

18 Therefore just as one man's trespass led to condemnation for all, so one man's act of righteousness leads to justification and life for all. 19 For just as by the one man's disobedience the many were made sinners, so by the one man's obedience the many will be made righteous. 20 But law came in, with the result that the trespass multiplied; but where sin increased, grace abounded all the more, 21 so that, just as sin exercised dominion in death, so grace might also exercise dominion through justification[b] leading to eternal life through Jesus Christ our Lord.

6 What then are we to say? Should we continue in sin in order that grace may abound? 2 By no means! How can we who died to sin go on living in it? 3 Do you not know that all of us who have been baptized into Christ Jesus were baptized into his death? 4 Therefore we have been buried with him by baptism into death, so that, just as Christ was raised from the dead by the glory of the Father, so we too might walk in newness of life.

5 For if we have been united with him in a death like his, we will certainly be united with him in a resurrection like his. 6 We know that our old self was crucified with him so that the body of sin might be destroyed, and we might no longer be enslaved to sin. 7 For whoever has died is freed from sin. 8 But if we have died with Christ, we believe that we will also live with him. 9 We know that Christ, being raised from the dead, will never die again; death no longer has dominion over him. 10 The death he died, he died to sin, once for all; but the life he lives, he lives to God. 11 So you also must consider yourselves dead to sin and alive to God in Christ Jesus.

12 Therefore, do not let sin exercise dominion in your mortal bodies, to make you obey their passions. 13 No longer present your members to sin as instruments[c] of wickedness, but present yourselves to God as those who have been brought from death to life, and present your members to God as instruments[c] of righteousness. 14 For sin will have no dominion over you, since you are not under law but under grace.

15 What then? Should we sin because we are not under law but under grace? By no means! 16 Do you not know that if you present yourselves to anyone as obedient slaves, you are slaves of the one whom you obey, either of sin, which leads to death, or of obedience, which leads to righteousness? 17 But thanks be to God that you, having once been slaves of sin, have become obedient from the heart to the form of teaching to which you were entrusted, 18 and that you, having been set free from sin, have become slaves of righteousness. 19 I am speaking in human terms because of

[a] Gk *the wrath* [b] Or *righteousness* [c] Or *weapons*

your natural limitations.[a] For just as you once
presented your members as slaves to impurity
and to greater and greater iniquity, so now present your members as slaves to righteousness for
sanctification.

20 When you were slaves of sin, you were
free in regard to righteousness. 21So what advantage did you then get from the things of which
you now are ashamed? The end of those things is
death. 22But now that you have been freed from
sin and enslaved to God, the advantage you get
is sanctification. The end is eternal life. 23For the
wages of sin is death, but the free gift of God is
eternal life in Christ Jesus our Lord.

7 Do you not know, brothers and sisters[b]—for
I am speaking to those who know the law—
that the law is binding on a person only during
that person's lifetime? 2Thus a married woman is
bound by the law to her husband as long as he
lives; but if her husband dies, she is discharged
from the law concerning the husband. 3Accord-
ingly, she will be called an adulteress if she lives
with another man while her husband is alive.
But if her husband dies, she is free from that law,
and if she marries another man, she is not an
adulteress.

4 In the same way, my friends,[b] you have died
to the law through the body of Christ, so that
you may belong to another, to him who has been
raised from the dead in order that we may bear
fruit for God. 5While we were living in the flesh,
our sinful passions, aroused by the law, were at
work in our members to bear fruit for death. 6But
now we are discharged from the law, dead to that
which held us captive, so that we are slaves not
under the old written code but in the new life of
the Spirit.

7 What then should we say? That the law is
sin? By no means! Yet, if it had not been for the
law, I would not have known sin. I would not have
known what it is to covet if the law had not said,
"You shall not covet." 8But sin, seizing an opportunity in the commandment, produced in me all
kinds of covetousness. Apart from the law sin lies
dead. 9I was once alive apart from the law, but
when the commandment came, sin revived 10and
I died, and the very commandment that promised
life proved to be death to me. 11For sin, seizing an
opportunity in the commandment, deceived me
and through it killed me. 12So the law is holy, and
the commandment is holy and just and good.

13 Did what is good, then, bring death to me?
By no means! It was sin, working death in me
through what is good, in order that sin might be
shown to be sin, and through the commandment
might become sinful beyond measure.

14 For we know that the law is spiritual; but I
am of the flesh, sold into slavery under sin.[c] 15I do
not understand my own actions. For I do not do
what I want, but I do the very thing I hate. 16Now
if I do what I do not want, I agree that the law is
good. 17But in fact it is no longer I that do it, but
sin that dwells within me. 18For I know that nothing good dwells within me, that is, in my flesh. I
can will what is right, but I cannot do it. 19For I
do not do the good I want, but the evil I do not
want is what I do. 20Now if I do what I do not
want, it is no longer I that do it, but sin that dwells
within me.

21 So I find it to be a law that when I want
to do what is good, evil lies close at hand. 22For I
delight in the law of God in my inmost self, 23but
I see in my members another law at war with the
law of my mind, making me captive to the law of
sin that dwells in my members. 24Wretched man
that I am! Who will rescue me from this body of
death? 25Thanks be to God through Jesus Christ
our Lord!

So then, with my mind I am a slave to the law
of God, but with my flesh I am a slave to the law
of sin.

8 There is therefore now no condemnation for
those who are in Christ Jesus. 2For the law of
the Spirit[d] of life in Christ Jesus has set you[e] free
from the law of sin and of death. 3For God has
done what the law, weakened by the flesh, could
not do: by sending his own Son in the likeness of

[a] Gk *the weakness of your flesh* [b] Gk *brothers* [c] Gk *sold under sin* [d] Or *spirit*
[e] Here the Greek word *you* is singular number; other ancient authorities read *me* or *us*

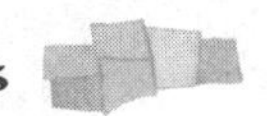

sinful flesh, and to deal with sin,[a] he condemned sin in the flesh, 4so that the just requirement of the law might be fulfilled in us, who walk not according to the flesh but according to the Spirit.[b] 5For those who live according to the flesh set their minds on the things of the flesh, but those who live according to the Spirit[b] set their minds on the things of the Spirit.[b] 6To set the mind on the flesh is death, but to set the mind on the Spirit[b] is life and peace. 7For this reason the mind that is set on the flesh is hostile to God; it does not submit to God's law—indeed it cannot, 8and those who are in the flesh cannot please God.

9 But you are not in the flesh; you are in the Spirit,[b] since the Spirit of God dwells in you. Anyone who does not have the Spirit of Christ does not belong to him. 10But if Christ is in you, though the body is dead because of sin, the Spirit[b] is life because of righteousness. 11If the Spirit of him who raised Jesus from the dead dwells in you, he who raised Christ[c] from the dead will give life to your mortal bodies also through[d] his Spirit that dwells in you.

12 So then, brothers and sisters,[e] we are debtors, not to the flesh, to live according to the flesh— 13for if you live according to the flesh, you will die; but if by the Spirit you put to death the deeds of the body, you will live. 14For all who are led by the Spirit of God are children of God. 15For you did not receive a spirit of slavery to fall back into fear, but you have received a spirit of adoption. When we cry, "Abba![f] Father!" 16it is that very Spirit bearing witness[g] with our spirit that we are children of God, 17and if children, then heirs, heirs of God and joint heirs with Christ—if, in fact, we suffer with him so that we may also be glorified with him.

18 I consider that the sufferings of this present time are not worth comparing with the glory about to be revealed to us. 19For the creation waits with eager longing for the revealing of the children of God; 20for the creation was subjected to futility, not of its own will but by the will of the one who subjected it, in hope 21that the creation itself will be set free from its bondage to decay and will obtain the freedom of the glory of the children of God. 22We know that the whole creation has been groaning in labor pains until now; 23and not only the creation, but we ourselves, who have the first fruits of the Spirit, groan inwardly while we wait for adoption, the redemption of our bodies. 24For in[h] hope we were saved. Now hope that is seen is not hope. For who hopes[i] for what is seen? 25But if we hope for what we do not see, we wait for it with patience.

26 Likewise the Spirit helps us in our weakness; for we do not know how to pray as we ought, but that very Spirit intercedes[j] with sighs too deep for words. 27And God,[k] who searches the heart, knows what is the mind of the Spirit, because the Spirit[l] intercedes for the saints according to the will of God.[m]

28 We know that all things work together for good[n] for those who love God, who are called according to his purpose. 29For those whom he foreknew he also predestined to be conformed to the image of his Son, in order that he might be the firstborn within a large family.[o] 30And those whom he predestined he also called; and those whom he called he also justified; and those whom he justified he also glorified.

31 What then are we to say about these things? If God is for us, who is against us? 32He who did not withhold his own Son, but gave him up for all of us, will he not with him also give us everything else? 33Who will bring any charge against God's elect? It is God who justifies. 34Who is to condemn? It is Christ Jesus, who died, yes, who was raised, who is at the right hand of God, who indeed intercedes for us.[p] 35Who will separate us

[a] Or *and as a sin offering* [b] Or *spirit* [c] Other ancient authorities read *the Christ* or *Christ Jesus* or *Jesus Christ* [d] Other ancient authorities read *on account of* [e] Gk *brothers* [f] Aramaic for *Father* [g] Or [15]*a spirit of adoption, by which we cry, "Abba! Father!"* [16]*The Spirit itself bears witness* [h] Or *by* [i] Other ancient authorities read *awaits* [j] Other ancient authorities add *for us* [k] Gk *the one* [l] Gk *he* or *it* [m] Gk *according to God* [n] Other ancient authorities read *God makes all things work together for good, or in all things God works for good* [o] Gk *among many brothers* [p] Or *Is it Christ Jesus . . . for us?*

from the love of Christ? Will hardship, or distress,
or persecution, or famine, or nakedness, or peril,
or sword? 36 As it is written,

"For your sake we are being killed all day
long;
we are accounted as sheep to be
slaughtered."

37 No, in all these things we are more than conquerors through him who loved us. 38 For I am
convinced that neither death, nor life, nor angels,
nor rulers, nor things present, nor things to come,
nor powers, 39 nor height, nor depth, nor anything
else in all creation, will be able to separate us from
the love of God in Christ Jesus our Lord.

Romans 8:28-39

Paul's assurance of the love of God is one of the most cherished texts for many Christians. Much less well-known, however, are the climactic lines that follow and to which Paul means to lead his reader, at 9:1-4. Paul would gladly renounce all the spiritual benefits he has just named for the sake of his fellow Israelites, for whom these benefits represent the "irrevocable" gifts and calling of God (11:29). His point is not to congratulate Gentile Christians but to model for them appropriate humility and concern for others.

—*NE*

9 I am speaking the truth in Christ—I am not
lying; my conscience confirms it by the Holy
Spirit— 2 I have great sorrow and unceasing anguish in my heart. 3 For I could wish that I myself
were accursed and cut off from Christ for the sake
of my own people,[a] my kindred according to the
flesh. 4 They are Israelites, and to them belong the
adoption, the glory, the covenants, the giving of
the law, the worship, and the promises; 5 to them
belong the patriarchs, and from them, according
to the flesh, comes the Messiah,[b] who is over all,
God blessed forever.[c] Amen.

6 It is not as though the word of God had
failed. For not all Israelites truly belong to Israel,
7 and not all of Abraham's children are his true
descendants; but "It is through Isaac that descendants shall be named for you." 8 This means
that it is not the children of the flesh who are the
children of God, but the children of the promise
are counted as descendants. 9 For this is what the
promise said, "About this time I will return and
Sarah shall have a son." 10 Nor is that all; something similar happened to Rebecca when she had
conceived children by one husband, our ancestor
Isaac. 11 Even before they had been born or had
done anything good or bad (so that God's purpose of election might continue, 12 not by works
but by his call) she was told, "The elder shall serve
the younger." 13 As it is written,

"I have loved Jacob,
but I have hated Esau."

14 What then are we to say? Is there injustice on God's part? By no means! 15 For he says
to Moses,

"I will have mercy on whom I have mercy,
and I will have compassion on whom I
have compassion."

16 So it depends not on human will or exertion,
but on God who shows mercy. 17 For the scripture
says to Pharaoh, "I have raised you up for the very
purpose of showing my power in you, so that my
name may be proclaimed in all the earth." 18 So
then he has mercy on whomever he chooses, and
he hardens the heart of whomever he chooses.

19 You will say to me then, "Why then does
he still find fault? For who can resist his will?"
20 But who indeed are you, a human being, to
argue with God? Will what is molded say to the
one who molds it, "Why have you made me like
this?" 21 Has the potter no right over the clay, to
make out of the same lump one object for special
use and another for ordinary use? 22 What if God,
desiring to show his wrath and to make known
his power, has endured with much patience the
objects of wrath that are made for destruction;
23 and what if he has done so in order to make
known the riches of his glory for the objects of

[a] Gk *my brothers* [b] Or *the Christ*

[c] Or *Messiah, who is God over all, blessed forever*; or *Messiah. May he who is God over all be blessed forever*

mercy, which he has prepared beforehand for
glory— 24including us whom he has called, not
from the Jews only but also from the Gentiles?
25As indeed he says in Hosea,

"Those who were not my people I will call
'my people,'
and her who was not beloved I will call
'beloved.'"

26 "And in the very place where it was said to
them, 'You are not my people,'
there they shall be called children of the
living God."

27 And Isaiah cries out concerning Israel,
"Though the number of the children of Israel
were like the sand of the sea, only a remnant of
them will be saved; 28for the Lord will execute
his sentence on the earth quickly and decisively."[a]
29And as Isaiah predicted,

"If the Lord of hosts had not left survivors[b]
to us,
we would have fared like Sodom
and been made like Gomorrah."

30 What then are we to say? Gentiles, who
did not strive for righteousness, have attained it,
that is, righteousness through faith; 31but Israel,
who did strive for the righteousness that is based
on the law, did not succeed in fulfilling that law.
32Why not? Because they did not strive for it on
the basis of faith, but as if it were based on works.
They have stumbled over the stumbling stone,
33as it is written,

"See, I am laying in Zion a stone that will
make people stumble, a rock that will
make them fall,
and whoever believes in him[c] will not be
put to shame."

10 Brothers and sisters,[d] my heart's desire
and prayer to God for them is that they
may be saved. 2I can testify that they have a zeal
for God, but it is not enlightened. 3For, being ignorant of the righteousness that comes from God,
and seeking to establish their own, they have not
submitted to God's righteousness. 4For Christ is
the end of the law so that there may be righteousness for everyone who believes.

5 Moses writes concerning the righteousness
that comes from the law, that "the person who
does these things will live by them." 6But the righteousness that comes from faith says, "Do not say
in your heart, 'Who will ascend into heaven?'"
(that is, to bring Christ down) 7"or 'Who will descend into the abyss?'" (that is, to bring Christ up
from the dead). 8But what does it say?

"The word is near you,
on your lips and in your heart"

(that is, the word of faith that we proclaim); 9be-
cause[e] if you confess with your lips that Jesus is
Lord and believe in your heart that God raised
him from the dead, you will be saved. 10For one
believes with the heart and so is justified, and one
confesses with the mouth and so is saved. 11The
scripture says, "No one who believes in him will
be put to shame." 12For there is no distinction between Jew and Greek; the same Lord is Lord of
all and is generous to all who call on him. 13For,
"Everyone who calls on the name of the Lord
shall be saved."

14 But how are they to call on one in whom
they have not believed? And how are they to believe in one of whom they have never heard? And
how are they to hear without someone to proclaim him? 15And how are they to proclaim him
unless they are sent? As it is written, "How beautiful are the feet of those who bring good news!"
16But not all have obeyed the good news;[f] for Isaiah says, "Lord, who has believed our message?"
17So faith comes from what is heard, and what is
heard comes through the word of Christ.[g]

18 But I ask, have they not heard? Indeed
they have; for

"Their voice has gone out to all the earth,
and their words to the ends of the world."

19Again I ask, did Israel not understand? First
Moses says,

"I will make you jealous of those who are not
a nation;

[a] Other ancient authorities read *for he will finish his work and cut it short in righteousness, because the Lord will make the sentence shortened on the earth* [b] Or *descendants*; Gk *seed* [c] Or *trusts in it* [d] Gk *Brothers* [e] Or *namely, that* [f] Or *gospel* [g] Or *about Christ*; other ancient authorities read *of God*

with a foolish nation I will make you
angry."
20 Then Isaiah is so bold as to say,
"I have been found by those who did not
seek me;
I have shown myself to those who did not
ask for me."
21 But of Israel he says, "All day long I have held
out my hands to a disobedient and contrary
people."

11 I ask, then, has God rejected his people?
By no means! I myself am an Israelite, a
descendant of Abraham, a member of the tribe
of Benjamin. 2 God has not rejected his people
whom he foreknew. Do you not know what the
scripture says of Elijah, how he pleads with God
against Israel? 3 "Lord, they have killed your
prophets, they have demolished your altars; I
alone am left, and they are seeking my life." 4 But
what is the divine reply to him? "I have kept for
myself seven thousand who have not bowed the
knee to Baal." 5 So too at the present time there is
a remnant, chosen by grace. 6 But if it is by grace,
it is no longer on the basis of works, otherwise
grace would no longer be grace.[a]

7 What then? Israel failed to obtain what it
was seeking. The elect obtained it, but the rest
were hardened, 8 as it is written,
"God gave them a sluggish spirit,
eyes that would not see
and ears that would not hear,
down to this very day."
9 And David says,
"Let their table become a snare and a trap,
a stumbling block and a retribution for
them;
10 let their eyes be darkened so that they cannot
see,
and keep their backs forever bent."

11 So I ask, have they stumbled so as to fall?
By no means! But through their stumbling[b] salvation has come to the Gentiles, so as to make
Israel[c] jealous. 12 Now if their stumbling[b] means
riches for the world, and if their defeat means
riches for Gentiles, how much more will their full
inclusion mean!

13 Now I am speaking to you Gentiles. Inasmuch then as I am an apostle to the Gentiles, I
glorify my ministry 14 in order to make my own
people[d] jealous, and thus save some of them.
15 For if their rejection is the reconciliation of the
world, what will their acceptance be but life from
the dead! 16 If the part of the dough offered as first
fruits is holy, then the whole batch is holy; and if
the root is holy, then the branches also are holy.

17 But if some of the branches were broken
off, and you, a wild olive shoot, were grafted in
their place to share the rich root[e] of the olive tree,
18 do not boast over the branches. If you do boast,
remember that it is not you that support the
root, but the root that supports you. 19 You will
say, "Branches were broken off so that I might be
grafted in." 20 That is true. They were broken off
because of their unbelief, but you stand only
through faith. So do not become proud, but stand
in awe. 21 For if God did not spare the natural
branches, perhaps he will not spare you.[f] 22 Note
then the kindness and the severity of God: severity toward those who have fallen, but God's kindness toward you, provided you continue in his
kindness; otherwise you also will be cut off. 23 And
even those of Israel,[g] if they do not persist in unbelief, will be grafted in, for God has the power
to graft them in again. 24 For if you have been
cut from what is by nature a wild olive tree and
grafted, contrary to nature, into a cultivated olive
tree, how much more will these natural branches
be grafted back into their own olive tree.

25 So that you may not claim to be wiser
than you are, brothers and sisters,[h] I want you to
understand this mystery: a hardening has come
upon part of Israel, until the full number of the
Gentiles has come in. 26 And so all Israel will be
saved; as it is written,
"Out of Zion will come the Deliverer;
he will banish ungodliness from Jacob."

[a] Other ancient authorities add *But if it is by works, it is no longer on the basis of grace, otherwise work would no longer be work*
[b] Gk *transgression* [c] Gk *them* [d] Gk *my flesh* [e] Other ancient authorities read *the richness* [f] Other ancient authorities read *neither will he spare you* [g] Gk lacks *of Israel* [h] Gk *brothers*

27 "And this is my covenant with them,
when I take away their sins."
28As regards the gospel they are enemies of God[a]
for your sake; but as regards election they are
beloved, for the sake of their ancestors; 29for
the gifts and the calling of God are irrevocable.
30Just as you were once disobedient to God but
have now received mercy because of their disobedience, 31so they have now been disobedient in
order that, by the mercy shown to you, they too
may now[b] receive mercy. 32For God has imprisoned all in disobedience so that he may be merciful to all.

33 O the depth of the riches and wisdom and
knowledge of God! How unsearchable are his
judgments and how inscrutable his ways!
34 "For who has known the mind of the Lord?
Or who has been his counselor?"
35 "Or who has given a gift to him,
to receive a gift in return?"
36For from him and through him and to him are
all things. To him be the glory forever. Amen.

12 I appeal to you therefore, brothers and
sisters,[c] by the mercies of God, to present your bodies as a living sacrifice, holy and
acceptable to God, which is your spiritual[d] worship. 2Do not be conformed to this world,[e] but be
transformed by the renewing of your minds, so
that you may discern what is the will of God—
what is good and acceptable and perfect.[f]

3 For by the grace given to me I say to everyone among you not to think of yourself more
highly than you ought to think, but to think with
sober judgment, each according to the measure of
faith that God has assigned. 4For as in one body
we have many members, and not all the members
have the same function, 5so we, who are many,
are one body in Christ, and individually we are
members one of another. 6We have gifts that differ according to the grace given to us: prophecy,
in proportion to faith; 7ministry, in ministering;
the teacher, in teaching; 8the exhorter, in exhortation; the giver, in generosity; the leader, in diligence; the compassionate, in cheerfulness.

9 Let love be genuine; hate what is evil, hold
fast to what is good; 10love one another with
mutual affection; outdo one another in showing
honor. 11Do not lag in zeal, be ardent in spirit, serve
the Lord.[g] 12Rejoice in hope, be patient in suffering, persevere in prayer. 13Contribute to the needs
of the saints; extend hospitality to strangers.

14 Bless those who persecute you; bless and
do not curse them. 15Rejoice with those who rejoice, weep with those who weep. 16Live in harmony with one another; do not be haughty, but
associate with the lowly;[h] do not claim to be wiser
than you are. 17Do not repay anyone evil for evil,
but take thought for what is noble in the sight of
all. 18If it is possible, so far as it depends on you,
live peaceably with all. 19Beloved, never avenge
yourselves, but leave room for the wrath of God;[i]
for it is written, "Vengeance is mine, I will repay,
says the Lord." 20No, "if your enemies are hungry,
feed them; if they are thirsty, give them something
to drink; for by doing this you will heap burning
coals on their heads." 21Do not be overcome by
evil, but overcome evil with good.

13 Let every person be subject to the governing authorities; for there is no authority
except from God, and those authorities that exist
have been instituted by God. 2Therefore whoever
resists authority resists what God has appointed,
and those who resist will incur judgment. 3For
rulers are not a terror to good conduct, but to
bad. Do you wish to have no fear of the authority? Then do what is good, and you will receive its
approval; 4for it is God's servant for your good.
But if you do what is wrong, you should be afraid,
for the authority[j] does not bear the sword in vain!
It is the servant of God to execute wrath on the
wrongdoer. 5Therefore one must be subject, not
only because of wrath but also because of conscience. 6For the same reason you also pay taxes,
for the authorities are God's servants, busy with
this very thing. 7Pay to all what is due them—

[a] Gk lacks *of God* [b] Other ancient authorities lack *now* [c] Gk *brothers* [d] Or *reasonable* [e] Gk *age* [f] Or *what is the good and acceptable and perfect will of God* [g] Other ancient authorities read *serve the opportune time* [h] Or *give yourselves to humble tasks* [i] Gk *the wrath* [j] Gk *it*

Romans 13:1-6

Paul's Roman citizenship (see Acts 22:25-28) was a privilege that allowed him to travel freely around the empire, spreading the gospel message. Benefiting from the Roman power that claimed to have secured the peace, it is understandable that Paul would support the prevailing political structures of his time. But he goes beyond the gospel message when he equates submission to the empire to submission to God. From this text derive such later heresies as the divine right of kings. For those conquered by empire, on the other hand, submission has often been tantamount to death, or solidarity with lethal institutions. If the message of Christ is abundant life, then to truly be a disciple of Christ is to be an enemy of all empires and all death-dealing social structures. One must choose between Christ and Caesar, for to love the one is to hate the other.

— *MDLT*

taxes to whom taxes are due, revenue to whom
revenue is due, respect to whom respect is due,
honor to whom honor is due.
8 Owe no one anything, except to love one
another; for the one who loves another has fulfilled the law. 9 The commandments, "You shall
not commit adultery; You shall not murder; You
shall not steal; You shall not covet"; and any other
commandment, are summed up in this word,
"Love your neighbor as yourself." 10 Love does no
wrong to a neighbor; therefore, love is the fulfilling of the law.
11 Besides this, you know what time it is,
how it is now the moment for you to wake from
sleep. For salvation is nearer to us now than when
we became believers; 12 the night is far gone, the
day is near. Let us then lay aside the works of
darkness and put on the armor of light; 13 let us
live honorably as in the day, not in reveling and
drunkenness, not in debauchery and licentiousness, not in quarreling and jealousy. 14 Instead,
put on the Lord Jesus Christ, and make no provision for the flesh, to gratify its desires.

14 Welcome those who are weak in faith,[a]
but not for the purpose of quarreling over
opinions. 2 Some believe in eating anything, while
the weak eat only vegetables. 3 Those who eat
must not despise those who abstain, and those
who abstain must not pass judgment on those
who eat; for God has welcomed them. 4 Who are
you to pass judgment on servants of another? It is
before their own lord that they stand or fall. And
they will be upheld, for the Lord[b] is able to make
them stand.
5 Some judge one day to be better than another, while others judge all days to be alike. Let
all be fully convinced in their own minds. 6 Those
who observe the day, observe it in honor of the
Lord. Also those who eat, eat in honor of the
Lord, since they give thanks to God; while those
who abstain, abstain in honor of the Lord and
give thanks to God.
7 We do not live to ourselves, and we do not
die to ourselves. 8 If we live, we live to the Lord,
and if we die, we die to the Lord; so then, whether
we live or whether we die, we are the Lord's. 9 For
to this end Christ died and lived again, so that he
might be Lord of both the dead and the living.
10 Why do you pass judgment on your
brother or sister?[c] Or you, why do you despise
your brother or sister?[c] For we will all stand before
the judgment seat of God.[d] 11 For it is written,

"As I live, says the Lord, every knee shall bow
to me,
and every tongue shall give praise to[e]
God."

12 So then, each of us will be accountable to
God.[f]
13 Let us therefore no longer pass judgment

[a] Or *conviction* [b] Other ancient authorities read *for God* [c] Gk *brother* [d] Other ancient authorities read *of Christ*
[e] Or *confess* [f] Other ancient authorities lack *to God*

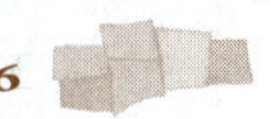

on one another, but resolve instead never to put
a stumbling block or hindrance in the way of another.[a] 14I know and am persuaded in the Lord
Jesus that nothing is unclean in itself; but it is
unclean for anyone who thinks it unclean. 15If
your brother or sister[b] is being injured by what
you eat, you are no longer walking in love. Do not
let what you eat cause the ruin of one for whom
Christ died. 16So do not let your good be spoken
of as evil. 17For the kingdom of God is not food
and drink but righteousness and peace and joy in
the Holy Spirit. 18The one who thus serves Christ
is acceptable to God and has human approval.
19Let us then pursue what makes for peace and
for mutual upbuilding. 20Do not, for the sake of
food, destroy the work of God. Everything is indeed clean, but it is wrong for you to make others
fall by what you eat; 21it is good not to eat meat
or drink wine or do anything that makes your
brother or sister[b] stumble.[c] 22The faith that you
have, have as your own conviction before God.
Blessed are those who have no reason to condemn themselves because of what they approve.
23But those who have doubts are condemned if
they eat, because they do not act from faith;[d] for
whatever does not proceed from faith[d] is sin.[e]

15 We who are strong ought to put up with
the failings of the weak, and not to please
ourselves. 2Each of us must please our neighbor
for the good purpose of building up the neighbor. 3For Christ did not please himself; but, as it
is written, "The insults of those who insult you
have fallen on me." 4For whatever was written in
former days was written for our instruction, so
that by steadfastness and by the encouragement
of the scriptures we might have hope. 5May the
God of steadfastness and encouragement grant
you to live in harmony with one another, in accordance with Christ Jesus, 6so that together you
may with one voice glorify the God and Father of
our Lord Jesus Christ.

7 Welcome one another, therefore, just as
Christ has welcomed you, for the glory of God.
8For I tell you that Christ has become a servant of
the circumcised on behalf of the truth of God in
order that he might confirm the promises given
to the patriarchs, 9and in order that the Gentiles
might glorify God for his mercy. As it is written,

"Therefore I will confess[f] you among the
Gentiles,
and sing praises to your name";

10and again he says,

"Rejoice, O Gentiles, with his people";

11and again,

"Praise the Lord, all you Gentiles,
and let all the peoples praise him";

12and again Isaiah says,

"The root of Jesse shall come,
the one who rises to rule the Gentiles;
in him the Gentiles shall hope."

13May the God of hope fill you with all joy and
peace in believing, so that you may abound in
hope by the power of the Holy Spirit.

14 I myself feel confident about you, my
brothers and sisters,[g] that you yourselves are
full of goodness, filled with all knowledge, and
able to instruct one another. 15Nevertheless on
some points I have written to you rather boldly
by way of reminder, because of the grace given
me by God 16to be a minister of Christ Jesus
to the Gentiles in the priestly service of the

Romans 15:14-16

Only at the end of this diplomatically framed letter does Paul reveal his ulterior motive. the Romans' response to his exhortation will guarantee the holiness of the "offering of the nations" (here translated "Gentiles"), that is, the collection that Paul has gathered from Greek cities and is about to deliver to serve "the poor among the saints at Jerusalem" (15:26). The collection is more than an instrument of economic mutuality: it represents the obedience of the nations that Isaiah prophesied for the last days.

— *NE*

[a] Gk *of a brother* [b] Gk *brother* [c] Other ancient authorities add *or be upset or be weakened* [d] Or *conviction*
[e] Other authorities, some ancient, add here 16.25–27 [f] Or *thank* [g] Gk *brothers*

gospel of God, so that the offering of the Gentiles may be acceptable, sanctified by the Holy
Spirit. 17 In Christ Jesus, then, I have reason to
boast of my work for God. 18 For I will not venture to speak of anything except what Christ has
accomplished[a] through me to win obedience
from the Gentiles, by word and deed, 19 by the
power of signs and wonders, by the power of the
Spirit of God,[b] so that from Jerusalem and as
far around as Illyricum I have fully proclaimed
the good news[c] of Christ. 20 Thus I make it my
ambition to proclaim the good news,[c] not where
Christ has already been named, so that I do not
build on someone else's foundation, 21 but as it is
written,

> "Those who have never been told of him shall
> see,
> and those who have never heard of him
> shall understand."

22 This is the reason that I have so often
been hindered from coming to you. 23 But now,
with no further place for me in these regions, I
desire, as I have for many years, to come to you
24 when I go to Spain. For I do hope to see you
on my journey and to be sent on by you, once
I have enjoyed your company for a little while.
25 At present, however, I am going to Jerusalem
in a ministry to the saints; 26 for Macedonia and
Achaia have been pleased to share their resources
with the poor among the saints at Jerusalem.
27 They were pleased to do this, and indeed they
owe it to them; for if the Gentiles have come to
share in their spiritual blessings, they ought also
to be of service to them in material things. 28 So,
when I have completed this, and have delivered
to them what has been collected,[d] I will set out
by way of you to Spain; 29 and I know that when
I come to you, I will come in the fullness of the
blessing[e] of Christ.

30 I appeal to you, brothers and sisters,[f] by
our Lord Jesus Christ and by the love of the Spirit,
to join me in earnest prayer to God on my behalf,
31 that I may be rescued from the unbelievers in
Judea, and that my ministry[g] to Jerusalem may be
acceptable to the saints, 32 so that by God's will
I may come to you with joy and be refreshed in
your company. 33 The God of peace be with all of
you.[h] Amen.

16 I commend to you our sister Phoebe, a
deacon[i] of the church at Cenchreae, 2 so
that you may welcome her in the Lord as is fitting
for the saints, and help her in whatever she may
require from you, for she has been a benefactor of
many and of myself as well.

3 Greet Prisca and Aquila, who work with me
in Christ Jesus, 4 and who risked their necks for
my life, to whom not only I give thanks, but also
all the churches of the Gentiles. 5 Greet also the
church in their house. Greet my beloved Epaene-
tus, who was the first convert[j] in Asia for Christ.
6 Greet Mary, who has worked very hard among
you. 7 Greet Andronicus and Junia,[k] my relatives[l]
who were in prison with me; they are prominent
among the apostles, and they were in Christ before I was. 8 Greet Ampliatus, my beloved in the
Lord. 9 Greet Urbanus, our co-worker in Christ,
and my beloved Stachys. 10 Greet Apelles, who is
approved in Christ. Greet those who belong to
the family of Aristobulus. 11 Greet my relative[m]
Herodion. Greet those in the Lord who belong
to the family of Narcissus. 12 Greet those workers
in the Lord, Tryphaena and Tryphosa. Greet the
beloved Persis, who has worked hard in the Lord.
13 Greet Rufus, chosen in the Lord; and greet his
mother—a mother to me also. 14 Greet Asyncri-
tus, Phlegon, Hermes, Patrobas, Hermas, and the
brothers and sisters[f] who are with them. 15 Greet
Philologus, Julia, Nereus and his sister, and
Olympas, and all the saints who are with them.
16 Greet one another with a holy kiss. All the
churches of Christ greet you.

17 I urge you, brothers and sisters,[f] to keep an
eye on those who cause dissensions and offenses,

[a] Gk *speak of those things that Christ has not accomplished* [b] Other ancient authorities read *of the Spirit* or *of the Holy Spirit*
[c] Or *gospel* [d] Gk *have sealed to them this fruit* [e] Other ancient authorities add *of the gospel* [f] Gk *brothers*
[g] Other ancient authorities read *my bringing of a gift* [h] One ancient authority adds 16.25–27 here [i] Or *minister*
[j] Gk *first fruits* [k] Or *Junias*; other ancient authorities read *Julia* [l] Or *compatriots* [m] Or *compatriot*

in opposition to the teaching that you have
learned; avoid them. 18 For such people do not
serve our Lord Christ, but their own appetites,[a]
and by smooth talk and flattery they deceive the
hearts of the simple-minded. 19 For while your
obedience is known to all, so that I rejoice over
you, I want you to be wise in what is good and
guileless in what is evil. 20 The God of peace will
shortly crush Satan under your feet. The grace of
our Lord Jesus Christ be with you.[b]

21 Timothy, my co-worker, greets you; so do
Lucius and Jason and Sosipater, my relatives.[c]

22 I Tertius, the writer of this letter, greet you
in the Lord.[d]

23 Gaius, who is host to me and to the whole
church, greets you. Erastus, the city treasurer, and
our brother Quartus, greet you.[e]

25 Now to God[f] who is able to strengthen
you according to my gospel and the proclamation
of Jesus Christ, according to the revelation of the
mystery that was kept secret for long ages 26 but is
now disclosed, and through the prophetic writings is made known to all the Gentiles, according to the command of the eternal God, to bring
about the obedience of faith— 27 to the only wise
God, through Jesus Christ, to whom[g] be the glory
forever! Amen.[h]

[a] Gk *their own belly* [b] Other ancient authorities lack this sentence [c] Or *compatriots* [d] Or *I Tertius, writing this letter in the Lord, greet you* [e] Other ancient authorities add verse 24, *The grace of our Lord Jesus Christ be with all of you. Amen.* [f] Gk *the one* [g] Other ancient authorities lack *to whom*. The verse then reads, *to the only wise God be the glory through Jesus Christ forever. Amen.* [h] Other ancient authorities lack 16.25–27 or include it after 14.23 or 15.33; others put verse 24 after verse 27

The First Letter of Paul to the Corinthians

Paul's Corinthian correspondence is the most lively, lengthy, and informative of his letters because of its vivid portrayal of the actual life situations and challenges of this community of believers. First-century CE Corinth was socially and politically stratified under the empire of Rome. The empire had destroyed the city in 146 BCE, and Julius Caesar resettled it a century later (44 BCE), mostly with an ethnically diverse population of freed slaves conscripted from Italy, Greece, Syria, Egypt, and Judea. Corinth, the capital of the Roman province of Achaia, was governed by a proconsul sent annually from Rome, and its municipal government was modeled on that of republican Rome.

Located on Greece's Peloponnesian peninsula, Corinth prospered as a trade and communication center. Its rapid rise to prominence was inspired in part by intense competition for commercial success—Corinth sponsored athletic games second only to the Olympic games—and the opportunity its lack of a hereditary class offered for upward mobility. But Corinth's success did not come without criticism. It gained a reputation as a sin city where "anything goes." Such was its fame that an Athenian comic-poet coined the verb "Corinthianize" (*korinthiazesthai*), which meant to engage in sexually immoral behavior. This openness was also evident in Corinth's religious diversity, which included a thriving Jewish community, a cult to the emperor, and temples dedicated to Greek and Egyptian deities. Added to this were a host of ideas imported along with material goods to the city's two ports from various parts of the ancient Mediterranean world. The religious diversity and ethnic complexity of Corinth destined it to evoke from Paul some impassioned and intense responses. The letters we call 1 and 2 Corinthians (another letter, lost to us, preceded 1 Corinthians; see 5:9) have long been viewed as primarily concerning theological or doctrinal issues, thus minimizing the cultural influences and social-political codes in them. Certainly Paul's responses were and are theological, because he brought to these matters his understanding of Scripture and the new reality brought about by Jesus Christ. Nevertheless, it is important to recognize that the Corinthians' beliefs and practices, and their challenges to Paul, were culturally informed and have their counterparts around the world today.

Paul wrote 1 Corinthians from Ephesus, most likely in 53 or 54 CE, to address various issues, which can be outlined in two parts: first, matters that "Chloe's people" reported to Paul (1:10—6:20), including factions in Corinth (1:10—4:21), incest and sexual transgressions (5:1-13), litigation before pagan courts (6:1-11), and sexual morality (6:12-20); and, second, the Corinthians' questions in their letter to Paul (7:1—15:58; see especially 7:1, 8:1, and 12:1), including marriage and celibacy, slavery and freedom (ch. 7), Christian liberty (especially Paul's refusal of the Corin-

thians' patronage, ch. 9) and the problems of idolatry (8:1—11:1), the dress and status of women in worship (11:2-16 and especially 14:33b-36), the practice of the Lord's Supper (11:17-34), the use of spiritual gifts in worship (chs. 12–14), and the future resurrection (ch. 15). In closing, Paul addresses some practical matters (ch. 16), including arrangements for the collection, travel plans, and final greetings.

The first readers or hearers of this letter would most likely have been familiar with these cultural practices: 1) rhetoric and rhetorical self-presentation, which was the basis of the Corinthians' allegiance to certain leaders, especially Apollos; 2) the practice of closely examining rhetoric—the basis of some Corinthians' negative evaluation of Paul's preaching (see chs. 4 and 9); 3) litigation in the courts, the foundation of Greco-Roman civil society; and 4) the buying of sacrificial meat in the marketplace, a practice common in Greco-Roman "pagan" society. What those first readers may have regarded as problematic innovations or violations of cultural boundaries were 1) Paul's teaching about sexual ethics—some Corinthians apparently believed those were matters of individual freedom, that "all things are lawful for me" (6:12; 10:23); 2) the (only slightly) elevated status Paul ascribed to women; 3) rituals such as baptism and the Lord's Supper; 4) Paul's assessment of rhetoric (he insists he is a *herald*, not an orator or rhetorician); and 5) his teaching on the resurrection.

While many of these ideas and practices seem alien to our modern social and cultural experiences, contemporary readers will spot some convergences: 1) the role of women in church and society remains a problem for some faith communities; 2) especially for persons of African descent living in the West—including me—the legacy and continuing effects of slavery and racism remain a concern; 3) church schisms and disagreements remain painful realities, and as a particular cause of these, 4) we see lively and often strained debate over the possibilities for a new sexual ethics that will include openness to and the affirming of loving same-gender and transgendered persons in church and society. Many of these issues, both in Paul's time and in ours, are not only theological but also relate in some degree to issues of culture and society.

— ***Demetrius K. Williams***

1 Paul, called to be an apostle of Christ Jesus by the will of God, and our brother Sosthenes,

2 To the church of God that is in Corinth, to those who are sanctified in Christ Jesus, called to be saints, together with all those who in every place call on the name of our Lord Jesus Christ, both their Lord[a] and ours:

3 Grace to you and peace from God our Father and the Lord Jesus Christ.

[a] Gk *theirs*

4 I give thanks to my[a] God always for you
because of the grace of God that has been given
you in Christ Jesus, 5 for in every way you have
been enriched in him, in speech and knowledge
of every kind— 6 just as the testimony of[b] Christ
has been strengthened among you— 7 so that you
are not lacking in any spiritual gift as you wait for
the revealing of our Lord Jesus Christ. 8 He will
also strengthen you to the end, so that you may
be blameless on the day of our Lord Jesus Christ.
9 God is faithful; by him you were called into the
fellowship of his Son, Jesus Christ our Lord.

10 Now I appeal to you, brothers and sisters,[c]
by the name of our Lord Jesus Christ, that all of
you be in agreement and that there be no divisions among you, but that you be united in the
same mind and the same purpose. 11 For it has
been reported to me by Chloe's people that there
are quarrels among you, my brothers and sisters.[d]
12 What I mean is that each of you says, "I belong to
Paul," or "I belong to Apollos," or "I belong to Cephas," or "I belong to Christ." 13 Has Christ been
divided? Was Paul crucified for you? Or were you
baptized in the name of Paul? 14 I thank God[e] that
I baptized none of you except Crispus and Gaius,
15 so that no one can say that you were baptized in
my name. 16 (I did baptize also the household of
Stephanas; beyond that, I do not know whether I
baptized anyone else.) 17 For Christ did not send
me to baptize but to proclaim the gospel, and not
with eloquent wisdom, so that the cross of Christ
might not be emptied of its power.

18 For the message about the cross is foolishness to those who are perishing, but to us who
are being saved it is the power of God. 19 For it
is written,

"I will destroy the wisdom of the wise,
and the discernment of the discerning I
will thwart."

20 Where is the one who is wise? Where is the
scribe? Where is the debater of this age? Has
not God made foolish the wisdom of the world?
21 For since, in the wisdom of God, the world did
not know God through wisdom, God decided,
through the foolishness of our proclamation, to
save those who believe. 22 For Jews demand signs
and Greeks desire wisdom, 23 but we proclaim
Christ crucified, a stumbling block to Jews and
foolishness to Gentiles, 24 but to those who are the
called, both Jews and Greeks, Christ the power
of God and the wisdom of God. 25 For God's foolishness is wiser than human wisdom, and God's
weakness is stronger than human strength.

26 Consider your own call, brothers and sisters:[c] not many of you were wise by human standards,[f] not many were powerful, not many were of
noble birth. 27 But God chose what is foolish in the
world to shame the wise; God chose what is weak
in the world to shame the strong; 28 God chose
what is low and despised in the world, things that
are not, to reduce to nothing things that are, 29 so
that no one[g] might boast in the presence of God.
30 He is the source of your life in Christ Jesus, who
became for us wisdom from God, and righteousness and sanctification and redemption, 31 in order that, as it is written, "Let the one who boasts,
boast in[h] the Lord."

1 Corinthians 1:27-29

Most people choose those who are wise and strong to lead, to be the representatives of their message, to entrust with important responsibilities. Yet God chooses those who are foolish and weak in the eyes of the dominant culture to bring about God's will. It is not the wise and strong who are entrusted by God, but the disenfranchised, the frail, the outcast. It is the stone rejected by those whom society admires that God uses as the foundation for God's work. In fact, salvation comes even to the powerful and privileged via the marginalized.

— *MDLT*

2 When I came to you, brothers and sisters,[c]
I did not come proclaiming the mystery[i] of
God to you in lofty words or wisdom. 2 For I de-

[a] Other ancient authorities lack *my* [b] Or *to* [c] Gk *brothers* [d] Gk *my brothers* [e] Other ancient authorities read *I am thankful* [f] Gk *according to the flesh* [g] Gk *no flesh* [h] Or *of* [i] Other ancient authorities read *testimony*

cided to know nothing among you except Jesus
Christ, and him crucified. 3And I came to you
in weakness and in fear and in much trembling.
4My speech and my proclamation were not with
plausible words of wisdom,[a] but with a demonstration of the Spirit and of power, 5so that your
faith might rest not on human wisdom but on the
power of God.

6 Yet among the mature we do speak wisdom, though it is not a wisdom of this age or of
the rulers of this age, who are doomed to perish.
7But we speak God's wisdom, secret and hidden,
which God decreed before the ages for our glory.
8None of the rulers of this age understood this;
for if they had, they would not have crucified the
Lord of glory. 9But, as it is written,

"What no eye has seen, nor ear heard,
nor the human heart conceived,
what God has prepared for those who love
him"—

10these things God has revealed to us through the
Spirit; for the Spirit searches everything, even the
depths of God. 11For what human being knows
what is truly human except the human spirit that
is within? So also no one comprehends what is
truly God's except the Spirit of God. 12Now we
have received not the spirit of the world, but the
Spirit that is from God, so that we may understand the gifts bestowed on us by God. 13And we
speak of these things in words not taught by human wisdom but taught by the Spirit, interpreting spiritual things to those who are spiritual.[b]

14 Those who are unspiritual[c] do not receive
the gifts of God's Spirit, for they are foolishness
to them, and they are unable to understand them
because they are spiritually discerned. 15Those
who are spiritual discern all things, and they are
themselves subject to no one else's scrutiny.

16 "For who has known the mind of the Lord
so as to instruct him?"

But we have the mind of Christ.

3 And so, brothers and sisters,[d] I could not
speak to you as spiritual people, but rather
as people of the flesh, as infants in Christ. 2I fed
you with milk, not solid food, for you were not
ready for solid food. Even now you are still not
ready, 3for you are still of the flesh. For as long as
there is jealousy and quarreling among you, are
you not of the flesh, and behaving according to
human inclinations? 4For when one says, "I belong to Paul," and another, "I belong to Apollos,"
are you not merely human?

5 What then is Apollos? What is Paul? Servants through whom you came to believe, as the
Lord assigned to each. 6I planted, Apollos watered, but God gave the growth. 7So neither the
one who plants nor the one who waters is anything, but only God who gives the growth. 8The
one who plants and the one who waters have a
common purpose, and each will receive wages according to the labor of each. 9For we are God's
servants, working together; you are God's field,
God's building.

10 According to the grace of God given to me,
like a skilled master builder I laid a foundation,
and someone else is building on it. Each builder
must choose with care how to build on it. 11For
no one can lay any foundation other than the one
that has been laid; that foundation is Jesus Christ.
12Now if anyone builds on the foundation with
gold, silver, precious stones, wood, hay, straw—
13the work of each builder will become visible,
for the Day will disclose it, because it will be revealed with fire, and the fire will test what sort of
work each has done. 14If what has been built on
the foundation survives, the builder will receive
a reward. 15If the work is burned up, the builder
will suffer loss; the builder will be saved, but only
as through fire.

16 Do you not know that you are God's temple and that God's Spirit dwells in you?[e] 17If anyone destroys God's temple, God will destroy that
person. For God's temple is holy, and you are that
temple.

18 Do not deceive yourselves. If you think
that you are wise in this age, you should become

[a] Other ancient authorities read *the persuasiveness of wisdom* or *comparing spiritual things with spiritual* [b] Or *interpreting spiritual things in spiritual language,* [c] Or *natural* [d] Gk *brothers* [e] In verses 16 and 17 the Greek word for *you* is plural

fools so that you may become wise. 19For the wisdom of this world is foolishness with God. For it
is written,

"He catches the wise in their craftiness,"
20and again,
"The Lord knows the thoughts of the wise,
that they are futile."

21So let no one boast about human leaders. For
all things are yours, 22whether Paul or Apollos or
Cephas or the world or life or death or the present or the future—all belong to you, 23and you
belong to Christ, and Christ belongs to God.

4 Think of us in this way, as servants of Christ
and stewards of God's mysteries. 2Moreover,
it is required of stewards that they be found trustworthy. 3But with me it is a very small thing that I
should be judged by you or by any human court.
I do not even judge myself. 4I am not aware of
anything against myself, but I am not thereby acquitted. It is the Lord who judges me. 5Therefore
do not pronounce judgment before the time, before the Lord comes, who will bring to light the
things now hidden in darkness and will disclose
the purposes of the heart. Then each one will receive commendation from God.

6 I have applied all this to Apollos and myself
for your benefit, brothers and sisters,[a] so that you
may learn through us the meaning of the saying,
"Nothing beyond what is written," so that none of
you will be puffed up in favor of one against another. 7For who sees anything different in you?[b]
What do you have that you did not receive? And
if you received it, why do you boast as if it were
not a gift?

8 Already you have all you want! Already you
have become rich! Quite apart from us you have
become kings! Indeed, I wish that you had become kings, so that we might be kings with you!
9For I think that God has exhibited us apostles as
last of all, as though sentenced to death, because
we have become a spectacle to the world, to angels and to mortals. 10We are fools for the sake of
Christ, but you are wise in Christ. We are weak,
but you are strong. You are held in honor, but we
in disrepute. 11To the present hour we are hungry
and thirsty, we are poorly clothed and beaten and
homeless, 12and we grow weary from the work
of our own hands. When reviled, we bless; when
persecuted, we endure; 13when slandered, we
speak kindly. We have become like the rubbish of
the world, the dregs of all things, to this very day.

1 Corinthians 4:8-13

Paul's scathing rebuke of the complacency among the Corinthians is doubtless directed to the comfortable members of the city's elite within the assembly. His words must sound just as scathing in the ears of comfortable Christians in the global north today. Given the long history of conquest, colonialism, and slavery, Paul's question, "What do you have that you did not receive?" might be rephrased for the prosperous north, "What do you have that was not taken from others?"

—*NE*

14 I am not writing this to make you
ashamed, but to admonish you as my beloved
children. 15For though you might have ten thousand guardians in Christ, you do not have many
fathers. Indeed, in Christ Jesus I became your father through the gospel. 16I appeal to you, then,
be imitators of me. 17For this reason I sent[c] you
Timothy, who is my beloved and faithful child
in the Lord, to remind you of my ways in Christ
Jesus, as I teach them everywhere in every church.
18But some of you, thinking that I am not coming
to you, have become arrogant. 19But I will come
to you soon, if the Lord wills, and I will find out
not the talk of these arrogant people but their
power. 20For the kingdom of God depends not
on talk but on power. 21What would you prefer?
Am I to come to you with a stick, or with love in
a spirit of gentleness?

5 It is actually reported that there is sexual immorality among you, and of a kind that is
not found even among pagans; for a man is liv-

[a] Gk *brothers* [b] Or *Who makes you different from another?* [c] Or *am sending*

ing with his father's wife. 2And you are arrogant!
Should you not rather have mourned, so that he
who has done this would have been removed
from among you?
3 For though absent in body, I am present in
spirit; and as if present I have already pronounced
judgment 4in the name of the Lord Jesus on the
man who has done such a thing.[a] When you
are assembled, and my spirit is present with the
power of our Lord Jesus, 5you are to hand this
man over to Satan for the destruction of the flesh,
so that his spirit may be saved in the day of the
Lord.[b]
6 Your boasting is not a good thing. Do you
not know that a little yeast leavens the whole
batch of dough? 7Clean out the old yeast so that
you may be a new batch, as you really are unleavened. For our paschal lamb, Christ, has been sacrificed. 8Therefore, let us celebrate the festival,
not with the old yeast, the yeast of malice and
evil, but with the unleavened bread of sincerity
and truth.
9 I wrote to you in my letter not to associate with sexually immoral persons— 10not at all
meaning the immoral of this world, or the greedy
and robbers, or idolaters, since you would then
need to go out of the world. 11But now I am writing to you not to associate with anyone who bears
the name of brother or sister[c] who is sexually immoral or greedy, or is an idolater, reviler, drunkard, or robber. Do not even eat with such a one.
12For what have I to do with judging those outside? Is it not those who are inside that you are to
judge? 13God will judge those outside. "Drive out
the wicked person from among you."

6 When any of you has a grievance against
another, do you dare to take it to court before the unrighteous, instead of taking it before
the saints? 2Do you not know that the saints will
judge the world? And if the world is to be judged
by you, are you incompetent to try trivial cases?
3Do you not know that we are to judge angels—
to say nothing of ordinary matters? 4If you have
ordinary cases, then, do you appoint as judges
those who have no standing in the church? 5I say
this to your shame. Can it be that there is no one
among you wise enough to decide between one
believer[c] and another, 6but a believer[c] goes to
court against a believer[c]—and before unbelievers
at that?
7 In fact, to have lawsuits at all with one another is already a defeat for you. Why not rather
be wronged? Why not rather be defrauded? 8But
you yourselves wrong and defraud—and believers[d] at that.
9 Do you not know that wrongdoers will not
inherit the kingdom of God? Do not be deceived!
Fornicators, idolaters, adulterers, male prostitutes, sodomites, 10thieves, the greedy, drunkards, revilers, robbers—none of these will inherit
the kingdom of God. 11And this is what some of
you used to be. But you were washed, you were
sanctified, you were justified in the name of the
Lord Jesus Christ and in the Spirit of our God.
12 "All things are lawful for me," but not all
things are beneficial. "All things are lawful for me,"
but I will not be dominated by anything. 13"Food
is meant for the stomach and the stomach for
food,"[e] and God will destroy both one and the
other. The body is meant not for fornication but
for the Lord, and the Lord for the body. 14And
God raised the Lord and will also raise us by his
power. 15Do you not know that your bodies are
members of Christ? Should I therefore take the
members of Christ and make them members of a
prostitute? Never! 16Do you not know that whoever is united to a prostitute becomes one body
with her? For it is said, "The two shall be one
flesh." 17But anyone united to the Lord becomes
one spirit with him. 18Shun fornication! Every sin
that a person commits is outside the body; but
the fornicator sins against the body itself. 19Or
do you not know that your body is a temple[f] of
the Holy Spirit within you, which you have from
God, and that you are not your own? 20For you
were bought with a price; therefore glorify God
in your body.

[a] Or *on the man who has done such a thing in the name of the Lord Jesus* [b] Other ancient authorities add *Jesus* [c] Gk *brother*
[d] Gk *brothers* [e] The quotation may extend to the word *other* [f] Or *sanctuary*

7 Now concerning the matters about which
you wrote: "It is well for a man not to touch a
woman." 2 But because of cases of sexual immorality, each man should have his own wife and each
woman her own husband. 3 The husband should
give to his wife her conjugal rights, and likewise
the wife to her husband. 4 For the wife does not
have authority over her own body, but the husband does; likewise the husband does not have
authority over his own body, but the wife does.
5 Do not deprive one another except perhaps by
agreement for a set time, to devote yourselves
to prayer, and then come together again, so that
Satan may not tempt you because of your lack of
self-control. 6 This I say by way of concession, not
of command. 7 I wish that all were as I myself am.
But each has a particular gift from God, one having one kind and another a different kind.

8 To the unmarried and the widows I say that
it is well for them to remain unmarried as I am.
9 But if they are not practicing self-control, they
should marry. For it is better to marry than to be
aflame with passion.

10 To the married I give this command—not
I but the Lord—that the wife should not separate
from her husband 11 (but if she does separate, let
her remain unmarried or else be reconciled to
her husband), and that the husband should not
divorce his wife.

12 To the rest I say—I and not the Lord—
that if any believer[a] has a wife who is an unbeliever, and she consents to live with him, he
should not divorce her. 13 And if any woman has
a husband who is an unbeliever, and he consents
to live with her, she should not divorce him. 14 For
the unbelieving husband is made holy through
his wife, and the unbelieving wife is made holy
through her husband. Otherwise, your children
would be unclean, but as it is, they are holy. 15 But
if the unbelieving partner separates, let it be so;
in such a case the brother or sister is not bound.
It is to peace that God has called you.[b] 16 Wife,
for all you know, you might save your husband.
Husband, for all you know, you might save
your wife.

17 However that may be, let each of you lead
the life that the Lord has assigned, to which God
called you. This is my rule in all the churches.
18 Was anyone at the time of his call already circumcised? Let him not seek to remove the marks
of circumcision. Was anyone at the time of his
call uncircumcised? Let him not seek circumcision. 19 Circumcision is nothing, and uncircumcision is nothing; but obeying the commandments
of God is everything. 20 Let each of you remain in
the condition in which you were called.

21 Were you a slave when called? Do not be
concerned about it. Even if you can gain your
freedom, make use of your present condition
now more than ever.[c] 22 For whoever was called
in the Lord as a slave is a freed person belonging to the Lord, just as whoever was free when

[a] Gk *brother* [b] Other ancient authorities read *us* [c] Or *avail yourself of the opportunity*

1 Corinthians 7:21-24

The fact that verse 21 can be translated in two opposite ways (see the textual note), and that the previous RSV translation preferred the alternative, should give us pause. Although broad generalizations about Paul's advocacy of the status quo have shaped translation habits here, the equally plausible alternative produces an opposite effect. Paul's point is *not* that everyone should remain "in whatever condition" they were called (7:20, 24), but that they should remain loyal to their *calling* (the Greek word *klēsis* never refers elsewhere to social location)—namely, their calling to peace (7:15) and to obedience to the commandments of God (7:19). Paul's qualifications throughout this chapter show that he never imagined God had "called" anyone to occupy a particular social location.

— *NE*

called is a slave of Christ. 23You were bought with
a price; do not become slaves of human masters.
24In whatever condition you were called, brothers and sisters,[a] there remain with God.

25 Now concerning virgins, I have no command of the Lord, but I give my opinion as one
who by the Lord's mercy is trustworthy. 26I think
that, in view of the impending[b] crisis, it is well for
you to remain as you are. 27Are you bound to a
wife? Do not seek to be free. Are you free from
a wife? Do not seek a wife. 28But if you marry,
you do not sin, and if a virgin marries, she does
not sin. Yet those who marry will experience distress in this life,[c] and I would spare you that. 29I
mean, brothers and sisters,[a] the appointed time
has grown short; from now on, let even those
who have wives be as though they had none,
30and those who mourn as though they were not
mourning, and those who rejoice as though they
were not rejoicing, and those who buy as though
they had no possessions, 31and those who deal
with the world as though they had no dealings
with it. For the present form of this world is passing away.

32 I want you to be free from anxieties. The
unmarried man is anxious about the affairs of the
Lord, how to please the Lord; 33but the married
man is anxious about the affairs of the world, how
to please his wife, 34and his interests are divided.
And the unmarried woman and the virgin are
anxious about the affairs of the Lord, so that they
may be holy in body and spirit; but the married
woman is anxious about the affairs of the world,
how to please her husband. 35I say this for your
own benefit, not to put any restraint upon you,
but to promote good order and unhindered devotion to the Lord.

36 If anyone thinks that he is not behaving properly toward his fiancée,[d] if his passions
are strong, and so it has to be, let him marry as
he wishes; it is no sin. Let them marry. 37But if
someone stands firm in his resolve, being under
no necessity but having his own desire under control, and has determined in his own mind to keep
her as his fiancée,[d] he will do well. 38So then, he
who marries his fiancée[d] does well; and he who
refrains from marriage will do better.

39 A wife is bound as long as her husband
lives. But if the husband dies,[e] she is free to marry
anyone she wishes, only in the Lord. 40But in my
judgment she is more blessed if she remains as
she is. And I think that I too have the Spirit of
God.

8 Now concerning food sacrificed to idols:
we know that "all of us possess knowledge."
Knowledge puffs up, but love builds up. 2Anyone
who claims to know something does not yet have
the necessary knowledge; 3but anyone who loves
God is known by him.

4 Hence, as to the eating of food offered to
idols, we know that "no idol in the world really
exists," and that "there is no God but one." 5In-
deed, even though there may be so-called gods
in heaven or on earth—as in fact there are many
gods and many lords— 6yet for us there is one
God, the Father, from whom are all things and
for whom we exist, and one Lord, Jesus Christ,
through whom are all things and through whom
we exist.

7 It is not everyone, however, who has this
knowledge. Since some have become so accustomed to idols until now, they still think of the
food they eat as food offered to an idol; and their
conscience, being weak, is defiled. 8"Food will
not bring us close to God."[f] We are no worse off if
we do not eat, and no better off if we do. 9But take
care that this liberty of yours does not somehow
become a stumbling block to the weak. 10For if
others see you, who possess knowledge, eating
in the temple of an idol, might they not, since
their conscience is weak, be encouraged to the
point of eating food sacrificed to idols? 11So by
your knowledge those weak believers for whom
Christ died are destroyed.[g] 12But when you thus
sin against members of your family,[h] and wound
their conscience when it is weak, you sin against
Christ. 13Therefore, if food is a cause of their

[a] Gk *brothers* [b] Or *present* [c] Gk *in the flesh* [d] Gk *virgin* [e] Gk *falls asleep* [f] The quotation may extend to the end of the verse [g] Gk *the weak brother . . . is destroyed* [h] Gk *against the brothers*

falling,[a] I will never eat meat, so that I may not
cause one of them[b] to fall.

9 Am I not free? Am I not an apostle? Have
I not seen Jesus our Lord? Are you not my
work in the Lord? 2If I am not an apostle to others, at least I am to you; for you are the seal of my
apostleship in the Lord.

3 This is my defense to those who would examine me. 4Do we not have the right to our food
and drink? 5Do we not have the right to be accompanied by a believing wife,[c] as do the other
apostles and the brothers of the Lord and Cephas? 6Or is it only Barnabas and I who have no
right to refrain from working for a living? 7Who
at any time pays the expenses for doing military
service? Who plants a vineyard and does not eat
any of its fruit? Or who tends a flock and does not
get any of its milk?

8 Do I say this on human authority? Does not
the law also say the same? 9For it is written in the
law of Moses, "You shall not muzzle an ox while
it is treading out the grain." Is it for oxen that God
is concerned? 10Or does he not speak entirely for
our sake? It was indeed written for our sake, for
whoever plows should plow in hope and whoever
threshes should thresh in hope of a share in the
crop. 11If we have sown spiritual good among
you, is it too much if we reap your material benefits? 12If others share this rightful claim on you,
do not we still more?

Nevertheless, we have not made use of this
right, but we endure anything rather than put an
obstacle in the way of the gospel of Christ. 13Do
you not know that those who are employed in the
temple service get their food from the temple,
and those who serve at the altar share in what
is sacrificed on the altar? 14In the same way, the
Lord commanded that those who proclaim the
gospel should get their living by the gospel.

15 But I have made no use of any of these
rights, nor am I writing this so that they may be
applied in my case. Indeed, I would rather die
than that—no one will deprive me of my ground
for boasting! 16If I proclaim the gospel, this gives
me no ground for boasting, for an obligation is
laid on me, and woe to me if I do not proclaim the
gospel! 17For if I do this of my own will, I have a
reward; but if not of my own will, I am entrusted
with a commission. 18What then is my reward?
Just this: that in my proclamation I may make the
gospel free of charge, so as not to make full use of
my rights in the gospel.

19 For though I am free with respect to all,
I have made myself a slave to all, so that I might
win more of them. 20To the Jews I became as a
Jew, in order to win Jews. To those under the law I
became as one under the law (though I myself am
not under the law) so that I might win those under the law. 21To those outside the law I became
as one outside the law (though I am not free from
God's law but am under Christ's law) so that I
might win those outside the law. 22To the weak I
became weak, so that I might win the weak. I have
become all things to all people, that I might by all
means save some. 23I do it all for the sake of the
gospel, so that I may share in its blessings.

24 Do you not know that in a race the runners all compete, but only one receives the prize?
Run in such a way that you may win it. 25Athletes
exercise self-control in all things; they do it to receive a perishable wreath, but we an imperishable
one. 26So I do not run aimlessly, nor do I box as
though beating the air; 27but I punish my body
and enslave it, so that after proclaiming to others
I myself should not be disqualified.

10 I do not want you to be unaware, brothers and sisters,[d] that our ancestors were
all under the cloud, and all passed through the
sea, 2and all were baptized into Moses in the
cloud and in the sea, 3and all ate the same spiritual food, 4and all drank the same spiritual drink.
For they drank from the spiritual rock that followed them, and the rock was Christ. 5Neverthe-
less, God was not pleased with most of them, and
they were struck down in the wilderness.

6 Now these things occurred as examples for
us, so that we might not desire evil as they did.
7Do not become idolaters as some of them did;

[a] Gk *my brother's falling* [b] Gk *cause my brother* [c] Gk *a sister as wife* [d] Gk *brothers*

as it is written, "The people sat down to eat and
drink, and they rose up to play." 8We must not indulge in sexual immorality as some of them did,
and twenty-three thousand fell in a single day.
9We must not put Christ[a] to the test, as some of
them did, and were destroyed by serpents. 10And
do not complain as some of them did, and were
destroyed by the destroyer. 11These things happened to them to serve as an example, and they
were written down to instruct us, on whom the
ends of the ages have come. 12So if you think you
are standing, watch out that you do not fall. 13No
testing has overtaken you that is not common to
everyone. God is faithful, and he will not let you
be tested beyond your strength, but with the testing he will also provide the way out so that you
may be able to endure it.

14 Therefore, my dear friends,[b] flee from the
worship of idols. 15I speak as to sensible people;
judge for yourselves what I say. 16The cup of
blessing that we bless, is it not a sharing in the
blood of Christ? The bread that we break, is it not
a sharing in the body of Christ? 17Because there
is one bread, we who are many are one body, for
we all partake of the one bread. 18Consider the
people of Israel;[c] are not those who eat the sacrifices partners in the altar? 19What do I imply
then? That food sacrificed to idols is anything, or
that an idol is anything? 20No, I imply that what
pagans sacrifice, they sacrifice to demons and not
to God. I do not want you to be partners with
demons. 21You cannot drink the cup of the Lord
and the cup of demons. You cannot partake of the
table of the Lord and the table of demons. 22Or
are we provoking the Lord to jealousy? Are we
stronger than he?

23 "All things are lawful," but not all things are
beneficial. "All things are lawful," but not all things
build up. 24Do not seek your own advantage, but
that of the other. 25Eat whatever is sold in the
meat market without raising any question on the
ground of conscience, 26for "the earth and its fullness are the Lord's." 27If an unbeliever invites you
to a meal and you are disposed to go, eat whatever
is set before you without raising any question on
the ground of conscience. 28But if someone says
to you, "This has been offered in sacrifice," then
do not eat it, out of consideration for the one who
informed you, and for the sake of conscience—
29I mean the other's conscience, not your own.
For why should my liberty be subject to the judgment of someone else's conscience? 30If I partake
with thankfulness, why should I be denounced
because of that for which I give thanks?

31 So, whether you eat or drink, or whatever
you do, do everything for the glory of God. 32Give
no offense to Jews or to Greeks or to the church
of God, 33just as I try to please everyone in everything I do, not seeking my own advantage, but
11 that of many, so that they may be saved.
1Be imitators of me, as I am of Christ.

2 I commend you because you remember
me in everything and maintain the traditions

[a] Other ancient authorities read *the Lord* [b] Gk *my beloved* [c] Gk *Israel according to the flesh*

1 Corinthians 10:20

Paul sets up a dangerous dichotomy here between Christianity and the faith of others. For him, the gods of other nations, cultures, and peoples are basically demons. This understanding, coupled with colonialism, has led to much suffering, misery, and death. Because the gods of the conquered were seen as demons and their followers as demon worshipers, the colonizers were emboldened to eliminate non-Christian cultures and murder those who chose to defend these "demon" gods. Paul's words prevent the possibility of learning how to disagree without destroying, for in the minds of those who followed Paul, there can never be any coexistence between the God of truth and purity and the demons of darkness that stand behind all other faith traditions.

—MDLT

just as I handed them on to you. 3But I want you
to understand that Christ is the head of every
man, and the husband[a] is the head of his wife,[b]
and God is the head of Christ. 4Any man who
prays or prophesies with something on his head
disgraces his head, 5but any woman who prays
or prophesies with her head unveiled disgraces
her head—it is one and the same thing as having
her head shaved. 6For if a woman will not veil
herself, then she should cut off her hair; but if
it is disgraceful for a woman to have her hair cut
off or to be shaved, she should wear a veil. 7For a
man ought not to have his head veiled, since he
is the image and reflection[c] of God; but woman
is the reflection[c] of man. 8Indeed, man was not
made from woman, but woman from man. 9Nei-
ther was man created for the sake of woman, but
woman for the sake of man. 10For this reason a
woman ought to have a symbol of[d] authority on
her head,[e] because of the angels. 11Nevertheless,
in the Lord woman is not independent of man
or man independent of woman. 12For just as
woman came from man, so man comes through
woman; but all things come from God. 13Judge
for yourselves: is it proper for a woman to pray to
God with her head unveiled? 14Does not nature
itself teach you that if a man wears long hair, it
is degrading to him, 15but if a woman has long
hair, it is her glory? For her hair is given to her
for a covering. 16But if anyone is disposed to be
contentious—we have no such custom, nor do
the churches of God.

17 Now in the following instructions I do not
commend you, because when you come together
it is not for the better but for the worse. 18For, to
begin with, when you come together as a church,
I hear that there are divisions among you; and to
some extent I believe it. 19Indeed, there have to
be factions among you, for only so will it become
clear who among you are genuine. 20When you
come together, it is not really to eat the Lord's
supper. 21For when the time comes to eat, each
of you goes ahead with your own supper, and
one goes hungry and another becomes drunk.
22What! Do you not have homes to eat and drink
in? Or do you show contempt for the church of
God and humiliate those who have nothing?
What should I say to you? Should I commend
you? In this matter I do not commend you!

1 Corinthians 11:17-22

Paul's words here are often invoked over bread and wine in Christian communion services, but the thrust of his rebuke is a devastating indictment of the worship practices of the privileged. The common meal is not really the Lord's Supper so long as some remain hungry when the meal is over. The disaster in Corinth was that the prosperous failed to make any connection between their worship and the poverty in their midst.

— *NE*

23 For I received from the Lord what I also
handed on to you, that the Lord Jesus on the
night when he was betrayed took a loaf of bread,
24and when he had given thanks, he broke it and
said, "This is my body that is for[f] you. Do this in
remembrance of me." 25In the same way he took
the cup also, after supper, saying, "This cup is the
new covenant in my blood. Do this, as often as
you drink it, in remembrance of me." 26For as often as you eat this bread and drink the cup, you
proclaim the Lord's death until he comes.

27 Whoever, therefore, eats the bread or
drinks the cup of the Lord in an unworthy manner will be answerable for the body and blood of
the Lord. 28Examine yourselves, and only then
eat of the bread and drink of the cup. 29For all
who eat and drink[g] without discerning the body,[h]
eat and drink judgment against themselves. 30For
this reason many of you are weak and ill, and
some have died.[i] 31But if we judged ourselves, we
would not be judged. 32But when we are judged

[a] The same Greek word means *man* or *husband* [b] Or *head of the woman* [c] Or *glory* [d] Gk lacks *a symbol of* [e] Or *have freedom of choice regarding her head* [f] Other ancient authorities read *is broken for* [g] Other ancient authorities add *in an unworthy manner,* [h] Other ancient authorities read *the Lord's body* [i] Gk *fallen asleep*

by the Lord, we are disciplined[a] so that we may
not be condemned along with the world.

33 So then, my brothers and sisters,[b] when
you come together to eat, wait for one another.
34If you are hungry, eat at home, so that when you
come together, it will not be for your condemnation. About the other things I will give instructions when I come.

12 Now concerning spiritual gifts,[c] brothers and sisters,[b] I do not want you to be
uninformed. 2You know that when you were pagans, you were enticed and led astray to idols that
could not speak. 3Therefore I want you to understand that no one speaking by the Spirit of God
ever says "Let Jesus be cursed!" and no one can
say "Jesus is Lord" except by the Holy Spirit.

4 Now there are varieties of gifts, but the same
Spirit; 5and there are varieties of services, but the
same Lord; 6and there are varieties of activities,
but it is the same God who activates all of them in
everyone. 7To each is given the manifestation of
the Spirit for the common good. 8To one is given
through the Spirit the utterance of wisdom, and
to another the utterance of knowledge according
to the same Spirit, 9to another faith by the same
Spirit, to another gifts of healing by the one Spirit,
10to another the working of miracles, to another
prophecy, to another the discernment of spirits,
to another various kinds of tongues, to another
the interpretation of tongues. 11All these are ac-
tivated by one and the same Spirit, who allots to
each one individually just as the Spirit chooses.

12 For just as the body is one and has many
members, and all the members of the body,
though many, are one body, so it is with Christ.
13For in the one Spirit we were all baptized into
one body—Jews or Greeks, slaves or free—and
we were all made to drink of one Spirit.

14 Indeed, the body does not consist of one
member but of many. 15If the foot would say,
"Because I am not a hand, I do not belong to the
body," that would not make it any less a part of
the body. 16And if the ear would say, "Because I
am not an eye, I do not belong to the body," that
would not make it any less a part of the body.
17If the whole body were an eye, where would
the hearing be? If the whole body were hearing,
where would the sense of smell be? 18But as it is,
God arranged the members in the body, each one
of them, as he chose. 19If all were a single member, where would the body be? 20As it is, there
are many members, yet one body. 21The eye cannot say to the hand, "I have no need of you," nor
again the head to the feet, "I have no need of you."
22On the contrary, the members of the body that
seem to be weaker are indispensable, 23and those
members of the body that we think less honorable we clothe with greater honor, and our less
respectable members are treated with greater
respect; 24whereas our more respectable members do not need this. But God has so arranged
the body, giving the greater honor to the inferior member, 25that there may be no dissension
within the body, but the members may have the
same care for one another. 26If one member suffers, all suffer together with it; if one member is
honored, all rejoice together with it.

27 Now you are the body of Christ and individually members of it. 28And God has appointed
in the church first apostles, second prophets,
third teachers; then deeds of power, then gifts
of healing, forms of assistance, forms of leadership, various kinds of tongues. 29Are all apostles?
Are all prophets? Are all teachers? Do all work
miracles? 30Do all possess gifts of healing? Do all
speak in tongues? Do all interpret? 31But strive
for the greater gifts. And I will show you a still
more excellent way.

13 If I speak in the tongues of mortals and
of angels, but do not have love, I am a
noisy gong or a clanging cymbal. 2And if I have
prophetic powers, and understand all mysteries
and all knowledge, and if I have all faith, so as to
remove mountains, but do not have love, I am
nothing. 3If I give away all my possessions, and if
I hand over my body so that I may boast,[d] but do
not have love, I gain nothing.

[a] Or *When we are judged, we are being disciplined by the Lord* [b] Gk *brothers* [c] Or *spiritual persons*
[d] Other ancient authorities read *body to be burned*

4 Love is patient; love is kind; love is not
envious or boastful or arrogant 5 or rude. It does
not insist on its own way; it is not irritable or resentful; 6 it does not rejoice in wrongdoing, but
rejoices in the truth. 7 It bears all things, believes
all things, hopes all things, endures all things.

8 Love never ends. But as for prophecies,
they will come to an end; as for tongues, they
will cease; as for knowledge, it will come to an
end. 9 For we know only in part, and we prophesy only in part; 10 but when the complete comes,
the partial will come to an end. 11 When I was a
child, I spoke like a child, I thought like a child, I
reasoned like a child; when I became an adult, I
put an end to childish ways. 12 For now we see in
a mirror, dimly,[a] but then we will see face to face.
Now I know only in part; then I will know fully,
even as I have been fully known. 13 And now faith,
hope, and love abide, these three; and the greatest of these is love.

14 Pursue love and strive for the spiritual
gifts, and especially that you may prophesy. 2 For those who speak in a tongue do not
speak to other people but to God; for nobody understands them, since they are speaking mysteries in the Spirit. 3 On the other hand, those who
prophesy speak to other people for their upbuilding and encouragement and consolation. 4 Those
who speak in a tongue build up themselves, but
those who prophesy build up the church. 5 Now I
would like all of you to speak in tongues, but even
more to prophesy. One who prophesies is greater
than one who speaks in tongues, unless someone
interprets, so that the church may be built up.

6 Now, brothers and sisters,[b] if I come to you
speaking in tongues, how will I benefit you unless I speak to you in some revelation or knowledge or prophecy or teaching? 7 It is the same way
with lifeless instruments that produce sound,
such as the flute or the harp. If they do not give
distinct notes, how will anyone know what is being played? 8 And if the bugle gives an indistinct
sound, who will get ready for battle? 9 So with
yourselves; if in a tongue you utter speech that
is not intelligible, how will anyone know what
is being said? For you will be speaking into the
air. 10 There are doubtless many different kinds
of sounds in the world, and nothing is without
sound. 11 If then I do not know the meaning of a
sound, I will be a foreigner to the speaker and the
speaker a foreigner to me. 12 So with yourselves;
since you are eager for spiritual gifts, strive to excel in them for building up the church.

13 Therefore, one who speaks in a tongue
should pray for the power to interpret. 14 For if
I pray in a tongue, my spirit prays but my mind
is unproductive. 15 What should I do then? I will
pray with the spirit, but I will pray with the mind
also; I will sing praise with the spirit, but I will
sing praise with the mind also. 16 Otherwise, if
you say a blessing with the spirit, how can anyone in the position of an outsider say the "Amen"
to your thanksgiving, since the outsider does not
know what you are saying? 17 For you may give
thanks well enough, but the other person is not
built up. 18 I thank God that I speak in tongues
more than all of you; 19 nevertheless, in church I
would rather speak five words with my mind, in
order to instruct others also, than ten thousand
words in a tongue.

20 Brothers and sisters,[b] do not be children
in your thinking; rather, be infants in evil, but in
thinking be adults. 21 In the law it is written,

"By people of strange tongues
and by the lips of foreigners
I will speak to this people;
yet even then they will not listen to me,"

says the Lord. 22 Tongues, then, are a sign not for
believers but for unbelievers, while prophecy is
not for unbelievers but for believers. 23 If, therefore, the whole church comes together and all
speak in tongues, and outsiders or unbelievers
enter, will they not say that you are out of your
mind? 24 But if all prophesy, an unbeliever or outsider who enters is reproved by all and called to
account by all. 25 After the secrets of the unbeliever's heart are disclosed, that person will bow
down before God and worship him, declaring,
"God is really among you."

26 What should be done then, my friends?[b]

[a] Gk *in a riddle* [b] Gk *brothers*

1 Corinthians 14:34-35

The factors that lead some scholars to regard these lines ("women should be silent in the churches...") as an interpolation—an insertion into Paul's letter by a later hand—are their similarity to the abrupt statement in 1 Tim 2:12-15; their interruption of what otherwise would be this coherent line of thought from 14:33 to 14:36 ("The spirits of prophets are subject to the prophets, for God is a God not of disorder but of peace.... Or did the word of God originate with you?"); their apparent contradiction of 11:5, where women are imagined leading in worship; and a few ancient manuscripts, from different centuries, that show in different ways that just these verses were bracketed as questionable by Christian scribes.

— NE

When you come together, each one has a hymn,
a lesson, a revelation, a tongue, or an interpretation. Let all things be done for building up. 27If
anyone speaks in a tongue, let there be only two
or at most three, and each in turn; and let one interpret. 28But if there is no one to interpret, let
them be silent in church and speak to themselves
and to God. 29Let two or three prophets speak,
and let the others weigh what is said. 30If a revelation is made to someone else sitting nearby,
let the first person be silent. 31For you can all
prophesy one by one, so that all may learn and all
be encouraged. 32And the spirits of prophets are
subject to the prophets, 33for God is a God not of
disorder but of peace.

(As in all the churches of the saints, 34women
should be silent in the churches. For they are not
permitted to speak, but should be subordinate, as
the law also says. 35If there is anything they desire
to know, let them ask their husbands at home. For
it is shameful for a woman to speak in church.[a]
36Or did the word of God originate with you? Or
are you the only ones it has reached?)

37 Anyone who claims to be a prophet, or
to have spiritual powers, must acknowledge that
what I am writing to you is a command of the
Lord. 38Anyone who does not recognize this is
not to be recognized. 39So, my friends,[b] be eager to prophesy, and do not forbid speaking in
tongues; 40but all things should be done decently
and in order.

15 Now I would remind you, brothers and
sisters,[c] of the good news[d] that I proclaimed to you, which you in turn received, in
which also you stand, 2through which also you
are being saved, if you hold firmly to the message
that I proclaimed to you—unless you have come
to believe in vain.

3 For I handed on to you as of first importance
what I in turn had received: that Christ died for
our sins in accordance with the scriptures, 4and
that he was buried, and that he was raised on the
third day in accordance with the scriptures, 5and
that he appeared to Cephas, then to the twelve.
6Then he appeared to more than five hundred
brothers and sisters[c] at one time, most of whom

1 Corinthians 15:3-8

Paul states that the first to see the risen Christ was Peter, then the others of the original twelve—including Judas?—then by more than 500 brothers, then James, then all the apostles—more than the original twelve?—and finally by Paul. Yet all four Gospels say that the first people told to proclaim the good news that Christ had risen were the women who discovered the empty tomb. The women are absent from Paul's earlier account, raising the possibility that he has written them out of the story. Those who have been disenfranchised are accustomed to being written out of history; they are remembered only when the "main characters" of the story reach down to save them, but seldom as the instruments by which those who enjoy privileges at their expense may be saved.

— MDLT

[a] Other ancient authorities put verses 34–35 after verse 40 [b] Gk *my brothers* [c] Gk *brothers* [d] Or *gospel*

are still alive, though some have died.[a] 7Then he
appeared to James, then to all the apostles. 8Last
of all, as to one untimely born, he appeared also to
me. 9For I am the least of the apostles, unfit to be
called an apostle, because I persecuted the church
of God. 10But by the grace of God I am what I am,
and his grace toward me has not been in vain. On
the contrary, I worked harder than any of them—
though it was not I, but the grace of God that is
with me. 11Whether then it was I or they, so we
proclaim and so you have come to believe.

12 Now if Christ is proclaimed as raised from
the dead, how can some of you say there is no resurrection of the dead? 13If there is no resurrection of the dead, then Christ has not been raised;
14and if Christ has not been raised, then our
proclamation has been in vain and your faith has
been in vain. 15We are even found to be misrepre-
senting God, because we testified of God that he
raised Christ—whom he did not raise if it is true
that the dead are not raised. 16For if the dead are
not raised, then Christ has not been raised. 17If
Christ has not been raised, your faith is futile and
you are still in your sins. 18Then those also who
have died[a] in Christ have perished. 19If for this
life only we have hoped in Christ, we are of all
people most to be pitied.

20 But in fact Christ has been raised from the
dead, the first fruits of those who have died.[a] 21For
since death came through a human being, the resurrection of the dead has also come through a human being; 22for as all die in Adam, so all will be
made alive in Christ. 23But each in his own order:
Christ the first fruits, then at his coming those
who belong to Christ. 24Then comes the end,[b]
when he hands over the kingdom to God the Father, after he has destroyed every ruler and every
authority and power. 25For he must reign until he
has put all his enemies under his feet. 26The last
enemy to be destroyed is death. 27For "God[c] has
put all things in subjection under his feet." But
when it says, "All things are put in subjection,"
it is plain that this does not include the one who
put all things in subjection under him. 28When
all things are subjected to him, then the Son himself will also be subjected to the one who put all
things in subjection under him, so that God may
be all in all.

29 Otherwise, what will those people do who
receive baptism on behalf of the dead? If the dead
are not raised at all, why are people baptized on
their behalf?

30 And why are we putting ourselves in
danger every hour? 31I die every day! That is as
certain, brothers and sisters,[d] as my boasting of
you—a boast that I make in Christ Jesus our Lord.
32If with merely human hopes I fought with wild
animals at Ephesus, what would I have gained by
it? If the dead are not raised,

"Let us eat and drink,
for tomorrow we die."

33Do not be deceived:

"Bad company ruins good morals."

34Come to a sober and right mind, and sin no
more; for some people have no knowledge of
God. I say this to your shame.

35 But someone will ask, "How are the dead
raised? With what kind of body do they come?"
36Fool! What you sow does not come to life unless it dies. 37And as for what you sow, you do not
sow the body that is to be, but a bare seed, perhaps of wheat or of some other grain. 38But God
gives it a body as he has chosen, and to each kind
of seed its own body. 39Not all flesh is alike, but
there is one flesh for human beings, another for
animals, another for birds, and another for fish.
40There are both heavenly bodies and earthly
bodies, but the glory of the heavenly is one thing,
and that of the earthly is another. 41There is one
glory of the sun, and another glory of the moon,
and another glory of the stars; indeed, star differs
from star in glory.

42 So it is with the resurrection of the dead.
What is sown is perishable, what is raised is imperishable. 43It is sown in dishonor, it is raised in
glory. It is sown in weakness, it is raised in power.
44It is sown a physical body, it is raised a spiritual
body. If there is a physical body, there is also a
spiritual body. 45Thus it is written, "The first man,
Adam, became a living being"; the last Adam

[a] Gk *fallen asleep* [b] Or *Then come the rest* [c] Gk *he* [d] Gk *brothers*

became a life-giving spirit. 46But it is not the
spiritual that is first, but the physical, and then
the spiritual. 47The first man was from the earth,
a man of dust; the second man is[a] from heaven.
48As was the man of dust, so are those who are of
the dust; and as is the man of heaven, so are those
who are of heaven. 49Just as we have borne the
image of the man of dust, we will[b] also bear the
image of the man of heaven.

50 What I am saying, brothers and sisters,[c]
is this: flesh and blood cannot inherit the kingdom of God, nor does the perishable inherit the
imperishable. 51Listen, I will tell you a mystery!
We will not all die,[d] but we will all be changed,
52in a moment, in the twinkling of an eye, at the
last trumpet. For the trumpet will sound, and the
dead will be raised imperishable, and we will be
changed. 53For this perishable body must put on
imperishability, and this mortal body must put on
immortality. 54When this perishable body puts
on imperishability, and this mortal body puts on
immortality, then the saying that is written will
be fulfilled:

"Death has been swallowed up in victory."
55 "Where, O death, is your victory?
Where, O death, is your sting?"

56The sting of death is sin, and the power of sin is
the law. 57But thanks be to God, who gives us the
victory through our Lord Jesus Christ.

58 Therefore, my beloved,[e] be steadfast, immovable, always excelling in the work of the Lord,
because you know that in the Lord your labor is
not in vain.

16 Now concerning the collection for the
saints: you should follow the directions I
gave to the churches of Galatia. 2On the first day
of every week, each of you is to put aside and save
whatever extra you earn, so that collections need
not be taken when I come. 3And when I arrive, I
will send any whom you approve with letters to
take your gift to Jerusalem. 4If it seems advisable
that I should go also, they will accompany me.

5 I will visit you after passing through Macedonia—for I intend to pass through Macedonia—
6and perhaps I will stay with you or even spend
the winter, so that you may send me on my way,
wherever I go. 7I do not want to see you now just in
passing, for I hope to spend some time with you, if
the Lord permits. 8But I will stay in Ephesus until
Pentecost, 9for a wide door for effective work has
opened to me, and there are many adversaries.

10 If Timothy comes, see that he has nothing
to fear among you, for he is doing the work of the
Lord just as I am; 11therefore let no one despise
him. Send him on his way in peace, so that he
may come to me; for I am expecting him with the
brothers.

12 Now concerning our brother Apollos,
I strongly urged him to visit you with the other
brothers, but he was not at all willing[f] to come
now. He will come when he has the opportunity.

13 Keep alert, stand firm in your faith, be
courageous, be strong. 14Let all that you do be
done in love.

15 Now, brothers and sisters,[c] you know that
members of the household of Stephanas were the
first converts in Achaia, and they have devoted
themselves to the service of the saints; 16I urge you
to put yourselves at the service of such people, and
of everyone who works and toils with them. 17I
rejoice at the coming of Stephanas and Fortunatus
and Achaicus, because they have made up for your
absence; 18for they refreshed my spirit as well as
yours. So give recognition to such persons.

19 The churches of Asia send greetings. Aquila and Prisca, together with the church in their
house, greet you warmly in the Lord. 20All the
brothers and sisters[c] send greetings. Greet one
another with a holy kiss.

21 I, Paul, write this greeting with my own
hand. 22Let anyone be accursed who has no love
for the Lord. Our Lord, come![g] 23The grace of the
Lord Jesus be with you. 24My love be with all of
you in Christ Jesus.[h]

[a] Other ancient authorities add *the Lord* [b] Other ancient authorities read *let us* [c] Gk *brothers* [d] Gk *fall asleep* [e] Gk *beloved brothers* [f] Or *it was not at all God's will for him* [g] Gk *Marana tha*. These Aramaic words can also be read *Maran atha*, meaning *Our Lord has come* [h] Other ancient authorities add *Amen*

The Second Letter of Paul to the Corinthians

Paul probably wrote 2 Corinthians in 55 CE, shortly after 1 Corinthians, in response to new developments within the community of believers involving even more acute issues related to the culture of Greco-Roman society. Competing missionaries and apostles had entered the Christian community at Corinth and their rhetorical eloquence and personal presence resonated with Corinth's cultural norms. In the closing of his previous letter to Corinth (1 Cor 16:1-9), Paul said he planned to stay in Ephesus until Pentecost, then travel to Corinth and possibly remain there for the winter. He changed his plans, deciding to visit Corinth two more times (2 Cor 1:15). But his next visit to the city was a humiliating and painful one (2:5; 7:12) because one Corinthian member supported those other apostles and opposed Paul's leadership. Paul cancelled the second proposed visit and rushed back to Ephesus, where he composed an important letter, delivered by Titus and written "out of much distress and anguish of heart and with many tears" (2:4; some believe that chs. 10–13 represent that letter). Desiring to hear how the Corinthians had received his tearful letter, Paul traveled to Macedonia to find Titus (2:12). Upon finding him, Paul learned that the community was on his side (7:5-16). His letter had been successful in persuading the Corinthians of his leadership and ensuring their continued support of the collection for the Jerusalem saints.

Traditional commentaries have been preoccupied with two questions about 2 Corinthians. Was it written as a single letter, or was it originally several letters in which Paul addressed different situations, which a later editor compiled as the letter that has come down to us? And who were these opponents who attack Paul's gospel and apostolic self-understanding? While many interpreters today uphold the original unity of 2 Corinthians, those who view it as a composite writing cite its unevenness and digressive structure. Whichever way one reads the letter, it reflects religious and cultural influences that were part of Paul's heritage as a Diaspora Jew. Moreover, 2 Corinthians is written in the Greek used by educated people of his day, and displays features of Hellenistic rhetoric (lists of suffering and achievements, invective, and comparison) and epistolary form. All these features represent Hellenistic (Greek) cultural influence and also Paul's "hybridity," the Hebrew-Hellenist mix that can be seen in the contrast between Paul's interpretation of Moses' veil (3:12-18, drawing on Exod 34) and the "fool's speech" of chapters 11–12.

Paul's oratorical encounter with those other apostles can also be viewed against the background of Hellenistic cultural influences. The wealthier members of the Corinthian community welcomed the "super-apostles" as guests at their house meetings (11:4-5, 13-15) and served as their patrons. These traveling apostles came to Corinth—Paul's mission field, at least from his perspective (10:15-16)—with "letters of recommendation" (3:1; 11:4-5) and were well received

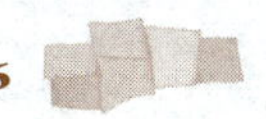

(11:4, 20). They, like Paul, are Hebrews, Israelites, seed of Abraham, and ministers of Christ (11:22-23a). Their hybridity, too, is evident: they are Greek-speaking, rhetorically competent Jewish-Christian missionaries. In the spirit of Hellenism, they viewed mission as competition and saw themselves as missionaries offering a competing model of rhetoric and apostleship (11:7-11; 12:13-15). For them success depended on the missionary's ability to express the divine in his or her performance—rhetorical eloquence, knowledge, and personal charisma.

These rivals and some in the Corinthian community felt that Paul did not measure up. He is unreliable. He changes his travel plans. He lacks letters of recommendation (3:1). He takes advantage of the Corinthians to enrich himself (7:2; 12:16). He is brave only from the safe distance from which he writes (10:1, 10). He is not a good orator (10:11; 11:6). He refuses financial support from the Corinthians, which must be evidence of his lack of love for them (11:7; 12:13). He is inferior to the super-apostles (11:5; 12:11). And he is not a "true apostle" (12:12).

If these charges are informed by Greek and Roman culture, Paul responds in kind, using well-known rhetorical techniques. But he also insists on the authority of Israel's Scripture and grounds his apostolic authority in his personal experience of humility, which he describes as strength in weakness ("for whenever I am weak, then I am strong," 12:10). His perspective is informed in light of the passion, death, and resurrection of Jesus Christ.

How should today's readers of 2 Corinthians view these issues? Some might recall contemporary televangelists who boast of charismatic powers—healings, words of knowledge, and ecstatic visions. Others might take notice of the rhetoric of some televangelists who proclaim a theology of personal success and material prosperity that can be had by all who have the proper faithpractice. A focus on contemporary competitiveness in Western capitalism and imperialistic politics in our contemporary world might gain the attention of other readers. Whatever perspective one takes, the issues in the time of Paul and the Corinthians and our time are not merely theological but also relate to issues of culture and society.

— ***Demetrius K. Williams***

1 Paul, an apostle of Christ Jesus by the will of God, and Timothy our brother,

To the church of God that is in Corinth, including all the saints throughout Achaia:

2 Grace to you and peace from God our Father and the Lord Jesus Christ.

3 Blessed be the God and Father of our Lord Jesus Christ, the Father of mercies and the God of
all consolation, 4who consoles us in all our afflic-
tion, so that we may be able to console those who
are in any affliction with the consolation with
which we ourselves are consoled by God. 5For
just as the sufferings of Christ are abundant for
us, so also our consolation is abundant through
Christ. 6If we are being afflicted, it is for your consolation and salvation; if we are being consoled,
it is for your consolation, which you experience

when you patiently endure the same sufferings
that we are also suffering. 7Our hope for you is
unshaken; for we know that as you share in our
sufferings, so also you share in our consolation.

8 We do not want you to be unaware, brothers and sisters,[a] of the affliction we experienced in
Asia; for we were so utterly, unbearably crushed
that we despaired of life itself. 9Indeed, we felt
that we had received the sentence of death so that
we would rely not on ourselves but on God who
raises the dead. 10He who rescued us from so
deadly a peril will continue to rescue us; on him
we have set our hope that he will rescue us again,
11as you also join in helping us by your prayers, so
that many will give thanks on our[b] behalf for the
blessing granted us through the prayers of many.

12 Indeed, this is our boast, the testimony
of our conscience: we have behaved in the world
with frankness[c] and godly sincerity, not by earthly
wisdom but by the grace of God—and all the
more toward you. 13For we write you nothing
other than what you can read and also understand; I hope you will understand until the end—
14as you have already understood us in part—that
on the day of the Lord Jesus we are your boast
even as you are our boast.

15 Since I was sure of this, I wanted to come
to you first, so that you might have a double favor;[d]
16I wanted to visit you on my way to Macedonia,
and to come back to you from Macedonia and have
you send me on to Judea. 17Was I vacillating when
I wanted to do this? Do I make my plans according
to ordinary human standards,[e] ready to say "Yes,
yes" and "No, no" at the same time? 18As surely as
God is faithful, our word to you has not been "Yes
and No." 19For the Son of God, Jesus Christ, whom
we proclaimed among you, Silvanus and Timothy
and I, was not "Yes and No"; but in him it is always
"Yes." 20For in him every one of God's promises is
a "Yes." For this reason it is through him that we
say the "Amen," to the glory of God. 21But it is
God who establishes us with you in Christ and has
anointed us, 22by putting his seal on us and giving
us his Spirit in our hearts as a first installment.

23 But I call on God as witness against me:
it was to spare you that I did not come again to
Corinth. 24I do not mean to imply that we lord it
over your faith; rather, we are workers with you
for your joy, because you stand firm in the faith.

2 1So I made up my mind not to make you another painful visit. 2For if I cause you pain,
who is there to make me glad but the one whom I
have pained? 3And I wrote as I did, so that when
I came, I might not suffer pain from those who
should have made me rejoice; for I am confident
about all of you, that my joy would be the joy of
all of you. 4For I wrote you out of much distress
and anguish of heart and with many tears, not to
cause you pain, but to let you know the abundant
love that I have for you.

5 But if anyone has caused pain, he has caused
it not to me, but to some extent—not to exaggerate it—to all of you. 6This punishment by the
majority is enough for such a person; 7so now instead you should forgive and console him, so that
he may not be overwhelmed by excessive sorrow.
8So I urge you to reaffirm your love for him. 9I
wrote for this reason: to test you and to know
whether you are obedient in everything. 10Any-
one whom you forgive, I also forgive. What I have
forgiven, if I have forgiven anything, has been for
your sake in the presence of Christ. 11And we do
this so that we may not be outwitted by Satan; for
we are not ignorant of his designs.

12 When I came to Troas to proclaim the
good news of Christ, a door was opened for me in
the Lord; 13but my mind could not rest because
I did not find my brother Titus there. So I said
farewell to them and went on to Macedonia.

14 But thanks be to God, who in Christ always
leads us in triumphal procession, and through us
spreads in every place the fragrance that comes
from knowing him. 15For we are the aroma of
Christ to God among those who are being saved
and among those who are perishing; 16to the one
a fragrance from death to death, to the other a fragrance from life to life. Who is sufficient for these
things? 17For we are not peddlers of God's word

[a] Gk *brothers* [b] Other ancient authorities read *your* [c] Other ancient authorities read *holiness* [d] Other ancient authorities read *pleasure* [e] Gk *according to the flesh*

> **2 Corinthians 2:14-16**
>
> Paul invokes the striking image of a triumphal procession in which prisoners of war are paraded publicly—often to their deaths. To the outside world, the apostles appear defeated victims, powerless and humiliated, reeking of death; but to those who anticipate God's future triumph, they are walking signs of Christ's power.
>
> —*NE*

like so many;[a] but in Christ we speak as persons
of sincerity, as persons sent from God and standing in his presence.

3 Are we beginning to commend ourselves
again? Surely we do not need, as some do,
letters of recommendation to you or from you,
do we? 2You yourselves are our letter, written on
our[b] hearts, to be known and read by all; 3and you
show that you are a letter of Christ, prepared by
us, written not with ink but with the Spirit of the
living God, not on tablets of stone but on tablets
of human hearts.

4 Such is the confidence that we have through
Christ toward God. 5Not that we are competent
of ourselves to claim anything as coming from us;
our competence is from God, 6who has made us
competent to be ministers of a new covenant, not
of letter but of spirit; for the letter kills, but the
Spirit gives life.

7 Now if the ministry of death, chiseled in
letters on stone tablets,[c] came in glory so that
the people of Israel could not gaze at Moses' face
because of the glory of his face, a glory now set
aside, 8how much more will the ministry of the
Spirit come in glory? 9For if there was glory in
the ministry of condemnation, much more does
the ministry of justification abound in glory!
10Indeed, what once had glory has lost its glory
because of the greater glory; 11for if what was set
aside came through glory, much more has the
permanent come in glory!

12 Since, then, we have such a hope, we act
with great boldness, 13not like Moses, who put a
veil over his face to keep the people of Israel from
gazing at the end of the glory that[d] was being set
aside. 14But their minds were hardened. Indeed,
to this very day, when they hear the reading of the
old covenant, that same veil is still there, since
only in Christ is it set aside. 15Indeed, to this very
day whenever Moses is read, a veil lies over their
minds; 16but when one turns to the Lord, the
veil is removed. 17Now the Lord is the Spirit, and
where the Spirit of the Lord is, there is freedom.
18And all of us, with unveiled faces, seeing the
glory of the Lord as though reflected in a mirror,
are being transformed into the same image from
one degree of glory to another; for this comes
from the Lord, the Spirit.

4 Therefore, since it is by God's mercy that we
are engaged in this ministry, we do not lose
heart. 2We have renounced the shameful things
that one hides; we refuse to practice cunning or
to falsify God's word; but by the open statement
of the truth we commend ourselves to the conscience of everyone in the sight of God. 3And
even if our gospel is veiled, it is veiled to those
who are perishing. 4In their case the god of this
world has blinded the minds of the unbelievers,
to keep them from seeing the light of the gospel
of the glory of Christ, who is the image of God.
5For we do not proclaim ourselves; we proclaim
Jesus Christ as Lord and ourselves as your slaves
for Jesus' sake. 6For it is the God who said, "Let
light shine out of darkness," who has shone in our
hearts to give the light of the knowledge of the
glory of God in the face of Jesus Christ.

7 But we have this treasure in clay jars, so
that it may be made clear that this extraordinary power belongs to God and does not come
from us. 8We are afflicted in every way, but not
crushed; perplexed, but not driven to despair;
9persecuted, but not forsaken; struck down, but
not destroyed; 10always carrying in the body the
death of Jesus, so that the life of Jesus may also be
made visible in our bodies. 11For while we live,
we are always being given up to death for Jesus'
sake, so that the life of Jesus may be made visible

[a] Other ancient authorities read *like the others* [b] Other ancient authorities read *your* [c] Gk *on stones* [d] Gk *of what*

in our mortal flesh. 12 So death is at work in us, but life in you.

13 But just as we have the same spirit of faith that is in accordance with scripture—"I believed, and so I spoke"—we also believe, and so we speak, 14 because we know that the one who raised the Lord Jesus will raise us also with Jesus, and will bring us with you into his presence. 15 Yes, everything is for your sake, so that grace, as it extends to more and more people, may increase thanksgiving, to the glory of God.

16 So we do not lose heart. Even though our outer nature is wasting away, our inner nature is being renewed day by day. 17 For this slight momentary affliction is preparing us for an eternal weight of glory beyond all measure, 18 because we look not at what can be seen but at what cannot be seen; for what can be seen is temporary, but what cannot be seen is eternal.

5 For we know that if the earthly tent we live in is destroyed, we have a building from God, a house not made with hands, eternal in the heavens. 2 For in this tent we groan, longing to be clothed with our heavenly dwelling— 3 if indeed, when we have taken it off[a] we will not be found naked. 4 For while we are still in this tent, we groan under our burden, because we wish not to be unclothed but to be further clothed, so that what is mortal may be swallowed up by life. 5 He who has prepared us for this very thing is God, who has given us the Spirit as a guarantee.

6 So we are always confident; even though we know that while we are at home in the body we are away from the Lord— 7 for we walk by faith, not by sight. 8 Yes, we do have confidence, and we would rather be away from the body and at home with the Lord. 9 So whether we are at home or away, we make it our aim to please him. 10 For all of us must appear before the judgment seat of Christ, so that each may receive recompense for what has been done in the body, whether good or evil.

11 Therefore, knowing the fear of the Lord, we try to persuade others; but we ourselves are well known to God, and I hope that we are also well known to your consciences. 12 We are not commending ourselves to you again, but giving you an opportunity to boast about us, so that you may be able to answer those who boast in outward appearance and not in the heart. 13 For if we are beside ourselves, it is for God; if we are in our right mind, it is for you. 14 For the love of Christ urges us on, because we are convinced that one has died for all; therefore all have died. 15 And he died for all, so that those who live might live no longer for themselves, but for him who died and was raised for them.

16 From now on, therefore, we regard no one from a human point of view;[b] even though we once knew Christ from a human point of view,[b] we know him no longer in that way. 17 So if anyone is in Christ, there is a new creation: everything old has passed away; see, everything has become new! 18 All this is from God, who reconciled us to himself through Christ, and has given us the ministry of reconciliation; 19 that is, in Christ God was reconciling the world to himself,[c] not counting their trespasses against them, and entrusting the message of reconciliation to us. 20 So we are ambassadors for Christ, since God is making his appeal through us; we entreat you on behalf of Christ, be reconciled to God. 21 For our sake he made him to be sin who knew no sin, so that in him we might become the righteousness of God.

6 As we work together with him,[d] we urge you also not to accept the grace of God in vain. 2 For he says,

"At an acceptable time I have listened to you,
and on a day of salvation I have helped
you."

See, now is the acceptable time; see, now is the day of salvation! 3 We are putting no obstacle in anyone's way, so that no fault may be found with our ministry, 4 but as servants of God we have commended ourselves in every way: through great endurance, in afflictions, hardships, calamities, 5 beatings, imprisonments, riots, labors, sleepless nights, hunger; 6 by purity, knowledge, patience,

[a] Other ancient authorities read *put it on* [b] Gk *according to the flesh* [c] Or *God was in Christ reconciling the world to himself*
[d] Gk *As we work together*

kindness, holiness of spirit, genuine love, 7truth-
ful speech, and the power of God; with the weapons of righteousness for the right hand and for
the left; 8in honor and dishonor, in ill repute and
good repute. We are treated as impostors, and yet
are true; 9as unknown, and yet are well known;
as dying, and see—we are alive; as punished, and
yet not killed; 10as sorrowful, yet always rejoicing; as poor, yet making many rich; as having
nothing, and yet possessing everything.
11 We have spoken frankly to you Corinthians; our heart is wide open to you. 12There is no
restriction in our affections, but only in yours.
13In return—I speak as to children—open wide
your hearts also.

14 Do not be mismatched with unbelievers.
For what partnership is there between righteousness and lawlessness? Or what fellowship is there
between light and darkness? 15What agreement
does Christ have with Beliar? Or what does a
believer share with an unbeliever? 16What agreement has the temple of God with idols? For we[a]
are the temple of the living God; as God said,

"I will live in them and walk among them,
and I will be their God,
and they shall be my people.
17 Therefore come out from them,
and be separate from them, says the Lord,
and touch nothing unclean;
then I will welcome you,
18 and I will be your father,
and you shall be my sons and daughters,
says the Lord Almighty."

7 Since we have these promises, beloved, let us
cleanse ourselves from every defilement of
body and of spirit, making holiness perfect in the
fear of God.

2 Make room in your hearts[b] for us; we have
wronged no one, we have corrupted no one, we
have taken advantage of no one. 3I do not say this
to condemn you, for I said before that you are in
our hearts, to die together and to live together. 4I
often boast about you; I have great pride in you;
I am filled with consolation; I am overjoyed in all
our affliction.
5 For even when we came into Macedonia,
our bodies had no rest, but we were afflicted in
every way—disputes without and fears within.
6But God, who consoles the downcast, consoled
us by the arrival of Titus, 7and not only by his
coming, but also by the consolation with which
he was consoled about you, as he told us of your
longing, your mourning, your zeal for me, so
that I rejoiced still more. 8For even if I made you
sorry with my letter, I do not regret it (though I
did regret it, for I see that I grieved you with that
letter, though only briefly). 9Now I rejoice, not
because you were grieved, but because your grief
led to repentance; for you felt a godly grief, so
that you were not harmed in any way by us. 10For
godly grief produces a repentance that leads to
salvation and brings no regret, but worldly grief
produces death. 11For see what earnestness this
godly grief has produced in you, what eagerness
to clear yourselves, what indignation, what alarm,
what longing, what zeal, what punishment! At every point you have proved yourselves guiltless in
the matter. 12So although I wrote to you, it was
not on account of the one who did the wrong, nor
on account of the one who was wronged, but in
order that your zeal for us might be made known
to you before God. 13In this we find comfort.
In addition to our own consolation, we rejoiced still more at the joy of Titus, because his
mind has been set at rest by all of you. 14For if I
have been somewhat boastful about you to him,
I was not disgraced; but just as everything we
said to you was true, so our boasting to Titus has
proved true as well. 15And his heart goes out all
the more to you, as he remembers the obedience
of all of you, and how you welcomed him with
fear and trembling. 16I rejoice, because I have
complete confidence in you.

8 We want you to know, brothers and sisters,[c]
about the grace of God that has been granted
to the churches of Macedonia; 2for during a severe
ordeal of affliction, their abundant joy and their

[a] Other ancient authorities read *you* [b] Gk lacks *in your hearts* [c] Gk *brothers*

extreme poverty have overflowed in a wealth of
generosity on their part. 3 For, as I can testify, they
voluntarily gave according to their means, and
even beyond their means, 4 begging us earnestly
for the privilege[a] of sharing in this ministry to the
saints— 5 and this, not merely as we expected;
they gave themselves first to the Lord and, by the
will of God, to us, 6 so that we might urge Titus
that, as he had already made a beginning, so he
should also complete this generous undertaking[b]
among you. 7 Now as you excel in everything—in
faith, in speech, in knowledge, in utmost eagerness, and in our love for you[c]—so we want you to
excel also in this generous undertaking.[b]

8 I do not say this as a command, but I am
testing the genuineness of your love against the
earnestness of others. 9 For you know the generous act[d] of our Lord Jesus Christ, that though
he was rich, yet for your sakes he became poor,
so that by his poverty you might become rich.
10 And in this matter I am giving my advice: it
is appropriate for you who began last year not
only to do something but even to desire to do
something— 11 now finish doing it, so that your
eagerness may be matched by completing it according to your means. 12 For if the eagerness is
there, the gift is acceptable according to what one
has—not according to what one does not have.
13 I do not mean that there should be relief for
others and pressure on you, but it is a question of
a fair balance between 14 your present abundance
and their need, so that their abundance may be
for your need, in order that there may be a fair
balance. 15 As it is written,

"The one who had much did not have too
much,
and the one who had little did not have
too little."

16 But thanks be to God who put in the heart
of Titus the same eagerness for you that I myself
have. 17 For he not only accepted our appeal, but
since he is more eager than ever, he is going to you
of his own accord. 18 With him we are sending the
brother who is famous among all the churches
for his proclaiming the good news;[e] 19 and not
only that, but he has also been appointed by the
churches to travel with us while we are administering this generous undertaking[b] for the glory of
the Lord himself[f] and to show our goodwill. 20 We
intend that no one should blame us about this
generous gift that we are administering, 21 for we
intend to do what is right not only in the Lord's
sight but also in the sight of others. 22 And with
them we are sending our brother whom we have
often tested and found eager in many matters, but
who is now more eager than ever because of his
great confidence in you. 23 As for Titus, he is my
partner and co-worker in your service; as for our
brothers, they are messengers[g] of the churches,
the glory of Christ. 24 Therefore openly before the
churches, show them the proof of your love and
of our reason for boasting about you.

9 Now it is not necessary for me to write you
about the ministry to the saints, 2 for I know
your eagerness, which is the subject of my boasting about you to the people of Macedonia, saying that Achaia has been ready since last year;
and your zeal has stirred up most of them. 3 But I
am sending the brothers in order that our boasting about you may not prove to have been empty
in this case, so that you may be ready, as I said
you would be; 4 otherwise, if some Macedonians
come with me and find that you are not ready, we
would be humiliated—to say nothing of you—in

2 Corinthians 8:13-15

Just as the early church was characterized by the common sharing of resources—what historians have called "apostolic communism"—so Paul invokes a central principle of Christian mutualism among the assemblies: a "fair balance" between abundance and need means that no one holds an inherent right to abundance while others are in need.

—*NE*

[a] Gk *grace* [b] Gk *this grace* [c] Other ancient authorities read *your love for us* [d] Gk *the grace* [e] Or *the gospel*
[f] Other ancient authorities lack *himself* [g] Gk *apostles*

this undertaking.[a] 5So I thought it necessary to urge the brothers to go on ahead to you, and arrange in advance for this bountiful gift that you have promised, so that it may be ready as a voluntary gift and not as an extortion.

6 The point is this: the one who sows sparingly will also reap sparingly, and the one who sows bountifully will also reap bountifully. 7Each of you must give as you have made up your mind, not reluctantly or under compulsion, for God loves a cheerful giver. 8And God is able to provide you with every blessing in abundance, so that by always having enough of everything, you may share abundantly in every good work. 9As it is written,

"He scatters abroad, he gives to the poor;
his righteousness[b] endures forever."

10He who supplies seed to the sower and bread for food will supply and multiply your seed for sowing and increase the harvest of your righteousness.[b] 11You will be enriched in every way for your great generosity, which will produce thanksgiving to God through us; 12for the rendering of this ministry not only supplies the needs of the saints but also overflows with many thanksgivings to God. 13Through the testing of this ministry you glorify God by your obedience to the confession of the gospel of Christ and by the generosity of your sharing with them and with all others, 14while they long for you and pray for you because of the surpassing grace of God that he has given you. 15Thanks be to God for his indescribable gift!

10 I myself, Paul, appeal to you by the meekness and gentleness of Christ—I who am humble when face to face with you, but bold toward you when I am away!— 2I ask that when I am present I need not show boldness by daring to oppose those who think we are acting according to human standards.[c] 3Indeed, we live as human beings,[d] but we do not wage war according to human standards;[c] 4for the weapons of our warfare are not merely human,[e] but they have divine power to destroy strongholds. We destroy arguments 5and every proud obstacle raised up against the knowledge of God, and we take every thought captive to obey Christ. 6We are ready to punish every disobedience when your obedience is complete.

7 Look at what is before your eyes. If you are confident that you belong to Christ, remind yourself of this, that just as you belong to Christ, so also do we. 8Now, even if I boast a little too much of our authority, which the Lord gave for building you up and not for tearing you down, I will not be ashamed of it. 9I do not want to seem as though I am trying to frighten you with my letters. 10For they say, "His letters are weighty and strong, but his bodily presence is weak, and his speech contemptible." 11Let such people understand that what we say by letter when absent, we will also do when present.

12 We do not dare to classify or compare ourselves with some of those who commend themselves. But when they measure themselves by one another, and compare themselves with one another, they do not show good sense. 13We, however, will not boast beyond limits, but will keep within the field that God has assigned to us, to reach out even as far as you. 14For we were not overstepping our limits when we reached you; we were the first to come all the way to you with the good news[f] of Christ. 15We do not boast beyond limits, that is, in the labors of others; but our hope is that, as your faith increases, our sphere of action among you may be greatly enlarged, 16so that we may proclaim the good news[f] in lands beyond you, without boasting of work already done in someone else's sphere of action. 17"Let the one who boasts, boast in the Lord." 18For it is not those who commend themselves that are approved, but those whom the Lord commends.

11 I wish you would bear with me in a little foolishness. Do bear with me! 2I feel a divine jealousy for you, for I promised you in marriage to one husband, to present you as a chaste virgin to Christ. 3But I am afraid that as the serpent

[a] Other ancient authorities add *of boasting* [b] Or *benevolence* [c] Gk *according to the flesh* [d] Gk *in the flesh* [e] Gk *fleshly* [f] Or *the gospel*

deceived Eve by its cunning, your thoughts will
be led astray from a sincere and pure[a] devotion
to Christ. 4 For if someone comes and proclaims
another Jesus than the one we proclaimed, or if
you receive a different spirit from the one you received, or a different gospel from the one you accepted, you submit to it readily enough. 5 I think
that I am not in the least inferior to these super-
apostles. 6 I may be untrained in speech, but not
in knowledge; certainly in every way and in all
things we have made this evident to you.

7 Did I commit a sin by humbling myself so
that you might be exalted, because I proclaimed
God's good news[b] to you free of charge? 8 I robbed
other churches by accepting support from them
in order to serve you. 9 And when I was with you
and was in need, I did not burden anyone, for my
needs were supplied by the friends[c] who came
from Macedonia. So I refrained and will continue
to refrain from burdening you in any way. 10 As
the truth of Christ is in me, this boast of mine
will not be silenced in the regions of Achaia.
11 And why? Because I do not love you? God
knows I do!

12 And what I do I will also continue to do, in
order to deny an opportunity to those who want
an opportunity to be recognized as our equals in
what they boast about. 13 For such boasters are
false apostles, deceitful workers, disguising themselves as apostles of Christ. 14 And no wonder!
Even Satan disguises himself as an angel of light.
15 So it is not strange if his ministers also disguise
themselves as ministers of righteousness. Their
end will match their deeds.

16 I repeat, let no one think that I am a fool;
but if you do, then accept me as a fool, so that I too
may boast a little. 17 What I am saying in regard
to this boastful confidence, I am saying not with
the Lord's authority, but as a fool; 18 since many
boast according to human standards,[d] I will also
boast. 19 For you gladly put up with fools, being
wise yourselves! 20 For you put up with it when
someone makes slaves of you, or preys upon you,
or takes advantage of you, or puts on airs, or gives
you a slap in the face. 21 To my shame, I must say,
we were too weak for that!

But whatever anyone dares to boast of—I am
speaking as a fool—I also dare to boast of that.
22 Are they Hebrews? So am I. Are they Israelites?
So am I. Are they descendants of Abraham? So
am I. 23 Are they ministers of Christ? I am talking like a madman—I am a better one: with far
greater labors, far more imprisonments, with
countless floggings, and often near death. 24 Five
times I have received from the Jews the forty
lashes minus one. 25 Three times I was beaten
with rods. Once I received a stoning. Three times
I was shipwrecked; for a night and a day I was
adrift at sea; 26 on frequent journeys, in danger
from rivers, danger from bandits, danger from my
own people, danger from Gentiles, danger in the
city, danger in the wilderness, danger at sea, danger from false brothers and sisters;[c] 27 in toil and
hardship, through many a sleepless night, hungry
and thirsty, often without food, cold and naked.
28 And, besides other things, I am under daily pressure because of my anxiety for all the churches.
29 Who is weak, and I am not weak? Who is made
to stumble, and I am not indignant?

30 If I must boast, I will boast of the things
that show my weakness. 31 The God and Father
of the Lord Jesus (blessed be he forever!) knows
that I do not lie. 32 In Damascus, the governor[e]
under King Aretas guarded the city of Damascus
in order to[f] seize me, 33 but I was let down in a
basket through a window in the wall,[g] and escaped from his hands.

12 It is necessary to boast; nothing is to be
gained by it, but I will go on to visions
and revelations of the Lord. 2 I know a person in
Christ who fourteen years ago was caught up to
the third heaven—whether in the body or out
of the body I do not know; God knows. 3 And I
know that such a person—whether in the body
or out of the body I do not know; God knows—
4 was caught up into Paradise and heard things
that are not to be told, that no mortal is permitted
to repeat. 5 On behalf of such a one I will boast,

[a] Other ancient authorities lack *and pure* [b] Gk *the gospel of God* [c] Gk *brothers* [d] Gk *according to the flesh*
[e] Gk *ethnarch* [f] Other ancient authorities read *and wanted to* [g] Gk *through the wall*

but on my own behalf I will not boast, except of
my weaknesses. 6 But if I wish to boast, I will not
be a fool, for I will be speaking the truth. But I
refrain from it, so that no one may think better
of me than what is seen in me or heard from me,
7 even considering the exceptional character of
the revelations. Therefore, to keep[a] me from being too elated, a thorn was given me in the flesh,
a messenger of Satan to torment me, to keep me
from being too elated.[b] 8 Three times I appealed
to the Lord about this, that it would leave me,
9 but he said to me, "My grace is sufficient for
you, for power[c] is made perfect in weakness."
So, I will boast all the more gladly of my weaknesses, so that the power of Christ may dwell in
me. 10 Therefore I am content with weaknesses,
insults, hardships, persecutions, and calamities
for the sake of Christ; for whenever I am weak,
then I am strong.

11 I have been a fool! You forced me to it.
Indeed you should have been the ones commending me, for I am not at all inferior to these
super-apostles, even though I am nothing. 12 The
signs of a true apostle were performed among
you with utmost patience, signs and wonders and
mighty works. 13 How have you been worse off
than the other churches, except that I myself did
not burden you? Forgive me this wrong!

14 Here I am, ready to come to you this third
time. And I will not be a burden, because I do not
want what is yours but you; for children ought
not to lay up for their parents, but parents for
their children. 15 I will most gladly spend and be
spent for you. If I love you more, am I to be loved
less? 16 Let it be assumed that I did not burden
you. Nevertheless (you say) since I was crafty, I
took you in by deceit. 17 Did I take advantage of
you through any of those whom I sent to you? 18 I
urged Titus to go, and sent the brother with him.
Titus did not take advantage of you, did he? Did
we not conduct ourselves with the same spirit?
Did we not take the same steps?

19 Have you been thinking all along that we
have been defending ourselves before you? We
are speaking in Christ before God. Everything
we do, beloved, is for the sake of building you up.
20 For I fear that when I come, I may find you not
as I wish, and that you may find me not as you
wish; I fear that there may perhaps be quarreling, jealousy, anger, selfishness, slander, gossip,
conceit, and disorder. 21 I fear that when I come
again, my God may humble me before you, and
that I may have to mourn over many who previously sinned and have not repented of the impurity, sexual immorality, and licentiousness that
they have practiced.

13 This is the third time I am coming to you.
"Any charge must be sustained by the
evidence of two or three witnesses." 2 I warned
those who sinned previously and all the others,
and I warn them now while absent, as I did when
present on my second visit, that if I come again, I
will not be lenient— 3 since you desire proof that
Christ is speaking in me. He is not weak in dealing with you, but is powerful in you. 4 For he was
crucified in weakness, but lives by the power of
God. For we are weak in him,[d] but in dealing with
you we will live with him by the power of God.

5 Examine yourselves to see whether you are
living in the faith. Test yourselves. Do you not
realize that Jesus Christ is in you?—unless, indeed, you fail to meet the test! 6 I hope you will
find out that we have not failed. 7 But we pray to
God that you may not do anything wrong—not
that we may appear to have met the test, but that
you may do what is right, though we may seem to
have failed. 8 For we cannot do anything against
the truth, but only for the truth. 9 For we rejoice
when we are weak and you are strong. This is what
we pray for, that you may become perfect. 10 So I
write these things while I am away from you, so
that when I come, I may not have to be severe in
using the authority that the Lord has given me for
building up and not for tearing down.

11 Finally, brothers and sisters,[e] farewell.[f] Put
things in order, listen to my appeal,[g] agree with

[a] Other ancient authorities read *To keep* [b] Other ancient authorities lack *to keep me from being too elated*
[c] Other ancient authorities read *my power* [d] Other ancient authorities read *with him* [e] Gk *brothers* [f] Or *rejoice*
[g] Or *encourage one another*

one another, live in peace; and the God of love
and peace will be with you. 12Greet one another
with a holy kiss. All the saints greet you.

13 The grace of the Lord Jesus Christ, the
love of God, and the communion of[a] the Holy
Spirit be with all of you.

[a] Or *and the sharing in*

The Letter of Paul to the Galatians

GALATIANS WAS WRITTEN in the middle of the first century CE. If Paul was writing to the ethnic Galatians who lived in north-central Asia Minor, the *region* called Galatia before the Roman conquests, the letter was written in the years 53–57 and from Ephesus or Madeconia. If he was writing to the churches in the *Roman province* of Galatia—a region extended by the Romans to include the southern cities of Lystra, Derbe, Iconium, and Pisidian Antioch—the dates would more probably be 48–49 from Syrian Antioch, or 51–53 from Corinth. On either account, this letter emerges in the midst of a cultural debate between Jewish Christians and some converted Gentiles, the fruits of Paul's mission to the Gentiles.

To understand the letter to the Galatians, we need to read it in its cultural context. Early Christianity emerged out of the Jesus movement's mission to bring restoration to Israel. Originally this mission did not include Gentiles (see Matt 10:5, 6). However, Jesus' mission and compassion to the outcasts of Israel soon were extended to those Gentiles who feared God. Their attraction to what (for the sake of convenience) we may call early Jewish Christianity developed into the mission to the Gentiles. This mission provoked a controversy among the first Christians, who debated whether Gentiles needed to become Jews first in order to be part of the Christian community. Were Gentile Christians supposed to observe the Jewish Sabbath, the separation of meals as clean or unclean, and circumcision? Different answers were given to these questions.

The letter to the Galatians gives evidence of two positions regarding the cultural identity markers of the Christian community. Many Jewish Christians wanted to require Gentile converts to be circumcised and keep the Mosaic Law, in addition to believing in Jesus as the Messiah (perhaps in the spirit of Jesus' teaching as reflected in Matt 5:17-20). Another less restrictive group was willing to require only the minimum: monotheism and Jewish morals. The book of Acts presents some of the stories of these Hellenistic Jewish Christians (chs. 6–9, 12). In Antioch of Syria, Hellenistic Jewish Christians spread the faith among Gentiles, and Christianity made big inroads among them; Paul became one of the leaders of the Antioch church (see Acts 11:25-30, 12:25—13:3, and Gal 2:11-14).

The letters of Paul are evidence of his openness to the Gentiles. From the letter to the Galatians we know that Peter and Barnabas were ambivalent about socializing and worshiping with Gentiles (2:11-14). It seems that the people of James, Jesus' brother, were powerful enough to intimidate Peter and Barnabas into submitting to a major Jewish religious and cultural requirement for the Gentiles: circumcision. Some Jewish Christian missionaries came to Galatia and were preaching a message contrary to what Paul had preached (1:6-9). We don't know the content of their message because we have only one side of the controversy. But given Paul's reaction it is evident that they advised the Galatians to accept circumcision and to observe (at least aspects of) the Jewish law (4:10; compare 5:2-4). The Galatians probably started to observe the law in part because these teachers said that Paul himself was preaching circumcision (Gal 5:11; 1 Cor 9:20-22). To confuse them even more, the Judaizing teachers may have also added that Paul was not a real apostle (Gal 1:1, 11-12)—not like Peter, James, or the other early leaders in Jerusalem who were law-abiding Christians and also preached circumcision (Gal 2:4, 6-7, 12, 14).

Paul replies with a strong defense of his apostolic authority (chs. 1–2) and assures the Gentiles that adding observance of the Jewish law will not enhance the salvation they have in Christ: "We know that a person is justified not by the works of the law but through faith in Jesus Christ" (2:16). Paul said Gentiles were justified before God only through Jesus. Therefore, justification was a *gift,* received from Jesus, "who loved me and gave himself for me" (2:20). The Gentiles did not need circumcision or to observe the law to be saved.

What Paul thinks of the Gentiles accepting circumcision is clear enough. What is less clear—and more controversial, given the long tradition of Christian theological anti-Judaism—is the extent to which Paul's statements set him in opposition to his ancestral religion, Judaism, or to the other apostles, whom Paul represents as agreeing with him on theological principle (2:1-10, 14-16). These remain lively questions in contemporary scholarship.

As a Puerto Rican, growing up both in New York and San Juan within a fundamentalist family, I learned to live in two worlds and bear the violence of religious intolerance. Later on, through the process of finding my cultural identity, becoming aware of oppression, encountering African American liberation theology and human rights theology for the homosexual community, I have learned to struggle and recognize the ambiguities of colonialism and the false certainties of religious intolerance. These experiences have given me a keen eye for equality, which I bring to my reading of Galatians.

— Ediberto López-Rodríguez

1 Paul an apostle—sent neither by human
commission nor from human authorities, but
through Jesus Christ and God the Father, who
raised him from the dead— 2 and all the members
of God's family[a] who are with me,
To the churches of Galatia:
3 Grace to you and peace from God our Father and the Lord Jesus Christ, 4 who gave himself
for our sins to set us free from the present evil age,
according to the will of our God and Father, 5 to
whom be the glory forever and ever. Amen.

6 I am astonished that you are so quickly
deserting the one who called you in the grace of
Christ and are turning to a different gospel— 7 not
that there is another gospel, but there are some

[a] Gk *all the brothers*

who are confusing you and want to pervert the gospel of Christ. 8 But even if we or an angel[a] from heaven should proclaim to you a gospel contrary to what we proclaimed to you, let that one be accursed! 9 As we have said before, so now I repeat, if anyone proclaims to you a gospel contrary to what you received, let that one be accursed!

10 Am I now seeking human approval, or God's approval? Or am I trying to please people? If I were still pleasing people, I would not be a servant[b] of Christ.

11 For I want you to know, brothers and sisters,[c] that the gospel that was proclaimed by me is not of human origin; 12 for I did not receive it from a human source, nor was I taught it, but I received it through a revelation of Jesus Christ.

13 You have heard, no doubt, of my earlier life in Judaism. I was violently persecuting the church of God and was trying to destroy it. 14 I advanced in Judaism beyond many among my people of the same age, for I was far more zealous for the traditions of my ancestors. 15 But when God, who had set me apart before I was born and called me through his grace, was pleased 16 to reveal his Son to me,[d] so that I might proclaim him among the Gentiles, I did not confer with any human being, 17 nor did I go up to Jerusalem to those who were already apostles before me, but I went away at once into Arabia, and afterwards I returned to Damascus.

18 Then after three years I did go up to Jerusalem to visit Cephas and stayed with him fifteen days; 19 but I did not see any other apostle except James the Lord's brother. 20 In what I am writing to you, before God, I do not lie! 21 Then I went into the regions of Syria and Cilicia, 22 and I was still unknown by sight to the churches of Judea that are in Christ; 23 they only heard it said, "The one who formerly was persecuting us is now proclaiming the faith he once tried to destroy." 24 And they glorified God because of me.

2 Then after fourteen years I went up again to Jerusalem with Barnabas, taking Titus along with me. 2 I went up in response to a revelation. Then I laid before them (though only in a private meeting with the acknowledged leaders) the gospel that I proclaim among the Gentiles, in order to make sure that I was not running, or had not run, in vain. 3 But even Titus, who was with me, was not compelled to be circumcised, though he was a Greek. 4 But because of false believers[e] secretly brought in, who slipped in to spy on the freedom we have in Christ Jesus, so that they might enslave us— 5 we did not submit to them even for a moment, so that the truth of the gospel might always remain with you. 6 And from those who were supposed to be acknowledged leaders (what they actually were makes no difference to me; God shows no partiality)—those leaders contributed nothing to me. 7 On the contrary, when they saw that I had been entrusted with the gospel for the uncircumcised, just as Peter had been entrusted with the gospel for the circumcised 8 (for he who worked through Peter making him an apostle to the circumcised also worked through me in sending me to the Gentiles), 9 and when James and Cephas and John, who were acknowledged pillars, recognized the grace that had been given to me, they gave to Barnabas and me the right hand of fellowship, agreeing that we should go to the Gentiles and they to the circumcised. 10 They asked only one thing, that we remember the poor, which was actually what I was[f] eager to do.

Galatians 2:10

It is easy to exaggerate the differences between Paul and the Jerusalem apostles. Here Paul seeks to minimize those differences, insisting that on matters of principle the apostles were all in agreement and that when differences arose, as with Peter in Antioch, it was because someone had failed to live up to that principle. Paul says the point over which the Jerusalem apostles were most concerned had nothing to do with circumcision; it was about care for the poor, something that was central to Paul's work as well (see Acts 11:29; Rom 15:25-28; 2 Cor 8–9).

—NE

[a] Or *a messenger* [b] Gk *slave* [c] Gk *brothers* [d] Gk *in me* [e] Gk *false brothers* [f] Or *had been*

11 But when Cephas came to Antioch, I
opposed him to his face, because he stood self-
condemned; 12for until certain people came from
James, he used to eat with the Gentiles. But after
they came, he drew back and kept himself separate for fear of the circumcision faction. 13And
the other Jews joined him in this hypocrisy, so
that even Barnabas was led astray by their hypocrisy. 14But when I saw that they were not acting
consistently with the truth of the gospel, I said
to Cephas before them all, "If you, though a Jew,
live like a Gentile and not like a Jew, how can you
compel the Gentiles to live like Jews?"[a]

15 We ourselves are Jews by birth and not
Gentile sinners; 16yet we know that a person is
justified[b] not by the works of the law but through
faith in Jesus Christ.[c] And we have come to believe in Christ Jesus, so that we might be justified
by faith in Christ,[d] and not by doing the works
of the law, because no one will be justified by the
works of the law. 17But if, in our effort to be justified in Christ, we ourselves have been found to be
sinners, is Christ then a servant of sin? Certainly
not! 18But if I build up again the very things that
I once tore down, then I demonstrate that I am a
transgressor. 19For through the law I died to the
law, so that I might live to God. I have been crucified with Christ; 20and it is no longer I who live,
but it is Christ who lives in me. And the life I now
live in the flesh I live by faith in the Son of God,[e]
who loved me and gave himself for me. 21I do not
nullify the grace of God; for if justification[f] comes
through the law, then Christ died for nothing.

3 You foolish Galatians! Who has bewitched
you? It was before your eyes that Jesus Christ
was publicly exhibited as crucified! 2The only
thing I want to learn from you is this: Did you
receive the Spirit by doing the works of the law
or by believing what you heard? 3Are you so foolish? Having started with the Spirit, are you now
ending with the flesh? 4Did you experience so
much for nothing?—if it really was for nothing.
5Well then, does God[g] supply you with the Spirit
and work miracles among you by your doing the
works of the law, or by your believing what you
heard?

6 Just as Abraham "believed God, and it was
reckoned to him as righteousness," 7so, you see,
those who believe are the descendants of Abraham. 8And the scripture, foreseeing that God
would justify the Gentiles by faith, declared the
gospel beforehand to Abraham, saying, "All the
Gentiles shall be blessed in you." 9For this reason,
those who believe are blessed with Abraham who
believed.

10 For all who rely on the works of the law
are under a curse; for it is written, "Cursed is everyone who does not observe and obey all the
things written in the book of the law." 11Now it
is evident that no one is justified before God by
the law; for "The one who is righteous will live
by faith."[h] 12But the law does not rest on faith;
on the contrary, "Whoever does the works of the
law[i] will live by them." 13Christ redeemed us from
the curse of the law by becoming a curse for us—
for it is written, "Cursed is everyone who hangs
on a tree"— 14in order that in Christ Jesus the
blessing of Abraham might come to the Gentiles,
so that we might receive the promise of the Spirit
through faith.

15 Brothers and sisters,[j] I give an example
from daily life: once a person's will[k] has been
ratified, no one adds to it or annuls it. 16Now the
promises were made to Abraham and to his offspring;[l] it does not say, "And to offsprings,"[m] as of
many; but it says, "And to your offspring,"[l] that is,
to one person, who is Christ. 17My point is this:
the law, which came four hundred thirty years
later, does not annul a covenant previously ratified by God, so as to nullify the promise. 18For if
the inheritance comes from the law, it no longer
comes from the promise; but God granted it to
Abraham through the promise.

[a] Some interpreters hold that the quotation extends into the following paragraph [b] Or *reckoned as righteous;* and so elsewhere [c] Or *the faith of Jesus Christ* [d] Or *the faith of Christ* [e] Or *by the faith of the Son of God* [f] Or *righteousness* [g] Gk *he* [h] Or *The one who is righteous through faith will live* [i] Gk *does them* [j] Gk *Brothers* [k] Or *covenant* (as in verse 17) [l] Gk *seed* [m] Gk *seeds*

19 Why then the law? It was added because
of transgressions, until the offspring[a] would come
to whom the promise had been made; and it was
ordained through angels by a mediator. 20Now a
mediator involves more than one party; but God
is one.

21 Is the law then opposed to the promises of
God? Certainly not! For if a law had been given
that could make alive, then righteousness would
indeed come through the law. 22But the scripture
has imprisoned all things under the power of sin,
so that what was promised through faith in Jesus
Christ[b] might be given to those who believe.

23 Now before faith came, we were imprisoned and guarded under the law until faith would
be revealed. 24Therefore the law was our disciplinarian until Christ came, so that we might be
justified by faith. 25But now that faith has come,
we are no longer subject to a disciplinarian,
26for in Christ Jesus you are all children of God
through faith. 27As many of you as were baptized
into Christ have clothed yourselves with Christ.
28There is no longer Jew or Greek, there is no longer slave or free, there is no longer male and female; for all of you are one in Christ Jesus. 29And
if you belong to Christ, then you are Abraham's
offspring,[a] heirs according to the promise.

Galatians 3:28

Taken as a whole, the liberating message of the biblical writings—even though some texts fall short of that message—is that in Christ there exists no difference between Jew or Gentile (racism), between a slave and a free person (classism), or between male or female (sexism). The structures that create these divisions, which privilege some at the expense of others due to race, ethnicity, class, or gender, must be dismantled, for they have no basis in Christ.

— *MDLT*

4 My point is this: heirs, as long as they are
minors, are no better than slaves, though
they are the owners of all the property; 2but they
remain under guardians and trustees until the
date set by the father. 3So with us; while we were
minors, we were enslaved to the elemental spirits[c] of the world. 4But when the fullness of time
had come, God sent his Son, born of a woman,
born under the law, 5in order to redeem those
who were under the law, so that we might receive
adoption as children. 6And because you are children, God has sent the Spirit of his Son into our[d]
hearts, crying, "Abba![e] Father!" 7So you are no
longer a slave but a child, and if a child then also
an heir, through God.[f]

8 Formerly, when you did not know God,
you were enslaved to beings that by nature are not
gods. 9Now, however, that you have come to know
God, or rather to be known by God, how can you
turn back again to the weak and beggarly elemental spirits?[g] How can you want to be enslaved to
them again? 10You are observing special days, and
months, and seasons, and years. 11I am afraid that
my work for you may have been wasted.

12 Friends,[h] I beg you, become as I am, for I
also have become as you are. You have done me no
wrong. 13You know that it was because of a physical
infirmity that I first announced the gospel to you;
14though my condition put you to the test, you did
not scorn or despise me, but welcomed me as an
angel of God, as Christ Jesus. 15What has become
of the goodwill you felt? For I testify that, had it
been possible, you would have torn out your eyes
and given them to me. 16Have I now become your
enemy by telling you the truth? 17They make much
of you, but for no good purpose; they want to exclude you, so that you may make much of them.
18It is good to be made much of for a good purpose
at all times, and not only when I am present with
you. 19My little children, for whom I am again in
the pain of childbirth until Christ is formed in you,
20I wish I were present with you now and could
change my tone, for I am perplexed about you.

[a] Gk *seed* [b] Or *through the faith of Jesus Christ* [c] Or *the rudiments* [d] Other ancient authorities read *your*
[e] Aramaic for *Father* [f] Other ancient authorities read *an heir of God through Christ* [g] Or *beggarly rudiments*
[h] Gk *Brothers*

21 Tell me, you who desire to be subject to
the law, will you not listen to the law? 22 For it is
written that Abraham had two sons, one by a slave
woman and the other by a free woman. 23 One,
the child of the slave, was born according to the
flesh; the other, the child of the free woman,
was born through the promise. 24 Now this is an
allegory: these women are two covenants. One
woman, in fact, is Hagar, from Mount Sinai, bearing children for slavery. 25 Now Hagar is Mount
Sinai in Arabia[a] and corresponds to the present
Jerusalem, for she is in slavery with her children.
26 But the other woman corresponds to the Jerusalem above; she is free, and she is our mother.
27 For it is written,

"Rejoice, you childless one, you who bear no
children,
burst into song and shout, you who endure
no birth pangs;
for the children of the desolate woman are
more numerous
than the children of the one who is
married."

28 Now you,[b] my friends,[c] are children of the promise, like Isaac. 29 But just as at that time the child
who was born according to the flesh persecuted
the child who was born according to the Spirit, so
it is now also. 30 But what does the scripture say?
"Drive out the slave and her child; for the child
of the slave will not share the inheritance with
the child of the free woman." 31 So then, friends,[c]
we are children, not of the slave but of the free
5 woman. 1 For freedom Christ has set us free.
Stand firm, therefore, and do not submit
again to a yoke of slavery.

2 Listen! I, Paul, am telling you that if you
let yourselves be circumcised, Christ will be of
no benefit to you. 3 Once again I testify to every
man who lets himself be circumcised that he is
obliged to obey the entire law. 4 You who want
to be justified by the law have cut yourselves off
from Christ; you have fallen away from grace.
5 For through the Spirit, by faith, we eagerly wait
for the hope of righteousness. 6 For in Christ Jesus
neither circumcision nor uncircumcision counts
for anything; the only thing that counts is faith
working[d] through love.

7 You were running well; who prevented you
from obeying the truth? 8 Such persuasion does
not come from the one who calls you. 9 A little
yeast leavens the whole batch of dough. 10 I am
confident about you in the Lord that you will not
think otherwise. But whoever it is that is confusing you will pay the penalty. 11 But my friends,[c]
why am I still being persecuted if I am still preaching circumcision? In that case the offense of the

[a] Other ancient authorities read *For Sinai is a mountain in Arabia* [b] Other ancient authorities read *we* [c] Gk *brothers*
[d] Or *made effective*

Galatians 4:22-31

Paul reads the two children of Abraham allegorically. The one born to the servant girl Hagar is the one who must be sent away, deprived of the father's heritage; the child born of Sarah is to participate fully in that heritage. Christians, Paul says, are sons not of the servant woman but of the free woman. The allegory is disturbing for contemporary readers, first because Paul is not troubled by the coercive aspect of the story: as an African slave girl, Hagar had no choice in having sex with her much older master; her body was taken because it belonged to him. The second concern is that most of us from disenfranchised communities are ourselves the children of servant girls, whether they are domestic help, maids, underpaid factory workers, or laborers in dead-end service jobs. The "Abrahams" of the world—the prosperous and powerful—have taken advantage of our mothers, too, whether economically or sexually. We often feel greater resonance with the children of Hagar than with the privileged and powerful children of Sarah.

—MDLT

cross has been removed. 12I wish those who unsettle you would castrate themselves!
13 For you were called to freedom, brothers
and sisters;[a] only do not use your freedom as an
opportunity for self-indulgence,[b] but through
love become slaves to one another. 14For the
whole law is summed up in a single commandment, "You shall love your neighbor as yourself."
15If, however, you bite and devour one another,
take care that you are not consumed by one another.
16 Live by the Spirit, I say, and do not gratify the desires of the flesh. 17For what the flesh
desires is opposed to the Spirit, and what the
Spirit desires is opposed to the flesh; for these
are opposed to each other, to prevent you from
doing what you want. 18But if you are led by the
Spirit, you are not subject to the law. 19Now the
works of the flesh are obvious: fornication, impurity, licentiousness, 20idolatry, sorcery, enmi-
ties, strife, jealousy, anger, quarrels, dissensions,
factions, 21envy,[c] drunkenness, carousing, and
things like these. I am warning you, as I warned
you before: those who do such things will not inherit the kingdom of God.
22 By contrast, the fruit of the Spirit is love,
joy, peace, patience, kindness, generosity, faithfulness, 23gentleness, and self-control. There is
no law against such things. 24And those who belong to Christ Jesus have crucified the flesh with
its passions and desires. 25If we live by the Spirit,
let us also be guided by the Spirit. 26Let us not become conceited, competing against one another,
envying one another.

6 My friends,[d] if anyone is detected in a transgression, you who have received the Spirit
should restore such a one in a spirit of gentleness.
Take care that you yourselves are not tempted.
2Bear one another's burdens, and in this way you
will fulfill[e] the law of Christ. 3For if those who are
nothing think they are something, they deceive
themselves. 4All must test their own work; then
that work, rather than their neighbor's work, will
become a cause for pride. 5For all must carry
their own loads.
6 Those who are taught the word must share
in all good things with their teacher.
7 Do not be deceived; God is not mocked,
for you reap whatever you sow. 8If you sow to
your own flesh, you will reap corruption from the
flesh; but if you sow to the Spirit, you will reap
eternal life from the Spirit. 9So let us not grow
weary in doing what is right, for we will reap
at harvest time, if we do not give up. 10So then,
whenever we have an opportunity, let us work
for the good of all, and especially for those of the
family of faith.

11 See what large letters I make when I am
writing in my own hand! 12It is those who want
to make a good showing in the flesh that try to
compel you to be circumcised—only that they
may not be persecuted for the cross of Christ.
13Even the circumcised do not themselves obey
the law, but they want you to be circumcised so
that they may boast about your flesh. 14May I
never boast of anything except the cross of our
Lord Jesus Christ, by which[f] the world has been
crucified to me, and I to the world. 15For[g] neither
circumcision nor uncircumcision is anything;
but a new creation is everything! 16As for those
who will follow this rule—peace be upon them,
and mercy, and upon the Israel of God.
17 From now on, let no one make trouble for
me; for I carry the marks of Jesus branded on my
body.
18 May the grace of our Lord Jesus Christ be
with your spirit, brothers and sisters.[a] Amen.

[a] Gk *brothers* [b] Gk *the flesh* [c] Other ancient authorities add *murder* [d] Gk *Brothers* [e] Other ancient authorities read *in this way fulfill* [f] Or *through whom* [g] Other ancient authorities add *in Christ Jesus*

The Letter of Paul to the Ephesians

EPHESIANS IS ONE OF THIRTEEN New Testament letters attributed to Paul. Most contemporary scholars question its Pauline authorship because it is noticeably dissimilar to the undisputed Pauline letters in vocabulary, writing style, and theology. An emerging consensus among scholars holds that the letter was probably written by an interpreter (or perhaps a disciple) of Paul to congregations in western Asia Minor, sometime in the late first century CE. This was a time when the church was emerging as a force in the Greco-Roman world.

The letter, which appears to have been written from a prison (4:1), confronts divisions in the church. Although Ephesians contains few explicit references to conflict between Jews and Gentiles, a good part of it highlights the author's attempts to promote harmonious relations between the two communities. Issues of identity, concern about factors that engendered strife, and the need for unity figure prominently in this letter.

Ephesians comprises a brief introduction followed by two distinct sections and a short closing. The salutation (1:1-2) greets the readers and identifies the writer. The first section (1:3—3:21) is doctrinal in nature and emphasizes the Christ event and its ability to unite Christians. The second section (4:1—6:20) offers ethical instructions. The writer seeks to promote unity among believers and exhorts readers to challenge principalities and powers. The book's final verses (6:21-24) include a benediction.

The doctrinal section declares that the Gentiles, who were alienated both from God and from the Jews, have been reconciled with both through the Christ event. The ethnic identities of Jews and Gentiles have hitherto divided their respective communities, but now the dividing wall has been brought down by Jesus, who has united them in God.

The ethical or paraenetic section of the letter exhorts readers to live out the unity made possible through Christ and to manifest it in interpersonal relations in familial, ecclesial, and social settings. This part of the letter emphasizes unifying factors such as the Christ event and seeks to attenuate dividing factors such as rigid aspects of the law. It also encourages an ethic of subordination of wives to husbands, children to parents, and slaves to masters that goes beyond what we see in the seven unquestioned letters of Paul (5:22—6:9; compare Col 3:18—4:1). Although this ethic appears under the apparently mutual rule "be subject to one another" (5:22), the instructions are not completely reciprocal, leading some readers to conclude that the unity envisioned here is achieved at a greater cost to some than to others. Can equality between Jew and Gentile be purchased only at the cost of inequality in other relationships?

The letter's rhetoric calls our attention to the destructive potential that a particular identity—whether ethnic, or grounded in some other difference—can play, and offers suggestions for

achieving a common identity, based on the Christ event, that can transcend all dividing walls. Because the dividing walls have been brought down, the readers are to create an inclusive community around the Christ event, which offers a transformational and unifying identity for the new community.

Most identity markers unite members of similar communities while simultaneously separating them from those that do not share that identity. I am a member of the Naidu community, a caste group in Andhra Pradesh, a south Indian state with a multiethnic and multicultural population. My identity as a Naidu unites me to this group, but given the troubled history of caste relations in this state, it has the potential to alienate me from members of other caste groups. The same issue applies to members of other castes. It is possible for different caste groups to transcend barriers and arrive at a unifying identity by focusing on their common language—Telugu. Yet even as Telugu might provide a unifying identity for people in the state, it would separate them from other linguistic groups in India and thus can cause strife. It appears that divisions between diverse groups stem primarily from the absence of *unifying identities* that can transcend all barriers. But divisions arise also when individuals and groups choose to focus on the divisive, rather than the unifying, aspects of an identity. The message and the exhortations of Ephesians are relevant wherever two or more communities are more aware of the differences that separate them than of what can and should unite them as equals.

— ***Raj Nadella***

1 Paul, an apostle of Christ Jesus by the will of
God,
To the saints who are in Ephesus and are faithful[a] in Christ Jesus:
2 Grace to you and peace from God our Father and the Lord Jesus Christ.

3 Blessed be the God and Father of our Lord
Jesus Christ, who has blessed us in Christ with every spiritual blessing in the heavenly places, 4just
as he chose us in Christ[b] before the foundation of
the world to be holy and blameless before him in
love. 5He destined us for adoption as his children
through Jesus Christ, according to the good pleasure of his will, 6to the praise of his glorious grace
that he freely bestowed on us in the Beloved. 7In
him we have redemption through his blood, the
forgiveness of our trespasses, according to the
riches of his grace 8that he lavished on us. With
all wisdom and insight 9he has made known to
us the mystery of his will, according to his good
pleasure that he set forth in Christ, 10as a plan
for the fullness of time, to gather up all things in
him, things in heaven and things on earth. 11In
Christ we have also obtained an inheritance,[c]
having been destined according to the purpose of
him who accomplishes all things according to his
counsel and will, 12so that we, who were the first
to set our hope on Christ, might live for the praise
of his glory. 13In him you also, when you had
heard the word of truth, the gospel of your salvation, and had believed in him, were marked with

[a] Other ancient authorities lack *in Ephesus*, reading *saints who are also faithful* [b] Gk *in him* [c] Or *been made a heritage*

the seal of the promised Holy Spirit; [14]this[a] is the pledge of our inheritance toward redemption as God's own people, to the praise of his glory.

15 I have heard of your faith in the Lord Jesus and your love[b] toward all the saints, and for this reason [16]I do not cease to give thanks for you as I remember you in my prayers. [17]I pray that the God of our Lord Jesus Christ, the Father of glory, may give you a spirit of wisdom and revelation as you come to know him, [18]so that, with the eyes of your heart enlightened, you may know what is the hope to which he has called you, what are the riches of his glorious inheritance among the saints, [19]and what is the immeasurable greatness of his power for us who believe, according to the working of his great power. [20]God[c] put this power to work in Christ when he raised him from the dead and seated him at his right hand in the heavenly places, [21]far above all rule and authority and power and dominion, and above every name that is named, not only in this age but also in the age to come. [22]And he has put all things under his feet and has made him the head over all things for the church, [23]which is his body, the fullness of him who fills all in all.

2 You were dead through the trespasses and sins [2]in which you once lived, following the course of this world, following the ruler of the power of the air, the spirit that is now at work among those who are disobedient. [3]All of us once lived among them in the passions of our flesh, following the desires of flesh and senses, and we were by nature children of wrath, like everyone else. [4]But God, who is rich in mercy, out of the great love with which he loved us [5]even when we were dead through our trespasses, made us alive together with Christ[d]—by grace you have been saved— [6]and raised us up with him and seated us with him in the heavenly places in Christ Jesus, [7]so that in the ages to come he might show the immeasurable riches of his grace in kindness toward us in Christ Jesus. [8]For by grace you have been saved through faith, and this is not your own doing; it is the gift of God— [9]not the result of works, so that no one may boast. [10]For we are what he has made us, created in Christ Jesus for good works, which God prepared beforehand to be our way of life.

11 So then, remember that at one time you Gentiles by birth,[e] called "the uncircumcision" by those who are called "the circumcision"—a physical circumcision made in the flesh by human hands— [12]remember that you were at that time without Christ, being aliens from the commonwealth of Israel, and strangers to the covenants of promise, having no hope and without God in the world. [13]But now in Christ Jesus you who once were far off have been brought near by the blood of Christ. [14]For he is our peace; in his flesh he has made both groups into one and has broken down the dividing wall, that is, the hostility between us. [15]He has abolished the law with its commandments and ordinances, that he might create in himself one new humanity in place of the two, thus making peace, [16]and might reconcile both groups to God in one body[f] through the cross, thus putting to death that hostility through it.[g] [17]So he came and proclaimed peace to you who were far off and peace to those who were near; [18]for through him both of us have access in one Spirit to the Father. [19]So then you are no longer strangers and aliens, but you are citizens

Ephesians 2:11-22

The author's moving rhetoric of unity across boundaries has inspired countless episodes of reconciliation. But hardheaded historical scrutiny raises questions: can the unity between Jew and Gentile really be accomplished only when "the law with its commandments and ordinances" is "abolished" (2:15)? Paul did not think so when he insisted, in Romans, that we do *not* "overthrow the law" (3:31; the Greek verb in the two verses is the same). If the unity in Ephesians is won at the cost of Jewish identity, what is its value?

—*NE*

[a] Other ancient authorities read *who* [b] Other ancient authorities lack *and your love* [c] Gk *He* [d] Other ancient authorities read *in Christ* [e] Gk *in the flesh* [f] Or *reconcile both of us in one body for God* [g] Or *in him*, or *in himself*

with the saints and also members of the household of God, 20built upon the foundation of the apostles and prophets, with Christ Jesus himself as the cornerstone.[a] 21In him the whole structure is joined together and grows into a holy temple in the Lord; 22in whom you also are built together spiritually[b] into a dwelling place for God.

3 This is the reason that I Paul am a prisoner for[c] Christ Jesus for the sake of you Gentiles— 2for surely you have already heard of the commission of God's grace that was given me for you, 3and how the mystery was made known to me by revelation, as I wrote above in a few words, 4a reading of which will enable you to perceive my understanding of the mystery of Christ. 5In former generations this mystery[d] was not made known to humankind, as it has now been revealed to his holy apostles and prophets by the Spirit: 6that is, the Gentiles have become fellow heirs, members of the same body, and sharers in the promise in Christ Jesus through the gospel.

7 Of this gospel I have become a servant according to the gift of God's grace that was given me by the working of his power. 8Although I am the very least of all the saints, this grace was given to me to bring to the Gentiles the news of the boundless riches of Christ, 9and to make everyone see[e] what is the plan of the mystery hidden for ages in[f] God who created all things; 10so that through the church the wisdom of God in its rich variety might now be made known to the rulers and authorities in the heavenly places. 11This was in accordance with the eternal purpose that he has carried out in Christ Jesus our Lord, 12in whom we have access to God in boldness and confidence through faith in him.[g] 13I pray therefore that you[h] may not lose heart over my sufferings for you; they are your glory.

14 For this reason I bow my knees before the Father,[i] 15from whom every family[j] in heaven and on earth takes its name. 16I pray that, according to the riches of his glory, he may grant that you may be strengthened in your inner being with power through his Spirit, 17and that Christ may dwell in your hearts through faith, as you are being rooted and grounded in love. 18I pray that you may have the power to comprehend, with all the saints, what is the breadth and length and height and depth, 19and to know the love of Christ that surpasses knowledge, so that you may be filled with all the fullness of God.

20 Now to him who by the power at work within us is able to accomplish abundantly far more than all we can ask or imagine, 21to him be glory in the church and in Christ Jesus to all generations, forever and ever. Amen.

4 I therefore, the prisoner in the Lord, beg you to lead a life worthy of the calling to which you have been called, 2with all humility and gentleness, with patience, bearing with one another in love, 3making every effort to maintain the unity of the Spirit in the bond of peace. 4There is one body and one Spirit, just as you were called to the one hope of your calling, 5one Lord, one faith, one baptism, 6one God and Father of all, who is above all and through all and in all.

7 But each of us was given grace according to the measure of Christ's gift. 8Therefore it is said,

"When he ascended on high he made
captivity itself a captive;
he gave gifts to his people."

9(When it says, "He ascended," what does it mean but that he had also descended[k] into the lower parts of the earth? 10He who descended is the same one who ascended far above all the heavens, so that he might fill all things.) 11The gifts he gave were that some would be apostles, some prophets, some evangelists, some pastors and teachers, 12to equip the saints for the work of ministry, for building up the body of Christ, 13until all of us come to the unity of the faith and of the knowledge of the Son of God, to maturity, to the measure of the full stature of Christ. 14We must no longer be children, tossed to and fro and blown about by every wind of doctrine,

[a] Or *keystone* [b] Gk *in the Spirit* [c] Or *of* [d] Gk *it* [e] Other ancient authorities read *to bring to light* [f] Or *by*
[g] Or *the faith of him* [h] Or *I* [i] Other ancient authorities add *of our Lord Jesus Christ* [j] Gk *fatherhood*
[k] Other ancient authorities add *first*

by people's trickery, by their craftiness in deceitful scheming. 15 But speaking the truth in love, we must grow up in every way into him who is the head, into Christ, 16 from whom the whole body, joined and knit together by every ligament with which it is equipped, as each part is working properly, promotes the body's growth in building itself up in love.

17 Now this I affirm and insist on in the Lord: you must no longer live as the Gentiles live, in the futility of their minds. 18 They are darkened in their understanding, alienated from the life of God because of their ignorance and hardness of heart. 19 They have lost all sensitivity and have abandoned themselves to licentiousness, greedy to practice every kind of impurity. 20 That is not the way you learned Christ! 21 For surely you have heard about him and were taught in him, as truth is in Jesus. 22 You were taught to put away your former way of life, your old self, corrupt and deluded by its lusts, 23 and to be renewed in the spirit of your minds, 24 and to clothe yourselves with the new self, created according to the likeness of God in true righteousness and holiness.

25 So then, putting away falsehood, let all of us speak the truth to our neighbors, for we are members of one another. 26 Be angry but do not sin; do not let the sun go down on your anger, 27 and do not make room for the devil. 28 Thieves must give up stealing; rather let them labor and work honestly with their own hands, so as to have something to share with the needy. 29 Let no evil talk come out of your mouths, but only what is useful for building up,[a] as there is need, so that your words may give grace to those who hear. 30 And do not grieve the Holy Spirit of God, with which you were marked with a seal for the day of redemption. 31 Put away from you all bitterness and wrath and anger and wrangling and slander, together with all malice, 32 and be kind to one another, tenderhearted, forgiving one another, as God in Christ has forgiven you.[b]

5 1 Therefore be imitators of God, as beloved children, 2 and live in love, as Christ loved us[c] and gave himself up for us, a fragrant offering and sacrifice to God.

3 But fornication and impurity of any kind, or greed, must not even be mentioned among you, as is proper among saints. 4 Entirely out of place is obscene, silly, and vulgar talk; but instead, let there be thanksgiving. 5 Be sure of this, that no fornicator or impure person, or one who is greedy (that is, an idolater), has any inheritance in the kingdom of Christ and of God.

6 Let no one deceive you with empty words, for because of these things the wrath of God comes on those who are disobedient. 7 Therefore do not be associated with them. 8 For once you were darkness, but now in the Lord you are light. Live as children of light— 9 for the fruit of the light is found in all that is good and right and true. 10 Try to find out what is pleasing to the Lord. 11 Take no part in the unfruitful works of darkness, but instead expose them. 12 For it is shameful even to mention what such people do secretly; 13 but everything exposed by the light becomes visible, 14 for everything that becomes visible is light. Therefore it says,

"Sleeper, awake!
Rise from the dead,
and Christ will shine on you."

15 Be careful then how you live, not as unwise people but as wise, 16 making the most of the time, because the days are evil. 17 So do not be foolish, but understand what the will of the Lord is. 18 Do not get drunk with wine, for that is debauchery; but be filled with the Spirit, 19 as you sing psalms and hymns and spiritual songs among yourselves, singing and making melody to the Lord in your hearts, 20 giving thanks to God the Father at all times and for everything in the name of our Lord Jesus Christ.

21 Be subject to one another out of reverence for Christ.

22 Wives, be subject to your husbands as you are to the Lord. 23 For the husband is the head of the wife just as Christ is the head of the church, the body of which he is the Savior. 24 Just as the

[a] Other ancient authorities read *building up faith* [b] Other ancient authorities read *us*
[c] Other ancient authorities read *you*

Ephesians 5:21-22

Professional social-work literature on women suffering domestic abuse showed that one of the anecdotally established indications that a woman was in imminent danger of suffering physical violence was that the man with whom she lived was quoting Paul's command that women be subject to their husbands.[72]

— *NE*

church is subject to Christ, so also wives ought to
be, in everything, to their husbands.
25 Husbands, love your wives, just as Christ
loved the church and gave himself up for her, 26 in
order to make her holy by cleansing her with the
washing of water by the word, 27 so as to present
the church to himself in splendor, without a spot
or wrinkle or anything of the kind—yes, so that
she may be holy and without blemish. 28 In the
same way, husbands should love their wives as they
do their own bodies. He who loves his wife loves
himself. 29 For no one ever hates his own body, but
he nourishes and tenderly cares for it, just as Christ
does for the church, 30 because we are members of
his body.[a] 31 "For this reason a man will leave his father and mother and be joined to his wife, and the
two will become one flesh." 32 This is a great mystery, and I am applying it to Christ and the church.
33 Each of you, however, should love his wife as
himself, and a wife should respect her husband.
6 Children, obey your parents in the Lord,[b]
for this is right. 2 "Honor your father and
mother"—this is the first commandment with a
promise: 3 "so that it may be well with you and
you may live long on the earth."
4 And, fathers, do not provoke your children
to anger, but bring them up in the discipline and
instruction of the Lord.
5 Slaves, obey your earthly masters with fear
and trembling, in singleness of heart, as you obey
Christ; 6 not only while being watched, and in order to please them, but as slaves of Christ, doing
the will of God from the heart. 7 Render service
with enthusiasm, as to the Lord and not to men
and women, 8 knowing that whatever good we
do, we will receive the same again from the Lord,
whether we are slaves or free.
9 And, masters, do the same to them. Stop
threatening them, for you know that both of you
have the same Master in heaven, and with him
there is no partiality.
10 Finally, be strong in the Lord and in the
strength of his power. 11 Put on the whole armor of
God, so that you may be able to stand against the
wiles of the devil. 12 For our[c] struggle is not against

[a] Other ancient authorities add *of his flesh and of his bones*
[b] Other ancient authorities lack *in the Lord*
[c] Other ancient authorities read *your*

Ephesians 6:5-9

In all the letters attributed to Paul, these must be the most troubling words to be read by slaves, whether of past generations or those who today work for slave wages. It is troublesome that the author does not call for justice. Instead, he demands that slaves do their work as if they are doing it unto Christ, and he asks masters not to be violent. He ignores the fact that this unequal relationship is based on institutionalized violence. The deprivation that leads to a short life and a slow death is as violent as the master's whip. Clothing the iron fist of oppression with a velvet glove does not make oppressive structures any more benign; it only masks the violence that is inherently present in the relationship. For slaves to work diligently as if they were working for the Lord only perpetuates the very injustices under which Jesus died. The author would have been more in line with the gospel message had he told the masters to set their captives free.

— *MDLT*

enemies of blood and flesh, but against the rulers,
against the authorities, against the cosmic powers of this present darkness, against the spiritual
forces of evil in the heavenly places. 13Therefore
take up the whole armor of God, so that you may
be able to withstand on that evil day, and having
done everything, to stand firm. 14Stand therefore,
and fasten the belt of truth around your waist,
and put on the breastplate of righteousness. 15As
shoes for your feet put on whatever will make you
ready to proclaim the gospel of peace. 16With all
of these,[a] take the shield of faith, with which you
will be able to quench all the flaming arrows of the
evil one. 17Take the helmet of salvation, and the
sword of the Spirit, which is the word of God.

18 Pray in the Spirit at all times in every
prayer and supplication. To that end keep alert
and always persevere in supplication for all the
saints. 19Pray also for me, so that when I speak, a
message may be given to me to make known with
boldness the mystery of the gospel,[b] 20for which
I am an ambassador in chains. Pray that I may declare it boldly, as I must speak.

21 So that you also may know how I am and
what I am doing, Tychicus will tell you everything. He is a dear brother and a faithful minister
in the Lord. 22I am sending him to you for this
very purpose, to let you know how we are, and to
encourage your hearts.

23 Peace be to the whole community,[c] and
love with faith, from God the Father and the Lord
Jesus Christ. 24Grace be with all who have an un-
dying love for our Lord Jesus Christ.[d]

[a] Or *In all circumstances* [b] Other ancient authorities lack *of the gospel* [c] Gk *to the brothers*
[d] Other ancient authorities add *Amen*

The Letter of Paul to the Philippians

Paul wrote this friendly missive to a community of Christians living in Philippi, the first church Paul founded in Europe (4:15; Acts 16:11-40). Philippi was an important Roman colony located in eastern Macedonia, now northeastern Greece, where many retired soldiers had received land. The city was located on the *Via Egnatia,* a main trade road of the region.

The letter to the Philippians expresses Paul's gratitude for the financial support they sent to him with Epaphroditus while Paul was in jail awaiting trial (1:2-26; 4:10-20). The letter also reassures the community that Paul is well and will soon be freed from prison (1:12-26). Paul responds to issues of selfishness and quarrels (1:27-28; 2:2, 14; 3:15; 4:2-3) and opposition to his gospel (1:15-17, 27-28; 3:1b-20). Paul writes that he intends to send Epaphroditus back to the Philippians and that he hopes to send Timothy to them as well (2:25-30).

The letter is organized as follows: After a salutation (1:1-2) and a thanksgiving (1:3-11), Paul reflects on his imprisonment (1:12-30), exhorts the Philippians to be humble in imitation of Jesus (2:1-18), and asks them to live in harmony even as Paul discredits the Judaizers and subordinates his own Jewish accomplishments to Christ (3:1b—4:9). Paul closes with a note of gratitude for the financial aid the congregation sent him (4:10-23).

Scholars have struggled to determine when and how this letter fits in the chronology of Paul's ministry in Acts. Depending on his imprisonment, Philippians could have been written from Ephesus around 56 CE (see Acts 20:31; 1 Cor 15:32; 2 Cor 1:8-10), from Rome, between 61 and 63 (see 1:13; 4:22; and Acts 28:11-31), or from Caesarea, between 58 and 60 (Acts 23–26). Some abrupt changes of subjects and emotions have led some scholars to argue that this letter is a composite, comprised of different letters (1:1—3:1a; 3:1b—4:1; 4:2-9; 4:10-20, 23). To others, however, Philippians reads as a single composition with natural and spontaneous thematic changes.

As a person born and raised in Venezuela, who moved to the United States and eventually became a U.S. citizen, I have learned to appreciate diverse ethnic experiences with their corresponding hopes and struggles. Therefore I tend to approach the Bible from angles and ideas that privilege the multi-colored and complex human experience. From this vantage point, a cross-cultural reading of Philippians brings to the fore some issues worth considering. Modeling Greco-Roman ways of expressing friendship, Paul writes this letter to strengthen his close relationship with the Philippians and evoke appropriate responses from them. The letter's fraternal imagery shows strong affectionate ties between the apostle and these Christians (1:7-8; 2:18; 4:1, 14). This invites reflection on how appropriate rhetoric can help to create a sense of community, especially in a diverse and fragmented society. Philippians offers glimpses of social reciprocity between Paul and this church on the matter of giving and receiving favors, particularly with respect to monetary support and the appropriate response to it (1:4, 7; 4:10, 14-15). And as we continue to create conditions for gender equality, the position and prominent roles played by women in Philippi is noteworthy. Although masculine language and ideology permeate this letter, Paul praises Euodia and Syntyche for the strong leadership they provided in this church's ministry (1:1; 4:2-7; see also Rom 16:3-5, 7, 12, 16).

Paul's attack on some unknown Jewish adversaries raises questions about religious and civil discourse in a multi-ethnic context (1:15-17, 27-28; 3:1b-20). He counteracts people who insist on having Gentile converts circumcised, denouncing such practice as "mutilation" and calling its advocates "dogs," "evil workers," and "enemies of the cross of Christ" (3:2; 3:18), and discounting several aspects of his Jewish pedigree as "rubbish" (3:8). We can understand Paul as shaming opponents in a situation of conflict and irreconcilable ideological differences, but in a contemporary context of boundary crossing, pluralism, and respect for others, do we think such rhetoric is appropriate for constructing religious (and especially Christian) identity? Paul also argues that Christian citizenship is heavenly (3:20), that Jesus is Lord and Savior (2:11; 3:8, 20), and that eventually all would be subjected to Jesus (1:28-30; 2:9-11, 15; 4:21). Such language would have challenged the views of people who were Roman citizens and believed that Caesar was the only lord and benefactor. Though not explicitly stated, the political and possibly counter-imperial implications of Paul's language seems clear.

As impoverished and persecuted communities experience hardships today, the joyful overtone of this letter encourages Christians to move forward with hope (1:4, 18-19, 25; 2:2, 17-19, 28; 3:1a; 4:1, 4, 10). The early hymn recorded in Phil 2:5-11 reveals how early Christians perceived the nature of Jesus, but also how they made such a perception a mediation of their faith and a point of encounter with the sacred. How do expressions of faith, including song writing and poetry, do something similar in contemporary worship?

— Aquiles Ernesto Martínez

1 Paul and Timothy, servants[a] of Christ Jesus,
To all the saints in Christ Jesus who are in
Philippi, with the bishops[b] and deacons:[c]
2 Grace to you and peace from God our Father and the Lord Jesus Christ.

3 I thank my God every time I remember
you, 4 constantly praying with joy in every one of
my prayers for all of you, 5 because of your sharing in the gospel from the first day until now. 6 I
am confident of this, that the one who began a
good work among you will bring it to completion
by the day of Jesus Christ. 7 It is right for me to
think this way about all of you, because you hold
me in your heart,[d] for all of you share in God's
grace[e] with me, both in my imprisonment and in

[a] Gk *slaves* [b] Or *overseers* [c] Or *overseers and helpers* [d] Or *because I hold you in my heart* [e] Gk *in grace*

the defense and confirmation of the gospel. 8 For
God is my witness, how I long for all of you with
the compassion of Christ Jesus. 9 And this is my
prayer, that your love may overflow more and
more with knowledge and full insight 10 to help
you to determine what is best, so that in the day
of Christ you may be pure and blameless, 11 having produced the harvest of righteousness that
comes through Jesus Christ for the glory and
praise of God.

12 I want you to know, beloved,[a] that what has
happened to me has actually helped to spread the
gospel, 13 so that it has become known throughout the whole imperial guard[b] and to everyone
else that my imprisonment is for Christ; 14 and
most of the brothers and sisters,[a] having been
made confident in the Lord by my imprisonment,
dare to speak the word[c] with greater boldness and
without fear.

15 Some proclaim Christ from envy and rivalry, but others from goodwill. 16 These proclaim
Christ out of love, knowing that I have been put
here for the defense of the gospel; 17 the others proclaim Christ out of selfish ambition, not
sincerely but intending to increase my suffering
in my imprisonment. 18 What does it matter?
Just this, that Christ is proclaimed in every way,
whether out of false motives or true; and in that
I rejoice.

Yes, and I will continue to rejoice, 19 for I know
that through your prayers and the help of the
Spirit of Jesus Christ this will turn out for my deliverance. 20 It is my eager expectation and hope
that I will not be put to shame in any way, but that
by my speaking with all boldness, Christ will be
exalted now as always in my body, whether by life
or by death. 21 For to me, living is Christ and dying is gain. 22 If I am to live in the flesh, that means
fruitful labor for me; and I do not know which I
prefer. 23 I am hard pressed between the two: my
desire is to depart and be with Christ, for that is
far better; 24 but to remain in the flesh is more
necessary for you. 25 Since I am convinced of this,
I know that I will remain and continue with all of
you for your progress and joy in faith, 26 so that I
may share abundantly in your boasting in Christ
Jesus when I come to you again.

27 Only, live your life in a manner worthy
of the gospel of Christ, so that, whether I come
and see you or am absent and hear about you, I
will know that you are standing firm in one spirit,
striving side by side with one mind for the faith
of the gospel, 28 and are in no way intimidated
by your opponents. For them this is evidence of
their destruction, but of your salvation. And this
is God's doing. 29 For he has graciously granted
you the privilege not only of believing in Christ,
but of suffering for him as well— 30 since you are
having the same struggle that you saw I had and
now hear that I still have.

2 If then there is any encouragement in Christ,
any consolation from love, any sharing in the
Spirit, any compassion and sympathy, 2 make my
joy complete: be of the same mind, having the
same love, being in full accord and of one mind.
3 Do nothing from selfish ambition or conceit,
but in humility regard others as better than yourselves. 4 Let each of you look not to your own
interests, but to the interests of others. 5 Let the
same mind be in you that was[d] in Christ Jesus,

Philippians 2:5-8

Paul instructs the followers of Jesus to imitate God. This imitation excludes holding on to power and privilege, or ruling over humans. Although Jesus had access to all the treasures and powers of heaven, he instead chose to be in solidarity with the least among humans, even assuming the role of a slave. This is the same pattern adopted by Moses centuries earlier. Although he was in Pharaoh's court, he cast his lot with the Hebrew slaves. The difficulty for the elite in finding salvation is usually their refusal to imitate Moses and Jesus in accompanying the disenfranchised in their daily struggle.

— MDLT

[a] Gk *brothers* [b] Gk *whole praetorium* [c] Other ancient authorities read *word of God* [d] Or *that you have*

6 who, though he was in the form of God,
did not regard equality with God
as something to be exploited,
7 but emptied himself,
taking the form of a slave,
being born in human likeness.
And being found in human form,
8 he humbled himself
and became obedient to the point of death—
even death on a cross.

9 Therefore God also highly exalted him
and gave him the name
that is above every name,
10 so that at the name of Jesus
every knee should bend,
in heaven and on earth and under the earth,
11 and every tongue should confess
that Jesus Christ is Lord,
to the glory of God the Father.

Philippians 2:12

The Christianity of the dominant culture often reduces salvation to a public confession of one's faith in Jesus Christ. Or salvation is reduced to a ritual, be it baptism or the confession of sin. Yet Paul instructs believers to work out their salvation in "fear and trembling," signifying a long and difficult process. Salvation, as usually understood by marginalized communities, is a lifelong process toward liberation—not only from the shortcomings of self but, just as important, liberation from the sinful structures that the dominant culture imposes to maintain power and privilege. The process of dismantling oppressive structures requires dangerous work that can cost one's livelihood or life, hence the need to do this work in fear and trembling.

— MDLT

12 Therefore, my beloved, just as you have
always obeyed me, not only in my presence, but
much more now in my absence, work out your
own salvation with fear and trembling; 13for it is
God who is at work in you, enabling you both to
will and to work for his good pleasure.

14 Do all things without murmuring and
arguing, 15so that you may be blameless and innocent, children of God without blemish in the
midst of a crooked and perverse generation,
in which you shine like stars in the world. 16It
is by your holding fast to the word of life that I
can boast on the day of Christ that I did not run
in vain or labor in vain. 17But even if I am being
poured out as a libation over the sacrifice and the
offering of your faith, I am glad and rejoice with
all of you— 18and in the same way you also must
be glad and rejoice with me.

19 I hope in the Lord Jesus to send Timothy
to you soon, so that I may be cheered by news of
you. 20I have no one like him who will be genuinely concerned for your welfare. 21All of them
are seeking their own interests, not those of Jesus
Christ. 22But Timothy's[a] worth you know, how
like a son with a father he has served with me in
the work of the gospel. 23I hope therefore to send
him as soon as I see how things go with me; 24and
I trust in the Lord that I will also come soon.

25 Still, I think it necessary to send to you
Epaphroditus—my brother and co-worker and
fellow soldier, your messenger[b] and minister to
my need; 26for he has been longing for[c] all of you,
and has been distressed because you heard that
he was ill. 27He was indeed so ill that he nearly
died. But God had mercy on him, and not only
on him but on me also, so that I would not have
one sorrow after another. 28I am the more eager
to send him, therefore, in order that you may rejoice at seeing him again, and that I may be less
anxious. 29Welcome him then in the Lord with
all joy, and honor such people, 30because he came
close to death for the work of Christ,[d] risking his
life to make up for those services that you could
not give me.

3 Finally, my brothers and sisters,[e] rejoice[f] in
the Lord.

[a] Gk *his* [b] Gk *apostle* [c] Other ancient authorities read *longing to see* [d] Other ancient authorities read *of the Lord*
[e] Gk *my brothers* [f] Or *farewell*

To write the same things to you is not troublesome to me, and for you it is a safeguard.
2 Beware of the dogs, beware of the evil workers, beware of those who mutilate the flesh![a] 3 For
it is we who are the circumcision, who worship in
the Spirit of God[b] and boast in Christ Jesus and
have no confidence in the flesh— 4 even though I,
too, have reason for confidence in the flesh.
If anyone else has reason to be confident in
the flesh, I have more: 5 circumcised on the eighth
day, a member of the people of Israel, of the
tribe of Benjamin, a Hebrew born of Hebrews; as
to the law, a Pharisee; 6 as to zeal, a persecutor of
the church; as to righteousness under the law,
blameless.
7 Yet whatever gains I had, these I have come
to regard as loss because of Christ. 8 More than
that, I regard everything as loss because of the
surpassing value of knowing Christ Jesus my
Lord. For his sake I have suffered the loss of all
things, and I regard them as rubbish, in order
that I may gain Christ 9 and be found in him, not
having a righteousness of my own that comes
from the law, but one that comes through faith
in Christ,[c] the righteousness from God based on
faith. 10 I want to know Christ[d] and the power of
his resurrection and the sharing of his sufferings
by becoming like him in his death, 11 if somehow I
may attain the resurrection from the dead.
12 Not that I have already obtained this or
have already reached the goal;[e] but I press on to
make it my own, because Christ Jesus has made
me his own. 13 Beloved,[f] I do not consider that I
have made it my own;[g] but this one thing I do:
forgetting what lies behind and straining forward
to what lies ahead, 14 I press on toward the goal
for the prize of the heavenly[h] call of God in Christ
Jesus. 15 Let those of us then who are mature be of
the same mind; and if you think differently about
anything, this too God will reveal to you. 16 Only
let us hold fast to what we have attained.
17 Brothers and sisters,[f] join in imitating
me, and observe those who live according to
the example you have in us. 18 For many live as
enemies of the cross of Christ; I have often told
you of them, and now I tell you even with tears.
19 Their end is destruction; their god is the belly;
and their glory is in their shame; their minds are
set on earthly things. 20 But our citizenship[i] is in
heaven, and it is from there that we are expecting
a Savior, the Lord Jesus Christ. 21 He will transform the body of our humiliation[j] that it may be
conformed to the body of his glory,[k] by the power
that also enables him to make all things subject
to himself.

4 1 Therefore, my brothers and sisters,[l] whom I love and long for, my joy and
crown, stand firm in the Lord in this way, my
beloved.
2 I urge Euodia and I urge Syntyche to be of
the same mind in the Lord. 3 Yes, and I ask you
also, my loyal companion,[m] help these women,
for they have struggled beside me in the work of
the gospel, together with Clement and the rest
of my co-workers, whose names are in the book
of life.
4 Rejoice[n] in the Lord always; again I will
say, Rejoice.[n] 5 Let your gentleness be known to
everyone. The Lord is near. 6 Do not worry about
anything, but in everything by prayer and supplication with thanksgiving let your requests be
made known to God. 7 And the peace of God,
which surpasses all understanding, will guard
your hearts and your minds in Christ Jesus.

8 Finally, beloved,[o] whatever is true, whatever is honorable, whatever is just, whatever is
pure, whatever is pleasing, whatever is commendable, if there is any excellence and if there is anything worthy of praise, think about[p] these things.
9 Keep on doing the things that you have learned
and received and heard and seen in me, and the
God of peace will be with you.
10 I rejoice[q] in the Lord greatly that now at
last you have revived your concern for me; indeed,

[a] Gk *the mutilation* [b] Other ancient authorities read *worship God in spirit* [c] Or *through the faith of Christ* [d] Gk *him*
[e] Or *have already been made perfect* [f] Gk *Brothers* [g] Other ancient authorities read *my own yet* [h] Gk *upward*
[i] Or *commonwealth* [j] Or *our humble bodies* [k] Or *his glorious body* [l] Gk *my brothers* [m] Or *loyal Syzygus*
[n] Or *Farewell* [o] Gk *brothers* [p] Gk *take account of* [q] Gk *I rejoiced*

you were concerned for me, but had no opportunity to show it.[a] 11Not that I am referring to being in need; for I have learned to be content with whatever I have. 12I know what it is to have little, and I know what it is to have plenty. In any and all circumstances I have learned the secret of being well-fed and of going hungry, of having plenty and of being in need. 13I can do all things through him who strengthens me. 14In any case, it was kind of you to share my distress.

15 You Philippians indeed know that in the early days of the gospel, when I left Macedonia, no church shared with me in the matter of giving and receiving, except you alone. 16For even when I was in Thessalonica, you sent me help for my needs more than once. 17Not that I seek the gift, but I seek the profit that accumulates to your account. 18I have been paid in full and have more than enough; I am fully satisfied, now that I have received from Epaphroditus the gifts you sent, a fragrant offering, a sacrifice acceptable and pleasing to God. 19And my God will fully satisfy every need of yours according to his riches in glory in Christ Jesus. 20To our God and Father be glory forever and ever. Amen.

21 Greet every saint in Christ Jesus. The friends[b] who are with me greet you. 22All the saints greet you, especially those of the emperor's household.

23 The grace of the Lord Jesus Christ be with your spirit.[c]

[a] Gk lacks *to show it* [b] Gk *brothers* [c] Other ancient authorities add *Amen*

The Letter of Paul to the Colossians

THIS LETTER TO THE "SAINTS AND FAITHFUL" at Colossae, a town east of Ephesus in Phrygia, Asia Minor, is a message of exhortation and encouragement. It commends the readers for their faith in Christ (1:4-7; 2:5-7), but also shows concern about the possible impact of an aberrant teaching (2:4, 8, 16, 18). Colossians highlights the sole supremacy of Christ throughout the cosmos and in the church (1:13-23). Christ is God's creative, reconciling, peacemaking, and saving power. Believers are to depend on Christ alone. All other claims to traditions, sources of wisdom, and forms of social ordering are dismissed as merely human (1:27-28; 2:2-15, 20; 3:1-4, 9-11, 15, 17). The letter emphasizes a communal life of moral and social virtue, especially a unifying love and a commitment to peace that embrace the cultural diversity of the peoples and nations (1:4, 27; 2:2; 3:5-16).

Seeking to extend Paul's apostolic authority and ministry (1:23—2:5; 4:3, 7-18), this letter—addressed to a believing assembly not founded or visited by Paul himself (1:7; 2:1)—was also intended to be read by the neighboring congregation in Laodicea (4:16). Colossians is set during a period of Paul's imprisonment (4:3, 10, 18). The immediate occasion of the letter is the return of the slave Onesimus back to his home community (4:7-9; see Philemon).

The letter follows the pattern of most Pauline letters: salutation (1:1-2); thanksgiving (1:3-8); prayer for the readers and a review of Paul's apostolic ministry, interlaced with affirmations of God's work in Christ that set the foundation for the subsequent main appeal of the letter (1:9—2:5); the letter's main body of warning, teaching, and exhortation (2:6—4:6); and a closing with greetings, information, instructions, and a benediction (4:7-18).

The teaching opposed in the letter is marked by rigorous self-denial (2:18, 23), special regulations regarding food, drink, and contact with physical objects (2:16, 21), observance of a possible sacred calendar (2:16-17), and the worship of angelic beings and cosmic forces (2:8, 15). The letter asserts that these practices represent an accommodation to dogma and regulations (2:14, 20, 21) and elemental cosmic principles or forces (2:8, 20), and are based on a philosophy that is merely "human" or "earthly" (2:8, 20, 22-23; 3:2) and of no worth in truly checking human self-indulgence (2:23).

In opposition to such practices, Colossians offers the full knowledge of God, wisdom, and life (1:9-11, 13, 20, 26-28; 2:2-4, 23; 3:3). It stresses moral, mental, and social transformation made possible through Christ (3:1—4:6), and calls on believers to avoid destructive impulses (3:5-9). They are to make real the "new self" and new humanity (3:10), by pursuing virtues that make for communal unity while celebrating diversity (3:10-15), engendering a liturgical life of mutual teaching, song, prayer, and thankfulness (3:16; 4:2-4), assessing all speech and conduct in the light of Christ (3:17; cf. 1:10-12, 28), following the traditional codes of domestic life (2:5; 3:18—4:1), and promoting wise and timely speech and conduct before outsiders (4:5-6). These exhortations are grounded in the sole supremacy of Christ as God's agent in creation and redemption—and in the redemptive transformation of the readers through their baptismal status (1:12-14, 21-23; 2:10-15, 20; 3:1-4, 9-10). They are dead to the former world and humanity but raised and made alive again with Christ.

If this letter was written or endorsed by Paul himself when he was imprisoned by the Roman imperial authorities in Ephesus, Colossians may have been written as early as 55 CE; or it may have been written as late as the mid-60s if it was composed during Paul's imprisonment in Rome. If written by a disciple writing in Paul's name after his death, as many scholars hold (due to differences in style, language, Christology, and the inclusion of the household codes), then the letter can be dated between 65 and 90 CE.

Twenty-first-century Christian readers will be mindful of the ambivalent potential of Colossians, and especially how it has been used to suppress indigenous cultural and religious practices in colonizing situations. That happens, for example, when people cite 2:8-23 to emphasize the exclusive supremacy of Christ over all human traditions while neglecting 1:27 ("how great among the Gentiles"), or 3:11 ("no longer Greek and Jew"). It happens when people use 1:16-20 and 2:10 to give legitimacy and encourage acquiescence to unjust rule and imperial domination, while ignoring 2:15 ("he disarmed the rulers"). It happens when people use 3:18—4:1 to promote oppressive social hierarchies or exclusions, while neglecting 3:9-11, Gal 3:26-28, and Philemon.

Growing up in Japan as the son of missionaries, my first memories are those of being a foreigner. That experience provided the trajectory toward my adult commitment to practice the Christian faith in an Anabaptist-Mennonite perspective, along with a concern for ecumenical and inter-faith exchange. Consciously and unconsciously, my experience has affected my reading of Colossians through the lens of sociocultural dynamics, both in understanding the past and in engaging the present. Serving four years in the Philippines as a visiting professor sharpened my interest in local readings and the public performance of Scripture, leaving me more attentive to both the integrity of the cultures of others and to the positive potential of respectful cultural interactions.

— ***Gordon Zerbe***

1 Paul, an apostle of Christ Jesus by the will of
God, and Timothy our brother,
2 To the saints and faithful brothers and sisters[a] in Christ in Colossae:
Grace to you and peace from God our Father.
3 In our prayers for you we always thank God,
the Father of our Lord Jesus Christ, 4 for we have
heard of your faith in Christ Jesus and of the love
that you have for all the saints, 5 because of the
hope laid up for you in heaven. You have heard

[a] Gk *brothers*

of this hope before in the word of the truth, the
gospel 6that has come to you. Just as it is bearing fruit and growing in the whole world, so it has
been bearing fruit among yourselves from the day
you heard it and truly comprehended the grace of
God. 7This you learned from Epaphras, our beloved fellow servant.[a] He is a faithful minister of
Christ on your[b] behalf, 8and he has made known
to us your love in the Spirit.

9 For this reason, since the day we heard it, we
have not ceased praying for you and asking that
you may be filled with the knowledge of God's[c]
will in all spiritual wisdom and understanding,
10so that you may lead lives worthy of the Lord,
fully pleasing to him, as you bear fruit in every
good work and as you grow in the knowledge
of God. 11May you be made strong with all the
strength that comes from his glorious power, and
may you be prepared to endure everything with
patience, while joyfully 12giving thanks to the Father, who has enabled[d] you[e] to share in the inheritance of the saints in the light. 13He has rescued
us from the power of darkness and transferred us
into the kingdom of his beloved Son, 14in whom
we have redemption, the forgiveness of sins.[f]

15 He is the image of the invisible God, the
firstborn of all creation; 16for in[g] him all things
in heaven and on earth were created, things visible and invisible, whether thrones or dominions
or rulers or powers—all things have been created
through him and for him. 17He himself is before
all things, and in[g] him all things hold together.
18He is the head of the body, the church; he is the
beginning, the firstborn from the dead, so that
he might come to have first place in everything.
19For in him all the fullness of God was pleased
to dwell, 20and through him God was pleased to
reconcile to himself all things, whether on earth
or in heaven, by making peace through the blood
of his cross.

21 And you who were once estranged and
hostile in mind, doing evil deeds, 22he has now
reconciled[h] in his fleshly body[i] through death,
so as to present you holy and blameless and ir-
reproachable before him— 23provided that you
continue securely established and steadfast in the
faith, without shifting from the hope promised by
the gospel that you heard, which has been proclaimed to every creature under heaven. I, Paul,
became a servant of this gospel.

24 I am now rejoicing in my sufferings for your
sake, and in my flesh I am completing what is lacking in Christ's afflictions for the sake of his body,
that is, the church. 25I became its servant according to God's commission that was given to me for
you, to make the word of God fully known, 26the
mystery that has been hidden throughout the ages
and generations but has now been revealed to his
saints. 27To them God chose to make known how
great among the Gentiles are the riches of the
glory of this mystery, which is Christ in you, the
hope of glory. 28It is he whom we proclaim, warning everyone and teaching everyone in all wisdom,
so that we may present everyone mature in Christ.
29For this I toil and struggle with all the energy
that he powerfully inspires within me.

2 For I want you to know how much I am
struggling for you, and for those in Laodicea,
and for all who have not seen me face to face. 2I
want their hearts to be encouraged and united in
love, so that they may have all the riches of assured understanding and have the knowledge of
God's mystery, that is, Christ himself,[j] 3in whom
are hidden all the treasures of wisdom and knowledge. 4I am saying this so that no one may deceive
you with plausible arguments. 5For though I am
absent in body, yet I am with you in spirit, and
I rejoice to see your morale and the firmness of
your faith in Christ.

6 As you therefore have received Christ
Jesus the Lord, continue to live your lives[k] in him,
7rooted and built up in him and established in
the faith, just as you were taught, abounding in
thanksgiving.

[a] Gk *slave* [b] Other ancient authorities read *our* [c] Gk *his* [d] Other ancient authorities read *called* [e] Other ancient authorities read *us* [f] Other ancient authorities add *through his blood* [g] Or *by* [h] Other ancient authorities read *you have now been reconciled* [i] Gk *in the body of his flesh* [j] Other ancient authorities read *of the mystery of God, both of the Father and of Christ* [k] Gk *to walk*

8 See to it that no one takes you captive
through philosophy and empty deceit, according to human tradition, according to the elemental spirits of the universe,[a] and not according to
Christ. 9 For in him the whole fullness of deity
dwells bodily, 10 and you have come to fullness in
him, who is the head of every ruler and authority. 11 In him also you were circumcised with a
spiritual circumcision,[b] by putting off the body
of the flesh in the circumcision of Christ; 12 when
you were buried with him in baptism, you were
also raised with him through faith in the power of
God, who raised him from the dead. 13 And when
you were dead in trespasses and the uncircumcision of your flesh, God[c] made you[d] alive together
with him, when he forgave us all our trespasses,
14 erasing the record that stood against us with its
legal demands. He set this aside, nailing it to the
cross. 15 He disarmed[e] the rulers and authorities
and made a public example of them, triumphing
over them in it.

16 Therefore do not let anyone condemn you
in matters of food and drink or of observing festivals, new moons, or sabbaths. 17 These are only a
shadow of what is to come, but the substance belongs to Christ. 18 Do not let anyone disqualify you,
insisting on self-abasement and worship of angels,
dwelling[f] on visions,[g] puffed up without cause by a
human way of thinking,[h] 19 and not holding fast to
the head, from whom the whole body, nourished
and held together by its ligaments and sinews,
grows with a growth that is from God.

20 If with Christ you died to the elemental
spirits of the universe,[a] why do you live as if you
still belonged to the world? Why do you submit
to regulations, 21 "Do not handle, Do not taste, Do
not touch"? 22 All these regulations refer to things
that perish with use; they are simply human
commands and teachings. 23 These have indeed
an appearance of wisdom in promoting self-
imposed piety, humility, and severe treatment of
the body, but they are of no value in checking self-
indulgence.[i]

3 So if you have been raised with Christ, seek
the things that are above, where Christ is,
seated at the right hand of God. 2 Set your minds
on things that are above, not on things that are on
earth, 3 for you have died, and your life is hidden
with Christ in God. 4 When Christ who is your[j]
life is revealed, then you also will be revealed with
him in glory.

5 Put to death, therefore, whatever in you is
earthly: fornication, impurity, passion, evil desire, and greed (which is idolatry). 6 On account
of these the wrath of God is coming on those who
are disobedient.[k] 7 These are the ways you also
once followed, when you were living that life.[l]
8 But now you must get rid of all such things—anger, wrath, malice, slander, and abusive[m] language
from your mouth. 9 Do not lie to one another, seeing that you have stripped off the old self with its
practices 10 and have clothed yourselves with the
new self, which is being renewed in knowledge
according to the image of its creator. 11 In that renewal[n] there is no longer Greek and Jew, circumcised and uncircumcised, barbarian, Scythian,
slave and free; but Christ is all and in all!

12 As God's chosen ones, holy and beloved,
clothe yourselves with compassion, kindness, humility, meekness, and patience. 13 Bear with one
another and, if anyone has a complaint against
another, forgive each other; just as the Lord[o] has
forgiven you, so you also must forgive. 14 Above
all, clothe yourselves with love, which binds everything together in perfect harmony. 15 And let
the peace of Christ rule in your hearts, to which
indeed you were called in the one body. And be
thankful. 16 Let the word of Christ[p] dwell in you
richly; teach and admonish one another in all

[a] Or *the rudiments of the world* [b] Gk *a circumcision made without hands* [c] Gk *he* [d] Other ancient authorities read *made us*; others, *made* [e] Or *divested himself of* [f] Other ancient authorities read *not dwelling* [g] Meaning of Gk uncertain [h] Gk *by the mind of his flesh* [i] Or *are of no value, serving only to indulge the flesh* [j] Other authorities read *our* [k] Other ancient authorities lack *on those who are disobedient* (Gk *the children of disobedience*) [l] Or *living among such people* [m] Or *filthy* [n] Gk *its creator,* [11]*where* [o] Other ancient authorities read *just as Christ* [p] Other ancient authorities read *of God*, or *of the Lord*

wisdom; and with gratitude in your hearts sing
psalms, hymns, and spiritual songs to God.[a]
17And whatever you do, in word or deed, do
everything in the name of the Lord Jesus, giving
thanks to God the Father through him.

18 Wives, be subject to your husbands, as is
fitting in the Lord. 19Husbands, love your wives
and never treat them harshly.

20 Children, obey your parents in everything,
for this is your acceptable duty in the Lord. 21Fa-
thers, do not provoke your children, or they may
lose heart. 22Slaves, obey your earthly masters[b] in
everything, not only while being watched and in
order to please them, but wholeheartedly, fearing
the Lord.[b] 23Whatever your task, put yourselves
into it, as done for the Lord and not for your masters,[c] 24since you know that from the Lord you
will receive the inheritance as your reward; you
serve[d] the Lord Christ. 25For the wrongdoer will
be paid back for whatever wrong has been done,
and there is no partiality.

4 1Masters, treat your
slaves justly and fairly, for you know that you
also have a Master in heaven.

2 Devote yourselves to prayer, keeping alert
in it with thanksgiving. 3At the same time pray
for us as well that God will open to us a door for
the word, that we may declare the mystery of
Christ, for which I am in prison, 4so that I may
reveal it clearly, as I should.

Colossians 3:18—4:1

In what are commonly called the "household codes," early Christian authors, some of them writing under Paul's name, called for an ethic of subordination within domestic relationships (see Eph 5:21—6:9; 1 Tim 2:11-15; 6:1-2; Titus 2:3-10). Ephesians frames this exhortation as a matter of mutuality—"be subject to one another" (5:21)—but how mutual is the relationship when one can command the other or even claim to own the other?

— NE

5 Conduct yourselves wisely toward outsiders, making the most of the time.[e] 6Let your speech
always be gracious, seasoned with salt, so that you
may know how you ought to answer everyone.

7 Tychicus will tell you all the news about
me; he is a beloved brother, a faithful minister,
and a fellow servant[f] in the Lord. 8I have sent
him to you for this very purpose, so that you may
know how we are[g] and that he may encourage
your hearts; 9he is coming with Onesimus, the
faithful and beloved brother, who is one of you.
They will tell you about everything here.

10 Aristarchus my fellow prisoner greets you,

[a] Other ancient authorities read *to the Lord* [b] In Greek the same word is used for *master* and *Lord* [c] Gk *not for men* [d] Or *you are slaves of*, or *be slaves of* [e] Or *opportunity* [f] Gk *slave* [g] Other authorities read *that I may know how you are*

Colossians 4:7-18

The names of several of Paul's co-workers are listed here (and in 1:1). If this group of people were staying with Paul while he was under house arrest in Rome, then it is an amazing illustration of a community of reconciliation. Jews and Gentiles were living together. Timothy's presence as a person of mixed Jewish and Greek heritage would typically have been offensive, but not in this case. Onesimus was an escaped slave, soon to be sent to his master in an act that Paul believed would transform their relationship to that of equal brothers (Phlm vv. 8-16). Mark, the cousin of Barnabas, had been the reason for the break between his cousin and Paul (Acts 15:36-39)—one of the most painful events in the story of the first-century church. His presence must symbolize a reunion between Paul and Barnabas. In the final days of his life the apostle Paul was still living out his core belief of reconciliation.

— CPD

as does Mark the cousin of Barnabas, concerning whom you have received instructions—if he
comes to you, welcome him. 11 And Jesus who is
called Justus greets you. These are the only ones
of the circumcision among my co-workers for the
kingdom of God, and they have been a comfort to
me. 12 Epaphras, who is one of you, a servant[a] of
Christ Jesus, greets you. He is always wrestling in
his prayers on your behalf, so that you may stand
mature and fully assured in everything that God
wills. 13 For I testify for him that he has worked
hard for you and for those in Laodicea and in
Hierapolis. 14 Luke, the beloved physician, and
Demas greet you. 15 Give my greetings to the
brothers and sisters[b] in Laodicea, and to Nympha
and the church in her house. 16 And when this letter has been read among you, have it read also in
the church of the Laodiceans; and see that you
read also the letter from Laodicea. 17 And say to
Archippus, "See that you complete the task that
you have received in the Lord."

18 I, Paul, write this greeting with my own
hand. Remember my chains. Grace be with you.[c]

[a] Gk *slave* [b] Gk *brothers* [c] Other ancient authorities add *Amen*

The First Letter of Paul to the Thessalonians

FROM PAUL'S VANTAGE POINT, the proclamation of the gospel in Thessalonica, the capital of the Roman province of Macedonia, brought multiple changes, some positive, some negative. Several Thessalonians warmly welcomed Paul (1:9), accepted his gospel (2:13), turned to God from idols (1:9), and began a new walk or way of life (2:12). Among the negative changes, Paul and his companions were separated from the Thessalonian assembly (the *ekklēsia,* usually translated "church" in English: 2:17), and the assembly itself—in kinship with assemblies in Judea—suffered from the relentless opposition of their own compatriots (2:14). Whether the Greek word (*thlipsis*) that describes the assembly's afflictions (1:6; 3:3, 4, 7)—here translated as "persecution"—refers to physical abuse or social alienation, Paul read his assembly's troubles as the typical and predictable afflictions of the tempting one and as apocalyptic end-time hindrances designed to steer the faithful off track (3:3-5).

In response, an anxious Paul first dispatched his trustworthy envoy, Timothy, to learn about his nascent followers and encourage them (3:2, 5). Hearing that the assembly had not been shaken apart by their travails (3:6), Paul then sent them what we know as 1 Thessalonians, an affectionate letter of exhortation written about 50 or 51 CE. This is Paul's first extant letter and indeed the earliest writing in the New Testament canon. The letter appears to have had two goals: to declare Paul's repeated thanks to God (1:2; 2:13; cf. 3:9) for the assembly's reception of his gospel and their continuing maturation; and to offer a description or image of group distinctiveness (4:1—5:22) designed to build up their new cultural identity and solidarity in opposition to their former one.

Paul's repeated thanksgiving models the consistency of fidelity to God that he hopes the assembly will maintain and increase (cf. 4:1, 10; 5:16-18). His message about group distinctiveness includes *sanctification* or being "set apart" (4:3-4; 5:23); the designation of the "Gentiles" as persons who do not know God (4:5), a Jewish cultural slur that in effect put distance between the assembly's present life and the ethnic profile by which Paul and other Jews would have earlier identified them (compare 1:10; 2:14); "we-they" markers that divided people into two groups: *those who really know eschatological realities* (for example, that the dead believers will arise [4:13] and that the day of the Lord, that is, the parousia or the return of Jesus will come like a thief in the night [5:2]) and *those who do not*; and a request for consistent love for each other and for all (3:12; cf. 5:15). This consistent love is by contrast something that outsiders in Thessalonica cannot be said to have given their neighbors (2:14).

As an African American, I identify with Paul's assembly in Thessalonica for several reasons: their minority status in an imperial world; their attempts to remain faithful to their God despite affliction caused by many of their compatriots; and their quest to love all, thus modeling a new and better way of life. But I find Paul's own ideology in the letter troubling for three reasons. First, his we-they rhetoric, even if helpful for group-solidarity purposes, can be co-opted by majority cultures to serve the status quo. Second, Paul's casting of the assembly simply as "brothers and sisters" (used thirteen times) can also be co-opted by majority cultures to erase ethnic cultural identities and support notions of a false universalism. Third, I find patriarchal rhetoric (the view of God as father, 1:1, 3; 3:11) problematic, because it can so easily be co-opted to christen a male-dominated society.

— ***Abraham Smith***

1 Paul, Silvanus, and Timothy,
To the church of the Thessalonians in God
the Father and the Lord Jesus Christ:
Grace to you and peace.

2 We always give thanks to God for all of
you and mention you in our prayers, constantly
3 remembering before our God and Father your
work of faith and labor of love and steadfastness of hope in our Lord Jesus Christ. 4 For we
know, brothers and sisters[a] beloved by God, that
he has chosen you, 5 because our message of the
gospel came to you not in word only, but also in
power and in the Holy Spirit and with full conviction; just as you know what kind of persons
we proved to be among you for your sake. 6 And
you became imitators of us and of the Lord, for
in spite of persecution you received the word
with joy inspired by the Holy Spirit, 7 so that you
became an example to all the believers in Macedonia and in Achaia. 8 For the word of the Lord
has sounded forth from you not only in Macedonia and Achaia, but in every place your faith
in God has become known, so that we have no
need to speak about it. 9 For the people of those
regions[b] report about us what kind of welcome
we had among you, and how you turned to God
from idols, to serve a living and true God, 10 and
to wait for his Son from heaven, whom he raised
from the dead—Jesus, who rescues us from the
wrath that is coming.

2 You yourselves know, brothers and sisters,[a]
that our coming to you was not in vain, 2 but
though we had already suffered and been shamefully mistreated at Philippi, as you know, we had
courage in our God to declare to you the gospel of
God in spite of great opposition. 3 For our appeal
does not spring from deceit or impure motives
or trickery, 4 but just as we have been approved
by God to be entrusted with the message of the
gospel, even so we speak, not to please mortals,
but to please God who tests our hearts. 5 As you
know and as God is our witness, we never came
with words of flattery or with a pretext for greed;
6 nor did we seek praise from mortals, whether
from you or from others, 7 though we might have
made demands as apostles of Christ. But we were
gentle[c] among you, like a nurse tenderly caring
for her own children. 8 So deeply do we care for
you that we are determined to share with you not
only the gospel of God but also our own selves,
because you have become very dear to us.

9 You remember our labor and toil, brothers and sisters;[a] we worked night and day, so
that we might not burden any of you while we
proclaimed to you the gospel of God. 10 You are
witnesses, and God also, how pure, upright, and
blameless our conduct was toward you believers.

[a] Gk *brothers* [b] Gk *For they* [c] Other ancient authorities read *infants*

11 As you know, we dealt with each one of you
like a father with his children, 12 urging and encouraging you and pleading that you lead a life
worthy of God, who calls you into his own kingdom and glory.
13 We also constantly give thanks to God for
this, that when you received the word of God that
you heard from us, you accepted it not as a human
word but as what it really is, God's word, which is
also at work in you believers. 14 For you, brothers
and sisters,[a] became imitators of the churches of
God in Christ Jesus that are in Judea, for you suffered the same things from your own compatriots as they did from the Jews, 15 who killed both
the Lord Jesus and the prophets,[b] and drove us
out; they displease God and oppose everyone
16 by hindering us from speaking to the Gentiles
so that they may be saved. Thus they have constantly been filling up the measure of their sins;
but God's wrath has overtaken them at last.[c]

1 Thessalonians 2:14-16

It is not clear what Paul, writing in the 50s, might have meant by the wrath of God overtaking the Jews of Judea "at last." The Roman war that subdued Judea and destroyed Jerusalem was almost two decades away. Because the statement is missing from some early Latin manuscripts, some scholars have proposed that this line was inserted into the letter by later copyists.

— *NE*

17 As for us, brothers and sisters,[a] when, for
a short time, we were made orphans by being
separated from you—in person, not in heart—
we longed with great eagerness to see you face to
face. 18 For we wanted to come to you—certainly
I, Paul, wanted to again and again—but Satan
blocked our way. 19 For what is our hope or joy
or crown of boasting before our Lord Jesus at his
coming? Is it not you? 20 Yes, you are our glory
and joy!

3 Therefore when we could bear it no longer,
we decided to be left alone in Athens; 2 and we
sent Timothy, our brother and co-worker for God
in proclaiming[d] the gospel of Christ, to strengthen
and encourage you for the sake of your faith, 3 so
that no one would be shaken by these persecutions. Indeed, you yourselves know that this is
what we are destined for. 4 In fact, when we were
with you, we told you beforehand that we were to
suffer persecution; so it turned out, as you know.
5 For this reason, when I could bear it no longer, I
sent to find out about your faith; I was afraid that
somehow the tempter had tempted you and that
our labor had been in vain.
6 But Timothy has just now come to us from
you, and has brought us the good news of your
faith and love. He has told us also that you always
remember us kindly and long to see us—just as
we long to see you. 7 For this reason, brothers
and sisters,[a] during all our distress and persecution we have been encouraged about you through
your faith. 8 For we now live, if you continue to
stand firm in the Lord. 9 How can we thank God
enough for you in return for all the joy that we
feel before our God because of you? 10 Night and
day we pray most earnestly that we may see you
face to face and restore whatever is lacking in
your faith.
11 Now may our God and Father himself and
our Lord Jesus direct our way to you. 12 And may
the Lord make you increase and abound in love
for one another and for all, just as we abound in
love for you. 13 And may he so strengthen your
hearts in holiness that you may be blameless
before our God and Father at the coming of our
Lord Jesus with all his saints.

4 Finally, brothers and sisters,[a] we ask and urge
you in the Lord Jesus that, as you learned from
us how you ought to live and to please God (as, in
fact, you are doing), you should do so more and
more. 2 For you know what instructions we gave
you through the Lord Jesus. 3 For this is the will
of God, your sanctification: that you abstain from
fornication; 4 that each one of you know how to

[a] Gk *brothers* [b] Other ancient authorities read *their own prophets* [c] Or *completely* or *forever* [d] Gk lacks *proclaiming*

control your own body[a] in holiness and honor,
5not with lustful passion, like the Gentiles who
do not know God; 6that no one wrong or exploit
a brother or sister[b] in this matter, because the
Lord is an avenger in all these things, just as we
have already told you beforehand and solemnly
warned you. 7For God did not call us to impurity
but in holiness. 8Therefore whoever rejects this
rejects not human authority but God, who also
gives his Holy Spirit to you.

9 Now concerning love of the brothers and
sisters,[c] you do not need to have anyone write to
you, for you yourselves have been taught by God
to love one another; 10and indeed you do love
all the brothers and sisters[c] throughout Macedonia. But we urge you, beloved,[c] to do so more
and more, 11to aspire to live quietly, to mind
your own affairs, and to work with your hands,
as we directed you, 12so that you may behave
properly toward outsiders and be dependent on
no one.

13 But we do not want you to be uninformed,
brothers and sisters,[c] about those who have died,[d]
so that you may not grieve as others do who have
no hope. 14For since we believe that Jesus died
and rose again, even so, through Jesus, God will
bring with him those who have died.[d] 15For this
we declare to you by the word of the Lord, that
we who are alive, who are left until the coming
of the Lord, will by no means precede those who
have died.[d] 16For the Lord himself, with a cry
of command, with the archangel's call and with
the sound of God's trumpet, will descend from
heaven, and the dead in Christ will rise first.
17Then we who are alive, who are left, will be
caught up in the clouds together with them to
meet the Lord in the air; and so we will be with
the Lord forever. 18Therefore encourage one another with these words.

5 Now concerning the times and the seasons,
brothers and sisters,[c] you do not need to have
anything written to you. 2For you yourselves
know very well that the day of the Lord will come
like a thief in the night. 3When they say, "There
is peace and security," then sudden destruction
will come upon them, as labor pains come upon
a pregnant woman, and there will be no escape!
4But you, beloved,[c] are not in darkness, for that
day to surprise you like a thief; 5for you are all
children of light and children of the day; we are
not of the night or of darkness. 6So then let us
not fall asleep as others do, but let us keep awake
and be sober; 7for those who sleep sleep at night,
and those who are drunk get drunk at night. 8But
since we belong to the day, let us be sober, and
put on the breastplate of faith and love, and for
a helmet the hope of salvation. 9For God has
destined us not for wrath but for obtaining salvation through our Lord Jesus Christ, 10who died
for us, so that whether we are awake or asleep we
may live with him. 11Therefore encourage one
another and build up each other, as indeed you
are doing.

1 Thessalonians 5:3

Paul offers the Thessalonian assembly a strange assurance: they will not be surprised by the sudden day of the Lord as will those who falsely proclaim "peace and security." The Latin *pax et securitas* was one of the prominent themes of the Emperor Claudius's propaganda.

— ***NE***

12 But we appeal to you, brothers and sisters,[c] to respect those who labor among you, and
have charge of you in the Lord and admonish
you; 13esteem them very highly in love because
of their work. Be at peace among yourselves.
14And we urge you, beloved,[c] to admonish the
idlers, encourage the fainthearted, help the weak,
be patient with all of them. 15See that none of you
repays evil for evil, but always seek to do good to
one another and to all. 16Rejoice always, 17pray
without ceasing, 18give thanks in all circumstances; for this is the will of God in Christ Jesus
for you. 19Do not quench the Spirit. 20Do not

[a] Or *how to take a wife for himself* [b] Gk *brother* [c] Gk *brothers* [d] Gk *fallen asleep*

despise the words of prophets,[a] 21 but test everything; hold fast to what is good; 22 abstain from every form of evil.

23 May the God of peace himself sanctify you entirely; and may your spirit and soul and body be kept sound[b] and blameless at the coming of our Lord Jesus Christ. 24 The one who calls you is faithful, and he will do this.

25 Beloved,[c] pray for us.

26 Greet all the brothers and sisters[d] with a holy kiss. 27 I solemnly command you by the Lord that this letter be read to all of them.[e]

28 The grace of our Lord Jesus Christ be with you.[f]

[a] Gk *despise prophecies* [b] Or *complete* [c] Gk *Brothers* [d] Gk *brothers* [e] Gk *to all the brothers* [f] Other ancient authorities add *Amen*

The Second Letter of Paul to the Thessalonians

Written at an uncertain date, this short letter of friendly exhortation presupposes the continuation of the hostilities faced by Paul's assembly in Thessalonica (1 Thess 1:4). Likewise, it presupposes that there is, within and around this relatively new Christian community, an ongoing conflict, with one group being *the afflicted* and another being *the afflicters* (1:6). The letter bears striking formal similarities with 1 Thessalonians in its use of a simple letter opening (2 Thess 1:2; compare 1 Thess 1:1), repeated thanksgivings (2 Thess 1:3; 2:13; compare 1 Thess 1:2; 2:13), and an intercessory prayer (2 Thess 2:16-17; compare 1 Thess 3:11-13). But 2 Thessalonians depicts a deity who will exact an everlasting revenge upon the assembly's afflicters (1:6-9). Also different is the letter's presupposition of a *parousia,* a return of Jesus at an unspecified future time (2 Thess 2:1-12)—as opposed to 1 Thessalonians' support for an imminent parousia (1 Thess 4:13-18). Yet another difference is an emphasis on firm adherence to a set of Pauline traditions (2:15) as a basis for intra-group critique: against false teaching (the view that the day of the Lord, or parousia, has already come, 2:2) on the one hand; and against dissident or unruly behavior that contradicted the self-sufficiency ethos modeled earlier by the apostles (3:6-12), on the other.

The similarities lead some scholars to assume that Paul indeed wrote the letter shortly after writing 1 Thessalonians, with the differences then explained as a development in Paul's own teaching. Others, however, consider the similarities with 1 Thessalonians and other Pauline letters as a deliberate attempt by a later follower of Paul to imitate the apostle's words and style. They also find it difficult to believe that Paul would support an imminent parousia in 1 Thessalonians, shift to a delayed one in 2 Thessalonians, and then return to an imminent one in later letters (for example, 1 Cor 7:29; Rom 13:11; Phil 4:5). That the development of such a set of traditions, including an overall Pauline writing style (3:17), would not have been available until after the apostle's letters were collected, perhaps late in the first-century CE, becomes yet another reason for relegating the work to the category of deutero-Pauline (that is, from a second generation of Pauline tradition).

As an African American, I resonate with the letter's emphasis on group distinctiveness, an often necessary move for struggle-laden communities. Intra-group critique is also necessary lest parts of such communities romanticize their affliction beyond any possible critique of their cultural values or behaviors. Troubling, though, are the letter's presuppositions about the nature of the assembly's God, the reach of its love, and the rigid defining of its boundaries. Can a group harbor for long an image of a God who seeks everlasting revenge (1:9)? In opposition to the intra-group and extra-group love presupposed in 1 Thessalonians (3:12; cf. 5:15), the extent of the reach of the audience's love presupposed in 2 Thessalonians seems introverted (1:3). So too does the letter's clear and solid

boundaries between the afflicted and the afflicters (1:6). The use of apocalyptic rhetoric can impede the efforts of struggling, culturally distinctive communities to form just the coalitions that might help them come together for the common good.

— ***Abraham Smith***

1 Paul, Silvanus, and Timothy,
To the church of the Thessalonians in God
our Father and the Lord Jesus Christ:
2 Grace to you and peace from God our[a] Father and the Lord Jesus Christ.
3 We must always give thanks to God for you,
brothers and sisters,[b] as is right, because your faith
is growing abundantly, and the love of every one
of you for one another is increasing. 4 Therefore
we ourselves boast of you among the churches
of God for your steadfastness and faith during all
your persecutions and the afflictions that you are
enduring.
5 This is evidence of the righteous judgment
of God, and is intended to make you worthy of
the kingdom of God, for which you are also suffering. 6 For it is indeed just of God to repay with
affliction those who afflict you, 7 and to give relief to the afflicted as well as to us, when the Lord
Jesus is revealed from heaven with his mighty
angels 8 in flaming fire, inflicting vengeance on
those who do not know God and on those who
do not obey the gospel of our Lord Jesus. 9 These
will suffer the punishment of eternal destruction, separated from the presence of the Lord and
from the glory of his might, 10 when he comes to
be glorified by his saints and to be marveled at
on that day among all who have believed, because
our testimony to you was believed. 11 To this end
we always pray for you, asking that our God will
make you worthy of his call and will fulfill by his
power every good resolve and work of faith, 12 so
that the name of our Lord Jesus may be glorified
in you, and you in him, according to the grace of
our God and the Lord Jesus Christ.

2 As to the coming of our Lord Jesus Christ
and our being gathered together to him, we
beg you, brothers and sisters,[b] 2 not to be quickly
shaken in mind or alarmed, either by spirit or by
word or by letter, as though from us, to the effect that the day of the Lord is already here. 3 Let
no one deceive you in any way; for that day will
not come unless the rebellion comes first and the
lawless one[c] is revealed, the one destined for destruction.[d] 4 He opposes and exalts himself above
every so-called god or object of worship, so that
he takes his seat in the temple of God, declaring
himself to be God. 5 Do you not remember that I
told you these things when I was still with you?

2 Thessalonians 2:3-7

The author obviously expects his audience to understand references to both the "lawless one" and the thing (or person) that restrains him. Some have proposed that the Roman Empire is the lawless one (pointing out that Gaius, "Caligula," sought to erect a statue of himself inside the Jerusalem temple); others, that the empire is itself the restraining force, delaying the descent into greater lawlessness.

— ***NE***

[a] Other ancient authorities read *the* [b] Gk *brothers* [c] Gk *the man of lawlessness;* other ancient authorities read *the man of sin* [d] Gk *the son of destruction*

6And you know what is now restraining him, so
that he may be revealed when his time comes.
7For the mystery of lawlessness is already at
work, but only until the one who now restrains
it is removed. 8And then the lawless one will be
revealed, whom the Lord Jesus[a] will destroy[b]
with the breath of his mouth, annihilating him
by the manifestation of his coming. 9The coming
of the lawless one is apparent in the working of
Satan, who uses all power, signs, lying wonders,
10and every kind of wicked deception for those
who are perishing, because they refused to love
the truth and so be saved. 11For this reason God
sends them a powerful delusion, leading them to
believe what is false, 12so that all who have not
believed the truth but took pleasure in unrighteousness will be condemned.

13 But we must always give thanks to God
for you, brothers and sisters[c] beloved by the
Lord, because God chose you as the first fruits[d]
for salvation through sanctification by the Spirit
and through belief in the truth. 14For this purpose he called you through our proclamation of
the good news,[e] so that you may obtain the glory
of our Lord Jesus Christ. 15So then, brothers and
sisters,[c] stand firm and hold fast to the traditions
that you were taught by us, either by word of
mouth or by our letter.

16 Now may our Lord Jesus Christ himself
and God our Father, who loved us and through
grace gave us eternal comfort and good hope,
17comfort your hearts and strengthen them in every good work and word.

3 Finally, brothers and sisters,[c] pray for us, so
that the word of the Lord may spread rapidly
and be glorified everywhere, just as it is among
you, 2and that we may be rescued from wicked
and evil people; for not all have faith. 3But the
Lord is faithful; he will strengthen you and guard
you from the evil one.[f] 4And we have confidence
in the Lord concerning you, that you are doing
and will go on doing the things that we command. 5May the Lord direct your hearts to the
love of God and to the steadfastness of Christ.

6 Now we command you, beloved,[c] in the
name of our Lord Jesus Christ, to keep away from
believers who are[g] living in idleness and not according to the tradition that they[h] received from
us. 7For you yourselves know how you ought to
imitate us; we were not idle when we were with
you, 8and we did not eat anyone's bread without
paying for it; but with toil and labor we worked
night and day, so that we might not burden any
of you. 9This was not because we do not have
that right, but in order to give you an example to
imitate. 10For even when we were with you, we
gave you this command: Anyone unwilling to
work should not eat. 11For we hear that some of
you are living in idleness, mere busybodies, not
doing any work. 12Now such persons we command and exhort in the Lord Jesus Christ to do
their work quietly and to earn their own living.
13Brothers and sisters,[i] do not be weary in doing
what is right.

14 Take note of those who do not obey what
we say in this letter; have nothing to do with them,
so that they may be ashamed. 15Do not regard
them as enemies, but warn them as believers.[j]

16 Now may the Lord of peace himself give
you peace at all times in all ways. The Lord be
with all of you.

17 I, Paul, write this greeting with my own
hand. This is the mark in every letter of mine; it
is the way I write. 18The grace of our Lord Jesus
Christ be with all of you.[k]

[a] Other ancient authorities lack *Jesus* [b] Other ancient authorities read *consume* [c] Gk *brothers* [d] Other ancient authorities read *from the beginning* [e] Or *through our gospel* [f] Or *from evil* [g] Gk *from every brother who is* [h] Other ancient authorities read *you* [i] Gk *Brothers* [j] Gk *a brother* [k] Other ancient authorities add *Amen*

The First Letter of Paul to Timothy

The first of the Pastoral Epistles is addressed to Timothy, Paul's coworker ("my loyal child in the faith," 1 Tim 1:2). In it, Paul describes his personal life as he ministers to other Christians. Some readers of 1 Timothy have criticized the letter because it appears to bow down to the surrounding culture. For example, it is urged that Christian women be silent and not teach (2:11-15), and that Christian slaves be subservient (6:1-2). These statements (which seem to refer to a later period of the church), differences in style and theological terms, and the lack of support in Acts (19:22) regarding Paul's request to Timothy "to remain in Ephesus" (1:3) have led some scholars to conclude that Paul could never have written this letter and to date it as late as the second century CE. Scholars who support Paul's authorship date it during his lifetime, usually between 62 and 64, assuming it was written after Paul was released from prison in Rome (see Acts 28:30-31) and before he was imprisoned a final time in Rome.

It is a letter of paradoxes, with positive exhortations to some and negative judgments to others (for example, 1:18-20). It advances love and mercy as well as orthodoxy.

The letter purports to be written by Paul to Timothy—that is, by one multicultural person to another multicultural person, for the sake of a multicultural church. Paul, a Jew and zealous enforcer of Jewish law, was reared in Tarsus, outside Judea, in the Diaspora. Tarsus, in Asia Minor, represented a harmonious balance of East and West; both Greek and Aramaic were spoken there. According to the Acts of the Apostles, Paul's parents were Roman citizens (Acts 22:28). Thus, Paul was reared in a multicultural setting, yet he traveled to Jerusalem to learn rabbinic law (Acts 22:3). Paul's coworker, Timothy, is a Jew on his mother's side, but his father is a Gentile (1 Tim 1:2; see Acts 16:1-3). He is also from Asia Minor (Lystra).

Ephesus (1:3) was itself a multicultural city. It was the greatest city of the province of Asia, set at a key intersection for trade. It had a synagogue (Acts 19:8) and Jews who were Roman citizens. Yet Ephesus also was well known for the study and practice of magic (Acts 19:18-19) and for the temple of the goddess Artemis, the largest temple of the ancient world. In the Roman period, the worship of Artemis represented a syncretistic (that is, a mixed or blended) belief system.

Although Paul and Timothy could be described as multicultural people living in multicultural settings, the doctrines to which Paul is represented here as urging Timothy to hold fast are not at all syncretistic (1:3-7; 6:3). In this letter of lessons in church guidance and opposition to false teachings, truth is an important theme, as is a "healthy" or "wholesome teaching" (phrases repeated throughout the letter). Elders or overseers are important for teaching truth (1:3; 3:2; 5:17). Some teachers at Ephesus were promoting myths, endless genealogies, speculations, fruitless discussions, godless chatter, and contradictions (1:3-6; 4:7; 6:3-4, 20). Timothy is urged to guard the message he has received and avoid false knowledge (6:20).

As a multicultural person myself (my mother is from Puerto Rico, my father is from the Netherlands, and I was born and reared in the Dominican Republic, but I have lived in the United States since sixth grade), I can affirm the multicultural aspect of the communication in 1 Timothy. Although the accommodation to the larger culture's codes of subordination poses a challenge for many today, we can regard the Paul who speaks here and the Timothy who is addressed as constructing a bridge to reach others in their different cultures. First, they affirm that despite differences among people, all can have the same Savior (God is "our Savior" and Jesus "our hope," 1:1). God bridges all cultures and desires everyone to be saved and to come to a knowledge of the truth (1:15; 2:3-6; 4:10). Second, prayer is for everyone, no matter their social, political, or economic class (2:1-2). The author even advocated that older widows be part of a praying order (5:5). Third, despite different cultures, all can share similar values. The descriptions for overseers (bishop) and ministers (deacons) are built on such widely accepted character attributes as godliness, not being quarrelsome, not loving money, not living for pleasure, and not being a gossip (2:2, 8-10; 3:2-8; 4:7-8; 5:6, 11, 13; 6:2-3, 5-10, 17-18). Being "above reproach" (3:2, 7; 5:7, 14, 25) would help believers lead a "quiet and peaceable life" (2:2) so that more of the Greek and Jewish people might indeed "come to the knowledge of the truth" (2:4). This letter holds firm on the basic truths of the gospel yet encourages the sorts of virtues that would help advance the proclamation of the gospel in the larger culture.

— ***Aída Besançon Spencer***

1 Paul, an apostle of Christ Jesus by the command of God our Savior and of Christ Jesus
our hope,
2 To Timothy, my loyal child in the faith:
Grace, mercy, and peace from God the Father
and Christ Jesus our Lord.

3 I urge you, as I did when I was on my way
to Macedonia, to remain in Ephesus so that you
may instruct certain people not to teach any different doctrine, 4and not to occupy themselves
with myths and endless genealogies that promote
speculations rather than the divine training[a] that
is known by faith. 5But the aim of such instruction is love that comes from a pure heart, a good
conscience, and sincere faith. 6Some people have
deviated from these and turned to meaningless
talk, 7desiring to be teachers of the law, without
understanding either what they are saying or the
things about which they make assertions.

8 Now we know that the law is good, if one
uses it legitimately. 9This means understanding
that the law is laid down not for the innocent but
for the lawless and disobedient, for the godless
and sinful, for the unholy and profane, for those
who kill their father or mother, for murderers,

[a] Or *plan*

10fornicators, sodomites, slave traders, liars, per-
jurers, and whatever else is contrary to the sound
teaching 11that conforms to the glorious gospel
of the blessed God, which he entrusted to me.

12 I am grateful to Christ Jesus our Lord, who
has strengthened me, because he judged me faithful and appointed me to his service, 13even though
I was formerly a blasphemer, a persecutor, and a
man of violence. But I received mercy because I
had acted ignorantly in unbelief, 14and the grace
of our Lord overflowed for me with the faith and
love that are in Christ Jesus. 15The saying is sure
and worthy of full acceptance, that Christ Jesus
came into the world to save sinners—of whom I
am the foremost. 16But for that very reason I received mercy, so that in me, as the foremost, Jesus
Christ might display the utmost patience, making
me an example to those who would come to believe in him for eternal life. 17To the King of the
ages, immortal, invisible, the only God, be honor
and glory forever and ever.[a] Amen.

18 I am giving you these instructions, Timothy, my child, in accordance with the prophecies
made earlier about you, so that by following them
you may fight the good fight, 19having faith and
a good conscience. By rejecting conscience, certain persons have suffered shipwreck in the faith;
20among them are Hymenaeus and Alexander,
whom I have turned over to Satan, so that they
may learn not to blaspheme.

2 First of all, then, I urge that supplications,
prayers, intercessions, and thanksgivings be
made for everyone, 2for kings and all who are in
high positions, so that we may lead a quiet and
peaceable life in all godliness and dignity. 3This
is right and is acceptable in the sight of God our
Savior, 4who desires everyone to be saved and to
come to the knowledge of the truth. 5For

there is one God;
there is also one mediator between God
and humankind,
Christ Jesus, himself human,
6 who gave himself a ransom for all

—this was attested at the right time. 7For this I
was appointed a herald and an apostle (I am telling the truth,[b] I am not lying), a teacher of the
Gentiles in faith and truth.

8 I desire, then, that in every place the men
should pray, lifting up holy hands without anger or argument; 9also that the women should
dress themselves modestly and decently in suitable clothing, not with their hair braided, or with
gold, pearls, or expensive clothes, 10but with
good works, as is proper for women who profess
reverence for God. 11Let a woman[c] learn in silence with full submission. 12I permit no woman[c]
to teach or to have authority over a man;[d] she
is to keep silent. 13For Adam was formed first,
then Eve; 14and Adam was not deceived, but the
woman was deceived and became a transgressor.

[a] Gk *to the ages of the ages* [b] Other ancient authorities add *in Christ* [c] Or *wife* [d] Or *her husband*

1 Timothy 2:1-2

The author instructs Timothy to pray for kings and all others in authority so that we may have a calm and quiet life. Many within the church have historically made an alliance with the state so that law and order can prevail. There is nothing wrong with law and order, but as those who have struggled for civil rights have asked, *whose* law and *whose* order? Preserving public tranquility has often been the justification used to maintain unjust social structures. Those who question kings and those in authority are quickly labeled "outside agitators." Those who lived privileged lives as Roman citizens (like Paul himself, according to Acts) could, if they chose, live a "quiet and peaceable life," but slaves and the conquered have no such choice. What they might have desired instead was to *disrupt* the quiet and peaceable life of the privileged! The disenfranchised may join the author of 1 Timothy in praying for the king and those in authority, but I suspect the content of their prayers will be somewhat different.

— MDLT

15 Yet she will be saved through childbearing, provided they continue in faith and love and holiness, with modesty.

3 The saying is sure:[a] whoever aspires to the office of bishop[b] desires a noble task. 2 Now a bishop[c] must be above reproach, married only once,[d] temperate, sensible, respectable, hospitable, an apt teacher, 3 not a drunkard, not violent but gentle, not quarrelsome, and not a lover of money. 4 He must manage his own household well, keeping his children submissive and respectful in every way— 5 for if someone does not know how to manage his own household, how can he take care of God's church? 6 He must not be a recent convert, or he may be puffed up with conceit and fall into the condemnation of the devil. 7 Moreover, he must be well thought of by outsiders, so that he may not fall into disgrace and the snare of the devil.

8 Deacons likewise must be serious, not double-tongued, not indulging in much wine, not greedy for money; 9 they must hold fast to the mystery of the faith with a clear conscience. 10 And let them first be tested; then, if they prove themselves blameless, let them serve as deacons. 11 Women[e] likewise must be serious, not slanderers, but temperate, faithful in all things. 12 Let deacons be married only once,[f] and let them manage their children and their households well; 13 for those who serve well as deacons gain a good standing for themselves and great boldness in the faith that is in Christ Jesus.

14 I hope to come to you soon, but I am writing these instructions to you so that, 15 if I am delayed, you may know how one ought to behave in the household of God, which is the church of the living God, the pillar and bulwark of the truth. 16 Without any doubt, the mystery of our religion is great:

He[g] was revealed in flesh,
vindicated[h] in spirit,[i]
seen by angels,
proclaimed among Gentiles,
believed in throughout the world,
taken up in glory.

4 Now the Spirit expressly says that in later[j] times some will renounce the faith by paying attention to deceitful spirits and teachings of demons, 2 through the hypocrisy of liars whose consciences are seared with a hot iron. 3 They forbid marriage and demand abstinence from foods, which God created to be received with thanksgiving by those who believe and know the truth. 4 For everything created by God is good, and nothing is to be rejected, provided it is received with thanksgiving; 5 for it is sanctified by God's word and by prayer.

6 If you put these instructions before the brothers and sisters,[k] you will be a good servant[l] of Christ Jesus, nourished on the words of the faith and of the sound teaching that you have followed. 7 Have nothing to do with profane myths and old wives' tales. Train yourself in godliness, 8 for, while physical training is of some value, godliness is valuable in every way, holding promise for both the present life and the life to come. 9 The saying is sure and worthy of full acceptance. 10 For

1 Timothy 4:7

In the third-century *Acts of Paul,* Thekla, who has been converted by Paul's preaching, travels independently of him but as a colleague and an equal, and her preaching draws women away from their pagan husbands, fiancés, and fathers. Some scholars have argued that the author of 1 Timothy seeks to suppress just such provocative narratives by dismissing them as "old wives' tales" and by seeking to limit the possibilities for women's independent action—and indeed to silence them in the context of the assembly.

— *NE*

[a] Some interpreters place these words at the end of the previous paragraph. Other ancient authorities read *The saying is commonly accepted* [b] Or *overseer* [c] Or *an overseer* [d] Gk *the husband of one wife* [e] Or *Their wives,* or *Women deacons* [f] Gk *be husbands of one wife* [g] Gk *Who;* other ancient authorities read *God;* others, *Which* [h] Or *justified* [i] Or *by the Spirit* [j] Or *the last* [k] Gk *brothers* [l] Or *deacon*

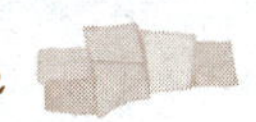

to this end we toil and struggle,[a] because we have
our hope set on the living God, who is the Savior
of all people, especially of those who believe.

11 These are the things you must insist on
and teach. 12Let no one despise your youth, but
set the believers an example in speech and conduct, in love, in faith, in purity. 13Until I arrive,
give attention to the public reading of scripture,[b]
to exhorting, to teaching. 14Do not neglect the
gift that is in you, which was given to you through
prophecy with the laying on of hands by the
council of elders.[c] 15Put these things into practice, devote yourself to them, so that all may see
your progress. 16Pay close attention to yourself
and to your teaching; continue in these things,
for in doing this you will save both yourself and
your hearers.

5 Do not speak harshly to an older man,[d] but
speak to him as to a father, to younger men as
brothers, 2to older women as mothers, to younger women as sisters—with absolute purity.

3 Honor widows who are really widows. 4If a
widow has children or grandchildren, they should
first learn their religious duty to their own family
and make some repayment to their parents; for
this is pleasing in God's sight. 5The real widow,
left alone, has set her hope on God and continues
in supplications and prayers night and day; 6but
the widow[e] who lives for pleasure is dead even
while she lives. 7Give these commands as well, so
that they may be above reproach. 8And whoever
does not provide for relatives, and especially for
family members, has denied the faith and is worse
than an unbeliever.

9 Let a widow be put on the list if she is not
less than sixty years old and has been married
only once;[f] 10she must be well attested for her
good works, as one who has brought up children,
shown hospitality, washed the saints' feet, helped
the afflicted, and devoted herself to doing good
in every way. 11But refuse to put younger widows
on the list; for when their sensual desires alienate them from Christ, they want to marry, 12and
so they incur condemnation for having violated
their first pledge. 13Besides that, they learn to be
idle, gadding about from house to house; and
they are not merely idle, but also gossips and
busybodies, saying what they should not say.
14So I would have younger widows marry, bear
children, and manage their households, so as to
give the adversary no occasion to revile us. 15For
some have already turned away to follow Satan.
16If any believing woman[g] has relatives who are
really widows, let her assist them; let the church
not be burdened, so that it can assist those who
are real widows.

17 Let the elders who rule well be considered
worthy of double honor,[h] especially those who labor in preaching and teaching; 18for the scripture
says, "You shall not muzzle an ox while it is treading out the grain," and, "The laborer deserves to
be paid." 19Never accept any accusation against
an elder except on the evidence of two or three
witnesses. 20As for those who persist in sin, rebuke them in the presence of all, so that the rest
also may stand in fear. 21In the presence of God
and of Christ Jesus and of the elect angels, I warn
you to keep these instructions without prejudice,
doing nothing on the basis of partiality. 22Do not
ordain[i] anyone hastily, and do not participate in
the sins of others; keep yourself pure.

23 No longer drink only water, but take a
little wine for the sake of your stomach and your
frequent ailments.

24 The sins of some people are conspicuous
and precede them to judgment, while the sins of
others follow them there. 25So also good works
are conspicuous; and even when they are not,
they cannot remain hidden.

6 Let all who are under the yoke of slavery
regard their masters as worthy of all honor,
so that the name of God and the teaching may
not be blasphemed. 2Those who have believing

[a] Other ancient authorities read *suffer reproach* [b] Gk *to the reading* [c] Gk *by the presbytery* [d] Or *an elder, or a presbyter* [e] Gk *she* [f] Gk *the wife of one husband* [g] Other ancient authorities read *believing man or woman;* others, *believing man* [h] Or *compensation* [i] Gk *Do not lay hands on*

masters must not be disrespectful to them on the
ground that they are members of the church;[a]
rather they must serve them all the more, since
those who benefit by their service are believers
and beloved.[b]

Teach and urge these duties. 3 Whoever teaches
otherwise and does not agree with the sound
words of our Lord Jesus Christ and the teaching
that is in accordance with godliness, 4 is conceited,
understanding nothing, and has a morbid craving for controversy and for disputes about words.
From these come envy, dissension, slander, base
suspicions, 5 and wrangling among those who are
depraved in mind and bereft of the truth, imagining that godliness is a means of gain.[c] 6 Of course,
there is great gain in godliness combined with
contentment; 7 for we brought nothing into the
world, so that[d] we can take nothing out of it; 8 but
if we have food and clothing, we will be content
with these. 9 But those who want to be rich fall
into temptation and are trapped by many senseless and harmful desires that plunge people into
ruin and destruction. 10 For the love of money is
a root of all kinds of evil, and in their eagerness to
be rich some have wandered away from the faith
and pierced themselves with many pains.

11 But as for you, man of God, shun all this;
pursue righteousness, godliness, faith, love, endurance, gentleness. 12 Fight the good fight of the
faith; take hold of the eternal life, to which you
were called and for which you made[e] the good
confession in the presence of many witnesses.
13 In the presence of God, who gives life to all
things, and of Christ Jesus, who in his testimony
before Pontius Pilate made the good confession,
I charge you 14 to keep the commandment without spot or blame until the manifestation of our
Lord Jesus Christ, 15 which he will bring about at
the right time—he who is the blessed and only
Sovereign, the King of kings and Lord of lords.
16 It is he alone who has immortality and dwells
in unapproachable light, whom no one has ever
seen or can see; to him be honor and eternal dominion. Amen.

17 As for those who in the present age are
rich, command them not to be haughty, or to set
their hopes on the uncertainty of riches, but rather
on God who richly provides us with everything
for our enjoyment. 18 They are to do good, to be
rich in good works, generous, and ready to share,
19 thus storing up for themselves the treasure of a
good foundation for the future, so that they may
take hold of the life that really is life.

20 Timothy, guard what has been entrusted
to you. Avoid the profane chatter and contradictions of what is falsely called knowledge; 21 by
professing it some have missed the mark as regards the faith.

Grace be with you.[f]

[a] Gk *are brothers* [b] Or *since they are believers and beloved, who devote themselves to good deeds*
[c] Other ancient authorities add *Withdraw yourself from such people* [d] Other ancient authorities read *world—it is certain that* [e] Gk *confessed*
[f] The Greek word for *you* here is plural; in other ancient authorities it is singular. Other ancient authorities add *Amen*

The Second Letter of Paul to

Timothy

TRADITIONALLY, 2 TIMOTHY IS CONSIDERED Paul's last letter before his death. On this view, Paul had been released from prison in Rome (Acts 28:30-31) but now has been imprisoned again in Rome after Nero has begun to persecute Christians (64–68 CE). Paul no longer expects to be released (2 Tim 4:6-8; cf. Phlm v. 22; Phil 2:24). Some scholars note some good reasons to accept Paul's authorship, particularly the personal elements in the correspondence. Nevertheless, based on chronological discrepancies between the imprisonments recounted in Acts and this letter (1:16, 17; 2:9; 4:16-17), other scholars question Paul's authorship of this letter.

Second Timothy has some themes in common with 1 Timothy and Titus, including sound teaching and truth (1:5, 13; 2:2, 14-15, 18, 24-25; 3:6-8, 10, 14-17; 4:2-4) and God as Savior (1:8-10; 2:10; 3:15). The virtues recommended for elders in those letters (1 Tim 3:2-3; Titus 1:7-9; 2:3, 5) are also recommended to Timothy here—good works, not being quarrelsome, apt teaching, and patience (2:21-24); similar problems in the church are addressed here—wrangling over words, profane chatter, senseless controversies, and myths (2:14, 16-17, 23; 3:2-8; 4:3-4); and the importance of conscience, self-control, faith, love, peace, and godliness are affirmed here as well (1:3, 7; 2:22; 3:2-5, 12, 16-17). These observations suggest to many scholars that the three letters came from the same hand—whether Paul's or another's.

But 2 Timothy is primarily about the need for community in the midst of suffering. This letter purports to be a personal communication from the apostle Paul to the evangelist Timothy to help him succeed as a Christian and as a minister. Thus, the author begins by calling Timothy "my beloved child," a term of endearment Paul uses in the singular only for Timothy (1:2; see 1 Cor 4:14, 17; Eph 5:1). Paul appears here to have an emotionally expressive relationship with Timothy. As his spiritual father, he does not hesitate to exhort Timothy: "I remind you" ... "Do not be ashamed" ... "Hold to the standard" ... "Guard" (1:6, 8, 13, 14). He also exhorts Timothy to remind and warn the church (2:14). These imperatives evidently flow from a warm relationship.

The author's main goal is to encourage Timothy to share in suffering with him (1:8; 2:3, 9; 4:5). We learn in Acts that Timothy was reared in Lystra as a devout Jew, though having a Gentile father (Acts 16:1), and that he was present at Antioch of Pisidia, Iconium, and Lystra when, after enthusiastic initial responses, unbelieving Jews stirred up persecution against Paul and Barnabas, eventually even stoning Paul almost to death (2 Tim 3:10-11; Acts 13:13—14:22). The letter reminds Timothy of those persecutions and how the Lord rescued him from all of them (2 Tim 3:11-12).

The author urges Timothy to recognize the importance of human community even when God strengthens the individual believer (2 Tim 4:17). Households were an important aspect of the early church. This letter provides some of the most intimate relational and familial language in the

Pauline corpus. Here we read that Paul deeply appreciates the household of Onesiphorus, who, not being ashamed that Paul was imprisoned, searched for him in Rome and many times "refreshed" him (1:16-17); Paul uses the same language to describe how Stephanas's household had refreshed him in Corinth (1 Cor 16:18). In other households, the author notes, some in the women's quarters have still not learned the truth (2 Tim 3:6-7; compare 1 Tim 2:11), but Prisca and Aquila remain constant (2 Tim 4:19), and Eunice and Lois have passed on their faith to their son and grandson Timothy (1:5; 3:15). Paul asks that the Lord repay Onesiphorus's household with the same mercy they displayed (2 Tim 1:16, 18). After all, Paul is a dangerous person to visit; his visitor might be imprisoned too. Even Timothy, when he arrives with Paul's winter cloak and parchment writing materials (4:13, 21), might be imprisoned (as eventually he is, according to Heb 13:23). Paul even seeks the company of Mark (4:11), whom, according to Acts, he once had not been willing to accept as a coworker (Acts 13:13; 15:37-40). Now, it would appear, they are reconciled, even though all Paul's friends from Asia have "turned away" from him (1:15). Demas, who had (according to Col 4:14) been with Paul in the first imprisonment, has now deserted him (4:10). Even Titus has left (4:10).

The letter ends with pathos: "Only Luke is with me" (4:11). At the end, the zealous Jew has only a Gentile Christian with him. During Paul's first imprisonment he was under house arrest (see Acts 28:30; Phil 1:12-13), but according to tradition, Paul's final imprisonment and execution took place in a former dungeon, the Tullianum.

When you are a multicultural person such as I, sometimes you may feel anomie—without country or a standard of truth. Second Timothy reminds us of the importance of the community we experience with family and church, as well as the importance that Scripture holds for Christians in any culture—especially in the midst of suffering for faith in Jesus Christ.

— Aída Besançon Spencer

1 Paul, an apostle of Christ Jesus by the will of
God, for the sake of the promise of life that is
in Christ Jesus,
2 To Timothy, my beloved child:
Grace, mercy, and peace from God the Father
and Christ Jesus our Lord.

3 I am grateful to God—whom I worship
with a clear conscience, as my ancestors did—
when I remember you constantly in my prayers
night and day. [4]Recalling your tears, I long to
see you so that I may be filled with joy. [5]I am reminded of your sincere faith, a faith that lived
first in your grandmother Lois and your mother
Eunice and now, I am sure, lives in you. [6]For this
reason I remind you to rekindle the gift of God
that is within you through the laying on of my
hands; [7]for God did not give us a spirit of cowardice, but rather a spirit of power and of love and
of self-discipline.
8 Do not be ashamed, then, of the testimony
about our Lord or of me his prisoner, but join
with me in suffering for the gospel, relying on the
power of God, [9]who saved us and called us with a

holy calling, not according to our works but according to his own purpose and grace. This grace
was given to us in Christ Jesus before the ages
began, 10but it has now been revealed through
the appearing of our Savior Christ Jesus, who
abolished death and brought life and immortality to light through the gospel. 11For this gospel
I was appointed a herald and an apostle and a
teacher,[a] 12and for this reason I suffer as I do. But
I am not ashamed, for I know the one in whom
I have put my trust, and I am sure that he is able
to guard until that day what I have entrusted to
him.[b] 13Hold to the standard of sound teaching
that you have heard from me, in the faith and
love that are in Christ Jesus. 14Guard the good
treasure entrusted to you, with the help of the
Holy Spirit living in us.

15 You are aware that all who are in Asia have
turned away from me, including Phygelus and
Hermogenes. 16May the Lord grant mercy to
the household of Onesiphorus, because he often
refreshed me and was not ashamed of my chain;
17when he arrived in Rome, he eagerly[c] searched
for me and found me 18—may the Lord grant
that he will find mercy from the Lord on that
day! And you know very well how much service
he rendered in Ephesus.

2 You then, my child, be strong in the grace
that is in Christ Jesus; 2and what you have
heard from me through many witnesses entrust
to faithful people who will be able to teach others as well. 3Share in suffering like a good soldier
of Christ Jesus. 4No one serving in the army gets
entangled in everyday affairs; the soldier's aim is
to please the enlisting officer. 5And in the case of
an athlete, no one is crowned without competing
according to the rules. 6It is the farmer who does
the work who ought to have the first share of the
crops. 7Think over what I say, for the Lord will
give you understanding in all things.

8 Remember Jesus Christ, raised from the
dead, a descendant of David—that is my gospel,
9for which I suffer hardship, even to the point of
being chained like a criminal. But the word of
God is not chained. 10Therefore I endure everything for the sake of the elect, so that they may
also obtain the salvation that is in Christ Jesus,
with eternal glory. 11The saying is sure:

If we have died with him, we will also live
with him;
12 if we endure, we will also reign with him;
if we deny him, he will also deny us;
13 if we are faithless, he remains faithful—
for he cannot deny himself.

14 Remind them of this, and warn them before God[d] that they are to avoid wrangling over
words, which does no good but only ruins those
who are listening. 15Do your best to present yourself to God as one approved by him, a worker
who has no need to be ashamed, rightly explaining the word of truth. 16Avoid profane chatter, for
it will lead people into more and more impiety,
17and their talk will spread like gangrene. Among
them are Hymenaeus and Philetus, 18who have
swerved from the truth by claiming that the
resurrection has already taken place. They are
upsetting the faith of some. 19But God's firm
foundation stands, bearing this inscription: "The
Lord knows those who are his," and, "Let everyone who calls on the name of the Lord turn away
from wickedness."

20 In a large house there are utensils not only
of gold and silver but also of wood and clay, some
for special use, some for ordinary. 21All who
cleanse themselves of the things I have mentioned[e]
will become special utensils, dedicated and useful
to the owner of the house, ready for every good
work. 22Shun youthful passions and pursue righteousness, faith, love, and peace, along with those
who call on the Lord from a pure heart. 23Have
nothing to do with stupid and senseless controversies; you know that they breed quarrels. 24And
the Lord's servant[f] must not be quarrelsome but
kindly to everyone, an apt teacher, patient, 25cor-
recting opponents with gentleness. God may
perhaps grant that they will repent and come to
know the truth, 26and that they may escape from

[a] Other ancient authorities add *of the Gentiles* [b] Or *what has been entrusted to me* [c] Or *promptly* [d] Other ancient authorities read *the Lord* [e] Gk *of these things* [f] Gk *slave*

the snare of the devil, having been held captive by
him to do his will.[a]

3 You must understand this, that in the last
days distressing times will come. 2For people
will be lovers of themselves, lovers of money,
boasters, arrogant, abusive, disobedient to their
parents, ungrateful, unholy, 3inhuman, impla-
cable, slanderers, profligates, brutes, haters of
good, 4treacherous, reckless, swollen with conceit, lovers of pleasure rather than lovers of God,
5holding to the outward form of godliness but denying its power. Avoid them! 6For among them
are those who make their way into households
and captivate silly women, overwhelmed by their
sins and swayed by all kinds of desires, 7who are
always being instructed and can never arrive at a
knowledge of the truth. 8As Jannes and Jambres
opposed Moses, so these people, of corrupt mind
and counterfeit faith, also oppose the truth. 9But
they will not make much progress, because, as in
the case of those two men,[b] their folly will become plain to everyone.

10 Now you have observed my teaching, my
conduct, my aim in life, my faith, my patience, my
love, my steadfastness, 11my persecutions, and
my suffering the things that happened to me in
Antioch, Iconium, and Lystra. What persecutions
I endured! Yet the Lord rescued me from all of
them. 12Indeed, all who want to live a godly life
in Christ Jesus will be persecuted. 13But wicked
people and impostors will go from bad to worse,
deceiving others and being deceived. 14But as
for you, continue in what you have learned and
firmly believed, knowing from whom you learned
it, 15and how from childhood you have known
the sacred writings that are able to instruct you
for salvation through faith in Christ Jesus. 16All
scripture is inspired by God and is[c] useful for
teaching, for reproof, for correction, and for
training in righteousness, 17so that everyone who
belongs to God may be proficient, equipped for
every good work.

4 In the presence of God and of Christ Jesus,
who is to judge the living and the dead,
and in view of his appearing and his kingdom, I
solemnly urge you: 2proclaim the message; be
persistent whether the time is favorable or unfavorable; convince, rebuke, and encourage, with
the utmost patience in teaching. 3For the time is
coming when people will not put up with sound
doctrine, but having itching ears, they will accu-
mulate for themselves teachers to suit their own
desires, 4and will turn away from listening to the
truth and wander away to myths. 5As for you, always be sober, endure suffering, do the work of
an evangelist, carry out your ministry fully.

6 As for me, I am already being poured out as
a libation, and the time of my departure has come.
7I have fought the good fight, I have finished the
race, I have kept the faith. 8From now on there
is reserved for me the crown of righteousness,
which the Lord, the righteous judge, will give me
on that day, and not only to me but also to all who
have longed for his appearing.

2 Timothy 4:6

Part of the pathos of this letter is the apostle's rather melancholy retrospective over his career—as if it is now finished. This might be the apostle's own reflection as he looks back at his life in anticipation of its end; or it might be the technique of a later writer who wishes to draw on the pathos of Paul's last days to bolster his own message—and in so doing augment the power of the apostle's developing legend.

—*NE*

9 Do your best to come to me soon, 10for Demas, in love with this present world, has deserted
me and gone to Thessalonica; Crescens has gone
to Galatia,[d] Titus to Dalmatia. 11Only Luke is
with me. Get Mark and bring him with you, for
he is useful in my ministry. 12I have sent Tychicus
to Ephesus. 13When you come, bring the cloak
that I left with Carpus at Troas, also the books,

[a] Or *by him, to do his* (that is, God's) *will* [b] Gk lacks *two men* [c] Or *Every scripture inspired by God is also*
[d] Other ancient authorities read *Gaul*

and above all the parchments. 14Alexander the
coppersmith did me great harm; the Lord will pay
him back for his deeds. 15You also must beware of
him, for he strongly opposed our message.

16 At my first defense no one came to my support, but all deserted me. May it not be counted
against them! 17But the Lord stood by me and
gave me strength, so that through me the message might be fully proclaimed and all the Gentiles might hear it. So I was rescued from the lion's
mouth. 18The Lord will rescue me from every evil
attack and save me for his heavenly kingdom. To
him be the glory forever and ever. Amen.

19 Greet Prisca and Aquila, and the household of Onesiphorus. 20Erastus remained in
Corinth; Trophimus I left ill in Miletus. 21Do
your best to come before winter. Eubulus sends
greetings to you, as do Pudens and Linus and
Claudia and all the brothers and sisters.[a]

22 The Lord be with your spirit. Grace be
with you.[b]

[a] Gk *all the brothers* [b] The Greek word for *you* here is plural. Other ancient authorities add *Amen*

The Letter of Paul to Titus

As with 1 and 2 Timothy, many scholars question whether the Apostle Paul himself wrote the letter to Titus. Because Crete is never mentioned in Paul's other letters—according to Acts, he was taken there only as a prisoner en route to Rome (Acts 27:7-13)—and because of differences in style and message from Paul's unquestioned writings similar to those evident in 1 and 2 Timothy, these scholars consider Titus a deutero-Pauline letter and date it as late as the second century CE, attributing it to the same hand that authored those letters. Scholars who hold to Pauline authorship date Titus to a time after Paul was released from prison in Rome (that is, between 62 and 64—or perhaps as late as 67).

Titus first appears in the narrative of Acts in Antioch in Syria, accompanying Paul on a relief visit to Jerusalem (Acts 11:29-30; see 15:2-4; Gal 2:1-3). As Paul's coworker and partner, he helped arrange the relief collection for the poor in Judea and was urged to go to Corinth as Paul's representative (2 Cor 2:13; 7:6-7; 8:6, 16-17, 23; 12:18). At Corinth he functions as a peacemaker and as a representative of the Corinthians to Paul (2 Cor 7:6-7, 15).

As the letter now represents the situation, Paul left Titus behind in Crete to "put in order what remained to be done," which included appointing elders for every city (Titus 1:5). He commands Titus to act "with all authority" and allow no one to "look down on you" (2:15). And no wonder, because Titus is an uncircumcised Greek who has to silence "those of the circumcision" (Titus 1:10-11; see Gal 2:3)! Paul further encourages Titus by addressing him as "my loyal child in the faith we share" (1:4; 1 Tim 1:2).

The problems in the churches at Crete (Titus 1:5, 12) are similar to those in Ephesus (according to 1 Tim 1:3-7) but are more clearly tied here to apparently Jewish opponents (see 1:10, 14). They involve rebelliousness and idle and deceptive talk. Lack of wisdom, self-control, honesty, and courtesy also seem to be problems (Titus 1:8; 2:2, 5-6, 9, 12; 3:1-3), and thus the author pointedly names God as the God "who never lies" (1:2). There appears to be a play here on a common cultural stereotype concerning the people of Crete. The island was reputed to be the home of notorious pirates; perhaps it is because of their influence that "to Cretanize" meant to lie, as Epimenides may have said (Titus 1:12). But the letter also speaks antagonistically of "those of the circumcision," of the proliferation of "Jewish myths," of the commandments of people who "reject the truth," and of quarrels about the law (Titus 1:10, 14; 3:9). Some scholars question whether the letter has actual Jews in view (although Jews had been at Crete for many years: see 1 Macc 15:19-23, referring to Gortyna, which lies in Crete, and Acts 2:11, which names Jews from Crete as present at Pentecost) or instead attacks the Judaizing practices of Gentiles (a problem against which the second-century bishop Ignatius of Antioch also inveighed).

Titus, 1 Timothy, Galatians, and 2 Corinthians are the only four letters in which the wrong thinking of the recipients (or the false teaching of opponents) has reached such proportions that no thanksgiving for the church appear at the letter opening. As in 1 and 2 Timothy, wholesome or "sound" teaching is very important for the author (Titus 1:9, 13; 2:1, 2, 8, 10). Elders (also called bishops) must have a "firm grasp" of the truth in order to teach and preach (1:9). The women elders must "teach what is good," and Titus himself is to have "integrity" and "gravity" in his teaching (2:3, 7). The gospel is summarized in a lengthy self-description in the letter salutation (1:1-3), including themes the author will develop in the letter, such as "knowledge of the truth" and recognizing God and Jesus as "our Savior," important themes also mentioned in 1 Timothy.

But an equally important concern is that the "word of God may not be discredited" (2:5, 8, 10). It is crucial that orthodoxy (right thinking) be reflected in orthopraxy (right practice: 1:16; 2:3, 7, 14; 3:1, 8, 14). A major theme of the letter is that "those who have come to believe in God may be careful to devote themselves to good works" (3:5, 8). Idleness can lead to idle talking.

As a minister and an intercultural person myself (of Hispanic and Dutch heritage), I am impressed that the letter represents Paul sending a *Gentile* to silence *Jews* (so I read "those of the circumcision"). Whether Jews or Gentiles adopting Jewish practices were the problem imagined by the author of Titus, the letter offers us an opportunity to recognize our own responsibility to minister across cultures today. Such cross-cultural engagement in our postmodern world requires *modeling* the truths and behaviors we teach and proclaim. Does Titus also suggest that we may also need, from time to time, to show errors, offer warning, and even seek to silence the voices of those who upset communities "for sordid gain" (1:11)? What might that responsibility entail?

— ***Aída Besançon Spencer***

1 Paul, a servant[a] of God and an apostle of
Jesus Christ, for the sake of the faith of God's
elect and the knowledge of the truth that is in accordance with godliness, 2in the hope of eternal
life that God, who never lies, promised before the
ages began— 3in due time he revealed his word
through the proclamation with which I have been
entrusted by the command of God our Savior,

4 To Titus, my loyal child in the faith we
share:

Grace[b] and peace from God the Father and Christ Jesus our Savior.

5 I left you behind in Crete for this reason,
so that you should put in order what remained
to be done, and should appoint elders in every
town, as I directed you: 6someone who is
blameless, married only once,[c] whose children
are believers, not accused of debauchery and
not rebellious. 7For a bishop,[d] as God's steward,
must be blameless; he must not be arrogant or
quick-tempered or addicted to wine or violent
or greedy for gain; 8but he must be hospitable,
a lover of goodness, prudent, upright, devout,
and self-controlled. 9He must have a firm grasp

[a] Gk *slave* [b] Other ancient authorities read *Grace, mercy,* [c] Gk *husband of one wife* [d] Or *an overseer*

of the word that is trustworthy in accordance with the teaching, so that he may be able both to preach with sound doctrine and to refute those who contradict it.

10 There are also many rebellious people, idle talkers and deceivers, especially those of the circumcision; 11 they must be silenced, since they are upsetting whole families by teaching for sordid gain what it is not right to teach. 12 It was one of them, their very own prophet, who said,

"Cretans are always liars, vicious brutes, lazy
gluttons."

13 That testimony is true. For this reason rebuke them sharply, so that they may become sound in the faith, 14 not paying attention to Jewish myths or to commandments of those who reject the truth. 15 To the pure all things are pure, but to the corrupt and unbelieving nothing is pure. Their very minds and consciences are corrupted. 16 They profess to know God, but they deny him by their actions. They are detestable, disobedient, unfit for any good work.

Titus 1:12-13

One way racism is manifested is when those from another culture are stereotyped. How many times have we heard it said or implied that members of the black or Hispanic community are liars, subhuman, sensual, or lazy. Most would be offended at such blatant bigotry. Yet Paul is represented here displaying his own bigotry when referring to the men of Crete. Not only does he repeat the slander of the Cretans—specifically that they are liars, vicious brutes, lazy gluttons—but he concludes that such an assessment is true, then goes on to suggest rebuking them so that they can be saved from their inferiority. Should we then be surprised that Christianity has had a history of those who saw themselves as racially superior paternalistically evangelizing their perceived inferiors?

— *MDLT*

2 But as for you, teach what is consistent with sound doctrine. 2 Tell the older men to be temperate, serious, prudent, and sound in faith, in love, and in endurance.

3 Likewise, tell the older women to be reverent in behavior, not to be slanderers or slaves to drink; they are to teach what is good, 4 so that they may encourage the young women to love their husbands, to love their children, 5 to be self-controlled, chaste, good managers of the household, kind, being submissive to their husbands, so that the word of God may not be discredited.

6 Likewise, urge the younger men to be self-controlled. 7 Show yourself in all respects a model of good works, and in your teaching show integrity, gravity, 8 and sound speech that cannot be censured; then any opponent will be put to shame, having nothing evil to say of us.

9 Tell slaves to be submissive to their masters and to give satisfaction in every respect; they are not to talk back, 10 not to pilfer, but to show complete and perfect fidelity, so that in everything they may be an ornament to the doctrine of God our Savior.

11 For the grace of God has appeared, bringing salvation to all,[a] 12 training us to renounce impiety and worldly passions, and in the present age to live lives that are self-controlled, upright, and godly, 13 while we wait for the blessed hope and the manifestation of the glory of our great God and Savior,[b] Jesus Christ. 14 He it is who gave himself for us that he might redeem us from all iniquity and purify for himself a people of his own who are zealous for good deeds.

15 Declare these things; exhort and reprove with all authority.[c] Let no one look down on you.

3 Remind them to be subject to rulers and authorities, to be obedient, to be ready for every good work, 2 to speak evil of no one, to avoid quarreling, to be gentle, and to show every courtesy to everyone. 3 For we ourselves were once foolish, disobedient, led astray, slaves to various passions and pleasures, passing our days in malice and envy, despicable, hating one another. 4 But when the goodness and loving kindness of God

[a] Or *has appeared to all, bringing salvation* [b] Or *of the great God and our Savior* [c] Gk *commandment*

our Savior appeared, 5 he saved us, not because of
any works of righteousness that we had done, but
according to his mercy, through the water[a] of rebirth and renewal by the Holy Spirit. 6 This Spirit
he poured out on us richly through Jesus Christ
our Savior, 7 so that, having been justified by his
grace, we might become heirs according to the
hope of eternal life. 8 The saying is sure.

I desire that you insist on these things, so
that those who have come to believe in God may
be careful to devote themselves to good works;
these things are excellent and profitable to everyone. 9 But avoid stupid controversies, genealogies, dissensions, and quarrels about the law, for
they are unprofitable and worthless. 10 After a first
and second admonition, have nothing more to do
with anyone who causes divisions, 11 since you
know that such a person is perverted and sinful,
being self-condemned.

12 When I send Artemas to you, or Tychicus,
do your best to come to me at Nicopolis, for I
have decided to spend the winter there. 13 Make
every effort to send Zenas the lawyer and Apollos on their way, and see that they lack nothing.
14 And let people learn to devote themselves to
good works in order to meet urgent needs, so that
they may not be unproductive.

15 All who are with me send greetings to you.
Greet those who love us in the faith.

Grace be with all of you.[b]

[a] Gk *washing* [b] Other ancient authorities add *Amen*

The Letter of Paul to

Philemon

The apostle Paul's letter to Philemon has been the cause for much debate about the complex matter of slavery in relation to the early church. The central person in this the third-shortest book in the New Testament (2 John has only 13 verses, and 3 John has 15), is apparently a runaway slave, Onesimus, who has fled from the household of his owner, Philemon (see vv. 11, 15). Biblical scholars have used the historical-critical method in their attempts to understand the original context and the theological significance for us of this letter. Unfortunately, interpreters have too often allowed the relatively modern aftermath of the transatlantic slave trade to serve as a definitive prism through which this epistle is to be understood. That has distorted the actual socio-political and economic issues of the first century CE. Although the protocols for Roman slavery are evident in this letter, many of the prevailing interpretations should be approached with caution.

This is one of the seven "prison epistles" among Paul's writings, that is, letters that purport to have been written from prison; the others in this category are Philippians, Colossians, Ephesians, 1 and 2 Timothy, and Titus. Of these, only Philemon and Philippians are universally regarded as unquestionably coming from Paul himself.

Several factors evidently moved Paul to write to Philemon regarding Onesimus. First, Paul had been responsible for converting Philemon, a wealthy slave owner in Asia Minor, while Paul was in Ephesus (so much is implied in the document itself—see v. 19—though there is no external evidence of this). Second, Paul then enjoyed a close friendship with Philemon and hoped to visit him after his release from prison. Third, it is clear that Onesimus has also become a Christian through the direct influence of Paul while in prison. Other, later letters will purport to have been carried by Onesimus traveling with Tychicus, one of Paul's virtual secretaries, to Ephesus, Colossae, and Laodicea. Paul's authoritative tone in the epistle stems from the simple fact that he was responsible for both master and slave becoming Christians.

That Paul wrote this letter from prison is clear enough (vv. 9, 13, 23), but the date of the letter is not. Rome, Caesarea, and Ephesus were sites where Paul was imprisoned. If Paul wrote from Rome, the letter must have been written about 61 CE; if from Caesarea, it would have been written about 58; and if from Ephesus, Paul would have written it in 55. The argument for Rome has the most merit, because many runaway slaves came to Rome rather than remain too near the place from which they had run. Those arguing for Ephesus claim that Paul's needing lodging with Philemon is a hint that Paul was nearby. But a runaway slave would most likely attempt to flee as far as possible from their master in order to avoid possible recapture. So Paul was most probably in Rome when he authored this epistle, sometime in the period 61–63.

The occasion and purpose for the letter appear straightforward. Paul wrote to Philemon because he wanted him to receive Onesimus back—certainly without penalty but also with a new status. A few modern interpreters have offered creative alternative views. One contemporary scholar has argued that the letter should not be regarded as a personal letter; it was actually written to a *congregation,* of which the addressee was a member (see v. 2). That is, Onesimus was no runaway but was sent to Paul on behalf of the church in Colossae. Paul writes to request that Onesimus now be released from his obligations in Colossae so that he might remain with Paul and work in Christian ministry as a free man. More recently, another scholar has argued that Philemon and Onesimus were blood brothers and that the issue of slavery thus had no bearing at all on the document. In my view, both these perspectives seem to go too far to deny Onesimus's identity as a slave, which seems to me irrefutable; it is because of Onesimus's conversion that Paul implores Philemon to accept him back as both a Christian and a free man.

The ancient but peculiar institution of slavery was a common practice during the Greco-Roman period. It was an acceptable form of socioeconomic and sociopolitical life. The rich owned slaves, and the slave had few if any rights. Even Aristotle contended that there were "natural slaves and natural masters." For him the structure of the human soul demands that some people be ruled as slaves. The early church did not deal in any uniform or persistent way with slavery as an ethical and theological issue. The seven undisputed Pauline epistles tend not to endorse slavery. But today one wishes, especially an African American like myself, that Paul had been more explicit in developing a clear and distinctive Christian position about slavery, that institution where one person is another's property.

Today commentators are careful not to assign Onesimus a racial or ethnic identity. Most biblical scholars now realize that in ancient times there was no *racial* policy that determined one's eligibility for slavery. Onesimus was likely not an African, as has so often been assumed. He probably was of the ethnic and racial identity of persons living in the Lycus Valley in Asia Minor. The letter to Philemon in fact has much less to do with slavery than it does with the radical difference Christianity should make when one becomes a Christian—a difference that would seem to leave no place for slaves or slavery. Paul has far too long been conveniently presented as a defender of slavery. Readers can judge for themselves the extent to which Philemon provides evidence to the contrary.

—***Cain Hope Felder***

1 Paul, a prisoner of Christ Jesus, and Timothy our brother,[a]

To Philemon our dear friend and co-worker,
2to Apphia our sister,[b] to Archippus our fellow soldier, and to the church in your house:

3 Grace to you and peace from God our Father and the Lord Jesus Christ.

4 When I remember you[c] in my prayers, I
always thank my God 5because I hear of your
love for all the saints and your faith toward the

[a] Gk *the brother* [b] Gk *the sister* [c] From verse 4 through verse 21, *you* is singular

Lord Jesus. [6]I pray that the sharing of your faith
may become effective when you perceive all the
good that we[a] may do for Christ. [7]I have indeed
received much joy and encouragement from your
love, because the hearts of the saints have been
refreshed through you, my brother.

8 For this reason, though I am bold enough
in Christ to command you to do your duty, [9]yet I
would rather appeal to you on the basis of love—
and I, Paul, do this as an old man, and now also
as a prisoner of Christ Jesus.[b] [10]I am appealing to
you for my child, Onesimus, whose father I have
become during my imprisonment. [11]Formerly
he was useless to you, but now he is indeed useful[c] both to you and to me. [12]I am sending him,
that is, my own heart, back to you. [13]I wanted to
keep him with me, so that he might be of service
to me in your place during my imprisonment for
the gospel; [14]but I preferred to do nothing without your consent, in order that your good deed
might be voluntary and not something forced.
[15]Perhaps this is the reason he was separated
from you for a while, so that you might have him
back forever, [16]no longer as a slave but more than
a slave, a beloved brother—especially to me but
how much more to you, both in the flesh and in
the Lord.

17 So if you consider me your partner, welcome him as you would welcome me. [18]If he has
wronged you in any way, or owes you anything,
charge that to my account. [19]I, Paul, am writing
this with my own hand: I will repay it. I say nothing about your owing me even your own self.
[20]Yes, brother, let me have this benefit from you
in the Lord! Refresh my heart in Christ. [21]Con-
fident of your obedience, I am writing to you,
knowing that you will do even more than I say.

22 One thing more—prepare a guest room
for me, for I am hoping through your prayers to
be restored to you.

23 Epaphras, my fellow prisoner in Christ
Jesus, sends greetings to you,[d] [24]and so do
Mark, Aristarchus, Demas, and Luke, my fellow
workers.

25 The grace of the Lord Jesus Christ be with
your spirit.[e]

[a] Other ancient authorities read *you* (plural) [b] Or *as an ambassador of Christ Jesus, and now also his prisoner*
[c] The name Onesimus means *useful* or (compare verse 20) *beneficial* [d] Here *you* is singular
[e] Other ancient authorities add *Amen*

Philemon 10-19

Paul sends a slave back to his master, asking the master to do his "duty" (v. 8)—but doesn't specify what that is. This silence is disturbing, especially for descendants of slaves. How could one send a slave back to his or her master simply trusting in the master's goodness? How could the runaway slave who has tasted freedom return to slavery simply for the sake of some perceived moral obligation to the master? And what about those who were not runaway slaves but stayed and kept working for the master? Recently some scholars have questioned whether Onesimus really was a runaway; others have detected in this letter a subtle but powerful demand that the master free his slave (the "duty" of v. 8). But for most of Christian history, this letter has been read in light of the "household codes" in other letters under the name of Paul (Eph 6:5-8; Col 3:22-25), where slaves are exhorted to obey their masters in fear and respect as if they were working for Christ. Is it any wonder that black gospel spirituals seldom, if ever, sing Paul's praises?

— MDLT

General Letters and Revelation

INTRODUCTION

Henry W. Morisada Rietz

Rome. Caesarea. Ephesus. Reading the General Letters (or Epistles) and Revelation in the context of *The Peoples' Bible* draws our attention to the peoples of the Bible in those places. Who are the people of the Bible? Certainly they are the authors *and* their communities, the original readers whom we imaginatively reconstruct as best we can. But the people of the Bible are also its present-day readers (whatever that present is), who actively participate in the creation of the Bible's meanings *today* and whose identities and social locations affect the construction of those meanings.

As a commentator on these biblical books, I am one of those people. I was born in Hawaíi in the 1960s. My mother was born in Germany to parents who were Jewish, French, and Hungarian gypsy. My father's ancestors emigrated from Japan to work in Hawaíi's sugar plantations. I am what we in Hawaíi call *hapa*—half—although I consider myself to be whole. I have spent much of my life in secrecy. In Hawaíi in the 1960s, it was a bold act for my father to marry a *haole*—literally "foreign," but now it has come to mean whites generally—woman and have a *hapa-haole* son. I now live and teach in a small, predominately white town in rural Iowa. I have experienced both alienation and the threat of assimilation, but as an educated, financially secure, healthy, heterosexual male who is a citizen of the United States, I also know the power of privilege.

My identities and misidentifications, my social locations and dislocations, lead me to value *particularity*—and similarity as well as difference. From my experience of privilege and discrimination, of being both insider and outsider, I have learned to espouse for myself a hermeneutic—that is, a method of interpretation—of self-critique; that is, I try to discern the ways that I may be implicated in the very critiques I make of other interpretations. The contractions and tensions that I embody sensitize me to listen for the tensions *within* the biblical texts, the conversations and arguments among the people *behind* the texts, and to make room for the various voices of the people who stand *in front of* the texts, reading them. Rather than seeking to resolve these tensions and trying to adopt fixed interpretations—which might involve silencing or alienating some voices, and assimilating others—I invite the reader to a practice of living within the tensions of multiple voices. Perhaps in this way we can all find nourishment for living within the diversities and ambiguities of life.

The General Letters and the Revelation to John represent a mixed collection of documents produced by the early followers of Jesus. Except for their having been gathered together at the end of the Christian canon, there is no inherent reason to treat these documents and collections together.

Hebrews, James, 1 and 2 Peter, 1–3 John, and Jude are called the General Letters, or sometimes the Catholic Epistles (from the Greek word *katholou*, meaning "general" or "universal"), since most of them do not name a specific addressee (2 John is addressed to "the elect lady and her children" and 3 John is addressed to "Gaius"). The English word "epistle" comes from the Greek word *epistolē*, which means "letter." The conventional form of a Greco-Roman letter included four elements:

an opening formula—*praescriptio*—that included the name of sender, the name of the addressee, and a greeting or salutation (often "greetings," or, in Jewish contexts, "peace");
an expression of thanksgiving;
the body of the letter; and
final greetings.

But not all of the General Letters are really epistles, that is, formal letters. While the ending of Hebrews resembles the final greetings of a letter (Heb 13:18-25), indicating that it was sent from one community to another, it lacks the opening formula and thanksgiving of a letter. Hebrews refers to itself as a "word of exhortation" (Heb 13:22), the phrase used in Acts 13:15 to refer to a sermon. 1 John also does not have the form of a letter; it is more of a theological treatise. The title "Revelation" translates the first word of the document, *apokalypsis,* but the author identifies what he has written as a "prophecy" (1:3; 22:18-19), and embedded within the work are letters to the seven churches (Rev 2–3). Nevertheless, modern interpreters have associated the book with a more specific genre called an apocalypse—a revelatory document mediated by an other-worldly agent.

Historically, these various documents come from diverse communities and contexts. Although there is some debate over their dating, most are generally assigned to the late first century CE or early in the second century (although some have argued for dating Jude in the 50s, which would make it one of the earliest Christian documents). They are thus mostly the products of second- or third-generation followers of Jesus (see, for example Heb 2:3, 1 Pet 1:8). The authorship of most of these books is disputed. Hebrews is anonymous, as are 1–3 John (although those documents are related to the community that composed the Gospel of John: see John 21:24). James, 1 Peter, and 2 Peter claim to have been written by the named apostles, but most scholars judge them to be written by followers of the disciples who wrote in their name; thus they are pseudonymous. It is possible that Jude was actually written by "Judas . . . brother of James" and thus also the brother of Jesus, but that is not certain. The author of Revelation was probably named John (1:1, 4, 9; 22:8), but which John we cannot be certain.

Literarily and historically, nothing demands that we treat these documents together. Nevertheless, perhaps it is in this diversity and even serendipity that our reflections may be sparked, since to some degree it reflects that of the Christian canon as a whole: Why *these* particular documents and not others? What happens when we place disparate and diverse voices side by side?

Many of these documents are struggling with issues of identity and reveal the complexity of ways that identity is negotiated and contested. While personal or group identities are often negotiated vis-à-vis an *other*, in reality there are *many* others and thus many identities. Since Jesus and his original followers were Jews, it is fair to say that Christianity emerges out of the Judaisms of the first century. The inclusion of Gentiles only happened after Jesus' death, and it was the source of much conflict. The Jewishness of the movement is evident in the language of James, which is addressed to "the twelve tribes in the Dispersion" (from the Greek word *diaspora*), and refers to the community's "assembly" or *sunagōgēn*, from which we get the English word "synagogue" (Jas 2:2). How do the followers of Jesus make sense of their experiences in light of the traditions they inherit—or steal?—from Judaism? First Peter is addressed to "the exiles of the Dispersion" (*diaspora*), who are also called "a chosen race, a royal priesthood, a holy nation, God's own people" (2:9), and who are now distinct from Gentiles (see 2:12). This is language that identifies the addressees as Jews. But there are also clear indications in 1 Peter that the addressees were born Gentiles (1:18; 2:10). Thus we see the centrality of Judaism—that one is either a Jew or a non-Jew, that is a Gentile—*assumed* among these followers of Jesus. As another example, the author of Hebrews compares Jesus to various traditions from the Hebrew Bible (or more probably a Greek translation of it) and from early Judaism—for example, the prophets (1:1-3), the angels (1:4-11), Moses (3:1-6), Joshua (4:1-11), the priesthood (4:14—5:10; 7:1-29), the covenant (8:1-13), the tabernacle (ch. 9), and the sacrifices (10:1-18). From the point of view of that author, those Jewish traditions prophetically anticipate or foreshadow the fulfillment or reality that Jesus represents. In doing so, an identity is constructed that degrades—but also is imbedded in—the Jewish *other*.

Some of the identity conflicts also occur within the community. Jude, 2 Peter, James, and 1–3 John all represent contestations within the movement. Reflecting the milieu of the ancient Mediterranean world, where religion was not focused on belief but on practice, these were not primarily theological or doctrinal controversies but arguments about praxis, what people should *do*. The author of Jude takes issue with other leaders within the movement—"intruders"—who are promoting licentiousness (vv. 4, 8, 16, 17-18). Jude responds to this situation, in part, by quoting as an authority *1 Enoch,* a Jewish document that most modern-day Jews and Christians do not recognize as biblical (vv. 14-15, quoting 1 En 1:9). The author of 2 Peter is also combating people he or she identifies as "false prophets" and "false teachers," who are likewise teaching freedom leading to licentiousness (2:1-2,18-22; 3:3-10). While the author of James doesn't explicitly address false teachers, that book's arguments nevertheless seem directed against particular ideas and notions, namely the privileging of faith over works (2:14-26). As is well known, Paul developed such a position in order to justify the inclusion of Gentiles among the early followers of Jesus, who were Jews (Gal 2:15-16). Interestingly, the argument in Jas 2:14-26 parallels Paul's argument in Rom 3:21—4:24, including the affirmation that "God is one" (Rom 3:30; Jas 2:19), an allusion to the *Shema* (Deut 6:4), and the example of Abraham, recalling Gen 15:6, "Abraham believed God, and it was reckoned to him as righteousness" (Rom 4:3 and Jas 2:21-23). A close reading of Paul shows that he himself was not a teacher of licentiousness, although it is easy to see how his opponents and even his own followers could interpret him that way (for example, 1 and 2 Corinthians).

One of the fiercest internal debates occurs within the community that produced the Gospel of John along with 1–3 John. Here the author's opponents are labeled as "antichrists" who "went out from us" (1 John 2:18-19), indicating that originally they were members of the community. These opponents deny that Jesus came "in the flesh" (1 John 4:2-3, 2 John v. 7), probably taking what would later be called a proto-docetic position, namely that Jesus was only a spirit being and not a physical human. This controversy is also reflected in the later editorial layers of the Gospel of John, such as the prologue, where it is asserted that "the Word became flesh and lived among us" (1:14), and resurrection scene with Thomas (20:24-29). In these controversies we see strong emphasis on materiality and praxis—Jesus cannot be just a theological affirmation and Christianity is more than a belief system. Flesh and blood matter; actions count. We cannot, of course, forget that we are only hearing certain sides of the arguments. The opponents also considered themselves to be faithful followers of Jesus and were trying to figure what that means and how to act accordingly.

These documents also reveal how imbedded they are within the cultural contexts of their times. Many of the documents were written to communities facing persecution (1 Pet 1:6, 17; Heb 10:32-34; Rev 13:5-10). These documents provide a variety of responses to persecutions, reflecting tensions between the need for civil order and perhaps enabling survival, and calls for resisting imperial forces and civil disobedience. First Peter encourages acceptance of suffering as punishment (1 Pet 4:1-2, 12-19). The persecutions experienced by the community may have been in response to the early Christian movement being considered a threat to Roman "family values" (Gal 3:28, 1 Cor 12:13, Col 3:11). The author of 1 Peter diminishes that threat by commanding submission to authority, whether authority of the emperor and other governmental rulers (2:13-17), slave masters (2:18-25), or husbands (3:1-6; 3:7). Thus, 1 Peter advocates for the traditional Roman patriarchal family structure that on the micro-level has the father at the head of the household, with wives, children, and slaves below him, and at the macro-level has the emperor over all the members of the Empire (see similar "household codes" in Col 3:18—4:1 and Eph 5:21—6:9). The assumption that individual families mirror the nation on the whole underlie much of the modern debate over family values and explains why, for some people, individual families are thought to threaten national security. Nevertheless, the endorsement of master-slave relationships in these biblical texts should counter any easy application of these texts as a model for Godly modern family relationships.

While 1 Pet 2:17 explicitly endorses the empire with even a slogan ("Honor everyone. Love the family of believers. Fear God. Honor the emperor."), Revelation is a testimony against imperial forces. When reading Revelation, it must be remembered that it was written for a specific place and time. It is addressed "to the seven churches that are in Asia" (1:4), namely Ephesus, Smyrna, Pergamum, Thyatira, Sardis, Philadelphia, and Laodicea, all within 150 miles of one another. Most scholars date Revelation to the time of the Roman emperor Domitian, who reigned 81–96 CE. From the point of view of the author, the events described are about to happen, "for the time is near" (1:3; cf. 22:20). Thus, Revelation was written for a specific place at a specific time, the Roman province of Asia Minor at the end of the first century. Revelation is not a blueprint or script for now in the twenty-first century or for future events. That does not mean, however, that it cannot have meaning for today. The hope of Revelation is a specific one. Steeped in Jewish tradition, Revelation anticipates the reconstitution of Israel. The 144,000 that are sealed include 12,000 from each of the twelve tribes of Israel (7:1-8). Alongside these representatives from Israel "was a great multitude . . . from every nation, from all tribes and peoples and languages" (7:9). But Israel is still at the center, a specificity that Gentile Christians must struggle with as we seek to appropriate this book.

Revelation is also a powerful witness to the reality of evil. Through its fantastic imagery and dependence upon mythical traditions, it testifies that evil is real and cosmic and has specific, concrete manifestations on earth. Steeped in the traditions of Israel, evil has manifested itself in the past through the imperial conquests of Babylon, and for the author now is manifested in the Roman Empire, which claims to bring *pax* (peace), but does so at the price of conquest, oppression, exploitation, and death. This is not peace. The "beast rising out of the sea" (13:1) is Rome, and its tens horns are its vassal rulers, client regimes it has set up to exploit the colonies. In this book, as one would expect in the first century, there is no dichotomy between religion and politics, or economics. Without the "mark of the beast" (16:2; 19:20)—whatever that was—"no one can buy or sell" (13:16-17). Evil permeates the imperial machine. At the beginning of the twenty-first century, imperial forces are alive and well, except that many of us find ourselves inextricably implicated in its machinery. For many, the empire now is the United States, or perhaps better, the complex system of global capitalism that is centered in the United States, propagated through electronic media, and enforced by its diplomatic and military forces and those of its clients.

Revelation's vision of the future reign of God is inspiring. It is not, ultimately, of an other-worldly, disembodied spiritual existence; rather it is an earthly vision of the transformation of the social, political, and ecological realities of this world. Offering an alternative to imperial Rome, Revelation envisions a new heaven and a new earth, centered in the new Jerusalem, where God and the Lamb will reign. This earthly hope of the Israelites restored to their land, restored to a sovereignty free from imperialism, parallels the hopes of many present-day indigenous peoples, from Palestinians, to Native American tribes, to the Kanaka Maoli (so-called native Hawaiians). Revelation affirms such particular dreams with a universalist pitch, where the nations will live together in peace, true peace free from oppression, exploitation, and death. The challenge to us is *how* to realize this vision; "Let... the righteous still do right" (22:11).

While coming from different perspectives and often taking different positions, hearing the voices of the people of the General Letters and Revelation can challenge and inspire us, today's people of the Bible. Let us not abdicate our responsibility as interpreters who seek to find meanings in these texts, but let us own our voices and the ethical choices we make based on those meanings. Let us also listen to the voices of other readers, who are also constructing their own meanings from these texts. Rather than too quickly relaxing the tensions and resolving the contradictions—moves that often do violence to the text as well as against others—let us dwell within them, for those are the tensions of living with other beings.

The Letter to the Hebrews

OF THE TWENTY-SEVEN WRITINGS that comprise the New Testament, the Letter to the Hebrews is arguably the most culturally specific. The social and religious experiences and beliefs of the Jewish people are so explicitly discussed in this writing that its title, "To Hebrews," found in the most ancient manuscripts of the work, seems well justified. At the same time, however, the message of the letter extends beyond Judaism because of what it teaches about Jesus. That message is that Jesus, the Son of God, became fully identified with all human experience so that his life, death, and resurrection could make access to God readily available to all who look to him as their Savior and exalted advocate. Here the Jewish Scriptures, the religious cultus of the tabernacle in the wilderness and, later, the temple, and historical Hebrew persons are all presented as provisional and prophetic in character, all pointing beyond themselves to what God has now made available to all people in the person and ministry of Jesus the Christ (the God-anointed One).

Among the many details specific to Jewish Scripture and tradition in the letter are references to the prophets (1:1); to the Hebrew people as descendants of Abraham (2:16; 6:13); to Moses and Joshua as exemplary leaders (chs. 3–4); to the nation's sojourn in the wilderness (ch. 4); to covenant concerns, the priestly system, and the necessity of sacrifices and offerings (chs. 5–10); and to a panoply of biblical heroes and heroines such as Abel, Enoch, and Noah (ch. 11). The Jewish flavor of the New Testament is nowhere more evident than in the Letter to the Hebrews, a writing whose understanding requires an awareness of the history, sacrificial system, Scriptures, beliefs, and covenantal obligations of the Hebrew people.

This close attention to aspects of Jewish belief and practice has convinced many readers that the letter must have been directed to Jews to attract them to faith in Jesus. For example, a 19th-century Christian commentator on the letter wrote that a Jew, reading Hebrews for the first time, "would be favourably impressed with the evident love and sympathy which the writer displays towards the Tabernacle, its ministers, and its ritual," and "would thus be led, insensibly and without offense, into a consideration of the argument that these symbols found in Christ their predestined and final fulfillment."[73]

Other scholars, however, have argued that the author's insistence that Christ has superseded aspects of the Jewish covenant must have come from, and been directed to, Gentile Christians. The first recipients of the Letter to the Hebrews cannot be stated with unquestioned certainty. But because *1 Clement,* written in Rome about 96 CE, quotes copiously from it, it may be that Jewish (or possibly, Gentile) members of the church in Rome were its intended audience.

In addition to Paul, many others have been suggested across the centuries as responsible for writing Hebrews. Most were members of the Pauline circle. They include Luke, Clement, Barnabas, Apollos, Priscilla (with her husband, Aquila), Epaphras, Timothy, and Silas. Although no final word can yet be given on its author, features of the letter suggest that its author was a Hellenistic (Greek-speaking) Jew who was skilled in rhetoric, seems acquainted with Paul's teaching but was an independent thinker, and was a second-generation Christian (2:3). The writer knew the group to which the letter was addressed (5:11-12; 6:9-10; 10:32; 13:7, 19). The writer also knew Timothy (13:23). As an African American preacher, the sermonic feel, especially the cadences of the biographical miniatures (11:1-39), causes me to resonate with the thought that perhaps the author was that first century African preacher Apollos.

Hebrews should be dated about 64 CE, and certainly prior to 70 and the destruction of Jerusalem, because mentioning that devastating event would have strengthened the writer's argument in chapters 7–10. Rome seems to match best what seems indicated in the letter as the locale of its intended recipients: 10:32 refers to the group's "hard struggle with sufferings," which could suggest the time when Emperor Claudius exiled Jews from Rome (chs. 49–50) or a severe period for Christians in the mid-to-late 60s under Nero's rule. Since further suffering was anticipated (12:3-4, 7, 12-13), the writer wanted to strengthen readers for a sustained faith in the mission and meaning of Jesus (10:15-19; 13:6, 20-21).

Concerned to encourage Christians as they faced persecution and slights, the writer reminds them anew that the Hebrew cultic forms actually pointed to the "new and living way" (10:20) opened by the expiatory death of Jesus, a death that grants believers an "eternal redemption" (9:12). The old covenant offered to Jews has been superseded by a new covenant offered to all people (10:16-18, citing invokes Jer 31:33-34). Backed by the Jewish Scriptures and the apostolic message, the writer explains that the animal sacrifices demanded under the old covenant really represented and foreshadowed the offering Jesus made of himself to God, and that because of this those sacrifices are no longer necessary, nor is the priesthood that administered them. A warning is voiced to trust fully the gospel they had received because it had been attested "by those who heard" the Lord Jesus (2:1-4). The readers are encouraged to "exhort one another" (3:13), remain confident in faith (3:14), hold fast to the Christian "confession" (4:14; 10:23), show "diligence" (6:11), and keep living by faith (10:36-39). They are to look steadily to Jesus (12:2) and not look back or return to an obsolete ritualistic order, since to do so would be to commit apostasy (6:4-6; 10:26-31). Under persecution, some persons have abandoned the fellowship (10:25), so the writer cautions all others against neglecting to gather together.

Hebrews is a dynamic restatement of the Christian faith. The conditions its first readers faced demanded such a treatment, and the writer prepared and sent it as an encouraging word flavored with the evident caring of a pastoral heart. Christians today continue to value the writing as a doctrinal manifesto about the meaning of Jesus and a strategic word of encouragement for believers beset by life and fretful or confused about what they see and experience in the world. Hebrews offers a needed word for believers facing difficulties *because* they are Christians.

Briefly outlined, the structured argument of Hebrews is as follows:

1. God's Son as God's supreme agent (1:1—4:13)
2. Jesus the great High Priest (4:14—10:39)
3. The meaning and necessity of faith (11:1—12:29)
4. Concluding remarks (13:1-25)

Hebrews appears in the oldest version of the New Testament canon. It won acceptance into the canon on the strength of the Eastern church's tradition that Paul wrote it or was otherwise somehow behind its creation. The churches in the West did not view the writing as Pauline, but they accepted Hebrews as authoritative, and it appears in our English versions immediately after Paul's writings rather than among them—an order influenced by that in the Latin Vulgate, the version on which the first English Bible was based.

— *James Earl Massey*

1 Long ago God spoke to our ancestors in
many and various ways by the prophets, 2but
in these last days he has spoken to us by a Son,[a]
whom he appointed heir of all things, through
whom he also created the worlds. 3He is the reflection of God's glory and the exact imprint of
God's very being, and he sustains[b] all things by
his powerful word. When he had made purification for sins, he sat down at the right hand of the
Majesty on high, 4having become as much superior to angels as the name he has inherited is
more excellent than theirs.

5 For to which of the angels did God ever
say,

"You are my Son;
today I have begotten you"?

Or again,

"I will be his Father,
and he will be my Son"?

6And again, when he brings the firstborn into the
world, he says,

"Let all God's angels worship him."

7Of the angels he says,

"He makes his angels winds,
and his servants flames of fire."

8But of the Son he says,

"Your throne, O God, is[c] forever and ever,
and the righteous scepter is the scepter of your[d] kingdom.
9 You have loved righteousness and hated wickedness;
therefore God, your God, has anointed you
with the oil of gladness beyond your companions."

10And,

"In the beginning, Lord, you founded the earth,
and the heavens are the work of your hands;
11 they will perish, but you remain;
they will all wear out like clothing;
12 like a cloak you will roll them up,
and like clothing[e] they will be changed.
But you are the same,
and your years will never end."

13But to which of the angels has he ever said,

"Sit at my right hand
until I make your enemies a footstool for your feet"?

14Are not all angels[f] spirits in the divine service,
sent to serve for the sake of those who are to inherit salvation?

[a] Or *the Son* [b] Or *bears along* [c] Or *God is your throne* [d] Other ancient authorities read *his* [e] Other ancient authorities lack *like clothing* [f] Gk *all of them*

2 Therefore we must pay greater attention
to what we have heard, so that we do not
drift away from it. 2 For if the message declared
through angels was valid, and every transgression
or disobedience received a just penalty, 3 how can
we escape if we neglect so great a salvation? It was
declared at first through the Lord, and it was attested to us by those who heard him, 4 while God
added his testimony by signs and wonders and
various miracles, and by gifts of the Holy Spirit,
distributed according to his will.

5 Now God[a] did not subject the coming
world, about which we are speaking, to angels.
6 But someone has testified somewhere,

"What are human beings that you are
mindful of them,[b]
or mortals, that you care for them?[c]
7 You have made them for a little while lower[d]
than the angels;
you have crowned them with glory and
honor,[e]
8 subjecting all things under their
feet."

Now in subjecting all things to them, God[a] left
nothing outside their control. As it is, we do not
yet see everything in subjection to them, 9 but
we do see Jesus, who for a little while was made
lower[f] than the angels, now crowned with glory
and honor because of the suffering of death, so
that by the grace of God[g] he might taste death for
everyone.

10 It was fitting that God,[a] for whom and
through whom all things exist, in bringing many
children to glory, should make the pioneer of
their salvation perfect through sufferings. 11 For
the one who sanctifies and those who are sanctified all have one Father.[h] For this reason Jesus[a]
is not ashamed to call them brothers and sisters,[i]
12 saying,

"I will proclaim your name to my brothers
and sisters,[i]
in the midst of the congregation I will
praise you."

13 And again,

"I will put my trust in him."

And again,

"Here am I and the children whom God has
given me."

14 Since, therefore, the children share flesh
and blood, he himself likewise shared the same
things, so that through death he might destroy
the one who has the power of death, that is, the
devil, 15 and free those who all their lives were
held in slavery by the fear of death. 16 For it is
clear that he did not come to help angels, but
the descendants of Abraham. 17 Therefore he
had to become like his brothers and sisters[i] in
every respect, so that he might be a merciful
and faithful high priest in the service of God, to
make a sacrifice of atonement for the sins of the
people. 18 Because he himself was tested by what
he suffered, he is able to help those who are being tested.

Hebrews 2:6-8

The language of God "subjecting all things" under the feet of human beings has introduced a dangerous paradigm that has been used to justify the degradation of our planet and the oppression of communities who depend on the land for their subsistence. Here human beings (and historically this has meant *men*) are described not as stewards of God's creation but as its rulers, who may use and abuse creation as they see fit. The imagery of subduing the land has been extended to the subjection of all those other men and women who fall short of being rulers, and their failure to rule creation has then been taken as proof that they are not really the human beings that the Bible is talking about—and hence that they deserve their subservient role, along with the rest of nature.

— *MDLT*

[a] Gk *he* [b] Gk *What is man that you are mindful of him?* [c] Gk *or the son of man that you care for him?* In the Hebrew of Psalm 8.4–6 both *man* and *son of man* refer to all humankind [d] Or *them only a little lower* [e] Other ancient authorities add *and set them over the works of your hands* [f] Or *who was made a little lower* [g] Other ancient authorities read *apart from God* [h] Gk *are all of one* [i] Gk *brothers*

3 Therefore, brothers and sisters,[a] holy partners in a heavenly calling, consider that
Jesus, the apostle and high priest of our confession, 2was faithful to the one who appointed
him, just as Moses also "was faithful in all[b] God's[c]
house." 3Yet Jesus[d] is worthy of more glory than
Moses, just as the builder of a house has more
honor than the house itself. 4(For every house
is built by someone, but the builder of all things
is God.) 5Now Moses was faithful in all God's[c]
house as a servant, to testify to the things that
would be spoken later. 6Christ, however, was
faithful over God's[c] house as a son, and we are
his house if we hold firm[e] the confidence and the
pride that belong to hope.

7 Therefore, as the Holy Spirit says,
"Today, if you hear his voice,
8 do not harden your hearts as in the rebellion,
as on the day of testing in the wilderness,
9 where your ancestors put me to the test,
though they had seen my works 10for forty
years.
Therefore I was angry with that generation,
and I said, 'They always go astray in their
hearts,
and they have not known my ways.'
11 As in my anger I swore,
'They will not enter my rest.' "
12Take care, brothers and sisters,[a] that none of
you may have an evil, unbelieving heart that turns
away from the living God. 13But exhort one another every day, as long as it is called "today," so
that none of you may be hardened by the deceit-
fulness of sin. 14For we have become partners of
Christ, if only we hold our first confidence firm to
the end. 15As it is said,
"Today, if you hear his voice,
do not harden your hearts as in the rebellion."
16Now who were they who heard and yet were
rebellious? Was it not all those who left Egypt
under the leadership of Moses? 17But with whom
was he angry forty years? Was it not those who
sinned, whose bodies fell in the wilderness?
18And to whom did he swear that they would not
enter his rest, if not to those who were disobedient? 19So we see that they were unable to enter
because of unbelief.

4 Therefore, while the promise of entering his
rest is still open, let us take care that none of
you should seem to have failed to reach it. 2For
indeed the good news came to us just as to them;
but the message they heard did not benefit them,
because they were not united by faith with those
who listened.[f] 3For we who have believed enter
that rest, just as God[g] has said,
"As in my anger I swore,
'They shall not enter my rest,' "
though his works were finished at the foundation
of the world. 4For in one place it speaks about
the seventh day as follows, "And God rested on
the seventh day from all his works." 5And again
in this place it says, "They shall not enter my
rest." 6Since therefore it remains open for some
to enter it, and those who formerly received the
good news failed to enter because of disobedience, 7again he sets a certain day—"today"—
saying through David much later, in the words
already quoted,
"Today, if you hear his voice,
do not harden your hearts."
8For if Joshua had given them rest, God[g] would
not speak later about another day. 9So then, a sabbath rest still remains for the people of God; 10for
those who enter God's rest also cease from their
labors as God did from his. 11Let us therefore
make every effort to enter that rest, so that no one
may fall through such disobedience as theirs.

12 Indeed, the word of God is living and active, sharper than any two-edged sword, piercing
until it divides soul from spirit, joints from marrow; it is able to judge the thoughts and intentions of the heart. 13And before him no creature
is hidden, but all are naked and laid bare to the
eyes of the one to whom we must render an account.

14 Since, then, we have a great high priest
who has passed through the heavens, Jesus, the

[a] Gk *brothers* [b] Other ancient authorities lack *all* [c] Gk *his* [d] Gk *this one* [e] Other ancient authorities add *to the end* [f] Other ancient authorities read *it did not meet with faith in those who listened* [g] Gk *he*

Son of God, let us hold fast to our confession.
15For we do not have a high priest who is unable
to sympathize with our weaknesses, but we have
one who in every respect has been tested[a] as we
are, yet without sin. 16Let us therefore approach
the throne of grace with boldness, so that we may
receive mercy and find grace to help in time of
need.

5 Every high priest chosen from among mortals is put in charge of things pertaining to
God on their behalf, to offer gifts and sacrifices
for sins. 2He is able to deal gently with the ignorant and wayward, since he himself is subject to
weakness; 3and because of this he must offer sacrifice for his own sins as well as for those of the
people. 4And one does not presume to take this
honor, but takes it only when called by God, just
as Aaron was.

5 So also Christ did not glorify himself in becoming a high priest, but was appointed by the
one who said to him,

"You are my Son,
today I have begotten you";

6as he says also in another place,

"You are a priest forever,
according to the order of Melchizedek."

7 In the days of his flesh, Jesus[b] offered up
prayers and supplications, with loud cries and
tears, to the one who was able to save him from
death, and he was heard because of his reverent
submission. 8Although he was a Son, he learned
obedience through what he suffered; 9and having
been made perfect, he became the source of eternal salvation for all who obey him, 10having been
designated by God a high priest according to the
order of Melchizedek.

11 About this[c] we have much to say that is
hard to explain, since you have become dull in
understanding. 12For though by this time you
ought to be teachers, you need someone to teach
you again the basic elements of the oracles of
God. You need milk, not solid food; 13for everyone who lives on milk, being still an infant, is unskilled in the word of righteousness. 14But solid
food is for the mature, for those whose faculties
have been trained by practice to distinguish good
from evil.

6 Therefore let us go on toward perfection,[d]
leaving behind the basic teaching about
Christ, and not laying again the foundation: repentance from dead works and faith toward God,
2instruction about baptisms, laying on of hands,
resurrection of the dead, and eternal judgment.
3And we will do[e] this, if God permits. 4For it is
impossible to restore again to repentance those
who have once been enlightened, and have tasted
the heavenly gift, and have shared in the Holy
Spirit, 5and have tasted the goodness of the word
of God and the powers of the age to come, 6and
then have fallen away, since on their own they are
crucifying again the Son of God and are holding
him up to contempt. 7Ground that drinks up the
rain falling on it repeatedly, and that produces
a crop useful to those for whom it is cultivated,
receives a blessing from God. 8But if it produces
thorns and thistles, it is worthless and on the verge
of being cursed; its end is to be burned over.

9 Even though we speak in this way, beloved,
we are confident of better things in your case,
things that belong to salvation. 10For God is not
unjust; he will not overlook your work and the
love that you showed for his sake[f] in serving the
saints, as you still do. 11And we want each one of
you to show the same diligence so as to realize
the full assurance of hope to the very end, 12so
that you may not become sluggish, but imitators
of those who through faith and patience inherit
the promises.

13 When God made a promise to Abraham,
because he had no one greater by whom to swear,
he swore by himself, 14saying, "I will surely bless
you and multiply you." 15And thus Abraham,[b]
having patiently endured, obtained the promise.
16Human beings, of course, swear by someone
greater than themselves, and an oath given as
confirmation puts an end to all dispute. 17In the
same way, when God desired to show even more
clearly to the heirs of the promise the unchange-

[a] Or *tempted* [b] Gk *he* [c] Or *him* [d] Or *toward maturity* [e] Other ancient authorities read *let us do*
[f] Gk *for his name*

able character of his purpose, he guaranteed it
by an oath, 18 so that through two unchangeable
things, in which it is impossible that God would
prove false, we who have taken refuge might be
strongly encouraged to seize the hope set before us. 19 We have this hope, a sure and steadfast
anchor of the soul, a hope that enters the inner
shrine behind the curtain, 20 where Jesus, a fore-
runner on our behalf, has entered, having become a high priest forever according to the order
of Melchizedek.

7 This "King Melchizedek of Salem, priest of
the Most High God, met Abraham as he was
returning from defeating the kings and blessed
him"; 2 and to him Abraham apportioned "one-
tenth of everything." His name, in the first place,
means "king of righteousness"; next he is also
king of Salem, that is, "king of peace." 3 Without
father, without mother, without genealogy, having neither beginning of days nor end of life, but
resembling the Son of God, he remains a priest
forever.

4 See how great he is! Even[a] Abraham the
patriarch gave him a tenth of the spoils. 5 And
those descendants of Levi who receive the
priestly office have a commandment in the law
to collect tithes[b] from the people, that is, from
their kindred,[c] though these also are descended
from Abraham. 6 But this man, who does not
belong to their ancestry, collected tithes[b] from
Abraham and blessed him who had received the
promises. 7 It is beyond dispute that the inferior
is blessed by the superior. 8 In the one case, tithes
are received by those who are mortal; in the
other, by one of whom it is testified that he lives.
9 One might even say that Levi himself, who receives tithes, paid tithes through Abraham, 10 for
he was still in the loins of his ancestor when
Melchizedek met him.

11 Now if perfection had been attainable
through the levitical priesthood—for the people
received the law under this priesthood—what
further need would there have been to speak of
another priest arising according to the order of
Melchizedek, rather than one according to the
order of Aaron? 12 For when there is a change in
the priesthood, there is necessarily a change in
the law as well. 13 Now the one of whom these
things are spoken belonged to another tribe, from
which no one has ever served at the altar. 14 For
it is evident that our Lord was descended from
Judah, and in connection with that tribe Moses
said nothing about priests.

15 It is even more obvious when another
priest arises, resembling Melchizedek, 16 one who
has become a priest, not through a legal requirement concerning physical descent, but through
the power of an indestructible life. 17 For it is attested of him,

"You are a priest forever,
according to the order of Melchizedek."

18 There is, on the one hand, the abrogation of an
earlier commandment because it was weak and
ineffectual 19 (for the law made nothing perfect);
there is, on the other hand, the introduction of a
better hope, through which we approach God.

20 This was confirmed with an oath; for others who became priests took their office without
an oath, 21 but this one became a priest with an
oath, because of the one who said to him,

"The Lord has sworn
and will not change his mind,
'You are a priest forever' "—

22 accordingly Jesus has also become the guarantee of a better covenant.

23 Furthermore, the former priests were
many in number, because they were prevented by
death from continuing in office; 24 but he holds
his priesthood permanently, because he continues forever. 25 Consequently he is able for all
time to save[d] those who approach God through
him, since he always lives to make intercession
for them.

26 For it was fitting that we should have such
a high priest, holy, blameless, undefiled, separated
from sinners, and exalted above the heavens.
27 Unlike the other[e] high priests, he has no need
to offer sacrifices day after day, first for his own
sins, and then for those of the people; this he did
once for all when he offered himself. 28 For the law

[a] Other ancient authorities lack *Even* [b] Or *a tenth* [c] Gk *brothers* [d] Or *able to save completely* [e] Gk lacks *other*

appoints as high priests those who are subject to
weakness, but the word of the oath, which came
later than the law, appoints a Son who has been
made perfect forever.

8 Now the main point in what we are saying
is this: we have such a high priest, one who
is seated at the right hand of the throne of the
Majesty in the heavens, 2 a minister in the sanctuary and the true tent[a] that the Lord, and not
any mortal, has set up. 3 For every high priest is
appointed to offer gifts and sacrifices; hence it is
necessary for this priest also to have something
to offer. 4 Now if he were on earth, he would not
be a priest at all, since there are priests who offer
gifts according to the law. 5 They offer worship in a
sanctuary that is a sketch and shadow of the heavenly one; for Moses, when he was about to erect
the tent,[a] was warned, "See that you make everything according to the pattern that was shown you
on the mountain." 6 But Jesus[b] has now obtained a
more excellent ministry, and to that degree he is
the mediator of a better covenant, which has been
enacted through better promises. 7 For if that first
covenant had been faultless, there would have
been no need to look for a second one.

8 God[c] finds fault with them when he says:
"The days are surely coming, says the
Lord,
when I will establish a new covenant with
the house of Israel
and with the house of Judah;
9 not like the covenant that I made with their
ancestors,
on the day when I took them by the hand
to lead them out of the land of
Egypt;
for they did not continue in my covenant,
and so I had no concern for them, says the
Lord.
10 This is the covenant that I will make with the
house of Israel
after those days, says the Lord:
I will put my laws in their minds,
and write them on their hearts,
and I will be their God,
and they shall be my people.
11 And they shall not teach one another
or say to each other, 'Know the Lord,'
for they shall all know me,
from the least of them to the greatest.
12 For I will be merciful toward their
iniquities,
and I will remember their sins no more."
13 In speaking of "a new covenant," he has made
the first one obsolete. And what is obsolete and
growing old will soon disappear.

9 Now even the first covenant had regulations
for worship and an earthly sanctuary. 2 For a
tent[a] was constructed, the first one, in which were
the lampstand, the table, and the bread of the
Presence;[d] this is called the Holy Place. 3 Behind
the second curtain was a tent[a] called the Holy of
Holies. 4 In it stood the golden altar of incense and
the ark of the covenant overlaid on all sides with
gold, in which there were a golden urn holding
the manna, and Aaron's rod that budded, and the
tablets of the covenant; 5 above it were the cherubim of glory overshadowing the mercy seat.[e] Of
these things we cannot speak now in detail.

6 Such preparations having been made, the
priests go continually into the first tent[a] to carry
out their ritual duties; 7 but only the high priest
goes into the second, and he but once a year,
and not without taking the blood that he offers
for himself and for the sins committed unintentionally by the people. 8 By this the Holy Spirit
indicates that the way into the sanctuary has not
yet been disclosed as long as the first tent[a] is still
standing. 9 This is a symbol[f] of the present time,
during which gifts and sacrifices are offered that
cannot perfect the conscience of the worshiper,
10 but deal only with food and drink and various
baptisms, regulations for the body imposed until
the time comes to set things right.

11 But when Christ came as a high priest of
the good things that have come,[g] then through the
greater and perfect[h] tent[a] (not made with hands,

[a] Or *tabernacle* [b] Gk *he* [c] Gk *He* [d] Gk *the presentation of the loaves* [e] Or *the place of atonement* [f] Gk *parable*
[g] Other ancient authorities read *good things to come* [h] Gk *more perfect*

that is, not of this creation), 12he entered once
for all into the Holy Place, not with the blood of
goats and calves, but with his own blood, thus obtaining eternal redemption. 13For if the blood of
goats and bulls, with the sprinkling of the ashes
of a heifer, sanctifies those who have been defiled
so that their flesh is purified, 14how much more
will the blood of Christ, who through the eternal
Spirit[a] offered himself without blemish to God,
purify our[b] conscience from dead works to worship the living God!

15 For this reason he is the mediator of a
new covenant, so that those who are called may
receive the promised eternal inheritance, because
a death has occurred that redeems them from the
transgressions under the first covenant.[c] 16Where
a will[c] is involved, the death of the one who made
it must be established. 17For a will[c] takes effect
only at death, since it is not in force as long as the
one who made it is alive. 18Hence not even the
first covenant was inaugurated without blood.
19For when every commandment had been told
to all the people by Moses in accordance with the
law, he took the blood of calves and goats,[d] with
water and scarlet wool and hyssop, and sprinkled
both the scroll itself and all the people, 20say-
ing, "This is the blood of the covenant that God
has ordained for you." 21And in the same way he
sprinkled with the blood both the tent[e] and all
the vessels used in worship. 22Indeed, under the
law almost everything is purified with blood, and
without the shedding of blood there is no forgiveness of sins.

23 Thus it was necessary for the sketches of
the heavenly things to be purified with these rites,
but the heavenly things themselves need better
sacrifices than these. 24For Christ did not enter
a sanctuary made by human hands, a mere copy
of the true one, but he entered into heaven itself,
now to appear in the presence of God on our behalf. 25Nor was it to offer himself again and again,
as the high priest enters the Holy Place year after
year with blood that is not his own; 26for then he
would have had to suffer again and again since the
foundation of the world. But as it is, he has appeared once for all at the end of the age to remove
sin by the sacrifice of himself. 27And just as it is
appointed for mortals to die once, and after that
the judgment, 28so Christ, having been offered
once to bear the sins of many, will appear a second time, not to deal with sin, but to save those
who are eagerly waiting for him.

10 Since the law has only a shadow of the
good things to come and not the true
form of these realities, it[f] can never, by the same
sacrifices that are continually offered year after
year, make perfect those who approach. 2Other-
wise, would they not have ceased being offered,
since the worshipers, cleansed once for all, would
no longer have any consciousness of sin? 3But
in these sacrifices there is a reminder of sin year
after year. 4For it is impossible for the blood of
bulls and goats to take away sins. 5Consequently,
when Christ[g] came into the world, he said,

"Sacrifices and offerings you have not
desired,
but a body you have prepared for me;
6 in burnt offerings and sin offerings
you have taken no pleasure.
7 Then I said, 'See, God, I have come to do
your will, O God'
(in the scroll of the book[h] it is written
of me)."

8When he said above, "You have neither desired
nor taken pleasure in sacrifices and offerings
and burnt offerings and sin offerings" (these are
offered according to the law), 9then he added,
"See, I have come to do your will." He abolishes
the first in order to establish the second. 10And
it is by God's will[i] that we have been sanctified
through the offering of the body of Jesus Christ
once for all.

11 And every priest stands day after day at
his service, offering again and again the same
sacrifices that can never take away sins. 12But
when Christ[j] had offered for all time a single

[a] Other ancient authorities read *Holy Spirit* [b] Other ancient authorities read *your* [c] The Greek word used here means both *covenant* and *will* [d] Other ancient authorities lack *and goats* [e] Or *tabernacle* [f] Other ancient authorities read *they* [g] Gk *he* [h] Meaning of Gk uncertain [i] Gk *by that will* [j] Gk *this one*

sacrifice for sins, "he sat down at the right hand
of God," 13 and since then has been waiting
"until his enemies would be made a footstool
for his feet." 14 For by a single offering he has
perfected for all time those who are sanctified.
15 And the Holy Spirit also testifies to us, for after saying,
16 "This is the covenant that I will make with
them
after those days, says the Lord:
I will put my laws in their hearts,
and I will write them on their minds,"
17 he also adds,
"I will remember[a] their sins and their lawless
deeds no more."
18 Where there is forgiveness of these, there is no
longer any offering for sin.
19 Therefore, my friends,[b] since we have
confidence to enter the sanctuary by the blood of
Jesus, 20 by the new and living way that he opened
for us through the curtain (that is, through his
flesh), 21 and since we have a great priest over
the house of God, 22 let us approach with a true
heart in full assurance of faith, with our hearts
sprinkled clean from an evil conscience and our
bodies washed with pure water. 23 Let us hold
fast to the confession of our hope without wavering, for he who has promised is faithful. 24 And
let us consider how to provoke one another to
love and good deeds, 25 not neglecting to meet
together, as is the habit of some, but encouraging
one another, and all the more as you see the Day
approaching.
26 For if we willfully persist in sin after having received the knowledge of the truth, there
no longer remains a sacrifice for sins, 27 but a
fearful prospect of judgment, and a fury of fire
that will consume the adversaries. 28 Anyone
who has violated the law of Moses dies without mercy "on the testimony of two or three
witnesses." 29 How much worse punishment do
you think will be deserved by those who have
spurned the Son of God, profaned the blood of
the covenant by which they were sanctified, and
outraged the Spirit of grace? 30 For we know the

Hebrews 10:26-27

The letter's theological argument concerning the heavenly action of Christ, of which earthly rites in the temple are only inferior copies, has a dramatic moral consequence. There is no longer any further sacrifice available for those who have come to Christ and then "willfully persist in sin" (or "fall away," 6:6). This teaching so alarmed some in the early church that the second-century prophet Hermas was moved to proclaim as revelation the offer of a single second chance at repentance—but no more (*Shepherd*, Mand. 3). Eventually the mainstream church developed a more complex—but less rigorous—penitential system.

— *NE*

one who said, "Vengeance is mine, I will repay."
And again, "The Lord will judge his people." 31 It
is a fearful thing to fall into the hands of the living God.
32 But recall those earlier days when, after
you had been enlightened, you endured a hard
struggle with sufferings, 33 sometimes being
publicly exposed to abuse and persecution, and
sometimes being partners with those so treated.
34 For you had compassion for those who were
in prison, and you cheerfully accepted the plundering of your possessions, knowing that you
yourselves possessed something better and more
lasting. 35 Do not, therefore, abandon that confidence of yours; it brings a great reward. 36 For you
need endurance, so that when you have done the
will of God, you may receive what was promised.
37 For yet
"in a very little while,
the one who is coming will come and will
not delay;
38 but my righteous one will live by faith.
My soul takes no pleasure in anyone who
shrinks back."
39 But we are not among those who shrink back
and so are lost, but among those who have faith
and so are saved.

[a] Gk *on their minds and I will remember* [b] Gk *Therefore, brothers*

11 Now faith is the assurance of things hoped
for, the conviction of things not seen. 2In-
deed, by faith[a] our ancestors received approval.
3By faith we understand that the worlds were
prepared by the word of God, so that what is seen
was made from things that are not visible.[b]

4 By faith Abel offered to God a more acceptable[c] sacrifice than Cain's. Through this he
received approval as righteous, God himself giving approval to his gifts; he died, but through his
faith[d] he still speaks. 5By faith Enoch was taken so
that he did not experience death; and "he was not
found, because God had taken him." For it was
attested before he was taken away that "he had
pleased God." 6And without faith it is impossible
to please God, for whoever would approach him
must believe that he exists and that he rewards
those who seek him. 7By faith Noah, warned by
God about events as yet unseen, respected the
warning and built an ark to save his household;
by this he condemned the world and became an
heir to the righteousness that is in accordance
with faith.

8 By faith Abraham obeyed when he was
called to set out for a place that he was to receive
as an inheritance; and he set out, not knowing
where he was going. 9By faith he stayed for a time
in the land he had been promised, as in a foreign
land, living in tents, as did Isaac and Jacob, who
were heirs with him of the same promise. 10For
he looked forward to the city that has foundations, whose architect and builder is God. 11By
faith he received power of procreation, even
though he was too old—and Sarah herself was
barren—because he considered him faithful who
had promised.[e] 12Therefore from one person, and
this one as good as dead, descendants were born,
"as many as the stars of heaven and as the innumerable grains of sand by the seashore."

13 All of these died in faith without having
received the promises, but from a distance they
saw and greeted them. They confessed that they
were strangers and foreigners on the earth, 14for
people who speak in this way make it clear that
they are seeking a homeland. 15If they had been
thinking of the land that they had left behind,
they would have had opportunity to return. 16But
as it is, they desire a better country, that is, a heavenly one. Therefore God is not ashamed to be
called their God; indeed, he has prepared a city
for them.

17 By faith Abraham, when put to the test, offered up Isaac. He who had received the promises
was ready to offer up his only son, 18of whom he
had been told, "It is through Isaac that descendants shall be named for you." 19He considered
the fact that God is able even to raise someone
from the dead—and figuratively speaking, he
did receive him back. 20By faith Isaac invoked
blessings for the future on Jacob and Esau. 21By
faith Jacob, when dying, blessed each of the sons
of Joseph, "bowing in worship over the top of
his staff." 22By faith Joseph, at the end of his life,
made mention of the exodus of the Israelites and
gave instructions about his burial.[f]

23 By faith Moses was hidden by his parents
for three months after his birth, because they
saw that the child was beautiful; and they were
not afraid of the king's edict.[g] 24By faith Moses,
when he was grown up, refused to be called a son
of Pharaoh's daughter, 25choosing rather to share
ill-treatment with the people of God than to enjoy the fleeting pleasures of sin. 26He considered
abuse suffered for the Christ[h] to be greater wealth
than the treasures of Egypt, for he was looking
ahead to the reward. 27By faith he left Egypt,
unafraid of the king's anger; for he persevered as
though[i] he saw him who is invisible. 28By faith
he kept the Passover and the sprinkling of blood,
so that the destroyer of the firstborn would not
touch the firstborn of Israel.[j]

29 By faith the people passed through the
Red Sea as if it were dry land, but when the Egyptians attempted to do so they were drowned. 30By

[a] Gk *by this* [b] Or *was not made out of visible things* [c] Gk *greater* [d] Gk *through it* [e] Or *By faith Sarah herself, though barren, received power to conceive, even when she was too old, because she considered him faithful who had promised.* [f] Gk *his bones* [g] Other ancient authorities add *By faith Moses, when he was grown up, killed the Egyptian, because he observed the humiliation of his people* (Gk *brothers*) [h] Or *the Messiah* [i] Or *because* [j] Gk *would not touch them*

faith the walls of Jericho fell after they had been
encircled for seven days. 31 By faith Rahab the
prostitute did not perish with those who were
disobedient,[a] because she had received the spies
in peace.

32 And what more should I say? For time
would fail me to tell of Gideon, Barak, Samson,
Jephthah, of David and Samuel and the prophets— 33 who through faith conquered kingdoms,
administered justice, obtained promises, shut the
mouths of lions, 34 quenched raging fire, escaped
the edge of the sword, won strength out of weakness, became mighty in war, put foreign armies
to flight. 35 Women received their dead by resurrection. Others were tortured, refusing to accept
release, in order to obtain a better resurrection.
36 Others suffered mocking and flogging, and even
chains and imprisonment. 37 They were stoned to
death, they were sawn in two,[b] they were killed by
the sword; they went about in skins of sheep and
goats, destitute, persecuted, tormented— 38 of
whom the world was not worthy. They wandered
in deserts and mountains, and in caves and holes
in the ground.

39 Yet all these, though they were commended
for their faith, did not receive what was promised, 40 since God had provided something better
so that they would not, apart from us, be made
perfect.

12 Therefore, since we are surrounded by
so great a cloud of witnesses, let us also
lay aside every weight and the sin that clings so
closely,[c] and let us run with perseverance the race
that is set before us, 2 looking to Jesus the pioneer
and perfecter of our faith, who for the sake of[d]
the joy that was set before him endured the cross,
disregarding its shame, and has taken his seat at
the right hand of the throne of God.

3 Consider him who endured such hostility
against himself from sinners,[e] so that you may
not grow weary or lose heart. 4 In your struggle
against sin you have not yet resisted to the point
of shedding your blood. 5 And you have forgotten
the exhortation that addresses you as children—

"My child, do not regard lightly the discipline
of the Lord,
or lose heart when you are punished by
him;
6 for the Lord disciplines those whom he
loves,
and chastises every child whom he
accepts."

7 Endure trials for the sake of discipline. God is
treating you as children; for what child is there
whom a parent does not discipline? 8 If you do
not have that discipline in which all children
share, then you are illegitimate and not his children. 9 Moreover, we had human parents to discipline us, and we respected them. Should we not
be even more willing to be subject to the Father
of spirits and live? 10 For they disciplined us for a
short time as seemed best to them, but he disciplines us for our good, in order that we may share
his holiness. 11 Now, discipline always seems painful rather than pleasant at the time, but later it
yields the peaceful fruit of righteousness to those
who have been trained by it.

12 Therefore lift your drooping hands and
strengthen your weak knees, 13 and make straight
paths for your feet, so that what is lame may not
be put out of joint, but rather be healed.

14 Pursue peace with everyone, and the holiness without which no one will see the Lord.
15 See to it that no one fails to obtain the grace
of God; that no root of bitterness springs up
and causes trouble, and through it many become defiled. 16 See to it that no one becomes
like Esau, an immoral and godless person, who
sold his birthright for a single meal. 17 You know
that later, when he wanted to inherit the blessing, he was rejected, for he found no chance to
repent,[f] even though he sought the blessing[g]
with tears.

18 You have not come to something[h] that
can be touched, a blazing fire, and darkness, and
gloom, and a tempest, 19 and the sound of a trum-

[a] Or *unbelieving* [b] Other ancient authorities add *they were tempted* [c] Other ancient authorities read *sin that easily distracts* [d] Or *who instead of* [e] Other ancient authorities read *such hostility from sinners against themselves* [f] Or *no chance to change his father's mind* [g] Gk *it* [h] Other ancient authorities read *a mountain*

pet, and a voice whose words made the hearers
beg that not another word be spoken to them.
20 (For they could not endure the order that was
given, "If even an animal touches the mountain,
it shall be stoned to death." 21 Indeed, so terrifying was the sight that Moses said, "I tremble with
fear.") 22 But you have come to Mount Zion and
to the city of the living God, the heavenly Jerusalem, and to innumerable angels in festal gathering, 23 and to the assembly[a] of the firstborn who
are enrolled in heaven, and to God the judge of
all, and to the spirits of the righteous made perfect, 24 and to Jesus, the mediator of a new covenant, and to the sprinkled blood that speaks a
better word than the blood of Abel.

25 See that you do not refuse the one who
is speaking; for if they did not escape when they
refused the one who warned them on earth, how
much less will we escape if we reject the one
who warns from heaven! 26 At that time his voice
shook the earth; but now he has promised, "Yet
once more I will shake not only the earth but also
the heaven." 27 This phrase, "Yet once more," indicates the removal of what is shaken—that is,
created things—so that what cannot be shaken
may remain. 28 Therefore, since we are receiving a kingdom that cannot be shaken, let us give
thanks, by which we offer to God an acceptable
worship with reverence and awe; 29 for indeed our
God is a consuming fire.

13 Let mutual love continue. 2 Do not neglect to show hospitality to strangers,
for by doing that some have entertained angels
without knowing it. 3 Remember those who are
in prison, as though you were in prison with
them; those who are being tortured, as though
you yourselves were being tortured.[b] 4 Let marriage be held in honor by all, and let the marriage
bed be kept undefiled; for God will judge fornicators and adulterers. 5 Keep your lives free from
the love of money, and be content with what you
have; for he has said, "I will never leave you or
forsake you." 6 So we can say with confidence,

"The Lord is my helper;
I will not be afraid.
What can anyone do to me?"

7 Remember your leaders, those who spoke
the word of God to you; consider the outcome
of their way of life, and imitate their faith. 8 Jesus
Christ is the same yesterday and today and forever. 9 Do not be carried away by all kinds of
strange teachings; for it is well for the heart to
be strengthened by grace, not by regulations
about food,[c] which have not benefited those
who observe them. 10 We have an altar from
which those who officiate in the tent[d] have no
right to eat. 11 For the bodies of those animals
whose blood is brought into the sanctuary by
the high priest as a sacrifice for sin are burned
outside the camp. 12 Therefore Jesus also suffered outside the city gate in order to sanctify
the people by his own blood. 13 Let us then go
to him outside the camp and bear the abuse
he endured. 14 For here we have no lasting city,
but we are looking for the city that is to come.
15 Through him, then, let us continually offer a
sacrifice of praise to God, that is, the fruit of lips
that confess his name. 16 Do not neglect to do
good and to share what you have, for such sacrifices are pleasing to God.

17 Obey your leaders and submit to them,
for they are keeping watch over your souls and
will give an account. Let them do this with joy
and not with sighing—for that would be harmful
to you.

18 Pray for us; we are sure that we have a
clear conscience, desiring to act honorably in all
things. 19 I urge you all the more to do this, so that
I may be restored to you very soon.

20 Now may the God of peace, who brought
back from the dead our Lord Jesus, the great
shepherd of the sheep, by the blood of the eternal covenant, 21 make you complete in everything
good so that you may do his will, working among
us[e] that which is pleasing in his sight, through
Jesus Christ, to whom be the glory forever and
ever. Amen.

[a] Or *angels, and to the festal gathering* [23]*and assembly* [b] Gk *were in the body* [c] Gk *not by foods* [d] Or *tabernacle*
[e] Other ancient authorities read *you*

22 I appeal to you, brothers and sisters,[a]
bear with my word of exhortation, for I have
written to you briefly. 23I want you to know that
our brother Timothy has been set free; and if he
comes in time, he will be with me when I see
you. 24Greet all your leaders and all the saints.
Those from Italy send you greetings. 25Grace be
with all of you.[b]

[a] Gk *brothers* [b] Other ancient authorities add *Amen*

The Letter of James

ALMOST HIDDEN among the many letters written by or attributed to Paul is James's brief letter to his churches. We who read this letter today are left with some unanswered—and possibly unanswerable—questions. We don't know who really wrote the letter or when it was written. Some biblical scholars think it was written by an anonymous author in the second century CE; others, that it was written by James, the brother of Jesus, which would put it in the 50s and make it contemporary with the letters of Paul of Tarsus. But this we can say with relative certainty: James is an *advice letter* to those James calls his "brothers and sisters" (1:2) and " my beloved" (1:16).

Children to whom God gave birth

James gives his community two striking identities. First he calls them the birth-children of God! This is a startling image, because Christians are used to identifying *Jesus* as God's begotten son and understanding themselves as God's *adopted* children. But James says God gave birth to the faithful by means of the "word of truth" so that they, like Christ, might be the "first fruits of his creatures" (1:18). Equally startling to me as a woman is the *femaleness* of James's God. James testifies that God, the source of wisdom (1:5), the giver of the royal law (2:8) and the law of freedom (1:25), is also the one who "gave us birth" (1:18); the metaphor depicts God as the community's birth-mother, laboring over the birthing stool to give them life!

James's people have another identity. He calls them "the twelve tribes in the Dispersion" (1:1). James probably does not mean that they are literally the people—or even the descendants of the people—who were exiled in 587 BCE. Rather, James is reminding his community that they are not "from here." Remembering that one is not from here is a constant theme in immigrant families such as my own. Even thirty years into my U.S. sojourn, I am reminded that my origins are with black and brown peoples outside the continental United States: from Africa, yes, but also of the Carib peoples and from the Indian subcontinent, all forcibly dispersed—exiled—in what the Rastafarians call Babylon, the islands of the British Caribbean.

To my immigrant ears, two of James's themes resonate. First, I am reminded that sojourners should be careful about whom they befriend. For as James remarks angrily, "friendship with the world is enmity with God" (4:4). Second, I am exhorted to endure when times are difficult, for although God "tempts no one" (1:13-14), this world in which we live can at times be a trial.

In light of the trials of life in exile, James in effect tells his community that "you must have that true religion." For James, true religion is marked by the person who prays, "Bridle my tongue; let my words edify," for James despises bragging, slander, grumbling, and other misuses of the tongue (3:2-5, 9; 4:1; 5:9). True religion requires an active faith that can be demonstrated in what one does (2:17). Importantly, true or "pure" religion means meeting the needs of the poor, the orphaned, and the widow (1:27). James excoriates the wealthy who oppress his people (5:1-6). In short, true religion, or what James calls "the wisdom from above" (3:17), is a life lived in worship of God, justice to others, and self-control. It is to this life that James's community, and all of us who understand life in exile, are called.

— Margaret Aymer Oget

1 James, a servant[a] of God and of the Lord
Jesus Christ,
To the twelve tribes in the Dispersion:
Greetings.

2 My brothers and sisters,[b] whenever you
face trials of any kind, consider it nothing but joy,
3because you know that the testing of your faith
produces endurance; 4and let endurance have its
full effect, so that you may be mature and complete, lacking in nothing.
5 If any of you is lacking in wisdom, ask God,
who gives to all generously and ungrudgingly,
and it will be given you. 6But ask in faith, never
doubting, for the one who doubts is like a wave
of the sea, driven and tossed by the wind; 7, 8for
the doubter, being double-minded and unstable
in every way, must not expect to receive anything
from the Lord.
9 Let the believer[c] who is lowly boast in being raised up, 10and the rich in being brought low,
because the rich will disappear like a flower in the
field. 11For the sun rises with its scorching heat
and withers the field; its flower falls, and its beauty
perishes. It is the same way with the rich; in the
midst of a busy life, they will wither away.
12 Blessed is anyone who endures temptation. Such a one has stood the test and will receive
the crown of life that the Lord[d] has promised to
those who love him. 13No one, when tempted,
should say, "I am being tempted by God"; for God
cannot be tempted by evil and he himself tempts
no one. 14But one is tempted by one's own desire,
being lured and enticed by it; 15then, when that
desire has conceived, it gives birth to sin, and that
sin, when it is fully grown, gives birth to death.
16Do not be deceived, my beloved.[e]
17 Every generous act of giving, with every
perfect gift, is from above, coming down from
the Father of lights, with whom there is no variation or shadow due to change.[f] 18In fulfillment
of his own purpose he gave us birth by the word
of truth, so that we would become a kind of first
fruits of his creatures.
19 You must understand this, my beloved:[e]
let everyone be quick to listen, slow to speak,

[a] Gk *slave* [b] Gk *brothers* [c] Gk *brother* [d] Gk *he*; other ancient authorities read *God* [e] Gk *my beloved brothers*
[f] Other ancient authorities read *variation due to a shadow of turning*

slow to anger; 20 for your anger does not produce
God's righteousness. 21 Therefore rid yourselves
of all sordidness and rank growth of wickedness,
and welcome with meekness the implanted word
that has the power to save your souls.

22 But be doers of the word, and not merely
hearers who deceive themselves. 23 For if any are
hearers of the word and not doers, they are like
those who look at themselves[a] in a mirror; 24 for
they look at themselves and, on going away, immediately forget what they were like. 25 But those
who look into the perfect law, the law of liberty,
and persevere, being not hearers who forget but
doers who act—they will be blessed in their
doing.

26 If any think they are religious, and do not
bridle their tongues but deceive their hearts, their
religion is worthless. 27 Religion that is pure and
undefiled before God, the Father, is this: to care
for orphans and widows in their distress, and to
keep oneself unstained by the world.

2 My brothers and sisters,[b] do you with your
acts of favoritism really believe in our glorious Lord Jesus Christ?[c] 2 For if a person with gold
rings and in fine clothes comes into your assembly,
and if a poor person in dirty clothes also comes in,
3 and if you take notice of the one wearing the fine
clothes and say, "Have a seat here, please," while
to the one who is poor you say, "Stand there," or,
"Sit at my feet,"[d] 4 have you not made distinctions
among yourselves, and become judges with evil
thoughts? 5 Listen, my beloved brothers and sisters.[e] Has not God chosen the poor in the world
to be rich in faith and to be heirs of the kingdom
that he has promised to those who love him? 6 But
you have dishonored the poor. Is it not the rich
who oppress you? Is it not they who drag you into
court? 7 Is it not they who blaspheme the excellent name that was invoked over you?

8 You do well if you really fulfill the royal
law according to the scripture, "You shall love
your neighbor as yourself." 9 But if you show partiality, you commit sin and are convicted by the
law as transgressors. 10 For whoever keeps the
whole law but fails in one point has become accountable for all of it. 11 For the one who said,
"You shall not commit adultery," also said, "You
shall not murder." Now if you do not commit
adultery but if you murder, you have become a
transgressor of the law. 12 So speak and so act as
those who are to be judged by the law of liberty.
13 For judgment will be without mercy to anyone who has shown no mercy; mercy triumphs
over judgment.

14 What good is it, my brothers and sisters,[e]
if you say you have faith but do not have works?
Can faith save you? 15 If a brother or sister is naked and lacks daily food, 16 and one of you says
to them, "Go in peace; keep warm and eat your
fill," and yet you do not supply their bodily needs,
what is the good of that? 17 So faith by itself, if it
has no works, is dead.

18 But someone will say, "You have faith and
I have works." Show me your faith apart from your
works, and I by my works will show you my faith.
19 You believe that God is one; you do well. Even
the demons believe—and shudder. 20 Do you
want to be shown, you senseless person, that faith
apart from works is barren? 21 Was not our ancestor Abraham justified by works when he offered
his son Isaac on the altar? 22 You see that faith was
active along with his works, and faith was brought

James 2:1-7

There are perhaps no words in the Bible more difficult than these for the prosperous churches of the global North, for whom increasing the congregational pledge base and denominational "market share" are constant preoccupations. James calls on the churches to find their true solidarity with the poor, not the oppressive rich, and condemns the feigned concern that masks a practiced indifference (2:14-17).

—NE

[a] Gk *at the face of his birth* [b] Gk *My brothers* [c] Or *hold the faith of our glorious Lord Jesus Christ without acts of favoritism*
[d] Gk *Sit under my footstool* [e] Gk *brothers*

to completion by the works. 23Thus the scripture
was fulfilled that says, "Abraham believed God,
and it was reckoned to him as righteousness," and
he was called the friend of God. 24You see that
a person is justified by works and not by faith
alone. 25Likewise, was not Rahab the prostitute
also justified by works when she welcomed the
messengers and sent them out by another road?
26For just as the body without the spirit is dead,
so faith without works is also dead.

3 Not many of you should become teachers,
my brothers and sisters,[a] for you know that
we who teach will be judged with greater strictness. 2For all of us make many mistakes. Anyone
who makes no mistakes in speaking is perfect,
able to keep the whole body in check with a bridle. 3If we put bits into the mouths of horses to
make them obey us, we guide their whole bodies.
4Or look at ships: though they are so large that
it takes strong winds to drive them, yet they are
guided by a very small rudder wherever the will
of the pilot directs. 5So also the tongue is a small
member, yet it boasts of great exploits.

How great a forest is set ablaze by a small fire!
6And the tongue is a fire. The tongue is placed
among our members as a world of iniquity; it
stains the whole body, sets on fire the cycle of
nature,[b] and is itself set on fire by hell.[c] 7For every species of beast and bird, of reptile and sea
creature, can be tamed and has been tamed by
the human species, 8but no one can tame the
tongue—a restless evil, full of deadly poison.
9With it we bless the Lord and Father, and with
it we curse those who are made in the likeness
of God. 10From the same mouth come blessing
and cursing. My brothers and sisters,[d] this ought
not to be so. 11Does a spring pour forth from the
same opening both fresh and brackish water?
12Can a fig tree, my brothers and sisters,[e] yield
olives, or a grapevine figs? No more can salt water
yield fresh.

13 Who is wise and understanding among
you? Show by your good life that your works are
done with gentleness born of wisdom. 14But if
you have bitter envy and selfish ambition in your
hearts, do not be boastful and false to the truth.
15Such wisdom does not come down from above,
but is earthly, unspiritual, devilish. 16For where
there is envy and selfish ambition, there will also
be disorder and wickedness of every kind. 17But
the wisdom from above is first pure, then peaceable, gentle, willing to yield, full of mercy and
good fruits, without a trace of partiality or hypocrisy. 18And a harvest of righteousness is sown in
peace for[f] those who make peace.

4 Those conflicts and disputes among you,
where do they come from? Do they not come
from your cravings that are at war within you?
2You want something and do not have it; so you

[a] Gk *brothers* [b] Or *wheel of birth* [c] Gk *Gehenna* [d] Gk *My brothers* [e] Gk *my brothers* [f] Or *by*

James 3

Frederick Douglass found the Letter of James particularly helpful as he tried to describe his understanding of true religion. In his most famous speech, "What to the Slave Is the Fourth of July?" he charges that ministers who uphold slavery

> make religion a cold and flinty-hearted thing. . . . It is a religion for oppressors, tyrants, man-stealers and thugs. It is not that "pure and undefiled religion" which is from above, and which is "first pure, then peaceable, easy to be entreated, full of mercy and good fruits, without partiality, and without hypocrisy."[74]

What is true religion to you?

—*MAO*

commit murder. And you covet[a] something and
cannot obtain it; so you engage in disputes and
conflicts. You do not have, because you do not
ask. 3You ask and do not receive, because you ask
wrongly, in order to spend what you get on your
pleasures. 4Adulterers! Do you not know that
friendship with the world is enmity with God?
Therefore whoever wishes to be a friend of the
world becomes an enemy of God. 5Or do you
suppose that it is for nothing that the scripture
says, "God[b] yearns jealously for the spirit that he
has made to dwell in us"? 6But he gives all the
more grace; therefore it says,

"God opposes the proud,
but gives grace to the humble."

7Submit yourselves therefore to God. Resist the
devil, and he will flee from you. 8Draw near to
God, and he will draw near to you. Cleanse your
hands, you sinners, and purify your hearts, you
double-minded. 9Lament and mourn and weep.
Let your laughter be turned into mourning and
your joy into dejection. 10Humble yourselves before the Lord, and he will exalt you.

11 Do not speak evil against one another, brothers and sisters.[c] Whoever speaks evil against another or judges another, speaks evil against the law
and judges the law; but if you judge the law, you are
not a doer of the law but a judge. 12There is one lawgiver and judge who is able to save and to destroy.
So who, then, are you to judge your neighbor?

13 Come now, you who say, "Today or tomorrow we will go to such and such a town and spend
a year there, doing business and making money."
14Yet you do not even know what tomorrow will
bring. What is your life? For you are a mist that
appears for a little while and then vanishes. 15In-
stead you ought to say, "If the Lord wishes, we
will live and do this or that." 16As it is, you boast
in your arrogance; all such boasting is evil. 17Any-
one, then, who knows the right thing to do and
fails to do it, commits sin.

5 Come now, you rich people, weep and wail
for the miseries that are coming to you. 2Your
riches have rotted, and your clothes are moth-
eaten. 3Your gold and silver have rusted, and their
rust will be evidence against you, and it will eat
your flesh like fire. You have laid up treasure[d] for
the last days. 4Listen! The wages of the laborers
who mowed your fields, which you kept back by
fraud, cry out, and the cries of the harvesters have
reached the ears of the Lord of hosts. 5You have
lived on the earth in luxury and in pleasure; you
have fattened your hearts in a day of slaughter.
6You have condemned and murdered the righteous one, who does not resist you.

7 Be patient, therefore, beloved,[c] until the
coming of the Lord. The farmer waits for the precious crop from the earth, being patient with it
until it receives the early and the late rains. 8You
also must be patient. Strengthen your hearts, for
the coming of the Lord is near.[e] 9Beloved,[f] do not
grumble against one another, so that you may not
be judged. See, the Judge is standing at the doors!
10As an example of suffering and patience, beloved,[c]
take the prophets who spoke in the name of the
Lord. 11Indeed we call blessed those who showed
endurance. You have heard of the endurance of
Job, and you have seen the purpose of the Lord,
how the Lord is compassionate and merciful.

12 Above all, my beloved,[c] do not swear, either by heaven or by earth or by any other oath,
but let your "Yes" be yes and your "No" be no, so
that you may not fall under condemnation.

13 Are any among you suffering? They should
pray. Are any cheerful? They should sing songs of
praise. 14Are any among you sick? They should call
for the elders of the church and have them pray
over them, anointing them with oil in the name
of the Lord. 15The prayer of faith will save the
sick, and the Lord will raise them up; and anyone
who has committed sins will be forgiven. 16There-
fore confess your sins to one another, and pray
for one another, so that you may be healed. The
prayer of the righteous is powerful and effective.
17Elijah was a human being like us, and he prayed
fervently that it might not rain, and for three
years and six months it did not rain on the earth.

[a] Or *you murder and you covet* [b] Gk *He* [c] Gk *brothers* [d] Or *will eat your flesh, since you have stored up fire*
[e] Or *is at hand* [f] Gk *Brothers*

18 Then he prayed again, and the heaven gave rain
and the earth yielded its harvest.
19 My brothers and sisters,[a] if anyone among
you wanders from the truth and is brought back
by another, 20 you should know that whoever
brings back a sinner from wandering will save the
sinner's[b] soul from death and will cover a multitude of sins.

[a] Gk *My brothers* [b] Gk *his*

The First Letter of Peter

THE FIRST LETTER OF PETER IS AN EXHORTATION written with the dual purpose of *encouraging* Christians going through difficult times due to the distinctiveness of their way of life and *witnessing* to them the "true grace of God" (5:12). The letter exhorts readers to rejoice even in time of unjust trials and suffering (1:6-7) and to maintain good behavior in the world (2:11-12; 4:7-11). It is directed to Christians in a broad region of Asia Minor whose social and religious identity made them "exiles" (1:2) and "aliens" (2:11) within the much larger non-Christian population. These terms had earlier been used to refer to Jews living outside Palestine, but now they refer to the dispersion of Christians. This experience of alienation is the result of their being called by the grace of God to be "a chosen race, a royal priesthood, a holy nation, God's own people, in order that you may proclaim the mighty acts of him who called you out of darkness into his marvelous light" (2:9; see Exod 19:5-6). God made these exiles and aliens into God's people (2:10; see Hos 1:6-9 and 2:23).

First Peter is usually dated sometime during the last quarter of the first century. It was probably written from Rome (5:13—"your sister church in Babylon") by someone who was ministered to and influenced by Peter. One reason for doubting Peter's own authorship has to do with the refined Greek used in the letter, unlikely the style of a Galilean fisherman. The letter follows the regular pattern of other letters in the New Testament: a greeting or opening formula (1:1-2); a blessing (1:3-12); the body of the letter (1:13—5:11), consisting of a call to holy living (1:13—2:10) and the adoption of appropriate behavior for Christians in a strange world (2:11—4:11), followed by an exhortation (4:12—5:11) and a closing formula (5:12-14).

First Peter calls Christians to recognize their distance and difference from the dominant culture and to resist cultural assimilation, even in times of repression and persecution (4:12-19). As a first-generation Latino from Puerto Rico, the identification of the letter's addressees as exiles gets my attention. Although the language may be used figuratively for the audience of the letter, for those whose experience of exile (voluntary or not) is a daily experience, this expression has a personal meaning. When the dominant culture discriminates and alienates people because of the color of their skin, their gender, their accent, or other cultural differences, the experience of exile becomes real and painful. As it happened to many Christians during the time of the Roman Empire, many immigrants now are discriminated against not because they are criminals but simply because they are different.

To the Christians suffering alienation in a strange land, 1 Peter declares that they have been chosen and destined by God and sanctified by the Spirit to be obedient to Jesus Christ (1:1). This community of believers are called to live not according to their former lives but as holy people, different from the common expected behavior of the time (1:13-16). These aliens are "God's own people," a "chosen race," a "royal priesthood," and a "holy nation," called to witness to God's grace (2:9-10).

Written for a people struggling in the midst of affliction, suffering in spite of their innocence, the letter encourages the believers to persevere and remain faithful. God is the hope, strength, and support of the discriminated and persecuted (5:10-11). Even the letter writer's "sister church in Babylon" (5:13) identify themselves as faithful partners with these aliens and strangers in struggle and in pilgrimage.

In our multicultural global context, we may read 1 Peter as a challenge to defy discrimination based on social-cultural markers and to find creative ways to celebrate our human diversity.

— David Cortés-Fuentes

1 Peter, an apostle of Jesus Christ,
To the exiles of the Dispersion in Pontus, Galatia, Cappadocia, Asia, and Bithynia, 2 who have
been chosen and destined by God the Father and
sanctified by the Spirit to be obedient to Jesus
Christ and to be sprinkled with his blood:
May grace and peace be yours in abundance.
3 Blessed be the God and Father of our Lord
Jesus Christ! By his great mercy he has given us
a new birth into a living hope through the resurrection of Jesus Christ from the dead, 4 and into
an inheritance that is imperishable, undefiled,
and unfading, kept in heaven for you, 5 who are
being protected by the power of God through
faith for a salvation ready to be revealed in the
last time. 6 In this you rejoice,[a] even if now for a
little while you have had to suffer various trials,
7 so that the genuineness of your faith—being
more precious than gold that, though perishable, is tested by fire—may be found to result in
praise and glory and honor when Jesus Christ is
revealed. 8 Although you have not seen[b] him, you
love him; and even though you do not see him
now, you believe in him and rejoice with an indescribable and glorious joy, 9 for you are receiving
the outcome of your faith, the salvation of your
souls.
10 Concerning this salvation, the prophets
who prophesied of the grace that was to be yours
made careful search and inquiry, 11 inquiring
about the person or time that the Spirit of Christ
within them indicated when it testified in advance
to the sufferings destined for Christ and the subsequent glory. 12 It was revealed to them that they
were serving not themselves but you, in regard
to the things that have now been announced to
you through those who brought you good news
by the Holy Spirit sent from heaven—things into
which angels long to look!
13 Therefore prepare your minds for action;[c]
discipline yourselves; set all your hope on the
grace that Jesus Christ will bring you when he is
revealed. 14 Like obedient children, do not be
conformed to the desires that you formerly had in
ignorance. 15 Instead, as he who called you is holy,
be holy yourselves in all your conduct; 16 for it is
written, "You shall be holy, for I am holy."
17 If you invoke as Father the one who judges
all people impartially according to their deeds,
live in reverent fear during the time of your exile.

[a] Or *Rejoice in this* [b] Other ancient authorities read *known* [c] Gk *gird up the loins of your mind*

18You know that you were ransomed from the futile ways inherited from your ancestors, not with
perishable things like silver or gold, 19but with the
precious blood of Christ, like that of a lamb without defect or blemish. 20He was destined before
the foundation of the world, but was revealed at
the end of the ages for your sake. 21Through him
you have come to trust in God, who raised him
from the dead and gave him glory, so that your
faith and hope are set on God.

22 Now that you have purified your souls
by your obedience to the truth[a] so that you have
genuine mutual love, love one another deeply[b]
from the heart.[c] 23You have been born anew, not
of perishable but of imperishable seed, through
the living and enduring word of God.[d] 24For

"All flesh is like grass
and all its glory like the flower of grass.
The grass withers,
and the flower falls,
25 but the word of the Lord endures forever."

That word is the good news that was announced
to you.

2 Rid yourselves, therefore, of all malice, and all
guile, insincerity, envy, and all slander. 2Like
newborn infants, long for the pure, spiritual milk,
so that by it you may grow into salvation— 3if indeed you have tasted that the Lord is good.

4 Come to him, a living stone, though rejected by mortals yet chosen and precious in
God's sight, and 5like living stones, let yourselves
be built[e] into a spiritual house, to be a holy priesthood, to offer spiritual sacrifices acceptable to
God through Jesus Christ. 6For it stands in scripture:

"See, I am laying in Zion a stone,
a cornerstone chosen and precious;
and whoever believes in him[f] will not be put
to shame."

7To you then who believe, he is precious; but for
those who do not believe,

"The stone that the builders rejected
has become the very head of the corner,"

8and

"A stone that makes them stumble,
and a rock that makes them fall."

They stumble because they disobey the word, as
they were destined to do.

9 But you are a chosen race, a royal priesthood, a holy nation, God's own people,[g] in order
that you may proclaim the mighty acts of him
who called you out of darkness into his marvelous light.

10 Once you were not a people,
but now you are God's people;
once you had not received mercy,
but now you have received mercy.

11 Beloved, I urge you as aliens and exiles to
abstain from the desires of the flesh that wage war
against the soul. 12Conduct yourselves honorably
among the Gentiles, so that, though they malign
you as evildoers, they may see your honorable
deeds and glorify God when he comes to judge.[h]

13 For the Lord's sake accept the authority of
every human institution,[i] whether of the emperor
as supreme, 14or of governors, as sent by him to
punish those who do wrong and to praise those
who do right. 15For it is God's will that by doing right you should silence the ignorance of the
foolish. 16As servants[j] of God, live as free people,
yet do not use your freedom as a pretext for evil.
17Honor everyone. Love the family of believers.[k]
Fear God. Honor the emperor.

18 Slaves, accept the authority of your masters with all deference, not only those who are
kind and gentle but also those who are harsh.
19For it is a credit to you if, being aware of God,
you endure pain while suffering unjustly. 20If you
endure when you are beaten for doing wrong,
what credit is that? But if you endure when you
do right and suffer for it, you have God's approval.
21For to this you have been called, because Christ
also suffered for you, leaving you an example, so
that you should follow in his steps.

[a] Other ancient authorities add *through the Spirit* [b] Or *constantly* [c] Other ancient authorities read *a pure heart* [d] Or *through the word of the living and enduring God* [e] Or *you yourselves are being built* [f] Or *it* [g] Gk *a people for his possession* [h] Gk *God on the day of visitation* [i] Or *every institution ordained for human beings* [j] Gk *slaves* [k] Gk *Love the brotherhood*

1 Peter 2:18-20

Prior to the American Civil War, Southern slaveholders used the Bible to justify slavery as a God-ordained institution. The Northern abolitionists could not point to any biblical verses that condemned the practice. Passages such as these instructed slaves to obey their masters even when the masters were cruel. According to 1 Peter, there was a certain redemptive quality to unjust suffering. But those who have suffered oppression would argue that there is nothing redemptive in pain received unjustly. All undeserved suffering is contrary to God's will and, as such, must be resisted, not obediently borne.

— *MDLT*

22 "He committed no sin,
and no deceit was found in his mouth."
23 When he was abused, he did not return abuse;
when he suffered, he did not threaten; but he entrusted himself to the one who judges justly. 24 He
himself bore our sins in his body on the cross,[a] so
that, free from sins, we might live for righteousness; by his wounds[b] you have been healed. 25 For
you were going astray like sheep, but now you
have returned to the shepherd and guardian of
your souls.

3 Wives, in the same way, accept the authority of your husbands, so that, even if some of
them do not obey the word, they may be won over
without a word by their wives' conduct, 2 when
they see the purity and reverence of your lives.
3 Do not adorn yourselves outwardly by braid-
ing your hair, and by wearing gold ornaments or
fine clothing; 4 rather, let your adornment be the
inner self with the lasting beauty of a gentle and
quiet spirit, which is very precious in God's sight.
5 It was in this way long ago that the holy women
who hoped in God used to adorn themselves by
accepting the authority of their husbands. 6 Thus
Sarah obeyed Abraham and called him lord. You
have become her daughters as long as you do
what is good and never let fears alarm you.

7 Husbands, in the same way, show consideration for your wives in your life together, paying honor to the woman as the weaker sex,[c] since
they too are also heirs of the gracious gift of life—
so that nothing may hinder your prayers.
8 Finally, all of you, have unity of spirit, sympathy, love for one another, a tender heart, and a
humble mind. 9 Do not repay evil for evil or abuse
for abuse; but, on the contrary, repay with a blessing. It is for this that you were called—that you
might inherit a blessing. 10 For
"Those who desire life
and desire to see good days,
let them keep their tongues from evil
and their lips from speaking deceit;
11 let them turn away from evil and do good;
let them seek peace and pursue it.
12 For the eyes of the Lord are on the righteous,
and his ears are open to their prayer.
But the face of the Lord is against those who
do evil."
13 Now who will harm you if you are eager to
do what is good? 14 But even if you do suffer for

1 Peter 3:1-7

Not only must wives obediently fall under their husbands' rule, even when poorly treated; but 1 Peter goes on to state that this subjugation is for women's benefit because, after all, they are the weaker vessel. The danger of rooting patriarchy in God's word is that it creates a dominant-subordinate model that moves beyond the male-female relationship. Those who are conquered become like women who need to be dominated for their own sake. Establishing a dominant-subordinate social structure becomes the "white man's burden": men of color are emasculated so that, like women, they can be subjected. Like women, they, too, are weaker vessels. Patriarchy is wrong because of how women of all ethnicities and races are treated and because it becomes the pattern by which men of color are also subjugated.

— *MDLT*

[a] Or *carried up our sins in his body to the tree* [b] Gk *bruise* [c] Gk *vessel*

doing what is right, you are blessed. Do not fear
what they fear,[a] and do not be intimidated, 15but
in your hearts sanctify Christ as Lord. Always be
ready to make your defense to anyone who demands from you an accounting for the hope that
is in you; 16yet do it with gentleness and reverence.[b] Keep your conscience clear, so that, when
you are maligned, those who abuse you for your
good conduct in Christ may be put to shame.
17For it is better to suffer for doing good, if suffering should be God's will, than to suffer for doing evil. 18For Christ also suffered[c] for sins once
for all, the righteous for the unrighteous, in order
to bring you[d] to God. He was put to death in the
flesh, but made alive in the spirit, 19in which also
he went and made a proclamation to the spirits in
prison, 20who in former times did not obey, when
God waited patiently in the days of Noah, during the building of the ark, in which a few, that is,
eight persons, were saved through water. 21And
baptism, which this prefigured, now saves you—
not as a removal of dirt from the body, but as an
appeal to God for[e] a good conscience, through
the resurrection of Jesus Christ, 22who has gone
into heaven and is at the right hand of God, with
angels, authorities, and powers made subject
to him.

4 Since therefore Christ suffered in the flesh,[f]
arm yourselves also with the same intention
(for whoever has suffered in the flesh has finished
with sin), 2so as to live for the rest of your earthly
life[g] no longer by human desires but by the will
of God. 3You have already spent enough time in
doing what the Gentiles like to do, living in licentiousness, passions, drunkenness, revels, carousing, and lawless idolatry. 4They are surprised that
you no longer join them in the same excesses of
dissipation, and so they blaspheme.[h] 5But they
will have to give an accounting to him who stands
ready to judge the living and the dead. 6For this is
the reason the gospel was proclaimed even to the
dead, so that, though they had been judged in the
flesh as everyone is judged, they might live in the
spirit as God does.

7 The end of all things is near;[i] therefore be
serious and discipline yourselves for the sake of
your prayers. 8Above all, maintain constant love
for one another, for love covers a multitude of
sins. 9Be hospitable to one another without complaining. 10Like good stewards of the manifold
grace of God, serve one another with whatever
gift each of you has received. 11Whoever speaks
must do so as one speaking the very words of God;
whoever serves must do so with the strength that
God supplies, so that God may be glorified in all
things through Jesus Christ. To him belong the
glory and the power forever and ever. Amen.

12 Beloved, do not be surprised at the fiery
ordeal that is taking place among you to test you,
as though something strange were happening
to you. 13But rejoice insofar as you are sharing
Christ's sufferings, so that you may also be glad
and shout for joy when his glory is revealed. 14If
you are reviled for the name of Christ, you are
blessed, because the spirit of glory,[j] which is the
Spirit of God, is resting on you.[k] 15But let none
of you suffer as a murderer, a thief, a criminal, or
even as a mischief maker. 16Yet if any of you suffers as a Christian, do not consider it a disgrace,
but glorify God because you bear this name.
17For the time has come for judgment to begin
with the household of God; if it begins with us,
what will be the end for those who do not obey
the gospel of God? 18And

"If it is hard for the righteous to be saved,
what will become of the ungodly and the
sinners?"

19Therefore, let those suffering in accordance
with God's will entrust themselves to a faithful
Creator, while continuing to do good.

5 Now as an elder myself and a witness of
the sufferings of Christ, as well as one who
shares in the glory to be revealed, I exhort the

[a] Gk *their fear* [b] Or *respect* [c] Other ancient authorities read *died* [d] Other ancient authorities read *us*
[e] Or *a pledge to God from* [f] Other ancient authorities add *for us*; others, *for you* [g] Gk *rest of the time in the flesh*
[h] Or *they malign you* [i] Or *is at hand* [j] Other ancient authorities add *and of power*
[k] Other ancient authorities add *On their part he is blasphemed, but on your part he is glorified*

elders among you 2 to tend the flock of God that
is in your charge, exercising the oversight,[a] not
under compulsion but willingly, as God would
have you do it[b]—not for sordid gain but eagerly.
3 Do not lord it over those in your charge, but
be examples to the flock. 4 And when the chief
shepherd appears, you will win the crown of
glory that never fades away. 5 In the same way,
you who are younger must accept the authority
of the elders.[c] And all of you must clothe yourselves with humility in your dealings with one
another, for

"God opposes the proud,
but gives grace to the humble."

6 Humble yourselves therefore under the
mighty hand of God, so that he may exalt you in
due time. 7 Cast all your anxiety on him, because
he cares for you. 8 Discipline yourselves, keep
alert.[d] Like a roaring lion your adversary the devil
prowls around, looking for someone to devour.
9 Resist him, steadfast in your faith, for you know
that your brothers and sisters[e] in all the world are
undergoing the same kinds of suffering. 10 And after you have suffered for a little while, the God of
all grace, who has called you to his eternal glory in
Christ, will himself restore, support, strengthen,
and establish you. 11 To him be the power forever
and ever. Amen.

12 Through Silvanus, whom I consider a
faithful brother, I have written this short letter to
encourage you and to testify that this is the true
grace of God. Stand fast in it. 13 Your sister church[f]
in Babylon, chosen together with you, sends you
greetings; and so does my son Mark. 14 Greet one
another with a kiss of love.

Peace to all of you who are in Christ.[g]

[a] Other ancient authorities lack *exercising the oversight* [b] Other ancient authorities lack *as God would have you do it*
[c] Or *of those who are older* [d] Or *be vigilant* [e] Gk *your brotherhood* [f] Gk *She who is*
[g] Other ancient authorities add *Amen*

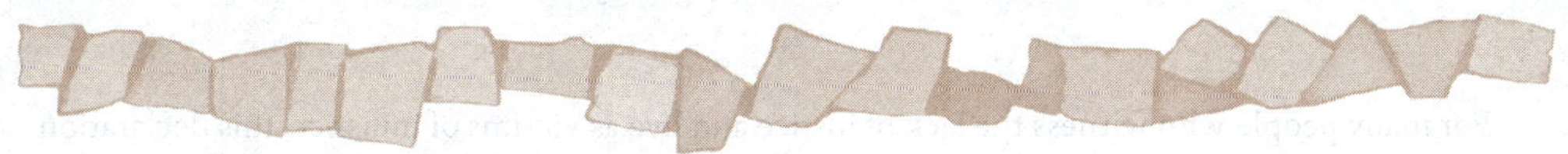

The Second Letter of Peter

SECOND PETER FOLLOWS THE FORM of a testament or farewell letter. The author uses it to remind readers of the teachings they have received and urges them to recall all of these things after his—the author's—death (1:12-15). He also warns them about false teachers (2:1-3) and encourages them to remain faithful and hopeful in a context of moral decay (2:10b-22).

The letter begins with a salutation (1:1-2), from Simeon Peter to fellow Christians, greeting them with grace and peace. The body of the letter (1:3—3:16) includes an exhortation to Christian character (1:3-15), the writer's claim of witnessing Christ's glory (1:16-21), a condemnation of false prophets and teachers (ch. 2), and a reminder of the coming of the Lord (3:1-16). The book concludes with an exhortation and blessing (3:17-18).

Although the author identifies himself as "Simeon Peter, a servant and apostle of Jesus Christ" (1:1), the letter reflects the language and concerns of a church of a much later period. The fact that the writer acknowledges Paul's letters (3:15-16) makes it clear that this letter was not written by Peter, since it is unlikely that Paul's letters had the status of Scripture during Peter's lifetime. Furthermore, the effort the author makes to show readers that his letter represents an authentic witness to the apostolic tradition (1:19-21; 3:2), the view of an eyewitness to the transfiguration of Jesus (1:16-18), and a sequel to an earlier letter they received from the same writer (3:1) all point to the pseudonymity of this letter—someone else writing in Peter's name. That was a common practice in antiquity, used by some to vest their writings with the authority of another author. The close similarity between this letter and the letter of Jude lends additional support to the argument that someone other than Peter was the author of 2 Peter.

The letter includes a denunciation and condemnation of false teachers and false prophets. It is directed against their greed, exploitation, and corrupt lifestyles as well as against their teachings (2:1-22; 3:1-13). The false teachers are similar to fallen angels, the people in the time of Noah, and the inhabitants of Sodom and Gomorrah (2:4-10). They deny the promise of the coming of the Lord, falsely contending that ever since the death of the earlier church leaders ("our ancestors") nothing has changed (3:1-7). The letter offers a more positive explanation of the delayed coming of the Lord: it is an extension of time, offering opportunity for repentance (2:8-9).

Second Peter is similar to the letter of Jude in its apocalyptic language and allusions to the stories of the Hebrew Bible as paradigms of the experience and struggles of the church. Especially distinctive is a statement that envisions a future similar to the one in the book of Revelation. Just before concluding the letter, the author urges the community to wait and hope "in accordance with his promise,... for new heavens and a new earth, where righteousness is at home" (3:13).

For many people who witness the lack of justice and live as victims of injustice, this declaration summarizes the hope of the letter and their own hope. The current system that perpetuates injustice by destroying natural resources, exploiting people, and putting too many resources in the hands of the few while too many people live in poverty and need cannot represent the final word of Scripture. This letter's call to faithfulness and hope is grounded in the certainty that believers will live "where righteousness is at home."

The hope expressed here for new heavens and a new earth finds its echo in the hope of many immigrants who come to the United States searching for a better life. My own experience as a first-generation Puerto Rican helps me understand this hope with a double perspective. First, I am keenly aware that not everyone experiences justice or enjoys the same opportunities to succeed. Second, I hear the message of the gospel as an invitation to continue the struggle for justice, and as an assurance that although there is still much to be done, God's promise is secure and firm. This hope sustains our struggles and strengthens our solidarity as people of God, waiting and working for a better future.

— David Cortés-Fuentes

1 Simeon[a] Peter, a servant[b] and apostle of Jesus
Christ,
To those who have received a faith as precious
as ours through the righteousness of our God and
Savior Jesus Christ:[c]
2 May grace and peace be yours in abundance
in the knowledge of God and of Jesus our Lord.
3 His divine power has given us everything
needed for life and godliness, through the knowledge of him who called us by[d] his own glory and
goodness. 4 Thus he has given us, through these
things, his precious and very great promises, so
that through them you may escape from the corruption that is in the world because of lust, and
may become participants of the divine nature.
5 For this very reason, you must make every effort to support your faith with goodness, and
goodness with knowledge, 6 and knowledge with
self-control, and self-control with endurance,
and endurance with godliness, 7 and godliness
with mutual[e] affection, and mutual[e] affection
with love. 8 For if these things are yours and are
increasing among you, they keep you from being
ineffective and unfruitful in the knowledge of our
Lord Jesus Christ. 9 For anyone who lacks these
things is short-sighted and blind, and is forgetful
of the cleansing of past sins. 10 Therefore, brothers
and sisters,[f] be all the more eager to confirm your
call and election, for if you do this, you will never
stumble. 11 For in this way, entry into the eternal
kingdom of our Lord and Savior Jesus Christ will
be richly provided for you.
12 Therefore I intend to keep on reminding you of these things, though you know them
already and are established in the truth that has
come to you. 13 I think it right, as long as I am
in this body,[g] to refresh your memory, 14 since I
know that my death[h] will come soon, as indeed
our Lord Jesus Christ has made clear to me.
15 And I will make every effort so that after my

[a] Other ancient authorities read *Simon* [b] Gk *slave* [c] Or *of our God and the Savior Jesus Christ* [d] Other ancient authorities read *through* [e] Gk *brotherly* [f] Gk *brothers* [g] Gk *tent* [h] Gk *the putting off of my tent*

departure you may be able at any time to recall
these things.
16 For we did not follow cleverly devised
myths when we made known to you the power
and coming of our Lord Jesus Christ, but we
had been eyewitnesses of his majesty. 17 For he
received honor and glory from God the Father
when that voice was conveyed to him by the
Majestic Glory, saying, "This is my Son, my Beloved,[a] with whom I am well pleased." 18 We ourselves heard this voice come from heaven, while
we were with him on the holy mountain.
19 So we have the prophetic message more
fully confirmed. You will do well to be attentive
to this as to a lamp shining in a dark place, until
the day dawns and the morning star rises in your
hearts. 20 First of all you must understand this,
that no prophecy of scripture is a matter of one's
own interpretation, 21 because no prophecy ever
came by human will, but men and women moved
by the Holy Spirit spoke from God.[b]

2 But false prophets also arose among the people, just as there will be false teachers among
you, who will secretly bring in destructive opinions. They will even deny the Master who bought
them—bringing swift destruction on themselves.
2 Even so, many will follow their licentious ways,
and because of these teachers[c] the way of truth
will be maligned. 3 And in their greed they will exploit you with deceptive words. Their condemnation, pronounced against them long ago, has not
been idle, and their destruction is not asleep.
4 For if God did not spare the angels when
they sinned, but cast them into hell[d] and committed them to chains[e] of deepest darkness to be kept
until the judgment; 5 and if he did not spare the
ancient world, even though he saved Noah, a herald of righteousness, with seven others, when he
brought a flood on a world of the ungodly; 6 and
if by turning the cities of Sodom and Gomorrah
to ashes he condemned them to extinction[f] and
made them an example of what is coming to the
ungodly;[g] 7 and if he rescued Lot, a righteous man
greatly distressed by the licentiousness of the lawless 8 (for that righteous man, living among them
day after day, was tormented in his righteous soul
by their lawless deeds that he saw and heard),
9 then the Lord knows how to rescue the godly
from trial, and to keep the unrighteous under
punishment until the day of judgment 10 —especially those who indulge their flesh in depraved
lust, and who despise authority.
Bold and willful, they are not afraid to slander
the glorious ones,[h] 11 whereas angels, though greater
in might and power, do not bring against them a
slanderous judgment from the Lord.[i] 12 These people, however, are like irrational animals, mere creatures of instinct, born to be caught and killed. They
slander what they do not understand, and when
those creatures are destroyed,[j] they also will be destroyed, 13 suffering[k] the penalty for doing wrong.
They count it a pleasure to revel in the daytime.
They are blots and blemishes, reveling in their dissipation[l] while they feast with you. 14 They have
eyes full of adultery, insatiable for sin. They entice
unsteady souls. They have hearts trained in greed.
Accursed children! 15 They have left the straight
road and have gone astray, following the road of
Balaam son of Bosor,[m] who loved the wages of doing wrong, 16 but was rebuked for his own transgression; a speechless donkey spoke with a human
voice and restrained the prophet's madness.
17 These are waterless springs and mists driven
by a storm; for them the deepest darkness has
been reserved. 18 For they speak bombastic nonsense, and with licentious desires of the flesh they
entice people who have just[n] escaped from those
who live in error. 19 They promise them freedom,
but they themselves are slaves of corruption; for
people are slaves to whatever masters them. 20 For

[a] Other ancient authorities read *my beloved Son* [b] Other ancient authorities read *but moved by the Holy Spirit saints of God spoke* [c] Gk *because of them* [d] Gk *Tartaros* [e] Other ancient authorities read *pits* [f] Other ancient authorities lack *to extinction* [g] Other ancient authorities read *an example to those who were to be ungodly* [h] Or *angels*; Gk *glories* [i] Other ancient authorities read *before the Lord*; others lack the phrase [j] Gk *in their destruction* [k] Other ancient authorities read *receiving* [l] Other ancient authorities read *love-feasts* [m] Other ancient authorities read *Beor* [n] Other ancient authorities read *actually*

if, after they have escaped the defilements of the
world through the knowledge of our Lord and
Savior Jesus Christ, they are again entangled in
them and overpowered, the last state has become
worse for them than the first. 21 For it would have
been better for them never to have known the
way of righteousness than, after knowing it, to
turn back from the holy commandment that was
passed on to them. 22 It has happened to them according to the true proverb,

"The dog turns back to its own vomit,"

and,

"The sow is washed only to wallow in the mud."

3 This is now, beloved, the second letter I am
writing to you; in them I am trying to arouse
your sincere intention by reminding you 2 that you
should remember the words spoken in the past by
the holy prophets, and the commandment of the
Lord and Savior spoken through your apostles.
3 First of all you must understand this, that in the
last days scoffers will come, scoffing and indulging
their own lusts 4 and saying, "Where is the promise
of his coming? For ever since our ancestors died,[a]
all things continue as they were from the beginning of creation!" 5 They deliberately ignore this
fact, that by the word of God heavens existed long
ago and an earth was formed out of water and by
means of water, 6 through which the world of that
time was deluged with water and perished. 7 But
by the same word the present heavens and earth
have been reserved for fire, being kept until the
day of judgment and destruction of the godless.

8 But do not ignore this one fact, beloved,
that with the Lord one day is like a thousand
years, and a thousand years are like one day. 9 The
Lord is not slow about his promise, as some think
of slowness, but is patient with you,[b] not wanting any to perish, but all to come to repentance.
10 But the day of the Lord will come like a thief,
and then the heavens will pass away with a loud
noise, and the elements will be dissolved with
fire, and the earth and everything that is done on
it will be disclosed.[c]

11 Since all these things are to be dissolved
in this way, what sort of persons ought you to be
in leading lives of holiness and godliness, 12 waiting for and hastening[d] the coming of the day of
God, because of which the heavens will be set
ablaze and dissolved, and the elements will melt
with fire? 13 But, in accordance with his promise,
we wait for new heavens and a new earth, where
righteousness is at home.

14 Therefore, beloved, while you are waiting for these things, strive to be found by him at
peace, without spot or blemish; 15 and regard the
patience of our Lord as salvation. So also our beloved brother Paul wrote to you according to the
wisdom given him, 16 speaking of this as he does in
all his letters. There are some things in them hard
to understand, which the ignorant and unstable
twist to their own destruction, as they do the other
scriptures. 17 You therefore, beloved, since you are
forewarned, beware that you are not carried away
with the error of the lawless and lose your own
stability. 18 But grow in the grace and knowledge
of our Lord and Savior Jesus Christ. To him be the
glory both now and to the day of eternity. Amen.[e]

2 Peter 3:1-10

In his 1963 manifesto for racial justice, James Baldwin charged that his countrymen had destroyed " hundreds of thousands of lives and do not know it and do not want to know it." "It is not permissible," he wrote, "that the authors of devastation should also be innocent. It is the innocence which constitutes the crime." Baldwin held out the prospect that the handful of "relatively conscious" blacks and whites might "end the racial nightmare" in the United States and "change the history of the world." The alternative, however, would be that "the fulfillment of that prophecy, re-created from the Bible in song by a slave, is upon us: *God gave Noah the rainbow sign, no more water, the fire next time!*"[75]

— *NE*

[a] Gk *our fathers fell asleep* [b] Other ancient authorities read *on your account* [c] Other ancient authorities read *will be burned up* [d] Or *earnestly desiring* [e] Other ancient authorities lack *Amen*

The First Letter of John

TRADITIONALLY, READERS ATTRIBUTED 1, 2, AND 3 JOHN to the anonymous author of the Fourth Gospel, who has conventionally been identified as the apostle John. But many scholars now debate that attribution. Because members of a theological "school" are more likely to share common ideas than a common style, I favor attributing the common style among these three epistles *and* the Fourth Gospel to a single author. In any case, all scholars use John's gospel as background for understanding these epistles and, although it is impossible to date them precisely, most scholars place them around the end of the first century, 90–110 CE.

Scholars also debate the background of these epistles beyond their apparent connection with the Fourth Gospel. Many think the author opposes an early form of what later became known as Gnosticism, because the opponents deny that Jesus truly "has come in the flesh" (1 John 4:2)—perhaps meaning that, in the eyes of the opponents, he only *seemed* to be human. Other scholars point out that we lack explicit evidence of Gnostics this early, although not of other theological opponents.

Some scholars suggest instead a situation in which local synagogues have expelled Jewish believers in Jesus, as John's gospel presupposes (John 9:22; 12:42; 16:2). In this case, those who "went out" and "denie[d] that Jesus is the Christ" (1 John 2:19, 22-23) might now be returning to the synagogues. But just as the seven churches of Asia Minor (Rev 2–3) faced a variety of situations, including conflicts with synagogues and compromises with immoral practices, we need not assume that these epistles address precisely the same situation as the Fourth Gospel.

Clearer indications of the background may be inferred from the Johannine epistles themselves. Some people have withdrawn from the fellowship of the community and no longer believe what the author considers the truth about Jesus. First John encourages believers not to let this departure by others shake their own faith. The Spirit within them assures them that they belong to Christ (1 John 3:24; 4:13; 5:7-8). The writer also offers a theological test by which believers can discern the true Spirit and Christ's true followers: they must believe in Jesus the incarnate Christ (1 John 2:22-23; 4:1-6; compare 2 John v. 7).

First John further offers a moral test: although the author knows that even believers sin sometimes, he graphically emphasizes that they must avoid sin, behaving righteously (1 John 2:3-4, 29; 3:4-10; 5:3, 18; 2 John v. 6). This righteous obedience to God's will especially involves loving their fellow believers (1 John 2:9-11; 3:10-17; see 2 John vv. 5-6). If faith and love are signs that one has eternal life (1 John 3:14-16, 23), the "mortal sin" (1 John 5:16) would be apostasy from faith and love.

Some issues that Christians debate today are more important than others. For John, recognizing that Jesus is Christ and Lord and that he fully shared our humanity are central and nonnegotiable tenets of Christian faith. But John also cares about ethics. By the time John wrote, the Christian movement was spreading among Gentiles (3 John v. 7). What does his teaching about love and remaining in fellowship say about Christians today who refuse to fellowship across racial or cultural lines? In addition to truly confessing Christ, a true Christian must love others who are Christ's. One who does not love one's brother or sister, God's children, cannot truly love God (1 John 4:20). If we are loyal to Christ, we share a deeper bond with fellow believers of different cultures, nations, or ethnicities than we do with others of our own culture who serve different lords. We must reject ethnocentrism (including all versions of apartheid) and chauvinistic nationalism.

A white convert from atheism to Christianity, I find John's message of cross-cultural love vital. In the time of my deepest brokenness, an African-American grandmother and her grandchildren welcomed me into their family. I found a spirit of strength in the black church, which knew how to deal with pain and nursed me back to wholeness. I was ordained in an African-American (National Baptist) church in North Carolina. Later I taught at an African Methodist Episcopal seminary. I continue to be nurtured spiritually by the black church. My wife was a refugee for eighteen months during war in the Congo. When ethnic strife between regions led to war, her family lost their home and nearly their lives. Painfully, such stories are not rare. Ethnic conflict, which is human selfishness on a corporate level, is widespread in the world. The ethnic reconciliation in Christ for which we work, on both my continent and hers, is for us a necessary expression of the love-in-action to which the Johannine epistles call us.

— Craig S. Keener

1 We declare to you what was from the beginning, what we have heard, what we have
seen with our eyes, what we have looked at and
touched with our hands, concerning the word of
life— 2this life was revealed, and we have seen it
and testify to it, and declare to you the eternal life
that was with the Father and was revealed to us—
3we declare to you what we have seen and heard
so that you also may have fellowship with us; and
truly our fellowship is with the Father and with
his Son Jesus Christ. 4We are writing these things
so that our[a] joy may be complete.

5 This is the message we have heard from him
and proclaim to you, that God is light and in him
there is no darkness at all. 6If we say that we have
fellowship with him while we are walking in darkness, we lie and do not do what is true; 7but if we
walk in the light as he himself is in the light, we
have fellowship with one another, and the blood
of Jesus his Son cleanses us from all sin. 8If we
say that we have no sin, we deceive ourselves, and
the truth is not in us. 9If we confess our sins, he
who is faithful and just will forgive us our sins and
cleanse us from all unrighteousness. 10If we say
that we have not sinned, we make him a liar, and
his word is not in us.

2 My little children, I am writing these things
to you so that you may not sin. But if anyone
does sin, we have an advocate with the Father,
Jesus Christ the righteous; 2and he is the aton-

[a] Other ancient authorities read *your*

ing sacrifice for our sins, and not for ours only but
also for the sins of the whole world.
3 Now by this we may be sure that we know
him, if we obey his commandments. 4Whoever
says, "I have come to know him," but does not
obey his commandments, is a liar, and in such
a person the truth does not exist; 5but whoever
obeys his word, truly in this person the love of
God has reached perfection. By this we may be
sure that we are in him: 6whoever says, "I abide in
him," ought to walk just as he walked.
7 Beloved, I am writing you no new commandment, but an old commandment that you
have had from the beginning; the old commandment is the word that you have heard. 8Yet I am
writing you a new commandment that is true in
him and in you, because[a] the darkness is passing away and the true light is already shining.
9Whoever says, "I am in the light," while hating a brother or sister,[b] is still in the darkness.
10Whoever loves a brother or sister[c] lives in the
light, and in such a person[d] there is no cause for
stumbling. 11But whoever hates another believer[e]
is in the darkness, walks in the darkness, and does
not know the way to go, because the darkness has
brought on blindness.

12 I am writing to you, little children,
because your sins are forgiven on account
of his name.
13 I am writing to you, fathers,
because you know him who is from the
beginning.
I am writing to you, young people,
because you have conquered the evil one.
14 I write to you, children,
because you know the Father.
I write to you, fathers,
because you know him who is from the
beginning.
I write to you, young people,
because you are strong
and the word of God abides in you,
and you have overcome the evil one.

15 Do not love the world or the things in the
world. The love of the Father is not in those who
love the world; 16for all that is in the world—the
desire of the flesh, the desire of the eyes, the pride
in riches—comes not from the Father but from
the world. 17And the world and its desire[f] are
passing away, but those who do the will of God
live forever.
18 Children, it is the last hour! As you have
heard that antichrist is coming, so now many antichrists have come. From this we know that it is
the last hour. 19They went out from us, but they
did not belong to us; for if they had belonged to
us, they would have remained with us. But by
going out they made it plain that none of them
belongs to us. 20But you have been anointed by
the Holy One, and all of you have knowledge.[g] 21I
write to you, not because you do not know the
truth, but because you know it, and you know that
no lie comes from the truth. 22Who is the liar but
the one who denies that Jesus is the Christ?[h] This
is the antichrist, the one who denies the Father
and the Son. 23No one who denies the Son has
the Father; everyone who confesses the Son has
the Father also. 24Let what you heard from the
beginning abide in you. If what you heard from
the beginning abides in you, then you will abide
in the Son and in the Father. 25And this is what he
has promised us,[i] eternal life.
26 I write these things to you concerning
those who would deceive you. 27As for you, the
anointing that you received from him abides in
you, and so you do not need anyone to teach you.
But as his anointing teaches you about all things,
and is true and is not a lie, and just as it has taught
you, abide in him.[j]
28 And now, little children, abide in him,
so that when he is revealed we may have confidence and not be put to shame before him at his
coming.
29 If you know that he is righteous, you may
be sure that everyone who does right has been
3 born of him. 1See what love the Father has
given us, that we should be called children
of God; and that is what we are. The reason the

[a] Or *that* [b] Gk *hating a brother* [c] Gk *loves a brother* [d] Or *in it* [e] Gk *hates a brother* [f] Or *the desire for it*
[g] Other ancient authorities read *you know all things* [h] Or *the Messiah* [i] Other ancient authorities read *you* [j] Or *it*

world does not know us is that it did not know him. 2Beloved, we are God's children now; what we will be has not yet been revealed. What we do know is this: when he[a] is revealed, we will be like him, for we will see him as he is. 3And all who have this hope in him purify themselves, just as he is pure.

4 Everyone who commits sin is guilty of lawlessness; sin is lawlessness. 5You know that he was revealed to take away sins, and in him there is no sin. 6No one who abides in him sins; no one who sins has either seen him or known him. 7Little children, let no one deceive you. Everyone who does what is right is righteous, just as he is righteous. 8Everyone who commits sin is a child of the devil; for the devil has been sinning from the beginning. The Son of God was revealed for this purpose, to destroy the works of the devil. 9Those who have been born of God do not sin, because God's seed abides in them;[b] they cannot sin, because they have been born of God. 10The children of God and the children of the devil are revealed in this way: all who do not do what is right are not from God, nor are those who do not love their brothers and sisters.[c]

11 For this is the message you have heard from the beginning, that we should love one another. 12We must not be like Cain who was from the evil one and murdered his brother. And why did he murder him? Because his own deeds were evil and his brother's righteous. 13Do not be astonished, brothers and sisters,[d] that the world hates you. 14We know that we have passed from death to life because we love one another. Whoever does not love abides in death. 15All who hate a brother or sister[c] are murderers, and you know that murderers do not have eternal life abiding in them. 16We know love by this, that he laid down his life for us—and we ought to lay down our lives for one another. 17How does God's love abide in anyone who has the world's goods and sees a brother or sister[e] in need and yet refuses help?

18 Little children, let us love, not in word or speech, but in truth and action. 19And by this we will know that we are from the truth and will reassure our hearts before him 20whenever our hearts condemn us; for God is greater than our hearts, and he knows everything. 21Beloved, if our hearts do not condemn us, we have boldness before God; 22and we receive from him whatever we ask, because we obey his commandments and do what pleases him.

23 And this is his commandment, that we should believe in the name of his Son Jesus Christ and love one another, just as he has commanded us. 24All who obey his commandments abide in him, and he abides in them. And by this we know that he abides in us, by the Spirit that he has given us.

4 Beloved, do not believe every spirit, but test the spirits to see whether they are from God; for many false prophets have gone out into the world. 2By this you know the Spirit of God: every spirit that confesses that Jesus Christ has come in the flesh is from God, 3and every spirit that does not confess Jesus[f] is not from God. And this is the spirit of the antichrist, of which you have heard that it is coming; and now it is already in the world. 4Little children, you are from God, and have conquered them; for the one who is in you is greater than the one who is in the world.

1 John 3:17

To Isaiah, God declared that true fasting meant the undoing of injustice and the sharing of bread with the hungry (58:6-7). To Amos, God spurned the people's sacrifices and called instead for justice to "roll down like waters" (5:21-24). James declared that "pure and undefiled" religion was "to care for orphans and widows in their distress" (1:27). And John asks how the love of God can be present in anyone who has the world's goods yet refuses to help those in need. How much easier it would be for us if the biblical God cared at all about our religiosity!

—*NE*

[a] Or *it* [b] Or *because the children of God abide in him* [c] Gk *his brother* [d] Gk *brothers* [e] Gk *brother*
[f] Other ancient authorities read *does away with Jesus* (Gk *dissolves Jesus*)

5They are from the world; therefore what they say
is from the world, and the world listens to them.
6We are from God. Whoever knows God listens
to us, and whoever is not from God does not listen to us. From this we know the spirit of truth
and the spirit of error.

7 Beloved, let us love one another, because
love is from God; everyone who loves is born of
God and knows God. 8Whoever does not love
does not know God, for God is love. 9God's love
was revealed among us in this way: God sent his
only Son into the world so that we might live
through him. 10In this is love, not that we loved
God but that he loved us and sent his Son to be
the atoning sacrifice for our sins. 11Beloved, since
God loved us so much, we also ought to love one
another. 12No one has ever seen God; if we love
one another, God lives in us, and his love is perfected in us.

13 By this we know that we abide in him and
he in us, because he has given us of his Spirit.
14And we have seen and do testify that the Father
has sent his Son as the Savior of the world. 15God
abides in those who confess that Jesus is the Son
of God, and they abide in God. 16So we have
known and believe the love that God has for us.

God is love, and those who abide in love abide
in God, and God abides in them. 17Love has been
perfected among us in this: that we may have
boldness on the day of judgment, because as he
is, so are we in this world. 18There is no fear in
love, but perfect love casts out fear; for fear has to
do with punishment, and whoever fears has not
reached perfection in love. 19We love[a] because he
first loved us. 20Those who say, "I love God," and
hate their brothers or sisters,[b] are liars; for those
who do not love a brother or sister[c] whom they
have seen, cannot love God whom they have not
seen. 21The commandment we have from him is
this: those who love God must love their brothers
and sisters[b] also.

5 Everyone who believes that Jesus is the
Christ[d] has been born of God, and everyone
who loves the parent loves the child. 2By this we
know that we love the children of God, when we
love God and obey his commandments. 3For the
love of God is this, that we obey his commandments. And his commandments are not burdensome, 4for whatever is born of God conquers the
world. And this is the victory that conquers
the world, our faith. 5Who is it that conquers the
world but the one who believes that Jesus is the
Son of God?

6 This is the one who came by water and
blood, Jesus Christ, not with the water only but
with the water and the blood. And the Spirit is
the one that testifies, for the Spirit is the truth.
7There are three that testify:[e] 8the Spirit and the
water and the blood, and these three agree. 9If we
receive human testimony, the testimony of God
is greater; for this is the testimony of God that he
has testified to his Son. 10Those who believe in
the Son of God have the testimony in their hearts.
Those who do not believe in God[f] have made him
a liar by not believing in the testimony that God
has given concerning his Son. 11And this is the
testimony: God gave us eternal life, and this life
is in his Son. 12Whoever has the Son has life;
whoever does not have the Son of God does not
have life.

13 I write these things to you who believe
in the name of the Son of God, so that you may
know that you have eternal life.

14 And this is the boldness we have in him,
that if we ask anything according to his will, he
hears us. 15And if we know that he hears us in
whatever we ask, we know that we have obtained
the requests made of him. 16If you see your
brother or sister[g] committing what is not a mortal
sin, you will ask, and God[h] will give life to such
a one—to those whose sin is not mortal. There
is sin that is mortal; I do not say that you should
pray about that. 17All wrongdoing is sin, but there
is sin that is not mortal.

18 We know that those who are born of God
do not sin, but the one who was born of God

[a] Other ancient authorities add *him*; others add *God* [b] Gk *brothers* [c] Gk *brother* [d] Or *the Messiah* [e] A few other authorities read (with variations) *7There are three that testify in heaven, the Father, the Word, and the Holy Spirit, and these three are one. 8And there are three that testify on earth:* [f] Other ancient authorities read *in the Son* [g] Gk *your brother* [h] Gk *he*

protects them, and the evil one does not touch
them. 19 We know that we are God's children, and
that the whole world lies under the power of the
evil one. 20 And we know that the Son of God has
come and has given us understanding so that we
may know him who is true;[a] and we are in him
who is true, in his Son Jesus Christ. He is the true
God and eternal life.

21 Little children, keep yourselves from idols.[b]

[a] Other ancient authorities read *know the true God* [b] Other ancient authorities add *Amen*

The Second Letter of John

SHORTER THAN 1 JOHN, 2 John shares its message and probably its author (see the introduction to 1 John). The writer offers a theological test by which Christ's true followers may be discerned: they must believe in Jesus the incarnate Christ (v. 7). They must also avoid sin, behaving righteously (v. 6). This righteous obedience to God's will especially involves loving their fellow believers (vv. 5-6).

— ***Craig S. Keener***

1 The elder to the elect lady and her children,
whom I love in the truth, and not only I but also
all who know the truth, 2 because of the truth that
abides in us and will be with us forever:

3 Grace, mercy, and peace will be with us
from God the Father and from[a] Jesus Christ, the
Father's Son, in truth and love.

4 I was overjoyed to find some of your children walking in the truth, just as we have been
commanded by the Father. 5 But now, dear lady, I
ask you, not as though I were writing you a new
commandment, but one we have had from the beginning, let us love one another. 6 And this is love,
that we walk according to his commandments;
this is the commandment just as you have heard
it from the beginning—you must walk in it.

7 Many deceivers have gone out into the world,
those who do not confess that Jesus Christ has
come in the flesh; any such person is the deceiver
and the antichrist! 8 Be on your guard, so that you
do not lose what we[b] have worked for, but may receive a full reward. 9 Everyone who does not abide
in the teaching of Christ, but goes beyond it, does
not have God; whoever abides in the teaching has
both the Father and the Son. 10 Do not receive into
the house or welcome anyone who comes to you
and does not bring this teaching; 11 for to welcome
is to participate in the evil deeds of such a person.

12 Although I have much to write to you,
I would rather not use paper and ink; instead I
hope to come to you and talk with you face to
face, so that our joy may be complete.

13 The children of your elect sister send you
their greetings.[c]

[a] Other ancient authorities add *the Lord*
[b] Other ancient authorities read *you*
[c] Other ancient authorities add *Amen*

The Third Letter of John

THE THIRD EPISTLE OF JOHN is the last and shortest of these epistles (see the introduction to 1 John). Though it shares with 1 and 2 John a common author, a common milieu, and a similar message, 3 John appears to address a different, nontheological division in the community. The principle at the heart of the author's message is nevertheless the same: loving one's fellow believers is central to the meaning of being a Christian (vv. 5-12).

— *Craig S. Keener*

1 The elder to the beloved Gaius, whom I
love in truth.
2 Beloved, I pray that all may go well with
you and that you may be in good health, just as
it is well with your soul. 3 I was overjoyed when
some of the friends[a] arrived and testified to your
faithfulness to the truth, namely how you walk in
the truth. 4 I have no greater joy than this, to hear
that my children are walking in the truth.
5 Beloved, you do faithfully whatever you do
for the friends,[a] even though they are strangers
to you; 6 they have testified to your love before
the church. You will do well to send them on in
a manner worthy of God; 7 for they began their
journey for the sake of Christ,[b] accepting no support from non-believers.[c] 8 Therefore we ought to
support such people, so that we may become co-
workers with the truth.
9 I have written something to the church; but
Diotrephes, who likes to put himself first, does
not acknowledge our authority. 10 So if I come, I
will call attention to what he is doing in spreading false charges against us. And not content with
those charges, he refuses to welcome the friends,[a]
and even prevents those who want to do so and
expels them from the church.

3 John

The French philosopher Alain Badiou observes that the collapse of the Berlin wall has not ushered in "a single world of freedom and democracy"; rather "the world's wall has simply shifted: instead of separating East and West it now divided the rich capitalist North from the poor and devastated South. New walls are being constructed all over the world... the 'unified world' of globalization is a sham."[76] In an economic order seemingly designed to divide and exclude, the Christian practice of hospitality has never been more urgent.

— *NE*

[a] Gk *brothers* [b] Gk *for the sake of the name* [c] Gk *the Gentiles*

11 Beloved, do not imitate what is evil but
imitate what is good. Whoever does good is
from God; whoever does evil has not seen God.
12Everyone has testified favorably about Demetrius, and so has the truth itself. We also testify for
him,[a] and you know that our testimony is true.

13 I have much to write to you, but I would
rather not write with pen and ink; 14instead I
hope to see you soon, and we will talk together
face to face.

15 Peace to you. The friends send you their
greetings. Greet the friends there, each by name.

[a] Gk lacks *for him*

The Letter of Jude

JUDE IS ONE OF THE BRIEFEST LETTERS of the New Testament. Its twenty-five verses are an apology—a defense—of the faith in response to threats from false teachings and the dangers posed to the church by teachers whose morality and ethical behavior do not conform to "the faith that was once for all entrusted to the saints" (v. 3b). In spite of its brevity, its passionate defense is an example of early Christian apologetic literature, written to encourage the church to remain faithful in times of uncertainty and moral decay.

Jude is often considered a circular letter, addressed not to a specific community but to all believers "who are called, who are beloved in God the Father and kept safe for Jesus Christ" (v. 1b). But the claim that the letter was intended for a particular community is also plausible, based on the reference in verse 4 to some strangers who had disrupted the community. It seems that the author's original purpose, to write about the common salvation he shared with the community of faith (v. 3), changed due to the crisis of the false teachers. He calls the people propagating the false doctrine "intruders" and "ungodly" (v. 4), "dreamers" (v. 8), "blemishes" (v. 12), and "waterless clouds carried along by the winds; autumn trees without fruit, twice dead, uprooted; wild waves of the sea, casting up the foam of their own shame; wandering stars, for whom the deepest darkness has been reserved forever" (v. 13).

The structure of the letter follows the pattern typical of early Christian letters, which in turn used a pattern common to letters of the Greco-Roman time. The opening formula (v. 1a) identifies the sender as "Jude, a servant of Jesus Christ, and brother of James." Later tradition identifies this Jude as a brother of the Lord mentioned in Mark 6:3 (Judas) and a plausible author of this letter—which if true could make Jude one of the earliest letters in the New Testament. The letter is addressed to "those who are called, who are beloved in God the Father and kept safe for Jesus Christ" (v. 1b). Immediately after this opening, the letter includes a salutation wishing the audience mercy, peace, and love (v. 2). As an introduction to the main body, the letter incorporates a statement of purpose: to appeal to the Christians to contend for their faith because of the false teachers infiltrating the church (vv. 3b-4).

The main body of the letter consists of an alternate description of the character of the false teachers and appeals to the faithful to avoid their mistakes. The letter uses examples from the Hebrew Scriptures and other early Jewish traditions (vv. 5-23). First the writer reminds readers of the exodus, the story of Sodom and Gomorrah, and of the fight for the body of Moses by the archangel Michael (vv. 5-10). Next he invokes the stories of Cain, Balaam, and Korah (vv. 11-13). Then the writer alludes to the mysterious character of Enoch and some prophecies preserved in an early Jewish apocalyptic text not included in the Bible (vv. 14-16). Also in this last section, the letter appeals

to prophecies of the apostles that announced the moral character of the people of the last days (vv. 17-19). The main body of the letter concludes with an exhortation to keep the faith and engage in works of kindness and compassion for the people (vv. 20-23). The letter closes with a doxology, praising God for caring for and strengthening the faithful in times of trial.

Although the letter begins with an apologetic tone, its main purpose is to urge the community to watch themselves, to avoid the mistakes of others, and above all to continue the fight for the faith. The last verses of the body of the letter (vv. 20-23) give readers some specifics on how they should conduct their fight for the faith: mutual support, common prayer, and mercy for those who waver.

I believe I am one of the few who finds the letter of Jude exciting. As a member of a so-called minority (a first-generation Puerto Rican), I find the exhortations of Jude fascinating. It seems easier to imitate and accommodate to the way of life of the dominant society, to assume their values, and be dragged into accusing and condemning the poor, the immigrants, and all those who are different for everything that goes wrong in our society. Jude reminds me that we are not alone in the struggle for justice, peace, and freedom. On the contrary, his witness, as that of many other Christians, sustains our faith and energizes our hope.

— ***David Cortés-Fuentes***

1 Jude,[a] a servant[b] of Jesus Christ and brother
of James,
To those who are called, who are beloved[c] in[d]
God the Father and kept safe for[d] Jesus Christ:
2 May mercy, peace, and love be yours in
abundance.

3 Beloved, while eagerly preparing to write to
you about the salvation we share, I find it necessary to write and appeal to you to contend for the
faith that was once for all entrusted to the saints.
4For certain intruders have stolen in among you,
people who long ago were designated for this
condemnation as ungodly, who pervert the grace
of our God into licentiousness and deny our only
Master and Lord, Jesus Christ.[e]
5 Now I desire to remind you, though you
are fully informed, that the Lord, who once for
all saved[f] a people out of the land of Egypt, afterward destroyed those who did not believe. 6And
the angels who did not keep their own position,
but left their proper dwelling, he has kept in eternal chains in deepest darkness for the judgment
of the great day. 7Likewise, Sodom and Gomorrah and the surrounding cities, which, in the same
manner as they, indulged in sexual immorality
and pursued unnatural lust,[g] serve as an example
by undergoing a punishment of eternal fire.
8 Yet in the same way these dreamers also defile the flesh, reject authority, and slander the glorious ones.[h] 9But when the archangel Michael
contended with the devil and disputed about the
body of Moses, he did not dare to bring a
condemnation of slander[i] against him, but said,

[a] Gk *Judas* [b] Gk *slave* [c] Other ancient authorities read *sanctified* [d] Or *by* [e] Or *the only Master and our Lord Jesus Christ* [f] Other ancient authorities read *though you were once for all fully informed, that Jesus* (or *Joshua*) *who saved* [g] Gk *went after other flesh* [h] Or *angels*; Gk *glories* [i] Or *condemnation for blasphemy*

"The Lord rebuke you!" 10 But these people slander whatever they do not understand, and they are destroyed by those things that, like irrational animals, they know by instinct. 11 Woe to them! For they go the way of Cain, and abandon themselves to Balaam's error for the sake of gain, and perish in Korah's rebellion. 12 These are blemishes[a] on your love-feasts, while they feast with you without fear, feeding themselves.[b] They are waterless clouds carried along by the winds; autumn trees without fruit, twice dead, uprooted; 13 wild waves of the sea, casting up the foam of their own shame; wandering stars, for whom the deepest darkness has been reserved forever.

14 It was also about these that Enoch, in the seventh generation from Adam, prophesied, saying, "See, the Lord is coming[c] with ten thousands of his holy ones, 15 to execute judgment on all, and to convict everyone of all the deeds of ungodliness that they have committed in such an ungodly way, and of all the harsh things that ungodly sinners have spoken against him." 16 These are grumblers and malcontents; they indulge their own lusts; they are bombastic in speech, flattering people to their own advantage.

17 But you, beloved, must remember the predictions of the apostles of our Lord Jesus Christ; 18 for they said to you, "In the last time there will be scoffers, indulging their own ungodly lusts." 19 It is these worldly people, devoid of the Spirit, who are causing divisions. 20 But you, beloved, build yourselves up on your most holy faith; pray in the Holy Spirit; 21 keep yourselves in the love of God; look forward to the mercy of our Lord Jesus Christ that leads to[d] eternal life. 22 And have mercy on some who are wavering; 23 save others by snatching them out of the fire; and have mercy on still others with fear, hating even the tunic defiled by their bodies.[e]

24 Now to him who is able to keep you from falling, and to make you stand without blemish in the presence of his glory with rejoicing, 25 to the only God our Savior, through Jesus Christ our Lord, be glory, majesty, power, and authority, before all time and now and forever. Amen.

[a] Or *reefs* [b] Or *without fear. They are shepherds who care only for themselves* [c] Gk *came* [d] Gk *Christ to*
[e] Gk *by the flesh*. The Greek text of verses 22–23 is uncertain at several points

The Revelation to John

The book of Revelation describes an "apocalypse" (1:1). As such, it narrates the revelation experience of one of Jesus' followers, John, to other followers in the Roman province of "Asia," today's western Turkey. In his vision John encounters the risen Jesus (1:9-20). Jesus dictates letters to seven churches scattered across Asia. Praising the churches for their faithfulness and admonishing them for their failures, Jesus promises eternal blessings for those who "conquer" in the face of the pressure to compromise their witness to Jesus. In his mystical state John enters the realm of heaven, where he visits the heavenly throne room, watches as the judgments of God unfold upon a violent world, observes Jesus' victory over the forces of imperialism and idolatry, and wonders as the New Jerusalem, the heavenly city, descends to earth. Revelation begins and ends by blessing those who see and hear the vision and do what it teaches (1:3; 22:18-19).

Many contemporary readers find Revelation hopelessly mysterious—or irrelevant. Their aversion is partly due to the bizarre ways in which self-made prophets today have distorted Revelation into a road map for the last days—always *these* days. Revelation's strange symbols also baffle modern audiences. Some people object to Revelation on ethical grounds as well, finding it too bloodthirsty, too vengeful, too world-denying, and misogynistic. Others simply cede Revelation to the "prophecy teachers," focusing their own attention instead on the more familiar stories of Jesus in the Gospels. Many of the self-styled prophecy teachers condemn ecumenical collaboration, environmental activism, global peacemaking, and a host of other causes as signs of satanic deception in the last days. Tragically, their influence continues to expand beyond North America to the rapidly growing churches of the global South.

But Revelation embodies perhaps the Bible's most forceful critique of imperial ideology, militarism, and commerce. Like many ancient Jewish and Christian literary apocalypses, Revelation speaks to the circumstances of its time and place, interpreting the ways of God for the crises of its own day. Not only does Jesus address seven actual churches made up of real people; Revelation insists that it reveals what "must soon take place" (1:1, 3, 19; 22:6, 10, 12). Even its most remarkable symbols—the dragon, the beast, and the whore—are familiar to readers of ancient Jewish and Christian literature. Revelation identifies the dragon as Satan (12:9), and it uses the beast and the whore to convey the wicked, idolatrous, and exploitative nature of Roman imperialism. The beast (prominent in ch. 13) and the whore (chs. 17–18) make war against "the saints." The beast is worshipped due to its surpassing power: "Who is like the beast, and who can fight against it?" (13:4). The whore generates unfathomable wealth for the few who benefit most from her commerce (18:11-13).

Revelation's most striking symbol applies to Jesus. In the heavenly throne room, John awaits the arrival of the "lion of the tribe of Judah," who has authority over the world's destiny. Yet the lion never appears. In its place stands the Lamb (5:5-6), who remains standing although it has been slaughtered. The Lamb conquers the forces of imperialism and evil through the word of its testimony—that is, by faithfully witnessing to the ways of God, even to the point of death. Revelation calls its audience to demonstrate their loyalty to the Lamb by following its example. They bear witness ("the word of their testimony") to the ways of justice and peace (12:11), and they resist the economic, political, and religious trappings of Roman imperialism (3:4; 18:4). Thus they endure in their faithful testimony to Jesus, the Lamb.

We know only a little about the churches John addresses. They must have been small, relatively powerless groups of believers. Some were wealthy (3:17), but far more would have been poor (2:9). Perhaps the churches included some merchants who benefited from imperial commerce. Revelation describes these little churches as under intense pressure, even persecution (1:9; 2:13; 6:9-11), from their neighbors. While we lack hard evidence for such persecution of Christians in Revelation's specific cultural context, Asia was well known for popular devotion to the cult of the emperor. Revelation's call for faithful witness and abstention from the imperial cults placed the churches at odds with their neighbors. The churches' emulation of Jesus cost them good will, economic and social benefits, and occasionally their lives.

I interpret Revelation as a citizen of the United States, the world's greatest military and economic empire today. As a young convert to Christianity, I adopted the virulent nationalism and militarism promoted by prophecy teachers. I believed that serving God and serving the nation went in lockstep. Then, in college and seminary, I encountered interpretations from Latin America and South Africa that emphasize how Revelation speaks out against imperial oppression. They challenged me to ask what is beast-ly in my nation and to bear faithful testimony to the ways of peace and truth.

— ***Greg Carey***

1 The revelation of Jesus Christ, which God
gave him to show his servants[a] what must
soon take place; he made[b] it known by sending
his angel to his servant[c] John, 2who testified to
the word of God and to the testimony of Jesus
Christ, even to all that he saw.
3 Blessed is the one who reads aloud the
words of the prophecy, and blessed are those who
hear and who keep what is written in it; for the
time is near.

4 John to the seven churches that are in Asia:
Grace to you and peace from him who is and
who was and who is to come, and from the seven
spirits who are before his throne, 5and from
Jesus Christ, the faithful witness, the firstborn

[a] Gk *slaves* [b] Gk *and he made* [c] Gk *slave*

of the dead, and the ruler of the kings of the
earth.
To him who loves us and freed[a] us from our
sins by his blood, 6and made[b] us to be a kingdom,
priests serving[c] his God and Father, to him be
glory and dominion forever and ever. Amen.

7 Look! He is coming with the clouds;
every eye will see him,
even those who pierced him;
and on his account all the tribes of the
earth will wail.
So it is to be. Amen.

8 "I am the Alpha and the Omega," says the
Lord God, who is and who was and who is to
come, the Almighty.

9 I, John, your brother who share with you
in Jesus the persecution and the kingdom and
the patient endurance, was on the island called
Patmos because of the word of God and the testimony of Jesus.[d] 10I was in the spirit[e] on the Lord's
day, and I heard behind me a loud voice like a
trumpet 11saying, "Write in a book what you see
and send it to the seven churches, to Ephesus, to
Smyrna, to Pergamum, to Thyatira, to Sardis, to
Philadelphia, and to Laodicea."

12 Then I turned to see whose voice it was
that spoke to me, and on turning I saw seven
golden lampstands, 13and in the midst of the
lampstands I saw one like the Son of Man, clothed
with a long robe and with a golden sash across his
chest. 14His head and his hair were white as white
wool, white as snow; his eyes were like a flame of
fire, 15his feet were like burnished bronze, refined
as in a furnace, and his voice was like the sound
of many waters. 16In his right hand he held seven
stars, and from his mouth came a sharp, two-
edged sword, and his face was like the sun shining with full force.

17 When I saw him, I fell at his feet as though
dead. But he placed his right hand on me, saying, "Do not be afraid; I am the first and the
last, 18and the living one. I was dead, and see, I
am alive forever and ever; and I have the keys of

Revelation 1:14-15

Many renditions of Jesus picture him with lily-white skin, blond hair, and even blue eyes. Jesus usually is represented looking like a European. Yet John, seeing Jesus in all his glory, describes him as having hair like wool and bronze-colored skin. John knew what Europeans looked like: after all, they represented the occupying forces of the empire. For him to have described Jesus looking like a European would have implied that he had been fathered by one of the soldiers or governmental officials of Rome stationed in Judea. But as a person indigenous to the land, Jesus would have had to be brown or black—closer in appearance to the way John describes him in this text.

— MDLT

Death and of Hades. 19Now write what you have
seen, what is, and what is to take place after this.
20As for the mystery of the seven stars that you
saw in my right hand, and the seven golden lampstands: the seven stars are the angels of the seven
churches, and the seven lampstands are the seven
churches.

2 "To the angel of the church in Ephesus write:
These are the words of him who holds the
seven stars in his right hand, who walks among
the seven golden lampstands:

2 "I know your works, your toil and your patient endurance. I know that you cannot tolerate
evildoers; you have tested those who claim to
be apostles but are not, and have found them to
be false. 3I also know that you are enduring patiently and bearing up for the sake of my name,
and that you have not grown weary. 4But I have
this against you, that you have abandoned the
love you had at first. 5Remember then from what
you have fallen; repent, and do the works you did
at first. If not, I will come to you and remove your
lampstand from its place, unless you repent. 6Yet
this is to your credit: you hate the works of the

[a] Other ancient authorities read *washed* [b] Gk *and he made* [c] Gk *priests to* [d] Or *testimony to Jesus*
[e] Or *in the Spirit*

Nicolaitans, which I also hate. 7Let anyone who
has an ear listen to what the Spirit is saying to the
churches. To everyone who conquers, I will give
permission to eat from the tree of life that is in the
paradise of God.

8 "And to the angel of the church in Smyrna
write: These are the words of the first and the last,
who was dead and came to life:

9 "I know your affliction and your poverty,
even though you are rich. I know the slander on
the part of those who say that they are Jews and
are not, but are a synagogue of Satan. 10Do not
fear what you are about to suffer. Beware, the
devil is about to throw some of you into prison
so that you may be tested, and for ten days you
will have affliction. Be faithful until death, and I
will give you the crown of life. 11Let anyone who
has an ear listen to what the Spirit is saying to the
churches. Whoever conquers will not be harmed
by the second death.

12 "And to the angel of the church in Pergamum write: These are the words of him who has
the sharp two-edged sword:

13 "I know where you are living, where Satan's throne is. Yet you are holding fast to my
name, and you did not deny your faith in me[a]
even in the days of Antipas my witness, my faithful one, who was killed among you, where Satan
lives. 14But I have a few things against you: you
have some there who hold to the teaching of Balaam, who taught Balak to put a stumbling block
before the people of Israel, so that they would eat
food sacrificed to idols and practice fornication.
15So you also have some who hold to the teaching of the Nicolaitans. 16Repent then. If not,
I will come to you soon and make war against
them with the sword of my mouth. 17Let anyone
who has an ear listen to what the Spirit is saying
to the churches. To everyone who conquers I will
give some of the hidden manna, and I will give a
white stone, and on the white stone is written a
new name that no one knows except the one who
receives it.

18 "And to the angel of the church in Thyatira
write: These are the words of the Son of God,
who has eyes like a flame of fire, and whose feet
are like burnished bronze:

19 "I know your works—your love, faith,
service, and patient endurance. I know that your
last works are greater than the first. 20But I have
this against you: you tolerate that woman Jezebel,
who calls herself a prophet and is teaching and
beguiling my servants[b] to practice fornication and
to eat food sacrificed to idols. 21I gave her time to
repent, but she refuses to repent of her fornication. 22Beware, I am throwing her on a bed, and
those who commit adultery with her I am throwing into great distress, unless they repent of her
doings; 23and I will strike her children dead. And
all the churches will know that I am the one who
searches minds and hearts, and I will give to each
of you as your works deserve. 24But to the rest of
you in Thyatira, who do not hold this teaching,
who have not learned what some call 'the deep
things of Satan,' to you I say, I do not lay on you
any other burden; 25only hold fast to what you
have until I come. 26To everyone who conquers
and continues to do my works to the end,

I will give authority over the nations;
27 to rule[c] them with an iron rod,
as when clay pots are shattered—

28even as I also received authority from my Father. To the one who conquers I will also give the
morning star. 29Let anyone who has an ear listen
to what the Spirit is saying to the churches.

3 "And to the angel of the church in Sardis
write: These are the words of him who has
the seven spirits of God and the seven stars:

"I know your works; you have a name of being
alive, but you are dead. 2Wake up, and strengthen
what remains and is on the point of death, for I
have not found your works perfect in the sight of
my God. 3Remember then what you received and
heard; obey it, and repent. If you do not wake up,
I will come like a thief, and you will not know at
what hour I will come to you. 4Yet you have still
a few persons in Sardis who have not soiled their

[a] Or *deny my faith* [b] Gk *slaves* [c] Or *to shepherd*

clothes; they will walk with me, dressed in white,
for they are worthy. 5If you conquer, you will be
clothed like them in white robes, and I will not
blot your name out of the book of life; I will confess your name before my Father and before his
angels. 6Let anyone who has an ear listen to what
the Spirit is saying to the churches.

7 "And to the angel of the church in Philadelphia write:

These are the words of the holy one, the true
one,
who has the key of David,
who opens and no one will shut,
who shuts and no one opens:

8 "I know your works. Look, I have set before you an open door, which no one is able to
shut. I know that you have but little power, and
yet you have kept my word and have not denied
my name. 9I will make those of the synagogue of
Satan who say that they are Jews and are not, but
are lying—I will make them come and bow down
before your feet, and they will learn that I have
loved you. 10Because you have kept my word of
patient endurance, I will keep you from the hour
of trial that is coming on the whole world to test
the inhabitants of the earth. 11I am coming soon;
hold fast to what you have, so that no one may
seize your crown. 12If you conquer, I will make
you a pillar in the temple of my God; you will
never go out of it. I will write on you the name
of my God, and the name of the city of my God,
the new Jerusalem that comes down from my
God out of heaven, and my own new name. 13Let
anyone who has an ear listen to what the Spirit is
saying to the churches.

14 "And to the angel of the church in Laodicea write: The words of the Amen, the faithful
and true witness, the origin[a] of God's creation:

15 "I know your works; you are neither cold
nor hot. I wish that you were either cold or hot.
16So, because you are lukewarm, and neither
cold nor hot, I am about to spit you out of my
mouth. 17For you say, 'I am rich, I have prospered, and I need nothing.' You do not realize
that you are wretched, pitiable, poor, blind, and
naked. 18Therefore I counsel you to buy from
me gold refined by fire so that you may be rich;
and white robes to clothe you and to keep the
shame of your nakedness from being seen; and
salve to anoint your eyes so that you may see.
19I reprove and discipline those whom I love.
Be earnest, therefore, and repent. 20Listen! I am
standing at the door, knocking; if you hear my
voice and open the door, I will come in to you
and eat with you, and you with me. 21To the one
who conquers I will give a place with me on my
throne, just as I myself conquered and sat down
with my Father on his throne. 22Let anyone who
has an ear listen to what the Spirit is saying to
the churches."

4 After this I looked, and there in heaven a door
stood open! And the first voice, which I had
heard speaking to me like a trumpet, said, "Come
up here, and I will show you what must take
place after this." 2At once I was in the spirit,[b] and
there in heaven stood a throne, with one seated
on the throne! 3And the one seated there looks
like jasper and carnelian, and around the throne
is a rainbow that looks like an emerald. 4Around
the throne are twenty-four thrones, and seated
on the thrones are twenty-four elders, dressed in
white robes, with golden crowns on their heads.
5Coming from the throne are flashes of lightning,
and rumblings and peals of thunder, and in front
of the throne burn seven flaming torches, which
are the seven spirits of God; 6and in front of the
throne there is something like a sea of glass, like
crystal.

Around the throne, and on each side of the
throne, are four living creatures, full of eyes in
front and behind: 7the first living creature like
a lion, the second living creature like an ox, the
third living creature with a face like a human face,
and the fourth living creature like a flying eagle.
8And the four living creatures, each of them with
six wings, are full of eyes all around and inside.
Day and night without ceasing they sing,

[a] Or *beginning* [b] Or *in the Spirit*

"Holy, holy, holy,
the Lord God the Almighty,
who was and is and is to come."
9And whenever the living creatures give glory
and honor and thanks to the one who is seated
on the throne, who lives forever and ever, 10the
twenty-four elders fall before the one who is
seated on the throne and worship the one who
lives forever and ever; they cast their crowns before the throne, singing,
11 "You are worthy, our Lord and God,
to receive glory and honor and power,
for you created all things,
and by your will they existed and were
created."

5 Then I saw in the right hand of the one seated
on the throne a scroll written on the inside
and on the back, sealed[a] with seven seals; 2and I
saw a mighty angel proclaiming with a loud voice,
"Who is worthy to open the scroll and break its
seals?" 3And no one in heaven or on earth or under the earth was able to open the scroll or to look
into it. 4And I began to weep bitterly because no
one was found worthy to open the scroll or to
look into it. 5Then one of the elders said to me,
"Do not weep. See, the Lion of the tribe of Judah,
the Root of David, has conquered, so that he can
open the scroll and its seven seals."
6 Then I saw between the throne and the four
living creatures and among the elders a Lamb
standing as if it had been slaughtered, having
seven horns and seven eyes, which are the seven
spirits of God sent out into all the earth. 7He
went and took the scroll from the right hand of
the one who was seated on the throne. 8When he
had taken the scroll, the four living creatures and
the twenty-four elders fell before the Lamb, each
holding a harp and golden bowls full of incense,
which are the prayers of the saints. 9They sing a
new song:
"You are worthy to take the scroll
and to open its seals,
for you were slaughtered and by your blood
you ransomed for God
saints from[b] every tribe and language and
people and nation;
10 you have made them to be a kingdom and
priests serving[c] our God,
and they will reign on earth."
11 Then I looked, and I heard the voice of
many angels surrounding the throne and the
living creatures and the elders; they numbered
myriads of myriads and thousands of thousands,
12singing with full voice,
"Worthy is the Lamb that was slaughtered
to receive power and wealth and wisdom and
might
and honor and glory and blessing!"
13Then I heard every creature in heaven and on
earth and under the earth and in the sea, and all
that is in them, singing,
"To the one seated on the throne and to the
Lamb
be blessing and honor and glory and might
forever and ever!"
14And the four living creatures said, "Amen!" And
the elders fell down and worshiped.

6 Then I saw the Lamb open one of the seven
seals, and I heard one of the four living
creatures call out, as with a voice of thunder,
"Come!"[d] 2I looked, and there was a white horse!
Its rider had a bow; a crown was given to him, and
he came out conquering and to conquer.
3 When he opened the second seal, I heard
the second living creature call out, "Come!"[d]
4And out came[e] another horse, bright red; its
rider was permitted to take peace from the earth,
so that people would slaughter one another; and
he was given a great sword.
5 When he opened the third seal, I heard the
third living creature call out, "Come!"[d] I looked,
and there was a black horse! Its rider held a pair
of scales in his hand, 6and I heard what seemed to
be a voice in the midst of the four living creatures
saying, "A quart of wheat for a day's pay,[f] and
three quarts of barley for a day's pay,[f] but do not
damage the olive oil and the wine!"

[a] Or *written on the inside, and sealed on the back* [b] Gk *ransomed for God from* [c] Gk *priests to* [d] Or *"Go!"*
[e] Or *went* [f] Gk *a denarius*

7 When he opened the fourth seal, I heard
the voice of the fourth living creature call out,
"Come!"[a] 8 I looked and there was a pale green
horse! Its rider's name was Death, and Hades followed with him; they were given authority over
a fourth of the earth, to kill with sword, famine,
and pestilence, and by the wild animals of the
earth.

9 When he opened the fifth seal, I saw under
the altar the souls of those who had been slaughtered for the word of God and for the testimony
they had given; 10 they cried out with a loud voice,
"Sovereign Lord, holy and true, how long will it
be before you judge and avenge our blood on the
inhabitants of the earth?" 11 They were each given
a white robe and told to rest a little longer, until
the number would be complete both of their fellow servants[b] and of their brothers and sisters,[c]
who were soon to be killed as they themselves
had been killed.

12 When he opened the sixth seal, I looked,
and there came a great earthquake; the sun became black as sackcloth, the full moon became
like blood, 13 and the stars of the sky fell to the
earth as the fig tree drops its winter fruit when
shaken by a gale. 14 The sky vanished like a scroll
rolling itself up, and every mountain and island
was removed from its place. 15 Then the kings of
the earth and the magnates and the generals and
the rich and the powerful, and everyone, slave
and free, hid in the caves and among the rocks
of the mountains, 16 calling to the mountains and
rocks, "Fall on us and hide us from the face of the
one seated on the throne and from the wrath of
the Lamb; 17 for the great day of their wrath has
come, and who is able to stand?"

7 After this I saw four angels standing at the
four corners of the earth, holding back the
four winds of the earth so that no wind could blow
on earth or sea or against any tree. 2 I saw another
angel ascending from the rising of the sun, having
the seal of the living God, and he called with a
loud voice to the four angels who had been given
power to damage earth and sea, 3 saying, "Do not
damage the earth or the sea or the trees, until we
have marked the servants[b] of our God with a seal
on their foreheads."

4 And I heard the number of those who were
sealed, one hundred forty-four thousand, sealed
out of every tribe of the people of Israel:

5 From the tribe of Judah twelve thousand
sealed,
from the tribe of Reuben twelve thousand,
from the tribe of Gad twelve thousand,
6 from the tribe of Asher twelve thousand,
from the tribe of Naphtali twelve thousand,
from the tribe of Manasseh twelve thousand,
7 from the tribe of Simeon twelve thousand,
from the tribe of Levi twelve thousand,
from the tribe of Issachar twelve thousand,
8 from the tribe of Zebulun twelve thousand,
from the tribe of Joseph twelve thousand,
from the tribe of Benjamin twelve thousand sealed.

9 After this I looked, and there was a great
multitude that no one could count, from every
nation, from all tribes and peoples and languages,
standing before the throne and before the Lamb,
robed in white, with palm branches in their hands.
10 They cried out in a loud voice, saying,

"Salvation belongs to our God who is seated
on the throne, and to the Lamb!"

11 And all the angels stood around the throne and
around the elders and the four living creatures,
and they fell on their faces before the throne and
worshiped God, 12 singing,

"Amen! Blessing and glory and wisdom
and thanksgiving and honor
and power and might
be to our God forever and ever! Amen."

13 Then one of the elders addressed me, saying, "Who are these, robed in white, and where
have they come from?" 14 I said to him, "Sir, you
are the one that knows." Then he said to me,
"These are they who have come out of the great
ordeal; they have washed their robes and made
them white in the blood of the Lamb.

[a] Or *"Go!"* [b] Gk *slaves* [c] Gk *brothers*

15 For this reason they are before the throne of God,
and worship him day and night within his temple,
and the one who is seated on the throne will shelter them.
16 They will hunger no more, and thirst no more;
the sun will not strike them,
nor any scorching heat;
17 for the Lamb at the center of the throne will be their shepherd,
and he will guide them to springs of the water of life,
and God will wipe away every tear from their eyes."

8 When the Lamb opened the seventh seal,
there was silence in heaven for about half
an hour. 2 And I saw the seven angels who stand
before God, and seven trumpets were given to
them.
3 Another angel with a golden censer came
and stood at the altar; he was given a great quantity of incense to offer with the prayers of all the
saints on the golden altar that is before the throne.
4 And the smoke of the incense, with the prayers
of the saints, rose before God from the hand of
the angel. 5 Then the angel took the censer and
filled it with fire from the altar and threw it on
the earth; and there were peals of thunder, rumblings, flashes of lightning, and an earthquake.
6 Now the seven angels who had the seven
trumpets made ready to blow them.
7 The first angel blew his trumpet, and there
came hail and fire, mixed with blood, and they
were hurled to the earth; and a third of the earth
was burned up, and a third of the trees were
burned up, and all green grass was burned up.
8 The second angel blew his trumpet, and
something like a great mountain, burning with
fire, was thrown into the sea. 9 A third of the sea
became blood, a third of the living creatures in
the sea died, and a third of the ships were destroyed.
10 The third angel blew his trumpet, and a
great star fell from heaven, blazing like a torch,
and it fell on a third of the rivers and on the
springs of water. 11 The name of the star is Wormwood. A third of the waters became wormwood,
and many died from the water, because it was
made bitter.
12 The fourth angel blew his trumpet, and
a third of the sun was struck, and a third of the
moon, and a third of the stars, so that a third of
their light was darkened; a third of the day was
kept from shining, and likewise the night.
13 Then I looked, and I heard an eagle crying
with a loud voice as it flew in midheaven, "Woe,
woe, woe to the inhabitants of the earth, at the
blasts of the other trumpets that the three angels
are about to blow!"

9 And the fifth angel blew his trumpet, and
I saw a star that had fallen from heaven to
earth, and he was given the key to the shaft of the
bottomless pit; 2 he opened the shaft of the bottomless pit, and from the shaft rose smoke like

Revelation 7:9-10; 10:11

John had a vision of the kingdom of heaven in all of its glory, with the hosts of heaven surrounding the throne of God. A multicultural gathering ransomed "from every nation, from all tribes and peoples and languages" sang of the victories of the Lord. What John witnessed is the paradigm for Christians waiting to enter glory, and this glimpse of heavenly worship has become the model by which churches should pattern earthly worship. John is told to report back all that he has seen. The "white man's burden" has historically been to bring civilization, including the gospel message, to the margins of society. But the angel tells John to go back to his center and tell people there *about the margins*. The gospel is already thriving in the margins of society today. The real question facing the Euro-Americans is asked by the people at those margins: Will they join *our* diversity?!

— *MDLT*

the smoke of a great furnace, and the sun and the
air were darkened with the smoke from the shaft.
3Then from the smoke came locusts on the earth,
and they were given authority like the authority
of scorpions of the earth. 4They were told not to
damage the grass of the earth or any green growth
or any tree, but only those people who do not
have the seal of God on their foreheads. 5They
were allowed to torture them for five months, but
not to kill them, and their torture was like the torture of a scorpion when it stings someone. 6And
in those days people will seek death but will not
find it; they will long to die, but death will flee
from them.

7 In appearance the locusts were like horses
equipped for battle. On their heads were what
looked like crowns of gold; their faces were like
human faces, 8their hair like women's hair, and
their teeth like lions' teeth; 9they had scales like
iron breastplates, and the noise of their wings was
like the noise of many chariots with horses rushing into battle. 10They have tails like scorpions,
with stingers, and in their tails is their power to
harm people for five months. 11They have as king
over them the angel of the bottomless pit; his
name in Hebrew is Abaddon,[a] and in Greek he is
called Apollyon.[b]

12 The first woe has passed. There are still
two woes to come.

13 Then the sixth angel blew his trumpet, and
I heard a voice from the four[c] horns of the golden
altar before God, 14saying to the sixth angel who
had the trumpet, "Release the four angels who are
bound at the great river Euphrates." 15So the four
angels were released, who had been held ready
for the hour, the day, the month, and the year,
to kill a third of humankind. 16The number of
the troops of cavalry was two hundred million; I
heard their number. 17And this was how I saw the
horses in my vision: the riders wore breastplates
the color of fire and of sapphire[d] and of sulfur; the
heads of the horses were like lions' heads, and fire
and smoke and sulfur came out of their mouths.
18By these three plagues a third of humankind
was killed, by the fire and smoke and sulfur coming out of their mouths. 19For the power of the
horses is in their mouths and in their tails; their
tails are like serpents, having heads; and with
them they inflict harm.

20 The rest of humankind, who were not
killed by these plagues, did not repent of the works
of their hands or give up worshiping demons and
idols of gold and silver and bronze and stone and
wood, which cannot see or hear or walk. 21And
they did not repent of their murders or their sorceries or their fornication or their thefts.

10 And I saw another mighty angel coming
down from heaven, wrapped in a cloud,
with a rainbow over his head; his face was like
the sun, and his legs like pillars of fire. 2He held
a little scroll open in his hand. Setting his right
foot on the sea and his left foot on the land, 3he
gave a great shout, like a lion roaring. And when
he shouted, the seven thunders sounded. 4And
when the seven thunders had sounded, I was
about to write, but I heard a voice from heaven
saying, "Seal up what the seven thunders have
said, and do not write it down." 5Then the angel
whom I saw standing on the sea and the land

raised his right hand to heaven
6 and swore by him who lives forever and
ever,

who created heaven and what is in it, the earth and
what is in it, and the sea and what is in it: "There
will be no more delay, 7but in the days when the
seventh angel is to blow his trumpet, the mystery
of God will be fulfilled, as he announced to his
servants[e] the prophets."

8 Then the voice that I had heard from heaven
spoke to me again, saying, "Go, take the scroll
that is open in the hand of the angel who is standing on the sea and on the land." 9So I went to the
angel and told him to give me the little scroll;
and he said to me, "Take it, and eat; it will be bitter to your stomach, but sweet as honey in your
mouth." 10So I took the little scroll from the hand
of the angel and ate it; it was sweet as honey in
my mouth, but when I had eaten it, my stomach
was made bitter.

11 Then they said to me, "You must prophesy

[a] That is, *Destruction* [b] That is, *Destroyer* [c] Other ancient authorities lack *four* [d] Gk *hyacinth* [e] Gk *slaves*

again about many peoples and nations and languages and kings."

11 Then I was given a measuring rod like a staff, and I was told, "Come and measure the temple of God and the altar and those who worship there, 2 but do not measure the court outside the temple; leave that out, for it is given over to the nations, and they will trample over the holy city for forty-two months. 3 And I will grant my two witnesses authority to prophesy for one thousand two hundred sixty days, wearing sackcloth."

4 These are the two olive trees and the two lampstands that stand before the Lord of the earth. 5 And if anyone wants to harm them, fire pours from their mouth and consumes their foes; anyone who wants to harm them must be killed in this manner. 6 They have authority to shut the sky, so that no rain may fall during the days of their prophesying, and they have authority over the waters to turn them into blood, and to strike the earth with every kind of plague, as often as they desire.

7 When they have finished their testimony, the beast that comes up from the bottomless pit will make war on them and conquer them and kill them, 8 and their dead bodies will lie in the street of the great city that is prophetically[a] called Sodom and Egypt, where also their Lord was crucified. 9 For three and a half days members of the peoples and tribes and languages and nations will gaze at their dead bodies and refuse to let them be placed in a tomb; 10 and the inhabitants of the earth will gloat over them and celebrate and exchange presents, because these two prophets had been a torment to the inhabitants of the earth.

11 But after the three and a half days, the breath[b] of life from God entered them, and they stood on their feet, and those who saw them were terrified. 12 Then they[c] heard a loud voice from heaven saying to them, "Come up here!" And they went up to heaven in a cloud while their enemies watched them. 13 At that moment there was a great earthquake, and a tenth of the city fell; seven thousand people were killed in the earthquake, and the rest were terrified and gave glory to the God of heaven.

14 The second woe has passed. The third woe is coming very soon.

15 Then the seventh angel blew his trumpet, and there were loud voices in heaven, saying,

"The kingdom of the world has become the
    kingdom of our Lord
and of his Messiah,[d]
and he will reign forever and ever."

16 Then the twenty-four elders who sit on their thrones before God fell on their faces and worshiped God, 17 singing,

"We give you thanks, Lord God Almighty,
    who are and who were,
for you have taken your great power
    and begun to reign.
18 The nations raged,
    but your wrath has come,
    and the time for judging the dead,
for rewarding your servants,[e] the prophets
    and saints and all who fear your name,
    both small and great,
and for destroying those who destroy the
    earth."

19 Then God's temple in heaven was opened, and the ark of his covenant was seen within his temple; and there were flashes of lightning, rumblings, peals of thunder, an earthquake, and heavy hail.

12 A great portent appeared in heaven: a woman clothed with the sun, with the moon under her feet, and on her head a crown of twelve stars. 2 She was pregnant and was crying out in birth pangs, in the agony of giving birth. 3 Then another portent appeared in heaven: a great red dragon, with seven heads and ten horns, and seven diadems on his heads. 4 His tail swept down a third of the stars of heaven and threw them to the earth. Then the dragon stood before the woman who was about to bear a child, so that he might devour her child as soon as it was born. 5 And she gave birth to a son, a male child, who is

[a] Or *allegorically;* Gk *spiritually* [b] Or *the spirit* [c] Other ancient authorities read *I* [d] Gk *Christ* [e] Gk *slaves*

to rule[a] all the nations with a rod of iron. But her
child was snatched away and taken to God and to
his throne; 6and the woman fled into the wilderness, where she has a place prepared by God, so
that there she can be nourished for one thousand
two hundred sixty days.

7 And war broke out in heaven; Michael and
his angels fought against the dragon. The dragon
and his angels fought back, 8but they were defeated, and there was no longer any place for them
in heaven. 9The great dragon was thrown down,
that ancient serpent, who is called the Devil and
Satan, the deceiver of the whole world—he was
thrown down to the earth, and his angels were
thrown down with him.

10 Then I heard a loud voice in heaven, proclaiming,

"Now have come the salvation and the power
and the kingdom of our God
and the authority of his Messiah,[b]
for the accuser of our comrades[c] has been
thrown down,
who accuses them day and night before
our God.

11 But they have conquered him by the blood of
the Lamb
and by the word of their testimony,
for they did not cling to life even in the face
of death.

12 Rejoice then, you heavens
and those who dwell in them!
But woe to the earth and the sea,
for the devil has come down to you
with great wrath,
because he knows that his time is short!"

13 So when the dragon saw that he had been
thrown down to the earth, he pursued[d] the woman
who had given birth to the male child. 14But the
woman was given the two wings of the great eagle, so that she could fly from the serpent into the
wilderness, to her place where she is nourished
for a time, and times, and half a time. 15Then from
his mouth the serpent poured water like a river after the woman, to sweep her away with the flood.
16But the earth came to the help of the woman;
it opened its mouth and swallowed the river that
the dragon had poured from his mouth. 17Then
the dragon was angry with the woman, and went
off to make war on the rest of her children, those
who keep the commandments of God and hold
the testimony of Jesus.

18 Then the dragon[e] took his stand on the
13 sand of the seashore. 1And I saw a beast
rising out of the sea, having ten horns and
seven heads; and on its horns were ten diadems,
and on its heads were blasphemous names. 2And
the beast that I saw was like a leopard, its feet were
like a bear's, and its mouth was like a lion's mouth.
And the dragon gave it his power and his throne
and great authority. 3One of its heads seemed to
have received a death-blow, but its mortal wound[f]
had been healed. In amazement the whole earth
followed the beast. 4They worshiped the dragon,
for he had given his authority to the beast, and
they worshiped the beast, saying, "Who is like
the beast, and who can fight against it?"

5 The beast was given a mouth uttering
haughty and blasphemous words, and it was allowed to exercise authority for forty-two months.
6It opened its mouth to utter blasphemies against
God, blaspheming his name and his dwelling,
that is, those who dwell in heaven. 7Also it was
allowed to make war on the saints and to conquer
them.[g] It was given authority over every tribe
and people and language and nation, 8and all the
inhabitants of the earth will worship it, everyone whose name has not been written from the
foundation of the world in the book of life of the
Lamb that was slaughtered.[h]

9 Let anyone who has an ear listen:

10 If you are to be taken captive,
into captivity you go;
if you kill with the sword,
with the sword you must be killed.

Here is a call for the endurance and faith of the
saints.

[a] Or *to shepherd* [b] Gk *Christ* [c] Gk *brothers* [d] Or *persecuted* [e] Gk *Then he*; other ancient authorities read *Then I stood* [f] Gk *the plague of its death* [g] Other ancient authorities lack this sentence
[h] Or *written in the book of life of the Lamb that was slaughtered from the foundation of the world*

11 Then I saw another beast that rose out of the earth; it had two horns like a lamb and it spoke like a dragon. 12 It exercises all the authority of the first beast on its behalf, and it makes the earth and its inhabitants worship the first beast, whose mortal wound[a] had been healed. 13 It performs great signs, even making fire come down from heaven to earth in the sight of all; 14 and by the signs that it is allowed to perform on behalf of the beast, it deceives the inhabitants of earth, telling them to make an image for the beast that had been wounded by the sword[b] and yet lived; 15 and it was allowed to give breath[c] to the image of the beast so that the image of the beast could even speak and cause those who would not worship the image of the beast to be killed. 16 Also it causes all, both small and great, both rich and poor, both free and slave, to be marked on the right hand or the forehead, 17 so that no one can buy or sell who does not have the mark, that is, the name of the beast or the number of its name. 18 This calls for wisdom: let anyone with understanding calculate the number of the beast, for it is the number of a person. Its number is six hundred sixty-six.[d]

14 Then I looked, and there was the Lamb, standing on Mount Zion! And with him were one hundred forty-four thousand who had his name and his Father's name written on their foreheads. 2 And I heard a voice from heaven like the sound of many waters and like the sound of loud thunder; the voice I heard was like the sound of harpists playing on their harps, 3 and they sing a new song before the throne and before the four living creatures and before the elders. No one could learn that song except the one hundred forty-four thousand who have been redeemed from the earth. 4 It is these who have not defiled themselves with women, for they are virgins; these follow the Lamb wherever he goes. They have been redeemed from humankind as first fruits for God and the Lamb, 5 and in their mouth no lie was found; they are blameless.

6 Then I saw another angel flying in midheaven, with an eternal gospel to proclaim to those who live[e] on the earth—to every nation and tribe and language and people. 7 He said in a loud voice, "Fear God and give him glory, for the hour of his judgment has come; and worship him who made heaven and earth, the sea and the springs of water."

8 Then another angel, a second, followed, saying, "Fallen, fallen is Babylon the great! She has made all nations drink of the wine of the wrath of her fornication."

9 Then another angel, a third, followed them, crying with a loud voice, "Those who worship the beast and its image, and receive a mark on their foreheads or on their hands, 10 they will also drink the wine of God's wrath, poured unmixed into the cup of his anger, and they will be tormented with fire and sulfur in the presence of the holy angels and in the presence of the Lamb. 11 And the smoke of their torment goes up forever and ever. There is no rest day or night for those who worship the beast and its image and for anyone who receives the mark of its name."

12 Here is a call for the endurance of the saints, those who keep the commandments of God and hold fast to the faith of[f] Jesus.

13 And I heard a voice from heaven saying, "Write this: Blessed are the dead who from now on die in the Lord." "Yes," says the Spirit, "they will rest from their labors, for their deeds follow them."

14 Then I looked, and there was a white cloud, and seated on the cloud was one like the Son of Man, with a golden crown on his head, and a sharp sickle in his hand! 15 Another angel came out of the temple, calling with a loud voice to the one who sat on the cloud, "Use your sickle and reap, for the hour to reap has come, because the harvest of the earth is fully ripe." 16 So the one who sat on the cloud swung his sickle over the earth, and the earth was reaped.

17 Then another angel came out of the temple in heaven, and he too had a sharp sickle. 18 Then another angel came out from the altar, the angel who has authority over fire, and he called with a

[a] Gk *whose plague of its death* [b] Or *that had received the plague of the sword* [c] Or *spirit* [d] Other ancient authorities read *six hundred sixteen* [e] Gk *sit* [f] Or *to their faith in*

loud voice to him who had the sharp sickle, "Use
your sharp sickle and gather the clusters of the
vine of the earth, for its grapes are ripe." 19 So the
angel swung his sickle over the earth and gathered the vintage of the earth, and he threw it into
the great wine press of the wrath of God. 20 And
the wine press was trodden outside the city, and
blood flowed from the wine press, as high as a
horse's bridle, for a distance of about two hundred miles.[a]

15 Then I saw another portent in heaven,
great and amazing: seven angels with seven
plagues, which are the last, for with them the
wrath of God is ended.

2 And I saw what appeared to be a sea of glass
mixed with fire, and those who had conquered the
beast and its image and the number of its name,
standing beside the sea of glass with harps of God
in their hands. 3 And they sing the song of Moses,
the servant[b] of God, and the song of the Lamb:

"Great and amazing are your deeds,
    Lord God the Almighty!
Just and true are your ways,
    King of the nations![c]
4 Lord, who will not fear
    and glorify your name?
For you alone are holy.
    All nations will come
    and worship before you,
for your judgments have been revealed."

5 After this I looked, and the temple of the
tent[d] of witness in heaven was opened, 6 and out of
the temple came the seven angels with the seven
plagues, robed in pure bright linen,[e] with golden
sashes across their chests. 7 Then one of the
four living creatures gave the seven angels seven
golden bowls full of the wrath of God, who lives
forever and ever; 8 and the temple was filled with
smoke from the glory of God and from his power,
and no one could enter the temple until the seven
plagues of the seven angels were ended.

16 Then I heard a loud voice from the temple telling the seven angels, "Go and pour
out on the earth the seven bowls of the wrath of
God."

2 So the first angel went and poured his bowl
on the earth, and a foul and painful sore came on
those who had the mark of the beast and who
worshiped its image.

3 The second angel poured his bowl into the
sea, and it became like the blood of a corpse, and
every living thing in the sea died.

4 The third angel poured his bowl into the
rivers and the springs of water, and they became
blood. 5 And I heard the angel of the waters say,

"You are just, O Holy One, who are and were,
    for you have judged these things;
6 because they shed the blood of saints and
        prophets,
    you have given them blood to drink.
It is what they deserve!"

7 And I heard the altar respond,

"Yes, O Lord God, the Almighty,
    your judgments are true and just!"

8 The fourth angel poured his bowl on the
sun, and it was allowed to scorch people with fire;
9 they were scorched by the fierce heat, but they
cursed the name of God, who had authority over
these plagues, and they did not repent and give
him glory.

10 The fifth angel poured his bowl on the
throne of the beast, and its kingdom was plunged
into darkness; people gnawed their tongues in
agony, 11 and cursed the God of heaven because
of their pains and sores, and they did not repent
of their deeds.

12 The sixth angel poured his bowl on the
great river Euphrates, and its water was dried up
in order to prepare the way for the kings from
the east. 13 And I saw three foul spirits like frogs
coming from the mouth of the dragon, from the
mouth of the beast, and from the mouth of the
false prophet. 14 These are demonic spirits, performing signs, who go abroad to the kings of the
whole world, to assemble them for battle on the
great day of God the Almighty. 15 ("See, I am coming like a thief! Blessed is the one who stays awake

[a] Gk *one thousand six hundred stadia* [b] Gk *slave* [c] Other ancient authorities read *the ages* [d] Or *tabernacle*
[e] Other ancient authorities read *stone*

and is clothed,[a] not going about naked and exposed to shame.") 16And they assembled them at the place that in Hebrew is called Harmagedon.

17 The seventh angel poured his bowl into the air, and a loud voice came out of the temple, from the throne, saying, "It is done!" 18And there came flashes of lightning, rumblings, peals of thunder, and a violent earthquake, such as had not occurred since people were upon the earth, so violent was that earthquake. 19The great city was split into three parts, and the cities of the nations fell. God remembered great Babylon and gave her the wine-cup of the fury of his wrath. 20And every island fled away, and no mountains were to be found; 21and huge hailstones, each weighing about a hundred pounds,[b] dropped from heaven on people, until they cursed God for the plague of the hail, so fearful was that plague.

17 Then one of the seven angels who had the seven bowls came and said to me, "Come, I will show you the judgment of the great whore who is seated on many waters, 2with whom the kings of the earth have committed fornication, and with the wine of whose fornication the inhabitants of the earth have become drunk." 3So he carried me away in the spirit[c] into a wilderness, and I saw a woman sitting on a scarlet beast that was full of blasphemous names, and it had seven heads and ten horns. 4The woman was clothed in purple and scarlet, and adorned with gold and jewels and pearls, holding in her hand a golden cup full of abominations and the impurities of her fornication; 5and on her forehead was written a name, a mystery: "Babylon the great, mother of whores and of earth's abominations." 6And I saw that the woman was drunk with the blood of the saints and the blood of the witnesses to Jesus.

When I saw her, I was greatly amazed. 7But the angel said to me, "Why are you so amazed? I will tell you the mystery of the woman, and of the beast with seven heads and ten horns that carries her. 8The beast that you saw was, and is not, and is about to ascend from the bottomless pit and go to destruction. And the inhabitants of the earth, whose names have not been written in the book of life from the foundation of the world, will be amazed when they see the beast, because it was and is not and is to come.

9 "This calls for a mind that has wisdom: the seven heads are seven mountains on which the woman is seated; also, they are seven kings, 10of whom five have fallen, one is living, and the other has not yet come; and when he comes, he must remain only a little while. 11As for the beast that was and is not, it is an eighth but it belongs to the seven, and it goes to destruction. 12And the ten horns that you saw are ten kings who have not yet received a kingdom, but they are to receive authority as kings for one hour, together with the beast. 13These are united in yielding their power and authority to the beast; 14they will make war on the Lamb, and the Lamb will conquer them, for he is Lord of lords and King of kings, and those with him are called and chosen and faithful."

15 And he said to me, "The waters that you saw, where the whore is seated, are peoples and multitudes and nations and languages. 16And the ten horns that you saw, they and the beast will hate the whore; they will make her desolate and naked; they will devour her flesh and burn her up with fire. 17For God has put it into their hearts to carry out his purpose by agreeing to give their kingdom to the beast, until the words of God will be fulfilled. 18The woman you saw is the great city that rules over the kings of the earth."

18 After this I saw another angel coming down from heaven, having great authority; and the earth was made bright with his splendor. 2He called out with a mighty voice,

"Fallen, fallen is Babylon the great!
It has become a dwelling place of demons,
a haunt of every foul spirit,
a haunt of every foul bird,
a haunt of every foul and hateful beast.[d]

3 For all the nations have drunk[e]

[a] Gk *and keeps his robes* [b] Gk *weighing about a talent* [c] Or *in the Spirit* [d] Other ancient authorities lack the words *a haunt of every foul beast* and attach the words *and hateful* to the previous line so as to read *a haunt of every foul and hateful bird* [e] Other ancient authorities read *She has made all nations drink*

Revelation 18:1-2

The escapist apocalyptic fiction so popular among some North American Christian circles reflects a cynical politics of indifference. Protagonists rely on sophisticated electronics, jet travel, and high-tech military equipment, but disdain efforts at international peacemaking or solicitude for the poor as futile and dangerously misguided. Such "biblical" fiction reads like "we-told-you-so" fantasy on the part of those who feel their possessions and privileges are endangered. Their anxiety is understandable; after all, the angel announces that the glorious fall of the imperial city and the consequent liberation of creation are the will of God.

—*NE*

of the wine of the wrath of her fornication,
and the kings of the earth have committed
fornication with her,
and the merchants of the earth have grown
rich from the power[a] of her luxury."

4 Then I heard another voice from heaven
saying,
"Come out of her, my people,
so that you do not take part in her sins,
and so that you do not share in her plagues;
5 for her sins are heaped high as heaven,
and God has remembered her iniquities.
6 Render to her as she herself has rendered,
and repay her double for her deeds;
mix a double draught for her in the cup
she mixed.
7 As she glorified herself and lived luxuriously,
so give her a like measure of torment and
grief.
Since in her heart she says,
'I rule as a queen;
I am no widow,
and I will never see grief,'
8 therefore her plagues will come in a single
day—
pestilence and mourning and famine—
and she will be burned with fire;
for mighty is the Lord God who judges
her."

9 And the kings of the earth, who committed fornication and lived in luxury with her, will
weep and wail over her when they see the smoke
of her burning; 10they will stand far off, in fear of
her torment, and say,
"Alas, alas, the great city,
Babylon, the mighty city!
For in one hour your judgment has come."

11 And the merchants of the earth weep and
mourn for her, since no one buys their cargo anymore, 12cargo of gold, silver, jewels and pearls,
fine linen, purple, silk and scarlet, all kinds of
scented wood, all articles of ivory, all articles of
costly wood, bronze, iron, and marble, 13cinna-
mon, spice, incense, myrrh, frankincense, wine,
olive oil, choice flour and wheat, cattle and sheep,
horses and chariots, slaves—and human lives.[b]
14 "The fruit for which your soul longed
has gone from you,
and all your dainties and your splendor
are lost to you,
never to be found again!"
15The merchants of these wares, who gained
wealth from her, will stand far off, in fear of her
torment, weeping and mourning aloud,
16 "Alas, alas, the great city,
clothed in fine linen,
in purple and scarlet,
adorned with gold,
with jewels, and with pearls!
17 For in one hour all this wealth has been laid
waste!"
And all shipmasters and seafarers, sailors and
all whose trade is on the sea, stood far off 18and
cried out as they saw the smoke of her burning,
"What city was like the great city?"
19And they threw dust on their heads, as they
wept and mourned, crying out,
"Alas, alas, the great city,
where all who had ships at sea
grew rich by her wealth!
For in one hour she has been laid waste."

[a] Or *resources* [b] Or *chariots, and human bodies and souls*

20 Rejoice over her, O heaven, you saints and
apostles and prophets! For God has given judgment for you against her.
21 Then a mighty angel took up a stone like a
great millstone and threw it into the sea, saying,
"With such violence Babylon the great city
will be thrown down,
and will be found no more;
22 and the sound of harpists and minstrels and
of flutists and trumpeters
will be heard in you no more;
and an artisan of any trade
will be found in you no more;
and the sound of the millstone
will be heard in you no more;
23 and the light of a lamp
will shine in you no more;
and the voice of bridegroom and bride
will be heard in you no more;
for your merchants were the magnates of the
earth,
and all nations were deceived by your
sorcery.
24 And in you[a] was found the blood of prophets
and of saints,
and of all who have been slaughtered on
earth."

19 After this I heard what seemed to be the
loud voice of a great multitude in heaven,
saying,
"Hallelujah!
Salvation and glory and power to our God,
2 for his judgments are true and just;
he has judged the great whore
who corrupted the earth with her
fornication,
and he has avenged on her the blood of his
servants."[b]
3 Once more they said,
"Hallelujah!
The smoke goes up from her forever and ever."
4 And the twenty-four elders and the four living
creatures fell down and worshiped God who is
seated on the throne, saying,
"Amen. Hallelujah!"
5 And from the throne came a voice saying,
"Praise our God,
all you his servants,[b]
and all who fear him,
small and great."
6 Then I heard what seemed to be the voice of a
great multitude, like the sound of many waters
and like the sound of mighty thunderpeals, crying out,
"Hallelujah!
For the Lord our God
the Almighty reigns.
7 Let us rejoice and exult
and give him the glory,
for the marriage of the Lamb has come,
and his bride has made herself ready;
8 to her it has been granted to be clothed
with fine linen, bright and pure"—
for the fine linen is the righteous deeds of the
saints.
9 And the angel said[c] to me, "Write this:
Blessed are those who are invited to the marriage
supper of the Lamb." And he said to me, "These
are true words of God." 10 Then I fell down at his
feet to worship him, but he said to me, "You must
not do that! I am a fellow servant[d] with you and
your comrades[e] who hold the testimony of Jesus.[f]
Worship God! For the testimony of Jesus[f] is the
spirit of prophecy."

11 Then I saw heaven opened, and there was
a white horse! Its rider is called Faithful and True,
and in righteousness he judges and makes war.
12 His eyes are like a flame of fire, and on his head
are many diadems; and he has a name inscribed
that no one knows but himself. 13 He is clothed in
a robe dipped in[g] blood, and his name is called
The Word of God. 14 And the armies of heaven,
wearing fine linen, white and pure, were following him on white horses. 15 From his mouth
comes a sharp sword with which to strike down
the nations, and he will rule[h] them with a rod of
iron; he will tread the wine press of the fury of the

[a] Gk *her* [b] Gk *slaves* [c] Gk *he said* [d] Gk *slave* [e] Gk *brothers* [f] Or *to Jesus* [g] Other ancient authorities read *sprinkled with* [h] Or *will shepherd*

wrath of God the Almighty. 16On his robe and on
his thigh he has a name inscribed, "King of kings
and Lord of lords."

17 Then I saw an angel standing in the sun,
and with a loud voice he called to all the birds
that fly in midheaven, "Come, gather for the great
supper of God, 18to eat the flesh of kings, the
flesh of captains, the flesh of the mighty, the flesh
of horses and their riders—flesh of all, both free
and slave, both small and great." 19Then I saw the
beast and the kings of the earth with their armies
gathered to make war against the rider on the
horse and against his army. 20And the beast was
captured, and with it the false prophet who had
performed in its presence the signs by which he
deceived those who had received the mark of the
beast and those who worshiped its image. These
two were thrown alive into the lake of fire that
burns with sulfur. 21And the rest were killed by
the sword of the rider on the horse, the sword
that came from his mouth; and all the birds were
gorged with their flesh.

20 Then I saw an angel coming down from
heaven, holding in his hand the key to the
bottomless pit and a great chain. 2He seized the
dragon, that ancient serpent, who is the Devil and
Satan, and bound him for a thousand years, 3and
threw him into the pit, and locked and sealed it
over him, so that he would deceive the nations no
more, until the thousand years were ended. After
that he must be let out for a little while.

4 Then I saw thrones, and those seated on
them were given authority to judge. I also saw the
souls of those who had been beheaded for their
testimony to Jesus[a] and for the word of God.
They had not worshiped the beast or its image
and had not received its mark on their foreheads
or their hands. They came to life and reigned with
Christ a thousand years. 5(The rest of the dead
did not come to life until the thousand years were
ended.) This is the first resurrection. 6Blessed
and holy are those who share in the first resurrection. Over these the second death has no power,
but they will be priests of God and of Christ, and
they will reign with him a thousand years.

7 When the thousand years are ended, Satan
will be released from his prison 8and will come
out to deceive the nations at the four corners of
the earth, Gog and Magog, in order to gather
them for battle; they are as numerous as the sands
of the sea. 9They marched up over the breadth of
the earth and surrounded the camp of the saints
and the beloved city. And fire came down from
heaven[b] and consumed them. 10And the devil
who had deceived them was thrown into the lake
of fire and sulfur, where the beast and the false
prophet were, and they will be tormented day
and night forever and ever.

11 Then I saw a great white throne and the one
who sat on it; the earth and the heaven fled from
his presence, and no place was found for them.
12And I saw the dead, great and small, standing
before the throne, and books were opened. Also
another book was opened, the book of life. And
the dead were judged according to their works,
as recorded in the books. 13And the sea gave up
the dead that were in it, Death and Hades gave up
the dead that were in them, and all were judged
according to what they had done. 14Then Death
and Hades were thrown into the lake of fire. This
is the second death, the lake of fire; 15and anyone
whose name was not found written in the book of
life was thrown into the lake of fire.

21 Then I saw a new heaven and a new earth;
for the first heaven and the first earth had
passed away, and the sea was no more. 2And I saw
the holy city, the new Jerusalem, coming down
out of heaven from God, prepared as a bride
adorned for her husband. 3And I heard a loud
voice from the throne saying,

"See, the home[c] of God is among mortals.
He will dwell[d] with them;
they will be his peoples,[e]
and God himself will be with them;[f]

[a] Or *for the testimony of Jesus* [b] Other ancient authorities read *from God, out of heaven,* or *out of heaven from God*
[c] Gk *the tabernacle* [d] Gk *will tabernacle* [e] Other ancient authorities read *people*
[f] Other ancient authorities add *and be their God*

4 he will wipe every tear from their eyes.
Death will be no more;
mourning and crying and pain will be no
more,
for the first things have passed away."

5 And the one who was seated on the throne said, "See, I am making all things new." Also he said, "Write this, for these words are trustworthy and true." 6 Then he said to me, "It is done! I am the Alpha and the Omega, the beginning and the end. To the thirsty I will give water as a gift from the spring of the water of life. 7 Those who conquer will inherit these things, and I will be their God and they will be my children. 8 But as for the cowardly, the faithless,[a] the polluted, the murderers, the fornicators, the sorcerers, the idolaters, and all liars, their place will be in the lake that burns with fire and sulfur, which is the second death."

9 Then one of the seven angels who had the seven bowls full of the seven last plagues came and said to me, "Come, I will show you the bride, the wife of the Lamb." 10 And in the spirit[b] he carried me away to a great, high mountain and showed me the holy city Jerusalem coming down out of heaven from God. 11 It has the glory of God and a radiance like a very rare jewel, like jasper, clear as crystal. 12 It has a great, high wall with twelve gates, and at the gates twelve angels, and on the gates are inscribed the names of the twelve tribes of the Israelites; 13 on the east three gates, on the north three gates, on the south three gates, and on the west three gates. 14 And the wall of the city has twelve foundations, and on them are the twelve names of the twelve apostles of the Lamb.

15 The angel[c] who talked to me had a measuring rod of gold to measure the city and its gates and walls. 16 The city lies foursquare, its length the same as its width; and he measured the city with his rod, fifteen hundred miles;[d] its length and width and height are equal. 17 He also measured its wall, one hundred forty-four cubits[e] by human measurement, which the angel was using. 18 The wall is built of jasper, while the city is pure gold, clear as glass. 19 The foundations of the wall of the city are adorned with every jewel; the first was jasper, the second sapphire, the third agate, the fourth emerald, 20 the fifth onyx, the sixth carnelian, the seventh chrysolite, the eighth beryl, the ninth topaz, the tenth chrysoprase, the eleventh jacinth, the twelfth amethyst. 21 And the twelve gates are twelve pearls, each of the gates is a single pearl, and the street of the city is pure gold, transparent as glass.

22 I saw no temple in the city, for its temple is the Lord God the Almighty and the Lamb. 23 And the city has no need of sun or moon to shine on it, for the glory of God is its light, and its lamp is the Lamb. 24 The nations will walk by its light, and the kings of the earth will bring their glory into it. 25 Its gates will never be shut by day—and there will be no night there. 26 People will bring into it the glory and the honor of the nations. 27 But nothing unclean will enter it, nor anyone who practices abomination or falsehood, but only those who are written in the Lamb's book of life.

22 Then the angel[f] showed me the river of the water of life, bright as crystal, flowing from the throne of God and of the Lamb 2 through the middle of the street of the city. On either side of the river is the tree of life[g] with its twelve kinds of fruit, producing its fruit each month; and the leaves of the tree are for the healing of the nations. 3 Nothing accursed will be found there any more. But the throne of God and of the Lamb will be in it, and his servants[h] will worship him; 4 they will see his face, and his name will be on their foreheads. 5 And there will be no more night; they need no light of lamp or sun, for the Lord God will be their light, and they will reign forever and ever.

6 And he said to me, "These words are trustworthy and true, for the Lord, the God of the spirits of the prophets, has sent his angel to show his servants[h] what must soon take place."

7 "See, I am coming soon! Blessed is the one who keeps the words of the prophecy of this book."

[a] Or *the unbelieving* [b] Or *in the Spirit* [c] Gk *He* [d] Gk *twelve thousand stadia* [e] That is, almost seventy-five yards
[f] Gk *he* [g] Or *the Lamb. 2In the middle of the street of the city, and on either side of the river, is the tree of life* [h] Gk *slaves*

8 I, John, am the one who heard and saw
these things. And when I heard and saw them, I
fell down to worship at the feet of the angel who
showed them to me; 9but he said to me, "You
must not do that! I am a fellow servant[a] with
you and your comrades[b] the prophets, and with
those who keep the words of this book. Worship
God!"

10 And he said to me, "Do not seal up the
words of the prophecy of this book, for the time is
near. 11Let the evildoer still do evil, and the filthy
still be filthy, and the righteous still do right, and
the holy still be holy."

12 "See, I am coming soon; my reward is with
me, to repay according to everyone's work. 13I am
the Alpha and the Omega, the first and the last,
the beginning and the end."

14 Blessed are those who wash their robes,[c]
so that they will have the right to the tree of life
and may enter the city by the gates. 15Outside are
the dogs and sorcerers and fornicators and murderers and idolaters, and everyone who loves and
practices falsehood.

16 "It is I, Jesus, who sent my angel to you
with this testimony for the churches. I am the
root and the descendant of David, the bright
morning star."

17 The Spirit and the bride say, "Come."
And let everyone who hears say, "Come."
And let everyone who is thirsty come.
Let anyone who wishes take the water of life
as a gift.

18 I warn everyone who hears the words
of the prophecy of this book: if anyone adds to
them, God will add to that person the plagues described in this book; 19if anyone takes away from
the words of the book of this prophecy, God will
take away that person's share in the tree of life and
in the holy city, which are described in this book.

20 The one who testifies to these things says,
"Surely I am coming soon."

Amen. Come, Lord Jesus!

21 The grace of the Lord Jesus be with all the
saints. Amen.[d]

[a] Gk *slave* [b] Gk *brothers* [c] Other ancient authorities read *do his commandments*

[d] Other ancient authorities lack *all*; others lack *the saints*; others lack *Amen*

Acknowledgments

GALLERY

Fig. 1: mural from tomb in Beni-Hassan, Egypt (nineteenth century BCE); Kunsthistorisches Museum, Vienna, Austria; photo © Erich Lessing/Art Resource, NY.

Fig. 2: Sandals from the Egyptian New Kingdom, Museo Egizio, Turin; photo Erich Lessing/Art Resource, N.Y.

Fig. 3: *Bible Quilt* (1898) by Harriet Powers; photo © 2007 Museum of Fine Arts, Boston.

Fig. 4: *Finding of Moses* by He Qi (China). For more information and art by He Qi, please visit www.heqigallery.com.

Fig. 5: *Grapes of Canaan* (Kappazuri dyed stencil print on paper, 6/100, 23 × 26 inches, 1983) by Sadao Watanabe (1913-1996). University Fund Purchase. Brauer Museum of Art 85.02.005. Valparaiso University. Photo © Brauer Museum of Art.

Fig. 6: Meeting of Solomon and the Queen of Sheba from *The History of the Queen of Sheba* (Ge'ez and Amharic); photo © Bildarchiv Preussischer Kulturbesitz/Art Resource, N.Y.

Fig. 7: *The Song of Solomon* by He Qi (China). For more information and art by He Qi, please visit www.heqigallery.com.

Fig. 8: *Nativity* by Lu Lan; © Lu Lan.

Fig. 9: *Feeding of the 5,000* by Laura James; © Laura James. Used by permission.

Fig. 10: *The Last Supper* (Japanese stencil, 1973) by Sadao Watanabe (1913-1996) from *Biblical Prints of Sadao Watanabe*. Reprinted with permission of Shinko Publishing Company.

Fig. 11: *Peter Repentant* from Ethiopian Octateuch (late seventeenth century); photo © British Library. All rights reserved. OR 481, folio 104v.

Fig. 12: *Mount Calvary* by William H. Johnson (oil on paperboard, c. 1944); photo © Smithsonian American Art Museum/Art Resource, N.Y.

Fig. 13: *Golgotha* by Romare Bearden from the Metropolitan Museum of Art, Bequest of Margaret Seligman Lewisohn, in memory of her husband, Sam A. Lewisoh, 1954 (54.143.9); image © The Metropolitan Museum of Art.

Fig. 14: *Mother and Child* by Michael Escoffery (oil on canvas, 2001); © Artist Rights Society (ARS), New York. Photo © Art Resource, N.Y.

Fig. 15: *Pieta* by Käthe Kollwitz (1867-1945); lithograph © Artist Rights Society (ARS), New York. Photo © Bildarchiv Preussischer Kulturbesitz/Art Resource, N.Y.

Fig. 16: *Head of Christ* by Warner Sallman (1892-1968); © 1941 Warner Press, Inc., Anderson, Ind. Used by permission.

Fig. 17: portrait of Jesus from BBC One's documentary *Son of God*, based on forensic anthropologists' research; illustration © BBC Photo Library. Used by permission.

Fig. 18: *Jesus of the People* by Janet McKenzie. "Through my inclusive painting *Jesus of the People* I hoped to remind that we are all created equally and beautifully in God's image." Copyright © 1999 Janet McKenzie, www. janetmckenzie.com.

Fig. 19: Romanized Christ as Shepherd from the catacombs of St. Priscilla, Rome, Italy (fresco); photo © Erich Lessing/Art Resource, N.Y.

Fig. 20: Christ as sun god Apollo from St. Peter's Basilica, Vatican State (mosaic); photo © Scala/Art Resource, N.Y.

Fig. 21: Christ as Judge enthroned with two angels from S. Apollinare Nuovo, Ravenna, Italy (mosaic); photo © Erich Lessing/Art Resource, N.Y.

Fig. 22: Mural of Black Jesus by Devon Cunninham, St. Cecelia's Catholic Church, Detroit, Mich.: photo © Jim West/The Image Works.

Fig. 23: Dust Bowl refugees; photo © Bettmann/CORBIS.

Fig. 24: Migrant workers pick tomatoes in a field in Camarillo, Calif., Tuesday, Oct. 26, 2004; photo © Damian Dovarganes/Associated Press.

Fig. 25: *Cherokee Trail of Tears* by John Guthrie; © John Guthrie.

Fig. 26: Japanese-American evacuees in Washington State; photo by Wartime Civil Control Administration, 1942.

Fig. 27: 1919 photo of execution of Charlemagne Peralte in Haiti by U.S. Marines Corps. http://static.wikipedia.org/new/wikipedia/en/articles/p/e/r/Image~Peraltebody.jpg_b176.html

Fig. 28: Bodies of the assassinated Jesuits; photo © Patrick Chauvel/Sygma/Corbis.

Fig. 29: Assassinated Oscar Romero; photo © Perez Garcia/Bettmann/Corbis.

Fig. 30: Underground Railroad; photo © Art Resource, N.Y.

Fig. 31: Family of eight flees East Germany, 1962; photo Will McBride; Bildarchiv Preussischer Kulturbesitz/Art Resource, N.Y.

Fig. 32: Berlin Wall in front of the Brandenburg Gate, Nov. 10, 1989; photo Klaus Lehnartz; Bildarchiv Preussischer Kulturbesitz/Art Resource, N.Y.

Fig. 33: South Africans waiting to vote, c. 1994; photo © David Turnley/CORBIS.

Fig. 34: *The First Supper* by Jane Evershed; © 1989 Jane Evershed.

Notes

THE BIBLE AT THE CROSSROAD OF CULTURES

1 Dag Hammarskjöld, *Markings*, trans. Leif Sjoberg and W. H. Auden (New York: Alfred Knopf, 1965), 205.
2 Huston Smith, *The Religions of Man* (New York: Harper and Row, 1965), 62.
3 Martin Buber, *The Eclipse of God: Studies in the Relation between Religion and Philosophy* (New York: Harper, 1957), 28.
4 Eduard Schweizer, *Luke, a Challenge to Present Theology*, trans. David Green (Atlanta: John Knox, 1982), 58.

THE OLD TESTAMENT

Genesis

5 Cain H. Felder, "Racial Ambiguities in the Biblical Narratives," in *The Church and Racism* (Concilium 151), ed. Gregory Baum and John Coleman (Edinburgh: T&T Clark, 1982), 18.
6 Robert E. Meagher, "Strangers at the Gate," *Parabola* 2, no. 4 (1977): 11; quoted in Parker J. Palmer, *The Company of Strangers* (New York: Crossroad, 1981), 67.
7 Kwok Pui-lan, "Fishing the Asia Pacific: Transnational Feminist Theologies in the Asia Pacific," *WJK Academic Update* 2 (2007–2008): 38. Reprinted in WJKAU from Rita Nakashima et al., eds., *Off the Menu: Asian and Asian North American Women's Religion and Theology* (Louisville: Westminster John Knox, 2007).
8 Gerhard Hoffmann, "Solidarity with Strangers as Part of the Mission of the Church," *International Review of Mission* 78 (1989): 54.
9 Steven Charleston, "The Old Testament of Native America," in *Constructing Christian Theologies from the Underside*, ed. Susan Brooks Thistlewaite and Mary Potter Engel (San Francisco: Harper SanFrancisco, 1990), 54.

Exodus

10 Willie K. Smith, "Dr. Martin Luther King, Jr.: The Politics of Sounds and Feelings," in *Leadership in America: Consensus, Corruption, and Charisma*, ed. Peter Dennis Bathory (New York: Longman, 1978), 98.
11 Helmut Frenz, "Human Rights: A Christian Viewpoint," *Gettysburg Lutheran Theological Seminary Bulletin* 56, no. 3 (August 1976): 38.
12 Gerhard Hoffmann, "Solidarity with Strangers as Part of the Mission of the Church," *International Review of Mission* 78 (1989): 57.
13 George V. Pixley, "A Latin American Perspective: The Option for the Poor in the OT," in *Voices from the Margin: Interpreting the Bible in the Third World*, ed. R. S. Sugirtharajah (Maryknoll: Orbis, 1991), 232.

Exodus *continued*

14 Naim Stifan Ateek, "A Palestinian Perspective: The Bible and Liberation," in *Voices from the Margin: Interpreting the Bible in the Third World*, ed. R. S. Sugirtharajah (Maryknoll: Orbis, 1991), 283.

15 Robert Allen Warrior, "A Native American Perspective: Canaanites, Cowboys and Indians," in *Voices from the Margin: Interpreting the Bible in the Third World*, ed. R. S. Sugirtharajah (Maryknoll: Orbis, 1991), 289.

Leviticus

16 Paul Tournier, *A Listening Ear* (Minneapolis: Augsburg, 1986), 117–118.

17 Michael Knoch, "Os Sem Terra—the Landless," *International Review of Mission* 78 (1989): 74; Qu'chua quotation from José Luís Caravias, *Lutar pela terra: inspirações bíblicas para as comunidades camponesas* (São Paulo: Edições Loyola, 1985).

Numbers

18 Michael Walzer, *Exodus and Revolution* (New York: Basic, 1985), 3–4.

Deuteronomy

19 Parker J. Palmer, *The Company of Strangers* (New York: Crossroad, 1981), 68. Quotation from Henri Nouwen, *Reaching Out* (Garden City: Doubleday, 1975), 51.

20 Gerhard Hoffmann, "Solidarity with Strangers as Part of the Mission of the Church," *International Review of Mission* 78 (1989): 57–58.

Judges

21 Peggy L. Day, "The Story of Jephthah's Daughter," in *Gender and Difference in Ancient Israel*, ed. Peggy L. Day (Minneapolis: Fortress Press, 1989), 66.

Ruth

22 See Robert D. Maldonado, "Reading Malinche Reading Ruth: Toward a Hermeneutic of Betrayal," *Semeia* 72 (1997): 99–100; and Francisco Garcia-Treto, "Mixed Messages: Encountering *Mestizaje* in the Old Testament," *Princeton Seminary Bulletin* 22, no. 2 (NS, 2001): 165.

23 Alan Neely, "God's People: A Community without Walls," *Princeton Seminary Bulletin* 14, no. 3 (NS, 2003): 160.

1 Kings

24 Michael Knoch, "Os Sem Terra—the Landless," *International Review of Mission* 78 (1989): 70–71.

2 Kings

25 Clarice J. Martin, "The African-American Christian Heritage: Its Witness and Promise," *Princeton Seminary Bulletin* 10, no. 3 (NS, 1989): 263; quoting C. Eric Lincoln, *Race, Religion, and the Continuing American Dilemma* (New York: Hill and Wang, 1984), 20f.

2 Chronicles

26 Katherine Doob Sakenfeld, "In the Wilderness, Awaiting the Land: the Daughters of Zelophehad and Feminist Interpretation," *Princeton Seminary Bulletin* 9, no. 3 (NS, 1988): 195.

Nehemiah

27 News release, Religious News Service, January 7, 1994.

28 Alan Neely, "God's People: A Community without Walls," *Princeton Seminary Bulletin* 14, no. 3 (NS, 2003): 153–154; quoting Paul D. Hanson, *The People Called* (San Francisco: Harper & Row, 1986), 297.

Job

29 Barbara Jurgensen, review of Karen Lebacqz, *Justice in an Unjust World, Trinity Seminary Review* 12, no. 1 (1990): 45.

30 Gustavo Gutiérrez, *On Job: God-talk and the Suffering of the Innocent* (Maryknoll: Orbis, 1987), 34.

Psalms

31 Barbara Ehrenreich, *Dancing in the Streets: A History of Collective Joy* (New York: Henry Holt, 2007).

32 Kathleen Norris, "Why the Psalms Scare Us," *Christianity Today* 40, no. 8 (July 15, 1996): 20–21.

33 Su Yon Pak, Unzu Lee, Jung Ha Kim, and Myung Ji Cho, *Singing the Lord's Song in a New Land: Korean American Practices of Faith* (Louisville: Westminster John Knox, 2005), 36.

34 Willie K. Smith, "Dr. Martin Luther King, Jr.: The Politics of Sounds and Feelings," in *Leadership in America: Consensus, Corruption, and Charisma,* ed. Peter Dennis Bathory (New York: Longman, 1978), 108.

35 Willie K. Smith, "Dr. Martin Luther King, Jr.: The Politics of Sounds and Feelings," in *Leadership in America: Consensus, Corruption, and Charisma,* ed. Peter Dennis Bathory (New York: Longman, 1978), 100.

36 Gustavo Gutiérrez, quoted without citation in Harvey Cox, *Religion in the Secular City* (New York: Simon & Schuster, 1984), 159.

37 John W. de Gruchy et al., eds., *The Kairos Document: Challenge to the Church, A Theological Comment on the Political Crisis in South Africa* (Grand Rapids: Eerdmans, 1985), 38–40.

38 Stephen Breck Reid, *Listening In: A Multicultural Reading of the Psalms* (Nashville: Abingdon, 1997), 88.

39 *On Naboth* 2; 45. *Corpus scriptorum ecclesiasticorum latinorum* 32.2.469.

40 Robert C. Fulton, "Victory from Death: What Makes the Rejects Sing!," *Currents in Theology and Mission* 14, no. 4 (August 1987): 278, 281.

41 *Economic Justice for All,* cited from David J. O'Brien and Thomas A. Shannon, *Catholic Social Thought: The Documentary Heritage* (Maryknoll: Orbis, 1992), 573–75.

Proverbs

42 Elizabeth A. Johnson, "Naming God She: The Theological Implications," *Princeton Seminary Bulletin* 22, no. 2 (NS, 2001): 144–145.

43 Susan E. Schreiner, "Educating the Congregation," *The Christian Century* (Nov 1, 1989): 987.

44 Harvey Cox, *Religion in the Secular City* (New York: Simon & Schuster, 1984), 143–145.

45 Jon Sobrino, *No Salvation Outside the Poor: Prophetic-Utopian Essays* (Maryknoll: Orbis, 2008), 48, citing John Paul II, *Pastores Gregis,* October 16, 2007, no. 67.

46 Thulisiwe Ndelu Beresford, review of Michael Battle, Reconciliation: *The Ubuntu Theology of Desmond Tutu, Trinity Seminary Review* 20, no. 1 (1998): 57.

Ecclesiastes

47 Lee Cormie, "The Churches and Economic Crisis," *The Ecumenist* 21, no. 3 (March–April 1983): 36.

Isaiah

48 Parker J. Palmer, *The Company of Strangers* (New York: Crossroad, 1981), 65.

49 Peter J. Paris, *The Social Teaching of the Black Churches* (Philadelphia: Fortress Press, 1985), 114–115.

50 John Dellis, "Light Illuminating Shadows," *Partners* 24 (2008): 14–15.

Jeremiah

51 Wayne Stumme, review of Bryant L. Myers, *Walking with the Poor: Principles and Practices of Transformational Development, Trinity Seminary Review* 22, no. 1 (2000): 56.

52 Clarice J. Martin, "The African-American Christian Heritage: Its Witness and Promise," *Princeton Seminary Bulletin* 10, no. 3 (NS, 1989): 265.

53 Janet K. Larson, "Margaret Atwood's Testaments: Resisting the Gilead Within," *The Christian Century* (May 20–27, 1987): 498.

Lamentations

54 Richard McCall, "Poverty and International Agencies," *Gettysburg Lutheran Theological Seminary Bulletin* 61, no. 4 (Fall 1981): 4.

55 Robert Lekachman, "A Decent Job—A Decent Income," *Gettysburg Lutheran Theological Seminary Bulletin* 56, no. 3 (August 1976): 52.

56 Larry Rasmussen, "The Persistence of Hunger," *Currents in Theology and Mission* 14, no. 4 (August 1987): 247, 251.

Ezekiel

57 Helmut Frenz, "Human Rights: A Christian Viewpoint," *Gettysburg Lutheran Theological Seminary Bulletin* 56, no. 3 (August 1976): 39.

58 Clark Pinnock, "A Call for Liberation for North American Christians," *Sojourners* (Sept. 1976): 23–24.

Joel

59 Tissa Balasuriya, *The Eucharist and Human Liberation* (Maryknoll, N.Y.: Orbis, 1979), 66–67.

Amos

60 Peter J. Paris, *The Social Teaching of the Black Churches* (Philadelphia: Fortress Press, 1985), 95–96. Quotation from George A. Singleton, *The Romance of African Methodism* (New York: Exposition, 1952), 150–151.

Micah

61 Ernesto Cardenal, "Epistle to Monseñor Casaldaliga," 1974, in Harvey Cox, *Religion in the Secular City* (New York: Simon & Schuster, 1984), 83.

62 Tissa Balasuriya, *The Eucharist and Human Liberation* (Maryknoll, N.Y.: Orbis, 1979), 14.

Malachi

63 Virgil Elizondo, "A Report on Racism: A Mexican American in the United States," in *The Church and Racism* (*Concilium* 151), ed. Gregory Baum and John Coleman (Edinburgh: T&T Clark, 1982), 62–63.

GALLERY

64 See Colleen McDannell, *Material Christianity: Religion and Popular Culture in America* (New Haven: Yale University Press, 1998), 190.

65 Ignacio Ellacuría, "The Crucified People," 580–604 in *Mysterium Liberationis: Fundamental Concepts of Liberation Theology,* ed. Ignacio Ellacuría and Jon Sobrino. (Maryknoll: Orbis, 1993).

66 Barbara Ehrenreich, *Dancing in the Streets: A History of Collective Joy* (New York: Metropolitan Books, 2007).

THE NEW TESTAMENT

Matthew

67 Justo L. González, *Mañana: Christian Theology from a Hispanic Perspective* (Nashville: Abingdon, 1990), 78.

68 Allan Boesak, *The Tenderness of Conscience: African Renaissance and the Spirituality of Politics* (Stellenbosch, South Africa: Sun Press, 2005), 201.

Mark

69 Kuribayashi Teruo, "Recovering Jesus for Outcasts in Japan," in R.S. Sugirtharajah, ed., *Frontiers in Asian Christian Theology: Emerging Trends* (Maryknoll: Orbis, 1994), 15.

Luke

70 Howard Thurman, *Jesus and the Disinherited* (New York: Abingdon-Cokesbury, 1949), 13.

71 Tissa Balasuriya, *The Eucharist and Human Liberation* (Maryknoll, NY: Orbis, 1979), xii.

Ephesians

72 R. Emerson Dobash and Russell Dobash, *Violence against Wives* (New York: Free Press, 1979), ch. 3.

Hebrews

73 F. W. Farrar, *The Epistle of Paul the Apostle to the Hebrews* (Cambridge: Cambridge University, 1891), 19.

James

74 "What to the Slave Is the Fourth of July," *Oration, Delivered in Corinthian Hall, Rochester, July 5, 1852,* reprinted in *The Frederick Douglass Papers*: 1847–54 (vol. 2 of *The Frederick Douglass Papers*; Series 1: Speeches, Debates and Interviews, ed. J. W. Blassingame (New Haven and London: Yale University Press, 1982).

2 Peter

75 James Baldwin, *The Fire Next Time* (New York: Vintage, 1963), 5–6, 104–5.

3 John

76 Alain Badiou, "The Communist Hypothesis," *NLR* 49 (2008): 38.

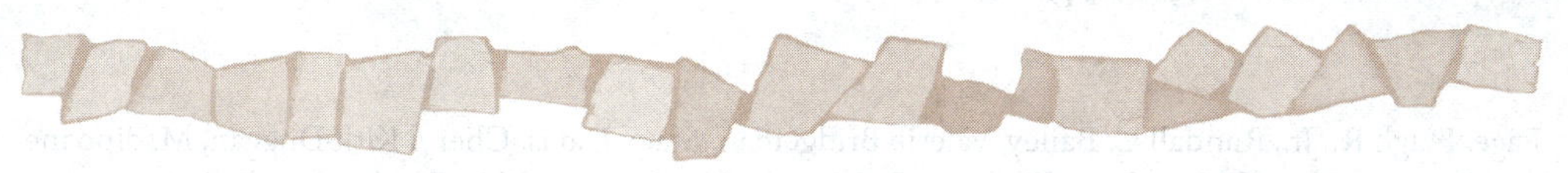

Select Bibliography

ON CULTURALLY AWARE INTERPRETATION OF THE BIBLE

Bellis, Alice Ogden, and Joel S. Kaminsky, eds. *Jews, Christians, and the Theology of the Hebrew Scriptures.* Atlanta: Society of Biblical Literature, 2000.

Blount, Brian K. *Cultural Interpretation: Reorienting New Testament Criticism.* Minneapolis: Fortress, 1995.

Blount, Brian K., Cain Hope Felder, Clarice J. Martin, and Emerson B. Powery, eds. *True to Our Native Land: An African American New Testament Commentary.* Minneapolis: Fortress, 2007.

Brooks, Roger, and John J. Collins, eds. *Hebrew Bible or Old Testament: Studying the Bible in Judaism and Christianity.* Notre Dame: Notre Dame University Press, 1990.

Choi, Hee An, and Katheryn Pfisterer Darr, eds. *Engaging the Bible: Critical Readings from Contemporary Women.* Minneapolis: Fortress, 2006.

Coote, Robert B., and Mary P. Coote. *Power, Politics, and the Making of the Bible: An Introduction.* Minneapolis: Fortress, 1990.

De La Torre, Miguel. *Reading the Bible from the Margins.* Maryknoll, N.Y.: Orbis, 2002.

Deloria, Vine, Jr. *God Is Red: A Native View of Religion.* Rev. ed. Golden, Colo.: Fulcrum, 2003.

Dube, Musa W. *Postcolonial Feminist Interpretation of the Bible.* St. Louis: Chalice, 2000.

Felder, Cain Hope, ed. *Stony the Road We Trod: African American Biblical Interpretation.* Minneapolis: Fortress, 1991.

Foskett, Mary F. and Jeffrey Kah-jin Kuan, eds. *Ways of Being, Ways of Reading: Asian American Biblical Interpretation.* St. Louis: Chalice, 2006.

Freire, Paolo. *The Pedagogy of the Oppressed.* Translated by Myra Bergman Ramos. New York: Seabury, 1968.

Gottwald, Norman K. *The Hebrew Bible: A Socio-Literary Introduction.* Philadelphia: Fortress, 1985.

Gottwald, Norman K., and Richard A. Horsley, eds. *The Bible and Liberation: Political and Social Hermeneutics.* Rev. ed. Maryknoll, N.Y.: Orbis, 1993.

Horsley, Richard A., ed. *In the Shadow of Empire: Reclaiming the Bible as a History of Resistance.* Louisville: Westminster John Knox, 2008.

Jobling, David, Peggy L. Day, and Gerald T. Sheppard, eds. *The Bible and the Politics of Exegesis.* Cleveland: Pilgrim, 1991.

Kelley, Shawn. *Racializing Jesus: Race, Ideology, and the Formation of Modern Biblical Scholarship.* London: Routledge, 2002.

Kwok, Pui-lan. *Discovering the Bible in the Non-biblical World.* Bible and Liberation Series. Maryknoll, N.Y.: Orbis, 1995.

Malina, Bruce. *The New Testament World: Insights from Cultural Anthropology.* 3rd ed. Louisville: Westminster John Knox, 2001.

Page, Hugh R., Jr., Randall C. Bailey, Valerie Bridgeman, Stacy Davis, Cheryl Kirk-Duggan, Madipoane Masenya, Samuel Murrell, and Rodney Sadler, eds. *The Africana Bible: Reading Israel's Scriptures from Africa and the African Diaspora.* Minneapolis: Fortress, 2009.

Patte, Daniel, J. Severino Croatto, Nicole Wilkinson Duran, Teresa Okure, and Archie Chi Chung Lee, eds. *Global Bible Commentary.* Nashville: Abingdon, 2004.

Prior, Michael. *The Bible and Colonialism: A Moral Critique.* Biblical Seminar 48. Sheffield, England: Sheffield Academic Press, 1997.

Schüssler Fiorenza, Elisabeth. *The Power of the Word: Scripture and the Rhetoric of Empire.* Minneapolis: Fortress, 2007.

———. *Rhetoric and Ethic: The Politics of Biblical Studies.* Minneapolis: Fortress, 1999.

Segovia, Fernando F. *Decolonizing Biblical Studies: A View from the Margins.* Maryknoll, N.Y.: Orbis, 2000.

Segovia, Fernando F., and Mary Ann Tolbert, eds. *Reading from This Place: Social Location and Biblical Interpretation in Global Perspective.* 2 vols. Minneapolis: Fortress, 1995, 2000.

———. *Teaching the Bible: The Discourses and Politics of Biblical Pedagogy.* Maryknoll, N.Y.: Orbis, 1998.

Segovia, Fernando F., and R. S. Sugirtharajah, eds. *A Postcolonial Commentary on the New Testament Writings.* London: T. & T. Clark, 2007.

Sugirtharajah, R. S. *Asian Biblical Hermeneutics and Postcolonialism: Contesting the Interpretations.* Maryknoll, N.Y.: Orbis, 1998.

———. *The Bible and the Third World: Precolonial, Colonial, and Postcolonial Encounters.* Cambridge, England: Cambridge University Press, 2001.

Tinker, George E. *"Indian Cultures and Interpreting the Christian Bible."* Pages 88–99 in *Spirit and Resistance: Political Theology and American Indian Liberation.* Minneapolis: Fortress, 2004.

van Wijk-Bos, Johanna W. H. *Making Wise the Simple: The Torah in Christian Faith and Practice.* Grand Rapids, Mich.: Eerdmans, 2005.

Vander Stichele, Caroline, and Todd Penner, eds. *Her Master's Tools? Feminist and Postcolonial Engagements of Historical-Critical Discourse.* Global Perspectives on Biblical Scholarship, Series 9. Atlanta: Society of Biblical Literature, 2005.

Von Kellenbach, Katharina. *Anti-Judaism in Feminist Religious Writings.* Atlanta: Scholars Press, 1994.